The Broadview Anthology of

AMERICAN LITERATURE

Volume B
1820 to Reconstruction

The Broadview Anthology of
AMERICAN LITERATURE

Volume B
1820 to Reconstruction

GENERAL EDITORS:

Derrick R. Spires, Cornell University
Rachel Greenwald Smith, Saint Louis University
Joseph Rezek, Boston University
Christina Roberts, Seattle University
Justine S. Murison, University of Illinois, Urbana-Champaign
Laura L. Mielke, University of Kansas
Christopher Looby, University of California, Los Angeles
Rodrigo Lazo, University of California, Irvine
Alisha Knight, Washington College
Hsuan L. Hsu, University of California, Davis
Michael Everton, Simon Fraser University
Christine Bold, University of Guelph

broadview press

BROADVIEW PRESS – www.broadviewpress.com
Peterborough, Ontario, Canada

Founded in 1985, Broadview Press remains a wholly independent publishing house. Broadview's focus is on academic publishing: our titles are accessible to university and college students as well as scholars and general readers. With over 800 titles in print, Broadview has become a leading international publisher in the humanities, with world-wide distribution. Broadview is committed to environmentally responsible publishing and fair business practices.

Library and Archives Canada Cataloguing in Publication

Title: The Broadview anthology of American literature / general editors: Derrick Spires, Cornell University [and 11 others].
Other titles: Beginnings to Reconstruction
Names: Spires, Derrick Ramon, editor.
Description: Includes bibliographical references and index.
Identifiers: Canadiana (print) 20220161925 | Canadiana (ebook) 20220161984 | ISBN 9781039301573 (set) | ISBN
      9781554814657 (Volume B ; softcover) | ISBN 9781770488274 (set ; PDF) | ISBN 9781770488267 (Volume B ; PDF)
Subjects: LCSH: American literature. | LCGFT: Literature.
Classification: LCC PS507 .B76 2022 | DDC 810.8—dc23

Broadview Press handles its own distribution in North America:
PO Box 1243, Peterborough, Ontario K9J 7H5, Canada
555 Riverwalk Parkway, Tonawanda, NY 14150, USA
Tel: (705) 743-8990; Fax: (705) 743-8353
email: customerservice@broadviewpress.com

For all territories outside of North America, distribution is handled by Eurospan Group.

Broadview Press acknowledges the financial support of the
Government of Canada for our publishing activities.

Canada

Cover design by Lisa Brawn
Typesetting by Alexandria Stuart

PRINTED IN CANADA

CONTRIBUTING EDITORS AND WRITERS

MANAGING EDITORS:	Laura Buzzard, Don LePan
DEVELOPMENTAL EDITORS AND STAFF WRITERS:	Jennifer McCue, Brett McLenithan, Nora Ruddock, Helena Snopek, Maxwell Uphaus
GENERAL ACADEMIC AND TEXTUAL EDITORS:	Joe Davies, Michel Pharand
DESIGN COORDINATOR:	Alexandria Stuart

ASSOCIATE GENERAL EDITORS:

Gina Caison   Koritha Mitchell
Drew Lopenzina   Benjamin Railton
John Marsh   Kelly Wisecup

CONTRIBUTING EDITORS:

David Anthony   Clayton McCarl   Ashley Reed
Kristin Boudreau   Laura K. Muñoz   Christopher B. Teuton
Scott Cave   Tiffany Potter   Willow White
Matthew Cohen   Birgit Brander Rasmussen Caroline Wigginton
Alejandra Dubcovsky   David Read   Kelly Wisecup
Jenny Marie Forsythe

CONTRIBUTING WRITERS:

Tim Cassedy   Rodrigo Lazo   Joseph Rezek
Michael Everton   John Marsh   Siân Silyn Roberts
Emily Farrell   Zoe McKenna   Jason Shaffer
Jenny Marie Forsythe Laura Mielke   Alexandria Stuart
John R. Funchion   Bethany Qualls   Kelly Wisecup
Christopher Hager   Ashley Reed   Braedan Zimmer
Genevieve Kirk   Andrew Reszitnyk

LAYOUT AND TYPESETTING:
Alexandria Stuart

PRODUCTION COORDINATORS:
Tara Lowes   Tara Trueman

PERMISSIONS COORDINATOR:
Jacqueline Kwan

PROOFREADERS:

Joe Davies   Judith Earnshaw   Michel Pharand
Bethany Qualls

TEXT PREPARATION:

Caileigh Broach   Genevieve Kirk   Jennifer McCue
Alexandria Stuart   Braedan Zimmer

Reiner Smolinski, Georgia State University
Carole Lynn Stewart, Brock University
Matthew Teutsch, Piedmont University
Margaret Thickstun, Hamilton College
Zachary Turpin, University of Idaho
Abram Van Engen, Washington University in
    St. Louis
Lindsay Van Tine, Gilder Lehrman Institute of
    American History

Megan Walsh, St. Bonaventure University
James Warren, Washington and Lee University
Ed White, Tulane University
Edward Whitley, Lehigh University
Maria Windell, University of Colorado Boulder
Chad Wriglesworth, University of Waterloo
Jonathan Yeager, University of Tennessee at
    Chattanooga
Michael Ziser, University of California, Davis

Contents

This anthology's online component is available at sites.broadviewpress.com/baalonline/

[Note to Instructors: *The Last of the Mohicans* is among over 400 available editions from Broadview, any one of which may be packaged together with this anthology volume.]

[Note to Instructors: *The Scarlet Letter* is among over 400 available editions from Broadview, any one of which may be packaged together with this anthology volume.]

[Note to Instructors: *Billy Budd, Sailor (An Inside Narrative)* is among over 400 available editions from Broadview, any one of which may be packaged together with this anthology volume.]

[Note to Instructors: *Little Women* is among over 400 available editions from Broadview, any one of which may be packaged together with this anthology volume.]

[Note to Instructors and Students: See the anthology's companion website for further supplemental resources, including a selection of historical maps and an interactive timeline.]

PREFACE

A Fresh Approach

To those with some awareness of the abundance of fresh material and lively debate in the field of American literary studies in recent decades, it may seem surprising that this abundance has not been more fully reflected in the number of multi-volume anthologies. Shorter anthologies have come and gone, but the decades since the first appearance of *The Norton Anthology of American Literature* in 1979 have seen the publication of only one other anthology of comparable size, *The Heath Anthology of American Literature*—which, like the Norton, has long been available in five volumes. There has, in short, been no expansion in the range of available multi-volume anthologies to match the expansion of content and of approach that has characterized the discipline itself; the number of writing guides and business communication textbooks has multiplied steadily (to the point where there are literally hundreds of available choices), while the number of comprehensive anthologies of American literature has remained at two.

For those of us who have been working for the past three years on *The Broadview Anthology of American Literature*, it is not difficult to understand why. The very expansion of the discipline has made the task of assembling and editing an anthology that fully and vibrantly reflects the ways in which American literary traditions are studied and taught an extraordinarily daunting one. The sheer amount of work involved is enormous, but so too is the amount of expertise that must be called on. With that background very much in mind, we decided when we embarked on this project to involve a large number of contributors in the process (as the pages following the title page to this volume attest), and to encourage a high degree of collaboration at every level. First and foremost have been the distinguished academics who serve as General Editors for the anthology, but in all there have been hundreds of people involved at various stages in advising, researching, drafting headnotes or annotations,

reviewing material, editing material, and carrying out the work of designing and typesetting the texts and other materials. That approach has allowed us to prepare a large anthology of high quality with unusual speed—but we have throughout remained acutely aware of the importance of maintaining a high degree of consistency. Material has been reviewed and revised in-house at Broadview, by outside editors, and by a variety of academics with an extraordinarily diverse range of backgrounds and academic specialities, as well as by members of the group of General Editors for the project as a whole. The aim has been not only to ensure accuracy but also to make sure that the same standards are applied throughout the anthology to matters such as extent and coverage in author introductions, level of annotation, tone of writing, and student accessibility.

The General Editors have throughout taken the lead in the process of making selections for the anthology. Along the way we have been guided by several core principles. We have endeavored to provide a selection that is broadly representative, while also being mindful of the importance of choosing texts that have the capacity to engage readers' interest today. We have included a select number of longer works (among them Mary Rowlandson's *Narrative*, Benjamin Franklin's *Autobiography*, Elizabeth Ashbridge's *Account*, Susanna Rowson's *Slaves in Algiers*, Hannah Webster Foster's *The Coquette*, Black Hawk's *Life*, Frederick Douglass's *Narrative*, Henry David Thoreau's *Walden*, Herman Melville's *Benito Cereno*, and Rebecca Harding Davis's *Life in the Iron Mills*) in their entirety. On the other hand, where inexpensive high-quality editions of particular works are available in our series of Broadview Editions, we have often decided to omit these works here, on the grounds that those wishing to teach one or more such works may easily order them in a special-price combination package with the anthology; on these grounds we have decided against including Hawthorne's *The Scarlet Letter*, for example. With a number of works (among them Olaudah Equiano's *Interesting Narrative*, Thomas Paine's *Common Sense*,

Harriet Beecher Stowe's *Uncle Tom's Cabin*, Harriet Jacobs's *Incidents in the Life of a Slave Girl*, and Herman Melville's *Moby-Dick*), we have provided a substantial selection of excerpts.

Overall, our aim has always been to present American literature in the round—literature from the South and West as well as the Northeast, literature by a wide range of black and Indigenous as well as white writers, literature by Hispanic writers, literature reflective of different sexual orientations, and popular literature as well as literature established by scholarly and pedagogical convention as "literary." We have aimed to represent all genres—including oral literature and oratory (for which we include a special section in Volume B) as well as prose non fiction, fiction, poetry, and drama. Throughout, we have aimed to include a wide range of selections by lesser-known writers as well as a full selection of works long accepted as part of the canon. From Elizabeth Ashbridge and Venture Smith to Absalom Jones and Lemuel Haynes, and from José María Heredia to Elias Boudinot and Margaret Jane Mussey Sweat, you will find many writers here who are not represented in most general anthologies of American literature. Nor is the anthology's expanded range a matter only of including writers who have never been part of the established canon of American literature. We have also taken a fresh look at the history of the canon in other ways; we acknowledge, for example, the central place that Henry Wadsworth Longfellow held in the literary imagination of nineteenth- and early twentieth-century America by according him more space than has any general anthology of American literature for at least a half century.

By this point, readers of this preface may well be wondering if the anthology could possibly manage to find space for the works they have long been accustomed to teaching, and have no wish to stop teaching: works by the likes of Bradstreet, Emerson, Poe, Hawthorne, Melville, Dickinson, and Whitman. The short answer is yes; indeed, the selection of works by these writers is, overall, at least as great as that in existing anthologies. The Melville section, for example, runs to over 140 pages, the Dickinson section to over 90 pages, the Whitman to over 120 pages.

But surely no anthology can offer *both* such an abundance of material by canonical writers *and* a much broader selection of underrepresented writers? How is such a sleight of hand possible? In part, the inclusion of a greater range of material is made possible simply by the format we have adopted; a two-column, large trim-size format allows us to include, in a similar number of pages, a greater amount of material than do the formats adopted by other anthologies. But even using a larger trim-size, no anthology that limited itself to two bound-book volumes covering the Beginnings to Reconstruction (a further three projected volumes will provide coverage to the present) could possibly do an adequate job of representing American literature so fully. The key point here is that the Broadview is emphatically *not* simply a bound-book anthology; for these first two periods the website component of the anthology includes well over a thousand pages of material. These website selections are not "add-ons" prepared to a lower editorial standard and meant to be accorded a subsidiary status; as their inclusion in the anthology's main table of contents suggests, they are an integral part of the anthology itself, presented in the same format, and edited and annotated according to the same principles as the material included in the bound book volumes. Our research has suggested that most of the authors and works which we have included as part of the anthology's website component are likely to be taught somewhat less frequently than are the authors and works included in the bound book volumes. But we fully expect that a majority of instructors will wish to teach at least *some* of the selections that are to be found in the anthology's online component rather than in the bound books. (In some cases, too, we have gone against what our research has suggested about current pedagogical practice, and have included in the bound-book volumes work by lesser-known writers who we believe deserve to be more widely taught—just as, in the other direction, we have included in the anthology's website component a number of works that have long been part of the established canon.) In the end, of course, instructors will make their own choices, with the needs of their own students in mind; our aim is simply to provide instructors with the widest possible range of materials to choose from, prepared to a high editorial standard, and accompanied by the widest possible range of contextual materials.

How does this hybrid approach work in practice? A few examples may help to make plain the various ways in which it can work. In volume A, excerpts from Cotton Mather's *The Wonders of the Invisible World* are included in the bound book, while a substantial package of contextual materials relating to the Salem Witch Trials is included in the anthology's online component; Parts 1 and 2 of Franklin's *Autobiography* are included in the bound book (together with "Remarks Concerning the Savages of North America" and "On the Slave Trade"), while the full *Autobiography* is made available in the anthology's website component. Four of Crèvecoeur's *Letters from an American Farmer* are included in the bound book, together with a small selection of contextual materials, while two more of the letters (and a good deal more contextual material) are included in the anthology's website component. In volume B, Catharine Maria Sedgwick's "Cacoethes Scribendi" is included in the bound book, while "Berkeley Jail," excerpts from *Hope Leslie*, and excerpts from "Slavery in New England" appear in the anthology's website component; substantial excerpts from Thoreau's *Walden* (together with "Resistance to Civil Government") are included in the bound book, while the complete text of *Walden* is made available in the anthology's website component, together with contextual materials and a number of other works (among them "A Plea for Captain John Brown," excerpts from *The Maine Woods*, excerpts from the journals, and excerpts from *A Yankee in Canada*). In a small number of cases, audio selections are included in the online component alongside written texts, in recognition of the value of oral traditions.

The online component of the anthology is also important when it comes to the overview introductions to each volume. At the request of the large number of instructors we consulted on this matter, these overviews cover significant developments in American history as well as developments in American literary history. Indeed (and somewhat to our surprise), a substantial majority of those we surveyed felt that it was more important to include overviews of key aspects of the historical background in the bound book volumes than it was to include overviews of the literary genres. The genre introductions for each period are thus included (together with certain of the historical overview sections, and with an overview of the development of language during the period) in the anthology's website component.

The way in which we have treated the poets George Moses Horton and Sarah Piatt is a good example of the degree to which a hybrid approach makes possible unprecedented opportunities for an anthology to be truly inclusive. Neither of these two writers has at this point a clearly established place in the canon; there is no handful of poems by either poet that have become familiar to all Americanists and that are included again and again in anthologies. Horton, author of the first book by a black Southerner and one of the most interesting poetic voices of the mid-nineteenth century, is rarely included in anthologies of any sort; even *The Norton Anthology of African American Literature* accords him only four pages. Piatt is more widely recognized, and is now represented by at least one or two poems in most anthologies of American literature—but, with the partial exception of "The Palace-Burner," there is no consensus on which of her poems most deserve to be read and studied. For each of these poets we present well over a dozen selections—some in the bound book, others as part of the anthology's online component. Our hope is that this approach may facilitate wider reading by both instructors and students, perhaps leading to some lively class discussions as to which poems by each poet are most engaging, most interesting—and most deserving of finding a place in the American literary canon.

One further point about a "hybrid" anthology such as this one deserves to be made; when an anthology comprises both bound book and website components, there is no need to remove any author or any work from the anthology—ever. Almost every academic who has been teaching for a few years has experienced the frustration that occurs when a new edition of a favorite anthology appears—and some of the selections that have *made* it a favorite anthology have been removed. With this anthology (as with Broadview's acclaimed anthology of British literature), any selections that, upon publication of a new edition, no longer appear in the bound book anthology, will readily be found in the anthology's website component.

In a number of cases the distinctive format of the anthology facilitates the presentation of content in an engaging and practical fashion. Notably, the adoption of a two-column format allows for different versions of texts to be presented in parallel column format. That provides an opportunity for ready comparison, for example, of the *Bay Psalm Book* version of Psalm 21 with the King James version; of Thomas Jefferson's original draft of the Declaration of Independence with the final text; and of various different versions of several of Emily Dickinson's poems. It provides an opportunity as well to show translated material alongside the original. We present several of Sor Juana's poems both in the Spanish originals and in a facing-column translation; we present Jane Johnston Schoolcraft's Ojibwe-language poems with her own English translations; we present Longfellow's English and Italian versions of "The Old Bridge at Florence" side by side; and we present the original Spanish text of Heredia's "To Washington" alongside an English translation specially prepared for this anthology. The translated material in the "Popular Literature and Print Culture" section of Volume B—Wilhelm Weitling's "The Little Communist" and an excerpt from Ignace Nau's poem of Haiti, "Dessalines"—is presented in the same way. Readers are thus provided with an accessible translation while at the same time being able to experience something of the flavor of the original, in a format that provides for maximum convenience in comparing the two.

The large trim-size, two-column format also allows for greater flexibility in the presentation of visual materials. Throughout we have aimed to make this an anthology that is fully alive to the visual aspects of print culture, and, more broadly, to the connections between literary and visual culture. Readers will thus find an abundance of illustrations from the original texts, of facsimiles of title pages, of newspaper clippings of relevant articles, and of other pertinent images. Wherever possible we include with each author headnote an image of the author—and, with authors such as Truth, Douglass, Whitman, and Longfellow, we include a portfolio of other author images. In all there are hundreds of black-and-white illustrations in each volume—and we include in each volume as well twelve pages of color images.

Visual materials are also a key component of the background contextual materials that form an important part of the anthology. These materials are presented in two ways. Several "Contexts" sections on particular topics or themes appear in each volume of the anthology, presented independent of any particular text or author. These include broadly based groupings of material on such topics as "Slavery and Resistance," "Gender and Sexuality," and "Expansion, Native American Expulsions, and 'Manifest Destiny.'" Groups of "In Context" materials, on the other hand, each relate to a particular text or author. They range from the "Indigenous Experiences of Metacom's War" (presented as "In Context" material accompanying Rowlandson's *Narrative*); to "Images of Rip Van Winkle"; to a fugitive slave advertisement for Harriet Jacobs; to a selection of materials on the California Gold Rush (presented as "In Context" material accompanying excerpts from the memoirs of Vicente Pérez Rosales); to a selection of "Nineteenth-Century Images of Whales and Whaling" and "The Story of the Essex" (both presented as "In Context" material accompanying the anthology's substantial selection of *Moby-Dick* excerpts).

For the most part these contextual materials are, as the word suggests, included purely with a view to setting texts in their broader literary, historical, and cultural context. In some cases, however, the materials included in "Contexts" sections are themselves literary works of considerable stature; such is the case, for example, with Boyrereau Brinch's memoirs of life as an enslaved person in New England (excerpted in the volume A section "Contexts: Slavery and Resistance"); with Gottlieb Mittelberger's account of his time in America (excerpted in the volume A section "Contexts: Immigration and Indentured Servitude"); with William Wells Brown's history of the Haitian Revolution and Joseph Plumb Martin's narrative of everyday life as a soldier during the Revolutionary War (both of which are excerpted in the volume A section "Contexts: Rebellions and Revolutions"); with *The Narrative of Bethany Veney: A Slave Woman* (excerpted in the volume B section "Contexts: Slavery and Abolition"); with Susan Fenimore Cooper's *Rural Hours* (excerpted in the volume B section "Contexts: Nature and the Environment"), and with the various excerpts of works by Frederick Law Olmsted that are included as contextual material. In the inclusion of texts such as these, as well as in other ways, the anthology aims to encourage readers to explore the boundaries of the literary and the non-literary, and the issue of what constitutes a "literary text."

We also take a rather different approach to popular literature than do competing anthologies. For decades now, the leading college-level anthologies of American literature have been making some space for texts that were popular in the eighteenth or nineteenth centuries but dropped from view in the early twentieth; works such as *The Coquette*, *Clotel*, and *Ruth Hall* have found their way into anthologies—as, of course, has *Uncle Tom's Cabin*. This renewed interest in popular and influential works of other eras, though, has often not extended to works that remained highly popular well into the twentieth century. This is particularly true of poems; works such as Longfellow's *Hiawatha* and "Paul Revere's Ride" and Whitman's "O Captain, My Captain," which were etched into the memories of generations of Americans, have been considered somehow inappropriate for inclusion in twenty-first-century anthologies. That is not the approach we take here; *The Coquette*, *Clotel*, *Ruth Hall*, and *Uncle Tom's Cabin* are certainly to be found in this anthology, but so too are *Hiawatha*, "Paul Revere's Ride," and "O Captain, My Captain." And so too are dozens of other works of popular literature—some within author entries, others in the substantial "Popular Literature and Print Culture" sections that are included in both of these first two volumes. From early poems such as the anonymous broadsheet "New England Bravery, Being a Full and True Account of the Taking of the City of Louisbourg by the New England Forces," Mary Nelson's "Forty Shillings Reward," and James Revel's "The Poor, Unhappy, Transported Felon"; to John Greenleaf Whittier's "Snow-Bound" and Elizabeth Oakes Smith's "The Drowned Mariner"; from Susanna Rowson's *Charlotte Temple*, Lydia Maria Child's *Hobomok*, and the anonymously authored "Theresa, a Haytien Tale" to Solomon Northup's *Twelve Years a Slave*, Ann S. Stephens's *Malaeska: Indian Wife of the White Hunter*, George Lippard's *The Quaker City, or, The Monks of Monk Hall*, and John Rollin Ridge's *The Life and Adventures of Joaquín Murieta: The Celebrated California Bandit*, an extraordinarily wide range of popular texts is presented. Our aim is to provide a broad-ranging representation of American literature that includes as full a sense as possible of American literary history and print culture.

Nor does the anthology neglect oral literature and oral culture. We provide a remarkably wide-ranging selection of Indigenous and African American oral literatures, and we incorporate a diverse array of speeches in both volumes. In anthologizing oral literatures in written form, we have aimed to be as transparent as possible in identifying when—and by whom—the oral works were recorded, and where possible we have included versions produced by writers from the communities to whom the stories belong. In the case of Indigenous traditions, we have also included a variety of visual pieces (such as wampum, story poles, and painted boxes). Indigenous oral and visual literatures are concentrated at the beginning of the anthology's first volume in recognition of Indigenous cultural precedence, but we have also endeavored to recognize the continued presence of Indigenous peoples and the continuing vitality of these forms—both by including some stories in contemporary versions and by including further examples of Indigenous oral and visual literature throughout the anthology volumes.

"AMERICAN": "American" is of course a slippery term. As used in expressions such as "American history" and "American literature," "American" is typically understood to mean "relating to the United States of America," rather than to all of the Americas, from Cape Horn to the North Pole. But we adopt a broad definition of "American" in this anthology, offering coverage that begins with the literatures of the people who inhabited what is now the United States, and contiguous areas; we include the literatures of Indigenous peoples first of all, and then those of settler colonists from Spain, France, and elsewhere as well as from Britain.

The fact that the United States of America as an independent nation existed first on the eastern seaboard has traditionally led to a strong emphasis in the teaching of early American literature on the literature of the east coast—and especially of the Northeast. Americanists in recent decades have pushed to broaden that scholarly and pedagogical focus, and those efforts have been reflected in recent editions of the main anthologies. This anthology partakes of that broadening, and carries it further. In our coverage of Indigenous literatures, for example, we provide a range of materials from groups in the South, the Southwest, and the Northwest as well as from the East and Northeast. Similarly, the "Civilizations in Contact" section includes extensive coverage of civilizations in contact throughout North America. Hispanic authors—among them Sor Juana Inés de la Cruz, José María Heredia, Vicente Pérez Rosales, and the anonymous author of *Xicoténcatl*—are here given considerably more space than they are conventionally accorded. More space too is provided for Indigenous voices. And, whereas many anthologies of the past have treated the writings of Indigenous authors primarily as contextual material, we have chosen to accord author entries to a significant number of Indigenous authors, including Canassatego, Sagoyewatha, Tecumseh, Jane Johnston Schoolcraft / Bamewawagezhikaquay, Mà-ka-tai-me-she-kià-kiàk / Black Hawk, Elias Boudinot / Gallegina, and John Rollin Ridge / Yellow Bird.

CHRONOLOGY, PERIODIZATION, AND REPRESENTATION: Like the other major anthologies of American literature, this anthology uses chronology as its primary organizing principle. But we nevertheless aim to challenge established conventions of periodization in important ways. Significantly, we end the first two volumes not at 1865 but rather with Reconstruction; we include in volume B a wide selection of material covering the 1865–77 period. The most common point at which to break the two halves of an American Literature survey course has long been the end of the Civil War in 1865, and all other American literature anthologies use 1865 as a break point. Why take a different approach? One reason is simply that the amount of literary material any full survey course must at least touch on keeps expanding. Some of that expansion occurs as a result of the ongoing process of recovering lesser-known antebellum authors and texts, but the majority occurs simply as a result of the march of time. Moving the break from 1865 to 1877 runs the risk of giving short shrift to some important pre-bellum writers and texts. On balance, however, more and more Americanists are coming round to the view that the higher priority is to give somewhat more weight to more recent material; it

is in part for that reason that an increasing number of institutions now break the survey at 1877 rather than 1865.

But achieving an appropriate balance between the more recent past and earlier eras is not the only reason for choosing 1877 rather than 1865 as a break point. The two dates send different messages as to the arc of American history—and of American literary history. Choosing 1865 as a break point suggests a new beginning, a fresh start, with America having finally put the wrenching issue of slavery behind it. Choosing the end of Reconstruction as a break point suggests, arguably, something closer to reality: that, much as slavery itself may have ended, the legacy of slavery carried on as an enormously powerful shaping force in American history and literature. In making this choice, we recognize that historians no longer see 1877 as representing a clean break point, a precise moment at which Reconstruction's hopes of achieving equality were dashed and Reconstruction's ideals finally betrayed. They and we see it rather as one important moment in a continuum. But choosing such a moment emphasizes the importance of that continuum to the history and the literature of America. That is not to suggest that other topics that have received more emphasis in other anthologies—industrialization and urbanization, for example, or realism and regionalism[1]—are unimportant; far from it. We are confident that the coverage we provide of these and other related topics compares favorably to that of any other available anthology. But throughout the anthology we accord a place of utmost

---

[1] Through to the end of the twentieth century, the degree to which anthologies of American literature placed very little emphasis on racial inequality after the end of the Civil War is striking. Through to at least its 1994 fourth edition, for example, *The Norton Anthology of American Literature* included in its introduction to the history and literature of 1865–1914 America just one short paragraph on "the problem of racial inequality, more specifically what came to be known as the 'Negro problem.'" The 11-line paragraph—included almost at the end of the introduction—includes a brief discussion of Booker T. Washington and W.E.B. Du Bois; in the rest of the introduction, the only mention of a black author is the appearance of Charles Chesnutt in a list of "southern local colorists." The introduction's emphasis is entirely on the economic "transformation of a nation" ushered in by the Civil War—on industrialization and urbanization, in short—and, in literature, on realism and naturalism and regionalism. The authors never use the word "slavery"—or, indeed, the word "Reconstruction."

significance to slavery, the legacy of slavery, and, more generally, the ongoing struggle for equality.

In taking this approach, we recognize that a majority of institutions still break the survey course at 1865; for that reason, we will also include material covering the period 1865–77 in the forthcoming volume C (the first volume covering the second half of the survey). Much as the editors of this anthology may feel that the end of Reconstruction is a more appropriate break point than 1865, we have no desire to inconvenience those working within the traditional framework of the American Literature survey.

At several points in the anthology, we challenge the traditional periodization of—and the traditional emphases on—the scholarship and the pedagogy of American literature through departures from strict chronology. The first three authors we included in volume B, for example, are William Apess, Catharine Sedgwick, and James Fenimore Cooper—in that order. Had we followed strict chronology according to each author's birthdate (the guideline through most of the anthology), that order would be reversed, with Cooper appearing first (just as he appears before Sedgwick and Apess in the Norton and in other leading anthologies). Cooper was born a few months earlier than Sedgwick in 1789, and Apess was born almost a decade later—in 1798. In part, it can be argued, Apess might justifiably precede the other two, despite having been born later, on the grounds that his best-known work, the memoir *A Son of the Forest*, recalls an earlier time—his childhood and youth in the very early years of the century. But we felt there was a more important reason for beginning with an Indigenous writer such as Apess. Presentation involves issues of representation, and this anthology aims to represent Indigenous perspectives—like those of African Americans and other previously under-represented groups—more fully and more prominently than has traditionally been done in presenting the chronology of American literature. Foregrounding Apess rather than Cooper at the opening of a volume is one important signal. Including Sedgwick before Cooper is another—a sign that we feel it to be at *least* as important to represent the traditions in nineteenth-century American literature that Sedgwick was so influential in forging as it is

to represent the influence of Cooper and his famous "Leatherstocking" series.

One other point is worth making about the presentation of William Apess in this anthology. We have chosen to foreground in the bound book portion of the anthology his "An Indian's Looking-Glass for the White Man" and excerpts from his *Eulogy on King Philip*; we do include excerpts from *Son of the Forest* in the anthology, but in the website component rather than in the bound book. That is not to suggest anything negative about *Son of the Forest* itself. But it is to run counter to what has long been a powerful tendency in anthologizing authors from underrepresented groups. Far too often, in our view, such authors (and such groups) are represented exclusively by memoirs and other autobiographical writings, while their analytical or argumentative works are ignored. Here as in other respects we aim to present American literature more fully and fairly than it often has been presented—and to represent Indigenous writers, black writers, and so on more fully and fairly than they have been represented. Readers will find an abundance of autobiographical writings in the pages of this anthology, by writers traditionally underrepresented as well as by canonical writers such as Jacobs and Douglass. But they will also find fiction, poetry, and analytic and argumentative writings by such authors as Lemuel Haynes, Elias Boudinot, Harriet Wilson, George Moses Horton, Maria Stewart, David Walker, Martin R. Delany, and John Rollin Ridge.

AMERICAN LITERATURE AND AMERICAN HISTORY IN THE TWENTY-FIRST CENTURY: This anthology is being published at a time when, in many parts of the U.S., broad-minded approaches to the teaching of American history, culture, and literature are under severe pressure. Most notably, it is argued in numerous states that the teaching of "divisive concepts" (as the phrasing of Oklahoma's legislation puts it) is to be discouraged in public institutions—at the post-secondary level as well as in schools. Students, it is argued, should not be exposed to "overly negative" portrayals of America— by which is often implied portrayals of the nation's checkered history with respect to gender equality, its dispossession and mistreatment of Indigenous peoples, and its long history of racial oppression. Even a cursory glance through the contents of this anthology will be enough to make clear we do not share that view. In these as in other respects, we have made every effort to present American literature in the context of a full and honest presentation of American culture and American history—which, in our view, has to include a full acknowledgment of the central role that settler colonialism, slavery, and racial oppression have played in that history, from the arrival of enslaved people in St. Augustine in 1565 and in Jamestown in 1619 through to our own time. But we do not present only the negative: far from it. Throughout the anthology we present a wide range of the texts that have reflected—and have shaped—the development of American ideals. Yes, we present Crèvecoeur's farmer's reflections on slavery and his jaundiced comments on the American Revolution—but we present too the glowing reflections on the American character that he puts forward in his "What Is an American?" letter. Yes, we provide the background on how the matter of slavery came to be omitted from the Declaration of Independence—but, in presenting Jefferson's original draft as well as the final text, we encourage a full and open discussion of the document that has been foundational in shaping American ideals. Literature that is straightforwardly expressive of the highest of those ideals—from John Winthrop and Roger Williams, to Phillis Wheatley and Canassatego and Benjamin Franklin, and on to Abraham Lincoln, Julia Ward Howe, Walt Whitman, and many others—features prominently in the anthology. But we believe too that many of the high points in American history and literature have been moments of resistance. From Thomas Paine and Absalom Jones to Lemuel Haynes and Judith Sargent Murray, from Tecumseh and William Apess to Lydia Maria Child and Margaret Fuller, from Henry David Thoreau to William Lloyd Garrison, the Grimké sisters, and Sojourner Truth, and on to David Walker, Frederick Douglass, Rebecca Harding Davis, Frances Harper—the list is a long one—some of America's finest literature has come from writers who struggled for justice and, in doing so, placed themselves in eloquent opposition to the tendencies of their time.[1] Authors such as

these are featured prominently throughout the anthology; in this as in other respects, we have striven to take a broad view, and to present American literature—and America—in the round.

COURSE TEXT OPTIONS: Our primary aim has been to provide an anthology of extraordinary quality and extraordinary range for use in American Literature survey courses of the sort that are found in the vast majority of North American colleges and universities; we envisage the two-volume package of volumes A and B as being a popular choice for any course surveying American literature from its beginnings to 1865 (or, as some courses now do, to 1877). The breadth and depth of coverage provided in the hybrid anthology also make it an excellent choice for upper-year courses of various sorts—courses covering narrower periods, thematic courses, and so on. For courses surveying Transatlantic Literature rather than American Literature only, an attractive option may be to create a custom text (either electronically or through Broadview's bound custom coursepack option), bringing together an instructor's preferred readings from this anthology and from *The Broadview Anthology of British Literature*—the format of which is almost identical to that of *The Broadview Anthology of American Literature*. Together, these anthologies offer several thousand pages of material to choose from in assembling your own custom course text. (We offer an easy and intuitive Custom Text Builder, and our Custom Text Administrator welcomes inquiries.)

Even for many teaching a standard American Literature survey course, the Broadview custom text option may be an appealing one. If, for example, you typically build your survey course around a small number of complete works, together with a relatively modest number of poems, short stories, essays, etc., you might bring together the shorter materials in a custom text of 200 pages or so, and then choose a special price package of Broadview editions. (Broadview's American literature editions list now includes more

---

[1]   We give considerably less prominence to the authors who reflect sides of the American character that virtually everyone today finds deeply repugnant—but even these we do not entirely hide from

view. In certain Contexts sections and as part of the anthology's website component readers can find, for example, excerpts from racist "anti-Indian" writings, excerpts from "anti-Tom" novels written in defense of slavery, and so on. Here too, our aim is to further in every way possible students' understanding of the literatures of America, both in the context of today and in their historical context.

than 80 titles, from *The Female American*, Equiano's *Interesting Narrative*, and Paine's *Common Sense* to Wharton's *The Age of Innocence* and Fitzgerald's *The Great Gatsby*.) Editions may be packaged together for a special discount—or, if you decide to choose just one or two editions for use with the anthology, the edition(s) may be packaged together with the anthology for a nominal additional charge.

EDITORIAL PROCEDURES, CONVENTIONS, AND APPARATUS

The in-house set of editorial guidelines for *The Broadview Anthology of American Literature* now runs to over 40 pages, covering everything from conventions for the spacing of marginal notes, to the use of small caps for the abbreviations CE and BCE, to the approach we have adopted to references in author headnotes to name changes. Perhaps the most important core principle in the introductions to the various volumes, in the headnotes for each author, in the introductions in "Contexts" sections, and in annotations throughout the anthology, is to endeavor to provide a sufficient amount of information to enable students to read and interpret these texts, but without making evaluative judgments or imposing particular interpretations. In practice that is all a good deal more challenging than it sounds; it is often extremely difficult to describe why a particular author is considered to be important without using language that verges on the interpretive or the evaluative. But it is a fine line that we have all agreed is worth trying to walk; we hope that readers will find that the anthology achieves an appropriate balance.

INTRODUCTIONS AND AUTHOR HEADNOTES:
Introductory headnotes are provided for each author included in the anthology; each "Contexts" section includes its own substantial introduction; and each volume includes an introduction to the period as a whole. The overview introductions to each volume of the anthology endeavor to provide a sense not only of the broad picture of literary developments in the period, but also of the historical, social, and political background, and of the cultural climate. Readers should be cautioned that, while there is inevitably some overlap between information presented here and information presented in the author headnotes, an effort has been made to avoid such repetition as much as possible; the introduction to each period should thus be read in conjunction with the author headnotes and the introductions to the Contexts sections.

We aim throughout to be factual in the information we provide in author headnotes, and not to direct students' response with a particular evaluative or interpretive emphasis. But at the same time, we aim to engage student interest by making clear the degree to which and the ways in which a particular author's works have provoked a deep response or excited controversy, whether in their own day or in more recent times. Of necessity we provide something by way of conventional biographies of the authors—an overview of each author's life and works. But we strive as well in each case to provide what might be called a biography of the texts themselves: a summary of the reception history for key works, and an indication of why—in their own day, in our era, and in the intervening decades—the works have been considered worthy of attention and engagement (or, in some cases, have been unjustly neglected).

ANNOTATION: It is also often difficult to make judgments as to where it is appropriate to provide an explanatory annotation for a word or phrase. Our policy has been to annotate where we believe that most second-year undergraduates are likely to have difficulty understanding the denotative meaning. (We have made it a practice not to provide notes discussing connotative meanings.) But in practice the vocabularies of undergraduates at any given level may vary enormously, both from institution to institution and within any given college or university class. Where a word might not be known to many students but is not extraordinarily unusual or obscure, we will leave it to students unfamiliar with the word to look up its meaning. In the other direction, we make it a practice to annotate seemingly familiar words where they are being used in a text in ways that many undergraduates may not be familiar with; if a child is described as having grown up in "mean circumstances," we will gloss *mean* as *humble, impoverished*. On the whole, we provide somewhat more annotation than most competitors, and somewhat less interpretation. Again, we hope that readers will find that the anthology has struck an appropriate balance.

SPELLING AND PUNCTUATION: The level of capitalization in many seventeenth-, eighteenth-, and early nineteenth-century texts can be a distraction for students coming for the first time to the literature of these periods—as can the ways in which such texts are often punctuated. Our general policy has been to use modern conventions of capitalization, and to lightly modernize spelling and punctuation, while also providing samples of important texts in the original (and indicating in the margin where the original spelling and punctuation have been retained). Where capitalization and italicization are concerned, we have made an exception in the case of certain authors and texts—Benjamin Franklin's *Autobiography* is a notable example[1]—where spelling and punctuation choices are known (or believed on reliable authority) to represent conscious choice on the part of the author rather than simply reflecting the common practice of the time.

Much as spelling and punctuation in the great majority of texts included in the anthology are lightly modernized, we aim to provide for readers a real sense of the historical development of the language and of print culture. To that end we have included in each volume many examples of texts in their original form—in some cases through the use of pages shown in facsimile, in others by providing short passages in original spelling and punctuation as described above. We have also included a section on the history of the language as part of the introduction to each volume. And throughout the anthology we include materials—visual as well as textual—relating to the history of print culture. While the anthology is intended for English-language courses, we have also made an effort through facsimile pages and facing-column translations to gesture toward the diversity of languages that are encompassed in American literature, including Spanish, French, and Indigenous languages such as Ojibwe and Massachusett.

We of course use modern conventions of American spelling and punctuation in all material newly prepared for the anthology (period introductions, author headnotes, annotations, etc.). We have not, however, "Americanized" all spellings in the texts themselves; texts from earlier periods of course use spellings that we would now categorize as British rather than American, which have been retained. (Instructors who wish to discuss with their students the development of American spelling can thus find in the anthology a wealth of material that is relevant.)

THE ETHICS AND POLITICS OF ANNOTATION, CAPITALIZATION, ETC.: Anthologies of American literature have traditionally allowed many offensive words or phrases (racist, sexist, anti-Semitic, anti-Muslim, anti-gay, etc.) either to pass entirely without comment, or to be glossed with apologist comments that leave the impression that such terms were excusable in the past, and may even be unobjectionable in the present. Most obviously, many anthologies print "the n-word" where it appears in various texts without remarking on its presence; our view is that, where such terms appear, they should be annotated, with a footnote making clear the degree to which such terms are highly offensive—and saying something as well about the history of their use. Derogatory comments about Jews and money and about the supposed cultural inferiority of Indigenous peoples are other examples. *The Broadview Anthology* endeavors in such cases, first of all, not to allow such words and phrases to pass without comment; and second, to gloss without glossing over. A few unacceptable slurs—such as the word "savage"—are unfortunately so omnipresent that we have elected not to gloss them at every usage.

Issues of ethics and politics often arise as well over debated points of present-day usage. Some of these—such as the decision whether or not to use "slave"—involve word choice. Our policy has been to avoid the use of this noun wherever possible; "enslaved people" may be somewhat more wordy than "slaves," but it has the advantage of emphasizing the essential humanity of those being referred to.

Other issues involve capitalization. As is the case with many other issues in the often-fraught history of racial and ethnic terminology, there may here be

---

[1]   For those who may prefer to teach the *Autobiography* with modernized spelling and punctuation, we provide a lightly modernized text in the anthology's website component.

reasonable arguments that point in somewhat different directions. After much discussion, we have decided to capitalize the word "Indigenous" wherever it has been judged an appropriate term to use, but to refer wherever possible to specific groups (Ojibwe, Diné, etc.). We have chosen not to capitalize "black," however (except, of course, where it is capitalized in the literary texts themselves); though many respected media outlets have in recent years made it a policy to capitalize "black," our view is that the capitalization of "black" may be taken to implicitly encourage the highly questionable assumption that a single, monolithic "black" ethnicity or culture exists.

TEXTS: Each author entry concludes with a note on the text(s), addressing issues regarding different versions and source texts. In some cases, we have also used footnotes to clarify one or more textual issues or to indicate what translation has been used. Copyright information for texts and translations that are not in the public domain is provided on the website and within the bound books, in a section listing Permissions Acknowledgments.

We make it a practice to include the date when the work was first made public, whether through publication in print or, in the case of dramatic works, made public through the first performance of the play (or in the case of oratory, when the speech was first delivered). Where that date is known to differ substantially from the date of composition, a note to this effect is included in parentheses.

TIMELINES: The "Texts and Contexts" timelines provide in each volume a convenient parallel reference guide to the dates of literary texts and historical developments.

GLOSSARY: Here we have adopted an integrated approach, including political and religious terms along with literary ones in a convenient general glossary. While we recognize that googling for information of this sort is often the student's first resort (and we recognize too the value of searching the web for the wealth of background reference information available there), we also recognize that information culled from the Internet is often far from reliable; it is our intent, through this glossary, through our introductions and headnotes, and through the wealth of accessible annotation in the anthology, to provide as part of the anthology a reliable core of information in the most convenient and accessible form possible.

MAPS: Also appearing within each of the bound books are a selection of maps specially prepared for this anthology.

ONLINE COMPANION MATERIALS: In addition to the website component of the anthology itself, the main anthology website includes a range of companion materials. "Reading Poetry" provides a concise but comprehensive introduction to the study of poetry; it includes discussions of diction, imagery, poetic figures, and of various poetic forms, as well as offering an introduction to prosody. We provide as well a comprehensive glossary of poetic terms. Also appearing online is a selection of historical maps; these may supplement the maps in the bound book volumes in a variety of interesting ways. Additional companion materials on the anthology website include an interactive timeline and lists of the anthology's contents grouped by theme and author background.

ACKNOWLEDGMENTS

In addition to those whose assistance is acknowledged formally on the contributors' pages following the title page of this anthology, and those who were kind enough to grant permission to reprint copyrighted material (listed in the Permissions Acknowledgments at the back of each volume) the General Editors and all of us in-house at Broadview owe an enormous debt of gratitude to the hundreds of academics who have offered advice and assistance at various stages of this project. In particular, we would like to express our appreciation and our thanks to the following:

Mary Grace Albanese, Binghamton University, State University of New York

Christopher Apap, Oakland University

Stephen Arch, Michigan State University

Marybeth Baggett, Liberty University

Brad Bannon, University of Tennessee, Knoxville

Margarita Barcelo, Metropolitan State University of Denver

Wesley Beal, Lyon College

Phillip Beard, Auburn University

William Bedford Clark, Texas A&M University

Ann Beebe, University of Texas at Tyler

Martin Bickman, University of Colorado, Boulder

John Blair, Texas State University

Anne Boyd Rioux, University of New Orleans

Nicholas Bradley, University of Victoria

Ashlee Brand, Cuyahoga Community College

Vince Brewton, University of North Alabama

Miriam Brown Spiers, Kennesaw State University

Michelle Burnham, Santa Clara University

Sandra Burr, Northern Michigan University

Cari Carpenter, West Virginia University

Vincent Casaregola, St. Louis University

John Casey, University of Illinois, Chicago

Abigail Chandler, University of Massachusetts Lowell

Mary Chapman, University of British Columbia

Schuyler Chapman, Glenville State College

Ben Child, Colgate University

Amanda Claybaugh, Harvard

Jim Coby, Indiana University

Michael Cohen, University of California, Los Angeles

Jeffrey Lamar Coleman, St. Mary's College of Maryland

Melissa Daniels-Rauterkus, University of Southern California

Clark Davis, University of Denver

David Davis, Mercer University

Richard De Prospo, Washington College

Christopher Diller, Berry College

Joseph A. Dimuro, University of California, Los Angeles

Don Dingledine, University of Wisconsin, Oshkosh

Kathleen Donegan, University of California, Berkeley

Virginia Dow, Liberty University

Paul Downes, University of Toronto

J. Michael Duvall, College of Charleston

Amy Earhart, Texas A&M University

S. Max Edelson, University of Virginia

Gregory Eiselein, Kansas State University

Berton Emerson, Whitworth University

Anna Esquivel, Jackson State Community College

Vera Foley, Gustavus Adolphus College

Laura Furlan, University of Massachusetts, Amherst

Brian Gazaille, University of Oregon

Lisa Gordis, Barnard College

Robin Grey, University of Illinois, Chicago

John Griffith, University of Washington

Christopher Hager, Trinity College

Kenneth Haley, Paris Junior College

Faye Halpern, University of Calgary

William Hammersmith, Liberty University

Lawrence Hanley, San Francisco State University

Lucas Hardy, Youngstown State University

Tamara Harvey, George Mason University

Jason Haslam, Dalhousie University

Heather Hathaway, Marquette University

John Hay, University of Las Vegas, Nevada
Desiree Henderson, University of Texas at Arlington
Melvin Hill, University of Tennessee at Martin
Andrew Hoberek, University of Missouri
Michael Hoberman, Fitchburg State University
Larry Howe, Roosevelt University
Zach Hutchins, Colorado State University
Coleman Hutchison, University of Texas at Austin
Gordon Hutner, University of Illinois
Mark Kamrath, University of Central Florida
Amelia Katanski, Kalamazoo College
Pam Kingsbury, University of North Alabama
Dana Kinnison, University of Missouri
Nadine M. Knight, College of the Holy Cross
Andrew Kopec, Purdue University, Fort Wayne
Cynthia Kuhn, Metropolitan State University, Denver
Kimberli Lawson, Brigham Young University
William Lawton, James Madison University
Hellen Lee, California State University, Sacramento
Lisa Logan, University of Central Florida
Laura Lorhan, University of California, Los Angeles
Christopher Love, University of Alabama
David Magill, Longwood University
Joshua Masters, University of West Georgia
Kristin Matthews, Brigham Young University
Barbara McCaskill, University of Georgia
Gabrielle McIntire, Queen's University
Diego Millan, Washington and Lee University
Keith Mitchell, University of Massachusetts, Lowell
Lisa Moody, Southeastern Louisiana University
Heather Moulton, Central Arizona College
Erich Nunn, Auburn University
Nadia Nurhussein, Johns Hopkins University
Jeffrey Ostler, University of Oregon
Keri Overall, Weatherford College
Robert Dale Parker, University of Illinois, Urbana-Champaign
Jason Payton, University of Georgia
KJ Peters, Loyola Marymount University
Arthur Redding, York University
Peter Reed, University of Mississippi
James Riemer, Marshall University
Siân Silyn Roberts, Queens College

Elizabeth Robinson, Tennessee Technological University
Karen Roggenkamp, Texas A&M University-Commerce
Eric Russell, Central Michigan University
Elissa Minor Rust, Portland Community College
Debra Ryals, Pensacola State College
James Salazar, Temple University
Jennifer Schell, University of Alaska, Fairbanks
Sarah Schuetze, University of Wisconsin, Green Bay
Susan Schulten, University of Denver
Ormond Seavey, George Washington University
Jason Shaffer, United States Naval Academy
Cherene Sherrard-Johnson, University of Wisconsin-Madison
Mark Silverberg, Cape Breton University
Scott Simkins, Auburn University
Avery Slater, University of Toronto
Scott Slawinski, Western Michigan University
Angela Sorby, Marquette University
Sunny Stalter-Pace, Auburn University
Nicole Stamant, Agnes Scott College
Jordan Alexander Stein, Fordham University
Carole Lynn Stewart, Brock University
Nancy Sweet, California State University, Sacramento
Brynnar Swenson, Butler University
Matthew Teutsch, Auburn University
Brianna Thompson, Kenyon College
David Thoreen, Assumption University
Michael Thurston, Smith College
Kathryn Walkiewicz, University of California, San Diego
Sarah Wasserman, University of Delaware
Ed White, Tulane University
Natasha Whitton, Southeastern Louisiana University
Caroline Wigginton, University of Mississippi
Maria Windell, University of Colorado, Boulder
Nathan Wolff, Tufts University
Chad Wriglesworth, University of Waterloo
Joan Wylie Hall, University of Mississippi
Hilary Wyss, Trinity College
Elissa Zellinger, Texas Tech University
Michael Ziser, University of California, Davis

AMERICA AND AMERICAN LITERATURE, 1820 TO RECONSTRUCTION

[Overview introductory sections on the following topics appear in the website component of the anthology:

Money and Machines, Capital and Labor
Individualism and Self-Reliance
Religion and Culture, 1820 to Reconstruction
The Civil War and Its Literature
Reconstruction and the Literature of Reconstruction
Language in America, 1820 to Reconstruction

Literary Genres, 1820 to Reconstruction
Poetry
Prose Fiction
Prose Non-fiction
Drama]

CHANGING VIEWS OF AMERICAN LITERATURE

In October 1840, the first issue appeared of what was termed by a British newspaper "an American periodical without a parallel in the history of the world." This was the *Lowell Offering*, "a repository of original articles on various subjects written by factory operatives," specifically, "females employed in the mills."[1] Though this publication survived for only a few years, it seems to have gained a surprisingly wide readership—and certainly it gained extraordinary respect, lauded in dozens of newspapers and magazines on both sides of the Atlantic, including in a review by Charles Dickens. With its mix of stories and poems (including pieces on such highly charged subjects as British oppression of Ireland as well as many on more familiar "poetical" subjects), together with essays on subjects ranging from nature, the arts, aesthetics, and astronomy, to "Time," "Contentment," "Indolence and Industry," and "The Nature of Man," the publication succeeded magnificently in challenging readers' assumptions as to what young working-class women might be capable of.

That challenge to conventional assumptions was made explicit by "A Factory Girl," the pseudonym of an unknown Lowell worker who set out, in the lead article of the *Lowell Offering*'s second issue, to rebut a characterization of female factory employees like herself that had been made by Orestes Brownson, an important figure in New England's intellectual establishment. Brownson had asserted that the phrase "She has worked in a factory, *is sufficient to damn to infamy the most worthy and virtuous girl.*" "A Factory Girl" scathingly refuted Brownson's assertion, thereby demonstrating, in her own words, that "*a factory girl* is not afraid to oppose herself to the *Editor of the Boston Quarterly Review.*" She was not afraid of opposing the influential arbiter of taste Sara Josepha Hale either. In the following issue of the *Lowell Offering* appeared "Gold Watches," in which "A Factory Girl"[2] took issue with Hale's lament that, with even some Lowell working girls having taken to wearing gold watches, all markers of class distinction were in danger of disappearing. In challenging Hale, "A Factory Girl" replied with an essay of strikingly incisive class commentary:

> Those who do not labor for their living have more time for the improvement of their minds, for the cultivation of conversational powers, and graceful manners; if, with all these advantages, they still need richer dress to distinguish them from us, the fault must be their own. ... [The factory girls] see things more as they really are, and not through the false medium which misleads the aristocracy.

The *Lowell Offering* was itself subject to challenging criticisms; some accused it of being, in its eagerness to "show what factory girls had power to do," too upbeat about working-class circumstances, too

---

[1] The city of Lowell, Massachusetts, founded in the 1820s as a planned manufacturing center for textiles, was the first large-scale factory town in the United States and a center of the industrial revolution in America.

[2] Most *Lowell Offering* contributions were anonymous; the most common practice was for authors to be identified by their first names or their initials. It is possible that the pieces by an author identified as "A Factory Girl" were in fact by different authors, but given the similarities in theme, tone, and style, it seems likely that they were written by the same author.

Cover of the May 1845 issue of the *Lowell Offering*.

keen to present "only one side of the question," too reluctant to "expose all the evils, and miseries, and mortifications attendant upon a factory life." But the fact that the *Lowell Offering* was widely read, praised, and reviewed is a testament to the diversity and openness that American literature was capable of in the 1820–Reconstruction period. Even the most partial of lists gives some sense of that range and openness: from Frederick Douglass's *North Star* in Rochester, New York to the *North Star* in Danville, Vermont that reprinted the *Lowell Offering* story "Abby's Year in Lowell"; from the popular prose of Fanny Fern, Bret Harte, and Mark Twain and the popular poetry of Lydia Sigourney and Henry Longfellow to the political writings of David Walker, Angelina Grimké, and Lydia Maria Child; from the sermons of Theodore Parker to the speeches of Abraham Lincoln; from the groundbreaking works of George Copway and John Rollin Ridge to the impassioned poetry of George Moses Horton and Frances Harper; from William Alcott's *Vegetable Diet* to Louisa May Alcott's *Little Women*; from the reformist prose of William Lloyd Garrison

and the reformist poetry of John Greenleaf Whittier to the reactionary prose of William Gilmore Simms; from the poems of the Seminole Wars to the 1867 anthology *Slave Songs of the United States*; from New Englander Richard Henry Dana Jr.'s enormously popular 1840 account of sailing to California and back to Chilean Vicente Pérez Rosales's equally engaging account of the California Gold Rush. Even in the face of the sort of censorship and repression that made *Uncle Tom's Cabin* unavailable in the South and led William Wells Brown to publish *Clotel* in England rather than America, American literature may fairly be said to have undergone an astonishing expansion and diversification in the 1820–Reconstruction period. Driven by an array of technological, economic, demographic, infrastructural, and educational changes, the number and variety of publications, and the speed and volume with which they could be circulated around the country, increased massively. And that in turn enabled many more Americans from all communities and walks of life, including people like the Lowell "Factory Girl," to join the national literary conversation.

In a passage from his 1849 novel *Redburn*, one of the writers who has come to be seen as central to nineteenth-century American literature, Herman Melville, powerfully conveys the expansiveness and diversity of that literature, and of nineteenth-century America as a whole. The passage reflects on America's identity as a nation of immigrants:

> Settled by the people of all nations, all nations may claim [America] for their own. You cannot spill a drop of American blood without spilling the blood of the whole world. Be he Englishman, Frenchman, German, Dane, or Scot; the European who scoffs at an American, calls his own brother *Raca*, and stands in danger of the judgment.[1] We are not a narrow tribe of men[.] ... No: our blood is as the flood of the Amazon, made up of a

---

1   Melville here alludes to Matthew 5.22, part of Jesus's Sermon on the Mount, in which Jesus quotes the Ten Commandments' injunction "Thou shalt not kill" and then continues: "But I say unto you, That whosoever is angry with his brother without a cause shall be in danger of the judgment; and whosoever shall say to his brother, Raca, shall be in danger of the council." "Raca" is the Greek rendering of a word in Aramaic, the language spoken by Jesus, that means "empty-headed" or "foolish."

thousand noble currents all pouring into one. We are not a nation, so much as a world.

Like America as a whole, as Melville describes it here, nineteenth-century American literature, as it took shape through the contributions of writers as different as Melville and "A Factory Girl," could be said to consist of "a thousand noble currents all pouring into one," and in that sense to be "not a nation, so much as a world."

A century later, though, literary scholars had considerably narrowed down their view of nineteenth-century American literature from the breadth and variety of Melville's vision in *Redburn*. By the mid-twentieth century, scholars came to see American literature of the time of *Redburn* and the *Lowell Offering* in exactly the way that *Redburn* rejects in describing America as a whole: as consisting of, or at least exemplified by, "a narrow tribe of men." Within this "narrow tribe" of canonized nineteenth-century authors—most of them white, upper-class men—Melville himself, ironically, was given an integral place, while the likes of the Lowell factory girl, and the many other nineteenth-century writers who made the literature of that period so multifaceted and capacious, were minimized or forgotten altogether. One of the main stories of nineteenth-century American literature is thus the story of how it grew to become a "world" in its own time; how twentieth-century scholars shrank it down to a "narrow tribe"; and how, since the mid-twentieth century, it has expanded again.

The United States in the early and mid-nineteenth century was, to an extent possibly unparalleled by any previous society in history, a nation of readers and writers. Developments in printing technology in the early decades of the century, especially the invention of cast-iron printing presses and steam-powered printing, lowered the production costs of books, newspapers, and periodicals and increased the speed and volume with which they could be published, while new transportation technologies such as the railroad and steamship greatly heightened how far and how fast such publications could be distributed. The nation's lax copyright laws afforded authors, especially international ones, little control over their works after publication, thereby encouraging a "culture of reprinting" that further fed the proliferation of printed material.

Albert Sands Southworth and/or Josiah Johnson Hawes, *Classroom in the Emerson School for Girls*, c. 1850. This school—established in 1823 by George Barrell Emerson, second cousin of Ralph Waldo Emerson—was the most prominent girls' school in Boston.

At the same time, the U.S. was becoming one of the most literate countries in the world. Public schools were rapidly established in the northern states after the Revolution; universal, free, compulsory primary education was introduced in the mid-nineteenth century, and every state had tax-subsidized elementary schools by 1870. These educational measures further raised a literacy rate that in some regions—and among white Americans—already exceeded 90 per cent at the start of the century.[1]

The result of this congruence of developments was a large and growing popular demand for printed material and a burgeoning publishing industry to feed that popular demand. This interconnected expansion of print culture and readership is perhaps best exemplified

---

[1] Literacy rates in the North far outstripped those among white Southerners in the decades leading up to the Civil War. During these same decades, the Southern states, in turn, steadily restricted the already limited ability of enslaved African Americans to learn to read and write.

by the growth, beginning in the 1830s, of the "penny press": a new variety of mass-produced newspaper, priced at one cent rather than the six cents that traditional newspapers cost. Such papers made news media affordable for the first time to the urban working classes and brought about a concomitant change in journalistic practices, as well as in ideas about what "the news" was.[1] However, the country's expanding print culture did not just create more readers; it also created more writers. As Catharine Maria Sedgwick's 1830 short story "Cacoethes Scribendi" satirically illustrates, the proliferation of books, periodicals, newspapers, and other kinds of publication both reflected and fostered the growth of an "irresistible urge to write" (the English translation of the story's Latin title) among numerous Americans, including many people—such as the homebound women of Sedgwick's story—who had previously been discouraged or excluded from authorship.

Alexander Gardner, *Virginia. Newspaper Vendor and Cart in Camp*, 1863. This depiction of a seller of "Philadelphia, N.Y. and Baltimore papers" to soldiers of the U.S. Army during the Civil War illustrates the extent of newspaper distribution and consumption by the 1860s.

---

[1]   Important penny papers included the *Transcript* in Boston (founded in 1830), the *Picayune* in New Orleans (1837), and the *Sun* (1833), *Herald* (1835), *Tribune* (1841), and *Daily Times* (1851) in New York—this last the progenitor of today's *New York Times*.

Sedgwick was part of a significant surge in literary production in the 1820s. This surge yielded the first cohort of major post-Revolutionary American writers, including Sedgwick, James Fenimore Cooper, William Cullen Bryant, Lydia Maria Child, and their older contemporary Washington Irving (who appears in the previous volume of this anthology). All these writers met with great popular success between 1819 and 1829 and quickly became among the most highly regarded and highest-selling authors of their day, a status they retained for much of the nineteenth century. Notably, they achieved this status in Europe, especially Britain, as well as in America. The writers of the 1820s thereby counteracted European prejudices against American literature as crude and derivative and won recognition for it, at least in some quarters, as a body of writing that could stand on par with that of any other country. In 1820, the English critic Sydney Smith had famously mocked American literature with his rhetorical question, "In the four quarters of the globe, who reads an American book?" By 1847, however, an article in the British periodical *Bentley's Miscellany*, which serialized work by both Cooper and Sedgwick, could assert with only some degree of exaggeration that American books—specifically, Cooper's—were read all over the world: "He has been the chosen companion of the prince and the peasant on the borders of the Volga, the Danube, and the Guadalquivir, by the Indus and the Ganges, the Paraguay and the Amazon." While plenty of Europeans would continue to look down on American literature for decades to come (if not longer), the literary generation of the 1820s firmly established the idea, both domestically and internationally, that a distinctive, reputable American literature existed and deserved further cultivation. It could fairly be said of this generation collectively what *Bentley's* said in 1847 of Cooper's *The Spy* (1821): "it gave an extraordinary impulse to literature in the United States, more than anything that had before occurred; it roused the people from their feelings of intellectual dependence."

One of the primary venues whereby this "impulse to literature" was cultivated was the literary society; these sprang up all over the country during this period, especially among the working classes. Typically, members of these societies paid a regular fee, which was used to subscribe jointly to newspapers and journals or to stock a library. Literary societies provided opportunities for their members to teach and learn from one another; to read and discuss a range of literary works; and frequently to compose, share, and even publish their own writing. The *Lowell Offering*, for example, was an outgrowth of the seven "Mutual Self-Improvement Clubs" that the Lowell factory workers had founded by the early 1840s, in which they met to read original compositions to one another. The Lowell literary societies, and the periodical they gave rise to, helped launch the career of at least one significant literary figure: the poet Lucy Larcom, who began working at a Lowell mill at age eleven, first printed her work in the *Offering*, and went on to become one of only three nineteenth-century American female poets to have a volume of her collected poems published in her lifetime.

Literary societies were also an important part of the lives of free African Americans in the North, for whom they played an equally significant intellectual, social, and political role. Black men in Philadelphia formed the Reading Room Society for Men of Colour in 1828, and many other such societies quickly followed in the ensuing years, including societies for black women. Speaking in 1837, James Forten Jr., a leading figure in Philadelphia's black community, summed up the significance literary societies held for African Americans:

> As soon as we engage in any enterprise having for its foundation the mighty principles of mental illumination, we are at once noticed and respected. Thus we see that, whatever tends to disseminate the principles of education, tends to raise us above the tide of popular prejudice; and whatever tends to raise us above the chilling influence of prejudice, must of reason tend to elevate our condition. ... Such, I conceive, our Literary Institutions to have the power of doing.

African American literary societies were often venues not just for "reading, ... examining, ... [and] exercising the great faculty of thinking," in Forten's words, but also for writing. In an 1832 article, the white abolitionist William Lloyd Garrison described the Female Literary Association of Philadelphia, the members of which "assemble[d] every Tuesday evening for the purpose of mutual improvement in moral and literary pursuits": "Nearly all of them write, almost weekly,

original pieces, which are put anonymously into a box, and afterward criticized by a committee." With the members' permission, Garrison printed some of their compositions in his newspaper, the *Liberator*, but other participants in black literary societies published their work on their own initiative. For example, Sarah Forten, a member of the Female Literary Association and the sister of James Forten Jr., regularly published her essays and poetry in the *Liberator* and other such periodicals—albeit under the pen names "Ada" and "Magawisca" (the latter a name she had gleaned from the writing of Catharine Sedgwick).

Even members of groups as comprehensively marginalized or subordinated as Indigenous Americans and enslaved people asserted their ability and right to participate in the country's enormous literary expansion, and furthered that expansion in significant ways. The same vast growth in the pace, volume, and variety of publication that produced the penny papers and the *Lowell Offering* also enabled the founding, in 1828, of the *Cherokee Phoenix*, the first Native American-run newspaper (printed in both English and Cherokee), as well as the printing of the first published Native American autobiography, the Pequot minister and writer William

Alfred R. Waud, *"Zion" School for Colored Children, Charleston, South Carolina*, 1866. The Zion School was one of several schools founded by Northern missionaries for recently emancipated people in Charleston in the wake of the Civil War. The caption that accompanied this illustration when it was published in *Harper's Weekly* in December 1866 noted, "It is a peculiarity of this school that it is entirely under the superintendence of colored teachers."

Apess's *A Son of the Forest* (1829). Enslaved people in the South were legally barred not just from printing their own newspapers or publishing their life stories but from learning to read and write at all, but they still seized whatever opportunities they could to educate themselves and enter the literary sphere. One of the most striking examples of this was the career of George Moses Horton, a self-taught enslaved poet in North Carolina who had three volumes of his work published between 1829 and 1865. Similar aspirations are evident in the "sabbath school" that Frederick Douglass organized before his escape from slavery in 1838, in which he surreptitiously taught "my loved fellow-slaves how to read," and in the intense desire for education that emancipated African Americans demonstrated after the Civil War: what Booker T. Washington described as "a whole race trying to go to school." And outside the circles of formal education and print culture, enslaved people created a rich and powerful oral literature of their own—one that, once it began to see its way into print, swiftly became a major influence on the further development of America's written literature.

Popular understandings of literature throughout the early and mid-nineteenth century were broader and more fluid than the definition of the literary that, in the twentieth century, would shape the formation of the nineteenth-century canon. The folktales, work songs, and spirituals circulated orally by enslaved African Americans highlight the limitations, even the arbitrariness, of a conception of literature tied exclusively to print culture and literacy. Even within the sphere of literate print culture, though, nineteenth-century notions of what counted as literature were malleable and expansive. The supposedly firm boundary between "high culture" and "popular culture" that would become so important to twentieth-century conceptions of the literary was much more porous in the nineteenth century: poetry and popular song shaded into each other, and the self-consciously artistic fiction of such writers as Melville, Nathaniel Hawthorne, and Edgar Allan Poe was shaped by, and even arose out of, mass-market "sensation literature," with its fixation on adventure, sexuality, and violence. Similarly, most nineteenth-century Americans would have recognized no hard-and-fast distinction between, for example, a historical study or devotional tract, on the one hand,

and a novel or poem on the other. Novels and poems could equally be vehicles of moral or historical instruction, and history books and religious tracts could equally be manifestations of linguistic artistry and sources of diversion and pleasure.

In this extensive, diverse, and expanding literary field, with its broad ideas about what constituted "the literary," the authors who would be canonized in the twentieth century were for the most part seen as quite marginal.[1] Poe barely eked out a living from his pen and was known more for his criticism than his creative writing; Melville perplexed and frustrated readers and critics by turning away from the popular travel narratives with which he began his career and sank into obscurity; and Henry David Thoreau and Walt Whitman won notoriety but only a limited readership. Even Hawthorne—whose *The Scarlet Letter* (1850) was an instant success that sold out its initial 2,500-volume print run in just ten days—felt unappreciated in comparison to more popular female writers such as Harriet Beecher Stowe and Maria Susanna Cummins, infamously complaining in 1855 that "America is now given over to a damned mob of scribbling women, and I should have no chance of success while the public taste is occupied with their trash—and should be ashamed of myself if I did succeed." The institutionalization by twentieth-century scholars of Hawthorne's sense of the superior merit of his work, and that of fellow figures like his admirer Melville, has long obscured the extent to which female writers such as Stowe and Cummins actually became among the most celebrated authors of the time, or the fact that African Americans such as Frederick Douglass and William Wells Brown achieved a popularity overseas, especially in Britain, that outstripped that of many white American writers.

The elevation of the likes of Hawthorne and Melville above the likes of Stowe, Douglass, and Brown, and the reconceptualization of nineteenth-century American

---

[1]   The writers of the generation of the 1820s discussed above *were* immediately recognized as major literary figures, and most of them have continued to be recognized as such ever since—although Catharine Sedgwick, for one, was sidelined in the twentieth century and has only been restored to prominence relatively recently.

Among the now canonical mid-century writers, Emily Dickinson is of course a special case, given that she published fewer than a dozen of her poems during her lifetime, all anonymously, and was otherwise read until the 1890s by only a small circle of family and acquaintants.

literature in terms of this narrow, elevated canon, took some time. Anthologies of American literature published in the early twentieth century tended to include a relatively capacious selection of nineteenth-century writers (as long as those writers were white) in a way that approximated the full breadth and variety of the early and mid-nineteenth century literary scene, as well as the breadth of what "the literary" encompassed during that period. During the early twentieth century, however, few American universities required students to take courses in American literature, and its study was widely looked down upon: in 1936, one scholar of American literature called his subject "the orphan child of the curriculum." Making American literature respectable in the eyes of the academic establishment required demonstrating that American literature could be both aesthetically and politically edifying, and in order to do that, scholars narrowed their focus to those works and authors who best matched their own conceptions of what "great literature" was, and of what America was.

The most important contribution to this narrower reconceptualization of nineteenth-century American literature in the mid-twentieth century was the Harvard scholar F.O. Matthiessen's 1941 book *American Renaissance*, which remains one of the single most influential books on American literature ever written. Matthiessen argued that mid-nineteenth-century American literature was best understood in terms of a "renaissance" exemplified by the works of just five writers, all of them white men from New England or New York: Ralph Waldo Emerson, Thoreau, Hawthorne, Whitman, and Melville.[1] According to Matthiessen, these five writers best exemplified "devotion to the possibilities of democracy" and thus "provide[d] a culture commensurate with America's political opportunity" in a way that warranted putting them at the core of the nineteenth-century American canon.[2] This project

of narrowing nineteenth-century American literature down to those figures deemed to have best enshrined, in literary form, a vision of America amenable to the nation's mid-twentieth-century cultural and political establishment also reflected the agenda of the United States government, which strongly promoted the study and teaching of American literature, at home and abroad, as a way of defending and elevating the nation's status during World War II and the Cold War. As a result of these scholarly and governmental efforts, American literature exploded as an academic subject in the 1940s and 50s, but the body of literature studied and taught became much more constricted than it had been earlier in the century. After World War II, for example, it became common practice for survey courses to include only eight writers from the 1820–Reconstruction period: Matthiessen's five plus Poe, Dickinson, and Mark Twain. A strong tendency to concentrate on this authorial canon—expanded slightly with the eventual inclusion of figures such as Douglass—persisted for much of the rest of the twentieth century and lingers into the twenty-first.

Ironically, though, this twentieth-century narrowing-down of nineteenth-century literature was driven, in part, by one of the same forces that also drove the original development of nineteenth-century literature, in all its true expansive diversity: American cultural nationalism. In and through their studies of nineteenth-century literature, mid-twentieth-century scholars such as Matthiessen sought to define a distinctive American national identity and culture. Many nineteenth-century American writers had similar motives. The first half of the nineteenth century was a period in which Americans sought earnestly to assert the distinctiveness and value of their national culture—to create, or demonstrate the existence of, an American literature that would not stand in Europe's shadow and would represent the originality, uniqueness, importance, and greatness that they saw in themselves. As the influential writer, editor, critic, and literary promoter John Neal—whose 1824 essay series on "American Writers" can claim to be the first history of American literature—put it in 1828, numerous Americans felt the need

---

[1]   Matthiessen's conception of the "American Renaissance" was even narrower than this list itself suggests: his exploration of these five writers focused on the works they published in a span of just six years, from 1850 to 1855.

[2]   While *American Renaissance* played a crucial part in this narrowing of the American literary canon, it should also be noted that Matthiessen himself—as a gay man whose fear of persecution for his left-wing political views during the McCarthy era contributed to his death by suicide in 1950—resisted the exclusionary forces at work in

---

American politics and culture during his time and represented some of the people and views those forces sought to exclude.

to announce "another Declaration of Independence, in the great *Republic of Letters*."

Such literary declarations of independence resound across the breadth of early and mid-nineteenth-century American literature—including in most of the examples given so far in this introduction. One of the Lowell "Factory Girl's" most withering critiques of Orestes Brownson was that his disrespect for industrial labor blurred the difference between European and American factory workers and perpetuated aristocratic European attitudes: "we often hear the condition of the factory population of England, and the station which the operatives hold in society there, referred to as descriptive of *our* condition. As well might it be said, as say the *nobility* of England, that *labor itself* is disgraceful, and that all

Portrait of John Neal by Sarah Miriam Peale, 1823. A leading American literary nationalist, Neal called for "faithful representations of native character" in American literature, urging American writers to cultivate the "abundant and hidden sources of fertility … in the northern, as well as the southern Americas." His literary criticism helped launch the careers of John Greenleaf Whittier, Edgar Allan Poe, Henry Wadsworth Longfellow, and Nathaniel Hawthorne.

who work should be consigned to contempt, if not to infamy." Melville's description of immigration and American national character in *Redburn* trumpets America's diverse expansiveness as the basis of the country's difference from the "narrow tribes" of Europe and cautions Europeans against "scoff[ing] at" Americans. Much of the work of the generation of the 1820s was devoted to Americanizing European literary genres, such as the historical novel, and to exploring stories and themes that could be considered distinctively American, such as the history of contact and conflict between Indigenous peoples and European settlers. And black and white writers alike singled out African American literature—in particular, the slave narrative—as the best basis for an American claim to literary independence, in both negative and positive terms: Frederick Douglass wrote of one slave narrative that "America has the melancholy honor of being the sole producer of books such as this," while the white abolitionist Theodore Parker posited that, because slave narratives best represented the urge for freedom at the core of American identity, "all the original romance of Americans is in them, not in the white man's novel." These writers, like most of their fellow Americans, would have rejected the idea that American literature could or should be completely *separate* from the European literary tradition: Douglass, for one, made a point, in the newspapers he edited, of printing works by both black and white American writers alongside the work of British authors. But an urge to establish American equality and distinctiveness within that ongoing conversation with European literature lay at the core of much nineteenth-century American literary creation, forming one of the unifying threads amid that literature's multifarious diversity.

This diversity began to be recovered in the latter decades of the twentieth century. Indeed, "recovery" could serve as the characteristic keyword for the prevailing scholarly approach to nineteenth-century literature in the late twentieth century and into the twenty-first, in the same way that "narrowing" can serve as a keyword for the prevailing mid-twentieth-century approach. Increasingly, as dominant assumptions about American history, culture, and identity came to be challenged, scholars began as well to challenge the established canon of nineteenth-century literature and to recover the writers and works that the process of canon-formation had marginalized, neglected, or forgotten. This recovery effort started with the works of white women, propelled by the rise of feminist theory in the 1970s and 80s; as post-colonial theory and queer theory developed in the ensuing decades, African American, Indigenous, and queer writing (including queer elements in canonical works) began to be recovered as well. At the same time, scholars went "beneath the American Renaissance"—to quote the title of one important 1988 study—to uncover the ways in which the canonical authors of the early and mid-nineteenth century were influenced by the vast array of other writing that existed around them. Scholarship on print culture and book history highlighted the diversity of that vast array of nineteenth-century writing and the speed with which it was changing during the period; more recently, digitization and related methods have made that huge nineteenth-century archive more accessible, thereby further facilitating recovery; and "hemispheric" approaches have recovered the suppressed political, cultural, and literary ties between the United States and the rest of the Americas, thereby prompting fundamental redefinition of what "American" literature is. All these developments, and more, continue to yield new views of nineteenth-century American literature, expanding and sharpening our picture of that literature's expansive "world."

RACE, SLAVERY, AND AMERICA, 1820–1860[1]

By 1820, settler colonists had been enslaving Africans and their descendants in what is now the United States for well over two hundred years.[2] Over that time chattel slavery and modern racism had developed together and become mutually reinforcing: white people enslaved black people because most white people viewed black people as inferior, and most white people viewed black people as inferior in part because most black people were enslaved. This connection between slavery and racism strengthened during the first half of the nineteenth century. In 1787, Thomas Jefferson, in his *Notes on the State of Virginia*, hedged his assertion that "the blacks … are inferior to the whites in the endowments both of body and mind," advancing this thought as "a suspicion only"; like many of America's founders, he also anticipated that slavery would come to a gradual end. By the 1850s, racist ideas had become more dogmatic and proslavery voices less apologetic—not just in the South but in the North as well. In 1852, for example, New York *Herald* publisher James Gordon Bennett proclaimed that "the negro is and always will be, to the end of time, inferior to the white race, and, therefore, doomed to subjection,"[3] while in 1854 the leading antislavery activist William Lloyd Garrison reported that, in "justification of slaveholding," a dozen reasons "are popularly urged in all parts of the country," the most common being simply that "the victims are black" and that they thereby "belong to an inferior race."

As these interconnected ideas about race and slavery became more deep-seated and pervasive in the proslavery camp, so too did opposition to them grow. "No compromise with Slavery!" was the ringing call of Garrison and other abolitionists; "Liberty for each, for all, forever!" The battle-lines, then, were clear. Yet within each camp, and between the two, a wide variety of complex and sometimes contradictory views about race and slavery continued to proliferate.

When Jefferson drafted the Declaration of Independence, the northern as well as the southern colonies all still enslaved black people. The self-proclaimed Vermont Republic abolished slavery outright in 1777, and the rest of the Northern states had by 1804 adopted measures to end slavery, though most states implemented abolition gradually (in some cases, *very* gradually). Slavery was also forbidden in the Northwest Territory—the recently-settled area between the Appalachian Mountains, the Great Lakes, and the Ohio

---

[1]   Please note that a "Contexts" section on the topic "Slavery and Abolition" appears in the body of this volume.

[2]   The first recorded Africans to be enslaved in the Thirteen Colonies arrived at Jamestown, Virginia, in 1619. The enslavement of Africans in the Spanish colonies founded in present-day South Carolina and Florida had begun much earlier; Spanish settler colonists brought enslaved people to the short-lived colony of San Miguel de Gualdape (at Winyah Bay, South Carolina) in 1526, where these enslaved Africans staged the first known slave rebellion in what would become the continental United States.

[3]   The context is interesting: Bennett was drawing a parallel between what he saw as the permanently inferior status of women (on account purely of their biological sex) and what he saw as the permanently inferior status of black people to "the white race." The woman is happier in a state of subjection "than she would be in any other condition," he concluded, "because it is the law of her nature."

and Mississippi Rivers—and in the new states created from it. In the South, by contrast, economic and technological developments reinforced slavery's hold. The success in the Carolinas of wetlands systems of cultivating rice (the know-how for which had been brought from Africa by enslaved workers) was making Carolina plantation owners wealthier and wealthier. The invention of the cotton engine (or "cotton gin") in 1793 facilitated the production of cotton fiber for textiles on an industrial scale—but the cotton mills required an ever-larger supply of cotton, picked by hand by an ever-growing population of enslaved people in an ever-expanding area across the "Deep South." And (in territory that would before long become part of the United States) the introduction into Louisiana in 1795 of the technology for sugar granulation led to tremendous growth of sugar plantations, whose owners likewise relied on a large enslaved workforce. (Especially large numbers of enslaved workers were required to support the Louisiana sugar industry, because the horrendous conditions the workers were forced to endure led to extraordinarily high death rates.) The growth of the cotton and sugar industries spread slavery westward from its original base on the Atlantic seaboard in Virginia, Georgia, and the Carolinas, into Alabama, Mississippi, and Louisiana in particular.[1]

At first, the crucial divergence between Northern "free states" and Southern "slave states" (as the states in which slavery was outlawed and those in which it was permitted were respectively termed) was accompanied by relatively little national conversation about slavery itself. In the words of historian John Jay Chapman, the issue of slavery in the late eighteenth and early nineteenth centuries was for the white majority "a sleeping serpent"—an issue that "was always in everyone's *mind*" but "not always on his tongue." The ban on slavery in the Northwest Territory had been passed in 1787 without much controversy, and twenty years later Congress outlawed the international slave trade as soon

as it was constitutionally permitted to do so,[2] also with little controversy.[3] The addition of new states to the union similarly took place in an uncontentious, carefully evenhanded way, in free state–slave state pairs, so as to preserve the overall balance of power between North and South.

The "sleeping serpent" was loudly roused during the 1818–1820 debate over the proposed entry of Missouri into the union as a slave state. Missouri had been created out of federal territory, as opposed to land previously claimed by existing states; however, unlike the Northwest Territory, Congress had not made any ruling on slavery's legality in the territory acquired in the 1803 Louisiana Purchase, including Missouri.[4] Missouri's admission to the union thus became an important and divisive test case of the federal government's ability to regulate slavery's expansion into new states. Northerners generally wished to limit the expansion of slavery westwards and thus favored a broad interpretation of the government's authority to do so, whereas white Southerners generally supported a narrow interpretation. The debate was resolved by the 1820 Missouri Compromise, which balanced Missouri's admission as a slave state with that of Maine as a free state and

---

[1]   In 1860 the United States cotton crop was valued at $217,000,000, the sugar cane crop at $39,000,000; the value of the rice crop ($3,200,000), however, had grown by only a million dollars since 1800. By comparison, the leading crops in the North were wheat (valued in 1860 at $151,000,000) and corn (valued in 1860 at $69,000,000).

[2]   The question of whether and how the U.S. Constitution would deal with the slave trade and—more centrally—with slavery itself was the most contentious issue at the 1787 constitutional convention. The compromises that resulted from these debates included the lack of any specific constitutional mention of slavery as such; the inclusion of a provision permitting Congress to ban the importation of enslaved people into the country after an interval of twenty years; the adoption of a so-called "fugitive slave clause" mandating the return of people "held to service or labor" who escaped into another state; and the infamous "Three Fifths Compromise" that based congressional representation on "the whole Number of free Persons" in each state plus "three fifths of all other Persons"—i.e., of enslaved people. This "representation" of enslaved people did not allow them any political voice, but it gave slave states, and thus enslavers, far more seats and influence in the federal government than they would otherwise have had.

[3]   In Congress, the ban was promoted by Thomas Jefferson and had substantial support from other white Southerners—especially in Virginia, where the economy was transitioning from a tobacco economy to one based on the cultivation of wheat and other crops that required less labor to grow, as well as on profits from the internal slave trade (the sale of "surplus" enslaved people to markets in the Deep South).

[4]   The future state of Louisiana itself, in which slavery was well-established by 1803, was an exception.

The ongoing efforts by enslaved people themselves to resist their bondage also became more prominent in the post-1820 political environment. News of the debate about Missouri's admission—which seemed to indicate to many people in the South, black as well as white, that slavery itself was under threat—may have helped inspire the planned revolt of enslaved people in Charleston, South Carolina, supposedly organized by the freed black man Denmark Vesey, that was preemptively quashed by white authorities in 1822.[1] In 1831 Nat Turner, an enslaved preacher in Southampton County, Virginia, led a revolt by around 70 enslaved people. He believed that the right time to rise up had now come: as he (reportedly) put it, "the great day of judgment" was at hand and the time was "fast approaching when the first should be last and the last should be first."

Turner's rebellion was bloodily suppressed, with terrified and vengeful white mobs arbitrarily murdering large numbers of black people in Virginia and throughout the South, and in its wake the slave states intensified efforts to regulate enslaved people and stamp out potential resistance—for example, by forbidding enslaved people from learning to read and write. News of Turner's rebellion circulated widely, however, and later uprisings by enslaved people on the slave ships *Amistad* in 1839 and *Creole* in 1841 were more successful. Both of these later uprisings resulted in high-profile court cases. In the *Amistad* case, Northern abolitionists argued before the U.S. Supreme Court on behalf of the enslaved people who had rebelled and taken over the ship—and won their case.

The "Underground Railroad" that developed in the 1840s and grew considerably in the 1850s was a much broader effort to help enslaved people win their freedom. This was an informal but extensive network of secret routes, safe houses, and personal connections within and between local groups (made up both of free blacks and of white abolitionists) that in one way or another helped thousands of enslaved people—according to one estimate, as many as 100,000—to escape to the free states, to Canada, or, in some cases, to Mexico.

As antislavery agitation in the North intensified, so too did Southern enslavers' insistence on slavery's necessity and value. Slavery became ever more crucial to the Southern economy; by the time the Civil War began, it has been estimated that over twenty percent of private wealth in the U.S. was in the form of enslaved people. In the first decades of the nineteenth century, most enslavers had still tended to characterize slavery in the way that Jefferson had done in 1787: as a necessary evil which they were reluctantly obliged to maintain, at least for the time being. But by the 1830s enslavers were increasingly praising slavery as altruistic, civilizing, and altogether beneficial. This so-called "positive good" depiction of slavery began to circulate around the time of the Missouri Compromise. It was expanded upon in the 1830s by Southern politicians such as John C. Calhoun, who became the most influential proponent of the view that (as he expressed it in an 1837 speech)

> in the present state of civilization, where two races of different origin, and distinguished by colour, and other physical differences, as well as intellectual, are brought together, the relation now existing in the slaveholding states between the two [races] is, instead of an evil, a good—a positive good.

Enslavers such as Calhoun continued to propound such views of slavery, in ever-more-hyperbolic terms, down to the Civil War, thereby further widening the gulf between them and their Northern antislavery opponents.

The vehemence of the rhetoric of "free states" versus "slave states," which proliferated at the time and has remained common ever since, should not be allowed to obscure the differences that existed within these regions—or the fact that the divide between them was in some respects a good deal blurrier than the rhetoric suggests. The stereotype of the antebellum white Southern family is that of a rich plantation owner with dozens or even hundreds of enslaved workers. Such families did exist, and the men who headed them wielded enormous power over the entire South

---

[1] Recently, some historians have proposed that the Missouri Compromise and its aftermath inspired the Vesey "conspiracy" in a different way: namely, that the anxiety about the survival of slavery that the compromise prompted in white enslavers drove them to concoct evidence of an intended revolt by enslaved people that did not actually exist, so as to give them an excuse for clamping down on enslaved African Americans and thus reasserting their hegemony.

and indeed the entire nation. Only a small minority of Southern white families fit that description, however. Even in 1860, when the population of enslaved people had reached a high of four million (one-third of the overall Southern population of twelve million), only about a quarter of free families in the slave states owned enslaved people, and most of those who did own enslaved people owned fewer than five.[1] The social division between the enslaving class, especially the large enslavers, and the so-called "poor whites" was and would remain a significant factor in Southern politics, intensifying but also complicating the fundamental racial divide between free whites and enslaved blacks.

An equally important distinction existed between more northerly slave states such as Kentucky, Virginia, and Maryland—the so-called "Upper South"—and the "Deep South," consisting of South Carolina, Georgia, Alabama, Mississippi, Louisiana, Florida, and Texas. Cotton cultivation, and that of other large-scale plantation crops such as sugar, indigo, and rice, flourished in the Deep South but, by the 1820s, scarcely existed in the Upper South, where environmental conditions for it were unsuitable (and where, in many cases, the soil had been exhausted by up to two centuries of intensive plantation agriculture). As a result, the economy of the Upper South came to rely increasingly on the sale of enslaved people born there to the large, labor-intensive plantations of the Deep South. Because the condition and treatment of enslaved people on such Deep Southern plantations tended to be even worse, and because sellers and traders of enslaved people frequently broke up the families of the people they dealt in, being "sold south"—or "sold down the river," in reference to the Mississippi—became a fate that enslaved people in the Upper South greatly feared for themselves and their loved ones. Nearly one million African Americans, however, were forced to endure it. Meanwhile, the economic distinction between Upper South and Deep South took on increasing political significance. It is telling that, while all seven states of the Deep South seceded in the winter of 1860–61, four

of the Upper South states (Virginia, North Carolina, Tennessee, and Arkansas) did not join them until several months later, and the other four (Missouri, Kentucky, Maryland, and Delaware) never did secede.[2]

The North, for its part, had its own important regional differentiations. The Puritan and Quaker traditions of New England and Pennsylvania lent strength to abolitionism in those states, and abolitionist sentiment was strong as well in parts of the former Northwest Territory that had been settled largely by New Englanders. Other areas of Ohio, Indiana, and

Timothy H. O'Sullivan, *Five generations on Smith's Plantation, Beaufort, South Carolina*, 1862. O'Sullivan took this photograph of an African American family whose members had been enslaved on the plantation of J.J. Smith, on one of the Sea Islands off the coast of South Carolina, shortly after the U.S. Army occupied the area early in the Civil War, liberating its enslaved population.

---

[1] These statistics should be qualified in two ways. First, many white farm families who could not afford ownership rented enslaved people at certain times of the year. Second, many white men who neither owned nor rented enslaved people seem nevertheless to have had no objection to the institution of slavery—with many aspiring to become enslavers themselves.

[2] Substantial popular opinion against secession also persisted even in parts of the Upper South states that did secede—for example, in eastern Tennessee and northwestern Virginia (which, when Virginia seceded, promptly seceded from Virginia, becoming the new state of West Virginia). These areas tended to have particularly low numbers of enslaved people and enslavers.

Illinois, however, had been settled by Southerners, and popular sentiment in those areas, as well as local laws, remained friendly to slavery. Much of the North, including New England, also retained a strong economic interest in slavery: enslaved labor provided cotton for northern textile mills such as those of Lowell, Massachusetts, while the banking, shipping, and manufacturing sectors of New York City—far and away the North's, and the nation's, biggest city—were all closely linked to slavery. An anonymous black member of the Female Literary Association of Philadelphia, writing in the 25 August 1832 issue of *The Liberator* under the pen name "Bera," emphasized these connections when she reminded "residents in the non-slaveholding states" who "consume[d] the produce of slave labor" that they too were implicated in slavery's crimes: "every citizen of the United States who withholds any exertion [against slavery that is] in his power to make," she insisted, "is in reality a kidnapper, a slave-trader, and a slaveholder."

It should be pointed out as well that various forms of involuntary servitude, including outright slavery, persisted even in the "free states." Indenture lingered as a labor arrangement well into the nineteenth century, and—as works by black Northerners such as Austin Reed's *Life and Adventures of a Haunted Convict* (c. 1858) and Harriet Wilson's *Our Nig* (1859) attest—it was frequently racialized and was in some cases virtually indistinguishable from slavery. Penal servitude (also documented in Austin Reed's remarkable memoir), which expanded significantly in the nineteenth century, could also in practice be very similar to slavery. And it should not be forgotten that the gradualism of the abolition laws passed by most Northern states meant that some African Americans remained enslaved there for decades after the legislation had been passed. New Jersey, the final Northern state to adopt an abolition measure, began a process of gradual emancipation in 1804, but the last enslaved people in the state were not freed until 1865, when the Thirteenth Amendment abolished slavery nationwide.

Above all, racism seems to have been just as pervasive among white Northerners as it was among white Southerners; indeed, some observers found white Northerners to be even more virulent in their racism, or at least more outspoken. The French traveler Alexis de Tocqueville, for instance, wrote in the wake of his 1831–32 visit to the United States, "The prejudice of race appears to be stronger in the states that have abolished slavery than those where it still exists." Racial prejudice shaped and was reflected by such popular cultural institutions in the North as blackface minstrelsy, as well as by laws such as Pennsylvania's disenfranchisement in 1838 of its black male population (the wealthier among whom, at least, had previously been able to vote). The decades between 1820 and 1860 also saw specific white Northern communities, including working-class men (both native-born and immigrants) and middle-class women, become more strongly invested in their whiteness. For members of these segments of the population—both of which were relatively disempowered or marginalized, albeit in different ways—emphasizing their whiteness provided a way of claiming empowerment and privilege by differentiating themselves from even more disempowered or marginalized non-white people. Whiteness offered a particularly important path to acceptance and empowerment for Irish immigrants—targets of both religious and racialized prejudice during this period. The views expressed in an 1852 article in the *Buffalo Morning Express* on the subject of immigration were widely shared among native-born white Americans:

> The Germans show their Teutonic blood by becoming land holders as soon as they settle among us. This is a remarkably good feature, as it leads to permanent location, stability of industry, and a thrifty method of living. The Irish lack this disposition, much to their detriment.

Over the course of the nineteenth century the Irish slowly but steadily became more accepted by the white establishment, in part by espousing antiblack racism and supporting slavery.[1]

---

1   Habits of racial classification in the nineteenth century were (and are) often confusing. Though many used the word "race" when referring to perceived national or ethnic characteristics (e.g., "Anglo-Saxon race," "Teutonic race," "Irish race"), all these groups were usually understood to be part of the wider "white race"—and certainly they were classed as such in the census. The Irish were by far the largest group of immigrants in the first half of the nineteenth century. The 1850 census, for instance, reported the following totals for "citizens of foreign birth": Ireland 961,719; Germany 573,225; England 278,675; British America 147,700; Scotland 70,550.

Given the obstacles, it is remarkable how many African Americans achieved great success during the 1820–Reconstruction period. Pictured on the right is Frances Ellen Watkins Harper; employed as a seamstress and domestic worker when in her teens, she published her first book at around the age of 20, and in 1854 became the first black woman to be hired by an antislavery society as a lecturer, eventually becoming a distinguished writer and campaigner for gender equality and racial equality (see her author entry in the body of this volume). Pictured on the left is Mifflin Wistar Gibbs, a Philadelphian who worked first as a carpenter, became a leading figure in the antislavery movement, moved to San Francisco during the 1849 Gold Rush, moved to Canada in 1858 in the face of discriminatory laws and became the first black person elected to public office in British Columbia before moving back to the U.S., where he settled in Arkansas, became an attorney and, in 1873, the first black judge elected in the U.S. His final public post was as American Consul in Madagascar.

Racial prejudice among white Northerners not infrequently prompted violent opposition to the abolitionist movement. William Lloyd Garrison was nearly lynched by a Boston mob in 1835, and two years later another high-profile antislavery activist, Elijah P. Lovejoy, was murdered by proslavery citizens of Alton, Illinois. Conversely, even some abolitionists or abolitionist sympathizers remained hostile to the notion that black people—or Indigenous Americans—could be accorded equal status. The British phrenologist[1] George Combe, for example, who visited the U.S. in 1838–39, described Native Americans and African Americans in the following terms in 1842: "The one is like the wolf or the fox, the other like the dog. In both

the brain is inferior in size, particularly in the moral and intellectual regions, to that of the Anglo-Saxon race, and hence the foundation of the natural superiority of the latter over both." Yet Combe was repulsed by slavery; he wrote of the enslaved people from the *Amistad* that he found it "impossible to look without horror and indignation on these young and unoffending men and children deprived of their liberty, reduced to slavery, and converted into mere 'property,' by *Christians*."

A combination of dislike for slavery and racial prejudice was also widespread in the colonization movement, which sought to emancipate enslaved black people and then resettle them out of the country, primarily to Liberia in West Africa. Represented in particular by the American Colonization Society, an organization founded in 1816 by an uneasy alliance of Northern abolitionists and Southern enslavers, colonization was overwhelmingly opposed by

---

[1]   Phrenology was a pseudoscience, widely popular throughout the nineteenth century, that claimed to be able to identify inherent differences in the character and capacities both of different individuals and different races from the shape of human skulls; it contributed greatly to the growth of "scientific" racism during this period.

African Americans but long remained popular with white Americans; Abraham Lincoln backed it as late as 1862 (and even in the preliminary version of his Emancipation Proclamation). Near the end of her 1859 autobiographical novel *Our Nig*, the black New Englander Harriet Wilson offered a withering commentary on such "professed abolitionists, who didn't want slaves at the South, nor [black people] in their own houses, North."

As hostile as many white Northerners thus were to African American equality and even to the existence of free African Americans in the United States, and as comfortable as many of them were with enslaving black people, opposition to Southern slavery continued to rise in the North, if often for reasons that had little to do with the sufferings or aspirations of enslaved people themselves. To many in the North, the slaveholding South constituted a threatening "Slave Power": the quasi-aristocratic social order in the slave states made the South fundamentally undemocratic, and the economic importance of "King Cotton," together with the extra sway in the federal government the South held as a result of the Constitution's "Three Fifths Clause" (allotting disproportionate representation to slave states), made Northerners fear that Southern slavery would ultimately destroy democracy in the nation as a whole. These fears particularly motivated Northern opposition to slavery's expansion—an issue that came to the fore again in the 1840s in response to the massive territorial acquisitions the U.S. made in that decade, especially from Mexico. By the 1840s, the question of slavery—and particularly that of its expansion—was causing the country's existing two-party political system to break down; in the North, antislavery members of both major political parties, the Whigs and Democrats, formed in 1848 the Free Soil Party, dedicated to keeping slavery out of the new western territories. Bitter debate ensued between Free Soil Northerners and Southern enslavers committed to the institution's expansion, in the course of which some Southern extremists began seriously to advocate secession.[1]

This renewed debate resulted in a new compromise, the Compromise of 1850, which admitted California as a free state (but required it to send one proslavery and one antislavery senator to Congress so as to preserve the free state–slave state balance of power in the Senate); empowered the inhabitants of other western territories to decide for themselves whether or not slavery would be permitted there; banned the slave trade in the District of Columbia; and—most controversially—implemented a new, much more draconian Fugitive Slave Act. By effectively requiring all citizens to assist in the capture and return of escapees from slavery, the 1850 Fugitive Slave Act inflamed popular opinion in the North and insured that, the compromise notwithstanding, the national divide regarding slavery would only deepen further in the ensuing decade.

The key signposts of this deepening divide can be briefly enumerated. In 1852, Harriet Beecher Stowe's antislavery novel *Uncle Tom's Cabin* became an enormous bestseller, strengthening opposition to slavery in the North and prompting proslavery writers to pen numerous would-be rebuttals. In 1854, the Kansas–Nebraska Act gave the settlers of those territories the

Eastman Johnson, *A Ride for Liberty—The Fugitive Slaves*, 1862. Johnson (1824–1906), an artist who had acquired a national reputation by the late 1850s, created three versions of this painting, which he based on a scene he claimed to have witnessed firsthand near Manassas, Virginia, during the Civil War.

---

[1] Seceding from the union was not, however, a course of action contemplated only in the slave states: some abolitionists supported Northern secession from the United States under the slogan "No Union with Slaveholders," which William Lloyd Garrison added to the masthead of *The Liberator*.

authority to vote for or against the existence of slavery there, resulting in years of bloodshed between pro- and antislavery factions in Kansas—a mini-civil war that has come to be called "Bleeding Kansas." In 1857, the Supreme Court's decision in *Dred Scott v. Sandford* declared that African Americans were not U.S. citizens under the Constitution, that the Missouri Compromise was unconstitutional, and that the federal government had no ability to restrict the expansion of slavery at all. In 1859, John Brown, an abolitionist who had fought in Kansas, mounted an armed raid on Harpers Ferry, Virginia, in an attempt to galvanize a mass resistance movement by enslaved people throughout the South; the failed raid, and Brown's subsequent trial and execution by the state of Virginia, polarized the country even more. And in 1860, the presidential election was won by Abraham Lincoln, the candidate of the new Republican Party (into which the Free Soil Party had evolved), who ran on a platform opposed to slavery's further expansion and who did not even appear on the ballot in slave states. Lincoln's election convinced the states of the Deep South that slavery's continued existence was at stake; even before Lincoln had taken office, they began to secede. Lincoln mobilized federal troops to suppress their rebellion, and four other slave states joined them, thus bringing on the Civil War.

By the time the war began, the great national debate about race and slavery that precipitated it had taken some participants to startling extremes. The Virginian social theorist George Fitzhugh, for example, argued that slavery was simply the best way of organizing labor for all people, white as well as black: he contended that Northern industrial workers would be better off enslaved outright than in their current condition of supposed "wage slavery" and called it "a libel on white men to say they are unfit for slavery." Other white commentators in both halves of the country had taken to racializing the country's division itself, by questioning whether the white inhabitants of the country's other half were, in fact, truly "white." A January 1860 article entitled "The Basis of Northern Hostility to the South" published in *De Bow's Review*, a New Orleans periodical, asserted that, in comparison to white Northerners, their Southern counterparts were a superior "race of the pure Anglo-Saxon blood"; another 1860 article in the *Southern Literary Messenger* similarly claimed that white Northerners belonged to a "branch of the human family" that had "acquired differences so marked as almost to constitute them a 'permanent variety' in the classification of Race." Conversely, the English artist Barbara Bodichon, who visited the South in 1857–58, declared that Southern enslavement of African Americans had deracinated Southern whites: "There is a recklessness and carelessness about these Southerners which I did not think the Anglo-Saxon race could attain under any circumstances." Such opinions should not be taken as broadly representative of popular feeling in either the North or the South, but they are a telling measure of how profoundly divisive slavery had become.

As the Civil War progressed, many long-held views began to be altered—not least of all those of Lincoln. Over the course of the war, the battle on the Union side was not only against the secessionist states but also—in part at least—against prejudice in the North. And it was fought within the hearts and minds of individuals as well as in society as a whole. When in 1863 Frederick Douglass petitioned the President to provide equal wages and equal treatment for black troops fighting in the federal army, Lincoln equivocated (according to Douglass's account),

> saying that the employment of colored troops at all was a great gain to the colored people; that the measure could not have been successfully adopted at the beginning of the war; that the wisdom of making colored men soldiers was still doubted; that their enlistment was a serious offense to popular prejudice.

By war's end Lincoln (and many others) had come round on this point, as he had come round on the question of "recolonization" and on other issues; black troops were finally receiving equal wages and equal rations, and with the Thirteenth Amendment of 1865, slavery was finally brought to an end. But "popular prejudice" against people of color would continue to plague America—and to distance it from the realization of its ideals.

EXPANSION, EXPULSION, AND "MANIFEST DESTINY"[1]

From the very start of their colonization of the Americas, Europeans conceived of that colonization as a providential process and used such conceptions to legitimize their dispossession of the Americas' Indigenous inhabitants. Such ideas took root in the thirteen colonies and became integral to the identity of the new nation formed from those colonies, which in the eyes of many of its citizens seemed "destined by Divine Providence"—as future president John Quincy Adams put it in an 1811 letter to his father, former president John Adams—to encompass "the whole continent of North America." Adams's claim reflected the way in which his young country had in fact been expanding energetically since its inception: in the first four decades of its existence, the United States began colonizing the vast territories between the Appalachian Mountains and the Mississippi River, crushing Indigenous resistance there in the Northwest Indian War (1785–95), Tecumseh's War (1810–13), and the Creek War (1813–14); purchased from France the even vaster Louisiana Territory west of the Mississippi in 1803; negotiated joint occupation, with the British-chartered Hudson's Bay Company, of the Oregon Country on the Pacific coast in 1818;[2] and obtained Florida by treaty with Spain in 1819.

Beginning in the 1820s, the westward push of the U.S.'s territory and population became more formalized, more concerted, and more intense than ever before—as did the expulsion, subordination, or outright destruction of the communities that resisted U.S. expansion or simply stood in its way, be they Native Americans or descendants of other European colonial empires. This accelerated expansionism was driven by the same fundamental dynamics that had propelled settler colonialism in North America from its beginning: the ready availability of abundant and therefore cheap land, which white colonists—disregarding the

Indigenous peoples already occupying it—believed to be theirs for the taking, and the perception that settling such land could provide a fresh start, especially to those who lacked economic opportunities in their place of origin.[3] Contrary to the claims of its propagandists at the time, however, American expansion, and the horrendous cruelties it entailed for those who stood in its way, were neither destined nor inevitable. Mid-century expansionism emerged in tandem with "Jacksonian democracy"—the populist political movement spearheaded by Andrew Jackson, who rose from relatively humble origins to serve two terms as President, from 1829 to 1837. Jackson championed the "common man" against what he characterized as a political and economic establishment dominated by aristocratic elites. His administration encouraged intensified migration westward, promising rapid access to cheap land for all migrants (in contrast to the more measured pace of settlement—in which public land would be sold at a price high enough to cover the federal government's costs—that was favored by Jackson's opponents).

Jackson's pro-expansionary policy gained additional strength after the financial crisis known as the Panic of 1837. During the economic depression that followed, members of Jackson's Democratic Party advocated westward migration, and the territorial annexation that would facilitate it, as a "safety-valve" for the labor unrest and class conflict they feared were brewing among the afflicted working classes in the industrializing Northeast. This supposed interest of the industrial North in westward expansion paralleled the longstanding desire of slaveholders in the South to extend slavery to new territories—something that Southern enslavers deemed necessary for the survival of their plantation economy (which quickly exhausted the soil and thus required the regular acquisition of fertile new land). Mississippi senator Albert G. Brown epitomized such

---

[1]   Please note that a "Contexts" section on this topic appears in the body of this volume.

[2]   This was a territory much larger than present-day Oregon; it included all of what are now the states of Washington, Oregon, and Idaho, together with parts of present-day Montana and Wyoming, and substantial portions of what is now the Canadian province of British Columbia. The British referred to the territory (which remained jointly occupied until 1846) as the Columbia District.

[3]   The myth of western settlement as offering endless opportunity for poor, landless people to become self-sufficient proprietors did not always match its reality. Of the 38 million acres of recently colonized public lands that were sold between 1835 and 1837, for example, 29 million ended up in the hands of real estate speculators rather than independent farmers. And according to one 1846 observer in the recently settled state of Indiana, one-third of that state's voters were "tenants or day laborers or young men who have acquired no property." Newly colonized territory in the South, meanwhile, came under the grip of the most inequitable and disempowering economic system of all: plantation slavery.

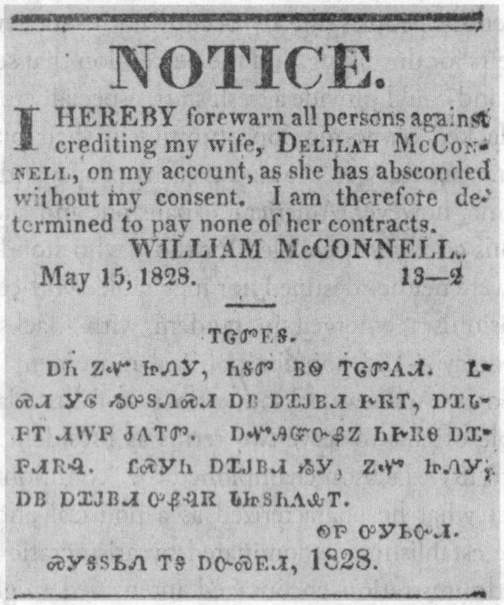

NOTICE.

I HEREBY forewarn all persons against crediting my wife, DELILAH McCONNELL, on my account, as she has absconded without my consent. I am therefore determined to pay none of her contracts.
WILLIAM McCONNELL.
May 15, 1828.   13—4

TGⱯFES.

DᏋ Z·Ꮴ· ᏂᎪᎩ, ᏂᏍᏬ ᏴᎾ ᎢᏔᏟᎭᎵ. ᏝᏬ ᏏᎵ ᎩᏋ ᏈᎾᏚᎵᏏᎵ ᎠᏈ ᎠᎢᎫᏔᎵ ᏛᏁᎢ, ᎠᎵᏞ ᏩᏔ ᎵᏬᏢ ᎫᎵᏙᎭ. ᎠᏫᎴᏇᎪᎬᏃᏕ ᏂᎵᏚ ᎠᎢᎴ ᏣᎵᏣ. ᏟᎶᎩᏂ ᎠᎢᏚᏋᎵ ᎪᎩ, ZᏬᏫ· ᏂᎪᎩᎸ ᎠᏈ ᎠᎢᏚᏔᎵ ᎤᏐᏏᏔᏯ ᎤᎴᏏᏂᎪᏬᎢ.

Ꭳ�P ᎤᎩᏃᏟᎵ.

ᏕᎩᏚᏚᏞᏂ ᎢᏏ ᏙᎤᎶᏕᎵ, 1828.

This bilingual notice announcing a husband's refusal to pay the debts of his "absconded" wife was published in 1828 in the *Cherokee Phoenix*, the Cherokee national newspaper, in both English and Cherokee script.

proslavery expansionism in an 1858 speech urging the wholesale annexation of Mexican and other Latin American territory, a decade after the U.S. had already wrested vast areas from Mexico: "I want Cuba[.] … I want Tamaulipas, Potosi, and one or two other Mexican States; and I want them all … for the planting or spreading of slavery. … I would spread the blessings of slavery, like the religion of our Divine Master, to the uttermost ends of the earth."

The first major target of Jacksonian America's drive to expand was the remaining territory of the Indigenous nations east of the Mississippi. By the 1820s, despite several wars and numerous territorial cessions, nearly 100,000 Native Americans still lived on millions of acres between the Great Lakes and the Gulf of Mexico.[1] Many of them had formed close economic and familial ties with their white neighbors and—in line with federal policies that officially encouraged their assimilation—had adopted such Euro-American institutions and practices as they thought would benefit them. They learned to speak and write English (and, in the case of the Cherokee, devised a writing system for their own language); they formed centralized governments with written constitutions; they participated in the market economy; and they often adopted Christianity. The so-called "Five Civilized Tribes" in the South (the Choctaw, Chickasaw, Cherokee, Muscogee [Creek], and Seminole) led the way in this acceptance of white American norms, which in their case extended to the enslavement, by their wealthiest citizens, of African Americans.[2] Even as members of these nations developed a form of plantation slavery themselves, however, the slaveholding white elites around them coveted their lands and feared that the continued existence of such well-organized, autonomous non-white communities in the South would weaken white supremacy there. Other white Americans with no vested interest in slavery wanted to open up Indigenous land to white settlement, and many expressed the view—some out of pure self-interest, others out of misguided but sincerely held philanthropic beliefs—that Indigenous people could not survive in close contact with whites and needed to be "removed" for their own good.

This mixture of motivations gave rise to a course of action that the Choctaw leader George Colbert called an "act of usurpation … unparalleled in history": the systematic, state-administered deportation beyond the bounds of the United States of the entire Indigenous population east of the Mississippi. In 1830, Congress passed the Indian Removal Act, which mandated that the Indigenous nations east of the Mississippi either cede their remaining lands and relocate to an allotted "Indian Territory" farther west or accept the jurisdiction of the states in which they lived—a measure that entailed their dissolution as autonomous nations. Many Indigenous people strenuously protested this measure, aided by considerable numbers of white American allies. Such protests notwithstanding, between 1831 and 1838, most members of the five Indigenous nations in the south, and numerous smaller nations in the north, were forced to move (for the Indigenous nations practicing slavery, the deportees included enslaved African

---

[1] 25,000 Native Americans lived north of the Ohio River and 66,000 south of it.

[2] By 1830, enslaved African Americans made up over five percent of the combined population of these five nations. The Cherokee nation contained the largest number of enslaved people; seven to eight percent of Cherokee families were slaveowners. As was the general case throughout the South, only a further small fraction of this enslaving minority owned more than a few enslaved people. The large majority of Cherokee enslavers claimed some white ancestry.

Wabokieshiek (c. 1794–c. 1841), a spiritual leader of the Sauk and Ho-Chunk nations of the upper Mississippi Valley. Wabokieshiek (also known as White Cloud) called for the preservation of traditional Indigenous ways of life and played a major part in Black Hawk's War (1832), the campaign waged by members of the Sauk and allied nations to retain their lands east of the Mississippi. George Catlin, a white American artist known for his depictions of Native Americans, painted this portrait in 1832.

Americans). During their various long journeys to the new territories designated for them, the deportees suffered from disease, harsh weather, meager rations, and administrative incompetence; thousands died. These deadly treks westward have come to be known, in American memory, by the name originally coined for the last and most famous deportation, that of the Cherokee: the Trail of Tears. Some Indigenous people from several nations, in both the north and the south, took up arms—unsuccessfully—against their expulsion; others managed to avoid being expelled, and

members of some expelled nations continue to live in or near their traditional eastern territories today. However, the scope and scale of the expulsions of the 1830s, and the way in which they geographically segregated the expelled nations from the bulk of the American populace, fundamentally transformed Indigenous–U.S. relations and set the course of those relations for at least the rest of the century.[1]

During the same decades in which "Indian Removal" was conceived and executed, U.S. expansionism also started to impinge on the territory of a different non-Anglo-American nation: Mexico. Beginning in the 1820s, substantial numbers of white American settlers, mainly from the South, immigrated to Texas, then a state of Mexico. The first American settlers in Texas came at the invitation of the state government, but many others arrived without official sanction. By the 1820s, many *Tejanos* (descendants of the original Hispanic colonists of Texas) were already agitating for greater political autonomy within Mexico. The American settlers also wanted to distance themselves from the authority of the Mexican government—and to form strong ties to the United States. They engaged in widespread defiance of Mexican authority and law—including, in particular, Mexico's abolition of slavery in 1829. These pressures, together with the Mexican government's corresponding fear of losing control of Texas, led in 1835 to the conflict known as the Texas Revolution; the American settlers, together with the Tejanos, took arms against the Mexican government. The bloodshed included the annihilation of the Texan garrison of the Alamo (a former Spanish mission in San Antonio), the massacre of several hundred Texan prisoners at Goliad, and the Texan slaughter of Mexican soldiers at the climactic Battle of San Jacinto. By the end of April 1836, Mexico had been defeated and Texas had declared its independence—which, however, the Mexican government refused to recognize. In part because of the persistence of tense relations between Texas and Mexico that resulted, Tejanos in the new Republic of Texas, including those who had fought for independence, were often ill treated; one of them, Juan Seguín—who had carried the Alamo defenders' final

---

[1] For a fuller discussion of Native American expulsion and resistance during the 1830s, see the following section of this introduction.

Carl Nebel, *General Scott's Entrance into Mexico*, 1851. This painting depicts American troops led by General Winfield Scott occupying Mexico City in 1847 during the Mexican–American War.

message requesting reinforcements—described himself as "a foreigner in my native land."

The vast majority of independent Texas's Anglo-American inhabitants favored annexation by the United States, as did American President John Tyler, but the fact that Texas was a slaveholding region whose entry into the union would upset the delicate balance of slave and free states made this a highly contentious issue in America. The debate over whether to annex Texas featured prominently in the 1844 presidential election, which was won by James K. Polk, a Jacksonian Democrat, slaveholding Southerner, and strong proponent of national expansion. Texas was accordingly admitted into the union in 1845—the first step in the enormous expansion of U.S. territory that the Polk administration oversaw. In the 1844 election some elements in Polk's party had demanded that the United States annex large tracts of territory in the Pacific Northwest as well, including what is now the Canadian province of British Columbia to the border

of Russian America (today's Alaska) at latitude 54°40'; "fifty-four forty or fight" became an annexationist rallying cry. In the other direction, the British claimed all territory south to the mouth of the Columbia River. In 1846, with war looming against Mexico over the annexation of Texas (which Mexico still claimed), Polk did not want to risk conflict on two different fronts; instead, he negotiated a treaty that divided the Oregon Country, leaving in American hands what are today the states of Oregon, Washington, and Idaho, as well as parts of Montana and Wyoming. The compromise was widely considered to be a negotiating victory for the United States, but it left those in Polk's own Democratic Party who had demanded the acquisition of "all of Oregon" less than fully satisfied.

That same year, Polk used a dispute over the Texas–Mexico boundary to provoke the long-anticipated war with Mexico. The Mexican–American War lasted for two years and remains, in terms of the percentage of military fatalities, the second-deadliest war in U.S.

Daniel A. Jenks, *Camp 100—Humbolt River*, 1859. This drawing of an emigrant encampment on the Humboldt River, in what is now western Nevada, comes from the sketchbook that Jenks kept of his journey overland to California.

history (exceeded only by the Civil War). Over 13,000 American soldiers—nearly seventeen percent of those who served—died in the war, while as many as 25,000 Mexicans perished, including an estimated 4,000 civilians.[1] The war, which Polk's opponents in the Whig Party justifiably characterized as a war of aggression, was deeply unpopular with much of the civilian population and even with many soldiers, thousands of whom deserted—including a significant number who switched sides to fight for Mexico.[2] The United States, however, was the clear victor, and when U.S. forces occupied the Mexican heartland and captured Mexico City, some of the same Americans who had demanded "all of Oregon" called for the annexation of "all of Mexico." Polk did not go quite that far, but when the war ended in 1848, Mexico was forced not only to surrender its claim to Texas but also to cede to the United States a vast amount of additional land, including all or most of the present-day states of California, Nevada, Utah, Arizona, New Mexico, and Colorado.[3]

As had been the case with Texas, Americans began colonizing the huge territories the U.S. took over during the Polk administration well before those territories formally became U.S. possessions. American missionaries, followed by small groups of emigrants, began journeying to the Oregon Country along the 2,170-mile route that would come to be called the Oregon Trail in the mid-1830s; the first large body of settlers traversed the route in 1843, and by 1869, about 400,000 westward migrants had used it. A further 300,000 people from the U.S. and around the world surged into California after gold was discovered there in January 1848, shortly before California was officially ceded to the U.S. The first group of the approximately

---

[1] As was typically the case during this period, most military deaths were due to disease.

[2] Most of the U.S. soldiers who did so were immigrants; Irish Catholic troops, who shared a religious affiliation with their Catholic Mexican opponents and who faced considerable anti-immigrant and anti-Catholic prejudice in the U.S., were especially likely to change sides. (Most U.S. soldiers in the Mexican–American War had been born outside the U.S.; about a quarter were Irish.)

[3] The 1848 Mexican Cession, which amounted to one-third of Mexico's original territory, also included portions of what is now Texas, Oklahoma, Kansas, and Wyoming. In return, the U.S. paid $15 million (the equivalent of over $400 million today) and assumed $3.25 million worth of Mexican state debt owed to U.S. citizens. The continental U.S. reached its present-day form a few years later with the Gadsden Purchase (1853), in which Mexico sold a further small portion of what is now Arizona and New Mexico.

70,000 Mormons who escaped persecution in the eastern U.S. by moving to Utah arrived there in 1847, at a time when it too was still nominally Mexican territory. These numbers attest to the tremendous appeal of the new western territories and the opportunities they afforded to many Americans. Many others, though, suffered from the risks, sacrifices, disruptions, and costs inevitably involved in such transcontinental migrations. One such person, a woman named Elizabeth Cress, who moved with her husband from North Carolina to Illinois but then refused to accompany him further westward, wrote a letter to her parents in 1851 that provides another perspective on, and another part of the story of, mid-nineteenth-century American expansion: "my old man has left me & has gone to California and took my wagon and left me and my Children in a bad situation."

The roughly 80,000 Hispanic inhabitants of the territories taken from Mexico experienced even more profound disruptions. Contempt for this Hispanic population featured prominently in U.S. expansionary thinking, according to which the Hispanic Mexicans were—as Richard Henry Dana put it in *Two Years Before the Mast* (1840), his account of his voyage to California by sea in the 1830s—"an idle, thriftless

Edward Vischer, *A Californian Magnate in His Home*, 1865. By the time this painting of Los Angeles landowner General Don Andres Pico was made, many such large Californio estates had been taken over, broken up, or whittled away by white American settlers.

people" who could "make nothing for themselves."[1] Many in the U.S. felt it to be only just that the land of these Hispanic settlers be taken over by supposedly more industrious and politically enlightened white Americans. The 1848 treaty that ended the Mexican–American War theoretically extended full U.S. citizenship to former Mexican citizens, and it also would have guaranteed property rights for holders of Mexican land grants; however, Congress removed this last provision from the treaty, stipulating instead that property rights would be guaranteed only to those who could prove ownership—a stipulation that was often difficult and financially ruinous to meet. Racialized prejudice and lack of adequate legal protections combined to relegate most Mexican Americans to the status of second-class citizens, and the influx of white American settlers to California and Texas soon also made them a minority. Mariano Guadalupe Vallejo, a prominent Californio who initially supported California's entrance into the U.S., voiced the resulting bitterness of many Hispanic Americans in his 1875 memoirs, in which he castigated "the swollen torrent of shysters, who came from Missouri and other states of the Union" in the Gold Rush: "[T]hese legal thieves, clothed in the robes of the law, took from us our lands and our houses and without the least scruple enthroned themselves in our homes like so many powerful kings." Similar injustices drove the Tejano Juan Cortina to armed resistance; in September 1859, he briefly occupied the border town of Brownsville, Texas, with a force of seventy men, issuing a proclamation that asserted the right of Mexican Americans to defend themselves against those who "persecute and rob us without reason and for no other motive or crime than that of being of Mexican origin" and avowed, "Our personal enemies will not possess our land, except by paying for it with their own blood."

Racialized discrimination was by no means confined to Hispanic Mexicans. Californian legislation such as the 1850 foreign miners' tax and the 1855 anti-vagrancy laws imposed restrictions on those of Mexican, Asian, Indigenous, and African backgrounds. Oregon's

---

[1]   Dana's comparisons of the lives of the Hispanic colonizers with those of the Indigenous peoples of California are of considerable interest: "Among the Mexicans," he observed, "there is no working class; (the Indians being slaves and doing all the hard work); and every rich man looks like a grandee, and every poor scamp like a broken-down gentleman."

original Negro Exclusion Law and additional exclusion laws of 1862 (levying special taxes on Hawaiians, Asians, and those of mixed race as well as on blacks) made it clear that, while Oregon might not be a slave state, it was emphatically not a state in which all were welcome or would be treated equally.

Arguably the greatest injustices were directed toward the Indigenous nations of the U.S.'s new western acquisitions; much of what had occurred to Native Americans east of the Mississippi up until the 1830s was repeated after 1848 in the West—in some cases, on an even larger and more terrible scale. When the Dakota of Minnesota rose up in 1862 in response to neglect and abuse by federal authorities, the rebellion was viciously suppressed; the American response included the largest mass execution in American history—the hanging of 38 Dakota men.[1] In 1864, the Navajo of the southwest followed in the footsteps of the Cherokee and so many other eastern nations when, in the "Long Walk of the Navajo," they too were deported *en masse* from their traditional territories (although unlike their eastern counterparts, they were eventually able to return). The Cherokee expulsion had been precipitated, in part, by the discovery of gold on their lands in Georgia in 1829; two decades later, the much larger gold rush in California had even grimmer consequences for California's Indigenous peoples. By 1900, the massacres and enslavement perpetrated by white American settlers, and the disease and starvation they spread, had reduced an Indigenous Californian population that numbered as high as 150,000 in 1848 to just 16,000.

One phrase introduced during the Polk administration has come to define American expansionism, a phrase that was used again and again both to celebrate the progress of expansion and to gloss over or rationalize the many wrongs committed in pursuing it: "manifest destiny." The phrase first appeared, more or less in passing, in an 1845 article advocating the annexation of Texas that was published in *The United States Magazine and Democratic Review*, a Jacksonian Democratic periodical edited by the Irish American journalist John L. O'Sullivan. The article proclaimed that Texas's incorporation into the U.S. was key to "the

Wife and two children of Little Crow, one of the leaders of the 1862 Dakota uprising in Minnesota, during their internment after the uprising's suppression; photograph by Benjamin Upton, 1864. Little Crow himself was killed by white settlers in 1863.

fulfillment of our manifest destiny to overspread the continent allotted by Providence for the free development of our yearly multiplying millions." This first use of the term "manifest destiny" did not have much immediate impact, but when the phrase appeared again in another *Democratic Review* article a few months later that asserted the U.S.'s right, in its dispute with Britain over the Oregon Country, to claim "the whole of Oregon," it began to catch on.[2] The idea of an American "manifest destiny" was cited by both

---

1   A further 265 Dakota prisoners had their death sentences commuted by President Lincoln.

2   As the phrase "manifest destiny" became more and more widespread, its origins were forgotten, and the *Democratic Review*'s role in coining it was not recognized until 1927. The two articles in which the phrase first appeared were both published anonymously; they have traditionally been credited to O'Sullivan, but several scholars have posited that the first, at least, was actually written by Jane Cazneau, a journalist for the *Democratic Review* and other periodicals and an avid expansionist.

sides in the congressional debate over the Oregon issue in early 1846, and in the late 1840s and 1850s the term became ubiquitous. By 1858, the writer and Army wife Teresa Griffin Vielé could use it as a commonplace to describe how, in her eyes, Anglo-American settlement in Texas displayed "the marks of inevitable progress ... otherwise called 'manifest destiny.'" Other writers repurposed the phrase to refer not to the supposed inevitability of (white) American expansion but to the supposed inevitability of Native American disappearance in the face of that expansion—a fate that Mary Eastman, in her 1849 book *Dahcotah; or, Life and Legends of the Sioux Around Fort Snelling*, termed the "manifest destiny of the aborigines."

In context, however, Eastman's use of "manifest destiny" demonstrates trepidation about, rather than confidence in, "the giant strides of civilization" before which Indigenous people supposedly were "receding rapidly, and with feeble resistance": "We should be better reconciled to this manifest destiny of the aborigines, if the inroads of civilization were worthy of it." Such misgivings were widespread: if many Americans enthusiastically endorsed and sought to realize their self-proclaimed "manifest destiny" to possess the continent and dispossess those who preceded them there, many others were troubled by this idea or opposed it outright. In the 1820s and 1830s, "Indian Removal" met with fervent opposition. In 1829, for example, a group of women (including the poet Lydia Sigourney and the educator Catharine Beecher, sister of Harriet Beecher Stowe) organized a grassroots campaign against Native American expulsion that resulted in almost 1,500 women submitting anti-removal petitions to Congress, in what has been identified as a landmark moment in the history of women's activism in the U.S. Even figures as reactionary as the Southern writer William Gilmore Simms, a strong supporter of slavery, condemned what, in 1845, he called "the reckless and unsparing hand with which we have smitten [Indigenous people] in their habitations, and expelled them from their country." Other commentators specifically warned against justifying the country's "unsparing" policies toward Native Americans by abstract invocations of destiny. As the pioneering anthropologist Lewis Henry Morgan put it in 1851: "It cannot be forgotten, that in after years our Republic must render

an account, to the civilized world, for the disposal which it makes of the Indian. It is not sufficient, before this tribunal, to plead inevitable destiny."

Aggression toward Mexico, the other major means whereby the U.S. pursued its "manifest destiny," was opposed just as strongly, sometimes in surprising ways or by surprising voices. John Quincy Adams, for example, whose 1811 characterization of American expansion as "destined by Divine Providence" was quoted earlier, had by 1836 become one of the staunchest opponents of American expansionism, as he demonstrated in an impassioned speech to his fellow members of the House of Representatives:

> What will be your *cause* in such a war [with Mexico]? Aggression, conquest, and the re-establishment of slavery where it has been abolished. In that war, Sir, the banners of *freedom* will be the banners of Mexico; and your banners—I blush to speak the word—will be the banners of *slavery*.

When the U.S. eventually went to war with Mexico a decade later, many New Englanders opposed the war because, like Adams, they considered it an attempt to expand slavery. Many white Southerners opposed it as well—on the grounds either that it would be too difficult to reimpose slavery in Mexico or that incorporating a large non-white (and non-Protestant) population into the United States would undermine white supremacy.[1] The common thread linking opposition to Indigenous expulsion and to war with Mexico, as parallel attempts to seize the rightful patrimony of others, was highlighted by the use, in both causes, of the biblical story of Naboth's vineyard, in which the Israelite King Ahab is condemned by God for arranging the death of his neighbor Naboth in order to obtain his vineyard, which Naboth had refused to sell.[2] In 1825, the New

---

[1]   The Mexican–American War, and the accompanying debates about whether to annex Mexican territory (and if so, how much), highlighted inherent, unresolved tensions in the concept of "manifest destiny" itself. Was America's destiny associated primarily with its supposed political superiority, as a constitutional democracy, or its supposed racial superiority, as an ostensibly "Anglo-Saxon" nation? Was America called to spread the benefits of its democratic political institutions (an argument made by proponents of annexing all of Mexico) or to consolidate and extend white supremacy (one of the arguments used to oppose that course of action)?

[2]   See 1 Kings 21.

York newspaper editor William Leete Stone likened the Georgia state government's attempts to dispossess the Muscogee (Creek) to Ahab "wickedly wresting from Naboth *the inheritance of his fathers*," while in 1848, the abolitionist minister Theodore Parker compared Ahab's designs on Naboth's vineyard to President Polk's designs on Mexico in his "Sermon of the Mexican War"—a piece of oratory that, scholars have suggested, helped inspire Herman Melville's *Moby-Dick* (1851).

African Americans had an especially complicated relationship with the idea of "manifest destiny." Many black people identified slavery as the root of U.S. expansionism and condemned it accordingly, as did Mary Ann Shadd in *A Plea for Emigration* (1852), her treatise advocating black emigration to Canada: "The pro-slavery party of the United States is the aggressive party on this continent. It is the serpent that aims to swallow all others." But "manifest destiny" thinking appealed to other African Americans. In 1848, for example, the clergyman Henry Highland Garnet celebrated the U.S. victory over Mexico as an event that would augment America's diversity and thereby make it more peaceful and democratic: "This republic, and this continent, are to be the theatre in which the grand drama of our triumphant Destiny is to be enacted." Still other black thinkers appropriated the language of "manifest destiny" to voice black separatist aspirations: the poet James Monroe Whitfield, arguing like Shadd in favor of African American emigration, asserted in 1853, "I ... consider it a part of [black people's] 'manifest destiny' to possess all the tropical regions of this continent," and the abolitionist minister Richard Harvey Cain entitled his 1862 lecture advocating the creation of an African American colony in Africa "Manifest Destiny of the African Race." As African Americans elaborated these various responses to the concept of manifest destiny, the question of whether slavery was to be permitted in the new western territories became more and more polarizing, bringing the country closer and closer to civil war.

The debates over national expansion and Native American expulsion that consumed the country as a whole between the 1820s and the Civil War also took place in and through American literature. These issues took center stage, in particular, in the wave of novels about Indigenous–settler relations that swept the national literary scene in the 1820s and 30s, including (among many others) Lydia Maria Child's *Hobomok* (1824), Catharine Maria Sedgwick's *Hope Leslie* (1827), William Gilmore Simms's *The Yemassee* (1835), and James Fenimore Cooper's Leatherstocking Tales (1823–41). While most of these works were set during colonial times a century or more previously, their subject-matter unavoidably resonated with the crisis in U.S.–Native American relations that was unfolding when they were published, and their popularity thrust the questions at stake in that crisis upon readers who otherwise might not have had to confront them. Cooper's *The Last of the Mohicans* (1827), for example, evokes the burgeoning issue of "Indian Removal" in passages such as the following, in which an Indigenous character denounces white expansionism: "[The white man's] gluttony makes him sick. God gave him enough, and yet he wants all. Such are the pale-faces!" It should be noted, though, that this speech is delivered by Magua, the novel's Huron (Wendat) villain; such novels' perspectives on the matters they address are far from consistent or univocal. If some writers, such as Child, outspokenly condemned Indigenous expulsion, others, such as Cooper, could voice reservations about the march of white civilization, and sympathetically portray Indigenous resistance to it, while also doing as much as anyone to foster the myths—of intrepid backwoodsmen, regenerative violence, and Native Americans who were either noble or savage but, in either case, inevitably doomed—that helped motivate and sustain American expansionism.

Similar ambivalence on the question of national expansion pervades the mid-nineteenth-century American literary canon. Many of the writers at the core of this canon endorsed and perpetuated ideas of American exceptionalism, of America's special destiny, and even of America's providential right to claim the continent. William Cullen Bryant and Walt Whitman, in their capacity as editors of Jacksonian Democratic newspapers, supported Indigenous expulsion and the Mexican–American War, respectively. Herman Melville was largely supportive of the idea of American exceptionalism, which the protagonist of his 1850 novel *White-Jacket; or, The World in a Man-of-War* endorses in ringing terms: "Americans are the peculiar, the chosen people—the Israel of our time; we bear the ark of the liberties of the world. God has pre-destined, mankind expects, great things from our race; and great things we feel in our souls."[1] Ralph Waldo Emerson declared that "Nature says to the American ... 'I give you the land and sea, the forest and the mine, the elemental forces'"; and Henry David Thoreau celebrated "the westward tendency" that he saw as "the prevailing tendency of my countrymen." Yet Whitman also came to consider Mexico "the only one to whom we have ever really done wrong"; Thoreau went to jail rather than pay a tax to fund the Mexican–American War; Emerson called invocations of "*Manifest Destiny, Democracy, Freedom*" "fine names for an ugly thing"; and Melville's writing also includes numerous condemnations of imperialism, including U.S. imperialism, and the prejudice that propelled it, from the negative portrayals of white incursions on Indigenous Pacific Islander life in *Typee* (1846) to the searing portrait of an obsessive, genocidal "Indian-hater" in *The Confidence-Man* (1857).

But to read the works of these canonical writers—most of whom had little firsthand acquaintance with what was occurring in the course of their country's enlargement—is barely to scratch the surface of nineteenth-century American literature's engagement with national expansion. Westward migration and settlement also generated a large body of writing, to which women, in particular, contributed significantly. Many depictions of newly colonized areas were promotional, meant to encourage western settlement and guide settlers in their new life; notable examples include *Texas: Observations, Historical, Geographical and Descriptive* (1833) by Mary Austin Holley—cousin of Stephen F. Austin, the founder of the first major Anglo-American colony in Texas—and *Life in Prairie Land* (1846) by Eliza Farnham. Margaret Fuller's *Summer on the Lakes* (1844), an account of a tour of newly colonized areas in the Great Lakes region in 1843, is promotional as well, but Fuller—a notable Transcendentalist and women's rights advocate—also documented settler colonialism's impact on Native Americans (albeit from the widely held white perspective that saw Indigenous people as

inevitably bound for "speedy extinction"). Fuller also registers environmental concern for the land itself, recording her fears that the settlers' "mode of cultivation will, in the course of twenty, perhaps ten years, obliterate the natural expression of the country." Other writers pushed back against promotional literature in their efforts to realistically depict the struggle and privation of settler life. Caroline Kirkland's *A New Home— Who'll Follow?* (1839), a lightly fictionalized portrayal of colonizer life in a new settlement in Michigan, became an acclaimed bestseller as it generated intense controversy for its unromanticized truth-telling; Alice Cary's *Clovernook; Or Recollections of Our Neighborhood in the West* (1852), also a bestseller, followed suit some years later.

The West became a common setting in the sentimental and domestic fiction that rose to popularity in the 1850s. Works such as Maria Susanna Cummins's *Mabel Vaughan* (1857) and Caroline Soule's *The Pet of the Settlement* (1860) celebrated the West as a place where, in the words of the latter novel, "struggling, debt-ridden, homeless and hungry men and women from the crowded cities of the older States" could find regeneration in cohesive rural communities. Similarly, in Mary Hayden Pike's *Ida May* (1854) and E.D.E.N. Southworth's *India: The Pearl of Pearl River* (1856), the free soil of the West redeems Southerners from the taint of slavery. Sensation fiction—the frequently lurid and violent, stereotypically "masculine" counterpart to stereotypically "feminine" sentimental fiction—also gravitated westward and dealt with national expansion in ways that are often more nuanced than readers might expect. The hero of *The Volunteer: or, the Maid of Monterey* (1847), by the prolific and influential popular writer Ned Buntline (the pen name of E.Z.C. Judson), calls the Mexican–American War a "war of invasion," and a character in Southworth's *The Hidden Hand* (1859) reflects similarly on his participation in the war: "what had I to do with invading another's country?" Such works prefigured the rise, in the 1860s, of the dime novel, a new form of cheap popular literature priced, as its name suggests, at ten cents; the titles of some of the first dime novels—*Malaeska, the Indian Wife of the White Hunter* and *Seth Jones; or, The Captives of the Frontier* (both 1860)—attest to the way in which western expansion was integral to this genre

---

[1]   This oft-quoted passage is prompted by a commentary on the practice of flogging on board ship; White-Jacket, the protagonist and narrator, is directly addressing the reader as he argues that America need not and should not follow the example of other nations: "in things of this kind England should be nothing to us, except an example to be shunned."

Cover of *Esther: A Story of the Oregon Trail* (1862), by the prolific dime novelist Ann S. Stephens.

from its start. And as the following passage from Ann S. Stephens's *Esther: A Story of the Oregon Trail* (1862) demonstrates, dime novels could reflect on "manifest destiny" and Indigenous expulsion in ways that were multifaceted and ambivalent, quite as much as could more canonical literary works:

> The star that leads civilization westward shines sadly upon the graves of a people almost extinct— a people that have been hunted ruthlessly from their greenwood haunts till every year has seen their graves multiplying thicker and thicker in the wilderness. Then the Anglo-Saxon comes to plow it up and plant corn above the dead warriors, stopping now and then to pick up a stone arrowhead from his furrow, and examine it curiously, as if he did not know what soil his sacrilegious plow was upturning. … Yon star that leads westward has no halting place for him till it sets on the calm Pacific, writing on its blue waters the history of a people that have perished.

These popular works, like their "highbrow" canonical counterparts, were largely written and published in the East, which remained the location of the country's literary establishment, but a vibrant literary and publishing scene quickly arose in the West as well. Western migrants brought nineteenth-century America's robust, deep-rooted print culture with them to their new homes, founding newspapers and printing shops and publishing a tremendous variety of journalism, essays, fiction, and poetry. By 1867, California had developed a literary culture big enough and busy enough to yield an anthology—*Poetry of the Pacific*, published in San Francisco—that was more than 400 pages long and featured the work of over sixty poets (half of them women). One of the leading Californian writers was Bret Harte, who moved there in 1853. Harte gained a reputation in the 1860s for his colorful, frequently satirical depictions of Gold Rush life—as well as for his condemnations of violence against Indigenous Californians, which earned him death threats from some of his white compatriots. The young Missourian Samuel Clemens, who spent the Civil War years in Nevada Territory and then California (where he met Harte), similarly made a name for himself in the West with his writing, in his case literally: his publications in Nevada newspapers in the 1860s included his first use of the pen name "Mark Twain." A different kind of Western writing is exemplified by the work of Eliza R. Snow, the so-called "Mormon poetess"—and plural wife (first of Joseph Smith, the Mormon founder, and then of Brigham Young, the leader of the Mormon exodus to Utah)—whose poetic depictions of Mormon westward migration and life in their new settlements filled two volumes, the first published in Britain in 1856 and the second in Salt Lake City in 1877.

The experience of U.S. expansion also gave rise to a rich and varied body of literature among America's Indigenous peoples and among the Hispanic inhabitants of the territories taken from Mexico. The petitions, essays, letters, poems, and narratives written during the expulsion crisis by members of those Indigenous nations that had adopted literacy and written languages are an eloquent record of Native Americans' various attempts to resist, survive, or come to terms with their dispossession. These texts run the gamut from the polished political prose of John Ross, the

Eliza R. Snow, c. 1852.

Cherokee Principal Chief, to the blunt, world-weary verse penned by an anonymous Choctaw during his nation's deportation: "On my way to the Arkansas / God damn the white mans laws / O come and go along with me / O come and go along with me." A particular standout among this corpus is the autobiography of Black Hawk, the Sauk chieftain who led an attempt to reclaim his nation's lands in Illinois and Wisconsin in the 1832 war named after him. Black Hawk dictated his autobiography to a U.S. government interpreter during his imprisonment after the war; published in 1833, it became a frequently reprinted bestseller. Alongside this written literature, Native Americans enshrined and interpreted their experiences in oral stories, many of which continue to be related today.

Mid-nineteenth-century Hispanic American literary culture is also characterized by both a vibrant written literature and a popular, largely oral counterpart. This culture includes, at one end of the spectrum, the memoirs of elite figures such as Mariano Guadalupe Vallejo and Juan Seguín, and the fiction of María Ruiz de Burton, a Californio woman from a similarly elite background who was the first female Mexican American author to write in English; her first novel,

Who Would Have Thought It? (1872), critiques white American racial hypocrisy and "manifest destiny" doctrine. At the other end of the spectrum, Hispanic American literature comprises popular dramas, such as the play *Los Tejanos* (probably written between 1841 and 1846), and anonymous corridos (ballads), such as the many composed about Joaquín Murrieta, a legendary Californio outlaw who is supposed to have fought back against Anglo-American injustice during the Gold Rush. These works also attest to Hispanic American grievances and resistance: *Los Tejanos*, which depicts a failed Texan expedition into New Mexico (then still part of Mexico) in 1841, ends with a Hispanic character telling a captured Anglo-American Texan general, "Die, you dog! Now you are going to pay for all the evil you had planned," while one of the Murrieta corridos pushes back against white American avowals of their "manifest destiny" in its declaration that "California is Mexico's / Because God wanted it that way."

Such ballads provided inspiration for a writer who brings together Native American, Hispanic American, and white American literary cultures in one complex combination: the Cherokee author John Rollin Ridge (Chees-quat-a-law-ny). The son and grandson of prominent Cherokee who were killed by fellow members of their nation for their support for, and role in bringing about, Cherokee "removal," Ridge was born on the Cherokee's traditional lands in Georgia but ended up in California, where he embarked on a career in journalism and literature. While he wrote poetry and essays, his most significant work was *The Life and Adventures of Joaquín Murieta: The Celebrated California Bandit* (1854), the first published Native American novel and the first novel written in California, which codified the Murrieta corridos in what would prove to be a popular and influential form. The novel condemns white American racism toward Mexican Americans, but is virtually silent about the treatment of California's Indigenous population. While Ridge occasionally spoke out against their mistreatment, his writing also traffics in the degrading characterization of Indigenous Californians as primitive "Diggers,"[1] a stereotype that helped drive their

---

1   This derogatory term reflected the contempt that white American settlers felt for the hunter-gatherer way of life—including digging up roots to eat—practiced by many of California's Indigenous peoples; the term is today rightly considered highly offensive.

near-total extermination. Ridge, as a Native American writer who adapted Hispanic American material and who suffered from, criticized, and participated in settler colonialism, arguably exemplifies more fully than any other single writer of the period the complex history of U.S. expansion.

NATIVE AMERICAN WRITING—AND WRITING ABOUT NATIVE AMERICANS

The complex case of John Rollin Ridge exemplifies a larger truth about American literature of the 1820–Reconstruction period: namely, that this literature cannot be understood apart from the violence visited upon Indigenous communities and the vital, persistent expression of Native Americans whose writings contradicted settler narratives about the supposed disappearance of Indigenous people and cultures. The United States pursued its grand narrative of settler rule, or self-proclaimed "manifest destiny," through a strategy of Indigenous expulsion that was then referred to as *Indian removal*—a polite term for the pilfering of Indigenous lands through questionable and broken treaties, and the forced relocation of approximately 100,000 Indigenous people from their homelands east of the Mississippi River to insufficient territories to the west. The strategy of expulsion went back to the beginnings of colonialism in North America, but its pursuit as official federal policy was a nineteenth-century phenomenon—articulated by Thomas Jefferson, passed narrowly by the House and Senate in 1830, signed into law by President Andrew Jackson, and implemented over subsequent decades.

Expulsion was always controversial; Native American leaders and non-Indigenous allies questioned it on both political and moral grounds. President Jackson—whose reputation stemmed, in part, from the brutal military campaigns he had conducted against the Muscogee (Creek) in 1813–14 and the Seminole in 1818—expressed his frustration over such protest, asking in his 1830 address to Congress, "What good man would prefer a country covered with forests and ranged by a few thousand savages to our extensive Republic, studded with cities, towns, and prosperous farms embellished with all the improvements which art can devise or industry execute, occupied by more than 12,000,000 happy people, and filled with all the blessings of liberty, civilization and religion?" Opponents of expulsion posed their own questions. In a petition to the U.S. Congress in December 1829, the Cherokee Nation queried, "what better right can a people have to a country, than the right of *inheritance* and *immemorial peaceable possession?*" No less an authority than the U.S. Supreme Court upheld the sovereignty of the Cherokee Nation in its 1832 *Worcester v. Georgia* decision, but ultimately to little effect: as Andrew Jackson is said—probably apocryphally—to have commented after the ruling was issued, "John Marshall [the Chief Justice] has made his decision; now let him enforce it!"

The most famous, or infamous, expulsion is the Cherokee Trail of Tears, in which, over the course of six months in 1838–39, approximately 16,000 members of the Cherokee Nation were forcibly removed from the southeast to lands in what had been designated as "Indian Territory" (a large and vaguely-defined area west of the Mississippi, centering on what is now Oklahoma). At least 4,000 died as a direct result. The basis for Cherokee expulsion was the controversial Treaty of New Echota (1835), signed by a faction of Cherokee leaders who, in contradiction of Principal Chief John Ross, had concluded that the nation's options for political resistance had run out. The federal government also expelled members of the Muscogee (Creek), Chickasaw, Choctaw, Sauk (Sac), Meskwaki (Fox), Seminole, Kickapoo, Shawnee, Ho-Chunk (Winnebago), and Potawatomi nations, among others, in deportations that were often as deadly as that of the Cherokee.

Native Americans resisted these efforts in a variety of ways. In the south, members of the Muscogee nation took up arms in the Second Creek War (1836), while the Seminole of Florida—including associated groups of African American escapees from slavery, the so-called Black Seminole—resisted until 1842. The Second Seminole War, the longest and most expensive (in both human and monetary terms) of all U.S.–Native American conflicts, cost the lives of 1,466 U.S. soldiers and an unknown number of militia members, as well as between thirty and forty million dollars, an unheard-of amount of money at the time; as many as a thousand Seminole—a number that would amount to twenty percent of their total population—were killed,

Henry Lewis, *The Battle of Bad Axe*, 1857. In his 2020 book *Surviving Genocide*, Jeffrey Ostler describes this image as "an especially striking example of colonial evasion; the caption refers to the event as a battle," but what is being portrayed in the image "is clearly a massacre."

and 3,824 were eventually deported. In the north, the Sauk leader Black Hawk and his band of warriors from several Indigenous nations defended their land holdings with force in 1832. But they were badly outnumbered, and the brief war ended with a massacre near the mouth of the Bad Axe River in what is now Wisconsin. When they surrendered, the Sauk and their allies were forced to sign a document ceding "to the United States forever all the lands to which the said tribes have title or claims"; the American government termed the document a "Treaty of Peace, Friendship, and Cession." In an autobiographical account dictated after his capture and detention by federal forces, Black Hawk commented on this sort of deceptive language: "How smooth must be the language of the whites, when they can make right look like wrong, and wrong like right." The hypocrisy of U.S. actions was a theme reiterated by all who spoke, wrote, and took up arms in defense of Indigenous sovereignty.

One of the most powerful critics of settler ideology in this era was the Pequot activist, orator, and minister William Apess, who insisted on a biblical basis for racial equality. In essays, and speeches, and his autobiography, Apess declared that the U.S., in dispossessing Indigenous people and enslaving Africans, was in violation of God's law. His brilliant "An Indian's Looking-Glass for the White Man" (1833) challenged white Americans to engage in self-reckoning regarding the "blackness" of their sins. In *Eulogy on King Philip* (1836), Apess linked seventeenth-century colonial violence with that of antebellum America, and confronted his audience directly: "Who, my dear sirs, were wanting of the name of savages—whites, or Indians? Let justice answer." Apess's inversion of the white framework of savagery and civilization echoes through political writings by settler activists, from Jeremiah Evarts's "William Penn" essays (1829) to Ralph Waldo Emerson's April 1838 letter to President Martin Van Buren, in which he angrily asked, "Sir, does this government think that the people of the United States are become savage and mad?"

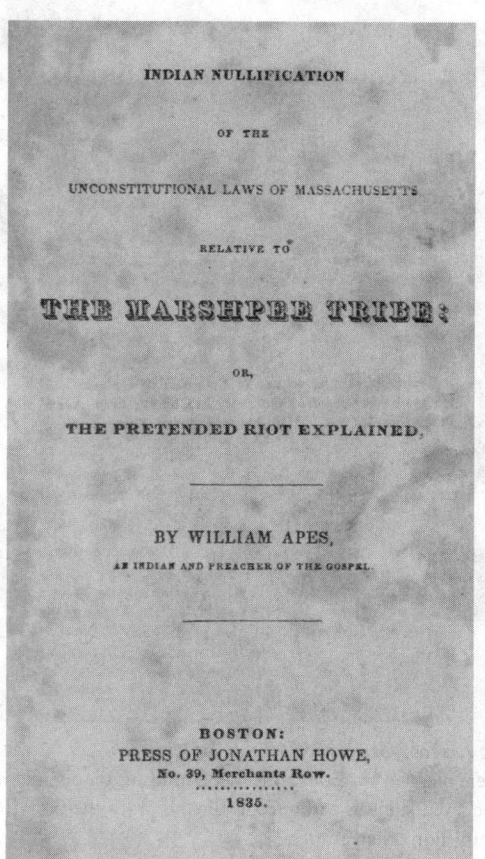

INDIAN NULLIFICATION

OF THE

UNCONSTITUTIONAL LAWS OF MASSACHUSETTS

RELATIVE TO

THE MARSHPEE TRIBE:

OR,

THE PRETENDED RIOT EXPLAINED,

BY WILLIAM APES,

AN INDIAN AND PREACHER OF THE GOSPEL.

BOSTON:
PRESS OF JONATHAN HOWE,
No. 39, Merchants Row.
1835.

Title page of William Apess's *Indian Nullification of the Unconstitutional Laws of Massachusetts Relative to the Marshpee Tribe* (1835).

William Apess was just one of a growing number of Indigenous authors who, in the years prior to the Civil War, produced periodicals, histories, collections of tales and songs, life writing, poetry, and fiction, in Indigenous languages as well as English. After Sequoyah (George Gist) completed a syllabary for the Cherokee language in 1821, the Cherokee Nation adopted it as an official writing system. That syllabary led to the publication of the bilingual *Cherokee Phoenix*, edited by Elias Boudinot (Buck Watie) from 1828 to 1834. The first newspaper in an Indigenous language, the *Phoenix* was read not only by most Cherokee households but also by subscribers across the U.S. and in Europe. Other newspapers followed—among them the Shawnee-language *Siwinowe Kesibwi*

(*The Shawnee Sun*) in 1835, *The Choctaw Telegraph* in 1848, and the bilingual Sioux and English *Iapi Oaye, the Word Carrier* in 1871. Indigenous people also began to write novels, beginning with John Rollin Ridge's *The Life and Adventures of Joaquín Murieta* (1854).

During this period, Indigenous historians also made efforts to document Indigenous history and traditional literatures from the perspective of their own peoples. Tuscarora writer and artist David Cusick was among the first to do so in print with *Sketches of Ancient History of the Six Nations* (1828), offering an Indigenous history of the people of the Haudenosaunee (Iroquois Confederacy) that combines Haudenosaunee and English literary traditions. George Copway (Ojibwe) achieved literary celebrity with his volumes of Ojibwe history and memoir, including *Life, History, and Travels of Kah-ge-ga-gah-bowh* (1847) and *The Traditional History and Characteristic Sketches of the Ojibway Nation* (1850).

Ojibwe author Jane Johnston Schoolcraft (Bamewa-wagezhikaquay) composed poetry in both English and Ojibwe, and translated a number of traditional oral stories into written English. Though she circulated much of her work in manuscript form rather than print, Schoolcraft's impact on nineteenth-century literary culture was profound. Her linguistic and cultural knowledge informed publications by her white husband, Henry Rowe Schoolcraft, beginning with an 1839 collection of Ojibwe oral traditions titled *Algic Researches*, to which her contributions were so extensive that her colleague Elizabeth Oakes Smith described her as "unquestionably, nearly, if not quite" its author. Henry's work, which failed to give adequate credit to his wife, inspired Henry Wadsworth Longfellow's 1855 epic *The Song of Hiawatha*.

This abundance of Native American literary production served as a demonstration of Indigenous humanity in the face of dehumanizing U.S. policy, and affirmed cultural and political sovereignty in a prolonged period of upheaval. Such work existed in conjunction with the variety of nonalphabetic Indigenous literacies including basketry, pictographs, wampum, tattoos, beadwork, scrolls, oral traditions, and orations. Most of these literacies had existed long before contact with Europeans, but some developed later. For example, the ledger art of the Cheyenne, Lakota, Kiowa, and other

THE FLYING HEAD PUT TO FLIGHT BY A WOMAN PARCHING ACORNS.

David Cusick, "The Flying Head Put to Flight by a Woman Parching Acorns," *Sketches of Ancient History of the Six Nations*, 1828. This drawing by Cusick illustrates a story in which the people were plagued by monstrous flying heads until, one night, one of the monsters saw a woman parching acorns and mistakenly believed she was eating coals directly from the fire. The flying heads were so frightened by the sight that they left the community alone thereafter.

Plains Indigenous people adapted the traditions of narrative painting to a nineteenth-century context. Before the pressures of colonization dramatically reduced buffalo populations, buffalo hides had been the most common material for narrative painting on the Plains; in the latter half of the nineteenth century, many artists replaced hides with paper from ledger books obtained from government agents and other settlers, integrating Euro-American drawing and painting implements into their artistic practice.

The interest of non-Indigenous people in Indigenous culture was fostered by U.S. cultural nationalism—somewhat ironically, given the close relationship between ideas of American exceptionalism and "manifest destiny." White Americans appropriated the images, histories, material objects, and languages of Native Americans as fodder for the creation of uniquely "American" art, from painting to music to literature.

This was an era in which an ever-growing number of white authors—among them James Fenimore Cooper, Catharine Maria Sedgwick, Washington Irving, William Gilmore Simms, Henry David Thoreau, Lydia Howard Sigourney, William Cullen Bryant, Margaret Fuller, Lydia Maria Child, and Henry Wadsworth Longfellow—recounted their travels into "Indian country" or spun fictional narratives of often noble Native Americans offering courageous but futile resistance in the face of European conquest. Stereotypes of the "noble savage," of the doomed "Indian warrior," and of the beautiful "Indian princess" pervade these texts. The presentation of Indigenous people in these ways often signaled authorial sympathy for the nations targeted for displacement, yet collectively these works reinforced a myth of the inevitability of Indigenous disappearance and white settlement and conquest, from the Atlantic to the Pacific.

Sitting Bull Counting Coup on an Indian Enemy, c. 1870. This copy of an illustration by the Lakota leader Sitting Bull (c. 1831–90) was drawn on the back of a roster sheet for the U.S. Army's Thirty-First Infantry Regiment. The illustration depicts Sitting Bull's first "coup"—an exploit in which a warrior touched an enemy in battle and escaped unharmed, thereby winning great prestige—at the age of fourteen.

Among the most famous and influential examples of what is sometimes called the "vanishing Indian" myth is Cooper's novel *The Last of the Mohicans: A Narrative of 1757* (1826). As the title suggests, the novel imagines the inevitable demise of the people Cooper calls Mohicans; the culture he imagines combines traits of the Mohican and Mohegan peoples, both of whom in fact continue to survive in the twenty-first century. The novel is admiring in its portrayal of most of its Indigenous characters and poignantly laments the loss of their cultures, but it also presents that loss as a foregone conclusion: at the novel's tragic end, the Lenni Lenape sage Tamenund declares that "The pale-faces are masters of the earth, and the time of the red-men has not yet come again. My day has been too long." *The Last of the Mohicans* retained its popularity and

influence into the twentieth century and has been adapted for film and television numerous times. The myth of the "vanishing Indian" that it helped to popularize persists in twenty-first-century popular culture, from Hollywood films to professional sports—and is present throughout the U.S. Capitol building.

A notable counterpoint to Cooper's work is Herman Melville's 1857 satirical novel *The Confidence-Man*, which focused not on the romanticized Native American but the inverse: Melville exposed the nation's reliance on narratives of the "Indian Hater," a "captain in the vanguard of conquering civilization" whose metaphysics entail "that a brother is to be loved, and an Indian to be hated." Melville knew that works such as Robert Montgomery Bird's *Nick of the Woods* (1837) and Simms's *The Yemassee* (1844) gave expression to the nation's genocidal impulse through the reduction of human beings to caricatures of evil incarnate. In *Nick of the Woods*, for example, the white Quaker Nathan Slaughter roams the Kentucky forest disguised as a monster, murdering Indigenous people to avenge the death of his family. Yet it is Slaughter's Shawnee enemy, the chief Wenonga, whom Bird villainizes. The racism inherent in the portrayal of Wenonga is crude and virulent; at one point Wenonga is portrayed as saying this to Slaughter: "'Me kill all white-man! Me Wenonga: me drink white-man blood; me no heart!'"

Ultimately, the appetite for the Indian Hater narrative and the perpetual representation of Native Americans in non-Indigenous literature, oratory, drama, visual art, music, and even place names, points to a deep disease—and a deep unease—at the heart of white America. The abundance of Indigenous writing and performance in a period of supposed Native American disappearance confirms the foundational role of Indigenous peoples at the moment of American literature's invention.

William H. Powell, *Discovery of the Mississippi by De Soto*, 1855, one of eight historical paintings commissioned by Congress and displayed in the U.S. Capitol rotunda. The painting depicts Hernando De Soto (1500–42) arriving at the shore of the Mississippi near Natchez, 8 May 1541.

THE NEW WORLD.

PARK BENJAMIN, EDITOR.

J. WINCHESTER, PUBLISHER.

"No pent-up Utica contracts our powers; For the whole boundless continent is ours."

EXTRA SERIES.   OFFICE 30 ANN STREET.   NUMBERS 27, 28.

VOLUME II.   NEW-YORK, OCTOBER, 1842.   NUMBERS 3, 4.

Original American Novel.

Entered according to Act of Congress, in the year 1842,
BY PARK BENJAMIN,
In the Clerk's Office of the Southern District of New York.

THE
WESTERN CAPTIVE;
OR,
THE TIMES OF TECUMSEH.

BY MRS. SEBA SMITH.

"Hearing oftentimes
The still, sad music of humanity."—WORDSWORTH.

TO THOSE OF HER SEX,
WHOM THE DESIRE FOR UTTERANCE, OR THE NECESSITIES OF LIFE,
HAVE CALLED FROM THE SANCTITY OF WOMANLY SECLUSION,
THESE PAGES ARE RESPECTFULLY INSCRIBED BY
THE AUTHOR.

CHAPTER I.—FREEDOM.

"Thy birth-right was not given by human hands
Thou wert twin-born with man. In pleasant fields,
While yet our race was few, thou satt'st with him,
To tend the quiet flock and watch the stars."   BRYANT.

THE greatness of an enterprise is to be tested, not by the splendor of its achievement, but by the magnitude of difficulties overcome in its conception. Patriots have struggled and fallen, having accomplished nothing, it may be, in their career, except to add one more impulsive throb to the great beating of the universal heart for freedom—yet time may fail to reveal how essential was that one throb to the high interests of humanity. We may deplore the fate of the individual, at the same time that we rejoice for man. History is full of illustration—slowly but surely is the race advancing to a goal where the chain shall of itself fall from the free limb; and the eye, wandering backward through the long vista of despotism and revolution, shall behold how strong men were stricken in the race, that they might become heralds and guide-marks for others. Such was the fate of Tecumseh—doomed, not to realize the high designs he had conceived, but to add one more to the list of those who have labored for the enfranchisement of a people, and to prove that, in every grade of society, the yearnings of the heart are still for freedom; and that the first and great principles of legislation have their elements in the mind itself; and therefore, the untutored savage being nearer the threshold of truth, may be better able to expound her doctrines, than the statesman, enveloped by custom and the huge intricacies of government.

Tecumseh beheld with dismay the encroachment of the white man upon the soil of his people, and saw that their system of purchase, as it was called, would soon leave them scarce a place for burial, while the infusion of vice among a primitive people was rapidly sealing their destruction. Thence, his active and powerful mind conceived the vast plan of union and peace between those western tribes, occupying the great valley of the Mississippi. He proposed consolidating them into one grand confederation, one of the principle articles of which should be, the non-bartering of their lands. Vast as was the design, it scarcely exceeded the personal sacrifices and hazards necessary to put it in execution.

At the period of the Council of Fort Wayne, in which several of the tribes ceded their lands to our Government under the agency of General Harrison, Tecumseh was absent upon a mission to the southern tribes, that he might obtain their assent to the terms of the league, which had already been obtained from all their northern brethren.

The ceding of lands, therefore, at the Council of Wayne, was in violation of a solemn pledge, and was thence not binding in itself, but also exposed the recreant leaders to the vengeance of the remaining tribes. The followers of Tecumseh and of Elskwatawa, "the open door," or, as he is most commonly called, "The Prophet," remained at their town upon the Tippecanoe, gloomy and inactive, waiting the return of the great chief from his southern crusade. They held little communication with the chiefs of the seceding tribes, regarding them as traitors to the common cause, and unworthy to partake of the high destiny reserved, even now, degenerate and weakened as they were, for the proud and independent children of the woods. They waited impatiently the return of that remarkable man, who united in his own person the bravery and skill of an accomplished warrior, the far-seeing and truth-discerning spirit of a reformer, with the power and persuasive eloquence of the orator. The chiefs of the several tribes had bound themselves by solemn vows and severe penalties, never to part with a foot of their land to the white man, to resume as far as possible the primitive habits of their people, and thus to throw off their yoke of dependence upon the white intruders. All the tribes bordering upon the great lakes of the north, those upon the Mississippi and its noble tributaries, even to the wilderness of the far west, had bound themselves by a like oath; and now the eloquent warrior was preaching his crusade at the south, confident of returning with a like pledge from those distant and excitable people. Skilful were the weapons to be used, and persuasive the tongue which was to give utterance to the conceptions of a great mind, about to realize the hopes and expectations of a patriotism, pure and engrossing, as ever swayed the bosom of a Roman in the proudest days of her freedom. He could not fail of success, for he was a Shawanee, and endowed with even more than the ordinary share of the hardihood and talent belonging to that extraordinary people. He could bring up the traditions of their old men, when the Shawanee dwelt upon the beautiful savannas of the south, and hunted game where the wild grape hung in festoons upon the palmetto, and the moss waved solemnly in the wind, as if a gray

---

First page of the serialization of Elizabeth Oakes Smith, *The Western Captive; or, The Times of Tecumseh*, 1842. Smith, a popular novelist and poet and an acquaintance of Jane Johnston Schoolcraft and Henry Rowe Schoolcraft, was influenced by the Schoolcrafts' work in her depictions of Indigenous lives and cultures. Her novel *The Western Captive* is unusual in its portrayal of Indigenous people not as inevitable casualties of history but as vital participants in an ongoing American struggle. She presents the Shawnee Chief Tecumseh as a "patriot," writing that

> slowly but surely is the race advancing to a goal where the chain shall of itself fall from the free limb; and the eye, wandering backward through the long vista of despotism and revolution, shall behold how strong men were stricken in the race, that they might become heralds and guide-marks for others. Such was the fate of Tecumseh[.]

While Oakes Smith's writings do not partake in the sort of hostile stereotyping of Indigenous peoples that permeates the writing of so many white writers of this period, they are sometimes informed by Rousseauian "noble savage" stereotypes, however; later in the same passage, for example, she comments that "the untutored savage being nearer the threshold of truth, may be better able to expound her doctrines."

WOMEN'S RIGHTS AND WOMEN'S ROLES[1]

Insofar as gender is defined by the law, it is not unreasonable to suggest that women barely existed in early nineteenth-century America. For the first half of the century, marriage was in most of the country governed by the law of coverture, by which all of a woman's property was subsumed under that of her husband upon marriage. The injustice of this law was captured in the 1848 "Declaration of Sentiments," a pioneering women's-rights manifesto: "[man] has made [woman], if married, in the eye of the law, civilly dead." The practice of coverture, a hold-over from English common law, essentially rendered married women, with few exceptions, legally dependent upon their husbands, with no ability to own property in their own names. A married woman could, in a limited number of situations, sue for divorce, but if successful she could not claim custody of the couple's children, except under extreme circumstances.

Though there was little by way of an organized movement for women's rights before the 1840s, some legal changes began to take place in the 1830s; beginning in 1839, several states began passing laws marginally increasing married women's rights to own property under limited circumstances. A significant stride came in April 1848, when the state of New York enacted the Married Women's Property Act, enabling married women to own property and financial assets under their own names. This legislation (which was a direct result of the petitioning of activists such as Elizabeth Cady Stanton and Ernestine Rose) became a model for similar acts passed throughout the United States in subsequent months and years.[2]

By this time increasing numbers of women were beginning to call for far more wide-reaching change. In 1843, Margaret Fuller published her monumental essay "The Great Lawsuit," calling for acknowledgment of women's intellectual equality and challenging her era's conventional conceptions of gender. Most famously, a formalized women's rights movement began to take shape at the Seneca Falls Convention in July 1848. The document that resulted from the convention, the Declaration of Sentiments, took the Declaration of Independence as its model, claiming that "all men and women are created equal" and structuring itself as a demand for government with the consent of the governed. Its signatories included sixty-eight women, including such leading activists as Elizabeth Cady Stanton and Lucretia Mott, and thirty-two men, including Frederick Douglass.

Elizabeth Cady Stanton with her sons Daniel and Henry, 1848.

Even among the group of activists attending the convention, the question of women's *suffrage* remained at this time highly controversial. The Declaration of Sentiments included a demand for women's suffrage rights, but only after robust debate; Frederick Douglass was among the delegates of the Seneca Falls Convention who argued most vigorously and persuasively for the inclusion of this demand in the document.

The only African American at Seneca Falls was Douglass; not a single black woman was invited to attend the convention. Often excluded from activist

---

[1]   Please note that "Contexts: Gender and Sexuality," elsewhere in this volume, addresses women's rights in further detail.

[2]   Not all women saw such laws as a complete victory, however. New York poet Frances Sargent Locke Osgood lamented in 1848 that the bill offered only financial protection to women, and therefore only improved the lives of those who had access to wealth in the first place—doing little to protect women who were poor, or "whose all of wealth / Is in their souls and faces."

organizations on account of their race, gender, or both, black women nonetheless found means to make their voices heard in favor of progressive causes. The extent of the barriers they faced is suggested by the fact that the Colored National Convention did not allow the participation of women delegates until 1848—and that the woman allowed to speak at the convention that year to persuade them to do so, Rebecca Sanford, was white. Despite such barriers, one of the best-remembered women's rights campaigners of the era was Sojourner Truth, who addressed the question of universal suffrage again and again in the 1850s, 60s, and 70s: "There is a great stir about colored men getting their rights, but not a word about the colored women; and if colored men get their rights, and not colored women theirs, you see the colored men will be masters over the women, and it will be just as bad as it was before."

The struggle against the oppression of women and the struggle to end slavery were indeed closely linked during this period; as Fuller remarked in 1843, "the warmest appeal in behalf of women" came from abolitionists, "partly in consequence of a natural following out of principles, partly because many women have been prominent in that cause." Yet women were often excluded from participation in formal abolitionist meetings and conventions, most famously from the 1840 World Anti-Slavery Convention. This exclusion not only triggered a split in the abolitionist movement but also, in many ways, triggered the development of the formalized women's rights movement.

That said, much as there tended to be strong lines of connection between the various progressive causes—most notably, abolitionism and women's rights—we should not assume that there was any *necessary* connection. In fact, several of the most prominent white women's rights leaders were lukewarm in their support of rights for African Americans—or outright opposed the idea that black men might obtain the vote before white women. Elizabeth Cady Stanton, for example, lamented in 1868, "To what a depth of degradation must the women of this nation have fallen to be willing to stand aside, silent and indifferent spectators in the reconstruction of the nation, while all the lower stratas of manhood are to legislate in their interests." On the other hand, the popular poet Lydia Sigourney—who

was strongly supportive of abolition, opposed the Mexican–American war, and spoke out against child labor—was reluctant to support the cause of women's rights; in "Women's patriotism," which appeared in the same year that the Seneca Falls convention took place, Sigourney wrote against the "loud clamor" for "women's rights" (a term she put in quotation marks), and recommended instead that the truly patriotic American woman stay "In her own place, the hearth beside."

There is a powerful irony in the path that the struggle for equitable gender roles took over the course of this period: progressive notions were given greater currency in public conversation at mid-century, but for the most part they were brought no closer to realization in society at large. Speakers and writers received considerable attention when they argued, for example, that women should be free to vote or should receive equal pay for equal work, or when they asserted (as Lucy Stone did) that women should not be required to give up their names upon marriage. But while such notions of equality were being circulated more widely, in its actual practices with regard to gender roles in the mid-to-late nineteenth century, mainstream American society was arguably becoming more restrictive rather than less so.

The middle decades of the nineteenth century saw the crystallization of the ideology of separate spheres: the concept that men and women could best contribute to their communities and attain self-fulfilment by committing themselves to the "spheres" on their respective sides of the gender binary—the public sphere for men, and the private or domestic sphere for women. While women's participation in the public sphere—including politics and the marketplace—had been frequently discouraged by the dominant social norms of much of western history, during the nineteenth century this ideology became increasingly mythologized. "The cult of true womanhood," as it was defined by historian Barbara Welter in the 1960s, was a set of cultural values that defined women as essentially domestic, family-oriented, emotional, physically weak, and selfless beings; women who did not conform to these ideals were often considered to be either morally deficient or simply unfortunate anomalies.

As Sarah Moore Grimké pointed out in the 1830s, marriage was "often held up to the view of girls as the *sine qua non* of human happiness and human existence." As early as 1819, Washington Irving's "The Wife" gave succinct expression to the nineteenth-century feminine ideal as it was beginning to take shape. The story, which tells of a newly married couple who unexpectedly fall into poverty, presents the view that "woman, who is the mere dependant and ornament of man in his happier hours, should be his stay and solace when smitten with sudden calamity …, tenderly supporting the drooping head, and binding up the broken heart." Two decades later, the doctrine of separate spheres was summarized—and applauded—by French social theorist Alexis de Tocqueville, in his monumental *Democracy in America* (1835–40):

In no country has such constant care been taken as in America to trace two clearly distinct lines of action for the two sexes, and to make them keep pace one with the other, but in two pathways which are always different. American women never manage the outward concerns of the family, or conduct a business, or take a part in political life; nor are they, on the other hand, ever compelled to perform the rough labor of the fields, or to make any of those laborious exertions which demand the exertion of physical strength. No families are so poor as to form an exception to this rule. If on

"Little Lessons for Little Ladies," *Harper's New Monthly Magazine*, August 1851. "Fan-ny Fal-lal, al-though she was not rich, nor a per-son of rank, was a ve-ry fine La-dy. She would pass all her time reading novels and work-ing cro-chet, but would neg-lect her house-hold du-ties; so her hus-band, who was a ve-ry nice man, and fond of a nice din-ner, be-came a mem-ber of a Club, and used to stop out ve-ry late at night, which led to ma-ny quar-rels. How fool-ish it was of Fan-ny to neg-lect her house-hold du-ties, and not to make her Al-bert hap-py at home."

the one hand an American woman cannot escape from the quiet circle of domestic employments, on the other hand she is never forced to go beyond it. Hence it is that the women of America, who often exhibit a masculine strength of understanding and a manly energy, generally preserve great delicacy of personal appearance and always retain the manners of women, although they sometimes show that they have the hearts and minds of men.

The shift toward hard-and-fast gender roles is closely connected to the shift toward a more urban society gathering steam during this period. Whereas between 1790 and 1820 the percentage of city-dwelling Americans increased only slightly (from 5.1% to 7.2%), by 1870 25.7% of Americans lived in cities. That is of course a long way from twenty-first-century America (in which roughly 80% are urban dwellers),

Albert Sands Southworth and/or Josiah Johnson Hawes, *Girl with Portrait of George Washington*, c. 1850. Women activists began in the 1840s and 1850s to rethink the ideas of the founders on the matter of gender equality; as Elizabeth Cady Stanton put it in her *Declaration of Sentiments*, "we hold these truths to be self-evident, that all men and women are created equal."

but it nonetheless represented a substantial movement away from American conventions of farm life circa 1800, which often involved husband and wife toiling together in the fields.

By the 1830s the ideology of separate spheres was strengthening even in rural areas. But for many families, the gendered ideal remained by necessity primarily aspirational in nature. In his assertion that no family was "so poor as to form an exception to this rule," de Toqueville was clearly mistaken. In the 1830s many women did indeed contribute to the "rough labor of the fields," and many were compelled to leave home to find paid employment. Moreover, since many employers were reluctant to hire women, paid work was often undertaken from the home. Sarah Moore Grimké described this difficult situation in one of her *Letters on the Equality of the Sexes*: "I have known a widow, left with four or five children to provide for, unable to leave home because her helpless babes demand her attention, compelled to earn a scanty subsistence, by making coarse shirts at 12 ½ cents a piece, or by taking in washing, for which she was paid by some wealthy persons 12 ½ cents per dozen."

The transition from rural to urban family life is often imagined to have resulted in the husband finding paid work and the wife taking care of the home and the children. Though such arrangements were not uncommon, it was common as well for the young women of the family to be the first to take up paid employment in the city. Indeed, one of the first templates for factory employment in the United States, the scheme developed by Francis Cabot Lowell, was intended specifically for young women. Lowell intended his scheme to be a more humane and forward-looking alternative to the English system, in which factory girls were often overworked, underpaid, and generally exploited. Factories that made use of this scheme—most famously the textile mills in Lowell, Massachusetts—initially promised their employees (relatively) good wages, clean and comfortable housing (the vast majority of female employees lived communally in on-site boarding houses), and a companionable environment in which the "mill girls" were given broader educational and cultural opportunities than would normally have been available to them. The scheme offered an allure of independence for young women that seemed almost

Winslow Homer, *New England Factory Life—"Bell Time,"* in *Harper's Weekly*, 25 July 1868.

revolutionary at the time. But by the mid-1830s, facing increased competition, many such mills began lowering the young women's wages, and conditions began deteriorating in other ways. In 1845 the mill employees formed the Female Labor Reform Organization, but to little avail. Factory work was not without stigma, either (as noted in the opening paragraphs of this introduction). By 1850, most of the factory owners, seeking ever-cheaper labor, had begun hiring immigrants instead of native-born women.

As the world of work became more and more organized into separate spheres, certain occupations became female-gendered to such an extent that men were regarded with amusement, suspicion, or distrust if they were so employed. Many retail sales jobs, for example, came to be considered the province of "shop girls"; though men often worked in such jobs, the pay was not enough to support a family, and the handling of fabric and other domestic items was a far cry from the rough physical labor that was considered the province of working-class men. The 1860 poem "Opening Day" makes the stereotype clear in its lament for the dry goods salesmen said to grow "thinner, weaker, feebler" through their employment:

> Ah, would they try
> To live—or die—
> By manly toil, despairing never!
> But no, each soul
> Plays woman's role,
> And tape and yardstick rule forever![1]

In many areas of nineteenth-century America, women were more likely to work in domestic service than any other occupation. A life "in service" in the nineteenth century is stereotypically associated with Victorian Britain, but statistics suggest that the percentage of the population employed as domestic servants in the U.S. in 1870—7.7%—may well have been as high as in Britain at the time. Employment as a governess, however (a situation common throughout

---

1   For more on dry-goods salesmen and on ideas of masculinity during this period, see "Contexts: Gender and Sexuality" elsewhere in this volume.

Britain during this period), was far less common in the United States.

The ideology of separate spheres, and related ideas of women's physical capabilities, did not apply to enslaved women, who often performed excruciatingly hard work. Many activists picked up on this double standard—particularly activists who had experience of slavery, such as Sojourner Truth. In her famous 1851 speech, Truth pointed out, "I have as much muscle as any man, and can do as much work as any man. I have plowed and reaped and husked and chopped and mowed, and can any man do more than that?" Yet, while enslaved women's gender was not considered when they were exploited in the fields, their gender *was* considered when their enslavers exploited them for their sexual and reproductive abilities. Formerly enslaved abolitionist Harriet Jacobs wrote that "Slavery is terrible for men; but it is far more terrible for women. Superadded to the burden common to all, they have wrongs, and sufferings, and mortifications peculiarly their own."

In the other direction, white attitudes toward slavery were gendered to a significant degree. Indeed, if Harriet Martineau is to be believed, it is entirely possible that a majority of the overall population of the South was in fact opposed to slavery. On the basis of her extensive travels in the United States in 1834, the famed British writer reported that she had "never met a lady of Southern origin who did not speak of slavery as a sin and a curse—the burden which oppressed their lives." If it were indeed the case that a majority of white Southern women were in fact quietly opposed to slavery, they, together with the roughly one-third of the population who were black,[1] would have constituted well over 50 per cent of the population of the South.

What Martineau does not make clear is that many of the white Southern women who detested slavery did so not because of fellow-feeling with enslaved African Americans, but in disgust at the damage to their own families caused by slaveholding men who routinely raped the women and girls they had enslaved. "God forgive us, but ours is a monstrous system," Mary Chesnut lamented: "our men live all in one house with their wives and their concubines, and the mulattoes one sees in every family exactly resemble the white children—and every lady tells you who is the father of all mulatto children in everybody's household, but those in her own she seems to think drop from the clouds, or pretends so to think."

Another subject of debate commonly linked to nineteenth-century women activists is the temperance movement, which played a vitally important role in the shaping of American social and political life from the 1820s onwards. In the twenty-first century, the puritanical temperance crusader demanding that people abstain from alcohol has become a quaint stereotype—but such a position seems far from absurd when one looks at the numbers. In 1790 the average American adult consumed 2.5 gallons of ethanol annually—very close to today's level of 2.4 gallons. But by 1810 Americans' per capita consumption had risen to 4.5 gallons, and by 1830 to a level far higher than that of any nation in the twenty-first century—7.1 gallons; those Americans who drank alcohol were on average consuming the equivalent of almost two bottles of whisky every week. The toll on family life was unprecedented.

It should not surprise us, then, that the fight for women's rights and the belief that women should work as society's moral leaders were tied closely to the movement for temperance. Among the most prominent temperance activists were Elizabeth Cady Stanton, Susan B. Anthony, and the poet Frances Harper. Harper, known today largely for her abolitionist and anti-racist writings, also wrote myriad poems on the subject of temperance (among them "The Drunkard's Child" and "The Revel") and spoke on the subject extensively in the years following the Civil War.

At the beginning of the 1820–Reconstruction period, Washington Irving was proving that it was possible for a man to earn a living by his pen in America. By the end of it, a very considerable number of women had proven that the same was possible for them. In the middle decades of the century, indeed, the leading women writers were at least as successful as the men. Though works such as Hawthorne's

---

[1] The ratio of black people to white people in the South remained quite consistent throughout the period, even as the overall population increased. In 1820 enslaved African Americans constituted 33 per cent of the total population (4,507,845) of the Southern states, with free people of color comprising an additional 3 per cent; in 1860 enslaved African Americans constituted 32 per cent of the overall population of 12,240,293, with free people of color comprising an additional 2 per cent.

Scarlet Letter, Melville's *Moby-Dick*, and Whitman's *Leaves of Grass* have become central to the canon of American literature, they did not sell overly well at the time. Far more successful were Harriet Beecher Stowe's *Uncle Tom's Cabin* (1851–52) and Susan Warner's *The Wide, Wide World* (1850), a novel of a young woman who struggles to find her way after the death of her mother; the book was issued in fourteen editions in its first two years. Fiction writers Susanna Cummins, E.D.E.N. Southworth, Elizabeth Oakes Smith, and Ann Sophia Stephens were hugely successful as well, as was the poet Lydia Sigourney; by the 1850s there could be no question that women were just as capable as men of earning a living out of literature. Yet women who wrote for publication were still frowned upon by some more conservative members of society (leading many women, especially at the beginnings of their careers, to publish anonymously or pseudonymously). And—as Louisa May Alcott makes clear in *Little Women*—there were still significant barriers for women to overcome if they wished to make writing their career. Writers such as Sigourney—who wrote both on conventional poetic themes and on issues such as slavery and the oppression of Indigenous peoples, and whose writing often provided the main source of income in a household in which the husband suffered various financial reverses—had to work hard to maintain a veneer of middle-class feminine respectability. When Sigourney published a volume of verse without her husband's knowledge, his response told much of the era's conception of women: "Who wants, or would value, a wife who is to be the public property of the whole community?"

Nathaniel Currier, *The Drunkard's Progress. From the First Glass to the Grave*, 1846. "Step 1. A glass with a Friend. "Step 2. A glass to keep the cold out." "Step 3. A glass too much." "Step 4. Drunk and riotous." "Step 5. The summit attained. Jolly companions. A confirmed drunkard." "Step 6. Poverty and Disease." "Step 7. Forsaken by Friends." "Step 8. Desperation and crime." "Step 9. Death by suicide."

Much is often made in discussions of gender in mid-nineteenth-century America of women's clothing of the era and of dress reform movements such as the development of bloomers in the 1850s. Named after their first prominent proponent, Amelia Bloomer, bloomers (loose-fitting trousers inspired by Turkish fashions, designed to be worn under knee-length skirts) did represent—for the middle and upper classes, at least—a strikingly different new option. But the backlash against women who challenged conventional gender norms through their dress was so extreme that the vast majority of bloomer-wearers abandoned the garment after a few years; as with votes for women and other matters of women's rights, it would not be until well into the twentieth century that more practical clothing for women in certain social or occupational classes became socially acceptable.

Bloomers represented one approach to the matter of how to design practical clothing for women. Others tried to adopt a more straightforward approach—wearing clothing designed for men. Yet in many jurisdictions, and increasingly as the century progressed, wearing garments conventionally associated with the opposite sex was punishable by law. The famous journalist Fanny Fern spoke out against such absurd laws, and herself experimented with wearing her husband's clothing for rainy walks. Fern's is far from the only case of a woman dressing in men's clothing during this period. But for the most part these were driven by concerns very far from a wish to enjoy greater comfort in everyday life; the largest number of women dressing as men during the period was probably during the Civil War, when numerous cases were reported of women assuming men's garb in order to enlist.[1] The majority of women, to be sure, dressed in ways that adhered strictly to the period's norms. But as these examples suggest, various women in this period cross-dressed in a number of different ways and for a variety of different reasons: some passed as men in daily life, some wore men's clothes without attempting to pass as men; some were women in romantic or sexual relationships with other women; some who consistently passed as men did so to travel more safely or to pursue careers

Nathaniel Currier, *The Bloomer Costume*, 1851.

not open to women, while others did so because they considered themselves men.[2]

MARRIAGE AND SEXUALITY[3]

At the beginning of the nineteenth century the idea that most people have an innate, fixed sexual orientation had not yet surfaced in public discourse. By the end of the century, that idea was taking root strongly in America (as in Britain and elsewhere)—but there is disagreement both as to when exactly it began to do so, and about how quickly the change occurred. Undoubtedly, a key point in the development of the idea of discrete homosexual and heterosexual identities is the coining of the words "homosexual" and "heterosexual" themselves; they are first recorded as having been used by the Austrian writer Karl-Maria Kertbeny

---

[1] Similar behavior was at least as common during the Revolutionary War in the late eighteenth century, but it seems to have entirely died out by the time of the First and Second World Wars in the twentieth.

[2] Because the word "transgender" was coined in the twentieth century, it can be difficult to determine what language should apply to people of earlier centuries whose experience of gender does not appear to have matched the gender they were assigned at birth. For real and fictional examples of such lives, see "Contexts: Gender and Sexuality" elsewhere in this volume.

[3] Please note that a "Contexts" section on the topic of "Gender and Sexuality" appears in the body of this volume.

in the late 1860s, but they took decades to become established in the English language. (The first modern usage of "bisexual" followed in the 1880s.) Before this, other terms existed to describe people who engaged in same-sex sexual activity; terms such as "lesbian" and "sapphic" are recorded as early as the mid-eighteenth century, and for men "sodomite" was long the term most commonly used. "Sodomite" and "homosexual" are, however, far from precise equivalents. Whereas the term "homosexual" references an inherent desire for sexual activity with members of one's own sex, the term "sodomy" references a particular act—an act that, as an early nineteenth-century Maryland law put it, "involved the penetration of a penis inside the rectum of an animal, woman or girl, or another man or a boy." To be sure, "sodomy" and "sodomite" seem often to have been used with particular reference to acts involving two men, but it was often assumed that those who engaged in such acts would have preferred an encounter with a woman—or alternatively, as in the arguments put forward in one newspaper in 1859 concerning the alleged proclivity of Chinese immigrants in San Francisco for sodomy, that it was a vice which one could be induced to abandon, so long as one had the good example of others to follow.

One result of these views is that same-sex sexuality was in many respects heavily regulated—both socially and, for men, legally, in that sodomy was a crime carrying long prison sentences and, under some circumstances, the threat of execution. Some environments (such as the navy) were more permissive than others, but there was always a threat of both legal and extra-legal punishment; in 1854, for example, a Presbyterian minister convicted of sodomy in Mobile, Alabama, was forced to "flee from the city or risk the chances of life in the hands of an infuriated mob." Yet despite such repressive norms, the absence of clearly defined sexual orientations also meant that individuals' experiences and expressions of desire were in some respects more fluid than they would be in the following century. Individuals might engage in same-sex intimacy—forbidden or otherwise—in ways that do not quite map on to later models of homo-, bi-, or heterosexuality. And not all forms of same-sex passion were forbidden: especially for young women, passionate connections of great intensity were permitted and even welcome.

Women in such friendships might openly kiss, cuddle, and share a bed, though it was expected that their physical intimacy would stop there—and in individual cases it is often difficult to determine whether it did or not.

The eroticism of passionate friendship—and its limits—are articulated by the writer Margaret Sweat in

Frances Shimer and Cindarella Gregory, 1869. Shimer and Gregory co-founded Mount Carroll Seminary—a pioneering higher-education institution in northwestern Illinois—in 1853 and ran it together until 1870; they had an extremely close relationship that one modern scholar has characterized as a "passionate friendship." Shimer married in 1857; she and her husband lived in separate quarters throughout their marriage.

her only novel, *Ethel's Love Life* (1859), whose description of a woman's connections with other women extends further into erotic territory than is typical of discussions of romantic friendship. When in that novel Ethel writes to her fiancé Ernest that "women often love each other with as much fervor and excitement as they do men," she also specifies that such love is "[f]reed from all the grosser elements of passion, as it exists between the sexes," while "it retains its energy, its abandonment, its flush, its eagerness, its palpitation, and its rapture." While a twenty-first-century reader might be tempted to speculate as to where Sweat would draw the line between "the grosser elements of passion" and the "rapture" that remained, it would be difficult to argue that there is nothing sexual in the novel's vision of same-sex love:

I have had my passionate attachments among women, which swept like whirlwinds over me, sometimes scorching me with a furnace blast[.] … I have loved so intensely that the daily and nightly communion I have held with my beloved ones has not sufficed to slake my thirst for them, nor the lavishness of their love for me been able to satisfy the demands of my exacting nature.

A high percentage of the most canonical of mid- and late-nineteenth-century American authors—including Dickinson, Emerson, and Melville as well as Whitman and James—have been thought by many of their biographers to have felt or, in some cases, acted on same-sex desires. Of these, it was Whitman who became most famous for foregrounding what he referred to in 1856 in a letter to Emerson as "manly friendship." At

Daguerreotype of two women, c. 1859. The woman on the right has been identified as Catherine Mary ("Kate") Scott Turner, an old friend of Sue Gilbert Dickinson, who (along with Austin Dickinson, her husband and Emily's brother) lived next door to Emily Dickinson. Some have argued that the figure on the left is Emily Dickinson. Kate Scott Turner and Emily Dickinson developed a warm friendship beginning in January 1859, but had a falling out in 1860. Turner's husband had died in 1857; in 1866 she married John Hone Anthon (and is thus also often referred to as Kate Anthon).

that time, he complained, there was little or nothing to be heard on the subject: "As to manly friendship, everywhere observed in the States, there is not the first breath of it to be observed in print." That would change in subsequent decades, as same-sex romantic friendship would become a commonplace element in literary fiction by the end of the century. Whitman's own view of such friendships was perhaps more sexual and certainly more ideological than that of most of his contemporaries. In *Democratic Vistas* (1871) he praised the "fervid comradeship" of same-sex love, and described it as a "counterbalance and offset of our materialistic and vulgar American democracy, and for the spiritualization thereof."

Whitman's poetry aroused substantial controversy among Americans in the nineteenth century—but not for the reasons we might assume today. Indeed, Whitman's most controversial poems appear not to have been those we are likely to interpret as homoerotic but rather those that celebrated too openly things such as heterosexual intercourse and prostitution, such as the

Portrait of Bayard Taylor by Thomas Hicks, 1855. A well-known author and lecturer in the mid-nineteenth century, Taylor gained fame as a poet and travel writer; his accounts of his journeys to the Middle East and to other locations prompted Hicks to paint him in Arab attire in this portrait. While traveling in Egypt, Taylor lived on a boat on the Nile with a middle-aged German business-man, later describing their time together as "happy and care-free as two Adams in a Paradise without Eves." Taylor is perhaps best-known today for his 1870 novel *Joseph and His Friend*, which has been described as "America's first gay novel"; Taylor addressed it to those "who believe in the truth and tenderness of man's love for man."

Herman Melville, c. 1860; Elizabeth Shaw Melville, c. 1860. He was an occasionally disloyal and some-times abusive husband; she copied and edited his manuscripts and is said to have remained devoted to him.

Anonymous, *The Plantation*, 1825.

Deborah Goldsmith, *Family Portrait*, c. 1832. Deborah Goldsmith (1808–36) earned her living as a traveling portrait painter in New York State—a very unusual career for a woman at the time. While she worked predominantly in watercolor, the family portrait reproduced here was painted with oils. The woman depicted holding a baby in the upper left corner would have been a servant rather than enslaved, as slavery had been abolished in New York in the 1820s.

"A token of love from me, to thee."

S. M. Douglass.

Sarah Mapps Douglass, *A Token of Love from Me to Thee*, 1833. Especially popular among younger women of the mid-nineteenth century, friendship albums are collections of poems and drawings—sometimes original, sometimes copied—contributed by the owner's friends. The painting included here, an original work by educator, writer, and activist Sarah Mapps Douglass, appears in the album of her friend and fellow activist Amy Cassey; Cassey and Douglass were both members of the Philadelphia Female Anti-Slavery Society, a mixed-race abolitionist organization, and of the Female Literary Association, a society of women intellectuals from Philadelphia's flourishing free black community. Mapps Douglass and the other middle-class black women in her circle laid claim to arts, such as writing and floral painting, that were in most of America considered the province of white women.

Thomas Cole, *The Course of Empire: The Consummation of Empire*, 1836. In 1833, Cole, an English-born painter, began work on a series of five allegorical paintings that would, in his words, show the changes "effected by man in his progress from Barbarism to Civilization, to Luxury, the Vicious state or state of destruction and to the state of Ruin & Desolation." The series' title was taken from a line from an eighteenth-century poem, "Verses on the Prospect of Planting Arts and Learning in America," that was frequently cited by nineteenth-century exponents of American national expansion: "Westward the Course of Empire takes its way." Each painting in the series depicts the same riverbank location, first as a village of nomadic hunters, then as a small agricultural settlement; in this painting, the third, the setting has developed into a magnificent—but also militaristic and decadent—imperial capital.

Thomas Cole, *The Course of Empire: Destruction*, 1836. This, the fourth painting in Cole's series, depicts the great city shown in the previous painting being sacked by a hostile army. *Destruction*, like the rest of *The Course of Empire*, was greeted with acclaim when the full series was exhibited in New York in 1836; the *New-York Mirror* wrote that it portrayed "the merited downfall of all the empires which the earth has heretofore known." Like some of his literary and artistic peers, Cole harbored fears of the U.S. experiencing a similar fate. In an 1835 journal entry, he wrote of his fears that the republic of America could face its downfall as a result of internal division and conflict: "I have of late felt a presentiment that the Institutions of the U[nited] States will ere long undergo a change—that there will be a separation of the States."

George Catlin, *Wi-jún-jon, Pigeon's Egg Head (The Light) Going to and Returning from Washington*, 1837–39. Catlin made it his artistic mission to create a visual record of traditional Native American ways of life—which, like many nineteenth-century white Americans, he believed to be headed for inevitable extinction. In the course of several journeys through the American West in the 1830s, Catlin created hundreds of portraits and other depictions of Native Americans, assembling them in what he called his "Indian Gallery." This painting is a double portrait of Ah-jon-jon, a leader of the Assiniboine nation of the northern Great Plains whose name, meaning "The Light," Catlin mistranslated as "Pigeon's Egg Head." The Light visited Washington, D.C. in 1831–32; while there, in Catlin's words, he "exchanged his beautifully garnished and classic costume" for a U.S.-style military uniform. "In this fashion," Catlin continued, "was poor Wi-jun-jon metamorphosed."

Edmonia Lewis, *Hiawatha*, 1868. A sculptor of black and Ojibwe parentage, Edmonia Lewis spent much of her career in a community of women artists in Rome, where she said she was "practically driven" because "the land of liberty had no room for a colored sculptor." Lewis sometimes took up subject matter that capitalized on her American audience's fascination with her racial background. The bust represented here depicts the Haudenosaunee (Iroquois) leader Hiawatha; Lewis paired it with a bust of Minnehaha, his fictional beloved in Longfellow's famous poem *The Song of Hiawatha* (1855).

Robert S. Duncanson, *Uncle Tom and Little Eva*, 1853. Born to a free black family in New York State, Robert S. Duncanson achieved international acclaim as, in the words of one American critic, "the best landscape painter in the West." The painting reproduced here, of characters from *Uncle Tom's Cabin*, is unusual in that Duncanson did not generally comment directly on racial issues in his work, although he did paint other scenes drawn from literature. *Uncle Tom's Cabin* was a common source of inspiration for mid-nineteenth-century artists, who were especially drawn to this scene in which Tom and Eva discuss religion; see Stowe's author section for further examples of art inspired by her novel.

Winslow Homer, *The Veteran in a New Field*, 1865. New England artist Winslow Homer spent part of the Civil War on the front lines as an illustrator depicting events for *Harper's Weekly*; following this experience, he produced a number of paintings reflecting on the war and its meaning. In this painting, completed a few months after the war ended, the figure is identified as a Union veteran by his jacket and canteen in the bottom right corner, almost obscured by the stalks of grain he is harvesting.

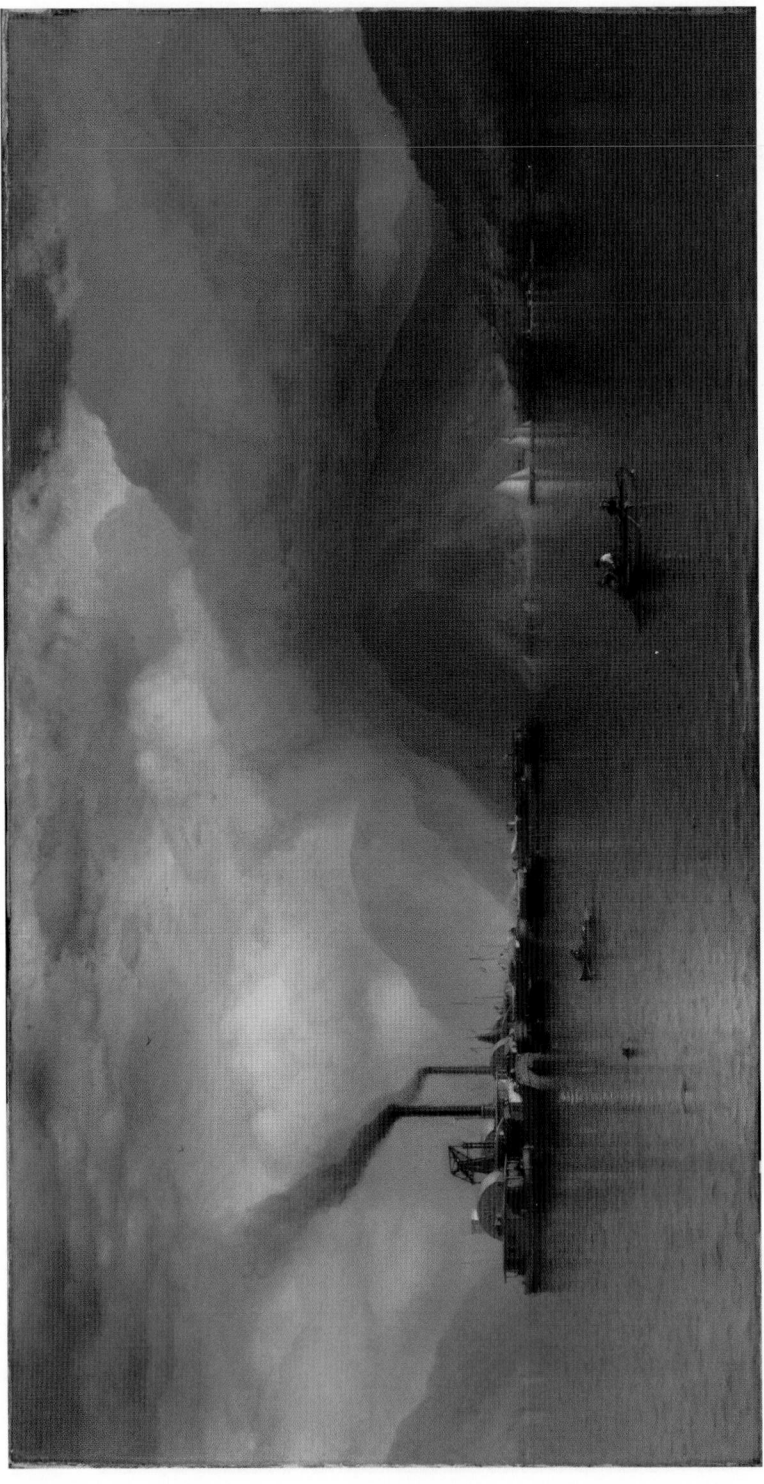

Samuel Colman Jr., *Storm King on the Hudson*, 1866. Colman belonged to the so-called "second generation" of the Hudson River School, an artistic movement founded in the 1820s and 30s that sought to capture what its practitioners considered to be the unique power of the American natural landscape—and the drama of its (white) human settlement. By the 1860s, many Hudson River School artists had taken to depicting scenes from (or inspired by) the trans-Mississippi West, but this painting maintains the school's traditional focus on the northeastern Hudson Valley landscapes. By the time Colman painted this depiction of the Hudson River near Storm King Mountain (a peak famous for dramatic weather), steam technology was transforming the river's extensive commercial traffic—as the painting illustrates.

Emily Dickinson, Seq. 32, *Herbarium*, c. 1839–46. When she was about nine years old, Emily Dickinson began to keep a detailed herbarium of flowers labeled with their Latin names and carefully pressed into a clothbound book. By the time she completed the book, around the age of sixteen, she had accumulated more than sixty pages of preserved flowers. The flowers on the page depicted here include *Solanum tuberosum* (the potato flower; upper left), *Veronica serpyllifolia* (thyme-leaved speedwell; middle row, second from left), and *Digitalis purpurea* (common foxglove; upper right). For additional pages from the herbarium, see Dickinson's author entry in this anthology.

After John Gast, *American Progress*, c. 1873 (painting produced 1872). *American Progress*, the best-known painting by Brooklyn-based artist John Gast, was commissioned by the publisher George Crofutt, who distributed it widely as the color print reproduced here and used it as a frontispiece in one of his popular tourist guides to the American West. In an advertisement offering the print to his subscribers, Crofutt describes it as a

> beautiful picture, which ... represents the United States' portion of the American Continent in its beauty and variety, from the Atlantic to the Pacific Ocean, illustrating at a glance the grand drama of Progress in the civilization, settlement and history of this country.
>
> In the foreground, the central and principal figure, a beautiful and charming female, is floating westward through the air, bearing on her forehead the "Star of Empire." ... In her right hand she carries a book—common schools—the emblem of education and the testimonial of our national enlightenment, while with the left hand she unfolds and stretches the slender wires of the telegraph, that are to flash intelligence throughout the land. On the right of the picture, is a city, steamships, manufactures, schools and churches, over which beams of light are streaming and filling the air—indicative of civilization. The general tone of the picture on the left, declares darkness, waste and confusion. ... Fleeing from "Progress," and towards the blue waters of the Pacific, ... are the Indians, buffaloes, wild horses, bears, and other game, moving westward—ever westward—the Indians ... turn their despairing faces towards, as they flee from, the presence of the wondrous vision. The "Star" is *too much for them*. ...

Howling Wolf, *At the Sand Creek Massacre*, 1874–75. Southern Cheyenne warrior and artist Howling Wolf was one of his era's most important practitioners of ledger art, a form that adapted Plains Indigenous painting styles and methods to Euro-American materials, including the ledger paper that was commonly used by traders and government officials. Howling Wolf here depicts the Sand Creek Massacre (1864), where a U.S. government force of 675 soldiers attacked a Cheyenne and Arapaho camp on a reservation, ignoring the inhabitants' clear attempts to surrender. While most of the estimated 150 to 230 people the soldiers killed were children and unarmed civilians, Howling Wolf was one of a small number of Cheyenne and Arapaho warriors who attempted to defend their community—but with little success, as they possessed only bows and rifles while the U.S. forces were well-armed with heavy artillery at their disposal. The soldiers scalped and mutilated the bodies of those they had killed, and the extraordinary brutality of the event evoked national disgust; their colonel, John Chivington, was condemned by a congressional committee for leading "a foul and dastardly massacre." Survivors of the massacre preserved its history in oral literature, and in hide paintings and other visual works such as the one reproduced here.

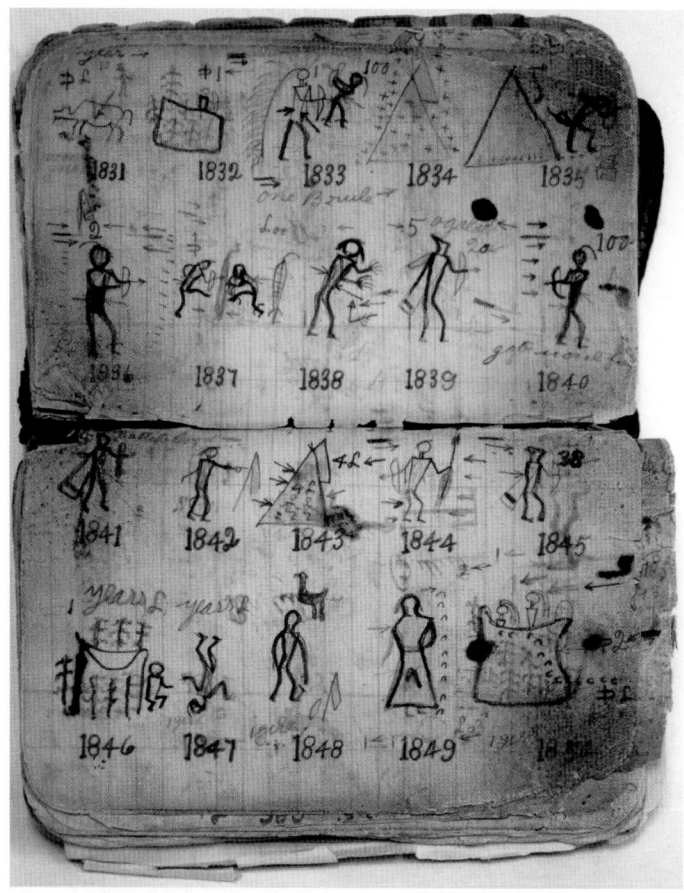

Battiste Good / Wapostangi, page of a winter count documenting 1831–52 (copy produced 1880). Winter counts, kept by Lakota, Kiowa, and other Plains peoples, are community records. In a Lakota winter count, each year is marked at the end of winter by a symbol indicating what the community has determined to be the most memorable event of that year; this symbol, drawn by the winter count's keeper, serves as a record of the year's name and a memory aid for the telling of the community's history. Winter counts were initially kept on buffalo hides and, increasingly as buffalo became scarce, cloth or paper. Battiste Good (Wapostangi), a winter count keeper of the Sicangu Lakota, kept his community's count on cloth, but the page reproduced here is drawn from a ledger-paper copy he made for a white collector. Many year names reference deaths, injuries, and battles; a selection of the year names for this page as given by Good may be translated as follows:

1830–31: "Shot-many-white-buffalo-cows winter"

1832–33: "Stiff-Leg-with-War-Bonnet-on-died winter," during which Stiff Leg died in a battle with Pawnee warriors

1833–34: "Storm-of-stars winter," the year of an exceptional meteor shower

1834–35: "Killed-the-Cheyenne-who-came-to-camp winter"

1839–40: "Came-home-from-the-starve-to-death-war-path winter," during which many Lakota peoples united against the Pawnee, succeeding in battle but nearly starving in the process

1845–46: "Broke-out-on-faces-had-sore-throats-and-camped-under-the-bluff winter"

1847–48: "The-Teal-broke-his-leg winter," the symbol for which shows The Teal's arm pointing toward the fractured leg, with a teal (a species of bird) near his head to suggest his identity

The Longfellows with friends, Newport, Rhode Island, 1852. Henry Wadsworth Longfellow is to the right, Frances ("Fanny") Longfellow in the center. The photo is a reminder of how tightly knit much of nineteenth-century literary society was; the Longfellows and the Melvilles were well acquainted with each other; Frances Appleton (as she had been before she married Longfellow) and Elizabeth Shaw had grown up in the same neighborhood of Boston. Another friend was poet Julia Ward Howe, the woman in the photograph with her hand on Fanny Longfellow's shoulder.

sexually explicit "A Woman Waits for Me." That said, Whitman has long been celebrated by many as a gay poet, especially since the late twentieth century, with his "Calamus" series in particular now well-known for its lyrical depiction of same-sex love.

When it came to sexuality between men and women, social norms largely restricted its expression to the confines of marriage. Women risked much more than men by contravening these norms—not only the possibility of pregnancy but also, especially for middle- and upper-class women, social ostracism. This is not to say, however, that sexual purity mores were not applied to men at all. Social reformer Sylvester Graham was among those who zealously advocated that men refrain from indulging their sexual impulses outside marriage, and his *Lecture to Young Men, on Chastity* (1837) also vigorously condemns what he calls "the worst form of venereal indulgence," masturbation. The disgust with which masturbation was considered by those who were willing to publicly mention it speaks to the profound suspicion with which all sexual activity outside the bounds of what was considered "natural"—i.e., inter-course between a married man and woman, engaged in primarily to produce children—was widely viewed at the time.

As to marriage, a wide variety of conduct books offered advice. Matthew Hale Smith's *Counsels Addressed to Young Ladies and Young Men* (1846), for example, advised those contemplating marriage not to "expect, nor insist upon, perfection," and not to be "misled by beauty, rank, or wealth; they are not to be despised, but they cannot alone make you happy." A young person was advised not to marry

unless there is … a sincere attachment. Sordid, conventional marriages, or marriages for convenience, are frightful things. … [But] if your hearts are bound together by love; if both are yielding and true; if both cultivate the spirit of meekness, forbearance, and kindness, you will be blessed in your home and in the journey of life.

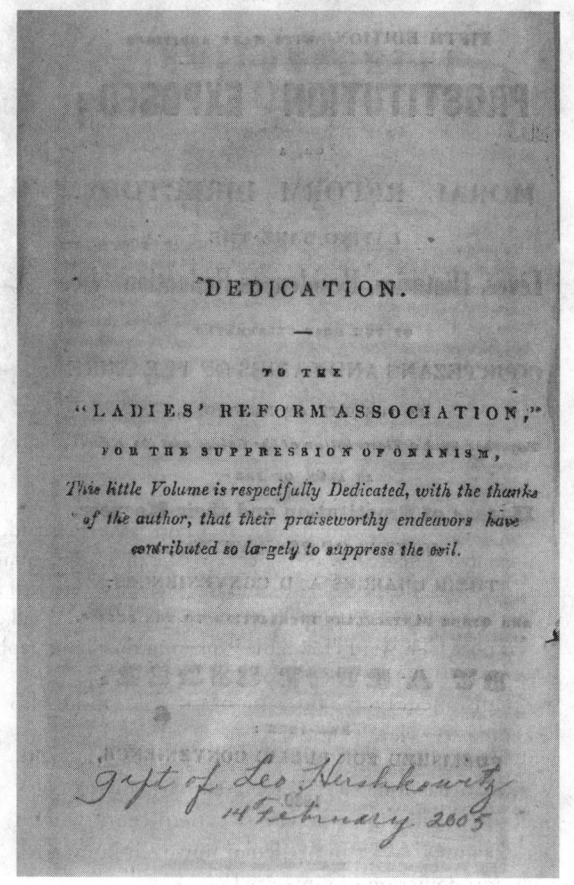

Pages from *Prostitution Exposed* (1839), the earliest known American brothel guide. These publications, marketed to middle- or upper-class men, provided directories of houses of prostitution in major cities (in the case of *Prostitution Exposed*, New York City), together with brief descriptions of the establishments. The dedication page of *Prostitution Exposed* parodies the rhetoric of contemporary moral reformers—specifically, those who sought to prevent the practice of masturbation—by dedicating the book "to the 'Ladies' Reform Association,' for the suppression of onanism," i.e., masturbation; the implication is that the "ladies" in question are sex workers, who prevent "onanism" by offering sexual services to men.

Daguerreotype of Edgar Allan Poe, 1848; daguerreotype of Sara Helen Whitman, c. 1856. The two were engaged to be married in 1848, but broke off the engagement. Whitman, a widow, was herself an accomplished poet; after Poe's death she became active in the struggle for women's rights, and did not again marry.

Such was the ideal—and yet both the conduct books and the marriage vows also made clear to young women that, in Hale-Smith's words, that they must "be obedient. So God expressly commands. … The head of the woman is the man; he must control and direct." In most American jurisdictions the law permitted corporal punishment by the husband of the wife, and it also accepted the view of the famous seventeenth-century British jurist Matthew Hale, who had ruled during the colonial period that a "husband cannot be guilty of rape committed by himself upon his lawful property throughout the marriage."

Among the most interesting opponents of such views was Lucy Stone; when she married abolitionist Henry Blackwell in 1855 the couple refused to make any reference to obedience in their marriage vows, and they prepared a special statement to be read at the ceremony. (Thomas Wentworth Higginson, who read the statement and performed the marriage, later encouraged others to follow the same principles.) Stone and Blackwell also negotiated a private agreement regarding sexual and reproductive rights; following principles that had been set out in Henry C. Wright's highly unconventional manual *Marriage and Parentage; or The Reproductive Element in Man, as a Means to His Elevation and Happiness* (1854), the two agreed that the woman should be in control of "the reproductive element."

Divorce also became more common during the nineteenth century, as the power to grant divorce shifted from the legislature to the judiciary and the conditions for being granted a divorce expanded in most states. At mid-century, the United States had the highest divorce rate in the western world.[1] In this regard as well, men and women were held to different standards, especially when it came to adultery and the custody of children, and laws varied widely across the

---

[1]   The rate was 0.3 divorces per 1,000 Americans in the 1860s; by the end of the century it had climbed to 0.7 per 1,000. (The rate peaked in the late 1970s at 5.1 per 1,000; by 2017 it had fallen to just under 3.0 per 1,000.)

country. States in New England and especially in the West had, on the whole, the most liberal divorce laws.

Black Americans, especially those who were enslaved, had far less choice when it came to marriage. Under both federal and state law, indeed, there could be no such thing as a marriage between two enslaved people; their status as property precluded any acknowledgment under law of familial ties. There was thus no legal obstacle to the breaking up of families. It has been estimated that at least one third of enslaved children in the Upper South experienced the breakup of family life through their own sale or the sale of one or more parents or siblings, and the figure may well have been higher in the Deep South, where conditions for enslaved people were, in many ways, even worse. When we read a poem such as Frances Harper's "The Fugitive's Wife," we are movingly reminded of the reality of life for those who could never be legally married, and whose children could never legally belong to them.

Daguerreotype, Unidentified couple, c. 1864. Even after emancipation (as historian Tera Hunter has detailed), numerous barriers to marriage for black people continued to be erected in many states.

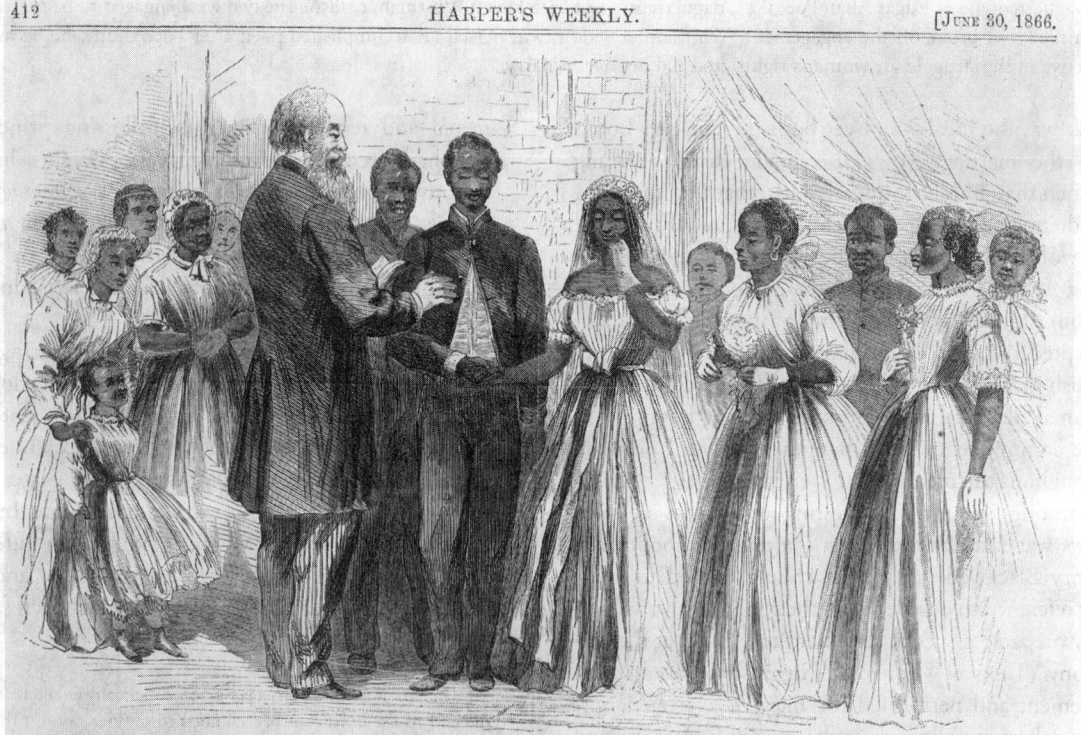

412   HARPER'S WEEKLY.   [JUNE 30, 1866.

Alfred R. Waud, *Marriage of a Colored Soldier at Vicksburg by Chaplain Warren of the Freedmen's Bureau,* 1866.

Herbert Gleason, *Walden Pond in Winter*. Gleason spent many years following Thoreau's footsteps and photographing scenes described in *Walden* and other writings; over 100 of his photographs were included in the 1906 edition of *The Writings of Henry David Thoreau*. The above image shows Walden Pond in winter; in the background is a passing train—or, as Thoreau described it, an "iron horse" that can "make the hills echo with his snort like thunder, shaking the earth with his feet, and breathing fire and smoke from his nostrils." (Additional Gleason images are included as "In Context" material in the Thoreau author section.)

Nature and the Environment[1]

To think of nature and the environment in the context of mid-nineteenth-century America is to think first and foremost of Emerson and Thoreau—and, in the visual arts, of Thomas Cole, Frederick Church, and Albert Bierstadt—figures who invested an idealized Nature with near-spiritual qualities, who saw Nature as standing apart from humanity, but also as possessing restorative powers for the human soul. "In the woods," as Emerson famously put it, "we return to reason and faith. There I feel that nothing can befall me ... which nature cannot repair."

Emerson and Thoreau were far from alone; nature writing became during this period a mainstay of American literature. The prose (as well as the art) of John James Audubon broke new ground scientifically as well as aesthetically. And—very much in the same spirit as Emerson and Thoreau—increasing numbers of poets sang nature's praises in much of their work. William Cullen Bryant wrote of the prairies that "man hath no part in all this glorious work" and called forest groves "God's first temples"; in similar fashion later in the century, Longfellow (in "My Cathedral") likened the "stately pines" to "cathedral towers," and John Greenleaf Whittier regarded "the wood giant" with a blending of "Pagan awe" and "Christian reverence."

But as Thoreau was retreating from the world to commune with nature at Walden Pond, General

---

[1] Please note that a "Contexts" section on this topic appears in the body of this volume.

Stephen Watts Kearny was leading the Army of the West into California, charged not only with defeating any Mexicans in his path but also with clearing a road through the mountains and forests across which settlers could travel. As put into words in a poem by Thomas D'Arcy McGee that celebrates the mission and extends it into a metaphor for western expansion in general, the goal of "the Army of the West"—both the literal army and its metaphorical counterpart in the "army" of westward-moving American settlers—was not only to "lay low the foes of liberty" (the Mexicans) and "annex their lands"; it was also to "pluck the primal forests up, and sow their sites with corn," to clear the way for "the plough that frees the soil." To McGee the forest was a "tangled waste"—and nowhere does he acknowledge it to be already inhabited by Indigenous peoples. It would be hard to imagine a literary work more antithetical to the sorts of values that we now call environmentalism.

The set of attitudes with which McGee approached the "tangled waste" of the California forest in verse—and with which Kearny approached California itself—is not often reflected in the literature that is most frequently taught today, but it was the dominant mode of thinking in America throughout this period. Trees were to be felled, and the earth was to be exploited without restriction for its mineral wealth. In 1840 the number of tons of coal mined in America exceeded 1 million for the first time; by 1860 the total had reached 20 million tons, and by 1880, 80 million tons. Non-human animals too were to be exploited for the benefit of humans; Bronson Alcott was almost alone in not only finding the consumption by humans of other animals morally repugnant but also environmentally unsound. ("It is calculated," he and his collaborator Charles Lane wrote in 1843, "that if no animal food were consumed, one-fourth of the land now used would suffice for human sustenance.") The building of mills and ironworks and factories was to be encouraged—as was the growth of cities—without regard to the effect they might have on the land, the air, and the water. Canals, steamships, and railways made the exploitation of the land and the waterways ever easier. In 1850 there were 9,000 miles of railway track in America; by 1880 that number had risen to 93,200.

Settler colonists steadily moved westward, and as they did so, imposed a new order on the land,

using the grid system that had been first proposed by Thomas Jefferson as a model. They expressed little concern as to the ways in which they might damage the environment, but many—following the naturalist and western explorer Josiah Gregg—expressed unbounded optimism as to the ways in which their activity would improve not only the land but also the climate. Gregg argued in his 1844 *Commerce of the Prairies, or, The Journal of a Santa Fe Trader* that "the extensive cultivation of the earth" on the high plains might "operate a change … upon the seasons" and "might contribute to the multiplication of showers." Later in the century some prominent agriculturalists lent spurious academic support to these ideas, hypothesizing that the soil would be better able to absorb the rain once it had been broken by the plough, that the absorbed moisture would then slowly evaporate, and that the result would be increased rainfall. The science turned out to be wrong, but generations of settlers bought the idea that "rain follows the plough."

A few commentators offered spirited resistance to the easy acceptance of environmental degradation in the face of "progress." Lydia Sigourney, for example, described in her 1854 poem "Fallen Forests" the terrible toll of "Man's warfare on the trees," and passionately lamented the loss of old-growth forests: "every echo of the axe doth hew / The iron heart of centuries away." The painter and poet Thomas Cole lamented such loss too—and was explicit in blaming human greed for the destruction: "each hill and dale," he wrote, had "become / An altar unto Mammon." But—particularly before 1850—the voices raised in support of conservation tended to be drowned out by those raised in support of the unbridled pursuit of material wealth.

Not everyone, of course, was allowed to share in that pursuit equally; the pursuit of wealth (and wealth itself—especially in the form of land) were in effect reserved for white men. The government soon reneged on the "40 acres and a mule" promise it made in 1865 to emancipated African Americans, and the Homestead Acts that resulted in the granting of almost 250 million acres of western land to homesteaders at virtually no cost effectively applied only to white people. Native Americans, for their part, were pushed by government fiat ever further westward into "Indian Country"— land supposedly reserved for them by the government,

Thomas Cole, *The Falls of the Kaaterskill*, 1826. On the rocky ledge beside the falls, Cole depicts an Indigenous man, face upraised, calling. By the time Cole painted the picture, the Indigenous peoples of the area had been almost entirely displaced; the painting dates from the same year in which James Fenimore Cooper's *The Last of the Mohicans* was published. Three years earlier, Cooper had included in *The Pioneers* a passage in which Natty Bumppo, a white scout who has lived among Native Americans, describes the view from the falls:

"There's a place in them hills that I used to climb to, when I wanted to see the carryings on of the world. ... The place I mean is next to the river, where one of the ridges juts out a little from the rest, and where the rocks fall for the best part of a thousand feet. ..."

"What see you when you get there?" asked Edwards.

"Creation!" said Natty, dropping the end of his rod into the water, and sweeping one hand around him in a circle— "all creation, lad. ..."

but under terms that kept shifting and that proved to be entirely unreliable. These "removals" were in many cases driven at least as much by issues of land use as they were by simple growth of the non-Indigenous population. In much of the South, for example, land was in capitalist terms undervalued; white plantation owners had invested little in the land they occupied, but often paid large amounts to create an enslaved labor force. When the cotton fields had exhausted the fertility of the soil (as cotton monocultures, with the limited fertilizers available at the time, tended to do fairly quickly), plantation owners looked to relocate to fresh land. What stood in their way initially were the agreements the government had made with peoples such as the Chickasaw, Choctaw, Muscogee (Creek), and Cherokee, giving them the right to occupy much of the land between the Appalachians and the Mississippi. The plantation owners lobbied the government to have Indigenous peoples forced west of the Mississippi—and successive American administrations (most notably that of Andrew Jackson) were happy to oblige.

The amount of land that constituted "Indian Country" was still fairly large at the beginning of this period; "Indian Country" in 1834 included most of the land between the Mississippi and the Rockies, and from the 49th parallel to the Mexican border. But by 1854 "Indian Country" constituted little more than the present state of Oklahoma. The remnants of more than a dozen peoples had been forced to relocate there—and the original Indigenous peoples of the region had been forced to share their space with the influx of newcomers. (In 1889, that territory too would be taken from Native Americans.) Indigenous peoples were prevented from controlling even the smaller and smaller parcels of land that they had been allotted. In a landmark 1823 decision, the Supreme Court ruled that Native Americans could deal only with the federal government regarding the purchase or sale of any land; no private transactions would be allowed.

Not all whites acquiesced in these moves. A significant minority of white Americans deplored the continuing annexation of Native American land—and many more acknowledged it to be a tragedy. But for most it was a tragedy with an air of inevitability to it; Indigenous people would simply have to make

way for progress as settlers took over more and more of the land. Even early on in the century, displaced Indigenous people were often portrayed as adding color to the landscape, picturesque additions to grand images of the wilderness. So it is that a lone Native American stands by the waterfall in Thomas Cole's 1826 *Falls of the Kaaterskill*. William Cullen Bryant assumed a Native American voice as he imagined the end point of continuous westward pressure on the Indigenous population: "... they shall fill the land, and we /Are driven to the western sea." White Antelope is said to have provided a blunter summary just before his death at Wounded Knee: "Nothing lives long. Only the earth and the mountains."

A few voices during this period also began to insist that the wilderness itself must be preserved. Increasingly, "the wilderness" came to be associated with the West. Thoreau's 1862 maxim on "wildness" is often quoted; less often noted is the degree to which he associated that wildness with the American West: "The West of which I speak is but another name for the Wild; and what I have been preparing to say is, that in Wildness is the preservation of the world."

John Muir's 1869 visit to the Sierra Nevada mountains was in this connection a key moment in American environmental history. A direct line can be drawn between the feelings the wilderness engendered in the young Muir during that summer and the landmark conservation efforts of the late nineteenth and early twentieth centuries that involved Muir, Theodore Roosevelt, and many others.[1] More important during the 1820–Reconstruction period, however, were the calls to action of George Perkins Marsh. Marsh shared the sense of loss expressed by Cole, Sigourney, and others at the loss of the old growth forests, but, as a congressman (and former farmer, lawyer, and businessman) he brought to bear on the matter a

---

1   In such contexts the word "wilderness" should arguably always appear in quotation marks, for in almost all cases it was used to denote land that was in fact inhabited to a greater extent than white explorers and adventurers were keen to acknowledge. John Muir, for example, described the flora of the Bloody Cañon of the Sierra Nevada as being "as yet untrodden" when he first beheld it in 1869—yet later in the same passage he describes an encounter with several local "Mono Indians," whom he describes as "mostly ugly, and some of them altogether hideous. ... Somehow they seemed to have no right place in the landscape."

practical ecological perspective that has led some to call him America's first environmentalist. In an 1847 lecture Marsh offered practical reasons (including the value of trees to "succeeding generations") why "trees are no longer what they were in our fathers' time, an incumbrance." And in the same lecture he warned that "climate itself has in many instances" been "gradually changed and ameliorated or deteriorated by human action." Marsh's ideas—summed up in his influential 1864 book *Man and Nature: or, Physical Geography as Modified by Human Action*—had much to do with the marked increase in environmental awareness beginning around mid-century; it was not entirely by coincidence that in the same year *Man and Nature* was published, Abraham Lincoln set aside the Yosemite region for "public use, resort and recreation," or that, early in the following decade, Ulysses S. Grant made Yellowstone the first national park. There may have been more degradation than preservation of the American environment between the 1820s and the 1870s, but the hardy seeds of American environmentalism had also been sown.

They had been sown in the cities as well as in the wild. Here the key figure of the period is Frederick Law Olmstead, famous as one of the most important individuals shaping the American urban environment in the nineteenth century—the moving force behind the designs of Central Park in New York, Franklin Park in Boston, and Jackson Park in Chicago. Less well known is that Olmstead was also a leading voice for the preservation of nonhuman American environments. His 1865 report on Yosemite laid out the principle of setting aside scenery that "shall never be private property but that … shall be held solely for public purposes." In the same document, Olmstead took issue with the destructive aspects of capitalism's driving force, recognizing that the duty of government was "to provide means of protection for all its citizens in the pursuit of happiness against the obstacles, otherwise insurmountable, which the selfishness of individuals or combinations of individuals is liable to interpose to that pursuit." Environmental issues, Olmstead realized, were inextricably intertwined with America's economic and political structures—and with its psyche.

Texts and Contexts:
A Chronological Chart

In the chart below, dates generally refer to the year when a work was first made public, whether published in print or, in the case of speeches and plays, made public through the first performance. Where that date is known to differ substantially from the date of composition, the difference is generally noted; for manuscript works whose exact date of composition is unknown, we have provided an estimated date range.

For the convenience of those who may wish to look slightly beyond the chronological boundaries of this volume, the following chart begins before 1820, with Thomas Jefferson's election to the presidency at the turn of the century.

⌘⌘⌘

	Texts		Contexts
		1800	Thomas Jefferson elected president
		1803	Louisiana Purchase
		1804	Haitian Declaration of Independence
		1804–06	Lewis and Clark expedition, aided by Shoshone guide Sacagawea
1805	Sagoyewatha, "Reply to the Missionary Jacob Cram"		
		1807	United States Congress passes Act Prohibiting Importation of Slaves (went into effect 1808)
			Britain passes Act for the Abolition of the Slave Trade (went into effect 1808)
1808	Leonora Sansay, *Secret History; or, the Horrors of St. Domingo*	1808	Under the leadership of Tecumseh and proclaiming the teachings of Tenskwatawa, Tecumseh's confederacy evolves to promote tribal unity and the rejection of English-American culture
		1810	Mexican War of Independence begins
		1812–14	War of 1812
		1813–14	Creek War

1826	Elias Boudinot, "An Address to the Whites"
	James Fenimore Cooper, *The Last of the Mohicans*
	Jane Johnston Schoolcraft begins to publish poems in *The Literary Voyager*
1827	James John Audubon begins to publish *The Birds of America*
	David Cusick, *Sketches of Ancient History of the Six Nations*
	Lydia Sigourney, *Poems*
	Catharine Sedgwick, *Hope Leslie*
1829	William Apess, *A Son of the Forest*
	David Walker, *An Appeal to the Coloured Citizens of the World*
	Cherokee Council, "Memorial of the Cherokees"
	George Moses Horton, *The Hope of Liberty*
1831	Edgar Allan Poe, *Poems*

1826	American Temperance Society founded
	Landscapes by Thomas Cole exhibited at the American Academy of the Fine Arts
1827	Last enslaved people in New York state freed
	Freedom's Journal founded
1827–28	The newspaper *The Cherokee Phoenix* founded (Elias Boudinot, editor)
1828	First performances of "Jump Jim Crow" by Thomas Dartmouth Rice
1829	First steam locomotive to operate on a U.S. railroad, "The Stourbridge Lion"
	Slavery abolished in Mexico
1830	Indian Removal Act
	Opening of Baltimore and Ohio Railroad (first U.S. railway chartered for commercial transportation)
	Louis A. Godey begins publishing *The Lady's Book* (subsequently known as *Godey's Lady's Book* and as *Godey's Magazine and Lady's Book*)
1831	William Lloyd Garrison begins publishing *The Liberator*
	Nat Turner leads a slave rebellion in Virginia; 55 white people are killed, and roughly 200 black people are either executed or killed by white mobs in retaliation
	Tim Rice escapes from slavery in Kentucky into Ohio. Over the next 34 years many thousands of enslaved people are aided in their escape north, often to Canada

		1832	New York and Harlem Railroad begins service (a harbinger of rapid mass transit)
			Samuel Morse applies for a patent for an electric telegraph
1833	Black Hawk, *Life of Ma-ka-tai-me-she-kia-kiak, or Black Hawk*	1833	American Anti-Slavery Society founded
	Lydia Maria Child, *An Appeal in Favor of That Class of Americans Called Africans*		Britain: Slavery Abolition Act passed (begins to take effect in 1834)
			Benjamin Day founds the *New York Sun*, ushering in the era of the penny press
1835	First volume of *Democracy in America*, by Alexis de Tocqueville	1835	Texas Revolution begins
	First *Davy Crockett Almanac* published		Second Seminole War begins
	William Gilmore Simms, *The Yemassee: A Romance of Carolina*		
1836	Angelina Grimké, *Appeal to the Christian Women of the South*	1836	Samuel Colt obtains a patent for a revolver
	Ralph Waldo Emerson, *Nature*		Migrant wagon train organized in Missouri; travel begins on what becomes known as the Oregon Trail
			Republic of Texas established, formally requests annexation by the United States
1837	Nathaniel Hawthorne, *Twice-Told Tales*	1837	Panic of 1837 initiates an economic depression that lasts until the mid-1840s
	Victor Séjour, "Le Mulatre" ("The Mulatto")		
		1838–39	Trail of Tears: Approximately 60,000 Cherokee, Muscogee, Seminole, Chickasaw, Choctaw, and other Indigenous people are forcibly removed by federal troops and relocated to Indian Territory in modern-day Oklahoma
		1839	*Amistad* Rebellion
1840	Richard Henry Dana Jr., *Two Years before the Mast*		
1841	Ralph Waldo Emerson, "Self Reliance"	1841	Experiment in communal living at Brook Farm begins
		1842	Term "underground railroad" appears in *The Liberator*
			Harriet Jacobs escapes to the Northern States

1860   Ann S. Stephens, *Malaeska* (1839 serial) republished as the first dime novel

Edward S. Ellis, *Seth Jones; Or, the Captives of the Frontier*

1861   Harriet Jacobs, *Incidents in the Life of a Slave Girl*

Rebecca Harding Davis, *Life in the Iron-Mills*

Frederick Law Olmstead, *The Cotton Kingdom*

Elizabeth Stoddard, *The Morgesons*

Emily Dickinson, "I taste a liquor never brewed –" published in the *Springfield Daily Republican* under the title "The May-Wine." (Of the many hundreds of poems Dickinson wrote, only ten were published in her lifetime.)

1862   Louisa May Alcott, "The Brothers" (later republished as "My Contraband")

1865   Mark Twain, "The Celebrated Jumping Frog of Calaveras County"

Henry James, "The Story of a Year"

1866   John Greenleaf Whittier, *Snow-Bound: A Winter Idyl*

1867   Horatio Alger, *Ragged Dick; or Street Life in New York with the Boot Blacks* serialized (book publication in 1868)

Slave Songs of the United States (earliest published collection of African-American spirituals)

1860   South Carolina secedes from the Union

1861   Abraham Lincoln becomes 16th president

Southern states variously secede from the Union and form the Confederate States of America; Civil War begins

1862   Land-Grant Colleges Act (leading ultimately to the establishment of 102 state colleges and universities)

1863   Emancipation Proclamation

Battle of Gettysburg

1864   Yosemite Grant (first instance of land being set aside by the Federal government for preservation and public use)

Sand Creek Massacre

1865   Lincoln is assassinated

The Ku Klux Klan is formed

Major General Gordon Granger advises the people of Texas that "all slaves are free"

Thirteenth Amendment abolishes slavery

1866   Civil Rights Act (first federal law to define citizenship)

1868   Fourteenth Amendment redefines citizenship to include those born with "slave" status

1869   Completion of the Pacific Railroad (the first transcontinental railroad in the United States)

1870   Fifteenth Amendment grants black men the right to vote

        John D. Rockefeller incorporates Standard Oil

1871   Great Chicago Fire

1872   Yellowstone becomes first national park

1874   Gold discovered in South Dakota; U.S. troops invade the Black Hills territory despite treaty

1876   Battle of the Little Bighorn (Greasy Grass)

        Alexander Graham Bell patents his telephone

1877   Thomas Edison patents his phonograph

        Anna Sewell's *Black Beauty* is published in London; by 1880 more than one million copies are circulating in the U.S.

        Great Sioux War ends; Sitting Bull escapes to Canada; Crazy Horse killed

        Compromise of 1877 leads to the end of Reconstruction

William Apess

1798 – 1839

Near the end of his renowned 1836 speech on King Philip's War, Pequot writer and activist William Apess declared:

> We want trumpets that sound like thunder, and men to act as though they were going at war with those corrupt and degrading principles that rob one of all rights, merely because he is ignorant and of a little different color. Let us have principles that will give everyone his due; and then shall wars cease, and the weary find rest.

In that speech, the apex of a remarkable career, he laid claim to Indigenous history, finding in King Philip (also known by his Massachusett name of Metacom) an exemplary forefather—and a focus for his ongoing critique of the injustice and brutality of colonization. As a preacher, Apess harnessed Christian principles to call for racial equality and to condemn colonial hypocrisy. As a historian, memoirist, and political activist, he was among the early nineteenth century's most eloquent defenders of the principle of Indigenous self-determination, powerfully challenging the white settler myth that the Euro-American colonial project was the destined will of God.

Almost all that we know of Apess's early life comes from his own account in his first published work, the autobiographical *A Son of the Forest* (1829). He was born in Colrain, Massachusetts, in 1798, and was of mixed white, Pequot, and possibly African American ancestry. Following his parents' early separation, he was sent to live with his maternal grandparents in Colchester, Connecticut, where he and his siblings endured dire poverty and frequent abuse until Apess was removed from the home by neighbors. He lived for a time as a "ward" of the town in the care of the white Furman family, and after a year was sold to them as an indentured servant—an extremely common circumstance for Indigenous children in the region.

Apess's account of his time with the Furmans (whom he describes as "poor" but who were also sufficiently financially comfortable to have several servants, and possibly enslaved people, in their household) is deeply ambivalent. Mr. and Mrs. Furman are described at different points as akin both to surrogate parents and to masters, and Mr. Furman clearly subjected Apess to regular (and often racially motivated) abuse, including teaching Apess to fear Indigenous people, thereby inflicting profound psychological trauma. Under their care, Apess received "six successive winters" of formal education, roughly the minimum that the Furmans would have been legally required to provide. Mrs. Furman also introduced him to the principles of Christianity, which soon took an intense hold on him, especially after he began attending Methodist camp meetings—a habit to which the Baptist Mr. Furman eventually put an end. When Apess was eleven years old, the Furmans sold his indenture to a new master, who promptly ended his formal schooling. After a few years, Apess ran away to New York, where he was conscripted into the army by a press gang (who gave his age as seventeen rather than fifteen). The War of 1812 was already well underway when he was enlisted, and he served until its conclusion in 1815.

Apess returned to Colrain in 1818 and was officially baptized into the Methodist Church, embarking then on an informal career as a preacher and missionary. In 1829 he released his autobiography, *A Son of the Forest*, a work heavily influenced by the popular genre of the conversion narrative as well as by the slave narrative. It also represented Apess's first published foray into historical writing; the appendix, which constitutes half the book, is an exploration of the history of Indigenous peoples and of European colonization. While Apess may also have included Indigenous oral history in his research, this appendix largely repurposes the scholarship of white colonists such as Elias Boudinot, whose 1816 book *A Star in the West* argues that North American Indigenous peoples are the descendants of the biblical lost tribes of Israel. Despite making use of such narratives, Apess is painfully aware of their inadequacy:

> The Indian character, I have observed before, has been greatly misrepresented. Justice has not and, I may add, justice cannot be fully done to them by the historian. My people have had no press to record their sufferings or to make known their grievances; on this account many a tale of blood and woe has never been known to the public.

Apess was ordained as a minister in 1831; he spent the following years traveling around the northeastern states, where he frequently spoke in Indigenous and mixed-race communities, forming connections with intellectuals in Indigenous and antislavery resistance movements and developing his ideas regarding religion, justice, and racial equality. For Apess, these issues were connected; as he had written in his autobiography, he was "convinced that Christ died for all mankind—that age, sect, colour, country, or situation, made no difference." Apess also collaborated with four other Pequot Christians in 1833 to produce a collection of short conversion narratives entitled *The Experiences of Five Christian Indians of the Pequod Tribe*. The text concludes with "An Indian's Looking-Glass for the White Man," a damning essay criticizing white Christians for their hypocritical treatment of Native Americans. In its arguments and rhetorical strategies, this essay displays the influence of abolitionist writers and speakers such as David Walker, as well as of Indigenous figures such as Cherokee editor and anti-Removal activist Elias Boudinot/Gallegina (named for the white politician mentioned above).

Later that year, Apess arrived in Mashpee, Massachusetts, where he became involved in agitating for the rights of the Mashpee tribe. Apess acquired regional notoriety for his role in helping draft what is sometimes known as the Mashpee Indian Declaration of Independence—a document that called for Mashpee self-government and jurisdiction over resources. He was briefly imprisoned and given a hefty fine of $100 following a non-violent confrontation over logging rights, but the Mashpee struggle was ultimately successful, and the tribe obtained some degree of self-government and resource control. Apess, who was adopted as a member of the tribe, described the Mashpee's accomplishments in *The Indian Nullification of the Unconstitutional Laws of Massachusetts, Relative to the Marshpee Tribe; or, the Pretended Riot Explained* (1835), where he recounts the tribe's resolution: "That we, as a tribe, will rule ourselves, and have the right to do so; for all men are born free and equal, says the Constitution of the country."

In 1836, Apess delivered a lecture at the Odeon in Boston on King Philip's War (1675–78), the conflict that had broken out between the Wampanoag and English Puritans after a longstanding peace treaty was repeatedly violated by the English settlers. Notorious for its high death toll, the war's violence disproportionately affected the Indigenous population, nearly eliminating the Wampanoag and their allies. King Philip's War already loomed large in American historical narratives—narratives in which the Wampanoag leader Metacom, or "King Philip," seemed to have only two possible roles. To some he personified the villainous "savage," described by Puritan historian Thomas Church as a "great, naked, dirty beast" in *The Entertaining History of King Philip's War* (1716); to others he was the embodiment of the "vanishing Indian," tragically representing a noble but inevitably declining race. (The latter approach is exemplified in John Augustus Stone's play *Metamora: or, The Last of the Wampanoags* [1829], whose title character is based on Metacom.) Apess's lecture powerfully re-envisioned this history, representing Metacom as a military hero. The speech's condemnation of the unchristian conduct of the Puritan settlers—and its linking of the same conduct to the ongoing oppression of people of color in America—made such an impression that Apess was asked to speak again two weeks later. The speech was published as *Eulogy on King Philip* (1836) and released in a second edition the following year; Apess also took the *Eulogy* on tour to several other cities.

Apess spent most of the last years of his life in New York City, during which time he made public appearances there and in Washington to speak about politics, religion, and Indigenous history. Upon his death in 1839, Apess was mentioned in a small handful of obituaries, which acknowledged him as a preacher and the author of a work on Metacom, but which did not mention his political activism in New England, or give any sense of the range and importance of his intellectual output. For many decades Apess's work was largely left out of the narrative of American history and literature. Since the 1990s, he has been increasingly acknowledged as a leading figure in the nineteenth century's culture of reform and activism and celebrated for his penetrating exposition of American racism and hypocrisy. Today he is widely seen as a visionary thinker, writer, and speaker, who broke new ground with his autobiographical self-fashioning and his radical reworking of the narratives of Indigenous history.

NOTE ON THE TEXTS: The texts included below are based upon the first Boston printings of *The Experiences of Five Christian Indians of the Pequod Tribe* (1833) and *Eulogy on King Philip, as Pronounced at the Odeon, in Federal Street, Boston, by the Rev. William Apess, An Indian* (1836). Spelling and punctuation have been modernized in accordance with the practices of this anthology.

⌘ ⌘ ⌘

An Indian's Looking-Glass for the White Man[1]

Having a desire to place a few things before my fellow creatures who are traveling with me to the grave, and to that God who is the maker and pre-server both of the white man and the Indian, whose abilities are the same, and who are to be judged by one God, who will show no favor to outward appear-ances, but will judge righteousness. Now I ask if deg-radation has not been heaped long enough upon the Indians? And if so, can there not be a compromise; is it right to hold and promote prejudices? If not, why not put them all away? I mean here amongst those who are civilized. It may well be that many are igno-rant of the situation of many of my brethren within the limits of New England. Let me for a few moments turn your attention to the reservations in the different states of New England, and, with but few exceptions, we shall find them as follows: The most mean, abject,

miserable race of beings in the world—a complete place of prodigality[2] and prostitution.

Let a gentleman and lady of integrity and respect-ability visit these places, and they would be surprised; as they wandered from one hut to the other they would view with the females who are left alone, children half starved, and some almost as naked as they came into the world. And it is a fact that I have seen them as much so—while the females are left without protec-tion, and are seduced by white men, and are finally left to be common prostitutes for them, and to be destroyed by that burning, fiery curse, that has swept millions, both of red and white men, into the grave with sorrow and disgrace—Rum. One reason why they are left so is, because their most sensible and active men are absent at sea.[3] Another reason is, because they are made to believe they are minors[4] and have not the abilities given them from God, to take care of them-selves, without it is to see to a few little articles, such

2   *prodigality* Wastefulness.

3   *most sensible ... absent at sea* Whaling was at the time a lucra-tive, though highly dangerous, industry that attracted many highly skilled Indigenous men. Few of these men, however, were ever granted positions of significant authority, and few were as well-remu-nerated as white whalers, especially since they were often obligated to give a percentage of their earnings to white overseers.

4   *minors* American law designated Indigenous people as legal minors.

1   This text is Apess's epilogue to a longer collaborative work, *The Experiences of Five Christian Indians of the Pequod Tribe* (1833), which contains brief conversion narratives from Apess and his wife Mary, as well as three others.

as baskets and brooms. Their land is in common stock, and they have nothing to make them enterprising.

Another reason is because those men who are Agents,[1] many of them are unfaithful, and care not whether the Indians live or die; they are much imposed upon by their neighbors who have no principle. They would think it no crime to go upon Indian lands and cut and carry off their most valuable timber, or anything else they chose; and I doubt not but they think it clear gain.[2] Another reason is because they have no education to take care of themselves; if they had, I would risk them[3] to take care of their own property.

Now I will ask, if the Indians are not called the most ingenious people amongst us? And are they not said to be men of talents? And I would ask, could there be a more efficient way to distress and murder them by inches than the way they have taken? And there is no people in the world but who may be destroyed in the same way. Now if these people are what they are held up in our view to be, I would take the liberty to ask why they are not brought forward and pains taken to educate them? to give them all a common education, and those of the brightest and first-rate talents put forward and held up to office? Perhaps some unholy, unprincipled men would cry out, the skin was not good enough; but stop friends—I am not talking about the skin, but about principles. I would ask if there cannot be as good feelings and principles under a red skin as there can be under a white? And let me ask, is it not on the account of a bad principle, that we who are red children have had to suffer so much as we have? And let me ask, did not this bad principle proceed from the whites or their forefathers? And I would ask, is it worth while to nourish it any longer? If not, then let us have a change; although some men no doubt will spout their corrupt principles against it, that are in the halls of legislation and elsewhere. But I presume this kind of talk will seem surprising and horrible. I do not see why it

should so long as they (the whites) say that they think as much of us as they do of themselves.

This I have heard repeatedly, from the most respectable gentlemen and ladies—and having heard so much precept, I should now wish to see the example. And I would ask who has a better right to look for these things than the naturalist[4] himself—the candid man would say none.

I know that many say that they are willing, perhaps the majority of the people, that we should enjoy our rights and privileges as they do. If so, I would ask why are not we protected in our persons and property throughout the Union? Is it not because there reigns in the breast of many who are leaders, a most unrighteous, unbecoming and impure black principle, and as corrupt and unholy as it can be—while these very same unfeeling, self-esteemed characters pretend to take the skin as a pretext to keep us from our unalienable and lawful rights? I would ask you if you would like to be disfranchised from all your rights, merely because your skin is white, and for no other crime? I'll venture to say, these very characters who hold the skin to be such a barrier in the way, would be the first to cry out, injustice! awful injustice!

But, reader, I acknowledge that this is a confused world, and I am not seeking for office; but merely placing before you the black inconsistency that you place before me—which is ten times blacker than any skin that you will find in the Universe. And now let me exhort you to do away that principle, as it appears ten times worse in the sight of God and candid men, than skins of color—more disgraceful than all the skins that Jehovah ever made. If black or red skins, or any other skin of color is disgraceful to God, it appears that he has disgraced himself a great deal—for he has made fifteen colored people to one white, and placed them here upon this earth.

Now let me ask you, white man, if it is a disgrace for to eat, drink and sleep with the image of God,[5] or sit, or walk and talk with them? Or have you the folly to think that the white man, being one in fifteen or sixteen, are the only beloved images of God? Assemble all nations together in your imagination, and then let

---

1   *Agents* White overseers appointed by the federal government to enforce federal policy in Indigenous communities and to represent Indigenous individuals in legal matters. Agents were ostensibly supposed to care for Indigenous people, whom white authorities deemed incapable of self-government, but many agents exploited their extreme power for personal gain.

2   *clear gain* I.e., gain without accompanying debt, loss, or legal burden.

3   *risk them* I.e., trust them.

4   *naturalist* I.e., Indigenous person.

5   *image of God* See Genesis 1.26: "And God said, Let us make man in our image, after our likeness."

the whites be seated amongst them, and then let us look for the whites, and I doubt not it would be hard finding them; for to the rest of the nations, they are still but a handful. Now suppose these skins were put together, and each skin had its national crimes written upon it—which skin do you think would have the greatest? I will ask one question more. Can you charge the Indians with robbing a nation almost of their whole Continent, and murdering their women and children, and then depriving the remainder of their lawful rights, that nature and God require them to have? And to cap the climax, rob another nation[1] to till their grounds, and welter out their days under the lash with hunger and fatigue under the scorching rays of a burning sun? I should look at all the skins, and I know that when I cast my eye upon that white skin, and if I saw those crimes written upon it, I should enter my protest against it immediately, and cleave to that which is more honorable. And I can tell you that I am satisfied with the manner of my creation, fully—whether others are or not.

But we will strive to penetrate more fully into the conduct of those who profess to have pure principles, and who tell us to follow Jesus Christ and imitate him and have his Spirit. Let us see if they come anywhere near him and his ancient disciples. The first thing we are to look at, are his precepts, of which we will mention a few. "Thou shalt love the Lord thy God with all thy heart, with all thy soul, with all thy mind, and with all thy strength. The second is like unto it. Thou shalt love thy neighbor as thyself. On these two precepts hang all the law and the prophets."—Matt. xxii. 37, 38, 39, 40. "By this shall all men know that they are my disciples, if ye have love one to another."—John xiii. 35. Our Lord left this special command with his followers, that they should love one another.

Again, John in his Epistles says, "He who loveth God, loveth his brother also."—iv. 21. "Let us not love in word but in deed."—iii. 18. "Let your love be without dissimulation. See that ye love one another with a pure heart fervently."—1. Peter viii. 22. "If any man say, I love God, and hateth his brother, he is a liar."—John iv. 20. "Whosoever hateth his brother is a murderer, and no murderer hath eternal life abiding in him." The first thing that takes our attention, is the saying of

Jesus, "Thou shalt love," &c. The first question I would ask my brethren in the ministry, as well as that of the membership, What is love, or its effects? Now if they who teach are not essentially affected with pure love, the love of God, how can they teach as they ought? Again, the holy teachers of old said, "Now if any man have not the spirit of Christ, he is none of his."—Rom. viii. 9. Now my brethren in the ministry, let me ask you a few sincere questions. Did you ever hear or read of Christ teaching his disciples that they ought to despise one because his skin was different from theirs? Jesus Christ being a Jew, and those of his Apostles certainly were not whites—and did not he who completed the plan of salvation complete it for the whites as well as for the Jews, and others? And were not the whites the most degraded people on the earth at that time, and none were more so; for they sacrificed their children to dumb idols! And did not St. Paul labor more abundantly for building up a Christian nation amongst you than any of the Apostles. And you know as well as I that you are not indebted to a principle beneath a white skin for your religious services, but to a colored one.

What then is the matter now; is not religion the same now under a colored skin as it ever was? If so I would ask why is not a man of color respected; you may say as many say, we have white men enough. But was this the spirit of Christ and his Apostles? If it had been, there would not have been one white preacher in the world—for Jesus Christ never would have imparted his grace or word to them, for he could forever have withheld it from them. But we find that Jesus Christ and his Apostles never looked at the outward appearances. Jesus in particular looked at the hearts, and his Apostles through him being discerners of the spirit, looked at their fruit without any regard to the skin, color or nation; as St. Paul himself speaks, "Where there is neither Greek nor Jew, circumcision nor uncircumcision, Barbarian nor Scythian, bond nor free—but Christ is all and in all."[2] If you can find a spirit like Jesus Christ and his Apostles prevailing now in any of the white congregations, I should like to know it. I ask, is it not the case that everybody that is not white

---

1   *another nation* I.e., the African continent.

2   *Where there is … in all* See Colossians 3.11; *Greek* Gentile; non-Jewish person; *Scythian* Eurasian nomadic ethnic group, often used in ancient rhetoric as an example of "barbaric" peoples.

is treated with contempt and counted as barbarians? And I ask if the word of God justifies the white man in so doing? When the prophets prophesied, of whom did they speak? When they spoke of heathens, was it not the whites and others who were counted Gentiles? And I ask if all nations with the exception of the Jews were not counted heathens? and according to the writings of some, it could not mean the Indians, for they are counted Jews.[1] And now I would ask, why is all this distinction made among these Christian societies? I would ask what is all this ado about Missionary Societies, if it be not to Christianize those who are not Christians? And what is it for? To degrade them worse, to bring them into society where they must welter out their days in disgrace, merely because their skin is of a different complexion. What folly it is to try to make the state of human society worse than it is. How astonished some may be at this—but let me ask, is it not so? Let me refer you to the churches only. And my brethren, is there any agreement? Do brethren and sisters love one another? Do they not rather hate one another? Outward forms and ceremonies, the lusts of the flesh, the lusts of the eye and pride of life is of more value to many professors,[2] than the love of God shed abroad in their hearts, or an attachment to his altar, to his ordinances or to his children. But you may ask who are the children of God? perhaps you may say none but white. If so, the word of the Lord is not true.

I will refer you to St. Peter's precepts—Acts 10. "God is no respecter of persons"—&c. Now if this is the case, my white brother, what better are you than God? And if no better, why do you who profess his gospel and to have his spirit, act so contrary to it? Let me ask why the men of a different skin are so despised, why are not they educated and placed in your pulpits? I ask if his services well performed are not as good as if a white man performed them? I ask if a marriage or a funeral ceremony, or the ordinance of the Lord's house would not be as acceptable in the sight of God as though he was white? And if so, why is it not to you? I ask again, why is it not acceptable to have men to exercise their office in one place as well as in another? Perhaps you

will say that if we admit you to all of these privileges you will want more. I expect that I can guess what that is—Why, say you, there would be intermarriages. How that would be I am not able to say—and if it should be, it would be nothing strange or new to me; for I can assure you that I know a great many that have intermarried, both of the whites and the Indians—and many are their sons and daughters—and people too of the first respectability. And I could point to some in the famous city of Boston and elsewhere. You may now look at the disgraceful act in the statute law passed by the Legislature of Massachusetts,[3] and behold the fifty pound fine levied upon any Clergyman or Justice of the Peace that dare to encourage the laws of God and nature by a legitimate union in holy wedlock between the Indians and whites. I would ask how this looks to your law makers. I would ask if this corresponds with your sayings—that you think as much of the Indians as you do of the whites. I do not wonder that you blush many of you while you read; for many have broken the ill-fated laws made by man to hedge up the laws of God and nature. I would ask if they who have made the law have not broken it—but there is no other state in New England that has this law but Massachusetts; and I think as many of you do not, that you have done yourselves no credit.

But as I am not looking for a wife, having one of the finest cast,[4] as you no doubt would understand while you read her experience and travail of soul in the way to heaven, you will see that it is not my object. And if I had none, I should not want anyone to take my right from me and choose a wife for me; for I think that I or any of my brethren have a right to choose a wife for themselves as well as the whites—and as the whites have taken the liberty to choose my brethren, the Indians, hundreds and thousands of them as partners in life, I believe the Indians have as much right to choose their partners amongst the whites if they wish. I would ask you if you can see anything inconsistent in your conduct and talk about the Indians? And if

---

[1] *the Indians … counted Jews*   Some early racial theories posited that North American Indigenous peoples were descended from one of the Ten Lost Tribes of Israel.

[2] *professors*   I.e., people who profess to follow Christianity.

[3] *disgraceful act … Legislature of Massachusetts*   Massachusetts had banned intermarriage between whites and those defined as "negro or mulatto" in 1705, and in 1786 it expanded this law to apply to Indigenous people as well. Interracial marriage was not legalized in Massachusetts until 1843.

[4] *cast*   Character; also complexion or physical form.

you do, I hope you will try to become more consistent. Now if the Lord Jesus Christ, who is counted by all to be a Jew, and it is well known that the Jews are a colored people, especially those living in the East, where Christ was born—and if he should appear amongst us, would he not be shut out of doors by many, very quickly? and by those too, who profess religion?

By what you read, you may learn how deep your principles are. I should say they were skin deep. I should not wonder if some of the most selfish and ignorant would spout a charge of their principles now and then at me. But I would ask, how are you to love your neighbors as yourself? Is it to cheat them? Is it to wrong them in anything? Now to cheat them out of any of their rights is robbery. And I ask, can you deny that you are not robbing the Indians daily, and many others? But at last you may think I am what is called a hard and uncharitable man. But not so. I believe there are many who would not hesitate to advocate our cause; and those too who are men of fame and respectability—as well as ladies of honor and virtue. There is a Webster, an Everett, and a Wirt,[1] and many others who are distinguished characters—besides an host of my fellow citizens, who advocate our cause daily. And how I congratulate such noble spirits—how they are to be prized and valued; for they are well calculated to promote the happiness of mankind. They well know that man was made for society, and not for hissing stocks[2] and outcasts. And when such a principle as this lies within the hearts of men, how much it is like its God—and how it honors its Maker—and how it imitates the feelings of the good Samaritan, that had his wounds bound up, who had been among thieves and robbers.[3]

Do not get tired, ye noble-hearted—only think how many poor Indians want their wounds done up daily;

the Lord will reward you, and pray you stop not till this tree of distinction shall be levelled to the earth, and the mantle of prejudice torn from every American heart—then shall peace pervade the Union.

WILLIAM APES.[4]

—1833

from *Eulogy on King Philip*[5]

I do not arise to spread before you the fame of a noted warrior, whose natural abilities shone like those of the great and mighty Philip of Greece, or of Alexander the Great, or like those of Washington[6]—whose virtues and patriotism are engraven on the hearts of my audience. Neither do I approve of war as being the best method of bowing to the haughty tyrant, MAN, and civilizing the world. No, far from me be such a thought. But it is to bring before you beings made by the God of Nature, and in whose hearts and heads he has planted sympathies that shall live forever in the memory of the world, whose brilliant talents shone in the display of natural things, so that the most cultivated, whose powers shone with equal luster, were not able to prepare mantles to cover the burning elements of an uncivilized world. What, then—shall we cease to mention the mighty of the earth, the noble work of God?

Yet those purer virtues remain untold. Those noble traits that marked the wild man's course lie buried in the shades of night; and who shall stand? I appeal to the lovers of liberty. But those few remaining descendants who now remain as the monument of the cruelty of those who came to improve our race, and correct our errors; and as the immortal Washington lives

[1] *Webster* Daniel Webster (1782–1852), orator, lawyer, and Massachusetts senator, who spoke for the defense of Muscogee lands against Georgia State's expansionist ambitions; *Everett* Edward Everett (1794–1865), Massachusetts governor and Harvard professor, who opposed the Indian Removal Act; *Wirt* William Wirt (1772–1834), the longest-serving Attorney General in United States history, who represented (unsuccessfully) the Cherokee nation in the case *Cherokee Nation v. Georgia* (1831).

[2] *for hissing stocks* To be objects of scorn or mockery (i.e., "laughing stocks").

[3] *the good Samaritan ... and robbers* See Luke 10.30–37.

[4] *WILLIAM APES* Apess began adding the second "s" to his surname around the summer of 1836; this has since become the standard spelling.

[5] *King Philip* Known in the Massachusett language as Metacom (1638–76), a Wampanoag sachem who led his people into a war of resistance against English colonists; Apess forwarded the claim that Metacom was his direct paternal ancestor.

[6] *Philip of Greece ... Washington* Three famous and well-respected military leaders: King Philip II of Macedon (382–336 BCE); Philip's son Alexander III of Macedon (356–323 BCE), who established one of the largest empires in ancient history; and George Washington (1732–99).

This engraving (the artist is unknown) was presented opposite the frontispiece of the 1836 and 1837 editions of
the Eulogy. Under the heading "Errata" that appears at the end of the text, Apess includes the following note:
"In the Frontispiece, the man at the head of Philip should be an Indian."

endeared and engraven on the hearts of every white
in America, never to be forgotten in time—even such
is the immortal Philip honored, as held in memory
by the degraded, but yet grateful descendants, who
appreciate his character; so will every patriot, especially in this enlightened age, respect the rude[1] yet all-
accomplished son of the forest, that died a martyr to
his cause, though unsuccessful, yet as glorious as the
American Revolution. Where, then, shall we place the
hero of the wilderness?

Justice and humanity for the remaining few prompt
me to vindicate the character of him who yet lives in
their hearts and, if possible, melt the prejudice that
exists in the hearts of those who are in the possession of his soil, and only by the right of conquest—is
the aim of him who proudly tells you, the blood of a
denominated[2] savage runs in his veins. It is, however,
true, that there are many who are said to be honorable
warriors, who, in the wisdom of their civilized legislation, think it no crime to wreak their vengeance upon
whole nations and communities, until the fields are
covered with blood, and the rivers turned into purple

fountains, while groans, like distant thunder, are heard
from the wounded, and the tens of thousands of the
dying, leaving helpless families depending on their
cares and sympathies for life; while a loud response is
heard floating through the air from the ten thousand
Indian children and orphans, who are left to mourn
the honorable acts of a few—civilized men. …

The first inquiry is, Who is Philip? He was the
descendant of one of the most celebrated chiefs in the
known world,[3] for peace and universal benevolence
towards all men; for injuries upon injuries, and the
most daring robberies and barbarous deeds of death
that were ever committed by the American Pilgrims,[4]

---

[1]   *rude* Uncultivated.

[2]   *denominated* Named; so-called.

[3]   *one of the … known world* Metacom's father Ousamequin (c.
1581–1661), frequently referred to by his title of Massasoit ("Great
Sachem"). He was widely respected as a leader and had been committed to maintaining peace between his people and the colonists,
having initiated the first treaty between the Wampanoag and the
Plymouth settlers in March 1621.

[4]   *for injuries … American Pilgrims* Apess may have in mind the
atrocities committed by colonial (Massachusetts Bay, Plymouth, and
Saybrook) forces during the Pequot War (1636–38), during which
hundreds of Pequot were massacred or enslaved. For more on the
Pequot War, see William Bradford's account in volume A of this
anthology; see also the In Context materials appended to Bradford
entitled "Mapping Colonial Conflict."

were with patience and resignation borne, in a manner that would do justice to any Christian nation or being in the world—especially when we realize that it was voluntary suffering on the part of the good old chief. His country extensive—his men numerous, so as the wilderness was enlivened by them, say a thousand to one of the white men, and they, also, sick and feeble—where, then, shall we find one nation submitting so tamely to another, with such a host at their command? For injuries of much less magnitude have the people called Christians slain their brethren, till they could sing, like Sampson, "With a jaw bone of an ass have we slain our thousands, and laid them in heaps."[1] It will be well for us to lay those deeds and depredations committed by whites upon Indians before the civilized world, and then they can judge for themselves. ...

December (O.S.[2]) 1620, the Pilgrims landed at Plymouth, and without asking liberty from anyone, they possessed themselves of a portion of the country, and built themselves houses, and then made a treaty, and commanded them[3] to accede to it. This, if now done, would be called an insult, and every white man would be called to go out and act the part of a patriot, to defend their country's rights; and if every intruder were butchered, it would be sung upon every hilltop in the Union, that victory and patriotism was the order of the day. And yet the Indians (though many were dissatisfied), without the shedding of blood, or imprisoning anyone, bore it. And yet for their kindness and resignation towards the whites, they were called savages, and made by God on purpose for them to destroy. We might say, God understood his work better than this. But to proceed, it appears that a treaty was made by the Pilgrims and the Indians, which treaty was kept during forty years; the young chiefs during this time were showing the Pilgrims how to live in their country, and find support for their wives and little ones; and for all this, they were receiving the applauses of being savages. The two gentleman chiefs were Squanto and Samoset,[4] that were so good to the Pilgrims. ...

The history of New England writers say, that our tribes were large and respectable. How then, could it be otherwise, but their safety rested in the hands of friendly Indians. In 1647, the pilgrims speak of large and respectable tribes. But let us trace them for a few moments. How have they been destroyed, is it by fair means? No. How then? By hypocritical proceedings, by being duped and flattered; flattered by informing the Indians that their God was a going to speak to them, and then place them before the cannon's mouth in a line, and then putting the match to it and kill thousands of them. We might suppose that meek Christians had better gods and weapons than cannon; weapons that were not carnal, but mighty through God, to the pulling down of strong holds. These are the weapons that modern Christians profess to have; and if the pilgrims did not have them, they ought not to be honored as such. But let us again review their weapons, to civilize the nations of this soil. What were they: rum and powder, and ball, together with all the diseases, such as the small pox, and every other disease immaginable; and in this way sweep off thousands and tens of thousands. And then it has been said, that these men who were free from these things, that they could not live among civilized people. We wonder how a virtuous people could live in a sink of diseases, a people who had never been used to them.

And who is to account for those destructions upon innocent families and helpless children? It was said by some of the New England writers, that living babes were found at the breast of their dead mothers. What an awful sight! and to think too, that these diseases were carried among them on purpose to destroy them. Let the children of the Pilgrims blush, while the son of the forest drops a tear, and groans over the fate of his murdered and departed fathers. He would say to the

original spelling / punctuation

---

1 *slain their brethren ... in heaps* In the Book of Judges, the Israelite leader Samson, who is repeatedly visited by bursts of super-human strength, kills a thousand Philistines using only the jawbone of a donkey, in retaliation for the Philistines' murder of his wife and father-in-law. See Judges 15.15–16.

2 *O.S.* Old Style; indicates that the date was recorded according to the Julian calendar, which in England and the colonies was not replaced by the Gregorian calendar until 1752.

3 *them* I.e., the Indigenous peoples inhabiting the area.

---

4 *Squanto and Samoset* Tisquantum, or Squanto (d. 1622), was a Patuxet who, prior to the arrival of the Pilgrims, had been captured by English explorers and sold into slavery in Europe, where he learned English; following his eventual return to North America, he provided crucial assistance to the New England colonists. Samoset, an Abenaki, was the first Indigenous person to reach out in diplomacy upon the arrival of the Pilgrims, and his work paved the way for later diplomacy between the settlers and Ousamequin.

sons of the Pilgrims (as Job said about his birth day[1]), let the day be dark, the 22nd of December, 1622;[2] let it be forgotten in your celebration, in your speeches, and by the burying of the Rock that your fathers first put their foot upon. For be it remembered, although the gospel is said to be glad tidings to all people, yet we poor Indians never have found those who brought it as messengers of mercy, but contrawise. We say, therefore, let every man of color wrap himself in mourning, for the 22nd of December and the 4th of July are days of mourning and not of joy. (I would here say, there is an error in my book; it speaks of the 25th of December, but it should be the 22d. See *Indian Nullification*.[3]) Let them rather fast and pray to the great Spirit, the Indian's God, who deals out mercy to his red children, and not destruction.

Oh, Christians, can you answer for those beings that have been destroyed by your hostilities, and beings too that lie endeared to God as yourselves? his Son being their Savior as well as yours, and alike to all men? And will you presume to say that you are executing the judgments of God by so doing, or as many really are approving the works of their fathers to be genuine, as it is certain that every time they celebrate the day of the Pilgrims they do? Although in words they deny it, yet in works they approve of the iniquities of their fathers. And as the seed of iniquity and prejudice was sown in that day, so it still remains; and there is a deep-rooted popular opinion in the hearts of many, that Indians were made, &c. on purpose for destruction, to be driven out by white Christians, and they to take their places; and that God had decreed it from all eternity. If such theologians would only study the works of nature more, they would understand the purposes of good better than they do. That the favor of the Almighty

was good and holy, and all his nobler works were made to adorn his image, by being his grateful servants, and admiring each other as angels, and not, as they say, to drive and devour each other. …

But having laid a mass of history and exposition before you, the purpose of which is to show that Philip and all the Indians generally felt indignantly towards whites, whereby they were more easily allied together by Philip, their King and Emperor, we come to notice more particularly his history. As to his Majesty, King Philip, it was certain that his honor was put to the test, and it was certainly to be tried, even at the loss of his life and country. It is a matter of uncertainty about his age; but his birth-place was at Mount Hope, Rhode Island, where Massasoit, his father, lived, till 1656, and died, as also his brother, Alexander, by the governor's ill-treating him (that is, Winthrop[4]), which caused his death, as before mentioned, in 1662; after which, the kingdom fell into the hands of Philip, the greatest man that ever lived upon the American shores. Soon after his coming to the throne, it appears he began to be noticed, though, prior to this, it appears that he was not forward in the councils of war or peace. When he came into office it appears that he knew there was great responsibility resting upon himself and country; that it was likely to be ruined by those rude intruders around him, though he appears friendly, and is willing to sell them lands for almost nothing, as we shall learn from dates of the Plymouth Colony, which commence June 23, 1664. …

In the year 1668 Philip made a complaint against one Weston, who had wronged one of his men of a gun and some swine; and we have no account that he got any justice for his injured brethren. And, indeed, it would be a strange thing for poor unfortunate Indians to find justice in those Courts of the pretended pious, in those days, or even since; and for a proof of my assertion I will refer the reader or hearer to the records of Legislatures and Courts throughout New England; and also to my book, *Indian Nullification*.

We would remark still further; who stood up in those days, and since, to plead Indian rights? Was it the friend of the Indian? No, it was his enemies who rose; his enemies, to judge and pass sentence. And

---

[1]   *as Job … birth day*   In the Book of Job, God allows Satan to test the virtuous Job's faith through a series of terrible misfortunes; in his misery, Job curses the day he was born (see Job 3.1), but his faith is never fully shaken.

[2]   *22nd of December, 1622*   The purported date on which the Pilgrims arrived at Plymouth Rock in Massachusetts, where they began to establish a colony. In fact, the *Mayflower* arrived at the shores of North America in 1620.

[3]   *Indian Nullification*   Apess's account of his participation in the Mashpee struggle for self-government, published in 1835. See the In Context materials for Apess in the website component of this anthology.

[4]   *Winthrop*   John Winthrop (c. 1587–1649), English Puritan colonist and governor of the Massachusetts Bay Colony.

we know that such kind of characters as the Pilgrims were, in regard to the Indians' rights, who, as they say, had none, must certainly always give verdict against them, as, generally speaking, they always have. Prior to this insult it appears that Philip had met with great difficulty with the Pilgrims; that they appeared to be suspicious of him in 1671; and the Pilgrims sent for him, but he did not appear to move as though he cared much for their messenger, which caused them to be still more suspicious. What grounds the Pilgrims had is not ascertained, unless it is attributed to a guilty conscience for wrongs done to Indians. It appears that Philip, when he got ready, goes near to them and sends messengers to Taunton, to invite the Pilgrims to come and treat with him; but the governor being either too proud, or afraid, sends messengers to him to come to their residence at Taunton, to which he complied. Among these messengers was the Honorable Roger Williams,[1] a Christian and a patriot and a friend to the Indians, for which we rejoice. Philip, not liking to trust the Pilgrims, left some of the whites in his stead, to warrant his safe return. When Philip and his men had come near the place, some of the Plymouth people were ready to attack him; this rashness was, however, prevented by the Commissioner of Massachusetts, who met there with the Governor, to treat with Philip; and it was agreed upon to meet in the meetinghouse. Philip's complaint was that the Pilgrims had injured the planting grounds of his people. The Pilgrims acting as umpires say the charges against them were not sustained; and because it was not, to their satisfaction, the whites wanted that Philip should order all his men to bring in his arms and ammunition; and the Court was to dispose of them as they pleased. The next thing was that Philip must pay the cost of the treaty, which was four hundred dollars. The pious Dr. Mather[2] says that Philip was appointed to pay a sum of money to defray the charges that his insolent clamors had put the Colony to. We wonder if the Pilgrims were as ready to pay the Indians for the trouble they put them to.

If they were, it was with the instruments of death. It appears that Phillip did not wish to make war with them, but compromised with them; and in order to appease the Pilgrims he actually did order his men, whom he could not trust, to deliver them up; but his own men withheld, with the exception of a very few.

Now, what an unrighteous act this was in the people, who professed to be friendly and humane, and peaceable to all men. It could not be that they were so devoid of sense as to think these illiberal acts would produce peace; but contrawise, continual broils. And in fact it does appear that they courted war instead of peace, as it appears from a second council that was held by order of the Governor, at Plymouth, September 13, 1671. It appears that they sent again for Philip; but he did not attend, but went himself and made complaint to the governor, which made him write to the council, and ordered them to desist, to be more mild, and not to take such rash measures. But it appears that on the 24th, the scene changed; that they held another council, and the disturbers of the peace, the intruders upon a peaceable people, say they find Philip guilty of the following charges:

1. That he had neglected to bring in his arms, although competent time had been given him.

2. That he had carried insolently and proudly towards us on several occasions, in refusing to come down to our courts (when sent for) to procure a right understanding betwixt us.

What an insult this was to his Majesty, and independent Chief of a powerful nation, should come at the beck and call of his neighbors whenever they pleased to have him do it. Besides, did not Philip do as he agreed, at Taunton, that is in case there was more difficulty they were to leave it to Massachusetts, to be settled there in the high council, and both parties were to abide by their decision; but did the Pilgrims wait? No. But being infallible, of course they could not err.

The third charge was harboring diverse Indians; not his own men, but vagabond Indians.

Now what a charge this was to bring against a King, calling his company vagabonds, because it did not happen to please them; and what right had they to find fault with his company? I do

---

[1] *Roger Williams* Puritan minister, writer on Indigenous languages, and founder of the Colony of Rhode Island and Providence Plantations (1603–83).

[2] *Dr. Mather* Influential Puritan minister Increase Mather, who wrote an account of the war entitled *A Brief History of the War with the Indians in New-England* (1676).

not believe that Philip ever troubled himself about the white people's company, and prefer charges[1] against them for keeping company with whom they pleased. Neither do I believe he called their company vagabonds, for he was more noble than that.

The fourth charge is that he went to Massachusetts with his council, and complained against them, and turned their brethren against them.

This was more a complaint against themselves than Philip, inasmuch as it represents that Philip's story was so correct, that they were blamable.

5. That he had not been quite so civil as they wished him to be.

We presume that Philip felt himself much troubled by these intruders, and of course put them off from time to time, or did not take much notice of their proposals. Now such charges as those, we think are to no credit of the Pilgrims. However, this council ended much as the other did, in regard to disarming the Indians, which they never were able to do. Thus ended the events of 1671.

But it appears that the Pilgrims could not be contented with what they had done, but they must send an Indian, and a traitor, to preach to Philip and his men, in order to convert him and his people to Christianity. The preacher's name was Sassamon.[2] I would appeal to this audience, is it not certain that the Plymouth people strove to pick a quarrel with Philip and his men? What could have been more insulting than to send a man to them who was false, and looked upon as such; for it is most certain that a traitor was above all others, the more to be detested than any other. And not only so; it was the laws of the Indians, that such a man must die; that he had forfeited his life; and when he made his appearance among them, Philip would have killed him upon the spot, if his council had not persuaded

him not to. But it appears that in March, 1674, one of Philip's men killed him, and placed him beneath the ice in a certain pond near Plymouth; doubtless by the order of Philip. After this, search was made for him, and they found there a certain Indian, by the name of Patuckson; Tobias, also, his son were apprehended and tried. Tobias was one of Philip's counselors, as it appears from the records that the trial did not end here, that it was put over, and that two of the Indians entered into bonds for $400, for the appearance of Tobias at the June term; for which a mortgage of land was taken to that amount, for his safe return. June having arrived, three instead of one are arraigned. There was no one but Tobias suspected at the previous Court. Now two others are arraigned, tried, condemned and executed (making three in all), on June the 8th, 1675, by hanging and shooting. It does not appear that any more than one was guilty, and it was said that he was known to acknowledge it; but the other two persisted in their innocency to the last.

This murder of the preacher brought on the war a year sooner than it was anticipated by Philip. But this so exasperated King Philip, that from that day he studied to be revenged of the Pilgrims; judging that his white intruders had nothing to do in punishing his people for any crime, and that it was in violation of treaties of ancient date. But when we look at this, how bold and how daring it was to Philip, as though they would bid defiance to him and all his authority, we do not wonder at his exasperation. When the Governor finds that his Majesty was displeased, he then sends messengers to him, and wishes to know why he would make war upon him (as if he had done all right), and wished to enter into a new treaty with him. The King answered them thus: "Your governor is but a subject of King Charles of England,[3] I shall not treat with a subject; I shall treat of peace only with a King, my brother; when he comes, I am ready."

This answer of Philip's to the messengers, is worthy of note throughout the world. And never could a prince answer with more dignity in regard to his official authority than he did; disdaining the idea of placing himself upon a par of the minor subjects of a King; letting them

---

1   *prefer charges*   Suggest to an authority that charges be made.

2   *Sassamon* Wussausmon, also known in English as John Sassamon, was a Christian Massachusett preacher who worked as a diplomat between various Indigenous groups and the colonists, and had warned the Plymouth governor of an impending attack by the Wampanoag.

3   *King Charles of England*   Charles II, who ruled England, Scotland, and Ireland (and thereby the English colonies) from 1660 to 1685.

know at the same time, that he felt his independence more than they thought he did. And indeed it was time for him to wake up, for now the subjects of King Charles had taken one of his counselors and killed him, and he could no longer trust them. Until the execution of these three Indians, supposed to be the murderers of Sassamon, no hostility was committed by Philip or his warriors. About the time of their trial, he was said to be marching his men up and down the country in arms; but when it was known, he could no longer restrain his young men, who, upon the 24th of June, provoked the people of Swansea, by killing their cattle and other injuries, which was a signal to commence the war, and what they had desired, as a superstitious notion prevailed among the Indians, that whoever fired the first gun of either party, would be conquered. Doubtless a notion they had received from the Pilgrims. It was upon a fast day[1] too, when the first gun was fired; and as the people were returning from church, they were fired upon by the Indians, when several of them were killed. It is not supposed that Philip directed this attack, but was opposed to it. Though it is not doubted that he meant to be revenged upon his enemies; for during some time he had been cementing his countrymen together, as it appears that he had sent to all the disaffected tribes, who also had watched the movements of the comers from the new world,[2] and were as dissatisfied as Philip himself was with their proceedings.

Now around the council fires they meet,
    The young nobles for to greet;
Their tales of woe and sorrows to relate,
    About the Pilgrims, their wretched foes.

And while their fires were blazing high,
    Their King and Emperor to greet;
His voice like lightning fires their hearts,
    To stand the test or die.

See those Pilgrims from the world unknown,
    No love for Indians do know:

Although our fathers fed them well
    With venison rich, of precious kinds.

No gratitude to Indians now is shown,
    From people saved by them alone;
All gratitude that poor Indians do know,
    Is, we are robbed of all our rights.[3]

At this council it appears that Philip made the following speech to his chiefs, counselors, and warriors:

Brothers,—You see this vast country before us, which the great Spirit gave to our fathers and us; you see the buffalo and deer that now are our support.—Brothers, you see these little ones, our wives and children, who are looking to us for food and raiment; and you now see the foe before you, that they have grown insolent and bold; that all our ancient customs are disregarded; the treaties made by our fathers and us are broken, and all of us insulted; our council fires disregarded, and all the ancient customs of our fathers; our brothers murdered before our eyes, and their spirits cry to us for revenge. Brothers, these people from the unknown world will cut down our groves, spoil our hunting and planting grounds, and drive us and our children from the graves of our fathers, and our council fires, and enslave our women and children.

This famous speech of Philip was calculated to arouse them to arms, to do the best they could in protecting and defending their rights. The blow had now been struck, the die was cast, and nothing but blood and carnage was before them. And we find Philip as active as the wind, as dextrous as a giant, firm as the pillows of heaven, and fierce as a lion, a powerful foe to contend with indeed; and as swift as an eagle, gathering together his forces to prepare them for the battle. And as it would swell our address too full to mention all the tribes in Philip's train of warriors, suffice it to say that from six to seven were with him at different times. When he begins the war, he goes forward and musters about 500 of his men, and arms them complete, and

---

[1] *fast day*   Day officially set aside for public penitence; fast days were often declared during times of war, pestilence, famine, or other hardship, on the assumption that collective penitence would prompt the sympathy and aid of God.

[2] *comers from the new world*   Either an unintended error (the colonists having arrived from what is conventionally referred to as the "Old World"), or a conscious inversion of conventional language.

[3] *Now around ... our rights*   The author of the poem is unknown; it may have been written by Apess himself.

about 900 of the other, making in all about fourteen hundred warriors when he commenced. It must be recollected that this war was legally declared by Philip, so that the colonies had a fair warning. It was no savage war of surprise as some suppose, but one sorely provoked by the Pilgrims themselves. But when Philip and his men fought, as they were accustomed to do, and according to their mode of war, it was no more than what could be expected. But we hear no particular acts of cruelty committed by Philip during the siege. But we find more manly nobility in him, than we do in all the head Pilgrims put together, as we shall see during this quarrel between them. Philip's young men were eager to do exploits, and to lead captive their haughty lords. It does appear that every Indian heart had been lighted up at the council fires, at Philip's speech, and that the forest was literally alive with this injured race. And now town after town fell before them. The Pilgrims with their forces were marching ever in one direction, while Philip and his forces were marching in another, burning all before them, until Middleborough, Taunton, and Dartmouth were laid in ruins, and forsaken by its inhabitants.

At the great fight at Pocasset,[1] Philip commanded in person, where he also was discovered with his host in a dismal swamp. He had retired here with his army to secure a safe retreat from the Pilgrims, who were in close pursuit of him, and their numbers were so powerful they thought the fate of Philip was sealed. They surrounded the swamp, in hopes to destroy him and his army. At the edge of the swamp Philip had secreted a few of his men to draw them into ambush, upon which the Pilgrims showed fight; Philip's men retreating and the whites pursuing them till they were surrounded by Philip, and nearly all cut off. This was a sorry time to them; the Pilgrims, however, reinforced, but ordered a retreat, supposing it impossible for Philip to escape; and knowing his forces to be great, it was conjectured by some to build a fort to starve him out, as he had lost but few men in the fight. The situation of Philip was rather peculiar, as there was but one outlet to the swamp, and a river before him nearly seven miles to descend. The Pilgrims placed a guard around the swamp for 13 days, which gave Philip and his men time to prepare canoes to make good his retreat; in which he

did, to the Connecticut river, and in his retreat lost but fourteen men. We may look upon this move of Philip's to be equal, if not superior, to that of Washington crossing the Delaware.[2] ...

The Pilgrims determined to break down Philip's power, if possible, with the Narragansetts:[3] thus they raised an army of 1,500 strong to go against them and destroy them if possible. In this, Massachusetts, Plymouth, and Connecticut all join in severally to crush Philip. Accordingly, in December, in 1675, the Pilgrims set forward to destroy them. Preceding their march, Philip had made all arrangements for the winter, and had fortified himself beyond what was common for his countrymen to do, upon a small island near South Kingston, R.I. Here he intended to pass the winter with his warriors, and their wives and children. About 500 Indian houses was erected of a superior kind, in which was deposited all their stores, tubs of corn, and other things, piled up to a great height, which rendered it bullet proof. It was supposed that about 3,000 persons had taken up their residence in it. (I would remark that Indians took better care of themselves in those days than they have been able to since.) Accordingly, on the 19th day of December, after the Pilgrims had been out in the extreme cold for nearly one month, lodging in tents, and their provision being short, and the air full of snow, they had no other alternative than to attack Philip in the fort. Treachery, however, hastened his ruin; one of his men, by hope of reward from the deceptive Pilgrims, betrayed his country into their hands. The traitor's name was Peter. No white man was acquainted with the way, and it would have been almost impossible for them to have found it, much less to have captured it. There was

---

[1]   *great fight at Pocasset*   On 18 July 1675.

[2]   *Washington crossing the Delaware*   On the night and early morning of 25–26 December 1776, George Washington led a secret military crossing of the Delaware River to surprise British forces in Trenton, New Jersey; the successful operation was highly dangerous and is considered to have been one of the defining moments of the Revolutionary War.

[3]   *Narragansetts*   The Narragansett had remained largely neutral during the course of the war, but were drawn into the conflict in part because of their refusal to surrender to colonial forces the Wampanoag women and children to whom they had given refuge. They began to engage in small-scale raids on colonial strongholds following what is sometimes called the Great Swamp Massacre, in which hundreds of Narragansett were killed and much of the tribe's winter stores were destroyed.

but one point where it could have been entered or assailed with any success, and this was fortified much like a block house, directly in front of the entrance, and also flankers[1] to cover a cross fire. Besides high palisades, an immense hedge of fallen trees of nearly a rod in thickness. Thus surrounded by trees and water, there was but one place that the Pilgrims could pass. Nevertheless, they made the attempt. Philip now had directed his men to fire, and every platoon of the Indians swept every white man from the path one after another, until six captains, with a great many of the men had fallen. In the meantime, one Captain Moseley with some of his men had somehow or other gotten into the fort in another way, and surprised them; by which the Pilgrims were enabled to capture the fort, at the same time setting fire to it, and hewing down men, women and children indiscriminately. Philip, however, was enabled to escape with many of his warriors. It is said at this battle eighty whites were killed, and one hundred and fifty wounded; many of whom died of their wounds afterwards, not being able to dress them till they had marched 18 miles; also leaving many of their dead in the fort. It is said that 700 of the Narragansetts perished. The greater part of them being women and children. …

It appears that one of the whites had married one of Philip's countrymen; and they, the Pilgrims, said he was a traitor, and therefore they said he must die. So they quartered him; and as history informs us, they said, he being a heathen, but a few tears were shed at his funeral. Here, then, because a man would not turn and fight against his own wife and family, or leave them, he was condemned as an heathen. We presume that no honest men will commend those ancient fathers for such absurd conduct. Soon after this, Philip and his men left that part of the country and retired farther back, near the Mohawks; where, in July 1676, some of his men were slain by the Mohawks. Notwithstanding this, he strove to get them to join him; and here it is said that Philip did not do that which was right; that he killed some of the Mohawks and laid it to[2] the whites, in order that he might get them to join him. If so, we cannot consistently believe he did right. But he was so exasperated that nothing but revenge would

satisfy him. All this act was no worse than our political men do in our days, of their strife to wrong each other, who profess to be enlightened; and all for the sake of carrying their points. Heathen-like, either by the sword, calumny or deception of every kind; and the late duels among the [so-]called high men of honor, is sufficient to warrant my statements. But while we pursue our history in regard to Philip, we find that he made many successful attempts against the Pilgrims, in surprising and driving them from their posts, during the year 1676, in February, and through till August, in which time many of the Christian Indians joined him. It is thought by many that all would have joined him if they had been left to their choice, as it appears they did not like their white brethren very well. It appears that Philip treated his prisoners with a great deal more Christian-like spirit than the Pilgrims did; even Mrs. Rolandson,[3] although speaking with bitterness sometimes of the Indians, yet in her journal she speaks not a word against him. Philip even hires her to work for him, and pays her for her work, and then invites her to dine with him and to smoke with him. And we have many testimonies that he was kind to his prisoners; and when the English wanted to redeem Philip's prisoners, they had the privilege. …

But we have another dark and corrupt deed for the sons of the pilgrims to look at, and that is the fight and capture of Philip's son and wife, and many of his warriors, in which Philip lost about 130 men killed and wounded; this was in August 1676. But the most horrid act was in taking Philip's son, about ten years of age, and selling him to be a slave away from his father and mother. While I am writing, I can hardly restrain my feelings, to think a people calling themselves Christians, should conduct so scandalous, so outrageous, making themselves appear so despicable in the eyes of the Indians; and even now in this audience, I doubt not but there is men honorable enough to despise the conduct of those pretended Christians. And surely none but such as believe they did right,

---

1   *flankers*   Protective structures.

2   *laid it to*   Blamed it on.

3   *Mrs. Rolandson*   Mary Rowlandson was a colonist taken prisoner by a group of Narragansett during the war, and was for several months held captive among a group of Narragansett, Nipmuc, and Wampanoag. Following her release, Rowlandson published *The Sovereignty and Goodness of God* (1682), which sold extremely well throughout the colonies; the narrative describes several encounters with Metacom, who treated Rowlandson with relative kindness.

will ever go and undertake to celebrate that day of their landing, the 22nd of December. Only look at it, then stop and pause. My fathers came here for liberty themselves, and then they must go and chain that mind, that image they professed to serve; not content to rob and cheat the poor ignorant Indians, but must take one of the King's sons, and make a slave of him. Gentlemen and ladies, I blush at these tales, if you do not, especially when they professed to be a free and humane people. Yes, they did; they took a part of my tribe, and sold them to the Spaniards in Bermuda, and many others; and then on the Sabbath day, these people would gather themselves together, and say that God is no respecter of persons; while the divines would pour forth, "he that says he loves God and hates his brother, is a liar, and the truth is not in him."[1] And at the same time they hating and selling their fellow men in bondage. And there is no manner of doubt but that all my countrymen would have been enslaved if they had tamely submitted. But no sooner would they butcher every white man that come in their way, and even put an end to their own wives and children, and that was all that prevented them from being slaves; yes, *all*. It was not the good will of those holy pilgrims that prevented, no. But I would speak, and I could wish it might be like the voice of thunder, that it might be heard afar off, even to the ends of the earth. He that will advocate slavery is worse than a beast, is a being devoid of shame; and has gathered around him the most corrupt and debasing principles in the world; and I care not whether he be a minister or member of any church in the world; no, not excepting the head men of the nation. And he that will not set his face against its corrupt principles is a coward, and not worthy of being numbered among men and Christians. And conduct too that libels the laws of the country, and the word of God, that men profess to believe in.

After Philip had his wife and son taken, sorrow filled his heart; but notwithstanding, as determined as ever to be revenged, though was pursued by the duped Indians and Church, into a swamp; one of the men proposing to Philip that he had better make peace with the enemy, upon which he slew him upon the spot.

And the pilgrims being also repulsed[2] by Philip, were forced to retreat with the loss of one man in particular, whose name was Thomas Lucas, of Plymouth. We rather suspect that he was some related to Lucas and Hedge,[3] who made their famous speeches against the poor Marshpees in 1834, in the Legislature in Boston, against freeing them from slavery, that their fathers, the pilgrims, had made of them for years.

Philip's forces had now become very small, so many having been duped away by the whites, and killed, that it was now easy surrounding him. Therefore, upon the 12th of August, Captain Church[4] surrounded the swamp where Philip and his men had encamped, early in the morning, before they had risen, doubtless led on by an Indian who was either compelled or hired to turn traitor. Church had now placed his guard so that it was impossible for Philip to escape without being shot. It is doubtful, however, whether they would have taken him if he had not been surprised. Suffice it to say, however, this was the case. A sorrowful morning to the poor Indians, to lose such a valuable man. When coming out of the swamp, he was fired upon by an Indian, and killed dead upon the spot.

I rejoice that it was even so, that the Pilgrims did not have the pleasure of tormenting him. The white man's gun missing fire lost the honor of killing the truly great man, Philip. The place where Philip fell was very muddy. Upon this news, the Pilgrims gave three cheers; then Church ordering his body to be pulled out of the mud, while one of those tender-hearted Christians exclaims, "What a dirty creature he looks like." And we have also Church's speech upon that subject, as follows: "For as much as he has caused many a Pilgrim to lie above ground unburied, to rot, not one of his bones shall be buried." With him fell five of his best and most trusty men; one the son of a chief, who fired the first gun in the war.

Captain Church now orders him to be cut up. Accordingly, he was quartered and hung up upon four trees; his head and one hand given to the Indian who

---

[1]   *God is ... of persons* See Acts 10.34;   *he that says ... not in him* See 1 John 4.20.

[2]   *repulsed* I.e., driven back.

[3]   *Lucas and Hedge* Men mentioned by Apess in his book *Indian Nullification* (1835) as resisting the Mashpee struggle for self-government, a struggle in which Apess had been an important leader.

[4]   *Captain Church* Benjamin Church (1639–1718), a captain of what would one day become the United States Army Rangers.

shot him, to carry about to show. At which sight it so overjoyed the Pilgrims, that they would give him money for it; and in this way obtained a considerable sum. After which, his head was sent to Plymouth, and exposed upon a gibbet[1] for twenty years; and his hand to Boston, where it was exhibited in savage triumph; and his mangled body denied a resting place in the tomb, and thus adds the poet,

> Cold with the beast he slew, he sleeps,
> O'er him no filial spirit weeps.[2]

I think that as a matter of honor, that I can rejoice that no such evil conduct is recorded of the Indians; that they never hung up any of the white warriors who were head men. And we add the famous speech of Dr. Increase Mather; he says, during the bloody contest, the pious fathers wrestled hard and long with their God, in prayer, that he would prosper their arms, and deliver their enemies into their hands. And when upon stated days of prayer, the Indians got the advantage, it was considered as a rebuke of divine providence (we suppose the Indian prayed best then), which stimulated them to more ardor. ...

I do not hesitate to say that through the prayers, preaching, and examples of those pretended pious, has been the foundation of all the slavery and degradation in the American Colonies towards colored people. Experience has taught me that this has been a most sorry and wretched doctrine to us poor ignorant Indians. I will mention two or three things to amuse you a little; that is, as I was passing through Connecticut, about 15 years ago, where they are so pious that they kill the cats for killing rats, and whip the beer barrels for working upon the Sabbath, that in a severe cold night, when the face of the earth was one glare of ice, dark and stormy, I called at a man's house to know if I could not stay with him, it being about nine miles to the house where I then lived, and knowing him to be a rich man, and withal very pious, knowing if he had a mind he could do it comfortably, and withal we were both members of one church. My reception, however, was almost as

cold as the weather, only he did not turn me out of doors; if he had I know not but I should have frozen to death. My situation was a little better than being out, for he allowed a little wood, but no bed, because I was an Indian. Another Christian asked me to dine with him, and put my dinner behind the door; I thought this a queer compliment indeed. ...

But who was Philip, that made all this display in the world; that put an enlightened nation to flight, and won so many battles? It was a son of nature; with nature's talents alone. And who did he have to contend with? With all the combined arts of cultivated talents of the old and new world. It was like putting one talent against a thousand. And yet Philip with that accomplished more than all of them. Yea, he out-did the well-disciplined forces of Greece, under the command of Philip, the Grecian Emperor; for he never was enabled to lay such plans of allying the tribes of the earth together, as Philip of Mount Hope did. And even Napoleon patterned after him, in collecting his forces and surprising the enemy. Washington, too, pursued many of his plans in attacking the enemy, and thereby enabled him to defeat his antagonists and conquer them. What, then, shall we say; shall we not do right to say that Philip, with his one talent, out-strips them all with their ten thousand? No warrior of any age, was ever known to pursue such plans as Philip did. And it is well known that Church and nobody else could have conquered, if his people had not used treachery, which was owing to their ignorance; and after all, it is a fact, that it was not the Pilgrims that conquered him, it was Indians. And as to his benevolence, it was very great; no one in history can accuse Philip of being cruel to his conquered foes; that he used them with more hospitality than they, the Pilgrims, did, cannot be denied; and that he had knowledge and forethought, cannot be denied. As Mr. Gooking,[3] in speaking of Philip, says,

---

[1] *gibbet* Upright post from which the bodies of criminals were hung for display after execution.

[2] *Cold with ... spirit weeps* From *An Ode Pronounced before the Inhabitants of Boston* (1830) by American poet Charles Sprague.

[3] *Mr. Gooking* Daniel Gookin (1612–87), Irish settler who performed substantial missionary work in the Massachusetts Bay Colony and became a strong advocate for the so-called Praying Indians—the name given to groups of Indigenous people who converted to Christianity and lived in Christian communities called praying towns. His books *Historical Collections of the Indians in New England* (1792) and *The Doings and Sufferings of the Christian Indians* (1836) were written partially in response to what he perceived as the erasure of the Praying Indians from colonial histories of New England and of King Philip's War.

that he was a man of good understanding and knowledge in the best things. Mr. Gooking it appears was a benevolent man and a friend to Indians.

How deep then was the thought of Philip, when he could look from Maine to Georgia, and from the ocean to the lakes, and view with one look all his brethren withering before the more enlightened to come; and how true his prophesy, that the white people would not only cut down their groves, but would enslave them. Had the inspiration of Isaiah[1] been there, he could not have been more correct. Our groves and hunting grounds are gone, our dead are dug up, our council-fires are put out, and a foundation was laid in the first Legislature, to enslave our people,[2] by taking from them all rights which has been strictly adhered to ever since.[3] Look at the disgraceful laws, disfranchising us as citizens. Look at the treaties made by Congress, all broken. Look at the deep-rooted plans laid, when a territory becomes a State, that after so many years, the laws shall be extended over the Indians that live within their boundaries. Yea, every charter that has been given, was given with the view of driving the Indians out of the States, or dooming them to become chained under desperate laws, that would make them drag out a miserable life as one chained to the galley; and this is the course that has been pursued for nearly two hundred years. A fire, a canker, created by the Pilgrims from across the Atlantic, to burn and destroy my poor unfortunate brethren, and it cannot be denied. What then shall we do, shall we cease crying, and say it is all wrong, or shall we bury the hatchet and those unjust laws, and Plymouth Rock together, and become friends? And will the sons of the Pilgrims aid in putting out the fire and destroying the canker that will ruin all that their fathers left behind them to destroy? (By this we see how true Philip spake.) If so, we hope we shall

not hear it said from ministers and church members, that we are so good no other people can live with us, as you know it is a common thing for them to say, Indians cannot live among Christian people; no, even the President of the United States tells the Indians they cannot live among civilized people, and we want your lands and must have them, and will have them.[4] As if he had said to them, "we want your land for our use to speculate upon, it aids us in paying off our national debt and supporting us in Congress, to drive you off.

"You see, my red children, that our fathers carried on this scheme of getting your lands for our use, and we have now become rich and powerful; and we have a right to do with you just as we please; we claim to be your fathers. And we think we shall do you a great favor, my dear sons and daughters, to drive you out, to get you away out of the reach of our civilized people, who are cheating you, for we have no law to reach them, we cannot protect you although you be our children. So it is no use, you need not cry, you must go, even if the lions devour you, for we promised the land you have to somebody else long ago, perhaps twenty or thirty years; and we did it without your consent, it is true. But this has been the way our fathers first brought us up, and it is hard to depart from it; therefore you shall have no protection from us." Now while we sum up this subject. Does it not appear that the cause of all wars from beginning to end, was and is for the want of good usage? That the whites have always been the aggressors, and the wars, cruelties and bloodshed is a job of their own seeking, and not the Indians? Did you ever know of Indians' hurting those who was kind to them? No. We have a thousand witnesses to the contrary. Yea, every male and female declare it to be the fact. We often hear of the wars breaking out upon the frontiers, and it is because the same spirit reigns there that reigned here in New England; and wherever there are any Indians, that spirit still reigns; and at present, there is no law to stop it. What, then, is to be done;

---

[1]   *Isaiah*   Biblical prophet.

[2]   *a foundation ... our people*   The 1641 Body of Liberties of Massachusetts is considered the first formal legal code in the New England colonies; it established a set of individual rights for colonists—as well as the right to enslave "captives taken in just wars" and "strangers ... [that] are sold to us."

[3]   *first Legislature ... ever since*   Following the termination of the genocidal Pequot War (1636–37), many of the surviving Pequot people—children as well as adults—were sold into slavery in Bermuda. The subsequent Treaty of Hartford (1638) outlawed the use of the Pequot name, in an attempt to declare the people extinct.

[4]   *even the President ... have them*   Apess refers to the devastating Indian Removal policies of U.S. President Andrew Jackson (in office 1829–37), which forced Indigenous peoples to abandon their homelands and migrate westwards to what was called Indian Territory, in order to clear land for white settlers. Jackson justified the Indian Removal Act by claiming that Indigenous cultures were incompatible with white American "civilization." Thousands of Indigenous people died during their forced migration.

let every friend of the Indians now seize the mantle of Liberty and throw it over those burning elements that has spread with such fearful rapidity, and at once extinguish them forever. It is true that now and then a feeble voice has been raised in our favor. Yes, we might speak of distinguished men, but they fall so far short in the minority, that it is heard but at a small distance. We want trumpets that sound like thunder, and men to act as though they were going at war with those corrupt and degrading principles that robs one of all rights, merely because he is ignorant, and of a little different color. Let us have principles that will give everyone his due; and then shall wars cease, and the weary find rest. Give the Indian his rights, and you may be assured war will cease.

But, by this time you have been enabled to see that Philip's prophesy has come to pass; therefore, as a man of natural abilities, I shall pronounce him the greatest man that was ever in America; and so it will stand, until he is proved to the contrary, to the everlasting disgrace of the Pilgrims' fathers.

We will now give you his language in the Lord's Prayer.[1]

Noo-chun kes-uk-qut-tiam-at-am unch koo-we-su-onk, kuk-ket-as-soo-tam-oonk pey-au-moo-utch, keet-te-nan-tam-oo-onk ne nai; ne-ya-ne ke-suk-qutkah oh-ke-it; aos-sa-ma-i-in-ne-an ko-ko-ke-suk-o-da-e nut-as-e-suk-ok-kefu-tuk-qun-neg; kah ah-quo-an-tam-a-i-in-ne-an num-match-e-se-ong-an-on-ash, ne-match-ene-na-mun wonk neet-ah-quo-antam-au-o-un-non-og nish-noh pasuk noo-na-mortuk-quoh-who-nan, kah chaque sag-kom-pa-ginne-an en qutch-e-het-tu-ong-a-nit, qut poh-qud-wus-sin-ne-an watch match-i-tut.

Having now given historical facts, and an exposition in relation to ancient times, by which we have been enabled to discover the foundation which destroyed our common fathers, in their struggle together; it was indeed nothing more than the spirit of avarice and usurpation of power, that has brought people in all ages to hate and devour each other. And I cannot for one

moment look back upon what is past, and call it religion. No, it has not the least appearance like it. Do not then wonder, my dear friends, at my bold and unpolished statements; though I do not believe that truth wants any polishing whatever. And I can assure you, that I have no design to tell an untruth, but facts alone. Oft have I been surprised at the conduct of those who pretend to be Christians, to see how they were affected towards those who were of a different cast, professing one faith. Yes, the spirit of degradation has always been exercised towards us poor and untaught people. If we cannot read, we can see and feel; and we find no excuse in the Bible for Christians conducting towards us as they do.

It is said that in the Christian's guide, God is merciful, and they that are his followers are like him. How much mercy do you think has been shown towards Indians, their wives and their children? Not much, we think. No. And ye fathers, I will appeal to you that are white. Have you any regard for your wives and children, for those delicate sons and daughters? Would you like to see them slain and laid in heaps, and their bodies devoured by the vultures and wild beasts of prey? And their bones bleaching in the sun and air, till they molder away, or were covered by the falling leaves of the forest, and not resist? No. Your hearts would break with grief, and with all the religion and knowledge you have, it would not impede your force to take vengeance upon your foe, that had so cruelly conducted thus, although God has forbid you in so doing. For he has said, "Vengeance is mine, and I will repay."[2] What, then, my dear affectionate friends, can you think of those who have been so often betrayed, routed and stripped of all they possess, of all their kindred in the flesh? Can, or do you think we have no feeling? The speech of Logan,[3] the white man's friend, is no doubt fresh in your memory, that he intended to live and die the friend of the white man; that he always fed them and gave them the best his cabin afforded;

---

[1] *Lord's Prayer* Commonly recited Christian prayer; see Matthew 6.9–13 and Luke 11.2–4.

[2] *Vengeance is … will repay* See Romans 12.19: "Dearly beloved, avenge not yourselves, but rather give place unto wrath: for it is written, Vengeance is mine; I will repay, saith the Lord."

[3] *Logan* Cayuga orator from the Iroquois Confederacy (c. 1723–80) who had advocated peaceful relations with white settlers until the murder of his family by English soldiers in a raid on his village; he delivered a renowned speech, sometimes known as "Logan's Lament," in 1774.

and he appealed to them if they had not been well used; to which they never denied. After which, they murdered all of his family in cool blood; which roused his passions to be revenged upon the whites. This circumstance is but one in a thousand.

Upon the banks of Ohio, a party of two hundred white warriors, in 1757, or about that time, came across a settlement of Christian Indians, and falsely accused them of being warriors; to which they denied, but all to no purpose; they were determined to massacre them all. They, the Indians, then asked liberty to prepare for the fatal hour. The white savages then gave them one hour, as the historian said. They then prayed together; and in tears and cries, upon their knees, begged pardon of each other, of all they had done. After which, they informed the white savages that they were now ready. One white man then begun with a mallet, and knocked them down, and continued his work until he had killed fifteen, with his own hand; then saying it ached, he gave his commission to another. And thus they continued till they had massacred nearly ninety men, women and children, all these innocent of any crime. What sad tales are these for us to look upon the massacre of our dear fathers, mothers, brothers and sisters; and if we speak, we are then called savages for complaining. Our affections for each other, are the same as yours; we think as much of ourselves as you do of yourselves. When our children are sick, we do all we can for them; they lie buried deep in our affections; if they die, we remember it long, and mourn in after years. Children also cleave to their parents; they look to them for aid; they do the best they know how to do for each other; and when strangers come among us, we use them as well as we know how; we feel honest in whatever we do, we have no desire to offend anyone. But when we are so deceived, it spoils all our confidence in our visitors. And although I can say that I have some dear, good friends among white people, yet I eye them with a jealous eye, for fear they will betray me. Having been deceived so much by them, how can I help it; being brought up to look upon white people as being enemies and not friends, and by the whites treated as such, who can wonder? Yes, in vain have I looked for the Christian to take me by the hand, and bid me welcome to his cabin, as my fathers did them, before we were born; and if they did, it was only to

satisfy curiosity, and not to look upon me as a man and a Christian. And so all of my people have been treated, whether Christians or not. I say then, a different course must be pursued, and different laws must be enacted, and all men must operate under one general law. And while you ask yourselves, "What do they, the Indians, want?" you have only to look at the unjust laws made for them, and say, "They want what I want," in order to make men of them, good and wholesome citizens. And this plan ought to be pursued by all missionaries, or not pursued at all. That is not only to make Christians of us, but men; which plan as yet has never been pursued. And when it is, I will then throw my might upon the side of missions, and do what I can to favor it. But this work must begin here first, in New England.

Having now closed, I would say that many thanks is due from me to you, though an unworthy speaker, for your kind attention; and I wish you to understand that we are thankful for every favor; and you and I have to rejoice that we have not to answer for our fathers' crimes, neither shall we do right to charge them one to another. We can only regret it, and flee from it, and from henceforth, let peace and righteousness be written upon our hearts and hands forever, is the wish of a poor Indian.

—1836

Advertisement, *The Times*, Hartford, 5 March 1836.

CATHARINE MARIA SEDGWICK
1789 – 1867

In 1846, Edgar Allan Poe wrote of Catharine Maria Sedgwick that she "is not only one of our most celebrated and most meritorious writers, but attained reputation at a period when *American* reputation in letters was regarded as a phenomenon." As one of the United States' first literary celebrities, Sedgwick played a major role in defining a distinctively American nineteenth-century literature and spearheading its growth. Sedgwick was a pioneer in reinventing originally European genres, such as the novel of manners and the historical novel, in an American context as a means of realistically expressing specifically American experiences and ideas. She thereby helped create and shape an American tradition of literary realism. Her efforts to depict American life often center on members of groups that her country continued to marginalize, including religious dissenters, black Americans, Indigenous Americans, and women.

Born in the western Massachusetts town of Stockbridge in 1789, Sedgwick belonged to an elite New England family. Her father, Theodore Sedgwick, was an eminent Federalist politician who served  in both houses of Congress; he also took part in the dispossession of Stockbridge's original Indigenous inhabitants by buying up much of the land that had been allotted to them there. Sedgwick's mother, Pamela Dwight Sedgwick, suffered from severe depression, and Sedgwick's two older sisters both married while she was still young, so the dominant influences on her early life were her father and her four brothers. When he was not away pursuing his political career, her father read to the family and cultivated Sedgwick's love of books. Sedgwick later characterized this informal literary schooling as her "only education," claiming that what formal education she received was by comparison "a waste." Later in her life, her brothers encouraged and assisted her literary career, and she maintained a close relationship with them. Counterpointing these elite male influences was the role of Elizabeth Freeman, a formerly enslaved black woman who had gained her freedom with Theodore Sedgwick's assistance and subsequently worked for the family as a housekeeper, becoming Sedgwick's surrogate mother. Sedgwick paid tribute to Freeman in her 1853 essay "Slavery in New England" as well as in her autobiography, where she describes the enduring impact of Freeman's "strong love of justice" and "incorruptible integrity."

In 1822, Sedgwick made an immediately successful literary debut with her novel *A New-England Tale*. An account of a young woman's social and spiritual education as she progresses from servant, to schoolteacher, to wife of a wealthy Quaker philanthropist, *A New-England Tale* draws on the English novel of manners, as honed by writers such as Jane Austen, but develops an American version of that genre by carefully representing the distinguishing features of New England society, especially its fluid, mutable class structure. *A New-England Tale* also reflects Sedgwick's own conversion from the dominant Calvinism of Massachusetts's Puritan founders to the more liberal Unitarian movement; the novel's heroine eventually rejects what the book depicts as Calvinism's dogmatism, repressiveness, and hypocrisy in favor of a more humane, authentic Christianity represented by characters belonging to other Protestant denominations, including Methodists and Quakers. Despite its negative portrayal of Calvinism, *A New-England Tale* won praise for its scrupulous and well-wrought portrait of contemporary American life, as did its follow-up, *Redwood* (1824). The success of these two novels rapidly elevated Sedgwick to the level of America's other emerging literary luminaries: James Fenimore Cooper, for example, praised the realism of *A New-England Tale* and, when *Redwood* was published in France, found himself mistakenly identified as its author, much to Sedgwick's amusement.

Sedgwick's newfound parity—and rivalry—with writers such as Cooper influenced her turn in her third novel, *Hope Leslie* (1827), from contemporary New England to the region's colonial history. Set in the wake of the seventeenth-century war between Puritan colonists and the Indigenous Pequot nation, *Hope Leslie* joins novels such as Cooper's *Last of the Mohicans* (1826) and Lydia Maria Child's *Hobomok* (1824) in Americanizing the historical novel, a genre initially popularized by British writers such as Maria Edgeworth and Sir Walter Scott. Like Cooper and Child, Sedgwick explores the history of contact and conflict between settlers and Indigenous Americans, in the belief that this history formed the best basis for a distinctively American national literature. In adopting this focus, *Hope Leslie* also spoke to the debates surrounding U.S. policy toward Indigenous peoples and the push for further national expansion at their expense going on in the 1820s. The novel centers on two independent-minded women, the Puritan Hope Leslie and her Pequot counterpart Magawisca, both of whom defy the gender norms of their own time as well as their author's era. *Hope Leslie*'s centering of women in general, and sympathetic portrayal of an Indigenous woman in particular, bemused some of its initial reviewers: the *North American Review* judged that Sedgwick held "a decided partiality for her own sex," while the *Western Monthly Review* refused to credit her positive depiction of Magawisca: "we should have looked in any place for such a character, rather than in an Indian wigwam." Both reviews, however, ultimately endorsed the critical and popular consensus that the novel was another success, and today it is widely regarded as Sedgwick's masterpiece.

Sedgwick followed *Hope Leslie* with one of the first American urban novels, *Clarence* (1830), which skewers the growing commercialism of contemporary American society. Her next novel, *The Linwoods* (1835), is a narrative of the American Revolution that, in its celebratory portrayal of the country's founding generation, counterbalances *Hope Leslie*'s critique of New England's Puritan settlers. Sedgwick further solidified her literary stature with her abundant short fiction. In all, she published more than a hundred "tales and sketches," some of which further explore themes from her novels; for instance, "Berkeley Jail" (1832) continues *Hope Leslie*'s consideration of Indigenous–settler relations. Others treat matters of more personal import to Sedgwick—in "Cacoethes Scribendi" (1830), for example, a woman's choice between marriage and writing. In her own life, Sedgwick chose the latter: though she was engaged twice, she never chose to marry, instead devoting herself to, and supporting herself by, her literary career. The role of marriage in women's lives also provides the central question underlying her final novel, *Married or Single?* (1857); while the protagonist does marry at the novel's conclusion, its preface frames the story as an argument against "the miserable cant that matrimony is essential to the feebler sex."

Sedgwick largely refrained from extending her literary advocacy for marginalized groups to political advocacy. Unlike her fellow novelist Lydia Maria Child, she did not move from writing fiction decrying past dispossessions of Indigenous people to opposing the policy of "Indian removal" in the present. Similarly, she resisted attempts by Child and others to enlist her open support for the abolition of slavery, claiming that she found some abolitionists to be "foolish and doubtful zealots" and fearing that their efforts would destroy the union. From the mid-1830s on, though, she devoted extensive time and energy to other forms of social advocacy, especially work for the New York Women's Prison Association, of which she served as the first "directress" from 1848 to 1863. This work, which included teaching Bible classes, giving readings to convicts, and helping released women prisoners reenter society, reflected Sedgwick's longstanding interest in class dynamics and her conviction that "the favored class of society owe an immense debt to Providence, which can only be discharged by attempting to rescue the vicious and ignorant from misery and degradation." This commitment to social and moral uplift also animated much of her writing after the mid-1830s, which included "domestic novellas" emphasizing moral responsibility and instruction—some of which, such as *The Rich Poor Man and the Poor Rich Man* (1836) and *Live and Let Live; or, Domestic Service Illustrated* (1837), became her most popular works. In the latter part of her career, she also wrote advice manuals, numerous works for children, two biographies, and a European travelogue. She died of paralysis in 1867.

Sedgwick's work remained popular throughout the nineteenth century, and she was enormously influential. As what Nathaniel Hawthorne called "our most truthful novelist," she laid much of the groundwork for realism in American literature. Writers such as Hawthorne and Herman Melville benefited from the prestige she won for American letters—as the *Literary World* put it in 1850, Sedgwick "promote[d] Melville's and Hawthorne's reputation by association with her"—and built on her foundational depictions of American society, both past and present: Hawthorne's *The Scarlet Letter*, for example, owes much to the portrayal of Puritan New England in *Hope Leslie*. For other writers, Sedgwick's work provided models and inspirations for radical political critique, as can be seen, for instance, in the African American abolitionist writer Sarah Louisa Forten's occasional use of the pen name "Magawisca."

In an 1829 review, Lydia Maria Child celebrated the stature Sedgwick had achieved with her first three novels, predicting that "an hundred years hence, when other and gifted competitors have crowded into the field, our country will still be proud of her name." "An hundred years hence," however, Sedgwick had become critically neglected; in the early twentieth century, as American literary scholarship became increasingly male-dominated, the later male "competitors" who had "crowded into the field" in her wake were permitted to crowd her out of the American canon. Feminist scholarship in the 1970s and 80s recovered Sedgwick from obscurity, and critics since then have debated the politics of her work while reaffirming and consolidating her central place in the literary history of the early United States.

NOTE ON THE TEXT: The text presented here is based on the first published edition of "Cacoethes Scribendi," from the 1830 issue of the *Atlantic Souvenir*. Spelling and punctuation have been modernized according to the practices of this anthology.

⌘⌘⌘

Cacoethes Scribendi[1]

Glory and gain the industrious tribe provoke.[2]

POPE

The little secluded and quiet village of H. lies at no great distance from our "literary emporium."[3] It was never remarked or remarkable for anything, save one mournful preeminence, to those who sojourned within its borders—it was duller even than common villages. The young men of the better class all emigrated. The most daring spirits adventured on the sea. Some went to Boston; some to the south; and some to the west; and left a community of women who lived like nuns, with the advantage of more liberty and fresh air, but without the consolation and excitement of a religious vow. Literally, there was not a single young gentleman in the village—nothing in manly shape to which these desperate circumstances could give the form and quality and use of a beau.[4] Some dashing city blades,[5] who once strayed from the turnpike to this sequestered spot, averred that the girls stared at them as if, like Miranda, they would have exclaimed—

What i'st? a spirit?
Lord, how it looks about! Believe me, sir,
It carries a brave form—But 'tis a spirit.[6]

---

[1]   *Cacoethes Scribendi*   Latin: Irresistible urge to write (*cacoethes* carries the additional meaning of "bad habit" or "malignant disease"). The phrase comes from the Roman poet Juvenal's *Satires* 7.52: "the incurable itch for writing affects many."

[2]   *Glory … provoke*   From *The Dunciad* (1728, revised 1743), a mock-heroic poem by the English poet Alexander Pope. The poem satirizes the literary culture of Pope's time, especially what Pope saw as its abundance of untalented hack authors, whom the poem portrays as courtiers of the goddess Dulness. The passage from which Sedgwick's epigraph is taken specifically targets "stationers," i.e., booksellers: "With authors, stationers obeyed the call, / (The field of glory is a field for all). / Glory and gain the industrious tribe provoke; / And gentle Dulness ever loves a joke."

[3]   *literary emporium*   Boston, which by the 1830s had acquired a reputation as a cultural center and was widely known by this phrase; *emporium*   Major marketplace or commercial hub.

[4]   *beau*   Male sweetheart or suitor.

[5]   *blades*   Gallant, good-natured fellows.

[6]   *What i'st … a spirit*   From Shakespeare's *The Tempest* 1.2.488–90. The character of Miranda, who has spent her life on a deserted island with limited human contact, says this after first laying eyes on the shipwrecked Prince Ferdinand, whom she later marries; *brave*   Fine.

A peculiar fatality hung over this devoted[1] place. If death seized on either head of a family, he was sure to take the husband; every woman in H. was a widow or maiden; and it is a sad fact, that when the holiest office of the church[2] was celebrated, they were compelled to borrow deacons from an adjacent village. But, incredible as it may be, there was no great diminution of happiness in consequence of the absence of the nobler sex.[3] Mothers were occupied with their children and housewifery, and the young ladies read their books with as much interest as if they had lovers to discuss them with, and worked their frills and capes as diligently, and wore them as complacently, as if they were to be seen by manly eyes. Never were there pleasanter gatherings or parties (for that was the word even in their nomenclature) than those of the young girls of H. There was no mincing—no affectation—no hope of passing for what they were not—no envy of the pretty and fortunate—no insolent triumph over the plain and demure and neglected—but all was good will and good humour. They were a pretty circle of girls—a garland of bright fresh flowers. Never were there more sparkling glances—never sweeter smiles—nor more of them. Their present was all health and cheerfulness; and their future, not the gloomy perspective of dreary singleness, for somewhere in the passage of life they were sure to be mated. Most of the young men who had abandoned their native soil, as soon as they found themselves *getting along*, loyally returned to lay their fortunes at the feet of the companions of their childhood.

The girls made occasional visits to Boston, and occasional journeys to various parts of the country, for they were all enterprising and independent, and had the characteristic New England avidity for seizing a "privilege"; and in these various ways, to borrow a phrase of their good grandames,[4] "a door was opened for them," and in due time they fulfilled the destiny of women.

We spoke strictly, and à la lettre,[5] when we said that in the village of H. there was not a single *beau*. But on the outskirts of the town, at a pleasant farm, embracing hill and valley, upland and meadow land; in a neat house, looking to the south, with true economy of sunshine and comfort, and overlooking the prettiest winding stream that ever sent up its sparkling beauty to the eye, and flanked on the north by a rich maple grove, beautiful in spring and summer, and glorious in autumn, and the kindest defence in winter—on this farm and in this house dwelt a youth, to fame unknown,[6] but known and loved by every inhabitant of H., old and young, grave and gay, lively and severe. Ralph Hepburn was one of nature's favourites. He had a figure that would have adorned courts and cities; and a face that adorned human nature, for it was full of good humour, kindheartedness, spirit, and intelligence; and driving the plough or wielding the scythe, his cheek flushed with manly and profitable exercise, he looked as if he had been moulded in a poet's fancy—as farmers look in Georgics and Pastorals.[7] His gifts were by no means all external. He wrote verses in every album[8] in the village, and very pretty album verses they were, and numerous too—for the number of albums was equivalent to the whole female population. He was admirable at pencil sketches; and once with a little paint, the refuse[9] of a house painting, he achieved an admirable portrait of his grandmother and her cat. There was, to be sure, a striking likeness between the two figures, but he was limited to the same colours for both; and besides, it was not out of nature, for the old lady and her cat had purred together in the chimney corner, till their physiognomies bore an obvious resemblance to each other. Ralph had a talent for music too. His voice was the sweetest of all the Sunday choir, and one would have fancied, from the bright eyes that were turned on him from the long line and double lines of treble and counter singers,[10] that Ralph Hepburn was a note book, or that the girls listened with their eyes as well as their ears. Ralph did not

---

1   *devoted* Doomed.

2   *the holiest ... church* Communion.

3   *nobler sex* I.e., men.

4   *grandames* Grandmothers.

5   *à la lettre* French: according to the letter, i.e., literally.

6   *a youth ... unknown* See "Elegy Written in a Country Churchyard" (1751), by the English poet Thomas Gray.

7   *Georgics and Pastorals* Genres of poetry concerning rural life.

8   *album* Book containing signatures, quotations, and other inscriptions left by visitors, kept by its owner as a keepsake.

9   *refuse* Leftovers.

10   *treble and counter singers* Here, types of female singers; treble singers sing the highest part in a musical composition, while counter singers sing lower parts.

restrict himself to psalmody.[1] He had an ear so exquisitely susceptible to the "touches of sweet harmony"[2] that he discovered, by the stroke of his axe, the musical capacities of certain species of wood, and he made himself a violin of chestnut, and drew strains from it, that if they could not create a soul under the ribs of death,[3] could make the prettiest feet and the lightest hearts dance, an achievement far more to Ralph's taste than the aforesaid miracle. In short, it seemed as if nature, in her love of compensation, had showered on Ralph all the gifts that are usually diffused through a community of beaux. Yet Ralph was no prodigy; none of his talents were in excess, but all in moderate degree. No genius was ever so good humoured, so useful, so practical; and though, in his small and modest way, a Crichton,[4] he was not, like most universal geniuses, good for nothing for any particular office in life. His farm was not a pattern farm[5]—a prize farm for an agricultural society—but in wonderful order considering his miscellaneous pursuits. He was the delight of his grandfather for his sagacity in hunting bees—the old man's favourite, in truth his only pursuit. He was so skilled in woodcraft that the report[6] of his gun was as certain a signal of death as the tolling of a church bell.[7] The fish always caught at his bait. He manufactured half his farming utensils, improved upon old inventions, and struck out some new ones; tamed partridges—the most untameable of all the feathered tribe; domesticated squirrels; rivalled

Scheherazade[8] herself in telling stories, strange and long—the latter quality being essential at a country fireside; and, in short, Ralph made a perpetual holiday of a life of labour.

Every girl in the village street knew when Ralph's wagon or sleigh traversed it; indeed, there was scarcely a house to which the horses did not, as if by instinct, turn up while their master greeted its fair tenants. This state of affairs had continued for two winters and two summers since Ralph came to his majority and, by the death of his father, to the sole proprietorship of the "Hepburn farm"—the name his patrimonial acres had obtained from the singular circumstance (in our *moving* country) of their having remained in the same family for four generations. Never was the matrimonial destiny of a young lord, or heir just come to his estate, more thoroughly canvassed than young Hepburn's by mothers, aunts, daughters, and nieces. But Ralph, perhaps from sheer good heartedness, seemed reluctant to give to one the heart that diffused rays of sunshine through the whole village.

With all decent people he eschewed the doctrines of a certain erratic female lecturer on the odious monopoly of marriage,[9] yet Ralph, like a tender hearted judge, hesitated to place on a single brow the crown matrimonial which so many deserved, and which, though Ralph was far enough from a coxcomb,[10] he could not but see so many coveted.

Whether our hero perceived that his mind was becoming elated or distracted with this general favour, or that he observed a dawning of rivalry among the fair competitors, or whatever was the cause, the fact was, that he by degrees circumscribed his visits, and finally concentrated them in the family of his aunt Courland.

Mrs. Courland was a widow, and Ralph was the kindest of nephews to her, and the kindest of cousins to her children. To their mother he seemed their guardian angel. That the five lawless, daring little urchins did not drown themselves when they were

[1] *psalmody* Singing of psalms or other kinds of religious vocal music.

[2] *touches … harmony* From Shakespeare's *The Merchant of Venice* 5.1.65.

[3] *create … death* See John Milton's *Comus* (1634): "I was all ear, / And took in strains that might create a soul / Under the ribs of Death" (560–62).

[4] *Crichton* James Crichton (1560–82), a Scottish scholar and traveler whose extraordinary gifts and attainments in a multitude of different fields earned him the title "the Admirable Crichton."

[5] *pattern farm* Model farm used for experimenting with and demonstrating new agricultural techniques.

[6] *report* Resounding noise, especially that caused by the discharge of a gun.

[7] *tolling of a church bell* Reference to the practice of ringing church bells to mark deaths and funerals.

[8] *Scheherazade* Legendary storyteller of the *One Thousand and One Nights*.

[9] *the doctrines … marriage* Reference to Frances "Fanny" Wright (1795–1852), a Scottish-born lecturer and writer who became notorious for her advocacy of sexual freedom and opposition to traditional marriage, among many other radical causes; *erratic* Eccentric.

[10] *coxcomb* Vain, conceited person.

swimming, nor shoot themselves when they were shooting, was, in her eyes, Ralph's merit; and then "he was so attentive to Alice, her only daughter—a brother could not be kinder." But who would not be kind to Alice? she was a sweet girl of seventeen, not beautiful, not handsome perhaps, but pretty enough—with soft hazel eyes, a profusion of light brown hair, always in the neatest trim, and a mouth that could not but be lovely and loveable, for all kind and tender affections were playing about it. Though Alice was the only daughter of a doting mother, the only sister of five loving boys, the only niece of three single, fond aunts, and, last and greatest, the only cousin of our only beau, Ralph Hepburn, no girl of seventeen was ever more disinterested,[1] unassuming, unostentatious, and unspoiled. Ralph and Alice had always lived on terms of cousinly affection—an affection of a neutral tint that they never thought of being shaded into the deep dye of a more tender passion.[2] Ralph rendered her all cousinly offices. If he had twenty damsels to escort, not an uncommon case, he never forgot Alice. When he returned from any little excursion, he always brought some graceful offering to Alice.

He had lately paid a visit to Boston. It was at the season of the periodical inundation of annuals.[3] He brought two of the prettiest to Alice. Ah! little did she think they were to prove Pandora's box[4] to her. Poor simple girl! she sat down to read them, as if an annual were meant to be read, and she was honestly interested and charmed. Her mother observed her delight. "What have you there, Alice?" she asked. "Oh the prettiest story, mamma! Two such tried faithful lovers, and married at last! It ends beautifully: I hate love stories that don't end in marriage."

"And so do I, Alice," exclaimed Ralph, who entered at the moment, and for the first time Alice felt her cheeks tingle at his approach. He had brought a basket, containing a choice plant he had obtained for her, and she laid down the annual and went with him to the garden to see it set by his own hand.

Mrs. Courland seized upon the annual with avidity. She had imbibed a literary taste in Boston, where the best and happiest years of her life were passed. She had some literary ambition too. She read the North American Review[5] from beginning to end, and she fancied no conversation could be sensible or improving that was not about books. But she had been effectually prevented, by the necessities of a narrow income, and by the unceasing wants of five teasing[6] boys, from indulging her literary inclinations; for Mrs. Courland, like all New England women, had been taught to consider domestic duties as the first temporal[7] duties of her sex. She had recently seen some of the native productions with which the press is daily teeming, and which certainly have a tendency to dispel our early illusions about the craft of authorship. She had even felt some obscure intimations, within her secret soul, that she might herself become an author. The annual was destined to fix her fate. She opened it—the publisher had written the names of the authors of the anonymous pieces against their productions.[8] Among them she found some of the familiar friends of her childhood and youth.

If, by a sudden gift of second sight, she had seen them enthroned as kings and queens, she would not have been more astonished. She turned to their pieces, and read them, as perchance no one else ever did, from beginning to end—faithfully. Not a sentence—a sentence! not a word was skipped. She paused to consider commas, colons, and dashes. All the art and magic of authorship were made level to her comprehension, and when she closed the book, she *felt a call*[9] to become an author, and before she retired to bed she obeyed the call, as if it had been, in truth, a divinity stirring within her. In the morning she presented an article

---

1   *disinterested*   Not self-interested; modest, humble.

2   *Ralph ... passion*   Marriage between first cousins was legal and unremarkable throughout the United States and Europe in the late eighteenth and early nineteenth centuries.

3   *annuals*   I.e., literary annuals, also known as gift books: collections of essays, short fiction, and poetry that were published annually. They were often lavishly decorated and were intended for gift-giving. *The Atlantic Souvenir*, in the 1830 issue of which "Cacoethes Scribendi" was first published, was one such gift book.

4   *Pandora's box*   In Greek myth, a box that contained all human evils, said to have been opened by a girl named Pandora.

5   *North American Review*   First literary magazine in the United States, founded in Boston in 1815.

6   *teasing*   Irritating, vexing.

7   *temporal*   Earthly, as opposed to spiritual.

8   *against their productions*   I.e., next to their works.

9   *she ... call*   Sedgwick's language here echoes the Christian sense of "call" as a divine prompting to service.

to *her* public, consisting of her own family and a few select friends. All applauded, and every voice, save one, was unanimous for publication—that one was Alice. She was a modest, prudent girl; she feared failure, and feared notoriety still more. Her mother laughed at her childish scruples. The piece was sent off, and in due time graced the pages of an annual. Mrs. Courland's fate was now decided. She had, to use her own phrase, started in the career of letters, and she was no Atalanta[1] to be seduced from her straight onward way. She was a social, sympathetic, good hearted creature too, and she could not bear to go forth in the golden field to reap alone.

She was, besides, a prudent woman, as most of her countrywomen are, and the little pecuniary equivalent[2] for this delightful exercise of talents was not overlooked. Mrs. Courland, as we have somewhere said, had three single sisters—worthy women they were—but nobody ever dreamed of their taking to authorship. She, however, held them all in sisterly estimation.[3] Their talents were magnified as the talents of persons who live in a circumscribed sphere are apt to be, particularly if seen through the dilating[4] medium of affection.

Miss Anne, the oldest, was fond of flowers, a successful cultivator, and a diligent student of the science of botany. All this taste and knowledge, Mrs. Courland thought, might be turned to excellent account; and she persuaded Miss Anne to write a little book entitled "Familiar[5] Dialogues on Botany." The second sister, Miss Ruth, had a turn for education ("bachelor's wives and maid's children are always well taught"[6]), and Miss Ruth undertook a popular treatise on that subject. Miss Sally, the youngest, was the saint of the family, and she doubted about the propriety of a literary occupation,

till her scruples were overcome by the fortunate suggestion that her coup d'essai[7] should be a Saturday night book[8] entitled "Solemn Hours"—and solemn hours they were to their unhappy readers. Mrs. Courland next besieged her old mother. "You know, mamma," she said, "you have such a precious fund of anecdotes of the revolution and the French war,[9] and you talk just like the 'Annals of the Parish,'[10] and I am certain you can write a book fully as good."

"My child, you are distracted![11] I write a dreadful poor hand, and I never learned to spell—no girls did in my time."

"Spell! that is not of the least consequence—the printers correct the spelling."

But the honest old lady would not be tempted on the crusade, and her daughter consoled herself with the reflection that if she would not write, she was an admirable subject to be written about, and her diligent fingers worked off three distinct stories in which the old lady figured.

Mrs. Courland's ambition, of course, embraced within its widening circle her favourite nephew Ralph. She had always thought him a genius, and genius in her estimation was the philosopher's stone.[12] In his youth she had laboured to persuade his father to send him to Cambridge,[13] but the old man uniformly replied that Ralph "was a smart lad on the farm, and steady, and by that he knew he was no genius." As Ralph's character was developed, and talent after talent broke forth, his

---

[1]   *Atalanta* In Greek mythology, a follower of Artemis, the goddess of hunting and virginity. Atalanta's father ordered her to marry, and she made a bargain with him that she would only marry a suitor who defeated her in a footrace. Aphrodite aided the successful suitor by providing him with golden apples, which he dropped throughout the race to slow Atalanta as she picked them up.

[2]   *pecuniary equivalent* I.e., payment.

[3]   *estimation* Esteem.

[4]   *dilating* Amplifying, enlarging.

[5]   *Familiar* Friendly; casual; readily comprehensible.

[6]   *bachelor's ... taught* Proverb implying that "old maids" like Ruth fancy themselves experts on raising children because they have none of their own.

[7]   *coup d'essai* French: first attempt.

[8]   *Saturday night book* Collection of religious meditations intended to be studied on Saturday nights, in preparation for church on Sunday morning.

[9]   *French war* I.e., the French and Indian War (1754–63), a conflict between Britain and its North American colonies and Indigenous allies, on one side, and France and its North American colonies and Indigenous allies, on the other.

[10]   *Annals of the Parish* 1821 novel by the Scottish writer John Galt. The novel takes the form of a year-by-year chronicle of events in a fictional Scottish parish from 1760 to 1810.

[11]   *distracted* Insane.

[12]   *philosopher's stone* Legendary substance believed to turn any metal into gold; by extension, something capable of transforming common materials into precious items.

[13]   *to Cambridge* I.e., to Harvard College, which at the time was the most prestigious institution of higher education in the United States. Harvard is located in Cambridge, a town just north of Boston.

aunt renewed her lamentations over his ignoble destiny. That Ralph was useful, good, and happy—the most difficult and rare results achieved in life—was nothing, so long as he was but a farmer in H. Once she did half persuade him to turn painter, but his good sense and filial duty triumphed "over her eloquence," and suppressed the hankerings after distinction that are innate in every human breast, from the little ragged chimneysweep that hopes to be a *boss*, to the political aspirant whose bright goal is the presidential chair.

Now Mrs. Courland fancied Ralph might climb the steep of fame without quitting his farm; occasional authorship was compatible with his vocation. But alas! she could not persuade Ralph to pluck the laurels[1] that she saw ready grown to his hand. She was not offended, for she was the best natured woman in the world, but she heartily pitied him, and seldom mentioned his name without repeating that stanza of Gray's, inspired for the consolation of hopeless obscurity:

> Full many a gem of purest ray serene, &c.[2]

Poor Alice's sorrows we have reserved to the last, for they were heaviest. "Alice," her mother said, "was gifted; she was well educated, well informed; she was everything necessary to be an author." But Alice resisted; and, though the gentlest, most complying of all good daughters, she would have resisted to the death—she would as soon have stood in a pillory[3] as appeared in print. Her mother, Mrs. Courland, was not an obstinate woman, and gave up in despair. But still our poor heroine was destined to be the victim of this *cacoethes scribendi*; for Mrs. Courland divided the world into two classes, or rather parts—authors and subjects for authors; the one active, the other passive. At first blush one would have thought the village of H. rather a barren field for such a reaper as Mrs. Courland, but her zeal and indefatigableness worked

wonders. She converted the stern scholastic divine of H. into as much of a La Roche[4] as she could describe; a tall wrinkled bony old woman, who reminded her of Meg Merrilies,[5] sat for a witch; the school master for an Ichabod Crane;[6] a poor half witted boy was made to utter as much pathos and sentiment and wit as she could put into his lips; and a crazy vagrant was a Godsend to her. Then every "wide spreading elm," "blasted pine," or "gnarled oak," flourished on her pages. The village church and school house stood there according to their actual dimensions. One old *pilgrim* house[7] was as prolific as haunted tower or ruined abbey.[8] It was surveyed outside, ransacked inside, and again made habitable for the reimbodied spirits of its founders.

The most kind hearted of women, Mrs. Courland's interests came to be so at variance with the prosperity of the little community of H., that a sudden calamity, a death, a funeral, were fortunate events to her. To do her justice she felt them in a twofold capacity. She wept as a woman, and exulted as an author. The days of the calamities of authors have passed by. We have all wept over Otway and shivered at the thought of Tasso.[9] But times are changed. The lean sheaf is devouring the full one.[10] A new class of sufferers has arisen, and there is

---

[1] *laurels*   In ancient Greece, laurel wreaths were given in recognition of high achievement.

[2] *Full … serene, &c.*   See Gray's "Elegy Written in a Country Churchyard." The full stanza Sedgwick alludes to reads "Full many a gem of purest ray serene, / The dark unfathomed caves of ocean bear: / Full many a flow'r is born to blush unseen, / And waste its sweetness on the desert air."

[3] *pillory*   Wooden framework used to restrain people for punishment by public humiliation and abuse.

[4] *La Roche*   Kindly widowed clergyman and loving father in "The Story of La Roche" (1779), a short story by the Scottish writer Henry Mackenzie.

[5] *Meg Merrilies*   Romani character with supernatural associations in *Guy Mannering* (1815), by the Scottish writer Sir Walter Scott. She is also the subject of a poem by the English poet John Keats (1795–1821).

[6] *Ichabod Crane*   Fictional schoolmaster who is the protagonist of "The Legend of Sleepy Hollow" (1820), by the American writer Washington Irving.

[7] *pilgrim house*   I.e., house dating back to the period of the Pilgrims, who in 1620 founded the first English colony in what would become Massachusetts.

[8] *haunted … abbey*   Stock locations of Gothic fiction, which was widely popular in Europe and America in the late eighteenth and early nineteenth centuries.

[9] *Otway*   Thomas Otway (1652–85), English writer of tragic dramas, who experienced numerous misfortunes and privations and ultimately died in poverty;   *Tasso*   Torquato Tasso, Italian poet, who achieved great success with his epic poem *Jerusalem Delivered* (1581) but whose creativity and productivity were cut short by mental illness.

[10] *The lean … full one*   See Genesis 41.5–7, where this image appears in a dream foretelling a period of famine.

nothing more touching in all the memoirs Mr. D'Israeli[1] has collected, than the trials of poor Alice, tragi-comic though they were. Mrs. Courland's new passion ran most naturally in the worn channel of maternal affection. Her boys were too purely boys for her art—but Alice, her sweet Alice, was preeminently lovely in the new light in which she now placed every object. Not an incident of her life but was inscribed on her mother's memory, and thence transferred to her pages, by way of precept, or example, or pathetic or ludicrous circumstance. She regretted now, for the first time, that Alice had no lover whom she might introduce among her dramatis personae.[2] Once her thoughts did glance on Ralph, but she had not quite merged the woman in the author; she knew instinctively that Alice would be particularly offended at being thus paired with Ralph. But Alice's *public life* was not limited to her mother's productions. She was the darling niece of her three aunts. She had studied botany with the eldest, and Miss Anne had recorded in her private diary all her favourite's clever remarks during their progress in the science. This diary was now a mine of gold to her, and faithfully worked up for a circulating medium. But, most trying of all to poor Alice, was the attitude in which she appeared in her aunt Sally's "solemn hours." Every aspiration of piety to which her young lips had given utterance was there printed. She felt as if she were condemned to say her prayers in the marketplace.[3] Every act of kindness, every deed of charity, she had ever performed, were produced to the public. Alice would have been consoled if she had known how small that public was; but, as it was, she felt like a modest country girl when she first enters an apartment hung on every side with mirrors, when, shrinking from observation, she sees in every direction her image multiplied and often distorted; for, notwithstanding Alice's dutiful respect for her good aunts, and her consciousness of their affectionate intentions, she could not but perceive that they were unskilled painters. She grew afraid

to speak or to act, and from being the most artless, frank, and, at home, social little creature in the world, she became as silent and as stiff as a statue. And, in the circle of her young associates, her natural gaiety was constantly checked by their winks and smiles, and broader allusions to her multiplied portraits; for they had instantly recognized them through the thin veil of feigned[4] names of persons and places. They called her a blue stocking[5] too; for they had the vulgar notion that everybody must be tinged that lived under the same roof with an author. Our poor victim was afraid to speak of a book—worse than that, she was afraid to touch one, and the last Waverley novel[6] actually lay in the house a month before she opened it. She avoided wearing even a blue ribbon, as fearfully as a forsaken damsel shuns the colour of green.[7]

It was during the height of this literary fever in the Courland family, that Ralph Hepburn, as has been mentioned, concentrated all his visiting there. He was of a compassionate disposition, and he knew Alice was, unless relieved by him, in solitary possession of their once social parlour, while her mother and aunts were driving their quills[8] in their several apartments.

Oh! what a changed place was that parlour! Not the tower of Babel,[9] after the builders had forsaken it, exhibited a sadder reverse; not a Lancaster school,[10]

---

[1] *Mr. D'Israeli* Isaac D'Israeli, British essayist and biographer, known for books such as *Calamities of Authors* (1812–13) and *Quarrels of Authors* (1814).

[2] *dramatis personae* Latin: cast of characters.

[3] *say … marketplace* See Matthew 6.5: "And when thou prayest, thou shalt not be as the hypocrites are: for they love to pray standing in the synagogues and in the corners of the streets, that they may be seen of men. Verily I say unto you, They have their reward."

[4] *feigned* Made-up.

[5] *blue stocking* Woman with literary tastes and inclinations. The term comes from the Blue Stockings Society, a mid-eighteenth-century English literary discussion club in which both women and men participated. By the 1830s, the term had acquired pejorative connotations.

[6] *the last Waverley novel* The Waverley novels (1814–31) were a wildly popular series of novels by Sir Walter Scott. At the time "Cacoethes Scribendi" was published, the most recent Waverley novel was *Anne of Geierstein, or, The Maiden in the Mist* (1829).

[7] *a forsaken … green* Green was widely believed to symbolize fickleness and to be unlucky.

[8] *driving their quills* I.e., writing.

[9] *tower of Babel* In the Book of Genesis, tower built by people who wished to reach Heaven. For their presumption, God caused them all to speak different languages, so that they could not communicate well enough to continue to build the tower. See Genesis 11.1–9.

[10] *Lancaster school* School operating according to the educational system devised by the English educationist Joseph Lancaster (1778–1838). In Lancasterian schools, students who had learned the material were rewarded for helping to pass it on to their [continued ...]

when the boys have left it, a more striking contrast. Mrs. Courland and her sisters were all "talking women," and too generous to encroach on one another's rights and happiness. They had acquired the power to hear and speak simultaneously. Their parlour was the general gathering place, a sort of village exchange, where all the innocent gossips, old and young, met together. "There are tongues in trees,"[1] and surely there seemed to be tongues in the very walls of that vocal parlour. Everything there had a social aspect. There was something agreeable and conversable in the litter of netting and knitting work, of sewing implements, and all the signs and shows[2] of happy female occupation.

Now, all was as orderly as a town drawing room in company hours.[3] Not a sound was heard there save Ralph's and Alice's voices, mingling in soft and suppressed murmurs, as if afraid of breaking the chain of their aunt's ideas, or, perchance, of too rudely jarring a tenderer chain. One evening, after tea, Mrs. Courland remained with her daughter, instead of retiring, as usual, to her writing desk. "Alice, my dear," said the good mother, "I have noticed for a few days past that you look out of spirits. You will listen to nothing I say on that subject; but if you would try it, my dear, if you would only try it, you would find there is nothing so tranquillizing[4] as the occupation of writing."

"I shall never try it, mamma."

"You are afraid of being called a blue stocking. Ah! Ralph, how are you?"—Ralph entered at this moment.—"Ralph, tell me honestly, do you not think it a weakness in Alice to be so afraid of blue stockings?"

"It would be a pity, aunt, to put blue stockings on such pretty feet as Alice's."

Alice blushed and smiled, and her mother said— "Nonsense, Ralph; you should bear in mind the celebrated saying of the Edinburgh wit—'no matter how blue the stockings are, if the petticoats are long enough to hide them.'"[5]

"Hide Alice's feet! Oh aunt, worse and worse!"

"Better hide her feet, Ralph, than her talents—that is a sin for which both she and you will have to answer. Oh! you and Alice need not exchange such significant glances! You are doing yourselves and the public injustice, and you have no idea how easy writing is."

"Easy writing, but hard reading, aunt."

"That's false modesty, Ralph. If I had but your opportunities to collect materials"—Mrs. Courland did not know that in literature, as in some species of manufacture, the most exquisite productions are wrought from the smallest quantity of raw material—"There's your journey to New York, Ralph," she continued, "you might have made three capital articles out of that. The revolutionary officer would have worked up for the 'Legendary'; the mysterious lady for the 'Token'; and the man in black for the 'Remember Me'[6]—all founded on fact, all romantic and pathetic."[7]

"But mamma," said Alice, expressing in words what Ralph's arch smile expressed almost as plainly, "you know the officer drank too much; and the mysterious lady turned out to be a runaway milliner;[8] and the man in black—oh! what a theme for a pathetic story!—the man in black was a widower, on his way to Newhaven,[9] where he was to select his third wife from three *recommended* candidates."

"Pshaw! Alice: do you suppose it is necessary to tell things precisely as they are?"

"Alice is wrong, aunt, and you are right; and if she will open her writing desk for me, I will sit down this moment, and write a story—a true story—true from beginning to end; and if it moves you, my dear aunt, if it meets your approbation,[10] my destiny is decided."

---

peers, a method known as "mutual instruction." The system spread in both Britain and America in the early nineteenth century but soon acquired a reputation for poor standards and harsh discipline.

[1]   *There are ... trees*   See Shakespeare's *As You Like It* 2.1.15–17: "And this our life, exempt from public haunt, / Finds tongues in trees, books in the running brooks, / Sermons in stones, and good in everything."

[2]   *shows*   Appearances.

[3]   *company hours*   Hours designated for receiving visitors.

[4]   *tranquillizing*   Calming.

[5]   *the celebrated ... hide them*   Saying attributed to Francis Jeffrey, Lord Jeffrey (1773–1850), Scottish judge and literary critic. Jeffrey supposedly said this to a woman writer who had remarked to him, "I fear my *cacoethes scribendi* forms no recommendation in your sight."

[6]   *the 'Legendary' ... the 'Remember Me'*   Mrs. Courland refers to the titles of three literary annuals.

[7]   *romantic*   Imaginatively compelling; *pathetic*   Emotionally affecting.

[8]   *milliner*   Hat-maker.

[9]   *Newhaven*   I.e., New Haven, a city in Connecticut.

[10]   *approbation*   Approval.

Mrs. Courland was delighted; she had slain the giant, and she saw fame and fortune smiling on her favourite. She arranged the desk for him herself; she prepared a folio sheet[1] of paper, folded the ominous margins; and was so absorbed in her bright visions, that she did not hear a little by-talk[2] between Ralph and Alice, nor see the tell-tale flush on their cheeks, nor notice the perturbation with which Alice walked first to one window and then to another, and finally settled herself to that best of all sedatives—hemming a ruffle. Ralph chewed off the end of his quill, mended his pen twice, though his aunt assured him "printers did not mind the penmanship," and had achieved a single line when Mrs. Courland's vigilant eye was averted by the entrance of her servant girl, who put a packet into her hands. She looked at the direction,[3] cut the string, broke the seals, and took out a periodical fresh from the publisher. She opened at the first article—a strangely mingled current of maternal pride and literary triumph rushed through her heart and brightened her face. She whispered to the servant a summons to all her sisters to the parlour, and an intimation, sufficiently intelligible to them, of her joyful reason for interrupting them.

Our readers will sympathize with her, and with Alice too, when we disclose to them the secret of her joy. The article in question was a clever composition written by our devoted Alice when she was at school. One of her fond aunts had preserved it; and aunts and mother had combined in the pious fraud of giving it to the public, unknown to Alice. They were perfectly aware of her determination never to be an author. But they fancied it was the mere timidity of an unfledged bird; and that when, by their innocent artifice, she found that her opinions could soar in a literary atmosphere, she would realize the sweet fluttering sensations they had experienced at their first flight. The good souls all hurried to the parlour, eager to witness the coup de théatre.[4] Miss Sally's pen stood emblematically erect in her turban; Miss Ruth, in her haste, had overset her inkstand, and the drops were trickling down her white dressing, or, as she now called it, writing gown; and

Miss Anne had a wild flower in her hand, as she hoped, of an undescribed species, which, in her joyful agitation, she most unluckily picked to pieces. All bit their lips to keep impatient congratulation from bursting forth. Ralph was so intent on his writing, and Alice on her hemming, that neither noticed the irruption;[5] and Mrs. Courland was obliged twice to speak to her daughter before she could draw her attention.

"Alice, look here—Alice, my dear."

"What is it, mamma? something new of yours?"

"No; guess again, Alice."

"Of one of my aunts, of course?"

"Neither, dear, neither. Come and look for yourself, and see if you can then tell whose it is."

Alice dutifully laid aside her work, approached and took the book. The moment her eye glanced on the fatal page, all her apathy vanished—deep crimson overspread her cheeks, brow, and neck. She burst into tears of irrepressible vexation, and threw the book into the blazing fire.

The gentle Alice! Never had she been guilty of such an ebullition[6] of temper. Her poor dismayed aunts retreated; her mother looked at her in mute astonishment; and Ralph, struck with her emotion, started from the desk, and would have asked an explanation, but Alice exclaimed—"Don't say anything about it, mamma—I cannot bear it now."

Mrs. Courland knew instinctively that Ralph would sympathize entirely with Alice, and quite willing to avoid an éclaircissement,[7] she said—"Some other time, Ralph, I'll tell you the whole. Show me now what you have written. How have you begun?"

Ralph handed her the paper with a novice's trembling hand.

"Oh! how very little! and so scratched and interlined! but never mind—'c'est le premier pas qui coute.'"[8]

While making these general observations, the good mother was getting out and fixing her spectacles, and Alice and Ralph had retreated behind her. Alice rested her head on his shoulder, and Ralph's lips were not far from her ear. Whether he was soothing her ruffled

---

[1] *folio sheet* Single large page.

[2] *by-talk* Talk taking place on the margin of the main conversation; side talk.

[3] *direction* Address.

[4] *coup de théatre* French: sudden dramatic event.

[5] *irruption* Abrupt incursion, i.e., of Mrs. Courland's sisters.

[6] *ebullition* Boiling over, outburst.

[7] *éclaircissement* Explanation.

[8] *c'est ... coute* French: it is only the first step that costs, i.e., getting started is the hardest part.

spirit, or what he was doing, is not recorded. Mrs. Courland read and re-read the sentence. She dropped a tear on it. She forgot her literary aspirations for Ralph and Alice—forgot she was herself an author—forgot everything but the mother; and rising, embraced them both as her dear children, and expressed, in her raised and moistened eye, consent to their union, which Ralph had dutifully and prettily asked in that short and true story of his love for his sweet cousin Alice.

In due time the village of H. was animated with the celebration of Alice's nuptials: and when her mother and aunts saw her the happy mistress of the Hepburn farm, and the happiest of wives, they relinquished, without a sigh, the hope of ever seeing her an AUTHOR.
—1830

JAMES FENIMORE COOPER
1789 – 1851

James Fenimore Cooper was one of the most popular U.S. novelists of the nineteenth century. The author of more than thirty novels, he was the first to adapt Walter Scott's genre of the historical novel to an American context, with *The Spy* (1821), and he founded the popular genre of the sea tale with *The Pilot* (1824). Cooper is most famous and celebrated for his Leatherstocking Tales (1823–41), a series of historical novels that depict the life and times of Natty Bumppo, a soldier and hunter who makes his way on the edge of Anglo-American settlements during the colonial era and early national period. As a simple-spoken, illiterate, brave, self-reliant, and sharp-shooting white adventurer who rejects civilization, Natty Bumppo became the prototype for the mascu-line heroes of the American Western. Cooper earned fame and fortune around the world for his celebration of U.S. national identity and his representations of Native Americans, who appear in many of his novels. One of the first U.S. writers to succeed as a professional author, Cooper fashioned himself as an international man of letters, writing about politics, culture, history, and the law; he was in his day, as he is now, a polarizing figure in American culture.

Born in Burlington, New Jersey, Cooper spent his early life in Otsego, New York—later called "Cooperstown" in honor of his father, the village's first settler and founder. As a young man, Cooper studied briefly at Yale University and then spent time as a sailor on merchant ships and in the U.S. Navy. A sizable inheritance from his father, received in 1809, allowed him to retire from the Navy, and in 1811, he married Susan DeLancey, the daughter of a well-established New York family. Over the next eight years, Cooper experienced a series of family deaths and business failures; the ensuing financial troubles may have led him to seek his fortune with novel writing. In 1820, Cooper published his first novel, *Precaution*, an imitation of the English domestic novel. It was a moderate success, but nothing compared to his best-selling next novel, *The Spy*, a tale of a double agent operating between British and Continental armies during the American Revolution. Inspired by Scott—who fictionalized great historical events through the perspective of ordinary characters—Cooper turned to American history.

Cooper's third novel, *The Pioneers* (1823), inaugurated the Leatherstocking Tales and was the first to feature Natty Bumppo. Set in the 1790s in a New York village modeled loosely on Cooperstown, this novel reckoned with historical changes in the settlements from the perspective of Judge Temple, a figure for Cooper's father, and from the perspective of Bumppo and his Indigenous friend, Chingachgook, who resist the encroaching laws, culture, and institutions of the modern nation-state. Later Leatherstocking tales included *The Last of the Mohicans* (1826), *The Prairie* (1827), *The Pathfinder* (1840), and *The Deerslayer* (1841). These works were some of the first American novels to express concern about the destruction of the natural world at the hands of human beings.

For his depictions of Native Americans, Cooper drew on the writings of other Anglo-Americans, especially John Heckewelder, a Moravian missionary to the Lenape. At times Cooper's work commu-nicates a sympathy for Indigenous peoples, but overall his novels reinforce damaging stereotypes and inaccurate myths, including the notion that Native Americans were incapable of integrating into or coexisting with white society. Such ideas were challenged by a few of Cooper's Anglo-American contem-poraries, especially Lydia Maria Child and Catharine Maria Sedgwick, who offer alternative portraits of Indigenous peoples in their respective historical romances *Hobomok* (1824) and *Hope Leslie* (1827). On the whole, however, Cooper's work helped to popularize the belief that Native American cultures were inevitably in decline—a position that was used by nineteenth-century politicians to justify the forced migration and extermination of Indigenous populations.

Cooper's fourth novel, *The Pilot* (1824), is widely considered the first major work of nautical fiction. It has had many successors, including novels by Herman Melville and Joseph Conrad. Although Cooper was initially celebrated in the United States—New York chief justice James Kent called him "the genius which has rendered our native soil classic ground"—some American critics soon soured on his work. A staunch backer of Andrew Jackson and the Democratic party, Cooper was made the target of a smear campaign by reviewers affiliated with the anti-Jacksonian Whig party. To these reviewers, Cooper was motivated solely by greed; he was a class traitor for lending his support to Jackson's efforts to reign in the power of moneyed elites and increase popular sovereignty. "[A]ll that I see and hear gives me reason to believe that there is a great falling off in popular favor at home," Cooper wrote in an 1832 letter from Europe, where he and his family—his wife and their five children—had by that time been living for six years. "I rarely see my name mentioned even with respect in any American publication."

Cooper returned to America in 1833, and was soon living again at Cooperstown, but he had been sufficiently stung by the criticisms of his work that, in his 1834 *Letter to His Countrymen*, he declared his intention to renounce his career as a writer. The resolution proved hard to keep; he was soon publishing more works of non-fiction, including a history of the U.S. Navy, and by the end of the decade he had begun writing the last two of his Leatherstocking tales, *The Pathfinder* and *The Deerslayer*. In another series, the "Littlepage" novels—including *Satanstoe* (1845), *The Chainbearer* (1845), and *The Redskins* (1846)—Cooper defended landowners against tenants, now earning the ire of Democrats who accused him of the worst kind of aristocratic values. Despite such controversies, Cooper's novels continued to sell astonishingly well in the U.S., in Britain, and on the European Continent. After his death in 1851, he was lionized by fellow literary giants Washington Irving, Herman Melville, and Ralph Waldo Emerson. His major works were then republished in New York in a lavish edition illustrated by F.O.C. Darley in 1859–61, which solidified Cooper's stature in the canon of American literature.

Mark Twain famously ridiculed Cooper in his 1895 satire "Fenimore Cooper's Literary Offenses." But Twain, who also hated Walter Scott, in fact owed many debts to both novelists, and his opinion went against the grain of the common consensus. In the twentieth century, Marxist literary theorist Georg Lukács ranked Cooper along with historical novelists Balzac and Tolstoy, calling him the only "worthy successor" to Scott in the English language, while D.H. Lawrence, in *Studies in Classic American Literature* (1923), compared the Leatherstocking Tales to the *Odyssey* and praised Cooper's romantic depictions of nature: "No man could sufficiently praise the beauty and glamorous magnificence of Cooper's presentation of the aboriginal American landscape, the New World." Cooper's reputation declined significantly with the rise of Modernism. But it was his vision of the magnificence of nature, and his placement of the white settler and outcast seemingly alone at its center, that lasted far into the twentieth century and that marks Cooper's major contribution to the myth of American innocence.

NOTE ON THE TEXT: The text presented below is based on that of the first 1826 edition of *The Last of the Mohicans; a Narrative of 1757*. Spelling and punctuation have been modernized in accordance with the practices of this anthology.

⌘⌘⌘

from *The Last of the Mohicans;*
a Narrative of 1757

Set in the Province of New York during the 1754–63 conflict known by Anglo-Americans as the French and Indian War, *The Last of the Mohicans* (1826) was the second published installment of Cooper's Leatherstocking Tales (though chronologically its storyline precedes that of *The Pioneers* by several decades). Like the other Leatherstocking Tales, the novel is defined by the presence of character Nathaniel "Natty" Bumppo, who also bears the nicknames Hawk-eye, La Longue Carabine, and Leatherstocking. A white hunter and adventurer who was raised in a Lenape community, he now works as a British Army scout with his Mohican companions Chingachgook and his son Uncas. The novel takes place in the days leading up to and following the Siege of Fort William Henry (1757), part of the French and Indian War (1754–63), a territorial dispute in which French colonists and a diverse group of Indigenous allies fought British colonists and their Indigenous allies, including Mohican fighters.

The novel begins at Ford Edward, where half-sisters Alice and Cora Munro are preparing for a journey to meet their father, Colonel George Munro, at Fort William Henry. Along with their escort, Major Duncan Heyward, the party soon meet a Huron named Magua, who offers to guide them through the woods; they are also joined by an eccentric and out-of-place psalmodist named David Gamut. After they encounter Hawk-eye and his companions in the forest, it is revealed that Magua—who holds a personal grudge against Colonel Munro—has been intentionally leading the group astray. In the brawl that follows, Magua kidnaps the sisters, intending to force Cora to marry him. The rest of the novel follows the adventures of Hawk-eye, Uncas, and Heyward as they seek to rescue the captives from Magua and his fellow Huron, who are depicted as treacherous and villainous. Uncas, the eponymous "last of the Mohicans," emerges as a powerful leader of the favorably depicted Lenape, heroically motivated by his love for Cora. The portrayals of Uncas and Cora (who is eventually revealed to be of partially African ancestry) would become the prototypes for many depictions of Indigenous and mixed-race characters in later American literature.

VOLUME 2

from CHAPTER 12

[At this point in the narrative, Hawk-eye, Heyward, Alice, and Cora are in hiding from Magua and the Hurons at a Lenape camp; Magua arrives, and seeks to convince the Lenape to give up those he considers to be his lawful prisoners.]

"The Spirit that made men, colored them differently," commenced the subtle Huron.[1] "Some are blacker than the sluggish bear. These he said should be slaves; and he ordered them to work forever, like the beaver. You may hear them groan, when the south wind blows, louder than the lowing buffaloes, along the shores of the great salt water, where the big canoes come and go with them in droves. Some he made with faces paler than the ermine[2] of the forests, and these he ordered to be traders; dogs to their women, and wolves to their slaves. He gave this people the nature of the pigeon: wings that never tire; young, more plentiful than the leaves on the trees, and appetites to devour the earth. He gave them tongues like the false call of the wildcat; hearts like rabbits; the cunning of the hog (but none of the fox); and arms longer than the legs of the moose. With his tongue he stops the ears of the Indians; his heart teaches him to pay warriors to fight his battles; his cunning tells him how to get together the goods of the earth; and his arms enclose the land from the shores of the salt water, to the islands of the great lake. His gluttony makes him sick. God gave him enough, and yet he wants all. Such are the pale faces.

"Some the Great Spirit made with skins brighter and redder than yonder sun," continued Magua, pointing impressively upward to the lurid luminary, which was struggling through the misty atmosphere of the horizon; "and these did he fashion to his own mind. He gave them this island as he had made it, covered with trees, and filled with game. The wind made their clearings; the sun and rain ripened their fruits; and the snows came to tell them to be thankful. What need had they of roads to journey by! They saw through the

---

[1] *subtle Huron* Magua, who is also known by the French nickname "le Renard subtil," or "the cunning fox,"

[2] *ermine* Species of weasel known for its white winter coat.

hills! When the beavers worked, they lay in the shade, and looked on. The winds cooled them in summer; in winter, skins kept them warm. If they fought among themselves, it was to prove that they were men. They were brave; they were just; they were happy."

Here the speaker paused, and again looked around him, to discover if his legend had touched the sympathies of his listeners. He met everywhere with eyes riveted on his own, heads erect, and nostrils expanded, as if each individual present felt himself able and willing, singly, to redress the wrongs of his race.

"If the Great Spirit gave different tongues to his red children," he continued, in a low, still, melancholy voice, "it was that all animals might understand them. Some he placed among the snows, with their cousin, the bear. Some he placed near the setting sun, on the road to the happy hunting grounds. Some on the lands around the great fresh waters; but to his greatest, and most beloved, he gave the sands of the salt lake. Do my brothers know the name of this favored people?"

"It was the Lenape!" exclaimed twenty eager voices in a breath.

"It was the Lenni Lenape," returned Magua, affecting to bend his head in reverence to their former greatness. "It was the tribes of the Lenape! The sun rose from the water that was salt, and set in water that was sweet, and never hid himself from their eyes. But why should I, a Huron of the woods, tell a wise people their own traditions? Why remind them of their injuries; their ancient greatness; their deeds; their glory; their happiness—their losses; their defeats; their misery? Is there not one among them who has seen it all, and who knows it to be true? I have done. My tongue is still, but my ears are open."

[Though the elderly Lenape sage Tamenund considers Magua's arguments, in Chapter 13 he declares Uncas to be a rightful leader of the Lenape. Uncas is free to take back Hawk-eye, Heyward, and Alice, but Cora—with whom Uncas has now fallen in love—remains in Magua's grasp.]

from Chapter 15

"'Tis the maiden!"[1] shouted the scout. "Courage, lady; we come—we come."

The chase was renewed with a diligence rendered tenfold encouraging, by this glimpse of the captive. But the way was now rugged, broken, and, in spots, nearly impassable. Uncas abandoned his rifle, and leaped forward with headlong precipitation. Heyward rashly imitated his example, though both were, a moment afterwards, admonished of its madness, by hearing the bellowing of a piece,[2] that the Hurons found time to discharge down the passage in the rocks, the bullet from which even gave the young Mohican a slight wound.

"We must close!" said the scout, passing his friends by a desperate leap; "the knaves will pick us all off at this distance; and see, they hold the maiden so as to shield themselves!"

Though his words were unheeded, or rather unheard, his example was followed by his companions, who, by incredible exertions, got near enough to the fugitives to perceive that Cora was borne along between the two warriors, while Magua prescribed the direction and manner of their flight. At this moment, the forms of all four were strongly drawn against an opening in the sky, and then they disappeared. Nearly frantic with disappointment, Uncas and Heyward increased efforts that already seemed superhuman, and they issued from the cavern on the side of the mountain, in time to note the route of the pursued. The course lay up the ascent, and still continued hazardous and laborious.

Encumbered by his rifle, and, perhaps, not sustained by so deep an interest in the captive as his companions, the scout suffered the latter to precede him a little, Uncas, in his turn, taking the lead of Heyward. In this manner, rocks, precipices, and difficulties, were surmounted, in an incredibly short space, that at another time, and under other circumstances, would have been deemed almost insuperable. But the impetuous young men were rewarded, by finding, that, encumbered with Cora, the Hurons were rapidly losing ground in the race.

---

[1] *the maiden* Cora.

[2] *a piece* I.e., a rifle.

"Stay, dog of the Wyandots!" exclaimed Uncas, shaking his bright tomahawk at Magua; "a Delaware girl calls stay!"

"I will go no farther," cried Cora, stopping unexpectedly on a ledge of rocks, that overhung a deep precipice, at no great distance from the summit of the mountain. "Kill me if thou wilt, detestable Huron, I will go no farther!"

The supporters of the maiden raised their ready tomahawks with the impious joy that fiends are thought to take in mischief, but Magua suddenly stayed their uplifted arms. The Huron chief, after casting the weapons he had wrested from his companions over the rock, drew his knife, and turned to his captive, with a look in which conflicting passions fiercely contended.

"Woman," he said, "choose; the wigwam or the knife of le Subtil!"

Cora regarded him not; but dropping on her knees, with a rich glow suffusing itself over her features, she raised her eyes and stretched her arms towards Heaven, saying, in a meek and yet confiding voice—

"I am thine! do with me as thou seest best!"

"Woman," repeated Magua, hoarsely, and endeavouring in vain to catch a glance from her serene and beaming eye, "choose."

But Cora neither heard nor heeded his demand. The form of the Huron trembled in every fibre, and he raised his arm on high, but dropped it again, with a wild and bewildered air, like one who doubted. Once more he struggled with himself, and lifted the keen weapon again—but just then a piercing cry was heard above them, and Uncas appeared, leaping frantically, from a fearful height, upon the ledge. Magua recoiled a step, and one of his assistants, profiting by the chance, sheathed his own knife in the bosom of the maiden.

The Huron sprang like a tiger on his offending and already retreating countryman, but the falling form of Uncas separated the unnatural combatants. Diverted from his object by this interruption, and maddened by the murder he had just witnessed, Magua buried his weapon in the back of the prostrate Delaware, uttering an unearthly shout, as he committed the dastardly deed. But Uncas arose from the blow, as the wounded panther turns upon his foe, and struck the murderer of Cora to his feet, by an effort, in which the last of his failing strength was expended. Then, with a stern and

steady look, he turned to le Subtil, and indicated, by the expression of his eye, all that he would do, had not the power deserted him. The latter seized the nerveless arm of the unresisting Delaware, and passed his knife into his bosom three several times, before his victim, still keeping his gaze riveted on his enemy with a look of inextinguishable scorn, fell dead at his feet.

"Mercy! mercy! Huron," cried Heyward, from above, in tones nearly choked by horror; "give mercy, and thou shalt receive it!"

Whirling the bloody knife up at the imploring youth, the victorious Magua uttered a cry, so fierce, so wild, and yet so joyous, that it conveyed the sounds of savage triumph to the ears of those who fought in the valley, a thousand feet below. He was answered by an appalling burst from the lips of the scout, whose tall person was just then seen moving swiftly towards him, along those dangerous crags, with steps as bold and reckless, as if he possessed the power to move in middle air. But when the hunter reached the scene of the ruthless massacre, the ledge was tenanted only by the dead.

His keen eye took a single look at the victims, and then shot its glances over the difficulties of the ascent in his front. A form stood at the brow of the mountain, on the very edge of the giddy height, with uplifted arms, in an awful attitude of menace. Without stopping to consider his person, the rifle of Hawk-eye was raised, but a rock, which fell on the head of one of the fugitives below, exposed the indignant and glowing countenance of the honest Gamut. Then Magua issued from a crevice, and, stepping with calm indifference over the body of the last of his associates, he leaped a wide fissure, and ascended the rocks at a point where the arm of David could not reach him. A single bound would carry him to the brow of the precipice, and assure his safety. Before taking the leap, however, the Huron paused, and shaking his hand at the scout, he shouted—

"The pale-faces are dogs! the Delawares women! Magua leaves them on the rocks, for the crows!"

Laughing hoarsely, he made a desperate leap, and fell short of his mark; though his hands grasped a shrub on the verge of the height. The form of Hawk-eye had crouched like a beast about to take its spring, and his frame trembled so violently with eagerness, that the muzzle of the half raised rifle played like a leaf fluttering in the wind. Without exhausting himself with fruitless efforts, the cunning Magua suffered[1] his body to drop to the length of his arms, and found a fragment for his feet to rest upon. Then, summoning all his powers, he renewed the attempt, and so far succeeded, as to draw his knees on the edge of the mountain. It was now, when the body of his enemy was most collected together, that the agitated weapon of the scout was drawn to his shoulder. The surrounding rocks, themselves, were not steadier than the piece became for the single instant that it poured out its contents.

The arms of the Huron relaxed, and his body fell back a little, while his knees still kept their position. Turning a relentless look on his enemy, he shook a hand in grim defiance. But his hold loosened, and his dark person was seen cutting the air with its head downward, for a fleeting instant, until it glided past the fringe of shrubbery which clung to the mountain, in its rapid flight to destruction.

—1826

[NOTE: The final chapter of *The Last of the Mohicans* is included in the online component of this anthology.]

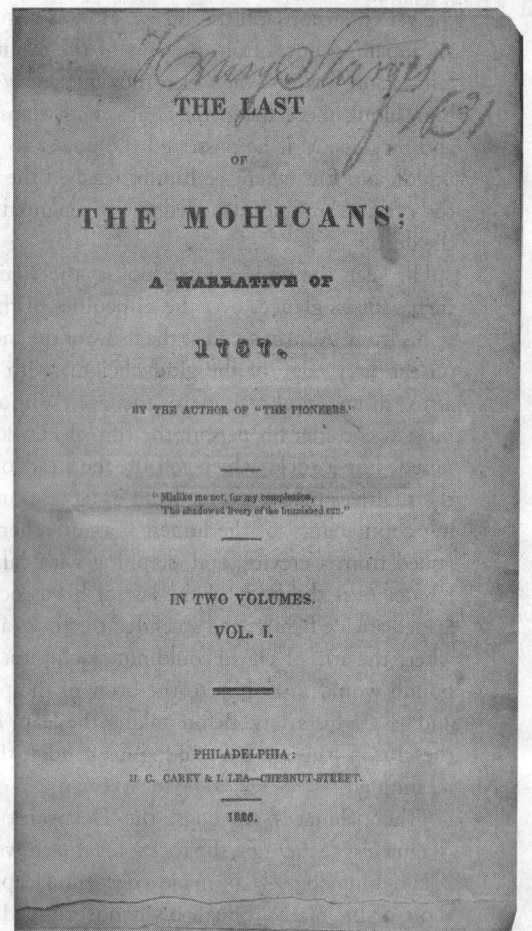

Title page of volume 1 of the 1826 first edition of *The Last of the Mohicans*. The quotation—"Mislike me not, for my complexion, / The shadowed livery of the burnished sun"—is from a speech in Shakespeare's *The Merchant of Venice* by the dark-skinned Prince of Morocco, who is attempting to woo the light-skinned Portia.

---

1   *suffered* Allowed.

LYDIA HUNTLEY SIGOURNEY
1791 – 1865

One of the first American literary superstars, Lydia Sigourney had a tremendous impact on nineteenth-century popular culture. An adept professional, she established herself as an icon of middle-class American womanhood and repurposed European Romantic forms for an American audience. Her prolific body of work includes fifteen volumes of poetry, as well as works of history, children's books, conduct manuals, a novel, and over two thousand articles in nearly three hundred different periodicals. Deftly exploiting the popular appeal of the sentimental mode, she wrote on a wide range of politically and socially important subjects, including the environment, the role of women, and government policies that she felt threatened the integrity of the union, such as slavery and the genocide of Indigenous peoples.

Sigourney was born in Norwich, Connecticut, the only child of Ezekiel and Zerviah Huntley. The Huntleys lived in the mansion of the wealthy Lathrop family, for whom Ezekiel Huntley was a gardener. Mrs. Lathrop took a keen interest in the development of Lydia's intelligence, and Lydia received one of the best educations available to girls at this time. She studied both at home and at various local schools, where she learned the usual domestic skills taught to girls, as well as mathematics, grammar, literature, and classical languages. At the age of twenty, she opened her own school.

Sigourney thrived as a teacher, and, in 1814 moved to Hartford, where she ran a school for the daughters of wealthy families. The following year, she published her first book: *Moral Pieces, in Prose and Verse*, a collection of poems, advice, and homilies addressed to young women. This volume's emphasis on nature, subjectivity, originality, and deep feeling reflects Sigourney's extensive reading in British sentimental and Romantic literature, particularly the works of evangelical poets such as Hannah More and William Cowper. In *Moral Pieces*, however, as in many of her later works, Sigourney adapts Romantic aesthetics and poetic forms to American cultural, political, and religious life, particularly the lives of American women and children, and to the American landscape.

In 1819 Sigourney accepted the proposal of Charles Sigourney, an upper-class businessperson. Social mores required her to abandon teaching for a married upper-class woman's domestic duties. Charles also disapproved of her literary ambitions and persuaded her to publish anonymously; this would remain a source of conflict for much of their marriage. In the first three years of their marriage, the couple conceived three children, all of whom died at birth or shortly afterwards. In 1824, she published—anonymously—the long poem *Traits of the Aborigines of America*. In this and her other poems about Indigenous peoples, Sigourney takes part in her culture's propensity to romanticize and elegize Indigenous people, thereby participating in their erasure, but she also turns a fierce critical eye on the cruelty and greed of white settlers, acting, as she did on many subjects, as a kind of national conscience for the American middle and upper classes.

In 1827, Sigourney published *Poems*, by "the Author of 'Moral Pieces in Prose and Verse,'" without informing her husband. His response was furious: "Who wants or would value, a wife who is to be the public property of the whole community?" Sigourney tried and failed to convince Charles to agree to a formal separation, and in the end she agreed to his demands that she slow down her literary activity and bear children; by 1830, she had borne a daughter and a son. In her writing during this period, she came increasingly to represent herself as an exemplar of feminine virtue, shifting her focus to women's domestic duties in works such as *Letters to Young Ladies* (1833). To build on the popular success of *Letters to Young Ladies*, she began to publish under her own name, achieving widespread international fame with *Poems* (1834).

Sigourney's philanthropic activity also gained momentum in these years. In 1828 she helped found the Hartford campaign to aid in the Greek War of Independence; in 1829 she formed the Hartford Female African Society and the Hartford County Temperance Society, as well as a protest movement, the "Ladies' Circular" to petition against the Indian Removal Act (which was passed in 1830). While Sigourney opposed slavery and viewed it as a stain on the republic, she argued that enslaved people should be freed and then helped to emigrate to Africa, rather than being accorded citizenship in America.

In 1836 her husband's business interests began to suffer, and Sigourney's income as a writer took on more importance to the family's finances. She produced a great deal of material, much of which appeared in magazines and was then repurposed for inclusion in books. She also continued to write for the lucrative "advice" or "conduct" book market, publishing volumes such as *Letters to Mothers* (1838), a discussion of women's place in the republic. In works such as these, Sigourney located women's influence in the home and in philanthropic endeavors; she did not advocate for suffrage or for other political power for women. Meanwhile, rumors circulated that Charles denied food and writing paper to Sigourney, that he had threatened her with a sword, and that his daughters (from his previous marriage) attempted to poison her and her baby. In 1840 Sigourney signed a note Charles had written stating that these rumors were untrue. She then departed to Europe for a long reading tour that expanded her transatlantic audience.

After returning home, Sigourney published a travel memoir, *Pleasant Memories of Pleasant Lands* (1842). She also began to write collections of verse that her readers could copy out in their own scrapbooks or letters: poems in *The Voice of Flowers* (1846), for example, could be inscribed in valentines, while *The Weeping Willow* (1847) contained elegies for use in funeral readings or sympathy cards. She also collected her poems on certain social topics; *Water-Drops* (1843) contains her verses on temperance, and *Poetry for Seamen* (1845) collects poems aimed at reforming the morality of sailors. Her middle- and upper-class readership thereby connected to her poems in an intimate way, sharing them among themselves on the defining occasions of their lives, and looking to Sigourney for moral leadership.

Sigourney's later publications include *The Faded Hope* (1850), a memoir of her son who had died of tuberculosis, as well as several collections of her writing for periodicals and an advice book about aging, *Past Meridian* (1854). She died in Hartford in 1865, and her autobiography *Letters of Life* (1866) was published posthumously. Her fame, while greatest in America, was transatlantic, and by the time she died, countless societies and organizations had been named after her, as had a town in Iowa.

During Sigourney's lifetime, most critics praised her for the devout morality underlying her poetry, and for her feminine, sentimental style: as one critic phrased it, "Her womanly delicacy gilds every page traced by her pen, and sheds a beautiful halo around her genius. … [H]er name has become a household word in all lands where Christian virtues are cherished." As tastes changed toward the end of the nineteenth century, however, her reputation declined rapidly. With the rise of literary modernism, the critical establishment largely dismissed Sigourney, viewing her achievement as saccharine, feminine, and didactic. It was not until the 1970s that interest in Sigourney's work was revived, as attention turned to the important role that nineteenth-century sentimentalism played in spurring social reform, and to the role that Sigourney in particular played in shaping American cultural identity. Interest in Sigourney's work has since flourished, uncovering her importance as a professional writer, political activist, and advocate for domestic and sentimental values.

NOTE ON THE TEXTS: The texts of all poems included here are based upon their earliest printings in book form. The texts of "Death of an Infant" and "The Suttee" are based on those published in *Poems, by the Author of Moral Pieces in Prose and Verse* (1827); the texts of "Indian Names" and "Slavery" are based on those published in *Poems* (1834); the text of "The Indian's Welcome to the Pilgrim Fathers" is based on the version printed in *Zinzendorff and Other Poems* (1835); the text of "To a Shred of Linen" is based on those published in *Select Poems* (1838). Spelling and punctuation have been modernized in accordance with the practices of this anthology.

⌘ ⌘ ⌘

Death of an Infant

Death found strange beauty on that cherub brow,
  And dashed it out. There was a tint of rose
On cheek and lip; he touched the veins with ice,
And the rose faded. Forth from those blue eyes
5 There spake a wishful tenderness, a doubt
Whether to grieve or sleep, which innocence
Alone can wear. With ruthless haste he bound
The silken fringes of those curtaining lids
Forever. There had been a murmuring sound,
10 With which the babe would claim its mother's ear,
Charming her even to tears. The spoiler set
His seal of silence. But there beamed a smile
So fixed and holy from that marble brow,
Death gazed and left it there; he dared not steal
15 The signet-ring[1] of Heaven.
    —1827

The Suttee[2]

She sat upon the pile° by her dead lord,   *pyre*
  And in her full, dark eye, and shining hair
Youth revelled. The glad murmur of the crowd
Applauding her consent to the dread doom,
5 And the hoarse chanting of infuriate priests
She heeded not, for her quick ear had caught
An infant's wail. Feeble and low that moan,
Yet it was answered in her heaving heart,
For the mimosa[3] in its shrinking fold
10 From the rude pressure, is not half so true,
So tremulous, as is a mother's soul
Unto her wailing babe. There was such woe
In her imploring aspect, in her tones
Such thrilling agony, that even the hearts
15 Of the flame-kindlers softened, and they laid
The famished infant on her yearning breast.

There with his tear-wet cheek he lay and drew
Plentiful nourishment from that full fount
Of infant happiness—and long he prest
20 With eager lip the chalice of his joy.
And then his little hands he stretched to grasp
His mother's flower-wove tresses, and with smile
And gay caress embraced his bloated sire,
As if kind Nature taught that innocent one
25 With fond delay to cheat the hour which sealed
His hopeless orphanage. But those were near
Who mocked such dalliance, as that Spirit malign
Who twined his serpent length mid Eden's bowers
Frowned on our parents' bliss.[4] The victim marked
30 Their harsh intent, and clasped the
    unconscious° babe   *unknowing*
With such convulsive force, that when they tore
His writhing form away, the very nerves
Whose deep-sown fibers rack the inmost soul
Uprooted seemed.
35   With voice of high command
Tossing her arms, she bade them bring her son,
And then in maniac rashness sought to leap
Among the astonished throng. But the rough cord
Compressed her slender limbs, and bound her fast
40 Down to her loathsome partner. Quick the fire
In showers was hurled upon the reeking pile;
But yet amid the wild, demoniac shout
Of priest and people, mid the thundering yell
Of the infernal gong, was heard to rise
45 Thrice a dire death-shriek. And the men who stood
Near the red pile and heard that fearful cry,
Called on their idol-gods, and stopped their ears,
And oft amid their nightly dream would start
As frighted Fancy echoed in her cell
50 That burning mother's scream.
    —1827

---

1   *signet-ring*   Engraved ring, usually with initials or another personal mark that could be pressed into a wax seal as confirmation of the bearer's identity.

2   *Suttee*   Hindu widow who, following a custom legally abolished in 1829, immolates herself on her husband's funeral pyre.

3   *mimosa*   Also known as the "sensitive plant," the mimosa has leaves that fold into themselves when touched.

---

4   *Spirit malign … parents' bliss*   Reference to Satan's temptation of Adam and Eve, the first humans, to commit the first sin in the garden of Eden (see Genesis 3).

Indian Names[1]

"How can the red men be forgotten, while so many of our
states and territories, bays, lakes and rivers, are indelibly
stamped by names of their giving?"

Ye say they all have passed away,
   That noble race and brave,
That their light canoes have vanished
   From off the crested wave;
5 That, 'mid the forests where they roamed,
   There rings no hunter shout,
But their name is on your waters,
   Ye may not wash it out.

'Tis where Ontario's billow°   *wave*
10 Like Ocean's surge is curled,
Where strong Niagara's thunders wake
   The echo of the world.
Where red Missouri bringeth
   Rich tribute from the west,
15 And Rappahannock[2] sweetly sleeps
   On green Virginia's[3] breast.

Ye say their cone-like cabins,[4]
   That clustered o'er the vale,
Have fled away like withered leaves
20   Before the autumn gale,
But their memory liveth on your hills,
   Their baptism on your shore,
Your everlasting rivers speak
   Their dialect of yore.

25 Old Massachusetts wears it,
   Within her lordly crown,
And broad Ohio bears it,
   Amid his young renown;
Connecticut hath wreathed it

30   Where her quiet foliage waves,
And bold Kentucky breathes it hoarse
   Through all her ancient caves.

Wachuset[5] hides its lingering voice
   Within his rocky heart,
35 And Alleghany[6] graves° its tone   *engraves*
   Throughout his lofty chart;[7]
Monadnock,[8] on his forehead hoar°   *gray*
   Doth seal the sacred trust,
Your mountains build their monument,
40   Though ye destroy their dust.

Ye call these red-brown brethren
   The insects of an hour,
Crushed like the noteless° worm amid   *unnoticed*
   The regions of their power;
45 Ye drive them from their father's lands,
   Ye break of faith the seal,
But can ye from the court of Heaven
   Exclude their last appeal?

Ye see their unresisting tribes
50   With toilsome step and slow,
On through the trackless desert pass,
   A caravan of woe;[9]
Think ye the Eternal's ear is deaf?
   His sleepless vision dim?
55 Think ye the *soul's blood* may not cry
   From that far land to him?
—1834

---

[5] *Wachuset* Mountain in Massachusetts.

[6] *Alleghany* Mountain range in the eastern United States and
Canada.

[7] *chart* Outline, especially as recorded on a map.

[8] *Monadnock* Mountain in New Hampshire.

[9] *unresisting tribes … caravan of woe* The 1830 Indian Removal
Act, signed into law by President Andrew Jackson, forced southeastern Indigenous tribes—the Chickasaw, Cherokee, Muscogee
(Creek), Seminole, and Choctaw—to leave their ancestral lands and
move west of the Mississippi river. This forced removal of 60,000
people, known as the Trail of Tears, has been described as cultural
genocide, and thousands of people died of disease and starvation
during the journey or shortly afterward. Sigourney's description of
the removals as "unresisting," however, is not true; the Cherokee,
in particular, put forward strong resistance, but were ultimately
unsuccessful.

---

[1] This poem was republished in *Selections from the American Poets*
(1840), with the last two stanzas omitted.

[2] *Rappahannock* River in eastern Virginia.

[3] *Virginia* Unlike the other place names mentioned in this
poem, Virginia does not derive from Indigenous languages, but is
derived from the Latin "virgo," which means "virgin" or "maiden."

[4] *cone-like cabins* I.e., tepees, traditional dwellings of many
Indigenous tribes from the Great Plains.

Slavery

"Slavery is a dark shade on the map of
the United States."
—La Fayette[1]

WRITTEN FOR THE CELEBRATION OF THE
FOURTH OF JULY

We have a goodly clime,
    Broad vales and streams we boast,
Our mountain frontiers frown sublime,
    Old Ocean guards our coast;
5 Suns bless our harvest fair,
    With fervid° smile serene,   *glowing*
But a dark shade is gathering there—
    What can its blackness mean?

We have a birthright proud,
10   For our young sons to claim,
An eagle soaring o'er the cloud,
    In freedom and in fame;
We have a scutcheon[2] bright,
    By our dead fathers bought,
15 A fearful blot distains° its white—   *stains*
    Who hath such evil wrought?

Our banner o'er the sea
    Looks forth with starry eye,
Emblazoned, glorious, bold and free,
20   A letter on the sky,
What hand with shameful stain
    Hath marred its heavenly blue?
The yoke, the fasces,[3] and the chain,
    Say, are these emblems true?

25 This day[4] doth music rare
    Swell through our nation's bound,
But Afric's wailing mingles there,
    And Heaven doth hear the sound:
O God of power! we turn
30   In penitence to thee,
Bid our loved land the lesson learn—
    To bid the slave *be free.*
      —1834

The Indian's Welcome to the Pilgrim Fathers

"On Friday, March 16th, 1622, while the colonists were
busied in their usual labors, they were much surprised to see
a savage walk boldly towards them, and salute them with,
'much welcome, English, much welcome, Englishmen.'"[5]

Above them spread a stranger sky;
    Around, the sterile plain;
The rock-bound coast rose frowning nigh,
    Beyond—the wrathful main:°   *sea*
5 Chill remnants of the wintry snow
    Still choked the encumbered soil,
Yet forth those Pilgrim Fathers go
    To mark their future toil.

'Mid yonder vale their corn must rise
10   In summer's ripening pride,
And there the church-spire woo the skies
    Its sister-school beside.
Perchance 'mid England's velvet green
    Some tender thought reposed,
15 Though nought upon their stoic mien°   *bearing*
    Such soft regret disclosed.

When sudden from the forest wide
    A red-browed chieftain came,

---

[1] *La Fayette* The Marquis de Lafayette (1757–1834) fought in
the American Revolution commanding American troops; he also
supported the French Revolution and was a prominent abolitionist
throughout his life. The quoted statement was widely attributed to
him.

[2] *scutcheon* Coat of arms represented on a shield.

[3] *fasces* Group of rods, often birch rods, with an axe in the
middle. The symbol is prominent in American iconography, including, for example, the seal of the Senate and the frieze of the Supreme
Court. It represents the power of unity and order of law, but has also
long been associated with corporal punishment.

[4] *This day* I.e., the fourth of July.

[5] *On Friday … Englishmen* Several accounts by Plymouth settlers record the encounter described here; the visitor described was
Samoset (c. 1590–1653), sagamore of the Pemaquid Abenaki people
who lived in what is now Maine. His coming to Plymouth, and the
diplomacy that he helped foster between the Pilgrims and Massasoit
(c. 1581–1661), sachem of the Wampanoag, ensured peaceful relations
between the settlers and the Wampanoag during Massasoit's lifetime.

With towering form, and haughty stride,
20   And eye like kindling flame:
No wrath he breathed, no conflict sought,
    To no dark ambush drew,
But simply *to the Old World brought*
    The welcome of the New.

25 That *welcome* was a blast° and ban°   *blight | curse*
    Upon thy race unborn;
Was there no seer, thou fated° man!   *doomed*
    Thy lavish zeal to warn?
Thou in thy fearless faith didst hail
30   A weak, invading band,
But who shall heed thy children's wail
    Swept from their native land?

Thou gav'st the riches of thy streams,
    The lordship o'er thy waves,
35 The region of thine infant dreams
    And of thy fathers' graves,
But who to yon proud mansions, piled
    With wealth of earth and sea,
Poor outcast from thy forest wild,
40   *Say, who shall welcome thee?*
—1835

To a Shred of Linen

Would they swept cleaner!
    Here's a littering shred
Of linen left behind—a vile reproach
To all good housewifery. Right glad am I,
That no neat lady, trained in ancient times
5 Of pudding-making, and of sampler-work,[1]
And speckless sanctity of household care,
Hath happened here, to spy thee. She, no doubt,
Keen looking through her spectacles, would say,
" *This comes of reading books*": or some spruce[2] beau
10 Essenced and lily-handed, had he chanced
To scan thy slight superfices,°   *outward appearance*
    'twould be

"*This comes of writing poetry.*" Well—well—
Come forth—offender!—hast thou aught to say?
Canst thou by merry thought, or quaint conceit,[3]
15 Repay this risk, that I have run for thee?
—Begin at alpha,[4] and resolve thyself
Into thine elements. I see the stalk
And bright, blue flower of flax,[5] which
    erst° o'erspread   *formerly*
That fertile land, where mighty Moses stretched
20 His rod miraculous.[6] I see thy bloom
Tinging, too scantly, these New England vales.
But, lo! the sturdy farmer lifts his flail,[7]
To crush thy bones unpitying, and his wife
With 'kerchiefed head, and eyes brimful of dust,
25 Thy fibrous nerves, with hatchel-tooth[8] divides.
—I hear a voice of music—and behold!
The ruddy damsel singeth at her wheel,[9]
While by her side the rustic lover sits.
Perchance, his shrewd eye secretly doth count
30 The mass of skeins, which, hanging on the wall,
Increaseth day by day. Perchance his thought
(*For men have deeper minds than women—sure!*)
Is calculating what a thrifty wife
The maid will make; and how his dairy shelves
35 Shall groan beneath the weight of golden cheese,
Made by her dexterous hand, while many a keg
And pot of butter, to the market borne,
May, transmigrated, on his back appear,
In new thanksgiving coats.
                    Fain would I ask,
40 Mine own New England, for thy once loved wheel,

---

1   *sampler-work*   Type of needlework done to display one's expertise in embroidery.

2   *spruce*   Tidy and good-looking.

3   *quaint conceit*   Ingenious metaphor.

4   *alpha*   The first letter of the Greek alphabet; i.e., the beginning.

5   *flax*   Linen is woven from flax fibers.

6   *fertile land … rod miraculous*   See Exodus 9.23: "And Moses stretched forth his rod toward heaven: and the Lord sent thunder and hail, and the fire ran along upon the ground; and the Lord rained hail upon the land of Egypt." Exodus 9.31 describes the hail damage: "And the flax and the barley was smitten: for the barley was in the ear, and the flax was bolled [ripe]."

7   *flail*   Instrument used for threshing.

8   *hatchel-tooth*   Instrument with sharp teeth used to comb out flax.

9   *wheel*   Spinning-wheel, used to create thread out of the combed flax.

By sofa and piano quite displaced.
Why dost thou banish from thy parlor-hearth
That old Hygeian harp,[1] whose magic ruled
Dyspepsia,° as the minstrel-shepherd's skill   *indigestion*
45 Exorcised Saul's ennui?[2] There was no need,
In those good times, of trim callisthenics,
And there was less of gadding,° and far more   *gallivanting*
Of home-born, heart-felt comfort, rooted strong
In industry, and bearing such rare fruit,
50 As wealth might never purchase.
                                        But come back,
Thou shred of linen. I did let thee drop,
In my harangue, as wiser ones have lost
The thread of their discourse. What was thy lot
When the rough battery of the loom had stretched
55 And knit thy sinews, and the chemist sun
Thy brown complexion bleached?
                                        Methinks I scan
Some idiosyncrasy, that marks thee out
A defunct pillow-case. Did the trim guest,

To the best chamber ushered, e'er admire
60 The snowy whiteness of thy freshened youth
Feeding thy vanity? or some sweet babe
Pour its pure dream of innocence on thee?
Say, hast thou listened to the sick one's moan,
When there was none to comfort? or shrunk back
65 From the dire tossings of the proud man's brow?
Or gathered from young beauty's restless sigh
A tale of untold love?
                                        Still, close and mute!
Wilt tell no secrets, ha? Well then, go down,
With all thy churl-kept[3] hoard of curious lore,
70 In majesty and mystery, go down
Into the paper-mill,[4] and from its jaws,
Stainless and smooth, emerge. Happy shall be
The renovation, if on thy fair page
Wisdom and truth, their hallowed lineaments
75 Trace for posterity. So shall thine end
Be better than thy birth, and worthier bard
Thine apotheosis[5] immortalize.
                                        —1838

---

[1] *Hygeian harp* I.e., spinning-wheel. In Greek mythology, Hygeia is a goddess of health and cleanliness; the implication is that the activity of spinning could prevent illnesses associated with luxury or idleness.

[2] *minstrel-shepherd's ... Saul's ennui* See 1 Samuel 16.23: "And it came to pass, when the evil spirit from God was upon Saul, that David took an harp, and played with his hand: so Saul was refreshed, and was well, and the evil spirit departed from him."

---

[3] *churl-kept* Stingily kept. "Churl" could also refer to a rural or unrefined person.

[4] *paper-mill* Scraps of cloth would be shredded and reused to make paper.

[5] *apotheosis* Transformation into a god; deification.

William Cullen Bryant

1794 – 1878

Throughout much of the nineteenth century, William Cullen Bryant was among the most well-respected and widely celebrated poets in the United States. Sometimes referred to as an American Romantic or as "the American Wordsworth," Bryant earned a reputation both as a skilled imitator of British literary traditions and as a poet who adapted and fundamentally reworked those traditions for an American context.

Bryant was born in the Berkshires region of Massachusetts in 1794 to Sarah Snell Bryant and Peter Bryant, a country physician and literary enthusiast. Bryant began writing poetry in childhood, mainly in imitation of classical poets and of eighteenth-century British poets such as Alexander Pope; some of these early efforts were printed in *The Hampshire Gazette* in 1807. The following year, Bryant's long poem *The Embargo; or, Sketches of the Times* was published as a pamphlet. A vicious satire of the recent economic policies of President Thomas Jefferson, the poem was strongly influenced by the political views of the poet's father. Nevertheless, readers were both amused and impressed by the precocious talents of the thirteen-year-old author, and *The Embargo* caused a minor sensation in New England, where frustration with the Jefferson administration was widespread.

It became apparent that the family finances would not support a literary career, and Bryant entered the legal profession in 1815 at the instigation of his father, but he continued to be drawn toward poetry. At some point between 1810 and 1815, Bryant wrote the early versions of two poems that would before long establish his literary career: "Thanatopsis" (published 1817) and "To a Waterfowl" (published 1818). Radically different from his juvenile output, these poems suggested the stylistic and thematic influence of more recent English writers such as William Wordsworth, William Cowper, and Robert Southey, whose work was often characterized by a focus on the speaker's communion with nature. Published in the newly established but respectable literary journal the *North American Review*, both poems were lauded by critics. "Thanatopsis" in particular was seen as a milestone in American writing; *North American Review* editor Richard Henry Dana is said to have dismissed the poem at first as a British production, having claimed that "no one on this side of the Atlantic is capable of writing such verses."

The success of these and other poems led to the publication in 1821 of a collection titled simply *Poems*. Sales were slow, but the collection was widely praised within literary circles. Bryant had by then also begun to make a name for himself as a critic in the *North American Review*, where he advised writers on how best to contribute to the national literary culture. He emphasized that a good poet should not blindly imitate English verse: "Let me counsel you to draw your images," he wrote in an 1838 letter, "in describing Nature, from what you observe around you[.] … The skylark is an English bird, and an American who has never visited Europe has no right to be in raptures about it."

Bryant married Frances Fairchild in 1821, and their daughter Fanny was born soon thereafter. In 1824, increasingly frustrated by the legal system, he ceased working as a lawyer and set his sights on the growing metropolis of New York City in the hopes of furthering his career in criticism and journalism. He moved there in 1825 (joined by Frances and Fanny a few months later), and soon shared a circle with several of the city's present and future literary celebrities, including James Fenimore Cooper, Washington Irving, and Catharine Sedgwick. In 1826, he was hired as the assistant editor of the prestigious daily paper the *New York Evening Post*; by 1829 he was editor-in-chief, a position he would retain for almost five decades.

During his tenure at the *Post*, Bryant released numerous collections of poetry, including several more successful editions of *Poems*. Journalism, however, became a major intellectual outlet for him, and the *Post*—which, like many other newspapers during the period, was often unabashedly partisan—offered a platform for his political views. In the 1830s Bryant was a vocal supporter of Andrew Jackson and the newly established Democratic Party; later in the century he supported the Free Soil Party, and as the question of slavery became more nationally divisive mid-century he switched his allegiance to the antislavery Republican Party. Bryant often wrote in support of causes such as free trade, increased rights for immigrants, and the right to organized labor. He was also, however, a staunch supporter of the Indian Removal Act intended to expel several Indigenous nations from their homelands. In a number of editorials, Bryant extoled the proposed Act as both humane and nationally beneficial; in 1830 he claimed that it would entail "no shedding of blood, no 'driving them from the graves of their fathers'; no abridgement of their means of happiness." (This statement was, of course, false, and thousands of Indigenous people would die during the forced relocation or shortly afterward.) Poems such as "An Indian at the Burial-Place of His Fathers" (1824) and "The Prairies" (1833) hint at Bryant's enthusiasm for American expansion and at his troubling views of Native Americans, of whom he wrote that "a great deal might be done" as literary symbols.

By mid-century Bryant was widely recognized as a literary and cultural authority. In 1860, he introduced Abraham Lincoln to the crowds in New York before Lincoln's famous Cooper Union Speech, and in April 1865 his elegy to the assassinated President, "The Death of Lincoln," was read aloud at the funeral ceremony in Union Square, Manhattan. In his final decade, Bryant turned to translation; his renditions of Homer's *Iliad* (1870) and *Odyssey* (1871–72) were well-received. Bryant suffered a fall in 1878 while speaking at the unveiling of a monument in Central Park; he died shortly thereafter.

Throughout his career, acclaim for Bryant's poetry came from many quarters, including from a young Walt Whitman, who wrote in 1846 that Bryant stood "among the first [poets] in the world," as well as from Edgar Allan Poe (who clarified, however, that it would "never do to claim for Bryant a genius of the loftiest order"). But by the 1870s, Bryant's literary stature was so firmly established that he had come to be seen by some newer writers as old-fashioned and uninventive; praise often came in the style of that published in *The Aldine* in June 1871:

> Rejecting with disdain the innovations in orthography of his contemporaries … Mr. Bryant has kept the faith with the grand old mother-tongue, which, unfortunately, between the lexicographers and the laureates of "dialect," is rapidly losing in character on this side of the Atlantic.

By the early twentieth century, Bryant's association with the so-called "Schoolroom Poets"—a small group of frequently anthologized American poets whose works were commonly memorized and recited in classrooms—made him seem distinctly outdated and irrelevant. The 1917 *Cambridge History of American Literature* relegated him to a chapter titled "Bryant and the Minor Poets," and, in an otherwise modestly appreciative assessment, called his ideas the "common property of simple minds." Nevertheless, Bryant's poetry remains central to the discussion of what it means for poetry to be distinctly "American"; twenty-first-century scholars increasingly engage with his work for its interpretations of Romanticism and for its influence on how American landscapes are perceived and valued.

NOTE ON THE TEXTS: The texts of the poems reprinted below are based on those appearing in the last authorized edition of Bryant's *Poems*, published in 1871. Spelling and punctuation have been modernized in accordance with the practices of this anthology.

⌘⌘⌘

Thanatopsis[1]

To him who in the love of Nature holds
Communion with her visible forms, she speaks
A various° language; for his gayer hours   *changeable*
She has a voice of gladness, and a smile
5   And eloquence of beauty, and she glides
Into his darker musings, with a mild
And healing sympathy, that steals away
Their sharpness, ere he is aware. When thoughts
Of the last bitter hour come like a blight
10   Over thy spirit, and sad images
Of the stern agony, and shroud, and pall,[2]
And breathless darkness, and the narrow house,
Make thee to shudder, and grow sick at heart—
Go forth, under the open sky, and list°   *listen*
15   To Nature's teachings, while from all around—
Earth and her waters, and the depths of air—
Comes a still voice—Yet a few days, and thee
The all-beholding sun shall see no more
In all his course; nor yet in the cold ground,
20   Where thy pale form was laid, with many tears,
Nor in the embrace of ocean, shall exist
Thy image. Earth, that nourished thee, shall claim
Thy growth, to be resolved to earth again,
And, lost each human trace, surrendering up
25   Thine individual being, shalt thou go
To mix forever with the elements,
To be a brother to the insensible rock
And to the sluggish clod, which the rude swain[3]
Turns with his share,[4] and treads upon. The oak
30   Shall send his roots abroad, and pierce thy mould.[5]

Yet not to thine eternal resting-place
Shalt thou retire alone—nor couldst thou wish
Couch more magnificent. Thou shalt lie down
With patriarchs of the infant world—with kings,

35   The powerful of the earth—the wise, the good,
Fair forms, and hoary[6] seers of ages past,
All in one mighty sepulchre. The hills
Rock-ribbed and ancient as the sun—the vales
Stretching in pensive quietness between;
40   The venerable woods—rivers that move
In majesty, and the complaining brooks
That make the meadows green; and, poured round all,
Old ocean's gray and melancholy waste—
Are but the solemn decorations all
45   Of the great tomb of man. The golden sun,
The planets, all the infinite host of heaven,
Are shining on the sad abodes of death,
Through the still lapse of ages. All that tread
The globe are but a handful to the tribes
50   That slumber in its bosom. Take the wings
Of morning pierce the Barcan[7] wilderness,
Or lose thyself in the continuous woods
Where rolls the Oregon,[8] and hears no sound,
Save his own dashings—yet the dead are there:
55   And millions in those solitudes, since first
The flight of years began, have laid them down
In their last sleep—the dead reign there alone.
So shalt thou rest and what if thou withdraw
In silence from the living, and no friend
60   Take note of thy departure? All that breathe
Will share thy destiny. The gay will laugh
When thou art gone, the solemn brood of care
Plod on, and each one as before will chase
His favourite phantom; yet all these shall leave
65   Their mirth and their employments, and shall come
And make their bed with thee. As the long train
Of ages glide away, the sons of men,
The youth in life's green spring, and he who goes
In the full strength of years matron, and maid,
70   The speechless babe, and the gray-headed man—
Shall one by one be gathered to thy side,
By those, who in their turn shall follow them.

So live, that when thy summons comes to join
The innumerable caravan, which moves

---

[1]   *Thanatopsis* This title was devised by the editors of the *North American Review*, where the poem was first published; derived from Ancient Greek, the coinage means roughly "a contemplation of death."

[2]   *pall* Cloth placed over a coffin.

[3]   *clod* Lump or tract of earth; *rude* Coarse, unsophisticated; *swain* Country laborer.

[4]   *share* Blade of a plow.

[5]   *mould* Body (especially when considered as mingled with rotting earth).

---

[6]   *hoary* White-haired.

[7]   *Barcan* Barca was an ancient city on the coast of what is now Libya.

[8]   *Oregon* I.e., the Columbia River (which runs largely through Oregon).

₇₅ To that mysterious realm, where each shall take
His chamber in the silent halls of death,
Thou go not, like the quarry-slave at night,
Scourged to his dungeon, but, sustained and soothed
By an unfaltering trust, approach thy grave,
₈₀ Like one who wraps the drapery of his couch
About him, and lies down to pleasant dreams.
—1817 (REVISED 1821)

To a Waterfowl

Whither, midst falling dew,
    While glow the heavens with the last steps of day,
Far, through their rosy depths, dost thou pursue
    Thy solitary way?

₅   Vainly the fowler's[1] eye
Might mark thy distant flight to do thee wrong,
As, darkly seen against the crimson sky,
    Thy figure floats along.

    Seek'st thou the plashy° brink   *marshy*
₁₀ Of weedy lake, or marge° of river wide,   *shore*
Or where the rocking billows° rise and sink   *waves*
    On the chafed ocean-side?

    There is a Power whose care
Teaches thy way along that pathless coast—
₁₅ The desert° and illimitable air—   *empty*
    Lone wandering, but not lost.

    All day thy wings have fanned,
At that far height, the cold, thin atmosphere,
Yet stoop not, weary, to the welcome land,
₂₀   Though the dark night is near.

And soon that toil shall end;
Soon shalt thou find a summer home, and rest,
And scream among thy fellows; reeds shall bend,
    Soon, o'er thy sheltered nest.

₂₅   Thou'rt gone, the abyss of heaven
Hath swallowed up thy form; yet, on my heart
Deeply hath sunk the lesson thou hast given,
    And shall not soon depart.

    He who, from zone to zone,
₃₀ Guides through the boundless sky thy certain flight,
In the long way that I must tread alone,
    Will lead my steps aright.
—1818, 1871

To Cole, the Painter, Departing for Europe[2]

Thine eyes shall see the light of distant skies;
    Yet, Cole! thy heart shall bear to Europe's
        strand°   *shore*
    A living image of our own bright land,
Such as upon thy glorious canvas lies;
₅ Lone lakes—savannas where the bison roves—
    Rocks rich with summer garlands—solemn streams—
    Skies, where the desert eagle wheels and screams—
Spring bloom and autumn blaze of boundless groves,
Fair scenes shall greet thee where thou goest—fair,
₁₀   But different—everywhere the trace of men,
    Paths, homes, graves, ruins, from the lowest glen
To where life shrinks from the fierce Alpine air,
    Gaze on them, till the tears shall dim thy sight,
    But keep that earlier, wilder image bright.
—1829, 1871

---

¹   *fowler*   Hunter of wild birds.

---

²   Bryant's friend Thomas Cole (1801–48) was a founding member
of the Hudson River School of painters. He was known for portraying American landscapes, such as Niagara Falls and the Catskill
Mountains, with a sensibility inspired by the Romantic movement
in Europe. Cole embarked on a tour of Europe, the subject of this
poem, in 1829. See the color insert and "Contexts: Nature and the
Environment," elsewhere in this volume, for paintings by Cole.

Nature and the Environment

Contexts

Across Europe, the late eighteenth and early nineteenth centuries saw dramatic changes in the ways in which humans conceived of the world around them. William Wordsworth and other Romantic poets, and Caspar David Friedrich and other Romantic painters, led the way in seeing nature with fresh eyes—sometimes glorifying nature, sometimes idealizing nature, often finding in nature new value for humans as a source of aesthetic and spiritual energy that could counteract the deadening effects of urbanization and industrialization. Between the early nineteenth century and the Reconstruction era, these new currents of thought brought changes as well to the ways in which Americans viewed the natural environment, as did a cascade of other artistic, social, cultural, economic, technological, and scientific developments. Drawing on European Romanticism, poets such as William Cullen Bryant and painters such as Thomas Cole formulated American visions of nature that foregrounded the sublime and offered the possibility of a quasi-religious connection with nature for the person "who in the love of Nature holds—Communion with her visible forms," as Bryant put it in his famous poem "Thanatopsis" (first published in 1817).

To be sure, twenty-first-century readers should not expect to find a full-fledged equivalent of a modern-day environmental ethic in the nineteenth century, even from the period's most progressive thinkers. Even as norm-defying a figure as the women's-rights activist Elizabeth Cady Stanton could characterize, in an 1869 speech, "the love of acquisition and [the love of] conquest, ... when expended on the earth, the sea, the elements, the riches and forces of Nature" as "the very pioneers of civilization." Stanton was far from alone in holding such a view of the subordination of nature as the basis of "civilization": for many Americans, the U.S.'s rapid (if uneven) industrialization between the 1820s and the 1870s simply intensified a deep-seated belief that nature existed for human use, and that the domination and exploitation of nonhuman environments was therefore entirely legitimate, even praiseworthy. Other Americans, however, were adopting quite different ways of looking at the natural world. John James Audubon's dramatically realized detail; Edward Hicks's Quaker religiosity; William Cullen Bryant's Romantic perspective on nature as a source of moral improvement and inspiration; and Charles Lane and Bronson Alcott's utopian emphasis on physical and spiritual health (with its idiosyncratic blend of scientific thinking and mysticism)—all these and more yielded views of the natural environment and nonhuman life as vibrantly autonomous and deserving of reverence or protection.

Susan Fenimore Cooper's *Rural Hours* (1850) synthesizes several of these perspectives, including Romanticism and traditional religiosity, with the kind of pragmatic, utilitarian assessment of the economic value of natural resources that also helped propel the Industrial Revolution. Cooper used this synthesis to make a multifaceted, prescient argument for conserving the Northeast's rapidly diminishing forests—an argument that may have influenced Henry David Thoreau, whose *Walden; or Life in the Woods* (1854) has long been established as *the* canonical American environmental text of the nineteenth century.

From the 1820s through at least the 1850s, arguably the most important expressions of a new way of seeing American nature were the works of the so-called Hudson River School, one of the first major homegrown American fine art movements. In line with the emerging appreciation of "the wilderness" in American culture from the 1820s on, the painters associated with this school (the name "Hudson River School" was initially a pejorative one) sought to portray the beauty and power they identified in American landscapes: at first the eastern landscapes of the Hudson Valley itself and the neighboring mountain ranges and river valleys of New York and New England, and later the even more dramatic landscapes west of the Mississippi. Their artistic renderings of these landscapes frequently combine (or juxtapose) naturalism and idealization, symbolism and realistic detail, conflict and harmony, glorification of untamed nature and celebration of its conquest by humans. Several of the Hudson River School artists enjoyed extraordinary popularity in their day—thousands of people paid 25 cents a head (a considerable sum at the time) to view Frederic Edwin Church's *Niagara* (1857), while Albert Bierstadt's *The Rocky Mountains, Lander's Peak* (1863) set a new price record for American art—and the legacy of their reinterpretation of American nature continues to be felt.

A different but equally novel way of viewing the American environment was from the 1840s onwards provided by the emerging medium of photography. Landscape photography was integral to the medium from its very beginning, and nineteenth-century photographers—from Hugh Lee Pattinson, through Carleton Watkins and Timothy O'Sullivan, to Marion Hooper Adams—crafted evocative depictions of American landscapes that attest to the transformations such landscapes were undergoing due to tourism, westward expansion, warfare, and the kind of industrial and technological development that photography itself formed part of.

One of the foremost manifestations of such technological development, with its environmental repercussions, were the revolutions in transportation that took place in the nineteenth century. The canals cut and railways laid down by nineteenth-century Americans not only dramatically modified the landscape themselves; they also propelled and accelerated patterns of land settlement, urban growth, and industrialization that further altered the environment in massive, unprecedented ways. Two very different but equally human-made products of such transformations, both of which became the subject of considerable discussion and debate, were the industrializing cities that were most thickly concentrated in the Northeast and the cotton and other monoculture plantations of the South. As industrialization and the urbanization that accompanied it spread across the country, the effect that these urban industrial environments had on the people who were obliged to live in them became a subject of growing concern. One of the strategies with which reformers sought to improve the physical and moral condition of the urban poor was to bring facsimiles of the supposedly healthful, uplifting, or edifying natural landscapes that writers and artists were starting to extol into the midst of the cities themselves. New York's Central Park, designed in the 1850s by the landscape architect Frederick Law Olmsted, exemplifies this strategy—and the fact that this "green oasis for the refreshment of the city's soul and body" (as the park's Board of Commissioners described it) was built on the site of a thriving African American community that the city authorities displaced to make way for it embodies the strategy's complications.

As the excerpt from his *The Cotton Kingdom* (1861) included in this section demonstrates, Olmsted also took a leading part in the debate about the environmental consequences of the South's system of slave-labor-based plantation agriculture. By the time the Civil War began, what we would now call the unsustainability of this agricultural system—the way in which it methodically exhausted the soil on which it relied—had been abundantly attested to: by Northern observers such as Olmsted, by African Americans such as Charles Ball who had been forced to labor in the system, and even by Southern plantation owners themselves (although the solutions such planters envisioned for the environmental problem they recognized tended to involve either developing ways to restore soil fertility or acquiring fresh land at the expense of Native American or Latin American nations). The subsection on this topic presented below, which includes excerpts from Olmsted's and Ball's works as well as from T.B. Thorpe's celebratory 1854 article on "Cotton and Its Cultivation," shows how this environmental debate fed into, and provided another dimension to, the era's overriding moral and political question: the status and future of American slavery.

Like so many other aspects of mid-nineteenth-century American life, Americans' engagement with these intensifying environmental issues pointed many of them toward the vast territories west of the Mississippi that their country was coming to dominate. It was in the West that, in the eyes of many advocates of westward migration, the industrialized East's urban masses were to be rejuvenated by returning to a supposedly healthier agrarian lifestyle; it was in the West that many Southerners sought to give their unsustainable system of plantation agriculture and chattel slavery a new lease on life; and it was in the West that writers, artists, and burgeoning environmentalists found the quintessence of the "wilderness" that they were teaching their compatriots to revere. Frederick Law Olmsted went from creating Central Park and demonstrating the environmentally disastrous effects of plantation agriculture to making a case for protecting California's Yosemite Valley that would become a conceptual foundation for the national park system, while John Muir's time in the Sierra Nevada in 1869 helped give rise to the ideas about the importance and value of natural landscapes that would make him one of America's most influential environmentalist thinkers. The western environments that such figures were so awed by, however, were not actually any "wilder" or more untouched than their eastern counterparts had been, and Olmsted and Muir's celebrations of and efforts to conserve such spaces did little to counteract the frequent efforts of settler colonizers and of the United States government to displace, and in many instances to exterminate, the Indigenous peoples who lived in and used them—peoples who had their own distinct and ancient ways of envisioning their relationship to their environment. Indigenous perspectives on the American environment—as recorded in works such as the illustrations of Plains ledger artists and Chief Seattle's disputed 1854 speech—compellingly counterpoint the various ways of viewing and relating to the natural world espoused by the Euro-Americans who, during these decades, were steadily overwhelming the American environment's original human inhabitants.

⌘⌘⌘

Nature and the Environment: Changing Views

John James Audubon, Bird Paintings (1827–38)

In the 1820s, John James Audubon (1785–1851), a Franco-American ornithologist, naturalist, and painter, undertook a massive project: a book that would compile paintings of every species of bird in North America, based on fourteen years of field observations and drawings. The completed book, *The Birds of America*, comprises 435 images (printed in installments from 1827 to 1838) of 497 bird species; it was hailed internationally as a great scientific and artistic accomplishment. While aspects of Audubon's methods and accuracy have been called into question, as has his character as an enslaver, his work wielded enormous influence on how subsequent nineteenth-century scientists and artists alike viewed and represented the natural world.

John James Audubon, *Great Horned Owl,* 1827.

John James Audubon, *Golden Eagle,* 1833–34.

Hugh Lee Pattinson, *Horseshoe Falls,* 1840. Pattinson (1796–1858), an English chemist and entrepreneur, took this photograph while visiting Canada in 1840; the image is the first known photograph of Niagara Falls as well as the first photograph known to have been taken in Canada.

Edward Hicks, *The Peaceable Kingdom,* c. 1848. Hicks (1780–1849) was a Quaker minister as well as a painter. Between about 1820 and his death, he painted 62 versions of *The Peaceable Kingdom,* drawing inspiration and imagery from the famous description of the kingdom of God in Isaiah 11.6–7: "The wolf also shall dwell with the lamb, and the leopard shall lie down with the kid; and the calf and the young lion and the fatling together; and a little child shall lead them. … [A]nd the lion shall eat straw like the ox."

from Susan Fenimore Cooper, *Rural Hours* (1850)

Susan Augusta Fenimore Cooper (1813–94) was the daughter of the famous novelist James Fenimore Cooper, whom she assisted as a secretary in her later years; he in turn encouraged her in her own writing. By far the most successful and influential of her diverse works was *Rural Hours*, her second book. First published anonymously in 1850, it was reprinted multiple times in the ensuing decades, including in an 1855 British edition. Based on the diary Cooper kept of her observations of the environment around her home in Cooperstown, New York, *Rural Hours* was a pioneering work of nature writing and conservationist advocacy, preceding by four years Henry David Thoreau's more well-known *Walden* (1854). The book's detailed, attentive natural descriptions—which earned the admiration of Charles Darwin—and presciently conservationist message have in recent years helped it to win recognition as a milestone in American environmentalist literature. The text of the excerpt given here is based on the 1850 first edition.

Saturday, 28th [July 1849].—Passed the afternoon in the woods. What a noble gift to man are the forests! What a debt of gratitude and admiration we owe for their utility and their beauty!

How pleasantly the shadows of the wood fall upon our heads, when we turn from the glitter and turmoil of the world of man! The winds of heaven seem to linger amid these balmy branches, and the sunshine falls like a blessing upon the green leaves; the wild breath of the forest, fragrant with bark and berry, fans the brow with grateful freshness; and the beautiful wood-light, neither garish nor gloomy, full of calm and peaceful influences, sheds repose over the spirit. The view is limited, and the objects about us are uniform in character; yet within the bosom of the woods the mind readily lays aside its daily littleness, and opens to higher thoughts, in silent consciousness that it stands alone with the works of God. The humble moss beneath our feet, the sweet flowers, the varied shrubs, the great trees, and the sky gleaming above in sacred blue, are each the handiwork of God. They were all called into

being by the will of the Creator, as we now behold them, full of wisdom and goodness. Every object here has a deeper merit than our wonder can fathom; each has a beauty beyond our full perception; the dullest insect crawling about these roots lives by the power of the Almighty; and the discolored shreds of last year's leaves wither away upon the lowly herbs in a blessing of fertility. But it is the great trees, stretching their arms above us in a thousand forms of grace and strength, it is more especially the trees which fill the mind with wonder and praise.

Of the infinite variety of fruits which spring from the bosom of the earth, the trees of the wood are the greatest in dignity. Of all the works of the creation which know the changes of life and death, the trees of the forest have the longest existence. Of all the objects which crown the gray earth, the woods preserve unchanged, throughout the greatest reach of time, their native character: the works of man are ever varying their aspect; his towns and his fields alike reflect the unstable opinions, the fickle wills and fancies of each passing generation; but the forests on his borders remain today the same they were ages of years since. Old as the everlasting hills, during thousands of seasons they have put forth and laid down their verdure[1] in calm obedience to the decree which first bade them cover the ruins of the Deluge.[2]

But, although the forests are great and old, yet the ancient trees within their bounds must each bend individually beneath the doom of every earthly existence; they have their allotted period when the mosses of Time gather upon their branches; when, touched by decay, they break and crumble to dust. Like man, they are decked in living beauty; like man, they fall a prey to death; and while we admire their duration, so far beyond our own brief years, we also acknowledge that especial interest which can only belong to the graces of life and to the desolation of death. We raise our eyes, and we see collected in one company vigorous trunks, the oak, the ash, the pine, firm in the strength of maturity; by their side stand a young group, elm, and birch, and maple, their supple branches playing in

---

1 *verdure* Vegetation, greenery.

2 *the Deluge* I.e., the catastrophic flood described in Genesis Chapters 6–9, which is said to have destroyed all life on earth except for that preserved by Noah in his Ark.

the breezes, gay and fresh as youth itself; and yonder, rising in unheeded gloom, we behold a skeleton trunk, an old fir, every branch broken, every leaf fallen—dull, still, sad, like the finger of Death. …

These hills, and the valleys at their feet, lay for untold centuries one vast forest; unnumbered seasons, ages of unrecorded time passed away while they made part of the boundless wilderness of woods. The trees waved over the valleys, they rose upon the swelling knolls, they filled the hollows, they crowded the narrow glens, they shaded the brooks and springs, they washed their roots in the lakes and rivers, they stood upon the islands, they swept over the broad hills, they crowned the heads of all the mountains. The whole land lay slumbering in the twilight of the forest. Wild dreams made up its half-conscious existence. The hungry cry of the beast of prey, or the fierce deed of savage man, whoop and dance, triumph and torture, broke in fitful bursts upon the deep silence, and then died away, leaving the breath of life to rise and fall with the passing winds.

Every rocky cliff on the hillside, every marshy spot on the lowlands, was veiled in living, rustling folds of green. Here a dark wave of pine, hemlock, and balsam ran through a ravine, on yonder knoll shone the rich glossy verdure of oak, and maple, and chestnut; upon the breast of the mountain stood the birch, the elm, and the aspen, in light and airy tufts. Leaves of every tint of green played in the summer sunshine, leaves fluttered in the moonlight, and the showers of heaven fell everywhere upon the green leaves of the unbroken forest.

Sixty years have worked a wonderful[1] change; the forest has fallen upon the lowlands, and there is not a valley about us which has not been opened. Another half century may find the country bleak and bare; but as yet the woods have not all been felled, and within the circle which bounds our view, there is no mountain which has been wholly shorn, none presents a bald front to the sky; upon the lake shore, there are several hills still wrapped in wood from the summit to the base. He who takes pleasure in the forest, by picking his way, and following a winding course, may yet travel many a long mile over a shady path, such as the red man loved. …

In these times, the hewers of wood are an unsparing race. The first colonists looked upon a tree as an enemy, and to judge from appearances, one would think that something of the same spirit prevails among their descendants at the present hour. It is not surprising, perhaps, that a man whose chief object in life is to make money should turn his timber into bank-notes with all possible speed; but it is remarkable that any one at all aware of the value of wood, should act so wastefully as most men do in this part of the world. Mature trees, young saplings, and last year's seedlings, are all destroyed at one blow by the axe or by fire; the spot where they have stood is left, perhaps, for a lifetime without any attempt at cultivation, or any endeavor to foster new wood. One would think that by this time, when the forest has fallen in all the valleys—when the hills are becoming more bare every day—when timber and fuel are rising in prices, and new uses are found for even indifferent[2] woods—some forethought and care in this respect would be natural in people laying claim to common sense. The rapid consumption of the large pine timber among us should be enough to teach a lesson of prudence and economy[3] on this subject. It has been calculated that 60,000 acres of pine woods are cut every year in our own State[4] alone; and at this rate, it is said that in twenty years, or about 1870, these trees will have disappeared from our part of the country![5] But unaccountable as it may appear, few American farmers are aware of the full value and importance of wood. They seem to forget the relative value of the forests. It has been reported in the State of New York, that the produce of tilled lands carried to tide-water by the Erie Canal, in one year, amounted to $8,170,000 dollars worth of property; that of animals, or farm-stock, for the same year, is given at $3,230,000; that of the forests, lumber, staves, etc., at $4,770,000.[6] Thus the forest yielded more than the stock, and more than half as much as the farm lands; and when the comparative expense of the two is considered, their value will be brought still nearer together.

---

1   *wonderful*   I.e., eliciting wonder; astonishing, incredible.

2   *indifferent*   Of mediocre or inferior quality.

3   *economy*   Carefulness, resourcefulness.

4   *our own State*   I.e., New York state.

5   [Cooper's note]   Dr. Torrey's State Botany. [I.e., the report on the flora of New York state prepared by John Torrey, the official state botanist, published in two volumes in 1843.]

6   [Cooper's note]   See State Reports for 1835. [The monetary values given in this sentence are all equivalent to well over a hundred million dollars in twenty-first-century currency; *staves*   Sticks of wood.]

Peltries[1] were not included in this account. Our people seldom remember that the forests, while they provide food and shelter for the wildest savage tribes, make up a large amount of the wealth of the most civilized nations. The first rude devices of the barbarian are shaped in wood, and the cedar of Lebanon ranks with the gold of Ophir[2] within the walls of palaces. ...

But independently of their market price in dollars and cents, the trees have other values: they are connected in many ways with the civilization of a country; they have their importance in an intellectual and in a moral sense. After the first rude stage of progress is past in a new country—when shelter and food have been provided—people begin to collect the conveniences and pleasures of a permanent home about their dwellings, and then the farmer generally sets out a few trees before his door. This is very desirable, but it is only the first step in the track; something more is needed; the preservation of fine trees, already standing, marks a farther progress, and this point we have not yet reached. It frequently happens that the same man who yesterday planted some half dozen branchless saplings before his door, will today cut down a noble elm, or oak, only a few rods[3] from his house, an object which was in itself a hundred-fold more beautiful than any other in his possession. In very truth, a fine tree near a house is a much greater embellishment than the thickest coat of paint that could be put on its walls, or a whole row of wooden columns to adorn its front; nay, a large shady tree in a door-yard is much more desirable than the most expensive mahogany and velvet sofa in the parlor. Unhappily, our people generally do not yet see things in this light. But time is a very essential element, absolutely indispensable, indeed, in true civilization; and in the course of years we shall, it is to be hoped, learn further lessons of this kind. ...

How easy it would be to improve most of the farms in the country by a little attention to the woods and trees, improving their appearance and adding to their market value at the same time! Thinning woods and not

blasting them; clearing only such ground as is marked for immediate tillage; preserving the wood on the hilltops and rough sidehills; encouraging a coppice on this or that knoll; permitting bushes and young trees to grow at will along the brooks and watercourses; sowing, if need be, a grove on the bank of the pool, such as are found on many of our farms; sparing an elm or two about the spring; with a willow also to overhang the well; planting one or two chestnuts, or oaks, or beeches, near the gates or bars; leaving a few others scattered about every field to shade the cattle in summer, as is frequently done, and setting out others, in groups, or singly, to shade the house—how little would be the labor and expense required to accomplish this, and how desirable would be the result! Assuredly, the pleasing character thus given to a farm and a neighborhood is far from being beneath the consideration of a sensible man.

But there is also another view of the subject. A careless indifference to any good gift of our gracious Maker, shows a want of thankfulness, as any abuse or waste, betrays a reckless spirit of evil. It is, indeed, strange that one claiming to be a rational creature should not be thoroughly ashamed of the spirit of destructiveness, since the principle itself is clearly an evil one. Let us remember that it is the Supreme Being who is the Creator, and in how many ways do we see his gracious providence, his Almighty economy,[4] deigning to work progressive renovation in the humblest objects when their old forms have become exhausted by Time! There is also something in the care of trees which rises above the common labors of husbandry,[5] and speaks of a generous mind. We expect to wear the fleece from our flocks, to drink the milk of our herds, to feed upon the fruits of our fields; but in planting a young wood, in preserving a fine grove, a noble tree, we look beyond ourselves to the band of household friends, to our neighbors—ay, to the passing wayfarer and stranger who will share with us the pleasure they give, and it becomes a grateful reflection that long after we are gone, those trees will continue a good to our fellow-creatures for more years, perhaps, than we can tell.

---

[1] *Peltries* Animal pelts, i.e., furs and skins, which would predominately have been harvested from forested areas.

[2] *the cedar ... Ophir* In the Hebrew Bible (the Old Testament), immensely valuable materials used in the construction of the temple in Jerusalem and the palace of the Israelite kings.

[3] *rods* A rod is a unit of measurement equivalent to about five and a half yards.

---

[4] *economy* In this context, God's divine government of the world, but also with connotations of resourceful management.

[5] *husbandry* Cultivation, agriculture.

Marian Hooper Adams, *Umbrella Tree at Smith's Point,* 1883. Adams (1843–85), who was married to the renowned historian Henry Adams and known to friends and family as "Clover" Adams, was admired for both her portraits and her landscape photographs.

The Hudson River School

The mode of representing natural scenes developed by the artists of the Hudson River School—realistic but also idealized and symbolically rich, and attuned to both the beneficent and the threatening sides of nature (or, as Romantic aesthetic theory termed them, the beautiful and the sublime)—is especially well-exemplified by Thomas Cole's *View from Mount Holyoke, Northampton, Massachusetts, after a Thunderstorm—The Oxbow.* This painting by Cole (1801–48), an English-born artist typically considered the founder of the Hudson River School, depicts the Oxbow, a well-known landscape created by a bend of the Connecticut River in western Massachusetts, as seen from a nearby mountaintop. With its combination of sweeping natural vista and wealth of symbolic detail, it has become one of the most famous and representative Hudson River School paintings.

After Cole's untimely death in 1848, his older contemporary Asher Durand (1796–1886) inherited his widely acknowledged status as the leader of what was becoming an emerging school of New York-based landscape artists. Durand paid tribute to Cole shortly after the latter's death in his *Kindred Spirits,* which was commissioned by the New York businessman and art patron Jonathan Sturges as a gift for the poet William Cullen Bryant, a friend of Cole's. As Sturges explained to Bryant, he had "requested Mr. Durand to paint a picture in which he should associate our departed friend and yourself as kindred spirits." The painting portrays Cole and Bryant surveying a landscape based on Kaaterskill Clove, a valley in the Catskill Mountains of New York state that was frequently painted by Hudson River School artists and that Bryant also described in his poetry. After receiving the painting, Bryant noted to Durand that "everybody admires it greatly," and it was praised by critics when it was exhibited publicly in 1849.

Nearly a decade after Durand used it as the basis for *Kindred Spirits*, Harriet Cany Peale (1799–1869) also depicted Kaaterskill Clove in her own painting of that name. Cany had studied with Rembrandt Peale, a member of a famous artistic family whom she later married, and her association with him and his family long overshadowed her own accomplishments. After her death, she was largely remembered only as a copyist, but she has recently begun to gain increased recognition as more of her original work is rediscovered.

The achievements of Cole, Durand, and Cany Peale's generation were built on by the second generation of Hudson River School artists. Emerging in the 1850s, this second generation perpetuated the Hudson River School into the post-Civil War period; many of them extended the school's aesthetic approach to the western landscapes being intensively opened up during that period. Robert S. Duncanson (1821–72), a Cincinnati, Ohio-based African American painter with no formal art education, was one of these; in 1861, the *Daily Cincinnati Gazette* dubbed him "the best landscape painter in the west," and another Cincinnati newspaper called his *Landscape with Rainbow* "one of the most beautiful pictures painted on this side of the [Allegheny] mountains." *Landscape with Rainbow*, together with Duncanson's other landscape paintings of the 1850s and 60s, helped him become the first black American artist to achieve an international reputation, winning acclaim in Canada and Britain as well as the United States.

Thomas Cole, *View from Mount Holyoke, Northampton, Massachusetts, after a Thunderstorm—The Oxbow*, 1836.

Asher Durand, *Kindred Spirits,* 1849. The right-hand figure pointing to the landscape is the painter Thomas Cole; the poet William Cullen Bryant is on the left.

Harriet Cany Peale, *Kaaterskill Clove,* 1858.

Robert S. Duncanson, *Landscape with Rainbow,* 1859.

Transportation and the Environment

As is well known, nineteenth-century technology made human travel vastly easier and faster—a development epitomized by the completion of the transcontinental railroad, which reduced travel time across the continent from months to mere days. Innovations in transportation also had dramatic effects on the U.S. economy, and on its environment. The building of canals—most notably the Erie Canal, which opened in 1825—and later, of a network of railroads, together with the development of steamships, made it possible to ship agricultural products in large quantities from rural areas to markets in the more heavily populated cities of the east, as well as to export markets. With each major transportation advance, the availability of goods was greatly increased and their prices greatly reduced. And, in a seemingly never-ending cycle, each great advance in transportation spurred further economic growth and expansion, accelerating the settlement of western

lands (divided into neat squares according to the grid pattern that had been first proposed by Thomas Jefferson, and had been codified into law by Congress in 1785) and the expulsion of Indigenous people from them.

The new transportation methods also had an enormous effect on the land itself, enabling the clearing of forests and encouraging a different mix of crops on the land farmed by settler colonists. With the advent of grain elevators as well as of inexpensive means of long-distance transportation, wheat became the leading cash crop from Ohio to Iowa and Kansas—and bread figured ever more largely in the American diet. The transcontinental railroad, in particular, ushered in the definitive transformation of the Great Plains from an environment dominated by huge herds of bison and the Native Americans who lived off of them—an environment that the first white Americans to explore it dismissed as "the Great American Desert"—to a vast breadbasket that exported grain around the world, and from which bison had been almost entirely eradicated.

The Erie Canal

The Erie Canal at Little Falls, New York, c. 1880. A train is visible in the distance to the left. As the large grain elevator suggests, storage technology was important to the development of canals as well as to that of railroads—and that of farmland. Steam-powered grain elevators, first introduced in 1842, greatly increased the capability of canals and railroads to transport crops in bulk.

from "The Canal Policy of the State of New York: Report," *The Buffalo Commercial* (12 August 1867)

The construction of the Erie Canal was commenced in 1817. It was opened for transportation of property in 1825. From the very commencement, the national character of the work was recognized, and it was foreseen that a navigable communication between Lake Erie and the Atlantic Ocean would promote, to use language then employed by the legislature, "agriculture, manufactures and commerce between the States." The experience of almost half a century has fully approved the statesmanship which originally adopted our canal policy, which was, to improve the natural advantages of our geographical position—to pass through our State the then undeveloped commerce of the West, and gradually to improve the facilities afforded to a degree requisite to meet the requirements of its growth. The sagacity and foresight of the early friends of the Erie Canal enabled them to see clearly in the future the necessity which would require this commercial highway. It was a gigantic enterprise, and only those who have studied the history of the times are able fully to appreciate its magnitude. Once completed, it immediately gave promise of future successes, and comparatively little difficulty was found in securing its enlargement. So plain was the necessity, and so palpable the benefits which it conferred, that the work was pushed forward with enthusiasm. Of course, the patronage attending so large an expenditure of public money was accompanied by the usual amount of corruption, from which no government has ever yet been exempted, for no pure government has ever yet existed on this earth, except in the dreams of such visionaries as Sir Thomas More, in his Utopia.[1]

---

[1]   *Utopia*   Book published in 1516 by the English writer, jurist, and politician Sir Thomas More, in which he describes an imaginary ideal society.

The Transcontinental Railroad

This photograph, taken on 28 April 1869, shows workers for the Central Pacific Railroad, one of two railway lines—the Central Pacific, built eastwards from California, and the Union Pacific, built westwards from Iowa—that together formed America's first transcontinental railroad. Shortly after this photograph was taken, the two lines met at Promontory, Utah. See also "Money and Machines, Capital and Labor" in the anthology's online component.

from "Pacific Railroad Completed," *The National Republican* (11 May 1869)

Yesterday at two o'clock and forty-eight minutes p.m., the last spike necessary to complete the Pacific railroad was driven, and the Atlantic and the Pacific were connected by a band of iron that, in coming time, will work a revolution in the commerce of our country. This event, which will mark an era in our nation's history, took place at Promontory Point, some one hundred and eighty miles west of Salt Lake, and was performed with befitting ceremonies.

Preparations had been made to announce the precise time at which the event occurred all over the country simultaneously. The stations upon the vast network of wires of the Western Union Telegraph Company was placed by mechanical repeaters in direct communication with the operator at Promontory Point, and with the hammer which was to strike the blow to drive the last spike home.

Two o'clock, New York time, was the hour set for the last blow, but owing to some delay the time was postponed to 2:35. A large number of people were assembled at the telegraph office in this city, and we presume at every other office, to witness the announcement of this important event.

A little after 2 o'clock the wires were all in readiness, and after some conversation between Chicago, Omaha, New York and Promontory Point, and other stations, Omaha, at 2:25, Washington time, gave the order "keep quiet. When the spike is driven Promontory Point will say 'done'; don't break but watch."

At 2:30 Promontory Point sent the following: "Almost ready; prayer is being offered." ...

At 2:40, "Now they have got done praying and are presenting the spike," came from Promontory Point.

At 2:42, he telegraphed "The signal given a minute before the striking of the first blow will be three dots."

Five minutes later, and one, two, three rung out upon the little bell in the Washington office, as it did also all over the country. There was breathless silence, and the spectators counted the seconds upon their watches as the hand moved round. The sixty seconds passed, and the blow was not recorded. One or perhaps two minutes more and Chicago announced that *he* had received the strokes, and that the great work was completed. The offices on the wire east of Chicago had missed the blows of the hammer, but the news that the road was completed was sufficient to allay the disappointment felt by the spectators in not seeing, as it were, the blow struck.

Advertisement, *Cincinnati Enquirer*, 20 December 1872. This advertisement appeared numerous times in the same paper in 1872, as well as in newspapers in Chicago and other cities.

The Far West—Shooting Buffalo on the Line of the Kansas-Pacific Railroad, 1871. This illustration of the mass slaughter of bison that the building of railroads through the Great Plains enabled and encouraged was printed in *Frank Leslie's Illustrated Newspaper* on 3 June 1871.

The Mississippi River

The Mississippi and its tributaries continued throughout this period to be of major importance to transportation, and their use as a transportation artery had significant environmental consequences. As these photographs from the 1870s suggest, Mississippi River steamboats were a pivotal part of the economic network that sustained and was sustained by Southern cotton production—the environmental consequences of which are described elsewhere in this Contexts section.

Urban and Industrial Environments

1839 poster circulated in Philadelphia to discourage the coming of the railroad.

Thomas H. Johnson, *Inclined Plane G*, c. 1863–65. This photograph is one of a series taken by Johnson, a photographer based in Scranton, Pennsylvania, documenting the operations of the Delaware & Hudson Canal and Gravity Railroad, an infrastructural network in northeastern Pennsylvania and southeastern New York that conveyed coal from the Pennsylvania coalfields to the Hudson River, where it could be shipped downriver to New York City. In 1829, Honesdale, Pennsylvania, where the gravity railroad from the coalfields met the canal, was the starting point for the first commercial steam locomotive run on rails in the United States.

from Matthew Hale Smith, *Sunshine and Shadow in New York* (1868)

Matthew Hale Smith (1810–79) served as a Calvinist minister before taking up the practice of law in New York City at about age forty. He subsequently also branched out into journalism; *Sunshine and Shadow in New York*, first published in 1868, is one of the fruits of his endeavors in this vein. (Another excerpt from this book can be found in the website portion of this section.)

FROM CHAPTER 42: LIFE AMONG THE LOWLY

HOMES OF THE LOWLY

The extreme value of land in the city makes tenement-houses a necessity. Usually they occupy a lot of twenty-five by one hundred feet, six stories high, with apartments for four families on each floor. These houses resemble barracks more than dwellings for families. One standing on a lot fifty by two hundred and fifty feet has apartments for one hundred and twenty-six families. Nearly all the apartments are so situated that the sun can never touch the windows. In a cloudy day it is impossible to have sunlight enough to read or see. A narrow room and bedroom comprise an apartment. Families keep boarders in these narrow quarters. Two or three families live in one apartment frequently. Not one of the one hundred and twenty-six rooms can be properly ventilated. The vaults and water-closets are disgusting and shameful. They are accessible not only to the five or six hundred occupants of the building, but to all who choose to go in from the street. The water-closets are without doors, and privacy is impossible. Into these vaults every imaginable abomination is poured. The doors from the cellar open in the vault, and the whole house is impregnated with a stench that would poison cattle.

A NIGHT TRAMP

With a lantern and an officer, a visit to the cellars where the poor of New York sleep may be undertaken with safety. Fetid odors and pestiferous smells greet you as you descend. There bunks are built on the side of the room; beds filthier than can be imagined, and crowded with occupants. No regard is paid to age or sex. Men, women, and children are huddled together in one disgusting mass. Without a breath of air from without, these holes are hotbeds of pestilence. The landlord was asked, in one cellar, "How many can you lodge?" "We can lodge twenty-five; if we crowd, perhaps thirty."

The lodgers in these filthy dens seem to be lost to all moral feeling, and to all sense of shame. They are not as decent as the brutes. Drunken men, debased women, young girls, helpless children, are packed together in a filthy, underground room, destitute of light or ventilation, reeking with filth, and surrounded with a poisoned atmosphere. The decencies of life are abandoned, and blasphemy and ribald talk fill the place.

Thomas M. Easterly, *Chouteau's Mill Creek, East from Thirteenth and Gratiot, Showing Construction of Mill Creek Sewer. Man Sitting on Pipe Over Stream,* 1868. This picture, taken in St. Louis, Missouri, depicts work underway on St. Louis's Mill Creek Sewer, which drained an area on the city's western edge formerly occupied by Chouteau's Pond, a lake that had become polluted and unhealthy. Rail lines and massive railyards were subsequently built in the drained area, fueling the city's further growth.

Slavery, Plantation Agriculture, and the Environment

from Charles Ball, *Slavery in the United States: A Narrative of the Life and Adventures of Charles Ball, A Black Man* (1837)

Charles Gross—the real name of the man whose life story was published under the name "Charles Ball"—was born into slavery in Maryland around 1780. In 1805, he was sold to a new enslaver in South Carolina, separating him from his wife and children, then was given as a present to yet another enslaver in Georgia. He eventually escaped and returned to his family in Maryland in 1810, where he served in the U.S. Navy during the War of 1812. In 1830, he was caught and returned to slavery in Georgia, only to escape again, after which he settled in Pennsylvania. *Slavery in the United States* was first published by a local Pennsylvania printer in 1836; it was reprinted by New York abolitionists in 1837, and re-edited versions of the book, some considerably abridged, were subsequently published in 1846 and 1858. Ball/Gross's later life is unknown, as are the date and circumstances of his death.

The text of the below excerpts from *Slavery in the United States* is based on the book's 1837 edition. The latter two excerpts describe scenes from Ball's journey from Maryland to South Carolina in 1805.

FROM CHAPTER I

... It has been supposed, by many, that the state of the Southern slaves is constantly becoming better; and that the treatment which they receive at the hands of their masters, is progressively milder and more humane; but the contrary of all this is unquestionably the truth; for, under the bad culture[1] which is practised in the South, the land is constantly becoming poorer, and the means of getting food, more and more difficult. So long as the land is new and rich, and produces corn and sweet potatoes abundantly, the black people seldom suffer greatly for food; but, when the ground is all cleared, and planted in rice, or cotton, corn and potatoes become scarce; *and when corn has to be bought on a cotton plantation, the people must expect to make acquaintance with hunger.* ...

FROM CHAPTER 3

... Before night we crossed the Potomac,[2] at Hoe's Ferry, and bade farewell to Maryland. At night we stopped at the house of a poor gentleman, at least he appeared to wish my master to consider him a gentleman; and he had no difficulty in establishing his claim to poverty. He lived at the side of the road, in a framed house, which had never been plastered within—the weather-boards being the only wall. He had about fifty acres of land enclosed by a fence, the remains of a farm which had once covered two or three hundred acres; but the cedar bushes had encroached upon all sides, until the cultivation had been confined to its present limits. The land was the very picture of sterility, and there was neither barn nor stable on the place. The owner was ragged, and his wife and children were in a similar plight. It was with difficulty that we obtained a bushel of corn, which our master ordered us to parch at a fire made in the yard, and to eat for our supper. Even this miserable family possessed two slaves, half-starved, half-naked wretches, whose appearance bespoke them familiar with hunger, and victims of the lash[.] ...

FROM CHAPTER 4

... The ground over which we had travelled, since we crossed the Potomac, had generally been a strong reddish clay, with an admixture of sand, and was of the same quality with the soil of the counties of Chester, Montgomery and Bucks, in Pennsylvania. It had originally been highly fertile and productive, and had it been properly treated, would doubtlessly have continued to yield abundant and prolific crops; but the gentlemen who became the early proprietors of this fine region, supplied themselves with slaves from Africa, cleared large plantations of many thousands of acres—cultivated tobacco—and became suddenly wealthy; built spacious houses and numerous

---

[1]   *culture* Agricultural system.

[2]   *Potomac* River that forms the boundary between Maryland and Virginia.

churches[;] … but, regardless of[1] their true interest, they valued their lands less than their slaves, exhausted the kindly soil by unremitting crops of tobacco, declined in their circumstances, and finally grew poor, upon the very fields that had formerly made their possessors rich; abandoned one portion after another, as not worth planting any longer, and, pinched by necessity, at last sold their slaves to Georgian planters, to procure a subsistence; and when all was gone, took refuge in the wilds of Kentucky, again to act the same melancholy drama, leaving their native land to desolation and poverty. … Virginia has become poor by the folly and wickedness of slavery, and dearly has she paid for the anguish and sufferings she has inflicted upon our injured, degraded, and fallen race. …

from T.B. Thorpe, "Cotton and Its Cultivation," *Harper's New Monthly Magazine* (March 1854)

> Born in Massachusetts, Thomas Bangs Thorpe (1815–78) moved in 1837 to Baton Rouge, Louisiana, for health reasons. He made his name as the writer of humorous stories and sketches depicting Southern life, but he was far from an uncritical celebrant of his adopted region's society and culture; for example, his body of work also includes an antislavery novel, *The Master's House* (1854).

How unpretending is the cotton-plant, however luxuriantly it may flourish! Its soft, pithy wood, its delicate looking leaves, its quickly-fading blossoms, are characteristics that would not make it a favorite in the highly-cultivated garden; yet the gossamer filament, that envelops its hardy seeds, binds together great nations through the ameliorating pursuits of commerce, and gives subsistence to half of the profitable industry of the world. …

One of the amusing incidents connected with the growth of cotton is the interest taken in procuring "fancy" varieties of seed. The wise planter knows the full value of using seed that is procured from a distance, and thus secures himself against the deterioration of his crop, resulting from replanting continually that which is produced upon his own field. But occasionally favorable circumstances cause the cotton plant to yield more than the usual amount to the planted acre, and instantly it is announced that a new variety of cotton has made its advent upon the earth, and the local newspapers teem with advertisements, and the commission houses are filled with the magic seed. No wonder is it that the planter should rejoice at any improvement in the growth of his favorite plant, or that he should allow his hopes to carry his reason captive. When, with the usual amount of labor, the prospect of increased production presents itself, the consequences to him and the commercial interests of the world are too great to be contemplated with a cold and philosophic eye.

… [I]magine what must be the feelings of many who, cultivating cotton, and admiring it for its money-producing value, hear florid reports of new varieties of seed, that, regardless of the manner of being sown, or of excellence of soil or care of cultivation, spring into plants, from which flows the rich cotton as from an overfilled basket. The "White Seed," "the Petite Gulf," "the Okra," "the Multibolled," "the Mastodon," "the Sugar-loaf," and "the Prolific," are the fanciful names of these wonderful germinators, which have for a time commanded admiration, and then sunk into obscurity; the universal law still prevailing, that good land, with judicious cultivation and the blessings of Providence, are the only securities for a good crop. …

The cotton region, extending as it does over more than two-thirds of the geographical division of the Union, possesses therefore every variety of scenery, and, consequently, cotton plantations, unlike sugar estates, are made picturesque by the combinations of hill and dale. Some favorite site, which commands a view of the surrounding country, is generally chosen for the "residence," while a gushing spring hard by[2] will form the nucleus of the "quarters." The roads follow the favorable suggestion of the surface of the country, and, of course, wind pleasantly through the cultivated fields and untouched woodland. …

On some plantations there is no "overseer"; the owner manages his place with the help of a skillful and trustworthy negro, termed the "driver." These drivers are very ambitious, and are, like their masters,

---

[1] *regardless of* I.e., without regard for; disregarding.

[2] *hard by* Nearby.

exceedingly sensitive if a stranger, or other disinterested person, gives an unfavorable opinion of the general appearance of the crop under their management. If much grass is seen in the cotton field, it is supposed to be an unfavorable testimony of the industry or skill of the driver. Upon a certain occasion, a gentleman riding along a cotton field remarked to the negro manager, "You have a good deal of grass in your crop." The negro felt mortified, and, anxious to break the force of the insinuation, coolly replied, "It is poor ground, master, that won't bring grass." The finest intellect could not, under the circumstances, have said a better thing.

… The announcement of the "first blossom" of the neighborhood is a matter of general interest; it is the unfailing sign of the approach of the busy season of fall; it is the evidence that soon the labor of man will, under a kind Providence, receive its reward.

It should perhaps here be remarked, that the color of cotton in its perfection is precisely that of the blossom—a beautiful light, but warm cream color. In buying cotton cloth, the "bleached" and "unbleached" are perceptibly different qualities to the most casual observer; but the dark hues and harsh look of the "unbleached domestic" comes from the handling of the artisan and the soot of machinery. If cotton, pure as it looks in the field, could be wrought into fabrics, they would have a brilliancy and beauty never yet accorded to any other material in its natural or artificial state. …

The appearance of a well-cultivated cotton field, if it has escaped the ravages of insects and the destruction of the elements, is of singular beauty. Although it may be a mile in extent, still it is as carefully wrought as is the mould of the limited garden of the coldest climate. The cotton leaf is of a delicate green, large and luxuriant; the stalk indicates rapid growth, yet it has a firm and healthy look. Viewed from a distance, the perfecting plant has a warm and glowing expression. The size of the cotton-plant depends upon the accident of climate and soil. The cotton of Tennessee bears very little resemblance to the luxuriant growth of Alabama and Georgia; but even in those favored states the cotton-plant is not everywhere the same, for in the rich bottom lands it grows to a commanding size, while in the more barren regions it is an humble shrub. In the rich alluvium of the Mississippi the cotton will tower beyond the reach of the tallest "picker," and a single plant will contain hundreds of perfect "bolls";[1] in the neighboring "piney-woods" it lifts its humble head scarcely above the knee, and is proportionably meagre in its produce of fruit. …

The cultivation of the soil being the earliest as well as the noblest of pursuits, it seems to create a manliness and patriotism in those who follow it. The Southern planter presents the agriculturist in the most dignified form. He directs, he plows, he sows, he reaps, and yet he does nothing of mere physical labor. He has all the advantages that come from a familiarity with the open fields, combined with all the accomplishments that flow from elegant leisure. Surrounded with an overabundance of the necessaries of life, and, from his isolated position, ever glad to see the face of a friend or stranger, he has become proverbial throughout the world for his accomplished manners and unbounded hospitality. …

Within the last few years the cotton planters have had "their conventions," and we have in these "signs of the times"—whatever may have been the result— an evidence of a growing community of feeling, that is bound to increase until the cotton-growing states understand and practice what is to their true interests.

Georgia has set an example of wisdom, and very soon she will possess within herself so completely all the elements of empire, that she might be forever separated from the surrounding world, and yet flourish with unexampled[2] prosperity. Upon her hilltops begin to smoke the wealth-achieving furnace; the buzz of the cotton spindle mingles with the whisperings of her clear blue streams; the "iron horse" is far and wide circulating her products; her heretofore isolated population is beginning to feel that a market is created for "home industry," and that Georgia could, if the demand was made, make her shipments of unginned cotton as obsolete as is now the shipment of cotton in the seed. What cares such a state whether a foreign country enriches itself by spinning her cotton? The staple is produced by the wearing labor of the muscles of men, defiant of malaria, and regardless of fever-breeding heat—the easier, and *quadruply* more profitable work of manufacturing, by the never-tiring

---

[1]   *bolls* Protective fiber cases that grow around the seeds of the cotton plant, from which cotton is extracted.

[2]   *unexampled* Unparalleled.

engine, and the sinews of the spindle and loom, is at her command. Georgia has but to grasp the sceptre, and she is commercially free.

Will her sister states, so rich in agricultural products, and which are equally interested with her in the cultivation of the "great staple," imitate her example? If they do so, "the South" will become, in the natural course of things, the most independent portion of our extending empire, and thus forever hold the benefits of a great cotton monopoly in her hands.

J.H. Lakin, *Picking Cotton Near Montgomery, Alabama*, c. 1860.

from Frederick Law Olmsted, *The Cotton Kingdom* (1861)

Frederick Law Olmsted (1822–1903) is most famous today as a pioneering American landscape architect, responsible for designing Central Park in New York City as well as many other parks and public spaces throughout the U.S. and Canada; he was also an early conservationist, and one of his most important works in that vein is excerpted later in this section. His first career, however, was journalism, in which capacity he was commissioned in 1852 by the *New York Daily Times* (progenitor of today's *New York Times*) to undertake a reporting trip through the South. Olmsted eventually spent five years traveling in the region; his reports were published in three volumes from 1856 to 1860 and then republished in 1861, in abridged form, as *The Cotton Kingdom: A Traveller's Observations on Cotton and Slavery in the American Slave States*. The book critiqued plantation slavery's regressive social and economic consequences, as well as the adverse environmental effects of that system's mode of cultivation—something the excerpt given here illustrates by quoting Southern authorities themselves. (Another excerpt from the book can be found in the website portion of this Contexts section.)

FROM VOLUME 2

FROM CHAPTER 8: THE CONDITION AND CHARACTER OF THE PRIVILEGED CLASSES OF THE SOUTH

... The following is a graphic sketch by a native Georgian of the present appearance of what was once the most productive cotton land of the State:

"The classic hut occupied a lovely spot, overshadowed by majestic hickories, towering poplars, and strong-armed oaks. The little plain on which it stood was terminated, at the distance of about fifty feet from the door, by the low brow of a hill, which descended rather abruptly to a noble spring, that gushed joyously forth from among the roots of a stately beech, at its foot. The stream from this fountain scarcely burst into view, before it hid itself in the dark shade of a field of cane, which overspread the dale through which it flowed, and marked its windings, until it turned from sight, among vine-covered hills, at a distance far beyond that to which the eye could have traced it, without the help of its evergreen belt. A remark of the captain's, as we viewed this lovely country, will give the reader my apology for the minuteness of the foregoing description: 'These lands,' said he, 'will never wear out. Where they lie level, they will be just as good, fifty years hence, as they are now.' Forty-two years afterwards, I visited the spot on which he stood when he made the remark. The sun poured his whole strength upon the bald hill which once supported the sequestered school-house; many a deep-washed gully met at a sickly bog, where had gushed the limpid[1] fountain; a dying willow rose from the soil which had nourished the venerable beech; flocks wandered among the dwarf pines, and cropped a scanty meal from the vale where the rich cane had bowed and rustled to every breeze, and all around was barren, dreary, and cheerless."[2]

I will quote from graver authority: Fenner's Southern Medical Reports:[3]

"The native soil of Middle Georgia is a rich argillaceous[4] loam, resting on a firm clay foundation. In some of the richer counties, nearly all the lands have been cut down, and appropriated to tillage: a large maximum of which have been worn out, leaving a desolate picture for the traveller to behold. Decaying tenements, red, old hills, stripped of their native growth and virgin soil, and washed into deep gullies, with here and there patches of Bermuda grass and stunted pine shrubs, struggling for subsistence on what was once one of the richest soils in America."

Let us go on to Alabama, which was admitted as a State of the Union only so long ago as 1818.

In an address before the Chunnenuggee Horticultural Society, by Hon. C. C. Clay, Jr., reported by the author in De Bow's "Review," December, 1855, I find the following passage. I need add not a word to it to show how the political experiment of the Carolinas, and Georgia, is being repeated to the same cursed result in young Alabama. The author, it is fair to say, is devoted to the sustentation[5] of Slavery, and would not, for the world, be suspected of favouring any scheme for arresting this havoc[6] of wealth, further than by chemical science:

"I can show you, with sorrow, in the older portions of Alabama, and in my native county of Madison, the sad memorials of the artless and exhausting culture of cotton. Our small planters, after taking the cream off their lands, unable to restore them by rest, manures, or otherwise, are going further west and south, in search of other virgin lands, which they may and will despoil and impoverish in like manner. *Our wealthier planters, with greater means and no more skill, are buying out their poorer neighbours, extending their plantations, and adding to their slave force. The wealthy few, who are able to live on smaller profits, and to give their blasted fields some rest, are thus pushing off the many, who are merely independent.*[7]

... "*[A] country in its infancy, where, fifty years ago, scarce a forest tree had been felled by the axe of the pioneer is already exhibiting the painful signs of senility and decay, apparent in Virginia and the Carolinas; the freshness of its agricultural glory is gone; the vigour of its youth is extinct, and the spirit of desolation seems brooding over it.*"

What inducement has capital in railroads or shops or books or tools to move into districts like this, or which are to become like this? Why, rather, I shall be asked, does it not withdraw more completely? Why do not all, who are able, remove from a region so desolate? Why was not its impoverishment more complete, more simultaneous? How is it that any slaveholders yet remain? The "venerable Edmund

---

[1]   *limpid*   Clear.

[2]   [Olmsted's note] "Georgia Scenes," by the Rev. and Hon. Judge Longstreet, now President of the University of Mississippi. Harper's edition, p. 76. [The Georgian minister, judge, and educator Augustus Baldwin Longstreet self-published *Georgia Scenes*, a depiction of the rural Georgia of his youth, in 1835; the book was republished in New York in 1840.]

[3]   *Fenner's ... Reports*   The New Orleans-based physician Erasmus Darwin Fenner edited and published the *Southern Medical Reports*, a collection of articles on health conditions and medical practices in the South, from 1848 to 1850.

[4]   *argillaceous*   Consisting of clay.

[5]   *sustentation*   Maintenance, preservation.

[6]   *havoc*   Destruction.

[7]   *merely independent*   I.e., just making enough to get by, in contrast to the surplus profits of the "wealthy few."

Ruffin," president of the Virginia State Agricultural Society, shall answer:[1]

"The causes are not all in action at once, and in equal progress. The labours of exhausting culture,[2] also, are necessarily suspended as each of the cultivators' fields is successively worn out. And when tillage so ceases, and any space is thus left at rest, nature immediately goes to work to recruit[3] and replace as much as possible of the wasted fertility, until another destroyer, after many years, shall return, again to waste, and in much shorter time than before, the smaller stock of fertility so renewed. Thus the whole territory, so scourged, is not destroyed at one operation. But though these changes and partial recoveries are continually, to some extent, counteracting the labours for destruction, still the latter work is in general progress. It may require (as it did in my native region) more than two hundred years, from the first settlement, to reach the lowest degradation. But that final result is not the less certainly to be produced by the continued action of the causes." …

The West

Carleton Watkins, *Sequoia "Grizzly Giant" Mariposa*, c. 1865–66. Watkins (1829–1916) moved in 1851 with the Gold Rush to California, where he took up photography. He first visited the Yosemite Valley in 1861; the photographs he took of its scenery over the next few years were some of the first images of Yosemite to be seen in the East and played a significant role— as described in Frederick Law Olmsted's report on Yosemite excerpted in this section—in Yosemite's designation as a federally protected area.

---

[1]   [Olmsted's note]   Address before the South Carolina Institute. [The Virginian plantation owner Edmund Ruffin III (1794–1865) conducted intensive studies of how to preserve and improve soil productivity; he became known as "the father of soil science" in the United States. An outspoken supporter of slavery, he championed Southern secession in the years leading up to the Civil War and supposedly fired the first shot of the war in the Confederate bombardment of Fort Sumter. Because of his advanced age by the time the war began, newspaper coverage of him invariably referred to him as "the venerable Edmund Ruffin."]

[2]   *culture*   Agriculture.

[3]   *recruit*   Recuperate.

Frances Bond Palmer, *The Rocky Mountains, Emigrants Crossing the Plain*, 1866. Palmer (1812–76) created over 200 works for the Currier & Ives lithograph company; many of these were widely reproduced in greeting cards and calendars, and used in advertisements. *The Rocky Mountains, Emigrants Crossing the Plain* was one of her most popular images. Born and raised in England, Palmer emigrated to the United States in the 1840s; she never visited the American West.

Henry Lewis, *Falls of Saint Anthony, Upper Mississippi*, 1847. Lewis (1819–1904), a self-taught English-born artist, painted the Falls of Saint Anthony—today the site of Minneapolis, Minnesota—after a trip down the Mississippi River in the summer of 1847. The Falls of Saint Anthony was a popular tourist attraction in the mid-nineteenth century and was frequently depicted in works of art, including paintings by George Catlin (1871) and Albert Bierstadt (c. 1880–87).

from Frederick Law Olmsted, "The Yosemite Valley and the Mariposa Big Tree Grove" (1865)

The noted landscape architect Frederick Law Olmsted, who had gone west to California in 1863, was one of several prominent Californians who—awed by the scenery of the Yosemite Valley, which had only recently become known to white settlers—petitioned the federal government to preserve the valley's landscapes. In 1864, President Lincoln signed a bill granting Yosemite (together with the nearby Mariposa Grove of giant sequoia trees) to the state of California "for public use, resort and recreation." Olmsted served on the Board of Commissioners set up to administer the area; at the end of his term he delivered a report, excerpted below, which has become a landmark document in the history of the conservation movement in the United States.

... It was during one of the darkest hours [of the Civil War], ... when the paintings of Bierstadt and the photographs of Watkins,[1] both productions of the war time, had given to the people on the Atlantic some idea of the sublimity of the Yosemite, and of the stateliness of the neighboring Sequoia grove, that consideration was first given to the danger that such scenes might become private property and through the false taste, the caprice or the requirements of some industrial speculation of their holders, their value to posterity be injured. To secure them against this danger Congress passed an act providing that the premises should be segregated from the general domain of the public lands, and devoted forever to popular resort and recreation[.][2] ...

Two classes of considerations may be assumed to have influenced the action of Congress. The first and less important is the direct and obvious pecuniary advantage which comes to a commonwealth from the fact that it possesses objects which cannot be taken out of its domain, that are attractive to travellers and the enjoyment of which is open to all. ...

A more important class of considerations, however, remains to be stated. These are considerations of a political duty of grave importance to which seldom if ever before has proper respect been paid by any government in the world but the grounds of which rest on the same eternal base of equity and benevolence with all other duties of republican government. It is the main duty of government, if it is not the sole duty of government, to provide means of protection for all its citizens in the pursuit of happiness against the obstacles, otherwise insurmountable, which the selfishness of individuals or combinations of individuals is liable to interpose to that pursuit.

It is a scientific fact that the occasional contemplation of natural scenes of an impressive character, particularly if this contemplation occurs in connection with relief from ordinary cares, change of air and change of habits, is favorable to the health and vigor of men and especially to the health and vigor of their intellect beyond any other conditions which can be offered them, that it not only gives pleasure for the time being but increases the subsequent capacity for happiness and the means of securing happiness. The want[3] of such occasional recreation where men and women are habitually pressed by their business or household cares often results in a class of disorders the characteristic quality of which is mental disability, sometimes taking the severe forms of softening of the brain, paralysis, palsy, monomania, or insanity, but more frequently of mental and nervous excitability, moroseness, melancholy or irascibility, incapacitating the subject for the proper exercise of the intellectual and moral forces.

It is well established that where circumstances favor the use of such means of recreation as have been indicated, the reverse of this is true. ...

---

[1] *the paintings ... Watkins* German–American painter Albert Bierstadt (1830–1902) and American photographer Carleton Watkins (1829–1916) both visited the Yosemite Valley during the Civil War years, creating images of it in their respective mediums whose exhibition in the eastern United States helped galvanize attempts to protect Yosemite's landscapes.

[2] *Congress passed ... recreation* The Yosemite Grant, by which the Yosemite Valley was set aside for preservation and public use, passed both houses of Congress and was signed by President Lincoln in 1864. The grant set the precedent for the creation of the first national park, Yellowstone, eight years later; Yosemite itself was not declared a national park until 1890.

[3] *want* Lack.

...[I]n this country at least it is not those who have the most important responsibilities in state affairs or in commerce, who suffer most from the lack of recreation; women suffer more than men, and the agricultural class is more largely represented in our insane asylums than the professional, and for this, and other reasons, it is these classes to which the opportunity for such recreation is the greatest blessing. ...

The power of scenery to affect men is, in a large way, proportionate to the degree of their civilization and the degree in which their taste has been cultivated. Among a thousand savages there will be a much smaller number who will show the least sign of being so affected than among a thousand persons taken from a civilized community. This is only one of the many channels in which a similar distinction between civilized and savage men is to be generally observed. The whole body of the susceptibilities of civilized men, and with their susceptibilities their powers, are on the whole enlarged. ...

...[T]here is a special reason why the reinvigoration of those parts which are stirred into conscious activity by natural scenery is more effective upon the general development and health than that of any other, which is this: The severe and excessive exercise of the mind which leads to the greatest fatigue and is the most wearing upon the whole constitution is almost entirely caused by application to the removal of something to be apprehended in the future, or to interests beyond those of the moment, or of the individual; to the laying up of wealth, to the preparation of something, to accomplishing something in the mind of another, and especially to small and petty details which are uninteresting in themselves and which engage the attention at all only because of the bearing they have on some general end of more importance which is seen ahead.

In the interest which natural scenery inspires there is the strongest contrast to this. It is for itself and at the moment it is enjoyed. The attention is aroused and the mind occupied without purpose, without a continuation of the common process of relating the present action, thought or perception to some future end. There is little else that has this quality so purely. There are few enjoyments with which regard for something outside and beyond the enjoyment of the moment can ordinarily be so little mixed. ...

... [T]he enjoyment of scenery employs the mind without fatigue and yet exercises it; tranquilizes it and yet enlivens it; and thus, through the influence of the mind over the body, gives the effect of refreshing rest and reinvigoration to the whole system.

Men who are rich enough and who are sufficiently free from anxiety with regard to their wealth can and do provide places of this needed recreation for themselves. ... The enjoyment of the choicest natural scenes in the country and the means of recreation connected with them is thus a monopoly, in a very peculiar manner, of a very few, very rich people. The great mass of society, including those to whom it would be of the greatest benefit, is excluded from it. In the nature of the case private parks can never be used by the mass of the people in any country nor by any considerable number even of the rich, except by the favor of a few, and in dependence on them.

Thus without means are taken[1] by government to withhold them from the grasp of individuals, all places favorable in scenery to the recreation of the mind and body will be closed against the great body of the people. For the same reason that the water of rivers should be guarded against private appropriation and the use of it for the purpose of navigation and otherwise protected against obstruction, portions of natural scenery may therefore properly be guarded and cared for by government. To simply reserve them from monopoly by individuals, however, it will be obvious, is not all that is necessary. It is necessary that they should be laid open to the use of the body of the people.

The establishment by government of great public grounds for the free enjoyment of the people under certain circumstances, is thus justified and enforced as a political duty.

Such a provision, however, having regard to the whole people of a state, has never before been made and the reason it has not is evident.

It has always been the conviction of the governing classes of the old world that it is necessary that the large mass of all human communities should spend their lives in almost constant labor and that the power of enjoying beauty either of nature or of art in any high degree, requires a cultivation of certain faculties, which is impossible to these humble toilers. Hence it is

---

[1] *without means are taken*   I.e., if means are not taken.

thought better, so far as the recreations of the masses of a nation receive attention from their rulers, to provide artificial pleasure for them, such as theatres, parades, and promenades where they will be amused by the equipages[1] of the rich and the animation of crowds.

It is unquestionably true that excessive and persistent devotion to sordid interests cramps and distorts the power of appreciating natural beauty and destroys the love of it which the Almighty has implanted in every human being, and which is so intimately and mysteriously associated with the moral perceptions and intuition, but it is not true that exemption from toil, much leisure, much study, much wealth, are necessary to the exercise of the esthetic and contemplative faculties. It is the folly of laws which have permitted and favored the monopoly by privileged classes of many of the means supplied in nature for the gratification, exercise and education of the esthetic faculties that has caused the appearance of dullness and weakness and disease of these faculties in the mass of the subjects of kings. And it is against the limitation of the means of such education to the rich that the wise legislation of free governments must be directed. …

It was in accordance with these views of the destiny of the New World and the duty of the republican government that Congress enacted that the Yosemite should be held, guarded and managed for the free use of the whole body of the people forever, and that the care of it, and the hospitality of admitting strangers from all parts of the world to visit it and enjoy it freely, should be a duty of dignity and be committed only to a sovereign state. …

The first point to be kept in mind then is the preservation and maintenance as exactly as is possible of the natural scenery; the restriction, that is to say, within the narrowest limits consistent with the necessary accommodations of visitors, of all artificial constructions and the prevention of all constructions markedly inharmonious with the scenery or which would unnecessarily obscure, distort or detract from the dignity of the scenery.

In addition to the more immediate and obvious arrangements by which this duty is enforced there are two considerations which should not escape attention.

First: the value of the district is in its present condition as a museum of natural science and the danger, indeed the certainty, that without care many of the species of plants now flourishing upon it will be lost and many interesting objects be defaced or obscured if not destroyed.

… Many of the finer specimens of the most important trees in the scenery of the Yosemite have been already destroyed and the proclamation of the Governor, issued after the passage of the Act of Congress, forbidding the destruction of trees in the district, alone prevented the establishment of a saw mill within it. Notwithstanding the proclamation many fine trees have been felled and others girdled within a year. Indians and others have set fire to the forests and herbage and numbers of trees have been killed by these fires; the giant tree before referred to as probably the noblest tree now standing on the earth[2] has been burned completely through the bark near the ground for a distance of more than one hundred feet of its circumference; not only have trees been cut, hacked, barked and fired in prominent positions,[3] but rocks in the midst of the most picturesque natural scenery have been broken, painted and discolored by fires built against them. In travelling to the Yosemite and within a few miles of the nearest point at which it can be approached by a wheeled vehicle, the Commissioners saw other picturesque rocks stencilled over with advertisements of patent medicines and found the walls of the Bower Cave, one of the most beautiful natural objects in the state, already so much broken and scratched by thoughtless visitors that it is evident that unless the practice should be prevented not many years will pass before its natural charms will be quite destroyed.

Second: it is important that it should be remembered that in permitting the sacrifice of anything that would be of the slightest value to future visitors to the convenience, bad taste, playfulness, carelessness, or

---

[1]   *equipages*   Horses and carriages.

[2]   *the giant … earth*   The so-called Grizzly Giant, a giant sequoia in Mariposa Grove, still living in the early twenty-first century. A photograph of this tree by Carleton Watkins is included elsewhere in this Contexts section.

[3]   *Many of … positions*   For a different perspective on the felling of giant sequoias and other trees in California, see Walt Whitman's poem "Song of the Redwood Tree," included in the Whitman section of this anthology volume.

wanton destructiveness of present visitors, we probably yield in each case the interest of uncounted millions to the selfishness of a few individuals. ...

It is but sixteen years since the Yosemite was first seen by a white man, several visitors have since made a journey of several thousand miles at large cost to see it, and notwithstanding the difficulties which now interpose, hundreds resort to it annually. Before many years if proper facilities are offered, these hundreds will become thousands and in a century the whole number of visitors will be counted by the millions. An injury to the scenery so slight that it may be unheeded by any visitor now, will be one of deplorable magnitude when its effect upon each visitor's enjoyment is multiplied by these millions. But again, the slight harm which the few hundred visitors of this year might do, if no care were taken to prevent it, would not be slight if it should be repeated by millions.

At some time, therefore, laws to prevent an unjust use by individuals, of that which is not individual but public property must be made and rigidly enforced. The principle of justice involved is the same now that it will be then; such laws as this principle demands will be more easily enforced, and there will be less hardship in their action, if the abuses they are designed to prevent are never allowed to become customary but are checked while they are yet of unimportant consequence.

It should, then, be made the duty of the Commission to prevent a wanton or careless disregard on the part of anyone entering the Yosemite or the Grove, of the rights of posterity as well as of contemporary visitors, and the Commission should be clothed with proper authority and given the necessary means for this purpose. ...

Next to this, and for a similar reason preceding all other duties of the state in regard to this trust, is that of aiding to make this appropriation of Congress available as soon and as generally[1] as may be economically practicable to those whom it is designed to benefit.

People of Yosemite: The Photographic Record

It was on land from which Indigenous people had very largely been removed that Yosemite Park was created. The Yosemite area was inhabited in the mid-nineteenth century by the Ahwahneechee people (a subset of the Southern Sierra Miwok) and also by the Northern Paiute and Mono peoples. During the Gold Rush-era conflict that became known as the Mariposa War, white settler militias killed or drove away many of the Indigenous inhabitants; others were forcibly relocated to a reservation. The number of Indigenous people who managed to remain represented only a small percentage of the numbers that had inhabited the area prior to the arrival of white miners and settlers.

Eadweard Muybridge, *A Native American Gathering Near a Cedar-bark u'macha Near the Merced River in the Yosemite Valley*, 1872. An *u'macha* is a home constructed of cedar poles woven together with vines and covered with cedar bark; these are the traditional homes of the Ahwahneechee tribe of Miwok people. Muybridge (1830–1904), an English photographer who lived for some time in the American West, is nowadays best known for his late 1870s photographs of animal movement; he made his reputation with an 1868 series of photographs of Yosemite.

---

[1] *generally* Widely.

Ma-ha-la of the Yosemite Band.

George Fiske, *Ma-ha-la of the Yosemite Band*, c. 1885. Fiske (1835–1918) is one of the best known of the early Yosemite photographers; he and his wife moved there in 1879. The vast majority of the photographs he took are of the landscape, but in the 1880s he also took a number of photographs of Ma-ha-la and other local inhabitants.

Julius Theodore Boysen, *Susie McGowan, of the Paiute tribe, with Daughter Sadie in Cradleboard in Yosemite Valley*, c. 1901. Boysen (1869–1939), together with his wife, Mabel Boysen, operated a photographic studio in Yosemite for many years—first in a tent in Yosemite Valley, later in permanent premises in Yosemite Village. Mabel is said to have maintained close relations with many of the area's remaining Indigenous inhabitants; she recounted in a 1934 interview that she "would have been very lonely when I came here if it had not been for the Indians. They were good to me, and there were often several of them sitting around the rooms of my house."

from John Muir, *My First Summer in the Sierra* (1911)

The Scottish-American naturalist, writer, and ecological thinker John Muir (1838–1914) is a towering figure in American environmental history, who played a crucial part in the formulation of ideas largely taken for granted today, in America and around the world, about the value of natural landscapes and the importance of preserving them. At the same time, his writing contains derogatory descriptions of the Indigenous people who had, from time immemorial, inhabited and used the "wilderness" he idealized and wished to conserve. (Muir's work also includes racist depictions of African Americans.) Both of these aspects of Muir are on display in the following excerpt from *My First Summer in the Sierra*, a book based on the journals Muir kept of his first experience, in 1869, of California's Sierra Nevada mountains.

FROM CHAPTER NINE: BLOODY CAÑON AND MONO LAKE

August 21—Have just returned from a fine wild excursion across the range to Mono Lake, by way of the Mono or Bloody Cañon Pass.[1] Mr. Delaney has been good to me all summer, lending a helping, sympathizing hand at every opportunity, as if my wild notions and rambles and studies were his own. He is one of those remarkable California men who have been overflowed and denuded and remodeled by the excitements of the gold fields, like the Sierra landscapes by grinding ice, bringing the harder bosses and ridges of character into relief ... —lots of good in him, shining out now and then in this mountain light. Recognizing my love of wild places, he told me one evening that I ought to go through Bloody Cañon, for he was sure I should find it wild enough. He had not been there himself, he said, but had heard many of his mining friends speak of it as the wildest of all the Sierra passes. Of course I was glad to go. It lies just to the east of our

camp and swoops down from the summit of the range to the edge of the Mono desert, making a descent of about four thousand feet in a distance of about four miles. It was known and traveled as a pass by wild animals and the Indians long before its discovery by white men in the gold year of 1858, as is shown by old trails which come together at the head of it. The name may have been suggested by the red color of the metamorphic slates in which the cañon abounds, or by the blood stains on the rocks from the unfortunate animals that were compelled to slide and shuffle over the sharp-angled boulders.

Early in the morning I tied my notebook and some bread to my belt, and strode away full of eager hope, feeling that I was going to have a glorious revel. The glacier meadows that lay along my way served to soothe my morning speed, for the sod was full of blue gentians and daisies, kalmia and dwarf vaccinium, calling for recognition as old friends[.] ...

Near the summit at the head of the pass I found a species of dwarf willow lying perfectly flat on the ground, making a nice, soft, silky gray carpet, not a single stem or branch more than three inches high; but the catkins,[2] which are now nearly ripe, stand erect and make a close, nearly regular gray growth, being larger than all the rest of the plants. Some of these interesting dwarfs have only one catkin—willow bushes reduced to their lowest terms. I found patches of dwarf vaccinium also forming smooth carpets, closely pressed to the ground or against the sides of stones, and covered with round pink flowers in lavish abundance as if they had fallen from the sky like hail. A little higher, almost at the very head of the pass, I found the blue arctic daisy and purple-flowered bryanthus, the mountain's own darlings, gentle mountaineers face to face with the sky, kept safe and warm by a thousand miracles, seeming always the finer and purer the wilder and stormier their homes. The trees, tough and resiny, seem unable to go a step farther; but up and up, far above the tree-line, these tender plants climb, cheerily spreading their gray and pink carpets right up to the very edges of the snow-banks in deep hollows and shadows. Here, too, is the familiar robin, tripping on the flowery lawns, bravely singing the same cheery song I first

---

[1]   *Mono Lake* Alkaline salt lake in California, on the eastern edge of the Sierra Nevada near the present-day state border with Nevada; *Mono ... Pass* Pass through the Sierra Nevada that connects the Yosemite Valley (today the site of Yosemite National Park) and Mono Lake.

[2]   *catkins* Slim, cylindrical flower clusters found in many plant families, including the willow.

heard when a boy in Wisconsin newly arrived from old Scotland. In this fine company sauntering enchanted, taking no heed of time, I at length entered the gate of the pass, and the huge rocks began to close around me in all their mysterious impressiveness. Just then I was startled by a lot of queer, hairy, muffled creatures coming shuffling, shambling, wallowing toward me as if they had no bones in their bodies. Had I discovered them while they were yet a good way off, I should have tried to avoid them. What a picture they made contrasted with the others I had just been admiring. When I came up to them, I found that they were only a band of Indians from Mono[1] on their way to Yosemite for a load of acorns. They were wrapped in blankets made of the skins of sage-rabbits. The dirt on some of the faces seemed almost old enough and thick enough to have a geological significance; some were strangely blurred and divided into sections by seams and wrinkles that looked like cleavage joints, and had a worn abraded look as if they had lain exposed to the weather for ages. I tried to pass them without stopping, but they wouldn't let me; forming a dismal circle about me, I was closely besieged while they begged whiskey or tobacco, and it was hard to convince them that I hadn't any. How glad I was to get away from the gray, grim crowd and see them vanish down the trail! Yet it seems sad to feel such desperate repulsion from one's fellow beings, however degraded. To prefer the society of squirrels and woodchucks to that of our own species must surely be unnatural. So with a fresh breeze and a hill or mountain between us I must wish them Godspeed and try to pray and sing with Burns, "It's coming yet, for a' that, that man to man, the world o'er, shall brothers be for a' that."[2]

How the day passed I hardly know. By the map I have come only about ten or twelve miles, though the sun is already low in the west, showing how long I must have lingered, observing, sketching, taking notes among the glaciated rocks and moraines and Alpine flower-beds.

[1]   *Indians from Mono*   The Kucadikadi, a band of the Northern Paiute people, live near Mono Lake; they are especially known today for their artistry in basket-weaving.

[2]   *Burns ... a' that*   Final lines of "A Man's a Man for A' That," also known as "Is There for Honest Poverty," a 1795 poem and song by the Scottish poet Robert Burns.

At sundown the sombre crags and peaks were inspired with the ineffable beauty of the alpenglow, and a solemn, awful stillness hushed everything in the landscape. Then I crept into a hollow by the side of a small lake near the head of the cañon, smoothed a sheltered spot, and gathered a few pine tassels for a bed. After the short twilight began to fade I kindled a sunny fire, made a tin cupful of tea, and lay down to watch the stars. Soon the night-wind began to flow from the snowy peaks overhead, at first only a gentle breathing, then gaining strength, in less than an hour rumbled in massive volume something like a boisterous stream in a boulder-choked channel, roaring and moaning down the cañon as if the work it had to do was tremendously important and fateful; and mingled with these storm tones were those of the waterfalls on the north side of the cañon, now sounding distinctly, now smothered by the heavier cataracts of air, making a glorious psalm of savage wildness. My fire squirmed and struggled as if ill at ease, for though in a sheltered nook, detached masses of icy wind often fell like icebergs on top of it, scattering sparks and coals, so that I had to keep well back to avoid being burned. But the big resiny roots and knots of the dwarf pine could neither be beaten out nor blown away, and the flames, now rushing up in long lances, now flattened and twisted on the rocky ground, roared as if trying to tell the storm stories of the trees they belonged to, as the light given out was telling the story of the sunshine they had gathered in centuries of summers.

The stars shone clear in the strip of sky between the huge dark cliffs; and as I lay recalling the lessons of the day, suddenly the full moon looked down over the cañon wall, her face apparently filled with eager concern, which had a startling effect, as if she had left her place in the sky and had come down to gaze on me alone, like a person entering one's bedroom. It was hard to realize that she was in her place in the sky, and was looking abroad on half the globe, land and sea, mountains, plains, lakes, rivers, oceans, ships, cities with their myriads of inhabitants sleeping and waking, sick and well. No, she seemed to be just on the rim of Bloody Cañon and looking only at me. This was indeed getting near to Nature. I remember watching the harvest moon rising above the oak trees in Wisconsin apparently as big as a cart-wheel and not farther than half a mile distant. With these exceptions I might say I never before had seen the moon, and this night she seemed so full of life and so near, the effect was marvelously impressive and made me forget the Indians, the great black rocks above me, and the wild uproar of the winds and waters making their way down the huge jagged gorge. Of course I slept but little and gladly welcomed the dawn over the Mono Desert. By the time I had made a cupful of tea the sunbeams were pouring through the cañon, and I set forth, gazing eagerly at the tremendous walls of red slates savagely hacked and scarred and apparently ready to fall in avalanches great enough to choke the pass and fill up the chain of lakelets. But soon its beauties came to view, and I bounded lightly from rock to rock, admiring the polished bosses shining in the slant sunshine with glorious effect in the general roughness of moraines and avalanche taluses, even toward the head of the cañon near the highest fountains of the ice. Here, too, are most of the lowly plant people seen yesterday on the other side of the divide now opening their beautiful eyes. None could fail to glory in Nature's tender care for them in so wild a place. The little ouzel is flitting from rock to rock along the rapid swirling Cañon Creek, diving for breakfast in icy pools, and merrily singing as if the huge rugged avalanche-swept gorge was the most delightful of all its mountain homes. Besides a high fall on the north wall of the cañon, apparently coming direct from the sky, there are many narrow cascades, bright silvery ribbons zigzagging down the red cliffs, tracing the diagonal cleavage joints of the metamorphic slates, now contracted and out of sight, now leaping from ledge to ledge in filmy sheets through which the sunbeams sift. And on the main Cañon Creek, to which all these are tributary, is a series of small falls, cascades, and rapids extending all the way down to the foot of the cañon, interrupted only by the lakes in which the tossed and beaten waters rest. One of the finest of the cascades is outspread on the face of a precipice, its waters separated into ribbon-like strips, and woven into a diamond-like pattern by tracing the cleavage joints of the rock, while tufts of bryanthus, grass, sedge, saxifrage form beautiful fringes. Who could imagine beauty so fine in so savage a place? Gardens are blooming in all sorts of nooks and hollows—at the head alpine eriogonums, erigerons, saxifrages, gentians, cowania, bush primula;

in the middle region larkspur, columbine, orthocarpus, castilleia, harebell, epilobium, violets, mints, yarrow; near the foot sunflowers, lilies, brier rose, iris, lonicera, clematis. …

Looking up the cañon from the warm sunny edge of the Mono plain my morning ramble seems a dream, so great is the change in the vegetation and climate. The lilies on the bank of Moraine Lake are higher than my head, and the sunshine is hot enough for palms. Yet the snow round the arctic gardens at the summit of the pass is plainly visible, only about four miles away, and between lie specimen zones of all the principal climates of the globe. In little more than an hour one may swoop down from winter to summer, from an arctic to a torrid[1] region, through as great changes of climate as one would encounter in traveling from Labrador to Florida.

The Indians I had met near the head of the cañon had camped at the foot of it the night before they made the ascent, and I found their fire still smoking on the side of a small tributary stream near Moraine Lake; and on the edge of what is called the Mono Desert, four or five miles from the lake, I came to a patch of elymus, or wild rye, growing in magnificent waving clumps six or eight feet high, bearing heads six to eight inches long. The crop was ripe, and Indian women were gathering the grain in baskets by bending down large handfuls, beating out the seed, and fanning it in the wind. The grains are about five eighths of an inch long, dark-colored and sweet. I fancy the bread made from it must be as good as wheat bread. A fine squirrelish employment this wild grain gathering seems, and the women were evidently enjoying it, laughing and chattering and looking almost natural, though most Indians I have seen are not a whit more natural in their lives than we civilized whites. Perhaps if I knew them better I should like them better. The worst thing about them is their uncleanliness. Nothing truly wild is unclean. Down on the shore of Mono Lake I saw a number of their flimsy huts on the banks of streams that dash swiftly into that dead sea—mere brush tents where they lie and eat at their ease. Some of the men were feasting on buffalo berries, lying beneath the tall bushes now red with fruit. The berries are rather insipid,[2] but they

---

1   *torrid* Tropical.

2   *insipid* Flavorless.

must needs be wholesome, since for days and weeks the Indians, it is said, eat nothing else. In the season they in like manner depend chiefly on the fat larvæ of a fly that breeds in the salt water of the lake,[1] or on the big fat corrugated caterpillars of a species of silkworm that feeds on the leaves of the yellow pine. Occasionally a grand rabbit-drive is organized and hundreds are slain with clubs on the lake shore, chased and frightened into a dense crowd by dogs, boys, girls, men and women, and rings of sage brush fire, when of course they are quickly killed. The skins are made into blankets. In the autumn the more enterprising of the hunters bring in a good many deer, and rarely a wild sheep from the high peaks. Antelopes used to be abundant on the desert at the base of the interior mountain-ranges. Sage hens, grouse, and squirrels help to vary their wild diet of worms; pine nuts also from the small interesting *Pinus monophylla*,[2] and good bread and good mush are made from acorns and wild rye. Strange to say, they seem to like the lake larvæ best of all. Long windrows[3] are washed up on the shore, which they gather and dry like grain for winter use. It is said that wars, on account of encroachments on each other's worm-grounds, are of common occurrence among the various tribes and families. Each claims a certain marked portion of the shore. The pine nuts are delicious—large quantities are gathered every autumn. The tribes of the west flank of the range trade acorns for worms and pine nuts. The squaws[4] carry immense loads on their backs across the rough passes and down the range, making journeys of about forty or fifty miles each way.

The desert around the lake is surprisingly flowery. In many places among the sage bushes I saw mentzelia, abronia, aster, bigelovia, and gilia, all of which seemed to enjoy the hot sunshine. The abronia, in particular, is a delicate, fragrant, and most charming plant.

Opposite the mouth of the cañon a range of volcanic cones extends southward from the lake, rising abruptly out of the desert like a chain of mountains. The largest of the cones are about twenty-five hundred feet high above the lake level, have well-formed craters, and all of them are evidently comparatively recent additions to the landscape. At a distance of a few miles they look like heaps of loose ashes that have never been blessed by either rain or snow, but, for a' that and a' that,[5] yellow pines are climbing their gray slopes, trying to clothe them and give beauty for ashes. A country of wonderful contrasts. Hot deserts bounded by snow-laden mountains—cinders and ashes scattered on glacier-polished pavements—frost and fire working together in the making of beauty. In the lake are several volcanic islands, which show that the waters were once mingled with fire.

Glad to get back to the green side of the mountains, though I have greatly enjoyed the gray east side and hope to see more of it. Reading these grand mountain manuscripts displayed through every vicissitude of heat and cold, calm and storm, upheaving volcanoes and down-grinding glaciers, we see that everything in Nature called destruction must be creation—a change from beauty to beauty. ...

---

[1] *they ... lake* The name "Kucadikadi" means "eaters of the brine fly pupae."

[2] *Pinus monophylla* Type of pine tree native to the Great Basin and the southwestern United States.

[3] *windrows* Heaped-up rows.

[4] *squaws* Offensive term for Indigenous women; while it carried negative connotations by the mid-nineteenth century, the term continued to be used frequently even by those who did not intend it derogatorily.

[5] *for ... a' that* Another allusion to Burns's "A Man's a Man for A' That."

Timothy H. O'Sullivan, *Ancient Ruins in the Cañon de Chelle, N.M.,* 1873. O'Sullivan (c. 1840–82) took some of the first photographs of pre-contact Indigenous ruins in the American Southwest—among them this image of the so-called "White House Ruins" in Canyon de Chelly, a canyon in what is now Arizona that is one of the oldest continuously inhabited landscapes in North America.

Helen Henderson Chain, *Royal Gorge,* c. 1890. Chain (1849–92) was for several decades a leading figure in the art world of Colorado, where she moved following her marriage to James Chain. In Denver he opened a bookstore and art supply shop, and she became an art teacher as well as an artist; together with her students she often climbed local peaks, and she and her husband traveled throughout much of the Southwest, painting such scenes as the Grand Canyon, Yosemite, Yellowstone, and the Pueblos of New Mexico.

Helen Henderson Chain painting in the woods, c. 1880.

Indigenous Perspectives

from Chief Seattle, Speech, 1854

Chief Seattle (c. 1786–1866) was a leader of the Suquamish and Duwamish peoples, the Indigenous inhabitants of the area on Puget Sound, in Washington state, that is today the site of Seattle, Washington (a city named after Chief Seattle). "Seattle" is the traditional Anglicization of a name in Lushootseed, the language spoken by the Suquamish and Duwamish, that would more accurately be rendered Sealth or Si'ahl. Chief Seattle is most famous today for a speech he reportedly gave in 1854 to an audience that included Isaac Stevens, the recently-appointed governor of Washington Territory, who had been empowered to negotiate the cession of Indigenous lands in the territory. The earliest-known text of the speech was published in 1887 in the *Seattle Sunday Star* by Dr. Henry A. Smith, one of the early settlers of the city of Seattle; Smith claimed to have heard Chief Seattle speak in 1854 and to have transcribed "a fragment" of the speech from notes he took at the time. Smith's rendition of the speech was reprinted in 1891 in Frederic James Grant's *History of Seattle, Washington* and then was reprinted again, with additions, by several writers in the 1930s. The speech's massive modern popularity, however, dates from the late 1960s and 1970s, when it was rewritten and republished several times, in versions that bore increasingly little resemblance to Smith's original version (which itself was over thirty years removed from Seattle's actual speech). These later, almost completely invented versions of the speech included overtly environmentalist ideas and language and gained widespread circulation; they formed the basis, for example, for a popular 1993 children's book, *Brother Eagle, Sister Sky: A Message from Chief Seattle*.

The accuracy and fidelity of Smith's 1887 text of the speech is today a subject of scholarly debate: some scholars contend that Smith likely fabricated it, while others are persuaded that at least some of it derives from Seattle's actual words in 1854 (possibly blended with reports of a later speech of Seattle's).

If the 1887 text may contain at least a kernel of authenticity, the versions of the speech—or,

as it is sometimes called, Seattle's "letter" to the president—that began to circulate in the 1970s are entirely artificial. This very artificiality, though, makes Seattle's speech an important and revealing case study in the way that the modern environmental movement mythologized Indigenous perspectives on the environment and their relationship with it. An excerpt of Smith's original 1887 version of the speech appears below (the text of which is based on that published in *History of Seattle* in 1891); the text of one of the rewritten twentieth-century versions of the speech can be found in the website portion of this Contexts section.

... The great, and I presume also good, white chief sends us word that he wants to buy our lands but is willing to allow us to reserve enough to live on comfortably. This indeed appears generous, for the red man no longer has rights that he need respect,[1] and the offer may be wise, also, as we are no longer in need of a great country. There was a time when our people covered the whole land as the waves of a wind-ruffled sea cover its shell-paved floor. But that time has long since passed away with the greatness of tribes almost forgotten. I will not mourn over our untimely decay, nor reproach my pale-face brothers with hastening it, for we, too, may have been somewhat to blame. ...

... Your God loves your people and hates mine; he folds his strong arms lovingly around the white man and leads him as a father leads his infant son, but he has forsaken his red children; he makes your people wax strong every day, and soon they will fill the land; while our people are ebbing away like a fast-receding tide, that will never flow again. The white man's God cannot love his red children or he would protect them. They seem to be orphans and can look nowhere for help. How then can we become brothers? How can your father become our father and bring us prosperity and awaken in us dreams of returning greatness?

Your God seems to us to be partial. He came to the white man. We never saw Him; never even heard His voice; He gave the white man laws but He had

---

1   *the red man ... respect*   This rendering of Seattle's words echoes the infamous assertion in the Supreme Court's 1857 *Dred Scott* decision—issued three years after Seattle spoke but thirty years before Smith's version of the speech was published—that African Americans had "no rights which the white man was bound to respect."

no word for His red children whose teeming millions filled this vast continent as the stars fill the firmament.[1] No, we are two distinct races and must ever remain so. There is little in common between us. The ashes of our ancestors are sacred and their final resting place is hallowed ground, while you wander away from the tombs of your fathers seemingly without regret. …

Your dead cease to love you and the homes of their nativity as soon as they pass the portals of the tomb. They wander far off beyond the stars, are soon forgotten and never return. Our dead never forget the beautiful world that gave them being. They still love its winding rivers, its great mountains and its sequestered vales, and they ever yearn in tenderest affection over the lonely hearted living and often return to visit and comfort them.

Day and night cannot dwell together. The red man has ever fled the approach of the white man, as the morning mists on the mountain side flee before the blazing morning sun.

However, your proposition seems a just one, and I think that my folks will accept it and will retire to the reservation you offer them, and we will dwell apart and in peace, for the words of the great white chief seem to be the voice of nature speaking to my people out of the thick darkness that is fast gathering around them like a dense fog floating inward from a midnight sea.

It matters but little where we pass the remainder of our days. They are not many. The Indian's night promises to be dark. No bright star hovers about the horizon. Sad-voiced winds moan in the distance. Some grim Nemesis of our race is on the red man's trail, and wherever he goes he will still hear the sure approaching footsteps of the fell[2] destroyer and prepare to meet his doom, as does the wounded doe that hears the approaching footsteps of the hunter. A few more moons, a few more winters and not one of all the mighty hosts that once filled this broad land or that now roam in fragmentary bands through these vast solitudes will remain to weep over the tombs of a people once as powerful and as hopeful as your own.

But why should we repine? Why should I murmur at the fate of my people? Tribes are made up of individuals and are no better than they. Men come and go like the waves of the sea. A tear, a tamanamus,[3] a dirge, and they are gone from our longing eyes forever. Even the white man, whose God walked and talked with him, as friend to friend, is not exempt from the common destiny. We *may* be brothers after all. We will see.

We will ponder your proposition, and when we have decided we will tell you. But should we accept it, I here and now make this the first condition: That we will not be denied the privilege, without molestation, of visiting at will the graves of our ancestors and friends. Every part of this country is sacred to my people. Every hillside, every valley, every plain and grove has been hallowed by some fond memory or some sad experience of my tribe. Even the rocks that seem to lie dumb as they swelter in the sun along the silent seashore in solemn grandeur thrill with memories of past events connected with the fate of my people, and the very dust under your feet responds more lovingly to our footsteps than to yours, because it is the ashes of our ancestors, and our bare feet are conscious of the sympathetic touch, for the soil is rich with the life of our kindred.

The sable braves, and fond mothers, and glad-hearted maidens, and the little children who lived and rejoiced here, and whose very names are now forgotten, still love these solitudes, and their deep fastnesses at eventide grow shadowy with the presence of dusky spirits. And when the last red man shall have perished from the earth and his memory among white men shall have become a myth, these shores shall swarm with the invisible dead of my tribe, and when your children's children shall think themselves alone in the field, the store, the shop, upon the highway or in the silence of the woods they will not be alone. In all the earth there is no place dedicated to solitude. At night, when the streets of your cities and villages shall be silent, and you think them deserted, they will throng with the returning hosts that once filled and still love this beautiful land. The white man will never be alone. Let him be just and deal kindly with my people, for the dead are not altogether powerless.

---

[1] *firmament* Sky or heavens.

[2] *Nemesis* Agent of destruction or downfall (originally the name, in classical mythology, of the goddess of retribution or vengeance); *fell* Cruel.

[3] *tamanamus* In the culture of the Native Americans of the Pacific Northwest, a song or ceremony performed by a shaman on behalf of an ill, dying, or dead person.

Plains Ledger Art

The Indigenous peoples of the Great Plains have a rich artistic tradition that, in the mid-nineteenth century, included a variety of different kinds of painting on bison and other animal hides. By convention, types of hide painting were apportioned by gender: women traditionally painted abstract, geometrical designs, while men painted representational art, including scenes of combat and hunting, depictions of important events such as treaty signings, renderings of supernatural visions, and pictorial calendars (known as winter counts) in which individual years were represented by pictograms.

Starting in the 1860s, as the United States began settling the Great Plains in earnest and clamping down on the autonomous existence of the region's Indigenous inhabitants, these artistic practices began to change dramatically. As the great bison herds of the Plains were systematically destroyed by industrial hunting, Indigenous artists largely had to shift from hides to paper, often taken from accounting ledger books—because of which this transitional art form has come to be called "ledger art." The content of this art changed as well. In addition to the conventional representation of hunting and warfare, Indigenous artists depicted the Euro-American people and technologies that were radically altering their way of life and environment, and they also began increasingly to portray rituals and other aspects of their daily life from before intensive Euro-American encroachment began, as a way of both documenting these threatened aspects of their traditional way of life and asserting continuity with a past from which official U.S. policy was striving to sever them. Similar aims also guided the Indigenous artists who revived ledger art in the 1960s and 70s and who continue to practice it into the twenty-first century.

As an art form that both depicts and was shaped by profound cultural and environmental change—including the near-eradication of bison that necessitated the use of ledger paper in the first place—Plains ledger art provides a rich record of how the Indigenous people of this region related to and used their environment before Euro-American intrusion into it, as well as of how they adapted to this environment's dramatic transformation.

Shave Head (O-uk-ste-uh), *Hunting Buffalo*, 1875–78. Shave Head, also known as John Wicks, was a Cheyenne man in his twenties who was one of seventy-two men and one woman from various Indigenous nations of the Great Plains (mainly Cheyenne, Kiowa, and Comanche) incarcerated at Fort Marion, Florida, from 1875 to 1878. During their imprisonment, the fort commander provided them with art supplies; twenty-six of the prisoners took up drawing, including Shave Head. In the image reproduced here, four Cheyenne warriors are depicted hunting a herd of bison (four of which have been wounded), while a fifth warrior above them is wounding a lone elk. All five warriors wear full headdresses, and four of them carry elaborate, symbolically powerful mountain lion bows and quivers, indicating the hunt's ceremonial importance.

BLACK HAWK, IMAGES FROM THE BLACK HAWK LEDGER (1880–81)

Black Hawk (Čhetáŋ Sápa' or Cetan Sapa, c. 1832–90)[1] was a medicine man and spiritual leader of the Sans Arc (Itázipčho) Lakota. During the very severe winter of 1880–81, William Edward Caton, a trader at the Cheyenne River reservation in what is now South Dakota, commissioned Black Hawk—who, according to Caton's son, "was in great straits," having "absolutely nothing, no food, and would not beg"—to create a series of drawings based on "a wonderful dream" Black Hawk was said to have had. Caton paid Black Hawk 50 cents per drawing (at the time, a generous compensation) and had the 76 completed drawings bound into a book; the collection was later lost and was not rediscovered until 1993. Black Hawk himself is believed to have been killed in the Wounded Knee Massacre in 1890.

The Black Hawk Ledger, as it is now called, contains depictions of warfare, rituals, and supernatural visions, and is regarded as a valuable visual record of Lakota religion and culture. The ledger also contains seventeen scenes of animal life, including the first image reproduced below. The view of non-human animals underlying such scenes is well described by the twentieth-century Lakota medicine man Archie Fire Lame Deer (Tȟáȟča Hušté): "all wild animals have power because Wakan Tanka [the Great Spirit] dwells in all of them, even in a tiny ant. The white man has built a wall between himself and that power. To understand what the animals are telling us needs time and patience, and the white man never has time."

The second image presented here, one of the ledger's many ceremonial depictions, portrays what has been described as a "buffalo transformation ceremony": a ritual in which members of a society of holy men called "Buffalo Dreamers" don bison masks, initiating a process whereby they are believed to acquire the animal's identity and power.

Black Hawk, *Great Horned Owls, Sandhill Crane, Crow.*

---

[1] *Black Hawk … 90* Not to be confused with Black Hawk (Mà-ka-tai-me-she-kià-kiàk [1767–1838]), the famous Sauk leader.

Black Hawk, *Buffalo Dreamers*.

GEORGE MOSES HORTON

c. 1797 – after 1867

George Moses Horton aptly summarized his own importance in American literary history in a letter he wrote in 1852: "I am the only public or recognized poet of color in my native state or perhaps in the union, born in slavery but yet craving that scope and expression whereby my literary labor of the night may be circulated throughout the whole world." Horton was not only one of the first published African American poets, but also the only one to have multiple volumes of poetry published while enslaved, arguably the first one to advocate openly for release from enslavement in his work, and the first black person to publish a book of any kind in the American South. In a literary career that spanned five decades, Horton explored a wide variety of subjects in an equally wide variety of verse forms and poetic styles, leaving behind a body of work that would be significant by any standard but is all the more so considering the circumstances in which it was produced. His poetry balances the conventional and the colloquial, the influence of the white-dominated literary canon and the poet's own experiences of racialization and enslavement, in a way that makes it a major contribution to the development of a distinctively American poetry in the mid-nineteenth century—a development that Horton advocated and in which he saw himself as an integral participant.

Horton was enslaved from his birth, in 1797 or 98, on the North Carolina estate of William Horton, a small tobacco farmer who, as was common, imposed his surname on the people he enslaved; the names of Horton's parents are unknown. As a child, Horton was put to work herding cattle, but he quickly exhibited an inclination toward books. He taught himself to read by acquiring "old parts of spelling books" and laboriously working through them in his free time on Sundays and by night. In his autobiographical introduction to his second poetry collection, which is one of the few sources of information about his life, Horton vividly describes this labor: "by close application to my book at night, my visage became considerably emaciated by extreme perspiration[.] … I had to sit sweating and smoking over my incompetent bark or brush light, almost exhausted by the heat of the fire, and almost suffocated with smoke." From spelling books, he moved on to the New Testament, Methodist hymns, and especially poetry. Soon, being able to read but not yet able to write, he was composing his own poetry in his head.

In the 1820s, Horton found a market for this skill at the University of North Carolina in Chapel Hill, where he would walk on Sundays from his enslaver's farm to sell produce. Horton quickly became acquainted with students at the university, who would frequently force him, as a prank, to deliver off-the-cuff speeches for them but also began paying him to compose poems to order. Horton came to specialize in acrostic poems on the names of his clients' love interests; he charged between 25 and 75 cents a poem and eventually was making three to four dollars a week—a considerable amount of money at the time. This income enabled him to buy his own time from his enslaver and spend more time in Chapel Hill. Some of the university students he knew gave him books, including works by Homer, Virgil, Shakespeare, Milton, and Byron, which influenced his emerging style. Horton's burgeoning literary career was further assisted by his friendship with Caroline Lee Hentz, the wife of a university faculty member, who helped him get his first poems into print in 1828. (Ironically, Hentz would later have her own literary career as a proslavery novelist.)

The wider attention these first publications won for Horton provided the impetus for his first collection, *The Hope of Liberty* (1829)—a booklet that appears to have been produced without Horton's participation, or possibly even his knowledge. The publisher of *The Hope of Liberty* was a member of the American Colonization Society (ACS), an organization that sought to resettle free black Americans in the African colony of Liberia; he seems to have had Horton's work distributed for free, in the hope of obtaining sufficient charitable contributions to buy Horton's freedom and send him to the colony. (It is unclear whether or not Horton himself, at this time, had any interest in emigrating to Liberia.) As the volume's title suggests, Horton's resistance to his enslavement and desire for release from it provide the collection's main theme, evident in poems such as "The Slave's Complaint" and "On Hearing of the Intention of a Gentleman to Purchase the Poet's Freedom." The collection also incorporates poems on numerous other topics, including love lyrics, reflections on nature, and religious meditations. Besides exhibiting Horton's range, this thematic variety helped make the collection publishable in North Carolina, as did the way in which, in his poems addressing enslavement, Horton concentrates on his personal situation and aspirations rather than condemning slavery more broadly. A more sustained and open poetic attack on slavery as an institution, especially coming from an author who was himself enslaved, would likely have been suppressed—and the volume's publisher appears to have edited Horton's more aggrieved or forceful descriptions of his condition accordingly. Even so, *The Hope of Liberty* did not garner enough contributions to the ACS to pay for Horton's freedom.

Instead, Horton's ambiguous life as an enslaved professional poet continued for another three-and-a-half decades. Although marriages between enslaved people were illegal, he married sometime in the 1830s and had two children. He also finally learned to write in the early 1830s and continued to hire his time from his enslaver, despite the fact that, during these years, North Carolina made it illegal to teach enslaved people to read and write—and illegal to allow them to buy their own time. The growing restrictions Horton faced in the 1830s and 40s, as slavery in North Carolina became ever more stringent, are indirectly reflected in his second collection, *The Poetical Works of George M. Horton* (1845). This volume was not an ACS venture, and Horton was actively involved in its publication, even penning an autobiographical introduction for it, but it shared the same goal as *The Hope of Liberty*: raising sufficient money to buy Horton out of enslavement. Unlike *The Hope of Liberty*, however, *The Poetical Works* contains hardly any direct references to slavery and nowhere openly expresses a desire for freedom. Such desire, though, can be glimpsed in Horton's treatment of other subjects, such as his celebration of the intellectual freedom enjoyed by the white students at UNC in "On the Pleasures of College Life." *The Poetical Works* also includes poems in a more colloquial style on such everyday topics as drinking, indebtedness, and itching skin, which Horton treats with humane detail and wry, often self-deprecating humor. This second collection once again demonstrates Horton's range and versatility, but it fell short of its financial goal.

Horton remained enslaved up until the arrival of Union troops in North Carolina in the spring of 1865, at the end of the Civil War. After his emancipation, Horton, then nearly seventy, became friends with a Union officer, William H.S. Banks, who sponsored the publication of Horton's third and final collection, *Naked Genius* (1865). Horton's newfound freedom enabled him to return, in these poems, to direct reflections on slavery and liberation, but the volume also expresses a sense of age and decline, as in "George Moses Horton, Myself," and a feeling of displacement, as in "The Southern Refugee." Subsequently, Horton went north to Philadelphia, where he published at least two more poems in local newspapers. He disappears from the historical record in 1866, and his ultimate fate is unknown. According to one testimony, he was still living in Philadelphia in 1883 and died later that year, but recent scholarship suggests that he ended up emigrating to Liberia after all, arriving in 1867 and likely dying there.

Horton was a strong defender of American literature and proponent of its further growth. As he wrote in an 1849 letter to a North Carolina newspaper, "I am for developing *our own* resources, and cherishing native genius. … Why *go abroad* for poetry when we have an infinitely superior article of domestic manufacture?" He went on to say that "I am too modest to speak of my own [poetry]" as a case in point, but he clearly did think of himself as an American poet who was playing a part in cultivating a "native" poetic canon. It took well over a century, however, for literary scholarship to see Horton in the way that he saw himself. In what is probably the last evaluation of Horton written during his lifetime, the Philadelphia *Evening Telegraph* described him in 1866 as "a profound and prolific writer" with "an intelligence, a bright intellectual fire, that would have made an imperishable name for him had he enjoyed the benefits of an ordinary education," but such positive, if patronizing, assessments of him did not long endure. Up through the 1960s, the few formal studies of Horton that were undertaken, all by white scholars, tended to be openly condescending and even racist in their treatment of him, acknowledging the significance of the fact that he wrote but largely dismissing the value of his work itself. Horton's rehabilitation began in the 1970s and is ongoing: new writing by him continues to be discovered in archival collections, and his critical reputation, together with appreciation of his importance to American literature, continues to grow. Horton is now increasingly recognized as one of the figures who helped bring mid-nineteenth-century American poetry into its own.

NOTE ON THE TEXTS: The texts of Horton's poems presented here are mainly based on the first editions of the three collections of Horton's poetry published in his lifetime. "The Lover's Farewell," "On Liberty and Slavery," "The Slave's Complaint," and "On Hearing of the Intention of a Gentleman to Purchase the Poet's Freedom" are based on the versions of these poems printed in *The Hope of Liberty* (1829); "The Fearful Traveller in the Haunted Castle," "Imploring to Be Resigned at Death," and "Division of an Estate" are based on the versions printed in *The Poetical Works of George M. Horton* (1845); and "George Moses Horton, Myself," "The Southern Refugee," "The Obstructions of Genius," and "Death of an Old Carriage Horse" are based on the versions printed in *Naked Genius* (1865). The text of "Lines to My —" is based on the version printed in the *Southern Literary Messenger* 9.4 (April 1843). The text of "For the Fair Miss M.M. McLean" is based on the manuscript of the poem held in the library of the University of North Carolina at Charlotte, a digitized version of which is available on the library's website. Spelling and punctuation have been modernized according to the practices of this anthology, except in the case of "For the Fair Miss M.M. McLean," in which the original spelling has been retained in order to assist in the reading of the accompanying manuscript facsimile.

⌘ ⌘ ⌘

The Lover's Farewell

And wilt thou, love, my soul display,
And all my secret thoughts betray?
I strove but could not hold thee fast,
My heart flies off with thee at last.

5   The favorite daughter of the dawn,
On love's mild breeze will soon be gone;
I strove, but could not cease to love,
Nor from my heart the weight remove.

And wilt thou, love, my soul beguile,
10 And gull° thy favorite with a smile?   trick, deceive
Nay, soft affection answers, nay,
And beauty wings my heart away.

I steal on tiptoe from these bowers,°   wooded enclosures
All spangled° with a thousand flowers;   adorned
15 I sigh, yet leave them all behind,
To gain the object of my mind.

And wilt thou, love, command my soul,
And waft° me with a light control?—   carry, propel
Adieu to all the blooms of May,
20 Farewell—I fly with love away!

I leave my parents here behind,
And all my friends—to love resigned—
'Tis grief to go, but death to stay:
Farewell—I'm gone with love away!
—1829

On Liberty and Slavery

Alas! and am I born for this,
To wear this slavish chain?
Deprived of all created bliss,
Through hardship, toil and pain!

5   How long have I in bondage lain,
And languished to be free!
Alas! and must I still complain—
Deprived of liberty.

Oh, Heaven! and is there no relief
10 This side the silent grave—
To soothe the pain—to quell the grief
And anguish of a slave?

Come Liberty, thou cheerful sound,
Roll through my ravished[1] ears!

---

[1]   *ravished*   Overwhelmed with delight or ecstasy; or, forcibly stolen.

15 Come, let my grief in joys be drowned,
    And drive away my fears.

    Say unto foul oppression, Cease:
    Ye tyrants rage no more,
    And let the joyful trump° of peace,   *trumpet*
20 Now bid the vassal soar.

    Soar on the pinions° of that dove   *wings*
    Which long has cooed for thee,
    And breathed her notes from Afric's° grove,   *Africa's*
    The sound of Liberty.

25 Oh, Liberty! thou golden prize,
    So often sought by blood—
    We crave thy sacred sun to rise,
    The gift of nature's God:[1]

    Bid Slavery hide her haggard face,
30 And barbarism fly:
    I scorn to see the sad disgrace
    In which enslaved I lie.

    Dear Liberty! upon thy breast,
    I languish to respire;°   *rest*
35 And like the swan unto her nest,
    I'd to thy smiles retire.

    Oh, blest asylum—heavenly balm!
    Unto thy boughs I flee—
    And in thy shades the storm shall calm,
40 With songs of Liberty!
    —1829

The Slave's Complaint

Am I sadly cast aside,
On misfortune's rugged° tide?   *stormy*
Will the world my pains deride
    Forever?

5   Must I dwell in Slavery's night,
    And all pleasure take its flight,

Far beyond my feeble sight,
    Forever?

Worst of all, must Hope grow dim,
10 And withhold her cheering beam?
    Rather let me sleep and dream
    Forever!

Something still my heart surveys,°   *perceives*
Groping through this dreary maze;
15 Is it Hope?—then burn and blaze
    Forever!

Leave me not a wretch confined,
Altogether lame and blind—
Unto gross[2] despair consigned,
20 Forever!

Heaven! in whom can I confide?
Canst thou not for all provide?
Condescend° to be my guide   *graciously consent*
    Forever:

25 And when this transient life shall end,
    Oh, may some kind eternal friend
    Bid me from servitude ascend,
    Forever!
    —1829

On Hearing of the Intention of a Gentleman to Purchase the Poet's Freedom

When on life's ocean first I spread my sail,
    I then implored° a mild auspicious gale;   *prayed to*
And from the slippery strand° I took my flight,   *shore*
And sought the peaceful haven° of delight.   *harbor*

5   Tyrannic storms arose upon my soul,
    And dreadful did their mad'ning[3] thunders roll;
    The pensive° muse[4] was shaken from her sphere, *anxious*
    And hope, it vanished in the clouds of fear.

---

[1] *nature's God* The introduction to the Declaration of Independence asserts that the American colonies are entitled to independence by "the Laws of Nature and of Nature's God."

[2] *gross* Enormous; thick; deep.

[3] *mad'ning* So overwhelming as to cause madness.

[4] *muse* Figure of inspiration for poetry or art, so called after the nine Muses, classical goddesses who presided over the arts and learning.

At length a golden sun broke through the gloom,
10   And from his smiles arose a sweet perfume—
A calm ensued, and birds began to sing,
And lo! the sacred muse resumed her wing.

With frantic° joy she chanted as she flew,   *delirious*
And kissed the clement° hand that bore her   *merciful*
    through
15   Her envious foes did from her sight retreat,
Or prostrate fall beneath her burning feet.

'Twas like a proselyte,° allied to Heaven—   *converted person*
Or rising spirits' boast of sins forgiven,
Whose shout dissolves the adamant[1] away
20   Whose melting[2] voice the stubborn rocks obey.

'Twas like the salutation of the dove,
Borne on the zephyr[3] through some lonesome grove,
When Spring returns, and Winter's chill is past,
And vegetation smiles above the blast.

25   'Twas like the evening of a nuptial pair,[4]
When love pervades the hour of sad despair—
'Twas like fair Helen's sweet return to Troy,
When every Grecian bosom swelled with joy.[5]

The silent harp which on the osiers° hung,   *willow trees*
30   Was then attuned,° and manumission[6] sung: *tuned*
Away by hope the clouds of fear were driven,
And music breathed my gratitude to Heaven.

Hard was the race to reach the distant goal,
The needle oft was shaken from the pole;[7]
35   In such distress, who could forbear to weep?[8]
Tossed by the headlong billows° of the deep!   *waves*

The tantalizing beams which shone so plain,
Which turned my former pleasures into pain—
Which falsely promised all the joys of fame,
40   Gave way, and to a more substantial flame.

Some philanthropic souls as from afar,
With pity strove to break the slavish bar;
To whom my floods of gratitude shall roll,
And yield with pleasure to their soft control.

45   And sure of Providence this work begun—
He shod my feet this rugged° race to run;   *strenuous*
And in despite° of all the swelling tide,   *defiance*
Along the dismal path will prove my guide.

Thus on the dusky° verge of deep despair,   *dark*
50   Eternal Providence was with me there;
When pleasure seemed to fade on life's gay dawn,
And the last beam of hope was almost gone.
—1829

Lines to My ——

I would be thine when morning breaks
    On my enraptured view;
When every star her tow'r forsakes
And every tuneful bird awakes,
5   And bids the night adieu.
I would be thine, when Phœbus[9] speeds
    His chariot up the sky,
Or on the heel of night he treads,
And through the heavens refulgence° spreads—   *radiance*
10   Thine would I live or die.

---

1   *adamant*   Stone or mineral of extraordinary hardness.

2   *melting*   I.e., causing to melt.

3   *zephyr*   West wind, synonymous with a gentle and pleasant breeze. In Greek mythology, Zephyrus, the god of the west wind, was considered to be the messenger of spring.

4   *nuptial pair*   Newly married couple.

5   *'Twas like … joy*   Horton's reference to the story of Helen and the Trojan War here seems muddled: according to the story, Helen was seduced away from her husband, the Greek king Menelaus, by the Trojan prince Paris, and the Greeks attacked Troy in order to win her back.

6   *manumission*   Release from enslavement.

7   *The needle … pole*   I.e., the compass needle was frequently driven to point in other directions than north (towards "the pole"). Many enslaved people in America escaped to northern free states, or further north to Canada.

8   *forbear to weep*   Refrain from weeping.

9   *Phœbus*   Name applied to the Greek god Apollo in his role as sun god. Each day, he drives the chariot of the sun across the sky.

I would be thine, thou fairest one,
    And hold thee as my boon,°   *gift, blessing*
When full the morning's race is run,
And half the fleeting day is gone,
15   Thine let me rest at noon.
I would be thine when evening's veil
    O'er-mantles all the plain,
When Cynthia[1] smiles on every dale,
And spreads like thee, her nightly sail
20   To dim the starry train.°   *procession*
Let me be thine, although I take
    My exit from this world;
And when the heavens with thunder shake,
And all the wheels of time shall break,
25   With globes to nothing hurled,
    I would be thine.
      —1843

The Fearful Traveller in the Haunted Castle

Oft do I hear those windows ope°   *open*
    And shut with dread surprise,
And spirits murmur as they grope,
    But break not on the eyes.

5 Still fancy° spies the winding sheet,[2]   *imagination*
    The phantom and the shroud,
And bids the pulse of horror beat
    Throughout my ears aloud.

Some unknown finger thumps the door,
    From one of faltering voice,
10 Till someone seems to walk the floor
    With an alarming noise.

The drum of horror holds her sound,
    Which will not let me sleep,
15 When ghastly breezes float around,
    And hidden goblins creep.

Methinks I hear some constant groan,
    The din of all the dead,

While trembling thus I lie alone,
20   Upon this restless bed.

At length the blaze of morning broke
    On my impatient view,
And truth or fancy told the joke,
    And bade the night adieu.

25 'Twas but the noise of prowling rats,
    Which ran with all their speed,
Pursued in haste by hungry cats,
    Which on the vermin feed.

The cat growled as she held her prey,
30   Which shrieked with all its might,
And drove the balm of sleep away
    Throughout the live-long night.

Those creatures crumbling off the cheese
    Which on the table lay;
35 Some cats, too quick the rogues to seize,
    With rumbling lost their prey.

Thus man is often his own elf,[3]
    Who makes the night his ghost,
And shrinks with horror from himself,
40   Which is to fear the most.
    —1845

Imploring to Be Resigned at Death

Let me die and not tremble at death,
    But smile at the close of my day,
And then at the flight of my breath,
    Like a bird of the morning in May,
5   Go chanting away.

Let me die without fear of the dead,
    No horrors my soul shall dismay,
And with faith's pillow under my head,
    With defiance to mortal decay,
10   Go chanting away.

Let me die like a son of the brave,
    And martial distinction display,

---

[1] *Cynthia* Classical goddess of the moon.
[2] *winding sheet* Burial shroud.

[3] *elf* Supernatural creature; demon.

Nor shrink from a thought of the grave,
   No, but with a smile from the clay,
15   Go chanting away.

Let me die glad, regardless of pain,
   No pang to this world to betray;
And the spirit cut loose from its chain,
   So loath° in the flesh to delay,   *unwilling*
20   Go chanting away.

Let me die, and my worst foe forgive,
   When death veils the last vital ray;[1]
Since I have but a moment to live,
   Let me, when the last debt I pay,
25   Go chanting away.
      —1845

Division of an Estate

It well bespeaks a man beheaded, quite
Divested of the laurel[2] robe of life,
When every member° struggles for its base,   *body part*
The head; the power of order now recedes,
5 Unheeded efforts rise on every side,
With dull emotion rolling through the brain
Of apprehending° slaves. The flocks and herds,   *fearful*
In sad confusion, now run to and fro,
And seem to ask, distressed, the reason why
10 That they are thus prostrated. Howl, ye dogs!
Ye cattle, low! ye sheep, astonished, bleat!
Ye bristling swine, trudge squealing through the glades,
Void of an owner to impart your food!
Sad horses, lift your heads and neigh aloud,
15 And caper frantic from the dismal scene;
Mow the last food upon your grass-clad lea,°   *pasture*
And leave a solitary home behind,
In hopeless widowhood no longer gay!
The trav'ling sun of gain his journey ends
20 In unavailing pain; he sets with tears;
A king sequestered[3] sinking from his throne,

Succeeded by a train° of busy friends,   *assembly, retinue*
Like stars which rise with smiles, to mark the flight
Of awful° Phoebus[4] to another world;   *awe-inspiring*
25 Stars after stars in fleet° succession rise   *swift*
Into the wide empire of fortune clear,
Regardless of the donor of their lamps,
Like heirs forgetful of parental care,
Without a grateful smile or filial tear,[5]
30 Redound in rev'rence to expiring age.
But soon parental benediction flies
Like vivid meteors; in a moment gone,
As though they ne'er had been. But O! the state,
The dark suspense in which poor vassals°   *slaves*
   stand, servants,
35 Each mind upon the spire of chance hangs fluctuant;
The day of separation is at hand;
Imagination lifts her gloomy curtains,
Like evening's mantle° at the flight of day,   *cloak*
Through which the trembling pinnacle we spy,
40 On which we soon must stand with hopeful smiles,
Or apprehending frowns; to tumble on
The right or left forever.[6]
      —1845

For the Fair Miss M.M. McLean
An Acrostic[7]

May this inspired acrostic prove
A perfect token of my love
Return thy torch allmost expired
Yet find by whom thou art admired

5 My soul of love would fly to thee
Constrained thy winning form to see

---

[1] *vital ray* Ray of life. Some nineteenth-century scientists claimed that living beings are animated by a "vital spark" that departs at death.

[2] *laurel* I.e., honored, distinguished. In ancient Greece and Rome, laurel wreaths were given in recognition of high achievement.

[3] *sequestered* Removed from office.

[4] *Phoebus* Name applied to the Greek god Apollo in his role as sun god. Each day, he drives the chariot of the sun across the sky.

[5] *filial tear* I.e., the tears befitting a child on the loss of their parent.

[6] *The right … forever* See Matthew Chapter 25.32–33, which describes how, in the Last Judgment, God will separate saved from damned souls "as a shepherd divideth his sheep from the goats: And he shall set the sheep on his right hand, but the goats on the left."

[7] Richard Allison Torrance, a student at the University of North Carolina in Chapel Hill, commissioned Horton to write this poem, which Horton signed in Torrance's name. The poem here appears in its original spelling, accompanied by a reproduction of the manuscript.

Like Pan[1] whose destiny was grief
Exploring nature for relief
And sure when thee my love has found
10   Nought els in life can heal the wound

When on the constelations
i cast my eyes afar
Then i can tell
My bonny° belle   *comely, beautiful*
15   The queen of every star

When i look from the mountain
Or nature's lofty tower
Then i can tell
My bonny belle
20   The queen of ever flower

When gazing from the window
On blooms both low and tall
Then i can tell
My charming belle
25   The fairest one of all
—c. 1854

George Moses Horton, Myself

I feel myself in need
Of the inspiring strains° of ancient lore,   *melodies*
My heart to lift, my empty mind to feed,
    And all the world explore.

5   I know that I am old
    And never can recover what is past,
But for the future may some light unfold
    And soar from ages blast.[2]

I feel resolved to try,
10   My wish to prove, my calling to pursue,
Or mount up from the earth into the sky,

To show what Heaven can do.
My genius[3] from a boy,
    Has fluttered like a bird within my heart;
15   But could not thus confined her powers employ,
    Impatient to depart.

She like a restless bird,
    Would spread her wing, her power to be unfurled,
And let her songs be loudly heard,
20   And dart from world to world.
—1865

The Southern Refugee

What sudden ill the world await,
    From my dear residence I roam;
I must deplore the bitter fate,
    To straggle from my native home.

5   The verdant° willow droops her head,   *green*
    And seems to bid a fare thee well;
The flowers with tears their fragrance shed,
    Alas! their parting tale to tell.

'Tis like the loss of Paradise,
10   Or Eden's garden left in gloom,
Where grief affords us no device,°   *plan*
    Such is thy lot, my native home.

I never, never shall forget,
    My sad departure far away,
15   Until the sun of life is set,
    And leaves behind no beam of day.

How can I from my seat remove
    And leave my ever devoted home,
And the dear garden which I love,
20   The beauty of my native home.

Alas! sequestered,° set aside,   *secluded, confiscated*
    It is a mournful tale to tell;

---

[1]   *Pan*   Ancient Greek god of the wild, shepherds and flocks, and rustic music, also frequently associated with sexuality. Several myths about him involve his unsuccessful pursuit of nymphs with whom he has become infatuated.

[2]   *ages blast*   I.e., blasted (withered or destroyed) ages.

[3]   *genius*   Attendant spirit that accompanies a soul from birth to death and shapes an individual's character; also, exceptional creative power or ability.

Manuscript page, "For the Fair Miss M.M. McLean," c. 1854.

'Tis like a lone deserted bride
    That bade her bridegroom fare thee well.

25 I trust I soon shall dry the tear
    And leave forever hence to roam,
Far from a residence so dear,
    The place of beauty—my native home.
    —1865

The Obstructions of Genius

I am surveyed by envy's eye,
    By white and colored all the same,
Which oft draws out a secret sigh,
    To feel the ills that bother fame.

5 Throughout my life I've tried the path,
    Which seemed as leading out of gloom,
Beneath my feet still kindled wrath,
    Genius seemed leading to a tomb.

No cultivating hand was found,
10   To urge[1] the night improving[2] slave,
Never by freedom's laurel crowned,[3]
    But pushed through hardship to the grave.

Has philanthropic vigor slept,
    So long in cells of disregard,
15 While genius in his fetters wept,
    Devoid of favors or reward?

They often fly to trivial pleas,
    To interdict° the important cause,   *prohibit, suppress*
To crush the negligent[4] disease,
20   And kill the force of humane laws.

---

[1] *urge* Stimulate; motivate.

[2] *night improving* Making full use of the night; or, improving oneself at night. In his autobiographical introduction to his 1845 collection *The Poetical Works of George M. Horton*, Horton describes how he devoted his nights as a boy to learning to read and the physical toll this took on him.

[3] *freedom's laurel crowned* Crowns of laurels were conferred upon poets in ancient Greece as a mark of honor.

[4] *negligent* Careless, especially in a way that is contrary to moral law.

Why did the Gods of Afric° sleep,   *Africa*
    Forgetful of their guardian love,
When the white traitors of the deep,°   *ocean*
    Betrayed him in the palmy grove?

25 Let us the evil now forget,
    Which darkened the Columbian shore,[5]
Till sun shall fail to rise and set,
    And slavery's cries are heard no more.
    —1865

Death of an Old Carriage Horse

I was a harness horse,
    Constrained to travel weak or strong,
With orders from oppressing force,
    Push along, push along.

5 I had no space of rest,
    And took at forks the roughest prong,
Still by the cruel driver pressed,
    Push along, push along.

Vain strove the idle bird
10 To charm me with her artless° song,   *simple, sincere*
But pleasure lingered from the word,
    Push along, push along.

The order of the day
    Was push, the peal of every tongue,
15 The only word was all the way,
    Push along, push along.

Thus to my journey's end,
    Had I to travel right or wrong,
'Till death, my sweet and favored friend,
20 Bade me from life to push along.
    —1865

---

[5] *Columbian shore* I.e., the United States, or the Americas more generally (the term is derived from Christopher Columbus).

John Brown

1800 – 1859

According to Frederick Douglass, John Brown was "the man of this nineteenth century." By taking up arms against slavery, first in Kansas Territory and then in a failed raid on Harpers Ferry, Virginia, Brown helped bring to a boiling point the long-simmering tensions between abolitionist and proslavery factions in America. Indeed, historians view his armed resistance as a key trigger of the Civil War,

nineteenth-century America's defining conflict. Cutting to the heart of the question sundering his country, Brown instantly became, and has always remained, an intensely polarizing figure. The passionately religious and deeply personal fervor of his abolitionism, and his conviction that armed struggle against slavery was necessary for its eradication, have led Brown's critics throughout history to characterize him as a violent, fanatical madman, but his advocates have viewed those same attributes as evidence of a perceptive, even visionary outlook, for it did take a terrible war to end slavery in America. Brown was an eloquent spokesperson for his cause—Ralph Waldo Emerson ranked his so-called "Last Speech" with the Gettysburg Address as "the two best specimens of eloquence we have had in this country"—but his vision was played out more fully in his actions, through which he sought to bring into being a rejuvenated America, free of slavery. As two modern scholars of Brown have put it, he had "a rich imagination—a sense of alternate reality more common to writers and artists than to militant political leaders." Not surprisingly, Brown captured the imaginations of many of the foremost literary figures of his era—Douglass, Emerson, Henry David Thoreau, Herman Melville, Walt Whitman, Lydia Maria Child, and John Greenleaf Whittier, to name a few—who responded powerfully to him in their own work.

Abolitionism was part of Brown's upbringing from his birth in Connecticut in 1800. His father, Owen Brown, was a stern New England Calvinist and a vocal opponent of slavery; after moving his family to Ohio in 1805, he operated a safe house on the Underground Railroad, as his son was also later to do. John Brown was educated at an abolitionist-run academy and briefly studied for the ministry before setting up as a tanner (his father's trade). In 1837, the widely-publicized murder of the antislavery clergyman and newspaper editor Elijah Lovejoy caused Brown to declare that "from this time, I consecrate my life to the destruction of slavery." As Brown became more involved in the national antislavery movement, however, he came to disagree with the white abolitionist establishment, whose commitment to emancipation through nonviolent persuasion he deemed "hopeless": he once voiced a desire that the leading abolitionist orators would have their tongues cut out, so that, being no longer able to say anything, they would be forced to "do something." Instead, Brown preferred to align himself with black abolitionists and formerly enslaved people, whose stake in the struggle against slavery was more personal and urgent. He drew inspiration particularly from the ideas and tactics of black revolutionaries such as Nat Turner, Joseph Cinqué, and Toussaint L'Ouverture.

Brown first acted on these ideas amid the civil strife between pro- and antislavery settlers in the Kansas Territory in the 1850s, a period that became known as "Bleeding Kansas." Brown moved to Kansas in 1855, after learning about the apparent helplessness of the antislavery settlers (known as Free-Staters) in the face of proslavery violence. This aggression came to a head on 21 May 1856, when proslavery raiders sacked the Free-State town of Lawrence. To avenge the raid and pre-empt further such attacks, Brown and his followers, including four of his sons, murdered five proslavery settlers at Pottawatomie Creek on the night of 23–24 May. The brutality of these killings, and Brown's role in and motivation for them, remain a source of controversy. Brown went on to stage a brave but unsuccessful defense of the Free-State town of Osawatomie against a much larger proslavery force, and by late 1856 his actions in Kansas had gained him nationwide prominence.

After returning east in the autumn of 1856, Brown began enlisting support for a more ambitious plan. He proposed establishing a guerilla force in the Appalachian Mountains of western Virginia, modeled on the "Maroon" communities of fugitive blacks in the Caribbean, which would stage raids into the surrounding lowlands to free enslaved people. Brown maintained that as more and more enslaved people joined this group, and as other groups sprang up to emulate it, the whole slave system would eventually break down. As part of the preparation for this plan, and while staying in the home of Frederick Douglass, Brown wrote a "Provisional Constitution" that would govern his guerilla organization and provide the basis for a new government for the United States in the wake of slavery's collapse. The constitution condemned slavery as a betrayal of the country's founding ideals and as an institutionalization of a state of war between one group of citizens and another. It also set forth a vision of a new society organized on egalitarian and explicitly religious principles, in which "filthy conversation" would be forbidden, the Sabbath universally observed, all property held in common, and all people—male and female alike—encouraged to bear arms and to "labor in some way for the general good." (Brown practiced what he preached in his own household, requiring his sons as well as his daughters—he had a total of twenty children by two marriages—to share in domestic chores.) The constitution helped Brown raise funding from white abolitionist backers, but his plans were viewed with skepticism by Douglass, who believed the scheme was doomed by Brown's lack of firsthand acquaintance with the region and the enslaved people living there.

Douglass's fears came to pass when Brown and his followers launched their plan on 16 October 1859 with a raid on Harpers Ferry, Virginia, which housed a federal armory from which Brown intended to equip the enslaved people he believed would join him. Brown's party seized the armory and took hostages (whom he treated well, including ordering them breakfast from the town's hotel) but was cut off and surrounded by local militia and then by U.S. Marines, who crushed the raiders and captured Brown on 18 October. The raid resulted in seventeen deaths, including Brown's sons Watson and Oliver and eight others from Brown's party, and electrified the nation, as did Brown's subsequent trial by the state of Virginia for murder, treason, and incitement of slave insurrection. Brown refused his defense team's attempt to present his provisional constitution as evidence of his insanity, and in his "Last Speech," after being found guilty on all counts, he denied any criminal intent, defended his actions as motivated by the Golden Rule, and declared himself ready to die a martyr for his cause. He held to this intention up to his execution on 2 December 1859, rejecting a friend's attempt to spring him from jail. On his way to be hanged, he handed one of his jailers a note: "I, John Brown, am now quite certain that the crimes of this guilty land will never be purged away but with blood."

Brown and his actions immediately inspired contradictory interpretations and have remained divisive ever since. Opponents of abolition viewed Brown as, in Nathaniel Hawthorne's words, a "blood-stained fanatic," and the Harpers Ferry raid caused panic about potential slave revolts throughout the South, convincing many Southerners that Northern abolitionism threatened not just their livelihoods but their lives. Conversely, Northern abolitionists—including many committed to pacifism—came to hail Brown as a Christ-like martyr: Emerson said that Brown's hanging would "make the gallows glorious like the cross," while Thoreau called him "meteor-like, flashing through the darkness in which we live." (Later, Whitman and Melville both wrote poems about Brown's execution in which they echoed Thoreau's meteor image.) As the nation careened toward civil war, these competing interpretations of Brown made him an ongoing force; in the words of the "John Brown Song," popular in the Union during the war and later rewritten by poet Julia Ward Howe as "The Battle Hymn of the Republic," Brown's "soul" kept "marching on."

In the late nineteenth and early twentieth centuries, many white Americans embraced a view of the Civil War as a tragic, unnecessary fratricide, and the depiction of Brown as an unhinged perpetrator of needless violence accordingly became dominant. Later in the twentieth century, Brown was variously praised and condemned all across the political spectrum: he has been claimed as a model for revolutionary armed resistance by the right-wing terrorist Timothy McVeigh and the left-wing Weather Underground group, and castigated as a progenitor of American domestic terrorism by mainstream and extremist voices alike. Many African American activists, from Harriet Tubman to W.E.B. Du Bois to Malcolm X, have seen Brown as a clear-eyed opponent of the systemic, state-supported terrorism that was slavery. Present-day scholarship continues to debate Brown and his legacy, paying particular attention to his provisional constitution as an important landmark in a long history of grassroots American attempts to change what the country was and re-envision what it could be.

NOTE ON THE TEXT: The text included here of "John Brown's Last Speech" is based on the transcript printed in the *New York Herald* on 3 November 1859; the text of the speech included in *John Brown's Trial*, by Brian McGinty (2009), was also consulted. Spelling and punctuation have been modernized in accordance with the practices of this anthology.

⌘ ⌘ ⌘

John Brown's Last Speech[1]

I have, may it please the Court, a few words to say.

In the first place, I deny everything but what I have all along admitted, of a design on my part to free slaves. I intended certainly to have made a clean thing of that matter, as I did last winter, when I went into Missouri, and there took slaves without the snapping of a gun on either side, moving them through the country, and finally leaving them in Canada.[2] I designed to have done the same thing again on a larger scale. That was all I intended. I never did intend murder or treason, or the destruction of property, or to excite or incite slaves to rebellion, or to make insurrection.[3]

I have another objection, and that is that it is unjust that I should suffer such a penalty. Had I interfered in the manner in which I admit, and which I admit has been fairly proved—for I admire the truthfulness and candor of the greater portion of the witnesses who have testified in this case—had I so interfered in behalf of the rich, the powerful, the intelligent, the so-called great, or in behalf of any of their friends, either father, mother, brother, sister, wife or children, or any of that class, and suffered and sacrificed what I have in this interference, it would have been all right; every man in this court would have deemed it an act worthy of reward rather than punishment.

This court acknowledges, too, as I suppose, the validity of the law of God. I see a book kissed, which I suppose to be the Bible, or at least the New Testament, which teaches me that all things whatsoever I would that men should do to me, I should do even so to them.[4] It teaches me, further, to remember them that are in bonds, as bound with them.[5] I endeavored to act up to that instruction. I say I am yet too young to understand that God is any respecter of persons. I believe that to have interfered as I have done, as I

[1] Brown gave this speech in court before being sentenced to death on 2 November 1859 on charges of murder, treason, and inciting a slave insurrection resulting from his raid on Harpers Ferry, Virginia. He had just been invited by the clerk of the court to "say why sentence should not be pronounced upon him." The extent to which Brown had prepared the speech in advance is not clear; in a subsequent letter, he claimed that "I was taken wholly by surprise" by the clerk's invitation. According to some eyewitnesses, Brown spoke "timidly—hesitatingly, indeed," but others found him "composed" and judged that he spoke "with perfect calmness of voice and mildness of manner." Newspaper reporters transcribed his words as he spoke, and in the ensuing days they were widely printed around the country.

[2] *as I did ... Canada* Brown refers here to a raid he led into the slave state of Missouri in December 1858, during which his party liberated eleven enslaved people and led them to Canada. Contrary to Brown's assertion, this raid was not entirely free of violence, as one enslaver was killed during it.

[3] *I never ... insurrection* This claim led hostile observers to accuse Brown of lying, since aiding enslaved people to revolt was his avowed

purpose in undertaking the Harpers Ferry raid. When Brown's prosecuting attorney pointed out this contradiction to him during the month between Brown's trial and execution, Brown replied in a letter that, in the "hurry of the moment" when he was called on to speak, he "did not consider the full bearing of what I then said." He went on to admit that his aim at Harpers Ferry had in fact been to arm enslaved people in the South rather than to "run them out of the slave States."

[4] *all things ... them* See Matthew 7.12.

[5] *remember ... them* See Hebrews 13.3.

have always freely admitted I have done, in behalf of His despised poor, is no wrong, but right. Now, if it is deemed necessary that I should forfeit my life for the furtherance of the ends of justice, and mingle my blood further with the blood of my children[1] and with the blood of millions in this slave country, whose rights are disregarded by wicked, cruel, and unjust enactments, I say let it be done.

Let me say one word further. I feel entirely satisfied with the treatment I have received on my trial. Considering all the circumstances, it has been more generous than I expected; but I feel no consciousness of guilt. I have stated from the first what was my intention and what was not. I never had any design against the liberty of any person, nor any disposition to commit treason or excite slaves to rebel or make any general insurrection. I never encouraged any man to do so, but always discouraged any idea of that kind.

Let me say also, in regard to the statements made by some of those who were connected with me. I fear it has been stated by some of them that I have induced them to join me, but the contrary is true. I do not say this to injure them, but as regretting their weakness. Not one joined me but of his own accord, and the greater part of them at their own expense. A number of them I never saw and never had a word of conversation with till the day they came to me, and that was for the purpose I have stated.

Now, I have done.

—1859

---

[1] *the blood of my children*   Two of Brown's sons had been killed when federal troops put down his Harpers Ferry raid; another son had been killed by proslavery militia in Kansas three years earlier.

Jane Johnston Schoolcraft /
Bamewawagezhikaquay
1800 – 1842

Bamewawagezhikaquay, also known as Jane Johnston Schoolcraft, translated her Ojibwe name into English as "Woman of the Sound the Stars Make Rushing through the Sky." A Métis writer well-educated in both Ojibwe and British traditions, she created a sophisticated body of writing that is at once Métis, Ojibwe, and Euro-American in its content and style. She wrote formal English poetry, translations of traditional Ojibwe stories and love songs, and original poetry in Ojibwe—the first poetry known to have been composed in writing by an Indigenous author in an Indigenous language. Although little of her work was formally published in her lifetime, and her career was overshadowed by that of her husband, the ethnographer Henry Rowe Schoolcraft, her significance is coming to be appreciated in the twenty-first century.

Schoolcraft was born Jane Johnston in Sault Ste. Marie, in what is now the state of Michigan's upper peninsula, in 1800. Her mother, Ozhaguscodaywayquay, also known as Susan Johnston, was part of a prominent Ojibwe family; her father, John Johnston, was a Scotch-Irish trader. Schoolcraft was thus born into a Métis culture—a midwestern culture blending Indigenous, French, and Anglo ancestries and traditions—that was already well established in the area. Each of her parents preserved their own traditions and languages, and Schoolcraft and her seven siblings all received thorough Ojibwe- and English-language educations at home, where their father amassed an unusually extensive library of literature, theology, and history (despite their rural location, the family owned about a thousand books). Schoolcraft traveled to Ireland in 1809 and may have received a few months of formal schooling there, but a change in the family's finances prompted an early return to the Sault in 1810.

Schoolcraft probably began to write literature in her teens, and continued to write for most of her life; her oldest surviving dated poem was completed when she was fifteen years old. Many poems appear only in Ojibwe or, more often, English, while in some cases she composed the same content in English and Ojibwe versions. Most of her English poetry employs the formal conventions and style of Euro-American Romanticism; her Ojibwe poetry, on the other hand, tends to use formal techniques drawn from Ojibwe oral traditions. While her translations of Ojibwe traditional songs are sometimes literal, without a new poetic form imposed, others adapt the content to the Euro-American verse forms that Schoolcraft's English-language readers would have recognized as poetry. Similarly, Schoolcraft appears to have varied her approach to the translation of traditional Ojibwe stories. Some appear to preserve the original narrative structure, giving the impression of a direct translation, while others are creative adaptations employing the tone and structure of Euro-American folk stories, suggesting the influence of the Brothers Grimm and other Romantic-era collectors of folk and fairytales.

Schoolcraft's work was deeply entwined with her husband's. She met Henry Rowe Schoolcraft in 1822 when he came to the Sault as a United States Indian agent; they were married in 1823. They had four children, though the eldest, William, died before age three. As writers, she and Henry had a complex and mutually influential relationship: her expertise shaped much of the ethnographic work on Indigenous peoples that made him famous, and he encouraged and preserved her writing—some of which he published, often without clear attribution, as part of his own books. Henry, whose attitude toward Native Americans was generally condescending, appears to have enjoyed his wife's combination of Indigeneity and Euro-American refinement; in his *Personal Memoirs* (1851), he describes their reception during a 1824–25 trip to New York as "something like a sensation in every circle," observing that many wanted "to see the northern Pocahontas" who was educated, had traveled abroad, and wrote with "grammatical skill and taste." Henry's commentary offers a glimpse of the patronizing, exoticizing attitudes Schoolcraft often faced at home and abroad.

During her lifetime, Jane Schoolcraft's work appeared only once in a "publication" under her own name. This was in a handwritten magazine edited by Henry during the winter of 1826–27, which he titled *The Muzzeniegun, or Literary Voyager*. The *Muzzeniegun* (Ojibwe: "book") circulated among their friends, and it included at least nine poems and five Ojibwe stories by Jane (some appearing under pseudonyms), including the poem "By an Ojibwa Female Pen," the story "Mishōsha, or the Magician and His Daughters," and poems about her eldest son's death. One recipient, the Schoolcrafts' friend Charles Christopher Trowbridge, praised "the pathos of style and the singular felicity of expression" of Schoolcraft's poem "To My Ever Beloved & Lamented Son William Henry" and asked for permission to have it published, but his request appears to have been declined.

In 1833, the Schoolcrafts moved to Michigan's Mackinac Island, separating Jane Schoolcraft from her mother and siblings. Henry, who became Superintendent of Indian Affairs for Michigan in 1836, began to travel more extensively to support his political career (which included the negotiation of a treaty that deprived the Ojibwe of a vast portion of their land). In a letter to her husband, Schoolcraft describes herself as "chained at home … like a domestic bear, who ever & anon, growls out his dissatisfaction at his circumscribed limits." During this period, she was also frequently ill and became addicted to the opium mixture doctors prescribed to treat her pain.

In 1839, Henry published some of Jane's English versions of traditional Ojibwe oral stories in the collection *Algic Researches*. He did not identify her translations specifically—though he did acknowledge "Mrs. Henry R. Schoolcraft" as one of the volume's contributors—and she may have been involved in the preparation of the rest of the book as well. After Henry was dismissed from his role as superintendent, the Schoolcrafts moved to New York City to start afresh in 1841. The following year, Jane Schoolcraft died unexpectedly while visiting her sister in Dundas, a town in what is now Ontario, Canada. The writer Margaret Fuller, a friend of the Schoolcrafts, lamented that "by the premature death of Mrs. Schoolcraft was lost a mine of poesy, to which few had access."

After Schoolcraft's death, her husband continued to publish her work—generally in his own books and periodicals, though with some direct acknowledgment of her authorship. He also gathered a collection of her poetry that appears to have been intended for publication but was never printed. He did, however, save much of her work in manuscript form, and it would probably not have survived if not for its inclusion in archive collections dedicated to his writings. Though some of these materials are in her handwriting, many more were copied out by Henry and probably revised by him. Because he is known to have freely intervened in the revision and translation of her work—and whether he did so with or without her approval is unclear—it is often difficult to determine how closely the surviving documents reflect their original author's intentions.

For a century, Schoolcraft's importance was barely acknowledged in print, though her work in *Algic Researches* would exert a significant influence on Henry Wadsworth Longfellow's famous poem *The Song of Hiawatha* (1855). She began to receive some recognition in 1962, when Philip P. Mason edited a print edition of *Literary Voyager*, which included footnotes clarifying the extent of her contributions. No collection dedicated to her writing was released until 2007, when the scholar Robert Dale Parker collected her work in *The Sound the Stars Make Rushing through the Sky: The Writings of Jane Johnston Schoolcraft*. Parker's recovery efforts brought Schoolcraft to broader attention and quickly established her as a writer of significance, important not only for her erudition in multiple languages and traditions but also for her skill and versatility as a poet and storyteller.

NOTE ON THE TEXTS: The following texts are based upon those appearing in Robert Dale Parker's collection of Schoolcraft's writings, *The Sound the Stars Make Rushing through the Sky* (2007); the original sources employed by Parker are noted in footnotes at the beginning of each text. In Schoolcraft's time, Ojibwe did not yet have a standardized orthography, and her work in Ojibwe thus employs spelling and word divisions that differ significantly from those of the present day. Her original spellings have been preserved in the Ojibwe texts, while the English texts have been modernized in accordance with the practices of this anthology.

⌘ ⌘ ⌘

To the Pine Tree

*on first seeing it
on returning from Europe*[1]

Shing wauk! Shing wauk! nin ge ik id,
Waish kee wau bum ug, shing wauk
Tuh quish in aun nau aub, ain dak nuk i yaun.
Shing wauk, shing wauk No sa
5 Shi e gwuh ke do dis au naun
Kau gega way zhau wus co zid.

Mes ah nah, shi egwuh tah gwish en aung
Sin da mik ke aum baun
Kag ait suh, ne meen wain dum
10 Me nah wau, wau bun dah maun
Gi yut wi au, wau bun dah maun een
Shing wauk, shing wauk nosa
Shi e gwuh ke do dis au naun.

Ka ween ga go, kau wau bun duh e yun
15 Tib isht co, izz henau gooz ze no an
Shing wauk wah zhau wush co zid
Ween Ait ah kwanaudj e we we
Kau ge gay wa zhau soush ko zid
—2007 (WRITTEN 1822–40)

Translation[2]

The pine! the pine! I eager cried,
The pine, my father! see it stand,
As first that cherished tree I spied,
Returning to my native land.
5 The pine! the pine! oh lovely scene!
The pine, that is forever green.

Ah beauteous tree! ah happy sight!
That greets me on my native strand°   shore
And hails me, with a friend's delight,
10 To my own dear bright mother land
Oh 'tis to me a heart-sweet scene,
The pine—the pine! that's ever green.

Not all the trees of England bright,
Not Erin's° lawns of green and light   Ireland's
15 Are half so sweet to memory's eye,
As this dear type of northern sky
Oh 'tis to me a heart-sweet scene,
The pine—the pine! that ever green.
—2007 (WRITTEN 1822–40)

---

[1] *returning from Europe*   Schoolcraft visited Ireland and England with her father in 1809, returning to her native North America in 1810.

[2] The translation reprinted here is Schoolcraft's own.

The Contrast[1]

With pen in hand, I shall contrast,
    The present moments with the past
And mark difference, not by grains,
But weighed by feelings, joys and pains.
5 Calm, tranquil—far from fashion's gaze,
Passed all my earliest, happy days
Sweetly flew the golden hours,
In St. Mary's woodland bowers
Or my father's simple hall,
10 Oped° to whomsoe'er might call   *opened*
Pains or cares we seldom knew
All the hours so peaceful flew
Concerts sweet we oft enjoyed,
Books our leisure time employed
15 Friends on every side appeared
From whose minds no ill I feared
If by chance, one gave me pain
The wish to wound me not again
Quick expressed in accents kind
20 Cast a joy throughout my mind
That, to have been a moment pained,
Seemed like bliss but just attained.
Whene'er in fault, to be reproved,
With gratitude my heart was moved,
25 So mild and gentle were their words
It seemed as soft as song of birds
For well I knew, that each behest,
Was warmed by love—convincing test.

     Thus passed the morning of my days,
30 My only wish, to gain the praise
Of friends I loved, and neighbours kind,
And keep a calm and heavenly mind.
My efforts, kindly were received,
Nor grieved, nor was myself aggrieved.
35 But ah! how changed is every scene,
Our little hamlet, and the green,
The long rich green, where warriors played,
And often, breezy elm-wood shade.
How changed, since full of strife and fear,
40 The world hath sent its votaries here.

The tree cut down—the cot° removed,   *cottage*
The cot the simple Indian loved,
The busy strife of young and old
To gain one sordid bit of gold
45 By trade's o'er done plethoric moil,[2]
And lawsuits, meetings, courts and toil.

Adieu, to days of homebred ease,
When many a rural care could please,
We trim our sail[3] anew, to steer
50 By shoals we never knew were here,
And with the star flag, raised on high
Discover a new dominion nigh,
And half in joy, half in fear,
Welcome the proud Republic here.[4]
—2007 (WRITTEN AFTER 1823)

By an Ojibwa Female Pen[5]

*Invitation to sisters to a walk in the Garden, after a
  shower*

Come, sisters come! the shower's past,
    The garden walks are drying fast,
The Sun's bright beams are seen again,
And nought within, can now detain.
5 The rain drops tremble on the leaves,
Or drip expiring, from the eaves;
But soon the cool and balmy air,

---

[1] An earlier version of this poem, dated March 1823, has a different
title. This version is from a bound manuscript of Schoolcraft's poems
prepared by her husband after her death.

[2] *plethoric moil* Excessive hard work.

[3] *trim our sail* To trim a ship's sail is to adjust its position to
adapt to changes in the wind.

[4] *Discover a new ... Republic here* Although Indigenous peoples
had gathered in the area for thousands of years, the growing French
settlement of Sault Ste. Marie was given its European name in 1688;
its strategic location made the river a site of conflict between the
British and French into the nineteenth century. The Treaty of the
Sault (1820) turned control of the area over to the United States in
1823, with Fort Brady built to protect it from British invasions from
Canada; *proud Republic* United States.

[5] This poem appeared in the first issue of *The Muzzeniegun, or
Literary Voyager*, a handwritten manuscript magazine edited by
Henry Rowe Schoolcraft in 1826 and 1827, under the pseud-
onym "Rosa." This magazine seems to have circulated among the
Schoolcrafts' friends in the region, and the poem was not formally
published until 1962.

Shall dry the gems that sparkle there,
With whisp'ring breath shake ev'ry spray,
10 And scatter every cloud away.

Thus sisters! shall the breeze of hope,
Through sorrow's clouds a vista ope;°   open
Thus, shall affliction's surly blast,
By faith's bright calm be stilled at last;
15 Thus, pain and care—the tear and sigh,
Be chased from every dewy eye;
And life's mixed scene itself, but cease,
To show us realms of light and peace.
—1962 (WRITTEN BEFORE 1826)

To My Ever Beloved and Lamented Son
William Henry[1]

Who was it, nestled on my breast,
"And on my cheek sweet kisses prest"[2]
And in whose smile I felt so blest?
                              Sweet Willy.
5 Who hailed my form as home I stept,
And in my arms so eager leapt,
And to my bosom joyous crept?
                              My Willy.
Who was it, wiped my tearful eye,
10 And kissed away the coming sigh,
And smiling bid me say "good boy"?
                              Sweet Willy.
Who was it, looked divinely fair,
Whilst lisping sweet the evening prayer,
15 Guileless and free from earthly care?
                              My Willy.
Whither has fled the rose's hue?
The lily's whiteness blending grew,
Upon thy cheek—so fair to view.
20   My Willy.
Oft have I gazed with rapt delight,
Upon those eyes that sparkled bright,

Emitting beams of joy and light!
                              Sweet Willy.
25 Oft have I kissed that forehead high,
Like polished marble to the eye,
And blessing, breathed an anxious sigh.
                              For Willy.
My son! Thy coral lips are pale,
30 Can I believe the heart-sick tale,
That I, thy loss must ever wail?
                              My Willy.
The clouds in darkness seemed to low'r,
The storm has passed with awful pow'r,
35 And nipped my tender, beauteous flow'r!
                              Sweet Willy.
But soon my spirit will be free,
And I, my lovely son shall see,
For God, I know, did this decree!
40   My Willy.
—1827

Mishösha, or the Magician and His Daughters[3]
A Chippewa Tale or Legend

In an early age of the world, when there were fewer inhabitants in the earth than there now are, there lived an Indian, who had a wife and two children, in a remote situation. Buried in the solitude of the forest, it was not often that he saw any one, out of the circle of his own family. Such a situation seemed favorable for his pursuits; and his life passed on in uninterrupted happiness, till he discovered a wanton disposition in his wife.

---

1   *William Henry*   Schoolcraft's son, who was less than three years old when he died of croup in 1827.

2   *And on … prest*   From English poet Ann Taylor's "My Mother" (1804), a popular poem in which a child praises its mother. Schoolcraft here employs the same form as Taylor's poem but replaces the original refrain, "My mother," with "My Willy" or "Sweet Willy."

3   The first part of this tale, signed "Bame-wa-wa-ge-zhik-a-quay," appeared in the January 1827 issue of *The Muzzeniegun, or Literary Voyager*, a manuscript magazine edited by Henry Rowe Schoolcraft; the following issue, presumably with its ending, has not survived. Another version, with the elder brother named Panigwun, appears in Henry's *Algic Researches* (1839) and *The Myth of Hiawatha, and Other Oral Legends, Mythologic and Allegoric, of the North American Indians* (1856). The version included here follows Robert Dale Parker in reprinting the first half of the narrative from the surviving *Muzzeniegun* text and the second half from a manuscript version transcribed by Jane's brother William Johnston; these versions appear to be closer to the author's intentions than other versions of the story.

This woman secretly cherished a passion for a young man whom she accidentally met in the woods, and she lost no opportunity of courting his approaches. She even planned the death of her husband, who, she justly concluded, would put her to death, should he discover her infidelity. But this design was frustrated by the alertness of the husband, who having cause to suspect her, determined to watch narrowly, to ascertain the truth, before he should come to a determination how to act. He followed her silently one day, at a distance, and hid himself behind a tree. He soon beheld a tall, handsome man approach his wife, and lead her away.

He was now convinced of her crime, and thought of killing her the moment she returned. In the meantime he went home and pondered on his situation. At last he came to the determination of leaving her forever, thinking that her own conscience would, in the end, punish her sufficiently; and relying on her maternal feelings to take care of the two boys, whom he determined to leave behind.

When the wife returned, she was disappointed in not finding her husband, having concerted a plan to dispatch him. When she saw that day after day passed, and he did not return, she at last guessed the true cause of his absence. She then returned to her paramour, leaving the two helpless boys behind, telling them that she was going a short distance and would return; but determined never to see them more.

The children thus abandoned, soon made way with the food that was left in the lodge, and were compelled to quit[1] it, in search of more. The eldest boy possessed much intrepidity, as well as great tenderness for his little brother, frequently carrying him when he became weary, and gathering all the wild fruit he saw. Thus they went deeper into the forest, soon losing all traces of their former habitation, till they were completely lost in the labyrinths of the wilderness.

The elder boy fortunately had a knife, with which he made a bow and arrows, and was thus enabled to kill a few birds for himself and [his] brother. In this way they lived some time, still pressing on, they knew not whither. At last they saw an opening through the woods and were shortly after delighted to find themselves on the borders of a broad lake. Here the elder boy busied himself in picking the seed pods of the wild rose. In

the meanwhile the younger amused himself by shooting some arrows into the sand, one of which happened to fall into the lake. The elder brother, not willing to lose his time in making another, waded into the water to reach it. Just as he was about to grasp the arrow, a canoe passed by him with the rapidity of lightning. An old man, sitting in the centre, seized the affrighted youth and placed him in the canoe. In vain the boy addressed him. "My grandfather" (a term of respect for old people) "pray take my little brother also. Alone, I cannot go with you; he will starve if I leave him." The old magician (for such was his real character) laughed at him. Then giving his canoe a slap, and commanding it to go, it glided through the water with inconceivable swiftness. In a few minutes they reached the habitation of Mishösha, standing on an island in the centre of the lake. Here he lived, with his two daughters, the terror of all the surrounding country.

Leading the young man up to the lodge, "Here my eldest daughter," said he, "I have brought a young man who shall become your husband." The youth saw surprise depicted in the countenance of the daughter, but she made no reply, seeming thereby to acquiesce in the commands of her father. In the evening he overheard the daughters in conversation. "There again": said the elder daughter, "our father has brought another victim, under the pretence of giving me a husband. When will his enmity to the human race cease; or when shall we be spared witnessing such scenes of vice and wickedness as we are daily compelled to behold."

When the old magician was asleep, the youth told the elder daughter how he had been carried off and compelled to leave his helpless brother on the shore. She told him to get up and take her father's canoe, and using the charm he had observed, it would carry him quickly to his brother. That he could carry him food, prepare a lodge for him, and return by morning. He did in everything as he had been directed, and after providing for the subsistence of his brother, told him that in a short time he should come for him. Then returning to the enchanted island, resumed his place in the lodge before the magician awoke. Once during the night Mishösha awoke, and not seeing his son-in-law, asked his eldest daughter what had become of him. She replied that he had merely stepped out, and would be back soon. This satisfied him. In the morning, finding

---

[1]   *quit* Leave.

the young man in the lodge, his suspicions were completely lulled. "I see, my daughter, you have told me the truth."

As soon as the sun rose, Mishösha thus addressed the young man. "Come, my son, I have a mind to gather gulls' eggs. I am acquainted with an island where there are great quantities; and I wish your aid in gathering them." The young man saw no reasonable excuse, and getting into the canoe, the magician gave it a slap, and bidding it go, in an instant they were at the island. They found the shore covered with gulls' eggs, and the island surrounded with birds of this kind. "Go, my son," said the old man, "and gather them while I remain in the canoe." But the young man was no sooner ashore than Mishösha pushed his canoe a little from land and exclaimed: "Listen ye gulls: you have long expected something from me. I now give you an offering. Fly down, and devour him." Then striking his canoe, left the young man to his fate.

The birds immediately came in clouds around their victim, darkening all the air with their numbers. But the youth, seizing the first that came near him, and drawing his knife, cut off its head, and immediately skinning the bird, hung the feathers as a trophy on his breast. "Thus," he exclaimed, "will I treat every one of you who approaches me. Forbear, therefore, and listen to my words. It is not for you to eat human food.[1] You have been given by the Great Spirit as food for man. Neither is it in the power of that old magician to do you any good. Take me on your beaks and carry me to his lodge, and you shall see that I am not ungrateful."

The gulls obeyed, collecting in a cloud for him to rest upon, and quickly flew to the lodge, where they arrived before the magician. The daughters were surprised at his return, but Mishösha conducted as if nothing extraordinary had taken place.

On the following day he again addressed the youth. "Come, my son," said he. "I will take you to an island covered with the most beautiful pebbles, looking like silver. I wish you to assist me in gathering some of them. They will make handsome ornaments, and are possessed of great virtues."[2] Entering the canoe, the magician made use of his charm, and they were carried in a few moments to a solitary bay in an island, where there was a smooth sandy beach. The young man went ashore as usual. "A little further, a little further," cried the old man. "Up on that rock you will get some finer ones." Then pushing his canoe from land, "Come thou great king of fishes," cried he, "you have long expected an offering from me. Come, and eat the stranger I have put ashore on your island." So saying, he commanded his canoe to return, and was soon out of sight. Immediately a monstrous fish shoved his long snout from the water, moving partially on the beach, and opening wide his jaws to receive his victim.

"When" exclaimed the young man, drawing his knife and placing himself in a threatening attitude, "when did you ever taste human food. Have a care of yourself. You were given by the Great Spirit to man, and if you, or any of your tribes, taste human flesh, you will fall sick and die. Listen not to the words of that wicked old man, but carry me back to his island, in return for which, I shall present you a piece of red cloth."

The fish complied, raising his back out of water to allow the young man to get on. Then taking his way through the lake, landed his charge safely at the island before the return of the magician.

The daughters were still more surprised to see him thus escaped a second time from the arts of their father. But the old man maintained his taciturnity. He could not, however, help saying to himself, "What manner of boy is this, who ever escapes from my power. His spirit shall not however save him. I will entrap him tomorrow. Ha! ha! ha!"

The next day the magician addressed the young man as follows: "Come, my son," said he "you must go with me to procure some young eagles. I wish to tame them. I have discovered an island where they exist in great abundance." When they had reached the island, Mishösha led him inland till they came to the foot of a tall pine, upon which the nests were. "Now, my son," said he, "climb up this tree, and bring down the birds." The young man obeyed, and when he had with great effort got up near the nests—"Now," exclaimed the magician, addressing the tree "stretch yourself up, and be very tall." The tree rose up at the command. "Listen ye eagles," continued the old man, "you have long expected a gift from me. I now present you this boy who has had the presumption to molest your young.

---

[1] *It is not ... human food* I.e., the gulls should not eat human beings.

[2] *virtues* Supernatural powers.

Stretch forth your claws and seize him." So saying he left the young man to his fate, and returned.

But the intrepid youth, drawing his knife, and cutting off the head of the first eagle that menaced him, raised his voice and exclaimed—"Thus will I deal with all who come near me. What right have you, ye ravenous birds, to eat living flesh? Is it because that old cowardly old magician has bid you do so? He is an old woman. He can neither do you good nor harm. See! I have already slain one of your number. Respect my bravery, and carry me back to the lodge of the old man, that I may show you how I shall treat him."

The eagles, pleased with the spirit of the young man, assented, and clustering around him, formed a seat with their backs, and flew towards the enchanted Island. As they crossed the water they passed the magician lying half asleep in his canoe and treated him with great indignity.

The return of the young man was hailed with joy by the daughters, but excited the ire of the magician, who taxed his wits for some new mode of ridding himself of a youth so powerfully aided by his spirit. He therefore invited him to go a hunting. Taking his canoe, they proceeded to an island, and built a lodge to shelter themselves during the night. In the meantime, the magician caused a deep fall of snow and a storm of wind with severe cold.

According to custom the young man pulled off his moccasins and leggons,[1] and hung them before the fire. After he had gone to sleep, the magician, watching his opportunity, got up, and taking one moccasin and one leggon, threw them into the fire. He then went to sleep. In the morning, stretching himself as he arose, and uttering an exclamation of surprise, he exclaimed "My son, what has become of your moccasin and leggon? I believe this is the moon in which fire attracts, and I fear they have been drawn in." The young man suspected the true cause of his loss, and rightly attributed it to a design of the magician to freeze him to death on their march. But he maintained the strictest silence, and drawing his blanket over his head, thus communed with himself. "I have full faith in my spirit, who has preserved me thus far, and I do

not fear that he will now forsake me. Great is the power of my Manito;[2] and he shall prevail against this wicked old enemy of mankind."

Then drawing on the remaining moccasin and leggon, he took a coal from the fire and invoking his spirit to give it efficacy, blackened the foot and leg as far as the lost garment usually reached. Then rising announced himself ready for the march. In vain the magician led him through snow and over morasses, hoping to see the lad sink at every moment. But in this he was disappointed, and they for the first time returned home together.

Taking courage from this the young man now determined to try his own power, having previously consulted with the daughters. They all agreed that the life the old man led was detestable, and that whoever would rid the world of him would entitle himself to the thanks of the human race. On the following day the young man thus addressed the magician. "My grandfather, I have often gone with you on perilous excursions, and never murmured. I must now request that you will accompany me, I wish to visit my little brother and to bring him home with me." They accordingly went on a visit to the main land and found the little lad in the spot where he had been left. After taking him into the canoe, the young man again addressed the magician: "My grandfather, will you go and cut me a few of those red willows on the bank. I wish to prepare some smoking mixture."[3] "Certainly, my son," replied the old man "What you wish, is not very hard. Ha! ha! ha! do you think me too old to get up there?"

No sooner was the magician ashore, than the young man placing himself in the proper position, struck the canoe and repeated the charm *N'chimaun*[4] *Pall*. And immediately the canoe flew through the water on its passage to the island. It was evening when the two brothers arrived; but the elder daughter informed the young man, that unless he sat up and watched the canoe and kept his hand upon it, such was the power of their father it would slip off and return to him.

---

[1]   *moccasins*   Shoes made of soft leather;   *leggons*   In the traditional style of Ojibwe leggings, the legs are not connected to each other, but each is tied separately to a belt at the waist.

[2]   *Manito*   Manitou; spirit.

[3]   *some smoking mixture*   Red willow bark (from the red osier dogwood tree, *miskwaabiimag* in contemporary Ojibwe) is an ingredient in some traditional Native American herbal smoking mixtures.

[4]   *N'chimaun*   Ojibwe: My canoe. The meaning of "pall" is unclear.

The young man watched faithfully till near the dawn of day, when he could no longer resist the drowsiness which oppressed him and suffered himself to nod for a moment. In an instant the canoe slipped off, and sought its master, who soon returned in high glee; "Ha! ha! ha! my son," said he; "you thought to play me a trick; it was very clever; but you see I am too old for you."

A short time after, the youth again addressed the magician. "My grandfather, I wish to try my skill in hunting. It is said there is plenty of game on an island not far off and I have to request that you will take me there in your canoe." They accordingly spent the day in hunting, and night coming on, they put up a temporary lodge. When the magician had sunk into a profound sleep, the young man got up, and taking a moccasin and leggon of Mishösha's from the place where they hung before the fire, threw them in; thus retaliating the artifice before played upon himself. He had discovered by some secret means that the foot and leg were the only assailable parts of the magician's body which could not be guarded by the spirits who served him and treated him with great indignity.

The return of the young man was hailed with joy by the daughters. He then besought his Manito to cause a storm of snow, with cold wind and icy sleet, and then laid himself down beside the old man. Consternation was depicted in the countenance of the latter, when he awoke in the morning and found his moccasin and leggon missing. "I believe, my grandfather," said the young man, "that this is the moon in which fire attracts, and I fear your clothes have been drawn in." Then rising and bidding the old man follow, he began the morning's hunt; frequently he turned his head to see how Mishösha kept up. He saw him faltering at every step and almost benumbed with cold. But encouraged him to follow, saying we shall soon be through and reach the shore. But still leading him round about ways to let the frost take complete effect. At length the old man reached the brink of the island, where the woods are succeeded by a border of smooth sand. But he could go no further: his legs became stiff and refused all motion, and he found himself fixed to the spot, but he still kept stretching out his arms and swinging his body to and fro. Every moment he found the numbness creeping higher he felt his legs growing

downwards like roots, the feathers on his head turned to leaves, and in a few seconds he stood a tall and stiff sycamore,[1] leaning towards the water.

The young man getting into the canoe, and pronouncing the charm, was soon transported to the island, where he related his victory to the daughters. They applauded the deed, agreed to put on mortal shapes, become wives to the young men, and forever quit the enchanted island. They immediately passed over to the main land, where they lived in happiness and peace.

—1827

Invocation

To my Maternal Grandfather on hearing his descent from Chippewa ancestors misrepresented[2]

Rise bravest chief! of the mark of the noble deer,[3]
    With eagle glance,
    Resume thy lance,
And wield again thy warlike spear!
    The foes of thy line,
    With coward design,
Have dared with black envy to garble the truth,
5 And stain with a falsehood thy valorous youth.

They say when a child, thou wert ta'en from the Sioux,[4]
    And with impotent aim,

---

1 *sycamore* I.e., a North American hardwood tree that can grow over one hundred feet tall.

2 *To my Maternal ... misrepresented* Schoolcraft's grandfather Waubojeeg (1747–93) was a famous Ojibwe leader and war chief. This poem first appeared under the pseudonym "Rosa" in the thirteenth issue of *The Muzzeniegun, or Literary Voyager*, a handwritten manuscript magazine edited by Henry Rowe Schoolcraft in 1826 and 1827; the version reprinted here appeared in the *Southern Literary Messenger* in 1860; *Chippewa* Ojibwe.

3 *noble deer* Waubojeeg was a member of the caribou clan.

4 *They say ... Sioux* In the early 1700s, the Ojibwe expanded their territory westward into modern-day Minnesota and Wisconsin. In the 1730s they came into contact with the Santee Dakota (referred to as the Sioux by French traders) and began to fight over [continued ...] the region around Lake Superior; this conflict continued well into the 1800s.

10   To lessen thy fame
Thy warlike lineage basely abuse;
            For they know that our band,
            Tread a far distant land,
And thou noble chieftain art nerveless and dead,
15 Thy bow all unstrung, and thy proud spirit fled.

Can the sports of thy youth, or thy deeds ever fade?
            Or those e'er forget,
            Who are mortal men yet,
The scenes where so bravely thou'st lifted the blade,
20   Who have fought by thy side,
            And remember thy pride,
When rushing to battle, with valour and ire,
Thou saw'st the fell° foes of thy nation expire?   *cruel, deadly*

Can the warrior forget how sublimely you rose?
25   Like a star in the west,
            When the sun's sunk to rest,
That shines in bright splendour to dazzle our foes?
            Thy arm and thy yell,
            Once the tale could repel
30 Which slander invented, and minions detail,
And still shall thy actions refute the false tale.

Rest thou, noblest chief! in thy dark house of clay,
            Thy deeds and thy name,
            Thy child's child shall proclaim,
35 And make the dark forests resound with the lay;°   *song*
            Though thy spirit has fled,
            To the hills of the dead,
Yet thy name shall be held in my heart's warmest core,
And cherished till valour and love be no more.
40 —1827 (WRITTEN 1823?)

Lines Written at Castle Island,[1]
Lake Superior[2]

Here in my native inland sea[3]
From pain and sickness would I flee
And from its shores and island bright
Gather a store of sweet delight.
5 Lone island of the saltless sea!
How wide, how sweet, how fresh and free
How all transporting—is the view
Of rocks and skies and waters blue
Uniting, as a song's sweet strains
10 To tell, here nature only reigns.
Ah, nature! here forever sway
Far from the haunts of men away
For here, there are no sordid fears,
No crimes, no misery, no tears
15 No pride of wealth; the heart to fill,
No laws to treat my people ill.
—2007 (WRITTEN 1838?)

---

[1]   *Castle Island* Now Little Presque Isle, near Marquette, Michigan.

[2]   Though this poem was originally written in Ojibwe by Schoolcraft, none of these versions have survived. It was translated into English by either Jane or Henry Schoolcraft, with all extant versions written in Henry's hand.

[3]   *native inland sea* Lake Superior, the farthest north and west of the five Great Lakes, is the world's largest freshwater lake by surface area. Its Ojibwe name, gichigami, loosely translates to "big sea."

On Leaving My Children John and Jane at School, in the Atlantic States, and Preparing to Return to the Interior

In 1839, the eldest living Schoolcraft children were sent to elite, predominately white boarding schools in Philadelphia and Princeton when Jane (called Janee) was eleven and Johnston (called John) nine years old. Though the forced enrollment of Native American children in boarding schools would become a tool of cultural assimilation in the later nineteenth century, this was not yet a commonplace practice; the Schoolcraft children went to boarding school following the wishes of their father.

The following poem appeared in Henry Rowe Schoolcraft's *Personal Memoirs of a Residence of Thirty Years with the Indian Tribes on the American Frontiers* (1851), where he introduced them with the statement that "Mrs. Schoolcraft, having left her children at school, at Philadelphia and Princeton, remained pensive, and wrote the following lines in the Indian tongue, on parting from them, which I thought so just that I made a translation of them." Henry subtitles his version a "Free Translation," and it diverges in many respects from Jane's Ojibwe original. A twenty-first-century translation more faithful to the original text, prepared by Dennis Jones, Heidi Stark, and James Vukelich for *The Sound the Stars Make Rushing through the Sky*, appears in facing column with the Ojibwe; it is followed by Henry's English version.

Nyau nin de nain dum
May kow e yaun in
Ain dah nuk ki yaun
Waus sa wa kom eg
5 Ain dah nuk ki yaun

Ne dau nis ainse e
Ne gwis is ainse e
Ishe nau gun ug wau
Waus sa wa kom eg

10 She gwau go sha ween
Ba sho waud e we
Nin zhe ka we yea
Ishe ez hau jau yaun
Ain dah nuk ke yaun

15 Ain dah nuk ke yaun
Nin zhe ke we yea
Ishe ke way aun e
Nyau ne gush kain dum
—1851 (WRITTEN 1839)

As I am thinking
When I find you
My land
Far in the west
5 My land

My little daughter
My little son
I leave them behind
Far away land

10 [emphatically] But soon
It is close however
To my home I shall return
That is the way that I am, my being
My land

15 My land
To my home I shall return
I begin to make my way home
Ahh but I am sad
—2007

Free Translation

Ah! when thought reverts to my country so dear,
My heart fills with pleasure, and throbs with a fear:
My country, my country, my own native land,
So lovely in aspect, in features so grand,
5   Far, far in the West. What are cities to me,
Oh! land of my mother, compared unto thee?

Fair land of the lakes! thou are blest to my sight,
With thy beaming bright waters, and landscapes of
      light;
The breeze and the murmur, the dash and the roar,
10 That summer and autumn cast over the shore,
They spring to my thoughts, like the lullaby tongue,
That soothed me to slumber when youthful and
      young.

One feeling more strongly still binds me to thee,
There roved my forefathers, in liberty free—
15 There shook they the war lance, and sported the
      plume,
Ere Europe had cast o'er this country a gloom;

Nor thought they that kingdoms more happy could be,
White lords of a land so resplendent and free.

Yet it is not alone that my country is fair,
20 And my home and my friends are inviting me there;
While they beckon me onward, my heart is still here,
With my sweet lovely daughter, and bonny boy dear;
And oh! what's the joy that a home can impart,
Removed from the dear ones who cling to my heart.

25 It is learning that calls them; but tell me, can schools
Repay for my love, or give nature new rules?
They may teach them the lore of the wit and the sage,
To be grave in their youth, and be gay in their age;
But ah! my poor heart, what are schools to thy view,
30 While severed from children thou lovest so true!

I return to my country, I haste on my way,
For duty commands me, and duty must sway;
Yet I leave the bright land where my little ones dwell,
With a sober regret, and a bitter farewell;
35 For there I must leave the dear jewels I love,
The dearest of gifts from my Master above.
—1851

José María Heredia

1803 – 1839

In 1888, José Martí, a Cuban poet and political exile, declared José María Heredia "the first poet of America." A leader of the Romantic movement in Spanish-language literature, and now the national poet of Cuba, Heredia was a pioneering figure in hemispheric American literary history whose innova-

tive poetry responded to locations and histories specific to the Americas. Heredia was also an important "poet of America" in a narrower sense, in that he spent a short but formative part of his life in the United States, where he published the first edition of his only poetry collection to appear in his lifetime, *Poesías* (*Poems*, 1825). Heredia's time in the U.S. strengthened his commitment to independence for all the Americas, especially Cuba, and his encounters with the U.S. literary scene and with North American landscapes shaped some of his most characteristic and famous poems, such as "Niágara" ("Niagara," 1825). Heredia's poetry, in turn, was celebrated and translated by U.S. writers. Accordingly, his work claims a place in U.S. literary history, highlighting the connections between U.S.-American literature and the multi-lingual and multi-national literatures of the rest of the Americas.

Born in the Cuban city of Santiago de Cuba on the last day of 1803, Heredia belonged to the elite ruling class of Spain's American colonies. His family came from the Spanish colony of Santo Domingo, where they had owned coffee plantations worked by enslaved laborers. When the Haitian Revolution broke out in the neighboring French portion of the island, the family fled to Cuba. Heredia's father, a Spanish colonial magistrate, went on to hold a succession of posts in Florida, Venezuela, and Mexico as well as Cuba, so Heredia spent his early years moving frequently throughout Spanish America. During this itinerant upbringing, Heredia received a classical education and soon proved himself something of a child prodigy: capable, when he was only eight, of translating from Latin the work of the Roman poet Horace. Heredia's burgeoning poetic imagination was also fed, in a different way, by the wars of independence being waged throughout Spanish America during his youth. The ongoing freedom struggles he witnessed in Venezuela and Mexico aligned with his own spontaneous, creative temperament to give rise to what would become his central commitment to *libertad* (liberty) in all forms, personal and literary as well as public and political. This emerging commitment shaped the poetry Heredia began writing in his teens, as well as the political activity he undertook as a law student in Cuba in the early 1820s, which included advocating for Cuban independence and the abolition of slavery. In 1823, charged with participation in an anti-colonial conspiracy, he had to flee Cuba and went into exile in the United States.

Heredia's time in the U.S. is amply documented in his letters, which describe the genesis of much of his poetry together with his personal sufferings and aspirations as an exile, his dislike of the English language and northern winters, and his admiration for U.S. political institutions and for the places he saw in the course of his travels. After arriving in Boston in the dead of winter, he stated his intention, in one of his first letters, "to deal head on with the English language, or to work a bit more on my poetry" before noting that "I don't know whether you will understand these last paragraphs because the ink is well nigh frozen." He quickly resettled in New York City and began dealing "head on" with English by translating into Spanish an array of English-language works, including the poetry of Lord Byron and the republican political rhetoric of the U.S. orator Daniel Webster. Heredia's translating spurred his own poetry-writing, as did his travels throughout the U.S.: a visit to sites from the country's revolutionary history, including Philadelphia and Mount Vernon, inspired his "Ode to Washington," while a trip to Niagara Falls prompted "Niágara."

Heredia's poetry was further encouraged by—and capitalized on—a surge of U.S.-American interest in Spanish language and literature; as one New York newspaper put it at the time, "The great business of the day is learning Spanish and Italian." The publishing houses of New York and Philadelphia also did extensive business printing Spanish-language books for distribution in Latin America. When Heredia's *Poesías* appeared in New York in the summer of 1825, it was targeted at domestic as well as international markets: a foreword in both Spanish and English explained that Heredia had endeavored "to make these poems useful to Americans learning the Spanish language," but the publisher also set aside copies for sale in Cuba and Mexico.

Poesías showcases Heredia's classical roots, as well as the qualities that made him a trailblazing American Romantic. He worked largely in established poetic forms, especially the *silva*, a form popular with Heredia's poetic generation that consists of hendecasyllabic (eleven-syllable) lines, together with occasional heptasyllabic (seven-syllable) lines; Spanish poets of the period—Heredia very much included—built intricate variations of rhyme and stanza length into this form. (Both of the poems by Heredia included below are *silvas*.) Heredia's poetry, however, balances formal polish with a deliberately unrefined diction and style. He used *cultismos* (learned words) and classical allusions sparingly, aiming instead for a freer, more direct poetic style that hews closer to living, spoken language. This goal aligns with Heredia's poetic emphasis on spontaneity, emotional sincerity, and depth of feeling. In these respects, Heredia's poetry reflects the Romanticism that, by the time he started writing, was well-established in British and German literature but was only beginning to make itself felt in both Spanish-language literature and the literatures of the Americas. A further quintessentially Romantic aspect of Heredia's poetry is his receptiveness to nature and the sublime—a quality abundantly on display in poems such as "Niágara."

Yet Heredia's poetry differentiates itself from its European Romantic antecedents by its focus on distinctively American locations and features: not just Niagara Falls, but also the hurricanes of his native Caribbean, as in "En una tempestad" ("In a Storm," 1822), or the pyramids and volcanos of Mexico, as in "En el teocalli de Cholula" ("In the Pyramid of Cholula," 1820). As Martí contended when hailing Heredia as "the first poet of America," "Only he has put in his verses the sublimity, pomp, and fire of [America's] nature. He is volcanic like its core, and serene like its heights." In addition, Heredia's poetry reinvents, in a specifically American form, another hallmark of much European literary Romanticism: its revolutionary politics. Heredia transmutes this aspect of his literary inheritance into a consistent call for anticolonial liberation, in Cuba and throughout the Americas. In the words of an 1849 U.S.-American review of Heredia's work, "Thoughts of sorrow or of hope for Cuba underlie almost all his poems."

Poesías met with acclaim in the United States and throughout the Americas, as well as in Western Europe. As Heredia himself put it in a letter to his mother, "These poems have been rather well received here; and the periodicals have praised them to exaggeration." The *New-York American* described the poems as possessing "traits of the truest genius" and went on to print a lengthy Spanish review asserting that Heredia "may be as sure of the esteem of his compatriots as he is the hatred of tyrants." Heredia's work was also applauded by fellow Latin American exiles and by Spanish intellectuals. This international acclaim brought to a close Heredia's U.S. period: at the personal invitation of the Mexican president, he left the U.S. in August 1825 for Mexico, where he spent most of the rest of his life. In Mexico, Heredia served in various governmental and educational positions, wrote and staged plays, edited literary reviews and newspapers, translated English-language works such as Sir Walter Scott's *Waverley*, and revised and expanded *Poesías*, a second edition of which was published in 1832. His continued involvement in plots to liberate Cuba from Spain earned him a death sentence *in absentia* in 1831, but near the end of his life he was able to make an arrangement with the colonial authorities that allowed him to visit Cuba to see his mother. He died of tuberculosis in Mexico in 1839.

If Heredia's time in the U.S. played a pivotal role in his literary career, his poetry also had an impact on U.S. literary culture. Through at least the mid-nineteenth century, U.S. critics continued to praise Heredia as, in the words of one 1849 reviewer, one of "the noblest and loftiest poets of Spanish America" and "first among the poets of his country." In particular, William Cullen Bryant, a leading U.S. poet, was influenced by Heredia's work, which he greatly admired. Bryant used a free translation of "En una tempestad" as the basis for his poem "The Hurricane," and he was also involved in writing a popular, anonymously published translation of "Niágara" that helped disseminate Heredia's poetry in North America. In Latin America, and especially in Cuba, Heredia's reputation went from strength to strength: new editions of his poetry appeared consistently throughout the nineteenth century and into the twentieth, and today, "El Cantor del Niagara," as he is known, is securely canonized within Latin American literary history. Scholarly interest in Heredia's U.S. period and the poetry resulting from it began to increase in the mid-twentieth century, and contemporary scholarship continues to explore his work's implications for evolving definitions of "American" literature and for efforts to trace the enduring links among the literatures of the Americas.

———————————

NOTE ON THE TEXTS: Two different versions of "Niágara" were published in Heredia's lifetime, in the 1825 and 1832 editions of *Poesías*. The English-language version of the poem presented below is based on the translation of the 1825 version, by Thatcher Taylor Payne and William Cullen Bryant, that was printed anonymously in *The United States Review and Literary Gazette* in 1827. The text of this translation has been modernized in accordance with the practices of this anthology. The full Spanish-language text of the 1832 version of "Niágara" appears in the anthology's website portion, along with the scholar Frederick Luciani's 2020 translation of this version.

The text of the original Spanish excerpt of Heredia's "A Washington" ("To Washington") included below is based on that of the 1832 edition of *Poesías*, in which this poem was first printed; we present this Spanish-language excerpt together with a new English translation, completed especially for this anthology by Rodrigo Lazo.

⌘ ⌘ ⌘

Niagara

From the Spanish of José Maria Heredia

My lyre![1] give me my lyre! my bosom feels
The glow of inspiration. Oh how long
Have I been left in darkness since this light
Last visited my brow. Niagara!
5 Thou with thy rushing waters dost restore
The heavenly gift that sorrow took away.

Tremendous torrent! for an instant hush
The terrors of thy voice and cast aside
Those wide involving° shadows, that my eyes   *enveloping*
10 May see the fearful beauty of thy face!
I am not all unworthy of thy sight,
For from my very boyhood have I loved,
Shunning the meaner° track of common minds,   *cruder*
To look on nature in her loftier moods.
15 At the fierce rushing of the hurricane,
At the near bursting of the thunderbolt
I have been touched with joy; and when the sea,

Lashed by the wind, hath rocked my bark°   *ship*
and showed
Its yawning caves beneath me, I have loved
20 Its dangers and the wrath of elements.
But never yet the madness of the sea
Hath moved me as thy grandeur moves me now.

Thou flowest on in quiet, till thy waves
Grow broken 'midst the rocks; thy current then
25 Shoots onward like the irresistible course
Of destiny. Ah, terribly they rage—
The hoarse and rapid whirlpools there! My brain
Grows wild, my senses wander, as I gaze
Upon the hurrying waters, and my sight
30 Vainly would follow, as toward the verge
Sweeps the wide torrent—waves innumerable
Meet there and madden—waves innumerable
Urge on and overtake the waves before,
And disappear in thunder and in foam.

35 They reach—they leap the barrier—the abyss
Swallows insatiable the sinking waves.
A thousand rainbows arch them, and woods
Are deafened with the roar. The violent shock
Shatters to vapor the descending sheets—

———————————

[1] *lyre* Stringed instrument resembling a harp, traditionally used (for example, in ancient Greece) to accompany song or the performance of poetry.

40 A cloudy whirlwind fills the gulf, and heaves
The mighty pyramid of circling mist
To heaven. The solitary hunter near
Pauses with terror in the forest shades.

What seeks my restless eye? Why are not here,
45 About the jaws of this abyss, the palms—
Ah—the delicious° palms, that on the plains   *delightful*
Of my own native Cuba, spring and spread
Their thickly foliaged summits to the sun,
And, in the breathings of the ocean air,
50 Wave soft beneath the heaven's unspotted blue?

But no, Niagara—thy forest pines
Are fitter coronal° for thee. The palm,   *garland, crown*
The effeminate myrtle, and frail rose may grow
In gardens, and give out their fragrance there,
55 Unmanning him who breathes it. Thine it is
To do a nobler office. Generous minds
Behold thee, and are moved, and learn to rise
Above earth's frivolous pleasures; they partake
Thy grandeur at the utterance of thy name.

60 God of all truth! in other lands I've seen
Lying philosophers,[1] blaspheming men,
Questioners of thy mysteries, that draw
Their fellows deep into impiety,
And therefore doth my spirit seek thy face
65 In earth's majestic solitudes. Even here
My heart doth open all itself to thee.
In this immensity of loneliness
I feel thy hand upon me. To my ear
The eternal thunder of the cataract brings
70 Thy voice, and I am humbled as I hear.

Dread torrent! that with wonder and with fear
Dost overwhelm the soul of him that looks

Upon thee, and dost bear it from itself,
Whence hast thou thy beginning? Who supplies,
75 Age after age, thy unexhausted springs?
What power hath ordered, that, when all thy weight
Descends into the deep, the swollen waves
Rise not, and roll to overwhelm the earth?

The Lord hath opened his omnipotent hand,
80 Covered thy face with clouds, and given his voice
To thy down-rushing waters; he hath girt
Thy terrible forehead with his radiant bow.[2]
I see thy never-resting waters run,
And I bethink me how the tide of time
85 Sweeps to eternity. So pass of man—
Pass, like a noon-day dream—the blossoming days,
And he awakes to sorrow. I, alas!
Feel that my youth is withered, and my brow
Ploughed early with the lines of grief and care.

90 Never have I so deeply felt as now
The hopeless solitude, the abandonment,
The anguish of a loveless life. Alas!
How can the impassioned, the unfrozen heart
Be happy without love? I would that one
95 Beautiful—worthy to be loved and joined
In love with me—now shared my lonely walk
On this tremendous brink. 'T were sweet to see
Her dear face touched with paleness, and become
More beautiful from fear, and overspread
100 With a faint smile while clinging to my side!
Dreams—dreams. I am an exile, and for me
There is no country and there is no love.

Hear, dread Niagara, my latest voice!
Yet a few years and the cold earth shall close
105 Over the bones of him who sings thee now
Thus feelingly. Would that this, my humble verse,
Might be like thee, immortal. I, meanwhile,
Cheerfully passing to the appointed rest,
Might raise my radiant forehead in the clouds
110 To listen to the echoes of my fame.
—1825 (TRANSLATION PUBLISHED 1827)

---

1   *God ... Lying philosophers*   In the revised version of "Niágara"
that Heredia published in the 1832 edition of *Poesías*, an additional
eight lines appear between these two. These further lines, which
Heredia either composed later and added to the 1832 version of the
poem or deliberately excluded from the poem's 1825 publication, are
translated as follows in Frederick Luciani's 2020 translation of the
1832 version (which appears in full in the website portion of this
anthology): "I have seen execrable men / Your holy name blaspheme,
/ Impious fanaticism sow, / Fields engulf in blood and tears, / Lay
waste in war the very earth, / And turn brother into foe. / I saw these,
and my heart would swell / In righteous wrath."

2   *What power ... bow*   See Genesis 9.9–17, in which, after the
Flood, God makes the rainbow the sign of his promise to never again
send another flood to destroy all life.

from *To Washington*

A Washington

(Escrita en Monte Vernon)

Primero en paz y en guerra.
primero en el afecto de tu patria
Y en la veneración del universo.
Viva imagen de Dios sobre la tierra,
5 libertador, legislador y justo,
Washington inmortal, oye benigno
el débil canto de tu gloria indigno,
con que voy a ensalzar tu nombre augusto.

¿Te pintaré indignado
10 a la voz de la patria dolorida
volar al arduo campo de la gloria,
y como Jove en el Olimpo, armado,
a la suerte mandar y a la victoria?
Magnánimo apareces;
15 ríndese Boston, y respira libre.
Vanamente el tirano
cuarenta mil esclavos lanza fiero
para extirpar el nombre americano.

To Washington[1]

(Composed at Mount Vernon[2])

"First in war, first in peace,
first in the hearts of your countrymen,"[3]
and the veneration of the globe.
A liberator, a legislator, a just leader,
5 living image of God on earth,
immortal Washington, kindly hear
my humble and unworthy song
which will exalt your respected name.

Should I portray you alarmed
10 at your country's suffering cry,
flying to the glory of the battlefield,
armed, like Jove on Olympus,[4]
to command fortune and victory?
Benevolent you appear;
15 Boston surrenders and breathes freely.[5]
Vainly does the proud tyrant
send forty-thousand slave-troops[6]
to erase the name "American."

---

1   Translated by Rodrigo Lazo for Broadview Press, 2021.

2   *Mount Vernon*   Washington's plantation estate on the banks of the Potomac River in Virginia, which he owned from 1761 until his death in 1799. At the time of Heredia's stay in the United States, the estate was still owned by the Washington family but was falling into disrepair.

3   *First … countrymen*   Heredia's opening lines play on a well-known passage from Washington's funeral oration, delivered in 1799 by Henry Lee: "First in war, first in peace, and first in the hearts of his countrymen."

4   *Jove on Olympus*   "Jove" is a Roman name for Zeus, king of the Greek gods, said to dwell on Mount Olympus.

5   *Boston … freely*   After the outbreak of the Revolutionary War in April 1775, American militia laid siege to the British troops occupying Boston; Washington took command of the besieging forces in July 1775, and the British were eventually forced out of the city in March 1776.

6   *slave-troops*   In the nineteenth century, the word "slavery" was commonly used in general terms, including by Heredia and his circle, to describe subjugation to tyrannical authority. Heredia is here characterizing the troops sent to America by King George III as servile subjects of such authority.

[A Washington *cont'd*]

Tú, sin baldón, al número cediste,
20 y acallando el espíritu guerrero,
a tu gloria, la patria, preferiste.
Así del pueblo eterno los caudillos
al vencedor Aníbal contemplaron
con inmutable frente,
25 y la invasión rugiente
a la púnica rechazaron.

Mas luego, una noche de feliz memoria,
del Delaware el vacilante hielo
ofreció a tu valor y patrio celo,
30 el camino del triunfo y de la gloria.
La sobervia británica humillada
es por ultimo en York, y su caudillo
tinde a tus pies la ponderosa espada.
El universo atónito saluda
35 a la triunfante América, y te adora,

[To Washington *cont'd*]

With honor, you retreat before the number[1]
20 and, tempering the martial spirit,
Protect your true glory, your country.
Just so, the leaders of the Eternal City
looked down on triumphant Hannibal,
keeping a calm front,[2]
25 and on the Punic coast turned away
the bellowing invasion.[3]

And later, on a memorable brilliant night,
the unsteady ice on the Delaware
honored your bravery and love of country,
30 opening a route to triumph and glory.[4]
Proud Britain is finally trampled
at York,[5] and her kingpin[6]
yields the sword at your feet.
The astonished world salutes
35 triumphant America, and adores you,

---

[1] *you ... number*   In the summer and fall of 1776, Washington gradually withdrew his Continental Army from New York City and its vicinity in the face of a much larger British force.

[2] [Translator's note]   My use of "front" here draws from the Spanish "frente," which can also mean forehead.

[3] *Just so ... invasion*   In the Second Punic War (218–201 BCE), the second of three wars between Rome ("the Eternal City") and the North African city-state of Carthage, Carthaginian (also known as Punic) forces led by the general Hannibal invaded Roman territory in Italy. Hannibal won several significant victories, but the Romans were eventually able to wear his army down by avoiding major battles and waging a prolonged war of attrition; in the meantime, another Roman army attacked Carthaginian territory ("the Punic coast"), compelling Hannibal to leave Italy and pursue them there, where he was conclusively defeated. Heredia is here comparing Washington's strategic withdrawals in the face of overwhelming British strength to the delaying tactics that ultimately enabled Rome to defeat Hannibal.

[4] *And later ... glory*   Reference to Washington's famous crossing of the icy Delaware River on the night of 25–26 December 1776, a daring move that enabled him to launch a successful surprise attack on the garrison of Hessians (German mercenaries fighting for the British) in Trenton, New Jersey, the following day.

[5] *Proud Britain ... York*   Reference to Washington's victory at the Battle of Yorktown (1781), the final British defeat of the Revolutionary War, which compelled the British to recognize American independence.

[6] *kingpin*   The Spanish word Heredia uses here, "caudillo," connotes an authoritarian ruler who wields power arbitrarily and coercively.

[A Washington *cont'd*]

mientras que la metrópoli sañuda
tu gloria bella y su baldón devora.
Mas cuando por la paz inutil viste
de libertad la espada en tu alta mano,
40 el poder soberano
como insufrible carga depusiste.

Alzado a la primer magistratura,
de tu patria la suerte coronaste,
y en cimientos eternos afirmaste
45 la paz, la libertad sublime y pura. …

En la tumba modesta,
que guarda tus cenizas por Tesoro,
ni luce el mármol, ni centella el oro,
ni entallado laurel ni palmas veo.
50 ¿Para qué, si es un mundo
a tu gloria inmortal digno trofeo?
Con estupor profundo
por tu genio creador lo miro alzado
hasta la cumbre de moral grandeza.
55 Potente y con virtud; libre y tranquilo;
esclavo de las leyes;[1]
del universe asilo;
Asombro de naciones y de reyes.
—1832 (WRITTEN 1824)

[To Washington *cont'd*]

while the empire chokes on its disgrace,
rages at your beautiful glory.
But when peace covers with liberty
The sword in your august hand,
40 Sovereign power over the land
You decline as insufferable misery.

Elected to the highest office,
you crowned your country with prosperity
and set an eternal foundation of peace
45 based on pure and sublime liberty. …

At your humble tomb[2]
that guards your ashes as a treasure,
I see neither laurel nor palm[3]
Neither gold nor marble adornments.
50 Why bother, if your trophy
is a world of immortal glory?
With profound modesty, I watch
Your ingenious creation rise
to the summit of moral greatness.
55 Peace, liberty and virtue disburse
Laws that bring cooperation;
Refuge for the universe;
Astonishment for monarchs and nations.
—2021

---

[1] [Translator's note] Heredia invokes slavery to emphasize subservience to laws in the new republic. An alternate interpretation and potential translation would take the word "esclavo" as an enslaved person under the new constitution, and thus that image would clash with the veneration of the new country in the surrounding lines. [Washington enslaved African Americans throughout his life, but—unlike most other slaveholding founders—he emancipated all enslaved people he owned in his will. By the time of Heredia's stay in the United States, both pro- and antislavery factions were claiming Washington's legacy to support their own positions. Heredia voiced antislavery sentiments elsewhere in his work, but his writing from his U.S. period is silent on the subject of American slavery.]

---

[2] *your humble tomb* Washington was initially buried in a modest family vault at Mount Vernon. He had left instructions for the construction of a new funeral vault in his will, but this was not carried out until 1831.

[3] *neither laurel nor palm* In ancient Greece and Rome, laurel wreaths were given in recognition of high achievement, including victory in battle; palm leaves are also traditional symbols of victory and honor.

Vicente Pérez Rosales
1807 – 1886

In 1886, Chilean lawyer and historian Luis Montt, writing in the prologue to the third edition of Vicente Pérez Rosales's memoir *Recuerdos del Pasado* (*Memories from the Past*), mused: "[T]here would have been profound shock had an astrologer predicted the great ups and downs in fortune to be experienced by this child born in 1807, in a town whose residents usually only traveled as far as their nearby farms in the summer." Indeed, over the course of his eventful life, Pérez Rosales would travel from his native Chile to Argentina and Brazil, to Paris to finish his schooling, to the gold mines of California, and eventually to Germany and beyond as a Chilean government official. A prolific writer, Pérez Rosales published numerous books and essays, leaving an impressive corpus that provides considerable insight into an important and tumultuous century in Chile's history. Perhaps the most important of his works is the Gold Rush diary in which Pérez Rosales provides a vivid record of Californian life during the Gold Rush period—and details the persecution inflicted at the time upon the large number of Chileans then living in California.

Pérez Rosales was born in Santiago on 5 April 1807 to José Joaquín Pérez y Salas and Mercedes Rosales Larraín; his extended family was wealthy, well-educated, and politically well-connected. On his mother's side, he was descended from the Larraíns, a Basque dynasty that had put down roots in Chile in the seventeenth century. His father died when he was young, and his mother soon remarried Felipe Santiago de Solar, a wealthy banker, merchant, and politician. When Chilean independence from Spain was declared in 1810, Pérez Rosales was just a toddler. The ensuing convulsion, the Spanish reconquest in 1814, and the Chilean civil wars that followed would have a significant impact on the trajectory of Pérez Rosales's life; several of his relatives were exiled or imprisoned. At age eleven, Pérez Rosales and his family fled to Mendoza, Argentina as political refugees, where he witnessed the execution of the brothers of José Miguel Carrera, the aristocrat who had been responsible for the first constitution of independent Chile.

In spite of the incessant political turmoil, Pérez Rosales enjoyed the benefits of his privileged upbringing. His mother, who was fluent in French and English, taught him those languages in addition to Spanish, and Pérez Rosales was provided with private tutors to complement his education in private schools in Santiago. As a teenager, he was put on a ship bound for England but got no further than Rio de Janeiro; he witnessed the celebrations when Brazil declared its independence in 1822—and he witnessed too the horrors of the slave trade. Sailing back to Santiago the following year on the *Doris*, he met Maria Graham, a British travel writer and illustrator and the wife of the ship's captain. She would write of her "particular interest in Vicente" in her *Journal of a Residence in Chile* (1824), describing him as "a clever child." In 1825, Pérez Rosales, now eighteen, traveled to Paris with five half-siblings, two cousins, and twenty-seven other children of Chilean aristocrats; here he studied at the prestigious Maison d'Education and later at the Liceo Hispanoamericano (under the tutelage of Leandro Fernández Moratín, an important literary figure in the Spanish Enlightenment).

By the time Pérez Rosales returned to Chile after France's July Revolution of 1830, his stepfather was a political exile; the other members of his family had lost their estate and were living in reduced circumstances. Pérez Rosales became resourceful; at various times over the next thirty years he earned his living working in retail sales, tobacco smuggling, distilling and bootlegging, quack medicine, and farming. He had as well a short-lived career as a journalist, which ended abruptly after he was sued and fined for accusing a local priest of fraud. In 1846 he co-founded the newspaper *El Mosaico*, a weekly publication that reported on European artistic, literary, philosophical, and scientific developments as well as local news; in total twelve issues were published.

In 1848 Pérez Rosales and several of his brothers (together with several servants) ventured to California to seek their fortune in the Gold Rush—a move that tens of thousands of other Chileans were making as well. People from around the world were of course being drawn to California in large numbers at this time; that a disproportionate number of them were Chilean had less to do with tales of immense wealth being particularly persuasive in Chile than it did with the Chilean city of Valparaiso being the South American port that any ship on its way to California from Europe or the eastern United States would routinely stop at—sometimes for extended periods to repair damage incurred rounding the perilous Cape Horn in these pre-Panama Canal days.

Pérez Rosales kept an illustrated journal of his time as a '49er, and for the better part of thirty years afterward he published occasional newspaper or magazine articles recounting aspects of his Gold Rush experiences. In 1878 he published *Viaje a California: Recuerdos de 1848, 1849, 1850* (*Travels in California: Memories of 1848, 1849, 1850*), and a few years later he followed that up with a longer memoir, *Recuerdos del Pasado* (*Memories from the Past*) (1882, 1886), the story of his life from 1814 to 1860.

There are many accounts of California during the frenzy of the Gold Rush years; the most interesting and most widely read include those of William Swain and of Alonzo Delano (excerpted in the website component of this anthology as "In Context" material). Pérez Rosales' account, though, is at least as engaging, even in translation—and, unlike the great majority of the accounts in English, it is not strongly tainted by expressions of anti-Indigenous and/or anti-Hispanic prejudice. The perspective he brings to bear on the Gold Rush years—and on the degree to which crude nativist feelings came to the fore, with horrific consequences for Chileans and other minority groups—provides a welcome corrective to the ways in which the mid-century history of California has often been presented.

A disillusioned Pérez Rosales returned to Chile in 1850 and turned to a life of civil service and politics, first with the Chilean Conservative Party and later with the National Party. He worked as a colonization agent, founding settlements in the country's remote southern regions in Llanquihue and Valdivia and promoting German immigration to the area. As he recounted in his memoirs, he once paid an Indigenous guide named Pichi-Juan thirty pesos to burn down a large area of native forest in order to clear the area for farmland that could be offered to German immigrants.

Pérez Rosales was promoted to Consul General in 1855 and traveled to Hamburg to continue promoting German immigration. He spent four years abroad, visited England and Denmark, and authored several essays and technical manuals in the course of this work.

The year 1861 was an eventful one in Pérez Rosales's life. At fifty-four years of age, he married a wealthy widow and old family friend named Antonia Urrutia. That same year his cousin José Joaquín Pérez became president of Chile, and Pérez Rosales was elected to the Chamber of Deputies in the Chilean congress, though because he was suffering from a bout of poor health he was not able to take his seat until that August. From 1876 to 1881 he served in the Chilean senate, and during the same period he published a series of satirical articles in the periodicals *La Revista Chilena* and *Los Lunes*, writing comic "definitions" for words that provide ironically insightful commentary on Chilean society. These were later collected and posthumously published as *El Diccionario del Entrometido* (*Dictionary of a Busybody*) in 1946.

Pérez Rosales died on 6 September 1886, aged seventy-nine, of complications from a stroke he had suffered the previous year. Chile's oldest national park, founded in 1926 in Llanquihue, is named after him, and in honor of the 100th anniversary of the Gold Rush in 1949, his California diary was published in Santiago.

NOTE ON THE TEXT: The translation presented below is by Edwin A. Beilhartz and Carlos U. López, first published in their collection *We Were 49ers: Chilean Accounts of the Californian Gold Rush* (1976). Beilhartz and López use what remains of Pérez Rosales's diary (*Diario de un Viaje a California*) as their base text for the initial portions of the account (translating from the manuscript in the National Archives of Chile). Only the first 48 pages of the diary have survived, however; at the point where the text stops Beilhartz and López begin using Pérez Rosales's 1878 account (as found in *Viaje a California: Recuerdos de 1848, 1849, 1850*) as their base text.

⌘ ⌘ ⌘

from *Diary of Travels in California*

[Pérez Rosales and his companions are on their way
to the gold fields at Sutter's Mill.]

March 16, 1849

The road became steeper and more tortuous every
moment, and we were much afraid a wheel might
break. Although the axle was iron, as were also the
wheel rims, the iron was so worn it could give way any
minute. The hills with their ups and downs followed
one another endlessly, and the bogs between them
made the job even harder. ...

We soon realized that not knowing the road would
have been no handicap to us. There was a trail of bottles strewn along the whole way. If you want to locate
a Yankee, follow the empty cognac bottles and you are
sure to find him. ...

At dawn of the next day every one of us took a good
hot drink and, some leading the pack animals on
ahead, we set out once more to climb and descend the
most intricate hills that formed the little tableland of
the mountain we had climbed the day before.

The country appeared the same, but the pines grew
steadily larger and the ground was a veritable garden.
The third fork of the Weber Creek, the last stream we
had to cross, runs through a beautiful meadow. We
saw signs of life there. There was a half-house, half-
inn made of logs on the other side of the stream, and
it was apparently much frequented. This was shown
by the presence of a number of adventurers of all
nationalities, on foot and on horseback, with the look

of bandits, who were seen to be entering and coming
out contented. There were also piles of broken bottles
adjoining the entrance of this horrible tavern.

A party of Indian women came down the hill close
by, naked, and squatted down to make themselves
as inconspicuous as possible. One man, who seemed
to be more forward, came towards us to offer some
acorns, a unique and favorite food of those aborigines.
We could not help laughing at his odd and unexpected
appearance.

Casil and some others tried to approach the Indian
women, but when this was observed by them and their
male companions they all took off, running like deer
back up the hill. ...

After another climb of two hours we found ourselves
on a beautiful high mesa. From there we could see the
high snowy mountains in whose bowels, it is said, there
is so much gold. We were told we had almost reached
our destination, and there would be no more climbing.

It was true. We started down a smooth, inclined slope
and came, in good spirits, to another residence-inn,
which looked better than the previous one. It was set,
as in an amphitheater, in a beautiful, marshy meadow.
Many Indians of both sexes were at work washing gold
from the mud of a small spring. We went among them
to watch them work, and their extraordinary skill was
surprising.

The men wore only a kind of loincloth or a shirt, or
perhaps a ragged and dirty jacket, next to their skins.
The women were dressed in an identical or similar way,
but they exposed completely those parts of their persons which are carefully covered in less liberal or more
evil-minded lands.

None of them could speak any but his native tongue,
so it was no use asking them anything. The only reply

Un resultado de poco más de tres onzas de oro no era ciertamente pª lisonjear, sin embargo nos recojimos como siempre

they could make was "Bueno," and they accompanied this word with a stupid kind of laugh.

The division of labor they followed was this: the men dug and gave the mud to the children, who then carried it in baskets to the women. The women, lined up along the stream, then washed it in grass baskets of the most perfect construction. The gold was tied in rags, in amounts more or less equal, and they use these little parcels to trade with just as if they were money. After spending some time, amused and half-scandalized by the carelessness[1] and innocence of these bare-breasted Indian women, we went on our way toward the village at the mill. It is a nice-looking place, not far away, and the path is downhill, easy to walk on and shaded by very tall pine trees.

When we got there, we set to work in haste and high spirits to set up our camp. Here, as in Sacramento, it attracted attention by the amount of ground it covered and by the completeness and good order of our equipment.

This place ought to be a city and not, as it is now, just an area in the wilderness with a name. It is a very small valley ringed with high hills and thick pine forest, situated on the bank of the south fork of the American River not far from the point where it flows into the main stream. This is the place where the discovery occurred that brought us here. At the southern end was a site suitable for a mill race, and it was there that Mr. Sutter planned to build his saw mill. In digging the channel for it, the workers found gold dust and nuggets in such abundance they could not believe it was the real thing. ... The news, gathering speed, spread down the river, to San Jose, San Francisco, and Monterrey. The people there, stunned by the reports, left their homes, families, and property, and soon turned all the area around the mill upside down. ...

There are only two wooden buildings in this place: the mill and a store. The others are all tents and lean-tos. This is no longer considered a mining area; it is just a stopping point on the road to the mines of the north and middle forks. ... We decided, for good or ill, to busy ourselves with looking over and reworking the abandoned diggings. ... We worked until dark, some digging, some carrying the soil, and others washing it. Our success was not brilliant, but we felt happy when we got back to camp and weighed our gold. It turned out to be only an ounce, but that was because we did not know the terrain.

—1849

---

[1] *carelessness* I.e., carefreeness.

from *Travels in California: Memories of 1848, 1849, 1850*

My brother Federico left his work on three occasions—to look for some excitement, he said. The first two times he came back with his pockets full of bits of quartz with little specks of gold in them. On the third occasion, he returned with a nugget of solid gold weighing 17 ¼ ounces that he had found at the bottom of a gully among the rocks.

In early April we were all in danger of being wiped out in a general uprising of the Indians. They wanted to get rid of the intruders, who would not leave them in peace anywhere. They had planned it so secretly that, had it not been for a traitor who sold them out, I might not be here now to tell what happened.

An immediate meeting was called. Everyone left his work, and in a few hours, a body of one hundred seventy riflemen and eighteen horsemen were on their way to find the Indians. Because I had not gone to the meeting, something that really surprised them about a Frenchman (that is what they thought I was), their committee came looking for me. They found me, *naturally*, very sick but strongly desirous of accompanying them. They did not demand such a sacrifice but were content to accept from the valiant fellow-countryman of Lafayette[1] a contribution of gunpowder and lead.

Two days later the expedition returned with one hundred and forty captives, men, women, and children. They were made to stand for two hours on the bank of the river while an improvised jury decided their fate. Then the man who acted as commander, followed by some riflemen, addressed himself to the miserable wretches and said, "Now you have seen, one and all, what we are able to do and know how to do. If you behave from now on you have nothing to fear. I am going to show you what will happen to you if you behave badly. Then you'll be let go so you can tell your chiefs." With that they shot fifteen wretches who had been led apart previously, leaving their bodies strewn over the ground.

I have told this bloody tale as quickly as it happened, for I saw in it, translated anew in vigorous terms, the favorite maxim of the Yankees: "Time is Money!"

The impression this swift and horrifying punishment left on the minds of the hardy adventurers of Coloma lasted only two hours. We had scarcely lost sight of the Indians who had been set free and who were loudly wailing in misery as they disappeared in the pine-covered hills that surrounded the valley when the report of another gold strike on the other side of the river took possession of all minds. Nobody could talk of anything else. ...

... No one has time to get sick in California, so two days of quick convalescing [after a bout of food poisoning] were enough. Then a boat of Gillespie's, stocked with all the necessities, took me down to San Francisco. I arrived there twelve days after leaving the mines, weak and crippled, it is true, but full of good humor and high resolve.

How different San Francisco was from what it had been when I left it to go into the interior. Instead of an "Araucanian"[2] village with foundations marked off here and there on which buildings were to rise, now those buildings were finished, and others were under rapid construction. The tents, huts, and windbreaks of old were now lined up beside streets in the suburbs. But, by the look of things, all these suburbs too would soon be built over and become part of a beautiful town. Building lots were already being laid out and measured in feet there, and prices had gone out of sight!

What a mistake we had made in not acquiring land in the towns at prices that would almost have made them gifts. It was depressing to me now to see how much they had increased in value in so short a time! Here I want to say something, without meaning to offend anyone: the men who made fortunes in California were gentlemen who lacked the hardihood to go prospecting for gold all out, scorning hunger, weariness, and danger. It was those who acquired valuable building sites either by just taking them or buying them at low prices; or those men who happened, without meaning to do so, to bring merchandise into the area to sell. Such men found themselves wealthy overnight.

---

[1]   *Lafayette*   Gilbert du Motier, Marquis de Lafayette (1757–1834), French military hero who fought alongside the Continental Army in the American Revolutionary War.

[2]   *Araucanian*   Collective name for three ethnic groups indigenous to Chile: the Picunche, Huilliche, and Mapuche peoples.

The bay was full of ships, all of them abandoned. Their passengers and crews had swelled the town's population to thirty thousand souls; and, whether permanent residents or transient, their activity was so great that the city seemed to change and expand as if by enchantment. Long piers, supported on redwood piles, were being constructed or were being further extended at the end of every street that ran down to the beach. These carried the street out over the tidal flat and provided roadways and foundations for additional buildings. At one place a lack of ready materials for piers had been solved by piling boxes and sacks of earth across the muddy beach; at the other locations, so as not to lose time, piers had been improvised by grounding ships side by side at the ends of streets and laying beams up to them; and there, too, shops and offices were built.

One of the first to transform his ship into a home ashore was a young Chilean, Wenceslao Urbistondo. He had taken advantage of an unusually high tide to beach his deserted and useless bark[1] at the end of the last street to the north of town; then he had laid his masts and spars to form a bridge across the mud so he could get back and forth.

The sidewalks along the streets were made with bales of jerky because it was the cheapest and most readily available material.[2] The bales were pushed down into the mud along the front of the buildings so one could get around without sinking into mud up to the knees.

Business was at the mercy of shifting tides in that city. Sometimes the high water invaded everything, reducing the value of the highest quality merchandise; at other times it left everything high and dry. The most provident merchant was not safe from ruinous effects an unexpected high or low tide might produce. One man might get rich with no idea how it

happened. Another would be ruined despite precautions of the most meticulous sort. I remember, for example, that because there was a shortage of housing in San Francisco, they asked that prefabricated houses be brought from Chile. When these arrived, houses were so plentiful in San Francisco that those who had ordered the houses had to pay to get them landed and then had to pay someone to accept them. I am witness and victim of what I am describing.

Nobody, however, was discouraged. Even the lowest-priced items could be given scarcity value by arranging for convenient fires. We saw such fires break out all over town day after day, posing the danger of a general conflagration.

In this theater, where the most uproarious international fair that memory records was in process, no actor played the role his lot would have assigned him in his native country. Masters were transformed into servants; a lawyer might be a freight agent; a doctor, a stevedore;[3] sailors found themselves digging excavations; and philosophers, having abandoned the realm of the abstract, were working with the most concrete materials. I have seen, without surprise and with the just pride of a Chilean, a soft and effeminate dandy from Santiago, with the same gold vest chain he wore at dances in our capital city still hanging from the buttonhole of a sweaty wool shirt, standing in water up to his waist and carrying the baggage of a tarred and brawny sailor with a smile on his face; and then, after having got paid for that job, offering his services to some other oaf.

The most ostentatious signs had been hung up everywhere. A wooden barracks bore the name, "Hotel Frémont." One man had a sign that said: "So-and-so, Physician and Surgeon" painted on the flap of his tent, though he had never been more than a gravedigger. An insurance salesman from Valparaíso had a hut that bore two signs: "So-and-so, Attorney at Law," and "So-and-so and Company, General Insurance Brokers." An arbor made of poles called itself, "French Hotel"; it belonged to an old Santiago barber. This sort of thing was done by Chileans of prominent families— few of which were not represented by family members in California.

---

1 *bark* Small boat.

2 *bales of jerky … material* The cattle industry was central to the growth of the Californian economy in the first half of the nineteenth century, but what was of economic value in an animal was not so much its meat (which at the time could not easily be shipped over long distances) but its hide and tallow from its fat (used to make candles and soap); beef hides and beef tallow were exported in huge quantities from California. Meat that could not be sold fresh was often dried and offered for sale as jerky, but as this passage suggests, in parts of California oversupply would sometimes mean that the jerky had little or no economic value.

---

3 *stevedore* Dockworker tasked with loading and unloading cargo from ships.

The crowds of men—and only men, because that creature called woman was not yet in fashion there—had made it necessary to set up at least a makeshift kind of civil government in that Babylon.[1]

They had an official they called an alcalde.[2] He was a factotum[3] whose duties were precisely like those of our old "subdelegates," with this difference: the orders and decrees of our subdelegates, whether just or unjust, were carried out, while those of the California or San Francisco alcalde were carried out only if convenient. With justices and trials of this sort, it is not surprising that lawsuits and appeals are often decided with pistol or dagger.

The relations between Chileans and Americans were anything but cordial. When General Persifer Smith[4] sent a decree from Panamá to the effect that, after that date, no foreigner was to be allowed to exploit gold mines in California, that decree brought to a head all the hostility shown to peaceful and defenseless Chileans.

Merchants and traders were alarmed by this, and the authorities proposed to the aliens that they become full United States citizens; they were to be charged only ten dollars, a small sum for such an imposing title. But this safe-conduct was only halfway effective: it worked only where it was accepted. In other places, it was treated as a joke. A little later on, the provisional government in San José made a ruling that an alien could work the mines on payment of twenty dollars a month in advance. A receipt would serve as sufficient authorization for the right to work. But how many clashes there were that arose from that agreement between collectors and contributors.

The ill will of the Yankee rabble against the sons of other nations and, especially, Chileans, was rising by that time. They offered a simple and conclusive argument: Chileans were descended from Spaniards; Spaniards were of Moorish[5] ancestry; therefore, a Chilean was at the best something like a Hottentot,[6] or, to put it more gently, something like the humbled but dangerous Californio.[7] They could not stomach the fearlessness of the Chilean, who might be submissive in his own country but did not behave that way abroad. A Chilean would face up to a loaded pistol at his chest if he had his hand on the haft of his knife. For his part, the Chilean detested the Yankee and constantly referred to him as a coward. This mutual bad feeling explains the bloody hostilities and atrocities we witnessed every day in this land of gold and hope.

It was not long in San Francisco until an organized group of bandits appeared, called the Hounds. They were vagrants, gamblers, or drunks, drawn together in a fellowship of crime; and they had as their motto, "We can get away with it." Fear and hatred spread in advance of their appearance, and they deliberately generated these feelings by their provocations. Everywhere they went they established their control by quarrelsomeness and violence.

They did not always "get away with it," though. One morning when they were passing by a little point of land to the north of town where a sort of Little Chile had grown up, separated from the center of the city, these vicious Hounds decided to give it a savage going over. Because in California, time is money, these merciless ruffians in large numbers charged the Chileans there with pistols and clubs. You can imagine the shouting and uproar this brutal and unprovoked attack brought on. The Chileans rallied and counterattacked by hurling stones. One respectable Chilean gentleman, not being able to escape through the front of his tent because it was jammed with a threatening band of Hounds, brought one of them down with a pistol shot as he came towards him then, slashing with his dagger the cloth of his tent, managed to escape through the improvised exit and join his friends in safety.

Brannan, the ex-Mormon[8] owner of the unforgettable Daice-may-nana, informed by some Chileans of

---

[1] *Babylon* Ancient Mesopotamian city known as a bustling and diverse metropolis and associated in many nineteenth-century minds with corruption and decadence.

[2] *alcalde* Town government official with administrative and judicial powers.

[3] *factotum* Person in charge of a variety of tasks.

[4] *General Persifer Smith* Persifor Frazer Smith (1798–1858), American army officer who briefly served as military governor in California in 1849.

[5] *Moorish* North African.

[6] *Hottentot* Derogatory (but formerly common) term for a member of the Khoekhoe people of southern Africa.

[7] *Californio* Native Californian of Hispanic descent.

[8] *Mormon* Member of The Church of Jesus Christ of Latter-day Saints.

what was happening in Little Chile, climbed up on top of his own house in just indignation and shouted in a loud voice for the people to come. Then, in a short but forceful speech, he declared it was time to make an example of those who had perpetrated such unheard-of atrocities against the sons of a friendly country, a country that had day after day supplied the city of San Francisco with its best flour, as well as the most skillful arms in the world when it came to making adobe bricks! "I propose," he said, "that to take care of this once and for all, the Chileans of goodwill, led by citizens of the United States, go at once to the scene and arrest these disturbers of the peace!" A general "hurrah!" was raised, and the almost instantaneous appearance of the defenders of order at the point put an end to the savagery that could have brought on the most terrible consequences. …

… I have already described the enormous swarms of poisonous and persistent mosquitoes that infest the swampy shores of the Sacramento and San Joaquín Rivers, especially where the two rivers join.

We protected ourselves as best we could, swatting them with our handkerchiefs and, finally, taking cover under some bushes that faced a dry grassless area. This area was covered with small holes like those made by our cururos[1] in the dry area beyond the Maule River. We were there about an hour before we noticed little sticks, about three inches long, that were lying there, one beside each hole, in a manner that could not be accidental. I became curious then and walked out to look at them more closely—then backed up in a fright, yelling, "They are snakes!"

I have roamed through many solitary regions in the course of my life, but I cannot remember seeing anywhere a land with so many vipers and other snakes as golden California possesses. The coral snake and the rattler can be found almost anywhere, along with a multitude of other ophidians of all different types and sizes. These are not all poisonous, but they are enough to frighten a traveler into making a detour wherever he finds one lying across the path sunning himself. The snakes we had found were not the dangerous sort. None of the many we killed had scales on its head. They looked rather like the Chilean snake which, instead of scales, has a shell that resembles the back of a turtle.

We spent a good deal of time beating these creatures to death with clubs, and then bombarding with rocks the turtles that were lined up on tree trunks floating in the water. We were at the same time being attacked by such clouds of mosquitoes that they blocked our view, as well as tore us to pieces with their bites. They could not be driven off by hand waving, fanning with branches, or even by smoke. It was late in the afternoon by the time we got back to the ship.

There are certain sights so horrifying you can never forget them. Martínez was lying motionless, monstrously swollen, the blanket at his feet—no doubt kicked there in some convulsive movement. His whole body, including his head, was covered with a disgusting and bloody layer of mosquitoes, hovering, bloated and heavy, over their miserable victim; at least an inch thick, it seemed to us. When we saw that, we ran to him, shook him, and brushed off so many thousands of mosquitoes that our hands were covered with blood. But it was too late: Martínez was dead!

We had no tools to dig a grave for him. There was no point in carrying him on to Sacramento. And the thought of leaving him ashore was, of course, unendurable to us, for he would be eaten by coyotes. After a sad night, the waters of the Sacramento River received, along with our tears, the lifeless body of the unhappy young man who only the day before had been friend and companion.

The life of a California miner closely resembled that of a soldier on a campaign. A tear may sometimes moisten the bronzed face of a soldier as he grimly shakes the hand of a dead comrade for the last time, but that tear quickly dries when he is faced with new dangers or elated by the enthusiasm victory brings.

The cool breeze of morning, the disappearance of the mosquitoes swept away by the wind, the impressive vision of the tranquil waters of Suisun Bay, the gracious hills and forests of its faraway shore, with happy passengers—and, perhaps, also the thought that tears are useless when shed over misfortunes that cannot be altered—all these things reawakened in our sad spirits their dormant energies. …

… In California there was so little difference between planning and carrying out a project that not even a line of the compass could measure it. We joined with two

---

[1] *cururos* Burrowing rodents endemic to Chile.

sons of General Lastra[1] in organizing a company; they had tried out various ways of getting ahead, just as we had. We bought a lot on Dupont Street for three thousand pesos, equipped ourselves with lumber and carpenters' tools, and set to work. A Yankee day-laborer helped us. We sawed, planed, and chiseled with such energy that in a few days (months are like centuries there) we had put up a handsome coffin-like structure with a parlor and three rooms on the first floor and four on the second. We also built a private, intimate convivence that looked like a sentry box and set it a prudent distance away from the building; this was a luxury in San Francisco at that time. I mention this little room because many Chileans, among them our fine countryman, J.M.I, spent many nights sitting in it because they did not have a better place to sleep; and slept there as well as the Prince of the Asturias could have done in a soft bed.

A well was dug for drinking water, and the job was assigned to the miner, Juan Nepomuceno Espejo. He had exchanged the manipulation of his graceful and illustrious pen for the handling of a heavy crowbar, but he did it better than the strongest rustic. He dug at the bottom of the shaft, filling a bucket, which I lowered to him, with soil and stones, and getting his head covered with the cascades of mud that dropped as I drew it up. I remember that when the water got to his knees, he called up to me in a sepulchral voice, "Vicente, it's deep enough. Look, I'm being swept away by the—" I broke in to say, "Just go on working, my friend. I'm not paying you for doing nothing!"

We hired a famous French cook called Monsieur Michel, who got, besides board and room that was worth two hundred dollars a month, a salary of five hundred dollars; that is to say eighty-four hundred dollars a year. That is a good deal more than the Secretary of State earns in Chile. We hung over the door of our cafe a large sign, "Citizen's Restaurant," and got underway with a full force in the summer of 1849.

In the beginning, needless to say, the business went well—everything went well at first in California; it was only when things reached the middle that they collapsed. We were, at one and the same time, the masters and servants of the restaurant. Barring some lapses of memory, excusable because we were new at the work, we did not do badly as servants.

We had a mulatto[2] among our customers who had recently taken on the status of a gentleman but still had a good deal of the cow pasture about him. He shouted his orders in an arrogant way, and his whole manner was unpleasant. Milk had been up to that time an exotic luxury in San Francisco. I had not had any since that which was given us with so much amiability and goodwill by the sire of the horse we bought in Sacramento. I was tempted by Satan one morning and almost finished in two swallows the milk reserved for the lunch of our gentlemanly customer. I replaced what I had drunk with water and went about my usual duties.

I was serving a cocktail to a customer when I had to drop everything and run to my brother Federico because of the vile oaths and imprecations being heaped on him by our loud-mouthed friend because of the kind of milk served him. The mood and behavior of the man made Federico forget his role as a waiter, and he was doubling up his fist. I intervened just in time to save the good name of our restaurant. I applied the most exaggerated and polished courtesies, took away the modified water that had been served as milk. I took it out to the kitchen, poured it into another mug, and brought it back to the customer immediately. The grandson of Africa, mollified by this, then exclaimed, "At last; this is more like it, waiter!" A cat can be passed off as a rabbit with many customers if it is done properly.

When the restaurant was closed late at night, we all sat on the floor and did the dishes. Then one of us was designated to sprinkle and sweep the floor and get everything ready for the next day, while the rest of us went happily to bed like any other innkeepers.

That is what our life was like during the brief time we ran the restaurant. As the business did not need all of us to manage it, and I could not forget the trick I had pulled with regard to the milk, I gave the excuse that I wanted to enlarge our sphere of activity and got from my comrades the permission to make a trip to Monterey.

---

[1]   *General Lastra* Francisco de la Lastra (1777–1852), Santiago-born politician and military officer during the Chilean War of Independence who served as the first Supreme Director of Chile from March to July 1814.

[2]   *mulatto* Term (now considered derogatory) used to refer to a mixed-race person.

I admit my real object was to get down to that town so I could drink all the milk I wanted.

On a cool and lovely July morning, rifle on my shoulder, pistols and a slender snake of gold at my waist, wearing a dirty cloth hat, a sarape,[1] and a beard down to my chest, I set out on foot through the hills around San Francisco toward the old capital of Alta California.

I crossed the first slopes of what is called the Coast Range, accompanied by a number of men from Sonora who were returning disillusioned to their homes, and entered a wide valley covered with grass and flowers. Birds and squirrels were so abundant it seemed as though they sprouted from the ground about our feet. Herds of deer acted like our guanacos:[2] they would come close, scamper away at the least movement— only to stop all of a sudden and come toward us again. The height and value as lumber of the trees surprise one here in this valley as they do in all areas of this privileged land. Oaks, pines, and birches seem inexhaustible in number. The coast opposite San Francisco is covered with redwoods; they are similar to our "alerce."[3] These trees certainly do not yield in size to the giants of our southern forest. In my earlier wandering I had occasion to view admiringly the marvelous conifers that grow in the Mariposa mining area. There I saw trees that measured from two hundred to two hundred twenty feet in height, and from sixty to sixty-five feet in circumference at the base. What is more surprising is that lateral branches some one hundred feet from the ground were more than six feet through. This portentous representative of the vegetable kingdom is called by scientists the "Sequoia Gigantea." But it has many names in California, so many that a visitor does not know which one to use. Some call it "the Grizzly Giant"; others the "redwood." English gringos call it "The Wellington"; Yankees, "The Washington." Perhaps we ought to call it "The San Martín."[4]

We slept in the shelter of an oak tree, and all night long we were bothered by the visits of coyotes. This is a variety of wolf that, although smaller than the European wolf, is as ravenous and vicious. It was fear of coyotes that drove Señor O.A. from California. He was a recognized Argentinian socialite, well known in Santiago. He set out to do what everyone else was doing, going out prospecting on his own, and the coyotes chased him without a pause until they had driven him screaming into camp. These accursed animals did not even leave us any breakfast the next morning, for they got away with what was left of the deer we had shot for food, even though it was lying right beside us.

In this, as in my previous encounters with Mexicans and Spanish Californians, I had to marvel at the candor with which these poor people talked about the invasion and take-over of their country by the Yankees. They were sure they could not by themselves drive out "the tyrants," as they, with justice, referred to the Yankees. But they firmly believed, having seen the vigorous resistance Chileans put up to the brutality and strength of the Yankees, that we Chileans could drive them out! They seemed to feel safe from being molested while traveling in my company—almost as if they were being guarded by the devil himself. But when the time came for us to part, I confess the devil was as uneasy as they were at finding himself alone.

On the afternoon of the third day of my journey (which I had begun to regret undertaking), I saw the white tower of Monterey and made up my mind to reach it before nightfall.

Monterey, the port, is one of the best on the coast. Monterey, the town, considered up to that time as the capital of California, was a village rather similar to our Casa Blanca in 1840, with a total population of not more than two thousand. However, the nature of the countryside around it and, in general, of the whole district together with that of Santa Cruz, makes it the best and most fertile area I have found as yet in the state of California.

The setting of this charming town was made more cheerful by many small orchards full of beautiful trees; and although the buildings were of the sort that our heavy country houses were a half-century ago, still,

---

1 *sarape*   Colorful blanket worn as a shawl or cloak.

2 *guanacos*   Wild South American llamas with red-brown wool coats.

3 *alerce*   Giant South American evergreen cypress tree.

4 *Wellington*   Arthur Wellesley, 1st Duke of Wellington (1769–1852), Anglo-Irish military hero who famously defeated Napoleon at the Battle of Waterloo; *San Martín* José de San Martín

(1778–1850), Argentinian general who figured prominently in the South American wars for independence from the Spanish Empire.

their wide-arched porticoes[1] facing the street demonstrated the characteristic hospitality of the Spanish race.

Night was falling fast, and as neither my appearance nor my dress was respectable enough to enable me to ask for lodgings, I decided to take shelter in one of those porticoes. I chose a house with windows closed and the door slightly ajar because I thought these conditions were evidence that the family was away. But as I approached the house the door slammed noisily. "Bad," I said to myself; "It's impossible to think they hadn't seen me. What did that slamming mean?" I went into the corridor nevertheless and knocked with three light raps in the Spanish manner on the door. No one answered, and, remembering I was in California, I then used the butt of my rifle on the unresponsive door. Two blows secured an immediate reaction. Someone within said, "Who is it?" It was the voice of an old and frail woman. "*Deo gratias*,[2] señora," I replied, "I am a man of peace who only asks permission to spread my sarape on the floor of your corridor for one night, nothing more." Then I heard some quick movements of several persons inside, and a woman's voice said, "It is not a Yankee; it's a Spaniard." I answered, "Forever," very slowly; and cautiously opened the door. I was met by a gentleman of about forty-five, simply and decently dressed. He greeted me and asked what he could do for me. When he heard me speak, he burst out with an expression of the most complete joy, "May God forgive you, my friend, for the fright you gave us. When we saw you coming we thought you were one of those scoundrels who infest our roads and towns ever since peace brought us a change of masters. Enter, señor, enter."

He was right to have taken precautions. Only a Californio house owner could know how many wrongs they had been forced to endure without hope of appeal since the invasion of the "barbarians of the north," as they called the Yankees.

You should have seen the general contentment that awakened in that amiable and hospitable family—made up of a gentleman, his lovely wife, and two sisters-in-law who would have been thought beautiful by any man but seemed like angels to me—when they realized they were dealing not only with a decent man but actually with a Chilean.

A Chilean who had been at the diggings in the high mountains was a guarantee of personal security, a scarecrow to frighten off Yankees and their misdeeds, and a brother to whom one should always extend one's hand.

Confidence and goodwill were not long in settling over these kind people and the recent arrival whom they bombarded with innumerable questions: about Chile, about the Chileans in San Francisco, about my misadventures, and about my reason for coming to Monterey. I thought they would die laughing when I told the ladies my chief reason for coming to Monterey was to gorge myself on milk.

The master of the house, Don Juan Alvarado, taking me by the hand, led me to his private room; and, making me promise I would stay with him as long as I could, he then begged me strongly and even violently to accept a linen shirt and a coat from him. He did not want to be constantly reminded by my appearance of the intruders he disliked so much. He left me alone then, and I was like a new Don Quixote,[3] changing my clothes in the palace of the duke. After a marvelous bath and a clean shave, I enjoyed the indescribable sense of well-being a fine, freshly ironed shirt gives a man, especially if his skin has been chafed for a good long time by wearing wool.

I actually slept that night in a bed with sheets and pillows! And on the following day, what did I find waiting for me beside the arcade that opened out into a fine patio filled with flowers?—two beautiful cows! I had all the milk I could drink, glass after glass passed to me in my insatiable thirst by the delicate hands of the two sisters-in-law. If, as they say, there is a "seventh heaven," then I was in it! Really to know what rest is, you have to be tired first; in the same way, really to appreciate comfort, you should be a California prospector.

Through Don Juan, I arranged with a ranchero to deliver twelve milk cows and eight oxen in San Francisco. I decided a relaxing vacation of eight days

---

[1]   *porticoes*   Colonnade porches, typically at the entrance to a building.

[2]   *Deo gratias*   Latin: Thanks be to God.

[3]   *Don Quixote*   Title character of a Spanish comic romance (1605, 1615) by Miguel de Cervantes. In Chapter 31 of Part 2 of the book, Don Quixote has just met a duke and duchess who have invited him to stay with them at their castle. They end up playing a series of tricks on him, but as he arrives at the castle he is given a royal welcome and is invited to change into a fine, new shirt.

was enough self-indulgence for me, and I told the family I would leave the next day. I was met by protests such as only those of the Latin race know how to make to guests, so I stayed for one more day for a party they arranged for me. The day after that I got ready to leave with all my gear in good shape. The entire hospitable family saw me out to the corridor facing the street, and there a fine mule waiting for me. It had a rich saddle of velvet embroidered with gold; the pommel[1] was an eagle's head of solid silver of the sort so much admired by those who have visited Mexico. It was impossible to resist the insistence of Don Juan that I accept this souvenir—this trinket, as he called it. After protestations and a very affectionate goodbye, I set out with real reluctance from this oasis in my journey through the deserts of selfishness and indifference, and, full of hope and resolution, directed my steps toward new adventures.

On my arrival at San Francisco, I found the town full of new Chilean arrivals. As I have said, there were no well-known Chilean families that did not have a legitimate representative in California. These were somewhat lost when they first landed. An activity that brought invariable success yesterday would yield only failure today. In the midst of these disillusionments and lamentations, my companions and I were trying vainly to swim against a tidal wave of discouragement that carried everything before it.

I sold my mule for six hundred pesos and my elegant saddle for seven hundred. Felipe Ramírez was put in charge of selling milk to the hotels, while my brother, César, did the milking and took charge of street sales. Federico was to go back to Chile to provide company for our excellent mother. The rest of us, including myself, would attend to the restaurant.

Then, everything in San Francisco took on a new aspect.

Up to that time, as has been said, we had engaged in dealings only with men because no women were to be found on the streets.

The mercantile spirit that speculates even with immorality did not lose much time in seeking out substitutes for the fair sex. Paintings of women totally nude and very badly drawn were hung in the best cafes in the city. These nauseating pictures that covered the walls of the saloons would have put the most wanton satyr[2] to flight in any other place; but here, offered along with gambling tables and liquor, they filled the pockets of their lucky owners with gold. With such a precedent to go on, it was only to be expected that the mercantile spirit would not lose much time in producing the real thing, of flesh and blood, as repulsive as are the painted representations.

The passenger ship from Panamá on its first voyage brought two daughters of Eve of the sort called "liberated." Those who went down to watch the steamer come in at the western headland, when they saw the hats and sunshades of women, became so enthusiastic and ran down to the pier so fast that they drew in everyone they passed; so a thousand men were waiting on the beach. No sooner had the anchor been dropped than there broke out a noisy quarrel between the two damsels and the purser.[3] They wanted to come ashore at once; the purser said the arrangement had been that they would pay their passage as soon as they reached the city. The more spirited of the two Yankee girls, acting on the principle that "time is money," said the purser would be held responsible for damages and losses, plus interest, caused by the delay. Whereupon two of the waiting crowd, tired of marking time, clambered on board the ship, and, throwing a bag of gold at the feet of the greedy purser, came back to land with the girls to a general "Hooray!" from the crowd.

The joyful crowd opened a path, and the girls on the arms of their two deliverers, waving greetings and receiving "hurrahs" in turn, quickly disappeared into the crossroads that led to the cribs, followed at a distance by the lascivious and envious eyes of those who had not given the maxim, time is money, its legitimate importance.

It was to be expected that shipowners, noting the high passage rate feminine merchandise could command on arrival at San Francisco, set out to procure and did procure the embarkation of as much of this kind of merchandise as they could find. On the next

---

[1]   *pommel*   Raised arch on the front end of a saddle, also known as a saddlebow; in this case, an ornamental knob on the saddlebow.

[2]   *satyr*   Half man, half beast (usually goat or horse) of classical mythology. In classical art and literature, satyrs are often depicted in the lustful pursuit of nymphs.

[3]   *purser*   Naval officer in charge of a ship's financial accounting.

voyage, seven more arrived and were received with the same gallantry.

The cafe owners were alarmed by the competition that their badly painted monstrosities had to meet from these real monstrosities who kept on arriving. They planned and carried out the most incredible and obscene projects that human shamelessness can improvise in such situations. They hired these creatures, at a gold peso each, to pose in plastic displays in the café dining halls. They sat up platforms on both sides of the room, and on them placed, totally nude, and assuming indecent poses, these exemplifications of California modesty and decency.

The doors of the exhibition were opened at eight in the evening to the sound of music. Curious men, who had left a good part of their gold dust at the door, were pushed rapidly through to the exits by those coming on behind them before they had time to look. They came tumbling out the rear door, cursing like fiends. I remember that a Chilean of good family, Don J.E., whose name I will not further clarify, said to me, "My friend, the devil tempted me, and then cleaned me out of all the gold I had in my purse, a half-pound! I was pouring onto the scale enough to pay for my entrance when a shove from behind made me dump it all, and then I was pushed on forward so I couldn't get back to recover the extra gold."

This enterprise could be kept going only for a month, though, because the steamers began coming not with a few but with whole cargoes of women on board, all under the agreement to pay for their passage before disembarking, or, at least, the next day afterward.

If the scenes described to this point are repugnant, those I will sketch next, before closing this page of my notes, are no less to be wondered at.

At the door of the room each one of these first Messalinas[1] had on arrival, fights with clubs and pistol broke out every night between those who wanted to get in first to meet them. The women knew very well there was no profit to be had from men who were beaten up or dead, so they would rush out to pacify the combatants, using kinds of arguments that shame prevents me from revealing.

The demand for women had slackened somewhat because the ships were bringing in so many; so, to keep profits up, the captains decided to sell the unpaid passage bills at auction. The highest bidder got to carry off his prize, and the captain pocketed whatever he got over the cost of the passage.

The strangest, coarsest scenes developed as a result of this.

The objects to be auctioned off were assembled in the cabin of the poop deck with all their meretricious ornaments. The man who was to conduct the auction would take one of these shameless creatures by the hand, and, after praising her figure, her youth, and beauty, he would call out in a loud voice, "Gentlemen, what are you willing to pay, any one of you, right now, to have this pretty dame, fresh from New York, pay you a very special visit?" The bidding began at once, and the highest bidder, as soon as the hammer fell, handed over the gold dust and carried away his property. …

… In all fairness, however, it must be said that not everything in San Francisco was chaotic. Some thought was also given to the future political status of the area in the midst of all the hurly-burly. The strong spirit of liberty incarnate in every one of the adventurers who intended to make his home permanently in California had long before led to the rejection of military government. These people wanted the new territory elevated immediately to the rank of a sovereign state. Overt steps were already being taken in Washington to bring this about. To add weight to this just aspiration, which was being expressed more and more strongly, it was proposed to elect the members of the legislature to meet in San José; where, instead of Monterey as in the past, the capital was to be located and the governor was to reside. …

… California had by this time lost almost all its attractiveness for venturesome foreigners, concerning the opportunities that had drawn so many people of such different types to her shores. This followed the wavering policy of support or lack of support by Governor Smith. What was needed there now was not foreigners striving to achieve success by their own labor and for their own profit, but rather men who would work for salaries and wages. It is not surprising,

---

[1] *Messalinas*   Devious, licentious women, called so after the third wife of the Roman emperor Claudius, Messalina Valeria, who was executed after she wed one of her lovers, the senator Gaius Silius, allegedly in an attempt to seize power.

then, that those who had considerable capital at their disposal either lost it or resigned themselves to leaving the country in disillusionment. We were thinking of doing the same thing, when fate, which had treated us so badly, gave us the *coup de grace*.[1] What drove us out of this ex-land of promise with so harsh a dismissal was one of those terrible fires, wiping everything out, that broke out in the last months of 1850.

We had been in bed about two hours, after having made up our minds to go back to Chile, when a flickering red light coming through the windowpanes threw a glow into the room where we were sleeping. The fire had been set deliberately, as so many were, in the hotel already mentioned as having the infamous display of living nudes. We never would have imagined that a fire more than three blocks away from our building could have brought us any damage. We were rejoicing over the evil end being put to all that ugliness, and calculating the increase in the price of our building as a result of the shortage that was to follow, when, about an hour and a half later, fate demonstrated to us that shining thought of profit may continue to be shining but cease to be profitable. The fire spread in all directions with the same reckless speed that we had seen it spread through our wheat fields in Chile at harvest time. In the midst of that immense and roaring bonfire enlivened by exploding gunpowder casks in the stores, with the air filled with sparks and burning bits of wood, and the blazing walls fanned by the wind, the whole region was involved. We were hemmed in by flames on every side, and we, like everyone else, owed our escape solely to the swiftness of our flight.

Two and a half months later, in the garb of seamen, we were in peaceful Chile tenderly embracing our mother, poor as ever, but satisfied that we had not abandoned the fort before the last shot was fired.

AFTERTHOUGHTS

Before closing this brief glimpse of California, I believe that I should try to give you some idea of its government and the critical and abnormal conditions that Chileans were facing in that country at the time of my departure.

There is certainly much to admire and much to criticize in the behavior of the new owners of California. However, much as we may feel tempted to present them at one extreme as models worthy of imitation, or at the other as deserving condemnation by all civilized peoples, we will limit ourselves simply to the facts and leave it to our readers to draw their own conclusions.

There were no more than five hundred North American Californians in the summer of 1845. The country was under military law. This was administered by Colonel Mason, the acting Provisional Governor. California was a sorry spectacle: it was being regenerated in spite of itself, setting the inert force of its old customs against the innovative spirit that had invaded it. The people of California, considerably increased by immigration, presented a heterogeneous mass of usages and customs, of languages and religions; they would require, it seemed, a good many years of living together, and much wisdom, to reach the stage one finds there today. The men in authority there were unfamiliar with Spanish law. The Californios were equally ignorant of North American law. They did not know what rules they were to observe, nor how to defend their rights and make their just claims prevail. Interpreters were paid in a gold dollar, and almost always tipped the scales on the side of the new masters. These rulers wanted to rectify things and put an end to the difficulties arbitrary rule brought, but the only solution they could think of was to call the magistrate in the towns by the title of the alcalde. The North American laws remained in force, though, even if masked and obscured with certain Spanish procedures. This system satisfied neither the Californios nor the North Americans. The latter were disoriented, and all transactions were conducted in an atmosphere of uncertainty and suspicion.

The arbitrary nature of the taxes, and the military duties on trade that were put into force in October of 1847, tended to absorb all profits and fatten the military treasury uselessly while drawing all the coinage out of circulation. This imposed the greatest difficulties on trade. Because gold dust was not acceptable for payment of taxes, it lost value and brought only six dollars an ounce.

Such a state of affairs could not last. Everywhere it was felt that the highest need of the area was for a

---

[1] *coup de grace*   French: finishing blow.

provisional government. The heavy labor in the gold fields of 1848 had scarcely ended when the people who were concentrated in the towns, who possessed a good deal of gold but were without any form of civil government that would protect their property, decided to act. Without halting their material constructions, which were astonishing in their enormous extent, the people began to hold repeated meetings for the election of deputies to a constitutional convention. The difficulties in carrying out so important an object as this were enough to frighten a people less used to governing themselves.

Nevertheless, on September 1, 1849, to the amazement of all, the memorable assembly opened in Monterey, and in only one and a half months it bequeathed to the country a government, a constitution, and a national representation. Its achievement was received with general approval. …

… From that time on, the administration, regularized and complete in all its parts, began to exercise its powers in conformity with what was laid down in the constitution. It also asked that the government in Washington admit this most beautiful of its territories as an independent state of the Union. …

… While the tireless North American was laboring to acquire riches, and building a government for his adopted state that would create security through the strength of its institutions, what were the foreigners doing in California?

They had arrived from all parts of the world, flocking to the great fair nature had opened up from the human race. They had come to a land where, it was said, the generous immigration laws had removed the word stranger from the vocabulary. None of them was destitute, as were thousands of North Americans, and all of them believed they could make their fortunes because wealth was so easy to acquire.

To raw and empty California, their imports and industry ought to have been as beneficial and as welcome as gifts from heaven. But, needless to say, they were not viewed in that light. Foreigners had to conclude that either North Americans had changed their

Tando de enebrar una campaña

nature in California, or it was a lie to say immigrants got a fraternal welcome on the Atlantic coast.

I will deal only with Chileans because they made a very major contribution, because they came to California in great numbers, and because the kinds of mistreatment they suffered caught the attention of the whole world. What caused the conquerors of California to pick the Chileans as the target of their hatred and brutal violence is to me, even today, an incomprehensible mystery. The beginning of San Francisco's economic development was entirely attributable to the sons of Chile. It was Chileans from Concepción and Valparaíso who built the first houses there. Prior to the great fire that destroyed a large part of the city, you could count all the buildings that were not made of Chilean lumber. Because there was not enough wood, Chileans were hired to manufacture adobes,[1] as they were the only persons skilled at this and willing to work as reasonable wages. There is scarcely a well in the city Chileans did not dig. Chile also supplied the necessities of ready-made clothing, shoes, and bread, along with a host of other goods to that land, which was inhospitable to them alone.

Many Chileans took jobs on the promise of wages but got only blows and insults. If they had the effrontery to complain to those in authority, they found there such weighted injustice and such extortion on the part of the interpreters that it would have been better for them to have swallowed their indignation. From the early months of 1849 on, the Chilean was looked upon as a pariah; he was viewed by most Yankees very much the way a Jew was by a Knight Templar[2] in the Middle Ages. The inexplicable prejudice was not restricted to the cities. Outrages of a lighter or a more serious nature were also perpetrated against them in the goldfields. Wherever the Chileans were outnumbered by their enemies they were dispossessed and driven out with the most fearful threats. …

… Scattered and persecuted Chileans trickled down into Sacramento and Stockton every day. They had no one they could call upon for help, no money to continue their journey, and nothing to sell but their labor—for which they were paid little or nothing. Exposed in their need to the disease-ridden climate of summer, many caught yellow fever. Chile lost many of her sons there.

All outcry was useless. The interpreters, the collectors of customs, the freight handlers, and the merchants all wanted immigration to continue so it would keep on providing them with victims they could exploit. So they played down the malignity of the situation and called attention instead to the continuing richness and the great number of strikes being made in the mining areas.

The defense the unfortunate Chileans put up to save their own hide intensified the rancor of their tormentors to such a pitch that they decided to wipe out the rest of the outlawed race once and for all. The city of San Francisco was a witness to that incredible undertaking on the part of the Hounds. They attacked with banner and drums and were guilty of horrible excesses. What is most strange, some of them spoke Spanish they had picked up in Chile, where they had been treated with cordial and fraternal hospitality.

May I say in passing for the benefit of those who applaud the efforts of the Union authorities in San Francisco, that the least of the crimes that gang committed included robbery, arson, and murder. Any one of these by itself was a capital crime. Despite that, the heaviest penalty given to them was a mock trial and an order to leave the city; and most of the perpetrators of those outrages walked the streets of San Francisco unpunished and without fear.

After that event, the only things Chileans had to fear in San Francisco were the exactions of the police, the dishonesty of the interpreters and customs collectors, and the constant bias of the judges. In the mines, however, there continued to be an endless succession of violent dispossessions and murders. Men were whipped, cruelly mutilated, and hung.[3]

The authorities were not able to stop these crimes perpetrated against the peaceful sons of a friendly nation, but they could at least have disavowed them

---

[1] *adobes* Bricks made of a mixture of sand, clay, and straw.

[2] *Knight Templar* Member of the Poor Fellow-Soldiers of Christ and of the Temple of Solomon, more commonly known as the Knights Templar (after a medieval military and religious order of knighthood that had enormous military and financial influence during the Crusades). The comment also refers more generally to the persecution faced by Jews in medieval Christian Europe.

---

[3] [Pérez Rosales's note] At Sutter's Mill [where gold was discovered in January 1848, setting off the California Gold Rush], I saw them hang an Indian by the neck on a rope, and afterward let him fall so they could force him to make a statement. The same thing was done to a poor Chilean in San Francisco, and to Senór D. José María Alvarez.

in the newspapers, ... Chile was not favored by even this disavowal by either the authorities of the United States or those of the state, though it would have been politically wise, courteous, and would have cost little.

The press itself, a major force in North America, and one surely not controlled by mobsters, disregarded both the interests of trade and the duties of humanity on a false point of honor and fed the flames of discord by setting off their atrocities with the alarming headline: "*North American Blood Shed By Chileans!*" As if the conduct of a mere handful of valiant men, exasperated by atrocities, in fighting off a group of bandits, reflected the least dishonor upon their compatriots! ... —1878

In Context

The California Gold Rush

[Additional "In Context" materials appear as part of the anthology's website component.]

Images of Gold Rush Days

The Treaty of Guadalupe Hidalgo was signed on 2 February 1848, formally ending the Mexican-American War and making California an official possession of the United States. A mere eight days earlier, on 24 January, gold had been discovered at Sutter's Mill on the American River near Coloma, instigating the Gold Rush. At the beginning of 1848 the non-Hispanic population of the region had totalled fewer than 1,000, the native Californios of Hispanic descent between 6,500 and 7,000, and the Native American population between 110,000 and 150,000. By the mid-1850s some 300,000 new settlers had arrived from around the world—and the Native American population had been greatly reduced, with tens of thousands dying from disease and violence.

1849 handbill advertisement. Through an 1846 treaty, the United States had obtained transit rights across the isthmus of Panama. Though a canal would not finally be built until the early twentieth century, a considerable amount of the traffic between California and the American east coast during the Gold Rush was via Panama; an overland journey was sandwiched between two steamship journeys.

"Yerba Buena Cove," 1850. [San Francisco harbor]

Studio photograph of an unidentified miner, 1851.

Unidentified miners posed against a photographic studio backdrop.

Unidentified woman outside a California daguerreotype studio, 1852. The daguerreotype process reverses an image; unless a daguerreotypist attached a special device to the lens, what was printed would be a mirror image of what was seen.

Miners working for Sterrett and Company, 1852. Individuals staking their claims predominated in the early days of the Gold Rush, but in the early 1850s corporate interests began to play a much larger role. Though the Gold Rush is considered to have continued until 1855, the spirit of "the '49ers" was by then largely a thing of the past.

Unidentified Californian, 1854. In the early days of the Gold Rush, lawlessness and vigilantism flourished in the absence of any official government or means of enforcing order in the newly acquired territory. And, as Vicente Pérez Rosales observes, even the establishment of a police force and a judicial system brought little improvement for many.

Newspaper Reports

The following letter, dated July 2, was first published in a Philadelphia newspaper, the *North American and U.S. Gazette*, on 14 September 1848. It was subsequently reprinted in the Baltimore *Commercial Journal*, the Augusta, Georgia *Daily Constitutionalist and Republic*, the *Buffalo Courier*, and other newspapers across the country, helping to spark the Gold Rush frenzy.

In the *New York Daily Herald* of 21 December 1848, the lead article on "Californian Emigration" was followed by letters on the subject, beginning with the letter from a Seneca Falls, NY, correspondent excerpted below.

Monterrey, Upper California, July 2nd, 1848

Messrs. Editors—The mineral wealth of California is being daily developed. Mines of silver, quicksilver, copper, zinc, and lead have been found in our mountains ....

But a recent gold discovery has thrown all others into the shade. The sands which border Feather River and the American Fork[1] abound in particles of gold—resembling in shape snowflakes. These are separated from the sand by stirring them in water in a basin or bowl. A person will collect by this simple process from one to two ounces of gold a day—some have gone as high as six and eight ounces. I have just been conversing with a man who, in six days, gathered five hundred dollars worth. He has one piece which weighs an ounce.

There are probably now not less than five thousand persons, whites and Indians, gathering this gold. San Francisco, Sonoma, Santa Cruz and San Jose are literally deserted by their inhabitants; all have gone to the gold regions. The farmers have thrown aside their ploughs, the lawyers their briefs, the doctors their pills, the priests their prayer books, and all are now digging gold. The diamond-broached gentleman and the clouted[2] Indian work side by side, lovingly, as if they had been rocked in the same cradle. Tin pans to wash the sparking sand in have sold as high as eight dollars a piece—shovels for ten and wooden bowls for five! ...

The tract of land where the gold is found covers a hundred miles in one direction and fifty in another. It is said that ten thousand men in ten years could not exhaust it. ...

We want, in California, some good school books, a few good teachers, and a few off-hand preachers. All these would find persons to read and to listen. We are gathering the elements of a great and influential community—if we are not ruined by this gold excitement. There was never yet a people strong in wealth and sound in morals in the midst of gold and silver mines.

You talk of farmers; why, I saw a farmer here brand last week a thousand calves, all of one year's growth, and he is considered here rather a small farmer. You reckon by acres, and we by miles and leagues. Your sheep produce one lamb a year—ours always two, and often four. Your streams have a few minnows in them, and ours are paved with gold! How are my Philadelphia friends? I expect to leave this El Dorado in a few months, and be among them.

Very truly yours, W.C.

from the *New York Daily Herald*, 21 December 1848

California Emigration

Emigration to the gold region from the United States, as far as we can ascertain from various ... sources within our reach, has been as yet exceedingly small ... but if the persons who have resolved to seek their fortunes there make good their resolutions, the list of gold diggers will, in less than

---

[1] *American Fork* Gold was discovered on the South Fork of the American River.

[2] *clouted* Clothed in ragged or patchy garments.

a year, fill an enormous parchment. ... The number of vessels up for the Pacific, at this port, has not been enlarged since yesterday; at Boston, Philadelphia, and Baltimore, we do not hear of any additional movements of interest. The owners of the *Crescent City*, which leaves on Saturday for Chagres,[1] have made an engagement with a gentleman who has crossed the isthmus several times, to proceed by express to Panama. It is his intention to make all possible arrangements at Panama for the despatch of passengers to San Francisco, and, by arrangements along the road, to facilitate the transit of the isthmus.

_____

Seneca Falls, Dec. 18, 1848

The gold fever runs ahead of the cholera, by tens of thousands, in this district. A perfect diarrhoea of emigration threatens to bring down all western New York upon the torrid zone,[2] and thence transmit its excited inhabitants to California. ... If the excitement in other portions of the country only approximates to the intensity of feeling in this region, something must be done by Congress to protect the populating of these "old free States." Every individual in our village ... has been seized by this deep, consuming fever. ...

You know we have always been somewhat given to a diverted state of mind in this peculiar locality, giving birth to or violently supporting every new light—moral, political, religious, or otherwise—that has made its appearance during the last twenty years. ... Land speculation was in our midst from 1830 until 1838 to a fearful extent. ... The original Mormons first commenced their labors in this interesting neighborhood.[3] ... But it was reserved for the summer of 1848 to complete the great moral triumph we have always been gaining. Friend Lucretia Mott of Philadelphia; that clever but saucy n—, Frederick Douglass; the Hon. Ansel Bascom; and a highly talented lady in our village, called a convention and struck boldly for the great cause of woman's rights,[4] as they are, in some particulars, understood and enunciated[.] ... But all the feeling upon the sundry subjects of ... anti-masonry, land speculation, Mormonism, temperance, free soil,[5] woman's rights etc. was nothing to the tornado of excitement now caused by this new discovery of America. ...

from William Swain, letter to his mother, 12 August 1850

In April 1849, William Swain (1821–1904), a well educated, twenty-seven-year-old farmer from Youngstown, New York, left his wife and small child behind to seek gold in California. Taking the overland route, he suffered numerous hardships and did not arrive in the gold fields until December. In the letter below he describes the disappointment that so many suffered when their dreams of wealth did not pan out.

By November Swain had made only $500; he decided to return home, and booked a passage via the isthmus of Panama, reaching New York on 30 January 1850.

_____

[1] *Chagres*   Then the main port on the Atlantic coast of Panama.

[2] *torrid zone*   I.e., the Tropics.

[3] *The original Mormons ... interesting neighborhood*   The Church of Jesus Christ of Latter-day Saints was founded (as the Church of Christ) in Fayette, New York, in 1830.

[4] *Friend Lucretia Mott ... woman's rights*   The writer refers to the Seneca Falls Convention of 1848, an event often seen as having launched the formal women's rights movement. Attendees of the convention included Lucretia Mott (referred to here as "Friend" because she was a member of the Religious Society of Friends, or Quakers) and the abolitionist orator Frederick Douglass.

[5] *free soil*   Reference to the Free Soil Party, an abolitionist political party whose focus was on preventing the expansion of slavery into the western territories.

Dear Mother

As an expressman has just gone by our door and will return in an hour, I take my pen to write a line to let you know that I am and have been well since I last wrote, and as the sickly season is almost over, I am in hopes I shall escape any sickness this summer. There is considerable sickness of fevers and ague[1] in the valley of Sacramento and some in the mountains and some mountain fever, but generally the miners are well as to physical [condition]. But nine-tenths of them are sick at heart! Ay!! Downhearted and discouraged!!! And many of them have great reason to be discouraged. Thousands who one month ago felt certain that their chances were sure for a fortune are at this time without money or any chance of any, and [are] hundreds of dollars in debt. Certainly such a turn of fortune is enough to sicken the heart of any man.

The cause of this is the failure of the claims on the rivers. All were induced to believe that a claim or place where the river … bed could be worked for gold would yield ample reward to those who worked it. In keeping with that, miners universally sought places in which to operate in that way, and spent the winter and spring in cutting races, building dams, and preparing to reap an immediate fortune when the water fell. *That time has come!* And nine out of ten of the locations have not worked out, and the operators with dark forebodings behold their bright daydreams of golden wealth vanish like the dreams of night. …

Since I wrote last …, I have been in company with Henry Hill on the Kanaka Bar[2] and have done middling well, making some $200. So you see that I am plodding my slow length along toward making a thousand. …

If it was two months later, I think I would bid these terrible hills a long farewell and vamoose to the cities. But not till the fall comes. Then I think if I am not doing extremely well I shall quit this hellish life of a miner and try the valley, for I assure you I believe California has a little for me, anyway. I am quite satisfied with the way she has used[3] me so far, and a satisfied mind is a great deal in this country. I think that *time* is all that is necessary, in this country, to get money—that is, if a man has his health; but it is a terrible place to be sick in.

I shall hang like death to what money I have got and get what I can. Time and circumstances only will enable me to say when I shall start for home.

Mother, you must kiss little Sis for me. Tell Sabrina that I hope I shall be able to come home this fall with thousands. But the expressman is here and I must close. Tell George that he must save all the money he can from his office.

Yours with affection,
William Swain

---

[1] *ague* Shaking.

[2] *Kanaka Bar* Located on the middle fork of the Feather River.

[3] *used* Treated.

Lydia Maria Child

1802 – 1880

Lydia Maria Child's work was so diverse, so prolific, and so widely read that, as her first biographer wrote, "she seemed to supply a sufficient literature for any family through her own unaided pen" as the author of novels, domestic handbooks, stories for children, and more. But Child rapidly fell from the height of her popularity when she began to publish abolitionist writing far too radical for the mainstream taste she had served. For portions of her career, her uncompromising articulation of her views on slavery—and on other matters such as interracial marriage, Indigenous-settler relations, gender roles, and the equality of religions—garnered her boycotts and mainstream derision. It also produced an incisive and rich body of fiction and nonfiction addressing the concerns most pertinent to nineteenth-century American society.

Child was born in Massachusetts in 1802, the youngest daughter of Convers and Susannah Rand Francis. Her devoutly Calvinist parents generally disapproved of academic pursuits—especially for girls—so her formal education was limited to that offered by local public schools. Her literary interests were encouraged, however, by her elder brother Convers. In 1815, following the deaths of her mother and several other family members, Child was sent to live with a married elder sister in rural Maine, where Child worked briefly as a schoolteacher but was expected primarily to cultivate her domestic skills. In 1821, however, she had the opportunity to live again with her brother Convers near Boston; here she became increasingly immersed in the study of literature, history, religion, and philosophy, and met other future literary luminaries such as Ralph Waldo Emerson.

As early as the publication of her first novel, *Hobomok: A Tale of Early Times* (1824), Child began to court both the controversy and the popularity that together would define her career. The novel, which she wrote in a matter of weeks, was set in early colonial Massachusetts and largely inspired by Child's encounter with J.W. Eastburn and R.C. Sands's epic poem *Yamoyden: A Tale of the Wars of King Philip* (1820). *Hobomok* itself dramatized the settler-Indigenous relations of early colonial Massachusetts and Plymouth, and depicted a short-lived marriage between its Puritan heroine and the Native American Hobomok. It was this element that was perceived as scandalous by many white readers, who balked at the depiction of an interracial marriage as well as at Child's generally sympathetic—if stereotypical—portrayal of Massachusett Indigenous culture. One article in the *North American Review* called the subject matter "revolting," and initial sales of the book's one-thousand-copy print run were slow. Nevertheless, *Hobomok* was received favorably by an influential minority. Child actively sought out the support of respected literary scholar George Ticknor; he took her on as a protégée, and she soon became a minor celebrity in Boston circles.

Buoyed by the support of the Boston literary establishment and motivated to achieve financial independence, Child continued to mine the increasingly popular field of colonial history for her subsequent publications. Her novel *The Rebels, or Boston before the Revolution* (1825) centered on the American Revolution; *The First Settlers of New England* (1828) was a nonfiction book aimed at children. Child furthered her reputation by founding *The Juvenile Miscellany*, a very successful magazine in the burgeoning genre of children's literature, and she cemented her celebrity in 1829 with *The Frugal Housewife*, a wildly popular handbook whose topics encompassed cookery, domestic economy, and parenting. In 1828 she married David Lee Child, a struggling lawyer and journalist; together they edited *The Massachusetts Journal*, while Child's more lucrative publications continued to provide their primary income. By the time Child released *The Mother's Book*, a parenting handbook, in 1831, she was one of the most popular writers in the country; as a critic for the *North American Review* asserted in July 1833, Child was, as an author and public figure, "just the woman we want for the mothers and daughters of the present generation."

A month after that review was published, Child released *An Appeal in Favor of that Class of Americans Called Africans*—a work unlike anything she had published before. Partially instigated by Child's recent friendship with radical abolitionist William Lloyd Garrison, the *Appeal* was the result of three years' study, informed by abolitionist editorials, Southern newspaper reports and registers of enslaved people, and histories of Africa and of the slave trade. While Child's writings had previously hinted at moderately antislavery sentiments, the majority of her audience were unprepared for the exhaustively researched and fervently articulated abolitionism of her *Appeal*. The work condemned Southern slavery in the strongest terms, denounced racism in the North, and went so far as to express sympathy for enslaved people who engaged in violent resistance, comparing it to the "blood [shed] for the sake of liberty" during the American Revolution. The influence on her argument of African American writers such as David Walker—whose *Appeal to the Colored Citizens of the World* had caused a storm of controversy in 1829—was clear. Readers were scandalized, and many canceled their subscriptions to the *Juvenile Miscellany* in response, causing Child to relinquish her editorial position; she also lost the patronage of Ticknor. At the same time, the abolitionist press welcomed the text; numerous anecdotes were shared of enslavers who had "converted" to the abolitionist cause upon reading her work. Child's *Appeal* would prove to be among the most influential antislavery texts of the era. One review in *The Unionist* called it "altogether one of the most valuable publications which have for a long time fallen under our eye."

Child continued to be a household name, but her sphere of influence changed and her work was for several decades dominated by antislavery activism, as well as by a wide range of other influential nonfiction works such as *History of the Condition of Women, In Various Ages and Nations* (1835). She also continued to write short stories, many of them centered on the subjects of slavery and racism, for various publications. In 1841, she began writing for New York City's *National Anti-Slavery Standard*, to which she contributed a popular column that came to be known as "Letters from New York"; her 1843 collection of these letters sold out within months. The epistles covered a wide variety of social, moral, and philosophical topics that were generally deemed inappropriate for women writers, including prison reform, prostitution, and gender equality. Child also vehemently criticized Indian Removal and other federal policies concerning Native Americans, though her proposed alternatives were often paternalistic and assimilationist, grounded in the view that Indigenous people were inherently equal to but "less advanced" than Europeans.

As the Civil War broke out, Child often expressed frustration with the Lincoln administration for its emphasis on preserving the Union over abolishing slavery; during Reconstruction, she criticized the regressive racial policies that characterized much of the post-slavery nation. Her 1865 reader *The Freedmen's Book* was a diverse collection of inspirational biographies, poems, and other writings by both white and African American authors, dedicated by Child "to the freedmen" with the hope that readers would "derive fresh strength and courage from this true record of what colored men have accomplished, under great disadvantages." Child published her final novel, *A Romance of the Republic*, in 1867; it returned to the subject of interracial marriage, this time envisioning a positive future relationship between African Americans and white Americans.

Child died in 1880, two years after the death of her husband. A funeral address was given by abolitionist and orator Wendell Phillips, who celebrated both her literary achievements and her lifelong pursuit of social justice. In the late nineteenth century, a decline in interest in abolitionist figures led to reduced attention to Child's work, but the breadth of her intellectual contributions helped to ensure that she was regularly discussed—as an essayist, as a novelist, as a writer for children—throughout much of the twentieth century and into the twenty-first. Recent criticism has focused increasingly on her fiction, addressing the ways in which her depictions of colonialism and Indigenous societies both challenge and conform to nineteenth-century prejudices. Yet Child's nonfiction remains central to her importance—and her *Appeal* in particular remains a seminal work of historical scholarship, as well as a salient condemnation of racism and a prescient analysis of the social, political, and economic effects of slavery on the United States.

NOTE ON THE TEXTS: The texts of the New York letters "Women's Rights" and "The Indians" presented here are based on those in the 1843 edition of Child's *Letters from New-York*. The text of "The Quadroons" is based on the version of the story printed in Child's collection *Fact and Fiction* (1846). The text of *The Duty of Disobedience to the Fugitive Slave Act* is based on the first published edition. Spelling and punctuation have been modernized in accordance with the practices of this anthology.

⌘ ⌘ ⌘

The Quadroons[1]

I promised thee a sister tale
Of man's perfidious cruelty;
Come then and hear what cruel wrong
Befell the dark Ladie.[2] — *Coleridge*

Not far from Augusta, Georgia, there is a pleasant place called Sand-Hills, appropriated almost exclusively to summer residences for the wealthy inhabitants of the neighboring city. Among the beautiful cottages that adorn it was one far retired from the public roads, and almost hidden among the trees. It was a perfect model of rural beauty. The piazzas that surrounded it were covered with clematis and passionflower. The pride of China[3] mixed its oriental-looking foliage with the majestic magnolia, and the air was redolent with the fragrance of flowers, peeping out from every nook, and nodding upon you in bye places, with a most unexpected welcome. The tasteful hand of Art had not learned to *imitate* the lavish beauty and harmonious disorder of Nature, but they lived together in loving unity, and spoke in according tones. The gateway rose in a Gothic arch, with graceful tracery in iron-work, surmounted by a cross, around which fluttered and played the mountain fringe, that lightest and most fragile of vines.

The inhabitants of this cottage remained in it all the year round; and perhaps enjoyed most the season that left them without neighbours. To one of the parties, indeed, the fashionable summer residents that came and went with the butterflies were merely neighbors-in-law. The edicts of society had built up a wall of separation between her and them; for she was a quadroon; the daughter of a wealthy merchant of New Orleans, highly cultivated in mind and manners, graceful as an antelope, and beautiful as the evening star. She had early attracted the attention of a handsome and wealthy young Georgian; and as their acquaintance increased, the purity and bright intelligence of her mind inspired him with a far deeper sentiment than belongs merely to excited passion. It was in fact Love in its best sense—that most perfect landscape of our complex nature, where earth everywhere kisses the sky, but the heavens embrace all; and the lowliest dew-drop reflects the image of the highest star.

The tenderness of Rosalie's conscience required an outward form of marriage; though she well knew that a union with her proscribed race was unrecognized by law,[4] and therefore the ceremony gave her no legal hold on Edward's constancy. But her high, poetic nature regarded the reality rather than the semblance of things; and when he playfully asked how she could keep him if he wished to run away, she replied, "Let the

---

[1]   *Quadroons*   Term commonly used in the nineteenth century to classify individuals of mixed racial background, generally those who had one black and three white grandparents.

[2]   *I promised … Ladie*   From "Ballad of the Dark Ladie" (1799) by English poet Samuel Taylor Coleridge.

[3]   *pride of China*   Also called the Chinese flame tree, which produces dramatic sprays of yellow flowers that turn to reddish fruit.

[4]   *a union … by law*   Many states legally prohibited marriage between people of different races, especially white and African American people; Georgia passed its first law to this effect in 1750, and marriages between white and black or Indigenous people remained illegal in the state until 1972. In some states, anyone with at least one-eighth black ancestry was prohibited from marrying a white person, while in other states this prohibition applied to anyone with any black ancestry whatsoever.

church that my mother loved sanction our union, and my own soul will be satisfied, without the protection of the state. If your affections fall from me, I would not, if I could, hold you by a legal fetter."

It was a marriage sanctioned by Heaven, though unrecognized on earth. The picturesque cottage at Sand-Hills was built for the young bride under her own directions; and there they passed ten as happy years as ever blessed the heart of mortals. It was Edward's fancy to name their eldest child Xarifa, in commemoration of a Spanish song[1] which had first conveyed to his ears the sweet tones of her mother's voice. Her flexile form and nimble motions were in harmony with the breezy sound of the name; and its Moorish[2] origin was most appropriate to one so emphatically "a child of the sun." Her complexion, of a still lighter brown than Rosalie's, was rich and glowing as an autumnal leaf. The iris of her large, dark eye had the melting, mezzotinto[3] outline which remains the last vestige of African ancestry, and gives that plaintive expression, so often observed, and so appropriate to that docile and injured race.

Xarifa learned no lessons of humility or shame within her own happy home; for she grew up in the warm atmosphere of father's and mother's love, like a flower open to the sunshine, and sheltered from the winds. But in summer walks with her beautiful mother, her young cheek often mantled[4] at the rude gaze of the young men, and her dark eye flashed fire, when some contemptuous epithet met her ear, as white ladies passed them by, in scornful pride and ill-concealed envy.

Happy as Rosalie was in Edward's love, and surrounded by an outward environment of beauty so well adapted to her poetic spirit, she felt these incidents with inexpressible pain. For herself, she cared but little; for she had found a sheltered home in Edward's heart, which the world might ridicule, but had no power to profane. But when she looked at her beloved Xarifa, and reflected upon the unavoidable and dangerous position which the tyranny of society had awarded her, her soul was filled with anguish. The rare loveliness of the child increased daily, and was evidently ripening into most marvellous beauty. The father rejoiced in it with unmingled pride; but in the deep tenderness of the mother's eye there was an indwelling sadness, that spoke of anxious thoughts and fearful foreboding.

When Xarifa entered her ninth year, these uneasy feelings found utterance in earnest solicitations that Edward would remove to France, or England. This request excited but little opposition, and was so attractive to his imagination that he might have overcome all intervening obstacles, had not "a change come o'er the spirit of his dream."[5] He still loved Rosalie; but he was now twenty-eight years old, and, unconsciously to himself, ambition had for some time been slowly gaining an ascendancy over his other feelings. The contagion of example had led him into the arena where so much American strength is wasted; he had thrown himself into political excitement with all the honest fervor of youthful feeling. His motives had been unmixed with selfishness, nor could he ever define to himself when or how sincere patriotism took the form of personal ambition. But so it was, that at twenty-eight years old, he found himself an ambitious man, involved in movements which his frank nature would have once abhorred, and watching the doubtful[6] game of mutual cunning with all the fierce excitement of a gambler.

Among those on whom his political success most depended was a very popular and wealthy man, who had an only daughter. His visits to the house were at first of a purely political nature; but the young lady was pleasing, and he fancied he discovered in her a sort of timid preference for himself. This excited his vanity, and awakened thoughts of the great worldly advantages connected with a union. Reminiscences of his first love kept these vague ideas in check for several months; but Rosalie's image at last became an unwelcome intruder, for with it was associated the idea of restraint. Moreover Charlotte, though inferior in beauty, was yet a pretty contrast to her rival. Her light hair fell in silken profusion, her blue eyes were gentle,

---

[1]   *Xarifa ... Spanish song*   Xarifa is the heroine of a fifteenth-century Spanish ballad, "The Bridal of Andalla," translated into English by John Gibson Lockhart in 1841.

[2]   *Moorish*   Of the Moors, a European term for the Muslim cultures of North Africa and the Iberian Peninsula.

[3]   *mezzotinto*   Of a shade neither dark nor light.

[4]   *mantled*   Blushed.

[5]   *a change ... his dream*   See Lord Byron's poem "The Dream" (1816).

[6]   *doubtful*   Of uncertain morality.

though inexpressive, and her healthy cheeks were like opening rose-buds.

He had already become accustomed to the dangerous experiment of resisting his own inward convictions; and this new impulse to ambition, combined with the strong temptation of variety in love, met the ardent young man weakened in moral principle, and unfettered by laws of the land. The change wrought upon him was soon noticed by Rosalie.

> In many ways does the full heart reveal
> The presence of the love it would conceal;
> But in far more the estranged heart lets know
> The absence of the love, which yet it fain would show.[1]

At length the news of his approaching marriage met her ear. Her head grew dizzy, and her heart fainted within her; but, with a strong effort at composure, she inquired all the particulars; and her pure mind at once took its resolution. Edward came that evening, and though she would have fain met him as usual, her heart was too full not to throw a deep sadness over her looks and tones. She had never complained of his decreasing tenderness, or of her own lonely hours; but he felt that the mute appeal of her heart-broken looks was more terrible than words. He kissed the hand she offered, and with a countenance almost as sad as her own, led her to a window in the recess shadowed by a luxuriant passionflower. It was the same seat where they had spent the first evening in this beautiful cottage, consecrated to their youthful loves. The same calm, clear moonlight looked in through the trellis. The vine then planted had now a luxuriant growth; and many a time had Edward fondly twined its sacred blossoms with the glossy ringlets of her raven hair. The rush of memory almost overpowered poor Rosalie; and Edward felt too much oppressed and ashamed to break the long, deep silence. At length, in words scarcely audible, Rosalie said, "Tell me, dear Edward, are you to be married next week?" He dropped her hand, as if a rifle-ball had struck him; and it was not until after long hesitation, that he began to make some reply about the necessity of circumstances. Mildly, but earnestly, the poor girl

begged him to spare apologies. It was enough that he no longer loved her, and that they must bid farewell. Trusting to the yielding tenderness of her character, he ventured, in the most soothing accents, to suggest that as he still loved her better than all the world, she would ever be his real wife, and they might see each other frequently. He was not prepared for the storm of indignant emotion his words excited. Hers was a passion too absorbing to admit of partnership; and her spirit was too pure to form a selfish league with crime.

At length this painful interview came to an end. They stood together by the Gothic gate, where they had so often met and parted in the moonlight. Old remembrances melted their souls. "Farewell, dearest Edward," said Rosalie. "Give me a parting kiss." Her voice was choked for utterance, and the tears flowed freely, as she bent her lips toward him. He folded her convulsively in his arms, and imprinted a long, impassioned kiss on that mouth, which had never spoken to him but in love and blessing.

With effort like a death-pang, she at length raised her head from his heaving bosom, and turning from him with bitter sobs, she said, "It is our *last*. To meet thus is henceforth crime. God bless you. I would not have you so miserable as I am. Farewell. A *last* farewell." "The *last*!" exclaimed he, with a wild shriek. "Oh God, Rosalie, do not say that!" and covering his face with his hands, he wept like a child.

Recovering from his emotion, he found himself alone. The moon looked down upon him mild, but very sorrowful, as the Madonna[2] seems to gaze on her worshipping children, bowed down with consciousness of sin. At that moment he would have given worlds to have disengaged himself from Charlotte; but he had gone so far, that blame, disgrace, and duels with angry relatives, would now attend any effort to obtain his freedom. Oh, how the moonlight oppressed him with its friendly sadness! It was like the plaintive eye of his forsaken one—like the music of sorrow echoed from an unseen world.

Long and earnestly he gazed at that dwelling, where he had so long known earth's purest foretaste of heavenly bliss. Slowly he walked away; then turned again to look on that charmed spot, the nestling-place of his young affections. He caught a glimpse of Rosalie,

---

[1]   *In many ... would show*   See Samuel Taylor Coleridge's "Prose in Rhyme: or, Epigrams, Moralities and Things Without a Name" (1828).

[2]   *the Madonna*   I.e., the Virgin Mary.

weeping beside a magnolia, which commanded a long view of the path leading to the public road. He would have sprung toward her, but she darted from him, and entered the cottage. That graceful figure, weeping in the moonlight, haunted him for years. It stood before his closing eyes, and greeted him with the morning dawn.

Poor Charlotte! had she known all, what a dreary lot would hers have been; but fortunately, she could not miss the impassioned tenderness she had never experienced; and Edward was the more careful in his kindness, because he was deficient in love. Once or twice she heard him murmur, "dear Rosalie," in his sleep; but the playful charge she brought was playfully answered, and the incident gave her no real uneasiness. The summer after their marriage, she proposed a residence at Sand-Hills, little aware what a whirlwind of emotion she excited in her husband's heart. The reasons he gave for rejecting the proposition appeared satisfactory; but she could not quite understand why he was never willing that their afternoon drives should be in the direction of those pleasant rural residences, which she had heard him praise so much. One day, as their barouche[1] rolled along a winding road that skirted Sand-Hills, her attention was suddenly attracted by two figures among the trees by the way-side; and touching Edward's arm, she exclaimed, "Do look at that beautiful child!" He turned, and saw Rosalie and Xarifa. His lips quivered, and his face became deadly pale. His young wife looked at him intently, but said nothing. There were points of resemblance in the child, that seemed to account for his sudden emotion. Suspicion was awakened, and she soon learned that the mother of that lovely girl bore the name of Rosalie; with this information came recollections of the "dear Rosalie," murmured in uneasy slumbers. From gossiping tongues she soon learned more than she wished to know. She wept, but not as poor Rosalie had done, for she never had loved, and been beloved, like her; and her nature was more proud. Henceforth a change came over her feelings and her manners; and Edward had no further occasion to assume a tenderness in return for hers. Changed as he was by ambition, he felt the wintry chill of her polite propriety, and sometimes in agony of heart, compared it with the gushing love of her who was indeed his wife.

But these, and all his emotions, were a sealed book to Rosalie, of which she could only guess the contents. With remittances for her and her child's support, there sometimes came earnest pleadings that she would consent to see him again; but these she never answered, though her heart yearned to do so. She pitied his fair young bride, and would not be tempted to bring sorrow into her household by any fault of hers. Her earnest prayer was that she might never know of her existence. She had not looked on Edward since she watched him under the shadow of the magnolia, until his barouche passed her in her rambles some months after. She saw the deadly paleness of his countenance, and had he dared to look back, he would have seen her tottering with faintness. Xarifa brought water from a little rivulet, and sprinkled her face. When she revived, she clasped the beloved child to her heart with a vehemence that made her scream. Soothingly she kissed away her fears, and gazed into her beautiful eyes with a deep, deep sadness of expression, which Xarifa never forgot. Wild were the thoughts that pressed around her aching heart, and almost maddened her poor brain; thoughts which had almost driven her to suicide the night of that last farewell. For her child's sake she conquered the fierce temptation then; and for her sake, she struggled with it now. But the gloomy atmosphere of their once happy home overclouded the morning of Xarifa's life.

She from her mother learnt the trick of grief,
    And sighed among her playthings.[2]

Rosalie perceived this, and it gave her gentle heart unutterable pain. At last, the conflicts of her spirit proved too strong for the beautiful frame in which it dwelt. About a year after Edward's marriage, she was found dead in her bed, one bright autumnal morning. She had often expressed to her daughter a wish to be buried under a spreading oak that shaded a rustic garden-chair, in which she and Edward had spent many happy evenings. And there she was buried, with a small white cross at her head, twined with the cypress vine. Edward came to the funeral, and wept long, very long, at the grave. Hours after midnight, he sat in the

---

1   *barouche* Fashionable four-wheeled carriage.

2   *She from … playthings* From Book One of William Wordsworth's long poem *The Excursion* (1814).

recess-window, with Xarifa folded to his heart. The poor child sobbed herself to sleep on his bosom; and the convicted murderer had small reason to envy that wretched man, as he gazed on the lovely countenance, that so strongly reminded him of his early and his only love.

From that time, Xarifa was the central point of all his warmest affections. He employed an excellent old negress to take charge of the cottage, from which he promised his darling child that she should never be removed. He employed a music master, and dancing master, to attend upon her; and a week never passed without a visit from him, and a present of books, pictures, or flowers. To hear her play upon the harp, or repeat some favorite poem in her mother's earnest accents and melodious tones, or to see her flexile figure float in the garland-dance, seemed to be the highest enjoyment of his life. Yet was the pleasure mixed with bitter thoughts. What would be the destiny of this fascinating young creature, so radiant with life and beauty? She belonged to a proscribed race; and though the brown color on her soft cheek was scarcely deeper than the sunny side of a golden pear, yet was it sufficient to exclude her from virtuous society. He thought of Rosalie's wish to carry her to France; and he would have fulfilled it, had he been unmarried. As it was, he inwardly resolved to make some arrangement to effect it, in a few years, even if it involved separation from his darling child.

But alas for the calculations of man! From the time of Rosalie's death, Edward had sought relief for his wretched feelings in the free use of wine. Xarifa was scarcely fifteen when her father was found dead by the road-side, having fallen from his horse, on his way to visit her. He left no will; but his wife, with kindness of heart worthy of a happier domestic fate, expressed a decided reluctance to change any of the plans he had made for the beautiful child at Sand-Hills.

Xarifa mourned her indulgent father; but not as one utterly desolate. True she had lived "like a flower deep hid in rocky cleft";[1] but the sunshine of love had already peeped in upon her. Her teacher on the harp was a handsome and agreeable young man of twenty, the only son of an English widow. Perhaps Edward

had not been altogether unmindful of the result, when he first invited him to the flowery cottage. Certain it is, he had more than once thought what a pleasant thing it would be, if English freedom from prejudice should lead him to offer legal protection to his graceful and winning child. Being thus encouraged, rather than checked, in his admiration, George Elliot could not be otherwise than strongly attracted toward his beautiful pupil. The lonely and unprotected state in which her father's death left her deepened this feeling into tenderness. And lucky was it for her enthusiastic and affectionate nature; for she could not live without an atmosphere of love. In her innocence, she knew nothing of the dangers in her path; and she trusted George with an undoubting simplicity, that rendered her sacred to his noble and generous soul. It seemed as if that flower-embosomed nest was consecrated by the Fates to Love. The French have well named it *La Belle Passion*; for without it life were "a year without spring, or a spring without roses."[2] Except the loveliness of infancy, what does earth offer so much like Heaven, as the happiness of two young, pure, and beautiful beings, living in each other's hearts?

Xarifa inherited her mother's poetic and impassioned temperament; and to her, above others, the first consciousness of these sweet emotions was like a golden sunrise on the sleeping flowers.

> Thus stood she at the threshold of the scene
> Of busy life.　　*　　*　　*　　*
> How fair it lay in solemn shade and sheen!
> And he beside her, like some angel, posted
> To lead her out of childhood's fairy land,
> On to life's glancing summit, hand in hand.[3]

Alas, the tempest was brooding over their young heads. Rosalie, though she knew it not, had been the daughter of a slave, whose wealthy master, though he remained attached to her to the end of her days, had carelessly omitted to have papers of manumission recorded. His heirs had lately failed, under

---

[1] *like a flower ... cleft* From Rann Kennedy's "A Poem on the Death of Her Royal Highness, the Princess Charlotte of Wales" (1817).

[2] *a year ... without roses* Quotation attributed to King Francis I of France (1494–1547), who is reported to have said this of "a court without the presence of the fair sex."

[3] *Thus stood ... in hand* See Friedrich Schiller's play *The Death of Wallenstein* 4.12 (1799).

circumstances which greatly exasperated their creditors; and in an unlucky hour, they discovered their claim on Angelique's grand-child.

The gentle girl, happy as the birds in spring-time, accustomed to the fondest indulgence, surrounded by all the refinements of life, timid as a young fawn, and with a soul full of romance, was ruthlessly seized by a sheriff, and placed on the public auction-stand in Savannah. There she stood, trembling, blushing, and weeping; compelled to listen to the grossest language, and shrinking from the rude hands that examined the graceful proportions of her beautiful frame. "Stop that!" exclaimed a stern voice, "I bid two thousand dollars for her, without asking any of their d—d questions." The speaker was probably about forty years of age, with handsome features, but a fierce and proud expression. An older man, who stood behind him, bid two thousand five hundred. The first bid higher; then a third, a dashing young man, bid three thousand; and thus they went on, with the keen excitement of gamblers, until the first speaker obtained the prize, for the moderate sum of five thousand dollars.[1]

And where was George, during this dreadful scene? He was absent on a visit to his mother, at Mobile. But, had he been at Sand-Hills, he could not have saved his beloved from the wealthy profligate, who was determined to obtain her at any price. A letter of agonized entreaty from her brought him home on the wings of the wind. But what could he do? How could he ever obtain a sight of her, locked up as she was in the princely mansion of her master? At last, by bribing one of the slaves, he conveyed a letter to her, and received one in return. As yet, her purchaser treated her with respectful gentleness, and sought to win her favor, by flattery and presents; but she dreaded every moment, lest the scene should change, and trembled at the sound of every footfall. A plan was laid for escape. The slave agreed to drug his master's wine; a ladder of ropes was prepared, and a swift boat was in readiness. But the slave, to obtain a double reward, was treacherous. Xarifa had scarcely given an answering signal to the low, cautious whistle of her lover, when the sharp sound of a rifle was followed by a deep groan, and a heavy fall on the pavement of the court-yard. With frenzied eagerness she swung herself down by the ladder of ropes, and, by the glancing light of lanterns, saw George, bleeding and lifeless at her feet. One wild shriek, that pierced the brains of those who heard it, and she fell senseless by his side.

For many days she had a confused consciousness of some great agony, but knew not where she was, or by whom she was surrounded. The slow recovery of her reason settled into the most intense melancholy, which moved the compassion even of her cruel purchaser. The beautiful eyes, always pleading in expression, were now so heart-piercing in their sadness, that he could not endure to look upon them. For some months, he sought to win her smiles by lavish presents, and delicate attentions. He bought glittering chains of gold, and costly bands of pearl. His victim scarcely glanced at them, and the slave laid them away, unheeded and forgotten. He purchased the furniture of the cottage at Sand-Hills, and one morning Xarifa found her harp at the bed-side, and the room filled with her own books, pictures, and flowers. She gazed upon them with a pang unutterable, and burst into an agony of tears; but she gave her master no thanks, and her gloom deepened.

At last his patience was exhausted. He grew weary of her obstinacy, as he was pleased to term it; and threats took the place of persuasion.

*   *   *   *   *   *   *

In a few months more, Xarifa was a raving maniac. That pure temple was desecrated; that loving heart was broken; and that beautiful head fractured against the wall in the frenzy of despair. Her master cursed the useless expense she had cost him; the slaves buried her; and no one wept at the grave of her who had been so carefully cherished, and so tenderly beloved.

Reader, do you complain that I have written fiction? Believe me, scenes like these are of no unfrequent occurrence at the South. The world does not afford such materials for tragic romance, as the history of the Quadroons.

—1842

---

[1] *five thousand dollars* More than ten times the average price to purchase an enslaved person in 1840.

from *Letters from New-York*

LETTER 34
WOMAN'S RIGHTS

January, 1843

You ask what are my opinions about "Woman's Rights." I confess a strong distaste for the subject, as it has been generally treated. On no other theme, probably, has there been uttered so much of false, mawkish sentiment, shallow philosophy, and sputtering, farthing-candle wit. If the style of its advocates has often been offensive to taste, and unacceptable to reason, assuredly that of its opponents have been still more so. College boys have amused themselves with writing dreams in which they saw women in hotels, with their feet hoisted, and chairs tilted back, or growling and bickering at each other in legislative halls, or fighting at the polls, with eyes blackened by fisticuffs. But it never seems to have occurred to these facetious writers that the proceedings which appear so ludicrous and improper in women are also ridiculous and disgraceful in men. It were well that men should learn not to hoist their feet above their heads, and tilt their chairs backward, not to growl and snap in the halls of legislation, or give each other black eyes at the polls.

Maria Edgeworth[1] says, "We are disgusted when we see a woman's mind overwhelmed with a torrent of learning; that the tide of literature has passed over it should be betrayed only by its fertility." This is beautiful and true; but is it not likewise applicable to man? The truly great never seek to display themselves. If they carry their heads high above the crowd, it is only made manifest to others by accidental revelations of their extended vision. "Human duties and proprieties do not lie so very far apart," said Harriet Martineau;[2] "if

they did, there would be two gospels, and two teachers, one for man, and another for woman."

It would seem, indeed, as if men were willing to give women the exclusive benefit of gospel-teaching. "Women should be gentle," say the advocates of subordination; but when Christ said, "Blessed are the meek," did he preach to women only? "Girls should be modest," is the language of common teaching, continually uttered in words and customs. Would it not be an improvement for men, also, to be scrupulously pure in manners, conversation and life? Books addressed to young married people abound with advice to the wife, to control her temper, and never to utter wearisome complaints, or vexatious words, when the husband comes home fretful or unreasonable, from his out-of-door conflicts with the world. Would not the advice be as excellent and appropriate, if the husband were advised to conquer his fretfulness, and forbear his complaints, in consideration of his wife's ill-health, fatiguing cares, and the thousand disheartening influences of domestic routine? In short, whatsoever can be named as loveliest, best, and most graceful in woman, would likewise be good and graceful in man. You will perhaps remind me of courage? If you use the word in its highest signification, I answer that woman, above others, hath abundant need of it, in her pilgrimage; and the true woman wears it with a quiet grace. If you mean mere animal courage, that is not mentioned in the sermon on the Mount, among those qualities which enable us to inherit the earth, or become the children of God. That the feminine ideal approaches much nearer to the gospel standard than the prevalent idea of manhood is shown by the universal tendency to represent the Saviour and his most beloved disciple with mild, meek expression, and feminine beauty. None speak of the bravery, the might, or the intellect of Jesus; but the devil is always imagined as a being of acute intellect, political cunning, and the fiercest courage. These universal and instinctive tendencies of the human mind reveal much.

That the present position of women in society is the result of physical force is obvious enough; whosoever doubts it, let her reflect why she is afraid to go out in the evening without the protection of a man. What

---

[1] *Maria Edgeworth* Anglo-Irish writer who wrote widely on subjects such as education and the intellectual equality of women; Child may be alluding to a passage from Edgeworth's *Letters for Literary Ladies* (1795): "When you say that men of superior understanding dislike the appearance of extraordinary strength of mind in the fair sex, you probably mean that the display of that strength is disgusting."

[2] *Harriet Martineau* English writer and social theorist who had written in support of Child's abolitionist writing in 1838. Child is

likely paraphrasing from Martineau's *Society in America* (1837), which was written after her extended tour of the United States.

constitutes the danger of aggression? Superior physical strength, uncontrolled by the moral sentiments. If physical strength were in complete subjection to moral influence, there would be no need of outward protection. That animal instinct and brute force now govern the world is painfully apparent in the condition of women everywhere; from the Morduan Tartars,[1] whose ceremony of marriage consists in placing the bride on a mat, and consigning her to the bridegroom, with the words, "Here, wolf, take thy lamb"—to the German remark, that "stiff ale, stinging tobacco, and a girl in her smart dress, are the best things." The same thing, softened by the refinements of civilization, peeps out in Stephen's remark, that "woman never looks so interesting, as when leaning on the arm of a soldier";[2] and in Hazlitt's complaint that "it is not easy to keep up a conversation with women in company. It is thought a piece of rudeness to differ from them; it is not quite fair to ask them a reason for what they say."[3]

This sort of politeness to women is what men call gallantry; an odious word to every sensible woman, because she sees that it is merely the flimsy veil which foppery[4] throws over sensuality, to conceal its grossness.[5] So far is it from indicating sincere esteem and affection for women, that the profligacy of a nation may, in general, be fairly measured by its gallantry. This taking away rights, and condescending to grant privileges, is an old trick of the physical force principle; and with the immense majority, who only look on the surface of things, this mask effectually disguises an ugliness, which would otherwise be abhorred. The most inveterate slave-holders are probably those who take most pride in dressing their household servants handsomely, and who would be most ashamed to have the name of being unnecessarily cruel. And profligates, who form the lowest and most sensual estimate of women, are the very ones to treat them with an excess of outward deference.

There are few books which I can read through without feeling insulted as a woman; but this insult is almost universally conveyed through that which was intended for praise. Just imagine, for a moment, what impression it would make on men if women authors should write about their "rosy lips," and "melting eyes," and "voluptuous forms," as they write about us! That women in general do not feel this kind of flattery to be an insult, I readily admit; for, in the first place, they do not perceive the gross chattel-principle,[6] of which it is the utterance; moreover, they have, from long habit, become accustomed to consider themselves as household conveniences, or gilded toys. Hence, they consider it feminine and pretty to abjure all such use of their faculties as would make them co-workers with man in the advancement of those great principles, on which the progress of society depends. "There is perhaps no animal," says Hannah More,[7] "so much indebted to subordination, for its good behaviour, as woman." Alas, for the animal age, in which such utterance could be tolerated by public sentiment!

Martha More, sister of Hannah, describing a very impressive scene at the funeral of one of her Charity School teachers, says, "The spirit within seemed struggling to speak, and I was in a sort of agony; but I recollected that I had heard, somewhere, a woman must not speak in the church. Oh, had she been buried in the church-yard, a messenger from Mr. Pitt[8] himself should not have restrained me; for I seemed to have received a message from a higher Master within."

This application of theological teaching carries its own commentary.

I have said enough to show that I consider prevalent opinions and customs highly unfavourable to the moral and intellectual development of women: and I need not say that, in proportion to their true culture,[9]

---

[1]   *Morduan Tartars*   Turkic ethnic group residing in central Asia.

[2]   *Stephen's remark ... soldier*   Paraphrased from American explorer and diplomat John Lloyd Stephen's *Incidents of Travel in the Russian and Turkish Empires* (1839).

[3]   *Hazlitt's ... they say*   From English writer William Hazlitt's essay "On the Conversation of Authors" (1820).

[4]   *foppery*   Affected elegance.

[5]   *grossness*   Unrefined nature.

[6]   *chattel-principle*   I.e., the principle that women are the property of men.

[7]   *Hannah More*   English poet, playwright, and religious writer (1745–1833) who advocated education for women but also criticized many of the proto-feminist writings of her era. More and her sister Martha ran a number of so-called "Charity Schools" for the poor. The quotation is from a 1793 letter More wrote to the Earl of Orford.

[8]   *Mr. Pitt*   William Pitt the Younger, English politician who served as Prime Minister of Great Britain from 1783 to 1801 and of the United Kingdom from 1801 to 1806.

[9]   *culture*   I.e., cultivation.

women will be more useful and happy, and domestic life more perfected. True culture in them, as in men, consists in the full and free development of individual character, regulated by their own perceptions of what is true, and their own love of what is good.

This individual responsibility is rarely acknowledged, even by the most refined, as necessary to the spiritual progress of women. I once heard a very beautiful lecture from R.W. Emerson, on Being and Seeming.[1] In the course of many remarks, as true as they were graceful, he urged women to be, rather than seem. He told them that all their laboured education of forms, strict observance of genteel etiquette, tasteful arrangement of the toilette,[2] etc., all this seeming would not gain hearts like being truly what God made them; that earnest simplicity, the sincerity of nature, would kindle the eye, light up the countenance, and give an inexpressible charm to the plainest features.

The advice was excellent, but the motive by which it was urged brought a flush of indignation over my face. Men were exhorted to be, rather than to seem, that they might fulfil the sacred mission for which their souls were embodied; that they might, in God's freedom, grow up into the full stature of spiritual manhood; but women were urged to simplicity and truthfulness, that they might become more pleasing.

Are we not all immortal beings? Is not each one responsible for himself and herself? There is no measuring the mischief done by the prevailing tendency to teach women to be virtuous as a duty to man, rather than to God—for the sake of pleasing the creature,[3] rather than the Creator. "God is thy law, thou mine,"[4] said Eve to Adam. May Milton be forgiven for sending that thought "out into everlasting time" in such a jewelled setting. What weakness, vanity, frivolity, infirmity of moral purpose, sinful flexibility of principle—in a

word, what soul-stifling, has been the result of thus putting man in the place of God!

But while I see plainly that society is on a false foundation, and that prevailing views concerning women indicate the want of wisdom and purity, which they serve to perpetuate—still, I must acknowledge that much of the talk about women's rights offends both my reason and my taste. I am not of those who maintain there is no sex in souls; nor do I like the results deducible from that doctrine. Kinmont,[5] in his admirable book, called *The Natural History of Men*, speaking of the warlike courage of the ancient German women, and of their being respectfully consulted on important public affairs, says, "You ask me if I consider all this right, and deserving of approbation; or that women were here engaged in their appropriate tasks? I answer, yes; it is just as right that they should take this interest in the honour of their country, as the other sex. Of course, I do not think that women were made for war and battle; neither do I believe that men were. But since the fashion of the times had made it so, and settled it that war was a necessary element of greatness, and that no safety was to be procured without it, I argue that it shows a healthful state of feeling in other respects, that the feelings of both sexes were equally enlisted in the cause; that there was no division in the house, or the State; and that the serious pursuits and objects of the one were also the serious pursuits and objects of the other."

The nearer society approaches to divine order, the less separation will there be in the characters, duties, and pursuits of men and women. Women will not become less gentle and graceful, but men will become more so. Women will not neglect the care and education of their children, but men will find themselves ennobled and refined by sharing those duties with them; and will receive, in return, co-operation and sympathy in the discharge of various other duties, not deemed inappropriate to women. The more women become rational companions, partners in business and in thought, as well as in affection and amusement, the more highly will men appreciate home—that blessed word, which opens to the human heart the most perfect glimpse of

---

[1]   *R.W. Emerson ... Seeming*   Child alludes to a lecture given in Boston by Transcendentalist thinker Ralph Waldo Emerson on 10 January 1838.

[2]   *toilette*   Dressing and personal grooming.

[3]   *creature*   Created being.

[4]   *God is ... mine*   See Book 4 of *Paradise Lost* (1667, 1674), John Milton's epic poem about the fall of Adam and Eve from the Garden of Eden: "God is thy law, thou mine: To know no more / Is woman's happiest knowledge, and her praise."

[5]   *Kinmont*   Alexander Kinmont, Scottish-American ethnologist. Child refers to his collection *Twelve Lectures on the Natural History of Man* (1839).

Heaven, and helps to carry it thither, as on an angel's wings.

> Domestic bliss,
> That can, the world eluding, be itself
> A world enjoyed; that wants no witnesses
> But its own sharers, and approving heaven;
> That, like a flower deep hid in rocky cleft,
> Smiles, though 'tis looking only at the sky.[1]

Alas, for these days of Astor houses, and Tremonts, and Albions![2] where families exchange comforts for costliness, fireside retirement for flirtation and flaunting, and the simply, healthful, cozy meal, for gravies and gout, dainties and dyspepsia. There is no characteristic of my countrymen which I regret so deeply, as their slight degree of adhesiveness to home. Closely intertwined with this instinct is the religion of a nation. The home and the church bear a near relation to each other. The French have no such word as home in their language, and I believe they are the least reverential and religious of all the Christian nations. A Frenchman had been in the habit of visiting a lady constantly for several years, and being alarmed at a report that she was sought in marriage, he was asked why he did not marry her himself. "Marry her!" exclaimed he; "good heavens! where should I spend my evenings?" The idea of domestic happiness was altogether a foreign idea to his soul, like a word that conveyed no meaning. Religious sentiment in the French leads the same roving life as the domestic affections; breakfasting at one restaurateur's, and supping at another's. When some wag in Boston reported that Louis-Philippe[3] had sent over for Dr. Channing[4] to manufacture a religion for the French people, the witty significance of the joke was generally appreciated.

There is a deep spiritual reason why all that relates to the domestic affections should ever be found in close proximity with religious faith. The age of chivalry was likewise one of unquestioning veneration, which led to the crusade for the holy sepulchre.[5]

The French Revolution, which tore down churches, and voted that there was no God, likewise annulled marriage; and the doctrine that there is no sex in souls has usually been urged by those of infidel tendencies. Carlyle[6] says, "But what feeling it was in the ancient, devout, deep soul, which of marriage made a sacrament; this, of all things in the world, is what Diderot will think of for aeons without discovering; unless, perhaps, it were to increase the vestry fees."[7]

The conviction that woman's present position in society is a false one, and therefore re-acts disastrously on the happiness and improvement of man, is pressing, by slow degrees, on the common consciousness, through all the obstacles of bigotry, sensuality, and selfishness. As man approaches to the truest life, he will perceive more and more that there is no separation or discord in their mutual duties. They will be one; but it will be as affection and thought are one; the treble and bass of the same harmonious tune.

LETTER 36
THE INDIANS

March, 1843

I went, a few evenings ago, to the American Museum,[8] to see fifteen Indians fresh from the western forest. Sacs, Fox, and Iowas,[9] really important people in their respective tribes. Nan-Nouce-Fush-E-To, which means the Buffalo King, is a famous Sac chief, sixty years old, covered with scars, and grim as a Hindoo god,

---

[1] *Domestic bliss ... the sky* From Scottish-born poet Rann Kennedy's "A Poem on the Death of Her Royal Highness, the Princess Charlotte of Wales" (1817).

[2] *Astor houses ... Albions!* Names of well-known, elegant hotels.

[3] *Louis-Philippe* King of France from 1830 to 1848.

[4] *Dr. Channing* William Ellery Channing (1780–1842), an influential Unitarian preacher known for his liberal and tolerant religious views.

[5] *holy sepulchre* Site of Jesus' burial, in Jerusalem.

[6] *Carlyle* Thomas Carlyle, English essayist. The following paraphrase is from his 1833 essay on Denis Diderot (1713–84), in which he strongly criticizes the French Enlightenment philosopher.

[7] *vestry fees* Fees paid for the use of chapels or other special seats in a church.

[8] *American Museum* Barnum's American Museum was an attraction in lower Manhattan opened by entrepreneur P.T. Barnum in 1841. The venue contained exhibitions ranging from scientific curiosities and hoaxes to exploitative human displays, including exhibitions of Indigenous Americans.

[9] *Sacs, Fox, and Iowas* I.e., people of the Sauk, Meskwaki (Fox), and Ioway nations.

or pictures of the devil on a Portuguese contribution box,[1] to help sinners through purgatory. It is said that he has killed with his own hand one hundred Osages, three Mohawks, two Kas, two Sioux, and one Pawnee; and if we may judge by his organ of destructiveness,[2] the story is true; a more enormous bump I never saw in that region of the skull. He speaks nine Indian dialects, has visited almost every existing tribe of his race, and is altogether a very remarkable personage. Mon-To-Gah, the White Bear, wears a medal from President Monroe,[3] for certain services rendered to the whites. Wa-Con-To-Kitch-Er, is an Iowa chief, of grave and thoughtful countenance, held in much veneration as the prophet of his tribe. He sees visions, which he communicates to them for their spiritual instruction. Among the squaws[4] is No-Nos-See, the She Wolf, a niece of the famous Black Hawk,[5] and very proud of the relationship; and Do-Hum-Me, the Productive Pumpkin, a very handsome woman, with a great deal of heart and happiness in her countenance.

> Smiles settled on her sun-flecked cheeks,
> Like noon upon the mellow apricot.[6]

She was married about a fortnight ago, at Philadelphia, to Cow-Hick-He, son of the principal chief of the

Iowas, and as noble a specimen of manhood as I ever looked upon. Indeed, I have never seen a group of human beings so athletic, well-proportioned, and majestic. They are a keen satire on our civilized customs, which produce such feeble forms and pallid faces. The unlimited pathway, the broad horizon, the free grandeur of the forest, has passed into their souls, and so stands revealed in their material forms.

We who have robbed the Indians of their lands, and worse still, of *themselves*, are very fond of proving their inferiority. We are told that the *facial angle*[7] in the

Caucasian race is	*	*	* 85	degrees.
Asiatic	*	*	* 78	"
American Indian	*	*	* 73	"
Ethiopian[8]	*	*	* 70	"
Ourang Outang	*	*	* 67	"

This simply proves that the Caucasian race, through a succession of ages, has been exposed to influences eminently calculated to develop the moral and intellectual faculties. That they started first in the race might have been owing to a finer and more susceptible nervous organization, originating in climate, perhaps, but serving to bring the physical organization into more harmonious relation with the laws of spiritual reception. But by whatever agency it might have been produced, the nation or race that perceived even one spiritual idea in advance of others, would necessarily go on improving in geometric ratio, through the lapse of ages. For our past, we have the oriental fervour, gorgeous imagery, and deep reverence of the Jews, flowing from that high fountain, the perception of the oneness and invisibility of God. From the Greeks we receive the very Spirit of Beauty, flowing into all forms of philosophy and art, encircled by a golden halo of Platonism,[9] which

---

1   *contribution box*   Box for collecting church donations.

2   *organ of destructiveness*   The pseudoscience of phrenology, which was prominent (though controversial) in American discourse throughout much of the nineteenth century, held that the mind was divided into distinct "organs" that ruled distinct mental and psychological faculties, and whose respective sizes could be determined by the shape of the skull. Discussions of phrenology were prominent in racist discourse.

3   *President Monroe*   James Monroe, who was president from 1817 to 1825.

4   *squaws*   Offensive term for Indigenous women; while it carried negative connotations by this point, the term continued to be used frequently by English speakers well into the twentieth century, even by those who did not intend it derogatorily.

5   *Black Hawk*   Sauk war chief and prominent leader in what later became known as the Black Hawk War, an 1832 resistance movement against colonial encroachment on Sauk land. Black Hawk became famous after being toured as a prisoner of war following the conflict, and he dictated a popular memoir, *Life of Black Hawk* (1833).

6   *Smiles settled … apricot*   From English poet Philip James Bailey's long poem *Festus* (1839); in their original context the lines describe the "lasses" at a village feast.

7   *facial angle*   Another racist phrenological concept, the "facial angle" refers to the vertical angle between the forehead and chin; a wider angle was considered both more "beautiful" and indicative of greater intelligence.

8   *Ethiopian*   In the nineteenth century, this term was used as a vague racial and cultural designation that could include all Africans and people of African descent.

9   *Platonism*   Philosophical system derived from the work of the ancient Greek Plato (c. 427–c. 347 BCE), whose ideas about the essentially immaterial origins of true reality were later adapted to Christian ideas by the Neoplatonists.

Far over many a land and age hath shone,
And mingles with the light that beams from God's
    own throne.[1]

These have been transmitted to us in their own forms, and again reproduced through the classic strength and high cultivation of Rome, and the romantic minstrelsy and rich architecture of the Middle Ages. Thus we stand, a congress of ages, each with a glory on its brow, peculiar to itself, yet in part reflected from the glory that went before.

But what have the African savage and the wandering Indian for their past? To fight for food, and grovel in the senses, has been the employment of their ancestors. The past reproduced in them mostly belongs to the animal part of our mixed nature. They have indeed come in contact with the race on which had dawned higher ideas; but how have they come in contact? As victims, not as pupils. Rum, gunpowder, the horrors of slavery, the unblushing knavery of trade, these have been their teachers! And because these have failed to produce a high degree of moral and intellectual cultivation, we coolly declare that the negroes are made for slaves, that the Indians cannot be civilized; and that when either of the races come in contact with us, they must either consent to be our beasts of burden, or be driven to the wall, and perish.

That the races of mankind are different, spiritually as well as physically, there is, of course, no doubt; but it is the difference between trees of the same forest, not as between trees and minerals. The facial angle and shape of the head is various in races and nations; but these are the effects of spiritual influences, long operating on character, and in their turn becoming causes; thus intertwining, as past and future ever do.

But it is urged that Indians who have been put to schools and colleges still remain attached to a roving life, away from all these advantages,

His blanket tied with yellow strings, the Indian of the
    forest went.[2]

And what if he did? Do not white young men, who have been captured by savages in infancy, show an equally strong disinclination to take upon themselves the restraints of civilized life? Does anybody urge that this well-known fact proves the white race incapable of civilization?

You ask, perhaps, what becomes of my theory that races and individuals are the product of ages, if the influences of half a life produce the same effects on the Caucasian and the Indian? I answer, that white children brought up among Indians, though they strongly imbibe the habits of the race, are generally prone to be the geniuses and prophets of their tribe. The organization of nerve and brain has been changed by a more harmonious relation between the animal and the spiritual; and this comparative harmony has been produced by the influences of Judea, and Greece, and Rome, and the age of chivalry; though of all these things the young man never heard.

Similar influences brought to bear on the Indians or the Africans, as a race, would gradually change the structure of their skulls, and enlarge their perceptions of moral and intellectual truth. The same influences cannot be brought to bear upon them; for their past is not our past; and of course never can be. But let ours mingle with theirs, and you will find the result variety, without inferiority. They will be flutes on different notes, and so harmonize the better.

And how is this elevation of all races to be effected? By that which worketh all miracles, in the name of Jesus—the law of love. We must not teach as superiors; we must love as brothers. Here is the great deficiency in all our efforts for the ignorant and the criminal. We stand apart from them, and expect them to feel grateful for our condescension in noticing them at all. We do not embrace them warmly with our sympathies, and put our souls into their soul's stead.

But even under this great disadvantage—accustomed to our smooth, deceitful talk, when we want their lands, and to the cool villainy with which we break treaties when our purposes are gained; receiving gunpowder and rum from the very hands which retain from them all the better influences of civilized life; cheated by knavish agents, cajoled by government, and hunted with bloodhounds—still, under all these disadvantages, the Indians have shown that they can

---

[1] *Far over ... own throne* See William Cullen Bryant's poem "The Ages" (1821).

[2] *His blanket ... went* Final lines of Philip Freneau's "The Indian Student: or, Force of Nature" (1788). In the poem, a Native American attends college but rejects Euro-American education to return to his traditional lifeways.

be civilized. Of this, the Choctaws and Cherokees are admirable proofs.[1] Both these tribes have a regularly-organized, systematic government, in the democratic form, and a printed constitution. The right of trial by jury, and other principles of a free government, are established on a permanent basis. They have good farms, cotton-gins, saw-mills, schools, and churches. Their dwellings are generally comfortable, and some of them are handsome. The last annual message of the chief of the Cherokees is a highly-interesting document, which would not compare disadvantageously with any of our governors' messages. It states that more than £625,000 are due to them from the United States; and recommends that this sum be obtained, and in part distributed among the people; but that the interest of the school fund be devoted to the maintenance of schools, and the diffusion of knowledge.

There was a time when our ancestors, the ancient Britons, went nearly without clothing, painted their bodies in fantastic fashion, offered up human victims to uncouth idols, and lived in hollow trees, or rude habitations, which we should now consider unfit for cattle. Making all due allowance for the different state of the world, it is much to be questioned whether they made more rapid advancement than the Cherokees and Choctaws.

It always fills me with sadness to see Indians surrounded by the false environment of civilized life; but I never felt so deep a sadness, as I did in looking upon these western warriors; for they were evidently the noblest of their dwindling race, unused to restraint, accustomed to sleep beneath the stars. And here they were, set up for a two-shilling show, with monkeys, flamingoes, dancers, and buffoons! If they understood our modes of society well enough to be aware of their degraded position, they would doubtless quit it with burning indignation at the insult. But as it is, they allow women to examine their beads, and children to play with their wampum, with the most philosophic indifference. In their imperturbable countenances, I thought I could once or twice detect a slight expression of scorn at the eager curiosity of the crowd. The

Albiness,[2] a short woman, with pink eyes, and hair like white floss, was the only object that visibly amused them. The young chiefs nodded to her often, and exchanged smiling remarks with each other, as they looked at her. Upon all the buffooneries and legerdemain[3] tricks of the Museum, they gazed as unmoved as John Knox[4] himself could have done. I would have given a good deal to know their thoughts, as mimic cities, and fairy grottoes, and mechanical dancing figures, rose and sunk before them. The mechanical figures were such perfect imitations of life, and went through so many wonderful evolutions, that they might well surprise even those accustomed to the marvels of mechanism. But Indians, who pay religious honours to venerable rocks and moss-grown trees, who believe that brutes[5] have souls as well as men, and that all nature is filled with spirits, might well doubt whether there was not here some supernatural agency, either good or evil. I would suffer almost anything, if my soul could be transmigrated into the She Wolf, or the Productive Pumpkin, and their souls pass consciously into my frame, for a few days, that I might experience the fashion of their thoughts and feelings. Was there ever such a foolish wish! The soul is Me, and is Thee. I might as well put on their blankets as their bodies, for purposes of spiritual insight. In that other world, shall we be enabled to know exactly how heaven, and earth, and hell, appear to other persons, nations, and tribes? I would it might be so; for I have an intense desire for such revelations. I do not care to travel to Rome, or St. Petersburg, because I can only look at people; and I want to look into them, and through them; to know how things appear to their spiritual eyes, and sound to their spiritual ears. This is a universal want; hence the intense interest taken in autobiography, by all classes of readers. Oh, if anyone had but the courage to write the whole truth of himself, undisguised, as it appears before the eye of God and angels, the World would read it, and it would soon be translated into all the dialects of the universe.

---

[1] *the Choctaws … proofs* Prior to their forced migration westwards under the 1830 Indian Removal Act, the Choctaw and Cherokee were categorized by the U.S. government as among the five "civilized tribes" because of their adoption of various European cultural practices.

[2] *Albiness* Woman with albinism.

[3] *legerdemain* Sleight of hand; conjuring tricks.

[4] *John Knox* Scottish theologian and leader in the Protestant Reformation (1514–72).

[5] *brutes* Non-human animals.

But these children of the forest do not even give us glimpses of their inner life; for they consider that the body was given to conceal the emotions of the soul. The stars look down into their hearts, as into mine, the broad ocean, glittering in the moonbeams, speaks to them of the infinite; and doubtless the wild flowers and the sea-shells, "talk to them a thought." But what thoughts, what revelations of the infinite? This would I give the world to know; but the world cannot buy an answer.

How foreign is my soul to that of the beautiful Do-Hum-Me! How helpless should I be in situations where she would be a heroine; and how little could she comprehend my eager thought, which seeks the creative three-in-one[1] throughout the universe, and finds it in every blossom, and every mineral. Between Wa-Con-To-Kitch-Er and the German Herder,[2] what a distance! Yet are they both prophets; and though one looks through nature with the pitch-pine torch of the wilderness, and the other is lighted by a whole constellation of suns, yet have both learned, in their degree, that matter is only the time-garment of the spirit. The stammering utterance with which the Iowa seer reveals this, it were worth a kingdom to hear, if we could but borrow the souls of his tribe, while they listen to his visions.

It is a general trait with the Indian tribes to recognise the Great Spirit in every little child. They rarely refuse a child anything. When their revenge is most implacable, a little one is often sent to them, adorned with flowers and shells, and taught to lisp a prayer that the culprit may be forgiven; and such mediation is rarely without effect, even on the sternest warrior. This trait alone is sufficient to establish their relationship with Herder, Richter,[3] and other spirits of angel-stature. Nay, if we could look back a few centuries, we should find the ancestors of Shakspeare, and the fastidiously-refined Goëthe, with painted cheeks, wolves' teeth for jewels, and boars' hides for garments. Perhaps the universe could not have passed before the vision of those star-like spirits, except through the forest life of such wild ancestry.

Some theorists say that the human brain, in its formation, "changes with a steady rise, through a likeness to one animal and then another, till it is perfected in that of man, the highest animal."[4] It seems to be so with the nations, in their progressive rise out of barbarism. I was never before so much struck with the animalism of Indian character, as I was in the frightful war-dance of these chiefs. Their gestures were as furious as wild-cats, they howled like wolves, screamed like prairie dogs, and tramped like buffaloes. Their faces were painted fiery red, or, with cross-bars of green and red, and they were decorated with all sorts of uncouth trappings of hair, and bones, and teeth. That which regulated their movements, in lieu of music, was a discordant clash; and altogether they looked and acted more like demons from the pit, than anything I ever imagined. It was the natural and appropriate language of war. The wolfish howl, and the wild-cat leap, represent it more truly than graceful evolutions, and the Marseilles hymn. That music rises above mere brute vengeance; it breathes, in fervid ecstasy, the soul's aspiration after freedom—the struggle of will with fate. It is the future setting sail from old landings, and merrily piping all hands on board. It is too noble a voice to belong to physical warfare; the shrill howl of old Nan-Nouce-Fush-E-To, is good enough for such brutish work; it clove the brain like a tomahawk, and was hot with hatred.

In truth, that war-dance was terrific both to eye and ear. I looked at the door, to see if escape were easy, in case they really worked themselves up to the scalping point. For the first time, I fully conceived the sacrifices and perils of Puritan settlers. Heaven have mercy on the mother who heard those dreadful yells when they really foreboded murder! or who suddenly met such a group of grotesque demons in the loneliness of the forest!

But instantly I felt that I was wronging them in my thought. Through paint and feathers, I saw gleams of right honest and friendly expression; and I said, we are children of the same Father, seeking the same home. If the Puritans suffered from their savage hatred, it was

---

1   *the creative three-in-one*   I.e., the Christian God, whom most denominations hold to be simultaneously one and three—the Father, the Son, and the Holy Spirit.

2   *German Herder*   German philosopher and theologian Johann Gottfried von Herder (1744–1803).

3   *Richter*   Johann Paul Friedrich Richter (1763–1825), German Romantic writer and humorist.

4   *changes ... highest animal*   From James Russell Lowell, "Song-Writing" (1843).

because they met them with savage weapons, and a savage spirit. Then I thought of William Penn's treaty with the Indians;[1] "the only one ever formed without an oath, and the only one that was never broken." I thought of the deputation of Indians, who, some years ago, visited Philadelphia, and knelt with one spontaneous impulse round the monument of Penn.

Again, I looked at the yelling savages in their grim array, stamping through the war-dance, with a furious energy that made the floor shake, as by an earthquake; and I said, These, too, would bow, like little children, before the persuasive power of Christian love! Alas, if we had but faith in this divine principle, what mountains of evil might be removed into the depths of the sea.

P.S. Alas, poor, Do-Hum-Me is dead; so is No-See, Black Hawk's niece; and several of the chiefs are indisposed. Sleeping by hot anthracite fires, and then exposed to the keen encounters of the wintry wind; one hour, half stifled in the close atmosphere of theatres and crowded saloons, and the next, driving through snowy streets and the midnight air; this is a process which kills civilized people by inches, but savages at a few strokes.

Do-Hum-Me was but nineteen years old, in vigorous health, when I saw her a few days since, and obviously so happy in her newly wedded love, that it ran over at her expressive eyes, and mantled her handsome face like a veil of sunshine. Now she rests among the trees, in Greenwood Cemetery; not the trees that whispered to her childhood. Her coffin was decorated according to Indian custom, and deposited with the ceremonies peculiar to her people. Alas, for the handsome one, how lonely she sleeps here! Far, far away from him, to whom her eye turned constantly, as the sunflower to the light!

Sick, and sad at heart, this noble band of warriors, with melancholy steps, left the pestilential city last week, for their own broad prairies in the West. Do-Hum-Me was the pride and idol of them all. The old Iowa chief, the head of the deputation, was her father; and notwithstanding the stoicism of Indian character, it is said that both he and the bereaved young husband were overwhelmed with an agony of grief. They obviously loved each other most strongly. May the Great Spirit grant them a happy meeting in their "fair hunting grounds" beyond the sky.

—1843

from *The Duty of Disobedience to the Fugitive Slave Act:*[2] *An Appeal to the Legislators of Massachusetts*[3]

I feel there is no need of apologizing to the Legislature of Massachusetts because a woman addresses them. Sir Walter Scott[4] says: "The truth of Heaven was never committed to a tongue, however feeble, but it gave a right to that tongue to announce mercy, while it declared judgment." And in view of all that women have done, and are doing, intellectually and morally, for the advancement of the world, I presume no enlightened legislator will be disposed to deny that the "truth of Heaven" *is* often committed to them, and that they sometimes utter it with a degree of power that greatly influences the age in which they live.

I therefore offer no excuses on that score. But I do feel as if it required some apology to attempt to convince men of ordinary humanity and common sense that the Fugitive Slave Bill is utterly wicked, and consequently ought never to be obeyed. Yet Massachusetts consents to that law! Some shadow of justice she grants, inasmuch as her Legislature have passed what is called a Personal Liberty Bill, securing trial by jury to those claimed as slaves. Certainly it is *something* gained, especially for those who may get brown by working in the sunshine, to prevent our Southern masters from

---

[1] *William Penn's ... Indians* William Penn (1644–1718), founder of Pennsylvania, negotiated an exchange with the Lenape whose territory he colonized, trading goods for signed documents ceding land to the colonists. The relationship between the Pennsylvanians and the Lenape was remarkably peaceful for the period and was seen as representative of ideal Indigenous-settler relations; nevertheless, Penn and his settlers displaced the Lenape and forced them to conform to the needs of the colony.

[2] *Fugitive Slave Act* Enacted by U.S. Congress in 1850, the Fugitive Slave Act mandated increased efforts on the part of free states to hunt down and arrest fugitives from slavery, while also imposing fines and jail time on anyone who assisted such fugitives.

[3] The text presented here is based on that of the pamphlet published by the American Anti-Slavery Society in 1860.

[4] *Sir Walter Scott* Popular Scottish writer; the quotation that follows is from his novel *The Fair Maid of Perth, or St. Valentine's Day* (1828).

taking any of us, at a moment's notice, and dragging us off into perpetual bondage. It is *something* gained to require legal proof that a man is a slave, before he is given up to arbitrary torture and unrecompensed toil. But is *that* the measure of justice becoming the character of a free Commonwealth? "*Prove* that the man is property, according *your* laws, and I will drive him into your cattle-pen with sword and bayonet," is what Massachusetts practically says to Southern tyrants. "Show me a Bill of Sale from the Almighty!" is what she *ought* to say. No other proof should be considered valid in a Christian country.

One thousand five hundred years ago, Gregory,[1] a Bishop in Asia Minor, preached a sermon in which he rebuked the sin of slaveholding. Indignantly he asked, "Who can be the possessor of human beings save God? Those men that you say belong to you, did not God create them free? Command the brute creation; that is well. Bend the beasts of the field beneath your yoke. But are your fellow-men to be bought and sold, like herds of cattle? Who can pay the value of a being created in the image of God? The whole world itself bears no proportion to the value of a soul, on which the Most High has set the seal his likeness. This world will perish, but the soul of man is immortal. Show me, then, your titles of possession. Tell me whence you derive this strange claim. Is not your own nature the same with that of those you call your slaves? Have they not the same origin with yourselves? Are they not born to the same immortal destinies?"

Thus spake a good old Bishop, in the early years of Christianity. Since then, thousands and thousands of noble souls have given their bodies to the gibbet[2] and the stake, to help onward the slow progress of truth and freedom; a great unknown continent has been opened as a new, free starting point for the human race; printing has been invented, and the command, "Whatsoever ye would that men should do unto you, do ye even so unto them," has been sent abroad in all the languages of the earth. And here, in the noon-day of light the nineteenth century, in a nation claiming to be the freest and most enlightened on the face of the globe, a portion the population of fifteen States have

thus agreed among themselves: "Other men shall work for us, without wages, while we smoke, and drink, and gamble, and race horses, and fight. We will have their wives and daughters for concubines, and sell their children in the market with horses and pigs. If they make any objection to this arrangement, we will break them into subjection with the cow-hide and the bucking-paddle. They shall not be permitted to read or write, because that would be likely to 'produce dissatisfaction in their minds.'[3] If they attempt to run away from us, our blood-hounds shall tear the flesh from their bones, and any man who sees them may shoot them down like mad dogs. If they succeed in getting beyond our frontier, into States where it is the custom to pay men for their work, and to protect their wives and children from outrage, we will compel the people of those States to drive them back into the jaws of our blood-hounds."

And what do the people of the other eighteen States of that enlightened country answer to this monstrous demand? What says Massachusetts, with the free blood of the Puritans coursing in her veins, and with the sword uplifted in her right hand, to procure "peaceful repose under liberty"?[4] Massachusetts answers: "O yes. We will be your blood-hounds, and pay our own expenses. Only prove to our satisfaction that the stranger who has taken refuge among us is one of the men you have agreed among yourselves to whip into working without wages, and we will hunt him back for you. Only prove to us that this woman, who has run away from your harem, was bought for a concubine, that you might get more drinking-money by the sale of the children she bears you, and our soldiers will hunt her back with alacrity."

Shame on my native State! Everlasting shame! Blot out the escutcheon[5] of the brave old Commonwealth! Instead of the sword uplifted to protect liberty, let the slave-driver's whip be suspended over a blood-hound, and take for your motto, Obedience to tyrants is the highest law. …

---

[1] *Gregory* Saint Gregory of Nyssa (c. 335–c. 395), bishop who was among the earliest Christian voices to denounce slavery.

[2] *gibbet* Gallows.

[3] *produce … minds* Paraphrased from North Carolina's Act to Prevent All Persons from Teaching Slaves to Read or Write, the Use of Figures Excepted (1830). Many states had similar laws.

[4] *peaceful repose under liberty* Reference to the Latin motto of the Commonwealth of Massachusetts, sometimes translated as "By the sword she seeks peaceful repose under Liberty."

[5] *escutcheon* Shield on which a coat of arms is displayed.

Legislators of Massachusetts! if *you* had been thus continually robbed of your rights by the hand of violence, what would *you* think of the compact between North and South to perpetuate your wrongs, and transmit them to your posterity? Would you not regard it as a league between highwaymen, who had "no rights that you were bound to respect"?[1] I put the question plainly and directly to your consciences and your common sense, and they will not allow you to answer, No. Are you, then, doing right to sustain the validity of a law for *others*, which you would vehemently reject for *yourselves*, in the name of outraged justice and humanity? …

It is well known that Southerners have repeatedly declared they do not demand fugitives merely to recover articles of property, or for the sake of making an example of them, to inspire terror in other runaways; that they have a still stronger motive, which is to humiliate the North; to make them feel that no latitude limits their mastership. Have we no honest pride, that we so tamely submit to this? What lethargic disease has fallen on Northern souls, that they dare not be as bold for Freedom as tyrants are for Slavery? It was not thus with our fathers, whose sepulchres we whiten.[2] If old Ben Franklin[3] had stood as near Boston Court House as his statue does, do you believe *he* would have remained passive, while Sims,[4] the intelligent mechanic, was manacled and driven through the streets, guiltless of

any crime, save that of wishing to be free? *My* belief is that the brave old printer of '76[5] would have drawn down the lightning out of heaven upon that procession, with a vengeance. …

If you resort to the alleged legal obligation to return fugitives, it has more plausibility, but has it in reality any firm foundation? Americans boast of making their own laws, and of amending them whenever circumstances render it necessary. How, then, can they excuse themselves, or expect the civilized world to excuse them, for making, or sustaining, unjust and cruel laws? The Fugitive Slave Act has none of the attributes of law. If two highwaymen agreed between themselves to stand by each other in robbing helpless men, women and children, should we not find it hard work to "conquer our prejudices"[6] so far as to dignify their bargain with the name of *law*? That is the light in which the compact between North and South presents itself to the minds of intelligent slaves, and we should view it in the same way, if we were in their position. …

Moreover, there is wrong done, even to the humblest individual, when he is compelled to be ashamed of his country. When the judge passed under chains into Boston Court House, and when Anthony Burns[7] was sent back into slavery, I wept for my native State, as a daughter weeps for the crimes of a beloved mother. It seemed to me that I would gladly have died to have saved Massachusetts from that sin and that shame. The tears of a secluded woman, who has no vote to give, may appear to you of little consequence. But assuredly it is not well with any Commonwealth, when her daughters weep over her degeneracy and disgrace.

In the name of oppressed humanity, of violated religion, of desecrated law, of tarnished honor, of our own freedom endangered, of the moral sense of our people degraded by these evil influences, I respectfully,

---

1   *no rights … respect*   Paraphrased from the Supreme Court decision *Dred Scott v. Sandford*, in which the Court stated that black people were "of an inferior order and altogether unfit to associate with the white race, either in social or political relations, and so far inferior that they had no rights which the white man was bound to respect." The plaintiff, Dred Scott, an enslaved man, had argued that upon leaving a slave state and entering a free territory he should be considered legally free; the Court determined that his suit automatically failed because he had no rights of citizenship.

2   *whose sepulchres we whiten*   See Matthew 23.27: "Woe unto you, scribes and Pharisees, hypocrites! for ye are like unto whited sepulchres, which indeed appear beautiful outward, but are within full of dead men's bones, and of all uncleanness."

3   *Ben Franklin*   Benjamin Franklin, though he owned a number of enslaved people prior to 1770, became increasingly critical of slavery in later years, and in 1785 was elected president of the Pennsylvania Abolition Society.

4   *Sims*   Thomas Sims, an enslaved man who escaped to Massachusetts in 1851 but was sent back to slavery in Georgia after a court hearing.

5   *printer of '76*   Reference to Franklin's career as a printer as well as to his involvement in the drafting of the Declaration of Independence in 1776.

6   *conquer our prejudices*   Paraphrased from a 29 April 1850 speech by Massachusetts senator Daniel Webster in which he suggests that the state should "conquer her own prejudices" by obeying its duty to the South and enforcing the Fugitive Slave Act.

7   *Anthony Burns*   Born into slavery in Virginia, Burns fled north to Boston in 1853, only to be captured and sent back the following year. His freedom was eventually purchased by Northern abolitionists, after which he emigrated to Upper Canada.

but most urgently, entreat you to annul this infamous enactment, so far as the jurisdiction of Massachusetts extends. Our old Commonwealth has been first and foremost in many good works; let her lead in this also. And deem it not presumptuous, if I ask it likewise for my own sake. I am a humble member of the community; but I am deeply interested in the welfare and reputation of my native State, and that gives me some claim to be heard. I am growing old; and on this great question of equal rights I have toiled for years, sometimes with a heart sickened by "hope deferred."[1] I beseech you to let me die on Free Soil! Grant me the satisfaction of saying, ere I go hence—

Slaves cannot breathe among us. If their lungs
Receive *our* air, that moment they are free!
They touch *our* country, and their shackles fall![2]

If you cannot be induced to reform this great wickedness, for the sake of outraged justice and humanity, then do it for the honor of the State, for the political welfare of our own people, for the moral character of our posterity. For, as sure as there is a Righteous Ruler in the heavens, if you continue to be accomplices in violence and fraud, God will *not* "save the Commonwealth of Massachusetts."

L. MARIA CHILD

—1860

---

[1]   *hope deferred*   See Proverbs 13.12: "Hope deferred maketh the heart sick: but when the desire cometh, it is a tree of life."

[2]   *Slaves cannot … shackles fall!*   Allusion to *The Task* (1785) by English antislavery poet William Cowper. The original poem reads "Slaves cannot breathe in England" in reference to a 1772 court ruling (known as Somersett's Case) that effectively outlawed the keeping of enslaved people in England, even as English people continued to own enslaved people elsewhere in the British Empire.

Expansion, Native American Expulsion, and "Manifest Destiny"

CONTEXTS

By the start of the nineteenth century, Euro-American settlers had been steadily dispossessing Native Americans of what had become the eastern United States for nearly two hundred years. With the adoption of the Indian Removal Act of 1830, which mandated the wholesale expulsion of the eastern U.S.'s Indigenous communities, this steady dispossession reached a dreadful climax. Indigenous people throughout the U.S. were facing the immediate threats of the country's westward expansion well before the Removal Act was signed into law, however. By 1820, the Indigenous nations of the Old Northwest (the region bounded by the Appalachian Mountains, the Great Lakes, and the Ohio and Mississippi Rivers) had been fragmented and marginalized by the tide of white settlement. The larger Indigenous nations in the South—the Choctaw, Chickasaw, Cherokee, Muscogee (Creek), and Seminole—more successfully maintained their cohesion while adopting many Euro-American institutions and practices, because of which white Americans dubbed them the "Five Civilized Tribes," but that did not prevent them from facing intense pressure, like their fellow Indigenous peoples to the north, to surrender their territories and relocate west of the Mississippi. This pressure not infrequently took the form of outright aggression, as in the 1818 attack by white militia on a friendly Muscogee community described in the newspaper article "Destruction of Chehaw Village." Some Native Americans gave in to the pressures directed toward them—including the parents of Catharine Brown, a young Cherokee convert to Christianity, as she describes in the letter included below. As the petitions addressed by Cherokee women to their leaders in 1817 and 1818 make clear, though, many other Indigenous people were firmly opposed to "part[ing] with any more of our land."

Calls to open up the remaining Indigenous territory east of the Mississippi to white settlement, and to move its inhabitants out of the way of that settlement, continued to increase during the 1820s. A wide variety of groups and individuals at different levels of government and civil society joined in advocating for Indigenous expulsion: state and territorial governors, U.S. congressional committees, citizen groups, religious organizations, Indian agents, the heads of the federal Office of Indian Affairs (later the Bureau of Indian Affairs), and even some Indigenous leaders. This widespread, decentered movement for expulsion came to a head, and received powerful centralized endorsement, when Andrew Jackson became president in 1829. Jackson had made his name, in part, as the leader of brutal military campaigns against Native Americans, and his administration made "Indian removal"—as the plan for Indigenous expulsion was euphemistically termed—a policy priority. Debate about this policy quickly came to the forefront of the national conversation. Some of the policy's strongest supporters were Southern enslavers (such as Jackson himself), who wanted to spread plantation slavery onto Indigenous land, but "removal" was also championed in the North by members of Jackson's Democratic Party, as the poet and newspaper editor William Cullen Bryant's editorials on the topic demonstrate. This nationwide support enabled the passage of the Removal Act, according to which all Indigenous people east of the Mississippi had to either cede their remaining lands and relocate to designated "Indian Territory" west of the river or accept the jurisdiction of the U.S. states in which they lived. In December 1830, Jackson himself—whose name has remained indelibly associated with Indigenous expulsion ever since—applauded this act, and defended the policy underlying it, in his "Message to Congress on Indian Removal."

The Indian Removal Act only passed Congress by a very narrow margin, however, and many white Americans, especially in the North, opposed the government's plans to deport Native Americans (a fact that Bryant's editorials acknowledge). One of the leaders of this opposition was the well-known poet Lydia Sigourney, who helped organize the so-called "Ladies' Circular" campaign that petitioned Congress to reject the Removal Act—a milestone in the history of American female political advocacy. After the act passed, Sigourney then lamented its consequences, as she imagined them, in "The Cherokee Mother," a poem she published in 1831 in *The Cherokee Phoenix*, the Cherokee national newspaper.

Despite such opposition, the federal government, empowered by the Removal Act, quickly began negotiating removal treaties—many of dubious legitimacy—with Indigenous nations and then deporting them piecemeal. The first nation to be expelled was the Choctaw people of Mississippi and Alabama; part of their deportation, which occurred between 1831 and 1833 and caused thousands of Choctaw deaths, was witnessed by the visiting French writer Alexis de Tocqueville, who recorded its "air of ruin and destruction." The Muscogee (Creek) and Chickasaw in the South, and numerous nations in the North, followed suit in the next few years. The Cherokee strenuously protested their own planned expulsion, even after a minority of Cherokee leaders formally ceded their nation's land—despite lacking the legal authority to do so—in the Treaty of New Echota in 1835. John Ross, the Cherokee Principal Chief, led the Cherokee opposition to "removal," making its case in documents such as the 1836 petition to Congress written by Ross and signed by thousands of other Cherokee. Joining the Cherokee in these efforts were white allies such as Ralph Waldo Emerson, whose open letter to Jackson's successor as president, Martin Van Buren, was written early in 1838. Such protests notwithstanding, the Cherokee were deported in 1838, the last major "removal" to take place. Two accounts of the ensuing "Trail of Tears" appear below: the testimony of Eliza Whitmire, an enslaved African American whose family made the deadly trek to Indian Territory along with their Cherokee enslavers, and a narrative by the modern-day Cherokee storyteller Freeman Owle.

Because the Cherokee and their fellow Southeastern nations were the largest, wealthiest, and most politically prominent Indigenous nations, and because their expulsion involved a massive movement of people over a vast distance, their case commanded public attention at the time and has often been taken to be representative of "Indian removal" ever since. Many other Indigenous nations besides the five major Southeastern ones, though, were deported during the 1820s and 30s: the Shawnee, for instance, were expelled from their homelands in the Old Northwest just as thoroughly as the Cherokee and were moved just as far, but their expulsion inspired nothing like as intense of a public debate. Indigenous expulsion in other parts of the country also often took a quite different form than it did in the South. The expulsion of the Ojibwe, for example, involved many local, small-scale relocations or confinements and took them a much shorter distance from their traditional territories than the Cherokee, Shawnee, or other nations were forced to move.

Expulsion undoubtedly was an enormous, traumatic rupture for the Indigenous people who underwent it, and it decisively moved most of the Indigenous population of the eastern U.S. beyond the sphere of daily lived experience for the bulk of the country's white population. By no means, however, should expulsion be seen as the end of the story. The deported nations survived and in some cases even thrived, and an important part of the history of Indigenous expulsion is the history of what Indigenous people did after it: re-establish livelihoods, including farms and plantations, and institutions, including schools and academies, printing offices, and governments, in their new territories, and envision and negotiate new political relationships, both between deported nations that found themselves living next to one another and between deportees and the local Indigenous communities whose lands, in some cases, the deportees were now occupying.

The expulsions of the 1830s also sparked several wars, as various groups of Native Americans throughout the country fought back against the effort to expel them. U.S. forces were tasked with quelling armed resistance by members of the Sauk and allied nations, led by Black Hawk, in Illinois and Wisconsin and by members of the Muscogee nation in Alabama. The longest and costliest conflict was the war fought against the Seminole of Florida, who took up arms in 1835 and held out until 1842, when the remaining few hundred Seminole who had not been killed or deported were permitted to remain on an unofficial reservation. (Further white encroachment onto this residual territory led to another U.S.–Seminole war, the third, from 1855 to 1858.) The war's great expense in both money and lives, together with its flimsy moral justification, made it unpopular both with many civilians and many soldiers—as is attested by some of the documents presented in this section, including the diary of U.S. Army officer

Ethan Allen Hitchcock (in the section's website component) and the political cartoon criticizing the tactics used against the Seminole by General Zachary Taylor.

At the same time as the Seminole War was breaking out, another conflict erupted on one of the other fronts of American expansion: Texas. By the 1830s, large numbers of white Americans had settled in that territory, then part of Mexico, and their resistance to Mexican authority—together with the desire for greater political autonomy of many Hispanic Tejanos—led to war in 1835. After initial defeats at the Alamo, where a small Texan garrison fought to the death, and Goliad, where Mexican troops executed several hundred Texan prisoners, Texan forces ultimately prevailed in the spring of 1836, gaining the Republic of Texas *de facto* independence. Among the texts included in this section's website component, R.M. Potter's "Hymn of the Alamo" extols the defense of the Alamo as a self-sacrificial stand that helped win "Freedom," while U.S. Senator Daniel S. Dickinson's 1845 speech likens the Texas Revolution to America's Revolutionary War in the course of an argument in favor of annexing the Republic of Texas to the United States.

The heated debate over Texas annexation that occasioned Dickinson's speech also gave rise to the term that has come to epitomize American expansion: "manifest destiny." This term first appeared in an article, entitled "Annexation," published in 1845 in *The United States Magazine and Democratic Review*, a Jacksonian Democratic periodical that had already made clear its commitment to American exceptionalism and its exalted view of American national destiny in its 1839 article "The Great Nation of Futurity." The term quickly caught on among advocates of national expansion, but the idea that America had an expansionary destiny that legitimized its seizure of others' territory was just as quickly condemned—for example, by Democratic Congressman Charles Goodyear, who gave a speech in early 1846 in which he scathingly characterized "manifest destiny" as "the robber's title."

The stakes of this debate became even higher when war broke out with Mexico later in 1846—largely at U.S. provocation—over the annexation of Texas, which Mexico still claimed. Some Americans, including a young Walt Whitman in his editorials for the *Brooklyn Daily Eagle*, welcomed the war as an opportunity for the country to realize its "manifest destiny" at Mexico's expense, while others opposed the war as an unjustified imperialistic land-grab. U.S. forces swiftly surpassed the goals set for them by the likes of Whitman, conquering New Mexico and California before invading the Mexican heartland; the account of Rosalía Vallejo (in this section's online component), describing her experiences at the hands of the white American settlers in California who rebelled against Mexican rule at the beginning of the war, provides a Hispanic perspective on these conquests. After Mexico was defeated and gave up these and other vast stretches of its territory in 1848, the Irish American politician and poet Thomas D'Arcy McGee elaborated the campaign waged during the war by the U.S. "Army of the West," in his poem of that title, into a metaphor for American westward expansion and colonization writ large.

During the 1850s, in the wake of the enormous territorial acquisitions that had occurred between 1845 and 1848, the idea of "manifest destiny" further proliferated and diversified. The African American poet James Monroe Whitfield's 1853 open letter to Frederick Douglass advocating black emigration out of the United States illustrates how widely the term had spread and the different uses to which it was being put. The conventional white American understanding of the country's "manifest destiny" also continued to run strong in the 1850s. However, as the Whig presidential administrations of Zachary Taylor and Millard Fillmore moved away from overtly expansionist policies, and as the debate over the extension of slavery into the western territories intensified, attempts to continue the country's expansion during that decade generally took the unofficial form of "filibustering": the practice by U.S. citizens of inciting insurrections in Latin American countries, frequently with the aim of enabling U.S. annexation of the country in question in the insurrection's wake. This practice is skewered in the popular 1854 poem "Filibustering Ethics," which also serves as a withering critique of "manifest destiny" thinking more generally. A different kind of critique of such thinking, from the point of view of one of the communities recently taken over by American expansion, can be seen in Francisco Ramírez's 1855 editorial from *El Clamor Público*, his pioneering Spanish-language Californian newspaper.

The two chronologically latest pieces in this section, by John Rollin Ridge (in the bound book) and Henry David Thoreau (in the website component), exemplify the variety and complexity of the ways in which Americans of all stripes responded to American national expansion, its justifications, and its consequences. Ridge's "Poem (Delivered at Commencement of Oakland College, California, June 6th 1861)" demonstrates how Ridge—the son and grandson of Cherokee leaders killed in the internal Cherokee dispute over their nation's "removal"—could imbue certain of his works with "manifest destiny" ideas, even as others criticize the effects of U.S. expansion on some of the people it subordinated. Thoreau's essay "Walking" demonstrates the powerful appeal that the idea of America's "westward tendency" had even for such a writer as Thoreau, whose uncompromising opposition to the Mexican–American War had landed him in jail. By the time Ridge's poem was written and Thoreau's essay published, the debate over how to incorporate the new western territories—specifically, whether or not slavery would be allowed there—had helped precipitate the Civil War: a further consequence of the great national "westering" that both works, in their different ways, celebrate.

⌘ ⌘ ⌘

Catharine Brown (Kä tý), letter to Loring S. Williams and Matilda Loomis Williams, 5 July 1819

By late 1818, the family of Catharine Brown (c. 1800–23), having suffered repeated acts of theft and violence on their land from encroaching settlers, had determined to move westwards in the hopes of escaping further white aggression. For Catharine, however—a Cherokee student at the American Board of Commissioners for Foreign Missions school in Brainerd, Tennessee, and a recent convert to Christianity—moving west would mean leaving behind the Christian community to which she now felt profoundly connected. Brown was herself a minor celebrity, known throughout the United States both for her renowned piety and for her letters to missionary friends, which were widely published in newspapers and religious periodicals. Though her parents temporarily removed her from the Brainerd school in November 1818, their move westwards ultimately did not take place until after Brown's death. Nevertheless, her letters from the period vividly recount the agony of having to choose between what she had come to think of as her two families. A larger selection of Brown's correspondence is included in the website component of this anthology.

TO MR. AND MRS. WILLIAMS
Brainerd, July 5, 1819

My dear Brother and Sister,[1]

Although I have long omitted answering your affectionate letters, my heart has been often with you. Yes, dear brother and sister, I do not forget you, and all the pleasant meetings we had together, when you were here. But pain is mixed with pleasure when I think they are gone, no more to return! When I remember the kind instruction I received from you, before you left this place, my heart swells with gratitude. I feel much indebted to you, but more particularly to that God, who sent you here to instruct the poor ignorant Indians in the way that leads to everlasting life. Oh, my dear friends, may the Lord ever bless you, and make you the instrument of doing great good where he has called you.

You may pass through many trials; but remember, beloved brother and sister, all our trials here will only make us richer there when we arrive at our home. A few more days, and then, I hope, our weary souls will be at rest in our Saviour's kingdom, where we shall enjoy His blessed presence forever.

---

1   *Brother and Sister*   Like many devout Christians at the time, Brown refers to all of her fellow believers as brothers and sisters, not just her siblings by blood.

When I wrote you before, I expected to go to the Arkansas,[1] and never to see this place again. But the Lord has in mercy ordered it otherwise. He has permitted me to live with the dear missionaries here again, though my parents could not bear to think of leaving me behind. My mother said, if I remained here, she did not expect to see me again in this world. Indeed, she wished she had never sent me to this school, and that I had never received religious instruction. I told her, if she was a Christian, she would not feel so: she would be willing to give me, and all she had, up to Christ. I told her I did not wish to stay on account of my own pleasure, but that I wished to get more instruction, so that it might be for her good, as well as for mine.

I felt very sorry for my poor parents. I thought it was my duty to go in obedience to their commands, and commit myself to the will of God. I knew the Lord could change the hearts of my parents.

They are now perfectly willing that I should stay here two years longer. I left them in March. They expected to set out in that month for the Arkansas. They had already prepared for the journey. But the Lord has so ordered, that they have concluded not to go until next fall. I don't know whether they will go then. I hope you will pray for them, and also for me, that I may be useful to their immortal souls. O that I might be made the means of turning many souls from darkness unto marvellous light.[2] My dear brother and sister, I love you much, and feel that the time is short when we shall sit down with our Saviour, and experience that love which no words can describe.

From your affectionate sister in Christ,

Catharine Brown

---

[1] *the Arkansas* I.e., Arkansas Territory, which became the state of Arkansas in 1836. Groups of Cherokee had begun relocating there as early as the Revolutionary era, and a substantial number, who became known as the "Old Settlers," moved to the territory after the federal government established a Cherokee reservation there in 1815.

[2] *turning ... unto marvellous light* See Acts 26.18: "To open their eyes, and to turn them from darkness to light, and from the power of Satan unto God, that they may receive forgiveness of sins, and inheritance among them which are sanctified by faith that is in me."

Cherokee Women's Petitions (1817, 1818, 1831)

The Cherokee traditionally accorded an important place to women, not just symbolically but also socially and economically. The Cherokee kinship system was matrilineal, meaning descent was traced through women; in addition, Cherokee women were responsible for agriculture, which gave them significant economic status. As the Cherokee adopted Euro-American culture and institutions in the early nineteenth century, Cherokee society became more overtly male-dominated. However, Cherokee women still wielded substantial influence (even if this was often overlooked) and frequently acted as preservers of traditional values. These roles are particularly on display in the three petitions that, between 1817 and 1831, Cherokee women presented to the male leaders of the Cherokee Nation in response to white American pressure for Cherokee "removal." All three petitions oppose removal or the relinquishment of further Cherokee land, but they frame this opposition in different ways that reflect the development of Cherokee society, and women's place in it, throughout the early nineteenth century.

The text of the petitions is based on their original manuscript (1817) or published (1818 and 1831) versions.

PETITION (2 MAY 1817)

The Cherokee ladies now being present at the meeting of their chiefs and warriors in council have thought it their duty as mothers to address their beloved chiefs and warriors now assembled.

Our beloved children and head men of the Cherokee Nation, we address you as warriors in council. We have raised all of you on the land which we now have, which God gave us to inhabit and raise provisions. We know that our country has once been extensive, but by repeated sales has become circumscribed to a small track, and [we] never have thought it our duty to interfere in the disposition[3] of it till now. If a father or mother was to sell all their lands which they had to depend on, which their children had to raise their living on, which would be indeed bad and to be

---

[3] *disposition* Administration, disposal.

removed to another country. We do not wish to go [to] an unknown country [to] which we have understood some of our children wish to go over the Mississippi, but this act of our children would be like destroying your mothers.

Your mothers, your sisters ask and beg of you not to part with any more of our land. We say ours. You are our descendants; take pity on our request. But keep it for our growing children, for it was the good will of our creator to place us here, and you know our father, the great president,[1] will not allow his white children to take our country away. Only keep your hands off of paper talks for it's our own country. For [if] it was not, they would not ask you to put your hands to paper, for it would be impossible to remove us all. For as soon as one child is raised, we have others in our arms, for such is our situation and will consider our circumstance.

Therefore, children, don't part with any more of our lands but continue on it and enlarge your farms and cultivate and raise corn and cotton and we, your mothers and sisters, will make clothing for you which our father the president has recommended to us all. We don't charge anybody for selling any lands, but we have heard such intentions of our children. But your talks become true at last; it was our desire to forewarn you all not to part with our lands.

Nancy Ward[2] to her children: Warriors to take pity and listen to the talks of your sisters. Although I am very old yet cannot but pity the situation in which you will hear of their minds. I have great many grandchildren which [I] wish them to do well on our land.

---

[1]   *the great president*   At the time of this petition, the President of the United States was James Monroe.

[2]   *Nancy Ward*   English name of Nanyehi (c. 1738–1822 or 1824), a Cherokee political leader. In recognition for battlefield heroism during her youth, she was named a "Beloved Woman," a Cherokee title conferring great honor and responsibility: Beloved Women headed the Council of Women, could vote in the Council of Chiefs, decided the fate of prisoners taken in war, and could serve as ambassadors on behalf of the Cherokee Nation. As a Beloved Woman, Nanyehi was known for her support for the American colonists during the Revolutionary War (at a time when most Cherokee supported the British) and for her advocacy of peaceful coexistence with white Americans.

PETITION (30 JUNE 1818)

Beloved Children,

We have called a meeting among ourselves to consult on the different points now before the council, relating to our national affairs. We have heard with painful feelings that the bounds of the land we now possess are to be drawn into very narrow limits. The land was given to us by the Great Spirit above as our common right, to raise our children upon, and to make support for our rising generations. We therefore humbly petition our beloved children, the head men and warriors, to hold out to the last in support of our common rights, as the Cherokee nation have been the first settlers of this land; we therefore claim the right of the soil.

We well remember that our country was formerly very extensive, but by repeated sales it has become circumscribed to the very narrow limits we have at present. Our Father the President advised us to become farmers, to manufacture our own clothes, and to have our children instructed. To this advice we have attended in everything as far as we were able. Now the thought of being compelled to remove to the other side of the Mississippi is dreadful to us, because it appears to us that we, by this removal, shall be brought to a savage state[3] again, for we have, by the endeavor of our Father the President, become too much enlightened to throw aside the privileges of a civilized life.

We therefore unanimously join in our meeting to hold our country in common as hitherto.

Some of our children have become Christians. We have missionary schools among us. We have heard the gospel in our nation. We have become civilized and enlightened, and are in hopes that in a few years our nation will be prepared for instruction in other branches of sciences and arts, which are both useful and necessary in civilized society.

There are some white men among us, who have been raised in our country from their youth, are connected with us by marriage, and have considerable families, who are very active in encouraging the emigration of

---

[3]   *savage state*   The authors of this petition have here assimilated the use of the derogatory term "savage," common among white Americans in the nineteenth century, to characterize Indigenous society and culture.

our nation. These ought to be our truest friends but prove our worst enemies. They seem to be only concerned how to increase their riches, but do not care what becomes of our Nation, nor even of their own wives and children.

PETITION (17 OCTOBER 1831[1])

To the Committee and Council,

We the females, residing in Salequoree and Pine Log,[2] believing that the present difficulties and embarrassments under which this nation is placed demands a full expression of the mind of every individual, on the subject of emigrating to Arkansas,[3] would take upon ourselves to address you. Although it is not common for our sex to take part in public measures, we nevertheless feel justified in expressing our sentiments on any subject where our interest is as much at stake as any other part of the community.

We believe the present plan of the General Government to effect our removal West of the Mississippi, and thus obtain our lands for the use of the State of Georgia, to be highly oppressive, cruel and unjust. And we sincerely hope there is no consideration which can induce our citizens to forsake the land of our fathers of which they have been in possession from time immemorial, and thus compel us, against our will, to undergo the toils and difficulties of removing with our helpless families hundreds of miles to unhealthy and unproductive country. We hope therefore the Committee and Council will take into deep consideration our deplorable situation, and do everything in their power to avert such a state of things. And we trust by a prudent course their transactions with the General Government will enlist in our behalf the sympathies of the good people of the United States.

---

[1] *1831* This petition, dated "1821" in its original text, was published as a letter in the *Cherokee Phoenix* on 12 November 1831; the 1821 dating is almost certainly a typographical error.

[2] *Salequoree and Pine Log* Cherokee communities in northern Georgia.

[3] *Arkansas* I.e., Arkansas Territory, which became the state of Arkansas in 1836. Groups of Cherokee had begun relocating there as early as the Revolutionary era, and a substantial number, who became known as the "Old Settlers," moved to the territory after the federal government established a Cherokee reservation there in 1815.

Andrew Jackson, message to Congress on Indian Removal (1830)

One of the most famous of Andrew Jackson's numerous defenses of the policy of Native American expulsion is the portion excerpted below of his annual message to Congress on 6 December 1830, after the passage of the Indian Removal Act earlier that year. The text of the excerpt is based on that contained in the U.S. National Archives (in the Records of the United States Senate, 1789–1990) and published on the National Archives website.

It gives me pleasure to announce to Congress that the benevolent policy of the Government, steadily pursued for nearly thirty years, in relation to the removal of the Indians beyond the white settlements is approaching to a happy consummation. Two important tribes have accepted the provision made for their removal at the last session of Congress,[4] and it is believed that their example will induce the remaining tribes also to seek the same obvious advantages.

The consequences of a speedy removal will be important to the United States, to individual States, and to the Indians themselves. The pecuniary advantages which it promises to the Government are the least of its recommendations. It puts an end to all possible danger of collision between the authorities of the General and State Governments on account of the Indians. It will place a dense and civilized population in large tracts of country now occupied by a few savage hunters. By opening the whole territory between Tennessee on the north and Louisiana on the south to the settlement of the whites it will incalculably strengthen the southwestern frontier and render the adjacent States strong enough to repel future invasions without remote aid. It will relieve the whole State of Mississippi and the western part of Alabama of Indian occupancy, and enable those States to advance rapidly in population, wealth, and power. It will separate the Indians from immediate contact with settlements of whites; free them from the

---

[4] *Two important ... Congress* At the time Jackson spoke, elements of the leadership of the Chickasaw and Choctaw nations had signed removal treaties in August and September 1830, respectively. (The Chickasaw later deemed the land allotted to them west of the Mississippi unacceptable and renegotiated a new treaty in 1832.)

power of the States; enable them to pursue happiness in their own way and under their own rude[1] institutions; will retard the progress of decay, which is lessening their numbers, and perhaps cause them gradually, under the protection of the Government and through the influence of good counsels, to cast off their savage habits and become an interesting,[2] civilized, and Christian community.

What good man would prefer a country covered with forests and ranged by a few thousand savages to our extensive Republic, studded with cities, towns, and prosperous farms embellished with all the improvements which art can devise or industry execute, occupied by more than 12,000,000 happy people, and filled with all the blessings of liberty, civilization and religion?

The present policy of the Government is but a continuation of the same progressive change by a milder process. The tribes which occupied the countries now constituting the Eastern States were annihilated or have melted away to make room for the whites. The waves of population and civilization are rolling to the westward, and we now propose to acquire the countries occupied by the red men of the South and West by a fair exchange, and, at the expense of the United States, to send them to land where their existence may be prolonged and perhaps made perpetual. Doubtless it will be painful to leave the graves of their fathers; but what do they more than our ancestors did or than our children are now doing? To better their condition in an unknown land our forefathers left all that was dear in earthly objects. Our children by thousands yearly leave the land of their birth to seek new homes in distant regions. Does Humanity weep at these painful separations from everything, animate and inanimate, with which the young heart has become entwined? Far from it. It is rather a source of joy that our country affords scope where our young population may range unconstrained in body or in mind, developing the power and facilities of man in their highest perfection. These remove[3] hundreds and almost thousands of miles at their own expense, purchase the lands they occupy, and support themselves at their new homes from the moment of their arrival. Can it be cruel in

this Government when, by events which it cannot control, the Indian is made discontented in his ancient home to purchase his lands, to give him a new and extensive territory, to pay the expense of his removal, and support him a year in his new abode? How many thousands of our own people would gladly embrace the opportunity of removing to the West on such conditions! If the offers made to the Indians were extended to them, they would be hailed with gratitude and joy.

Andrew Jackson as the Great Father, c. 1835. "Great Father" was a title frequently used in the context of Indigenous–settler relations, by both Euro-American authorities and Indigenous people, to refer to the leaders of settler-colonial nations, including the Kings of France and Britain and later the U.S. President. The title was meant to evoke the President or other Euro-American leader's supposedly beneficent care for his Indigenous "children"—an idea literalized by this cartoon's unknown illustrator. The framed painting in the top right-hand corner of the illustration depicts Columbia—the allegorical female personification of the United States—standing with her foot on the head of a subjugated foe.

---

[1] *rude* Uncivilized.

[2] *interesting* Important, worthy of consideration.

[3] *remove* Relocate.

And is it supposed that the wandering savage has a stronger attachment to his home than the settled, civilized Christian? Is it more afflicting to him to leave the graves of his fathers than it is to our brothers and children? Rightly considered, the policy of the General Government toward the red man is not only liberal, but generous. He is unwilling to submit to the laws of the States and mingle with their population. To save him from this alternative, or perhaps utter annihilation, the General Government kindly offers him a new home, and proposes to pay the whole expense of his removal and settlement.

Lydia Sigourney, "The Cherokee Mother" (1831)

By the time of the Indian Removal Act, the celebrated white American poet Lydia Huntley Sigourney had already demonstrated, in poems such as *Traits of the Aborigines of America* (1822), a sympathetic—if also romanticizing and condescending—interest in Indigenous people and history. This poem, written in response to the Removal Act and published in 1831 in *The Cherokee Phoenix*, the Cherokee national newspaper, further exemplifies that interest. The poem was never republished in any of Sigourney's collections.

Ye bid us hence.[1] These vales are dear,
    To infant hope, to patriot pride,
These streamlets tuneful to our ear,
Where our light shallops[2] peaceful glide.

5 Beneath yon consecrated mounds
Our fathers' treasured ashes rest,
Our hands have tilled these corn-clad grounds,
Our children's birth these homes have blest.

Here, on our souls a Saviour's love
10 First beamed with renovating° ray,   *regenerating, redeeming*
Why should we from these haunts° remove?   *habitations*
But still you warn us hence away.

Child, ask not where! I cannot tell,
Save where wide wastes uncultured° spread,   *uncultivated*

15 Where unknown waters fiercely roll,
And savage monsters howling tread;

Where no blest Church with hallowed train,[3]
Nor hymns of praise, nor voice of prayer,
Like angels soothe the wanderer's pain;
20 Ask me no more. I know not where.

Go seek thy Sire. The anguish charm[4]
That shades his brow like frowning wrath,
Divide the burden from his arm,[5]
And gird him for his pilgrim-path.

25 Come, moaning babe! Thy mother's arms
Shall bear thee on our weary course,
Shall be thy shield from midnight harms,
And baleful dews, and tempests hoarse.°   *rough*

John Ross, letter to the Senate and House of Representatives, 28 September 1836

As the momentum for expulsion intensified in the wake of the Indian Removal Act and Andrew Jackson's landslide re-election in 1832, the leadership of the Cherokee Nation became divided over how to respond. A majority, headed by Principal Chief John Ross (1790–1866), remained strongly opposed to giving up their traditional lands. However, a minority of Cherokee, including some influential leaders, decided that it was in the nation's best interest to come to terms with the federal government; this faction became known as the "Treaty Party." In late 1835, without any sanction from Ross or the Cherokee National Council, members of the Treaty Party separately negotiated the Treaty of New Echota with federal representatives, whereby they consented to removal. The outraged response of the Cherokee majority, and their continued opposition to removal even after the Treaty of New Echota was ratified by the Senate in May 1836, is illustrated by the following petition, addressed to the U.S. Congress in September 1836 by Ross and thousands of other Cherokee.

---

1 *Ye bid us hence* I.e., you command us to leave.

2 *shallops* Shallow-water boats.

3 *train* Assembly of people.

4 *The anguish charm* I.e., charm away the anguish.

5 *Divide ... arm* I.e., take a share of the "burden" he is carrying.

Red Clay Council Ground,[1] Cherokee Nation
September 28, 1836

Most respectfully, and most humbly showeth: That your memorialists,[2] the Chiefs, National Committee and Council, and people of the Cherokee Nation in General Council assembled, solicit permission to approach your honorable bodies, under circumstances peculiar in the history of nations; circumstances of distress and anxiety beyond our power to express. We earnestly bespeak your patience, therefore, while we lay before you a brief epitome[3] of our griefs.

It is well known that for a number of years past we have been harassed by a series of vexations, which it is deemed unnecessary to recite in detail, but the evidence of which our delegation will be prepared to furnish. With a view to bringing our troubles to a close, a delegation was appointed on the 23rd of October, 1835, by the General Council of the nation, clothed with full powers to enter into arrangements with the Government of the United States, for the final adjustment of all our existing difficulties. The delegation, failing to effect an arrangement with the United States commissioner then in the nation, proceeded, agreeably to[4] their instructions in that case, to Washington City, for the purpose of negotiating a treaty with the authorities of the United States.

After the departure of the Delegation, a contract was made by the Rev. John F. Schermerhorn,[5] and certain individual Cherokees, purporting to be a "treaty, concluded at New Echota, in the State of Georgia, on the 29th day of December, 1835, by General William Carroll and John F. Schermerhorn, commissioners on the part of the United States, and the chiefs, headmen, and people of the Cherokee tribes of Indians." A spurious Delegation, in violation of a special injunction of the general council of the nation, proceeded to Washington city with this pretended treaty, and by false and fraudulent representations supplanted in the favor of the Government the legal and accredited Delegation of the Cherokee people, and obtained for this instrument, after making important alterations in its provisions, the recognition of the United States Government. And now it is presented to us as a treaty, ratified by the Senate, and approved by the President Andrew Jackson, and our acquiescence in its requirements demanded, under the sanction of the displeasure of the United States, and the threat of summary compulsion, in case of refusal. It comes to us, not through our legitimate authorities, the known and usual medium of communication between the Government of the United States and our nation, but through the agency of a complication[6] of powers, civil and military.

By the stipulations of this instrument, we are despoiled of our private possessions, the indefeasible property of individuals. We are stripped of every attribute of freedom and eligibility for legal self-defence. Our property may be plundered before our eyes; violence may be committed on our persons; even our lives may be taken away, and there is none to regard our complaints. We are denationalized; we are disfranchised. We are deprived of membership in the human family! We have neither land nor home, nor resting place that can be called our own. And this is effected by the provisions of a compact which assumes the venerated, the sacred appellation of treaty.

We are overwhelmed! Our hearts are sickened, our utterance is paralyzed, when we reflect on the condition in which we are placed, by the audacious practices of unprincipled men, who have managed their stratagems with so much dexterity as to impose on[7] the Government of the United States, in the face of our earnest, solemn, and reiterated protestations.

The instrument in question is not the act of our Nation; we are not parties to its covenants; it has not received the sanction of our people. The makers of

---

[1] *Red Clay Council Ground* Capital of the Cherokee Nation, located in extreme southeastern Tennessee, just north of the state border with Georgia. Because of laws passed by the state of Georgia restricting the right of the Cherokee to hold public meetings, the Cherokee had officially moved their seat of government from New Echota, Georgia, to Red Clay Council Ground in 1832.

[2] *memorialists* Petitioners.

[3] *epitome* Summary.

[4] *agreeably to* In accordance with.

[5] *Rev. John F. Schermerhorn* Minister and personal friend of Andrew Jackson, whom Jackson appointed as an Indian Commissioner in 1832 with a mandate to accomplish the removal of the Cherokee and Chickasaw nations.

[6] *complication* Complex combination.

[7] *impose on* Deceive.

it sustain no office nor appointment in our Nation, under the designation of Chiefs, Head men, or any other title, by which they hold, or could acquire, authority to assume the reins of Government, and to make bargain and sale of our rights, our possessions, and our common country. And we are constrained solemnly to declare, that we cannot but contemplate the enforcement of the stipulations of this instrument on us, against our consent, as an act of injustice and oppression, which, we are well persuaded, can never knowingly be countenanced by the Government and people of the United States; nor can we believe it to be the design of these honorable and highminded individuals, who stand at the head of the Government, to bind a whole Nation, by the acts of a few unauthorized individuals. And, therefore, we, the parties to be affected by the result, appeal with confidence to the justice, the magnanimity, the compassion, of your honorable bodies, against the enforcement, on us, of the provisions of a compact, in the formation of which we have had no agency.

In truth, our cause is your own; it is the cause of liberty and of justice; it is based upon your own principles, which we have learned from yourselves; for we have gloried to count your George Washington and your Thomas Jefferson our great teachers; we have read their communications to us with veneration; we have practised their precepts with success. And the result is manifest. The wildness of the forest has given place to comfortable dwellings and cultivated fields, stocked with the various domestic animals. Mental culture, industrious habits, and domestic enjoyments, have succeeded the rudeness of the savage[1] state.

We have learned your religion also. We have read your Sacred books. Hundreds of our people have embraced their doctrines, practised the virtues they teach, cherished the hopes they awaken, and rejoiced in the consolations which they afford. To the spirit of your institutions, and your religion, which has been imbibed by our community, is mainly to be ascribed that patient endurance which has characterized the conduct of our people, under the laceration of their keenest woes. For assuredly, we are not ignorant of our condition; we are not insensible to our sufferings. We feel them! we groan under their pressure! And anticipation[2] crowds our breasts with sorrows yet to come. We are, indeed, an afflicted people! Our spirits are subdued! Despair has well nigh seized upon our energies! But we speak to the representatives of a Christian country; the friends of justice; the patrons of the oppressed. And our hopes revive, and our prospects brighten, as we indulge the thought. On your sentence, our fate is suspended; prosperity or desolation depends on your word. To you, therefore, we look! Before your august assembly we present ourselves, in the attitude of deprecation,[3] and of entreaty. On your kindness, on your humanity, on your compassion, on your benevolence, we rest our hopes. To you we address our reiterated prayers. Spare our people! Spare the wreck of our prosperity! Let not our deserted homes become the monuments of our desolation! But we forbear! We suppress the agonies which wring our hearts, when we look at our wives, our children, and our venerable sires! We restrain the forebodings of anguish and distress, of misery and devastation and death, which must be the attendants on the execution of this ruinous compact.

In conclusion, we commend to your confidence and favor, our well-beloved and trustworthy brethren and fellow-citizens, John Ross, Principal Chief, Richard Taylor, Samuel Gunter, John Benge, George Sanders, Walter S. Adair, Stephen Foreman, and Kalsateehee of Aquohee, who are clothed with full powers to adjust all our existing difficulties by treaty arrangements with the United States, by which our destruction may be averted, impediments to the advancement of our people removed, and our existence perpetuated as a living monument, to testify to posterity the honor, the magnanimity, the generosity of the United States. And your memorialists, as in duty bound, will ever pray. Signed by Ross, George Lowrey, Edward Gunter, Lewis Ross, thirty-one members of the National Committee and National Council, and 2,174 others.

---

[1] *rudeness* Ignorance; lack of refinement; primitiveness; *savage* Ross here adopts the common nineteenth-century use of the disparaging term "savage" by white Americans to describe the society and culture of Indigenous peoples.

---

[2] *anticipation* Fear.

[3] *august* Exalted; *deprecation* Sincere plea.

Ralph Waldo Emerson, letter to Martin Van Buren, 23 April 1838

After the ratification of the Treaty of New Echota, the U.S. government set a deadline of 23 May 1838 for the Cherokee to voluntarily remove in accordance with the treaty, after which they would be forcibly expelled. As the deadline approached, opponents of the treaty continued to petition the government not to enforce removal. One of the most prominent such petitioners was Ralph Waldo Emerson, who addressed this open letter on the subject directly to President Martin Van Buren. Judging by his journals, Emerson composed this letter with a great deal of difficulty, and he himself doubted its efficacy: he called it "merely a scream," before adding that "sometimes a scream is better than a thesis." A similar ambivalence about the letter was exhibited by its first publishers, the editors of the Washington, D.C., *Daily National Intelligencer*, who printed it "with some reluctance" on 14 May 1838. The present text is based on that reprinted in the *New-Bedford Mercury* on 25 May 1838.

Letter to Martin Van Buren, President of the United States

A Protest Against the Removal of the Cherokee Indians from the State of Georgia

SAY, what is Honour? 'Tis the finest sense
Of justice which the human mind can frame,
Intent each lurking frailty to disclaim,
And guard the way of life from all offence,
Suffered or done.[1]

Concord, Mass.
April 23, 1838

SIR:

The seat you fill places you in a relation of credit and nearness to every citizen. By right and natural position, every citizen is your friend. Before any acts contrary to his own judgment or interest have repelled the affections of any man, each may look with trust and living anticipation to your government. Each has the highest right to call your attention to such subjects as are of a public nature, and properly belong to the chief magistrate;[2] and the good magistrate will feel a joy in meeting such confidence. In this belief and at the instance[3] of a few of my friends and neighbors, I crave of your patience a short hearing for their sentiments and my own: and the circumstance that my name will be utterly unknown to you will only give the fairer chance to your equitable construction[4] of what I have to say.

Sir, my communication respects the sinister rumors that fill this part of the country concerning the Cherokee people. The interest always felt in the aboriginal population—an interest naturally growing as that decays[5]—has been heightened in regard to this tribe. Even in our distant State some good rumor of their worth and civility has arrived. We have learned with joy their improvement in the social arts. We have read their newspapers. We have seen some of them in our schools and colleges. In common with the great body of the American people, we have witnessed with sympathy the painful labors of these red men to redeem their own race from the doom of eternal inferiority, and to borrow and domesticate in the tribe the arts and customs of the Caucasian race. And notwithstanding the unaccountable apathy with which of late years the Indians have been sometimes abandoned to their enemies, it is not to be doubted that it is the good pleasure and the understanding of all humane persons in the Republic, of the men and the matrons sitting in the thriving independent families all over the land, that they shall be duly cared for; that they shall taste justice

---

[1]   *SAY … done*   From one of the "Sonnets Dedicated to Liberty" (1802–03) by the English poet William Wordsworth.

[2]   *chief magistrate*   I.e., president. This term was used frequently to refer to the President of the United States in the early decades of the nation's existence but is rare today.

[3]   *instance*   Urging.

[4]   *equitable construction*   Fair interpretation.

[5]   *as that decays*   I.e., as "the aboriginal population" declines. A belief that Native Americans were in terminal decline and inevitably bound for extinction—an idea known as the "vanishing Indian" trope—was widespread among white Americans in the nineteenth century, even those such as Emerson who sympathized with Indigenous people and sought to prevent their further dispossession.

and love from all to whom we have delegated the office of dealing with them.

The newspapers now inform us that, in December, 1835, a treaty contracting for the exchange of all the Cherokee territory was pretended to be made by an agent on the part of the United States with some persons appearing on the part of the Cherokees; that the fact afterwards transpired that these deputies did by no means represent the will of the nation; and that, out of eighteen thousand souls composing the nation, fifteen thousand six hundred and sixty-eight have protested against the so-called treaty. It now appears that the government of the United States choose to hold the Cherokees to this sham treaty, and are proceeding to execute the same. Almost the entire Cherokee Nation stand up and say, "This is not our act. Behold us. Here are we. Do not mistake that handful of deserters for us"; and the American President and the Cabinet, the Senate and the House of Representatives, neither hear these men nor see them, and are contracting to put this active nation into carts and boats, and to drag them over mountains and rivers to a wilderness at a vast distance beyond the Mississippi. And a paper purporting to be an army order fixes a month from this day as the hour for this doleful removal.

In the name of God, sir, we ask you if this be so. Do the newspapers rightly inform us? Men and women with pale and perplexed faces meet one another in the streets and churches here, and ask if this be so. We have inquired if this be a gross misrepresentation from the party opposed to the government[1] and anxious to blacken it with the people. We have looked in the newspapers of different parties[2] and find a horrid confirmation of the tale. We are slow to believe it. We hoped the Indians were misinformed, and that their remonstrance was premature, and will turn out to be a needless act of terror.

The piety, the principle that is left in the United States, if only in its coarsest form, a regard to the speech of men—forbid us to entertain it as a fact. Such a dereliction of all faith and virtue, such a denial of justice, and such deafness to screams for mercy were never heard of in times of peace and in the dealing of a nation with its own allies and wards,[3] since the earth was made. Sir, does this government think that the people of the United States are become savage and mad? From their mind are the sentiments of love and a good nature wiped clean out? The soul of man, the justice, the mercy that is the heart's heart in all men, from Maine to Georgia, does abhor this business.

In speaking thus the sentiments of my neighbors and my own, perhaps I overstep the bounds of decorum. But would it not be a higher indecorum coldly to argue a matter like this? We only state the fact that a crime is projected that confounds our understandings by its magnitude—a crime that really deprives us as well as the Cherokees of a country, for how could we call the conspiracy that should crush these poor Indians our government, or the land that was cursed by their parting and dying imprecations our country, any more? You, sir, will bring down that renowned chair in which you sit into infamy if your seal is set to this instrument of perfidy; and the name of this nation, hitherto the sweet omen of religion and liberty, will stink to the world.

You will not do us the injustice of connecting this remonstrance with any sectional and party feeling. It is in our hearts the simplest commandment of brotherly love. We will not have this great and solemn claim upon national and human justice huddled aside under

---

[1] *the party opposed to the government* I.e., the Whig Party, the main opposition party in the United States at the time; Van Buren and his predecessor, Andrew Jackson, were both Democrats. The Whigs took shape in the 1830s in opposition to Jackson's presidency; they tended to oppose both an overly powerful executive branch and territorial expansion and drew their support mainly from the urban middle classes, in contrast to the poor farmers and working-class men who formed the Democrats' base.

[2] *the newspapers of different parties* Most U.S. newspapers in the 1830s had explicit partisan affiliations.

[3] *wards* Dependants—people (such as minor children) under the protection or custody of someone else. Emerson's characterization here of the relationship between the U.S. government and Indigenous nations reflects the idea—widespread among white Americans at the time—that this relationship was one of guardianship or tutelage of weaker, supposedly more "childlike" people by a stronger, supposedly more "mature" state. This view can be seen, for example, in the common portrayal—as in the political cartoon of Andrew Jackson included elsewhere in this Contexts section—of Indigenous people as "children" of the "Great Father" (i.e., the U.S. president); it was also enshrined in federal law, for instance in Supreme Court Chief Justice John Marshall's ruling in *Cherokee Nation v. Georgia* (1831), which asserted that the relationship of Indigenous nations to the U.S. resembled "that of a ward to their guardian."

the flimsy plea of its being a party act. Sir, to us the questions upon which the government and the people have been agitated during the past year, touching the prostration of the currency and of trade,[1] seem but motes[2] in comparison. These hard times, it is true, have brought the discussion home to every farmhouse and poor man's house in this town; but it is the chirping of grasshoppers beside the immortal question whether justice shall be done by the race of civilized to the race of savage man—whether all the attributes of reason, of civility, of justice, and even of mercy, shall be put off by the American people, and so vast an outrage upon the Cherokee Nation and upon human nature shall be consummated.

One circumstance lessens the reluctance with which I intrude at this time on your attention, my conviction that the government ought to be admonished of a new historical fact, which the discussion of this question has disclosed, namely, that there exists in a great part of the Northern people a gloomy diffidence[3] in the *moral* character of the government.

On the broaching of this question, a general expression of despondency, of disbelief that any good will accrue from a remonstrance on an act of fraud and robbery, appeared in those men to whom we naturally turn for aid and counsel. Will the American government steal? Will it lie? Will it kill?—We ask triumphantly. Our counsellors and old statesmen here say that ten years ago they would have staked their lives on the affirmation that the proposed Indian measures could not be executed; that the unanimous country would put them down. And now the steps of this crime follow each other so fast, at such fatally quick time, that the millions of virtuous citizens, whose agents the government are, have no place to interpose, and must shut their eyes until the last howl and wailing of these tormented villages and tribes shall afflict the ear of the world.

I will not hide from you, as an indication of this alarming distrust, that a letter addressed as mine is, and suggesting to the mind of the Executive the plain obligations of man, has a burlesque character in the apprehensions[4] of some of my friends. I, sir, will not beforehand treat you with the contumely[5] of this distrust. I will at least state to you this fact, and show you how plain and humane people, whose love would be honor, regard the policy of the government, and what injurious inferences they draw as to the minds of the governors. A man with your experience in affairs must have seen cause to appreciate the futility of opposition to the moral sentiment. However feeble the sufferer and however great the oppressor, it is in the nature of things that the blow should recoil upon the aggressor. For God is in the sentiment, and it cannot be withstood. The potentate and the people perish before it; but with it, and as its executor, they are omnipotent.

I write thus, sir, to inform you of the state of mind these Indian tidings have awakened here, and to pray with one voice more that you, whose hands are strong with the delegated power of fifteen millions of men, will avert with that might the terrific[6] injury which threatens the Cherokee tribe.

With great respect, sir, I am your fellow citizen, Ralph Waldo Emerson.

from Eliza Whitmire, interview (1936)

One of the white American institutions assimilated by the so-called "Five Civilized Tribes," especially the Cherokee, as they adapted to the settler-colonial culture encroaching upon them in the early nineteenth century was African American chattel slavery. When the remaining Cherokee were expelled in 1838, the small minority who owned enslaved people brought their "property" with them. Among the enslaved African Americans caught up in the Cherokee expulsion was the family of Eliza Whitmire, who was about five years old at the time. Nearly

---

[1]   *the prostration … trade* In 1837, various economic developments (including a sharp drop in the price of cotton and a collapsing land bubble) sparked a severe financial crisis, known as the Panic of 1837. The panic caused an economic depression that lasted into the mid-1840s.

[2]   *motes* Trifles.

[3]   *diffidence* Distrust.

[4]   *burlesque* Grotesquely comic; *apprehensions* Understandings.

[5]   *beforehand* I.e., in anticipation (of the president not being worthy of his trust); *contumely* Insolent contempt.

[6]   *terrific* I.e., terrible.

a century later, she was interviewed as part of an oral history project conducted by the federal Works Progress Administration under the New Deal, during which she gave the account of the Cherokee expulsion presented below.

My name is Eliza Whitmire. I live on a farm near Estella[1] where I settled shortly after the Civil War and where I have lived ever since. I was born in slavery in the state of Georgia, my parents having belonged to a Cherokee Indian of the name of George Sanders who owned a large plantation in the old Cherokee Nation in Georgia. He also owned a large number of slaves but I was too young to remember how many he owned.

I do not know the exact date of my birth, although my mother told me I was about five years old when President Andrew Jackson[2] ordered General Scott[3] to proceed to the Cherokee country in Georgia, with two thousand troops and remove the Cherokees by force to the Indian Territory. This bunch of Indians were called the Eastern Emigrants. The Old Settler Cherokees had moved themselves in 1835 when the order was first given to the Cherokees to move out.

The weeks that followed General Scott's order to remove the Cherokees were filled with horror and suffering for the unfortunate Cherokees and their slaves. The women and children were driven from their homes, sometimes with blows, and close on the heels of the retreating Indians came greedy whites to pillage the Indians' homes, drive off their cattle, horses and hogs, and they even rifled the graves for any jewelry or other ornaments that might have been buried with the dead.

The Cherokees, after being driven from their homes, were divided into detachments of nearly equal size and late in October, 1838, the first detachment started, the others following one by one. The aged, sick and the young children rode in the wagons, which carried the provisions and bedding, while others went on foot. The trip was made in the dead of winter and many died from exposure from sleet and snow, and all who lived to make this trip, or had parents who made it, will long remember it as a bitter memory.

Freeman Owle, "The Trail of Tears" (1996)

Born in 1947, Freeman Owle is a member of the Eastern Band of Cherokee Indians, who are descended from Cherokee living in the mountains of southwestern North Carolina who managed to escape expulsion. He grew up hearing and learning his family's traditional stories and eventually became a storyteller himself. He related the story below, which combines a family history of the Trail of Tears with an account of the origin of the Cherokee Eastern Band, in October 1996; the story was collected in *Living Stories of the Cherokee*, edited by Barbara R. Duncan (1998), on which the present text is based.

I found that out[4] as I was growing up,
and my parents began to tell me this story of the
    Trail of Tears.
And you look at me and you say,
    "Well, he's probably as much Scots-Irish[5] as I am."
Yes, I am.
But I am Oogoku tsiskayi Tsalagi ashkaya.[6]

---

[1] *Estella* Town in the Cherokee Nation, in the northeastern portion of what is now the state of Oklahoma.

[2] *President Andrew Jackson* Although Jackson was the most prominent advocate of "Indian removal" and is the president most closely associated with the policy, the expulsion of the Cherokee was in fact carried out under the authority of Jackson's successor, Martin Van Buren, who became president in 1837.

[3] *General Scott* Winfield Scott (1786–1866), Army general who oversaw the Cherokee expulsion. The combined force of militiamen, Army regulars, and volunteers with which Scott enforced the expulsion totaled 7,000, far more than the 2,000 Whitmire goes on to estimate.

[4] *I found that out* A segue from the previous story Owle told in the session at which this story was collected, which ends with the affirmation that "Never again will there be a person like you in this world[.] … [W]e're all very, very special."

[5] *Scots-Irish* Descendants of Protestants from Scotland and England who settled in Ulster, the northern province of Ireland, during the seventeenth century, many of whom then re-emigrated to the American colonies. In America, most Scots-Irish settled in the Appalachian Mountains from Pennsylvania southward, where they lived in close proximity to Native Americans, including the Cherokee, and frequently intermarried with them.

[6] *Oogoku … ashkaya* Cherokee: Owl Birdtown Cherokee man. (The editors wish to thank Professor Christopher Teuton of the Cherokee Nation for his translation of this line.)

My name is Owle, I live in Birdtown,[1]
   and I happened to grow up on the reservation.
Sort of like a little story that Marsha was reading to
   our daughter last night
      about the zebra.
Says, "Are you white with black stripes or black with
   white stripes?"
Are you Scots-Irish with Indian, or Indian with
   Scots-Irish?
I don't know, I really don't.
All I know is I'm different from anyone who's ever
   lived,
      and different than anyone who ever will.
And my fingerprints are different, so I must be special.
They told me that
   my family was, in 1838, in a log cabin near
      Murphy, North Carolina.
And all of a sudden,
   someone was banging on the door
   early that morning.
And they opened up the door and they looked out,
   and fifty Georgia soldiers were standing in the yard.
They said,
   "Come out of the cabin."
And when my great-grandfather—
   I'll just call him grandfather—
   did,
   they burned the cabin to the ground.
He and his wife and small baby were taken to
   Murphy, North Carolina,
      put into a stockade,
      stayed there for six weeks.
There was no roof, only a line of poles
   encircling the stockade.
They say that
   the mud was deep,
   there wasn't much food,
   no one had anything to cover themselves with,
   but the baby survived because the mother was
      feeding it.
Early one morning,
   on that October morning
   when the frost was heavy

and the ground was frozen hard enough for
   wagons to travel,
   General Winfield Scott[2] began to march the
      people out of this fort.
So he marched them across the frozen ground
   and across the Santeetlah Mountains
   into Tennessee.
There was a woman by the name of Martha Ross,
   Scots-Irish and Cherokee.
She had a beautiful coat,
   and she began to look, late that night,
   and the rain was coming down, and it was cold,
   and she heard a baby crying.
She went to the sound of the baby and found the child
   very cold
   and wet—
   it had pneumonia.
She covered the child with her coat,
   and two days later she died of pneumonia herself.
It is people like this
   who have made contributions to the Cherokee
      society.
It is people like the people of North Carolina
   who allowed those people living in North Carolina
      to remain there.
The history is written,
   the history says
   that North Carolina did not remove its
      Cherokees.[3]
They were called the Oconaluftee Cherokees.
And you go see *Unto These Hills*,[4] it doesn't mention
   this.

---

[1] *Birdtown* Town in the Qualla Boundary, the area in south-western North Carolina that is the territory of the Eastern Band of Cherokee Indians, held in trust for them by the federal government.

[2] *Winfield Scott* Army general (1786–1866) who oversaw the Cherokee expulsion.

[3] *It is people like the people … its Cherokees* Several hundred Cherokee living in the remote mountains of southwestern North Carolina were able to evade the troops sent to round them up for deportation; others managed to negotiate exemptions from being expelled, in some cases under the condition that they give up Cherokee citizenship and assimilate as U.S. and North Carolina citizens. The name "Oconaluftee Cherokees," which Owle gives in the following line, comes from the Oconaluftee River, along which most of the North Carolina Cherokee who escaped expulsion lived and which the Cherokee consider to be sacred.

[4] *Unto These Hills* Historical drama about Cherokee history up to the Trail of Tears. The drama has been staged consistently at an outdoor theater in Cherokee, North Carolina, the headquarters of the Eastern Band, since 1950.

But they didn't make them leave.
The other fifteen thousand began to march on toward
 Oklahoma.
When they got to the Mississippi, they asked my
 grandfather
  if he would count the Cherokees who crossed the
   river.
And he said,
 "Yes, I will."
But he told his wife in Cherokee,
  "Go hide in the cane brake and take the baby with
   you.
  And I will tell them you're here.
  And we'll go back home."
So he counted the Cherokees as they crossed the
 flatboat across the Mississippi,
  and he told the soldiers,
  "All the Cherokees are accounted for."
And they said,
 "Are you sure?
 Go back to the river and check again."
And this was what he wanted,
 and he goes back to the river,
 and he looks into the bushes and the brush,
 and all of a sudden he leaps into the water.
They come running behind, and they shoot many
 times into the water.
They look into the black, swirling waters of the
 Mississippi,
  and this Cherokee doesn't surface.
So—for a long time.
And they give him up as being dead.
He's breathing through a reed all this time.
And after he gives the soldiers time enough to go away,
 he comes up and he swims back
 across the Mississippi.
He looks for his wife on the other side,
 and—she heard the gunshots.
She ran
 with the baby in her arms,
 she would run all night long,
 and then find a briar patch to sleep in in the
  daytime,
 or a farmer's haystack.
 Took her several weeks to get back home,

but she came on back to the old burned-out cabin
 site
because that's all she knew as home.
She waited there week after week,
 and her husband didn't return.
She went down to the village,
 to the Scots-Irish settlers,
 and they gladly gave her food.
And they were feeding those Cherokees
 that were hiding in the mountains.
If the North Carolina people had been caught by the
 Georgia guard
  handing out food to the Cherokees,
  they too would have lost their land and been put
   in prison
  as Cherokee sympathizers.
But the Scots-Irish people were feeding her
 one morning, a year later,
 when she heard a noise up on the hill,
 and she looked and there was someone coming.
And so she ran and hid with the baby.
And after a while it was her husband
 coming out of the woods.
They were reunited,
 and we still live
 in a little place where they came and rebought
  with their own money
 called Birdtown.
And the reason they were able to rebuy it was:
 there was a wagon train coming through here,
 and it had a little baby on it—
 a little white child
 who was very sick.
And the parents were smart enough to say,
 "If we go on with this child, it's going to die."
And they said—
 have you ever heard the term, "Give it to the
  Indians"?[1]
 They gave the child to the Indians.

---

[1] *Give it ... Indians* Variation of "Give it back to the Indians," a phrase that was widespread in white American usage in the mid- and late twentieth century. The phrase was used of a place or thing that had become so spoiled or run-down as to be undesirable, with the implication either that it was now fit only for Indigenous people or that it would be better off in the hands of Indigenous people, who would take better care of it than white Americans had. The phrase was popularized by a 1939 Broadway show tune, "Give [continued ...]

Chief Yonaguska[1] made the child better.
His name was William Holland Thomas.[2]
Will Thomas was already a citizen of the United
    States,
        and the Cherokees could go and buy up land
        and put it in this child's name
        by the thousands of acres,
        and we are still here.
But in the early 1920s
    ·   my grandfather, Solomon Owle,
        was living in this little place called Birdtown
        and paying his taxes to Swain County,[3]
        and I think was a good citizen.
The federal government looked down and said,
        "This can't be.
        This bunch of savages are not supposed to be able
            to take care of themselves."
And they came down and took the deeds away from
    those people
        and set up what they called the Qualla Indian
            Boundary.
They couldn't call it a reservation,
        because a reservation is land that is given to the
            Indians,
        and the Indians are forced upon it.
This land was bought back
        under Will Thomas's name—
        see, it's not a reservation
        it's a little different.
You know, I came here tonight to tell you
        that the Cherokee people don't really hold any
            hatred

or animosity in their heart
    for those things that happened in the past.
We can take our hats off to the past,
    but as one great gentleman said,
    "We should take our shirts off to the future."
The reason the Cherokee people survived
    is because they loved their neighbors
    and were good neighbors.
The Cherokees of today
    still welcome even all the visitors in the '41 Chevys
    and the '40 Ford coupes
    and the bears and everything—
    they were glad to see the tourists come.
And we're glad to see the tourists come, even today.

from John O'Sullivan or Jane Cazneau, "Annexation," *The United States Magazine and Democratic Review* (1845)

The first recorded appearance of the term "manifest destiny" was in the article below, published in the July–August 1845 issue of *The United States Magazine and Democratic Review*, a Jacksonian Democratic periodical founded by the Irish American editor John L. O'Sullivan (1813–95). The article, which makes the case for the U.S. annexation of what was then the independent Republic of Texas (a hotly debated issue at the time), was originally published anonymously; it has traditionally been credited to O'Sullivan, but several historians have posited that it was actually written by Jane Cazneau (1807–78), a journalist for the *Democratic Review* and other periodicals who was an avid expansionist.

It is now time for the opposition to the Annexation of Texas to cease, all further agitation of the waters of bitterness and strife, at least in connection with this question—even though it may perhaps be required of us as a necessary condition of the freedom of our institutions, that we must live on forever in a state of unpausing struggle and excitement upon some subject of party division or other. But, in regard to Texas, enough has now been given to party. It is time for the common duty of Patriotism to the Country to succeed—or if this claim will not be recognized, it is at

---

It Back to the Indians," which jocularly proposes returning New York City to the Indigenous people from whom it was first purchased.

[1] *Yonaguska* Cherokee chief (1759–1839) whose name translates to "Drowning Bear"; he led the North Carolina Cherokee who managed to avoid expulsion and remain on their homelands, where they eventually reorganized as the Eastern Band of Cherokee Indians.

[2] *William Holland Thomas* White adopted son of Yonaguska (1805–93) who negotiated on behalf of the North Carolina Cherokee with the federal government, purchased land in North Carolina to be used by the Cherokee, and eventually succeeded Yonaguska as chief of the Eastern Band, despite the fact that he had no Cherokee ancestry himself. The written historical record of the circumstances of Thomas's adoption by Yonaguska does not match the version related in this story.

[3] *Swain County* County in the southwestern corner of North Carolina on the border with Tennessee.

James S. Baillie, *Hunting Indians in Florida with Blood Hounds,* 1848. This lithograph by Baillie, a prolific mid-nineteenth-century lithograph artist, was printed by opponents of Zachary Taylor's successful 1848 presidential campaign. The lithograph criticizes Taylor's conduct during his period (1838–40) as commander of U.S. military forces in the Second Seminole War—specifically, his use of bloodhounds against the Seminole. In fact, bloodhounds were used only to track Seminole through the Florida wetlands (often unsuccessfully), not—as depicted here—to physically attack them, but the misconception reflects the revulsion many white Americans felt toward the war and the country's treatment of Native Americans in general. Taylor's speech bubble reads: "Hurra! Captain, we've got them at last, the dogs are at them—now forward with the Rifle and Bayonet and 'give them Hell Brave Boys,' let not a red nigger escape—, show no mercy—, exterminate them,—this day we'll close the Florida War, and write its history in the blood of the Seminole—but remember Captn., as I have written to our Government to say that the dogs are intended to ferret out the Indians, (not to worry [i.e., bite] them) for the sake of consistency and the appearance of Humanity, you will appear not to notice the devastation they commit."

Charles Bird King, *Tuko-See-Mathla, a Seminole Chief,* 1844. Also known as John Hicks, Tuko-See-Mathla was a member of a Seminole delegation to Washington, D.C. in 1826, where King painted his portrait. This lithograph, based on King's portrait, was later printed as part of *History of the Indian Tribes of North America,* a three-volume collection of biographies of Indigenous leaders, with accompanying portraits, published by Thomas McKenney and James Hall; the collection remains an important source for biographical and visual information about early nineteenth-century Native American life.

least time for common sense to acquiesce with decent grace in the inevitable and the irrevocable.

Texas is now ours. Already, before these words are written, her Convention has undoubtedly ratified the acceptance, by her Congress, of our proffered invitation into the Union; and made the requisite changes in her already republican form of constitution to adapt it to its future federal relations. Her star and her stripe may already be said to have taken their place in the glorious blazon of our common nationality; and the sweep of our eagle's wing already includes within its circuit the wide extent of her fair and fertile land. She is no longer to us a mere geographical space—a certain combination of coast, plain, mountain, valley, forest and stream. She is no longer to us a mere country on the map. She comes within the dear and sacred designation of Our Country; no longer a "*pays*," she is a part of "*la patrie*";[1] and that which is at once a sentiment and a virtue, Patriotism, already begins to thrill for her too within the national heart. ... The next session of Congress will see the representatives of the new young State in their places in both our halls of national legislation, side by side with those of the old Thirteen. Let their reception into "the family" be frank, kindly, and cheerful, as befits such an occasion, as comports not less with our own self-respect than patriotic duty towards them. Ill betide those foul birds that delight to file[2] their own nest, and disgust the ear with perpetual discord of ill-omened croak.

Why, were other reasoning wanting, in favor of now elevating this question of the reception of Texas into the Union, out of the lower region of our past party dissensions, up to its proper level of a high and broad nationality, it surely is to be found, found abundantly, in the manner in which other nations have undertaken to intrude themselves into it, between us and the proper parties to the case, in a spirit of hostile interference against us, for the avowed object of thwarting our policy and hampering our power, limiting our greatness and checking the fulfillment of our manifest destiny to overspread the continent allotted by Providence for the free development of our yearly multiplying millions. This we

have seen done by England, our old rival and enemy; and by France, strangely coupled with her against us[.][3] ... The zealous activity with which this effort to defeat us was pushed by the representatives of those governments, together with the character of intrigue accompanying it, fully constituted that case of foreign interference, which Mr. Clay[4] himself declared should and would unite us all in maintaining the common cause of our country against foreigner and the foe. ...

It is wholly untrue, and unjust to ourselves, the pretence that the Annexation has been a measure of spoliation, unrightful and unrighteous—of military conquest under forms of peace and law—of territorial aggrandizement at the expense of justice, and justice due by a double sanctity to the weak. This view of the question is wholly unfounded[.] ... The independence of Texas was complete and absolute. It was an independence, not only in fact, but of right. No obligation of duty towards Mexico tended in the least degree to restrain our right to effect the desired recovery of the fair province once our own—whatever motives of policy might have prompted a more deferential consideration of her feelings and her pride, as involved in the question. If Texas became peopled with an American population, it was by no contrivance of our government, but on the express invitation of that of Mexico herself[.] ... [Texas] was released, rightfully and absolutely released, from all Mexican allegiance, or duty of cohesion to the Mexican political body, by the acts and fault of Mexico herself, and Mexico alone.[5] There never was a clearer case. ... What then can be more preposterous than all this clamor by Mexico and the Mexican interest, against Annexation, as a violation of any rights of hers, any duties of ours?...

---

1   *pays ... la patrie*   In French, "pays" means "land," while "patrie" means "fatherland," i.e., nation.

2   *file*   Defile, pollute. The phrase "It's a foul bird that files its own nest" was proverbial.

3   *England ... us*   When the administration of U.S. President John Tyler began to push for the annexation of Texas in 1844, Britain and France attempted to forestall it by proposing a treaty between Texas and Mexico whereby Mexico would recognize Texan independence and Texas would agree not to seek incorporation into the United States.

4   *Mr. Clay*   Henry Clay (1777–1852), politician from Kentucky. As a leading figure in the generally anti-expansionist Whig Party who was the party's candidate in the 1844 presidential election, Clay strongly opposed Texas annexation.

5   *If Texas ... Mexico alone*   See the section on "Expansion, Expulsion, and Manifest Destiny" in the introduction to this anthology volume for an overview of the history of American settlement in Texas and of Texas's revolt against Mexican rule referred to here.

Nor is there any just foundation for the charge that Annexation is a great pro-slavery measure—calculated to increase and perpetuate that institution. Slavery had nothing to do with it. Opinions were and are greatly divided, both at the North and South, as to the influence to be exerted by it on Slavery and the Slave States. ...

... The country which was the subject of Annexation in this case, from its geographical position and relations, happens to be—or rather the portion of it now actually settled, happens to be—a slave country. But a similar process might have taken place in proximity to a different section of our Union; and indeed there is a great deal of Annexation yet to take place, within the life of the present generation, along the whole line of our northern border. Texas has been absorbed into the Union in the inevitable fulfilment of the general law which is rolling our population westward; the connection of which with that ratio of growth in population which is destined to swell our numbers to the enormous population of *two hundred and fifty millions* (if not more), is too evident to leave us in doubt of the manifest design of Providence in regard to the occupation of this continent. It was disintegrated from Mexico in the natural course of events, by a process perfectly legitimate on its own part, blameless on ours; and in which all the censures due to wrong, perfidy and folly, rest on Mexico alone. And possessed as it was by a population which was in truth but a colonial detachment from our own, and which was still bound by myriad ties of the very heart-strings to its old relations, domestic and political, their incorporation into the Union was not only inevitable, but the most natural, right and proper thing in the world—and it is only astonishing that there should be any among ourselves to say it nay. ...

... With no friendship for slavery, though unprepared to excommunicate to eternal damnation, with bell, book, and candle, those who are, we see nothing in the bearing of the Annexation of Texas on that institution to awaken a doubt of the wisdom of that measure, or a compunction for the humble part contributed by us towards its consummation.

California will, probably, next fall away from the loose adhesion which, in such a country as Mexico, holds a remote province in a slight equivocal kind of dependence on the metropolis. Imbecile[1] and distracted, Mexico never can exert any real governmental authority over such a country. The impotence of the one and the distance of the other, must make the relation one of virtual independence; unless, by stunting the province of all natural growth, and forbidding that immigration which can alone develop its capabilities and fulfil the purposes of its creation, tyranny may retain a military dominion, which is no government in the legitimate sense of the term. In the case of California this is now impossible. The Anglo-Saxon[2] foot is already on its borders. Already the advance guard of the irresistible army of Anglo-Saxon emigration has begun to pour down upon it, armed with the plough and the rifle, and marking its trail with schools and colleges, courts and representative halls, mills and meeting-houses.[3] A population will soon be in actual occupation of California, over which it will be idle for Mexico to dream of dominion. They will necessarily become independent. All this without agency of our government, without responsibility of our people—in the natural flow of events, the spontaneous working of principles, and the adaptation of the tendencies and wants of the human race to the elemental circumstances in the midst of which they find themselves placed. And they will have a right to independence—to self-government—to the possession of the homes conquered from the wilderness by their own labors and dangers, sufferings and sacrifices—a better and a truer right than the artificial title of sovereignty in Mexico, a thousand miles distant, inheriting from Spain a title good only against those who have none better. Their right to independence will be the natural right of self-government belonging to any community strong enough to maintain it—distinct in position, origin and character, and free from any mutual obligations of membership of a common

---

[1] *Imbecile* Weak (though also with derogatory connotations of intellectual deficiency).

[2] *Anglo-Saxon* This term, which originally referred to the Germanic cultural group that settled in and ruled England in the early Middle Ages, was widely used in both Britain and the United States in the nineteenth century to refer to white people inhabiting or stemming from England (or the British Isles more generally). In such contexts, the term often carried—and still carries—racist connotations of inherent racial superiority.

[3] *meeting-houses* I.e., churches, specifically those of Protestant denominations.

political body, binding it to others by the duty of loyalty and compact of public faith. This will be their title to independence; and by this title, there can be no doubt that the population now fast streaming down upon California will both assert and maintain that independence. Whether they will then attach themselves to our Union or not, is not to be predicted with any certainty. Unless the projected railroad across the continent to the Pacific be carried into effect, perhaps they may not; though even in that case, the day is not distant when the Empires of the Atlantic and Pacific would again flow together into one, as soon as their inland border should approach each other. But that great work, colossal as appears the plan on its first suggestion, cannot remain long unbuilt. Its necessity for this very purpose of binding and holding together in its iron clasp our fast-settling Pacific region with that of the Mississippi valley—the natural facility[1] of the route—the ease with which any amount of labor for the construction can be drawn in from the overcrowded populations of Europe, to be paid in the lands made valuable by the progress of the work itself—and its immense utility to the commerce of the world with the whole eastern coast of Asia, alone almost sufficient for the support of such a road—these considerations give assurance that the day cannot be distant which shall witness the conveyance of the representatives from Oregon and California to Washington within less time than a few years ago was devoted to a similar journey by those from Ohio; while the magnetic telegraph will enable the editors of the "San Francisco Union," the "Astoria Evening Post," or the "Nootka Morning News,"[2] to set up in type the first half of the President's Inaugural before the echoes of the latter half shall have died away beneath the lofty porch of the Capitol, as spoken from his lips.

---

[1]   *facility* Ease, expediency.

[2]   *Astoria … News* Astoria and Nootka are both places in the Pacific Northwest. While Astoria is in what would become the U.S. state of Oregon, Nootka Island is adjacent to Vancouver Island, which today belongs to the Canadian province of British Columbia. A year after this article was published, the so-called Oregon Country was divided between Britain and the U.S. along the 49th parallel, with all territory to the south of the parallel entering the U.S. and all territory to the north of it remaining in British hands (and eventually becoming part of Canada). As the article makes clear, however, expansionist Americans in the early 1840s desired and expected to annex the entire Pacific Northwest.

Away, then, with all idle French talk of *balances of power* on the American Continent. There is no growth in Spanish America! Whatever progress of population there may be in the British Canadas, is only for their own early severance of their present colonial relation to the little island three thousand miles across the Atlantic; soon to be followed by Annexation, and destined to swell the still accumulating momentum of our progress. And whosoever may hold the balance, though they should cast into the opposite scale all the bayonets and cannon, not only of France and England, but of Europe entire, how would it kick the beam against the simple, solid weight of the two hundred and fifty, or three hundred millions—and American millions—destined to gather beneath the flutter of the stripes and stars, in the fast hastening year of the Lord 1945!

from Walt Whitman, *Brooklyn Daily Eagle* editorials

In 1846, Walt Whitman, then twenty-seven years old, took over the editorship of *The Brooklyn Daily Eagle and Kings County Democrat*, a newspaper with strong Democratic Party affiliations. As editor, Whitman authored a series of columns that year that enthusiastically endorsed "manifest destiny" thinking: the editorials supported the Mexican–American War and advocated the annexation of Mexican territory, especially California. However, Whitman soon grew more uneasy about the war, and particularly about the possibility that slavery would be extended to the areas seized from Mexico; he supported the Wilmot Proviso—Democratic Congressman David Wilmot's unsuccessful attempt to ban slavery in conquered Mexican territory—and was eventually fired from the *Daily Eagle* for his embrace of such "free soil" policies. The text of the excerpts from Whitman's editorials given below is based on their original newspaper publications.

SHALL WE FIGHT IT OUT? (11 MAY 1846)

Yes: Mexico must be thoroughly chastised! We have reached a point, in our intercourse[3] with that

---

[3]   *intercourse* Interactions.

Frances Flora Bond Palmer, *Across the Continent: "Westward the Course of Empire Takes Its Way,"* 1868. The title of this lithograph, produced for the popular Currier and Ives printmaking firm that sold inexpensive colored engravings to a mass audience, alludes to both a line from a 1726 poem, "Verses on the Prospect of Planting Arts and Learning in America," by the British philosopher George Berkeley, and a well-known mural, painted in 1861 for the U.S. Capitol Building by the artist Emmanuel Leutze, that took Berkeley's line for its title. (Another example of the widespread quotation and misquotation of the line in nineteenth-century American culture occurs in Henry David Thoreau's essay 'Walking' (1862), excerpted in the website portion of this Contexts section.) Born and raised in Britain, Frances Palmer (1812–76) moved to the U.S. in the 1840s, where she became a successful illustrator; another of her lithographs appears in the "Nature and the Environment" Contexts section elsewhere in this anthology volume.

country, when prompt and effectual demonstrations of force are enjoined upon us by every dictate of right and policy. The news of yesterday[1] has added the last argument wanted to prove the necessity of an immediate Declaration of War by our government toward its southern neighbor.

We are justified in the face of the world, in having treated Mexico with more forbearance than we have ever yet treated an enemy—for Mexico, though contemptible in many respects, is an enemy deserving a vigorous "lesson." We have coaxed, excused, listened with deaf ears to the insolent gasconade[2] of her government, submitted thus far to a most offensive rejection of an Ambassador personifying the American nation, and waited for years without payment of the claims of our injured merchants. We have sought peace through

---

[1]   *news of yesterday* In late April 1846, Mexican forces attacked a U.S. patrol in the territory between the Nueces and Rio Grande rivers—territory that was disputed between Mexico, which claimed the Nueces as Texas's boundary (and refused to recognize Texan independence from Mexico in any case), and the U.S., which claimed the Rio Grande as the boundary. U.S. President James K. Polk had ordered U.S. troops to move into the disputed area, fully aware that this would likely provoke conflict. News of the clash reached the U.S. east coast in early May (by which time Mexican and U.S. troops in the disputed region had fought several other battles), and Congress declared war on Mexico on 13 May.

[2]   *gasconade* Extravagant boasting.

every avenue, and shut our eyes to many things, which, had they come from England or France, the President would not have dared to pass over without stern and speedy resentment. We have dammed up our memory, of what has passed in the South years ago—of the devilish massacres of some of our bravest and noblest sons, the children not of the South alone, but of the North and the West—massacres, not only in defiance of ordinary humanity, but in violation of all the rules of war.[1] Who has read the sickening story of those brutal wholesale massacres, so useless for any purpose except gratifying the cowardly appetite of a nation of bravos,[2] willing to shoot down men by the hundred in cold blood—without panting for the day when the prayer of that blood should be listened to[3]—when the vengeance of a retributive God should be meted out to those who so ruthlessly and needlessly slaughtered His image?

That day has arrived. We think there can be no doubt of the truth of yesterday's news; and we are sure the people here, ten to one, are for prompt and *effectual* hostilities. … Let our arms now be carried with a spirit which shall teach the world that, while we are not forward with a quarrel, America knows how to crush, as well as how to expand!

from OUR TERRITORY ON THE PACIFIC (7 JULY 1846)

However soon the passage-at-arms between this republic and Mexico be closed, we hope—since things have resolved themselves into the state they now hold—that the United States will (in some way) fix their mark of ownership on the American coast of the Pacific[.] …

We love to indulge in thoughts of the future extent and power of this republic—because all its increase is the increase of human happiness and liberty. Therefore hope we that the U.S. will keep a fast grip on California. What has miserable, inefficient Mexico—with her superstition, her burlesque[4] of freedom, her actual tyranny by the few over the many—what has she to do with the great mission of peopling the new world with a noble race? Be it ours, to achieve that mission! Be it ours to roll down all of the upstart leaven[5] of old despotism, that comes in our way!

Alfred Jones, *Mexican News*, 1851. Jones (1819–1900), an Anglo-American engraver, made this copy of an 1848 painting, *War News from Mexico*, by the artist Richard Caton Woodville, Sr. (1825–55); the copy was distributed to members of the American Art-Union, a subscription-based organization founded to promote awareness of (and the sale of) work by American artists. Both the original painting and this copy effectively convey the intensity with which Americans followed, and debated, the Mexican–American War, and the works' metaphorically rich composition and detail have made them enduringly famous.

---

1   *We have dammed up … war*   Reference to the battles of the Alamo and Goliad, fought between the Mexican Army and rebel Texans during the Texan Revolution in 1836. At the Alamo, the entire Texan garrison of between 182 and 257 men was killed, several of them after they had surrendered; at Goliad, hundreds of Texan prisoners (the exact number is unknown) were executed. Whitman later included a description of the Goliad Massacre in his poem "Song of Myself," first published in 1855.

2   *bravos*   Men who fight and kill for hire.

3   *when … listened to*   See Genesis 4.10, in which God tells Cain, who has just murdered his brother Abel, "the voice of thy brother's blood crieth unto me from the ground."

4   *burlesque*   Ridiculous parody.

5   *leaven*   Undesirable holdover. See 1 Corinthians 5.7: "Purge out therefore the old leaven, that ye may be a new lump, as ye are unleavened."

Thomas D'Arcy McGee, "The Army of the West" (c. 1849)

During the Mexican–American War, an American military unit called the Army of the West, commanded by General Stephen Watts Kearny, marched west from Fort Leavenworth, Kansas, to invade New Mexico and California. The army was charged not only with defeating any Mexicans in its path but also with clearing a road through the mountains and forests across which settlers could travel. The poem presented below, by the Irish-born politician and writer Thomas D'Arcy McGee (1825–68), takes the Army of the West's successful campaign as its backdrop but broadens and deepens the actual army's metaphorical significance. McGee, whose advocacy for Irish revolution against British rule forced him to move to the U.S. in 1848, supported Irish American settlement in the west as a way of preserving Irish Catholic identity from dilution in the big eastern cities— as well as protecting Irish Catholics themselves from the anti-immigrant and anti-Catholic prejudice they frequently encountered there. McGee's own experiences in the U.S. eventually soured him on American-style democracy and republicanism, and in the 1850s he abandoned revolutionary politics in favor of Irish Catholic conservatism. He left the U.S. in 1857 and moved to Montreal, where he became a strong advocate of Canadian confederation and an outspoken critic of American expansionism. His opposition to the Fenians—Irish American radicals who sought to strike a blow against the British Empire by seizing Canada from Britain—probably led to his assassination in 1868, one year after he had helped bring about a confederated Canada.

"The Army of the West" was first published in 1849 in the New York *Nation*, an Irish American newspaper McGee edited. The text presented below is based on that published in *The Poems of Thomas D'Arcy McGee* (1870).

We fight upon a new-found plan, our Army of the West—
Our brave brigades, along the line, will leave the foe no rest—

Our battle-axes, bright and keen, with every day's swift sands,
Lay low the foes of Liberty, and then annex their lands;
5 On, onward through the Western woods our standard saileth ever
And shadows many a nameless peak and unbaptizèd river—
The Army of the Future we, the champions of the Unborn—
We pluck the primal forests up, and sow their sites with corn.

That ruggèd standard beareth the royal arms of toil—
10 The axe, and pike, and ponderous sledge, and plough that frees the soil—
The field is made of stripes, and the stars the crest supplies,
And the living eagles hover round the flagstaffs where it flies.
And thus beneath our standard, right merrily we go,
The Future for our heritage, the tangled Waste our foe:
15 The Army of the Future we, the champions of the Unborn—
We pluck the primal forests up, and sow their sites with corn.

Down in yon glade the anvil rings beneath the arching oaks,
Behind yon hills our neighbors drive young oxen in the yokes,
Yon laughing boys now boating down the rapid river's tide,
20 Go to the learnèd man who keeps the log-house on its side—
Like suckers° of the pine they grow,   *offshoots* elastic, rugged, tall,
They will hit a swallow on the wing with a single rifle ball—
The cadets of our army they, from "the West-Point"[1] of the unborn,
They too will pluck the forests up, and sow their sites with corn.

---

1 *West-Point* Since 1802, West Point, New York, has been the site of the United States Military Academy, where cadets are trained to become officers in the U.S. Army.

25   Oh ye who dwell in cities, in the self-conceited East,
      Do you ever think how by our toils your comforts are
          increased?
      When you walk upon your carpets, and sit on your
          easy chairs,
      And read self-applauding stories, and give yourselves
          such airs—
      Do you ever think upon us, Backwoodsmen of the
          West,
30   Who, from the Lakes[1] to Texas, have given the foe no
          rest?
      On the Army of the Future, and the champions of the
          Unborn,
      Who pluck the primal forests up, and sow their sites
          with corn?

from J.M. Whitfield in reply to F. Douglass [Letter on Emigration], 25 September 1853

The African American poet James Monroe
Whitfield (1822–71) wrote the letter excerpted
below in response to Frederick Douglass's criticism of a call by Martin Delany—like Douglass,
a friend and patron of Whitfield's—for a convention to discuss potential African American
emigration out of the United States. The letter
initiated an extended public debate between
Whitfield, on one side, and Douglass and his
allies, on the other, over the necessity and efficacy of African American emigration. The text
of the excerpt from Whitfield's letter presented
here is based on that published by Whitfield
in *Arguments, Pro and Con, on the Call for a
National Emigration Convention* (1854); the full
text of the letter can be found under the author
section on Whitfield in the website component
of this anthology.

...   [C]olored men can never be fully and
           fairly respected as the equals of the
whites, in this country, or any other, until they are
able to show in some part of the world, men of their
own race occupying a primary and independent
position, instead of a secondary and inferior one, as
is now the case everywhere. In short, that they must
show a powerful nation in which the black is the

ruling element, capable of maintaining a respectable
position among the *great* nations of the earth; and I
believe that the reflex influence of such a power with
the increased activity that its reaction will excite in the
colored people of this country will be the only thing
sufficiently powerful to remove the prejudices which
ages of unequal oppression have engendered, unless the
bleaching theory of Henry Clay should prevail,[2] and be
carried into practice, by which the negro race in this
country is to be absorbed, and its identity lost in that
of the Caucasian—a consummation in my opinion
not to be wished for.[3] I believe it to be the destiny of
the negro to develop a higher order of civilization and
Christianity than the world has yet seen. I also consider it a part of his "manifest destiny" to possess all
the tropical regions of this continent, with the adjacent
islands. That the negro is to be the predominant race in
all that region in regard to numbers, is beyond doubt.
The only question is, shall they exercise the power and
influence their numbers entitle them to, and become
the ruling political element of the land in which they
live? Or shall they, as too many of our brethren in this
country seem to be willing to do, tamely submit to the
usurpation of a white aristocracy, naturally inferior to
themselves in physical, moral, and mental power, and
devote their lives to building up a power whose every
energy will be wielded to crush them?

anonymous, "Filibustering Ethics" (1854)

First published in a San Francisco newspaper
(exactly which one is a matter of dispute), this
comic parody of "filibustering"—the practice by
Americans of attempting to foment instability
in, and then seize, Latin American countries—
quickly   went   the   mid-nineteenth-century

---

[1]   *the Lakes*   I.e., the Great Lakes.

[2]   *the bleaching … prevail*   Henry Clay was a prominent politician
who, as senator for Kentucky, had recently helped put together the
Compromise of 1850, an arrangement between slave states and free
states that was regarded by abolitionists as a sellout. Clay enslaved
African Americans throughout his life but supported the gradual
abolition of slavery; however, he believed a multiracial society was
impossible and that free African Americans would therefore either
have to merge with white Americans or leave the country.

[3]   *a consummation … wished for*   See Shakespeare's *Hamlet* 3.1.71–
72, in which Hamlet calls death "a consummation / Devoutly to be
wished."

equivalent of viral: during the first five months of 1854, it was reprinted (under various titles) from Wisconsin to Louisiana and as far afield as Honolulu, in newspapers that ran the political gamut from abolitionism to the defense of "Southern Rights." The text given below is based on that printed in the *Milwaukee Daily Sentinel*, 20 May 1854.

S ays Captain Robb to Farmer Cobb,
    "Your farm is very fine, sir;
Please give me up your title-deeds,
    I claim it all as mine, sir."
5 "Pray, how can it be thine?" says Cobb;
    "I'm sure I never sold it:
'Twas left me by my father, sir;
    I only ought to hold it."

"Nay, Cobb, the 'march of destiny'—
10   'Tis strange you don't perceive it—
Is sure to make it mine someday,
    I solemnly believe it."
"But have you not already got
    More land than you can till, sir?
15 More rocks than you can ever blast?
    More weeds than you can kill, sir?"

"Aye, Cobb; but something whispers me—
    A sort of inspiration—
That I've a *right* to every farm
20   Not under cultivation.
I'm of the 'Anglo-Saxon race,'[1]
    A people known to fame, sir;
But you—what right have you to land?
    Who ever heard your name, sir?

25 "I deem you, Cobb, a lazy lout,
    Poor, trodden down, and blind, sir;
And if I take your useless land,
    You ought to think it kind, sir!
And with my scientific skill,

30   I set it down as true, sir,
That I can gather from the farm
    Full twice as much as you, sir.

"To be explicit: 'Tis an age
    Of freedom and progression;
35 No longer, dog in manger-like,[2]
    Can you retain possession.
The farm you long since forfeited
    Because you failed to till it;
To me it clearly now belongs,
40   Simply because—*I will it.*

"My logic if you disapprove,
    Or fail of comprehending,
Or do not feel convinced that I
    Your welfare am attending,
45 I've plenty more of arguments
    To which I can resort, sir!
Six-shooters, rifles, bowie-knives,[3]
    Will indicate the sort, sir.

"So prithee, Cobb, take my advice;
50   Make over your domains, sir;
Or, sure as I am Captain Robb,
    Will I blow out your brains, sir!"
Poor Cobb can only grind his teeth
    And grumble protestations
55 That *might* should be the rule of *right*
    Among *enlightened nations.*

---

[1] *Anglo-Saxon race* The term "Anglo-Saxon," which originally referred to the Germanic cultural group that settled in and ruled England in the early Middle Ages, was widely used in both Britain and the United States in the nineteenth century as a name for white people inhabiting or stemming from England (or the British Isles more generally). In such contexts, the term often carried—and still carries—racist connotations of inherent racial superiority.

[2] *dog in manger-like* Reference to a traditional fable about a dog lying in a manger, who does not eat the grain contained in the manger but, by lying there, also prevents a horse from eating it. The fable is typically used to criticize someone who has no use for an object or resource in their possession but who prevents others, for whom it would be useful, from accessing it.

[3] *bowie-knives* Type of fighting-knife associated with the American South. It was created for and named after Jim Bowie (c. 1796–1836), a soldier and slave trader who gained a reputation in the South for his violent exploits; he later moved to Texas, where he became a leader in the Texas Revolution and was killed at the Alamo.

This 1848 political cartoon caricatures Lewis Cass (1782–1866), the Democratic candidate in that year's presidential election. Cass had had a long political career up to that point, serving, among many other capacities, as Andrew Jackson's Secretary of War; he was one of the primary architects and leading exponents of Native American expulsion and had become known as a strong advocate of American expansion. The cartoon depicts Cass holding a bloodstained sword labeled "Manifest Destiny"; his leg, along with many other parts of his body, is a cannon firing "Gas" (a reference to Cass's nickname, "General Gas"); and his speech bubble lays out his annexationist agenda: "New Mexico, California, Chihuahua, Zacatecas, MEXICO, Peru, Yucatan, Cuba."

Francisco P. Ramírez, editorial from *El Clamor Público*, 24 July 1855

Born in Los Angeles, California, Francisco Ramírez (1837–1908) was just seventeen when, in 1855, he founded *El Clamor Público* ("The Public Outcry"), southern California's first Spanish-language newspaper. The paper was created, as Ramírez put it in 1856, "to serve as an organ for the general perspective of the Spanish race as a means of manifesting the atrocious injuries of which they have been victims in this country where they were born and in which they now live in a state inferior to the poorest of their persecutors." In his writing for the newspaper, Ramírez consistently celebrated the values enshrined in the U.S. Constitution, especially freedom of expression and freedom of the press,

while tirelessly condemning the hypocrisy with which the white Americans who had come to dominate his native land applied these values. His stewardship of the paper, which shut down in 1859, made *El Clamor Público* a landmark in the development of a Hispanic American ethnic and political consciousness in the United States. Ramírez later came to support the Republican Party because of its opposition to the expansion of slavery; he was active in Republican state politics until 1880, when he fled to Mexico to avoid a charge of bank fraud, never returning to California.

The editorial presented below exemplifies Ramírez's critique of white American racism and "manifest destiny" doctrine. The editorial was written, in part, in response to the passage of California's Anti-Vagrancy Act, which authorized the incarceration of all "vagrants," defined as people who did not have or accept employment, as well as sex workers and alcoholics. Section Two of the act specifically singled out "All persons who are commonly known as 'Greasers' or the issue of Spanish and Indian blood" as especially worthy of suspicion and prosecution; this racist provision led to the law being dubbed "the Greaser Act." The present text is based on a translation of the editorial first published by Arte Público Press and reprinted in *Herencia: The Anthology of Hispanic Literature of the United States* (2001).

The United States' conception of freedom is truly curious. This much-lauded freedom is imaginary. We think that a man is not truly free when he is obligated to pay a tax for so many doors and windows, even for the air he breathes. In our opinion, freedom is what all rational creation has a right to make use of as it sees fit, conforming to reason and justice. There are three species of freedom: natural, civil, and political, or rather, freedom of man, freedom of the citizen, and freedom of the nation. Natural freedom is the right man enjoys by nature to make use of it according to his free will, in keeping with the purpose for which he was raised. Civil freedom is the right that links all citizens to society so that they can do as they please when it is not to the contrary of the established laws. And lastly, political or national freedom is the right that all nations have to work for themselves independently of another nation, to be subject or servile to no tyrant. But here in this fabulous[1] country, he who robs and assassinates the most is he who enjoys freedom. Certain people have no kind of freedom—this freedom, we say, is that which the courts deny to all individuals of color. To buy a man for money, to hang or burn him alive arbitrarily, is another great liberty which any individual has here, according to his likes. This happens in the United States, where slavery is tolerated, where the most vile despotism reigns unchecked—in the middle of a nation that they call the "Model Republic." It is enough that these institutions are unique in a country that tries to consume everything due to its "Manifest Destiny." Ultimately, we here in California have been favored by our "Model Legislature," with two laws so original that they have no equal in the annals of any civilized nation. These are the Sunday law[2] and the famous vagrant law. The former prohibits dances and other innocent diversions on Sunday, on pain of incarceration and fine for all those who infringe on the decree, as if to force people to stay at home to fast and pray to the Almighty for our welfare. (Wouldn't it be better to pray so that he would free us from such legislatures?) The supposition that people are made more moral by taking away their pastimes and diversions is truly ridiculous. The latter is that which affects our Californian and Mexican population directly. They particularly distinguish us by the title of Greasers. This law has served to widen the gap that has existed for some time between the foreigners and the natives.

from John Rollin Ridge, "Poem (Delivered at Commencement of Oakland College, California, June 6th 1861)" (1861)

John Rollin Ridge (1827–67) was the son and grandson of prominent Cherokee signatories to the Treaty of New Echota, the 1836 treaty—unsanctioned by the Cherokee leadership—that ceded the Cherokee's traditional lands and agreed that the Cherokee people would relocate west of the Mississippi. Because of this, both were killed in 1839 by supporters of John Ross, the Cherokee Principal Chief and an opponent of removal; Ridge, then twelve years old, witnessed his father's murder. Ridge's writing after his move to California in the 1850s includes poetry and journalism as well as the first novel by an Indigenous author, *The Life and Adventures of Joaquín Murieta* (1854). His work contains condemnations of white American racism and advocacy for California's Indigenous population, but he was also capable of espousing the expansionism and condescension toward Indigenous Californians that typified the white settler-colonial society he had joined—as the poem presented here (the text of which is based on that printed in 1868 in *The Poems of John Rollin Ridge*) demonstrates.

A larger selection of Ridge's work can be found in the author section for him elsewhere in this anthology volume.

The waves that murmur at our feet,
Through many an age had rolled
Ere fortune found her favorite seat
Within this land of gold.

5 The Digger,[3] searching for his roots,
Here roamed the region wide—
Or, wearied with the day's pursuits,
Slept by this restless tide.

The dream of greatness never rose
10 Upon his simple brain;
The wealth on which a nation grows,
And builds its power to reign,

All darkly lay beneath his tread,
Where many a stream did wind,
15 Deep slumbering in its yellow bed,
The charm that rules mankind.

---

[1] *fabulous* I.e., fabled; of mythological reputation.

[2] *the Sunday law* Lobbying by Protestant religious leaders among the white American settlers in California led to the passage of California's first "Sunday law," outlawing noisy amusements on Sundays, in 1855. A more stringent version of the law, outlawing all business on Sundays, was passed in 1858 and was not repealed until 1883.

[3] *Digger* Highly derogatory term for the Indigenous peoples of California, stemming from the hunter-gatherer way of life—including digging up roots to eat—practiced by many of them. The term epitomizes the contempt that many American settlers in California felt for Indigenous Californians, a contempt which greatly facilitated the near-total extermination of California's Indigenous population during the decades following the Gold Rush.

Had he and his dark brethren known
Of gold the countless worth,
They now beyond that power had grown
20   Which sweeps them from the earth.

But happier he perchance, by far,
Still digging for his roots,
Than thousand paler wanderers are
Whose toil hath had no fruits. ...

25   Far off among the mountains stern,
Shall thousands meet with blight,
And many a raven lock shall turn
To hairs of frosty white;

And many a lonely grave shall hide
30   The mouldering form of him
For whom sad eyes are never dried,
With age and sorrow dim.

Yet, though the wayside all be strewn
With sorrows and with graves,
35   The glory of the race is shown
By what it does and braves.

What though the desert's mouldering heaps
Affright the startled eye—
What though in wilds the venturer sleeps,
40   His bones uncovered lie,

'Tis not the living that have won
Alone the victory:
But each dead soldier, too, has done
His part as loftily.

45   'Tis they—the living and the dead—
Who have redeemed our land;
Have cities reared, the arts have spread,
And placed us where we stand.

As led Adventure bold before,
50   The Arts and Learning came;
And now, behold I upon this shore
They have a place and name.

Where roamed erewhile the rugged bear
Amid these oaks of green,
55   And wandering from his mountain lair
The cougar's steps were seen,

Lo! Peace hath built her quiet nest;
And "mild-eyed Science"[1] roves,
As was her wont° when Greece was blest,   habit
60   In Academic groves.[2]

Oh! tranquil be these shades for aye,°   forever
These groves forever green;
And youth and age still bless their day
That here their steps have been.

65   May Learning here still have her seat,
Her empire of the mind
The home of Genius, Wit's Retreat,
Whate'er is pure refined.

And thus the proudest boast shall be
70   Of young Ambition crowned—
"The woods of Oakland sheltered me,
Their leaves my brow have bound."[3]

---

[1]   *mild-eyed Science*   Ridge may be thinking of the English writer and academic Robert Blakey's translation, published in 1845, of "Lines on the Burning of the Alexandrian Library" by Saint Ammon, a fourth-century Christian ascetic, in which these words appear.

[2]   *Academic groves*   The words "academic" and "academy" come from *Akademia*, the name for a sacred grove of olive trees outside of Athens that was the site of the philosophical school (also called the Academy) founded by the Greek philosopher Plato (c. 427–347 BCE).

[3]   *Their leaves ... bound*   In ancient Greece, oak trees were sacred to the god Zeus, and the wearing of oak leaf crowns symbolized wisdom.

Sarah Moore Grimké

1792 – 1873

Born into the height of privilege on a plantation in South Carolina, Sarah Moore Grimké defied convention to become, in the 1830s, one of the most influential abolitionists in the United States, as well as a progressive thinker on women's rights. Working closely with her sister Angelina, Grimké drew on the Bible, on contemporary political and sociological writings, and on her own experiences in the slaveholding South in building her arguments against racial prejudice and gender constraints in nineteenth-century America; her writings, which often utilized the popular epistolary form, would go on to influence later writers and activists, including Harriet Beecher Stowe and Elizabeth Cady Stanton.

Sarah Moore Grimké was born in Charleston in 1792, the sixth child of Mary and John Grimké. The family divided their time between fashionable Charleston and their large cotton plantation in the north of the state. As a child, Grimké expressed discomfort with her family's slaveholding practices, and she was once punished for teaching her enslaved handmaid to read (a violation of South Carolina law); it was not until much later in life, though, that she began unequivocally to oppose slavery as an institution. She took private lessons with her brother Thomas until 1805, when he left the state to enter Yale College; her parents discouraged her from pursuing further "unfeminine" education. Angelina Grimké was born not long thereafter; Grimké was, at her own request, named Angelina's godmother, initiating a close bond that would endure until the end of her life.

In her twenties, Grimké began seeking religious fulfilment outside the Episcopalian Church of her family, experiencing an emotionally exhausting cycle of mystical visions, conversions, and relapses that lasted many years. Drawn initially to the Presbyterian Church, she was introduced to the Society of Friends (the Quakers) in 1818, while on a visit to Philadelphia. Though initially put off by the Quakers' somber ethos and outsider status, Grimké was by 1821 sufficiently moved by the faith to return to Philadelphia and take up residence with a Quaker family; she was an official member of the Society of Friends by 1823. Private spiritual concerns continued to dominate Grimké's life over the following years, but she began too to contemplate larger social issues, and on her occasional returns to South Carolina she found her sister increasingly beginning to probe the religious and ethical questions surrounding plantation slavery. Grimké was joined by Angelina in Philadelphia in 1829; it was Angelina who would ultimately push her to embrace the abolitionist cause in the coming decade.

Though the Society of Friends had for over a century been officially opposed to slavery, and though its doctrines upheld the spiritual equality of all people, the Grimké sisters found themselves often frustrated by the relative indifference to slavery of most Quaker individuals, and by the frequency with which they were, as women, expected to keep especially silent on the topic. Sarah herself remained hesitant to speak on the matter or to attend abolitionist meetings until mid-1835. A diary entry for May 12 of that year records her change of heart: "Truly," she wrote, "I often feel ready to go to prison or to death in this cause of justice, mercy, and love; and I do fully believe if I am called to return to Carolina, it will not be long before I shall suffer persecution of some kind or other." In late 1836, she incurred the anger of the Philadelphia Quakers by accompanying Angelina to New York, where the sisters then became the first female agents for the American Anti-Slavery Society; the following three years would comprise the most productive period of Grimké's abolitionist activism.

Grimké's first abolitionist work, *An Epistle to the Clergy of the Southern States*, was published by the American Anti-Slavery Society that year. A theologically charged admonition to Southern religious authorities to relinquish their support of slavery, the text emphasizes biblical arguments—refuting the biblical defenses of slavery often put forward in the South—but also shows Grimké's familiarity with Thomas Jefferson's *Notes on the State of Virginia* (1787) and other secular works describing American slavery. Grimké and her sister began to hold "parlor meetings" on slavery in the North—attended, controversially, by both men and women—and spent much of 1837 on a speaking tour of New England, aiming particularly to draw women into the abolitionist movement.

During this period Grimké began working on a series of letters in which she further developed her theory of women's rights; these letters were eventually published in *The New England Spectator* and the abolitionist newspaper *The Liberator*. Her arguments addressed matters of class as well as race and gender, highlighting issues such as the pay gap between laboring men and women. The series was deeply influenced by Lydia Maria Child's recent *The History of the Condition of Women in Various Ages and Nations* (1835); Grimké had had little opportunity to read other works on women's rights, and she opened the collection by describing her topic as "nearly untrodden ground." The letters were later published as a single volume titled *Letters on the Equality of the Sexes* (1838).

In 1839, the sisters collaborated with abolitionist Theodore Weld (whom Angelina had married the previous year) to publish *American Slavery as It Is: Testimony of a Thousand Witnesses*, a monumental work to which Grimké contributed substantial research as well as numerous accounts of slavery on her family's plantation. The book was enormously influential, providing abolitionists with an invaluable trove of incontrovertible evidence (the raw material was derived from personal testimony, from thousands of newspaper reports, and—tellingly—from advertisements that had been placed in newspapers by the slaveholders themselves). In turn, the book helped to provide raw material for some of the most influential abolitionist works of fiction later in the century—chief among them Stowe's *Uncle Tom's Cabin*.

Grimké lived with the Welds for the rest of her life. The household eventually expanded to include not only the Welds's children but also two nephews, Archibald and Francis James Grimké, mixed-race sons of Henry Grimké and his enslaved mistress; both men would become prominent African American rights activists in the late nineteenth and early twentieth centuries. *American Slavery* was Grimké's last published work to be widely influential, but she continued to be involved in the fight for social justice, including in the burgeoning women's suffrage movement, until late in her life. Her private writings reveal a continuing engagement with early feminist works (including Elizabeth Barrett Browning's *Aurora Leigh* [1856] and John Stuart Mill's *The Subjection of Women* [1869]). Her translation of Lamartine's biography of Joan of Arc was published with a small print run in 1867. Her unpublished writings include a novel, now lost, about an interracial marriage.

Throughout much of her life, Grimké's accomplishments were frequently overshadowed by those of her more outspoken and oratorically talented sister. Both Grimkés were in 1885 the subject of a biography (written by Catherine Birney), but they were thereafter largely neglected in twentieth-century scholarship of the abolitionist movement—as were most female and African American abolitionists. Dwight Dumond's 1961 *Antislavery: The Crusade for Freedom in America* devotes a chapter to Angelina Grimké, but makes little mention of Sarah. It was not until the publication of Gerda Lerner's landmark *The Grimké Sisters from South Carolina: Pioneers for Women's Rights and Abolition* in 1967 that Sarah Grimké's achievements as a pioneering feminist as well as an abolitionist began to receive renewed attention from scholars.

NOTE ON THE TEXT: The text of "Letter 8: On the Condition of Women in the United States" is based on that published in the first edition of Sarah Moore Grimké's *Letters on the Equality of the Sexes* (1838). Spelling and punctuation have been modernized in accordance with the practices of this anthology.

⌘ ⌘ ⌘

from *Letters on the Equality of the Sexes and the Condition of Woman*

LETTER 8
ON THE CONDITION OF WOMEN
IN THE UNITED STATES

Brookline, 1837

My dear Sister[1]—I have now taken a brief survey of the condition of woman in various parts of the world. I regret that my time has been so much occupied by other things, that I have been unable to bestow that attention upon the subject which it merits, and that my constant change of place has prevented me from having access to books, which might probably have assisted me in this part of my work. I hope that the principles I have asserted will claim the attention of some of my sex, who may be able to bring into view, more thoroughly than I have done, the situation and degradation of woman. I shall now proceed to make a few remarks on the condition of women in my own country.

During the early part of my life, my lot was cast among the butterflies of the *fashionable* world; and of this class of women, I am constrained to say, both from experience and observation, that their education is miserably deficient; that they are taught to regard marriage as the one thing needful, the only avenue to distinction; hence to attract the notice and win the attentions of men, by their external charms, is the chief business of fashionable girls. They seldom think that men will be allured by intellectual acquirements, because they find, that where any mental superiority exists, a woman is generally shunned and regarded as stepping out of her "appropriate sphere," which, in their view, is to dress, to dance, to set out to the best possible advantage her person,[2] to read the novels which inundate the press, and which do more to destroy her character

as a rational creature, than anything else. Fashionable women regard themselves, and are regarded by men, as pretty toys or as mere instruments of pleasure; and the vacuity of mind, the heartlessness, the frivolity which is the necessary result of this false and debasing estimate of women, can only be fully understood by those who have mingled in the folly and wickedness of fashionable life; and who have been called from such pursuits by the voice of the Lord Jesus, inviting their weary and heavy laden souls to come unto Him and learn of Him, that they may find something worthy of their immortal spirit, and their intellectual powers; that they may learn the high and holy purposes of their creation, and consecrate themselves unto the service of God; and not, as is now the case, to the pleasure of man.

There is another and much more numerous class in this country who are withdrawn by education or circumstances from the circle of fashionable amusements, but who are brought up with the dangerous and absurd idea that *marriage* is a kind of preferment;[3] and that to be able to keep their husband's house, and render his situation comfortable, is the end of her being. Much that she does and says and thinks is done in reference to this situation; and to be married is too often held up to the view of girls as the *sine qua non*[4] of human happiness and human existence. For this purpose, more than for any other, I verily believe the majority of girls are trained. This is demonstrated by the imperfect education which is bestowed upon them, and the little pains[5] taken to cultivate their minds, after they leave school, by the little time allowed them for reading, and by the idea being constantly inculcated, that although all household concerns should be attended to with scrupulous punctuality at particular seasons, the improvement of their intellectual capacities is only a secondary consideration, and may serve as an occupation to fill up the odds and ends of time. In most families, it is considered a matter of far more consequence to call a girl off from making a pie, or a pudding, than to interrupt her whilst engaged in her studies. This mode of training necessarily exalts, in their view, the animal above the intellectual and spiritual nature, and teaches women to regard themselves as a kind of machinery,

---

[1] *My dear Sister* The letters in this book, which were first published individually in *The New England Spectator*, were addressed to Mary S. Parker, who was then president of the Boston Female Anti-Slavery Society. Grimké's habit of addressing people as "Sister" or "Brother," and her occasional use of the pronouns "thee," "thou," and "thine," stemmed in part from Quaker customs.

[2] *person* I.e., body; physical appearance.

[3] *preferment* Promotion.

[4] *sine qua non* Latin: indispensable attribute.

[5] *pains* Effort.

necessary to keep the domestic engine in order, but of little value as the *intelligent* companions of men.

Let no one think, from these remarks, that I regard a knowledge of housewifery as beneath the acquisition of women. Far from it: I believe that a complete knowledge of household affairs is an indispensable requisite in a woman's education—that by the mistress of a family, whether married or single, doing her duty thoroughly and *understandingly*, the happiness of the family is increased to an incalculable degree, as well as a vast amount of time and money saved. All I complain of is that our education consists so almost exclusively in culinary and other manual operations. I do long to see the time, when it will no longer be necessary for women to expend so many precious hours in furnishing "a well spread table," but that their husbands will forego some of their accustomed indulgences in this way, and encourage their wives to devote some portion of their time to mental cultivation, even at the expense of having to dine sometimes on baked potatoes, or bread and butter.

I believe the sentiment expressed by the author of *Live and Let Live*[1] is true:

> Other things being equal, a woman of the highest mental endowments will always be the best housekeeper, for domestic economy,[2] is a science that brings into action the qualities of the mind, as well as the graces of the heart. A quick perception, judgment, discrimination, decision and order are high attributes of mind, and are all in daily exercise in the well ordering of a family. If a sensible woman, an intellectual woman, a woman of genius, is not a good housewife, it is not because she is either, or all of those, but because there is some deficiency in her character, or some omission of duty which should make her very humble, instead of her indulging in any secret self-complacency on account of a certain superiority, which only aggravates her fault.

The influence of women over the minds and character of *children* of both sexes is allowed[3] to be far greater than that of men. This being the case by the very ordering of nature, women should be prepared by education for the performance of their sacred duties as mothers and as sisters. A late American writer,[4] speaking on this subject, says in reference to an article in the *Westminster Review*:

> I agree entirely with the writer in the high estimate which he places on female education, and have long since been satisfied that the subject not only merits, but *imperiously demands* a thorough reconsideration. The whole scheme must, in my opinion, be reconstructed. The great elements of usefulness and duty are too little attended to. Women ought, in my view of the subject, to approach to the best education now given to men (I except mathematics and the classics), far more I believe than has ever yet been attempted. Give me a host of educated, pious mothers and sisters, and I will do more to revolutionize a country, in moral and religious taste, in manners and in social virtues and intellectual cultivation, than I can possibly do in double or treble the time, with a similar host of educated men. I cannot but think that the miserable condition of the great body of the people in all ancient communities, is to be ascribed in a very great degree to the degradation of women.

There is another way in which the general opinion, that women are inferior to men, is manifested, that bears with tremendous effect on the laboring class, and indeed on almost all who are obliged to earn a subsistence, whether it be by mental or physical exertion—I allude to the disproportionate value set on the time and labor of men and women. A man who is engaged in teaching, can always, I believe, command a higher price for tuition than a woman—even when he teaches the same branches, and is not in any respect superior to the woman. This I know is the case in boarding and other schools with which I have been acquainted, and it is so in every occupation in which the sexes engage indiscriminately. As for example, in tailoring, a man has twice or three times as much, for making a waistcoat

---

1   *the author of* Live and Let Live   American novelist Catharine Maria Sedgwick (1789–1867); this 1837 novel focuses on the experiences of domestic servants and other working-class women.

2   *domestic economy*   Household management.

3   *allowed*   Admitted; acknowledged.

4   [Grimké's note]   Thomas S. Grimke. [Grimké here refers to her elder brother, with whom she had studied as a child, and who had died in 1834. As a lawyer and noted orator, Thomas Grimké was known for supporting various reform movements, including that of women's education (though he was far less radical than either of his sisters on the topic of abolition).]

or pantaloons, as a woman, although the work done by each may be equally good. In those employments which are peculiar to women, their time is estimated at only half the value of that of men. A woman who goes out to wash[1] works as hard in proportion as a wood sawyer, or a coal heaver, but she is not generally able to make more than half as much by a day's work. The low remuneration which women receive for their work has claimed the attention of a few philanthropists, and I hope it will continue to do so until some remedy is applied for this enormous evil. I have known a widow, left with four or five children to provide for, unable to leave home because her helpless babes demand her attention, compelled to earn a scanty subsistence, by making coarse shirts at 12 ½ cents a piece, or by taking in washing, for which she was paid by some wealthy persons 12 ½ cents per dozen. All these things evince the low estimation in which woman is held. There is yet another and more disastrous consequence arising from this unscriptural notion—women being educated, from earliest childhood, to regard themselves as inferior creatures, have not that self-respect which conscious equality would engender, and hence when their virtue[2] is assailed, they yield to temptation with facility, under the idea that it rather exalts than debases them to be connected with a superior being.

There is another class of women in this country to whom I cannot refer without feelings of the deepest shame and sorrow. I allude to our female slaves. Our southern cities are whelmed beneath a tide of pollution; the virtue of female slaves is wholly at the mercy of irresponsible tyrants, and women are bought and sold in our slave markets, to gratify the brutal lust of those who bear the name of Christians. In our slave states, if amid all her degradation and ignorance, a woman desires to preserve her virtue unsullied, she is either bribed or whipped into compliance, or if she dares resist her seducer, her life by the laws of some of the slave states may be, and has actually been sacrificed to the fury of disappointed passion. Where such laws

do not exist, the power which is necessarily vested in the master over his property leaves the defenceless slave entirely at his mercy, and the sufferings of some females on this account, both physical and mental, are intense. Mr. Gholson, in the House of Delegates of Virginia, in 1832, said, "He really had been under the impression that he owned his slaves. He had lately purchased four women and ten children, in whom he thought he had obtained a great bargain; for he supposed they were his own property, *as were his brood mares*." But even if any laws existed in the United States, as in Athens formerly, for the protection of female slaves, they would be null and void, because the evidence of a colored person is not admitted against a white, in any of our Courts of Justice in the slave states. "In Athens, if a female slave had cause to complain of any want[3] of respect to the laws of modesty, she could seek the protection of the temple, and demand a change of owners; and such appeals were never discountenanced, or neglected by the magistrate." In Christian America, the slave has no refuge from unbridled cruelty and lust.

S.A. Forrall,[4] speaking of the state of morals at the South, says, "Negresses, when young and likely,[5] are often employed by the planter, or his friends, to administer to their sensual desires. This frequently is a matter of speculation, for if the offspring, a mulatto, be a handsome female, 800 or 1000 dollars may be obtained for her in the New Orleans market. It is an occurrence of no uncommon nature to see a Christian father sell his own daughter, and the brother his own sister." The following is copied by the *N.Y. Evening Star* from the *Picayune*, a paper published in New Orleans. "A very beautiful girl, belonging to the estate of John French, a deceased gambler at New Orleans, was sold a few days since for the round sum of $7,000. An ugly-looking bachelor named Gouch, a member of the Council of one of the Principalities, was the purchaser. The girl is a brunette; remarkable for her beauty and intelligence, and there was considerable contention, who should be the purchaser. She was, however, persuaded to accept Gouch, he having made

---

[1]   *wash* I.e., launder clothing. In middle- or upper-class households, this task—which, carried out without the help of modern implements, was very physically demanding—was usually performed by servants or hired launderers. Laundering was one of few options available to women who needed to earn money, and was often considered particularly lowly work.

[2]   *virtue* I.e., chastity.

[3]   *want* Lack.

[4]   *S.A. Forrall* Author of the 1832 book *A Ramble of Six Thousand Miles Through the United States of America*, from which the following quotation is taken.

[5]   *likely* Attractive.

her princely promises." I will add but one more from the numerous testimonies respecting the degradation of female slaves, and the licentiousness of the South. It is from the *Circular* of the Kentucky Union, for the moral and religious improvement of the colored race. "To the female character among our black population, we cannot allude but with feelings of the bitterest shame. A similar condition of moral pollution and utter disregard of a pure and virtuous reputation, is to be found *only without the pale of Christendom.* That such a state of society should exist in a Christian nation, claiming to be the most enlightened upon earth, without calling forth any *particular attention* to its existence, though ever before our eyes and *in our* families, is a moral phenomenon at once unaccountable and disgraceful." Nor does the colored woman suffer alone: the moral purity of the white woman is deeply contaminated. In the daily habit of seeing the virtue of her enslaved sister sacrificed without hesitancy or remorse, she looks upon the crimes of seduction and illicit intercourse without horror, and although not personally involved in the guilt, she loses that value for innocence in her own, as well as the other sex, which is one of the strongest safeguards to virtue. She lives in habitual intercourse[1] with men, whom she knows to be polluted by licentiousness, and often is she compelled to witness in her own domestic circle, those disgusting and heart-sickening jealousies and strifes which disgraced and distracted the family of Abraham.[2] In addition to all this, the female slaves suffer every species of degradation and cruelty, which the most wanton barbarity can inflict; they are indecently divested of their clothing, sometimes tied up and severely whipped, sometimes prostrated on the earth, while their naked bodies are torn by the scorpion lash.

The whip on WOMAN's shrinking flesh!
    Our soil yet reddening with the stains
Caught from her scourging warm and fresh.[3]

Can any American woman look at these scenes of shocking licentiousness and cruelty, and fold her hands in apathy, and say, "I have nothing to do with slavery"? *She cannot and be guiltless.*

I cannot close this letter without saying a few words on the benefits to be derived by men, as well as women, from the opinions I advocate relative to the equality of the sexes. Many women are now supported, in idleness and extravagance, by the industry of their husbands, fathers, or brothers, who are compelled to toil out their existence at the counting house, or in the printing office, or some other laborious occupation, while the wife and daughters and sisters take no part in the support of the family, and appear to think that their sole business is to spend the hard bought earnings of their male friends. I deeply regret such a state of things, because I believe that if women felt their responsibility, for the support of themselves, or their families, it would add strength and dignity to their characters, and teach them more true sympathy for their husbands, than is now generally manifested—a sympathy which would be exhibited by actions as well as words. Our brethren may reject my doctrine, because it runs counter to common opinions, and because it wounds their pride; but I believe they would be "partakers of the benefit" resulting from the Equality of the Sexes, and would find that woman, as their equal, was unspeakably more valuable than woman as their inferior, both as a moral and an intellectual being.

Thine in the bonds of womanhood,
SARAH M. GRIMKÉ

—1837

---

[1]   *intercourse* Communication; contact.

[2]   *jealousies and strifes … Abraham* In the Book of Genesis, the patriarch Abraham is described as having one wife, Sarah, and two concubines, Hagar and Keturah. Abraham's fathering of Ishmael by Hagar when Sarah was unable to conceive causes considerable tension in their household; eventually, this leads to the exile of Ishmael and Hagar.

[3]   *The whip … and fresh* From "Stanzas" by American Quaker antislavery poet John Greenleaf Whittier (1807–92).

RALPH WALDO EMERSON

1803 – 1882

In 1885, poet Oliver Wendell Holmes wrote that Ralph Waldo Emerson was "the poet whom some admired without understanding, a few understood, or thought they did, without admiring, and many both understood and admired—among these there being not a small number who went far beyond admiration, and lost themselves in devout worship." Even today, few nineteenth-century American figures are as frequently discussed, paraphrased, quoted, and even idolized as the New England orator, philosopher, and poet—though some critics have seen him, in the words of Edgar Allan Poe, as a "mystic for mysticism's sake." Partly because of the complex and sometimes self-contradictory qualities of Emerson's essays, his name is frequently invoked by writers, thinkers, and politicians in disparate realms, from environmentalism to economics, and for varied, even conflicting, ends. His writings themselves espouse not so much a certain set of values as a certain understanding of the relationship between the self and the external world, as well as between the self and the divine. It is in large part through Emerson's influence that the values of individualism, anti-traditionalism, and anti-institutionalism have come to dominate so much of American literary and political culture. And Emerson's Americanism has itself been influential; his work posed a prominent challenge to the idea that in order for Americans to develop a literary tradition, they needed to imitate the English one.

Emerson was born in 1803 to Bostoners William and Ruth Haskins Emerson. He followed in the footsteps of his minister father and grandfather when he himself joined the Unitarian ministry as a young man; it was largely from his mother Ruth's influence that he developed strong religious feeling. Emerson's aunt, Mary Moody Emerson—a significant writer and diarist in her own right—was also an important educational influence, and though they later disagreed on many religious principles, Emerson would continue to cite Mary Moody as his best early teacher. The Emersons lived in poverty for many years following William's early death, but Ruth managed to earn enough money to send the Emerson children to Harvard College; Emerson performed unexceptionally, but developed a voracious literary appetite outside class, and kept detailed journals of his readings; he would later call these journals the "Wide World."

Emerson entered Harvard's Divinity School in 1825, and soon met Ellen Louisa Tucker, with whom he appears to have had a profound and spiritual relationship. They married in 1829, and that same year he accepted a post as assistant pastor in Boston's Second Church. The next several years would be fraught with private difficulty, however, as Ellen died of tuberculosis in 1831, less than two years into their marriage. During the same period, Emerson became increasingly dissatisfied with Unitarian theology and conventional Christian rites in general, writing in 1832 that "The profession [of minister] is antiquated. In an altered age, we worship in the dead forms of our forefathers." Emerson formally broke with the Church, and, in December of 1832, he embarked on a tour of Europe that lasted until the following autumn. Traveling to popular cultural centers in Italy, Switzerland, France, and Britain, he met many of the leading literary and intellectual figures of the day, among them the Romantic poets Wordsworth and Coleridge—whose *Aids to Reflection* (1825) would prove highly influential in Emerson's future works—and the essayist and translator Thomas Carlyle, with whom he would maintain a lasting correspondence.

The year after his return to the United States in 1833, Emerson received his late wife's legacy, an annual sum of over one thousand dollars that granted him the financial freedom to pursue his re-invigorated intellectual interests. Inspired as much by the literature of the Romantics as by contemporary developments in natural science, Emerson was increasingly engrossed by ideas about the relationship between nature and the soul. Having come home to a New England just beginning to be taken over by the Lyceum movement (which aimed to disseminate knowledge among the general population by providing public lectures on the ethical, intellectual, and scientific questions of the day), he entered himself into the ranks of public educators. His lectures were the early anchors of Emerson's future success; well into his career as a writer, he was known as much for his passionate and invigorating delivery at the podium as for the ideas he delivered on paper.

During this period Emerson met Lydia (later Lidian) Jackson, whom he married in 1835; the couple then moved to Concord. The following year, Emerson published his first book, *Nature*—a work that laid the groundwork for the Transcendentalist thought with which he would be associated for the rest of his life. A loose company of intellectuals drawn to the philosophy of *Nature* began to gather, designating Emerson as their informal leader. The members of the Transcendental Club, though varying in their philosophical approaches, shared with Emerson essential beliefs in the primacy of the individual, in the ability to apprehend truth through the synthesis of the self with nature, and in the immanent divinity of nature and the human soul. *Nature* weaves together intellectual threads from an extraordinarily wide array of sources, ranging from the scientific mysticism of Emanuel Swedenborg to the novels and letters of Madame de Staël; from classical philosophy and Neoplatonism to Quakerism; from English and German Romanticism to Hindu mythology and scripture. *Nature* abounds with quotations, misquotations, and paraphrases from all these, woven into a uniquely Emersonian work.

While *Nature* began almost immediately to be influential, it did not make Emerson well-known among the general public. He first attracted wide public notice in 1837, after he had delivered a speech before the Phi Beta Kappa students graduating from Harvard College. The speech, now known as "The American Scholar," encouraged his audience not to succumb to unreflective bookishness and academic hero-worship, but to trust the genius that could be found within their own selves. His next major speech, the "Divinity School Address," was delivered at Harvard in 1838. The Harvard Divinity School was then considered a center of Unitarian theology, and Emerson's speech provoked controversy by challenging many tenets of Unitarianism and appearing to utterly undermine the authority of Christian traditions and texts. He condemned what he called "historical Christianity" for its obsession with "the personal, the positive, the ritual," and for dwelling overly on Jesus as a "*person*" and miracle-worker, rather than simply as a prophet of the divine. Many were shocked by the speech, and a public debate over what came to be known as the "miracles controversy" ensued.

Though scandalous, the event helped crystallize Emerson's status as an important and innovative American voice. The Transcendentalist movement continued to grow, and in 1840 the Club—whose members now included such New England intellectuals as Margaret Fuller, Elizabeth Peabody, Amos Bronson Alcott, and Henry David Thoreau—established a periodical called *The Dial* (1840–44), for which Emerson wrote the introduction to the first issue. In 1841, Emerson cemented his growing international renown with *Essays* (later retitled *Essays: First Series*), a volume of writings drawn largely from lectures he had previously delivered. The volume, which included the now-classic essay "Self-Reliance," was a popular as well as a critical success in both the United States and Europe.

Emerson again faced personal tragedy, however, when his son Waldo died of scarlet fever in 1842, at the age of five. Wrestling with sorrow, Emerson wrote the essay "Experience" (1844), in which he attempted to reconcile the optimistic self-assuredness of his previous writings with the apparent impotency of human effort against the "lords of life." Around this time Emerson began more seriously engaging with Eastern religion and philosophy, and especially with Hindu texts such as the *Bhagavad Gita* and the *Vishnu Purana*; their influence can be seen in his first volume of poetry, *Poems* (1846), as well as in later work.

In 1847 Emerson embarked again on a tour of Europe, this time as a famous speaker and writer, and in Scotland and England he delivered numerous lectures. These provided raw material for successful books such as *Representative Men* (1850), a collection of semi-biographical pieces on influential historical figures—all men—each of whom are posited as representatives of a particular human virtue or type (among them Plato as the "philosopher," Shakespeare as the "poet," and Swedenborg as the "mystic"). The collection was influenced by Carlyle's similarly structured *On Heroes, Hero-Worship, and The Heroic in History* (1841), which expounded what is sometimes known as the "great man theory" of history.

Emerson long defined himself as "a seeing eye and not a useful hand," and his suspicions of social institutions and of conformity held him back from associating himself with the various social and political movements of the day. Partly thanks to the influence of his wife Lidian, however, Emerson eventually came to support the abolitionist movement. He became more strongly committed to the abolitionist cause after the passing of the Fugitive Slave Law in 1850, and delivered multiple addresses against slavery throughout the 1850s. He welcomed the outbreak of the Civil War in 1861, believing it to be the crisis that would lead America to a new age. (Emerson's dedication to abolitionism, like that of many white activists of the era, should not be misconstrued as implying an unqualified egalitarianism; he continued throughout his life to hold many false ideas regarding racial hierarchy.)

Though he began to experience degenerative memory problems and his output slowed after the War, Emerson continued to lecture and write until not long before his death. He died of pneumonia-related complications in 1882, and was buried in Sleepy Hollow Cemetery, Concord. Emerson's many journals, edited by his son Edward Waldo, were published posthumously; these private writings have contributed greatly to scholarly understanding of Emerson's personal, professional, and philosophical development.

It is difficult to overstate Emerson's importance to American intellectual history—or his influence on American literature. The extraordinary degree to which he lent emotional as well as intellectual force to other leading nineteenth-century writers is suggested in a comment made by Walt Whitman, who sent Emerson a copy of his first volume of poetry, *Leaves of Grass* (1855). "I was simmering, simmering, simmering," Whitman later wrote; "Emerson brought me to a boil."

NOTE ON THE TEXTS: The selections presented here are based on the following editions and printings: *Nature* (1836); "Self-Reliance" in *Essays: First Series* (1841); "The Poet" in *Essays: Second Series* (1844); "Original Hymn [Concord Hymn]" on the broadside printed in 1837; "Each in All" on the version published in *Western Messenger* in 1839; "The Snow-Storm" on the version published in *The Dial* in January 1841; and "Brahma" on the version that appeared in the *Atlantic Monthly* in 1857.

Spelling and punctuation have been modernized in accordance with the practices of this anthology; Emerson's original capitalization has, however, for the most part been preserved.

⌘ ⌘ ⌘

from *Nature*

Nature is but an image or imitation of wisdom, the
last thing of the soul; nature being a thing which doth
only do, but not know.
PLOTINUS[1]

[1] *PLOTINUS* Roman-Egyptian philosopher (205–270 CE) whose theories of emanation postulated the existence of one supreme source that creates the possibility of all other existences; this philosophical system, which was largely derived from the earlier Greek philosopher Plato (c. 427–c. 347 BCE), was named Neoplatonism by medieval scholars. In his 1849 edition of *Nature*, Emerson replaced this epigraph with lines from his own poem, "Nature": "A subtle chain of countless rings / The next unto the farthest brings; / The eye reads omens where it goes, / And speaks all languages the rose; /

INTRODUCTION

Our age is retrospective. It builds the sepulchres of the fathers. It writes biographies, histories, and criticism. The foregoing generations beheld God and nature face to face; we, through their eyes. Why should not we also enjoy an original relation to the universe? Why should not we have a poetry and philosophy of insight and not of tradition, and a religion by revelation to us, and not the history of theirs? Embosomed for a season in nature, whose floods of life stream around and through us, and invite us by the powers

---

And, striving to be man, the worm / Mounts through all the spires of form."

they supply, to action proportioned to nature, why should we grope among the dry bones of the past, or put the living generation into masquerade out of its faded wardrobe? The sun shines today also. There is more wool and flax in the fields. There are new lands, new men, new thoughts. Let us demand our own works and laws and worship.

Undoubtedly we have no questions to ask which are unanswerable. We must trust the perfection of the creation so far, as to believe that whatever curiosity the order of things has awakened in our minds, the order of things can satisfy. Every man's condition is a solution in hieroglyphic to those inquiries he would put. He acts it as life, before he apprehends it as truth. In like manner, nature is already, in its forms and tendencies, describing its own design. Let us interrogate the great apparition, that shines so peacefully around us. Let us inquire, to what end[1] is nature?

All science has one aim, namely, to find a theory of nature. We have theories of races and of functions, but scarcely yet a remote approximation to an idea of creation. We are now so far from the road to truth, that religious teachers dispute and hate each other, and speculative men are esteemed unsound and frivolous. But to a sound judgment, the most abstract truth is the most practical. Whenever a true theory appears, it will be its own evidence. Its test is, that it will explain all phenomena. Now many are thought not only unexplained but inexplicable; as language, sleep, dreams, beasts, sex.

Philosophically considered, the universe is composed of Nature and the Soul. Strictly speaking, therefore, all that is separate from us, all which Philosophy distinguishes as the NOT ME, that is, both nature and art, all other men and my own body, must be ranked under this name, NATURE. In enumerating the values of nature and casting up their sum, I shall use the word in both senses—in its common and in its philosophical import. In inquiries so general as our present one, the inaccuracy is not material; no confusion of thought will occur. *Nature*, in the common sense, refers to essences unchanged by man; space, the air, the river, the leaf. *Art* is applied to the mixture of his will with the same things, as in a house, a canal, a statue, a picture. But his operations taken together are so insignificant,

a little chipping, baking, patching, and washing, that in an impression so grand as that of the world on the human mind, they do not vary the result.

CHAPTER 1
NATURE

To go into solitude, a man needs to retire as much from his chamber as from society. I am not solitary whilst I read and write, though nobody is with me. But if a man would be alone, let him look at the stars. The rays that come from those heavenly worlds, will separate between him and vulgar things. One might think the atmosphere was made transparent with this design, to give man, in the heavenly bodies, the perpetual presence of the sublime. Seen in the streets of cities, how great they are! If the stars should appear one night in a thousand years, how would men believe and adore; and preserve for many generations the remembrance of the city of God which had been shown! But every night come out these preachers of beauty, and light the universe with their admonishing smile.

The stars awaken a certain reverence, because though always present, they are always inaccessible; but all natural objects make a kindred impression, when the mind is open to their influence. Nature never wears a mean[2] appearance. Neither does the wisest man extort all her secret, and lose his curiosity by finding out all her perfection. Nature never became a toy to a wise spirit. The flowers, the animals, the mountains, reflected all the wisdom of his best hour, as much as they had delighted the simplicity of his childhood.

When we speak of nature in this manner, we have a distinct but most poetical sense in the mind. We mean the integrity of impression made by manifold natural objects. It is this which distinguishes the stick of timber of the wood-cutter, from the tree of the poet. The charming landscape which I saw this morning is indubitably made up of some twenty or thirty farms. Miller owns this field, Locke that, and Manning[3] the woodland beyond. But none of them owns the landscape. There is a property in the horizon which no man has but he whose eye can integrate all the parts, that is,

---

[1]   *end* Purpose.

[2]   *mean* Lowly or insignificant.

[3]   *Miller ... Manning* Common, generic surnames in Emerson's area.

the poet. This is the best part of these men's farms, yet to this their land-deeds give them no title.

To speak truly, few adult persons can see nature. Most persons do not see the sun. At least they have a very superficial seeing. The sun illuminates only the eye of the man, but shines into the eye and the heart of the child. The lover of nature is he whose inward and outward senses are still truly adjusted to each other; who has retained the spirit of infancy even into the era of manhood. His intercourse with heaven and earth becomes part of his daily food. In the presence of nature, a wild delight runs through the man, in spite of real sorrows. Nature says—he is my creature, and maugre[1] all his impertinent griefs, he shall be glad with me. Not the sun or the summer alone, but every hour and season yields its tribute of delight; for every hour and change corresponds to and authorizes a different state of the mind, from breathless noon to grimmest midnight. Nature is a setting that fits equally well a comic or a mourning piece. In good health, the air is a cordial of incredible virtue. Crossing a bare common,[2] in snow puddles, at twilight, under a clouded sky, without having in my thoughts any occurrence of special good fortune, I have enjoyed a perfect exhilaration. Almost I fear to think how glad I am. In the woods too, a man casts off his years, as the snake his slough, and at what period soever of life, is always a child. In the woods, is perpetual youth. Within these plantations of God, a decorum and sanctity reign, a perennial festival is dressed, and the guest sees not how he should tire of them in a thousand years. In the woods, we return to reason and faith. There I feel that nothing can befall me in life—no disgrace, no calamity (leaving me my eyes) which nature cannot repair. Standing on the bare ground—my head bathed by the blithe air, and uplifted into infinite space—all mean egotism vanishes. I become a transparent eyeball. I am nothing. I see all. The currents of the Universal Being circulate through me; I am part or particle of God. The name of the nearest friend sounds then foreign and accidental.[3] To be brothers, to be acquaintances, master or servant, is then a trifle and a disturbance. I am the lover of uncontained and immortal beauty. In the wilderness, I find something more dear and connate[4] than in streets or villages. In the tranquil landscape, and especially in the distant line of the horizon, man beholds somewhat[5] as beautiful as his own nature.

The greatest delight which the fields and woods minister, is the suggestion of an occult[6] relation between man and the vegetable.[7] I am not alone and unacknowledged. They nod to me and I to them. The waving of the boughs in the storm, is new to me and old. It takes me by surprise, and yet is not unknown. Its effect is like that of a higher thought or a better emotion coming over me, when I deemed I was thinking justly or doing right.

Yet it is certain that the power to produce this delight, does not reside in nature, but in man, or in a harmony of both. It is necessary to use these pleasures with great temperance. For, nature is not always tricked in holiday attire, but the same scene which yesterday breathed perfume and glittered as for the frolic of the nymphs, is overspread with melancholy today. Nature always wears the colors of the spirit. To a man laboring under calamity, the heat of his own fire hath sadness in it. Then, there is a kind of contempt of the landscape felt by him who has just lost by death a dear friend. The sky is less grand as it shuts down over less worth in the population. —1836

[NOTE: The full text of *Nature* is included in the online component of this anthology.]

---

1   *maugre*   In spite of.

2   *common*   Tract of land belonging collectively to the public.

3   *accidental*   Inessential.

4   *connate*   Inborn; corresponding deeply with one's inner being.

5   *somewhat*   Something.

6   *occult*   Mysterious; secret.

7   *vegetable*   I.e., vegetation; plants.

IN CONTEXT: ILLUSTRATIONS OF EMERSON'S *NATURE*

Artist and poet Christopher Cranch (1813–92) ardently embraced Emerson's ideas and abandoned his intended career as a Unitarian minister in favor of Transcendentalist artistic and intellectual circles. The drawing reproduced here, commonly known as "the transparent eyeball," is his best-known work. As Cranch would later write, the drawing had its origin in a series of casually drawn "comic illustrations of some of Emerson's quaint sentences"; he then expanded the project into a bound manuscript titled *Illustrations of the New Philosophy*, a collection of caricatures based on statements quoted from Emerson's writings. These drawings remained in manuscript form until they were published in the mid-twentieth century.

"I expand and live in the warm day, like corn & melons." From Christopher Cranch, *Illustrations of the New Philosophy*, manuscript c. 1837–39 (MS Am 1506, Houghton Library, Harvard University).

"Few grown-up persons see the Sun." From Christopher Cranch, *Illustrations of the New Philosophy* (MS Am 1506, Houghton Library, Harvard University).

"Standing on the bare ground,—my head bathed by the blithe air, & uplifted into infinite space,—all mean egotism vanishes. I become a Transparent Eyeball." From Christopher Cranch, *Illustrations of the New Philosophy* (MS Am 1506, Houghton Library, Harvard University).

Original Hymn [Concord Hymn]¹

By the rude bridge that arched the flood,
　　Their flag to April's breeze unfurled,
Here, once, the embattled farmers stood
　　And fired the shot heard round the world.

5　The foe long since, in silence slept;
　　Alike, the conqueror silent sleeps;
And Time the ruined bridge has swept
　　Down the dark stream which seaward creeps.

On this green bank, by this soft stream,
10　　We place with joy a votive stone;
That memory may their deed redeem,
　　When, like our sires, our sons are gone.

O Thou who made those heroes dare²
　　To die, or leave their children free,
15　Bid Time and Nature gently spare
　　The shaft we raise to them and Thee.
　　　　　—1837

Each in All

Little thinks, in the field, yon red-cloaked
　　clown°   *peasant*
Of thee from the hill-top looking down;
And the heifer° that lows in the upland farm   *cow*
Far heard, lows not thine ear to charm;
The sexton³ tolling his bell at noon
5　Dreams not that great Napoleon

Stops his horse, and lists° with delight,   *listens*
Whilst his files sweep round yon Alpine height;
Nor knowest thou what argument
10　Thy life to thy neighbor's creed has lent.
All are needed by each one;
Nothing is fair or good alone.

I thought the sparrow's note from heaven,
Singing at dawn on the alder bough;
15　I brought him home in his nest at even°—   *evening*
He sings the song, but it pleases not now,
For I did not bring home the river and sky,
He sang to my ear, these sang to my eye.
The delicate shells lay on the shore—
20　The bubbles of the latest wave
Fresh pearls to their enamel gave,
And the bellowing of the savage sea
Greeted their safe escape to me.
I wiped away the weeds and foam,
25　I fetched my sea-born treasures home,
But the poor, unsightly, noisome⁴ things
Had left their beauty on the shore,
With the sun, and the sand, and the wild uproar.
Nor rose, nor stream, nor bird is fair,
30　Their concord is beyond compare.

The lover watched his graceful maid
As 'mid the virgin train she strayed,
Nor knew her beauty's best attire
Was woven still by that snow-white quire.°   *choir*
35　At last, she came to his hermitage,
Like the bird from the woodlands to the cage—
The gay enchantment was undone—
A gentle wife, but fairy none.
Then I said, "I covet truth;
40　Beauty is unripe childhood's cheat;
I leave it behind with the games of youth."
—As I spoke, beneath my feet
The ground-pine curled its pretty wreath,
Running over the hair-cap burs;
45　I inhaled the violet's breath;
Around me stood the oaks and firs;
Pine-cones and acorns lay on the ground.
Over me soared the eternal sky,
Full of light and of deity;

---

¹　Emerson wrote this poem for the 19 April 1837 unveiling in Concord, Massachusetts, of the Obelisk, a monument commemorating the Battle of Concord (19 April 1775). The Battles of Lexington and Concord, begun on the same day, were the first battles of the American Revolution.

　　The 1837 broadside printing of this poem, which came to be known as "Concord Hymn," was first entitled "Original Hymn"; it was sung to the popular tune of "Old Hundredth."

²　*O Thou … dare*   Later editions of this line read "Spirit, that made those heroes dare."

³　*sexton*   Church officer who oversees material affairs, such as ringing bells and digging graves.

---

⁴　*noisome*   Disagreeable; foul-smelling.

50 Again I saw—again I heard,
    The rolling river, the morning bird:
    Beauty through my senses stole—
    I yielded myself to the perfect Whole.
    —1839

The Snow-Storm

Announced by all the trumpets of the sky
Arrives the snow, and driving o'er the fields,
Seems nowhere to alight: the whited air
Hides hills and woods, the river, and the heaven,
5   And veils the farm-house at the garden's end.
    The sled and traveller stopped, the courier's feet
    Delayed, all friends shut out, the housemates sit
    Around the radiant fireplace, enclosed
    In a tumultuous privacy of storm.

10   Come see the north-wind's masonry.
    Out of an unseen quarry evermore
    Furnished with tile, the fierce artificer
    Curves his white bastions with projected roof
    Round every windward stake, or tree, or door.
15 Speeding, the myriad-handed, his wild work
    So fanciful, so savage, nought cares he
    For number or proportion. Mockingly
    On coop or kennel he hands Parian[1] wreaths;
    A swan-like form invests the hidden thorn;
20 Fills up the farmer's lane from wall to wall,
    Maugre° the farmer's sighs, and at the gate   *despite*
    A tapering turret overtops the work.
    And when his hours are numbered, and the world
    Is all his own, retiring, as he were not,
25 Leaves, when the sun appears, astonished Art
    To mimic in slow structures, stone by stone,
    Built in an age, the mad wind's night-work,
    The frolic architecture of the snow.
    —1841

---

1   *Parian*   Resembling the fine, white marble of the Greek island of Paros.

Self-Reliance

Ne te quaesiveris extra.[2]

Man is his own star, and the soul that can
Render an honest and a perfect man,
Command all light, all influence, all fate,
Nothing to him falls early or too late.
Our acts our angels are, or good or ill,
Our fatal shadows that walk by us still.
    Epilogue to Beaumont and Fletcher's *Honest Man's
    Fortune.*[3]

Cast the bantling° on the rocks,   *infant*
Suckle him with the she-wolf's teat:
Wintered with the hawk and fox,
Power and speed be hands and feet.[4]

I read the other day some verses written by an eminent painter[5] which were original and not conventional. Always the soul hears an admonition in such lines, let the subject be what it may. The sentiment they instill is of more value than any thought they may contain. To believe your own thought, to believe that what is true for you in your private heart, is true for all men—that is genius. Speak your latent conviction and it shall be the universal sense; for always the inmost becomes the outmost—and our first thought is rendered back to us by the trumpets of the Last Judgment. Familiar as the voice of the mind is to each, the highest merit we ascribe to Moses, Plato, and Milton,[6] is that they set at naught books and traditions, and spoke not what men but what they thought. A man should learn to detect and watch that gleam of light which flashes across his mind from within, more than the lustre of the

---

2   *Ne te quaesiveris extra*   Latin: Do not search outside yourself. See *Satire* 1.7 by Roman poet Persius (34–62 CE).

3   *Epilogue to … Man's Fortune*   A slight misattribution; *The Honest Man's Fortune* (written c. 1613) was most likely written by John Fletcher in collaboration with Nathan Field and Philip Massinger.

4   *Cast the … and feet*   Stanza written by Emerson.

5   *eminent painter*   Likely Washington Allston (1779–1843), American painter and poet.

6   *Moses*   Old Testament prophet; *Plato*   Greek philosopher (c. 427–c. 347 BCE); *Milton*   English poet John Milton (1608–74).

firmament[1] of bards and sages. Yet he dismisses without notice his thought, because it is his. In every work of genius we recognize our own rejected thoughts: they come back to us with a certain alienated majesty. Great works of art have no more affecting lesson for us than this. They teach us to abide by our spontaneous impression with good humored inflexibility then most when the whole cry of voices is on the other side. Else, tomorrow a stranger will say with masterly good sense precisely what we have thought and felt all the time, and we shall be forced to take with shame our own opinion from another.

There is a time in every man's education when he arrives at the conviction that envy is ignorance; that imitation is suicide; that he must take himself for better, for worse, as his portion; that though the wide universe is full of good, no kernel of nourishing corn can come to him but through his toil bestowed on that plot of ground which is given to him to till. The power which resides in him is new in nature, and none but he knows what that is which he can do, nor does he know until he has tried. Not for nothing one face, one character, one fact makes much impression on him, and another none. It is not without pre-established harmony, this sculpture in the memory. The eye was placed where one ray should fall, that it might testify of that particular ray. We but half express ourselves, and are ashamed of that divine idea which each of us represents. It may be safely trusted as proportionate and of good issues, so it be faithfully imparted, but God will not have his work made manifest by cowards. It needs a divine man to exhibit anything divine. A man is relieved and gay when he has put his heart into his work and done his best; but what he has said or done otherwise shall give him no peace. It is a deliverance which does not deliver. In the attempt his genius deserts him; no muse befriends; no invention, no hope.

Trust thyself:[2] every heart vibrates to that iron string. Accept the place the divine Providence has found for you; the society of your contemporaries, the connection of events. Great men have always done so and confided themselves childlike to the genius of their age, betraying their perception that the Eternal was stirring at their heart, working through their hands, predominating in all their being. And we are now men, and must accept in the highest mind the same transcendent destiny; and not pinched in a corner, not cowards fleeing before a revolution, but redeemers and benefactors, pious aspirants to be noble clay, plastic[3] under the Almighty effort, let us advance and advance on Chaos and the Dark.

What pretty oracles nature yields us on this text in the face and behavior of children, babes and even brutes. That divided and rebel mind, that distrust of a sentiment because our arithmetic has computed the strength and means opposed to our purpose, these have not. Their mind being whole, their eye is as yet unconquered, and when we look in their faces, we are disconcerted. Infancy conforms to nobody: all conform to it, so that one babe commonly makes four or five out of the adults who prattle and play to it. So God has armed youth and puberty and manhood no less with its own piquancy and charm, and made it enviable and gracious and its claims not to be put by, if it will stand by itself. Do not think the youth has no force because he cannot speak to you and me. Hark![4] in the next room, who spoke so clear and emphatic? Good Heaven! it is he! it is that very lump of bashfulness and phlegm which for weeks has done nothing but eat when you were by, that now rolls out these words like bell-strokes. It seems he knows how to speak to his contemporaries. Bashful or bold, then, he will know how to make us seniors very unnecessary.

The nonchalance of boys who are sure of a dinner, and would disdain as much as a lord to do or say aught to conciliate one, is the healthy attitude of human nature. How is a boy the master of society; independent, irresponsible, looking out from his corner on such people and facts as pass by, he tries and sentences them on their merits, in the swift summary way of boys, as good, bad, interesting, silly, eloquent, troublesome. He cumbers himself never about consequences, about interests: he gives an independent, genuine verdict. You must court him: he does not court you. But the man is, as it were, clapped into jail by his consciousness. As soon as he has once acted or spoken

---

1   *firmament*   Sky; the heavens.

2   *Trust thyself*   Variation of the famous ancient Greek maxim "know thyself."

3   *plastic*   Flexible; able to be molded.

4   *Hark!*   Listen!

with éclat,[1] he is a committed person, watched by the sympathy or the hatred of hundreds whose affections must now enter into his account. There is no Lethe[2] for this. Ah, that he could pass again into his neutral, godlike independence! Who can thus lose all pledge, and having observed, observe again from the same unaffected, unbiased, unbribable, unaffrighted innocence, must always be formidable, must always engage the poet's and the man's regards. Of such an immortal youth the force would be felt. He would utter opinions on all passing affairs, which being seen to be not private but necessary, would sink like darts into the ear of men, and put them in fear.

These are the voices which we hear in solitude, but they grow faint and inaudible as we enter into the world. Society everywhere is in conspiracy against the manhood of every one of its members. Society is a joint-stock company[3] in which the members agree, for the better securing of his bread to each shareholder, to surrender the liberty and culture of the eater. The virtue in most request is conformity. Self-reliance is its aversion. It loves not realities and creators, but names and customs.

Whoso would be a man must be a nonconformist. He who would gather immortal palms[4] must not be hindered by the name of goodness, but must explore if it be goodness. Nothing is at last sacred but the integrity of our own mind. Absolve you to yourself, and you shall have the suffrage[5] of the world. I remember an answer which when quite young I was prompted to make to a valued adviser who was wont[6] to importune me with the dear old doctrines of the church. On my saying, What have I to do with the sacredness of traditions, if I live wholly from within? my friend suggested—"But these impulses may be from below, not from above." I replied, "They do not seem to me to be such; but if I am the devil's child, I will live then from the devil." No law can be sacred to me but that of my nature. Good and bad are but names very readily transferable to that or this; the only right is what is after my constitution, the only wrong what is against it. A man is to carry himself in the presence of all opposition as if everything were titular[7] and ephemeral but he. I am ashamed to think how easily we capitulate to badges and names, to large societies and dead institutions. Every decent and well-spoken individual affects and sways me more than is right. I ought to go upright and vital, and speak the rude[8] truth in all ways. If malice and vanity wear the coat of philanthropy, shall that pass? If an angry bigot assumes this bountiful cause of Abolition, and comes to me with his last news from Barbados,[9] why should I not say to him, "Go love thy infant; love thy wood-chopper: be good-natured and modest: have that grace; and never varnish your hard, uncharitable ambition with this incredible tenderness for black folk a thousand miles off. Thy love afar is spite at home." Rough and graceless would be such greeting, but truth is handsomer than the affectation of love. Your goodness must have some edge to it—else it is none. The doctrine of hatred must be preached as the counteraction of the doctrine of love when that pules[10] and whines. I shun father and mother and wife and brother, when my genius calls me. I would write on the lintels of the door-post, *Whim*.[11] I hope it is somewhat better than whim at last, but we cannot spend the day in explanation. Expect me not to show cause why I seek or why I exclude company. Then, again, do not tell me, as a good man did today, of my obligation to put all poor men in good situations. Are they *my* poor?

---

1 *éclat* Brilliance.

2 *Lethe* In Classical mythology, river in the underworld that causes forgetfulness, so that the dead may forget their earthly existence.

3 *joint-stock company* Company in which capital is divided into a common, shared fund.

4 *palms* I.e., honors.

5 *suffrage* Support; prayers.

6 *was wont* Had the tendency.

7 *titular* I.e., possessing a seemingly important title but having no real importance.

8 *rude* Unembellished.

9 *Barbados* Slavery had been abolished in most of the British Empire with the Slavery Abolition Act of 1833. The Act's passage was in large part motivated by a series of rebellions held by enslaved people in British territories, including one in Barbados in 1816. Before Emerson became a committed abolitionist in the years leading up to the Civil War, he expressed ambivalence about the matter, as can be seen here.

10 *pules* Cries or whimpers.

11 *I would … Whim* See Exodus 12, in which God instructs the Israelites to mark their lintels (or doorframes) with blood to identify their homes so that he can spare them when he punishes the Egyptians with a plague.

I tell thee, thou foolish philanthropist, that I grudge the dollar, the dime, the cent I give to such men as do not belong to me and to whom I do not belong. There is a class of persons to whom by all spiritual affinity I am bought and sold; for them I will go to prison, if need be; but your miscellaneous popular charities; the education at college of fools; the building of meeting-houses to the vain end to which many now stand; alms to sots; and the thousandfold Relief Societies—though I confess with shame I sometimes succumb and give the dollar, it is a wicked dollar which by-and-by I shall have the manhood to withhold.

Virtues are in the popular estimate rather the exception than the rule. There is the man *and* his virtues. Men do what is called a good action, as some piece of courage or charity, much as they would pay a fine in expiation of daily non-appearance on parade.[1] Their works are done as an apology or extenuation of their living in the world—as invalids and the insane pay a high board. Their virtues are penances. I do not wish to expiate, but to live. My life is not an apology, but a life. It is for itself and not for a spectacle. I much prefer that it should be of a lower strain, so it be genuine and equal, than that it should be glittering and unsteady. I wish it to be sound and sweet, and not to need diet and bleeding.[2] My life should be unique; it should be an alms, a battle, a conquest, a medicine. I ask primary evidence that you are a man, and refuse this appeal from the man to his actions. I know that for myself it makes no difference whether I do or forbear those actions which are reckoned excellent. I cannot consent to pay for a privilege where I have intrinsic right. Few and mean[3] as my gifts may be, I actually am, and do not need for my own assurance or the assurance of my fellows any secondary testimony.

What I must do, is all that concerns me, not what the people think. This rule, equally arduous in actual and in intellectual life, may serve for the whole distinction between greatness and meanness. It is the harder, because you will always find those who think they know what is your duty better than you know it. It is

easy in the world to live after the world's opinion; it is easy in solitude to live after our own; but the great man is he who in the midst of the crowd keeps with perfect sweetness the independence of solitude.

The objection to conforming to usages that have become dead to you is that it scatters your force. It loses your time and blurs the impression of your character. If you maintain a dead church, contribute to a dead Bible Society, vote with a great party either for the Government or against it, spread your table like base housekeepers—under all these screens, I have difficulty to detect the precise man you are. And, of course, so much force is withdrawn from your proper life. But do your thing, and I shall know you. Do your work, and you shall reinforce yourself. A man must consider what a blindman's-buff is this game of conformity. If I know your sect, I anticipate your argument. I hear a preacher announce for his text and topic the expediency of one of the institutions of his church. Do I not know beforehand that not possibly can he say a new and spontaneous word? Do I not know that with all this ostentation of examining the grounds of the institution, he will do no such thing? Do I not know that he is pledged to himself not to look but at one side; the permitted side, not as a man, but as a parish minister? He is a retained attorney, and these airs of the bench are the emptiest affectation. Well, most men have bound their eyes with one or another handkerchief, and attached themselves to some one of these communities of opinion. This conformity makes them not false in a few particulars, authors of a few lies, but false in all particulars. Their every truth is not quite true. Their two is not the real two, their four not the real four: so that every word they say chagrins us, and we know not where to begin to set them right. Meantime nature is not slow to equip us in the prison-uniform of the party to which we adhere. We come to wear one cut of face and figure, and acquire by degrees the gentlest asinine expression. There is a mortifying experience in particular which does not fail to wreak itself also in the general history; I mean, "the foolish face of praise,"[4] the forced smile which we put on in company where we do not feel at ease in answer to conversation which does not interest us. The muscles, not spontaneously moved, but

---

[1]   *daily non-appearance on parade*   Failure of military personnel to appear in uniform for daily drills or inspection.

[2]   *bleeding*   Archaic medical treatment in which a person's blood is extracted.

[3]   *mean*   Lowly.

[4]   *the foolish face of praise*   See "Epistle to Dr. Arbuthnot" (1735) by English satirical poet Alexander Pope.

moved by a low usurping willfulness, grow tight about the outline of the face and make the most disagreeable sensation, a sensation of rebuke and warning which no brave young man will suffer twice.

For non-conformity the world whips you with its displeasure. And therefore a man must know how to estimate a sour face. The bystanders look askance on him in the public street or in the friend's parlor. If this aversation[1] had its origin in contempt and resistance like his own, he might well go home with a sad countenance; but the sour faces of the multitude, like their sweet faces, have no deep cause, disguise no god, but are put on and off as the wind blows, and a newspaper directs. Yet is the discontent of the multitude more formidable than that of the senate and the college. It is easy enough for a firm man who knows the world to brook the rage of the cultivated classes. Their rage is decorous and prudent, for they are timid as being very vulnerable themselves. But when to their feminine rage the indignation of the people is added, when the ignorant and the poor are aroused, when the unintelligent brute force that lies at the bottom of society is made to growl and mow,[2] it needs the habit[3] of magnanimity and religion to treat it godlike as a trifle of no concernment.

The other terror that scares us from self-trust is our consistency; a reverence for our past act or word, because the eyes of others have no other data for computing our orbit than our past acts, and we are loath to disappoint them.

But why should you keep your head over your shoulder? Why drag about this monstrous corpse of your memory, lest you contradict somewhat you have stated in this or that public place? Suppose you should contradict yourself; what then? It seems to be a rule of wisdom never to rely on your memory alone, scarcely even in acts of pure memory, but to bring the past for judgment into the thousand-eyed present, and live ever in a new day. Trust your emotion. In your metaphysics you have denied personality to the Deity: yet when the devout motions of the soul come, yield to them heart and life, though they should clothe God with shape and color. Leave your theory as Joseph his coat in the hand of the harlot,[4] and flee.

A foolish consistency is the hobgoblin of little minds, adored by little statesmen and philosophers and divines. With consistency a great soul has simply nothing to do. He may as well concern himself with his shadow on the wall. Out upon your guarded lips! Sew them up with packthread, do. Else, if you would be a man, speak what you think today in words as hard as cannon balls, and tomorrow speak what tomorrow thinks in hard words again, though it contradict everything you said today. Ah, then, exclaim the aged ladies, you shall be sure to be misunderstood. Misunderstood! It is a right fool's word. Is it so bad then to be misunderstood? Pythagoras was misunderstood, and Socrates, and Jesus, and Luther, and Copernicus, and Galileo, and Newton,[5] and every pure and wise spirit that ever took flesh. To be great is to be misunderstood.

I suppose no man can violate his nature. All the sallies[6] of his will are rounded in by the law of his being as the inequalities[7] of Andes and Himmaleh[8] are insignificant in the curve of the sphere. Nor does it matter how you gauge and try him. A character is like

---

1   *aversation*   Rejection.

2   *mow*   Grimace.

3   *habit*   Clothing.

4   *as Joseph ... the harlot*   Joseph, who has been sold into slavery by his jealous brothers, flees from his master's wife when she tries to seduce him. See Genesis 39.12: "And she caught him by his garment, saying, Lie with me: and he left his garment in her hand, and fled, and got him out."

5   *Pythagoras*   Ancient Greek philosopher, mathematician, and mystic (c. 570–c. 495 BCE); *Socrates*   Ancient Greek philosopher and teacher (c. 470–399 BCE) who was famously executed by the Athenian authorities for his supposed crimes of impiety and of corrupting the minds of his students; *Luther*   Martin Luther (1483–1546), German theologian and foremost leader of the Protestant Reformation who in 1520 was excommunicated by the Pope for his controversial writings; *Copernicus*   Nicolaus Copernicus (1473–1543), Polish-Prussian astronomer who posited that the Sun, not the Earth, is at the center of the solar system; *Galileo*   Galileo Galilei (1564–1642), Italian astronomer and physicist who was considered a heretic for his championing of the Copernican model of the Solar System; *Newton*   Sir Isaac Newton (1642–1727), English physicist who formulated a number of revolutionary theories about the physical world, including the law of gravity.

6   *sallies*   Ventures forth (the term especially refers to a military force attacking from a position of retreat).

7   *inequalities*   I.e., peaks and valleys.

8   *Andes and Himmaleh*   Large mountain ranges in South America and Asia.

an acrostic or Alexandrian stanza[1]—read it forward, backward, or across, it still spells the same thing. In this pleasing contrite wood-life which God allows me, let me record day by day my honest thought without prospect or retrospect, and, I cannot doubt, it will be found symmetrical, though I mean it not, and see it not. My book should smell of pines and resound with the hum of insects. The swallow over my window should interweave that thread or straw he carries in his bill into my web also. We pass for what we are. Character teaches above our wills. Men imagine that they communicate their virtue or vice only by overt actions and do not see that virtue or vice emit a breath every moment.

Fear never but you shall be consistent in whatever variety of actions, so they be each honest and natural in their hour. For of one will, the actions will be harmonious, however unlike they seem. These varieties are lost sight of at a little distance, at a little height of thought. One tendency unites them all. The voyage of the best ship is a zigzag line of a hundred tacks. This is only microscopic criticism. See the line from a sufficient distance, and it straightens itself to the average tendency. Your genuine action will explain itself and will explain your other genuine actions. Your conformity explains nothing. Act singly, and what you have already done singly, will justify you now. Greatness always appeals to the future. If I can be great enough now to do right and scorn eyes, I must have done so much right before, as to defend me now. Be it how it will, do right now. Always scorn appearances, and you always may. The force of character is cumulative. All the foregone days of virtue work their health into this. What makes the majesty of the heroes of the senate and the field, which so fills the imagination? The consciousness of a train of great days and victories behind. There they all stand and shed an united light on the advancing actor. He is attended as by a visible escort of angels to every man's eye. That is it which throws thunder into Chatham's[2] voice, and dignity into Washington's[3] port, and

America into Adams's[4] eye. Honor is venerable to us because it is no ephemeris.[5] It is always ancient virtue. We worship it today, because it is not of today. We love it and pay it homage, because it is not a trap for our love and homage, but is self-dependent, self-derived, and therefore of an old immaculate pedigree, even if shown in a young person.

I hope in these days we have heard the last of conformity and consistency. Let the words be gazetted[6] and ridiculous henceforward. Instead of the gong for dinner, let us hear a whistle from the Spartan fife.[7] Let us bow and apologize never more. A great man is coming to eat at my house. I do not wish to please him: I wish that he should wish to please me. I will stand here for humanity, and though I would make it kind, I would make it true. Let us affront and reprimand the smooth mediocrity and squalid contentment of the times, and hurl in the face of custom, and trade, and office, the fact which is the upshot of all history, that there is a great responsible Thinker and Actor moving wherever moves a man; that a true man belongs to no other time or place, but is the centre of things. Where he is, there is nature. He measures you, and all men, and all events. You are constrained to accept his standard. Ordinarily everybody in society reminds us of somewhat else or of some other person. Character, reality, reminds you of nothing else. It takes place of the whole creation. The man must be so much that he must make all circumstances indifferent—put all means into the shade. This all great men are and do. Every true man is a cause, a country, and an age; requires infinite spaces and numbers and time fully to accomplish his thought—and posterity seem to follow his steps as a procession. A man Caesar is born, and for ages after, we have a Roman Empire. Christ is born, and millions of minds so grow and cleave to his genius, that he is confounded with virtue and the possible of man. An institution is the lengthened shadow of one man; as, the Reformation, of Luther; Quakerism, of

[1] *Alexandrian stanza* Here, a palindrome, a word or line that reads the same forwards or backwards; usually, an "Alexandrian" is a poetic line with twelve syllables.

[2] *Chatham* William Pitt, first Earl of Chatham (1708–78), British prime minister known for his oratorical skills.

[3] *Washington* George Washington (1732–99).

[4] *Adams* Probably John Adams (1735–1826), second president of the United States and one of the nation's founders.

[5] *ephemeris* Ephemeral thing.

[6] *gazetted* Announced in a newspaper.

[7] *Spartan fife* Military flute of the Spartans, an ancient Greek people known for their emphasis on strength and military prowess.

Fox; Methodism, of Wesley; Abolition, of Clarkson.[1] Scipio,[2] Milton called "the height of Rome";[3] and all history resolves itself very easily into the biography of a few stout and earnest persons.

Let a man then know his worth, and keep things under his feet. Let him not peep or steal, or skulk up and down with the air of a charity-boy, a bastard, or an interloper, in the world which exists for him. But the man in the street finding no worth in himself which corresponds to the force which built a tower or sculptured a marble god, feels poor when he looks on these. To him a palace, a statue, a costly book have an alien and forbidding air, much like a gay equipage,[4] and seem to say like that, "Who are you, sir?" Yet they all are his, suitors for his notice, petitioners to his faculties that they will come out and take possession. The picture waits for my verdict: it is not to command me, but I am to settle its claims to praise. That popular fable of the sot who was picked up dead drunk in the street, carried to the duke's house, washed and dressed and laid in the duke's bed, and, on his waking, treated with all obsequious ceremony like the duke, and assured that he had been insane,[5] owes its popularity to the fact that it symbolizes so well the state of man, who is in the world a sort of sot, but now and then wakes up, exercises his reason, and finds himself a true prince.

Our reading is mendicant[6] and sycophantic. In history, our imagination makes fools of us, plays us false. Kingdom and lordship, power and estate are a gaudier vocabulary than private John and Edward in a small house and common day's work: but the things of life are the same to both: the sum total of both is the same. Why all this deference to Alfred, and Scanderbeg, and Gustavus?[7] Suppose they were virtuous: did they wear out virtue? As great a stake depends on your private act today, as followed their public and renowned steps. When private men shall act with vast views, the lustre will be transferred from the actions of kings to those of gentlemen.

The world has indeed been instructed by its kings, who have so magnetized the eyes of nations. It has been taught by this colossal symbol the mutual reverence that is due from man to man. The joyful loyalty with which men have everywhere suffered the king, the noble, or the great proprietor to walk among them by a law of his own, make his own scale of men and things, and reverse theirs, pay for benefits not with money but with honor, and represent the Law in his person, was the hieroglyphic by which they obscurely signified their consciousness of their own right and comeliness, the right of every man.

The magnetism which all original action exerts is explained when we inquire the reason of self-trust. Who is the Trustee? What is the aboriginal[8] Self on which a universal reliance may be grounded? What is the nature and power of that science-baffling star, without parallax,[9] without calculable elements, which shoots a ray of beauty even into trivial and impure actions, if the least mark of independence appear? The inquiry leads us to that source, at once the essence of genius, the essence of virtue, and the essence of life, which we call Spontaneity or Instinct. We denote this primary wisdom as Intuition, whilst all later teachings are tuitions. In that deep force, the last fact behind which analysis cannot go, all things find their common origin. For the sense of being which in calm hours rises, we know not how, in the soul, is not diverse from things, from space, from light, from time, from man, but one with them, and proceedeth obviously from the same source whence their life and being also proceedeth. We first share the life by which

---

[1] *Fox* George Fox (1624–91), founder of the Religious Society of Friends, more commonly known as the Quakers; *Wesley* John Wesley (1703–91), founder of Methodism; *Clarkson* Thomas Clarkson (1760–1846), prominent English abolitionist.

[2] *Scipio* Publius Cornelius Scipio Africanus (236–183 BCE), Roman general who conquered Spain and Carthage and defeated Hannibal in the Punic Wars.

[3] *the height of Rome* See *Paradise Lost* 9.510.

[4] *equipage* Carriage and horses, with attendants.

[5] *That popular … been insane* See Shakespeare's *The Taming of the Shrew*, "Induction."

[6] *mendicant* Like a beggar.

[7] *Alfred* King Alfred the Great of England (849–99); *Scanderbeg* Albanian military commander (1405–68) who rebelled against the Turkish occupation of Albania; *Gustavus* King Gustavus Adolphus of Sweden (1594–1632).

[8] *aboriginal* Inherent.

[9] *parallax* Change in an object's apparent position caused by an actual change in the position from which it is being observed, such as the apparent movement of the stars caused by the movement of the Earth.

things exist, and afterwards see them as appearances in nature, and forget that we have shared their cause. Here is the fountain of action and the fountain of thought. Here are the lungs of that inspiration which giveth man wisdom, of that inspiration of man which cannot be denied without impiety and atheism. We lie in the lap of immense intelligence, which makes us organs of its activity and receivers of its truth. When we discern justice, when we discern truth, we do nothing of ourselves, but allow a passage to its beams. If we ask whence this comes, if we seek to pry into the soul that causes—all metaphysics, all philosophy is at fault. Its presence or its absence is all we can affirm. Every man discerns between the voluntary acts of his mind, and his involuntary perceptions. And to his involuntary perceptions, he knows a perfect respect is due. He may err in the expression of them, but he knows that these things are so, like day and night, not to be disputed. All my willful actions and acquisitions are but roving—the most trivial reverie, the faintest native emotion, are domestic and divine. Thoughtless people contradict as readily the statement of perceptions as of opinions, or rather much more readily; for they do not distinguish between perception and notion. They fancy that I choose to see this or that thing. But perception is not whimsical, but fatal.[1] If I see a trait, my children will see it after me, and in course of time, all mankind—although it may chance that no one has seen it before me. For my perception of it is as much a fact as the sun.

The relations of the soul to the divine spirit are so pure that it is profane to seek to interpose helps. It must be that when God speaketh, he should communicate not one thing, but all things; should fill the world with his voice; should scatter forth light, nature, time, souls, from the centre of the present thought; and new date and new create the whole. Whenever a mind is simple, and receives a divine wisdom, old things pass away—means, teachers, texts, temples fall; it lives now and absorbs past and future into the present hour. All things are made sacred by relation to it—one as much as another. All things are dissolved to their centre by their cause, and in the universal miracle petty and particular miracles disappear. This is and must be. If, therefore, a man claims to know and speak of God,

and carries you backward to the phraseology of some old mouldered nation in another country, in another world, believe him not. Is the acorn better than the oak which is its fullness and completion? Is the parent better than the child into whom he has cast his ripened being? Whence then this worship of the past? The centuries are conspirators against the sanity and majesty of the soul. Time and space are but physiological colors which the eye maketh, but the soul is light; where it is, is day; where it was, is night; and history is an impertinence and an injury, if it be anything more than a cheerful apologue[2] or parable of my being and becoming.

Man is timid and apologetic. He is no longer upright. He dares not say "I think," "I am," but quotes some saint or sage. He is ashamed before the blade of grass or the blowing rose. These roses under my window make no reference to former roses or to better ones; they are for what they are; they exist with God today. There is no time to them. There is simply the rose; it is perfect in every moment of its existence. Before a leaf-bud has burst, its whole life acts; in the full-blown flower, there is no more; in the leafless root, there is no less. Its nature is satisfied, and it satisfies nature, in all moments alike. There is no time to it. But man postpones or remembers; he does not live in the present, but with reverted eye laments the past, or, heedless of the riches that surround him, stands on tiptoe to foresee the future. He cannot be happy and strong until he too lives with nature in the present, above time.

This should be plain enough. Yet see what strong intellects dare not yet hear God himself, unless he speak the phraseology of I know not what David, or Jeremiah, or Paul.[3] We shall not always set so great a price on a few texts, on a few lives. We are like children who repeat by rote the sentences of grandames and tutors, and, as they grow older, of the men of talents and character they chance to see, painfully recollecting the exact words they spoke; afterwards, when they come into the point of view which those had who uttered these sayings, they understand them, and are willing to let the words go; for, at any time, they can

---

[1]   *fatal* I.e., determined by fate.

[2]   *apologue* Allegory.

[3]   *David, or Jeremiah, or Paul* Biblical King of Israel, biblical prophet, and one of Jesus' apostles, all of whom have been credited with the authorship of portions of the Bible.

use words as good, when occasion comes. So was it with us, so will it be, if we proceed. If we live truly, we shall see truly. It is as easy for the strong man to be strong, as it is for the weak to be weak. When we have new perception, we shall gladly disburden the memory of its hoarded treasures as old rubbish. When a man lives with God, his voice shall be as sweet as the murmur of the brook and the rustle of the corn.

And now at last the highest truth on this subject remains unsaid; probably, cannot be said; for all that we say is the far off remembering of the intuition. That thought, by what I can now nearest approach to say it, is this. When good is near you, when you have life in yourself, it is not by any known or appointed way; you shall not discern the footprints of any other; you shall not see the face of man; you shall not hear any name; the way, the thought, the good shall be wholly strange and new. It shall exclude all other being. You take the way from man not to man. All persons that ever existed are its fugitive ministers. There shall be no fear in it. Fear and hope are alike beneath it. It asks nothing. There is somewhat low even in hope. We are then in vision. There is nothing that can be called gratitude nor properly joy. The soul is raised over passion. It seeth identity and eternal causation. It is a perceiving that Truth and Right are. Hence it becomes a Tranquillity out of the knowing that all things go well. Vast spaces of nature; the Atlantic Ocean, the South Sea; vast intervals of time, years, centuries, are of no account. This which I think and feel, underlay that former state of life and circumstances, as it does underlie my present, and will always all circumstance, and what is called life, and what is called death.

Life only avails, not the having lived. Power ceases in the instant of repose; it resides in the moment of transition from a past to a new state; in the shooting of the gulf; in the darting to an aim. This one fact the world hates, that the soul *becomes*; for that forever degrades the past; turns all riches to poverty; all reputation to shame; confounds the saint with the rogue; shoves Jesus and Judas[1] equally aside. Why then do we prate of self-reliance? Inasmuch as the soul is present, there will be power not confident but agent. To talk of reliance is a poor external way of speaking. Speak rather of that which relies, because it works and is. Who has more soul than I, masters me, though he should not raise his finger. Round him I must revolve by the gravitation of spirits; who has less, I rule with like facility. We fancy it rhetoric when we speak of eminent virtue. We do not yet see that virtue is Height, and that a man or a company of men plastic and permeable to principles, by the law of nature must overpower and ride all cities, nations, kings, rich men, poets, who are not.

This is the ultimate fact which we so quickly reach on this as on every topic, the resolution of all into the ever blessed One. Virtue is the governor, the creator, the reality. All things real are so by so much of virtue as they contain. Hardship, husbandry, hunting, whaling, war, eloquence, personal weight, are somewhat, and engage my respect as examples of the soul's presence and impure action. I see the same law working in nature for conservation and growth. The poise of a planet, the bended tree recovering itself from the strong wind, the vital resources of every vegetable and animal, are also demonstrations of the self-sufficing, and therefore self-relying soul. All history from its highest to its trivial passages is the various record of this power.

Thus all concentrates; let us not rove; let us sit at home with the cause. Let us stun and astonish the intruding rabble of men and books and institutions by a simple declaration of the divine fact. Bid them take the shoes from off their feet, for God is here within.[2] Let our simplicity judge them, and our docility to our own law demonstrate the poverty of nature and fortune beside our native riches.

But now we are a mob. Man does not stand in awe of man, nor is the soul admonished to stay at home, to put itself in communication with the internal ocean, but it goes abroad to beg a cup of water of the urns of men. We must go alone. Isolation must precede true society. I like the silent church before the service begins, better than any preaching. How far off, how cool, how chaste the persons look, begirt[3] each one with a precinct or sanctuary. So let us always sit. Why should we assume the faults of our friend, or wife, or father, or child, because they sit around our hearth, or are said to have the same blood? All men have my blood, and I have all

---

[1] *Judas* The apostle who is said to have betrayed Jesus to the authorities.

[2] *Bid them … here within* See Exodus 3.5: "put off thy shoes from off thy feet, for the place whereon thou standest is holy ground."

[3] *begirt* Surround.

men's. Not for that will I adopt their petulance or folly, even to the extent of being ashamed of it. But your isolation must not be mechanical, but spiritual, that is, must be elevation. At times the whole world seems to be in conspiracy to importune you with emphatic trifles. Friend, client, child, sickness, fear, want, charity, all knock at once at thy closet door and say, "Come out unto us." Do not spill thy soul; do not all descend; keep thy state; stay at home in thine own heaven; come not for a moment into their facts, into their hubbub of conflicting appearances, but let in the light of thy law on their confusion. The power men possess to annoy me, I give them by a weak curiosity. No man can come near me but through my act. "What we love that we have, but by desire we bereave ourselves of the love."[1]

If we cannot at once rise to the sanctities of obedience and faith, let us at least resist our temptations, let us enter into the state of war, and wake Thor and Woden,[2] courage and constancy in our Saxon breasts. This is to be done in our smooth times by speaking the truth. Check[3] this lying hospitality and lying affection. Live no longer to the expectation of these deceived and deceiving people with whom we converse. Say to them, O father, O mother, O wife, O brother, O friend, I have lived with you after appearances hitherto. Henceforward I am the truth's. Be it known unto you that henceforward I obey no law less than the eternal law. I will have no covenants but proximities. I shall endeavor to nourish my parents, to support my family, to be the chaste husband of one wife—but these relations I must fill after a new and unprecedented way. I appeal from your customs. I must be myself. I cannot break myself any longer for you, or you. If you can love me for what I am, we shall be the happier. If you cannot, I will still seek to deserve that you should. I must be myself. I will not hide my tastes or aversions. I will so trust that what is deep is holy, that I will do strongly before the sun and moon whatever inly rejoices me, and the heart appoints. If you are noble, I will love you; if you are not, I will not hurt you and

myself by hypocritical attentions. If you are true, but not in the same truth with me, cleave to your companions; I will seek my own. I do this not selfishly, but humbly and truly. It is alike your interest and mine and all men's, however long we have dwelt in lies, to live in truth. Does this sound harsh today? You will soon love what is dictated by your nature as well as mine, and if we follow the truth, it will bring us out safe at last.—But so you may give these friends pain. Yes, but I cannot sell my liberty and my power, to save their sensibility. Besides, all persons have their moments of reason when they look out into the region of absolute truth; then will they justify me and do the same thing.

The populace think that your rejection of popular standards is a rejection of all standard, and mere antinomianism;[4] and the bold sensualist will use the name of philosophy to gild his crimes. But the law of consciousness abides. There are two confessionals, in one or the other of which we must be shriven. You may fulfill your round of duties by clearing yourself in the *direct*, or, in the *reflex* way. Consider whether you have satisfied your relations to father, mother, cousin, neighbor, town, cat, and dog; whether any of these can upbraid you. But I may also neglect this reflex standard, and absolve me to myself. I have my own stern claims and perfect circle. It denies the name of duty to many offices that are called duties. But if I can discharge its debts, it enables me to dispense with the popular code. If anyone imagines that this law is lax, let him keep its commandment one day.

And truly it demands something godlike in him who has cast off the common motives of humanity, and has ventured to trust himself for a task-master. High be his heart, faithful his will, clear his sight, that he may in good earnest be doctrine, society, law to himself, that a simple purpose may be to him as strong as iron necessity is to others.

If any man consider the present aspects of what is called by distinction *society*, he will see the need of these ethics. The sinew and heart of man seem to be drawn out, and we are become timorous desponding whimperers. We are afraid of truth, afraid of fortune,

---

[1] *What we ... the love* Emerson's own loose translation of the first line of "Love and Desire" by German poet Friedrich Schiller (1759–1805).

[2] *Thor and Woden* Norse gods associated with strength and warfare.

[3] *Check* Stop; restrain.

[4] *antinomianism* Doctrine held to by some Christians that salvation is derived from faith and divine grace alone, and that therefore the saved are not bound by moral laws such as those of the Ten Commandments.

afraid of death, and afraid of each other. Our age yields no great and perfect persons. We want men and women who shall renovate life and our social state, but we see that most natures are insolvent; cannot satisfy their own wants, have an ambition out of all proportion to their practical force, and so do lean and beg day and night continually. Our housekeeping is mendicant, our arts, our occupations, our marriages, our religion we have not chosen, but society has chosen for us. We are parlor soldiers. The rugged battle of fate, where strength is born, we shun.

If our young men miscarry[1] in their first enterprises, they lose all heart. If the young merchant fails, men say he is *ruined*. If the finest genius studies at one of our colleges, and is not installed in an office within one year afterwards in the cities or suburbs of Boston or New York, it seems to his friends and to himself that he is right in being disheartened and in complaining the rest of his life. A sturdy lad from New Hampshire or Vermont, who in turn tries all the professions, who *teams it*,[2] *farms it*, *peddles*, keeps a school, preaches, edits a newspaper, goes to Congress, buys a township, and so forth, in successive years, and always, like a cat, falls on his feet, is worth a hundred of these city dolls. He walks abreast with his days, and feels no shame in not "studying a profession," for he does not postpone his life, but lives already. He has not one chance, but a hundred chances. Let a stoic arise who shall reveal the resources of man, and tell men they are not leaning willows, but can and must detach themselves; that with the exercise of self-trust, new powers shall appear; that a man is the word made flesh,[3] born to shed healing to the nations,[4] that he should be ashamed of our compassion, and that the moment he acts from himself, tossing the laws, the books, idolatries, and customs out of the window, we pity him no more but thank and revere him—and that teacher shall restore the life of man to splendor, and make his name dear to all History.

It is easy to see that a greater self-reliance—a new respect for the divinity in man—must work a revolution in all the offices and relations of men; in their religion; in their education; in their pursuits; their modes of living; their association; in their property; in their speculative views.

1. In what prayers do men allow themselves! That which they call a holy office, is not so much as brave and manly. Prayer looks abroad and asks for some foreign addition to come through some foreign virtue, and loses itself in endless mazes of natural and supernatural, and mediatorial and miraculous. Prayer that craves a particular commodity—anything less than all good—is vicious. Prayer is the contemplation of the facts of life from the highest point of view. It is the soliloquy of a beholding and jubilant soul. It is the spirit of God pronouncing his works good. But prayer as a means to effect a private end, is theft and meanness. It supposes dualism and not unity in nature and consciousness. As soon as the man is at one with God, he will not beg. He will then see prayer in all action. The prayer of the farmer kneeling in his field to weed it, the prayer of the rower kneeling with the stroke of his oar, are true prayers heard throughout nature, though for cheap ends. Caratach, in Fletcher's *Bonduca*,[5] when admonished to inquire the mind of the god Audate, replies,

> His hidden meaning lies in our endeavors,
> Our valors are our best gods.

Another sort of false prayers are our regrets. Discontent is the want of self-reliance: it is infirmity of will. Regret calamities, if you can thereby help the sufferer; if not, attend your own work, and already the evil begins to be repaired. Our sympathy is just as base. We come to them who weep foolishly, and sit down and cry for company, instead of imparting to them truth and health in rough electric shocks, putting them once more in communication with the soul. The secret of fortune is joy in our hands. Welcome evermore to gods and men is the self-helping man. For him all doors are flung wide. Him all tongues greet, all honors crown, all eyes follow with desire. Our love goes out to him and embraces him, because he did not need it. We solicitously and apologetically caress and celebrate him, because he held on his way and scorned our

---

1   *miscarry* Fail.

2   *teams it* Drives a team of horses or other animals.

3   *word made flesh* Phrase applied to Jesus in John 1.14.

4   *shed healing to the nations* See Revelation 2.22: "on either side of the river [of life], was there the tree of life … and the leaves of the tree were for the healing of the nations."

5   *Fletcher's Bonduca* See *Bonduca* 3.1 (c. 1613) by John Fletcher.

disapprobation. The gods love him because men hated him. "To the persevering mortal," said Zoroaster,[1] "the blessed Immortals are swift."

As men's prayers are a disease of the will, so are their creeds a disease of the intellect. They say with those foolish Israelites, "Let not God speak to us, lest we die. Speak thou, speak any man with us, and we will obey."[2] Everywhere I am bereaved of meeting God in my brother, because he has shut his own temple doors, and recites fables merely of his brother's, or his brother's brother's God. Every new mind is a new classification. If it prove a mind of uncommon activity and power, a Locke, a Lavoisier, a Hutton, a Bentham, a Spurzheim,[3] it imposes its classification on other men, and lo! a new system. In proportion always to the depth of the thought, and so to the number of the objects it touches and brings within reach of the pupil, is his complacency. But chiefly is this apparent in creeds and churches, which are also classifications of some powerful mind acting on the elemental thought of Duty, and man's relation to the Highest. Such is Calvinism, Quakerism, Swedenborgianism.[4] The pupil takes the same delight in subordinating everything to the new terminology that a girl does who has just learned botany, in seeing a new earth and new seasons thereby. It will happen for a time that the pupil will feel a real debt to the teacher—will find his intellectual power has grown by the study of his writings. This will continue until he has exhausted his master's mind. But in all unbalanced minds, the classification is idolized, passes for the end, and not for a speedily exhaustible means, so that the walls of the system blend to their eye in the remote horizon with the walls of the universe; the luminaries of heaven seem to them hung on the arch their master built. They cannot imagine how you aliens have any right to see—how you can see; "It must be somehow that you stole the light from us." They do not yet perceive that light, unsystematic, indomitable, will break into any cabin, even into theirs. Let them chirp awhile and call it their own. If they are honest and do well, presently their neat new pinfold[5] will be too strait and low, will crack, will lean, will rot and vanish, and the immortal light, all young and joyful, million-orbed, million-colored, will beam over the universe as on the first morning.

2. It is for want of self-culture that the idol of Travelling, the idol of Italy, of England, of Egypt, remains for all educated Americans. They who made England, Italy, or Greece venerable in the imagination, did so not by rambling round creation as a moth round a lamp, but by sticking fast where they were, like an axis of the earth. In manly hours, we feel that duty is our place, and that the merrymen of circumstance should follow as they may. The soul is no traveller: the wise man stays at home with the soul, and when his necessities, his duties, on any occasion call him from his house, or into foreign lands, he is at home still, and is not gadding abroad from himself, and shall make men sensible by the expression of his countenance, that he goes the missionary of wisdom and virtue, and visits cities and men like a sovereign, and not like an interloper or a valet.

I have no churlish[6] objection to the circumnavigation of the globe, for the purposes of art, of study, and benevolence, so that the man is first domesticated, or does not go abroad with the hope of finding somewhat greater than he knows. He who travels to be amused, or to get somewhat which he does not carry, travels away from himself, and grows old even in youth among old things. In Thebes, in Palmyra,[7] his will and mind have become old and dilapidated as they. He carries ruins to ruins.

Travelling is a fool's paradise. We owe to our first journeys the discovery that place is nothing. At home I dream that at Naples, at Rome, I can be intoxicated with beauty, and lose my sadness. I pack my trunk,

---

[1]   *Zoroaster*   Ancient Persian prophet who founded the religion of Zoroastrianism.

[2]   *Let not … will obey*   See Exodus 20.19.

[3]   *Locke*   John Locke (1632–1704), English philosopher;   *Lavoisier* Antoine Lavoisier (1743–97), French chemist;   *Hutton*   James Hutton (1726–97), Scottish geologist;   *Bentham*   Jeremy Bentham (1748–1832), English utilitarian philosopher;   *Spurzheim*   Johann Gaspar Spurzheim (1776–1832), proponent of the popular pseudoscience of phrenology. Emerson amended the 1847 edition of this text to refer to French mathematician Joseph Fourier instead of Spurzheim, as phrenology was losing its credibility in the United States.

[4]   *Calvinism, Quakerism, Swedenborgianism*   Schools of Christian thought.

[5]   *pinfold*   Enclosure for livestock.

[6]   *churlish*   Lowly or boorish.

[7]   *Thebes … Palmyra*   Ancient, ruined cities in Egypt and what is now Syria.

embrace my friends, embark on the sea, and at last wake up in Naples, and there beside me is the stern Fact, the sad self, unrelenting, identical, that I fled from. I seek the Vatican, and the palaces. I affect to be intoxicated with sights and suggestions, but I am not intoxicated. My giant goes with me wherever I go.

3. But the rage of travelling is itself only a symptom of a deeper unsoundness affecting the whole intellectual action. The intellect is vagabond, and the universal system of education fosters restlessness. Our minds travel when our bodies are forced to stay at home. We imitate; and what is imitation but the travelling of the mind? Our houses are built with foreign taste; our shelves are garnished with foreign ornaments; our opinions, our tastes, our whole minds lean, and follow the Past and the Distant, as the eyes of a maid follow her mistress. The soul created the arts wherever they have flourished. It was in his own mind that the artist sought his model. It was an application of his own thought to the thing to be done and the conditions to be observed. And why need we copy the Doric or the Gothic[1] model? Beauty, convenience, grandeur of thought, and quaint expression are as near to us as to any, and if the American artist will study with hope and love the precise thing to be done by him, considering the climate, the soil, the length of the day, the wants of the people, the habit and form of the government, he will create a house in which all these will find themselves fitted, and taste and sentiment will be satisfied also.

Insist on yourself; never imitate. Your own gift you can present every moment with the cumulative force of a whole life's cultivation; but of the adopted talent of another, you have only an extemporaneous, half possession. That which each can do best, none but his Maker can teach him. No man yet knows what it is, nor can, till that person has exhibited it. Where is the master who could have taught Shakespeare? Where is the master who could have instructed Franklin, or Washington, or Bacon,[2] or Newton? Every great man is an unique. The Scipionism of Scipio is precisely

that part he could not borrow. If anybody will tell me whom the great man imitates in the original crisis[3] when he performs a great act, I will tell him who else than himself can teach him. Shakespeare will never be made by the study of Shakespeare. Do that which is assigned thee, and thou canst not hope too much or dare too much. There is at this moment, there is for me an utterance bare and grand as that of the colossal chisel of Phidias,[4] or trowel of the Egyptians, or the pen of Moses, or Dante,[5] but different from all these. Not possibly will the soul all rich, all eloquent, with thousand-cloven tongue, deign to repeat itself; but if I can hear what these patriarchs say, surely I can reply to them in the same pitch of voice: for the ear and the tongue are two organs of one nature. Dwell up there in the simple and noble regions of thy life, obey thy heart, and thou shalt reproduce the Foreworld[6] again.

4. As our Religion, our Education, our Art look abroad, so does our spirit of society. All men plume themselves on the improvement of society, and no man improves.

Society never advances. It recedes as fast on one side as it gains on the other. Its progress is only apparent, like the workers of a treadmill.[7] It undergoes continual changes: it is barbarous, it is civilized, it is christianized, it is rich, it is scientific; but this change is not amelioration. For everything that is given, something is taken. Society acquires new arts and loses old instincts. What a contrast between the well-clad, reading, writing, thinking American, with a watch, a pencil, and a bill of exchange in his pocket, and the naked New Zealander, whose property is a club, a spear, a mat, and an undivided twentieth of a shed to sleep under. But compare the health of the two men, and you shall see that his aboriginal strength the white man has lost. If the traveller tell us truly, strike the savage with a broad axe, and in a day or two the flesh shall unite and heal

---

1 *Doric or the Gothic* Traditional modes of architecture from ancient Greece and medieval Europe, respectively.

2 *Where is ... or Washington* Neither Benjamin Franklin (1706–90) nor George Washington (1732–99) received extensive formal education; *Bacon* Francis Bacon (1561–1626), English philosopher.

3 *crisis* Critically important stage; turning point.

4 *Phidias* Ancient Greek sculptor and architect (c. 480–430 BCE) involved in many renowned projects, such as the construction of the Parthenon in Athens.

5 *Dante* Italian poet Dante Alighieri (1265–1321).

6 *Foreworld* I.e., the past.

7 *treadmill* In the nineteenth century, treadmills were used to power mills and other machines; they were also operated as a punishment for prisoners sentenced to hard labor.

as if you struck the blow into soft pitch, and the same blow shall send the white to his grave.

The civilized man has built a coach, but has lost the use of his feet. He is supported on crutches, but loses so much support of muscle. He has got a fine Geneva watch, but he has lost the skill to tell the hour by the sun. A Greenwich nautical almanac[1] he has, and so being sure of the information when he wants it, the man in the street does not know a star in the sky. The solstice he does not observe; the equinox he knows as little; and the whole bright calendar of the year is without a dial in his mind. His notebooks impair his memory; his libraries overload his wit; the insurance office increases the number of accidents; and it may be a question whether machinery does not encumber; whether we have not lost by refinement some energy, by a christianity entrenched in establishments and forms, some vigor of wild virtue. For every stoic[2] was a stoic; but in Christendom where is the Christian?

There is no more deviation in the moral standard than in the standard of height or bulk. No greater men are now than ever were. A singular equality may be observed between the great men of the first and of the last ages; nor can all the science, art, religion and philosophy of the nineteenth century avail to educate greater men than Plutarch's[3] heroes, three or four and twenty centuries ago. Not in time is the race progressive. Phocion, Socrates, Anaxagoras, Diogenes,[4] are great men, but they leave no class. He who is really of their class will not be called by their name, but be wholly his own man, and in his turn the founder of a sect. The arts and inventions of each period are only its costume, and do not invigorate men. The harm of the improved machinery may compensate

its good. Hudson and Behring[5] accomplished so much in their fishing-boats, as to astonish Parry and Franklin,[6] whose equipment exhausted the resources of science and art. Galileo, with an opera-glass,[7] discovered a more splendid series of facts than anyone since. Columbus found the New World in an undecked boat. It is curious to see the periodical disuse and perishing of means and machinery which were introduced with loud laudation, a few years or centuries before. The great genius returns to essential man. We reckoned the improvements of the art of war among the triumphs of science, and yet Napoleon conquered Europe by the Bivouac,[8] which consisted of falling back on naked valor, and disencumbering it of all aids. The Emperor held it impossible to make a perfect army, says Las Casas,[9] "without abolishing our arms, magazines, commissaries, and carriages, until in imitation of the Roman custom, the soldier should receive his supply of corn, grind it in his hand-mill, and bake his bread himself."

Society is a wave. The wave moves onward, but the water of which it is composed does not. The same particle does not rise from the valley to the ridge. Its unity is only phenomenal. The persons who make up a nation today, next year die, and their experience with them.

And so the reliance on Property, including the reliance on governments which protect it, is the want of self-reliance. Men have looked away from themselves and at things so long that they have come to esteem what they call the soul's progress, namely, the religious, learned, and civil institutions, as guards of property, and they deprecate assaults on these, because they feel them to be assaults on property. They measure their esteem of each other, by what each has, and not by what each is. But a cultivated man becomes ashamed

---

[1]   *Greenwich nautical almanac*   Published by the Royal Greenwich Observatory, almanac providing the data needed to determine one's longitude at sea.

[2]   *stoic*   Follower of stoicism, an ancient Greek philosophy that emphasized virtue and the importance of intellectual pursuits over emotional and bodily concerns.

[3]   *Plutarch*   Greek writer (c. 46–c. 120 CE) best known for *Lives of the Noble Greeks and Romans*, a collection of biographies focused on the moral character of historical figures.

[4]   *Phocion* Athenian politician (402–318 BCE); *Anaxagoras* Ancient Greek philosopher (c. 510–c. 428 BCE); *Diogenes* Ancient Greek philosopher (c. 412–323 BCE).

[5]   *Hudson and Behring*   Henry Hudson (c. 1565–1611), English Arctic explorer who sought the Northwest Passage, and Vitus Bering (1681–1741), Danish explorer who led two Russian expeditions exploring the ocean around China and Siberia.

[6]   *Parry and Franklin*   William Edward Parry (1790–1855) and John Franklin (1786–1847), English Arctic explorers who sought the Northwest Passage.

[7]   *Galileo, with an opera-glass*   Galileo made landmark discoveries in astronomy using small, basic telescopes.

[8]   *Bivouac*   Temporary, makeshift encampment.

[9]   *Las Casas* Emmanuel, comte de Las Cases; the quotation is from his *Mémorial de Sainte-Hélène* (1823), a record of his conversations with Napoleon.

of his property, ashamed of what he has, out of new respect for his being. Especially he hates what he has, if he see that it is accidental—came to him by inheritance, or gift, or crime; then he feels that it is not having; it does not belong to him, has no root in him, and merely lies there, because no revolution or no robber takes it away. But that which a man is, does always by necessity acquire, and what the man acquires is permanent and living property, which does not wait the beck of rulers, or mobs, or revolutions, or fire, or storm, or bankruptcies, but perpetually renews itself wherever the man is put. "Thy lot or portion of life," said the Caliph Ali,[1] "is seeking after thee; therefore be at rest from seeking after it." Our dependence on these foreign goods leads us to our slavish respect for numbers. The political parties meet in numerous conventions; the greater the concourse, and with each new uproar of announcement, The delegation from Essex! The Democrats from New Hampshire! The Whigs of Maine! the young patriot feels himself stronger than before by a new thousand of eyes and arms. In like manner the reformers summon conventions, and vote and resolve in multitude. But not so, O friends! will the God deign to enter and inhabit you, but by a method precisely the reverse. It is only as a man puts off from himself all external support, and stands alone, that I see him to be strong and to prevail. He is weaker by every recruit to his banner. Is not a man better than a town? Ask nothing of men, and in the endless mutation, thou only firm column must presently appear the upholder of all that surrounds thee. He who knows that power is in the soul, that he is weak only because he has looked for good out of him and elsewhere, and so perceiving, throws himself unhesitatingly on his thought, instantly rights himself, stands in the erect position, commands his limbs, works miracles; just as a man who stands on his feet is stronger than a man who stands on his head.

So use all that is called Fortune. Most men gamble with her, and gain all, and lose all, as her wheel rolls. But do thou leave as unlawful these winnings, and deal with Cause and Effect, the chancellors of God. In the Will work and acquire, and thou hast chained the wheel of Chance, and shalt always drag her after

thee. A political victory, a rise of rents, the recovery of your sick, or the return of your absent friend, or some other quite external event, raises your spirits, and you think good days are preparing for you. Do not believe it. It can never be so. Nothing can bring you peace but yourself. Nothing can bring you peace but the triumph of principles.

—1841

from *The Poet*

A moody child and wildly wise
Pursued the game with joyful eyes,
Which chose, like meteors, their way,
And rived° the dark with private ray: split
They overleapt the horizon's edge,
Searched with Apollo's[2] privilege;
Through man, and woman, and sea, and star,
Saw the dance of nature forward far;
Through worlds, and races, and terms, and times,
Saw musical order, and pairing rhymes.

Olympian bards[3] who sung
Divine ideas below,
Which always find us young,
And always keep us so.

Those who are esteemed umpires of taste, are often persons who have acquired some knowledge of admired pictures or sculptures, and have an inclination for whatever is elegant; but if you inquire whether they are beautiful souls, and whether their own acts are like fair pictures, you learn that they are selfish and sensual. Their cultivation is local, as if you should rub a log of dry wood in one spot to produce fire, all the rest remaining cold. Their knowledge of the fine arts is some study of rules and particulars, or some limited judgment of color or form, which is exercised for amusement or for show. It is a proof of the shallowness of the doctrine of beauty, as it lies in the minds of our amateurs, that men seem to have lost the perception of

---

[1] *Caliph Ali* Ali ibn Abi Talib (c. 600–61 CE), early Muslim leader; the quoted line is attributed to him in Simon Ockley's *History of the Saracens* (1708–18).

[2] *Apollo* In Greek mythology, Apollo was god of music, poetry, and the sun.

[3] *Olympian bards* Divine poets. In Greek mythology, Mount Olympus was the home of the gods.

the instant dependence of form upon soul. There is no doctrine of forms[1] in our philosophy. We were put into our bodies, as fire is put into a pan, to be carried about; but there is no accurate adjustment between the spirit and the organ, much less is the latter the germination of the former. So in regard to other forms, the intellectual men do not believe in any essential dependence of the material world on thought and volition. Theologians think it a pretty air-castle to talk of the spiritual meaning of a ship or a cloud, of a city or a contract, but they prefer to come again to the solid ground of historical evidence; and even the poets are contented with a civil and conformed manner of living, and to write poems from the fancy, at a safe distance from their own experience. But the highest minds of the world have never ceased to explore the double meaning, or, shall I say, the quadruple, or the centuple, or much more manifold meaning, of every sensuous fact: Orpheus, Empedocles, Heraclitus, Plato, Plutarch, Dante, Swedenborg,[2] and the masters of sculpture, picture, and poetry. For we are not pans and barrows,[3] nor even porters of the fire and torch-bearers, but children of the fire, made of it, and only the same divinity transmuted, and at two or three removes, when we know least about it. And this hidden truth, that the fountains whence all this river of Time, and its creatures, floweth, are intrinsically ideal and beautiful, draws us to the consideration of the nature and functions of the Poet, or the man of Beauty, to the means and materials he uses, and to the general aspect of the art in the present time.

The breadth of the problem is great, for the poet is representative. He stands among partial men for the complete man, and apprises us not of his wealth, but of the commonwealth. The young man reveres men of genius, because, to speak truly, they are more himself than he is. They receive of the soul as he also receives, but they more. Nature enhances her beauty, to the eye of loving men, from their belief that the poet is beholding her shows at the same time. He is isolated among his contemporaries, by truth and by his art, but with this consolation in his pursuits, that they will draw all men sooner or later. For all men live by truth, and stand in need of expression. In love, in art, in avarice, in politics, in labor, in games, we study to utter our painful secret. The man is only half himself, the other half is his expression.

Notwithstanding this necessity to be published,[4] adequate expression is rare. I know not how it is that we need an interpreter; but the great majority of men seem to be minors, who have not yet come into possession of their own, or mutes, who cannot report the conversation they have had with nature. There is no man who does not anticipate a supersensual[5] utility in the sun, and stars, earth, and water. These stand and wait to render him a peculiar[6] service. But there is some obstruction, or some excess of phlegm[7] in our constitution, which does not suffer them to yield the due effect. Too feeble fall the impressions of nature on us to make us artists. Every touch should thrill. Every man should be so much an artist, that he could report in conversation what had befallen him. Yet, in our experience, the rays or appulses[8] have sufficient force to arrive at the

---

1   *doctrine of forms*   Platonic philosophy posits an ideal realm of forms, with the perceivable, physical world a mere shadow of these forms.

2   *Orpheus*   In Greek mythology, Orpheus was a poet and prophet whose music could charm trees, stones, and wild animals into following his will; *Empedocles* Greek philosopher (c. 494–c. 434 BCE); *Heraclitus* Greek philosopher (c. 535–475 BCE); *Plato* Greek philosopher (c. 427–c. 347 BCE) whose system of philosophy—which argues for the essentially immaterial origins of reality—had a shaping influence on Western thought; *Plutarch* Greek essayist, biographer, and Platonic philosopher whose book *Parallel Lives of Noble Greeks and Romans* (c. second century CE) Emerson described as a "bible for heroes"; *Dante* Dante Alighieri was a Renaissance Italian poet whose *Divine Comedy* (c. 1308–20) is widely acknowledged as a major work of world literature; *Swedenborg* Swedish scientist and mystic Emanuel Swedenborg. His work, particularly the spiritual vision in his *Heaven and Hell* (1758), strongly influenced Emerson and the Transcendentalist movement more generally.

3   *barrows*   Tools for carrying loads, i.e., stretchers or wheelbarrows.

4   *to be published*   To be heard, to be made public.

5   *supersensual*   I.e., beyond the material; spiritual.

6   *peculiar*   Particular, distinctive.

7   *excess of phlegm*   Phlegm was considered one of the "bodily humors," four fluids which, according to classical and medieval medical theory, must be balanced within the body in order for a person to be healthy. According to this theory, when one fluid predominates, the temperament associated with it is exacerbated; a person suffering an excess of phlegm was thought to become apathetic, lacking the energy to act.

8   *appulses*   Propelled motions, such as those that govern the planets and stars.

senses, but not enough to reach the quick,[1] and compel the reproduction of themselves in speech. The poet is the person in whom these powers are in balance, the man without impediment, who sees and handles that which others dream of, traverses the whole scale of experience, and is representative of man, in virtue of being the largest power to receive and to impart.

For the Universe has three children, born at one time, which reappear, under different names, in every system of thought, whether they be called cause, operation, and effect; or, more poetically, Jove, Pluto, Neptune;[2] or, theologically, the Father, the Spirit, and the Son; but which we will call here, the Knower, the Doer, and the Sayer. These stand respectively for the love of truth, for the love of good, and for the love of beauty. These three are equal. Each is that which he is essentially, so that he cannot be surmounted or analyzed, and each of these three has the power of the others latent in him, and his own patent.

The poet is the sayer, the namer, and represents beauty. He is a sovereign, and stands on the centre. For the world is not painted, or adorned, but is from the beginning beautiful; and God has not made some beautiful things, but Beauty is the creator of the universe. Therefore the poet is not any permissive potentate, but is emperor in his own right. Criticism is infested with a cant of materialism, which assumes that manual skill and activity is the first merit of all men, and disparages such as say and do not, overlooking the fact, that some men, namely, poets, are natural sayers, sent into the world to the end[3] of expression, and confounds them with those whose province is action, but who quit it to imitate the sayers. But Homer's[4] words are as costly and admirable to Homer, as Agamemnon's victories are to Agamemnon.[5] The poet does not wait for the hero or the sage, but, as they act and think primarily, so he writes primarily what will and must be spoken, reckoning the others, though primaries also, yet, in respect

to him, secondaries and servants; as sitters or models in the studio of a painter, or as assistants who bring building materials to an architect.

For poetry was all written before time was, and whenever we are so finely organized that we can penetrate into that region where the air is music, we hear those primal warblings, and attempt to write them down, but we lose ever and anon[6] a word, or a verse, and substitute something of our own, and thus miswrite the poem. The men of more delicate ear write down these cadences more faithfully, and these transcripts, though imperfect, become the songs of the nations. For nature is as truly beautiful as it is good, or as it is reasonable, and must as much appear, as it must be done, or be known. Words and deeds are quite indifferent modes of the divine energy. Words are also actions, and actions are a kind of words.

The sign and credentials of the poet are, that he announces that which no man foretold. He is the true and only doctor;[7] he knows and tells; he is the only teller of news, for he was present and privy to the appearance which he describes. He is a beholder of ideas, and utterer of the necessary and causal. For we do not speak now of men of poetical talents, or of industry and skill in metre, but of the true poet. …

For it is not metres, but a metre-making argument, that makes a poem—a thought so passionate and alive, that, like the spirit of a plant or an animal, it has architecture of its own, and adorns nature with a new thing. The thought and the form are equal in the order of time, but in the order of genesis the thought is prior to the form. The poet has a new thought: he has a whole new experience to unfold; he will tell us how it was with him, and all men will be the richer in his fortune. For, the experience of each new age requires a new confession, and the world seems always waiting for its poet. … We know that the secret of the world is profound, but who or what shall be our interpreter, we know not. A mountain ramble, a new style of face, a new person, may put the key into our hands. Of course, the value of genius to us is in the veracity of its report. Talent may frolic and juggle; genius realizes and adds. Mankind, in good earnest, have arrived so far in

---

1   *quick*   Vital part, the life-blood.

2   *Jove, Pluto, Neptune*   Roman gods of the sky, the underworld, and the sea, respectively.

3   *end*   Purpose.

4   *Homer*   Traditionally said to be the author of the ancient Greek epic poems the *Iliad* and the *Odyssey*.

5   *Agamemnon*   Commander of the Greek army that lays siege to the city of Troy in Homer's *Iliad*.

6   *ever and anon*   I.e., every now and then.

7   *doctor*   Expert, teacher.

understanding themselves and their work, that the foremost watchman on the peak announces his news. It is the truest word ever spoken and the phrase will be the fittest, most musical, and the unerring voice of the world for that time.

All that we call sacred history attests that the birth of a poet is the principal event in chronology. Man, never so often deceived, still watches for the arrival of a brother who can hold him steady to a truth, until he has made it his own. With what joy I begin to read a poem, which I confide in as an inspiration! And now my chains are to be broken; I shall mount about these clouds and opaque airs in which I live—opaque, though they seem transparent—and from the heaven of truth I shall see and comprehend my relations. That will reconcile me to life, and renovate nature, to see trifles animated by a tendency,[1] and to know what I am doing. Life will no more be a noise; now I shall see men and women, and know the signs by which they may be discerned from fools and satans. This day shall be better than my birthday: then I became an animal: now I am invited into the science of the real. Such is the hope, but the fruition is postponed. Oftener it falls, that this winged man, who will carry me into the heaven, whirls me into mists, then leaps and frisks about with me from cloud to cloud, still affirming that he is bound heavenward; and I, being myself a novice, am slow in perceiving that he does not know the way into the heavens, and is merely bent that I should admire his skill to rise, like a fowl or a flying fish, a little way from the ground or the water; but the all-piercing, all-feeding, and ocular[2] air of heaven, that man shall never inhabit. I tumble down again soon into my old nooks, and lead the life of exaggerations as before, and have lost some faith in the possibility of any guide who can lead me thither where I would be.

But leaving these victims of vanity, let us, with new hope, observe how nature, by worthier impulses, has ensured the poet's fidelity to his office of announcement and affirming, namely, by the beauty of things, which becomes a new, and higher beauty, when expressed. Nature offers all her creatures to him as a picture-language. Being used as a type, a second wonderful value appears in the object, far better than its old value, as the carpenter's stretched cord,[3] if you hold your ear close enough, is musical in the breeze. "Things more excellent than every image," says Jamblichus,[4] "are expressed through images." Things admit of being used as symbols, because nature is a symbol, in the whole, and in every part. ...

The Universe is the externization of the soul. Wherever the life is, that bursts into appearance around it. Our science is sensual, and therefore superficial. The earth, and the heavenly bodies, physics, and chemistry, we sensually treat, as if they were self-existent; but these are the retinue of that Being we have. "The mighty heaven," said Proclus, "exhibits, in its transfigurations, clear images of the splendor of intellectual perceptions; being moved in conjunction with the unapparent periods of intellectual natures." Therefore, science always goes abreast with the just elevation of the man, keeping step with religion and metaphysics; or, the state of science is an index of our self-knowledge. Since everything in nature answers to a moral power, if any phenomenon remains brute and dark, it is because the corresponding faculty in the observer is not yet active.

No wonder, then, if these waters be so deep, that we hover over them with a religious regard. The beauty of the fable proves the importance of the sense; to the poet, and to all others; or, if you please, every man is so far a poet as to be susceptible of these enchantments of nature; for all men have the thoughts whereof the universe is the celebration. I find that the fascination resides in the symbol. Who loves nature? Who does not? Is it only poets, and men of leisure and cultivation, who live with her? No; but also hunters, farmers, grooms, and butchers, though they express their affection in their choice of life, and not in their choice of words. The writer wonders what the coachman or the hunter values in riding, in horses, and dogs. It is not superficial qualities. When you talk with him, he holds these at as slight a rate as you. His worship is sympathetic; he has no definitions, but he is commanded in nature, by the living power which he feels to be there present. No imitation, or playing of these things, would content him; he loves the earnest of the north

---

[1] *tendency* Conscious aim or purpose.

[2] *ocular* Visible.

[3] *carpenter's ... cord* Cord that is stretched taut for use as a measuring tool.

[4] *Jamblichus* Iamblichus (c. 242–325) was a Syrian Neoplatonist philosopher.

wind, of rain, of stone, and wood, and iron. A beauty not explicable, is dearer than a beauty which we can see to the end of. It is nature the symbol, nature certifying the supernatural, body overflowed by life, which he worships, with coarse, but sincere rites.

The inwardness, and mystery, of this attachment, drive men of every class to the use of emblems. The schools of poets, and philosophers, are not more intoxicated with their symbols, than the populace with theirs. In our political parties, compute the power of badges and emblems. See the great ball which they roll from Baltimore to Bunker hill![1] In the political processions, Lowell goes in a loom, and Lynn in a shoe, and Salem[2] in a ship. Witness the cider-barrel, the log-cabin, the hickory-stick, the palmetto, and all the cognizances[3] of party. See the power of national emblems. Some stars, lilies, leopards, a crescent, a lion, an eagle, or other figure, which came into credit God knows how, on an old rag of bunting, blowing in the wind, on a fort, at the ends of the earth, shall make the blood tingle under the rudest, or the most conventional exterior. The people fancy they hate poetry, and they are all poets and mystics!

… We are far from having exhausted the significance of the few symbols we use. We can come to use them yet with a terrible simplicity. It does not need that a poem should be long. Every word was once a poem. Every new relation is a new word. …

For, as it is dislocation and detachment from the life of God, that makes things ugly, the poet, who re-attaches things to nature and the Whole—re-attaching even artificial things, and violations of nature, to nature, by a deeper insight—disposes very easily of the most disagreeable facts. Readers of poetry see the factory-village, and the railway, and fancy that the poetry of the landscape is broken up by these, for these works of art are not yet consecrated in their reading; but the poet sees them fall within the great Order not less than the bee-hive, or the spider's geometrical web. Nature adopts them very fast into her vital circles, and the gliding train of cars she loves like her own. …

… We are symbols, and inhabit symbols; workmen, work, and tools, words and things, birth and death, all are emblems; but we sympathize with the symbols, and, being infatuated with the economical uses of things, we do not know that they are thoughts. The poet, by an ulterior intellectual perception, gives them power which makes their old use forgotten, and puts eyes, and a tongue, into every dumb[4] and inanimate object. … All the facts of the animal economy,[5] sex, nutriment, gestation, birth, growth, are symbols of the passage of the world into the soul of man, to suffer there a change, and reappear a new and higher fact. He uses forms according to the life, and not according to the form. This is true science. The poet alone knows astronomy, chemistry, vegetation, and animation,[6] for he does not stop at these facts, but employs them as signs. He knows why the plain, or meadow of space, was strown with these flowers we call suns, and moons, and stars; why the great deep is adorned with animals, with men, and gods; for, in every word he speaks he rides on them as the horses of thought.

By virtue of this science the poet is the Namer, or Language-maker, naming things sometimes after their appearance, sometimes after their essence, and giving to every one its own name and not another's, thereby rejoicing the intellect, which delights in detachment or boundary. The poets made all the words, and therefore language is the archives of history, and, if we must say it, a sort of tomb of the muses. For, though the origin of most of our words is forgotten, each word was at a stroke of genius, and obtained currency, because for the moment it symbolized the world to the first speaker

---

[1] *great ball … Bunker hill* In the 1840 election, the Whigs, seeking to unseat President Martin Van Buren, used various songs, slogans, and campaign stunts, one of which was rolling balls made of twine and paper called "Harrison balls"—named after the Whig presidential candidate William Henry Harrison—down the streets of towns. This activity was inspired by campaign slogans such as "Keep the Ball Rolling." The balls were at times as big as twelve feet in diameter.

[2] *Lowell … Salem* Three cities in Massachusetts, each here accompanied by a symbol of their primary industry: textiles for Lowell; shoemaking for Lynn; and shipping for Salem.

[3] *cider-barrel … log-cabin* Symbols used by William Henry Harrison in his presidential campaign, as an effort to connect to the common people; *hickory-stick* Symbol associated with President Andrew Jackson (1767–1845), also known as "Old Hickory," who defended himself against assassination in 1835 with a cane of hickory wood; *palmetto* The palmetto tree is a symbol associated with the state of South Carolina; *cognizances* Badges.

[4] *dumb* Silent.

[5] *economy* In this context, the organization of the body.

[6] *animation* Art of bringing things to life.

and to the hearer. The etymologist finds the deadest word to have been once a brilliant picture. Language is fossil poetry. As the limestone of the continent consists of infinite masses of the shells of animalcules,[1] so language is made up of images, or tropes, which now, in their secondary use, have long ceased to remind us of their poetic origin. But the poet names the thing because he sees it, or comes one step nearer to it than any other. This expression, or naming, is not art, but a second nature, grown out of the first, as a leaf out of a tree. What we call nature, is a certain self-regulated motion, or change; and nature does all things by her own hands, and does not leave another to baptise her, but baptises herself; and this through the metamorphosis again. ...

... The poet knows that he speaks adequately, then, only when he speaks somewhat wildly, or, "with the flower of the mind"; not with the intellect, used as an organ, but with the intellect released from all service, and suffered to take its direction from its celestial life; or, as the ancients were wont to express themselves, not with intellect alone, but with the intellect inebriated by nectar. ...

This is the reason why bards love wine, mead, narcotics, coffee, tea, opium, the fumes of sandalwood and tobacco, or whatever other species of animal exhilaration. All men avail themselves of such means as they can, to add this extraordinary power to their normal powers; and to this end they prize conversation, music, pictures, sculpture, dancing, theatres, travelling, war, mobs, fires, gaming, politics, or love, or science, or animal intoxication, which are several coarser or finer *quasi*-mechanical substitutes for the true nectar, which is the ravishment of the intellect by coming nearer to the fact. These are auxiliaries to the centrifugal tendency of a man, to his passage out into free space, and they help him to escape the custody of that body in which he is pent up, and of that jail-yard of individual relations in which he is enclosed. Hence a great number of such as were professionally expressors of Beauty, as painters, poets, musicians, and actors, have been more than others wont to lead a life of pleasure and indulgence; all but the few who received the true nectar; and, as it was a spurious mode of attaining freedom, as it was an emancipation not into the heavens, but into the freedom of baser places, they were punished for that advantage they won, by a dissipation and deterioration. But never can any advantage be taken of nature by a trick. The spirit of the world, the great calm presence of the creator, comes not forth to the sorceries of opium or of wine. The sublime vision comes to the pure and simple soul in a clean and chaste body. ... It is with this as it is with toys. We fill the hands and nurseries of our children with all manner of dolls, drums, and horses, withdrawing their eyes from the plain face and sufficing objects of nature, the sun, and moon, the animals, the water, and stones, which should be their toys. So the poet's habit of living should be set on a key so low and plain, that the common influences should delight him. His cheerfulness should be the gift of the sunlight; the air should suffice for his inspiration, and he should be tipsy with water. ... If thou fill thy brain with Boston and New York, with fashion and covetousness, and wilt stimulate thy jaded senses with wine and French coffee, thou shalt find no radiance of wisdom in the lonely waste of the pinewoods.

If the imagination intoxicates the poet, it is not inactive in other men. The metamorphosis excites in the beholder an emotion of joy. The use of symbols has a certain power of emancipation and exhilaration for all men. We seem to be touched by a wand, which makes us dance and run about happily, like children. We are like persons who come out of a cave or cellar into the open air. This is the effect on us of tropes, fables, oracles, and all poetic forms. Poets are thus liberating gods. Men have really got a new sense, and found within their world, another world, or nest of worlds; for, the metamorphosis once seen, we divine that it does not stop. ...

The poets are thus liberating gods. The ancient British bards had for the title of their order, "Those who are free throughout the world." They are free, and they make free. An imaginative book renders us much more service at first, by stimulating us through its tropes, than afterward, when we arrive at the precise sense of the author. I think nothing is of any value in books, excepting the transcendental and extraordinary. ...

There is good reason why we should prize this liberation. The fate of the poor shepherd, who, blinded and lost in the snowstorm, perishes in a drift within a

---

[1]   *animalcules* Small organisms.

few feet of his cottage door, is an emblem of the state of man. On the brink of the waters of life and truth, we are miserably dying. The inaccessibleness of every thought but that we are in, is wonderful. What if you come near to it—you are as remote, when you are nearest, as when you are farthest. Every thought is also a prison; every heaven is also a prison. Therefore we love the poet, the inventor, who in any form, whether in an ode, or in an action, or in looks and behavior, has yielded us a new thought. He unlocks our chains, and admits us to a new scene.

This emancipation is dear to all men, and the power to impart it, as it must come from greater depth and scope of thought, is a measure of intellect. Therefore all books of the imagination endure, all which ascend to that truth, that the writer sees nature beneath him, and uses it as his exponent. Every verse or sentence, possessing this virtue, will take care of its own immortality. The religions of the world are the ejaculations[1] of a few imaginative men. …

I look in vain for the poet whom I describe. We do not, with sufficient plainness, or sufficient profoundness, address ourselves to life, nor dare we chaunt our own times and social circumstance. If we filled the day with bravery, we should not shrink from celebrating it. Time and nature yield us many gifts, but not yet the timely man, the new religion, the reconciler, whom all things await. Dante's praise is, that he dared to write his autobiography in colossal cipher, or into universality. We have yet had no genius in America, with tyrannous eye, which knew the value of our incomparable materials, and saw, in the barbarism and materialism of the times, another carnival of the same gods whose picture he so much admires in Homer; then in the middle age; then in Calvinism.[2] Banks and tariffs, the newspaper and caucus, methodism and unitarianism,[3] are flat and dull to dull people, but rest on the same

foundations of wonder as the town of Troy, and the temple of Delphos,[4] and are as swiftly passing away. Our logrolling, our stumps[5] and their politics, our fisheries, our Negroes, and Indians, our boasts, and our repudiations, the wrath of rogues, and the pusillanimity of honest men, the northern trade, the southern planting, the western clearing, Oregon, and Texas, are yet unsung. Yet America is a poem in our eyes; its ample geography dazzles the imagination, and it will not wait long for metres.[6] If I have not found that excellent combination of gifts in my countrymen which I seek, neither could I aid myself to fix the idea of the poet by reading now and then in Chalmers's collection of five centuries of English poets.[7] These are wits, more than poets, though there have been poets among them. But when we adhere to the ideal of the poet, we have our difficulties even with Milton and Homer. Milton is too literary, and Homer too literal and historical.

But I am not wise enough for a national criticism, and must use the old largeness a little longer, to discharge my errand from the muse to the poet concerning his art.

Art is the path of the creator to his work. The paths, or methods, are ideal and eternal, though few men ever see them, not the artist himself for years, or for a lifetime, unless he come into the conditions. The painter, the sculptor, the composer, the epic rhapsodist, the orator, all partake one desire, namely, to express themselves symmetrically and abundantly, not dwarfishly and fragmentarily. They found or put themselves in certain conditions, as, the painter and sculptor before some impressive human figures; the orator, into the assembly of the people; and the others, in such scenes as each has found exciting to his intellect; and each presently feels the new desire. He hears a voice, he sees a beckoning. Then he is apprised, with wonder, what herds of daemons hem him in. He can no more rest; he says, with the old painter, "By God, it is in me, and must go forth of me." He pursues a beauty, half

---

[1] *ejaculations* Brief, often spontaneous prayers or expressions of emotion.

[2] *Calvinism* Branch of Protestant belief based on the teachings of French dissenter John Calvin (1509–64); many of the Puritans who settled in America followed Calvinistic doctrine.

[3] *methodism and unitarianism* Protestant denominations that began to take root in America in the latter half of the eighteenth century; both of these more liberal denominations rejected some of the harsher tenets of Calvinism, such as that of predestination (the idea that one is unalterably destined by God for heaven or hell).

---

[4] *temple of Delphos* The temple at Delphi was dedicated to Apollo, the Greek god of the sun, music, and poetry. It was also the location of the Pythia, a renowned oracle.

[5] *stumps* Stumps of big trees were used as platforms for oratory.

[6] *metres* I.e., lines of poetry.

[7] *Chalmers's … English poets* Alexander Chalmers's collection *The Works of the English Poets, from Chaucer to Cowper* (1801).

seen, which flies before him. The poet pours out verses in every solitude. Most of the things he says are conventional, no doubt; but by and by he says something which is original and beautiful. That charms him. He would say nothing else but such things. In our way of talking, we say, "That is yours, this is mine"; but the poet knows well that it is not his; that it is as strange and beautiful to him as to you; he would fain hear the like eloquence at length. Once having tasted this immortal ichor,[1] he cannot have enough of it, and, as an admirable creative power exists in these intellections, it is of the last importance that these things get spoken. What a little of all we know is said! What drops of all the sea of our science are baled up! and by what accident it is that these are exposed, when so many secrets sleep in nature! Hence the necessity of speech and song; hence these throbs and heart-beatings in the orator, at the door of the assembly, to the end, namely, that thought may be ejaculated as Logos,[2] or Word.

Doubt not, O poet, but persist. Say, "It is in me, and shall out." Stand there, baulked and dumb, stuttering and stammering, hissed and hooted, stand and strive, until, at last, rage draw out of thee that dream-power which every night shows thee is thine own; a power transcending all limit and privacy, and by virtue of which a man is the conductor of the whole river of electricity. Nothing walks, or creeps, or grows, or exists, which must not in turn arise and walk before him as exponent of his meaning. Comes he to that power, his genius is no longer exhaustible. All the creatures, by pairs and by tribes, pour into his mind as into a Noah's ark, to come forth again to people a new world. This is like the stock of air for our respiration, or for the combustion of our fireplace, not a measure of gallons, but the entire atmosphere if wanted. And therefore the rich poets, as Homer, Chaucer, Shakespeare, and Raphael,[3] have obviously no limits to their works, except the limits of their lifetime, and resemble a mirror carried through the street, ready to render an image of every created thing.

O poet! a new nobility is conferred in groves and pastures, and not in castles, or by the sword-blade, any longer. The conditions are hard, but equal. Thou shalt leave the world, and know the muse only. Thou shalt not know any longer the times, customs, graces, politics, or opinions of men, but shalt take all from the muse. For the time of towns is tolled from the world by funereal chimes, but in nature the universal hours are counted by succeeding tribes of animals and plants, and by growth of joy on joy. God wills also that thou abdicate a manifold and duplex life, and that thou be content that others speak for thee. Others shall be thy gentlemen, and shall represent all courtesy and worldly life for thee; others shall do the great and resounding actions also. Thou shalt lie close hid with nature, and canst not be afforded to the Capitol or the Exchange. The world is full of renunciations and apprenticeships, and this is thine: thou must pass for a fool and a churl for a long season. This is the screen and sheath in which Pan[4] has protected his well-beloved flower, and thou shalt be known only to thine own, and they shall console thee with tenderest love. And thou shalt not be able to rehearse the names of thy friends in thy verse, for an old shame before the holy ideal. And this is the reward: that the ideal shall be real to thee, and the impressions of the actual world shall fall like summer rain, copious, but not troublesome, to thy invulnerable essence. Thou shalt have the whole land for thy park and manor, the sea for thy bath and navigation, without tax and without envy; the woods and the rivers thou shalt own; and thou shalt possess that wherein others are only tenants and boarders. Thou true landlord! sea-lord! air-lord! Wherever snow falls, or water flows, or birds fly, wherever day and night meet in twilight, wherever the blue heaven is hung by clouds, or sown with stars, wherever are forms with transparent boundaries, wherever are outlets into celestial space, wherever is danger, and awe, and love, there is Beauty, plenteous as rain, shed for thee, and though thou shouldest walk the world over, thou shalt not be able to find a condition inopportune or ignoble.

—1844

---

[1]   *immortal ichor*   In Greek mythology, the fluid that runs through the veins of the gods.

[2]   *Logos*   Greek word meaning both "reason" and "word"; it also has specialized meanings in classical and Christian theology.

[3]   *Raphael*   Italian Renaissance painter (1483–1520).

[4]   *Pan*   In Greek mythology, Pan was the god of the wilderness, often depicted with a pipe or flute. He was associated with the land and fertility.

Brahma[1]

If the red slayer[2] think he slays,
Or if the slain think he is slain,
They know not well the subtle ways
I keep, and pass, and turn again.[3]

5 Far or forgot to me is near,
Shadow and sunlight are the same,
The vanished gods to me appear,
And one to me are shame and fame.

10 They reckon ill who leave me out;
When me they fly, I am the wings;
I am the doubter and the doubt,
And I the hymn the Brahmin[4] sings.

The strong gods[5] pine for my abode,
And pine in vain the sacred Seven;[6]
15 But thou, meek lover of the good!
Find me, and turn thy back on heaven.
    —1857

IN CONTEXT

Emerson and the Lyceum Movement

In 1829, Josiah Holbrook, a teacher and amateur scientist, published a book called *American Lyceum*, which describes his vision for a series of educational institutions in the cities, towns, and villages of America:

> A Town Lyceum is a voluntary association of individuals disposed to improve each other in useful knowledge, and to advance the interests of their schools. To gain the first object, they hold weekly or other stated meetings, for reading, conversation, discussion, illustrating the sciences, or other exercises designed for their mutual benefit; and, as it is found convenient, they collect a cabinet, consisting of apparatus for illustrating the sciences, books, minerals, plants, or other natural or artificial productions.

Holbrook started the first lyceum in Millbury, Massachusetts, in 1826, and he advocated for the advantages these institutions could bring to a community, including better conversation, educational opportunities for children and adults, and increased use of libraries. His ideas proved popular: a National Lyceum organization was created in 1831, and by the mid-1830s there were more than 3,000 lyceums across the United States.

---

[1] *Brahma* Here Emerson may be conflating two concepts in Hinduism: Brahma, the Hindu creator god, and Brahman, the unifying principle that pervades all reality, simultaneously creative and unchanging. Emerson was familiar with discussions of Brahman in ancient Sanskrit texts such as the *Katha Upanishad* and the *Bhagavad Gita*.

[2] *red slayer* Rudra, a terrifying god whose name may derive from the Sanskrit word for "red"; Rudra is sometimes identified with Shiva, a major deity associated with destruction.

[3] *If the … turn again* See *Katha Upanishad* 1.2.19; the stanza bears a resemblance to lines from other Hindu texts as well.

[4] *Brahmin* Member of the Brahmin caste, the highest caste in Hinduism, associated with priesthood.

[5] *strong gods* Devas, divine beings in Hinduism.

[6] *sacred Seven* Highly extolled sages or saints, sometimes known as the saptarishis, who appear in Hindu literature.

The lyceums would put on lectures and other events, and local people would come to speak; national figures—politicians and intellectuals—would also tour the country speaking at various lyceums, on what was known as the "circuit." Abraham Lincoln gave his first public speech in a lyceum, and many other politicians, ministers, and activists honed their oratorical skills on the circuit. The lectures and events were attended by most classes of society, including professionals, intellectuals, farmers, and artisans, and included women as well as men.

The lyceum in Concord, Massachusetts, was particularly vibrant, and Ralph Waldo Emerson attended it frequently and gave lectures, as did Henry David Thoreau. Emerson was so highly valued as a speaker that he toured the circuit regularly, giving over fifteen hundred public lectures over his career, developing his ideas and sharing them with audiences across the country. Many of his lectures were then published in his collections of essays.

The Lyceum Movement steadily gained in popularity, reaching a crescendo in the years before the Civil War, and giving way to other forms of popular entertainment in the decades that followed. It is believed that the movement contributed a great deal to the education of Americans in the nineteenth century. The first of the following selections, from Emerson's personal writings, articulates some of his views on the lyceum circuit and on the lecture as an art form; the remaining excerpts are taken from reviews and memoirs of Emerson as a public speaker.

from Ralph Waldo Emerson, *Journals and Miscellaneous Notebooks, Volume 7: 1838–1842*

Why should we write dramas, & epics, & sonnets, & novels in two volumes? Why not write as variously as we dress and think? A lecture is a new literature, which leaves aside all tradition, time, place, circumstance, & addresses an assembly as mere human beings—no more—it has never yet been well done. It is an organ of sublime power a panharmonicon[1] for variety of note. …

I look on the Lecture Room as the true Church of the coming time … For here is all that the true orator will ask, namely, a convertible audience—an audience coming up to the house, not knowing what shall befall them there, but uncommitted and willing victims to reason and love. There is no topic that may not be treated, and no method excluded. *Here* everything is admissible, philosophy, ethics, divinity, criticism, poetry, humor, fun, mimicry, anecdotes, jokes, ventriloquism. All the breadth & versatility of the most liberal conversation highest and lowest personal local topics, all are permitted, and all may be combined in one speech; it is a panharmonicon—every note on the longest gamut,[2] from the explosion of the cannon, to the tinkle of a guitar. Let us try if Folly, Custom, Convention & Phlegm[3] cannot hear our sharp artillery. Here is the pulpit that makes other pulpits tame & ineffectual—with their cold mechanical preparation for a delivery the most decorous—fine things, pretty things, wise things, but no arrows, no axes, no nectar, no growling, no transpiercing, no loving, no enchantment. Here he may lay himself out utterly, large, enormous, prodigal, on the subject of the hour. Here he may dare to hope for ecstasy and eloquence.

from anonymous, "Emerson as a Lecturer," *Boston Post* (25 January 1849)

We listened to Mr. Ralph Waldo Emerson's second lecture[4] on Monday evening, as we always listen to him, with admiration and delight. Yet it is quite out of character to say Mr. Emerson

---

1   *panharmonicon*   Mechanical device that can imitate a variety of instruments and other sounds.

2   *gamut*   Full scale of musical notes.

3   *Phlegm*   Used here figuratively to mean "apathy" or "dullness."

4   *second lecture*   "The Relation of Intellect to Natural Science," part of Emerson's *Mind and Manners of the Nineteenth Century* series of lectures.

lectures—he does no such thing. He drops nectar—he chips out sparks—he exhales odors—he lets off mental skyrockets and fireworks—he spouts fire, and conjurer like, draws ribbons out of his mouth. He smokes, he sparkles, he improvises, he shouts, he sings, he explodes like a bundle of crackers, he goes off in fiery eruptions like a volcano, but he does not *lecture*. …

He exhibited on Monday evening a wealth of imagination, an opulence of imagery, and of original and peculiar thought which amounted to a surfeit. He went swiftly over the ground of knowledge with a Damascus blade, severing every thing from its bottom, leaving one in doubt whether any thing would ever grow again. So that, after all, we are inclined to think no great harm has been done. He comes and goes like a spirit of whom one just hears the rustle of his wings. He is a vitalized speculation—a talking essence—a sort of celestial emanation—a bit of transparency broken from the spheres—a spiritual prism through which we see all beautiful rays of immaterial existences. His leaping fancy mounts upward like an India rubber ball, and drifts and falls like a snow-flake or feather. He moves in the regions of similitudes. … He inverts the rainbow and uses it for a swing—now sweeping the earth, and now clapping his hands among the stars.

We wonder if he will ever die like other men? It seems to us he will find some way of slipping out of the world and shutting the door behind him before any body knows he is going. We cannot believe he will be *translated*, for this would be too gross a method of exit. He is more likely to be evaporated some sunshiny day, or to be exhaled like a perfume. He will certainly not be seen to go—he will only *vanish*.

from George Willis Cooke, *Ralph Waldo Emerson: His Life, Writings, and Philosophy* (1881)

On the lecture platform Emerson seems to be unconscious of his audience, is not disturbed by inter-ruptions of any kind[.] … He usually begins in a slow and spiritless manner, in a low tone; and he is not fluent of speech, or passionate in manner. As he proceeds, he becomes earnest and magnetic; while the thrilling intensity of his voice deeply affects and rivets the attention of his audience. He is full of mannerisms in expression and in bodily attitude, seldom makes a gesture, and has little variation of voice. He secures the interest of his hearers by the simple grandeur of his thought[.] …

He hesitates for words, and seems to find it difficult to secure the precise expression he desires. He speaks on the lecture-platform much as he converses[.] … In his conversation, there is the same antithesis and abrupt transition to be found as in his books. He does not think continuously; he does not in conversa-tion follow a subject through, but hesitates, skips intervening ideas, is unable, apparently, to hold his mind to all the links of thought. It is not natural for him to do so. He does not think logically, but intuitively, sees and seizes at a glance, in bold generalizations, but is unable to follow and arrange the intervening steps from premise to conclusion.

from Edward Waldo Emerson, *Emerson in Concord: A Memoir* (1889)

[Emerson] held to the faith that all "differences are superficial, that they all have one fundamental nature," which it was for him to find and awaken. And his confidence was justified. In a paper full of interesting reminiscences Mr. Albee mentions talking with a Concord farmer who said he had heard all Mr. Emerson's lectures before the Lyceum and added—"and understood 'em too."

But I must also tell that Mrs. Storer relates that her mother, Madam Hoar, seeing Ma'am Bemis, a neighbor who came in to work for her, drying her hands and rolling down her sleeves one afternoon somewhat earlier than usual, asked her if she was going so soon: "Yes, I've got to go now. I'm going to Mr. Emerson's lecture." "Do you understand Mr. Emerson?" "Not a word, but I like to go and see him stand up there and look as if he thought everyone was as good as he was."

MÀ-KA-TAI-ME-SHE-KIÀ-KIÀK / BLACK HAWK
<u>1767?</u> – 1838

The year 1833 saw the publication of a searing account of Native American removal: *Life of Ma-Ka-Tai-Me-She-Kia-Kiak or Black Hawk*, significantly subtitled "Dictated by Himself." The book told the story of Black Hawk, a Sauk leader who had recently come to celebrity—or, in the views of some, to notoriety—for his involvement in a movement of resistance to the enforced migration of his people. The narrative was indeed based upon a dictation by Black Hawk, who was, at the time of the dictation, nearing the end of his term of imprisonment for his role in what became known as the Black Hawk War; the recording of his story was a joint effort shared by Antoine LeClaire, a Pottawatomi and French-Canadian government interpreter, and John Barton Patterson, a Virginian newspaper editor. In the context of a literary scene gripped by "frontier" romances such as James Fenimore Cooper's *The Last of the Mohicans* (1826)—which were narrated from the colonial point of view and tended to depict the suppression of Native American life and culture as tragic but inevitable—*Life of Black Hawk* stood out as monumental in its depiction of the active fight for the preservation of Sauk land, autonomy, and culture, and in the vital challenge Black Hawk presented to colonial assumptions regarding land rights, Native American culture, and the presumed national destiny.

Mà-ka-tai-me-she-kià-kiàk, whose name translates roughly to Black Sparrow Hawk or simply Black Hawk, was probably born around 1767, based on estimates of his age at the time he dictated his *Life*. His native village was Saukenuk, on Rock Island (now Arsenal Island), Illinois. The opening pages of Black Hawk's narrative recount the first stages of his people's relationship with white settlers as well as the ancestral origin of his own claim to Sauk Chiefdom. He says nothing of his childhood; his account of his own life begins around age fifteen, when he participated in his first battle against the Osages, a longstanding enemy of the Sauk. Though Black Hawk was neither a hereditary nor an elected civil chief, he was clearly a charismatic leader and a highly competent warrior, and is often referred to as a war chief in recognition of his leadership role. After siding with the British in the War of 1812—a war which was divisive among the Sauk—Black Hawk and his "British band" entered into a period of rising conflict with American settlers, which eventually led to the enforced migration of the Sauk out of their traditional territory, to which Black Hawk led a movement of resistance in the early 1830s.

The Black Hawk War (also known as the U.S.–Sauk War), may be understood in relation to President Andrew Jackson's genocidal "Indian removal" policies, which sought to banish numerous Native American tribes from their homelands to lands west of the Mississippi River. More narrowly, the origin of this particular 1832 conflict can be traced to the 1804 Treaty of St. Louis, which Black Hawk openly condemns in his *Life*. The treaty stipulated the ceding of millions of acres of Sauk land east of the Mississippi River to the United States, in exchange for a supply of provisions and a $1000 annuity. Black Hawk continually insisted on the invalidity of this treaty: deviating from the precedent afforded by earlier treaties, and from the consensus-based political practices of the Sauk, it had been signed by only four delegates from the Sauk nation and one member of the closely allied Meskwaki (referred to throughout the *Life* as the Fox), all of whom were reportedly intoxicated at the time of the signing and none of whom is believed to have understood the full extent and consequences of the treaty's claims. Though the tribe was for a time permitted to continue living and hunting upon the land, its members came into frequent conflict with white settlers and were eventually forced out when the land was officially sold to colonists. While many Sauk—including those following the leadership of Black Hawk's rival, Ke-o-kuck—complied with this demand, Black Hawk and his band continually resisted expulsion, making numerous attempts to return to their homeland. Black Hawk's band was finally defeated in August 1832 after a brutal struggle at Bad Axe, in which U.S. forces fired upon families who were trying to cross the Mississippi. Approximately 150 to 300 members of Black Hawk's band died in the massacre; the U.S. forces lost five men.

Three weeks after the events at Bad Axe, Black Hawk surrendered himself to U.S. forces. Along with several fellow leaders, he was held in captivity at the Jefferson Barracks in Missouri for eight months, a period he describes in his *Life* as tedious and degrading. Following this, Black Hawk's life took an extraordinary turn; though released from prison, he was compelled to go on a tour of the northeastern states under continued military custody. He was both shown to the American public and introduced to various political and military figures. The intention behind the enforced tour is unclear: it may have been a show of American military prowess and social superiority, and it may have been designed to further humiliate Black Hawk by publicly displaying him as a kind of trophy. To the inhabitants of New York, Philadelphia, Baltimore, and other northeastern cities, Black Hawk was evidently a spectacle to behold, and crowds gathered to meet and gawk at him. Nevertheless, it is evident from Black Hawk's own narrative that he enjoyed much of his time on tour, and that he used it as an opportunity to learn about U.S. culture and society. After several months—during which he crossed paths a number of times with President Jackson, and was once introduced to him—Black Hawk was finally released.

It is likely that some of the people Black Hawk met during this period encouraged him to have his story recorded. Though all documentation regarding the origins of his collaboration with LeClaire and Patterson has been lost, LeClaire claims in his introductory note to the *Life* that it was Black Hawk himself who first approached him with the intention of sharing his version of events. LeClaire was the official government interpreter for the Sauk and Meskwaki nations; Patterson was a Virginian newspaper editor, and was likely responsible for many editorial modifications, such as bracketed insertions, italicized words and phrases, and exclamation marks. Many reviewers at the time of *Life*'s publication thought the work had to be a hoax; many others, however, received it as the first published work to give expression to a truly "Indian" voice. (In so doing, they drew a contrast between the *Life* and earlier works written by literate Native Americans such as William Apess, whom such readers considered to be too fully assimilated to be capable of authentic cultural expression.)

Life of Black Hawk was an instant success, going through five editions in its first year. For the next few years of his life Black Hawk was something of a celebrity, and became a popular subject for portraits by artists such as George Catlin. The year 1838 saw the publication of another biography, *Life and Adventures of Black Hawk*, by Benjamin Drake, and he was the central figure of an 1839 long poem entitled *Ma-ka-tai-me-she-kia-kiak; or, Black Hawk, and Scenes in the West* by Elbert H. Smith. In 1882 J.B. Patterson, this time acting on his own rather than with LeClaire, released a new edition of the *Life* which further modified the text's language and introduced new narrative elements (now believed to be complete fabrications).

Another new edition appeared in 1916, with annotations and a new preface and introduction by historian Milo Milton Quaife. Quaife saw the story of Black Hawk as illuminating, "as with a flash of lightning, the viewpoint and state of mind of a typical representative of the vanquished race," but his appreciation of Black Hawk's autobiography was colored throughout by prejudice; he took it as a given that "the red man" was, "as measured by civilized standards …, vastly the white man's inferior"; that whatever wisdom a Native American might possess was "the wisdom of the child of the forest"; and that the conquest of the American Indian was "an essential accompaniment to the progress of the human race." Similar views held sway among white historians and literary historians well into the second half of the twentieth century; as recently as 1995 the sixth edition of *The Oxford Companion to American Literature* continued to reprint James D. Hart's summation of Black Hawk's story from the 1943 first edition, portraying him as a leader who "refused to accept" the provisions of a legitimate treaty, and "instead, made war in frontier settlements." By then, however, a fuller and fairer interpretation of Black Hawk's life and writings had begun to emerge, most notably with the publication of Roger L. Nichols's *Black Hawk and the Warrior's Path* (1992, second edition 2017). New editions of the *Life* edited by Nichols (1999) and by J.

Gerald Kennedy (2008) have furthered our understanding of the degree to which Black Hawk's story, in Kennedy's words, "exposes the dark side of America's blind faith in its own sacred destiny."

Black Hawk died in 1838 while living in Iowa; his body was buried on a friend's farm. His remains were stolen the following year, and kept on display at the Burlington Geological and Historical Society in Iowa until 1855, when the building burned down. *Life* is a testament to Black Hawk's persistent defense of Sauk land and culture.

NOTE ON THE TEXT: The text presented below is based on that of the first edition of *Life of Ma-Ka-Tai-Me-She-Kia-Kiak or Black Hawk, Embracing the Tradition of His Nation* (1833). Bracketed words or phrases in this text represent editorial additions on the parts of Patterson and LeClaire. Spelling and punctuation have been modernized in accordance with the practices of this anthology. The full text of Black Hawk's *Life* is included in the website component of this anthology.

⌘ ⌘ ⌘

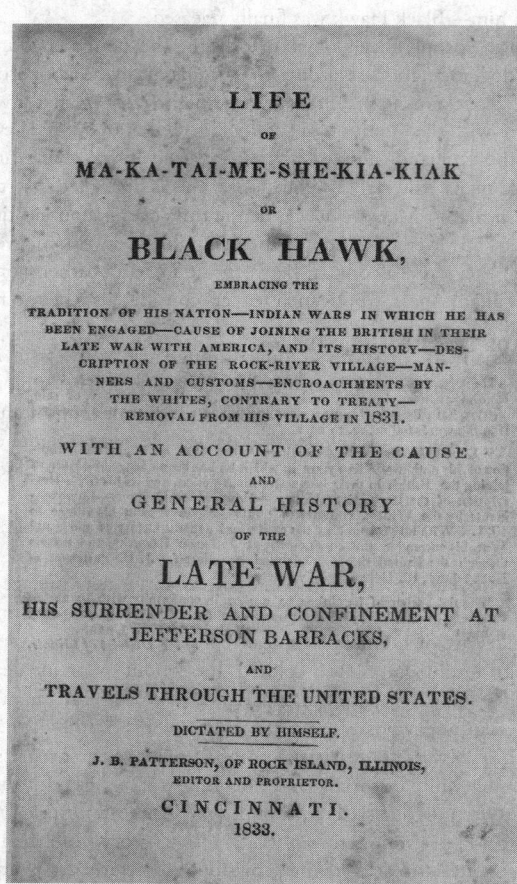

LIFE

OF

MA-KA-TAI-ME-SHE-KIA-KIAK

OR

BLACK HAWK,

EMBRACING THE

TRADITION OF HIS NATION—INDIAN WARS IN WHICH HE HAS BEEN ENGAGED—CAUSE OF JOINING THE BRITISH IN THEIR LATE WAR WITH AMERICA, AND ITS HISTORY—DESCRIPTION OF THE ROCK-RIVER VILLAGE—MANNERS AND CUSTOMS—ENCROACHMENTS BY THE WHITES, CONTRARY TO TREATY—REMOVAL FROM HIS VILLAGE IN 1831.

WITH AN ACCOUNT OF THE CAUSE

AND

GENERAL HISTORY

OF THE

LATE WAR,

HIS SURRENDER AND CONFINEMENT AT JEFFERSON BARRACKS,

AND

TRAVELS THROUGH THE UNITED STATES.

DICTATED BY HIMSELF.

J. B. PATTERSON, OF ROCK ISLAND, ILLINOIS, EDITOR AND PROPRIETOR.

CINCINNATI.
1833.

from *Life of Ma-Ka-Tai-Me-She-Kia-Kiak, or Black Hawk*

[By this point in Black Hawk's narrative, the War of 1812 has come to an end. The Sauk have been invited to Portage des Sioux to participate in the peace treaty signing, but their chief dies along the way, and his successor refuses to continue the journey, angering the U.S. leaders. The excerpt below picks up just after an interlude in which Black Hawk recounts a story shared to him by his Potawatomi friend Gomo, about a young Potawatomi man killed when his hunting party had been violently attacked by a group of white cattle herders.]

Here Gomo ended his story. I could relate many similar ones that have come within my own knowledge and observation; but I dislike to look back and bring on sorrow afresh. I will resume my narrative.

The great chief at St. Louis[1] having sent word for us to go down and confirm the treaty of peace, we did not hesitate, but started immediately, that we might smoke the *peace-pipe* with him. On our arrival, we met the great chiefs in council. They explained to us the words of our Great Father at Washington, accusing us of heinous crimes and diverse[2] misdemeanors, particularly in not coming down when first invited. We knew very well that *our Great Father had deceived us*, and thereby *forced* us to join the British, and could not believe that he had put this speech into the mouths of these chiefs to deliver to us. I was not a civil chief, and consequently made no reply: but our chiefs told the commissioners that "what they had said was a *lie*! That our Great Father had sent no such speech, he knowing the situation in which we had been placed had been *caused by him*!" The white chiefs appeared very angry at this reply, and said they "would break off the treaty with us, and *go to war*, as they would not be insulted."

Our chiefs had no intention of insulting them, and told them so—"that they merely wished to explain to them that *they had told a lie*, without making them angry; in the same manner that the whites do, when

they do not believe what is told them!" The council then proceeded, and the pipe of peace was smoked.

Here, for the first time, I touched the goose quill to the treaty—not knowing, however, that, by that act, I consented to give away my village. Had that been explained to me, I should have opposed it, and never would have signed their treaty, as my recent conduct will clearly prove.[3]

What do we know of the manner of the laws and customs of the white people? They might buy our bodies for dissection, and we would touch the goose quill to confirm it, without knowing what we are doing. This was the case with myself and people in touching the goose quill the first time.

We can only judge of what is proper and right by our standard of right and wrong, which differs widely from the whites, if I have been correctly informed. The whites *may do bad* all their lives, and then, if they are *sorry for it* when about to die, *all is well*! But with us it is different: we must continue throughout our lives to do what we conceive to be good. If we have corn and meat, and know of a family that have none, we divide with them. If we have more blankets than sufficient, and others have not enough, we must give to them that want. But I will presently explain our customs, and the manner we live.

We were friendly treated by the white chiefs, and started back to our village on Rock River. Here we found that troops had arrived to build a fort at Rock Island.[4] This, in our opinion, was a contradiction to what we had done—"to prepare for war in time of peace." We did not, however, object to their building their fort on the island, but were very sorry, as this was the best island on the Mississippi, and had long been the resort of our young people during the summer. It was our garden (like the white people have near to their big villages) which supplied us with strawberries, blackberries, gooseberries, plums, apples, and nuts of different kinds; and its waters supplied us with fine fish, being situated in the rapids of the river. In my early life, I spent many happy days on this island. A good spirit had care of it, who lived in a cave in the

---

1   *great chief at St. Louis* William Clark (1770–1838), Missouri governor who had famously explored western North America with Meriwether Lewis.

2   *diverse* Various.

3   *Here, for the … clearly prove* Unbeknownst to Black Hawk, this peace treaty also reaffirmed the terms of the 1804 treaty.

4   *build a fort at Rock Island* This was to become Fort Armstrong, construction of which began in 1816.

rocks immediately under the place where the fort now stands, and has often been seen by our people. He was white, with large wings like a *swan's*, but ten times larger. We were particular not to make much noise in that part of the island which he inhabited, for fear of disturbing him. But the noise of the fort has since driven him away, and no doubt a *bad spirit* has taken his place!

Our village was situate on the north side of Rock River, at the foot of its rapids, and on the point of land between Rock River and the Mississippi. In its front, a prairie extended to the bank of the Mississippi; and in our rear, a continued bluff, gently ascending from the prairie. On the side of this bluff we had our corn-fields, extending about two miles up, running parallel with the Mississippi; where we joined those of the Foxes, whose village was on the bank of the Mississippi, opposite the lower end of Rock Island, and three miles distant from ours. We had about eight hundred acres in cultivation, including what we had on the islands of Rock River. The land around our village, uncultivated, was covered with blue-grass, which made excellent pasture for our horses. Several fine springs broke out of the bluff, nearby, from which we were supplied with good water. The rapids of Rock River furnished us with an abundance of excellent fish, and the land, being good, never failed to produce good crops of corn, beans, pumpkins, and squashes. We always had plenty—our children never cried with hunger, nor our people were never in want. Here our village had stood for more than a hundred years, during all which time we were the undisputed possessors of the valley of the Mississippi, from the Ouisconsin to the Portage des Sioux, near the mouth of the Missouri, being about seven hundred miles in length.

At this time we had very little intercourse with the whites, except our traders. Our village was healthy, and there was no place in the country possessing such advantages, nor no hunting grounds better than those we had in possession. If another prophet had come to our village in those days, and told us what has since taken place, none of our people would have believed him. What! to be driven from our village and hunting grounds, and not even permitted to visit the graves of our forefathers, and relations, and friends!

This hardship is not known to the whites. With us it is a custom to visit the graves of our friends, and keep them in repair for many years. The mother will go alone to weep over the grave of her child! The brave, with pleasure, visits the grave of his father, after he has been successful in war, and repaints the post that shows where he lies! There is no place like that where the bones of our forefathers lie, to go to when in grief. Here the Great Spirit will take pity on us!

But, how different is our situation now, from what it was in those days! Then were we as happy as the buffalo on the plains—but now, we are as miserable as the hungry howling wolf in the prairie! But I am digressing from my story. Bitter reflection crowds upon my mind, and must find utterance.

When we returned to our village in the spring, from our wintering grounds, we would finish trading with our traders, who always followed us to our village. We purposely kept some of our fine furs for this trade; and, as there was great opposition among them, who should get these skins, we always got our goods cheap. After this trade was over, the traders would give us a few kegs of rum, which was generally promised in the fall, to encourage us to make a good hunt, and not go to war. They would then start with their furs and peltries for their homes. Our old men would take a frolic (at this time our young men never drank). When this was ended, the next thing to be done was to bury our dead (such as had died during the year). This is a great *medicine feast*. The relations of those who have died, give all the goods they have purchased, as presents to their friends—thereby reducing themselves to poverty, to show the Great Spirit that they are humble, so that he will take pity on them. We would next open the caches, and take out corn and other provisions, which had been put up in the fall—and then commence repairing our lodges. As soon as this is accomplished, we repair the fences around our fields, and clean them off, ready for planting corn. This work is done by our women. The men, during this time, are feasting on dried venison, bear's meat, wild fowl, and corn, prepared in different ways; and recounting to each other what took place during the winter.

Our women plant the corn, and as soon as they get done, we make a feast and dance the *crane* dance, in which they join us, dressed in their best, and decorated with feathers. At this feast our young braves select the young woman they wish to have for a wife. He then informs his mother, who calls on the mother of the girl, when the arrangement is made, and the time appointed for him to come. He goes to the lodge when all are asleep (or pretend to be), lights his matches, which have been provided for the purpose, and soon finds where his intended sleeps. He then awakens her, and holds the light to his face that she may know him—after which he places the light close to her. If she blows it out, the ceremony is ended, and he appears in the lodge the next morning, as one of the family. If she does not blow out the light, but leaves it to burn out, he retires from the lodge. The next day he places himself in full view of it, and plays his flute. The young women go out, one by one, to see who he is playing for. The tune changes, to let them know he is not playing for them. When his intended makes her appearance at the door, he continues his *courting* tune, until she returns to the lodge. He then gives over playing, and makes another trial at night, which generally turns out favorable. During the first year they ascertain whether they can agree with each other, and can be happy—if not, they part, and each looks out again. If we were to live together and disagree we should be as foolish as the whites. No indiscretion can banish a woman from her parental lodge—no difference how many children she may bring home, she is always welcome—the kettle is over the fire to feed them.

The crane dance often lasts two or three days. When this is over, we feast again, and have our *national dance*. The large square in the village is swept and prepared for the purpose. The chiefs and old warriors, take seats on mats which have been spread at the upper end of the square—the drummers and singers come next, and the braves and women form the sides, leaving a large space in the middle. The drums beat, and the singers commence. A warrior enters the square, keeping time with the music. He shows the manner he started on a war party—how he approached the enemy—he strikes, and describes the way he killed him. All join in applause. He then leaves the square, and another enters and takes his place. Such of our young men as have not been out in war parties, and killed an enemy, stand back ashamed—not being able to enter the square. I remember that I was ashamed to look where

our young women stood, before I could take my stand in the square as a warrior.

What pleasure it is to an old warrior, to see his son come forward and relate his exploits—it makes him feel young, and induces him to enter the square, and "fight his battles o'er again."[1]

This national dance makes our warriors. When I was travelling last summer, on a steam boat, on a large river, going from New York to Albany, I was shown the place where the Americans dance their national dance [West Point[2]]; where the old warriors recount to their young men, what they have done, to stimulate them to go and do likewise. This surprised me, as I did not think the whites understood our way of making braves.

When our national dance is over—our corn-fields hoed, and every weed dug up, and our corn about knee-high, all our young men would start in a direction towards sundown, to hunt deer and buffalo—being prepared also to kill Sioux, if any are found on our hunting grounds—a part of our old men and women to the lead mines to make lead—and the remainder of our people start to fish, and get mat stuff.[3] Everyone leaves the village, and remains about forty days. They then return: the hunting party bringing in dried buffalo and deer meat, and sometimes *Sioux scalps*, when they are found trespassing on our hunting grounds. At other times they are met by a party of Sioux too strong for them, and are driven in. If the Sioux have killed the Sacs last, they expect to be retaliated upon, and will fly before them, and vice versa. Each party knows that the other has a right to retaliate, which induces those who have killed last, to give way before their enemy—as neither wish to strike, except to avenge the death of their relatives. All our wars are predicated by the relatives of those killed; or by aggressions upon our hunting grounds.

The party from the lead mines bring lead, and the others dried fish, and mats for our winter lodges. Presents are now made by each party; the first, giving to the others dried buffalo and deer, and they, in exchange, presenting them with lead, dried fish and

---

[1] *fight his battles o'er again* Loose quotation from John Dryden's *Alexander's Feast* (1697), evidently an insertion on the part of LeClaire or Patterson.

[2] *West Point* Large military academy in New York.

[3] *mat stuff* I.e., material for making mats for the lodges.

mats. This is a happy season of the year—having plenty of provisions, such as beans, squashes, and other produce, with our dried meat and fish, we continue to make feasts and visit each other, until our corn is ripe. Some lodge in the village makes a feast daily, to the Great Spirit. I cannot explain this so that the white people would comprehend me, as we have no regular standard among us. Everyone makes his feast as he thinks best, to please the Great Spirit, who has the care of all beings created. Others believe in two Spirits: one good and one bad, and make feasts for the Bad Spirit, *to keep him quiet*! If they can make peace with him, the Good Spirit will not hurt them! For my part, I am of opinion, that so far as we have *reason*, we have a right to use it, in determining what is right or wrong; and should pursue that path which we believe to be right— believing, that "whatever is, is right." If the Great and Good Spirit wished us to believe and do as the whites, he could easily change our opinions, so that we would see, and think, and act as they do. We are *nothing* compared to His power, and we feel and know it. We have men among us, like the whites, who pretend to know the right path, but will not consent to show it without *pay*! I have no faith in their paths—but believe that every man must make his own path!

When our corn is getting ripe, our young people watch with anxiety for the signal to pull roasting ears—as none dare touch them until the proper time. When the corn is fit to use, another great ceremony takes place, with feasting, and returning thanks to the Great Spirit for giving us corn.

I will here relate the manner in which corn first came. According to tradition, handed down to our people, a beautiful woman was seen to descend from the clouds, and alight upon the earth, by two of our ancestors, who had killed a deer, and were sitting by a fire, roasting a part of it to eat. They were astonished at seeing her, and concluded that she must be hungry, and had smelt the meat—and immediately went to her, taking with them a piece of the roasted venison. They presented it to her, and she eat—and told them to return to the spot where she was sitting, at the end of one year, and they would find a reward for their kindness and generosity. She then ascended to the clouds, and disappeared. The two men returned to their village, and explained to the nation what they

had seen, done, and heard—but were laughed at by their people. When the period arrived, for them to visit this consecrated ground, where they were to find a reward for their attention to the beautiful woman of the clouds, they went with a large party, and found, where her right hand had rested on the ground, *corn* growing—and where the left hand had rested, *beans*, and immediately where she had been seated, *tobacco*.

The two first have, ever since, been cultivated by our people, as our principal provisions—and the last used for smoking. The white people have since found out the latter, and seem to relish it as much as we do—as they use it in different ways, viz. smoking, snuffing and eating![1]

We thank the Great Spirit for all the benefits he has conferred upon us. For myself, I never take a drink of water from a spring, without being mindful of his goodness.

We next have our great ball play—from three to five hundred on a side, play this game. We play for horses, guns, blankets, or any other kind of property we have. The successful party take the stakes, and all retire to our lodges in peace and friendship.

We next commence horse-racing, and continue our sport and feasting, until the corn is all secured. We then prepare to leave our village for our hunting grounds. The traders arrive, and give us credit for such articles as we want to clothe our families, and enable us to hunt. We first, however, hold a council with them, to ascertain the price they will give for our skins, and what they will charge us for goods. We inform them where we intend hunting—and tell them where to build their houses. At this place, we deposit part of our corn, and leave our old people. The traders have always been kind to them and relieved them when in want. They were always much respected by our people—and never since we have been a nation, has one of them been killed by any of our people.

We disperse, in small parties, to make our hunt, and as soon as it is over, we return to our traders establishment, with our skins, and remain feasting, playing cards, and other pastimes, until near the close of the winter. Our young men then start on the beaver hunt; others to hunt racoons and muskrats—and the remainder of our people go to the sugar camps to make

---

[1]   *eating*   I.e., chewing.

sugar. All leave our encampment, and appoint a place to meet on the Mississippi, so that we may return to our village together, in the spring. We always spent our time pleasantly at the sugar camp. It being the season for wild fowl, we lived well, and always had plenty, when the hunters came in, that we might make a feast for them. After this is over, we return to our village, accompanied, sometimes, by our traders. In this way, the year rolled round happily. But these are times that were!

On returning in the spring, from our hunting ground, I had the pleasure of meeting our old friend, the trader of Peoria, at Rock Island. He came up in a boat from St. Louis, not as a trader, as in times past, but as our *agent*. We were all pleased to see him. He told us, that he narrowly escaped falling into the hands of Dixon. He remained with us a short time, gave us good advice, and then returned to St. Louis.

The Sioux having committed depredations on our people, we sent out war parties that summer who succeeded in killing *fourteen*. I paid several visits to Fort Armstrong during the summer, and was always well treated. We were not as happy then in our village as formerly. Our people got more liquor than customary. I used all my influence to prevent drunkenness, but without effect. As the settlements progressed towards us, we became worse off, and more unhappy. Many of our people, instead of going to their old hunting grounds, where game was plenty, would go near to the settlements to hunt—and, instead of saving their skins to pay the trader for goods furnished them in the fall, would sell them to the settlers for whisky! and return in the spring without the means of getting anything for them.

About this time my eldest son was taken sick and died. He had always been a dutiful child, and had just grown to manhood. Soon after, my youngest daughter, an interesting and affectionate child, died also. This was a hard stroke, because I loved my children. In my distress, I left the noise of the village, and built my lodge on a mound in my corn-field, and enclosed it with a fence, around which I planted corn and beans. Here I was with my family alone. I gave everything I had away, and reduced myself to poverty. The only covering I retained, was a piece of buffalo robe. I resolved on blacking my face and fasting, for two years, for the loss of my two children—drinking only of water in the middle of the day, and eating sparingly of boiled corn at sunset. I fulfilled my promise, hoping that the Great Spirit would take pity on me.

My nation had now some difficulty with the Ioways, with whom we wished to be at peace. Our young men had repeatedly killed some of the Ioways; and these breaches had always been made up by giving presents to the relations of those killed. But the last council we had with them, we promised that, in case any more of their people were killed ours, instead of presents, we would give up the person, or persons, that had done the injury. We made this determination known to our people; but, notwithstanding, one of our young men killed an Ioway the following winter.

A party of our people were about starting for the Ioway village to give the young man up. I agreed to accompany them. When we were ready to start, I called at the lodge for the young man to go with us. He was sick, but willing to go. His brother, however, prevented him, and insisted on going to die in his place, as his brother was unable to travel. We started, and on the seventh day arrived in sight of the Ioway village, and when within a short distance of it, halted and dismounted. We all bid farewell to our young brave, who entered the village alone, singing his *death-song*, and sat down in the square in the middle of the village. One of the Ioway chiefs came out to us. We told him that we had fulfilled our promise—that we had brought the brother of the young man who had killed one of their people—that he had volunteered to come in his place, in consequence of his brother being unable to travel from sickness. We had no further conversation, but mounted our horses and rode off. As we started, I cast my eye towards the village, and observed the Ioways coming out of their lodges with spears and war clubs. We took our trail back, and travelled until dark—then encamped and made a fire. We had not been here long, before we heard the sound of horses coming towards us. We seized our arms; but instead of an enemy, it was our young brave with two horses. He told me that after we had left him, they menaced him with death for sometime—then gave him something to eat—smoked the pipe with him—and made him a present of the two horses and some goods, and started him after us. When we arrived at our village, our people were much pleased; and for the noble and generous conduct of the Ioways, on this occasion, not one of their people has been killed since by any of our nation.

That fall I visited Malden[1] with several of my band, and were well treated by our British father, who gave us a variety of presents. He also gave me a medal, and told me there never would be war between England and America again; but, for my fidelity to the British during the war that had terminated sometime before, requested me to come with my band every year and get presents, as Col. Dixon had promised me.

I returned, and hunted that winter on the Two Rivers. The whites were now settling the country fast. I was out one day hunting in a bottom,[2] and met three white men. They accused me of killing their hogs; I denied it; but they would not listen to me. One of them took my gun out of my hand and fired it off—then took out the flint, gave back my gun, and commenced beating me with sticks, and ordered me off. I was so much bruised that I could not sleep for several nights.

Some time after this occurrence, one of my camp cut a bee-tree,[3] and carried the honey to his lodge. A party of white men soon followed, and told him that the bee-tree was theirs, and that he had no right to cut it. He pointed to the honey, and told them to take it; they were not satisfied with this, but took all the packs of skins that he had collected during the winter, to pay his trader and clothe his family with in the spring, and carried them off!

How could we like such people, who treated us so unjustly? We determined to break up our camp, for fear that they would do worse—and when we joined our people in the spring, a great many of them complained of similar treatment.

This summer our agent[4] came to live at Rock Island. He treated us well, and gave us good advice. I visited him and the trader very often during the summer, and, for the first time, heard talk of our having to leave my village. The trader explained to me the terms of the treaty that had been made, and said we would be obliged to leave the Illinois side of the Mississippi, and advised us to select a good place for our village, and remove to it in the spring. He pointed out the difficulties we would have to encounter, if we remained at our village on Rock River. He had great influence with the principal Fox chief (his adopted brother), and persuaded him to leave his village, and go to the west side of the Mississippi River, and build another—which he did the spring following.

Nothing was now talked of but leaving our village. Ke-o-kuck had been persuaded to consent to go; and was using all his influence, backed by the war chief at fort Armstrong, and our agent and trader at Rock Island, to induce others to go with him. He sent the crier through the village to inform our people that it was the wish of our Great Father that we should remove to the west side of the Mississippi—and recommended the Ioway River[5] as a good place for the new village—and wished his party to make such arrangements, before they started on their winter's hunt, as to preclude the necessity of their returning to the village in the spring.

The party opposed to removing, called upon me for my opinion. I gave it freely—and after questioning Quàsh-quà-me about the sale of the lands, he assured me that he "never had consented to the sale of our village." I now promised this party to be their leader, and raised the standard of opposition to Ke-o-kuck, with a full determination not to leave my village. I had an interview with Ke-o-kuck, to see if this difficulty could not be settled with our Great Father—and told him to propose to give other land (any that our Great Father might choose, even our *lead mines*), to be peaceably permitted to keep the small point of land on which our village and fields were situate. I was of opinion that the white people had plenty of land, and would never take our village from us. Ke-o-kuck promised to make an exchange if possible; and applied to our agent, and the great chief at St. Louis (who has charge of all the agents), for permission to go to Washington to see our Great Father for that purpose. This satisfied us for some time. We started to our hunting grounds, in good hopes that something would be done for us. During the winter, I received information that three families of whites had arrived at our village, and destroyed some

---

[1]   *Malden* British-held fort located in present-day Ontario, visited annually by Black Hawk and his band.

[2]   *bottom* Valley or lowland.

[3]   *bee-tree* Tree in which honeybees have built their hive.

[4]   *our agent* This would have been English trader George Davenport (1783–1845), a close friend of Antoine LeClaire.

[5]   *Ioway River* I.e., the Iowa River.

of our lodges, and were making fences and dividing our corn-fields for their own use—*and were quarrelling among themselves about their lines, in the division*! I immediately started for Rock River, a distance of ten day's travel, and on my arrival, found the report to be true. I went to my lodge, and saw a family occupying it. I wished to talk with them, but they could not understand me. I then went to Rock Island, and (the agent being absent) told the interpreter what I wanted to say to those people, viz: "Not to settle on our lands—nor trouble our lodges or fences—that there was plenty of land in the country for them to settle upon—and they must leave our village, as we were coming back to it in the spring." The interpreter wrote me a paper, and I went back to the village, and showed it to the intruders, but could not understand their reply. I expected, however, that they would remove, as I requested them. I returned to Rock Island, passed the night there, and had a long conversation with the trader. He again advised me to give up, and make my village with Ke-o-kuck, on the Ioway River. I told him that I would not. The next morning I crossed the Mississippi, on very bad ice—but the Great Spirit made it strong, that I might pass over safe. I travelled three days farther to see the Winnebago sub-agent, and converse with him on the subject of our difficulties. He gave me no better news than the trader had done. I started then, by way of Rock River, to see the prophet,[1] believing that he was a man of great knowledge. When we met, I explained to him everything as it was. He at once agreed that I was right, and advised me never to give up our village, for the whites to plough up the bones of our people. He said, that if we remained at our village, the whites would not trouble us—and advised me to get Ke-o-kuck, and the party that had consented to go with him to the Ioway in the spring, to return, and remain at our village.

I returned to my hunting ground, after an absence of one moon, and related what I had done. In a short time we came up to our village, and found that the whites had not left it—but that others had come, and that the greater part of our corn-fields had been enclosed. When we landed, the whites appeared displeased because we had come back. We repaired the lodges that had been left standing, and built others. Ke-o-kuck came to the village; but his object was to persuade others to follow him to the Ioway. He had accomplished nothing towards making arrangements for us to remain, or to exchange other lands for our village. There was no more friendship existing between us. I looked upon him as a coward, and no brave, to abandon his village to be occupied by strangers. What *right* had these people to our village, and our fields which the Great Spirit had given us to live upon?

My reason teaches me that *land cannot be sold*. The Great Spirit gave it to his children to live upon, and cultivate, as far as is necessary for their subsistence; and so long as they occupy and cultivate it, they have the right to the soil—but if they voluntarily leave it, then any other people have a right to settle upon it. Nothing can be sold, but such things as can be carried away.

In consequence of the improvements of the intruders on our fields, we found considerable difficulty to get ground to plant a little corn. Some of the whites permitted us to plant small patches in the fields they had fenced, keeping all the best ground for themselves. Our women had great difficulty in climbing their fences (being unaccustomed to the kind), and were ill-treated if they left a rail down.

One of my old friends thought he was safe. His corn-field was on a small island of Rock River. He planted his corn; it came up well—but the white man saw it! He wanted the island, and took his team over, ploughed up the corn, and re-planted it for himself! The old man shed tears; not for himself, but the distress his family would be in if they raised no corn.

The white people brought whisky into our village, made our people drunk, and cheated them out of their homes, guns and traps! This fraudulent system was carried to such an extent that I apprehended serious difficulties might take place, unless a stop was put to it. Consequently, I visited all the whites and begged them not to sell whisky to my people. One of them continued the practice openly. I took a party of my young men, went to his house, and took out his barrel and broke in the head and turned out the whisky. I did this for fear some of the whites might be killed by my people when drunk.

---

[1] *the prophet* This would have been the influential medicine man Wabokieshiek (c. 1794–c. 1841), also known as White Cloud and as the Winnebago Prophet.

Our people were treated badly by the whites on many occasions. At one time, a white man beat one of our women cruelly, for pulling a few suckers[1] of corn out of his field, to suck, when hungry! At another time, one of our young men was beat with clubs by two white men for opening a fence which crossed our road, to take his horse through. His shoulder blade was broken, and his body badly bruised, from which he soon after *died*!

Bad, and cruel, as our people were treated by the whites, not one of them was hurt or molested by any of my band. I hope this will prove that we are a peaceable people—having permitted ten men to take possession of our corn-fields; prevent us from planting corn; burn and destroy our lodges; ill-treat our women; and *beat to death* our men, without offering resistance to their barbarous cruelties. This is a lesson worthy for the white man to learn: to use forbearance when injured.

We acquainted our agent daily with our situation, and through him, the great chief at St. Louis—and hoped that something would be done for us. The whites were *complaining* at the same time that *we* were *intruding* upon *their rights*! THEY made themselves out the *injured* party, and *we* the *intruders*! and called loudly to the great war chief to protect *their* property!

How smooth must be the language of the whites, when they can make right look like wrong, and wrong like right.

During this summer, I happened at Rock Island, when a great chief arrived, whom I had known as the great chief of Illinois [governor Cole[2]], in company with another chief, who, I have been told, is a great writer [judge Jas. Hall[3]]. I called upon them, and begged to explain to them the grievances under which me and my people were laboring, hoping that they could do something for us. The great chief, however, did not seem disposed to council with me. He said he was no longer the chief of Illinois—that his children had selected another father in his stead, and that he now only ranked as they did. I was surprised at this talk, as

I had always heard that he was a good, brave, and great chief. But the white people never appear to be satisfied. When they get a good father, they hold councils (at the suggestion of some bad, ambitious man, who wants the place himself), and conclude, among themselves, that this man, or some other equally ambitious, would make a better father than they have, and nine times out of ten they don't get as good a one again.

I insisted on explaining to these two chiefs the true situation of my people. They gave their assent: I rose and made a speech, in which I explained to them the treaty made by Quàsh-quà-me, and three of our braves, according to the manner the trader and others had explained it to me. I then told them that Quàsh-quà-me and his party *denied*, positively, having ever sold my village; and that, as I had never known them to *lie*, I was determined to keep it in possession.

I told them that the white people had already entered our village, *burnt our lodges, destroyed our fences, ploughed up our corn, and beat our people*: that they had brought *whisky* into our country, *made our people drunk*, and taken from them their *horses, guns*, and *traps*; and that I had borne all this injury, without suffering any of my braves to raise a hand against the whites.

My object in holding this council was to get the opinion of these two chiefs, as to the best course for me to pursue. I had appealed in vain, time after time, to our agent, who regularly represented our situation to the great chief at St. Louis, whose duty it was to call upon our Great Father to have justice done to us; but instead of this, we are told *that the white people want our country, and we must leave it to them*!

I did not think it possible that our Great Father wished us to leave our village, where we had lived so long, and where the bones of so many of our people had been laid. The great chief said that, as he was no longer a chief, he could do nothing for us; and felt sorry that it was not in his power to aid us—nor did he know how to advise us. Neither of them could do anything for us; but both evidently appeared very sorry. It would give me great pleasure, at all times, to take these two chiefs by the hand.

That fall I paid a visit to the agent, before we started to our hunting grounds, to hear if he had any good news for me. He had news! He said that the land on

---

1   *suckers*   Young shoots growing from the base of the stalk.

2   *governor Cole*   Edward Coles (1786–1868), secretary to President James Madison and governor of Illinois from 1822 to 1826.

3   *judge Jas. Hall*   James Hall (1793–1868), who published a collection of biographical sketches of significant Native Americans between 1836 and 1844.

which our village stood was now ordered to be sold to individuals; and that, when sold, *our right* to remain, by treaty, would be at an end, and that if we returned next spring, we would be *forced* to remove!

We learned during the winter, that *part* of the lands where our village stood had been sold to individuals, and that the *trader* at Rock Island had bought the greater part that had been sold.[1] The reason was now plain to me, why *he* urged us to remove. His object, we thought, was to get our lands. We held several councils that winter to determine what we should do, and resolved, in one of them, to return to our village in the spring, as usual: and concluded, that if we were removed by force, that the *trader*, agent, and others, must be the cause; and that, if found guilty of having us driven from our village, they should be *killed!* The trader stood foremost on this list. He had purchased the land on which my lodge stood, and that of our *graveyard* also! Ne-a-pope proposed to kill him, and the agent, interpreter, the great chief at St. Louis, the war chief at fort Armstrong, Rock Island, and Ke-o-kuck—these being the principal persons to blame for endeavoring to remove us.

Our women received bad accounts from the women that had been raising corn at the new village—the difficulty of breaking the new prairie with hoes—and the small quantity of corn raised. We were nearly in the same situation in regard to the latter, it being the first time I ever knew our people to be in want of provision.

I prevailed upon some of Ke-o-kuck's band to return this spring to the Rock River village. Ke-o-kuck would not return with us. I hoped that we would get permission to go to Washington to settle our affairs with our Great Father. I visited the agent at Rock Island. He was displeased because we had returned to our village, and told me that we *must* remove to the west of the Mississippi. I told him plainly that we *would not!* I visited the interpreter at his house, who advised me to do as the agent had directed me. I then went to see the trader, and upbraided him for buying our lands. He said that if he had not purchased them, some person else would, and that if our Great Father would make an exchange with us, he would willingly give up the land he had purchased to the government. This I

thought was fair, and began to think that he had not acted as badly as I had suspected. We again repaired our lodges, and built others, as most of our village had been burnt and destroyed. Our women selected small patches to plant corn (where the whites had not taken them within their fences), and worked hard to raise something for our children to subsist upon.

I was told that, according to the treaty, we had no *right* to remain on the lands *sold*, and that the government would *force* us to leave them. There was but a small portion, however, that *had been sold*; the balance, remaining in the hands of the government, we claimed the right (if we had no other) to "live and hunt upon, as long as it remained the property of the government," by a stipulation in the same treaty that required us to evacuate it *after* it had been sold. This was the land that we wished to inhabit, and thought we had the best right to occupy.

I heard that there was a great chief on the Wabash, and sent a party to get his advice. They informed him that we had not sold our village. He assured them then, that if we had not sold the land on which our village stood, our Great Father would not take it from us.

I started early to Malden to see the chief of my British Father, and told him my story. He gave the same reply that the chief on the Wabash had given; and, in justice to him, I must say, that he never gave me any bad advice: but advised me to apply to our American Father, who, he said, would do us justice. I next called on the great chief at Detroit,[2] and made the same statement to him that I had to the chief of our British father. He gave me the same reply. He said, if we had not sold our lands, and would remain peaceably on them, that we would not be disturbed. This assured me that I was right, and determined me to hold out, as I had promised my people.

I returned from Malden late in the fall. My people were gone to their hunting ground, whither I followed. Here I learned that they had been badly treated all summer by the whites; and that a treaty had been held at Prairie du Chien. Ke-o-kuck and some of our people attended it, and found out that our Great Father had exchanged a small strip of the land that was ceded by Quàsh-quà-me and his party, with the Pottowatomies,

---

[1]   *the trader ... been sold* Davenport purchased the land on Rock Island around 1829.

[2]   *great chief at Detroit* Lewis Cass (1782–1866), territorial governor of Michigan.

for a portion of their land, near Chicago; and that the object of this treaty was to get it back again; and that the United States had agreed to give them *sixteen thousand dollars a year forever*, for this small strip of land— it being less than the twentieth part of that taken from our nation, for *one thousand dollars a year*! This bears evidence of something I cannot explain. This land, they say, belonged to the United States. What reason, then, could have induced them to exchange it with the Pottowatomies? If it was so valuable, why not keep it? Or, if they found that they had made a bad bargain with the Pottowatomies, why not take back their land at a fair proportion of what they gave our nation for it? If this small portion of the land that they took from us for *one thousand dollars* a year, be worth *sixteen thousand dollars a year forever*, to the Pottowatomies, then the whole tract of country taken from us ought to be worth, to our nation, *twenty times* as much as this small fraction.

Here I was again puzzled to find out how the white people reasoned; and began to doubt whether they had any standard of right and wrong!

—1833

ELIAS BOUDINOT / GALLEGINA

c. 1804 – 1839

Cherokee speaker, printer, and journalist Elias Boudinot was among the most influential Indigenous writers of his day. As editor of America's first Native American newspaper—and the first American paper to be published in an Indigenous language—Boudinot facilitated a lively written discourse on pertinent social issues within the Cherokee Nation, and contributed to a broader awareness of contemporary Cherokee society and its relationship to American settler culture.

Elias Boudinot was born Gallegina, or "Buck," Watie, in Oothcalga, Georgia in around 1804. His father Oo'Watie, or David Watie, had been among the founding figures of Oothcalga in the post-Revolutionary period, during which many Cherokee had begun to move away from their former village system onto small, independent homesteads. (The U.S. government enthusiastically supported such moves, seeing them as signs of the progressing "assimilation" of Indigenous peoples.) Gallegina was first educated in a Moravian missionary school, where Indigenous children were not only taught religious and academic subjects but were also encouraged to learn "civilized" arts such as farming, weaving, and sewing. Seen as a promising student, Gallegina was sent north in 1817 to continue his education at the American Board of Commissioners Foreign Mission School in Cornwall, Connecticut. It was on his way there that he met the respected lawyer and politician Elias Boudinot, whose name he adopted as a mark of respect.

The ABC Foreign Mission School aimed to educate and Christianize youth from foreign nations (including Hawaii and China), with the expectation that they would eventually return to their home communities and spread Christianity there themselves. As with the Moravian mission, the focus was at least as much on teaching students European-style agricultural practices as it was on academic learning. Boudinot excelled as a student, and was considered a strong candidate for entry into the Andover Theological Seminary in Massachusetts; in 1822, however, a severe illness caused him to return temporarily to his family home in Georgia.

While in Georgia, Boudinot kept up a written correspondence with Harriet Gold (whose family were involved in the running of the Foreign Mission School). The public announcement of their engagement in 1825 caused an uproar in Cornwall, where newspapers denounced the interracial relationship, and effigies of the couple were burned in the street. The Gold family at first refused to give their consent to the marriage, but when Harriet herself became severely ill they saw it as a sign from God and relented; Gold and Boudinot married in 1826. The Foreign Mission School never recovered from the scandal, with former white supporters now seeing the school as a breeding ground for interracial marriage. It closed permanently not long thereafter.

Now married, the Boudinots established a home in New Echota, Georgia, then the capital of the Cherokee Nation. Boudinot was subsequently appointed by the Cherokee Council to return to the northeast on a speaking tour to raise funds for a Cherokee national academy and printing press. Boudinot's lectures centered on subjects such as racial equality, and also emphasized the "progress" made in recent years by the Cherokee Nation in adopting many aspects of Euro-American political, agricultural, and social life. The lectures were heavily attended; he went on to publish a pamphlet, *An Address to the Whites* (1826)—based on a speech given in Philadelphia—with the aim of spreading awareness to an even wider audience.

The tour was a modest financial success; sufficient funds were raised for the Nation to launch a newspaper, the *Cherokee Phoenix*, in early 1828, with Boudinot as editor. The *Cherokee Phoenix* was remarkable for printing its content both in English and in Cherokee, using the recently invented Cherokee syllabary. The paper's subscription base came to include most households in the Cherokee Nation, as well as numerous non-Indigenous subscribers in America and Europe. Its content included poetry, religious writings, local reporting, and editorials written by Boudinot on subjects such as racism, Cherokee progress, and Indian removal.

For the first two years of his position as editor, Boudinot fervently opposed removal, describing Georgia's calls for Cherokee relocation as "tyrannical and unchristian," and writing that they threatened "to blast all [the Cherokee's] rising hopes and expectations." As Georgia's actions against the Cherokee Nation grew more aggressive, Boudinot gradually changed his position, seeing peaceful coexistence between the Cherokee and white settlers as impossible, and compliance with the state's demands, however unjust they might have been, as being in the Nation's best interests. By 1832, pressure from the anti-removal Cherokee Council led to Boudinot's resignation. Partly due to a sudden loss of federal government funding, the *Cherokee Phoenix* ceased publication indefinitely in 1834. (A version of the paper was revived as *The Cherokee Advocate* from 1844 to 1906, and it operates today under its original name.)

In December 1835, Boudinot held a conference in his home with U.S. treaty commissioners and a group of Cherokee known as the Treaty Party, which consisted of around two hundred members—less than two per cent of the Nation's population. The resultant Treaty of New Echota—which ceded all Cherokee land east of the Mississippi to Georgia—was protested by the Cherokee Council, who asserted that they represented the majority of the Cherokee population and petitioned the Supreme Court to declare the document invalid. Nevertheless, removal was enforced in 1838. Some four thousand Cherokee died either in internment camps or on the trail to Indian Territory, which would come to be known as the Trail of Tears. Boudinot would continue to defend his actions regarding removal for the rest of his life; in an 1837 letter he wrote, "I cannot hesitate. Whether it is right and justifiable on the part of the United States that the Cherokees should remove, is not now the question. That it is right for the Cherokees to save themselves from destruction, bears no question in my opinion."

Harriet Gold died of complications related to childbirth in 1836; Boudinot married a New England missionary, Delight Sargent, the following year, and moved with his family to Oklahoma before the U.S. enforcement of removal. He was attacked and killed in 1839 by a group of Cherokee men, in compliance with a Cherokee Nation law that punished with death anyone who sold Cherokee lands without the Council's approval. Boudinot's complex and changing positions on some of the most important social and political issues of his age have ensured that he remains a controversial but widely discussed writer to this day.

NOTE ON THE TEXTS: The text of Boudinot's *An Address to the Whites. Delivered in the First Presbyterian Church on the 26th of May, 1826* is based on that of the pamphlet printed in Philadelphia in 1826. The text of "To the Public" is based on that printed in the first issue of the *Cherokee Phoenix* on 21 February 1828. Spelling and punctuation have been modernized in accordance with the practices of this anthology; Boudinot's inconsistency in his use of American and British spellings, however, has been retained.

⌘ ⌘ ⌘

An Address to the Whites

To those who are unacquainted with the manners, habits, and improvements of the aborigines of this country, the term *Indian* is pregnant with ideas the most repelling and degrading. But such impressions, originating, as they frequently do, from infant prejudices, although they hold too true when applied to some, do great injustices to many of this race of beings.

Some there are, perhaps even in this enlightened assembly, who at the bare sight of an Indian, or at the mention of the name, would throw back their imaginations to ancient times, to the savages of savage warfare, to the yells pronounced over the mangled bodies of women and children, thus creating an opinion, inapplicable and highly injurious to those for whose temporal interest and eternal welfare, I come to plead.

What is an Indian? Is he not formed of the same materials with yourself? For "Of one blood God created all the nations that dwell on the face of the earth."[1] Though it be true that he is ignorant, that he is a heathen, that he is a savage, yet he is no more than all others have been under similar circumstances. Eighteen centuries ago, what were the inhabitants of Great Britain?

You here behold an *Indian*, my kindred are *Indians*, and my fathers sleeping in the wilderness grave—they too were Indians. But I am not as my fathers were—broader means and nobler influences have fallen upon me. Yet I was not born as thousands are, in a stately dome and amid the congratulations of the great, for on a little hill, in a lonely cabin, overspread by the forest oak, I first drew my breath; and in a language unknown to learned and polished nations, I learnt to lisp my fond mother's name. In after days, I have had greater advantages than most of my race; and I now stand before you delegated by my native country to seek her interest, to labour for her respectability, and by my public efforts to assist in raising her to an equal standing with other nations of the earth.

The time has arrived when speculations and conjectures as to the practicability of civilizing the Indians must forever cease. A period is fast approaching when the stale remark, "Do what you will, an Indian will still be an Indian," must be placed no more in speech. With whatever plausibility this popular objection may have heretofore been made, every candid[2] mind must now be sensible that it can no longer be uttered, except by those who are uninformed with respect to us, who are strongly prejudiced against us, or who are filled with vindictive feelings towards us; for the present history of the Indians, particularly of that nation to which I belong, most incontrovertibly establishes the fallacy of this remark. I am aware of the difficulties which have ever existed to Indian civilization; I do not deny the almost insurmountable obstacles which we ourselves have thrown in the way of this improvement, nor do I say that difficulties no longer remain; but facts will permit me to declare that there are none which may not easily be overcome, by strong and continued exertions. It needs not abstract reasoning to prove this position. It needs not the display of language to prove to the minds of good men, that Indians are susceptible of attainments necessary to the formation of polished society. It needs not the power of argument on the nature of man, to silence forever the remark that "it is the purpose of the Almighty that the Indians should be exterminated." It needs only that the world should know what we have done in the last few years, to foresee what yet we may do with the assistance of our white brethren, and that of the common Parent of us all.

It is not necessary to present to you a detailed account of the various aborigine tribes, who have been known to you only on the pages of history, and there but obscurely known. They have gone; and to revert back to their days, would be only to disturb their oblivious sleep; to darken these walls with deeds at which humanity must shudder; to place before your eyes the scenes of Muskingum Sahta-goo and the plains of Mexico, to call up the crimes of the bloody Cortes and his infernal host;[3] and to describe the animosity and vengeance which have overthrown, and hurried into the shades of death those numerous tribes. But

---

1   *Of one … earth*   See Acts 17.26.

2   *candid*   Fair or unbiased.

3   *Muskingum Sahta-goo*   Probable reference to the Gnadenhutten Massacre of 1782, in which 96 unarmed Christian Lenape were killed by a U.S. militia band in their village near the Muskingum River; *plains of Mexico … infernal host*   Reference to Hernán Cortés (1485–1547), Spanish Conquistador who led the conquest of the Aztec Empire, during which tens of thousands of people from the Aztec and allied nations were killed.

here let me say that, however guilty these unhappy nations may have been, yet many and unreasonable were the wrongs they suffered, many the hardships they endured, and many their wanderings through the trackless wilderness. Yes, "Notwithstanding the obloquy[1] [with] which the early historians of the colonies have overshadowed the character of the ignorant and unfortunate natives, some bright gleams will occasionally break through, that throw a melancholy lustre on their memories. Facts are occasionally to be met with in their rude annals, which though recorded with all the colouring of prejudice and bigotry, yet speak for themselves, and will be dwelt upon with applause and sympathy when prejudice shall have passed away."[2]

Nor is it my purpose to enter largely into the consideration of the remnants, of those who have fled with time and are no more. They stand as monuments of the Indian's fate. And should they ever become extinct, they must move off the earth, as did their fathers. My design is to offer a few disconnected facts relative to the present improved state, and to the ultimate prospects of that particular tribe called Cherokees to which I belong.

The Cherokee Nation lies within the chartered limits of the states of Georgia, Tennessee, and Alabama. Its extent as defined by treaties is about 200 miles in length from East to West, and about 120 in breadth. This country which is supposed to contain about 10,000,000 of acres exhibits great varieties of surface, the most part being hilly and mountainous, affording soil of no value. The valleys, however, are well watered and afford excellent land, in many parts, particularly on the large streams, that of the first quality. The climate is temperate and healthy; indeed I would not be guilty of exaggeration were I to say that the advantages which this country possesses to render it salubrious are many and superior. Those lofty and barren mountains, defying the labour and ingenuity of man, and supposed by some as placed there only to exhibit omnipotence, contribute to the healthiness and beauty of the surrounding plains, and give us to that free air and pure water which distinguish our country. These advantages, calculated to make the inhabitants healthy, vigorous,

and intelligent, cannot fail to cause this country to become interesting. And there can be no doubt that the Cherokee Nation, however obscure and trifling it may now appear, will finally become, if not under its present occupants, one of the garden spots of America. And here, let me be indulged in the fond wish, that she may thus become under those who now possess her; and ever be fostered, regulated and protected by the generous government of the United States.

The population of the Cherokee Nation increased, from the year 1810 to that of 1824, 2000, exclusive of those who emigrated in 1818 and 19 to the west of the Mississippi—of those who reside on the Arkansas the number is supposed to be about 5000.

The rise of these people in their movement toward civilization, may be traced as far back as the relinquishment of their towns, when game became incompetent to their support,[3] by reason of the surrounding white population. They then betook themselves to the woods, commenced the opening of small clearings, and the raising of stock; still however following the chase. Game has since become so scarce that little dependence for subsistence can be placed upon it. They have gradually and I could almost say universally forsaken their ancient employment. In fact, there is not a single family in the nation that can be said to subsist on the slender support which the wilderness would afford. The love and the practice of hunting are not now carried to a higher degree, than among all frontier people whether white or red. It cannot be doubted, however, that there are many who have commenced a life of agricultural labour from mere necessity, and if they could, would gladly resume their former course of living. But these are individual failings and ought to be passed over.

On the other hand, it cannot be doubted that the nation is improving, rapidly improving in all those particulars which must finally constitute the inhabitants an industrious and intelligent people.

It is a matter of surprise to me, and must be to all those who are properly acquainted with the condition of the Aborigines of this country, that the Cherokees have advanced so far and so rapidly in civilization. But there are yet powerful obstacles, both within and

---

[1]   *obloquy* Public reproach.

[2]   *Notwithstanding … passed away* Boudinot here quotes from the essay "Traits of Indian Character" (1814) by Washington Irving.

[3]   *when game … their support* I.e., when they could no longer sufficiently support themselves by hunting wild game.

without, to be surmounted in the march of improvement. The prejudices in regard to them in the general community are strong and lasting. The evil effects of their intercourse with their immediate white neighbours, who differ from them chiefly in name, are easily to be seen, and it is evident that from this intercourse proceed those demoralizing practices which in order to surmount, peculiar and unremitting efforts are necessary. In defiance, however, of these obstacles, the Cherokees have improved and are still rapidly improving. To give you a further view of their condition, I will here repeat some of the articles of the two statistical tables taken at different periods.

In 1810 there were 19,500 cattle; 6,100 horses; 19,600 swine; 1,037 sheep; 467 looms; 1,600 spinning wheels; 30 wagons; 500 ploughs; 3 saw-mills; 13 grist-mills, etc. At this time there are 22,000 cattle; 7,600 horses; 46,000 swine; 2,500 sheep; 762 looms; 2,488 spinning wheels; 172 wagons; 2,943 ploughs; 10 saw-mills; 31 grist-mills; 62 blacksmith shops; 8 cotton machines; 18 schools; 18 ferries; and a number of public roads. In one district there were, last winter, upwards of 1000 volumes of good books, and 11 different periodical papers, both religious and political, which were taken and read. On the public roads there are many decent inns, and few houses, for convenience, etc., would disgrace any country. Most of the schools are under the care and tuition of Christian missionaries, of different denominations, who have been of great service to the nation, by inculcating moral and religious principles into the minds of the rising generation. In many places the word of God is regularly preached and explained, both by missionaries and natives; and there are numbers who have publicly professed their belief in the merits of the great Savior of the world. It is worthy of remark, that in no ignorant country have the missionaries undergone less trouble and difficulty in spreading a knowledge of the Bible than in this. Here, they have been welcomed and encouraged by the proper authorities of the nation, their persons have been protected, and in very few instances have some individual vagabonds threatened violence to them. Indeed it may be said with truth, that among no heathen people has the faithful minister of God experienced greater success, greater reward for his labour, than in this. He is surrounded by attentive hearers; the words which flow from his lips are not spent in vain. The Cherokees have had no established religion of their own, and perhaps to this circumstance we may attribute, in part, the facilities with which missionaries have pursued their ends. They cannot be called idolaters; for they never worshipped Images. They believed in a Supreme Being, the Creator of all, the God of the white, the red, and the black man. They also believed in the existence of an evil spirit who resided, as they thought, in the setting sun, the future place of all who in their life time had done iniquitously. Their prayers were addressed alone to the Supreme Being, and which if written would fill a large volume, and display much sincerity, beauty and sublimity. When the ancient customs of the Cherokees were in their full force, no warrior thought himself secure, unless he had addressed his guardian angel; no hunter could hope for success, unless before the rising sun he had asked the assistance of his God, and on his return at eve he had offered his sacrifice to him.

There are three things of late[1] occurrence which must certainly place the Cherokee Nation in a fair light, and act as a powerful argument in favor of Indian improvement.

First. The invention of letters.[2]

Second. The translation of the New Testament into Cherokee.[3]

And Third. The organization of a Government.[4]

The Cherokee mode of writing lately invented by George Guest, who could not read any language nor speak any other than his own, consists of eighty-six characters, principally syllabic, the combinations of which form all the words of the language. Their terms may be greatly simplified, yet they answer all the purposes of writing, and already many natives use them.

The translation of the New Testament, together with Guest's mode of writing, has swept away that barrier

---

1   *late*   Recent.

2   *The invention of letters*   The Cherokee syllabary was developed by Sequoyah (known in English as George Guess or Guest) in the 1810s and 20s. The system was widely and rapidly adopted throughout the Cherokee Nation.

3   *The translation ... into Cherokee*   The New Testament was translated into Cherokee in 1825 by Cherokee clergyman David Brown.

4   *The organization of a Government*   The Cherokee developed a centralized government in the 1790s, establishing the position of Principal Chief in 1794; the first Principal Chief of the Cherokee was Little Turkey (1758–1801).

which has long existed, and opened a spacious channel for the instruction of adult Cherokees. Persons of all ages and classes may now read the precepts of the Almighty in their own language. Before it is long, there will scarcely be an individual in the nation who can say, "I know not God neither understand I what thou sayest,"[1] for all shall know him, from the greatest to the least. The aged warrior over whom has rolled three score and ten years of savage life, will grace the temple of God with his hoary head; and the little child yet on the breast of its pious mother shall learn to lisp its Maker's name.

The shrill sound of the Savage yell shall die away as the roaring of far distant thunder; and Heaven-wrought music will gladden the affrighted wilderness. "The solitary place will be glad for them, and the desert shall rejoice and blossom as a rose."[2] Already do we see the morning star, forerunner of approaching dawn, rising over the tops of deep forests in which for ages have echoed the warrior's whoop. But has not God said it, and will he not do it? The Almighty decrees his purposes, and man cannot with all his ingenuity and device countervail them. They are more fixed in their course than the rolling sun—more durable than the everlasting mountains.

The Government, though defective in many respects, is well suited to the condition of the inhabitants. As they rise in information and refinement, changes in it must follow, until they arrive at that state of advancement, when I trust they will be admitted into all the privileges of the American family.

The Cherokee Nation is divided into eight districts, in each of which are established courts of justice, where all disputed cases are decided by a jury, under the direction of a circuit Judge, who has jurisdiction over two districts. Sheriffs and other public officers are appointed to execute the decisions of the courts, collect debts, and arrest thieves and other criminals. Appeals may be taken to the Superior Court, held annually at the seat of Government. The Legislative authority is vested in General Court, which consists of the National Committee and Council. The National Committee consists of thirteen members who are generally men of sound sense and fine talents. The National Council

consists of thirty-two members, beside the speaker, who act as the representatives of the people. Every bill, passing these two bodies, becomes the law of the land. Clerks are appointed to do the writings, and record the proceedings of the Council. The executive power is vested in two principal chiefs, who hold their office during good behaviour, and sanction all the decisions of the legislative council. Many of the laws display some degree of civilization, and establish the respectability of the nation.

Polygamy is abolished. Female chastity and honor are protected by law. The Sabbath is respected by the Council during session. Mechanics are encouraged by law. The practice of putting aged persons to death for witchcraft is abolished and murder has now become a governmental crime.

From what I have said, you will form but a faint opinion of the true state and prospects of the Cherokees. You will, however, be convinced of three important truths.

First, that the means which have been employed for the Christianization and civilization of this tribe have been greatly blessed. Second, that the increase of these means will meet with final success. Third, that it has now become necessary that efficient and more than ordinary means should be employed.

Sensible of this last point, and wishing to do something for themselves, the Cherokees have thought it advisable that there should be established a printing press and a seminary of respectable character; and for these purposes your aid and patronage are now solicited. They wish the types,[3] as expressed in their resolution, to be composed of English letters and Cherokee characters. Those characters have now become extensively used in the nation; their religious songs are written in them; there is an astonishing eagerness in people of all classes and ages to acquire a knowledge of them; and the New Testament has been translated into their language. All this impresses on them the immediate necessity of procuring types. The most informed and judicious of our nation believe that such a press would go further to remove ignorance, and her offspring superstition and prejudice, than all other means. The adult part of the nation will probably grovel on in ignorance and die in ignorance, without any fair trial

---

[1] *I know ... thou sayest* See Mark 14.68.

[2] *The solitary ... a rose* See Isaiah 35.1.

[3] *types* I.e., blocks used for printing text.

upon them, unless the proposed means are carried into effect. The simplicity of this method of writing, and the eagerness to obtain a knowledge of it, are evinced by the astonishing rapidity with which it is acquired, and by the numbers who do so. It is about two years since its introduction, and already there are a great many who can read it. In the neighbourhood in which I live, I do not recollect a male Cherokee, between the ages of fifteen and twenty-five, who is ignorant of this mode of writing. But in connection with those for Cherokee characters, it is necessary to have type for English letters. There are many who already speak and read the English language, and can appreciate the advantages which would result from the publication of their laws and transactions in a well conducted newspaper. Such a paper, comprising a summary of religious and political events, etc., on the one hand; and on the other, exhibiting the feelings, disposition, improvements, and prospects of the Indians; their traditions, their true character, as it once was and as it now is; the ways and means most likely to throw the mantle of civilization over all tribes; and such other matters as will tend to diffuse proper and correct impressions in regard to their condition—such a paper could not fail to create much interest in the American community, favourable to the aborigines, and to have a powerful influence on the advancement of the Indians themselves. How can the patriot or the philanthropist devise efficient means, without full and correct information as to the subjects of their labour? And I am inclined to think, after all that has been said of the aborigines, after all that has been written in narratives, professedly to elucidate the leading traits of their character, that the public knows little of that character. To obtain a correct and complete knowledge of these people, there must exist a vehicle of Indian intelligence, altogether different from those which have heretofore been employed. Will not a paper published in an Indian country, under proper and judicious regulations, have the desired effect? I do not say that Indians will produce learned and elaborate dissertations in explanation and vindication of their own character; but they may exhibit specimens of their intellectual efforts, of their eloquence, of their moral, civil and physical advancement, which will do quite as much to remove prejudice and to give profitable information.

The Cherokees wish to establish their Seminary upon a footing which will insure to it all the advantages that belong to such institutions in the states. Need I spend one moment in arguments in favor of such an institution; need I speak one word of the utility, of the necessity, of an institution of learning; need I do more than simply to ask the patronage of benevolent hearts, to obtain that patronage?

When before did a nation of Indians step forward and ask for the means of civilization? The Cherokee authorities have adopted the measures already stated with a sincere desire to make their nation an intelligent and a virtuous people, and with a full hope that those who have already pointed out to them the road of happiness, will now assist them to pursue it. With that assistance, what are the prospects of the Cherokees? Are they not indeed glorious, compared to that deep darkness in which the nobler qualities of their souls have slept? Yes, methinks I can view my native country rising from the ashes of her degradation, wearing her purified and beautiful garments, and taking her seat with the nations of the earth. I can behold her sons bursting the fetters of ignorance and unshackling her from the vices of heathenism. She is at this instant risen like the first morning sun, which grows brighter and brighter, until it reaches its fulness of glory.

She will become not a great, but a faithful ally of the United States. In times of peace she will plead the common liberties of America. In time of war her intrepid sons will sacrifice their lives in your defence. And because she will be useful to you in coming time, she asks you to assist her in her present struggles. She asks not for greatness; she seeks not wealth; she pleads only for assistance to become respectable as a nation, to enlighten and ennoble her sons, and to ornament her daughters with modesty and virtue. She pleads for this assistance, too, because on her destiny hangs that of many nations. If she completes her civilization—then may we hope that all our nations will—then, indeed, may true patriots be encouraged in their efforts to make this world of the West, one continuous abode of enlightened, free, and happy people.

But if the Cherokee Nation fail in her struggle, if she die away, then all hopes are blasted, and falls the fabric of Indian civilization. Their fathers were born in darkness, and have died in darkness; without your assistance so will their sons. You, see, however, where the probability rests. Is there a soul whose narrowness will not permit the exercise of charity on such an occasion? Where is he that can withhold his mite[1] from an object so noble? Who can prefer a little of his silver and gold, to the welfare of nations of his fellow beings? Human wealth perishes with our clay,[2] but that wealth gained in charity still remains on earth, to enrich our names, when we are gone, and will be remembered in Heaven, when the miser and his coffers have mouldered together in their kindred earth. The works of a generous mind sweeten the cup of affliction; they enlighten the dreary way to the cold tomb; they blunt the sting of death, and smooth his passage to the unknown world. When all the kingdoms of this earth shall die away and their beauty and power shall perish, his name shall live and shine as a twinkling star; those for whose benefit he did his deeds of charity shall call him blessed, and they shall add honor to his immortal head.

There are, with regard to the Cherokees and other tribes, two alternatives; they must either become civilized and happy, or sharing the fate of many kindred nations, become extinct. If the General Government continue its protection, and the American people assist them in their humble efforts, they will, they must rise. Yes, under such protection, and with such assistance, the Indian must rise like the Phoenix, after having wallowed for ages in ignorant barbarity. But should this Government withdraw its care, and the American people their aid, then, to use the words of a writer, "They will go the way that so many tribes have gone before them; for the hordes that still linger about the shores of Huron, and the tributary streams of the Mississippi, will share the fate of those tribes that once lorded it along the proud banks of the Hudson; of that gigantic race that [is] said to have existed on the borders of the Susquehanna; of those various nations that flourished about the Potomac and the Rappahannoc, and that peopled the forests of the vast valley of Shenandoah. They will vanish like a vapour from the face of the earth, their very history will be lost in forgetfulness, and the places that now know them will know them no more."[3]

There is, in Indian history, something very melancholy, and which seems to establish a mournful precedent for the future events of the few sons of the forest, now scattered over this vast continent. We have seen everywhere the poor aborigines melt away before the white population. I merely speak of the fact, without at all referring to the cause. We have seen, I say, one family after another, one tribe after another, nation after nation, pass away, until only a few solitary creatures are left to tell the sad story of extinction.

Shall this precedent be followed? I ask you, shall red men live, or shall they be swept from the earth? With you and this public at large, the decision chiefly rests. Must they perish? Must they all, like the unfortunate Creeks[4] (victims of the unchristian policy of certain persons), go down in sorrow to their graves?

They hang upon your mercy as to a garment. Will you push them from you, or will you save them? Let humanity answer.

—1826

To the Public

New Echota
Thursday, February 21, 1828

We are happy in being able, at length, to issue the first number of our paper, although after a longer delay than we anticipated. This delay has been owing to unavoidable circumstances, which, we think, will be sufficient to acquit us, and though our readers and patrons may be wearied in the expectation of gratifying their eyes on this paper of no ordinary novelty,

---

1   *mite* Small donation, see Mark 12.41–44: "And Jesus sat over against the treasury, and beheld how the people cast money into the treasury; and many that were rich cast in much. And there came a certain poor widow and she threw in two mites, which make a farthing. And he called unto him his disciples, and saith unto them, Verily I say unto you, That this poor widow hath cast more in, than all they which have cast into the treasury. For all they did cast is of their abundance, but she of her want did cast in all that she had, even all her living."

2   *clay* I.e., physical bodies.

3   *They will … no more* From Washington Irving, "Traits of Indian Character."

4   *like the unfortunate Creeks* Presumably referring to the events of the Creek War (1813–14). Beginning as an internal conflict between different factions of the Creek, or Muscogee, people, the Creek War eventually became drawn into the War of 1812, with certain members of the Creek allying with the United States, the Choctaw, and the Cherokee to fight the Red Stick Creek, who resisted settler encroachment on their lands. With the end of the war, the Creek were forced to cede twenty-three million acres of their territory to the United States.

yet we hope their patience will not be so exhausted, but that they will give it a calm perusal, and pass upon it a candid[1] judgment. It is far from our expectation that it will meet with entire and universal approbation, particularly from those who consider learning and science necessary to the merits of newspapers. Such must not expect to be gratified here, for the merits (if merits they can be called) on which our paper is expected to exist, are not alike with those which keep alive the political and religious papers of the day. We lay no claim to extensive information; and we sincerely hope this public disclosure will save us from the severe criticisms to which our ignorance of many things will frequently expose us, in the future course of our editorial labors. Let the public but consider our motives, and the design[2] of this paper, which is, the benefit of the Cherokees, and we are sure, those who wish well to the Indian race, will keep out of view all the failings and deficiencies of the Editor, and give a prompt support to the first paper ever published in an Indian country, and under the direction of some of the remnants of those who by the most mysterious course of providence have dwindled into oblivion. To prevent us from the like destiny, is certainly a laudable undertaking, which the Christian, the Patriot, and the Philanthropist will not be ashamed to aid. Many are now engaged, by various means and with various success, in attempting to rescue, not only us, but all our kindred tribes, from the impending danger which has been so fatal to our forefathers; and we are happy to be in a situation to tender them our public acknowledgements for their unwearied efforts. Our present undertaking is intended to be nothing more than a feeble auxiliary to these efforts. Those, therefore, who are engaged for the good of the Indians of every tribe, and who pray that salvation, peace, and the comforts of civilized life may be extended to every Indian fireside on this continent, will consider us as co-workers together in their benevolent labors. To them we make our appeal for patronage, and pledge ourselves to encourage and assist them, in whatever appears to be for the benefit of the Aborigines.

In the commencement of our labours, it is due to our readers that we should acquaint them with the general principles which we have prescribed to ourselves as rules in conducting this paper. These principles we shall accordingly state briefly. It may, however, be proper to observe that the establishment which has been lately purchased, principally with the charities of our white brethren, is the property of the Nation,[3] and that the paper, which is now offered to the public, is patronized by, and under the direction of, the Cherokee Legislature, as will be seen in the Prospectus already before the public. As servants we are bound to that body, from which, however, we have not received any instructions, but are left at liberty to form such regulations for our conduct as will appear to us most conducive to the interests of the people, for whose benefit this paper has been established.

As the *Phoenix* is a national paper, we shall feel ourselves bound to devote it to national purposes. "The laws and public documents of the Nation," and matters relating to the welfare and condition of the Cherokees as a people, will be faithfully published in English and Cherokee.

As the liberty of the press is so essential to the improvement of the mind, we shall consider our paper a *free paper*, with, however, proper and usual restrictions. We shall reserve to ourselves the liberty of rejecting such communications as tend to evil, and such as are too intemperate and too personal. But the columns of this paper shall always be open to free and temperate discussions on matters of politics, religion, etc.

We shall avoid as much as possible controversy on disputed doctrinal points in religion. Though we have our particular belief on this important subject, and perhaps are as strenuous upon it, as some of our brethren of a different faith, yet we conscientiously think—and in this thought we are supported by men of judgment—that it would be injudicious, perhaps highly pernicious, to introduce to this people the various minor differences of Christians. Our object is not sectarian; and if we had a wish to support, in our paper, the denomination with which we have the honor and privilege of being connected, yet we know our incompetency for the task.

We will not unnecessarily intermeddle with the politics and affairs of our neighbors. As we have no particular interest in the concerns of the surrounding

---

[1]   *candid* Unbiased.

[2]   *design* Purpose.

[3]   *the Nation* I.e., the Cherokee Nation.

states, we shall only expose ourselves to contempt and ridicule by improper intrusion. And though at times we should do ourselves injustice to be silent on matters of great interest to the Cherokees, yet we will not return railing for railing, but consult mildness, for we have been taught to believe, that "A soft answer turneth away wrath; but grievous words stir up anger."[1] The unpleasant controversy existing with the state of Georgia,[2] of which many of our readers are aware, will frequently make our situation trying, by having hard sayings and threatenings thrown out against us, a specimen of which will be found in our next. We pray God that we may be delivered from such spirit.

In regard to the controversy with Georgia, and the present policy of the General Government, in removing and concentrating the Indians out of the limits of any state, which, by the way, appears to be gaining strength, we will invariably and faithfully state the feelings of the majority of our people. Our views, as a people, on this subject, have been most sadly misrepresented. These views we do not wish to conceal, but are willing that the public should know what we think of this policy, which, in our opinion, if carried into effect, will prove pernicious to us.

We have been asked which side of the Presidential question[3] we should take. Our answer is, we think best to take a neutral stand, and we know that such a course is most prudent, as we have no vote on the question,[4] and although we have our individual choice, yet it would be folly for us to spend words and time on a subject which has engrossed very much the attention of the public already.

In fine, we shall pay a sacred regard to truth, and avoid, as much as possible, that partiality to which we shall be exposed. In relating facts of a local nature, whether political, moral, or religious, we shall take care that exaggeration shall not be our crime. We shall also feel ourselves bound to correct all misstatements relating to the present condition of the Cherokees.

How far we shall be successful in advancing the improvement of our people is not now for us to decide. We hope, however, our efforts will not be altogether in vain. Now is the moment when mere speculation on the practicability of civilizing us is out of the question. Sufficient and repeated evidence has been given, that Indians can be reclaimed from a savage state, and that with proper advantages, they are as capable of improvement in mind as any other people; and let it be remembered, notwithstanding the assertions of those who talk to the contrary, that this improvement can be made, not only by the Cherokees, but by all the Indians, *in their present locations*. We are rendered bold in making this assertion, by considering the history of our people within the last fifteen years. There was a time within our remembrance, when darkness was sadly prevalent, and ignorance abounded amongst us—when strong and deep-rooted prejudices were directed against many things relating to civilized life and when it was thought a disgrace for a Cherokee to appear in the costume of a white man. We mention these things not by way of boasting, but to show to our readers that it is not a visionary thing to attempt to civilize and Christianize all the Indians, but highly practicable.

It is necessary for our white patrons to know that this paper is not intended to be a source of profit, and that its continuance must depend, in a great measure, on the liberal support which they may be pleased to grant us. Though our object is not gain, yet we wish as much patronage, as will enable us to support the establishment without subjecting it to pecuniary difficulties. Those of our friends who have done so much already for us by instructing us in the arts of civilized life, and enabling us to enjoy the blessings of education, and

---

[1]   *A soft ... anger*   See Proverbs 15.1.

[2]   *The unpleasant ... Georgia*   I.e., the efforts on the part of the state and federal governments to arrange for the removal of the Cherokee people from their land in Georgia to "Indian territory," to which the vast majority of Cherokee were opposed.

[3]   *the Presidential question*   The two main candidates of the 1828 presidential election were the incumbent President John Quincy Adams, leader of the National Republican Party, and Andrew Jackson, leader of the Democratic Party. Jackson, a staunch proponent of Indian Removal, won the election in December 1828; he remained in office until 1837.

[4]   *we have ... the question*   The right to vote was withheld from the vast majority of Native Americans until the passage of the Indian Citizenship Act in 1924, which granted birthright citizenship to all Native Americans born after its passage. Prior to that time, citizenship could only be attained by Indigenous individuals if they were considered to be fully "assimilated" and to have abandoned any tribal affiliations. Even after 1924, voter suppression prevented many Native Americans from voting in state and federal elections;

only with the passage of the Voting Rights Act in 1965 did Native Americans attain full voting rights.

the comforts of religion, and to whose exertions may be attributed the present means of improvement in this Nation, will not think it a hard matter that their aid should now be respectfully requested. In order that our paper may have an extensive circulation in this Nation and out of it, we have fixed upon the most liberal terms possible; such, in our opinion, as will render it as cheap as most of the Southern papers; and in order that our subscribers may be prompt in their remittances, we have made considerable difference between the first and the last payments. Those who have any experience in the management of periodicals will be sensible how important it is that the payments of subscribers should be prompt and regular, particularly where the existence of a paper depends upon its own income. We sincerely hope that we shall never have any occasion to complain of the delinquency of any of our patrons.

We would now commit our feeble efforts to the good will and indulgence of the public, praying that God will attend them with his blessings, and hoping for that happy period when all the Indian tribes of America shall arise, Phoenix-like, from their ashes, and when the terms, "Indian depredation," "war whoop," "scalping knife," and the like, shall become obsolete, and forever be "buried deep under ground."

—1828

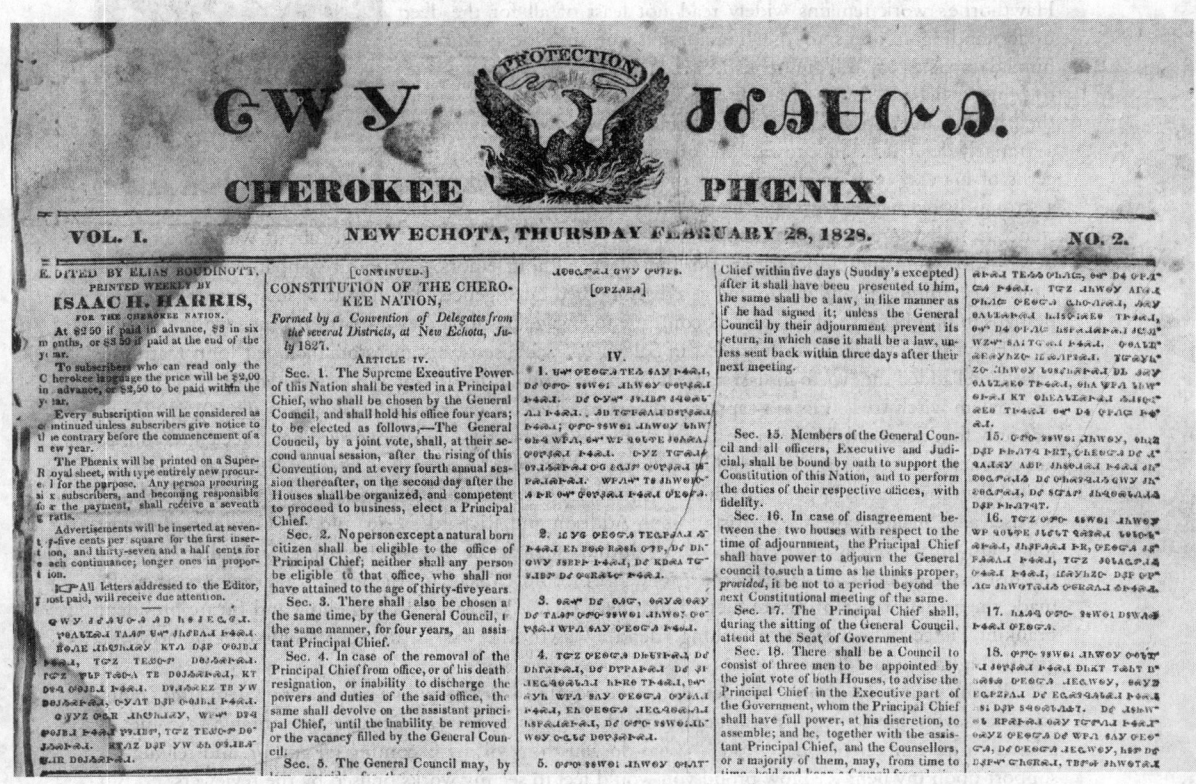

Front page of the second issue of the *Cherokee Phoenix*, with content in both English and Cherokee.

Nathaniel Hawthorne

1804 – 1864

Descended from a long line of Massachusetts Puritan settlers, Nathaniel Hawthorne was born into a cultural and psychological inheritance that deeply affected a body of work that has long been accorded a central place in American literature. His fiction is renowned for its psychological depth, for its dark and richly symbolic character, and for its evocative historical portrayals. Novels such as *The Scarlet Letter* (1850) and *The House of the Seven Gables* (1851) and stories such as "Young Goodman Brown" (1835) and "My Kinsman, Major Molineux" (1832) depict imagined moments of the American past, interrogating and re-interpreting the American legacy of Puritan beliefs and values; our understanding of early colonial society continues to be substantially shaped by Hawthorne's depictions. So too does our sense of the human psyche, and what it is capable of; Hawthorne's work remains widely read not least of all for the deep understanding it offers to the human sense of sinfulness—and the human capacity for self-righteousness. But his fiction also continues to provoke debate, and to spin off questions in rich profusion. For all their historical and psychological depth, Hawthorne's writings embody a strangely detached stance toward the pressing ethical and societal concerns of his era; even on the topic of the Civil War, his work shows a strong disinclination to make themes clear or morals obvious. That

stance troubled some of his contemporaries—his enigmatic 1862 essay "Chiefly about War Matters" was described by one contemporary as "pure intellect, without emotion, without sympathy, without principles … as unhuman and passionless as a disembodied intelligence." Yet in spite of such detachment—or perhaps in part because of it—readers continue to engage passionately with Hawthorne's work.

Hawthorne was born in July 1804 in Salem, Massachusetts; his ancestors included John Hathorne (Nathaniel added the "w" to his last name later in life), one of the fiercest and least repentant judges in the 1692 Salem witch trials. His sea-captain father died of yellow fever while in Suriname when Hawthorne was only four years old; Hawthorne's mother, Elizabeth, was forced to move with her three children into her parents' home—a large household that included her two unmarried sisters and her several brothers. Here Hawthorne had a large library at his disposal, from which he read English authors such as Edmund Spenser and Shakespeare, the satirists Joseph Addison and Richard Steele, and the Christian allegorist John Bunyan, as well as more contemporary authors such as the Scottish Romantic Sir Walter Scott. At the insistence of an uncle, Hawthorne attended Bowdoin College in Maine from 1821 to 1825; there he made the acquaintance of future literary luminary Henry Wadsworth Longfellow and future president Franklin Pierce (who became a lifelong friend). Hawthorne was an unexceptional student, however, graduating in the middle of his class.

By this point Hawthorne had determined to become a writer, and he returned to Salem after graduation to devote himself to his new ambition. He appears to have anticipated the struggle to come: in a letter to his mother he once wrote, "What do you think of my becoming an author, and relying for support upon my pen? … How proud you would feel to see my works praised by the reviewers. … But authors are always poor devils, and therefore Satan may take them."

Hawthorne lived comfortably with his mother's family, but with little income of his own. For several years he struggled agonizingly—once burning a manuscript in frustration—to enter a literary market in which there seemed to be little demand for American fiction. American publishers had an easy time acquiring the rights to reprint works from Britain and Europe, while few readers or critics took seriously the idea of American "literature" (popular New York writers Washington Irving and James

Fenimore Cooper were among the few recognized as having made distinctive contributions). In 1828 Hawthorne published—privately, anonymously, and at his own expense—the novel *Fanshawe*. Heavily autobiographical and influenced by eighteenth-century British Romanticism, Gothicism, and literary melodrama, the novel sold poorly and received very mixed reviews; Hawthorne destroyed all the copies he could get his hands on, and later refused to acknowledge his authorship.

Despite this evidently profound disappointment, Hawthorne did not abandon his literary pursuits. He had a minor triumph in 1830 with the publication of "The Hollow of the Three Hills" in a periodical, and continued throughout the decade to find outlets for his short works in newspapers, magazines, and gift books. He developed a talent for historical settings and symbolic imagery with stories such as "My Kinsman, Major Molineux" and "Young Goodman Brown." Such stories provided a notable contrast to the often sentimental and light-hearted contents of gift books such as *The Token*. Hawthorne seems to have endured some anxiety over his association with this "feminine" literature, which may help explain why he published anonymously throughout this period.

Recognizing that Hawthorne's fiction deserved another chance at stand-alone publication, in 1837 a Bowdoin friend, Horatio Bridge, secretly gave a publisher $250 to finance the publication of the first volume of Hawthorne's collection *Twice-Told Tales* (a second volume appeared in 1842). *Twice-Told Tales* was his first real critical success; those praising the book included Edgar Allan Poe.

In 1838 Hawthorne worked briefly as a "weigher and gauger" at the Boston Custom House; despite the humble job description the position was something of a political sinecure, with a substantial salary of $1,200 a year. In the same year he became engaged to Sophia Peabody, an accomplished artist whose better-known sister Elizabeth was a prominent Transcendentalist (and would become a leading progressive educator).

Hawthorne resigned from his Custom House position in 1841 to spend a period of several months working at Brook Farm, a utopian Transcendentalist community and joint-stock company that he had invested in. In July 1842 he and Sophia were finally married; they rented the Old Manse in Concord, Massachusetts, and moved in immediately. In Concord, they befriended leading Transcendentalists such as Ralph Waldo Emerson, Henry David Thoreau, and Margaret Fuller, though Hawthorne never became fully integrated into this group or its ideals—and at times expressed distaste for Fuller's feminism.

By 1844 the family had begun to grow (Una, the first of their three children, was born that year), but their financial resources had shrunk, and they were forced to give up the large house in Concord and return to Salem. Hawthorne's third collection, *Mosses from an Old Manse* (1846), did little to alleviate the growing family's financial burden. Through his connection with Pierce and other Democrats he obtained another Custom House appointment, this time in Salem to the more senior position of surveyor. The work was remunerative, but Hawthorne found it unfulfilling.

The year 1849 marked a low point for him. The 1848 electoral defeat of the Democrats led to the dismissal of many political appointees in 1849; Hawthorne received word on June 8 that he had lost his job. He protested vigorously but unsuccessfully (arguing that he had in fact acted above party politics while in the position), and the unauthorized publication of one of his letters led to a substantial controversy over the matter. Hawthorne felt he had been dragged down among "the common political brawlers" (as he termed them in a letter to Longfellow), and he became alienated from many of his old acquaintances in Salem. The controversy had not yet died down when, in late July, his mother died; Hawthorne described it as "the darkest hour I ever lived."

In the ensuing grief and financial distress, Hawthorne began work on his first full-length novel, *The Scarlet Letter: A Romance*. Published the following year, the "romance" was prefaced by "The Custom-House: Introductory to *The Scarlet Letter*," a satirical sketch based on his own experiences in Salem and bearing little connection (at least on the surface) to the body of the work. (Then, as now, critics have disagreed as to the degree to which strong connections between the two do in fact exist.) A historical novel, *The Scarlet Letter* was a full-length treatment of themes such as sinfulness, guilt, and Puritan social hypocrisy that had sounded throughout Hawthorne's shorter work. The story of Hester Prynne—a young woman accused of (and punished for) adultery—was likely inspired by stories of other Puritan women persecuted for their sexual relationships; laws punishing adultery with the enforced wearing of a letter

"A" had existed in Plymouth, for instance. The novel's "revolting subject," as it was deemed by a writer for the *North American Review*, was controversial, even though the narrative never explicitly condemned the social code under which Hester was punished; indeed, one reviewer commended the novel for the "great moral lesson" it provided against the sin of adultery. Nevertheless, the novel was a popular success, and most critics admired its power. The London magazine *The Athenaeum* declared Hawthorne "among the most original and peculiar writers of American fiction," and the *Boston Transcript* speculated that not only was he among the best American writers of the "last half century," but that he had "not been eclipsed by the higher class of European minds which have led the way in that department to which his genius belongs."

Having at last established a reputation, over the following decade Hawthorne continued to focus on longer works. *The Scarlet Letter* was followed by two more works of fiction that have come to be regarded as classics: *The House of the Seven Gables* (1851), a historical novel in the Gothic mode; and *The Blithedale Romance* (1852), a novel touching on a wide range of the most controversial issues of the day, among them the fight for prison reform and the nascent struggle for women's rights. *The Blithedale Romance* had clearly been partially inspired by his time living communally at Brook Farm, but Hawthorne intended it (as he wrote in a preface) to be read as "a little removed" from "the actual events of real lives" and to imply no conclusion, "favorable or otherwise, in respect to Socialism."

Also in 1852, Hawthorne published *The Life of Franklin Pierce*, a campaign biography of the presidential candidate and Hawthorne's great friend from Bowdoin College. Pierce ran as a Democrat (which in those days meant support for American expansionism—as a military commander Pierce had played a significant role in the Mexican–American War—and opposition to any measures that might threaten the institution of slavery). In supporting Pierce, Hawthorne was very clear in his opposition to the abolitionists, suggesting that it might be wise to regard slavery

> as one of those evils which divine Providence does not leave to be remedied by human contrivances, but which, in its own good time, by some means impossible to be anticipated, but of the simplest and easiest operation, when all its uses shall have been fulfilled, it causes to vanish like a dream.

Pierce won the election, taking office in 1853; later that year Hawthorne was appointed American Consul at Liverpool, England, the center of the cotton trade. It was a sinecure, but Hawthorne took his duties seriously. Once again, politics led to the loss of his position; Hawthorne resigned in 1857 after Pierce had been defeated in his bid for re-nomination as presidential candidate of the Democratic Party.

Hawthorne and his family spent a good deal of 1858 and 1859 in Europe, with extended stays in Rome and Florence; his next novel, *The Marble Faun* (1860), was set in a romanticized Italy and inspired by their travels.

As the Civil War took hold in America, Hawthorne became even more distanced from the political stance taken by many of his fellow New Englanders. Unlike friends such as Emerson—who had been openly wary of causes and movements earlier in his career but was eventually persuaded by the injustice of slavery to join the abolitionist cause—Hawthorne stayed clear of the fray. In 1862 he wrote his only piece on the Civil War, "Chiefly about War Matters," in which he dismissed Lincoln, criticized the war, and appeared completely uninterested in the conflict's causes. Scholars continue to wrestle with the meanings of this layered and iconoclastic piece.

The last work published during Hawthorne's lifetime was *Our Old Home* (1863), a series of English travel sketches dedicated—controversially—to Pierce. Toward the following year Hawthorne's health started to decline; he died in the spring of 1864, aged fifty-nine, during a trip with Pierce to the White Mountains of New Hampshire.

In 1847, Edgar Allan Poe had remarked that Hawthorne was "*the* example ... in this country, of the privately-admired and publicly-underappreciated man of genius." But by the time he died his reputation had grown considerably. An appreciative piece published in *The Atlantic Monthly* in 1870 gave expression to what had become the prevailing view of Hawthorne's unique talent:

[H]is genius, as all the world knows, was of masculine force and sweep. But, on the other hand, no man had more of the feminine element than he. He was feminine in his quick perceptions, his fine insight, his sensibility to beauty, his delicate reserve, his purity of feeling. No man comprehended woman more perfectly; none has painted woman with a more exquisite and ethereal pencil. ... *The Scarlet Letter, The Blithedale Romance, The House of the Seven Gables, The Marble Faun*, and many of his smaller stories, have one marked characteristic in common, which maybe defined a taste for studying and delineating the night-side of human nature. He had a passion for exploring the crypts and caverns of the soul. ... *The Scarlet Letter* is the highest expression of his genius in this respect—a work of prodigious power, but so painful in the impression that it leaves that many can never read it a second time.

By the end of the century, though, many saw the dark symbolism of Hawthorne's "romances" as out of step with the trend toward realism in fiction; Henry James, for one, faulted *The Scarlet Letter* for what seemed to him a lack "of reality" and for "superficial symbolism." It was not until the mid-twentieth century that Hawthorne's reputation was fully restored. The critic F.O. Matthiessen, in setting out an array of enormously influential historical/aesthetic concepts, devoted almost 200 of the 650 pages of his *American Renaissance* (1941) to Hawthorne—to the importance of allegory and symbolism in his works, and to the importance of Hawthorne himself in American literature.

In the late twentieth and early twenty-first centuries feminist, deconstructionist, and new historicist critics have opened many other windows onto Hawthorne and his work in the context of his era. Particularly notable has been the work of Nina Baym, whose arguments for reading "Hawthorne as a feminist writer" have sparked lively discussion among literary scholars (many of whom have perceived ambivalence rather than feminism in his presentation of female characters). There continues to be lively discussion as well over Hawthorne's treatment of slavery and other ethical/political issues—a discussion given new life in the late twentieth century by Eric Cheyfitz's suggestion that Hawthorne scholars have too often felt the need to "explain, that is, complicate" what to Cheyfitz was a plain fact—"Hawthorne's simply reprehensible stand on the slavery issue." Few in the twenty-first century have defended that stand—but many have continued to draw nuanced distinctions between the author and the aesthetic and affective aspects of his work.

NOTE ON THE TEXTS: Unless otherwise noted, the texts of the works presented here are based on their first published appearances. Spelling and punctuation have been modernized in accordance with the practices of this anthology.

⌘ ⌘ ⌘

My Kinsman, Major Molineux

After the kings of Great Britain had assumed the right of appointing the colonial governors, the measures of the latter seldom met with the ready and generous approbation, which had been paid to those of their predecessors, under the original charters.[1] The people looked with most jealous scrutiny to the exercise of power, which did not emanate from themselves, and they usually rewarded the rulers with slender gratitude for the compliances by which, in softening their instructions from beyond the sea, they had incurred the reprehension of those who gave them. The annals of Massachusetts Bay will inform us that of six governors, in the space of about forty years from the surrender of the old charter, under James II, two were imprisoned by a popular insurrection; a third, as Hutchinson[2] inclines to believe, was driven from the province by the whizzing of a musket ball; a fourth, in the opinion of the same historian, was hastened to his grave by continual bickerings with the house of representatives; and the remaining two, as well as their successors, till the Revolution, were favored with few and brief intervals of peaceful sway. The inferior members of the court party, in times of high political excitement, led scarcely a more desirable life. These remarks may serve as a preface to the following adventures, which chanced upon a summer night, not far from a hundred years ago. The reader, in order to avoid a long and dry detail of colonial affairs, is requested to dispense with an account of the train of circumstances, that had caused much temporary inflammation of the popular mind.

It was near nine o' clock of a moonlight evening, when a boat crossed the ferry with a single passenger, who had obtained his conveyance, at that unusual hour, by the promise of an extra fare. While he stood on the landing-place, searching in either pocket for the means of fulfilling his agreement, the ferryman lifted a lantern, by the aid of which, and the newly risen moon, he took a very accurate survey of the stranger's figure. He was a youth of barely eighteen years, evidently country-bred, and now, as it should seem, upon his first visit to town.[3] He was clad in a coarse grey coat, well worn, but in excellent repair; his under garments[4] were durably constructed of leather, and sat tight to a pair of serviceable and well-shaped limbs; his stockings of blue yarn were the incontrovertible handiwork of a mother or a sister; and on his head was a three-cornered hat, which in its better days had perhaps sheltered the graver brow of the lad's father. Under his left arm was a heavy cudgel, formed of an oak sapling, and retaining a part of the hardened root; and his equipment was completed by a wallet,[5] not so abundantly stocked as to incommode the vigorous shoulders on which it hung. Brown, curly hair, well-shaped features, and bright, cheerful eyes, were nature's gifts, and worth all that art could have done for his adornment.

The youth, one of whose names was Robin, finally drew from his pocket the half of a little province-bill of five shillings, which, in the depreciation in that sort of currency, did but satisfy the ferryman's demand, with the surplus of a sexangular piece of parchment valued at three pence.[6] He then walked forward into the town, with as light a step, as if his day's journey had not already exceeded thirty miles, and with as eager an eye, as if he were entering London city, instead of the little metropolis of a New England colony. Before Robin had proceeded far, however, it occurred to him, that he knew not whither to direct his steps; so he paused, and looked up and down the narrow street, scrutinizing the small and mean wooden buildings that were scattered on either side.

---

[1] *After the kings … original charters* Until 1684, the Colony of Massachusetts Bay elected its own governors; this changed after King Charles II (r. 1649–85) revoked the colony's charter, in an effort to bring it more firmly under the monarchy's rule. His successor James II (r. 1685–88) first asserted the right to appoint senior government officials in 1685, as did later monarchs. The colony became the Province of Massachusetts Bay in 1692, at the establishment of a new charter.

[2] *Hutchinson* Thomas Hutchinson, last colonial governor of the Province of Massachusetts Bay, as well as a historian who wrote *History of the Province of Massachusetts Bay* (1764–67).

[3] *town* Boston.

[4] *under garments* I.e., trousers (*under* in this context means *lower*).

[5] *wallet* Knapsack; traveler's bag.

[6] *finally drew … three pence* I.e., Robin paid with a five shilling note—which was worth less than he had expected—and received only three pence in change; in the early days of paper money, it was often valued at considerably less than its nominal value; *province-bill* I.e., note issued by the Massachusetts province; different colonies issued their own currencies, whose values varied from one another.

"This low hovel cannot be my kinsman's dwelling," thought he, "nor yonder old house, where the moonlight enters at the broken casement; and truly I see none hereabouts that might be worthy of him. It would have been wise to inquire my way of the ferryman, and doubtless he would have gone with me, and earned a shilling from the Major for his pains. But the next man I meet will do as well."

He resumed his walk, and was glad to perceive that the street now became wider, and the houses more respectable in their appearance. He soon discerned a figure moving on moderately in advance, and hastened his steps to overtake it. As Robin drew nigh, he saw that the passenger was a man in years, with a full periwig[1] of grey hair, a wide-skirted coat of dark cloth, and silk stockings rolled about his knees. He carried a long and polished cane, which he struck down perpendicularly before him, at every step; and at regular intervals he uttered two successive hems, of a peculiarly solemn and sepulchral[2] intonation. Having made these observations, Robin laid hold of the skirt of the old man's coat, just when the light from the open door and windows of a barber's shop, fell upon both their figures.

"Good evening to you, honored Sir," said he, making a low bow, and still retaining his hold of the skirt. "I pray you tell me whereabouts is the dwelling of my kinsman, Major Molineux?"

The youth's question was uttered very loudly; and one of the barbers, whose razor was descending on a well-soaped chin, and another who was dressing a Ramillies wig,[3] left their occupations, and came to the door. The citizen, in the meantime, turned a long-favored countenance upon Robin, and answered him in a tone of excessive anger and annoyance. His two sepulchral hems, however, broke into the very centre of his rebuke, with most singular effect, like a thought of the cold grave obtruding among wrathful passions.

"Let go my garment, fellow! I tell you. I know not the man you speak of. What! I have authority, I have—hem, hem—authority; and if this be the respect you show for your betters, your feet shall be brought acquainted with the stocks,[4] by daylight, tomorrow morning!"

Robin released the old man's skirt, and hastened away, pursued by an ill-mannered roar of laughter from the barber's shop. He was at first considerably surprised by the result of his question, but, being a shrewd youth, soon thought himself able to account for the mystery.

"This is some country representative," was his conclusion, "who has never seen the inside of my kinsman's door, and lacks the breeding to answer a stranger civilly. The man is old, or verily—I might be tempted to turn back and smite him on the nose. Ah, Robin, Robin! even the barber's boys laugh at you, for choosing such a guide! You will be wiser in time, friend Robin."

He now became entangled in a succession of crooked and narrow streets, which crossed each other, and meandered at no great distance from the waterside. The smell of tar was obvious to his nostrils, the masts of vessels pierced the moonlight above the tops of the buildings, and the numerous signs, which Robin paused to read, informed him that he was near the centre of business. But the streets were empty, the shops were closed, and lights were visible only in the second stories of a few dwelling-houses. At length, on the corner of a narrow lane, through which he was passing, he beheld the broad countenance of a British hero swinging before the door of an inn, whence proceeded the voices of many guests. The casement of one of the lower windows was thrown back, and a very thin curtain permitted Robin to distinguish a party at supper, round a well-furnished table. The fragrance of the good cheer steamed forth into the outer air, and the youth could not fail to recollect, that the last remnant of his travelling stock of provision had yielded to his morning appetite, and that noon had found, and left him, dinnerless.

"Oh, that a parchment three-penny[5] might give me a right to sit down at yonder table," said Robin, with a sigh. "But the Major will make me welcome to the best

---

[1] *in years* I.e., elderly; *periwig* Wig.

[2] *hems* Coughs; *sepulchral* Funereal; gloomy.

[3] *Ramillies wig* Eighteenth-century style of wig worn with a braid down the back, often tied with bows.

[4] *stocks* Instruments of punishment (often used in public in order to humiliate) consisting of two wooden planks between which one's ankles would be confined.

[5] *parchment three-penny* Three pence note.

of his victuals; so I will even step boldly in, and inquire my way to his dwelling."

He entered the tavern, and was guided by the murmur of voices, and the fumes of tobacco, to the public room. It was a long and low apartment, with oaken walls, grown dark in the continual smoke, and a floor, which was thickly sanded, but of no immaculate purity. A number of persons, the larger part of whom appeared to be mariners, or in some way connected with the sea, occupied the wooden benches, or leather-bottomed chairs, conversing on various matters, and occasionally lending their attention to some topic of general interest. Three or four little groups were draining as many bowls of punch,[1] which the West India trade had long since made a familiar drink in the colony. Others, who had the aspect of men who lived by regular and laborious handicraft, preferred the insulated bliss of an unshared potation,[2] and became more taciturn under its influence. Nearly all, in short, evinced a predilection for the Good Creature[3] in some of its various shapes, for this is a vice, to which, as Fast Day[4] sermons of a hundred years ago will testify, we have a long hereditary claim. The only guests to whom Robin's sympathies inclined him were two or three sheepish countrymen, who were using the inn somewhat after the fashion of a Turkish Caravansary;[5] they had gotten themselves into the darkest corner of the room, and, heedless of the Nicotian[6] atmosphere, were supping on the bread of their own ovens, and the bacon cured in their own chimney-smoke. But though Robin felt a sort of brotherhood with these strangers, his eyes were attracted from them, to a person who stood near the door, holding whispered conversation with a group of ill-dressed associates. His features were

separately striking almost to grotesqueness, and the whole face left a deep impression in the memory. The forehead bulged out into a double prominence, with a vale between; the nose came boldly forth in an irregular curve, and its bridge was of more than a finger's breadth; the eyebrows were deep and shaggy, and the eyes glowed beneath them like fire in a cave.

While Robin deliberated of whom to inquire respecting his kinsman's dwelling, he was accosted by the innkeeper, a little man in a stained white apron, who had come to pay his professional welcome to the stranger. Being in the second generation from a French protestant, he seemed to have inherited the courtesy of his parent nation; but no variety of circumstances was ever known to change his voice from the one shrill note in which he now addressed Robin.

"From the country, I presume, Sir?" said he, with a profound bow. "Beg to congratulate you on your arrival, and trust you intend a long stay with us. Fine town here, Sir, beautiful buildings, and much that may interest a stranger. May I hope for the honor of your commands in respect to supper?"

"The man sees a family likeness! the rogue has guessed that I am related to the Major!" thought Robin, who had hitherto experienced little superfluous civility.

All eyes were now turned on the country lad, standing at the door, in his worn three-cornered hat, grey coat, leather breeches, and blue yarn stockings, leaning on an oaken cudgel, and bearing a wallet on his back. Robin replied to the courteous innkeeper, with such an assumption of consequence, as befitted the Major's relative.

"My honest friend," he said, "I shall make it a point to patronize your house on some occasion, when—" here he could not help lowering his voice—"I may have more than a parchment three-pence in my pocket. My present business," continued he, speaking with lofty confidence, "is merely to inquire the way to the dwelling of my kinsman, Major Molineux."

There was a sudden and general movement in the room, which Robin interpreted as expressing the eagerness of each individual to become his guide. But the innkeeper turned his eyes to a written paper on the wall, which he read, or seemed to read, with occasional recurrences to the young man's figure.

---

1 *punch* Rum-based drink made in the West Indies, which became especially popular with colonial sailors.

2 *potation* Drink.

3 *Good Creature* Rum, or alcohol more generally.

4 *Fast Day* It was fairly common practice in colonial America to declare special days of public penitence which involved fasting, prayer, and "humiliation," in response to various social crises such as plagues, epidemics, and even wars; the understanding was that God would alleviate the burdens of society if they were sufficiently penitent for the sins that had presumably caused their suffering.

5 *Caravansary* Form of inn where travelers could put up their own caravans to rest for the night.

6 *Nicotian* Tobacco-filled.

"What have we here?" said he, breaking his speech into little dry fragments. "'Left the house of the sub-scriber, bounden servant,[1] Hezekiah Mudge—had on, when he went away, grey coat, leather breeches, master's third-best hat. One pound currency reward to whoever shall lodge him in any jail in the province.' Better trudge, boy, better trudge."

Robin had begun to draw his hand towards the lighter end of the oak cudgel, but a strange hostility in every countenance, induced him to relinquish his purpose of breaking the courteous innkeeper's head. As he turned to leave the room, he encountered a sneering glance from the bold-featured personage whom he had before noticed; and no sooner was he beyond the door, than he heard a general laugh, in which the innkeeper's voice might be distinguished, like the dropping of small stones into a kettle.

"Now is it not strange," thought Robin, with his usual shrewdness, "is it not strange, that the confession of an empty pocket, should outweigh the name of my kinsman, Major Molineux? Oh, if I had one of those grinning rascals in the woods, where I and my oak sapling grew up together, I would teach him that my arm is heavy, though my purse be light!"

On turning the corner of the narrow lane, Robin found himself in a spacious street, with an unbroken line of lofty houses on each side, and a steepled build-ing at the upper end, whence the ringing of a bell announced the hour of nine. The light of the moon, and the lamps from numerous shop windows, dis-covered people promenading on the pavement, and amongst them, Robin hoped to recognize his hitherto inscrutable[2] relative. The result of his former inquiries made him unwilling to hazard another, in a scene of such publicity, and he determined to walk slowly and silently up the street, thrusting his face close to that of every elderly gentleman, in search of the Major's lineaments. In his progress, Robin encountered many gay[3] and gallant figures. Embroidered garments of showy colors, enormous periwigs, gold-laced hats, and silver-hilted swords, glided past him and dazzled his optics. Travelled youths, imitators of the European fine gentlemen of the period, trod jauntily along, half-dancing to the fashionable tunes which they hummed, and making poor Robin ashamed of his quiet and nat-ural gait. At length, after many pauses to examine the gorgeous display of goods in the shop windows, and after suffering some rebukes for the impertinence of his scrutiny into people's faces, the Major's kinsman found himself near the steepled building, still unsuccessful in his search. As yet, however, he had seen only one side of the thronged street; so Robin crossed, and con-tinued the same sort of inquisition down the opposite pavement, with stronger hopes than the philosopher seeking an honest man,[4] but with no better fortune. He had arrived about midway towards the lower end, from which his course began, when he overheard the approach of someone, who struck down a cane on the flag-stones at every step, uttering, at regular intervals, two sepulchral hems.

"Mercy on us!" quoth Robin, recognising the sound.

Turning a corner, which chanced to be close at his right hand, he hastened to pursue his researches, in some other part of the town. His patience was now wearing low, and he seemed to feel more fatigue from his rambles since he crossed the ferry, than from his journey of several days on the other side. Hunger also pleaded loudly within him, and Robin began to balance the propriety of demanding, violently and with lifted cudgel, the necessary guidance from the first solitary passenger, whom he should meet. While a resolution to this effect was gaining strength, he entered a street of mean appearance, on either side of which, a row of ill-built houses was straggling towards the harbor. The moonlight fell upon no passenger along the whole extent, but in the third domicile which Robin passed, there was a half-opened door, and his keen glance detected a woman's garment within.

"My luck may be better here," said he to himself.

Accordingly, he approached the door, and beheld it shut closer as he did so; yet an open space remained, sufficing for the fair occupant to observe the stranger, without a corresponding display on her part. All that

---

1   *bounden servant*   Indentured servant; person bound by contract to work for an employer, without wages, for a set period of time, often in exchange for passage from Europe to the colonies.

2   *inscrutable*   Unable to be found; elusive.

3   *gay*   Brightly colored or dazzling.

---

4   *philosopher seeking an honest man*   Reference to Greek phi-losopher Diogenes (c. 412–323 BCE), who was known to walk about Athens with a lamp in full daylight, claiming to be seeking an honest man.

Robin could discern was a strip of scarlet petticoat, and the occasional sparkle of an eye, as if the moonbeams were trembling on some bright thing.

"Pretty mistress,"—for I may call her so with a good conscience, thought the shrewd youth, since I know nothing to the contrary—"my sweet pretty mistress, will you be kind enough to tell me whereabouts I must seek the dwelling of my kinsman, Major Molineux?"

Robin's voice was plaintive and winning, and the female, seeing nothing to be shunned in the handsome country youth, thrust open the door, and came forth into the moonlight. She was a dainty little figure, with a white neck, round arms, and a slender waist, at the extremity of which her scarlet petticoat jutted out over a hoop, as if she were standing in a balloon. Moreover, her face was oval and pretty, her hair dark beneath the little cap, and her bright eyes possessed a sly freedom, which triumphed over those of Robin.

"Major Molineux dwells here," said this fair woman. Now her voice was the sweetest Robin had heard that night, the airy counterpart of a stream of melted silver; yet he could not help doubting whether that sweet voice spoke gospel truth. He looked up and down the mean street, and then surveyed the house before which they stood. It was a small, dark edifice of two stories, the second of which projected over the lower floor; and the front apartment had the aspect of a shop for petty commodities.

"Now truly I am in luck," replied Robin, cunningly, "and so indeed is my kinsman, the Major, in having so pretty a housekeeper. But I prithee trouble him to step to the door; I will deliver him a message from his friends in the country, and then go back to my lodgings at the inn."

"Nay, the Major has been a-bed this hour or more," said the lady of the scarlet petticoat; "and it would be to little purpose to disturb him tonight, seeing his evening draught was of the strongest. But he is a kind-hearted man, and it would be as much as my life's worth, to let a kinsman of his turn away from the door. You are the good old gentleman's very picture, and I could swear that was his rainy-weather hat. Also, he has garments very much resembling those leather—But come in, I pray, for I bid you hearty welcome in his name."

So saying, the fair and hospitable dame took our hero by the hand; and though the touch was light, and the force was gentleness, and though Robin read in her eyes what he did not hear in her words, yet the slender-waisted woman, in the scarlet petticoat, proved stronger than the athletic country youth. She had drawn his half-willing footsteps nearly to the threshold, when the opening of a door in the neighborhood, startled the Major's housekeeper, and, leaving the Major's kinsman, she vanished speedily into her own domicile. A heavy yawn preceded the appearance of a man, who, like the Moonshine of Pyramus and Thisbe,[1] carried a lantern, needlessly aiding his sister luminary in the heavens. As he walked sleepily up the street, he turned his broad, dull face on Robin, and displayed a long staff, spiked at the end.

"Home, vagabond, home!" said the watchman, in accents that seemed to fall asleep as soon as they were uttered. "Home, or we'll set you in the stocks by peep of day!"

"This is the second hint of the kind," thought Robin. "I wish they would end my difficulties, by setting me there tonight."

Nevertheless, the youth felt an instinctive antipathy towards the guardian of midnight order, which at first prevented him from asking his usual question. But just when the man was about to vanish behind the corner, Robin resolved not to lose the opportunity, and shouted lustily after him—

"I say, friend! will you guide me to the house of my kinsman, Major Molineux?"

The watchman made no reply, but turned the corner and was gone; yet Robin seemed to hear the sound of drowsy laughter stealing along the solitary street. At that moment, also, a pleasant titter saluted him from the open window above his head; he looked up, and caught the sparkle of a saucy eye; a round arm beckoned to him, and next he heard light footsteps descending the staircase within. But Robin, being of the household of a New England clergyman, was a good youth, as well as a shrewd one; so he resisted temptation, and fled away.

He now roamed desperately, and at random, through the town, almost ready to believe that a spell was on

---

[1]   *like the Moonshine … and Thisbe*   See the play-within-the-play in Shakespeare's *A Midsummer Night's Dream* (1596), in which Robin Starveling plays the Moonshine, carrying a lantern to illuminate the tragic lovers Pyramus and Thisbe.

him, like that, by which a wizard of his country, had once kept three pursuers wandering, a whole winter night, within twenty paces of the cottage which they sought. The streets lay before him, strange and desolate, and the lights were extinguished in almost every house. Twice, however, little parties of men, among whom Robin distinguished individuals in outlandish attire, came hurrying along, but though on both occasions they paused to address him, such intercourse did not at all enlighten his perplexity. They did but utter a few words in some language of which Robin knew nothing, and perceiving his inability to answer, bestowed a curse upon him in plain English, and hastened away. Finally, the lad determined to knock at the door of every mansion that might appear worthy to be occupied by his kinsman, trusting that perseverance would overcome the fatality which had hitherto thwarted him. Firm in this resolve, he was passing beneath the walls of a church, which formed the corner of two streets, when, as he turned into the shade of its steeple, he encountered a bulky stranger, muffled in a cloak. The man was proceeding with the speed of earnest business, but Robin planted himself full before him, holding the oak cudgel with both hands across his body, as a bar to further passage.

"Halt, honest man, and answer me a question," said he, very resolutely, "Tell me, this instant, whereabouts is the dwelling of my kinsman, Major Molineux?"

"Keep your tongue between your teeth, fool, and let me pass," said a deep, gruff voice, which Robin partly remembered. "Let me pass, I say, or I'll strike you to the earth!"

"No, no, neighbor!" cried Robin, flourishing his cudgel, and then thrusting its larger end close to the man's muffled face. "No, no, I'm not the fool you take me for, nor do you pass, till I have an answer to my question. Whereabouts is the dwelling of my kinsman, Major Molineux?"

The stranger, instead of attempting to force his passage, stepped back into the moonlight, unmuffled his own face, and stared full into that of Robin.

"Watch here an hour, and Major Molineux will pass by," said he.

Robin gazed with dismay and astonishment on the unprecedented physiognomy[1] of the speaker. The fore-

head with its double prominence, the broad-hooked nose, the shaggy eyebrows, and fiery eyes, were those which he had noticed at the inn, but the man's complexion had undergone a singular, or more properly, a two-fold change. One side of the face blazed of an intense red, while the other was black as midnight, the division line being in the broad bridge of the nose; and a mouth, which seemed to extend from ear to ear, was black or red, in contrast to the color of the cheek. The effect was as if two individual devils, a fiend of fire and a fiend of darkness, had united themselves to form this infernal visage. The stranger grinned in Robin's face, muffled his party-colored features, and was out of sight in a moment.

"Strange things we travellers see!" ejaculated Robin.

He seated himself, however, upon the steps of the church-door, resolving to wait the appointed time for his kinsman's appearance. A few moments were consumed in philosophical speculations, upon the species of the *genus homo*, who had just left him, but having settled this point shrewdly, rationally, and satisfactorily, he was compelled to look elsewhere for amusement. And first he threw his eyes along the street; it was of more respectable appearance than most of those into which he had wandered, and the moon, "creating, like the imaginative power, a beautiful strangeness in familiar objects," gave something of romance to a scene that might not have possessed it in the light of day. The irregular, and often quaint architecture of the houses, some of whose roofs were broken into numerous little peaks; while others ascended, steep and narrow, into a single point; and others again were square; the pure milk-white of some of their complexions, the aged darkness of others, and the thousand sparklings, reflected from bright substances in the walls of many; these matters engaged Robin's attention for awhile, and then began to grow wearisome. Next he endeavored to define the forms of distant objects, starting away with almost ghostly indistinctness, just as his eye appeared to grasp them; and finally he took a minute survey of an edifice, which stood on the opposite side of the street, directly in front of the church-door, where he was stationed. It was a large, square mansion, distinguished from its neighbors by a balcony, which rested on tall pillars,

---

[1] *physiognomy* Facial features.

and by an elaborate Gothic window, communicating therewith.[1]

"Perhaps this is the very house I have been seeking," thought Robin.

Then he strove to speed away the time by listening to a murmur which swept continually along the street, yet was scarcely audible, except to an unaccustomed ear like his; it was a low, dull, dreamy sound, compounded of many noises, each of which was at too great a distance to be separately heard. Robin marvelled at this snore of a sleeping town, and marvelled more, whenever its continuity was broken, by now and then a distant shout, apparently loud where it originated. But altogether it was a sleep-inspiring sound, and, to shake off its drowsy influence, Robin arose, and climbed a window-frame, that he might view the interior of the church. There the moonbeams came trembling in, and fell down upon the deserted pews, and extended along the quiet aisles. A fainter, yet more awful radiance was hovering round the pulpit, and one solitary ray had dared to rest upon the open page of the great Bible. Had Nature, in that deep hour, become a worshipper in the house, which man had builded? Or was that heavenly light the visible sanctity of this place, visible because no earthly and impure feet were within the walls? The scene made Robin's heart shiver with a sensation of loneliness, stronger than he had ever felt in the remotest depths of his native woods; so he turned away, and sat down again before the door. There were graves around the church, and now an uneasy thought obtruded into Robin's breast. What if the object of his search, which had been so often and so strangely thwarted, were all the time mouldering in his shroud? What if his kinsman should glide through yonder gate, and nod and smile to him in passing dimly by?

"Oh, that any breathing thing were here with me!" said Robin.

Recalling his thoughts from this uncomfortable track, he sent them over forest, hill, and stream, and attempted to imagine how that evening of ambiguity and weariness, had been spent by his father's household. He pictured them assembled at the door, beneath the tree, the great old tree, which had been spared for its huge twisted trunk, and venerable shade, when a thousand leafy brethren fell. There, at the going down of the summer sun, it was his father's custom to perform domestic worship, that the neighbors might come and join with him like brothers of the family, and that the wayfaring man might pause to drink at that fountain, and keep his heart pure by freshening the memory of home. Robin distinguished the seat of every individual of the little audience; he saw the good man in the midst, holding the scriptures in the golden light that shone from the western clouds; he beheld him close the book, and all rise up to pray. He heard the old thanksgivings for daily mercies, the old supplications for their continuance, to which he had so often listened in weariness, but which were now among his dear remembrances. He perceived the slight inequality[2] of his father's voice when he came to speak of the Absent One; he noted how his mother turned her face to the broad and knotted trunk; how his elder brother scorned, because the beard was rough upon his upper lip, to permit his features to be moved; how his younger sister drew down a low hanging branch before her eyes; and how the little one of all, whose sports had hitherto broken the decorum of the scene, understood the prayer for her playmate, and burst into clamorous grief. Then he saw them go in at the door; and when Robin would have entered also, the latch tinkled into its place, and he was excluded from his home.

"Am I here, or there?" cried Robin, starting; for all at once, when his thoughts had become visible and audible in a dream, the long, wide, solitary street shone out before him.

He aroused himself, and endeavored to fix his attention steadily upon the large edifice which he had surveyed before. But still his mind kept vibrating between fancy and reality; by turns, the pillars of the balcony lengthened into the tall, bare stems of pines, dwindled down to human figures, settled again into their true shape and size, and then commenced a new succession of changes. For a single moment, when he deemed himself awake, he could have sworn that a visage, one which he seemed to remember, yet could not absolutely name as his kinsman's, was looking towards him from the gothic window. A deeper sleep wrestled with, and nearly overcame him, but fled at the sound of footsteps along the opposite pavement.

---

[1]   *communicating therewith* I.e., the window opened onto the balcony.

[2]   *inequality* Unevenness.

Robin rubbed his eyes, discerned a man passing at the foot of the balcony, and addressed him in a loud, peevish, and lamentable cry.

"Halloo, friend! must I wait here all night for my kinsman, Major Molineux?"

The sleeping echoes awoke, and answered the voice; and the passenger, barely able to discern a figure sitting in the oblique shade of the steeple, traversed the street to obtain a nearer view. He was himself a gentleman in his prime, of open, intelligent, cheerful, and altogether prepossessing countenance. Perceiving a country youth, apparently homeless and without friends, he accosted him in a tone of real kindness, which had become strange to Robin's ears.

"Well, my good lad, why are you sitting here?" inquired he. "Can I be of service to you in any way?"

"I am afraid not, Sir," replied Robin, despondingly; "yet I shall take it kindly, if you'll answer me a single question. I've been searching half the night for one Major Molineux; now, Sir, is there really such a person in these parts, or am I dreaming?"

"Major Molineux! The name is not altogether strange to me," said the gentleman, smiling. "Have you any objection to telling me the nature of your business with him?"

Then Robin briefly related that his father was a clergyman, settled on a small salary, at a long distance back in the country, and that he and Major Molineux were brothers' children. The Major, having inherited riches, and acquired civil and military rank, had visited his cousin in great pomp a year or two before; had manifested much interest in Robin and an elder brother, and, being childless himself, had thrown out hints respecting the future establishment of one of them in life. The elder brother was destined to succeed to the farm, which his father cultivated, in the interval of sacred duties; it was therefore determined that Robin should profit by his kinsman's generous intentions, especially as he had seemed to be rather the favorite, and was thought to possess other necessary endowments.

"For I have the name of being a shrewd youth," observed Robin, in this part of his story.

"I doubt not you deserve it," replied his new friend, good naturedly; "but pray proceed."

"Well, Sir, being nearly eighteen years old, and well grown, as you see," continued Robin, raising himself to his full height, "I thought it high time to begin the world. So my mother and sister put me in handsome trim, and my father gave me half the remnant of his last year's salary, and five days ago I started for this place, to pay the Major a visit. But, would you believe it, Sir? I crossed the ferry a little after dusk, and have yet found nobody that would show me the way to his dwelling; only an hour or two since, I was told to wait here, and Major Molineux would pass by."

"Can you describe the man who told you this?" inquired the gentleman.

"Oh, he was a very ill-favored fellow, Sir," replied Robin, "with two great bumps on his forehead, a hook nose, fiery eyes, and, what struck me as the strangest, his face was of two different colors. Do you happen to know such a man, Sir?"

"Not intimately," answered the stranger, "but I chanced to meet him a little time previous to your stopping me. I believe you may trust his word, and that the Major will very shortly pass through this street. In the meantime, as I have a singular curiosity to witness your meeting, I will sit down here upon the steps, and bear you company."

He seated himself accordingly, and soon engaged his companion in animated discourse. It was but of brief continuance, however, for a noise of shouting, which had long been remotely audible, drew so much nearer, that Robin inquired its cause.

"What may be the meaning of this uproar?" asked he. "Truly, if your town be always as noisy, I shall find little sleep, while I am an inhabitant."

"Why, indeed, friend Robin, there do appear to be three or four riotous fellows abroad tonight," replied the gentleman. "You must not expect all the stillness of your native woods, here in our streets. But the watch will shortly be at the heels of these lads, and—"

"Aye, and set them in the stocks by peep of day," interrupted Robin, recollecting his own encounter with the drowsy lantern-bearer. "But, dear Sir, if I may trust my ears, an army of watchmen would never make head against such a multitude of rioters. There were at least a thousand voices went up to make that one shout."

"May not a man have several voices, Robin, as well as two complexions?" said his friend.

"Perhaps a man may; but heaven forbid that a woman should!" responded the shrewd youth, thinking of the seductive tones of the Major's housekeeper.

The sounds of a trumpet in some neighboring street, now became so evident and continual, that Robin's curiosity was strongly excited. In addition to the shouts, he heard frequent bursts from many instruments of discord, and a wild and confused laughter filled up the intervals. Robin rose from the steps, and looked wistfully towards a point, whither several people seemed to be hastening.

"Surely some prodigious merrymaking is going on," exclaimed he. "I have laughed very little since I left home, Sir, and should be sorry to lose an opportunity. Shall we step round the corner by that darkish house, and take our share of the fun?"

"Sit down again, sit down, good Robin," replied the gentleman, laying his hand on the skirt of the grey coat. "You forget that we must wait here for your kinsman; and there is reason to believe that he will pass by, in the course of a very few moments."

The near approach of the uproar had now disturbed the neighborhood; windows flew open on all sides; and many heads, in the attire of the pillow,[1] and confused by sleep suddenly broken, were protruded to the gaze of whoever had leisure to observe them. Eager voices hailed each other from house to house, all demanding the explanation, which not a soul could give. Half-dressed men hurried towards the unknown commotion, stumbling as they went over the stone steps, that thrust themselves into the narrow foot-walk. The shouts, the laughter, and the tuneless bray, the antipodes[2] of music, came onward with increasing din, till scattered individuals, and then denser bodies, began to appear round a corner, at a distance of a hundred yards.

"Will you recognize your kinsman, Robin, if he passes in this crowd?" inquired the gentleman.

"Indeed, I can't warrant it, Sir; but I'll take my stand here, and keep a bright lookout," answered Robin, descending to the outer edge of the pavement.

A mighty stream of people now emptied into the street, and came rolling slowly towards the church. A single horseman wheeled the corner in the midst of them, and close behind him came a band of fearful wind-instruments, sending forth a fresher discord, now that no intervening buildings kept it from the ear. Then a redder light disturbed the moonbeams, and a dense multitude of torches shone along the street, concealing by their glare whatever object they illuminated. The single horseman, clad in a military dress, and bearing a drawn sword, rode onward as the leader, and, by his fierce and variegated countenance, appeared like war personified; the red of one cheek was an emblem of fire and sword; the blackness of the other betokened the mourning which attends them. In his train were wild figures in the Indian dress, and many fantastic shapes without a model, giving the whole march a visionary air, as if a dream had broken forth from some feverish brain, and were sweeping visibly through the midnight streets. A mass of people, inactive, except as applauding spectators, hemmed the procession in, and several women ran along the sidewalks, piercing the confusion of heavier sounds with their shrill voices of mirth or terror.

"The double-faced fellow has his eye upon me," muttered Robin, with an indefinite but uncomfortable idea, that he was himself to bear a part in the pageantry.

The leader turned himself in the saddle, and fixed his glance full upon the country youth, as the steed went slowly by. When Robin had freed his eyes from those fiery ones, the musicians were passing before him, and the torches were close at hand; but the unsteady brightness of the latter formed a veil which he could not penetrate. The rattling of wheels over the stones sometimes found its way to his ear, and confused traces of a human form appeared at intervals, and then melted into the vivid light. A moment more, and the leader thundered a command to halt; the trumpets vomited a horrid breath, and held their peace; the shouts and laughter of the people died away, and there remained only an universal hum, nearly allied to silence. Right before Robin's eyes was an uncovered cart. There the torches blazed the brightest, there the moon shone out like day, and there, in tar-and-feathery[3] dignity, sat his kinsman, Major Molineux!

---

[1]   *attire of the pillow* I.e., nightclothes.

[2]   *antipodes* Opposite.

---

[3]   *tar-and-feathery* To be stripped naked, covered in hot tar, and then strewn with feathers, was a common form of torture and public humiliation, especially in the context of mob violence.

He was an elderly man, of large and majestic person, and strong, square features, betokening a steady soul; but steady as it was, his enemies had found the means to shake it. His face was pale as death, and far more ghastly; the broad forehead was contracted in his agony, so that the eyebrows formed one dark grey line; his eyes were red and wild, and the foam hung white upon his quivering lip. His whole frame was agitated by a quick and continual tremor, which his pride strove to quell, even in those circumstances of overwhelming humiliation. But perhaps the bitterest pang of all was when his eyes met those of Robin; for he evidently knew him on the instant, as the youth stood witnessing the foul disgrace of a head grown grey in honor. They stared at each other in silence, and Robin's knees shook, and his hair bristled, with a mixture of pity and terror. Soon, however, a bewildering excitement began to seize upon his mind; the preceding adventures of the night, the unexpected appearance of the crowd, the torches, the confused din, and the hush that followed, the spectre of his kinsman reviled by that great multitude, all this, and more than all, a perception of tremendous ridicule in the whole scene, affected him with a sort of mental inebriety. At that moment a voice of sluggish merriment saluted Robin's ears; he turned instinctively, and just behind the corner of the church stood the lantern-bearer, rubbing his eyes, and drowsily enjoying the lad's amazement. Then he heard a peal of laughter like the ringing of silvery bells; a woman twitched his arm, a saucy eye met his, and he saw the lady of the scarlet petticoat. A sharp, dry cachinnation[1] appealed to his memory, and, standing on tiptoe in the crowd, with his white apron over his head, he beheld the courteous little innkeeper. And lastly, there sailed over the heads of the multitude a great, broad laugh, broken in the midst by two sepulchral hems; thus—

"Haw, haw, haw—hem, hem—haw, haw, haw, haw!"

The sound proceeded from the balcony of the opposite edifice, and thither Robin turned his eyes. In front of the Gothic window stood the old citizen, wrapped in a wide gown, his grey periwig exchanged for a nightcap, which was thrust back from his forehead, and his silk stockings hanging down about his legs. He supported himself on his polished cane in a fit of convulsive merriment, which manifested itself on his solemn old features, like a funny inscription on a tomb-stone. Then Robin seemed to hear the voices of the barbers; of the guests of the inn; and of all who had made sport of him that night. The contagion was spreading among the multitude, when, all at once, it seized upon Robin, and he sent forth a shout of laughter that echoed through the street; every man shook his sides, every man emptied his lungs, but Robin's shout was the loudest there. The cloud-spirits peeped from their silvery islands, as the congregated mirth went roaring up the sky! The Man in the Moon heard the far bellow; "Oho," quoth he, "the old Earth is frolicsome tonight!"

When there was a momentary calm in that tempestuous sea of sound, the leader gave the sign, and the procession resumed its march. On they went, like fiends that throng in mockery round some dead potentate,[2] mighty no more, but majestic still in his agony. On they went, in counterfeited pomp, in senseless uproar, in frenzied merriment, trampling all on an old man's heart. On swept the tumult, and left a silent street behind.

"Well, Robin, are you dreaming?" inquired the gentleman, laying his hand on the youth's shoulder.

Robin started, and withdrew his arm from the stone post, to which he had instinctively clung, while the living stream rolled by him. His cheek was somewhat pale, and his eye not quite so lively as in the earlier part of the evening.

"Will you be kind enough to show me the way to the ferry?" said he, after a moment's pause.

"You have then adopted a new subject of inquiry?" observed his companion, with a smile.

"Why, yes, Sir," replied Robin, rather dryly. "Thanks to you, and to my other friends, I have at last met my kinsman, and he will scarce desire to see my face again. I begin to grow weary of a town life, Sir. Will you show me the way to the ferry?"

"No, my good friend Robin, not tonight, at least," said the gentleman. "Some few days hence, if you continue to wish it, I will speed you on your journey. Or, if you prefer to remain with us, perhaps, as you are a shrewd youth, you may rise in the world, without the help of your kinsman, Major Molineux."

—1832

---

[1] *cachinnation* Excess of laughter.

[2] *potentate* Ruler.

Young Goodman Brown

Young Goodman[1] Brown came forth, at sunset, into the street of Salem village, but put his head back, after crossing the threshold, to exchange a parting kiss with his young wife. And Faith, as the wife was aptly named, thrust her own pretty head into the street, letting the wind play with the pink ribbons of her cap, while she called to Goodman Brown.

"Dearest heart," whispered she, softly and rather sadly, when her lips were close to his ear, "pr'y thee, put off your journey until sunrise, and sleep in your own bed tonight. A lone woman is troubled with such dreams and such thoughts, that she's afeard of herself, sometimes. Pray, tarry with me this night, dear husband, of all nights in the year!"

"My love and my Faith," replied young Goodman Brown, "of all nights in the year, this one night must I tarry away from thee. My journey, as thou callest it, forth and back again, must needs be done 'twixt now and sunrise. What, my sweet, pretty wife, dost thou doubt me already, and we but three months married?"

"Then God bless you!" said Faith, with the pink ribbons, "and may you find all well, when you come back."

"Amen!" cried Goodman Brown. "Say thy prayers, dear Faith, and go to bed at dusk, and no harm will come to thee."

So they parted; and the young man pursued his way, until, being about to turn the corner by the meeting-house, he looked back, and saw the head of Faith still peeping after him, with a melancholy air, in spite of her pink ribbons.

"Poor little Faith!" thought he, for his heart smote him. "What a wretch am I, to leave her on such an errand! She talks of dreams, too. Methought, as she spoke, there was trouble in her face, as if a dream had warned her what work is to be done tonight. But, no, no! 't would kill her to think it. Well, she's a blessed angel on earth; and after this one night, I'll cling to her skirts and follow her to Heaven."

With this excellent resolve for the future, Goodman Brown felt himself justified in making more haste on his present evil purpose. He had taken a dreary road, darkened by all the gloomiest trees of the forest, which barely stood aside to let the narrow path creep through, and closed immediately behind. It was all as lonely as could be; and there is this peculiarity in such a solitude, that the traveler knows not who may be concealed by the innumerable trunks and the thick boughs overhead; so that, with lonely footsteps, he may yet be passing through an unseen multitude.

"There may be a devilish Indian behind every tree," said Goodman Brown, to himself; and he glanced fearfully behind him, as he added, "What if the devil himself should be at my very elbow!"

His head being turned back, he passed a crook of the road, and looking forward again, beheld the figure of a man, in grave and decent attire, seated at the foot of an old tree. He arose, at Goodman Brown's approach, and walked onward, side by side with him.

"You are late, Goodman Brown," said he. "The clock of the Old South was striking as I came through Boston; and that is full fifteen minutes agone."[2]

"Faith kept me back a while," replied the young man, with a tremor in his voice caused by the sudden appearance of his companion, though not wholly unexpected.

It was now deep dusk in the forest, and deepest in that part of it where these two were journeying. As nearly as could be discerned, the second traveler was about fifty years old, apparently in the same rank of life as Goodman Brown, and bearing a considerable resemblance to him, though perhaps more in expression than features. Still, they might have been taken for father and son. And yet, though the elder person was as simply clad as the younger, and as simple in manner too, he had an indescribable air of one who knew the world, and would not have felt abashed at the governor's dinner-table, or in King William's[3] court, were it possible that his affairs should call him thither. But the only thing about him that could be fixed upon as remarkable was his staff, which bore the likeness of a great black snake, so curiously wrought, that it might almost be seen to twist and wriggle itself, like a living

---

[1]   *Goodman*   Respectful title for the male head of a household.

[2]   *The clock ... minutes agone*   Reference to the Old South Church in Boston; to have walked the sixteen miles from Boston to Salem in fifteen minutes suggests unnatural power;   *agone*   Ago.

[3]   *King William*   William III (r. 1689–1702), monarch of England along with his wife, Mary II (r. 1689–94).

serpent. This, of course, must have been an ocular deception, assisted by the uncertain light.

"Come, Goodman Brown!" cried his fellow traveler, "this is a dull pace for the beginning of a journey. Take my staff, if you are so soon weary."

"Friend," said the other, exchanging his slow pace for a full stop, "having kept covenant by meeting thee here, it is my purpose now to return whence I came. I have scruples, touching the matter thou wot'st[1] of."

"Sayest thou so?" replied he of the serpent, smiling apart. "Let us walk on, nevertheless, reasoning as we go; and if I convince thee not, thou shalt turn back. We are but a little way in the forest, yet."

"Too far, too far!" exclaimed the Goodman, unconsciously resuming his walk. "My father never went into the woods on such an errand, nor his father before him. We have been a race of honest men and good Christians, since the days of the martyrs.[2] And shall I be the first of the name of Brown, that ever took this path, and kept—"

"Such company, thou wouldst say," observed the elder person, interpreting his pause. "Good, Goodman Brown! I have been as well acquainted with your family as with ever a one among the Puritans; and that's no trifle to say. I helped your grandfather, the constable, when he lashed the Quaker woman so smartly through the streets of Salem.[3] And it was I that brought your father a pitch-pine knot, kindled at my own hearth, to set fire to an Indian village, in King Philip's War.[4] They were my good friends, both; and many a pleasant walk have we had along this path, and returned merrily after midnight. I would fain be friends with you, for their sake."

"If it be as thou sayest," replied Goodman Brown, "I marvel they never spoke of these matters. Or, verily, I marvel not, seeing that the least rumor of the sort would have driven them from New England. We are a people of prayer, and good works to boot, and abide[5] no such wickedness."

"Wickedness or not," said the traveler with the twisted staff, "I have a very general acquaintance here in New England. The deacons of many a church have drunk the communion wine with me; the selectmen of diverse[6] towns make me their chairman; and a majority of the Great and General Court[7] are firm supporters of my interest. The governor and I, too—but these are state secrets."

"Can this be so!" cried Goodman Brown, with a stare of amazement at his undisturbed companion. "Howbeit, I have nothing to do with the governor and council; they have their own ways, and are no rule for a simple husbandman,[8] like me. But, were I to go on with thee, how should I meet the eye of that good old man, our minister, at Salem village? Oh, his voice would make me tremble, both Sabbath day and lecture day!"[9]

Thus far, the elder traveler had listened with due gravity, but now burst into a fit of irrepressible mirth, shaking himself so violently, that his snake-like staff actually seemed to wriggle in sympathy.

"Ha! ha! ha!" shouted he, again and again; then composing himself, "Well, go on, Goodman Brown, go on; but, pr'y thee, don't kill me with laughing!"

"Well, then, to end the matter at once," said Goodman Brown, considerably nettled, "there is my wife, Faith. It would break her dear little heart; and I'd rather break my own!"

"Nay, if that be the case," answered the other, "e'en go thy ways, Goodman Brown. I would not, for twenty old women like the one hobbling before us, that Faith should come to any harm."

As he spoke, he pointed his staff at a female figure on the path, in whom Goodman Brown recognized a very pious and exemplary dame who had taught him

---

1   *wot'st*   Wotest; knows.

2   *days of the martyrs*   I.e., the period during which Protestants were persecuted in Europe, especially, in England, during the reign (1553–58) of the Catholic Mary I.

3   *your grandfather ... of Salem*   Hawthorne's ancestor William Hathorne was an oppressive Puritan leader in 1600s Salem, and was also known to have had a Quaker woman publicly lashed.

4   *pitch-pine*   Type of coniferous tree which produces pitch or turpentine; *King Philip's War*   Conflict between English settlers and the Wanpanoag and other Native American tribes of the region; the Wanpanoag leader Metacom (1638–76) was called "King Philip" by some of the English.

5   *to boot, and abide*   As well, and tolerate.

6   *diverse*   Various.

7   *Great and General Court*   Legislative bodies.

8   *husbandman*   Holder of a small farm or simply a man of common status.

9   *lecture day*   Sermon day held during the week, rather than on a Sunday.

his catechism[1] in youth, and was still his moral and spiritual adviser, jointly with the minister and deacon Gookin.[2]

"A marvel, truly, that Goody Cloyse[3] should be so far in the wilderness, at nightfall!" said he. "But, with your leave, friend, I shall take a cut through the woods, until we have left this Christian woman behind. Being a stranger to you, she might ask whom I was consorting with, and whither I was going."

"Be it so," said his fellow traveler. "Betake you to the woods, and let me keep the path."

Accordingly, the young man turned aside, but took care to watch his companion, who advanced softly along the road, until he had come within a staff's length of the old dame. She, meanwhile, was making the best of her way, with singular speed for so aged a woman, and mumbling some indistinct words, a prayer, doubtless, as she went. The traveler put forth his staff, and touched her withered neck with what seemed the serpent's tail.

"The devil!" screamed the pious old lady.

"Then Goody Cloyse knows her old friend?" observed the traveler, confronting her, and leaning on his writhing stick.

"Ah, forsooth, and is it your worship, indeed?" cried the good dame. "Yea, truly is it, and in the very image of my old gossip, Goodman Brown, the grandfather of the silly fellow that now is. But, would your worship believe it? my broomstick hath strangely disappeared, stolen, as I suspect, by that unhanged witch, Goody Cory,[4] and that, too, when I was all anointed with the juice of smallage and cinque-foil and wolf's bane[5]—"

"Mingled with fine wheat and the fat of a new-born babe," said the shape of old Goodman Brown.

"Ah, your worship knows the receipt,"[6] cried the old lady, cackling aloud. "So, as I was saying, being all ready for the meeting, and no horse to ride on, I made up my mind to foot it; for they tell me, there is a nice young man to be taken into communion[7] tonight. But now your good worship will lend me your arm, and we shall be there in a twinkling."

"That can hardly be," answered her friend. "I may not spare you my arm, Goody Cloyse, but here is my staff, if you will."

So saying, he threw it down at her feet, where, perhaps, it assumed life, being one of the rods which its owner had formerly lent to the Egyptian Magi.[8] Of this fact, however, Goodman Brown could not take cognizance. He had cast up his eyes in astonishment, and looking down again, beheld neither Goody Cloyse nor the serpentine staff, but his fellow-traveler alone, who waited for him as calmly as if nothing had happened.

"That old woman taught me my catechism!" said the young man; and there was a world of meaning in this simple comment.

They continued to walk onward, while the elder traveler exhorted his companion to make good speed and persevere in the path, discoursing so aptly, that his arguments seemed rather to spring up in the bosom of his auditor, than to be suggested by himself. As they went, he plucked a branch of maple, to serve for a walking stick, and began to strip it of the twigs and little boughs, which were wet with evening dew. The moment his fingers touched them, they became strangely withered and dried up, as with a week's sunshine. Thus the pair proceeded, at a good free pace, until suddenly, in a gloomy hollow of the road, Goodman Brown sat himself down on the stump of a tree, and refused to go any farther.

"Friend," said he, stubbornly, "my mind is made up. Not another step will I budge on this errand. What if a wretched old woman do choose to go to the devil, when I thought she was going to Heaven! Is that any

---

[1]   *catechism*   Formal Christian instruction given to children, often given from church-ordained books.

[2]   *deacon Gookin*   Daniel Gookin (1612–87) was a Boston politician; *deacon*   Church officer.

[3]   *Goody Cloyse*   A woman named Sarah Cloyse was among the people imprisoned for witchcraft during the Salem witch trials; *Goody*   Short form of *goodwife*, female variant of the title Goodman.

[4]   *Goody Cory*   Martha Cory or Corey was hanged for witchcraft in Salem in 1692.

[5]   *smallage ... wolf's bane*   Herbs associated with witchcraft.

[6]   *receipt*   Recipe.

[7]   *communion*   Ordinarily, Christian ceremony initiating a young person into the ceremonies of the church.

[8]   *it assumed life ... Egyptian Magi*   See Exodus 7.11, where the Egyptian magi copy Aaron's feat by throwing their rods before the Pharaoh and turning them into serpents.

reason why I should quit my dear Faith, and go after her?"

"You will think better of this, by-and-by," said his acquaintance, composedly. "Sit here and rest yourself awhile; and when you feel like moving again, there is my staff to help you along."

Without more words, he threw his companion the maple stick, and was as speedily out of sight as if he had vanished into the deepening gloom. The young man sat a few moments by the roadside, applauding himself greatly, and thinking with how clear a conscience he should meet the minister, in his morning walk, nor shrink from the eye of good old deacon Gookin. And what calm sleep would be his, that very night, which was to have been spent so wickedly, but so purely and sweetly now, in the arms of Faith! Amidst these pleasant and praiseworthy meditations, Goodman Brown heard the tramp of horses along the road, and deemed it advisable to conceal himself within the verge of the forest, conscious of the guilty purpose that had brought him thither, though now so happily turned from it.

On came the hoof tramps and the voices of the riders, two grave old voices, conversing soberly as they drew near. These mingled sounds appeared to pass along the road, within a few yards of the young man's hiding place; but owing, doubtless, to the depth of the gloom at that particular spot, neither the travelers nor their steeds were visible. Though their figures brushed the small boughs by the wayside, it could not be seen that they intercepted, even for a moment, the faint gleam from the strip of bright sky, athwart which they must have passed. Goodman Brown alternately crouched and stood on tiptoe, pulling aside the branches, and thrusting forth his head as far as he durst,[1] without discerning so much as a shadow. It vexed him the more because he could have sworn, were such a thing possible, that he recognized the voices of the minister and deacon Gookin, jogging along quietly, as they were wont to do, when bound to some ordination or ecclesiastical council. While yet within hearing, one of the riders stopped to pluck a switch.

"Of the two, reverend Sir," said the voice like the deacon's, "I had rather miss an ordination dinner than tonight's meeting. They tell me that some of our community are to be here from Falmouth and beyond, and others from Connecticut and Rhode Island; besides several of the Indian powows[2] who, after their fashion, know almost as much deviltry as the best of us. Moreover, there is a goodly young woman to be taken into communion."

"Mighty well, deacon Gookin!" replied the solemn old tones of the minister. "Spur up, or we shall be late. Nothing can be done, you know, until I get on the ground."

The hoofs clattered again, and the voices, talking so strangely in the empty air, passed on through the forest, where no church had ever been gathered, nor solitary Christian prayed. Whither, then, could these holy men be journeying, so deep into the heathen wilderness? Young Goodman Brown caught hold of a tree, for support, being ready to sink down on the ground, faint and overburdened with the heavy sickness of his heart. He looked up to the sky, doubting whether there really was a Heaven above him. Yet, there was the blue arch, and the stars brightening in it.

"With Heaven above, and Faith below, I will yet stand firm against the devil!" cried Goodman Brown.

While he still gazed upward, into the deep arch of the firmament, and had lifted his hands to pray, a cloud, though no wind was stirring, hurried across the zenith, and hid the brightening stars. The blue sky was still visible, except directly overhead, where this black mass of cloud was sweeping swiftly northward. Aloft in the air, as if from the depths of the cloud, came a confused and doubtful sound of voices. Once, the listener fancied that he could distinguish the accents of townspeople of his own, men and women, both pious and ungodly, many of whom he had met at the communion table, and had seen others rioting at the tavern. The next moment, so indistinct were the sounds, he doubted whether he had heard aught but the murmur of the old forest, whispering without a wind. Then came a stronger swell of those familiar tones, heard daily in the sunshine at Salem village, but never, until now, from a cloud of night. There was one voice, of a young woman, uttering lamentations, yet with an uncertain sorrow, and entreating for some favor, which, perhaps, it would grieve her to obtain. And all the unseen multitude, both saints and sinners, seemed to encourage her onward.

---

1   *durst* Dared.

2   *powows* Medicine men; shamans.

"Faith!" shouted Goodman Brown, in a voice of agony and desperation; and the echoes of the forest mocked him, crying—"Faith! Faith!" as if bewildered wretches were seeking her, all through the wilderness.

The cry of grief, rage, and terror was yet piercing the night, when the unhappy husband held his breath for a response. There was a scream, drowned immediately in a louder murmur of voices, fading into far-off laughter, as the dark cloud swept away, leaving the clear and silent sky above Goodman Brown. But something fluttered lightly down through the air, and caught on the branch of a tree. The young man seized it, and beheld a pink ribbon.

"My Faith is gone!" cried he, after one stupefied moment. "There is no good on earth; and sin is but a name. Come, devil! for to thee is this world given."

And maddened with despair, so that he laughed loud and long, did Goodman Brown grasp his staff and set forth again, at such a rate, that he seemed to fly along the forest path, rather than to walk or run. The road grew wilder and drearier, and more faintly traced, and vanished at length, leaving him in the heart of the dark wilderness, still rushing onward, with the instinct that guides mortal man to evil. The whole forest was peopled with frightful sounds; the creaking of the trees, the howling of wild beasts, and the yell of Indians; while, sometimes, the wind tolled like a distant church bell, and sometimes gave a broad roar around the traveler, as if all Nature were laughing him to scorn. But he was himself the chief horror of the scene, and shrank not from its other horrors.

"Ha! ha! ha!" roared Goodman Brown, when the wind laughed at him. "Let us hear which will laugh loudest! Think not to frighten me with your deviltry! Come witch, come wizard, come Indian powow, come devil himself! and here comes Goodman Brown. You may as well fear him as he fear you!"

In truth, all through the haunted forest, there could be nothing more frightful than the figure of Goodman Brown. On he flew, among the black pines, brandishing his staff with frenzied gestures, now giving vent to an inspiration of horrid blasphemy, and now shouting forth such laughter, as set all the echoes of the forest laughing like demons around him. The fiend[1] in his own shape is less hideous than when he rages in the breast of man. Thus sped the demoniac on his course, until, quivering among the trees, he saw a red light before him, as when the felled trunks and branches of a clearing have been set on fire, and throw up their lurid blaze against the sky, at the hour of midnight. He paused, in a lull of the tempest that had driven him onward, and heard the swell of what seemed a hymn, rolling solemnly from a distance, with the weight of many voices. He knew the tune; it was a familiar one in the choir of the village meeting-house. The verse died heavily away, and was lengthened by a chorus, not of human voices, but of all the sounds of the benighted wilderness, pealing in awful harmony together. Goodman Brown cried out; and his cry was lost to his own ear, by its unison with the cry of the desert.[2]

In the interval of silence he stole forward, until the light glared full upon his eyes. At one extremity of an open space, hemmed in by the dark wall of the forest, arose a rock, bearing some rude, natural resemblance either to an altar or a pulpit, and surrounded by four blazing pines, their tops aflame, their stems untouched, like candles at an evening meeting. The mass of foliage that had overgrown the summit of the rock was all on fire, blazing high into the night, and fitfully illuminating the whole field. Each pendent twig and leafy festoon was in a blaze. As the red light arose and fell, a numerous congregation alternately shone forth, then disappeared in shadow, and again grew, as it were, out of the darkness, peopling the heart of the solitary woods at once.

"A grave and dark-clad company!" quoth Goodman Brown.

In truth, they were such. Among them, quivering to-and-fro between gloom and splendor, appeared faces that would be seen, next day, at the council board of the province, and others which, Sabbath after Sabbath, looked devoutly heavenward, and benignantly over the crowded pews, from the holiest pulpits in the land. Some affirm that the lady of the governor was there. At least, there were high dames well known to her, and wives of honored husbands, and widows, a great multitude, and ancient maidens, all of excellent repute, and fair young girls who trembled lest their mothers should espy them. Either the sudden gleams of light, flashing over the obscure field, bedazzled Goodman Brown, or

---

[1] *The fiend* I.e., the devil.

[2] *desert* Wilderness.

he recognized a score of the church members of Salem village, famous for their especial sanctity. Good old deacon Gookin had arrived, and waited at the skirts of that venerable saint, his revered pastor. But, irreverently consorting with these grave, reputable, and pious people, these elders of the church, these chaste dames and dewy virgins, there were men of dissolute lives and women of spotted fame, wretches given over to all mean and filthy vice, and suspected even of horrid crimes. It was strange to see that the good shrank not from the wicked, nor were the sinners abashed by the saints. Scattered, also, among their pale-faced enemies, were the Indian priests, or powows, who had often scared their native forest with more hideous incantations than any known to English witchcraft.

"But, where is Faith?" thought Goodman Brown; and, as hope came into his heart, he trembled.

Another verse of the hymn arose, a slow and solemn strain such as the pious love, but joined to words which expressed all that our nature can conceive of sin, and darkly hinted at far more. Unfathomable to mere mortals is the lore of fiends. Verse after verse was sung, and still the chorus of the desert swelled between, like the deepest tone of a mighty organ. And, with the final peal of that dreadful anthem, there came a sound, as if the roaring wind, the rushing streams, the howling beasts, and every other voice of the unconverted wilderness, were mingling and according with the voice of guilty man, in homage to the prince of all. The four blazing pines threw up a loftier flame, and obscurely discovered shapes and visages of horror on the smoke wreaths, above the impious assembly. At the same moment, the fire on the rock shot redly forth, and formed a glowing arch above its base, where now appeared a figure. With reverence be it spoken, the figure bore no slight similitude, both in garb and manner, to some grave divine of the New England churches.

"Bring forth the converts!" cried a voice, that echoed through the field and rolled into the forest.

At the word, Goodman Brown stepped forth from the shadow of the trees, and approached the congregation, with whom he felt a loathful brotherhood, by the sympathy of all that was wicked in his heart. He could have well nigh sworn that the shape of his own dead father beckoned him to advance, looking downward from a smoke wreath, while a woman, with dim features of despair, threw out her hand to warn him back.[1] Was it his mother? But he had no power to retreat one step, nor to resist, even in thought, when the minister and good old deacon Gookin, seized his arms, and led him to the blazing rock. Thither came also the slender form of a veiled female, led between Goody Cloyse, that pious teacher of the catechism, and Martha Carrier,[2] who had received the devil's promise to be queen of hell. A rampant hag was she! And there stood the proselytes, beneath the canopy of fire.

"Welcome, my children," said the dark figure, "to the communion of your race![3] Ye have found, thus young, your nature and your destiny. My children, look behind you!"

They turned; and flashing forth, as it were, in a sheet of flame, the fiend worshippers were seen; the smile of welcome gleamed darkly on every visage.

"There," resumed the sable[4] form, "are all whom ye have reverenced from youth. Ye deemed them holier than yourselves, and shrank from your own sin, contrasting it with their lives of righteousness, and prayerful aspirations heavenward. Yet, here are they all, in my worshipping assembly! This night it shall be granted you to know their secret deeds; how hoary bearded elders of the church have whispered wanton words to the young maids of their households; how many a woman, eager for widows' weeds,[5] has given her husband a drink at bedtime, and let him sleep his last sleep in her bosom; how beardless youths have made haste to inherit their fathers' wealth; and how fair damsels— blush not, sweet ones!—have dug little graves in the garden, and bidden me, the sole guest, to an infant's funeral. By the sympathy of your human hearts for sin,

---

[1] *shape of … him back* Allusion to the belief in "spectral evidence" during the witch trials. Many of the accusers claimed to have seen or been attacked by the "specters" of the accused, proving them to be witches; spectral evidence became less accepted as people suspected that the devil could also take the shape of the innocent.

[2] *Martha Carrier* Another of the accused in the Salem witch trials. She vehemently denied all accusations against herself; nevertheless, she was hanged in 1692. In his summary of her trial, Cotton Mather called Carrier a "rampant hag" and asserted that "the Devil had promised her, she should be Queen of Hell."

[3] *race* Appearing as "grave" in the original printing, this was corrected in *Mosses from an Old Manse* (1846).

[4] *sable* Dark.

[5] *widow's weeds* Mourning clothes of a widow.

ye shall scent out all the places—whether in church, bedchamber, street, field, or forest—where crime has been committed, and shall exult to behold the whole earth one stain of guilt, one mighty blood spot. Far more than this! It shall be yours to penetrate, in every bosom, the deep mystery of sin, the fountain of all wicked arts, and which, inexhaustibly supplies more evil impulses than human power—than my power, at its utmost!—can make manifest in deeds. And now, my children, look upon each other."

They did so; and, by the blaze of the hell-kindled torches, the wretched man beheld his Faith, and the wife her husband, trembling before that unhallowed altar.

"Lo! there ye stand, my children," said the figure, in a deep and solemn tone, almost sad, with its despairing awfulness, as if his once angelic nature could yet mourn for our miserable race. "Depending upon one another's hearts, ye had still hoped, that virtue were not all a dream. Now are ye undeceived! Evil is the nature of mankind. Evil must be your only happiness. Welcome, again, my children, to the communion of your race!"

"Welcome!" repeated the fiend worshippers, in one cry of despair and triumph.

And there they stood, the only pair, as it seemed, who were yet hesitating on the verge of wickedness, in this dark world. A basin was hollowed, naturally, in the rock. Did it contain water, reddened by the lurid light? or was it blood? or, perchance, a liquid flame? Herein did the Shape of Evil dip his hand, and prepare to lay the mark of baptism upon their foreheads, that they might be partakers of the mystery of sin, more conscious of the secret guilt of others, both in deed and thought, than they could now be of their own. The husband cast one look at his pale wife, and Faith at him. What polluted wretches would the next glance show them to each other, shuddering alike at what they disclosed and what they saw!

"Faith! Faith!" cried the husband, "look up to Heaven, and resist the Wicked One!"

Whether Faith obeyed, he knew not. Hardly had he spoken, when he found himself amid calm night and solitude, listening to a roar of the wind, which died heavily away through the forest. He staggered against the rock and felt it chill and damp, while a hanging twig, that had been all on fire, besprinkled his cheek with the coldest dew.

The next morning, young Goodman Brown came slowly into the street of Salem village, staring around him like a bewildered man. The good old minister was taking a walk along the graveyard, to get an appetite for breakfast and meditate his sermon, and bestowed a blessing, as he passed, on Goodman Brown. He shrank from the venerable saint, as if to avoid an anathema.[1] Old deacon Gookin was at domestic worship, and the holy words of his prayer were heard through the open window. "What God doth the wizard pray to?" quoth Goodman Brown. Goody Cloyse, that excellent old Christian, stood in the early sunshine, at her own lattice, catechising a little girl who had brought her a pint of morning's milk. Goodman Brown snatched away the child, as from the grasp of the fiend himself. Turning the corner by the meeting-house, he spied the head of Faith, with the pink ribbons, gazing anxiously forth, and bursting into such joy at sight of him that she skipped along the street, and almost kissed her husband before the whole village.[2] But, Goodman Brown looked sternly and sadly into her face, and passed on without a greeting.

Had Goodman Brown fallen asleep in the forest, and only dreamed a wild dream of a witch-meeting?

Be it so, if you will. But, alas! it was a dream of evil omen for young Goodman Brown. A stern, a sad, a darkly meditative, a distrustful, if not a desperate man did he become, from the night of that fearful dream. On the Sabbath day, when the congregation were singing a holy psalm, he could not listen, because an anthem of sin rushed loudly upon his ear, and drowned all the blessed strain. When the minister spoke from the pulpit, with power and fervid eloquence, and, with his hand on the open Bible, of the sacred truths of our religion, and of saint-like lives and triumphant deaths, and of future bliss or misery unutterable, then did Goodman Brown turn pale, dreading, lest the roof should thunder down upon the gray blasphemer and his hearers. Often, waking suddenly at midnight, he

---

1 *anathema* Curse denouncing a person, and excommunicating them from church and God.

2 *almost kissed … village* Publicly kissing one's spouse was generally frowned upon, and even punishable by law, in seventeenth-century Massachusetts.

shrank from the bosom of Faith, and at morning or eventide, when the family knelt down at prayer, he scowled, and muttered to himself, and gazed sternly at his wife, and turned away. And when he had lived long, and was borne to his grave, a hoary corpse, followed by Faith, an aged woman, and children and grandchildren, a goodly procession, besides neighbors, not a few, they carved no hopeful verse upon his tombstone; for his dying hour was gloom.

—1835

The Minister's Black Veil

A Parable[1]

The sexton stood in the porch of Milford[2] meeting house, pulling busily at the bell-rope. The old people of the village came stooping along the street. Children, with bright faces, tripped merrily beside their parents, or mimicked a graver gait, in the conscious dignity of their Sunday clothes. Spruce bachelors looked sidelong at the pretty maidens, and fancied that the sabbath sunshine made them prettier than on weekdays. When the throng had mostly streamed into the porch, the sexton began to toll the bell, keeping his eye on the Reverend Mr. Hooper's door. The first glimpse of the clergyman's figure was the signal for the bell to cease its summons.

"But what has good Parson Hooper got upon his face?" cried the sexton in astonishment.

All within hearing immediately turned about, and beheld the semblance of Mr. Hooper, pacing slowly his meditative way towards the meeting house. With one accord they started, expressing more wonder than if some strange minister were coming to dust the cushions of Mr. Hooper's pulpit.

"Are you sure it is our parson?" inquired Goodman[3] Gray of the sexton.

"Of a certainty it is good Mr. Hooper," replied the sexton. "He was to have exchanged pulpits with Parson Shute of Westbury; but Parson Shute sent to excuse himself yesterday, being to preach a funeral sermon."

The cause of so much amazement may appear sufficiently slight. Mr. Hooper, a gentlemanly person of about thirty, though still a bachelor, was dressed with due clerical neatness, as if a careful wife had starched his band,[4] and brushed the weekly dust from his Sunday's garb. There was but one thing remarkable in his appearance. Swathed about his forehead, and hanging down over his face, so low as to be shaken by his breath, Mr. Hooper had on a black veil. On a nearer view, it seemed to consist of two folds of crape,[5] which entirely concealed his features, except the mouth and chin, but probably did not intercept his sight, farther than to give a darkened aspect to all living and inanimate things. With this gloomy shade before him, good Mr. Hooper walked onward, at a slow and quiet pace, stooping somewhat and looking on the ground, as is customary with abstracted men, yet nodding kindly to those of his parishioners who still waited on the meeting house steps. But so wonder-struck were they, that his greeting hardly met with a return.

"I can't really feel as if good Mr. Hooper's face was behind that piece of crape," said the sexton.

"I don't like it," muttered an old woman, as she hobbled into the meeting house. "He has changed himself into something awful,[6] only by hiding his face."

"Our parson has gone mad!" cried Goodman Gray, following him across the threshold.

A rumor of some unaccountable phenomenon had preceded Mr. Hooper into the meeting house, and set all the congregation astir. Few could refrain from twisting their heads towards the door; many stood upright, and turned directly about; while several little boys clambered upon the seats, and came down again with a terrible racket. There was a general bustle, a rustling of the women's gowns and shuffling of the men's feet, greatly at variance with that hushed repose which

---

1 [Hawthorne's note] Another clergyman in New-England, Mr. Joseph Moody, of York, Maine, who died about eighty years since, made himself remarkable by the same eccentricity that is here related of the Reverend Mr. Hooper. In his case, however, the symbol had a different import. In early life he had accidentally killed a beloved friend; and from that day till the hour of his own death, he hid his face from men.

2 *sexton* Officer responsible for maintaining a church; *Milford* Town in Massachusetts, near Boston.

3 *Goodman* Respectful title for the male head of a household.

4 *band* Collar (usually white) worn by a cleric.

5 *crape* Thin, gauzy fabric frequently used for mourning attire.

6 *awful* Inspiring of awe and reverential fear.

should attend the entrance of the minister. But Mr. Hooper appeared not to notice the perturbation of his people. He entered with an almost noiseless step, bent his head mildly to the pews on each side, and bowed as he passed his oldest parishioner, a white-haired great-grandsire, who occupied an armchair in the centre of the aisle. It was strange to observe how slowly this venerable man became conscious of something singular in the appearance of his pastor. He seemed not fully to partake of the prevailing wonder, till Mr. Hooper had ascended the stairs, and showed himself in the pulpit, face to face with his congregation, except for the black veil. That mysterious emblem was never once withdrawn. It shook with his measured breath as he gave out the psalm; it threw its obscurity between him and the holy page, as he read the Scriptures; and while he prayed, the veil lay heavily on his uplifted countenance. Did he seek to hide it from the dread Being whom he was addressing?

Such was the effect of this simple piece of crape, that more than one woman of delicate nerves was forced to leave the meeting house. Yet perhaps the pale-faced congregation was almost as fearful a sight to the minister, as his black veil to them.

Mr. Hooper had the reputation of a good preacher, but not an energetic one: he strove to win his people heavenward by mild, persuasive influences, rather than to drive them thither by the thunders of the Word. The sermon which he now delivered was marked by the same characteristics of style and manner as the general series of his pulpit oratory. But there was something, either in the sentiment of the discourse itself, or in the imagination of the auditors, which made it greatly the most powerful effort that they had ever heard from their pastor's lips. It was tinged, rather more darkly than usual, with the gentle gloom of Mr. Hooper's temperament. The subject had reference to secret sin, and those sad mysteries which we hide from our nearest and dearest, and would fain conceal from our own consciousness, even forgetting that the Omniscient can detect them. A subtle power was breathed into his words. Each member of the congregation, the most innocent girl, and the man of hardened breast, felt as if the preacher had crept upon them, behind his awful veil, and discovered their hoarded iniquity of deed or thought. Many spread their clasped hands on their bosoms. There was nothing terrible in what Mr. Hooper said, at least, no violence; and yet, with every tremor of his melancholy voice, the hearers quaked. An unsought pathos came hand in hand with awe. So sensible were the audience of some unwonted attribute in their minister, that they longed for a breath of wind to blow aside the veil, almost believing that a stranger's visage would be discovered, though the form, gesture, and voice were those of Mr. Hooper.

At the close of the services, the people hurried out with indecorous confusion, eager to communicate their pent-up amazement, and conscious of lighter spirits the moment they lost sight of the black veil. Some gathered in little circles, huddled closely together, with their mouths all whispering in the centre; some went homeward alone, wrapped in silent meditation; some talked loudly, and profaned the Sabbath day with ostentatious laughter. A few shook their sagacious heads, intimating that they could penetrate the mystery; while one or two affirmed that there was no mystery at all, but only that Mr. Hooper's eyes were so weakened by the midnight lamp, as to require a shade. After a brief interval, forth came good Mr. Hooper also, in the rear of his flock. Turning his veiled face from one group to another, he paid due reverence to the hoary heads, saluted the middle aged with kind dignity as their friend and spiritual guide, greeted the young with mingled authority and love, and laid his hands on the little children's heads to bless them. Such was always his custom on the Sabbath day. Strange and bewildered looks repaid him for his courtesy. None, as on former occasions, aspired to the honor of walking by their pastor's side. Old Squire Saunders, doubtless by an accidental lapse of memory, neglected to invite Mr. Hooper to his table, where the good clergyman had been wont to bless the food almost every Sunday since his settlement. He returned, therefore, to the parsonage, and, at the moment of closing the door, was observed to look back upon the people, all of whom had their eyes fixed upon the minister. A sad smile gleamed faintly from beneath the black veil, and flickered about his mouth, glimmering as he disappeared.

"How strange," said a lady, "that a simple black veil, such as any woman might wear on her bonnet, should become such a terrible thing on Mr. Hooper's face!"

"Something must surely be amiss with Mr. Hooper's intellects," observed her husband, the physician of the village. "But the strangest part of the affair is the effect of this vagary, even on a sober-minded man like myself. The black veil, though it covers only our pastor's face, throws its influence over his whole person, and makes him ghostlike from head to foot. Do you not feel it so?"

"Truly do I," replied the lady; "and I would not be alone with him for the world. I wonder he is not afraid to be alone with himself!"

"Men sometimes are so," said her husband.

The afternoon service was attended with similar circumstances. At its conclusion, the bell tolled for the funeral of a young lady. The relatives and friends were assembled in the house, and the more distant acquaintances stood about the door, speaking of the good qualities of the deceased, when their talk was interrupted by the appearance of Mr. Hooper, still covered with his black veil. It was now an appropriate emblem. The clergyman stepped into the room where the corpse was laid, and bent over the coffin, to take a last farewell of his deceased parishioner. As he stooped, the veil hung straight down from his forehead, so that, if her eyelids had not been closed forever, the dead maiden might have seen his face. Could Mr. Hooper be fearful of her glance, that he so hastily caught back the black veil? A person who watched the interview between the dead and living, scrupled not to affirm that, at the instant when the clergyman's features were disclosed, the corpse had slightly shuddered, rustling the shroud and muslin cap, though the countenance retained the composure of death. A superstitious old woman was the only witness of this prodigy. From the coffin, Mr. Hooper passed into the chamber of the mourners, and thence to the head of the staircase, to make the funeral prayer. It was a tender and heart-dissolving prayer, full of sorrow, yet so imbued with celestial hopes, that the music of a heavenly harp, swept by the fingers of the dead, seemed faintly to be heard among the saddest accents of the minister. The people trembled, though they but darkly understood him when he prayed that they, and himself, and all of mortal race, might be ready, as he trusted this young maiden had been, for the dreadful hour that should snatch the veil from their faces. The bearers went heavily forth, and the mourners followed, saddening all the street, with the dead before them, and Mr. Hooper in his black veil behind.

"Why do you look back?" said one in the procession to his partner.

"I had a fancy," replied she, "that the minister and the maiden's spirit were walking hand in hand."

"And so had I, at the same moment," said the other.

That night, the handsomest couple in Milford village were to be joined in wedlock. Though reckoned a melancholy man, Mr. Hooper had a placid cheerfulness for such occasions, which often excited a sympathetic smile where livelier merriment would have been thrown away. There was no quality of his disposition which made him more beloved than this. The company at the wedding awaited his arrival with impatience, trusting that the strange awe which had gathered over him throughout the day would now be dispelled. But such was not the result. When Mr. Hooper came, the first thing that their eyes rested on was the same horrible black veil, which had added deeper gloom to the funeral, and could portend nothing but evil to the wedding. Such was its immediate effect on the guests, that a cloud seemed to have rolled duskily from beneath the black crape, and dimmed the light of the candles. The bridal pair stood up before the minister. But the bride's cold fingers quivered in the tremulous hand of the bridegroom, and her deathlike paleness caused a whisper that the maiden who had been buried a few hours before was come from her grave to be married. If ever another wedding were so dismal, it was that famous one where they tolled the wedding knell.[1] After performing the ceremony, Mr. Hooper raised a glass of wine to his lips, wishing happiness to the new-married couple in a strain of mild pleasantry that ought to have brightened the features of the guests, like a cheerful gleam from the hearth. At that instant, catching a glimpse of his figure in the looking-glass, the black veil involved his own spirit in the horror with which it overwhelmed all others. His frame shuddered—his lips grew white—he spilt the untasted wine upon the carpet—and rushed forth into the darkness. For the Earth, too, had on her Black Veil.

---

[1] *that famous ... wedding knell* Allusion to Hawthorne's own story *The Wedding Knell*, first published along with this story in the gift-book *The Token* in 1836; *knell* Sound of a funeral bell.

The next day, the whole village of Milford talked of little else than Parson Hooper's black veil. That, and the mystery concealed behind it, supplied a topic for discussion between acquaintances meeting in the street, and good women gossiping at their open windows. It was the first item of news that the tavern-keeper told to his guests. The children babbled of it on their way to school. One imitative little imp covered his face with an old black handkerchief, thereby so affrighting his playmates that the panic seized himself, and he well nigh lost his wits by his own waggery.[1]

It was remarkable that, of all the busybodies and impertinent people in the parish, not one ventured to put the plain question to Mr. Hooper, wherefore he did this thing. Hitherto, whenever there appeared the slightest call for such interference, he had never lacked advisers, nor shown himself averse to be guided by their judgment. If he erred at all, it was by so painful a degree of self-distrust, that even the mildest censure would lead him to consider an indifferent action as a crime. Yet, though so well acquainted with this amiable weakness, no individual among his parishioners chose to make the black veil a subject of friendly remonstrance. There was a feeling of dread, neither plainly confessed nor carefully concealed, which caused each to shift the responsibility upon another, till at length it was found expedient to send a deputation to the church, in order to deal with Mr. Hooper about the mystery, before it should grow into a scandal. Never did an embassy so ill discharge its duties. The minister received them with friendly courtesy, but became silent after they were seated, leaving to his visitors the whole burden of introducing their important business. The topic, it might be supposed, was obvious enough. There was the black veil swathed round Mr. Hooper's forehead, and concealing every feature above his placid mouth, on which, at times, they could perceive the glimmering of a melancholy smile. But that piece of crape, to their imagination, seemed to hang down before his heart, the symbol of a fearful secret between him and them. Were the veil but cast aside, they might speak freely of it, but not till then. Thus they sat a considerable time, speechless, confused, and shrinking uneasily from Mr. Hooper's eye, which they felt to be fixed upon them with an invisible glance. Finally, the deputies returned

abashed to their constituents, pronouncing the matter too weighty to be handled, except by a council of the churches, if, indeed, it might not require a general synod.[2]

But there was one person in the village unappalled by the awe with which the black veil had impressed all besides herself. When the deputies returned without an explanation, or even venturing to demand one, she, with the calm energy of her character, determined to chase away the strange cloud that appeared to be settling round Mr. Hooper, every moment more darkly than before. As his plighted wife, it should be her privilege to know what the black veil concealed. At the minister's first visit, therefore, she entered upon the subject with a direct simplicity, which made the task easier both for him and her. After he had seated himself, she fixed her eyes steadfastly upon the veil, but could discern nothing of the dreadful gloom that had so overawed the multitude: it was but a double fold of crape, hanging down from his forehead to his mouth, and slightly stirring with his breath.

"No," she said aloud, and smiling, "there is nothing terrible in this piece of crape, except that it hides a face which I am always glad to look upon. Come, good sir, let the sun shine from behind the cloud. First lay aside your black veil: then tell me why you put it on."

Mr. Hooper's smile glimmered faintly.

"There is an hour to come," said he, "when all of us shall cast aside our veils. Take it not amiss, beloved friend, if I wear this piece of crape till then."

"Your words are a mystery, too," returned the young lady. "Take away the veil from them, at least."

"Elizabeth, I will," said he, "so far as my vow may suffer[3] me. Know, then, this veil is a type[4] and a symbol, and I am bound to wear it ever, both in light and darkness, in solitude and before the gaze of multitudes, and as with strangers, so with my familiar friends. No mortal eye will see it withdrawn. This dismal shade must separate me from the world: even you, Elizabeth, can never come behind it!"

"What grievous affliction hath befallen you," she earnestly inquired, "that you should thus darken your eyes forever?"

---

[1]   *waggery*   Mischievousness.

[2]   *synod*   Large assemblage of the clergy of a given church.

[3]   *suffer*   Allow.

[4]   *type*   Embodiment of a religious theme.

"If it be a sign of mourning," replied Mr. Hooper, "I, perhaps, like most other mortals, have sorrows dark enough to be typified by a black veil."

"But what if the world will not believe that it is the type of an innocent sorrow?" urged Elizabeth. "Beloved and respected as you are, there may be whispers that you hide your face under the consciousness of secret sin. For the sake of your holy office, do away this scandal!"

The color rose into her cheeks as she intimated the nature of the rumors that were already abroad in the village. But Mr. Hooper's mildness did not forsake him. He even smiled again—that same sad smile, which always appeared like a faint glimmering of light, proceeding from the obscurity beneath the veil.

"If I hide my face for sorrow, there is cause enough," he merely replied; "and if I cover it for secret sin, what mortal might not do the same?"

And with this gentle but unconquerable obstinacy did he resist all her entreaties. At length Elizabeth sat silent. For a few moments she appeared lost in thought, considering, probably, what new methods might be tried to withdraw her lover from so dark a fantasy, which, if it had no other meaning, was perhaps a symptom of mental disease. Though of a firmer character than his own, the tears rolled down her cheeks. But, in an instant, as it were, a new feeling took the place of sorrow: her eyes were fixed insensibly on the black veil, when, like a sudden twilight in the air, its terrors fell around her. She arose, and stood trembling before him.

"And do you feel it then at last?" said he mournfully.

She made no reply, but covered her eyes with her hand, and turned to leave the room. He rushed forward and caught her arm.

"Have patience with me, Elizabeth!" cried he passionately. "Do not desert me, though this veil must be between us here on earth. Be mine, and hereafter there shall be no veil over my face, no darkness between our souls! It is but a mortal veil—it is not for eternity! Oh! you know not how lonely I am, and how frightened to be alone behind my black veil. Do not leave me in this miserable obscurity forever!"

"Lift the veil but once, and look me in the face," said she.

"Never! It cannot be!" replied Mr. Hooper.

"Then farewell!" said Elizabeth.

She withdrew her arm from his grasp, and slowly departed, pausing at the door, to give one long, shuddering gaze, that seemed almost to penetrate the mystery of the black veil. But, even amid his grief, Mr. Hooper smiled to think that only a material emblem had separated him from happiness, though the horrors which it shadowed forth must be drawn darkly between the fondest of lovers.

From that time no attempts were made to remove Mr. Hooper's black veil, or, by a direct appeal, to discover the secret which it was supposed to hide. By persons who claimed a superiority to popular prejudice, it was reckoned merely an eccentric whim, such as often mingles with the sober actions of men otherwise rational, and tinges them all with its own semblance of insanity. But with the multitude, good Mr. Hooper was irreparably a bugbear.[1] He could not walk the street with any peace of mind, so conscious was he that the gentle and timid would turn aside to avoid him, and that others would make it a point of hardihood to throw themselves in his way. The impertinence of the latter class compelled him to give up his customary walk, at sunset, to the burial ground; for when he leaned pensively over the gate, there would always be faces behind the gravestones, peeping at his black veil. A fable went the rounds, that the stare of the dead people drove him thence. It grieved him, to the very depth of his kind heart, to observe how the children fled from his approach, breaking up their merriest sports, while his melancholy figure was yet afar off. Their instinctive dread caused him to feel, more strongly than aught else, that a preternatural horror was interwoven with the threads of the black crape. In truth, his own antipathy to the veil was known to be so great, that he never willingly passed before a mirror, nor stooped to drink at a still fountain, lest, in its peaceful bosom, he should be affrighted by himself. This was what gave plausibility to the whispers, that Mr. Hooper's conscience tortured him for some great crime too horrible to be entirely concealed, or otherwise than so obscurely intimated. Thus, from beneath the black veil, there rolled a cloud into the sunshine, an ambiguity of sin or sorrow, which enveloped the poor minister, so that love or sympathy could never reach him. It was said that ghost and fiend

---

[1] *bugbear* Creature that causes great fear or anxiety.

consorted with him there. With self-shudderings and outward terrors, he walked continually in its shadow, groping darkly within his own soul, or gazing through a medium that saddened the whole world. Even the lawless wind, it was believed, respected his dreadful secret, and never blew aside the veil. But still good Mr. Hooper sadly smiled at the pale visages of the worldly throng as he passed by.

Among all its bad influences, the black veil had the one desirable effect, of making its wearer a very efficient clergyman. By the aid of his mysterious emblem—for there was no other apparent cause—he became a man of awful power over souls that were in agony for sin. His converts always regarded him with a dread peculiar to themselves, affirming, though but figuratively, that, before he brought them to celestial light, they had been with him behind the black veil. Its gloom, indeed, enabled him to sympathize with all dark affections. Dying sinners cried aloud for Mr. Hooper, and would not yield their breath till he appeared; though ever, as he stooped to whisper consolation, they shuddered at the veiled face so near their own. Such were the terrors of the black veil, even when death had bared his visage! Strangers came long distances to attend service at his church, with the mere idle purpose of gazing at his figure, because it was forbidden them to behold his face. But many were made to quake ere they departed! Once, during Governor Belcher's administration, Mr. Hooper was appointed to preach the election sermon.[1] Covered with his black veil, he stood before the chief magistrate, the council, and the representatives, and wrought so deep an impression that the legislative measures of that year were characterized by all the gloom and piety of our earliest ancestral sway.

In this manner Mr. Hooper spent a long life, irreproachable in outward act, yet shrouded in dismal suspicions; kind and loving, though unloved, and dimly feared; a man apart from men, shunned in their health and joy, but ever summoned to their aid in mortal anguish. As years wore on, shedding their snows above his sable veil, he acquired a name throughout the New England churches, and they called him Father Hooper.

Nearly all his parishioners, who were of mature age when he was settled, had been borne away by many a funeral: he had one congregation in the church, and a more crowded one in the churchyard; and having wrought so late into the evening, and done his work so well, it was now good Father Hooper's turn to rest.

Several persons were visible by the shaded candlelight, in the death chamber of the old clergyman. Natural connections[2] he had none. But there was the decorously grave, though unmoved, physician, seeking only to mitigate the last pangs of the patient whom he could not save. There were the deacons, and other eminently pious members of his church. There, also, was the Reverend Mr. Clark, of Westbury, a young and zealous divine, who had ridden in haste to pray by the bedside of the expiring minister. There was the nurse, no hired handmaiden of death, but one whose calm affection had endured thus long in secrecy, in solitude, amid the chill of age, and would not perish, even at the dying hour. Who, but Elizabeth! And there lay the hoary head of good Father Hooper upon the death pillow, with the black veil still swathed about his brow and reaching down over his face, so that each more difficult gasp of his faint breath caused it to stir. All through life that piece of crape had hung between him and the world: it had separated him from cheerful brotherhood and woman's love, and kept him in that saddest of all prisons, his own heart; and still it lay upon his face, as if to deepen the gloom of his darksome chamber, and shade him from the sunshine of eternity.

For some time previous, his mind had been confused, wavering doubtfully between the past and the present, and hovering forward, as it were, at intervals, into the indistinctness of the world to come. There had been feverish turns, which tossed him from side to side, and wore away what little strength he had. But in his most convulsive struggles, and in the wildest vagaries of his intellect, when no other thought retained its sober influence, he still showed an awful solicitude lest the black veil should slip aside. Even if his bewildered soul could have forgotten, there was a faithful woman at his pillow, who, with averted eyes, would have covered that aged face, which she had last beheld in the comeliness of manhood. At length the death-stricken

---

[1]   *Governor Belcher ... election sermon*   Jonathan Belcher (1682–1757) was governor of Massachusetts and New Hampshire. Election sermons were preached at the beginning of a governor's administration, upon election.

[2]   *Natural connections*   I.e., blood relations; family.

old man lay quietly in the torpor of mental and bodily exhaustion, with an imperceptible pulse, and breath that grew fainter and fainter, except when a long, deep, and irregular inspiration seemed to prelude the flight of his spirit.

The minister of Westbury approached the bedside.

"Venerable Father Hooper," said he, "the moment of your release is at hand. Are you ready for the lifting of the veil, that shuts in time from eternity?"

Father Hooper at first replied merely by a feeble motion of his head; then, apprehensive, perhaps, that his meaning might be doubtful, he exerted himself to speak.

"Yea," said he, in faint accents; "my soul hath a patient weariness until that veil be lifted."

"And is it fitting," resumed the Reverend Mr. Clark, "that a man so given to prayer, of such a blameless example, holy in deed and thought, so far as mortal judgment may pronounce; is it fitting that a father in the church should leave a shadow on his memory, that may seem to blacken a life so pure? I pray you, my venerable brother, let not this thing be! Suffer us to be gladdened by your triumphant aspect as you go to your reward. Before the veil of eternity be lifted, let me cast aside this black veil from your face!"

And thus speaking, the Reverend Mr. Clark bent forward to reveal the mystery of so many years. But, exerting a sudden energy, that made all the beholders stand aghast, Father Hooper snatched both his hands from beneath the bedclothes, and pressed them strongly on the black veil, resolute to struggle, if the minister of Westbury would contend with a dying man.

"Never!" cried the veiled clergyman. "On earth, never!"

"Dark old man!" exclaimed the affrighted minister, "with what horrible crime upon your soul are you now passing to the judgment?"

Father Hooper's breath heaved; it rattled in his throat; but, with a mighty effort, grasping forward with his hands, he caught hold of life, and held it back till he should speak. He even raised himself in bed; and there he sat, shivering with the arms of death around him, while the black veil hung down, awful, at that last moment, in the gathered terrors of a lifetime. And yet the faint, sad smile, so often there, now seemed to glimmer from its obscurity, and linger on Father Hooper's lips.

"Why do you tremble at me alone?" cried he, turning his veiled face round the circle of pale spectators. "Tremble also at each other! Have men avoided me, and women shown no pity, and children screamed and fled, only for my black veil? What, but the mystery which it obscurely typifies, has made this piece of crape so awful? When the friend shows his inmost heart to his friend; the lover to his best-beloved; when man does not vainly shrink from the eye of his Creator, loathsomely treasuring up the secret of his sin; then deem me a monster, for the symbol beneath which I have lived, and die! I look around me, and lo! on every visage a black veil!"

While his auditors shrank from one another, in mutual affright, Father Hooper fell back upon his pillow, a veiled corpse, with a faint smile lingering on the lips. Still veiled, they laid him in his coffin, and a veiled corpse they bore him to the grave. The grass of many years has sprung up and withered on that grave; the burial stone is moss-grown, and good Mr. Hooper's face is dust; but awful is still the thought that it moldered beneath the black veil!

—1836

The Birthmark

In the latter part of the last century, there lived a man of science—an eminent proficient in every branch of natural philosophy—who, not long before our story opens, had made experience of a spiritual affinity, more attractive than any chemical one. He had left his laboratory to the care of an assistant, cleared his fine countenance from the furnace smoke, washed the stain of acids from his fingers, and persuaded a beautiful woman to become his wife. In those days, when the comparatively recent discovery of electricity, and other kindred mysteries of nature, seemed to open paths into the region of miracle, it was not unusual for the love of science to rival the love of woman, in its depth and absorbing energy. The higher intellect, the imagination, the spirit, and even the heart, might all find their congenial aliment in pursuits which, as some of their ardent votaries[1] believed, would ascend from one step of powerful intelligence to another, until the philosopher should lay his hand on the secret of creative force, and perhaps make new worlds for himself. We know not whether Aylmer possessed this degree of faith in man's ultimate control over nature. He had devoted himself, however, too unreservedly to scientific studies, ever to be weaned from them by any second passion. His love for his young wife might prove the stronger of the two; but it could only be by intertwining itself with his love of science, and uniting the strength of the latter to his own.

Such a union accordingly took place, and was attended with truly remarkable consequences, and a deeply impressive moral. One day, very soon after their marriage, Aylmer sat gazing at his wife, with a trouble in his countenance that grew stronger, until he spoke.

"Georgiana," said he, "has it never occurred to you that the mark upon your cheek might be removed?"

"No, indeed," said she, smiling; but perceiving the seriousness of his manner, she blushed deeply. "To tell you the truth, it has been so often called a charm, that I was simple enough to imagine it might be so."

"Ah, upon another face, perhaps it might," replied her husband. "But never on yours! No, dearest Georgiana, you came so nearly perfect from the hand of Nature, that this slightest possible defect—which we hesitate whether to term a defect or a beauty—shocks me, as being the visible mark of earthly imperfection."

"Shocks you, my husband!" cried Georgiana, deeply hurt; at first reddening with momentary anger, but then bursting into tears. "Then why did you take me from my mother's side? You cannot love what shocks you!"

To explain this conversation, it must be mentioned that, in the centre of Georgiana's left cheek, there was a singular mark, deeply interwoven, as it were, with the texture and substance of her face. In the usual state of her complexion—a healthy, though delicate, bloom—the mark wore a tint of deeper crimson, which imperfectly defined its shape amid the surrounding rosiness. When she blushed, it gradually became more indistinct, and finally vanished amid the triumphant rush of blood that bathed the whole cheek with its brilliant glow. But, if any shifting emotion caused her to turn pale, there was the mark again, a crimson stain upon the snow, in what Aylmer sometimes deemed an almost fearful distinctness. Its shape bore not a little similarity to the human hand, though of the smallest pigmy size. Georgiana's lovers were wont to say that some fairy, at her birth hour, had laid her tiny hand upon the infant's cheek, and left this impress there, in token of the magic endowments that were to give her such sway over all hearts. Many a desperate swain would have risked life for the privilege of pressing his lips to the mysterious hand. It must not be concealed, however, that the impression wrought by this fairy sign-manual varied exceedingly, according to the difference of temperament in the beholders. Some fastidious persons—but they were exclusively of her own sex—affirmed that the Bloody Hand, as they chose to call it, quite destroyed the effect of Georgiana's beauty, and rendered her countenance even hideous. But it would be as reasonable to say, that one of those small blue stains, which sometimes occur in the purest statuary marble, would convert the Eve of Powers[2] to a monster. Masculine observers, if the birthmark did not heighten their admiration, contented themselves with wishing it away, that the world might possess one living specimen of ideal loveliness, without the semblance of a flaw. After his marriage—for he thought little or nothing of the matter before—Aylmer discovered that this was the case with himself.

Had she been less beautiful—if Envy's self could have found aught else to sneer at—he might have felt his affection heightened by the prettiness of this mimic hand, now vaguely portrayed, now lost, now stealing forth again, and glimmering to-and-fro with every pulse of emotion that throbbed within her heart. But, seeing her otherwise so perfect, he found this one defect grow more and more intolerable, with every moment of their united lives. It was the fatal flaw of humanity, which Nature, in one shape or another, stamps ineffaceably on all her productions, either to imply that they are temporary and finite, or that their perfection must be wrought by toil and pain. The Crimson Hand expressed the ineludible grip, in which mortality clutches the highest and purest of earthly

---

[1] *aliment* Nourishment; *votaries* Devotees.

[2] *Eve of Powers* Marble sculpture (variously known as *Eve Before the Fall* or *Eve Tempted*) by American sculptor Hiram Powers (1805–73).

mould, degrading them into kindred with the lowest, and even with the very brutes, like whom their visible frames return to dust. In this manner, selecting it as the symbol of his wife's liability to sin, sorrow, decay, and death, Aylmer's sombre imagination was not long in rendering the birthmark a frightful object, causing him more trouble and horror than ever Georgiana's beauty, whether of soul or sense, had given him delight.

At all the seasons which should have been their happiest, he invariably, and without intending it—nay, in spite of a purpose to the contrary—reverted to this one disastrous topic. Trifling as it at first appeared, it so connected itself with innumerable trains of thought, and modes of feeling, that it became the central point of all. With the morning twilight, Aylmer opened his eyes upon his wife's face, and recognized the symbol of imperfection; and when they sat together at the evening hearth, his eyes wandered stealthily to her cheek, and beheld, flickering with the blaze of the wood fire, the spectral Hand that wrote mortality where he would fain have worshipped. Georgiana soon learned to shudder at his gaze. It needed but a glance, with the peculiar expression that his face often wore, to change the roses of her cheek into a deathlike paleness, amid which the Crimson Hand was brought strongly out, like a *bas-relief*[1] of ruby on the whitest marble.

Late, one night, when the lights were growing dim, so as hardly to betray the stain on the poor wife's cheek, she herself, for the first time, voluntarily took up the subject.

"Do you remember, my dear Aylmer," said she, with a feeble attempt at a smile—"have you any recollection of a dream, last night, about this odious Hand?"

"None! none whatever!" replied Aylmer, starting; but then he added in a dry, cold tone, affected for the sake of concealing the real depth of his emotion—"I might well dream of it; for, before I fell asleep, it had taken a pretty firm hold of my fancy."

"And you did dream of it," continued Georgiana, hastily; for she dreaded lest a gush of tears should interrupt what she had to say—"A terrible dream! I wonder that you can forget it. Is it possible to forget this one expression? 'It is in her heart now—we must have it

out!' Reflect, my husband; for by all means I would have you recall that dream."

The mind is in a sad state, when Sleep, the all-involving, cannot confine her spectres within the dim region of her sway, but suffers them to break forth, affrighting this actual life with secrets that perchance belong to a deeper one. Aylmer now remembered his dream. He had fancied himself, with his servant Aminidab, attempting an operation for the removal of the birthmark. But the deeper went the knife, the deeper sank the Hand, until at length its tiny grasp appeared to have caught hold of Georgiana's heart; whence, however, her husband was inexorably resolved to cut or wrench it away.

When the dream had shaped itself perfectly in his memory, Aylmer sat in his wife's presence with a guilty feeling. Truth often finds its way to the mind close-muffled in robes of sleep, and then speaks with uncompromising directness of matters in regard to which we practise an unconscious self-deception, during our waking moments. Until now, he had not been aware of the tyrannizing influence acquired by one idea over his mind, and of the lengths which he might find in his heart to go, for the sake of giving himself peace.

"Aylmer," resumed Georgiana, solemnly, "I know not what may be the cost to both of us, to rid me of this fatal birthmark. Perhaps its removal may cause cureless deformity. Or, it may be, the stain goes as deep as life itself. Again, do we know that there is a possibility, on any terms, of unclasping the firm grip of this little Hand, which was laid upon me before I came into the world?"

"Dearest Georgiana, I have spent much thought upon the subject," hastily interrupted Aylmer—"I am convinced of the perfect practicability of its removal."

"If there be the remotest possibility of it," continued Georgiana, "let the attempt be made, at whatever risk. Danger is nothing to me; for life—while this hateful mark makes me the object of your horror and disgust—life is a burden which I would fling down with joy. Either remove this dreadful Hand, or take my wretched life! You have deep science! All the world bears witness of it. You have achieved great wonders! Cannot you remove this little, little mark, which I cover with the tips of two small fingers? Is this beyond

---

[1]   *bas-relief*   Low relief sculpture, characterized by slightly raised features that project from a flat background.

your power, for the sake of your own peace, and to save your poor wife from madness?"

"Noblest—dearest—tenderest wife!" cried Aylmer, rapturously. "Doubt not my power. I have already given this matter the deepest thought—thought which might almost have enlightened me to create a being less perfect than yourself. Georgiana, you have led me deeper than ever into the heart of science. I feel myself fully competent to render this dear cheek as faultless as its fellow; and then, most beloved, what will be my triumph, when I shall have corrected what Nature left imperfect, in her fairest work! Even Pygmalion, when his sculptured woman assumed life,[1] felt not greater ecstasy than mine will be."

"It is resolved, then," said Georgiana, faintly smiling. "And, Aylmer, spare me not, though you should find the birthmark take refuge in my heart at last."

Her husband tenderly kissed her cheek—her right cheek, not that which bore the impress of the Crimson Hand.

The next day, Aylmer apprized his wife of a plan that he had formed, whereby he might have opportunity for the intense thought and constant watchfulness, which the proposed operation would require; while Georgiana, likewise, would enjoy the perfect repose essential to its success. They were to seclude themselves in the extensive apartments occupied by Aylmer as a laboratory, and where, during his toilsome youth, he had made discoveries in the elemental powers of nature, that had roused the admiration of all the learned societies in Europe. Seated calmly in this laboratory, the pale philosopher had investigated the secrets of the highest cloud-region, and of the profoundest mines; he had satisfied himself of the causes that kindled and kept alive the fires of the volcano; and had explained the mystery of fountains, and how it is that they gush forth, some so bright and pure, and others with such rich medicinal[2] virtues, from the dark bosom of the earth. Here, too, at an earlier period, he had studied the wonders of the human frame, and attempted to fathom the very process by which Nature assimilates all her precious influences from earth and air, and from the spiritual world, to create and foster Man, her masterpiece. The latter pursuit, however, Aylmer had long laid aside, in unwilling recognition of the truth, against which all seekers sooner or later stumble, that our great creative Mother, while she amuses us with apparently working in the broadest sunshine, is yet severely careful to keep her own secrets, and, in spite of her pretended openness, shows us nothing but results. She permits us, indeed, to mar, but seldom to mend, and, like a jealous patentee,[3] on no account to make. Now, however, Aylmer resumed these half-forgotten investigations; not, of course, with such hopes or wishes as first suggested them; but because they involved much physiological truth, and lay in the path of his proposed scheme for the treatment of Georgiana.

As he led her over the threshold of the laboratory, Georgiana was cold and tremulous. Aylmer looked cheerfully into her face, with intent to reassure her, but was so startled with the intense glow of the birthmark upon the whiteness of her cheek, that he could not restrain a strong convulsive shudder. His wife fainted.

"Aminidab! Aminidab!" shouted Aylmer, stamping violently on the floor.

Forthwith, there issued from an inner apartment a man of low stature, but bulky frame, with shaggy hair hanging about his visage, which was grimed with the vapors of the furnace. This personage had been Aylmer's underworker during his whole scientific career, and was admirably fitted for that office by his great mechanical readiness, and the skill with which, while incapable of comprehending a single principle, he executed all the practical details of his master's experiments. With his vast strength, his shaggy hair, his smoky aspect, and the indescribable earthiness that incrusted him, he seemed to represent man's physical nature; while Aylmer's slender figure, and pale, intellectual face, were no less apt a type of the spiritual element.

"Throw open the door of the boudoir, Aminidab," said Aylmer, "and burn a pastille."[4]

---

[1] *Pygmalion … assumed life* In Greek myth—best known from Ovid's *Metamorphoses*—Pygmalion sculpted a woman of ivory so beautiful that he fell in love with her; upon hearing his lovelorn prayers, the goddess Aphrodite brought the sculpture to life.

[2] *medicinal* Appearing as "medical" in the first 1843 printing, this was corrected when the story was reprinted in *Mosses from an Old Manse* (1846).

[3] *jealous* Suspicious and overprotective; *patentee* Someone who holds a patent on an invention.

[4] *pastille* Small tablet which releases a fragrance when burned, often for therapeutic purposes.

"Yes, master," answered Aminadab, looking intently at the lifeless form of Georgiana; and then he muttered to himself—"If she were my wife, I'd never part with that birthmark."

When Georgiana recovered consciousness, she found herself breathing an atmosphere of penetrating fragrance, the gentle potency of which had recalled her from her deathlike faintness. The scene around her looked like enchantment. Aylmer had converted those smoky, dingy, sombre rooms, where he had spent his brightest years in recondite pursuits, into a series of beautiful apartments,[1] not unfit to be the secluded abode of a lovely woman. The walls were hung with gorgeous curtains, which imparted the combination of grandeur and grace, that no other species of adornment can achieve; and as they fell from the ceiling to the floor, their rich and ponderous folds, concealing all angles and straight lines, appeared to shut in the scene from infinite space. For aught Georgiana knew, it might be a pavilion among the clouds. And Aylmer, excluding the sunshine, which would have interfered with his chemical processes, had supplied its place with perfumed lamps, emitting flames of various hue, but all uniting in a soft, empurpled radiance. He now knelt by his wife's side, watching her earnestly, but without alarm; for he was confident in his science, and felt that he could draw a magic circle round her, within which no evil might intrude.

"Where am I? Ah, I remember!" said Georgiana, faintly; and she placed her hand over her cheek, to hide the terrible mark from her husband's eyes.

"Fear not, dearest!" exclaimed he, "Do not shrink from me! Believe me, Georgiana, I even rejoice in this single imperfection, since it will be such rapture to remove it."

"Oh, spare me!" sadly replied his wife—"Pray do not look at it again. I never can forget that convulsive shudder."

In order to soothe Georgiana, and, as it were, to release her mind from the burden of actual things, Aylmer now put in practice some of the light and playful secrets which science had taught him among its profounder lore. Airy figures, absolutely bodiless ideas, and forms of unsubstantial beauty, came and danced before her, imprinting their momentary footsteps on beams of light. Though she had some indistinct idea of the method of these optical phenomena, still the illusion was almost perfect enough to warrant the belief that her husband possessed sway over the spiritual world. Then again, when she felt a wish to look forth from her seclusion, immediately, as if her thoughts were answered, the procession of external existence flitted across a screen. The scenery and the figures of actual life were perfectly represented, but with that bewitching, yet indescribable difference, which always makes a picture, an image, or a shadow, so much more attractive than the original. When wearied of this, Aylmer bade her cast her eyes upon a vessel, containing a quantity of earth. She did so, with little interest at first, but was soon startled to perceive the germ of a plant, shooting upward from the soil. Then came the slender stalk—the leaves gradually unfolded themselves—and amid them was a perfect and lovely flower.

"It is magical!" cried Georgiana, "I dare not touch it."

"Nay, pluck it," answered Aylmer, "pluck it, and inhale its brief perfume while you may. The flower will wither in a few moments, and leave nothing save its brown seed-vessels—but thence may be perpetuated a race as ephemeral as itself."

But Georgiana had no sooner touched the flower than the whole plant suffered a blight, its leaves turning coal-black, as if by the agency of fire.

"There was too powerful a stimulus," said Aylmer thoughtfully.

To make up for this abortive[2] experiment, he proposed to take her portrait by a scientific process of his own invention. It was to be effected by rays of light striking upon a polished plate of metal. Georgiana assented—but, on looking at the result, was affrighted to find the features of the portrait blurred and indefinable; while the minute figure of a hand appeared where the cheek should have been. Aylmer snatched the metallic plate, and threw it into a jar of corrosive acid.

Soon, however, he forgot these mortifying failures. In the intervals of study and chemical experiment, he came to her, flushed and exhausted, but seemed invigorated by her presence, and spoke in glowing language of the resources of his art. He gave a history of the long dynasty of the Alchemists, who spent so many ages in

---

1 *apartments* Rooms.

2 *abortive* Unfulfilled.

quest of the universal solvent, by which the Golden Principle might be elicited from all things vile and base.[1] Aylmer appeared to believe that, by the plainest scientific logic, it was altogether within the limits of possibility to discover this long-sought medium; but, he added, a philosopher who should go deep enough to acquire the power, would attain too lofty a wisdom to stoop to the exercise of it. Not less singular were his opinions in regard to the Elixir Vitae.[2] He more than intimated that it was at his option to concoct a liquid that should prolong life for years—perhaps interminably—but that it would produce a discord in nature, which all the world, and chiefly the quaffer of the immortal nostrum,[3] would find cause to curse.

"Aylmer, are you in earnest?" asked Georgiana, looking at him with amazement and fear; "it is terrible to possess such power, or even to dream of possessing it!"

"Oh, do not tremble, my love!" said her husband, "I would not wrong either you or myself by working such inharmonious effects upon our lives. But I would have you consider how trifling, in comparison, is the skill requisite to remove this little Hand."

At the mention of the birthmark, Georgiana, as usual, shrank, as if a red-hot iron had touched her cheek.

Again Aylmer applied himself to his labors. She could hear his voice in the distant furnace-room, giving directions to Aminidab, whose harsh, uncouth, misshapen tones were audible in response, more like the grunt or growl of a brute than human speech. After hours of absence, Aylmer re-appeared, and proposed that she should now examine his cabinet of chemical products, and natural treasures of the earth. Among the former he showed her a small vial, in which, he remarked, was contained a gentle, yet most powerful fragrance, capable of impregnating all the breezes that blow across a kingdom. They were of inestimable value, the contents of that little vial; and, as he said so,

he threw some of the perfume into the air, and filled the room with piercing and invigorating delight.

"And what is this?" asked Georgiana, pointing to a small crystal globe, containing a gold-colored liquid. "It is so beautiful to the eye, that I could imagine it the Elixir of Life."

"In one sense it is," replied Aylmer, "or rather the Elixir of Immortality. It is the most precious poison that ever was concocted in this world. By its aid, I could apportion the lifetime of any mortal at whom you might point your finger. The strength of the dose would determine whether he were to linger out years, or drop dead in the midst of a breath. No king, on his guarded throne, could keep his life, if I, in my private station, should deem that the welfare of millions justified me in depriving him of it."

"Why do you keep such a terrific[4] drug?" inquired Georgiana in horror.

"Do not mistrust me, dearest!" said her husband, smiling; "its virtuous potency is yet greater than its harmful one. But, see! here is a powerful cosmetic. With a few drops of this, in a vase of water, freckles may be washed away as easily as the hands are cleansed. A stronger infusion would take the blood out of the cheek, and leave the rosiest beauty a pale ghost."

"Is it with this lotion that you intend to bathe my cheek?" asked Georgiana anxiously.

"Oh, no!" hastily replied her husband—"this is merely superficial. Your case demands a remedy that shall go deeper."

In his interviews with Georgiana, Aylmer generally made minute inquiries as to her sensations, and whether the confinement of the rooms, and the temperature of the atmosphere, agreed with her. These questions had such a particular drift, that Georgiana began to conjecture that she was already subjected to certain physical influences, either breathed in with the fragrant air, or taken with her food. She fancied, likewise—but it might be altogether fancy—that there was a stirring up of her system—a strange, indefinite sensation creeping through her veins, and tingling, half painfully, half pleasurably, at her heart. Still, whenever she dared to look into the mirror, there she beheld herself, pale as a white rose, and with the crimson

---

[1] *Alchemists ... vile and base* Alchemy was a protoscientific school, widespread during the medieval and Early Modern periods, which sought to discover the nature of physical substances and how to transform them, particularly how to transform "baser" materials into gold.

[2] *Elixir Vitae* Elixir of Life; another substance sought by the Alchemists, thought to delay death indefinitely.

[3] *nostrum* Concoction.

[4] *terrific* I.e., terrible; of awe-inspiring power.

birthmark stamped upon her cheek. Not even Aylmer now hated it so much as she.

To dispel the tedium of the hours which her husband found it necessary to devote to the processes of combination and analysis, Georgiana turned over the volumes of his scientific library. In many dark old tomes, she met with chapters full of romance and poetry. They were the works of the philosophers of the middle ages, such as Albertus Magnus, Cornelius Agrippa, Paracelsus, and the famous friar who created the prophetic Brazen Head.[1] All these antique naturalists stood in advance of their centuries, yet were imbued with some of their[2] credulity, and therefore were believed, and perhaps imagined themselves, to have acquired from the investigation of nature a power above nature, and from physics a sway over the spiritual world. Hardly less curious and imaginative were the early volumes of the Transactions of the Royal Society,[3] in which the members, knowing little of the limits of natural possibility, were continually recording wonders, or proposing methods whereby wonders might be wrought.

But, to Georgiana, the most engrossing volume was a large folio from her husband's own hand, in which he had recorded every experiment of his scientific career, with its original aim, the methods adopted for its development, and its final success or failure, with the circumstances to which either event was attributable. The book, in truth, was both the history and emblem of his ardent, ambitious, imaginative, yet practical and laborious life. He handled physical details, as if there were nothing beyond them; yet spiritualized them all, and redeemed himself from materialism by his strong and eager aspiration towards the infinite. In his grasp, the veriest clod of earth assumed a soul. Georgiana, as she read, reverenced Aylmer, and loved him more profoundly than ever, but with a less entire

dependence on his judgment than heretofore. Much as he had accomplished, she could not but observe that his most splendid successes were almost invariably failures, if compared with the ideal at which he aimed. His brightest diamonds were the merest pebbles, and felt to be so by himself, in comparison with the inestimable gems which lay hidden beyond his reach. The volume, rich with achievements that had won renown for its author, was yet as melancholy a record as ever mortal hand had penned. It was the sad confession, and continual exemplification, of the short-comings of the composite man—the spirit burdened with clay and working in matter—and of the despair that assails the higher nature, at finding itself so miserably thwarted by the earthly part. Perhaps every man of genius, in whatever sphere, might recognise the image of his own experience in Aylmer's journal.

So deeply did these reflections affect Georgiana, that she laid her face upon the open volume, and burst into tears. In this situation she was found by her husband.

"It is dangerous to read in a sorcerer's books," said he, with a smile, though his countenance was uneasy and displeased. "Georgiana, there are pages in that volume which I can scarcely glance over and keep my senses. Take heed lest it prove as detrimental to you!"

"It has made me worship you more than ever," said she.

"Ah! wait for this one success," rejoined he, "then worship me if you will. I shall deem myself hardly unworthy of it. But, come! I have sought you for the luxury of your voice. Sing to me, dearest!"

So she poured out the liquid music of her voice to quench the thirst of his spirit. He then took his leave, with a boyish exuberance of gaiety, assuring her that her seclusion would endure but a little longer, and that the result was already certain. Scarcely had he departed, when Georgiana felt irresistibly impelled to follow him. She had forgotten to inform Aylmer of a symptom, which, for two or three hours past, had begun to excite her attention. It was a sensation in the fatal birthmark, not painful, but which induced a restlessness throughout her system. Hastening after her husband, she intruded, for the first time, into the laboratory.

The first thing that struck her eye was the furnace, that hot and feverish worker, with the intense glow of

---

1   *Albertus Magnus ... Brazen Head*   European scientists and philosophers of the Middle Ages and Renaissance, whose works were associated with alchemy and the occult (although any alchemical texts associated with Magnus have likely been misattributed); the Brazen Head, a talking head which could answer questions, was reputedly created by the medieval scholar Roger Bacon.

2   *their*   This was corrected from "its" in *Mosses from an Old Manse.*

3   *Royal Society*   Scientific community founded in London in the mid-1600s.

its fire, which, by the quantities of soot clustered above it, seemed to have been burning for ages. There was a distilling apparatus in full operation. Around the room were retorts, tubes, cylinders, crucibles,[1] and other apparatus of chemical research. An electrical machine stood ready for immediate use. The atmosphere felt oppressively close, and was tainted with gaseous odors, which had been tormented forth by the processes of science. The severe and homely simplicity of the apartment, with its naked walls and brick pavement, looked strange, accustomed as Georgiana had become to the fantastic elegance of her boudoir. But what chiefly, indeed almost solely, drew her attention, was the aspect of Aylmer himself.

He was pale as death, anxious, and absorbed, and hung over the furnace as if it depended upon his utmost watchfulness whether the liquid, which it was distilling, should be the draught of immortal happiness or misery. How different from the sanguine and joyous mien that he had assumed for Georgiana's encouragement!

"Carefully now, Aminidab! Carefully, thou human machine! Carefully, thou man of clay!" muttered Aylmer, more to himself than his assistant. "Now, if there be a thought too much or too little, it is all over!"

"Hoh! hoh!" mumbled Aminadab—"look, master, look!"

Aylmer raised his eyes hastily, and at first reddened, then grew paler than ever, on beholding Georgiana. He rushed towards her, and seized her arm with a grip that left the print of his fingers upon it.

"Why do you come hither? Have you no trust in your husband?" cried he impetuously. "Would you throw the blight of that fatal birthmark over my labors? It is not well done. Go, prying woman, go!"

"Nay, Aylmer," said Georgiana, with the firmness of which she possessed no stinted endowment, "it is not you that have a right to complain. You mistrust your wife! You have concealed the anxiety with which you watch the development of this experiment. Think not so unworthily of me, my husband! Tell me all the risk we run; and fear not that I shall shrink, for my share in it is far less than your own!"

"No, no, Georgiana!" said Aylmer impatiently, "it must not be."

"I submit," replied she, calmly. "And, Aylmer, I shall quaff whatever draught you bring me; but it will be on the same principle that would induce me to take a dose of poison, if offered by your hand."

"My noble wife," said Aylmer, deeply moved, "I knew not the height and depth of your nature, until now. Nothing shall be concealed. Know, then, that this Crimson Hand, superficial as it seems, has clutched its grasp into your being, with a strength of which I had no previous conception. I have already administered agents powerful enough to do aught except to change your entire physical system. Only one thing remains to be tried. If that fail us, we are ruined!"

"Why did you hesitate to tell me this?" asked she.

"Because, Georgiana," said Aylmer, in a low voice, "there is danger!"

"Danger? There is but one danger—that this horrible stigma shall be left upon my cheek!" cried Georgiana. "Remove it! remove it!—whatever be the cost—or we shall both go mad!"

"Heaven knows, your words are too true," said Aylmer, sadly. "And now, dearest, return to your boudoir. In a little while, all will be tested."

He conducted her back, and took leave of her with a solemn tenderness, which spoke far more than his words how much was now at stake. After his departure, Georgiana became rapt in musings. She considered the character of Aylmer, and did it completer justice than at any previous moment. Her heart exulted, while it trembled, at his honorable love, so pure and lofty that it would accept nothing less than perfection, nor miserably make itself contented with an earthlier nature than he had dreamed of. She felt how much more precious was such a sentiment, than that meaner kind which would have borne with the imperfection for her sake, and have been guilty of treason to holy love, by degrading its perfect idea to the level of the actual. And, with her whole spirit, she prayed that, for a single moment, she might satisfy his highest and deepest conception. Longer than one moment, she well knew, it could not be; for his spirit was ever on the march— ever ascending—and each instant required something that was beyond the scope of the instant before.

---

1   *retorts* Vessels used to distill liquids; *crucibles* Heat-resistant vessels for the fusing of molten metals.

The sound of her husband's footsteps aroused her. He bore a crystal goblet, containing a liquor colorless as water, but bright enough to be the draught of immortality. Aylmer was pale; but it seemed rather the consequence of a highly wrought state of mind, and tension of spirit, than of fear or doubt.

"The concoction of the draught has been perfect," said he, in answer to Georgiana's look. "Unless all my science have deceived me, it cannot fail."

"Save on your account, my dearest Aylmer," observed his wife, "I might wish to put off this birthmark of mortality by relinquishing mortality itself, in preference to any other mode. Life is but a sad possession to those who have attained precisely the degree of moral advancement at which I stand. Were I weaker and blinder, it might be happiness. Were I stronger, it might be endured hopefully. But, being what I find myself, methinks I am of all mortals the most fit to die."

"You are fit for heaven without tasting death!" replied her husband. "But why do we speak of dying? The draught cannot fail. Behold its effect upon this plant!"

On the window-seat there stood a geranium, diseased with yellow blotches, which had overspread all its leaves. Aylmer poured a small quantity of the liquid upon the soil in which it grew. In a little time, when the roots of the plant had taken up the moisture, the unsightly blotches began to be extinguished in a living verdure.

"There needed no proof," said Georgiana, quietly. "Give me the goblet. I joyfully stake all upon your word."

"Drink, then, thou lofty creature!" exclaimed Aylmer, with fervid admiration. "There is no taint of imperfection on thy spirit. Thy sensible frame, too, shall soon be all perfect!"

She quaffed the liquid, and returned the goblet to his hand.

"It is grateful," said she, with a placid smile. "Methinks it is like water from a heavenly fountain; for it contains I know not what of unobtrusive fragrance and deliciousness. It allays a feverish thirst, that had parched me for many days. Now, dearest, let me sleep. My earthly senses are closing over my spirit, like the leaves around the heart of a rose, at sunset."

She spoke the last words with a gentle reluctance, as if it required almost more energy than she could command to pronounce the faint and lingering syllables. Scarcely had they loitered through her lips, ere she was lost in slumber. Aylmer sat by her side, watching her aspect with the emotions proper to a man, the whole value of whose existence was involved in the process now to be tested. Mingled with this mood, however, was the philosophic investigation, characteristic of the man of science. Not the minutest symptom escaped him. A heightened flush of the cheek—a slight irregularity of breath—a quiver of the eyelid—a hardly perceptible tremor through the frame—such were the details which, as the moments passed, he wrote down in his folio[1] volume. Intense thought had set its stamp upon every previous page of that volume; but the thoughts of years were all concentrated upon the last.

While thus employed, he failed not to gaze often at the fatal Hand, and not without a shudder. Yet once, by a strange and unaccountable impulse, he pressed it with his lips. His spirit recoiled, however, in the very act, and Georgiana, out of the midst of her deep sleep, moved uneasily and murmured, as if in remonstrance. Again, Aylmer resumed his watch. Nor was it without avail. The Crimson Hand, which at first had been strongly visible upon the marble paleness of Georgiana's cheek, now grew more faintly outlined. She remained not less pale than ever; but the birthmark, with every breath that came and went, lost somewhat of its former distinctness. Its presence had been awful;[2] its departure was more awful still. Watch the stain of the rainbow fading out of the sky, and you will know how that mysterious symbol passed away.

"By Heaven, it is well nigh gone!" said Aylmer to himself, in almost irrepressible ecstasy. "I can scarcely trace it now. Success! Success! And now it is like the faintest rose-color. The slightest flush of blood across her cheek would overcome it. But she is so pale!"

He drew aside the window-curtain, and suffered the light of natural day to fall into the room, and rest upon her cheek. At the same time, he heard a gross, hoarse chuckle, which he had long known as his servant Aminidab's expression of delight.

---

[1] *folio* Ledger or notebook.

[2] *awful* Awe-inspiring.

"Ah, clod! Ah, earthly mass!" cried Aylmer, laughing in a sort of frenzy. "You have served me well! Matter and Spirit—Earth and Heaven—have both done their part in this! Laugh, thing of the senses! You have earned the right to laugh."

These exclamations broke Georgiana's sleep. She slowly unclosed her eyes, and gazed into the mirror, which her husband had arranged for that purpose. A faint smile flitted over her lips, when she recognized how barely perceptible was now that Crimson Hand, which had once blazed forth with such disastrous brilliancy as to scare away all their happiness. But then her eyes sought Aylmer's face, with a trouble and anxiety that he could by no means account for.

"My poor Aylmer!" murmured she.

"Poor? Nay, richest! Happiest! Most favored!" exclaimed he. "My peerless bride, it is successful! You are perfect!"

"My poor Aylmer!" she repeated, with a more than human tenderness. "You have aimed loftily! you have done nobly! Do not repent that, with so high and pure a feeling, you have rejected the best that earth could offer. Aylmer—dearest Aylmer—I am dying!"

Alas, it was too true! The fatal Hand had grappled with the mystery of life, and was the bond by which an angelic spirit kept itself in union with a mortal frame. As the last crimson tint of the birthmark—that sole token of human imperfection—faded from her cheek, the parting breath of the now perfect woman passed into the atmosphere, and her soul, lingering a moment near her husband, took its heavenward flight. Then a hoarse, chuckling laugh was heard again! Thus ever does the gross Fatality of Earth exult in its invariable triumph over the immortal essence, which, in this dim sphere of half-development, demands the completeness of a higher state. Yet, had Alymer reached a profounder wisdom, he need not thus have flung away the happiness, which would have woven his mortal life of the self-same texture with the celestial. The momentary circumstance was too strong for him; he failed to look beyond the shadowy scope of Time, and living once for all in Eternity, to find the perfect Future in the present.

—1843

from *The House of the Seven Gables, A Romance*

PREFACE[1]

When a writer calls his work a Romance, it need hardly be observed that he wishes to claim a certain latitude,[2] both as to its fashion and material, which he would not have felt himself entitled to assume, had he professed to be writing a novel. The latter form of composition is presumed to aim at a very minute fidelity, not merely to the possible, but to the probable and ordinary course of man's experience. The former—while, as a work of art, it must rigidly subject itself to laws, and while it sins unpardonably so far as it may swerve aside from the truth of the human heart—has fairly a right to present that truth under circumstances, to a great extent, of the writer's own choosing or creation. If he think fit, also, he may so manage his atmospherical medium as to bright out or mellow the lights, and deepen and enrich the shadows, of the picture. He will be wise, no doubt, to make a very moderate use of the privileges here stated, and, especially, to mingle the Marvellous[3] rather as a slight, delicate, and evanescent flavor, than as any portion of the actual substance of the dish offered to the public. He can hardly be said, however, to commit a literary crime even if he disregard this caution.

In the present work, the author has proposed to himself—but with what success, fortunately, it is not for him to judge—to keep undeviatingly within his immunities.[4] The point of view in which this tale comes

---

[1] Hawthorne's second novel, *The House of the Seven Gables* (1851), centers on several members of the Pyncheon family, who live on land that was seized in the seventeenth century by an ancestor, Colonel Pyncheon, who wrongfully accused its original owner of witchcraft. The Preface is a frequent reference point in discussions of realism and romance in fiction; the novel itself employs numerous flashbacks and supernatural occurrences to suggest that the Pyncheons are cursed with the inherited guilt of the greedy Colonel.

[2] *latitude* I.e., range or scope.

[3] *Marvellous* Fantastical; improbable.

[4] *immunities* I.e., his right to claim immunity from criticism for presenting the truth under circumstances of his own choice, without aiming for a "minute fidelity" to experience, so long as he presents the truth of the human heart.

under the Romantic definition lies in the attempt to connect a bygone time with the very present that is flitting away from us. It is a legend, prolonging itself, from an epoch now gray in the distance, down into our own broad daylight, and bringing along with it some of its legendary mist, which the reader, according to his pleasure, may either disregard, or allow it to float almost imperceptibly about the characters and events, for the sake of a picturesque effect. The narrative, it may be, is woven of so humble a texture as to require this advantage,[1] and, at the same time, to render it the more difficult of attainment.

Many writers lay very great stress upon some definite moral purpose at which they profess to aim their works. Not to be deficient in this particular, the author has provided himself with a moral—the truth, namely, that the wrong-doing of one generation lives into the successive ones, and, divesting itself of every temporary advantage, becomes a pure and uncontrollable mischief; and he would feel it a singular gratification if this romance might effectually convince mankind—or, indeed, any one man—of the folly of tumbling down an avalanche of ill-gotten gold, or real estate, on the heads of an unfortunate posterity, thereby to maim and crush them, until the accumulated mass shall be scattered abroad in its original atoms. In good faith, however, he is not sufficiently imaginative to flatter himself with the slightest hope of this kind. When romances do really teach anything, or produce any effective operation, it is usually through a far more subtle process than the ostensible one. The author has considered it hardly worth his while, therefore, relentlessly to impale the story with its moral, as with an iron rod—or, rather, as by sticking a pin through a butterfly[2]—thus at once depriving it of life, and causing it to stiffen in an ungainly and unnatural attitude. A high truth, indeed,

fairly, finely, and skilfully wrought out, brightening at every step, and crowning the final development of a work of fiction, may add an artistic glory, but is never any truer, and seldom any more evident, at the last page than at the first.

The reader may perhaps choose to assign an actual locality to the imaginary events of this narrative. If permitted by the historical connection—which, though slight, was essential to his plan—the author would very willingly have avoided anything of this nature. Not to speak of other objections, it exposes the romance to an inflexible and exceedingly dangerous species of criticism, by bringing his fancy-pictures almost into positive contact with the realities of the moment. It has been no part of his object, however, to describe local manners, nor in any way to meddle with the characteristics of a community for whom he cherishes a proper respect and a natural regard. He trusts not to be considered as unpardonably offending by laying out a street that infringes upon nobody's private rights, and appropriating a lot of land which had no visible owner, and building a house, of materials long in use for constructing castles in the air. The personages of the tale—though they give themselves out to be of ancient stability and considerable prominence—are really of the author's own making, or, at all events, of his own mixing; their virtues can shed no lustre, nor their defects redound, in the remotest degree, to the discredit of the venerable town of which they profess to be inhabitants. He would be glad, therefore, if—especially in the quarter to which he alludes—the book may be read strictly as a Romance, having a great deal more to do with the clouds overhead than with any portion of the actual soil of the County of Essex.

LENNOX, *January 27,* 1851.

—1851

---

1   *this advantage*   I.e., the picturesque effect.

2   *sticking ... butterfly*   I.e., when mounting a specimen for study or display.

Henry Wadsworth Longfellow

1807 – 1882

Throughout the second half of the nineteenth century there could be no doubt as to the identity of the best-known, most widely read and most highly esteemed American poet: Henry Wadsworth Longfellow. In a century when accentual syllabic meters dominated the world of English-language poetry, Longfellow was an accomplished versifier in virtually every accentual syllabic form. In an era when short lyric poetry had not yet crowded out longer narrative forms, Longfellow was an acknowledged master of narrative in verse. In a nation that largely looked to its poets to clothe in romance a history too often driven by acquisitiveness and cruelty, Longfellow shaped a sense of gentle and cooperative nationhood—and shaped it in words that adults and schoolchildren alike could readily commit to memory. When, as President, Lincoln asked his friend Noah Brooks to recite part of "The Building of the Ship," Lincoln's "eyes filled with tears and his cheeks were wet" as Brooks delivered the final section ("sail on, O ship of State / Sail on, O Union, strong and great"); Lincoln was so moved that he "did not speak for several minutes. He finally said, with simplicity, 'It is a wonderful gift, to be able to stir men like that.'"

Longfellow's background was one of privilege. He was born in Portland, Maine (at a time when Maine was still a district within the state of Massachusetts) on 27 February, 1807. His mother, the former Zilpah Wadsworth, was an accomplished pianist whose family could trace their ancestors to the families who had come to America on the *Mayflower* in 1620, and his father, Stephen Longfellow, was one of Maine's leading citizens—a Harvard graduate and a lawyer who would later serve as a judge and as a member of Congress. Longfellow's childhood was quiet and bookish, and his literary ambitions were evident early on; his first poem was published in the *Portland Gazette* when he was just thirteen. At fifteen he entered Maine's leading college, Bowdoin (where his father, a former overseer of the school, remained a trustee). Not long after his graduation in 1825, Longfellow successfully applied for the post of professor of Modern Languages at Bowdoin—though the appointment was conditional on his willingness to spend several years abroad familiarizing himself with the languages he would be expected to teach. Longfellow spent the next three years traveling and studying in Europe, and retuned to Bowdoin to take up his professorship in 1829, by then conversant with the languages and literatures of France, Italy, Spain, and Germany. In 1831 he married Mary Potter, a friend of his sister's who, like Longfellow, was of a distinguished legal family. And within a few years he had published a number of textbooks, as well as numerous articles on European literatures—and he had written a good deal of poetry, most of it in the form of translations.

From the beginning, Longfellow had grand aspirations that he felt could not be realized among the "dust and cobwebs of this country college"—as he described Bowdoin. He had cultivated a relationship with George Ticknor, Harvard's distinguished Professor of Modern Languages, and when Ticknor retired in 1834, Longfellow (at the age of 27) was offered the post. He followed his previous pattern of going abroad for an extended period to immerse himself in foreign languages and literatures, this time spending a year and a half in Europe.

When he returned from Europe to take up his Harvard post, Longfellow was a widower; Mary had died in 1835, following a miscarriage. Eight months after Mary's death, however, while still traveling in Europe, he had met Frances ("Fanny") Appleton, a well-educated and witty young woman from an established and very wealthy Massachusetts family. Appleton rejected Longfellow when, in 1837, he first proposed marriage to her—and she was further alienated when in 1839 he published *Hyperion*, a prose romance informed by the history of their relationship that enjoyed little success. Longfellow's 1839 volume of verse, *Voices of the Night*, however, was met with an enthusiastic reception; one of the poems included in it, "A Psalm of Life," became one of nineteenth-century America's most frequently recited poems. Popular too was his 1841 volume, *Ballads and Other Poems*; of the poems in that volume, "The Wreck of the Hesperus," "The Village Blacksmith," and "Excelsior" received particular praise, with "Excelsior" being reprinted in newspapers across America and becoming popular too in a version set to music.

Longfellow's passion for Appleton remained undimmed through these years, and eventually he won her over. The two were married in 1843, and Longfellow's father purchased for them the large, historic house in Cambridge, Massachusetts in which Longfellow had until then been renting rooms.

The previous year, with little fanfare, Longfellow had published a pamphlet of antislavery verse, *Poems on Slavery*, which was widely distributed by abolitionist societies. Though he steered clear thereafter of public engagement in the controversial political issues of the day, his abolitionist commitment was unwavering; during the 1850s he is now known to have purchased the freedom of a number of enslaved people.

For the next twelve years Longfellow combined his professorship with a prolific output, and became more popular with each passing year. His long narrative poems *Evangeline* (1847) and *The Song of Hiawatha* (1855) were particular successes (by 1857 the former had sold close to 36,000 copies and the latter over 50,000 copies) and they were critical successes as well, in Britain as well as in America. His poems were acclaimed above all for their sonorousness and for their affective qualities—for instilling in readers a love of nature and (though Longfellow always eschewed crude or overtly jingoistic appeals) an appreciation of America and its history. They were acclaimed too for the sincere goodwill that they were felt to convey—and for the moral effect that such goodwill was felt to exert upon readers. The view of Longfellow and his poetry that was expressed by the *Huntington Democrat* may seem extravagant to twenty-first-century sensibilities, but it was not untypical: "No person has ever read his writings without feeling bettered thereby, and without feeling filled with a love for the good, true, and pure."

By the late 1850s Longfellow was firmly established as one of America's leading literary figures—sufficiently so that he felt able to resign his professorship at Harvard in order to focus exclusively on his writing. His marriage was a happy one, and the couple had six children. On 9 July 1861, however, the family was devastated by a catastrophic accident. As the *New York Times* reported it,

> [Mrs. Fanny Longfellow was] seated at her library table, making seals for the entertainment of her two youngest children. A match or a piece of lighted paper caught her dress, and she was in a moment enveloped in flames. Professor Longfellow, who was in his study, ran to her assistance, and succeeded in extinguishing the flames, with considerable injury to himself, but too late for the rescue of her life.

Over the next several years Longfellow increasingly turned to translation, though he continued to publish original work as well throughout the 1860s and 1870s. When he died, aged 75, he was mourned throughout America, and his passing was soon commemorated in Poets' Corner, Westminster Abbey, in London; he was the first American to be so honored.

Poems such as "A Psalm of Life" and "Paul Revere's Ride" continued to be memorized by schoolchildren well into the twentieth century, and continued to be enormously popular among adults as well; when a National Poetry Poll to choose America's favorite poem was run in over 250 newspapers in 1929, two Longfellow poems placed in the top ten ("A Psalm of Life" at number 1, and *Evangeline* at number 6), and no fewer than ten Longfellow poems were among the top fifty. In the literary and scholarly community, however, Longfellow's sonorousness was more and more devalued, and the substance of his poetry was more and more often dismissed as shallow, simplistic, and sentimental. Even in the late nineteenth century educated opinion had often expressed reservations about Longfellow's supposed greatness as a poet. An obituary that appeared on 25 March 1882 in the Philadelphia *Times*, for example, delicately qualified its praise for his poetic accomplishment:

His verse, while it is not always artistically exact, has always a natural ease, a graceful movement, that conveys the impression of great elevation of thought, even where the thought does
not really rise very far from earth.

By the mid-twentieth century, Longfellow's importance was widely viewed as being merely historical; it was considered to be to his credit that he had come "nearer than anyone else to being the voice of the [nineteenth-century] man in the street and on the farm" (as Henry Seidel Canby put it in 1947), but the poems themselves (with the exception of a few lyrics) came to be less and less thought of as an important part of the canon of American literature. In his influential *Oxford Companion to American Literature* (which went through six editions between 1944 and 1995), James D. Hart dismissed Longfellow as "lacking in passion and high imagination, and ... too decorous, benign, and sweet."

The twenty-first century has brought new questions as to Longfellow's place in American literature. In 1947 it was con-sidered a sign of the breadth of a writer's appeal if he could be described as "the voice of the man in the street"; by the twenty-first century the maleness and the presumed whiteness of the "voice of the man in the street" paradigm was becoming increas-ingly evident—and Longfellow's vision as a highly privileged white male has come on those grounds to seem if anything even more limited than it did to mid-twentieth-century critics.

Several other twenty-first-century trends have worked in the other direction, though, and have helped to renew serious interest in Longfellow as a poet of real importance. One is simply the increased interest in literary history that has characterized literary studies since the early 1990s. A second has been a revival of interest in the force that appeals to the emotions can exert in the interplay between a text and an audience; whereas modernism and postmodernism tended to distrust or to disparage overt expressions of sentiment in literary works, sentiment has become a topic of considerable interest to many twenty-first-century critics. And a third has been a renewed interest in traditional poetic forms. That renewed interest has led to a renewed appreciation of the extraordinary range of Longfellow's formal accomplishment, even in unusual and highly challenging meters. Finally, increased engagement with transatlantic and transnational approaches to literature has fostered a greater appreciation of Longfellow's lifelong interest in reaching across cultural and linguistic barriers. Where Longfellow will settle into the canon of American literature as it continues to be re-shaped in the twenty-first century remains a question of considerable interest, with no clear answer.

Longfellow Entertainment.

On Monday evening next, Feb. 27th, The King's Daughters will give a Long-fellow Entertainment, at the Presbyterian Manse, in honor of the birthday of this favorite poet. The programme will be as follows :

Sketch of Longfellow's Life.
Vocal Solo.   The Bridge   *Longfellow.*
Selections from Miles Standish.
                                    Longfellow.
Piano Solo. Rando Capricise.
                                    Mendelssohn.
Vocal Solo. The Day is Done.
                                    Longfellow.
Hiawatha's Wooing.   *Longfellow.*
Vocal Solo. The Rainy Day. *Longfellow.*
Piano Solo. Invitation to the Dance.
                                    Weber.
The Wreck of the Hesperus. *Longfellow.*
Vocal Solo. Beware.   *Longfellow.*
Selections of Shorter Poems by
                                    Longfellow.
Vocal Solo. Isbotan Arrow. *Longfellow.*
Piano Duet. 2nd Rhapsodie.   *Liszt.*

Newspaper notice of "Longfellow Entertainment," from the *Carolina Watchman* (Salisbury, Carolina), 23 February 1888. Events of this sort were common throughout the United States in the years following Longfellow's death.

NOTE ON THE TEXTS: Where possible we have based our text on the first-published text. Longfellow's poetry presents few large textual issues, but with several of his best-known poems the texts of the originally published magazine versions differ in some respects from those of the versions published later in bound book collections. In a number of such cases, we have drawn attention in the footnotes to significant differences between the texts. Where no magazine version exists, we have used the first published version in book form as our base text, while also consulting other editions—notably the Cambridge *Complete Poetical Works* (1893), edited by H.E. Scudder, and the Library of America *Poems and Other Writings* (2000), edited by J.D. McClatchy. Spelling and punctua-tion have been modernized in accordance with the practices of this anthology.

⌘ ⌘ ⌘

A Psalm of Life[1]

What the Heart of the Young Man Said to the Psalmist[2]

Tell me not, in mournful numbers,[3]
 Life is but an empty dream!
For the soul is dead that slumbers,
 And things are not what they seem.

5 Life is real! Life is earnest![4]
 And the grave is not its goal;
Dust thou art, to dust returnest,[5]
 Was not spoken of the soul.

Not enjoyment, and not sorrow,
10 Is our destined end or way;

But to act,[6] that each tomorrow
 Find us farther than today.

Art is long, and Time is fleeting,
 And our hearts, though stout° and brave,   resolute
15 Still, like muffled drums, are beating
 Funeral marches to the grave.

In the world's broad field of battle,
 In the bivouac of Life,
Be not like dumb,° driven cattle!   silent
20 Be a hero in the strife!

Trust no Future, howe'er pleasant!
 Let the dead Past bury its dead!
Act—act in the living Present!
 Heart within, and God o'erhead!

25 Lives of great men all remind us
 We can make our[7] lives sublime,
And, departing, leave behind us
 Footprints on the sands of time;

Footprints,[8] that perhaps another,
30 Sailing o'er life's solemn main,°   ocean
A forlorn and shipwrecked brother,
 Seeing, shall take heart again.

Let us, then, be up and doing,
 With a heart for any fate;
35 Still achieving, still pursuing,
 Learn to labor and to wait.
—1838, 1839

1 When first published (in the September 1838 issue of *The Knickerbocker: or, New-York Monthly Magazine*) the poem was prefaced by three lines adapted from seventeenth-century English poet Richard Crashaw's "Wishes to His (Supposed) Mistress": "[I wish her] life that shall send / A challenge to its end, And when it comes, say, 'Welcome, friend.'" (Longfellow either misremembered two words from the Crashaw stanza, or intentionally altered them; Crashaw's poem reads "dares send" in the first line, and "his end" in the second.) The magazine version numbered the stanzas with the Roman numerals I to IX. Longfellow removed the epigram and the stanza numbers when the poem was published in *Voices of the Night* (1839), and altered some of the punctuation; that version became one of the best-known poems of the nineteenth and early twentieth centuries. Longfellow, who had written the poem soon after the death of his first wife, later said that he had "kept it some time in manuscript, unwilling to show it to anyone, it being a voice from my inmost heart, at a time when I was rallying from depression."

2 *the Psalmist*   David is traditionally said to have been the author of many of the psalms in the biblical Book of Psalms—including Psalm 103, which includes these lines: "… the Lord has compassion on those who fear him; / for he knows how we are formed, / he remembers that we are dust. / The life of mortals is like grass, they flourish like a flower of the field; / the wind blows over it and it is gone, and its place remembers it no more."

3 *numbers*   In its metrical pattern, any accentual-syllabic poem is divisible into numbers—regularly patterned groups of stressed and unstressed syllables.

4 *Life is real … earnest*   The 1838 *Knickerbocker* version has dashes rather than exclamation marks in this line.

5 *Dust … returnest*   The phrase "earth to earth, ashes to ashes, dust to dust" occurs in the text of the funeral service in the *Book of Common Prayer*. The phrase has its roots in biblical verses such as Ecclesiastes 3.20: "All go unto one place; all are of the dust, and all turn to dust again." See also above regarding Psalm 103.

6 *act*   In the 1838 *Knickerbocker* version this word is italicized.

7 *our*   In the 1838 *Knickerbocker* version this word is italicized.

8 *Footprints*   In both the 1838 *Knickerbocker* version and the 1839 *Voices of the Night* version, footsteps rather than *footprints*. Longfellow revised to *footprints* for his 1850 two-volume *Poems*, and "footprints on the sands of time" became one of the most often quoted lines of American poetry.

The Wreck of the Hesperus[1]

It was the schooner Hesperus,
    That sailed the wintry sea;
And the skipper had taken his little daughter,
    To bear him company.

5   Blue were her eyes as the fairy-flax,
        Her cheeks like the dawn of day,
    And her bosom white as the hawthorn buds,
        That ope in the month of May.

    The skipper he stood beside the helm,
10   His pipe was in his mouth,
    And he watched how the veering flaw° did blow   *gust*
        The smoke now West, now South.

    Then up and spake an old Sailòr,
        Had sailed to the Spanish Main,[2]
15 "I pray thee, put into yonder port,
        For I fear a hurricane.

    "Last night, the moon had a golden ring,
        And tonight no moon we see!"
    The skipper, he blew a whiff from his pipe,
20   And a scornful laugh laughed he.[3]

Colder and louder blew the wind,
    A gale from the Northeast.
The snow fell hissing in the brine,
    And the billows frothed like yeast.

25 Down came the storm, and smote amain°   *quickly*
        The vessel in its strength;
    She shuddered and paused, like a frighted steed,
        Then leaped her cable's length.

    "Come hither! come hither! my little daughter,
30   And do not tremble so;
    For I can weather the roughest gale
        That ever wind did blow."

    He wrapped her warm in his seaman's coat
        Against the stinging blast;
35 He cut a rope from a broken spar,
        And bound her to the mast.

    "O father! I hear the church-bells ring,
        O say, what may it be?"
    "'Tis a fog-bell on a rock-bound coast!"—
40   And he steered for the open sea.

    "O father! I hear the sound of guns,
        O say, what may it be?"
    "Some ship in distress, that cannot live
        In such an angry sea!"

45 "O father! I see a gleaming light,
        O say, what may it be?"
    But the father answered never a word,
        A frozen corpse was he.

    Lashed to the helm, all stiff and stark,
50   With his face turned to the skies,
    The lantern gleamed through the gleaming snow
        On his fixed and glassy eyes.

    Then the maiden clasped her hands and prayed
        That savèd she might be;
55 And she thought of Christ, who stilled the wave,
        On the Lake of Galilee.[4]

---

[1]   First published 11 January 1840 in *The New World* (a New York weekly newspaper), this ballad had by the end of that year been widely published in other American newspapers, as well as in Britain in the literary magazine *Bentley's Miscellany*. It became one of Longfellow's most popular poems, and remained so until the second half of the twentieth century, when the ballad form fell from fashion. The poem was twice made into a film (in 1927, and in 1948).
    Though the story of Longfellow's ballad is fiction, it has some basis in fact. The poet made this entry in his journal on 17 December 1839: "News of shipwrecks horrible on the coast. Twenty bodies washed ashore near Gloucester, one lashed to a piece of the wreck. There is a reef called Norman's Woe where many of these took place; among others the schooner *Hesperus*. Also the *Sea-flower* on Black Rock. I must write a ballad upon this."

[2]   *Spanish Main*   Northern coast of South America.

[3]   *laughed he*   An additional stanza appears at this point in the *New World* version: "I would not put into yonder port, / Nor yet into yonder bay / Though it blew a gale, with fiery hail, / As on the Judgment Day!" This stanza does not appear in later versions— including in the text of the poem as it was published in other newspapers later in the same year.

[4]   *Christ … Galilee*   See Matthew 8, Mark 4, and Luke 8; all three gospels recount this incident, in which Jesus is reported to have miraculously calmed the waves when a great storm has blown up on the Sea of Galilee.

And fast through the midnight dark and drear,
    Through the whistling sleet and snow,
Like a sheeted ghost, the vessel swept
60   Tow'rds the reef of Norman's Woe.[1]

And ever the fitful gusts between
    A sound came from the land;
It was the sound of the trampling surf
    On the rocks and the hard sea-sand.

65 The breakers were right beneath her bows,
    She drifted a dreary wreck,
And a whooping billow swept the crew
    Like icicles from her deck.

She struck where the white and fleecy waves
70   Looked soft as carded wool,[2]
But the cruel rocks, they gored her side
    Like the horns of an angry bull.

Her rattling shrouds, all sheathed in ice,
    With the masts went by the board;
75 Like a vessel of glass, she stove and sank,
    Ho! ho! the breakers roared!

At daybreak, on the bleak sea-beach,
    A fisherman stood aghast,
To see the form of a maiden fair,
80   Lashed close to a drifting mast.

The salt sea was frozen on her breast,
    The salt tears in her eyes;
And he saw her hair, like the brown sea-weed,
    On the billows fall and rise.

85 Such was the wreck of the Hesperus,
    In the midnight and the snow!
Christ save us all from a death like this,
    On the reef of Norman's Woe!
—1840

D. Huntington, Illustration for "The Wreck of the Hesperus," *Poems* (Carey and Hart edition), 1845.

---

[1] *Norman's Woe* Reef off the shore of Cape Ann, Gloucester, Massachusetts; the site of many shipwrecks.

[2] *carded wool* Unprocessed wool that has been cleaned and disentangled.

John Gilbert, Illustration for "The Wreck of the Hesperus," *Longfellow's Poetical Works* (Ticknor & Fields edition), 1856.

from *Poems on Slavery* [1]

During the six months Longfellow spent in Europe in 1842 he met with his German translator, Ferdinand Freiligrath, a political radical who was a vehement opponent of slavery. He also corresponded with his close friend Charles Sumner (later to become a leading figure among the Radical Republicans in the American Senate); Sumner suggested that Longfellow write some antislavery poems—"some stirring words that shall move the whole land."

Longfellow liked to steer clear of controversy, but he clearly felt strongly about slavery; for years he made a practice of devoting a portion of his earnings to purchasing freedom for enslaved African Americans, and he predicted following the execution

of John Brown in 1859 that a new revolution was coming—"a new Revolution quite as much needed" as that of 1776 had been.

Longfellow published the antislavery poems on their own as a slim volume in 1842. He prefaced the volume with a brief note regarding the death of William Ellery Channing, a leading abolitionist, a leading figure in the Unitarian Church, and one of America's most influential intellectuals. The first of Longfellow's eight poems is dedicated to Channing. The others in the group, as Longfellow noted in his preface, "were written at sea, in the latter part of October, 1842."

The Slave's Dream

Beside the ungathered rice[2] he lay,
　　His sickle in his hand;
His breast was bare, his matted hair
　　Was buried in the sand.
5　Again, in the mist and shadow of sleep,
　　He saw his Native Land.

Wide through the landscape of his dreams
　　The lordly Niger[3] flowed;
Beneath the palm-trees on the plain
10　　Once more a king he strode;
And heard the tinkling caravans
　　Descend the mountain-road.[4]

He saw once more his dark-eyed queen
　　Among her children stand;
15　They clasped his neck, they kissed his cheeks,
　　They held him by the hand!—
A tear burst from the sleeper's lids
　　And fell into the sand.

---

[1]　Three of the eight poems are included in these pages; the complete *Poems on Slavery* is included in the website component of this anthology.

---

[2]　*ungathered rice*　Conditions for enslaved workers were notoriously brutal on American plantations in the South—for workers assigned to harvest rice as much as for those forced to pick cotton or cut sugar cane.

[3]　*Niger*　The largest river in West Africa.

[4]　*the tinkling caravans … road*　Trade caravans from the ancient Ghana and Mali empires in the upper reaches of the Niger traveled south and west to the Atlantic coast; north to Marrakech and Morocco; and east to Egypt and Ethiopia. Such caravans operated into the twentieth century.

And then at furious speed he rode
20   Along the Niger's bank;
His bridle-reins were golden chains,
      And, with a martial clank,
At each leap he could feel his scabbard of steel
      Smiting his stallion's flank.

25 Before him, like a blood-red flag,
      The bright flamingoes flew;
From morn till night he followed their flight,
      O'er plains where the tamarind grew,
Till he saw the roofs of Caffre[1] huts,
30   And the ocean rose to view.

At night he heard the lion roar,
      And the hyena scream,
And the river-horse,[2] as he crushed the reeds
      Beside some hidden stream;
35 And it passed, like a glorious roll of drums,
      Through the triumph of his dream.

The forests, with their myriad tongues,
      Shouted of liberty;
And the Blast of the Desert cried aloud,
40   With a voice so wild and free,
That he started in his sleep and smiled
      At their tempestuous glee.

He did not feel the driver's whip,
      Nor the burning heat of day;
45 For Death had illumined the Land of Sleep,
      And his lifeless body lay
A worn-out fetter, that the soul
      Had broken and thrown away!
—1842

The Slave Singing at Midnight

Loud he sang the psalm of David!
He, a Negro and enslaved,
Sang of Israel's victory,
Sang of Zion,° bright and free.[3]   *Israel*

5   In that hour, when night is calmest,
Sang he from the Hebrew Psalmist,
In a voice so sweet and clear
That I could not choose but hear,

Songs of triumph, and ascriptions,
10 Such as reached the swart° Egyptians,   *swarthy*
When upon the Red Sea coast
Perished Pharaoh and his host.°   *multitude*

And the voice of his devotion
Filled my soul with strange emotion;
15 For its tones by turns were glad,
Sweetly solemn, wildly sad.

Paul and Silas, in their prison,
Sang of Christ, the Lord arisen,
And an earthquake's arm of might
20 Broke their dungeon-gates at night.[4]

But, alas! what holy angel
Brings the Slave this glad evangel?[5]
And what earthquake's arm of might
Breaks his dungeon-gates at night?
—1842

---

[1] *Caffre* Term (also spelled "Kaffir") widely used in the nineteenth century to denote sub-Saharan African peoples. (In the twentieth century the term came to be used almost exclusively in pejorative ways, and it is now considered extremely offensive.)

[2] *river-horse* The roots of the word "hippopotamus" are the ancient Greek words for "horse" and "river."

[3] *the psalm ... and free* Several of the biblical psalms (traditionally attributed to David) reference the escape of the Israelites from slavery in Egypt, across the Red Sea to freedom; the story has it that God parts the waters of the sea, allowing the Israelites to cross unharmed. When the Egyptian Pharaoh and his forces try to follow, however, the waters close up again, and they perish.

[4] *Paul and Silas ... at night* As recounted in Acts 16.25–31, the apostles Paul and Silas, who had been imprisoned unjustly, prayed for deliverance; the prison was soon shaken by an earthquake, and they were able to escape.

[5] *glad evangel* Good news.

The Quadroon[1] Girl

The slaver in the broad lagoon
    Lay moored with idle sail;
He waited for the rising moon,
    And for the evening gale.

5 Under the shore his boat was tied,
    And all her listless crew
Watched the gray alligator slide
    Into the still bayou.

Odors of orange-flowers, and spice,
10   Reached them from time to time,
Like airs that breathe from Paradise
    Upon a world of crime.

The planter, under his roof of thatch,
    Smoked thoughtfully and slow;
15 The slaver's thumb was on the latch,
    He seemed in haste to go.

He said, "My ship at anchor rides
    In yonder broad lagoon;
I only wait the evening tides,
20   And the rising of the moon."

Before them, with her face upraised,
    In timid attitude,
Like one half curious, half amazed,
    A quadroon maiden stood.

25 Her eyes were large, and full of light,
    Her arms and neck were bare;
No garment she wore save° a kirtle[2] bright,   *except*
    And her own long, raven hair.

And on her lips there played a smile
30   As holy, meek, and faint,
As lights in some cathedral aisle
    The features of a saint.

"The soil is barren—the farm is old,"
    The thoughtful planter said;
35 Then looked upon the slaver's gold,
    And then upon the maid.

His heart within him was at strife
    With such accursed gains:
For he knew whose passions gave her life,
40   Whose blood ran in her veins.

But the voice of nature was too weak;
    He took the glittering gold!
Then pale as death grew the maiden's cheek,
    Her hands as icy cold.

45 The slaver led her from the door,
    He led her by the hand,
To be his slave and paramour
    In a strange and distant land!
—1842

Resolution passed by the Worcester County Anti-Slavery Society at their annual meeting, held Friday 12 January 1844 (as reported in *The Liberator*, 26 January 1844). A wider selection of In Context materials pertaining to Longfellow's *Poems on Slavery* is provided as part of the anthology's website component.

---

1   *Quadroon* Term commonly used in the nineteenth century to classify a person of mixed racial background—specifically, someone with one black and three white grandparents.

2   *kirtle* Simple, one-piece garment.

Mezzo Cammin[1]

WRITTEN AT BOPPARD ON THE RHINE, AUGUST 25, 1842, JUST BEFORE LEAVING FOR HOME

Half of my life is gone, and I have let
The years slip from me and have not fulfilled
    The aspiration of my youth, to build
    Some tower of song with lofty parapet.
5 Not indolence, nor pleasure, nor the fret
    Of restless passions that would not be stilled,
    But sorrow, and a care that almost killed,
    Kept me from what I may accomplish yet;
Though, half-way up the hill, I see the Past
10   Lying beneath me with its sounds and sights—
    A city in the twilight dim and vast,
With smoking roofs, soft bells, and gleaming lights—
    And hear above me on the autumnal blast
    The cataract of Death far thundering from the
      heights.
—1886 (WRITTEN 1842)

The Arrow and the Song

I shot an arrow into the air,
It fell to earth, I knew not where;
For, so swiftly it flew, the sight
Could not follow it in its flight.

5 I breathed a song into the air,
It fell to earth, I knew not where;
For who has sight so keen and strong,
That it can follow the flight of song?

Long, long afterward, in an oak
10 I found the arrow, still unbroke;
And the song, from beginning to end,
I found again in the heart of a friend.
—1845

---

[1] *Mezzo Cammin* Italian: The middle of the journey. Longfellow is referencing the opening of Dante's *Divine Comedy*: "Nel mezzo del cammin di nostra vita / mi ritrovai per una selva oscura, / chè la diritta via era smarrita." ["Half way through our life's journey / I found myself in a shadowy forest, / having lost my way."] The poem was published only after Longfellow's death.

The Day Is Done

The day is done, and the darkness
    Falls from the wings of Night,
As a feather is wafted downward
    From an eagle in his flight.

5 I see the lights of the village
    Gleam through the rain and the mist,
And a feeling of sadness comes o'er me
    That my soul cannot resist:

A feeling of sadness and longing,
10   That is not akin to pain,
And resembles sorrow only
    As the mist resembles the rain.

Come, read to me some poem,
    Some simple and heartfelt lay,[2]
15 That shall soothe this restless feeling,
    And banish the thoughts of day.

Not from the grand old masters,
    Not from the bards sublime,
Whose distant footsteps echo
20   Through the corridors of Time.

For, like strains of martial music,
    Their mighty thoughts suggest
Life's endless toil and endeavor;
    And tonight I long for rest.

25 Read from some humbler poet,
    Whose songs gushed from his heart,
As showers from the clouds of summer,
    Or tears from the eyelids start;

Who, through long days of labor,
30   And nights devoid of ease,
Still heard in his soul the music
    Of wonderful melodies.

Such songs have power to quiet
    The restless pulse of care,

---

[2] *lay* Medieval term for a lyric poem that recounts a narrative.

35   And come like the benediction
        That follows after prayer.

     Then read from the treasured volume
        The poem of thy choice,
     And lend to the rhyme of the poet
40   The beauty of thy voice.

And the night shall be filled with music,
   And the cares, that infest the day,
Shall fold their tents, like the Arabs,
   And as silently steal away.[1]
—1845

from *Evangeline: A Tale of Acadie*

The germ out of which the first of Longfellow's three book-length poems of American history developed was a tale recounted by a Boston minister over dinner at the Longfellows; Horace L. Conolly told the story, saying that he had heard it from an unnamed French Canadian. At the heart of the story as Longfellow tells it is the search of Evangeline for her lost love, Gabriel. The two become separated on what was to have been their wedding day in the Acadian village of Grand Pré, Nova Scotia (presented by the poet as an idyllic, egalitarian community, in complete harmony with nature). They are caught up in the 1755–64 expulsion of the Acadians from "Acadia"—the area in what are now the Canadian provinces of Nova Scotia and New Brunswick, together with portions of Maine in which French-speaking settlers were concentrated. These areas had all been controlled by the British since the early 1700s, but the Acadians outnumbered English-speaking settlers by a considerable margin in many areas; they had remained suspicious of the British, and many were determined never to swear an oath of allegiance to the British monarch. In 1755 (as the great struggle of the Seven Years' War between Britain and France was about to begin), the colonial militia began to forcibly remove the Acadian population; some were shipped south to the thirteen colonies, others overseas. Many eventually made their way to Louisiana—so many that French-speaking "Cajuns" (a corruption of "Acadians") became a significant part of the population of that state.

Evangeline's epic search for Gabriel carries her across much of the continent, including to Louisiana and to Texas. Eventually giving up her search, she settles in Philadelphia, and takes up work among the poor as a Sister of Mercy. Years go by; eventually an unnamed "pestilence" falls on the city. As she is ministering to the afflicted, Evangeline discovers the dying Gabriel, in "the form of an old man"; the reunion between the two lasts only a moment but Evangeline expresses gratitude to her God as all is ended—"the hope, and the fear, and the sorrow."

Evangeline was an immediate success, and a lasting one. The epic was praised for its poetical qualities (particularly its descriptive passages—reviewers were less sure as to the success of the rhythms of its long lines[2]), and praised as well for the scope of its vision. With its idyllic portrayal of an American society "where all men were equal, and all were brothers and sisters," and its broad geographical scope, Longfellow's poem touched a chord with a vast number of Americans; in this

---

[1]   *fold their tents … steal away*   One Arabic group in particular—the Bedouin (or Bedu), have a long tradition of nomadic living; given the extreme heat of the desert of the Arabian Peninsula, they would often pitch their tents during the day and travel by night. As early as the fourteenth century their culture was celebrated (and idealized) by Arabic thinkers such as Ibn Khaldun, who saw in their spare, nomadic lifestyle a purity that he contrasted with the clutter and corruption of urban life. Whether Longfellow was aware of that line of thinking is unclear, but he would certainly have been aware of the nineteenth-century Orientalist conception of desert peoples

(and Arabic peoples in particular) as possessing an unusual capacity for silent movement. That view could take on pejorative shadings (implying that such peoples are naturally "stealthy," with all the negative implications that that word carries); Longfellow does not appear to have intended such negative connotations here, however.

[2]   In imitation of the rhythms of Homeric epics in ancient Greek, Longfellow chose to write the poem in dactylic hexameter; a line typically consists of six groups of syllables, with each group typically consisting of a stressed syllable followed by two unstressed syllables.

epic poem, as *The American Review* observed, Longfellow had made his subject "wholly national in character."

In addition to the tragic story of the betrothed couple as it had been recounted to him over dinner, Longfellow drew on a number of written sources.[1] He never visited either the old Acadian areas of Nova Scotia, the bayous of Louisiana, or many of the other scenes described in the poem. He did, however, twice attend Boston showings of John Banyard's popular "Diorama of the Mississippi and Missouri" in December 1846.

A brief excerpt from Part the First is included here; much more substantial excerpts from both parts of *Evangeline* are included in the website component of this anthology.

from PART THE FIRST

[PROLOGUE]

This is the forest primeval.[2] The murmuring pines and the hemlocks,
Bearded with moss, and in garments green, indistinct in the twilight,
Stand like Druids of eld,[3] with voices sad and prophetic,
Stand like harpers hoar,[4] with beards that rest on their bosoms.
5   Loud from its rocky caverns, the deep-voiced neighboring ocean
Speaks, and in accents disconsolate answers the wail of the forest.

This is the forest primeval; but where are the hearts that beneath it
Leaped like the roe,[5] when he hears in the woodland the voice of the huntsman?
Where is the thatch-roofed village, the home of Acadian farmers—
10   Men whose lives glided on like rivers that water the woodlands,
Darkened by shadows of earth, but reflecting an image of heaven?
Waste are those pleasant farms, and the farmers forever departed!
Scattered like dust and leaves, when the mighty blasts of October
Seize them, and whirl them aloft, and sprinkle them far o'er the ocean.
15   Naught but tradition remains of the beautiful village of Grand-Pré.[6]

Ye who believe in affection that hopes, and endures, and is patient,
Ye who believe in the beauty and strength of woman's devotion,
List° to the mournful tradition still sung by the pines of the forest;   *listen*
List to a Tale of Love in Acadie, home of the happy.

---

[1]   He relied heavily on Thomas Haliburton's *An Historical and Statistical Account of Nova Scotia* (1829), on William Darby's *Geographical Description of the State of Louisiana* (1816); and on John Fanning Watson's *Annals of Philadelphia: Being a Collection of Memoirs, Anecdotes, and Incidents of the City and Its Inhabitants* (1830).

[2]   *primeval*   Ancient, undisturbed.

[3]   *Druids*   In ancient Celtic cultures, members of a group who served as religious leaders, judges, and repositories of cultural knowledge;   *eld*   Old.

[4]   *hoar*   Gray-haired, old.

[5]   *roe*   Species of small deer.

[6]   *Grand-Pré*   Village in Nova Scotia, located by the Bay of Fundy near the present-day town of Wolfville; the French "Grand Pré" means "Great Meadow."

I

20 In the Acadian land, on the shores of the Basin of Minas,[1]
    Distant, secluded, still, the little village of Grand-Pré
    Lay in the fruitful valley. Vast meadows stretched to the eastward,
    Giving the village its name, and pasture to flocks without number.
    Dikes, that the hands of the farmers had raised with labor incessant,
25 Shut out the turbulent tides; but at stated seasons the flood-gates
    Opened and welcomed the sea to wander at will o'er the meadows.
    West and south there were fields of flax, and orchards and cornfields
    Spreading afar and unfenced o'er the plain; and away to the northward
    Blomidon[2] rose, and the forests old, and aloft on the mountains
30 Sea-fogs pitched their tents, and mists from the mighty Atlantic
    Looked on the happy valley, but ne'er from their station descended.
    There, in the midst of its farms, reposed the Acadian village.
    Strongly built were the houses, with frames of oak and of hemlock,
    Such as the peasants of Normandy built in the reign of the Henries.[3]
35 Thatched were the roofs, with dormer-windows;[4] and gables projecting
    Over the basement below protected and shaded the doorway.
    There in the tranquil evenings of summer, when brightly the sunset
    Lighted the village street, and gilded the vanes on the chimneys,
    Matrons and maidens sat in snow-white caps and in kirtles[5]
40 Scarlet and blue and green, with distaffs[6] spinning the golden
    Flax for the gossiping looms, whose noisy shuttles[7] within doors
    Mingled their sound with the whir of the wheels[8] and the songs of the maidens.
    Solemnly down the street came the parish priest, and the children
    Paused in their play to kiss the hand he extended to bless them.
45 Reverend walked he among them; and up rose matrons and maidens.
    Hailing his slow approach with words of affectionate welcome.
    Then came the laborers home from the field, and serenely the sun sank
    Down to his rest, and twilight prevailed. Anon from the belfry[9]
    Softly the Angelus[10] sounded, and over the roofs of the village

---

[1] *Basin of Minas*   Eastern inlet of Nova Scotia's coast along the Bay of Fundy; Grand-Pré is located on a peninsula on the southern shore of the Basin of Minas.

[2] *Blomidon*   Headland at the entrance of the Basin of Minas.

[3] *reign of the Henries*   British monarchs Henry IV (r. 1399–1413), Henry V (r. 1413–22), and Henry VI (r. 1422–61). (At the time Britain controlled substantial territory in what is now France.)

[4] *dormer-windows*   Windows at the end of dormers (i.e., that project outward from a sloped roof).

[5] *kirtles*   Long gowns.

[6] *distaffs*   Devices used to hold unspun fibers while spinning.

[7] *shuttles*   Boat-shaped tools used to weave thread horizontally.

[8] *wheels*   I.e., spinning wheels.

[9] *Anon*   Presently;   *belfry*   Bell-tower of a church.

[10] *Angelus*   Church bells rung three times daily to call Catholics to recite the prayer of the same name which commemorates the angel Gabriel's visit to the Virgin Mary.

50   Columns of pale blue smoke, like clouds of incense ascending,
    Rose from a hundred hearths, the homes of peace and contentment.
    Thus dwelt together in love these simple Acadian farmers—
    Dwelt in the love of God and of man. Alike were they free from
    Fear, that reigns with the tyrant, and envy, the vice of republics.
55   Neither locks had they to their doors, nor bars to their windows;
    But their dwellings were open as day and the hearts of the owners;
    There the richest was poor, and the poorest lived in abundance.

      Somewhat apart from the village, and nearer the Basin of Minas,
    Benedict Bellefontaine, the wealthiest farmer of Grand Pré,
60   Dwelt on his goodly acres; and with him, directing his household,
    Gentle Evangeline lived, his child, and the pride of the village.
    Stalworth[1] and stately in form was the man of seventy winters;
    Hearty and hale[2] was he, an oak that is covered with snow-flakes;
    White as the snow were his locks, and his cheeks as brown as the oak-leaves.
65   Fair was she to behold, that maiden of seventeen summers;
    Black were her eyes as the berry that grows on the thorn by the wayside,
    Black, yet how softly they gleamed beneath the brown shade of her tresses!
    Sweet was her breath as the breath of kine[3] that feed in the meadows.
    When in the harvest heat she bore to the reapers at noon-tide
70   Flagons of home-brewed ale, ah! fair in sooth[4] was the maiden.
    Fairer was she when, on Sunday morn, while the bell from its turret
    Sprinkled with holy sounds the air, as the priest with his hyssop[5]
    Sprinkles the congregation, and scatters blessings upon them,
    Down the long street she passed, with her chaplet of beads and her missal,[6]
75   Wearing her Norman cap and her kirtle of blue, and the ear-rings
    Brought in the olden times from France, and since, as an heirloom,
    Handed down from mother to child, through long generations.
    But a celestial brightness—a more ethereal beauty—
    Shone on her face and encircled her form, when, after confession,
80   Homeward serenely she walked with God's benediction upon her.
    When she had passed, it seemed like the ceasing of exquisite music.

      Firmly builded with rafters of oak, the house of the farmer
    Stood on the side of a hill commanding the sea; and a shady
    Sycamore grew by the door, with a woodbine[7] wreathing around it.
85   Rudely carved was the porch, with seats beneath; and a footpath

---

1   *Stalworth*   Strong.

2   *hale*   Healthy.

3   *kine*   Cattle.

4   *sooth*   Truth.

5   *hyssop*   Plant used for sprinkling holy water in religious ceremonies.

6   *chaplet of beads*   Beaded garland used for prayer, similar to a rosary;   *missal*   Christian mass- or prayer-book.

7   *woodbine*   Climbing vine or shrub.

Led through an orchard wide, and disappeared in the meadow.
Under the sycamore-tree were hives overhung by a penthouse,[1]
Such as the traveller sees in regions remote by the roadside,
Built o'er a box for the poor, or the blessed image of Mary.
90 Farther down, on the slope of the hill, was the well with its moss-grown
Bucket, fastened with iron, and near it a trough for the horses.
Shielding the house from storms, on the north, were the barns and the farm-yard;
There stood the broad-wheeled wains and the antique ploughs and the harrows;[2]
There were the folds for the sheep; and there, in his feathered seraglio,[3]
95 Strutted the lordly turkey, and crowed the cock, with the selfsame
Voice that in ages of old had startled the penitent Peter.[4]
Bursting with hay were the barns, themselves a village. In each one
Far o'er the gable projected a roof of thatch; and a staircase,
Under the sheltering eaves, led up to the odorous corn-loft.
100 There too the dove-cot[5] stood, with its meek and innocent inmates
Murmuring ever of love; while above in the variant breezes
Numberless noisy weathercocks[6] rattled and sang of mutation.

Thus, at peace with God and the world, the farmer of Grand-Pré
Lived on his sunny farm, and Evangeline governed his household.
105 Many a youth, as he knelt in the church and opened his missal,
Fixed his eyes upon her as the saint of his deepest devotion;
Happy was he who might touch her hand or the hem of her garment!
Many a suitor came to her door, by the darkness befriended,
And as he knocked and waited to hear the sound of her footsteps,
110 Knew not which beat the louder, his heart or the knocker of iron;
Or, at the joyous feast of the Patron Saint of the village,
Bolder grew, and pressed her hand in the dance as he whispered
Hurried words of love, that seemed a part of the music.
But among all who came young Gabriel only was welcome;
115 Gabriel Lajeunesse,[7] the son of Basil the blacksmith,
Who was a mighty man in the village, and honoured of all men;
For since the birth of time, throughout all ages and nations,
Has the craft of the smith been held in repute by the people.
Basil was Benedict's friend. Their children from earliest childhood

---

[1] *penthouse* Small, sloped, protective roof.

[2] *wains* Large horse-drawn wagons; *harrows* Spiked agricultural tools used to smooth the surface of plowed soil.

[3] *seraglio* Harem.

[4] *startled the penitent Peter* Biblical allusion to Peter's denial of Jesus (an episode that appears in all four gospels). In Matthew 26.74–75: "Then began he to curse and to swear, saying, I know not the man. And immediately the cock crew. And Peter remembered the word of Jesus, which said unto him, Before the cock crow, thou shalt deny me thrice. And he went out, and wept bitterly." See also Mark 14.66–72; Luke 22.55–62; John 18.17–27.

[5] *dove-cot* Structure for doves and pigeons to roost.

[6] *weathercocks* Weathervanes shaped like roosters.

[7] *Lajeunesse* Gabriel's surname translates as "The youth."

120 Grew up together as brother and sister; and Father Felician,
    Priest and pedagogue[1] both in the village, had taught them their letters
    Out of the selfsame book, with the hymns of the church and the plain-song.[2]
    But when the hymn was sung, and the daily lesson completed,
    Swiftly they hurried away to the forge of Basil the blacksmith.
125 There at the door they stood, with wondering eyes to behold him
    Take in his leathern lap the hoof of the horse as a plaything,
    Nailing the shoe in its place; while near him the tire of the cart-wheel
    Lay like a fiery snake, coiled round in a circle of cinders.
    Oft on autumnal eves, when without° in the gathering darkness   *outside*
130 Bursting with light seemed the smithy,[3] through every cranny and crevice,
    Warm by the forge within they watched the labouring bellows,[4]
    And as its panting ceased, and the sparks expired in the ashes,
    Merrily laughed, and said they were nuns going into the chapel.
    Oft on sledges in winter, as swift as the swoop of the eagle,
135 Down the hillside bounding, they glided away o'er the meadow.
    Oft in the barns they climbed to the populous nests on the rafters,
    Seeking with eager eyes that wondrous stone, which the swallow
    Brings from the shore of the sea to restore the sight of its fledglings;
    Lucky was he who found that stone in the nest of the swallow!
140 Thus passed a few swift years, and they no longer were children.
    He was a valiant youth, and his face, like the face of the morning,
    Gladdened the earth with its light, and ripened thought into action.
    She was a woman now, with the heart and hopes of a woman.
    "Sunshine of Saint Eulalie"[5] was she called; for that was the sunshine
145 Which, as the farmers believed, would load their orchards with apples;
    She too would bring to her husband's house delight and abundance,
    Filling it full of love and the ruddy faces of children.
    …
    —1847

---

1 *pedagogue* Schoolmaster.

2 *plain-song* Religious chants intended to be sung a cappella and in unison.

3 *smithy* Blacksmith's workshop or forge.

4 *bellows* Devices that, when compressed, blow air on a fire so as to make it burn hotter.

5 *Sunshine of Saint Eulalie* Allusion to a French weather proverb: "Si le soleil rit le jour de la Sainte-Eulalie, / Il y aura pommes et cidre à folie." In English: "If the sun shines on Saint Eulalia's day [12 February], there will be plenty of apples, and cider enough."

from *The Building of the Ship*

In all, "The Building of the Ship" is a poem of almost 400 lines; excerpted here are 37 lines from early on in the poem, together with the poem's final section. In addition to recounting the various stages in the building of a ship called the *Union*, Longfellow tells the tale of a romance between a young man and the daughter of the ship's master builder—their marriage echoing "the bridal day / Of beauty and of strength" that is to take place with the launch of the vessel, as well as the union of the (female) ship with her "bridegroom," the sea.

    ...

The sun was rising o'er the sea,
   And long the level shadows lay,
As if they, too, the beams would be
Of some great, airy argosy,[1]
5 Framed and launched in a single day.
That silent architect, the sun,
Had hewn and laid them every one,
Ere the work of man was yet begun.
Beside the Master, when he spoke,
10 A youth, against an anchor leaning,
Listened, to catch his slightest meaning.
Only the long waves, as they broke
In ripples on the pebbly beach,
Interrupted the old man's speech.
15 Beautiful they were, in sooth,°   *truth*
The old man and the fiery youth!
The old man, in whose busy brain
Many a ship that sailed the main
Was modelled o'er and o'er again—
20 The fiery youth, who was to be
The heir of his dexterity,
The heir of his house, and his daughter's hand,
When he had built and launched from land
What the elder head had planned.

25 "Thus," said he, "will we build this ship!
Lay square the blocks upon the slip,[2]
And follow well this plan of mine.
Choose the timbers with greatest care;

---

1   *argosy* Large cargo-carrying ship.

2   *slip* Boat launch; slipway.

Of all that is unsound beware;
30 For only what is sound and strong
To this vessel shall belong.
Cedar of Maine and Georgia pine
Here together shall combine.
A goodly frame, and a goodly fame,
35 And the Union be her name!
For the day that gives her to the sea
Shall give my daughter unto thee!"
    ...
Then the Master,
With a gesture of command,
40 Waved his hand;
And at the word,
Loud and sudden there was heard,
All around them and below,
The sound of hammers, blow on blow,
45 Knocking away the shores and spurs.
And see! she stirs!
She starts—she moves—she seems to feel
The thrill of life along her keel,
And, spurning with her foot the ground,
50 With one exulting, joyous bound,
She leaps into the ocean's arms!

And lo! from the assembled crowd
There rose a shout, prolonged and loud,
That to the ocean seemed to say,
55 "Take her, O bridegroom, old and gray,
Take her to thy protecting arms,
With all her youth and all her charms!"

How beautiful she is! How fair
She lies within those arms, that press
60 Her form with many a soft caress
Of tenderness and watchful care!
Sail forth into the sea, O ship!
Through wind and wave, right onward steer!
The moistened eye, the trembling lip,
65 Are not the signs of doubt or fear.

Sail forth into the sea of life,
O gentle, loving, trusting wife,
And safe from all adversity
Upon the bosom of that sea
70 Thy comings and thy goings be!

For gentleness and love and trust
Prevail o'er angry wave and gust;
And in the wreck of noble lives
Something immortal still survives!

75 Thou, too, sail on, O Ship of State!
Sail on, O Union, strong and great!
Humanity with all its fears,
With all the hopes of future years,
Is hanging breathless on thy fate!
80 We know what Master laid thy keel,
What Workmen wrought thy ribs of steel,
Who made each mast, and sail, and rope,
What anvils rang, what hammers beat,
In what a forge and what a heat
85 Were shaped the anchors of thy hope!
Fear not each sudden sound and shock,
'Tis of the wave and not the rock;
'Tis but the flapping of the sail,
And not a rent° made by the gale!   rip, tear
90 In spite of rock and tempest's roar,
In spite of false lights on the shore,
Sail on, nor fear to breast° the sea!   push through
Our hearts, our hopes, are all with thee,
Our hearts, our hopes, our prayers, our tears,
95 Our faith triumphant o'er our fears,
Are all with thee—are all with thee!
    —1849

The Jewish Cemetery at Newport[1]

How strange it seems! These Hebrews in their
        graves,
    Close by the street of this fair seaport town,
Silent beside the never-silent waves,
    At rest in all this moving up and down!

5 The trees are white with dust, that o'er their sleep
        Wave their broad curtains in the south-wind's
        breath,
While underneath these leafy tents they keep
    The long, mysterious Exodus of Death.

And these sepulchral stones, so old and brown,
10   That pave with level flags their burial-place,
Seem like the tablets of the Law, thrown down
    And broken by Moses at the mountain's base.[2]

The very names recorded here are strange,
    Of foreign accent, and of different climes;
15 Alvares and Rivera[3] interchange

---

1 Longfellow visited this cemetery while in Newport, Rhode Island in 1852; the poem was first published in *Putnam's Magazine* in July of that year. The synagogue was founded in 1763 by Isaac Touro; by the end of the century, however (according to an 1869 *Harper's* report, the Jews' Newport "temple was deserted, though from time to time a few of their race congregated to celebrate a feast, a marriage, or funeral; for they reverently brought back their dead, and laid them to rest with the ashes of their forefathers." One of those ceremonies occurred earlier in 1854; Judah Touro (younger son of Isaac) died 28 January 1854; he had long been a resident of New Orleans, but he asked that his remains be buried in Newport. His death and burial were was widely reported, though it is not clear if Longfellow read of them.

2 *the tablets ... mountain's base* See Exodus 32.19. In the biblical story, Moses has ascended Mount Sinai to receive the stone tablets from God (with the commandments inscribed upon them); when he discovers that the Israelites have been worshipping a golden calf—an idol—he becomes infuriated and smashes the tablets.

3 *Alvares and Rivera* The name "Alvares" (like the name "Touro") is of Portuguese origin, the name "Rivera" of Spanish origin. Both countries expelled their Jewish populations, beginning in the 1490s (as England had done two centuries earlier); Jews from Portugal or Spain had the option of converting to Christianity or leaving their homeland. Many emigrated as a result (to various Mediterranean destinations, as well as across the Atlantic), and emigration continued over the next two hundred years, as many Marranos (those who had converted to Christianity under duress, and who [continued ...]

With Abraham and Jacob of old times.

"Blessed be God! for he created Death!"
    The mourners said, "and Death is rest and peace";
Then added, in the certainty of faith,
20   "And giveth Life that nevermore shall cease."[1]

Closed are the portals of their Synagogue,
    No Psalms of David now the silence break,
No Rabbi reads the ancient Decalogue[2]
    In the grand dialect the Prophets spake.

25 Gone are the living, but the dead remain,
    And not neglected; for a hand unseen,[3]
Scattering its bounty, like a summer rain,
    Still keeps their graves and their remembrance
        green.

How came they here? What burst of Christian hate,
30   What persecution, merciless and blind,
Drove o'er the sea—that desert desolate—
    These Ishmaels and Hagars[4] of mankind?

They lived in narrow streets and lanes obscure,
    Ghetto and Judenstrass,[5] in mirk and mire;

35 Taught in the school of patience to endure
    The life of anguish and the death of fire.

All their lives long, with the unleavened bread
    And bitter herbs of exile[6] and its fears,
The wasting famine of the heart they fed,
40   And slaked its thirst with marah[7] of their tears.

Anathema maranatha![8] was the cry
    That rang from town to town, from street to
        street;
At every gate the accursed Mordecai[9]
    Was mocked and jeered, and spurned by Christian
        feet.

45 Pride and humiliation hand in hand
    Walked with them through the world where'er
        they went;
Trampled and beaten were they as the sand,
    And yet unshaken as the continent.

For in the background figures vague and vast
50   Of patriarchs and of prophets rose sublime,
And all the great traditions of the Past
    They saw reflected in the coming time.

And thus forever with reverted look
    The mystic volume of the world they read,
55 Spelling it backward, like a Hebrew book,[10]
    Till life became a Legend of the Dead.

---

still faced considerable discrimination) continued to become alienated from the other residents of their Spanish and Portuguese homelands.

[1] *Blessed be ... shall cease* The Jewish funeral service involves prayers such as the Tziduk Hadin, which includes these lines: "He brings death and restores life, brings down to the grave and raises up from there. ... Righteous are You, Lord, to bring death and to restore life, for in Your hands are entrusted all spirits."

[2] *Decalogue* The Ten Commandments.

[3] *a hand unseen* Abraham Touro, one of the sons of Isaac Touro, the founder of the Touro synagogue, made a bequest to the town of Newport when he died in 1822, in order that the cemetery, the synagogue, and the adjacent street be kept in good repair in perpetuity. In 1854 the *Providence Journal* reported (in an article reporting the death of his brother, Judah) that the "Touro Fund" had grown to "more than $15,000"—in those days a very large sum.

[4] *Ishmaels and Hagars* Outcasts. See Genesis 21 for the story of how Hagar and her son Ishmael are forced to leave their home.

[5] *Ghetto and Judenstrass* In parts of Europe where anti-Semitism had not led to the outright expulsion of Jews, Jews nevertheless faced substantial discrimination. Forms of employment were severely restricted, as was residency; in many cities Jews were restricted to a single, small neighborhood, where cramped conditions prevailed.

Venice created the first such neighborhood in 1516, and called it a new "ghetto"; soon the name was being used to denote Jewish areas in Florence, Rome, and many other cities; *Judenstrass* German: Jews street.

[6] *unleavened bread ... herbs of exile* Bitter herbs and unleavened bread are among the foods traditionally eaten at Passover, commemorating the Exodus—the Jews' escape from slavery across the Red Sea into Egypt.

[7] *marah* Bitter water; see Exodus 15.22–25.

[8] *Anathema maranatha!* See 1 Corinthians 21–22; the apostle Paul calls for anyone who does not love Jesus Christ to be cursed ("Anathema Maranatha").

[9] *Mordecai* A central figure in the biblical book of Esther—but here, simply a common Jewish name.

[10] *Spelling ... Hebrew book* Lines of Hebrew are read right to left.

But ah! what once has been shall be no more!   Brings forth its races, but does not restore,
The groaning earth in travail and in pain   60   And the dead nations never rise again.
—1854

IN CONTEXT

"The Jews at Newport"

from Henry T. Tuckerman, "The Graves at Newport," *Harper's New Monthly Magazine* (August 1869)

> Tuckerman's long article touches on "the Indian mounds, few of which are now discoverable," and discusses various Christian cemeteries at length. Much of his treatment of the Jewish cemetery was excerpted in *The Israelite* (Cincinnati, Ohio), 13 August 1869, under the heading "The Jews at Newport": "We lay before our readers the scholastic essay on the subject of 'The Graves at Newport,' and various incidents concerning the old Jewish residents, by Mr. Henry T. Tuckerman, from *Harper's* magazine for August." *The Israelite* included all four of the stanzas of Longfellow that Tuckerman had quoted.

The memorials of Hebrew sojourn in Newport are unique among the relics of bygone times in New England, and among the most striking evidences of the triumphant conservatism of the race. The freshness and order that characterize the abandoned synagogue and unvisited cemetery reproach the neglected temples and sepulchers of those who trust to local attachment and living kindred to guard their shrines and ashes. With that prevailing and indominable fidelity which has kept the scattered people intact and their faith vital through ages of exile and oppression, the wealthier survivor, by testamentary provision, kept "decently and in order" the graves and place of worship. ... Touro Street perpetuates the name of the testator, whose thoughtful care for the departed of his race daily suggests itself as a benign evidence of ancient civilization. After the terrible earthquake at Lisbon, a company of Jews embarked thence for America[.] ... Adverse and violent winds led them to seek refuge in Narragansett Bay. Allured by the tolerant laws and spirit of Newport, the Israelite emigrants determined to remain there—thus adding a new element to the already curious diversity of faith and nativity which signalized the colony.[1]

... Neat, silent, and shaded, the little enclosure [of the cemetery] is passed with a careless glance by crowds of summer sojourners; but a poet's eye gleaned an impressive picture and sacred lesson from the "Jewish Cemetery at Newport":[2] [quotes first four stanzas]

Other Jewish emigrants from the west Indies followed their Portuguese brethren to Newport; and in 1763, when 60 families of wealth had settled there, the synagogue was erected at a little distance from the cemetery, farther down Touro Street. ...

---

[1]   *the already curious diversity ... the colony*   Unlike most of the colonies along the Eastern seaboard, Rhode Island had been founded without any established religion, on the basis of an explicit separation of church and state. As a result, people from a wide range of faiths settled there—and also people born in a wide range of places, since those fleeing religious persecution elsewhere kept arriving in Rhode Island;   *curious*   Unusual, surprising.

[2]   [Tuckerman's note]   On the 24th of August, 1694, a ship arrived at Newport, Rhode Island, then the principal port of entry, from one of the West India islands, with a number of Jewish families on board, of wealth and respectability, who settled there. In a few years a congregation of sixty worshipped at the synagogue, which at length boasted of eleven hundred and seventy-five worshippers. Gradually emigrating to new states, not a resident Jew is now found at Newport—only their sepulchers remain.

Both the advent and the exodus of the Jews at Newport is characteristic, and so are the few glimpses contemporary annals afford of their enterprise and influence. ...

The war of the revolution dispersed the Jewish merchants. Their ships were nearly all taken by the enemy. And in 1799 their temple was deserted, though from time to time a few of their race congregated to celebrate a feast, a marriage, or funeral; for they reverently brought back their dead, and laid them to rest with the ashes of their forefathers. ... Thus departed from the old town one after another of the once busy and genial Hebrews, whose memorials are so faithfully conserved. ...

IN CONTEXT

Rebekah Hyneman, Poems on Death

There are few Jewish poets of note in mid-nineteenth-century America; Rebekah Gumpert Hyneman (1812–75) is one—and one who, though she did not compose any poem on the subject of a cemetery, wrote frequently on the theme of death and dying. Hyneman was born Rebekah Gumpert in Philadelphia to a Jewish-German shopkeeper and his wife, and was largely self-educated. She was married in 1835 to Benjamin Hyneman, an itinerant jewelry seller, but he died in 1839 (he was presumed to have been murdered, while on a business trip to Texas). Hyneman began in the 1840s to publish her literary work (prose fiction and essays as well as poetry) in *The Occident and American Jewish Advocate* and other newspapers. In 1853 she published *The Leper and Other Poems*, and in the same year her gothic mystery *The Fatal Cosmetic* was serialized in the *Masonic Mirror and Keystone*. Her two sons both predeceased her—Baron from disease in 1864 and Elias Leon from starvation in the Andersonville Confederate Prison in 1865.

In addition to writing extensively on the subject of death and dying, Hyneman wrote a good deal of poetry on religious themes (including a series of poems on women of the Bible).

"The Unforgotten" (1853)

Far, far away, in a distant land
   Beneath the light of another sky,
Thy grave unadorned by a kindred hand—
   Thy death unwept by a kindred eye.

5 Thou art laid to rest! And the rank grass waves
   In wild luxuriance o'er thy bed—
That lonely bed among stranger graves
   The lowly though unforgotten dead.

Those graves may be watered by tears of love
10   May be decked with fair and blooming flowers,
And many a scene where mourners rove
   May serve to solace their saddest hours.

For there, too, have wandered the loved ones fled,
   And there some link of the mighty chain

15 That bound the heart of the living and the dead,
    May recall those happier hours again.

But where on this cold, bleak earth, art thou laid?
    What spot on its bosom, oh! Tempest-tossed,
Can we point to, and say that there has been made
20   The grave of the erring friend we have lost?

We never shall know it! Time tolls on,
    And death may sever our household band,
But we never shall know where that desolate one
    Met his lone death-hour, in a strange land.

"Now Let Me Die" (1853)

Now let me die!
The bloom of earth has passed away,
Its pleasures pall, its flowers decay—
The hopes that lured with dazzling ray,
5   Low, withered lie.

Bury me deep,
That no foot profane disturb my rest;
But place no stone above my breast—
Too heavily life's burden prest,
10   And banished sleep.

Ask me now why
I long for my deep, lonely grave;
Ask me now why, I only crave
A release from life, the boon it gave
15   Was misery.

Oh! placid sleep,
I sink at length in thy embrace;
My task is done—a weary race
Was mine on earth; let my resting-place
20   Be lone and deep.

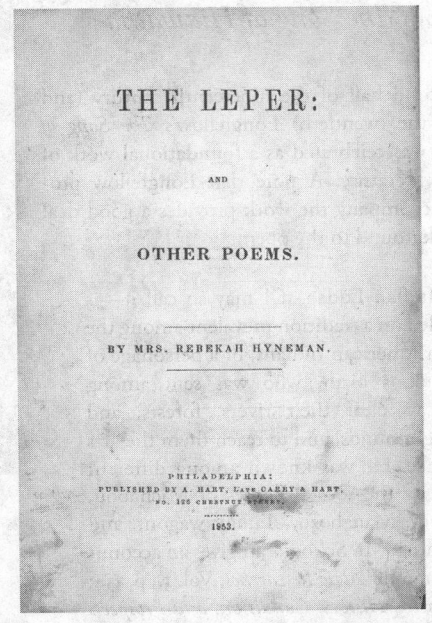

Title page, *The Leper and Other Poems*, 1863.

from *The Song of Hiawatha*

In the second half of the nineteenth century (and well into the twentieth) Longfellow's *The Song of Hiawatha* was celebrated as a foundational work of American literature. A note that Longfellow provided to accompany the work provides a good deal of the background to the poem:

> This Indian Edda—if I may so call it—is founded on a tradition prevalent among the North American Indians, of a personage of miraculous birth, who was sent among them to clear their rivers, forests, and fishing-grounds, and to teach them the arts of peace. He was known among different tribes by the several names of Michabou, Chiabo, Manabozo, Tarenyawagon, and Hiawatha. Mr. Schoolcraft gives an account of him in his *Algic Researches*, Vol. 1., p. 134; and in his *History, Condition, and Prospects of the Indian Tribes of the United States*, Part 3., p. 314, may be found the Iroquois form of the tradition, derived from the verbal narrations of an Onondaga chief.
>
> Into this old tradition I have woven other curious Indian legends, drawn chiefly from the various and valuable writings of Mr. Schoolcraft, to whom the literary world is greatly indebted for his indefatigable zeal in rescuing from oblivion so much of the legendary lore of the Indians.
>
> The scene of the poem is among the Ojibways on the southern shore of Lake Superior, in the region between the Pictured Rocks and the Grand Sable.

The "Edda" that Longfellow refers to is a collection of medieval Old Norse poems known as *The Poetic Edda*. In addition to being influenced by the heroic tone of such poems, Longfellow was influenced by the form; the unusual meter that he chose for *The Song of Hiawatha*—trochaic tetrameter[1]—has some affinities with the rhythms of old Scandinavian verse. For the subject matter of his poem, Longfellow largely relied, as he says, on the writings of Henry Rowe Schoolcraft—who had himself relied extensively on the work of his wife, Jane Johnston Schoolcraft, the daughter of an Ojibwe mother and a Scotch-Irish father. (See Jane Johnston Schoolcraft's author entry elsewhere in this anthology.)

As is now universally accepted by historians, there was a historical figure named Hiawatha, who played a central role in bringing peace to his people.[2] Longfellow's poem, however, is as much about myth and legend as it is about history. As he had discovered in Schoolcraft's writings, the "personage of miraculous birth, … sent to teach the arts of peace" was a traditional mythic figure who went by different names in many different native traditions. Drawing on the mythology of the "Noble Savage" that had become established in white culture, as well as on Indigenous myths and traditions (in particular, those of the Ojibwe), Longfellow crafted a poem that millions of readers on both sides of the Atlantic found deeply affecting. The exuberant response of the reviewer of the *Aberdeen Journal* (who had obtained an advance copy in November 1855) gives some sense of the degree of enthusiasm that *The Song of Hiawatha* inspired in many quarters:

> As we read [the sections of the poem], at every line we become enchanted more and more with their wild and mystic, yet simple and homely beauty. Each of them, after the first two, relates a separate adventure of Hiawatha, the hero of the poem. This Hiawatha is a kind of demigod—a semi-mythical personage. …

Situating his poem in a semi-mythical past made it possible for Longfellow to steer clear of the pressing controversies of his own time regarding the settler colonists and the Indigenous peoples of America.

---

1   *trochaic tetrameter*   In verse written in trochaic tetrameter, a line typically consists of four groups of syllables, with each group typically consisting of a stressed syllable followed by an unstressed syllable.

2   *Hiawatha … his people*   Following a long period of conflict within the Iroquois Confederacy, the prophet Dekanawida and his disciple Hayonhwatha (variously spelled Deganawida and Hiawatha) arranged a series of meetings of the feuding Iroquois nations, and managed to negotiate a lasting peace accord—the Great Law of Peace. Modern historians have not reached a consensus of precisely when these momentous developments occurred; some are of the view that the peace accord was reached in the sixteenth century CE, others that it occurred some centuries earlier. But all agree that the legend of Deganawida and Hiawatha is based on a series of historical events—events that were crucial to the formation of what became the most powerful and influential Indigenous group in the northeast of the continent.

The Song of Hiawatha ends with the arrival of white people in North America, and Hiawatha experiences a vague vision of how the settler colonialists will sweep across the continent:

> In the woodlands rang their axes,
> Smoked their towns in all the valleys,
> Over all the lakes and rivers
> Rushes their great canoes of thunder.

A partial exception has been made with this poem to the anthology policy of modernizing spelling and punctuation; Longfellow often capitalizes words such as "Winter" or "Prairie" in the poem; though in many cases these entities are not clearly personified, it seems likely that he intended there to be a suggestion of personification; on that assumption we have retained such capitalizations in the text provided here.

One chapter of *The Song of Hiawatha* is included in these pages; a much more substantial set of excerpts is included as part of the website component of this anthology.

14
PICTURE-WRITING[1]

In those days said Hiawatha,
"Lo! how all things fade and perish!
From the memory of the old men
Pass away the great traditions,
5　The achievements of the warriors,
The adventures of the hunters,
All the wisdom of the Medas,
All the craft of the Wabenos,
All the marvellous dreams and visions
10　Of the Jossakeeds, the Prophets![2]

"Great men die and are forgotten,
Wise men speak; their words of wisdom
Perish in the ears that hear them,

Do not reach the generations
15　That, as yet unborn, are waiting
In the great, mysterious darkness
Of the speechless days that shall be!

"On the grave-posts of our fathers
Are no signs, no figures painted;
20　Who are in those graves we know not,
Only know they are our fathers.
Of what kith[3] they are and kindred,
From what old, ancestral Totem,
Be it Eagle, Bear, or Beaver,[4]
25　They descended, this we know not,
Only know they are our fathers.

"Face to face we speak together,
But we cannot speak when absent,
Cannot send our voices from us
30　To the friends that dwell afar off;
Cannot send a secret message,
But the bearer learns our secret,
May pervert it, may betray it,
May reveal it unto others."

35　Thus said Hiawatha, walking
In the solitary forest,
Pondering, musing in the forest,
On the welfare of his people.

From his pouch he took his colors,
40　Took his paints of different colors,
On the smooth bark of a birch-tree
Painted many shapes and figures,
Wonderful and mystic figures,
And each figure had a meaning,
45　Each some word or thought suggested.

Gitche Manito[5] the Mighty,
He, the Master of Life, was painted
As an egg, with points projecting
To the four winds of the heavens.
50　Everywhere is the Great Spirit,
Was the meaning of this symbol.

Mitche Manito the Mighty,

1　Longfellow draws heavily in this section of the poem on information provided by George Copway in his 1850 book, *The Traditional History and Characteristic Sketches of the Ojibway Nation.* (See Volume A of this anthology for excerpts from Copway's work.)

2　*All the wisdom … the Prophets* According to Henry Rowe Schoolcraft (whose writings Longfellow relied on), the Medas, Wabenos, and Jossakeeds were members of mystical secret societies respectively practicing medicine, magic, and prophecy.

3　*kith* Friends, neighbors, acquaintances.

4　*ancestral Totem … Beaver* Totems are objects emblematic of a particular native group—most commonly, of clans within a particular tribe. Eagle, Bear, and Beaver clans may all be found within the Ojibwe (and the broader Anishinaabe group); the word *totem* itself derives from the Ojibwe language.

5　*Gitche Manito* Algonquian term for "great spirit."

He the dreadful Spirit of Evil,
As a serpent was depicted,
55 As Kenabeek, the great serpent.
Very crafty, very cunning,
Is the creeping Spirit of Evil,
Was the meaning of this symbol.
  Life and Death he drew as circles,
60 Life was white, but Death was darkened;
Sun and moon and stars he painted,
Man and beast, and fish and reptile,
Forests, mountains, lakes, and rivers.
  For the earth he drew a straight line,
65 For the sky a bow above it;
White the space between for daytime,
Filled with little stars for nighttime;
On the left a point for sunrise,
On the right a point for sunset,
70 On the top a point for noontide,
And for rain and cloudy weather
Waving lines descending from it.
  Footprints pointing towards a wigwam
Were a sign of invitation,
75 Were a sign of guests assembling;
Bloody hands with palms uplifted
Were a symbol of destruction,
Were a hostile sign and symbol.
  All these things did Hiawatha
80 Show unto his wondering people,
And interpreted their meaning,
And he said: "Behold, your grave-posts
Have no mark, no sign, nor symbol,
Go and paint them all with figures;
85 Each one with its household symbol,
With its own ancestral Totem;
So that those who follow after
May distinguish them and know them."
  And they painted on the grave-posts
90 On the graves yet unforgotten,
Each his own ancestral Totem,
Each the symbol of his household;
Figures of the Bear and Reindeer,
Of the Turtle, Crane, and Beaver,
95 Each inverted as a token
That the owner was departed,
That the chief who bore the symbol
Lay beneath in dust and ashes.

And the Jossakeeds, the Prophets,
100 The Wabenos, the Magicians,
And the Medicine-men, the Medas,
Painted upon bark and deer-skin
Figures for the songs they chanted,
For each song a separate symbol,
105 Figures mystical and awful,
Figures strange and brightly colored;
And each figure had its meaning,
Each some magic song suggested.
  The Great Spirit, the Creator,
110 Flashing light through all the heaven;
The Great Serpent, the Kenabeek,
With his bloody crest erected,
Creeping, looking into heaven;
In the sky the sun, that listens,
115 And the moon eclipsed and dying;
Owl and eagle, crane and hen-hawk,
And the cormorant, bird of magic;
Headless men, that walk the heavens,
Bodies lying pierced with arrows,
120 Bloody hands of death uplifted,
Flags on graves, and great war-captains
Grasping both the earth and heaven!
  Such as these the shapes they painted
On the birch-bark and the deer-skin;
125 Songs of war and songs of hunting,
Songs of medicine and of magic,
All were written in these figures,
For each figure had its meaning,
Each its separate song recorded.
130   Nor forgotten was the Love-Song,
The most subtle of all medicines,
The most potent spell of magic,
Dangerous more than war or hunting!
Thus the Love-Song was recorded,
135 Symbol and interpretation.
  First a human figure standing,
Painted in the brightest scarlet;
'Tis the lover, the musician,
And the meaning is, "My painting
140 Makes me powerful over others."
  Then the figure seated, singing,
Playing on a drum of magic,
And the interpretation, "Listen!
'Tis my voice you hear, my singing!"

145 Then the same red figure seated
In the shelter of a wigwam,
And the meaning of the symbol,
"I will come and sit beside you
In the mystery of my passion!"
150 Then two figures, man and woman,
Standing hand in hand together,
With their hands so clasped together
That they seemed in one united,
And the words thus represented
155 Are, "I see your heart within you,
And your cheeks are red with blushes!"
  Next the maiden on an island,
In the centre of an island;
And the song this shape suggested
160 Was, "Though you were at a distance,
Were upon some far-off island,
Such the spell I cast upon you,
Such the magic power of passion,
I could straightway draw you to me!"
165 Then the figure of the maiden
Sleeping, and the lover near her,
Whispering to her in her slumbers,
Saying, "Though you were far from me
In the land of Sleep and Silence,
170 Still the voice of love would reach you!"
  And the last of all the figures
Was a heart within a circle,
Drawn within a magic circle;
And the image had this meaning:
175 "Naked lies your heart before me,
To your naked heart I whisper!"
  Thus it was that Hiawatha,
In his wisdom, taught the people
All the mysteries of painting,
180 All the art of Picture-Writing,
On the smooth bark of the birch-tree,
On the white skin of the reindeer,
On the grave-posts of the village.
  —1855

Nature

As a fond mother, when the day is o'er,
 Leads by the hand her little child to bed,
 Half willing, half reluctant to be led,
 And leave his broken playthings on the floor,
5 Still gazing at them through the open door,
 Nor wholly reassured and comforted
 By promises of others in their stead,
 Which, though more splendid, may not please
  him more;
So Nature deals with us, and takes away
10 Our playthings one by one, and by the hand
 Leads us to rest so gently, that we go
Scarce knowing if we wish to go or stay,
 Being too full of sleep to understand
 How far the unknown transcends the what we
  know.
—1877

My Cathedral

Like two cathedral towers these stately pines
 Uplift their fretted summits tipped with cones;
 The arch beneath them is not built with stones,
 Not Art but Nature traced these lovely lines,
5 And carved this graceful arabesque[1] of vines;
 No organ but the wind here sighs and moans,
 No sepulchre conceals a martyr's bones.
 No marble bishop on his tomb reclines.
Enter! the pavement, carpeted with leaves,
10 Gives back a softened echo to thy tread!
 Listen! the choir is singing; all the birds,
In leafy galleries beneath the eaves,
 Are singing! listen, ere the sound be fled,
 And learn there may be worship without words.
—1880

---

1 *arabesque* Complex decorative design.

IN CONTEXT

Images of Longfellow

Albert Sands Southworth and Josiah Johnson Hawes, Henry Wadsworth Longfellow, 1850.

Henry Wadsworth Longfellow, 1858.

Photographer unknown, Longfellow Family, c. 1849. Pictured along with Longfellow are his wife, Frances "Fanny" Appleton Longfellow, and their sons Charles and Ernest.

Julia Margaret Cameron, Henry Wadsworth Longfellow, 1868. This famous photograph was taken when Longfellow visited Alfred, Lord Tennyson at his home on the Isle of Wight. Julia Margaret Cameron, who was already becoming recognized as an extraordinary photographer, was a neighbor of Tennyson's, and had photographed the famous British poet several times; it was at Tennyson's suggestion that Cameron photographed Longfellow.

Longfellow grew a beard after his face had been burned when he attempted to rescue his wife from the flames in 1861.

ABRAHAM LINCOLN

1809 – 1865

Revered by many for his leadership of the United States during the Civil War, Abraham Lincoln is scarcely less renowned for his oratorical accomplishments. The elegant balance of his sentences and the gentle but insistent repetitions embedded within them bring clarity to ideas and engender an emotional response among those reading or hearing them. Lincoln's reputation as a skilled rhetorician was well established before the election of 1860, but it was the speeches he delivered as president—especially the Gettysburg Address and the Second Inaugural Address (the latter delivered mere weeks before his assassination)—that cemented his reputation as one of history's most extraordinary orators. As President, Lincoln saw the nation through the most dramatic crisis it had yet experienced, and his memorable expressions of that crisis shaped the way subsequent generations came to understand the Civil War.

The story of Lincoln's youth is widely known. His parents were poor farmers in southwestern Kentucky who later moved to Indiana and then Illinois. Lincoln was bookishly inclined from an early age, much to the chagrin of his father, who often beat young Abraham for neglecting his farm duties in order to read books. In his early twenties, Lincoln left his family for town life in New Salem, Illinois, where he purchased a shop and became a popular local figure (with a reputation for telling exceptionally vulgar jokes). Following a brief period serving in the Black Hawk War, Lincoln ran for and was elected to the Illinois General Assembly (while he was at the same time studying to become a lawyer). By 1837 he had moved to the state capital of Springfield, where he established a successful law practice while serving in the state legislature. It was in Springfield that he met Mary Todd, whose parents were members of an illustrious slaveholding Kentucky family. Todd and Lincoln married in 1842.

Lincoln continued to engage in politics throughout the 1840s, and served for one term in the U.S. House of Representatives; but in 1849 he chose not to run for re-election, and it appeared that he had finished with political life. The passage of the controversial Kansas-Nebraska Act in 1854 drew Lincoln back into politics. As a vocal, if moderate, critic of slavery, Lincoln was infuriated by the new legislation and decided to seek election to the U.S. Senate.

From this point onward, Lincoln's national reputation grew rapidly. In 1856 he was significantly involved in the creation of the new Republican Party of Illinois, and in 1858, he was pitted against Democratic leader Stephen A. Douglas—one of the primary voices behind the Kansas-Nebraska Act—in the campaign to represent Illinois in the Senate. The now-famous seven debates in which Lincoln and Douglas engaged were particularly remarkable for their highly public nature; the telegraph, the railroad, and the greater prevalence of shorthand in journalism made possible the widespread dissemination of Lincoln's and Douglas's words even to those who could not attend the events. Slavery was the predominant topic. Lincoln, perhaps more so than any major American politician before him, insisted that the future of slavery was a moral question. Yet in the face of Douglas's accusations that he was an "abolitionist," Lincoln asserted repeatedly that he had no intention of interfering with the institution of slavery in areas where it was already established. Lincoln also repeatedly denied Douglas's allegations that he desired full political and social equality for African Americans.

The Illinois legislature awarded Douglas the Senate seat—though it was clear that, if the popular vote had determined the state's senator (as would not be the case until after the Seventeenth Amendment was enacted in 1913), Lincoln would have emerged victorious. Lincoln's impressive performance in the debates was followed by his Cooper Union address in New York City in early 1860—a long and intensely researched oration arguing (contrary to the claims of Democrats such as Douglas) that the Founders had included no clause in the Constitution that would prevent Congress from forbidding the extension of slavery. The speech's success made it clear that Lincoln was a contender for the presidency. He was nominated at the Republican Convention that spring; on November 6 he was elected as the sixteenth President (and first Republican President) of the United States.

By the time Lincoln took office in March of 1861, however, the country was in turmoil. South Carolina seceded from the Union in December 1860, and six other Southern states quickly followed; little more than a month after Lincoln's inauguration in 1861, the Civil War broke out.

As the incoming president of a broken nation, Lincoln's overriding goal was not to end slavery but to preserve the Union. His first inaugural address repeated sentiments he had expressed during the Douglas debates: "I have no purpose, directly or indirectly, to interfere with the institution of slavery in the States where it exists. I believe I have no lawful right to do so, and I have no inclination to do so." In a personal letter dated 22 August 1862, over a year after the war had begun, Lincoln wrote, "If I could save the Union without freeing any slave I would do it, and if I could save it by freeing all the slaves I would do it." As the war dragged on, however, the second of those alternatives came to the fore. On 1 January 1863 Lincoln issued the Emancipation Proclamation, an executive order declaring the freedom of all enslaved residents of the Confederacy (this did not include the enslaved in states that had not seceded: Kentucky, Missouri, Maryland, and Delaware), and inviting all emancipated men to join the Union Army. That August Lincoln met for the first time with the prominent black abolitionist Frederick Douglass to discuss the treatment of black Union soldiers. And in January 1865, the Thirteenth Amendment passed, ending slavery in all states.

The occasion for the most memorable of all Lincoln's speeches was the dedication in November 1863 before a crowd of some 15,000 people of a national cemetery at Gettysburg, Pennsylvania, which the previous summer had been the site of one of the most violent battles of the war. Lincoln followed a two-and-a-half-hour speech given by celebrated orator Edward Everett with a two-and-a-half-minute address that stunned the audience with its brevity. Everett wrote the president the next day, "I should be glad if I could flatter myself that I came as near to the central idea of the occasion, in two hours, as you did in two minutes." Lincoln's Gettysburg Address was being anthologized in texts on elocution within the next two years.

Lincoln delivered his Second Inaugural Address on 4 March 1865, as the war was nearing its end. Though the ground outside the Capitol building (with its newly completed dome) was muddy following weeks of rain, many thousands turned out to hear the President's speech. Among them was John Wilkes Booth, an actor and proslavery radical, who would assassinate Lincoln just a few weeks later. Of all Lincoln's speeches, the Second Inaugural most eloquently frames the moral crisis at the center of the Civil War; Frederick Douglass described the speech as a "sacred effort."

Less than two months after the inauguration, Lincoln was shot in the back of the head by Booth while attending a theater performance with his wife; he died the following morning. The assassination of Lincoln seemed to many a martyrdom. Walt Whitman penned four poems in memory of Lincoln, picturing him as a fallen ship's captain, a drooping star, a dear commander, and a gentle, just man. The abolitionist preacher Henry Ward Beecher, brother to Harriet Beecher Stowe, evoked the biblical narrative of Moses in his eulogy for the fallen President, claiming that Lincoln had been sent by God "to lead them [the enslaved] out of the land of bondage." The eloquent president did indeed die as slavery legally ended. However, the struggle for African American equality turned out to be very far from over.

NOTE ON THE TEXTS: The text of the speech popularly known as "A House Divided" is based on that printed in the *Chicago Tribune* for 19 June 1858; this is the version of the speech Lincoln sent to the editors of an 1860 edition of the Lincoln-Douglas debates. The version of the Gettysburg Address reproduced here (of which Lincoln wrote five drafts) is known as the Bliss copy, after Colonel Alexander Bliss. It is the only version to have been signed and dated by Lincoln, and it is also the version etched into the wall of the Lincoln Memorial. The text of the Second Inaugural Address is based on the handwritten manuscript, which is thought to have been the copy used by Lincoln when he delivered the speech; scans of this manuscript are available online through the Library of Congress. Spelling and punctuation have been lightly modernized.

⌘ ⌘ ⌘

from *Speech delivered at the Republican State Convention in Springfield, Illinois* [*"A House Divided"*]

The speech excerpted below, popularly known as the "House Divided" speech for the biblical metaphor used in its opening lines, is often considered to have initiated the famous Lincoln-Douglas debates. It was delivered immediately following Lincoln's nomination by the Illinois Republican Party for the position of state senator, against incumbent Democratic senator Stephen A. Douglas. Both Lincoln and Douglas referred back to the ideas of the "House Divided" speech several times over the course of their series of debates.

If we could first know where we are, and whither we are tending, we could better judge what to do, and how to do it. We are now far into the fifth year, since a policy was initiated with the avowed object, and confident promise, of putting an end to slavery agitation.[1] Under the operation of that policy, that agitation has not only not ceased, but has constantly augmented. In my opinion, it will not cease, until a crisis shall have been reached and passed. "A house divided against itself cannot stand."[2] I believe this government cannot endure permanently half slave and half free. I do not expect the Union to be dissolved—I do not expect the house to fall—but I do expect it will cease to be divided. It will become all one thing, or all the other. Either the opponents of slavery will arrest the further spread of it, and place it where the public mind shall rest in the belief that it is in the course of ultimate extinction; or its advocates will push it forward, till it shall become alike lawful in all the States, old as well as new—North as well as South.

Have we no tendency to the latter condition?

Let anyone who doubts, carefully contemplate that now almost complete legal combination—piece of machinery so to speak—compounded of the Nebraska doctrine, and the Dred Scott decision.[3] ...

... Put this and that together, and we have another nice little niche, which we may, ere long, see filled with another Supreme Court decision, declaring that the Constitution of the United States does not permit a *State* to exclude slavery from its limits. And this may especially be expected if the doctrine of "care not whether slavery be voted down or voted up"[4] shall gain

---

[1] *a policy ... slavery agitation* Lincoln refers to the Kansas-Nebraska Act of May 1854, which had been drafted by Stephen Douglas; it repealed the Missouri Compromise and allowed new states to determine by popular vote whether or not they would allow slavery. To the surprise of Douglas, President Franklin Pierce, and other supporters of the Act, it had virtually the opposite effect to ending the national debate over slavery, and led to the period of violence between proslavery and antislavery agitators popularly known as "Bleeding Kansas."

[2] *A house ... cannot stand* See Mark 3.25: "And if a house be divided against itself, that house cannot stand."

[3] *Dred Scott decision* 1857 Supreme Court decision in which it was declared that persons of African descent, whether free or enslaved, could not be considered American citizens, and thereby had no legal standing in court. The decision came after the formerly enslaved Dred Scott attempted to secure the court's further confirmation of his freedom so that the children of his deceased former owner could not claim inherited ownership of Scott's daughters.

[4] *care not ... voted up* Statement made in a speech by Stephen Douglas referring to his support of popular sovereignty on the question of slavery as Kansas sought to enter the Union.

upon the public mind sufficiently to give promise that such a decision can be maintained when made.

Such a decision is all that slavery now lacks of being alike lawful in all the States. Welcome or unwelcome, such decision is probably coming, and will soon be upon us, unless the power of the present political dynasty shall be met and overthrown. We shall lie down pleasantly dreaming that the people of Missouri are on the verge of making their State free, and we shall awake to the reality, instead, that the Supreme Court has made Illinois a slave state. To meet and overthrow the power of that dynasty, is the work now before all those who would prevent that consummation. That is what we have to do. ...

... Two years ago the Republicans of the nation mustered over thirteen hundred thousand strong. We did this under the single impulse of resistance to a common danger, with every external circumstance against us. Of strange, discordant, and even hostile elements, we gathered from the four winds, and formed and fought the battle through, under the constant hot fire of a disciplined, proud and pampered enemy. Did we brave all them to falter now? now, when that same enemy is wavering, dissevered and belligerent? The result is not doubtful. We shall not fail—if we stand firm, we *shall not fail*. Wise counsels may accelerate, or mistake delay it, but, sooner or later, the victory is sure to come. —1858

The "Bliss copy" of the Gettysburg Address. This is the last known version of the speech written in Lincoln's hand, and the only one that bears his signature

Address Delivered at the Dedication of the Cemetery at Gettysburg

Four score and seven years ago our fathers brought forth on this continent, a new nation, conceived in Liberty, and dedicated to the proposition that all men are created equal.

Now we are engaged in a great civil war, testing whether that nation, or any nation so conceived and so dedicated, can long endure. We are met on a great battle-field of that war. We have come to dedicate a portion of that field, as a final resting place for those who here gave their lives, that that nation might live. It is altogether fitting and proper that we should do this.

But, in a larger sense, we cannot dedicate—we cannot consecrate—we cannot hallow—this ground. The brave men, living and dead, who struggled here, have consecrated it, far above our poor power to add or detract. The world will little note, nor long remember what we say here, but it can never forget what they did here. It is for us the living, rather, to be dedicated here to the unfinished work which they who fought here have thus far so nobly advanced. It is rather for us to be here dedicated to the great task remaining before us—that from these honored dead we take increased devotion to that cause for which they gave the last full measure of devotion—that we here highly resolve that these dead shall not have died in vain—that this nation, under God, shall have a new birth of freedom—and that government of the people, by the people, for the people, shall not perish from the earth.

—1863

Second Inaugural Address

Fellow-Countrymen:

At this second appearing to take the oath of the presidential office, there is less occasion for an extended address than there was at the first.[1] Then a statement, somewhat in detail, of a course to be pursued, seemed fitting and proper. Now, at the expiration of four years, during which public declarations have been constantly called forth on every point and phase of the great contest which still absorbs the attention, and engrosses the energies of the nation, little that is new could be presented. The progress of our arms,[2] upon which all else chiefly depends, is as well known to the public as to myself; and it is, I trust, reasonably satisfactory and encouraging to all. With high hope for the future, no prediction in regard to it is ventured.

On the occasion corresponding to this four years ago, all thoughts were anxiously directed to an impending civil war. All dreaded it—all sought to avert it. While the inaugural address was being delivered from this place, devoted altogether to *saving* the Union without war, insurgent agents[3] were in the city seeking to *destroy* it without war—seeking to dissolve the Union, and divide effects,[4] by negotiation. Both parties deprecated war;[5] but one of them would *make* war rather than let the nation survive; and the other would *accept* war rather than let it perish. And the war came.

One eighth of the whole population were colored slaves, not distributed generally over the Union, but localized in the Southern part of it. These slaves constituted a peculiar and powerful interest. All knew that this interest was, somehow, the cause of the war. To strengthen, perpetuate, and extend this interest was the object for which the insurgents would rend the Union,

---

[1] *less occasion … the first* Lincoln's first inaugural address, delivered on 4 March 1861, was, at over three-and-a-half thousand words, far longer than the second one; it is included in full in the website component of this anthology.

[2] *of our arms* Of the Union forces in the Civil War.

[3] *insurgent agents* Representatives attempting to undermine the government.

[4] *effects* Possessions (of the United States as a whole).

[5] *Both parties deprecated war* Both Northerners and Southerners expressed their disapproval of the idea of going to war.

Photograph taken at the United States Capitol during the delivery of Lincoln's Second Inaugural Address, by the Scottish-American photographer Alexander Gardner; Lincoln can be seen at the center of the photograph with the manuscript of his speech in hand.

even by war, while the government claimed no right to do more than to restrict the territorial enlargement of it. Neither party expected for the war, the magnitude, or the duration, which it has already attained. Neither anticipated that the *cause* of the conflict might cease with, or even before, the conflict itself should cease. Each looked for an easier triumph, and a result less fundamental and astounding. Both read the same Bible, and pray to the same God; and each invokes His aid against the other. It may seem strange that any men should dare to ask a just God's assistance in wringing their bread from the sweat of other men's faces; but let us judge not that we be not judged.[1] The prayers of both could not be answered; that of neither has been answered fully. The Almighty has His own purposes. "Woe unto the world because of offences! for it must needs be that offences come; but woe to that man by whom the offence cometh!"[2] If we shall suppose that American slavery is one of those offenses which, in the providence of God, must needs come, but which, having continued through His appointed time, He now wills to remove, and that He gives to both North and South this terrible war, as the woe due to those by whom the offence came, shall we discern therein any departure from those divine attributes which the believers in a living God always ascribe to Him? Fondly do we hope—fervently do we pray—that this mighty scourge of war may speedily pass away. Yet, if God wills that it continue, until all the wealth piled by the bondsman's two hundred and fifty years of unrequited toil shall be sunk, and until every drop of blood drawn with the lash, shall be paid by another drawn with the sword, as was said three thousand years ago, so still it must be said "the judgments of the Lord, are true and righteous altogether."[3]

With malice toward none; with charity for all; with firmness in the right, as God gives us to see the right, let us strive on to finish the work we are in; to bind up the nation's wounds; to care for him who shall have borne the battle, and for his widow, and his orphan—to do all which may achieve and cherish a just and a lasting peace, among ourselves, and with all nations. —1865

---

[1]   *let us ... not judged*   See Matthew 7.1.

[2]   *Woe unto ... cometh*   See Matthew 18.7.

[3]   *the judgments ... altogether*   See Psalm 9.19.

EDGAR ALLAN POE
1809 – 1849

Edgar Allan Poe is a legendary figure in popular culture, a writer famous for his alienation, his madness and substance abuse, and his mastery of eerie and gruesome tales. Poe broadened, through his critical writings as well as through the example of his own fiction, the expressive powers of the American short story. Yet, during his own lifetime, he barely scraped by on his earnings as a writer and rarely experienced more than modest popular success. What renown he did earn prior to his death rested largely on his work as a literary critic; in 1845 poet James Russell Lowell called him "the most discriminating, philosophical, and fearless critic upon imaginative works who has written in America." In the years following his death, however, his fiction and poetry found enthusiastic adherents (as well as detractors), and his influence on literature and popular culture ever since has been profound: he is widely considered an originator of the detective story, wrote several pioneering tales of science fiction, and penned some of the most evocative and disturbing tales of the supernatural and macabre to be found in nineteenth-century literature.

Edgar Poe was born in Boston in 1809 to itinerant stage actors Elizabeth Arnold and David Poe, but after his father left the family and his mother died, Poe was brought up by John and Frances Allan, a wealthy Virginian merchant couple. Poe spent most of his childhood in Richmond, Virginia, but the family also lived in London for a few years. He entered the University of Virginia in 1826, where he excelled academically, though numerous letters sent home reveal Poe's distress at John Allan's inadequate financial support, which at times left Poe seriously impoverished. He also fell into the institution's rampant drinking and gambling culture, incurring significant debts. After intense quarreling with Allan, who cut him off financially, Poe left the university after one year and departed Richmond for Boston.

It is unclear when exactly Poe began writing seriously, but by 1827 he had composed enough poems to make up a short volume. His first published collections, *Tamerlane and Other Poems* (1827, published anonymously) and its expanded edition, *Al Aaraaf, Tamerlane, and Minor Poems* (1829), were virtually ignored by critics and were acknowledged by Poe himself to be of generally indifferent quality. Already evident in this early work, however, is Poe's debt to German and British Romanticism—particularly to the work of Lord Byron and Thomas Moore—and to such poets' fascination with the art and culture of the Middle East. Poe achieved slightly more critical (but not popular) success with his third collection, *Poems by Edgar A. Poe* (1831). Many of these poems reflect their author's increasing preoccupation with the theme of death—especially that of a beloved or beautiful woman, which he would later describe as "the most poetical topic in the world." After the financial failure of *Poems*, Poe began to experiment with the short story, publishing his first tale in 1832.

Poe was one of the first Americans to live solely, and precariously, on the profits of his writing, and he considered himself a "magazinist," contributing fiction, poetry, and criticism to periodicals as well as taking on editorial roles. By mid-decade Poe was working as an editorial assistant at the *Southern Literary Messenger* back in Richmond, while also continuing to contribute poems and stories to various journals and annual gift books. Over the course of his career, Poe worked for several magazines and earned a good deal of both respect and notoriety for his literary reviews. Frustrated by an American reviewing practice that he saw as overly moralizing and didactic, Poe advocated a rigorously analytical practice. Indeed, he believed that his role as a critic meant exposing bad writing, and his ruthless reviews sparked notoriously combative relationships with many of his contemporaries. Among them were many intellectual figures from New England, a region which Poe saw as disproportionately represented in literary media and whose most prominent authors—among them Emerson, Longfellow, and Whittier—he often dismissed as unimaginative and overly regional in their literary vision. Poe sometimes used his critical platform to praise the works of other Southerners whom he saw as unjustly overlooked by the New England literary establishment, such as William Gilmore Simms—whose "Murder Will Out" Poe called the "best ghost-story ever written by an American"—Philip Pendleton Cooke, and John Pendleton Kennedy.

In 1836, Poe moved to Baltimore and married his first cousin, Virginia Clemm, who was then only thirteen years old—though on their marriage certificate her age was given as twenty-one (closer to the average age of a bride in the nineteenth century). Virginia was passionately devoted to Poe, who claimed to love her "as no man ever loved before." The ongoing threat of severe poverty, however, posed difficulties, as did Poe's continuing struggles with depression and alcohol abuse and Virginia's failing health due to tuberculosis, of which she died in 1847. In popular accounts of Poe's life, Virginia's early death is often framed as precipitating a decline into alcoholism and madness, and as inspiring the macabre content for which he is famous; in fact, he had already written his best-known Gothic pieces before she died, and while he grieved her loss deeply, he was in the midst of planning a second marriage at the time of his own death less than three years after hers.

Unable to find a publisher interested in a collection of his short stories, Poe turned to the more popular novel form, and managed to secure the publication of *The Narrative of Arthur Gordon Pym of Nantucket* in 1838. The short novel—whose protagonist was dubbed "the American Robinson Crusoe" by a London reviewer—owed much to the genre of the sea tale (popularized by New York writer James Fenimore Cooper) as well as to the travel literature then popular. Today, the novel is deemed by some to be among Poe's best works; it also, however, gives expression to the racist views that Poe held throughout his life. John Allan's business relied on enslaved people for its operation, and at eighteen Poe expressed to his father outrage at being subjected to the "authority of the blacks" in the household. Poe rarely stated opinions on slavery directly in his writing, but as a critic he disparaged abolitionist works for their "fanaticism" and "misrepresentation" of how the enslaved were treated. Relatively few scholars drew attention to Poe's racism until the 1980s, when it became a focus of academic discussion; interest in Poe's treatment of race intensified in 1993, when Toni Morrison argued that Poe had been instrumental in developing white American ideas of blackness. Following Morrison, many scholars have been less interested in determining the extent of Poe's personal racism than in considering what Poe's depictions of servile black characters, racialized monsters, and tyrannical white oppressors suggest about white American anxieties surrounding blackness and slavery.

In 1840 Poe published *Tales of the Grotesque and Arabesque*, a short-story collection that, like so much of his earlier work, sold poorly but was critically well received. Many of Poe's most famous stories were released either in this collection or in periodicals over the next few years, during which he wrote comic and satirical tales as well as the dark, Gothic, and horror-inducing fiction he would come to be most strongly associated with. Poe's dark humor—his delight in hoaxes, word play, and subversive mockery—is present, to varying degrees, in much of his work. His remarkably influential series of mystery stories, featuring the detective C. Auguste Dupin, initiated the trope of the crime-solving protagonist who uses painstaking rational inquiry to solve complex or dramatic crimes. Stories such as Poe's "The Fall of the House of Usher" (1839)—with its ruined manor house, gloomy landscape, and a psychologically tortured character—build on the late eighteenth-century Gothic tradition developed by writers such as Ann Radcliffe. Though such Gothic elements were mainly drawn from British and other European literature, Poe also had American predecessors and contemporaries, including Charles Brockden Brown, William Dunlap, and James Kirke. He was also influenced by the African American ghost stories he heard as a child from the enslaved woman, Judith or Juliet (the record is unclear), who helped raise him in the Allan household.

Poe's greatest success in his lifetime was "The Raven" (1845), a poem whose speaker is a psychologically tortured student grieving the loss of his beloved. The poem was reprinted widely in both the United States and Britain; among its many enthusiastic readers was poet Elizabeth Barrett Browning, who wrote that it had "produced a sensation, a 'fit of horror,' here in England." Following up on the poem's popularity, Poe wrote "The Philosophy of Composition," which professed to detail his writing process. By his account, "The Raven" appears to have been a culmination of all his artistic aims; Poe claimed to value "unity of impression" (a work should ideally be short enough to be read in one sitting), a near-mathematical degree of attention to aesthetic and compositional detail, and the evocation of pleasure and beauty rather than of realism or truth. Due to ineffective copyright laws, "The Raven" earned Poe little money, leaving him and his wife as deeply in poverty as ever.

In 1848, Poe published the prose poem *Eureka*, a work in which he put forward his intuitive understanding of "the material and spiritual universe"; audiences were largely bewildered by the book's mysticism, though Poe himself claimed it was his most important work. In October of the following year, Poe was found delirious in Baltimore. He died in a hospital a few days later; the cause of his death remains unclear. Poe's character was torn apart in a scathing *New York Tribune* obituary, in which literary critic Rufus Griswold described him as a "naturally unamiable" cynic who "walked the streets, in madness or melancholy, with lips moving in indistinct curses." Griswold wrote a further memoir about Poe that emphasized his alcoholism and dishonesty, though even he had to acknowledge Poe's force of character, reporting that his conversation was "supra-mortal in its eloquence." For decades, controversy surrounded Poe's character, and many interpreted his tales of horror and melancholy as direct reflections of his own psyche.

Poe's work, however, became increasingly renowned in Europe—and especially in France, where the poet Charles Baudelaire translated much of his work in the mid-nineteenth century. The French Symbolists were heavily influenced by Poe, as were writers in the Aesthetic movement, whose motto "Art for Art's Sake" had been anticipated by Poe in a posthumously published essay, "The Poetic Principle" (1850), in which he praises the nobility of a "poem written solely for the poem's sake." The Anglo-American literary scene was slower to warm up to Poe, but in these countries, too, his influence grew. American authors from H.P. Lovecraft and Shirley Jackson to Richard Wright were indebted to Poe's legacy, as was the film director Alfred Hitchcock. In England, Sir Arthur Conan Doyle acknowledged Poe as a key precursor for his Sherlock Holmes tales: "Where was the detective story until Poe breathed the breath of life into it?" Indeed, the genres of detective fiction, horror fiction, and science fiction all find in Poe a significant influence, as do related genres in film and television. While Poe's work continues to find detractors and skeptics, the balance over the last hundred years has swung decidedly in his favor, and his stories, poems, and essays continue to be read and reinterpreted by both literary critics and a wide general readership.

NOTE ON THE TEXTS: Poe often revised his stories and poems, particularly as he prepared for book publication works that had originally appeared in periodicals. Texts reprinted in this anthology are based upon his latest authorized versions, as these include his corrections and additions. The texts of "The Tell-Tale Heart," "The Imp of the Perverse," and "Hop-Frog" are based upon the versions printed in Griswold's 1850–56 four-volume edition, *The Works of the Late Edgar Allan Poe*. The texts of "The Fall of the House of Usher," "The Man of the Crowd," and "The Murders in the Rue Morgue" are based upon the versions appearing in the 1845 *Tales by Edgar Allan Poe*. The text of "Sonnet—To Science" is based upon that published in *The Raven and Other Poems* (1845). The version of "The Raven" reprinted here is based upon the text that appeared in the *Richmond Semi-Weekly Examiner* on 25 September 1849, and "The Philosophy of Composition" is based on the version printed in *Graham's Magazine* in 1846. For "Annabel Lee," the editors have consulted the "Griswold" manuscript, the version Poe sent to his editor in May 1849. Unless otherwise noted, spelling and punctuation have been modernized in accordance with the practices of this anthology.

⌘⌘⌘

Sonnet—To Science

Science! true daughter of Old Time thou art!
   Who alterest all things with thy peering eyes.
Why preyest thou thus upon the poet's heart,
      Vulture,[1] whose wings are dull realities?
5 How should he love thee? or how deem thee wise?
      Who wouldst not leave him in his wandering
To seek for treasure in the jewelled skies,
      Albeit he soared with an undaunted wing?[2]
Hast thou not dragged Diana[3] from her car?
10   And driven the Hamadryad[4] from the wood
To seek a shelter in some happier star?
      Hast thou not torn the Naiad[5] from her flood,
The Elfin[6] from the green grass, and from me
The summer dream beneath the tamarind tree?
—1829

---

[1] *Why preyest … Vulture* Allusion to Prometheus, a Greek mythical figure who stole fire from the gods to give to humankind; for this, his punishment was to be chained to a rock while a vulture (in some versions, an eagle) devoured his liver each day.

[2] *Albeit … wing* Allusion to the Greek myth of Icarus, a young man who flew using wings made from wax. When he ascended too close to the sun, the wax melted, and Icarus fell to his death.

[3] *Diana* Roman goddess of chastity, childbirth, wilderness, and the hunt. As she is here, she is often equated with the moon goddess Selene, who rides a chariot across the sky.

[4] *Hamadryad* In Greek mythology, a nymph whose life is bound to a tree.

[5] *Naiad* Nymph associated with small bodies of water such as streams or springs.

[6] *Elfin* I.e., elf.

The Fall of the House of Usher

Son coeur est un luth suspendu;
Sitôt qu'on le touche il résonne.[7]
            De Béranger.

During the whole of a dull, dark, and soundless day in the autumn of the year, when the clouds hung oppressively low in the heavens, I had been passing alone, on horseback, through a singularly dreary tract of country; and at length found myself, as the shades of the evening drew on, within view of the melancholy House of Usher. I know not how it was—but, with the first glimpse of the building, a sense of insufferable gloom pervaded my spirit. I say insufferable; for the feeling was unrelieved by any of that half-pleasurable, because poetic, sentiment, with which the mind usually receives even the sternest natural images of the desolate or terrible. I looked upon the scene before me—upon the mere house, and the simple landscape features of the domain—upon the bleak walls—upon the vacant eye-like windows—upon a few rank sedges—and upon a few white trunks of decayed trees—with an utter depression of soul which I can compare to no earthly sensation more properly than to the after-dream of the reveller upon opium—the bitter lapse into every-day life—the hideous dropping off of the veil. There was an iciness, a sinking, a sickening of the heart—an unredeemed dreariness of thought which no goading of the imagination could torture into aught of the sublime. What was it—I paused to think—what was it that so unnerved me in the contemplation of the House of Usher? It was a mystery all insoluble; nor could I grapple with the shadowy fancies that crowded upon me as I pondered. I was forced to fall back upon the unsatisfactory conclusion, that while, beyond doubt, there *are* combinations of very simple natural objects which have the power of thus affecting us, still the analysis of this power lies among considerations beyond our depth. It was possible, I reflected, that a mere different arrangement of the particulars of the scene, of the details of the picture, would be sufficient to modify, or

---

[7] *Son coeur … résonne* French: His or her heart is a suspended lute; it resounds as soon as it is touched. The quotation is slightly altered from Pierre Jean de Béranger's song "Le Refus" (1830).

perhaps to annihilate its capacity for sorrowful impression; and, acting upon this idea, I reined my horse to the precipitous brink of a black and lurid tarn[1] that lay in unruffled lustre by the dwelling, and gazed down—but with a shudder even more thrilling than before—upon the re-modelled and inverted images of the gray sedge, and the ghastly tree-stems, and the vacant and eye-like windows.

Nevertheless, in this mansion of gloom I now proposed to myself a sojourn of some weeks. Its proprietor, Roderick Usher, had been one of my boon companions in boyhood; but many years had elapsed since our last meeting. A letter, however, had lately reached me in a distant part of the country—a letter from him—which, in its wildly importunate nature, had admitted of no other than a personal reply. The MS.[2] gave evidence of nervous agitation. The writer spoke of acute bodily illness—of a mental disorder which oppressed him—and of an earnest desire to see me, as his best, and indeed his only personal friend, with a view of attempting, by the cheerfulness of my society, some alleviation of his malady. It was the manner in which all this, and much more, was said—it was the apparent *heart* that went with his request—which allowed me no room for hesitation; and I accordingly obeyed forthwith what I still considered a very singular summons.

Although, as boys, we had been even intimate associates, yet I really knew little of my friend. His reserve had been always excessive and habitual. I was aware, however, that his very ancient family had been noted, time out of mind, for a peculiar sensibility of temperament, displaying itself, through long ages, in many works of exalted art, and manifested, of late, in repeated deeds of munificent yet unobtrusive charity, as well as in a passionate devotion to the intricacies, perhaps even more than to the orthodox and easily recognizable beauties, of musical science. I had learned, too, the very remarkable fact, that the stem of the Usher race, all time-honored as it was, had put forth, at no period, any enduring branch; in other words, that the entire family lay in the direct line of descent, and had always, with very trifling and very temporary variation, so lain. It was this deficiency, I considered, while running over in thought the perfect keeping

of the character of the premises with the accredited character of the people, and while speculating upon the possible influence which the one, in the long lapse of centuries, might have exercised upon the other—it was this deficiency, perhaps, of collateral issue,[3] and the consequent undeviating transmission, from sire to son, of the patrimony with the name, which had, at length, so identified the two as to merge the original title of the estate in the quaint and equivocal appellation of the "House of Usher"—an appellation which seemed to include, in the minds of the peasantry who used it, both the family and the family mansion.

I have said that the sole effect of my somewhat childish experiment—of looking down within the tarn—had been to deepen the first singular impression. There can be no doubt that the consciousness of the rapid increase of my superstition—for why should I not so term it?—served mainly to accelerate the increase itself. Such, I have long known, is the paradoxical law of all sentiments having terror as a basis. And it might have been for this reason only, that, when I again uplifted my eyes to the house itself, from its image in the pool, there grew in my mind a strange fancy—a fancy so ridiculous, indeed, that I but mention it to show the vivid force of the sensations which oppressed me. I had so worked upon my imagination as really to believe that about the whole mansion and domain there hung an atmosphere peculiar to themselves and their immediate vicinity—an atmosphere which had no affinity with the air of heaven, but which had reeked up from the decayed trees, and the gray wall, and the silent tarn—a pestilent and mystic vapor, dull, sluggish, faintly discernible, and leaden-hued.

Shaking off from my spirit what *must* have been a dream, I scanned more narrowly the real aspect[4] of the building. Its principal feature seemed to be that of an excessive antiquity. The discoloration of ages had been great. Minute fungi overspread the whole exterior, hanging in a fine tangled web-work from the eaves. Yet all this was apart from any extraordinary dilapidation. No portion of the masonry had fallen; and there appeared to be a wild inconsistency between its still perfect adaptation of parts, and the crumbling

---

[1] *tarn* Small mountain lake.

[2] *MS.* Manuscript; also, handwriting.

[3] *collateral issue* Blood relatives outside the direct line of descent, i.e., siblings, cousins, aunts, uncles, etc.

[4] *aspect* Physical appearance.

condition of the individual stones. In this there was much that reminded me of the specious totality of old wood-work which has rotted for long years in some neglected vault, with no disturbance from the breath of the external air. Beyond this indication of extensive decay, however, the fabric[1] gave little token of instability. Perhaps the eye of a scrutinizing observer might have discovered a barely perceptible fissure, which, extending from the roof of the building in front, made its way down the wall in a zig-zag direction, until it became lost in the sullen waters of the tarn.

Noticing these things, I rode over a short causeway to the house. A servant in waiting took my horse, and I entered the Gothic archway of the hall. A valet,[2] of stealthy step, thence conducted me, in silence, through many dark and intricate passages in my progress to the *studio* of his master. Much that I encountered on the way contributed, I know not how, to heighten the vague sentiments of which I have already spoken. While the objects around me—while the carvings of the ceilings, the sombre tapestries of the walls, the ebon blackness of the floors, and the phantasmagoric[3] armorial trophies which rattled as I strode, were but matters to which, or to such as which, I had been accustomed from my infancy—while I hesitated not to acknowledge how familiar was all this—I still wondered to find how unfamiliar were the fancies which ordinary images were stirring up. On one of the staircases, I met the physician of the family. His countenance, I thought, wore a mingled expression of low cunning and perplexity. He accosted me with trepidation and passed on. The valet now threw open a door and ushered me into the presence of his master.

The room in which I found myself was very large and lofty. The windows were long, narrow, and pointed, and at so vast a distance from the black oaken floor as to be altogether inaccessible from within. Feeble gleams of encrimsoned light made their way through the trellissed panes,[4] and served to render sufficiently distinct the more prominent objects around; the eye, however, struggled in vain to reach the remoter angles of the chamber, or the recesses of the vaulted and fretted ceiling. Dark draperies hung upon the walls. The general furniture was profuse, comfortless, antique, and tattered. Many books and musical instruments lay scattered about, but failed to give any vitality to the scene. I felt that I breathed an atmosphere of sorrow. An air of stern, deep, and irredeemable gloom hung over and pervaded all.

Upon my entrance, Usher rose from a sofa upon which he had been lying at full length, and greeted me with a vivacious warmth which had much in it, I at first thought, of an overdone cordiality—of the constrained effort of the *ennuyé*[5] man of the world. A glance, however, at his countenance convinced me of his perfect sincerity. We sat down; and for some moments, while he spoke not, I gazed upon him with a feeling half of pity, half of awe. Surely, man had never before so terribly altered, in so brief a period, as had Roderick Usher! It was with difficulty that I could bring myself to admit the identity of the wan[6] being before me with the companion of my early boyhood. Yet the character of his face had been at all times remarkable. A cadaverousness of complexion; an eye large, liquid, and luminous beyond comparison; lips somewhat thin and very pallid, but of a surpassingly beautiful curve; a nose of a delicate Hebrew model, but with a breadth of nostril unusual in similar formations; a finely moulded chin, speaking, in its want of prominence, of a want of moral energy; hair of a more than web-like softness and tenuity; these features, with an inordinate expansion above the regions of the temple,[7] made up altogether a countenance not easily to be forgotten. And now in the mere exaggeration of the prevailing character of these features, and of the expression they were wont to

---

1   *fabric*   Frame of the building.

2   *valet*   Gentleman's servant.

3   *phantasmagoric*   Illusory, continuously transforming; here the word describes optical illusions created by the reflection of light off metal, in this case off armor or weaponry that is displayed on the walls of the house.

4   *trellissed panes*   Gothic-style windows with tracery—decorative stonework that keeps the glass in place.

5   *ennuyé*   French: bored.

6   *wan*   Pale and sickly.

7   *inordinate expansion ... temple*   In the pseudoscience of phrenology, according to which the shape of one's skull indicates one's personality traits, a person whose skull is enlarged above the temple is particularly strong in the trait of "ideality" (i.e., imagination, especially the capacity to imagine and appreciate perfection).

convey, lay so much of change that I doubted to whom I spoke. The now ghastly pallor of the skin, and the now miraculous lustre of the eye, above all things startled and even awed me. The silken hair, too, had been suffered to grow all unheeded, and as, in its wild gossamer texture, it floated rather than fell about the face, I could not, even with effort, connect its Arabesque[1] expression with any idea of simple humanity.

In the manner of my friend I was at once struck with an incoherence—an inconsistency; and I soon found this to arise from a series of feeble and futile struggles to overcome an habitual trepidancy—an excessive nervous agitation. For something of this nature I had indeed been prepared, no less by his letter, than by reminiscences of certain boyish traits, and by conclusions deduced from his peculiar physical conformation and temperament. His action was alternately vivacious and sullen. His voice varied rapidly from a tremulous indecision (when the animal spirits seemed utterly in abeyance) to that species of energetic concision—that abrupt, weighty, unhurried, and hollow-sounding enunciation—that leaden, self-balanced and perfectly modulated guttural utterance, which may be observed in the lost drunkard, or the irreclaimable eater of opium, during the periods of his most intense excitement.

It was thus that he spoke of the object of my visit, of his earnest desire to see me, and of the solace he expected me to afford him. He entered, at some length, into what he conceived to be the nature of his malady. It was, he said, a constitutional and a family evil, and one for which he despaired to find a remedy—a mere nervous affection, he immediately added, which would undoubtedly soon pass off. It displayed itself in a host of unnatural sensations. Some of these, as he detailed them, interested and bewildered me; although, perhaps, the terms, and the general manner of the narration had their weight. He suffered much from a morbid acuteness of the senses; the most insipid food was alone endurable; he could wear only garments of certain texture; the odors of all flowers were oppressive; his eyes were tortured by even a faint light; and there were but peculiar sounds, and these from stringed instruments, which did not inspire him with horror.

To an anomalous species of terror I found him a bounden slave. "I shall perish," said he, "I *must* perish in this deplorable folly. Thus, thus, and not otherwise, shall I be lost. I dread the events of the future, not in themselves, but in their results. I shudder at the thought of any, even the most trivial, incident, which may operate upon this intolerable agitation of soul. I have, indeed, no abhorrence of danger, except in its absolute effect—in terror. In this unnerved—in this pitiable condition—I feel that the period will sooner or later arrive when I must abandon life and reason together, in some struggle with the grim phantasm, FEAR."

I learned, moreover, at intervals, and through broken and equivocal hints, another singular feature of his mental condition. He was enchained by certain superstitious impressions in regard to the dwelling which he tenanted, and whence, for many years, he had never ventured forth—in regard to an influence whose supposititious force was conveyed in terms too shadowy here to be re-stated—an influence which some peculiarities in the mere form and substance of his family mansion, had, by dint of long sufferance, he said, obtained over his spirit—an effect which the *physique* of the gray walls and turrets, and of the dim tarn into which they all looked down, had, at length, brought about upon the *morale* of his existence.

He admitted, however, although with hesitation, that much of the peculiar gloom which thus afflicted him could be traced to a more natural and far more palpable origin—to the severe and long-continued illness—indeed to the evidently approaching dissolution—of a tenderly beloved sister—his sole companion for long years—his last and only relative on earth. "Her decease," he said, with a bitterness which I can never forget, "would leave him (him the hopeless and the frail) the last of the ancient race of the Ushers." While he spoke, the lady Madeline (for so was she called) passed slowly through a remote portion of the apartment, and, without having noticed my presence, disappeared. I regarded her with an utter astonishment not unmingled with dread—and yet I found it impossible to account for such feelings. A sensation of stupor oppressed me, as my eyes followed her retreating steps.

---

[1]   *Arabesque*   Ornate, especially with a complex interweaving pattern; the term can also refer to things perceived to possess "Arabian" qualities.

When a door, at length, closed upon her, my glance sought instinctively and eagerly the countenance of the brother—but he had buried his face in his hands, and I could only perceive that a far more than ordinary wanness had overspread the emaciated fingers through which trickled many passionate tears.

The disease of the lady Madeline had long baffled the skill of her physicians. A settled apathy, a gradual wasting away of the person, and frequent although transient affections of a partially cataleptical character,[1] were the unusual diagnosis. Hitherto she had steadily borne up against the pressure of her malady, and had not betaken herself finally to bed; but, on the closing in of the evening of my arrival at the house, she succumbed (as her brother told me at night with inexpressible agitation) to the prostrating power of the destroyer; and I learned that the glimpse I had obtained of her person would thus probably be the last I should obtain—that the lady, at least while living, would be seen by me no more.

For several days ensuing, her name was unmentioned by either Usher or myself; and, during this period I was busied in earnest endeavors to alleviate the melancholy of my friend. We painted and read together; or I listened, as if in a dream, to the wild improvisations of his speaking guitar. And thus, as a closer and still closer intimacy admitted me more unreservedly into the recesses of his spirit, the more bitterly did I perceive the futility of all attempt at cheering a mind from which darkness, as if an inherent positive quality, poured forth upon all objects of the moral and physical universe, in one unceasing radiation of gloom.

I shall ever bear about me a memory of the many solemn hours I thus spent alone with the master of the House of Usher. Yet I should fail in any attempt to convey an idea of the exact character of the studies, or of the occupations, in which he involved me, or led me the way. An excited and highly distempered ideality threw a sulphureous[2] lustre over all. His long improvised dirges[3] will ring for ever in my ears. Among other things, I bear painfully in mind a certain singular

perversion and amplification of the wild air of the last waltz of Von Weber.[4] From the paintings over which his elaborate fancy brooded, and which grew, touch by touch, into vaguenesses at which I shuddered the more thrillingly, because I shuddered knowing not why—from these paintings (vivid as their images now are before me) I would in vain endeavor to educe[5] more than a small portion which should lie within the compass of merely written words. By the utter simplicity, by the nakedness, of his designs, he arrested and overawed attention. If ever mortal painted an idea, that mortal was Roderick Usher. For me at least—in the circumstances then surrounding me—there arose out of the pure abstractions which the hypochondriac contrived to throw upon his canvass, an intensity of intolerable awe, no shadow of which felt I ever yet in the contemplation of the certainly glowing yet too concrete reveries of Fuseli.[6]

One of the phantasmagoric conceptions of my friend, partaking not so rigidly of the spirit of abstraction, may be shadowed forth, although feebly, in words. A small picture presented the interior of an immensely long and rectangular vault or tunnel, with low walls, smooth, white, and without interruption or device.[7] Certain accessory points of the design served well to convey the idea that this excavation lay at an exceeding depth below the surface of the earth. No outlet was observed in any portion of its vast extent, and no torch, or other artificial source of light was discernible; yet a flood of intense rays rolled throughout, and bathed the whole in a ghastly and inappropriate splendor.

I have just spoken of that morbid condition of the auditory nerve which rendered all music intolerable to the sufferer, with the exception of certain effects of stringed instruments. It was, perhaps, the narrow limits to which he thus confined himself upon the guitar, which gave birth, in great measure, to the fantastic character of his performances. But the fervid

---

[1] *affections ... cataleptical character* Medical complaints that involve loss of consciousness, such as fainting spells, trances, and seizures.

[2] *sulphureous* I.e., smoky, unclear; also, more figuratively, hellish.

[3] *dirges* Somber, funereal songs.

[4] *Von Weber* Carl Maria von Weber (1786–1826) German Romantic composer, to whom "Von Weber's Last Waltz" was long attributed; the piece was in fact composed by Carl Gottlieb Reissiger (1798–1859).

[5] *educe* Draw out; come up with.

[6] *Fuseli* Swiss painter Henry Fuseli (1741–1825), known for depictions of dark, Gothic, and supernatural subjects.

[7] *device* Design; carving or other decoration.

facility of his *impromptus* could not be so accounted for. They must have been, and were, in the notes, as well as in the words of his wild fantasias (for he not unfrequently accompanied himself with rhymed verbal improvisations), the result of that intense mental collectedness and concentration to which I have previously alluded as observable only in particular moments of the highest artificial excitement. The words of one of these rhapsodies I have easily remembered. I was, perhaps, the more forcibly impressed with it, as he gave it, because, in the under or mystic current of its meaning, I fancied that I perceived, and for the first time, a full consciousness on the part of Usher, of the tottering of his lofty reason upon her throne. The verses, which were entitled "The Haunted Palace,"[1] ran very nearly, if not accurately, thus:

1.

In the greenest of our valleys,
    By good angels tenanted,
Once a fair and stately palace—
    Radiant palace—reared its head.
5 In the monarch Thought's dominion—
    It stood there!
Never seraph° spread a pinion°   angel / wing
    Over fabric half so fair.

2.

Banners yellow, glorious, golden,
10   On its roof did float and flow;
(This—all this—was in the olden
    Time long ago)
And every gentle air that dallied,
    In that sweet day,
15 Along the ramparts plumed and pallid,
    A winged odor went away.

3.

Wanderers in that happy valley
    Through two luminous windows saw
Spirits moving musically
20   To a lute's well-tunèd law,

Round about a throne, where sitting
    (Porphyrogene![2])
In state his glory well befitting,
    The ruler of the realm was seen.

4.

25 And all with pearl and ruby glowing
    Was the fair palace door,
Through which came flowing, flowing, flowing,
    And sparkling evermore,
A troop of Echoes whose sole duty
30   Was but to sing,
In voices of surpassing beauty,
    The wit and wisdom of their king.

5.

But evil things, in robes of sorrow,
    Assailed the monarch's high estate;
35 (Ah, let us mourn, for never morrow
    Shall dawn upon him, desolate!)
And, round about his home, the glory
    That blushed and bloomed
Is but a dim-remembered story
40   Of the old time entombed.

6.

And travellers now within that valley,
    Through the red-litten windows, see
Vast forms that move fantastically
    To a discordant melody;
45 While, like a rapid ghastly river,
    Through the pale door,
A hideous throng rush out forever,
    And laugh—but smile no more.

I well remember that suggestions arising from this ballad, led us into a train of thought wherein there became manifest an opinion of Usher's which I mention not so much on account of its novelty (for other men[3] have thought thus) as on account of the per-

---

1 *The Haunted Palace* An endnote in the original *Burton's* publication of this story reads as follows: "The ballad of 'The Haunted Palace,' introduced in this tale, was published separately, some months ago, in the Baltimore 'Museum.'"

2 *Porphyrogene* Born into purple (the color of royalty); of noble birth.

3 [Poe's note] Watson, Dr. Percival, Spallanzani, and especially the Bishop of Landaff. See "Chemical Essays," vol. v. [Poe refers to Richard Watson, Bishop of Landaff (1737–1816), who wrote extensively on chemistry and other sciences as well as on theology; Thomas Percival (1740–1804), English writer on [continued …]]

tinacity with which he maintained it. This opinion, in its general form, was that of the sentience of all vegetable things. But, in his disordered fancy, the idea had assumed a more daring character, and trespassed, under certain conditions, upon the kingdom of inorganization.[1] I lack words to express the full extent, or the earnest *abandon* of his persuasion. The belief, however, was connected (as I have previously hinted) with the gray stones of the home of his forefathers. The condition of the sentience had been here, he imagined, fulfilled in the method of collocation of these stones—in the order of their arrangement, as well as in that of the many *fungi* which overspread them, and of the decayed trees which stood around—above all, in the long undisturbed endurance of this arrangement, and in its reduplication in the still waters of the tarn. Its evidence—the evidence of the sentience—was to be seen, he said (and I here started as he spoke), in the gradual yet certain condensation of an atmosphere of their own about the waters and the walls. The result was discoverable, he added, in that silent, yet importunate and terrible influence which for centuries had moulded the destinies of his family, and which made *him* what I now saw him—what he was. Such opinions need no comment, and I will make none.

Our books—the books which, for years, had formed no small portion of the mental existence of the invalid—were, as might be supposed, in strict keeping with this character of phantasm. We pored together over such works as the Ververt et Chartreuse of Gresset; the Belphegor of Machiavelli; the Heaven and Hell of Swedenborg; the Subterranean Voyage of Nicholas Klimm de Holberg; the Chiromancy of Robert Flud, of Jean D'Indaginé, and of De la Chambre; the Journey into the Blue Distance of Tieck; and the City of the Sun of Campanella.[2] One favorite volume was a small

octavo edition of the *Directorium Inquisitorium,* by the Dominican Eymeric de Gironne; and there were passages in Pomponius Mela, about the old African Satyrs and œgipans,[3] over which Usher would sit dreaming for hours. His chief delight, however, was found in the earnest and repeated perusal of an exceedingly rare and curious book in quarto Gothic—the manual of a forgotten church—the *Vigiliae Mortuorum secundum Chorum Ecclesiae Maguntinae.*[4]

I could not help thinking of the wild ritual of this work, and of its probable influence upon the hypochondriac, when, one evening, having informed me abruptly that the lady Madeline was no more, he stated his intention of preserving her corpse for a fortnight (previously[5] to its final interment) in one of the numerous vaults within the main walls of the building. The worldly reason, however, assigned for this singular proceeding, was one which I did not feel at liberty to dispute. The brother had been led to his resolution (so he told me) by consideration of the unusual character of the malady of the deceased, of certain obtrusive and eager inquiries on the part of her medical men, and of the remote and exposed situation of the burial ground of the family. I will not deny that when I called to mind the sinister countenance of the person whom I met upon the staircase, on the day of my arrival at the house, I had no desire to oppose what I regarded as

---

medical ethics; and Lazzaro Spallanzani (1729–99), Italian biologist and Catholic priest. All three writers speculated on the possibility that plant matter may be sensitive or in some way perceptive.]

[1]   *kingdom of inorganization*   World of inanimate matter.

[2]   *Our books ... Campanella*   The narrator lists works (many of them rather obscure) whose themes include religion, science, mysticism, and the supernatural; the authors are French poet Jean-Baptiste-Louis Gresset (1709–77), Italian political philosopher Niccolò Machiavelli (1469–1527), Swedish scientist and mystic Emanuel Swedenborg (1688–1772), Danish-Norwegian playwright and philosopher Ludvig Holberg (1684–1754), English scientist and

occultist Robert Fludd (1574–1637), German astrologer Johannes Indagine (c. 1467–1537), French writer on palmistry Maria Cireau de la Chambre (1594–1669), German poet Ludwig Tieck (1773–1853), and Italian Utopian philosopher Tommaso Campanella (1568–1639); *Chiromancy*   Palm-reading.

[3]   *octavo*   Small book size, created by folding sheets of paper so as to produce eight pages per sheet; *Directorium Inquisitorium*   Written by Spanish theologian Nicholas Eymeric de Gerone (c. 1316–99), the *Directorium Inquisitorum* was a definitive text on Inquisitorial procedure and the means of extracting confessions from suspected heretics (especially through torture); *Pomponius Mela*   Roman geographer (c. 43 CE) who wrote about bizarre foreign mythological creatures; *Satyrs and œgipans*   Mythological creatures who are half human and half goat.

[4]   *quarto*   Book size created by folding sheets of paper so as to produce four pages per sheet; *Gothic*   Ornate type face also known as black letter; *Vigiliae ... Maguntinae*   Roman Catholic book of prayers for the dead, printed c. 1500.

[5]   *previously*   Prior.

at best but a harmless, and by no means an unnatural, precaution.[1]

At the request of Usher, I personally aided him in the arrangements for the temporary entombment. The body having been encoffined, we two alone bore it to its rest. The vault in which we placed it (and which had been so long unopened that our torches, half smothered in its oppressive atmosphere, gave us little opportunity for investigation) was small, damp, and utterly without means of admission for light; lying, at great depth, immediately beneath that portion of the building in which was my own sleeping apartment. It had been used, apparently, in remote feudal times, for the worst purposes of a donjon-keep,[2] and, in later days, as a place of deposit for powder, or some other highly combustible substance, as a portion of its floor, and the whole interior of a long archway through which we reached it, were carefully sheathed with copper. The door, of massive iron, had been, also, similarly protected. Its immense weight caused an unusually sharp grating sound, as it moved upon its hinges.

Having deposited our mournful burden upon trestles[3] within this region of horror, we partially turned aside the yet unscrewed lid of the coffin, and looked upon the face of the tenant. A striking similitude between the brother and sister now first arrested my attention; and Usher, divining, perhaps, my thoughts, murmured out some few words from which I learned that the deceased and himself had been twins, and that sympathies of a scarcely intelligible nature had always existed between them. Our glances, however, rested not long upon the dead—for we could not regard her unawed. The disease which had thus entombed the lady in the maturity of youth, had left, as usual in all maladies of a strictly cataleptical character, the mockery of a faint blush upon the bosom and the face, and that suspiciously lingering smile upon the lip which is so terrible in death. We replaced and screwed down the lid, and, having secured the door of iron, made our way, with toil, into the scarcely less gloomy apartments of the upper portion of the house.

And now, some days of bitter grief having elapsed, an observable change came over the features of the mental disorder of my friend. His ordinary manner had vanished. His ordinary occupations were neglected or forgotten. He roamed from chamber to chamber with hurried, unequal, and objectless step. The pallor of his countenance had assumed, if possible, a more ghastly hue—but the luminousness of his eye had utterly gone out. The once occasional huskiness of his tone was heard no more; and a tremulous quaver, as if of extreme terror, habitually characterized his utterance. There were times, indeed, when I thought his unceasingly agitated mind was laboring with some oppressive secret, to divulge which he struggled for the necessary courage. At times, again, I was obliged to resolve all into the mere inexplicable vagaries of madness, for I beheld him gazing upon vacancy for long hours, in an attitude of the profoundest attention, as if listening to some imaginary sound. It was no wonder that his condition terrified—that it infected me. I felt creeping upon me, by slow yet certain degrees, the wild influences of his own fantastic yet impressive superstitions.

It was, especially, upon retiring to bed late in the night of the seventh or eighth day after the placing of the lady Madeline within the donjon, that I experienced the full power of such feelings. Sleep came not near my couch—while the hours waned and waned away. I struggled to reason off the nervousness which had dominion over me. I endeavored to believe that much, if not all of what I felt, was due to the bewildering influence of the gloomy furniture of the room—of the dark and tattered draperies, which, tortured into motion by the breath of a rising tempest, swayed fitfully to and fro upon the walls, and rustled uneasily about the decorations of the bed. But my efforts were fruitless. An irrepressible tremor gradually pervaded my frame; and, at length, there sat upon my very heart an incubus[4] of utterly causeless alarm. Shaking this off with a gasp and a struggle, I uplifted myself upon the pillows, and, peering earnestly within the intense darkness of the chamber, harkened—I know not why,

---

[1] *The worldly reason ... precaution* Grave-robbing was common in nineteenth-century America, as the rise of medicine produced an increasing need for bodies to be dissected for study; fresh graves were thus more susceptible. Usher may also have been concerned over the possibility of premature burial—in case Madeline were not actually dead, but in a deep coma—which was a rare but not unheard-of occurrence during this period.

[2] *donjon-keep* Dungeon.

[3] *trestles* Braces for supporting the coffin.

[4] *incubus* Evil spirit said to sit upon people's chests in their sleep, causing nightmares.

except that an instinctive spirit prompted me—to certain low and indefinite sounds which came, through the pauses of the storm, at long intervals, I knew not whence. Overpowered by an intense sentiment of horror, unaccountable yet unendurable, I threw on my clothes with haste (for I felt that I should sleep no more during the night) and endeavored to arouse myself from the pitiable condition into which I had fallen, by pacing rapidly to and fro through the apartment.

I had taken but few turns in this manner, when a light step on an adjoining staircase arrested my attention. I presently recognized it as that of Usher. In an instant afterwards he rapped, with a gentle touch, at my door, and entered, bearing a lamp. His countenance was, as usual, cadaverously wan—but, moreover, there was a species of mad hilarity in his eyes—an evidently restrained *hysteria* in his whole demeanor. His air appalled me—but anything was preferable to the solitude which I had so long endured, and I even welcomed his presence as a relief.

"And you have not seen it?" he said abruptly, after having stared about him for some moments in silence—"you have not then seen it? But, stay! you shall." Thus speaking, and having carefully shaded his lamp, he hurried to one of the casements,[1] and threw it freely open to the storm.

The impetuous fury of the entering gust nearly lifted us from our feet. It was, indeed, a tempestuous yet sternly beautiful night, and one wildly singular in its terror and its beauty. A whirlwind had apparently collected its force in our vicinity; for there were frequent and violent alterations in the direction of the wind; and the exceeding density of the clouds (which hung so low as to press upon the turrets of the house) did not prevent our perceiving the life-like velocity with which they flew careering from all points against each other, without passing away into the distance. I say that even their exceeding density did not prevent our perceiving this—yet we had no glimpse of the moon or stars, nor was there any flashing forth of the lightning. But the under surfaces of the huge masses of agitated vapor, as well as all terrestrial objects immediately around us, were glowing in the unnatural light of a faintly luminous and distinctly visible gaseous exhalation which hung about and enshrouded the mansion.

"You must not—you shall not behold this!" said I, shuddering, to Usher, as I led him, with a gentle violence, from the window to a seat. "These appearances, which bewilder you, are merely electrical phenomena not uncommon—or it may be that they have their ghastly origin in the rank miasma of the tarn. Let us close this casement—the air is chilling and dangerous to your frame. Here is one of your favorite romances.[2] I will read, and you shall listen—and so we will pass away this terrible night together."

The antique volume which I had taken up was the "Mad Trist" of Sir Launcelot Canning[3]—but I had called it a favorite of Usher's more in sad jest than in earnest; for, in truth, there is little in its uncouth and unimaginative prolixity which could have had interest for the lofty and spiritual ideality of my friend. It was, however, the only book immediately at hand; and I indulged a vague hope that the excitement which now agitated the hypochondriac might find relief (for the history of mental disorder is full of similar anomalies) even in the extremeness of the folly which I should read. Could I have judged, indeed, by the wild, overstrained air of vivacity with which he harkened, or apparently harkened, to the words of the tale, I might well have congratulated myself upon the success of my design.

I had arrived at that well-known portion of the story where Ethelred, the hero of the Trist, having sought in vain for peaceable admission into the dwelling of the hermit, proceeds to make good an entrance by force. Here, it will be remembered, the words of the narrative run thus:

"And Ethelred, who was by nature of a doughty heart, and who was now mighty withal, on account of the powerfulness of the wine which he had drunken, waited no longer to hold parley with the hermit, who, in sooth,[4] was of an obstinate and maliceful turn, but, feeling the rain upon his shoulders, and fearing the rising of the tempest, uplifted his mace outright, and, with blows, made quickly room in the plankings of the door for his gauntleted hand; and now pulling therewith sturdily, he so cracked, and ripped, and tore all

---

1   *casements* Window panes that open outward.

2   *romances* I.e., heroic tales of adventure and chivalry.

3   *"Mad Trist" ... Launcelot Canning* Both the book and its author are fictional;   *Trist* Meeting or encounter.

4   *sooth* Truth.

asunder, that the noise of the dry and hollow-sounding wood alarummed[1] and reverberated throughout the forest."

At the termination of this sentence I started, and for a moment, paused; for it appeared to me (although I at once concluded that my excited fancy had deceived me)—it appeared to me that, from some very remote portion of the mansion, there came, indistinctly, to my ears, what might have been, in its exact similarity of character, the echo (but a stifled and dull one certainly) of the very cracking and ripping sound which Sir Launcelot had so particularly described. It was, beyond doubt, the coincidence alone which had arrested my attention; for, amid the rattling of the sashes of the casements, and the ordinary commingled noises of the still increasing storm, the sound, in itself, had nothing, surely, which should have interested or disturbed me. I continued the story:

"But the good champion Ethelred, now entering within the door, was sore enraged and amazed to perceive no signal of the maliceful hermit; but, in the stead thereof, a dragon of a scaly and prodigious demeanor, and of a fiery tongue, which sate in guard before a palace of gold, with a floor of silver; and upon the wall there hung a shield of shining brass with this legend enwritten—

Who entereth herein, a conqueror hath bin,
Who slayeth the dragon, the shield he shall win.

And Ethelred uplifted his mace, and struck upon the head of the dragon, which fell before him, and gave up his pesty[2] breath, with a shriek so horrid and harsh, and withal so piercing, that Ethelred had fain to close his ears with his hands against the dreadful noise of it, the like whereof was never before heard."

Here again I paused abruptly, and now with a feeling of wild amazement—for there could be no doubt whatever that, in this instance, I did actually hear (although from what direction it proceeded I found it impossible to say) a low and apparently distant, but harsh, protracted, and most unusual screaming or grating sound—the exact counterpart of what my fancy had already conjured up as the sound of the dragon's unnatural shriek as described by the romancer.

Oppressed, as I certainly was, upon the occurrence of this second and most extraordinary coincidence, by a thousand conflicting sensations, in which wonder and extreme terror were predominant, I still retained sufficient presence of mind to avoid exciting, by any observation, the sensitive nervousness of my companion. I was by no means certain that he had noticed the sounds in question; although, assuredly, a strange alteration had, during the last few minutes, taken place in his demeanor. From a position fronting my own, he had gradually brought round his chair, so as to sit with his face to the door of the chamber; and thus I could but partially perceive his features, although I saw that his lips trembled as if he were murmuring inaudibly. His head had dropped upon his breast—yet I knew that he was not asleep, from the wide and rigid opening of the eye, as I caught a glance of it in profile. The motion of his body, too, was at variance with this idea—for he rocked from side to side with a gentle yet constant and uniform sway. Having rapidly taken notice of all this, I resumed the narrative of Sir Launcelot, which thus proceeded:

"And now, the champion, having escaped from the terrible fury of the dragon, bethinking himself of the brazen[3] shield, and of the breaking up of the enchantment which was upon it, removed the carcass from out of the way before him, and approached valorously over the silver pavement of the castle to where the shield was upon the wall; which in sooth tarried not for his full coming, but fell down at his feet upon the silver floor, with a mighty great and terrible ringing sound."

No sooner had these syllables passed my lips, than—as if a shield of brass had indeed, at the moment, fallen heavily upon a floor of silver—I became aware of a distinct, hollow, metallic, and clangorous, yet apparently muffled reverberation. Completely unnerved, I leaped to my feet; but the measured rocking movement of Usher was undisturbed. I rushed to the chair in which he sat. His eyes were bent fixedly before him, and throughout his whole countenance there reigned a stony rigidity. But, as I laid my hand upon his shoulder, there came a strong shudder over his whole person; a sickly smile quivered about his lips; and I saw that he

---

1   *alarummed* Rang out; sounded loudly.

2   *pesty* Putrid.

3   *brazen* Brass.

spoke in a low, hurried, and gibbering murmur, as if unconscious of my presence. Bending closely over his person, I at length drank in the hideous import of his words.

"Not hear it? yes, I hear it, and *have* heard it. Long—long—long—many minutes, many hours, many days, have I heard it—yet I dared not—oh, pity me, miserable wretch that I am!—I dared not—*I dared* not speak! *We have put her living in the tomb!* Said I not that my senses were acute? I *now* tell you that I heard her first feeble movements in the hollow coffin. I heard them—many, many days ago—yet I dared not—*I dared not speak!* And now—tonight—Ethelred—ha! ha!—the breaking of the hermit's door, and the death-cry of the dragon, and the clangor of the shield! say, rather, the rending of the coffin, and the grating of the iron hinges, and her struggles within the coppered archway of the vault! Oh whither shall I fly? Will she not be here anon? Is she not hurrying to upbraid me for my haste? Have I not heard her footstep on the stair? Do I not distinguish that heavy and horrible beating of her heart? Madman!"—here he sprang furiously to his feet, and shrieked out his syllables, as if in the effort he were giving up his soul—"*Madman! I tell you that she now stands without*[1] *the door!*"

As if in the superhuman energy of his utterance there had been found the potency of a spell—the huge antique panels to which the speaker pointed, threw slowly back, upon the instant, their ponderous and ebony jaws. It was the work of the rushing gust—but then without those doors there *did* stand the lofty and enshrouded figure of the lady Madeline of Usher. There was blood upon her white robes, and the evidence of some bitter struggle upon every portion of her emaciated frame. For a moment she remained trembling and reeling to and fro upon the threshold—then, with a low moaning cry, fell heavily inward upon the person of her brother, and in her violent and now final death-agonies, bore him to the floor a corpse, and a victim to the terrors he had anticipated.

From that chamber, and from that mansion, I fled aghast. The storm was still abroad in all its wrath as I found myself crossing the old causeway. Suddenly there shot along the path a wild light, and I turned to see whence a gleam so unusual could have issued; for

the vast house and its shadows were alone behind me. The radiance was that of the full, setting, and blood-red moon, which now shone vividly through that once barely-discernible fissure, of which I have before spoken as extending from the roof of the building, in a zig-zag direction, to the base. While I gazed, this fissure rapidly widened—there came a fierce breath of the whirlwind—the entire orb of the satellite burst at once upon my sight—my brain reeled as I saw the mighty walls rushing asunder—there was a long tumultuous shouting sound like the voice of a thousand waters—and the deep and dank tarn at my feet closed sullenly and silently over the fragments of the "*House of Usher*."
—1839 (REVISED 1845)

The Man of the Crowd

Ce grand malheur, de ne pouvoir être seul.[2]
La Bruyère.

It was well said of a certain German book that "*er lässt sich nicht lesen*"—it does not permit itself to be read. There are some secrets which do not permit themselves to be told. Men die nightly in their beds, wringing the hands of ghostly confessors, and looking them piteously in the eyes—die with despair of heart and convulsion of throat, on account of the hideousness of mysteries which will not *suffer themselves* to be revealed. Now and then, alas, the conscience of man takes up a burden so heavy in horror that it can be thrown down only into the grave. And thus the essence of all crime is undivulged.

Not long ago, about the closing in of an evening in autumn, I sat at the large bow window of the D——Coffee-House in London. For some months I had been ill in health, but was now convalescent, and, with returning strength, found myself in one of those happy moods which are so precisely the converse of *ennui*—moods of the keenest appetency,[3] when the

---

[1]   *without* Outside.

[2]   *Ce grand … seul* French: This great misfortune, of not being able to be alone. A loose paraphrase from *Les Caractères* (1688) by French philosopher Jean de La Bruyère.

[3]   *appetency* Appetite.

film from the mental vision departs—the αχλυς ος πριν επηεν[1]—and the intellect, electrified, surpasses as greatly its everyday condition, as does the vivid yet candid reason of Leibnitz, the mad and flimsy rhetoric of Gorgias.[2] Merely to breathe was enjoyment; and I derived positive pleasure even from many of the legitimate sources of pain. I felt a calm but inquisitive interest in everything. With a cigar in my mouth and a newspaper in my lap, I had been amusing myself for the greater part of the afternoon, now in poring over advertisements, now in observing the promiscuous[3] company in the room, and now in peering through the smoky panes into the street.

This latter is one of the principal thoroughfares of the city, and had been very much crowded during the whole day. But, as the darkness came on, the throng momently increased; and, by the time the lamps were well lighted, two dense and continuous tides of population were rushing past the door. At this particular period of the evening I had never before been in a similar situation, and the tumultuous sea of human heads filled me, therefore, with a delicious novelty of emotion. I gave up, at length, all care of things within the hotel, and became absorbed in contemplation of the scene without.[4]

At first my observations took an abstract and generalizing turn. I looked at the passengers in masses, and thought of them in their aggregate relations. Soon, however, I descended to details, and regarded with minute interest the innumerable varieties of figure, dress, air, gait, visage, and expression of countenance.

By far the greater number of those who went by had a satisfied business-like demeanor, and seemed to be thinking only of making their way through the press. Their brows were knit, and their eyes rolled quickly; when pushed against by fellow-wayfarers they evinced no symptom of impatience, but adjusted their clothes and hurried on. Others, still a numerous class, were restless in their movements, had flushed faces, and talked and gesticulated to themselves, as if feeling in solitude on account of the very denseness of the company around. When impeded in their progress, these people suddenly ceased muttering, but redoubled their gesticulations, and awaited, with an absent and overdone smile upon the lips, the course of the persons impeding them. If jostled, they bowed profusely to the jostlers, and appeared overwhelmed with confusion. There was nothing very distinctive about these two large classes beyond what I have noted. Their habiliments belonged to that order which is pointedly termed the decent. They were undoubtedly noblemen, merchants, attorneys, tradesmen, stock-jobbers[5]—the Eupatrids[6] and the common-places of society—men of leisure and men actively engaged in affairs of their own—conducting business upon their own responsibility. They did not greatly excite my attention.

The tribe of clerks was an obvious one and here I discerned two remarkable divisions. There were the junior clerks of flash houses[7]—young gentlemen with tight coats, bright boots, well-oiled hair, and supercilious lips. Setting aside a certain dapperness of carriage, which may be termed *deskism* for want of a better word, the manner of these persons seemed to me an exact facsimile of what had been the perfection of *bon ton*[8] about twelve or eighteen months before. They wore the cast-off graces of the gentry—and this, I believe, involves the best definition of the class.

The division of the upper clerks of staunch firms, or of the "steady old fellows," it was not possible to mistake. These were known by their coats and pantaloons of black or brown, made to sit comfortably, with white cravats and waistcoats, broad solid-looking shoes, and thick hose or gaiters. They had all slightly bald heads, from which the right ears, long used to pen-holding, had an odd habit of standing off on end.

---

[1] αχλυς … επηεν Greek: the haze that was once upon them; from Homer's *Iliad* 5.127.

[2] *Leibnitz … Gorgias* Poe compares the work of highly regarded Enlightenment philosopher and mathematician Gottfried Wilhelm Leibniz (1646–1716) to that of ancient Greek sophist Gorgias (c. 483–375 BCE), who was strongly criticized by Plato and whose surviving works are often characterized by confusing and ambiguous arguments.

[3] *promiscuous* Varied; diverse.

[4] *without* Outside.

[5] *stock-jobbers* People who buy and sell stocks quickly in order to turn a profit.

[6] *Eupatrids* Members of the upper class; term alluding to the ancient Athenian class system.

[7] *flash houses* Pretentious upstart businesses; this term can also refer to brothels or to taverns where criminals spend time.

[8] *bon ton* French: good taste or manners; also refers to fashionable society as a whole.

I observed that they always removed or settled their hats with both hands, and wore watches, with short gold chains of a substantial and ancient pattern. Theirs was the affectation of respectability—if indeed there be an affectation so honorable.

There were many individuals of dashing appearance, whom I easily understood as belonging to the race of swell pick-pockets, with which all great cities are infested. I watched these gentry with much inquisitiveness, and found it difficult to imagine how they should ever be mistaken for gentlemen by gentlemen themselves. Their voluminousness of wristband, with an air of excessive frankness, should betray them at once.

The gamblers, of whom I descried not a few, were still more easily recognisable. They wore every variety of dress, from that of the desperate thimble-rig[1] bully, with velvet waistcoat, fancy neckerchief, gilt chains, and filagreed buttons, to that of the scrupulously inornate clergyman, than which nothing could be less liable to suspicion. Still all were distinguished by a certain sodden swarthiness of complexion, a filmy dimness of eye, and pallor and compression of lip. There were two other traits, moreover, by which I could always detect them—a guarded lowness of tone in conversation, and a more than ordinary extension of the thumb in a direction at right angles with the fingers. Very often, in company with these sharpers,[2] I observed an order of men somewhat different in habits, but still birds of a kindred feather. They may be defined as the gentlemen who live by their wits. They seem to prey upon the public in two battalions—that of the dandies and that of the military men. Of the first grade the leading features are long locks and smiles; of the second frogged coats[3] and frowns.

Descending in the scale of what is termed gentility, I found darker and deeper themes for speculation. I saw Jew pedlars, with hawk eyes[4] flashing from countenances whose every other feature wore only an expression of abject humility; sturdy professional street beggars scowling upon mendicants of a better stamp, whom despair alone had driven forth into the night for charity; feeble and ghastly invalids, upon whom death had placed a sure hand, and who sidled and tottered through the mob, looking everyone beseechingly in the face, as if in search of some chance consolation, some lost hope; modest young girls returning from long and late labor to a cheerless home, and shrinking more tearfully than indignantly from the glances of ruffians, whose direct contact, even, could not be avoided; women of the town[5] of all kinds and of all ages—the unequivocal beauty in the prime of her womanhood, putting one in mind of the statue in Lucian, with the surface of Parian marble, and the interior filled with filth[6]—the loathsome and utterly lost leper in rags—the wrinkled, bejewelled and paint-begrimed beldame,[7] making a last effort at youth—the mere child of immature form, yet, from long association, an adept in the dreadful coquetries of her trade, and burning with a rabid ambition to be ranked the equal of her elders in vice; drunkards innumerable and indescribable—some in shreds and patches, reeling, inarticulate, with bruised visage and lack-lustre eyes—some in whole although filthy garments, with a slightly unsteady swagger, thick sensual lips, and hearty-looking rubicund faces—others clothed in materials which had once been good, and which even now were scrupulously well brushed—men who walked with a more than naturally firm and springy step, but whose countenances were fearfully pale, whose eyes hideously wild and red, and who clutched with quivering fingers, as they strode through the crowd, at every object which came within their reach; beside these, pie-men, porters, coal-heavers, sweeps;[8] organ-grinders, monkey-exhibiters and ballad mongers, those who vended with those who sang; ragged artisans and exhausted laborers of every description, and all full of a noisy and

---

1   *thimble-rig*   Cheating game played with thimbles or other hollow objects, similar to the three-card trick.

2   *sharpers*   Fraudulent gamblers.

3   *frogged coats*   Coats with frogs—fastenings that consist of a long button secured to a loop on the other side of the coat. Ornamental frogs are commonly used on military uniforms.

4   *Jew pedlars ... eyes*   Beginning with this anti-Semitic image, this paragraph makes extensive use of stereotypes commonly held in nineteenth-century America regarding the poor, women, and other oppressed groups.

5   *women of the town*   I.e., prostitutes.

6   *statue in Lucian ... filth*   Poe alludes to a passage from *Somnium* by Syrian-Greek writer Lucian of Samosata (c. 125–c. 180 CE), which mentions a beautiful sculpture stuffed with rags.

7   *beldame*   Derogatory word for an old woman; a hag.

8   *sweeps*   Chimney sweepers.

inordinate vivacity which jarred discordantly upon the ear, and gave an aching sensation to the eye.

As the night deepened, so deepened to me the interest of the scene; for not only did the general character of the crowd materially alter (its gentler features retiring in the gradual withdrawal of the more orderly portion of the people, and its harsher ones coming out into bolder relief, as the late hour brought forth every species of infamy from its den), but the rays of the gas-lamps, feeble at first in their struggle with the dying day, had now at length gained ascendancy, and threw over everything a fitful and garish lustre. All was dark yet splendid—as that ebony to which has been likened the style of Tertullian.[1]

The wild effects of the light enchained me to an examination of individual faces; and although the rapidity with which the world of light flitted before the window, prevented me from casting more than a glance upon each visage, still it seemed that, in my then peculiar mental state, I could frequently read, even in that brief interval of a glance, the history of long years.

With my brow to the glass, I was thus occupied in scrutinizing the mob, when suddenly there came into view a countenance (that of a decrepit old man, some sixty-five or seventy years of age)—a countenance which at once arrested and absorbed my whole attention, on account of the absolute idiosyncrasy of its expression. Anything even remotely resembling that expression I had never seen before. I well remember that my first thought, upon beholding it, was that Retzsch, had he viewed it, would have greatly preferred it to his own pictural incarnations of the fiend.[2] As I endeavored, during the brief minute of my original survey, to form some analysis of the meaning conveyed, there arose confusedly and paradoxically within my mind, the ideas of vast mental power, of caution, of penuriousness, of avarice, of coolness, of malice, of

blood-thirstiness, of triumph, of merriment, of excessive terror, of intense—of supreme despair. I felt singularly aroused, startled, fascinated. "How wild a history," I said to myself, "is written within that bosom!" Then came a craving desire to keep the man in view—to know more of him. Hurriedly putting on an overcoat, and seizing my hat and cane, I made my way into the street, and pushed through the crowd in the direction which I had seen him take; for he had already disappeared. With some little difficulty I at length came within sight of him, approached, and followed him closely, yet cautiously, so as not to attract his attention.

I had now a good opportunity of examining his person. He was short in stature, very thin, and apparently very feeble. His clothes, generally, were filthy and ragged; but as he came, now and then, within the strong glare of a lamp, I perceived that his linen, although dirty, was of beautiful texture; and my vision deceived me, or, through a rent in a closely-buttoned and evidently second-handed *roquelaire*[3] which enveloped him, I caught a glimpse both of a diamond and of a dagger. These observations heightened my curiosity, and I resolved to follow the stranger whithersoever he should go.

It was now fully nightfall, and a thick humid fog hung over the city, soon ending in a settled and heavy rain. This change of weather had an odd effect upon the crowd, the whole of which was at once put into new commotion, and overshadowed by a world of umbrellas. The waver, the jostle, and the hum increased in a tenfold degree. For my own part I did not much regard the rain—the lurking of an old fever in my system rendering the moisture somewhat too dangerously pleasant. Tying a handkerchief about my mouth, I kept on. For half an hour the old man held his way with difficulty along the great thoroughfare; and I here walked close at his elbow through fear of losing sight of him. Never once turning his head to look back, he did not observe me. By and bye he passed into a cross street, which, although densely filled with people, was not quite so much thronged as the main one he had quitted. Here a change in his demeanor became evident. He walked more slowly and with less object than before—more hesitatingly. He crossed and re-crossed the way repeatedly without apparent aim; and the press

---

[1] *Tertullian* Early Christian theologian (c. 155–c. 240 CE) from Roman Carthage (what is now Tunisia). The French writer Balzac (1799–1850), in a letter to his editor, described his fondness for Tertullian's writing style: "I have found in his writings that black light, which is mentioned in one of the ancient poets; and I look upon his obscurity with the same pleasure as that of ebony which is very bright and neatly wrought."

[2] *Retzsch … the fiend* German painter Moritz Retzsch (1779–1857) was known particularly for his depictions of scenes from Goethe's *Faust* (1808), in which Dr. Faust sells his soul to the devil.

[3] *roquelaire* Knee-length cloak.

was still so thick that, at every such movement, I was obliged to follow him closely. The street was a narrow and long one, and his course lay within it for nearly an hour, during which the passengers had gradually diminished to about that number which is ordinarily seen at noon in Broadway near the Park[1]—so vast a difference is there between a London populace and that of the most frequented American city. A second turn brought us into a square, brilliantly lighted, and overflowing with life. The old manner of the stranger reappeared. His chin fell upon his breast, while his eyes rolled wildly from under his knit brows, in every direction, upon those who hemmed him in. He urged his way steadily and perseveringly. I was surprised, however, to find, upon his having made the circuit of the square, that he turned and retraced his steps. Still more was I astonished to see him repeat the same walk several times—once nearly detecting me as he came round with a sudden movement.

In this exercise he spent another hour, at the end of which we met with far less interruption from passengers than at first. The rain fell fast; the air grew cool; and the people were retiring to their homes. With a gesture of impatience, the wanderer passed into a bye-street comparatively deserted. Down this, some quarter of a mile long, he rushed with an activity I could not have dreamed of seeing in one so aged, and which put me to much trouble in pursuit. A few minutes brought us to a large and busy bazaar, with the localities of which the stranger appeared well acquainted, and where his original demeanor again became apparent, as he forced his way to and fro, without aim, among the host of buyers and sellers.

During the hour and a half, or thereabouts, which we passed in this place, it required much caution on my part to keep him within reach without attracting his observation. Luckily I wore a pair of caoutchouc[2] over-shoes, and could move about in perfect silence. At no moment did he see that I watched him. He entered shop after shop, priced nothing, spoke no word, and looked at all objects with a wild and vacant stare. I was now utterly amazed at his behaviour, and firmly resolved that we should not part until I had satisfied myself in some measure respecting him.

A loud-toned clock struck eleven, and the company were fast deserting the bazaar. A shop-keeper, in putting up a shutter, jostled the old man, and at the instant I saw a strong shudder come over his frame. He hurried into the street, looked anxiously around him for an instant, and then ran with incredible swiftness through many crooked and people-less lanes, until we emerged once more upon the great thoroughfare whence we had started—the street of the D—— Hotel. It no longer wore, however, the same aspect. It was still brilliant with gas;[3] but the rain fell fiercely, and there were few persons to be seen. The stranger grew pale. He walked moodily some paces up the once populous avenue, then, with a heavy sigh, turned in the direction of the river, and, plunging through a great variety of devious ways, came out, at length, in view of one of the principal theatres. It was about being closed, and the audience were thronging from the doors. I saw the old man gasp as if for breath while he threw himself amid the crowd; but I thought that the intense agony of his countenance had, in some measure, abated. His head again fell upon his breast; he appeared as I had seen him at first. I observed that he now took the course in which had gone the greater number of the audience—but, upon the whole, I was at a loss to comprehend the waywardness of his actions.

As he proceeded, the company grew more scattered, and his old uneasiness and vacillation were resumed. For some time he followed closely a party of some ten or twelve roisterers;[4] but from this number one by one dropped off, until three only remained together, in a narrow and gloomy lane little frequented. The stranger paused, and, for a moment, seemed lost in thought; then, with every mark of agitation, pursued rapidly a route which brought us to the verge of the city, amid regions very different from those we had hitherto traversed. It was the most noisome quarter of London, where everything wore the worst impress of the most deplorable poverty, and of the most desperate crime. By the dim light of an accidental lamp, tall, antique, worm-eaten, wooden tenements were seen tottering to their fall, in directions so many and capricious

----

[1]   *the Park*   I.e., City Hall Park, in Poe's day one of the liveliest parts of New York City.

[2]   *caoutchouc* Rubber.

[3]   *gas*   I.e., gas streetlamps.

[4]   *roisterers* Boisterous partiers.

that scarce the semblance of a passage was discernible between them. The paving-stones lay at random, displaced from their beds by the rankly-growing grass. Horrible filth festered in the dammed-up gutters. The whole atmosphere teemed with desolation. Yet, as we proceeded, the sounds of human life revived by sure degrees, and at length large bands of the most abandoned of a London populace were seen reeling to and fro. The spirits of the old man again flickered up, as a lamp which is near its death-hour.[1] Once more he strode onward with elastic[2] tread. Suddenly a corner was turned, a blaze of light burst upon our sight, and we stood before one of the huge suburban temples of Intemperance[3]—one of the palaces of the fiend, Gin.

It was now nearly day-break; but a number of wretched inebriates still pressed in and out of the flaunting entrance. With a half shriek of joy the old man forced a passage within, resumed at once his original bearing, and stalked backward and forward, without apparent object, among the throng. He had not been thus long occupied, however, before a rush to the doors gave token that the host was closing them for the night. It was something even more intense than despair that I then observed upon the countenance of the singular being whom I had watched so pertinaciously. Yet he did not hesitate in his career, but, with a mad energy, retraced his steps at once, to the heart of the mighty London. Long and swiftly he fled, while I followed him in the wildest amazement, resolute not to abandon a scrutiny in which I now felt an interest all-absorbing. The sun arose while we proceeded, and, when we had once again reached that most thronged mart of the populous town, the street of the D—— Hotel, it presented an appearance of human bustle and activity scarcely inferior to what I had seen on the evening before. And here, long, amid the momently increasing confusion, did I persist in my pursuit of the stranger. But, as usual, he walked to and fro, and during the day did not pass from out the turmoil of that street. And, as the shades of the second evening came on, I grew wearied unto death, and, stopping fully in front of the wanderer, gazed at him steadfastly in the face. He

noticed me not, but resumed his solemn walk, while I, ceasing to follow, remained absorbed in contemplation. "This old man," I said at length, "is the type and the genius of deep crime. He refuses to be alone. *He is the man of the crowd.* It will be in vain to follow; for I shall learn no more of him, nor of his deeds. The worst heart of the world is a grosser[4] book than the 'Hortulus Animæ,'[5] and perhaps it is but one of the great mercies of God that '*er lässt sich nicht lesen.*'"

—1840

The Murders in the Rue Morgue

What song the Syrens sang, or what name Achilles assumed when he hid himself among women, although puzzling questions, are not beyond *all* conjecture.[6]

Sir Thomas Browne

The mental features discoursed of as the analytical, are, in themselves, but little susceptible of analysis. We appreciate them only in their effects. We know of them, among other things, that they are always to their possessor, when inordinately possessed, a source of the liveliest enjoyment. As the strong man exults in his physical ability, delighting in such exercises as call his muscles into action, so glories the analyst in that moral activity which *disentangles.* He derives pleasure from even the most trivial occupations bringing his talent into play. He is fond of enigmas, of conundrums, of hieroglyphics; exhibiting in his solutions of each a degree of *acumen* which appears to the ordinary

---

1   *as a lamp ... death-hour* The light emitted by a lamp running out of gas glows more brightly just prior to extinguishing.

2   *elastic* Buoyant; uplifted.

3   *Intemperance* Excessive alcohol consumption.

4   *grosser* Denser.

5   [Poe's note] The "*Hortulus Animæ cum Oratiunculis Aliquibus Superadditis*" of Grünninger. [The *Hortulus Animae* was a Catholic prayer book popular in Germany in the early sixteenth century. Poe probably encountered the title in Isaac D'Israeli's *Curiosities of Literature* (1791–1823), in which D'Israeli describes a Latin edition issued by the German printer John Grunninger in 1500; D'Israeli calls the prayers themselves "as puerile as they are superstitious" and condemns the illustrations as "licentious" and "ridiculous."]

6   *What song ... conjecture* From Browne's nonfiction work *Hydriotaphia, Urn Burial* (1658); the Sirens are mythological female monsters from Greek mythology, while Achilles is the hero of Homer's war epic, the *Iliad*.

apprehension preternatural. His results, brought about by the very soul and essence of method, have, in truth, the whole air of intuition.

The faculty of re-solution is possibly much invigorated by mathematical study, and especially by that highest branch of it which, unjustly, and merely on account of its retrograde operations, has been called, as if *par excellence*, analysis. Yet to calculate is not in itself to analyse. A chess-player, for example, does the one without effort at the other. It follows that the game of chess, in its effects upon mental character, is greatly misunderstood. I am not now writing a treatise, but simply prefacing a somewhat peculiar narrative by observations very much at random; I will, therefore, take occasion to assert that the higher powers of the reflective intellect are more decidedly and more usefully tasked by the unostentatious game of draughts[1] than by all the elaborate frivolity of chess. In this latter, where the pieces have different and *bizarre* motions, with various and variable values, what is only complex is mistaken (a not unusual error) for what is profound. The *attention* is here called powerfully into play. If it flag for an instant, an oversight is committed, resulting in injury or defeat. The possible moves being not only manifold but involute,[2] the chances of such oversights are multiplied; and in nine cases out of ten it is the more concentrative rather than the more acute player who conquers. In draughts, on the contrary, where the moves are *unique* and have but little variation, the probabilities of inadvertence[3] are diminished, and the mere attention being left comparatively unemployed, what advantages are obtained by either party are obtained by superior *acumen*. To be less abstract— Let us suppose a game of draughts where the pieces are reduced to four kings, and where, of course, no oversight is to be expected. It is obvious that here the victory can be decided (the players being at all equal) only by some *recherché*[4] movement, the result of some strong exertion of the intellect. Deprived of ordinary resources, the analyst throws himself into the spirit of his opponent, identifies himself therewith, and not

unfrequently sees thus, at a glance, the sole methods (sometimes indeed absurdly simple ones) by which he may seduce into error or hurry into miscalculation.

Whist[5] has long been noted for its influence upon what is termed the calculating power; and men of the highest order of intellect have been known to take an apparently unaccountable delight in it, while eschewing chess as frivolous. Beyond doubt there is nothing of a similar nature so greatly tasking the faculty of analysis. The best chess-player in Christendom *may* be little more than the best player of chess; but proficiency in whist implies capacity for success in all those more important undertakings where mind struggles with mind. When I say proficiency, I mean that perfection in the game which includes a comprehension of *all* the sources whence legitimate advantage may be derived. These are not only manifold but multiform, and lie frequently among recesses of thought altogether inaccessible to the ordinary understanding. To observe attentively is to remember distinctly; and, so far, the concentrative chess-player will do very well at whist; while the rules of Hoyle[6] (themselves based upon the mere mechanism of the game) are sufficiently and generally comprehensible. Thus to have a retentive memory, and to proceed by "the book," are points commonly regarded as the sum total of good playing. But it is in matters beyond the limits of mere rule that the skill of the analyst is evinced. He makes, in silence, a host of observations and inferences. So, perhaps, do his companions; and the difference in the extent of the information obtained, lies not so much in the validity of the inference as in the quality of the observation. The necessary knowledge is that of *what* to observe. Our player confines himself not at all; nor, because the game is the object, does he reject deductions from things external to the game. He examines the countenance of his partner, comparing it carefully with that of each of his opponents. He considers the mode of assorting the cards in each hand; often counting trump by trump, and honor by honor, through the glances

---

[1] *draughts* Checkers.

[2] *involute* Complex, intricate.

[3] *probabilities of inadvertence* I.e., likelihood of mistake through lack of attention.

[4] *recherché* French: researched; studied or well-planned.

[5] *Whist* Card game popular during the eighteenth and nineteenth centuries that is similar to the modern game of bridge. Whist has simple rules but high potential for complexity depending on the players' skills and level of engagement.

[6] *Hoyle* Edmond Hoyle (1672–1769), widely considered an authority on card games.

bestowed by their holders upon each. He notes every variation of face as the play progresses, gathering a fund of thought from the differences in the expression of certainty, of surprise, of triumph, or of chagrin. From the manner of gathering up a trick he judges whether the person taking it can make another in the suit. He recognises what is played through feint, by the air with which it is thrown upon the table. A casual or inadvertent word; the accidental dropping or turning of a card, with the accompanying anxiety or carelessness in regard to its concealment; the counting of the tricks, with the order of their arrangement; embarrassment, hesitation, eagerness or trepidation—all afford, to his apparently intuitive perception, indications of the true state of affairs. The first two or three rounds having been played, he is in full possession of the contents of each hand, and thenceforward puts down his cards with as absolute a precision of purpose as if the rest of the party had turned outward the faces of their own.

The analytical power should not be confounded with simple ingenuity; for while the analyst is necessarily ingenious, the ingenious man is often remarkably incapable of analysis. The constructive or combining power, by which ingenuity is usually manifested, and to which the phrenologists (I believe erroneously) have assigned a separate organ,[1] supposing it a primitive faculty, has been so frequently seen in those whose intellect bordered otherwise upon idiocy, as to have attracted general observation among writers on morals. Between ingenuity and the analytic ability there exists a difference far greater, indeed, than that between the fancy and the imagination, but of a character very strictly analogous. It will be found, in fact, that the ingenious are always fanciful, and the *truly* imaginative never otherwise than analytic.

The narrative which follows will appear to the reader somewhat in the light of a commentary upon the propositions just advanced.

Residing in Paris during the spring and part of the summer of 18—, I there became acquainted with a Monsieur C. Auguste Dupin. This young gentleman was of an excellent—indeed of an illustrious family, but, by a variety of untoward events, had been reduced to such poverty that the energy of his character succumbed beneath it, and he ceased to bestir himself in the world, or to care for the retrieval of his fortunes. By courtesy of his creditors, there still remained in his possession a small remnant of his patrimony; and, upon the income arising from this, he managed, by means of a rigorous economy, to procure the necessaries of life, without troubling himself about its superfluities. Books, indeed, were his sole luxuries, and in Paris these are easily obtained.

Our first meeting was at an obscure library in the Rue Montmartre, where the accident of our both being in search of the same very rare and very remarkable volume, brought us into closer communion. We saw each other again and again. I was deeply interested in the little family history which he detailed to me with all that candor which a Frenchman indulges whenever mere self is his theme. I was astonished, too, at the vast extent of his reading; and, above all, I felt my soul enkindled within me by the wild fervor, and the vivid freshness of his imagination. Seeking in Paris the objects I then sought, I felt that the society of such a man would be to me a treasure beyond price; and this feeling I frankly confided to him. It was at length arranged that we should live together during my stay in the city; and as my worldly circumstances were somewhat less embarrassed than his own, I was permitted to be at the expense of renting, and furnishing in a style which suited the rather fantastic gloom of our common temper, a time-eaten and grotesque mansion, long deserted through superstitions into which we did not inquire, and tottering to its fall in a retired and desolate portion of the Faubourg St. Germain.[2]

Had the routine of our life at this place been known to the world, we should have been regarded as madmen—although, perhaps, as madmen of a harmless nature. Our seclusion was perfect. We admitted no visitors. Indeed the locality of our retirement had been carefully kept a secret from my own former associates; and it had been many years since Dupin had ceased

---

1   *phrenologists ... organ*   The pseudoscience of phrenology, widely influential (but nevertheless controversial) during the nineteenth century, held that the mind was divided into distinct "organs" that ruled distinct mental and psychological faculties, and whose respective sizes determined the strength or weakness of those faculties in individuals.

---

2   *Faubourg St. Germain*   District of Paris historically populated by members of the French aristocracy, though many of them abandoned their homes there following the events of the July Revolution in 1830.

to know or be known in Paris. We existed within ourselves alone.

It was a freak of fancy in my friend (for what else
shall I call it?) to be enamored of the Night for her
own sake; and into this *bizarrerie*, as into all his others,
I quietly fell; giving myself up to his wild whims with
a perfect *abandon*. The sable[1] divinity would not herself dwell with us always; but we could counterfeit her
presence. At the first dawn of the morning we closed
all the massy[2] shutters of our old building; lighting a
couple of tapers which, strongly perfumed, threw out
only the ghastliest and feeblest of rays. By the aid of
these we then busied our souls in dreams—reading,
writing, or conversing, until warned by the clock of the
advent of the true Darkness. Then we sallied forth into
the streets, arm in arm, continuing the topics of the
day, or roaming far and wide until a late hour, seeking,
amid the wild lights and shadows of the populous city,
that infinity of mental excitement which quiet observation can afford.

At such times I could not help remarking and admiring (although from his rich ideality I had been prepared to expect it) a peculiar analytic ability in Dupin.
He seemed, too, to take an eager delight in its exercise—if not exactly in its display—and did not hesitate
to confess the pleasure thus derived. He boasted to me,
with a low chuckling laugh, that most men, in respect
to himself, wore windows in their bosoms, and was
wont to follow up such assertions by direct and very
startling proofs of his intimate knowledge of my own.
His manner at these moments was frigid and abstract;
his eyes were vacant in expression; while his voice,
usually a rich tenor, rose into a treble which would
have sounded petulantly but for the deliberateness
and entire distinctness of the enunciation. Observing
him in these moods, I often dwelt meditatively upon
the old philosophy of the Bi-Part Soul,[3] and amused
myself with the fancy of a double Dupin—the creative
and the resolvent.

Let it not be supposed, from what I have just said,
that I am detailing any mystery, or penning any

romance.[4] What I have described in the Frenchman,
was merely the result of an excited, or perhaps of a diseased intelligence. But of the character of his remarks
at the periods in question an example will best convey
the idea.

We were strolling one night down a long dirty street,
in the vicinity of the Palais Royal.[5] Being both, apparently, occupied with thought, neither of us had spoken
a syllable for fifteen minutes at least. All at once Dupin
broke forth with these words:

"He is a very little fellow, that's true, and would do
better for the *Théâtre des Variétés*."[6]

"There can be no doubt of that," I replied unwittingly, and not at first observing (so much had I been
absorbed in reflection) the extraordinary manner in
which the speaker had chimed in with my meditations.
In an instant afterward I recollected myself, and my
astonishment was profound.

"Dupin," said I, gravely, "this is beyond my comprehension. I do not hesitate to say that I am amazed, and
can scarcely credit my senses. How was it possible you
should know I was thinking of ——?" Here I paused,
to ascertain beyond a doubt whether he really knew of
whom I thought.

—— "of Chantilly," said he, "why do you pause?
You were remarking to yourself that his diminutive
figure unfitted him for tragedy."

This was precisely what had formed the subject of
my reflections. Chantilly was a *quondam*[7] cobbler of
the Rue St. Denis, who, becoming stage-mad, had
attempted the *rôle* of Xerxes,[8] in Crébillon's tragedy
so called, and been notoriously Pasquinaded[9] for his
pains.

"Tell me, for Heaven's sake," I exclaimed, "the
method—if method there is—by which you have been
enabled to fathom my soul in this matter." In fact I was
even more startled than I would have been willing to
express.

---

1   *sable*   Dark.

2   *massy*   Large, weighty, or imposing.

3   *Bi-Part Soul*   Though described here as an "old philosophy," the
idea of the bi-part soul as put forward here is largely an invention of
Poe's, and remerges in his other works featuring C. Auguste Dupin.

4   *romance*   I.e., tale of magic or fantasy.

5   *Palais Royal*   Famous and well-respected playhouse.

6   *Théâtre des Variétés*   Parisian playhouse historically known for
lighthearted and comic performances.

7   *quondam*   Former.

8   *Xerxes*   Character in the tragic play *Xerxes* (1714) by Prosper
Joylot de Crébillon.

9   *Pasquinaded*   Satirized.

"It was the fruiterer," replied my friend, "who brought you to the conclusion that the mender of soles was not of sufficient height for Xerxes *et id genus omne*."[1]

"The fruiterer! You astonish me—I know no fruiterer whomsoever."

"The man who ran up against you as we entered the street—it may have been fifteen minutes ago."

I now remembered that, in fact, a fruiterer, carrying upon his head a large basket of apples, had nearly thrown me down, by accident, as we passed from the Rue C—— into the thoroughfare where we stood; but what this had to do with Chantilly I could not possibly understand.

There was not a particle of *charlatânerie*[2] about Dupin. "I will explain," he said, "and that you may comprehend all clearly, we will first retrace the course of your meditations, from the moment in which I spoke to you until that of the *rencontre*[3] with the fruiterer in question. The larger links of the chain run thus— Chantilly, Orion, Dr. Nichols, Epicurus, Stereotomy,[4] the street stones, the fruiterer."

There are few persons who have not, at some period of their lives, amused themselves in retracing the steps by which particular conclusions of their own minds have been attained. The occupation is often full of interest; and he who attempts it for the first time is astonished by the apparently illimitable distance and incoherence between the starting-point and the goal. What, then, must have been my amazement when I heard the Frenchman speak what he had just spoken, and when I could not help acknowledging that he had spoken the truth. He continued:

"We had been talking of horses, if I remember aright, just before leaving the Rue C——. This was the last subject we discussed. As we crossed into this street, a fruiterer, with a large basket upon his head, brushing

quickly past us, thrust you upon a pile of paving-stones collected at a spot where the causeway is undergoing repair. You stepped upon one of the loose fragments, slipped, slightly strained your ankle, appeared vexed or sulky, muttered a few words, turned to look at the pile, and then proceeded in silence. I was not particularly attentive to what you did; but observation has become with me, of late, a species of necessity.

"You kept your eyes upon the ground—glancing, with a petulant expression, at the holes and ruts in the pavement (so that I saw you were still thinking of the stones), until we reached the little alley called Lamartine, which has been paved, by way of experiment, with the overlapping and riveted blocks. Here your countenance brightened up, and, perceiving your lips move, I could not doubt that you murmured the word 'stereotomy,' a term very affectedly applied to this species of pavement. I knew that you could not say to yourself 'stereotomy' without being brought to think of atomies, and thus of the theories of Epicurus; and since, when we discussed this subject not very long ago, I mentioned to you how singularly, yet with how little notice, the vague guesses of that noble Greek had met with confirmation in the late nebular cosmogony, I felt that you could not avoid casting your eyes upward to the great *nebula* in Orion, and I certainly expected that you would do so. You did look up; and I was now assured that I had correctly followed your steps. But in that bitter *tirade* upon Chantilly, which appeared in yesterday's '*Musée*,' the satirist, making some disgraceful allusions to the cobbler's change of name upon assuming the buskin,[5] quoted a Latin line about which we have often conversed. I mean the line

Perdidit antiquum litera prima sonum.[6]

I had told you that this was in reference to Orion, formerly written Urion; and, from certain pungencies connected with this explanation, I was aware that you could not have forgotten it. It was clear, therefore, that you would not fail to combine the two ideas of Orion and Chantilly. That you did combine them I saw by

---

1   *et id genus omne*   Latin: and everything else of that sort.

2   *charlatânerie*   Quackery; deceptiveness.

3   *rencontre*   French: meeting, encounter.

4   *Orion*   Constellation named after the Greek mythological hunter Orion; *Dr. Nichols*   John Pringle Nichol (1804–59) was a Scottish astronomer and economist; *Epicurus*   Greek philosopher (341–270 BCE) who supported the theory that all matter is composed of small, imperceptible particles called "atoms"; *Stereotomy*   Art of cutting stones and placing them in geometric patterns.

5   *assuming the buskin*   Acting in a tragedy (a buskin was a style of boot worn by tragic actors in classical Athens).

6   *Perdidit ... sonum*   Latin: The first letter lost its original sound. From Roman poet Ovid's *Fasti*, Book 5.

the character of the smile which passed over your lips. You thought of the poor cobbler's immolation.[1] So far, you had been stooping in your gait; but now I saw you draw yourself up to your full height. I was then sure that you reflected upon the diminutive figure of Chantilly. At this point I interrupted your meditations to remark that as, in fact, he *was* a very little fellow— that Chantilly—he would do better at the *Théâtre des Variétés*."

Not long after this, we were looking over an evening edition of the "Gazette des Tribunaux," when the following paragraphs arrested our attention.

EXTRAORDINARY MURDERS. This morning, about three o'clock, the inhabitants of the Quartier St. Roch were aroused from sleep by a succession of terrific shrieks, issuing, apparently, from the fourth story of a house in the Rue Morgue, known to be in the sole occupancy of one Madame L'Espanaye, and her daughter, Mademoiselle Camille L'Espanaye. After some delay, occasioned by a fruitless attempt to procure admission in the usual manner, the gateway was broken in with a crowbar, and eight or ten of the neighbors entered, accompanied by two *gendarmes*.[2] By this time the cries had ceased; but, as the party rushed up the first flight of stairs, two or more rough voices, in angry contention, were distinguished, and seemed to proceed from the upper part of the house. As the second landing was reached, these sounds, also, had ceased, and everything remained perfectly quiet. The party spread themselves, and hurried from room to room. Upon arriving at a large back chamber in the fourth story (the door of which, being found locked, with the key inside, was forced open), a spectacle presented itself which struck every one present not less with horror than with astonishment.

The apartment was in the wildest disorder—the furniture broken and thrown about in all directions. There was only one bedstead; and from this the bed had been removed, and thrown into the middle of the floor. On a chair

lay a razor, besmeared with blood. On the hearth were two or three long and thick tresses of grey human hair, also dabbled in blood, and seeming to have been pulled out by the roots. Upon the floor were found four Napoleons,[3] an earring of topaz, three large silver spoons, three smaller of *métal d'Alger*,[4] and two bags, containing nearly four thousand francs in gold. The drawers of a *bureau*, which stood in one corner, were open, and had been, apparently, rifled, although many articles still remained in them. A small iron safe was discovered under the *bed* (not under the bedstead).[5] It was open, with the key still in the door. It had no contents beyond a few old letters, and other papers of little consequence.

Of Madame L'Espanaye no traces were here seen; but an unusual quantity of soot being observed in the fireplace, a search was made in the chimney, and (horrible to relate!) the corpse of the daughter, head downward, was dragged therefrom; it having been thus forced up the narrow aperture for a considerable distance. The body was quite warm. Upon examining it, many excoriations were perceived, no doubt occasioned by the violence with which it had been thrust up and disengaged. Upon the face were many severe scratches, and, upon the throat, dark bruises, and deep indentations of finger nails, as if the deceased had been throttled to death.

After a thorough investigation of every portion of the house, without farther discovery, the party made its way into a small paved yard in the rear of the building, where lay the corpse of the old lady, with her throat so entirely cut that, upon an attempt to raise her, the head fell off. The body, as well as the head, was fearfully mutilated—the former so much so as scarcely to retain any semblance of humanity.

To this horrible mystery there is not as yet, we believe, the slightest clue.

The next day's paper had these additional particulars.

---

1   *immolation*   Sacrificial slaughter.

2   *gendarmes*   Police officers.

3   *Napoleons*   Gold coins.

4   *métal d'Alger*   Cheap metal alloy resembling silver.

5   *bed ... bedstead*   I.e., the safe was under the mattress, not the bedframe.

The Tragedy in the Rue Morgue. Many individuals have been examined in relation to this most extraordinary and frightful affair. [The word '*affaire*' has not yet, in France, that levity of import which it conveys with us.[1]] But nothing whatever has transpired to throw light upon it. We give below all the material testimony elicited.

Pauline Dubourg, laundress, deposes that she has known both the deceased for three years, having washed for them during that period. The old lady and her daughter seemed on good terms—very affectionate towards each other. They were excellent pay. Could not speak in regard to their mode or means of living. Believed that Madame L. told fortunes for a living. Was reputed to have money put by. Never met any persons in the house when she called for the clothes or took them home. Was sure that they had no servant in employ. There appeared to be no furniture in any part of the building except in the fourth story.

Pierre Moreau, tobacconist, deposes that he has been in the habit of selling small quantities of tobacco and snuff[2] to Madame L'Espanaye for nearly four years. Was born in the neighborhood, and has always resided there. The deceased and her daughter had occupied the house in which the corpses were found, for more than six years. It was formerly occupied by a jeweller, who under-let the upper rooms to various persons. The house was the property of Madame L. She became dissatisfied with the abuse of the premises by her tenant, and moved into them herself, refusing to let any portion. The old lady was childish. Witness had seen the daughter some five or six times during the six years. The two lived an exceedingly retired life—were reputed to have money. Had heard it said among the neighbors that Madame L. told fortunes—did not believe it. Had never seen any person enter the door except the old lady and her daughter, a porter once or twice, and a physician some eight or ten times.

Many other persons, neighbors, gave evidence to the same effect. No one was spoken of as frequenting the house. It was not known whether there were any living connections of Madame L. and her daughter. The shutters of the front windows were seldom opened. Those in the rear were always closed, with the exception of the large back room, fourth story. The house was a good house—not very old.

Isidore Musèt, *gendarme*, deposes that he was called to the house about three o'clock in the morning, and found some twenty or thirty persons at the gateway, endeavoring to gain admittance. Forced it open, at length, with a bayonet—not with a crowbar. Had but little difficulty in getting it open, on account of its being a double or folding gate, and bolted neither at bottom nor top. The shrieks were continued until the gate was forced—and then suddenly ceased. They seemed to be screams of some person (or persons) in great agony—were loud and drawn out, not short and quick. Witness led the way up stairs. Upon reaching the first landing, heard two voices in loud and angry contention—the one a gruff voice, the other much shriller—a very strange voice. Could distinguish some words of the former, which was that of a Frenchman. Was positive that it was not a woman's voice. Could distinguish the words "*sacré*" and "*diable*."[3] The shrill voice was that of a foreigner. Could not be sure whether it was the voice of a man or of a woman. Could not make out what was said, but believed the language to be Spanish. The state of the room and of the bodies was described by this witness as we described them yesterday.

Henri Duval, a neighbor, and by trade a silver-smith, deposes that he was one of the party who first entered the house. Corroborates the testimony of Musèt in general. As soon as they forced an entrance, they reclosed the door, to keep out the crowd, which collected very fast, notwithstanding the lateness of the hour. The shrill voice, this witness thinks, was that of an Italian. Was certain it was not French. Could

---

[1]   *The word ... with us*   In nineteenth-century American English, "affair" could carry an air of condescension or belittlement.

[2]   *snuff*   Ground tobacco inhaled through the nostrils.

[3]   *sacré ... diable*   French exclamations meaning "holy" and "devil."

not be sure that it was a man's voice. It might have been a woman's. Was not acquainted with the Italian language. Could not distinguish the words, but was convinced by the intonation that the speaker was an Italian. Knew Madame L. and her daughter. Had conversed with both frequently. Was sure that the shrill voice was not that of either of the deceased.

—— *Odenheimer, restaurateur.* This witness volunteered his testimony. Not speaking French, was examined through an interpreter. Is a native of Amsterdam. Was passing the house at the time of the shrieks. They lasted for several minutes—probably ten. They were long and loud—very awful and distressing. Was one of those who entered the building. Corroborated the previous evidence in every respect but one. Was sure that the shrill voice was that of a man—of a Frenchman. Could not distinguish the words uttered. They were loud and quick—unequal—spoken apparently in fear as well as in anger. The voice was harsh—not so much shrill as harsh. Could not call it a shrill voice. The gruff voice said repeatedly "*sacré*," "*diable*," and once "*mon Dieu*."[1]

Jules Mignaud, banker, of the firm of Mignaud et Fils, Rue Deloraine. Is the elder Mignaud. Madame L'Espanaye had some property. Had opened an account with his banking house in the spring of the year —— (eight years previously). Made frequent deposits in small sums. Had checked for nothing until the third day before her death, when she took out in person the sum of 4000 francs. This sum was paid in gold, and a clerk sent home with the money.

Adolphe Le Bon, clerk to Mignaud et Fils, deposes that on the day in question, about noon, he accompanied Madame L'Espanaye to her residence with the 4000 francs, put up in two bags. Upon the door being opened, Mademoiselle L. appeared and took from his hands one of the bags, while the old lady relieved him of the other. He then bowed and departed. Did not see

any person in the street at the time. It is a bye-street[2]—very lonely.

William Bird, tailor, deposes that he was one of the party who entered the house. Is an Englishman. Has lived in Paris two years. Was one of the first to ascend the stairs. Heard the voices in contention. The gruff voice was that of a Frenchman. Could make out several words, but cannot now remember all. Heard distinctly "*sacré*" and "*mon Dieu*." There was a sound at the moment as if of several persons struggling—a scraping and scuffling sound. The shrill voice was very loud—louder than the gruff one. Is sure that it was not the voice of an Englishman. Appeared to be that of a German. Might have been a woman's voice. Does not understand German.

Four of the above-named witnesses, being recalled, deposed that the door of the chamber in which was found the body of Mademoiselle L. was locked on the inside when the party reached it. Everything was perfectly silent—no groans or noises of any kind. Upon forcing the door no person was seen. The windows, both of the back and front room, were down and firmly fastened from within. A door between the two rooms was closed, but not locked. The door leading from the front room into the passage was locked, with the key on the inside. A small room in the front of the house, on the fourth story, at the head of the passage, was open, the door being ajar. This room was crowded with old beds, boxes, and so forth. These were carefully removed and searched. There was not an inch of any portion of the house which was not carefully searched. Sweeps were sent up and down the chimneys. The house was a four story one, with garrets (*mansardes*). A trap-door on the roof was nailed down very securely—did not appear to have been opened for years. The time elapsing between the hearing of the voices in contention and the breaking open of the room door, was variously stated by the witnesses. Some made it as short as three minutes—some as long as five. The door was opened with difficulty.

---

[1]   *mon Dieu* French: my God.

[2]   *bye-street* Side street or alley.

Alfonzo Garcio, undertaker, deposes that he resides in the Rue Morgue. Is a native of Spain. Was one of the party who entered the house. Did not proceed up stairs. Is nervous, and was apprehensive of the consequences of agitation. Heard the voices in contention. The gruff voice was that of a Frenchman. Could not distinguish what was said. The shrill voice was that of an Englishman—is sure of this. Does not understand the English language, but judges by the intonation.

Alberto Montani, confectioner, deposes that he was among the first to ascend the stairs. Heard the voices in question. The gruff voice was that of a Frenchman. Distinguished several words. The speaker appeared to be expostulating. Could not make out the words of the shrill voice. Spoke quick and unevenly. Thinks it the voice of a Russian. Corroborates the general testimony. Is an Italian. Never conversed with a native of Russia.

Several witnesses, recalled, here testified that the chimneys of all the rooms on the fourth story were too narrow to admit the passage of a human being. By "sweeps" were meant cylindrical sweeping-brushes, such as are employed by those who clean chimneys. These brushes were passed up and down every flue in the house. There is no back passage by which anyone could have descended while the party proceeded up stairs. The body of Mademoiselle L'Espanaye was so firmly wedged in the chimney that it could not be got down until four or five of the party united their strength.

Paul Dumas, physician, deposes that he was called to view the bodies about day-break. They were both then lying on the sacking of the bedstead in the chamber where Mademoiselle L. was found. The corpse of the young lady was much bruised and excoriated. The fact that it had been thrust up the chimney would sufficiently account for these appearances. The throat was greatly chafed. There were several deep scratches just below the chin, together with a series of livid spots which were evidently the impression of fingers. The face was fearfully discolored, and the eyeballs protruded. The tongue had been partially bitten through. A large bruise was discovered upon the pit of the stomach, produced, apparently, by the pressure of a knee. In the opinion of M. Dumas, Mademoiselle L'Espanaye had been throttled to death by some person or persons unknown. The corpse of the mother was horribly mutilated. All the bones of the right leg and arm were more or less shattered. The left *tibia* much splintered, as well as all the ribs of the left side. Whole body dreadfully bruised and discolored. It was not possible to say how the injuries had been inflicted. A heavy club of wood, or a broad bar of iron—a chair—any large, heavy, and obtuse weapon would have produced such results, if wielded by the hands of a very powerful man. No woman could have inflicted the blows with any weapon. The head of the deceased, when seen by witness, was entirely separated from the body, and was also greatly shattered. The throat had evidently been cut with some very sharp instrument—probably with a razor.

Alexandre Etienne, surgeon, was called with M. Dumas to view the bodies. Corroborated the testimony, and the opinions of M. Dumas.

Nothing farther of importance was elicited, although several other persons were examined. A murder so mysterious, and so perplexing in all its particulars, was never before committed in Paris—if indeed a murder has been committed at all. The police are entirely at fault[1]—an unusual occurrence in affairs of this nature. There is not, however, the shadow of a clue apparent.

The evening edition of the paper stated that the greatest excitement still continued in the Quartier St. Roch—that the premises in question had been carefully re-searched, and fresh examinations of witnesses instituted, but all to no purpose. A postscript, however, mentioned that Adolphe Le Bon had been arrested and imprisoned—although nothing appeared to criminate him, beyond the facts already detailed.

Dupin seemed singularly interested in the progress of this affair—at least so I judged from his manner, for

---

[1]   *at fault* Baffled.

he made no comments. It was only after the announcement that Le Bon had been imprisoned, that he asked me my opinion respecting the murders.

I could merely agree with all Paris in considering them an insoluble mystery. I saw no means by which it would be possible to trace the murderer.

"We must not judge of the means," said Dupin, "by this shell of an examination. The Parisian police, so much extolled for *acumen*, are cunning, but no more. There is no method in their proceedings, beyond the method of the moment. They make a vast parade of measures; but, not unfrequently, these are so ill adapted to the objects proposed, as to put us in mind of Monsieur Jourdain's calling for his *robe-de-chambre—pour mieux entendre la musique*.[1] The results attained by them are not unfrequently surprising, but, for the most part, are brought about by simple diligence and activity. When these qualities are unavailing, their schemes fail. Vidocq,[2] for example, was a good guesser, and a persevering man. But, without educated thought, he erred continually by the very intensity of his investigations. He impaired his vision by holding the object too close. He might see, perhaps, one or two points with unusual clearness, but in so doing he, necessarily, lost sight of the matter as a whole. Thus there is such a thing as being too profound. Truth is not always in a well.[3] In fact, as regards the more important knowledge, I do believe that she is invariably superficial. The depth lies in the valleys where we seek her, and not upon the mountain-tops where she is found. The modes and sources of this kind of error are well typified in the contemplation of the heavenly bodies. To look at a star by glances—to view it in a side-long way, by turning toward it the exterior portions of the *retina* (more susceptible of feeble impressions of light than the interior), is to behold the star distinctly—is to

have the best appreciation of its lustre—a lustre which grows dim just in proportion as we turn our vision *fully* upon it. A greater number of rays actually fall upon the eye in the latter case, but, in the former, there is the more refined capacity for comprehension. By undue profundity we perplex and enfeeble thought; and it is possible to make even Venus[4] herself vanish from the firmament by a scrutiny too sustained, too concentrated, or too direct.

"As for these murders, let us enter into some examinations for ourselves, before we make up an opinion respecting them. An inquiry will afford us amusement," [I thought this an odd term, so applied, but said nothing] "and, besides, Le Bon once rendered me a service for which I am not ungrateful. We will go and see the premises with our own eyes. I know G——, the Prefect of Police, and shall have no difficulty in obtaining the necessary permission."

The permission was obtained, and we proceeded at once to the Rue Morgue. This is one of those miserable thoroughfares which intervene between the Rue Richelieu and the Rue St. Roch. It was late in the afternoon when we reached it; as this quarter is at a great distance from that in which we resided. The house was readily found; for there were still many persons gazing up at the closed shutters, with an objectless curiosity, from the opposite side of the way. It was an ordinary Parisian house, with a gateway, on one side of which was a glazed watch-box, with a sliding panel in the window, indicating a *loge de concierge*. Before going in we walked up the street, turned down an alley, and then, again turning, passed in the rear of the building—Dupin, meanwhile, examining the whole neighborhood, as well as the house, with a minuteness of attention for which I could see no possible object.

Retracing our steps, we came again to the front of the dwelling, rang, and, having shown our credentials, were admitted by the agents in charge. We went up stairs—into the chamber where the body of Mademoiselle L'Espanaye had been found, and where both the deceased still lay. The disorders of the room had, as usual, been suffered to exist. I saw nothing beyond what had been stated in the "Gazette des Tribunaux." Dupin scrutinized everything—not excepting the bodies of the victims. We then went into

---

[1]   *pour mieux … la musique* French: to better hear the music. The phrase is an allusion to French playwright Molière's *Bourgeois gentilhomme* (1670), in which the foolish protagonist, Mr. Jourdain, calls for his "robe de chambre," or dressing gown, in order to better appreciate chamber music.

[2]   *Vidocq* Eugène François Vidocq (1775–1857), former convict who eventually became head of the French police force and a private detective.

[3]   *Truth is … well* Reference to the proverbial statement "truth lies at the bottom of a well," often attributed to the ancient Greek philosopher Democritus (c. 460–c. 370 BCE).

[4]   *Venus* One of the brightest objects in the night sky.

the other rooms, and into the yard; a *gendarme* accompanying us throughout. The examination occupied us until dark, when we took our departure. On our way home my companion stepped in for a moment at the office of one of the daily papers.

I have said that the whims of my friend were manifold, and that *Je les ménagais*[1]—for this phrase there is no English equivalent. It was his humor, now, to decline all conversation on the subject of the murder, until about noon the next day. He then asked me, suddenly, if I had observed any thing *peculiar* at the scene of the atrocity.

There was something in his manner of emphasizing the word "peculiar," which caused me to shudder, without knowing why.

"No, nothing *peculiar*," I said; "nothing more, at least, than we both saw stated in the paper."

"The 'Gazette,'" he replied, "has not entered, I fear, into the unusual horror of the thing. But dismiss the idle opinions of this print. It appears to me that this mystery is considered insoluble, for the very reason which should cause it to be regarded as easy of solution—I mean for the *outré*[2] character of its features. The police are confounded by the seeming absence of motive—not for the murder itself—but for the atrocity of the murder. They are puzzled, too, by the seeming impossibility of reconciling the voices heard in contention, with the facts that no one was discovered up stairs but the assassinated Mademoiselle L'Espanaye, and that there were no means of egress without the notice of the party ascending. The wild disorder of the room; the corpse thrust, with the head downward, up the chimney; the frightful mutilation of the body of the old lady; these considerations, with those just mentioned, and others which I need not mention, have sufficed to paralyze the powers, by putting completely at fault the boasted *acumen*, of the government agents. They have fallen into the gross but common error of confounding the unusual with the abstruse. But it is by these deviations from the plane of the ordinary, that reason feels its way, if at all, in its search for the true. In investigations such as we are now pursuing, it should not be so much asked 'what has occurred,' as 'what has occurred that has never occurred before.' In fact, the

facility with which I shall arrive, or have arrived, at the solution of this mystery, is in the direct ratio of its apparent insolubility in the eyes of the police."

I stared at the speaker in mute astonishment.

"I am now awaiting," continued he, looking toward the door of our apartment—"I am now awaiting a person who, although perhaps not the perpetrator of these butcheries, must have been in some measure implicated in their perpetration. Of the worst portion of the crimes committed, it is probable that he is innocent. I hope that I am right in this supposition; for upon it I build my expectation of reading the entire riddle. I look for the man here—in this room—every moment. It is true that he may not arrive; but the probability is that he will. Should he come, it will be necessary to detain him. Here are pistols; and we both know how to use them when occasion demands their use."

I took the pistols, scarcely knowing what I did, or believing what I heard, while Dupin went on, very much as if in a soliloquy. I have already spoken of his abstract manner at such times. His discourse was addressed to myself; but his voice, although by no means loud, had that intonation which is commonly employed in speaking to some one at a great distance. His eyes, vacant in expression, regarded only the wall.

"That the voices heard in contention," he said, "by the party upon the stairs, were not the voices of the women themselves, was fully proved by the evidence. This relieves us of all doubt upon the question whether the old lady could have first destroyed the daughter, and afterward have committed suicide. I speak of this point chiefly for the sake of method; for the strength of Madame L'Espanaye would have been utterly unequal to the task of thrusting her daughter's corpse up the chimney as it was found; and the nature of the wounds upon her own person entirely preclude the idea of self-destruction. Murder, then, has been committed by some third party; and the voices of this third party were those heard in contention. Let me now advert—not to the whole testimony respecting these voices—but to what was *peculiar* in that testimony. Did you observe anything peculiar about it?"

I remarked that, while all the witnesses agreed in supposing the gruff voice to be that of a Frenchman,

---

[1]   *Je les ménagais*   French: I humored them.

[2]   *outré*   Outrageous, abnormal.

there was much disagreement in regard to the shrill, or, as one individual termed it, the harsh voice.

"That was the evidence itself," said Dupin, "but it was not the peculiarity of the evidence. You have observed nothing distinctive. Yet there *was* something to be observed. The witnesses, as you remark, agreed about the gruff voice; they were here unanimous. But in regard to the shrill voice, the peculiarity is—not that they disagreed—but that, while an Italian, an Englishman, a Spaniard, a Hollander, and a Frenchman attempted to describe it, each one spoke of it as that *of a foreigner.* Each is sure that it was not the voice of one of his own countrymen. Each likens it—not to the voice of an individual of any nation with whose language he is conversant—but the converse. The Frenchman supposes it the voice of a Spaniard, and 'might have distinguished some words *had he been acquainted with the Spanish.'* The Dutchman maintains it to have been that of a Frenchman; but we find it stated that '*not understanding French this witness was examined through an interpreter.'* The Englishman thinks it the voice of a German, and '*does not understand German.'* The Spaniard 'is sure' that it was that of an Englishman, but 'judges by the intonation' altogether, '*as he has no knowledge of the English.'* The Italian believes it the voice of a Russian, but '*has never conversed with a native of Russia.'* A second Frenchman differs, moreover, with the first, and is positive that the voice was that of an Italian; but, *not being cognizant of that tongue*, is, like the Spaniard, 'convinced by the intonation.' Now, how strangely unusual must that voice have really been, about which such testimony as this *could* have been elicited! in whose *tones*, even, denizens of the five great divisions of Europe could recognise nothing familiar! You will say that it might have been the voice of an Asiatic—of an African. Neither Asiatics nor Africans abound in Paris; but, without denying the inference, I will now merely call your attention to three points. The voice is termed by one witness 'harsh rather than shrill.' It is represented by two others to have been 'quick and *unequal.'* No words—no sounds resembling words— were by any witness mentioned as distinguishable.

"I know not," continued Dupin, "what impression I may have made, so far, upon your own understanding; but I do not hesitate to say that legitimate deductions even from this portion of the testimony—the portion respecting the gruff and shrill voices—are in themselves sufficient to engender a suspicion which should give direction to all farther progress in the investigation of the mystery. I said 'legitimate deductions'; but my meaning is not thus fully expressed. I designed to imply that the deductions are the *sole* proper ones, and that the suspicion arises *inevitably* from them as the single result. What the suspicion is, however, I will not say just yet. I merely wish you to bear in mind that, with myself, it was sufficiently forcible to give a definite form—a certain tendency—to my inquiries in the chamber.

"Let us now transport ourselves, in fancy, to this chamber. What shall we first seek here? The means of egress employed by the murderers. It is not too much to say that neither of us believe in preternatural events. Madame and Mademoiselle L'Espanaye were not destroyed by spirits. The doers of the deed were material, and escaped materially. Then how? Fortunately, there is but one mode of reasoning upon the point, and that mode *must* lead us to a definite decision. Let us examine, each by each, the possible means of egress. It is clear that the assassins were in the room where Mademoiselle L'Espanaye was found, or at least in the room adjoining, when the party ascended the stairs. It is then only from these two apartments that we have to seek issues. The police have laid bare the floors, the ceilings, and the masonry of the walls, in every direction. No *secret* issues could have escaped their vigilance. But, not trusting to *their* eyes, I examined with my own. There were, then, *no* secret issues. Both doors leading from the rooms into the passage were securely locked, with the keys inside. Let us turn to the chimneys. These, although of ordinary width for some eight or ten feet above the hearths, will not admit, throughout their extent, the body of a large cat. The impossibility of egress, by means already stated, being thus absolute, we are reduced to the windows. Through those of the front room no one could have escaped without notice from the crowd in the street. The murderers *must* have passed, then, through those of the back room. Now, brought to this conclusion in so unequivocal a manner as we are, it is not our part, as reasoners, to reject it on account of apparent impossibilities. It is only left for us to prove that these apparent 'impossibilities' are, in reality, not such.

"There are two windows in the chamber. One of them is unobstructed by furniture, and is wholly visible. The lower portion of the other is hidden from view by the head of the unwieldy bedstead which is thrust close up against it. The former was found securely fastened from within. It resisted the utmost force of those who endeavored to raise it. A large gimlet-hole[1] had been pierced in its frame to the left, and a very stout nail was found fitted therein, nearly to the head. Upon examining the other window, a similar nail was seen similarly fitted in it; and a vigorous attempt to raise this sash, failed also. The police were now entirely satisfied that egress had not been in these directions. And, *therefore*, it was thought a matter of supererogation[2] to withdraw the nails and open the windows.

"My own examination was somewhat more particular, and was so for the reason I have just given—because here it was, I knew, that all apparent impossibilities *must* be proved to be not such in reality.

"I proceeded to think thus—à posteriori.[3] The murderers *did* escape from one of these windows. This being so, they could not have re-fastened the sashes from the inside, as they were found fastened; the consideration which put a stop, through its obviousness, to the scrutiny of the police in this quarter. Yet the sashes *were* fastened. They *must*, then, have the power of fastening themselves. There was no escape from this conclusion. I stepped to the unobstructed casement, withdrew the nail with some difficulty, and attempted to raise the sash. It resisted all my efforts, as I had anticipated. A concealed spring must, I now knew, exist; and this corroboration of my idea convinced me that my premises, at least, were correct, however mysterious still appeared the circumstances attending the nails. A careful search soon brought to light the hidden spring. I pressed it, and, satisfied with the discovery, forbore to upraise the sash.

"I now replaced the nail and regarded it attentively. A person passing out through this window might have reclosed it, and the spring would have caught—but the nail could not have been replaced. The conclusion was

plain, and again narrowed in the field of my investigations. The assassins *must* have escaped through the other window. Supposing, then, the springs upon each sash to be the same, as was probable, there *must* be found a difference between the nails, or at least between the modes of their fixture. Getting upon the sacking of the bedstead, I looked over the headboard minutely at the second casement. Passing my hand down behind the board, I readily discovered and pressed the spring, which was, as I had supposed, identical in character with its neighbor. I now looked at the nail. It was as stout as the other, and apparently fitted in in the same manner—driven in nearly up to the head.

"You will say that I was puzzled; but, if you think so, you must have misunderstood the nature of the inductions. To use a sporting phrase, I had not been once 'at fault.' The scent had never for an instant been lost. There was no flaw in any link of the chain. I had traced the secret to its ultimate result—and that result was *the nail*. It had, I say, in every respect, the appearance of its fellow in the other window; but this fact was an absolute nullity (conclusive as it might seem to be) when compared with the consideration that here, at this point, terminated the clue. 'There *must* be something wrong,' I said, 'about the nail.' I touched it; and the head, with about a quarter of an inch of the shank, came off in my fingers. The rest of the shank was in the gimlet-hole, where it had been broken off. The fracture was an old one (for its edges were incrusted with rust), and had apparently been accomplished by the blow of a hammer, which had partially embedded, in the top of the bottom sash, the head portion of the nail. I now carefully replaced this head portion in the indentation whence I had taken it, and the resemblance to a perfect nail was complete—the fissure was invisible. Pressing the spring, I gently raised the sash for a few inches; the head went up with it, remaining firm in its bed. I closed the window, and the semblance of the whole nail was again perfect.

"The riddle, so far, was now unriddled. The assassin had escaped through the window which looked upon the bed. Dropping of its own accord upon his exit (or perhaps purposely closed), it had become fastened by the spring; and it was the retention of this spring which had been mistaken by the police for that of the nail—farther inquiry being thus considered unnecessary.

---

1 *gimlet-hole* Hole made with a small drilling tool.

2 *supererogation* Performance of a task that is above and beyond what is required.

3 *à posteriori* Latin: from the later; i.e., knowledge derived by working backwards from available evidence.

"The next question is that of the mode of descent. Upon this point I had been satisfied in my walk with you around the building. About five feet and a half from the casement in question there runs a lightning-rod. From this rod it would have been impossible for anyone to reach the window itself, to say nothing of entering it. I observed, however, that the shutters of the fourth story were of the peculiar kind called by Parisian carpenters *ferrades*—a kind rarely employed at the present day, but frequently seen upon very old mansions at Lyons and Bordeaux. They are in the form of an ordinary door (a single, not a folding door), except that the lower half is latticed or worked in open trellis—thus affording an excellent hold for the hands. In the present instance these shutters are fully three feet and a half broad. When we saw them from the rear of the house, they were both about half open—that is to say, they stood off at right angles from the wall. It is probable that the police, as well as myself, examined the back of the tenement; but, if so, in looking at these *ferrades* in the line of their breadth (as they must have done), they did not perceive this great breadth itself, or, at all events, failed to take it into due consideration. In fact, having once satisfied themselves that no egress could have been made in this quarter, they would naturally bestow here a very cursory examination. It was clear to me, however, that the shutter belonging to the window at the head of the bed, would, if swung fully back to the wall, reach to within two feet of the lightning-rod. It was also evident that, by exertion of a very unusual degree of activity and courage, an entrance into the window, from the rod, might have been thus effected. By reaching to the distance of two feet and a half (we now suppose the shutter open to its whole extent) a robber might have taken a firm grasp upon the trellis-work. Letting go, then, his hold upon the rod, placing his feet securely against the wall, and springing boldly from it, he might have swung the shutter so as to close it, and, if we imagine the window open at the time, might even have swung himself into the room.

"I wish you to bear especially in mind that I have spoken of a *very* unusual degree of activity as requisite to success in so hazardous and so difficult a feat. It is my design to show you, first, that the thing might possibly have been accomplished—but, secondly and *chiefly*, I wish to impress upon your understanding the

very extraordinary—the almost preternatural character of that agility which could have accomplished it.

"You will say, no doubt, using the language of the law, that 'to make out my case,' I should rather undervalue, than insist upon a full estimation of the activity required in this matter. This may be the practice in law, but it is not the usage of reason. My ultimate object is only the truth. My immediate purpose is to lead you to place in juxtaposition, that *very unusual* activity of which I have just spoken, with that *very peculiar* shrill (or harsh) and *unequal* voice, about whose nationality no two persons could be found to agree, and in whose utterance no syllabification could be detected."

At these words a vague and half-formed conception of the meaning of Dupin flitted over my mind. I seemed to be upon the verge of comprehension, without power to comprehend—as men, at times, find themselves upon the brink of remembrance, without being able, in the end, to remember. My friend went on with his discourse.

"You will see," he said, "that I have shifted the question from the mode of egress to that of ingress. It was my design to convey the idea that both were effected in the same manner, at the same point. Let us now revert to the interior of the room. Let us survey the appearances here. The drawers of the bureau, it is said, had been rifled, although many articles of apparel still remained within them. The conclusion here is absurd. It is a mere guess—a very silly one—and no more. How are we to know that the articles found in the drawers were not all these drawers had originally contained? Madame L'Espanaye and her daughter lived an exceedingly retired life—saw no company—seldom went out—had little use for numerous changes of habiliment. Those found were at least of as good quality as any likely to be possessed by these ladies. If a thief had taken any, why did he not take the best—why did he not take all? In a word, why did he abandon four thousand francs in gold to encumber himself with a bundle of linen? The gold *was* abandoned. Nearly the whole sum mentioned by Monsieur Mignaud, the banker, was discovered, in bags, upon the floor. I wish you, therefore, to discard from your thoughts the blundering idea of *motive*, engendered in the brains of the police by that portion of the evidence which speaks of money delivered at the door of the house.

Coincidences ten times as remarkable as this (the delivery of the money, and murder committed within three days upon the party receiving it), happen to all of us every hour of our lives, without attracting even momentary notice. Coincidences, in general, are great stumbling-blocks in the way of that class of thinkers who have been educated to know nothing of the theory of probabilities—that theory to which the most glorious objects of human research are indebted for the most glorious of illustration. In the present instance, had the gold been gone, the fact of its delivery three days before would have formed something more than a coincidence. It would have been corroborative of this idea of motive. But, under the real circumstances of the case, if we are to suppose gold the motive of this outrage, we must also imagine the perpetrator so vacillating an idiot as to have abandoned his gold and his motive together.

"Keeping now steadily in mind the points to which I have drawn your attention—that peculiar voice, that unusual agility, and that startling absence of motive in a murder so singularly atrocious as this—let us glance at the butchery itself. Here is a woman strangled to death by manual strength, and thrust up a chimney, head downward. Ordinary assassins employ no such modes of murder as this. Least of all, do they thus dispose of the murdered. In the manner of thrusting the corpse up the chimney, you will admit that there was something *excessively outré*—something altogether irreconcilable with our common notions of human action, even when we suppose the actors the most depraved of men. Think, too, how great must have been that strength which could have thrust the body *up* such an aperture so forcibly that the united vigor of several persons was found barely sufficient to drag it *down*!

"Turn, now, to other indications of the employment of a vigor most marvellous. On the hearth were thick tresses—very thick tresses—of grey human hair. These had been torn out by the roots. You are aware of the great force necessary in tearing thus from the head even twenty or thirty hairs together. You saw the locks in question as well as myself. Their roots (a hideous sight!) were clotted with fragments of the flesh of the scalp—sure token of the prodigious power which had been exerted in uprooting perhaps half a million of hairs

at a time. The throat of the old lady was not merely cut, but the head absolutely severed from the body: the instrument was a mere razor. I wish you also to look at the *brutal* ferocity of these deeds. Of the bruises upon the body of Madame L'Espanaye I do not speak. Monsieur Dumas, and his worthy coadjutor Monsieur Etienne, have pronounced that they were inflicted by some obtuse instrument; and so far these gentlemen are very correct. The obtuse instrument was clearly the stone pavement in the yard, upon which the victim had fallen from the window which looked in upon the bed. This idea, however simple it may now seem, escaped the police for the same reason that the breadth of the shutters escaped them—because, by the affair of the nails, their perceptions had been hermetically sealed against the possibility of the windows having ever been opened at all.

"If now, in addition to all these things, you have properly reflected upon the odd disorder of the chamber, we have gone so far as to combine the ideas of an agility astounding, a strength superhuman, a ferocity brutal, a butchery without motive, a *grotesquerie* in horror absolutely alien from humanity, and a voice foreign in tone to the ears of men of many nations, and devoid of all distinct or intelligible syllabification. What result, then, has ensued? What impression have I made upon your fancy?"

I felt a creeping of the flesh as Dupin asked me the question. "A madman," I said, "has done this deed—some raving maniac, escaped from a neighboring *Maison de Santé*."[1]

"In some respects," he replied, "your idea is not irrelevant. But the voices of madmen, even in their wildest paroxysms, are never found to tally with that peculiar voice heard upon the stairs. Madmen are of some nation, and their language, however incoherent in its words, has always the coherence of syllabification. Besides, the hair of a madman is not such as I now hold in my hand. I disentangled this little tuft from the rigidly clutched fingers of Madame L'Espanaye. Tell me what you can make of it."

"Dupin!" I said, completely unnerved; "this hair is most unusual—this is no *human* hair."

---

[1] *Maison de Santé* French: House of health; an asylum for the mentally ill.

"I have not asserted that it is," said he; "but, before we decide this point, I wish you to glance at the little sketch I have here traced upon this paper. It is a *facsimile* drawing of what has been described in one portion of the testimony as 'dark bruises, and deep indentations of finger nails,' upon the throat of Mademoiselle L'Espanaye, and, in another (by Messrs. Dumas and Etienne), as a 'series of livid spots, evidently the impression of fingers.'

"You will perceive," continued my friend, spreading out the paper upon the table before us, "that this drawing gives the idea of a firm and fixed hold. There is no *slipping* apparent. Each finger has retained—possibly until the death of the victim—the fearful grasp by which it originally imbedded itself. Attempt, now, to place all your fingers, at the same time, in the respective impressions as you see them."

I made the attempt in vain.

"We are possibly not giving this matter a fair trial," he said. "The paper is spread out upon a plane surface; but the human throat is cylindrical. Here is a billet of wood, the circumference of which is about that of the throat. Wrap the drawing around it, and try the experiment again."

I did so; but the difficulty was even more obvious than before. "This," I said, "is the mark of no human hand."

"Read now," replied Dupin, "this passage from Cuvier."[1]

It was a minute anatomical and generally descriptive account of the large fulvous Ourang-Outang[2] of the East Indian Islands. The gigantic stature, the prodigious strength and activity, the wild ferocity, and the imitative propensities of these mammalia are sufficiently well known to all. I understood the full horrors of the murder at once.

"The description of the digits," said I, as I made an end of reading, "is in exact accordance with this drawing. I see that no animal but an Ourang-Outang, of the species here mentioned, could have impressed the indentations as you have traced them. This tuft of tawny hair, too, is identical in character with that of the beast of Cuvier. But I cannot possibly comprehend the particulars of this frightful mystery. Besides, there were *two* voices heard in contention, and one of them was unquestionably the voice of a Frenchman."

"True; and you will remember an expression attributed almost unanimously, by the evidence, to this voice—the expression, '*mon Dieu!*' This, under the circumstances, has been justly characterized by one of the witnesses (Montani, the confectioner) as an expression of remonstrance or expostulation. Upon these two words, therefore, I have mainly built my hopes of a full solution of the riddle. A Frenchman was cognizant of the murder. It is possible—indeed it is far more than probable—that he was innocent of all participation in the bloody transactions which took place. The Ourang-Outang may have escaped from him. He may have traced it to the chamber; but, under the agitating circumstances which ensued, he could never have re-captured it. It is still at large. I will not pursue these guesses—for I have no right to call them more—since the shades of reflection upon which they are based are scarcely of sufficient depth to be appreciable by my own intellect, and since I could not pretend to make them intelligible to the understanding of another. We will call them guesses then, and speak of them as such. If the Frenchman in question is indeed, as I suppose, innocent of this atrocity, this advertisement, which I left last night, upon our return home, at the office of 'Le Monde' (a paper devoted to the shipping interest, and much sought by sailors), will bring him to our residence."

He handed me a paper, and I read thus:

Caught—*In the Bois de Boulogne,*[3] *early in the morning of the* —— *inst.* (the morning of the murder), *a very large, tawny Ourang-Outang of the Bornese species. The owner (who is ascertained to be a sailor, belonging to a Maltese vessel), may have the animal again, upon identifying it satisfactorily, and paying a few charges arising from its capture and keeping. Call at No.* ——, *Rue* ——, *Faubourg St. Germain—au troisiême.*[4]

---

1   *Cuvier* Georges Cuvier (1769–1832), French naturalist and paleontologist.

2   *fulvous Ourang-Outang* Reddish-yellow orangutan.

3   *Bois de Boulogne* Large city park in Paris.

4   *au troisiême* French: on the third (floor).

"How was it possible," I asked, "that you should know the man to be a sailor, and belonging to a Maltese vessel?"

"I do *not* know it," said Dupin. "I am not *sure* of it. Here, however, is a small piece of ribbon, which from its form, and from its greasy appearance, has evidently been used in tying the hair in one of those long *queues*[1] of which sailors are so fond. Moreover, this knot is one which few besides sailors can tie, and is peculiar to the Maltese. I picked the ribbon up at the foot of the lightning-rod. It could not have belonged to either of the deceased. Now if, after all, I am wrong in my induction from this ribbon, that the Frenchman was a sailor belonging to a Maltese vessel, still I can have done no harm in saying what I did in the advertisement. If I am in error, he will merely suppose that I have been misled by some circumstance into which he will not take the trouble to inquire. But if I am right, a great point is gained. Cognizant although innocent of the murder, the Frenchman will naturally hesitate about replying to the advertisement—about demanding the Ourang-Outang. He will reason thus: 'I am innocent; I am poor; my Ourang-Outang is of great value—to one in my circumstances a fortune of itself—why should I lose it through idle apprehensions of danger? Here it is, within my grasp. It was found in the Bois de Boulogne—at a vast distance from the scene of that butchery. How can it ever be suspected that a brute beast should have done the deed? The police are at fault—they have failed to procure the slightest clue. Should they even trace the animal, it would be impossible to prove me cognizant of the murder, or to implicate me in guilt on account of that cognizance. Above all, *I am known*. The advertiser designates me as the possessor of the beast. I am not sure to what limit his knowledge may extend. Should I avoid claiming a property of so great value, which it is known that I possess, I will render the animal at least, liable to suspicion. It is not my policy to attract attention either to myself or to the beast. I will answer the advertisement, get the Ourang-Outang, and keep it close until this matter has blown over.'"

At this moment we heard a step upon the stairs.

"Be ready," said Dupin, "with your pistols, but neither use them nor show them until at a signal from myself."

The front door of the house had been left open, and the visitor had entered, without ringing, and advanced several steps upon the staircase. Now, however, he seemed to hesitate. Presently we heard him descending. Dupin was moving quickly to the door, when we again heard him coming up. He did not turn back a second time, but stepped up with decision, and rapped at the door of our chamber.

"Come in," said Dupin, in a cheerful and hearty tone.

A man entered. He was a sailor, evidently—a tall, stout, and muscular-looking person, with a certain dare-devil expression of countenance, not altogether unprepossessing. His face, greatly sunburnt, was more than half hidden by whisker and *mustachio*. He had with him a huge oaken cudgel, but appeared to be otherwise unarmed. He bowed awkwardly, and bade us "good evening," in French accents, which, although somewhat Neufchatel-ish,[2] were still sufficiently indicative of a Parisian origin.

"Sit down, my friend," said Dupin. "I suppose you have called about the Ourang-Outang. Upon my word, I almost envy you the possession of him; a remarkably fine, and no doubt a very valuable animal. How old do you suppose him to be?"

The sailor drew a long breath, with the air of a man relieved of some intolerable burden, and then replied, in an assured tone:

"I have no way of telling—but he can't be more than four or five years old. Have you got him here?"

"Oh no; we had no conveniences for keeping him here. He is at a livery stable[3] in the Rue Dubourg, just by. You can get him in the morning. Of course you are prepared to identify the property?"

"To be sure I am, sir."

"I shall be sorry to part with him," said Dupin.

"I don't mean that you should be at all this trouble for nothing, sir," said the man. "Couldn't expect it.

---

[1] *queues*   Long braids or ponytails worn at the back of the head.

[2] *Neufchatel-ish*   I.e., provincial; Neufchâtel is a northern French town known for cheesemaking.

[3] *livery stable*   Stable where stalls are available for hire, usually for horses.

Am very willing to pay a reward for the finding of the animal—that is to say, any thing in reason."

"Well," replied my friend, "that is all very fair, to be sure. Let me think! what should I have? Oh! I will tell you. My reward shall be this. You shall give me all the information in your power about these murders in the Rue Morgue."

Dupin said the last words in a very low tone, and very quietly. Just as quietly, too, he walked toward the door, locked it, and put the key in his pocket. He then drew a pistol from his bosom and placed it, without the least flurry, upon the table.

The sailor's face flushed up as if he were struggling with suffocation. He started to his feet and grasped his cudgel; but the next moment he fell back into his seat, trembling violently, and with the countenance of death itself. He spoke not a word. I pitied him from the bottom of my heart.

"My friend," said Dupin, in a kind tone, "you are alarming yourself unnecessarily—you are indeed. We mean you no harm whatever. I pledge you the honor of a gentleman, and of a Frenchman, that we intend you no injury. I perfectly well know that you are innocent of the atrocities in the Rue Morgue. It will not do, however, to deny that you are in some measure implicated in them. From what I have already said, you must know that I have had means of information about this matter—means of which you could never have dreamed. Now the thing stands thus. You have done nothing which you could have avoided—nothing, certainly, which renders you culpable. You were not even guilty of robbery, when you might have robbed with impunity. You have nothing to conceal. You have no reason for concealment. On the other hand, you are bound by every principle of honor to confess all you know. An innocent man is now imprisoned, charged with that crime of which you can point out the perpetrator."

The sailor had recovered his presence of mind, in a great measure, while Dupin uttered these words; but his original boldness of bearing was all gone.

"So help me God," said he, after a brief pause, "I *will* tell you all I know about this affair; but I do not expect you to believe one half I say—I would be a fool indeed if I did. Still, I *am* innocent, and I will make a clean breast if I die for it."

What he stated was, in substance, this. He had lately made a voyage to the Indian Archipelago. A party, of which he formed one, landed at Borneo, and passed into the interior on an excursion of pleasure. Himself and a companion had captured the Ourang-Outang. This companion dying, the animal fell into his own exclusive possession. After great trouble, occasioned by the intractable ferocity of his captive during the home voyage, he at length succeeded in lodging it safely at his own residence in Paris, where, not to attract toward himself the unpleasant curiosity of his neighbors, he kept it carefully secluded, until such time as it should recover from a wound in the foot, received from a splinter on board ship. His ultimate design was to sell it.

Returning home from some sailors' frolic on the night, or rather in the morning of the murder, he found the beast occupying his own bedroom, into which it had broken from a closet adjoining, where it had been, as was thought, securely confined. Razor in hand, and fully lathered, it was sitting before a looking-glass, attempting the operation of shaving, in which it had no doubt previously watched its master through the keyhole of the closet. Terrified at the sight of so dangerous a weapon in the possession of an animal so ferocious, and so well able to use it, the man, for some moments, was at a loss what to do. He had been accustomed, however, to quiet the creature, even in its fiercest moods, by the use of a whip, and to this he now resorted. Upon sight of it, the Ourang-Outang sprang at once through the door of the chamber, down the stairs, and thence, through a window, unfortunately open, into the street.

The Frenchman followed in despair; the ape, razor still in hand, occasionally stopping to look back and gesticulate at its pursuer, until the latter had nearly come up with it. It then again made off. In this manner the chase continued for a long time. The streets were profoundly quiet, as it was nearly three o'clock in the morning. In passing down an alley in the rear of the Rue Morgue, the fugitive's attention was arrested by a light gleaming from the open window of Madame L'Espanaye's chamber, in the fourth story of her house. Rushing to the building, it perceived the lightning-rod, clambered up with inconceivable agility, grasped the shutter, which was thrown fully back against the wall, and, by its means, swung itself directly upon the headboard of the bed. The whole feat did not occupy a minute. The shutter was kicked open again by the Ourang-Outang as it entered the room.

The sailor, in the meantime, was both rejoiced and perplexed. He had strong hopes of now recapturing the brute, as it could scarcely escape from the trap into which it had ventured, except by the rod, where it might be intercepted as it came down. On the other hand, there was much cause for anxiety as to what it might do in the house. This latter reflection urged the man still to follow the fugitive. A lightning-rod is ascended without difficulty, especially by a sailor; but, when he had arrived as high as the window, which lay far to his left, his career was stopped; the most that he could accomplish was to reach over so as to obtain a glimpse of the interior of the room. At this glimpse he nearly fell from his hold through excess of horror. Now it was that those hideous shrieks arose upon the night, which had startled from slumber the inmates of the Rue Morgue. Madame L'Espanaye and her daughter, habited in their night clothes, had apparently been occupied in arranging some papers in the iron chest already mentioned, which had been wheeled into the middle of the room. It was open, and its contents lay beside it on the floor. The victims must have been sitting with their backs toward the window; and, from the time elapsing between the ingress of the beast and the screams, it seems probable that it was not immediately perceived. The flapping-to of the shutter would naturally have been attributed to the wind.

As the sailor looked in, the gigantic animal had seized Madame L'Espanaye by the hair (which was loose, as she had been combing it), and was flourishing the razor about her face, in imitation of the motions of a barber. The daughter lay prostrate and motionless; she had swooned. The screams and struggles of the old lady (during which the hair was torn from her head) had the effect of changing the probably pacific purposes of the Ourang-Outang into those of wrath. With one determined sweep of its muscular arm it nearly severed her head from her body. The sight of blood inflamed its anger into phrenzy. Gnashing its teeth, and flashing fire from its eyes, it flew upon the body of the girl, and imbedded its fearful talons in her throat, retaining its grasp until she expired. Its wandering and wild glances fell at this moment upon the head of the bed, over which the face of its master, rigid with horror, was just discernible. The fury of the beast, who no doubt bore still in mind the dreaded whip, was instantly converted into fear. Conscious of having deserved punishment, it seemed desirous of concealing its bloody deeds, and skipped about the chamber in an agony of nervous agitation; throwing down and breaking the furniture as it moved, and dragging the bed from the bedstead. In conclusion, it seized first the corpse of the daughter, and thrust it up the chimney, as it was found; then that of the old lady, which it immediately hurled through the window headlong.

As the ape approached the casement with its mutilated burden, the sailor shrank aghast to the rod, and, rather gliding than clambering down it, hurried at once home—dreading the consequences of the butchery, and gladly abandoning, in his terror, all solicitude about the fate of the Ourang-Outang. The words heard by the party upon the staircase were the Frenchman's exclamations of horror and affright, commingled with the fiendish jabberings of the brute.

I have scarcely anything to add. The Ourang-Outang must have escaped from the chamber, by the rod, just before the breaking of the door. It must have closed the window as it passed through it. It was subsequently caught by the owner himself, who obtained for it a very large sum at the *Jardin des Plantes*.[1] Le Bon was instantly released, upon our narration of the circumstances (with some comments from Dupin) at the *bureau* of the Prefect of Police. This functionary, however well disposed to my friend, could not altogether conceal his chagrin at the turn which affairs had taken, and was fain to indulge in a sarcasm or two, about the propriety of every person minding his own business.

"Let him talk," said Dupin, who had not thought it necessary to reply. "Let him discourse; it will ease his conscience. I am satisfied with having defeated him in his own castle. Nevertheless, that he failed in the solution of this mystery, is by no means that matter for wonder which he supposes it; for, in truth, our friend the Prefect is somewhat too cunning to be profound.

---

[1] *Jardin des Plantes* Major botanical garden in Paris, which also contains a zoo.

In his wisdom is no *stamen*.[1] It is all head and no body, like the pictures of the Goddess Laverna[2]—or, at best, all head and shoulders, like a codfish. But he is a good creature after all. I like him especially for one master stroke of cant, by which he has attained his reputation for ingenuity. I mean the way he has '*de nier ce qui est, et d'expliquer ce qui n'est pas.*'[3]

—1841 (REVISED 1845)

The Tell-Tale Heart[4]

TRUE!—nervous—very, very dreadfully nervous I had been and am; but why *will* you say that I am mad? The disease had sharpened my senses—not destroyed—not dulled them. Above all was the sense of hearing acute. I heard all things in the heaven and in the earth. I heard many things in hell. How, then, am I mad? Hearken! and observe how healthily—how calmly I can tell you the whole story.

It is impossible to say how first the idea entered my brain; but once conceived, it haunted me day and night. Object there was none. Passion there was none. I loved the old man. He had never wronged me. He had never given me insult. For his gold I had no desire. I think it was his eye! yes, it was this! One of his eyes resembled that of a vulture—a pale blue eye, with a film over it. Whenever it fell upon me, my blood ran cold; and so by degrees—very gradually—I made up my mind to take the life of the old man, and thus rid myself of the eye forever.

Now this is the point. You fancy me mad. Madmen know nothing. But you should have seen *me*. You should have seen how wisely I proceeded—with what caution—with what foresight—with what dissimulation I went to work! I was never kinder to the old man than during the whole week before I killed him. And

every night, about midnight, I turned the latch of his door and opened it—oh, so gently! And then, when I had made an opening sufficient for my head, I put in a dark lantern, all closed, closed, so that no light shone out, and then I thrust in my head. Oh, you would have laughed to see how cunningly I thrust it in! I moved it slowly—very, very slowly, so that I might not disturb the old man's sleep. It took me an hour to place my whole head within the opening so far that I could see him as he lay upon his bed. Ha!—would a madman have been so wise as this? And then, when my head was well in the room, I undid the lantern cautiously—oh, so cautiously—cautiously (for the hinges creaked)—I undid it just so much that a single thin ray fell upon the vulture eye. And this I did for seven long nights—every night just at midnight—but I found the eye always closed; and so it was impossible to do the work; for it was not the old man who vexed me, but his Evil Eye. And every morning, when the day broke, I went boldly into the chamber, and spoke courageously to him, calling him by name in a hearty tone, and inquiring how he had passed the night. So you see he would have been a very profound old man, indeed, to suspect that every night, just at twelve, I looked in upon him while he slept.

Upon the eighth night I was more than usually cautious in opening the door. A watch's minute hand moves more quickly than did mine. Never before that night, had I *felt* the extent of my own powers—of my sagacity. I could scarcely contain my feelings of triumph. To think that there I was, opening the door, little by little, and he not even to dream of my secret deeds or thoughts. I fairly chuckled at the idea; and perhaps he heard me; for he moved on the bed suddenly, as if startled. Now you may think that I drew back—but no. His room was as black as pitch with the thick darkness, (for the shutters were close fastened, through fear of robbers,) and so I knew that he could not see the opening of the door, and I kept pushing it on steadily, steadily.

I had my head in, and was about to open the lantern, when my thumb slipped upon the tin fastening, and the old man sprang up in the bed, crying out—"Who's there?"

I kept quite still and said nothing. For a whole hour I did not move a muscle, and in the mean time I did

---

[1] *stamen* Male reproductive organ of a flower; by implication, vitality.

[2] *Goddess Laverna* Roman goddess of thieves, depicted in ancient art as a head with no body.

[3] [Poe's note] Rousseau — *Nouvelle Heloise* [1761]. [French: To deny that which is, and to explain that which is not.]

[4] Diverging from this anthology's standard practice, spelling and punctuation have been left unmodernised throughout this story.

not hear him lie down. He was still sitting up in the bed, listening;—just as I have done, night after night, hearkening to the death watches[1] in the wall.

Presently I heard a slight groan, and I knew it was the groan of mortal terror. It was not a groan of pain or of grief—oh, no!—it was the low stifled sound that arises from the bottom of the soul when overcharged with awe. I knew the sound well. Many a night, just at midnight, when all the world slept, it has welled up from my own bosom, deepening, with its dreadful echo, the terrors that distracted me. I say I knew it well. I knew what the old man felt, and pitied him, although I chuckled at heart. I knew that he had been lying awake ever since the first slight noise, when he had turned in the bed. His fears had been ever since growing upon him. He had been trying to fancy them causeless, but could not. He had been saying to himself—"It is nothing but the wind in the chimney—it is only a mouse crossing the floor," or "it is merely a cricket which has made a single chirp." Yes, he had been trying to comfort himself with these suppositions: but he had found all in vain. *All in vain*; because Death, in approaching him, had stalked with his black shadow before him, and enveloped the victim. And it was the mournful influence of the unperceived shadow that caused him to feel—although he neither saw nor heard—to *feel* the presence of my head within the room.

When I had waited a long time, very patiently, without hearing him lie down, I resolved to open a little—a very, very little crevice in the lantern. So I opened it—you cannot imagine how stealthily, stealthily—until, at length, a single dim ray, like the thread of the spider, shot from out the crevice and fell upon the vulture eye.

It was open—wide, wide open—and I grew furious as I gazed upon it. I saw it with perfect distinctness—all a dull blue, with a hideous veil over it that chilled the very marrow in my bones; but I could see nothing else of the old man's face or person: for I had directed the ray as if by instinct, precisely upon the damned spot.

And now have I not told you that what you mistake for madness is but over acuteness of the senses?—now,

I say, there came to my ears a low, dull, quick sound, such as a watch makes when enveloped in cotton. I knew *that* sound well, too. It was the beating of the old man's heart. It increased my fury, as the beating of a drum stimulates the soldier into courage.

But even yet I refrained and kept still. I scarcely breathed. I held the lantern motionless. I tried how steadily I could maintain the ray upon the eye. Meantime the hellish tattoo of the heart increased. It grew quicker and quicker, and louder and louder every instant. The old man's terror *must* have been extreme! It grew louder, I say, louder every moment!—do you mark[2] me well? I have told you that I am nervous: so I am. And now at the dead hour of the night, amid the dreadful silence of that old house, so strange a noise as this excited me to uncontrollable terror. Yet, for some minutes longer I refrained and stood still. But the beating grew louder, louder! I thought the heart must burst. And now a new anxiety seized me—the sound would be heard by a neighbor! The old man's hour had come! With a loud yell, I threw open the lantern and leaped into the room. He shrieked once—once only. In an instant I dragged him to the floor, and pulled the heavy bed over him. I then smiled gaily, to find the deed so far done. But, for many minutes, the heart beat on with a muffled sound. This, however, did not vex me; it would not be heard through the wall. At length it ceased. The old man was dead. I removed the bed and examined the corpse. Yes, he was stone, stone dead. I placed my hand upon the heart and held it there many minutes. There was no pulsation. He was stone dead. His eye would trouble me no more.

If still you think me mad, you will think so no longer when I describe the wise precautions I took for the concealment of the body. The night waned, and I worked hastily, but in silence. First of all I dismembered the corpse. I cut off the head and the arms and the legs.

I then took up three planks from the flooring of the chamber, and deposited all between the scantlings.[3] I then replaced the boards so cleverly, so cunningly, that no human eye—not even *his*—could have detected any thing wrong. There was nothing to wash out—no

---

[1] *death watches* Beetles that bore into wood, especially the wood of old buildings. They make a tapping sound that resembles the ticking of a watch, and their presence is thought by some to be an omen of death.

---

[2] *mark* Attend, listen to.

[3] *scantlings* Joists; supporting beams.

stain of any kind—no blood-spot whatever. I had been too wary for that. A tub had caught all—ha! ha!

When I had made an end of these labors, it was four o'clock—still dark as midnight. As the bell sounded the hour, there came a knocking at the street door. I went down to open it with a light heart,—for what had I *now* to fear? There entered three men, who introduced themselves, with perfect suavity, as officers of the police. A shriek had been heard by a neighbor during the night; suspicion of foul play had been aroused; information had been lodged at the police office, and they (the officers) had been deputed to search the premises.

I smiled,—for *what* had I to fear? I bade the gentlemen welcome. The shriek, I said, was my own in a dream. The old man, I mentioned, was absent in the country. I took my visiters all over the house. I bade them search—search *well*. I led them, at length, to *his* chamber. I showed them his treasures, secure, undisturbed. In the enthusiasm of my confidence, I brought chairs into the room, and desired them *here* to rest from their fatigues, while I myself, in the wild audacity of my perfect triumph, placed my own seat upon the very spot beneath which reposed the corpse of the victim.

The officers were satisfied. My *manner* had convinced them. I was singularly at ease. They sat, and while I answered cheerily, they chatted of familiar things. But, ere long, I felt myself getting pale and wished them gone. My head ached, and I fancied a ringing in my ears: but still they sat and still they chatted. The ringing became more distinct:—it continued and became more distinct: I talked more freely to get rid

of the feeling: but it continued and gained definitiveness—until, at length, I found that the noise was *not* within my ears.

No doubt I now grew *very* pale;—but I talked more fluently, and with a heightened voice. Yet the sound increased—and what could I do? It was *a low, dull, quick sound—much such a sound as a watch makes when enveloped in cotton*. I gasped for breath—and yet the officers heard it not. I talked more quickly—more vehemently; but the noise steadily increased. I arose and argued about trifles, in a high key and with violent gesticulations; but the noise steadily increased. Why *would* they not be gone? I paced the floor to and fro with heavy strides, as if excited to fury by the observations of the men—but the noise steadily increased. Oh God! what *could* I do? I foamed—I raved—I swore! I swung the chair upon which I had been sitting, and grated it upon the boards, but the noise arose over all and continually increased. It grew louder—louder—*louder*! And still the men chatted pleasantly, and smiled. Was it possible they heard not? Almighty God!—no, no! They heard!—they suspected!—they *knew*!—they were making a mockery of my horror!—this I thought, and this I think. But anything was better than this agony! Anything was more tolerable than this derision! I could bear those hypocritical smiles no longer! I felt that I must scream or die!—and now—again!—hark! louder! louder! louder! *louder*!—

"Villains!" I shrieked, "dissemble[1] no more! I admit the deed!—tear up the planks!—here, here!—it is the beating of his hideous heart!"

—1843

---

[1]   *dissemble*   Pretend.

The Raven

Once upon a midnight dreary, while I pondered, weak and weary,
Over many a quaint and curious volume of forgotten lore—
While I nodded, nearly napping, suddenly there came a tapping,
As of someone gently rapping, rapping at my chamber door—
"'Tis some visitor," I muttered, "tapping at my chamber door—
5   Only this and nothing more."

Ah, distinctly I remember it was in the bleak December;
And each separate dying ember wrought its ghost upon the floor.
Eagerly I wished the morrow; vainly I had tried to borrow
From my books surcease° of sorrow—sorrow for the lost Lenore—   *stoppage*
10 For the rare and radiant maiden whom the angels name Lenore—
     Nameless *here* for evermore.

And the silken, sad, uncertain rustling of each purple curtain
Thrilled me—filled me with fantastic terrors never felt before;
So that now, to still the beating of my heart, I stood repeating
15 "'Tis some visitor entreating entrance at my chamber door—
Some late visitor entreating entrance at my chamber door;—
     This it is and nothing more."

Presently my soul grew stronger; hesitating then no longer,
20 "Sir," said I, "or Madam, truly your forgiveness I implore;
But the fact is I was napping, and so gently you came rapping,
And so faintly you came tapping, tapping at my chamber door,
That I scarce was sure I heard you"—here I opened wide the door;
     Darkness there and nothing more.

25 Deep into that darkness peering, long I stood there wondering, fearing,
Doubting, dreaming dreams no mortal ever dared to dream before;
But the silence was unbroken, and the darkness gave no token,
And the only word there spoken was the whispered word, "Lenore?"
This I whispered, and an echo murmured back the word, "Lenore!"
30   Merely this and nothing more.

Back into the chamber turning, all my soul within me burning,
Soon I heard again a tapping somewhat louder than before.
"Surely," said I, "surely that is something at my window lattice;
Let me see, then, what thereat is, and this mystery explore—
35 Let my heart be still a moment and this mystery explore—
     'Tis the wind, and nothing more!"

Open here I flung the shutter, when, with many a flirt° and flutter,   *dart, flick*
In there stepped a stately Raven of the saintly days of yore;
Not the least obeisance made he; not an instant stopped or stayed he;

40   But, with mien of lord or lady, perched above my chamber door—
    Perched upon a bust of Pallas[1] just above my chamber door—
        Perched, and sat, and nothing more.

    Then this ebony bird beguiling my sad fancy into smiling,
    By the grave and stern decorum of the countenance it wore,
45   "Though thy crest be shorn and shaven, thou," I said, "art sure no craven,[2]
    Ghastly grim and ancient Raven wandering from the Nightly shore—
    Tell me what thy lordly name is on the Night's Plutonian[3] shore!"
        Quoth the Raven "Nevermore."

    Much I marvelled this ungainly fowl to hear discourse so plainly,
50   Though its answer little meaning—little relevancy bore;
    For we cannot help agreeing that no living human being
    Ever yet was blessed with seeing bird above his chamber door—
    Bird or beast upon the sculptured bust above his chamber door,
        With such name as "Nevermore."

55   But the Raven, sitting lonely on the placid bust, spoke only
    That one word, as if his soul in that one word he did outpour.
    Nothing farther then he uttered—not a feather then he fluttered—
    Till I scarcely more than muttered "Other friends have flown before—
    On the morrow *he* will leave me, as my Hopes have flown before."
60   Then the bird said "Nevermore."

    Startled at the stillness broken by reply so aptly spoken,
    "Doubtless," said I, "what it utters is its only stock and store
    Caught from some unhappy master whom unmerciful Disaster
    Followed fast and followed faster till his songs one burden[4] bore—
65   Till the dirges[5] of his Hope that melancholy burden bore
        Of 'Never—nevermore.'"

    But the Raven still beguiling all my sad fancy into smiling,
    Straight I wheeled a cushioned seat in front of bird, and bust and door;
    Then upon the velvet sinking, I betook myself to linking
70   Fancy unto fancy, thinking what this ominous bird of yore—
    What this grim, ungainly, ghastly, gaunt, and ominous bird of yore
        Meant in croaking "Nevermore."

    This I sat engaged in guessing, but no syllable expressing
    To the fowl whose fiery eyes now burned into my bosom's core;

---

1   *bust* Sculpture of the head and shoulders; *Pallas* Epithet of Athena, Greek goddess of wisdom, warfare, and art.

2   *Though thy crest … craven* Reference to the practice of punishing cowardly knights by shaving their heads.

3   *Plutonian* Dark or gloomy, alluding to Pluto as the Roman god of the underworld.

4   *burden* Refrain, chorus.

5   *dirges* Funeral songs.

75 This and more I sat divining, with my head at ease reclining
   On the cushion's velvet lining that the lamp-light gloated o'er,
   But whose velvet-violet lining with the lamp-light gloating o'er,
      She shall press, ah, nevermore!

Then, methought, the air grew denser, perfumed from an unseen censer[1]
80 Swung by seraphim° whose footfalls tinkled on the tufted° floor.   *angels / carpeted*
   "Wretch," I cried, "thy God hath lent thee—by these angels he hath sent thee
   Respite—respite and nepenthe[2] from thy memories of Lenore;
   Quaff,[3] oh quaff this kind nepenthe and forget this lost Lenore!"
      Quoth the Raven "Nevermore."

85 "Prophet!" said I, "thing of evil! prophet still, if bird or devil!
   Whether Tempter sent, or whether tempest tossed thee here ashore,
   Desolate yet all undaunted, on this desert land enchanted—
   On this home by Horror haunted—tell me truly, I implore—
   Is there—*is* there balm in Gilead?[4]—tell me—tell me, I implore!"
90   Quoth the Raven "Nevermore."

"Prophet!" said I, "thing of evil! prophet still, if bird or devil!
   By that Heaven that bends above us—by that God we both adore—
   Tell this soul with sorrow laden if, within the distant Aidenn,°   *Eden*
   It shall clasp a sainted maiden whom the angels name Lenore—
95 Clasp a rare and radiant maiden whom the angels name Lenore."
      Quoth the Raven "Nevermore."

"Be that word our sign of parting, bird or fiend!" I shrieked, upstarting—
   "Get thee back into the tempest and the Night's Plutonian shore!
   Leave no black plume° as a token of that lie thy soul hath spoken!   *feather*
100 Leave my loneliness unbroken! quit the bust above my door!
   Take thy beak from out my heart, and take thy form from off my door!"
      Quoth the Raven "Nevermore."

And the Raven, never flitting, still is sitting, *still* is sitting
   On the pallid bust of Pallas just above my chamber door;
105 And his eyes have all the seeming of a demon's that is dreaming,
   And the lamp-light o'er him streaming throws his shadow on the floor;
   And my soul from out that shadow that lies floating on the floor
      Shall be lifted—nevermore!
   —1845 (REVISED 1849)

---

1   *censer*   Incense burner.

2   *nepenthe*   Legendary drug supposed to banish sorrow by inducing forgetfulness.

3   *Quaff*   Drink quickly and deeply.

4   *balm in Gilead*   See Jeremiah 8.22: "Is there no balm in Gilead?" Balm is a medicinal ointment, and, proverbially, the balm of Gilead is a powerful cure; Christian interpretation identifies the balm with Christ.

IN CONTEXT

"The Raven" in Nineteenth-Century Visual Culture

Widely considered one of the most famous poems in history, "The Raven" began early on to be interpreted, celebrated, and parodied by artists in a variety of media, including engravings, drawings, and paintings. This fascination continued through the twentieth century and into the twenty-first, with new literary interpretations emerging as well as graphic novels, films, and television adaptations. "The Raven" was also translated widely, contributing to Poe's international reputation—especially in France, where the following illustrations of the poem originate. Poe's fame became so closely entwined with his poem that he was nicknamed "Mr. Raven," and depictions of him in popular culture often included a raven perched nearby.

Edouard Manet, "Once Upon a Midnight Dreary." Illustration from Stéphane Mallarmé's translation of *Le Corbeau* [*The Raven*], 1875.

This edition had a considerable impact. Manet's fellow post-Impressionist Paul Gauguin, for example, included Poe's raven in his 1891 engraving of Manet—as well as in *Mana'o tupapa'u* (1892) and several other of his well-known paintings of the 1890s.

Edouard Manet, "Design for the poster and cover." Illustration to Stéphane Mallarmé's translation of *Le Corbeau* [*The Raven*], 1875.

Gustave Doré, "Illustration 14," *The Raven*, 1884. Doré's engravings of *The Raven* have proved enduringly popular; his illustrated version of the poem was widely distributed in America and in Europe.

"Edgar A. Poe," Great Americans cigarette card, 1888. Poe's fame led to his appearance as one of fifty "great Americans" illustrated in an 1888 series of cards included in packs of W. Duke, Sons & Co. cigarettes. The raven perched on the statue of Pallas is conspicuous in the background.

The Imp of the Perverse[1]

In the consideration of the faculties and impulses—of the *prima mobilia*[2] of the human soul, the phrenologists[3] have failed to make room for a propensity[4] which, although obviously existing as a radical, primitive, irreducible sentiment, has been equally overlooked by all the moralists who have preceded them. In the pure arrogance of the reason,[5] we have all overlooked it. We have suffered its existence to escape our senses, solely through want of belief—of faith; whether it be faith in Revelation, or faith in the Kabbala.[6] The idea of it has never occurred to us, simply because of its supererogation.[7] We saw no need of the impulse—for the propensity. We could not perceive its necessity. We could not understand, that is to say, we could not have understood, had the notion of this *primum mobile* ever obtruded itself; we could not have understood in what manner it might be made to further the objects of humanity, either temporal or eternal. It cannot be denied that phrenology and, in great measure, all metaphysicianism, have been concocted *à priori*.[8] The intellectual or logical man, rather than the understanding or observant man, set himself to imagine designs—to dictate purposes to

God. Having thus fathomed, to his satisfaction, the intentions of Jehovah, out of these intentions he built his innumerable systems of mind. In the matter of phrenology, for example, we first determined, naturally enough, that it was the design of the Deity that man should eat. We then assigned to man an organ of alimentiveness,[9] and this organ is the scourge with which the Deity compels man, willy-nilly, into eating. Secondly, having settled it to be God's will that man should continue his species, we discovered an organ of amativeness,[10] forthwith. And so with combativeness, with ideality, with causality, with constructiveness[11]—so, in short, with every organ, whether representing a propensity, a moral sentiment, or a faculty of the pure intellect. And in these arrangements of the *principia*[12] of human action, the Spurzheimites,[13] whether right or wrong, in part, or upon the whole, have but followed, in principle, the footsteps of their predecessors; deducing and establishing everything from the preconceived destiny of man, and upon the ground of the objects of his Creator.[14]

It would have been wiser, it would have been safer to classify, (if classify we must), upon the basis of what man usually or occasionally did, and was always occasionally doing, rather than upon the basis of what we took it for granted the Deity intended him to do. If we cannot comprehend God in his visible works, how then in his inconceivable thoughts, that call the works into being? If we cannot understand him in his objective creatures, how then in his substantive[15] moods and phases of creation?

---

[1]   *Perverse*   Irrational, persistently contrary, or deliberately immoral.

[2]   *prima mobilia*   Latin: first mover, i.e., first motivation.

[3]   *phrenologists*   Pseudo-scientists who studied the shape of the head and delineated character traits from their observations (known as phrenology). The idea was that a person's character was shaped by several "organs" found in the brain; the phrenologist would measure the degree of development of these "organs" and draw conclusions about the individual's personality therefrom. Phrenological principles were often invoked to justify belief in the inherent propensity of some people to become criminals, and in the superiority of some people over others, often reinforcing race, class, gender, and other prejudices.

[4]   *propensity*   Character trait, tendency to do a certain thing.

[5]   *the reason*   I.e., the faculty of reason.

[6]   *Revelation*   Divine knowledge as revealed in the Bible; *Kabbala*   Secret, mystical, or unwritten knowledge; the term is traditionally applied to interpretation of the Old Testament.

[7]   *supererogation*   Excessiveness, superfluity.

[8]   *metaphysicianism*   Speculation about matters beyond the physical world; *à priori*   Logically deduced from abstract principles, rather than through observation.

[9]   *organ of alimentiveness*   Phrenological "organ" in the brain that governs the appetite for food.

[10]   *organ of amativeness*   Phrenological "organ" in the brain that governs the appetite for sex.

[11]   *ideality*   Beauty; *causality*   Logical thinking; *constructiveness*   Creativity. Phrenologists assigned "organs" in the brain for each of these qualities.

[12]   *principia*   Latin: origins.

[13]   *Spurzheimites*   Followers of Dr. Johann Gaspar Spurzheim (1776–1832), one of the most prominent popularizers of phrenology in Europe and America.

[14]   *upon the ground ... of his Creator*   Upon the foundation of the intentions of God.

[15]   *objective creatures*   Material creations; *substantive*   Essential, inherent.

Induction, *à posteriori*,[1] would have brought phrenology to admit, as an innate and primitive principle of human action, a paradoxical something, which we may call perverseness, for want of a more characteristic term. In the sense I intend, it is, in fact, a *mobile without motive, a motive not motivirt*.[2] Through its promptings we act without comprehensible object; or, if this shall be understood as a contradiction in terms, we may so far modify the proposition as to say, that through its promptings we act, for the reason that we should *not*. In theory, no reason can be more unreasonable; but, in fact, there is none more strong. With certain minds, under certain conditions, it becomes absolutely irresistible. I am not more certain that I breathe, than that the assurance of the wrong or error of any action is often the one unconquerable *force* which impels us, and alone impels us to its prosecution. Nor will this overwhelming tendency to do wrong for the wrong's sake, admit of analysis, or resolution into ulterior elements.[3] It is a radical, a primitive impulse—elementary. It will be said, I am aware, that when we persist in acts because we feel we should *not* persist in them, our conduct is but a modification of that which ordinarily springs from the *combativeness* of phrenology. But a glance will show the fallacy of this idea. The phrenological combativeness has for its essence, the necessity of self-defence. It is our safeguard against injury. Its principle regards our well-being; and thus the desire to be well, is excited simultaneously with its development. It follows, that the desire to be well must be excited simultaneously with any principle which shall be merely a modification of combativeness, but in the case of that something which I term *perverseness*, the desire to be well is not only not aroused, but a strongly antagonistical sentiment exists.

An appeal to one's own heart is, after all, the best reply to the sophistry just noticed.[4] No one who trustingly consults and thoroughly questions his own soul, will be disposed to deny the entire radicalness of the propensity in question.[5] It is not more incomprehensible than distinctive. There lives no man who at some period, has not been tormented, for example, by an earnest desire to tantalize a listener by circumlocution.[6] The speaker is aware that he displeases; he has every intention to please; he is usually curt, precise, and clear; the most laconic and luminous language is struggling for utterance upon his tongue; it is only with difficulty that he restrains himself from giving it flow; he dreads and deprecates the anger of him whom he addresses; yet, the thought strikes him, that by certain involutions and parentheses, this anger may be engendered. That single thought is enough. The impulse increases to a wish, the wish to a desire, the desire to an uncontrollable longing, and the longing (to the deep regret and mortification of the speaker, and in defiance of all consequences) is indulged.

We have a task before us which must be speedily performed. We know that it will be ruinous to make delay. The most important crisis of our life calls, trumpet-tongued, for immediate energy and action. We glow, we are consumed with eagerness to commence the work, with the anticipation of whose glorious result our whole souls are on fire. It must, it shall be undertaken today, and yet we put it off until to-morrow, and why? There is no answer, except that we feel *perverse*, using the word with no comprehension of the principle. Tomorrow arrives, and with it a more impatient anxiety to do our duty, but with this very increase of anxiety arrives, also, a nameless, a positively fearful, because unfathomable craving for delay. This craving gathers strength as the moments fly. The last hour for action is at hand. We tremble with the violence of the conflict within us—of the definite with the indefinite—of the substance with the shadow. But, if the contest have proceeded thus far, it is the shadow which prevails—we struggle in vain. The clock strikes, and is the knell[7] of our welfare. At the same time, it is the

---

[1] *Induction, à posteriori* I.e., reasoning based on observation (rather than abstract principles).

[2] *mobile without motive* Motivation without motive; *motivirt* German: motivation. An obscure literary term used to denote the motive assigned by playwrights to their characters in a drama.

[3] *resolution into ulterior elements* Reduction into underlying components.

[4] *sophistry* Plausible but unsound argument; *noticed* Mentioned.

[5] *entire radicalness … in question* Fundamental nature of the impulse being discussed.

[6] *circumlocution* Talking in a long-winded, circular manner.

[7] *knell* Sound of a bell being tolled, particularly the "death-knell," the slow tolling of a bell to commemorate a death.

chanticleer-note[1] to the ghost that has so long over-awed us. It flies—it disappears—we are free. The old energy returns. We will labor *now*. Alas, it is *too late!*

We stand upon the brink of a precipice. We peer into the abyss—we grow sick and dizzy. Our first impulse is to shrink from the danger. Unaccountably we remain. By slow degrees our sickness and dizziness, and horror become merged in a cloud of unnameable feeling. By gradations, still more imperceptible, this cloud assumes shape, as did the vapor from the bottle out of which arose the genius in the Arabian Nights.[2] But out of this, *our* cloud, upon the precipice's edge, there grows into palpability, a shape, far more terrible than any genius, or any demon of a tale, and yet it is but a thought, although a fearful one, and one which chills the very marrow of our bones with the fierceness of the delight of its horror. It is merely the idea of what would be our sensations during the sweeping precipitancy of a fall from such a height. And this fall—this rushing annihilation—for the very reason that it involves that one most ghastly and loathsome of all the most ghastly and loathsome images of death and suffering which have ever presented themselves to our imagination—for this very cause do we now the most vividly desire it. And because our reason violently deters us from the brink, *therefore*, do we the most impetuously approach it. There is no passion in nature so demoniacally impatient, as that of him, who shuddering upon the edge of a precipice, thus meditates a plunge. To indulge for a moment, in any attempt at thought, is to be inevitably lost; for reflection but urges us to forbear, and therefore it is, I say, that we cannot. If there be no friendly arm to check us, or if we fail in a sudden effort to prostrate ourselves backward from the abyss, we plunge, and are destroyed.

Examine these and similar actions as we will, we shall find them resulting solely from the spirit of the *Perverse*. We perpetrate them merely because we feel that we should not. Beyond or behind this, there is no intelligible principle: and we might, indeed, deem

this perverseness a direct instigation of the arch-fiend,[3] were it not occasionally known to operate in furtherance of good.

I have said thus much, that in some measure I may answer your question—that I may explain to you why I am here—that I may assign to you something that shall have at least the faint aspect of a cause for my wearing these fetters,[4] and for my tenanting this cell of the condemned. Had I not been thus prolix,[5] you might either have misunderstood me altogether, or, with the rabble, have fancied me mad. As it is, you will easily perceive that I am one of the many uncounted victims of the Imp of the Perverse.

It is impossible that any deed could have been wrought with a more thorough deliberation. For weeks, for months, I pondered upon the means of the murder. I rejected a thousand schemes, because their accomplishment involved a chance of detection. At length, in reading some French memoirs, I found an account of a nearly fatal illness that occurred to Madame Pilau,[6] through the agency of a candle accidentally poisoned. The idea struck my fancy at once. I knew my victim's habit of reading in bed. I knew, too, that his apartment was narrow and ill-ventilated. But I need not vex you with impertinent details. I need not describe the easy artifices by which I substituted, in his bedroom candle-stand, a wax-light of my own making, for the one which I there found. The next morning he was discovered dead in his bed, and the Coroner's verdict was, "Death by the visitation of God."

Having inherited his estate, all went well with me for years. The idea of detection never once entered my brain. Of the remains of the fatal taper,[7] I had myself carefully disposed. I had left no shadow of a clue by which it would be possible to convict, or even to suspect me of the crime. It is inconceivable how

---

[1] *chanticleer-note*   Wake-up call (chanticleer is a literary name for a rooster). According to some folk traditions, ghosts must return to their graves at the crowing of the rooster.

[2] *vapor … Arabian Nights*   In "The Fisherman and the Jinni," a folktale in the Middle Eastern collection *One Thousand and One Nights*, a fisher opens a copper jar to find that a genie emerges in a trail of smoke.

[3] *the arch-fiend*   I.e., the devil.

[4] *fetters*   Shackles, chains.

[5] *prolix*   Wordy, long-winded.

[6] *Madame Pilau*   See Catherine Gore, "An Oddity of the Seventeenth Century," *The New Monthly Magazine* (1839). According to this article, probably Poe's source, Madame Pilau was a prominent French society woman who was poisoned by a candle intended for someone else; Louis XIV sent his best doctor to take care of her, and she recovered, living to an "extreme old age."

[7] *taper*   Candle.

rich a sentiment of satisfaction arose in my bosom as I reflected upon my absolute security. For a very long period of time, I was accustomed to revel in this sentiment. It afforded me more real delight than all the mere worldly advantages accruing from my sin. But there arrived at length an epoch, from which the pleasurable feeling grew, by scarcely perceptible gradations, into a haunting and harassing thought. It harassed because it haunted. I could scarcely get rid of it for an instant. It is quite a common thing to be thus annoyed with the ringing in our ears, or rather in our memories, of the burden[1] of some ordinary song, or some unimpressive snatches from an opera. Nor will we be the less tormented if the song in itself be good, or the opera air meritorious. In this manner, at last, I would perpetually catch myself pondering upon my security, and repeating, in a low, under-tone, the phrase, "I am safe."

One day, whilst sauntering along the streets, I arrested myself in the act of murmuring, half aloud, these customary syllables. In a fit of petulance, I remodelled them thus: "I am safe—I am safe—yes—if I be not fool enough to make open confession!"

No sooner had I spoken these words, than I felt an icy chill creep to my heart. I had had some experience in these fits of perversity (whose nature I have been at some trouble to explain), and I remembered well, that in no instance, I had successfully resisted their attacks. And now my own casual self-suggestion, that I might possibly be fool enough to confess the murder of which I had been guilty, confronted me, as if the very ghost of him whom I had murdered—and beckoned me on to death.

At first, I made an effort to shake off this nightmare of the soul. I walked vigorously—faster—still faster—at length I ran. I felt a maddening desire to shriek aloud. Every succeeding wave of thought overwhelmed me with new terror, for, alas! I well, too well understood that, to *think*, in my situation, was to be lost. I still quickened my pace. I bounded like a madman through the crowded thoroughfares. At length, the populace took the alarm, and pursued me. I felt *then* the consummation of my fate. Could I have torn out my tongue, I would have done it—but a rough voice resounded in my ears—a rougher grasp seized me by the shoulder. I turned—I gasped for breath. For a

moment I experienced all the pangs of suffocation; I became blind, and deaf, and giddy; and then some invisible fiend, I thought, struck me with his broad palm upon the back. The long-imprisoned secret burst forth from my soul.

They say that I spoke with a distinct enunciation, but with marked emphasis and passionate hurry, as if in dread of interruption before concluding the brief but pregnant sentences that consigned me to the hangman and to hell.

Having related all that was necessary for the fullest judicial conviction, I fell prostrate in a swoon.

But why shall I say more? Today I wear these chains, and am *here*! Tomorrow I shall be fetterless!—*but where*?
—1845

from *The Philosophy of Composition*

...Nothing is more clear than that every plot, worth the name, must be elaborated to its *dénouement* before anything be attempted with the pen. It is only with the *dénouement* constantly in view that we can give a plot its indispensable air of consequence, or causation, by making the incidents, and especially the tone at all points, tend to the development of the intention.

There is a radical error, I think, in the usual mode of constructing a story. Either history affords a thesis[2]—or one is suggested by an incident of the day—or, at best, the author sets himself to work in the combination of striking events to form merely the basis of his narrative—designing, generally, to fill in with description, dialogue, or authorial comment, whatever crevices of fact, or action, may, from page to page, render themselves apparent.

I prefer commencing with the consideration of an *effect*. Keeping originality *always* in view—for he is false to himself who ventures to dispense with so obvious and so easily attainable a source of interest—I say to myself, in the first place, "Of the innumerable effects, or impressions, of which the heart, the intellect, or (more generally) the soul is susceptible, what one shall I, on the present occasion, select?" Having chosen

---

[1] *burden* Here, chorus.

[2] *thesis* Theme.

a novel, first, and secondly a vivid effect, I consider whether it can best be wrought by incident or tone—whether by ordinary incidents and peculiar tone, or the converse, or by peculiarity both of incident and tone—afterward looking about me (or rather within) for such combinations of event, or tone, as shall best aid me in the construction of the effect. …

… If any literary work is too long to be read at one sitting, we must be content to dispense with the immensely important effect derivable from unity of impression—for, if two sittings be required, the affairs of the world interfere, and everything like totality is at once destroyed. But since, *ceteris paribus*,[1] no poet can afford to dispense with *anything* that may advance his design, it but remains to be seen whether there is, in extent, any advantage to counterbalance the loss of unity which attends it. Here I say no, at once. What we term a long poem is, in fact, merely a succession of brief ones—that is to say, of brief poetical effects. It is needless to demonstrate that a poem is such, only inasmuch as it intensely excites, by elevating, the soul; and all intense excitements are, through a psychal[2] necessity, brief. For this reason, at least one half of the "Paradise Lost"[3] is essentially prose—a succession of poetical excitements interspersed, *inevitably*, with corresponding depressions—the whole being deprived, through the extremeness of its length, of the vastly important artistic element, totality, or unity, of effect.

It appears evident, then, that there is a distinct limit, as regards length, to all works of literary art—the limit of a single sitting—and that, although in certain classes of prose composition, such as "Robinson Crusoe"[4] (demanding no unity), this limit may be advantageously overpassed, it can never properly be overpassed in a poem. Within this limit, the extent of a poem may be made to bear mathematical relation to its merit—in other words, to the excitement or elevation—again in other words, to the degree of the true poetical effect which it is capable of inducing; for it is clear that the brevity must be in direct ratio of the intensity of the intended effect: this, with one proviso—that a certain degree of duration is absolutely requisite for the production of any effect at all. …

—1846

Hop-Frog

I never knew any one so keenly alive to a joke as the king was. He seemed to live only for joking. To tell a good story of the joke kind, and to tell it well, was the surest road to his favor. Thus it happened that his seven ministers were all noted for their accomplishments as jokers. They all took after the king, too, in being large, corpulent, oily men, as well as inimitable jokers. Whether people grow fat by joking, or whether there is something in fat itself which predisposes to a joke, I have never been quite able to determine; but certain it is that a lean joker is a *rara avis in terris*.[5]

About the refinements, or, as he called them, the "ghosts" of wit, the king troubled himself very little. He had an especial admiration for *breadth* in a jest, and would often put up with *length*, for the sake of it. Over-niceties wearied him. He would have preferred Rabelais's "Gargantua," to the "Zadig" of Voltaire:[6] and, upon the whole, practical jokes suited his taste far better than verbal ones.

At the date of my narrative, professing[7] jesters had not altogether gone out of fashion at court. Several of the great continental "powers" still retained their "fools," who wore motley,[8] with caps and bells, and who were expected to be always ready with sharp witticisms, at a moment's notice, in consideration of the crumbs that fell from the royal table.[9]

---

1 *ceteris paribus* Latin: all things being equal.

2 *psychal* Psychological.

3 *Paradise Lost* 1667 epic poem by John Milton, often ranked among the most important works of English literature.

4 *Robinson Crusoe* Influential 1719 novel by Daniel Defoe.

5 *rara avis in terris* Latin: a rare bird on this earth; in Roman poet Juvenal's *Satires* (c. 100 CE), the phrase refers to a black swan (proverbially impossible to find).

6 *Rabelais's … Voltaire* François Rabelais's long series of novels *Gargantua and Pantagruel* (1532–64) is full of crude and scatological humor, while Voltaire's novella *Zadig* (1747) is brief and philosophical in tone.

7 *professing* Professional.

8 *motley* Many-colored costumes.

9 *the crumbs … royal table* I.e., trifling rewards given out by the wealthy royal guests. See Luke 16.19–21, which describes "a certain rich man, which was clothed in purple and fine linen, and fared sumptuously every day" and a beggar who wishes "to be fed with the crumbs which fell from the rich man's table."

Our king, as a matter of course, retained his "fool." The fact is, he *required* something in the way of folly— if only to counterbalance the heavy wisdom of the seven wise men who were his ministers—not to mention himself.

His fool, or professional jester, was not *only* a fool, however. His value was trebled in the eyes of the king, by the fact of his being also a dwarf and a cripple. Dwarfs were as common at court, in those days, as fools; and many monarchs would have found it difficult to get through their days (days are rather longer at court than elsewhere) without both a jester to laugh *with*, and a dwarf to laugh *at*. But, as I have already observed, your jesters, in ninety-nine cases out of a hundred, are fat, round and unwieldy—so that it was no small source of self-gratulation with our king that, in Hop-Frog (this was the fool's name), he possessed a triplicate treasure in one person.

I believe the name "Hop-Frog" was *not* that given to the dwarf by his sponsors at baptism, but it was conferred upon him, by general consent of the seven ministers, on account of his inability to walk as other men do. In fact, Hop-Frog could only get along by a sort of interjectional gait—something between a leap and a wriggle—a movement that afforded illimitable amusement, and of course consolation, to the king, for (notwithstanding the protuberance of his stomach and a constitutional swelling of the head) the king, by his whole court, was accounted a capital figure.

But although Hop-Frog, through the distortion of his legs, could move only with great pain and difficulty along a road or floor, the prodigious muscular power which nature seemed to have bestowed upon his arms, by way of compensation for deficiency in the lower limbs, enabled him to perform many feats of wonderful dexterity, where trees or ropes were in question, or anything else to climb. At such exercises he certainly much more resembled a squirrel, or a small monkey, than a frog.

I am not able to say, with precision, from what country Hop-Frog originally came. It was from some barbarous region, however, that no person ever heard of—a vast distance from the court of our king. Hop-Frog, and a young girl very little less dwarfish than himself (although of exquisite proportions, and a marvellous dancer), had been forcibly carried off from their respective homes in adjoining provinces, and sent as presents to the king, by one of his ever-victorious generals.

Under these circumstances, it is not to be wondered at that a close intimacy arose between the two little captives. Indeed, they soon became sworn friends. Hop-Frog, who, although he made a great deal of sport, was by no means popular, had it not in his power to render Trippetta many services; but *she*, on account of her grace and exquisite beauty (although a dwarf) was universally admired and petted: so she possessed much influence; and never failed to use it, whenever she could, for the benefit of Hop-Frog.

On some grand state occasion—I forget what—the king determined to have a masquerade; and whenever a masquerade, or anything of that kind, occurred at our court, then the talents both of Hop-Frog and Trippetta were sure to be called in play. Hop-Frog, in especial, was so inventive in the way of getting up pageants, suggesting novel characters, and arranging costume, for masked balls, that nothing could be done, it seems, without his assistance.

The night appointed for the *fête*[1] had arrived. A gorgeous hall had been fitted up, under Trippetta's eye, with every kind of device which could possibly give *éclàt*[2] to a masquerade. The whole court was in a fever of expectation. As for costumes and characters, it might well be supposed that everybody had come to a decision on such points. Many had made up their minds (as to what *rôles* they should assume) a week, or even a month, in advance; and, in fact, there was not a particle of indecision anywhere—except in the case of the king and his seven ministers. Why *they* hesitated I never could tell, unless they did it by way of a joke. More probably, they found it difficult, on account of being so fat, to make up their minds. At all events, time flew; and, as a last resource, they sent for Trippetta and Hop-Frog.

When the two little friends obeyed the summons of the king, they found him sitting at his wine with the seven members of his cabinet council; but the monarch appeared to be in a very ill humor. He knew that Hop-Frog was not fond of wine, for it excited the poor cripple almost to madness; and madness is no comfortable

---

1 *fête* French: party.

2 *éclàt* French: sparkle, brilliance.

feeling. But the king loved his practical jokes, and took pleasure in forcing Hop-Frog to drink and (as the king called it) "to be merry."

"Come here, Hop-Frog," said he, as the jester and his friend entered the room: "swallow this bumper[1] to the health of your absent friends [here Hop-Frog sighed] and then let us have the benefit of your invention. We want characters—*characters*, man—something novel—out of the way. We are wearied with this everlasting sameness. Come, drink! the wine will brighten your wits."

Hop-Frog endeavored, as usual, to get up a jest in reply to these advances from the king; but the effort was too much. It happened to be the poor dwarf's birthday, and the command to drink to his "absent friends" forced the tears to his eyes. Many large, bitter drops fell into the goblet as he took it, humbly, from the hand of the tyrant.

"Ah! ha! ha! ha!" roared the latter, as the dwarf reluctantly drained the beaker. "See what a glass of good wine can do! Why, your eyes are shining already!"

Poor fellow! his large eyes *gleamed*, rather than shone; for the effect of wine on his excitable brain was not more powerful than instantaneous. He placed the goblet nervously on the table, and looked round upon the company with a half-insane stare. They all seemed highly amused at the success of the king's "*joke*."

"And now to business," said the prime minister, a *very* fat man.

"Yes," said the king; "come, Hop-Frog, lend us your assistance. Characters, my fine fellow; we stand in need of characters—all of us—ha! ha! ha!" and as this was seriously meant for a joke, his laugh was chorused by the seven.

Hop-Frog also laughed, although feebly and somewhat vacantly.

"Come, come," said the king, impatiently, "have you nothing to suggest?"

"I am endeavoring to think of something *novel*," replied the dwarf, abstractedly, for he was quite bewildered by the wine.

"Endeavoring!" cried the tyrant, fiercely; "what do you mean by *that*? Ah, I perceive. You are sulky, and want more wine. Here, drink this!" and he poured out

another goblet full and offered it to the cripple, who merely gazed at it, gasping for breath.

"Drink, I say!" shouted the monster, "or by the fiends—"

The dwarf hesitated. The king grew purple with rage. The courtiers smirked. Trippetta, pale as a corpse, advanced to the monarch's seat, and, falling on her knees before him, implored him to spare her friend.

The tyrant regarded her, for some moments, in evident wonder at her audacity. He seemed quite at a loss what to do or say—how most becomingly to express his indignation. At last, without uttering a syllable, he pushed her violently from him, and threw the contents of the brimming goblet in her face.

The poor girl got up as best she could, and, not daring even to sigh, resumed her position at the foot of the table.

There was a dead silence for about a half a minute, during which the falling of a leaf, or of a feather, might have been heard. It was interrupted by a low, but harsh and protracted *grating* sound which seemed to come at once from every corner of the room.

"What—what—*what* are you making that noise for?" demanded the king, turning furiously to the dwarf.

The latter seemed to have recovered, in great measure, from his intoxication, and looking fixedly but quietly into the tyrant's face, merely ejaculated:

"I—I? How could it have been me?"

"The sound appeared to come from without," observed one of the courtiers. "I fancy it was the parrot at the window, whetting his bill upon his cage-wires."

"True," replied the monarch, as if much relieved by the suggestion; "but, on the honor of a knight, I could have sworn that it was the gritting of this vagabond's teeth."

Hereupon the dwarf laughed (the king was too confirmed a joker to object to anyone's laughing), and displayed a set of large, powerful, and very repulsive teeth. Moreover, he avowed his perfect willingness to swallow as much wine as desired. The monarch was pacified; and having drained another bumper with no very perceptible ill effect, Hop-Frog entered at once, and with spirit, into the plans for the masquerade.

"I cannot tell what was the association of idea," observed he, very tranquilly, and as if he had never

---

[1] *bumper* Cup filled to the brim.

tasted wine in his life, "but *just after* your majesty had struck the girl and thrown the wine in her face—*just after* your majesty had done this, and while the parrot was making that odd noise outside the window, there came into my mind a capital diversion—one of my own country frolics—often enacted among us, at our masquerades: but here it will be new altogether. Unfortunately, however, it requires a company of eight persons, and—"

"Here we *are*!" cried the king, laughing at his acute discovery of the coincidence; "eight to a fraction—I and my seven ministers. Come! what is the diversion?"

"We call it," replied the cripple, "the Eight Chained Ourang-Outangs, and it really is excellent sport if well enacted."

"*We* will enact it," remarked the king, drawing himself up, and lowering his eyelids.

"The beauty of the game," continued Hop-Frog, "lies in the fright it occasions among the women."

"Capital!" roared in chorus the monarch and his ministry.

"*I* will equip you as ourang-outangs," proceeded the dwarf; "leave all that to me. The resemblance shall be so striking, that the company of masqueraders will take you for real beasts—and of course, they will be as much terrified as astonished."

"O, this is exquisite!" exclaimed the king. "Hop-Frog! I will make a man of you."

"The chains are for the purpose of increasing the confusion by their jangling. You are supposed to have escaped, *en masse*, from your keepers. Your majesty cannot conceive the *effect* produced, at a masquerade, by eight chained ourang-outangs, imagined to be real ones by most of the company; and rushing in with savage cries, among the crowd of delicately and gorgeously habited men and women. The *contrast* is inimitable."

"It *must* be," said the king: and the council arose hurriedly (as it was growing late), to put in execution the scheme of Hop-Frog.

His mode of equipping the party as ourang-outangs was very simple, but effective enough for his purposes. The animals in question had, at the epoch of my story, very rarely been seen in any part of the civilized world; and as the imitations made by the dwarf were sufficiently beast-like and more than sufficiently hideous, their truthfulness to nature was thus thought to be secured.

The king and his ministers were first encased in tight-fitting stockinet[1] shirts and drawers. They were then saturated with tar. At this stage of the process, someone of the party suggested feathers; but the suggestion was at once overruled by the dwarf, who soon convinced the eight, by ocular demonstration, that the hair of such a brute as the ourang-outang was much more efficiently represented by *flax*. A thick coating of the latter was accordingly plastered upon the coating of tar. A long chain was now procured. First, it was passed about the waist of the king, *and tied*; then about another of the party, and also tied; then about all successively, in the same manner. When this chaining arrangement was complete, and the party stood as far apart from each other as possible, they formed a circle; and to make all things appear natural, Hop-Frog passed the residue of the chain, in two diameters, at right angles, across the circle, after the fashion adopted, at the present day, by those who capture Chimpanzees, or other large apes, in Borneo.

The grand saloon in which the masquerade was to take place, was a circular room, very lofty, and receiving the light of the sun only through a single window at top. At night (the season for which the apartment was especially designed) it was illuminated principally by a large chandelier, depending by a chain from the centre of the sky-light, and lowered, or elevated, by means of a counter-balance as usual; but (in order not to look unsightly) this latter passed outside the cupola[2] and over the roof.

The arrangements of the room had been left to Trippetta's superintendence; but, in some particulars, it seems, she had been guided by the calmer judgment of her friend the dwarf. At his suggestion it was that, on this occasion, the chandelier was removed. Its waxen drippings (which, in weather so warm, it was quite impossible to prevent) would have been seriously detrimental to the rich dresses of the guests, who, on account of the crowded state of the saloon, could not *all* be expected to keep from out its centre—that is to say, from under the chandelier. Additional sconces were set in various parts of the hall, out of the way;

---

1   *stockinet* Tightly knit fabric with considerable stretch.

2   *cupola* Dome.

and a flambeau,[1] emitting sweet odor, was placed in the right hand of each of the Caryatides[2] that stood against the wall—some fifty or sixty altogether.

The eight ourang-outangs, taking Hop-Frog's advice, waited patiently until midnight (when the room was thoroughly filled with masqueraders) before making their appearance. No sooner had the clock ceased striking, however, than they rushed, or rather rolled in, all together—for the impediment of their chains caused most of the party to fall, and all to stumble as they entered.

The excitement among the masqueraders was prodigious, and filled the heart of the king with glee. As had been anticipated, there were not a few of the guests who supposed the ferocious-looking creatures to be beasts of *some* kind in reality, if not precisely ourang-outangs. Many of the women swooned with affright; and had not the king taken the precaution to exclude all weapons from the saloon, his party might soon have expiated their frolic in their blood. As it was, a general rush was made for the doors; but the king had ordered them to be locked immediately upon his entrance; and, at the dwarf's suggestion, the keys had been deposited with *him*.

While the tumult was at its height, and each masquerader attentive only to his own safety (for, in fact, there was much *real* danger from the pressure of the excited crowd), the chain by which the chandelier ordinarily hung, and which had been drawn up on its removal, might have been seen very gradually to descend, until its hooked extremity came within three feet of the floor.

Soon after this, the king and his seven friends, having reeled about the hall in all directions, found themselves, at length, in its centre, and, of course, in immediate contact with the chain. While they were thus situated, the dwarf, who had followed closely at their heels, inciting them to keep up the commotion, took hold of their own chain at the intersection of the two portions which crossed the circle diametrically and at right angles. Here, with the rapidity of thought, he inserted the hook from which the chandelier had been

wont to depend; and, in an instant, by some unseen agency, the chandelier-chain was drawn so far upward as to take the hook out of reach, and, as an inevitable consequence, to drag the ourang-outangs together in close connection, and face to face.

The masqueraders, by this time, had recovered, in some measure, from their alarm; and, beginning to regard the whole matter as a well-contrived pleasantry, set up a loud shout of laughter at the predicament of the apes.

"Leave them to *me*!" now screamed Hop-Frog, his shrill voice making itself easily heard through all the din. "Leave them to *me*. I fancy *I* know them. If I can only get a good look at them, *I* can soon tell who they are."

Here, scrambling over the heads of the crowd, he managed to get to the wall; when, seizing a flambeau from one of the Caryatides, he returned, as he went, to the centre of the room—leaped, with the agility of a monkey, upon the king's head—and thence clambered a few feet up the chain—holding down the torch to examine the group of ourang-outangs, and still screaming, "*I* shall soon find out who they are!"

And now, while the whole assembly (the apes included) were convulsed with laughter, the jester suddenly uttered a shrill whistle; when the chain flew violently up for about thirty feet—dragging with it the dismayed and struggling ourang-outangs, and leaving them suspended in mid-air between the sky-light and the floor. Hop-Frog, clinging to the chain as it rose, still maintained his relative position in respect to the eight maskers, and still (as if nothing were the matter) continued to thrust his torch down towards them, as though endeavoring to discover who they were.

So thoroughly astonished were the whole company at this ascent, that a dead silence, of about a minute's duration, ensued. It was broken by just such a low, harsh, *grating* sound, as had before attracted the attention of the king and his councillors, when the former threw the wine in the face of Trippetta. But, on the present occasion, there could be no question as to *whence* the sound issued. It came from the fang-like teeth of the dwarf, who ground them and gnashed them as he foamed at the mouth, and glared, with an expression of maniacal rage, into the upturned countenances of the king and his seven companions.

---

[1] *flambeau* Torch.

[2] *Caryatides* Sculpted female figures serving as columns. Originating in ancient Greece, they experienced a revival in European architecture during and after the Renaissance.

"Ah, ha!" said at length the infuriated jester. "Ah, ha! I begin to see who these people *are*, now!" Here, pretending to scrutinize the king more closely, he held the flambeau to the flaxen coat which enveloped him, and which instantly burst into a sheet of vivid flame. In less than half a minute the whole eight ourang-outangs were blazing fiercely, amid the shrieks of the multitude who gazed at them from below, horror-stricken, and without the power to render them the slightest assistance.

At length the flames, suddenly increasing in virulence, forced the jester to climb higher up the chain, to be out of their reach; and, as he made this movement, the crowd again sank, for a brief instant, into silence. The dwarf seized his opportunity, and once more spoke:

"I now see *distinctly*," he said, "what manner of people these maskers are. They are a great king and his seven privy-councillors—a king who does not scruple to strike a defenceless girl, and his seven councillors who abet him in the outrage. As for myself, I am simply Hop-Frog, the jester—and *this is my last jest*."

Owing to the high combustibility of both the flax and the tar to which it adhered, the dwarf had scarcely made an end of his brief speech before the work of vengeance was complete. The eight corpses swung in their chains, a fetid, blackened, hideous, and indistinguishable mass. The cripple hurled his torch at them, clambered leisurely to the ceiling, and disappeared through the sky-light.

It is supposed that Trippetta, stationed on the roof of the saloon, had been the accomplice of her friend in his fiery revenge, and that, together, they effected their escape to their own country: for neither was seen again.

—1849

Annabel Lee

It was many and many a year ago,
    In a kingdom by the sea,
That a maiden there lived whom you may know
    By the name of Annabel Lee;
5 And this maiden she lived with no other thought
    Than to love and be loved by me.

I was a child and *she* was a child,
    In a kingdom by the sea;
But we loved with a love that was more than love—
10   I and my Annabel Lee—
With a love that the wingèd seraphs° in Heaven   *angels*
    Coveted her and me.

And this was the reason that, long ago,
    In this kingdom by the sea,
15 A wind blew out of a cloud, chilling
    My beautiful Annabel Lee;
So that her high-born kinsmen came
    And bore her away from me,
To shut her up in a sepulchre,
20   In this kingdom by the sea.

The angels, not half so happy in Heaven,
    Went envying her and me—
Yes!—that was the reason (as all men know,
    In this kingdom by the sea)
25 That the wind came out of the cloud by night,
    Chilling and killing my Annabel Lee.

But our love it was stronger by far than the love
    Of those who were older than we—
    Of many far wiser than we—
30 And neither the angels in Heaven above,
    Nor the demons down under the sea,
Can ever dissever my soul from the soul
    Of the beautiful Annabel Lee:

For the moon never beams, without bringing me
  dreams
35   Of the beautiful Annabel Lee;
And the stars never rise, but I feel the bright eyes
    Of the beautiful Annabel Lee:
And so, all the night-tide, I lie down by the side
Of my darling—my darling—my life and my bride,
40   In her sepulchre there by the sea—
    In her tomb by the sounding sea.

—1849

NINETEENTH-CENTURY ORATORY

In 1810, future U.S. president John Quincy Adams—who had just completed a three-year term as Harvard College's first Boylston Professor of Rhetoric and Oratory—predicted a dawning golden age of oratory for his young country: "[Our] own nation is at this time precisely under the same circumstances which were so propitious to the advancement of rhetoric and oratory among the Greeks. ... Persuasion, or the influence of reason and of feeling, is the great if not the only instrument whose operation can affect the acts of all our corporate bodies; of towns, cities, counties, states, and of the whole confederated empire." Adams's prediction was borne out by a diverse, extensive, and thriving culture of oratory throughout nineteenth-century America; indeed, by the middle of the century, oratory had greater importance and centrality, and was studied and practiced more systematically and intensively, than at arguably any time in American history since.

The rhetorical arts of public debate and persuasion played an indispensable role in America's democratic institutions, and nineteenth-century Americans—for all the considerable limitations and deficiencies of their democracy in practice—took the exercise of these arts seriously. In addition, in a world without any of the electronic mass media that would so completely transform life in the twentieth and twenty-first centuries, public speaking was not just fundamental to politics but was a crucial way in which nineteenth-century Americans received their education, kept abreast of current events, and entertained themselves. The recording and dissemination of oratory was greatly facilitated by the use of shorthand—or, as it was known in the nineteenth century, "phonography"—which enabled reporters to transcribe speeches verbatim; several phonographic systems flourished during the period, including Pitman shorthand, first introduced in 1837, which came to prominence in America in 1858 when it was used to record the Lincoln–Douglas debates. Thanks to phonography, full texts of speeches—often including descriptions of audience reaction, as a number of the speech texts included in this section do—were frequently reprinted in newspapers, where they were read avidly by those who had not been able to hear them in person. Cultural and educational institutions also helped make oratory an integral part of daily life: lyceums (local institutions for continuing education) brought celebrated orators to cities and small towns across the country, and oratorical training was an integral part of primary education. Students learned public speaking in the classroom, and they studied well-regarded speeches in popular anthologies—such as the *Columbian Orator*, first published in 1797 and reprinted numerous times throughout the nineteenth century—which allowed instructors to teach speaking, reading, and patriotic values simultaneously. Ralph Waldo Emerson aptly summarized the importance of oratory in the lives of his contemporaries when he said of the orator that "[a]ll other fame must hush before his. He is the true potentate."

Precisely because of its omnipresence and importance, however, oratory was also the subject of considerable controversy, concern, and contention. The prevailing way in which oratory was theorized and taught valued an overtly "genteel" rhetorical style: polished, ornate, and (in the words of the French observer Alexis de Tocqueville) occasionally "inflated." This rhetorical style was embodied by such celebrity orator-politicians as Edward Everett—whom Emerson called "aloof and uncommon as a star"—John C. Calhoun, and Daniel Webster: not coincidentally, all privileged white men. For women, by contrast, speaking in public—especially in front of "mixed" audiences, that is, ones including men as well as women—was frowned upon, and the trailblazers of nineteenth-century women's oratory, such as Frances Wright and Maria Stewart, garnered intense controversy. In addition to women, members of the working class and African Americans also found themselves discouraged or outright excluded from the practice of oratory and had to fight to claim a place for themselves in the rhetorical sphere; as they did so, they often developed oratorical styles that did not conform to the conventions of the "genteel" rhetoric cultivated in privileged, formally educated spheres, but that many listeners came to find more effective and powerful.

As Walt Whitman put it, "Talking of oratory, why is it that the unsophisticated practices often strike deeper than the train'd ones?"

As African American oratory in particular demonstrates, however, standard or culturally privileged rhetorical practices and more marginal, less-privileged ones were not always mutually exclusive. Many black orators readily and even eagerly assimilated the conventions and archive of Euro-American oratory, from its classical Greco-Roman roots to the speeches of America's white founders. As an enslaved boy of twelve, for example, Frederick Douglass paid fifty cents for his own copy of the *Columbian Orator* and later described his encounter with this anthology as a pivotal event in his life, from which he derived not just oratorical aspirations and skills but strengthened conviction: some of the speeches contained in the anthology, he wrote, demonstrated "bold and powerful denunciation of oppression and a most brilliant vindication of the rights of man." (The degree of influence the *Columbian Orator* actually wielded on Douglass's own oratory, however, is a matter of dispute among scholars.) African American oratory also drew on the distinctive rhetorical conventions and practices black people had developed for and among themselves, including the prophetic biblical language of the black church and the call-and-response structure of much African American oral literature—both of which, for instance, are on display in the 1866 speech by Bayley Wyat presented below. The interaction of, and tension between, these two lines of influence is an especially illuminating thread to trace through nineteenth-century African American oratory.

While many voices outside the dominant white culture of oratory had to create audiences and find creative ways to make themselves heard, the case of Indigenous oratory was slightly different, as white culture did, however condescendingly, appreciate the excellence of Indigenous speech-making. Indigenous peoples had their own rich and ancient rhetorical traditions, developed in many cases out of the value they placed on fostering consensus in political decision-making. The genuine power of Indigenous rhetoric, mingled with the longstanding Enlightenment idealization of "noble savages," gave rise to a widespread Euro-American view of Native Americans as naturally eloquent. White Americans eagerly seized on actual examples of Indigenous oratory—even or especially ones condemning white Americans' own aggression against Indigenous nations—as evidence of this belief. Indigenous speeches were frequently reprinted and anthologized, were memorized and recited in schools, and in some cases became widely influential. As the *American Pioneer* proclaimed in 1842 of an especially famous Indigenous speech, "no piece of composition ever did more, if so much, as the speech of Logan ... to form the mind and develop the latent energies of the youthful American orator." Because white Americans were particularly inclined to celebrate Indigenous descriptions of their own victimization, however, the popularity of Indigenous oratory helped entrench the damaging stereotype of the "vanishing Indian." The 1822 speech by "The Pawnee Chief" included below notably pushes back against this stereotype—which did not prevent it, too, from becoming widely popular.

The debates over who could take part in oratory, and why, were connected to another nineteenth-century controversy, namely how far orators should go in stirring up the emotions of their audiences. While standard rhetorical theory emphasized the importance of appealing to an audience's passions or emotions as well as to its intellect and reason, many cultural commentators worried about the effect on audiences of too much emotional intensity. At what point did the necessary work of arousing listeners' feelings and engaging their imaginative sympathy shade over into emotional manipulation or rabble-rousing? In the words of one 1854 article criticizing the allegedly overheated rhetoric of abolitionist orators, "Is it a subject of surprise that, thus appealed to, ... and assailed by every device of hypocrisy and fanaticism, a large portion of the people of the north, should, by all degrees, lose all respect for the laws, and resort to violent opposition on any occasion of excitement?" Even within movements such as the campaigns for abolition and women's rights, reformers argued intensely among themselves over what rhetorical strategies would most effectively promote change. (Disagreement on this score was one factor in the falling-out between Frederick Douglass and William Lloyd Garrison—a quarrel so bitter that they eventually stopped speaking to each other.) Were such reform causes best served by more restrained attempts to win opponents over using logical argumentation and a refined and civil oratorical style? Or were they best served by taking the rhetorical gloves off and engaging—as the famed abolitionist orator

Wendell Phillips put it—in "denunciation, and ridicule, and every other weapon that the human mind knows"?

The speeches presented below and in the website portion of this section—as well as the numerous other oratorical works included elsewhere in this anthology—showcase different answers to these and other questions as they attest to the vibrancy, diversity, and power of American oratory during its mid-nineteenth-century heyday.

⌘ ⌘ ⌘

MRS JULI ANN JANE TILLMAN

Alfred M. Hoffy (artist) and Peter S. Duval (printer), *Mrs. Juliann Jane Tillman*, 1844. Little is known about Tillman, except that she was a lay preacher in the African Methodist Episcopal Church whose oratory was evidently popular enough to warrant the publication of this (often-reproduced) lithograph of her. She is one of several black female preachers of the late eighteenth and early nineteenth centuries whose public speaking has not been recorded but was an important component of the nineteenth-century oratorical scene.

Illustration from *Sanders' School Speaker: A Comprehensive Course of Instruction in the Principles of Oratory*, 1857, one of the many textbooks, primers, and anthologies that were used to teach elocution and oratory in nineteenth-century schools. This illustration comes from the book's section on how to use gesture to accentuate delivery; according to the illustration's key, "Fig. 9 represents the speaker as addressing some grand imposing object; ... Fig. 10 represents the speaker, as though filled with wonder; ... Fig. 11 represents the speaker as in a state of rapturous delight; ... Fig. 12 represents the speaker as making an earnest appeal to conscience."

Petalesharo or Sharitarish, "Speech of 'The Pawnee Chief'"

Between late 1821 and early 1822, a delegation of leaders of Indigenous nations from the upper Missouri River region visited Washington, D.C. The delegation was organized by Major Benjamin O'Fallon, the federal Indian agent for the upper Missouri. The star of the delegation was Petalesharo (c. 1797–c. 1836), a young chief of the Skidi band of the Pawnee nation, who had become a celebrity among white Americans for preventing the human sacrifice of young female captives from other Indigenous nations at the Morning Star ceremony, an important ritual in Pawnee religion. (The Pawnee were one of the few Indigenous nations north of Mexico to practice human sacrifice.) The speech printed below was given during the Indigenous delegates' meeting with President James Monroe at the White House on 5 February 1822; it was the first Indigenous speech given in response to Monroe's opening remarks. It is not known who translated or first recorded the speech (because of which some historians have doubted its authenticity). The earliest surviving text of the speech, published by the British diplomat James Buchanan in his *Sketches of the North American Indians* (1824), identifies its speaker simply as "The Pawnee Chief"; it has usually been ascribed to Petalesharo, but a more probable candidate is Sharitarish, a chief from another Pawnee band, the Chaui, who was the senior delegate of the Pawnee and thus more likely to have the privilege of being the first Indigenous delegate to respond to Monroe. Whoever originally gave it, the speech has become one of the most famous examples of nineteenth-century Indigenous oratory.

My Great Father: I have travelled a great distance to see you—I have seen you and my heart rejoices. I have heard your words—they have entered one ear and shall not escape the other, and I will carry them to my people as pure as they came from your mouth.

My Great Father: I am going to speak the truth. The Great Spirit looks down upon us, and I call *Him* to witness all that may pass between us on this occasion. If I am here now and have seen your people, your houses, your vessels on the big lake, and a great many wonderful things far beyond my comprehension, which appear to have been made by the Great Spirit and placed in your hands, I am indebted to my Father here, who invited me from home, under whose wings I have been protected.[1] Yes, my Great Father, I have travelled with your chief; I have followed him, and trod in his tracks; but there is still *another* Great Father *to whom I am much indebted—it is the Father of us all*. Him who made us and placed us on this earth. I feel grateful to the Great Sprit for strengthening my heart for such an undertaking, and for preserving the life which he gave me. The Great Spirit made us all— he made my skin red, and yours white; he placed us on this earth, and intended that we should live differently from each other.

He made the whites to cultivate the earth, and feed on domestic animals; but he made us, red skins, to rove through the uncultivated woods and plains; to feed on wild animals; and to dress with their skins. He also intended that we should go to war—to take scalps— *steal horses from* and triumph over our enemies—cultivate peace at home, and promote the happiness of each other. I believe there are no people of any colour on this earth who do not believe in the Great Spirit—in rewards, and in punishments. We worship him, but we worship him not as you do. We differ from you in appearance and manners as well as in our customs; and we differ from you in our religion; we have no large houses as you have to worship the Great Spirit in; if we had them today, we should want others tomorrow, for we have not, like you, a fixed habitation—we have no settled home except our villages, where we remain but two moons in twelve. We, like animals, rove through the country, whilst you whites reside between us and heaven; but still, my Great Father, we love the Great Spirit—we acknowledge his supreme power—our peace, our health, and our happiness depend upon him, and our lives belong to him—he made us and he can destroy us.

My Great Father: Some of your good chiefs, as they are called (missionaries), have proposed to send some of their good people among us to change our habits, to

---

[1]   [Buchanan's note]   Pointing to Major O'Fallon.

make us work and live like the white people. I will not tell a lie—I am going to tell the truth. You love your country—you love your people—you love the manner in which they live, and you think your people are brave. I am like you, my Great Father, I love my country—I love my people—I love the manner in which we live, and think myself and warriors brave. Spare me then, my Father; let me enjoy my country, and pursue the buffalo, and the beaver, and the other wild animals of our country, and I will trade their skins with your people. I have grown up, and lived thus long without work—I am in hopes you will suffer me to die without it. We have plenty of buffalo, beaver, deer and other wild animals—we have also an abundance of horses—we have everything we want—we have plenty of land, if you will keep your people off of it. My father[1] has a piece on which he lives (Council Bluffs)[2] and we wish him to enjoy it—we have enough without it—but we wish him to live near us to give us good counsel—to keep our ears and eyes open that we may continue to pursue the right road—the road to happiness. He settles all differences between us and the whites, between the red skins themselves—he makes the whites do justice to the red skins, and he makes the red skins do justice to the whites. He saves the effusion of human blood, and restores peace and happiness on the land. You have already sent us a father; it is enough he knows us and we know him—we have confidence in him—we keep our eye constantly upon him, and since we have heard your words, we will listen more attentively to *his*.

It is too soon, my Great Father, to send those good men among us. *We are not starving yet*—we wish you to permit us to enjoy the chase until the game of our country is exhausted—until the wild animals become extinct. Let us exhaust our present resources before you make us toil and interrupt our happiness—let me continue to live as I have done, and after I have passed to the Good or Evil Spirit from off the wilderness of my present life, the subsistence of my children may become so precarious as to need and embrace the assistance of those good people.

There was a time when we did not know the whites—our wants were then fewer than they are now. They were always within our control—we had then seen nothing which we could not get. Before our intercourse[3] with the *whites* (who have caused such a destruction in our game), we could lie down to sleep, and when we awoke we would find the buffalo feeding around our camp—but we are now killing them for their skins,[4] and feeding the wolves with their flesh, to make our children cry over their bones.

Here, my Great Father, is a pipe which I present you, as I am accustomed to present pipes to all the red skins in peace with us. It is filled with such tobacco as we were accustomed to smoke before we knew the white people. It is pleasant, and the spontaneous growth of the most remote parts of our country. I know that the robes, leggings, moccasins, bear-claws, etc., are of little value to you, but we wish you to have them deposited and preserved in some conspicuous part of your lodge, so that when we are gone and the sod turned over our bones, if our children should visit this place, as we do now, they may see and recognize with pleasure the deposits of their fathers; and reflect on the times that are past.

—1822

Maria W. Stewart, "Lecture Delivered at Franklin Hall"

Maria W. Stewart (1803–79) is one of the first American women known to have publicly addressed mixed-gender, interracial audiences, as well as one of the first African American female orators whose speeches were recorded and survive. (The oratory of Stewart's forerunners, who include the renowned black female preachers Rebecca Cox Jackson, Jarena Lee, and Zilpha Elaw, was, unfortunately, never written down.) Stewart was born Maria Miller into a free black family in Hartford, Connecticut. After being completely orphaned at the age of three, she was brought up by a minister and his family;

---

1   *My father*   I.e., Major O'Fallon.

2   *Council Bluffs*   I.e., Fort Atkinson, a military post on the Missouri River, twenty miles northwest of the present-day city of Council Bluffs, Iowa, that was O'Fallon's upriver headquarters as Indian Agent for the upper Missouri.

3   *intercourse*   Interaction.

4   *but we … skins*   I.e., killing the buffalo purely in order to trade their hides to white traders, rather than for subsistence as previously.

the only education she received was Sabbath School before Sunday church services. She married James W. Stewart, a Boston shipping agent, in 1826 but was widowed three years later, whereupon his executors denied her any share of his estate—an experience that galvanized her to begin challenging the unequal treatment of women, particularly African American women. Stewart was also inspired by David Walker, a prominent black Bostonian whose incendiary *Appeal to the Coloured Citizens of the World*, issued in 1829, called for African American resistance to slavery. These influences sparked a combined spiritual-political awakening in Stewart, who began writing religious essays—published as pamphlets by *The Liberator*, a leading abolitionist newspaper—and then moved into public speaking. She is known to have delivered four speeches between 1832 and 1833, all of which were also printed in *The Liberator*; the speech included below was given to a meeting of the New England Anti-Slavery Society at Franklin Hall, Boston, on 21 September 1832. Stewart's propensity to challenge not just the white but also the black members of her audiences won her little popularity, and she retired from public speaking in 1833. She subsequently moved to New York City, Baltimore, and finally Washington, D.C., working as a schoolteacher and hospital nurse while remaining involved in the abolition movement. She re-emerged into the public eye in 1879, when she published an expanded edition of her essays and speeches, *Meditations from the Pen of Mrs. Maria W. Stewart*; she died in Washington later that year.

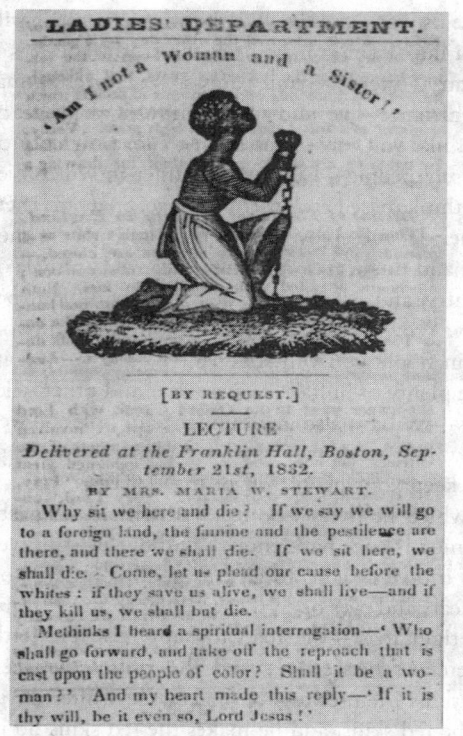

The beginning of Maria Stewart's "Lecture Delivered at Franklin Hall," as printed in *The Liberator* (17 November 1832).

Methinks I heard a spiritual interrogation—"Who shall go forward, and take off the reproach that is cast upon the people of color? Shall it be a woman?" And my heart made this reply—"If it is thy will, be it even so, Lord Jesus!"

I have heard much respecting the horrors of slavery; but may Heaven forbid that the generality of my color throughout these United States should experience any more of its horrors than to be a servant of servants, or hewers of wood and drawers of water![2] Tell us no more of southern slavery; for with few exceptions, although

Why sit ye here and die? If we say we will go to a foreign land, the famine and the pestilence are there, and there we shall die. If we sit here, we shall die. Come let us plead our cause before the whites: if they save us alive, we shall live—and if they kill us, we shall but die.[1]

---

1   *Why sit ... die*   See 2 Kings 7.3–4. In this biblical passage, four lepers sitting outside the gates of Samaria, a city besieged by a Syrian army and afflicted by famine, decide that if they remain as outcasts, they will die of their disease, and if they enter the city, they will die of famine, so they will go to ask for help from the Syrians. In the ensuing verses, the Syrians hear, instead of the approaching lepers, an approaching army and flee, abandoning their treasure and saving the city.

2   *a servant ... water*   Stewart alludes to two biblical descriptions of servitude. In Genesis 9.25 (a passage frequently drawn on by pro-slavery writers seeking to justify African American slavery on biblical grounds), Noah curses his grandson Canaan, due to an indiscretion by Canaan's father Ham: "Cursed be Canaan; a servant of servants shall he be unto his brethren." In Joshua 9.23, the Israelite leader Joshua tells a group of captured opponents, "Now therefore ye are cursed, and there shall none of you be freed from being bondmen, and hewers of wood and drawers of water."

I may be very erroneous in my opinion, yet I consider our condition but little better than that. Yet, after all, methinks there are no chains so galling as the chains of ignorance—no fetters so binding as those that bind the soul, and exclude it from the vast field of useful and scientific knowledge. O, had I received the advantages of early education, my ideas would, ere now, have expanded far and wide; but, alas! I possess nothing but moral capability—no teachings but the teachings of the Holy Spirit.

I have asked several individuals of my sex, who transact business for themselves, if providing our girls were to give them the most satisfactory references, they would not be willing to grant them an equal opportunity with others? Their reply has been—for their own part, they had no objection; but as it was not the custom, were they to take them into their employ, they would be in danger of losing the public patronage.

And such is the powerful force of prejudice. Let our girls possess what amiable qualities of soul they may; let their characters be fair and spotless as innocence itself; let their natural taste and ingenuity be what they may; it is impossible for scarce an individual of them to rise above the condition of servants. Ah! why is this cruel and unfeeling distinction? Is it merely because God has made our complexion to vary? If it be, O shame to soft, relenting[1] humanity! "Tell it not in Gath! publish it not in the streets of Askelon!"[2] Yet, after all, methinks were the American free people of color to turn their attention more assiduously to moral worth and intellectual improvement, this would be the result: prejudice would gradually diminish, and the whites would be compelled to say, unloose those fetters!

Though black their skins as shades of night,
Their hearts are pure, their souls are white.[3]

Few white persons of either sex, who are calculated[4] for anything else, are willing to spend their lives and bury their talents in performing mean, servile labor. And such is the horrible idea that I entertain respecting a life of servitude, that if I conceived of there being no possibility of my rising above the condition of a servant, I would gladly hail death as a welcome messenger. O, horrible idea, indeed! to possess noble souls aspiring after high and honorable acquirements, yet confined by the chains of ignorance and poverty to lives of continual drudgery and toil. Neither do I know of any who have enriched themselves by spending their lives as house-domestics, washing windows, shaking carpets, brushing boots, or tending upon gentlemen's tables. I can but die for expressing my sentiments; and I am as willing to die by the sword as the pestilence—for I am a true born American—your blood flows in my veins, and your spirit fires my breast.

I observed a piece in the *Liberator* a few months since, stating that the colonizationists[5] had published a work respecting us, asserting that we were lazy and idle. I confute them on that point. Take us generally as a people, we are neither lazy nor idle; and considering how little we have to excite or stimulate us, I am almost astonished that there are so many industrious and ambitious ones to be found; although I acknowledge, with extreme sorrow, that there are some who never were and never will be serviceable to society. And have you not a similar class among yourselves?

Again—It was asserted that we were "a ragged set, crying for liberty." I reply to it, the whites have so long and so loudly proclaimed the theme of equal rights and privileges, that our souls have caught the flame also, ragged as we are. As far as our merit deserves, we feel a common desire to rise above the condition of servants and drudges. I have learnt, by bitter experience,

---

[1] *relenting* Forgiving, merciful.

[2] *Tell it … Askelon* See 2 Samuel 1.20. In this passage, the Israelite King David rhetorically laments the defeat and death of his predecessor Saul, and Saul's son Jonathan, at the hands of the Philistines, declaring that if this defeat is made known in the Philistine cities of Gath and Askelon, it will shame the Israelites. In the same way, Stewart avers, the fact of race-based prejudice shames America.

[3] *Though black … white* This couplet, which also appears elsewhere in Stewart's work, seems to be of her own composition; however, it echoes a line from "The Little Black Boy" (1789), by the English poet William Blake: "I am black, but O! my soul is white."

[4] *calculated* Prepared or suited.

[5] *colonizationists* Members or supporters of the American Colonization Society, an organization established in 1817 that aimed at relocating free African Americans to a number of proposed colonies in Africa (primarily Liberia, which was founded by the ACS in 1822). Members of the ACS portrayed it as a benevolent society (although its membership included numerous slaveholders or defenders of slavery), and the goal of African American colonization was widely supported by white Americans throughout the early nineteenth century; many abolitionists and black Americans, however, condemned the colonization project.

that continual hard labor deadens the energies of the soul, and benumbs the faculties of the mind; the ideas become confined, the mind barren, and, like the scorching sands of Arabia, produces nothing; or, like the uncultivated soil, brings forth thorns and thistles.

Again, continual hard labor irritates our tempers and sours our dispositions; the whole system becomes worn out with toil and fatigue; nature herself becomes almost exhausted, and we care but little whether we live or die. It is true, that the free people of color throughout these United States are neither bought nor sold, nor under the lash of the cruel driver; many obtain a comfortable support; but few, if any, have an opportunity of becoming rich and independent; and the employments we most pursue are as unprofitable to us as the spider's web or the floating bubbles that vanish into air. As servants, we are respected; but let us presume to aspire any higher, our employer regards us no longer. And were it not that the King eternal has declared that Ethiopia shall stretch forth her hands unto God,[1] I should indeed despair.

I do not consider it derogatory, my friends, for persons to live out to service. There are many whose inclination leads them to aspire no higher; and I would highly commend the performance of almost any thing for an honest livelihood; but where constitutional strength is wanting, labor of this kind, in its mildest form, is painful. And doubtless many are the prayers that have ascended to Heaven from Afric's[2] daughters for strength to perform their work. Oh, many are the tears that have been shed for the want of that strength! Most of our color have dragged out a miserable existence of servitude from the cradle to the grave. And what literary acquirements can be made, or useful knowledge derived, from either maps, books or charts, by those who continually drudge from Monday morning until Sunday noon? O, ye fairer sisters, whose hands are never soiled, whose nerves and muscles are never strained, go learn by experience! Had we had the opportunity that you have had, to improve our moral and mental faculties, what would have hindered our intellects from being as bright, and our manners from being as dignified as yours? Had it been our lot to have been nursed in the lap of affluence and ease, and to have basked beneath the smiles and sunshine of fortune, should we not have naturally supposed that we were never made to toil? And why are not our forms as delicate, and our constitutions as slender, as yours? Is not the workmanship as curious and complete? Have pity upon us, have pity upon us, O ye who have hearts to feel for other's woes; for the hand of God has touched us. Owing to the disadvantages under which we labor, there are many flowers among us that are

"born to bloom unseen,
And waste their fragrance on the desert air."[3]

My beloved brethren, as Christ has died in vain for those who will not accept of offered mercy, so will it be vain for the advocates of freedom to spend their breath in our behalf, unless with united hearts and souls you make some mighty efforts to raise your sons and daughters from the horrible state of servitude and degradation in which they are placed. It is upon you that woman depends; she can do but little besides using her influence; and it is for her sake and yours that I have come forward and made myself a hissing and a reproach among the people;[4] for I am also one of the wretched and miserable daughters of the descendants of fallen Africa. Do you ask, why are you wretched and miserable? I reply, look at many of the most worthy and interesting of us doomed to spend our lives in gentlemen's kitchens. Look at our young men, smart, active and energetic, with souls filled with ambitious fire; if they look forward, alas! what are their prospects? They can be nothing but the humblest laborers, on account of their dark complexions; hence many of them lose their ambition, and become worthless. Look at our middle-aged men, clad in their rusty plaids and coats; in winter, every cent they earn goes to buy their wood and pay their rents; their poor wives also toil beyond

---

[1]   *the King ... unto God*   See Psalm 68.31 (a line frequently invoked by nineteenth-century abolitionists): "Ethiopia shall soon stretch out her hands unto God." The name "Ethiopia" at this period was often used to refer generally to all of Africa, and to all people of African descent.

[2]   *Afric*   I.e., Africa.

[3]   *born ... air*   See the English poet Thomas Gray's "Elegy Written in a Country Churchyard" (1751), lines 55–56. The passage from which these lines are taken describes how poverty and marginalization thwart the development or expression of creative talents.

[4]   *a hissing ... people*   See Jeremiah 29.18.

their strength, to help support their families. Look at our aged sires, whose heads are whitened with the frosts of seventy winters, with their old wood-saws on their backs. Alas, what keeps us so? Prejudice, ignorance and poverty. But ah! methinks our oppression is soon to come to an end; yea, before the Majesty of heaven, our groans and cries have reached the ears of the Lord of Sabaoth.[1] As the prayers and tears of Christians will avail the finally impenitent nothing; neither will the prayers and tears of the friends of humanity avail us any thing, unless we possess a spirit of virtuous emulation within our breasts. Did the pilgrims, when they first landed on these shores, quietly compose themselves, and say, "the Britons have all the money and all the power, and we must continue their servants forever"? Did they sluggishly sigh and say, "our lot is hard, the Indians own the soil, and we cannot cultivate it"? No; they first made powerful efforts to raise themselves, and then God raised up those illustrious patriots, Washington and Lafayette,[2] to assist and defend them. And, my brethren, have you made a powerful effort? Have you prayed the Legislature for mercy's sake to grant you all the rights and privileges of free citizens, that your daughters may rise to that degree of respectability which true merit deserves, and your sons above the servile situations which most of them fill?

—1832

from Michael Walsh, "An Abridgment of the Speech at the Great County Meeting in Tammany Hall"

The politician and journalist Michael Walsh (1810–59) was born in Ireland and immigrated to the United States with his parents as a small child. By the 1840s, he had become one of the most prominent and popular leaders of New York City's working-class men—many of them Irish immigrants like himself—and a forceful practitioner of the city's chaotic, frequently violent politics. He founded the Spartan Association, a Democratic working-men's society, doubling as a street gang, that opposed—and sometimes came to blows with—both the rival Whig Party and supporters of the wealthy coterie that, at the time, controlled Tammany Hall, the political organization dominating New York Democratic politics. (At the time, the Democrats were the more populist of the two major political parties, but the leaders of the party in New York in the 1830s and early 1840s generally only paid lip service to the interests of the working class and were just starting to recognize the potential political power of the city's large and growing number of Irish immigrants.) A colorful figure known for sporting ragged clothing together with a silver-tipped cane and a diamond ring, Walsh was also an eloquent orator whose speeches resoundingly condemned corrupt, careerist politicians and exploitative, oblivious elites and laid out a radically anti-capitalist political vision. His cutting, combative oratorical style carried over into his journalistic work: his editorship of the newspaper *The Subterranean* caused him to be imprisoned for libel. Walsh eventually won enough support from Tammany Hall to be elected to the New York state legislature, where he pushed for a reform agenda that included shorter working hours, the right to strike, and measures against child labor. He was then elected to the U.S. Congress, but after his single congressional term ended in 1855, his career declined and he sank into alcoholism, dying in suspicious circumstances in 1859. His leadership and advocacy, however, helped the largely-immigrant working class he represented obtain, by the time of his death, an unprecedented degree of power in New York politics.

The text of the excerpt given below is based on the text of the speech as printed in *Sketches of the Speeches and Writings of Michael Walsh* (1843), which compiled its collection of Walsh's speeches from the transcriptions of them in New York newspapers.

---

[1] *our groans ... Lord of Sabaoth*   See James 5.4: "Behold, the hire of the labourers who have reaped down your fields, which is of you kept back by fraud, crieth: and the cries of them which have reaped are entered into the ears of the Lord of Sabaoth." The expression "Lord of Sabaoth," meaning "Lord of Hosts" or "God of armies," is a biblical term used to refer to God in his capacity as a military leader of either the Israelite army or the heavenly host of angels.

[2] *Lafayette*   Gilbert du Motier, Marquis de Lafayette (1757–1834), French aristocrat and general who led American troops in the Revolutionary War.

Campaign poster for Michael Walsh, 1847.

Mr. Walsh was rejected by the Democratic Nominating Committee, because he indignantly refused to censure the conduct of three thousand honest working men, who assembled at a public meeting and unanimously recommended him to the favorable notice of the Committee, as the most honest, fearless, talented and high-minded representative that the City of New York could send to the State Legislature; and one in whom the working classes had the most unbounded confidence. Mike was determined to appeal to the people at the County Meeting. …

… On coming forward he was greeted with the most enthusiastic shouts, cheers, hisses and all sorts of noises. He threw down his hat, calmly surveyed the living mass of undulating beings beneath and around him—smiled, and then, addressing himself to those who were hissing and crying out "turn him out," "chuck him out of the window," et cetera, he then quietly exclaimed, in an ironical tone:

"Keep still, gentlemen—don't tire yourselves. You must hear what I have to tell you before you hear anyone else; so you might as well swallow it quietly—we can interrupt others as well as you can interrupt me; and, if I mistake not, a *leetle* better."

Quiet being now somewhat restored he proceeded as follows:

"My friends—Almost every person of my description when about to address an assemblage of their fellow citizens usually preface their remarks with a humble confession of their entire incompetency for the task. Some plead youth, some ignorance, and others their low position in society. I too might, with equal propriety, plead youth and the lowness of my state, but I deem these no disqualifications, and as I wish to be as plain, candid and straight forward as possible, the only apology I shall make for intruding upon your time and patience is that of a pure, fervent, disinterested and devoted desire to do all that lays within my humble means to promote the glorious principles which form our great and common cause. My principles, which hundreds present can attest, are not to be swayed like the position of a weathercock by every passing breeze; they were born in me—education has confirmed what nature implanted, and a close observation of men and measures from childhood has forever cemented them. For the truth of this I now appeal to those among you who were companions of my childhood—you who have watched the gradual development of my mind and principles. Was I not in boyhood the advocate and champion of the same glorious principles which I now profess and practise? ["You were," by some thousand voices]—principles which are looked upon as treasonable by that favored portion of the human family whose interest it is to degrade and oppress the producing classes of mankind for their own elevation and aggrandizement, but which in reality are as immutable as the laws which govern the Universe. [Tremendous cheering.] …

"… I wish you to distinctly understand me when I tell you that Tammany Hall belongs to us—we being the only honest, virtuous portion of the Democratic Party, and I wish you also to distinctly understand that we are determined to keep possession of it until you are able to dispossess us—and that I believe is as good as a lease for life, isn't it boys? [Terrific cheering, hisses and cries of "yes," mingled with "go it Mike," "turn him out etc.," which finally ended in two or three beautiful fights. The uproar was here so great, that the reporters were unable to note a word for several minutes.] …

"Oh, suffering, patient, persecuted, deluded and degraded man—from the first dawn of my reason, from the first hour at which I was capable of contemplating thy character, and comprehending thy many wrongs, I have consecrated my life to thy redemption. For this I have been persecuted, vilified and traduced, even by men who are realizing fortunes through false and hypocritical professions of devotion to my principles, and for it I would willingly sacrifice my existence. Would to God that I could make every working man feel the same on those subjects as I do. That day oppression and injustice would be known in the world only as things which once had an existence—that day unprincipled demagogues would cease to ride into power, place and fortune, by insultingly pretending to love the people who they are humbugging and plundering from year to year—that day millions of the human race who now live worse than the fowl of the air, the fish of the sea, or the beast of the forest, while their lazy plundering oppressors revel in luxury and magnificence, would shake off their manacles—walk forth in the dignity of human nature, and feel that they are men in something more than name. I have, thank Heaven, moulded many to my views, and from a close intimacy with all classes of men I can boldly assert that mankind in the mass only require to know their rights to *obtain* and *maintain* them. Yes, my friends, I must candidly acknowledge that I am one of those wild youthful enthusiasts who are just foolish enough to believe that every rule ought to work both ways, and that if the Democratic Party will but stick to their text—if they will but carry out their principles and creed to the letter, without consulting expediency—if they will oppose all charter monopolies and repeal those in existence—if they will cease to contract the public work out for a bonus to unprincipled favorites, who amass fortunes by driving round in their gigs,[1] abusing, goading, and driving almost to death the poor half-starved wretches; the chief part of the proceeds of whose labor they are enabled by this plundering contract process to pocket. If they will wage war against all exclusive privileges and special legislation—set their faces against everything which is calculated to elevate the rich, and degrade and oppress the poor—if they will do all in their power to break down the hoary-headed[2] errors of ages—errors which have loaded the mass of the human race for centuries upon centuries with sorrow, suffering and chains, for the aggrandizement of the lazy idle few, and simply practise what they preach—if they will but do all this, they need never apprehend a defeat. The laboring classes with the exception of a few poor paltry unprincipled, heartless, soulless, spiritless wretches, will support them to a man—yes, and lay down their lives for them if necessary. We must purify our own party—we must pin them to their professions;[3] and until we do, we may carry a thousand elections without gaining half a victory. In all the elections we have gained since my recollection, so far as principle is concerned it would have been a blessing to have lost them. Like all the revolutions on the earth, they have been for the elevation of one class, and the pulling down of another. But both of those classes are our oppressors, each in their turn as they acquire the power. We are the instruments by which these great revolutions have been always effected, and yet we have been invariably excluded from the benefits of each change. Look at the thousand bloody fields which have been fought in the old world—where men have carried desolation and death to each other's doors and families, for the *worthy and noble* purpose of deciding which should wear their crown and be their tyrant, Dick or Tom. If the working classes would only use one tenth of the exertion, and make one tenth of the sacrifice to get rid of masters entirely, that they do in trying to have their own choice of that burdensome article, both slaves and tyrants would soon be compelled to mingle—and a middle and happier class would be formed, by blending the two extremes. [Great cheers and cries of "True."] And what have we gained by the numberless political triumphs which we have achieved? Nothing but a change of masters! We have had to bear all the evils of legislation—and its benefits have never yet reached us. We have been humbugged from year to year—from election to election, by a set of selfish demagogues who possess no feeling in common with us, and who laugh in their sleeves at our credulity in believing them sincere, when they preach for pay, doctrines which they

---

[1] *gigs* Type of carriage.

[2] *hoary-headed* Gray-haired.

[3] *professions* I.e., things that the party has publicly proclaimed ("professed") itself to stand for.

secretly hate at heart and openly oppose in practice. Destroy every sinecure[1]—abolish party patronage, do away with every useless office and reduce the pay of all to something near what the incumbents' talents and services would command in a private sphere—cease to give out the public work by contract and you'll reduce the number of brawling patriots nine tenths. [Cheers and cries of "True!" ...]

"The great and fruitful source of crime and misery on earth is the *inequality of society*—the abject dependence of honest, willing industry upon idle and dishonest capitalists. The more that wealth is concentrated in the hands of the few, the more miserable must be the many. You may do as they did in England—first make laws to reduce the poor to starvation, and then pass laws to hang them for stealing a loaf of bread to lull to sleep the starvation which by this means is brought upon them; but will this stop crime—will it benefit mankind in the mass? No! Look at the blood-stained records of law-made and law-murdered poverty in England, and you will see that the laws became more severe as poverty increased, and that crime kept pace with the severity of the laws. There is no tyranny on earth so oppressive as the tyranny of wealth—and no slavery so great as the slavery of poverty! So long as one portion of mankind are wallowing in wealth, idleness and luxury, the rest will never be satisfied with toil, want and degradation! ..."

Nothing could surpass the enthusiastic burst of applause which followed this speech; all opposition was neutralized for the time, and on taking the question on the names presented by the nominating committee, the name of a pettifogger[2] named Field, who was never heard of before was immediately stricken off, and that of Mike's substituted in its stead, after which, nine tremendous cheers were given for Mike Walsh the champion of the young democracy. Notwithstanding this, and the decisions of the Hon. Churchill C. Cambreleng, who was chairman, that Mr. Walsh was regularly nominated, ... a number of ...

low politicians, old clo' dealers[3] and dangerous lodging house keepers, thieves and defaulters, got together, and by the most villainous means succeeded in defeating him. In consequence of their bribing the regular reporters, no verbatim report of it appeared at the time. Every independent paper in the city spoke of it, as did Cambreleng, Vanderpoel and others at the meeting, as one of the greatest efforts ever made.

This abridged report, as now published, was purchased from O.J. Pinckney, who was paid for suppressing it.

—1841

from Henry Highland Garnet, "Address to the Slaves of the United States of America"

Henry Highland Garnet (1815–82) was born into slavery in Maryland and escaped along with ten other members of his family in 1824. Educated at the distinguished African Free School in New York City and later at other schools in New Hampshire and New York, Garnet became a schoolteacher and then, in 1842, a Presbyterian minister, developing a reputation as a powerful orator. He also became involved in the abolition movement and quickly came to believe that more direct and forceful measures would be required to end slavery—a stance that brought him into opposition with such leaders of the movement as Frederick Douglass and William Lloyd Garrison, who were committed to peaceful moral persuasion. These differences came to a head in 1843, when Garnet presented the address below to the National Convention of Colored Citizens in Buffalo, New York. The address sparked intense debate (as is described in the convention minutes, included in the website portion of this Contexts section); the convention delegates eventually voted against endorsing the address by a margin of a single vote. Garnet later supported African American emigration out of the United States, although he withdrew from this position when the Civil War broke out. In February 1865, Garnet became the first African American to speak on the floor of the

---

[1]   *sinecure* Position that requires little or no actual work, often granted as a political spoil by a successful electoral candidate to someone who helped elect them.

[2]   *pettifogger* Unskilled or unscrupulous person of no account.

[3]   *old clo' dealers* I.e., dealers in second-hand clothes; disreputable or undistinguished people.

U.S. Capitol when he preached a sermon to the House of Representatives in commemoration of the passage of the Thirteenth Amendment abolishing slavery. He was serving as U.S. ambassador to Liberia when he died in 1882.

AN ADDRESS

TO THE SLAVES OF THE UNITED STATES OF AMERICA

(REJECTED BY THE NATIONAL CONVENTION, 1843.)

BY HENRY HIGHLAND GARNET.

PREFACE.

The following Address was first read at the National Convention held at Buffalo, N.Y., in 1843. Since that time it has been slightly modified, retaining, however, all of its original doctrine. The document elicited more discussion than any other paper that was ever brought before that, or any other deliberative body of colored persons, and their friends. Gentlemen who opposed the Address, based their objections on these grounds. 1. That the document was war-like, and encouraged insurrection; and 2. That if the Convention should adopt it, that those delegates who lived near the borders of the slave states, would not dare to return to their homes. The Address was rejected by a small majority; and now in compliance with the earnest request of many who heard it, and in conformity to the wishes of numerous friends who are anxious to see it, the author now gives it to the public, praying God that this little book may be borne on the four winds of heaven, until the principles it contains shall be understood and adopted by every slave in the Union.

H.H.G.

Troy, N.Y., April 15, 1848.

An Address to the Slaves of the United States of America, Buffalo, N.Y., 1843

Brethren and Fellow-Citizens: Your brethren of the North, East, and West have been accustomed to meet together in National Conventions, to sympathize with each other, and to weep over your unhappy condition. In these meetings we have addressed all classes of the free, but we have never, until this time, sent a word of consolation and advice to you. We have been contented in sitting still and mourning over your sorrows, earnestly hoping that before this day your sacred liberties would have been restored. But, we have hoped in vain. Years have rolled on, and tens of thousands have been borne on streams of blood and tears, to the shores of eternity. While you have been oppressed, we have also been partakers with you; nor can we be free while you are enslaved. We, therefore, write to you as being bound with you.

Many of you are bound to us, not only by the ties of a common humanity, but we are connected by the more tender relations of parents, wives, husbands, children, brothers, and sisters, and friends. As such we most affectionately address you.

Slavery has fixed a deep gulf between you and us, and while it shuts out from you the relief and consolation which your friends would willingly render, it afflicts and persecutes you with a fierceness which we might not expect to see in the fiends of hell. But still the Almighty Father of mercies has left to us a glimmering ray of hope, which shines out like a lone star in a cloudy sky. Mankind are becoming wiser, and better— the oppressor's power is fading, and you, every day, are becoming better informed, and more numerous. Your grievances, brethren, are many. We shall not attempt, in this short address, to present to the world all the dark catalogue of this nation's sins, which have been committed upon an innocent people. Nor is it indeed necessary, for you feel them from day to day, and all the civilized world look upon them with amazement.

Two hundred and twenty-seven years ago, the first of our injured race were brought to the shores of America.[1] They came not with glad spirits to select their homes in the New World. They came not with their own consent, to find an unmolested enjoyment of the blessings of this fruitful soil. The first dealings they had with men calling themselves Christians, exhibited to them the worst features of corrupt and sordid hearts: and convinced them that no cruelty is too great, no villainy and no robbery too abhorrent for even enlightened men to perform, when influenced by

---

[1]   *Two hundred ... America*   The first enslaved Africans known to have been brought to the English colonies in North America arrived at Jamestown, Virginia, in 1619.

avarice and lust. Neither did they come flying upon the wings of Liberty, to a land of freedom. But they came with broken hearts, from their beloved native land, and were doomed to unrequited toil and deep degradation. Nor did the evil of their bondage end at their emancipation by death. Succeeding generations inherited their chains, and millions have come from eternity into time, and have returned again to the world of spirits, cursed and ruined by American slavery.

The propagators of the system, or their immediate ancestors, very soon discovered its growing evil, and its tremendous wickedness, and secret promises were made to destroy it. The gross inconsistency of a people holding slaves, who had themselves "ferried o'er the wave"[1] for freedom's sake, was too apparent to be entirely overlooked. The voice of Freedom cried, "Emancipate your slaves." Humanity supplicated with tears for the deliverance of the children of Africa. Wisdom urged her solemn plea. The bleeding captive pleaded his innocence, and pointed to Christianity who stood weeping at the cross. Jehovah frowned upon the nefarious institution, and thunderbolts, red with vengeance, struggled to leap forth to blast the guilty wretches who maintained it. But all was vain. Slavery had stretched its dark wings of death over the land, the Church stood silently by—the priests prophesied falsely, and the people loved to have it so. Its throne is established, and now it reigns triumphant. …

The colonists threw the blame upon England. They said that the mother country entailed[2] the evil upon them, and that they would rid themselves of it if they could. The world thought they were sincere, and the philanthropic pitied them. But time soon tested their sincerity. In a few years the colonists grew strong, and severed themselves from the British Government. Their independence was declared, and they took their station among the sovereign powers of the earth. The declaration was a glorious document. Sages admired it, and the patriotic of every nation reverenced the God-like sentiments which it contained. When the power of Government returned to their hands, did they emancipate the slaves? No; they rather added new links to our chains. Were they ignorant of the principles of Liberty? Certainly they were not. The sentiments of their revolutionary orators fell in burning eloquence upon their hearts, and with one voice they cried, *Liberty or Death*. Oh what a sentence was that! It ran from soul to soul like electric fire, and nerved the arm of thousands to fight in the holy cause of Freedom. Among the diversity of opinions that are entertained in regard to physical resistance, there are but a few found to gainsay that stern declaration. We are among those who do not.

Slavery! How much misery is comprehended in that single word. What mind is there that does not shrink from its direful effects? Unless the image of God be obliterated from the soul, all men cherish the love of Liberty. The nice[3] discerning political economist does not regard the sacred right more than the untutored African who roams in the wilds of Congo. Nor has the one more right to the full enjoyment of his freedom than the other. In every man's mind the good seeds of liberty are planted, and he who brings his fellow down so low, as to make him contented with a condition of slavery, commits the highest crime against God and man. Brethren, your oppressors aim to do this. They endeavor to make you as much like brutes as possible. When they have blinded the eyes of your mind—when they have embittered the sweet waters of life—when they have shut out the light which shines from the word of God—then, and not till then, has American slavery done its perfect work.

To such Degradation it is sinful in the Extreme for you to make voluntary Submission. The divine commandments you are in duty bound to reverence and obey. If you do not obey them, you will surely meet with the displeasure of the Almighty. He requires you to love him supremely, and your neighbor as yourself—to keep the Sabbath day holy—to search the Scriptures—and bring up your children with respect for his laws, and to worship no other God but him. But slavery sets all these at nought, and hurls defiance in the face

---

[1]   *ferried … wave*   See Book II, line 38, of *The Task* (1785), by the English poet William Cowper. The passage from which this line comes directly criticizes the United States for its hypocrisy in maintaining slavery: "We have no slaves at home.—Then why abroad? / And they themselves once ferried o'er the wave / That parts us, are emancipate and loos'd." This portion of Cowper's poem was frequently quoted by antislavery writers.

[2]   *entailed*   Bestowed; passed down as an irrevocable inheritance. (An estate that was legally "entailed" could not be disposed of at will by the person who inherited it, but rather had to remain as an inalienable possession.)

[3]   *nice*   Overly particular; also, overly refined or fastidious.

of Jehovah. The forlorn condition in which you are placed, does not destroy your moral obligation to God. ... The diabolical injustice by which your liberties are cloven down, *neither God; nor angels, or just men, command you to suffer for a single moment. Therefore it is your solemn and imperative duty to use every means, both moral, intellectual and physical that promises success.* If a band of heathen men should attempt to enslave a race of Christians, and to place their children under the influence of some false religion, surely, Heaven would frown upon the men who would not resist such aggression, even to death. If, on the other hand, a band of Christians should attempt to enslave a race of heathen men, and to entail slavery upon them, and to keep them in heathenism in the midst of Christianity, the God of heaven would smile upon every effort which the injured might make to disenthral themselves.

Brethren, it is as wrong for your lordly oppressors to keep you in slavery, as it was for the man-thief to steal our ancestors from the coast of Africa. You should therefore now use the same manner of resistance, as would have been just in our ancestors, when the bloody footprints of the first remorseless soul-thief was placed upon the shores of our fatherland. The humblest peasant is as free in the sight of God as the proudest monarch that ever swayed a sceptre. Liberty is a spirit sent out from God, and like its great Author, is no respecter of persons.

Brethren, the time has come when you must act for yourselves. It is an old and true saying that, "if hereditary bondmen would be free, they must themselves strike the blow."[1] You can plead your own cause, and do the work of emancipation better than any others. ... Look around you, and behold the bosoms of your loving wives heaving with untold agonies! Hear the cries of your poor children! Remember the stripes[2] your fathers bore. Think of the torture and disgrace of your noble mothers. Think of your wretched sisters, loving virtue and purity, as they are driven into concubinage and are exposed to the unbridled lusts of incarnate devils. Think of the undying glory that hangs around the ancient name of Africa—and forget not that you are native-born American citizens, and as such, you are justly entitled to all the rights that are granted to the freest. Think how many tears you have poured out upon the soil which you have cultivated with unrequited toil and enriched with your blood; and then go to your lordly enslavers and tell them plainly, that you *are determined to be free.* Appeal to their sense of justice, and tell them that they have no more right to oppress you, than you have to enslave them. Entreat them to remove the grievous burdens which they have imposed upon you, and to remunerate you for your labor. Promise them renewed diligence in the cultivation of the soil, if they will render to you an equivalent for your services. Point them to the increase of happiness and prosperity in the British West Indies since the Act of Emancipation.[3] Tell them in language which they cannot misunderstand, of the exceeding sinfulness of slavery, and of a future judgment, and of the righteous retributions of an indignant God. Inform them that all you desire is *freedom*, and that nothing else will suffice. Do this, and for ever after cease to toil for the heartless tyrants, who give you no other reward but stripes and abuse. If they then commence the work of death, they, and not you, will be responsible for the consequences. You had far better all die—*die immediately,* than live slaves, and entail your wretchedness upon your posterity. If you would be free in this generation, here is your only hope. However much you and all of us may desire it, there is not much hope of redemption without the shedding of blood. If you must bleed, let it all come at once—rather *die freemen, than live to be the slaves.* It is impossible, like the children of Israel, to make a grand exodus from the land of bondage. The Pharaohs are on both sides of the blood-red waters![4] You cannot move *en masse*, to the dominions of the British Queen—nor can you pass through Florida and overrun Texas,[5] and at last find

---

[1] *if hereditary ... blow* See Canto II, stanza 76, lines 28–29 of *Childe Harold's Pilgrimage* (1812–18), by the English Romantic poet George Gordon, Lord Byron: "Hereditary bondsmen! know ye not / Who would be free themselves must strike the blow?"

[2] *stripes* I.e., wounds caused by being whipped.

[3] *the British ... Emancipation* Slavery in the British colonies in the Caribbean (and throughout the British Empire) was abolished by an 1833 act of Parliament, which took effect in 1834.

[4] *It is impossible ... blood-red waters* Reference to the biblical Book of Exodus, which tells the story of the Israelites' divinely-mandated escape from slavery in Egypt, at the climax of which they cross the Red Sea when God miraculously parts its waters, which then drown their Egyptian pursuers.

[5] *overrun Texas* In 1843, Texas, which had seceded from Mexico in 1836, was still an independent republic and had not yet joined the United States (which it would in 1845).

peace in Mexico. The propagators of American slavery are spending their blood and treasure, that they may plant the black flag in the heart of Mexico and riot in the halls of the Montezumas.[1] …

Fellow-men! Patient sufferers! Behold your dearest rights crushed to the earth! See your sons murdered, and your wives, mothers and sisters doomed to prostitution. In the name of the merciful God, and by all that life is worth, let it no longer be a debatable question, whether it is better to choose *Liberty* or *death*.[2] …

Brethren, arise, arise! Strike for your lives and liberties. Now is the day and the hour. Let every slave throughout the land do this, and the days of slavery are numbered. You cannot be more oppressed than you have been—you cannot suffer greater cruelties than you have already. *Rather die freemen than live to be slaves.* Remember that you are *four millions!*

It is in your power so to torment the God-cursed slaveholders, that they will be glad to let you go free. If the scale was turned, and black men were the masters and white men the slaves, every destructive agent and element would be employed to lay the oppressor low. Danger and death would hang over their heads day and night. Yes, the tyrants would meet with plagues more terrible than those of Pharaoh.[3]

---

[1]   *The propagators … Montezumas*   Northern opponents of slavery frequently considered designs for American territorial expansion at Mexican expense (culminating in the Mexican–American War of 1846–48) to be the work of Southern slaveholders seeking to expand slavery into new territories;   *riot* Indulge themselves wildly and without restraint;   *Montezumas* I.e., rulers of the Aztec Empire, the Indigenous civilization that controlled much of Mexico at the time of its conquest by Spain.

[2]   *Liberty or death*   Title of the proclamation issued in 1804 by Jean-Jacques Dessalines, one of the leaders of the Haitian Revolution (the successful revolt, beginning in 1791, of the enslaved black population of the French colony of Saint-Domingue). The proclamation defended the massacres in 1804 of the former colony's white inhabitants and claimed that Dessalines had "avenged America" by taking action against white slaveholders. Many African American abolitionists supported the aims of the Haitian Revolution and its leaders such as Dessalines, although the violence that occurred in Haiti was more controversial and divisive. In the omitted portion of the speech that follows, Garnet surveys the history of enslaved people's armed resistance to slavery in the United States, from Denmark Veazie's abortive revolt in Charleston, South Carolina, in 1822, through Nat Turner's supressed rebellion in Virginia in 1831, to the successful uprisings on slave ships led by Joseph Cinque in 1839 and Madison Washington in 1841.

[3]   *the tyrants … Pharaoh* Another reference to the Book of Exodus, according to which, before Egypt's Pharaoh finally permits

But you are a patient people. You act as though you were made for the special use of these devils. You act as though your daughters were born to pamper the lusts of your masters and overseers. And worse than all, you tamely submit while your lords tear your wives from your embraces and defile them before your eyes. In the name of God, we ask, are you men? Where is the blood of your fathers? Has it all run out of your veins? Awake, awake; millions of voices are calling you! Your dead fathers speak to you from their graves. Heaven, as with a voice of thunder, calls on you to arise from the dust.

Let your motto be resistance! *resistance*! *resistance*! No oppressed people have ever secured their liberty without resistance. What kind of resistance you had better make, you must decide by the circumstances that surround you, and according to the suggestion of expediency. Brethren, adieu! Trust in the living God. Labor for the peace of the human race, and remember that you are *four millions*.

—1843

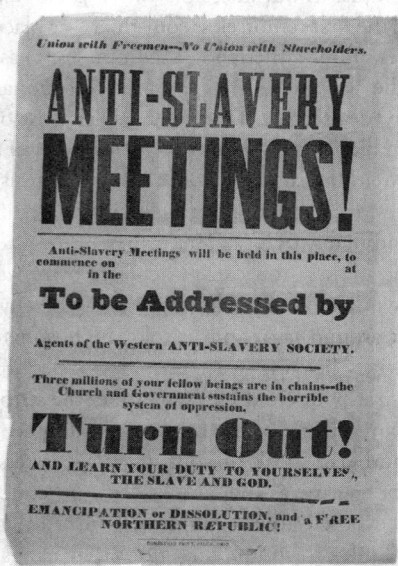

This broadside, printed by an antislavery society in Ohio in 1850, is a blank announcement template that could be filled in with details of specific events featuring abolitionist orators.

---

the enslaved Israelites to depart, his stubbornness causes the infliction of ten devastating plagues on Egypt.

OUTRAGE.

Fellow Citizens,

AN
ABOLITIONIST,

of the most revolting character is among you, exciting the feelings of the North against the South. A seditious Lecture is to be delivered

THIS EVENING,

at 7 o'clock, at the Presbyterian Church in Cannon-street.

You are requested to attend and unite in putting down and silencing by peaceable means this tool of evil and fanaticism.

Let the rights of the States guaranteed by the Constitution be protected.

Feb. 27, 1837.   *The Union forever!*

Handbill circulated by opponents of abolitionism in New York in 1837 to organize the disruption of an abolitionist lecture.

from Elizabeth Cady Stanton, "Address on Woman's Rights"

Elizabeth Cady Stanton (1815–1902) was one of the most prominent figures in the nineteenth-century U.S. women's rights movement. She helped organize the 1848 Seneca Falls Convention, the first public meeting solely dedicated to the issue of women's rights, and she continued to help lead the fight for legal gender equality for over half a century while also working on behalf of other progressive causes, including abolitionism. Stanton gave the speech excerpted below, which she called her "first speech," on at least two occasions in September and October 1848, in the wake of the Seneca Falls Convention in July of that year. On the basis of the publication of a revised text of the speech in 1870 under the title *Address of Mrs. Elizabeth Cady Stanton, Delivered at Seneca Falls and Rochester, N.Y., July 19th and Aug. 2d, 1848*, it has often been presented as Stanton's "keynote address" at the Seneca Falls Convention itself. There is a great deal of historical evidence against this, however, and the original manuscript of the speech discusses Seneca Falls in the past tense. While it was

probably not actually delivered at Seneca Falls, the speech does give eloquent voice to some of the core beliefs, arguments, and demands of the women's movement at the moment of its emergence onto the national stage.

The text presented below is based on the revised version of the speech published in 1870, which is the most commonly reprinted version today; however, important differences between this version and the original manuscript have been identified by footnotes.

I should feel exceedingly diffident to appear before you at this time, having never before spoken in public, were I not nerved by a sense of right and duty, did I not feel the time had fully come for the question of woman's wrongs to be laid before the public, did I not believe that woman herself must do this work; for woman alone can understand the height, the depth, the length, and the breadth of her own degradation. Man cannot speak for her, because he has been educated to believe that she differs from him so materially, that he cannot judge of her thoughts, feelings, and opinions by his own. Moral beings can only judge of others by themselves. The moment they assume a different nature for any of their own kind, they utterly fail. …

Among the many important questions which have been brought before the public, there is none that more vitally affects the whole human family than that which is technically called Woman's Rights. Every allusion to the degraded and inferior position occupied by women all over the world has been met by scorn and abuse. From the man of highest mental cultivation to the most degraded wretch who staggers in the streets do we meet ridicule, and coarse jests, freely bestowed upon those who dare assert that woman stands by the side of man, his equal, placed here by her God, to enjoy with him the beautiful earth, which is her home as it is his, having the same sense of right and wrong, and looking to the same Being for guidance and support. So long has man exercised tyranny over her, injurious to himself and benumbing her faculties, that few can nerve themselves to meet the storm; and so long has the chain been about her that she knows not there is a remedy. …

As the nations of the earth emerge from a state of barbarism, the sphere of woman gradually becomes wider, but not even under what is thought to be the full blaze of the sun of civilization is it what God designed it to be. In every country and clime does man assume the responsibility of marking out the path for her to tread. In every country does he regard her as a being inferior to himself, and one whom he is to guide and control. …

We have met here today to discuss our rights and wrongs, civil and political, and not, as some have supposed, to go into the detail of social life alone. We do not propose to petition the legislature to make our husbands just, generous and courteous, to seat every man at the head of a cradle, and to clothe every woman in male attire. None of these points, however important they may be considered by leading men, will be touched upon[.] … But we are assembled to protest against a form of government, existing without the consent of the governed—to declare our right to be free as man is free, to be represented in the government which we are taxed to support, to have such disgraceful laws as give man the power to chastise and imprison his wife, to take the wages which she earns, the property which she inherits, and, in case of separation, the children of her love; laws which make her the mere dependent on his bounty. It is to protest against such unjust laws as these that we are assembled today, and to have them, if possible, forever erased from our statute-books, deeming them a shame and a disgrace to a Christian republic in the nineteenth century. … And, strange as it may seem to many, we now demand our right to vote according to the declaration of the government under which we live. This right no one pretends to deny. We need not prove ourselves equal to Daniel Webster[1] to enjoy this privilege, for the ignorant Irishman in the ditch has all the civil rights he has. We need not prove our muscular power equal to this same Irishman to enjoy this privilege, for the most tiny, weak, ill-shaped stripling[2] of twenty-one, has all the civil rights of the Irishman. We have no objection to discuss the question of equality, for we feel that the weight of argument lies wholly with us, but we wish the question of equality kept distinct from the question of rights, for the proof of the one does not determine the truth of the other. All white men[3] in this country have the same rights, however they may differ in mind, body or estate. The right is ours. The question now is, how shall we get possession of what rightfully belongs to us. We should not feel so sorely grieved if no man who had not attained the full stature of a Webster, Clay, Van Buren, or Gerrit Smith[4] could claim the right of the elective franchise. But to have drunkards, idiots, horse-racing, rum-selling rowdies, ignorant foreigners and silly boys fully recognized, while we ourselves are thrust out from all the rights that belong to citizens, it is too grossly insulting to the dignity of woman to be longer quietly submitted to. The right is ours. Have it, we must. Use it, we will. The pens, the tongues, the fortunes, the indomitable wills of many women are already pledged to secure this right. The great truth, that no just government can be formed without the consent of the governed, we shall

---

[1] *Daniel Webster* Prominent lawyer and politician renowned for his oratory (1782–1852).

[2] *stripling* Youth.

[3] *All white men* The manuscript version of this speech here reads, "All men."

[4] *Clay* Henry Clay (1777–1852), influential American politician; *Van Buren* Martin Van Buren, politician who served as president from 1837 to 1841; *Gerrit Smith* Reformist politician (1797–1874) who supported various progressive causes, including the temperance movement and abolitionism.

echo and re-echo in the ears of the unjust judge, until by continual coming we shall weary him. ...

But what would woman gain by voting? Men must know the advantages of voting, for they all seem very tenacious about the right. Think you, if woman had a voice in this government, that all those laws affecting her interests would so entirely violate every principle of right and justice? Had woman a vote to give, might not the office holders and seekers propose some change in her condition? Might not Woman's Rights become as great a question as free soil?[1]

"But are you not already represented by your fathers, husbands, brothers and sons?" Let your statute books answer the question. We have had enough of such representation. In nothing is woman's true happiness consulted. Men like to call her an angel—to feed her on what they think sweet food—nourishing her vanity; to make her believe that her organization is so much finer than theirs, that she is not fitted to struggle with the tempests of public life, but needs their care and protection!! Care and protection—such as the wolf gives the lamb—such as the eagle the hare he carries to his eyrie!! Most cunningly he entraps her, and then takes from her all those rights which are dearer to him than life itself—rights which have been baptized in blood—and the maintenance of which is even now rocking to their foundations the kingdoms of the Old World.[2]

The most discouraging, the most lamentable aspect our cause wears is the indifference, indeed, the contempt with which women themselves regard the movement. Where the subject is introduced, among those even who claim to be intelligent and educated, it is met by the scornful curl of the lip, and by expression of ridicule and disgust. But we shall hope better things of them when they are enlightened in regard to their present position. When women know the laws and constitutions under which they live, they will not publish[3] their degradation, by declaring themselves satisfied, nor their ignorance, by declaring they have all the rights they want. ...

Let woman live as she should. Let her feel her accountability to her Maker. Let her know that her spirit is fitted for as high a sphere as man's, and that her soul requires food as pure and exalted as his. Let her live first for God, and she will not make imperfect man an object of reverence and awe. Teach her her responsibility as a being of conscience and reason, that all earthly support is weak and unstable, that her only safe dependence is the arm of omnipotence,[4] and that true happiness springs from duty accomplished. Thus will she learn the lesson of individual responsibility for time and eternity: that neither father, husband, brother or son, however willing they may be, can discharge her high duties of life, or stand in her stead when called into the presence of the great Searcher of Hearts at the last day. ...

... There seems now to be a kind of moral stagnation in our midst. Philanthropists have done their utmost to rouse the nation to a sense of its sins. War, slavery, drunkenness, licentiousness, gluttony, have been dragged naked before the people, and all their abominations and deformities fully brought to light, yet with idiotic laugh we hug those monsters to our breasts and rush on to destruction. Our churches are multiplying on all sides, our missionary societies, Sunday schools, and prayer meetings and innumerable charitable and reform organizations are all in operation, but still the tide of vice is swelling, and threatens the destruction of everything, and the battlements of righteousness are weak against the raging elements of sin and death. Verily, the world waits the coming of some new element, some purifying power, some spirit of mercy and love. The voice of woman has been

---

[1] *free soil* I.e., the attempt, led by the antislavery factions of the two main political parties at the time, the Whigs and Democrats, to prevent the expansion of slavery into the country's western territories—in particular, those won from Mexico in the Mexican–American War of 1846–48. In the late 1840s and 1850s, the debate over whether slavery would be permitted in these territories came to dominate national politics, contributing significantly to the outbreak of the Civil War.

[2] *the maintenance ... Old World* In 1848, a wave of revolutions swept across much of Europe. The revolutionaries, who sprang mainly from the middle and working classes, had various (sometimes conflicting) aims, but in general they sought to replace authoritarian monarchies with more democratic forms of government and to create independent nation-states in places, such as Germany and Italy, where they did not yet exist. The revolutions were largely suppressed or their gains reversed, but they exposed the fundamental instability of many European regimes.

[3] *publish* Reveal publicly; display.

[4] *Teach her ... omnipotence* The manuscript adds here, "Teach her there is no sex in mind," i.e., that men and women have the same mental attributes and capacities.

silenced in the state, the church, and the home, but man cannot fulfill his destiny alone, he cannot redeem his race unaided. There are deep and tender chords of sympathy and love in the hearts of the downfallen and oppressed that woman can touch more skillfully than man. The world has never yet seen a truly great and virtuous nation, because in the degradation of woman the very fountains of life are poisoned at their source. It is vain to look for silver and gold from mines of copper and lead. It is the wise mother that has the wise son. So long as your women are slaves you may throw your colleges and churches to the winds. You can't have scholars and saints so long as your mothers are ground to powder between the upper and nether millstone of tyranny and lust. … We do not expect our path will be strewn with the flowers of popular applause, but over the thorns of bigotry and prejudice will be our way, and on our banners will beat the dark storm-clouds of opposition from those who have entrenched themselves behind the stormy bulwarks of custom and authority, and who have fortified their position by every means, holy and unholy. But we will steadfastly abide the result. Unmoved we will bear it aloft. Undauntedly we will unfurl it to the gale, for we know that the storm cannot rend from it a shred, that the electric flash will but more clearly show to us the glorious words inscribed upon it, "Equality of Rights."
—1848

Yᴱ MAY SESSION OF Yᴱ WOMAN'S RIGHTS CONVENTION—Yᴱ ORATOR OF Yᴱ DAY DENOUNCING Yᴱ LORDS OF CREATION.

HARPER'S WEEKLY   [JUNE 11, 1859.

This cartoon, published in *Harper's Weekly* in 1859, satirizes women's-rights conventions—specifically, the venue they provided for female oratory.

Bayley Wyat, "Speech by a Virginia Freedman"

In the immediate aftermath of the Civil War, many newly emancipated African Americans expected to be able to make an independent living on lands that had formerly belonged to their enslavers—and judged that they had a right to do so. These expectations were abetted by the Freedmen's Bureau, a U.S. government agency established to provide essential services for the "freedmen" (formerly enslaved people), including food, medical care, employment, locating and communicating with family members, and education. The bill establishing the bureau authorized it to lease forty-acre tracts of land abandoned by plantation owners to formerly-enslaved people, a provision that gave rise to the expression that epitomized the "freedmen's" aspirations: "forty acres and a mule." However, the Freedmen's Bureau lacked the power to confiscate land owned by Confederate supporters, while the exceptionally lenient policies adopted toward ex-Confederates by President Andrew Johnson enabled them to reclaim much of the abandoned or confiscated plantation land on which the formerly enslaved had hoped to make a start for themselves.

The speech presented below was given by a formerly-enslaved man named Bayley Wyat at a meeting held in southern Virginia to discuss these issues in December 1866. The speech was recorded by a white official, Jacob Vining, and published by a Northern Quaker organization, the Friends' Association of Philadelphia, to raise funds "for the relief of colored freedmen." Vining transcribed Wyat's speech in an "eye-dialect" (a form of written English using deliberately non-standard spelling and grammar) crafted to represent on the page what both Vining and the white Northern audience for whose consumption the speech was published would have assumed was a typical African American manner of speaking. Such conventionalized, even stereotypical white American renderings of African American speech were extremely common throughout the nineteenth century (and beyond); as is often the case with such renderings, Vining's representation of Wyat's speech reveals as much, if not more, about Vining—especially his assumptions about Wyat and his assessment of Wyat's oratory—as it does about Wyat himself.

A FREEDMAN'S SPEECH.

In a letter from Yorktown, Va., dated 12th month 15, 1866, Jacob H. Vining, Superintendent of Friends'[1] Freedmen's Schools, writes:

"I enclose for publication the substance of a speech made by Bayley Wyat, a colored man, living near here. It was delivered at a Mass Meeting of colored freedmen held in our large school-house. The meeting was called at the close of one held the preceding evening by the Freedmen's Bureau, on the subject of removing the camps. The former meeting was addressed by Gen. Armstrong, Lieut. Massey[2] and myself, advising them to seek homes in the adjoining counties and elsewhere; the latter meeting was held to consider of and reply to our advice. I was present by special invitation, heard their deliberations, and felt that their arguments were unanswerable. I think I never heard more touching eloquence than that which characterized this simple speech. I was chained to the spot as I listened, and could not refrain from mingling tears with the crowd, who were often melted into tears by the pathetic[3] allusions of the speaker to their past and present experiences. I saw in this speech so much naked, simple truth, and natural pathos and oratory, that I sent to the speaker, and got him to come to my place and repeat to me the substance of his speech, while I wrote it down. It comes far short of doing justice to him, but there are facts and forces in it which should command the respect and sympathy of all, and especially of legislators."

BAYLEY WYAT'S SPEECH

Taking notice of the address the gemmen[4] gave us last night concerning leavin' the camps in which we are

---

[1] *Friends'*   The formal name of the Quakers, a Christian denomination noted for its pacifism and resistance to slavery, is "the Society of Friends."

[2] *Gen. Armstrong, Lieut. Massey*   Army officers who were officials in the Freedmen's Bureau.

[3] *pathetic*   I.e., eliciting pathos; moving.

[4] *gemmen*   Gentlemen.

now settled, and thrown back to the adjinin' counties where we came from, it seems that it had been told the gemmen that if we would go back to the counties we came from, we should be taken care of as well as in the place where we are now located. But we have full satisfaction, if we turns back to them counties or the lands we came from, under the present situation of the rebels and the unsettled situation of the United States, we shall be forebber made hewers of wood and drawers of water.[1]

But when we looks back and sees our former state, when education was kept from us; and though we was made like men by God as other men, we was kept in bondage—we made bricks without straw under old Pharo;[2] and you all 'members de home house and de wife house,[3] how de wife house was often eight or ten miles from de home house, and we would go there Saturday night expectin' to see de wife we had left and she would be gone!—sent down South, nebber to come back, and de little cabin shut up and desolate; den we would fold our arms and cry, "O Lord, how long!" and dat was all we could say. And we was not able to own even our names, as men among other men. For this cause we now looks on our present situation, and we believes it is by the overrulin' providence of God, and not of men, that we enjoys freedom—that we are placed in this most pleasant situation.

And we first thanks God for this great blessin' we now has; second, we thanks our friends from de North for the great sacrifice which dey have made for our benefition;[4] and we feels so well satisfied that we has God on our side—that we has some friends that through God's assistance will intercede for us and assist us, yet wishes to be all the aid we can be to the United States as men.

And as to our dear friends, de Quakers to de North, we does consider dem our best earthly friends, for de great sacrifice dey has made and is making for us; we does tank dem most kindly; and as to de great North, for de sacrifices of treasures, of lives, and of blood, we now consider dem our affectionate friends, and we heartily tank dem.

We now, as a people, desires to be elevated, and we desires to do all we can to be educated, and we hope our friends will aid us all dey can.

As to our going back to the counties we came from and to the rebels again, we knows for the truth, by thousands of witnesses, the sight of the darkies who left the rebels in the time of war is now as a dose of pizen[5] in their eyes, because we left the rebels and went to the Yankees.

We now feels unprotected against de rebels, and we feels unprotected wid dem; and though de rebels have and do scoff us for calling de North our friends we hope we shall nebber lose our confidence in dem—I mean our friends in the North.

Oh, most respectable Friends ob de North, please consider our interests; we feels sometimes as if our welfare in dis life depends on you.

Mr Vining, the Superintender of Schools, held a mass meeting on Friday night, and he departed[6] to us some very good, perm'ent instructions, such as we believes are based on the very foundations of Truth; and immegiately we agrees with him to take his counsel, believing it is for our benefit, and we has every reason to believe he is a friend of ours.

I may state to all our friends, and to all our enemies, that we has a right to the land where we are located. For why? I tell you. Our wives, our children, our husbands, has been sold over and over again to purchase the lands we now locates upon; for that reason we have a divine right to the land.

Den again, the United States, by deir officers, told us if we would leave the Rebs and come to de Yankees and help de Government, we should have de land where dey put us as long as we live; and dey told us dat we

---

[1] *hewers … water* See Joshua 9.23: "Now therefore ye are cursed, and there shall none of you be freed from being bondmen, and hewers of wood and drawers of water for the house of my God."

[2] *we made … Pharo* In the Book of Exodus, after Moses first begins demanding the release of the Israelites enslaved in Egypt, the Egyptian Pharaoh responds by depriving the enslaved Israelites of the straw necessary for the bricks they are required to make, thereby making their labor much more difficult and time-consuming. See Exodus 5.1–19.

[3] *de home … house* Because marriages between enslaved people had no legal status, enslaved men were often forced to live separately from their wives and children.

[4] *benefition* I.e., benefit.

[5] *pizen* Poison.

[6] *departed* I.e., imparted; communicated.

should be see'd after and cared for by de Government, and placed in a position to become men among men.

And de Government furder promised to protect us from de rebels as long as we lived, and we sacrificed all we had, and left de rebels and came to the Yankees.

Some of us had some money to buy our freedom, and some of us had a house, and some of us had cattle with which we hoped sometimes to buy ourselves; but we left all depending on de promises of de Yankees.

Dey told us dese lands was 'fiscated from the Rebs, who was fightin' de United States to keep us in slavery and to destroy the Government. De Yankee officers say to us: "Now, dear friends, colored men, come and go with us; we will gain de victory, and by de proclamation of our President you have your freedom, and you shall have the 'fiscated lands."

And now we feels disappointed dat dey has not kept deir promise. O educated men! men of principle, men of honor, as we once considered you was! Now we don't seem to know what to consider, for de great confidence we had seems to be shaken, for now we has orders to leave dese lands by the Superintender of the Bureau.

We was first ordered to pay rent, and we paid de rent; now we has orders to leave, or have our log cabins torn down over our heads. Dey say "de lands has been 'stored to de old owners, and dey must have it."

And now where shall we go? Shall we go into the streets, or into de woods, or into de ribber? We has nowhere to go! and we now wants to know what we can do?

I is not here to ask de Government to help me nor my family. I has never asked any help from de Government nor from friends, and I never has received any. I has got a living by honest, hard work since I came to the Yankees, and I has saved something besides. *I* owes no man any thing, but my people cannot all do this. Dey has been bought and sold like horses; dey has been kept in ignorance; dey has been sold for lands, for horses, for carriages, and for every thing their old masters had. I want some gemmen to tell me of one ting that our people hasn't been sold to buy for deir owners.

And den didn't we clear the land, and raise de crops of corn, ob cotton, ob tobacco, ob rice, ob sugar, ob ebery ting. And den didn't dem large cities in de North grow up on de cotton and de sugars and de rice dat we

made? Yes! I appeal to de South and to de North if I hasn't spoken de words of truth?

I say dey has grown rich, and my people is poor. We lives in slab cabins, on ground for floor, and many of us has not food, and we goes ragged and most naked.

God heard our groans. He saw our afflictions, and he came down and delivered us; but anudder king is now risen—Andy Johnson![1] I will not call him king or President; he is not our friend; he has forgotten the afflictions of Joseph,[2] if he ever knowed them, and we are now turned back to the old taskmasters. Our cabins are threatened to be turned down over our heads if we do not go, and we must be drove about from place to place, and chased as hounds chase rabbits. And we must go; and I ask again, where shall we go, and who shall we trust?

I tell you who we is to trust. We is to trust God, and he will bring us all out ob de wilderness,[3] somehow, and sometime, and somewhere. I cannot tell how nor when He'll do it, but I'm bound to believe He will do it. Gemmen, we must not depend on the warlike nations around us to help us; dey have all deceived us; dey has combined against us to keep us out of de promised land.

Now, we must be united; we must take care of ourselves, and protect ourselves, and must support ourselves. We must form societies to help each other who cannot help demselves, and we must show to the nations dat we can support ourselves, and dat we can

---

[1]   *Andy Johnson*   Andrew Johnson, U.S. president from 1865 to 1869. A Tennessee politician and enslaver, Johnson supported the Union when his state seceded. In a bid to obtain the support of the Southern Unionists Johnson represented, President Lincoln made Johnson his running mate in the 1864 presidential election; as vice-president, Johnson then assumed the presidency after Lincoln's assassination. During his presidency, Johnson opposed federal attempts to protect and promote the rights of formerly enslaved people and supported the reestablishment of white supremacist governments in the Southern states on the grounds of "states' rights."

[2]   *the afflictions of Joseph*   Chapters 37–50 of the Book of Genesis relate how Joseph, one of the twelve sons of the Israelite patriarch Jacob, is sold by his jealous brothers into slavery in Egypt, where he endures injustice and hardship before eventually rising to become a high government official.

[3]   *wilderness*   According to the Bible, the Israelites wandered for forty years in the wilderness after their escape from slavery in Egypt before finally entering into the "promised land" under the leadership of Joshua.

protect ourselves wid the help of God; and dat He will do. He has done it, and I know He will help us one time more, if we looks to Him.

I know de times looks hard and berry dark to some of us, who is hungry and cold. Like all de chillen of Israel, our soul is dried away, and we 'members de flesh-pots and de leeks and de onions of Egypt, and we is ready to say, "Oh, dat our graves had been dere!" for we tinks dat our Moses has left us and we has lost our confidence in him.[1] But I stands here tonight to tell you dat God has not forgotten us, and He is just, and He will bring us along bimeby.[2]

We deserves hard times, we deserves hunger and cold, and we deserves enemies, because we is not all honest, and we doesn't do de best we can. We doesn't help ourselves; and I tell you dat God won't help those dat won't help themselves. You know when Joshua went to fight Ai, he was beat, and his men got killed, and was driven back, and poor Joshua didn't know what was de matter; but God did know dat something was wrong with Joshua's men. Some of dem did steal a coat, and some did steal money, and God knowed it, and he telled Joshua, and den Joshua find it so; and he punish and kill de tief and de liar, and den his enemies could not stand against him.[3] Now we has liars, and we has thieves, and knows it; and we all suffer as a people, as dere is sin wid us. God ain't gwine to help de wicked and bless dem. No sir! God ain't gwine to do any sich thing. He is gwine to 'flict us some way, long as we is wicked; long as we don't speak de truth; long as we steal; long as we doesn't believe Him; long as we is lazy; long as we don't help ourselves, He won't help us.
—1866

---

[1] *Like all ... in him*   See Exodus 16.2–3, which describes how, after escaping from Egypt, "the children of Israel murmured against Moses ... in the wilderness": "Would to God we had died by the hand of the Lord in the land of Egypt, when we sat by the flesh pots, and when we did eat bread to the full; for ye have brought us forth into this wilderness, to kill this whole assembly with hunger." "Flesh pots" in this context are cooking pots for meat.

[2] *bimeby*   By and by.

[3] *You know ... against him*   For the full account of this episode from the Israelites' conquest of Canaan (their "promised land") at the end of their Exodus from Egypt, see Joshua 7–8.

MARGARET FULLER

1810 – 1850

At the peak of her career in the 1840s, writer, journalist, and literary critic Margaret Fuller was among the most influential nonfiction writers in America. She was an important friend of the Transcendentalist school that sprouted in Massachusetts in late 1830s, but her career also took her beyond the scope of that movement, and into the arena of social and political reform. Praised by her friend and fellow Transcendentalist Ralph Waldo Emerson as "the greatest woman, I believe, of ancient or modern times," Fuller was remarkable not least of all for achieving literary prominence and independent financial success at a time when many considered the quietude of the domestic sphere to be the only appropriate place for women. But the range of Fuller's writing, the scope of her ambition, and her profound enthusiasm for the life of the mind were also recognized as being extraordinary for any human being, male or female. The admiration expressed by Scottish writer Thomas Carlyle was widely shared: "Such a predetermination to eat this big universe as her oyster or her egg, and to be absolute empress of all height and glory in it that her heart could conceive, I have not before seen in any human soul."

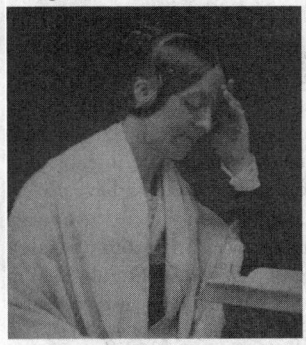

Born in Cambridgeport, Massachusetts in May 1810, Sarah Margaret Fuller was the eldest child of Timothy and Margarett Crane Fuller. Timothy seems to have had few, if any, qualms about providing his daughter with an education most of his peers would have seen as "unfeminine" at best, and thus set about educating Margaret in the rigorous manner commonly imposed upon boys of the era. By four she was reading *Aesop's Fables*; by seven she was reading the classics of Greek and Latin philosophy and literature; and by her teens she rose daily before five in the morning to begin a twelve-hour study schedule. Similarly intensive instruction was not uncommon for boys of her era, who often entered college around the age of fifteen, and Fuller had a natural zeal to learn and to improve her mind that was well nurtured by these high expectations. But if her education provided her with the grounds for her future success, some would say it also underlaid a great deal of her future personal anguish. Throughout her childhood, Fuller suffered from hallucinations, nightmares, and episodes of somnambulism, and she continued to exhibit "nervous" tendencies and frequent headaches in adulthood.

Beginning in 1819, Fuller was enrolled in a series of private schools, beginning with the Cambridgeport Private Grammar School and including two "finishing schools" for young ladies. She returned to live with her family in 1826, where she continued to study from her father's library. When not reading, Fuller began in earnest to write; fascinated by German Romanticism, she completed her first translation of Goethe in 1833, and in 1834 published a first essay, "In Defense of Brutus," in the *Boston Daily Advertiser*.

Fuller's father died the following year; the sudden need to contribute financially to the family brought a temporary end to her scholarly ambitions, and she spent a little over a year working as a school-teacher. Fuller was beloved by many of her students, but the work did not fully engage her; after resigning from her post, she found a more fulfilling outlet for her teaching abilities in the "Conversations" she began holding in Boston—a series of intellectual seminars for women, held between 1839 and 1844, and addressing various topics including literature, ethics, pedagogy, and the place of women in society. The Conversations brought Fuller her first dose of fame, and at their peak became so popular that she was impelled to allow men to join her audience. The same year she began holding the Conversations, Fuller published the first English translation of *Conversations with Goethe* by Johann Peter Eckermann, to a good deal of acclaim.

In 1840, the Transcendental Movement coalesced to form *The Dial* (1840–44), the periodical that had been long envisioned by Ralph Waldo Emerson and his companions. Fuller was chosen as the magazine's first editor, and she published one of her most significant works in its pages; "The Great Lawsuit. Man *versus* Men. Woman *versus* Women" appeared in the July 1843 issue. In this long essay Fuller not only demands equal treatment of the sexes, but also explores the very concept of gender, suggesting that there may be masculine women and feminine men. The piece caught the eye of *New-York Tribune* editor Horace Greeley, who contacted Fuller and encouraged her to expand the work into book form: the result was *Woman in the Nineteenth Century* (1845). Though not without its detractors, the work was praised by many, and has since come to be regarded as a classic of American writing on gender and women's rights.

Greeley hired Fuller on as a critic for the *Tribune* in 1844. Over the span of less than two years she wrote well over two hundred articles for the paper, which was among the most widely-read papers in the nation. She developed a deeper interest in dominant social issues of the age, among them the incarceration of women, the treatment of mental patients, prostitution, and abolition. Her position with the *Tribune* also took Fuller abroad for the first time in her life. In 1846 she sailed for Britain and France, and she traveled to Italy the following year. When revolutions began to sweep the Italian states in 1848, Fuller reported on these events for the *Tribune*, while also participating in running a military hospital in Rome. Here Fuller met and fell in love with revolutionary Giovanni Angelo Ossoli, with whom she had a son. The family set sail for America in 1850; their ship was wrecked just off the New York coast, killing all on board, and Fuller's body was never found.

Fuller's death was a blow to her intellectual community at home, as was the loss of her rumored final work, a history of the Italian Revolution. The work left behind, however, was more than enough to secure her place in the canon of nineteenth-century American writers. In the first volume of their *History of Woman Suffrage* (1881), Elizabeth Cady Stanton and her co-authors concluded that Fuller had done more to influence "the thought of American women than any woman previous to her time." To be sure, there was a period in the late nineteenth and early twentieth centuries when Fuller's star was in decline. Literary historian Barrett Wendell, for example, wrote in 1925 of the Transcendentalists that "few have proved immortal. Bronson Alcott and Theodore Parker seem fading with Margaret Fuller into mere memories." By the second half of the twentieth century, however, Fuller's importance was again becoming widely acknowledged. When the first edition of *The Norton Anthology of American Literature* was published in 1979, she was one of only three women writers from the 1820–65 period to be included. In the twenty-first century, the publication of the concluding volume of Charles Capper's acclaimed *Margaret Fuller: An American Romantic Life* helped to confirm her reputation as (in scholar Mary Kelley's words) "one of America's most expansive intellectuals."

NOTE ON THE TEXT: The text of "The Great Lawsuit: Man *versus* Men. Woman *versus* Women" presented below is based on that published in volume 4 of *The Dial* in July 1843. Spelling and punctuation have been modernized in accordance with the practices of this anthology.

⌘ ⌘ ⌘

The Great Lawsuit: Man versus *Men.*
Woman versus *Women.*

This great suit has now been carried on through many ages, with various results. The decisions have been numerous, but always followed by appeals to still higher courts. How can it be otherwise, when the law itself is the subject of frequent elucidation, constant revision? Man has, now and then, enjoyed a clear, triumphant hour, when some irresistible conviction warmed and purified the atmosphere of his planet. But, presently, he sought repose after his labors, when the crowd of pygmy adversaries bound him in his sleep. Long years of inglorious imprisonment followed, while his enemies revelled in his spoils, and no counsel could be found to plead his cause, in the absence of that all-promising glance, which had, at times, kindled the poetic soul to revelation of his claims, of his rights.

Yet a foundation for the largest claim is now established. It is known that his inheritance consists in no partial sway, no exclusive possession, such as his adversaries desire. For they, not content that the universe is rich, would, each one for himself, appropriate treasure; but in vain! The many-colored garment, which clothed with honor an elected son,[1] when rent asunder for the many, is a worthless spoil. A band of robbers cannot live princely in the prince's castle; nor would he, like them, be content with less than all, though he would not, like them, seek it as fuel for riotous enjoyment, but as his principality, to administer and guard for the use of all living things therein. He cannot be satisfied with any one gift of the earth, any one department of knowledge, or telescopic peep at the heavens. He feels himself called to understand and aid nature, that she may, through his intelligence, be raised and interpreted; to be a student of, and servant to, the universe-spirit; and only king of his planet, that, as an angelic minister, he may bring it into conscious harmony with the law of that spirit.

Such is the inheritance of the orphan prince, and the illegitimate children of his family will not always be able to keep it from him, for, from the fields which they sow with dragon's teeth, and water with blood, rise monsters, which he alone has power to drive away.

But it is not the purpose now to sing the prophecy of his jubilee. We have said that, in clear triumphant moments, this has many, many times been made manifest, and those moments, though past in time, have been translated into eternity by thought. The bright signs they left hang in the heavens, as single stars or constellations, and, already, a thickly-sown radiance consoles the wanderer in the darkest night. Heroes have filled the zodiac of beneficent labors, and then given up their mortal part[2] to the fire without a murmur. Sages and lawgivers have bent their whole nature to the search for truth, and thought themselves happy if they could buy, with the sacrifice of all temporal ease and pleasure, one seed for the future Eden. Poets and priests have strung the lyre with heart-strings, poured out their best blood upon the altar which, reared anew from age to age, shall at last sustain the flame which rises to highest heaven. What shall we say of those who, if not so

---

[1] *The many-colored … elected son* Allusion to the coat of many colors, which Jacob gives to his favored son Joseph. Joseph's envious brothers subsequently sell him into slavery in Egypt. See Genesis 37.

[2] [Fuller's note] Jupiter alloquitur,

        Sed enim, ne pectora vano
Fida metun paveant, Œteas spernite flammas,
Omnia qui vieit, vincet, quos cernitis, ignes;
Nec nisi maternâ Vulcanum parte potentem
Sentiet. Aeternum est, à me quod traxit, et expers
Atque immune necis, nullaque domabile flamma
Idque ego defunctum terrâ cœlestibus oris
Accipiam, cunctisque meum lætabile factum
Dis fore confide. Si quis tamen, Hercule, si quis
Fortè Deo doliturus erit, data prœmia nollet;
Sed meruisse dari sciet, invitusque probabit.
Assensêre Dei.

Ovid, Apotheosis of Hercules, translated into clumsy English by Mr. Gay, as follows.

    Jove said,
        Be all your fears forborne,
Th' Œtean fires do thou, great hero, scorn;
Who vanquished all things, shall subdue the flame;
The part alone of gross *maternal* frame,
Fire shall devour, while that from me he drew
Shall live immortal, and its force renew;
That, when he's dead, I'll raise to realms above,
May all the powers the righteous act approve.
If any God dissent, and judge too great
The sacred honors of the heavenly seat,
Even he shall own his deeds deserve the sky,
Even he, reluctant, shall at length comply.
Th' assembled powers assent.

[From Ovid's *Metamorphoses* (first century CE), translated by English poet John Gay (1685–1732).]

directly, or so consciously, in connection with the central truth, yet, led and fashioned by a divine instinct, serve no less to develop and interpret the open secret of love passing into life, the divine energy creating for the purpose of happiness—of the artist, whose hand, drawn by a preexistent harmony to a certain medium, moulds it to expressions of life more highly and completely organized than are seen elsewhere, and, by carrying out the intention of nature, reveals her meaning to those who are not yet sufficiently matured to divine it; of the philosopher, who listens steadily for causes, and, from those obvious, infers those yet unknown; of the historian, who, in faith that all events must have their reason and their aim, records them, and lays up archives from which the youth of prophets may be fed. The man of science dissects the statement, verifies the facts, and demonstrates connection even where he cannot its purpose.

Lives, too, which bear none of these names, have yielded tones of no less significance. The candlestick, set in a low place, has given light as faithfully, where it was needed, as that upon the hill.[1] In close[2] alleys, in dismal nooks, the Word has been read as distinctly, as when shown by angels to holy men in the dark prison. Those who till a spot of earth, scarcely larger than is wanted for a grave, have deserved that the sun should shine upon its sod till violets answer.

So great has been, from time to time, the promise that, in all ages, men have said the Gods themselves came down to dwell with them; that the All-Creating wandered on the earth to taste in a limited nature the sweetness of virtue, that the All-Sustaining incarnated himself, to guard, in space and time, the destinies of his world; that heavenly genius dwelt among the shepherds, to sing to them and teach them how to sing. Indeed,

Der stets den Hirten gnädig sich bewies.[3]

He has constantly shown himself favorable to shepherds.

And these dwellers in green pastures and natural students of the stars, were selected to hail, first of all, the holy child, whose life and death presented the type of excellence, which has sustained the heart of so large a portion of mankind in these later generations.

Such marks have been left by the footsteps of man, whenever he has made his way through the wilderness of men. And whenever the pygmies stepped in one of these, they felt dilate within the breast somewhat that promised larger stature and purer blood. They were tempted to forsake their evil ways, to forsake the side of selfish personal existence, of decrepit skepticism, and covetousness of corruptible possessions. Conviction flowed in upon them. They, too, raised the cry: God is living, all is his, and all created beings are brothers, for they are his children. These were the triumphant moments; but as we have said, man slept and selfishness awoke.

Thus he is still kept out of his inheritance, still a pleader, still a pilgrim. But his reinstatement is sure. And now, no mere glimmering consciousness, but a certainty, is felt and spoken, that the highest ideal man can form of his own capabilities is that which he is destined to attain. Whatever the soul knows how to seek, it must attain. Knock, and it shall be opened; seek, and ye shall find.[4] It is demonstrated, it is a maxim. He no longer paints his proper nature in some peculiar form and says, "Prometheus[5] had it," but "Man must have it." However disputed by many, however ignorantly used, or falsified, by those who do receive it, the fact of an universal, unceasing revelation has been too clearly stated in words to be lost sight of in thought, and sermons preached from the text, "Be ye perfect,"[6] are the only sermons of a pervasive and deep-searching influence.

---

[1]   *The candlestick ... upon the hill* See Matthew 5.14–15: "Ye are the light of the world. A city that is set on an hill cannot be hid. Neither do men light a candle, and put it under a bushel, but on a candlestick; and it giveth light unto all that are in the house."

[2]   *close* Narrow.

[3]   *Der stets ... bewies* From Friedrich Schiller's *Die Jungfrau von Orleans* ("The Maid of Orleans," 1801). Fuller provides an English translation below.

[4]   *Knock ... shall find* See Matthew 7.7.

[5]   *Prometheus* In Greek mythology, the Titan responsible both for the creation of humans out of clay and for stealing fire from the gods and giving it to humankind for their own use (for which Prometheus was sentenced to eternal torment).

[6]   *Be ye perfect* See Matthew 5.48: "Be perfect, therefore, as your heavenly Father is perfect."

But among those who meditate upon this text, there is great difference of view, as to the way in which perfection shall be sought.

Through the intellect, say some: Gather from every growth of life its seed of thought; look behind every symbol for its law. If thou canst *see* clearly, the rest will follow.

Through the life, say others: Do the best thou knowest today. Shrink not from incessant error, in this gradual, fragmentary state. Follow thy light for as much as it will show thee, be faithful as far as thou canst, in hope that faith presently will lead to sight. Help others, without blame that they need thy help. Love much, and be forgiven.

It needs not intellect, needs not experience, says a third. If you took the true way, these would be evolved in purity. You would not learn through them, but express through them a higher knowledge. In quietness, yield thy soul to the casual soul. Do not disturb its teachings by methods of thine own. Be still, seek not, but wait in obedience. Thy commission will be given.

Could we, indeed, say what we want, could we give a description of the child that is lost, he would be found. As soon as the soul can say clearly, that a certain demonstration is wanted, it is at hand. When the Jewish prophet described the Lamb,[1] as the expression of what was required by the coming era, the time drew nigh. But we say not, see not, as yet, clearly what we would. Those who call for a more triumphant expression of love, a love that cannot be crucified, show not a perfect sense of what has already been expressed. Love has already been expressed, that made all things new, that gave the worm its ministry as well as the eagle; a love, to which it was alike to descend into the depths of hell, or to sit at the right hand of the Father.

Yet, no doubt, a new manifestation is at hand, a new hour in the day of man. We cannot expect to see him a completed being, when the mass of men lie so entangled in the sod, or use the freedom of their limbs only with wolfish energy. The tree cannot come to flower till its root be freed from the cankering worm, and its whole growth open to air and light. Yet something new shall presently be shown of the life of man, for hearts crave it now, if minds do not know how to ask it.

Among the strains of prophecy, the following, by an earnest mind of a foreign land, written some thirty years ago, is not yet outgrown; and it has the merit of being a positive appeal from the heart, instead of a critical declaration what man shall *not* do.

The ministry of man implies, that he must be filled from the divine fountains which are being engendered through all eternity, so that, at the mere name of his Master, he may be able to cast all his enemies into the abyss; that he may deliver all parts of nature from the barriers that imprison them; that he may purge the terrestrial atmosphere from the poisons that infect it; that he may preserve the bodies of men from the corrupt influences that surround, and the maladies that afflict them; still more, that he may keep their souls pure from the malignant insinuations which pollute, and the gloomy images that obscure them; that we may restore its serenity to the Word, which false words of men fill with mourning and sadness; that he may satisfy the desires of the angels, who await from him the development of the marvels of nature; that, in fine, his world may be filled with God, as eternity is.[2]

Another attempt we will give, by an obscure observer of our own day and country, to draw some lines of the desired image. It was suggested by seeing the design of Crawford's Orpheus,[3] and connecting with the circumstance of the American, in his garret at Rome, making choice of this subject, that of Americans here at home, showing such ambition to represent the character, by calling their prose and verse, Orphic sayings, Orphics.[4] Orpheus was a lawgiver by theocratic commission. He understood nature, and made all her forms move to his music. He told her secrets in the form of hymns, nature as seen in the mind of God. Then it is the

---

[1]   *the Lamb* I.e., Jesus.

[2]   [Fuller's note]   St. Martin. [See *The Ministry of Man and Spirit* (1802) by French mystic philosopher Louis Claude de Saint-Martin.]

[3]   *Crawford's Orpheus* 1839 sculpture by American sculptor Thomas Crawford, who spent much of his career living in Rome, The Greek mythological musician Orpheus journeys to the underworld to rescue his dead wife Eurydice, but inadvertently loses her again when, against the orders of the gods Hades and Persephone, he looks back at her before both have reached the upper world.

[4]   *Orphics* Massachusetts Transcendentalist Amos Bronson Alcott (1799–1888) wrote a series of philosophical essays called "Orphic Sayings."

prediction, that to learn and to do, all men must be lovers, and Orpheus was, in a high sense, a lover. His soul went forth towards all beings, yet could remain sternly faithful to a chosen type of excellence. Seeking what he loved, he feared not death nor hell, neither could any presence daunt his faith in the power of the celestial harmony that filled his soul.

It seemed significant of the state of things in this country that the sculptor should have chosen the attitude of shading his eyes. When we have the statue here, it will give lessons in reverence.

> Each Orpheus must to the depths descend,
> For only thus the poet can be wise,
> Must make the sad Persephone[1] his friend,
> And buried love to second life arise;
> Again his love must lose through too much love,
> Must lose his life by living life too true,
> For what he sought below is passed above,
> Already done is all that he would do;
> Must tune all being with his single lyre,
> Must melt all rocks free from their primal pain,
> Must search all nature with his one soul's fire,
> Must bind anew all forms in heavenly chain.
> If he already sees what he must do,
> Well may he shade his eyes from the far-shining view.[2]

Meanwhile, not a few believe—and men themselves have expressed the opinion—that the time is come when Euridice is to call for an Orpheus, rather than Orpheus for Euridice; that the idea of man, however imperfectly brought out, has been far more so than that of woman, and that an improvement in the daughters will best aid the reformation of the sons of this age.

It is worthy of remark that, as the principle of liberty is better understood and more nobly interpreted, a broader protest is made in behalf of woman. As men become aware that all men have not had their fair chance, they are inclined to say that no women have had a fair chance. The French Revolution, that strangely disguised angel, bore witness in favor of woman, but interpreted her claims no less ignorantly than those of man. Its idea of happiness did not rise

beyond outward enjoyment, unobstructed by the tyranny of others. The title it gave was *Citoyen, Citoyenne*,[3] and it is not unimportant to woman that even this species of equality was awarded her. Before, she could be condemned to perish on the scaffold for treason, but not as a citizen, but a subject. The right with which this title then invested a human being, was that of bloodshed and license. The Goddess of Liberty was impure. Yet truth was prophesied in the ravings of that hideous fever induced by long ignorance and abuse. Europe is conning[4] a valued lesson from the blood-stained page. The same tendencies, farther unfolded, will bear good fruit in this country.

Yet, in this country—as by the Jews, when Moses was leading them to the promised land—everything has been done that inherited depravity could, to hinder the promise of heaven from its fulfilment.[5] The cross, here as elsewhere, has been planted only to be blasphemed by cruelty and fraud. The name of the Prince of Peace has been profaned by all kinds of injustice towards the Gentile[6] whom he said he came to save. But I need not speak of what has been done towards the red man, the black man. These deeds are the scoff of the world; and they have been accompanied by such pious words, that the gentlest would not dare to intercede with, "Father forgive them, for they know not what they do."[7]

Here, as elsewhere, the gain of creation consists always in the growth of individual minds, which live

---

[1]   *sad Persephone*   Persephone became goddess of the underworld when she was abducted and brought there by Hades.

[2]   *Each Orpheus … far-shining view*   Poem written by Fuller.

[3]   *Citoyen, Citoyenne*   French: masculine and feminine forms of "citizen," used as class-less terms of address during and immediately after the French Revolution.

[4]   *conning*   Learning.

[5]   *in this country—as by the Jews … fulfilment*   When Moses was leading the Jews to the land God had promised them, some were mistrustful and disobedient, and as a result the entire group was barred from entering the promised land. In like fashion, Fuller suggests, the people of America have not been following the ways of God; in America's case, she identifies in particular the cruelties practiced by Christians against black Americans and Native Americans— as contravening the ways of God.

[6]   *Prince of Peace*   Jesus, who offered salvation to all who had faith in him;   *Gentile*   Non-Jew. The term derives from medieval Latin versions of the Bible and, in societies where almost all non-Jews are Christian, it has often been used as a virtual synonym for "Christian" (sometimes with pejorative connotations regarding Jews, though Fuller does not appear to be using the term in that fashion here).

[7]   *Father … they do*   See Luke 23.34; said by Christ of those responsible for his crucifixion.

and aspire, as flowers bloom and birds sing, in the midst of morasses; and in the continual development of that thought, the thought of human destiny, which is given to eternity to fulfil, and which ages of failure only seemingly impede. Only seemingly, and whatever seems to the contrary, this country is as surely destined to elucidate a great moral law, as Europe was to promote the mental culture of man.

Though the national independence be blurred by the servility of individuals; though freedom and equality have been proclaimed only to leave room for a monstrous display of slave dealing, and slave keeping; though the free American so often feels himself free, like the Roman, only to pamper his appetites and his indolence through the misery of his fellow beings, still it is not in vain, that the verbal statement has been made, "All men are born free and equal." There it stands, a golden certainty, wherewith to encourage the good, to shame the bad. The new world may be called clearly to perceive that it incurs the utmost penalty, if it rejects the sorrowful brother. And if men are deaf, the angels hear. But men cannot be deaf. It is inevitable that an external freedom, such as has been achieved for the nation, should be so also for every member of it. That, which has once been clearly conceived in the intelligence, must be acted out. It has become a law, irrevocable as that of the Medes[1] in their ancient dominion. Men will privately sin against it, but the law so clearly expressed by a leading mind of the age,

Tutti fatti a sembianza d' un Solo;
Figli tutti d' un solo riscatto,
In qual ora, in qual parte del suolo
Trascorriamo quest' aura vital,
Siam fratelli, siam stretti ad un patto:
Maladetto colui che lo infrange,
Che s' innalza sul fiacco che piange,
Che contrista uno spirto immortal.[2]

All made in the likeness of the One,
All children of one ransom,
In whatever hour, in whatever part of the soil

We draw this vital air,
We are brothers, we must be bound by one compact,
Accursed he who infringes it,
Who raises himself upon the weak who weep,
Who saddens an immortal spirit.

cannot fail of universal recognition.

We sicken no less at the pomp than at the strife of words. We feel that never were lungs so puffed with the wind of declamation, on moral and religious subjects, as now. We are tempted to implore these "word-heroes," these word-Catos,[3] word-Christs, to beware of cant[4] above all things; to remember that hypocrisy is the most hopeless as well as the meanest[5] of crimes, and that those must surely be polluted by it, who do not keep a little of all this morality and religion for private use.[6] We feel that the mind may "grow black and rancid in the smoke"[7] even of altars. We start up from the harangue to go into our closet and shut the door. But, when it has been shut long enough, we remember that where there is so much smoke, there must be some fire; with so much talk about virtue and freedom must be mingled some desire for them; that it cannot be in vain that such have become the common topics of conversation among men; that the very newspapers should proclaim themselves Pilgrims, Puritans, Heralds of Holiness. The king that maintains so costly a retinue cannot be a mere Count of Carabbas[8] fiction. We have

---

1 *Medes* People of ancient Iran.

2 [Fuller's note] Manzoni. [From *Il Conte de Carmagnola* by Italian novelist Alessandro Manzoni (1785–1873). The translation appears to be Fuller's own.]

3 *word-Catos* I.e., those who look to emulate the likes of Cato in their words, but not their deeds. Cato the Younger (95–46 BCE) was known for his integrity and refusal to take bribes, and for defending the Roman Republic against Julius Caesar, ultimately dying by suicide in protest against his rule.

4 *cant* Jargon; empty language.

5 *meanest* Lowliest.

6 [Fuller's note] Dr. Johnson's one piece of advice should be written on every door: "Clear your mind of cant." But Byron, to whom it was so acceptable, in clearing away the noxious vine, shook down the building too. Stirling's emendation is note-worthy: "Realize your cant, not cast it off." [*Dr. Johnson* Samuel Johnson, English writer, whose many witticisms are famously recorded in James Boswell's biography *Life of Samuel Johnson* (1791); *Byron* English Romantic poet George Gordon, Lord Byron (1788–1824); *Stirling* John Sterling (1806–44), Scottish writer.]

7 *grow black … the smoke* The source of this quotation is unclear.

8 *Count of Carabbas* In Charles Perrault's fairytale "Puss in Boots" (1697), the deceitful cat tells the king that his poor master is the Master of Carabas.

waited here long in the dust; we are tired and hungry, but the triumphal procession must appear at last.

Of all its banners, none has been more steadily upheld, and under none has more valor and willingness for real sacrifices been shown, than that of the champions of the enslaved African. And this band it is, which, partly in consequence of a natural following out of principles, partly because many women have been prominent in that cause, makes, just now, the warmest appeal in behalf of woman.

Though there has been a growing liberality on this point, yet society at large is not so prepared for the demands of this party, but that they are, and will be for some time, coldly regarded as the Jacobins[1] of their day.

"Is it not enough," cries the sorrowful trader, "that you have done all you could to break up the national Union, and thus destroy the prosperity of our country, but now you must be trying to break up family union, to take my wife away from the cradle, and the kitchen hearth, to vote at polls, and preach from a pulpit? Of course, if she does such things, she cannot attend to those of her own sphere. She is happy enough as she is. She has more leisure than I have, every means of improvement, every indulgence."

"Have you asked her whether she was satisfied with these indulgences?"

"No, but I know she is. She is too amiable to wish what would make me unhappy, and too judicious to wish to step beyond the sphere of her sex. I will never consent to have our peace disturbed by any such discussions."

"'Consent'—you? it is not consent from you that is in question, it is assent from your wife."

"Am not I the head of my house?"

"You are not the head of your wife. God has given her a mind of her own."

"I am the head and she the heart."

"God grant you play true to one another then. If the head represses no natural pulse of the heart, there can be no question as to your giving your consent. Both will be of one accord, and there needs but to present any question to get a full and true answer. There is no need of precaution, of indulgence, or consent. But our doubt is whether the heart consents with the head, or only acquiesces in its decree; and it is to ascertain the truth on this point, that we propose some liberating measures."

Thus vaguely are these questions proposed and discussed at present. But their being proposed at all implies much thought, and suggests more. Many women are considering within themselves what they need that they have not, and what they can have, if they find they need it. Many men are considering whether women are capable of being and having more than they are and have, and whether, if they are, it will be best to consent to improvement in their condition.

The numerous party, whose opinions are already labelled and adjusted too much to their mind to admit of any new light, strive, by lectures on some model-woman of bridal-like beauty and gentleness, by writing or lending little treatises, to mark out with due precision the limits of woman's sphere, and woman's mission, and to prevent other than the rightful shepherd from climbing the wall, or the flock from using any chance gap to run astray.

Without enrolling ourselves at once on either side, let us look upon the subject from that point of view which today offers. No better, it is to be feared, than a high house-top. A high hill-top, or at least a cathedral spire, would be desirable.

It is not surprising that it should be the Anti-Slavery party that pleads for woman, when we consider merely that she does not hold property on equal terms with men; so that, if a husband dies without a will, the wife, instead of stepping at once into his place as head of the family, inherits only a part of his fortune, as if she were a child, or ward only, not an equal partner.

We will not speak of the innumerable instances in which profligate or idle men live upon the earnings of industrious wives; or if the wives leave them and take with them the children, to perform the double duty of mother and father, follow from place to place, and threaten to rob them of the children, if deprived of the rights of a husband, as they call them, planting themselves in their poor lodgings, frightening them into paying tribute by taking from them the children, running into debt at the expense of these otherwise so overtasked helots. Though such instances abound, the public opinion of his own sex is against the man, and

---

[1]   *Jacobins*   Members of a revolutionary political sect during the French Revolution (1789–99), who became known for their leading role in the period of mass executions known as the Reign of Terror.

when cases of extreme tyranny are made known, there is private action in the wife's favor. But if woman be, indeed, the weaker party, she ought to have legal protection, which would make such oppression impossible.

And knowing that there exists, in the world of men, a tone of feeling towards women as towards slaves, such as is expressed in the common phrase, "Tell that to women and children"; that the infinite soul can only work through them in already ascertained limits; that the prerogative of reason, man's highest portion, is allotted to them in a much lower degree; that it is better for them to be engaged in active labor, which is to be furnished and directed by those better able to think, etc. etc.; we need not go further, for who can review the experience of last week, without recalling words which imply, whether in jest or earnest, these views, and views like these? Knowing this, can we wonder that many reformers think that measures are not likely to be taken in behalf of women, unless their wishes could be publicly represented by women?

That can never be necessary, cry the other side. All men are privately influenced by women; each has his wife, sister, or female friends, and is too much biased by these relations to fail of representing their interests. And if this is not enough, let them propose and enforce their wishes with the pen. The beauty of home would be destroyed, the delicacy of the sex be violated, the dignity of halls of legislation destroyed, by an attempt to introduce them there. Such duties are inconsistent with those of a mother; and then we have ludicrous pictures of ladies in hysterics at the polls, and senate chambers filled with cradles.

But if, in reply, we admit as truth that woman seems destined by nature rather to the inner circle, we must add that the arrangements of civilized life have not been as yet such as to secure it to her. Her circle, if the duller, is not the quieter. If kept from excitement, she is not from drudgery. Not only the Indian[1] carries the burdens of the camp, but the favorites of Louis the Fourteenth accompany him in his journeys,[2] and the washerwoman stands at her tub and carries home her work at all seasons, and in all states of health.

As to the use of the pen, there was quite as much opposition to woman's possessing herself of that help to free-agency as there is now to her seizing on the rostrum[3] or the desk; and she is likely to draw, from a permission to plead her cause that way, opposite inferences to what might be wished by those who now grant it.

As to the possibility of her filling, with grace and dignity, any such position, we should think those who had seen the great actresses, and heard the Quaker preachers[4] of modern times, would not doubt, that woman can express publicly the fulness of thought and emotion, without losing any of the peculiar beauty of her sex.

As to her home, she is not likely to leave it more than she now does for balls, theatres, meetings for promoting missions, revival meetings, and others to which she flies, in hope of an animation for her existence, commensurate with what she sees enjoyed by men. Governors of Ladies' Fairs are no less engrossed by such a charge, than the Governor of the State by his; presidents of Washingtonian societies,[5] no less away from home than presidents of conventions. If men look straitly to it, they will find that, unless their own lives are domestic, those of the women will not be. The female Greek, of our day, is as much in the street as the male, to cry, What news? We doubt not it was the same in Athens of old. The women, shut out from the market-place, made up for it at the religious festivals. For human beings are not so constituted that they can live without expansion; and if they do not get it one way, must another, or perish.

And, as to men's representing women fairly, at present, while we hear from men who owe to their wives not only all that is comfortable and graceful, but all that is wise in the arrangement of their lives, the frequent remark, "You cannot reason with a woman," when from those of delicacy, nobleness, and poetic culture, the contemptuous phrase, "Women and children," and that in no light sally of the hour, but in works intended to give a permanent statement of the best experiences;

---

1   *the Indian* I.e., Native American women. (The impression among nineteenth-century white Americans that most manual labor in Indigenous communities was performed by women was often used to negatively compare the treatment of women in Indigenous cultures to that in "civilized" cultures.)

2   *the favorites … his journeys* Reference to the many mistresses, both official and unofficial, of Louis XIV of France (1638–1715).

3   *rostrum* Podium.

4   *Quaker preachers* Quakers were notable as one of the only Christian denominations that allowed public preaching by women.

5   *Washingtonian societies* Fellowships aimed at promoting temperance and helping alcoholics achieve sobriety.

when not one man in the million, shall I say, no, not in the hundred million, can rise above the view that woman was made *for man*—when such traits as these are daily forced upon the attention, can we feel that man will always do justice to the interests of woman? Can we think that he takes a sufficiently discerning and religious view of her office[1] and destiny, ever to do her justice, except when prompted by sentiment; accidentally or transiently, that is, for his sentiment will vary according to the relations in which he is placed. The lover, the poet, the artist, are likely to view her nobly. The father and the philosopher have some chance of liberality; the man of the world, the legislator for expediency, none.

Under these circumstances, without attaching importance in themselves to the changes demanded by the champions of woman, we hail them as signs of the times. We would have every arbitrary barrier thrown down. We would have every path laid open to woman as freely as to man. Were this done, and a slight temporary fermentation allowed to subside, we believe that the Divine would ascend into nature to a height unknown in the history of past ages, and nature, thus instructed, would regulate the spheres not only so as to avoid collision, but to bring forth ravishing harmony.

Yet then, and only then, will human beings be ripe for this, when inward and outward freedom for woman, as much as for man, shall be acknowledged as a right, not yielded as a concession. As the friend of the negro assumes that one man cannot, by right, hold another in bondage, so should the friend of woman assume that man cannot, by right, lay even well-meant restrictions on woman. If the negro be a soul, if the woman be a soul, apparelled in flesh, to one master only are they accountable. There is but one law for all souls, and, if there is to be an interpreter of it, he comes not as man, or son of man, but as Son of God.

Were thought and feeling once so far elevated that man should esteem himself the brother and friend, but nowise the lord and tutor of woman, were he really bound with her in equal worship, arrangements as to function and employment would be of no consequence. What woman needs is not as a woman to act or rule, but as a nature to grow, as an intellect to discern, as a soul to live freely, and unimpeded to unfold such powers as were given her when we left our common home. If fewer talents were given her, yet, if allowed the free and full employment of these, so that she may render back to the giver his own with usury, she will not complain, nay, I dare to say she will bless and rejoice in her earthly birthplace, her earthly lot.

Let us consider what obstructions impede this good era, and what signs give reason to hope that it draws near.

I was talking on this subject with Miranda,[2] a woman who, if any in the world, might speak without heat or bitterness of the position of her sex. Her father was a man who cherished no sentimental reverence for woman, but a firm belief in the equality of the sexes. She was his eldest child, and came to him at an age when he needed a companion. From the time she could speak and go[3] alone, he addressed her not as a plaything, but as a living mind. Among the few verses he ever wrote were a copy addressed to this child, when the first locks were cut from her head, and the reverence expressed on this occasion for that cherished head he never belied. It was to him the temple of immortal intellect. He respected his child, however, too much to be an indulgent parent. He called on her for clear judgment, for courage, for honor and fidelity, in short for such virtues as he knew. In so far as he possessed the keys to the wonders of this universe, he allowed free use of them to her, and by the incentive of a high expectation he forbade, as far as possible, that she should let the privilege lie idle.

Thus this child was early led to feel herself a child of the spirit. She took her place easily, not only in the world of organized being, but in the world of mind. A dignified sense of self-dependence was given as all her portion, and she found it a sure anchor. Herself securely anchored, her relations with others were established with equal security. She was fortunate, in a total absence of those charms which might have drawn to her bewildering flatteries, and of a strong electric

---

[1]   *office* Duties.

[2]   *Miranda* The experiences attributed to "Miranda" in the following passage closely resemble those of Fuller herself. The name itself is an allusion to the character Miranda from Shakespeare's *The Tempest*; Shakespeare's Miranda is highly learned, but also extremely sheltered and naïve, having spent most of her life on an isolated island accompanied only by her controlling father, the native man he enslaves, and a magical sprite.

[3]   *go* Walk.

nature, which repelled those who did not belong to her, and attracted those who did. With men and women her relations were noble; affectionate without passion, intellectual without coldness. The world was free to her, and she lived freely in it. Outward adversity came, and inward conflict, but that faith and self-respect had early been awakened, which must always lead at last to an outward serenity, and an inward peace.

Of Miranda I had always thought as an example, that the restraints upon the sex were insuperable only to those who think them so, or who noisily strive to break them. She had taken a course of her own, and no man stood in her way. Many of her acts had been unusual, but excited no uproar. Few helped, but none checked her; and the many men, who knew her mind and her life, showed to her confidence as to a brother, gentleness as to a sister. And not only refined, but very coarse men approved one in whom they saw resolution and clearness of design. Her mind was often the leading one, always effective.

When I talked with her upon these matters, and had said very much what I have written, she smilingly replied, And yet we must admit that I have been fortunate, and this should not be. My good father's early trust gave the first bias, and the rest followed of course. It is true that I have had less outward aid, in after years, than most women, but that is of little consequence. Religion was early awakened in my soul, a sense that what the soul is capable to ask it must attain, and that, though I might be aided by others, I must depend on myself as the only constant friend. This self-dependence, which was honored in me, is deprecated as a fault in most women. They are taught to learn their rule from without, not to unfold it from within.

This is the fault of man, who is still vain, and wishes to be more important to woman than by right he should be.

Men have not shown this disposition towards you, I said.

No, because the position I early was enabled to take, was one of self-reliance. And were all women as sure of their wants as I was, the result would be the same. The difficulty is to get them to the point where they shall naturally develop self-respect, the question how it is to be done.

Once I thought that men would help on this state of things more than I do now. I saw so many of them wretched in the connections they had formed in weakness and vanity. They seemed so glad to esteem women whenever they could!

But early I perceived that men never, in any extreme of despair, wished to be women. Where they admired any woman they were inclined to speak of her as above her sex. Silently I observed this, and feared it argued a rooted skepticism, which for ages had been fastening on the heart, and which only an age of miracles could eradicate.

Ever I have been treated with great sincerity; and I look upon it as a most signal instance of this, that an intimate friend of the other sex said in a fervent moment, that I deserved in some star to be a man. Another used as highest praise, in speaking of a character in literature, the words "a manly woman."

It is well known that of every strong woman they say she has a masculine mind.

This by no means argues a willing want[1] of generosity towards woman. Man is as generous towards her, as he knows how to be.

Wherever she has herself arisen in national or private history, and nobly shone forth in any ideal of excellence, men have received her, not only willingly, but with triumph. Their encomiums indeed are always in some sense mortifying, they show too much surprise.

In everyday life the feelings of the many are stained with vanity. Each wishes to be lord in a little world, to be superior at least over one; and he does not feel strong enough to retain a life-long ascendant over a strong nature. Only a Brutus would rejoice in a Portia.[2] Only Theseus could conquer before he wed the Amazonian Queen.[3] Hercules wished rather to rest from his labors

---

[1] *want* Lack.

[2] *Brutus … Portia* Allusion to Shakespeare's *Julius Caesar*, in which Brutus, who has just been involved in a plot to murder the would-be dictator Julius Caesar, comes home to find his wife Portia dead, having died by suicide in distress over his persistent absence from home.

[3] *Only Theseus … Amazonian Queen* There are differing versions of the Greek myths about the Athenian hero Theseus and the Amazons, a race of powerful warrior women—including versions in which Theseus rapes or abducts their queen—but Fuller may be thinking of the story recounted in Shakespeare's *A Midsummer Night's Dream*, which centers on the consensual marriage between Theseus and the Amazonian queen Hippolyta.

with Dejanira, and received the poisoned robe, as a fit guerdon.[1] The tale should be interpreted to all those who seek repose with the weak.

But not only is man vain and fond of power, but the same want of development, which thus affects him morally in the intellect, prevents his discerning the destiny of woman. The boy wants no woman, but only a girl to play ball with him, and mark his pocket handkerchief.

Thus in Schiller's Dignity of Woman,[2] beautiful as the poem is, there is no "grave and perfect man," but only a great boy to be softened and restrained by the influence of girls. Poets, the elder brothers of their race, have usually seen further; but what can you expect of everyday men, if Schiller was not more prophetic as to what women must be? Even with Richter[3] one foremost thought about a wife was that she would "cook him something good."

The sexes should not only correspond to and appreciate one another, but prophesy to one another. In individual instances this happens. Two persons love in one another the future good which they aid one another to unfold. This is very imperfectly done as yet in the general life. Man has gone but little way, now he is waiting to see whether woman can keep step with him, but instead of calling out like a good brother: You can do it if you only think so; or impersonally: Anyone can do what he tries to do; he often discourages with school-boy brag: Girls can't do that, girls can't play ball. But let anyone defy their taunts, break through, and be brave and secure, they rend the air with shouts.

No! man is not willingly ungenerous. He wants faith and love, because he is not yet himself an elevated being. He cries with sneering skepticism: Give us a sign. But if the sign appears, his eyes glisten, and he offers not merely approval, but homage.

The severe nation which taught that the happiness of the race was forfeited through the fault of a woman, and showed its thought of what sort of regard man owed her, by making him accuse her on the first question to his God, who gave her to the patriarch as a handmaid,[4] and, by the Mosaical law,[5] bound her to allegiance like a serf, even they greeted, with solemn rapture, all great and holy women as heroines, prophetesses, nay judges in Israel; and, if they made Eve listen to the serpent, gave Mary to the Holy Spirit. In other nations it has been the same down to our day. To the woman who could conquer, a triumph was awarded. And not only those whose strength was recommended to the heart by association with goodness and beauty, but those who were bad, if they were steadfast and strong, had their claims allowed. In any age a Semiramis,[6] an Elizabeth of England, a Catharine of Russia[7] makes her place good, whether in a large or small circle.

How has a little wit, a little genius, always been celebrated in a woman! What an intellectual triumph was that of the lonely Aspasia,[8] and how heartily acknowledged! She, indeed, met a Pericles. But what annalist, the rudest of men, the most plebeian of husbands, will spare from his page one of the few anecdotes of Roman women? Sappho, Eloisa![9] The names are of thread-bare celebrity. The man habitually most narrow towards women will be flushed, as by the worst assault on Christianity, if you say it has made no improvement in her condition. Indeed, those most opposed to new

---

[1] *Hercules wished … fit guerdon* In Greek myth, Dejanira, the wife of Hercules, sought to regain her husband's love by giving him a robe soaked in a love potion; the potion turned out to be a poison, burning Hercules's flesh, and both Hercules and Dejanira subsequently died by suicide; *guerdon* Reward.

[2] *Schiller's Dignity of Woman* 1796 poem by the German Romantic poet Friedrich Schiller (1759–1805).

[3] *Richter* Johann Paul Friedrich Richter (1763–1825), German writer. His novels were known for their frequently empathetic portrayals of female characters, but also for the frequent appearance of misogynistic humor.

[4] *the happiness … handmaid* See Genesis 3.12, in which Adam says to God of Eve: "The woman you put here with me—she gave me some fruit from the tree, and I ate it."

[5] *Mosaical law* Collection of laws set down in the Torah, or the first five books of the Old Testament.

[6] *Semiramis* Legendary queen of Assyria.

[7] *Catharine of Russia* Catherine II, Empress of Russia from 1762 to 1796, during which Russia came to be known as a great international power.

[8] *Aspasia* Resident of Classical Athens, partner of the politician Pericles, whose home became an intellectual center and who was greatly admired by Socrates.

[9] *Sappho* Ancient Greek lyric poet (c. 630–570 BCE) from the island of Lesbos, where she led a group of artistic women; *Eloisa* Also spelled Héloïse (c. 1100–64), French nun and scholar, best known for her scandalous love affair with the philosopher and theologian Peter Abelard.

acts in her favor are jealous of the reputation of those which have been done.

We will not speak of the enthusiasm excited by actresses, improvisatrici,[1] female singers, for here mingles the charm of beauty and grace, but female authors, even learned women, if not insufferably ugly and slovenly, from the Italian professor's daughter, who taught behind the curtain, down to Mrs. Carter and Madame Dacier,[2] are sure of an admiring audience, if they can once get a platform on which to stand.

But how to get this platform, or how to make it of reasonably easy access is the difficulty. Plants of great vigor will almost always struggle into blossom, despite impediments. But there should be encouragement, and a free, genial atmosphere for those of more timid sort, fair play for each in its own kind. Some are like the little, delicate flowers, which love to hide in the dripping mosses by the sides of mountain torrents, or in the shade of tall trees. But others require an open field, a rich and loosened soil, or they never show their proper hues.

It may be said man does not have his fair play either; his energies are repressed and distorted by the interposition of artificial obstacles. Aye, but he himself has put them there; they have grown out of his own imperfections. If there is a misfortune in woman's lot, it is in obstacles being interposed by men, which do *not* mark her state, and if they express her past ignorance, do not her present needs. As every man is of woman born, she has slow but sure means of redress, yet the sooner a general justness of thought makes smooth the path, the better.

Man is of woman born, and her face bends over him in infancy with an expression he can never quite forget. Eminent men have delighted to pay tribute to this image, and it is a hackneyed observation, that most men of genius boast some remarkable development in the mother. The rudest tar[3] brushes off a tear with his coat-sleeve at the hallowed name. The other day I met a decrepit old man of seventy, on a journey, who challenged the stage-company to guess where he was going.

They guessed aright, "To see your mother." "Yes," said he, "she is ninety-two, but has good eyesight still, they say. I've not seen her these forty years, and I thought I could not die in peace without." I should have liked his picture painted as a companion piece to that of a boisterous little boy, whom I saw attempt to declaim at a school exhibition.

> O that those lips had language! Life has passed
> With me but roughly since I heard thee last.[4]

He got but very little way before sudden tears shamed him from the stage.

Some gleams of the same expression which shone down upon his infancy, angelically pure and benign, visit man again with hopes of pure love, of a holy marriage. Or if not before, in the eyes of the mother of his child they again are seen, and dim fancies pass before his mind, that woman may not have been born for him alone, but have come from heaven, a commissioned soul, a messenger of truth and love.

In gleams, in dim fancies, this thought visits the mind of common men. It is soon obscured by the mists of sensuality, the dust of routine, and he thinks it was only some meteor or ignis fatuus[5] that shone. But, as a Rosicrucian lamp,[6] it burns unwearied, though condemned to the solitude of tombs. And, to its permanent life, as to every truth, each age has, in some form, borne witness. For the truths, which visit the minds of careless men only in fitful gleams, shine with radiant clearness into those of the poet, the priest, and the artist.

Whatever may have been the domestic manners of the ancient nations, the idea of woman was nobly manifested in their mythologies and poems, where she

---

[1] *improvisatrici* Female performers of improvised poetry.

[2] *Mrs. Carter* Elizabeth Carter (1717–1806), English scholar and translator; *Madame Dacier* Anne Dacier (1647–1720), French Classicist.

[3] *tar* Sailor.

[4] *O that ... thee last* See William Cowper, "On the Receipt of My Mother's Picture Out of Norfolk" (1798).

[5] *ignis fatuus* Latin: foolish fire; phosphorescent light that hovers above marshy ground and is believed to be caused by the spontaneous combustion of gases emitted from the marsh; in folklore the phenomenon was sometimes believed to represent dangerous or misleading aspirations.

[6] *Rosicrucian lamp* Symbol of a seventeenth-century esoteric order, whose founder's body was supposedly found buried with a still-burning lamp, a century after his death.

appeared as Sita in the Ramayana,[1] a form of tender purity, in the Egyptian Isis,[2] of divine wisdom never yet surpassed. In Egypt, too, the Sphinx, walking the earth with lion tread, looked out upon its marvels in the calm, inscrutable beauty of a virgin's face, and the Greek could only add wings to the great emblem.[3] In Greece, Ceres and Proserpine,[4] significantly termed "the goddesses," were seen seated, side by side. They needed not to rise for any worshipper or any change; they were prepared for all things, as those initiated to their mysteries knew. More obvious is the meaning of those three forms, the Diana, Minerva, and Vesta.[5] Unlike in the expression of their beauty, but alike in this—that each was self-sufficing. Other forms were only accessories and illustrations, none the complement to one like these. Another might indeed be the companion, and the Apollo[6] and Diana set off one another's beauty. Of the Vesta, it is to be observed, that not only deep-eyed, deep-discerning Greece, but ruder Rome, who represents the only form of good man (the always busy warrior) that could be indifferent to woman, confided the permanence of its glory to a tutelary goddess, and her wisest legislator spoke of Meditation as a nymph.

In Sparta, thought, in this respect as all others, was expressed in the characters of real life, and the women of Sparta were as much Spartans as the men. The Citoyen, Citoyenne, of France, was here actualized. Was not the calm equality they enjoyed well worth the honors of chivalry? They intelligently shared the ideal life of their nation.

Generally, we are told of these nations, that women occupied there a very subordinate position in actual life. It is difficult to believe this, when we see such range and dignity of thought on the subject in the mythologies, and find the poets producing such ideals as Cassandra, Iphigenia, Antigone, Macaria[7] (though it is not unlike our own day, that men should revere those heroines of their great princely houses at theatres, from which their women were excluded), where Sibylline priestesses[8] told the oracle of the highest god, and he could not be content to reign with a court of less than nine Muses. Even Victory wore a female form.[9]

But whatever were the facts of daily life, I cannot complain of the age and nation which represents its thought by such a symbol as I see before me at this moment. It is a zodiac of the busts of gods and goddesses, arranged in pairs. The circle breathes the music of a heavenly order. Male and female heads are distinct in expression, but equal in beauty, strength, and calmness. Each male head is that of a brother and a king, each female of a sister and a queen. Could the thought, thus expressed, be lived out, there would be nothing more to be desired. There would be unison in variety, congeniality in difference.

Coming nearer our own time, we find religion and poetry no less true in their revelations. The rude man, but just disengaged from the sod,[10] the Adam, accuses woman to his God, and records her disgrace to their posterity. He is not ashamed to write that he could be drawn from heaven by one beneath him. But in the same nation, educated by time, instructed by successive prophets, we find woman in as high a position as she has ever occupied. And no figure, that has ever arisen

---

[1] *Sita in the Ramayana* Protagonist of the Sanskrit epic the *Ramayana*, associated with chastity and courage.

[2] *Isis* Powerful ancient Egyptian goddess associated with, among other things, fertility, the sky, and the afterlife.

[3] *the Greek … great emblem* The Sphinx of Greek mythology is conceptually very similar to that of the Egyptians, but is usually depicted with wings.

[4] *Ceres and Proserpine* Roman goddess of agriculture and her daughter, the goddess of the Underworld.

[5] *Diana* Roman goddess of virginity and the hunt; *Minerva* Roman goddess of wisdom and strategic warfare; *Vesta* Roman goddess of the hearth and home.

[6] *Apollo* Twin brother of Diana, god of the arts.

[7] *Cassandra* In Greek mythology, a woman given the power of prophecy by Apollo (though, as a result of a subsequent curse, her prophesies were not believed); *Iphigenia* Daughter of Mycenaean king Agamemnon, who is offered by her father as a sacrifice to the goddess Artemis (the Greek equivalent of Diana) in order to ensure the success of the Greek army during the Trojan War (in some versions of the myth, Artemis saves Iphigenia at the last moment); *Antigone* Daughter of Oedipus, who bravely defied orders not to give her brother Polynices an honorable burial and was executed for her defiance; *Macaria* Daughter of Hercules, who sacrifices herself in order to prevent the deaths of her siblings at the hands of the vengeful king Eurystheus.

[8] *Sibylline priestesses* Divinely inspired prophetesses of Greek mythology.

[9] *Victory wore a female form* The goddess Victoria was a personification of victory in ancient Rome; her Greek equivalent was Nike.

[10] *rude* Rough, uncultivated; rudimentary; *but just … sod* Only recently emerged from the earth.

to greet our eyes, has been received with more fervent reverence than that of the Madonna.[1] Heine calls her the Dame du Comptoir[2] of the Catholic Church, and this jeer well expresses a serious truth.

And not only this holy and significant image was worshipped by the pilgrim, and the favorite subject of the artist, but it exercised an immediate influence on the destiny of the sex. The empresses who embraced the cross converted sons and husbands.[3] Whole calendars of female saints, heroic dames of chivalry, binding the emblem of faith on the heart of the best-beloved, and wasting the bloom of youth in separation and loneliness for the sake of duties they thought it religion to assume, with innumerable forms of poesy, trace their lineage to this one. Nor, however imperfect may be the action, in our day, of the faith thus expressed, and though we can scarcely think it nearer this ideal than that of India or Greece was near their ideal, is it in vain that the truth has been recognised, that woman is not only a part of man, bone of his bone and flesh of his flesh, born that men might not be lonely, but in themselves possessors of and possessed by immortal souls. This truth undoubtedly received a greater outward stability from the belief of the church, that the earthly parent of the Saviour of souls was a woman.

The Assumption of the Virgin,[4] as painted by sublime artists, Petrarch's[5] Hymn to the Madonna, cannot have spoken to the world wholly without result, yet oftentimes those who had ears heard not.

Thus, the Idea of woman has not failed to be often and forcibly represented. So many instances throng on the mind, that we must stop here, lest the catalogue be swelled beyond the reader's patience.

Neither can she complain that she has not had her share of power. This, in all ranks of society except the lowest, has been hers to the extent that vanity could crave, far beyond what wisdom would accept. In the very lowest, where man, pressed by poverty, sees in woman only the partner of toils and cares, and cannot hope, scarcely has an idea of a comfortable home, he maltreats her often, and is less influenced by her. In all ranks, those who are amiable and uncomplaining suffer much. They suffer long, and are kind; verily, they have their reward. But wherever man is sufficiently raised above extreme poverty, or brutal stupidity, to care for the comforts of the fireside, or the bloom and ornament of life, woman has always power enough, if she choose to exert it, and is usually disposed to do so in proportion to her ignorance and childish vanity. Unacquainted with the importance of life and its purposes, trained to a selfish coquetry and love of petty power, she does not look beyond the pleasure of making herself felt at the moment, and governments are shaken and commerce broken up to gratify the pique of a female favorite. The English shopkeeper's wife does not vote, but it is for her interest that the politician canvasses by the coarsest flattery. France suffers[6] no woman on her throne, but her proud nobles kiss the dust at the feet of Pompadour and Dubarry,[7] for such flare in the lighted foreground where a Roland[8] would modestly aid in the closet. Spain shuts up her women

---

[1] *the Madonna* The Virgin Mary.

[2] *Heine … Dame du Comptoir* German Romantic poet and essayist Heinrich Heine referred to the Virgin Mary by this French phrase in his 1835 essay *Die romantische Schule,* or *The Romantic School.* The term means saleswoman (literally, "lady of the counter") and was meant to suggest that the idea of the Virgin Mary was being used to "sell" Catholicism to her devotees.

[3] *The empresses … and husbands* This may refer to any number of early Christian matriarchs, but perhaps particularly to Roman empress Helena (c. 246–c. 330), who is said to have discovered the True Cross (a relic of the cross on which Jesus was crucified) and thereafter to have converted to Christianity. Her son, Constantine the Great, became the first Roman emperor to convert to Christianity shortly before his death in the year 337, and some believe that her husband Constantius (c. 250–306) was secretly also a Christian.

[4] *The Assumption of the Virgin* Mary's "assumption," or ascension, into Heaven upon death, a popular subject of Christian art and iconography.

[5] *Petrarch* Italian Renaissance poet and scholar (1304–74).

[6] *suffers* Allows.

[7] *Pompadour and Dubarry* Two famous mistresses of French King Louis XV, Jeanne Antoinette Poisson, Marquise de Pompadour (1721–64) and Jeanne Bécu, Comtesse du Barry (1743–93). Both women were highly influential in the French court prior to the French Revolution, were villainized during the Revolution (du Barry was executed during the Reign of Terror), and became important figures of popular culture during the nineteenth century.

[8] *Roland* Marie-Jeanne Roland de la Platière (1754–93), French intellectual. Though an influential proponent of the French Revolution, she differed from many other female revolutionaries in her relative conservativism on the subject of women's social and political rights; she was executed during the Reign of Terror.

in the care of duennas,[1] and allows them no book but the Breviary;[2] but the ruin follows only the more surely from the worthless favorite of a worthless queen.

It is not the transient breath of poetic incense that women want; each can receive that from a lover. It is not life-long sway;[3] it needs but to become a coquette, a shrew, or a good cook, to be sure of that. It is not money, nor notoriety, nor the badges of authority that men have appropriated to themselves. If demands made in their behalf lay stress on any of these particulars, those who make them have not searched deeply into the need. It is for that which at once includes all these and precludes them; which would not be forbidden power, lest there be temptation to steal and misuse it; which would not have the mind perverted by flattery from a worthiness of esteem. It is for that which is the birthright of every being capable to receive it—the freedom, the religious, the intelligent freedom of the universe, to use its means, to learn its secret as far as nature has enabled them, with God alone for their guide and their judge.

Ye cannot believe it, men; but the only reason why women ever assume what is more appropriate to you, is because you prevent them from finding out what is fit for themselves. Were they free, were they wise fully to develop the strength and beauty of woman, they would never wish to be men, or manlike. The well-instructed moon flies not from her orbit to seize on the glories of her partner. No; for she knows that one law rules, one heaven contains, one universe replies to them alike. It is with women as with the slave.

> Vor dem Sklaven, wenn er die Kette bricht,
> Vor dem freien Menschen erzittert nicht.[4]

> Tremble not before the free man, but before the slave
>   who has chains to break.

In slavery, acknowledged slavery, women are on a par with men. Each is a work-tool, an article of property—no more! In perfect freedom, such as is painted in Olympus,[5] in Swedenborg's angelic state,[6] in the heaven where there is no marrying nor giving in marriage,[7] each is a purified intelligence, an enfranchised soul—no less!

> Jene himmlissche Gestalten
> Sie fragen nicht nach Mann und Weib,
> Und keine Kleider, keine Falten
> Umgeben den verkläten Leib.[8]

The child who sang this was a prophetic form, expressive of the longing for a state of perfect freedom, pure love. She could not remain here, but was transplanted to another air. And it may be that the air of this earth will never be so tempered, that such can bear it long. But, while they stay, they must bear testimony to the truth they are constituted to demand.

That an era approaches which shall approximate nearer to such a temper than any has yet done, there are many tokens, indeed so many that only a few of the most prominent can here be enumerated.

The reigns of Elizabeth of England and Isabella of Castile[9] foreboded this era. They expressed the beginning of the new state, while they forwarded its progress. These were strong characters, and in harmony with the wants of their time. One showed that this strength did not unfit a woman for the duties of a wife and

---

mother; the other, that it could enable her to live and die alone.[1] Elizabeth is certainly no pleasing example. In rising above the weakness, she did not lay aside the weaknesses ascribed to her sex; but her strength must be respected now, as it was in her own time.

We may accept it as an omen for ourselves, that it was Isabella who furnished Columbus with the means of coming hither.[2] This land must pay back its debt to woman, without whose aid it would not have been brought into alliance with the civilized world.

The influence of Elizabeth on literature was real, though, by sympathy with its finer productions, she was no more entitled to give name to an era than Queen Anne.[3] It was simply that the fact of having a female sovereign on the throne affected the course of a writer's thoughts. In this sense, the presence of a woman on the throne always makes its mark. Life is lived before the eyes of all men, and their imaginations are stimulated as to the possibilities of woman. "We will die for our King, Maria Theresa,"[4] cry the wild warriors, clashing their swords, and the sounds vibrate through the poems of that generation. The range of female character in Spenser alone might content us for one period. Britomart and Belphoebe have as much room in the canvass as Florimel; and where this is the case, the haughtiest Amazon will not murmur that Una should be felt to be the highest type.[5]

Unlike as was the English Queen to a fairy queen, we may yet conceive that it was the image of a queen before the poet's mind that called up this splendid court of women.

Shakespeare's range is also great, but he has left out the heroic characters, such as the Macaria of Greece, the Britomart of Spenser. Ford and Massinger[6] have, in this respect, shown a higher flight of feeling than he. It was the holy and heroic woman they most loved, and if they could not paint an Imogen, a Desdemona, a Rosalind,[7] yet in those of a stronger mould, they showed a higher ideal, though with so much less poetic power to represent it, than we see in Portia or Isabella.[8] The simple truth of Cordelia,[9] indeed, is of this sort. The beauty of Cordelia is neither male nor female; it is the beauty of virtue.

The ideal of love and marriage rose high in the mind of all the Christian nations who were capable of grave and deep feeling. We may take as examples of its English aspect, the lines,

I could not love thee, dear, so much,
Loved I not honor more.[10]

The address of the Commonwealth's man to his wife as she looked out from the Tower window to see him for the last time on his way to execution. "He stood up in the cart, waved his hat, and cried, 'To Heaven, my love, to Heaven! and leave you in the storm!'"[11]

---

[1] *One showed ... die alone*   Isabella I had seven children with her husband, King Ferdinand II, five of whom lived past childhood; Elizabeth I famously remained unmarried (earning her the widely used title "The Virgin Queen").

[2] *it was Isabella ... hither*   Isabella I sponsored Christopher Columbus's first westward voyage in 1492.

[3] *Queen Anne*   Anne I, who reigned from 1702 to 1714, and whose name was given to various styles of the era (Queen Anne style architecture, Queen Anne style furniture, etc.).

[4] *We will ... Maria Theresa*   Maria Theresa was queen of the Habsburg dominions (which included Hungary, Austria, and the region of Bohemia) from 1745 to 1765; as Habsburg tradition did not allow for female rulers, Maria Theresa was officially known as "king."

[5] *The range ... highest type*   Fuller alludes to Edmund Spenser's epic poem *The Faerie Queene* (1590–96), an allegory of the reign of Elizabeth I. Its wide cast of allegorical female characters includes the female knight Britomart, an allegory of Chastity; the beautiful and virtuous Belphoebe; the brave Florimell, who faces numerous trials in pursuit of her beloved; and Una, who symbolizes Truth and the True (that is, the Protestant) Church.

[6] *Ford and Massinger*   English playwrights John Ford (1586–c. 1639) and Philip Massinger (1583–1640).

[7] *an Imogen, a Desdemona, a Rosalind*   Female characters in Shakespeare's *Cymbeline*, *Othello*, and *As You Like It* respectively, all depicted as highly virtuous.

[8] *Isabella*   Chaste and virtuous heroine in Shakespeare's *Measure for Measure*.

[9] *Cordelia*   Heroine in Shakespeare's *King Lear*.

[10] *I could not ... honor more*   See Richard Lovelace's poem "To Lucasta, Going to the Wars" (1649).

[11] *The address ... the storm!*   Colonel John Hutchinson (1615–64) was a supporter of the Parliamentarians during the English Civil War, and one of the signatories of King Charles I's death warrant; the source of the quotation here is unclear, though it may allude to something written in *Memoirs of the Life of Colonel Hutchinson*, the biography written by Hutchinson's wife Lucy Hutchinson and published posthumously in 1806.

Such was the love of faith and honor, a love which stopped, like Colonel Hutchinson's, "on this side idolatry,"[1] because it was religious. The meeting of two such souls Donne describes as giving birth to an "abler soul."[2]

Lord Herbert wrote to his love,

> Were not our souls immortal made,
> Our equal loves can make them such.[3]

In Spain the same thought is arrayed in a sublimity, which belongs to the sombre and passionate genius of the nation. Calderon's Justina resists all the temptation of the Demon, and raises her lover with her above the sweet lures of mere temporal happiness.[4] Their marriage is vowed at the stake, their souls are liberated together by the martyr flame into "a purer state of sensation and existence."

In Italy, the great poets wove into their lives an ideal love which answered to the highest wants. It included those of the intellect and the affections, for it was a love of spirit for spirit. It was not ascetic and superhuman, but interpreting all things, gave their proper beauty to details of the common life, the common day; the poet spoke of his love not as a flower to place in his bosom, or hold carelessly in his hand, but as a light towards which he must find wings to fly, or "a stair to heaven." He delighted to speak of her not only as the bride of his heart, but the mother of his soul, for he saw that, in cases where the right direction has been taken, the greater delicacy of her frame, and stillness of her life, left her more open to spiritual influx than man is. So he did not look upon her as betwixt him and earth, to serve his temporal needs, but rather betwixt him and heaven, to purify his affections and lead him to wisdom through her pure love. He sought in her not so much the Eve as the Madonna.

In these minds the thought, which glitters in all the legends of chivalry, shines in broad intellectual effulgence, not to be misinterpreted. And their thought is reverenced by the world, though it lies so far from them as yet, so far, that it seems as though a gulf of Death lay between.

Even with such men the practice was often widely different from the mental faith. I say mental, for if the heart were thoroughly alive with it, the practice could not be dissonant. Lord Herbert's was a marriage of convention, made for him at fifteen; he was not discontented with it, but looked only to the advantages it brought of perpetuating his family on the basis of a great fortune. He paid, in act, what he considered a dutiful attention to the bond; his thoughts travelled elsewhere, and, while forming a high ideal of the companionship of minds in marriage, he seems never to have doubted that its realization must be postponed to some other stage of being. Dante, almost immediately after the death of Beatrice, married a lady chosen for him by his friends.[5]

Centuries have passed since, but civilized Europe is still in a transition state about marriage, not only in practice, but in thought. A great majority of societies and individuals are still doubtful whether earthly marriage is to be a union of souls, or merely a contract of convenience and utility. Were woman established in the rights of an immortal being, this could not be. She would not in some countries be given away by her father, with scarcely more respect for her own feelings than is shown by the Indian chief, who sells his daughter for a horse, and beats her if she runs away from her new home. Nor, in societies where her choice is left free, would she be perverted, by the current of opinion that seizes her, into the belief that she must marry, if it be only to find a protector, and a home of her own.

---

[1]   *on this side idolatry*   Allusion to Ben Jonson's statement in the short piece "On Shakespeare," published in the posthumous volume *Timber, or Discoveries made upon men and matter.* "I loved the man [Shakespeare], and do honour his memory on this side idolatry as much as any."

[2]   *The meeting ... abler soul*   See "The Ecstasy" (1633) by English poet John Donne.

[3]   *Were not ... them such*   See "An Ode upon a Question Moved, Whether Love Should Continue for Ever?" (1665) by English poet Edward Herbert, 1st Baron of Cherbury.

[4]   *Calderon's Justina ... temporal happiness*   Fuller alludes to a brave and pious female character in *El mágico prodigioso* ("The Mighty Magician," 1637) by Spanish playwright Pedro Calderón de la Barca.

[5]   *Dante ... his friends*   Italian poet Dante Alighieri (c. 1265–1321) immortalized his childhood sweetheart Beatrice Portinari (1265–90) in his epic Christian allegory *The Divine Comedy*, where she serves as the protagonist's guide through Paradise. Dante was betrothed to Gemma Donati around the age of eleven, and married her around 1285.

Neither would man, if he thought that the connection was of permanent importance, enter upon it so lightly. He would not deem it a trifle, that he was to enter into the closest relations with another soul, which, if not eternal in themselves, must eternally affect his growth.

Neither, did he believe woman capable of friendship, would he, by rash haste, lose the chance of finding a friend in the person who might, probably, live half a century by his side. Did love to his mind partake of infinity, he would not miss his chance of its revelations, that he might the sooner rest from his weariness by a bright fireside, and have a sweet and graceful attendant, "devoted to him alone." Were he a step higher, he would not carelessly enter into a relation, where he might not be able to do the duty of a friend, as well as a protector from external ill, to the other party, and have a being in his power pining for sympathy, intelligence, and aid, that he could not give.

Where the thought of equality has become pervasive, it shows itself in four kinds.

The household partnership. In our country the woman looks for a "smart but kind" husband, the man for a "capable, sweet-tempered" wife.

The man furnishes the house, the woman regulates it. Their relation is one of mutual esteem, mutual dependence. Their talk is of business, their affection shows itself by practical kindness. They know that life goes more smoothly and cheerfully to each for the other's aid; they are grateful and content. The wife praises her husband as a "good provider," the husband in return compliments her as a "capital housekeeper." This relation is good as far as it goes.

Next comes a closer tie which takes the two forms, either of intellectual companionship, or mutual idolatry. The last, we suppose, is to no one a pleasing subject of contemplation. The parties weaken and narrow one another; they lock the gate against all the glories of the universe that they may live in a cell together. To themselves they seem the only wise, to all others steeped in infatuation, the gods smile as they look forward to the crisis of cure, to men the woman seems an unlovely siren,[1] to women the man an effeminate boy.

The other form, of intellectual companionship, has become more and more frequent. Men engaged in public life, literary men, and artists have often found in their wives companions and confidants in thought no less than in feeling. And, as in the course of things the intellectual development of woman has spread wider and risen higher, they have, not unfrequently, shared the same employment. As in the case of Roland and his wife,[2] who were friends in the household and the nation's councils, read together, regulated home affairs, or prepared public documents together indifferently.

It is very pleasant, in letters begun by Roland and finished by his wife, to see the harmony of mind and the difference of nature, one thought, but various ways of treating it.

This is one of the best instances of a marriage of friendship. It was only friendship, whose basis was esteem; probably neither party knew love, except by name.

Roland was a good man, worthy to esteem and be esteemed, his wife as deserving of admiration as able to do without it. Madame Roland is the fairest specimen we have yet of her class, as clear to discern her aim, as valiant to pursue it, as Spenser's Britomart, austerely set apart from all that did not belong to her, whether as woman or as mind. She is an antetype[3] of a class to which the coming time will afford a field, the Spartan[4] matron, brought by the culture of a book-furnishing age to intellectual consciousness and expansion.

Self-sufficing strength and clear-sightedness were in her combined with a power of deep and calm affection. The page of her life is one of unsullied dignity.

Her appeal to posterity is one against the injustice of those who committed such crimes in the name of liberty. She makes it in behalf of herself and her husband. I would put beside it on the shelf a little volume, containing a similar appeal from the verdict of contemporaries to that of mankind, that of Godwin in behalf of his wife, the celebrated, the by most men detested

---

[1]   *siren* Mythical creature, part woman and part bird, whose enchanted song is said to lure sailors to their destruction.

[2]   *Roland and his wife* Fuller refers again to Marie-Jeanne Roland de la Platière and to her husband, French revolutionary Jean-Marie Roland de la Platière (1734–93).

[3]   *antetype* Predecessor.

[4]   *Spartan* With the spirit of the ancient Greek culture known for valuing bravery and militarism.

Mary Wollstonecraft.[1] In his view it was an appeal from the injustice of those who did such wrong in the name of virtue.

Were this little book interesting for no other cause, it would be so for the generous affection evinced under the peculiar circumstances. This man had courage to love and honor this woman in the face of the world's verdict, and of all that was repulsive in her own past history. He believed he saw of what soul she was, and that the thoughts she had struggled to act out were noble. He loved her and he defended her for the meaning and tendency of her inner life. It was a good fact.

Mary Wollstonecraft, like Madame Dudevant[2] (commonly known as George) in our day, was a woman whose existence better proved the need of some new interpretation of woman's rights, than anything she wrote. Such women as these, rich in genius, of most tender sympathies, and capable of high virtue and a chastened harmony, ought not to find themselves by birth in a place so narrow, that in breaking bonds they become outlaws. Were there as much room in the world for such, as in Spenser's poem for Britomart, they would not run their heads so wildly against its laws. They find their way at last to purer air, but the world will not take off the brand it has set upon them. The champion of the rights of woman found in Godwin one who pleads her own cause like a brother. George Sand smokes, wears male attire, wishes to be addressed as *Mon frère*;[3] perhaps, if she found those who were as brothers indeed, she would not care whether she were brother or sister.

We rejoice to see that she, who expresses such a painful contempt for men in most of her works, as shows she must have known great wrong from them, in *La Roche Mauprat*,[4] depicting one raised, by the workings of love, from the depths of savage sensualism to a moral and intellectual life. It was love for a pure object, for a steadfast woman, one of those who, the Italian said, could make the stair to heaven.

Women like Sand will speak now, and cannot be silenced; their characters and their eloquence alike foretell an era when such as they shall easier learn to lead true lives. But though such forebode, not such shall be the parents of it. Those who would reform the world must show that they do not speak in the heat of wild impulse; their lives must be unstained by passionate error; they must be severe lawgivers to themselves. As to their transgressions and opinions, it may be observed, that the resolve of Eloisa to be only the mistress of Abelard, was that of one who saw the contract of marriage a seal of degradation. Wherever abuses of this sort are seen, the timid will suffer, the bold protest. But society is in the right to outlaw them till she has revised her law, and she must be taught to do so, by one who speaks with authority, not in anger and haste.

If Godwin's choice of the calumniated authoress of the "Rights of Woman," for his honored wife, be a sign of a new era, no less so is an article of great learning and eloquence, published several years since in an English review, where the writer, in doing full justice to Eloisa, shows his bitter regret that she lives not now to love him, who might have known better how to prize her love than did the egotistical Abelard.

These marriages, these characters, with all their imperfections, express an onward tendency. They speak of aspiration of soul, of energy of mind, seeking clearness and freedom. Of a like promise are the tracts now publishing by Goodwyn Barmby (the European Pariah as he calls himself) and his wife Catharine.[5] Whatever we may think of their measures, we see them in wedlock, the two minds are wed by the only contract that can permanently avail, of a common faith, and a common purpose.

We might mention instances, nearer home, of minds, partners in work and in life, sharing together, on equal terms, public and private interests, and which

---

[1]   *Godwin … Mary Wollstonecraft* Mary Wollstonecraft's 1792 *A Vindication of the Rights of Woman* was among the most influential works to argue for women's education and intellectual rights in the eighteenth century. Her husband, philosopher William Godwin, published the biography *Memoirs of the Author of A Vindication of the Rights of Woman* in 1798 after her death, inciting controversy in Britain for his frank treatment of her unconventional life.

[2]   *Madame Dudevant* Reference to the popular French novelist Amantine Lucile Aurore Dupin (married to Casimir Dudevant until their separation in 1835), famous for wearing men's clothes and for adopting the masculine pseudonym George Sand.

[3]   *Mon frère* French: My brother.

[4]   *La Roche Mauprat* 1837 novel by Sand.

[5]   *Goodwyn Barmby … his wife Catharine* English philosophers and supporters of socialism and women's rights (1820–81 and 1816–53, respectively).

have not on any side that aspect of offence which characterizes the attitude of the last named; persons who steer straight onward, and in our freer life have not been obliged to run their heads against any wall. But the principles which guide them might, under petrified or oppressive institutions, have made them warlike, paradoxical, or, in some sense, Pariahs. The phenomenon is different, the law the same, in all these cases. Men and women have been obliged to build their house from the very foundation. If they found stone ready in the quarry, they took it peaceably, otherwise they alarmed the country by pulling down old towers to get materials.

These are all instances of marriage as intellectual companionship. The parties meet mind to mind, and a mutual trust is excited which can buckler[1] them against a million. They work together for a common purpose, and, in all these instances, with the same implement, the pen.

A pleasing expression in this kind is afforded by the union in the names of the Howitts. William and Mary Howitt[2] we heard named together for years, supposing them to be brother and sister; the equality of labors and reputation, even so, was auspicious, more so, now we find them man and wife. In his late work on Germany, Howitt mentions his wife with pride, as one among the constellation of distinguished English women, and in a graceful, simple manner.

In naming these instances we do not mean to imply that community of employment is an essential to union of this sort, more than to the union of friendship. Harmony exists in difference no less than in likeness, if only the same keynote govern both parts. Woman the poem, man the poet; woman the heart, man the head; such divisions are only important when they are never to be transcended. If nature is never bound down, nor the voice of inspiration stifled, that is enough. We are pleased that women should write and speak, if they feel the need of it, from having something to tell; but silence for a hundred years would be as well, if that silence be from divine command, and not from man's tradition.

While Goetz von Berlichingen[3] rides to battle, his wife is busy in the kitchen; but difference of occupation does not prevent that community of life, that perfect esteem, with which he says,

Whom God loves, to him gives he such a wife!

Manzoni thus dedicates his *Adelchi*:[4]

To his beloved and venerated wife, Enrichetta Luigia Blondel, who, with conjugal affections and maternal wisdom, has preserved a virgin mind, the author dedicates this Adelchi, grieving that he could not, by a more splendid and more durable monument, honor the dear name and the memory of so many virtues.

The relation could not be fairer, nor more equal, if she too had written poems. Yet the position of the parties might have been the reverse as well; the woman might have sung the deeds, given voice to the life of the man, and beauty would have been the result, as we see in pictures of Arcadia[5] the nymph singing to the shepherds, or the shepherd with his pipe allures the nymphs, either makes a good picture. The sounding lyre requires not muscular strength, but energy of soul to animate the hand which can control it. Nature seems to delight in varying her arrangements, as if to show that she will be fettered by no rule, and we must admit the same varieties that she admits.

I have not spoken of the higher grade of marriage union, the religious, which may be expressed as pilgrimage towards a common shrine. This includes the others; home sympathies, and household wisdom, for these pilgrims must know how to assist one another to carry their burdens along the dusty way; intellectual communion, for how sad it would be on such a journey to have a companion to whom you could not communicate thoughts and aspirations, as they sprang to life, who would have no feeling for the more and more glorious prospects that open as we advance, who would

---

[1] *buckler* Shield.

[2] *William and Mary Howitt* English authors and translators (1792–1879 and 1799–1888, respectively) who worked closely together throughout their careers.

[3] *Goetz von Berlichingen* Famed German knight and mercenary (1480–1562), depicted by Goethe in his 1773 play of the same name, from which Fuller quotes below.

[4] *Adelchi* Tragic 1822 play written by Alessandro Manzoni.

[5] *Arcadia* Region of Greece, often depicted as a bucolic paradise in classical literature.

never see the flowers that may be gathered by the most industrious traveler. It must include all these. Such a fellow pilgrim Count Zinzendorf[1] seems to have found in his countess of whom he thus writes.

> Twenty-five years' experience has shown me that just the help-mate whom I have is the only one that could suit my vocation. Who else could have so carried through my family affairs? Who lived so spotlessly before the world? Who so wisely aided me in my rejection of a dry morality? Who so clearly set aside the Pharisaism[2] which, as years passed, threatened to creep in among us? Who so deeply discerned as to the spirits of delusion which sought to bewilder us? Who would have governed my whole economy so wisely, richly, and hospitably when circumstances commanded? Who have taken indifferently the part of servant or mistress, without on the one side affecting an especial spirituality, on the other being sullied by any worldly pride? Who, in a community where all ranks are eager to be on a level, would, from wise and real causes, have known how to maintain inward and outward distinctions? Who, without a murmur, have seen her husband encounter such dangers by land and sea? Who undertaken with him and sustained such astonishing pilgrimages? Who amid such difficulties always held up her head, and supported me? Who found so many hundred thousands and acquitted them on her own credit? And, finally, who, of all human beings, would so well understand and interpret to others my inner and outer being as this one, of such nobleness in her way of thinking, such great intellectual capacity, and free from the theological perplexities that enveloped me?

An observer[3] adds this testimony.

We may in many marriages regard it as the best arrangement, if the man has so much advantage over his wife that she can, without much thought of her own, be, by him, led and directed, as by a father. But it was not so with the Count and his consort. She was not made to be a copy; she was an original; and, while she loved and honored him, she thought for herself on all subjects with so much intelligence, that he could and did look on her as sister and friend also.

Such a woman is the sister and friend of all beings, as the worthy man is their brother and helper.

Another sign of the time is furnished by the triumphs of female authorship. These have been great and constantly increasing. They have taken possession of so many provinces for which men had pronounced them unfit, that though these still declare there are some inaccessible to them, it is difficult to say just *where* they must stop.

The shining names of famous women have cast light upon the path of the sex, and many obstructions have been removed. When a Montague[4] could learn better than her brother, and use her lore to such purpose afterwards as an observer, it seemed amiss to hinder women from preparing themselves to see, or from seeing all they could when prepared. Since Somerville[5] has achieved so much, will any young girl be prevented from attaining a knowledge of the physical sciences, if she wishes it? De Staël's[6] name was not so clear of offence; she could not forget the woman in the thought; while she was instructing you as a mind, she wished to be admired as a woman; sentimental tears often dimmed the eagle glance. Her intellect, too, with all its splendor, trained in a drawing room, fed on flattery, was tainted and flawed; yet its beams make the obscurest school house in New England warmer and lighter to the little rugged girls, who are gathered together on

---

1   *Count Zinzendorf* Nikolaus Ludwig, Count von Zinzendorf (1700–60), German Protestant religious leader, bishop of the Moravian Church. His first wife was hymnodist Erdmuthe Dorothea (1700–56).

2   *Pharisaism* Hypocrisy; reference to the Pharisees, an ancient orthodox Jewish sect often referred to in the New Testament as overly invested in religious law.

3   [Fuller's note] Spangenberg. [August Gottlieb Spangenberg (1704–92), German theologian, who became bishop of the Moravian Church after the death of Count Zinzendorf.]

4   *Montague* Lady Mary Wortley Montagu (1689–1762), English writer particularly known for her letters about life and culture—especially about the lives of women—in the Ottoman Empire, where she lived for a period with her ambassador husband.

5   *Somerville* Mary Somerville (1780–1872), Scottish scientist and mathematician.

6   *De Staël* Germaine de Staël (1766–1817), commonly known as Madame de Staël, French intellectual, salon leader, and proponent of the Romantic movement.

its wooden bench. They may never through life hear her name, but she is not the less their benefactress.

This influence has been such that the aim certainly is how, in arranging school instruction for girls, to give them as fair a field as boys. These arrangements are made as yet with little judgment or intelligence, just as the tutors of Jane Grey,[1] and the other famous women of her time, taught them Latin and Greek, because they knew nothing else themselves, so now the improvement in the education of girls is made by giving them gentlemen as teachers, who only teach what has been taught themselves at college, while methods and topics need revision for those new cases, which could better be made by those who had experienced the same wants. Women are often at the head of these institutions, but they have as yet seldom been thinking women, capable to organize a new whole for the wants of the time, and choose persons to officiate in the departments. And when some portion of education is got of a good sort from the school, the tone of society, the much larger proportion received from the world, contradicts its purport. Yet books have not been furnished, and a little elementary instruction been given in vain. Women are better aware how large and rich the universe is, not so easily blinded by the narrowness and partial views of a home circle.

Whether much or little has or will be done, whether women will add to the talent of narration, the power of systematizing, whether they will carve marble as well as draw, is not important. But that it should be acknowledged that they have intellect which needs developing, that they should not be considered complete, if beings of affection and habit alone, is important.

Yet even this acknowledgment, rather obtained by woman than proffered by man, has been sullied by the usual selfishness. So much is said of women being better educated [so] that they may be better companions and mothers *of men*! They should be fit for such companionship, and we have mentioned with satisfaction instances where it has been established. Earth knows no fairer, holier relation than that of a mother.

But a being of infinite scope must not be treated with an exclusive view to any one relation. Give the soul free course, let the organization be freely developed, and the being will be fit for any and every relation to which it may be called. The intellect, no more than the sense of hearing, is to be cultivated, [not][2] that she may be a more valuable companion to man, but because the Power who gave a power by its mere existence signifies that it must be brought out towards perfection.

In this regard, of self-dependence and a greater simplicity and fulness of being, we must hail as a preliminary the increase of the class contemptuously designated as old maids.

We cannot wonder at the aversion with which old bachelors and old maids have been regarded. Marriage is the natural means of forming a sphere, of taking root on the earth: it requires more strength to do this without such an opening, very many have failed of this, and their imperfections have been in everyone's way. They have been more partial, more harsh, more officious and impertinent than others. Those who have a complete experience of the human instincts, have a distrust as to whether they can be thoroughly human and humane, such as is hinted at in the saying, "Old maids' and bachelors' children are well cared for," which derides at once their ignorance and their presumption.

Yet the business of society has become so complex, that it could now scarcely be carried on without the presence of these despised auxiliaries, and detachments from the army of aunts and uncles are wanted to stop gaps in every hedge. They rove about, mental and moral Ishmaelites,[3] pitching their tents amid the fixed and ornamented habitations of men.

They thus gain a wider, if not so deep, experience. They are not so intimate with others, but thrown more upon themselves, and if they do not there find peace and incessant life, there is none to flatter them that they are not very poor and very mean.

A position which so constantly admonishes may be of inestimable benefit. The person may gain, undistracted by other relationships, a closer communion

---

1   *Jane Grey* English noblewoman famous for her nine days' reign as Queen of England (10–19 July 1553), after which she was deposed by Mary Tudor (subsequently Mary I) and eventually executed. Prior to her reign she was also famous for her learnedness, especially for her proficiency in languages—though she is said to have lamented the strictness of her education and upbringing.

2   *not* Omitted from the original in an apparent error.

3   *Ishmaelites* Outcasts or wanderers; in the Book of Genesis, Abraham casts out his mistress Hagar and his illegitimate son Ishmael, after which the mother and son roam the wilderness for an extended period.

with the One. Such a use is made of it by saints and sibyls. Or she may be one of the lay sisters of charity, or more humbly only the useful drudge of all men, or the intellectual interpreter of the varied life she sees.

Or she may combine all these. Not "needing to care that she may please a husband," a frail and limited being, all her thoughts may turn to the centre, and by steadfast contemplation enter into the secret of truth and love, use it for the use of all men, instead of a chosen few, and interpret through it all the forms of life.

Saints and geniuses have often chosen a lonely position, in the faith that, if undisturbed by the pressure of near ties, they could give themselves up to the inspiring spirit, it would enable them to understand and reproduce life better than actual experience could.

How many old maids take this high stand, we cannot say; it is an unhappy fact that too many of those who come before the eye are gossips rather, and not always good-natured gossips. But, if these abuse, and none make the best of their vocation, yet it has not failed to produce some good fruit. It has been seen by others, if not by themselves, that beings likely to be left alone need to be fortified and furnished within themselves, and education and thought have tended more and more to regard beings as related to absolute Being, as well as to other men. It has been seen that as the loss of no bond ought to destroy a human being, so ought the missing of none to hinder him from growing. And thus a circumstance of the time has helped to put woman on the true platform. Perhaps the next generation will look deeper into this matter, and find that contempt is put on old maids, or old women at all, merely because they do not use the elixir which will keep the soul always young. No one thinks of Michael Angelo's Persican Sibyl, or St. Theresa, or Tasso's Leonora, or the Greek Electra[1] as an old maid, though all had reached the period in life's course appointed to take that degree.

Even among the North American Indians, a race of men as completely engaged in mere instinctive life as almost any in the world, and where each chief, keeping many wives as useful servants, of course looks with no kind eye on celibacy in woman, it was excused in the following instance mentioned by Mrs. Jameson.[2] A woman dreamt in youth that she was betrothed to the sun. She built her a wigwam apart, filled it with emblems of her alliance and means of an independent life. There she passed her days, sustained by her own exertions, and true to her supposed engagement.

In any tribe, we believe, a woman, who lived as if she was betrothed to the sun, would be tolerated, and the rays which made her youth blossom sweetly would crown her with a halo in age.

There is on this subject a nobler view than heretofore, if not the noblest, and we greet improvement here, as much as on the subject of marriage. Both are fertile themes, but time permits not here to explore them.

If larger intellectual resources begin to be deemed necessary to woman, still more is a spiritual dignity in her, or even the mere assumption of it listened to with respect. Joanna Southcote, and Mother Ann Lee[3] are sure of a band of disciples; Ecstatica, Dolorosa,[4] of enraptured believers who will visit them in their lowly huts, and wait for hours to revere them in their trances. The foreign noble traverses land and sea to hear a few words from the lips of the lowly peasant girl, whom he believes especially visited by the Most High. Very beautiful in this way was the influence of the invalid of St. Petersburg, as described by De Maistre.[5]

To this region, however misunderstood and ill-developed, belong the phenomena of Magnetism, or

---

[1] *Michael Angelo's Persican Sibyl* Legendary prophetess, depicted in Michelangelo's painting in the Sistine Chapel; *St. Theresa* Spanish mystic and Carmelite nun (1515–82); *Tasso's Leonora* Eleonora d'Este (1515–75), Italian noblewoman rumored to have been the lover of the poet Torquato Tasso (1544–95); *Greek Electra* Character of Classical literature, who kills her mother Clytemnestra and Clytemnestra's lover Aegisthus as revenge for the murder of her father, Agamemnon. Electra later marries Pylades.

[2] *Mrs. Jameson* Anglo-Irish art historian and traveler Anna Brownell Jameson, author of the travel memoir *Winter Studies and Summer Rambles in Canada* (1838).

[3] *Joanna Southcote* English religious leader and self-described prophet Joanna Southcott (1750–1814), who founded a religious sect that continued after her death; *Mother Ann Lee* Founder of the Shaker religious movement, officially known as the United Society of Believers in Christ's Second Appearing (1736–84).

[4] *Ecstatica, Dolorosa* Latin: (religious) ecstasy and grief or suffering; used here as symbolic female names to represent religious ideals.

[5] *the invalid … De Maistre* The exact reference here is unclear; Joseph de Maistre (1753–1821) was a French counter-Enlightenment philosopher and monarchist.

Mesmerism,[1] as it is now often called, where the trance of the Ecstatica purports to be produced by the agency of one human being on another, instead of, as in her case, direct from the spirit.

The worldling has his sneer here as about the services of religion. "The churches can always be filled with women." "Show me a man in one of your magnetic states, and I will believe."

Women are indeed the easy victims of priestcraft, or self-delusion, but this might not be, if the intellect was developed in proportion to the other powers. They would then have a regulator and be in better equipoise, yet must retain the same nervous susceptibility, while their physical structure is such as it is.

It is with just that hope that we welcome everything that tends to strengthen the fibre and develop the nature on more sides. When the intellect and affections are in harmony, when intellectual consciousness is calm and deep, inspiration will not be confounded with fancy.

The electrical, the magnetic element in woman has not been fairly developed at any period. Everything might be expected from it; she has far more of it than man. This is commonly expressed by saying that her intuitions are more rapid and more correct.

But I cannot enlarge upon this here, except to say that on this side is highest promise. Should I speak of it fully, my title should be Cassandra, my topic the Seeress of Prevorst,[2] the first, or the best observed subject of magnetism in our times, and who, like her ancestresses at Delphos,[3] was roused to ecstasy or frenzy by the touch of the laurel.

In such cases worldlings sneer, but reverent men learn wondrous news, either from the person observed, or by the thoughts caused in themselves by the observation.

Fenelon learns from Guyon,[4] Kerner from his Seeress what we fain would know. But to appreciate such disclosures one must be a child, and here the phrase, "women children," may perhaps be interpreted aright, that only little children shall enter into the kingdom of heaven.[5]

All these motions of the time, tides that betoken a waxing moon, overflow upon our own land. The world at large is readier to let woman learn and manifest the capacities of her nature than it ever was before, and here is a less encumbered field, and freer air than anywhere else. And it ought to be so; we ought to pay for Isabella's[6] jewels.

The names of nations are feminine. Religion, Virtue, and Victory are feminine. To those who have a superstition as to outward signs, it is not without significance that the name of the Queen of our mother-land should at this crisis be Victoria.[7] Victoria the First. Perhaps to us it may be given to disclose the era there outwardly presaged.

Women here are much better situated than men. Good books are allowed with more time to read them. They are not so early forced into the bustle of life, nor so weighed down by demands for outward success. The perpetual changes, incident to our society, make the blood circulate freely through the body politic, and, if not favorable at present to the grace and bloom of life, they are so to activity, resource, and would be to reflection but for a low materialist tendency, from which the women are generally exempt.

They have time to think, and no traditions chain them, and few conventionalities compared with what must be met in other nations. There is no reason why the fact of a constant revelation should be hid from them, and when the mind once is awakened by that, it will not be restrained by the past, but fly to seek the seeds of a heavenly future.

---

1   *Magnetism, or Mesmerism*   Natural energy transmission or hypnosis, a theory of which was developed by German doctor Franz Mesmer in the eighteenth century, and which became widely popular in the nineteenth.

2   *Seeress of Prevorst*   Reference to the German mystic Friederike Hauffe (1801–29), who was known as the Seeress of Prevorst. Her trances were described by the physician and poet Justinius Kerner in his book *The Seeress of Prevorst* (1829).

3   *Delphos*   Delphi, site of the Temple of Apollo in ancient Greece, presided over by a priestess known as the Oracle of Delphi.

4   *Fenelon learns from Guyon*   Jeanne Guyon (1648–1717) was a French mystic, accused of heresy by the Catholic Church; her cousin François Fénelon (1651–1715), a Catholic archbishop, was among her most ardent supporters.

5   *little children ... of heaven*   See Matthew 19.14: "But Jesus said, Suffer little children, and forbid them not, to come unto me: for of such is the kingdom of heaven." See also Mark 10.14–15.

6   *Isabella*   I.e., Isabella I of Castile—referring, again, to her sponsoring of the "discovery" of the American continent.

7   *Victoria*   Queen Victoria (r. 1837–1901).

Their employments are more favorable to the inward life than those of the men.

Woman is not addressed religiously here, more than elsewhere. She is told to be worthy to be the mother of a Washington, or the companion of some good man. But in many, many instances, she has already learnt that all bribes have the same flaw; that truth and good are to be sought for themselves alone. And already an ideal sweetness floats over many forms, shines in many eyes.

Already deep questions are put by young girls on the great theme, What shall I do to inherit eternal life?[1]

Men are very courteous to them. They praise them often, check[2] them seldom. There is some chivalry in the feelings towards "the ladies," which gives them the best seats in the stage-coach, frequent admission not only to lectures of all sorts, but to courts of justice, halls of legislature, reform conventions. The newspaper editor "would be better pleased that the Lady's Book[3] were filled up exclusively by ladies. It would then, indeed, be a true gem, worthy to be presented by young men to the mistresses of their affections." Can gallantry go farther?

In this country is venerated, wherever seen, the character which Goethe spoke of as an Ideal. "The excellent woman is she who, if the husband dies, can be a father to the children." And this, if rightly read, tells a great deal.

Women who speak in public, if they have a moral power, such as has been felt from Angelina Grimke and Abby Kelly,[4] that is, if they speak for conscience' sake, to serve a cause which they hold sacred, invariably subdue the prejudices of their hearers, and excite an interest proportionate to the aversion with which it had been the purpose to regard them.

A passage in a private letter so happily illustrates this, that I take the liberty to make use of it, though there is not opportunity to ask leave either of the writer or owner of the letter. I think they will pardon me when they see it in print; it is so good, that as many as possible should have the benefit of it.

Abby Kelly in the Town-House of——

The scene was not unheroic—to see that woman, true to humanity and her own nature, a centre of rude eyes and tongues, even gentlemen feeling licensed to make part of a species of mob around a female out of her sphere. As she took her seat in the desk amid the great noise, and in the throng full, like a wave, of something to ensue, I saw her humanity in a gentleness and unpretension, tenderly open to the sphere around her, and, had she not been supported by the power of the will of genuineness and principle, she would have failed. It led her to prayer, which, in woman especially, is childlike; sensibility and will going to the side of God and looking up to him; and humanity was poured out in aspiration.

She acted like a gentle hero, with her mild decision and womanly calmness. All heroism is mild and quiet and gentle, for it is life and possession, and combativeness and firmness show a want of actualness. She is as earnest, fresh, and simple as when she first entered the crusade. I think she did much good, more than the men in her place could do, for woman feels more as being and reproducing; this brings the subject more into home relations. Men speak through and mostly from intellect, and this addresses itself in others, which creates and is combative.

Not easily shall we find elsewhere, or before this time, any written observations on the same subject, so delicate and profound.

The late Dr. Channing,[5] whose enlarged and tender and religious nature shared every onward impulse of his time, though his thoughts followed his wishes with a deliberative caution, which belonged to his habits and temperament, was greatly interested in these expectations for women. His own treatment of them

---

[1]   *What shall ... eternal life?*   See Matthew 19.16: "And, behold, one came and said unto him, Good Master, what good thing shall I do, that I may have eternal life?"

[2]   *check* Criticize.

[3]   *Lady's Book* Allusion to literary periodicals such as *Godey's Lady's Book*, which were aimed particularly at female readers but whose contributing authors were men at least as often as they were women.

[4]   *Angelina Grimke and Abby Kelly* Prominent abolitionists and women's rights activists (1805–79 and 1811–87, respectively), famous as orators during a time when political oratory was almost exclusively the field of men.

[5]   *The late Dr. Channing* William Ellery Channing (1780–1842), prominent Unitarian preacher.

was absolutely and thoroughly religious. He regarded them as souls, each of which had a destiny of its own, incalculable to other minds, and whose leading it must follow, guided by the light of a private conscience. He had sentiment, delicacy, kindness, taste, but they were all pervaded and ruled by this one thought, that all beings had souls, and must vindicate their own inheritance. Thus all beings were treated by him with an equal, and sweet, though solemn courtesy. The young and unknown, the woman and the child, all felt themselves regarded with an infinite expectation, from which there was no reaction to vulgar prejudice. He demanded of all he met, to use his favorite phrase, "great truths."

His memory, every way dear and reverend, is by many especially cherished for this intercourse of unbroken respect.

At one time when the progress of Harriet Martineau[1] through this country, Angelina Grimke's appearance in public, and the visit of Mrs. Jameson had turned his thoughts to this subject, he expressed high hopes as to what the coming era would bring to woman. He had been much pleased with the dignified courage of Mrs. Jameson in taking up the defence of her sex in a way from which women usually shrink, because, if they express themselves on such subjects with sufficient force and clearness to do any good, they are exposed to assaults whose vulgarity makes them painful. In intercourse with such a woman, he had shared her indignation at the base injustice, in many respects, and in many regions done to the sex; and been led to think of it far more than ever before. He seemed to think that he might some time write upon the subject. That his aid is withdrawn from the cause is a subject of great regret, for on this question, as on others, he would have known how to sum up the evidence and take, in the noblest spirit, middle ground. He always furnished a platform on which opposing parties could stand, and look at one another under the influence of his mildness and enlightened candor.

Two younger thinkers, men both, have uttered noble prophecies, auspicious for woman. Kinmont,[2] all whose thoughts tended towards the establishment of the reign of love and peace, thought that the inevitable means of this would be an increased predominance given to the idea of woman. Had he lived longer to see the growth of the peace party, the reforms in life and medical practice which seek to substitute water for wine and drugs, pulse for animal food,[3] he would have been confirmed in his view of the way in which the desired changes are to be effected.

In this connection I must mention Shelley,[4] who, like all men of genius, shared the feminine development, and unlike many, knew it. His life was one of the first pulse-beats in the present reform-growth. He, too, abhorred blood and heat, and, by his system and his song, tended to reinstate a plant-like gentleness in the development of energy. In harmony with this his ideas of marriage were lofty, and of course no less so of woman, her nature, and destiny.

For woman, if by a sympathy as to outward condition she is led to aid the enfranchisement of the slave, must no less so, by inward tendency, to favor measures which promise to bring the world more thoroughly and deeply into harmony with her nature. When the lamb takes place of the lion as the emblem of nations, both women and men will be as children of one spirit, perpetual learners of the word and doers thereof, not hearers only.

A writer in a late number of the New York Pathfinder, in two articles headed "Femality," has uttered a still more pregnant word than any we have named. He views woman truly from the soul, and not from society, and the depth and leading of his thoughts is proportionably remarkable. He views the feminine nature as a harmonizer of the vehement elements, and this has often been hinted elsewhere; but what he expresses most forcibly is the lyrical, the inspiring and inspired apprehensiveness of her being.

---

[1] *Harriet Martineau* British sociologist who described her tour of the United States in 1834 in the influential (and controversial) text *Society in America* (1837).

[2] *Kinmont* Scottish educator Alexander Kinmont (1799–1838).

[3] *pulse for animal food* It was beginning to be recognized in the 1840s that humans could obtain needed protein from plant food—in particular, from pulses such as beans and chickpeas—rather than from eating other animals. (A small group of vegetarians became vocal in New England in the 1840s; Transcendentalist thinker Amos Bronson Alcott, who was what would today be described as vegan, was the best known of the group.)

[4] *Shelley* English Romantic poet Percy Bysshe Shelley (1792–1822), husband of novelist Mary Shelley (1797–1851) and proponent of various reform movements such as vegetarianism and nonviolence.

Had I room to dwell upon this topic, I could not say anything so precise, so near the heart of the matter, as may be found in that article; but, as it is, I can only indicate, not declare, my view.

There are two aspects of woman's nature, expressed by the ancients as Muse[1] and Minerva. It is the former to which the writer in the Pathfinder looks. It is the latter which Wordsworth[2] has in mind, when he says,

> With a placid brow,
> Which woman ne'er should forfeit, keep thy vow.

The especial genius of woman I believe to be electrical in movement, intuitive in function, spiritual in tendency. She is great not so easily in classification, or re-creation, as in an instinctive seizure of causes, and a simple breathing out of what she receives that has the singleness of life, rather than the selecting or energizing of art.

More native to her is it to be the living model of the artist, than to set apart from herself any one form in objective reality; more native to inspire and receive the poem than to create it. In so far as soul is in her completely developed, all soul is the same; but as far as it is modified in her as woman, it flows, it breathes, it sings, rather than deposits soil, or finishes work, and that which is especially feminine flushes in blossom the face of earth, and pervades like air and water all this seeming solid globe, daily renewing and purifying its life. Such may be the especially feminine element, spoken of as Femality. But it is no more the order of nature that it should be incarnated pure in any form, than that the masculine energy should exist unmingled with it in any form.

Male and female represent the two sides of the great radical dualism. But, in fact, they are perpetually passing into one another. Fluid hardens to solid, solid rushes to fluid. There is no wholly masculine man, no purely feminine woman.

History jeers at the attempts of physiologists to bind great original laws by the forms which flow from them. They make a rule; they say from observation, what can and cannot be. In vain! Nature provides exceptions to every rule. She sends women to battle, and sets Hercules spinning;[3] she enables women to bear immense burdens, cold, and frost; she enables the man, who feels maternal love, to nourish his infant like a mother. Of late she plays still gayer pranks. Not only she deprives organizations, but organs, of a necessary end. She enables people to read with the top of the head, and see with the pit of the stomach. Presently she will make a female Newton,[4] and a male Siren.

Man partakes of the feminine in the Apollo, woman of the masculine as Minerva.

Let us be wise and not impede the soul. Let her work as she will. Let us have one creative energy, one incessant revelation. Let it take what form it will, and let us not bind it by the past to man or woman, black or white. Jove sprang from Rhea, Pallas from Jove.[5] So let it be.

If it has been the tendency of the past remarks to call woman rather to the Minerva side—if I, unlike the more generous writer, have spoken from society no less than the soul—let it be pardoned. It is love that has caused this, love for many incarcerated souls that might be freed could the idea of religious self-dependence be established in them, could the weakening habit of dependence on others be broken up.

Every relation, every gradation of nature, is incalculably precious, but only to the soul which is poised upon itself, and to whom no loss, no change, can bring dull discord, for it is in harmony with the central soul.

If any individual live too much in relations, so that he becomes a stranger to the resources of his own nature, he falls after a while into a distraction,[6] or imbecility, from which he can only be cured by a time of isolation, which gives the renovating fountains time to rise up. With a society it is the same. Many minds, deprived of the traditionary or instinctive means of passing a

---

[1]   *Muse*   One of the nine female personifications of art and inspiration described in Greek and Roman mythology.

[2]   *Wordsworth*   English Romantic poet William Wordsworth (1770–1850); Fuller quotes from his 1829 poem "Liberty" below.

[3]   *sets Hercules spinning*   Several Greek and Roman myths describe a period during which the hero Hercules was made a servant to the Lydian queen Omphale, who forced him to perform traditionally feminine tasks such as spinning wool.

[4]   *Newton*   Reference to the English scientist and mathematician Isaac Newton (1642–1726).

[5]   *Jove … Jove*   In Greek and Roman mythology, the Titaness Rhea is the mother of Zeus (known by the Romans as Jove); Athena, often referred to with the honorific Pallas, was born from the head of Zeus.

[6]   *distraction*   Distress or madness.

cheerful existence, must find help in self-impulse or perish. It is therefore that while any elevation, in the view of union, is to be hailed with joy, we shall not decline celibacy as the great fact of the time. It is one from which no vow, no arrangement, can at present save a thinking mind. For now the rowers are pausing on their oars, they wait a change before they can pull together. All tends to illustrate the thought of a wise contemporary. Union is only possible to those who are units. To be fit for relations in time, souls, whether of man or woman, must be able to do without them in the spirit.

It is therefore that I would have woman lay aside all thought, such as she habitually cherishes, of being taught and led by men. I would have her, like the Indian girl, dedicate herself to the Sun, the Sun of Truth, and go nowhere if his beams did not make clear the path. I would have her free from compromise, from complaisance, from helplessness, because I would have her good enough and strong enough to love one and all beings, from the fulness, not the poverty of being.

Men, as at present instructed, will not help this work, because they also are under the slavery of habit. I have seen with delight their poetic impulses. A sister is the fairest ideal, and how nobly Wordsworth, and even Byron,[1] have written of a sister.

There is no sweeter sight than to see a father with his little daughter. Very vulgar men become refined to the eye when leading a little girl by the hand. At that moment the right relation between the sexes seems established, and you feel as if the man would aid in the noblest purpose, if you ask him in behalf of his little daughter. Once two fine figures stood before me, thus. The father of very intellectual aspect, his falcon eye softened by affection as he looked down on his fair child, she the image of himself, only more graceful and brilliant in expression. I was reminded of Southey's Kehama,[2] when lo, the dream was rudely broken. They were talking of education, and he said,

"I shall not have Maria brought too forward. If she knows too much, she will never find a husband; superior women hardly ever can."

"Surely," said his wife, with a blush, "you wish Maria to be as good and wise as she can, whether it will help her to marriage or not."

"No," he persisted, "I want her to have a sphere and a home, and someone to protect her when I am gone."

It was a trifling incident, but made a deep impression. I felt that the holiest relations fail to instruct the unprepared and perverted mind. If this man, indeed, would have looked at it on the other side, he was the last that would have been willing to have been taken himself for the home and protection he could give, but would have been much more likely to repeat the tale of Alcibiades with his phials.

But men do *not* look at both sides, and women must leave off asking them and being influenced by them, but retire within themselves, and explore the groundwork of being till they find their peculiar secret. Then when they come forth again, renovated and baptized, they will know how to turn all dross[3] to gold, and will be rich and free though they live in a hut, tranquil if in a crowd. Then their sweet singing shall not be from passionate impulse, but the lyrical overflow of a divine rapture, and a new music shall be elucidated from this many-chorded world.

Grant her then for a while the armor and the javelin. Let her put from her the press of other minds and meditate in virgin loneliness. The same idea shall reappear in due time as Muse, or Ceres, the all-kindly, patient Earth-Spirit.

I tire everyone with my Goethean illustrations. But it cannot be helped.

Goethe, the great mind which gave itself absolutely to the leadings of truth, and let rise through him the waves which are still advancing through the century, was its intellectual prophet. Those who know him see, daily, his thought fulfilled more and more, and they must speak of it, till his name weary and even nauseate, as all great names have in their time. And I cannot spare the reader, if such there be, his wonderful sight as to the prospects and wants of women.

---

[1] *Wordsworth, and even Byron* Both Wordsworth and Lord Byron wrote poetry addressed to their beloved sisters (in Byron's case a half-sister) Dorothy Wordsworth (1771–1855) and Augusta Mary Leigh (1783–1851), respectively. (Byron is also known, however, for his numerous affairs and his occasionally abusive relationships with women.)

[2] *Southey's Kehama* Reference to Robert Southey's epic poem *The Curse of Kehama* (1810).

[3] *dross* Waste matter produced during the smelting process.

As his Wilhelm grows in life and advances in wisdom, he becomes acquainted with women of more and more character, rising from Mariana to Macaria.[1]

Macaria, bound with the heavenly bodies in fixed revolutions, the centre of all relations, herself unrelated, expresses the Minerva side.

Mignon, the electrical, inspired lyrical nature.

All these women, though we see them in relations, we can think of as unrelated. They all are very individual, yet seem nowhere restrained. They satisfy for the present, yet arouse an infinite expectation.

The economist Theresa, the benevolent Natalia,[2] the fair Saint, have chosen a path, but their thoughts are not narrowed to it. The functions of life to them are not ends, but suggestions.

Thus to them all things are important, because none is necessary. Their different characters have fair play, and each is beautiful in its minute indications, for nothing is enforced or conventional, but everything, however slight, grows from the essential life of the being.

Mignon and Theresa wear male attire when they like, and it is graceful for them to do so, while Macaria is confined to her arm chair behind the green curtain, and the Fair Saint could not bear a speck of dust on her robe.

All things are in their places in this little world because all is natural and free, just as "there is room for everything out of doors." Yet all is rounded in by natural harmony which will always arise where Truth and Love are sought in the light of freedom.

Goethe's book bodes an era of freedom like its own, of "extraordinary generous seeking," and new revelations. New individualities shall be developed in the actual world, which shall advance upon it as gently as the figures come out upon his canvass.

A profound thinker has said "no married woman can represent the female world, for she belongs to her husband. The idea of woman must be represented by a virgin."[3]

But that is the very fault of marriage, and of the present relation between the sexes, that the woman does belong to the man, instead of forming a whole with him. Were it otherwise there would be no such limitation to the thought.

Woman, self-centred, would never be absorbed by any relation; it would be only an experience to her as to man. It is a vulgar error that love, *a* love to woman is her whole existence; she also is born for Truth and Love in their universal energy. Would she but assume her inheritance, Mary would not be the only Virgin Mother. Not Manzoni alone would celebrate in his wife the virgin mind with the maternal wisdom and conjugal affections. The soul is ever young, ever virgin.

And will not she soon appear? The woman who shall vindicate their birthright for all women; who shall teach them what to claim, and how to use what they obtain? Shall not her name be for her era Victoria, for her country and her life Virginia? Yet predictions are rash; she herself must teach us to give her the fitting name.

—1843

---

[1] *As his Wilhelm ... Macaria*   Here and over the next few paragraphs, Fuller references numerous female characters from Goethe's *Wilhelm Meister's Apprenticeship.*

[2] *Natalia*   Natalia of Nicomedia, wife of the martyr Saint Adrian (d. 306).

[3] *no married ... a virgin*   The source of this quotation is unknown.

David Walker

c. 1785/96 – 1830

First published in 1829, David Walker's *Appeal to the Coloured Citizens of the World* was among the most controversial publications of the antebellum period. Written in language as impassioned as it is deliberate, the pamphlet is an incisive condemnation of the institution of slavery and all who profited from it, calling for immediate emancipation and for the rise of a nationwide racial consciousness among both enslaved and free African Americans. Perceived by many at the time as dangerously radical, the *Appeal* was immediately vilified by Southern slaveholders as well as by moderate Northern abolitionists, its author deemed by detractors to be at best misguided and at worst a threat to the very foundations of American society. To threaten and overthrow those cruel and unjust foundations, however, was one of Walker's primary aims. The *Appeal*, which helped usher in abolitionism as one of the most important concerns of nineteenth-century America, has been influential in the struggle for racial justice ever since its publication, and echoes of it can be heard in the work of Maria W. Stewart, Frederick Douglass, W.E.B. Du Bois, Martin Luther King Jr., and Malcolm X, among others.

Though Walker's father had been enslaved, his mother was free and therefore Walker himself was born into freedom. Nevertheless, the legal and social restraints experienced by even free African Americans in the antebellum South were severe. At an unknown date he left his native North Carolina for Charleston, South Carolina, where he joined the African Methodist Episcopal Church—a leading force in the fight for racial justice throughout the nineteenth century—and likely encountered the formerly enslaved Denmark Vesey, whose radical, revolutionary approach to abolitionism would see echoes in Walker's later work. After traveling numerous Southern and Western states, Walker settled in Boston, where, though black people continued to experience severe discrimination and outright violence, there was nonetheless a flourishing black intellectual and political community. Here he purchased a used-clothing store and married Eliza Butler. Walker joined the influential Prince Hall Masonic Lodge, which advocated for black education rights among other causes; helped found the Massachusetts General Colored Association, before which he frequently lectured; wrote for and helped distribute *Freedom's Journal*, the first African American-owned newspaper in the country; and used his shop and home as a shelter, often for those escaping slavery via the Underground Railroad.

Published in 1829, *Walker's Appeal, in Four Articles, together with a Preamble, to the Coloured Citizens of the World*, was a consummation of years of antislavery thought, calling upon African Americans to recognize and resist the oppression under which they lived, and invoking ancient and biblical examples of slavery to demonstrate the historically exceptional injustice of the American institution. In part, Walker's text was a response to Thomas Jefferson's influential *Notes on the State of Virginia* (1787)—often considered a foundational expression of American political culture—in which Jefferson defends slavery on the basis of the "real distinctions which nature has made" between black and white people, and claims that African Americans should, if free, be "removed beyond the reach of mixture" with whites. Walker addresses the way this latter infamous claim had recently been taken up by the American Colonization Society, which advocated for the deportation of black people to Africa; from the 1820s to the 1840s the Society sent thousands of African Americans to colonize Liberia, where more than half died.

Though *Walker's Appeal* was not the first standalone publication of its sort—a number of abolitionist tracts had, for instance, been previously published by Boston's African Society—it was among the most ambitious. Anticipating the negative response his pamphlet would likely elicit among white authorities if distributed conventionally, Walker used a varied network of supporters to circulate the *Appeal* among people who would otherwise have been unable to access it, and to read it aloud to those who were illiterate; this network may have included sympathetic sailors and ship workers—a large proportion of whom were free blacks—as well as activists and ministers to whom Walker mailed crates of the pamphlet directly. The pamphlet soon reached thousands of people around the country, with copies found as far south as New Orleans. In 1830 the work was already in its third revised edition, with each revision featuring additional material, as well as a shift towards increasingly radical language.

By this point the pamphlet had attracted the notice of many outraged Southern slaveholders, who took quick action to suppress knowledge of the text among the people they enslaved. Southern newspapers reported on the pamphlet extensively, and proslavery Southerners called for Walker's capture and execution—with a large reward offered to those willing to do the deed. Georgia's Governor Gilmer accused Boston of harboring "highly inflammatory" literature and demanded that the pamphlet's circulation be brought to an end (the city's mayor declined to take such action). The legislature of North Carolina met secretly about the *Appeal* and passed harsh laws forbidding anyone from teaching enslaved people how to read or write, and from circulating what was considered seditious literature. On the whole, many Southern states saw a surge in racist legislation during the early 1830s, likely in part as a response to the increasingly vigorous antislavery resistance represented by texts like the *Appeal*. White abolitionists, too, were disturbed by the forceful language of the pamphlet: Benjamin Lundy, for instance, declared the *Appeal* "a labored attempt to rouse the worst passions of human nature, and inflame the minds of those to whom it is addressed," while William Lloyd Garrison commented that "We deprecate its circulation, though we cannot but wonder at the bravery and intelligence of its author." (Though Garrison's personal response to the *Appeal* was mixed, the text appears to have influenced his own growing support for immediate abolition—and his rejection of the aims of the American Colonization Society.)

Despite the attempts to suppress its influence, Walker's *Appeal* was an important catalyst for the explosion of abolitionist culture throughout the country in the post-1830 era. It had a profound influence on the abolitionist and feminist work of Walker's protégée Maria Stewart, who built upon Walker's rhetoric of racial uplift even while rejecting his controversial endorsement of violent means. The slave rebellion led by Nat Turner in 1831—a struggle for freedom in which rebels killed fifty-five whites, widely depicted as a massacre in the South—reflected Walker's revolutionary rhetoric, though we cannot be certain that Turner himself had encountered Walker's work. While the *Appeal* was somewhat forgotten over the following decade, it experienced a revival in 1848, when it was republished by black Northern abolitionist Henry Highland Garnet, who wrote in his brief "Sketch" of the author, "They said that he went too far, and was making trouble. So the Jews spoke of Moses." Walker's fiery rhetoric, and his openness to armed revolt as an appropriate response to slavery, have led some historians to see his work as influential in the development of the later Black Power and Black Nationalist movements.

Walker died unexpectedly not long after the release of the *Appeal*'s third edition. The cause of his death has long been disputed and never resolved—many in Boston's black community believed he had been murdered, though the official cause of death was recorded as tuberculosis. Walker's only child to live to adulthood, Edward Garrison Walker, was born after his father's death; in 1866 he became one of the first black men elected to the Massachusetts State Legislature.

NOTE ON THE TEXT: The text of the work presented here is based on the third edition of the *Appeal*, the last edition published during Walker's lifetime, with the full title *Walker's Appeal, in Four Articles, together with a Preamble, to the Coloured Citizens of the World, but in particular, and very expressly, to those of The United States of America* (1830). Spelling and punctuation have been modernized in accordance with the practices of this anthology. Inconsistencies in the use of American and British spelling conventions have not been corrected.

⌘ ⌘ ⌘

from *Walker's Appeal, in Four Articles*

APPEAL, ETC.

My dearly beloved Brethren and Fellow Citizens.
Having travelled over a considerable portion of these United States, and having, in the course of my travels, taken the most accurate observations of things as they exist—the result of my observations has warranted the full and unshaken conviction, that we (coloured people of these United States) are the most degraded, wretched, and abject set of beings that ever lived since the world began; and I pray God that none like us ever may live again until time shall be no more. They tell us of the Israelites in Egypt, the Helots in Sparta,[1] and of the Roman Slaves, which last were made up from almost every nation under heaven, whose sufferings under those ancient and heathen nations, were, in comparison with ours, under this enlightened and Christian nation, no more than a cypher[2]—or, in other words, those heathen nations of antiquity, had but little more among them than the name and form of slavery; while wretchedness and endless miseries were reserved, apparently in a phial, to be poured out upon our fathers, ourselves and our children, by *Christian* Americans!

These positions I shall endeavour, by the help of the Lord, to demonstrate in the course of this *Appeal*, to the satisfaction of the most incredulous mind—and may God Almighty, who is the Father of our Lord Jesus Christ, open your hearts to understand and believe the truth.

The *causes*, my brethren, which produce our wretchedness and miseries, are so very numerous and aggravating, that I believe the pen only of a Josephus or a Plutarch,[3] can well enumerate and explain them. Upon subjects, then, of such incomprehensible magnitude, so impenetrable, and so notorious, I shall be obliged to omit a large class of, and content myself with giving you an exposition of a few of those, which do indeed rage to such an alarming pitch, that they cannot but be a perpetual source of terror and dismay to every reflecting mind.

I am fully aware, in making this appeal to my much afflicted and suffering brethren, that I shall not only be assailed by those whose greatest earthly desires are, to keep us in abject ignorance and wretchedness, and who are of the firm conviction that Heaven has designed us and our children to be slaves and *beasts of burden* to them and their children. I say, I do not only expect to be held up to the public as an ignorant, impudent and restless disturber of the public peace, by such avaricious creatures, as well as a mover of insubordination—and perhaps put in prison or to death, for giving a superficial exposition of our miseries, and exposing tyrants. But I am persuaded, that many of my brethren, particularly those who are ignorantly in league with slaveholders or tyrants, who acquire their daily bread by the blood and sweat of their more ignorant brethren—and not a few of those too, who are too ignorant to see an inch beyond their noses, will rise up and call me cursed—Yea, the jealous ones among us will perhaps use more abject subtlety, by affirming that this work is not worth perusing, that we are well situated, and there is no use in trying to better our condition, for we cannot. I will ask one question here. Can our condition be any worse? Can it be more mean[4] and abject? If there are any changes, will they not be for the better, though they may appear for the worst at first? Can they get us any lower? Where can they get us? They are afraid to treat us worse, for they know well, the day they do it they are gone. But against all accusations which may or can be preferred against me, I appeal to Heaven for my motive in writing—who knows that my object is, if possible, to awaken in the breasts of my afflicted, degraded and slumbering brethren, a spirit of

---

[1] *Israelites in Egypt ... in Sparta* Historical examples of slavery. The Israelites' enslavement to the Egyptians, and their subsequent emancipation through the intervention of God, is the primary subject of the Book of Exodus. The Helots were a class of people in Spartan society; their exact status has been the subject of historical debate, with some uncertainty as to whether they were fully considered slaves by the Spartans or whether they occupied a status between slave and citizen.

[2] *cypher* Literally, the digit zero; i.e., of no comparative importance.

[3] *Josephus* Roman-Jewish scholar (37–100 CE) best known for his works on Jewish history; *Plutarch* Influential Greek essayist and biographer (46–120 CE).

[4] *mean* Base, impoverished.

inquiry and investigation respecting our miseries and wretchedness in this *Republican Land of Liberty!!!!!!*

The sources from which our miseries are derived, and on which I shall comment, I shall not combine in one, but shall put them under distinct heads and expose them in their turn; in doing which, keeping truth on my side, and not departing from the strictest rules of morality, I shall endeavour to penetrate, search out, and lay them open for your inspection. If you cannot or will not profit by them, I shall have done *my* duty to you, my country and my God.

And as the inhuman system of *slavery* is the *source* from which most of our miseries proceed, I shall begin with that *curse to nations*, which has spread terror and devastation through so many nations of antiquity, and which is raging to such a pitch at the present day in Spain and in Portugal.[1] It had one tug in England, in France, and in the United States of America;[2] yet the inhabitants thereof, do not learn wisdom, and erase it entirely from their dwellings and from all with whom they have to do. The fact is, the labour of slaves comes so cheap to the avaricious usurpers, and is (as they think) of such great utility to the country where it exists, that those who are actuated by sordid avarice only, overlook the evils, which will as sure as the Lord lives, follow after the good. In fact, they are so happy to keep in ignorance and degradation, and to receive the homage and labour of the slaves, they forget that God rules in the armies of heaven and among the inhabitants of the earth, having his ears continually open to the cries, tears and groans of his oppressed people; and being a just and holy Being will at one day appear fully in behalf of the oppressed, and arrest the progress of the avaricious oppressors; for although the destruction of the oppressors God may not effect by the oppressed, yet the Lord our God will bring other destructions upon them—for not unfrequently will he cause them to rise up one against another, to be split and divided, and to oppress each other, and sometimes to open hostilities with sword in hand. Some may ask, what is the matter with this united and happy people? Some say it is the cause of political usurpers, tyrants, oppressors, &c. But has not the Lord an oppressed and suffering people among them? Does the Lord condescend to hear their cries and see their tears in consequence of oppression? Will he let the oppressors rest comfortably and happy always? Will he not cause the very children of the oppressors to rise up against them, and oftimes put them to death? "God works in many ways his wonders to perform."[3] ...

All persons who are acquainted with history, and particularly the Bible, who are not blinded by the God of this world, and are not actuated by avarice—who are able to lay aside prejudice long enough to view candidly and impartially, things as they were, are, and probably will be—who are willing to admit that God made man to serve Him *alone*, and that man should have no other Lord or Lords but Himself—that God Almighty is the *sole proprietor* or *master* of the WHOLE human family, and will not on any consideration admit of a colleague, being unwilling to divide his glory with another—and who can dispense with prejudice long enough to admit that we are *men*, notwithstanding our *improminent noses* and *woolly heads*, and believe that we feel for our fathers, mothers, wives and children, as well as the whites do for theirs. I say, all who are permitted to see and believe these things, can easily recognize the judgments of God among the Spaniards. Though others may lay the cause of the fierceness with which they cut each other's throats, to some other circumstance, yet they who believe that God is a God of justice, will believe that SLAVERY *is the principal cause.*

---

[1] *And as ... in Portugal* Walker is referring to the theory that slavery, as a morally corrupt institution, would inherently lead to dissolution and unrest within the societies that upheld it; as an example, he alludes to the bloody civil conflicts and economic crises that occurred in the formerly slave-trading countries of Spain and Portugal in the first few decades of the nineteenth century. (Both countries also lost possession of slaveholding colonies in the early decades of the nineteenth century; though in most cases these colonies were established as non-slaveholding nations, the formerly Portuguese colony Brazil did not abolish slavery until 1888.)

[2] *It had one tug ... of America* The Atlantic slave trade was abolished by the United Kingdom in 1807, and in the United States the importation of enslaved people was banned that same year. Slavery was abolished, re-instated, and then re-abolished by France between 1794 and 1826. Though considered an important victory by abolitionists, the abolition of the Atlantic slave trade did not ban the actual possession and sale of enslaved people within the U.S. or within British and French colonies, nor did it stop the illegal importation of enslaved people into the country.

[3] *God works ... to perform* Paraphrase of the opening lines of English poet William Cowper's abolitionist hymn "Light Shining Out of Darkness" (1773).

While the Spaniards are running about upon the field of battle cutting each other's throats, has not the Lord an afflicted and suffering people in the midst of them, whose cries and groans in consequence of oppression are continually pouring into the ears of the God of justice? Would they not cease to cut each other's throats, if they could? But how can they? The very support which they draw from government to aid them in perpetrating such enormities, does it not arise in a great degree from the wretched victims of oppression among them? And yet they are calling for *Peace! Peace!!* Will any peace be given unto them? Their destruction may indeed be procrastinated awhile, but can it continue long, while they are oppressing the Lord's people? Has He not the hearts of all men in His hand? Will he suffer one part of his creatures to go on oppressing another like brutes always, with impunity? And yet, those avaricious wretches are calling for *Peace!!!!* I declare, it does appear to me, as though some nations think God is asleep, or that he made the Africans for nothing else but to dig their mines and work their farms, or they cannot believe history, sacred or profane. I ask every man who has a heart, and is blessed with the privilege of believing—Is not God a God of justice to *all* his creatures? Do you say he is? Then if he gives peace and tranquility to tyrants, and permits them to keep our fathers, our mothers, ourselves and our children in eternal ignorance and wretchedness, to support them and their families, would he be to us a God of *justice?* I ask, O ye *Christians!!!* who hold us and our children in the most abject ignorance and degradation, that ever a people were afflicted with since the world began—I say, if God gives you peace and tranquility, and suffers you thus to go on afflicting us, and our children, who have never given you the least provocation—would he be to us *a God of justice?* If you will allow that we are MEN, who feel for each other, does not the blood of our fathers and of us their children, cry aloud to the Lord of Sabaoth[1] against you, for the cruelties and murders with which you have, and do continue to afflict us. But it is time for me to close my remarks on the suburbs, just to enter more fully into the interior of this system of cruelty and oppression.

ARTICLE I.
OUR WRETCHEDNESS IN CONSEQUENCE OF SLAVERY.

My beloved brethren: The Indians of North and of South America—the Greeks—the Irish, subjected under the king of Great Britain—the Jews, that ancient people of the Lord—the inhabitants of the islands of the sea—in fine,[2] all the inhabitants of the earth (except however, the sons of Africa) are called *men*, and of course are, and ought to be free. But we (coloured people) and our children are *brutes!!* and of course are, and *ought to be* SLAVES to the American people and their children forever!! to dig their mines and work their farms; and thus go on enriching them, from one generation to another with our *blood* and our *tears!!!!*

I promised in a preceding page to demonstrate to the satisfaction of the most incredulous, that we (coloured people of these United States of America) are the *most wretched, degraded* and *abject* set of beings that *ever lived* since the world began, and that the white Americans having reduced us to the wretched state of *slavery,* treat us in that condition *more cruel* (they being an enlightened and Christian people), than any heathen nation did any people whom it had reduced to our condition. These affirmations are so well confirmed in the minds of all unprejudiced men, who have taken the trouble to read histories, that they need no elucidation from me. But to put them beyond all doubt, I refer you in the first place to the children of Jacob,[3] or of Israel in Egypt, under Pharaoh and his people. Some of my brethren do not know who Pharaoh and the Egyptians were—I know it to be a fact, that some of them take the Egyptians to have been a gang of *devils,* not knowing any better, and that they (Egyptians) having got possession of the Lord's people, treated them *nearly* as cruel as *Christian Americans* do us, at the present day. For the information of such, I would only mention that the Egyptians, were Africans or coloured people, such as we are—some of them yellow and others dark—a mixture of Ethiopians and the natives of Egypt—about the same as you see the coloured people of the United States at the present day. I say, I call your attention then, to the children

---

[1] *Lord of Sabaoth* Lord of Hosts or God of armies; used to refer to God in his capacity as a military leader of the heavenly host.

[2] *in fine* To summarize.

[3] *the children of Jacob* I.e., the Israelites; Jacob is an Israelite patriarch also referred to by the name "Israel."

of Jacob, while I point out particularly to you his son Joseph,[1] among the rest, in Egypt.

"And Pharaoh, said unto Joseph, thou shalt be over my house, and according unto thy word shall all my people be ruled: only in the throne will I be greater than thou."[2]

"And Pharaoh said unto Joseph, see, I have set thee over all the land of Egypt."[3]

"And Pharaoh said unto Joseph, I am Pharaoh, and without thee shall no man lift up his hand or foot in all the land of Egypt."[4]

Now I appeal to heaven and to earth, and particularly to the American people themselves, who cease not to declare that our condition is not *hard*, and that we are comparatively satisfied to rest in wretchedness and misery, under them and their children. Not, indeed, to show me a coloured President, a Governor, a Legislator, a Senator, a Mayor, or an Attorney at the Bar. But to show me a man of colour, who holds the low office of a Constable, or one who sits in a Juror Box, even on a case of one of his wretched brethren, throughout this great Republic!! But let us pass Joseph the son of Israel a little farther in review, as he existed with that heathen nation.

"And Pharaoh called Joseph's name Zaphnath-paaneah; and he gave him to wife Asenath the daughter of Potipherah priest of On. And Joseph went out over all the land of Egypt."[5]

Compare the above, with the American institutions. Do they not institute laws to prohibit us from marrying among the whites?[6] I would wish, candidly, however, before the Lord, to be understood, that I would not give a *pinch of snuff* to be married to any white person I ever saw in all the days of my life. And I do say it, that

the black man, or man of colour, who will leave his own colour (provided he can get one, who is good for any thing) and marry a white woman, to be a double slave to her, just because she is *white*, ought to be treated by her as he surely will be, viz:[7] as a NIGER ! ! ! ![8] It is not, indeed, what I care about inter-marriages with the whites, which induced me to pass this subject in review; for the Lord knows, that there is a day coming when they will be glad enough to get into the company of the blacks, notwithstanding, we are, in this generation, levelled by them, almost on a level with the brute creation: and some of us they treat even worse than they do the brutes that perish. I only made this extract to show how much lower we are held, and how much more cruel we are treated by the Americans, than were the children of Jacob, by the Egyptians.—We will notice the sufferings of Israel some further, under *heathen Pharaoh*, compared with ours under the *enlightened Christians of America*.

"And Pharaoh spake unto Joseph, saying, thy father and thy brethren are come unto thee:

"The land of Egypt is before thee: in the best of the land make thy father and brethren to dwell; in the land of Goshen let them dwell: and if thou knowest any men of activity among them, then make them rulers over my cattle."[9]

I ask those people who treat us so *well*, Oh! I ask them, where is the most barren spot of land which they have given unto us? Israel had the most fertile land in all Egypt. Need I mention the very notorious fact, that I have known a poor man of colour, who laboured night and day, to acquire a little money, and having acquired it, he vested it in a small piece of land, and got him a house erected thereon, and having paid for the whole, he moved his family into it, where he was suffered to remain but nine months, when he was cheated out of his property by a white man, and driven out of door! And is not this the case generally? Can a man of colour buy a piece of land and keep it peaceably? Will

—original spelling—

original spelling —

---

[1]   *Joseph*   One of Jacob's twelve sons, Joseph is sold into slavery to a man named Potiphar by his jealous brothers. The Book of Genesis narrates the story of Joseph's rise from slavery to the status of vizier, second only to the Pharaoh in power.

[2]   [Walker's note]   See Genesis, chap. xli. v. 40.

[3]   [Walker's note]   v. 41.

[4]   [Walker's note]   v. 44.

[5]   [Walker's note]   v. 45.

[6]   *Do they not … the whites?*   Numerous anti-miscegenation laws were in place in the United States in this period in both the South and the North (Massachusetts, for instance, first enacted legislation barring black people from intermarrying with whites in 1705, and did not repeal the law until 1843).

---

[7]   *viz:*   Abbreviation for the Latin *videlicet*, meaning "namely" or "that is to say."

[8]   *NIGER*   As the context here suggests, the "n word" had by this time firmly established itself in the vernacular as an emphatically pejorative alternative to the then-more-neutral term "negro." This spelling (with a single g) remained in occasional use until the mid-nineteenth century.

[9]   [Walker's note]   Genesis, xlvii.—v. 5–6.

not some white man try to get it from him, even if it is in a *mud hole*? I need not comment any farther on a subject, which all, both black and white, will readily admit. But I must, really, observe that in this very city, when a man of colour dies, if he owned any real estate it most generally falls into the hands of some white person. The wife and children of the deceased may weep and lament if they please, but the estate will be kept snug enough by its white possessor.

But to prove farther that the condition of the Israelites was better under the Egyptians than ours is under the whites. I call upon the professing Christians, I call upon the philanthropist, I call upon the very tyrant himself, to show me a page of history, either sacred or profane, on which a verse can be found, which maintains, that the Egyptians heaped the *insupportable insult* upon the children of Israel, by telling them that they were not of the *human family*. Can the whites deny this charge? Have they not, after having reduced us to the deplorable condition of slaves under their feet, held us up as descending originally from the tribes of *Monkeys*, or *Orang-Outangs*? O! my God! I appeal to every man of feeling—is not this insupportable? Is it not heaping the most gross insult upon our miseries, because they have got us under their feet and we cannot help ourselves? Oh! pity us we pray thee, Lord Jesus, Master. Has Mr. Jefferson declared to the world, that we are inferior to the whites, both in the endowments of our bodies and of minds?[1] It is indeed surprising, that a man of such great learning, combined with such excellent natural parts, should speak so of a set of men in chains. I do not know what to compare it to, unless, like putting one wild deer in an iron cage, where it will be secured, and hold another by the side of the same, then let it go, and expect the one in the cage to run as fast as the one at liberty. So far, my brethren, were the Egyptians from heaping these insults upon their slaves, that Pharaoh's daughter took Moses, a son of Israel for her own, as will appear by the following.

"And Pharaoh's daughter said unto her, [Moses' mother] take this child away, and nurse it for me, and I will pay thee thy wages. And the woman took the child [Moses] and nursed it.

"And the child grew, and she brought him unto Pharaoh's daughter and he became her son. And she called his name Moses: and she said because I drew him out of the water."[2]

In all probability, Moses would have become Prince Regent to the throne, and no doubt, in process of time but he would have been seated on the throne of Egypt. But he had rather suffer shame, with the people of God, than to enjoy pleasures with that wicked people for a season. O! that the coloured people were long since of Moses' excellent disposition, instead of courting favour with, and telling news and lies to our *natural enemies*, against each other—aiding them to keep their hellish chains of slavery upon us. Would we not long before this time, have been respectable men, instead of such wretched victims of oppression as we are? Would they be able to drag our mothers, our fathers, our wives, our children and ourselves, around the world in chains and hand-cuffs as they do, to dig up gold and silver for them and theirs? This question, my brethren, I leave for you to digest; and may God Almighty force it home to your hearts. Remember that unless you are united, keeping your tongues within your teeth, you will be afraid to trust your secrets to each other, and thus perpetuate our miseries under the *Christians!!!!!* ᴔ ADDITION.— Remember, also to lay humble at the feet of our Lord and Master Jesus Christ, with prayers and fastings. Let our enemies go on with their butcheries, and at once fill up their cup. Never make an attempt to gain our freedom or *natural right*, from under our cruel oppressors and murderers, until you see your way clear[3]—when

---

[1]   *Mr. Jefferson ... of minds?*   Here and throughout the text Walker refers to Thomas Jefferson's *Notes on the State of Virginia* (1787). A work of political commentary on subjects such as the separation of church and state, individual liberty, and freedom of speech, the book also expresses Jefferson's racialist scientific theories on what he considered to be the "natural" inequality of white and black people. Jefferson presents these theories to support his argument that Virginia should not yet emancipate its enslaved people.

[2]   [Walker's note]   See Exodus, chap. II. v. 9, 10.

[3]   [Walker's note]   It is not to be understood here, that I mean for us to wait until God shall take us by the hair of our heads and drag us out of abject wretchedness and slavery, nor do I mean to convey the idea for us to wait until our enemies shall make preparations, and call us to seize those preparations, take it away from them, and put everything before us to death, in order to gain our freedom which God has given us. For you must remember that we are men as well as they. God has been pleased to give us two eyes, two hands, two feet, and some sense in our heads as well as they. They have no more right to hold us in slavery than we have to hold them, we have just as much right, in the sight of God, to hold them and their children in slavery and wretchedness, as they have to hold us, and no more.

that hour arrives and you move, be not afraid or dismayed; for be you assured that Jesus Christ the King of heaven and of earth who is the God of justice and of armies, will surely go before you. And those enemies who have for hundreds of years stolen our *rights*, and kept us ignorant of Him and His divine worship, he will remove. Millions of whom, are this day, so ignorant and avaricious, that they cannot conceive how God can have an attribute of justice, and show mercy to us because it pleased Him to make us black—which colour, Mr. Jefferson calls unfortunate!!!!!! As though we are not as thankful to our God, for having made us as it pleased himself, as they (the whites) are for having made them white. They think because they hold us in their infernal chains of slavery, that we wish to be white, or of their color—but they are dreadfully deceived—we wish to be just as it pleased our Creator to have made us, and no avaricious and unmerciful wretches, have any business to make slaves of, or hold us in slavery. How would they like for us to make slaves of, and hold them in cruel slavery, and murder them as they do us? But is Mr. Jefferson's assertion true? viz. "that it is unfortunate for us that our Creator has been pleased to make us *black*." We will not take his say so, for the fact. The world will have an opportunity to see whether it is unfortunate for us, that our Creator *has made us* darker than the *whites*.

Fear not the number and education of our *enemies*, against whom we shall have to contend for our lawful right; guaranteed to us by our Maker; for why should we be afraid, when God is, and will continue (if we continue humble) to be on our side?

The man who would not fight under our Lord and Master Jesus Christ, in the glorious and heavenly cause of freedom and of God—to be delivered from the most wretched, abject and servile slavery, that ever a people was afflicted with since the foundation of the world, to the present day—ought to be kept with all of his children or family, in slavery, or in chains, to be butchered by his *cruel enemies*. 🐟

I saw a paragraph, a few years since, in a South Carolina paper, which, speaking of the barbarity of the Turks, it said: "The Turks are the most barbarous people in the world—they treat the Greeks more like *brutes* than human beings." And in the same paper was an advertisement, which said: "Eight well built

Virginia and Maryland *Negro fellows* and four *wenches* will positively be *sold* this day, *to the highest bidder!*" And what astonished me still more was, to see in this same *humane* paper!! the cuts of three men, with clubs and budgets[1] on their backs, and an advertisement offering a considerable sum of money for their apprehension and delivery. I declare, it is really so amusing to hear the Southerners and Westerners of this country talk about *barbarity*, that it is positively, enough to make a man *smile*.

The suffering of the Helots among the Spartans, were somewhat severe, it is true, but to say that theirs, were as severe as ours among the Americans, I do most strenuously deny—for instance, can any man show me an article on a page of ancient history which specifies, that, the Spartans chained, and hand-cuffed the Helots, and dragged them from their wives and children, children from their parents, mothers from their suckling babes, wives from their husbands, driving them from one end of the country to the other? Notice the Spartans were heathens, who lived long before our Divine Master made his appearance in the flesh. Can Christian Americans deny these barbarous cruelties? Have you not, Americans, having subjected us under you, added to these miseries, by insulting us in telling us to our face, because we are helpless, that we are not of the human family? I ask you, O! Americans, I ask you, in the name of the Lord, can you deny these charges? Some perhaps may deny, by saying, that they never thought or said that we were not men. But do not actions speak louder than words? Have they not made provisions for the Greeks, and Irish?[2] Nations who have never done the least thing for them, while *we*, who have enriched their country with our blood and tears—have dug up gold and silver for them and their children, from generation to generation, and are in more miseries than any other people under heaven, are not seen, but by comparatively, a handful of the American people? There are indeed, more ways to kill a dog, besides choking it to death with butter. Further—The Spartans or Lacedemonians, had some frivolous pretext, for enslaving the Helots, for they (Helots) while being free inhabitants of Sparta, stirred

---

1   *cuts* I.e., woodcuts; engravings;   *budgets* Leather bags.

2   *made provisions … Irish* I.e., provided them with rights.

up an intestine[1] commotion, and were, by the Spartans subdued, and made prisoners of war. Consequently they and their children were condemned to perpetual slavery.[2]

I have been for years troubling the pages of historians, to find out what our fathers have done to the *white Christians of America*, to merit such condign[3] punishment as they have inflicted on them, and do continue to inflict on us their children. But I must aver, that my researches have hitherto been to no effect. I have therefore, come to the immovable conclusion, that they (Americans) have, and do continue to punish us for nothing else, but for enriching them and their country. For I cannot conceive of anything else. Nor will I believe otherwise, until the Lord shall convince me.

The world knows, that slavery as it existed among the Romans, (which was the primary cause of their destruction) was, comparatively speaking, no more than a *cypher*, when compared with ours under the Americans. Indeed I should not have noticed the Roman slaves, had not the very learned and penetrating Mr. Jefferson said, "when a master was murdered, all his slaves in the same house, or within hearing, were condemned to death."[4] Here let me ask Mr. Jefferson, (but he is gone to answer at the bar of God, for the deeds done in his body while living), I therefore ask the whole American people, had I not rather die, or be put to death, than to be a slave to any tyrant, who takes not only my own, but my wife and children's lives by the inches? Yea, would I meet death with avidity far! far!! in preference to such *servile submission* to the murderous hands of tyrants. Mr. Jefferson's very severe remarks on us have been so extensively argued upon by men whose attainments in literature, I shall never be able to reach, that I would not have meddled with it, were it not to solicit each of my brethren, who has the spirit of a man, to buy a copy of Mr. Jefferson's "Notes on Virginia," and put it in the hand of his son. For let no one of us suppose that the refutations which have been written

by our white friends are enough—they are *whites*, we are *blacks*. We, and the world wish to see the charges of Mr. Jefferson refuted by the blacks *themselves*, according to their chance; for we must remember that what the whites have written respecting this subject, is other men's labours, and did not emanate from the blacks. I know well, that there are some talents and learning among the coloured people of this country, which we have not a chance to develop, in consequence of oppression; but our oppression ought not to hinder us from acquiring all we can. For we will have a chance to develop them by and by. God will not suffer us, always to be oppressed. Our sufferings will come to an *end*, in spite of all the Americans this side of *eternity*. Then we will want all the learning and talents among ourselves, and perhaps more, to govern ourselves. "Every dog must have its day," the American's is coming to an end.

But let us review Mr. Jefferson's remarks respecting us some further. Comparing our miserable fathers, with the learned philosophers of Greece, he says: "Yet notwithstanding these and other discouraging circumstances among the Romans, their slaves were often their rarest artists. They excelled too, in science, insomuch as to be usually employed as tutors to their master's children; Epictetus, Terence and Phaedrus,[5] were slaves—but they were of the race of whites. It is not their *condition* then, but *nature*, which has produced the distinction."[6] See this, my brethren!! Do you believe that this assertion is swallowed by millions of the whites? Do you know that Mr. Jefferson was one of as great characters as ever lived among the whites? See his writings for the world, and public labours for the United States of America. Do you believe that the assertions of such a man, will pass away into oblivion unobserved by this people and the world? If you do you are much mistaken—See how the American people treat us—have we souls in our bodies? Are we men who have any spirits at all? I know that there are many *swell-bellied* fellows among us, whose greatest object is to fill their stomachs. Such

---

[1]   *intestine*   Internal, as in a civil conflict.

[2]   [Walker's note]   See Dr. Goldsmith's *History of Greece*—page 9. See also, Plutarch's *Lives*. The Helots [were] subdued by Agis, king of Sparta.

[3]   *condign*   Deserved; fitting.

[4]   [Walker's note]   See his *Notes on Virginia*, page 210.

[5]   *Epictetus*   Greek stoic philosopher (c. 55–135 CE) who was born enslaved in Phrygia but later became free; *Terence*   Roman playwright (c. 195–159 BCE), enslaved by a Roman senator and later freed; *Phaedrus*   Probably Gaius Julius Phaedrus, a first-century Roman writer of fables who was born enslaved and likely freed under the reign of Augustus.

[6]   [Walker's note]   See his Notes on Virginia, page 211.

I do not mean—I am after those who know and feel, that we are MEN, as well as other people; to them, I say, that unless we try to refute Mr. Jefferson's arguments respecting us, we will only establish them.

But the slaves among the Romans. Everybody who has read history, knows, that as soon as a slave among the Romans obtained his freedom, he could rise to the greatest eminence in the State, and there was no law instituted to hinder a slave from buying his freedom. Have not the Americans instituted laws to hinder us from obtaining our freedom? Do any deny this charge? Read the laws of Virginia, North Carolina, &c. Further: have not the Americans instituted laws to prohibit a man of colour from obtaining and holding any office whatever, under the government of the United States of America? Now, Mr. Jefferson tells us, that our condition is not so hard, as the slaves' were under the Romans!!!!!!

It is time for me to bring this article to a close. But before I close it, I must observe to my brethren that at the close of the first Revolution in this country, with Great Britain, there were but thirteen States in the Union, now there are twenty-four, most of which are slave-holding States, and the whites are dragging us around in chains and in hand-cuffs, to their new States and Territories to work their mines and farms, to enrich them and their children—and millions of them believing firmly that we being a little darker than they, were made by our Creator to be an inheritance to them and their children forever—the same as a parcel of *brutes*.

Are we MEN!!—I ask you, O my brethren! are we MEN? Did our Creator make us to be slaves to dust and ashes like ourselves? Are they not dying worms as well as we? Have they not to make their appearance before the tribunal of Heaven, to answer for the deeds done in the body, as well as we? Have we any other Master but Jesus Christ alone? Is he not their Master as well as ours? What right then, have we to obey and call any other Master, but Himself? How we could be so *submissive* to a gang of men, whom we cannot tell whether they are *as good* as ourselves or not, I never could conceive. However, this is shut up with the Lord, and we cannot precisely tell—but I declare, we judge men by their works.

The whites have always been an unjust, jealous, unmerciful, avaricious and blood-thirsty set of beings, always seeking after power and authority. We view them all over the confederacy of Greece, where they were first known to be anything (in consequence of education) we see them there, cutting each other's throats—trying to subject each other to wretchedness and misery—to effect which, they used all kinds of deceitful, unfair, and unmerciful means. We view them next in Rome, where the spirit of tyranny and deceit raged still higher. We view them in Gaul, Spain, and in Britain. In fine, we view them all over Europe, together with what were scattered about in Asia and Africa, as heathens, and we see them acting more like devils than accountable men. But some may ask, did not the blacks of Africa, and the mulattoes of Asia,[1] go on in the same way as did the whites of Europe. I answer, no—they never were half so avaricious, deceitful and unmerciful as the whites, according to their knowledge.

But we will leave the whites or Europeans as heathens, and take a view of them as Christians, in which capacity we see them as cruel, if not more so than ever. In fact, take them as a body, they are ten times more cruel, avaricious and unmerciful than ever they were; for while they were heathens, they were bad enough it is true, but it is positively a fact that they were not quite so audacious as to go and take vessel loads of men, women and children, and in cold blood, and through devilishness, throw them into the sea, and murder them in all kind of ways. While they were heathens, they were too ignorant for such barbarity. But being Christians, enlightened and sensible, they are completely prepared for such hellish cruelties. Now suppose God were to give them more sense, what would they do? If it were possible, would they not *dethrone* Jehovah and seat themselves upon his throne? I therefore, in the name and fear of the Lord God of Heaven and of earth, divested of prejudice either on the side of my colour or that of the whites, advance my suspicion of them, whether they are *as good by nature* as we are or not. Their actions, since they were known as a people, have been the reverse, I do indeed suspect them, but

---

1   *mulattoes of Asia* Though the term "mulatto" (which is today considered archaic and offensive) generally referred to people of mixed black and white parentage, it would occasionally be used to refer more vaguely to persons of other ethnicities perceived to have a skin tone between black and white.

this, as I before observed, is shut up with the Lord, we cannot exactly tell, it will be proved in succeeding generations. The whites have had the essence of the gospel as it was preached by my master and his apostles—the Ethiopians have not, who are to have it in its meridian[1] splendor—the Lord will give it to them to their satisfaction. I hope and pray to my God, that they will make good use of it, that it may be well with them.[2]

from ARTICLE 4.
OUR WRETCHEDNESS IN CONSEQUENCE OF THE COLONIZING PLAN.[3]

My dearly beloved brethren: This is a scheme on which so many able writers, together with that very judicious coloured Baltimorean,[4] have commented, that I feel my delicacy about touching it. But as I am compelled to do the will of my Master, I declare, I will give you my sentiments upon it. Previous, however, to giving my sentiments, either for or against it, I shall give that of Mr. Henry Clay, together with that of Mr. Elias B. Caldwell,[5] Esq. of the District of Columbia, as extracted from the *National Intelligencer*, by Dr. Torrey, author of a series of "Essays on Morals, and the Diffusion of Useful Knowledge."

At a meeting which was convened in the District of Columbia, for the express purpose of agitating the subject of colonizing us in some part of the world, Mr. Clay was called to the chair, and having been seated a little while, he rose and spake, in substance, as follows: says he[6]—"That class of the mixt population of our country [coloured people] was peculiarly situated; they neither enjoyed the immunities of freemen, nor were they subjected to the incapacities of slaves, but partook, in some degree, of the qualities of both. From their condition, and the unconquerable prejudices resulting from their colour, they never could amalgamate with the free whites of this country. It was desirable, therefore, as it respected them, and the residue of the population of the country, to drain them off. Various schemes of colonization had been thought of, and a part of our continent, it was supposed by some, might furnish a suitable establishment for them. But, for his part, Mr. C. said, he had a decided preference for some part of the Coast of Africa. There ample provision might be made for the colony itself, and it might be rendered instrumental to the introduction into that extensive quarter of the globe, of the arts, civilization, and Christianity." [Here I ask Mr. Clay, what kind of Christianity? Did he mean such as they have among the Americans—distinction, whip, blood and oppression? I pray the Lord Jesus Christ to forbid it.] "There," said he, "was a peculiar, a moral fitness, in restoring them to the land of their fathers, and if instead of the evils and sufferings which we had been the innocent cause of inflicting upon the inhabitants of Africa, we can transmit to her the blessings of our arts, our civilization, and our religion. May we not hope that America will extinguish a great portion of that moral debt which she has contracted to that unfortunate continent? Can there be

---

[1] *meridian* Highest; zenith.

[2] [Walker's note]   It is my solemn belief, that if ever the world becomes Christianized, (which must certainly take place before long) it will be through the means, under God of the *Blacks*, who are now held in wretchedness, and degradation, by the white *Christians* of the world, who before they learn to do justice to us before our Maker—and be reconciled to us, and reconcile us to them, and by that means have clear consciences before God and man. Send out Missionaries to convert the Heathens, many of whom after they cease to worship gods, which neither see nor hear, become ten times more the children of Hell, than ever they were, why what is the reason? Why the reason is obvious, they must learn to do justice at home, before they go into distant lands, to display their charity, Christianity, and benevolence; when they learn to do justice, God will accept their offering (no man may think that I am against Missionaries for I am not, my object is to see justice done at home, before we go to convert the Heathens).

[3] *THE COLONIZING PLAN* The American Colonization Society, founded by a group of white politicians in 1816, aimed to deport free African Americans to the newly established colony of Liberia. The society's leaders included both supporters of slavery and abolitionists; though its supporters claimed that colonization would benefit black people, many black activists, and later some white abolitionists, were strongly opposed to the endeavor, believing it to be a means of protecting the institution of slavery from the influence of free African Americans. The mortality rate in the colony of Liberia was extremely high.

[4] *coloured Baltimorean* William Watkins (1801–58), antislavery and anti-colonization speaker who wrote numerous articles for the abolitionist newspapers *The Liberator* and *The Genius of Universal Emancipation* under the alias "The Colored Baltimorean."

[5] *Mr. Henry Clay … Elias B. Caldwell* White politicians who were involved in the establishment of the American Colonization Society.

[6] [Walker's note]   See Dr. Torrey's *Portraiture of Domestic Slavery in the United States*, page 85, 86.

a nobler cause than that which, whilst it proposes, &c. * * * * * * * [you know what this means.]¹ contemplates the spreading of the arts of civilized life, and the possible redemption from ignorance and barbarism of a benighted quarter of the globe?"

Before I proceed any further, I solicit your notice, brethren, to the foregoing part of Mr. Clay's speech, in which he says, (☞ look above) "and if, instead of the evils and sufferings, which we had been the innocent cause of inflicting," &c. What this very learned statesman could have been thinking about, when he said in his speech, "we had been the innocent cause of inflicting," &c., I have never been able to conceive. Are Mr. Clay and the rest of the Americans, innocent of the blood and groans of our fathers and us, their children? Every individual may plead innocence, if he pleases, but God will, before long, separate the innocent from the guilty, unless something is speedily done—which I suppose will hardly be, so that their destruction may be sure. Oh Americans! let me tell you, in the name of the Lord, it will be good for you, if you listen to the voice of the Holy Ghost, but if you do not, you are ruined!!! Some of you are good men; but the will of my God must be done. Those avaricious and ungodly tyrants among you, I am awfully afraid will drag down the vengeance of God upon you. When God Almighty commences his battle on the continent of America, for the oppression of his people, tyrants will wish they never were born.

But to return to Mr. Clay, whence I digressed. He says, "It was proper and necessary distinctly to state, that he understood it constituted no part of the object of this meeting, to touch or agitate in the slightest degree, a delicate question, connected with another portion of the coloured population of our country. It was not proposed to deliberate upon or consider at all, any question of emancipation, or that which was connected with the abolition of slavery. It was upon that condition alone, he was sure, that many gentlemen from the South and the West, whom he saw present,

had attended, or could be expected to co-operate. It was upon that condition only, that he himself had attended." That is to say, to fix a plan to get those of the coloured people, who are said to be free, away from among those of our brethren whom they unjustly hold in bondage, so that they may be enabled to keep them the more secure in ignorance and wretchedness, to support them and their children, and consequently they would have the more obedient slaves. For if the free are allowed to stay among the slaves, they will have intercourse together, and, of course, the free will learn² the slaves *bad habits*, by teaching them that they are MEN, as well as other people, and certainly *ought* and *must* be FREE. ...

The Americans of North and of South America, including the West India Islands—no trifling portion of whom were, for stealing, murdering, &c. compelled to flee from Europe, to save their necks or banishment,³ have effected their escape to this continent, where God blessed them with all the comforts of life—He gave them a plenty of every thing calculated to do them good—not satisfied with this, however, they wanted slaves, and wanted us for their slaves, who belong to the Holy Ghost, and no other, who we shall have to serve us instead of tyrants. I say, the Americans want us, the property of the Holy Ghost, to serve them. But there is a day fast approaching, when (unless there is a universal repentance on the part of the whites, which will scarcely take place, they have got to be so hardened in consequence of our blood, and so wise in their own conceit). To be plain and candid with you, Americans! I say that the day is fast approaching, when there will be a greater time on the continent of America, than ever was witnessed upon this earth, since it came from the hand of its Creator. Some of you have done us so much injury, that you will never be able to repent. Your cup must be filled. You want us for your slaves, and shall have enough of us—God is just, *who will give you your fill of us.* ...

---

1   *&c. ... [you know what this means.]* Clay's original 1816 speech here reads, "... whilst it proposes to rid our own country of a useless and pernicious, if not a dangerous portion of its population." In Walker's source for this passage, Jesse Torrey—a white supporter of colonization—euphemistically omits this portion of the sentence and replaces it with "&c." Walker himself added the asterisks and bracketed comment.

2   *intercourse* I.e., interactions, communication; *learn* Teach.

3   *The Americans ... banishment* Walker is referring to the practice of penal transportation, whereby people convicted of crimes in their home countries (especially Britain) were deported to one of that country's colonies. (This practice ceased in the United States after the American Revolution.)

I shall now pass in review of the speech of Mr. Elias B. Caldwell, Esq. of the District of Columbia, extracted from the same page on which Mr. Clay's will be found. Mr. Caldwell, giving his opinion respecting us, at that ever memorable meeting, he says: "The more you improve the condition of these people, the more you cultivate their minds, the more miserable you make them in their present state. You give them a higher relish for those privileges which they can never attain, and turn what we intend for a blessing into a curse." Let me ask this benevolent man, what he means by a blessing intended for us? Did he mean sinking us and our children into ignorance and wretchedness, to support him and his family? What he meant will appear evident and obvious to the most ignorant in the world. ☞ See Mr. Caldwell's intended blessings for us, O! my Lord! ! "No," said he, "if they must remain in their present situation, keep them in the *lowest state of degradation and ignorance*. The nearer you bring them to the condition of brutes, the better chance do you give them of possessing their *apathy*." Here I pause to get breath, having laboured to extract the above clause of this gentleman's speech, at that colonizing meeting. I presume that everybody knows the meaning of the word "*apathy*"—if any do not, let him get Sheridan's Dictionary, in which he will find it explained in full. I solicit the attention of the world, to the foregoing part of Mr. Caldwell's speech, that they may see what man will do with his fellow men, when he had them under his feet. To what length will not man go in iniquity when given up to a hard heart, and reprobate mind, in consequence of blood and oppression? The last clause of this speech, which was written in a very artful manner, and which will be taken for the speech of a friend, without close examination and deep penetration, I shall now present. He says, "surely, Americans ought to be the last people on earth, to advocate such slavish doctrines, to cry peace and contentment to those who are deprived of the privileges of civil liberty, they who have so largely partaken of its blessings, who know so well how to estimate its value, ought to be among the foremost to extend it to others." The real sense and meaning of the last part of Mr. Caldwell's speech is, get the free people of colour away to Africa, from among the slaves, where they may at once be blessed and happy, and those who we hold in slavery,

will be contented to rest in ignorance and wretchedness, to dig up gold and silver for us and our children. Men have indeed got to be so cunning, these days, that it would take the eye of a Solomon[1] to penetrate and find them out. ...

God will show the whites what we are, yet. I say, from the beginning, I do not think that we were natural enemies to each other. But the whites having made us so wretched, by subjecting us to slavery, and having murdered so many millions of us, in order to make us work for them, and out of devilishness—and they taking our wives, whom we love as we do ourselves—our mothers, who bore the pains of death to give us birth—our fathers and dear little children, and ourselves, and strip and beat us one before the other—chain, hand-cuff, and drag us about like rattle-snakes—shoot us down like wild bears, before each other's faces, to make us submissive to, and work to support them and their families. They (the whites) know well, if we are *men*—and there is a secret monitor in their hearts which tells them we are—they know, I say, if we *are* men, and see them treating us in the manner they do, that there can be nothing in our hearts but death alone, for them, notwithstanding we may appear cheerful, when we see them murdering our dear mothers and wives, because we cannot help ourselves. ... Consequently they, themselves, (and not us) render themselves our natural enemies, by treating us so cruel. They keep us miserable now, and call us their property, but some of them will have enough of us by and by—their stomachs shall run over with us; they want us for their slaves, and shall have us to their fill. We are all in the world together!! I said above, because we cannot help ourselves, (viz. we cannot help the whites murdering our mothers and our wives) but this statement is incorrect—for we can help ourselves; for, if we lay aside abject servility, and be determined to act like men, and not brutes—the murderers among the whites would be afraid to show their cruel heads. But O, my God!—in sorrow I must say it, that my colour, all over the world, have a mean, servile spirit. They yield in a moment to the whites, let them be right or wrong—the reason they are able to keep their feet on our throats. Oh! my coloured brethren, all over the world, when shall we arise from this death-like apathy?—And be men!! You will notice, if

---

[1]   *Solomon*   Ancient King of Israel, known for his great wisdom.

ever we become men, I mean *respectable* men, such as other people are, we must exert ourselves to the full. For remember, that it is the greatest desire and object of the greater part of the whites, to keep us ignorant, and make us work to support them and their families.—Here now, in the Southern and Western sections of this country, there are at least three coloured persons for one white, why is it, that those few weak, good-for-nothing whites, are able to keep so many able men, one of whom, can put to flight a dozen whites, in wretchedness and misery? It shows at once, what the blacks are, we are ignorant, abject, servile and mean—and the whites know it—they know that we are too servile to assert our rights as men—or they would not fool with us as they do. Would they fool with any other people as they do with us? No, they know too well, that they would get themselves ruined. Why do they not bring the inhabitants of Asia to be body servants to them? They know they would get their bodies rent and torn from head to foot. Why do they not get the Aborigines of this country to be slaves to them and their children, to work their farms and dig their mines? They know well that the Aborigines of this country, or (Indians) would tear them from the earth. The Indians would not rest day or night, they would be up all times of night, cutting their cruel throats. But my colour, (some, not all,) are willing to stand still and be murdered by the cruel whites. In some of the West-India Islands, and over a large part of South America, there are six or eight coloured persons for one white.[1] Why

do they not take possession of those places? Who hinders them? It is not the avaricious whites—for they are too busily engaged in laying up money—derived from the blood and tears of the blacks. The fact is, they are too servile, they love to have Masters too well!! ...

... Will any of us leave our homes and go to Africa? I hope not.[2] Let them commence their attack upon us as they did on our brethren in Ohio,[3] driving and beating us from our country, and my soul for theirs, they will have enough of it. Let no man of us budge one step, and let slave-holders come to beat us from our country. America is more our country, than it is the whites'—we have enriched it with our *blood and tears*. The greatest riches in all America have arisen from our blood and tears—and will they drive us from our property and homes, which we have earned with our *blood*? They must look sharp or this very thing will bring swift destruction upon them. The Americans have got so fat on our blood and groans, that they have almost forgotten the God of armies. But let them go on. ...

---

[1]   [Walker's note]   For instance in the two States of Georgia, and South Carolina, there are, perhaps, not much short of six or seven hundred thousand persons of colour; and if I was a gambling character, I would not be afraid to stake down upon the board FIVE CENTS against TEN, that there are in the single State of Virginia, five or six hundred thousand coloured persons. Four hundred and fifty thousand of whom (let them be well equipt for war) I would put against every white person on the whole continent of America. (Why? why because I know that the Blacks, once they get involved in a war, had rather die than to live, they either kill or be killed.) The whites know this too, which makes them quake and tremble. To show the world further, how servile the coloured people are, I will only hold up to view, the one Island of Jamaica, as a specimen of our meanness.

In that Island, there are three hundred and fifty thousand souls—of whom fifteen thousand are whites, the remainder, three hundred and thirty-five thousand are coloured people! and this Island is ruled by the white people!!!!!!!! (15,000) ruling and tyrannizing over 335,000 persons!!!!!!!!—O! coloured men!! O! coloured

men!!! O! coloured men!!!! Look!! look!!! at this!!!! and, tell me if we are not abject and servile enough, how long, O! how long my colour shall we be dupes and dogs to the cruel whites?—I only passed Jamaica, and its inhabitants, in review as a specimen to show the world, the condition of the Blacks at this time, now coloured people of the whole world, I beg you to look at the (15000 white,) and (Three Hundred and Thirty-Five Thousand coloured people) in that Island, and tell me how can the white tyrants of the world but say that we are not men, but were made to be slaves and Dogs to them and their children forever!!!!!!!—why my friends only look at the thing!!!! (15000) whites keeping in wretchedness and degradation (335000) viz. 22 coloured persons for one white!!!!!!!!) when at the same time, an equal number (15000) Blacks, would almost take the whole of South America, because where they go as soldiers to fight death follows in their train.

[2]   [Walker's note]   Those who are ignorant enough to go to Africa, the coloured people ought to be glad to have them go, for if they are ignorant enough to let the whites *fool* them off to Africa, they would be no small injury to us if they reside in this country.

[3]   *Let them ... in Ohio*   Although Ohio had been established as a free state in 1803, shortly thereafter the state passed laws known as "Black Codes" or "Black Laws," severely restricting black immigration into the state as well as the movement and employment of free black people within the state. Free black people found in the state without free papers and other such documents (which could cost as much as $500 to obtain) would be subject to severe prosecution. The year 1829 in particular saw a rise in anti-black violence, and a number of riots resulted in the burning down of numerous black communities.

And now, brethren, having concluded these four Articles, I submit them, together with my Preamble, dedicated to the Lord, for your inspection, in language so very simple, that the most ignorant, who can read at all, may easily understand—of which you may make the best you possibly can.[1] Should tyrants take it into their heads to emancipate any of you, remember that your freedom is your natural right. You are men, as well as they, and instead of returning thanks to them for your freedom, return it to the Holy Ghost, who is our rightful owner. ...

—1829, 1830

[NOTE: The full text of *Walker's Appeal, in Four Articles* is included in the online component of this anthology.]

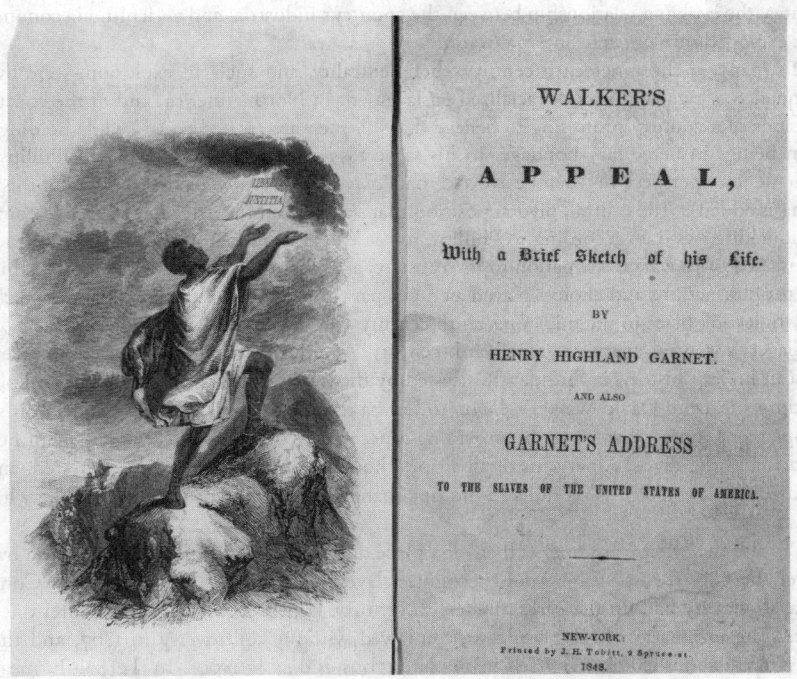

Walker's Appeal was reprinted by black abolitionist Henry Highland Garnet in 1848, in an edition that also featured Garnet's *Address to the Slaves of the United States of America*. That edition also included this engraving as a new "frontispiece" to Walker's pamphlet. The identity of the artist is not known.

---

1 [Walker's note] Some of my brethren, who are sensible, do not take an interest in enlightening the minds of our more ignorant brethren respecting this Book, and in reading it to them, just as though they will not have either to stand or fall by what is written in this book. Do they believe that I would be so foolish as to put out a book of this kind without strict—ah! very strict commandments of the Lord? Surely the blacks and whites must think that I am ignorant enough. Do they think that I would have the audacious wickedness to take the name of my God in vain? Notice, I said in the concluding clause of Article 3 [omitted here]—I call God, I call Angels, I call men to witness, that the destruction of the Americans is at hand, and will be speedily consummated unless they repent. Now I wonder if the world think that I would take the name of God in this way in vain? What do they think I take God to be? Do they suppose that I would trifle with that God who will not have his Holy name taken in vain? He will show you and the world, in due time, whether this book is for his glory, or written by me through envy to the whites, as some have represented.

SLAVERY AND ABOLITION
CONTEXTS

In 1853, the abolitionist orator Wendell Phillips called the question of slavery—its morality, its status, its future—"the question of this generation." This characterization is hard to dispute. By the time of Phillips's 1853 speech, the debate about slavery had come to dominate the nation's politics and pervade its literature; the debate intersected with or subsumed all sorts of other urgent issues of the time—westward expansion, regional and sectional rivalries, the distribution of power between the federal government and the states, the evolving relationship between the country's industrial and agricultural economies—and in 1861 it exploded into outright internal warfare.

To many in the nineteenth century, such centrality, and such an explosion, were the inevitable consequence of two centuries of racialized enslavement in North America, and of the constitutive contradictions of a country professing to believe that "all men are created equal" while holding millions of human beings in hereditary bondage. In his same 1853 speech, however, Wendell Phillips provided a complementary perspective when he avowed that "*Slavery has been made* the question of this generation" (emphasis added).[1] The central, pivotal position that slavery, and the drive to end it, had come to occupy in national life was due, according to Phillips, to the efforts of numerous people—white and black, free and enslaved—"to waken the nation to its real state, and chain it to the consideration of this one duty." These peoples' actions and choices played a crucial part in bringing on the great national reckoning with slavery that took place in the mid-nineteenth century.

Slavery's central place in nineteenth-century America, and specifically in nineteenth-century American literary history, is abundantly attested by the many works throughout this anthology volume that address it, from David Walker's *Appeal* to Louisa May Alcott's "My Contraband." This section aims to supplement those other works by providing a necessarily brief and selective survey of how, between the 1820s and the 1870s, Americans of all stripes thought about, wrote about, contested, and defended race-based slavery, and of what did and did not change for enslaved people, and for the whole country, as a result.

Despite the intense arguments that took place during the constitutional convention over how and whether the U.S. Constitution would recognize slavery—arguments that shaped the Constitution in key ways—slavery had, in the early nineteenth century, largely receded from the forefront of national politics. The international slave trade was outlawed without controversy in 1807, and the Northern states steadily abolished slavery itself in the late 1700s and early 1800s. In the South, meanwhile, the invention of the cotton gin in the 1790s, and the subsequent massive growth of the cotton industry, made slavery newly important, even vital, to the region's economy. This re-entrenchment of slavery in the South, however, did not substantively affect the national political scene until 1820, when the dispute surrounding Missouri's admission to the Union as a slave state, resulting in the Missouri Compromise, brought the conflicting interests and divergent trajectories of the so-called "slave" and "free" states into the open.

One major contributor to these divergent trajectories was the growth in the North, in the years after the Missouri Compromise, of "modern abolitionism" (as the activist William Goodell termed it): a movement, building on the transatlantic campaign against the international slave trade in the eighteenth and early nineteenth centuries, that sought to end slavery in the United States on moral grounds. Abolitionism drew from and incorporated various communities, including free Northern black people, such as Samuel Cornish and John Russwurm, the editors of the first African American-run newspaper, *Freedom's Journal*; white members of various antislavery Christian denominations, such as Quakers and Unitarians; and

---

[1]   Phillips's speech can be found in the website component of this anthology's Nineteenth-Century Oratory section.

escapees from slavery such as Frederick Douglass and Harriet Jacobs. Abolitionist activism also took a huge variety of forms, some of which are represented in the bound book and website portions of this section, including sentimental appeals such as Annie Parker's poem "Story Telling"; rigorous legal and constitutional argumentation, as in Goodell's *The American Slave Code in Theory and Practice* and Douglass's *The Dred Scott Decision*; and impassioned, unflinching documentation of slavery's inhumanity, as in the enormously influential collection *American Slavery as It Is*. This diversity of abolitionist voices gave rise to occasional internal fissures: the movement split between supporters and opponents of armed resistance to slavery, as well as between those such as Goodell and Douglass who believed slavery could be ended under the Constitution as it existed and those, such as William Lloyd Garrison, who held that the Constitution, and indeed the whole country in its current form, were irreparably tainted by slavery.

Abolitionism existed alongside, and sometimes augmented or joined forces with, the efforts to escape, defy, or overthrow slavery undertaken by enslaved people in the South. Many thousands of enslaved people made difficult and dangerous journeys to freedom in the Northern states or in Canada, assisted by the extensive infrastructure of the "Underground Railroad" and the abolitionists who maintained it. The many different forms such journeys could take are illustrated in this section by the anonymous poem "Escape from Slavery of Henry Box Brown" and the selections from *Narratives of Fugitive Slaves in Canada*. A smaller but still significant number of enslaved people made even more difficult and dangerous journeys southward to freedom in Mexico, as the website excerpt from Frederick Law Olmsted's *A Journey Through Texas* attests. Still other enslaved people rose up against their enslavement or plotted to do so, including Denmark Vesey in South Carolina in 1822, Nat Turner in Virginia in 1831, Joseph Cinqué on the *Amistad* in 1839, and Madison Washington on the *Creole* in 1841. Similar, smaller-scale acts of defiance—no less powerful, and even more poignant, for the hopeless circumstances in which they were undertaken—are documented below in the excerpts from Bethany Veney's slave narrative and the newspaper article "Arrest of Fugitive Slaves" covering the famous case of Margaret Garner, who chose to kill her children rather than let them be taken back to slavery.

Faced with the condemnation of abolitionists and the active resistance, in various forms, of enslaved people themselves, enslavers and supporters of slavery increasingly sought to defend the institution and combat attempts to restrict, escape, or resist it. These efforts of enslavers and their allies also took a wide variety of forms, including the advertisements for fugitives placed in newspapers; the justifications of slavery penned by writers such as Zephaniah Kingsley, John P. Kennedy, and Caroline Lee Hentz; and political and legal mandates such as the 1850 Fugitive Slave Act and the 1857 *Dred Scott* decision. Slavery, and the racism which allowed it to endure, were further bolstered by—and left deep imprints on—institutions and cultural practices in the North. As the excerpt from Austin Reed's memoir *The Life and Adventures of a Haunted Convict* included in the website portion of this section demonstrates, often-racialized forms of involuntary servitude, including indenture and forced convict labor, continued in the North after slavery per se was abolished there (and the Thirteenth Amendment would later explicitly permit the continuation of penal servitude even as it abolished slavery per se nationwide). The massive popularity of blackface minstrelsy also helped the cause of slavery in the "free" states: the idealization of slavery and derogatory depiction of enslaved people in minstrel songs such as "Old Uncle Ned" (also included in this section's website portion) did much to make especially working-class white Northerners—many of whom felt threatened by the prospect of abolition, which they believed would increase competition for low-wage jobs—sympathetic towards slavery. While numerous white Northerners thus came to passively or actively support slavery, some white Southerners with daily, face-to-face acquaintance with the institution, such as the diarist Mary Chesnut, came to dislike it—albeit in Chesnut's case for reasons that centered on the opportunities for the sexual exploitation of enslaved women that slavery afforded to white men, and the attendant shame this brought on white women like herself.

The slavery debate came to a head in the 1850s in a series of escalating crises, including the bitter disputes over slavery's expansion into the western territories, the passage of and response to the Fugitive Slave Act, the argument surrounding Harriet Beecher Stowe's *Uncle Tom's Cabin*, the violence of "Bleeding Kansas," and the *Dred Scott* decision. In 1860, this chain of crises resulted in Southern secession. The ensuing Civil War brought about the downfall of slavery, though in a contingent, haphazard way: a contingency and haphazardness evident in the two versions, preliminary and final, of President Lincoln's Emancipation Proclamation, which reveal the political calculations that went into this epochal measure and the limitations of its scope and efficacy. Victory over secession in 1865 made emancipation a reality for enslaved African Americans throughout the South, but their legal status remained unclear until slavery was formally and universally abolished by the Thirteenth Amendment, which did not take effect until December 1865—and then it took two more constitutional amendments, in 1868 and 1870, to legally ensure the citizenship and voting rights of formerly enslaved people (or at least of formerly enslaved men).

The struggle between emancipated African Americans (and their allies) and erstwhile enslavers continued after the end of the Civil War. Formerly enslaved people sought to make the most of their newfound—but often only nominal—freedom, while former enslavers sought to restrict that freedom and reimpose a social and economic system as much like slavery as possible. This section tells this continuing story through documents such as Jourdon Anderson's witheringly deadpan response to his former enslaver's request for his continued labor; the advertisements placed by formerly enslaved people trying to reunite their broken, dispersed families; and examples of the many attempts made by white Southerners, by means of oratory, legal codes, and terrorist violence alike, to keep African Americans subordinated. By the 1870s—despite the ongoing efforts of such African American champions of civil rights as Robert B. Elliott and Frederick Douglass—these white Southern attempts to reimpose legalized racial subordination in another form had met with substantial success. Opponents of such racism would have to build on the activism of abolitionists into the Reconstruction era and beyond, as they pursued a vision of an America in which all citizens could be free, prosperous, and equal before the law.

⌘⌘⌘

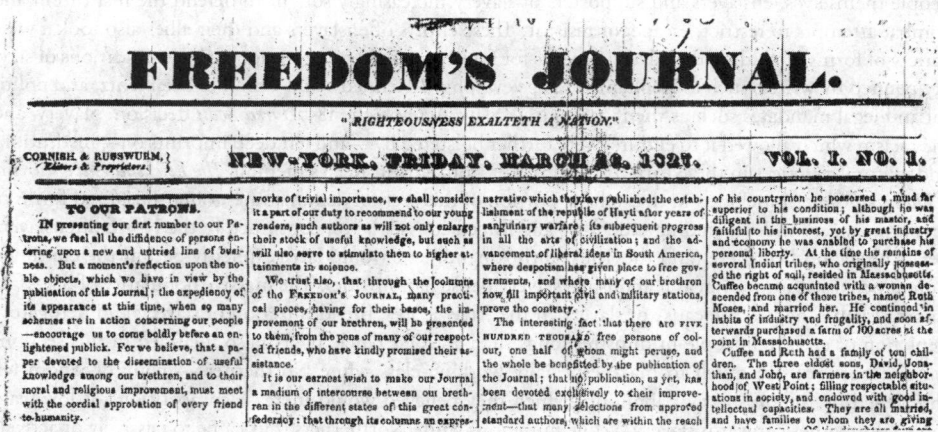

Masthead and opening of the first issue (16 March 1827) of *Freedom's Journal*, a pioneering African American newspaper that greatly influenced the development of the abolitionist movement. For the full text of the introductory editorial, "To Our Patrons," the beginning of which appears here, see the first selection below.

Samuel Cornish and John B. Russwurm, "To Our Patrons," *Freedom's Journal* (16 March 1827)

Founded in 1827 by leaders of the free black community in New York City, *Freedom's Journal* was the first newspaper owned and operated by African Americans to be published in the United States. The paper's initial editors were Samuel Cornish (1795–1858) and John B. Russwurm (1799–1851). Cornish was the first African American to become a Presbyterian minister; after *Freedom's Journal* ceased publication in 1829, he founded a new paper, *The Rights of All*. Russwurm was the second African American to have earned a bachelor's degree from a U.S. university. In addition to regional, national, and international news, the paper—which circulated in eleven states and the District of Columbia, as well as in Haiti, Europe, and Canada—published editorials opposing slavery, lynching, and other manifestations of white American racism; biographical and historical information relevant to African Americans; and announcements of births, marriages, and deaths in the New York black community. The paper folded in 1829, but it wielded a lasting influence on the abolitionist movement, as well as on the political consciousness of its African American readers: for example, David Walker, the antislavery activist who published his landmark *Appeal to the Coloured Citizens of the World* in 1829, was one of *Freedom's Journal*'s subscription agents.

The rationale, agenda, and contents of *Freedom's Journal* are aptly summarized in Cornish and Russwurm's introductory editorial to its first issue, presented below.

In presenting our first number to our patrons, we feel all the diffidence of persons entering upon a new and untried line of business. But a moment's reflection upon the noble objects which we have in view by the publication of this journal; the expediency of its appearance at this time, when so many schemes are in action concerning our people—encourage us to come boldly before an enlightened public. For we believe that a paper devoted to the dissemination of useful knowledge among our brethren, and to their moral and religious improvement, must meet with the cordial approbation of every friend to humanity.

The peculiarities of this journal render it important that we should advertise to the world the motives by which we are actuated, and the objects which we contemplate.

We wish to plead our own cause. Too long have others spoken for us. Too long has the public been deceived by misrepresentations, in things which concern us dearly, though in the estimation of some mere trifles; for though there are many in society who exercise towards us benevolent feelings; still (with sorrow we confess it) there are others who make it their business to enlarge upon the least trifle which tends to the discredit of any person of colour; and pronounce anathemas and denounce our whole body for the misconduct of this guilty one. We are aware that there are many instances of vice among us, but we avow that it is because no one has taught its subjects to be virtuous; many instances of poverty, because no sufficient efforts accommodated to minds contracted by slavery and deprived of early education have been made, to teach them how to husband their hard earnings, and to secure to themselves comforts.

Education being an object of the highest importance to the welfare of society, we shall endeavour to present just and adequate views of it, and to urge upon our brethren the necessity and expediency of training their children, while young, to habits of industry, and thus forming them for becoming useful members of society. It is surely time that we should awake from this lethargy of years, and make a concentrated effort for the education of our youth. We form a spoke in the human wheel, and it is necessary that we should understand our pendence[1] on the different parts, and theirs on us, in order to perform our part with propriety.

Though not desirous of dictating, we shall feel it our incumbent duty to dwell occasionally upon the general principles and rules of economy. The world has grown too enlightened, to estimate any man's character by his personal appearance. Though all men acknowledge

---

[1] *pendence* I.e., dependence.

the excellency of Franklin's maxims,[1] yet comparatively few practise upon them. We may deplore when it is too late, the neglect of these self-evident truths,[2] but it avails little to mourn. Ours will be the task of admonishing our brethren on these points.

The civil rights of a people being of the greatest value, it shall ever be our duty to vindicate our brethren, when oppressed; and to lay the case before the public. We shall also urge upon our brethren (who are qualified by the laws of the different states) the expediency of using their elective franchise;[3] and of making an independent use of the same. We wish them not to become the tools of party.

And as much time is frequently lost, and wrong principles instilled, by the perusal of works of trivial importance, we shall consider it a part of our duty to recommend to our young readers such authors as will not only enlarge their stock of useful knowledge, but such as will also serve to stimulate them to higher attainments in science.[4]

We trust also, that through the columns of the Freedom's Journal, many practical pieces, having for their bases the improvement of our brethren, will be presented to them, from the pens of many of our respected friends, who have kindly promised their assistance.

It is our earnest wish to make our journal a medium of intercourse[5] between our brethren in the different states of this great confederacy: that through its columns an expression of our sentiments, on many interesting subjects which concern us, may be offered to the public: that the plans which apparently are beneficial may be candidly discussed and properly weighed; if worthy, receive our cordial approbation; if not, our marked disapprobation.

Useful knowledge of every kind, and everything that relates to Africa, shall find a ready admission into our columns; and as that vast continent becomes daily more known, we trust that many things will come to light, proving that the natives of it are neither so ignorant nor stupid as they have generally been supposed to be.

And while these important subjects shall occupy the columns of the Freedom's Journal, we would not be unmindful of our brethren who are still in the iron fetters of bondage. They are our kindred by all the ties of nature; and though but little can be effected by us, still let our sympathies be poured forth, and our prayers in their behalf ascend to Him who is able to succour them.

From the press and the pulpit we have suffered much by being incorrectly represented. Men whom we equally love and admire have not hesitated to represent us disadvantageously, without becoming personally acquainted with the true state of things, nor discerning between virtue and vice among us. The virtuous part of our people feel themselves sorely aggrieved under the existing state of things—they are not appreciated.

Our vices and our degradation are ever arrayed against us, but our virtues are passed by unnoticed. And what is still more lamentable, our friends, to whom we concede all the principles of humanity and religion, from these very causes seem to have fallen into the current of popular feeling and are imperceptibly floating on the stream—actually living in the practice of prejudice, while they abjure it in theory, and feel it not in their hearts. Is it not very desirable that such should know more of our actual condition; and of our efforts and feelings, that in forming or advocating plans for our amelioration, they may do it more understandingly? In the spirit of candor and humility we intend by a simple representation of facts to lay our case before the public, with a view to arrest the progress of prejudice, and to shield ourselves against the consequent evils. We wish to conciliate all and to

---

[1] *Franklin's maxims*   I.e., the aphorisms and tips regarding how to manage one's economic affairs that the American colonial politician, intellectual, and writer Benjamin Franklin published in the yearly issues of his *Poor Richard's Almanack* (1732–58) and later collected in his essay "The Way to Wealth" (1758). Many of these maxims, such as "A penny saved is a penny earned" and "Early to bed, and early to rise, makes a man healthy, wealthy and wise," counsel industry and frugality and have become commonplaces in modern American vernacular.

[2] *self-evident truths*   See the second sentence of the Declaration of Independence: "We hold these truths to be self-evident, that all men are created equal, that they are endowed by their Creator with certain unalienable Rights, that among these are Life, Liberty and the pursuit of Happiness."

[3] *using … franchise*   I.e., voting.

[4] *science*   Intellectual study.

[5] *intercourse*   Communication.

irritate none, yet we must be firm and unwavering in our principles, and persevering in our efforts.

If ignorance, poverty and degradation have hitherto been our unhappy lot; has the eternal decree gone forth, that our race alone are to remain in this state, while knowledge and civilization are shedding their enlivening rays over the rest of the human family? The recent travels of Denham and Clapperton in the interior of Africa, and the interesting narrative which they have published;[1] the establishment of the republic of Haiti after years of sanguinary warfare;[2] its subsequent progress in all the arts of civilization; and the advancement of liberal ideas in South America, where despotism has given place to free governments,[3] and where many of our brethren now fill important civil and military stations, prove the contrary.

The interesting fact that there are five hundred thousand free persons of colour, one half of whom might peruse, and the whole be benefitted by the publication of the journal; that no publication, as yet, has been devoted exclusively to their improvement— that many selections from approved standard authors, which are within the reach of few, may occasionally be made—and more important still, that this large body of our citizens have no public channel—all serve to prove the real necessity, at present, for the appearance of the Freedom's Journal.

It shall ever be our desire so to conduct the editorial department of our paper as to give offence to none of our patrons; as nothing is farther from us than to make it the advocate of any partial[4] views, either in politics or religion. What few days we can number have been devoted to the improvement of our brethren; and it is our earnest wish that the remainder may be spent in the same delightful service.

In conclusion, whatever concerns us as a people will ever find a ready admission into the Freedom's Journal, interwoven with all the principal news of the day.

And while everything in our power shall be performed to support the character of our journal, we would respectfully invite our numerous friends to assist by their communications, and our coloured brethren to strengthen our hands by their subscriptions, as our labour is one of common cause, and worthy of their consideration and support. And we do most earnestly solicit the latter, that if at any time we should seem to be zealous, or too pointed in the inculcation of any important lesson, they will remember that they are equally interested in the cause in which we are engaged, and attribute our zeal to the peculiarities of our situation; and our earnest engagedness in their well-being.

THE EDITORS.

from Zephaniah Kingsley, *A Treatise on the Patriarchal, or Cooperative System of Society* (1828)

> Zephaniah Kingsley (1765–1843), an English-born Quaker, merchant, and slave trader, settled in Florida, then a Spanish colony, in 1803, where he became a major plantation owner; after Spain ceded Florida to the United States in 1821, he helped mediate Florida's transition to U.S. administration. Kingsley published *A Treatise on the Patriarchal, or Co-operative System of Society as It Exists in Some Governments and Colonies in America, and in the United States, Under the Name of Slavery, with Its Necessity and Advantages*—to give the work its full title—in 1828. The treatise defended the institution of slavery, albeit in terms that were heavily influenced by Kingsley's experience in Spanish Florida, where enslaved people were often encouraged to purchase their freedom and free black people were tolerated and permitted

---

[1] *The recent travels ... published* Between 1822 and 1825, the British military officers Dixon Denham and Hugh Clapperton traveled from Tripoli, on the Mediterranean coast of what is now Libya, to present-day Nigeria and back. Their account of the journey, *Narrative of Travels and Discoveries in Northern and Central Africa in the Years 1822–23 and 1824*, was published in 1826.

[2] *the establishment ... warfare* The Haitian Revolution began in 1791 in what was then the French colony of Saint Domingue (also known as St. Domingo), when the colony's enslaved black population rose in revolt. After over a decade of conflict, the Republic of Haiti won its independence in 1804, making the revolution the first successful large-scale rebellion by enslaved people in modern history. As such, the Haitian Revolution loomed large in the imagination of early nineteenth-century African Americans, including the founders and editors of *Freedom's Journal*.

[3] *the advancement ... free governments* By 1827, all of the Spanish colonies in mainland North, Central, and South America had achieved independence from Spain.

[4] *partial* Biased; unduly favoring one party over others.

some civil rights. Kingsley—who took four of his enslaved women as common-law wives or concubines, all of whom he eventually freed—was troubled by Florida's transition to the U.S.'s more rigid form of race-based slavery, in which the existence of free black people was viewed as a threat, and he left the state for Haiti in the 1830s. His treatise was reprinted in 1829, 1833, and 1834; despite some criticism of Kingsley's support for a class of free black people existing alongside enslaved people, the treatise continued to inform Southern defenses of slavery as a "positive good" down to the Civil War.

The treatise's preface, summarizing its main arguments, is presented below; the text is based on the treatise's 1829 second edition. A longer excerpt from the body of the work can be found in the website portion of this anthology.

PREFACE

It will be allowed[1] by everyone that agriculture is the great foundation of the wealth and prosperity of our Southern states. This important science has already attracted some share of attention from men of the first talents, by whose improvements in cultivation several valuable productions promise, from their superiority, to maintain a preference in foreign markets; and the recent introduction of new articles of tropical produce into the southern districts, where they bid fair to succeed, offers still greater incitements to agricultural enterprise, and opens a new and extensive range for future speculation.

While this great field of wealth and independence promises now to be well understood and duly appreciated, the primary cause and means by which alone it can be realized, has either escaped attention, or been designedly overlooked: I mean the perpetuation of that kind of labor which now produces it, and which seems best adapted, under all circumstances, to render it profitable to the Southern capitalist.

The idea of slavery, when associated with cruelty and injustice, is revolting to every philanthropic mind; but when that idea is associated with justice and benevolence, slavery, commonly so called, easily amalgamates with the ordinary conditions of life.

To counteract the existing prejudice against slavery, by making it evident that the condition of slaves may be equally happy and more independent of the ordinary evils of life, than that of the common class of whites denominated free—that they are now equally virtuous, moral and less corrupted than the ordinary class of laboring whites—that their labor is far more

Robert Douglass, Jr., *The Booroom Slave,* 1834. This pen-and-ink wash drawing by Douglass (1809–87), a Philadelphia-based African American artist, appears on one of the first pages of the friendship album of Mary Anne Dickerson, another black Philadelphian. (Friendship albums were scrapbooks in which friends of the album's owner could leave notes, poems, sketches, or other keepsakes.) The image reworks a well-known abolitionist painting by the English artist Henry Thomson. The lines underneath, taken from a 1744 poem by the English writer William Shenstone, read "When the grim lion urged his cruel chase, / When the stern panther sought his midnight prey, / What fate reserved me for this Christian race? / A race more polished, more severe than they!"

---

[1]   *allowed* Admitted.

productive—that they yield more support and benefit to the State; which, under a well regulated system of management, is better fitted to endure a state of war than it would be with an equal number of free white people of ordinary means and condition; and, finally, that the slave or patriarchal system of society (so often commiserated[1] as a subject of deep regret) which constitutes the bond of social compact of the southern seaboard of the United States, is better adapted for strength, durability and independence, than any other state of society hitherto adopted. To endeavor to prove all this, and to destroy the prejudice existing against slavery, under the circumstances with which it is now associated in the South, is the object of the present essay; dedicated to the people of Florida, and to political economists throughout the Southern states, by a votary of rational policy, and

most respectfully

their humble servant,

Z. KINGSLEY

from Theodore Dwight Weld, Angelina Grimké Weld, and Sarah Grimké, *American Slavery as It Is: Testimony of a Thousand Witnesses* (1839)

A compendious, impassioned compilation of firsthand testimony about slavery, *American Slavery as It Is* influenced the development of the American abolitionist movement more than quite possibly any other single work. The degree of the book's importance can be measured by the fact that its primary rival for the title of most influential abolitionist work, Harriet Beecher Stowe's *Uncle Tom's Cabin* (1852), relied heavily on it. The book was co-authored by Theodore Dwight Weld (1803–95), a prominent abolitionist during the movement's formative years in the 1830s and 40s, and the Grimké sisters, Angelina (1805–79) and Sarah (1792–1873), antislavery activists originally from South Carolina (Angelina Grimké was also Weld's wife). Weld and the Grimkés put together the book largely from numerous direct descriptions of, or examples of, slavery's brutality, most of

them written by observers in the slave states and especially by enslavers themselves; newspaper advertisements offering rewards for fugitive enslaved people were a particularly useful resource. (The book emphasized the accounts of enslavers over those of enslaved people, because, as its authors put it, "That [enslavers] should utter falsehoods, for the sake of proclaiming their own infamy, is not probable.") The book's impact thus derived not just from its array of factual evidence about what slavery was actually like, but specifically from the way in which it derived this evidence in large part from enslavers' own words.

... It is assumed by slaveholders that "public opinion" at the South[2] so frowns on cruelty to the slaves, that *fear of disgrace* would restrain from the infliction of it, were there no other consideration.

Now, that this is sheer fiction is shown by the fact that the newspapers in the slaveholding states teem with advertisements for runaway slaves, in which the masters and mistresses describe their men and women as having been "branded with a hot iron," on their "cheeks," "jaws," "breasts," "arms," "legs," and "thighs"; also as "scarred," "very much scarred," "cut up," "marked," etc. "with the whip," also with "iron collars on," "chains," "bars of iron," "fetters," "bells," "horns,"[3] "shackles," etc. They also describe them as having been wounded by "buckshot," "rifle-balls," etc. fired at them by their "owners," and others when in pursuit; also, as having "notches" cut in their ears, the tops or bottoms of their ears "cut off," or "slit," or "one ear cut off," or "both ears cut off," etc. etc. The masters and mistresses who thus advertise their runaway slaves coolly sign their names to their advertisements, giving the street and number of their residences, if in cities, their post office address, etc. if in the country; thus making public proclamation as widely as possible that *they* "brand,"

---

[1] *commiserated* Lamented.

[2] *at the South* I.e., in the South.

[3] *bells, horns* Enslaved people—especially those who had previously attempted to escape—were sometimes forced to wear metal collars with bells attached, often known as a "bell and horns," to prevent further escape attempts. Moses Roper's *Narrative of the Adventures and Escape of Moses Roper, from American Slavery* (1838) described the use of "iron horns, with bells, attached to the back of the slave's neck," calling such implements (which could be several feet in height) an "instrument of torture."

"scar," "gash," "cut up," etc. the flesh of their slaves; load them with irons, cut off their ears, etc.; they speak of these things with the utmost *sang froid*,[1] not seeming to think it possible that any one will esteem them at all the less because of these outrages upon their slaves; further, these advertisements swarm in many of the largest and most widely circulated political and commercial papers that are published in the slave states. The editors of those papers constitute the main body of the literati of the slave states; they move in the highest circle of society, are among the "popular" men in the community, and *as a class*, are more influential than any other; yet these editors publish these advertisements with iron indifference. So far from proclaiming to such felons, homicides, and murderers, that they will not be their bloodhounds, to hunt down the innocent and mutilated victims who have escaped from their torture, they freely furnish them with every facility,[2] become their accomplices and share their spoils; and instead of outraging "public opinion" by doing it, they are the men after its own heart, its organs, its representatives, its *self*.

To show that the "public opinion" of the slave states towards the slaves is absolutely *diabolical,* we will insert a few, out of a multitude, of similar advertisements from a variety of southern papers now before us.

The North Carolina Standard, of July 18, 1838, contains the following:

"TWENTY DOLLARS REWARD. Ran away from the subscriber, a negro woman and two children; the woman is tall and black, and *a few days before she went off,* I burnt her with a hot iron on the left side of her face; I tried to make the letter M, *and she kept a cloth over her head and face and a fly bonnet on her head so as to cover the burn;* her children are both boys, the oldest is in his seventh year; he is a *mulatto*[3] and has blue eyes; the youngest is black and is in his fifth year. The woman's name is Betty, commonly called Bet.

MICAJAH RICKS.

Nash County, July 7, 1838."

---

[1]   *sang froid*   French: cold blood.

[2]   *facility*   Opportunity, accommodation.

[3]   *mulatto*   Term, now universally regarded as offensive, that was widely used in the nineteenth century to classify individuals of mixed racial background—typically, someone with one white parent and one parent of African descent.

Hear the wretch tell his story, with as much indifference as if he were describing the cutting of his initials in the bark of a tree.

"*I burnt her with a hot iron on the left side of her face,*" "*I tried to make the letter M,*" and this he says in a newspaper, and puts his name to it, and the editor of the paper, who is also its proprietor, publishes it for him and pockets his fee. ...

J.P. Ashford advertises as follows in the "Natchez Courier," August 24, 1838.

"Ran away, a negro girl called Mary, has a small scar over her eye, a *good many teeth missing,* the letter A. *is branded on her cheek and forehead.*"

A.B. Metcalf thus advertises a woman in the same paper, June 15, 1838.

"Ran away, Mary, a black woman, has a *scar* on her back and right arm near the shoulder, *caused by a rifle ball.*"

John Henderson, in the "Grand Gulf Advertiser," August 29, 1838, advertises Betsey.

"Ran away, a black woman Betsey, has an *iron bar on her right leg.*"

Robert Nicoll, whose residence is in Mobile, in Dauphin street, between Emmanuel and Conception streets, thus advertises a woman in the "Mobile Commercial Advertiser."

"TEN DOLLARS REWARD will be given for my negro woman Liby. The said Liby is about 30 years old, and VERY MUCH SCARRED ABOUT THE NECK AND EARS, occasioned by whipping, had on a handkerchief tied round her ears, as she COMMONLY wears it to HIDE THE SCARS."

To show that slaveholding brutality now is the same that it was the eighth of a century ago, we publish the following advertisement from the "Charleston (S.C.) Courier," of 1825.

"TWENTY DOLLARS REWARD—Ran away from the subscriber, on the 14th instant,[4] a negro girl named Molly.

"The said girl was sold by Messrs. Wm. Payne & Sons, as the property of an estate of a Mr. Gearrall, and purchased by a Mr. Moses, and sold by him to a Thomas Prisley, of Edgefield District, of whom I

---

[4]   *instant*   Anglicization of the Latin "instante mense," meaning "[of] this month."

bought her on the 17th of April, 1819. She is 16 or 17 years of age, slim made, LATELY BRANDED ON THE LEFT CHEEK, THUS, R, and a piece taken off of her ear on the same side; the same letter on the inside of both her legs.

ABNER ROSS, Fairfield District."

But instead of filling pages with similar advertisements, illustrating the horrible brutality of slaveholders towards their slaves, the reader is referred to the preceding pages of this work, to the scores of advertisements written by slaveholders, printed by slaveholders, published by slaveholders, in newspapers edited by slaveholders, and patronized by slaveholders; advertisements describing not only men and boys, but women, aged and middle-aged, matrons and girls of tender years, their necks chafed with iron collars with prongs, their limbs galled with iron rings, and chains, and bars of iron, iron hobbles and shackles, all parts of their persons scarred with the lash, and branded with hot irons, and torn with rifle bullets, pistol balls and buck shot, and gashed with knives, their eyes out, their ears cut off, their teeth drawn out, and their bones broken. He is referred also to the cool and shocking indifference with which these slaveholders, "gentlemen" and "ladies," Reverends, and Honorables, and Excellencies, write and print, and publish and pay, and take money for, and read and circulate, and sanction, such infernal barbarity. Let the reader ponder all this, and then lay it to heart, that this is that "public opinion" of the slaveholders which protects their slaves from all injury, and is an effectual guarantee of personal security. ...

But we are not yet quite ready to dismiss this protector, "Public Opinion." To illustrate the hardened brutality with which slaveholders regard their slaves, the shameless and apparently unconscious indecency with which they speak of their female slaves, examine their persons, and describe them, under their own signatures, in newspapers, hand-bills, etc. just as they would describe the marks of cattle and swine, on all parts of their bodies; we will make a few extracts from southern papers. Reader, as we proceed to these extracts, remember our motto—"True humanity consists *not* in a squeamish ear."

Mr. P. Abdie, of New Orleans, advertises in the New Orleans Bee, of January 29, 1838, for one of his female slaves, as follows;

"Ran away, the negro wench[1] named Betsey, aged about 22 years, handsome-faced, and good countenance; having the marks of the whip behind her neck, and several others on her rump. The above reward ($10) will be given to whoever will bring that wench to P. Abdie." ...

Mr. William Robinson, Georgetown, District of Columbia, advertised for his slave in the National Intelligencer, of Washington City, Oct. 2, 1837, as follows:

"Eloped from my residence a young negress, 22 years old, of a chesnut, or brown color. She has a very singular mark—this mark, to the best of my recollection, covers a part of her *breasts*, *body*, and *limbs*; and when her neck and arms are uncovered, is very perceptible; she has been frequently seen east and south of the Capitol Square, and is harbored by ill-disposed persons, of every complexion, for her services."

Mr. John C. Beasley, near Huntsville, Alabama, thus advertises a young girl of eighteen, in the Huntsville Democrat, of August 1st, 1837. "Ran away Maria, about 18 years old, *very far advanced with child.*" He then offers a reward to any one who will commit this young girl, in this condition, *to jail*. ...

The above are a few specimens of the gross[2] details, in describing the persons of females, of all ages, and the marks upon all parts of their bodies; proving incontestably, that slaveholders are in the habit not only of stripping their female slaves of their clothing, and inflicting punishment upon their "shrinking flesh,"[3] but of subjecting their naked persons to the most minute and revolting inspection, and then of publishing to the world the results of their examination, as well as the scars left by their own inflictions upon them, their length, size, and exact position on the body; and all this without impairing in the least, the standing in the community of the shameless wretches who thus proclaim their own abominations. That such things should not at all affect the standing of such persons in

---

1   *wench*   In American usage, this word, a now-derogatory term for a female servant, was exclusively applied to black women.

2   *gross*   Repulsively immoral or uncivilized.

3   *shrinking flesh*   See the abolitionist poet John Greenleaf Whittier's "Stanzas," later retitled "Expostulation" (1834): "What, ho!—*our* countrymen in chains! / The whip on woman's shrinking flesh!"

society, is certainly no marvel: how could they affect it, when the same communities enact laws *requiring* their own legal officers to inspect minutely the persons and bodily marks of all slaves taken up as runaways, and to publish in the newspapers a particular description of all such marks and peculiarities of their persons, their size, appearance, position on the body, etc. Yea, verily, when the "public opinion" of the community, in the solemn form of law, commands jailors, sheriffs, captains of police, etc. to divest of their clothing aged matrons and young girls, minutely examine their naked persons, and publish the results of their examination—who can marvel, that the same "public opinion" should tolerate the slaveholders themselves, in doing the same things to their own property, which they have appointed legal officers to do as their proxies.[1] ...

Runaway Advertisements

For nearly two centuries, advertisements for fugitive enslaved people—posted either by enslavers offering rewards for their return or by authorities announcing their capture—were an extremely common feature of American newspapers. Such advertisements began to appear almost as soon as the first newspapers were founded in the American colonies, and they continued to be printed—as the final example below indicates—even after the official abolition of slavery, as the so-called "Black Codes" (bodies of law introduced immediately after the Civil War in many Southern states that imposed numerous restrictions on the freedom of emancipated African Americans, including labor requirements) attempted to perpetuate legal African American servitude in a different form. The examples of runaway advertisements from the early and mid-nineteenth century included here provide insight into how enslavers thought about their "property"; they also offer small but valuable windows into the lives of enslaved people who may otherwise have left no trace in the historical record.

FROM THE *RALEIGH REGISTER AND NORTH CAROLINA WEEKLY ADVERTISER* (19 MAY 1820)

RUNAWAY NEGROES

On the 10th of this month I bought at a Sheriff's sale, a stout black negro woman by the name of Sooky, considerably advanced in years, and her female child, called Olive, about four years old. They were sold as the property of Samuel G. Briggs, of Raleigh. They formerly belonged to a Miss Hart, who lived in Mr. Briggs's family, and were, as I understand, brought from Northampton County. They were at my house in the night after the sale, and apparently contented, but in the morning were missing. Whether they have attempted to make their way to Northampton; or whether they are harbored in or about Raleigh; or what has become of them, I am at a loss to conjecture.

Any useful information on this subject will be thankfully received; and I will give a reward of ten dollars to any person who will deliver the negroes to me, together with a suitable reward for any services beyond my present expectation.

HENRY POTTER.
Raleigh, May 18, 1820.

---

[1] [Authors' note] As a sample of these laws, we give the following extract from one of the laws of Maryland, where slaveholding "public opinion" exists in its mildest form.

"It shall be the duty of the sheriffs of the several counties of this state, upon any runaway servant or slave being committed to his custody, to cause the same to be advertised, etc. and to make particular and minute descriptions of the *person and bodily marks* of such runaway." –*Laws of Maryland of* 1802, Chap. 96, Sec. 1 and 2.

That the sheriffs, jailors, etc. do not neglect this part of their official "duty" is plain from the minute description which they give in the advertisements of marks upon all parts of the persons of females, as well as males; and also from the occasional declaration "no scars discoverable on any part," or "no marks discoverable *about* her"; which last is taken from an advertisement in the Milledgeville (Geo.) Journal, June 26, 1838, signed "T.S. Densler, Jailor."

FROM THE *MOBILE COMMERCIAL REGISTER*
(2 JUNE 1826)

NOTICE.

COMMITTED to the Jail of Mobile County, on the 23d of January last, a Negro Man, named GUY, five feet, eight inches high, with a scar on his right cheek, & also a small scar on the right side of his nose. Appears to be 35 years of age, says he came from Monticello, in Mississippi, to this place, and professes to be free. If he is not taken out in the time prescribed by law, he will be sold to pay jail fees.

James P. Bates,
Sheriff.

$100 Reward.

RUN AWAY from the subscriber living in Walker county, Georgia, a negro boy named ESSEX, about 28 or 29 years old, 5 feet 8 or 9 inches high, spare made, dark complexion, quick spoken, and intelligent, and disposed to converse with any person who will converse with him, can read and write his name; he left me during Christmas holidays, in the year 1839; on one of his ancles or feet he had a scar produced by the cut of an axe. He was principally raised in Elbert county, by James Mann, and afterwards taken to Gwinnett county, and is supposed to be harbored by some person in that region of country.

Fifty Dollars reward will be given to any person who will deliver said boy to me, or lodge him in some jail so that I get him, and Fifty Dollars more for the thief or harborer with sufficient testimony to convict him.

JAMES GORDEN.

Lafayette, Walker co., Ga., May 20, 1841. 50—4t

☞ The Southern Whig, Athens, will give the above four insertions, and forward their account to me.

J. G.

Runaway advertisement from the *Milledgeville Federal Union*, 8 June 1841.

FROM THE *MILLEDGEVILLE FEDERAL UNION*
(1 NOVEMBER 1853)

$400 Reward.

RAN AWAY or stolen from my negro mart in Columbus,[1] in December last, TWO NEGRO MEN, one named Simon, the other named John, both carpenters. Simon is a yellow[2] copper-colored man, about forty years old, middling height, stout built, he has a scar in one corner of his mouth cut with a knife; since his departure he has been seen lurking about Mr. Bowin's in Coweta County, where he has a wife. He was purchased of E.C. Bowin in the neighborhood of Griffin; he may be in that section, or he may be in Carroll County. John is a mulatto about 45 or 50 years of age, middling height, stout built, in a previous runaway scrape he tried to pass himself off as a Frenchman, he can talk French a little. A few days previous to his leaving he received a severe scar on his forehead in a fight with a negro. I presume the scar is still to be seen; he is considerably gray, perhaps half gray, the black hairs are very black. It is not likely that he will acknowledge himself a slave. When he was apprehended before, he claimed to be a free Frenchman, and threatened to prosecute the party that took him for unlawfully detaining him. They were on the point of releasing him, when he was recognized by a carpenter that he had worked for. The above reward will be given for the delivery of the two negroes if stolen with sufficient proof to convict the thief, or ONE HUNDRED DOLLARS for either of the negroes, if delivered to me by the fifteenth of November next, or FIFTY DOLLARS, if delivered any time after the 15th of November or placed in any jail so that I can get them.

H.H. LOWE.

---

[1] *negro mart* I.e., establishment of a trader and seller of enslaved people; *Columbus* City in western Georgia. Milledgeville, where this newspaper was published, was at the time the Georgia state capital.

[2] *yellow* Term, now considered offensive except in African American usage, for a (usually mixed-race) African American with light brown skin.

TWENTY-FIVE DOLLARS REWARD—For the apprehension of the griffe[1] woman JOSEPHINE, about 34 years of age, of medium height, some teeth missing, and rather polite or modest. She formerly lived at Algiers,[2] and was until recently owned by Mr. J.C. Wilson at the Balize,[3] where she has a daughter about 16 years of age, of whom she appears to be very fond.

She left on Friday last, 18th inst.,[4] about 2 o'clock P.M., was dressed ordinarily, had no shoes on and appeared to be intoxicated.

The above reward will be paid by

MAJOR HARBIN, 169 Gravier street, or at No. 30 Poydras street.

Runaway—GEORGE WASHINGTON, a negro boy aged about 15 years who was indentured to the undersigned by the Assistant Superintendent of the Freedmen's Bureau[5] on the 25th day of September, 1865, has absconded from my service and employment, without any just cause or provocation. This is to forewarn all persons against harboring or employing the said indentured boy, as in such cases the law will be rigidly enforced against those so employing or harboring the said George. And for the apprehension and return of him to me in Greensboro[6] a reasonable reward will be paid.

JAMES F. PEARCE.

anonymous, "Escape from Slavery of Henry Box Brown" (c. 1849)

Henry Brown (c. 1815–97), an enslaved Virginian man, resolved to escape in August 1848, when his wife Nancy and their three children were all sold away to North Carolina. With the help of two citizens of Richmond, Virginia, one of whom was a free black man, Brown arranged to have himself shipped in a box from Richmond to the office of an abolitionist Quaker merchant in Philadelphia. His journey in the box, which measured three feet long, two and a half feet deep, and two feet wide, took place in March 1849 and lasted just over a full day before he arrived safely in Philadelphia. During Brown's subsequent tour on the abolitionist lecture circuit, he added "Box" to his name. The first of two published versions of Brown's life story, *Narrative of Henry Box Brown*, appeared in Boston in 1849, and Brown used his share of its proceeds to fund a live theatrical experience, *Henry Box Brown's Mirror of Slavery*, which featured a moving panorama—a very long canvas with a series of paintings that was progressively unrolled on stage—together with music and narration. He toured with the panorama throughout New England and—after the Fugitive Slave Act was passed in 1850—Great Britain, where he settled and where the second version of his narrative was published. In his later life, Brown made his living as a magician and entertainer; after returning to the U.S. in 1875, he moved to Canada in 1886 and died there in 1897.

One of the many renditions of Brown's famous escape that circulated, in various mediums, in the years after it took place was the song given below, the lyrics to which were printed (probably in the summer of 1849) in Boston as a broadside, here reproduced in facsimile. The song was composed to the tune of—and satirically rewrites the lyrics of—a minstrel song, "Old Uncle Ned," the words to which can be found in the website portion of this section.

---

[1]   *griffe* Term for a person with three-quarters black and one-quarter white ancestry. Like all such nineteenth-century terms classifying people in terms of their racial background, it is today considered archaic and offensive.

[2]   *Algiers* Neighborhood in New Orleans, Louisiana, the second-oldest neighborhood in the city.

[3]   *the Balize* La Balize, Louisiana, a community at the mouth of the Mississippi River; it was abandoned in 1860 after being destroyed by a hurricane.

[4]   *inst.* Abbreviation of Latin "instante mense," meaning "[of] this month."

[5]   *Freedmen's Bureau* U.S. government agency established after the Civil War to provide essential services to formerly enslaved people ("freedmen"), including food, medical care, education, locating and communicating with family members, and employment.

[6]   *Greensboro* Town in North Carolina.

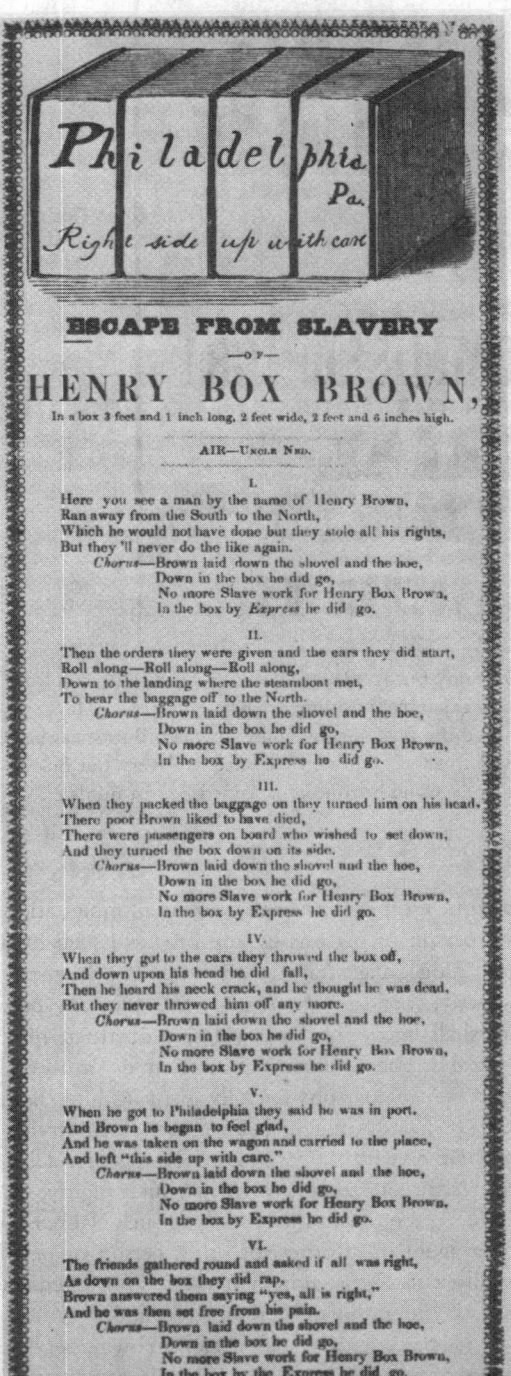

from the Fugitive Slave Act (1850)

The right of enslavers to apprehend enslaved people who had escaped into another state and to have them returned to slavery was codified in the so-called "Fugitive Slave Clause" of the U.S. Constitution, and was further enforced by a Fugitive Slave Act passed in 1793. By the 1840s, however, the steady stream of enslaved people escaping to the North, the extent of the assistance they were receiving from Northern abolitionists, and various measures taken by local and state courts and legislatures in the North, and by the U.S. Supreme Court, that made it more difficult for enslavers to reclaim fugitive "property" in other states all convinced many Southerners that a more rigorous update of the 1793 act was needed. The resultant 1850 Fugitive Slave Act formed a key part of the Compromise of 1850, a package of laws designed to settle the intensifying disputes between North and South over slavery and its westward expansion (or, as many Northern abolitionists saw it, to appease the South). The act penalized anyone—not just law enforcement officers but common citizens—who sought to aid fugitive enslaved people or did not cooperate in their capture; gave officials financial incentives to return fugitives to slavery; and denied alleged fugitives the right to a jury trial or even to testify on their own behalf—a provision that resulted in free black Northerners being kidnapped, accused of being fugitives, and enslaved. The Fugitive Slave Act convinced many African Americans that they could not live safely anywhere in the United States, while the act's attempt, in effect, to make every American citizen responsible for enforcing slavery intensified the antislavery commitment of abolitionists and pushed many white Northerners who had previously believed slavery was no concern of theirs to oppose the institution.

... Sec. 6. *And be it further enacted*, That when a person held to service or labor in any State or Territory of the United States, has heretofore or shall hereafter escape into another State or Territory of the United States, the person or persons to whom such service or labor may be due, or his, her, or their agent

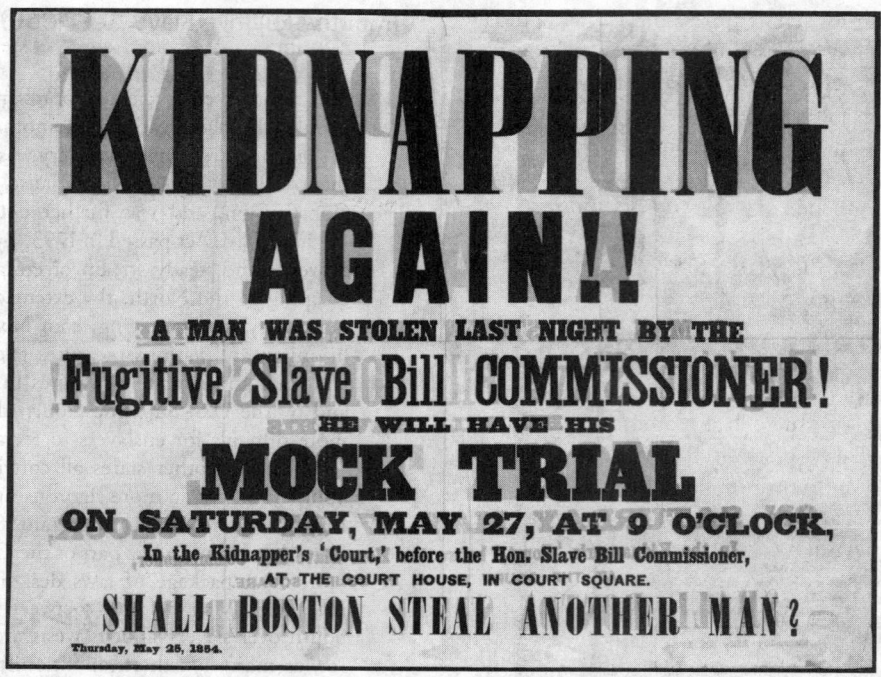

KIDNAPPING AGAIN!!
A MAN WAS STOLEN LAST NIGHT BY THE
Fugitive Slave Bill COMMISSIONER!
HE WILL HAVE HIS
MOCK TRIAL
ON SATURDAY, MAY 27, AT 9 O'CLOCK,
In the Kidnapper's 'Court,' before the Hon. Slave Bill Commissioner,
AT THE COURT HOUSE, IN COURT SQUARE.
SHALL BOSTON STEAL ANOTHER MAN?
Thursday, May 25, 1854.

This broadside, distributed in Boston in 1854, publicizes the case of Anthony Burns (1834–62), who escaped to Boston from slavery in Virginia. His capture under the 1850 Fugitive Slave Act sparked intense opposition; on the evening of 26 May 1854, the day after this broadside was printed, a group of abolitionists attacked the Boston courthouse in which Burns was held in an unsuccessful attempt to free him. With the aid of federal troops, Burns was eventually returned to slavery, but Boston sympathizers later purchased his freedom. He then attended Oberlin College and became an ordained Baptist minister.

or attorney, duly authorized, by power of attorney, in writing, … may pursue and reclaim such fugitive person, either by procuring a warrant from some one of the courts, judges, or commissioners aforesaid, … or by seizing and arresting such fugitive, where the same can be done without process, and by taking, or causing such person to be taken, forthwith before such court, judge, or commissioner, whose duty it shall be to hear and determine the case of such claimant in a summary manner[.][1] … In no trial or hearing under this act shall the testimony of such alleged fugitive be admitted in evidence; and the certificates in this and the first [fourth] section mentioned, shall be conclusive of the right of the person or persons in whose favor granted, to remove such fugitive to the State or Territory from

which he escaped, and shall prevent all molestation of such person or persons by any process issued by any court, judge, magistrate, or other person whomsoever.

Sec. 7. *And be it further enacted,* That any person who shall knowingly and willingly obstruct, hinder, or prevent such claimant, his agent or attorney, or any person or persons lawfully assisting him, her, or them, from arresting such a fugitive from service or labor, either with or without process as aforesaid, or shall rescue, or attempt to rescue, such fugitive from service or labor, from the custody of such claimant, his or her agent or attorney, or other person or persons lawfully assisting as aforesaid, when so arrested, pursuant to the authority herein given and declared; or shall aid, abet, or assist such person so owing service or labor as aforesaid, directly or indirectly, to escape from such claimant, his agent or attorney, or other person or

[1]   *in a summary manner*   Quickly, without jury trial or other usual judicial procedures.

persons legally authorized as aforesaid; or shall harbor or conceal such fugitive, so as to prevent the discovery and arrest of such person, after notice or knowledge of the fact that such person was a fugitive from service or labor as aforesaid, shall, for either of said offences, be subject to a fine not exceeding one thousand dollars, and imprisonment not exceeding six months, by indictment and conviction before the District Court of the United States for the district in which such offence may have been committed, or before the proper court of criminal jurisdiction, if committed within any one of the organized Territories of the United States; and shall moreover forfeit and pay, by way of civil damages to the party injured by such illegal conduct, the sum of one thousand dollars for each fugitive so lost as aforesaid, to be recovered by action of debt, in any of the District or Territorial Courts aforesaid, within whose jurisdiction the said offence may have been committed.

Sec. 8. *And be it further enacted*, That the marshals, their deputies, and the clerks of the said District and Territorial Courts, shall be paid, for their services, the like fees as may be allowed for similar services in other cases; ... and in all cases where the proceedings are before a commissioner, he shall be entitled to a fee of ten dollars in full for his services in each case, upon the delivery of the said certificate[1] to the claimant, his agent or attorney; or a fee of five dollars in cases where the proof shall not, in the opinion of such commissioner, warrant such certificate and delivery, inclusive of all services incident to such arrest and examination, to be paid, in either case, by the claimant, his or her agent or attorney. ...

from Bethany Veney, *The Narrative of Bethany Veney: A Slave Woman* (1889)

Bethany Veney (c. 1815–1916) was born into slavery on a plantation in the Shenandoah Valley, in Virginia. She endured a forced separation from her first husband, Jerry Fickland, when he was sold further south; many years

later, she was to dedicate her *Narrative* to Fickland. Veney herself endured being sold to several plantation owners before she was purchased in the 1850s by a Northern entrepreneur and abolitionist who freed her and her son. This purchase, while it gave Veney and her child freedom, led to Veney's permanent separation from her second husband, Frank Veney. The selection below from Bethany Veney's memoir, which she dictated in the 1880s, describes her separation from Fickland; a longer excerpt, detailing the couple's courtship and marriage, is included in the website component of this anthology.

CHAPTER 5
MEETING—A LAST INTERVIEW—SEPARATION

The place where I was to meet Jerry[2] was, as I have said, across the run,[3] in a corn-field, near the blacksmith's shop, the time Friday night.

It had rained hard all day, and the stream was swollen, and pouring and rushing at a fearful rate. I waited till everybody was in bed and asleep, when I lighted my pine knot,[4] and started for the Pass. It was still raining, and the night was very dark. Only by my torch could I see a step before me; and, when I attempted to wade in, as I did in many different places, I found it was no use. I should surely be drowned if I persisted. So, disappointed and grieved, I gave up and went home. The next morning I was able to get over on horseback to milk the cows, but I neither heard nor saw anything of Jerry.

Saturday night came. I knew well that, if not caught by White,[5] Jerry would be round. At last, everyone was in bed, and all was still. I waited and listened. I listened and waited. Then I heard his step at the door. I hurriedly opened it, and he came in. His clothes were

---

[1] *the said certificate* I.e., the certificate mentioned in Section 6 authorizing the enslaver or their representative(s) to remove the captured fugitive or fugitives back to the state or territory in which they were enslaved.

[2] *The place ... Jerry* In the previous chapter of Veney's *Narrative*, included in the website portion of this section, she and Jerry discover that he is to be sold to help pay the debts of his enslaver's family. Jerry is permitted to visit his wife before being sent south; during the visit, they decide that he will try to escape and hide in the mountains, where Bethany will meet him to discuss their further course of action.

[3] *run* Creek, stream.

[4] *pine knot* Piece of pinewood carried as a torch.

[5] *White* Frank White, the slave trader to whom Jerry has been sold.

still damp and stiff from the rain of yesterday. He was frightened and uneasy. He had been hiding around in different places, constantly fearing detection. He had seen me from behind the old blacksmith's shop when I had tried the night before, with my pine knot, to ford the stream; and he was glad, he said, when he saw me go back, for he knew I should be carried down by the current and be drowned, if I had persisted. I went to my mistress's bedroom, and asked her if I might go to the cellar. She knew at once what I meant, and whispered softly, "Betty, has Jerry come?" then, without waiting for reply, added, "get him some milk and light bread and butter." I was not long in doing so; and the poor fellow ate like one famishing. Then he wanted to know all that had happened, and what White had said when he found he was gone. We talked a long time, and tried to devise some plans for our mutual safety and possible escape from slavery altogether; but, every way we looked, the path was beset with danger and exposure. We were both utterly disheartened. But sleep came at last and, for the time being, relieved us of our fears.

In the morning, which was Sunday, we had our breakfast together, and, as the hours passed, began to feel a little comforted. After dinner, we walked out to the field and strolled about for some time; and, when ready to go back to the house, we each took an armful of fodder along for the horses. As we laid it down and turned to go into the house, David McCoy[1] rode up on horseback. He saw Jerry at once, and called him to come to the fence. The excitement of the last days— the fasting and the fear—had completely cowed and broken whatever of manhood, or even of brute courage, a slave might by any possibility be presumed at any time to be possessed of, and the last remains of these qualities in poor Jerry were gone. He mutely obeyed; and when, with an oath, McCoy commanded him to mount the horse behind him, he mutely seated himself there. McCoy then called to me to go to the house and bring Jerry's clothes. "Never," I screamed back to him—"never, not to save your miserable life." But Jerry said: "O Betty, 'tis no use. We can't help it." I knew this was so. I stifled my anger and my grief, brought his little bundle, into which I tucked a testament and catechism

someone had given me, and shook hands "good-bye" with him. So we *parted forever*, in this world.

from "Arrest of Fugitive Slaves," *Cincinnati Gazette* (29 January 1856)

One especially well-publicized case of an enslaved person's attempt to escape or resist enslavement was that of Margaret Garner, an enslaved woman who escaped from northern Kentucky along with her husband Robert, her four children—the three younger of whom were most likely fathered by her enslaver, Archibald Gaines—and a group of relatives and other enslaved families. When the Garners were caught outside Cincinnati, Ohio, Margaret—in an attempt to prevent her children from being taken back to slavery—killed her two-year-old daughter Mary with a butcher's knife and wounded her other children before being subdued. In the hearing that followed, Margaret's defenders, who included the prominent women's-rights activist Lucy Stone, argued that she should stand trial in Ohio rather than being immediately returned to slavery in Kentucky, but she was eventually returned to her enslaver, who then sent her and her husband "down the river" to the Deep South; she died in Mississippi in 1858. Margaret Garner's case became instantly famous and has inspired numerous literary and artistic responses ever since, from Frances Harper's 1859 poem "The Slave Mother: A Tale of Ohio" to Toni Morrison's renowned 1987 novel *Beloved*.

This article reporting on the case, originally published in the *Cincinnati Gazette*, was reprinted in the 2 February 1856 issue of *The Anti-Slavery Bugle*, an abolitionist Ohio newspaper, on which the text presented below is based. In its accompanying editorial, the *Bugle* wrote, "Let the spirit of this despairing mother seize upon her oppressed race over the South and the whole Union cannot enslave them."

---

[1]   *David McCoy* Another slave trader, with whom Frank White has made an agreement to find Jerry and send him along to White.

Lewis Miller, *Slave Trader, Sold to Tennessee*, 1850. This watercolor sketch comes from *Sketchbook of Landscapes in the State of Virginia*, in which Miller (1796–1882), a Pennsylvanian, documented his visits to Virginia, where he had family. The sketch depicts a group of recently-sold enslaved people being marched—barefoot—to their new enslaver in Tennessee. Miller's accompanying caption notes that such sights were common in Virginia, "with the negro's in droves Sold." The lines Miller wrote above the scene put a seemingly positive spin on it: they contain an injunction to "weep no more" and call the location of the people's new enslavement "that happy shore."

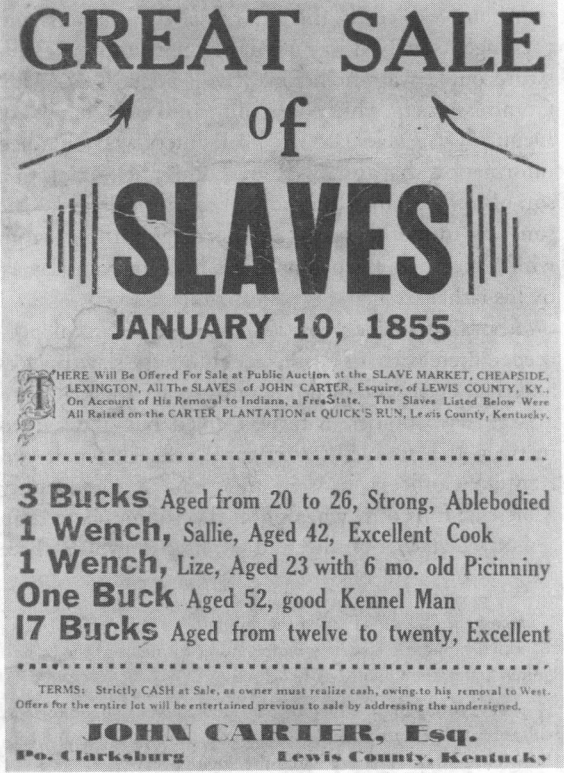

Poster advertising an auction of enslaved people in Kentucky, 1855. The poster exemplifies the demeaning racist terminology often used to categorize enslaved African Americans: "buck" and "wench" for men and women, respectively, and "picinniny" (also spelled various other ways) for children.

ARREST OF FUGITIVE SLAVES.

A SLAVE MOTHER MURDERS HER CHILD RATHER THAN SEE IT RETURNED TO SLAVERY.

Great excitement existed throughout the city the whole of yesterday, in consequence of the arrest of a party of slaves, and the murder of her child by a slave mother, while the officers were in the act of making the arrest. A party of seventeen slaves escaped from Boone and Kenton counties, in Kentucky (about sixteen miles from the Ohio), on Sunday night last, and taking with them two horses and a sled, drove that night to the Ohio River, opposite to Western Row, in this city. Leaving the horses and sled standing there, they crossed the river on foot on the ice.[1]

Five of them were the slaves of Archibald K. Gaines, three of John Marshall, both living in Boone County, a short distance beyond Florence, and six of Levi F. Daugherty, of Kenton County. We have not learned who claims the other three.

About 7 o'clock this morning the masters and their agents arrived in pursuit of their property. They swore out a warrant before J.L. Pendery, Esq., U.S. Commissioner, which was put into the hands of Deputy U.S. Marshal Geo. S. Bennet, who obtained information that they were in a house belonging to a son of Jo. Kite, the third house beyond Millcreek. The son was formerly owned in the neighborhood from which they had escaped and was bought from slavery by his father.

About 10 o'clock the Deputy U.S. Marshal proceeded there with his posse,[2] including the slave owners and their agent and Major Murphy, a Kentuckian, and a large slave holder. Kite was called out and agreed to open the door, but afterwards refused, when two Kentucky officers, assisted by some of the Deputy Marshals, forced it, whereupon the young negro man Simon, the father of the children, fired a revolver three times before he was overpowered. By one of these shots, Special Marshal John Patterson, who raised his arm to reach the pistol, had two of his fingers of his right hand shot off, the ball afterward striking his lip.

In the house were found four adults, viz:[3] old Simon and his wife, and young Simon and his wife and four children of the latter, the oldest near six years and the youngest a babe of about nine months. One of these, however, was lying on the floor dying, its head cut almost entirely off. There was also a gash about four inches long in the throat of the eldest, and a wound on the head of the other boy.

The officers state that when they questioned the boys about their wounds they said the folks threw them down and tried to kill them.

The young woman, Peggy, and her four children belonged to Marshall, and her husband and the old man Simon and the old woman Mary to Gaines. Old Simon and Mary are the parents of young Simon.

The other nine of the party, we were informed, were put upon the cars yesterday, by a director of the underground railway, and furnished with through tickets.[4]

Those arrested in Kite's house were taken to the U.S. Court Rooms about 12 o'clock, and guarded there until 3 o'clock, when Commissioner Pendery came and opened his Court.

Gaines appeared to claim his negroes. Marshall was represented by his son, but as he has no power of attorney from his father, the case was postponed until 9 o'clock this morning, in order to give him time to supply this omission.

The fugitives were then taken to the Hammond Street station house to be kept overnight. The Marshal attempted to get a hack to carry them there, but the crowd frightened all the hackmen[5] that were called so that they declined. They were afraid their carriages would be broken by the mob.

About an hour after they were taken there Mr. Gaines came along with the dead body of the murdered

---

[1] *they crossed … ice* During the famously severe winter of 1855–56, which brought record low temperatures to much of the eastern United States, the Ohio River froze over.

[2] *posse* Group of local men that a sheriff could call upon to assist with various law enforcement duties: in this case, pursuing and capturing escapees from slavery under the Fugitive Slave Act.

[3] *viz.* Abbreviation of the Latin "videlicet," meaning "namely" or "that is to say."

[4] *put upon … through tickets* The author of this article is here elaborating on the metaphor of the "Underground Railroad": i.e., the escapees were secretly helped further north toward Canada by abolitionist sympathizers.

[5] *hack* Hired coach; *hackmen* People hired to drive carriages and transport goods.

child. He was taking it to Covington[1] for interment that it might rest in ground consecrated to slavery.[2] ...

It is said that it can be proven that these slaves have frequently been in Ohio in company with their masters, and the question will be raised ... whether such bringing them into a free State has not rendered them free.

from *The Narratives of Fugitive Slaves in Canada* (1856)

The only collection ever compiled of first-hand interviews of black people who had escaped slavery by taking the Underground Railroad to Canada, *The Narratives of Fugitive Slaves in Canada* was published in 1856 by the Massachusetts abolitionist Benjamin Drew (1812–1903). The book—the full title of which is *A North-Side View of Slavery. The Refugee: or the Narratives of Fugitive Slaves in Canada*—was partially a response to *A South-Side View of Slavery* (1855), a book by Drew's fellow white Massachusetts writer Nehemiah Adams that described the supposed moral and religious benefits that enslavement conferred on African Americans and criticized the abolition movement's ostensible radicalism. In order to rebut Adams's arguments, Drew traveled widely in Canada West (the present-day Canadian province of Ontario), interviewing some of the thousands of escapees from slavery who had settled there and recording their accounts of their lives in slavery, their journeys to freedom, and their experiences in Canada.

A larger sample of narratives from this book can be found in the website portion of this anthology.

WILLIAM JOHNSON

I look upon slavery as I do upon a deadly poison. The slaves are not contented nor happy in their lot. Neither on the farm where I was in Virginia, nor in the neighborhood were the slaves satisfied. The man I belonged to did not give us enough to eat. My feet were frostbitten on my way North, but I would rather have died on the way than to go back.

It would not do to stop at all about our work—if the people should try to get a little rest, there would be a cracking spell amongst them.[3] I have had to go through a great deal of affliction; I have been compelled to work when I was sick. I used to have rheumatism,[4] and could not always do so much work as those who were well—then I would sometimes be whipped. I have never seen a runaway that wanted to go back—I have never heard of one.

I knew a very smart young man—he was a fellow-servant of mine, who had recently professed religion[5]—who was tied up by a quick-tempered overseer, and whipped terribly. He died not long after, and the people there believed it was because of the whipping. Some of the slaves told the owner, but he did not discharge the overseer. He will have to meet it at the day of judgment.

I had grown up quite large, before I thought anything about liberty. The fear of being sold South[6] had more influence in inducing me to leave than any other thing. Master used to say, that if we didn't suit him, he would put us in his pocket quick—meaning he would sell us. He never gave me a great coat[7] in his life—he said he knew he ought to do it, but that he couldn't get ahead far enough. His son had a child by a colored woman, and he would have sold it—his own grandchild—if the other folks hadn't opposed it.

I have found good friends in Canada, but have been able to do no work on account of my frozen feet—I lost two toes from my right foot. My determination is to go to work as soon as I am able. I have been about

---

[1] *Covington* City in Kentucky, just across the Ohio River from Cincinnati.

[2] *ground ... slavery* I.e., in the soil of a slave state.

[3] *there would ... amongst them* I.e., they would be beaten severely.

[4] *rheumatism* Term for a class of disorders affecting the joints, such as arthritis.

[5] *professed religion* Publicly embraced Christianity.

[6] *The fear ... South* Conditions for enslaved people in the Deep South, where most large-scale cotton cultivation took place, were generally much worse than in the more northerly slave states; consequently, enslaved people in "Upper South" states such as Virginia greatly feared being sold to new enslavers in the Deep South.

[7] *great coat* Long, warm overcoat.

among the colored people in St. Catharines[1] considerably, and have found them industrious and frugal. No person has offered me any liquor since I have been here: I have seen no colored person use it. I have been trying to learn to read since I came here, and I know a great many fugitives who are trying to learn.

HARRIET TUBMAN[2]

I grew up like a neglected weed—ignorant of liberty, having no experience of it. Then I was not happy or contented: every time I saw a white man, I was afraid of being carried away. I had two sisters carried away in a chain-gang—one of them left two children. We were always uneasy. Now I've been free, I know what a dreadful condition slavery is. I have seen hundreds of escaped slaves, but I never saw one who was willing to go back and be a slave. I have no opportunity to see my friends in my native land. We would rather stay in our native land, if we could be as free there as we are here. I think slavery is the next thing to hell. If a person would send another into bondage, he would, it appears to me, be bad enough to send him into hell, if he could.

MRS. CHRISTOPHER HAMILTON

I left Mississippi about fourteen years ago. I was raised a house servant, and was well used,[3] but I saw and heard a great deal of the cruelty of slavery. I saw more than I wanted to—I never want to see so much again. The slaveholders say their slaves are better off than if they were free, and that they prefer slavery to freedom. I do not, and never saw one that wished to go back. It would be a hard trial to make me a slave again. I had

HARRIET TUBMAN.

Harriet Tubman as she appeared during the Civil War, in which she served as a scout and spy for the U.S. Army. Tubman guided federal troops on an 1863 raid on plantations along the Combahee River in South Carolina, an action in which more than 750 enslaved people were freed. This image was printed as a frontispiece to *Scenes in the Life of Harriet Tubman* (1869).

rather live in Canada, on one potato a day, than to live in the South with all the wealth they have got. I am now my own mistress, and need not work when I am sick. I can do my own thinkings, without having any one to think for me—to tell me when to come, what to do, and to sell me when they get ready. I wish I could have my relatives here. I might say a great deal more against slavery—nothing for it.

The people who raised me failed; they borrowed money and mortgaged me. I went to live with people whose ways did not suit me, and I thought it best to come to Canada, and live as I pleased.

BEN BLACKBURN

I was born in Maysville, Ky. I got here last Tuesday evening, and spent the Fourth of July in Canada. I felt as big and free as any man could feel, and I worked part of the day for my own benefit: I guess my master's

---

[1] *St. Catharines* Town in what is now the Canadian province of Ontario, not far from the U.S. border, that became a center of abolitionist activity and a place of refuge and settlement for enslaved people who took the Underground Railroad to Canada. By the mid-1850s, about 800 black people lived there, out of a total population of approximately 6,000.

[2] *HARRIET TUBMAN* African American abolitionist and activist (c. 1822–1913) who was one of the most famous "conductors" on the Underground Railroad. After herself escaping from slavery in Maryland in 1849, she guided first her family and then numerous other enslaved people to freedom, for which she became known as "Moses." Tubman lived in St. Catharines from 1851 to 1858.

[3] *well used* I.e., well treated.

time is out. Seventeen came away in the same gang that I did.

LYDIA ADAMS

[Mrs. A. lives in a very comfortable log-house on the road from Windsor to the Refugees' Home.[1]]

I am seventy or eighty years old. I was from Fairfax County, old Virginia. I was married and had three children when I left there for Wood County, where I lived twenty years: thence to Missouri, removing with my master's family. One by one they sent four of my children away from me, and sent them to the South: and four of my grandchildren all to the South but one. My oldest son, Daniel—then Sarah—all gone. "It's no use to cry about it," said one of the young women, "she's got to go." That's what she said when Esther went away. Esther's husband is here now, almost crazy about her: they took her and sold her away from him. They were all Methodist people—great Methodists—all belonged to the church. My master died—he left no testimony whether he was willing to go or not. ... I have been in Canada about one year, and like it as far as I have seen.

I've been wanting to be free ever since I was a little child. I said to them I didn't believe God ever meant me to be a slave, if my skin was black—at any rate not all my lifetime: why not have it as in old times, seven years' servants?[2] Master would say, "No, you were made to wait on white people: what was niggers[3] made for? Why, just to wait on us all."

I am afraid the slaveholders will go to a bad place—I am really afraid they will. I don't think any slaveholder can get to the kingdom.[4]

DAVID GRIER

I was born free in Maryland—was stolen and sold in Kentucky, when between eight and nine years old. In Kentucky I was set free by will,[5] and as they were trying to break the will up, some of my claimant's friends persuaded me to come off to Ohio. From Ohio, I came here on account of the oppressive laws demanding security for good behavior[6]—I was a stranger and could not give it. I had to leave my family in Kentucky.

I came in 1831. I have cleared land on lease for five or six years, then have to leave it, and go into the bush again. I worked so about thirteen years. I could do no better, and the white people, I believe, took advantage of it to get the land cleared. This has kept me poor. I guess I have cleared not short of seventy or eighty acres, and got no benefit. I have now six acres cleared.

from Roger Taney, the *Dred Scott* Decision (1857)

> In 1846, Dred Scott, an enslaved Missouri man, sued for his freedom (assisted by white abolitionists), arguing that because he had been taken by his enslavers for extended periods to Illinois and Wisconsin Territory, where slavery was illegal, he had automatically become free. The St. Louis Circuit Court ruled in favor of Scott, but the Missouri Supreme Court reversed that ruling, whereupon Scott sued again in federal court; the case reached the U.S. Supreme Court, as *Dred Scott v. Sandford*, in 1856. In a 7–2 decision issued on 6 March 1857, the Court

---

[1] *on the road ... Refugees' Home* In 1851, the Refugee Home Society, an international Canadian–American abolitionist organization, founded a settlement for fugitive enslaved people twenty miles from Windsor, a Canadian city directly across the U.S.–Canada border from Detroit, Michigan.

[2] *why not ... servants* Reference to the practice of indentured servitude, widespread during the early colonial period, according to which the indentured person was obliged to perform unpaid labor for a fixed period of time—usually four to seven years—after which they would be free.

[3] *niggers* By the nineteenth century, as the context here suggests, "the n-word" (today universally acknowledged to be an utterly unacceptable expression of racism) had achieved its current, emphatically pejorative meaning in white American vernacular.

[4] *the kingdom* The kingdom of God—i.e., heaven.

[5] *by will* I.e., according to the written will of his enslaver after his enslaver's death.

[6] *the oppressive ... good behavior* Ohio's so-called "Black Laws," passed in 1807 in order to discourage African American migration to the state, required, among other things, that black residents find at least two people who would guarantee a surety of five hundred dollars—an amount of money designed to be prohibitively expensive—for their good behavior.

ruled that African Americans were not recognized as U.S. citizens under the Constitution and that federal courts therefore had no jurisdiction in the case and no right to end Scott's enslavement under Missouri law. In addition, the majority decision, written by Chief Justice Roger Taney, went on to declare any attempt by the federal government to impose restrictions on the expansion of slavery unconstitutional. The decision, which the Court had hoped would definitively settle the debate surrounding slavery, was predictably hailed in the slave states and bitterly decried in the free states, thereby further deepening the national polarization that would spark civil war a few years later.

... The question is simply this: Can a negro, whose ancestors were imported into this country, and sold as slaves, become a member of the political community formed and brought into existence by the Constitution of the United States, and as such become entitled to all the rights, and privileges, and immunities, guaranteed by that instrument to the citizen? One of which rights is the privilege of suing in a court of the United States in the cases specified in the Constitution. ...

In the opinion of the court, the legislation and histories of the times, and the language used in the Declaration of Independence, show that neither the class of persons who had been imported as slaves, nor their descendants, whether they had become free or not, were then acknowledged as a part of the people, nor intended to be included in the general words used in that memorable instrument.

It is difficult at this day to realize the state of public opinion in relation to that unfortunate race, which prevailed in the civilized and enlightened portions of the world at the time of the Declaration of Independence, and when the Constitution of the United States was framed and adopted. But the public history of every European nation displays it in a manner too plain to be mistaken.

They had for more than a century before been regarded as beings of an inferior order, and altogether unfit to associate with the white race, either in social or political relations; and so far inferior, that they had no rights which the white man was bound to respect; and that the negro might justly and lawfully be reduced to slavery for his benefit. He was bought and sold, and treated as an ordinary article of merchandise and traffic,[1] whenever a profit could be made by it. This opinion was at that time fixed and universal in the civilized portion of the white race. It was regarded as an axiom in morals as well as in politics, which no one thought of disputing, or supposed to be open to dispute; and men in every grade and position in society daily and habitually acted upon it in their private pursuits, as well as in matters of public concern, without doubting for a moment the correctness of this opinion. ...

No one, we presume, supposes that any change in public opinion or feeling, in relation to this unfortunate race, in the civilized nations of Europe or in this country, should induce the court to give to the words of the Constitution a more liberal construction in their favor than they were intended to bear when the instrument was framed and adopted. Such an argument would be altogether inadmissible in any tribunal called on to interpret it. If any of its provisions are deemed unjust, there is a mode prescribed in the instrument itself by which it may be amended; but while it remains unaltered, it must be construed now as it was understood at the time of its adoption. ...

Upon the whole, therefore, it is the judgment of this court, ... that the plaintiff in error is not a citizen of Missouri, in the sense in which that word is used in the Constitution; and that the Circuit Court of the United States, for that reason, had no jurisdiction in the case, and could give no judgment in it. Its judgment for the defendant must, consequently, be reversed, and a mandate issued, directing the suit to be dismissed for want[2] of jurisdiction.

---

[1] *traffic* Trade.

[2] *want* Lack.

from Mary Chesnut, Diary, 18 March 1861

The Civil War diary of Mary Boykin Chesnut (1823–86) is widely considered by modern historians to be a masterpiece of the diary genre. The wife of a wealthy Southern planter, Senator, and eventual aide to Jefferson Davis, president of the secessionist Southern government during the Civil War, Chesnut kept a journal from February 1861 through July 1865 in which she chronicled her wartime experiences. Though she belonged to the South's enslaving elite, Chesnut herself disliked slavery; many of her diary entries reveal passionate opposition to the institution, although more because of what she perceived as its ill effects on white enslavers, especially white women, than out of any strong sympathy with enslaved people themselves. (In fact, the diary makes it painfully clear that Chesnut shared many of her society's racist prejudices.) Chesnut revised her wartime diary in the 1880s, though she died before she could complete this project; it was this version that was first published in the early 1900s and earned Chesnut literary acclaim. An authoritative scholarly edition published in 1981 made available much of her original wartime writing; the excerpt presented below is based on one of these original diary entries.

March 18, 1861

… I wonder if it be a sin to think slavery a curse to any land. Sumner[1] said not one word of this hated institution which is not true. Men and women are punished when their masters and mistresses are brutes and not when they do wrong—and then we live surrounded by prostitutes.[2] An abandoned woman[3] is sent out of any decent house elsewhere. Who thinks any worse of a negro or mulatto[4] woman for being a thing we can't name? God forgive us, but ours is a *monstrous* system and wrong and iniquity. Perhaps the rest of the world is as bad—this *only* I see. Like the patriarchs of old[5] our men live all in one house with their wives and their concubines, and the mulattoes one sees in every family exactly resemble the white children—and every lady tells you who is the father of all the mulatto children in everybody's household, but those in her own she seems to think drop from the clouds, or pretends so to think. Good women we have, *but* they talk of all *nastiness* … —but they are, I believe, in conduct the purest women God ever made. Thank God for my countrywomen—alas for the men! No worse than men everywhere, but the lower their mistresses, the more degraded they must be. …

Mr. Harris said it was so patriarchal. So it is—flocks and herds and slaves—and wife Leah does not suffice. Rachel must be *added*, if not *married*.[6] And all the time they seem to think themselves patterns—models of husbands and fathers.

… And again I say, my countrywomen are as pure as angels, though surrounded by another race who are the social evil![7] …

---

1   *Sumner* Charles Sumner (1811–74), U.S. Senator for Massachusetts noted for his fervent opposition to slavery.

2   *prostitutes* Though the core meaning of prostitute is *person who engages in sexual activity in exchange for money*, enslaved women were of course not paid for the sexual acts they were coerced into taking part in with their enslavers. Then (as now) the word was often used loosely as a slur against any woman who had engaged in sexual activity considered to be inappropriate—whether coerced or not, whether for payment or not.

3   *An abandoned woman* I.e., a woman who has been seduced or sexually exploited and then deserted.

4   *mulatto* Term used in the nineteenth century, today considered archaic and offensive, to refer to an individual of mixed racial background—typically, someone with one white parent and one parent of African descent.

5   *patriarchs of old* Reference to the male figures of the biblical book of Genesis, who are typically described as ruling over large tribal households that include one or more wives as well as concubines (unmarried women, often enslaved, who are kept as sexual partners).

6   *wife Leah … married* Chestnut refers here to the story of Jacob (later renamed Israel), one of the biblical patriarchs and the traditional ancestor of the Israelites, who fell in love with Rachel, was tricked by her father into marrying her older sister Leah instead, but was eventually able to marry Rachel as well. See Genesis 29.

7   *the social evil* In the nineteenth century, this phrase was often used to refer specifically to prostitution.

Wilson.

Branded Slave from New Orleans.

LEARNING IS WEALTH.

WILSON, CHARLEY, REBECCA & ROSA.

Slaves from New Orleans

Charles Paxson, *Wilson. Branded Slave from New Orleans* and *Learning Is Wealth. Wilson, Charley, Rebecca & Rosa. Slaves from New Orleans*, 1863–64. These photographs depict formerly enslaved people freed when the U.S. Army occupied New Orleans, Louisiana during the Civil War. The first photograph portrays Wilson Chinn, "about 60 years old," posing with instruments of restraint and torture commonly used on enslaved people, including a collar, a whipping paddle, and chains. Chinn appears again in the second photograph, together with three mixed-race children, Charles Taylor, Rebecca Huger, and Rosina Downs; this second photograph exemplifies the genre of "white slave propaganda," in which images or descriptions of enslaved people who appeared white were used to shock white audiences. The photographs, and others like them, were reproduced and copies of them sold to raise funds for the education of emancipated people, and more generally to build support for abolition.

from Abraham Lincoln, Emancipation Proclamation, 1 January 1863

Opposition to slavery, and especially to its expansion, formed one of the cornerstones of Abraham Lincoln's Republican Party. After the Civil War broke out, however, President Lincoln long resisted taking any broad or systematic steps to end slavery, due largely to political considerations: he was mindful of the fact that most Northerners saw the war—as he himself at first saw it—as a war to preserve the Union and would likely resist an attempt to redefine it as a war for abolition. He also feared that any federal measures against slavery would drive the four slave states that had remained in the Union (Missouri, Kentucky, Maryland, and Delaware) to secede and join the other secessionist slave states. These considerations also shaped the Emancipation Proclamation that Lincoln eventually did issue in September 1862, and which was formalized on 1 January 1863. The Proclamation's scope was further limited by Lincoln's sense that he lacked any constitutional authority to take unilateral measures against slavery beyond that which he possessed as Commander-in-Chief of the U.S. armed forces in time of war.

The text of the final Emancipation Proclamation, given below, bears comparison to the so-called "Preliminary" Emancipation Proclamation, the text of which appears in the website portion of this section.

By the President of the United States
of America:
A Proclamation.

Whereas, on the twenty-second day of September, in the year of our Lord one thousand eight hundred and sixty-two, a proclamation was issued by the President of the United States, containing, among other things, the following, to wit:

"That on the first day of January, in the year of our Lord one thousand eight hundred and sixty-three, all persons held as slaves within any State or designated part of a State, the people whereof shall then be in rebellion against the United States, shall be then, thenceforward,

and forever free; and the Executive Government of the United States, including the military and naval authority thereof, will recognize and maintain the freedom of such persons, and will do no act or acts to repress such persons, or any of them, in any efforts they may make for their actual freedom. ..."

Now, therefore, I, Abraham Lincoln, President of the United States, by virtue of the power in me vested as Commander-in-Chief, of the Army and Navy of the United States in time of actual armed rebellion against the authority and government of the United States, and as a fit and necessary war measure for suppressing said rebellion, do, on this first day of January, in the year of our Lord one thousand eight hundred and sixty-three, and in accordance with my purpose so to do publicly proclaimed for the full period of one hundred days, from the day first above mentioned, order and designate as the States and parts of States wherein the people thereof respectively are this day in rebellion against the United States, the following, to wit:

Arkansas, Texas, Louisiana (except the Parishes of St. Bernard, Plaquemines, Jefferson, St. John, St. Charles, St. James Ascension, Assumption, Terrebonne, Lafourche, St. Mary, St. Martin, and Orleans, including the City of New Orleans),[1] Mississippi, Alabama, Florida, Georgia, South Carolina, North Carolina, and Virginia (except the forty-eight counties designated as West Virginia, and also the counties of Berkley, Accomac, Northampton, Elizabeth City, York, Princess Ann, and Norfolk, including the cities of Norfolk and Portsmouth),[2] and which excepted parts are for the present left precisely as if this proclamation were not issued.

And by virtue of the power and for the purpose aforesaid, I do order and declare that all persons held

---

[1]   *the Parishes … New Orleans* Portions of the state of Louisiana that were, at the time the Emancipation Proclamation was issued, under Union military occupation.

[2]   *except the forty-eight … Portsmouth* In 1861, after Virginia seceded from the Union, what was then the northwestern portion of the state, which had a very small enslaved population and correspondingly low support for secession, broke away in turn from Virginia (aided by the fact that the Union Army had occupied the region). The area was admitted to the Union as the new state of West Virginia on 20 June 1863. The other parts of Virginia named in this parenthesis were all portions of the state that Union forces had also occupied.

as slaves within said designated States, and parts of States, are and henceforward shall be free; and that the Executive government of the United States, including the military and naval authorities thereof, will recognize and maintain the freedom of said persons.

And I hereby enjoin upon the people so declared to be free to abstain from all violence, unless in necessary self-defence; and I recommend to them that, in all cases when allowed, they labor faithfully for reasonable wages.

And I further declare and make known, that such persons of suitable condition will be received into the armed service of the United States to garrison forts, positions, stations, and other places, and to man vessels of all sorts in said service.

And upon this act, sincerely believed to be an act of justice, warranted by the Constitution, upon military necessity, I invoke the considerate judgment of mankind, and the gracious favor of Almighty God.

In witness whereof, I have hereunto set my hand and caused the seal of the United States to be affixed.

Done at the City of Washington, this first day of January, in the year of our Lord one thousand eight hundred and sixty-three, and of the Independence of the United States of America the eighty-seventh.

By the President: Abraham Lincoln
William H. Seward, Secretary of State.

Jourdon Anderson, "Letter from a Freedman to His Old Master" (1865)

Jourdon Anderson (1825–1907) was enslaved for nearly three decades on a plantation in Wilson County, Tennessee. In 1848, he married Amanda (Mandy) McGregor, with whom he eventually had eleven children. They and their family gained their freedom in 1864, when U.S. Army troops camped at the plantation of their enslaver, Patrick Henry Anderson. By the summer of 1865, Jourdon Anderson and his family were living in Dayton, Ohio, where Patrick contacted him with a request that he return to work on the plantation, which was in deep financial trouble. Anderson, who was illiterate, dictated his response to this request

to his employer, the Dayton banker and abolitionist Valentine Winters, who published it in the *Cincinnati Commercial*. The letter quickly became a sensation and was widely reprinted, including in the *New York Daily Tribune* and in Lydia Maria Child's anthology *The Freedmen's Book* (1865); it even appeared in French translation in Switzerland. Anderson spent the remaining forty years of his life in Dayton, working as a janitor, coachman, hostler, and church sexton; his former enslaver was forced to sell his estate in September 1865 and died two years later.

DAYTON, Ohio, August 7, 1865.

To my Old Master, Col. P.H. ANDERSON, *Big Spring, Tennessee.*

Sir: I got your letter and was glad to find that you had not forgotten Jordan, and that you wanted me to come back and live with you again, promising to do better for me than anybody else can. I have often felt uneasy about you. I thought the Yankees would have hung you long before this for harboring Rebs they found at your house. I suppose they never heard about your going to Col. Martin's to kill the Union soldier that was left by his company in their stable. Although you shot at me twice before I left you, I did not want to hear of your being hurt, and am glad you are still living. It would do me good to go back to the dear old home again and see Miss Mary and Miss Martha[1] and Allen, Esther, Green, and Lee. Give my love to them all, and tell them I hope we will meet in the better world, if not in this. I would have gone back to see you all when I was working in the Nashville Hospital, but one of the neighbors told me Henry[2] intended to shoot me if he ever got a chance.

I want to know particularly what the good chance is you propose to give me. I am doing tolerably well here; I get $25 a month, with victuals and clothing; have a comfortable home for Mandy (the folks here call her Mrs. Anderson), and the children, Milly Jane and Grundy, go to school and are learning well; the teacher says Grundy has a head for a preacher. They go

---

[1]   *Miss ... Martha*   Patrick Henry Anderson's wife and daughter.

[2]   *Henry*   Probably Patrick Henry Anderson's son, Patrick Henry Jr., who was generally known as Henry.

to Sunday School, and Mandy and me attend church regularly. We are kindly treated; sometimes we overhear others saying, "Them colored people were slaves" down in Tennessee. The children feel hurt when they hear such remarks, but I tell them it was no disgrace in Tennessee to belong to Col. Anderson. Many darkies would have been proud, as I used to was, to call you master. Now, if you will write and say what wages you will give me, I will be better able to decide whether it would be to my advantage to move back again.

As to my freedom, which you say I can have, there is nothing to be gained on that score, as I got my free papers in 1864 from the Provost-Marshal-General of the Department of Nashville. Mandy says she would be afraid to go back without some proof that you are sincerely disposed to treat us justly and kindly—and we have concluded to test your sincerity by asking you to send us our wages for the time we served you. This will make us forget and forgive old scores, and rely on your justice and friendship in the future. I served you faithfully for thirty-two years, and Mandy twenty years. At $25 a month for me, and $2 a week for Mandy, our earnings would amount to $11,680. Add to this the interest for the time our wages has been kept back and deduct what you paid for our clothing and three doctor's visits to me, and pulling a tooth for Mandy, and the balance will show what we are in justice entitled to. Please send the money by Adams Express, in care of V. Winters,[1] esq., Dayton, Ohio. If you fail to pay us for faithful labors in the past we can have little faith in your promises in the future. We trust the good Maker has opened your eyes to the wrongs which you and your fathers have done to me and my fathers, in making us toil for you for generations without recompense. Here I draw my wages every Saturday night, but in Tennessee there was never any pay-day for the Negroes any more than for the horses and cows. Surely there will be a day of reckoning for those who defraud the laborer of his hire.[2]

In answering this letter please state if there would be any safety for my Milly and Jane, who are now grown up and both good-looking girls. You know how it was with poor Matilda and Catherine. I would rather stay here and starve and die if it come to that than have my girls brought to shame by the violence and wickedness of their young masters. You will also please state if there has been any schools opened for the colored children in your neighborhood, the great desire of my life now is to give my children an education, and have them form virtuous habits.

From your old servant, Jourdon Anderson.

P.S. Say howdy to George Carter,[3] and thank him for taking the pistol from you when you were shooting at me.

from William Marvin, Speech to the Freedmen of Marianna, 17 September 1865

> William Marvin (1808–1902), a native New Yorker, moved to Florida in the 1830s, where he served as a U.S. attorney and district court judge; he remained loyal to the Union when Florida seceded. In July 1865, President Andrew Johnson appointed him Provisional Governor of Florida. Marvin gave the speech excerpted below to an audience of more than a thousand formerly enslaved people in the northern Florida city of Marianna.

With this war you had nothing to do; you neither commenced it, nor did you end it, nor is the result attributable to you at all. It was a white man's war. It is true that a few colored men were enlisted in the army of the U.S., but they fought no battles; or if [they] engaged at all in such, they were trifling affairs.[4] Indeed, you had nothing to do with it; you remained at home, worked, behaved yourselves, and the blood of no man is on your hands. …

At the beginning, the war was neither intended nor prosecuted … to liberate you from slavery. Neither

---

[1] *V. Winters* Jourdon Anderson's employer, Valentine Winters; Anderson and his wife later named one of their sons after him, who grew up to become a friend and collaborator of the African American author Paul Laurence Dunbar.

[2] *Surely … his hire* Anderson here echoes several Bible verses, including Leviticus 19.13 and James 5.4.

[3] *George Carter* A carpenter in Wilson County, Tennessee.

[4] *It is true … trifling affairs* African American Union troops took part in a battle in Marianna itself on 27 September 1864, just a year before Marvin gave this speech.

the Northern white man nor the Southern white man expected nor intended such a result; neither, therefore, is entitled to your thanks or gratitude. … To a higher power should you feel grateful for your freedom—the Providence and tender mercies of Almighty God. You are free—as free as the white man—and never again so long as the U.S. exist … will you be reduced to slavery. …

If you ask me the question, whether the white man of the North or the white man of the South is your friend, I will answer you by saying that I hope and believe both of them are; but if it comes to a question of certainty as to which of the two is your better friend, I shall answer plainly and tell you: the white man of the South. I was born in the North, raised and educated there, but I have spent the last thirty years of my life in the South, and I consider myself capable of judging between the two people, particularly in reference to yourselves. I know the Northern man, or Yankee, as you call him, from the crown of his head to the sole of his foot, and I tell you today as your friend, that the Southern white man, with whom you were raised and who is acquainted with your habits and customs, is the best friend you have. …

I know, that though I am here as the governor of the state, and tell you that you are free, that you will not believe it. You are prepared to say that you remain on the same plantations and are controlled and directed by the same owners, for whom, as before, you have to work, and that you do not understand by such facts that you are free.[1] And on and after the first of January next,[2] I know, as well as if I witnessed it now, what you will do. You will leave your old homes—drift about the country—float from plantation to plantation; hundreds of you will come to town, and everywhere

you will be looking for freedom, and it will only be when your old masters and mistresses do not pursue you that you will be convinced that you are no longer slaves. And when you shall find as you will that you are free—find it with hungry stomachs and with nothing to eat, with the fact that none cares for you, and that you are driven more than ever to care for yourselves, you will then begin wisely to consider what is best to be done. …

My advice is to remain on the plantations where you have been accustomed to work, with your former owners if they will make a contract with you. Make the best contract you can with them, and show to them that you are willing to work better, now that you are compensated for your work, than you ever have done before. Be faithful, be truthful, be honest, be interested in the affairs of the plantation; see that the mules are well fed, that the hogs get good attention and that the things entrusted to you be not neglected. …

Your masters, influenced by interest aside from human feelings, which none question many of them having, have fed you, clothed you, and when sick have nursed you and when necessary have employed medical attendance. The raising of your children has received almost their exclusive care; they furnished the old women to watch over them during the absence of their mothers, who came two or three times to nurse them during the day. Now, as freed men and women, you are by your work to feed yourselves, clothe yourselves, employ medical attendance, [and] raise and educate your children. …

Do not think that, because you are free, you have a right to be impudent, uncivil, or impolite to white people. You have no such right. Impoliteness is not justifiable in anyone. You should be as civil, as polite as you always have been. … You do not wish to make white people hate you. It is to them that you are to look for almost everything: you want to be instructed by them; you want to learn from them; so you must be polite and civil to them, and don't put on airs and flaunt and look insolent at them, and don't, as I have heard has been done in places, jostle, or rub, or shove up against them when passing them on the road. Such a course is highly wrong and will get you into trouble. Some of the most polite men I have ever seen were colored men who have been raised in good families. They

---

[1]   *You are prepared … free*   Florida, like many other former secessionist slave states, imposed so-called "Black Codes" in the immediate aftermath of the Civil War. Among numerous other restrictions on the freedom of formerly enslaved people, these laws mandated annual labor contracts, which kept many African Americans working for their former enslavers on terms that were frequently little better than slavery. (An example of Mississippi's Black Code can be found in the website portion of this section.)

[2]   *on and after … next*   Marvin delivered this speech in part to refute rumors circulating among formerly enslaved people that, in January 1866, they were to receive distributions of land belonging to their former enslavers.

SCENES IN MEMPHIS, TENNESSEE, DURING THE RIOT—SHOOTING DOWN NEGROES ON THE MORNING OF MAY 2, 1866.—[SKETCHED BY A. R. W.]

Alfred Waud, *Scenes in Memphis, Tennessee, During the Riot—Shooting Down Negroes on the Morning of May 2, 1866*, 1866. This illustration by Waud—an English-born artist who had previously sketched many combat scenes during the Civil War—was published in the 26 May 1866 issue of *Harper's Weekly*. It depicts the massacre that had occurred earlier that month in Memphis, Tennessee: a coordinated assault in which, over the first three days of May, a white mob, including many police officers, killed over forty black citizens of the city and destroyed numerous black churches, schools, and private homes. The Memphis Massacre typified the white supremacist violence whereby, over the next decade, white Southerners would reimpose their hegemony over emancipated African Americans. A selection of firsthand accounts of the Memphis Massacre can be found in the website component of this section.

were naturally polite and knew well how to be so, and it is so with you. You can be as polite as anyone, and you ought not to be otherwise. It is a duty which is due to yourselves; it is gentlemanly and ladylike, and, now that you are free, you should try and be gentlemen and ladies. You have a greater inducement now than you ever had before, and if you wish to be esteemed as ladies and gentlemen, you must conduct yourselves accordingly. Call your old master, Master, and your old mistress, Mistress. It is right that you should; it is proper, it is polite. You do not mean, by calling them so, that you belong to them, but that you wish to be respectful and polite, and to give no cause for offence, but rather desire to please. I don't say that you must call them Master or Mistress, but

I say it is civil and polite in you to do it, and you ought, therefore, to do it. I have known many white servants; and there are thousands in the North where I was raised, and it is so in England, too; who call those who employ them Master and Mistress. It is a term of respect and deference, and they call them thus because this is so. There they, as I said before, are white servants, and they till the land, feed the stock and do other work that is done here, and they are respected and all of them find employment, as you may do if you will conduct yourselves properly. …

[Do not conclude that] the mantle of freedom makes you the equal of the white man. [For that to happen] you would have to be able to write a book, build a railroad, a steam engine, a steamboat and thousands of other things. ... [It would be foolish] to think they are not superior to you and will ever be. ...

Before the war each one of you was worth, in dollars and cents to your owners, eight hundred, or a thousand, or fifteen hundred dollars—worth more than fifty acres, or eighty acres of land and a mule thrown in. Well, the president[1] has, in giving you your freedom, taken so many dollars and cents from your old masters, and he thinks, as I do, they have lost enough, and you by it have had enough given to you. If he were to give you more it would prove a curse to you. God has directed the president how much to give you and he will give no more. ...

Will you promise me to do the best you can, be kindly disposed to all, to be good men and women? ("We will.") ... God help you do it.

Advertisements Taken Out by Formerly Enslaved People Seeking Family Members

> In the years after the end of slavery, thousands of advertisements were placed in African American newspapers throughout the country by formerly enslaved people searching for family members from whom they had been separated, usually by sale into the domestic slave trade. The advertisements were typically published in special sections titled "Information Wanted," "Last Seen," or (as in the *Southwestern Christian Advocate*) "Lost Friends," and were also frequently read aloud in churches; they were a fixture of black periodicals for decades and continued to appear into the twentieth century. How many such advertisements resulted in reunions it is impossible to know, but that at least some proved successful is demonstrated by the final example included below.

FROM THE *COLORED TENNESSEAN* (24 MARCH 1866)

Information Wanted

Of my daughter, Martha James. When last heard from was in Montgomery, Ala., but is supposed to have gone to Mobile. She formerly belonged to Dr. Barnett, Princeton, Ky., and was sold to Mr. John James, Nashville, Tenn., about nine years ago, since which time she has not been seen by me. Information of her will be thankfully received by her mother by addressing Colored Tennessean, Box 1150, Nashville, Tenn.

HANNAH BARNETT ...

Of our five children, whom we have not seen for four years. Their names are as follows, viz.:[2] Josephine, aged 20 years; Celia, aged 14 years; Caroline, aged 13 years; Ellen, aged 10 years; and Augusta, aged 8 years. They were in Charlotte, N.C., or at Rock Hill[3] when we last heard from them.

Any information concerning these children will be thankfully received by their mother. Our address is, Augusta, Ga.

AUGUSTUS BRYANT
LUTITIA BRYANT

N.B.—These persons were formerly owned by John L. and Virginia Moon, of Augusta, Ga.

FROM THE *CHRISTIAN RECORDER*[4] (24 MARCH 1866)

Information Wanted

By Lucy Walker, of my husband, Anderson Walker. The last time I saw him was on September 2, 1864, at Athens, Georgia. His former owner was Ferdinand

---

[1] *the president* Andrew Johnson, U.S. President from 1865 to 1869. A Tennessee politician and enslaver, Johnson supported the Union when his state seceded. In a bid to obtain the support of the Southern Unionists Johnson represented, President Lincoln made Johnson his running mate in the 1864 presidential election; as vice-president, Johnson then assumed the presidency after Lincoln's assassination. During his presidency, Johnson opposed federal attempts to protect and promote the rights of formerly enslaved people and supported the reestablishment of white supremacist governments in the Southern states on the grounds of "states' rights."

[2] *viz.* Abbreviation of the Latin "videlicet," meaning "namely" or "that is to say."

[3] *Rock Hill* City in northern South Carolina, about twenty-five miles south of Charlotte.

[4] *CHRISTIAN RECORDER* Official newspaper, published in Philadelphia, of the African Methodist Episcopal Church; founded in 1848, it is the oldest continuously-published African American periodical in the United States.

Phirwell. Lucy was owned by Marcella Bloomfield. Any information will be thankfully received by the undersigned. Address

Lucy Walker
Care of Rev. Cyrus Boey,
Elder of Bethel Church,
Oswego City, N.Y.

FROM THE *CHRISTIAN RECORDER* (28 JANUARY 1871)

Information wanted of my sister Rosanna. We parted in Richmond, Va., thirty-five years ago. Learned that she was carried to Alabama by a man named Templeman. She is now about 58 years old. My name then was Anthony Terrill. Also, information wanted of Harriet Chapman, mother of Sidney Oliver. When last heard from she was at Chapman's Mill, Monroe County, Ga., upward of 40 years ago. Any information address,

Anthony Fleming,
Plaquemine, La.

FROM THE *SOUTHWESTERN CHRISTIAN ADVOCATE*[1] (12 JULY 1877)

I am searching for my mother, whose name is Mary Hall. In 1859 she belonged to Bill Lawson, in Wharton County;[2] he sold her to a cousin of his, whose name I think was also Lawson, and that he lived near Powderhorn, Texas. My name was formerly Henry Hall, I had a sister named Caroline. Address, Henry Wharton, San Filipe, Texas.

FROM THE *SOUTHWESTERN CHRISTIAN ADVOCATE* (24 APRIL 1884)

Mr. Editor—I have got a letter from Turner Petty's people through the inquiry in the paper. God bless the paper. It is bringing the people together.

W.H. JACKSON.
Brenham, Texas.

Bureau Refugees, Freedmen and Abandoned Lands.

By the authority of Circular No. 5, dated ASSISTANT COMMISSIONER'S OFFICE KY. AND TENN., Nashville, Feb. 26, 1866, I certify that I have this day united Joseph Provines and Mary Provines to belong to U.S. Hall. colored, in the bonds of matrimony, they having been living together as man and wife for about Twenty and years past, and have had, as the result thereof, the following children, viz:

Stephen Provines   Aged about 19 years. Stephen went off with Genl. Willess command of U.S. troops in 1863, and was heard from at Louisville Ky soon after Morby's raid to Nashville, probably went by the name of Sanders or Calhoun

In witness whereof, I have hereunto set my hand in duplicate at office in Lebanon, Wilson County, Tennessee, April 23, 1866.

S. B. F. C. BARR, Sup't
Wilson County.

This certificate, issued by the Wilson County, Tennessee office of the federal Freedmen's Bureau on 23 April 1866, formalizes the marriage of Joseph and Mary Province, formerly enslaved people who had, according to the certificate, "been living together as man and wife for about twenty-one years" and had a nineteen-year-old son. Because marriages between enslaved people were not recognized under slavery, emancipated African Americans frequently asked for and received such certificates from Freedmen's Bureau agents, legalizing marriages that had often existed informally for many years. The bureau also helped African Americans find spouses or other family members from whom they had been separated during slavery.

---

[1] *SOUTHWESTERN … ADVOCATE* Newspaper published in New Orleans, Louisiana.

[2] *Wharton County* County in southeast Texas.

from Robert B. Elliott, Speech to the House of Representatives, 6 January 1874

Robert Brown Elliott (1842–84) was one of the first African American men to win a seat in Congress in the wake of the abolition of slavery and the passage of the Fourteenth Amendment. Elliott's early life is obscure, but he was likely born and educated in England before settling in South Carolina in 1867, where he practiced law (and helped form the first known African American law firm), served in state government, and led the South Carolina National Guard in its efforts to suppress the Ku Klux Klan. He was elected to the U.S. House of Representatives in 1870 and was reelected in 1872. In Congress, he opposed granting amnesty to former secessionists and worked to pass legislation to weaken the KKK. He made his greatest impact with the speech excerpted below, given in support of a proposed Civil Rights Bill to outlaw discrimination in public transportation, public accommodations, and schools. Elliott's forceful defense of the cause of civil rights, and his eloquence on behalf of his formerly enslaved compatriots, won praise across the country. The Civil Rights Bill passed Congress and was signed into law in 1875, though it went largely unenforced as white supremacist governments regained control of the South. The same reimposition of white hegemony in the South also put an end to Elliott's political career, and he died in poverty in New Orleans in 1884.

While I am sincerely grateful for this high mark of courtesy that has been accorded to me by this House, it is a matter of regret to me that it is necessary at this day that I should rise in the presence of an American Congress to advocate a bill which simply asserts equal rights and equal public privileges for all classes of American citizens. I regret, sir, that the dark hue of my skin may lend a color to the imputation that I am controlled by motives personal to myself in my advocacy of this great measure of national justice. Sir, the motive that impels me is restricted by no such narrow boundary, but is as broad as your Constitution. I advocate it, sir, because it is right. The bill, however,

not only appeals to your justice, but it demands a response from your gratitude. …

… The negro, true to that patriotism and love of country that have ever characterized and marked his history on this continent, came to the aid of the government in its efforts to maintain the Constitution. To that government he now appeals; that Constitution he now invokes for protection against outrage and unjust prejudices founded upon caste.

But, sir, we are told by the distinguished gentleman from Georgia [Mr. Stephens[1]] that Congress has no power under the Constitution to pass such a law, and that the passage of such an act is in direct contravention of the rights of the states. I cannot assent to any such proposition. The constitution of a free government ought always to be construed in favor of human rights. Indeed, the Thirteenth, Fourteenth, and Fifteenth Amendments, in positive words, invest Congress with the power to protect the citizen in his civil and political rights. …

These amendments, one and all, are … declared to have as their all-pervading design and end the security to the recently enslaved race, not only their nominal freedom, but their complete protection from those who had formerly exercised unlimited dominion over them. It is in this broad light that all these amendments must be read: the purpose to secure the perfect equality before the law of all citizens of the United States. What you give to one class you must give to all; what you deny to one class you shall deny to all[.] …

… [I]n this discussion I cannot and I will not forget that the welfare and rights of my whole race in this country are involved. When, therefore, the honorable gentleman from Georgia lends his voice and influence to defeat this measure, I do not shrink from saying that it is not from him that the American House of Representatives should take lessons in matters touching human rights or the joint relations of the state and national governments. While the honorable gentleman contented himself with harmless speculations in his study, or in the columns of a newspaper, we might well smile at the impotence of his efforts to turn back

---

[1]   *Mr. Stephens*   Alexander H. Stephens (1812–83), politician from Georgia who served as vice-president of the secessionist Southern government throughout the Civil War. After the war, he was briefly imprisoned before being elected, in 1873, to the U.S. House of Representatives, in which he had also served before the war.

the advancing tide of opinion and progress; but, when he comes again upon this national arena, and throws himself with all his power and influence across the path which leads to the full enfranchisement of my race, I meet him only as an adversary; nor shall age or any other consideration restrain me from saying that he now offers this government, which he has done his utmost to destroy, a very poor return for its magnanimous treatment, to come here and seek to continue, by the assertion of doctrines obnoxious to the true principles of our Government, the burdens and oppressions which rest upon five millions of his countrymen who never failed to lift their earnest prayers for the success of this government when the gentleman was seeking to break up the Union of these states and to blot the American republic from the galaxy of nations. [Loud applause.]

Sir, it is scarcely twelve years since that gentleman shocked the civilized world by announcing the birth of a government which rested on human slavery as its cornerstone.[1] The progress of events has swept away that *pseudo*-government which rested on greed, pride, and tyranny; and the race whom he then ruthlessly spurned and trampled on are here to meet him in debate, and to demand that the rights which are enjoyed by their former oppressors—who vainly sought to overthrow a government which they could not prostitute to the base uses of slavery—shall be accorded to those who even in the darkness of slavery kept their allegiance true to freedom and the Union. ...

... Technically, this bill is to decide upon the civil status of the colored American citizen: a point disputed at the very formation of our present government, when by a short-sighted policy, a policy repugnant to true republican government, one negro counted as three-fifths of a man.[2] The logical result of this mistake of the framers of the Constitution strengthened the cancer of slavery, which finally spread its poisonous tentacles over the southern portion of the body-politic. To arrest its growth and save the nation we have passed through the harrowing operation of intestine[3] war, dreaded at all times, resorted to at the last extremity, like the surgeon's knife, but absolutely necessary to extirpate the disease which threatened with the life of the nation the overthrow of civil and political liberty on this continent. In that dire extremity the members of the race which I have the honor in part to represent—the race which pleads for justice at your hands today, forgetful of their inhuman and brutalizing servitude at the South, their degradation and ostracism at the North—flew willingly and gallantly to the support of the national government. Their sufferings, assistance, privations, and trials in the swamps and in the rice-fields, their valor on the land and on the sea, is a part of the ever-glorious record which makes up the history of a nation preserved, and might, should I urge the claim, incline you to respect and guarantee their rights and privileges as citizens of our common republic. But I remember that valor, devotion, and loyalty are not always rewarded according to their just deserts, and that after the battle some who have borne the brunt of the fray may, through neglect or contempt, be assigned to a subordinate place, while the enemies in war may be preferred to the sufferers.

The results of the war, as seen in reconstruction, have settled forever the political status of my race. The passage of this bill will determine the civil status, not only of the negro, but of any other class of citizens who may feel themselves discriminated against. It will form the capstone of that temple of liberty, begun on this continent under discouraging circumstances, carried on in spite of the sneers of monarchists and the

---

[1] *it is ... cornerstone* On 21 March 1861, Alexander Stephens gave a speech explaining and interpreting the new constitution of the Confederate States of America—as the government formed by the secessionist states called itself—in which he declared that the Confederacy's "foundations are laid, its cornerstone rests, upon the great truth, that the negro is not equal to the white man; that slavery—subordination to the superior race—is his natural and normal condition." The speech—which, after the war, Stephens attempted to revise and downplay—became known as "The Cornerstone Speech"; excerpts of it can be found in the Contexts section on the Civil War elsewhere in this anthology volume.

[2] *one ... man* Reference to the so-called "Three-Fifths Compromise" made during the drafting of the U.S. Constitution. According to the compromise, each enslaved person in states permitting slavery would count as three-fifths of a person when determining that state's representation in the House of Representatives (and, by extension, its number of electoral votes in the Electoral College). The compromise was enshrined in Article 1, Section 2, Clause 3 of the Constitution but was superseded and repudiated by the Fourteenth Amendment in 1868.

[3] *intestine* Internal, as in a civil conflict.

cavils of pretended friends of freedom, until at last it stands in all its beautiful symmetry and proportions, a building the grandest of which the world has ever seen, realizing the most sanguine expectations and the highest hopes of those who, in the name of equal, impartial, and universal liberty, laid the foundation stones.

The Holy Scriptures tell us of an humble handmaiden who long, faithfully, and patiently gleaned in the rich fields of her wealthy kinsman; and we are told further that at last, in spite of her humble antecedents, she found complete favor in his sight.[1] For over two centuries our race had "reaped down your fields." The cries and woes which we have uttered have "entered into the ears of the Lord of Sabaoth,"[2] and we are at last politically free. The last vesture only is needed—civil rights. Having gained this, we may, with hearts overflowing with gratitude, and thankful that our prayer has been granted, repeat the prayer of Ruth: "entreat me not to leave thee, or to return from following after thee; for whither thou goest, I will go; and where thou lodgest, I will lodge; thy people shall be my people, and thy god my God; where thou diest, will I die, and there will I be buried; the Lord do so to me, and more also, if aught but death part thee and me."[3] [Great applause.]

---

[1] *The Holy … his sight* Elliott here briefly summarizes the biblical Book of Ruth; *gleaned* Gathered the grain left behind after the fields were harvested. This was a means of obtaining food for poor or marginalized people that was explicitly identified as a legal right of theirs in the biblical books of Leviticus and Deuteronomy and, later, in parts of medieval and early modern Europe.

[2] *For over … Sabaoth* See James 5.4: "Behold, the hire of the labourers who have reaped down your fields, which is of you kept back by fraud, crieth: and the cries of them which have reaped are entered into the ears of the Lord of Sabaoth." The expression "Lord of Sabaoth," meaning "Lord of Hosts" or "God of armies," is a biblical term used to refer to God in his capacity as a military leader of either the Israelite army or the heavenly host of angels.

[3] *entreat … thee and me* See Ruth 1.16–17. In this passage, Ruth, a Moabite—i.e., non-Israelite—woman who married an Israelite and has now been widowed, tells her mother-in-law Naomi that she still intends to follow and remain loyal to her, even now that her husband, Naomi's son, is dead; *aught* Anything.

WILLIAM LLOYD GARRISON

1805 – 1879

In the early 1830s, abolitionism had not yet become the sweeping force in American social and political discourse that it would become during the next two decades. Massachusetts-based newspaper editor William Lloyd Garrison, however, had by this time adopted what was considered a radical antislavery stance: he advocated immediate abolition (rather than the gradual emancipation promoted by most other early activists), and rejected the proposals of colonizationists, who aimed to resettle free African Americans in overseas colonies. Over the following years, Garrison's Boston-based weekly newspaper, *The Liberator*, became one of the leading platforms in the United States for the expression of radical abolitionism.

Garrison was born in Newburyport, Massachusetts in 1805, and lived in relative poverty for several years after his father abandoned the family. As a young man he enjoyed only a limited education before entering the workforce, being briefly apprenticed to a shoemaker, then a cabinetmaker, and finally working as a typesetter for the *Newburyport Herald*, to which he was soon contributing articles.

In 1828, after having tried and failed to run several other news publications, Garrison was introduced to the Quaker newspaper editor Benjamin Lundy, an advocate of gradual abolition; Garrison, to whom slavery had as yet been only an abstract, theoretical wrong, was won over wholeheartedly to the abolitionist cause. Lundy hired Garrison to coedit his Baltimore antislavery newspaper *The Genius of Universal Emancipation*, which had been established in 1821 and was thus one of the first papers of its kind in the country. Garrison quickly became more radical than his mentor in his approach to the cause; he began to advocate immediate emancipation and to reject Lundy's support of the American Colonization Society (a group whose activities, many critics suggested, had the fundamental effect of protecting slavery where it continued to exist in the South). Lundy and Garrison continued to work side by side in amicable disagreement until 1830, when Garrison's penchant for inflammatory antislavery rhetoric led to their both being charged with libel. Lundy was ultimately acquitted, but Garrison spent several weeks in prison near the end of that year, after which the men mutually decided to end their partnership.

Undeterred, Garrison relocated to Boston in early 1831 and founded his own antislavery platform, *The Liberator*. The passionate language and uncompromising tone of the publication's famous inaugural letter signaled its radical aims; the project appeared to herald a new era for Garrison and, in many ways, for abolitionism as a whole. The paper's actual subscription base, usually hovering around 3,000, was not large, but it quickly gained significant support from black readers, and its articles were frequently reprinted in other publications throughout the country (including in the South, where publishers often pointed to the *Liberator* as an example of Northern fanaticism). Such recirculation was common practice in nineteenth-century newspaper culture across the country; Garrison's paper, likewise, would often reprint content from Southern papers, with a view to exposing or condemning the sentiments expressed. As a result of this frequent recirculation, as well as of the paper's innovative use of advertising—integrating moral evangelism with capitalism by advertising free-labor products—the *Liberator* became the most successful periodical associated with the abolitionist movement. (Indeed, its success came somewhat at the expense of other black-run abolitionist papers of the era, which rarely achieved the same level of cross-racial renown that the *Liberator* did. The most successful African American-run newspaper of the era was *The North Star*, launched by Garrison's former protégé Frederick Douglass in 1847; Garrison conspicuously withheld his support from this endeavor.)

One product of this success was the American Anti-Slavery Society, founded by Garrison and associates in 1833 and boasting over 250,000 members by 1838. By mid-decade Garrison had lent his name to a whole school of activism. The "Garrisonian" approach was characterized by pacifism; by anticlericalism; by an emphasis on moral suasion rather than direct political activity; by a refusal to participate in elections; by opposition to the American Constitution (on the grounds that it was an inherently proslavery document); and, consequently, by promotion of the idea that the Northern states should secede from the Union. Garrison's profoundly Christian sense of moral perfectionism led him to reject and condemn most forms of organized Christianity, and his public burning of a copy of the Constitution in 1854 scandalized many. Unsurprisingly, these Garrisonian measures alienated many members of the community, who saw them variously as too extreme, too idealistic, or as simply unhelpful. Some saw secession as a path to ensuring the continuation of slavery in the South. Others, meanwhile, saw Garrison's pacifism as an increasingly impracticable ideal in the years leading up to the Civil War. Garrison came to be seen as overly controlling by some members of the community, especially by African American members such as Douglass, whose friendship with Garrison broke down in the 1850s. (Interestingly enough, however, it was Garrison's promotion of women's involvement in the movement that finally caused the society to fragment in 1840, leading to the formation of the more politically and socially conservative American and Foreign Anti-Slavery Society, as well as of several abolitionist political parties.)

Though a pacifist at heart, Garrison reluctantly embraced Lincoln's presidency and the Union Cause when the Civil War broke out in 1861. After the end of the War and the 1865 passage of the Thirteenth Amendment, Garrison continued to support the fight for equal rights for the African American community, though he ended his publication of the *Liberator* and stepped down as president of the AASS, believing the primary goals of both newspaper and association to have been achieved. This view became a cause of significant contention within the society, which continued to operate under the leadership of Wendell Phillips until the granting of black suffrage in 1870.

Garrison died at his home in 1879, and was eulogized by many prominent activists, his efforts widely recognized as having been instrumental in shaping the abolitionist culture that fought and flourished in antebellum America. His deeply moral approach—reflecting the overarching evangelical reform culture dominant in the nineteenth century—had influence beyond American borders; the Russian author Leo Tolstoy was among those who expressed admiration of Garrisonian pacifism. In his eulogy for Garrison, Frederick Douglass—who had remained estranged from his former mentor in the years leading up to his death—addressed Garrison's polemical nature and claimed that he "revolted at halfness, abhorred compromise, and demanded that men should be either hot or cold." In the post-reconstruction era, however, Douglass pronounced, the nation would "sorely miss the mind and voice of William Lloyd Garrison."

NOTE ON THE TEXT: The text of "To the Public" presented here is based on that printed in the first issue of *The Liberator*, published on 1 January 1831. Spelling and punctuation have been modernized in accordance with the practices of this anthology.

⌘ ⌘ ⌘

To the Public

In the month of August, I issued proposals for publishing THE LIBERATOR in Washington city; but the enterprise, though hailed in different sections of the country, was palsied[1] by public indifference. Since that time, the removal of the *Genius of Universal Emancipation*[2] to the Seat of Government has rendered less imperious the establishment of a similar periodical in that quarter.

During my recent tour for the purpose of exciting the minds of the people by a series of discourses on the subject of slavery, every place that I visited gave fresh evidence of the fact, that a greater revolution in public sentiment was to be effected in the free states—*and particularly in New-England*—than at the south. I found contempt more bitter, opposition more active, detraction more relentless, prejudice more stubborn, and apathy more frozen, than among slave-owners themselves. Of course, there were individual exceptions to the contrary. This state of things afflicted, but did not dishearten me. I determined, at every hazard, to lift up the standard of emancipation in the eyes of the nation, *within sight of Bunker Hill*[3] *and in the birth place of liberty*. That standard is now unfurled; and long may it float, unhurt by the spoliations of time or the missiles of a desperate foe—yea, till every chain be broken, and every bondman set free! Let southern oppressors tremble—let their secret abettors tremble—let their northern apologists tremble—let all the enemies of the persecuted blacks tremble.

I deem the publication of my original Prospectus unnecessary, as it has obtained a wide circulation. The principles therein inculcated will be steadily pursued in this paper, excepting that I shall not array myself as the political partisan of any man. In defending the great cause of human rights, I wish to derive the assistance of all religions and of all parties.

Assenting to the "self-evident truth" maintained in the American Declaration of Independence, "that all men are created equal, and endowed by their Creator with certain inalienable rights—among which are life, liberty and the pursuit of happiness," I shall strenuously contend for the immediate enfranchisement of our slave population. In Park Street Church,[4] on the Fourth of July, 1829, in an address on slavery, I unreflectingly assented to the popular but pernicious doctrine of *gradual* abolition. I seize this opportunity to make a full and unequivocal recantation, and thus publicly to ask pardon of my God, of my country, and of my brethren the poor slaves, for having uttered a sentiment so full of timidity, injustice and absurdity. A similar recantation, from my pen, was published in the *Genius of Universal Emancipation* at Baltimore, in September, 1829. My conscience is now satisfied.

I am aware, that many object to the severity of my language; but is there not cause for severity? I *will be* as harsh as truth, and as uncompromising as justice. On this subject, I do not wish to think, or speak, or write, with moderation. No! no! Tell a man whose house is on fire to give a moderate alarm; tell him to moderately rescue his wife from the hands of the ravisher; tell the mother to gradually extricate her babe from the fire into which it has fallen—but urge me not to use moderation in a cause like the present. I am in earnest—I will not equivocate—I will not excuse—I will not retreat a single inch—AND I WILL BE HEARD. The apathy of the people is enough to make every statue leap from its pedestal, and to hasten the resurrection of the dead.

It is pretended, that I am retarding the cause of emancipation by the coarseness of my invective, and the precipitancy of my measures. *The charge is not true*. On this question my influence—humble as it is—is felt at this moment to a considerable extent, and shall be felt in coming years—not perniciously, but beneficially—not as a curse, but as a blessing; and posterity will bear testimony that I was right. I desire to thank God, that he enables me to disregard "the fear of man which bringeth a snare,"[5] and to speak

---

[1] *palsied* Paralyzed; rendered ineffectual ("palsy" is a term given to a medical condition involving trembling and/or partial paralysis).

[2] *Genius of Universal Emancipation* Newspaper founded by Quaker abolitionist Benjamin Lundy in 1821; Garrison briefly served as its editor. Lundy, who—unlike Garrison—supported gradual emancipation, tried unsuccessfully to relocate the newspaper to Washington, D.C. in 1830.

[3] *Bunker Hill* Site of the Battle of Bunker Hill (1775) in Massachusetts, a significant event of the Revolutionary War.

[4] *Park Street Church* In Boston, Massachusetts.

[5] *the fear … a snare* See Proverbs 29.25.

his truth in its simplicity and power. And here I close with this fresh dedication:

> Oppression! I have seen thee, face to face,
> And met thy cruel eye and cloudy brow;
> But thy soul-withering glance I fear not now—
> For dread to prouder feelings doth give place
> Of deep abhorrence! Scorning the disgrace
> Of slavish knees that at thy footstool bow,
> I also kneel—but with far other vow
> Do hail thee and thy herd of hirelings base:—

> I swear, while life-blood warms my throbbing veins,
> Still to oppose and thwart, with heart and hand,
> Thy brutalising sway—till Afric's chains
> Are burst, and Freedom rules the rescued land,—
> Trampling Oppression and his iron rod:
> *Such is the vow I take*—SO HELP ME GOD![1]

William Lloyd Garrison
Boston, January 1, 1831

—1831

Mastheads from *The Liberator*, 9 March 1834 and 7 October 1859.

---

[1]   *Oppression! … SO HELP ME GOD!*   From the poem "To Oppression" by Scottish poet and abolitionist Thomas Pringle (1789–1834).

SOJOURNER TRUTH

c. 1797 – 1883

Abolitionist and women's rights activist Sojourner Truth was among the most celebrated and compelling orators of nineteenth-century America. Born into slavery near the turn of the century, Truth spent the first seventeen years of her free life working as a domestic servant in New York City before undergoing the spiritual transformation that, in 1843, compelled her to begin a career as an itinerant evangelist. Truth soon became a national celebrity, renowned both for her moving religious exhortations and for her uniquely powerful campaigning for racial and gender equality. Throughout her career, Truth thought and spoke about the intersections of race, class, and gender in a way that few of her fellow activists fully appreciated. Truth never learned to read or write herself; her ideas have come down to us primarily through the accounts of her contemporaries—a fact that has for decades challenged scholars seeking an "authentic" account of this exceptionally charismatic figure.

Isabella (Truth's birth name) was born to parents Elizabeth and James Baumfree or Bomefree around 1797 in Ulster County, two years before the passage of New York State's Gradual Abolition Act, and three decades before that act would take effect for all enslaved people in the state. Speaking Low Dutch as her first language, Isabella learned English when she was sold to an English-speaker, John Neely, around the age of nine. She lived under five different enslavers over the course of her enslaved life, enduring forced separation from her family as well as numerous instances of severe abuse. Forbidden from marrying her first love, Robert, because he belonged to another owner, Isabella was instead arranged to be married to Thomas, with whom she had five children.

Isabella's final enslaver was John Dumont, under whom some scholars speculate she experienced sexual abuse, and with whom she lived for sixteen years until the autumn of 1826. When Dumont broke a promise he had made to emancipate her that summer, Isabella emancipated herself. Leaving in the early hours of the morning, she walked twelve miles to a Quaker settlement with her youngest daughter in tow, leaving her other children with their father, who did not join her. The Quakers provided shelter for Isabella, and provided for her purchase from Dumont when he later came to demand her return. She was taken into the household of Isaac Van Wagenen, for whom she worked voluntarily—though legally still enslaved—as a domestic helper over the course of the next year. While working for Van Wagenen, Isabella discovered that her five-year-old son Peter had been illegally sold into slavery in Alabama by Dumont. When the Gradual Abolition Act came into effect and she was officially freed, Isabella sued to regain custody of her son, and, remarkably, succeeded.

In 1828 Isabella underwent a conversion experience, upon which she moved to New York City; she lived there for the next fifteen years, working as a domestic servant, preaching in various contexts including within the Methodist Church and at revivalist camp meetings, and briefly becoming involved in a controversial cult called the Kingdom of Matthias. She underwent a second religious experience in 1843; leaving behind what she now believed to be a sinful city, Isabella adopted the new name Sojourner Truth and began her travels to spread God's word.

Truth discovered a talent for oratory and religious ministry, and soon became something of a regional celebrity. As her fame increased, Truth took to posing for photographs, which she had printed in the popular form of *cartes de visite* that she then sold to collectors to fund her missionary travels. Though she did not initially demonstrate a vocal interest in either abolitionism or women's rights, the religious circles in which she moved often had a strongly antislavery bent. In the mid-1840s, Truth began living at the Northampton Association for Education and Industry, one of the era's many utopian, reform-minded communities. Here she met several prominent abolitionists—among them William Lloyd Garrison, David Ruggles, and, perhaps most significantly, the formerly enslaved orator Frederick Douglass. Douglass and Truth, though very different in their personalities, made profound impressions on one another here; it was at this point that Truth seems to have dedicated herself to the antislavery cause.

Around 1848, Garrison encouraged Truth to compose an autobiography focused on her time in slavery, in the vein of similar slave narratives by individuals such as Douglass. Having never learned to read or write, Truth dictated her life story to abolitionist Olive Gilbert, and had it published in 1850 as *The Narrative of Sojourner Truth, A Northern Slave*. It was printed cheaply, and sold in large numbers at abolitionist conferences. The *Narrative* contributed to Truth's growing abolitionist fame; she began speaking publicly on the subject that fall.

In May 1851, Truth spoke at a women's rights conference held at a church in Akron, Ohio, at which she appears to have been the only African American woman in attendance. In contemporary records of the speech, Truth affirmed the physical capabilities of women, using herself as an example; argued for their intellectual rights; and sharply repudiated the biblically derived objections to the equality of women that opponents of women's rights commonly offered. In the best-known contemporaneous report of the speech, Marius Robinson claimed that it was "impossible to transfer it to paper, or convey any adequate idea of the effect [Truth's speech] produced upon the audience." Another account of Truth's speech, however, eventually became more famous; it was produced in 1863, over a decade after the speech had been given, by Frances Dana Gage, who had presided over the Akron convention. In her version, Gage significantly expanded upon the content of Truth's speech, portraying her as speaking in a strong dialect reflective of stereotypical Southern "slave" accents. (Truth, as a native Dutch speaker from the North, would almost certainly not have spoken with such an accent.) Gage also added the famous refrain, "Ar'n't I a Woman?," which has since lent the speech its popular name. Gage's version appeared in revised editions of Truth's *Narrative* published in the 1870s and 1880s, as well as in the first volume of Elizabeth Cady Stanton's monumental *History of Woman Suffrage* (1881); it remained throughout much of the twentieth century the most widely known and reproduced.

Truth's speeches continued to garner her influence and notoriety. Her highly animated, song-filled lectures were the subject of much comment, as was her physical appearance; she stood nearly six feet tall, and is said to have bared both her arms and her breasts on stage to prove her strength and womanhood to skeptics. She was regularly discussed in abolitionist and feminist media; Harriet Beecher Stowe famously wrote of her in *The Atlantic* in 1863, describing her as "the Libyan Sibyl."

Though a pacifist at heart, Truth welcomed the Civil War as a national spiritual purge. She met (and posed for a photograph with) Abraham Lincoln during the period at which the Emancipation Proclamation was being drafted, and, after the end of the war, she provided aid and advice to newly emancipated men and women. Over the following years she agitated for healthcare, housing, and land reform for African Americans; for the desegregation of transportation; for temperance; for the abolition of capital punishment; and for universal suffrage.

Truth died in 1883, at the age of eighty-six, having by then established a vivid presence in the American public imagination. She had often aroused puzzlement in her admirers, including in Frederick Douglass, who described her as a "strange compound of wit and wisdom, of wild enthusiasm and flint-like common sense. She was a genuine specimen of the uncultured negro. She cared very little for elegance of speech or refinement of manners." Long after her death, monikers such as "the Negro Joan of Arc" remained associated with her name. Later scholarship has often pivoted on the question of authenticity, especially as it relates to her apparently intentional rejection of conventional literacy; on her highly dynamic lectures; and on her intersectional politics. Her life, career, and words continue to both challenge and fascinate.

NOTE ON THE TEXTS: The text of Truth's narrative is taken from the first edition of the *Narrative of Sojourner Truth, a Northern Slave, emancipated from bodily servitude by the state of New York, in 1828* (1850). Truth's famous 1851 speech is presented in two versions: the first is based on that printed in *The Anti-Slavery Bugle* on 21 June 1851, transcribed with commentary by Marius Robinson; the second is based on that published in the 1875 edition *Narrative of Sojourner Truth; A Bondswoman of Olden Time, emancipated by the New York Legislature in the early part of the present century; with a history of her Labors and Correspondence, drawn from her "Book of life,"* edited by Frances Titus with reminiscences by Frances Dana Gage. Spelling and punctuation have been lightly modernized in accordance with the practices of this anthology, but any writing that aims to reproduce (authentically or not) Truth's speech patterns remains unaltered.

⌘ ⌘ ⌘

from *The Narrative of Sojourner Truth, A Northern Slave*

Her Religious Instruction

Isabella[1] and Peter (her youngest brother) remained, with their parents, the legal property of Charles Ardinburgh till his decease, which took place when Isabella was near nine years old.

After this event, she was often surprised to find her mother in tears; and when, in her simplicity, she inquired, "Mau-mau, what makes you cry?" she would answer, "Oh, my child, I am thinking of your brothers and sisters that have been sold away from me." And she would proceed to detail many circumstances respecting them. But Isabella long since concluded that it was the impending fate of her only remaining children, which her mother but too well understood, even then, that called up those memories from the past, and made them crucify her heart afresh.

In the evening, when her mother's work was done, she would sit down under the sparkling vault of heaven, and calling her children to her, would talk to them of the only Being that could effectually aid or protect them. Her teachings were delivered in Low Dutch, her only language, and, translated into English, ran nearly as follows:

"My children, there is a God, who hears and sees you."

"A *God*, mau-mau! Where does he live?" asked the children.

"He lives in the sky," she replied; "and when you are beaten, or cruelly treated, or fall into any trouble, you must ask help of him, and he will always hear and help you." She taught them to kneel and say the Lord's Prayer. She entreated them to refrain from lying and stealing, and to strive to obey their masters.

At times, a groan would escape her, and she would break out in the language of the Psalmist—"Oh Lord, how long?[2] Oh Lord, how long?" And in reply to Isabella's question—"What ails you, mau-mau?" her only answer was, "Oh, a good deal ails me—Enough ails me." Then again, she would point them to the stars, and say, in her peculiar language, "Those are the same stars, and that is the same moon, that look down upon your brothers and sisters, and which they see as they look up to them, though they are ever so far away from us, and each other."

Thus, in her humble way, did she endeavor to show them their Heavenly Father, as the only being who could protect them in their perilous condition; at the same time, she would strengthen and brighten the chain of family affection, which she trusted extended itself sufficiently to connect the widely scattered members of her precious flock. These instructions of the mother were treasured up and held sacred by Isabella, as our future narrative will show.

The Auction

At length, the never-to-be-forgotten day of the terrible auction arrived, when the "slaves, horses, and other cattle" of Charles Ardinburgh, deceased, were to be

---

[1]   *Isabella*   Truth's birth name.

[2]   *Oh Lord, how long?*   See Psalm 13.1: "How long wilt thou forget me, O Lord? for ever? how long wilt thou hide thy face from me?"

put under the hammer, and again change masters. Not only Isabella and Peter, but their mother, were now destined to the auction block, and would have been struck off with the rest to the highest bidder, but for the following circumstance: A question arose among the heirs, "Who shall be burdened with Bomefree, when we have sent away his faithful Mau-mau Bett?"[1] He was becoming weak and infirm; his limbs were painfully rheumatic and distorted—more from exposure and hardship than from old age, though he was several years older than Mau-mau Bett; he was no longer considered of value, but must soon be a burden and care to some one. After some contention on the point at issue, none being willing to be burdened with him, it was finally agreed, as most expedient for the heirs, that the price of Mau-mau Bett should be sacrificed, and she receive her freedom, on condition that she take care of and support her faithful James—faithful, not only to her as a husband, but proverbially faithful as a slave to those who would not willingly sacrifice a dollar for *his* comfort, now that he had commenced his descent into the dark vale of decrepitude and suffering. This important decision was received as joyful news indeed to our ancient couple, who were the objects of it, and who were trying to prepare their hearts for a severe struggle, and one altogether new to them, as they had never before been separated; for, though ignorant, helpless, crushed in spirit, and weighed down with hardship and cruel bereavement, they were still human, and their human hearts beat within them with as true an affection as ever caused a human heart to beat. And their anticipated separation now, in the decline of life, after the last child had been torn from them, must have been truly appalling. Another privilege was granted them—that of remaining occupants of the same dark, humid cellar I have before described: otherwise, they were to support themselves as they best could. And as her mother was still able to do considerable work, and her father a little, they got on for some time very comfortably. The strangers who rented the house were humane people, and very kind to them; they were not rich, and owned no slaves. How long this state of things continued, we are unable to say, as Isabella had

not then sufficiently cultivated her organ[2] of time to calculate years, or even weeks or hours. But she thinks her mother must have lived several years after the death of Master Charles. She remembers going to visit her parents some three or four times before the death of her mother, and a good deal of time seemed to her to intervene between each visit.

At length her mother's health began to decline—a fever-sore made its ravages on one of her limbs, and the palsy[3] began to shake her frame; still, she and James tottered about, picking up a little here and there, which, added to the mites[4] contributed by their kind neighbors, sufficed to sustain life, and drive famine from the door. …

THE CAUSE OF HER LEAVING THE CITY

The first years spent by Isabella in the city, she accumulated more than enough to satisfy all her wants, and she placed all the overplus in the Savings Bank. Afterwards, while living with Mr. Pierson,[5] he prevailed on her to take it all thence, and invest it in a common fund which he was about establishing, as a fund to be drawn from by all the faithful; the faithful, of course, were the handful that should subscribe to his peculiar creed. This fund, commenced by Mr. Pierson, afterwards became part and parcel of the kingdom of which Matthias assumed to be head;[6] and at the breaking up of the kingdom, her little property was merged in the general ruin—or went to enrich those who profited by the loss of others, if any such there were. Mr. Pierson and others had so assured her that the fund would supply all her wants, at all times, and in all emergencies, and to the end of life, that she became perfectly careless on the subject—asking for no interest when she drew her money from the bank, and

---

1   *Bomefree* Truth's father, James Baum-free; *Mau-mau Bett* Truth's mother Elizabeth.

2   *organ* Mental sense.

3   *palsy* Paralysis or tremor.

4   *mites* Small donations.

5   *Mr. Pierson* Isabella's employer, businessperson Elias Pierson.

6   *the kingdom … head* Elias Pierson had been converted by itinerant preacher Robert Matthews, also known as Matthias, in the 1830s, following which he helped fund a new religious cult called the Kingdom of Matthias. Matthias became a notorious figure both for his unorthodox—and rampantly misogynistic—theology and for the controversy that surrounded his cult's dissolution.

taking no account of the sum she placed in the fund. She recovered a few articles of the furniture from the wreck of the kingdom, and received a small sum of money from Mr. B. Folger, as the price of Mrs. Folger's attempt to convict her of murder.[1] With this to start upon, she commenced anew her labors, in the hope of yet being able to accumulate a sufficiency to make a little home for herself, in her advancing age. With this stimulus before her, she toiled hard, working early and late, doing a great deal for a little money, and turning her hand to almost anything that promised good pay. Still, she did not prosper, and somehow, could not contrive to lay by a single dollar for a "rainy day."

When this had been the state of her affairs some time, she suddenly paused, and taking a retrospective view of what had passed, inquired within herself why it was that, for all her unwearied labors, she had nothing to show; why it was that others, with much less care and labor, could hoard up treasures for themselves and children? She became more and more convinced, as she reasoned, that everything she had undertaken in the city of New York had finally proved a failure; and where her hopes had been raised the highest, there she felt the failure had been the greatest, and the disappointment most severe.

After turning it in her mind for some time, she came to the conclusion that she had been taking part in a great drama, which was, in itself, but one great system of robbery and wrong. "Yes," she said, "the rich rob the poor, and the poor rob one another." True, she had not received labor from others, and stinted their pay, as she felt had been practised against her; but she had taken their work from them, which was their only means to get money, and was the same to them in the end. For instance—a gentleman where she lived would give her a dollar to hire a poor man to clear the new-fallen snow from the steps and sidewalks. She would arise early, and perform the labor herself, putting the money into her own pocket. A poor man would come along, saying she ought to have let him have the job; he was poor, and needed the pay for his family. She would harden her heart against him, and

answer—"I am poor too, and I need it for mine." But, in her retrospection, she thought of all the misery she might have been adding to, in her selfish grasping, and it troubled her conscience sorely; and this insensibility to the claims of human brotherhood, and the wants of the destitute and wretched poor, she now saw, as she never had done before, to be unfeeling, selfish and wicked. These reflections and convictions gave rise to a sudden revulsion of feeling in the heart of Isabella, and she began to look upon money and property with great indifference, if not contempt—being at that time unable, probably, to discern any difference between a miserly grasping at and hoarding of money and means, and a true use of the good things of this life for one's own comfort, and the relief of such as she might be enabled to befriend and assist. One thing she was sure of—that the precepts, "Do unto others as ye would that others should do unto you," "Love your neighbor as yourself,"[2] and so forth, were maxims that had been but little thought of by herself, or practised by those about her.

Her next decision was that she must leave the city; it was no place for her; yea, she felt called in spirit to leave it, and to travel east and lecture. She had never been further east than the city, neither had she any friends there of whom she had particular reason to expect anything; yet to her it was plain that her mission lay in the east, and that she would find friends there. She determined on leaving; but these determinations and convictions she kept close locked in her own breast, knowing that if her children and friends were aware of it, they would make such an ado about it as would render it very unpleasant, if not distressing to all parties. Having made what preparations for leaving she deemed necessary—which was, to put up a few articles of clothing in a pillow-case, all else being deemed an unnecessary incumbrance—about an hour before she left, she informed Mrs. Whiting, the woman of the house where she was stopping, that her name was no longer Isabella, but SOJOURNER, and that she was going east. And to her inquiry, "What are you going east for?" her answer was, "The Spirit calls me there, and I must go."

---

[1] *Mr. B. Folger ... murder* The Kingdom of Matthias fell apart after Pierson died under suspicious circumstances, upon which both Matthias and Isabella were accused of his murder. Isabella successfully sued their accusers, the Folgers, for libel.

[2] *Do unto others ... as yourself* See Luke 6.31 and Mark 12.31, respectively.

She left the city on the morning of the 1st of June, 1843, crossing over to Brooklyn, L.I.;[1] and taking the rising sun for her only compass and guide, she "remembered Lot's wife,"[2] and hoping to avoid her fate, she resolved not to look back till she felt sure the wicked city from which she was fleeing was left too far behind to be visible in the distance; and when she first ventured to look back, she could just discern the blue cloud of smoke that hung over it, and she thanked the Lord that she was thus far removed from what seemed to *her* a second Sodom.

She was now fairly started on her pilgrimage; her bundle in one hand, and a little basket of provisions in the other, and two York shillings[3] in her purse— her heart strong in the faith that her true work lay before her, and that the Lord was her director; and she doubted not he would provide for and protect her, and that it would be very censurable in her to burden herself with anything more than a moderate supply for her then present needs. Her mission was not merely to travel east, but to "lecture," as she designated it, "testifying of the hope that was in her"—exhorting the people to embrace Jesus, and refrain from sin, the nature and origin of which she explained to them in accordance with her own most curious and original views. Through her life, and all its chequered changes, she has ever clung fast to her first permanent impressions on religious subjects.

Wherever night overtook her, there she sought for lodgings—free, if she might—if not, she paid; at a tavern, if she chanced to be at one—if not, at a private dwelling; with the rich, if they would receive her—if not, with the poor.

But she soon discovered that the largest houses were nearly always full; if not quite full, company was soon expected; and that it was much easier to find an unoccupied corner in a small house than in a large one; and if a person possessed but a miserable roof over his head, you might be sure of a welcome to part of it.

But this, she had penetration enough to see, was quite as much the effect of a want of sympathy as of benevolence; and this was also very apparent in her religious conversations with people who were strangers to her. She said, "she never could find out that the rich had any religion. If *I* had been rich and accomplished, I could; for the rich could always find religion in the rich, and *I* could find it among the poor."

At first, she attended such meetings as she heard of, in the vicinity of her travels, and spoke to the people as she found them assembled. Afterwards, she advertised meetings of her own, and held forth to large audiences, having, as she said, "a good time."

When she became weary of travelling, and wished a place to stop a while and rest herself, she said some opening for her was always near at hand; and the first time she needed rest, a man accosted her as she was walking, inquiring if she was looking for work. She told him that was not the object of her travels, but that she would willingly work a few days, if anyone wanted. He requested her to go to his family, who were sadly in want of assistance, which he had been thus far unable to supply. She went to the house where she was directed, and was received by his family, one of whom was ill, as a "Godsend"; and when she felt constrained to resume her journey, they were very sorry, and would fain have detained her longer; but as she urged the necessity of leaving, they offered her what seemed in her eyes a great deal of money as a remuneration for her labor, and an expression of their gratitude for her opportune assistance; but she would only receive a very little of it; enough, as she says, to enable her to pay tribute to Cæsar,[4] if it was demanded of her; and two or three York shillings at a time were all she allowed herself to take; and then, with purse replenished, and strength renewed, she would once more set out to perform her mission.

---

[1] *L.I.* Long Island.

[2] *remembered Lot's wife* In Genesis 19, the virtuous man Lot and his unnamed wife are permitted by God to flee the city of Sodom, which God is about to destroy because its inhabitants have been sinful; Lot and his wife are instructed not to look back upon the burning city, but Lot's wife disobeys, and as a punishment is turned into a pillar of salt. The story is referenced in the New Testament; Luke 17.32 instructs Christians to "Remember Lot's wife."

[3] *York shillings* Colonial form of currency still then in circulation in New York; one shilling was the equivalent of approximately twelve cents.

[4] *pay tribute to Cæsar* Truth is likely referencing the biblical saying regarding taxation, "Render unto Caesar the things that are Caesar's, and unto God the things that are God's" (Matthew 22.21); the "things that are Caesar's" referred to taxes or other fees relating to secular matters. In other words, Truth will accept only as much money as she needs to pay for the demands of earthly life, which may have included road and bridge taxes as well as things such as food and shelter.

THE CONSEQUENCES OF REFUSING A TRAVELLER A NIGHT'S LODGING

As she drew near the centre of the Island,[1] she commenced, one evening at nightfall, to solicit the favor of a night's lodging. She had repeated her request a great many, it seemed to her some twenty times, and as many times she received a negative answer. She walked on, the stars and the tiny horns of the new moon shed but a dim light on her lonely way, when she was familiarly accosted by two Indians, who took her for an acquaintance. She told them they were mistaken in the person; she was a stranger there, and asked them the direction to a tavern. They informed her it was yet a long way— some two miles or so—and inquired if she were alone. Not wishing for their protection, or knowing what might be the character of their kindness, she answered, "No, not exactly," and passed on. At the end of a weary way, she came to the tavern—rather, to a large building, which was occupied as a courthouse, tavern, and jail—and on asking for a night's lodging, was informed she could stay, if she would consent to be locked in. This to her mind was an insuperable objection. To have a key turned on her was a thing not to be thought of, at least not to be endured, and she again took up her line of march, preferring to walk beneath the open sky, to being locked up by a stranger in such a place. She had not walked far, before she heard the voice of a woman under an open shed; she ventured to accost her, and inquired if she knew where she could get in for the night. The woman answered that she did not, unless she went home with them; and turning to her "good man," asked him if the stranger could not share their home for the night, to which he cheerfully assented. Sojourner thought it evident he had been taking a drop too much, but as he was civil and good-natured, and she did not feel inclined to spend the night alone in the open air, she felt driven to the necessity of accepting their hospitality, whatever it might prove to be. The woman soon informed her that there was a ball in the place, at which they would like to drop in a while, before they went to their home.

Balls being no part of Sojourner's mission, she was not desirous of attending; but her hostess could be satisfied with nothing short of a taste of it, and she was forced to go with her, or relinquish their company at once, in which move there might be more exposure than in accompanying her. She went, and soon found herself surrounded by an assemblage of people, collected from the very dregs of society, too ignorant and degraded to understand, much less entertain, a high or bright idea—in a dirty hovel, destitute of every comfort, and where the fumes of whiskey were abundant and powerful.

Sojourner's guide there was too much charmed with the combined entertainments of the place to be able to tear herself away, till she found her faculties for enjoyment failing her, from a too free use of liquor; and she betook herself to bed till she could recover them. Sojourner, seated in a corner, had time for many reflections, and refrained from lecturing them, in obedience to the recommendation, "Cast not your pearls,"[2] etc. When the night was far spent, the husband of the sleeping woman aroused the sleeper, and reminded her that she was not very polite to the woman she had invited to sleep at her house, and of the propriety of returning home. They once more emerged into the pure air, which to our friend Sojourner, after so long breathing the noisome air of the ballroom, was most refreshing and grateful. Just as day dawned, they reached the place they called their home. Sojourner now saw that she had lost nothing in the shape of rest by remaining so long at the ball, as their miserable cabin afforded but one bunk or pallet for sleeping; and had there been many such, she would have preferred sitting up all night to occupying one like it. They very politely offered her the bed, if she would use it; but civilly declining, she waited for morning with an eagerness of desire she never felt before on the subject, and was never more happy than when the eye of day shed its golden light once more over the earth. She was once more free, and while daylight should last, independent, and needed no invitation to pursue her journey. Let these facts teach us that every pedestrian in the world is not a vagabond, and that it is a dangerous thing to compel anyone to receive that hospitality from the vicious and abandoned which they should

---

[1]   *the Island*   I.e., Long Island.

[2]   *Cast not your pearls*   See Matthew 7.6: "Give not that which is holy unto the dogs, neither cast ye your pearls before swine, lest they trample them under their feet, and turn again and rend you."

have received from us—as thousands can testify, who have thus been caught in the snares of the wicked.

The fourth of July, Isabella arrived at Huntingdon; from thence she went to Cold Springs, where she found the people making preparations for a mass temperance meeting. With her usual alacrity, she entered into their labors, getting up dishes *à la New York*,[1] greatly to the satisfaction of those she assisted. After remaining at Cold Springs some three weeks, she returned to Huntingdon, where she took boat for Connecticut. Landing at Bridgeport, she again resumed her travels towards the northeast, lecturing some, and working some, to get wherewith to pay tribute to Cæsar, as she called it; and in this manner she presently came to the city of New Haven, where she found many meetings, which she attended—at some of which, she was allowed to express her views freely, and without reservation. She also called meetings expressly to give herself an opportunity to be heard; and found in the city many true friends of Jesus, as she judged, with whom she held communion of spirit, having no preference for one sect more than another, but being well satisfied with all who gave her evidence of having known or loved the Saviour.

After thus delivering her testimony in this pleasant city, feeling she had not as yet found an abiding place, she went from thence to Bristol, at the request of a zealous sister who desired her to go to the latter place and hold a religious conversation with some friends of hers there. She went as requested, found the people kindly and religiously disposed, and through them she became acquainted with several very interesting persons.

A spiritually-minded brother in Bristol, becoming interested in her new views and original opinions, requested as a favor that she would go to Hartford, to see and converse with friends of his there. Standing ready to perform any service in the Lord, she went to Hartford as desired, bearing in her hand the following note from this brother:

SISTER—I send you this living messenger, as I believe her to be one that God loves. Ethiopia is stretching forth her hands unto God.[2] You can see by this sister, that God does by his Spirit alone teach his own children things to come. Please receive her, and she will tell you some new things. Let her tell her story without interrupting her, and give close attention, and you will see she has got the lever of truth, that God helps her to pry where but few can. She cannot read or write, but the law is in her heart.

Send her to brother—brother—and where she can do the most good.

From your brother,   H.L.B.

SOME OF HER VIEWS AND REASONINGS

As soon as Isabella saw God as an all-powerful, all-pervading spirit, she became desirous of hearing all that had been written of him, and listened to the account of the creation of the world and its first inhabitants, as contained in the first chapters of Genesis, with peculiar interest. For some time she received it all literally, though it appeared strange to her that "God worked by the day, got tired, and stopped to rest," etc. But after a little time, she began to reason upon it, thus—"Why, if God works by the day, and one day's work tires him, and he is obliged to rest, either from weariness or on account of darkness, or if he waited for the 'cool of the day to walk in the garden,'[3] because he was inconvenienced by the heat of the sun, why then it seems that God cannot do as much as *I* can; for *I* can bear the sun at noon, and work several days and nights in succession without being much tired. Or, if he rested nights because of the darkness, it is very queer that he should make the night so dark that he could not see himself. If *I* had been God, I would have made the night light enough for my own convenience, surely." But the moment she placed this idea of God by the side

---

[1] *getting up dishes à la New York* Preparing meals in New York style. The expression "à la New York" is tongue-in-cheek; nineteenth-century American cuisine was typically quite unrefined, but restaurants often tried to suggest a higher level of sophistication by dressing up the dishes they served with French or other European names (*potatoes Parisienne, macaroni à la Milanese*, etc.).

[2] *Ethiopia ... unto God* See Psalm 68.31: "Princes shall come out of Egypt; Ethiopia shall soon stretch out her hands unto God." In the nineteenth century, this biblical line was often referenced by abolitionists, with "Ethiopia" being used as a shorthand for the African continent and African-descended people as a whole.

[3] *cool of ... the garden* See Genesis 3.8: "And they [Adam and Eve] heard the voice of the Lord God walking in the garden in the cool of the day."

of the impression she had once so suddenly received of his inconceivable greatness and entire spirituality, that moment she exclaimed mentally, "No, God does not stop to rest, for he is a spirit, and cannot tire; he cannot want for light, for he hath all light in himself. And if 'God is all in all,' and 'worketh all in all,'[1] as I have heard them read, then it is impossible he should rest at all; for if he did, every other thing would stop and rest too; the waters would not flow, and the fishes could not swim; and all motion must cease. God could have no pauses in his work, and he needed no Sabbaths of rest. Man might need them, and he should take them when he needed them, whenever he required rest. As it regarded the worship of God, he was to be worshipped at all times and in all places; and one portion of time never seemed to her more holy than another."

These views, which were the results of the workings of her own mind, assisted solely by the light of her own experience and very limited knowledge, were, for a long time after their adoption, closely locked in her own breast, fearing lest their avowal might bring upon her the imputation of "infidelity"—the usual charge preferred by all religionists, against those who entertain religious views and feelings differing materially from their own. If, from their own sad experience, they are withheld from shouting the cry of "infidel," they fail not to see and to feel, ay, and to say, that the dissenters are not of the right spirit, and that their spiritual eyes have never been unsealed.

While travelling in Connecticut, she met a minister, with whom she held a long discussion on these points, as well as on various other topics, such as the origin of all things, especially the origin of evil, at the same time bearing her testimony strongly against a paid ministry. He belonged to that class, and, as a matter of course, as strongly advocated his own side of the question.

I had forgotten to mention, in its proper place, a very important fact, that when she was examining the scriptures, she wished to hear them without comment; but if she employed adult persons to read them to her, and she asked them to read a passage over again, they invariably commenced to explain, by giving her their version of it; and in this way, they tried her feelings exceedingly. In consequence of this, she ceased to ask

adult persons to read the Bible to her, and substituted children in their stead. Children, as soon as they could read distinctly, would re-read the same sentence to her, as often as she wished, and without comment—and in that way she was enabled to see what her own mind could make out of the record, and that, she said, was what she wanted, and not what others thought it to mean. She wished to compare the teachings of the Bible with the witness within her; and she came to the conclusion, that the spirit of truth spoke in those records, but that the recorders of those truths had intermingled with them ideas and suppositions of their own. This is one among the many proofs of her energy and independence of character.

When it became known to her children that Sojourner had left New York, they were filled with wonder and alarm. Where could she have gone, and why had she left? were questions no one could answer satisfactorily. Now, their imaginations painted her as a wandering maniac—and again they feared she had been left to commit suicide; and many were the tears they shed at the loss of her.

But when she reached Berlin, Conn., she wrote to them by amanuensis, informing them of her whereabouts, and waiting an answer to her letter; thus quieting their fears, and gladdening their hearts once more with assurances of her continued life and her love.
—1850

Speech at the Akron, Ohio Women's Right Convention, 1851

On the 29th of May 1851, Sojourner Truth attended a women's rights convention held at the Old Stone Church in Akron, Ohio, where she ventured before the crowd, apparently spontaneously, and delivered what would become one of the most famous speeches of the burgeoning women's rights movement. Numerous reports of her speech were published in newspapers at the time; most notable among them was that written by Marius Robinson for the Salem *Anti-Slavery Bugle*. Nearly twelve years later, another account was published in the 23 April 1863 issue of the *New York Independent*, written by Frances Dana Gage, who had presided over the 1851 Akron event. This version differed substantially from the earlier

---

[1]   *God is ... in all*   See 1 Corinthians 12.6: "And there are diversities of operations, but it is the same God which worketh all in all."

transcription, portraying Truth as speaking with a dialect that modern scholars argue was almost certainly not representative of her actual mode of speaking. Nevertheless, Gage's version was reprinted in an 1875 edition of the *Narrative of Sojourner Truth; A Bondswoman of Olden Time*, and again in Volume 1 of Elizabeth Cady Stanton's *History of Woman Suffrage* (1881). It prevailed as the standard rendition of Truth's speech well into the twentieth century.

[*1851 version*]

WOMEN'S RIGHTS CONVENTION

SOJOURNER TRUTH

One of the most unique and interesting speeches of the Convention was made by Sojourner Truth, an emancipated slave. It is impossible to transfer it to paper, or convey any adequate idea of the effect it produced upon the audience. Those only can appreciate it who saw her powerful form, her whole-souled, earnest gesture, and listened to her strong and truthful tones. She came forward to the platform and addressing the President said with great simplicity:

May I say a few words? Receiving an affirmative answer, she proceeded: I want to say a few words about this matter. I am a woman's rights. I have as much muscle as any man, and can do as much work as any man. I have plowed and reaped and husked and chopped and mowed, and can any man do more than that? I have heard much about the sexes being equal; I can carry as much as any man, and can eat as much too, if I can get it. I am as strong as any man that is now. As for intellect, all I can say is, if woman have a pint and man a quart—why can't she have her little pint full? You need not be afraid to give us our rights for fear we will take too much—for we can't take more than our pint'll hold. The poor men seem to be all in confusion, and don't know what to do. Why children, if you have woman's rights give it to her and you will feel better. You will have your own rights, and they won't be so much trouble. I can't read, but I can hear. I have heard the Bible and have learned that Eve caused man to sin. Well if woman upset the world, do give her a chance to set it right side up again. The Lady has spoken about

Jesus, how he never spurned woman from him, and she was right. When Lazarus died, Mary and Martha came to him with faith and love and besought him to raise their brother. And Jesus wept—and Lazarus came forth.[1] And how came Jesus into the world? Through God who created him and woman who bore him. Man, where is your part? But the women are coming up blessed by God and a few of the men are coming up with them. But man is in a tight place, the poor slave is on him, woman is coming on him, and he is surely between a hawk and a buzzard.

—1851

[*1875 version*]

The cause [of women's rights] was unpopular then. The leaders of the movement trembled on seeing a tall, gaunt black woman, in a gray dress and white turban, surmounted by an uncouth sun-bonnet, march deliberately into the church, walk with the air of a queen up the aisle, and take her seat upon the pulpit steps. A buzz of disapprobation was heard all over the house, and such words as these fell upon listening ears:

"An abolition affair!" "Woman's rights and niggers!" "We told you so!" "Go it, old darkey!"

I chanced upon that occasion to wear my first laurels in public life as president of the meeting. At my request, order was restored and the business of the hour went on. The morning session was held; the evening exercises came and went. Old Sojourner, quiet and reticent as the "Libyan Statue,"[2] sat crouched against the wall on the corner of the pulpit stairs, her sun-bonnet shading her eyes, her elbows on her knees, and her chin resting upon her broad, hard palm. At intermission she was busy, selling "The Life of Sojourner Truth," a narrative of her own strange and adventurous life. Again and again timorous and trembling ones came to me and said with earnestness, "Don't let her speak, Mrs.

---

[1] *When Lazarus ... came forth* In John 11, Jesus is asked by Mary and Martha of Bethany to come to the aid of their ailing brother Lazarus. Jesus arrives in Bethany four days after Lazarus' death, but because of the sisters' faith, Jesus raises Lazarus from the dead.

[2] *Libyan Statue* Reference to an 1861 marble sculpture by William Wetmore Story; see the contextual materials in the website component of this anthology.

Gage, it will ruin us. Every newspaper in the land will have our cause mixed with abolition and niggers, and we shall be utterly denounced." My only answer was, "We shall see when the time comes."

The second day the work waxed warm. Methodist, Baptist, Episcopal, Presbyterian, and Universalist ministers came in to hear and discuss the resolutions presented. One claimed superior rights and privileges for man on the ground of superior intellect; another, because of the manhood of Christ. "If God had desired the equality of woman, he would have given some token of his will through the birth, life, and death of the Saviour." Another gave us a theological view of the sin of our first mother. There were few women in those days that dared to "speak in meeting," and the august teachers of the people were seeming to get the better of us, while the boys in the galleries and the sneerers among the pews were hugely enjoying the discomfiture, as they supposed, of the "strong minded." Some of the tender-skinned friends were on the point of losing dignity, and the atmosphere of the convention betokened a storm.

Slowly from her seat in the corner rose Sojourner Truth, who, till now, had scarcely lifted her head. "Don't let her speak!" gasped half a dozen in my ear. She moved slowly and solemnly to the front, laid her old bonnet at her feet, and turned her great, speaking eyes to me. There was a hissing sound of disapprobation above and below. I rose and announced "Sojourner Truth," and begged the audience to keep silence for a few moments. The tumult subsided at once, and every eye was fixed on this almost Amazon[1] form, which stood nearly six feet high, head erect, and eye piercing the upper air, like one in a dream. At her first word, there was a profound hush. She spoke in deep tones, which, though not loud, reached every ear in the house, and away through the throng at the doors and windows:

"Well, chilern, whar dar is so much racket dar must be something out o' kilter. I tink dat 'twixt de niggers of de Souf and de women at de Norf all a talkin' 'bout rights, de white men will be in a fix pretty soon. But what's all dis here talkin' 'bout? Dat man ober dar say dat women needs to be helped into carriages, and lifted

ober ditches, and to have de best place every whar. Nobody eber help me into carriages, or ober mud puddles, or gives me any best place," and raising herself to her full height and her voice to a pitch like rolling thunder, she asked, "and ar'n't I a woman? Look at me! Look at my arm!" And she bared her right arm to the shoulder, showing her tremendous muscular power. "I have plowed, and planted, and gathered into barns, and no man could head me—and ar'n't I a woman? I could work as much and eat as much as a man (when I could get it), and bear de lash as well—and ar'n't I a woman? I have borne thirteen chilern and seen 'em mos' all sold off into slavery,[2] and when I cried out with a mother's grief, none but Jesus heard—and ar'n't I a woman? Den dey talks 'bout dis ting in de head—what dis dey call it?" "Intellect," whispered some one near. "Dat's it honey. What's dat got to do with women's rights or nigger's rights? If my cup won't hold but a pint and yourn holds a quart, would n't ye be mean[3] not to let me have my little half-measure full?" And she pointed her significant finger and sent a keen glance at the minister who had made the argument. The cheering was long and loud.

"Den dat little man in black dar, he say woman can't have as much rights as man, cause Christ want[4] a woman. Whar did your Christ come from?" Rolling thunder could not have stilled that crowd as did those deep, wonderful tones, as she stood there with outstretched arms and eye of fire. Raising her voice still louder, she repeated, "Whar did your Christ come from? From God and a woman. Man had nothing to do with him." Oh! what a rebuke she gave the little man.

Turning again to another objector, she took up the defense of mother Eve.[5] I cannot follow her through

---

[2]   *I have ... into slavery*   In fact, as Truth relates in her *Narrative*, she had only five children, all of whom were born into slavery, and all of whom she lived with until she left Dumont's farm in 1826. (One son was sold—illegally—to a slaveholder in Alabama shortly before New York emancipated all its enslaved inhabitants, but Truth successfully sued for his return.)

[3]   *mean*   Selfish; small-minded.

[4]   *want*   Wasn't.

[5]   *defense of mother Eve*   I.e., an attack against Christian arguments by which Eve is considered to have introduced sin to the world through her actions in the Garden of Eden, and thereby to have rendered all women sinful.

---

[1]   *Amazon*   Legendary race of tall, strong women warriors in Greek mythology.

it all. It was pointed, and witty, and solemn, eliciting at almost every sentence deafening applause; and she ended by asserting that "if de fust woman God ever made was strong enough to turn the world upside down, all 'lone, dese togedder," and she glanced her eye over us, "ought to be able to turn it back and get it right side up again, and now dey is asking to do it, de men better let em." Long continued cheering. "Bleeged[1] to ye for hearin' on me, and now ole Sojourner ha'n't got nothing more to say."

Amid roars of applause, she turned to her corner, leaving more than one of us with streaming eyes and hearts beating with gratitude. She had taken us up in her strong arms and carried us safely over the slough of difficulty, turning the whole tide in our favor. I have never in my life seen anything like the magical influence that subdued the mobbish spirit of the day and turned the jibes and sneers of an excited crowd into notes of respect and admiration. Hundreds rushed up to shake hands, and congratulate the glorious old mother and bid her God speed on her mission of "testifying again concerning the wickedness of this 'ere people."

—1875

IN CONTEXT

Sojourner Truth's *cartes de visite*

In the 1860s, Sojourner Truth started regularly posing for photographs, which she printed in mass and sold at speeches and events to fund her activist travels. In 1864 she began having her photographs copyrighted under her own name—as opposed to that of the photographer—and adding the distinctive caption: "I sell the Shadow to Support the Substance." Many of her early portraits were printed in the form of *cartes de visite*, small (approximately the size of modern playing cards), inexpensive photo cards that in the 1860s became hugely popular as collectors' items, especially those that depicted politicians and celebrities. The *carte de visite* was among several innovations in early photography that led many at the time to praise photography as democratizing the tradition of portraiture, both by making it more accessible and affordable and by making portraits easier to reproduce and share. In the late 1870s the *cartes de visite* format was largely supplanted by that of the somewhat larger cabinet card, and Truth adapted her practice to suit. She continued posing for and selling her photographs until not long before her death.

---

[1] *Bleeged* Obliged.

Photographer unknown. The first known extant photograph of Truth, this 1861 portrait depicts Truth just prior to her appearance at an event in Indiana, whose state constitution included an article forbidding African Americans from traveling into the state. Some reports suggest that Truth's unusual outfit, consisting of numerous layers of heavy, padded, red-white-and-blue garments, was given her by her white colleagues as a sort of coat of soft armor against the disorderly and potentially hostile crowd. Truth was also escorted to the event by the state's Home Guard. She was arrested and released several times over the course of her Indiana speaking tour, but her abolitionist following also grew with every speech.

Photographer unknown, 1864. This photograph is among the few which clearly show Truth's right hand, which had lost part of its index finger in an accident during her time enslaved by John Dumont.

I SELL THE SHADOW TO SUPPORT THE SUBSTANCE.
SOJOURNER TRUTH.

I Sell the Shadow to Support the Substance.
SOJOURNER TRUTH.

Photographer unknown, 1864. Knitting exploded in popularity during the Civil War, with many women knitting garments, especially socks, to be sent to the soldiers. Several photographs depict Truth with her knitting.

Photographer unknown, 1866. The framed portrait sitting on her lap is a photograph of her grandson, James Caldwell, who had fought with the 54th Massachusetts Regiment during the Civil War.

Randall Studio, circa 1870. The backdrop in this photograph (which would have been supplied by the studio) is among the most ornate of those to be seen in Truth's portraits.

AFRICAN AMERICAN ORAL LITERATURE

In a famous passage in his 1845 *Narrative of the Life of Frederick Douglass, an American Slave*, Douglass pays tribute to the vital importance that the music and oral literature created by enslaved African Americans had for his life, politics, and writing. He relates how his fellow enslaved people on a Maryland plantation "would compose and sing as they went along": "Every tone was a testimony against slavery[.] ... Those songs still follow me, to deepen my hatred of slavery, and quicken my sympathies for my brethren in bonds." Douglass's sense of the power of such oral creations has today become nearly universal: African American oral literature is now commonly valued as a rich and compelling artform. This genre of music and oral storytelling attests to how enslaved people resisted dehumanization, maintained their creativity, and fostered a culture of their own, and it has wielded incalculable influence on the subsequent course of not just African American literature but the whole of American literature, culture, and language.

African American oral literature comprises a huge array of different forms, including spirituals (or, as W.E.B. Du Bois termed them, "sorrow songs"), work songs, and a variety of more irreverent or lighthearted songs and poems, as well as animal fables, supernatural tales, tall tales, and anecdotal narratives both serious and comic.[1] This varied body of literature stems from an equally wide array of sources. In the twentieth century, many scholars of slavery (including both white writers such as historian Stanley Elkins and black writers such as sociologist E. Franklin Frazier) argued that the experience of the Middle Passage and subsequent enslavement completely severed enslaved Africans from their previous identities and cultural traditions. While enslavement certainly constituted a profound culture shock, however, it is clear—as many African Americans had always known, and as black writers such as Du Bois and historian Carter G. Woodson were already emphasizing in the late nineteenth and early twentieth centuries—that enslaved people did in fact preserve and perpetuate stories, myths, characters, and traditions of storytelling, performance, and recitation from various African cultures. These African elements in African American oral literature include trickster tales centering on mythological figures such as the spider Anansi (who survived as Ah Nancy in the Gullah communities of the South Carolina and Georgia coast), the West African deities Eshu and Legba, and the trickster hares found in South, Central, and East African folklore—one potential source for the stories of Brer Rabbit.

The development of African American oral literature was also shaped by African institutions and practices such as the call-and-response mode of group recitation. In their explanation of this practice, the white editors of *Slave Songs of the United States* (1867), the first published collection of such songs, describe how call-and-response could serve as a form of improvisatory composition as well as performance: "the leading singer starts the words of each verse, often improvising, and the others, who 'base' him, as it is called, strike in with the refrain, or even join in the solo, when the words are familiar." Oral literature, which by definition requires the simultaneous presence of a speaker or speakers and a hearer or hearers, is inherently communal in a way that written literature is not; the solitary reader, privately taking in the disembodied written words of someone far distant from them in space, time, or both, has no equivalent in an oral-literary world. Call-and-response, by involving the whole group in the work of oral creation, amplifies this inherently communal nature. As a participatory, communal form that blurs the line between leader or speaker and audience and emphasizes (in the words of African American linguist Geneva Smitherman) "group cohesiveness, cooperation, and the collective common good," call-and-response embodies the creation and affirmation of community among enslaved people that was a core aim of black oral literature.

---

[1] Though it is not included in the following section, being instead represented in the Nineteenth-Century Oratory section as well as in individual author entries, African American oratory also certainly merits consideration as another variety of African American oral literature.

Alongside such enduring African legacies, the stories and songs of enslaved people also attest to the encounter with different cultural traditions that took place in America. Similarities between African American oral narratives (such as "Why Brer Possum Has No Hair on His Tail," a modern version of which is presented below) and Native American stories (such as "Why the Possum's Tail Is Bare," which appears in the first volume of this anthology) have been noted ever since the former were first collected in the late nineteenth century; debate continues as to the primary direction of cultural transmission between African American and Native American oral literatures, but that there was cross-fertilization between the two literatures seems clear. Additionally, the culture of enslaved African Americans was shaped in more overt and immediate ways by that of Euro-American enslavers. The genre of the spiritual exemplifies how enslaved people took one of the centerpieces of the Euro-American culture imposed on them, Christianity, and made it into a source of consolation, an expression of their deepest aspirations, and even a means of resistance.

African American oral literature often repurposes the materials it draws from various different cultural traditions to codify and express the experience of living through slavery, as well as the hope of escape. Spirituals, for instance, abundantly attest to enslaved people's yearning for freedom, in their ubiquitous expressions of longing for deliverance from hardship and suffering and their frequent references to the biblical story of the Israelites' escape from slavery in Egypt. In addition, particular songs such as "Swing Low, Sweet Chariot" and "Steal Away" have been interpreted as coded messages referring specifically to escape plans or attempts. (Whether enslaved people actually used such so-called "Underground Railroad songs" in these ways, though, has been disputed.) Similarly, a longstanding interpretation of trickster tales such as those of Brer Rabbit—in which smaller and weaker creatures such as rabbits consistently escape and even prevail over larger, more powerful predators by means of their wits—views them as describing the means whereby enslaved people could survive and resist their enslavers; as Abigail Christensen, one of the first collectors of these tales, succinctly put it, "The Rabbit represents the colored man." More recent interpreters, however, have called into question this view as well, pointing to the fact that the weaker animals in these stories sometimes behave just as unscrupulously, obtusely, and even cruelly as the predators, in ways that complicate any easy correspondence to enslavers and enslaved.

Whether or not it specifically addressed the circumstances of life under slavery, enslaved people's oral literature was crucial for surviving enslavement and for imagining—and enacting—an identity not defined or confined by it. In their oral creations, enslaved black people used what was available to them, from their own cultural pasts as well as from the other cultural traditions they had assimilated, to forge community, wield agency, and show that there was more to them than the fact of their enslavement. It is in this sense, even more than on the level of content, that, in Douglass's words, "every tone" of his fellow enslaved people's songs "was a testimony against slavery." In this way, black oral literature is intrinsically a literature of hope and resistance. The strategies, mentalities, and practices that fostered and were fostered by enslaved people's oral culture would go on to inform the attitudes of African Americans towards literacy and written literature, according to which—as the scholar Gholdy Muhammad has put it of the literary societies developed in the nineteenth century by black people in the North—literacy and literature were fundamentally about "liberation and power."

While the oral literature of enslaved people was first and foremost something they created among and for themselves, black oral culture—song in particular—was already appealing to certain white observers by the mid-eighteenth century. Samuel Davies, a Presbyterian minister who evangelized to enslaved people in Virginia from 1748 to 1759 (and whose missionary work likely inspired a spiritual, "Lord, I Want to be a Christian"), described the religious singing of his African American parishioners as "a torrent of sacred harmony" that "carried my mind away to Heaven," while Thomas Jefferson noted more clinically some years later that enslaved people "are more generally gifted than the whites with accurate ears for tune and time." Others were more dismissive: in 1819, the Philadelphia minister John Fanning Watson condemned as "a growing evil" the songs "composed and first sung by the illiterate *blacks* of the society," which he called "miserable as poetry, and senseless as matter." In the decades after Watson wrote, blackface minstrelsy, with its racist white representations and parodies of black musical culture, became an enormously popular genre of mass entertainment: the first—but certainly not the last—white American appropriation of a black American expressive form. Despite—or because of—minstrelsy's popularity (and despite the fact that certain African Americans performed in minstrel shows and even formed their own troupes), practically no examples of actual African American song were collected or published until the 1860s; Frederick Douglass's printing, in *My Bondage and My Freedom* (1855), of the slave song beginning "We raise de wheat," presented below, is one of the few exceptions.

The first intensive efforts to record black oral literature in print took place during, and because of, the Civil War, which brought large numbers of white Northern intellectuals—mainly abolitionists belonging to or accompanying the Union Army—into sustained contact with communities of enslaved or formerly-enslaved people for the first time. Some of these white observers admired the songs they heard from the black people they worked with and arranged for their publication. The words and music for two such songs, including "Poor Rosy, Poor Gal," were published in Philadelphia in 1862 by Lucy McKim, the twenty-year-old daughter of an antislavery Pennsylvania family. Five years later, McKim (who by then had married the son of the antislavery leader William Lloyd Garrison) collaborated with two other abolitionists, William Francis Allen and Charles Pickard Ware—both of whom, like her, had spent time during the war with the African American inhabitants of the Sea Islands off the South Carolina and Georgia coast—to publish *Slave Songs of the United States*. This pioneering collection assembled 136 African American songs from throughout the states practicing slavery, but primarily from the Sea Islands; most were spirituals, but the collection also included non-religious songs such as "Charleston Gals" and "Run, N—, Run!"

The musical, poetic dimension of African American oral literature was further popularized in the decade after the Civil War by the Fisk Jubilee Singers, an a cappella ensemble founded in 1871 to raise funds for Fisk University, a black educational institution in Nashville, Tennessee. The Singers' tours gave many white Americans their first real exposure to black music; according to one reviewer of the group, "Those who have only heard the burnt cork caricatures of negro minstrelsy have not the slightest conception of what it really is." (The Singers had, however, learned Euro-American musical and choral conventions from George White, the white Northern teacher who organized the group, and they were likely able to connect with white audiences in part because their manner of performing spirituals was adapted to these Euro-American conventions.) When the Singers began touring, many African Americans resisted disseminating spirituals beyond their own communities, though for divergent reasons. Some black people viewed spirituals as relics of an enslaved past that they did not wish to perpetuate, while others saw these songs as profoundly meaningful centerpieces of their own culture and hence resisted sharing them with white audiences, precisely because—as Ella Sheppard, one of the most prominent of the Jubilee Singers, put it—"they were sacred to our parents." The Singers themselves only reluctantly agreed to the idea of performing spirituals, when this was first broached by the white managers of the group, but once (in Sheppard's words) "we began to appreciate the wonderful beauty and power of our songs," they collected and arranged over one hundred for their repertoire, many of which were published in *The Story of the Jubilee Singers; With Their Songs* (1877). By then, the Jubilee Singers had become internationally popular, introducing spirituals to white audiences that included the likes of Mark Twain and Queen Victoria (while also experiencing constant racial discrimination in the process). How their popularization of spirituals was viewed by other African Americans is harder to gauge; black periodicals, notably, gave the Singers practically no coverage. The Singers did win the esteem of black leaders such as Douglass, however, and their efforts helped make the case within their own community, as well as beyond it, that this aspect of the black oral tradition had enduring value and could resonate with audiences very different from the groups that had birthed it.

Other collections of the song and poetry of enslaved people continued to appear into the twentieth century; a volume published in 1922 by the Fisk University chemistry professor Thomas W. Talley, *Negro Folk Rhymes: Wise and Otherwise*, deserves particular mention as the first such collection published by an African American scholar, as well as one of the first to emphasize other genres besides spirituals. In the meantime, another dimension of black oral literature had also been made extensively available to a mass readership: prose folktales. By far the most influential collector and transmitter of such tales was Joel Chandler Harris, a white Southerner whose 1880 book *Uncle Remus: His Songs and His Sayings: The*

Folk-lore of the Old Plantation threaded together stories Harris heard during the Civil War years from several enslaved people at a plantation in Georgia, presenting them in a frame story as narratives told to a young white boy by the fictional "Uncle Remus." The book, in which the exploits of Brer Rabbit featured prominently, was a bestseller, and Harris followed it up with eight other Uncle Remus collections (three of them posthumous). Undeniably significant in American literary history, Harris's work also remains deeply controversial: critics debate whether his collections should be primarily seen as works of preservation or appropriation, as well as how to weigh his commitment, as a politically-engaged journalist and editor, to racial reconciliation and equality in the Reconstruction-era South against his books' idealization of "the old plantation."

Harris, however, was neither the first nor the only collector of African American oral prose. Abigail Christensen, a folklorist who spent most of her life in South Carolina after moving there from Massachusetts with her abolitionist parents, published a version of the story of Brer Rabbit and the Tar-Baby that she heard on the Sea Islands (which appears below) in 1874, six years before Harris's first book appeared, leading an admirer to dub her "The Original Uncle Remus." Christensen's full collection, *Afro-American Folk Lore: Told Round Cabin Fires on the Sea Islands of South Carolina*, was published in 1892. Other notable collectors of black folktales during this period included Robert Roosevelt—uncle of future president Theodore Roosevelt, who also preceded Harris in the publication of Brer Rabbit stories—and Alcée Fortier, whose research into Louisiana Creole culture included documenting stories about that tradition's equivalent of Brer Rabbit, "Compair Lapin."

The work of studying and publishing the oral culture of enslaved black people continued into the twentieth century, carried forward by both white and black collectors. One of the best-known stories today to have come out of slavery, "All God's Chillen Had Wings," was recorded by the Ohio-born white writer John Bennett, who followed in Abigail Christensen's footsteps by moving to South Carolina and developing an interest in the language and culture of the local Gullah people. Bennett first heard a version of a widespread story of people flying away from slavery in 1907; however, his research scandalized Charleston's white upper-class society (into which he had married), and he did not publish this and other stories he collected until the 1940s. African American documenters of the oral literature of slavery include some of the foremost names in twentieth-century African American literature, such as W.E.B. Du Bois—who ended his epochal *The Souls of Black Folk* (1903) with an influential study of the nature and importance of the "sorrow songs"—and Zora Neale Hurston, an academically-trained anthropologist who collected black Southern folktales, including stories of slavery like "Big Sixteen," which she published in the collection *Mules and Men* (1935).

Hurston and Du Bois's work with black oral literature also highlights the degree to which, as a creative medium fundamentally tied to live speech or song, this literature eludes, and can even be distorted by, representation in print. Hurston's collections attest to this issue precisely because of the care she took to contextualize the stories she heard in the circumstances in which they were related; her attempts to bring readers as close to these circumstances as possible also have the effect of foregrounding the inevitable difference and distance between readers and hearers. Du Bois, for his part, identified something intangible in the "sorrow songs" that could be fully conveyed only in person, not on the page: "the true Negro folk-song … lives in the hearts of those who have heard them truly sung and in the hearts of the Negro people." The fact that, as oral literature, African American spirituals or folktales cannot be encapsulated by—or bound by—any one printed version of them has been embraced by such recent transmitters of this literature as Julius Lester, who rewrote Harris's "Uncle Remus" stories in the 1980s and 90s to make them better able to speak to a contemporary American audience—not least by removing the condescending if not demeaning aspects of Harris's renderings.

As the oral literature of enslaved people has undergone repeated revitalization and reinvention, this literature has also powerfully shaped American literature and culture from the late nineteenth century on. Just as it inspired Douglass, so black oral literature has galvanized the work of numerous African American writers since his time, from Du Bois and Hurston, through Langston Hughes, Ralph Ellison, and Richard Wright, to Alice Walker and Toni Morrison. In addition, some of the foremost white American writers, including Mark Twain and William Faulkner, owe a deep stylistic and thematic debt to African American oral culture. Brer Rabbit stories have become a cornerstone of modern children's literature (while also continuing to interest and delight adult readers); the words and themes of the spirituals are integrally woven into the fabric of American life and resonate around the world; and the musical traditions that originated in slavery have become one of the most all-pervasive forces in American culture, engendering gospel, the blues, and jazz (and thence rock 'n' roll and its descendants in modern popular culture), as well as influencing countless novelists and poets, including writers as different as T.S. Eliot and Allen Ginsberg. If, in the early twentieth century, John Bennett, disappointed by the initial reception of the Gullah folktales he had collected, could only hope that "maybe somebody, some day, will appreciate these really uncommon things," today that hope has been abundantly realized. Not only do the songs and stories crafted by enslaved people, in Douglass's words, "still follow" all Americans; in important respects, they have led the country on its ongoing literary, cultural, and political journey.

NOTE ON THE TEXTS: The works included in the following section were selected with an eye to conveying something of the breadth and diversity of African American oral literature: song and poetry as well as oral prose, non-religious as well as religious material, relatively obscure works as well as famous ones. The selections were also made to highlight works recorded earlier—as close as possible to their origins during slavery. The section includes songs and poems first, followed by prose stories; in both cases, the texts are ordered chronologically by date of their first publication. (Though it was published in the 1990s, Julius Lester's version of "Why Brer Possum Has No Hair on His Tail" appears before stories published by Zora Neale Hurston and John Bennett in the 1930s and 40s because it is a reworking of a story first published by Joel Chandler Harris in the late nineteenth century.) Some of the works included in this section, such as the songs from *Slave Songs of the United States* and "De Rabbit, de Wolf, an' de Tar Baby," were initially printed in a rendition—often, but not always, a white editor's or collector's rendition—of an African American dialect, while other works, such as the songs from *The Story of the Jubilee Singers* and "All God's Chillen Had Wings," were initially printed in standard English. In all cases, the style and form of a work's initial publication has been retained.

⌘ ⌘ ⌘

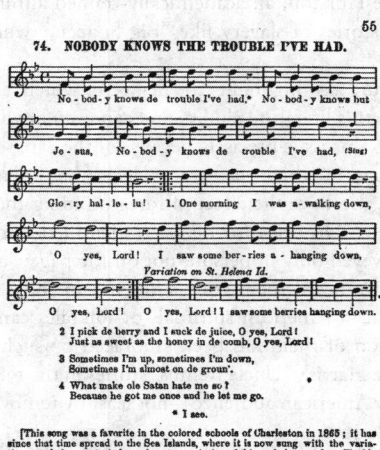

"Nobody Knows the Trouble I've Had," as printed in *Slave Songs of the United States* (1867). This song, under the alternate title "Nobody Knows the Trouble I've Seen," has since become one of the most famous and often-performed African American spirituals.

The Fisk Jubilee Singers, 1875.

[WE RAISE DE WHEAT]

as recorded by Frederick Douglass, *My Bondage and My Freedom* (1855)

We raise de wheat,
　　Dey gib us de corn;[1]
We bake de bread,
Dey gib us de cruss;
5　We sif de meal,°　　　　　　　　　　　　　*cornmeal*
Dey gib us de huss;°　　　　　　　　　　　*husk*
We peal de meat,
Dey gib us de skin,
And dat's de way
10　Dey takes us in.
We skim de pot,
Dey gib us the liquor,[2]
And say dat's good enough for nigger.[3]

15　Walk over! walk over!
Tom butter and de fat;
Poor nigger you can't get over dat;

　　Walk over!

POOR ROSY, POOR GAL

as recorded by Lucy McKim, *Songs of the Freedmen of Port Royal, Collected and Arranged by Miss Lucy McKim* (1862)

Poor Rosy, poor gal![4]
　　Poor Rosy, poor gal!
Poor Rosy, poor gal!
　　Heab'n shall-a be my home.
5　Poor Rosy, poor gal!
Poor Rosy, poor gal!
Poor Rosy, poor gal!
　　Heab'n shall-a be my home.
Before I spend one day in hell,
10　　Heab'n shall-a be my home
I sing and pray my soul away.
　　Heab'n shall-a be my home.

1　*corn* Corn was considered a lesser food than bread, and thus suitable for enslaved persons.

2　*We skim ... liquor* Pot liquor (sometimes colloquially spelled "pot likker") is the liquid by-product of boiling greens—all that was typically left for the enslaved people who cooked the greens for their enslavers. It has since become an important component of traditional Southern cuisine.

3　*nigger* By the mid-nineteenth century, this word, when used by white people of black people, had acquired the extremely derogatory connotations it carries today, but it had also become a term used by

African Americans, for and among themselves, in a neutral or positive way.

4　*Poor Rosy, poor gal* According to the editors of *Slave Songs of the United States*, alternate versions of this song replaced this line with "Poor Caesar, poor boy."

Poor Rosy, poor gal!
Poor Rosy, poor gal!
15   Poor Rosy, poor gal!
Heab'n shall-a be my home.

Got hard trial in my way!
Hard trial in my way,
Hard trial in my way,
20   Heab'n shall-a be my home.
O! when I talk I talk wid God.
Heab'n shall-a be my home.
O! when I talk I talk wid God.
Heab'n shall-a be my home.
25   Poor Rosy, poor gal!
Poor Rosy, poor gal!
Poor Rosy, poor gal!
Heab'n shall-a be my home.

I dunno what de people[1] want o' me,
30   Dunno what de people want o' me,
Dunno what de people want o' me,
Heab'n shall-a be my home.
O! dis day no holiday,
Heab'n shall-a be my home.
35   O! dis day no holiday,
Heab'n shall-a be my home.
Poor Rosy, poor gal!
Poor Rosy, poor gal!
Poor Rosy, poor gal!
40   Heab'n shall-a be my home.

A-singin' an' emb'acin', talkin' too,
Singin' an' emb'acin', talkin' too,
Singin' an' emb'acin', talkin' too,
Heab'n shall-a be my home.
45   O! when I walk, I walk wid God!
Heab'n shall-a be my home.
O! when I sleep, I sleep in God!
Heab'n shall-a be my home.
Poor Rosy, poor gal!
50   Poor Rosy, poor gal!
Poor Rosy, poor gal!
Heab'n shall-a be my home.

---

[1]   *people*   The editors of *Slave Songs of the United States* note that this song was also sung with the word "Massa" here.

ROLL, JORDAN, ROLL[2]
as recorded by Lucy McKim Garrison, William Francis Allen, and Charles Pickard Ware, *Slave Songs of the United States* (1867)

My brudder[3] sittin' on de tree of life,
An' he yearde° when Jordan[4] roll.   *hear*

[Chorus]
Roll, Jordan, Roll,
Roll, Jordan Roll!
5   O march de angel march,
O march de angel march;
O my soul arise in Heaven, Lord,
For to yearde when Jordan roll.

Little chil'en, learn to fear de Lord,
10   And let your days be long.

O, let no false nor spiteful word
Be found upon your tongue.

MICHAEL ROW THE BOAT ASHORE
as recorded by Lucy McKim Garrison, William Francis Allen, and Charles Pickard Ware, *Slave Songs of the United States* (1867)

Michael[5] row the boat ashore, Hallelujah!
Michael boat a gospel boat, Hallelujah!
I wonder where my mudder deh,° Hallelujah!   *there*

---

[2]   *ROLL, JORDAN, ROLL*   According to the editors of *Slave Songs of the United States*, "This spiritual probably extends from South Carolina to Florida, and is one of the best known and noblest of the songs."

[3]   *My brudder*   The editors of *Slave Songs of the United States* note, as variants of these words in other renditions of the song, "Parson Fuller, Deacon Henshaw, Brudder Mosey [Moses], Massa Linkum [Lincoln], etc."

[4]   *Jordan*   The Jordan River, which today forms the boundary between Israel and the West Bank, on one side, and Jordan, on the other, has great symbolic significance in the Jewish and Christian traditions. According to the Bible, the Israelites entered the Promised Land, after their escape from slavery in Egypt, by crossing the Jordan, and Jesus was later baptized in it at the beginning of his ministry. The Jordan was also frequently used to symbolize the transition from this world to the next.

[5]   *Michael*   According to Christian tradition, the archangel Michael conducts souls to the afterlife and protects the souls of the virtuous from Satan.

See my mudder on de rock gwine° home,   *goin*
  Hallelujah!
5 On de rock gwine home in Jesus' name, Hallelujah!
Michael boat a music boat, Hallelujah!
Gabriel blow de trumpet horn,[1] Hallelujah!
O you mind your boastin' talk, Hallelujah!
Boastin' talk will sink your soul, Hallelujah!
10 Brudder, lend a helpin' hand, Hallelujah!
Sister, help for trim dat boat, Hallelujah!
Jordan stream is wide and deep, Hallelujah!
Jesus stand on t' oder side, Hallelujah!
I wonder if my maussa deh, Hallelujah!
15 My fader gone to unknown land, Hallelujah!
O de Lord he plant his garden deh, Hallelujah!
He raise de fruit for you to eat, Hallelujah!
He dat eat shall neber die, Hallelujah!
When de riber overflow, Hallelujah!
20 O poor sinner, how you land? Hallelujah!
Riber run and darkness comin', Hallelujah!
Sinner row to save your soul, Hallelujah!

Words from Hilton Head[2]
Michael haul the boat ashore.
Then you'll hear the horn they blow.
Then you'll hear the trumpet sound.
Trumpet sound the world around.
Trumpet sound for rich and poor.
Trumpet sound the jubilee.[3]
Trumpet sound for you and me.

---

[1] *Gabriel ... horn* In Christian tradition, the second coming of Christ, and the consequent Last Judgment, will be heralded by a trumpet blown by the archangel Gabriel; this motif appears frequently in African American spirituals.

[2] *Hilton Head* Island off the coast of South Carolina, one of the Sea Islands that extend along the South Carolina, Georgia, and Florida coasts. The version of the song given previously was first recorded on St. Helena Island, another of the Sea Islands not far from Hilton Head.

[3] *jubilee* The biblical Book of Leviticus mandates a Jubilee year every fiftieth year, in which debts would be forgiven and slaves and prisoners set free: "Then shalt thou cause the trumpet of the jubilee to sound[.] ... And ye shall hallow the fiftieth year, and proclaim liberty throughout all the land unto all the inhabitants thereof: it shall be a jubilee unto you; and ye shall return every man unto his possession, and ye shall return every man unto his family" (Leviticus 25.9–10).

O'ER THE CROSSING[4]
as recorded by Lucy McKim Garrison, William Francis Allen, and Charles Pickard Ware, *Slave Songs of the United States* (1867)

Bendin' knees achin',
  Body racked wid pain,
I wish I was a child of God,
I'd git home bime-by.°   *by and by*

5 Keep prayin', I do believe
We're a long time waggin'° o' de crossin';   *waiting*
Keep prayin', I do believe
We'll git home to heaven bime-by.

O yonder's my ole mudder,
10 Been a waggin' at de hill so long;
It's about time she cross over,
Git home bime-by.

Keep prayin', I do believe, etc.

O hear dat lumberin' thunder
15 A-roll for do'° to do',   *door*
A-callin' de people home to God;
Dey'll git home bime-by.

Little chil'n, I do believe, etc.

O see dat forked lightnin'
20 A-jump from cloud to cloud,
A-pickin' up God's chil'n;
Dey'll git home bime-by.

Pray mourner, I do believe, etc.

---

[4] *O'ER THE CROSSING* The editors of *Slave Songs of the United States* describe this song as follows: "This 'infinitely quaint description of the length of the heavenly road,' as Col. Higginson styles it, is one of the most peculiar and widespread of the spirituals. It was sung as given above in Caroline Co., Virginia, and probably spread southward from this State, variously modified in different localities." Thomas Wentworth Higginson (1823–1911), an abolitionist minister and author, commanded an African American Union regiment during the Civil War; he recorded the songs sung by the regiment's soldiers and later contributed to *Slave Songs of the United States*.

RUN, N—, RUN![1]

as recorded by Lucy McKim Garrison, William Francis Allen, and Charles Pickard Ware, *Slave Songs of the United States* (1867)

O some tell me that a nigger won't steal,
But I've seen a nigger in my cornfield;
O run, nigger, run, for the patrol[2] will catch you,
O run, nigger, run, for 'tis almost day.

CHARLESTON GALS

as recorded by Lucy McKim Garrison, William Francis Allen, and Charles Pickard Ware, *Slave Songs of the United States* (1867)

As I walked down the new-cut road,
I met the tap[3] and then the toad;
The toad commenced to whistle and sing,
And the possum cut the pigeon-wing.[4]

5   Along come an old man riding by:
Old man, if you don't mind,[5] your horse will die;
If he dies I'll tan his skin,
And if he lives I'll ride him agin.

Hi ho, for Charleston gals!
10   Charleston gals are the gals for me.

As I went a-walking down the street,
Up steps Charleston gals to take a walk with me.
I kep' a-walking and they kep' a-talking,
I danced with a gal with a hole in her stocking.

SWING LOW, SWEET CHARIOT

as recorded in J.B.I. Marsh, ed., *The Story of the Jubilee Singers; With Their Songs* (1877)

[Chorus]
Swing low, sweet chariot,
Coming for to carry me home,[6]
Swing low, sweet chariot,
Coming for to carry me home.

5   I looked over Jordan, and what did I see,
Coming for to carry me home?
A band of angels coming after me,
Coming for to carry me home.

If you get there before I do,
10   Coming for to carry me home,
Tell all my friends I'm coming too,
Coming for to carry me home.

The brightest day that ever I saw,
Coming for to carry me home,
15   When Jesus washed my sins away,
Coming for to carry me home.

I'm sometimes up and sometimes down,
Coming for to carry me home,
But still my soul feels heavenly bound,
20   Coming for to carry me home.

---

[1] *RUN, N—, RUN* Because the title of this song, "Run, Nigger, Run," includes what is today an extremely derogatory racial slur whose use is rightly considered completely unacceptable, the editors of this anthology have chosen to edit the word's appearance in the title but—consistent with the anthology's general practices—not to edit its appearances in the song's lyrics. By the mid-nineteenth century, "the n-word," when used by white people of black people, had acquired the highly pejorative connotations it carries today, but it had also become a term used by African Americans, for and among themselves, in a neutral or positive way.

[2] *patrol* Slave patrols—whose members were known colloquially as patrollers, pattyrollers, or other variants—were armed white militias in the states practicing slavery, formed to keep enslaved people in place and subservient. The patrols were especially devoted to regulating enslaved people's travel beyond their enslavers' plantations and apprehending escapees. Pre-Civil War slave patrols helped give rise to the white supremacist paramilitary organizations, such as the KKK, that formed in the South after the Civil War, as well as to modern organized police forces.

[3] *tap* Terrapin, a type of turtle (often abbreviated "t'apin," and thence "tap").

[4] *cut the pigeon-wing* The "pigeon wing" was a dance move that imitated a bird.

[5] *if you don't mind* I.e., if you're not careful.

---

[6] *Swing ... home* In the Second Book of Kings, the great Israelite prophet Elijah, at the end of his life, is taken up to heaven by "a chariot of fire" in the view of his disciple and successor Elisha after crossing the River Jordan. See 2 Kings 2.1–12.

DIDN'T MY LORD DELIVER DANIEL

as recorded in J.B.I. Marsh, ed., *The Story of the Jubilee Singers; With Their Songs* (1877)

[Chorus]
Didn't my Lord deliver Daniel,
Deliver Daniel, deliver Daniel,
Didn't my Lord deliver Daniel,
And why not a every man?

5 He delivered Daniel from the lion's den,
Jonah from the belly of the whale,
And the Hebrew children from the fiery furnace,[1]
And why not every man?

The moon run down in a purple stream,
10 The sun forbear to shine,
And every star disappear,
King Jesus shall be mine.

The wind blows East, and the wind blows West,
It blows like the judgment day,[2]
15 And every poor soul that never did pray,
'll be glad to pray that day.

I set my foot on the Gospel ship,
And the ship it begin to sail,
It landed me over on Canaan's shore,[3]
20 And I'll never come back any more.

---

[1] *He delivered ... furnace* Episodes in the Hebrew Bible (the Old Testament) in which God saves from seemingly inescapable destruction either righteous people or people who have been chosen to do God's work. In Chapter 6 of the Book of Daniel, the Israelite prophet Daniel is thrown into a lion's den for praying to God, in defiance of a royal edict that all petitions must be addressed to the king, but God "shut[s] the lions' mouths"; in the Book of Jonah, Jonah miraculously survives for three days and nights in the belly of a huge fish that has swallowed him and is ultimately vomited back out when "the Lord spake unto the fish"; and in Daniel Chapter 3, three Hebrew youths named Shadrach, Meshach, and Abednego are thrown into a fiery furnace for refusing to worship an idol set up by the king, but survive unscathed.

[2] *judgment day* In Christian tradition, the day at the end of the world in which all the people who have ever lived will be judged by God.

[3] *Canaan's shore* In the Bible, Canaan, a region corresponding to modern-day Israel and Palestine, is considered to be the "Promised Land" which God has destined for the Israelites. At the end of their Exodus from enslavement in Egypt, the Israelites enter Canaan by

MANY THOUSAND GONE

as recorded in J.B.I. Marsh, ed., *The Story of the Jubilee Singers; With Their Songs* (1877)

No more auction block for me,
No more, no more;
No more auction block for me,
Many thousand gone.

5 No more peck o' corn[4] for me,
No more, no more;
No more peck o' corn for me,
Many thousand gone.

No more driver's lash for me,
10 No more, no more;
No more driver's lash for me,
Many thousand gone.

No more pint o' salt[5] for me,
No more, no more;
15 No more pint o' salt for me,
Many thousand gone.

No more hundred lash for me,
No more, no more;
No more hundred lash for me,
20 Many thousand gone.

No more mistress's call for me,
No more, no more;

---

crossing the Jordan River, which can also symbolically stand for the transition between this life and the next.

[4] *peck o' corn* A peck is a unit of measure equivalent to two gallons. A "peck of corn" would have been the ration of corn given to enslaved fieldworkers (corn being less valued than other foods).

[5] *pint o' salt* Compare Frederick Douglass's description, in his autobiography *The Life and Times of Frederick Douglass* (1881), of the rations at the plantation at which he was enslaved: "The men and the women slaves on Col. Lloyd's farm received as their monthly allowance of food, eight pounds of pickled pork, or its equivalent in fish. The pork was often tainted, and the fish were of the poorest quality. With their pork or fish, they had given them one bushel of Indian meal [corn] ... of which quite fifteen per cent. was more fit for pigs than for men. With this one pint of salt was given, and this was the entire monthly allowance of a full-grown slave, working constantly in the open field from morning till night every day in the month except Sunday."

No more mistress's call for me,
Many thousand gone.

STEAL AWAY

as recorded in J.B.I. Marsh, ed., *The Story of the Jubilee Singers; With Their Songs* (1877)

[Chorus]
Steal away, steal away, steal away to Jesus!
Steal away, steal away home, I hain't got long to
   stay here.

My Lord calls me,
He calls me by the thunder;
5 The trumpet sounds it[1] in my soul:
I hain't got long to stay here.

Green trees are bending,
Poor sinners stand trembling;
The trumpet sounds it in my soul:
10 I hain't got long to stay here.

My Lord calls me,
He calls me by the lightning;
The trumpet sounds it in my soul:
I hain't got long to stay here.

15 Tombstones are bursting,
Poor sinners are trembling;
The trumpet sounds it in my soul:
I hain't got long to stay here.

SLAVE MARRIAGE CEREMONY SUPPLEMENT

as recorded by Thomas W. Talley, *Negro Folk Rhymes: Wise and Otherwise, With a Study* (1922)

Dark an' stormy may come de wedder;
I jines dis he-male an' dis she-male togedder.
Let none, but Him dat makes de thunder,
Put dis he-male an' dis she-male asunder.
5 I darfore 'nounce you bofe de same.
Be good, go 'long, an' keep up yo' name.
De broomstick's jumped,[2] de worl's not wide.
She's now yo' own. Salute yo' bride!

PICK A BALE OF COTTON

as recorded in Langston Hughes and Arna Bontemps, *The Book of Negro Folklore* (1958)

Jump down, turn around to pick a bale of cotton.
Jump down, turn around, pick a bale a day.
Jump down, turn around to pick a bale of cotton.
Jump down, turn around, pick a bale a day.

5 Oh, Lordy, pick a bale of cotton!
Oh, Lordy, pick a bale a day!

Me and my gal can pick a bale of cotton,
Me and my gal can pick a bale a day. ...

Me and my wife can pick a bale of cotton,
10 Me and my wife can pick a bale a day. ...

Me and my friend can pick a bale of cotton,
Me and my friend can pick a bale a day. ...

Me and my poppa can pick a bale of cotton,
Me and my poppa can pick a bale a day.
15 Oh, Lordy, pick a bale of cotton!
Oh, Lordy, pick a bale a day!

---

[1] *The trumpet sounds it* In Christian tradition, the second coming of Christ, and the consequent Last Judgment, will be heralded by a trumpet blown by the archangel Gabriel; this motif appears frequently in African American spirituals.

[2] *De broomstick's jumped* During the 1840s and 50s, it became a widespread practice at marriages between enslaved people for the newly-married couple to jump over a broomstick. Because slave marriages were not legally recognized, jumping over the broomstick served as a public ceremony symbolizing the couple's commitment. The practice still forms part of some African American marriage ceremonies today.

De Rabbit, de Wolf an' de Tar Baby[1]

as recorded by A.M.H. [Abigail Mandana Holmes]
Christensen, *Afro-American Folk Lore: Told Round Cabin
Fires on the Sea Islands of South Carolina* (1892)

Now de Wolf, 'e bery wise man; but not so wise as de Rabbit. De Rabbit 'e mos' cunnin' man dat go on four leg. 'E lib in de brier-bush. Now, de Wolf 'e done plant corn one 'ear, but Rabbit 'e aint plant nuttin' tall.[2] 'E lib on Wolf corn all winter. Nex' 'ear Wolf aint plant corn, 'e tink corn crop too poo'; so 'e plant groun'-nut.[3] Rabbit, 'e do jes' de same as befo'.

Well, Wolf 'e biggin for tink someting wrong. 'E gone out in de mawnin' look at 'e groun'-nut patch, look bery hard at Rabbit track, say: "I 'spicion some-bordy ben a tief[4] my groun'-nut."

Nex' mawnin' 'e go 'gen, meet mo' groun'-nut gone, say same ting. Den 'e say, "I gwine mek one skeer-crow for set up in dis yere groun'-nut patch, for skeer de tief." So 'e mek one ol' skeer-crow an' set um in de middle ob de groun'-nut patch.

Dat night when Rabbit come wid 'e bag for git groun'-nut, 'e see de skeer-crow stan' bery white in de moonshine, an' 'e say, "Wha' dat?" Nobordy aint say anyting. "Wha' dat?" 'e say 'gen. Den nobordy aint say nuttin', an' he aint see nuttin' moobe, so 'e gone up leetle closer, an' leetle closer, tel 'e git *close* up ter um, den 'e put out 'e paw an' touch de skeer-crow. Den 'e say, "*You* aint nuttin' but on ol' bundle o' rag! Wolf tink I gwine fraid *you*? mus' be fool!" So 'e kick ober the skeer-crow an' fill 'e bag wid groun'-nut, an' he gone back home to de brier-bush.

Nex' mawnin' Wolf gone out for look at 'e groun'-nut patch, an' when 'e meet mo' groun'-nut gone an'

de skeer-crow knock down, 'e bery mad. 'E say, "Neber you min', I fix ol' Rabbit dat done tief all my groun'-nut. Jes' le' me show you!" So 'e mek one baby out o' tar, an' set up in 'e groun'-nut patch, an' say, "Jes' le' ol' Rabbit try for knock ober dis yere Tar Baby an' 'e 'll see! I jes' wan' um for try!"

Dat night, when Rabbit come 'gen wid 'e bag in 'e han' an' see de Tar Baby stan' bery black in de moon-shine, 'e say, "Wha' dat?—ol' Wolf done gone set up nodder skeer-crow? mus' be." So 'e moobe leetle nearer, an' say, "Dis yere enty no skeer-crow, dis yere mus' be one gal; I mus' study 'pon dis."

So 'e tu'n roun' an' spread out 'e bag an' sit down on um in de middle ob de groun'-nut patch an' look hard at de Tar Baby. Bimeby[5] 'e say, "Gal, wha' you name?" Gal aint say anyting. "Gal, why don' you speak me? wha' you da do dere?" Den 'e listen long time, aint hear anyting 'cept whip-poor-will in de swamp.

So 'e gone close ter um an' say, "Gal, you speak ter me, you min'! Gal, ef you aint speak to me I knock you! I knock you wid my right paw, den you tink it tunder!" Tar Baby aint say nuttin', so 'e knock um wid 'e right paw, and 'e paw stick!

Den 'e biggin for holler. "Gal, le' go me! I tell you, le' go me! Wha' for you da hol' me? Ef you aint le' go me I knock you wid my lef' paw; den you tink 'e tunder an' lighten too!" So 'e knock um 'gen wid 'e lef' paw, an' 'e lef' paw stick!

Den 'e say, "Gal, lef me loose! lef me loose, I tell you! Ef you don't I kick you wid my right foot; den you tink colt kick you!" So 'e kick um wid 'e right foot, an 'e right foot stick.

Den 'e say, "Now, gal, ef you aint tu'n me loose mighty quick I gwine kick you wid my lef' foot; den you tink hoss kick you!" So 'e kick um wid 'e lef' foot, an' 'e lef' foot stick.

Den 'e say, "Min' now, gal, I aint done nuttin' to you, wha' for you hol' me? tu'n me loose an I aint gwine meddle you 'gen sho'. Mebbe you tink I can't do nuttin' to you? aint you know I kin bite you do? Ef you aint tu'n me loose I gwine bit you sho'. Aint you know my bite wuss dan snake bite?" So 'e bite um, an' 'e nose stick!

Nex' mawnin', fo' sun-up, Wolf gone to de groun'-nut patch for see wha' he kin fin', an' dere 'e meet poo'

---

[1] *TAR BABY* I.e., a doll made out of tar. The term "tar baby" originates in Brer Rabbit stories such as this one; however, analogous folktales in which a sticky doll or artificial creature is used as a trap are extraordinarily widespread, with hundreds of similar stories having been identified around the world. The popularity of the Brer Rabbit stories in the late nineteenth and early twentieth centuries gave rise to the use of "tar baby" as a term for a difficult, inescapable situation that becomes worse the more one struggles with it. Simultaneously, the term also developed into a racial slur, and its use is increasingly considered to be unacceptable.

[2] *nuttin' tall* Nothing at all.

[3] [Christensen's note] Peanut.

[4] *somebordy ben a tief* Somebody has been stealing.

[5] *Bimeby* By and by.

Rabbit wid 'e paw an' 'e foot an' 'e nose all farsten on Tar Baby, an' 'e say, "Enty I done tol' you so? look a yawnder! I reckon Tar Baby done cotch ol' Rabbit dis time." So 'e tuk Rabbit off an' say, "You done tief half my groun'-nut; now what I gwine do wid you?"

Den Rabbit biggin for beg: "Oh, Maussa Wolf, do le' me go, an' I nebber tief groun'-nut no mo'." Wolf say, "No, Brudder Rabbit, you ben a tief my corn las' 'ear an' you ben a tief groun'-nut dis 'ear, an' now I gwine eat you up." Den Rabbit say, "Oh, Maussa Wolf, do don't do me so, but le' me beg you. You ma' roas' me, you ma' toas' me, you ma' cut me up, you ma' eat me, but do, Maussa Wolf, whatebber you do, don't t'row me in de brier-bush! Ef you t'row me in de brier-bush I gwine dead!"

So Wolf say, "You aint wan' me for t'row you in de brier-bush, enty? dat de bery ting I gwine do wid you, den." So 'e fling um in de brier-bush, an' *den* Rabbit laugh and say, "Hi! Maussa Wolf, aint you know I *lib* in de brier-bush? Aint you know all my farmbly bawn an' bred in de brier-bush? *Dat* what mek I tol' you for t'row me yere. How you is gwine get me 'gen?"

Den Wolf bery mad, 'cause 'e see Rabbit too wise man for him. 'E gone home, tell 'e wife, "No Rabbit soup for dinner today"; an' dey biggin for corntribe.[1] An' dey mek plan for git Rabbit for come to deir house.

So, one day, Wolf wife call Neighbor Dog an' tell um, "Neighbor Dog, I wan' for git you for do one errun' for me. I wan' you for git on you hoss an' ride fars' as you kin to Rabbit doo' an' tell Brudder Rabbit Brudder Wolf dead, an' fo' 'e die 'e leabe sorlum word 'e don' wan' nobordy else for lay um out[2] but Brudder Rabbit. An' do, Neighbor Dog, beg um for come ober quick as 'e kin possuble, so we all kin hab de funerul, for Wolf say 'e wont hab nobordy for lay um out but Brudder Rabbit."

So Neighbor Dog 'e git on 'e hoss an' ride fars' as 'e kin to Rabbit doo', den 'e knock an' say, "Brudder Rabbit, Brudder Wolf dead, an' 'e leabe sorlum word 'e wont hab nobordy for lay um out but Brudder Rabbit."

Rabbit say, "How! Brudder Wolf dead?" "Yes, 'e die lars' night, an' 'e say 'e don' wan' nobordy else for lay um out, an' Sister Wolf beg you for come ober an' lay

um out quick as you kin possuble, so dey all kin hab de settin'-up."[3]

So Rabbit git on 'e hoss an' ride to Wolf doo'; den 'e knock an' say, "How! I yeardy[4] Brudder Wolf dead."

Wolf wife say, "Yes, 'e dead for true, an' fo' 'e die 'e leabe sorlum word 'e don' wan' nobordy else for lay um out but Brudder Rabbit."

So den Rabbit say, "Kin I shum?"[5] So Wolf wife tuk um in de bedroom an' show um Wolf ben a lie on de bed, cober up wid sheet.

Rabbit lif' up de cornder ob de sheet an' peep at Wolf. Wolf nebber wink! So Rabbit tuk out 'e snuff-box an' drop one leetle grain ob snuff on Wolf nose, an' Wolf sneeze! Den Rabbit say, "Hi! how can *dead* man sneeze?"

So 'e gone out, *jump* on 'e hoss an' ride home fars' as 'e kin. An' Wolf see Rabbit too wise man for him, an' nebber try for cotch um no mo'.

WHY BRER POSSUM HAS NO HAIR ON HIS TAIL[6]
as rewritten by Julius Lester, *Uncle Remus: The Complete Tales* (1999)

There aren't too many tales about Brer Possum. That's because he never did that much. Why would he? Brer Possum is one of the laziest animals in creation. One time, though, his laziness got him in trouble.

On this particular day Brer Possum woke up hungry. If you and I wake up hungry, we go to the refrigerator, get a slice of cold pizza, and tell our stomachs that it is time to go to work. Brer Possum woke up hungry and

---

1   *corntribe*   Contrive.

2   *lay um out*   Prepare him for burial.

3   *settin'-up*   Ritual of sitting through the night with the body of the dead person.

4   *yeardy*   Hear.

5   [Christensen's note]   See him.

6   WHY ... TAIL   A version of this story first appeared in print, as "Why Mr. Possum Has No Hair on His Tail," in Joel Chandler Harris's *Uncle Remus: His Songs and Sayings, The Folk-Lore of the Old Plantation* (1886). The version presented here is that of the modern African American scholar Julius Lester (1939–2018), who rewrote Harris's Brer Rabbit stories in the 1980s and 90s, removing the stereotyped African American dialect in which Harris recorded the stories, as well as the framing he provided for them, and adding occasional references to features of late twentieth-century American life. This story bears comparison to the Cherokee story "Why the Possum's Tail Is Bare," which appears in the first volume of this anthology.

did not know what to do. He hung there in the tree, upside down, his tail curled around a limb, listening to his stomach. His stomach was saying, "Fool! Go find some cold pizza!"

Brer Possum was too lazy to go anywhere. He thought if he hung there long enough, food would come to him. He changed his mind, however, when he overheard his stomach tell Ol' Man Death, "Come get this fool!" Brer Possum decided it was time to do something.

He dropped out of the tree at the very minute Brer Rabbit was walking by, and almost landed on him.

"You trying to hit me?" Brer Rabbit hollered angrily.

"No, no, Brer Rabbit. Why would I do that? You and me always been the best of friends."

"That's true," Brer Rabbit agreed. "So tell me. How you be?"

"I'm hungry," said Brer Possum.

"A body has to be smart to keep a full stomach these days," Brer Rabbit agreed. "But I believe I know where you can get as much to eat as you want."

"Where's that?" Brer Possum asked eagerly.

"Brer Bear's apple orchard. Brer Bear don't care nothing about apples. He's a honey man. He watches the bees when they come to the apple blossoms. When the bees leave he follows them to their hives and gets the honey."

Brer Possum lit out for Brer Bear's apple orchard. Sure enough, the trees were full of the reddest, juiciest apples you can imagine. Brer Possum climbed to the top of the biggest tree and proceeded to do away with some apples.

While Brer Possum was getting fat on the apples, what do you think Brer Rabbit was doing? He was banging on Brer Bear's door.

"Brer Bear! Brer Bear! There's somebody in your apple trees."

Brer Bear came barreling out of the house. He couldn't afford to have somebody eating his apples. That's what he filled up on before he went into hibernation every winter. He lit out for the apple orchard.

Brer Possum thought he heard somebody coming. "Just one more apple."

He ate another one. He heard something again, and it was closer this time.

"Just one more."

The noise was closer now. Brer Possum looked out over the landscape and there was Brer Bear running toward the orchard like a runaway horse.

"Just one more," said Brer Possum.

That was one more too many.

Brer Possum was still chewing when Brer Bear started shaking the tree with all his strength, and down came Brer Possum like a leaf in a November wind.

But Brer Possum's feet were moving before he touched the ground, and when he did, those little legs shot him five feet down the road.

Brer Bear took off after him. Brer Bear may be big but he ain't slow. Uh-uh. It wasn't long before Brer Bear caught up to Brer Possum and grabbed him.

That didn't mean a thing to Brer Possum. Caught or not, Brer Possum didn't stop moving his legs. They were churning and turning and kicking up grass so bad that Brer Bear's grip was slipping. He bent over and grabbed Brer Possum's tail in his teeth.

That didn't slow Brer Possum down either. His little legs were still flinging dirt and grass back into Brer Bear's eyes. Brer Possum kicked and scratched and scratched and kicked until you would have thought a little tornado had landed. He kicked and scratched until he kicked and scratched his tail right out of Brer Bear's teeth. And all the hair on his tail came off in Brer Bear's mouth.

Brer Bear started coughing and gagging and he might've strangulated to death if Brer Rabbit hadn't come along and beat him on the back until Brer Possum's hair came out of his throat.

The hair may have come out of Brer Bear's throat, but it didn't go back on Brer Possum's tail. That's why, from that day to this, the Possum has no hair on his tail.

[BIG SIXTEEN][1]
as recorded by Zora Neale Hurston, *Mules and Men* (1935)

"A hm glad she gone," said Mah Honey. "She always pickin' fights and gittin beat. Dat 'oman hates peace and agreement." He looked after her a moment then yelled after her. "Hey, lady, you got all you' bust in de back!" Everybody laughed and Mah Honey went on. "She so mad now she'll stay way and let Mack tell Zora some lies. Gwan, Mack, you got de business."

"Aw, Ah feel lak singin'," Mack Ford said.

"Well nobody don't feel lak hearin' yuh, so g'wan tell dat lie on Big Sixteen. Ah never gits tired uh dat one."

"You ruther hear uh story, Zora?"

"Yeah, g'wan tell it. Dats jus' what Ah'm here for."

"Well alright then:

It was slavery time, Zora, when Big Sixteen was a man. They called 'im Sixteen 'cause dat was de number of de shoe he wore. He was big and strong and Ole Massa looked to him to do everything.

One day Ole Massa said, "Big Sixteen, Ah b'lieve Ah want you to move dem sills[2] Ah had hewed out down in de swamp."

"I yassuh, Massa."

Big Sixteen went down in de swamp and picked up dem 12x12's[3] and brought 'em on up to de house and stack 'em. No one man ain't never toted a 12x12 befo' nor since.

So Ole Massa said one day, "Go fetch in de mules. Ah want to look 'em over."

Big Sixteen went on down to de pasture and caught dem mules by de bridle but they was contrary and balky[4] and he tore de bridles to pieces

pullin' on 'em, so he picked one of 'em up under each arm and brought 'em up to Old Massa.

He says, "Big Sixteen, if you kin tote a pair of balky mules, you kin do anything. You kin ketch de Devil."

"Yassuh, Ah kin, if you git me a nine-pound hammer and a pick and shovel!"

Ole Massa got Sixteen de things he ast for and tole 'im to go ahead and bring him de Devil.

Big Sixteen went out in front of de house and went to diggin'. He was diggin' nearly a month befo' he got where he wanted. Then he took his hammer and went and knocked on de Devil's door. Devil answered de door hisself.

"Who dat out dere?"

"It's Big Sixteen."

"What you want?"

"Wanta have a word wid you for a minute."

Soon as de Devil poked his head out de door, Sixteen lammed him over de head wid dat hammer and picked 'im up and carried 'im back to Old Massa.

Ole Massa looked at de dead Devil and hollered, "Take dat ugly thing 'way from here, quick! Ah didn't think you'd ketch de Devil sho 'nuff."

So Sixteen picked up de Devil and throwed 'im back down de hole.

Way after while, Big Sixteen died and went up to Heben. But Peter looked at him and tole 'im to g'wan 'way from dere. He was too powerful. He might git outa order and there wouldn't be nobody to handle 'im. But he had to go somewhere so he went on to hell.

Soon as he got to de gate de Devil's children was playin' in de yard and they seen 'im and run to de house, says, "Mama, mama! Dat man's out dere dat kilt papa!"

So she called 'im in de house and shet de door. When Sixteen got dere she handed 'im a li'l piece of fire and said, "You ain't comin' in here. Here, take dis hot coal and g'wan off and start you a hell uh yo' own."

So when you see a Jack O'Lantern in de woods at night you know it's Big Sixteen wid his piece of fire lookin' for a place to go.

---

[1]   In Zora Neale Hurston's 1935 collection *Mules and Men*, this story appears (untitled) as part of Hurston's rendition of a "lyin' contest" held by inhabitants of a phosphate mining community in central Florida. Just before this, a woman called Good Bread has become involved in an altercation with other storytellers and has stormed out.

[2]   *sills*   Very large timber beams used as wall foundations or for windowsills.

[3]   *12x12's*   Long timber sills (see previous footnote) with a cross-section of 144 square inches.

[4]   *balky*   Resistant, perverse.

ALL GOD'S CHILLEN HAD WINGS
as recorded by John Bennett, *Doctor to the Dead* (1943, 1946)

Once all Africans could fly like birds; but owing to their many transgressions, their wings were taken away. There remained, here and there, in the Sea Islands and out-of-the-way places in the low country,[1] some who had been overlooked, and had retained the power of flight, though they looked like other men.

There was a cruel master on one of the sea islands who worked his people till they died. When they died he bought others to take their places. These also he killed with overwork in the burning summer sun, through the middle hours of the day, although this was against the law.

One day, when all the worn-out Negroes were dead of overwork, he bought, of a broker in the town, a company of native Africans just brought into the country, and put them at once to work in the cottonfield.

He drove them hard. They went to work at sunrise and did not stop until dark. They were driven with unsparing harshness all day long, men, women and children. There was no pause for rest during the unendurable heat of the midsummer noon, though trees were plenty and near. But through the hardest hours, when fair plantations gave their Negroes rest, this man's driver pushed the work along without a moment's stop for breath, until all grew weak with heat and thirst.

There was among them one young woman who had lately borne a child. It was her first; she had not fully recovered from bearing, and should not have been sent to the field until her strength had come back. She had her child with her, as the other women had, astraddle on her hip, or piggyback.

The baby cried. She spoke to quiet it. The driver could not understand her words. She took her breast with her hand and threw it over her shoulder that the child might suck and be content. Then she went back to chopping knot-grass; but being very weak, and sick with the great heat, she stumbled, slipped and fell.

The driver struck her with his lash until she rose and staggered on.

She spoke to an old man near her, the oldest man of them all, tall and strong, with a forked beard. He replied; but the driver could not understand what they said; their talk was strange to him.

She returned to work; but in a little while she fell again. Again the driver lashed her until she got to her feet. Again she spoke to the old man. But he said: "Not yet, daughter; not yet." So she went on working, though she was very ill.

Soon she stumbled and fell again. But when the driver came running with his lash to drive her on with her work, she turned to the old man and asked: "Is it time yet, daddy?" He answered: "Yes, daughter; the time has come. Go; and peace be with you!" … and stretched out his arms toward her … so.

With that she leaped straight up into the air and was gone like a bird, flying over field and wood.

The driver and overseer ran after her as far as the edge of the field; but she was gone, high over their heads, over the fence, and over the top of the woods, gone, with her baby astraddle of her hip, sucking at her breast.

Then the driver hurried the rest to make up for her loss; and the sun was very hot indeed. So hot that soon a man fell down. The overseer himself lashed him to his feet. As he got up from where he had fallen the old man called to him in an unknown tongue. My grandfather told me the words he said; but it was a long time ago, and I have forgotten them. But when he had spoken, the man turned and laughed at the overseer, and leaped up into the air, and was gone, like a gull, flying over field and wood.

Soon another man fell. The driver lashed him. He turned to the old man. The old man cried out to him, and stretched out his arms as he had done for the other two; and he, like them, leaped up, and was gone through the air, flying like a bird over field and wood.

Then the overseer cried to the driver, and the master cried to them both: "Beat the old devil! He is the doer!"

The overseer and the driver ran at the old man with lashes ready; and the master ran too, with a picket pulled from the fence, to beat the life out of the old man who had made those Negroes fly.

---

[1] *Sea Islands* Chain of islands off the coast of South Carolina, Georgia, and Florida; *low country* Coastal region of South Carolina and Georgia, including the Sea Islands as well as the mainland coastal plain. The enslaved African Americans brought to work on the cotton, indigo, and rice plantations of the Low Country developed a distinctive creole language, known as Gullah, and a culture that preserved many aspects of various African traditions.

But the old man laughed in their faces, and said something loudly to all the Negroes in the field, the new Negroes and the old Negroes.

And as he spoke to them they all remembered what they had forgotten, and recalled the power which once had been theirs. Then all the Negroes, old and new, stood up together; the old man raised his hands; and they all leaped up into the air with a great shout; and in a moment were gone, flying, like a flock of crows, over the field, over the fence, and over the top of the wood; and behind them flew the old man.

The men went clapping their hands; and the women went singing; and those who had children gave them their breasts; and the children laughed and sucked as their mothers flew, and were not afraid.

The master, the overseer, and the driver looked after them as they flew, beyond the wood, beyond the river, miles on miles, until they passed beyond the last rim of the world and disappeared in the sky like a handful of leaves. They were never seen again.

Where they went I do not know; I never was told. Nor what it was that the old man said ... that I have forgotten. But as he went over the last fence he made a sign in the master's face, and cried "Kuli-ba! Kuli-ba!" I don't know what that means.

But if I could only find the old wood sawyer,[1] he could tell you more; for he was there at the time, and saw the Africans fly away with their women and children. He is an old, old man, over ninety years of age, and remembers a great many things.

As told by Caesar Grant, of John's Island,[2] carter and laborer.

---

[1]   *wood sawyer*   Workman who saws wood.

[2]   *John's Island*   Coastal island near Charleston, South Carolina; the largest of the Sea Islands.

JAMES MONROE WHITFIELD

1822 – 1871

At the height of his literary career in the early 1850s, James Monroe Whitfield could claim a place in the first rank of American writers. His work appeared, for example, in the anthology *Autographs for Freedom*, published in 1853 as an abolitionist fundraiser, alongside writing by such luminaries as Catharine Sedgwick and Harriet Beecher Stowe. Whitfield's poetry, especially as collected in *America and Other Poems* (1853), powerfully articulated and contributed to the opposition to slavery that was gathering force during the 1850s; it undertakes a groundbreaking definition and exploration of American identity and forms an integral part of the wave of innovative American poetry that arose in the mid-nineteenth century. In addition, Whitfield's writing highlights the complexity and variety of nineteenth-century African American political thought, standing as an important literary harbinger of black nationalism.

Whitfield was born in Exeter, New Hampshire, in 1822. His father, James Whitfield, had escaped enslavement in Virginia, while his mother, Nancy Paul Whitfield, belonged to a distinguished family of free black New Englanders: two of her brothers were Baptist ministers who became nationally recognized abolitionists, and her brother-in-law was a famous Revolutionary War veteran who had been freed from slavery in recognition of his military service. Whitfield would draw on this family background in his poetry by condemning slavery as a betrayal of both Christian principles and the contributions African Americans had made during the Revolution. The biographical record of Whitfield's early life is scanty. Both of his parents had died by the time he was ten, and by the late 1830s he had moved to Buffalo, New York, where he was working as a barber—the trade he would follow for the rest of his life. Later admirers of Whitfield's poetry were distressed by the fact that he had to barber for a living, a necessity that Frederick Douglass called "painfully disheartening," and Whitfield's status as a barber-poet became central to his reputation and contributed to condescending assessments of his writing, both at the time and subsequently. As a barber, though, Whitfield was less a menial tradesperson than a successful entrepreneur: he came to own both his barbershop and his own home and seems to have been well-to-do by the standards of free black people at the time. Scholars have also speculated that the conversation and networking that would have gone on in Whitfield's barbershop may in some respects have assisted his writing, by providing inspiration for his poetry and helping him disseminate it.

During the 1840s and early 1850s, as Whitfield married, had three sons, and continued to establish himself in Buffalo society, he also became increasingly devoted to both politics and poetry. He took a leading role in a national African American convention when he was only sixteen, and his political activity continued apace from then on. He agitated against schemes to colonize free blacks in Africa, and in favor of voting rights and the abolition of slavery. Through his work for these causes, Whitfield befriended two of the most prominent African American leaders of the time: Frederick Douglass, the eminent abolitionist, and Martin Delany, a writer and physician who, during the late 1840s, collaborated with Douglass on the *North Star*, an abolitionist newspaper. Whitfield's first published poem, "Stanzas on the First of August," a commemoration of the abolition of slavery in the British West Indies, appeared in the *North Star* in 1849. Over the next few years, Whitfield published several other poems on a range of topics, both political and non-political, in the *North Star* (or, as it was retitled in 1851, *Frederick Douglass' Paper*). Douglass hailed Whitfield as a "son of genius," and Delany declared him "one of the purest poets in America."

Whitfield's growing reputation as a poet and abolitionist advocate was further bolstered by the publication of *America and Other Poems*. The book appeared at a moment when the debate about slavery had reached a new intensity, coming to dominate the national conversation. *America and Other Poems* furthered this debate by portraying slavery as both a betrayal and a foundational element of the United States' national identity—a deeply American evil, but also one that was part of a larger context, as an institution that the nation shared with neighbors such as the West Indies. In addition to making the abolitionist case in resonant new terms, the book also showcases Whitfield's range, erudition, and mastery of poetic form. Whitfield's wide array of inspirations, which included the Bible, classical mythology, Eastern religions, the British literary canon, and contemporary American writing, are reflected by the collection's diverse contents: its 24 poems include hymns, ballads, and odes and treat a wide variety of topics. In poems such as "The Misanthropist" and "Yes! Strike Again That Sounding String," Whitfield draws on the work of the English Romantic poet George Gordon, Lord Byron, while "Self-Reliance" recasts the philosophy of Ralph Waldo Emerson. The book's marriage of abolitionist sentiment and poetic style won it praise in the antislavery press: both *Frederick Douglass' Paper* and William Lloyd Garrison's *Liberator* again heralded Whitfield's "genius," while another abolitionist journal proclaimed that a copy of the book "should be in every family."

Shortly after *America and Other Poems* was published, Whitfield joined a debate that had arisen within the black abolitionist community, setting his two patrons, Douglass and Delany, at odds. By 1853, these two had come to hold different visions of the future of black people in the United States: Douglass believed they should remain committed to demanding their rightful equality within the country, whereas Delany, who was starting to doubt that these demands would ever be met, instead began to advocate for African Americans to establish a nation of their own by emigration to Central or South America. Whitfield had dedicated *America and Other Poems* to Delany, and in the wake of the book's appearance he publicly espoused Delany's emigrationism, joining with Delany to call for a national convention on the subject. When Douglass opposed this call, Whitfield then wrote a series of open letters to *Frederick Douglass' Paper* arguing for the necessity of black nationalism. He contended that "colored men can never be fully and fairly respected as the equals of the whites, in this country, or any other, until they are able to show in some part of the world, men of their own race occupying a primary and independent position, instead of a secondary and inferior one[.] … They must show a powerful nation in which the black is the *ruling* element, capable of maintaining a respectable position among the *great* nations of the earth." In 1854, Whitfield republished these letters, together with the responses of Douglass and his allies, as *Arguments, Pro and Con, on the Call for a National Emigration Convention*, and he attended the convention in question when it was held the same year.

Whitfield continued to support emigrationism into the 1860s: he was involved with two different plans to found African American emigrant colonies in Central America and Haiti (and may have traveled to one or both of these locations himself), and in 1862 he signed a pro-emigration petition to Congress. By then, however, Whitfield had himself relocated—not out of the country, but to California, where the local black community embraced him as a literary celebrity. He published poems and letters in newspapers in San Francisco (where he also established his barbering practice) while traveling widely throughout the American West. When the Civil War broke out, Whitfield, like Delany, turned from black nationalism to support the Union war effort and, in the Reconstruction era, the equitable integration of African Americans into national life. He championed these causes in poems that, throughout the 1860s, continued to be warmly received; for example, his public recitation in San Francisco in 1867 of a poem commemorating the Emancipation Proclamation, in which he laid out a grand vision of slavery and freedom as competing constitutive forces in American history, was "frequently interrupted by loud bursts of applause." Whitfield's last known published poem appeared in 1870, and he died of heart disease in 1871.

Despite the esteem in which he was held in the black community and abolitionist circles, Whitfield's work met with little commercial success during his lifetime, and after his death he was largely neglected, appearing, at best, as a marginal figure in histories of African American poetry. His legacy was kept alive, albeit indirectly, by Delany, who incorporated some of Whitfield's poems, without attribution, into his novel *Blake; or, The Huts of America* (1859, 1861–62); later, Whitfield's grand-niece, Pauline Hopkins, fictionalized aspects of his life in her 1900 novel *Contending Forces*. In recent decades, scholars have begun restoring Whitfield to prominence, arguing that he should be placed alongside Emily Dickinson and Walt Whitman as a major mid-nineteenth century poet who took American verse in important new directions. In particular, *America and Other Poems* bears comparison with Whitman's *Leaves of Grass* (first published two years later) as a book-length poetic exploration of American identity, but one that, unlike *Leaves of Grass*, puts slavery and race at the center of its vision of America. In addition, Whitfield's participation in the emigrationism debate makes him a pivotal figure in African American intellectual history as one of the first proponents, with Delany, of black nationalism; the extent to which *America and Other Poems* voices a black nationalist stance remains a topic of scholarly debate.

———

NOTE ON THE TEXTS: The texts of the poems by Whitfield included here are all based on the versions published in the first edition of *America and Other Poems* (1853). Spelling and punctuation have been modernized according to the practices of this anthology.

⌘⌘⌘

James Monroe Whitfield's signature at the end of the poem by him
included in the abolitionist anthology *Autographs for Freedom* (1853).

America

America, it is to thee,
Thou boasted land of liberty—
It is to thee I raise my song,
Thou land of blood, and crime, and wrong.[1]
5 It is to thee, my native land,
From whence has issued many a band°   shackle
To tear the black man from his soil,
And force him here to delve° and toil;   dig; labor
Chained on your blood-bemoistened sod,

10 Cringing beneath a tyrant's rod,
Stripped of those rights which Nature's God[2]
Bequeathed to all the human race,
Bound to a petty tyrant's nod,
Because he wears a paler face.
15 Was it for this, that freedom's fires
Were kindled by your patriot sires?
Was it for this, they shed their blood,
On hill and plain, on field and flood?
Was it for this, that wealth and life
20 Were staked upon that desperate strife,
Which drenched this land for seven long years
With blood of men, and women's tears?

———

1 *America ... wrong* See the opening of "America (My Country, 'Tis of Thee)," a popular patriotic song composed in 1831 by the clergyman Samuel Francis Smith: "My country, 'tis of thee, / Sweet land of liberty, / Of thee I sing."

2 *Nature's God* The preamble of the Declaration of Independence invokes "the Laws of Nature and of Nature's God," suggesting that such laws entitle the American people to separate from Britain.

When black and white fought side by side,[1]
Upon the well-contested field—
25 Turned back the fierce opposing tide,
And made the proud invader yield—
When, wounded, side by side they lay,
And heard with joy the proud hurrah
From their victorious comrades say
30 That they had waged successful war,
The thought ne'er entered in their brains
That they endured those toils and pains,
To forge fresh fetters, heavier chains
For their own children, in whose veins
35 Should flow that patriotic blood,
So freely shed on field and flood.
Oh no; they fought, as they believed,
For the inherent rights of man;
But mark,° how they have been deceived   observe
40 By slavery's accursed plan.
They never thought, when thus they shed
Their heart's best blood, in freedom's cause,
That their own sons would live in dread,
Under unjust, oppressive laws:
45 That those who quietly enjoyed
The rights for which they fought and fell,
Could be the framers of a code,°   body of law
That would disgrace the fiends of hell!
Could they have looked, with prophet's ken,°   sight
50 Down to the present evil time,
Seen free-born men, uncharged with crime,
Consigned unto a slaver's pen—
Or thrust into a prison cell,
With thieves and murderers to dwell—
55 While that same flag whose stripes and stars
Had been their guide through freedom's wars
As proudly waved above the pen
Of dealers in the souls of men!
Or could the shades° of all the dead,   spirits
60 Who fell beneath that starry flag,
Visit the scenes where they once bled,
On hill and plain, on vale and crag,
By peaceful brook, or ocean's strand,
By inland lake, or dark green wood,

65 Where'er the soil of this wide land
Was moistened by their patriot blood,
And then survey the country o'er,
From north to south, from east to west,
And hear the agonizing cry
70 Ascending up to God on high,
From western wilds to ocean's shore,
The fervent prayer of the oppressed;
The cry of helpless infancy
Torn from the parent's fond caress
75 By some base tool of tyranny,
And doomed to woe and wretchedness;
The indignant wail of fiery youth,
Its noble aspirations crushed,
Its generous zeal, its love of truth,
80 Trampled by tyrants in the dust;
The aerial piles[2] which fancy° reared,   imagination
And hopes too bright to be enjoyed,
Have passed and left his young heart seared,
And all its dreams of bliss destroyed.
85 The shriek of virgin purity,
Doomed to some libertine's° embrace,   licentious man's
Should rouse the strongest sympathy
Of each one of the human race;
And weak old age, oppressed with care,
90 As he reviews the scene of strife,
Puts up to God a fervent prayer,
To close his dark and troubled life.
The cry of fathers, mothers, wives,
Severed from all their hearts hold dear,
95 And doomed to spend their wretched lives
In gloom, and doubt, and hate, and fear;
And manhood, too, with soul of fire,
And arm of strength, and smothered ire,°   anger
Stands pondering with brow of gloom,
100 Upon his dark unhappy doom,
Whether to plunge in battle's strife,
And buy his freedom with his life,
And with stout heart and weapon strong,
Pay back the tyrant wrong for wrong,
105 Or wait the promised time of God,
When his Almighty ire shall wake,
And smite the oppressor in his wrath,
And hurl red ruin in his path,
And with the terrors of his rod,

---

1   *When black ... side* Black abolitionists frequently argued that African Americans had earned their own freedom by helping their country to win its freedom through their participation in the Revolutionary War.

---

2   *aerial piles* Imaginary edifices.

110 Cause adamantine° hearts to quake.   *extremely hard*
     Here Christian writhes in bondage still,
     Beneath his brother Christian's rod,
     And pastors trample down at will,
     The image of the living God.[1]
115 While prayers go up in lofty strains,°   *melodies*
     And pealing hymns ascend to heaven,
     The captive, toiling in his chains,
     With tortured limbs and bosom riven,
     Raises his fettered hand on high,
120 And in the accents of despair,
     To him who rules both earth and sky,
     Puts up a sad, a fervent prayer,
     To free him from the awful blast
     Of slavery's bitter galling shame—
125 Although his portion° should be cast   *fate, destiny*
     With demons in eternal flame!
     Almighty God! 't is this they call
     The land of liberty and law;
     Part of its sons in baser° thrall   *more degrading*
130 Than Babylon or Egypt[2] saw—
     Worse scenes of rapine,° lust and shame,   *plunder*
     Than Babylonian ever knew,[3]
     Are perpetrated in the name
     Of God, the holy, just, and true;
135 And darker doom than Egypt felt,[4]
     May yet repay this nation's guilt.
     Almighty God! thy aid impart,
     And fire anew each faltering heart,
     And strengthen every patriot's hand,
140 Who aims to save our native land.
     We do not come before thy throne,
     With carnal° weapons drenched in gore,   *murderous*
     Although our blood has freely flown,
     In adding to the tyrant's store.

145 Father! before thy throne we come,
     Not in the panoply° of war,   *armor*
     With pealing trump,° and rolling drum,   *trumpet*
     And cannon booming loud and far;
     Striving in blood to wash out blood,
150 Through wrong to seek redress for wrong;
     For while thou 'rt holy, just and good,
     The battle is not to the strong;[5]
     But in the sacred name of peace,
     Of justice, virtue, love and truth,
155 We pray, and never mean to cease,
     Till weak old age and fiery youth
     In freedom's cause their voices raise,
     And burst the bonds of every slave;
     Till, north and south, and east and west,
160 The wrongs we bear shall be redressed.
     —1853

Yes! Strike Again That Sounding String

Yes! strike again that sounding string,
     And let the wildest numbers[6] roll;
Thy song of fiercest passion sing—
It breathes responsive to my soul!

5 A soul, whose gentlest hours were nursed,
     In stern adversity's dark way,
     And o'er whose pathway never burst
     One gleam of hope's enlivening ray.

If thou wouldst soothe my burning brain,
10 Sing not to me of joy and gladness;
     'T will but increase the raging pain,
     And turn the fever into madness.

Sing not to me of landscapes bright,
     Of fragrant flowers and fruitful trees—
15 Of azure skies and mellow light,
     Or whisperings of the gentle breeze;

---

1   *image … God*   According to Genesis 1.27, humans were created "in the image of God."

2   *Babylon or Egypt*   Locations in which, in the Bible, the Israelites are at various times held captive or enslaved.

3   *Worse … knew*   In the Bible, Babylon is frequently associated with worldliness and evil. See, in particular, Revelation 17.5, where Babylon is described as "Babylon the Great, mother of harlots and abominations of the earth."

4   *darker … felt*   In the Book of Exodus, after the Egyptian pharaoh refuses to release the Israelites from enslavement, God punishes the people of Egypt with a series of ten plagues, culminating in the death of every firstborn son. See Exodus 7–12.

5   *The battle … strong*   See Ecclesiastes 9.11: "I returned, and saw under the sun, that the race is not to the swift, nor the battle to the strong."

6   *numbers*   Verses, of song or poetry.

But tell me of the tempest roaring
Across the angry foaming deep,°   *ocean*
Or torrents from the mountains pouring
20   Down precipices dark and steep.

Sing of the lightning's lurid flash,
The ocean's roar, the howling storm,
The earthquake's shock, the thunder's crash,
Where ghastly terrors teeming swarm.

25   Sing of the battle's deadly strife,
The ruthless march of war and pillage,
The awful waste of human life,
The plundered town, the burning village!

Of streets with human gore made red,
30   Of priests upon the altar slain;
The scenes of rapine,° woe and dread,   *plunder*
That fill the warriors' horrid train.°   *wake, path*

Thy song may then an echo wake,
Deep in this soul, long crushed and sad,
35   The direful° impressions shake   *terrible*
Which threaten now to drive it mad.
—1850

The North Star[1]

Star of the north! whose steadfast ray
Pierces the sable pall° of night,   *black shroud*
Forever pointing out the way

That leads to freedom's hallowed light:
5   The fugitive lifts up his eye
To where thy rays illume° the sky.   *illuminate*

That steady, calm, unchanging light,
Through dreary wilds and trackless dells,°   *valleys*
Directs his weary steps aright
10   To the bright land where freedom dwells;
And spreads, with sympathizing breast,
Her ægis[2] over the oppressed.

Though other stars may round thee burn,
With larger disk and brighter ray,
15   And fiery comets round thee turn,
While millions mark their blazing way;
And the pale moon and planets bright
Reflect on us their silvery light.

Not like that moon, now dark, now bright,
20   In phase and place forever changing;
Or planets with reflected light,
Or comets through the heavens ranging;
They all seem varying to our view,
While thou art ever fixed and true.

25   So may that other bright North Star,
Beaming with truth and freedom's light,
Pierce with its cheering ray afar,
The shades of slavery's gloomy night;
And may it never cease to be
30   The guard of truth and liberty.
—1849

---

1   [Whitfield's note]   Written for the North Star; a newspaper edited by a fugitive slave. [The eminent abolitionist Frederick Douglass, who had escaped from enslavement in 1838 and whose freedom was formally purchased in 1847, founded the *North Star*, an abolitionist newspaper, in 1847 and edited it until 1851, when he changed its name to *Frederick Douglass' Paper*. Whitfield's poem was first published in this venue in 1849. By 1853, when *America and Other Poems* was published, Whitfield and Douglass were beginning to part ways on the question of African American emigration, which Douglass opposed but Whitfield was coming to support.]

---

2   *ægis*   Protection, defense. The word is derived from the name for a shield or other defensive implement wielded in Greek mythology by the gods Zeus and Athena.

Stanzas for the First of August[1]

From bright West Indies' sunny seas,
  Comes, borne upon the balmy breeze,
The joyous shout, the gladsome tone,
  Long in those bloody isles unknown;
5 Bearing across the heaving wave
The song of the unfettered slave.

No charging squadrons shook the ground,
  When freedom here her claims obtained;
No cannon, with tremendous sound,
10 The noble patriot's cause maintained:
No furious battle-charger neighed,
No brother fell by brother's blade.

None of those desperate scenes of strife,
  Which mark the warrior's proud career,

15 The awful waste of human life,
  Have ever been enacted here;
But truth and justice spoke from heaven,
And slavery's galling chain was riven.

Twas moral force which broke the chain,
20 That bound eight hundred thousand men;
And when we see it snapped in twain,
  Shall we not join in praises then?—
And prayers unto Almighty God,
Who smote to earth the tyrant's rod?

25 And from those islands of the sea,
  The scenes of blood and crime and wrong,
The glorious anthem of the free,
  Now swells in mighty chorus strong;
Telling th' oppressed, where'er they roam,
30 Those islands now are freedom's home.
  —1849

---

[1] *First of August*   From the early 1840s onwards, emancipation celebrations and antislavery demonstrations on this date were widespread in the Northern states. In Britain and its possessions, the Slavery Abolition Act of 1833 had come into effect 1 August 1834. That date is often thought of as marking the end of slavery for the approximately 800,000 people who had been enslaved in Britain's colonies in the West Indies. It did not immediately free all those who had been enslaved, however; the status of enslaved people older than six years of age was altered to "apprentice," and they were forced to work without pay for their former slaveholders for a further four years, as compensation to the former slaveholders. There was thus good reason to celebrate the anniversary both of 1 August 1834 and of 1 August 1838. (For more on August First celebrations during this period, see the excerpts from William J. Wilson's 1859 August First speech that are included in the Popular Literature and Print Culture section of this volume.)

The fact that abolition in the British colonies was won by moral suasion rather than open warfare—although revolts by enslaved people, including the so-called Baptist War in Jamaica in 1831–32, helped push the British government toward abolition—was also celebrated by many. So too was the peaceful aftermath of abolition; slavery's proponents had predicted a bloodbath if those who had been enslaved were freed. (The relatively peaceful manner in which slavery was ended in Britain's Caribbean colonies contrasted strongly with the corresponding French Caribbean colony of Saint-Domingue, where the enslaved black population won its freedom and established the independent nation of Haiti only after over a decade of warfare [1791–1804]—an event that also powerfully affected the imagination of observers in the United States, both white and black.)

Whitfield read this poem at an August First gathering in Buffalo, New York in 1849.

Martin R. Delany
1812 – 1885

Martin R. Delany's associate and rival Frederick Douglass once commented, "I thank God for making me a man simply; but Delany always thanks God for making him a *black man*." One of the most powerful and provocative voices to emerge from the social and political unrest preceding the Civil War, the abolitionist and political activist Delany is today considered to have been among the earliest black nationalists. His career was extraordinarily wide-ranging—embracing the realms of journalism, medicine, the lecture and pamphlet-writing circuit, and the military—and his one published novel, *Blake* (1859, 1861–62), is often hailed as one of the masterpieces of nineteenth-century American literature. Delany provoked fiery disagreement as well as vehement admiration among the African American intellectual community, and his participation in some of the most important social debates of the mid-nineteenth century helped define the characteristics of the fight for black rights for decades to come.

Delany was born in Charles Town, Virginia (now West Virginia), to Pati and Samuel Delany, a free seamstress and an enslaved plantation worker. According to *partus* law, his mother's freedom was conferred upon him at birth; nevertheless, as Delany experienced throughout his life, the social and legal status of African Americans, whether free or enslaved, was constantly ambiguous and unstable. Pati was threatened with arrest in 1822 when it was found that her children had learned to read (Virginia prohibited the education of black people), and so fled with them northwards to Pennsylvania, where the family was joined by Samuel Delany once he had managed to purchase his freedom.

In 1831, at the age of nineteen, Delany moved to Pittsburgh to seek further education, and enrolled in a school associated with the African Methodist Episcopal (AME) Church. Here he started a literacy society, took up a medical apprenticeship (a career to which he would return at various stages throughout his life), attended black rights conventions, and engaged with black political leaders, including Lewis Woodson (who is sometimes described as the first black nationalist). In 1843 Delany founded the *Mystery*, an important African American newspaper. He dedicated the next several years of his life to this and related projects, before ceasing publication of the *Mystery* in 1847 to collaborate with Frederick Douglass on a new publication, the *North Star*. The *North Star* became very influential, but the collaboration was relatively brief. Douglass and Delany increasingly diverged in their approaches to abolitionism and black liberation, though they would continue to express respect for one another—sometimes begrudgingly— over the decades.

In November 1850, Delany was accepted into Harvard Medical School, and then promptly expelled following complaints from white students, who claimed that the admission of black classmates would damage the school's reputation (a smaller group of students counter-petitioned to let Delany remain, but Harvard faculty ignored this appeal). This personal humiliation proved something of a political catalyst for Delany, whose ideology became increasingly radical over the following years. The 1850s saw a number of regressive legislative decisions—beginning with the outrageous Fugitive Slave Act (1850)—that enraged the abolitionist community and confirmed the fears of many African Americans that the United States would never live up to its promises of democracy and equality. For Delany, the necessary resolution to the crisis was black emigration from the United States, and he put forward this view in *The Condition, Elevation, Emigration, and Destiny of the Colored People of the United States, Politically Considered* (1852). Two years later Delany sponsored the National Emigration Convention of Colored People in Cleveland, where he delivered an even more rousing address—published as *Political Destiny of the Colored Race on the American Continent* (1854)—calling on African Americans to recognize the profound oppression they faced in their country of birth and to respond by coming together to create a united, black-led nation of their own. At this point, Delany advocated emigration to South America; later he would change his focus to the African continent.

To Delany, it was essential to distinguish his plan from superficially similar projects that had been endorsed by various white political groups since earlier in the century. Most prominent was the white-led American Colonization Society, which had since 1821 encouraged thousands of free African Americans to migrate to the colony of Liberia. In Delany's view, Liberia was a "*burlesque* on government" that existed primarily to rid America of free African Americans and to ensure the continued enslavement of those who remained in bondage. (Historical records indicate, too, that the black colonists were often severely underfunded and insufficiently supported by their white American sponsors, which led to extreme mortality rates.)

Delany, by contrast, presented his plan as grounded in the pursuit of global black solidarity and liberation, and emphasized that the new nation he proposed would be governed by black leaders. Not everyone was convinced by the distinction, however. (Indeed, the text of *Political Destiny* was later used promotionally by white advocates of colonization.) Many black activists saw emigration as a betrayal of the struggle at home; in 1858 the Ohio Convention of Colored Men, under the leadership of William H. Day, resolved that "the amount of labor and self-sacrifice required to establish a home in a foreign land, would, if exercised here, redeem our native land from the grasp of slavery." Many others, however, did support Delany. African American priest James T. Holly, who would later settle in the Republic of Haiti, echoed Delany's ideas when he wrote that "[t]he social ostracism of the colored people in the United States is complete and irremediable. … They must escape as Lot from the guilty and doomed cities of the plain, not even looking back upon this accursed land." Emigration remained a subject of heated debate among African Americans for decades, with Delany often at the center.

In 1856, Delany moved to Canada, where he set up a medical practice, wrote for Mary Ann Shadd Cary's abolitionist newspaper *The Provincial Freeman* (which advocated emigration to Canada), met with white militant abolitionist John Brown, and further developed his plans for emigration. In 1859, he traveled to west Africa, where he met with the Alake (King) of the Egba and agreed on a treaty that would grant land to African American immigrants (the Alake would, however, soon rescind his support, possibly under pressure from the British).

At the end of the decade Delany wrote his first and only novel, *Blake; or, the Huts of America* (serialized in 1859 and 1861–62; not published in book form until 1970), which tells the story of self-emancipated Henry Blake, who flees his plantation, travels through the South sowing the seeds of rebellion among the enslaved, leads his wife's family to freedom in Canada, and eventually travels to Cuba, where he plans a revolution of enslaved people. The book was written partly in response to Harriet Beecher Stowe's extraordinarily popular *Uncle Tom's Cabin* (1852), which Delany criticized for its failure to embrace black self-determination and its advocacy of Christian forbearance instead of direct action in response to the evils of slavery. *Blake* received little attention at the time of its publication—with its intended audience perhaps preoccupied by the Civil War—and even less in the following decades. The novel experienced a revival in 1970, however, when it was re-released in an edition that placed it in dialogue with the contemporary Black Power and Black Arts movements. Since then, *Blake* has become highly regarded by many critics, for whom the novel's revolutionary consciousness positions it as a counter to its more sentimental contemporaries (such as William Wells Brown's *Clotel*), and who celebrate its insistence on collective action and on the right of black people to demand liberation.

The progress of the Civil War marked a change of direction for Delany's efforts, as the struggle against slavery became militarized. Delany returned to the United States and began recruiting black soldiers for the Union Army, and in 1865, following an audience with President Abraham Lincoln, was made America's first black field major. After the end of the war, Delany continued to engage in American politics, running for lieutenant governor of South Carolina in 1874; he also wrote advice pamphlets intended for newly emancipated African Americans. In 1880, he resumed his medical practice in order to support his children; he continued this work until his death in 1885.

Delany remained a focus of debate as well as of admiration in the years following his death. AME bishop Daniel Payne wrote in 1888 that Delany had been "too intensely African to be popular," and lamented that his "love for his race" had been greater than his "love for humanity." Douglass put it more harshly: he claimed Delany had "gone about the same length in favor of black, as the whites have in favor of the doctrine of white supremacy." For others, however, the same qualities that disconcerted some of Delany's associates made him, as James Holly wrote, "one of the great men of this age." His legacy would only grow throughout the twentieth century, influencing writers such as W.E.B. Du Bois, as well as movements such as the Pan-Africanist movement.

NOTE ON THE TEXT: The text of *Blake; or, the Huts of America* presented below is based on that published in *The Anglo-African Magazine* in 1859. Spelling and punctuation have been modernized in accordance with the practices of this anthology.

⌘ ⌘ ⌘

from *Blake; or, the Huts of America*

Delany's only novel, *Blake*, made little impact upon its serialized publication between 1859 and 1862, but it is today acknowledged by many critics as one of the most important and remarkable American novels of the nineteenth century. The work tells of Henry Holland (later known by the name Henry Blake), who flees slavery and endeavors to instigate a mass rebellion of the enslaved after the sudden sale of his wife, Maggie, to a northerner who plans to keep Maggie in slavery at her winter residence in Cuba. Over time, it is revealed that Henry was born free as "Henrico Blacus" in the West Indies, but was kidnapped and sold into slavery as a young man; Henry's sense of freedom as his birthright becomes a significant aspect of his leadership as he spreads the word of revolution, first throughout the southern United States, and later in Cuba.

Set roughly in the years 1852 to 1853, *Blake*, which regularly alludes to real-world people and events, is considered by some modern critics to be an early experiment with the genre of alternative history. The revolution promised in the novel's early chapters, however, never occurs; the final chapters of Part Two were likely published in the May 1862 issues of *The Weekly Anglo-African*, but those issues of the magazine have since been lost, and no manuscript copy of the text is extant. The work virtually disappeared from public consciousness until the mid-twentieth century; nevertheless, *Blake*'s radical interpretation

of Christianity, and its insistence that open resistance and even violence were appropriate means of achieving black liberation, make the novel itself revolutionary.

CHAPTER 1
THE PROJECT

On one of those exciting occasions, during a contest for the Presidency of the United States,[1] a number of gentlemen met in the city of Baltimore. They were few in number, and appeared little concerned about the affairs of the general government. Though men of intelligence, their time and attention appeared to be entirely absorbed in an adventure of self interest. They met for the purpose of completing arrangements for refitting the old ship *Merchantman*, which then lay in the harbor near Fells Point. Colonel Stephen Franks, Major James Armsted, Captain Richard Paul and Captain George Royer, composed those who represented the American side—Captain

---

[1]   *a contest ... United States* The presidential election of 1852, which saw the Democrat Franklin Pierce elected to the presidency; though he was a northerner who claimed to be morally opposed to slavery, Pierce did nothing to pursue abolition and in fact encouraged legislation that allowed the westward expansion of slavery. Pierce's main opponent was the Whig Winfield Scott, with a third party, the antislavery Free Soil Party, gaining approximately five per cent of the popular vote.

Juan Garcia and Captain Jose Castello, those of Cuban interest.[1]

Here a conversation ensued upon what seemed a point of vital importance to the company; it related to the place best suited for the completion of their arrangements. The Americans insisted on Baltimore as affording the greatest facilities, and having done more for the encouragement and protection of the trade than any other known place. Whilst the Cubans, on the other side, urged their objections on the ground that the continual increase of liberal principles in the various political parties, which were fast ushering into existence, made the objection beyond a controversy. Havana was contended for as a point best suited for adjusting their arrangements, and that too with many apparent reasons; but for some cause, the preference for Baltimore prevailed.

Subsequently to the adjustment of their affairs by the most complete arrangement for refitting the vessel, Col. Franks took leave of the party for his home in the distant State of Mississippi.

CHAPTER 2
COLONEL FRANKS AT HOME

On the return of Col. Stephen Franks to his home at Natchez, he met there Mrs. Arabella, the wife of Judge Ballard, an eminent jurist of one of the Northern states. She had arrived but a day before him, on a visit to some relatives, of whom Mrs. Franks was one. The conversation, as is customary on the meeting of Americans residing in such distant latitudes, readily turned on the general policy of the country.

Mrs. Ballard possessed the highest intelligence, and Mrs. Maria Franks was among the most accomplished of Southern ladies.

"Tell me, Madam Ballard, how will the North go in the present issue?"[2] enquired Franks.

"Give yourself no concern about that, Colonel," replied Mrs. Ballard, "you will find the North true to the country."

"What you consider true, may be false—that is, it might be true to you, and false to us," continued he.

"You do not understand me, Colonel," she rejoined, "we can have no interests separate from yours; you know the time-honored motto, 'united we stand,' and so forth, must apply to the American people under every policy in every section of the Union."

"So it should, but amidst the general clamor in the contest for ascendency, may you not lose sight of this important point?"

"How can we? You, I'm sure, Colonel, know very well that in our country commercial interests have taken precedence of all others, which is a sufficient guarantee of our fidelity to the South."

"That may be, madam, but we are still apprehensive."

"Well sir, we certainly do not know what more to do to give you assurance of our sincerity. We have as a plight of faith yielded Boston, New York, and Philadelphia—the intelligence and wealth of the North—in carrying out the Compromise measures for the interests of the South;[3] can we do more?"

"True, Madam Ballard, true! I yield the controversy. You have already done more than we of the South expected. I now remember that the Judge himself, tried the first case under the Act, in your city, by which the measures were tested."[4]

---

1   *an adventure ... Cuban interest*   The implication in this opening paragraph is that the men are gathering to strike a deal concerning the trade of enslaved people, using the *Merchantman* to illegally transport their human cargo. While the U.S. had ended its participation in the international slave trade in 1808, with the Act Prohibiting Importation of Slaves, such illicit transactions remained relatively commonplace due to the continued legality of both slavery and the international slave trade in Spanish-controlled Cuba (slavery there was not formally abolished until 1886). Many proslavery Americans in the 1840s and 1850s were in favor of annexing Cuba as a slave state, a movement that Franklin Pierce openly supported.

2   *the present issue*   I.e., the presidential election.

3   *We have ... the South*   Mrs. Ballard refers to the Compromise of 1850, a series of acts meant to defuse the increasing divergence of political interests between the North and the South, particularly on the matter of slavery. Most significantly, the Fugitive Slave Act mandated increased efforts on the part of free states to hunt down and arrest fugitives from slavery, while also imposing fines and jail time on anyone who assisted such fugitives. The Act was highly controversial throughout the North—even among whites who did not strongly oppose slavery, but who saw the new legislation as an encroachment of the Southern slave power upon the Northern states' rights.

4   *tried the first case ... tested*   Delany alludes to cases such as that of Thomas Sims, who fled enslavement in Georgia in 1851; Sims's trial in Boston, which saw him forcibly returned to enslavement, was among the first and most famous of such trials that took place in the early 1850s.

"He did, sir, and if you will not consider me unwomanly by telling you, desired me, on coming here, to seek every opportunity to give the fullest assurance that the judiciary are sound on that question. Indeed, so far as an individual might be concerned, his interests in another direction as you know, place him beyond suspicion," concluded Mrs. Ballard.

"I am satisfied, madam, and by your permission, arrest the conversation. My acknowledgements, madam!" bowed the Colonel, with true southern courtesy.

"Maria, my dear, you look careworn; are you indisposed?" inquired Franks of his wife, who during conversation sat silent.

"Not physically, Colonel," replied she, "but—"

Just at this moment a servant throwing open the door announced dinner.

Besides a sprightly black boy of some ten years of age, there was in attendance a prepossessing, handsome maidservant, who generally kept, as much as the occasion would permit, behind the chair of her mistress. A mutual attachment appeared to exist between them, the maid apparently disinclined to leave the mistress, who seemed to keep her as near her person as possible.

Now and again the fat cook, mammy Judy, would appear at the door of the dining room bearing a fresh supply for the table, who with a slight nod of the head, accompanied with an affectionate smile and the word "Maggie," indicated a tie much closer than that of mere fellow-servants.

Maggie had long been the favorite maidservant of her mistress, having attained the position through merit. She was also nurse and foster-mother to the two last children of Mrs. Franks, and loved them, to all appearance, as her own. The children reciprocated this affection, calling her "mammy."

Mammy Judy, who for years had occupied this position, ceded it to her daughter, she preferring, in consequence of age, the less active life of the culinary department.

The boy Tony would frequently cast a comic look upon Mrs. Ballard, then imploringly gaze in the face of his mistress. So intent was he in this, that twice did his master admonish him by a nod of the head.

"My dear," said the Colonel, "you are dull today; pray tell me what makes you sad?"

"I am not bodily afflicted, colonel Franks, but my spirit is heavy," she replied.

"How so? What is the matter?"

"That will best be answered at another time and place, colonel."

Giving his head an unconscious scratch accompanied with a slight twitch of the corner of the mouth, Franks seemed to comprehend the whole of it.

On one of her Northern tours to the watering places,[1] during a summer season some two years previous, having with her Maggie the favorite, Mrs. Franks visited the family of the Judge, at which time Mrs. Ballard first saw the maid. She was a dark mulatto[2] of a rich, yellow, autumn-like complexion, with a matchless, cushion-like head of hair, neither straight nor curly, but handsomer than either.

Mrs. Franks was herself a handsome lady of some thirty-five summers, but ten years less in appearance, a little above medium height, between the majestic and graceful, raven black hair, and dark, expressive eyes. Yet it often had been whispered that in beauty the maid equalled if not exceeded the mistress. Her age was twenty-eight.

The conduct of Mrs. Franks toward her servant was more like that of an elder sister than a mistress, and the mistress and maid sometimes wore dresses cut from the same web of cloth. Mrs. Franks would frequently adjust the dress and see that the hair of her maid was properly arranged. This to Mrs. Ballard was as unusual as it was an objectionable sight, especially as she imagined there was an air of hauteur in her demeanor. It was then she determined to subdue her spirit.

Acting from this impulse, several times in her absence, Mrs. Ballard took occasion to administer to the maid severities she had never experienced at the hands of her mistress, giving her at one time a severe slap on the cheek, calling her an "impudent jade."[3]

At this, Mrs. Franks, on learning, was quite surprised, but on finding that the maid gave no just cause

---

[1] *the watering places*   Resort towns located by the sea or by natural mineral springs.

[2] *mulatto*   Term used in the nineteenth century to refer to an individual of mixed racial background—typically, someone with one white parent and one parent of African descent. (It is today considered archaic and offensive.)

[3] *jade*   Derogatory term for a woman perceived to be rude or poorly behaved.

for it, took no further notice of it, designedly evading the matter. But before leaving, Mrs. Ballard gave her no rest until she gave her the most positive assurance that she would part with the maid on her next visit at Natchez.[1] And thus she is found pressing her suit at the residence of the Mississippi planter.

CHAPTER 3
THE FATE OF MAGGIE

After dinner colonel Franks again pressed the inquiry concerning the disposition of his lady. At this time the maid was in the culinary department taking her dinner. The children having been served, she preferred the company of her old mother, whom she loved, the children hanging around and upon her lap. There was no servant save the boy Tony present in the parlor.

"I can't, I won't let her go! she's a dear good girl!" replied Mrs. Franks. "The children are attached to her, and so am I; let Minny or any other of them go—but do not, for Heaven's sake, tear Maggie from me!"

"Maria, my dear, you've certainly lost your balance of mind! Do try and compose yourself," admonished the Colonel. "There's certainly no disposition to do contrary to your desires; try and be a little reasonable."

"I'm sure cousin, I see no cause for your importunity. No one that I know of designs to hurt the negro girl. I'm sure it's not me!" impatiently remarked Mrs. Ballard.

During this, the boy had several times gone into the hall, looking toward the kitchen, then meaningly into the parlor as if something unusual were going on.

Mammy Judy becoming suspicious, went into the hall and stood close beside the parlor door, listening at the conversation.

"Cousin, if you will listen for a moment, I wish to say a word to you," said Mrs. Ballard. "The Judge, as you know, has a country seat in Cuba near the city of Havana, where we design making every year our winter retreat. As we cannot take with us either free negroes or white servants, on account of the existing restrictions,[2]

I must have a slave, and of course I prefer a well-trained one, as I know all of yours to be. The price will be no object; as I know it will be none to you, it shall be none to me."

"I will not consent to part with her, cousin Arabella, and it is useless to press the matter any further!" emphatically replied Mrs. Franks.

"I am sure, cousin Maria, it was well understood between the Colonel and the Judge, that I was to have one of your best-trained maid servants!" continued Mrs. Ballard.

"The Colonel and the Judge! If any such understanding exist, it is without my knowledge and consent, and—"

"It is true, my dear," interposed the Colonel, "but—"

"Then," replied she, "heaven grant that I may go too! from—"

"Pah, pah! cousin Maria Franks, I'm really astonished at you to take on so about a negro girl! You really appear to have lost your reason. I would not behave so for all the negroes in Mississippi."

"My dear," said Franks, "I have been watching the conduct of that girl for some time past; she is becoming both disobedient and unruly, and as I have made it a rule of my life never to keep a disobedient servant, the sooner we part with her the better. As I never whip my servants, I do not want to depart from my rule in her case."

Maggie was true to her womanhood, and loyal to her mistress, having more than once communicated to her ears facts the sound of which reflected no credit in his. For several repulses, such as this, it was that she became obnoxious to her master.[3]

"Cousin Maria, you certainly have forgotten; I'm sure, when last at the North, you promised, in presence of the girl, that I was to have her, and I'm certain she's expecting it," explained Mrs. Ballard.

"This I admit," replied Mrs. Franks, "but you very well know, cousin Arabella, that that promise was a mere *ruse*, to reconcile an uneasiness which you informed me you discovered in her, after overhearing a conversation between her and some free negroes, at Saratoga Springs."

---

[1] *Natchez* City in Mississippi, notable for its many cotton plantations.

[2] *the existing restrictions* Cuba had implemented a ban on free people of color entering the colony in 1844, after an alleged antislavery conspiracy.

[3] *Maggie … her master* The implication is that Maggie had previously rejected Colonel Franks's sexual overtures.

"Well, cousin, you can do as you please," concluded Mrs. Ballard.

"Colonel, I'm weary of this conversation. What am I to expect?" inquired Mrs. Franks.

"It's a settled point, my dear, she must be sold!" decisively replied Franks.

"Then I must hereafter be disrespected by our own slaves! You know, Colonel, that I gave my word to Henry, her husband, your most worthy servant, that his wife should be here on his return. He had some misgiving that she was to be taken to Cuba before his return, when I assured him that she should be here. How can I bear to meet this poor creature, who places every confidence in what we tell him? He'll surely be frantic."

"Nonsense, cousin, nonsense," sneered Mrs. Ballard; "frantic, indeed! Why you speak of your negro slaves as if speaking of equals. Make him know that whatever you order, he must be contented with."

"I'll soon settle the matter with him, should he dare show any feelings about it!" interposed Franks; "when do you look for him, Maria?"

"I'm sure, Colonel you know more about the matter than I do. Immediately after you left, he took the horses to Baton Rouge, where at the last accounts, he was waiting the conclusion of the races. Judge Dilbreath had entered them according to your request one horse for each day's races. I look for him every day. Then there are more than him to reconcile. There's old mammy Judy, who will run mad about her. You know, Colonel, she thought so much of her, that she might be treated tenderly the old creature gave up her situation in the house as nurse and foster-mother to our children, going into the kitchen to do the harder work."

"Well, my dear, we'll detain your cousin till he comes. I'll telegraph the Judge that if not yet left, to start him home immediately."

"Colonel that will be still worse, to let him witness her departure; I would much rather she'd leave before his return. Poor thing!" she sighed.

"Then she may go!" replied he.

"And what of poor old mammy and his boy?"

"I'll soon settle the matter with old Judy."

Mrs. Franks looking him imploringly in the face, let drop her head, burying her face in the palms of her hands. Soon it was found necessary to place her under the care of a physician.

Old mammy Judy had long since beckoned her daughter, where both stood in breathless silence catching every word that passed.

At the conclusion, Maggie clasping her hands, exclaimed in suppressed tones—

"O mammy, O mammy! what shall I do? O, is there no hope for me? Can't you beg master—can't you save me!"

"Look to de Laud, my chile! him ony able to bring yeh out mo' nah conkeh!"[1] was the prayerful advice of the woe-stricken old mother; both hastening into the kitchen, falling upon their knees, invoked aloud the God of the oppressed.

Hearing in that direction an unusual noise, Franks hastened past the kitchen door, dropping his head, and clearing his throat as he went along. This brought the slaves to an ordinary mood, who trembled at his approach.

CHAPTER 4
DEPARTURE OF MAGGIE

The country-seat of Franks, or the "great house" of the cotton plantation, was but a short distance from the city. Mrs. Franks, by the advice of her physician, was removed there to avoid the disturbance of the town, when at the same time Mrs. Ballard left with her slave Maggie *en route* for Baltimore, whither she designed leaving her until ready to sail for Cuba.

"Fahwell, my chile! fahwell; may God A'mighty be wid you!" were the parting words of the poor old slave, who with streaming eyes gazed upon her parting child for the last time.

"O mammy! can't you save me? O Lord, what shall I do! O my husband! O my poor child! O my! O my!" were the only words, the sounds of which died upon the breeze, as the cab hastily bore her to a steamer then lying at the wharf.

Poor old mammy Judy sat at the kitchen door with elbow resting upon her knee, side of the face resting in the palm of the hand, tears streaming down, with a rocking motion, noticing nothing about her,

---

1   *mo' nah conkeh*   I.e., more than a conqueror; the allusion is to Romans 8.37: "Nay, in all these things we are more than conquerors through him [Christ] that loved us,"

but in sorrow moaning just distinctly enough to be understood:

"Po' me! po' me! po' me!"

The sight was enough to move the heart of anyone, and it so affected Franks, that he wished he had "never owned a negro."

Daddy Joe, the husband of mammy Judy, was a field hand on the cotton place,[1] visiting his wife at the town residence, every Saturday night. Colonel Franks was a fine, grave, senatorial looking man, of medium height, inclined to corpulency, black hair, slightly grey, and regarded by his slaves as a good master, and religiously as one of the best of men.

On their arrival at the great house, those working nearest, gathered around the carriage, among whom was daddy Joe.

"Wat a mautta wid missus?" was the general inquiry of the gang.

"Your mistress is sick, boys," replied the master.

"Maus,[2] whah's Margot?" enquired the old man, on seeing his mistress carried into the house without the attendance of her favorite maid-servant.

"She's in town, Joe," replied Franks.

"How's Judy, seh?"

"Judy is well."

"Tank'e seh!" politely concluded the old man, with a bow, turning away in the direction of his work, with a countenance expressive of anything but satisfaction from the interview.

The slaves, from their condition, are suspicious; any evasion or seeming design at suppressing the information sought by them, frequently arouses their greatest apprehensions.

Not unfrequently the mere countenance, a look, a word, or laugh of the master, is an unerring foreboding of misfortune to the slave. Ever on the watch for these things, they learn to read them with astonishing precision.

This day was Friday, and the old slave consoled himself with the thought that on the next evening he would be able to see and know for himself the true state of things about his master's residence in town. The few hours intervening were spent with great anxiety, which was even observed by his fellow-slaves.

At last came Saturday evening and with it, immediately after sunset, daddy Joe made his appearance at the hall door of the great house, tarrying only long enough to inquire "How's missus?" and receive the reply, "she's better," when a few moments found him quite out of sight, striding his way down the lane toward the road to the city.

The sudden and unexpected fate of Maggie had been noised among the slaves throughout the entire neighborhood; many who had the opportunity of doing so, repairing to the house to learn the facts.

In the lower part of the town, bordering on the river there is a depot or receptacle for the slave gangs brought by professional traders. This part of the town is known as "Natchez under the Hill." It is customary among the slaves when any of their number are sold, to say that they are gone "under the hill," and their common salutation through the day was that "Franks' Mag had gone under the hill."

As with quickened steps daddy Joe approached the town, his most fearful apprehensions became terribly realised when meeting a slave who informed him that "Margot had gone under the hill." Falling upon his knees, in the fence corner, the old man raised his voice in supplication of Divine aid:

"O Laud! dow has promis' in dine own wud, to be a fadah to de fadeless, an' husband do de widah![3] O Laud, let dy wud run an' be glorify! Sof'en de haud haut ob de presseh,[4] an' let my po' chile cum back! an'—"

"Stop that noise there, old nigger!" ordered a patrol approaching him; "who's boy are you?"

"Sahvant, mausta!" saluted the old slave, "I b'long to cunel Frank, seh!"

"Is this old Joe?"

"Dis is me maus Johnny."

"You had better trudge along home then, as it's likely old Judy wants to see you about this time."

"Tank'e seh," replied the old man, with a bow, feeling grateful that he was permitted to proceed.

"Devilish good, religious old negro," he remarked to his associates, as the old man left them in the road.

---

1   *the cotton place* I.e., the plantation.

2   *Maus* Master.

3   *fadah to ... de widah* See Psalm 68.5: "A father of the fatherless, and a judge of the widows, is God in his holy habitation."

4   *de haud ... presseh* The hard heart of the oppressor.

A few minutes more, and daddy Joe entered the kitchen door at his master's residence. Mammy Judy, on seeing him, gave vent afresh to bitter wailing, when the emotion became painfully mutual.

"O husban'! husban'! ouah po' chile is gone!" exclaimed the old woman, clasping him around the neck.

"Laud! dy will be done!" exclaimed he, "ole 'umin,[1] look to de Laud! as he am suffishen fah all tings." Both, falling on their knees, breathed in silence their desires to God.

"How long! how long! O Laud how long!" was the supplicating cry of the old woman, being overcome with devotion and sorrow.

Taking the little grandchild in his arms—"Po' chile," said the old man, "I wish yeh had nebeh been baun!" impressing upon it kisses whilst it slept.

After a fervent and earnest prayer to God for protection to themselves, the little grandson Joe, the return of his mother their only child, and blessings upon their master and the recovery of their mistress, the poor old slaves retired to rest for the evening, to forget their sorrows in the respite of sleep.

CHAPTER 5
A VACANCY

This morning the sun rose with that beauty known to a southern sky in the last month of autumn. The day was Sabbath, and with it was ushered in every reminiscence common to the customs of that day and locality.

That she might spend the day at church for the diversion of her mind, Mrs. Franks was brought into her city residence; and Natchez, which is usually gay, seemed more so on this day than on former occasions.

When the bells began to signalise the hour of worship, the fashionable people seemed *en masse* to crowd the streets. The carriages ran in every direction, bearing happy hearts and cheerful faces to the various places of worship—there to lay their offerings on the altar of The Most High for the blessings they enjoyed, whilst peering over every gate, out of every ally, or every kitchen door, could be seen the faithful black servants, who, staying at home to prepare them food and attend to other domestic duties, were satisfied to look smilingly upon their masters and families as they rode along, without for a moment dreaming that they had a right to worship the same God, with the same promise of life and salvation.

"God bless you, missus! pray fah me," was the honest request of many a simple-hearted slave who dared not aspire to the enjoyment of praying for themselves in the Temple of the living God.

But amidst these scenes of gaiety and pleasure, there was one much devoted to her church, who could not be happy that day, as there, to her, was a seeming vacancy which could not be filled—the seat of her favorite maidservant. The Colonel, as a husband and father, was affectionate and indulgent; but his *slave* had offended, disobeyed his commands, and consequently had to be properly punished, or he be disrespected by his own servants. The will of the master being absolute, his commands should be enforced, let them be what they may, and the consequences what they would. If slavery be right, the master is justifiable in enforcing obedience to his will; deny him this, and you at once deprive him of the right to hold a slave—the one is a necessary sequence of the other. Upon this principle colonel Franks acted, and the premise justified the conclusion.

When the carriage drove to the door, Mrs. Franks wept out most bitterly, refusing to enter because her favorite maid could not be an incumbent. Fears being entertained of seriousness in her case,[2] it was thought advisable to let her remain quietly at home.

Daddy Joe and mammy Judy were anxious spectators of all that transpired at the door of the mansion, and that night, on retiring to their humble bed, earnestly petitioned at the altar of Grace, that the Lord would continue upon her his afflictions, until their master, convinced of his wrongs, would order the return of their child.

This the Colonel would have most willingly done without the petition of Joe or Judy, but the case had gone too far, the offense was too great, and consequently there could be no reconsideration.

"Poor thing," uttered Mrs. Franks in a delirium, "she served him right! And this her only offense! Yes, she was true to me!"

---

1   *'umin* Woman.

2   *Fears being ... her case* I.e., it being feared that Mrs. Franks's condition of emotional agitation might be serious.

Little Joe, the son of Maggie, in consequence of her position to the white children—from whom her separation had been concealed—had been constantly with his grandmother, and called her "mammy." Accustomed to being without her, he was well satisfied so long as permitted to be with the old woman Judy.

So soon as her condition would permit, Mrs. Franks was returned to her country seat, to avoid the contingencies of the city.

Chapter 6
Henry's Return

Early on Monday morning, a steamer was heard puffing up the Mississippi. Many who reside near the river, by custom can tell the name of every approaching boat by the peculiar sound of the steam-pipe, the one in the present instance being the *Sultana*.[1]

Daddy Joe had risen and [was] just leaving for the plantation, but stopped a moment to be certain.

"Hush!" admonished mammy Judy, "hush! sho chile, do'n yeh heah how she hollah? Sholy dat's de wat's name! wat dat yeh call eh? *Suckana*, wat not; sho! I ain' gwine bautha my head long so—sho! See, ole man see! dah she come! See dat now! I tole yeh so, but yeh uden bleve[2] me!" And the old man and woman stood for some minutes in breathless silence, although the boat must have been some five miles distant, as the escape of steam can be heard on the western waters a great way off.

The approach toward sunrise admonished daddy Joe of demands for him at the cotton farm, when after bidding "good monin' ole umin," he hurried to the daily task which lie before him.

Mammy Judy had learned by the boy Tony that Henry was expected on the *Sultana*, and at the approach of every steamer, her head had been thrust out of the door or window to catch a distinct sound. In motionless attitude after the departure of her husband this morning, the old woman stood awaiting the steamer, when presently the boat arrived. But then to be certain that it was the expected vessel—now came the suspense.

The old woman was soon relieved from this most disagreeable of all emotions by the cry of news boys returning from the wharf—

"'Ere's the *Picayune*, *Atlas*, *Delta*![3] lates' news from New Orleans by the swift steamer *Sultana*!"

"Dah now!" exclaimed mammy Judy in soliloquy; "dah now! I tole yeh so! de wat's name come!" Hurrying into the kitchen, she waited with anxiety the arrival of Henry.

Busying about the breakfast for herself and other servants about the house—the white members of the family all being absent—mammy Judy for a time lost sight of the expected arrival. Soon, however, a hasty footstep arrested her attention, when on looking around it proved to be Henry who came smiling up the yard.

"How'd you go mammy! how's Mag' and the boy?" inquired he, grasping the old woman by the hand.

She burst into a flood of tears, throwing herself upon him.

"What is the matter!" exclaimed Henry, "is Maggie dead?"

"No, chile," with increased sobs she replied, "much betteh she wah."

"My God! has she disgraced herself?"[4]

"No, chile, may be betteh she dun so, den she bin heah now an' not sole. Maus Stephen sell eh case she!—I dun'o, reckon dat's da reason!"

"What! Do you tell me mammy she had better disgraced herself than been sold! By the—!"

"So, Henry! yeh ain' gwine swah![5] hope yeh ain' gwine lose yeh 'ligion? Do'n do so; put yeh trus' in de Laud, he is suffishen fah all!"

"Don't tell me about religion! What's religion to me? My wife is sold away from me by a man who is one of the leading members of the very church to which both she and I belong! Put my trust in the Lord! I have done

---

[1]   *the Sultana*   Reference to a real steamboat that operated on the Mississippi River in the 1850s. (The original *Sultana* was decommissioned and replaced by a new ship of the same name in 1863; it was that second *Sultana* that infamously exploded in 1865, killing hundreds.)

[2]   *uden bleve*   Wouldn't believe.

[3]   *Picayune … Delta*   Nineteenth-century New Orleans newspapers *The Times-Picayune*, *The Daily Atlas*, and *The Daily Delta*.

[4]   *disgraced herself*   I.e., had sexual relations with—or been raped by—Colonel Franks.

[5]   *gwine swah*   Going to swear.

so all my life nearly, and of what use is it to me? My wife is sold from me just the same as if I didn't. I'll—"

"Come, come, Henry, yeh mus'n talk so; we is po' weak an' bline cretehs, an' cah[1] see de way uh da Laud. He move' in a mystus way, his wundahs to puhfaum."[2]

"So he may, and what is all that to me? I don't gain anything by it, and—"

"Stop, Henry, stop! ain' de Laud bless yo' soul? ain' he take yeh foot out de miah an' clay, an' gib yeh hope da uddah side dis vale ub teahs?"[3]

"I'm tired looking the other side; I want a hope this side of the vale of tears. I want something on this earth as well as a promise of things in another world. I and my wife have been both robbed of our liberty, and you want me to be satisfied with a hope of heaven. I won't do any such thing: I have waited long enough on heavenly promises; I'll wait no longer. I—"

"Henry, wat de mauttah wid yeh? I neveh heah yeh talk so fo'[4]—yeh sin in de sight ub God; yeh gone clean back,[5] I reckon. De good Book tell us, a tousan' yeahs wid man, am but a day wid de Laud.[6] Boy, yeh got wait de Laud own pinted[7] time."

"Well mammy, it is useless for me to stand here and have the same gospel preached into my ears by you, that I have all my lifetime heard from my enslavers. My mind is made up, my course is laid out, and if life last, I'll carry it out. I'll go out to the place today, and let them know that I have returned."

"Sho boy! what yeh gwine do, bun house down? Bettah put yeh trus' in de Laud!" concluded the old woman.

"You have too much religion, mammy, for me to tell you what I intend doing," said Henry in conclusion.

After taking up his little son, impressing on his lips and cheeks kisses for himself and tears for his mother, the intelligent slave left the abode of the care-worn old woman, for that of his master at the cotton place.

Henry was a black—a pure negro—handsome, manly and intelligent, in size comparing well with his master, but neither so fleshy nor heavy-built in person. A man of good literary attainments—unknown to Col. Franks, though he was aware he could read and write—having been educated in the West Indies, and decoyed[8] away when young. His affection for wife and child was not excelled by colonel Franks for his. He was bold, determined and courageous, but always mild, gentle and courteous, though impulsive when an occasion demanded his opposition.

Going immediately to the place, he presented himself before his master. Much conversation ensued concerning the business which had been entrusted to his charge, all of which was satisfactorily transacted, and full explanations concerning the horses, but not a word was uttered concerning the fate of Maggie, the Colonel barely remarking "your mistress is unwell."

After conversing till a late hour, Henry was assigned a bed in the great house, but sleep was far from his eyes. He turned and changed upon his bed with restlessness and anxiety, impatiently awaiting a return of the morning.

CHAPTER 7
MASTER AND SLAVE

Early on Tuesday morning, in obedience to his master's orders, Henry was on his way to the city, to get the house in readiness for the reception of his mistress, Mrs. Franks having much improved in three or four days. Mammy Judy had not yet risen when he knocked at the door.

"Hi Henry! yeh heah ready![9] huccum yeh git up so soon; arter some mischif I reckon? Do'n reckon yeh arter any good!" saluted mammy Judy.

---

[1]   *bline cretehs* Blind creatures;   *cah* Can't.

[2]   *He move'… to puhfaum* Reference to a well-known 1773 hymn by English poet William Cowper, originally titled "Light Shining out of Darkness."

[3]   *he take … an' clay* See Psalm 40.2: "He brought me up also out of an horrible pit, out of the miry clay, and set my feet upon a rock, and established my goings";   *vale ub teahs* Vale of tears; Christian idiom signifying the world as a site of struggle and tragedy that can be escaped only in the afterlife.

[4]   *fo'* Foul.

[5]   *gone clean back* I.e., gone back on your religious faith.

[6]   *De good Book … de Laud* See 2 Peter 3.8: "But, beloved, be not ignorant of this one thing, that one day is with the Lord as a thousand years, and a thousand years as one day."

[7]   *pinted* Appointed.

[8]   *decoyed* Enticed or tricked (i.e., into his present position of slavery).

[9]   *heah ready* Here already.

"No mammy," replied he; "no mischief, but like a good slave such as you wish me to be, come to obey my master's will, just what you like to see."

"Sho boy! none yeh nonsens'; huccum I want yeh bey maus Stephen? Git dat nonsens' in yeh head las' night long so, I reckon! Wat dat yeh gwine do now?"

"I have come to dust and air the mansion for their reception. They have sold my wife away from me, and who else would do her work?" This reply excited the apprehension of mammy Judy.

"Wat yeh gwine go Henry? yeh arter no good; yeh ain' gwine 'tack maus Stephen is yeh?"

"What do you mean, mammy, strike him?"

"Yes! reckon yeh ain' gwine hit 'im?"

"Curse—!"

"Henry, Henry, membeh wat ye 'fess![1] fah de Laud sake, yeh ain gwine take to swahin?"[2] interrupted the old woman.

"I make no profession, mammy. I once did believe in religion, but now I have no confidence in it. My faith has been wrecked on the stony hearts of such pretended Christians as Stephen Franks, while passing through the stormy sea of trouble and oppression! and—"

"Hay, boy! yeh is gittin high! yeh call maussa 'Stephen'?"

"Yes, and I'll never call him 'master' again, except when compelled to do so."

"Bettah g'long ten' t' de house fo' wite folks come, an' nebeh mine talkin' 'bout fightin' 'long wid maus Stephen. Wat yeh gwine do wid white folks? Sho!"

"I don't intend to fight him, mammy Judy, but I'll attack him concerning my wife, if the words be my last! Yes, I'll—!" and pressing his lips to suppress the words, the outraged man turned away from the old slave mother, with such feelings as only an intelligent slave could realize.

The orders of the morning were barely executed, when the carriage came to the door. The bright eyes of the foot boy Tony sparkled when he saw Henry approaching the carriage.

"Well Henry! ready for us?" enquired his master.

"Yes sir," was the simple reply. "Mistress!" he saluted, politely bowing as he took her hand to assist her from the carriage.

"Come Henry, my man, get out the riding horses," ordered Franks after a little rest.

"Yes sir."

A horse for the Colonel and lady each was soon in readiness at the door, but none for himself, it always having been the custom in their morning rides, for the maid and manservant to accompany the mistress and master.

"Ready did you say?" enquired Franks on seeing but two horses standing at the stile.

"Yes sir."

"Where's the other horse?"

"What for sir?"

"What for? yourself to be sure!"

"Colonel Franks!" said Henry, looking him sternly in the face, "when I last rode that horse in company with you and lady, *my wife* was at my side, and I will not now go without her! Pardon me—my life for it, I won't go!"

"Not another word you black imp!" exclaimed Franks, with an uplifted staff in a rage, "or I'll strike you down in an instant!"

"Strike away if you will sir, I don't care—I won't go without my wife!"

"You impudent scoundrel! I'll soon put an end to your conduct! I'll put you on the auction block, and sell you to the negro traders."

"Just as soon as you please sir, the sooner the better, as I don't want to live with you any longer!"

"Hold your tongue sir, or I'll cut it out of your head! you ungrateful black dog! Really things have come to a pretty pass, when I must take impudence off my own negro! By gracious! God forgive me for the expression—I'll sell every negro I have first! I'll dispose of him to the hardest negro trader I can find!" said Franks in a rage.

"You may do your mightiest, colonel Franks. I'm not your slave, nor never was, and you know it! and but for my wife and her people, I never would have stayed with you till now. I was decoyed away when young, and then became entangled in such domestic relations as to induce me to remain with you; but now the tie is broken! I know that the odds are against me, but never mind!"

"Do you threaten me, sir! Hold your tongue, or I'll take your life instantly, you villain!"

---

[1] *'fess* Profess; referring to a profession of Christian faith.

[2] *swahin* Swearing.

"No sir, I don't threaten you, colonel Franks, but I do say that I won't be treated like a dog. You sold my wife away from me, after always promising that she should be free. And more than that, you sold her because——! and now you talk about whipping me. Shoot me, sell me, or do anything else you please, but don't lay your hands on me, as I will not suffer you to whip me!"

Running up to his chamber, colonel Franks seized a revolver, when Mrs. Franks, grasping hold of his arm, exclaimed—

"Colonel! what does all this mean?"

"Mean, my dear? It's rebellion! a plot—this is but the shadow of a cloud that's fast gathering around us! I see it plainly, I see it!" responded the Colonel, starting for the stairs.

"Stop, Colonel!" admonished his lady, "I hope you'll not be rash. For Heaven's sake, do not stain your hands in blood!"

"I do not mean to, my dear! I take this for protection!" Franks hastening downstairs, when Henry had gone into the back part of the premises.

"Dah now! dah now!' exclaimed mammy Judy as Henry entered the kitchen, "see wat dis gwine back done foh yeh! Bettah put yo' trus' in de Laud! Henry, yeh gone clean back t'de wuhl,[1] yeh knows it!"

"You're mistaken mammy, I do trust the Lord as much as ever, but I now understand him better than I use to, that's all. I don't intend to be made a fool of any longer by false preaching."

"Henry!" interrogated Daddy Joe, who, apprehending difficulties in the case, had managed to get back to the house, "yeh gwine lose all yo' ligion? Wat yeh mean boy!"

"Religion!" replied Henry rebukingly, "that's always the cry with black people. Tell me nothing about religion when the very man who hands you the bread at communion, has sold your daughter away from you!"

"Den yeh 'fen'[2] God case man 'fen' yeh! Take cah Henry, take cah! mine wat yeh 'bout; God is lookin' at yeh, an' if yeh no' willin' trus' 'im, yeh need'n call on 'im in time o' trouble."

"I don't intend, unless He does more for me then than he has done before. 'Time of need!'[3] If ever man needed his assistance, I'm sure I need it now."

"Yeh do'n know wat yeh need; de Laud knows bes'. On'y trus' in 'im, an' 'e bring yeh out mo' nah conkah. By de help o' God I's heah dis day, to gib yeh cumfut!"

"I have trusted in Him daddy Joe, all my life, as I told mammy Judy this morning, but——"

"Ah boy, yeh's gwine back! Dat on't do Henry, dat on't do!"

"Going back from what? my oppressor's religion! If I could only get rid of his inflictions as easily as I can his religion, I would be this day a free man, when you might then talk to me about 'trusting.'"

"Dis Henry, am one uh de ways ob de Laud; 'e fus 'flicks[4] us an' den he bless us."

"Then it's a way I don't like."

"Mine how yeh talk, boy!"

God moves in a myst'us way
His wundahs to pehfaum, an—"

"He moves too slow for me daddy Joe; I'm tired waiting so—"

"Come Henry, I hab no such talk like dat! yeh is gittin' rale weaked; yeh gwine let de debil take full 'session on[5] yeh! Take cah boy, mine how yeh talk!"

"It is not wickedness, daddy Joe; you don't understand these things at all. If a thousand years with us is but a day with God, do you think that I am required to wait all that time?"

"Don't Henry, don't! de wud say 'Stan' still an' see de salbation.'"[6]

"That's no talk for me daddy Joe, I've been 'standing still' long enough; I'll 'stand still' no longer."

"Den yeh no call t' bey God wud? Take cah boy, take cah!"

---

1   *t'de wuhl*   To the world; i.e., to worldly rather than spiritual concerns.

2   *'fen'*   Offend.

3   *Time of need*   See Hebrews 4.16: "Let us therefore come boldly unto the throne of grace, that we may obtain mercy, and find grace to help in time of need."

4   *'flicks*   Afflicts.

5   *weaked*   Wicked;   *'session on*   Possession of.

6   *Stan' still … salbation*   Words said by Moses to the Israelites before their departure from Egyptian slavery, in the Old Testament; see Exodus 14.13.

"Yes I have, and I intend to obey it, but that part was intended for the Jews, a people long since dead. I'll obey that intended for me."

"How yeh gwine bey it?"

"'Now is the accepted time, today is the day of salvation.'[1] So you see, daddy Joe, this is very different to standing still."

"Ah boy, I's feahd yeh's losen yeh 'ligion!"

"I tell you once for all daddy Joe, that I'm not only 'losing,' but I have altogether lost my faith in the religion of my oppressors. As they are our religious teachers, my estimate of the thing they give, is no greater than it is for those who give it."

With elbows upon his knees, and face resting in the palms of his hands, daddy Joe for some time sat with his eyes steadily fixed on the floor, whilst Ailcey, who for a part of the time had been an auditor to the conversation, went into the house about her domestic duties.

"Never mind, Henry! I hope it will not always be so with you. You have been kind and faithful to me and the Colonel, and I'll do anything I can for you!" sympathetically said Mrs. Franks, who having been a concealed spectator of the interview between Henry and the old people, had just appeared before them.

Wiping away the emblems of grief which stole down his face, with a deep-toned voice, upgushing from the recesses of a more than iron-pierced soul, he enquired—

"Madam, what can you do! Where is my wife?" To this, Mrs. Franks gave a deep sigh. "Never mind, never mind!" continued he, "yes, I will mind, and by—!"

"O! Henry, I hope you've not taken to swearing! I do hope you will not give over to wickedness! Our afflictions should only make our faith the stronger."

"'Wickedness!' Let the righteous correct the wicked, and the Christian condemn the sinner!"

"That is uncharitable in you Henry! as you know I have always treated you kindly, and God forbid that I should consider myself any less than a Christian! and I claim as much at least for the Colonel, though like frail mortals he is liable to err at times."

"Madam!" said he with a suppressed emotion—starting back a pace or two—"do you think there is

anything either in or out of hell so wicked, as that which colonel Franks has done to my wife, and now about to do to me? For myself I care not—my wife!"

"Henry!" said Mrs. Franks, gently placing her hand upon his shoulder, "there is yet a hope left for you, and you will be faithful enough I know, not to implicate any person; it is this: Mrs. Van Winter, a true friend of your race, is shortly going to Cuba on a visit, and I will arrange with her to purchase you through an agent on the day of your sale, and by that means you can get to Cuba, where probably you may be fortunate enough to get the master of your wife to become your purchaser."

"Then I have two chances!" replied Henry.

Just then Ailcey, thrusting her head in the door, requested the presence of her mistress in the parlor.

Chapter 8
The Sale

"Dah now, dah now!" exclaimed mammy Judy; "jis wat ole man been tellin' on yeh! Yeh go out yandah, yeh kick up yeh heel, git yeh head clean full proclamation an' sich like dat, an' let debil fool yeh, den go fool long wid wite folks long so, sho! Bettah go 'bout yeh bisness; been sahvin' God right, yeh no call t'do so eh reckon!"

"I don't care what comes! my course is laid out and my determination fixed, and nothing they can do can alter it. So you and daddy Joe, mammy, had just as well quit your preaching to me the religion you have got from your oppressors."

"Soul-driveh[2] git yeh, yeh cah git way fom dem eh doh recken! Sho chile, yeh, ain' dat mighty!" admonished mammy Judy.

"Henry my chile, look to de Laud! look to de Laud! case 'e 'lone am able t' bah us up in ouah[3] trouble! an—"

"Go directly sir, to captain John Harris' office and ask him to call immediately to see me at my house!" ordered Franks.

Politely bowing, Henry immediately left the premises on his errand.

1 *Now is ... of salvation* See 2 Corinthians 6.2 (in the New Testament).

2 *Soul-driveh* Person who works in the transport and sale of enslaved people.

3 *'e 'lone ... in ouah* He alone is able to bear us up in our.

"Laud a' messy[1] maus Stephen!" exclaimed mammy Judy, on hearing the name of John Harris the negro-trader; "hope yeh arteh no haum! gwine sell all on us to de tradehs?"

"Hoot-toot, hoot-toot! Judy, give yourself no uneasiness about that, till you have some cause for it. So you and Joe may rest contented Judy," admonished Franks.

"Tank'e maus Stephen! case ah heahn yeh tell Henry dat yeh sell de las' nig—"

"Hush! ole umin, hush! yeh tongue too long! Put yeh trus' in de Laud!" interrupted daddy Joe.

"I treat my black folks well," replied Franks; "and all they have to—"

Here the doorbell having been rung, he was interrupted with a message from Ailcey, that a gentleman awaited his presence in the parlor.

At the moment which the Colonel left the kitchen, Henry stepped over the stile into the yard, which at once disclosed who the gentleman was to whom the master had been summoned. Henry passed directly around and behind the house.

"See, ole man, see! reckon 'e gwine dah now!" whispered mammy Judy, on seeing Henry pass through the yard without going into the kitchen.

"Whah?" enquired daddy Joe.

"Dun'o out yandah, whah 'e gwine way from wite folks!" she replied.

The interview between Franks and the trader Harris was not over half an hour duration, the trader retiring, Franks being prompt and decisive in all of his transactions, making little ceremony.

So soon as the front door was closed, Ailcey smiling bore into the kitchen a half pint glass of brandy, saying that her master had sent it to the old people.

The old man received it with compliments to his master, pouring it into a black jug in which there was both tansy and garlic, highly recommending it as a "bitters" and certain antidote for worms, for which purpose he and the old woman took of it as long as it lasted, though neither had been troubled with that particular disease since the days of their childhood.

"Wat de gwine do wid yeh meh son?" enquired mammy Judy as Henry entered the kitchen.

"Sell me to the soul-drivers! what else would they do?"

"Yeh gwine 'tay 'bout till de git yeh?"

"I shan't move a step! and let them do their—!"

"Maus wants to see yeh in da front house Henry," interrupted Ailcey, he immediately obeying the summons.

"Heah dat now!" said mammy Judy, as Henry followed the maid out of the kitchen.

"Carry this note sir, directly to captain Jack Harris!" ordered Franks, handing to Henry a sealed note. Receiving it, he bowed politely, going out of the front door, directly to the slave prison of Harris.

"Eh heh! I see," said Harris on opening the note; "colonel Frank's boy; walk in here"; passing through the office into a room which proved to be the first department of the slave-prison. "No common negro I see! you're a shade higher. A pretty deep shade too! Can read, write, cipher;[2] a good religious fellow, and has a Christian[3] and surname. The devil you say! Who's your father! Can you preach?"

"I have never tried," was the only reply.

"Have you ever been a member of Congress?" continued Harris with ridicule.

To this Henry made no reply.

"Won't answer hey! beneath your dignity. I understand that you're of that class of gentry who don't speak to common folks! You're not quite well enough dressed for a gentleman of your cloth. Here! Mr. Henry, I'll present you with a set of ruffles: give yourself no trouble sir, as I'll dress you! I'm here for that purpose," said Harris, fastening upon the wrists of the manly bondman a heavy pair of handcuffs.

"You hurt my wrist!" admonished Henry.

"New clothing will be a little tight when first put on. Now sir!" continued the trader, taking him to the back door and pointing into the yard at the slave gang there confined; "as you have been respectably dressed, walk out and enjoy yourself among the ladies and gentlemen there; you'll find them quite a select company."

Shortly after this the sound of the bell-ringer's voice was heard—a sound which usually spread terror among the slaves: "Will be sold this afternoon at three o'clock by public outcry, at the slave-prison of captain John Harris, a likely choice negro-fellow, the best trained body servant in the state, trained to the business by

---

1   *messy* Mercy.

2   *cipher* I.e., calculate; do arithmetic.

3   *Christian* First (name).

the most accomplished lady and gentleman negro-trainers in the Mississippi Valley. Sale positive without a proviso."[1]

"Dah, dah! did'n eh tell yeh so? Ole man, ole man! heah dat now! Come heah. Dat jis what I been tellin on im, but 'e uden blieve me!" ejaculated old mammy Judy on hearing the bell ring and the hand bill read.

Falling upon their knees, the two old slaves prayed fervently to God, thanking him that it was as "well with them" as it was.

"Bless de Laud! my soul is happy!" cried out mammy Judy, being overcome with devotion, clapping her hands.

"Tang God, fah wat I feels in my soul!" responded daddy Joe.

Rising from their knees with tears trickling down their cheeks, the old slaves endeavored to ease their troubled souls by singing—

Oh, when shall my sorrows subside,
And when shall my troubles be ended;
And when to the bosom of Christ be conveyed,
To the mansions of joy and bliss;
To the mansions of joy and bliss![2]

"Wuhthy to be praise! blessed be de name uh de Laud! Po' black folks, de Laud o'ny knows wats t' come ob us!" exclaimed mammy Judy.

"Look to de Laud ole umin, 'e's able t' bah us out mo' neh conkeh. Keep de monin stah[3] in sight!" advised daddy Joe.

"Yes ole man, yes, dat I is done dis many long day, an' ah ain' gwine lose sight uh it now! No, God bein' my helpeh, I is gwine keep my eyes right on it, dat I is!"

As the hour of three drew near, many there were going in the direction of the slave-prison, a large number of persons having assembled at the sale.

"Draw near, gentlemen! draw near!" cried Harris; "the hour of sale is arrived; a positive sale with no proviso, cash down, or no sale at all!" A general laugh succeeded the introduction of the auctioneer.

"Come up here my lad!" continued the auctioneer, wielding a long red rawhide;[4] "mount this block, stand beside me, an' let's see which is the best-looking man! We have met before, but I never had the pleasure of introducing you. Gentlemen one and all, I take pleasure in introducing to you Henry—pardon me sir—Mr. Henry Holland, I believe—am I right sir?—Mr. Henry Holland, a good looking fellow you will admit.

"I am offered one thousand dollars; one thousand dollars for the best-looking negro in all Mississippi! If all the negro boys in the state was as good looking as him, I'd give two thousand dollars as him, I'd give two thousand dollars for 'em all myself!" This caused another laugh. "Who'll give me one thousand five—"

Just then a shower of rain came on.

"Gentlemen!" exclaimed the auctioneer; "without a place can be obtained large enough to shelter the people here assembled, the sale will have to be postponed. This is a proviso we couldn't foresee, an' therefore is not responsible for it." There was another hearty laugh.

A whisper went through the crowd, when presently a gentleman came forward saying that those concerned had kindly tendered the use of the Church which stood near by, in which to continue the sale.

"Here we are again, gentlemen! Who bids five hundred more for the likely negro fellow? I am offered fifteen hundred dollars for the finest negro servant in the state! Come, my boy, bestir yourself an' don't stan' there like a statue; can't you give us a jig? whistle us a song! I forgot, the negro fellow is religious; by the by, an excellent recommendation gentlemen. Perhaps he'll give us a sermon. Say, git up there old fellow, an' hold forth. Can't you give us a sermon on Abolition? I'm only offered fifteen hundred dollars for the likely negro boy! Fifteen, sixteen, sixteen hundred dollars, seventeen hundred, just agoing at—eighteen, eighteen, nineteen hundred, nineteen nineteen! Just agoing at nineteen hundred dollars for the best body servant in the State; just agoing at nineteen and without a better bid I'll—going! going! go—!"

1   *Sale positive ... proviso*   Phrase describing an auction in which the seller is obligated to complete a sale to the highest bidder (as opposed to an auction in which the seller may choose to back out of the sale).

2   *Oh, when ... and bliss*   Lines of a Christian hymn; in most published versions, the last line of the stanza quoted is rendered as "mansions of glory and peace."

3   *monin stah*   Morning star; see Revelation 22.16, where Jesus describes himself as "the bright and morning star."

4   *rawhide*   I.e., a whip.

Just at this point a note was passed up the aisle to the auctioneer, who after reading it said:

"Gentlemen! circumstances beyond my control make it necessary that the sale be postponed until one day next week; the time of continuance will be duly announced," when bowing he left the stand.

"That's another proviso not in the original bill!" exclaimed a voice as the auctioneer left the stand, at which there were peals of laughter.

To secure himself against contingency, Harris immediately delivered Henry over to Franks.

There were present at the sale, Crow, Slider, Walker, Borbridge, Simpson, Hurst, Spangler and Williams, all noted slave traders, eager to purchase, some on their return home, and some with their gangs *en route* for the southern markets.

The note handed the auctioneer read thus:

> CAPT. HARRIS—Having learned that there are private individuals at the sale, who design purchasing my negro man, Harry, for his own *personal advantage*, you will peremptorily postpone the sale—making such apology as the occasion demands—and effect a private sale with Richard Crow, Esq., who offers me two thousand dollars for him. Let the boy return to me. Believe me to be,
> Very respectfully,
>   STEPHEN FRANKS
> Capt. John Harris
> Natchez, Nov. 29th, 1852

"Now sir," said Franks to Henry, who had barely reached the house from the auction block; "take this pass and go to Jackson and Woodville, or anywhere else you wish to see your friends, so that you be back against Monday afternoon. I ordered a postponement of the sale, thinking that I would try you awhile longer, as I never had cause before to part with you. Now see if you can't be a better boy!"

Eagerly taking the note, thanking him with a low bow, turning away, Henry opened the paper, which read:

> Permit the bearer my boy Henry, sometimes calling himself Henry Holland—a kind of negro pride he has—to pass and repass wherever he wants to go, he behaving himself properly.
>   STEPHEN FRANKS

> To all whom it may concern.
> Natchez, Nov. 29th 1852

Carefully depositing the *charte volante*[1] in his pocket wallet, Henry quietly entered the hut of mammy Judy and daddy Joe.

[In the following chapter, Henry discovers that Franks has sold him to Richard Crow, and that the pass Franks has given him is merely a ruse to have Henry kidnapped. The discovery spurs Henry to escape slavery and declare himself a free man; he makes plans to have his son taken to Canada, while he himself determines to travel through the South and spread the word of revolution among the enslaved population. He implores Mammy Judy and Daddy Joe to escape to Canada as well, but they refuse, protesting that they are too old to make the journey or to adapt to a new life. It is revealed that Henry has amassed substantial savings by taking small amounts of money from Colonel Franks over the years.

Before his departure, Henry calls a secret meeting with two enslaved friends, Andy and Charles.]

CHAPTER 11
THE SHADOW

"Ah, boys! here you are, true to your promise," said Henry, as he entered a covert[2] in the thicket adjacent the cotton place, late on Sunday evening, "have you been waiting long?"

"Not very," replied Andy, "not mo' dan two-three ouahs."

"I was fearful you would not come, or if you did before me, that you would grow weary, and leave."

"Yeh no call to doubt us Henry, case yeh fine us true as ole steel!"

"I know it," answered he, "but you know, Andy, that when a slave is once sold at auction, all respect for him—"

"O pshaw! we ain' goin' to heah nothin' like dat a tall! case—"

"No!" interrupted Charles, "all you got to do, Henry, is to tell we boys what you want, an' we're your men."

---

1   *charte volante*   French: loose sheet.

2   *covert*   Sheltered area.

"That's the talk for me!"

"Well, what you doin' here?" enquired Charles.

"W'at brought yeh back from Jackson so soon?" further enquired Andy.

"How did you get word to meet me here?"

"By Ailcey; she give me the stone,[1] an' I give it to Andy, an' we both sent one apiece back. Didn't you git 'em?"

"Yes, that's the way I knew you intended to meet me," replied Henry.

"So we thought," said Charles, "but tell us, Henry, what you want us to do."

"I suppose you know all about the sale, that they had me on the auction block, but ordered a postponement, and—"

"That's the very pint we can't understand, although I'm in the same family with you,"[2] interrupted Charles.

"But tell us Henry, what yeh doin' here?" impatiently enquired Andy.

"Yes," added Charles, "we want to know."

"Well, I'm a *runaway*, and from this time forth, I swear—I do it religiously—that I'll never again serve any white man living!"

"That's the pint I wanted to git at before," explained Charles, "as I can't understan' why you run away, after your release from Jack Harris, an'—"

"Nah I, nuthah!" interrupted Andy.

"It seems to me," continued Charles, "that I'd 'ave went before they 'tempted to sell me, an' that you're safer now than before they had you on the block."

"Dat's da way I look at it," responded Andy.

"The stopping of the sale was to deceive his wife, mammy, and Daddy Joe, as he had privately disposed of me to a regular soul-driver by the name of Crow."

"I knows Dick Crow," said Andy, "'e come f'om Faginy, whah I did, da same town."

"So Ailcey said of him. Then you know him without any description from me," replied Henry.

"Yes 'n deed! an' I knows 'im to be a inhuman, mean, dead-po'[3] white man, dat's wat I does."

"Well, I was privately sold to him for two thousand dollars, then ordered back to Franks, as though I was still his slave, and by him given a pass, and requested to go to Woodville where there were arrangements to seize me and hold me, till Crow ordered me, which was to have been on Tuesday evening. Crow is not aware of me having been given a pass; Franks gave it to deceive his wife, in case of my not returning, to make the impression that I had run away, when in reality I was sold to the trader."

"Then our people had their merrymaking[4] all for nothin'," said Charles, "an' Franks got what 'e didn't deserve—their praise."

"No, the merrymaking was only to deceive Franks, that I might have time to get away. Daddy Joe, Mammy Judy, and Ailcey knew all about it, and proposed the feast to deceive him."

"Dat's good! sarve 'im right, da 'sarned ole scamp!" rejoined Andy.

"It couldn't be better!" responded Charles.

"Henry, uh wish we was in yo' place an' you none da wus by it," said Andy.

"Never mind, boys, give yourselves no uneasiness, as it won't be long before we'll all be together."

"You think so, Henry?" asked Charles.

"Well uh hope so, but den body can haudly 'spect it," responded Andy.

"Boys," said Henry, with great caution, and much emotion, "I am now about to approach an important subject, and as I have always found you true to me—and you can only be true to me by being true to yourselves—I shall not hesitate to impart it! But for Heaven's sake!—perhaps I had better not!"

"Keep nothin' back, Henry," said Charles, "as you know that we boys 'll die by our principles, that's settled!"

"Yes, I wants to die right now by mine; right heah, now!" sanctioned Andy.

---

1 *she give me the stone* Presumably a device used to communicate messages without the knowledge of one's enslavers.

2 *although I'm … with you* The exact meaning here is unclear, though the implication seems to be that Charles considers himself and Henry to be akin to family members, and is thus surprised not to instinctively understand Henry's situation.

3 *dead-po'* Dead poor.

4 *their merrymaking* In Chapter 10, "Merry Making," Mammy Judy and Daddy Joe host a celebration meant in part to hide the fact that they know about Henry's sale to Crow—and to distract Franks while Henry begins his escape.

"Well it is this—close, boys! close!" When they gathered in a huddle beneath an underbush, upon their knees, "you both go with me, but not now. I—"

"Why not now?" anxiously enquired Charles.

"Dat's wat I like to know!" responded Andy.

"Stop, boys, till I explain. The plans are mine and you must allow me to know more about them than you. Just here, for once, the slave-holding preacher's advice to the black man is appropriate, 'Stand still and see the salvation.'"

"Then let us hear it, Henry," asked Charles.

"Fah God sake!" said Andy, "let us heah w'at it is, anyhow, Henry; yeh keep a body in 'spence so long, till I's mose crazy to heah it. Dat's no way!"

"You shall have it, but I approach it with caution! Nay, with fear and trembling,[1] at the thought of what has been the fate of all previous matters of this kind. I approach it with religious fear, and hardly think us fit for the task; at least, I know I am not. But as no one has ever originated, or given us anything of the kind, I suppose I may venture."

"Tell it! tell it!" urged both in a whisper.

"Andy," said Henry, "let us have a word of prayer first!" When they bowed low, with their heads to the ground, Andy, who was a preacher of the Baptist persuasion among his slave brethren, offering a solemn and affecting prayer, in whispers to the Most High, to give them knowledge and courage in the undertaking, and success in the effort.

Rising from their knees, Andy commenced an anthem, by which he appeared to be much affected, in the following words:

> About our future destiny,
> There need be none debate—
> Whilst we ride on the tide,
> With our Captain and his mate.[2]

Clasping each other by the hand, standing in a band together, as a plight of their union and fidelity to each other, Henry said, "I now impart to you the secret, it is this: I have laid a scheme, and matured a plan for a general insurrection of the slaves in every State, and the successful overthrow of slavery!"

"Amen!" exclaimed Charles.

"God grant it!" responded Andy.

"Tell us, Henry, how's dis to be carried out?" enquired Andy.

"That's the thing which most concerns me, as it seems that it would be hard to do in the present ignorant state of our people in the slave States," replied Charles.

"Dat's jis wat I feah!" said Andy.

"This difficulty is obviated. It is so simple that the most stupid among the slaves will understand it as well as if he had been instructed for a year."

"What!" exclaimed Charles.

"Let's heah dat again!" asked Andy.

"It is so just as I told you! So simple is it that the trees of the forest or an orchard illustrate it; flocks of birds or domestic cattle, fields of corn, hemp or sugar cane; tobacco, rice or cotton, the whistling of the wind, rustling of the leaves, flashing of lightning, roaring of thunder, and running of streams all keep it constantly before their eyes and in their memory, so that they can't forget it if they would."

"Are we to know it now?" enquired Charles.

"I'm boun' to know it dis night befo' I goes home, 'case I been longin' fah ole Pottah[3] dis many day, an' uh mos' think uh got 'im now!"

"Yes boys, you've to know it before we part, but—"

"That's the talk!" said Charles.

"Good nuff talk fah me!" responded Andy.

"As I was about to say, such is the character of this organization, that punishment and misery are made the instruments for its propagation, so—"

"I can't understan' that part—"

"You know nothing at all about it Charles, and you must—"

"Stan' still an' see da salvation!" interrupted Andy.

"Amen!" responded Charles.

"God help you so to do, brethren!" admonished Henry.

"Go on Henry tell us! give it to us!" they urged.

"Every blow you receive from the oppressor impresses the organization upon your mind, making it

---

[1] *with fear and trembling* See Philippians 2.12: "Wherefore, my beloved, as ye have always obeyed, not as in my presence only, but now much more in my absence, work out your own salvation with fear and trembling."

[2] *About our ... his mate* Lines from the hymn "The People Called Christians."

[3] *ole Pottah* Charles and Andy's enslaver, the slaveholder Potter.

so clear that even Whitehead's Jack[1] could understand it as well as his master."

"We are satisfied! The secret, the secret!" they importuned.

"Well then, first to prayer, and then to the organization. Andy!" said Henry, nodding to him, when they again bowed low with their heads to the ground, whilst each breathed a silent prayer, which was ended with "Amen" by Andy.

Whilst yet upon their knees, Henry imparted to them the secrets of his organization.

"O, dat's da thing!" exclaimed Andy.

"Capital, capital!" responded Charles. "What fools we was that we didn't know it long ago!"

"I is mad wid myse'f now!" said Andy.

"Well, well, well! Surely God must be in the work," continued Charles.

"'E's heah; Heaven's nigh! Ah feels it! It's right heah!" responded Andy, placing his hand upon his chest, the tears trickling down his cheeks.

"Brethren," asked Henry, "do you understand it?"

"Understand it? Why, a child could understand, it's so easy!" replied Charles.

"Yes," added Andy, "ah not only undehstan' myse'f, but wid da knowledge I has uv it, ah could make Whitehead's Jack a Moses!"

"Stand still, then, and see!" said he.

"Dat's good Bible talk!" responded Andy.

"Well, what is we to do?" enquired Charles.

"You must now go on and organize continually. It makes no difference when, nor where you are, so that the slaves are true and trustworthy, as the scheme is adapted to all times and places."

"How we gwine do Henry, 'bout gittin' da things 'mong da boys?" enquired Andy.

"All you have to do, is to find one good man or woman—I don't care which, so that they prove to be the right person—on a single plantation, and hold a seclusion and impart the secret to them, and make them the organizers for their own plantation, and they in like manner impart it to some other next to them, and so on. In this way it will spread like smallpox among them."

"Henry, you is fit fah leadah ah see," complimentingly said Andy.

"I greatly mistrust myself, brethren, but if I can't command, I can at least plan."

"Is they anything else for us to do Henry?" enquired Charles.

"Yes, a very important part of your duties has yet to be stated. I now go as a runaway, and will be suspected of lurking about in the thickets, swamps and caves; then to make the ruse complete, just as often as you think it necessary, to make a good impression, you must kill a shoat, take a lamb, pig, turkey, goose, chickens, ham of bacon from the smoke house, a loaf of bread or crock of butter from the spring house, and throw them down into the old waste well at the back of the old quarters, always leaving the heads of the fowls lying about and the blood of the larger animals. Everything that is missed do not hesitate to lay it upon me, as a runaway, it will only cause them to have the less suspicion of your having such a design."

"That's it—the very thing!" said Charles, "an it so happens that they's an ole waste well on both Franks' and Potter's places, one for both of us."

"I hope Andy, you have no religious objections to this?"

"It's a paut ah my 'ligion, Henry, to do whateveh I bleve right, an' shall sholy do dis, God being my helpah!"

"Now he's talkin'!" said Charles.

"You must make your religion subserve your interests, as your oppressors do theirs!" advised Henry. "They use the Scriptures to make you submit, by preaching to you the texts of 'obedience to your masters'[2] and 'standing still to see the salvation,' and we must now begin to understand the Bible so as to make it of interest to us."

"Dat's gospel talk," sanctioned Andy. "Is da anything else yeh want tell us boss—I calls 'im *boss*, 'case 'e aint nothing else but 'boss'—so we can make 'ase an' git to wuck? 'case I feels like goin' at 'em now, me!"

"Having accomplished our object, I think I have done, and must leave you tomorrow."

---

1 *Whitehead's Jack* Probably a reference to English writer Charles Whitehead's novel *The Autobiography of Jack Ketch* (1835), about a famously brutal executioner.

2 *obedience to your masters* Various biblical passages exhort the faithful to obey their enslavers, including Ephesians 6.5: "Slaves, obey your earthly masters with respect and fear, and with sincerity of heart, just as you would obey Christ." See also Colossians 3.22, Titus 2.9, and 1 Peter 2.18.

"When shall we hear from you, Henry?" enquired Charles.

"Not until you shall see me again; when that will be, I don't know. You may see me in six months, and might not in eighteen. I am determined, now that I am driven to it, to complete an organization in every slave state before I return, and have fixed two years as my utmost limit."

"Henry, tell me before we part, do you know anything about little Joe?" enquired Charles.

"I do!"

"Wha's da chile?" enquired Andy.

"He's safe enough, on his way to Canada!" at which Charles and Andy laughed.

"Little Joe is on 'is way to Canada?" said Andy, "mighty young travelah!"

"Yes," replied Henry with a smile.

"You're a joking, Henry?" said Charles, enquiringly.

"I am serious, brethren," replied he. "I do not joke in matters of this kind. I smiled because of Andy's surprise."

"How did 'e go?" farther enquired Andy.

"In company with his 'mother' who was waiting on her 'mistress!'" replied he quaintly.

"Eh heh!" exclaimed Andy. "I knows all 'bout it now; but whah'd da 'mammy' come f'om?"

"I found one!"

"Aint 'e high!" said Andy.

"Well, brethren, my time is drawing to a close," said Henry, rising to his feet.

"O!" exclaimed Andy, "ah like to forgot, has yeh any money Henry?"

"Have either of you any?"

"We has."

"How much?"

"I got two-three hundred dollahs!" replied Andy.

"An' so has I, Henry!" added Charles.

"Then keep it, as I have two thousand dollars now around my waist, and you'll find use for all you've got, and more, as you will before long have an opportunity of testing. Keep this studiously in mind and impress it as an important part of the scheme of organization, that they must have money, if they want to get free. Money will obtain them everything necessary by which to obtain their liberty. The money is within all of their reach if they only knew it was right to take it. God told the Egyptian slaves to 'borrow from their neighbors'—meaning their oppressors—'all their jewels'; meaning to take their money and wealth wherever they could lay hands upon it, and depart from Egypt.[1] So you must teach them to take all the money they can get from their masters, to enable them to make the strike without a failure. I'll show you when we leave for the North, what money will do for you, right here in Mississippi. Bear this in mind; it is your certain *passport* through the *white gap*, as I term it."

"I means to take all ah can git; I bin doin' dat dis some time. Ev'ry time ole Pottah leave 'is money pus,[2] I borrys some, an' 'e all'as lays it on Miss Mary, but 'e think so much uh huh, dat anything she do is right wid 'im. Ef 'e 'spected me, an' Miss Mary say 'twant me, dat would be 'nough fah 'im."

"That's right!" said Henry, "I see you have been putting your own interpretation on the Scriptures, Andy, and as Charles will now have to take my place, he'll have still a much better opportunity than you, to 'borrow from his master.'"

"You needn't fear, I'll make good use of my time!" replied Charles.

The slaves now fell upon their knees in silent communion, all being affected to the shedding of tears, a period being put to their devotion by a sorrowful trembling of Henry's voice singing to the following touching words:

Farewell, farewell, farewell!
My loving friends farewell!
Farewell old comrades in the cause,
I leave you here, and journey on;
And if I never more return,
Farewell, I'm bound to meet you there![3]

"One word before we part," said Charles. "If we never should see you again, I suppose you intend to push on this scheme?"

"Yes!"

Insurrection shall be my theme!
My watchword "Freedom or the grave!"

---

[1] *God told ... depart from Egypt*   See Exodus 3.22.

[2] *pus*   Purse.

[3] *Farewell ... you there*   These words, Delany's own, follow the structure of the folk hymn "The Minister's Farewell."

Until from Rappahannock's stream,[1]
To where the Cuato[2] waters lave,
One simultaneous war cry
Shall burst upon the midnight air!
And rouse the tyrant but to sigh—
Mid sadness, wailing, and despair!

Grasping each eagerly by the hand, the tears gushing from his eyes, with an humble bow, he bid them finally "farewell!" and the runaway was off through the forest.
—1859

INDEX TO VOLUME I.

Index to *The Anglo-African Magazine*, Volume 1, 1859. The first portion of *Blake* appeared in this volume of the periodical, to which Delany also contributed articles on astronomy.

---

[1] *Rappahannock's stream*   The Rappahannock River in Virginia.

[2] [Delany's note]   A river in Cuba.

HARRIET BEECHER STOWE
1811 – 1896

Harriet Beecher Stowe's first novel, *Uncle Tom's Cabin* (1852), may well have excited more controversy than any other work of fiction in American history. In the 1850s it was welcomed by abolitionists for the impetus it gave to their movement—and met with furious indignation by white Southerners. Its characters and dramatic scenes were absorbed into the nation's consciousness, and the novel spawned—largely without Stowe's approval—a veritable industry of crude "Tom shows" whose characters hardened into racist cultural artefacts, at once wildly popular and routinely mocked. By the mid-twentieth century, *Uncle Tom's Cabin* was widely dismissed as irrelevant politically, a failure artistically, and—in what would have struck readers of the 1850s as an extraordinary irony—pervasively racist in its portrayal of black people. In our own century, its estimation as literature and as a political work engaged with the most serious political and moral questions of its era has continued to fluctuate wildly, although no one can deny its significance or popularity.

Harriet Beecher was born in Litchfield, Connecticut in 1811, the seventh child of Lyman Beecher, a Congregational minister, and Roxana Foote Beecher. Roxana died in 1816; her death (and subsequent idolization in the family's collective memory) had a lasting psychological impact upon Stowe. Lyman (who promptly remarried, and had four more children) was a strong shaping force in her life in large part through his passionate Calvinist religious convictions.

Stowe attended the Litchfield Female Academy and later her elder sister Catharine's Hartford Female Seminary, an influential and progressive institution that, in addition to teaching the "domestic arts," offered a level of academic instruction rarely available to young women in the early nineteenth century. Stowe proved an enthusiastic student with a particular talent for writing, especially on moral, philosophical, and religious themes. By 1827 her formal education was considered complete and she took on a teaching position at the Seminary, where she remained for five more years.

In 1832 the Beecher family moved to Cincinnati, Ohio, a rapidly growing city then considered the westernmost outpost of "civilized" America. The following year Harriet and Catharine together wrote and published a geography textbook, *Primary Geography for Children*, which sold well; they also helped form the Semi-Colon Club, an informal literary association where Stowe received encouragement to start writing sketches (some of which were published in the local *Western Monthly Magazine*). In 1836 she met and married Calvin Stowe, a teacher at the Lane Seminary where her father taught; they had their first children, twin daughters, later that year. The couple had a companionate, intellectually fulfilling relationship, though differences in their temperaments and Calvin's frequent trips away from home in the early years of their marriage led to recurring tensions.

In the mid-1830s, Cincinnati, just across the border from the slave state of Kentucky, saw an explosion in public debate over slavery, with radical abolitionists increasingly unwilling to tolerate the passive antislavery sentiments of respected community leaders such as Lyman Beecher. Several anti- and pro-slavery riots shook the city; in their aftermath, many of the Beecher children, including Stowe, began to distance themselves from their father's careful tolerance of slavery and to interest themselves in the movement for immediate abolition.

To supplement the income for her growing family, Stowe began in the late 1830s to write short fiction for commercial magazines, including the new and increasingly popular *Godey's Lady's Book*; she experimented with various genres including brief domestic sketches, tales of the frontier, and religious and morally instructive stories. Her stories were in sufficient demand that in 1843 a selection was published in Boston in book form as *The Mayflower*. Throughout much of the 1840s, however, Stowe wrote little fiction; tensions in her marriage were recurrent, and household duties were utterly exhausting (by the end of the 1840s she would have six children, five of them living; her seventh child was born in 1850).

At the end of the decade, two dramatic events combined to provide Stowe with the impetus to begin writing *Uncle Tom's Cabin*. The first was the death of her infant son, Charley, during a cholera epidemic in 1849; Stowe's grief and devastation would inform much of her depiction of the sufferings of enslaved women and mothers in the novel. The second was the passage of the Fugitive Slave Act in September 1850. Part of the Compromise of 1850—a package of federal legislation meant to diffuse the increasing political tensions between the North and the South—the Act protected the right of slaveowners to pursue individuals who had fled North and re-enslave them; more than that, it required Northerners to assist in the pursuit, and threatened substantial fines or jail time for those found to be assisting fugitives. The Act was widely hated in the North, and made the injustices of slavery impossible to ignore. Stowe, who was already a supporter of immediate abolition, was enraged by the Fugitive Slave Act—"I have felt almost choked sometimes with pent-up wrath that does no good," she wrote to her sister. But her rage was transformative. She turned toward what was arguably the most effective means for American women to have their say in moral and political affairs—the pen.

The first installment of *Uncle Tom's Cabin* was published in the Washington, D.C., abolitionist paper *The National Era* on 5 June 1851, the last on 1 April 1852. The novel follows the interrelated stories of several enslaved characters: George Harris, a mixed-race man who defies his cruel enslaver and escapes to Canada; his wife Eliza, who flees her otherwise "kind" enslaver when she discovers he intends to sell both her and her young son; and the titular Uncle Tom, a deeply pious middle-aged man who is sold onto a Louisiana plantation and defies slavery not through violence or escape but through Christian forbearance. The serialized novel was moderately successful, eliciting many passionate responses from readers who wrote Stowe to share their feelings. However, it was the novel's publication in book format on 20 March 1852 that turned *Uncle Tom's Cabin* into a phenomenon. "Reader, buy *Uncle Tom's Cabin*," commanded an 1852 review in the New Hampshire *Morning Star*; "By all means do not go out of this world without having read 'the Story of the Age.'" The two-volume book became a bestseller almost overnight, selling over ten thousand copies in its first few days and over 300,000 within the year in the United States alone. In Britain (which had abolished slavery in the 1830s), it sold over one million copies in its first year.

As influential literary figure Edwin Percy Whipple observed in an 1876 essay in *Harper's Monthly Magazine*, the publication of *Uncle Tom's Cabin* turned out to be "an important political event. It was one of the most powerful agencies in building up the Republican party, in electing Abraham Lincoln to the Presidency,[1] and in raising earnest volunteers for the great crusade against slavery." The novel was widely praised for its effective combination of political suasion, religious feeling, and sentiment. And, as one letter-writer put it, the story was "peculiarly calculated to enlist the moral and religious sympathies, and call to action the latent energies of the female heart." But while the novel's sentimental rhetoric in many ways sought to appeal to women particularly, male readers were clearly affected too: the story of prominent newspaper editor Horace Greeley, who was said to have sobbed his way through the book in a hotel room in Ohio, is far from unique. The narrative inspired writers such as William Wells Brown and Mary Hayden Green Pike to write abolitionist novels of their own, and it inspired poets as well—including Quaker abolitionist John Greenleaf Whittier and activist Frances Ellen Watkins Harper (whose 1854 "Eliza Harris" is directly based on the novel).

In the other direction, countless proslavery apologists characterized Stowe's novel as an "infamous book of lies," and some questioned the propriety of Stowe's delving into the subject at all—as a Northerner, and as a woman. As one reviewer for *The Southern Literary Messenger* put it, "It is a horrible

---

[1]   The most frequently recounted Stowe anecdote concerns Lincoln, who is said to have greeted her in 1862 with these words: "So you're the little woman who wrote the book that made this great war." But the anecdote, which originated decades after the fact in family lore, cannot be said to have any basis in fact. Stowe and Lincoln did meet in November of 1862, but there is no reliable record of their conversation.

thought that a woman should write or a lady should read such productions as those by which [Stowe's] celebrity has been acquired." Proslavery authors began writing "anti-Tom" novels—novels portraying a romanticized view of the South and of master-slave relations; Virginia author Mary Henderson Eastman's *Aunt Phillis's Cabin; or Southern Life as It Is* (1852) enjoyed considerable popularity in the North as well as in the South.

Though most abolitionists welcomed Stowe's success in awakening "the strongest compassion for the oppressed and the utmost abhorrence of the system which grinds them to the dust" (as William Lloyd Garrison put in *The Liberator*), Garrison and others were deeply uncomfortable with the degree to which Stowe portrayed passivity in the face of oppression to be appropriate for the enslaved; they found the portrayal of the titular Uncle Tom particularly troubling in this respect. The novel's conclusion—which appears to endorse the controversial, primarily white-led movement to transport free African Americans to the colony of Liberia—was also deeply troubling to many. (Stowe would renounce the colonizationist movement in later years, partly as a result of her correspondence with the black abolitionist and anti-colonizationist Frederick Douglass.)

In 1853, Stowe responded to charges that she was ill-qualified to tackle the subject of slavery with *A Key to Uncle Tom's Cabin*, in which she provided exhaustive documentation of the facts on which she had based her novel (and also revealed that the character of Uncle Tom had been heavily based on that of the formerly enslaved minister Josiah Henson). The Stowes subsequently embarked on a tour of England and continental Europe, where her novel's egalitarian themes resonated with many who had supported the various democratic revolutions of 1848.

Stowe's next book was a second novel, *Dred: A Tale of the Great Dismal Swamp* (1856), which offered a more radical view of the struggle against slavery; her detailed appendix of research sources made it clear that her title character was a composite of the early nineteenth-century slave revolt leaders Nat Turner and Denmark Vesey. *Dred* sold modestly well, but had far less impact on America than had *Uncle Tom's Cabin*. Stowe's fame nevertheless continued unabated; she wrote several more novels over the next decade, including *The Minister's Wooing* (1859), a work set in eighteenth-century New England that turned a critical eye on the legacy of Calvinism, and *A Pearl of Orr's Island: A Story of the Coast of Maine* (1862).

Stowe's career was sufficiently lucrative that Calvin decided to retire in early 1864. Stowe courted controversy again in 1869 with "The True Story of Lady Byron's Life," which discussed English poet Lord Byron's incestuous affair with his half sister; though rumors of the affair had been widespread for years, the article was nevertheless explosive, nearly ruining both the prestigious *Atlantic Monthly* magazine in which it had been published and Stowe's own reputation. For decades scholars and biographers puzzled over this turn in Stowe's literary career; in recent years some scholars have read "The True Story" and the subsequent *Lady Byron Vindicated* (1870) as proto-feminist explorations of nineteenth-century gender roles and of the subjugation of women in sexual relationships.

Stowe's final novel was the 1878 *Poganuc People*, a regional novel that evoked the New England of her childhood. Her physical and mental health deteriorated rapidly over the next few years, especially after Calvin's death in 1886; Stowe herself died in July 1896.

The legacy of *Uncle Tom's Cabin* in American culture far outlived Stowe herself. The first stage adaptation had been written shortly after the novel's publication by George Aiken, a white playwright who also starred in the production as the novel's mixed-race hero George Harris. The novel was adapted countless additional times over the following decades, with many productions substantially altering the plot and exaggerating the racial stereotypes that had underlain the original narrative. These stage plays came to be known as "Tom Shows," and though their popularity was waning by the 1930s, they were still occasionally encountered even in the North as late as the 1940s. Some Tom Shows were wildly melodramatic, while others added song-and-dance numbers and comic scenes, adopting racist tropes from the minstrel show genre.

The "Tom Shows" were disdained by the literary establishment, but the novel itself continued to have broad appeal through the late-nineteenth century and into the twentieth. It was admired by respected European novelists such as George Eliot, George Sand, and Leo Tolstoy, who in 1897 declared it as an example "of the highest art flowing from love of God and man." By the 1920s, however, the novel had begun to be dismissed by the literary establishment as a hackneyed work of sentimentalism, with little in the way of aesthetic or intellectual value, and by mid century it was being attacked as downright pernicious. In his famous 1955 essay "Everybody's Protest Novel," James Baldwin dismissed the novel's "self-righteous, virtuous sentimentality" and condemned its two-dimensional characters. Baldwin treated *Uncle Tom's Cabin* as the paradigmatical protest novel, and condemned all such novels for their sentimentality—"sentimentality is the mark of dishonesty, the inability to feel," he proclaimed—and for the way in which, as he saw it, they simplified and distorted complex psychological and cultural truths; in his view, Stowe's "self-righteous sentimentality" and "catalog of violence" left "unanswered and unnoticed the only question that actually matters: what it was, after all, that moved her [i.e., white] people to such deeds." In another famous essay published a year later, J.C. Furnas focused more narrowly on Stowe's portrayal of black people, crediting her work for contributing significantly to "the wrongheadedness, distortions and wishful thinkings about Negroes in general and American Negroes in particular that still plague us today."

The reception history of *Uncle Tom's Cabin* has continued to take new turns in the twenty-first century. The literature of sentiment and the literature of protest are being read more sympathetically than they were for much of the twentieth century. Since the 1970s, critics have come to take the works of many nineteenth-century female writers much more seriously—and to question the gendered biases that often underlaid twentieth-century dismissals of popular and sentimental fiction as unworthy of study. Increasingly, twenty-first-century critics are interested in examining *Uncle Tom's Cabin*'s strategies in the context of the 1850s and 1860s as well as its legacy for race relations in subsequent periods; some critics also use Stowe's novel as a springboard for discussions about the role of emotion in literature more generally. The novel continues to entrance, infuriate, and, most of all, intrigue readers and scholars into our own day.

NOTE ON THE TEXT: The excerpts presented below are based on the 1852 first edition of *Uncle Tom's Cabin; or, Life Among the Lowly*. Spelling and punctuation have been modernized in accordance with the practices of this anthology.

⌘ ⌘ ⌘

from *Uncle Tom's Cabin; or, Life Among the Lowly*

CHAPTER 1
IN WHICH THE READER IS INTRODUCED
TO A MAN OF HUMANITY

Late in the afternoon of a chilly day in February, two gentlemen were sitting alone over their wine, in a well-furnished dining parlor, in the town of P——, in Kentucky. There were no servants present, and the gentlemen, with chairs closely approaching, seemed to be discussing some subject with great earnestness.

For convenience sake, we have said, hitherto, two *gentlemen*. One of the parties, however, when critically examined, did not seem, strictly speaking, to come under the species. He was a short, thick-set man, with coarse, commonplace features, and that swaggering air of pretension which marks a low man who is trying to elbow his way upward in the world. He was much over-dressed, in a gaudy vest of many colors, a blue neckerchief, bedropped gayly with yellow spots, and arranged with a flaunting tie, quite in keeping with the general air of the man. His hands, large and coarse, were plentifully bedecked with rings; and he wore a heavy gold watch-chain, with a bundle of seals of portentous size, and a great variety of colors, attached to it—which, in the ardor of conversation, he was in the habit of flourishing and jingling with evident satisfaction. His conversation was in free and easy defiance of Murray's Grammar,[1] and was garnished at convenient

---

[1] *Murray's Grammar* American scholar Lindley Murray's widely used textbook *English Grammar* (1795), which dictated rules of grammar and usage.

intervals with various profane expressions, which not even the desire to be graphic in our account shall induce us to transcribe.

His companion, Mr. Shelby, had the appearance of a gentleman; and the arrangements of the house, and the general air of the housekeeping, indicated easy and even opulent circumstances. As we before stated, the two were in the midst of an earnest conversation.

"That is the way I should arrange the matter," said Mr. Shelby.

"I can't make trade that way—I positively can't, Mr. Shelby," said the other, holding up a glass of wine between his eye and the light.

"Why, the fact is, Haley, Tom is an uncommon fellow; he is certainly worth that sum anywhere— steady, honest, capable, manages my whole farm like a clock."

"You mean honest, as niggers[1] go," said Haley, helping himself to a glass of brandy.

"No; I mean, really, Tom is a good, steady, sensible, pious fellow. He got religion at a camp meeting,[2] four years ago; and I believe he really *did* get it. I've trusted him, since then, with everything I have—money, house, horses—and let him come and go round the country; and I always found him true and square in everything."

"Some folks don't believe there is pious niggers, Shelby," said Haley, with a candid flourish of his hand, "but *I do*. I had a fellow, now, in this yer last lot I took to Orleans—'t was as good as a meetin, now, really, to hear that critter pray; and he was quite gentle and quiet like. He fetched me a good sum, too, for I bought him cheap of a man that was 'bliged to sell out; so I realized six hundred on him. Yes, I consider religion a valeyable thing in a nigger, when it's the genuine article, and no mistake."

"Well, Tom's got the real article, if ever a fellow had," rejoined the other. "Why, last fall, I let him go to Cincinnati alone, to do business for me, and bring home five hundred dollars. 'Tom,' says I to him, 'I trust you, because I think you're a Christian—I know you wouldn't cheat.' Tom comes back, sure enough; I knew he would. Some low fellows, they say, said to him—'Tom, why don't you make tracks for Canada?'[3] 'Ah, master trusted me, and I couldn't,'—they told me about it. I am sorry to part with Tom, I must say. You ought to let him cover the whole balance of the debt; and you would, Haley, if you had any conscience."

"Well, I've got just as much conscience as any man in business can afford to keep—just a little, you know, to swear by, as 't were," said the trader, jocularly; "and, then, I'm ready to do anything in reason to 'blige friends; but this yer, you see, is a leetle too hard on a fellow—a leetle too hard." The trader sighed contemplatively, and poured out some more brandy.

"Well, then, Haley, how will you trade?" said Mr. Shelby, after an uneasy interval of silence.

"Well, haven't you a boy or gal that you could throw in with Tom?"

"Hum! none that I could well spare; to tell the truth, it's only hard necessity makes me willing to sell at all. I don't like parting with any of my hands, that's a fact."

Here the door opened, and a small quadroon[4] boy, between four and five years of age, entered the room. There was something in his appearance remarkably beautiful and engaging. His black hair, fine as floss silk, hung in glossy curls about his round, dimpled face, while a pair of large dark eyes, full of fire and softness, looked out from beneath the rich, long lashes, as he peered curiously into the apartment. A gay robe of scarlet and yellow plaid, carefully made and neatly fitted, set off to advantage the dark and rich style of his beauty; and a certain comic air of assurance, blended with bashfulness, showed that he had been not unused to being petted and noticed by his master.

---

[1] *nigger* By the mid-nineteenth century, this word, when used by white speakers, had acquired the extremely derogatory connotations it carries today, though it was sometimes used by African Americans without any derogatory intention; "negro" was, by contrast, considered a polite term by both black and white Americans.

[2] *camp meeting* Outdoor religious gathering; camp meetings were associated particularly with evangelical Christian denominations, and provided a form of worship that was more accessible to the enslaved communities of the South.

[3] *why don't ... for Canada?* Due to its location along the border between Kentucky and the free state of Ohio, Cincinnati was an important center of the Underground Railroad, a secret network that aided enslaved people escaping to freedom in Canada.

[4] *quadroon* Term commonly used in the nineteenth century to classify a person of mixed racial ancestry, generally with one black and three white grandparents.

"Hulloa, Jim Crow![1] said Mr. Shelby, whistling, and snapping a bunch of raisins towards him, "pick that up, now!"

The child scampered, with all his little strength, after the prize, while his master laughed.

"Come here, Jim Crow," said he. The child came up, and the master patted the curly head, and chucked him under the chin.

"Now, Jim, show this gentleman how you can dance and sing." The boy commenced one of those wild, grotesque songs common among the negroes, in a rich, clear voice, accompanying his singing with many comic evolutions of the hands, feet, and whole body, all in perfect time to the music.

"Bravo!" said Haley, throwing him a quarter of an orange.

"Now, Jim, walk like old Uncle Cudjoe, when he has the rheumatism," said his master.

Instantly the flexible limbs of the child assumed the appearance of deformity and distortion, as, with his back humped up, and his master's stick in his hand, he hobbled about the room, his childish face drawn into a doleful pucker, and spitting from right to left, in imitation of an old man.

Both gentlemen laughed uproariously.

"Now, Jim," said his master, "show us how old Elder Robbins leads the psalm." The boy drew his chubby face down to a formidable length, and commenced toning a psalm tune through his nose, with imperturbable gravity.

"Hurrah! bravo! what a young 'un!" said Haley; "that chap's a case, I'll promise. Tell you what," said he, suddenly clapping his hand on Mr. Shelby's shoulder, "fling in that chap, and I'll settle the business—I will. Come, now, if that ain't doing the thing up about the rightest!"

At this moment, the door was pushed gently open, and a young quadroon woman, apparently about twenty-five, entered the room.

There needed only a glance from the child to her, to identify her as its mother. There was the same rich, full, dark eye, with its long lashes; the same ripples of silky black hair. The brown of her complexion gave way on the cheek to a perceptible flush, which deepened as she saw the gaze of the strange man fixed upon her in bold and undisguised admiration. Her dress was of the neatest possible fit, and set off to advantage her finely moulded shape; a delicately formed hand and a trim foot and ankle were items of appearance that did not escape the quick eye of the trader, well used to run up at a glance the points of a fine female article.

"Well, Eliza?" said her master, as she stopped and looked hesitatingly at him.

"I was looking for Harry, please, sir"; and the boy bounded toward her, showing his spoils, which he had gathered in the skirt of his robe.

"Well, take him away, then," said Mr. Shelby; and hastily she withdrew, carrying the child on her arm.

"By Jupiter," said the trader, turning to him in admiration, "there's an article, now! You might make your fortune on that ar gal in Orleans, any day. I've seen over a thousand, in my day, paid down for gals not a bit handsomer."

"I don't want to make my fortune on her," said Mr. Shelby, dryly; and, seeking to turn the conversation, he uncorked a bottle of fresh wine, and asked his companion's opinion of it.

"Capital, sir—first chop!" said the trader; then turning, and slapping his hand familiarly on Shelby's shoulder, he added—

"Come, how will you trade about the gal? What shall I say for her—what'll you take?"

"Mr. Haley, she is not to be sold," said Shelby. "My wife would not part with her for her weight in gold."

"Ay, ay! women always say such things, cause they ha'nt no sort of calculation. Just show 'em how many watches, feathers, and trinkets, one's weight in gold would buy, and that alters the case, I reckon."

"I tell you, Haley, this must not be spoken of; I say no, and I mean no," said Shelby, decidedly.

"Well, you'll let me have the boy, though," said the trader; "you must own I've come down pretty handsomely for him."

"What on earth can you want with the child?" said Shelby.

"Why, I've got a friend that's going into this yer branch of the business—wants to buy up handsome boys to raise for the market. Fancy articles entirely—sell for waiters,[1] and so on, to rich 'uns, that can pay for handsome 'uns. It sets off one of yer great places—a real handsome boy to open door, wait, and tend. They fetch a good sum; and this little devil is such a comical, musical concern, he's just the article."

"I would rather not sell him," said Mr. Shelby, thoughtfully; "the fact is, sir, I'm a humane man, and I hate to take the boy from his mother, sir."

"O, you do? La! yes—something of that ar natur. I understand, perfectly. It is mighty onpleasant getting on with women, sometimes. I al'ays hates these yer screechin', screamin' times. They are *mighty* onpleasant; but, as I manages business, I generally avoids 'em, sir. Now, what if you get the girl off for a day, or a week, or so; then the thing's done quietly—all over before she comes home. Your wife might get her some earrings, or a new gown, or some such truck, to make up with her."

"I'm afraid not."

"Lor bless ye, yes! These critters an't like white folks, you know; they gets over things, only manage right. Now, they say," said Haley, assuming a candid and confidential air, "that this kind o' trade is hardening to the feelings; but I never found it so. Fact is, I never could do things up the way some fellers manage the business. I've seen 'em as would pull a woman's child out of her arms, and set him up to sell, and she screechin' like mad all the time; very bad policy—damages the article—makes 'em quite unfit for service sometimes. I knew a real handsome gal once, in Orleans, as was entirely ruined by this sort o' handling. The fellow that was trading for her didn't want her baby; and she was one of your real high sort, when her blood was up. I tell you, she squeezed up her child in her arms, and talked, and went on real awful. It kinder makes my blood run cold to think on't; and when they carried off the child, and locked her up, she jest went ravin' mad, and died in a week. Clear waste, sir, of a thousand dollars, just for want of management—there's where 't is. It's always best to do the humane thing, sir; that's been *my* experience." And the trader leaned back in his chair, and folded his arm, with an air of virtuous decision, apparently considering himself a second Wilberforce.[2]

The subject appeared to interest the gentleman deeply; for while Mr. Shelby was thoughtfully peeling an orange, Haley broke out afresh, with becoming diffidence, but as if actually driven by the force of truth to say a few words more.

"It don't look well, now, for a feller to be praisin' himself; but I say it jest because it's the truth. I believe I'm reckoned to bring in about the finest droves of niggers that is brought in—at least, I've been told so; if I have once, I reckon I have a hundred times—all in good case—fat and likely, and I lose as few as any man in the business. And I lays it all to my management, sir; and humanity, sir, I may say, is the great pillar of *my* management."

Mr. Shelby did not know what to say, and so he said, "Indeed!"

"Now, I've been laughed at for my notions, sir, and I've been talked to. They an't pop'lar, and they an't common; but I stuck to 'em, sir; I've stuck to 'em, and realized well on 'em; yes, sir, they have paid their passage, I may say," and the trader laughed at his joke.

There was something so piquant and original in these elucidations of humanity, that Mr. Shelby could not help laughing in company. Perhaps you laugh too, dear reader; but you know humanity comes out in a variety of strange forms now-a-days, and there is no end to the odd things that humane people will say and do.

Mr. Shelby's laugh encouraged the trader to proceed.

"It's strange, now, but I never could beat this into people's heads. Now, there was Tom Loker, my old partner, down in Natchez;[3] he was a clever fellow, Tom was, only the very devil with niggers—on principle 't was, you see, for a better hearted feller never broke bread; 't was his *system*, sir. I used to talk to Tom. 'Why, Tom,' I used to say, 'when your gals takes on and cry, what's the use o' crackin on 'em over the head, and knockin' on 'em round? It's ridiculous,' says I, 'and don't do no sort o' good. Why, I don't see no harm in their cryin',' says I; 'it's natur,' says I, 'and if natur can't blow off one way, it will another. Besides, Tom,' says

---

1   *waiters* Personal servants.

2   *Wilberforce* English politician and abolitionist William Wilberforce (1759–1833), a leading figure in the movement to end

British involvement in slavery and the slave trade; the Slavery Abolition Act of 1833 (which took effect in August, 1834) ended slavery in most of the British colonies.

3   *Natchez* City in Mississippi, an important center of plantation agriculture.

I, 'it jest spiles[1] your gals; they get sickly, and down in the mouth; and sometimes they gets ugly—particular yallow[2] gals do—and it's the devil and all gettin' on 'em broke in. Now,' says I, 'why can't you kinder coax 'em up, and speak 'em fair? Depend on it, Tom, a little humanity, thrown in along, goes a heap further than all your jawin' and crackin'; and it pays better,' says I, 'depend on't.' But Tom couldn't get the hang on 't; and he spiled so many for me, that I had to break off with him, though he was a good-hearted fellow, and as fair a business hand as is goin'."

"And do you find your ways of managing do the business better than Tom's?" said Mr. Shelby.

"Why, yes, sir, I may say so. You see, when I any ways can, I takes a leetle care about the onpleasant parts, like selling young uns and that—get the gals out of the way—out of sight, out of mind, you know—and when it's clean done, and can't be helped, they naturally gets used to it. 'Tan't, you know, as if it was white folks, that's brought up in the way of 'spectin' to keep their children and wives, and all that. Niggers, you know, that's fetched up properly, ha'n't no kind of 'spectations of no kind; so all these things comes easier."

"I'm afraid mine are not properly brought up, then," said Mr. Shelby.

"S'pose not; you Kentucky folks spile your niggers. You mean well by 'em, but 'tan't no real kindness, arter all. Now, a nigger, you see, what's got to be hacked and tumbled round the world, and sold to Tom, and Dick, and the Lord knows who, 'tan't no kindness to be givin' on him notions and expectations, and bringin' on him up too well, for the rough and tumble comes all the harder on him arter. Now, I venture to say, your niggers would be quite chop-fallen in a place where some of your plantation niggers would be singing and whooping like all possessed. Every man, you know, Mr. Shelby, naturally thinks well of his own ways; and I think I treat niggers just about as well as it's ever worthwhile to treat 'em."

"It's a happy thing to be satisfied," said Mr. Shelby, with a slight shrug, and some perceptible feelings of a disagreeable nature.

"Well," said Haley, after they had both silently picked their nuts for a season, "what do you say?"

"I'll think the matter over, and talk with my wife," said Mr. Shelby. "Meantime, Haley, if you want the matter carried on in the quiet way you speak of, you'd best not let your business in this neighborhood be known. It will get out among my boys, and it will not be a particularly quiet business getting away any of my fellows, if they know it, I'll promise you."

"O! certainly, by all means, mum! of course. But I'll tell you, I'm in a devil of a hurry, and shall want to know, as soon as possible, what I may depend on," said he, rising and putting on his overcoat.

"Well, call up this evening, between six and seven, and you shall have my answer," said Mr. Shelby, and the trader bowed himself out of the apartment.

"I'd like to have been able to kick the fellow down the steps," said he to himself, as he saw the door fairly closed, "with his impudent assurance; but he knows how much he has me at advantage. If anybody had ever said to me that I should sell Tom down south to one of those rascally traders, I should have said, 'Is thy servant a dog, that he should do this thing?'[3] And now it must come, for aught I see. And Eliza's child, too! I know that I shall have some fuss with wife about that; and, for that matter, about Tom, too. So much for being in debt—heigho! The fellow sees his advantage, and means to push it."

Perhaps the mildest form of the system of slavery is to be seen in the State of Kentucky. The general prevalence of agricultural pursuits of a quiet and gradual nature, not requiring those periodic seasons of hurry and pressure that are called for in the business of more southern districts, makes the task of the negro a more healthful and reasonable one; while the master, content with a more gradual style of acquisition, has not those temptations to hardheartedness which always overcome frail human nature when the prospect of sudden and rapid gain is weighed in the balance, with no heavier counterpoise than the interests of the helpless and unprotected.

Whoever visits some estates there, and witnesses the good-humored indulgence of some masters and mistresses, and the affectionate loyalty of some slaves, might be tempted to dream the oft-fabled poetic

---

1 *spiles* Spoils.

2 *yallow* Racial descriptor designating individuals of mixed racial ancestry with light brown skin.

---

3 *Is ... thing?* See 2 Kings 8.13: "But what, is thy servant a dog, that he should do this great thing?"

legend of a patriarchal institution,[1] and all that; but over and above the scene there broods a portentous shadow—the shadow of *law*. So long as the law considers all these human beings, with beating hearts and living affections, only as so many *things* belonging to a master—so long as the failure, or misfortune, or imprudence, or death of the kindest owner, may cause them any day to exchange a life of kind protection and indulgence for one of hopeless misery and toil—so long it is impossible to make anything beautiful or desirable in the best regulated administration of slavery.

Mr. Shelby was a fair average kind of man, good-natured and kindly, and disposed to easy indulgence of those around him, and there had never been a lack of anything which might contribute to the physical comfort of the negroes on his estate. He had, however, speculated largely and quite loosely; had involved himself deeply, and his notes[2] to a large amount had come into the hands of Haley; and this small piece of information is the key to the preceding conversation.

Now, it had so happened that, in approaching the door, Eliza had caught enough of the conversation to know that a trader was making offers to her master for somebody.

She would gladly have stopped at the door to listen, as she came out; but her mistress just then calling, she was obliged to hasten away.

Still she thought she heard the trader make an offer for her boy—could she be mistaken? Her heart swelled and throbbed, and she involuntarily strained him so tight that the little fellow looked up into her face in astonishment.

"Eliza, girl, what ails you today?" said her mistress, when Eliza had upset the wash-pitcher, knocked down the work-stand, and finally was abstractedly offering her mistress a long night-gown in place of the silk dress she had ordered her to bring from the wardrobe.

Eliza started. "O, missis!" she said, raising her eyes; then, bursting into tears, she sat down in a chair, and began sobbing.

"Why, Eliza, child! what ails you?" said her mistress.

"O! missis, missis," said Eliza, "there's been a trader talking with master in the parlor! I heard him."

"Well, silly child, suppose there has."

"O, missis, *do* you suppose mas'r would sell my Harry?" And the poor creature threw herself into a chair, and sobbed convulsively.

"Sell him! No, you foolish girl! You know your master never deals with those southern traders, and never means to sell any of his servants, as long as they behave well. Why, you silly child, who do you think would want to buy your Harry? Do you think all the world are set on him as you are, you goosie? Come, cheer up, and hook my dress. There now, put my back hair up in that pretty braid you learnt the other day, and don't go listening at doors anymore."

"Well, but, missis, *you* never would give your consent—to—to—"

"Nonsense, child! to be sure, I shouldn't. What do you talk so for? I would as soon have one of my own children sold. But really, Eliza, you are getting altogether too proud of that little fellow. A man can't put his nose into the door, but you think he must be coming to buy him."

Reassured by her mistress' confident tone, Eliza proceeded nimbly and adroitly with her toilet,[3] laughing at her own fears, as she proceeded.

Mrs. Shelby was a woman of a high class, both intellectually and morally. To that natural magnanimity and generosity of mind which one often marks as characteristic of the women of Kentucky, she added high moral and religious sensibility and principle, carried out with great energy and ability into practical results. Her husband, who made no professions to any particular religious character, nevertheless reverenced and respected the consistency of hers, and stood, perhaps, a little in awe of her opinion. Certain it was that he gave her unlimited scope in all her benevolent efforts for the comfort, instruction, and improvement of her servants, though he never took any decided part in them himself. In fact, if not exactly a believer in the doctrine of the efficiency of the extra good works of saints,[4] he really seemed somehow or other to fancy that his

---

1   *patriarchal institution*   I.e., an institution in which slaveowners are perceived as benevolent, fatherly figures.

2   *notes*   Documents outlining debt and repayment terms.

3   *toilet*   Dressing and personal grooming.

4   *the doctrine ... of saints*   Reference to the belief held by Catholics and some other Christians that the good works of the saints have direct benefits for the souls of the living (the importance of earthly "good works" was generally held in low esteem by nineteenth-century Calvinists in comparison with the inner quality of grace).

wife had piety and benevolence enough for two—to indulge a shadowy expectation of getting into heaven through her superabundance of qualities to which he made no particular pretension.

The heaviest load on his mind, after his conversation with the trader, lay in the foreseen necessity of breaking to his wife the arrangement contemplated—meeting the importunities and opposition which he knew he should have reason to encounter.

Mrs. Shelby, being entirely ignorant of her husband's embarrassments,[1] and knowing only the general kindliness of his temper, had been quite sincere in the entire incredulity with which she had met Eliza's suspicions. In fact, she dismissed the matter from her mind, without a second thought; and being occupied in preparations for an evening visit, it passed out of her thoughts entirely.

[The following chapters introduce the reader further to the novel's enslaved characters, including Uncle Tom and his wife Aunt Chloe, their children Pete and Mose, and Eliza's husband George Harris, who is enslaved on a neighboring plantation under a cruel master. Also introduced is young Master George, the Shelbys' son, a good-natured boy who enjoys spending his time at Uncle Tom's cabin. George Harris reveals to Eliza that he intends on escaping to Canada, with the hope of eventually purchasing Eliza and Harry their freedom. Meanwhile, Mr. Shelby reluctantly signs a contract selling Harry and Tom to the trader Haley.]

CHAPTER 5
SHOWING THE FEELINGS OF LIVING PROPERTY ON CHANGING OWNERS

Mr. and Mrs. Shelby had retired to their apartment for the night. He was lounging in a large easy-chair, looking over some letters that had come in the afternoon mail, and she was standing before her mirror, brushing out the complicated braids and curls in which Eliza had arranged her hair; for, noticing her pale cheeks and haggard eyes, she had excused her attendance that night, and ordered her to bed. The employment, naturally enough, suggested her conversation with the girl

in the morning; and, turning to her husband, she said, carelessly,

"By the by, Arthur, who was that low-bred fellow that you lugged in to our dinner-table today?"

"Haley is his name," said Shelby, turning himself rather uneasily in his chair, and continuing with his eyes fixed on a letter.

"Haley! Who is he, and what may be his business here, pray?"

"Well, he's a man that I transacted some business with, last time I was at Natchez," said Mr. Shelby.

"And he presumed on it to make himself quite at home, and call and dine here, ay?"

"Why, I invited him; I had some accounts with him," said Shelby.

"Is he a negro-trader?" said Mrs. Shelby, noticing a certain embarrassment in her husband's manner.

"Why, my dear, what put that into your head?" said Shelby, looking up.

"Nothing—only Eliza came in here, after dinner, in a great worry, crying and taking on, and said you were talking with a trader, and that she heard him make an offer for her boy—the ridiculous little goose!"

"She did, hey?" said Mr. Shelby, returning to his paper, which he seemed for a few moments quite intent upon, not perceiving that he was holding it bottom upwards.

"It will have to come out," said he, mentally; "as well now as ever."

"I told Eliza," said Mrs. Shelby, as she continued brushing her hair, "that she was a little fool for her pains, and that you never had anything to do with that sort of persons. Of course, I knew you never meant to sell any of our people—least of all, to such a fellow."

"Well, Emily," said her husband, "so I have always felt and said; but the fact is that my business lies so that I cannot get on without. I shall have to sell some of my hands."

"To that creature? Impossible! Mr. Shelby, you cannot be serious."

"I'm sorry to say that I am," said Mr. Shelby. "I've agreed to sell Tom."

"What! our Tom? that good, faithful creature! been your faithful servant from a boy! O, Mr. Shelby! and you have promised him his freedom, too—you and I have spoken to him a hundred times of it. Well, I

---

1 *embarrassments* Financial difficulties.

can believe anything now—I can believe *now* that you could sell little Harry, poor Eliza's only child!" said Mrs. Shelby, in a tone between grief and indignation.

"Well, since you must know all, it is so. I have agreed to sell Tom and Harry both; and I don't know why I am to be rated as if I were a monster for doing what everyone does every day."

"But why, of all others, choose these?" said Mrs. Shelby. "Why sell them, of all on the place, if you must sell at all?"

"Because they will bring the highest sum of any— that's why. I could choose another, if you say so. The fellow made me a high bid on Eliza, if that would suit you any better," said Mr. Shelby.

"The wretch!" said Mrs. Shelby, vehemently.

"Well, I didn't listen to it, a moment—out of regard to your feelings, I wouldn't—so give me some credit."

"My dear," said Mrs. Shelby, recollecting herself, "forgive me. I have been hasty. I was surprised, and entirely unprepared for this—but surely you will allow me to intercede for these poor creatures. Tom is a noble-hearted, faithful fellow, if he is black. I do believe, Mr. Shelby, that if he were put to it, he would lay down his life for you."

"I know it, I dare say; but what's the use of all this? I can't help myself."

"Why not make a pecuniary sacrifice? I'm willing to bear my part of the inconvenience. O, Mr. Shelby, I have tried—tried most faithfully, as a Christian woman should—to do my duty to these poor, simple, dependent creatures. I have cared for them, instructed them, watched over them, and known all their little cares and joys, for years; and how can I ever hold up my head again among them if, for the sake of a little paltry gain, we sell such a faithful, excellent, confiding creature as poor Tom, and tear from him in a moment all we have taught him to love and value? I have taught them the duties of the family, of parent and child, and husband and wife; and how can I bear to have this open acknowledgement that we care for no tie, no duty, no relation, however sacred, compared with money? I have talked with Eliza about her boy—her duty to him as a Christian mother, to watch over him, pray for him, and bring him up in a Christian way; and now what can I say, if you tear him away, and sell him, soul and body, to a profane, unprincipled man,

just to save a little money? I have told her that one soul is worth more than all the money in the world; and how will she believe me when she sees us turn round and sell her child? sell him, perhaps, to certain ruin of body and soul!"

"I'm sorry you feel so about it, Emily—indeed I am," said Mr. Shelby; "and I respect your feelings, too, though I don't pretend to share them to their full extent; but I tell you now, solemnly, it's of no use—I can't help myself. I didn't mean to tell you this, Emily; but, in plain words, there is no choice between selling these two and selling everything. Either they must go, or *all* must. Haley has come into possession of a mortgage, which, if I don't clear off with him directly, will take everything before it. I've raked, and scraped, and borrowed, and all but begged—and the price of these two was needed to make up the balance, and I had to give them up. Haley fancied the child; he agreed to settle the matter that way, and no other. I was in his power, and *had* to do it. If you feel so to have them sold, would it be any better to have *all* sold?"

Mrs. Shelby stood like one stricken. Finally, turning to her toilet, she rested her face in her hands, and gave a sort of groan.

"This is God's curse on slavery! a bitter, bitter, most accursed thing! a curse to the master and a curse to the slave! I was a fool to think I could make anything good out of such a deadly evil. It is a sin to hold a slave under laws like ours—I always felt it was—I always thought so when I was a girl—I thought so still more after I joined the church; but I thought I could gild it over—I thought, by kindness, and care, and instruction, I could make the condition of mine better than freedom—fool that I was!"

"Why, wife, you are getting to be an abolitionist, quite."

"Abolitionist! if they knew all I know about slavery, they *might* talk! We don't need them to tell us; you know I never thought that slavery was right—never felt willing to own slaves."

"Well, therein you differ from many wise and pious men," said Mr. Shelby. "You remember Mr. B.'s sermon, the other Sunday?"

"I don't want to hear such sermons; I never wish to hear Mr. B. in our church again. Ministers can't help the evil, perhaps—can't cure it, any more than we can—but defend it! it always went against my common sense. And I think you didn't think much of that sermon, either."

"Well," said Shelby, "I must say these ministers sometimes carry matters further than we poor sinners would exactly dare to do. We men of the world must wink pretty hard at various things, and get used to a deal that isn't the exact thing. But we don't quite fancy, when women and ministers come out broad and square, and go beyond us in matters of either modesty or morals, that's a fact. But now, my dear, I trust you see the necessity of the thing, and you see that I have done the very best that circumstances would allow."

"O yes, yes!" said Mrs. Shelby, hurriedly and abstractedly fingering her gold watch, "I haven't any jewelry of any amount," she added, thoughtfully; "but would not this watch do something? it was an expensive one, when it was bought. If I could only at least save Eliza's child, I would sacrifice anything I have."

"I'm sorry, very sorry, Emily," said Mr. Shelby, "I'm sorry this takes hold of you so; but it will do no good. The fact is, Emily, the thing's done; the bills of sale are already signed, and in Haley's hands; and you must be thankful it is no worse. That man has had it in his power to ruin us all—and now he is fairly off. If you knew the man as I do, you'd think that we had had a narrow escape."

"Is he so hard, then?"

"Why, not a cruel man, exactly, but a man of leather—a man alive to nothing but trade and profit—cool, and unhesitating, and unrelenting, as death and the grave. He'd sell his own mother at a good percentage—not wishing the old woman any harm, either."

"And this wretch owns that good, faithful Tom, and Eliza's child!"

"Well, my dear, the fact is that this goes rather hard with me; it's a thing I hate to think of. Haley wants to drive matters, and take possession tomorrow. I'm going to get out my horse bright and early, and be off. I can't see Tom, that's a fact; and you had better arrange a drive somewhere, and carry Eliza off. Let the thing be done when she is out of sight."

"No, no," said Mrs. Shelby; "I'll be in no sense accomplice or help in this cruel business. I'll go and see poor old Tom, God help him, in his distress! They shall see, at any rate, that their mistress can feel for and with

them. As to Eliza, I dare not think about it. The Lord forgive us! What have we done, that this cruel necessity should come on us?"

There was one listener to this conversation whom Mr. and Mrs. Shelby little suspected.

Communicating with their apartment was a large closet, opening by a door into the outer passage. When Mrs. Shelby had dismissed Eliza for the night, her feverish and excited mind had suggested the idea of this closet; and she had hidden herself there, and, with her ear pressed close against the crack of the door, had not lost a word of the conversation.

When the voices died into silence, she rose and crept stealthily away. Pale, shivering, with rigid features and compressed lips, she looked an entirely altered being from the soft and timid creature she had been hitherto. She moved cautiously along the entry, paused one moment at her mistress' door, and raised her hands in mute appeal to Heaven, and then turned and glided into her own room. It was a quiet, neat apartment, on the same floor with her mistress. There was the pleasant sunny window, where she had often sat singing at her sewing; there a little case of books, and various little fancy articles, ranged by them, the gifts of Christmas holidays; there was her simple wardrobe in the closet and in the drawers: here was, in short, her home; and, on the whole, a happy one it had been to her. But there, on the bed, lay her slumbering boy, his long curls falling negligently around his unconscious face, his rosy mouth half open, his little fat hands thrown out over the bedclothes, and a smile spread like a sunbeam over his whole face.

"Poor boy! poor fellow!" said Eliza; "they have sold you! but your mother will save you yet!"

No tear dropped over that pillow; in such straits as these, the heart has no tears to give—it drops only blood, bleeding itself away in silence. She took a piece of paper and a pencil, and wrote, hastily,

"O, Missis! dear Missis! don't think me ungrateful—don't think hard of me, any way—I heard all you and master said tonight. I am going to try to save my boy—you will not blame me! God bless and reward you for all your kindness!"

Hastily folding and directing this, she went to a drawer and made up a little package of clothing for her boy, which she tied with a handkerchief firmly round her waist; and, so fond is a mother's remembrance, that, even in the terrors of that hour, she did not forget to put in the little package one or two of his favorite toys, reserving a gayly painted parrot to amuse him, when she should be called on to awaken him. It was some trouble to arouse the little sleeper; but, after some effort, he sat up, and was playing with his bird, while his mother was putting on her bonnet and shawl.

"Where are you going, mother?" said he, as she drew near the bed, with his little coat and cap.

His mother drew near, and looked so earnestly into his eyes, that he at once divined that something unusual was the matter.

"Hush, Harry," she said; "mustn't speak loud, or they will hear us. A wicked man was coming to take little Harry away from his mother, and carry him 'way off in the dark; but mother won't let him—she's going to put on her little boy's cap and coat, and run off with him, so the ugly man can't catch him."

Saying these words, she had tied and buttoned on the child's simple outfit, and, taking him in her arms, she whispered to him to be very still; and, opening a door in her room which led into the outer verandah, she glided noiselessly out.

It was a sparkling, frosty, starlight night, and the mother wrapped the shawl close round her child, as, perfectly quiet with vague terror, he clung round her neck.

Old Bruno, a great Newfoundland who slept at the end of the porch, rose, with a low groan, as she came near. She gently spoke his name, and the animal, an old pet and playmate of hers, instantly, wagging his tail, prepared to follow her, though apparently revolving much, in his simple dog's head, what such an indiscreet midnight promenade might mean. Some dim ideas of imprudence or impropriety in the measure seemed to embarrass him considerably; for he often stopped, as Eliza glided forward, and looked wistfully, first at her and then at the house, and then, as if reassured by reflection, he pattered along after her again. A few minutes brought them to the window of Uncle Tom's cottage, and Eliza, stopping, tapped lightly on the window-pane.

The prayer-meeting at Uncle Tom's had, in the order of hymn-singing, been protracted to a very late hour; and, as Uncle Tom had indulged himself in a few lengthy solos afterwards, the consequence was, that, although it was now between twelve and one o'clock, he and his worthy helpmeet were not yet asleep.

"Good Lord! what's that?" said Aunt Chloe, starting up and hastily drawing the curtain. "My sakes alive, if it an't Lizy! Get on your clothes, old man, quick! there's old Bruno, too, a pawin' round; what on airth! I'm gwine to open the door."

And, suiting the action to the word, the door flew open, and the light of the tallow candle, which Tom had hastily lighted, fell on the haggard face and dark, wild eyes of the fugitive.

"Lord bless you! I'm skeered to look at ye, Lizy! Are ye tuck[1] sick, or what's come over ye?"

"I'm running away—Uncle Tom and Aunt Chloe—carrying off my child—Master sold him!"

"Sold him?" echoed both, lifting up their hands in dismay.

"Yes, sold him!" said Eliza, firmly; "I crept into the closet by Mistress' door tonight, and I heard Master tell Missis that he had sold my Harry, and you, Uncle Tom, both, to a trader; and that he was going off this morning on his horse, and that the man was to take possession today."

Tom had stood, during this speech, with his hands raised, and his eyes dilated, like a man in a dream. Slowly and gradually, as its meaning came over him, he collapsed, rather than seated himself, on his old chair, and sunk his head down upon his knees.

"The good Lord have pity on us!" said Aunt Chloe. "O! it don't seem as if it was true! What has he done, that Mas'r should sell *him*?"

"He hasn't done anything—it isn't for that. Master don't want to sell; and Missis—she's always good. I heard her plead and beg for us; but he told her 'twas no use; that he was in this man's debt, and that this man had got the power over him; and that if he didn't pay him off clear, it would end in his having to sell the place and all the people, and move off. Yes, I heard him say there was no choice between selling these two and selling all, the man was driving him so hard. Master said he was sorry; but oh, Missis—you ought to have heard her talk! If she an't a Christian and an angel, there never was one. I'm a wicked girl to leave her so; but, then, I can't help it. She said, herself, one soul

---

[1] *tuck* Took; taken.

was worth more than the world; and this boy has a soul, and if I let him be carried off, who knows what'll become of it? It must be right: but, if it an't right, the Lord forgive me, for I can't help doing it!"

"Well, old man!" said Aunt Chloe, "why don't you go, too? Will you wait to be toted down river, where they kill niggers with hard work and starving? I'd a heap rather die than go there, any day! There's time for ye—be off with Lizy—you've got a pass to come and go any time.[1] Come, bustle up, and I'll get your things together."

Tom slowly raised his head, and looked sorrowfully but quietly around, and said,

"No, no—I an't going. Let Eliza go—it's her right! I wouldn't be the one to say no—'tan't in *natur* for her to stay; but you heard what she said! If I must be sold, or all the people on the place, and everything go to rack, why, let me be sold. I s'pose I can b'ar it as well as any on 'em," he added, while something like a sob and a sigh shook his broad, rough chest convulsively. "Mas'r always found me on the spot—he always will. I never have broke trust, nor used my pass no ways contrary to my word, and I never will. It's better for me alone to go, than to break up the place and sell all. Mas'r an't to blame, Chloe, and he'll take care of you and the poor—"

Here he turned to the rough trundle-bed full of little woolly heads, and broke fairly down. He leaned over the back of the chair, and covered his face with his large hands. Sobs, heavy, hoarse and loud, shook the chair, and great tears fell through his fingers on the floor: just such tears, sir, as you dropped into the coffin where lay your first-born son; such tears, woman, as you shed when you heard the cries of your dying babe. For, sir, he was a man—and you are but another man. And, woman, though dressed in silk and jewels, you are but a woman, and, in life's great straits and mighty griefs, ye feel but one sorrow!

"And now," said Eliza, as she stood in the door, "I saw my husband only this afternoon, and I little knew then what was to come. They have pushed him to the very last standing-place, and he told me, today, that he was going to run away. Do try, if you can, to get word

to him. Tell him how I went, and why I went; and tell him I'm going to try and find Canada. You must give my love to him, and tell him, if I never see him again,"—she turned away, and stood with her back to them for a moment, and then added, in a husky voice, "tell him to be as good as he can, and try and meet me in the kingdom of heaven."

"Call Bruno in there," she added. "Shut the door on him, poor beast! He mustn't go with me!"

A few last words and tears, a few simple adieus and blessings, and, clasping her wondering and affrighted child in her arms, she glided noiselessly away.

Chapter 7
The Mother's Struggle

It is impossible to conceive of a human creature more wholly desolate and forlorn than Eliza, when she turned her footsteps from Uncle Tom's cabin.

Her husband's suffering and dangers, and the danger of her child, all blended in her mind, with a confused and stunning sense of the risk she was running, in leaving the only home she had ever known, and cutting loose from the protection of a friend whom she loved and revered. Then there was the parting from every familiar object—the place where she had grown up, the trees under which she had played, the groves where she had walked many an evening in happier days, by the side of her young husband—everything, as it lay in the clear, frosty starlight, seemed to speak reproachfully to her, and ask her whither could she go from a home like that?

But stronger than all was maternal love, wrought into a paroxysm of frenzy by the near approach of a fearful danger. Her boy was old enough to have walked by her side, and, in an indifferent case, she would only have led him by the hand; but now the bare thought of putting him out of her arms made her shudder, and she strained him to her bosom with a convulsive grasp, as she went rapidly forward.

The frosty ground creaked beneath her feet, and she trembled at the sound; every quaking leaf and fluttering shadow sent the blood backward to her heart, and quickened her footsteps. She wondered within herself at the strength that seemed to be come upon her; for she felt the weight of her boy as if it had been a feather,

---

[1]   *you've got ... any time*   In order to travel on their own, enslaved persons often required written documents from their enslavers, granting them permission to do so.

and every flutter of fear seemed to increase the supernatural power that bore her on, while from her pale lips burst forth, in frequent ejaculations,[1] the prayer to a Friend above—"Lord, help! Lord, save me!"

If it were *your* Harry, mother, or your Willie, that were going to be torn from you by a brutal trader, tomorrow morning—if you had seen the man, and heard that the papers were signed and delivered, and you had only from twelve o'clock till morning to make good your escape—how fast could *you* walk? How many miles could you make in those few brief hours, with the darling at your bosom—the little sleepy head on your shoulder—the small, soft arms trustingly holding on to your neck?

For the child slept. At first, the novelty and alarm kept him waking; but his mother so hurriedly repressed every breath or sound, and so assured him that if he were only still she would certainly save him, that he clung quietly round her neck, only asking, as he found himself sinking to sleep,

"Mother, I don't need to keep awake, do I?"

"No, my darling; sleep, if you want to."

"But, mother, if I do get asleep, you won't let him get me?"

"No! so may God help me!" said his mother, with a paler cheek, and a brighter light in her large dark eyes.

"You're *sure*, an't you, mother?"

"Yes, *sure*!" said the mother, in a voice that startled herself; for it seemed to her to come from a spirit within, that was no part of her; and the boy dropped his little weary head on her shoulder, and was soon asleep. How the touch of those warm arms, the gentle breathings that came in her neck, seemed to add fire and spirit to her movements! It seemed to her as if strength poured into her in electric streams, from every gentle touch and movement of the sleeping, confiding child. Sublime is the dominion of the mind over the body, that, for a time, can make flesh and nerve impregnable, and string the sinews like steel, so that the weak become so mighty.

The boundaries of the farm, the grove, the wood-lot, passed by her dizzily, as she walked on; and still she went, leaving one familiar object after another, slacking not, pausing not, till reddening daylight found her

many a long mile from all traces of any familiar objects upon the open highway.

She had often been, with her mistress, to visit some connections, in the little village of T——, not far from the Ohio River, and knew the road well. To go thither, to escape across the Ohio River, were the first hurried outlines of her plan of escape; beyond that, she could only hope in God.

When horses and vehicles began to move along the highway, with that alert perception peculiar to a state of excitement, and which seems to be a sort of inspiration, she became aware that her headlong pace and distracted air might bring on her remark and suspicion. She therefore put the boy on the ground and, adjusting her dress and bonnet, she walked on at as rapid a pace as she thought consistent with the preservation of appearances. In her little bundle she had provided a store of cakes[2] and apples, which she used as expedients for quickening the speed of the child, rolling the apple some yards before them, when the boy would run with all his might after it; and this ruse, often repeated, carried them over many a half-mile.

After a while, they came to a thick patch of woodland, through which murmured a clear brook. As the child complained of hunger and thirst, she climbed over the fence with him; and, sitting down behind a large rock which concealed them from the road, she gave him a breakfast out of her little package. The boy wondered and grieved that she could not eat; and when, putting his arms round her neck, he tried to wedge some of his cake into her mouth, it seemed to her that the rising in her throat would choke her.

"No, no, Harry darling! mother can't eat till you are safe! We must go on—on—till we come to the river!" And she hurried again into the road, and again constrained herself to walk regularly and composedly forward.

She was many miles past any neighborhood where she was personally known. If she should chance to meet any who knew her, she reflected that the well-known kindness of the family would be of itself a blind to suspicion, as making it an unlikely supposition that she could be a fugitive. As she was also so white as not to be known as of colored lineage, without a critical

---

[1]   *ejaculations* Outbursts; exclamations.

[2]   *cakes* Likely including leavened breads, corn cakes, and fruit cakes rather than confections.

survey, and her child was white also, it was much easier for her to pass on unsuspected.

On this presumption, she stopped at noon at a neat farmhouse, to rest herself, and buy some dinner for her child and self; for, as the danger decreased with the distance, the supernatural tension of the nervous system lessened, and she found herself both weary and hungry.

The good woman, kindly and gossiping, seemed rather pleased than otherwise with having somebody come in to talk with; and accepted, without examination, Eliza's statement, that she "was going on a little piece, to spend a week with her friends,"—all which she hoped in her heart might prove strictly true.

An hour before sunset, she entered the village of T——, by the Ohio River, weary and foot-sore, but still strong in heart. Her first glance was at the river, which lay, like Jordan, between her and the Canaan[1] of liberty on the other side.

It was now early spring, and the river was swollen and turbulent; great cakes of floating ice were swinging heavily to and fro in the turbid waters. Owing to the peculiar form of the shore on the Kentucky side, the land bending far out into the water, the ice had been lodged and detained in great quantities, and the narrow channel which swept round the bend was full of ice, piled one cake over another, thus forming a temporary barrier to the descending ice, which lodged, and formed a great, undulating raft, filling up the whole river, and extending almost to the Kentucky shore.

Eliza stood, for a moment, contemplating this unfavorable aspect of things, which she saw at once must prevent the usual ferry-boat from running, and then turned into a small public house[2] on the bank, to make a few inquiries.

The hostess, who was busy in various fizzing and stewing operations over the fire, preparatory to the evening meal, stopped, with a fork in her hand, as Eliza's sweet and plaintive voice arrested her.

"What is it?" she said.

"Isn't there any ferry or boat, that takes people over to B——, now?" she said.

"No, indeed!" said the woman; "the boats has stopped running."

Eliza's look of dismay and disappointment struck the woman, and she said, inquiringly,

"Maybe you're wanting to get over? anybody sick? Ye seem mighty anxious?"

"I've got a child that's very dangerous,"[3] said Eliza. "I never heard of it till last night, and I've walked quite a piece today, in hopes to get to the ferry."

"Well, now, that's onlucky," said the woman, whose motherly sympathies were much aroused; "I'm re'lly consarned for ye. Solomon!" she called, from the window, towards a small back building. A man, in leather apron and very dirty hands, appeared at the door.

"I say, Sol," said the woman, "is that ar man going to tote them bar'ls over tonight?"

"He said he should try, if 't was any way prudent," said the man.

"There's a man a piece down here, that's going over with some truck[4] this evening, if he durs' to; he'll be in here to supper tonight, so you'd better set down and wait. That's a sweet little fellow," added the woman, offering him a cake.

But the child, wholly exhausted, cried with weariness.

"Poor fellow! he isn't used to walking, and I've hurried him on so," said Eliza.

"Well, take him into this room," said the woman, opening into a small bedroom, where stood a comfortable bed. Eliza laid the weary boy upon it, and held his hands in hers till he was fast asleep. For her there was no rest. As a fire in her bones, the thought of the pursuer urged her on; and she gazed with longing eyes on the sullen, surging waters that lay between her and liberty.

Here we must take our leave of her for the present, to follow the course of her pursuers.

———

Though Mrs. Shelby had promised that the dinner should be hurried on table, yet it was soon seen, as the

1   *like Jordan … Canaan* In the Old Testament, Canaan is a prosperous region west of the Jordan River that is promised by God to the Israelites after their liberation from slavery in Egypt. "Crossing Jordan" became a widespread metaphor for escaping from slavery.

2   *public house* Business providing food, drink, and often accommodation.

3   *dangerous* I.e., dangerously ill.

4   *truck* Goods for transport.

thing has often been seen before, that it required more than one to make a bargain. So, although the order was fairly given out in Haley's hearing, and carried to Aunt Chloe by at least half a dozen juvenile messengers, that dignitary only gave certain very gruff snorts, and tosses of her head, and went on with every operation in an unusually leisurely and circumstantial manner.

For some singular reason, an impression seemed to reign among the servants generally that Missis would not be particularly disobliged by delay; and it was wonderful what a number of counter accidents occurred constantly, to retard the course of things. One luckless wight contrived to upset the gravy; and then gravy had to be got up *de novo*,[1] with due care and formality, Aunt Chloe watching and stirring with dogged precision, answering shortly, to all suggestions of haste, that she "warn't a going to have raw gravy on the table, to help nobody's catchings." One tumbled down with the water, and had to go to the spring for more; and another precipitated the butter into the path of events; and there was from time to time giggling news brought into the kitchen that "Mas'r Haley was mighty oneasy, and that he couldn't sit in his cheer no ways, but was a walkin' and stalkin' to the winders and through the porch."

"Sarves him right!" said Aunt Chloe, indignantly. "He'll get wus nor oneasy,[2] one of these days, if he don't mend his ways. *His* master'll be sending for him, and then see how he'll look!"

"He'll go to torment, and no mistake," said little Jake.

"He desarves it!" said Aunt Chloe, grimly; "he's broke a many, many, many hearts—I tell ye all!" she said, stopping, with a fork uplifted in her hands; "it's like what Mas'r George reads in Ravelations—souls a callin' under the altar! and a callin' on the Lord for vengeance on sich! and by and by the Lord he'll hear 'em—so he will!"[3]

Aunt Chloe, who was much revered in the kitchen, was listened to with open mouth; and, the dinner being now fairly sent in, the whole kitchen was at leisure to gossip with her, and to listen to her remarks.

"Sich'll be burnt up forever, and no mistake; won't ther?" said Andy.

"I'd be glad to see it, I'll be boun'," said little Jake.

"Chil'en!" said a voice, that made them all start. It was Uncle Tom, who had come in, and stood listening to the conversation at the door.

"Chil'en!" he said, "I'm afeard you don't know what ye're sayin'. Forever is a *dre'ful* word, chil'en; it's awful to think on't. You oughtenter wish that ar to any human crittur."

"We wouldn't to anybody but the soul-drivers,"[4] said Andy; "nobody can help wishing it to them, they's so awful wicked."

"Don't natur herself kinder cry out on em?" said Aunt Chloe. "Don't dey tear der suckin' baby right off his mother's breast, and sell him, and der little children as is crying and holding on by her clothes—don't dey pull 'em off and sells em? Don't dey tear wife and husband apart?" said Aunt Chloe, beginning to cry, "when it's jest takin' the very life on 'em? and all the while does they feel one bit—don't dey drink and smoke, and take it oncommon easy? Lor, if the devil don't get them, what's he good for?" And Aunt Chloe covered her face with her checked apron, and began to sob in good earnest.

"Pray for them that 'spitefully use you, the good book says,"[5] says Tom.

"Pray for 'em!" said Aunt Chloe; "Lor, it's too tough! I can't pray for 'em."

"It's natur, Chloe, and natur's strong," said Tom, "but the Lord's grace is stronger; besides, you oughter think what an awful state a poor crittur's soul's in that'll do them ar things—you oughter thank God that you an't *like* him, Chloe. I'm sure I'd rather be sold, ten thousand times over, than to have all that ar poor crittur's got to answer for."

---

[1]   *wight* Creature; person;   *de novo* Latin: once again.

[2]   *wus nor oneasy* I.e., worse than uneasy.

[3]   *it's like ... he will!"* See Revelation 6.9–10, in which Christ opens the seven seals of a book, instigating the beginning of the Apocalypse: "And when he had opened the fifth seal, I saw under the altar the souls of them that were slain for the word of God, and for the testimony which they held: / And they cried with a loud voice, saying, How long, O Lord, holy and true, dost thou not judge and avenge our blood on them that dwell on the earth?"

[4]   *soul-drivers* Phrase commonly used to refer either to slave traders or to plantation overseers.

[5]   *Pray for ... book says* See Matthew 5.44: "But I say unto you, Love your enemies, bless them that curse you, do good to them that hate you, and pray for them which despitefully use you, and persecute you," and Luke 6.28: "Bless them that curse you, and pray for them which despitefully use you."

"So'd I, a heap," said Jake. "Lor, *shouldn't* we cotch it, Andy?"

Andy shrugged his shoulders, and gave an acquiescent whistle.

"I'm glad Mas'r didn't go off this morning, as he looked to," said Tom; "that ar hurt me more than sellin', it did. Mebbe it might have been natural for him, but 't would have come desp't hard on me, as has known him from a baby; but I've seen Mas'r, and I begin ter feel sort o' reconciled to the Lord's will now. Mas'r couldn't help hisself; he did right, but I'm feared things will be kinder goin' to rack,[1] when I'm gone. Mas'r can't be spected to be a pryin' round everywhar, as I've done, a keepin' up all the ends. The boys all means well, but they's powerful car'less. That ar troubles me."

The bell here rang, and Tom was summoned to the parlor.

"Tom," said his master, kindly, "I want you to notice that I give this gentleman bonds to forfeit a thousand dollars if you are not on the spot when he wants you; he's going today to look after his other business, and you can have the day to yourself. Go anywhere you like, boy."

"Thank you, Mas'r," said Tom.

"And mind yerself," said the trader, "and don't come it over your master with any o' yer nigger tricks; for I'll take every cent out of him, if you an't thar. If he'd hear to me, he wouldn't trust any on ye—slippery as eels!"

"Mas'r," said Tom—and he stood very straight—"I was jist eight years old when ole Missis put you into my arms, and you wasn't a year old. 'Thar,' says she, 'Tom, that's to be *your* young Mas'r; take good care on him,' says she. And now I jist ask you, Mas'r, have I ever broke word to you, or gone contrary to you, 'specially since I was a Christian?"

Mr. Shelby was fairly overcome, and the tears rose to his eyes.

"My good boy," said he, "the Lord knows you say but the truth; and if I was able to help it, all the world shouldn't buy you."

"And sure as I am a Christian woman," said Mrs. Shelby, "you shall be redeemed as soon as I can any way bring together means. Sir," she said to Haley, "take good account of who you sell him to, and let me know."

"Lor, yes, for that matter," said the trader, "I may bring him up in a year, not much the wuss for wear, and trade him back."

"I'll trade with you then, and make it for your advantage," said Mrs. Shelby.

"Of course," said the trader, "all's equal with me; li'ves trade 'em up as down, so I does a good business. All I want is a livin', you know, ma'am; that's all any on us wants, I s'pose."

Mr. and Mrs. Shelby both felt annoyed and degraded by the familiar[2] impudence of the trader, and yet both saw the absolute necessity of putting a constraint on their feelings. The more hopelessly sordid and insensible he appeared, the greater became Mrs. Shelby's dread of his succeeding in recapturing Eliza and her child, and of course the greater her motive for detaining him by every female artifice. She therefore graciously smiled, assented, chatted familiarly, and did all she could to make time pass imperceptibly.

At two o'clock Sam and Andy[3] brought the horses up to the posts, apparently greatly refreshed and invigorated by the scamper of the morning.

Sam was there new oiled from dinner, with an abundance of zealous and ready officiousness. As Haley approached, he was boasting, in flourishing style, to Andy, of the evident and eminent success of the operation, now that he had "farly come to it."

"Your master, I s'pose, don't keep no dogs," said Haley, thoughtfully, as he prepared to mount.

"Heaps on 'em," said Sam, triumphantly; "thar's Bruno—he's a roarer! and, besides that, 'bout every nigger of us keeps a pup of some natur or uther."

"Poh!" said Haley—and he said something else, too, with regard to the said dogs, at which Sam muttered,

"I don't see no use cussin' on 'em, no way."

"But your master don't keep no dogs (I pretty much know he don't) for trackin' out niggers."

Sam knew exactly what he meant, but he kept on a look of earnest and desperate simplicity.

"Our dogs all smells round considable sharp. I spect they's the kind, though they han't never had no practice. They's *far* dogs, though, at most anything, if you'd get 'em started. Here, Bruno," he called, whistling to

1 *rack* Wreck.

2 *familiar* Inappropriately informal.

3 *Sam and Andy* Two other men enslaved by the Shelbys, commanded by Mr. Shelby to aid Haley in finding Eliza.

the lumbering Newfoundland, who came pitching tumultuously toward them.

"You go hang!" said Haley, getting up. "Come, tumble up now."

Sam tumbled up accordingly, dexterously contriving to tickle Andy as he did so, which occasioned Andy to split out into a laugh, greatly to Haley's indignation, who made a cut at him with his riding-whip.

"I's 'stonished at yer, Andy," said Sam, with awful gravity. "This yer's a seris bisness, Andy. Yer mustn't be a makin' game. This yer an't no way to help Mas'r."

"I shall take the straight road to the river," said Haley, decidedly, after they had come to the boundaries of the estate. "I know the way of all of 'em—they makes tracks for the underground."[1]

"Sartin," said Sam, "dat's de idee. Mas'r Haley hits de thing right in de middle. Now, der's two roads to de river—de dirt road and der pike[2]—which Mas'r mean to take?"

Andy looked up innocently at Sam, surprised at hearing this new geographical fact, but instantly confirmed what he said, by a vehement reiteration.

"Cause," said Sam, "I'd rather be 'clined to 'magine that Lizy'd take de dirt road, bein' it's the least travelled."

Haley, notwithstanding that he was a very old bird, and naturally inclined to be suspicious of chaff,[3] was rather brought up by this view of the case.

"If yer warn't both on yer such cussed liars, now!" he said, contemplatively, as he pondered a moment.

The pensive, reflective tone in which this was spoken appeared to amuse Andy prodigiously, and he drew a little behind, and shook so as apparently to run a great risk of falling off his horse, while Sam's face was immovably composed into the most doleful gravity.

"Course," said Sam, "Mas'r can do as he'd ruther; go de straight road, if Mas'r thinks best—it's all one to us. Now, when I study 'pon it, I think de straight road de best, *decidedly*."

"She would naturally go a lonesome way," said Haley, thinking aloud, and not minding Sam's remark.

"Dar an't no sayin'," said Sam; "gals is pecular; they never does nothin' ye thinks they will; mose gen'lly the contrar. Gals is nat'lly made contrary; and so, if you thinks they've gone one road, it is sartin you'd better go t' other, and then you'll be sure to find 'em. Now, my private 'pinion is, Lizy took der dirt road; so I think we'd better take de straight one."

This profound generic view of the female sex did not seem to dispose Haley particularly to the straight road; and he announced decidedly that he should go the other, and asked Sam when they should come to it.

"A little piece ahead," said Sam, giving a wink to Andy with the eye which was on Andy's side of the head; and he added, gravely, "but I've studded on de matter, and I'm quite clar we ought not to go dat ar way. I nebber been over it no way. It's despit[4] lonesome, and we might lose our way—whar we'd come to, de Lord only knows."

"Nevertheless," said Haley, "I shall go that way."

"Now I think on't, I think I hearn 'em tell that dat ar road was all fenced up and down by der creek, and thar, an't it, Andy?"

Andy wasn't certain; he'd only "hearn tell" about that road, but never been over it. In short, he was strictly noncommittal.

Haley, accustomed to strike the balance of probabilities between lies of greater or lesser magnitude, thought that it lay in favor of the dirt road aforesaid. The mention of the thing he thought he perceived was involuntary on Sam's part at first, and his confused attempts to dissuade him he set down to a desperate lying on second thoughts, as being unwilling to implicate Eliza.

When, therefore, Sam indicated the road, Haley plunged briskly into it, followed by Sam and Andy.

Now, the road, in fact, was an old one, that had formerly been a thoroughfare to the river, but abandoned for many years after the laying of the new pike. It was open for about an hour's ride, and after that it was cut across by various farms and fences. Sam knew this fact perfectly well—indeed, the road had been so long closed up, that Andy had never heard of it. He therefore rode along with an air of dutiful submission,

---

[1] *underground*   The Underground Railroad, a secret traveling network (and network of safe-houses) by means of which many enslaved persons escaped to the North.

[2] *pike*   Paid road; highway.

[3] *old bird … chaff*   Allusion to the proverbial phrase "You cannot catch old birds with chaff," meaning that those who are old and wise are not easily deceived;   *chaff*   Empty grain husks.

[4] *despit*   Desperate.

only groaning and vociferating occasionally that 't was "desp't rough, and bad for Jerry's[1] foot."

"Now, I jest give yer warning," said Haley, "I know yer; yer won't get me to turn off this yer road, with all yer fussin'—so you shet up!"

"Mas'r will go his own way!" said Sam, with rueful submission, at the same time winking most portentously to Andy, whose delight was now very near the explosive point.

Sam was in wonderful spirits—professed to keep a very brisk look-out—at one time exclaiming that he saw "a gal's bonnet" on the top of some distant eminence, or calling to Andy "if that thar wasn't 'Lizy' down in the hollow"; always making these exclamations in some rough or craggy part of the road, where the sudden quickening of speed was a special inconvenience to all parties concerned, and thus keeping Haley in a state of constant commotion.

After riding about an hour in this way, the whole party made a precipitate and tumultuous descent into a barnyard belonging to a large farming establishment. Not a soul was in sight, all the hands being employed in the fields; but, as the barn stood conspicuously and plainly square across the road, it was evident that their journey in that direction had reached a decided finale.

"Wan't dat ar what I told Mas'r?" said Sam, with an air of injured innocence. "How does strange gentleman spect to know more about a country dan de natives born and raised?"

"You rascal!" said Haley, "you knew all about this."

"Didn't I tell yer I *know'd*, and yer wouldn't believe me? I told Mas'r 't was all shet up, and fenced up, and I didn't spect we could get through—Andy heard me."

It was all too true to be disputed, and the unlucky man had to pocket his wrath with the best grace he was able, and all three faced to the right about, and took up their line of march for the highway.

In consequence of all the various delays, it was about three-quarters of an hour after Eliza had laid her child to sleep in the village tavern that the party came riding into the same place. Eliza was standing by the window, looking out in another direction, when Sam's quick eye caught a glimpse of her. Haley and Andy were two yards behind. At this crisis, Sam contrived to have his hat blown off, and uttered a loud and characteristic ejaculation, which startled her at once; she drew suddenly back; the whole train swept by the window, round to the front door.

A thousand lives seemed to be concentrated in that one moment to Eliza. Her room opened by a side door to the river. She caught her child, and sprang down the steps towards it. The trader caught a full glimpse of her, just as she was disappearing down the bank; and throwing himself from his horse, and calling loudly on Sam and Andy, he was after her like a hound after a deer. In that dizzy moment her feet to her scarce seemed to touch the ground, and a moment brought her to the water's edge. Right on behind they came; and, nerved with strength such as God gives only to the desperate, with one wild cry and flying leap, she vaulted sheer over the turbid current by the shore, on to the raft of ice beyond. It was a desperate leap—impossible to anything but madness and despair; and Haley, Sam, and Andy instinctively cried out, and lifted up their hands, as she did it.

The huge green fragment of ice on which she alighted pitched and creaked as her weight came on it, but she stayed there not a moment. With wild cries and desperate energy she leaped to another and still another cake; stumbling—leaping—slipping—springing upwards again! Her shoes are gone—her stockings cut from her feet—while blood marked every step; but she saw nothing, felt nothing, till dimly, as in a dream, she saw the Ohio side, and a man helping her up the bank.

"Yer a brave gal, now, whoever ye ar!" said the man, with an oath.

Eliza recognized the voice and face of a man who owned a farm not far from her old home.

"O, Mr. Symmes! save me—do save me—do hide me!" said Eliza.

"Why, what's this?" said the man. "Why, if 'tan't Shelby's gal!"

"My child! this boy! he'd sold him! There is his Mas'r," said she, pointing to the Kentucky shore. "O, Mr. Symmes, you've got a little boy!"

"So I have," said the man, as he roughly, but kindly, drew her up the steep bank. "Besides, you're a right brave gal. I like grit, wherever I see it."

When they had gained the top of the bank, the man paused.

---

[1]   *Jerry*   Andy's horse.

"I'd be glad to do something for ye," said he; "but then there's nowhar I could take ye. The best I can do is to tell ye to go *thar*," said he, pointing to a large white house which stood by itself, off the main street of the village. "Go thar; they're kind folks. Thar's no kind o' danger but they'll help you—they're up to all that sort o' thing."

"The Lord bless you!" said Eliza, earnestly.

"No 'casion, no 'casion in the world," said the man. "What I've done's of no 'count."

"And, oh, surely, sir, you won't tell anyone!"

"Go to thunder, gal! What do you take a feller for? In course not," said the man. "Come, now, go along like a likely,[1] sensible gal, as you are. You've arnt your liberty, and you shall have it, for all me."

The woman folded her child to her bosom, and walked firmly and swiftly away. The man stood and looked after her.

"Shelby, now, mebbe won't think this yer the most neighborly thing in the world; but what's a feller to do? If he catches one of my gals in the same fix, he's welcome to pay back. Somehow I never could see no kind o' critter a strivin' and pantin', and trying to clar theirselves, with the dogs arter 'em, and go agin 'em. Besides, I don't see no kind of 'casion for me to be hunter and catcher for other folks, neither."

So spoke this poor, heathenish Kentuckian, who had not been instructed in his constitutional relations,[2] and consequently was betrayed into acting in a sort of Christianized manner, which, if he had been better situated and more enlightened, he would not have been left to do.

Haley had stood a perfectly amazed spectator of the scene, till Eliza had disappeared up the bank, when he turned a blank, inquiring look on Sam and Andy.

"That ar was a tolable fair stroke of business," said Sam.

"The gal's got seven devils in her, I believe!" said Haley. "How like a wildcat she jumped!"

"Wal, now," said Sam, scratching his head, "I hope Mas'r'll 'scuse us tryin' dat ar road. Don't think I feel spry enough for dat ar, no way!" and Sam gave a hoarse chuckle.

"*You* laugh!" said the trader, with a growl.

"Lord bless you, Mas'r, I couldn't help it, now," said Sam, giving way to the long pent-up delight of his soul. "She looked so curi's, a leapin' and springin'—ice a crackin'—and only to hear her—plump! ker chunk! ker splash! Spring! Lord! how she goes it!" and Sam and Andy laughed till the tears rolled down their cheeks.

"I'll make ye laugh t'other side yer mouths!" said the trader, laying about their heads with his riding-whip.

Both ducked, and ran shouting up the bank, and were on their horses before he was up.

"Good evening, Mas'r!" said Sam, with much gravity. "I berry much spect Missis be anxious 'bout Jerry. Mas'r Haley won't want us no longer. Missis wouldn't hear of our ridin' the critters over Lizy's bridge tonight"; and, with a facetious poke into Andy's ribs, he started off, followed by the latter, at full speed—their shouts of laughter coming faintly on the wind.

CHAPTER 9
IN WHICH IT APPEARS THAT A SENATOR IS BUT A MAN

The light of the cheerful fire shone on the rug and carpet of a cozy parlor, and glittered on the sides of the teacups and well-brightened teapot, as Senator Bird was drawing off his boots, preparatory to inserting his feet in a pair of new handsome slippers, which his wife had been working for him while away on his senatorial tour. Mrs. Bird, looking the very picture of delight, was superintending the arrangements of the table, ever and anon mingling admonitory remarks to a number of frolicsome juveniles, who were effervescing in all those modes of untold gambol and mischief that have astonished mothers ever since the flood.[3]

"Tom, let the doorknob alone—there's a man! Mary! Mary! don't pull the cat's tail—poor pussy! Jim, you mustn't climb on that table—no, no! You don't know, my dear, what a surprise it is to us all, to see you here

---

[1]   *likely* Term suggesting strength or capability, but also frequently physical attractiveness.

[2]   *constitutional relations* The recently passed Fugitive Slave Act made it a federal crime to aid persons escaping from slavery, and placed increased pressures on ordinary citizens to aid in their capture.

[3]   *gambol* Playfulness; *ever since the flood* Reference to the great flood that God sends to destroy most life on Earth in Genesis 7; i.e., since the beginning of time.

tonight!" said she, at last, when she found a space to say something to her husband.

"Yes, yes, I thought I'd just make a run down, spend the night, and have a little comfort at home. I'm tired to death, and my head aches!"

Mrs. Bird cast a glance at a camphor-bottle,[1] which stood in the half-open closet, and appeared to meditate an approach to it, but her husband interposed.

"No, no, Mary, no doctoring! a cup of your good hot tea, and some of our good home living, is what I want. It's a tiresome business, this legislating!"

And the senator smiled, as if he rather liked the idea of considering himself a sacrifice to his country.

"Well," said his wife, after the business of the tea-table was getting rather slack, "and what have they been doing in the Senate?"

Now, it was a very unusual thing for gentle little Mrs. Bird ever to trouble her head with what was going on in the house of the state, very wisely considering that she had enough to do to mind her own. Mr. Bird, therefore, opened his eyes in surprise, and said,

"Not very much of importance."

"Well; but is it true that they have been passing a law forbidding people to give meat and drink to those poor colored folks that come along? I heard they were talking of some such law, but I didn't think any Christian legislature would pass it!"

"Why, Mary, you are getting to be a politician, all at once."

"No, nonsense! I wouldn't give a fip for all your politics, generally, but I think this is something downright cruel and unchristian. I hope, my dear, no such law has been passed."

"There has been a law passed forbidding people to help off the slaves that come over from Kentucky, my dear; so much of that thing has been done by these reckless Abolitionists, that our brethren in Kentucky are very strongly excited, and it seems necessary, and no more than Christian and kind, that something should be done by our state to quiet the excitement."

"And what is the law? It don't forbid us to shelter these poor creatures a night, does it, and to give 'em something comfortable to eat, and a few old clothes, and send them quietly about their business?"

"Why, yes, my dear; that would be aiding and abetting, you know."

Mrs. Bird was a timid, blushing little woman, of about four feet in height, and with mild blue eyes, and a peach-blow complexion, and the gentlest, sweetest voice in the world; as for courage, a moderate-sized cock-turkey had been known to put her to rout at the very first gobble, and a stout house-dog, of moderate capacity, would bring her into subjection merely by a show of his teeth. Her husband and children were her entire world, and in these she ruled more by entreaty and persuasion than by command or argument. There was only one thing that was capable of arousing her, and that provocation came in on the side of her unusually gentle and sympathetic nature; anything in the shape of cruelty would throw her into a passion, which was the more alarming and inexplicable in proportion to the general softness of her nature. Generally the most indulgent and easy to be entreated of all mothers, still her boys had a very reverent remembrance of a most vehement chastisement she once bestowed on them, because she found them leagued with several graceless boys of the neighborhood, stoning a defenceless kitten.

"I'll tell you what," Master Bill used to say, "I was scared that time. Mother came at me so that I thought she was crazy, and I was whipped and tumbled off to bed, without any supper, before I could get over wondering what had come about; and, after that, I heard mother crying outside the door, which made me feel worse than all the rest. I'll tell you what," he'd say, "we boys never stoned another kitten!"

On the present occasion, Mrs. Bird rose quickly, with very red cheeks, which quite improved her general appearance, and walked up to her husband, with quite a resolute air, and said, in a determined tone,

"Now, John, I want to know if you think such a law as that is right and Christian?"

"You won't shoot me, now, Mary, if I say I do!"

"I never could have thought it of you, John; you didn't vote for it?"

"Even so, my fair politician."

"You ought to be ashamed, John! Poor, homeless, houseless creatures! It's a shameful, wicked, abominable law, and I'll break it, for one, the first time I get a chance; and I hope I *shall* have a chance, I do! Things have got to a pretty pass, if a woman can't give

---

[1] *camphor-bottle* In the nineteenth century, camphor oil was used as a pain reliever.

a warm supper and a bed to poor, starving creatures, just because they are slaves, and have been abused and oppressed all their lives, poor things!"

"But, Mary, just listen to me. Your feelings are all quite right, dear, and interesting, and I love you for them; but, then, dear, we mustn't suffer our feelings to run away with our judgment; you must consider it's not a matter of private feeling—there are great public interests involved—there is such a state of public agitation rising, that we must put aside our private feelings."

"Now, John, I don't know anything about politics, but I can read my Bible; and there I see that I must feed the hungry, clothe the naked, and comfort the desolate;[1] and that Bible I mean to follow."

"But in cases where your doing so would involve a great public evil—"

"Obeying God never brings on public evils. I know it can't. It's always safest, all round, to *do as He* bids us."

"Now, listen to me, Mary, and I can state to you a very clear argument, to show—"

"O, nonsense, John! you can talk all night, but you wouldn't do it. I put it to you, John—would *you* now turn away a poor, shivering, hungry creature from your door, because he was a runaway? *Would* you, now?"

Now, if the truth must be told, our senator had the misfortune to be a man who had a particularly humane and accessible nature, and turning away anybody that was in trouble never had been his forte; and what was worse for him in this particular pinch of the argument was, that his wife knew it, and, of course, was making an assault on rather an indefensible point. So he had recourse to the usual means of gaining time for such cases made and provided; he said "ahem," and coughed several times, took out his pocket-handkerchief, and began to wipe his glasses. Mrs. Bird, seeing the defenceless condition of the enemy's territory, had no more conscience than to push her advantage.

"I should like to see you doing that, John—I really should! Turning a woman out of doors in a snowstorm, for instance; or, maybe you'd take her up and put her in jail, wouldn't you? You would make a great hand at that!"

"Of course, it would be a very painful duty," began Mr. Bird, in a moderate tone.

"Duty, John! don't use that word! You know it isn't a duty—it can't be a duty! If folks want to keep their slaves from running away, let 'em treat 'em well—that's my doctrine. If I had slaves (as I hope I never shall have), I'd risk their wanting to run away from me, or you either, John. I tell you folks don't run away when they are happy; and when they do run, poor creatures! they suffer enough with cold and hunger and fear, without everybody's turning against them; and, law or no law, I never will, so help me God!"

"Mary! Mary! My dear, let me reason with you."

"I hate reasoning, John—especially reasoning on such subjects. There's a way you political folks have of coming round and round a plain right thing; and you don't believe in it yourselves, when it comes to practice. I know *you* well enough, John. You don't believe it's right any more than I do; and you wouldn't do it any sooner than I."

At this critical juncture, old Cudjoe, the black man-of-all-work, put his head in at the door, and wished "Missis would come into the kitchen"; and our senator, tolerably relieved, looked after his little wife with a whimsical mixture of amusement and vexation, and, seating himself in the armchair, began to read the papers.

After a moment, his wife's voice was heard at the door, in a quick, earnest tone—"John! John! I do wish you'd come here, a moment."

He laid down his paper, and went into the kitchen, and started, quite amazed at the sight that presented itself: A young and slender woman, with garments torn and frozen, with one shoe gone, and the stocking torn away from the cut and bleeding foot, was laid back in a deadly swoon upon two chairs. There was the impress of the despised race on her face, yet none could help feeling its mournful and pathetic[2] beauty, while its stony sharpness, its cold, fixed, deathly aspect, struck a solemn chill over him. He drew his breath short, and stood in silence. His wife, and their only colored domestic, old Aunt Dinah, were busily engaged in restorative measures; while old Cudjoe had got the boy on his knee, and was busy pulling off his shoes and stockings, and chafing his little cold feet.

---

1   *feed … the desolate*   See Matthew 25.35–36: "For I was hungry, and ye gave me meat: I was thirsty, and ye gave me drink: I was a stranger, and ye took me in: Naked, and ye clothed me: I was sick, and ye visited me: I was in prison, and ye came unto me."

2   *pathetic*   I.e., arousing a sense of pathos.

"Sure, now, if she an't a sight to behold!" said old Dinah, compassionately; "'pears like 't was the heat that made her faint. She was tol'able peart[1] when she cum in, and asked if she couldn't warm herself here a spell; and I was just a askin' her where she cum from, and she fainted right down. Never done much hard work, guess, by the looks of her hands."

"Poor creature!" said Mrs. Bird, compassionately, as the woman slowly unclosed her large, dark eyes, and looked vacantly at her. Suddenly an expression of agony crossed her face, and she sprang up, saying, "O, my Harry! Have they got him?"

The boy, at this, jumped from Cudjoe's knee, and, running to her side, put up his arms. "O, he's here! he's here!" she exclaimed.

"O, ma'am!" said she, wildly, to Mrs. Bird, "do protect us! don't let them get him!"

"Nobody shall hurt you here, poor woman," said Mrs. Bird, encouragingly. "You are safe; don't be afraid."

"God bless you!" said the woman, covering her face and sobbing; while the little boy, seeing her crying, tried to get into her lap.

With many gentle and womanly offices,[2] which none knew better how to render than Mrs. Bird, the poor woman was, in time, rendered more calm. A temporary bed was provided for her on the settle, near the fire; and, after a short time, she fell into a heavy slumber, with the child, who seemed no less weary, soundly sleeping on her arm; for the mother resisted, with nervous anxiety, the kindest attempts to take him from her; and, even in sleep, her arm encircled him with an unrelaxing clasp, as if she could not even then be beguiled of her vigilant hold.

Mr. and Mrs. Bird had gone back to the parlor, where, strange as it may appear, no reference was made, on either side, to the preceding conversation; but Mrs. Bird busied herself with her knitting work, and Mr. Bird pretended to be reading the paper.

"I wonder who and what she is!" said Mr. Bird, at last, as he laid it down.

"When she wakes up and feels a little rested, we will see," said Mrs. Bird.

"I say, wife!" said Mr. Bird, after musing in silence over his newspaper.

"Well, dear!"

"She couldn't wear one of your gowns, could she, by any letting down,[3] or such matter? She seems to be rather larger than you are."

A quite perceptible smile glimmered on Mrs. Bird's face, as she answered, "We'll see."

Another pause, and Mr. Bird again broke out,

"I say, wife!"

"Well! What now?"

"Why, there's that old bombasine[4] cloak, that you keep on purpose to put over me when I take my afternoon's nap; you might as well give her that—she needs clothes."

At this instant, Dinah looked in to say that the woman was awake, and wanted to see Missis.

Mr. and Mrs. Bird went into the kitchen, followed by the two eldest boys, the smaller fry having, by this time, been safely disposed of in bed.

The woman was now sitting up on the settle, by the fire. She was looking steadily into the blaze, with a calm, heartbroken expression, very different from her former agitated wildness.

"Did you want me?" said Mrs. Bird, in gentle tones. "I hope you feel better now, poor woman!"

A long-drawn, shivering sigh was the only answer; but she lifted her dark eyes, and fixed them on her with such a forlorn and imploring expression, that the tears came into the little woman's eyes.

"You needn't be afraid of anything; we are friends here, poor woman! Tell me where you came from, and what you want," said she.

"I came from Kentucky," said the woman.

"When?" said Mr. Bird, taking up the interrogatory.

"Tonight."

"How did you come?"

"I crossed on the ice."

"Crossed on the ice!" said everyone present.

"Yes," said the woman, slowly, "I did. God helping me, I crossed on the ice; for they were behind me—right behind—and there was no other way!"

---

1 *peart* Lively.

2 *offices* Services.

3 *letting down* I.e., having the hems and seams altered so as to enlarge the garment.

4 *bombasine* Twill fabric combining silk or cotton with worsted wool.

"Law, Missis," said Cudjoe, "the ice is all in broken-up blocks, a swinging and a tetering up and down in the water!"

"I know it was—I know it!" said she, wildly; "but I did it! I wouldn't have thought I could—I didn't think I should get over, but I didn't care! I could but die, if I didn't. The Lord helped me; nobody knows how much the Lord can help 'em, till they try," said the woman, with a flashing eye.

"Were you a slave?" said Mr. Bird.

"Yes, sir; I belonged to a man in Kentucky."

"Was he unkind to you?"

"No, sir; he was a good master."

"And was your mistress unkind to you?"

"No, sir—no! my mistress was always good to me."

"What could induce you to leave a good home, then, and run away, and go through such dangers?"

The woman looked up at Mrs. Bird, with a keen, scrutinizing glance, and it did not escape her that she was dressed in deep mourning.

"Ma'am," she said, suddenly, "have you ever lost a child?"

The question was unexpected, and it was a thrust on a new wound; for it was only a month since a darling child of the family had been laid in the grave.

Mr. Bird turned around and walked to the window, and Mrs. Bird burst into tears; but, recovering her voice, she said,

"Why do you ask that? I have lost a little one."

"Then you will feel for me. I have lost two, one after another—left 'em buried there when I came away; and I had only this one left. I never slept a night without him; he was all I had. He was my comfort and pride, day and night; and, ma'am, they were going to take him away from me—to *sell* him—sell him down south, ma'am, to go all alone—a baby that had never been away from his mother in his life! I couldn't stand it, ma'am. I knew I never should be good for anything, if they did; and when I knew the papers were signed, and he was sold, I took him and came off in the night; and they chased me—the man that bought him, and some of Mas'r's folks—and they were coming down right behind me, and I heard 'em. I jumped right on to the ice; and how I got across, I don't know—but, first I knew, a man was helping me up the bank."

The woman did not sob nor weep. She had gone to a place where tears are dry; but everyone around her was, in some way characteristic of themselves, showing signs of hearty sympathy.

The two little boys, after a desperate rummaging in their pockets, in search of those pocket-handkerchiefs which mothers know are never to be found there, had thrown themselves disconsolately into the skirts of their mother's gown, where they were sobbing, and wiping their eyes and noses, to their hearts' content; Mrs. Bird had her face fairly hidden in her pocket-handkerchief; and old Dinah, with tears streaming down her black, honest face, was ejaculating, "Lord have mercy on us!" with all the fervor of a camp-meeting; while old Cudjoe, rubbing his eyes very hard with his cuffs, and making a most uncommon variety of wry faces, occasionally responded in the same key, with great fervor. Our senator was a statesman, and of course could not be expected to cry, like other mortals; and so he turned his back to the company, and looked out of the window, and seemed particularly busy in clearing his throat and wiping his spectacle-glasses, occasionally blowing his nose in a manner that was calculated to excite suspicion, had anyone been in a state to observe critically.

"How came you to tell me you had a kind master?" he suddenly exclaimed, gulping down very resolutely some kind of rising in his throat, and turning suddenly round upon the woman.

"Because he *was* a kind master; I'll say that of him, anyway—and my mistress was kind; but they couldn't help themselves. They were owing money; and there was some way, I can't tell how, that a man had a hold on them, and they were obliged to give him his will. I listened, and heard him telling mistress that, and she begging and pleading for me—and he told her he couldn't help himself, and that the papers were all drawn—and then it was I took him and left my home, and came away. I knew 't was no use of my trying to live, if they did it; for't 'pears like this child is all I have."

"Have you no husband?"

"Yes, but he belongs to another man. His master is real hard to him, and won't let him come to see me, hardly ever; and he's grown harder and harder upon us, and he threatens to sell him down south; it's like I'll never see *him* again!"

The quiet tone in which the woman pronounced these words might have led a superficial observer to think that she was entirely apathetic; but there was a calm, settled depth of anguish in her large, dark eye, that spoke of something far otherwise.

"And where do you mean to go, my poor woman?" said Mrs. Bird.

"To Canada, if I only knew where that was. Is it very far off, is Canada?" said she, looking up, with a simple, confiding air, to Mrs. Bird's face.

"Poor thing!" said Mrs. Bird, involuntarily.

"Is't a very great way off, think?" said the woman, earnestly.

"Much further than you think, poor child!" said Mrs. Bird; "but we will try to think what can be done for you. Here, Dinah, make her up a bed in your own room, close by the kitchen, and I'll think what to do for her in the morning. Meanwhile, never fear, poor woman; put your trust in God; he will protect you."

Mrs. Bird and her husband reentered the parlor. She sat down in her little rocking-chair before the fire, swaying thoughtfully to and fro. Mr. Bird strode up and down the room, grumbling to himself, "Pish! pshaw! confounded awkward business!" At length, striding up to his wife, he said.

"I say, wife, she'll have to get away from here, this very night. That fellow will be down on the scent bright and early tomorrow morning; if 't was only the woman, she could lie quiet till it was over; but that little chap can't be kept still by a troop of horse and foot,[1] I'll warrant me; he'll bring it all out, popping his head out of some window or door. A pretty kettle of fish it would be for me, too, to be caught with them both here, just now! No; they'll have to be got off tonight."

"Tonight! How is it possible? where to?"

"Well, I know pretty well where to," said the senator, beginning to put on his boots, with a reflective air; and, stopping when his leg was half in, he embraced his knee with both hands, and seemed to go off in deep meditation.

"It's a confounded awkward, ugly business," said he, at last, beginning to tug at his boot-straps again, "and that's a fact!" After one boot was fairly on, the senator sat with the other in his hand, profoundly studying the figure of the carpet. "It will have to be done, though, for aught I see—hang it all!" and he drew the other boot anxiously on, and looked out of the window.

Now, little Mrs. Bird was a discreet woman—a woman who never in her life said, "I told you so!" and, on the present occasion, though pretty well aware of the shape her husband's meditations were taking, she very prudently forbore to meddle with them, only sat very quietly in her chair, and looked quite ready to hear her liege lord's intentions, when he should think proper to utter them.

"You see," he said, "there's my old client, Van Trompe, has come over from Kentucky, and set all his slaves free; and he has bought a place seven miles up the creek, here, back in the woods, where nobody goes, unless they go on purpose; and it's a place that isn't found in a hurry. There she'd be safe enough; but the plague of the thing is, nobody could drive a carriage there tonight, but *me*."

"Why not? Cudjoe is an excellent driver."

"Ay, ay, but here it is. The creek has to be crossed twice; and the second crossing is quite dangerous, unless one knows it as I do. I have crossed it a hundred times on horseback, and know exactly the turns to take. And so, you see, there's no help for it. Cudjoe must put in the horses, as quietly as may be, about twelve o'clock, and I'll take her over; and then, to give color to the matter, he must carry me on to the next tavern, to take the stage for Columbus,[2] that comes by about three or four, and so it will look as if I had had the carriage only for that. I shall get into business bright and early in the morning. But I'm thinking I shall feel rather cheap there, after all that's been said and done; but, hang it, I can't help it!"

"Your heart is better than your head, in this case, John," said the wife, laying her little white hand on his. "Could I ever have loved you, had I not known you better than you know yourself?" And the little woman looked so handsome, with the tears sparkling in her eyes, that the senator thought he must be a decidedly clever fellow, to get such a pretty creature into such a passionate admiration of him; and so, what could he do but walk off soberly, to see about the carriage.

---

1   *troop of horse and foot*   I.e., an army.

2   *stage*   Stagecoach;   *Columbus*   Capital city of Ohio.

At the door, however, he stopped a moment, and then coming back, he said, with some hesitation,

"Mary, I don't know how you'd feel about it, but there's that drawer full of things—of—of—poor little Henry's." So saying, he turned quickly on his heel, and shut the door after him.

His wife opened the little bedroom door adjoining her room, and, taking the candle, set it down on the top of a bureau there; then from a small recess she took a key, and put it thoughtfully in the lock of a drawer, and made a sudden pause, while two boys, who, boy like, had followed close on her heels, stood looking, with silent, significant glances, at their mother. And oh! mother that reads this, has there never been in your house a drawer, or a closet, the opening of which has been to you like the opening again of a little grave? Ah! happy mother that you are, if it has not been so.

Mrs. Bird slowly opened the drawer. There were little coats of many a form and pattern, piles of aprons, and rows of small stockings; and even a pair of little shoes, worn and rubbed at the toes, were peeping from the folds of a paper. There was a toy horse and wagon, a top, a ball—memorials gathered with many a tear and many a heartbreak! She sat down by the drawer and, leaning her head on her hands over it, wept till the tears fell through her fingers into the drawer; then suddenly raising her head, she began, with nervous haste, selecting the plainest and most substantial articles, and gathering them into a bundle.

"Mamma," said one of the boys, gently touching her arm, "are you going to give away *those* things?"

"My dear boys," she said, softly and earnestly, "if our dear, loving little Henry looks down from heaven, he would be glad to have us do this. I could not find it in my heart to give them away to any common person— to anybody that was happy; but I give them to a mother more heartbroken and sorrowful than I am; and I hope God will send his blessings with them!"

There are in this world blessed souls whose sorrows all spring up into joys for others; whose earthly hopes, laid in the grave with many tears, are the seed from which spring healing flowers and balm for the desolate and the distressed. Among such was the delicate woman who sits there by the lamp, dropping slow tears, while she prepares the memorials of her own lost one for the outcast wanderer.

After a while, Mrs. Bird opened a wardrobe, and, taking from thence a plain, serviceable dress or two, she sat down busily to her work-table and, with needle, scissors, and thimble at hand, quietly commenced the "letting down" process which her husband had recommended, and continued busily at it till the old clock in the corner struck twelve, and she heard the low rattling of wheels at the door.

"Mary," said her husband, coming in, with his overcoat in his hand, "you must wake her up now; we must be off."

Mrs. Bird hastily deposited the various articles she had collected in a small plain trunk, and locking it, desired her husband to see it in the carriage, and then proceeded to call the woman. Soon, arrayed in a cloak, bonnet, and shawl, that had belonged to her benefactress, she appeared at the door with her child in her arms. Mr. Bird hurried her into the carriage, and Mrs. Bird pressed on after her to the carriage steps. Eliza leaned out of the carriage, and put out her hand—a hand as soft and beautiful as was given in return. She fixed her large, dark eyes, full of earnest meaning, on Mrs. Bird's face, and seemed going to speak. Her lips moved—she tried once or twice, but there was no sound—and pointing upward, with a look never to be forgotten, she fell back in the seat, and covered her face. The door was shut, and the carriage drove on.

What a situation, now, for a patriotic senator, that had been all the week before spurring up the legislature of his native state to pass more stringent resolutions against escaping fugitives, their harborers and abettors!

Our good senator in his native state had not been exceeded by any of his brethren at Washington in the sort of eloquence which has won for them immortal renown! How sublimely he had sat with his hands in his pockets, and scouted[1] all sentimental weakness of those who would put the welfare of a few miserable fugitives before great state interests!

He was as bold as a lion about it, and "mightily convinced" not only himself, but everybody that heard him; but then his idea of a fugitive was only an idea of the letters that spell the word—or, at the most, the image of a little newspaper picture of a man with a stick and bundle, with "Ran away from the subscriber" under it. The magic of the real presence of distress—the

---

[1]   *scouted* Scorned.

imploring human eye, the frail, trembling human hand, the despairing appeal of helpless agony—these he had never tried. He had never thought that a fugitive might be a hapless mother, a defenceless child—like that one which was now wearing his lost boy's little well-known cap; and so, as our poor senator was not stone or steel—as he was a man, and a downright noble-hearted one, too—he was, as everybody must see, in a sad case for his patriotism. And you need not exult over him, good brother of the Southern States; for we have some inklings that many of you, under similar circumstances, would not do much better. We have reason to know, in Kentucky, as in Mississippi, are noble and generous hearts, to whom never was tale of suffering told in vain. Ah, good brother! is it fair for you to expect of us services which your own brave, honorable heart would not allow you to render, were you in our place?

Be that as it may, if our good senator was a political sinner, he was in a fair way to expiate it by his night's penance. There had been a long continuous period of rainy weather, and the soft, rich earth of Ohio, as everyone knows, is admirably suited to the manufacture of mud—and the road was an Ohio railroad of the good old times.

"And pray, what sort of a road may that be?" says some eastern traveller, who has been accustomed to connect no ideas with a railroad, but those of smoothness or speed.

Know, then, innocent eastern friend, that in benighted regions of the west, where the mud is of unfathomable and sublime depth, roads are made of round rough logs, arranged transversely side by side, and coated over in their pristine freshness with earth, turf, and whatsoever may come to hand, and then the rejoicing native calleth it a road, and straightway essayeth to ride thereupon. In process of time, the rains wash off all the turf and grass aforesaid, move the logs hither and thither, in picturesque positions, up, down and crosswise, with diverse chasms and ruts of black mud intervening.

Over such a road as this our senator went stumbling along, making moral reflections as continuously as under the circumstances could be expected, the carriage proceeding along much as follows—bump! bump! bump! slush! down in the mud!—the senator, woman and child, reversing their positions so suddenly as to come, without any very accurate adjustment, against the windows of the downhill side. Carriage sticks fast, while Cudjoe on the outside is heard making a great muster among the horses. After various ineffectual pullings and twitchings, just as the senator is losing all patience, the carriage suddenly rights itself with a bounce—two front wheels go down into another abyss, and senator, woman, and child, all tumble promiscuously on to the front seat—senator's hat is jammed over his eyes and nose quite unceremoniously, and he considers himself fairly extinguished—child cries, and Cudjoe on the outside delivers animated addresses to the horses, who are kicking, and floundering, and straining, under repeated cracks of the whip. Carriage springs up, with another bounce—down go the hind wheels—senator, woman, and child, fly over on to the back seat, his elbows encountering her bonnet, and both her feet being jammed into his hat, which flies off in the concussion. After a few moments the "slough" is passed, and the horses stop, panting—the senator finds his hat, the woman straightens her bonnet and hushes her child, and they brace themselves firmly for what is yet to come.

For a while only the continuous bump! bump! intermingled, just by way of variety, with diverse side plunges and compound shakes; and they begin to flatter themselves that they are not so badly off, after all. At last, with a square plunge, which puts all on to their feet and then down into their seats with incredible quickness, the carriage stops—and, after much outside commotion, Cudjoe appears at the door.

"Please, sir, it's powerful bad spot, this yer. I don't know how we's to get clar out. I'm a thinkin' we'll have to be a gettin' rails."[1]

The senator despairingly steps out, picking gingerly for some firm foothold; down goes one foot an immeasurable depth—he tries to pull it up, loses his balance, and tumbles over into the mud, and is fished out, in a very despairing condition, by Cudjoe.

But we forbear, out of sympathy to our readers' bones. Western travellers, who have beguiled the midnight hour in the interesting process of pulling down rail fences, to pry their carriages out of mud holes, will

---

1   rails The boards from rail fences were sometimes removed to provide tracks to ease carriages through muddy terrain.

have a respectful and mournful sympathy with our unfortunate hero. We beg them to drop a silent tear, and pass on.

It was full late in the night when the carriage emerged, dripping and bespattered, out of the creek, and stood at the door of a large farmhouse.

It took no inconsiderable perseverance to arouse the inmates; but at last the respectable proprietor appeared, and undid the door. He was a great, tall, bristling Orson[1] of a fellow, full six feet and some inches in his stockings, and arrayed in a red flannel hunting-shirt. A very heavy *mat* of sandy hair, in a decidedly tousled condition, and a beard of some days' growth, gave the worthy man an appearance, to say the least, not particularly prepossessing. He stood for a few minutes holding the candle aloft, and blinking on our travellers with a dismal and mystified expression that was truly ludicrous. It cost some effort of our senator to induce him to comprehend the case fully; and while he is doing his best at that, we shall give him a little introduction to our readers.

Honest old John Van Trompe was once quite a considerable land-holder and slave-owner in the State of Kentucky. Having "nothing of the bear about him but the skin,"[2] and being gifted by nature with a great, honest, just heart, quite equal to his gigantic frame, he had been for some years witnessing with repressed uneasiness the workings of a system equally bad for oppressor and oppressed. At last, one day, John's great heart had swelled altogether too big to wear his bonds any longer; so he just took his pocket-book out of his desk, and went over into Ohio, and bought a quarter of a township of good, rich land, made out free papers for all his people—men, women, and children—packed them up in wagons, and sent them off to settle down; and then honest John turned his face up the creek, and sat quietly down on a snug, retired farm, to enjoy his conscience and his reflections.

---

[1] *Orson* Bear-like; from the French word for bear, *ours*. The term also alludes to the fifteenth-century French story "Orson and Valentine," in which the lost son (Orson) of a king is abandoned in the woods and raised by a bear.

[2] *nothing of … the skin* Oliver Goldsmith's description of Samuel Johnson, as quoted in James Boswell's *Life of Samuel Johnson* (1791): "Johnson, to be sure, has a roughness in his manner; but no man alive has a more tender heart. He has nothing of the bear but his skin."

"Are you the man that will shelter a poor woman and child from slave-catchers?" said the senator, explicitly.

"I rather think I am," said honest John, with some considerable emphasis.

"I thought so," said the senator.

"If there's anybody comes," said the good man, stretching his tall, muscular form upward, "why here I'm ready for him: and I've got seven sons, each six foot high, and they'll be ready for 'em. Give our respects to 'em," said John; "tell 'em it's no matter how soon they call—make no kinder difference to us," said John, running his fingers through the shock of hair that thatched his head, and bursting out into a great laugh.

Weary, jaded, and spiritless, Eliza dragged herself up to the door, with her child lying in a heavy sleep on her arm. The rough man held the candle to her face, and uttering a kind of compassionate grunt, opened the door of a small bedroom adjoining to the large kitchen where they were standing, and motioned her to go in. He took down a candle, and lighting it, set it upon the table, and then addressed himself to Eliza.

"Now, I say, gal, you needn't be a bit afeard, let who will come here. I'm up to all that sort o' thing," said he, pointing to two or three goodly rifles over the mantelpiece; "and most people that know me know that 't wouldn't be healthy to try to get anybody out o' my house when I'm agin it. So *now* you jist go to sleep now, as quiet as if yer mother was a rockin' ye," said he, as he shut the door.

"Why, this is an uncommon handsome un," he said to the senator. "Ah, well; handsome uns has the greatest cause to run, sometimes, if they has any kind o' feelin, such as decent women should. I know all about that."

The senator, in a few words, briefly explained Eliza's history.

"O! ou! aw! now, I want to know?" said the good man, pitifully; "sho! now sho! That's natur now, poor crittur! hunted down now like a deer—hunted down, jest for havin' natural feelin's, and doin' what no kind o' mother could help a doin'! I tell ye what, these yer things make me come the nighest to swearin', now, o' most anything," said honest John, as he wiped his eyes with the back of a great, freckled, yellow hand. "I tell yer what, stranger, it was years and years before I'd jine the church, 'cause the ministers round in our parts used to preach that the Bible went in for these ere cuttings up—and I couldn't be up to 'em with their Greek and Hebrew, and so I took up agin 'em, Bible and all. I never jined the church till I found a minister that was up to 'em all in Greek and all that, and he said right the contrary; and then I took right hold, and jined the church—I did now, fact," said John, who had been all this time uncorking some very frisky bottled cider, which at this juncture he presented.

"Ye'd better jest put up here, now, till daylight," said he, heartily, "and I'll call up the old woman, and have a bed got ready for you in no time."

"Thank you, my good friend," said the senator, "I must be along, to take the night stage for Columbus."

"Ah! well, then, if you must, I'll go a piece with you, and show you a cross road that will take you there better than the road you came on. That road's mighty bad."

John equipped himself, and, with a lantern in hand, was soon seen guiding the senator's carriage towards a road that ran down in a hollow, back of his dwelling. When they parted, the senator put into his hand a ten-dollar bill.

"It's for her," he said, briefly.

"Ay, ay," said John, with equal conciseness.

They shook hands, and parted.

CHAPTER 11
IN WHICH PROPERTY GETS INTO
AN IMPROPER STATE OF MIND

It was late in a drizzly afternoon that a traveller alighted at the door of a small country hotel, in the village of N——, in Kentucky. In the barroom he found assembled quite a miscellaneous company, whom stress of weather had driven to harbor, and the place presented the usual scenery of such reunions. Great, tall, raw-boned Kentuckians, attired in hunting-shirts, and trailing their loose joints over a vast extent of territory, with the easy lounge peculiar to the race—rifles stacked away in the corner, shot-pouches, game-bags, hunting-dogs, and little negroes, all rolled together in the corners—were the characteristic features in the picture. At each end of the fireplace sat a long-legged gentleman, with his chair tipped back, his hat on his head, and the heels of his muddy boots reposing sublimely on the mantelpiece—a position, we will inform our readers, decidedly favorable to the turn of reflection incident to western taverns, where travellers exhibit a decided preference for this particular mode of elevating their understandings.

Mine host, who stood behind the bar, like most of his countrymen, was great of stature, good-natured, and loose-jointed, with an enormous shock of hair on his head, and a great tall hat on the top of that.

In fact, everybody in the room bore on his head this characteristic emblem of man's sovereignty; whether it were felt hat, palm-leaf, greasy beaver, or fine new chapeau, there it reposed with true republican independence. In truth, it appeared to be the characteristic mark of every individual. Some wore them tipped rakishly to one side—these were your men of humor, jolly, free-and-easy dogs; some had them jammed independently down over their noses—these were your hard characters, thorough men, who, when they wore their hats, *wanted* to wear them, and to wear them just as they had a mind to; there were those who had them set far over back—wide-awake[1] men, who wanted a clear prospect; while careless men, who did not know, or care, how their hats sat, had them shaking about in all directions. The various hats, in fact, were quite a Shakespearean study.

Diverse negroes, in very free-and-easy pantaloons, and with no redundancy in the shirt line,[2] were scuttling about, hither and thither, without bringing to pass any very particular results, except expressing a generic willingness to turn over everything in creation generally for the benefit of Mas'r and his guests. Add to this picture a jolly, cracking, rollicking fire, going rejoicingly up a great wide chimney—the outer door and every window being set wide open, and the calico window-curtain flopping and snapping in a good stiff breeze of damp raw air—and you have an idea of the jollities of a Kentucky tavern.

Your Kentuckian of the present day is a good illustration of the doctrine of transmitted instincts and peculiarities. His fathers were mighty hunters—men who lived in the woods, and slept under the free, open heavens, with the stars to hold their candles; and their descendant to this day always acts as if the house were

---

1 *wide-awake* Reference to a style of man's hat known as the wideawake hat, with a broad brim and low crown.

2 *no redundancy in the shirt line* I.e., shirtless.

his camp—wears his hat at all hours, tumbles himself about, and puts his heels on the tops of chairs or mantelpieces, just as his father rolled on the green sward,[1] and put his upon trees and logs—keeps all the windows and doors open, winter and summer, that he may get air enough for his great lungs—calls everybody "stranger," with nonchalant bonhomie,[2] and is altogether the frankest, easiest, most jovial creature living.

Into such an assembly of the free and easy our traveller entered. He was a short, thick-set man, carefully dressed, with a round, good-natured countenance, and something rather fussy and particular in his appearance. He was very careful of his valise and umbrella, bringing them in with his own hands, and resisting, pertinaciously, all offers from the various servants to relieve him of them. He looked round the barroom with rather an anxious air, and, retreating with his valuables to the warmest corner, disposed them under his chair, sat down, and looked rather apprehensively up at the worthy whose heels illustrated the end of the mantelpiece, who was spitting from right to left, with a courage and energy rather alarming to gentlemen of weak nerves and particular habits.

"I say, stranger, how are ye?" said the aforesaid gentleman, firing an honorary salute of tobacco-juice in the direction of the new arrival.

"Well, I reckon," was the reply of the other, as he dodged, with some alarm, the threatening honor.

"Any news?" said the respondent, taking out a strip of tobacco and a large hunting-knife from his pocket.

"Not that I know of," said the man.

"Chaw?"[3] said the first speaker, handing the old gentleman a bit of his tobacco, with a decidedly brotherly air.

"No, thank ye—it don't agree with me," said the little man, edging off.

"Don't, eh?" said the other, easily, and stowing away the morsel in his own mouth, in order to keep up the supply of tobacco-juice, for the general benefit of society.

The old gentleman uniformly gave a little start whenever his long-sided brother fired in his direction; and this being observed by his companion, he very good-naturedly turned his artillery to another quarter, and proceeded to storm one of the fire-irons with a degree of military talent fully sufficient to take a city.

"What's that?" said the old gentleman, observing some of the company formed in a group around a large handbill.

"Nigger advertised!" said one of the company, briefly.

Mr. Wilson, for that was the old gentleman's name, rose up, and, after carefully adjusting his valise and umbrella, proceeded deliberately to take out his spectacles and fix them on his nose; and, this operation being performed, read as follows:

> Ran away from the subscriber, my mulatto boy, George. Said George six feet in height, a very light mulatto, brown curly hair; is very intelligent, speaks handsomely, can read and write; will probably try to pass for a white man; is deeply scarred on his back and shoulders; has been branded in his right hand with the letter H.
>
> I will give four hundred dollars for him alive, and the same sum for satisfactory proof that he has been killed.

The old gentleman read this advertisement from end to end, in a low voice, as if he were studying it.

The long-legged veteran, who had been besieging the fire-iron, as before related, now took down his cumbrous length, and rearing aloft his tall form, walked up to the advertisement, and very deliberately spit a full discharge of tobacco-juice on it.

"There's my mind upon that!" said he, briefly, and sat down again.

"Why, now, stranger, what's that for?" said mine host.

"I'd do it all the same to the writer of that ar paper, if he was here," said the long man, coolly resuming his old employment of cutting tobacco. "Any man that owns a boy like that, and can't find any better way o' treating on him, *deserves* to lose him. Such papers as these is a shame to Kentucky; that's my mind right out, if anybody wants to know!"

"Well, now, that's a fact," said mine host, as he made an entry in his book.

"I've got a gang of boys, sir," said the long man, resuming his attack on the fire-irons, "and I jest tells

---

1   *sward*   Grassy field.

2   *bonhomie*   Camaraderie; friendliness.

3   *Chaw*   Chewing tobacco.

'em—'Boys,' says I, '*run* now! dig! put! jest when ye want to! I never shall come to look after you!' That's the way I keep mine. Let 'em know they are free to run any time, and it jest breaks up their wanting to. More 'n all, I've got free papers[1] for 'em all recorded, in case I gets keeled up any o' these times, and they knows it; and I tell ye, stranger, there an't a fellow in our parts gets more out of his niggers than I do. Why, my boys have been to Cincinnati, with five hundred dollars' worth of colts, and brought me back the money, all straight, time and agin. It stands to reason they should. Treat 'em like dogs, and you'll have dogs' works and dogs' actions. Treat 'em like men, and you'll have men's works." And the honest drover, in his warmth, endorsed this moral sentiment by firing a perfect *feu de joie*[2] at the fireplace.

"I think you're altogether right, friend," said Mr. Wilson; "and this boy described here *is* a fine fellow— no mistake about that. He worked for me some half-dozen years in my bagging factory, and he was my best hand, sir. He is an ingenuous fellow, too: he invented a machine for the cleaning of hemp—a really valuable affair; it's gone into use in several factories. His master holds the patent of it."

"I'll warrant ye," said the drover, "holds it and makes money out of it, and then turns round and brands the boy in his right hand. If I had a fair chance, I'd mark him, I reckon, so that he'd carry it *one* while."

"These yer knowin' boys is allers aggravatin' and sarcy,"[3] said a coarse-looking fellow, from the other side of the room; "that's why they gets cut up and marked so. If they behaved themselves, they wouldn't."

"That is to say, the Lord made 'em men, and it's a hard squeeze getting 'em down into beasts," said the drover, dryly.

"Bright niggers isn't no kind of 'vantage to their masters," continued the other, well intrenched, in a coarse, unconscious obtuseness, from the contempt of his opponent; "what's the use o' talents and them things, if you can't get the use on 'em yourself? Why, all the use they make on 't is to get round you. I've had one or two

of these fellers, and I jest sold 'em down river. I knew I'd got to lose 'em, first or last, if I didn't."

"Better send orders up to the Lord, to make you a set, and leave out their souls entirely," said the drover.

Here the conversation was interrupted by the approach of a small one-horse buggy to the inn. It had a genteel appearance, and a well-dressed, gentlemanly man sat on the seat, with a colored servant driving.

The whole party examined the newcomer with the interest with which a set of loafers in a rainy day usually examine every newcomer. He was very tall, with a dark, Spanish complexion, fine, expressive black eyes, and close-curling hair, also of a glossy blackness. His well-formed aquiline nose, straight thin lips, and the admirable contour of his finely-formed limbs, impressed the whole company instantly with the idea of something uncommon. He walked easily in among the company, and with a nod indicated to his waiter where to place his trunk, bowed to the company, and, with his hat in his hand, walked up leisurely to the bar, and gave his name as Henry Butler, Oaklands, Shelby County. Turning, with an indifferent air, he sauntered up to the advertisement, and read it over.

"Jim," he said to his man, "seems to me we met a boy something like this, up at Bernan's, didn't we?"

"Yes, Mas'r," said Jim, "only I an't sure about the hand."

"Well, I didn't look, of course," said the stranger, with a careless yawn. Then, walking up to the landlord, he desired him to furnish him with a private apartment, as he had some writing to do immediately.

The landlord was all obsequious, and a relay of about seven negroes, old and young, male and female, little and big, were soon whizzing about, like a covey of partridges, bustling, hurrying, treading on each other's toes, and tumbling over each other, in their zeal to get Mas'r's room ready, while he seated himself easily on a chair in the middle of the room, and entered into conversation with the man who sat next to him.

The manufacturer, Mr. Wilson, from the time of the entrance of the stranger, had regarded him with an air of disturbed and uneasy curiosity. He seemed to himself to have met and been acquainted with him somewhere, but he could not recollect. Every few moments, when the man spoke, or moved, or smiled, he would start and fix his eyes on him, and then suddenly withdraw

---

[1] *free papers* Documents confirming a person's free status.

[2] *feu de joie* French: literally, joyous fire; a celebratory rifle salute—though in this case, the reference is to spitting tobacco juice.

[3] *sarcy* Saucy; insolent.

them, as the bright, dark eyes met his with such unconcerned coolness. At last, a sudden recollection seemed to flash upon him, for he stared at the stranger with such an air of blank amazement and alarm, that he walked up to him.

"Mr. Wilson, I think," said he, in a tone of recognition, and extending his hand. "I beg your pardon, I didn't recollect you before. I see you remember me— Mr. Butler, of Oaklands, Shelby County."

"Ye—yes—yes, sir," said Mr. Wilson, like one speaking in a dream.

Just then a negro boy entered, and announced that Mas'r's room was ready.

"Jim, see to the trunks," said the gentleman, negligently; then addressing himself to Mr. Wilson, he added—"I should like to have a few moments' conversation with you on business, in my room, if you please."

Mr. Wilson followed him, as one who walks in his sleep; and they proceeded to a large upper chamber, where a new-made fire was crackling, and various servants flying about, putting finishing touches to the arrangements.

When all was done, and the servants departed, the young man deliberately locked the door, and putting the key in his pocket, faced about, and folding his arms on his bosom, looked Mr. Wilson full in the face.

"George!" said Mr. Wilson.

"Yes, George," said the young man.

"I couldn't have thought it!"

"I am pretty well disguised, I fancy," said the young man, with a smile. "A little walnut bark has made my yellow skin a genteel brown, and I've dyed my hair black; so you see I don't answer to the advertisement at all."

"O, George! but this is a dangerous game you are playing. I could not have advised you to it."

"I can do it on my own responsibility," said George, with the same proud smile.

We remark, *en passant*,[1] that George was, by his father's side, of white descent. His mother was one of those unfortunates of her race, marked out by personal beauty to be the slave of the passions of her possessor, and the mother of children who may never know a father. From one of the proudest families in Kentucky he had inherited a set of fine European features, and a high, indomitable spirit. From his mother he had received only a slight mulatto tinge, amply compensated by its accompanying rich, dark eye. A slight change in the tint of the skin and the color of his hair had metamorphosed him into the Spanish-looking fellow he then appeared; and as gracefulness of movement and gentlemanly manners had always been perfectly natural to him, he found no difficulty in playing the bold part he had adopted—that of a gentleman travelling with his domestic.

Mr. Wilson, a good-natured but extremely fidgety and cautious old gentleman, ambled up and down the room, appearing, as John Bunyan hath it, "much tumbled up and down in his mind,"[2] and divided between his wish to help George, and a certain confused notion of maintaining law and order: so, as he shambled about, he delivered himself as follows:

"Well, George, I s'pose you're running away—leaving your lawful master, George—(I don't wonder at it)—at the same time, I'm sorry, George—yes, decidedly—I think I must say that, George—it's my duty to tell you so."

"Why are you sorry, sir?" said George, calmly.

"Why, to see you, as it were, setting yourself in opposition to the laws of your country."

"*My* country!" said George, with a strong and bitter emphasis; "what country have I, but the grave—and I wish to God that I was laid there!"

"Why, George, no—no—it won't do; this way of talking is wicked—unscriptural. George, you've got a hard master—in fact, he is—well he conducts himself reprehensibly—I can't pretend to defend him. But you know how the angel commanded Hagar to return to her mistress, and submit herself under her hand; and the apostle sent back Onesimus to his master."[3]

1   *en passant*   French: in passing.

2   *much tumbled ... his mind*   From *The Pilgrim's Progress* Part 2, Chapter 2.

3   *the angel ... her mistress*   In the Book of Genesis, Hagar is the servant of Abraham's wife, Sarah. Having failed so far to bear Abraham any children, Sarah gives him Hagar, whom she then abuses jealously after Hagar becomes pregnant; Hagar flees the household in distress, but God commands her to return so as to bear Abraham his son, Ishmael;   *the apostle ... his master*   In the Epistle of Paul to Philemon (in the New Testament), Paul implores Philemon to welcome the formerly enslaved Onesimus, now converted to Christianity, back into his household as a brother rather than as a slave.

"Don't quote Bible at me that way, Mr. Wilson," said George, with a flashing eye, "don't! for my wife is a Christian, and I mean to be, if ever I get to where I can; but to quote Bible to a fellow in my circumstances, is enough to make him give it up altogether. I appeal to God Almighty—I'm willing to go with the case to Him, and ask Him if I do wrong to seek my freedom."

"These feelings are quite natural, George," said the good-natured man, blowing his nose. "Yes they're natural, but it is my duty not to encourage 'em in you. Yes, my boy, I'm sorry for you, now; it's a bad case—very bad; but the apostle says, 'Let everyone abide in the condition in which he is called.'[1] We must all submit to the indications of Providence, George—don't you see?"

George stood with his head drawn back, his arms folded tightly over his broad breast, and a bitter smile curling his lips.

"I wonder, Mr. Wilson, if the Indians should come and take you a prisoner away from your wife and children, and want to keep you all your life hoeing corn for them, if you'd think it your duty to abide in the condition in which you were called. I rather think that you'd think the first stray horse you could find an indication of Providence—shouldn't you?"

The little old gentleman stared with both eyes at this illustration of the case; but, though not much of a reasoner, he had the sense in which some logicians on this particular subject do not excel—that of saying nothing, where nothing could be said. So, as he stood carefully stroking his umbrella, and folding and patting down all the creases in it, he proceeded on with his exhortations in a general way.

"You see, George, you know, now, I always have stood your friend; and whatever I've said, I've said for your good. Now, here, it seems to me, you're running an awful risk. You can't hope to carry it out. If you're taken, it will be worse with you than ever; they'll only abuse you, and half kill you, and sell you down river."

"Mr. Wilson, I know all this," said George. "I *do* run a risk, but—" he threw open his overcoat, and showed two pistols and a bowie-knife.[2] "There!" he said, "I'm ready for 'em! Down south I never *will* go. No! if it comes to that, I can earn myself at least six feet of free soil—the first and last I shall ever own in Kentucky!"

"Why, George, this state of mind is awful; it's getting really desperate, George. I'm concerned. Going to break the laws of your country!"

"My country again! Mr. Wilson, *you* have a country; but what country have *I*, or anyone like me, born of slave mothers? What laws are there for us? We don't make them—we don't consent to them—we have nothing to do with them; all they do for us is to crush us, and keep us down. Haven't I heard your Fourth-of-July speeches? Don't you tell us all, once a year, that governments derive their just power from the consent of the governed?[3] Can't a fellow *think*, that hears such things? Can't he put this and that together, and see what it comes to?"

Mr. Wilson's mind was one of those that may not unaptly be represented by a bale of cotton—downy, soft, benevolently fuzzy and confused. He really pitied George with all his heart, and had a sort of dim and cloudy perception of the style of feeling that agitated him; but he deemed it his duty to go on talking *good* to him, with infinite pertinacity.

"George, this is bad. I must tell you, you know, as a friend, you'd better not be meddling with such notions; they are bad, George, very bad, for boys in your condition—very"; and Mr. Wilson sat down to a table, and began nervously chewing the handle of his umbrella.

"See here, now, Mr. Wilson," said George, coming up and sitting himself determinately down in front of him; "look at me, now. Don't I sit before you, every way, just as much a man as you are? Look at my face— look at my hands—look at my body," and the young man drew himself up proudly; "why am I *not* a man, as much as anybody? Well, Mr. Wilson, hear what I can tell you. I had a father—one of your Kentucky gentlemen—who didn't think enough of me to keep me from being sold with his dogs and horses, to satisfy the estate, when he died. I saw my mother put up at sheriff's sale, with her seven children. They were sold before her eyes, one by one, all to different masters; and I was the youngest. She came and kneeled down before old Mas'r, and begged him to buy her with me, that she might have at least one child with her; and he kicked her away with his heavy boot. I saw him do it; and the last that I heard was her moans and screams,

1 *Let everyone ... is called* See 1 Corinthians 7.20.
2 *bowie-knife* Short-handled fighting knife.

3 *governments derive ... the governed* Among the opening lines of the Declaration of Independence.

when I was tied to his horse's neck, to be carried off to his place."

"Well, then?"

"My master traded with one of the men, and bought my oldest sister. She was a pious, good girl—a member of the Baptist church—and as handsome as my poor mother had been. She was well brought up, and had good manners. At first, I was glad she was bought, for I had one friend near me. I was soon sorry for it. Sir, I have stood at the door and heard her whipped, when it seemed as if every blow cut into my naked heart, and I couldn't do anything to help her; and she was whipped, sir, for wanting to live a decent Christian life,[1] such as your laws give no slave girl a right to live; and at last I saw her chained with a trader's gang, to be sent to market in Orleans—sent there for nothing else but that—and that's the last I know of her. Well, I grew up—long years and years—no father, no mother, no sister, not a living soul that cared for me more than a dog; nothing but whipping, scolding, starving. Why, sir, I've been so hungry that I have been glad to take the bones they threw to their dogs; and yet, when I was a little fellow, and laid awake whole nights and cried, it wasn't the hunger, it wasn't the whipping, I cried for. No, sir, it was for *my mother* and *my sisters*—it was because I hadn't a friend to love me on earth. I never knew what peace or comfort was. I never had a kind word spoken to me till I came to work in your factory. Mr. Wilson, you treated me well; you encouraged me to do well, and to learn to read and write, and to try to make something of myself; and God knows how grateful I am for it. Then, sir, I found my wife; you've seen her—you know how beautiful she is. When I found she loved me, when I married her, I scarcely could believe I was alive, I was so happy; and, sir, she is as good as she is beautiful. But now what? Why, now comes my master, takes me right away from my work, and my friends, and all I like, and grinds me down into the very dirt! And why? Because, he says, I forgot who I was; he says, to teach me that I am only a nigger! After all, and last of all, he comes between me and my wife, and says I shall give her up, and live with another woman. And all this your laws give him power to do, in spite of God or man. Mr. Wilson, look at it! There

isn't *one* of all these things, that have broken the hearts of my mother and my sister, and my wife and myself, but your laws allow, and give every man power to do, in Kentucky, and none can say to him nay! Do you call these the laws of *my* country? Sir, I haven't any country, any more than I have any father. But I'm going to have one. I don't want anything of *your* country, except to be let alone—to go peaceably out of it; and when I get to Canada, where the laws will own me and protect me, *that* shall be my country, and its laws I will obey. But if any man tries to stop me, let him take care, for I am desperate. I'll fight for my liberty to the last breath I breathe. You say your fathers did it; if it was right for them, it is right for me!"

This speech, delivered partly while sitting at the table, and partly walking up and down the room—delivered with tears, and flashing eyes, and despairing gestures—was altogether too much for the good-natured old body to whom it was addressed, who had pulled out a great yellow silk pocket-handkerchief, and was mopping up his face with great energy.

"Blast 'em all!" he suddenly broke out. "Haven't I always said so—the infernal old cusses! I hope I an't swearing, now. Well! go ahead, George, go ahead; but be careful, my boy; don't shoot anybody, George, unless—well—you'd *better* not shoot, I reckon; at least, I wouldn't *hit* anybody, you know. Where is your wife, George?" he added, as he nervously rose, and began walking the room.

"Gone, sir, gone, with her child in her arms, the Lord only knows where—gone after the north star; and when we ever meet, or whether we meet at all in this world, no creature can tell."

"Is it possible! astonishing! from such a kind family?"

"Kind families get in debt, and the laws of *our* country allow them to sell the child out of its mother's bosom to pay its master's debts," said George, bitterly.

"Well, well," said the honest old man, fumbling in his pocket: "I s'pose, perhaps, I an't following my judgment—hang it, I *won't* follow my judgment!" he added, suddenly; "so here, George," and, taking out a roll of bills from his pocket-book, he offered them to George.

"No, my kind, good sir!" said George, "you've done a great deal for me, and this might get you into trouble.

---

[1]   *for wanting … Christian life*   The implication here is that she refused to perform sexual services.

I have money enough, I hope, to take me as far as I need it."

"No; but you must, George. Money is a great help everywhere; can't have too much, if you get it honestly. Take it—*do* take it, *now*—do, my boy!"

"On condition, sir, that I may repay it at some future time, I will," said George, taking up the money.

"And now, George, how long are you going to travel in this way? not long or far, I hope. It's well carried on, but too bold. And this black fellow—who is he?"

"A true fellow, who went to Canada more than a year ago. He heard, after he got there, that his master was so angry at him for going off that he had whipped his poor old mother; and he has come all the way back to comfort her, and get a chance to get her away."

"Has he got her?"

"Not yet; he has been hanging about the place, and found no chance yet. Meanwhile, he is going with me as far as Ohio, to put me among friends that helped him, and then he will come back after her."

"Dangerous, very dangerous!" said the old man.

George drew himself up, and smiled disdainfully.

The old gentleman eyed him from head to foot, with a sort of innocent wonder.

"George, something has brought you out wonderfully. You hold up your head, and speak and move like another man," said Mr. Wilson.

"Because I'm a *freeman*!" said George, proudly. "Yes, sir; I've said Mas'r for the last time to any man. *I'm free!*"

"Take care! You are not sure—you may be taken."

"All men are free and equal *in the grave*, if it comes to that, Mr. Wilson," said George.

"I'm perfectly dumb-foundered with your boldness!" said Mr. Wilson, "to come right here to the nearest tavern!"

"Mr. Wilson, it is *so* bold, and this tavern is so near, that they will never think of it; they will look for me on ahead, and you yourself wouldn't know me. Jim's master don't live in this county; he isn't known in these parts. Besides, he is given up; nobody is looking after him, and nobody will take me up from the advertisement, I think."

"But the mark in your hand?"

George drew off his glove, and showed a newly-healed scar in his hand.

"That is a parting proof of Mr. Harris' regard," he said, scornfully. "A fortnight ago, he took it into his head to give it to me, because he said he believed I should try to get away one of these days. Looks interesting, doesn't it?" he said, drawing his glove on again.

"I declare, my very blood runs cold when I think of it—your condition and your risks!" said Mr. Wilson.

"Mine has run cold a good many years, Mr. Wilson; at present, it's about up to the boiling point," said George.

"Well, my good sir," continued George, after a few moments' silence, "I saw you knew me; I thought I'd just have this talk with you, lest your surprised looks should bring me out. I leave early tomorrow morning, before daylight; by tomorrow night I hope to sleep safe in Ohio. I shall travel by daylight, stop at the best hotels, go to the dinner-tables with the lords of the land. So, goodbye, sir; if you hear that I'm taken, you may know that I'm dead!"

George stood up like a rock, and put out his hand with the air of a prince. The friendly little old man shook it heartily, and after a little shower of caution, he took his umbrella, and fumbled his way out of the room.

George stood thoughtfully looking at the door, as the old man closed it. A thought seemed to flash across his mind. He hastily stepped to it, and opening it, said,

"Mr. Wilson, one word more."

The old gentleman entered again, and George, as before, locked the door, and then stood for a few moments looking on the floor, irresolutely. At last, raising his head with a sudden effort—

"Mr. Wilson, you have shown yourself a Christian in your treatment of me—I want to ask one last deed of Christian kindness of you."

"Well, George."

"Well, sir—what you said was true. I *am* running a dreadful risk. There isn't, on earth, a living soul to care if I die," he added, drawing his breath hard, and speaking with a great effort, "I shall be kicked out and buried like a dog, and nobody'll think of it a day after—*only my poor wife!* Poor soul! she'll mourn and grieve; and if you'd only contrive, Mr. Wilson, to send this little pin to her. She gave it to me for a Christmas present, poor child! Give it to her, and tell her I loved her to the last. Will you? *Will* you?" he added, earnestly.

"Yes, certainly—poor fellow!" said the old gentleman, taking the pin, with watery eyes, and a melancholy quiver in his voice.

"Tell her one thing," said George; "it's my last wish, if she *can* get to Canada, to go there. No matter how kind her mistress is—no matter how much she loves her home; beg her not to go back—for slavery always ends in misery. Tell her to bring up our boy a free man, and then he won't suffer as I have. Tell her this, Mr. Wilson, will you?"

"Yes, George, I'll tell her; but I trust you won't die; take heart—you're a brave fellow. Trust in the Lord, George. I wish in my heart you were safe through, though—that's what I do."

"*Is* there a God to trust in?" said George, in such a tone of bitter despair as arrested the old gentleman's words. "O, I've seen things all my life that have made me feel that there can't be a God. You Christians don't know how these things look to us. There's a God for you, but is there any for us?"

"O, now, don't—don't, my boy!" said the old man, almost sobbing as he spoke; "don't feel so! There is— there is; clouds and darkness are around about him, but righteousness and judgment are the habitation of his throne.[1] There's a *God*, George—believe it; trust in Him, and I'm sure He'll help you. Everything will be set right—if not in this life, in another."

The real piety and benevolence of the simple old man invested him with a temporary dignity and authority, as he spoke. George stopped his distracted walk up and down the room, stood thoughtfully a moment, and then said, quietly,

"Thank you for saying that, my good friend; I'll *think of that*."

[Meanwhile, Tom has been taken from the Shelbys by Haley. He has a tearful parting with Master George, who promises Tom that he will buy him back one day. Tom and Haley—who has purchased several more enslaved people at an auction along the way—board the riverboat *La Belle Rivière* to New Orleans, but on the journey, Tom rescues a white child named Eva St. Clare from drowning; at Eva's request, her father Augustine purchases Tom, and brings him home to their Louisiana estate. Two

years pass, during which period Tom is treated with relative kindness, especially by the pious young Eva, with whom he develops an affectionate friendship.

Chapter 26 picks up after Eva has grown seriously ill, and the family have moved to their summer residence on Lake Pontchartrain.]

CHAPTER 26
DEATH

Weep not for those whom the veil of the tomb,
  In life's early morning, hath hid from our eyes.[2]

Eva's bedroom was a spacious apartment, which, like all the other rooms in the house, opened on to the broad verandah. The room communicated, on one side, with her father and mother's apartment; on the other, with that appropriated to Miss Ophelia.[3] St. Clare had gratified his own eye and taste in furnishing this room in a style that had a peculiar keeping with the character of her for whom it was intended. The windows were hung with curtains of rose-colored and white muslin, the floor was spread with a matting which had been ordered in Paris, to a pattern of his own device, having round it a border of rose-buds and leaves, and a centrepiece with full-blown roses. The bedstead, chairs, and lounges were of bamboo, wrought in peculiarly graceful and fanciful patterns. Over the head of the bed was an alabaster bracket, on which a beautiful sculptured angel stood, with drooping wings, holding out a crown of myrtle-leaves. From this depended,[4] over the bed, light curtains of rose-colored gauze, striped with silver, supplying that protection from mosquitos which is an indispensable addition to all sleeping accommodation in that climate. The graceful bamboo lounges were amply supplied with cushions of rose-colored damask, while over them, depending from the hands of sculptured figures, were gauze curtains similar to those of the bed. A light, fanciful bamboo table stood in the middle of the room,

---

[1]   *clouds and ... his throne*   See Psalm 97.2.

[2]   *Weep not ... our eyes*   See "Weep Not for Those" by Irish poet Thomas Moore (1779–1852).

[3]   *Miss Ophelia*   Augustine St. Clare's Northern cousin, an abolitionist, who has come to stay with the family.

[4]   *depended*   Hung.

where a Parian vase,[1] wrought in the shape of a white lily, with its buds, stood, ever filled with flowers. On this table lay Eva's books and little trinkets, with an elegantly wrought alabaster writing-stand, which her father had supplied to her when he saw her trying to improve herself in writing. There was a fireplace in the room, and on the marble mantle above stood a beautifully wrought statuette of Jesus receiving little children, and on either side marble vases, for which it was Tom's pride and delight to offer bouquets every morning. Two or three exquisite paintings of children, in various attitudes,[2] embellished the wall. In short, the eye could turn nowhere without meeting images of childhood, of beauty, and of peace. Those little eyes never opened, in the morning light, without falling on something which suggested to the heart soothing and beautiful thoughts.

The deceitful strength which had buoyed Eva up for a little while was fast passing away; seldom and more seldom her light footstep was heard in the verandah, and oftener and oftener she was found reclined on a little lounge by the open window, her large, deep eyes fixed on the rising and falling waters of the lake.

It was towards the middle of the afternoon, as she was so reclining—her Bible half open, her little transparent fingers lying listlessly between the leaves—suddenly she heard her mother's voice, in sharp tones, in the verandah.

"What now, you baggage! what new piece of mischief! You've been picking the flowers, hey?" and Eva heard the sound of a smart slap.

"Law, Missis! they's for Miss Eva," she heard a voice say, which she knew belonged to Topsy.[3]

"Miss Eva! A pretty excuse! you suppose she wants *your* flowers, you good-for-nothing nigger! Get along off with you!"

In a moment, Eva was off from her lounge, and in the verandah.

"O, don't, mother! I should like the flowers; do give them to me; I want them!"

"Why, Eva, your room is full now."

"I can't have too many," said Eva. "Topsy, do bring them here."

Topsy, who had stood sullenly, holding down her head, now came up and offered her flowers. She did it with a look of hesitation and bashfulness, quite unlike the eldrich[4] boldness and brightness which was usual with her.

"It's a beautiful bouquet!" said Eva, looking at it.

It was rather a singular one, a brilliant scarlet geranium, and one single white japonica,[5] with its glossy leaves. It was tied up with an evident eye to the contrast of color, and the arrangement of every leaf had carefully been studied.

Topsy looked pleased, as Eva said, "Topsy, you arrange flowers very prettily. Here," she said, "is this vase I haven't any flowers for. I wish you'd arrange something every day for it."

"Well, that's odd!" said Marie. "What in the world do you want that for?"

"Never mind, mamma; you'd as lief[6] as not Topsy should do it—had you not?"

"Of course, anything you please, dear! Topsy, you hear your young mistress; see that you mind."

Topsy made a short courtesy, and looked down; and, as she turned away, Eva saw a tear roll down her dark cheek.

"You see, mamma, I knew poor Topsy wanted to do something for me," said Eva to her mother.

"O, nonsense! it's only because she likes to do mischief. She knows she mustn't pick flowers—so she does it; that's all there is to it. But, if you fancy to have her pluck them, so be it."

"Mamma, I think Topsy is different from what she used to be; she's trying to be a good girl."

"She'll have to try a good while before *she* gets to be good," said Marie, with a careless laugh.

"Well, you know, mamma, poor Topsy! everything has always been against her."

"Not since she's been here, I'm sure. If she hasn't been talked to, and preached to, and every earthly thing done that anybody could do—and she's just so

---

[1]   *Parian vase*   Vase made of a type of bisque porcelain, designed to imitate carved marble.

[2]   *attitudes*   Poses.

[3]   *Topsy*   A young enslaved girl who has recently been purchased by Augustine St. Clare; as recounted in Chapter 20 (included in the website component of this anthology), Topsy has spent most of her childhood living under extraordinary cruelty.

[4]   *eldrich*   Odd, or spooky.

[5]   *japonica*   Likely *camellia japonica*, an east Asian plant widely grown in the American South and bearing large, ornate flowers.

[6]   *lief*   Happily.

ugly, and always will be; you can't make anything of the creature!"

"But, mamma, it's so different to be brought up as I've been, with so many friends, so many things to make me good and happy; and to be brought up as she's been, all the time, till she came here!"

"Most likely," said Marie, yawning, "dear me, how hot it is!"

"Mamma, you believe, don't you, that Topsy could become an angel, as well as any of us, if she were a Christian?"

"Topsy! what a ridiculous idea! Nobody but you would ever think of it. I suppose she could, though."

"But, mamma, isn't God her father, as much as ours? Isn't Jesus her Saviour?"

"Well, that may be. I suppose God made everybody," said Marie. "Where is my smelling bottle?"[1]

"It's such a pity—oh! *such* a pity!" said Eva, looking out on the distant lake, and speaking half to herself.

"What's a pity?" said Marie.

"Why, that anyone, who could be a bright angel, and live with angels, should go all down, down, down, and nobody help them! oh, dear!"

"Well, we can't help it; it's no use worrying, Eva! I don't know what's to be done; we ought to be thankful for our own advantages."

"I hardly can be," said Eva, "I'm so sorry to think of poor folks that haven't any."

"That's odd enough," said Marie; "I'm sure my religion makes me thankful for my advantages."

"Mamma," said Eva, "I want to have some of my hair cut off—a good deal of it."

"What for?" said Marie.

"Mamma, I want to give some away to my friends, while I am able to give it to them myself. Won't you ask aunty to come and cut it for me?"

Marie raised her voice, and called Miss Ophelia, from the other room.

The child half rose from her pillow as she came in, and, shaking down her long golden-brown curls, said, rather playfully, "Come, aunty, shear the sheep!"

"What's that?" said St. Clare, who just then entered with some fruit he had been out to get for her.

"Papa, I just want aunty to cut off some of my hair; there's too much of it, and it makes my head hot. Besides, I want to give some of it away."

Miss Ophelia came, with her scissors.

"Take care—don't spoil the looks of it!" said her father; "cut underneath, where it won't show. Eva's curls are my pride."

"O, papa!" said Eva, sadly.

"Yes, and I want them kept handsome against the time I take you up to your uncle's plantation, to see Cousin Henrique," said St. Clare, in a gay tone.

"I shall never go there, papa; I am going to a better country. O, do believe me! Don't you see, papa, that I get weaker, every day?"

"Why do you insist that I shall believe such a cruel thing, Eva?" said her father.

"Only because it is *true*, papa: and, if you will believe it now, perhaps you will get to feel about it as I do."

St. Clare closed his lips, and stood gloomily eying the long, beautiful curls which, as they were separated from the child's head, were laid, one by one, in her lap. She raised them up, looked earnestly at them, twined them around her thin fingers, and looked, from time to time, anxiously at her father.

"It's just what I've been foreboding!" said Marie; "it's just what has been preying on my health, from day to day, bringing me downward to the grave, though nobody regards it. I have seen this, long. St. Clare, you will see, after a while, that I was right."

"Which will afford you great consolation, no doubt!" said St. Clare, in a dry, bitter tone.

Marie lay back on a lounge, and covered her face with her cambric handkerchief.

Eva's clear blue eye looked earnestly from one to the other. It was the calm, comprehending gaze of a soul half loosed from its earthly bonds; it was evident she saw, felt, and appreciated, the difference between the two.

She beckoned with her hand to her father. He came, and sat down by her.

"Papa, my strength fades away every day, and I know I must go. There are some things I want to say and do—that I ought to do; and you are so unwilling to have me speak a word on this subject. But it must come; there's no putting it off. Do be willing I should speak now!"

---

[1]   *smelling bottle*   I.e., bottle of smelling salts, a compound used to enliven people who are feeling faint.

"My child, I *am* willing!" said St. Clare, covering his eyes with one hand, and holding up Eva's hand with the other.

"Then, I want to see all our people together. I have some things I *must* say to them," said Eva.

"*Well*," said St. Clare, in a tone of dry endurance.

Miss Ophelia dispatched a messenger, and soon the whole of the servants were convened in the room.

Eva lay back on her pillows; her hair hanging loosely about her face, her crimson cheeks contrasting painfully with the intense whiteness of her complexion and the thin contour of her limbs and features, and her large, soul-like eyes fixed earnestly on everyone.

The servants were struck with a sudden emotion. The spiritual face, the long locks of hair cut off and lying by her, her father's averted face, and Marie's sobs, struck at once upon the feelings of a sensitive and impressible race; and, as they came in, they looked one on another, sighed, and shook their heads. There was a deep silence, like that of a funeral.

Eva raised herself, and looked long and earnestly round at everyone. All looked sad and apprehensive. Many of the women hid their faces in their aprons.

"I sent for you all, my dear friends," said Eva, "because I love you. I love you all; and I have something to say to you, which I want you always to remember. I am going to leave you. In a few more weeks, you will see me no more—"

Here the child was interrupted by bursts of groans, sobs, and lamentations, which broke from all present, and in which her slender voice was lost entirely. She waited a moment, and then, speaking in a tone that checked the sobs of all, she said,

"If you love me, you must not interrupt me so. Listen to what I say. I want to speak to you about your souls. . . . . . Many of you, I am afraid, are very careless. You are thinking only about this world. I want you to remember that there is a beautiful world, where Jesus is. I am going there, and you can go there. It is for you, as much as me. But, if you want to go there, you must not live idle, careless, thoughtless lives. You must be Christians. You must remember that each one of you can become angels, and be angels forever. . . . . If you want to be Christians, Jesus will help you. You must pray to him; you must read—"

The child checked herself, looked piteously at them, and said, sorrowfully,

"O, dear! you *can't* read[1]—poor souls!" and she hid her face in the pillow and sobbed, while many a smothered sob from those she was addressing, who were kneeling on the floor, aroused her.

"Never mind," she said, raising her face and smiling brightly through her tears, "I have prayed for you; and I know Jesus will help you, even if you can't read. Try all to do the best you can; pray every day; ask Him to help you, and get the Bible read to you whenever you can; and I think I shall see you all in heaven."

"Amen," was the murmured response from the lips of Tom and Mammy, and some of the elder ones, who belonged to the Methodist church. The younger and more thoughtless ones, for the time completely overcome, were sobbing, with their heads bowed upon their knees.

"I know," said Eva, "you all love me."

"Yes; oh, yes! indeed we do! Lord bless her!" was the involuntary answer of all.

"Yes, I know you do! There isn't one of you that hasn't always been very kind to me; and I want to give you something that, when you look at, you shall always remember me. I'm going to give all of you a curl of my hair; and, when you look at it, think that I loved you and am gone to heaven, and that I want to see you all there."

It is impossible to describe the scene, as, with tears and sobs, they gathered round the little creature, and took from her hands what seemed to them a last mark of her love. They fell on their knees; they sobbed, and prayed, and kissed the hem of her garment; and the elder ones poured forth words of endearment, mingled in prayers and blessings, after the manner of their susceptible race.

As each one took their gift, Miss Ophelia, who was apprehensive for the effect of all this excitement on her little patient, signed to each one to pass out of the apartment.

At last, all were gone but Tom and Mammy.

"Here, Uncle Tom," said Eva, "is a beautiful one for you. O, I am so happy, Uncle Tom, to think I shall see

---

[1]   *you can't read* Unlike Kentucky—but like most other slave states—Louisiana had strict legislation against teaching enslaved people to read or write.

you in heaven—for I'm sure I shall; and Mammy—dear, good, kind Mammy!" she said, fondly throwing her arms round her old nurse—"I know you'll be there, too."

"O Miss Eva, don't see how I can live without ye, no how!" said the faithful creature. "'Pears like it's just taking everything off the place to oncet!"[1] And Mammy gave way to a passion of grief.

Miss Ophelia pushed her and Tom gently from the apartment, and thought they were all gone; but, as she turned, Topsy was standing there.

"Where did you start up from?" she said, suddenly.

"I was here," said Topsy, wiping the tears from her eyes. "O, Miss Eva, I've been a bad girl; but won't you give *me* one, too?"

"Yes, poor Topsy! to be sure, I will. There—every time you look at that, think that I love you, and wanted you to be a good girl!"

"O, Miss Eva, I *is* tryin!" said Topsy, earnestly; "but, Lor, it's so hard to be good! 'Pears like I an't used to it, no ways!"

"Jesus knows it, Topsy; he is sorry for you; he will help you."

Topsy, with her eyes hid in her apron, was silently passed from the apartment by Miss Ophelia; but, as she went, she hid the precious curl in her bosom.

All being gone, Miss Ophelia shut the door. That worthy lady had wiped away many tears of her own, during the scene; but concern for the consequence of such an excitement to her young charge was uppermost in her mind.

St. Clare had been sitting, during the whole time, with his hand shading his eyes, in the same attitude. When they were all gone, he sat so still.

"Papa!" said Eva, gently, laying her hand on his.

He gave a sudden start and shiver; but made no answer.

"Dear papa!" said Eva.

"I *cannot*," said St. Clare, rising, "I *cannot* have it so! The Almighty hath dealt *very bitterly* with me!"[2] and St. Clare pronounced these words with a bitter emphasis, indeed.

"Augustine! has not God a right to do what he will with his own?" said Miss Ophelia.

"Perhaps so; but that doesn't make it any easier to bear," said he, with a dry, hard, tearless manner, as he turned away.

"Papa, you break my heart!" said Eva, rising and throwing herself into his arms; "you must not feel so!" and the child sobbed and wept with a violence which alarmed them all, and turned her father's thoughts at once to another channel.

"There, Eva—there, dearest! Hush! hush! I was wrong; I was wicked. I will feel anyway, do anyway—only don't distress yourself; don't sob so. I will be resigned; I was wicked to speak as I did."

Eva soon lay like a wearied dove in her father's arms; and he, bending over her, soothed her by every tender word he could think of.

Marie rose and threw herself out of the apartment into her own, when she fell into violent hysterics.

"You didn't give me a curl, Eva," said her father, smiling sadly.

"They are all yours, papa," said she, smiling—"yours and mamma's; and you must give dear aunty as many as she wants. I only gave them to our poor people myself, because you know, papa, they might be forgotten when I am gone, and because I hoped it might help them remember. . . . . . You are a Christian, are you not, papa?" said Eva, doubtfully.

"Why do you ask me?"

"I don't know. You are so good, I don't see how you can help it."

"What is being a Christian, Eva?"

"Loving Christ most of all," said Eva.

"Do you, Eva?"

"Certainly I do."

"You never saw him," said St. Clare.

"That makes no difference," said Eva. "I believe him, and in a few days I shall *see* him"; and the young face grew fervent, radiant with joy.

St. Clare said no more. It was a feeling which he had seen before in his mother; but no chord within vibrated to it.

Eva, after this, declined rapidly; there was no more any doubt of the event; the fondest hope could not be blinded. Her beautiful room was avowedly a sick room; and Miss Ophelia day and night performed the duties of a nurse—and never did her friends appreciate her value more than in that capacity. With so

---

[1]   *to oncet*   At once.

[2]   *The Almighty ... with me*   See Ruth 1.20.

well-trained a hand and eye, such perfect adroitness and practice in every art which could promote neatness and comfort, and keep out of sight every disagreeable incident of sickness—with such a perfect sense of time, such a clear, untroubled head, such exact accuracy in remembering every prescription and direction of the doctors—she was everything to him. They who had shrugged their shoulders at her little peculiarities and setnesses, so unlike the careless freedom of southern manners, acknowledged that now she was the exact person that was wanted.

Uncle Tom was much in Eva's room. The child suffered much from nervous restlessness, and it was a relief to her to be carried; and it was Tom's greatest delight to carry her little frail form in his arms, resting on a pillow, now up and down her room, now out into the verandah; and when the fresh sea-breezes blew from the lake—and the child felt freshest in the morning—he would sometimes walk with her under the orange-trees in the garden, or, sitting down in some of their old seats, sing to her their favorite old hymns.

Her father often did the same thing; but his frame was slighter, and when he was weary, Eva would say to him,

"O, papa, let Tom take me. Poor fellow! it pleases him; and you know it's all he can do now, and he wants to do something!"

"So do I, Eva!" said her father.

"Well, papa, you can do everything, and are everything to me. You read to me—you sit up nights—and Tom has only this one thing, and his singing; and I know, too, he does it easier than you can. He carries me so strong!"

The desire to do something was not confined to Tom. Every servant in the establishment showed the same feeling, and in their way did what they could.

Poor Mammy's heart yearned towards her darling; but she found no opportunity, night or day, as Marie declared that the state of her mind[1] was such, it was impossible for her to rest; and, of course, it was against her principles to let anyone else rest. Twenty times in a night, Mammy would be roused to rub her feet, to bathe her head, to find her pocket-handkerchief, to see what the noise was in Eva's room, to let down a curtain because it was too light, or to put it up because it was too dark; and, in the daytime, when she longed to have some share in the nursing of her pet, Marie seemed unusually ingenious in keeping her busy anywhere and everywhere all over the house, or about her own person; so that stolen interviews and momentary glimpses were all she could obtain.

"I feel it my duty to be particularly careful of myself, now," she would say, "feeble as I am, and with the whole care and nursing of that dear child upon me."

"Indeed, my dear," said St. Clare, "I thought our cousin relieved you of that."

"You talk like a man, St. Clare—just as if a mother *could* be relieved of the care of a child in that state; but, then, it's all alike—no one ever knows what I feel! I can't throw things off, as you do."

St. Clare smiled. You must excuse him, he couldn't help it—for St. Clare could smile yet. For so bright and placid was the farewell voyage of the little spirit—by such sweet and fragrant breezes was the small bark[2] borne towards the heavenly shores—that it was impossible to realize that it was death that was approaching. The child felt no pain—only a tranquil, soft weakness, daily and almost insensibly increasing; and she was so beautiful, so loving, so trustful, so happy, that one could not resist the soothing influence of that air of innocence and peace which seemed to breathe around her. St. Clare found a strange calm coming over him. It was not hope—that was impossible; it was not resignation; it was only a calm resting in the present, which seemed so beautiful that he wished to think of no future. It was like that hush of spirit which we feel amid the bright, mild woods of autumn, when the bright hectic flush is on the trees, and the last lingering flowers by the brook; and we joy in it all the more, because we know that soon it will all pass away.

The friend who knew most of Eva's own imaginings and foreshadowings was her faithful bearer, Tom. To him she said what she would not disturb her father by saying. To him she imparted those mysterious intimations which the soul feels, as the cords begin to unbind, ere it leaves its clay[3] forever.

---

[1] *the state of her mind* Marie suffers from a variety of physical and mental ailments that are strongly implied by the narrator to be of her own invention; her enslaved handmaid, Mammy, is forced to abandon her own children in order to attend to Marie day and night.

[2] *bark* Boat.

[3] *clay* Earthly body.

Tom, at last, would not sleep in his room, but lay all night in the outer verandah, ready to rouse at every call.

"Uncle Tom, what alive[1] have you taken to sleeping anywhere and everywhere, like a dog, for?" said Miss Ophelia. "I thought you was one of the orderly sort, that liked to lie in bed in a Christian way."

"I do, Miss Feely," said Tom, mysteriously. "I do, but now—"

"Well, what now?"

"We mustn't speak loud; Mas'r St. Clare won't hear on't; but Miss Feely, you know there must be somebody watchin' for the bridegroom."

"What do you mean, Tom?"

"You know it says in Scripture, 'At midnight there was a great cry made. Behold, the bridegroom cometh.'[2] That's what I'm spectin now, every night, Miss Feely—and I couldn't sleep out o' hearin, no ways."

"Why, Uncle Tom, what makes you think so?"

"Miss Eva, she talks to me. The Lord, he sends his messenger in the soul. I must be thar, Miss Feely; for when that ar blessed child goes into the kingdom, they'll open the door so wide, we'll all get a look in at the glory, Miss Feely."

"Uncle Tom, did Miss Eva say she felt more unwell than usual tonight?"

"No; but she told me, this morning, she was coming nearer—thar's them that tells it to the child, Miss Feely. It's the angels—'it's the trumpet sound afore the break o' day,'[3] said Tom, quoting from a favorite hymn.

This dialogue passed between Miss Ophelia and Tom, between ten and eleven, one evening, after her arrangements had all been made for the night, when, on going to bolt her outer door, she found Tom stretched along by it, in the outer verandah.

She was not nervous or impressible; but the solemn, heartfelt manner struck her. Eva had been unusually bright and cheerful, that afternoon, and had sat raised in her bed, and looked over all her little trinkets and precious things, and designated the friends to whom she would have them given; and her manner was more animated, and her voice more natural, than they had known it for weeks. Her father had been in, in the evening, and had said that Eva appeared more like her former self than ever she had done since her sickness; and when he kissed her for the night, he said to Miss Ophelia, "Cousin, we may keep her with us, after all; she is certainly better"; and he had retired with a lighter heart in his bosom than he had had there for weeks.

But at midnight—strange, mystic hour!—when the veil between the frail present and the eternal future grows thin—then came the messenger!

There was a sound in that chamber, first of one who stepped quickly. It was Miss Ophelia, who had resolved to sit up all night with her little charge, and who, at the turn of the night, had discerned what experienced nurses significantly call "a change." The outer door was quickly opened, and Tom, who was watching outside, was on the alert, in a moment.

"Go for the doctor, Tom! lose not a moment," said Miss Ophelia; and, stepping across the room, she rapped at St. Clare's door.

"Cousin," she said, "I wish you would come."

Those words fell on his heart like clods upon a coffin. Why did they? He was up and in the room in an instant, and bending over Eva, who still slept.

What was it he saw that made his heart stand still? Why was no word spoken between the two? Thou canst say, who hast seen that same expression on the face dearest to thee; that look indescribable, hopeless, unmistakable, that says to thee that thy beloved is no longer thine.

On the face of the child, however, there was no ghastly imprint—only a high and almost sublime expression—the overshadowing presence of spiritual natures, the dawning of immortal life in that childish soul.

They stood there so still, gazing upon her, that even the ticking of the watch seemed too loud. In a few moments, Tom returned, with the doctor. He entered, gave one look, and stood silent as the rest.

"When did this change take place?" said he, in a low whisper, to Miss Ophelia.

"About the turn of the night," was the reply.

---

1 *what alive* I.e., why on earth.

2 *the bridegroom cometh* See Matthew 25.1: "Then shall the kingdom of heaven be likened unto ten virgins, which took their lamps, and went forth to meet the bridegroom."

3 *it's the … o' day* Line from "The Wings of the Morning," a hymn commonly sung in camp meetings. The line is taken from Psalm 139.9.

Marie, roused by the entrance of the doctor, appeared, hurriedly, from the next room.

"Augustine! Cousin! O! what!" she hurriedly began.

"Hush!" said St. Clare, hoarsely; "*she is dying!*"

Mammy heard the words, and flew to awaken the servants. The house was soon roused—lights were seen, footsteps heard, anxious faces thronged the verandah, and looked tearfully through the glass doors; but St. Clare heard and said nothing—he saw only *that look* on the face of the little sleeper.

"O, if she would only wake, and speak once more!" he said; and, stooping over her, he spoke in her ear, "Eva, darling!"

The large blue eyes unclosed—a smile passed over her face; she tried to raise her head, and to speak.

"Do you know me, Eva?"

"Dear papa," said the child, with a last effort, throwing her arms about his neck. In a moment they dropped again; and, as St. Clare raised his head, he saw a spasm of mortal agony pass over the face—she struggled for breath, and threw up her little hands.

"O, God, this is dreadful!" he said, turning away in agony, and wringing Tom's hand, scarce conscious what he was doing. "O, Tom, my boy, it is killing me!"

Tom had his master's hands between his own; and, with tears streaming down his dark cheeks, looked up for help where he had always been used to look.

"Pray that this may be cut short!" said St. Clare, "this wrings my heart."

"O, bless the Lord! it's over—it's over, dear Master!" said Tom; "look at her."

The child lay panting on her pillows, as one exhausted—the large clear eyes rolled up and fixed. Ah, what said those eyes, that spoke so much of heaven? Earth was past, and earthly pain; but so solemn, so mysterious, was the triumphant brightness of that face, that it checked even the sobs of sorrow. They pressed around her, in breathless stillness.

"Eva," said St. Clare, gently.

She did not hear.

"O, Eva, tell us what you see! What is it?" said her father.

A bright, a glorious smile passed over her face, and she said, brokenly, "O! love, joy, peace!" gave one sigh, and passed from death unto life!

"Farewell, beloved child! the bright, eternal doors have closed after thee; we shall see thy sweet face no more. O, woe for them who watched thy entrance into heaven, when they shall wake and find only the cold gray sky of daily life, and thou gone forever!"

[Following Eva's death, several characters embrace Christianity, including Augustine, who resolves to eventually free those whom he enslaves. His plans fail, however, upon his death in a tavern fight, leading his wife to take control of the estate. Marie sells Tom to Simon Legree, an exceedingly cruel planter in rural Louisiana who takes a particular dislike to Tom because of his religious convictions. Tom is purchased alongside Emmeline, a young woman whom Legree clearly intends to force into sexual slavery, and at the plantation he meets the older Cassy, who suffered the same fate under Legree previously. With Tom's help, Emmeline and Cassy resolve to flee the plantation.]

CHAPTER 40
THE MARTYR

Deem not the just by Heaven forgot!
    Though life its common gifts deny—
Though, with a crushed and bleeding heart,
    And spurned of man, he goes to die!
For God hath marked each sorrowing day,
    And numbered every bitter tear;
And heaven's long years of bliss shall pay
    For all his children suffer here.[1]   BRYANT

The longest way must have its close—the gloomiest night will wear on to a morning. An eternal, inexorable lapse of moments is ever hurrying the day of the evil to an eternal night, and the night of the just to an eternal day. We have walked with our humble friend thus far in the valley of slavery; first through flowery fields of ease and indulgence, then through heartbreaking separations from all that man holds dear. Again, we have waited with him in a sunny island, where generous hands concealed his chains with flowers; and, lastly, we

---

[1] *Deem not ... suffer here* See "Blessed Are They that Mourn" (1832) by American poet and supporter of abolition William Cullen Bryant (1794–1878). The first line of this passage actually reads, "Nor let the good man's trust depart."

have followed him when the last ray of earthly hope went out in night, and seen how, in the blackness of earthly darkness, the firmament of the unseen has blazed with stars of new and significant lustre.

The morning-star now stands over the tops of the mountains, and gales and breezes, not of earth, show that the gates of day are unclosing.

The escape of Cassy and Emmeline irritated the before surly temper of Legree to the last degree; and his fury, as was to be expected, fell upon the defence-less head of Tom. When he hurriedly announced the tidings among his hands, there was a sudden light in Tom's eye, a sudden upraising of his hands, that did not escape him. He saw that he did not join the muster of the pursuers. He thought of forcing him to do it; but, having had, of old, experience of his inflexibility when commanded to take part in any deed of inhu-manity, he would not, in his hurry, stop to enter into any conflict with him.

Tom, therefore, remained behind, with a few who had learned of him to pray, and offered up prayers for the escape of the fugitives.

When Legree returned, baffled and disappointed, all the long-working hatred of his soul towards his slave began to gather in a deadly and desperate form. Had not this man braved him—steadily, powerfully, resistlessly—ever since he bought him? Was there not a spirit in him which, silent as it was, burned on him like the fires of perdition?

"I *hate* him!" said Legree, that night, as he sat up in his bed; "I *hate* him! And isn't he MINE? Can't I do what I like with him? Who's to hinder, I wonder?" And Legree clenched his fist, and shook it, as if he had something in his hands that he could rend in pieces.

But, then, Tom was a faithful, valuable servant; and, although Legree hated him the more for that, yet the consideration was still somewhat of a restraint to him.

The next morning, he determined to say nothing, as yet; to assemble a party, from some neighboring plan-tations, with dogs and guns; to surround the swamp, and go about the hunt systematically. If it succeeded, well and good; if not, he would summon Tom before him, and—his teeth clenched and his blood boiled—*then* he would break that fellow down, or—there was a dire inward whisper, to which his soul assented.

Ye say that the *interest* of the master is a sufficient safeguard for the slave. In the fury of man's mad will, he will wittingly, and with open eye, sell his own soul to the devil to gain his ends; and will he be more care-ful of his neighbor's body?

"Well," said Cassy, the next day, from the garret, as she reconnoitred through the knothole, "the hunt's going to begin again, today!"

Three or four mounted horsemen were curvetting[1] about on the space front of the house; and one or two leashes of strange dogs were struggling with the negroes who held them, baying and barking at each other.

The men are, two of them, overseers of plantations in the vicinity; and others were some of Legree's associ-ates at the tavern-bar of a neighboring city, who had come for the interest of the sport. A more hard-favored set, perhaps, could not be imagined. Legree was serving brandy, profusely, round among them, as also among the negroes, who had been detailed from the various plantations for this service; for it was an object to make every service of this kind, among the negroes, as much of a holiday as possible.

Cassy placed her ear at the knothole; and, as the morning air blew directly towards the house, she could overhear a good deal of the conversation. A grave sneer overcast the dark, severe gravity of her face, as she lis-tened, and heard them divide out the ground, discuss the rival merits of the dogs, give orders about firing, and the treatment of each, in case of capture.

Cassy drew back; and, clasping her hands, looked upward, and said, "O, great Almighty God! we are *all* sinners; but what have *we* done, more than all the rest of the world, that we should be treated so?"

There was a terrible earnestness in her face and voice, as she spoke.

"If it wasn't for *you*, child," she said, looking at Emmeline, "I'd *go* out to them; and I'd thank any one of them that *would* shoot me down; for what use will freedom be to me? Can it give me back my children, or make me what I used to be?"[2]

---

1   *curvetting* Leaping or frolicking.

2   *Can it ... to be?* Cassy was separated from her own children when she was purchased by Legree; she eventually became pregnant by him, and subsequently killed the child rather than have it suffer under slavery as well.

Emmeline, in her childlike simplicity, was half afraid of the dark moods of Cassy. She looked perplexed, but made no answer. She only took her hand, with a gentle, caressing movement.

"Don't!" said Cassy, trying to draw it away; "you'll get me to loving you; and I never mean to love anything, again!"

"Poor Cassy!" said Emmeline, "don't feel so! If the Lord gives us liberty, perhaps he'll give you back your daughter; at any rate, I'll be like a daughter to you. I know I'll never see my poor old mother again! I shall love you, Cassy, whether you love me or not!"

The gentle, childlike spirit conquered. Cassy sat down by her, put her arm round her neck, stroked her soft, brown hair; and Emmeline then wondered at the beauty of her magnificent eyes, now soft with tears.

"O, Em!" said Cassy, "I've hungered for my children, and thirsted for them, and my eyes fail with longing for them! Here! here!" she said, striking her breast, "it's all desolate, all empty! If God would give me back my children, then I could pray."

"You must trust him, Cassy," said Emmeline; "he is our Father!"

"His wrath is upon us," said Cassy; "he has turned away in anger."

"No, Cassy! He will be good to us! Let us hope in Him," said Emmeline—"I always have had hope."

———

The hunt was long, animated, and thorough, but unsuccessful; and, with grave, ironic exultation, Cassy looked down on Legree as, weary and dispirited, he alighted from his horse.

"Now, Quimbo," said Legree, as he stretched himself down in the sitting room, "you jest go and walk that Tom up here, right away! The old cuss is at the bottom of this yer whole matter; and I'll have it out of his old black hide, or I'll know the reason why!"

Sambo and Quimbo both, though hating each other, were joined in one mind by a no less cordial hatred of Tom. Legree had told them, at first, that he had bought him for a general overseer, in his absence; and this had begun an ill will, on their part, which had increased, in their debased and servile natures, as they saw him becoming obnoxious to their master's

displeasure. Quimbo, therefore, departed, with a will, to execute his orders.

Tom heard the message with a forewarning heart; for he knew all the plan of the fugitives' escape, and the place of their present concealment; he knew the deadly character of the man he had to deal with, and his despotic power. But he felt strong in God to meet death, rather than betray the helpless.

He sat his basket down by the row, and, looking up, said, "Into thy hands I commend my spirit! Thou hast redeemed me, oh Lord God of truth!"[1] and then quietly yielded himself to the rough, brutal grasp with which Quimbo seized him.

"Ay, ay!" said the giant, as he dragged him along; "ye'll cotch it, now! I'll boun' Mas'r's back's up *high*! No sneaking out, now! Tell ye, ye'll get it, and no mistake! See how ye'll look, now, helpin' Mas'r's niggers to run away! See what ye'll get!"

The savage words none of them reached that ear! A higher voice there was saying, "Fear not them that kill the body, and, after that, have no more that they can do."[2] Nerve and bone of that poor man's body vibrated to those words, as if touched by the finger of God; and he felt the strength of a thousand souls in one. As he passed along, the trees and bushes, the huts of his servitude, the whole scene of his degradation, seemed to whirl by him as the landscape by the rushing car. His soul throbbed—his home was in sight—and the hour of release seemed at hand.

"Well, Tom!" said Legree, walking up, and seizing him grimly by the collar of his coat, and speaking through his teeth, in a paroxysm of determined rage, "do you know I've made up my mind to KILL you?"

"It's very likely, Mas'r," said Tom, calmly.

"I *have*," said Legree, with grim, terrible calmness, "*done—just—that—thing*, Tom, unless you'll tell me what you know about these yer gals!"

Tom stood silent.

"D'ye hear?" said Legree, stamping, with a roar like that of an incensed lion. "Speak!"

---

[1] *Into thy hands ... truth* See Luke 23.46, the last words of Christ on the cross: "And when Jesus had cried with a loud voice, he said, Father, into thy hands I commend my spirit: and having said thus, he gave up the ghost."

[2] *Fear not ... can do* See Matthew 10.28: "And fear not them which kill the body, but are not able to kill the soul: but rather fear him which is able to destroy both soul and body in hell."

"*I han't got nothing to tell, Mas'r*," said Tom, with a slow, firm, deliberate utterance.

"Do you dare to tell me, ye old black Christian, ye don't *know*?" said Legree.

Tom was silent.

"Speak!" thundered Legree, striking him furiously. "Do you know anything?"

"I know, Mas'r; but I can't tell anything. *I can die!*"

Legree drew in a long breath; and, suppressing his rage, took Tom by the arm, and, approaching his face almost to his, said, in a terrible voice, "Hark 'e, Tom! Ye think, 'cause I've let you off before, I don't mean what I say; but, this time, I've *made up my mind*, and counted the cost. You've always stood it out agin' me: now, I'll *conquer ye, or kill ye!* one or t' other. I'll count every drop of blood there is in you, and take 'em, one by one, till ye give up!"

Tom looked up to his master, and answered, "Mas'r, if you was sick, or in trouble, or dying, and I could save ye, I'd *give* ye my heart's blood; and, if taking every drop of blood in this poor old body would save your precious soul, I'd give 'em freely, as the Lord gave his for me. O, Mas'r! don't bring this great sin on your soul! It will hurt you more than 't will me! Do the worst you can, my troubles 'll be over soon; but, if ye don't repent, yours won't *never* end!"

Like a strange snatch of heavenly music, heard in the lull of a tempest, this burst of feeling made a moment's blank pause. Legree stood aghast, and looked at Tom; and there was such a silence, that the tick of the old clock could be heard, measuring, with silent touch, the last moments of mercy and probation to that hardened heart.

It was but a moment. There was one hesitating pause—one irresolute, relenting thrill—and the spirit of evil came back, with seven-fold vehemence; and Legree, foaming with rage, smote his victim to the ground.

———

Scenes of blood and cruelty are shocking to our ear and heart. What man has nerve to do, man has not nerve to hear. What brother-man and brother-Christian must suffer, cannot be told us, even in our secret chamber, it so harrows up the soul! And yet, oh my country!

these things are done under the shadow of thy laws! O, Christ! thy church sees them, almost in silence!

But, of old, there was One whose suffering changed an instrument of torture, degradation and shame, into a symbol of glory, honor, and immortal life;[1] and, where His spirit is, neither degrading stripes, nor blood, nor insults, can make the Christian's last struggle less than glorious.

Was he alone, that long night, whose brave, loving spirit was bearing up, in that old shed, against buffeting and brutal stripes?

Nay! There stood by him One—seen by him alone—"like unto the Son of God."[2]

The tempter[3] stood by him, too—blinded by furious, despotic will—every moment pressing him to shun that agony by the betrayal of the innocent. But the brave, true heart was firm on the Eternal Rock.[4] Like his Master, he knew that, if he saved others, himself he could not save; nor could utmost extremity wring from him words, save of prayer and holy trust.

"He's most gone, Mas'r," said Sambo, touched, in spite of himself, by the patience of his victim.

"Pay away, till he gives up! Give it to him! give it to him!" shouted Legree. "I'll take every drop of blood he has, unless he confesses!"

Tom opened his eyes, and looked upon his master. "Ye poor miserable critter!" he said, "there an't no more ye can do! I forgive ye,[5] with all my soul!" and he fainted entirely away.

"I b'lieve, my soul, he's done for, finally," said Legree, stepping forward, to look at him. "Yes, he is! Well, his mouth's shut up, at last—that's one comfort!"

Yes, Legree; but who shall shut up that voice in thy soul? that soul, past repentance, past prayer, past

---

1   *One whose ... immortal life*   Reference to Christ's sacrifice on the cross.

2   *One ... of God*   I.e., God. See Hebrews 7.3: "Without father, without mother, without descent, having neither beginning of days, nor end of life; but made like unto the Son of God; abideth a priest continually."

3   *tempter*   Satan.

4   *Eternal Rock*   The "Rock of Ages" is a common metaphor for Christ, as well as the name of a popular Christian hymn.

5   *I forgive ye*   Words spoken by Christ at the beginning of his crucifixion; see Luke 23.34: "Then said Jesus, Father, forgive them; for they know not what they do. And they parted his raiment, and cast lots."

hope, in whom the fire that never shall be quenched is already burning!

Yet Tom was not quite gone. His wondrous words and pious prayers had struck upon the hearts of the imbruted blacks, who had been the instruments of cruelty upon him; and, the instant Legree withdrew, they took him down, and, in their ignorance, sought to call him back to life—as if *that* were any favor to him.

"Sartin, we's been doin' a drefful wicked thing!" said Sambo; "hopes Mas'r 'll have to 'count for it, and not we."

They washed his wounds—they provided a rude[1] bed of some refuse cotton for him to lie down on; and one of them, stealing up to the house, begged a drink of brandy of Legree, pretending that he was tired, and wanted it for himself. He brought it back, and poured it down Tom's throat.

"O, Tom!" said Quimbo, "we's been awful wicked to ye!"

"I forgive ye, with all my heart!" said Tom, faintly.

"O, Tom! do tell us who is *Jesus*, anyhow?" said Sambo; "Jesus, that's been a standin' by you so, all this night! Who is he?"

The word roused the failing, fainting spirit. He poured forth a few energetic sentences of that wondrous One—his life, his death, his everlasting presence, and power to save.

They wept—both the two savage men.

"Why didn't I never hear this before?" said Sambo; "but I do believe! I can't help it! Lord Jesus, have mercy on us!"

"Poor critters!" said Tom, "I'd be willing to bar' all I have, if it'll only bring ye to Christ! O, Lord! give me these two more souls, I pray!"

That prayer was answered!

CHAPTER 41
THE YOUNG MASTER

Two days after, a young man drove a light wagon up through the avenue of china trees,[2] and, throwing the reins hastily on the horses' neck, sprang out and inquired for the owner of the place.

It was George Shelby; and, to show how he came to be there, we must go back in our story.

The letter of Miss Ophelia to Mrs. Shelby[3] had, by some unfortunate accident, been detained, for a month or two, at some remote post-office, before it reached its destination; and, of course, before it was received, Tom was already lost to view among the distant swamps of the Red River.

Mrs. Shelby read the intelligence with the deepest concern; but any immediate action upon it was an impossibility. She was then in attendance on the sickbed of her husband, who lay delirious in the crisis of a fever. Master George Shelby, who, in the interval, had changed from a boy to a tall young man, was her constant and faithful assistant, and her only reliance in superintending his father's affairs. Miss Ophelia had taken the precaution to send them the name of the lawyer who did business for the St. Clares; and the most that, in the emergency, could be done, was to address a letter of inquiry to him. The sudden death of Mr. Shelby a few days after brought, of course, an absorbing pressure of other interests, for a season.

Mr. Shelby showed his confidence in his wife's ability, by appointing her sole executrix upon his estates; and thus immediately a large and complicated amount of business was brought upon her hands.

Mrs. Shelby, with characteristic energy, applied herself to the work of straightening the entangled web of affairs; and she and George were for some time occupied with collecting and examining accounts, selling property and settling debts; for Mrs. Shelby was determined that everything should be brought into tangible and recognizable shape, let the consequences to her prove what they might. In the meantime they received a letter from the lawyer to whom Miss Ophelia had referred them, saying that he knew nothing of the matter; that the man was sold at a public auction, and that, beyond receiving the money, he knew nothing of the affair.

---

[1]   *rude* Crude; rustic.

[2]   *china trees* Native to southeast Asia and Australia, the *Melia azedarach* is naturalized in the Southern United States and known for its long clusters of purple flowers and ornamental yellow fruit.

[3]   *The letter ... Mrs. Shelby* Before Tom's sale, and after unsuccessfully pleading with Marie St. Clare to grant Tom his freedom, Miss Ophelia had sent a letter to Mrs. Shelby, in the hopes that she could send funds for his purchase.

Neither George nor Mrs. Shelby could be easy at this result; and, accordingly, some six months after, the latter,[1] having business for his mother down the river, resolved to visit New Orleans in person and push his inquiries, in hopes of discovering Tom's whereabouts, and restoring him.

After some months of unsuccessful search, by the merest accident, George fell in with a man in New Orleans who happened to be possessed of the desired information; and with his money in his pocket, our hero took steamboat for Red River, resolving to find out and re-purchase his old friend.

He was soon introduced into the house, where he found Legree in the sitting room.

Legree received the stranger with a kind of surly hospitality.

"I understand," said the young man, "that you bought, in New Orleans, a boy, named Tom. He used to be on my father's place, and I came to see if I couldn't buy him back."

Legree's brow grew dark, and he broke out, passionately: "Yes, I did buy such a fellow—and a h—l of a bargain I had of it, too! The most rebellious, saucy, impudent dog! Set up my niggers to run away; got off two gals, worth eight hundred or a thousand dollars apiece. He owned to that, and, when I bid him tell me where they was, he up and said he knew, but he wouldn't tell; and stood to it, though I gave him the cussedest flogging I ever gave nigger yet. I b'lieve he's trying to die; but I don't know as he'll make it out."

"Where is he?" said George, impetuously. "Let me see him." The cheeks of the young man were crimson, and his eyes flashed fire; but he prudently said nothing, as yet.

"He's in dat ar shed," said a little fellow, who stood holding George's horse.

Legree kicked the boy, and swore at him; but George, without saying another word, turned and strode to the spot.

Tom had been lying two days since the fatal night; not suffering, for every nerve of suffering was blunted and destroyed. He lay, for the most part, in a quiet stupor; for the laws of a powerful and well-knit frame would not at once release the imprisoned spirit. By stealth, there had been there, in the darkness of the night, poor desolated creatures, who stole from their scanty hours' rest, that they might repay to him some of those ministrations of love in which he had always been so abundant. Truly, those poor disciples had little to give—only the cup of cold water;[2] but it was given with full hearts.

Tears had fallen on that honest, insensible face—tears of late repentance in the poor, ignorant heathen, whom his dying love and patience had awakened to repentance, and bitter prayers, breathed over him to a late-found Saviour, of whom they scarce knew more than the name, but whom the yearning ignorant heart of man never implores in vain.

Cassy, who had glided out of her place of concealment, and, by over-hearing, learned the sacrifice that had been made for her and Emmeline, had been there, the night before, defying the danger of detection; and, moved by the few last words which the affectionate soul had yet strength to breathe, the long winter of despair, the ice of years, had given way, and the dark, despairing woman had wept and prayed.

When George entered the shed, he felt his head giddy[3] and his heart sick.

"Is it possible—is it possible?" said he, kneeling down by him. "Uncle Tom, my poor, poor old friend!"

Something in the voice penetrated to the ear of the dying. He moved his head gently, smiled, and said,

Jesus can make a dying-bed
Feel soft as downy pillows are.[4]

Tears which did honor to his manly heart fell from the young man's eyes as he bent over his poor friend.

"O, dear Uncle Tom! do wake—do speak once more! Look up! Here's Mas'r George—your own little Mas'r George. Don't you know me?"

"Mas'r George!" said Tom, opening his eyes, and speaking in a feeble voice; "Mas'r George!" He looked bewildered.

---

1   *the latter* A slip: Stowe clearly intends "the former."

2   *the cup of cold water* See Matthew 10.42: "And whosoever shall give to drink unto one of these little ones a cup of cold water only in the name of a disciple, verily I say unto you, he shall in no wise lose his reward."

3   *giddy* Dizzy.

4   *Jesus can … pillows are* See "Hymn 31" by popular hymnodist Isaac Watts (1674–1748). In the nineteenth century, these lines were often used as gravestone epitaphs.

Slowly the idea seemed to fill his soul; and the vacant eye became fixed and brightened, the whole face lighted up, the hard hands clasped, and tears ran down the cheeks.

"Bless the Lord! it is—it is—it's all I wanted! They haven't forgot me. It warms my soul; it does my old heart good! Now I shall die content! Bless the Lord, oh my soul!"

"You shan't die! you *mustn't* die, nor think of it! I've come to buy you, and take you home," said George, with impetuous vehemence.

"O, Mas'r George, ye're too late. The Lord's bought me, and is going to take me home—and I long to go. Heaven is better than Kintuck."

"O, don't die! It'll kill me! It'll break my heart to think what you've suffered—and lying in this old shed, here! Poor, poor fellow!"

"Don't call me poor fellow!" said Tom, solemnly. "I *have* been poor fellow; but that's all past and gone, now. I'm right in the door, going into glory! O, Mas'r George! *Heaven has come!* I've got the victory! The Lord Jesus has given it to me! Glory be to His name!"

George was awestruck at the force, the vehemence, the power, with which these broken sentences were uttered. He sat gazing in silence.

Tom grasped his hand, and continued, "Ye mustn't, now, tell Chloe, poor soul! how ye found me—'t would be so drefful to her. Only tell her ye found me going into glory; and that I couldn't stay for no one. And tell her the Lord's stood by me everywhere and al'ays, and made everything light and easy. And oh, the poor chil'en, and the baby! my old heart's been most broke for 'em, time and agin! Tell 'em all to follow me— follow me! Give my love to Mas'r, and dear good Missis, and everybody in the place! Ye don't know! 'Pears like I loves 'em all! I loves every creatur', everywhar! it's nothing *but* love! O, Mas'r George! what a thing 't is to be a Christian!"

At this moment, Legree sauntered up to the door of the shed, looked in, with a dogged air of affected carelessness, and turned away.

"The old satan!" said George, in his indignation. "It's a comfort to think the devil will pay *him* for this, some of these days!"

"O, don't! oh, ye mustn't!" said Tom, grasping his hand; "he's a poor mis'able critter! it's awful to think

on 't! O, if he only could repent, the Lord would forgive him now; but I'm 'feared he never will!"

"I hope he won't!" said George; "I never want to see *him* in heaven!"

"Hush, Mas'r George! it worries me! Don't feel so! He an't done me no real harm—only opened the gate of the kingdom for me; that's all!"

At this moment, the sudden flush of strength which the joy of meeting his young master had infused into the dying man gave way. A sudden sinking fell upon him; he closed his eyes; and that mysterious and sublime change passed over his face, that told the approach of other worlds.

He began to draw his breath with long, deep inspirations; and his broad chest rose and fell, heavily. The expression of his face was that of a conqueror.

"Who—who—who shall separate us from the love of Christ?"[1] he said, in a voice that contended with mortal weakness; and, with a smile, he fell asleep.

George sat fixed with solemn awe. It seemed to him that the place was holy; and, as he closed the lifeless eyes, and rose up from the dead, only one thought possessed him—that expressed by his simple old friend— "What a thing it is to be a Christian!"

He turned: Legree was standing, sullenly, behind him.

Something in that dying scene had checked the natural fierceness of youthful passion. The presence of the man was simply loathsome to George; and he felt only an impulse to get away from him, with as few words as possible.

Fixing his keen dark eyes on Legree, he simply said, pointing to the dead, "You have got all you ever can of him. What shall I pay you for the body? I will take it away, and bury it decently."

"I don't sell dead niggers," said Legree, doggedly. "You are welcome to bury him where and when you like."

"Boys," said George, in an authoritative tone, to two or three negroes, who were looking at the body, "help me lift him up, and carry him to my wagon; and get me a spade."

---

[1] *Who … of Christ?* See Romans 8.35: "Who shall separate us from the love of Christ? shall tribulation, or distress, or persecution, or famine, or nakedness, or peril, or sword?"

One of them ran for a spade; the other two assisted George to carry the body to the wagon.

George neither spoke to nor looked at Legree, who did not countermand his orders, but stood, whistling, with an air of forced unconcern. He sulkily followed them to where the wagon stood at the door.

George spread his cloak in the wagon, and had the body carefully disposed of in it—moving the seat, so as to give it room. Then he turned, fixed his eyes on Legree, and said, with forced composure,

"I have not, as yet, said to you what I think of this most atrocious affair; this is not the time and place. But, sir, this innocent blood shall have justice. I will proclaim this murder.[1] I will go to the very first magistrate, and expose you."

"Do!" said Legree, snapping his fingers, scornfully. "I'd like to see you doing it. Where you going to get witnesses? how you going to prove it? Come, now!"

George saw, at once, the force of this defiance. There was not a white person on the place; and, in all southern courts, the testimony of colored blood is nothing. He felt, at that moment, as if he could have rent the heavens with his heart's indignant cry for justice; but in vain.

"After all, what a fuss, for a dead nigger!" said Legree.

The word was as a spark to a powder magazine.[2] Prudence was never a cardinal virtue of the Kentucky boy. George turned, and, with one indignant blow, knocked Legree flat upon his face; and, as he stood over him, blazing with wrath and defiance, he would have formed no bad personification of his great namesake triumphing over the dragon.[3]

Some men, however, are decidedly bettered by being knocked down. If a man lays them fairly flat in the dust, they seem immediately to conceive a respect for him; and Legree was one of this sort. As he rose, therefore, and brushed the dust from his clothes, he eyed the slowly retreating wagon with some evident consideration; nor did he open his mouth till it was out of sight.

Beyond the boundaries of the plantation, George had noticed a dry, sandy knoll, shaded by a few trees: there they made the grave.

"Shall we take off the cloak, Mas'r?" said the negroes, when the grave was ready.

"No, no—bury it with him! It's all I can give you, now, poor Tom, and you shall have it."

They laid him in; and the men shovelled away, silently. They banked it up, and laid green turf over it.

"You may go, boys," said George, slipping a quarter into the hand of each. They lingered about, however.

"If young Mas'r would please buy us—" said one.

"We'd serve him so faithful!" said the other.

"Hard times here, Mas'r!" said the first. "Do, Mas'r, buy us, please!"

"I can't! I can't!" said George, with difficulty, motioning them off; "it's impossible!"

The poor fellows looked dejected, and walked off in silence.

"Witness, eternal God!" said George, kneeling on the grave of his poor friend; "oh, witness, that, from this hour, I will do *what one man can* to drive out this curse of slavery from my land!"

There is no monument to mark the last resting-place of our friend. He needs none! His Lord knows where he lies, and will raise him up, immortal, to appear with him when he shall appear in his glory.

Pity him not! Such a life and death is not for pity! Not in the riches of omnipotence is the chief glory of God; but in self-denying, suffering love! And blessed are the men whom he calls to fellowship with him, bearing their cross after him with patience. Of such it is written, "Blessed are they that mourn, for they shall be comforted."[4]

[The story of George, Eliza, and Harry is concluded in the novel's final chapters. The family is reunited, and they successfully make their way to Canada, where they live in peace for several years. Over time,

---

[1]   *I will ... murder* As in other slave states, it was illegal in Louisiana to kill an enslaved person, or to punish an enslaved person with excessive cruelty. However, such crimes were almost never prosecuted, and offenders were if convicted punished only with modest fines; only a tiny number of instances have been recorded where slaveowners received the maximum punishment for murder. Furthermore, the testimony of another enslaved person or a free African American was not accepted in courts.

[2]   *powder magazine* Storehouse of gunpowder.

[3]   *his great namesake ... dragon* Reference to the legend of Saint George (c. 275–303), the Patron Saint of England, who is said to have slain a dragon that tyrannized a village, demanding human sacrifices.

[4]   *Blessed are ... be comforted* See Matthew 5.4, from Jesus' Sermon on the Mount.

however, George Harris finds himself uncomfortable with his position in a predominantly white community and yearning to connect with his African ancestry. The Harrises ultimately make their way to Liberia, an American colony in West Africa founded by whites as a settlement for free blacks.]

—1852

[NOTE: Chapters 1, 3–5, 7–12, 20, 26, 40, 41, and 45 are included in full in the website component of this anthology.]

IN CONTEXT

Visualizing *Uncle Tom's Cabin* in the Nineteenth Century

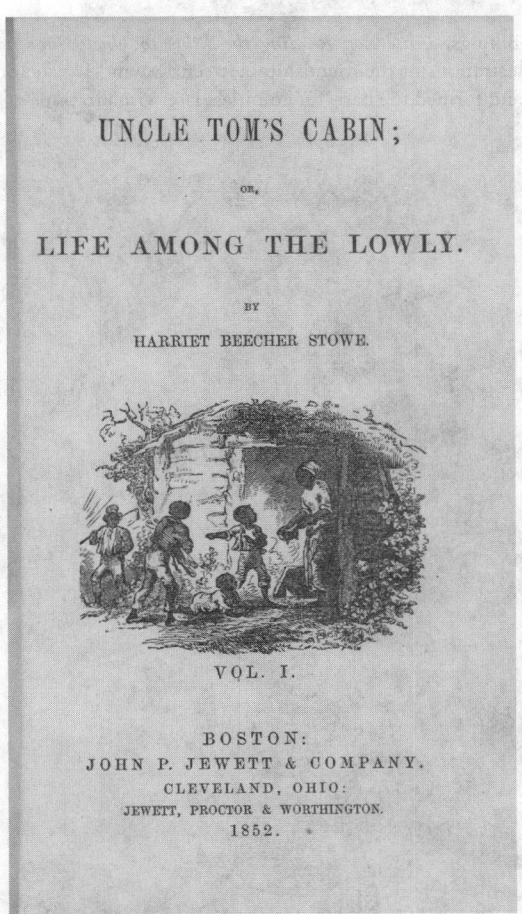

Frontispiece of the first edition of *Uncle Tom's Cabin*, which featured seven illustrations by Boston-based engraver Hammatt Billings (1818–74). Billings was already known for his work on the illustrated magazine *Gleason's Pictorial*, and in 1850 had redesigned the iconic masthead for the influential abolitionist newspaper *The Liberator*.

Hammatt Billings, *Little Eva Reading the Bible to Uncle Tom in the Arbor*, 1852. Billings's illustrations of the friendship between Eva and Uncle Tom were extremely influential and formed the basis for countless later visualizations of the novel.

Louisa Corbaux, *Eva and Topsy*, 1852. Colored lithograph.

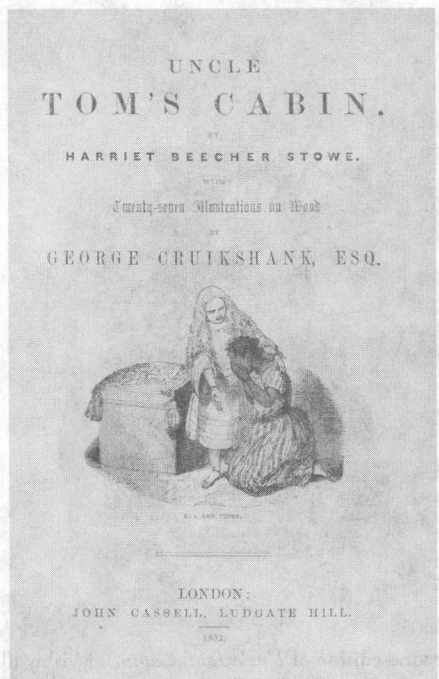

George Cruikshank, *Topsy with Miss Ophelia's Wardrobe*, 1852.

Frontispiece to the 1852 London edition, illustrated by George Cruikshank. Earlier in his career, Cruikshank (1792–1878) was best known as a caricaturist, his cartoons often targeting the royal family, contemporary fashions, and political ideologies on either side of the spectrum; interestingly, many of his cartoons targeted the abolitionist movement in particular, and were highly racist. He turned increasingly to book illustration in the 1830s, providing illustrations for several novels by Charles Dickens. The London edition featured twenty-seven engravings designed by Cruikshank.

George Cruikshank, *Eliza Crosses the Ohio on the Floating Ice*, 1852.

White actor Caroline Howard in blackface as the character of Topsy in the 1852 stage adaptation of *Uncle Tom's Cabin*, written by George Aiken. The play was produced by Caroline's father, George C. Howard, who himself starred as George Harris; other members of the Howard family also acted in the play.

For Christmas 1852, Jewett and Co. commissioned a second edition of *Uncle Tom's Cabin*, a lavishly illustrated "gift book" featuring over one hundred new images by Hammatt Billings. One of the last images in the edition is this one depicting a crowd of freed people reaching towards the African continent. The narrative of George and Eliza Harris in the novel concludes with them emigrating to Liberia, a colony that had been established by white politicians expressly for freed African Americans. The first edition of *Uncle Tom's Cabin* had sold for around $1.50; the Christmas edition sold for $15.

Advertisement for the 1881 stage play *Jay Rial's Ideal Uncle Tom's Cabin*. Eliza's dramatic escape over the Ohio was among the most popular scenes for stage adaptations of the novel, which often featured live bloodhounds—even though Eliza is not pursued by dogs in this scene in the original novel.

FANNY FERN

1811 – 1872

Over the course of her twenty-year writing career, Fanny Fern became one of the most popular, well-paid, and influential prose writers of her era. Her work was simultaneously beloved by those who found her frank and often comedic observations on mid-nineteenth-century society entertaining and refreshing, and censured by those who found her style and subject matter—as well as her financial independence and determined professionalism—to be unbecoming in a woman. Fern's informal, conversational prose and regular use of colloquialisms marked an important shift in the established literary conventions of nineteenth-century fiction and journalism.

Fern was born Sara Payson Willis in Portland, Maine in 1811, to Nathaniel and Hannah Parker Willis. Her education was completed at the renowned Hartford Female Seminary run by educational reformer Catharine Beecher; over the course of her time at the school she developed a reputation both for her wild behavior and for her lively intelligence and interest in writing, which her father, a printer of religious books and newspapers, later put to use by engaging her as a proofreader.

In 1837, at the age of twenty-six, Fern married Boston banker Charles Eldredge; the couple had three daughters before Eldredge died in 1845. His death was the last in a year-long string of tragedies during which Fern also lost a sister, her mother, and the couple's eldest daughter. Eldredge, who had been engaged in an expensive lawsuit at the point of his death, left the family severely in debt. The financial support Fern received from her father and her in-laws was minimal and reluctantly given. Instead, she was pressed to follow the conventional path of remarriage, to which she eventually capitulated, marrying widower Samuel Farrington in 1849. The marriage was a disaster. Farrington was controlling, emotionally abusive, and wildly jealous; less than two years after their marriage, Fern scandalized both their families by leaving him. Farrington would later obtain a divorce on grounds of desertion.

Having lost all financial support from her family, Fern struggled to earn money for herself and her two daughters through taking in sewing work. Eventually, Fern started writing articles. She submitted a few to her brother Nathaniel Parker Willis, now a prominent magazine editor, but he refused to publish her work or to publicly associate himself with a sister he felt had shamed him. Two Boston newspapers, however—the *Olive Branch* and the *True Flag*—began accepting her articles in late 1851.

Fern's writings included both snappy satires and opinion pieces (many of which poked fun at contemporary marriage conventions and gender roles), as well as sentimental sketches about family, death, childhood, and religion; all were written in relaxed, conversational language that stood out from the more formal prose style popular at the time. The articles elicited substantial debate about the identity of their author, especially on the matter of gender. Many readers doubted that a woman could be capable of writing so indelicately, though others noted how many of her articles spoke intimately of "feminine" subjects. The articles proved exceptionally popular, so much so that they were regularly pirated in competing newspapers—including newspapers owned by Parker Willis.

By the summer of 1852, Fern—who had now established "Fanny Fern" as her pen name—was sufficiently popular to have been offered an exclusive contract with the New York *Musical World and Times*; she would spend the rest of her career in New York City. In 1853, Fern published her first book, *Fern Leaves from Fanny's Portfolio*, a collection of her articles. This collection emphasized Fern's more sentimental sketches—though her more acerbic and humorous opinion pieces were at least as well known and popular. The collection sold astonishingly well, both in the United States and Britain. Fern was celebrated for popularizing a new prose style that was at once lively, casual, and intimate; in an 1854 review of her work, *Harper's Magazine* enthusiastically wrote that "the day for stilted rhetoric, scholastic refinements, and big dictionary words, the parade and pomp and pageantry of literature, is declining."

Near the end of 1854, Fern published her first novel, *Ruth Hall: A Domestic Tale of the Present Time*. The work is heavily autobiographical, telling the rags-to-riches story of its eponymous heroine who is widowed as a young woman, falls into dire poverty, and, despite the censure of her family, establishes a lucrative career as a columnist. The novel was an overwhelming success—again, notwithstanding the vocal criticism of those who felt its tone, as well as its focus on an independent, enterprising woman, to be unfeminine. A large number of *Ruth Hall*'s characters were clearly drawn from real life, including the unsympathetic character Hyacinth Ellet, whom many in the literary community recognized to be an accurate portrait of Nathaniel Parker Willis. The revelation of Fern's true identity by a spiteful former publisher in December 1854 fueled the novel's popularity, though it also added to the condemnations of critics who felt that "a woman that unsexes herself to abuse her parents and relatives, however much they may deserve it, is not a very agreeable personage."

Fern was continually aggravated by critics' tendencies to evaluate the personalities and private lives of female writers more so than the merits or demerits of their writing. Nevertheless, she continued to write boldly over the following years, developing a reputation for addressing provocative topics such as prostitution and sexual mores, prison reform, labor and the gendered pay gap, women's legal rights, education and childcare, and more, as well as reviewing literature; she was notable for her unqualified praise of Walt Whitman's innovative and controversial *Leaves of Grass* in 1855.

In 1855, Fern was offered a contract with *The New York Ledger*, whose owner, Robert Bonner, proposed the astounding sum of $100 per article. Fern's work for the *Ledger* over the next decade-and-a-half contributed to its becoming one of the most popular and influential newspapers of its era. The following year, Fern married the writer James Parton, who had befriended her early in her time in New York. At a time when the earnings of married women could legally be claimed by their husbands, the couple negotiated marriage terms ensuring that Fern's earnings would remain hers alone, to be inherited by her own children upon her death. A second novel, *Rose Clark*, was published that same year; a subplot follows a character whose experiences with an abusive husband closely mirror Fern's own.

The remainder of Fern's career was dominated by her work for the *Ledger*, though she also continued to release collections of her articles (now with somewhat less of an emphasis on sentimental sketches). She died of cancer in 1872, having continued to write regularly until days before her death.

Despite her immense popularity and influence in the nineteenth century, Fern was largely dismissed by critics in the early twentieth. Many literary scholars, focusing on her sentimental sketches rather than her social commentary and satire, employed the same dismissive tone they used in discussing other "sentimental" women writers (such as Fern's friend, Frances Osgood); Fred Lewis Pattee infamously wrote, in his 1940 work of literary criticism *The Feminine Fifties*, that Fern was the "most tearful and convulsingly 'female' moralizer of the whole modern blue-stocking school." Today, a good deal of Fern's work strikes readers as both remarkably forward-thinking and refreshingly readable; twenty-first-century scholarship often focuses on understanding and reconciling the seeming dichotomies of Fern's work, which was by turns sentimental and satirical, conventional and ground-breaking.

NOTE ON THE TEXTS: The versions of Fern's articles reprinted here are from the texts as they first appeared in her published collections, with four exceptions: the text of "Hints to Young Wives" is based on that which appeared in the 14 February 1852 issue of the *Olive Branch*, while the texts of "Male Criticism on Ladies' Books," "A Law More Nice than Just," and "Independence" are based on those that appeared in the *New York Ledger* in the 23 May 1857, the 10 July 1858, and the 30 July 1859 issues, respectively. Spelling and punctuation have been modernized in accordance with the practices of this anthology.

⌘ ⌘ ⌘

Hints to Young Wives

Shouldn't I like to make a bonfire of all the "Hints to Young Wives," "Married Woman's Friend," etc., and throw in the authors after them? I have a little neighbor who believes all they tell her is gospel truth, and lives up to it. The minute she sees her husband coming up the street, she makes for the door, as if she hadn't another minute to live, stands in the entry with her teeth chattering in her head till he gets all his coats and mufflers, and overshoes, and what-do-you-call-'ems off, then chases round (like a cat in a fit) after the boot-jack;[1] warms his slippers and puts 'em on, and dislocates her wrist carving at the table for fear it will tire him.

Poor little innocent fool! she imagines that's the way to preserve his affection. Preserve a fiddlestick! The consequence is, he's sick of the sight of her; snubs her when she asks him a question, and after he has eaten her good dinners takes himself off as soon as possible, bearing in mind the old proverb "that too much of a good thing is good for nothing." Now the truth is just this, and I wish all the women on earth had but one ear in common, so that I could put this little bit of gospel into it: Just so long as a man isn't quite as sure as if he knew for certain, whether nothing on earth could ever disturb your affection for him, he is your humble servant, but the very second he finds out (or thinks he does) that he has possession of every inch of your heart, and no neutral territory—he will turn on his heel and march off whistling "Yankee Doodle"!

Now it's no use to take your pocket handkerchief and go snivelling round the house with a pink nose and red eyes; not a bit of it! If you have made the interesting discovery that you were married for a sort of upper servant or housekeeper, just *fill that place and no other*, keep your temper, keep all his strings and buttons and straps on; and then keep him at a distance as a housekeeper should—"them's my sentiments!" I have seen one or two men in my life who could bear to be loved (as a woman with a soul knows how), without being spoiled by it, or converted into a tyrant—but they are rare birds, and should be caught, stuffed and handed over to Barnum![2] Now as the ministers say, "I'll close with an interesting little incident that came under my observation."

Mr. Fern[3] came home one day when I had such a crucifying headache that I couldn't have told whether I was married or single, and threw an old coat into my lap to mend. Well, I tied a wet bandage over my forehead, "left all flying," and sat down to it—he might as well have asked me to make a *new* one; however I new lined the sleeves, mended the buttonholes, sewed on new buttons down the front, and all over the coat tails—when finally it occurred to me (I believe it was a suggestion of Satan) that the *pocket* might need mending; so I turned it inside out, and *what do you think I found*? A *love-letter from him to my dress-maker*!! I dropped the coat, I dropped the work-basket, I dropped the buttons, I dropped the baby (it was a *female*, and I thought it just as well to put her out of future misery) and then I hopped into a chair in front of the looking-glass, and remarked to the young woman I saw there, "*F-a-n-n-y F-e-r-n! if you—are—ever—such—a—confounded fool again*"—and I wasn't.

—1852

A Practical Bluestocking[4]

"Have you called on your old friend, James Lee, since your return?" said Mr. Seldon to his nephew.

"No, sir; I understand he has the misfortune to have a bluestocking for a wife, and whenever I have thought of going there, a vision with inky fingers, frowzled hair, rumpled dress, and slip-shod heels[5] has come between me and my old friend—not to mention thoughts of

---

[1]   *boot-jack*   Tool used to assist in the removal of boots.

[2]   *Barnum*   Reference to the "American Museum" of entrepreneur P.T. Barnum (1810–91), which exhibited various scientific curiosities (many of which were hoaxes).

[3]   *Mr. Fern*   At the point at which this article was published, Fern was still legally married to the abusive Samuel Farrington, though she had left him early the previous year. Farrington eventually obtained a divorce on grounds of desertion.

[4]   *Bluestocking*   Literary or otherwise intellectually inclined woman, especially one who advocates for women's rights; the term often had a derogatory connotation in the nineteenth century.

[5]   *slip-shod heels*   Shoes worn down at the heel, or otherwise poorly taken care of.

a disorderly house, smoky puddings,[1] and dirty-faced children. Defend me from a wife who spends her time dabbling in ink, and writing for the papers. I'll lay a wager James hasn't a shirt with a button on it, or a pair of stockings that is not full of holes. Such a glorious fellow as he used to be, too!" said Harry, soliloquizingly, "so dependent upon somebody to love him. By Jove, it's a hard case."

"Harry, will you oblige me by calling there?" said Mr. Seldon with a peculiar smile.

"Well, yes, if you desire it; but these married men get so metamorphosed by their wives, that it's a chance if I recognize the melancholy remains of my old friend. A literary wife!" and he shrugged his shoulders contemptuously.

At one o'clock the next afternoon, Harry might have been seen ringing the bell of James Lee's door. He had a very ungracious look upon his face, as much as to say—"My mind is made up for the worst, and I must bear it for Jemmy's sake."

The servant ushered him into a pretty little sitting room, not expensively furnished, but neat and tasteful. At the further end of the room were some flowering plants, among which a sweet-voiced canary was singing. Harry glanced round the room; a little light-stand or Chinese table stood in the corner, with pen, ink, and papers scattered over it.

"I knew it," said Harry; "there's the sign! horror of horrors! an untidy, slatternly bluestocking! how I shall be disgusted with her! Jemmy's to be pitied."

He took up a book that lay upon the table, and a little manuscript copy of verses fell from between the leaves. He dropped the book as if he had been poisoned; then picking up the fallen manuscript with his thumb and forefinger, he replaced it with an impatient pshaw! Then he glanced round the room again—no! there was not a particle of dust to be seen, even by his prejudiced eyes; the windows were transparently clean; the hearth-rug was longitudinally and mathematically laid down; the pictures hung "plumb" upon the wall; the curtains were fresh and gracefully looped; and, what was a greater marvel, there was a child's dress half finished in a dainty little work-basket, and a thimble of fairy dimensions in the immediate neighborhood thereof. Harry felt a perverse inclination to examine the

stitches, but at the sound of approaching footsteps he braced himself up to undergo his mental shower-bath.

A little lady tripped lightly into the room, and stood smilingly before him; her glossy black hair was combed smoothly behind her ears, and knotted upon the back of a remarkably well-shaped head; her eyes were black and sparkling, and full of mirth; her dress fitted charmingly to a very charming little figure; her feet were unexceptionably small, and neatly gaitered;[2] the snowy fingers of her little hand had not the slightest "*soupçon*"[3] of ink upon them, as she extended them in token of welcome to her guest.

Harry felt very much like a culprit, and greatly inclined to drop on one knee, and make a clean breast of a confession, but his evil bachelor spirit whispered in his ear—"Wait a bit, she's fixed up for company; cloven foot[4] will peep out by and by!"

Well, they sat down! The lady knew enough—he heard that before he came; he only prayed that he might not be bored with her book-learning, or bluestockingism. It is hardly etiquette to report private conversations for the papers—so I will only say that when James Lee came home, two hours after, he found his old friend Harry in the finest possible spirits, *tête-à-tête*[5] with his "blue" wife. An invitation to dinner followed. Harry demurred—he had begun to look at the little lady through a very bewitching pair of spectacles, and he hated to be disenchanted—and a bluestocking dinner!

However, his objections, silent though they were, were overruled. There was no fault to be found with that tablecloth, or those snowy napkins; the glasses were clean, the silver bright as my lady's eyes; the meats cooked to a turn, the gravies and sauces perfect, and the dessert well got up and delicious. Mrs. Lee presided with ease and elegance; the custards and preserves were of her own manufacture, and the little prattler, who was introduced with them, fresh from her nursery bath, with moist ringlets, snowy robe, and dimpled shoulders, looked charmingly well cared for.

---

1   *smoky puddings*   I.e., burnt desserts.

2   *gaitered*   Covered with gaiters, cloth or leather coverings worn to protect shoes.

3   *soupçon*   French: tiny amount.

4   *cloven foot*   Sign of devilish intent.

5   *tête-à-tête*   In close conversation.

As soon as the two gentlemen were alone, Harry seized his friend's hand, saying, with a half smile, "James, I feel like an unmitigated scoundrel! I have heard your wife spoken of as a 'bluestocking,' and I came here prepared to pity you as the victim of an unshared heart, slatternly house, and indigestible cooking; but may I die an old bachelor if I don't wish that woman, who has just gone out, was my wife."

James Lee's eyes moistened with gratified pride. "You don't know half," said he. "Listen—some four years since[1] I became involved in business; at the same time my health failed me; my spirits were broken, and I was getting a discouraged man. Emma, unknown to me, made application as a writer to several papers and magazines. She soon became very popular; and not long after placed in my hands the sum of three hundred dollars, the product of her labor. During this time, no parental or household duty was neglected; and her cheerful and steady affection raised my drooping spirits, and gave me fresh courage to commence the world anew. She still continues to write, although, as you see, my head is above water. Thanks to her as my guardian angel, for she says, 'We must lay up something for a rainy day.' God bless her sunshiny face!"

The entrance of Emma put a stop to any further eulogy, and Harry took his leave in a very indescribable and penitential frame of mind, doing ample penance for his former unbelieving scruples, by being very uncomfortably in love with a "Bluestocking."

—1853

Soliloquy of a Housemaid

Oh, dear, dear! Wonder if my mistress *ever* thinks I am made of flesh and blood! Five times, within half an hour, I have trotted upstairs, to hand her things, that were only four feet from her rocking chair. Then, there's her son, Mr. George—it does seem to me, that a great able-bodied man like him, needn't call a poor tired woman up four pair of stairs to ask "what's the time of day?" Heigho! it's "*Sally* do this," and "*Sally* do that," till I wish I never had been baptized at all; and I might as well go farther back, while I am about it, and wish I had never been born.

Now, instead of ordering me round so like a dray horse,[2] if they would only look up smiling-like, now and then; or ask me how my "rheumatiz"[3] did; or say good morning, Sally; or show some sort of interest in a fellow-cretur, I could pluck up a bit of heart to work for them. A kind word would ease the wheels of my treadmill amazingly, and wouldn't cost *them* anything, either.

Look at my clothes, all at sixes and sevens.[4] I can't get a minute to sew on a string or button, except at night; and then I'm so sleepy it is as much as ever I can find the way to bed; and what a bed it is, to be sure! Why, even the pigs are now and then allowed clean straw to sleep on; and as to bedclothes, the less said about them the better; my old cloak serves for a blanket, and the sheets are as thin as a charity school soup. Well, well; one wouldn't think it, to see all the fine glittering things down in the drawing-room. Master's span of horses, and Miss Clara's diamond earrings, and mistress's rich dresses. I *try* to think it is all right, but it is no use.

Tomorrow is Sunday—"day of *rest*," I believe they *call* it. H-u-m-p-h! more cooking to be done—more company—more confusion than on any other day in the week. If I own a soul I have not heard how to take care of it for many a long day. Wonder if my master and mistress calculate to pay me for *that*, if I lose it? It is a *question* in my mind. Land of Goshen! I ain't sure I've got a mind—there's the bell again!

—1853

Male Criticism on Ladies' Books

Courtship and marriage, servants and children, these are the great objects of a woman's thoughts, and they necessarily form the staple topics of their writings and their conversation. We have no right to expect anything else in a woman's book.—*N.Y. Times*

---

[1] *since* Ago.

[2] *dray horse* Work horse.

[3] *rheumatiz* Rheumatism.

[4] *at sixes and sevens* In disarray.

Is it in feminine novels *only* that courtship, marriage, servants and children are the staple? Is not this true of all novels? Of Dickens, of Thackeray, of Bulwer[1] and a host of others? Is it peculiar to feminine pens, most astute and liberal of critics? Would a novel be a novel if it did not treat of courtship and marriage? and if it could be so recognized, would it find readers? When I see such a narrow, snarling criticism as the above, I always say to myself, the writer is some unhappy man, who has come up without the refining influence of mother, or sister, or reputable female friends; who has divided his migratory life between boarding houses, restaurants, and the outskirts of editorial sanctums; and who knows as much about reviewing a woman's book, as I do about navigating a ship, or engineering an omnibus[2] from the South Ferry, through Broadway, to Union Park. I think I see him writing that paragraph in a fit of spleen[3]—of *male* spleen—in his small boarding house upper chamber, by the cheerful light of a solitary candle, flickering alternately on cobwebbed walls, dusty washstand, begrimed bowl and pitcher, refuse cigar stumps, boot-jacks,[4] old hats, buttonless coats, muddy trousers, and all the wretched accompaniments of solitary, selfish male existence, not to speak of his own puckered, unkissable face; perhaps, in addition, his boots hurt, his cravat-bow persists in slipping under his ear for want[5] of a pin, and a wife to pin it (poor wretch!), or he has been refused by some pretty girl, as he deserved to be (narrow-minded old vinegar-cruet![6]), or snubbed by some lady authoress; or, more trying than all to the male constitution, has had a weak cup of coffee for that morning's breakfast.

But seriously—we have had quite enough of this shallow criticism (?) on lady-books. Whether the book which called forth the remark above quoted was a good book or a bad one, I know not: I should be inclined to think the *former* from the dispraise of such

a pen. Whether ladies can write novels or not, is a question I do not intend to discuss; but that some of them have no difficulty in finding either publishers or readers is a matter of history; and that gentlemen often write over feminine signatures would seem also to argue that feminine literature is, after all, in good odor[7] with the reading public. Granted that lady-novels are not all that they should be—is such shallow, unfair, wholesome, sneering criticism (?) the way to reform them? Would it not be better and more manly to point out a better way kindly, justly, *and, above all, respectfully*? or—what would be a much harder task for such critics—write a better book!
—1857

A Law More Nice[8] than Just

Here I have been sitting twiddling the morning paper between my fingers this half hour, reflecting upon the following paragraph in it: "Emma Wilson was arrested yesterday for wearing man's apparel."[9] Now, why this should be an actionable offense is past my finding out, or where's the harm in it, I am as much at a loss to see. Think of the old maids (and weep) who have to stay at home evening after evening, when, if they provided themselves with a coat, pants and hat, they might go abroad, instead of sitting there with their noses flattened against the window-pane, looking vainly for "the Coming Man."[10] Think of the married women who stay at home after their day's toil is done, waiting wearily for their thoughtless, truant husbands, when they might be taking the much needed independent walk in trousers, which custom forbids to petticoats. And this, I fancy, may be the secret of this famous law—who knows? It *wouldn't* be pleasant for some of them to be surprised by a touch on the shoulder from some dapper young fellow, whose familiar treble voice belied his corduroys.

---

[1] *Dickens ... Bulwer* Three popular male nineteenth-century novelists: Charles Dickens (1812–70), William Makepeace Thackeray (1811–63), and Edward Bulwer-Lytton (1803–73).

[2] *omnibus* Horse-drawn public carriage traveling a fixed route with set stops.

[3] *spleen* Bad temper.

[4] *boot-jacks* Implements to assist in the removal of boots.

[5] *want* Lack.

[6] *cruet* Bottle.

---

[7] *odor* Favor.

[8] *Nice* Proper; overly invested in the appearance of propriety.

[9] *Emma Wilson ... man's apparel* In the mid-to-late nineteenth century, many American municipalities had bylaws prohibiting individuals from dressing in garments conventionally associated with the opposite sex.

[10] *the Coming Man* I.e., a promising suitor.

That's it, now. What a fool I was not to think of it—not to remember that men who make the laws, make them to meet all these little emergencies.

Everybody knows what an everlasting drizzle of rain we have had lately, but nobody but a woman, and a woman who lives on fresh air and outdoor exercise, knows the thraldom of taking her daily walk through a three weeks' rain, with skirts to hold up, and umbrella to hold down, and puddles to skip over, and gutters to walk round, and all the time in a fright lest, in an unguarded moment, her calves should become visible to some one of those rainy-day philanthropists who are interested in the public study of female anatomy.

One evening, after a long rainy day of scribbling, when my nerves were in double-twisted knots, and I felt as if myriads of little ants were leisurely traveling over me, and all for want of the walk which is my daily salvation, I stood at the window, looking at the slanting, persistent rain, and took my resolve. "*I'll do it*," said I, audibly, planting my slipper upon the carpet. "Do what?" asked Mr. Fern,[1] looking up from a big book. "Put on a suit of your clothes and take a tramp with you," was the answer. "You dare not," was the rejoinder; "you are a little coward, only saucy on paper." It was the work of a moment, with such a challenge, to fly upstairs and overhaul my philosopher's wardrobe. Of course we had fun. Tailors[2] must be a stingy set, I remarked, to be so sparing of their cloth, as I struggled into a pair of their handiwork, undeterred by the vociferous laughter of the wretch who had solemnly vowed to "cherish me" through all my tribulations. "Upon my word, everything seems to be narrow where it ought to be broad, and the waist of this coat might be made for a hogshead;[3] and, ugh! this shirt collar is cutting my ears off, and you have not a decent cravat in the whole lot, and your vests are frights, and what am I to do with my hair?" Still no reply from Mr. Fern, who lay on the floor, faintly ejaculating, between his fits of laughter, "Oh, my! by Jove! oh! by Jupiter!"

Was that to hinder me? Of course not. Strings and pins, women's never-failing resort, soon brought broadcloth and kerseymere[4] to terms. I parted my hair on one side, rolled it under, and then secured it with hair pins; chose the best fitting coat, and capping the climax with one of those soft, cozy hats, looked in the glass,[5] where I beheld the very facsimile of a certain musical gentleman, whose photograph hangs this minute in Brady's entry.[6]

Well, Mr. Fern seized his hat, and out we went together. "Fanny," said he, "you must not take my arm; you are a fellow." "True," said I. "I forgot; and you must not help me over the puddles, as you did just now, and do, for mercy's sake, stop laughing. There, there goes your hat—I mean *my* hat; confound the wind! and down comes my hair; lucky 'tis dark, isn't it?" But oh, the delicious freedom of that walk, after we were well started! No skirts to hold up, or to draggle their wet folds against my ankles; no stifling veil flapping in my face, and blinding my eyes; no umbrella to turn inside out, but instead, the cool rain driving slap into my face, and the resurrectionized blood coursing through my veins, and tingling in my cheeks. To be sure, Mr. Fern occasionally loitered behind, and leaned up against the side of a house to enjoy a little private "guffaw," and I could now and then hear a gasping "Oh, Fanny! Oh, my!" but none of these things moved me, and if I don't have a nicely fitting suit of my own to wear rainy evenings, it is because—well, there *are* difficulties in the way. Who's the best tailor?

Now, if any male or female Miss Nancy[7] who reads this feels shocked, let 'em! Any woman who likes, may stay at home during a three weeks' rain, till her skin looks like parchment, and her eyes like those of a dead fish, or she may go out and get a consumption[8] dragging round wet petticoats; I won't—I positively declare I won't. I shall begin *evenings* when *that* suit is made, and take private walking lessons with Mr. Fern, and

---

1 *Mr. Fern* James Parton, whom Fern had married in 1856. She did not adopt his surname.

2 *Tailors* I.e., sewers of men's rather than women's clothing.

3 *hogshead* Large barrel.

4 *broadcloth* Fine wool material often used in men's jackets; *kerseymere* Fine twill wool material.

5 *glass* Mirror.

6 *a certain musical … Brady's entry* Fern is likely referring to her brother, the composer Richard Storrs Willis (1819–1900); "Brady" refers to the prominent New York-based photographer Mathew Brady (1822–96).

7 *Miss Nancy* Prudish individual.

8 *get a consumption* Contract tuberculosis (or, more loosely, get sick).

they who choose may crook their backs at home for fashion, and then send for the doctor to straighten them; I prefer to patronize my shoe-maker and tailor. I've as good a right to preserve the healthy body God gave me, as if I were not a woman.

—1858

Independence

"Fourth of July." Well—I don't feel patriotic. Perhaps I might if they would stop that deafening racket. Washington was very well, if he *couldn't* spell, and I'm glad we are all free; but as a woman—I shouldn't know it, didn't some orator tell me. Can I go out of an evening without a hat[1] at my side? Can I go out with one on my head without danger of a station-house?[2] Can I clap my hands at some public speaker when I am nearly bursting with delight? Can I signify the contrary when my hair stands on end with vexation? Can I stand up in the cars "like a gentleman" without being immediately invited "to sit down"? Can I get into an omnibus[3] without having my sixpence taken from my hand and given to the driver? Can I cross Broadway without having a policeman tackled to my helpless elbow? Can I go to see anything *pleasant*, like an execution or a dissection? Can I drive that splendid "Lantern,"[4] distancing—like his owner—all competitors? Can I have the nomination for "Governor of Vermont," like our other contributor, John G. Saxe?[5] Can I be a Senator, that I may hurry up that millennial International Copyright Law?[6] Can I *even* be President? Bah—you know I can't. "*Free*!" Humph!

—1859

IN CONTEXT

Contemporary Reviews of Fanny Fern's Work

Fanny Fern's rapid rise to fame and wealth during the early 1850s led to substantial discussion among journalists and literary critics. The 6 May 1854 issue of *The Musical World and New York Musical Times*, for which Fern wrote regularly and whose editor had helped publish her first two collections, included a full-page spread excerpting laudatory reviews of her work from numerous contemporary newspapers, including from influential papers such as *Harper's Magazine* and *Godey's Lady's Book*.

---

[1]   *a hat*   I.e., a man.

[2]   *Can I … station-house?*   Many jurisdictions in America had laws against cross-dressing; Fern implies that she could not go out wearing a man's hat without fear of being arrested (as had happened to other women).

[3]   *omnibus*   Horse-drawn public carriage traveling a fixed route with set stops.

[4]   *Lantern*   Reference to a racing horse owned by *New York Ledger* editor Robert Bonner.

[5]   *John G. Saxe*   American poet (1816–87) who unsuccessfully ran for governor of Vermont in 1859, whose works were published in the *Ledger*.

[6]   *International Copyright Law*   Prior to the 1886 Berne Convention for the Protection of Literary and Artistic Works, American authors had little or no legal protection against their works being copied and republished abroad without the authors being compensated.

$15,000 THE FIRST YEAR,

IS A PRETTY FAIR SUM FOR AN AUTHOR TO MAKE!!

Fanny Fern's popularity is still on the increase; the sale of her works continues unprecedented; it is with difficulty that the demand can be supplied. The secret of this success is perhaps hinted at in the subjoined notices of her works, which are selected at random from a peck or so now on our table. First, comes the opinion of that leviathan of literature, *Harpers' Magazine.*

A second series of *Fern Leaves from Fanny's Portfolio*, is published by Miller, Orton & Mulligan, which in many respects is superior to the former quaint and merry productions which have procured such a sudden access of fame to the lively authoress. Usually, we have little faith in these rapid growths of popularity. The temple of fame is not to be taken by storm, but must be approached by steep and winding ways. A desperate rush is apt to defeat itself. But Fanny Fern doubtless forms an exception to this rule. The favor with which her writings have been received—almost unprecedented in this country and in England—has a legitimate cause. She dips her pen in her heart, and writes out her own feelings and fancies. She is no imitator, no dealer in second-hand wares. Her inspiration comes from nature, not from books. She dares to be original. She has no fear of critics or of the public before her eyes. She conquers a peace with them by sheer force of audacity. Often verging on the bounds of wholesome conventionalities, she still shows a true and kindly nature—she has always the sympathy with suffering which marks the genuine woman—and her most petulant and frolicksome moods are softened by a perennial vein of tender humaneness. Fanny Fern is a poetess, though she avoids the use of rhyme. With all her sense of the indicrous, she knows how to seize the poetical aspects of life, and these are rendered in picturesque and melodious phrase, which lacks nothing but rhythm to be true poetry. Her rapid transitions from fun to pathos are very effective. Her pictures of domestic life, in its multiform relations, are so faithful to nature, as to excite alternate smiles and tears. We regard her extraordinary success as a good omen. She has won her way unmistakably to the hearts of the people; and this we interpret as a triumph of natural feeling. It shows that the day for stilted rhetoric, scholastic refinements, and big dictionary words, the parade, pomp, and pageantry of literature, is declining; and that the writer who is brave enough to build on universal human sympathies, is sure of the most grateful reward in unaffected popular appreciation.—*Harper's Magazine.*

Mrs. Swisshelm on Fanny Fern.—Mrs. Swisshelm, the able and conscientious editress of the *Pittsburgh Saturday Visitor*, who is so hard to please, so independent, so unflinchingly honest and bold in her utterance, thus discourses on the characteristics of "Our Fanny:" "Fanny Fern is a genius, and one who has told the world a great deal of wholesome truth which that same world very much needed to hear:—truth that, like the good seed, will bring forth good fruits in their season. Very grave objections are made to Fanny's style, in that it is not always according to Lindlay Murray; but one thing is certain; Fanny's language answers the original intent of that commodity, for it does convey ideas, and unlike many polished sentences, leaves no doubt as to the idea it was intended to convey. Fanny has a rare good gift of telling in a few words what she thinks, and thinking a great many times, something well worthy of being told. Her sentiment is no sham, for its utterance has that unmistakable sign of feeling, the power to awake an answering chord in other hearts. Her pages are more like bunches of mignonette than leaves of fern, for they are generally better than at first glance one might suppose—and under a plain, simple garb exhale a rare odor. To us they look like an amiable, beautiful and polished woman dressed in peasant's homespun—they exhibit the deep and exquisite sensibility draped in a plain, homely common sense; and to us her scraps are more refreshing, especially after some of the more elaborate compositions which afflict the public, and in which, or rather *on* which, sensibility spread as a varnish, is quite unable to hide selfishness within. Fanny is always talking about herself, but never conveys an idea of egotism,—she never obtrudes herself between you and the picture she presents for your inspection, but stands at your side and points it out. We do like Fanny for her genial temper, and for retaining the milk of human kindness in her heart, sweet and fresh through reverses of fortune, disappointments and troubles, which would have turned a common nature into vinegar. Her reproofs are often pungent but never sour or bitter. They often have a horse-radishy flavor, but never taste of wormwood, henbane or gall; and when she probes a wound, it is never with a poisoned arrow."—*Pittsburgh Sat. Visitor.*

Fanny Fern and Eliza Cook are sister spirits. Although Eliza is more versatile, Fanny, having enjoyed the birthright of freedom, possesses wilder spirits. She is the buxom nymph of sylvan shades and sunny nooks; she shoots her fiery darts at random, but they always hit the mark. Fern leaves, like the Chinese sensitive leaves, are magical tests of character—they sympathize only with congenial spirits; therefore Fanny may felicitate herself with this pleasurable assurance, that her reciprocating friends are as innumerable as the enchanted leaves she has scattered over the two hemispheres. Fanny's Portfolio is like the wizzard's—it contains a charm for everybody.—*N. Y. Mercantile Guide.*

Fern Leaves Second Series.—We welcome another volume of Fern Leaves. Where in the world are our male authors? To arms! authors who wear the unmentionables! The laurels are sliding from your brows! The best and most readable books are being written by women! You are a bold operator "Fanny," and we like you the better for it. There is no Homeopathy about you! no mixing, diluting and dosing. But have a care, "Fanny!" it is not every case that will bear your knife and caustic; for if you use them too unsparingly, you will kill as well as cure. There are some natures made of such contradictory stuff, that the more you chasten them, the more hardened they become; yet speak to them a soft and gentle word, persuade instead of deriding, and they will fall at your feet. The second series of Fern Leaves consists of 120 short articles, much resembling our author's first work under the same title published last summer. They are written with much spirit and sprightliness, and her woman's heart is seen through all nobly striving to denounce sin, and defend virtue, wherever found.—*Iowa Journal of Education.*

No writer in our country has ever, in so short a period, gained an equal celebrity, or touched so many of the heartstrings of the million. Keen, satirical, probing to the very depths of conventional wrongs; pricking the consciences of delinquent husbands, and scathing wayward wives and mothers; entering humble households, sympathising with all her womanly nature with human suffering, she has gone out from them and lashed with an unsparing hand the tyrannies of social life; she has been among the "upper ten" and the "lower millions," with no tongue of flattery for the faults of either; and yet all have fallen in with the gentle and kindly current of her thoughts. Blessings upon the head of Fanny Fern! and may she continue to pluck "leaves" that have so much moral fragrance. This new series is dedicated to a Lockport "boy,', or man we will call him, for his years now, and more than all, his praiseworthy self-elevation, well entitles him to all the prerogatives of manhood. Who would not be proud of such a dedication from such a source? "To my truest friend, Oliver Dyer, whose friendship never faltered in adversity; whose sympathy and encouragement cheered me when no bow of promise was set in my sky, this book is gratefully dedicated."—*Niagara Democrat.*

The success of Fanny Fern as a writer is one of the curiosities and marvels of literature. And yet it is all natural enough. She is an original and brilliant writer, and combines all those qualities which make up a formidable reputation—such as she now enjoys. Her Leaves contain passages that are witty, pathetic, satirical and also much that is genial and full of heart. If she is severe, it is only to rebuke some wrong, and if the dart of satire is thrown, it is merited. There is no malice, but rather justice in her writings. She seems to have all the flow of Irving, the polish of "Ike Marvel," and the edge of Dickens. In style she has nothing stiff or awkward, any more than she has in conversation. She writes like one who feels with intensity, whether she means to put roses or thorns into the mental heart. With a nice eye to the real or the sham, to those who *seem* and those who *are*, to merit or pretence, she deals with discrimination and effect. We know of no writer who writes with such a heart; who puts the very vim into the inkstand and upon paper. Always vivacious, earnest, energetic, she gives the public nothing that is not worth reading once, twice, and as many more times as a good thing is relished. Let all who wish for a work that will charm and improve, get this Second Series of Fern Leaves.—*Boston Bee.*

Another book from Fanny Fern! Yes, and another yet, if she continues to write as gracefully and prettily as she has been doing. Little did we think some years ago—we wont name the time—when we first saw Fanny's golden locks fluttering in the breeze on Boston Common, that she would stir up such a sensation in the hearts of the people. Why, she has already written the most pleasing and popular book of the day, the copies selling by tens of thousands; and here she must come out with another, to tempt our affections and our purses. We make it a point to read everything of Fanny's that our eyes greet, and we never yet failed to glean the most delectable pleasure from her pages.—*N. Y. Atlas.*

Every one—that is every one in the habit of reading the newspapers—has read, and consequently admired at least a few of the long and short *essays, paragraphs*, and memorable remarks, which, like *flashing meteors*, have shot athwart the literary firmament from time to time, to the amazement, in particular, of a certain class of quiet writers, who for a time have been left to wander in the gloom of the past. But, unlike meteors, which fade away after a brief flash, Fanny's flashes are designed for preservation, and are carefully collected together, and made to form a brilliant galaxy for permanent usefulness and lasting admiration. Her originality, industry and proficiency in all the departments of life and human knowledge, are wonderful, indeed, and therefore wonderfully widespread is her popularity. She is, besides, very bold and independent in her strictures on men, women, and every object else that comes in her way, and she has courage to say things which almost any common thinker might think, but which very few, perhaps, could put upon paper in the same nervous and striking language. Hence, no doubt, in a great measure, Fanny's popularity with the multitude of readers.—*Godey's Lady's Book.*

The secret of her power over the public mind, we apprehend, is, that she has a heart. Gifted with noble faculties by nature, and mellowed, if rumor says truly, by the furnace of affliction, she has come out of her trials, or we may say, forced her way out by her own indomitable courage—refined and quickened, instead of imbruted and deadened; and now pours forth from the rich fountain of her experience, with the ardor and sincerity of a child, the rich stores she had garnered there. In addition, she has point and wit, and of course is always on the side of humanity and justice, and in warm sympathy with the poor and the oppressed. That such a writer, with works made up of detached sketche, should have achieved the popularity she has, is a fragrant indication that the heart of humanity is budding, and, indeed, about to bloom.—*N. Y. Universe.*

Fanny is a genius, bright, sparkling, witty, racy and sensible withal. There is a vein of common sense underlying all her sarcasm, which makes her writings subservient to good morals and integrity. We trust her Leaves are for the cure of some follies, as well as instructive and amusing.—*Maine Farmer.*

Fern Leaves—Second Series—Fanny Fern's spicy, lively, heart-spoken productions, are most agreeable and racy specimens of composition. Everybody should read them, for everybody must enjoy their perusal.—*Utica Observer.*

HARRIET JACOBS
c. 1813 – 1897

For a hundred and twenty years, Harriet Jacobs's groundbreaking narrative, *Incidents in the Life of a Slave Girl* (1861), went largely unnoticed. When it did receive commentary, it was assumed that the narrative was not autobiography but fiction, and that its true author was the white abolitionist writer Lydia Maria Child (who in fact edited the volume). It was not until scholar Jean Fagan Yellin published a groundbreaking article on the narrative in 1981 that Jacobs's authorship was authenticated. This meant that Jacobs's gripping and eloquent narrative, one of the earliest written by an enslaved woman in the United States, did not impact American literature and history until late in the twentieth century. Since then, Jacobs's achievement as a writer and activist has been widely recognized, and her profound influence on American literature has taken firm root. Jacobs's *Incidents* is brave and revolutionary in that it openly discusses the  particular evils that slavery systemically inflicted on women—sexual abuse, rape, and the knowledge that any children born would be born enslaved. As critic Henry Gates Jr. wrote, "Whereas the black male slave narrators' accounts of sexual brutality remain suggestive, if gruesome, Jacobs's … charts in vivid detail precisely how the shape of her life and the choices she makes are defined by her reduction to a sexual object, an object to be raped, bred or abused." Jacobs herself put it very simply: "Slavery is terrible for men; but it is far more terrible for women."

Jacobs was born in Edenton, North Carolina; most biographers date her birth in 1813, though her tombstone states she was born in 1815. Her mother, Delilah Horniblow, was enslaved by Margaret Horniblow, and her father, Elijah Knox, was enslaved by Andrew Knox. As a young child, Jacobs was unaware of her own enslaved condition; her father, a skilled carpenter, was allowed to keep a portion of his earnings, and the family lived in tolerable independence. Jacobs's maternal grandmother, Molly Horniblow, was a formative influence and support to the family, particularly to Jacobs. "I was so fondly shielded," she recalled, "that I never dreamed I was a piece of merchandise." Jacobs's mother died when she was six, breaking up the family circle; Margaret Horniblow, who had owned Delilah and thus owned her daughter, brought Jacobs to her home. Jacobs was treated kindly, and Horniblow taught her to read, write, and sew. When Jacobs was almost twelve years old, Horniblow died. Although Jacobs had believed that her mistress would set her free, she was instead bequeathed to Horniblow's five-year-old niece. Jacobs came under the control of the girl's father, Dr. James Norcom (who is given the pseudonym Dr. Flint in *Incidents*), a cruel man who soon began persecuting Jacobs with unwanted sexual attention.

Norcom's harassment of Jacobs was persistent, and her life in his house became more and more unbearable, both because of the sexual pressure and because of Mrs. Norcom's jealousy. Jacobs was increasingly isolated by what she perceived to be the shame of her situation: she usually went to her grandmother for advice, but she did not want to communicate the sexual nature of Norcom's persecution. In an effort to find security, Jacobs took a lover, Samuel Tredwell Sawyer, a local white attorney. With Sawyer, Jacobs would have two children, Joseph and Louisa. "I knew nothing would enrage [Norcom] so much as to know that I favored another," Jacobs wrote, "and it was something to triumph over my tyrant even in that small way." This relationship did not free her, however, from Norcom's threats, and, in the summer of 1835, Jacobs ran away and hid in a small crawlspace just below her grandmother's roof. She spent seven years in this tiny garret, watching her children grow up through a small hole she made to peer through. She managed to sew and read the Bible, but those years in hiding were plagued by isolation, by discomfort brought on by the weather—cold, heat, and rain all made her hideaway a miserable place—and by illness. In 1842, Jacobs escaped and went by boat to Pennsylvania, and from there to New York City.

While Jacobs was in hiding, Sawyer, who had been elected to Congress in 1837, had managed to purchase his and Jacobs's two children from Norcom, and he had sent the girl, Louisa, to Brooklyn to work as a servant (he did not keep his promise to free the children). Jacobs settled in New York to be close to her daughter—her son also eventually joined them—and took a job as nursemaid in the house of Mary Stace Willis, wife of the well-known poet and editor Nathaniel Parker Willis. Periodically, Norcom would try to find Jacobs, and she would have to temporarily leave New York. On one such occasion in 1845, while Jacobs was hiding in Boston, her employer, Mary Willis, died; when Nathaniel Willis subsequently decided to take a trip to England with his daughter, Jacobs accepted his offer to go with them and act as nursemaid. Jacobs experienced little racism in England, and she was impressed that the poor people in that country had access to education. In 1849, again fleeing Norcom, Jacobs went to Rochester, New York, where she worked with her brother, John Jacobs, in an antislavery reading room and bookstore. Rochester was a thriving center for abolitionist and feminist activism—Jacobs and her brother's reading room was located above the offices of Frederick Douglass's newspaper—and Jacobs began to find likeminded friends there, including Amy Post, who encouraged Jacobs to write and publish her experience.

In the meantime, Nathaniel Parker Willis remarried, and his second wife, Cornelia Grinell, employed Jacobs as a nursemaid for her new baby. In 1852, when Jacobs was again threatened with capture, Cornelia bought her for $300, ensuring her freedom. Though it deflated Jacobs to be traded like merchandise, having her freedom was a significant relief, and in 1853 she began her writing career in earnest. She wrote anonymous letters to the *New York Tribune*, including "Letter from a Fugitive Slave. Slaves Sold under Peculiar Circumstances" (21 June 1853), which touches on what would become a central theme in *Incidents*: the sexual abuse faced by enslaved women, and the struggle enslaved mothers endured to attempt to protect their children. Jacobs wrote *Incidents* while still working as a nursemaid in the Willis household; she kept her writing private, because she was not convinced that Nathaniel Willis supported abolition (though his wife certainly did). In the summer of 1857, Jacobs wrote to Amy Post that she had finished "a true and just account of my own life in Slavery," and that she hoped it "might do something for the Antislavery Cause."

Jacobs faced hurdles, however, in publishing *Incidents*, traveling to England in 1858 in an unsuccessful search for a publisher. The Boston company Phillips and Samson eventually agreed to take the book if Willis, Jacobs's employer, or Harriet Beecher Stowe would write an introduction. Jacobs didn't feel Willis would support the book, so she asked Stowe, but Stowe rejected the idea of collaborating with Jacobs. A different publisher, Thayer and Eldridge, then agreed to publish, stipulating this time an introduction by Lydia Maria Child, and, though very reluctant to do so, Jacobs asked Child if she would contribute to the project. Child agreed to not only write an introduction, but to edit the book. Though many people thought Child's involvement was extensive, Jean Fagan Yellin's research makes it clear that Child did not exceed the role she herself described in the introduction to the volume: "I have not added anything to the incidents, or changed the import of [Jacobs's] very pertinent remarks. With trifling exceptions, both the ideas and the language are her own. I pruned excrescences a little, but otherwise I had no reason for changing her lively and dramatic way of telling her own story."

When Thayer and Eldridge dissolved as a company, Jacobs secured the typeset pages of *Incidents* and determined to publish it herself; it was finally published in 1860, followed by a British edition in 1861. Jacobs used a pseudonym, Linda Brent, and she changed the names of all the characters in the book to protect their anonymity. *Incidents* was warmly received by audiences in the North and across the Atlantic, but it was not financially successful, and the Civil War soon drew much of the public's attention. After the war, Jacobs's work fell into obscurity, and only since the 1980s have readership and scholarship of it flourished; it has since become one of the most often-taught and frequently-read slave narratives.

Jacobs's writing style was influenced by the Bible, by other slave narratives—such as those by Olaudah Equiano and Frederick Douglass—and by the work of various contemporary women writers, including Lydia Maria Child, Fanny Fern, and Harriet Beecher Stowe. Like Stowe, Jacobs uses the rhetorical tools of the sentimental novel to add emotional power to her attack on slavery, and to frame some of her own experiences. In sentimental novels such as Samuel Richardson's *Pamela* (1740), for example, a servant girl is persecuted by the sexual attentions of her master, whom she continually rejects, thereby preserving her virtue. Jacobs's persistence in escaping Norcom is presented within this framework, as she bravely and successfully keeps her abuser at bay; on the other hand, the shame she feels at having an unmarried affair with Sawyer is felt as a failure to live up to the idealization of what it means to be a virtuous young woman. While Jacobs clearly judged herself against such ideals, she also forcefully questions their application to a person who is trapped in the misery of slavery: "… in looking back, calmly, on the events of my life, I feel that the slave woman ought not to be judged by the same standard as others."

Jacobs's story, focusing as it does on the bonds of women and seeking as it does an inter-racial and inter-regional political alliance, has become a crucial feminist text. *Incidents* has also taken a vital place in the history of African American literature, influencing writers such as Toni Morrison, Alice Walker, bell hooks, Ta-Nehisi Coates, and Claudia Rankine, among many others. As writers consider what it means to lead a dignified life in an America still convulsed with sexism and racism, Jacobs's narrative is a touchstone and inspiration. It has been translated into many languages and is read and taught around the world.

Jacobs dedicated her life not only to exposing the sexual violence of slavery—a secret she said was "concealed like those of the Inquisition"—but also to bettering the condition of black people across the United States. Following the publication of *Incidents*, Jacobs delivered numerous speeches in support of abolition, nursed wounded black troops during the Civil War, and assisted newly-emancipated African Americans. In 1864, she established a school for black children in Alexandria, Virginia, where her daughter Louisa was a teacher. Jacobs died in Washington, D.C. in 1897 and was buried in Cambridge, Massachusetts, in Mount Auburn Cemetery.

NOTE ON THE TEXT: The excerpts presented here are based on the first 1861 Boston edition of Jacobs's *Incidents in the Life of a Slave Girl, Written by Herself*, edited by Lydia Maria Child.

⌘ ⌘ ⌘

from *Incidents in the Life of a Slave Girl, Written by Herself*

Northerners know nothing at all about Slavery. They think it is perpetual bondage only. They have no conception of the depth of *degradation* involved in that word, SLAVERY; if they had, they would never cease their efforts until so horrible a system was overthrown.

A WOMAN OF NORTH CAROLINA

Rise up, ye women that are at ease! Hear my voice, ye careless daughters! Give ear unto my speech.

ISAIAH 32.9

PREFACE BY THE AUTHOR

Reader, be assured this narrative is no fiction. I am aware that some of my adventures may seem incredible; but they are, nevertheless, strictly true. I have not exaggerated the wrongs inflicted by Slavery; on the contrary, my descriptions fall far short of the facts. I have concealed the names of places, and given persons fictitious names. I had no motive for secrecy on my own account, but I deemed it kind and considerate towards others to pursue this course.

I wish I were more competent to the task I have undertaken. But I trust my readers will excuse deficiencies in consideration of circumstances. I was born and reared in Slavery; and I remained in a Slave State twenty-seven years. Since I have been at the North, it has been necessary for me to work diligently for my own support, and the education of my children. This has not left me much leisure to make up for the loss of early opportunities to improve myself; and it has compelled me to write these pages at irregular intervals, whenever I could snatch an hour from household duties.

When I first arrived in Philadelphia, Bishop Paine[1] advised me to publish a sketch of my life, but I told him I was altogether incompetent to such an undertaking. Though I have improved my mind somewhat since that time, I still remain of the same opinion; but I trust my motives will excuse what might otherwise seem presumptuous. I have not written my experiences in order to attract attention to myself; on the contrary, it would have been more pleasant to me to have been silent about my own history. Neither do I care to excite sympathy for my own sufferings. But I do earnestly desire to arouse the women of the North to a realizing sense of the condition of two millions of women at the South, still in bondage, suffering what I suffered, and most of them far worse. I want to add my testimony to that of abler pens to convince the people of the Free States what Slavery really is. Only by experience can anyone realize how deep, and dark, and foul is that pit of abominations. May the blessing of God rest on this imperfect effort in behalf of my persecuted people!

Linda Brent[2]

INTRODUCTION BY THE EDITOR

The author of the following autobiography is personally known to me, and her conversation and manners inspire me with confidence. During the last seventeen years, she has lived the greater part of the time with a distinguished family in New York, and has so deported[3] herself as to be highly esteemed by them. This fact is sufficient, without further credentials of her character.

I believe those who know her will not be disposed to doubt her veracity, though some incidents in her story are more romantic[4] than fiction.

At her request, I have revised her manuscript; but such changes as I have made have been mainly for purposes of condensation and orderly arrangement. I have not added anything to the incidents, or changed the import of her very pertinent remarks. With trifling exceptions, both the ideas and the language are her own. I pruned excrescences a little, but otherwise I had no reason for changing her lively and dramatic way of telling her own story. The names of both persons and places are known to me; but for good reasons I suppress them.

It will naturally excite surprise that a woman reared in Slavery should be able to write so well. But circumstances will explain this. In the first place, nature endowed her with quick perceptions. Secondly, the mistress, with whom she lived till she was twelve years old, was a kind, considerate friend, who taught her to read and spell. Thirdly, she was placed in favorable circumstances after she came to the North; having frequent intercourse with intelligent persons, who felt a friendly interest in her welfare, and were disposed to give her opportunities for self-improvement.

I am well aware that many will accuse me of indecorum for presenting these pages to the public; for the experiences of this intelligent and much-injured woman belong to a class which some call delicate subjects, and others indelicate. This peculiar phase of Slavery[5] has generally been kept veiled; but the public ought to be made acquainted with its monstrous features, and I willingly take the responsibility of presenting them with the veil withdrawn. I do this for the sake of my sisters in bondage, who are suffering wrongs so foul, that our ears are too delicate to listen to them. I do it with the hope of arousing conscientious and reflecting women at the North to a sense of their duty in the exertion of moral influence on the question of Slavery, on all possible occasions. I do it with the hope that every man who reads this narrative will swear solemnly before God that, so far as he has power to prevent it, no fugitive from Slavery shall ever

---

[1] *Bishop Paine* Daniel Alexander Payne was a writer, educator, and bishop in the African Methodist Episcopal Church. In the early 1840s, he worked on the Philadelphia Vigilance Committee, which provided clothing and shelter for enslaved people escaping to the North.

[2] *Linda Brent* Harriet Jacobs's pseudonym.

[3] *deported* Conducted.

[4] *romantic* Unlikely or implausible.

[5] *peculiar phase of Slavery* I.e., the particular abuses, such as sexual violence, that slavery systemically encouraged and enabled.

be sent back to suffer in that loathsome den of corruption and cruelty.

L. Maria Child

CHAPTER 1. CHILDHOOD

I was born a slave; but I never knew it till six years of happy childhood had passed away. My father was a carpenter, and considered so intelligent and skillful in his trade, that, when buildings out of the common line were to be erected, he was sent for from long distances, to be head workman. On condition of paying his mistress two hundred dollars a year,[1] and supporting himself, he was allowed to work at his trade, and manage his own affairs. His strongest wish was to purchase his children; but, though he several times offered his hard earnings for that purpose, he never succeeded. In complexion my parents were a light shade of brownish yellow, and were termed mulattoes.[2] They lived together in a comfortable home; and, though we were all slaves, I was so fondly shielded that I never dreamed I was a piece of merchandise, trusted to them for safe keeping, and liable to be demanded of them at any moment. I had one brother, William, who was two years younger than myself—a bright, affectionate child. I had also a great treasure in my maternal grandmother, who was a remarkable woman in many respects. She was the daughter of a planter in South Carolina, who, at his death, left her mother and his three children free, with money to go to St. Augustine,[3] where they had relatives. It was during the Revolutionary War; and they were captured on their passage, carried back, and sold to different purchasers. Such was the story my grandmother used to tell me; but I do not remember all the particulars. She was a little girl when she was captured and sold to the keeper of a large hotel. I have often heard her tell how hard she fared during childhood. But as she grew older she evinced so much intelligence, and was so faithful, that her master and mistress could not help seeing it was

for their interest to take care of such a valuable piece of property. She became an indispensable personage in the household, officiating in all capacities, from cook and wet nurse to seamstress. She was much praised for her cooking; and her nice[4] crackers became so famous in the neighborhood that many people were desirous of obtaining them. In consequence of numerous requests of this kind, she asked permission of her mistress to bake crackers at night, after all the household work was done; and she obtained leave to do it, provided she would clothe herself and her children from the profits. Upon these terms, after working hard all day for her mistress, she began her midnight bakings, assisted by her two oldest children. The business proved profitable; and each year she laid by a little, which was saved for a fund to purchase her children. Her master died, and the property was divided among his heirs. The widow had her dower in the hotel, which she continued to keep open. My grandmother remained in her service as a slave; but her children were divided among her master's children. As she had five, Benjamin, the youngest one, was sold, in order that each heir might have an equal portion of dollars and cents. There was so little difference in our ages that he seemed more like my brother than my uncle. He was a bright, handsome lad, nearly white; for he inherited the complexion my grandmother had derived from Anglo-Saxon ancestors. Though only ten years old, seven hundred and twenty dollars were paid for him. His sale was a terrible blow to my grandmother; but she was naturally hopeful, and she went to work with renewed energy, trusting in time to be able to purchase some of her children. She had laid up three hundred dollars, which her mistress one day begged as a loan, promising to pay her soon. The reader probably knows that no promise or writing given to a slave is legally binding; for, according to Southern laws, a slave, being property, can hold no property. When my grandmother lent her hard earnings to her mistress, she trusted solely to her honor. The honor of a slaveholder to a slave!

To this good grandmother I was indebted for many comforts. My brother Willie and I often received portions of the crackers, cakes, and preserves, she made to sell; and after we ceased to be children we were indebted to her for many more important services.

---

1   *two hundred dollars a year*   Equivalent to about $6,000.

2   *mulattoes*   The term "mulatto," which is today considered archaic and offensive, was commonly used in the nineteenth century to classify individuals of mixed racial background—most frequently, those with one white and one black parent.

3   *St. Augustine*   City on the northeast coast of Florida.

4   *nice*   Tasty, delicate.

Such were the unusually fortunate circumstances of my early childhood. When I was six years old, my mother died; and then, for the first time, I learned, by the talk around me, that I was a slave. My mother's mistress was the daughter of my grandmother's mistress. She was the foster sister of my mother; they were both nourished at my grandmother's breast. In fact, my mother had been weaned at three months old, that the babe of the mistress might obtain sufficient food. They played together as children; and, when they became women, my mother was a most faithful servant to her whiter foster sister. On her death-bed her mistress promised that her children should never suffer for anything; and during her lifetime she kept her word. They all spoke kindly of my dead mother, who had been a slave merely in name, but in nature was noble and womanly. I grieved for her, and my young mind was troubled with the thought who would now take care of me and my little brother. I was told that my home was now to be with her mistress; and I found it a happy one. No toilsome or disagreeable duties were imposed upon me. My mistress was so kind to me that I was always glad to do her bidding, and proud to labor for her as much as my young years would permit. I would sit by her side for hours, sewing diligently, with a heart as free from care as that of any free-born white child. When she thought I was tired, she would send me out to run and jump; and away I bounded, to gather berries or flowers to decorate her room. Those were happy days—too happy to last. The slave child had no thought for the morrow; but there came that blight, which too surely waits on every human being born to be a chattel.

When I was nearly twelve years old, my kind mistress sickened and died. As I saw the cheek grow paler, and the eye more glassy, how earnestly I prayed in my heart that she might live! I loved her; for she had been almost like a mother to me. My prayers were not answered. She died, and they buried her in the little churchyard, where, day after day, my tears fell upon her grave.

I was sent to spend a week with my grandmother. I was now old enough to begin to think of the future; and again and again I asked myself what they would do with me. I felt sure I should never find another mistress so kind as the one who was gone. She had promised my dying mother that her children should never suffer for anything; and when I remembered that, and recalled her many proofs of attachment to me, I could not help having some hopes that she had left me free. My friends were almost certain it would be so. They thought she would be sure to do it, on account of my mother's love and faithful service. But, alas! we all know that the memory of a faithful slave does not avail much to save her children from the auction block.

After a brief period of suspense, the will of my mistress was read, and we learned that she had bequeathed me to her sister's daughter, a child of five years old. So vanished our hopes. My mistress had taught me the precepts of God's Word: "Thou shalt love thy neighbor as thyself." "Whatsoever ye would that men should do unto you, do ye even so unto them."[1] But I was her slave, and I suppose she did not recognize me as her neighbor. I would give much to blot out from my memory that one great wrong. As a child, I loved my mistress; and, looking back on the happy days I spent with her, I try to think with less bitterness of this act of injustice. While I was with her, she taught me to read and spell; and for this privilege, which so rarely falls to the lot of a slave, I bless her memory.

She possessed but few slaves; and at her death those were all distributed among her relatives. Five of them were my grandmother's children, and had shared the same milk that nourished her mother's children. Notwithstanding my grandmother's long and faithful service to her owners, not one of her children escaped the auction block. These God-breathing machines are no more, in the sight of their masters, than the cotton they plant, or the horses they tend.

CHAPTER 2. THE NEW MASTER AND MISTRESS

Dr. Flint, a physician in the neighborhood, had married the sister of my mistress, and I was now the property of their little daughter. It was not without murmuring[2] that I prepared for my new home; and what added to my unhappiness, was the fact that my

---

1   *Thou shalt … thyself*   The second of Christ's commandments, see Matthew 22.39; *Whatsoever ye would … unto them*   This saying is known as the "golden rule." See Leviticus 19.18 and Matthew 7.12.

2   *not without murmuring*   See Philippians 2.14–15: "Do all things without murmurings and disputings; / That ye may be blameless and harmless, the sons of God, without rebuke, in the midst of a crooked and perverse nation, among whom ye shine as lights in the world."

brother William was purchased by the same family. My father, by his nature, as well as by the habit of transacting business as a skillful mechanic, had more of the feelings of a freeman than is common among slaves. My brother was a spirited boy; and being brought up under such influences, he early detested the name of master and mistress. One day, when his father and his mistress both happened to call him at the same time, he hesitated between the two; being perplexed to know which had the strongest claim upon his obedience. He finally concluded to go to his mistress. When my father reproved him for it, he said, "You both called me, and I didn't know which I ought to go to first."

"You are *my* child," replied our father, "and when I call you, you should come immediately, if you have to pass through fire and water."[1]

Poor Willie! He was now to learn his first lesson of obedience to a master. Grandmother tried to cheer us with hopeful words, and they found an echo in the credulous hearts of youth.

When we entered our new home we encountered cold looks, cold words, and cold treatment. We were glad when the night came. On my narrow bed I moaned and wept, I felt so desolate and alone.

I had been there nearly a year, when a dear little friend of mine was buried. I heard her mother sob, as the clods fell on the coffin of her only child, and I turned away from the grave, feeling thankful that I still had something left to love. I met my grandmother, who said, "Come with me, Linda"; and from her tone I knew that something sad had happened. She led me apart from the people, and then said, "My child, your father is dead." Dead! How could I believe it? He had died so suddenly I had not even heard that he was sick. I went home with my grandmother. My heart rebelled against God, who had taken from me mother, father, mistress, and friend. The good grandmother tried to comfort me. "Who knows the ways of God?" said she. "Perhaps they have been kindly taken from the evil days to come." Years afterwards I often thought of this. She promised to be a mother to her grandchildren, so far as she might be permitted to do so; and

strengthened by her love, I returned to my master's. I thought I should be allowed to go to my father's house the next morning; but I was ordered to go for flowers, that my mistress's house might be decorated for an evening party. I spent the day gathering flowers and weaving them into festoons, while the dead body of my father was lying within a mile of me. What cared my owners for that? he was merely a piece of property. Moreover, they thought he had spoiled his children, by teaching them to feel that they were human beings. This was blasphemous doctrine for a slave to teach; presumptuous in him, and dangerous to the masters.

The next day I followed his remains to a humble grave beside that of my dear mother. There were those who knew my father's worth, and respected his memory.

My home now seemed more dreary than ever. The laugh of the little slave-children sounded harsh and cruel. It was selfish to feel so about the joy of others. My brother moved about with a very grave face. I tried to comfort him, by saying, "Take courage, Willie; brighter days will come by and by."

"You don't know anything about it, Linda," he replied. "We shall have to stay here all our days; we shall never be free."

I argued that we were growing older and stronger, and that perhaps we might, before long, be allowed to hire our own time, and then we could earn money to buy our freedom. William declared this was much easier to say than to do; moreover, he did not intend to buy his freedom. We held daily controversies upon this subject.

Little attention was paid to the slaves' meals in Dr. Flint's house. If they could catch a bit of food while it was going, well and good. I gave myself no trouble on that score, for on my various errands I passed my grandmother's house, where there was always something to spare for me. I was frequently threatened with punishment if I stopped there; and my grandmother, to avoid detaining me, often stood at the gate with something for my breakfast or dinner. I was indebted to her for all my comforts, spiritual or temporal. It was her labor that supplied my scanty wardrobe. I have a vivid recollection of the linsey-woolsey[2] dress given me

---

1   *pass through fire and water*   See Isaiah 43.2: "When thou passest through the waters, I will be with thee; and through the rivers, they shall not overflow thee: when thou walkest through the fire, thou shalt not be burned; neither shall the flame kindle upon thee."

2   *linsey-woolsey*   Coarse fabric made of the cheapest wool and linen.

every winter by Mrs. Flint. How I hated it! It was one of the badges of slavery.

While my grandmother was thus helping to support me from her hard earnings, the three hundred dollars she had lent her mistress were never repaid. When her mistress died, her son-in-law, Dr. Flint, was appointed executor. When grandmother applied to him for payment, he said the estate was insolvent, and the law prohibited payment. It did not, however, prohibit him from retaining the silver candelabra, which had been purchased with that money. I presume they will be handed down in the family, from generation to generation.

My grandmother's mistress had always promised her that, at her death, she should be free; and it was said that in her will she made good the promise. But when the estate was settled, Dr. Flint told the faithful old servant that, under existing circumstances, it was necessary she should be sold.

On the appointed day, the customary advertisement was posted up, proclaiming that there would be "a public sale of negroes, horses, &c." Dr. Flint called to tell my grandmother that he was unwilling to wound her feelings by putting her up at auction, and that he would prefer to dispose of her at private sale. My grandmother saw through his hypocrisy; she understood very well that he was ashamed of the job. She was a very spirited woman, and if he was base enough to sell her, when her mistress intended she should be free, she was determined the public should know it. She had for a long time supplied many families with crackers and preserves; consequently, "Aunt Marthy," as she was called, was generally known, and everybody who knew her respected her intelligence and good character. Her long and faithful service in the family was also well known, and the intention of her mistress to leave her free. When the day of sale came, she took her place among the chattels, and at the first call she sprang upon the auction-block. Many voices called out, "Shame! Shame! Who is going to sell *you*, Aunt Marthy? Don't stand there! That is no place for *you*." Without saying a word, she quietly awaited her fate. No one bid for her. At last, a feeble voice said, "Fifty dollars." It came from a maiden lady, seventy years old, the sister of my grandmother's deceased mistress. She had lived forty years under the same roof with my grandmother; she knew how faithfully she had served her owners, and how cruelly she had been defrauded of her rights; and she resolved to protect her. The auctioneer waited for a higher bid; but her wishes were respected; no one bid above her. She could neither read nor write; and when the bill of sale was made out, she signed it with a cross. But what consequence was that, when she had a big heart overflowing with human kindness? She gave the old servant her freedom.

At that time, my grandmother was just fifty years old. Laborious years had passed since then; and now my brother and I were slaves to the man who had defrauded her of her money, and tried to defraud her of her freedom. One of my mother's sisters, called Aunt Nancy, was also a slave in his family. She was a kind, good aunt to me; and supplied the place of both house-keeper and waiting maid to her mistress. She was, in fact, at the beginning and end of everything.

Mrs. Flint, like many southern women, was totally deficient in energy. She had not strength to superintend her household affairs; but her nerves were so strong, that she could sit in her easy chair and see a woman whipped, till the blood trickled from every stroke of the lash. She was a member of the church; but partaking of the Lord's supper[1] did not seem to put her in a Christian frame of mind. If dinner was not served at the exact time on that particular Sunday, she would station herself in the kitchen, and wait till it was dished, and then spit in all the kettles and pans that had been used for cooking. She did this to prevent the cook and her children from eking out their meagre fare with the remains of the gravy and other scrapings. The slaves could get nothing to eat except what she chose to give them. Provisions were weighed out by the pound and ounce, three times a day. I can assure you she gave them no chance to eat wheat bread from her flour barrel. She knew how many biscuits a quart of flour would make, and exactly what size they ought to be.

Dr. Flint was an epicure.[2] The cook never sent a dinner to his table without fear and trembling; for if there happened to be a dish not to his liking, he would

---

[1] *Lord's supper* I.e., sacrament of the Eucharist, in which the faithful drink wine and eat bread that is considered, symbolically, the blood and body of Christ.

[2] *epicure* Person devoted to sensual pleasure.

either order her to be whipped, or compel her to eat every mouthful of it in his presence. The poor, hungry creature might not have objected to eating it; but she did object to having her master cram it down her throat till she choked.

They had a pet dog, that was a nuisance in the house. The cook was ordered to make some Indian mush[1] for him. He refused to eat, and when his head was held over it, the froth flowed from his mouth into the basin. He died a few minutes after. When Dr. Flint came in, he said the mush had not been well cooked, and that was the reason the animal would not eat it. He sent for the cook, and compelled her to eat it. He thought that the woman's stomach was stronger than the dog's; but her sufferings afterwards proved that he was mistaken. This poor woman endured many cruelties from her master and mistress; sometimes she was locked up, away from her nursing baby, for a whole day and night.

When I had been in the family a few weeks, one of the plantation slaves was brought to town, by order of his master. It was near night when he arrived, and Dr. Flint ordered him to be taken to the work house, and tied up to the joist, so that his feet would just escape the ground. In that situation he was to wait till the doctor had taken his tea. I shall never forget that night. Never before, in my life, had I heard hundreds of blows fall, in succession, on a human being. His piteous groans, and his "O, pray don't, massa," rang in my ear for months afterwards. There were many conjectures as to the cause of this terrible punishment. Some said master accused him of stealing corn; others said the slave had quarrelled with his wife, in presence of the overseer, and had accused his master of being the father of her child. They were both black, and the child was very fair.

I went into the work house next morning, and saw the cowhide[2] still wet with blood, and the boards all covered with gore. The poor man lived, and continued to quarrel with his wife. A few months afterwards Dr. Flint handed them both over to a slave-trader. The guilty man put their value into his pocket, and had the satisfaction of knowing that they were out of sight and hearing. When the mother was delivered into the trader's hands, she said, "You *promised* to treat me

well." To which he replied, "You have let your tongue run too far; damn you!" She had forgotten that it was a crime for a slave to tell who was the father of her child.

From others than the master persecution also comes in such cases. I once saw a young slave girl dying soon after the birth of a child nearly white. In her agony she cried out, "O Lord, come and take me!" Her mistress stood by, and mocked at her like an incarnate fiend. "You suffer, do you?" she exclaimed. "I am glad of it. You deserve it all, and more too."

The girl's mother said, "The baby is dead, thank God; and I hope my poor child will soon be in heaven, too."

"Heaven!" retorted the mistress. "There is no such place for the like of her and her bastard."

The poor mother turned away, sobbing. Her dying daughter called her, feebly, and as she bent over her, I heard her say, "Don't grieve so, mother; God knows all about it; and HE will have mercy upon me."

Her sufferings, afterwards, became so intense, that her mistress felt unable to stay; but when she left the room, the scornful smile was still on her lips. Seven children called her mother. The poor black woman had but the one child, whose eyes she saw closing in death, while she thanked God for taking her away from the greater bitterness of life.

Chapter 5. The Trials of Girlhood

During the first years of my service in Dr. Flint's family, I was accustomed to share some indulgences with the children of my mistress. Though this seemed to me no more than right, I was grateful for it, and tried to merit the kindness by the faithful discharge of my duties. But I now entered on my fifteenth year—a sad epoch in the life of a slave girl. My master began to whisper foul words in my ear. Young as I was, I could not remain ignorant of their import. I tried to treat them with indifference or contempt. The master's age, my extreme youth, and the fear that his conduct would be reported to my grandmother, made him bear this treatment for many months. He was a crafty man, and resorted to many means to accomplish his purposes. Sometimes he had stormy, terrific[3] ways, that made his victims tremble; sometimes he assumed a gentleness that he thought must surely subdue. Of the two,

---

[1] *Indian mush* Porridge made of corn.

[2] *cowhide* Heavy whip made of cow's hide.

[3] *terrific* I.e., terrifying.

I preferred his stormy moods, although they left me trembling. He tried his utmost to corrupt the pure principles my grandmother had instilled. He peopled my young mind with unclean images, such as only a vile monster could think of. I turned from him with disgust and hatred. But he was my master. I was compelled to live under the same roof with him—where I saw a man forty years my senior daily violating the most sacred commandments of nature. He told me I was his property; that I must be subject to his will in all things. My soul revolted against the mean tyranny. But where could I turn for protection? No matter whether the slave girl be as black as ebony or as fair as her mistress. In either case, there is no shadow of law to protect her from insult, from violence, or even from death; all these are inflicted by fiends who bear the shape of men. The mistress, who ought to protect the helpless victim, has no other feelings towards her but those of jealousy and rage. The degradation, the wrongs, the vices, that grow out of slavery, are more than I can describe. They are greater than you would willingly believe. Surely, if you credited one half the truths that are told you concerning the helpless millions suffering in this cruel bondage, you at the north would not help to tighten the yoke.[1] You surely would refuse to do for the master, on your own soil, the mean and cruel work which trained bloodhounds and the lowest class of whites do for him at the south.

Everywhere the years bring to all enough of sin and sorrow; but in slavery the very dawn of life is darkened by these shadows. Even the little child, who is accustomed to wait on her mistress and her children, will learn, before she is twelve years old, why it is that her mistress hates such and such a one among the slaves. Perhaps the child's own mother is among those hated ones. She listens to violent outbreaks of jealous passion, and cannot help understanding what is the cause. She will become prematurely knowing in evil things. Soon she will learn to tremble when she hears her master's footfall. She will be compelled to realize that she

is no longer a child. If God has bestowed beauty upon her, it will prove her greatest curse. That which commands admiration in the white woman only hastens the degradation of the female slave. I know that some are too much brutalized by slavery to feel the humiliation of their position; but many slaves feel it most acutely, and shrink from the memory of it. I cannot tell how much I suffered in the presence of these wrongs, nor how I am still pained by the retrospect. My master met me at every turn, reminding me that I belonged to him, and swearing by heaven and earth that he would compel me to submit to him. If I went out for a breath of fresh air, after a day of unwearied toil, his footsteps dogged me. If I knelt by my mother's grave, his dark shadow fell on me even there. The light heart which nature had given me became heavy with sad forebodings. The other slaves in my master's house noticed the change. Many of them pitied me; but none dared to ask the cause. They had no need to inquire. They knew too well the guilty practices under that roof; and they were aware that to speak of them was an offence that never went unpunished.

I longed for someone to confide in. I would have given the world to have laid my head on my grandmother's faithful bosom, and told her all my troubles. But Dr. Flint swore he would kill me, if I was not as silent as the grave. Then, although my grandmother was all in all to me, I feared her as well as loved her. I had been accustomed to look up to her with a respect bordering upon awe. I was very young, and felt shamefaced about telling her such impure things, especially as I knew her to be very strict on such subjects. Moreover, she was a woman of a high spirit. She was usually very quiet in her demeanor; but if her indignation was once roused, it was not very easily quelled. I had been told that she once chased a white gentleman with a loaded pistol, because he insulted one of her daughters. I dreaded the consequences of a violent outbreak; and both pride and fear kept me silent. But though I did not confide in my grandmother, and even evaded her vigilant watchfulness and inquiry, her presence in the neighborhood was some protection to me. Though she had been a slave, Dr. Flint was afraid of her. He dreaded her scorching rebukes. Moreover, she was known and patronized by many people; and he did not wish to have his villainy made public. It was

---

[1]   *north ... yoke* Reference to the hope that Northerners would actively resist the terms of the Fugitive Slave Act of 1850, under which it became illegal for anyone, whether in the North or the South, to give aid to people escaping slavery; citizens throughout the country were expected to actively participate in the apprehension and return of fugitives to the South. The Fugitive Slave Act was fiercely resisted by Northern abolitionists, but it was not repealed until 1864.

lucky for me that I did not live on a distant plantation, but in a town not so large that the inhabitants were ignorant of each other's affairs. Bad as are the laws and customs in a slaveholding community, the doctor, as a professional man, deemed it prudent to keep up some outward show of decency.

O, what days and nights of fear and sorrow that man caused me! Reader, it is not to awaken sympathy for myself that I am telling you truthfully what I suffered in slavery. I do it to kindle a flame of compassion in your hearts for my sisters who are still in bondage, suffering as I once suffered.

I once saw two beautiful children playing together. One was a fair white child; the other was her slave, and also her sister. When I saw them embracing each other, and heard their joyous laughter, I turned sadly away from the lovely sight. I foresaw the inevitable blight that would fall on the little slave's heart. I knew how soon her laughter would be changed to sighs. The fair child grew up to be a still fairer woman. From childhood to womanhood her pathway was blooming with flowers, and overarched by a sunny sky. Scarcely one day of her life had been clouded when the sun rose on her happy bridal morning.

How had those years dealt with her slave sister, the little playmate of her childhood? She, also, was very beautiful; but the flowers and sunshine of love were not for her. She drank the cup of sin, and shame, and misery, whereof her persecuted race are compelled to drink.

In view of these things, why are ye silent, ye free men and women of the north? Why do your tongues falter in maintenance of the right? Would that I had more ability! But my heart is so full, and my pen is so weak! There are noble men and women who plead for us, striving to help those who cannot help themselves. God bless them! God give them strength and courage to go on! God bless those, everywhere, who are laboring to advance the cause of humanity!

CHAPTER 7. THE LOVER

Why does the slave ever love? Why allow the tendrils of the heart to twine around objects which may at any moment be wrenched away by the hand of violence? When separations come by the hand of death, the pious soul can bow in resignation, and say, "Not my will, but thine be done, O Lord!" But when the ruthless hand of man strikes the blow, regardless of the misery he causes, it is hard to be submissive. I did not reason thus when I was a young girl. Youth will be youth. I loved, and I indulged the hope that the dark clouds around me would turn out a bright lining. I forgot that in the land of my birth the shadows are too dense for light to penetrate. A land

> Where laughter is not mirth; nor thought the mind;
> Nor words a language; nor e'en men mankind.
> Where cries reply to curses, shrieks to blows,
> And each is tortured in his separate hell.[1]

There was in the neighborhood a young colored carpenter; a free born man. We had been well acquainted in childhood, and frequently met together afterwards. We became mutually attached, and he proposed to marry me. I loved him with all the ardor of a young girl's first love. But when I reflected that I was a slave, and that the laws gave no sanction to the marriage of such, my heart sank within me. My lover wanted to buy me; but I knew that Dr. Flint was too willful and arbitrary a man to consent to that arrangement. From him, I was sure of experiencing all sorts of opposition, and I had nothing to hope from my mistress. She would have been delighted to have got rid of me, but not in that way. It would have relieved her mind of a burden if she could have seen me sold to some distant state, but if I was married near home I should be just as much in her husband's power as I had previously been—for the husband of a slave has no power to protect her. Moreover, my mistress, like many others, seemed to think that slaves had no right to any family ties of their own; that they were created merely to wait upon the family of the mistress. I once heard her abuse a young slave girl, who told her that a colored man wanted to make her his wife. "I will have you peeled and pickled, my lady," said she, "if I ever hear you mention that subject again. Do you suppose that I will have you tending my children with the children of that nigger?" The girl to whom she said this had a mulatto

---

[1]   *Where laughter ... separate hell*   These lines are from Byron's "The Lament of Tasso," 4.84–87 (1817).

child, of course not acknowledged by its father. The poor black man who loved her would have been proud to acknowledge his helpless offspring.

Many and anxious were the thoughts I revolved in my mind. I was at a loss what to do. Above all things, I was desirous to spare my lover the insults that had cut so deeply into my own soul. I talked with my grandmother about it, and partly told her my fears. I did not dare to tell her the worst. She had long suspected all was not right, and if I confirmed her suspicions I knew a storm would rise that would prove the overthrow of all my hopes.

This love-dream had been my support through many trials; and I could not bear to run the risk of having it suddenly dissipated. There was a lady in the neighborhood, a particular friend of Dr. Flint's, who often visited the house. I had a great respect for her, and she had always manifested a friendly interest in me. Grandmother thought she would have great influence with the doctor. I went to this lady, and told her my story. I told her I was aware that my lover's being a free-born man would prove a great objection; but he wanted to buy me; and if Dr. Flint would consent to that arrangement, I felt sure he would be willing to pay any reasonable price. She knew that Mrs. Flint disliked me; therefore, I ventured to suggest that perhaps my mistress would approve of my being sold, as that would rid her of me. The lady listened, with kindly sympathy, and promised to do her utmost to promote my wishes. She had an interview with the doctor, and I believe she pleaded my cause earnestly; but it was all to no purpose.

How I dreaded my master now! Every minute I expected to be summoned to his presence; but the day passed, and I heard nothing from him. The next morning, a message was brought to me: "Master wants you in his study." I found the door ajar, and I stood a moment gazing at the hateful man who claimed a right to rule me, body and soul. I entered, and tried to appear calm. I did not want him to know how my heart was bleeding. He looked fixedly at me, with an expression which seemed to say, "I have half a mind to kill you on the spot." At last he broke the silence, and that was a relief to both of us.

"So you want to be married, do you?" said he, "and to a free nigger."

"Yes, sir."

"Well, I'll soon convince you whether I am your master, or the nigger fellow you honor so highly. If you *must* have a husband, you may take up with one of my slaves."

What a situation I should be in, as the wife of one of *his* slaves, even if my heart had been interested!

I replied, "Don't you suppose, sir, that a slave can have some preference about marrying? Do you suppose that all men are alike to her?"

"Do you love this nigger?" said he, abruptly.

"Yes, sir."

"How dare you tell me so!" he exclaimed, in great wrath. After a slight pause, he added, "I supposed you thought more of yourself; that you felt above the insults of such puppies."

I replied, "If he is a puppy I am a puppy, for we are both of the negro race. It is right and honorable for us to love each other. The man you call a puppy never insulted me, sir; and he would not love me if he did not believe me to be a virtuous woman."

He sprang upon me like a tiger, and gave me a stunning blow. It was the first time he had ever struck me; and fear did not enable me to control my anger. When I had recovered a little from the effects, I exclaimed, "You have struck me for answering you honestly. How I despise you!"

There was silence for some minutes. Perhaps he was deciding what should be my punishment; or, perhaps, he wanted to give me time to reflect on what I had said, and to whom I had said it. Finally, he asked, "Do you know what you have said?"

"Yes, sir; but your treatment drove me to it."

"Do you know that I have a right to do as I like with you—that I can kill you, if I please?"

"You have tried to kill me, and I wish you had; but you have no right to do as you like with me."

"Silence!" he exclaimed, in a thundering voice. "By heavens, girl, you forget yourself too far! Are you mad? If you are, I will soon bring you to your senses. Do you think any other master would bear what I have borne from you this morning? Many masters would have killed you on the spot. How would you like to be sent to jail for your insolence?"

"I know I have been disrespectful, sir," I replied; "but you drove me to it; I couldn't help it. As for the jail, there would be more peace for me there than there is here."

"You deserve to go there," said he, "and to be under such treatment, that you would forget the meaning of the word *peace*. It would do you good. It would take some of your high notions out of you. But I am not ready to send you there yet, notwithstanding your ingratitude for all my kindness and forbearance. You have been the plague of my life. I have wanted to make you happy, and I have been repaid with the basest ingratitude; but though you have proved yourself incapable of appreciating my kindness, I will be lenient towards you, Linda. I will give you one more chance to redeem your character. If you behave yourself and do as I require, I will forgive you and treat you as I always have done; but if you disobey me, I will punish you as I would the meanest slave on my plantation. Never let me hear that fellow's name mentioned again. If I ever know of your speaking to him, I will cowhide you both; and if I catch him lurking about my premises, I will shoot him as soon as I would a dog. Do you hear what I say? I'll teach you a lesson about marriage and free niggers! Now go, and let this be the last time I have occasion to speak to you on this subject."

Reader, did you ever hate? I hope not. I never did but once; and I trust I never shall again. Somebody has called it "the atmosphere of hell";[1] and I believe it is so.

For a fortnight[2] the doctor did not speak to me. He thought to mortify me; to make me feel that I had disgraced myself by receiving the honorable addresses of a respectable colored man, in preference to the base proposals of a white man. But though his lips disdained to address me, his eyes were very loquacious. No animal ever watched its prey more narrowly than he watched me. He knew that I could write, though he had failed to make me read his letters; and he was now troubled lest I should exchange letters with another man. After a while he became weary of silence; and I was sorry for it. One morning, as he passed through the hall, to leave the house, he contrived to thrust a note into my hand. I thought I had better read it, and spare myself the vexation of having him read it to me. It expressed regret

for the blow he had given me, and reminded me that I myself was wholly to blame for it. He hoped I had become convinced of the injury I was doing myself by incurring his displeasure. He wrote that he had made up his mind to go to Louisiana; that he should take several slaves with him, and intended I should be one of the number. My mistress would remain where she was; therefore I should have nothing to fear from that quarter. If I merited kindness from him, he assured me that it would be lavishly bestowed. He begged me to think over the matter, and answer the following day.

The next morning I was called to carry a pair of scissors to his room. I laid them on the table with the letter beside them. He thought it was my answer, and did not call me back. I went as usual to attend my young mistress to and from school. He met me in the street, and ordered me to stop at his office on my way back. When I entered, he showed me his letter, and asked me why I had not answered it. I replied, "I am your daughter's property, and it is in your power to send me, or take me, wherever you please." He said he was very glad to find me so willing to go, and that we should start early in the autumn. He had a large practice in the town, and I rather thought he had made up the story merely to frighten me. However that might be, I was determined that I would never go to Louisiana with him.

Summer passed away, and early in the autumn Dr. Flint's eldest son was sent to Louisiana to examine the country, with a view to emigrating. That news did not disturb me. I knew very well that I should not be sent with *him*. That I had not been taken to the plantation before this time, was owing to the fact that his son was there. He was jealous of his son; and jealousy of the overseer had kept him from punishing me by sending me into the fields to work. Is it strange that I was not proud of these protectors? As for the overseer, he was a man for whom I had less respect than I had for a bloodhound.

Young Mr. Flint did not bring back a favorable report of Louisiana, and I heard no more of that scheme. Soon after this, my lover met me at the corner of the street, and I stopped to speak to him. Looking up, I saw my master watching us from his window. I hurried home, trembling with fear. I was sent for, immediately, to go to his room. He met me with a blow. "When is mistress

---

[1]   *Somebody … hell* English writer Martin Farquhar Tupper wrote that "hatred is the atmosphere of hell" in his book *Proverbial Philosophy* (1838).

[2]   *a fortnight* Two weeks.

to be married?" said he, in a sneering tone. A shower of oaths and imprecations followed. How thankful I was that my lover was a free man! that my tyrant had no power to flog him for speaking to me in the street!

Again and again I revolved in my mind how all this would end. There was no hope that the doctor would consent to sell me on any terms. He had an iron will, and was determined to keep me, and to conquer me. My lover was an intelligent and religious man. Even if he could have obtained permission to marry me while I was a slave, the marriage would give him no power to protect me from my master. It would have made him miserable to witness the insults I should have been subjected to. And then, if we had children, I knew they must "follow the condition of the mother."[1] What a terrible blight that would be on the heart of a free, intelligent father! For *his* sake, I felt that I ought not to link his fate with my own unhappy destiny. He was going to Savannah to see about a little property left him by an uncle; and hard as it was to bring my feelings to it, I earnestly entreated him not to come back. I advised him to go to the Free States, where his tongue would not be tied, and where his intelligence would be of more avail to him. He left me, still hoping the day would come when I could be bought. With me the lamp of hope had gone out. The dream of my girlhood was over. I felt lonely and desolate.

Still I was not stripped of all. I still had my good grandmother, and my affectionate brother. When he put his arms round my neck, and looked into my eyes, as if to read there the troubles I dared not tell, I felt that I still had something to love. But even that pleasant emotion was chilled by the reflection that he might be torn from me at any moment, by some sudden freak of my master. If he had known how we loved each other, I think he would have exulted in separating us. We often planned together how we could get to the north. But, as William remarked, such things are easier said than done. My movements were very closely watched, and we had no means of getting any money to defray our expenses. As for grandmother, she was strongly opposed to her children's undertaking any such project. She had not forgotten poor Benjamin's sufferings,[2] and she was afraid that if another child tried to escape, he would have a similar or a worse fate. To me, nothing seemed more dreadful than my present life. I said to myself, "William *must* be free. He shall go to the north, and I will follow him." Many a slave sister has formed the same plans.

CHAPTER 8. WHAT SLAVES ARE TAUGHT TO THINK OF THE NORTH

Slaveholders pride themselves upon being honorable men; but if you were to hear the enormous lies they tell their slaves, you would have small respect for their veracity. I have spoken plain English. Pardon me. I cannot use a milder term. When they visit the north, and return home, they tell their slaves of the runaways they have seen, and describe them to be in the most deplorable condition. A slaveholder once told me that he had seen a runaway friend of mine in New York, and that she besought him to take her back to her master, for she was literally dying of starvation; that many days she had only one cold potato to eat, and at other times could get nothing at all. He said he refused to take her, because he knew her master would not thank him for bringing such a miserable wretch to his house. He ended by saying to me, "This is the punishment she brought on herself for running away from a kind master."

This whole story was false. I afterwards stayed with that friend in New York, and found her in comfortable circumstances. She had never thought of such a thing as wishing to go back to slavery. Many of the slaves believe such stories, and think it is not worthwhile to exchange slavery for such a hard kind of freedom. It

---

1   *follow ... mother*   From 1662 onwards, slave law in Britain and America had followed the doctrine that children followed the status of their mother (i.e., any child born to an enslaved woman would be themselves enslaved). This law meant that enslavers who fathered children with enslaved women were not held in any way accountable and in fact profited from the practice, as they could then exploit or sell their own children.

2   *Benjamin's sufferings*   In Chapter Four, "The Slave Who Dared to Feel Like a Man," the narrator relates the story of Benjamin, a character based on Joseph Horniblow, Jacobs's uncle, who, being close in age, "seemed more like my brother than my uncle." Joseph Horniblow ran away from his enslaver to avoid being whipped, was caught, paraded through town in chains, and put in jail, where his enslavers deliberately kept him in vermin-infested conditions in order to break his spirit. He was sold to a new enslaver in New Orleans and eventually escaped to New York. Jacobs and her brother both named their sons after Joseph Horniblow.

is difficult to persuade such that freedom could make them useful men, and enable them to protect their wives and children. If those heathen in our Christian land had as much teaching as some Hindoos, they would think otherwise. They would know that liberty is more valuable than life. They would begin to understand their own capabilities, and exert themselves to become men and women.

But while the Free States sustain a law[1] which hurls fugitives back into slavery, how can the slaves resolve to become men? There are some who strive to protect wives and daughters from the insults of their masters; but those who have such sentiments have had advantages above the general mass of slaves. They have been partially civilized and Christianized by favorable circumstances. Some are bold enough to *utter* such sentiments to their masters. O, that there were more of them!

Some poor creatures have been so brutalized by the lash that they will sneak out of the way to give their masters free access to their wives and daughters. Do you think this proves the black man to belong to an inferior order of beings? What would *you* be, if you had been born and brought up a slave, with generations of slaves for ancestors? I admit that the black man *is* inferior. But what is it that makes him so? It is the ignorance in which white men compel him to live; it is the torturing whip that lashes manhood out of him; it is the fierce bloodhounds of the South, and the scarcely less cruel human bloodhounds of the north, who enforce the Fugitive Slave Law. *They* do the work.

Southern gentlemen indulge in the most contemptuous expressions about the Yankees, while they,[2] on their part, consent to do the vilest work for them, such as the ferocious bloodhounds and the despised negro-hunters are employed to do at home. When southerners go to the north, they are proud to do them honor;[3] but the northern man is not welcome south of Mason Dixon's line, unless he suppresses every thought and feeling at variance with their "peculiar institution."[4] Nor is it enough to be silent. The masters are not pleased, unless they obtain a greater degree of subservience than that; and they are generally accommodated. Do they respect the northerner for this? I trow[5] not. Even the slaves despise "a northern man with southern principles"; and that is the class they generally see. When northerners go to the south to reside, they prove very apt scholars. They soon imbibe the sentiments and disposition of their neighbors, and generally go beyond their teachers. Of the two, they are proverbially the hardest masters.

They seem to satisfy their consciences with the doctrine that God created the Africans to be slaves. What a libel upon the heavenly Father, who "made of one blood all nations of men"![6] And then who are Africans? Who can measure the amount of Anglo-Saxon blood coursing in the veins of American slaves?

I have spoken of the pains slaveholders take to give their slaves a bad opinion of the north; but, notwithstanding this, intelligent slaves are aware that they have many friends in the Free States. Even the most ignorant have some confused notions about it. They knew that I could read; and I was often asked if I had seen anything in the newspapers about white folks over in the big north, who were trying to get their freedom for them. Some believe that the abolitionists have already made them free, and that it is established by law, but that their masters prevent the law from going into effect. One woman begged me to get a newspaper and read it over. She said her husband told her that the black people had sent word to the queen of 'Merica that they were all slaves; that she didn't believe it, and went to Washington city to see the president about it. They quarrelled; she drew her sword upon him, and swore that he should help her to make them all free.

That poor, ignorant woman thought that America was governed by a Queen, to whom the President was subordinate. I wish the President was subordinate to Queen Justice.

---

1   *Free States sustain a law*   See note 1 on page 629 above.

2   *Yankees*   In common American usage, this term referred originally to New Englanders, and later to Northerners in general—the sense in which Jacobs is using it here;   *they*   I.e., the Yankees.

3   *they … honor*   I.e., the Northerners are respectful of visiting Southerners.

4   *Mason Dixon's line*   Line separating parts of Pennsylvania and Delaware from parts of Maryland and Virginia; the phrase was used as shorthand for the boundary between the Northern free states and the Southern slave states;   *peculiar institution*   I.e., slavery.

5   *trow*   Believe.

6   *made … men*   See Acts 17.26.

Chapter 10. A Perilous Passage in the Slave Girl's Life

After my lover went away, Dr. Flint contrived a new plan. He seemed to have an idea that my fear of my mistress was his greatest obstacle. In the blandest tones, he told me that he was going to build a small house for me, in a secluded place, four miles away from the town. I shuddered; but I was constrained to listen, while he talked of his intention to give me a home of my own, and to make a lady of me. Hitherto, I had escaped my dreaded fate, by being in the midst of people. My grandmother had already had high words with my master about me. She had told him pretty plainly what she thought of his character, and there was considerable gossip in the neighborhood about our affairs, to which the open-mouthed jealousy of Mrs. Flint contributed not a little. When my master said he was going to build a house for me, and that he could do it with little trouble and expense, I was in hopes something would happen to frustrate his scheme; but I soon heard that the house was actually begun. I vowed before my Maker that I would never enter it. I had rather toil on the plantation from dawn till dark; I had rather live and die in jail, than drag on, from day to day, through such a living death. I was determined that the master, whom I so hated and loathed, who had blighted the prospects of my youth, and made my life a desert, should not, after my long struggle with him, succeed at last in trampling his victim under his feet. I would do anything, everything, for the sake of defeating him. What *could* I do? I thought and thought, till I became desperate, and made a plunge into the abyss.

And now, reader, I come to a period in my unhappy life, which I would gladly forget if I could. The remembrance fills me with sorrow and shame. It pains me to tell you of it; but I have promised to tell you the truth, and I will do it honestly, let it cost me what it may. I will not try to screen myself behind the plea of compulsion from a master; for it was not so. Neither can I plead ignorance or thoughtlessness. For years, my master had done his utmost to pollute my mind with foul images, and to destroy the pure principles inculcated by my grandmother, and the good mistress of my childhood. The influences of slavery had had the same effect on me that they had on other young girls;

they had made me prematurely knowing, concerning the evil ways of the world. I know what I did, and I did it with deliberate calculation.

But, O, ye happy women, whose purity has been sheltered from childhood, who have been free to choose the objects of your affection, whose homes are protected by law, do not judge the poor desolate slave girl too severely! If slavery had been abolished, I, also, could have married the man of my choice; I could have had a home shielded by the laws; and I should have been spared the painful task of confessing what I am now about to relate; but all my prospects had been blighted by slavery. I wanted to keep myself pure; and, under the most adverse circumstances, I tried hard to preserve my self-respect; but I was struggling alone in the powerful grasp of the demon Slavery; and the monster proved too strong for me. I felt as if I was forsaken by God and man; as if all my efforts must be frustrated; and I became reckless in my despair.

I have told you that Dr. Flint's persecutions and his wife's jealousy had given rise to some gossip in the neighborhood. Among others, it chanced that a white unmarried gentleman had obtained some knowledge of the circumstances in which I was placed. He knew my grandmother, and often spoke to me in the street. He became interested for me, and asked questions about my master, which I answered in part. He expressed a great deal of sympathy, and a wish to aid me. He constantly sought opportunities to see me, and wrote to me frequently. I was a poor slave girl, only fifteen years old.

So much attention from a superior person was, of course, flattering; for human nature is the same in all. I also felt grateful for his sympathy, and encouraged by his kind words. It seemed to me a great thing to have such a friend. By degrees, a more tender feeling crept into my heart. He was an educated and eloquent gentleman; too eloquent, alas, for the poor slave girl who trusted in him. Of course I saw whither all this was tending. I knew the impassable gulf between us; but to be an object of interest to a man who is not married, and who is not her master, is agreeable to the pride and feelings of a slave, if her miserable situation has left her any pride or sentiment. It seems less degrading to give one's self, than to submit to compulsion. There is something akin to freedom in having a lover who has no control over you, except that which he gains by kindness and attachment. A master may treat you as rudely as he pleases, and you dare not speak; moreover, the wrong does not seem so great with an unmarried man, as with one who has a wife to be made unhappy. There may be sophistry in all this; but the condition of a slave confuses all principles of morality, and, in fact, renders the practice of them impossible.

When I found that my master had actually begun to build the lonely cottage, other feelings mixed with those I have described. Revenge, and calculations of interest, were added to flattered vanity and sincere gratitude for kindness. I knew nothing would enrage Dr. Flint so much as to know that I favored another; and it was something to triumph over my tyrant even in that small way. I thought he would revenge himself by selling me, and I was sure my friend, Mr. Sands, would buy me. He was a man of more generosity and feeling than my master, and I thought my freedom could be easily obtained from him. The crisis of my fate now came so near that I was desperate. I shuddered to think of being the mother of children that should be owned by my old tyrant. I knew that as soon as a new fancy took him, his victims were sold far off to get rid of them; especially if they had children. I had seen several women sold, with his babies at the breast. He never allowed his offspring by slaves to remain long in sight of himself and his wife. Of a man who was not my master I could ask to have my children well supported; and in this case, I felt confident I should obtain the boon. I also felt quite sure that they would be made free. With all these thoughts revolving in my mind, and seeing no other way of escaping the doom I so much dreaded, I made a headlong plunge. Pity me, and pardon me, O virtuous reader! You never knew what it is to be a slave; to be entirely unprotected by law or custom; to have the laws reduce you to the condition of a chattel, entirely subject to the will of another. You never exhausted your ingenuity in avoiding the snares, and eluding the power of a hated tyrant; you never shuddered at the sound of his footsteps, and trembled within hearing of his voice. I know I did wrong. No one can feel it more sensibly than I do. The painful and humiliating memory will haunt me to my dying day. Still, in looking back, calmly, on the events of my life, I feel that the slave woman ought not to be judged by the same standard as others.

The months passed on. I had many unhappy hours. I secretly mourned over the sorrow I was bringing on my grandmother, who had so tried to shield me from harm. I knew that I was the greatest comfort of her old age, and that it was a source of pride to her that I had not degraded myself, like most of the slaves. I wanted to confess to her that I was no longer worthy of her love; but I could not utter the dreaded words.

As for Dr. Flint, I had a feeling of satisfaction and triumph in the thought of telling *him*. From time to time he told me of his intended arrangements, and I was silent. At last, he came and told me the cottage was completed, and ordered me to go to it. I told him I would never enter it. He said, "I have heard enough of such talk as that. You shall go, if you are carried by force; and you shall remain there." I replied, "I will never go there. In a few months I shall be a mother."

He stood and looked at me in dumb amazement, and left the house without a word. I thought I should be happy in my triumph over him. But now that the truth was out, and my relatives would hear of it, I felt wretched. Humble as were their circumstances, they had pride in my good character. Now, how could I look them in the face? My self-respect was gone! I had resolved that I would be virtuous, though I was a slave. I had said, "Let the storm beat! I will brave it till I die." And now, how humiliated I felt!

I went to my grandmother. My lips moved to make confession, but the words stuck in my throat. I sat down in the shade of a tree at her door and began to sew. I think she saw something unusual was the matter with me. The mother of slaves is very watchful. She knows there is no security for her children. After they have entered their teens she lives in daily expectation of trouble. This leads to many questions. If the girl is of a sensitive nature, timidity keeps her from answering truthfully, and this well-meant course has a tendency to drive her from maternal counsels. Presently, in came my mistress, like a mad woman, and accused me concerning her husband. My grandmother, whose suspicions had been previously awakened, believed what she said. She exclaimed, "O Linda! has it come to this? I had rather see you dead than to see you as you now are. You are a disgrace to your dead mother." She tore from my fingers my mother's wedding ring and her silver thimble. "Go away!" she exclaimed, "and never come to my house, again." Her reproaches fell so hot and heavy, that they left me no chance to answer. Bitter tears, such as the eyes never shed but once, were my only answer. I rose from my seat, but fell back again, sobbing. She did not speak to me; but the tears were running down her furrowed cheeks, and they scorched me like fire. She had always been so kind to me! So kind! How I longed to throw myself at her feet, and tell her all the truth! But she had ordered me to go, and never to come there again. After a few minutes, I mustered strength, and started to obey her. With what feelings did I now close that little gate, which I used to open with such an eager hand in my childhood! It closed upon me with a sound I never heard before.

Where could I go? I was afraid to return to my master's. I walked on recklessly, not caring where I went, or what would become of me. When I had gone four or five miles, fatigue compelled me to stop. I sat down on the stump of an old tree. The stars were shining through the boughs above me. How they mocked me, with their bright, calm light! The hours passed by, and as I sat there alone a chilliness and deadly sickness came over me. I sank on the ground. My mind was full of horrid thoughts. I prayed to die; but the prayer was not answered. At last, with great effort I roused myself, and walked some distance further, to the house of a woman who had been a friend of my mother. When I told her why I was there, she spoke soothingly to me; but I could not be comforted. I thought I could bear my shame if I could only be reconciled to my grandmother. I longed to open my heart to her. I thought if she could know the real state of the case, and all I had been bearing for years, she would perhaps judge me less harshly. My friend advised me to send for her. I did so; but days of agonizing suspense passed before she came. Had she utterly forsaken me? No. She came at last. I knelt before her, and told her the things that had poisoned my life; how long I had been persecuted; that I saw no way of escape; and in an hour of extremity I had become desperate. She listened in silence. I told her I would bear anything and do anything, if in time I had hopes of obtaining her forgiveness. I begged of her to pity me, for my dead mother's sake. And she did pity me. She did not say, "I forgive you"; but she looked at me lovingly, with her eyes full of tears. She laid her old hand gently on my head, and murmured, "Poor child! Poor child!"

[In the chapter omitted here, the narrator Linda is living at her Aunt Martha's house (though she is still owned by Dr. Flint). Linda falls ill and her baby boy is born early; it takes Linda a year to recover from her illness and the birth. Dr. Flint continues to persecute her with his attention even though she is no longer under his roof.]

Chapter 12. Fear of Insurrection

Not far from this time Nat Turner's insurrection[1] broke out; and the news threw our town into great commotion. Strange that they should be alarmed when their slaves were so "contented and happy"! But so it was.

It was always the custom to have a muster[2] every year. On that occasion every white man shouldered his musket. The citizens[3] and the so-called country gentlemen wore military uniforms. The poor whites took their places in the ranks in every-day dress, some without shoes, some without hats. This grand occasion had already passed; and when the slaves were told there was to be another muster, they were surprised and rejoiced. Poor creatures! They thought it was going to be a holiday. I was informed of the true state of affairs, and imparted it to the few I could trust. Most gladly would I have proclaimed it to every slave; but I dared not. All could not be relied on. Mighty is the power of the torturing lash.

By sunrise, people were pouring in from every quarter within twenty miles of the town. I knew the houses were to be searched; and I expected it would be done

---

[1] *Nat Turner's insurrection* In 1831, the enslaved preacher Nat Turner led an antislavery rebellion in Virginia; at least 51 white people were killed, and the rebellion was suppressed after four days of fighting, after which over a hundred black people were killed in retaliation. The revolt was widely depicted as a massacre in Southern media, and the events led to new restrictions on education for black people as well as to rules preventing enslaved people from meeting without a white person present.

[2] *muster* Gathering or roll-call for a militia unit, in order to count the number of persons available for potential military service.

[3] *citizens* Likely a reference to those who were entitled to vote—men in the community who paid taxes or owned property.

by country bullies and the poor whites. I knew nothing annoyed them so much as to see colored people living in comfort and respectability; so I made arrangements for them with especial care. I arranged everything in my grandmother's house as neatly as possible. I put white quilts on the beds, and decorated some of the rooms with flowers. When all was arranged, I sat down at the window to watch. Far as my eye could reach, it rested on a motley crowd of soldiers. Drums and fifes were discoursing[1] martial music. The men were divided into companies of sixteen, each headed by a captain. Orders were given, and the wild scouts rushed in every direction, wherever a colored face was to be found.

It was a grand opportunity for the low whites, who had no negroes of their own to scourge. They exulted in such a chance to exercise a little brief authority, and show their subserviency to the slaveholders; not reflecting that the power which trampled on the colored people also kept themselves in poverty, ignorance, and moral degradation. Those who never witnessed such scenes can hardly believe what I know was inflicted at this time on innocent men, women, and children, against whom there was not the slightest ground for suspicion. Colored people and slaves who lived in remote parts of the town suffered in an especial manner. In some cases the searchers scattered powder and shot among their clothes, and then sent other parties to find them, and bring them forward as proof that they were plotting insurrection. Everywhere men, women, and children were whipped till the blood stood in puddles at their feet. Some received five hundred lashes; others were tied hands and feet, and tortured with a bucking paddle,[2] which blisters the skin terribly. The dwellings of the colored people, unless they happened to be protected by some influential white person, who was nigh at hand, were robbed of clothing and everything else the marauders thought worth carrying away. All day long these unfeeling wretches went round, like a troop of demons, terrifying and tormenting the helpless. At night, they formed themselves into patrol bands, and

went wherever they chose among the colored people, acting out their brutal will. Many women hid themselves in woods and swamps, to keep out of their way. If any of the husbands or fathers told of these outrages, they were tied up to the public whipping post, and cruelly scourged for telling lies about white men. The consternation was universal. No two people that had the slightest tinge of color in their faces dared to be seen talking together.

I entertained no positive fears about our household, because we were in the midst of white families who would protect us. We were ready to receive the soldiers whenever they came. It was not long before we heard the tramp of feet and the sound of voices. The door was rudely pushed open; and in they tumbled, like a pack of hungry wolves. They snatched at everything within their reach. Every box, trunk, closet, and corner underwent a thorough examination. A box in one of the drawers containing some silver change was eagerly pounced upon. When I stepped forward to take it from them, one of the soldiers turned and said angrily, "What d'ye foller us fur? D'ye s'pose white folks is come to steal?"

I replied, "You have come to search; but you have searched that box, and I will take it, if you please."

At that moment I saw a white gentleman who was friendly to us; and I called to him, and asked him to have the goodness to come in and stay till the search was over. He readily complied. His entrance into the house brought in the captain of the company, whose business it was to guard the outside of the house, and see that none of the inmates left it. This officer was Mr. Litch, the wealthy slaveholder whom I mentioned, in the account of neighboring planters, as being notorious for his cruelty. He felt above soiling his hands with the search. He merely gave orders; and, if a bit of writing was discovered, it was carried to him by his ignorant followers, who were unable to read.

My grandmother had a large trunk of bedding and table cloths. When that was opened, there was a great shout of surprise; and one exclaimed, "Where'd the damned niggers git all dis sheet an' table clarf?"

My grandmother, emboldened by the presence of our white protector, said, "You may be sure we didn't pilfer 'em from *your* houses."

---

[1]   *fifes* Small flutes that are played along with drums in military music; *discoursing* Pouring forth.

[2]   *bucking paddle* Wooden paddle—also called a "spanking paddle"—with holes in it, designed to create blisters when repeatedly used to whip someone.

"Look here, mammy," said a grim-looking fellow without any coat, "you seem to feel mighty gran' 'cause you got all them 'ere fixens. White folks oughter have 'em all."

His remarks were interrupted by a chorus of voices shouting, "We's got 'em! We's got 'em! Dis 'ere yaller gal's[1] got letters!"

There was a general rush for the supposed letter, which, upon examination, proved to be some verses written to me by a friend. In packing away my things, I had overlooked them. When their captain informed them of their contents, they seemed much disappointed. He inquired of me who wrote them. I told him it was one of my friends. "Can you read them?" he asked. When I told him I could, he swore, and raved, and tore the paper into bits. "Bring me all your letters!" said he, in a commanding tone. I told him I had none. "Don't be afraid," he continued, in an insinuating way. "Bring them all to me. Nobody shall do you any harm." Seeing I did not move to obey him, his pleasant tone changed to oaths and threats. "Who writes to you? half free niggers?" inquired he. I replied, "O, no; most of my letters are from white people. Some request me to burn them after they are read, and some I destroy without reading."

An exclamation of surprise from some of the company put a stop to our conversation. Some silver spoons which ornamented an old-fashioned buffet had just been discovered. My grandmother was in the habit of preserving fruit for many ladies in the town, and of preparing suppers for parties; consequently she had many jars of preserves. The closet that contained these was next invaded, and the contents tasted. One of them, who was helping himself freely, tapped his neighbor on the shoulder, and said, "Wal done! Don't wonder de niggers want to kill all de white folks, when dey live on 'sarves" [meaning preserves]. I stretched out my hand to take the jar, saying, "You were not sent here to search for sweetmeats."

"And what *were* we sent for?" said the captain, bristling up to me. I evaded the question.

The search of the house was completed, and nothing found to condemn us. They next proceeded to the garden, and knocked about every bush and vine with no better success. The captain called his men together, and, after a short consultation, the order to march was given. As they passed out of the gate, the captain turned back, and pronounced a malediction on the house. He said it ought to be burned to the ground, and each of its inmates receive thirty-nine lashes. We came out of this affair very fortunately; not losing anything except some wearing apparel.

Towards evening the turbulence increased. The soldiers, stimulated by drink, committed still greater cruelties. Shrieks and shouts continually rent the air. Not daring to go to the door, I peeped under the window curtain. I saw a mob dragging along a number of colored people, each white man, with his musket upraised, threatening instant death if they did not stop their shrieks. Among the prisoners was a respectable old colored minister. They had found a few parcels of shot in his house, which his wife had for years used to balance her scales. For this they were going to shoot him on Court House Green. What a spectacle was that for a civilized country! A rabble, staggering under intoxication, assuming to be the administrators of justice!

The better class of the community exerted their influence to save the innocent, persecuted people; and in several instances they succeeded, by keeping them shut up in jail till the excitement abated. At last the white citizens found that their own property was not safe from the lawless rabble they had summoned to protect them. They rallied[2] the drunken swarm, drove them back into the country, and set a guard over the town.

The next day, the town patrols were commissioned to search colored people that lived out of the city; and the most shocking outrages were committed with perfect impunity. Every day for a fortnight, if I looked out, I saw horsemen with some poor panting negro tied to their saddles, and compelled by the lash to keep up with their speed, till they arrived at the jail yard. Those who had been whipped too unmercifully to walk were washed with brine, tossed into a cart, and carried to jail. One black man, who had not fortitude to endure scourging, promised to give information about the conspiracy. But it turned out that he knew nothing at all. He had not even heard the name of Nat Turner. The poor fellow had, however, made up a story,

---

[1]   *yaller gal*   I.e., mulatto girl.

[2]   *rallied*   Brought back together.

which augmented his own sufferings and those of the colored people.

The day patrol continued for some weeks, and at sundown a night guard was substituted. Nothing at all was proved against the colored people, bond or free. The wrath of the slaveholders was somewhat appeased by the capture of Nat Turner. The imprisoned were released. The slaves were sent to their masters, and the free were permitted to return to their ravaged homes. Visiting was strictly forbidden on the plantations. The slaves begged the privilege of again meeting at their little church in the woods, with their burying ground around it. It was built by the colored people, and they had no higher happiness than to meet there and sing hymns together, and pour out their hearts in spontaneous prayer. Their request was denied, and the church was demolished. They were permitted to attend the white churches, a certain portion of the galleries being appropriated to their use. There, when everybody else had partaken of the communion, and the benediction had been pronounced, the minister said, "Come down, now, my colored friends." They obeyed the summons, and partook of the bread and wine, in commemoration of the meek and lowly Jesus, who said, "God is your Father, and all ye are brethren."

[Linda relates how the slaveholders in her community try to use religion to instill obedience, and she explicates the hypocrisy of Christian slaveholders, particularly of Dr. Flint, who tries to convince Linda that sex with him—unlike sex with another enslaved person—wouldn't affect her virtue in God's eyes. Linda rejects this argument as not in keeping with her reading of the Bible.]

Chapter 14. Another Link to Life

I had not returned to my master's house since the birth of my child. The old man raved to have me thus removed from his immediate power; but his wife vowed, by all that was good and great, she would kill me if I came back; and he did not doubt her word. Sometimes he would stay away for a season. Then he would come and renew the old threadbare discourse about his forbearance and my ingratitude. He labored, most unnecessarily, to convince me that I had lowered

myself. The venomous old reprobate had no need of descanting on that theme. I felt humiliated enough. My unconscious babe was the ever-present witness of my shame. I listened with silent contempt when he talked about my having forfeited *his* good opinion; but I shed bitter tears that I was no longer worthy of being respected by the good and pure. Alas! slavery still held me in its poisonous grasp. There was no chance for me to be respectable. There was no prospect of being able to lead a better life.

Sometimes, when my master found that I still refused to accept what he called his kind offers, he would threaten to sell my child. "Perhaps that will humble you," said he.

Humble *me*! Was I not already in the dust? But his threat lacerated my heart. I knew the law gave him power to fulfil it; for slaveholders have been cunning enough to enact that "the child shall follow the condition of the *mother*," not of the *father*; thus taking care that licentiousness shall not interfere with avarice. This reflection made me clasp my innocent babe all the more firmly to my heart. Horrid visions passed through my mind when I thought of his liability to fall into the slave trader's hands. I wept over him, and said, "O my child! perhaps they will leave you in some cold cabin to die, and then throw you into a hole, as if you were a dog."

When Dr. Flint learned that I was again to be a mother, he was exasperated beyond measure. He rushed from the house, and returned with a pair of shears. I had a fine head of hair; and he often railed about my pride of arranging it nicely. He cut every hair close to my head, storming and swearing all the time. I replied to some of his abuse, and he struck me. Some months before, he had pitched me down stairs in a fit of passion; and the injury I received was so serious that I was unable to turn myself in bed for many days. He then said, "Linda, I swear by God I will never raise my hand against you again"; but I knew that he would forget his promise.

After he discovered my situation, he was like a restless spirit from the pit. He came every day; and I was subjected to such insults as no pen can describe. I would not describe them if I could; they were too low, too revolting. I tried to keep them from my grandmother's knowledge as much as I could. I knew she had enough to sadden her life, without having my troubles to bear. When she saw the doctor treat me with violence, and heard him utter oaths terrible enough to palsy a man's tongue, she could not always hold her peace. It was natural and motherlike that she should try to defend me; but it only made matters worse.

When they told me my new-born babe was a girl, my heart was heavier than it had ever been before. Slavery is terrible for men; but it is far more terrible for women. Superadded to the burden common to all, *they* have wrongs, and sufferings, and mortifications peculiarly their own.

Dr. Flint had sworn that he would make me suffer, to my last day, for this new crime against *him*, as he called it; and as long as he had me in his power he kept his word. On the fourth day after the birth of my babe, he entered my room suddenly, and commanded me to rise and bring my baby to him. The nurse who took care of me had gone out of the room to prepare some nourishment, and I was alone. There was no alternative. I rose, took up my babe, and crossed the room to where he sat. "Now stand there," said he, "till I tell you to go back!" My child bore a strong resemblance to her father, and to the deceased Mrs. Sands, her grandmother. He noticed this; and while I stood before him, trembling with weakness, he heaped upon me and my little one every vile epithet he could think of. Even the grandmother in her grave did not escape his curses. In the midst of his vituperations[1] I fainted at his feet. This recalled him to his senses. He took the baby from my arms, laid it on the bed, dashed cold water on my face, took me up, and shook me violently, to restore my consciousness before any one entered the room. Just then my grandmother came in, and he hurried out of the house. I suffered in consequence of this treatment; but I begged my friends to let me die, rather than send for the doctor. There was nothing I dreaded so much as his presence. My life was spared; and I was glad for the sake of my little ones. Had it not been for these ties to life, I should have been glad to be released by death, though I had lived only nineteen years.

Always it gave me a pang that my children had no lawful claim to a name. Their father offered his; but, if I had wished to accept the offer, I dared not while my master lived. Moreover, I knew it would not be accepted at their baptism. A Christian name they were at least entitled to; and we resolved to call my boy for our dear good Benjamin, who had gone far away from us.

My grandmother belonged to the church; and she was very desirous of having the children christened. I knew Dr. Flint would forbid it, and I did not venture to attempt it. But chance favored me. He was called to visit a patient out of town, and was obliged to be absent during Sunday. "Now is the time," said my grandmother; "we will take the children to church, and have them christened."

When I entered the church, recollections of my mother came over me, and I felt subdued in spirit. There she had presented me for baptism, without any reason to feel ashamed. She had been married, and had such legal rights as slavery allows to a slave. The vows had at least been sacred to *her*, and she had never violated them. I was glad she was not alive, to know under what different circumstances her grandchildren were presented for baptism. Why had my lot been so different from my mother's? *Her* master had died when she was a child; and she remained with her mistress till she married. She was never in the power of any master; and thus she escaped one class of the evils that generally fall upon slaves.

When my baby was about to be christened, the former mistress of my father stepped up to me, and proposed to give it her Christian name. To this I added the surname of my father, who had himself no legal right to it; for my grandfather on the paternal side was a white gentleman. What tangled skeins are the genealogies of slavery! I loved my father; but it mortified me to be obliged to bestow his name on my children.

When we left the church, my father's old mistress invited me to go home with her. She clasped a gold chain round my baby's neck. I thanked her for this kindness; but I did not like the emblem. I wanted no chain to be fastened on my daughter, not even if its links were of gold. How earnestly I prayed that she might never feel the weight of slavery's chain, whose iron entereth into the soul!

[Dr. Flint continues to terrorize and abuse Linda, threatening to sell her children, and at one point throwing her small son Benjamin across the room,

---

[1]   *vituperations*   Abusive rantings.

causing him to lose consciousness. The boy recovers, but Linda almost wanted him to die rather than be subject to the cruelties of slavery. Dr. Flint tells Linda she can either have sex with him or go to his son's plantation; Linda moves to the plantation with her daughter Ellen (Benjamin is too ill to go). Renewed threats to her children, and the cruelty of the younger Mr. Flint and his wife, determine Linda to escape.]

Chapter 17. The Flight

Mr. Flint was hard pushed for house servants, and rather than lose me he had restrained his malice. I did my work faithfully, though not, of course, with a willing mind. They were evidently afraid I should leave them. Mr. Flint wished that I should sleep in the great house instead of the servants' quarters. His wife agreed to the proposition, but said I mustn't bring my bed into the house, because it would scatter feathers on her carpet. I knew when I went there that they would never think of such a thing as furnishing a bed of any kind for me and my little one. I therefore carried my own bed, and now I was forbidden to use it. I did as I was ordered. But now that I was certain my children were to be put in their power, in order to give them a stronger hold on me, I resolved to leave them that night. I remembered the grief this step would bring upon my dear old grandmother; and nothing less than the freedom of my children would have induced me to disregard her advice. I went about my evening work with trembling steps. Mr. Flint twice called from his chamber door to inquire why the house was not locked up. I replied that I had not done my work. "You have had time enough to do it," said he. "Take care how you answer me!"

I shut all the windows, locked all the doors, and went up to the third story, to wait till midnight. How long those hours seemed, and how fervently I prayed that God would not forsake me in this hour of utmost need! I was about to risk everything on the throw of a die; and if I failed, O what would become of me and my poor children? They would be made to suffer for my fault.

At half past twelve I stole softly down stairs. I stopped on the second floor, thinking I heard a noise. I felt my way down into the parlor, and looked out of the window. The night was so intensely dark that I could see nothing. I raised the window very softly and jumped out. Large drops of rain were falling, and the darkness bewildered me. I dropped on my knees, and breathed a short prayer to God for guidance and protection. I groped my way to the road, and rushed towards the town with almost lightning speed. I arrived at my grandmother's house, but dared not see her. She would say, "Linda, you are killing me"; and I knew that would unnerve me. I tapped softly at the window of a room, occupied by a woman, who had lived in the house several years. I knew she was a faithful friend, and could be trusted with my secret. I tapped several times before she heard me. At last she raised the window, and I whispered, "Sally, I have run away. Let me in, quick." She opened the door softly, and said in low tones, "For God's sake, don't. Your grandmother is trying to buy you and de chillern. Mr. Sands was here last week. He tole her he was going away on business, but he wanted her to go ahead about buying you and de chillern, and he would help her all he could. Don't run away, Linda. Your grandmother is all bowed down wid trouble now."

I replied, "Sally, they are going to carry my children to the plantation tomorrow; and they will never sell them to anybody so long as they have me in their power. Now, would you advise me to go back?"

"No, chile, no," answered she. "When dey finds you is gone, dey won't want de plague ob de chillern; but where is you going to hide? Dey knows ebery inch ob dis house."

I told her I had a hiding-place, and that was all it was best for her to know. I asked her to go into my room as soon as it was light, and take all my clothes out of my trunk, and pack them in hers; for I knew Mr. Flint and the constable would be there early to search my room. I feared the sight of my children would be too much for my full heart; but I could not go out into the uncertain future without one last look. I bent over the bed where lay my little Benny and baby Ellen. Poor little ones! fatherless and motherless! Memories of their father came over me. He wanted to be kind to them; but they were not all to him, as they were to my womanly heart. I knelt and prayed for the innocent little sleepers. I kissed them lightly, and turned away.

As I was about to open the street door, Sally laid her hand on my shoulder, and said, "Linda, is you gwine all alone? Let me call your uncle."

"No Sally," I replied, "I want no one to be brought into trouble on my account."

I went forth into the darkness and rain. I ran on till I came to the house of the friend who was to conceal me.

Early the next morning Mr. Flint was at my grandmother's inquiring for me. She told him she had not seen me, and supposed I was at the plantation. He watched her face narrowly, and said, "Don't you know anything about her running off?" She assured him that she did not. He went on to say, "Last night she ran off without the least provocation. We had treated her very kindly. My wife liked her. She will soon be found and brought back. Are her children with you?" When told that they were, he said, "I am very glad to hear that. If they are here, she cannot be far off. If I find out that any of my niggers have had anything to do with this damned business, I'll give 'em five hundred lashes." As he started to go to his father's, he turned round and added, persuasively, "Let her be brought back, and she shall have her children to live with her."

The tidings made the old doctor rave and storm at a furious rate. It was a busy day for them. My grandmother's house was searched from top to bottom. As my trunk was empty, they concluded I had taken my clothes with me. Before ten o'clock every vessel northward bound was thoroughly examined, and the law against harboring fugitives was read to all on board. At night a watch was set over the town. Knowing how distressed my grandmother would be, I wanted to send her a message; but it could not be done. Everyone who went in or out of her house was closely watched. The doctor said he would take my children, unless she became responsible for them; which of course she willingly did. The next day was spent in searching. Before night, the following advertisement was posted at every corner, and in every public place for miles round:

"$300 REWARD! Ran away from the subscriber, an intelligent, bright, mulatto girl, named Linda, 21 years age. Five feet four inches high. Dark eyes, and black hair inclined to curl; but it can be made straight. Has a decayed spot on a front tooth. She can read and write, and in all probability will try to get to the Free States. All persons are forbidden, under penalty of the law, to harbor or employ said slave. $150 will be given to whoever takes her in the state, and $300 if taken out of the state and delivered to me, or lodged in jail.
DR. FLINT."

…

[Linda moves to new hiding places several times; Dr. Flint imagines she has gone North, and he goes to New York to find her. The father of Linda's children, Mr. Sands, uses an agent to buy the children and Linda's brother, William, from Dr. Flint. When Dr. Flint discovers who the buyer is, he is incensed and vows never to sell Linda. Linda needs to change hiding places again, and even spends a night hiding in the aptly named Snaky Swamp.]

CHAPTER 21. THE LOOPHOLE OF RETREAT

A small shed had been added to my grandmother's house years ago. Some boards were laid across the joists at the top, and between these boards and the roof was a very small garret, never occupied by anything but rats and mice. It was a pent roof, covered with nothing but shingles, according to the southern custom for such buildings. The garret was only nine feet long, and seven wide. The highest part was three feet high, and sloped down abruptly to the loose board floor. There was no admission for either light or air. My uncle Phillip, who was a carpenter, had very skillfully made a concealed trap door, which communicated with the storeroom. He had been doing this while I was waiting in the swamp. The storeroom opened upon a piazza.[1] To this hole I was conveyed as soon as I entered the house. The air was stifling; the darkness total. A bed had been spread on the floor. I could sleep quite comfortably on one side; but the slope was so sudden that I could not turn on the other without hitting the roof. The rats and mice ran over my bed; but I was weary, and I slept such sleep as the wretched may, when a tempest has passed over them. Morning came. I knew it only by the noises I heard; for in my small den day and night were all the same. I suffered for air even more than for light. But I

---
1 *piazza* Veranda.

was not comfortless. I heard the voices of my children. There was joy and there was sadness in the sound. It made my tears flow. How I longed to speak to them! I was eager to look on their faces; but there was no hole, no crack, through which I could peep. This continued darkness was oppressive. It seemed horrible to sit or lie in a cramped position day after day, without one gleam of light. Yet I would have chosen this, rather than my lot as a slave, though white people considered it an easy one; and it was so compared with the fate of others. I was never cruelly over-worked; I was never lacerated with the whip from head to foot; I was never so beaten and bruised that I could not turn from one side to the other; I never had my heel-strings cut to prevent my running away; I was never chained to a log and forced to drag it about, while I toiled in the fields from morning till night; I was never branded with hot iron, or torn by bloodhounds. On the contrary, I had always been kindly treated, and tenderly cared for, until I came into the hands of Dr. Flint. I had never wished for freedom till then. But though my life in slavery was comparatively devoid of hardships, God pity the woman who is compelled to lead such a life!

My food was passed up to me through the trap-door my uncle had contrived; and my grandmother, my uncle Phillip, and aunt Nancy would seize such opportunities as they could, to mount up there and chat with me at the opening. But of course this was not safe in the daytime. It must all be done in darkness. It was impossible for me to move in an erect position, but I crawled about my den for exercise. One day I hit my head against something, and found it was a gimlet.[1] My uncle had left it sticking there when he made the trap-door. I was as rejoiced as Robinson Crusoe[2] could have been in finding such a treasure. It put a lucky thought into my head. I said to myself, "Now I will have some light. Now I will see my children." I did not dare to begin my work during the daytime, for fear of attracting attention. But I groped round; and having found the side next the street, where I could frequently see my children, I stuck the gimlet in and waited for

evening. I bored three rows of holes, one above another; then I bored out the interstices between. I thus succeeded in making one hole about an inch long and an inch broad. I sat by it till late into the night, to enjoy the little whiff of air that floated in. In the morning I watched for my children. The first person I saw in the street was Dr. Flint. I had a shuddering, superstitious feeling that it was a bad omen. Several familiar faces passed by. At last I heard the merry laughing of children, and presently two sweet little faces were looking up at me, as though they knew I was there, and were conscious of the joy they imparted. How I longed to *tell* them I was there!

My condition was now a little improved. But for weeks I was tormented by hundreds of little red insects, fine as a needle's point, that pierced through my skin, and produced an intolerable burning. The good grandmother gave me herb teas and cooling medicines, and finally I got rid of them. The heat of my den was intense, for nothing but thin shingles protected me from the scorching summer's sun. But I had my consolations. Through my peeping-hole I could watch the children, and when they were near enough, I could hear their talk. Aunt Nancy brought me all the news she could hear at Dr. Flint's. From her I learned that the doctor had written to New York to a colored woman, who had been born and raised in our neighborhood, and had breathed his contaminating atmosphere. He offered her a reward if she could find out anything about me. I know not what was the nature of her reply; but he soon after started for New York in haste, saying to his family that he had business of importance to transact. I peeped at him as he passed on his way to the steamboat. It was a satisfaction to have miles of land and water between us, even for a little while; and it was a still greater satisfaction to know that he believed me to be in the Free States. My little den seemed less dreary than it had done. He returned, as he did from his former journey to New York, without obtaining any satisfactory information. When he passed our house next morning, Benny was standing at the gate. He had heard them say that he had gone to find me, and he called out, "Dr. Flint, did you bring my mother home? I want to see her." The doctor stamped his foot at him in a rage, and exclaimed, "Get out of the way, you little damned rascal! If you don't, I'll cut off your head."

---

[1]   *gimlet*   Tool used for boring holes.

[2]   *Robinson Crusoe*   Protagonist of Daniel Defoe's novel of the same name (1719). In the novel, Crusoe is shipwrecked on an uninhabited island and manages to build a dwelling and farm for himself with the few tools he successfully scavenges from the shipwreck.

Benny ran terrified into the house, saying, "You can't put me in jail again. I don't belong to you now." It was well that the wind carried the words away from the doctor's ear. I told my grandmother of it, when we had our next conference at the trap-door; and begged of her not to allow the children to be impertinent to the irascible old man.

Autumn came, with a pleasant abatement of heat. My eyes had become accustomed to the dim light, and by holding my book or work in a certain position near the aperture I contrived to read and sew. That was a great relief to the tedious monotony of my life. But when winter came, the cold penetrated through the thin shingle roof, and I was dreadfully chilled. The winters there are not so long, or so severe, as in northern latitudes; but the houses are not built to shelter from cold, and my little den was peculiarly comfortless. The kind grandmother brought me bed-clothes and warm drinks. Often I was obliged to lie in bed all day to keep comfortable; but with all my precautions, my shoulders and feet were frostbitten. O, those long, gloomy days, with no object for my eye to rest upon, and no thoughts to occupy my mind, except the dreary past and the uncertain future! I was thankful when there came a day sufficiently mild for me to wrap myself up and sit at the loophole to watch the passersby. Southerners have the habit of stopping and talking in the streets, and I heard many conversations not intended to meet my ears. I heard slave-hunters planning how to catch some poor fugitive. Several times I heard allusions to Dr. Flint, myself, and the history of my children, who, perhaps, were playing near the gate. One would say, "I wouldn't move my little finger to catch her, as old Flint's property." Another would say, "I'll catch *any* nigger for the reward. A man ought to have what belongs to him, if he *is* a damned brute." The opinion was often expressed that I was in the Free States. Very rarely did anyone suggest that I might be in the vicinity. Had the least suspicion rested on my grandmother's house, it would have been burned to the ground. But it was the last place they thought of. Yet there was no place, where slavery existed, that could have afforded me so good a place of concealment.

Dr. Flint and his family repeatedly tried to coax and bribe my children to tell something they had heard said about me. One day the doctor took them into a shop, and offered them some bright little silver pieces and gay handkerchiefs if they would tell where their mother was. Ellen shrank away from him, and would not speak; but Benny spoke up, and said, "Dr. Flint, I don't know where my mother is. I guess she's in New York; and when you go there again, I wish you'd ask her to come home, for I want to see her; but if you put her in jail, or tell her you'll cut her head off, I'll tell her to go right back."

[Linda continues to live in her roof-top garret, sewing for the children, suffering from the weather, falling ill and watching her children endure illness. Mr. Sands is elected to Congress; he promises to someday free the children but so far has not. Linda tricks Dr. Flint into thinking she is in Boston, which allows her to occasionally get out of her garret and stretch her legs.]

CHAPTER 29. PREPARATIONS FOR ESCAPE

I hardly expect that the reader will credit me, when I affirm that I lived in that little dismal hole, almost deprived of light and air, and with no space to move my limbs, for nearly seven years. But it is a fact; and to me a sad one, even now; for my body still suffers from the effects of that long imprisonment, to say nothing of my soul. Members of my family, now living in New York and Boston, can testify to the truth of what I say.

Countless were the nights that I sat late at the little loophole scarcely large enough to give me a glimpse of one twinkling star. There, I heard the patrols and slave-hunters conferring together about the capture of runaways, well knowing how rejoiced they would be to catch me.

Season after season, year after year, I peeped at my children's faces, and heard their sweet voices, with a heart yearning all the while to say, "Your mother is here." Sometimes it appeared to me as if ages had rolled away since I entered upon that gloomy, monotonous existence. At times, I was stupefied and listless; at other times I became very impatient to know when these dark years would end, and I should again be allowed to feel the sunshine, and breathe the pure air.

After Ellen left us, this feeling increased. Mr. Sands had agreed that Benny might go to the north whenever his uncle Phillip could go with him; and I was anxious to be there also, to watch over my children, and protect them so far as I was able. Moreover, I was likely to be drowned out of my den, if I remained much longer; for the slight roof was getting badly out of repair, and uncle Phillip was afraid to remove the shingles, lest someone should get a glimpse of me. When storms occurred in the night, they spread mats and bits of carpet, which in the morning appeared have been laid out to dry; but to cover the roof in the daytime might have attracted attention. Consequently, my clothes and bedding were often drenched; a process by which the pains and aches in my cramped and stiffened limbs were greatly increased. I revolved various plans of escape in my mind, which I sometimes imparted to my grandmother, when she came to whisper with me at the trap-door. The kind-hearted old woman had an intense sympathy for runaways. She had known too much of the cruelties inflicted on those who were captured. Her memory always flew back at once to the sufferings of her bright and handsome son, Benjamin, the youngest and dearest of her flock. So, whenever I alluded to the subject, she would groan out, "O, don't think of it, child. You'll break my heart." I had no good old aunt Nancy now to encourage me; but my brother William and my children were continually beckoning me to the north.

And now I must go back a few months in my story. I have stated that the first of January was the time for selling slaves, or leasing them out to new masters. If time were counted by heart-throbs, the poor slaves might reckon years of suffering during that festival so joyous to the free. On the New Year's day preceding my aunt's death, one of my friends, named Fanny, was to be sold at auction to pay her master's debts. My thoughts were with her during all the day, and at night I anxiously inquired what had been her fate. I was told that she had been sold to one master, and her four little girls to another master, far distant; that she had escaped from her purchaser, and was not to be found. Her mother was the old Aggie I have spoken of. She lived in a small tenement belonging to my grandmother, and built on the same lot with her own house. Her dwelling was searched and watched, and that brought the patrols so near me that I was obliged to keep very close in my den. The hunters were somehow eluded; and not

long afterwards Benny accidentally caught sight of Fanny in her mother's hut. He told his grandmother, who charged him never to speak of it, explaining to him the frightful consequences; and he never betrayed the trust. Aggie little dreamed that my grandmother knew where her daughter was concealed, and that the stooping form of her old neighbor was bending under a similar burden of anxiety and fear; but these dangerous secrets deepened the sympathy between the two old persecuted mothers.

My friend Fanny and I remained many weeks hidden within call of each other; but she was unconscious of the fact. I longed to have her share my den, which seemed a more secure retreat than her own; but I had brought so much trouble on my grandmother, that it seemed wrong to ask her to incur greater risks. My restlessness increased. I had lived too long in bodily pain and anguish of spirit. Always I was in dread that by some accident, or some contrivance, slavery would succeed in snatching my children from me. This thought drove me nearly frantic, and I determined to steer for the North Star at all hazards. At this crisis, Providence opened an unexpected way for me to escape. My friend Peter came one evening, and asked to speak with me. "Your day has come, Linda," said he. "I have found a chance for you to go to the Free States. You have a fortnight to decide." The news seemed too good to be true; but Peter explained his arrangements, and told me all that was necessary was for me to say I would go. I was going to answer him with a joyful yes, when the thought of Benny came to my mind. I told him the temptation was exceedingly strong, but I was terribly afraid of Dr. Flint's alleged power over my child, and that I could not go and leave him behind. Peter remonstrated earnestly. He said such a good chance might never occur again; that Benny was free, and could be sent to me; and that for the sake of my children's welfare I ought not to hesitate a moment. I told him I would consult with uncle Phillip. My uncle rejoiced in the plan, and bade me to go by all means. He promised, if his life was spared, that he would either bring or send my son to me as soon as I reached a place of safety. I resolved to go, but thought nothing had better be said to my grandmother till very near the time of departure. But my uncle thought she would feel it more keenly if I left her so suddenly. "I will reason with her," said he, "and convince her how necessary it is, not only for your sake, but for hers also. You cannot be blind to the fact that she is sinking under her burdens." I was not blind to it. I knew that my concealment was an ever-present source of anxiety, and that the older she grew the more nervously fearful she was of discovery. My uncle talked with her, and finally succeeded in persuading her that it was absolutely necessary for me to seize the chance so unexpectedly offered.

The anticipation of being a free woman proved almost too much for my weak frame. The excitement stimulated me, and at the same time bewildered me. I made busy preparations for my journey, and for my son to follow me. I resolved to have an interview with him before I went, that I might give him cautions and advice, and tell him how anxiously I should be waiting for him at the north. Grandmother stole up to me as often as possible to whisper words of counsel. She insisted upon my writing to Dr. Flint, as soon as I arrived in the Free States, and asking him to sell me to her. She said she would sacrifice her house, and all she had in the world, for the sake of having me safe with my children in any part of the world. If she could only live to know *that* she could die in peace. I promised the dear old faithful friend that I would write to her as soon as I arrived, and put the letter in a safe way to reach her; but in my own mind I resolved that not another cent of her hard earnings should be spent to pay rapacious slaveholders for what they called their property. And even if I had not been unwilling to buy what I had already a right to possess, common humanity would have prevented me from accepting the generous offer, at the expense of turning my aged relative out of house and home, when she was trembling on the brink of the grave.

I was to escape in a vessel; but I forbear to mention any further particulars. I was in readiness, but the vessel was unexpectedly detained several days. Meantime, news came to town of a most horrible murder committed on a fugitive slave, named James. Charity, the mother of this unfortunate young man, had been an old acquaintance of ours. I have told the shocking particulars of his death, in my description of some of the neighboring slaveholders. My grandmother, always nervously sensitive about runaways, was terribly frightened. She felt sure that a similar fate awaited me, if

I did not desist from my enterprise. She sobbed, and groaned, and entreated me not to go. Her excessive fear was somewhat contagious, and my heart was not proof against her extreme agony. I was grievously disappointed, but I promised to relinquish my project.

When my friend Peter was apprised of this, he was disappointed and vexed. He said, that judging from our past experience, it would be a long time before I had such another chance to throw away. I told him it need not be thrown away; that I had a friend concealed nearby, who would be glad enough to take the place that had been provided for me. I told him about poor Fanny, and the kind-hearted, noble fellow, who never turned his back upon anybody in distress, white or black, expressed his readiness to help her. Aggie was much surprised when she found that we knew her secret. She was rejoiced to hear of such a chance for Fanny, and arrangements were made for her to go on board the vessel the next night. They both supposed that I had long been at the north, therefore my name was not mentioned in the transaction. Fanny was carried on board at the appointed time, and stowed away in a very small cabin. This accommodation had been purchased at a price that would pay for a voyage to England. But when one proposes to go to fine old England, they stop to calculate whether they can afford the cost of the pleasure; while in making a bargain to escape from slavery, the trembling victim is ready to say, "Take all I have, only don't betray me!"

The next morning I peeped through my loophole, and saw that it was dark and cloudy. At night I received news that the wind was ahead,[1] and the vessel had not sailed. I was exceedingly anxious about Fanny, and Peter too, who was running a tremendous risk at my instigation. Next day the wind and weather remained the same. Poor Fanny had been half dead with fright when they carried her on board, and I could readily imagine how she must be suffering now. Grandmother came often to my den, to say how thankful she was I did not go. On the third morning she rapped for me to come down to the storeroom. The poor old sufferer was breaking down under her weight of trouble. She was easily flurried now. I found her in a nervous, excited state, but I was not

---

[1]   *wind was ahead*   I.e., there was a head wind, making it difficult to sail.

aware that she had forgotten to lock the door behind her, as usual. She was exceedingly worried about the detention of the vessel. She was afraid all would be discovered, and then Fanny, and Peter, and I, would all be tortured to death, and Phillip should be utterly ruined, and her house would be torn down. Poor Peter! If he should die such a horrible death as the poor slave James had lately done, and all for his kindness in trying to help me, how dreadful it would be for us all! Alas, the thought was familiar to me, and had sent many a sharp pang through my heart. I tried to suppress my own anxiety, and speak soothingly to her. She brought in some allusion to aunt Nancy, the dear daughter she had recently buried, and then she lost all control of herself. As she stood there, trembling and sobbing, a voice from the piazza called out, "Whar is you, aunt Marthy?" Grandmother was startled, and in her agitation opened the door, without thinking of me. In stepped Jenny, the mischievous housemaid, who had tried to enter my room, when I was concealed in the house of my white benefactress. "I's bin huntin ebery whar for you, aunt Marthy," said she. "My missis wants you to send her some crackers." I had slunk down behind a barrel, which entirely screened me, but I imagined that Jenny was looking directly at the spot, and my heart beat violently. My grandmother immediately thought what she had done, and went out quickly with Jenny to count the crackers locking the door behind her. She returned to me, in a few minutes, the perfect picture of despair. "Poor child!" she exclaimed, "my carelessness has ruined you. The boat ain't gone yet. Get ready immediately, and go with Fanny. I ain't got another word to say against it now; for there's no telling what may happen this day."

Uncle Phillip was sent for, and he agreed with his mother in thinking that Jenny would inform Dr. Flint in less than twenty-four hours. He advised getting me on board the boat, if possible; if not, I had better keep very still in my den, where they could not find me without tearing the house down. He said it would not do for him to move in the matter, because suspicion would be immediately excited; but he promised to communicate with Peter. I felt reluctant to apply to him again, having implicated him too much already; but there seemed to be no alternative. Vexed as Peter

had been by my indecision, he was true to his generous nature, and said at once that he would do his best to help me, trusting I should show myself a stronger woman this time.

He immediately proceeded to the wharf, and found that the wind had shifted, and the vessel was slowly beating downstream. On some pretext of urgent necessity, he offered two boatmen a dollar apiece to catch up with her. He was of lighter complexion than the boatmen he hired, and when the captain saw them coming so rapidly, he thought officers were pursuing his vessel in search of the runaway slave he had on board. They hoisted sails, but the boat gained upon them, and the indefatigable Peter sprang on board.

The captain at once recognized him. Peter asked him to go below, to speak about a bad bill he had given him. When he told his errand, the captain replied, "Why, the woman's here already; and I've put her where you or the devil would have a tough job to find her."

"But it is another woman I want to bring," said Peter. "She is in great distress, too, and you shall be paid anything within reason, if you'll stop and take her."

"What's her name?" inquired the captain.

"Linda," he replied.

"That's the name of the woman already here," rejoined the captain. "By George! I believe you mean to betray me."

"O!" exclaimed Peter, "God knows I wouldn't harm a hair of your head. I am too grateful to you. But there really is another woman in great danger. Do have the humanity to stop and take her!"

After a while they came to an understanding. Fanny, not dreaming I was anywhere about in that region, had assumed my name, though she called herself Johnson. "Linda is a common name," said Peter, "and the woman I want to bring is Linda Brent."

The captain agreed to wait at a certain place till evening, being handsomely paid for his detention.

Of course, the day was an anxious one for us all. But we concluded that if Jenny had seen me, she would be too wise to let her mistress know of it; and that she probably would not get a chance to see Dr. Flint's family till evening, for I knew very well what were the rules in that household. I afterwards believed that she did not see me; for nothing ever came of it, and she was one of those base characters that would have jumped to betray a suffering fellow being for the sake of thirty pieces of silver.[1]

I made all my arrangements to go on board as soon as it was dusk. The intervening time I resolved to spend with my son. I had not spoken to him for seven years, though I had been under the same roof, and seen him every day, when I was well enough to sit at the loophole. I did not dare to venture beyond the storeroom; so they brought him there, and locked us up together, in a place concealed from the piazza door. It was an agitating interview for both of us. After we had talked and wept together for a little while, he said, "Mother, I'm glad you're going away. I wish I could go with you. I knew you was here; and I have been so afraid they would come and catch you!"

I was greatly surprised, and asked him how he had found it out.

He replied, "I was standing under the eaves, one day, before Ellen went away, and I heard somebody cough up over the wood shed. I don't know what made me think it was you, but I did think so. I missed Ellen, the night before she went away; and grandmother brought her back into the room in the night; and I thought maybe she'd been to see *you*, before she went, for I heard grandmother whisper to her, 'Now go to sleep; and remember never to tell.'"

I asked him if he ever mentioned his suspicions to his sister. He said he never did; but after he heard the cough, if he saw her playing with other children on that side of the house, he always tried to coax her round to the other side, for fear they would hear me cough, too. He said he had kept a close lookout for Dr. Flint, and if he saw him speak to a constable, or a patrol, he always told grandmother. I now recollected that I had seen him manifest uneasiness, when people were on that side of the house, and I had at the time been puzzled to conjecture a motive for his actions. Such prudence may seem extraordinary in a boy of twelve years, but slaves, being surrounded by mysteries, deceptions, and dangers, early learn to be suspicious and watchful, and prematurely cautious and cunning. He had never asked a question of grandmother, or uncle Phillip, and I had often heard him chime in with other children, when they spoke of my being at the north.

I told him I was now really going to the Free States, and if he was a good, honest boy, and a loving child to his dear old grandmother, the Lord would bless him, and bring him to me, and we and Ellen would live together. He began to tell me that grandmother had not eaten anything all day. While he was speaking, the door was unlocked, and she came in with a small bag of money, which she wanted me to take. I begged her to keep a part of it, at least, to pay for Benny's being sent to the north; but she insisted, while her tears were falling fast, that I should take the whole. "You may be sick among strangers," she said, "and they would send you to the poorhouse to die." Ah, that good grandmother!

For the last time I went up to my nook. Its desolate appearance no longer chilled me, for the light of hope had risen in my soul. Yet, even with the blessed prospect of freedom before me, I felt very sad at leaving forever that old homestead, where I had been sheltered so long by the dear old grandmother; where I had dreamed my first young dream of love; and where, after that had faded away, my children came to twine themselves so closely round my desolate heart. As the hour approached for me to leave, I again descended to the storeroom. My grandmother and Benny were there. She took me by the hand, and said, "Linda, let us pray." We knelt down together, with my child pressed to my heart, and my other arm round the faithful, loving old friend I was about to leave forever. On no other occasion has it ever been my lot to listen to so fervent a supplication for mercy and protection. It thrilled through my heart, and inspired me with trust in God.

Peter was waiting for me in the street. I was soon by his side, faint in body, but strong of purpose. I did not look back upon the old place, though I felt that I should never see it again.

[Linda and Fanny make it safely to Philadelphia on the boat and soon after head to New York. Linda's children Ellen and Benny have in the meantime also both gone North, Ellen to live with a relation of Mr. Sands and Benny with Uncle Phillip. Linda finds on her arrival that Ellen was not going to school as planned but instead was working as a servant for a Mrs. Hobbs. Linda takes a job as nursemaid to a Mrs. Bruce, a very kind and considerate woman. Dr. Flint comes to New York to find Linda, and she goes to Boston for a month to avoid him. While on a trip

---

[1]   *thirty pieces of silver*   Before the Last Supper, Judas Iscariot betrays Jesus for thirty silver coins (see Matthew 26.15).

with Mrs. Bruce and the baby, Linda experiences the full extent of racism in the North, as she is treated scornfully and rudely. On their return, Dr. Flint returns again, as he had learned where Linda was staying, and she and her children flee to Boston for several months. On the death of Mrs. Bruce, Linda is distraught, but Mr. Bruce keeps her employed as a nurse for the child, Mary. They go to England, where Linda is impressed that the poor in that country have rights and access to education; she does not experience racism in England. Upon her return, she goes to Boston to look after her daughter Ellen.]

Chapter 39. The Confession

For two years my daughter and I supported ourselves comfortably in Boston. At the end of that time, my brother William offered to send Ellen to a boarding school. It required a great effort for me to consent to part with her, for I had few near ties, and it was her presence that made my two little rooms seem homelike. But my judgment prevailed over my selfish feelings. I made preparations for her departure. During the two years we had lived together I had often resolved to tell her something about her father; but I had never been able to muster sufficient courage. I had a shrinking dread of diminishing my child's love. I knew she must have curiosity on the subject, but she had never asked a question. She was always very careful not to say anything to remind me of my troubles. Now that she was going from me, I thought if I should die before she returned, she might hear my story from someone who did not understand the palliating circumstances; and that if she were entirely ignorant on the subject, her sensitive nature might receive a rude shock.

When we retired for the night, she said, "Mother, it is very hard to leave you alone. I am almost sorry I am going, though I do want to improve myself. But you will write to me often; won't you, mother?"

I did not throw my arms round her. I did not answer her. But in a calm, solemn way, for it cost me great effort, I said, "Listen to me, Ellen; I have something to tell you!" I recounted my early sufferings in slavery, and told her how nearly they had crushed me. I began to tell her how they had driven me into a great sin, when she clasped me in her arms, and exclaimed, "O, don't, mother! Please don't tell me anymore."

I said, "But, my child, I want you to know about your father."

"I know all about it, mother," she replied; "I am nothing to my father, and he is nothing to me. All my love is for you. I was with him five months in Washington, and he never cared for me. He never spoke to me as he did to his little Fanny. I knew all the time he was my father, for Fanny's nurse told me so; but she said I must never tell anybody, and I never did. I used to wish he would take me in his arms and kiss me, as he did Fanny; or that he would sometimes smile at me, as he did at her. I thought if he was my own father, he ought to love me. I was a little girl then, and didn't know any better. But now I never think anything about my father. All my love is for you." She hugged me closer as she spoke, and I thanked God that the knowledge I had so much dreaded to impart had not diminished the affection of my child. I had not the slightest idea she knew that portion of my history. If I had, I should have spoken to her long before; for my pent-up feelings had often longed to pour themselves out to someone I could trust. But I loved the dear girl better for the delicacy she had manifested towards her unfortunate mother.

The next morning, she and her uncle started on their journey to the village in New York, where she was to be placed at school. It seemed as if all the sunshine had gone away. My little room was dreadfully lonely. I was thankful when a message came from a lady, accustomed to employ me, requesting me to come and sew in her family for several weeks. On my return, I found a letter from brother William. He thought of opening an anti-slavery reading room in Rochester, and combining with it the sale of some books and stationery; and he wanted me to unite with him. We tried it, but it was not successful. We found warm anti-slavery friends there, but the feeling was not general enough to support such an establishment. I passed nearly a year in the family of Isaac and Amy Post, practical believers in the Christian doctrine of human brotherhood. They measured a man's worth by his character, not by his complexion. The memory of those beloved and honored friends will remain with me to my latest hour.

Chapter 40. The Fugitive Slave Law

My brother, being disappointed in his project, concluded to go to California; and it was agreed that Benjamin should go with him. Ellen liked her school, and was a great favorite there. They did not know her history, and she did not tell it, because she had no desire to make capital out of their sympathy. But when it was accidentally discovered that her mother was a fugitive slave, every method was used to increase her advantages and diminish her expenses.

I was alone again. It was necessary for me to be earning money, and I preferred that it should be among those who knew me. On my return from Rochester, I called at the house of Mr. Bruce, to see Mary, the darling little babe that had thawed my heart, when it was freezing into a cheerless distrust of all my fellow-beings. She was growing a tall girl now, but I loved her always. Mr. Bruce had married again, and it was proposed that I should become nurse to a new infant. I had but one hesitation, and that was my feeling of insecurity in New York, now greatly increased by the passage of the Fugitive Slave Law. However, I resolved to try the experiment. I was again fortunate in my employer. The new Mrs. Bruce was an American, brought up under aristocratic influences and still living in the midst of them; but if she had any prejudice against color, I was never made aware of it; and as for the system of slavery, she had a most hearty dislike of it. No sophistry of Southerners could blind her to its enormity. She was a person of excellent principles and a noble heart. To me, from that hour to the present, she has been a true and sympathizing friend. Blessings be with her and hers!

About the time that I reentered the Bruce family, an event occurred of disastrous import to the colored people. The slave Hamlin,[1] the first fugitive that came under the new law, was given up by the bloodhounds of the north to the bloodhounds of the south. It was the beginning of a reign of terror to the colored population. The great city rushed on in its whirl of excitement, taking no note of the "short and simple annals of the poor."[2] But while fashionables were listening to the thrilling voice of Jenny Lind[3] in Metropolitan Hall, the thrilling voices of poor hunted colored people went up, in an agony of supplication, to the Lord, from Zion's church. Many families, who had lived in the city for twenty years, fled from it now. Many a poor washerwoman, who, by hard labor, had made herself a comfortable home, was obliged to sacrifice her furniture, bid a hurried farewell to friends, and seek her fortune among strangers in Canada. Many a wife discovered a secret she had never known before— that her husband was a fugitive, and must leave her to ensure his own safety. Worse still, many a husband discovered that his wife had fled from slavery years ago, and as "the child follows the condition of its mother," the children of his love were liable to be seized and carried into slavery. Everywhere, in those humble homes, there was consternation and anguish. But what cared the legislators of the "dominant race" for the blood they were crushing out of trampled hearts?

When my brother William spent his last evening with me, before he went to California, we talked nearly all the time of the distress brought on our oppressed people by the passage of this iniquitous law; and never had I seen him manifest such bitterness of spirit, such stern hostility to our oppressors. He was himself free from the operation of the law; for he did not run from any Slaveholding State, being brought into the Free States by his master. But I was subject to it; and so were hundreds of intelligent and industrious people all around us. I seldom ventured into the streets; and when it was necessary to do an errand for Mrs. Bruce, or any of the family, I went as much as possible through back streets and by-ways. What a disgrace to a city calling itself free, that inhabitants, guiltless of offence, and seeking to perform their duties conscientiously, should be condemned to live in such incessant fear, and have nowhere to turn for protection! This state of things, of course, gave rise to many impromptu vigilance committees. Every colored

---

1   *Hamlin* James Hamlet was the first victim of the Fugitive Slave Act; he was arrested in Manhattan and sent to Baltimore in 1850. Hamlet insisted he was a free man, but a Mary Brown of Maryland succeeded in having the law seize hold of him, separating him from his wife and two children. Hamlet was then brought to the Baltimore slave market, where he was bought by his home community in Williamsburgh, Brooklyn for eight hundred dollars, after which he was able to return to his family and his job.

2   *short ... poor* Quotation is from line 32 of Thomas Gray's "Elegy Written in a Country Churchyard" (1751). The line refers to main life events—births, deaths, marriages, and christenings—that are recorded in parish registers.

3   *Jenny Lind* Renowned Swedish opera singer who, from 1850–52, toured the United States. The excitement surrounding her concerts came to be referred to as "Lind Mania."

person, and every friend of their persecuted race, kept their eyes wide open. Every evening I examined the newspapers carefully, to see what Southerners had put up at the hotels. I did this for my own sake, thinking my young mistress and her husband might be among the list; I wished also to give information to others, if necessary; for if many were "running to and fro," I resolved that "knowledge should be increased."[1]

This brings up one of my Southern reminiscences, which I will here briefly relate. I was somewhat acquainted with a slave named Luke, who belonged to a wealthy man in our vicinity. His master died, leaving a son and daughter heirs to his large fortune. In the division of the slaves, Luke was included in the son's portion. This young man became a prey to the vices growing out of the "patriarchal institution," and when he went to the north, to complete his education, he carried his vices with him. He was brought home, deprived of the use of his limbs, by excessive dissipation. Luke was appointed to wait upon his bed-ridden master, whose despotic habits were greatly increased by exasperation at his own helplessness. He kept a cowhide beside him, and, for the most trivial occurrence, he would order his attendant to bare his back, and kneel beside the couch, while he whipped him till his strength was exhausted. Some days he was not allowed to wear anything but his shirt, in order to be in readiness to be flogged. A day seldom passed without his receiving more or less blows. If the slightest resistance was offered, the town constable was sent for to execute the punishment, and Luke learned from experience how much more the constable's strong arm was to be dreaded than the comparatively feeble one of his master. The arm of his tyrant grew weak, and was finally palsied;[2] and then the constable's services were in constant requisition. The fact that he was entirely dependent on Luke's care, and was obliged to be tended like an infant, instead of inspiring any gratitude or compassion towards his poor slave, seemed only to increase his irritability and cruelty. As he lay there on his bed, a mere disgraced wreck of manhood, he took into his head the strangest freaks of despotism; and if Luke hesitated to submit to his orders, the constable was immediately sent for. Some of these freaks were of a nature too filthy to be repeated. When I fled from the house of bondage, I left poor Luke still chained to the bedside of this cruel and disgusting wretch.

One day, when I had been requested to do an errand for Mrs. Bruce, I was hurrying through back streets, as usual, when I saw a young man approaching, whose face was familiar to me. As he came nearer, I recognized Luke. I always rejoiced to see or hear of any one who had escaped from the black pit; but, remembering this poor fellow's extreme hardships, I was peculiarly glad to see him on Northern soil, though I no longer called it *free* soil. I well remembered what a desolate feeling it was to be alone among strangers, and I went up to him and greeted him cordially. At first, he did not know me; but when I mentioned my name, he remembered all about me. I told him of the Fugitive Slave Law, and asked him if he did not know that New York was a city of kidnappers.

He replied, "De risk ain't so bad for me, as 'tis fur you. 'Cause I runned away from de speculator,[3] and you runned away from de massa. Dem speculators vont spen dar money to come here fur a runaway, if dey ain't sartin sure to put dar hans right on him. An I tell you I's tuk good car 'bout dat. I had too hard times down dar, to let 'em ketch dis nigger."

He then told me of the advice he had received, and the plans he had laid. I asked if he had money enough to take him to Canada. "'Pend upon it, I hab," he replied. "I tuk car fur dat. I'd bin workin all my days fur dem cussed whites, an got no pay but kicks and cuffs. So I tought dis nigger had a right to money nuff to bring him to de Free States. Massa Henry he lib till ebery body vish him dead; an ven he did die, I knowed de debbil would hab him, an vouldn't vant him to bring his money 'long too. So I tuk some of his bills, and put 'em in de pocket of his ole trousers. An ven he was buried, dis nigger ask fur dem ole trousers, an dey gub 'em to me." With a low, chuckling laugh, he added, "You see I didn't *steal* it; dey *gub* it to me. I tell you, I had mighty hard time to keep de speculator from findin it; but he didn't git it."

---

1   *running … increased* These quotations are both from Daniel 12.4, where the prophet Daniel is finishing a description of what was revealed to him about the end of the world: "But thou, O Daniel, shut up the words, and seal the book, even to the time of the end: many shall run to and fro, and knowledge shall be increased."

2   *palsied* Affected by tremors and paralysis; rendered incapable.

3   *speculator* Interregional slave trader.

This is a fair specimen of how the moral sense is educated by slavery. When a man has his wages stolen from him, year after year, and the laws sanction and enforce the theft, how can he be expected to have more regard to honesty than has the man who robs him? I have become somewhat enlightened, but I confess that I agree with poor, ignorant, much-abused Luke, in thinking he had a *right* to that money, as a portion of his unpaid wages. He went to Canada forthwith, and I have not since heard from him.

All that winter I lived in a state of anxiety. When I took the children out to breathe the air, I closely observed the countenances of all I met. I dreaded the approach of summer, when snakes and slaveholders make their appearance. I was, in fact, a slave in New York, as subject to slave laws as I had been in a Slave State. Strange incongruity in a State called free!

Spring returned, and I received warning from the south that Dr. Flint knew of my return to my old place, and was making preparations to have me caught. I learned afterwards that my dress, and that of Mrs. Bruce's children, had been described to him by some of the Northern tools, which slaveholders employ for their base purposes, and then indulge in sneers at their cupidity and mean servility.

I immediately informed Mrs. Bruce of my danger, and she took prompt measures for my safety. My place as nurse could not be supplied immediately, and this generous, sympathizing lady proposed that I should carry her baby away. It was a comfort to me to have the child with me; for the heart is reluctant to be torn away from every object it loves. But how few mothers would have consented to have one of their own babes become a fugitive, for the sake of a poor, hunted nurse, on whom the legislators of the country had let loose the bloodhounds! When I spoke of the sacrifice she was making, in depriving herself of her dear baby, she replied, "It is better for you to have baby with you, Linda; for if they get on your track, they will be obliged to bring the child to me; and then, if there is a possibility of saving you, you shall be saved."

This lady had a very wealthy relative, a benevolent gentleman in many respects, but aristocratic and pro-slavery. He remonstrated with her for harboring a fugitive slave; told her she was violating the laws of her country; and asked her if she was aware of the penalty.

She replied, "I am very well aware of it. It is imprisonment and one thousand dollars fine. Shame on my country that it *is* so! I am ready to incur the penalty. I will go to the state's prison, rather than have any poor victim torn from *my* house, to be carried back to slavery."

The noble heart! The brave heart! The tears are in my eyes while I write of her. May the God of the helpless reward her for her sympathy with my persecuted people!

I was sent into New England, where I was sheltered by the wife of a senator, whom I shall always hold in grateful remembrance. This honorable gentleman would not have voted for the Fugitive Slave Law, as did the senator in "Uncle Tom's Cabin";[1] on the contrary, he was strongly opposed to it; but he was enough under its influence to be afraid of having me remain in his house many hours. So I was sent into the country, where I remained a month with the baby. When it was supposed that Dr. Flint's emissaries had lost track of me, and given up the pursuit for the present, I returned to New York.

Chapter 41. Free at Last

Mrs. Bruce, and every member of her family, were exceedingly kind to me. I was thankful for the blessings of my lot, yet I could not always wear a cheerful countenance. I was doing harm to no one; on the contrary, I was doing all the good I could in my small way; yet I could never go out to breathe God's free air without trepidation at my heart. This seemed hard; and I could not think it was a right state of things in any civilized country.

From time to time I received news from my good old grandmother. She could not write; but she employed others to write for her. The following is an extract from one of her last letters:

"Dear Daughter: I cannot hope to see you again on earth; but I pray to God to unite us above, where pain will no more rack this feeble body of mine; where sorrow and parting from my children will be no more. God has promised these things if we are faithful unto

---

[1] *senator in "Uncle Tom's Cabin"* In Harriet Beecher Stowe's novel *Uncle Tom's Cabin*, a state law prohibiting people from helping enslaved fugitives is signed by Senator Bird.

the end. My age and feeble health deprive me of going to church now; but God is with me here at home. Thank your brother for his kindness. Give much love to him, and tell him to remember the Creator in the days of his youth, and strive to meet me in the Father's kingdom. Love to Ellen and Benjamin. Don't neglect him. Tell him for me, to be a good boy. Strive, my child, to train them for God's children. May he protect and provide for you, is the prayer of your loving old mother."

These letters both cheered and saddened me. I was always glad to have tidings from the kind, faithful old friend of my unhappy youth; but her messages of love made my heart yearn to see her before she died, and I mourned over the fact that it was impossible. Some months after I returned from my flight to New England, I received a letter from her, in which she wrote, "Dr. Flint is dead. He has left a distressed family. Poor old man! I hope he made his peace with God."

I remembered how he had defrauded my grandmother of the hard earnings she had loaned; how he had tried to cheat her out of the freedom her mistress had promised her, and how he had persecuted her children; and I thought to myself that she was a better Christian than I was, if she could entirely forgive him. I cannot say, with truth, that the news of my old master's death softened my feelings towards him. There are wrongs which even the grave does not bury. The man was odious to me while he lived, and his memory is odious now.

His departure from this world did not diminish my danger. He had threatened my grandmother that his heirs should hold me in slavery after he was gone; that I never should be free so long as a child of his survived. As for Mrs. Flint, I had seen her in deeper afflictions than I supposed the loss of her husband would be, for she had buried several children; yet I never saw any signs of softening in her heart. The doctor had died in embarrassed circumstances, and had little to will to his heirs, except such property as he was unable to grasp. I was well aware what I had to expect from the family of Flints; and my fears were confirmed by a letter from the south, warning me to be on my guard, because Mrs. Flint openly declared that her daughter could not afford to lose so valuable a slave as I was.

I kept close watch of the newspapers for arrivals; but one Saturday night, being much occupied, I forgot to examine the Evening Express as usual. I went down into the parlor for it, early in the morning, and found the boy about to kindle a fire with it. I took it from him and examined the list of arrivals. Reader, if you have never been a slave, you cannot imagine the acute sensation of suffering at my heart, when I read the names of Mr. and Mrs. Dodge,[1] at a hotel in Courtland Street. It was a third-rate hotel, and that circumstance convinced me of the truth of what I had heard, that they were short of funds and had need of my value, as *they* valued me; and that was by dollars and cents. I hastened with the paper to Mrs. Bruce. Her heart and hand were always open to everyone in distress, and she always warmly sympathized with mine. It was impossible to tell how near the enemy was. He might have passed and repassed the house while we were sleeping. He might at that moment be waiting to pounce upon me if I ventured out of doors. I had never seen the husband of my young mistress, and therefore I could not distinguish him from any other stranger. A carriage was hastily ordered; and, closely veiled, I followed Mrs. Bruce, taking the baby again with me into exile. After various turnings and crossings and returnings, the carriage stopped at the house of one of Mrs. Bruce's friends, where I was kindly received. Mrs. Bruce returned immediately, to instruct the domestics what to say if any one came to inquire for me.

It was lucky for me that the evening paper was not burned up before I had a chance to examine the list of arrivals. It was not long after Mrs. Bruce's return to her house, before several people came to inquire for me. One inquired for me, another asked for my daughter Ellen, and another said he had a letter from my grandmother, which he was requested to deliver in person.

They were told, "She *has* lived here, but she has left."

"How long ago?"

"I don't know, sir."

"Do you know where she went?"

"I do not, sir." And the door was closed.

This Mr. Dodge, who claimed me as his property, was originally a Yankee peddler in the south; then he became a merchant, and finally a slaveholder. He managed to get introduced into what was called the first

---

[1]   *Mr. and Mrs. Dodge*   Dr. Flint's daughter and her husband.

society, and married Miss Emily Flint. A quarrel arose between him and her brother, and the brother cowhided him. This led to a family feud, and he proposed to remove to Virginia. Dr. Flint left him no property, and his own means had become circumscribed, while a wife and children depended upon him for support. Under these circumstances, it was very natural that he should make an effort to put me into his pocket.

I had a colored friend, a man from my native place, in whom I had the most implicit confidence. I sent for him, and told him that Mr. and Mrs. Dodge had arrived in New York. I proposed that he should call upon them to make inquiries about his friends at the south, with whom Dr. Flint's family were well acquainted. He thought there was no impropriety in his doing so, and he consented. He went to the hotel, and knocked at the door of Mr. Dodge's room, which was opened by the gentleman himself, who gruffly inquired, "What brought you here? How came you to know I was in the city?"

"Your arrival was published in the evening papers, sir; and I called to ask Mrs. Dodge about my friends at home. I didn't suppose it would give any offence."

"Where's that negro girl, that belongs to my wife?"

"What girl, sir?"

"You know well enough. I mean Linda, that ran away from Dr. Flint's plantation, some years ago. I dare say you've seen her, and know where she is."

"Yes, sir, I've seen her, and know where she is. She is out of your reach, sir."

"Tell me where she is, or bring her to me, and I will give her a chance to buy her freedom."

"I don't think it would be of any use, sir. I have heard her say she would go to the ends of the earth, rather than pay any man or woman for her freedom, because she thinks she has a right to it. Besides, she couldn't do it, if she would, for she has spent her earnings to educate her children."

This made Mr. Dodge very angry, and some high words passed between them. My friend was afraid to come where I was; but in the course of the day I received a note from him. I supposed they had not come from the south, in the winter, for a pleasure excursion; and now the nature of their business was very plain.

Mrs. Bruce came to me and entreated me to leave the city the next morning. She said her house was watched, and it was possible that some clue to me might be obtained. I refused to take her advice. She pleaded with an earnest tenderness, that ought to have moved me; but I was in a bitter, disheartened mood. I was weary of flying from pillar to post.[1] I had been chased during half my life, and it seemed as if the chase was never to end. There I sat, in that great city, guiltless of crime, yet not daring to worship God in any of the churches. I heard the bells ringing for afternoon service, and, with contemptuous sarcasm, I said, "Will the preachers take for their text, 'Proclaim liberty to the captive, and the opening of prison doors to them that are bound'?[2] or will they preach from the text, 'Do unto others as ye would they should do unto you'?"[3] Oppressed Poles and Hungarians could find a safe refuge in that city; John Mitchell was free to proclaim in the City Hall his desire for "a plantation well stocked with slaves";[4] but there I sat, an oppressed American, not daring to show my face. God forgive the black and bitter thoughts I indulged on that Sabbath day! The Scripture says, "Oppression makes even a wise man mad";[5] and I was not wise.

I had been told that Mr. Dodge said his wife had never signed away her right to my children, and if he could not get me, he would take them. This it was, more than anything else, that roused such a tempest in my soul. Benjamin was with his uncle William in California, but my innocent young daughter had come to spend a vacation with me. I thought of what I had suffered in slavery at her age, and my heart was like a tiger's when a hunter tries to seize her young.

---

1   *flying … post*   Futile traveling from place to place.

2   *Proclaim … bound*   See Isaiah 61.1: "The Spirit of the Lord God is upon me; because the Lord hath anointed me to preach good tidings unto the meek; he hath sent me to bind up the brokenhearted, to proclaim liberty to the captives, and the opening of the prison to them that are bound."

3   *Do unto others … unto you*   See Matthew 7.12: "Therefore all things whatsoever ye would that men should do to you, do ye even so to them: for this is the law and the prophets."

4   *John Mitchell … stocked with slaves*   John Mitchel was an Irish activist and journalist who escaped to America in 1853, where he became a proslavery Southern secessionist. In 1854 he claimed that he would like to have "a good plantation well-stocked with healthy negroes in Alabama."

5   *Oppression … mad*   See Ecclesiastes 7.7: "Surely oppression maketh a wise man mad; and a gift destroyeth the heart."

Dear Mrs. Bruce! I seem to see the expression of her face, as she turned away discouraged by my obstinate mood. Finding her expostulations unavailing, she sent Ellen to entreat me. When ten o'clock in the evening arrived and Ellen had not returned, this watchful and unwearied friend became anxious. She came to us in a carriage, bringing a well-filled trunk for my journey— trusting that by this time I would listen to reason. I yielded to her, as I ought to have done before.

The next day, baby and I set out in a heavy snow storm, bound for New England again. I received letters from the City of Iniquity,[1] addressed to me under an assumed name. In a few days one came from Mrs. Bruce, informing me that my new master was still searching for me, and that she intended to put an end to this persecution by buying my freedom. I felt grateful for the kindness that prompted this offer, but the idea was not so pleasant to me as might have been expected. The more my mind had become enlightened, the more difficult it was for me to consider myself an article of property; and to pay money to those who had so grievously oppressed me seemed like taking from my sufferings the glory of triumph. I wrote to Mrs. Bruce, thanking her, but saying that being sold from one owner to another seemed too much like slavery; that such a great obligation could not be easily cancelled; and that I preferred to go to my brother in California.

Without my knowledge, Mrs. Bruce employed a gentleman in New York to enter into negotiations with Mr. Dodge. He proposed to pay three hundred dollars down, if Mr. Dodge would sell me, and enter into obligations to relinquish all claim to me or my children forever after. He who called himself my master said he scorned so small an offer for such a valuable servant. The gentleman replied, "You can do as you choose, sir. If you reject this offer you will never get anything; for the woman has friends who will convey her and her children out of the country."

Mr. Dodge concluded that "half a loaf was better than no bread," and he agreed to the proffered terms. By the next mail I received this brief letter from Mrs. Bruce: "I am rejoiced to tell you that the money for your freedom has been paid to Mr. Dodge. Come home tomorrow. I long to see you and my sweet babe."

My brain reeled as I read these lines. A gentleman near me said, "It's true; I have seen the bill of sale." "The bill of sale!" Those words struck me like a blow. So I was *sold* at last! A human being *sold* in the free city of New York! The bill of sale is on record, and future generations will learn from it that women were articles of traffic in New York, late in the nineteenth century of the Christian religion. It may hereafter prove a useful document to antiquaries, who are seeking to measure the progress of civilization in the United States. I well know the value of that bit of paper; but much as I love freedom, I do not like to look upon it. I am deeply grateful to the generous friend who procured it, but I despise the miscreant who demanded payment for what never rightfully belonged to him or his.

I had objected to having my freedom bought, yet I must confess that when it was done I felt as if a heavy load had been lifted from my weary shoulders. When I rode home in the cars I was no longer afraid to unveil my face and look at people as they passed. I should have been glad to have met Daniel Dodge himself; to have had him seen me and known me, that he might have mourned over the untoward circumstances which compelled him to sell me for three hundred dollars.

When I reached home, the arms of my benefactress were thrown round me, and our tears mingled. As soon as she could speak, she said, "O Linda, I'm so glad it's all over! You wrote to me as if you thought you were going to be transferred from one owner to another. But I did not buy you for your services. I should have done just the same, if you had been going to sail for California tomorrow. I should, at least, have the satisfaction of knowing that you left me a free woman."

My heart was exceedingly full. I remembered how my poor father had tried to buy me, when I was a small child, and how he had been disappointed. I hoped his spirit was rejoicing over me now. I remembered how my good old grandmother had laid up her earnings to purchase me in later years, and how often her plans had been frustrated. How that faithful, loving old heart would leap for joy, if she could look on me and my children now that we were free! My relatives had been foiled in all their efforts, but God had raised me up a friend among strangers, who had bestowed on me the

---

[1] *City of Iniquity*   See Habakkuk 2.12: "Woe to him that buildeth a town with blood, and stablisheth a city by iniquity!"

precious, long-desired boon. Friend! It is a common word, often lightly used. Like other good and beautiful things, it may be tarnished by careless handling; but when I speak of Mrs. Bruce as my friend, the word is sacred.

My grandmother lived to rejoice in my freedom; but not long after, a letter came with a black seal. She had gone "where the wicked cease from troubling, and the weary are at rest."[1]

Time passed on, and a paper came to me from the south, containing an obituary notice of my uncle Phillip. It was the only case I ever knew of such an honor conferred upon a colored person. It was written by one of his friends, and contained these words: "Now that death has laid him low, they call him a good man and a useful citizen; but what are eulogies to the black man, when the world has faded from his vision? It does not require man's praise to obtain rest in God's kingdom." So they called a colored man a *citizen*! Strange words to be uttered in that region!

Reader, my story ends with freedom; not in the usual way, with marriage. I and my children are now free! We are as free from the power of slaveholders as are the white people of the north; and though that, according to my ideas, is not saying a great deal, it is a vast improvement in *my* condition. The dream of my life is not yet realized. I do not sit with my children in a home of my own. I still long for a hearthstone of my own, however humble. I wish it for my children's sake far more than for my own. But God so orders circumstances as to keep me with my friend Mrs. Bruce. Love, duty, gratitude, also bind me to her side. It is a privilege to serve her who pities my oppressed people, and who has bestowed the inestimable boon of freedom on me and my children.

It has been painful to me, in many ways, to recall the dreary years I passed in bondage. I would gladly forget them if I could. Yet the retrospection is not altogether without solace; for with those gloomy recollections come tender memories of my good old grandmother, like light, fleecy clouds floating over a dark and troubled sea.

—1861

---

[1] *where the wicked ... at rest*   See Job 3.17: "There the wicked cease from troubling; and there the weary be at rest."

IN CONTEXT

Fugitive Slave Advertisement for Harriet Jacobs

The following advertisement was placed by Dr. James Norcom in the *American Beacon* on 4 July 1835; in it, he offers a $100 dollar reward for the return of his "servant girl," Harriet Jacobs.

$100 REWARD

WILL be given for the apprehension and delivery of my Servant Girl HARRIET. She is a light mulatto, 21 years of age, about 5 feet 4 inches high, of a thick and corpulent habit, having on her head a thick covering of black hair that curls naturally, but which can be easily combed straight. She speaks easily and fluently, and has an agreeable carriage and address. Being a good seamstress, she has been accustomed to dress well, has a variety of very fine clothes, made in the prevailing fashion, and will probably appear, if abroad, tricked out in gay and fashionable finery. As this girl absconded from the plantation of my son without any known cause or provocation, it is probable she designs to transport herself to the North.

The above reward, with all reasonable charges, will be given for apprehending her, or securing her in any prison or jail within the U. States.

All persons are hereby forewarned against harboring or entertaining her, or being in any way instrumental in her escape, under the most rigorous penalties of the law.

JAMES NORCOM.

Edenton, N. C. June 30   tf2w

In Context

The "Peculiar Circumstances" of Slavery

Jacobs's career as a writer began with her anonymous "Letter from a Fugitive Slave," which was printed in the *New York Daily Tribune* in 1853. She was responding to a well-publicized conflict that took place in 1853 between two powerful women: the Duchess of Sutherland, a British aristocrat who had helped organize an effective and well-supported petition against slavery (it is known as the "Stafford House Address" or the "Address to the Christian Women of America") and Julia Tyler, who had been First Lady of the United States from 1841–45. Tyler penned a defense of slavery in response to the British petition, entitled "To the Duchess of Sutherland and the Ladies of England" (also known as "The Women of England versus the Women of America").

The "Stafford House Address" was originally drafted by the Earl of Shaftesbury, who had read Harriet Beecher Stowe's *Uncle Tom's Cabin* (1852) and was moved by it to political action. He then asked the Duchess of Sutherland, a close friend of Queen Victoria and an influential socialite, to join his effort, and she helped gather signatures for the petition from over half a million English women. As a "feminine" petition, it avoided political questions and protested specifically against the domestic evils of slavery (in particular, the fact that the system separated families). The full set of signatures was presented in twenty-six volumes to Harriet Beecher Stowe on 7 May 1853, when Stowe was in England on a visit. The petition was quickly published in United States newspapers, and Julia Tyler wrote her response, which was widely printed and praised; she declared that the separation of families was a "rare occurrence" attended by "peculiar circumstances"—a claim that spurred Jacobs to write a passionate, eloquent rebuttal, in which she explicates just how pervasive and destructive the practice of family separation was in the Southern slave states.

from Anthony Ashley Cooper, 7th Earl of Shaftesbury, with Harriet Sutherland-Leveson-Gower, Duchess of Sutherland, "The Affectionate and Christian Address of Many Thousands of Women of Great Britain and Ireland to Their Sisters the Women of the United States of America" (1853)

A common origin, a common faith, and, we sincerely, believe, a common cause, urge us, at the present moment, to address you on the subject of that system of negro slavery which still prevails so extensively, and, even under kindly disposed masters, with such frightful results, in many of the vast regions of the Western world.

We will not dwell on the ordinary topics—on the progress of civilization, on the advance of freedom everywhere, on the rights and requirements of the nineteenth century; but we appeal to you very seriously to reflect and to ask counsel of God how far such a state of things is in accordance with his Holy Word, the inalienable rights of immortal souls, and the pure and merciful spirit of the Christian religion. We do not shut our eyes to the difficulties, nay, the dangers, that might beset the immediate abolition of that long-established system. We see and admit the necessity of preparation for so great an event; but, in speaking of indispensable preliminaries, we cannot be silent on those laws of your country which, in direct contravention of God's own law, "instituted in the time of man's innocency,"[1] deny in effect to the slave the sanctity of marriage, with all its joys, rights, and obligations; which separate, at the will of the master, the wife from the husband and the children from the parents. Nor can we be silent on that awful

---

1   *instituted … innocency*   Phrase from the marriage service in the Anglican *Book of Common Prayer* (1549).

system which either by statute or by custom interdicts to any race of man or any portion of the human family education in the truths of the gospel and the ordinances of Christianity. A remedy applied to these two evils alone would commence the amelioration of their sad condition. We appeal to you, then, as sisters, as wives, and as mothers, to raise your voices to your fellow citizens and your prayers to God for the removal of this affliction and disgrace from the Christian world.

We do not say these things in a spirit of self-complacency, as though our nation were free from the guilt it perceives in others.

We acknowledge with grief and shame our heavy share in this great sin. We acknowledge that our fore-fathers introduced, nay, compelled the adoption of slavery in those mighty colonies. We humbly confess it before Almighty God; and it is because we so deeply feel and so unfeignedly avow our own complicity that we now venture to implore your aid to wipe away our common crime and our common dishonor. ...

from Julia Tyler, "To the Duchess of Sutherland and the Ladies of England," *Southern Literary Messenger* (February 1853)

... I must, moreover, in all frankness, declare to you, that the women of the South especially have not received your address in the kindest spirit. They regard it as entirely incompatible with all confidence in or consideration for them, to invoke the interposition of the women of what are called the Free States in a matter with which they have no more to do than have yourselves, and whose interference in the question can produce no other effect than to excite disturbance and agitation and ill will, and possibly in the end, a total annihilation of kind feeling between geographical sections. It is the province of the women of the Southern States to preside over the domestic economy[1] of the estates and plantations of their husbands; it is emphatically their province to visit the sick, and attend to the comfort of all the labourers upon such estates; and it is felt to be but a poor compliment to the women of the South to suppose it necessary to introduce other superintendence than their own over the condition of their dependents and servants. ... Governments and countries which are now looked upon as stars of the first magnitude will ere long, if the United States roll on in their present orbit, be secondary and tertiary in the political hemisphere. This is quite as thoroughly known by us as by you, women of England, and therefore you should not be in the slightest degree surprised at the suspicion with which your address is regarded by all the thinking women, not only of the South, but of the whole Union. We know that there is but one subject on which there is a possibility of wrecking the bark[2] of this Union—a possibility, however, which I trust is very remote—and to that very subject you have given your attention[.] ... Yes, you are altogether correct in ascribing whatever there is of immorality or crime, in the present condition of the Southern States, to your own England. ... It will be a very, very difficult matter to furnish us with satisfactory reasons for this great and sudden conversion of a whole people, after losing the American market, on the subject of the slave trade—and we women of the United States must ever receive with suspicion all interference in our domestic affairs on the part of the noble ladies of England, or any portion of her inhabitants. Such interference implies either a want of proper and becoming conduct on our part in the management of our negroes, or it seeks to enlist the sympathies of the world against us. ... In morals we believe ourselves quite your equals, and therefore it sounds harshly in our ears to be admonished by you of our sins, real or imaginary. There is a proud heart in the American breast, which rebels against all assumption on the part of others, although they may wear ducal coronets or be considered the stars of fashions in foreign courts. ... If you wish a suggestion as to the suitable occupation of your idle hours, I will point you to the true field of your philanthropy—the unsupplied wants of your own people of England. ... Go, my good Duchess of Sutherland, on an embassy of mercy to the poor, the stricken, the hungry and the naked of your own land—cast in their laps the superflux of your enormous wealth; a single jewel from your hair, a single gem from your dress, would relieve many a poor woman of England who is now cold and shivering

---

[1]   *domestic economy*   I.e., management of the domestic sphere.

[2]   *bark*   Ship.

and destitute. ... The negro of the South lives sumptuously in comparison with the 100,000 of the white population of London. He is clothed warmly in winter, and has his meat twice daily without stint of bread. ... Believe me that the human heart is quite as susceptible with us as with you. Moralists and dealers in fiction may artfully overdraw and give false colouring, as they are licensed to do; but be not deceived into the belief that the heart of man or woman, on this side of the Atlantic, is either more obdurate or cruel than on yours. There is no reason, then, why you should leave your fellow subjects in misery at home in order to take your seat by the side of the black man on the plantations of America. Even if you are horror-stricken at the highly coloured picture of human distress incident to the separation of husband and wife and parents and children under our system of negro slavery—a thing, by the way, of rare occurrence among us, and then attended by peculiar circumstances—you have no occasion to leave your own land for a similar, and still harsher and more unjust exercise of authority. ...

from Harriet Jacobs, *New York Daily Tribune* (21 June 1853)

LETTER FROM A FUGITIVE SLAVE. Slaves Sold under Peculiar Circumstances[1]

[We publish the subjoined communication exactly as written by the author, with the exception of corrections in punctuation and spelling, and the omission of one or two passages.—Ed.][2]

SIR: Having carefully read your paper for some months I became very much interested in some of the articles and comments written on Mrs. Tyler's Reply to the Ladies of England. Being a slave myself, I could not have felt otherwise. Would that I could write an article worthy of notice in your columns. As I never enjoyed the advantages of an education, therefore I could not study the arts of reading and writing, yet poor as it may be, I had rather give it from my own hand, than have it said that I employed others to do it for me. The truth can never be told so well through the second and third person as from yourself. But I am straying from the question. As Mrs. Tyler and her friend Bhains were so far used up,[3] that he could not explain what those peculiar circumstances were, let one whose peculiar sufferings justifies her in explaining it for Mrs. Tyler.

I was born a slave, reared in the Southern hot-bed until I was the mother of two children, sold at the early age of two and four years old. I have been hunted through all of the Northern States, but no, I will not tell you of my own suffering—no, it would harrow up my soul, and defeat the object that I wish to pursue. Enough—the dregs of that bitter cup[4] have been my bounty for many years.

And as this is the first time that I ever took my pen in hand to make such an attempt, you will not say that it is fiction, for had I the inclination I have neither the brain or talent to write it. But to this very peculiar circumstance under which slaves are sold.

My mother was held as property by a maiden lady; when she married my younger sister[5] was in her fourteenth year, whom they took into the family. She was as gentle as she was beautiful. Innocent and

---

[1] *Peculiar Circumstances*   Jacobs is here picking up on a phrase from Julia Tyler's letter, in which she describes the splitting up of enslaved families as being driven by "peculiar circumstances" (see above). The adjective "peculiar," when used in the context of slavery, carried a specific meaning in the United States at this point in history. Slavery was often referred to by slaveholders in the South as "our peculiar institution," a euphemism that came to be used by abolitionists, too, though with them it was used ironically (they recognized it as a cowardly expression invented by those who profited from slavery but didn't want to name it).

[2] *We ... Ed.*   Editorial note from the *New York Daily Tribune*.

[3] *so far used up*   I.e., they had exhausted their words.

[4] *dregs ... bitter cup*   See Alexander Pope's translation of the *Iliad* (1715–20), book 22, line 85: "The bitter dregs of fortune's cup to drain."

[5] *my younger sister*   Jacobs is not known to have had a sister, but some elements of the following account parallel events in Jacobs's autobiography in her *Incidents in the Life of a Slave Girl*.

guileless child, the light of our desolate hearth! But oh, my heart bleeds to tell you of the misery and degradation she was forced to suffer in slavery. The monster who owned her had no humanity in his soul. The most sincere affection that his heart was capable of, could not make him faithful to his beautiful and wealthy bride the short time of three months, but every stratagem was used to seduce my sister. Mortified and tormented beyond endurance, this child came and threw herself on her mother's bosom, the only place where she could seek refuge from her persecutor; and yet she could not protect her child that she bore into the world. On that bosom with bitter tears she told her troubles, and entreated her mother to save her. And oh, Christian mothers! you that have daughters of your own, can you think of your sable sisters without offering a prayer to that God who created all in their behalf! My poor mother, naturally high-spirited, smarting under what she considered as the wrongs and outrages which her child had to bear, sought her master, entreating him to spare her child. Nothing could exceed his rage at this what he called impertinence. My mother was dragged to jail, there remained twenty-five days, with Negro traders to come in as they liked to examine her, as she was offered for sale. My sister was told that she must yield, or never expect to see her mother again. There were three younger children; on no other condition could she be restored to them, without the sacrifice of one. That child gave herself up to her master's bidding, to save one that was dearer to her than life itself. And can you, Christian, find it in your heart to despise her? Ah, no! not even Mrs. Tyler; for though we believe that the vanity of a name would lead her to bestow her hand where her heart could never go with it,[1] yet, with all her faults and follies, she is nothing more than a woman. For if her domestic hearth is surrounded with slaves,[2] ere long before this she has opened her eyes to the evils of slavery, and that the mistress as well as the slave must submit to the indignities and vices imposed on them by their lords of body and soul. But to one of those peculiar circumstances.

At fifteen, my sister held to her bosom an innocent offspring of her guilt and misery. In this way she dragged a miserable existence of two years, between the fires of her mistress's jealousy and her master's brutal passion. At seventeen, she gave birth to another helpless infant, heir to all the evils of slavery.[3] Thus life and its sufferings was meted out to her until her twenty-first year. Sorrow and suffering has made its ravages upon her—she was less the object to be desired by the fiend who had crushed her to the earth; and as her children grew, they bore too strong a resemblance to him who desired to give them no other inheritance save Chains and Handcuffs, and in the dead hour of the night, when this young, deserted mother lay with her little ones clinging around her, little dreaming of the dark and inhuman plot that would be carried out into execution before another dawn, and when the sun rose on God's beautiful earth, that broken-hearted mother was far on her way to the capitol of Virginia.[4] That day should have refused her light to so disgraceful and inhuman an act in your boasted country of Liberty. Yet, reader, it is true, those two helpless children were the sons of one of your sainted Members in Congress;[5] that agonized mother, his victim and slave. And where she now is God only knows, who has kept a record on high of all that she has suffered on earth.

And, you would exclaim, Could not the master have been more merciful to his children? God is merciful to all of his children, but it is seldom that a slaveholder has any mercy for his slave child. And you will believe it when I tell you that mother and her children were sold to make room for another sister, who was now the age of that mother when she entered the family. And this selling appeased the mistress's wrath, and satisfied her desire for revenge, and made the path more smooth for her young rival at first.

[1] *Mrs. Tyler … with it* Reference to Julia Tyler's having married John Tyler, the former President, even though he was thirty years her senior.

[2] *if her … slaves* Julia Tyler and her husband held over sixty enslaved people at Sherwood Forest, their plantation in Virginia.

[3] *heir … slavery* From 1662 onwards, slavery law in Britain and America followed the doctrine that children followed the status of their mothers (i.e., any children born to enslaved women would be themselves enslaved).

[4] *on her way … Virginia* I.e., she was separated from her children and sent to be sold at the slave market in Richmond, Virginia.

[5] *one of … Congress* Jacobs's two children, Joseph and Louisa, were both fathered by Samuel Sawyer, who became a Member of Congress for North Carolina's 1st District in 1837.

For there is a strong rivalry between a handsome mulatto girl and a jealous and faded mistress, and her liege lord sadly neglects his wife or doubles his attentions, to save him being suspected by his wife. Would you not think that Southern Women had cause to despise that Slavery which forces them to bear so much deception practiced by their husbands? Yet all this is true, for a slaveholder seldom takes a white mistress, for she is an expensive commodity, not as submissive as he would like to have her, but more apt to be tyrannical; and when his passion seeks another object, he must leave her in quiet possession of all the gewgaws[1] that she has sold herself for. But not so with his poor slave victim, that he has robbed of everything that can make life desirable; she must be torn from the little that is left to bind her to life, and sold by her seducer and master, caring not where, so that it puts him in possession of enough to purchase another victim. And such are the peculiar circumstances of American Slavery—of all the evils in God's sight the most to be abhorred.

Perhaps while I am writing this you too, dear Emily, may be on your way to the Mississippi River,[2] for those peculiar circumstances occur every day in the midst of my poor oppressed fellow-creatures in bondage. And oh ye Christians, while your arms are extended to receive the oppressed of all nations, while you exert every power of your soul to assist them to raise funds, put weapons in their hands, tell them to return to their own country to slay every foe until they break the accursed yoke from off their necks,[3] not buying and selling; this they never do under any circumstances.

And because one friend of a slave has dared to tell of their wrongs you would annihilate her.[4] But in Uncle Tom's Cabin she has not told the half. Would that I had one spark from her store house of genius and talent I would tell you of my own sufferings—I would tell you of wrongs that Hungary has never inflicted, nor England ever dreamed of[5] in this free country where all nations fly for liberty, equal rights and protection under your stripes and stars. It should be stripes[6] and scars, for they go along with Mrs. Tyler's peculiar circumstances, of which I have told you only one.

A FUGITIVE SLAVE.

---

[1] *gewgaws* Trinkets.

[2] *Emily ... Mississippi River* Likely a reference to the character of Emmeline in *Uncle Tom's Cabin* (1852), a beautiful, fifteen-year-old girl whom the cruel plantation owner Legree enslaves for sex. To be "on her way" to the Mississippi River would be to be on her way to be sold at auction.

[3] *the accursed ... necks* In the Bible, the yoke appears frequently as an image of enslavement, or oppression. See, for example, Genesis 27.40 and Jeremiah 28.11.

[4] *her* I.e., Harriet Beecher Stowe, author of the novel *Uncle Tom's Cabin* (1852).

[5] *Hungary has never inflicted* Hungary was sympathetically perceived by Americans as a country suffering under imperial yoke, particularly after the Hungarian Revolution of 1848 was suppressed by both the Austro-Hungarian and Russian empires. Americans were interested in the fate of Hungary and its struggle for freedom, partly because, in 1851, Hungarian revolutionary leader Lajos Kossuth came to the United States for political asylum, at the invitation of the United States Congress; *nor England ever dreamed of* In sections excluded from the above selection of Julia Tyler's letter, she accuses England of what she considered to be worse crimes than slavery, particularly their treatment of the Irish people (the Irish Famine, in which the devastating effects of a potato blight were worsened by British colonial policies and laissez-faire capitalism, took place between 1845 and 1852).

[6] *stripes* In this context, lash marks left on the skin by a whip.

Jacobs Free School, Founded by Harriet Jacobs, 1864. A small "x" inscribed onto the photo indicates where Harriet Jacobs is standing.

WILLIAM WELLS BROWN

c. 1814 – 1884

William Wells Brown was a charismatic writer, orator, and leader in the antislavery cause. His literary and artistic work spans a wide variety of genres, including speeches, drawings, biography, drama, travel-writing, history, memoir, and the novel. Unlike fellow abolitionists Frederick Douglass and William Lloyd Garrison, who primarily appealed to men, Brown cultivated a diverse, predominantly female audience, making use of a wide array of dramatic conventions and rhetorical strategies to bring his arguments home to his auditors and readers. He spoke more directly than most men about the particular evils of slavery for women, as well as about the importance of female education. Popular and respected in his own time, Brown is now considered one of the foremost black writers of the nineteenth century; as Henry Louis Gates Jr. writes, "It is difficult to imagine any one of his contemporaries who contributed as much or as richly to so many genres as did William Wells Brown."

Brown was born in 1814 near Lexington, Kentucky; his mother, Elizabeth, was an enslaved woman, and his father was a white plantation owner, George W. Higgins. Elizabeth and all six of her children were enslaved by Dr. John Young (a relative of Higgins). When Brown was two years old, Young moved Elizabeth and her children to Missouri, where one of Brown's earliest traumatic memories included seeing his mother whipped for being a few minutes late for work. When Brown was a small boy, the Youngs adopted a nephew named William; they then changed Brown's first name to "Sandford," so there would be no confusing the young children (Brown had a light complexion). In 1827, when Brown was thirteen, Dr. Young moved to St. Louis, taking Elizabeth and Brown with him, but leaving four of Brown's siblings behind on the plantation. Over the next five years, Young made money by renting Brown's labor out to those willing to purchase it. He was thus subjected to an even wider range of the horrors of slavery: one of the men to whom Brown was leased, a vicious drunk, beat his workers and then suffocated them in a shed full of smoke, while another, a slave trader, gave Brown the heartbreaking task of preparing enslaved people for auction. There were, however, some positive experiences. For six months, Brown worked for a newspaper editor, the well-known abolitionist Elijah P. Lovejoy, whom Brown describes as "a very good man, and decidedly the best master that I had ever had." In the offices of Lovejoy's paper, the *St. Louis Times*, Brown wrote that he received "what little learning [he] obtained while in slavery," though this happier period ended when he was severely beaten by a white man who was furious that Brown had defended the office from a thieving gang of white boys. Brown also worked on Mississippi steamboats at this time; the experience of moving from place to place and seeing how others lived gave him an expanded sense of future possibility and solidified his determination to one day make an escape.

In 1833, Young decided to sell Brown and his sister, threatening to divide further the already scattered family. Determined not to be separated from his mother, Brown convinced her to escape with him. They were captured after eleven days, and Brown's mother was sold and sent to the Deep South, which often meant exposure to even harder labor, disease, and early death. Filled with remorse and grief, Brown was sold first to a tailor, Samuel Willi, for $500, and then to Enoch Price, a steamboat merchant, for $700. In January 1834, while aboard one of Price's steamboats that had stopped in Cincinnati, Brown escaped and met a Quaker named Wells Brown, who sheltered, fed, and clothed him. At this time, William rejected the name given him by his enslavers ("Sandford"), took back his original first name, and adopted the names of his benefactor, becoming William Wells Brown.

Once in the north, Brown worked several jobs to support himself, but his main source of income for the next nine years was from working seasonally on steamships on the Great Lakes. In 1834, he married Elizabeth Schooner, with whom he had two daughters, Clarissa and Josephine. He also launched himself into an intense program of self-education, while at the same time committing himself politically to the abolitionist cause. In 1836 the family moved to Buffalo, where Brown helped transport freedom-seeking enslaved people to Canada, as well as sheltering them in his home. Brown also began giving antislavery speeches; by 1843, he had quit his job stewarding ships and committed to working full-time as a traveling lecturer for the Western New York Anti-Slavery Society. He helped organize the 1843 National Convention of Colored Citizens in Buffalo, where he met fellow-abolitionist and keynote speaker Frederick Douglass, with whom he was to have a meaningful, if sometimes fraught, professional relationship. It was also in this momentous year that Brown published his first piece of writing, a letter to the editor in the *National Anti-Slavery Standard* arguing that abolition should be primarily a persuasive movement that would in time lead to a moral and political rejection of the institution.

Brown gained a national reputation as a gifted speaker and drew crowds of people to hear his lectures. As one reviewer in 1861 put it, Brown was a speaker of "unequalled attractive powers." Over time, Brown became more and more inventive in his presentations; in fact, it is more accurate to think of his lectures as examples of performance art, moving seamlessly between exhortation, storytelling, song, and panoramas of magic lantern slides. Some of his more famous speeches include *Lecture Delivered before the Female Anti-Slavery Society of Salem* (1847), *Speech Delivered in Croydon, England* (1849), and *St. Domingo: Its Revolutions and Its Patriots* (1854). Brown's dedication to the lecture circuit had a cost, however—his absences from home further deteriorated an already difficult relationship with his wife, leading to separation in 1847.

After the separation, Brown moved with his daughters to Boston, the national hub of antislavery activity and publication, where he started writing in earnest. His *Narrative of William W. Brown, A Fugitive Slave, Written by Himself* was published in 1847; the book proved popular, running to nine editions within the next three years. In *Narrative*, Brown uses a controlled, understated narrative voice to describe the dramatic and horrific incidents of his life in slavery, creating an ironic juxtaposition between the events described and the voice of description. This polished irony was a rhetorical tool Brown would use again and again to engage his largely white audience's sympathy without alienating them. Brown's portrayal of resistance in his *Narrative* also highlights the importance of outwitting the enslaver and the slave system, a different strategy from the more physical resistance exemplified in Douglass's famous *Narrative*, which had been published two years earlier, in 1845.

In 1849, Brown traveled to Europe; the passing of the Fugitive Slave Laws in 1850 made it unsafe to return to the United States, so Brown settled in England for the next five years, supporting himself by his lecturing. Brown also continued his education, reading widely and studying French, German, and Latin. He published four more books during this time abroad, including a travel narrative entitled *Three Years in Europe: or, Places I Have Seen and People I Have Met* (1852) and *Clotel, or The President's Daughter* (1853), his first and only novel. Upon publication, *Clotel* received a somewhat lackluster response, perhaps because it followed soon after Harriet Beecher Stowe's *Uncle Tom's Cabin* (1852), which had been a huge sensation the previous year (the impact of *Uncle Tom's Cabin* on the abolitionist movement was a key inspiration for Brown to try his own hand at novel-writing). *Clotel*'s story is grounded on rumors, prevalent at the time, that children were born to Thomas Jefferson and his enslaved servant Sally Hemings—rumors that have since been substantiated by DNA evidence. The novel thus exposes the narrow confines of what "freedom" meant for one of the authors of the Declaration of Independence, with Jefferson's hypocrisy serving as a microcosm for the larger hypocrisy of a free democracy built upon slavery. By focusing on the fate of a young African American woman, Brown also emphasized the particular dangers and suffering that women endured within this system.

For many years, critics saw *Clotel* as a work that tried to include too many elements and plot events into one literary space. But more recently, readers have celebrated the novel as a literary example of Brown's work as a performance artist, in which the crowding together of incident, song, poems, news clippings, and melodrama act together to attract and at times overwhelm the senses, leading to cathartic release. Critics are still unpacking the complex mixture of pleasure and discomfort that Brown elicits in this novel, even as he simultaneously makes vivid the horrors and hypocrisy of slavery; as critic Geoffrey Sanborn writes, "In [*Clotel*], anti-racism, still so often stereotyped and resisted as a joyless reformism, is capable of providing windfalls of psychic pleasure."

Brown returned to America with his daughters in 1854, after his freedom had been purchased by the British abolitionist Ellen Richardson. By this time, Brown's politics had become more radical, leaving behind the passivist ideals of Garrisonian abolitionism to support active—even violent—resistance to slavery. He began to write plays, including *Experience; or, How to Give a Northern Man a Backbone* in 1856, which he often performed at meetings and lectures, and *The Escape; or, A Leap for Freedom. A Drama in Five Acts* in 1858. Drawing heavily on Brown's own history, *The Escape* is noteworthy for its incisive exploration of moral hypocrisy and for its depiction of the increasing social tensions running up to the Civil War.

In 1860, Brown married again, and during the war he continued to write, focusing on histories and biographies aimed at celebrating the vital place of black people in America's past, present, and future. His historical works include *The Black Man; His Antecedents, His Genius, and His Achievements* (1862), *The Negro in the American Rebellion: His Heroism and His Fidelity* (1867), and *The Rising Son; or, The Antecedents and Advancement of the Colored Race* (1873). In his last autobiographical book, *My Southern Home: Or, The South and Its People* (1880) Brown records memories of his youth and also his impressions from a trip South in 1879–80, with particular attention on the deteriorating conditions for African Americans as the promise of Reconstruction faded; the book is considered an important precursor to W.E.B. Du Bois's *The Souls of Black Folk* (1903). Brown died in 1884, at the age of seventy, in Chelsea, Massachusetts.

For much of the twentieth century, Brown's work and legacy faded into the background, particularly when compared to his more famous colleague Frederick Douglass. Some of his strengths—his strategy of speaking particularly to women and of women, and his savviness in creating political performance art—run counter to the formalist aesthetics that determined literary fame in previous decades. Brown's rhetorical strategies are now, however, increasingly admired, as is his vast body of work, which touches on many subjects of contemporary scholarly interest, including racial identity, the literature of sentimentality, melodrama, minstrelsy, narrative fragmentation, and theatricality.

NOTE ON THE TEXT: The excerpts from *Clotel* presented here are based on the first printed edition of 1853. Spelling and punctuation have been modernized in accordance with the practices of this anthology.

⌘ ⌘ ⌘

from *Clotel; or,*
The President's Daughter: A Narrative of
Slave Life in the United States

CHAPTER I: THE NEGRO SALE

Why stands she near the auction stand,
    That girl so young and fair?
What brings her to this dismal place,
    Why stands she weeping there?[1]

With the growing population of slaves in the Southern States of America, there is a fearful increase of half whites, most of whose fathers are slaveowners, and their mothers slaves. Society does not frown upon the man who sits with his mulatto[2] child upon his knee, whilst its mother stands a slave behind his chair. The late Henry Clay,[3] some years since, predicted that the abolition of negro slavery would be brought about by the amalgamation of the races. John Randolph, a distinguished slaveholder of Virginia, and a prominent statesman, said in a speech in the legislature of his native state, that "the blood of the first American statesmen coursed through the veins of the slave of the South." In all the cities and towns of the slave states, the real negro, or clear black, does not amount to more than one in every four of the slave population. This fact is, of itself, the best evidence of the degraded and immoral condition of the relation of master and slave in the United States of America.

In all the slave states, the law says: "Slaves shall be deemed, sold, taken, reputed, and adjudged in law to be chattels personal in the hands of their owners and possessors, and their executors, administrators and assigns, to all intents, constructions, and purposes whatsoever." A slave is one who is in the power of a master to whom he belongs. The master may sell him, dispose of his person, his industry, and his labour. He can do nothing, possess nothing, nor acquire anything, but what must belong to his master. The slave is entirely subject to the will of his master, who may correct and chastise him, though not with unusual rigour, or so as to maim and mutilate him, or expose him to the danger of loss of life, or to cause his death. The slave, to remain a slave, must be sensible that there is no appeal from his master. Where the slave is placed by law entirely under the control of the man who claims him, body and soul, as property, what else could be expected than the most depraved social condition? The marriage relation, the oldest and most sacred institution given to man by his Creator, is unknown and unrecognised in the slave laws of the United States. Would that we could say, that the moral and religious teaching in the slave states were better than the laws; but, alas! we cannot. A few years since, some slaveholders became a little uneasy in their minds about the rightfulness of permitting slaves to take to themselves husbands and wives, while they still had others living, and applied to their religious teachers for advice; and the following will show how this grave and important subject was treated:

"Is a servant, whose husband or wife has been sold by his or her master into a distant country, to be permitted to marry again?"

The query was referred to a committee, who made the following report; which, after discussion, was adopted:

"That, in view of the circumstances in which servants in this country are placed, the committee are unanimous in the opinion, that it is better to permit servants thus circumstanced to take another husband or wife."

Such was the answer from a committee of the "Shiloh Baptist Association"; and instead of receiving light, those who asked the question were plunged into deeper darkness!

A similar question was put to the "Savannah River Association," and the answer, as the following will show, did not materially differ from the one we have already given:

---

[1]   *Why stands ... weeping there* First verse of "The Slave Auction—A Fact," an anonymous song included in William Wells Brown's collection *The Anti-Slavery Harp: A Collection of Songs for Anti-Slavery Meetings* (1848).

[2]   *mulatto* Term for a person with one white and one black parent; or, more loosely, a person with the appearance of being mixed-race. (The designation is today considered offensive.)

[3]   *Henry Clay* Politician (1777–1852) who represented Kentucky in Congress and served as Speaker of the House and later Secretary of State.

"Whether, in a case of involuntary separation, of such a character as to preclude all prospect of future intercourse, the parties ought to be allowed to marry again."

Answer—

"That such separation among persons situated as our slaves are, is civilly a separation by death; and they believe that, in the sight of God, it would be so viewed. To forbid second marriages in such cases would be to expose the parties, not only to stronger hardships and strong temptation, but to church-censure for acting in obedience to their masters, who cannot be expected to acquiesce in a regulation at variance with justice to the slaves, and to the spirit of that command which regulates marriage among Christians. The slaves are not free agents; and a dissolution by death is not more entirely without their consent, and beyond their control, than by such separation."

Although marriage, as the above indicates, is a matter which the slaveholders do not think is of any importance, or of any binding force with their slaves; yet it would be doing that degraded class an injustice, not to acknowledge that many of them do regard it as a sacred obligation, and show a willingness to obey the commands of God on this subject. Marriage is, indeed, the first and most important institution of human existence—the foundation of all civilization and culture—the root of church and state. It is the most intimate covenant of heart formed among mankind; and for many persons the only relation in which they feel the true sentiments of humanity. It gives scope for every human virtue, since each of these is developed from the love and confidence which here predominate. It unites all which ennobles and beautifies life—sympathy, kindness of will and deed, gratitude, devotion, and every delicate, intimate feeling. As the only asylum for true education, it is the first and last sanctuary of human culture. As husband and wife through each other become conscious of complete humanity, and every human feeling, and every human virtue; so children, at their first awakening in the fond covenant of love between parents, both of whom are tenderly concerned for the same object, find an image of complete humanity leagued in free love. The spirit of love which prevails between them acts with creative power upon the young mind, and awakens every germ of goodness within it. This invisible and incalculable influence of parental life acts more upon the child than all the efforts of education, whether by means of instruction, precept, or exhortation. If this be a true picture of the vast influence for good of the institution of marriage, what must be the moral degradation of that people to whom marriage is denied? Not content with depriving them of all the higher and holier enjoyments of this relation, by degrading and darkening their souls, the slaveholder denies to his victim even that slight alleviation of his misery, which would result from the marriage relation being protected by law and public opinion. Such is the influence of slavery in the United States, that the ministers of religion, even in the so-called free states, are the mere echoes, instead of the correctors, of public sentiment.

We have thought it advisable to show that the present system of chattel slavery in America undermines the entire social condition of man, so as to prepare the reader for the following narrative of slave life, in that otherwise happy and prosperous country.

In all the large towns in the Southern States, there is a class of slaves who are permitted to hire their time of their owners, and for which they pay a high price. These are mulatto women, or quadroons,[1] as they are familiarly known, and are distinguished for their fascinating beauty. The handsomest usually pays the highest price for her time. Many of these women are the favourites of persons who furnish them with the means of paying their owners, and not a few are dressed in the most extravagant manner. Reader, when you take into consideration the fact, that amongst the slave population no safeguard is thrown around virtue, and no inducement held out to slave women to be chaste, you will not be surprised when we tell you that immorality and vice pervade the cities of the Southern States in a manner unknown in the cities and towns of the Northern States. Indeed most of the slave women have no higher aspiration than that of becoming the finely-dressed mistress of some white man. And at negro balls and parties, this class of women usually cut the greatest figure.

---

[1] *quadroons* Term commonly used in the nineteenth century to classify individuals of mixed racial background, generally those who had one black and three white grandparents.

At the close of the year—the following advertisement appeared in a newspaper published in Richmond, the capital of the state of Virginia: "Notice: Thirty-eight negroes will be offered for sale on Monday, November 10th, at twelve o'clock, being the entire stock of the late John Graves, Esq. The negroes are in good condition, some of them very prime; among them are several mechanics, able-bodied field hands, plough-boys, and women with children at the breast, and some of them very prolific in their generating qualities, affording a rare opportunity to any one who wishes to raise a strong and healthy lot of servants for their own use. Also several mulatto girls of rare personal qualities: two of them very superior. Any gentleman or lady wishing to purchase, can take any of the above slaves on trial for a week, for which no charge will be made." Amongst the above slaves to be sold were Currer and her two daughters, Clotel and Althesa; the latter were the girls spoken of in the advertisement as "very superior." Currer was a bright mulatto, and of prepossessing appearance, though then nearly forty years of age. She had hired her time for more than twenty years, during which time she had lived in Richmond. In her younger days Currer had been the housekeeper of a young slaveholder; but of later years had been a laundress or washerwoman, and was considered to be a woman of great taste in getting up linen. The gentleman for whom she had kept house was Thomas Jefferson,[1] by whom she had two daughters. Jefferson being called to Washington to fill a government appointment, Currer was left behind, and thus she took herself to the business of washing, by which means she paid her master, Mr. Graves, and supported herself and two children. At the time of the decease of her master, Currer's daughters, Clotel and Althesa, were aged respectively sixteen and fourteen years, and both, like most of their own sex in America, were well grown. Currer early resolved to bring her daughters up as ladies, as she termed it, and therefore imposed little or no work upon them. As her daughters grew older, Currer had to pay a stipulated price for them; yet her notoriety as a laundress of the first class enabled her to put an extra price upon her charges, and thus she and her daughters lived in comparative luxury. To bring up Clotel and Althesa to attract attention, and especially at balls and parties, was the great aim of Currer. Although the term "negro ball" is applied to most of these gatherings, yet a majority of the attendants are often whites. Nearly all the negro parties in the cities and towns of the Southern States are made up of quadroon and mulatto girls, and white men. These are democratic gatherings, where gentlemen, shopkeepers, and their clerks, all appear upon terms of perfect equality. And there is a degree of gentility and decorum in these companies that is not surpassed by similar gatherings of white people in the Slave States. It was at one of these parties that Horatio Green, the son of a wealthy gentleman of Richmond, was first introduced to Clotel. The young man had just returned from college, and was in his twenty-second year. Clotel was sixteen, and was admitted by all to be the most beautiful girl, coloured or white, in the city. So attentive was the young man to the quadroon during the evening that it was noticed by all, and became a matter of general conversation; while Currer appeared delighted beyond measure at her daughter's conquest. From that evening, young Green became the favourite visitor at Currer's house. He soon promised to purchase Clotel, as speedily as it could be effected, and make her mistress of her own dwelling; and Currer looked forward with pride to the time when she should see her daughter emancipated and free. It was a beautiful moonlight night in August, when all who reside in tropical climes are eagerly gasping for a breath of fresh air, that Horatio Green was seated in the small garden behind Currer's cottage, with the object of his affections by his side. And it was here that Horatio drew from his pocket the newspaper, wet from the press, and read the advertisement for the sale of the slaves to which we have alluded; Currer and her two daughters being of the number. At the close of the evening's visit, and as the young man was leaving, he said to the girl, "You shall soon be free and your own mistress."

As might have been expected, the day of sale brought an unusual large number together to compete for the property to be sold. Farmers who make a business of raising slaves for the market were there; slave-traders and speculators were also numerously represented; and in the midst of this throng was one who felt a deeper interest in the result of the sale than any other of the

[1]   *Thomas Jefferson* Politician who played a leading role in the founding of the United States and later served as third U.S. president (in office from 1801 to 1809).

bystanders; this was young Green. True to his promise, he was there with a blank bank check in his pocket, awaiting with impatience to enter the list as a bidder for the beautiful slave. The less valuable slaves were first placed upon the auction block, one after another, and sold to the highest bidder. Husbands and wives were separated with a degree of indifference that is unknown in any other relation of life, except that of slavery. Brothers and sisters were torn from each other; and mothers saw their children leave them for the last time on this earth.

It was late in the day, when the greatest number of persons were thought to be present, that Currer and her daughters were brought forward to the place of sale. Currer was first ordered to ascend the auction stand, which she did with a trembling step. The slave mother was sold to a trader. Althesa, the youngest, and who was scarcely less beautiful than her sister, was sold to the same trader for one thousand dollars. Clotel was the last, and, as was expected, commanded a higher price than any that had been offered for sale that day. The appearance of Clotel on the auction block created a deep sensation amongst the crowd. There she stood, with a complexion as white as most of those who were waiting with a wish to become her purchasers; her features as finely defined as any of her sex of pure Anglo-Saxon; her long black wavy hair done up in the neatest manner; her form tall and graceful, and her whole appearance indicating one superior to her position. The auctioneer commenced by saying, that "Miss Clotel had been reserved for the last, because she was the most valuable. How much gentlemen? Real Albino,[1] fit for a fancy girl for anyone. She enjoys good health, and has a sweet temper. How much do you say?" "Five hundred dollars." "Only five hundred for such a girl as this? Gentlemen, she is worth a deal more than that sum; you certainly don't know the value of the article you are bidding upon. Here, gentlemen, I hold in my hand a paper certifying that she has a good moral character." "Seven hundred." "Ah, gentlemen, that is something like. This paper also states that she is very intelligent." "Eight hundred." "She is a devoted Christian, and perfectly trustworthy." "Nine

hundred." "Nine fifty." "Ten." "Eleven." "Twelve hundred." Here the sale came to a dead stand. The auctioneer stopped, looked around, and began in a rough manner to relate some anecdotes relative to the sale of slaves, which, he said, had come under his own observation. At this juncture the scene was indeed strange. Laughing, joking, swearing, smoking, spitting, and talking kept up a continual hum and noise amongst the crowd; while the slave-girl stood with tears in her eyes, at one time looking towards her mother and sister, and at another towards the young man whom she hoped would become her purchaser. "The chastity of this girl is pure; she has never been from under her mother's care, she is a virtuous creature." "Thirteen." "Fourteen." "Fifteen." "Fifteen hundred dollars," cried the auctioneer, and the maiden was struck for that sum. This was a Southern auction, at which the bones, muscles, sinews, blood, and nerves of a young lady of sixteen were sold for five hundred dollars; her moral character for two hundred; her improved intellect for one hundred; her Christianity for three hundred; and her chastity and virtue for four hundred dollars more. And this, too, in a city thronged with churches, whose tall spires look like so many signals pointing to heaven, and whose ministers preach that slavery is a God-ordained institution!

What words can tell the inhumanity, the atrocity, and the immorality of that doctrine which, from exalted office, commends such a crime to the favour of enlightened and Christian people? What indignation from all the world is not due to the government and people who put forth all their strength and power to keep in existence such an institution? Nature abhors it; the age repels it; and Christianity needs all her meekness to forgive it.

Clotel was sold for fifteen hundred dollars, but her purchaser was Horatio Green. Thus closed a negro sale, at which two daughters of Thomas Jefferson, the writer of the Declaration of American Independence, and one of the presidents of the great republic, were disposed of to the highest bidder!

"O God! my every heart-string cries,
    Dost thou these scenes behold
In this our boasted Christian land,
    And must the truth be told?

---

[1] *Real Albino* I.e., Truly white. Enslaved women with lighter complexions were highly valued at auction, particularly as potential sexual victims.

"Blush, Christian, blush! for e'en the dark,
    Untutored heathen see
Thy inconsistency; and, lo!
    They scorn thy God, and thee!"[1]

CHAPTER 2: GOING TO THE SOUTH

My country, shall thy honoured name,
    Be as a bye-word through the world?
Rouse! for, as if to blast thy fame,
    This keen reproach is at thee hurled;
The banner that above thee waves,
    Is floating o'er three million slaves.[2]

Dick Walker, the slave speculator, who had purchased Currer and Althesa, put them in prison until his gang[3] was made up, and then, with his forty slaves, started for the New Orleans market. As many of the slaves had been brought up in Richmond, and had relations residing there, the slave trader determined to leave the city early in the morning, so as not to witness any of those scenes so common where slaves are separated from their relatives and friends, when about departing for the Southern market. This plan was successful; for not even Clotel, who had been every day at the prison to see her mother and sister, knew of their departure. A march of eight days through the interior of the state, and they arrived on the banks of the Ohio river, where they were all put on board a steamer, and then speedily sailed for the place of their destination.

Walker had already advertised in the New Orleans papers, that he would be there at a stated time with "a prime lot of able-bodied slaves ready for field service; together with a few extra ones, between the ages of fifteen and twenty-five." But, like most who make a business of buying and selling slaves for gain, he often bought some who were far advanced in years, and would always try to sell them for five or ten years younger than they actually were. Few persons can arrive at anything like the age of a negro, by mere observation, unless they are well acquainted with the race. Therefore the slave trader very frequently carried out this deception with perfect impunity. After the steamer had left the wharf, and was fairly on the bosom of the Father of Waters,[4] Walker called his servant Pompey to him, and instructed him as to "getting the negroes ready for market." Amongst the forty negroes were several whose appearance indicated that they had seen some years, and had gone through some services. Their grey hair and whiskers at once pronounced them to be above the ages set down in the trader's advertisement. Pompey had long been with the trader, and knew his business; and if he did not take delight in discharging his duty, he did it with a degree of alacrity, so that he might receive the approbation of his master. "Pomp," as Walker usually called him, was of real negro blood, and would often say, when alluding to himself, "Dis nigger[5] is no countefit; he is de genewine artekil." Pompey was of low stature, round face, and, like most of his race, had a set of teeth, which for whiteness and beauty could not be surpassed; his eyes large, lips thick, and hair short and woolly. Pompey had been with Walker so long, and had seen so much of the buying and selling of slaves, that he appeared perfectly indifferent to the heartrending scenes which daily occurred in his presence. It was on the second day of the steamer's voyage that Pompey selected five of the old slaves, took them into a room by themselves, and commenced preparing them for the market. "Well," said Pompey, addressing himself to the company, "I is de gentman dat is to get you ready, so dat you will bring marser a good price in de Orleans market. How old is you?" addressing himself to a man who, from appearance, was not less than forty. "If I live to see next corn-planting time I will either be forty-five or fifty-five, I don't know which." "Dat may be," replied Pompey; "But now you is only thirty years old; dat is what marser says you is to be." "I know I is more den dat," responded the man. "I knows nothing about dat," said Pompey; "but when you get in

[1] *O God ... thee* Last two stanzas of "The Slave Auction—A Fact."

[2] *My country ... million slaves* First verse of "Freedom's Banner" by R.C. Wateson, a song included in William Wells Brown's collection *The Anti-Slavery Harp: A Collection of Songs for Anti-Slavery Meetings* (1848).

[3] *slave speculator* Interregional slave trader; *gang* Group of purchased enslaved people.

[4] *Father of Waters* I.e., Mississippi River; translation of the Ojibwe "misi-ziibi."

[5] *nigger* By the mid-nineteenth century, this word, when used by white people of black people, had acquired the extremely derogatory connotations it carries today, but it had also become a term used by African Americans for and among themselves in a neutral or positive way.

de market, an anybody axe you how old you is, an you tell 'em forty-five, marser will tie you up an gib you de whip like smoke. But if you tell 'em dat you is only thirty, den he wont." "Well den, I guess I will only be thirty when dey axe me," replied the chattel.

"What your name?" inquired Pompey. "Geemes," answered the man. "Oh, Uncle Jim, is it?" "Yes." "Den you must have off dem dare whiskers of yours, an when you get to Orleans you must grease dat face an make it look shiney." This was all said by Pompey in a manner which clearly showed that he knew what he was about. "How old is you?" asked Pompey of a tall, strong-looking man. "I was twenty-nine last potato-digging time," said the man. "What's your name?" "My name is Tobias, but dey call me 'Toby.'" "Well, Toby, or Mr. Tobias, if dat will suit you better, you is now twenty-three years old, an no more. Dus you hear dat?" "Yes," responded Toby. Pompey gave each to understand how old he was to be when asked by persons who wished to purchase, and then reported to his master that the "old boys" were all right. At eight o'clock on the evening of the third day, the lights of another steamer were seen in the distance, and apparently coming up very fast. This was a signal for a general commotion on the Patriot, and everything indicated that a steamboat race was at hand. Nothing can exceed the excitement attendant upon a steamboat on the Mississippi river. By the time the boats had reached Memphis, they were side by side, and each exerting itself to keep the ascendancy in point of speed. The night was clear, the moon shining brightly, and the boats so near to each other that the passengers were calling out from one boat to the other. On board the Patriot, the firemen were using oil, lard, butter, and even bacon, with the wood, for the purpose of raising the steam to its highest pitch. The blaze, mingled with the black smoke, showed plainly that the other boat was burning more than wood. The two boats soon locked, so that the hands of the boats were passing from vessel to vessel, and the wildest excitement prevailed throughout amongst both passengers and crew. At this moment the engineer of the Patriot was seen to fasten down the safety-valve, so that no steam should escape. This was, indeed, a dangerous resort. A few of the boat hands who saw what had taken place, left that end of the boat for more secure quarters.

The Patriot stopped to take in passengers, and still no steam was permitted to escape. At the starting of the boat cold water was forced into the boilers by the machinery, and, as might have been expected, one of the boilers immediately exploded. One dense fog of steam filled every part of the vessel, while shrieks, groans, and cries were heard on every hand. The saloons and cabins soon had the appearance of a hospital. By this time the boat had landed, and the Columbia, the other boat, had come alongside to render assistance to the disabled steamer. The killed and scalded (nineteen in number) were put on shore, and the Patriot, taken in tow by the Columbia, was soon again on its way.

It was now twelve o'clock at night, and instead of the passengers being asleep the majority were gambling in the saloons. Thousands of dollars change hand during a passage from Louisville or St. Louis to New Orleans on a Mississippi steamer, and many men, and even ladies, are completely ruined. "Go call my boy, steward," said Mr. Smith, as he took his cards one by one from the table. In a few moments a fine looking, bright-eyed mulatto boy, apparently about fifteen years of age, was standing by his master's side at the table. "I will see you, and five hundred dollars better," said Smith, as his servant Jerry approached the table. "What price do you set on that boy?" asked Johnson, as he took a roll of bills from his pocket. "He will bring a thousand dollars, any day, in the New Orleans market," replied Smith. "Then you bet the whole of the boy, do you?" "Yes." "I call you, then," said Johnson, at the same time spreading his cards out upon the table. "You have beat me," said Smith, as soon as he saw the cards. Jerry, who was standing on top of the table, with the bank notes and silver dollars round his feet, was now ordered to descend from the table. "You will not forget that you belong to me," said Johnson, as the young slave was stepping from the table to a chair. "No, sir," replied the chattel. "Now go back to your bed, and be up in time tomorrow morning to brush my clothes and clean my boots, do you hear?" "Yes, sir," responded Jerry, as he wiped the tears from his eyes.

Smith took from his pocket the bill of sale and handed it to Johnson; at the same time saying, "I claim the right of redeeming that boy, Mr. Johnson. My father gave him to me when I came of age, and I promised not to part with him." "Most certainly, sir, the boy shall be yours, whenever you hand me over a cool thousand," replied Johnson. The next morning, as the passengers were assembling in the breakfast saloons and upon the guards of the vessel, and the servants were seen running about waiting upon or looking for their masters, poor Jerry was entering his new master's stateroom with his boots. "Who do you belong to?" said a gentleman to an old black man, who came along leading a fine dog that he had been feeding. "When I went to sleep last night, I belonged to Governor Lucas; but I understand dat he is bin gambling all night, so I don't know who owns me dis morning." Such is the uncertainty of a slave's position. He goes to bed at night the property of the man with whom he has lived for years, and gets up in the morning the slave of someone whom he has never seen before! To behold five or six tables in a steamboat's cabin, with half-a-dozen men playing at cards, and money, pistols, bowie-knives, &c. all in confusion on the tables, is what may be seen at almost any time on the Mississippi river.

On the fourth day, while at Natchez, taking in freight and passengers, Walker, who had been on shore to see some of his old customers, returned, accompanied by a tall, thin-faced man, dressed in black, with a white neckcloth, which immediately proclaimed him to be a clergyman. "I want a good, trusty woman for house service," said the stranger, as they entered the cabin where Walker's slaves were kept. "Here she is, and no mistake," replied the trader. "Stand up, Currer, my gal; here's a gentleman who wishes to see if you will suit him." Althesa clung to her mother's side, as the latter rose from her seat. "She is a rare cook, a good washer, and will suit you to a T, I am sure." "If you buy me, I hope you will buy my daughter too," said the woman, in rather an excited manner. "I only want one for my own use, and would not need another," said the man in black, as he and the trader left the room. Walker and the parson went into the saloon, talked over the matter, the bill of sale was made out, the money paid over, and the clergyman left, with the understanding that the woman should be delivered to him at his house. It seemed as if poor Althesa would have wept herself to death, for the first two days after her mother had been torn from her side by the hand of the ruthless trafficker in human flesh. On the arrival of the boat at Baton Rouge, an additional number of passengers

were taken on board; and, amongst them, several persons who had been attending the races. Gambling and drinking were now the order of the day. Just as the ladies and gentlemen were assembling at the supper-table, the report of a pistol was heard in the direction of the Social Hall, which caused great uneasiness to the ladies, and took the gentlemen to that part of the cabin. However, nothing serious had occurred. A man at one of the tables where they were gambling had been seen attempting to conceal a card in his sleeve, and one of the party seized his pistol and fired; but fortunately the barrel of the pistol was knocked up, just as it was about to be discharged, and the ball passed through the upper deck, instead of the man's head, as intended. Order was soon restored; all went on well the remainder of the night, and the next day, at ten o'clock, the boat arrived at New Orleans, and the passengers went to the hotels and the slaves to the market!

Our eyes are yet on Afric's shores,
Her thousand wrongs we still deplore;
We see the grim slave trader there;
We hear his fettered victim's prayer;
And hasten to the sufferer's aid,
Forgetful of *our own 'slave trade.'*

The Ocean 'Pirate's' fiend like form
Shall sink beneath the vengeance-storm;
His heart of steel shall quake before
The battle-din and havoc roar:
The knave shall die, the Law hath said,
While it protects our own *'slave trade.'*

What earthly eye presumes to scan
The wily Proteas-heart[1] of man?—
What potent hand will e'er unroll
The mantled treachery of his soul!—
O where is he who hath surveyed
The horrors of *our own 'slave trade'?*

There is an eye that wakes in light,
There is a hand of peerless might;
Which, soon or late, shall yet assail
And rend dissimulation's veil:
Which *will* unfold the masquerade
Which justifies *our own 'slave trade.'*

---

[1]   *Proteas-heart*   Changeable heart. In Greek mythology, Proteus is a sea-god with the ability to change his physical form to elude capture.

CHAPTER 3: THE NEGRO CHASE

We shall now return to Natchez, where we left Currer in the hands of the Methodist parson. For many years, Natchez has enjoyed a notoriety for the inhumanity and barbarity of its inhabitants, and the cruel deeds perpetrated there, which have not been equalled in any other city in the Southern States. The following advertisements, which we take from a newspaper published in the vicinity, will show how they catch their negroes who believe in the doctrine that "all men are created free."

NEGRO DOGS.—The undersigned, having bought the entire pack of negro dogs (of the Hay and Allen stock), *he now proposes to catch runaway negroes*. His charges will be three dollars a day for hunting, and fifteen dollars for catching a runaway. He resides three and one half miles north of Livingston, near the lower Jones' Bluff Road.

WILLIAM GAMBREL.

Nov. 6, 1845.

NOTICE.—The subscriber, living on Carroway Lake, on Hoe's Bayou, in Carroll parish, sixteen miles on the road leading from Bayou Mason to Lake Providence, is ready with a pack of dogs to hunt runaway negroes at any time. These dogs are well trained, and are known throughout the parish. Letters addressed to me at Providence will secure immediate attention. My terms are five dollars per day for hunting the trails, whether the negro is caught or not. Where a twelve hours' trail is shown, and the negro not taken, no charge is made. For taking a negro, twenty-five dollars, and no charge made for hunting.

JAMES W. HALL.

Nov. 26, 1847.

These dogs will attack a negro at their master's bidding and cling to him as the bull-dog will cling to a beast. Many are the speculations, as to whether the negro will be secured alive or dead, when these dogs once get on his track. A slave hunt took place near Natchez, a few days after Currer's arrival, which was calculated to give her no favourable opinion of the people. Two slaves had run off owing to severe punishment. The dogs were put upon their trail. The slaves went into the swamps, with the hope that the dogs when put on their scent would be unable to follow them through the water. The dogs soon took to the swamp, which lies between the highlands, which was now covered with water, waist deep: here these faithful animals, *swimming* nearly all the time, followed the zigzag course, the tortuous twistings and windings of these two fugitives, who, it was afterwards discovered, were lost; sometimes scenting the tree wherein they had found a temporary refuge from the mud and water; at other places where the deep mud had pulled off a shoe, and they had not taken time to put it on again. For two hours and a half, for four or five miles, did men and dogs wade through this bushy, dismal swamp, surrounded with grim-visaged alligators, who seemed to look on with jealous eye at this encroachment of their hereditary domain; now losing the trail—then slowly and dubiously taking it off again, until they triumphantly threaded it out, bringing them back to the river, where it was found that the negroes had crossed their own trail, near the place of starting. In the meantime a heavy shower had taken place, putting out the trail. The negroes were now at least four miles ahead.

It is well known to hunters that it requires the keenest scent and best blood to overcome such obstacles, and yet these persevering and sagacious animals conquered every difficulty. The slaves now made a straight course for the Baton Rouge and Bayou Sara road, about four miles distant.

Feeling hungry now, after their morning walk, and perhaps thirsty, too, they went about half a mile off the road, and ate a good, hearty, substantial breakfast. Negroes must eat, as well as other people, but the dogs will tell on them. Here, for a moment, the dogs are at fault, but soon unravel the mystery, and bring them back to the road again; and now what before was wonderful, becomes almost a miracle. Here, in this common highway—the thoroughfare for the whole country around—through mud and through mire, meeting waggons and teams, and different solitary wayfarers, and, what above all is most astonishing, actually running through a gang of negroes, their favourite game, who were working on the road, they pursue the track of the two negroes; they even ran for eight miles to the very edge of the plain—the slaves near them for the last mile. At first they would fain believe it some hunter chasing deer. Nearer and nearer the whimpering pack presses on; the delusion begins to dispel; all at once the truth flashes upon them like a glare of light; their hair stands on end; 'tis Tabor with his dogs. The scent becomes warmer and warmer. What was an irregular cry, now deepens into one ceaseless roar, as the relentless pack rolls on after its human prey. It puts one in mind of Actæon and his dogs.[1] They grow desperate and leave the road, in the vain hope of shaking them off. Vain hope, indeed! The momentary cessation only adds new zest to the chase. The cry grows louder and louder; the yelp grows short and quick, sure indication that the game is at hand. It is a perfect rush upon the part of the hunters, while the negroes call upon their weary and jaded limbs to do their best, but they falter and stager beneath them. The breath of the hounds is almost upon their very heels, and yet they have a vain hope of escaping these sagacious animals. They can run no longer; the dogs are upon them; they hastily attempt to climb a tree, and as the last one is nearly out of reach, the catch-dog seizes him by the leg, and brings him to the ground; he sings out lustily and the dogs are called off. After this man was secured, the one in the tree was ordered to come down; this, however, he refused to do, but a gun being pointed at him, soon caused him to change his mind. On reaching the ground, the fugitive made one more bound, and the chase again commenced. But it was of no use to run and he soon yielded. While being tied, he committed an unpardonable offence: he resisted, and for that he must be made an example on their arrival home. A mob was collected together, and a Lynch court[2] was held, to determine what was best to be done with the negro who had had the impudence to raise his hand against a white man. The Lynch court decided that the negro should be burnt at the stake. A Natchez newspaper, the *Free Trader*, giving an account of it says,

"The body was taken and chained to a tree immediately on the banks of the Mississippi, on what is called Union Point. Faggots[3] were then collected and piled around him, to which he appeared quite indifferent. When the work was completed, he was asked what he had to say. He then warned all to take example by him, and asked the prayers of all around; he then called for a drink of water, which was handed to him; he drank it, and said, 'Now set fire—I am ready to go in peace!' The torches were lighted, and placed in the pile, which soon ignited. He watched unmoved the curling flame that grew, until it began to entwine itself around and feed upon his body; then he sent forth cries of agony painful to the ear, begging someone to blow his brains out; at the same time surging with almost superhuman strength, until the staple with which the chain was fastened to the tree (not being well secured) drew out, and he leaped from the burning pile. At that moment the sharp ringing of several rifles was heard: the body of the negro fell a corpse on the ground. He was picked up by some two or three, and again thrown into the fire, and consumed, not a vestige remaining to show that such a being ever existed."

Nearly 4,000 slaves were collected from the plantations in the neighbourhood to witness this scene. Numerous speeches were made by the magistrates and ministers of religion to the large concourse of slaves, warning them, and telling them that the same fate awaited them, if they should prove rebellious to their owners. There are hundreds of negroes who run away and live in the woods. Some take refuge in the swamps, because they are less frequented by human beings. A Natchez newspaper gave the following account of the hiding-place of a slave who had been captured:

A runaway's den was discovered on Sunday, near the Washington Spring, in a little patch of woods, where it had been for several months so artfully concealed under ground, that it was detected only by accident, though in sight of two or three houses, and near the road and fields where there has been constant daily passing. The entrance was concealed by a pile of pine straw, representing a hog-bed, which being removed, discovered a trap-door and steps that led to a room about six feet square, comfortably ceiled with plank, containing a small fire place, the flue of which was ingeniously conducted above ground and concealed by the straw. The inmates took the alarm, and made their escape; *but Mr. Adams and his excellent dogs being put upon the trail, soon run down and secured one of them*, which proved to be a negro-fellow who

---

[1] *Actæon and his dogs* In Greek mythology, Actæon was a hunter who accidentally saw the goddess Artemis bathing. Angered, she turned him into a stag, and his own hounds chased him down and tore him apart.

[2] *Lynch court* Group of people who mete out extralegal punishment, especially execution, which is then carried out by a mob outside official legal channels.

[3] *Faggots* Sticks bundled for use as kindling.

had been out about a year. He stated that the other occupant was a woman, who had been a runaway a still longer time. In the den was found a quantity of meal, bacon, corn, potatoes, &c. and various cooking utensils and wearing apparel.—*Vicksburgh Sentinel*, Dec. 6th, 1838.

Currer was one of those who witnessed the execution of the slave at the stake, and it gave her no very exalted opinion of the people of the cotton growing district.

Chapter 4: The Quadroon's Home

How sweetly on the hill-side sleeps
   The sunlight with its quickening rays!
The verdant trees that crown the steeps,
   Grow greener in its quivering blaze.[1]

About three miles from Richmond is a pleasant plain, with here and there a beautiful cottage surrounded by trees so as scarcely to be seen. Among them was one far retired from the public roads, and almost hidden among the trees. It was a perfect model of rural beauty. The piazzas that surrounded it were covered with clematis and passion flower. The pride of China mixed its oriental looking foliage with the majestic magnolia, and the air was redolent with the fragrance of flowers, peeping out of every nook and nodding upon you with a most unexpected welcome. The tasteful hand of art had not learned to imitate the lavish beauty and harmonious disorder of nature, but they lived together in loving amity, and spoke in accordant tones. The gateway rose in a gothic arch, with graceful tracery in iron work, surmounted by a cross, round which fluttered and played the mountain fringe, that lightest and most fragile of vines. This cottage was hired by Horatio Green for Clotel, and the quadroon girl soon found herself in her new home.

The tenderness of Clotel's conscience, together with the care her mother had with her and the high value she placed upon virtue, required an outward marriage; though she well knew that a union with her proscribed race was unrecognized by law, and therefore the ceremony would give her no legal hold on Horatio's constancy. But her high poetic nature regarded reality rather than the semblance of things; and when he playfully asked how she could keep him if he wished to run away, she replied, "If the mutual love we have for each other, and the dictates of your own conscience do not cause you to remain my husband, and your affections fall from me, I would not, if I could, hold you by a single fetter." It was indeed a marriage sanctioned by heaven, although unrecognised on earth. There the young couple lived secluded from the world, and passed their time as happily as circumstances would permit. It was Clotel's wish that Horatio should purchase her mother and sister, but the young man pleaded that he was unable, owing to the fact that he had not come into possession of his share of property, yet he promised that when he did, he would seek them out and purchase them. Their first-born was named Mary, and her complexion was still lighter than her mother. Indeed she was not darker than other white children. As the child grew older, it more and more resembled its mother. The iris of her large dark eye had the melting mezzotinto,[2] which remains the last vestige of African ancestry, and gives that plaintive expression, so often observed, and so appropriate to that docile and injured race. Clotel was still happier after the birth of her dear child; for Horatio, as might have been expected, was often absent day and night with his friends in the city, and the edicts of society had built up a wall of separation between the quadroon and them. Happy as Clotel was in Horatio's love, and surrounded by an outward environment of beauty, so well adapted to her poetic spirit, she felt these incidents with inexpressible pain. For herself she cared but little; for she had found a sheltered home in Horatio's heart, which the world might ridicule, but had no power to profane. But when she looked at her beloved Mary, and reflected upon the unavoidable and dangerous position which the tyranny of society had awarded her, her soul was filled with anguish. The rare loveliness of the child increased daily, and was evidently ripening into most marvellous beauty. The father seemed to rejoice in it with unmingled pride; but in the deep tenderness of the mother's eye, there was an indwelling sadness that spoke of anxious thoughts and fearful foreboding.

---

[1] *How sweetly ... blaze* First four lines of William H. Burleigh's poem "A Summer Morning in the Country" (1846).

[2] *mezzotinto* Italian for "half-tone," a gradient, in-between shade.

Clotel now urged Horatio to remove to France or England, where both her and her child would be free, and where colour was not a crime. This request excited but little opposition, and was so attractive to his imagination, that he might have overcome all intervening obstacles, had not "a change come over the spirit of his dreams." He still loved Clotel; but he was now becoming engaged in political and other affairs which kept him oftener and longer from the young mother; and ambition to become a statesman was slowly gaining the ascendancy over him.

Among those on whom Horatio's political success most depended was a very popular and wealthy man, who had an only daughter. His visits to the house were at first purely of a political nature; but the young lady was pleasing, and he fancied he discovered in her a sort of timid preference for himself. This excited his vanity, and awakened thoughts of the great worldly advantages connected with a union. Reminiscences of his first love kept these vague ideas in check for several months; for with it was associated the idea of restraint. Moreover, Gertrude, though inferior in beauty, was yet a pretty contrast to her rival. Her light hair fell in silken ringlets down her shoulders, her blue eyes were gentle though inexpressive, and her healthy cheeks were like opening rosebuds. He had already become accustomed to the dangerous experiment of resisting his own inward convictions; and this new impulse to ambition, combined with the strong temptation of variety in love, met the ardent young man weakened in moral principle, and unfettered by laws of the land. The change wrought upon him was soon noticed by Clotel.

from CHAPTER 5: THE SLAVE MARKET

What! mothers from their children riven!
   What! God's own image bought and sold!
Americans to market driven,
   And barter'd as the brute for gold.[1]—*Whittier*

Not far from Canal-street, in the city of New Orleans, stands a large two story flat building surrounded by a stone wall twelve feet high, the top of which is covered with bits of glass, and so constructed as to prevent even the possibility of any one's passing over it without sustaining great injury. Many of the rooms resemble cells in a prison. In a small room near the "office" are to be seen any number of iron collars, hobbles, handcuffs, thumbscrews, cowhides, whips, chains, gags, and yokes. A back yard enclosed by a high wall looks something like the playground attached to one of our large New England schools, and in which are rows of benches and swings. Attached to the back premises is a good-sized kitchen, where two old negresses are at work, stewing, boiling, and baking, and occasionally wiping the sweat from their furrowed and swarthy brows.

The slave-trader Walker, on his arrival in New Orleans, took up his quarters at this slave pen with his gang of human cattle; and the morning after, at ten o'clock, they were exhibited for sale. There, first of all, was the beautiful Althesa, whose pale countenance and dejected look told how many sad hours she had passed since parting with her mother at Natchez. There was a poor woman who had been separated from her husband and five children. Another woman, whose looks and manner were expressive of deep anguish, sat by her side. There, too, was "Uncle Geemes," with his whiskers off, his face shaved clean, and the grey hair plucked out, and ready to be sold for ten years younger than he was. Toby was also there, with his face shaved and greased, ready for inspection. The examination commenced, and was carried on in a manner calculated to shock the feelings of any one not devoid of the milk of human kindness. "What are you wiping your eyes for?" inquired a fat, red-faced man, with a white hat set on one side of his head, and a cigar in his mouth, of a woman who sat on one of the stools. "I s'pose I have been crying." "Why do you cry?" "Because I have left my man behind." "Oh, if I buy you I will furnish you with a better man than you left. I have lots of young bucks on my farm." "I don't want, and will never have, any other man," replied the woman. "What's your name?" asked a man in a straw hat of a tall negro man, who stood with his arms folded across his breast, and leaning against the wall. "My name is Aaron, sir." "How old are you?" "Twenty-five." "Where were you raised?" "In old Virginny, sir." "How many men have owned you?" "Four." "Do you enjoy good health?" "Yes, sir." "How long did you live with your first owner?"

---

[1]   *What ... gold* Lines 21–24 in John Greenleaf Whittier's poem "Stanzas," first published in *Voices of Freedom* (1846).

"Twenty years." "Did you ever run away?" "No, sir." "Did you ever strike your master." "No, sir." "Were you ever whipped much?" "No, sir, I s'pose I did not deserve it." "How long did you live with your second master?" "Ten years, sir." "Have you a good appetite?" "Yes, sir." "Can you eat your allowance?" "Yes, sir, when I can get it." "What were you employed at in Virginia?" "I worked in de terbacar feel." "In the tobacco field?" "Yes, sir." "How old did you say you were?" "I will be twenty-five if I live to see next sweet potater-digging time." "I am a cotton planter, and if I buy you, you will have to work in the cotton field. My men pick one hundred and fifty pounds a day, and the women one hundred and forty, and those who fail to pick their task receive five stripes from the cat[1] for each pound that is wanting. Now, do you think you could keep up with the rest of the hands?" "I don't know, sir, I 'spec I'd have to." "How long did you live with your third master?" "Three years, sir." "Why, this makes you thirty-three, I thought you told me you was only twenty-five?" Aaron now looked first at the planter, then at the trader, and seemed perfectly bewildered. He had forgotten the lesson given him by Pompey as to his age, and the planter's circuitous talk (doubtless to find out the slave's real age) had the negro off his guard. "I must see your back, so as to know how much you have been whipped, before I think of buying," said the planter. Pompey, who had been standing by during the examination, thought that his services were now required, and stepping forward with a degree of officiousness, said to Aaron, "Don't you hear de gentman tell you he want to zamon your limbs. Come, unharness yeself, old boy, an don't be standing dar." Aaron was soon examined and pronounced "sound"; yet the conflicting statement about the age was not satisfactory.

Fortunate for Althesa she was spared the pain of undergoing such an examination, Mr. Crawford, a teller in one of the banks, had just been married, and wanted a maid-servant for his wife; and passing through the market in the early part of the day, was pleased with the young slave's appearance and purchased her, and in his dwelling the quadroon found a much better home than often falls to the lot of a slave sold in the New Orleans market. The heart-rending and cruel traffic in slaves which has been so often described, is not confined to any particular class of persons. No one forfeits his or her character or standing in society, by buying or selling slaves; or even raising slaves for the market. The precise number of slaves carried from the slave-raising to the slave-consuming states,[2] we have no means of knowing. But it must be very great, as more than forty thousand were sold and taken out of the state of Virginia in one year. Known to God only is the amount of human agony and suffering which sends its cry from the slave markets and negro pens, unheard and unheeded by man, up to his ear; mothers weeping for their children, breaking the night-silence with the shrieks of their breaking hearts. From some you will hear the burst of bitter lamentation, while from others the loud hysteric laugh, denoting still deeper agony. Most of them leave the market for cotton or rice plantations,

> Where the slave-whip ceaseless swings,
> Where the noisome insect stings,
> Where the fever demon strews
> Poison with the falling dews,
> Where the sickly sunbeams glare
> Through the hot and misty air.[3]

…

from CHAPTER 15: TODAY A MISTRESS, TOMORROW A SLAVE

> I promised thee a sister tale
> Of man's perfidious cruelty;
> Come, then, and hear what cruel wrong
> Befel the dark ladie.[4]—*Coleridge*

Let us return for a moment to the home of Clotel. While she was passing lonely and dreary hours with none but her darling child, Horatio Green was trying

---

1 *the cat* Cat-o'-nine-tails; whip made of nine knotted ropes.

2 *slave-raising … states* Slave states in the Deep South had a shortage of labor, whereas the slave states further to the north, because they raised crops that were less labor-intensive, had an excess, leading to an active domestic slave trade from region to region.

3 *Where the slave-whip … misty air* Lines 3–8 in John Greenleaf Whittier's poem "The Farewell of a Virginia Slave Mother to Her Daughters Sold into Southern Bondage" (1838).

4 *I promised … dark ladie* Final stanza of Samuel Taylor Coleridge's poem "Introduction to the Tale of the Dark Ladie" (1799).

to find relief in that insidious enemy of man, the intoxicating cup. Defeated in politics, forsaken in love by his wife, he seemed to have lost all principle of honour, and was ready to nerve himself up to any deed, no matter how unprincipled. Clotel's existence was now well known to Horatio's wife, and both her and her father demanded that the beautiful quadroon and her child should be sold and sent out of the state. To this proposition he at first turned a deaf ear; but when he saw that his wife was about to return to her father's roof, he consented to leave the matter in the hands of his father-in-law. The result was, that Clotel was immediately sold to the slave-trader, Walker, who, a few years previous, had taken her mother and sister to the far South. But, as if to make her husband drink of the cup of humiliation to its very dregs, Mrs. Green resolved to take his child under her own roof for a servant. Mary was, therefore, put to the meanest work that could be found, and although only ten years of age, she was often compelled to perform labour, which, under ordinary circumstances, would have been thought too hard for one much older. One condition of the sale of Clotel to Walker was, that she should be taken out of the state, which was accordingly done. Most quadroon women who are taken to the lower countries to be sold are either purchased by gentlemen for their own use, or sold for waiting-maids; and Clotel, like her sister, was fortunate enough to be bought for the latter purpose. The town of Vicksburgh stands on the left bank of the Mississippi, and is noted for the severity with which slaves are treated. It was here that Clotel was sold to Mr. James French, a merchant.

Mrs. French was severe in the extreme to her servants. Well dressed, but scantily fed, and overworked were all who found a home with her. The quadroon had been in her new home but a short time ere she found that her situation was far different from what it was in Virginia. What social virtues are possible in a society of which injustice is the primary characteristic? in a society which is divided into two classes, masters and slaves? Every married woman in the far South looks upon her husband as unfaithful, and regards every quadroon servant as a rival. Clotel had been with her new mistress but a few days, when she was ordered to cut off her long hair. The negro, constitutionally, is fond of dress and outward appearance. He that has

short, woolly hair, combs it and oils it to death. He that has long hair, would sooner have his teeth drawn than lose it. However painful it was to the quadroon, she was soon seen with her hair cut as short as any of the full-blooded negroes in the dwelling.

Even with her short hair, Clotel was handsome. Her life had been a secluded one, and though now nearly thirty years of age, she was still beautiful. At her short hair, the other servants laughed, "Miss Clo needn't strut round so big, she got short nappy har well as I," said Nell, with a broad grin that showed her teeth. "She tinks she white, when she come here wid dat long har of hers," replied Mill. "Yes," continued Nell; "missus make her take down her wool so she no put it up today."

The fairness of Clotel's complexion was regarded with envy as well by the other servants as by the mistress herself. This is one of the hard features of slavery. Today the woman is mistress of her own cottage; tomorrow she is sold to one who aims to make her life as intolerable as possible. And be it remembered, that the house servant has the best situation which a slave can occupy. Some American writers have tried to make the world believe that the condition of the labouring classes of England is as bad as the slaves of the United States.

The English labourer may be oppressed, he may be cheated, defrauded, swindled, and even starved; but it is not slavery under which he groans. He cannot be sold; in point of law he is equal to the prime minister. "It is easy to captivate the unthinking and the prejudiced, by eloquent declamation about the oppression of English operatives being worse than that of American slaves, and by exaggerating the wrongs on one side and hiding them on the other. But all informed and reflecting minds, knowing that bad as are the social evils of England, those of Slavery are immeasurably worse." But the degradation and harsh treatment that Clotel experienced in her new home was nothing compared with the grief she underwent at being separated from her dear child. Taken from her without scarcely a moment's warning, she knew not what had become of her. The deep and heartfelt grief of Clotel was soon perceived by her owners, and fearing that her refusal to take food would cause her death, they resolved to sell her. Mr. French found no difficulty in getting a purchaser for the quadroon woman, for such are usually the most marketable kind of property. Clotel was sold at private sale to a young man for a housekeeper; but even he had missed his aim.

…

from CHAPTER 17: RETALIATION

I had a dream, a happy dream;
    I thought that I was free:
That in my own bright land again
    A home there was for me.[1]

With the deepest humiliation Horatio Green saw the daughter of Clotel, his own child, brought into his dwelling as a servant. His wife felt that she had been deceived, and determined to punish her deceiver. At first Mary was put to work in the kitchen, where she met with little or no sympathy from the other slaves, owing to the fairness of her complexion. The child was white, what should be done to make her look like other negroes, was the question Mrs. Green asked herself. At last she hit upon a plan: there was a garden at the back of the house over which Mrs. Green could look from her parlour window. Here the white slave-girl was put to work, without either bonnet or handkerchief upon her head. A hot sun poured its broiling rays on the naked face and neck of the girl, until she sank down in the corner of the garden, and was actually broiled to sleep. "Dat little nigger ain't working a bit, missus," said Dinah to Mrs. Green, as she entered the kitchen.

"She's lying in the sun, seasoning; she will work better by and by," replied the mistress. "Dees white niggers always tink dey sef good as white folks," continued the cook. "Yes, but we will teach them better; won't we, Dinah?" "Yes, missus, I don't like dees mularter niggers, no how; dey always want to set dey sef up for something big." The cook was black, and was not without that prejudice which is to be found among the negroes, as well as among the whites of the Southern States. The sun had the desired effect, for in less than a fortnight Mary's fair complexion had disappeared, and she was but little whiter than any other mulatto children running about the yard. But the close resemblance between the father and child annoyed the mistress more than the mere whiteness of the child's complexion. Horatio made proposition after proposition to have the girl sent away, for every time he beheld her countenance it reminded him of the happy days he had spent with Clotel. But his wife had commenced, and determined to carry out her unfeeling and fiendish designs. This child was not only white, but she was the granddaughter of Thomas Jefferson, the man who, when speaking against slavery in the legislature of Virginia, said,

The whole commerce between master and slave is a perpetual exercise of the most boisterous passions; *the most unremitting despotism on the one part, and degrading submission on the other.* With what execration should the statesman be loaded who, permitting one half the citizens thus to trample on the rights of the other, transforms those into despots and these into enemies, destroys the morals of the one part, and the *amor patriæ*[2] of the other! For if the slave can have a country in this world, it must be any other in preference to that in which he is born to live and labour for another; in which he must lock up the faculties of his nature, contribute as far as depends on his individual endeavours to the evanishment of the human race, or entail his own miserable condition on the endless generations proceeding from him. And can the liberties of a nation be thought secure when we have removed their only firm basis, a conviction in the minds of the people that these liberties are the gift of God? that they are not to be violated but with his wrath? Indeed, I tremble for my country when I reflect that God is just; that his justice cannot sleep for ever; that, considering numbers, nature, and natural means only, a revolution of the wheel of fortune, an exchange of situation, is among possible events; that it may become probable by supernatural interference! The Almighty has no attribute which can take side with us in such a contest.[3]

.   .   .   .

---

1   *I had a dream … for me*   First lines of William Caroll's song "The Slave's Dream" (1852).

2   *amor patriæ*   Latin: love of one's country.

3   *The whole commerce … contest*   From Thomas Jefferson's *Notes on the State of Virginia* (1785). This passage was not in fact spoken in the Virginia legislature.

What an incomprehensible machine is man! Who can endure toil, famine, stripes,[1] imprisonment, and death itself, in vindication of his own liberty, and the next moment be deaf to all those motives, whose power supported him through his trial, and inflict on his fellow men a bondage, *one hour of which is fraught with more misery than ages of that which he rose in rebellion to oppose!* But we must wait with patience the workings of an overruling Providence,[2] and hope that that is preparing the deliverance of these our suffering brethren. When the measure of their tears shall be full—when their tears shall have involved heaven itself in darkness—doubtless a God of justice will awaken to their distress, and by diffusing light and liberality among their oppressors, or at length by his exterminating thunder, manifest his attention to things of this world, and that they are not left to the guidance of blind fatality.[3]

The same man, speaking of the probability that the slaves might some day attempt to gain their liberties by a revolution, said,

> I tremble for my country, when I recollect that God is just, and that His justice cannot sleep for ever. The Almighty has no attribute that can take sides with us in such a struggle.[4]

But, sad to say, Jefferson is not the only American statesman who has spoken high-sounding words in favour of freedom, and then left his own children to die slaves.

...

from CHAPTER 19: ESCAPE OF CLOTEL

The fetters galled my weary soul—
    A soul that seemed but thrown away;
I spurned the tyrant's base control,
    Resolved at least the man to play.[5]

---

[1] *stripes* Marks left on the skin by a whip.

[2] *Providence* God's will; divine intervention.

[3] *What an ... fatality* From Thomas Jefferson's 26 June 1786 letter to French politician and writer Jean-Nicolas Démeunier.

[4] *I tremble ... struggle* These statements are drawn from *Notes on the State of Virginia* (1785), quoted above.

[5] *The fetters ... to play* Lines 1–4 of Elizur Wright's song "The Fugitive Slave to the Christian" (1844).

No country has produced so much heroism in so short a time, connected with escapes from peril and oppression, as has occurred in the United States among fugitive slaves, many of whom show great shrewdness in their endeavours to escape from this land of bondage. A slave was one day seen passing on the high road from a border town in the interior of the state of Virginia to the Ohio river. The man had neither hat upon his head or coat upon his back. He was driving before him a very nice fat pig, and appeared to all who saw him to be a labourer employed on an adjoining farm. "No negro is permitted to go at large in the Slave States without a written pass from his or her master, except on business in the neighbourhood." "Where do you live, my boy?" asked a white man of the slave, as he passed a white house with green blinds. "Jist up de road, sir," was the answer. "That's a fine pig." "Yes, sir, marser like dis choat[6] berry much." And the negro drove on as if he was in great haste. In this way he and the pig travelled more than fifty miles before they reached the Ohio river. Once at the river they crossed over; the pig was sold; and nine days after the runaway slave passed over the Niagara river, and, for the first time in his life, breathed the air of freedom. A few weeks later, and, on the same road, two slaves were seen passing; one was on horseback, the other was walking before him with his arms tightly bound, and a long rope leading from the man on foot to the one on horseback. "Oh, ho, that's a runaway rascal, I suppose," said a farmer, who met them on the road. "Yes, sir, he bin runaway, and I got him fast. Marser will tan his jacket for him nicely when he gets him." "You are a trustworthy fellow, I imagine," continued the farmer. "Oh yes, sir; marser puts a heap of confidence in dis nigger." And the slaves travelled on. When the one on foot was fatigued they would change positions, the other being tied and driven on foot. This they called "ride and tie." After a journey of more than two hundred miles they reached the Ohio river, turned the horse loose, told him to go home, and proceeded on their way to Canada. However they were not to have it all their own way. There are men in the Free States, and especially in the states adjacent to the Slave States, who make their living by catching the runaway slave, and returning him for the reward that may be offered.

---

[6] *choat* Shoat: piglet.

As the two slaves above mentioned were travelling on towards the land of freedom, led by the North Star, they were set upon by four of these slave-catchers, and one of them unfortunately captured. The other escaped. The captured fugitive was put under the torture, and compelled to reveal the name of his owner and his place of residence. Filled with delight, the kidnappers started back with their victim. Overjoyed with the prospect of receiving a large reward, they gave themselves up on the third night to pleasure. They put up at an inn. The negro was chained to the bed-post, in the same room with his captors. At dead of night, when all was still, the slave arose from the floor upon which he had been lying, looked around, and saw that the white men were fast asleep. The brandy punch had done its work. With palpitating heart and trembling limbs he viewed his position. The door was fast, but the warm weather had compelled them to leave the window open. If he could but get his chains off, he might escape through the window to the piazza, and reach the ground by one of the posts that supported the piazza. The sleeper's clothes hung upon chairs by the bedside; the slave thought of the padlock key, examined the pockets and found it. The chains were soon off, and the negro stealthily making his way to the window: he stopped and said to himself, "These men are villains, they are enemies to all who like me are trying to be free. Then why not I teach them a lesson?" He then undressed himself, took the clothes of one of the men, dressed himself in them, and escaped through the window, and, a moment more, he was on the high road to Canada. Fifteen days later, and the writer of this gave him a passage across Lake Erie, and saw him safe in her Britannic Majesty's dominions.

We have seen Clotel sold to Mr. French in Vicksburgh, her hair cut short, and everything done to make her realize her position as a servant. Then we have seen her re-sold, because her owners feared she would die through grief. As yet her new purchaser treated her with respectful gentleness, and sought to win her favour by flattery and presents, knowing that whatever he gave her he could take back again. But she dreaded every moment lest the scene should change, and trembled at the sound of every footfall. At every interview with her new master Clotel stoutly maintained that she had left a husband in Virginia, and would never think of taking another. The gold watch and chain, and other glittering presents which he purchased for her, were all laid aside by the quadroon, as if they were of no value to her. In the same house with her was another servant, a man, who had from time to time hired himself from his master. William was his name. He could feel for Clotel, for he, like her, had been separated from near and dear relatives, and often tried to console the poor woman. One day the quadroon observed to him that her hair was growing out again. "Yes," replied William, "you look a good deal like a man with your short hair." "Oh," rejoined she, "I have often been told that I would make a better looking man than a woman. If I had the money," continued she, "I would bid farewell to this place." In a moment more she feared that she had said too much, and smilingly remarked, "I am always talking nonsense." William was a tall, full-bodied negro, whose very countenance beamed with intelligence. Being a mechanic, he had, by his own industry, made more than what he paid his owner; this he laid aside, with the hope that some day he might get enough to purchase his freedom. He had in his chest one hundred and fifty dollars. His was a heart that felt for others, and he had again and again wiped the tears from his eyes as he heard the story of Clotel as related by herself. "If she can get free with a little money, why not give her what I have?" thought he, and then he resolved to do it. An hour after, he came into the quadroon's room, and laid the money in her lap, and said, "There, Miss Clotel, you said if you had the means you would leave this place; there is money enough to take you to England, where you will be free. You are much fairer than many of the white women of the South, and can easily pass for a free white lady." At first Clotel feared that it was a plan by which the negro wished to try her fidelity to her owner; but she was soon convinced by his earnest manner, and the deep feeling with which he spoke, that he was honest. "I will take the money only on one condition," said she; "and that is, that I effect your escape as well as my own." "How can that be done?" he inquired. "I will assume the disguise of a gentleman and you that of a servant, and we will take passage on a steamboat and go to Cincinnati, and thence to Canada."[1] Here William put in several objections to the plan. He feared detection, and he well knew that, when a slave is once caught when attempting to escape, if returned is sure to be worse treated than before. However, Clotel satisfied him that the plan could be carried out if he would only play his part.

The resolution was taken, the clothes for her disguise procured, and before night everything was in readiness for their departure. That night Mr. Cooper, their master, was to attend a party, and this was their opportunity. William went to the wharf to look out for a boat, and had scarcely reached the landing ere he heard the puffing of a steamer. He returned and reported the fact. Clotel had already packed her trunk, and had only to dress and all was ready. In less than an hour they were on board the boat. Under the assumed name of "Mr. Johnson," Clotel went to the clerk's office and took a private state room for herself, and paid her own and servant's fare. Besides being attired in a neat suit of black, she had a white silk handkerchief tied round her chin, as if she was an invalid. A pair of green glasses covered her eyes; and fearing that she would be talked to too much and thus render her liable to be detected, she assumed to be very ill. On the other hand, William was playing his part well in the servants' hall; he was talking loudly of his master's wealth. Nothing appeared as good on the boat as in his master's fine mansion. "I don't like dees steamboats no how," said William; "I hope when marser goes on a journey agin he will take de carriage and de hosses." Mr. Johnson (for such was the name by which Clotel now went) remained in his room, to avoid, as far as possible, conversation with others. After a passage of seven days they arrived at Louisville, and put up at Gough's Hotel. Here they had to await the departure of another boat for the North. They were now in their most critical position. They were still in a slave state, and John C. Calhoun,[2] a distinguished slave-owner, was a guest at this hotel. They feared, also, that trouble would attend their attempt to leave this place for the North, as all persons taking negroes with them have to give bail that such negroes are not runaway slaves. The law upon this point is very stringent: all steamboats and other public conveyances are liable to a fine for every slave that escapes by them, besides paying the full value for the slave. After a delay of four hours, Mr. Johnson and servant took passage on the steamer Rodolph, for Pittsburgh. It is usual, before the departure of the boats, for an officer to examine every part of the vessel to see that no slave secretes himself on board, "Where are you going?" asked the officer of William, as he was doing his duty on this occasion. "I am going with marser," was the quick reply. "Who is your master?" "Mr. Johnson, sir, a gentleman in the cabin." "You must take him to the office and satisfy that captain that all is right, or you can't go on this boat." William informed his master what the officer had said. The boat was on the eve of going, and no time could be lost, yet they knew not what to do. At last they went to the office, and Mr. Johnson, addressing the captain, said, "I am informed that my boy can't go with me unless I give security that he belongs to me." "Yes," replied the captain, "that is the law." "A very strange law indeed," rejoined Mr. Johnson, "that one can't take his property with him." After a conversation of some minutes, and a plea on the part of Johnson that he did not wish to be delayed owing to his illness, they were permitted to take their passage without farther trouble, and the boat was soon on its way up the river. The fugitives had now passed the Rubicon,[3] and the next place at which they would land would be in a Free State. Clotel called William to her room, and said to him, "We are now free, you can go on your way to Canada, and I shall go to Virginia in search of my daughter." The announcement that she was going to risk her liberty in a Slave State was unwelcome news to William. With all the eloquence he could command, he tried to persuade Clotel that she could not escape detection, and was only throwing her freedom away. But she had counted the cost, and made up her mind for the worst. In return for the

---

1   *disguise ... Canada* The story that follows of William and Clotel's escape is based on the experiences of William and Ellen Craft, who escaped from Macon, Georgia in 1848, though, unlike William and Clotel, the Crafts were a married couple.

2   *John C. Calhoun* Proslavery politician who served in the Senate and was the seventh Vice President of the United States from 1825 to 1832. He owned dozens of slaves in South Carolina.

3   *passed the Rubicon* Expression referring to crossing a boundary or to reaching a point of no return. By crossing the Rubicon—a stream that marked the boundary between Gaul and Italy—with his army in 49 BCE, Julius Caesar effectively declared war against Pompey.

money he had furnished, she had secured for him his liberty, and their engagement was at an end.

After a quick passage the fugitives arrived at Cincinnati, and there separated. William proceeded on his way to Canada, and Clotel again resumed her own apparel, and prepared to start in search of her child. As might have been expected, the escape of those two valuable slaves created no little sensation in Vicksburgh. Advertisements and messages were sent in every direction in which the fugitives were thought to have gone. It was soon, however, known that they had left the town as master and servant; and many were the communications which appeared in the newspapers, in which the writers thought, or pretended, that they had seen the slaves in their disguise. One was to the effect that they had gone off in a chaise;[1] one as master, and the other as servant. But the most probable was an account given by a correspondent of one of the Southern newspapers, who happened to be a passenger in the same steamer in which the slaves escaped, and which we here give:

One bright starlight night, in the month of December last, I found myself in the cabin of the steamer Rodolph, then lying in the port of Vicksburgh, and bound to Louisville. I had gone early on board, in order to select a good berth, and having got tired of reading the papers, amused myself with watching the appearance of the passengers as they dropped in, one after another, and I being a believer in physiognomy,[2] formed my own opinion of their characters.

The second bell rang, and as I yawningly returned my watch to my pocket, my attention was attracted by the appearance of a young man who entered the cabin supported by his servant, a strapping negro.

The man was bundled up in a capacious overcoat; his face was bandaged with a white handkerchief, and its expression entirely hid by a pair of enormous spectacles.

There was something so mysterious and unusual about the young man as he sat restless in the corner, that curiosity led me to observe him more closely.

He appeared anxious to avoid notice, and before the steamer had fairly left the wharf, requested, in a low, womanly voice, to be shown his berth, as he was

an invalid, and must retire early: his name he gave as Mr. Johnson. His servant was called, and he was put quietly to bed. I paced the deck until Tybee light grew dim in the distance, and then went to my berth.

I awoke in the morning with the sun shining in my face; we were then just passing St. Helena. It was a mild beautiful morning, and most of the passengers were on deck, enjoying the freshness of the air, and stimulating their appetites for breakfast. Mr. Johnson soon made his appearance, arrayed as on the night before, and took his seat quietly upon the guard of the boat.

From the better opportunity afforded by daylight, I found that he was a slight built, apparently handsome young man, with black hair and eyes, and of a darkness of complexion that betokened Spanish extraction. Any notice from others seemed painful to him; so to satisfy my curiosity, I questioned his servant, who was standing near, and gained the following information.

His master was an invalid—he had suffered for a long time under a complication of diseases, that had baffled the skill of the best physicians in Mississippi he was now suffering principally with the 'rheumatism,' and he was scarcely able to walk or help himself in any way. He came from Vicksburgh, and was now on his way to Philadelphia, at which place resided his uncle, a celebrated physician, and through whose means he hoped to be restored to perfect health.

This information, communicated in a bold, off-hand manner, enlisted my sympathies for the sufferer, although it occurred to me that he walked rather too gingerly for a person afflicted with so many ailments.

After thanking Clotel for the great service she had done him in bringing him out of slavery, William bade her farewell. The prejudice that exists in the Free States against coloured persons, on account of their colour, is attributable solely to the influence of slavery, and is but another form of slavery itself. And even the slave who escapes from the Southern plantations, is surprised when he reaches the North, at the amount and withering influence of this prejudice. William applied at the railway station for a ticket for the train going to Sandusky, and was told that if he went by that train he would have to ride in the luggage-van. "Why?" asked the astonished negro. "We don't send a Jim Crow carriage but once a day, and that went this morning." The "Jim Crow" carriage is the one in which the blacks

---

[1] *chaise* A light carriage.

[2] *physiognomy* Assessing someone's character based on physical appearance, particularly facial features.

have to ride. Slavery is a school in which its victims learn much shrewdness, and William had been an apt scholar. Without asking any more questions, the negro took his seat in one of the first-class carriages. He was soon seen and ordered out. Afraid to remain in the town longer, he resolved to go by that train; and consequently seated himself on a goods' box in the luggage-van. The train started at its proper time, and all went on well. Just before arriving at the end of the journey, the conductor called on William for his ticket. "I have none," was the reply. "Well, then, you can pay your fare to me," said the officer. "How much is it?" asked the black man. "Two dollars." "What do you charge those in the passenger-carriage?" "Two dollars." "And do you charge me the same as you do those who ride in the best carriages?" asked the negro. "Yes," was the answer. "I shan't pay it," returned the man. "You black scamp, do you think you can ride on this road without paying your fare?" "No, I don't want to ride for nothing; I only want to pay what's right." "Well, launch out two dollars, and that's right." "No, I shan't; I will pay what I ought, and won't pay any more." "Come, come, nigger, your fare and be done with it," said the conductor, in a manner that is never used except by Americans to blacks. "I won't pay you two dollars, and that enough," said William. "Well, as you have come all the way in the luggage-van, pay me a dollar and a half and you may go." "I shan't do any such thing." "Don't you mean to pay for riding?" "Yes, but I won't pay a dollar and a half for riding up here in the freight-van. If you had let me come in the carriage where others ride, I would have paid you two dollars." "Where were you raised? You seem to think yourself as good as white folks." "I want nothing more than my rights." "Well, give me a dollar, and I will let you off." "No, sir, I shan't do it." "What do you mean to do then—don't you wish to pay anything?" "Yes, sir, I want to pay you the full price." "What do you mean by full price?" "What do you charge per hundred-weight for goods?" inquired the negro with a degree of gravity that would have astonished Diogenes[1] himself. "A quarter of a dollar per hundred," answered the conductor. "I weigh just one hundred and fifty pounds," returned William, "and will pay you three-eighths of a dollar." "Do you expect

that you will pay only thirty-seven cents for your ride?" "This, sir, is your own price. I came in a luggage-van, and I'll pay for luggage." After a vain effort to get the negro to pay more, the conductor took the thirty-seven cents, and noted in his cash-book, "Received for one hundred and fifty pounds of luggage, thirty-seven cents." This, reader, is no fiction; it actually occurred in the railway above described.

Thomas Corwin, a member of the American Congress, is one of the blackest white men in the United States. He was once on his way to Congress, and took passage in one of the Ohio river steamers. As he came just at the dinner hour, he immediately went into the dining saloon, and took his seat at the table. A gentleman with his whole party of five ladies at once left the table. "Where is the captain," cried the man in an angry tone. The captain soon appeared, and it was sometime before he could satisfy the old gent. that Governor Corwin was not a nigger. The newspapers often have notices of mistakes made by innkeepers and others who undertake to accommodate the public, one of which we give below.

On the 6th inst.,[2] the Hon. Daniel Webster and family entered Edgartown, on a visit for health and recreation. Arriving at the hotel, without alighting from the coach, the landlord was sent for to see if suitable accommodation could be had. That dignitary appearing, and surveying Mr. Webster, while the hon. senator addressed him, seemed woefully to mistake the dark features of the traveller as he sat back in the corner of the carriage, and to suppose him a *coloured man,* particularly as there were two coloured servants of Mr. W. outside. So he promptly declared that there was no room for him and his family, and he could not be accommodated there—at the same time suggesting that he might perhaps find accommodation at some of the huts "up back," to which he pointed. So deeply did the prejudice of looks possess him, that he appeared not to notice that the stranger introduced himself to him as Daniel Webster, or to be so ignorant as not to have heard of such a personage; and turning away, he expressed to the driver his astonishment that he should bring *black* people there for *him* to take in. It was not till he had been repeatedly assured and made

---

[1] *Diogenes* Diogenes the Cynic (c. 412–323 BCE), a Greek philosopher.

[2] *inst.* Abbreviation for the Latin *instante mense,* meaning "[of] this month."

to understand that the said Daniel Webster was a real live senator of the United States, that he perceived his awkward mistake and the distinguished honour which he and his house were so near missing. …

William found, after all, that liberty in the so-called Free States was more a name than a reality; that prejudice followed the coloured man into every place that he might enter. The temples erected for the worship of the living God are no exception. The finest Baptist church in the city of Boston has the following paragraph in the deed that conveys its seats to pewholders:

> And it is a further condition of these presents, that if the owner or owners of said pew shall determine hereafter to sell the same, it shall first be offered, in writing, to the standing committee of said society for the time being, at such price as might otherwise be obtained for it; and the said committee shall have the right, for ten days after such offer, to purchase said pew for said society, at that price, first deducting therefrom all taxes and assessments on said pew then remaining unpaid. And if the said committee shall not so complete such purchase within said ten days, then the pew may be sold by the owner or owners thereof (after payment of all such arrears) to any one respectable *white person,* but upon the same conditions as are contained in this instrument; and immediate notice of such sale shall be given in writing, by the vendor, to the treasurer of said society.

Such are the conditions upon which the Rowe Street Baptist Church, Boston, disposes of its seats. The writer of this is able to put that whole congregation, minister and all, to flight, by merely putting his coloured face in that church. We once visited a church in New York that had a place set apart for the sons of Ham.[1] It was a dark, dismal looking place in one corner of the gallery, grated in front like a hen-coop, with a black border around it. It had two doors; over one was B. M.—black men; over the other B. W.—black women. …

---

[1] *sons of Ham* I.e., black people. Allusion to the Old Testament story in which Noah curses his son Ham's descendants, saying, "Cursed be Canaan; a servant of servants shall he be unto his brethren" (Genesis 9.25). Nineteenth-century misinterpretations of this story propagated the myth that Ham's descendants were "cursed" with dark skin, in addition to servitude, and this account was frequently used as a biblical justification for slavery.

from CHAPTER 24: THE ARREST

The fearful storm—it threatens lowering,
    Which God in mercy long delays;
Slaves yet may see their masters cowering,
    While whole plantations smoke and blaze![2]
                    Carter.

It was late in the evening when the coach arrived at Richmond, and Clotel once more alighted in her native city. She had intended to seek lodgings somewhere in the outskirts of the town, but the lateness of the hour compelled her to stop at one of the principal hotels for the night. She had scarcely entered the inn, when she recognised among the numerous black servants one to whom she was well known; and her only hope was, that her disguise would keep her from being discovered. The imperturbable calm and entire forgetfulness of self which induced Clotel to visit a place from which she could scarcely hope to escape, to attempt the rescue of a beloved child, demonstrate that over-willingness of woman to carry out the promptings of the finer feelings of her heart. True to woman's nature, she had risked her own liberty for another.

She remained in the hotel during the night, and the next morning, under the plea of illness, she took her breakfast alone. That day the fugitive slave paid a visit to the suburbs of the town, and once more beheld the cottage in which she had spent so many happy hours. It was winter, and the clematis and passionflower were not there; but there were the same walks she had so often pressed with her feet, and the same trees which had so often shaded her as she passed through the garden at the back of the house. Old remembrances rushed upon her memory, and caused her to shed tears freely. Clotel was now in her native-town, and near her daughter; but how could she communicate with her? How could she see her? To have made herself known, would have been a suicidal act; betrayal would have followed, and she arrested. Three days had passed away, and Clotel still remained in the hotel at which she had first put up; and yet she had got no tidings of her child. Unfortunately for Clotel, a disturbance had just

---

[2] *The fearful … blaze* Lines 13–16 of J.G. Carter's "Ye Sons of Freemen," published in Brown's collection *The Anti-Slavery Harp* (1848).

broken out amongst the slave population in the state of Virginia,[1] and all strangers were eyed with suspicion.

The evils consequent on slavery are not lessened by the incoming of one or two rays of light. If the slave only becomes aware of his condition, and conscious of the injustice under which he suffers, if he obtains but a faint idea of these things, he will seize the first opportunity to possess himself of what he conceives to belong to him. The infusion of Anglo-Saxon with African blood has created an insurrectionary feeling among the slaves of America hitherto unknown. Aware of their blood connection with their owners, these mulattoes labour under the sense of their personal and social injuries; and tolerate, if they do not encourage in themselves, low and vindictive passions. On the other hand, the slave owners are aware of their critical position, and are ever watchful, always fearing an outbreak among the slaves.

True, the Free States are equally bound with the Slave States to suppress any insurrectionary movement that may take place among the slaves. The Northern free-men are bound by their constitutional obligations to aid the slaveholder in keeping his slaves in their chains. Yet there are, at the time we write, four millions of bond slaves in the United States. The insurrection to which we now refer was headed by a full-blooded negro, who had been born and brought up a slave. He had heard the twang of the driver's whip, and saw the warm blood streaming from the negro's body; he had witnessed the separation of parents and children, and was made aware, by too many proofs, that the slave could expect no justice at the hand of the slave owner. He went by the name of "Nat Turner." He was a preacher amongst the negroes, and distinguished for his eloquence, respected by the whites, and loved and venerated by the negroes. On the discovery of the plan for the outbreak, Turner fled to the swamps, followed by those who had joined in the insurrection. Here the revolted negroes num-bered some hundreds, and for a time bade defiance to their oppressors. The Dismal Swamps cover many thou-sands of acres of wild land, and a dense forest, with wild animals and insects, such as are unknown in any other part of Virginia. Here runaway negroes usually seek a hiding-place, and some have been known to reside here for years. The revolters were joined by one of these. He was a large, tall, full-blooded negro, with a stern and savage countenance; the marks on his face showed that he was from one of the barbarous tribes in Africa, and claimed that country as his native land; his only cover-ing was a girdle around his loins, made of skins of wild beasts which he had killed; his only token of authority among those that he led, was a pair of epaulettes made from the tail of a fox, and tied to his shoulder by a cord. Brought from the coast of Africa when only fifteen years of age to the island of Cuba, he was smuggled from thence into Virginia. He had been two years in the swamps, and considered it his future home. He had met a negro woman who was also a runaway; and, after the fashion of his native land, had gone through the process of oiling her as the marriage ceremony. They had built a cave on a rising mound in the swamp; this was their home. His name was Picquilo. His only weapon was a sword, made from the blade of a scythe, which he had stolen from a neighbouring plantation. His dress, his character, his manners, his mode of fighting, were all in keeping with the early training he had received in the land of his birth. He moved about with the activity of a cat, and neither the thickness of the trees, nor the depth of the water could stop him. He was a bold, turbulent spirit; and from revenge imbrued his hands in the blood of all the whites he could meet. Hunger, thirst, fatigue, and loss of sleep he seemed made to endure as if by peculiarity of constitution. His air was fierce, his step oblique, his look sanguinary. Such was the character of one of the leaders in the Southampton insurrection. All negroes were arrested who were found beyond their master's threshold, and all strange whites watched with a great degree of alacrity.

Such was the position in which Clotel found affairs when she returned to Virginia in search of her Mary. Had not the slave-owners been watchful of strang-ers, owing to the outbreak, the fugitive could not have escaped the vigilance of the police; for advertisements, announcing her escape and offering a large reward for her arrest, had been received in the city previous to her arrival, and the officers were therefore on the look-out for the runaway slave. It was on the third day, as the qua-droon was seated in her room at the inn, still in the dis-guise of a gentleman, that two of the city officers entered

---

[1]   *a disturbance … Virginia*   Reference to the slave insurrection led by Nat Turner (1800–31) that took place in Southampton County, Virginia, in August 1831. More than fifty white people were killed, and well over a hundred black people were killed in retaliation. The revolt was widely depicted as a massacre in Southern media.

the room, and informed her that they were authorised to examine all strangers, to assure the authorities that they were not in league with the revolted negroes. With trembling heart the fugitive handed the key of her trunk to the officers. To their surprise, they found nothing but woman's apparel in the box, which raised their curiosity, and caused a further investigation that resulted in the arrest of Clotel as a fugitive slave. She was immediately conveyed to prison, there to await the orders of her master. For many days, uncheered by the voice of kindness, alone, hopeless, desolate, she waited for the time to arrive when the chains were to be placed on her limbs, and she returned to her inhuman and unfeeling owner.

The arrest of the fugitive was announced in all the newspapers, but created little or no sensation. The inhabitants were too much engaged in putting down the revolt among the slaves; and although all the odds were against the insurgents, the whites found it no easy matter, with all their caution. Every day brought news of fresh outbreaks. Without scruple and without pity, the whites massacred all blacks found beyond their owners' plantations: the negroes, in return, set fire to houses, and put those to death who attempted to escape from the flames. Thus carnage was added to carnage, and the blood of the whites flowed to avenge the blood of the blacks. These were the ravages of slavery. No graves were dug for the negroes; their dead bodies became food for dogs and vultures, and their bones, partly calcined by the sun, remained scattered about, as if to mark the mournful fury of servitude and lust of power. When the slaves were subdued, except a few in the swamps, bloodhounds were put in this dismal place to hunt out the remaining revolters. ...

"The Death of Clotel," frontispiece engraving from William Wells Brown's *Clotel*, 1853.

CHAPTER 25: DEATH IS FREEDOM

> I asked but freedom, and ye gave
> Chains, and the freedom of the grave.[1]—*Snelling*

There are, in the district of Columbia, several slave prisons, or "negro pens," as they are termed. These prisons are mostly occupied by persons to keep their slaves in, when collecting their gangs together for the New Orleans market. Some of them belong to the government, and one, in particular, is noted for having been the place where a number of free coloured persons have been incarcerated from time to time. In this district is situated the capitol of the United States. Any free coloured persons visiting Washington, if not provided with papers asserting and proving their right to be free, may be arrested and placed in one of these dens. If they succeed in showing that they are free, they are set at liberty, provided they are able to pay the expenses of their arrest and imprisonment; if they cannot pay these expenses, they are sold out. Through this unjust and oppressive law, many persons born in the Free States have been consigned to a life of slavery on the cotton, sugar, or rice plantations of the Southern States. By order of her master, Clotel was removed from Richmond and placed in one of these prisons, to await the sailing of a vessel for New Orleans. The prison in which she was put stands midway between the capitol at Washington and the president's house. Here the fugitive saw nothing but slaves brought in and taken out, to be placed in ships and sent away to the same part of the country to which she herself would soon be compelled to go. She had seen or heard nothing of her daughter while in Richmond, and all hope of seeing her now had fled. If she was carried back to New Orleans, she could expect no mercy from her master.

At the dusk of the evening previous to the day when she was to be sent off, as the old prison was being closed for the night, she suddenly darted past her keeper, and ran for her life. It is not a great distance from the prison to the Long Bridge, which passes from the lower part of the city across the Potomac, to the extensive forests and woodlands of the celebrated Arlington Place,

---

[1] *I asked ... the grave* Slightly altered lines from William J. Snelling's poem "Osceola" (1841), which originally read: "I asked but freedom—and ye gave / The freedom of the lonely grave."

occupied by that distinguished relative and descendant of the immortal Washington, Mr. George W. Curtis.[1] Thither the poor fugitive directed her flight. So unexpected was her escape, that she had quite a number of rods[2] the start before the keeper had secured the other prisoners, and rallied his assistants in pursuit. It was at an hour when, and in a part of the city where, horses could not be readily obtained for the chase; no bloodhounds were at hand to run down the flying woman; and for once it seemed as though there was to be a fair trial of speed and endurance between the slave and the slave-catchers. The keeper and his forces raised the hue and cry on her pathway close behind; but so rapid was the flight along the wide avenue, that the astonished citizens, as they poured forth from their dwellings to learn the cause of alarm, were only able to comprehend the nature of the case in time to fall in with the motley mass in pursuit, (as many a one did that night,) to raise an anxious prayer to heaven, as they refused to join in the pursuit, that the panting fugitive might escape, and the merciless soul dealer for once be disappointed of his prey. And now with the speed of an arrow—having passed the avenue—with the distance between her and her pursuers constantly increasing, this poor hunted female gained the "*Long Bridge*," as it is called, where interruption seemed improbable, and already did her heart begin to beat high with the hope of success. She had only to pass three-fourths of a mile across the bridge, and she could bury herself in a vast forest, just at the time when the curtain of night would close around her, and protect her from the pursuit of her enemies.

But God by his Providence had otherwise determined. He had determined that an appalling tragedy should be enacted that night, within plain sight of the President's house and the capital of the Union, which should be an evidence wherever it should be known, of the unconquerable love of liberty the heart may inherit; as well as a fresh admonition to the slave dealer, of the cruelty and enormity of his crimes. Just as the pursuers crossed the high draw for the passage of sloops, soon after entering upon the bridge, they beheld three men slowly approaching from the Virginia side. They immediately called to them to arrest the fugitive, whom they proclaimed a runaway slave. True to their Virginian instincts as she came near, they formed in line across the narrow bridge, and prepared to seize her. Seeing escape impossible in that quarter, she stopped suddenly, and turned upon her pursuers. On came the profane and ribald crew, faster than ever, already exulting in her capture, and threatening punishment for her flight. For a moment she looked wildly and anxiously around to see if there was no hope of escape. On either hand, far down below, rolled the deep foamy waters of the Potomac, and before and behind the rapidly approaching step and noisy voices of pursuers, showing how vain would be any further effort for freedom. Her resolution was taken. She clasped her *hands* convulsively, and raised *them*, as she at the same time raised her *eyes* towards heaven, and begged for that mercy and compassion there, which had been denied her on earth; and then, with a single bound, she vaulted over the railings of the bridge, and sunk for ever beneath the waves of the river!

Thus died Clotel, the daughter of Thomas Jefferson, a president of the United States; a man distinguished as the author of the Declaration of American Independence, and one of the first statesmen of that country.

Had Clotel escaped from oppression in any other land, in the disguise in which she fled from the Mississippi to Richmond, and reached the United States, no honour within the gift of the American people would have been too good to have been heaped upon the heroic woman. But she was a slave, and therefore out of the pale of their sympathy. They have tears to shed over Greece and Poland; they have an abundance of sympathy for "poor Ireland"; they can furnish a ship of war to convey the Hungarian refugees from a Turkish prison to the "land of the free and home of the brave."[3] They boast that America is the "cradle of liberty"; if it is, I fear they have rocked the child to death.

---

[1]   *Mr. George W. Curtis*   George Washington Parke Custis (1781–1857) was an Arlington (Virginia) plantation owner and a biographer of George Washington.

[2]   *rods*   Units of measurement equivalent to about 5.5 yards.

[3]   *Greece … Poland … poor Ireland … Hungarian refugees … home of the brave*   Americans in the mid-nineteenth century followed closely the revolutions and wars of independence that were taking place in Europe and supported those struggling for freedom, including welcoming refugees from these conflicts. Abolitionists often pointed out the hypocrisy of American support for freedom causes globally, while slavery still flourished within its borders.

The body of Clotel was picked up from the bank of the river, where it had been washed by the strong current, a hole dug in the sand, and there deposited, without either inquest being held over it, or religious service being performed. Such was the life and such the death of a woman whose virtues and goodness of heart would have done honour to one in a higher station of life, and who, if she had been born in any other land but that of slavery, would have been honoured and loved. ... A few days after the death of Clotel, the following poem appeared in one of the newspapers:

> Now, rest for the wretched! the long day is past,
> And night on you prison descendeth at last.
> Now lock up and bolt! Ha, jailor, look there!
> Who flies like a wild bird escaped from the snare?
>   A woman, a slave—up, out in pursuit,
>   While linger some gleams of day!
>   Let thy call ring out!—now a rabble rout
>   Is at thy heels—speed away!
>
> A bold race for freedom!—On, fugitive, on!
> Heaven help but the right, and thy freedom is won.
> How eager she drinks the free air of the plains;
> Every limb, every nerve, every fibre she strains;
>   From Columbia's glorious capitol,
>   Columbia's daughter flees
>   To the sanctuary God has given—
>   The sheltering forest trees.
>
> Now she treads the Long Bridge—joy lighteth her eye—
> Beyond her the dense wood and darkening sky—
> Wild hopes thrill her heart as she neareth the shore:
> O, despair! there are *men* fast advancing before!
>   Shame, shame on their manhood! they hear, they heed
>   The cry, her flight to stay,
>   And like demon forms with their outstretched arms,
>   They wait to seize their prey!
>
> She pauses, she turns! Ah, will she flee back?
> Like wolves, her pursuers howl loud on their track;
> She lifteth to Heaven one look of despair—
> Her anguish breaks forth in one hurried prayer—
>   Hark! her jailor's yell! like a bloodhound's bay
>   On the low night wind it sweeps!
>   Now, death or the chain! to the stream she turns,
>   And she leaps! O God, she leaps!
>
> The dark and the cold, yet merciful wave,
> Receives to its bosom the form of the slave:
> She rises—earth's scenes on her dim vision gleam,
> Yet she struggleth not with the strong rushing stream:
>   And low are the death-cries her woman's heart gives,
>   As she floats adown the river,
>   Faint and more faint grows the drowning voice,
>   And her cries have ceased for ever!
>
> Now back, jailor, back to thy dungeons, again,
> To swing the red lash and rivet the chain!
> The form thou would'st fetter—returned to its God;
>   The universe holdeth no realm of night
>   More drear than her slavery—
>   More merciless fiends than here stayed her flight
>   Joy! the hunted slave is free!
>
> That bond-woman's corse°—let Potomac's proud wave   *corpse*
> Go bear it along *by our Washington's grave*,
> And heave it high up on that hallowed strand,
> *To tell of the freedom he won for our land.*
>   A weak woman's corse, by freemen chased down;
>   Hurrah for our country! hurrah!
>   To freedom she leaped, through drowning and death—
>   Hurrah for our country! hurrah![1]

—1853

---

[1] *Now ... hurrah* Brown here quotes the entire poem "The Escape" (1844) by Sarah J. Clarke, who later published the same poem (omitting the final stanza) under her penname, Grace Greenwood, with the title "The Leap from the Long Bridge" (1851).

In Context

Advertisement for a Lecture by William Wells Brown

This broadside is for a lecture given by Brown in South Shields, England, sometime after 1852 and before Brown returned to the United States in 1854. Notice that the lecture features "Dissolving Views"—a magic lantern show in which one image fades away into the next. Rather than showing images of an idealized America, Brown's slides depict the realities of slavery, with titles such as "The Black Drivers and Their Victim" and "The Red Indian and the Fugitive Slave in the Burning Prairie."

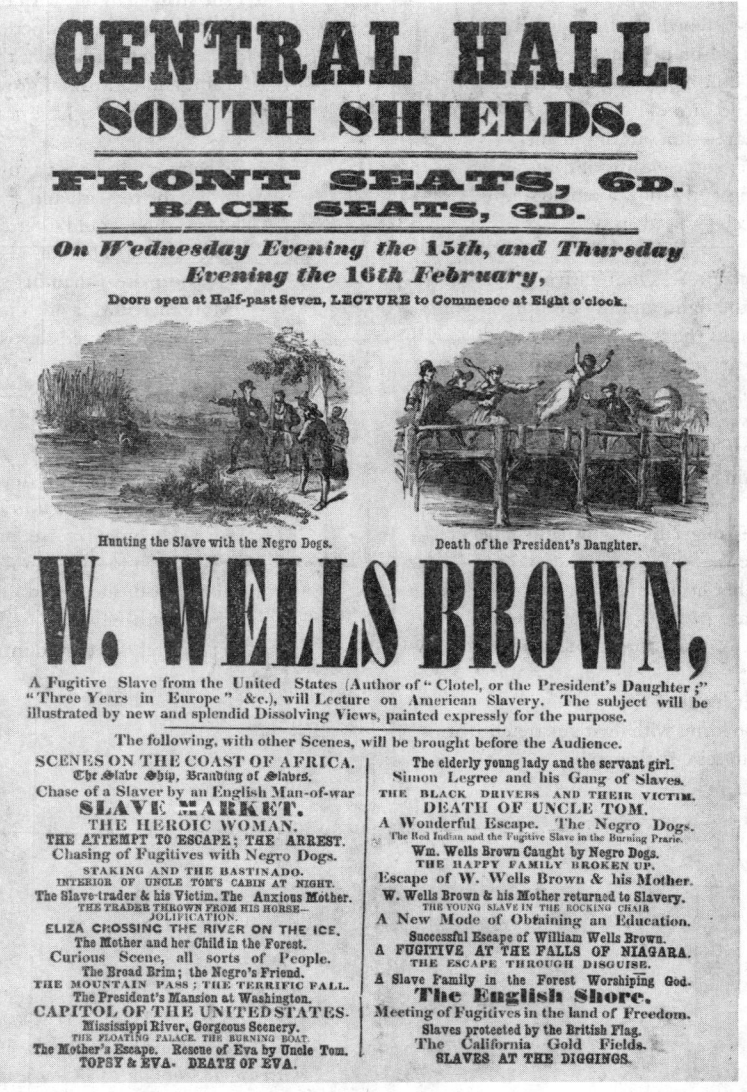

HENRY DAVID THOREAU

1817 – 1862

The works of Henry David Thoreau comprise the most influential outgrowth of the nineteenth-century Transcendentalist movement; from Thoreau's own day through to the twenty-first century they have taken on a life of their own, inspiring passionate engagement among generation after generation of readers. Thoreau's "Resistance to Civil Government" (1849) is a foundational text in the literature of non-violent political resistance. And *Walden; or, Life in the Woods* (1854), which has been read as a poetic meditation on nature and the spiritual life, as a work of social criticism, and as a philosophical tract, remains *the* foundational text of American environmental writing.

Thoreau's public literary career was inextricably entwined with the events of his private life, in which he endeavored to live according to his various dictums of anti-materialistic simplicity and moral integrity. Thoreau was one who set himself apart—in "Civil Disobedience," apart from the political mainstream, and in *Walden*, apart from his human neighbors and from "civilized life," answering what he felt to be an invitation to make his life equal in "simplicity, and … innocence, with Nature herself." But the setting-apart was performed very publicly; that is among the many paradoxes of Thoreau's writings, and of his life, that continue to provoke discussion and to engage readers. "Simplicity! Simplicity! Simplicity!" is his clarion call, yet it is impossible to escape complexity and paradox in his writing.

David Henry Thoreau (he started putting his middle name first shortly after college) was born in 1817 to Cynthia Dunbar—an enthusiastic member of an early antislavery society—and John Thoreau in Concord, Massachusetts. Thoreau spent four years at Harvard College, studying modern European and Indigenous American languages alongside the usual ancient Greek and Latin, after which he found work as a schoolteacher. But following a confrontation with a school board member (who insisted that Thoreau flog his students), he left the position. Sometime after this Thoreau met and befriended local preacher and intellectual Ralph Waldo Emerson. Emerson's *Nature* (1836) had recently energized the Transcendentalist movement with its rousing assertions about the relationship between the human self and the natural world; Emerson took on the younger man as a kind of intellectual protégé, initiating what would become a lifelong friendship. It was Emerson who first encouraged Thoreau to write a journal, a habit he would maintain for the rest of his life.

Massachusetts in the 1830s was simmering with the energy of the Lyceum Movement, which aimed to disseminate knowledge of science, art, literature, and philosophy to a wider and generalized audience. Thoreau was among those invited to lecture at the Concord Lyceum; he gave his first public talk there in 1838; his journal notes on the lecture (the full text of which has not survived) provide an early glimpse into Thoreau's ambitions as a thinker. Entitled "Society," the talk gave voice to his skepticism as to the efficacy of democracy in America, and his resistance to the Aristotelian idea that "man was made for society"; in Thoreau's view, "society was made for man."

In 1838 Thoreau accepted another teaching position—this time at the Concord Academy, where his brother, John Thoreau Jr., soon joined him as a teacher and co-director. Less than two years later, however, John's health had started to fail, and they closed the school. John's death on New Year's Day, 1842 was a devastating blow; Thoreau's first book, *A Week on the Concord and Merrimack Rivers* (1849), is in large part an elegy to John.

Throughout the 1840s, Thoreau contributed numerous poems, essays, and book reviews to *The Dial*, a Transcendentalist periodical launched in 1840 by Emerson, Margaret Fuller, and other local figures.

Some of Thoreau's contributions to the journal were prose meditations on the natural environment; many appeared in the *Dial*'s "Ethnical Scriptures" column, where Thoreau commented on various scriptural writings from Hinduism, Buddhism, Confucianism, and other Eastern traditions. Like Emerson, Thoreau was fascinated by the religions and philosophy of Asia and the Middle East, and ardently read translations of Indian texts such as the *Bhagavad Gita* and the Vedas.

By about 1845, Thoreau had in mind a book that would reflect on a boating journey he and his brother had taken together before John Thoreau Jr.'s death. It was partly in search of writerly solitude that Thoreau made his now-famous move to Walden Pond, a small, fairly secluded lake a couple of miles from the center of the village of Concord. There, on a tract of forested land owned by Emerson, he built a small cabin. This was not the first time he had considered some form of alternative lifestyle; earlier in the decade he had been urged to join two Utopian agricultural communities inspired by Transcendentalist principles—Brook Farm and Fruitlands. Both times he had said no. By the middle of the decade those communities had foundered; Thoreau embarked on a solitary initiative that would eventually have a far wider impact than either of those religiously-focused communal experiments.

Thoreau's solitary experiment began with little fanfare, though it sparked a good deal of interest among his Concord neighbors, who were puzzled by this eccentric Harvard graduate who had seemingly chosen to throw away his education and talents to live as a hermit in the woods. Thoreau ended up living at Walden Pond for two years (1845–47), spending his days reading, walking, observing Nature (unlike Emerson, Thoreau generally capitalized the noun), tending his bean fields, entertaining curious visitors, and beginning work on the only two books he would publish—first the elegiac *A Week on the Concord* and later *Walden*, an account of his present experiment.

A Week on the Concord (1849) was praised by friends for its powerful prose, but sold poorly. *Walden*, on the other hand, which was published five years later, sold well and for the most part received enthusiastic reviews, both in the United States and in England. English novelist George Eliot praised Thoreau's "deep poetic sensibility" and concluded that as readers "we feel throughout the book the presence of a refined as well as a hardy mind," while Emerson wrote (perhaps hyperbolically) that "all American kind are delighted with 'Walden' as far as they have dared say." Several reviewers predicted that *Walden* would hold a lasting place in American literature—and they have been proved right, though there was a period in the late nineteenth and early twentieth centuries when Thoreau's reputation dipped somewhat. Late nineteenth-century editions of *The American Cyclopedia* devote a page and a half to Emerson and over two pages to Hawthorne, but give Thoreau an entry less than a quarter page long. And Barrett Wendell's influential *A Literary History of America*, while praising *Walden* for the "artistic form" of its descriptions (the book "remains a vital bit of literature for anyone who loves to read about nature," Wendell concluded), lumps Thoreau together with Bronson Alcott in a chapter entitled "The Lesser Men of Concord." In the mid-twentieth century Thoreau and *Walden* came to be granted a more central place in the canon of American literature. Environmentalists such as Aldo Leopold were profoundly influenced by *Walden*, as were leading literary figures such as Annie Dillard (whose MA thesis was on the subject of Thoreau and *Walden*).

Much as Nature as a large concept was fundamental to Thoreau's thinking, so too did the details of the natural world come to fascinate him, and to occupy considerable space in his writing. Thoreau had become intrigued by Charles Darwin's *Journal of the Voyage of the Beagle* (1839) and other botanical and scientific writings, and that interest began to color both his daily pursuits and his writing; some of the best-loved and most widely cited passages from *Walden* involve detailed description of natural phenomena. At least one passage in the text—in which a battle between two species of ant is dramatically described—connects directly to similar descriptions of insect wars in Darwin's work.

In the years between leaving Walden Pond and writing *Walden*, Thoreau continued to expand on his reading as well as on the observations he had made of the natural world; in addition to numerous works of natural philosophy he absorbed the latest in American nature writing. (Among his influences were Susan Fenimore Cooper, author of *Rural Hours* [1850], and ornithologist John James Audubon.) Overall, *Walden* is noteworthy not least of all for paying far more attention to material, ecological details than had any of the nature writings of previous Transcendentalists. But the relationship within Thoreau's own mind between Nature as an idea and the natural world as a subject for detailed scientific interest was not without tension. His detailed observations brought him excitement but also, on occasion, concern; in an 1851 journal entry he wrote, "I fear that the character of my knowledge is from year to year becoming more distinct and scientific—that, in exchange for views as wide as heaven's cope, I am being narrowed down to the field of the microscope." Another, oft-quoted (and, like many of Thoreau's writings, oft-misquoted) line from an 1851 journal entry is his assertion that "the question is not what you look at, but what you see." It is often taken to be an unqualified endorsement of the value of sustained and observant engagement with the natural world—and his journal entry for that day does indeed include descriptions that exemplify such sustained and observant engagement. But the context of the famous quotation itself is one in which Thoreau is praising the poetic sensibility and dismissing the "mere science" of the astronomer who is blind to the true significance of the phenomena he is looking at.

Arguably, then, Thoreau's writing about Nature is in large part the product of ideas continually in tension within his own mind. Certainly *Walden* itself continues to command attention not least of all because of the tensions and paradoxes—even the contradictions—the text gives voice to. Even in the twenty-first century, *Walden* continues to excite not only interest, but heated debate; in 2015, for example, a passionate attack on Thoreau and *Walden* in *The New Yorker* by Pulitzer Prize-winning journalist Kathryn Schultz was met with equally passionate defenses (of both author and book) in other leading magazines by, among others, Columbia University law professor Jedediah Britton-Purdy. What seems to Schultz and some others as "an unnavigable thicket of contradiction" in *Walden* strikes others as an immensely readable and engaging expression of various ideas in tension with one another. What seems to some an unattractive degree of self-absorption in Thoreau's writing (Isaac Hecker, one of the few to review *Walden* negatively on its initial appearance, complained of what he read as Thoreau's "pride" and "pretension"), strikes others as lively individualism. *Walden* has become established as a central text in the canon of American literature in large part because of its continuing capacity to excite passionate debate.

While residing at Walden, Thoreau was embroiled in an unrelated controversy—arrested and briefly imprisoned in 1846 for refusing to pay his taxes. Although Thoreau was not the first local figure to be enmeshed in such a dispute—Concord teacher Amos Bronson Alcott, previously a leading member of Fruitlands, had been arrested on the same charge in 1843—curiosity and confusion regarding Thoreau's motives continued until well after his departure from the Walden cabin in 1847. The following year he returned to the Lyceum to speak about his decision to face imprisonment rather than pay the required fee. This lecture eventually grew into the essay "Resistance to Civil Government," an essay published in Transcendental educator Elizabeth Peabody's collection *Aesthetic Papers* in 1849. "Civil Disobedience" (as the essay is popularly known) posed an important question: how is it possible for an individual to retain moral integrity within the confines of an unjust society? Thoreau framed his action as a form of political protest against both slavery and the Mexican-American War. (The two were not unconnected; many opponents of the war regarded it as a means of extending the domain of American slavery.)

"Civil Disobedience" was among Thoreau's earliest public expressions of support for the abolitionist movement that would soon be coming to its crisis—though Thoreau would in some ways remain aloof from the movement itself. "Civil Disobedience" did little to dispel public disapproval of Thoreau's tax resistance, with one reviewer comparing Thoreau unfavorably to the "red republicans" of revolutionary France. But in the generations since, "Civil Disobedience" has been cited as inspiration by the Russian novelist and pacifist Leo Tolstoy, by the revolutionary Indian leader Mohandas Gandhi, and by the Civil Rights leader Martin Luther King Jr.; Thoreau's notion that "non-cooperation with evil is as much a moral obligation as is cooperation with good" continues to provoke heated debate—and to inspire resistance to authority.

Thoreau's participation on the New England lecture circuit increased following the favorable reception of *Walden*. He also worked with his mother in helping those fleeing slavery to escape along the Underground Railroad. Thoreau found his abolitionist zeal stimulated by the Fugitive Slave Act of 1850. In 1854 he delivered an acclaimed lecture, "Slavery in Massachusetts," in response to the Act and to the trial and re-enslavement of Anthony Burns; the lecture made Thoreau an abolitionist figure of some renown, and in the process solidified the reputation of Concord as a center of antebellum abolitionism.

Here too, however, some observers have detected tensions and paradoxes—one of the great exemplars of American individualists was sometimes perhaps an uneasy participant in community activism.

Thoreau's health began to fail in the early 1860s, and in 1862, not halfway into the Civil War, he succumbed to the tuberculosis that had troubled him since young adulthood. Numerous volumes of his lectures and writings were published posthumously—as were his collected journals in 1906, which contribute vastly to our understanding of his intellectual development and provide insight into some of his unrecorded lectures. After his death his old friend Emerson wrote of him that "few lives contain so many renunciations. … [H]e never married; he lived alone; he never went to church; he never voted; … he ate no flesh; he drank no wine; he never knew the use of tobacco; and, though a naturalist, he used neither trap nor gun."

Thoreau remains a vitally important reference point in discussions of the place of individual humans in human society as a whole, and of the place of humans (both individually and collectively) in the natural world. *Walden*—its status now secure as a foundational text of American nature writing and of twentieth- and twenty-first-century environmental movements—continues to strike a sympathetic chord among a wide range of readers. Thoreau at one and the same time posits Nature as a magnet attracting all that is best in humanity and presents a compelling vision of Nature as standing apart from humanity—even in opposition to human society. "I love Nature partly because she is not man, but a retreat from him," wrote Thoreau. "None of his institutions control or pervade her."

NOTE ON THE TEXTS: The text of "Resistance to Civil Government" presented here is based on its first published appearance in 1849 in Elizabeth Peabody's periodical *Aesthetic Papers*. The text of *Walden; or, Life in the Woods* presented here is based on that reproduced in *The Writings of Henry David Thoreau* (1906). Spelling and punctuation have been modernized in accordance with the practices of this anthology.

⌘ ⌘ ⌘

Resistance to Civil Government

In 1846, during the time he was living at Walden Pond, Thoreau was making a trip into the nearby town of Concord when he was arrested by Sam Staples, the local constable, for having failed to pay the local poll tax for the past several years. Staples initially offered to lend Thoreau enough money to pay the tax, but Thoreau refused, arguing that it was a matter of principle. He spent the night in jail—until the debt was paid, to his irritation, by an anonymous friend—and continued to make an issue of the principles involved, most notably in a lecture he gave in Concord on 26 January 1848, which was published as "Resistance to Civil Government" in 1849. The essay was later republished as "Civil Disobedience," and under that name has taken its place among the best known of all American essays. But the historical background to the famous piece remains unfamiliar to many modern readers.

In nineteenth-century America, a poll tax was a fixed annual amount charged to any individual who was eligible to go to the polls—to vote in an election. At the time, poll taxes were levied in several of the states; poll tax revenue accounted for at least a quarter of the total revenue of the state of Massachusetts. Though poll taxes were levied by the individual states, rather than by the federal government, Thoreau treated the state as a fundamental piece of the larger State—of American government as a whole. As a citizen, one was required to pay the poll tax in order to vote, whether for local, state, or federal positions, and Thoreau thus saw the politics of the United States as a whole as vitally relevant to the paying of the poll tax in the town of Concord, Massachusetts.

Thoreau's arguments were focused on two interconnected areas in which he saw America as having acted immorally—the Mexican–American War of 1846–47, and the American institution of slavery. He was not alone in seeing the two as connected; a substantial minority of Americans (and a majority in much of the North) suspected President James K. Polk, a slaveowner, of having provoked the war with the intent not only of adding new territory to the United States, but also of eventually increasing the number of states in which slavery was permitted, and thereby giving the slave states a controlling interest in the politics of the republic. Whether or not that was Polk's express intent,

it was certainly the case that the vast territory acquired by the United States as a result of the war lay almost entirely south of latitude 36°30'—the line that had been established under the terms of the 1820 Missouri Compromise as the northernmost limit of territory in which slavery would be permitted.

Opposition to the war (and to slavery) was particularly strong in the state of Massachusetts, where the government had in 1847 passed a resolution condemning the American government's actions. To Thoreau, however, words or resolutions on paper were not enough; those opposed to the war and to slavery should demonstrate their opposition through concrete actions. Above all, those opposing slavery should never be willing—as Massachusetts senator Daniel Webster was notoriously willing—to compromise with supporters of slavery.

The controversy over slavery and the new territories was further complicated for some time by passionate differences of opinion among those supporting slavery as to whether or not the nation should be interested in incorporating large parts of what had been Mexico into the United States. A significant faction was of the view that the racial "purity" of the American nation would be jeopardized if large numbers of dark-skinned Mexicans were allowed to live within American borders. It was only on the assurance that the territories being annexed were not heavily populated, and that they could readily be "Americanized," that majority opinion in America had swung unreservedly behind Polk.

The 1848 presidential election represented a dispiriting moment for opponents of the war, and of slavery. The issue of slavery in the newly acquired territories was a divisive one in both parties. Polk, a Democrat, chose not to run for another term, but his administration had been popular among a majority of Americans for having added to American territory through its prosecution of the war with Mexico, and it was widely expected that another Democrat would be elected. (That expectation remained strong even after a break-away faction of antislavery Democrats under the leadership of Martin Van Buren contested the election under a new antislavery banner as the Free Soil Party.) Many members of the Whig Party—the Democrats' main rival—had been highly critical of the war. But they had no confidence that anyone in their own ranks could stand a chance against almost any Democrat in the election. When the Whigs found that Zachary Taylor, a general who had led the American forces in the war effort but who had no discernable allegiance to Whig principles, was available as a candidate, they set principle to one side and nominated him at their convention. Taylor did indeed defeat the Democrats' nominee, Lewis Cass. (The 1848 popular vote was 47 per cent for Taylor and 43 per cent for Cass, with Van Buren's Free Soil Party taking 10 per cent.)

It was against this political background that Thoreau penned his famous essay on democratic principles.

I heartily accept the motto, "That government is best which governs least";[1] and I should like to see it acted up to more rapidly and systematically. Carried out, it finally amounts to this, which also I believe, "That government is best which governs not at all"; and when men are prepared for it, that will be the kind of government which they will have. Government is at best but an expedient; but most governments are usually, and all governments are sometimes, inexpedient. The objections which have been brought against a standing army, and they are many and weighty, and deserve to prevail, may also at last be brought against a standing government. The standing army is only an arm of the standing government. The government itself, which is only the mode which the people have chosen to execute their will, is equally liable to be abused and perverted before the people can act through it. Witness the present Mexican war,[2] the work of comparatively a few individuals using the standing government as their tool; for, in the outset, the people would not have consented to this measure.

This American government—what is it but a tradition, though a recent one, endeavoring to transmit itself unimpaired to posterity, but each instant losing some of its integrity? It has not the vitality and force of a single living man; for a single man can bend it to his will. It is a sort of wooden gun to the people themselves; and, if ever they should use it in earnest as

a real one against each other, it will surely split. But it is not the less necessary for this; for the people must have some complicated machinery or other, and hear its din, to satisfy that idea of government which they have. Governments show thus how successfully men can be imposed on, even impose on themselves, for their own advantage. It is excellent, we must all allow; yet this government never of itself furthered any enterprise, but by the alacrity with which it got out of its way. *It* does not keep the country free. *It* does not settle the West. *It* does not educate. The character inherent in the American people has done all that has been accomplished; and it would have done somewhat more, if the government had not sometimes got in its way. For government is an expedient by which men would fain succeed in letting one another alone; and, as has been said, when it is most expedient, the governed are most let alone by it. Trade and commerce, if they were not made of India rubber, would never manage to bounce over the obstacles which legislators are continually putting in their way; and, if one were to judge these men wholly by the effects of their actions, and not partly by their intentions, they would deserve to be classed and punished with those mischievous persons who put obstructions on the railroads.

But, to speak practically and as a citizen, unlike those who call themselves no-government men, I ask for, not at once no government, but *at once* a better government. Let every man make known what kind of government would command his respect, and that will be one step toward obtaining it.

After all, the practical reason why, when the power is once in the hands of the people, a majority are permitted, and for a long period continue, to rule, is not because they are most likely to be in the right, nor because this seems fairest to the minority, but because they are physically the strongest. But a government in which the majority rule in all cases cannot be based on justice, even as far as men understand it. Can there not be a government in which majorities do not virtually decide right and wrong, but conscience? in which majorities decide only those questions to which the rule of expediency is applicable? Must the citizen ever for a moment, or in the least degree, resign his conscience to the legislator? Why has every man a conscience, then? I think that we should be men first, and subjects

---

[1]   *That government … governs least*   Paraphrase of the motto of the *United States Magazine and Democratic Review*, which has often been erroneously attributed to Thomas Jefferson.

[2]   *Mexican war*   Many Northerners and abolitionists opposed the Mexican–American War, which had broken out in 1846, fearing that it would expand and strengthen the domain of Southern slavery.

afterward. It is not desirable to cultivate a respect for the law, so much as for the right. The only obligation which I have a right to assume, is to do at any time what I think right. It is truly enough said, that a corporation has no conscience;[1] but a corporation of conscientious men is a corporation *with* a conscience. Law never made men a whit more just; and, by means of their respect for it, even the well-disposed are daily made the agents of injustice. A common and natural result of an undue respect for law is, that you may see a file of soldiers, colonel, captain, corporal, privates, powder-monkeys[2] and all, marching in admirable order over hill and dale to the wars, against their wills, aye, against their common sense and consciences, which makes it very steep marching indeed, and produces a palpitation of the heart. They have no doubt that it is a damnable business in which they are concerned; they are all peaceably inclined. Now, what are they? Men at all? or small moveable forts and magazines,[3] at the service of some unscrupulous man in power? Visit the Navy Yard, and behold a marine, such a man as an American government can make, or such as it can make a man with its black arts, a mere shadow and reminiscence of humanity, a man laid out alive and standing, and already, as one may say, buried under arms with funeral accompaniments, though it may be

> Not a drum was heard, nor a funeral note,
> As his corse to the ramparts we hurried;
> Not a soldier discharged his farewell shot
> O'er the grave where our hero we buried.[4]

The mass of men serve the State thus, not as men mainly, but as machines, with their bodies. They are the standing army, and the militia, jailers, constables, *posse comitatus*,[5] &c. In most cases there is no free exercise whatever of the judgment or of the moral sense; but they put themselves on a level with wood and earth and stones; and wooden men can perhaps be manufactured that will serve the purpose as well. Such command no more respect than men of straw, or a lump of dirt. They have the same sort of worth only as horses and dogs. Yet such as these even are commonly esteemed good citizens. Others, as most legislators, politicians, lawyers, ministers, and office-holders, serve the State chiefly with their heads; and, as they rarely make any moral distinctions, they are as likely to serve the devil, without intending it, as God. A very few, as heroes, patriots, martyrs, reformers in the great sense, and men, serve the State with their consciences also, and so necessarily resist it for the most part; and they are commonly treated by it as enemies. A wise man will only be useful as a man, and will not submit to be "clay," and "stop a hole to keep the wind away,"[6] but leave that office to his dust at least:

> I am too high-born to be propertied,
> To be a secondary at control,
> Or useful serving-man and instrument
> To any sovereign state throughout the world.[7]

He who gives himself entirely to his fellow-men appears to them useless and selfish; but he who gives himself partially to them is pronounced a benefactor and philanthropist.

How does it become a man to behave toward this American government today? I answer that he cannot without disgrace be associated with it. I cannot for an instant recognize that political organization as *my* government which is the *slave's* government also.

All men recognize the right of revolution; that is, the right to refuse allegiance to and to resist the government, when its tyranny or its inefficiency are great and unendurable. But almost all say that such is not the case now. But such was the case, they think, in the Revolution of '75.[8] If one were to tell me that this was a bad government because it taxed certain foreign

---

[1]   *a corporation ... no conscience* Idea erroneously attributed to English jurist and politician Sir Edward Coke (1552–1634) by later English philosopher Jeremy Bentham (1748–1832).

[2]   *powder-monkeys* Boys hired to carry gunpowder from storage rooms to the guns.

[3]   *magazines* Military storehouses.

[4]   *Not a ... we buried* See "Burial of Sir John Moore at Corunna" by Irish poet Charles Wolfe (1791–1823);   *corse* Corpse.

[5]   *posse comitatus* Latin: enabling group of companions; temporary police force recruited from the general population.

[6]   *clay ... wind away* See Shakespeare's *Hamlet* 5.1.220–21.

[7]   *I am ... the world* See Shakespeare's *King John* 5.2.79–82.

[8]   *Revolution of '75* I.e., the American Revolutionary War; unjust taxation by the British government was one of the primary grievances among the revolution's leaders.

commodities brought to its ports, it is most probable that I should not make an ado about it, for I can do without them: all machines have their friction; and possibly this does enough good to counterbalance the evil. At any rate, it is a great evil to make a stir about it. But when the friction comes to have its machine, and oppression and robbery are organized, I say, let us not have such a machine any longer. In other words, when a sixth of the population of a nation which has undertaken to be the refuge of liberty are slaves, and a whole country is unjustly overrun and conquered by a foreign army, and subjected to military law, I think that it is not too soon for honest men to rebel and revolutionize. What makes this duty the more urgent is the fact, that the country so overrun is not our own, but ours is the invading army.

Paley,[1] a common authority with many on moral questions, in his chapter on the "Duty of Submission to Civil Government," resolves all civil obligation into expediency; and he proceeds to say, "that so long as the interest of the whole society requires it, that is, so long as the established government cannot be resisted or changed without public inconveniency, it is the will of God that the established government be obeyed, and no longer." "This principle being admitted, the justice of every particular case of resistance is reduced to a computation of the quantity of the danger and grievance on the one side, and of the probability and expense of redressing it on the other." Of this, he says, every man shall judge for himself. But Paley appears never to have contemplated those cases to which the rule of expediency does not apply, in which a people, as well as an individual, must do justice, cost what it may. If I have unjustly wrested a plank from a drowning man, I must restore it to him though I drown myself. This, according to Paley, would be inconvenient. But he that would save his life, in such a case, shall lose it.[2] This people must cease to hold slaves, and to make

war on Mexico, though it cost them their existence as a people.

In their practice, nations agree with Paley; but does anyone think that Massachusetts does exactly what is right at the present crisis?

> A drab of state, a cloth-o'-silver slut,
>   To have her train borne up, and her soul trail in the
>   dirt.[3]

Practically speaking, the opponents to a reform in Massachusetts are not a hundred thousand politicians at the South, but a hundred thousand merchants and farmers here, who are more interested in commerce and agriculture than they are in humanity, and are not prepared to do justice to the slave and to Mexico, *cost what it may*.[4] I quarrel not with far-off foes, but with those who, near at home, co-operate with, and do the bidding of those far away, and without whom the latter would be harmless. We are accustomed to say, that the mass of men are unprepared; but improvement is slow, because the few are not materially wiser or better than the many. It is not so important that many should be as good as you, as that there be some absolute goodness somewhere; for that will leaven the whole lump. There are thousands who are *in opinion* opposed to slavery and to the war, who yet in effect do nothing to put an end to them; who, esteeming themselves children of Washington and Franklin, sit down with their hands in their pockets, and say that they know not what to do, and do nothing; who even postpone the question of freedom to the question of free-trade, and quietly read

---

[1] *Paley* English theologian and philosopher William Paley (1743–1805); the quotation is from his *Principles of Moral and Political Philosophy* (1785).

[2] *But he … lose it* See Matthew 10.39: "He that findeth his life shall lose it: and he that loseth his life for my sake shall find it." The drowning man analogy stems from a question posed by Roman philosopher Cicero (106–43 BCE) in his book on ethics and moral philosophy, *De Officiis*.

[3] *A drab … the dirt* See *The Revenger's Tragedy* 4.4 by Thomas Middleton (1580–1627). The quotation suggests that a person whose soul is unclean cannot change their nature by dressing themselves in fine clothes. Massachusetts, Thoreau suggests, has dressed itself in fine clothes with its resolution against slavery, but its soul remains unclean. (The term "slut," in this context, refers to an unkempt or unclean person, and does not necessarily have derogatory sexual connotations.)

[4] *more interested … what it may* The legislature of Massachusetts had passed a resolution in 1847 condemning the war and the annexation of Mexican territories as a war "waged ingloriously, by a powerful nation against a weak neighbor, unnecessarily and without just cause … with the triple object of extending slavery … [and] of obtaining control of the Free States, under the Constitution of the United States." But few in Massachusetts were calling for concrete action beyond this.

the prices-current along with the latest advices from Mexico, after dinner, and, it may be, fall asleep over them both. What is the price-current of an honest man and patriot today? They hesitate, and they regret, and sometimes they petition; but they do nothing in earnest and with effect. They will wait, well disposed, for others to remedy the evil, that they may no longer have it to regret. At most, they give only a cheap vote, and a feeble countenance and Godspeed, to the right, as it goes by them. There are nine hundred and ninety-nine patrons of virtue to one virtuous man; but it is easier to deal with the real possessor of a thing than with the temporary guardian of it.

All voting is a sort of gaming, like chequers or backgammon, with a slight moral tinge to it, a playing with right and wrong, with moral questions; and betting naturally accompanies it. The character of the voters is not staked. I cast my vote, perchance, as I think right; but I am not vitally concerned that that right should prevail. I am willing to leave it to the majority. Its obligation, therefore, never exceeds that of expediency. Even voting *for the right* is *doing* nothing for it. It is only expressing to men feebly your desire that it should prevail. A wise man will not leave the right to the mercy of chance, nor wish it to prevail through the power of the majority. There is but little virtue in the action of masses of men. When the majority shall at length vote for the abolition of slavery, it will be because they are indifferent to slavery, or because there is but little slavery left to be abolished by their vote. *They* will then be the only slaves. Only *his* vote can hasten the abolition of slavery who asserts his own freedom by his vote.

I hear of a convention to be held at Baltimore,[1] or elsewhere, for the selection of a candidate for the Presidency, made up chiefly of editors, and men who are politicians by profession; but I think, what is it to any independent, intelligent, and respectable man what decision they may come to, shall we not have the advantage of his wisdom and honesty, nevertheless? Can we not count upon some independent votes? Are there not many individuals in the country who do not attend conventions? But no: I find that the respectable man, so called, has immediately drifted from his position, and despairs of his country, when his country has more reason to despair of him. He forthwith adopts one of the candidates thus selected as the only *available* one, thus proving that he is himself *available* for any purposes of the demagogue. His vote is of no more worth than that of any unprincipled foreigner or hireling native, who may have been bought. Oh for a man who is a *man*, and, as my neighbor says, has a bone in his back which you cannot pass your hand through! Our statistics are at fault: the population has been returned too large. How many *men* are there to a square thousand miles in this country? Hardly one. Does not America offer any inducement for men to settle here? The American has dwindled into an Odd Fellow[2]—one who may be known by the development of his organ of gregariousness, and a manifest lack of intellect and cheerful self-reliance; whose first and chief concern, on coming into the world, is to see that the alms-houses are in good repair; and, before yet he has lawfully donned the virile garb,[3] to collect a fund for the support of the widows and orphans that may be; who, in short, ventures to live only by the aid of the mutual insurance company, which has promised to bury him decently.

It is not a man's duty, as a matter of course, to devote himself to the eradication of any, even the most enormous wrong; he may still properly have other concerns to engage him; but it is his duty, at least, to wash his hands of it, and, if he gives it no thought longer, not to give it practically his support. If I devote myself to other pursuits and contemplations, I must first see, at least, that I do not pursue them sitting upon another man's shoulders. I must get off him first, that he may pursue his contemplations too. See what gross inconsistency is tolerated. I have heard some of my townsmen say, "I should like to have them order me out to help put down an insurrection of the slaves, or to march to Mexico—see if I would go"; and yet these very men have each, directly by their allegiance, and so indirectly, at least, by their money, furnished a substitute. The soldier is applauded who refuses to serve in an unjust war by those who do not refuse to sustain the

---

[1] *convention to ... at Baltimore* The 1848 Democratic National Convention. See the headnote to this essay for further information.

[2] *Odd Fellow* Ironic allusion to the Independent Order of Odd Fellows, a fraternal organization with benevolent social aims.

[3] *virile garb* The "toga virilis," robe donned by boys in ancient Rome upon reaching the age of adulthood.

unjust government which makes the war; is applauded by those whose own act and authority he disregards and sets at nought; as if the State were penitent to that degree that it hired one to scourge it while it sinned, but not to that degree that it left off sinning for a moment. Thus, under the name of order and civil government, we are all made at last to pay homage to and I support our own meanness. After the first blush of sin, comes its indifference; and from immoral it becomes, as it were, *un*moral, and not quite unnecessary to that life which we have made.

The broadest and most prevalent error requires the most disinterested virtue to sustain it. The slight reproach to which the virtue of patriotism is commonly liable, the noble are most likely to incur. Those who, while they disapprove of the character and measures of a government, yield to it their allegiance and support, are undoubtedly its most conscientious supporters, and so frequently the most serious obstacles to reform. Some are petitioning the State to dissolve the Union, to disregard the requisitions of the President. Why do they not dissolve it themselves—the union between themselves and the State—and refuse to pay their quota into its treasury? Do not they stand in the same relation to the State, that the State does to the Union? And have not the same reasons prevented the State from resisting the Union, which have prevented them from resisting the State?

How can a man be satisfied to entertain an opinion merely, and enjoy *it*? Is there any enjoyment in it, if his opinion is that he is aggrieved? If you are cheated out of a single dollar by your neighbor, you do not rest satisfied with knowing that you are cheated, or with saying that you are cheated, or even with petitioning him to pay you your due; but you take effectual steps at once to obtain the full amount, and see that you are never cheated again. Action from principle—the perception and the performance of right—changes things and relations; it is essentially revolutionary, and does not consist wholly with anything which was. It not only divides states and churches, it divides families; aye, it divides the *individual*, separating the diabolical in him from the divine.

Unjust laws exist: shall we be content to obey them, or shall we endeavor to amend them, and obey them until we have succeeded, or shall we transgress them at once? Men generally, under such a government as this, think that they ought to wait until they have persuaded the majority to alter them. They think that, if they should resist, the remedy would be worse than the evil. But it is the fault of the government itself that the remedy *is* worse than the evil. *It* makes it worse. Why is it not more apt to anticipate and provide for reform? Why does it not cherish its wise minority? Why does it cry and resist before it is hurt? Why does it not encourage its citizens to be on the alert to point out its faults, and *do* better than it would have them? Why does it always crucify Christ, and excommunicate Copernicus and Luther,[1] and pronounce Washington and Franklin rebels?

One would think, that a deliberate and practical denial of its authority was the only offence never contemplated by government; else, why has it not assigned its definite, its suitable and proportionate penalty? If a man who has no property refuses but once to earn nine shillings for the State, he is put in prison for a period unlimited by any law that I know, and determined only by the discretion of those who placed him there; but if he should steal ninety times nine shillings from the State, he is soon permitted to go at large again.

If the injustice is part of the necessary friction of the machine of government, let it go, let it go: perchance it will wear smooth—certainly the machine will wear out. If the injustice has a spring, or a pulley, or a rope, or a crank, exclusively for itself, then perhaps you may consider whether the remedy will not be worse than the evil; but if it is of such a nature that it requires you to be the agent of injustice to another, then, I say, break the law. Let your life be a counter friction to stop the machine. What I have to do is to see, at any rate, that I do not lend myself to the wrong which I condemn.

As for adopting the ways which the State has provided for remedying the evil, I know not of such ways. They take too much time, and a man's life will be gone. I have other affairs to attend to. I came into this world, not chiefly to make this a good place to live in, but to live in it, be it good or bad. A man has not everything to do, but something; and because he cannot do

---

1   *Copernicus and Luther* Renaissance astronomer Nicolaus Copernicus (1473–1543) and German theologian Martin Luther (1483–1546), who were both excommunicated from the church for their revolutionary ideas.

everything, it is not necessary that he should do *something* wrong. It is not my business to be petitioning the governor or the legislature any more than it is theirs to petition me; and, if they should not hear my petition, what should I do then? But in this case the State has provided no way: its very Constitution is the evil. This may seem to be harsh and stubborn and unconciliatory; but it is to treat with the utmost kindness and consideration the only spirit that can appreciate or deserves it. So is all change for the better, like birth and death which convulse the body.

I do not hesitate to say, that those who call themselves abolitionists should at once effectually withdraw their support, both in person and property, from the government of Massachusetts, and not wait till they constitute a majority of one, before they suffer the right to prevail through them. I think that it is enough if they have God on their side, without waiting for that other one. Moreover, any man more right than his neighbors, constitutes a majority of one already.

I meet this American government, or its representative the State government, directly, and face to face, once a year, no more, in the person of its tax-gatherer; this is the only mode in which a man situated as I am necessarily meets it; and it then says distinctly, Recognize me; and the simplest, the most effectual, and, in the present posture of affairs, the indispensablest mode of treating with it on this head, of expressing your little satisfaction with and love for it, is to deny it then. My civil neighbor, the tax-gatherer, is the very man I have to deal with—for it is, after all, with men and not with parchment that I quarrel—and he has voluntarily chosen to be an agent of the government. How shall he ever know well what he is and does as an officer of the government, or as a man, until he is obliged to consider whether he shall treat me, his neighbor, for whom he has respect, as a neighbor and well-disposed man, or as a maniac and disturber of the peace, and see if he can get over this obstruction to his neighborliness without a ruder and more impetuous thought or speech corresponding with his action? I know this well, that if one thousand, if one hundred, if ten men whom I could name—if ten *honest* men only—aye, if *one* HONEST man, in this State of Massachusetts, *ceasing to hold slaves*, were actually to withdraw from this co-partnership, and be locked up in the county jail therefore, it would be the abolition of slavery in America. For it matters not how small the beginning may seem to be: what is once well done is done for ever. But we love better to talk about it: that we say is our mission. Reform keeps many scores of newspapers in its service, but not one man. If my esteemed neighbor, the State's ambassador,[1] who will devote his days to the settlement of the question of human rights in the Council Chamber, instead of being threatened with the prisons of Carolina, were to sit down the prisoner of Massachusetts, that State which is so anxious to foist the sin of slavery upon her sister—though at present she can discover only an act of inhospitality to be the ground of a quarrel with her—the Legislature would not wholly waive the subject the following winter.

Under a government which imprisons any unjustly, the true place for a just man is also a prison. The proper place today, the only place which Massachusetts has provided for her freer and less desponding spirits, is in her prisons, to be put out and locked out of the State by her own act, as they have already put themselves out by their principles. It is there that the fugitive slave, and the Mexican prisoner on parole, and the Indian come to plead the wrongs of his race, should find them; on that separate, but more free and honorable ground, where the State places those who are not *with* her but *against* her—the only house in a slave-state in which a free man can abide with honor. If any think that their influence would be lost there, and their voices no longer afflict the ear of the State, that they would not be as an enemy within its walls, they do not know by how much truth is stronger than error, nor how much more eloquently and effectively he can combat injustice who has experienced a little in his own person. Cast your whole vote, not a strip of paper merely, but your whole influence. A minority is powerless while it conforms to the majority; it is not even a minority then; but it is irresistible when it clogs by its whole weight. If the alternative is to keep all just men in prison, or give up war and slavery, the State will not hesitate which to choose. If a thousand

---

[1] *my esteemed … State's ambassador* Samuel Hoar (1778–1856), Concord politician who in 1844 was forcibly expelled from South Carolina when he went there to protest the seizure of free black seamen from Massachusetts, whose freedom was not acknowledged by South Carolina and who were thus at risk of being sold into slavery.

men were not to pay their tax-bills this year, that would not be a violent and bloody measure, as it would be to pay them, and enable the State to commit violence and shed innocent blood. This is, in fact, the definition of a peaceable revolution, if any such is possible. If the tax-gatherer, or any other public officer, asks me, as one has done, "But what shall I do?" my answer is, "If you really wish to do anything, resign your office." When the subject has refused allegiance, and the officer has resigned his office, then the revolution is accomplished. But even suppose blood should flow. Is there not a sort of bloodshed when the conscience is wounded? Through this wound a man's real manhood and immortality flow out, and he bleeds to an everlasting death. I see this blood flowing now.

I have contemplated the imprisonment of the offender, rather than the seizure of his goods—though both will serve the same purpose—because they who assert the purest right, and consequently are most dangerous to a corrupt State, commonly have not spent much time in accumulating property. To such the State renders comparatively small service, and a slight tax is wont to appear exorbitant, particularly if they are obliged to earn it by special labor with their hands. If there were one who lived wholly without the use of money, the State itself would hesitate to demand it of him. But the rich man—not to make any invidious comparison—is always sold to the institution which makes him rich. Absolutely speaking, the more money, the less virtue; for money comes between a man and his objects, and obtains them for him; and it was certainly no great virtue to obtain it. It puts to rest many questions which he would otherwise be taxed to answer; while the only new question which it puts is the hard but superfluous one, how to spend it. Thus his moral ground is taken from under his feet. The opportunities of living are diminished in proportion as what are called the "means" are increased. The best thing a man can do for his culture when he is rich is to endeavour to carry out those schemes which he entertained when he was poor. Christ answered the Herodians according to their condition. "Show me the tribute-money," said he—and one took a penny out of his pocket—If you use money which has the image of Cæsar on it, and which he has made current and valuable, that is, *if you are men of the State*, and gladly enjoy the advantages of Cæsar's government, then pay him back some of his own when he demands it; "Render therefore to Cæsar that which is Cæsar's, and to God those things which are God's,"[1]—leaving them no wiser than before as to which was which; for they did not wish to know.

When I converse with the freest of my neighbors, I perceive that, whatever they may say about the magnitude and seriousness of the question, and their regard for the public tranquillity, the long and the short of the matter is, that they cannot spare the protection of the existing government, and they dread the consequences of disobedience to it to their property and families. For my own part, I should not like to think that I ever rely on the protection of the State. But, if I deny the authority of the State when it presents its tax-bill, it will soon take and waste all my property, and so harass me and my children without end. This is hard. This makes it impossible for a man to live honestly and at the same time comfortably in outward respects. It will not be worth the while to accumulate property; that would be sure to go again. You must hire or squat somewhere, and raise but a small crop, and eat that soon. You must live within yourself, and depend upon yourself, always tucked up and ready for a start, and not have many affairs. A man may grow rich in Turkey even, if he will be in all respects a good subject of the Turkish government. Confucius said, "If a State is governed by the principles of reason, poverty and misery are subjects of shame; if a State is not governed by the principles of reason, riches and honors are the subjects of shame."[2] No: until I want the protection of Massachusetts to be extended to me in some distant southern port, where my liberty is endangered, or until I am bent solely on building up an estate at home by peaceful enterprise, I can afford to refuse allegiance to Massachusetts, and her right to my property and life. It costs me less in every sense to incur the penalty of disobedience to the State, than it would to obey. I should feel as if I were worth less in that case.

---

[1] *Christ answered … are God's* See Matthew 22.16–21, in which the Herodians, in an attempt to slander him before the authorities, ask Jesus whether he thinks it lawful to pay taxes to Roman authorities.

[2] *If a … of shame* From the *Analects* 8.13 by Chinese philosopher Confucius (551–479 BCE).

Some years ago, the State met me in behalf of the church, and commanded me to pay a certain sum toward the support of a clergyman whose preaching my father attended, but never I myself. "Pay it," it said, "or be locked up in the jail." I declined to pay. But, unfortunately, another man saw fit to pay it. I did not see why the schoolmaster should be taxed to support the priest, and not the priest the schoolmaster; for I was not the State's schoolmaster, but I supported myself by voluntary subscription. I did not see why the lyceum should not present its tax-bill, and have the State to back its demand, as well as the church. However, at the request of the selectmen, I condescended to make some such statement as this in writing: "Know all men by these presents, that I, Henry Thoreau, do not wish to be regarded as a member of any incorporated society which I have not joined." This I gave to the town-clerk; and he has it. The State, having thus learned that I did not wish to be regarded as a member of that church, has never made a like demand on me since; though it said that it must adhere to its original presumption that time. If I had known how to name them, I should then have signed off in detail from all the societies which I never signed on to; but I did not know where to find a complete list.

I have paid no poll-tax for six years. I was put into a jail once on this account, for one night;[1] and, as I stood considering the walls of solid stone, two or three feet thick, the door of wood and iron, a foot thick, and the iron grating which strained the light, I could not help being struck with the foolishness of that institution which treated me as if I were mere flesh and blood and bones, to be locked up. I wondered that it should have concluded at length that this was the best use it could put me to, and had never thought to avail itself of my services in some way. I saw that, if there was a wall of stone between me and my townsmen, there was a still more difficult one to climb or break through, before they could get to be as free as I was. I did not for a moment feel confined, and the walls seemed a great waste of stone and mortar. I felt as if I alone of all my townsmen had paid my tax. They plainly did not know how to treat me, but behaved like persons who are underbred. In every threat and in every compliment there was a blunder; for they thought that my chief

desire was to stand the other side of that stone wall. I could not but smile to see how industriously they locked the door on my meditations, which followed them out again without let or hindrance, and *they* were really all that was dangerous. As they could not reach me, they had resolved to punish my body; just as boys, if they cannot come at some person against whom they have a spite, will abuse his dog. I saw that the State was half-witted, that it was timid as a lone woman with her silver spoons, and that it did not know its friends from its foes, and I lost all my remaining respect for it, and pitied it.

Thus the State never intentionally confronts a man's sense, intellectual or moral, but only his body, his senses. It is not armed with superior wit or honesty, but with superior physical strength. I was not born to be forced. I will breathe after my own fashion. Let us see who is the strongest. What force has a multitude? They only can force me who obey a higher law than I. They force me to become like themselves. I do not hear of *men* being *forced* to live this way or that by masses of men. What sort of life were that to live? When I meet a government which says to me, "Your money or your life," why should I be in haste to give it my money? It may be in a great strait, and not know what to do: I cannot help that. It must help itself; do as I do. It is not worth the while to snivel about it. I am not responsible for the successful working of the machinery of society. I am not the son of the engineer. I perceive that, when an acorn and a chestnut fall side by side, the one does not remain inert to make way for the other, but both obey their own laws, and spring and grow and flourish as best they can, till one, perchance, overshadows and destroys the other. If a plant cannot live according to its nature, it dies; and so a man.

The night in prison was novel and interesting enough. The prisoners in their shirt-sleeves were enjoying a chat and the evening air in the door-way, when I entered. But the jailer said, "Come, boys, it is time to lock up"; and so they dispersed, and I heard the sound of their steps returning into the hollow apartments. My room-mate was introduced to me by the jailer, as "a first-rate fellow and a clever man." When the door was locked, he showed me where to hang

---

[1]   *I was ... one night*   In July 1846.

my hat, and how he managed matters there. The rooms were whitewashed once a month; and this one, at least, was the whitest, most simply furnished, and probably the neatest apartment in the town. He naturally wanted to know where I came from, and what brought me there; and, when I had told him, I asked him in my turn how he came there, presuming him to be an honest man, of course; and, as the world goes, I believe he was. "Why," said he, "they accuse me of burning a barn; but I never did it." As near as I could discover, he had probably gone to bed in a barn when drunk, and smoked his pipe there; and so a barn was burnt. He had the reputation of being a clever man, had been there some three months waiting for his trial to come on, and would have to wait as much longer; but he was quite domesticated and contented, since he got his board for nothing, and thought that he was well treated.

He occupied one window, and I the other; and I saw, that, if one stayed there long, his principal business would be to look out the window. I had soon read all the tracts that were left there, and examined where former prisoners had broken out, and where a grate had been sawed off, and heard the history of the various occupants of that room; for I found that even here there was a history and a gossip which never circulated beyond the walls of the jail. Probably this is the only house in the town where verses are composed, which are afterward printed in a circular form,[1] but not published. I was shown quite a long list of verses which were composed by some young men who had been detected in an attempt to escape, who avenged themselves by singing them.

I pumped my fellow-prisoner as dry as I could, for fear I should never see him again; but at length he showed me which was my bed, and left me to blow out the lamp.

It was like traveling into a far country, such as I had never expected to behold, to lie there for one night. It seemed to me that I never had heard the town-clock strike before, nor the evening sounds of the village; for we slept with the windows open, which were inside the grating. It was to see my native village in the light of the middle ages, and our Concord was turned into a Rhine stream, and visions of knights and castles passed before me. They were the voices of old burghers that I heard in the streets. I was an involuntary spectator and auditor of whatever was done and said in the kitchen of the adjacent village-inn—a wholly new and rare experience to me. It was a closer view of my native town. I was fairly inside of it. I never had seen its institutions before. This is one of its peculiar institutions; for it is a shire town.[2] I began to comprehend what its inhabitants were about.

In the morning, our breakfasts were put through the hole in the door, in small oblong-square tin pans, made to fit, and holding a pint of chocolate, with brown bread, and an iron spoon. When they called for the vessels again, I was green enough to return what bread I had left; but my comrade seized it, and said that I should lay that up for lunch or dinner. Soon after, he was let out to work at haying in a neighboring field, whither he went every day, and would not be back till noon; so he bade me good-day, saying that he doubted if he should see me again.

When I came out of prison—for someone interfered, and paid the tax[3]—I did not perceive that great changes had taken place on the common, such as he observed who went in a youth, and emerged a tottering and gray-headed man; and yet a change had to my eyes come over the scene—the town, and State, and country— greater than any that mere time could effect. I saw yet more distinctly the State in which I lived. I saw to what extent the people among whom I lived could be trusted as good neighbors and friends; that their friendship was for summer weather only; that they did not greatly purpose to do right; that they were a distinct race from

---

1   *circular form* I.e., to be distributed among many people.

2   *shire town* County seat, meaning it held the county jail.

3   *for someone ... the tax* There has been a good deal of speculation as to the identity of this person, though no conclusions can be made; suggested persons have included Emerson, Samuel Hoar, and Thoreau's Aunt Maria.

me by their prejudices and superstitions, as the Chinamen and Malays are; that, in their sacrifices to humanity, they ran no risks, not even to their property; that, after all, they were not so noble but they treated the thief as he had treated them, and hoped, by a certain outward observance and a few prayers, and by walking in a particular straight though useless path from time to time, to save their souls. This may be to judge my neighbors harshly; for I believe that most of them are not aware that they have such an institution as the jail in their village.

It was formerly the custom in our village, when a poor debtor came out of jail, for his acquaintances to salute him, looking through their fingers, which were crossed to represent the grating of a jail window, "How do ye do?" My neighbors did not thus salute me, but first looked at me, and then at one another, as if I had returned from a long journey. I was put into jail as I was going to the shoemaker's to get a shoe which was mended. When I was let out the next morning, I proceeded to finish my errand, and, having put on my mended shoe, joined a huckleberry party, who were impatient to put themselves under my conduct; and in half an hour—for the horse was soon tackled—was in the midst of a huckleberry field, on one of our highest hills, two miles off; and then the State was nowhere to be seen.

This is the whole history of "My Prisons."[1]

I have never declined paying the highway tax, because I am as desirous of being a good neighbor as I am of being a bad subject; and, as for supporting schools, I am doing my part to educate my fellow-countrymen now. It is for no particular item in the tax-bill that I refuse to pay it. I simply wish to refuse allegiance to the State, to withdraw and stand aloof from it effectually. I do not care to trace the course of my dollar, if I could, till it buys a man, or a musket to shoot one with— the dollar is innocent—but I am concerned to trace the effects of my allegiance. In fact, I quietly declare war with the State, after my fashion, though I will still

make what use and get what advantage of her I can, as is usual in such cases.

If others pay the tax which is demanded of me, from a sympathy with the State, they do but what they have already done in their own case, or rather they abet injustice to a greater extent than the State requires. If they pay the tax from a mistaken interest in the individual taxed, to save his property or prevent his going to jail, it is because they have not considered wisely how far they let their private feelings interfere with the public good.

This, then, is my position at present. But one cannot be too much on his guard in such a case, lest his action be biased by obstinacy, or an undue regard for the opinions of men. Let him see that he does only what belongs to himself and to the hour.

I think sometimes, Why, this people mean well; they are only ignorant; they would do better if they knew how: why give your neighbors this pain to treat you as they are not inclined to? But I think, again, this is no reason why I should do as they do, or permit others to suffer much greater pain of a different kind. Again, I sometimes say to myself, When many millions of men, without heat, without ill-will, without personal feeling of any kind, demand of you a few shillings only, without the possibility, such is their constitution, of retracting or altering their present demand, and without the possibility, on your side, of appeal to any other millions, why expose yourself to this overwhelming brute force? You do not resist cold and hunger, the winds and the waves, thus obstinately; you quietly submit to a thousand similar necessities. You do not put your head into the fire. But just in proportion as I regard this as not wholly a brute force, but partly a human force, and consider that I have relations to those millions as to so many millions of men, and not of mere brute or inanimate things, I see that appeal is possible, first and instantaneously, from them to the Maker of them, and, secondly, from them to themselves. But, if I put my head deliberately into the fire, there is no appeal to fire or to the Maker of fire, and I have only myself to blame. If I could convince myself that I have any right to be satisfied with men as they are, and to treat them accordingly, and not according, in some respects, to my requisitions and expectations of what they and I

---

[1]   *My Prisons* Allusion to the prison memoir of Silvio Pellico (1788–1854).

ought to be, then, like a good Mussulman[1] and fatalist, I should endeavor to be satisfied with things as they are, and say it is the will of God. And, above all, there is this difference between resisting this and a purely brute or natural force, that I can resist this with some effect; but I cannot expect, like Orpheus,[2] to change the nature of the rocks and trees and beasts.

I do not wish to quarrel with any man or nation. I do not wish to split hairs, to make fine distinctions, or set myself up as better than my neighbors. I seek rather, I may say, even an excuse for conforming to the laws of the land. I am but too ready to conform to them. Indeed I have reason to suspect myself on this head; and each year, as the tax-gatherer comes round, I find myself disposed to review the acts and position of the general and state governments, and the spirit of the people, to discover a pretext for conformity. I believe that the State will soon be able to take all my work of this sort out of my hands, and then I shall be no better a patriot than my fellow-countrymen. Seen from a lower point of view, the Constitution, with all its faults, is very good; the law and the courts are very respectable; even this State and this American government are, in many respects, very admirable and rare things, to be thankful for, such as a great many have described them; but seen from a point of view a little higher, they are what I have described them; seen from a higher still, and the highest, who shall say what they are, or that they are worth looking at or thinking of at all?

However, the government does not concern me much, and I shall bestow the fewest possible thoughts on it. It is not many moments that I live under a government, even in this world. If a man is thought-free, fancy-free, imagination-free, that which *is not* never for a long time appearing *to be* to him, unwise rulers or reformers cannot fatally interrupt him.

I know that most men think differently from myself; but those whose lives are by profession devoted to the study of these or kindred subjects, content me as little as any. Statesmen and legislators, standing so completely within the institution, never distinctly and nakedly behold it. They speak of moving society, but have no resting-place without it. They may be men of a certain experience and discrimination, and have no doubt invented ingenious and even useful systems, for which we sincerely thank them; but all their wit and usefulness lie within certain not very wide limits. They are wont to forget that the world is not governed by policy and expediency. Webster[3] never goes behind government, and so cannot speak with authority about it. His words are wisdom to those legislators who contemplate no essential reform in the existing government; but for thinkers, and those who legislate for all time, he never once glances at the subject. I know of those whose serene and wise speculations on this theme would soon reveal the limits of his mind's range and hospitality. Yet, compared with the cheap professions of most reformers, and the still cheaper wisdom and eloquence of politicians in general, his are almost the only sensible and valuable words, and we thank Heaven for him. Comparatively, he is always strong, original, and, above all, practical. Still his quality is not wisdom, but prudence. The lawyer's truth is not Truth, but consistency, or a consistent expediency. Truth is always in harmony with herself, and is not concerned chiefly to reveal the justice that may consist with wrong-doing. He well deserves to be called, as he has been called, the Defender of the Constitution. There are really no blows to be given by him but defensive ones. He is not a leader, but a follower. His leaders are the men of '87.[4] "I have never made an effort," he says, "and never propose to make an effort; I have never countenanced an effort, and never mean to countenance an effort, to disturb the arrangement as originally made, by which the various States came into the Union." Still thinking of the sanction which the Constitution gives to slavery, he says, "Because it was a part of the original compact, let it stand." Notwithstanding his special acuteness and ability, he is unable to take a fact out

---

[1]   *Mussulman*   Antiquated term for a Muslim.

[2]   *Orpheus*   According to Ovid's *Metamorphoses*, Orpheus was able to charm trees, stones, and wild beasts into following him by the beautiful playing of his lyre.

[3]   *Webster*   Daniel Webster (1782–1852), Whig politician and at the time Senator from Massachusetts. Webster played a key role in persuading the Senate to accept the Compromise of 1850, under the terms of which California would be admitted to the Union as a free state, but Utah and New Mexico could choose if they wished to allow slavery. The Compromise also committed the government to strengthen the Fugitive Slave Act.

[4]   *men of '87*   Those who drafted the United States Constitution in 1787.

of its merely political relations, and behold it as it lies absolutely to be disposed of by the intellect—what, for instance, it behoves a man to do here in America today with regard to slavery—but ventures, or is driven, to make some such desperate answer as the following, while professing to speak absolutely, and as a private man—from which what new and singular code of social duties might be inferred? "The manner," says he, "in which the government of those States where slavery exists are to regulate it, is for their own consideration, under their responsibility to their constituents, to the general laws of propriety, humanity, and justice, and to God. Associations formed elsewhere, springing from a feeling of humanity, or any other cause, have nothing whatever to do with it. They have never received any encouragement from me, and they never will."[1]

They who know of no purer sources of truth, who have traced up its stream no higher, stand, and wisely stand, by the Bible and the Constitution, and drink at it there with reverence and humility; but they who behold where it comes trickling into this lake or that pool, gird up their loins once more, and continue their pilgrimage toward its fountain-head.

No man with a genius for legislation has appeared in America. They are rare in the history of the world. There are orators, politicians, and eloquent men, by the thousand; but the speaker has not yet opened his mouth to speak, who is capable of settling the much-vexed questions of the day. We love eloquence for its own sake, and not for any truth which it may utter, or any heroism it may inspire. Our legislators have not yet learned the comparative value of free-trade and of freedom, of union, and of rectitude, to a nation. They have no genius or talent for comparatively humble questions of taxation and finance, commerce and manufactures and agriculture. If we were left solely to the wordy wit of legislators in Congress for our guidance, uncorrected by the seasonable experience and the effectual complaints of the people, America would not long retain her rank among the nations. For eighteen hundred years, though perchance I have no right to say it, the New Testament has been written; yet where

is the legislator who has wisdom and practical talent enough to avail himself of the light which it sheds on the science of legislation?

The authority of government, even such as I am willing to submit to—for I will cheerfully obey those who know and can do better than I, and in many things even those who neither know nor can do so well—is still an impure one: to be strictly just, it must have the sanction and consent of the governed. It can have no pure right over my person and property but what I concede to it. The progress from an absolute to a limited monarchy, from a limited monarchy to a democracy, is a progress toward a true respect for the individual. Is a democracy, such as we know it, the last improvement possible in government? Is it not possible to take a step further towards recognizing and organizing the rights of man? There will never be a really free and enlightened State, until the State comes to recognize the individual as a higher and independent power, from which all its own power and authority are derived, and treats him accordingly. I please myself with imagining a State at last which can afford to be just to all men, and to treat the individual with respect as a neighbor; which even would not think it inconsistent with its own repose, if a few were to live aloof from it, not meddling with it, nor embraced by it, who fulfilled all the duties of neighbors and fellow-men. A State which bore this kind of fruit, and suffered it to drop off as fast as it ripened, would prepare the way for a still more perfect and glorious State, which also I have imagined, but not yet anywhere seen.

—1849

---

[1] [Thoreau's note] These extracts have been inserted since the Lecture was read. [Thoreau presumably refers to the two latter quotations, which are taken from speeches delivered by Webster before Congress in 1848.]

The woods around Walden Pond, with the former site of Thoreau's cabin marked by a stone cairn, 1908.

Herbert Wendell Gleason, *South shore of Walden Pond, from railroad; May 30, 1903*. For a larger selection of Gleason's photographs of the areas surrounding Walden Pond, see the "In Context" section below.

from *Walden; or, Life in the Woods*

In 1845, Thoreau made his now-famous move to Walden Pond, a small, fairly secluded lake a couple of miles from the center of the village of Concord. There, on a tract of forested land owned by Ralph Waldo Emerson, he built a small cabin. Thoreau ended up living at Walden Pond for two years, from 1845 to 1847, spending his days reading, walking, observing nature, tending his bean fields, entertaining curious visitors, and beginning work on the only two books he would ever publish—*A Week on the Concord*, an elegiac work reflecting on a boating journey he had taken with his brother John before his death, and *Walden*, an account of his life in the woods. *Walden* was published five years later; though it sold only moderately well at first, it was widely praised by reviewers and literary figures in both the United States and England.

Excerpts from *Walden* are included below; the full text is included as part of the website component of this anthology.

WALDEN;

OR,

LIFE IN THE WOODS.

By HENRY D. THOREAU,

AUTHOR OF "A WEEK ON THE CONCORD AND MERRIMACK RIVERS."

I do not propose to write an ode to dejection, but to brag as lustily as chanticleer in the morning, standing on his roost, if only to wake my neighbors up. — Page 92.

BOSTON:
TICKNOR AND FIELDS.
M DCCC LIV.

CHAPTER 1
ECONOMY

When I wrote the following pages, or rather the bulk of them, I lived alone, in the woods, a mile from any neighbor, in a house which I had built myself, on the shore of Walden Pond, in Concord, Massachusetts, and earned my living by the labor of my hands only. I lived there two years and two months. At present I am a sojourner in civilized life again.

I should not obtrude my affairs so much on the notice of my readers if very particular inquiries had not been made by my townsmen concerning my mode of life, which some would call impertinent, though they do not appear to me at all impertinent, but, considering the circumstances, very natural and pertinent. Some have asked what I got to eat; if I did not feel lonesome; if I was not afraid; and the like. Others have been curious to learn what portion of my income I devoted to charitable purposes; and some, who have large families, how many poor children I maintained. I will therefore ask those of my readers who feel no particular interest in me to pardon me if I undertake to answer some of these questions in this book. In most books, the *I*, or first person, is omitted; in this it will be retained; that, in respect to egotism, is the main difference. We commonly do not remember that it is, after all, always the first person that is speaking. I should not talk so much about myself if there were anybody else whom I knew as well. Unfortunately, I am confined to this theme by the narrowness of my experience. Moreover, I, on my side, require of every writer, first or last, a simple and sincere account of his own life, and not merely what he has heard of other men's lives; some such account as he would send to his kindred from a distant land; for if he has lived sincerely, it must have been in a distant land to me. Perhaps these pages are more particularly addressed to poor students. As for the rest of my readers, they will accept such portions as apply to them. I trust that none will stretch the seams in putting on the coat, for it may do good service to him whom it fits.

I would fain say something, not so much concerning the Chinese and Sandwich Islanders[1] as you who read these pages, who are said to live in New England;

something about your condition, especially your outward condition or circumstances in this world, in this town, what it is, whether it is necessary that it be as bad as it is, whether it cannot be improved as well as not. I have travelled a good deal in Concord; and everywhere, in shops, and offices, and fields, the inhabitants have appeared to me to be doing penance in a thousand remarkable ways. What I have heard of Bramins[2] sitting exposed to four fires and looking in the face of the sun; or hanging suspended, with their heads downward, over flames; or looking at the heavens over their shoulders "until it becomes impossible for them to resume their natural position, while from the twist of the neck nothing but liquids can pass into the stomach"; or dwelling, chained for life, at the foot of a tree; or measuring with their bodies, like caterpillars, the breadth of vast empires; or standing on one leg on the tops of pillars—even these forms of conscious penance are hardly more incredible and astonishing than the scenes which I daily witness. The twelve labors of Hercules[3] were trifling in comparison with those which my neighbors have undertaken; for they were only twelve, and had an end; but I could never see that these men slew or captured any monster or finished any labor. They have no friend Iolas to burn with a hot iron the root of the hydra's head,[4] but as soon as one head is crushed, two spring up.

I see young men, my townsmen, whose misfortune it is to have inherited farms, houses, barns, cattle, and farming tools; for these are more easily acquired than got rid of. Better if they had been born in the open pasture and suckled by a wolf, that they might have seen with clearer eyes what field they were called to labor in. Who made them serfs of the soil? Why should they eat their sixty acres, when man is condemned to eat only his peck of dirt? Why should they begin digging their graves as soon as they are born? They have got to live a

---

1   *Sandwich Islanders* Indigenous Hawaiians; the Hawaiian Islands were generally known to English speakers as the Sandwich Islands, after the British Earl of Sandwich, from 1778 until the mid-1800s.

2   *Bramins* Brahmins, members of the priest caste in Hindu culture. Thoreau's source for the following descriptions of Brahmin spiritual practices is James Mill's *The History of India* (1817).

3   *twelve labors of Hercules* The Greek mythological demigod Hercules was given twelve dangerous feats to perform.

4   *friend Iolas ... hydra's head* The hydra was a many-headed monster who could re-grow two heads from every one that was cut off; Hercules's friend Iolaus helped him defeat the monster.

man's life, pushing all these things before them, and get on as well as they can. How many a poor immortal soul have I met well nigh crushed and smothered under its load, creeping down the road of life, pushing before it a barn seventy-five feet by forty, its Augean stables[1] never cleansed, and one hundred acres of land, tillage, mowing, pasture, and wood-lot! The portionless, who struggle with no such unnecessary inherited encumbrances, find it labor enough to subdue and cultivate a few cubic feet of flesh.

But men labor under a mistake. The better part of the man is soon plowed into the soil for compost. By a seeming fate, commonly called necessity, they are employed, as it says in an old book, laying up treasures which moth and rust will corrupt and thieves break through and steal. It is a fool's life, as they will find when they get to the end of it, if not before. It is said that Deucalion and Pyrrha[2] created men by throwing stones over their heads behind them:

> Inde genus durum sumus, experiensque laborum,
> Et documenta damus quâ simus origine nati.

Or, as Raleigh[3] rhymes it in his sonorous way,

> From thence our kind hard-hearted is, enduring
>   pain and care,
> Approving that our bodies of a stony nature are.

So much for a blind obedience to a blundering oracle, throwing the stones over their heads behind them, and not seeing where they fell.

Most men, even in this comparatively free country, through mere ignorance and mistake, are so occupied with the factitious cares and superfluously coarse labors of life that its finer fruits cannot be plucked by them. Their fingers, from excessive toil, are too clumsy

---

[1] *Augean stables*   As one of his labors, Hercules had to clean the massive Augean stables.

[2] *Deucalion and Pyrrha*   In Greek mythology, Deucalion is the son of Prometheus who, like Noah, is warned of a coming flood, builds an ark, and so survives the devastation. He is then instructed to re-people the earth, together with his wife Pyrrha, by throwing stones over their shoulders; the cast stones will form men and women, respectively, according to the thrower's gender.

[3] *Raleigh*   English poet Sir Walter Ralegh (1554–1618), whose translation of Ovid's *Metamorphoses* (first century CE) is here quoted.

and tremble too much for that. Actually, the laboring man has not leisure for a true integrity day by day; he cannot afford to sustain the manliest relations to men; his labor would be depreciated in the market. He has no time to be anything but a machine. How can he remember well his ignorance—which his growth requires—who has so often to use his knowledge? We should feed and clothe him gratuitously sometimes, and recruit him with our cordials, before we judge of him. The finest qualities of our nature, like the bloom on fruits, can be preserved only by the most delicate handling. Yet we do not treat ourselves nor one another thus tenderly.

Some of you, we all know, are poor, find it hard to live, are sometimes, as it were, gasping for breath. I have no doubt that some of you who read this book are unable to pay for all the dinners which you have actually eaten, or for the coats and shoes which are fast wearing or are already worn out, and have come to this page to spend borrowed or stolen time, robbing your creditors of an hour. It is very evident what mean[4] and sneaking lives many of you live, for my sight has been whetted by experience; always on the limits, trying to get into business and trying to get out of debt, a very ancient slough, called by the Latins *æs alienum*, another's brass, for some of their coins were made of brass; still living, and dying, and buried by this other's brass; always promising to pay, promising to pay, tomorrow, and dying today, insolvent; seeking to curry favor, to get custom, by how many modes, only not state-prison offences; lying, flattering, voting, contracting yourselves into a nutshell of civility or dilating into an atmosphere of thin and vaporous generosity, that you may persuade your neighbor to let you make his shoes, or his hat, or his coat, or his carriage, or import his groceries for him; making yourselves sick, that you may lay up something against a sick day, something to be tucked away in an old chest, or in a stocking behind the plastering, or, more safely, in the brick bank; no matter where, no matter how much or how little.

I sometimes wonder that we can be so frivolous, I may almost say, as to attend to the gross but somewhat foreign form of servitude called Negro Slavery; there are so many keen and subtle masters that enslave both north and south. It is hard to have a southern overseer;

---

[4]   *mean*   Lowly.

it is worse to have a northern one; but worst of all when you are the slave-driver of yourself. Talk of a divinity in man! Look at the teamster on the highway, wending to market by day or night; does any divinity stir within him? His highest duty to fodder and water his horses! What is his destiny to him compared with the shipping interests? Does not he drive for Squire Make-a-stir? How godlike, how immortal, is he? See how he cowers and sneaks, how vaguely all the day he fears, not being immortal nor divine, but the slave and prisoner of his own opinion of himself, a fame won by his own deeds. Public opinion is a weak tyrant compared with our own private opinion. What a man thinks of himself, that it is which determines, or rather indicates, his fate. Self-emancipation even in the West Indian provinces of the fancy and imagination—what Wilberforce[1] is there to bring that about? Think, also, of the ladies of the land weaving toilet cushions[2] against the last day, not to betray too green an interest in their fates! As if you could kill time without injuring eternity.

The mass of men lead lives of quiet desperation. What is called resignation is confirmed desperation. From the desperate city you go into the desperate country, and have to console yourself with the bravery of minks and muskrats. A stereotyped but unconscious despair is concealed even under what are called the games and amusements of mankind. There is no play in them, for this comes after work. But it is a characteristic of wisdom not to do desperate things.

When we consider what, to use the words of the catechism, is the chief end of man,[3] and what are the true necessaries and means of life, it appears as if men had deliberately chosen the common mode of living because they preferred it to any other. Yet they honestly think there is no choice left. But alert and healthy natures remember that the sun rose clear. It is never too late to give up our prejudices. No way of thinking or doing, however ancient, can be trusted without proof. What everybody echoes or in silence passes by as true today may turn out to be falsehood tomorrow, mere smoke of opinion, which some had trusted for a cloud that would sprinkle fertilizing rain on their fields. What old people say you cannot do you try and find that you can. Old deeds for old people, and new deeds for new. Old people did not know enough once, perchance, to fetch fresh fuel to keep the fire a-going; new people put a little dry wood under a pot, and are whirled round the globe with the speed of birds, in a way to kill old people, as the phrase is. Age is no better, hardly so well, qualified for an instructor as youth, for it has not profited so much as it has lost. One may almost doubt if the wisest man has learned anything of absolute value by living. Practically, the old have no very important advice to give the young, their own experience has been so partial, and their lives have been such miserable failures, for private reasons, as they must believe; and it may be that they have some faith left which belies that experience, and they are only less young than they were. I have lived some thirty years on this planet, and I have yet to hear the first syllable of valuable or even earnest advice from my seniors. They have told me nothing, and probably cannot tell me anything to the purpose. Here is life, an experiment to a great extent untried by me; but it does not avail me that they have tried it. If I have any experience which I think valuable, I am sure to reflect that this my Mentors said nothing about.

One farmer says to me, "You cannot live on vegetable food solely, for it furnishes nothing to make bones with"; and so he religiously devotes a part of his day to supplying his system with the·raw material of bones; walking all the while he talks behind his oxen, which, with vegetable-made bones, jerk him and his lumbering plough along in spite of every obstacle. Some things are really necessaries of life in some circles, the most helpless and diseased, which in others are luxuries merely, and in others still are entirely unknown.

The whole ground of human life seems to some to have been gone over by their predecessors, both the heights and the valleys, and all things to have been

---

[1] *Wilberforce* William Wilberforce, English politician and abolitionist (1759–1833).

[2] *toilet cushions* Decorative cushions kept at one's dressing table or on the accompanying chair. (The noun "toilet" could refer either to the dressing room or table or to the action of getting dressed, doing one's hair, etc.)

[3] *the words … of man* The catechism is a church-authorized primer on Christian doctrine usually presented in the form of questions and conventionally accepted answers. The first question in *The New England Primer* is "What is the chief end of man?" with the answer being, "Man's chief end is to glorify God, and to enjoy him forever."

cared for. According to Evelyn,[1] "the wise Solomon prescribed ordinances for the very distances of trees; and the Roman prætors have decided how often you may go into your neighbor's land to gather the acorns which fall on it without trespass, and what share belongs to that neighbor." Hippocrates[2] has even left directions how we should cut our nails; that is, even with the ends of the fingers, neither shorter nor longer. Undoubtedly the very tedium and ennui which presume to have exhausted the variety and the joys of life are as old as Adam. But man's capacities have never been measured; nor are we to judge of what he can do by any precedents, so little has been tried. Whatever have been thy failures hitherto, "be not afflicted, my child, for who shall assign to thee what thou hast left undone?"[3]

We might try our lives by a thousand simple tests; as, for instance, that the same sun which ripens my beans illumines at once a system of earths like ours. If I had remembered this it would have prevented some mistakes. This was not the light in which I hoed them. The stars are the apexes of what wonderful triangles! What distant and different beings in the various mansions of the universe are contemplating the same one at the same moment! Nature and human life are as various as our several constitutions. Who shall say what prospect life offers to another? Could a greater miracle take place than for us to look through each other's eyes for an instant? We should live in all the ages of the world in an hour; ay, in all the worlds of the ages. History, Poetry, Mythology! I know of no reading of another's experience so startling and informing as this would be.

The greater part of what my neighbors call good I believe in my soul to be bad, and if I repent of anything, it is very likely to be my good behavior. What demon possessed me that I behaved so well? You may say the wisest thing you can, old man—you who have lived seventy years, not without honor of a kind—I hear an irresistible voice which invites me away from all that. One generation abandons the enterprises of another like stranded vessels.

I think that we may safely trust a good deal more than we do. We may waive just so much care of ourselves as we honestly bestow elsewhere. Nature is as well adapted to our weakness as to our strength. The incessant anxiety and strain of some is a well nigh incurable form of disease. We are made to exaggerate the importance of what work we do; and yet how much is not done by us! or, what if we had been taken sick? How vigilant we are! determined not to live by faith if we can avoid it; all the day long on the alert, at night we unwillingly say our prayers and commit ourselves to uncertainties. So thoroughly and sincerely are we compelled to live, reverencing our life, and denying the possibility of change. This is the only way, we say; but there are as many ways as there can be drawn radii from one centre. All change is a miracle to contemplate; but it is a miracle which is taking place every instant. Confucius said, "To know that we know what we know, and that we do not know what we do not know, that is true knowledge."[4] When one man has reduced a fact of the imagination to be a fact to his understanding, I foresee that all men at length establish their lives on that basis.

Let us consider for a moment what most of the trouble and anxiety which I have referred to is about, and how much it is necessary that we be troubled, or, at least, careful. It would be some advantage to live a primitive and frontier life, though in the midst of an outward civilization, if only to learn what are the gross necessaries of life and what methods have been taken to obtain them; or even to look over the old day-books of the merchants, to see what it was that men most commonly bought at the stores, what they stored, that is, what are the grossest groceries. For the improvements of ages have had but little influence on the essential laws of man's existence; as our skeletons, probably, are not to be distinguished from those of our ancestors.

By the words, *necessary of life*, I mean whatever, of all that man obtains by his own exertions, has been from the first, or from long use has become, so important to human life that few, if any, whether from savageness, or poverty, or philosophy, ever attempt to do without it. To many creatures there is in this sense but one

---

[1] *Evelyn* English diarist and gardener John Evelyn; the quotation is from his *Sylva; or, a Discourse of Forest Trees* (1679).

[2] *Hippocrates* Greek physician (c. 460–377 BCE).

[3] *be not afflicted ... undone?* From Horace Haymen Wilson's 1840 translation of *The Vishnu Purana*, a sacred Hindu text.

[4] *Confucius said ... knowledge* Thoreau's translation from Guillaume Pauthier's *Confucius et Mencius*, itself a French translation of the Confucian book *The Doctrine of the Mean*.

necessary of life, Food. To the bison of the prairie it is a few inches of palatable grass, with water to drink; unless he seeks the Shelter of the forest or the mountain's shadow. None of the brute creation requires more than Food and Shelter. The necessaries of life for man in this climate may, accurately enough, be distributed under the several heads of Food, Shelter, Clothing, and Fuel; for not till we have secured these are we prepared to entertain the true problems of life with freedom and a prospect of success. Man has invented, not only houses, but clothes and cooked food; and possibly from the accidental discovery of the warmth of fire, and the consequent use of it, at first a luxury, arose the present necessity to sit by it. We observe cats and dogs acquiring the same second nature. By proper Shelter and Clothing we legitimately retain our own internal heat; but with an excess of these, or of Fuel, that is, with an external heat greater than our own internal, may not cookery properly be said to begin? Darwin, the naturalist, says of the inhabitants of Tierra del Fuego, that while his own party, who were well clothed and sitting close to a fire, were far from too warm, these naked savages, who were farther off, were observed, to his great surprise, "to be streaming with perspiration at undergoing such a roasting."[1] So, we are told, the New Hollander[2] goes naked with impunity, while the European shivers in his clothes. Is it impossible to combine the hardiness of these savages with the intellectualness of the civilized man? According to Liebig,[3] man's body is a stove, and food the fuel which keeps up the internal combustion in the lungs. In cold weather we eat more, in warm less. The animal heat is the result of a slow combustion, and disease and death take place when this is too rapid; or for want of fuel, or from some defect in the draught, the fire goes out. Of course the vital heat is not to be confounded with fire; but so much for analogy. It appears, therefore, from the above list, that the expression, *animal life*, is nearly synonymous with the expression, *animal heat*; for while Food may be regarded as the Fuel which keeps up the fire

within us—and Fuel serves only to prepare that Food or to increase the warmth of our bodies by addition from without—Shelter and Clothing also serve only to retain the *heat* thus generated and absorbed.

The grand necessity, then, for our bodies, is to keep warm, to keep the vital heat in us. What pains we accordingly take, not only with our Food, and Clothing, and Shelter, but with our beds, which are our night-clothes, robbing the nests and breasts of birds to prepare this shelter within a shelter, as the mole has its bed of grass and leaves at the end of its burrow! The poor man is wont to complain that this is a cold world; and to cold, no less physical than social, we refer directly a great part of our ails. The summer, in some climates, makes possible to man a sort of Elysian[4] life. Fuel, except to cook his Food, is then unnecessary; the sun is his fire, and many of the fruits are sufficiently cooked by its rays; while Food generally is more various, and more easily obtained, and Clothing and Shelter are wholly or half unnecessary. At the present day, and in this country, as I find by my own experience, a few implements, a knife, an axe, a spade, a wheelbarrow, etc., and for the studious, lamplight, stationery, and access to a few books, rank next to necessaries, and can all be obtained at a trifling cost. Yet some, not wise, go to the other side of the globe, to barbarous and unhealthy regions, and devote themselves to trade for ten or twenty years, in order that they may live—that is, keep comfortably warm—and die in New England at last. The luxuriously rich are not simply kept comfortably warm, but unnaturally hot; as I implied before, they are cooked, of course à la mode.

Most of the luxuries, and many of the so-called comforts of life, are not only not indispensable, but positive hindrances to the elevation of mankind. With respect to luxuries and comforts, the wisest have ever lived a more simple and meagre life than the poor. The ancient philosophers, Chinese, Hindoo, Persian, and Greek, were a class than which none has been poorer in outward riches, none so rich in inward. We know not much about them. It is remarkable that we know so much of them as we do. The same is true of the more modern reformers and benefactors of their race. None can be an impartial or wise observer of human

---

[1]   *Darwin … roasting* See Charles Darwin's *Narrative of the Surveying Voyages of His Majesty's Ships Adventure and Beagle* (1839).

[2]   *New Hollander* Aboriginal Australian; Australia was named New Holland after its discovery by Dutch travelers in the seventeenth century.

[3]   *Liebig* German chemist Baron Justus von Liebig (1803–73).

[4]   *Elysian* Blissful. Referring to Elysium, where, according to classical mythology, the blessed reside after death.

life but from the vantage ground of what *we* should call voluntary poverty. Of a life of luxury the fruit is luxury, whether in agriculture, or commerce, or literature, or art. There are nowadays professors of philosophy, but not philosophers. Yet it is admirable to profess because it was once admirable to live. To be a philosopher is not merely to have subtle thoughts, nor even to found a school, but so to love wisdom as to live according to its dictates, a life of simplicity, independence, magnanimity, and trust. It is to solve some of the problems of life, not only theoretically, but practically. The success of great scholars and thinkers is commonly a courtier-like success, not kingly, not manly. They make shift to live merely by conformity, practically as their fathers did, and are in no sense the progenitors of a nobler race of men. But why do men degenerate ever? What makes families run out? What is the nature of the luxury which enervates and destroys nations? Are we sure that there is none of it in our own lives? The philosopher is in advance of his age even in the outward form of his life. He is not fed, sheltered, clothed, warmed, like his contemporaries. How can a man be a philosopher and not maintain his vital heat by better methods than other men?

When a man is warmed by the several modes which I have described, what does he want next? Surely not more warmth of the same kind, as more and richer food, larger and more splendid houses, finer and more abundant clothing, more numerous incessant and hotter fires, and the like. When he has obtained those things which are necessary to life, there is another alternative than to obtain the superfluities; and that is, to adventure on life now, his vacation from humbler toil having commenced. The soil, it appears, is suited to the seed, for it has sent its radicle[1] downward, and it may now send its shoot upward also with confidence. Why has man rooted himself thus firmly in the earth, but that he may rise in the same proportion into the heavens above?—for the nobler plants are valued for the fruit they bear at last in the air and light, far from the ground, and are not treated like the humbler esculents,[2] which, though they may be biennials, are cultivated only till they have perfected their root, and

often cut down at top for this purpose, so that most would not know them in their flowering season.

I do not mean to prescribe rules to strong and valiant natures, who will mind their own affairs whether in heaven or hell, and perchance build more magnificently and spend more lavishly than the richest, without ever impoverishing themselves, not knowing how they live—if, indeed, there are any such, as has been dreamed; nor to those who find their encouragement and inspiration in precisely the present condition of things, and cherish it with the fondness and enthusiasm of lovers—and, to some extent, I reckon myself in this number; I do not speak to those who are well employed, in whatever circumstances—and they know whether they are well employed or not—but mainly to the mass of men who are discontented, and idly complaining of the hardness of their lot or of the times, when they might improve them. There are some who complain most energetically and inconsolably of any, because they are, as they say, doing their duty. I also have in my mind that seemingly wealthy, but most terribly impoverished class of all, who have accumulated dross,[3] but know not how to use it, or get rid of it, and thus have forged their own golden or silver fetters.

If I should attempt to tell how I have desired to spend my life in years past, it would probably surprise those of my readers who are somewhat acquainted with its actual history; it would certainly astonish those who know nothing about it. I will only hint at some of the enterprises which I have cherished.

In any weather, at any hour of the day or night, I have been anxious to improve the nick of time, and notch it on my stick too; to stand on the meeting of two eternities, the past and future, which is precisely the present moment; to toe that line. You will pardon some obscurities, for there are more secrets in my trade than in most men's, and yet not voluntarily kept, but inseparable from its very nature. I would gladly tell all that I know about it, and never paint "No Admittance" on my gate.

I long ago lost a hound, a bay horse, and a turtledove, and am still on their trail. Many are the travellers I have spoken concerning them, describing their tracks

---

[1] *radicle* Root of a seedling.

[2] *esculents* Edibles.

[3] *dross* Substance left over from melting metals; more broadly, extraneous matter of little inherent value.

and what calls they answered to. I have met one or two who had heard the hound, and the tramp of the horse, and even seen the dove disappear behind a cloud, and they seemed as anxious to recover them as if they had lost them themselves.

To anticipate, not the sunrise and the dawn merely, but, if possible, Nature herself! How many mornings, summer and winter, before yet any neighbor was stirring about his business, have I been about mine! No doubt, many of my townsmen have met me returning from this enterprise, farmers starting for Boston in the twilight, or woodchoppers going to their work. It is true, I never assisted the sun materially in his rising, but, doubt not, it was of the last[1] importance only to be present at it.

So many autumn, ay, and winter days, spent outside the town, trying to hear what was in the wind, to hear and carry it express! I well-nigh sunk all my capital in it, and lost my own breath into the bargain, running in the face of it. If it had concerned either of the political parties, depend upon it, it would have appeared in the Gazette with the earliest intelligence. At other times watching from the observatory of some cliff or tree, to telegraph any new arrival; or waiting at evening on the hill-tops for the sky to fall, that I might catch something, though I never caught much, and that, manna-wise, would dissolve again in the sun.

For a long time I was reporter to a journal, of no very wide circulation, whose editor has never yet seen fit to print the bulk of my contributions, and, as is too common with writers, I got only my labor for my pains. However, in this case my pains were their own reward.

For many years I was self-appointed inspector of snow storms and rain storms, and did my duty faithfully; surveyor, if not of highways, then of forest paths and all across-lot routes, keeping them open, and ravines bridged and passable at all seasons, where the public heel had testified to their utility.

I have looked after the wild stock of the town, which give a faithful herdsman a good deal of trouble by leaping fences; and I have had an eye to the unfrequented nooks and corners of the farm; though I did not always know whether Jonas or Solomon worked in a particular field to-day; that was none of my business. I have

watered the red huckleberry, the sand cherry and the nettle tree, the red pine and the black ash, the white grape and the yellow violet, which might have withered else in dry seasons.

In short, I went on thus for a long time, I may say it without boasting, faithfully minding my business, till it became more and more evident that my townsmen would not after all admit me into the list of town officers, nor make my place a sinecure[2] with a moderate allowance. My accounts, which I can swear to have kept faithfully, I have, indeed, never got audited, still less accepted, still less paid and settled. However, I have not set my heart on that.

Not long since, a strolling Indian went to sell baskets at the house of a well-known lawyer in my neighborhood. "Do you wish to buy any baskets?" he asked. "No, we do not want any," was the reply. "What!" exclaimed the Indian as he went out the gate, "do you mean to starve us?" Having seen his industrious white neighbors so well off—that the lawyer had only to weave arguments, and by some magic, wealth and standing followed—he had said to himself; I will go into business; I will weave baskets; it is a thing which I can do. Thinking that when he had made the baskets he would have done his part, and then it would be the white man's to buy them. He had not discovered that it was necessary for him to make it worth the other's while to buy them, or at least make him think that it was so, or to make something else which it would be worth his while to buy. I too had woven a kind of basket of a delicate texture, but I had not made it worth any one's while to buy them. Yet not the less, in my case, did I think it worth my while to weave them, and instead of studying how to make it worth men's while to buy my baskets, I studied rather how to avoid the necessity of selling them. The life which men praise and regard as successful is but one kind. Why should we exaggerate any one kind at the expense of the others?

Finding that my fellow-citizens were not likely to offer me any room in the court house, or any curacy[3] or living anywhere else, but I must shift for myself, I turned my face more exclusively than ever to the woods, where I was better known. I determined to go into business at once, and not wait to acquire the usual

---

[1] *last* Greatest.

[2] *sinecure* Position that requires little or no actual work.

[3] *curacy* Ecclesiastical position.

capital, using such slender means as I had already got. My purpose in going to Walden Pond was not to live cheaply nor to live dearly there, but to transact some private business with the fewest obstacles; to be hindered from accomplishing which for want of a little common sense, a little enterprise and business talent, appeared not so sad as foolish.

I have always endeavored to acquire strict business habits; they are indispensable to every man. If your trade is with the Celestial Empire,[1] then some small counting house on the coast, in some Salem harbor, will be fixture enough. You will export such articles as the country affords, purely native products, much ice and pine timber and a little granite, always in native bottoms. These will be good ventures. To oversee all the details yourself in person; to be at once pilot and captain, and owner and underwriter; to buy and sell and keep the accounts; to read every letter received, and write or read every letter sent; to superintend the discharge of imports night and day; to be upon many parts of the coast almost at the same time—often the richest freight will be discharged upon a Jersey shore—to be your own telegraph, unweariedly sweeping the horizon, speaking all passing vessels bound coastwise; to keep up a steady despatch of commodities, for the supply of such a distant and exorbitant market; to keep yourself informed of the state of the markets, prospects of war and peace everywhere, and anticipate the tendencies of trade and civilization—taking advantage of the results of all exploring expeditions, using new passages and all improvements in navigation—charts to be studied, the position of reefs and new lights and buoys to be ascertained, and ever, and ever, the logarithmic tables to be corrected, for by the error of some calculator the vessel often splits upon a rock that should have reached a friendly pier—there is the untold fate of La Perouse[2]—universal science to be kept pace with, studying the lives of all great discoverers and navigators, great adventurers and merchants, from Hanno and the Phœnicians[3] down to our day; in

fine, account of stock to be taken from time to time, to know how you stand. It is a labor to task the faculties of a man—such problems of profit and loss, of interest, of tare and tret,[4] and gauging of all kinds in it, as demand a universal knowledge.

I have thought that Walden Pond would be a good place for business, not solely on account of the railroad and the ice trade; it offers advantages which it may not be good policy to divulge; it is a good port and a good foundation. No Neva marshes[5] to be filled; though you must every where build on piles of your own driving. It is said that a flood-tide, with a westerly wind, and ice in the Neva, would sweep St. Petersburg from the face of the earth.

As this business was to be entered into without the usual capital, it may not be easy to conjecture where those means, that will still be indispensable to every such undertaking, were to be obtained. As for Clothing, to come at once to the practical part of the question, perhaps we are led oftener by the love of novelty, and a regard for the opinions of men, in procuring it, than by a true utility. Let him who has work to do recollect that the object of clothing is, first, to retain the vital heat, and secondly, in this state of society, to cover nakedness, and he may judge how much of any necessary or important work may be accomplished without adding to his wardrobe. Kings and queens who wear a suit but once, though made by some tailor or dressmaker to their majesties, cannot know the comfort of wearing a suit that fits. They are no better than wooden horses to hang the clean clothes on. Every day our garments become more assimilated to ourselves, receiving the impress of the wearer's character, until we hesitate to lay them aside, without such delay and medical appliances and some such solemnity even as our bodies. No man ever stood the lower in my estimation for having a patch in his clothes; yet I am sure that there is greater anxiety, commonly, to have fashionable, or at least clean and unpatched clothes, than to have a sound conscience. But even if the rent is not mended, perhaps the worst vice betrayed is improvidence. I sometimes try my acquaintances by such tests as this: Who could wear a patch, or two extra seams only, over

---

[1] *Celestial Empire* . Term formerly used to refer to China.

[2] *La Perouse* French explorer Jean François de Galaup, comte de Lapérouse (1741–88).

[3] *Hanno* Carthaginian explorer of the west coast of Africa (c. fifth or sixth century BCE); *Phœnicians* Ancient inhabitants of the eastern Mediterranean region.

[4] *tare and tret* Deductions applied to weight of goods during shipping.

[5] *Neva marshes* Wetlands of the Neva river delta in Russia.

the knee? Most behave as if they believed that their prospects for life would be ruined if they should do it. It would be easier for them to hobble to town with a broken leg than with a broken pantaloon. Often if an accident happens to a gentleman's legs, they can be mended; but if a similar accident happens to the legs of his pantaloons, there is no help for it; for he considers, not what is truly respectable, but what is respected. We know but few men, a great many coats and breeches. Dress a scarecrow in your last shift, you standing shiftless by, who would not soonest salute the scarecrow? Passing a cornfield the other day, close by a hat and coat on a stake, I recognized the owner of the farm. He was only a little more weather-beaten than when I saw him last. I have heard of a dog that barked at every stranger who approached his master's premises with clothes on, but was easily quieted by a naked thief. It is an interesting question how far men would retain their relative rank if they were divested of their clothes. Could you, in such a case, tell surely of any company of civilized men, which belonged to the most respected class? When Madam Pfeiffer,[1] in her adventurous travels round the world, from east to west, had got so near home as Asiatic Russia, she says that she felt the necessity of wearing other than a travelling dress, when she went to meet the authorities, for she "was now in a civilized country, where … people are judged of by their clothes." Even in our democratic New England towns the accidental possession of wealth, and its manifestation in dress and equipage alone, obtain for the possessor almost universal respect. But they yield such respect, numerous as they are, are so far heathen, and need to have a missionary sent to them. Beside, clothes introduced sewing, a kind of work which you may call endless; a woman's dress, at least, is never done.[2]

A man who has at length found something to do will not need to get a new suit to do it in; for him the old will do, that has lain dusty in the garret[3] for an indeterminate period. Old shoes will serve a hero longer than they have served his valet—if a hero ever has a valet—bare feet are older than shoes, and he can make them do. Only they who go to soirées and legislative halls must have new coats, coats to change as often as the man changes in them. But if my jacket and trousers, my hat and shoes, are fit to worship God in, they will do; will they not? Who ever saw his old clothes—his old coat, actually worn out, resolved into its primitive elements, so that it was not a deed of charity to bestow it on some poor boy, by him perchance to be bestowed on some poorer still, or shall we say richer, who could do with less? I say, beware of all enterprises that require new clothes, and not rather a new wearer of clothes. If there is not a new man, how can the new clothes be made to fit? If you have any enterprise before you, try it in your old clothes. All men want, not something to *do with*, but something to *do*, or rather something to *be*. Perhaps we should never procure a new suit, however ragged or dirty the old, until we have so conducted, so enterprised or sailed in some way, that we feel like new men in the old, and that to retain it would be like keeping new wine in old bottles. Our moulting season, like that of the fowls, must be a crisis in our lives. The loon retires to solitary ponds to spend it. Thus also the snake casts its slough, and the caterpillar its wormy coat, by an internal industry and expansion; for clothes are but our outmost cuticle and mortal coil.[4] Otherwise we shall be found sailing under false colors, and be inevitably cashiered[5] at last by our own opinion, as well as that of mankind.

We don garment after garment, as if we grew like exogenous plants[6] by addition without. Our outside and often thin and fanciful clothes are our epidermis, or false skin, which partakes not of our life, and may be stripped off here and there without fatal injury; our thicker garments, constantly worn, are our cellular integument, or cortex; but our shirts are our liber or true bark, which cannot be removed without girdling and so destroying the man. I believe that all races at some seasons wear something equivalent to the shirt. It

---

[1]   *Madam Pfeiffer*   Austrian explorer Ida Laura Pfeiffer, née Reyer (1797–1858). The quotation that follows is from her *A Lady's Voyage Round the World* (1850).

[2]   *a woman's dress … never done*   Reference to the proverbial expression, "A woman's work is never done."

[3]   *garret*   Small, often unpleasant living space at the top of a building.

---

[4]   *mortal coil*   I.e., the body. See Shakespeare's *Hamlet* 3.1.74–76: "For in that sleep of death what dreams may come, / When we have shuffled off this mortal coil, / Must give us pause."

[5]   *cashiered*   Discredited; lowered in position.

[6]   *exogenous plants*   Plants that grow additional outer layers with each growth cycle, such as trees.

is desirable that a man be clad so simply that he can lay his hands on himself in the dark, and that he live in all respects so compactly and preparedly, that, if an enemy take the town, he can, like the old philosopher, walk out the gate empty-handed without anxiety. While one thick garment is, for most purposes, as good as three thin ones, and cheap clothing can be obtained at prices really to suit customers; while a thick coat can be bought for five dollars, which will last as many years, thick pantaloons for two dollars, cowhide boots for a dollar and a half a pair, a summer hat for a quarter of a dollar, and a winter cap for sixty-two and a half cents, or a better be made at home at a nominal cost, where is he so poor that, clad in such a suit, *of his own earning*, there will not be found wise men to do him reverence?

When I ask for a garment of a particular form, my tailoress tells me gravely, "They do not make them so now," not emphasizing the "They" at all, as if she quoted an authority as impersonal as the Fates, and I find it difficult to get made what I want, simply because she cannot believe that I mean what I say, that I am so rash. When I hear this oracular sentence, I am for a moment absorbed in thought, emphasizing to myself each word separately that I may come at the meaning of it, that I may find out by what degree of consanguinity *They* are related to *me*, and what authority they may have in an affair which affects me so nearly; and, finally, I am inclined to answer her with equal mystery, and without any more emphasis of the "they"—"It is true, they did not make them so recently, but they do now." Of what use this measuring of me if she does not measure my character, but only the breadth of my shoulders, as it were a peg to hang the coat on? We worship not the Graces, nor the Parcæ,[1] but Fashion. She spins and weaves and cuts with full authority. The head monkey at Paris puts on a traveller's cap, and all the monkeys in America do the same. I sometimes despair of getting anything quite simple and honest done in this world by the help of men. They would have to be passed through a powerful press first, to squeeze their old notions out of them, so that they would not soon get upon their legs again, and then there would be someone in the company with a maggot in his head, hatched from an egg deposited there nobody knows when, for not even fire kills these things, and you would have lost your labor. Nevertheless, we will not forget that some Egyptian wheat was handed down to us by a mummy.[2]

On the whole, I think that it cannot be maintained that dressing has in this or any country risen to the dignity of an art. At present men make shift to wear what they can get. Like shipwrecked sailors, they put on what they can find on the beach, and at a little distance, whether of space or time, laugh at each other's masquerade. Every generation laughs at the old fashions, but follows religiously the new. We are amused at beholding the costume of Henry VIII, or Queen Elizabeth, as much as if it was that of the King and Queen of the Cannibal Islands. All costume off a man is pitiful or grotesque. It is only the serious eye peering from and the sincere life passed within it, which restrain laughter and consecrate the costume of any people. Let Harlequin[3] be taken with a fit of the colic[4] and his trappings will have to serve that mood too. When the soldier is hit by a cannonball rags are as becoming as purple.

The childish and savage taste of men and women for new patterns keeps how many shaking and squinting through kaleidoscopes that they may discover the particular figure which this generation requires today. The manufacturers have learned that this taste is merely whimsical. Of two patterns which differ only by a few threads more or less of a particular color, the one will be sold readily, the other lie on the shelf, though it frequently happens that after the lapse of a season the latter becomes the most fashionable. Comparatively, tattooing is not the hideous custom which it is called. It is not barbarous merely because the printing is skin-deep and unalterable.

I cannot believe that our factory system is the best mode by which men may get clothing. The condition of the operatives is becoming every day more like that of the English; and it cannot be wondered at, since, as far as I have heard or observed, the principal object is, not that mankind may be well and honestly clad, but, unquestionably, that corporations may be enriched. In

---

1   *Graces* Greek goddesses of joy, charm, and beauty; *Parcæ* In Roman mythology, destiny, or The Fates.

2   *some Egyptian wheat … mummy* It was widely believed that seeds found in the tombs of ancient Egyptians could still germinate.

3   *Harlequin* Stock character in Italian stage comedies, known for his distinctive costume patterned in colorful diamond shapes.

4   *colic* Illness of the stomach or bowels.

the long run men hit only what they aim at. Therefore, though they should fail immediately, they had better aim at something high.

As for a Shelter, I will not deny that this is now a necessary of life, though there are instances of men having done without it for long periods in colder countries than this. Samuel Laing[1] says that "the Laplander[2] in his skin dress, and in a skin bag which he puts over his head and shoulders, will sleep night after night on the snow, in a degree of cold which would extinguish the life of one exposed to it in any woollen clothing." He had seen them asleep thus. Yet he adds, "They are not hardier than other people." But, probably, man did not live long on the earth without discovering the convenience which there is in a house, the domestic comforts, which phrase may have originally signified the satisfactions of the house more than of the family; though these must be extremely partial and occasional in those climates where the house is associated in our thoughts with winter or the rainy season chiefly, and two thirds of the year, except for a parasol, is unnecessary. In our climate, in the summer, it was formerly almost solely a covering at night. In the Indian gazettes[3] a wigwam was the symbol of a day's march, and a row of them cut or painted on the bark of a tree signified that so many times they had camped. Man was not made so large limbed and robust but that he must seek to narrow his world, and wall in a space such as fitted him. He was at first bare and out of doors; but though this was pleasant enough in serene and warm weather, by daylight, the rainy season and the winter, to say nothing of the torrid sun, would perhaps have nipped his race in the bud if he had not made haste to clothe himself with the shelter of a house. Adam and Eve, according to the fable, wore the bower before other clothes. Man wanted a home, a place of warmth, or comfort, first of physical warmth, then the warmth of the affections.

We may imagine a time when, in the infancy of the human race, some enterprising mortal crept into a hollow in a rock for shelter. Every child begins the world again, to some extent, and loves to stay outdoors, even in wet and cold. It plays house, as well as horse, having an instinct for it. Who does not remember the interest with which when young he looked at shelving rocks, or any approach to a cave? It was the natural yearning of that portion of our most primitive ancestor which still survived in us. From the cave we have advanced to roofs of palm leaves, of bark and boughs, of linen woven and stretched, of grass and straw, of boards and shingles, of stones and tiles. At last, we know not what it is to live in the open air, and our lives are domestic in more senses than we think. From the hearth to the field is a great distance. It would be well perhaps if we were to spend more of our days and nights without any obstruction between us and the celestial bodies, if the poet did not speak so much from under a roof, or the saint dwell there so long. Birds do not sing in caves, nor do doves cherish their innocence in dovecots.

However, if one designs to construct a dwelling house, it behooves him to exercise a little Yankee shrewdness, lest after all he find himself in a workhouse, a labyrinth without a clue, a museum, an almshouse, a prison, or a splendid mausoleum instead. Consider first how slight a shelter is absolutely necessary. I have seen Penobscot Indians, in this town, living in tents of thin cotton cloth, while the snow was nearly a foot deep around them, and I thought that they would be glad to have it deeper to keep out the wind. Formerly, when how to get my living honestly, with freedom left for my proper pursuits, was a question which vexed me even more than it does now, for unfortunately I am become somewhat callous,[4] I used to see a large box by the railroad, six feet long by three wide, in which the laborers locked up their tools at night, and it suggested to me that every man who was hard pushed might get such a one for a dollar, and, having bored a few auger holes in it, to admit the air at least, get into it when it rained and at night, and hook down the lid, and so have freedom in his love, and in his soul be free. This did not appear the worst, nor by any means a despicable alternative. You could

---

[1] *Samuel Laing* Scottish traveler and writer; Thoreau quotes from his 1837 *Journal of a Residence in Norway during the Years 1834, 1835, and 1836.*

[2] *Laplander* I.e., a Sami, or Indigenous person of northern Scandinavia; the term "Lapland" today refers more specifically to a region of northern Finland.

[3] *gazettes* Engravings.

---

[4] *callous* Hardened (with no suggestion of having become unfeeling toward the sufferings of others).

sit up as late as you pleased, and, whenever you got up, go abroad without any landlord or house-lord dogging you for rent. Many a man is harassed to death to pay the rent of a larger and more luxurious box who would not have frozen to death in such a box as this. I am far from jesting. Economy is a subject which admits of being treated with levity, but it cannot so be disposed of. A comfortable house for a rude and hardy race, that lived mostly out of doors, was once made here almost entirely of such materials as Nature furnished ready to their hands. Gookin,[1] who was superintendent of the Indians subject to the Massachusetts Colony, writing in 1674, says, "The best of their houses are covered very neatly, tight and warm, with barks of trees, slipped from their bodies at those seasons when the sap is up, and made into great flakes, with pressure of weighty timber, when they are green. The meaner sort are covered with mats which they make of a kind of bulrush, and are also indifferently tight and warm, but not so good as the former. Some I have seen, sixty or a hundred feet long and thirty feet broad. I have often lodged in their wigwams, and found them as warm as the best English houses." He adds, that they were commonly carpeted and lined within with well-wrought embroidered mats, and were furnished with various utensils. The Indians had advanced so far as to regulate the effect of the wind by a mat suspended over the hole in the roof and moved by a string. Such a lodge was in the first instance constructed in a day or two at most, and taken down and put up in a few hours; and every family owned one, or its apartment in one.

In the savage state[2] every family owns a shelter as good as the best, and sufficient for its coarser and simpler wants; but I think that I speak within bounds when I say that, though the birds of the air have their nests, and the foxes their holes,[3] and the savages their wigwams, in modern civilized society not more than one half the families own a shelter. In the large towns and cities, where civilization especially prevails, the number of those who own a shelter is a very small fraction of the whole. The rest pay an annual tax for this outside garment of all, become indispensable summer and winter, which would buy a village of Indian wigwams, but now helps to keep them poor as long as they live. I do not mean to insist here on the disadvantage of hiring[4] compared with owning, but it is evident that the savage owns his shelter because it costs so little, while the civilized man hires his commonly because he cannot afford to own it; nor can he, in the long run, any better afford to hire. But, answers one, by merely paying this tax the *poor* civilized man secures an abode which is a palace compared with the savage's. An annual rent of from twenty-five to a hundred dollars (these are the country rates) entitles him to the benefit of the improvements of centuries, spacious apartments, clean paint and paper, Rumford fireplace,[5] back plastering, Venetian blinds, copper pump, spring lock, a commodious cellar, and many other things. But how happens it that he who is said to enjoy these things is so commonly a poor civilized man, while the savage, who has them not, is rich as a savage? If it is asserted that civilization is a real advance in the condition of man—and I think that it is, though only the wise improve their advantages—it must be shown that it has produced better dwellings without making them more costly; and the cost of a thing is the amount of what I will call life which is required to be exchanged for it, immediately or in the long run. An average house in this neighborhood costs perhaps eight hundred dollars, and to lay up this sum will take from ten to fifteen years of the laborer's life, even if he is not encumbered with a family—estimating the pecuniary value of every man's labor at one dollar a day, for if some receive more, others receive less—so that he must have spent more than half his life commonly before *his* wigwam will be earned. If we suppose him to pay a rent instead, this is but a doubtful choice of evils. Would the savage have been wise to exchange his wigwam for a palace on these terms?

It may be guessed that I reduce almost the whole advantage of holding this superfluous property as

---

[1]   *Gookin* Irish-born Puritan settler Daniel Gookin (1612–87), who lived in Vermont and Massachusetts, and was known for his interest in and writings about Native American cultures.

[2]   *In the savage state*   In a state of simplicity (with no suggestion of being prone to savagery); living according to nature, without any of the trappings of civilization.

[3]   *the birds ... their holes* See Matthew 8.20: "The foxes have holes, and the birds of the air have nests, but the Son of man hath not where to lay his head."

[4]   *hiring* Renting.

[5]   *Rumford fireplace* Fireplace designed to prevent smoke from being carried downward by drafts.

a fund in store against the future, so far as the individual is concerned, mainly to the defraying of funeral expenses. But perhaps a man is not required to bury himself. Nevertheless this points to an important distinction between the civilized man and the savage; and, no doubt, they have designs on us for our benefit, in making the life of a civilized people an *institution*, in which the life of the individual is to a great extent absorbed, in order to preserve and perfect that of the race. But I wish to show at what a sacrifice this advantage is at present obtained, and to suggest that we may possibly so live as to secure all the advantage without suffering any of the disadvantage. What mean ye by saying that the poor ye have always with you, or that the fathers have eaten sour grapes, and the children's teeth are set on edge?

"As I live, saith the Lord God, ye shall not have occasion any more to use this proverb in Israel."

"Behold all souls are mine; as the soul of the father, so also the soul of the son is mine: the soul that sinneth, it shall die."[1]

When I consider my neighbors, the farmers of Concord, who are at least as well off as the other classes, I find that for the most part they have been toiling twenty, thirty, or forty years, that they may become the real owners of their farms, which commonly they have inherited with encumbrances, or else bought with hired money—and we may regard one third of that toil as the cost of their houses—but commonly they have not paid for them yet. It is true, the encumbrances sometimes outweigh the value of the farm, so that the farm itself becomes one great encumbrance, and still a man is found to inherit it, being well acquainted with it, as he says. On applying to the assessors, I am surprised to learn that they cannot at once name a dozen in the town who own their farms free and clear. If you would know the history of these homesteads, inquire at the bank where they are mortgaged. The man who has actually paid for his farm with labor on it is so rare that every neighbor can point to him. I doubt if there are three such men in Concord. What has been said of the merchants, that a very large majority, even ninety-seven in a hundred, are sure to fail, is equally true of the farmers. With regard to the merchants, however, one of them says pertinently that a great part

of their failures are not genuine pecuniary failures, but merely failures to fulfil their engagements, because it is inconvenient; that is, it is the moral character that breaks down. But this puts an infinitely worse face on the matter, and suggests, beside, that probably not even the other three succeed in saving their souls, but are perchance bankrupt in a worse sense than they who fail honestly. Bankruptcy and repudiation are the springboards from which much of our civilization vaults and turns its somersets,[2] but the savage stands on the unelastic plank of famine. Yet the Middlesex Cattle Show goes off here with éclat[3] annually, as if all the joints of the agricultural machine were suent.[4]

The farmer is endeavoring to solve the problem of a livelihood by a formula more complicated than the problem itself. To get his shoestrings[5] he speculates in herds of cattle. With consummate skill he has set his trap with a hair spring to catch comfort and independence, and then, as he turned away, got his own leg into it. This is the reason he is poor; and for a similar reason we are all poor in respect to a thousand savage comforts, though surrounded by luxuries. As Chapman sings,

> The false society of men—
> —for earthly greatness
> All heavenly comforts rarefies to air.[6]

And when the farmer has got his house, he may not be the richer but the poorer for it, and it be the house that has got him. As I understand it, that was a valid objection urged by Momus against the house which

---

[1]   *What mean ye ... shall die*   See Ezekiel 18.2–4.

[2]   *somersets*   Somersaults.

[3]   éclat   Dazzling effect.

[4]   *suent*   Running smoothly.

[5]   *shoestrings*   Generally made of leather in the 1800s.

[6]   *Chapman ... rarifies to air*   I.e., Human society leads us, for the sake of pursuing greatness on earth, to treat heavenly comforts as insubstantial. Chapman (1559–1634) was an English poet and dramatist; the quotation is from his *The Tragedy of Caesar and Pompey* 5.2; in which the character Sacrifice argues in a long speech that humans pay too much attention to expensive ornament and, more generally, to building in the outward, physical world; he expresses his own intent to "build all inward" and commends those who turn "their back to all the world / And only look at heaven."

Minerva[1] made, that she "had not made it movable, by which means a bad neighborhood might be avoided"; and it may still be urged, for our houses are such unwieldy property that we are often imprisoned rather than housed in them; and the bad neighborhood to be avoided is our own scurvy selves. I know one or two families, at least, in this town, who, for nearly a generation, have been wishing to sell their houses in the outskirts and move into the village, but have not been able to accomplish it, and only death will set them free.

Granted that the *majority* are able at last either to own or hire the modern house with all its improvements. While civilization has been improving our houses, it has not equally improved the men who are to inhabit them. It has created palaces, but it was not so easy to create noblemen and kings. *And if the civilized man's pursuits are no worthier than the savage's, if he is employed the greater part of his life in obtaining gross necessaries and comforts merely, why should he have a better dwelling than the former?*

But how do the poor *minority* fare? Perhaps it will be found, that just in proportion as some have been placed in outward circumstances above the savage, others have been degraded below him. The luxury of one class is counterbalanced by the indigence of another. On the one side is the palace, on the other are the almshouse and "silent poor."[2] The myriads who built the pyramids to be the tombs of the Pharaohs were fed on garlic, and it may be were not decently buried themselves. The mason who finishes the cornice of the palace returns at night perchance to a hut not so good as a wigwam. It is a mistake to suppose that, in a country where the usual evidences of civilization exist, the condition of a very large body of the inhabitants may not be as degraded as that of savages. I refer to the degraded poor, not now to the degraded rich. To know this I should not need to look farther than to the shanties which everywhere border our railroads, that last improvement in civilization; where I see in my daily walks human beings living in sties, and all winter with an open door, for the sake of light, without any visible, often imaginable, wood pile, and the forms of both old and young are permanently contracted by the long habit of shrinking from cold and misery, and the development of all their limbs and faculties is checked. It certainly is fair to look at that class by whose labor the works which distinguish this generation are accomplished. Such too, to a greater or less extent, is the condition of the operatives of every denomination in England, which is the great workhouse of the world. Or I could refer you to Ireland,[3] which is marked as one of the white or enlightened spots on the map. Contrast the physical condition of the Irish with that of the North American Indian, or the South Sea Islander, or any other savage race before it was degraded by contact with the civilized man. Yet I have no doubt that that people's rulers are as wise as the average of civilized rulers. Their condition only proves what squalidness may consist with civilization. I hardly need refer now to the laborers in our Southern States who produce the staple exports of this country, and are themselves a staple production of the South.[4] But to confine myself to those who are said to be in *moderate* circumstances.

Most men appear never to have considered what a house is, and are actually though needlessly poor all their lives because they think that they must have such a one as their neighbors have. As if one were to wear any sort of coat which the tailor might cut out for him, or, gradually leaving off palmleaf hat or cap of woodchuck skin, complain of hard times because he could not afford to buy him a crown! It is possible to invent a house still more convenient and luxurious than we have, which yet all would admit that man could not afford to pay for. Shall we always study to obtain more of these things, and not sometimes to be content with less? Shall the respectable citizen thus gravely teach, by precept and example, the necessity of the young man's providing a certain number of superfluous glow-shoes,[5] and umbrellas, and empty guest chambers for empty guests, before he dies? Why should not our furniture be as simple as the Arab's or the Indian's? When I think of the benefactors of the race, whom

---

[1] *Momus* Greek god of mockery and unfair criticism; *Minerva* Roman goddess of wisdom and strategic warfare (equivalent of the Greek Athena).

[2] *silent poor* Those who neither complain of their poverty nor seek charity.

[3] *Ireland* At the time of Thoreau's residence at Walden Pond, Ireland was going through the Great Famine, which resulted in the deaths of approximately one million people.

[4] *the laborers … the South* I.e., enslaved people.

[5] *glow-shoes* I.e., galoshes; rubber boots.

we have apotheosized as messengers from heaven, bearers of divine gifts to man, I do not see in my mind any retinue at their heels, any car-load of fashionable furniture. Or what if I were to allow—would it not be a singular allowance?—that our furniture should be more complex than the Arab's, in proportion as we are morally and intellectually his superiors! At present our houses are cluttered and defiled with it, and a good housewife would sweep out the greater part into the dust hole, and not leave her morning's work undone. Morning work! By the blushes of Aurora and the music of Memnon,[1] what should be man's *morning work* in this world? I had three pieces of limestone on my desk, but I was terrified to find that they required to be dusted daily, when the furniture of my mind was all undusted still, and I threw them out the window in disgust. How, then, could I have a furnished house? I would rather sit in the open air, for no dust gathers on the grass, unless where man has broken ground.

It is the luxurious and dissipated who set the fashions which the herd so diligently follow. The traveller who stops at the best houses, so called, soon discovers this, for the publicans presume him to be a Sardanapalus,[2] and if he resigned himself to their tender mercies he would soon be completely emasculated. I think that in the railroad car we are inclined to spend more on luxury than on safety and convenience, and it threatens without attaining these to become no better than a modern drawing room, with its divans, and ottomans, and sun-shades, and a hundred other oriental things, which we are taking west with us, invented for the ladies of the harem and the effeminate natives of the Celestial Empire, which Jonathan[3] should be ashamed to know the names of. I would rather sit on a pumpkin and have it all to myself than be crowded on a velvet cushion. I would rather ride on earth in an ox cart with a free circulation, than go to heaven in the fancy car of an excursion train and breathe a *malaria*[4] all the way.

The very simplicity and nakedness of man's life in the primitive ages imply this advantage at least, that they left him still but a sojourner in nature. When he was refreshed with food and sleep he contemplated his journey again. He dwelt, as it were, in a tent in this world, and was either threading the valleys, or crossing the plains, or climbing the mountain tops. But lo! men have become the tools of their tools. The man who independently plucked the fruits when he was hungry is become a farmer; and he who stood under a tree for shelter, a housekeeper. We now no longer camp as for a night, but have settled down on earth and forgotten heaven. We have adopted Christianity merely as an improved method of *agri*-culture.[5] We have built for this world a family mansion, and for the next a family tomb. The best works of art are the expression of man's struggle to free himself from this condition, but the effect of our art is merely to make this low state comfortable and that higher state to be forgotten. There is actually no place in this village for a work of *fine* art, if any had come down to us, to stand, for our lives, our houses and streets, furnish no proper pedestal for it. There is not a nail to hang a picture on, nor a shelf to receive the bust of a hero or a saint. When I consider how our houses are built and paid for, or not paid for, and their internal economy managed and sustained, I wonder that the floor does not give way under the visitor while he is admiring the gewgaws[6] upon the mantel-piece, and let him through into the cellar, to some solid and honest though earthy foundation. I cannot but perceive that this so called rich and refined life is a thing jumped at, and I do not get on in the enjoyment of the *fine* arts which adorn it, my attention being wholly occupied with the jump; for I remember that the greatest genuine leap, due to human muscles alone, on record, is that of certain wandering Arabs, who are said to have cleared twenty-five feet on level ground. Without factitious support, man is sure to come to earth again beyond that distance. The first question which I am tempted to put to the proprietor of such great impropriety is, Who bolsters you? Are you one of the ninety-seven who fail, or of the three who succeed? Answer me these questions, and then

---

[1] *Aurora* Roman goddess of the dawn; *Memnon* Mythological king of Ethiopia, son of Aurora; a statue built in his honor was said to have emitted a beautiful song every morning at dawn.

[2] *a Sardanapalus* I.e., as a king surrounded by his enemies, defeated; Sardanapalus was according to legend the last king of Assyria (c. seventh century BCE).

[3] *Jonathan* Generic name for a stereotypical American man.

[4] *a malaria* I.e., tainted, diseased air.

[5] *agri-culture* Play on words emphasizing the Latin root *agri*, meaning the tilling of fields.

[6] *gewgaws* Frivolous ornaments.

perhaps I may look at your baubles and find them ornamental. The cart before the horse is neither beautiful nor useful. Before we can adorn our houses with beautiful objects the walls must be stripped, and our lives must be stripped, and beautiful housekeeping and beautiful living be laid for a foundation: now, a taste for the beautiful is most cultivated out of doors, where there is no house and no housekeeper.

Old Johnson,[1] in his *Wonder-Working Providence*, speaking of the first settlers of this town, with whom he was contemporary, tells us that "they burrow themselves in the earth for their first shelter under some hillside, and, casting the soil aloft upon timber, they make a smoky fire against the earth, at the highest side." They did not "provide them houses," says he, "till the earth, by the Lord's blessing, brought forth bread to feed them," and the first year's crop was so light that "they were forced to cut their bread very thin for a long season." The secretary of the Province of New Netherland,[2] writing in Dutch, in 1650, for the information of those who wished to take up land there, states more particularly that "those in New Netherland, and especially in New England, who have no means to build farmhouses at first according to their wishes, dig a square pit in the ground, cellar fashion, six or seven feet deep, as long and as broad as they think proper, case the earth inside with wood all round the wall, and line the wood with the bark of trees or something else to prevent the caving in of the earth; floor this cellar with plank, and wainscot it overhead for a ceiling, raise a roof of spars clear up, and cover the spars with bark or green sods, so that they can live dry and warm in these houses with their entire families for two, three, and four years, it being understood that partitions are run through those cellars which are adapted to the size of the family. The wealthy and principal men in New England, in the beginning of the colonies, commenced their first dwelling houses in this fashion for two reasons; firstly, in order not to waste time in building, and not to want food the next season; secondly, in order not to discourage poor laboring people whom they brought over in numbers from Fatherland. In the course of three or four years, when the country became adapted to agriculture, they built themselves handsome houses, spending on them several thousands."

In this course which our ancestors took there was a show of prudence at least, as if their principle were to satisfy the more pressing wants first. But are the more pressing wants satisfied now? When I think of acquiring for myself one of our luxurious dwellings, I am deterred, for, so to speak, the country is not yet adapted to *human* culture, and we are still forced to cut our *spiritual* bread far thinner than our forefathers did their wheaten. Not that all architectural ornament is to be neglected even in the rudest periods; but let our houses first be lined with beauty, where they come in contact with our lives, like the tenement of the shell-fish, and not overlaid with it. But, alas! I have been inside one or two of them, and know what they are lined with.

Though we are not so degenerate but that we might possibly live in a cave or a wigwam or wear skins to-day, it certainly is better to accept the advantages, though so dearly bought, which the invention and industry of mankind offer. In such a neighborhood as this, boards and shingles, lime and bricks, are cheaper and more easily obtained than suitable caves, or whole logs, or bark in sufficient quantities, or even well-tempered clay or flat stones. I speak understandingly on this subject, for I have made myself acquainted with it both theoretically and practically. With a little more wit we might use these materials so as to become richer than the richest now are, and make our civilization a blessing. The civilized man is a more experienced and wiser savage. But to make haste to my own experiment.

Near the end of March, 1845, I borrowed an axe and went down to the woods by Walden Pond, nearest to where I intended to build my house, and began to cut down some tall, arrowy white pines, still in their youth, for timber. It is difficult to begin without borrowing, but perhaps it is the most generous course thus to permit your fellow-men to have an interest in your enterprise. The owner of the axe, as he released his hold on it, said that it was the apple of his eye; but I returned it sharper than I received it. It was a pleasant hillside

---

[1] *Old Johnson* Boston settler Edward Johnson, author of *A History of New England*, better known as *The Wonder-Working Providence of Sions Saviour in New England* (1654), from which Thoreau quotes.

[2] *Province of New Netherland* Region settled by the Dutch in the seventeenth century, which later became New York State.

where I worked, covered with pine woods, through which I looked out on the pond, and a small open field in the woods where pines and hickories were springing up. The ice in the pond was not yet dissolved, though there were some open spaces, and it was all dark-colored and saturated with water. There were some slight flurries of snow during the days that I worked there; but for the most part when I came out on to the railroad, on my way home, its yellow sand-heap stretched away gleaming in the hazy atmosphere, and the rails shone in the spring sun, and I heard the lark and pewee and other birds already come to commence another year with us. They were pleasant spring days, in which the winter of man's discontent[1] was thawing as well as the earth, and the life that had lain torpid began to stretch itself. One day, when my axe had come off and I had cut a green hickory for a wedge, driving it with a stone, and had placed the whole to soak in a pond hole in order to swell the wood, I saw a striped snake run into the water, and he lay on the bottom, apparently without inconvenience, as long as I stayed there, or more than a quarter of an hour; perhaps because he had not yet fairly come out of the torpid state. It appeared to me that for a like reason men remain in their present low and primitive condition; but if they should feel the influence of the spring of springs arousing them, they would of necessity rise to a higher and more ethereal life. I had previously seen the snakes in frosty mornings in my path with portions of their bodies still numb and inflexible, waiting for the sun to thaw them. On the 1st of April it rained and melted the ice, and in the early part of the day, which was very foggy, I heard a stray goose groping about over the pond and cackling as if lost, or like the spirit of the fog.

So I went on for some days cutting and hewing timber, and also studs and rafters, all with my narrow axe, not having many communicable or scholar-like thoughts, singing to myself,

> Men say they know many things;
> But lo! they have taken wings—
> The arts and sciences,
> And a thousand appliances;

The wind that blows
Is all that anybody knows.[2]

I hewed the main timbers six inches square, most of the studs on two sides only, and the rafters and floor timbers on one side, leaving the rest of the bark on, so that they were just as straight and much stronger than sawed ones. Each stick was carefully mortised or tenoned[3] by its stump, for I had borrowed other tools by this time. My days in the woods were not very long ones; yet I usually carried my dinner of bread and butter, and read the newspaper in which it was wrapped, at noon, sitting amid the green pine boughs which I had cut off, and to my bread was imparted some of their fragrance, for my hands were covered with a thick coat of pitch. Before I had done I was more the friend than the foe of the pine tree, though I had cut down some of them, having become better acquainted with it. Sometimes a rambler in the wood was attracted by the sound of my axe, and we chatted pleasantly over the chips which I had made.

By the middle of April, for I made no haste in my work, but rather made the most of it, my house was framed and ready for the raising. I had already bought the shanty of James Collins, an Irishman who worked on the Fitchburg Railroad, for boards. James Collins' shanty was considered an uncommonly fine one. When I called to see it he was not at home. I walked about the outside, at first unobserved from within, the window was so deep and high. It was of small dimensions, with a peaked cottage roof, and not much else to be seen, the dirt being raised five feet all around as if it were a compost heap. The roof was the soundest part, though a good deal warped and made brittle by the sun. Door-sill there was none, but a perennial passage for the hens under the door board. Mrs. C. came to the door and asked me to view it from the inside. The hens were driven in by my approach. It was dark, and had a dirt floor for the most part, dank, clammy, and aguish, only here a board and there a board which would not bear removal. She lighted a lamp to show me the inside of the roof and the walls, and also that the board floor extended under the bed, warning me not to step into

---

[1]   *winter of man's discontent*   See Shakespeare's *Richard III* I.I.I: "Now is the winter of our discontent."

[2]   *Men say … anybody knows*   The poem is Thoreau's own.

[3]   *mortised or tenoned*   Types of joint connecting two pieces of wood.

the cellar, a sort of dust hole two feet deep. In her own words, they were "good boards overhead, good boards all around, and a good window"—of two whole squares originally, only the cat had passed out that way lately. There was a stove, a bed, and a place to sit, an infant in the house where it was born, a silk parasol, gilt-framed looking-glass, and a patent new coffee mill nailed to an oak sapling, all told. The bargain was soon concluded, for James had in the meanwhile returned. I to pay four dollars and twenty-five cents tonight, he to vacate at five tomorrow morning, selling to nobody else meanwhile: I to take possession at six. It were well, he said, to be there early, and anticipate certain indistinct but wholly unjust claims on the score of ground rent and fuel. This he assured me was the only encumbrance. At six I passed him and his family on the road. One large bundle held their all,—bed, coffee-mill, looking-glass, hens—all but the cat, she took to the woods and became a wild cat, and, as I learned afterward, trod in a trap set for woodchucks, and so became a dead cat at last.

I took down this dwelling the same morning, drawing the nails, and removed it to the pond side by small cartloads, spreading the boards on the grass there to bleach and warp back again in the sun. One early thrush gave me a note or two as I drove along the woodland path. I was informed treacherously by a young Patrick[1] that neighbor Seeley, an Irishman, in the intervals of the carting, transferred the still tolerable, straight, and drivable nails, staples, and spikes to his pocket, and then stood when I came back to pass the time of day, and look freshly up, unconcerned, with spring thoughts, at the devastation; there being a dearth of work, as he said. He was there to represent spectatordom, and help make this seemingly insignificant event one with the removal of the gods of Troy.[2]

I dug my cellar in the side of a hill sloping to the south, where a woodchuck had formerly dug his burrow, down through sumach and blackberry roots, and the lowest stain of vegetation, six feet square by seven deep, to a fine sand where potatoes would not freeze in any winter. The sides were left shelving, and

not stoned; but the sun having never shone on them, the sand still keeps its place. It was but two hours' work. I took particular pleasure in this breaking of ground, for in almost all latitudes men dig into the earth for an equable temperature. Under the most splendid house in the city is still to be found the cellar where they store their roots as of old, and long after the superstructure has disappeared posterity remark its dent in the earth. The house is still but a sort of porch at the entrance of a burrow.

At length, in the beginning of May, with the help of some of my acquaintances, rather to improve so good an occasion for neighborliness than from any necessity, I set up the frame of my house. No man was ever more honored in the character of his raisers[3] than I. They are destined, I trust, to assist at the raising of loftier structures one day. I began to occupy my house on the 4th of July, as soon as it was boarded and roofed, for the boards were carefully feather-edged and lapped, so that it was perfectly impervious to rain; but before boarding I laid the foundation of a chimney at one end, bringing two cartloads of stones up the hill from the pond in my arms. I built the chimney after my hoeing in the fall, before a fire became necessary for warmth, doing my cooking in the meanwhile out of doors on the ground, early in the morning: which mode I still think is in some respects more convenient and agreeable than the usual one. When it stormed before my bread was baked, I fixed a few boards over the fire, and sat under them to watch my loaf, and passed some pleasant hours in that way. In those days, when my hands were much employed, I read but little, but the least scraps of paper which lay on the ground, my holder, or tablecloth, afforded me as much entertainment, in fact answered the same purpose as the *Iliad*.

It would be worth the while to build still more deliberately than I did, considering, for instance, what foundation a door, a window, a cellar, a garret, have in the nature of man, and perchance never raising any superstructure until we found a better reason for it than our temporal necessities even. There is some of the same fitness in a man's building his own house that there is

---

[1] *Patrick* Generic name for a stereotypical Irishman.

[2] *the removal … of Troy* Allusion to Virgil's *Aeneid*, in which Aeneas and his family escape Troy before its destruction, carrying with them their household gods.

[3] *his raisers* At least a half dozen others assisted Thoreau in raising his cabin—among them Ralph Waldo Emerson, Bronson Alcott, and William Ellery Channing.

in a bird's building its own nest. Who knows but if men constructed their dwellings with their own hands, and provided food for themselves and families simply and honestly enough, the poetic faculty would be universally developed, as birds universally sing when they are so engaged? But alas! we do like cowbirds and cuckoos, which lay their eggs in nests which other birds have built, and cheer no traveller with their chattering and unmusical notes. Shall we forever resign the pleasure of construction to the carpenter? What does architecture amount to in the experience of the mass of men? I never in all my walks came across a man engaged in so simple and natural an occupation as building his house. We belong to the community. It is not the tailor alone who is the ninth part of a man; it is as much the preacher, and the merchant, and the farmer. Where is this division of labor to end? and what object does it finally serve? No doubt another *may* also think for me; but it is not therefore desirable that he should do so to the exclusion of my thinking for myself.

True, there are architects so called in this country, and I have heard of one at least possessed with the idea of making architectural ornaments have a core of truth, a necessity, and hence a beauty, as if it were a revelation to him.[1] All very well perhaps from his point of view, but only a little better than the common dilettantism. A sentimental reformer in architecture, he began at the cornice, not at the foundation. It was only how to put a core of truth within the ornaments, that every sugar plum in fact might have an almond or caraway seed in it—though I hold that almonds are most wholesome without the sugar—and not how the inhabitant, the indweller, might build truly within and without, and let the ornaments take care of themselves. What reasonable man ever supposed that ornaments were something outward and in the skin merely—that the tortoise got his spotted shell, or the shell-fish its mother-o'-pearl tints, by such a contract as the inhabitants of Broadway their Trinity Church?[2] But a man

has no more to do with the style of architecture of his house than a tortoise with that of its shell: nor need the soldier be so idle as to try to paint the precise *color* of his virtue on his standard. The enemy will find it out. He may turn pale when the trial comes. This man seemed to me to lean over the cornice, and timidly whisper his half truth to the rude occupants who really knew it better than he. What of architectural beauty I now see, I know has gradually grown from within outward, out of the necessities and character of the indweller, who is the only builder—out of some unconscious truthfulness, and nobleness, without ever a thought for the appearance and whatever additional beauty of this kind is destined to be produced will be preceded by a like unconscious beauty of life. The most interesting dwellings in this country, as the painter knows, are the most unpretending, humble log huts and cottages of the poor commonly; it is the life of the inhabitants whose shells they are, and not any peculiarity in their surfaces merely, which makes them *picturesque*; and equally interesting will be the citizen's suburban box, when his life shall be as simple and as agreeable to the imagination, and there is as little straining after effect in the style of his dwelling. A great proportion of architectural ornaments are literally hollow, and a September gale would strip them off, like borrowed plumes, without injury to the substantials. They can do without *architecture* who have no olives nor wines in the cellar. What if an equal ado were made about the ornaments of style in literature, and the architects of our bibles spent as much time about their cornices as the architects of our churches do? So are made the *belles-lettres* and the *beaux-arts* and their professors. Much it concerns a man, forsooth, how a few sticks are slanted over him or under him, and what colors are daubed upon his box. It would signify somewhat, if, in any earnest sense, *he* slanted them and daubed it; but the spirit having departed out of the tenant, it is of a piece with constructing his own coffin—the architecture of the grave, and "carpenter" is but another name for "coffin-maker." One man says, in his despair or indifference to life, take up a handful of the earth at your feet, and paint your house that color. Is he thinking of his last and narrow house? Toss up a copper for it as well. What an abundance of leisure he must have! Why do you take up a handful of dirt? Better paint

---

[1]   *one at least ... revelation to him*   Horatio Greenough (1805–52), a sculptor and a friend of both Emerson and Thoreau, published several influential essays on architectural subjects; opposing unnecessary ornament, he defined beauty in architecture as "the promise of function."

[2]   *Trinity Church*   Heavily ornamented neo-Gothic style church, located at 79 Broadway in New York City. Completed in 1846, it remained the tallest building in the city until 1890.

your house your own complexion; let it turn pale or blush for you. An enterprise to improve the style of cottage architecture! When you have got my ornaments ready I will wear them.

Before winter I built a chimney, and shingled the sides of my house, which were already impervious to rain, with imperfect and sappy shingles made of the first slice of the log, whose edges I was obliged to straighten with a plane.

I have thus a tight shingled and plastered house, ten feet wide by fifteen long, and eight-feet posts, with a garret and a closet, a large window on each side, two trap doors, one door at the end, and a brick fireplace opposite. The exact cost of my house, paying the usual price for such materials as I used, but not counting the work, all of which was done by myself, was as follows; and I give the details because very few are able to tell exactly what their houses cost, and fewer still, if any, the separate cost of the various materials which compose them:

Boards	$ 8.03 ½,	mostly shanty boards.
Refuse shingles for roof and sides	4.00	
Laths	1.25	
Two second-hand windows with glass	2.43	
One thousand old brick	4.00	
Two casks of lime	2.40	That was high.
Hair	0.31	More than I needed.
Mantle-tree iron	0.15	
Nails	3.90	
Hinges and screws	0.14	
Latch	0.10	
Chalk	0.01	
Transportation	1.40	I carried a good part on my back.
In all	$28.12 ½	

These are all the materials, excepting the timber, stones, and sand, which I claimed by squatter's right. I have also a small wood-shed adjoining, made chiefly of the stuff which was left after building the house.

I intend to build me a house which will surpass any on the main street in Concord in grandeur and luxury,

as soon as it pleases me as much and will cost me no more than my present one.

I thus found that the student who wishes for a shelter can obtain one for a lifetime at an expense not greater than the rent which he now pays annually. If I seem to boast more than is becoming, my excuse is that I brag for humanity rather than for myself; and my shortcomings and inconsistencies do not affect the truth of my statement. Notwithstanding much cant and hypocrisy—chaff which I find it difficult to separate from my wheat, but for which I am as sorry as any man—I will breathe freely and stretch myself in this respect, it is such a relief to both the moral and physical system; and I am resolved that I will not through humility become the devil's attorney. I will endeavor to speak a good word for the truth. At Cambridge College[1] the mere rent of a student's room, which is only a little larger than my own, is thirty dollars each year, though the corporation had the advantage of building thirty-two side by side and under one roof, and the occupant suffers the inconvenience of many and noisy neighbors, and perhaps a residence in the fourth story. I cannot but think that if we had more true wisdom in these respects, not only less education would be needed, because, forsooth, more would already have been acquired, but the pecuniary expense of getting an education would in a great measure vanish. Those conveniences which the student requires at Cambridge or elsewhere cost him or somebody else ten times as great a sacrifice of life as they would with proper management on both sides. Those things for which the most money is demanded are never the things which the student most wants. Tuition, for instance, is an important item in the term bill, while for the far more valuable education which he gets by associating with the most cultivated of his contemporaries no charge is made. The mode of founding a college is, commonly, to get up a subscription of dollars and cents, and then following blindly the principles of a division of labor to its extreme, a principle which should never be followed but with circumspection—to call in a contractor who makes this a subject of speculation, and he employs Irishmen or other operatives actually to lay the foundations, while the students that

---

[1]   *Cambridge College* Harvard (located in Cambridge, Massachusetts).

are to be are said to be fitting themselves for it; and for these oversights successive generations have to pay. I think that it would be *better than this*, for the students, or those who desire to be benefited by it, even to lay the foundation themselves. The student who secures his coveted leisure and retirement by systematically shirking any labor necessary to man obtains but an ignoble and unprofitable leisure, defrauding himself of the experience which alone can make leisure fruitful. "But," says one, "you do not mean that the students should go to work with their hands instead of their heads?" I do not mean that exactly, but I mean something which he might think a good deal like that; I mean that they should not *play* life, or *study* it merely, while the community supports them at this expensive game, but earnestly *live* it from beginning to end. How could youths better learn to live than by at once trying the experiment of living? Methinks this would exercise their minds as much as mathematics. If I wished a boy to know something about the arts and sciences, for instance, I would not pursue the common course, which is merely to send him into the neighborhood of some professor, where anything is professed and practised but the art of life—to survey the world through a telescope or a microscope, and never with his natural eye; to study chemistry, and not learn how his bread is made, or mechanics, and not learn how it is earned; to discover new satellites to Neptune, and not detect the motes in his eyes,[1] or to what vagabond he is a satellite himself; or to be devoured by the monsters that swarm all around him, while contemplating the monsters in a drop of vinegar. Which would have advanced the most at the end of a month—the boy who had made his own jackknife from the ore which he had dug and smelted, reading as much as would be necessary for this—or the boy who had attended the lectures on metallurgy at the Institute in the meanwhile, and had received a Rodgers' penknife[2] from his father? Which would be most likely to cut his fingers? To my astonishment I was informed on leaving college that I had studied navigation! Why, if I had taken one turn down the harbor I should have known more about it. Even the *poor* student studies and is taught only *political* economy, while that economy of living which is synonymous with philosophy is not even sincerely professed in our colleges. The consequence is, that while he is reading Adam Smith, Ricardo, and Say,[3] he runs his father in debt irretrievably.

As with our colleges, so with a hundred "modern improvements"; there is an illusion about them; there is not always a positive advance. The devil goes on exacting compound interest to the last for his early share and numerous succeeding investments in them. Our inventions are wont to be pretty toys, which distract our attention from serious things. They are but improved means to an unimproved end, an end which it was already but too easy to arrive at; as railroads lead to Boston or New York. We are in great haste to construct a magnetic telegraph from Maine to Texas; but Maine and Texas, it may be, have nothing important to communicate. Either is in such a predicament as the man who was earnest to be introduced to a distinguished deaf woman, but when he was presented, and one end of her ear trumpet was put into his hand, had nothing to say. As if the main object were to talk fast and not to talk sensibly. We are eager to tunnel under the Atlantic and bring the old world some weeks nearer to the new; but perchance the first news that will leak through into the broad, flapping American ear will be that the Princess Adelaide[4] has the whooping cough. After all, the man whose horse trots a mile in a minute does not carry the most important messages; he is not an evangelist, nor does he come round eating locusts and wild honey. I doubt if Flying Childers[5] ever carried a peck[6] of corn to mill.

One says to me, "I wonder that you do not lay up money; you love to travel; you might take the cars and go to Fitchburg today and see the country." But I am wiser than that. I have learned that the swiftest traveller

---

[1] *detect ... his eyes* See Luke 6.41: "And why beholdest thou the mote that is in thy brother's eye, but perceivest not the beam that is in thine own eye?"

[2] *Rodgers' penknife* High quality penknife manufactured in England.

[3] *Adam Smith* Scottish economist (1723–90); *Ricardo* English economist David Ricardo (1772–1823); *Say* French economist Jean-Baptiste Say (1767–1832).

[4] *Princess Adelaide* Adelaide of Saxe-Meiningen, queen consort of the United Kingdom and Hanover until the death of her husband, King William IV, in 1837.

[5] *Flying Childers* Famous racehorse born in 1714.

[6] *peck* Unit of measurement for dry goods.

is he that goes afoot. I say to my friend, Suppose we try who will get there first. The distance is thirty miles; the fare ninety cents. That is almost a day's wages. I remember when wages were sixty cents a day for laborers on this very road. Well, I start now on foot, and get there before night; I have travelled at that rate by the week together. You will in the meanwhile have earned your fare, and arrive there some time tomorrow, or possibly this evening, if you are lucky enough to get a job in season. Instead of going to Fitchburg, you will be working here the greater part of the day. And so, if the railroad reached round the world, I think that I should keep ahead of you; and as for seeing the country and getting experience of that kind, I should have to cut your acquaintance altogether.

Such is the universal law, which no man can ever outwit, and with regard to the railroad even we may say it is as broad as it is long. To make a railroad round the world available to all mankind is equivalent to grading the whole surface of the planet. Men have an indistinct notion that if they keep up this activity of joint stocks and spades long enough all will at length ride somewhere, in next to no time, and for nothing; but though a crowd rushes to the depot, and the conductor shouts "All aboard!" when the smoke is blown away and the vapor condensed, it will be perceived that a few are riding, but the rest are run over—and it will be called, and will be, "A melancholy accident." No doubt they can ride at last who shall have earned their fare, that is, if they survive so long, but they will probably have lost their elasticity and desire to travel by that time. This spending of the best part of one's life earning money in order to enjoy a questionable liberty during the least valuable part of it, reminds me of the Englishman who went to India to make a fortune first, in order that he might return to England and live the life of a poet. He should have gone up garret[1] at once. "What!" exclaim a million Irishmen[2] starting up from all the shanties in the land, "is not this railroad which we have built a good thing?" Yes, I answer, *comparatively* good, that

---

[1] *gone up garret* I.e., become a poet. (The death of English poet Thomas Chatterton [1752–70] established in the public mind a long-lasting image of the poet as a dedicated soul who chooses to live in poverty in a tiny attic room.)

[2] *a million Irishmen* A substantial portion of laborers on the railroads of the nineteenth century were immigrants from Ireland.

is, you might have done worse; but I wish, as you are brothers of mine, that you could have spent your time better than digging in this dirt.

Before I finished my house, wishing to earn ten or twelve dollars by some honest and agreeable method, in order to meet my unusual expenses, I planted about two acres and a half of light and sandy soil near it chiefly with beans, but also a small part with potatoes, corn, peas, and turnips. The whole lot contains eleven acres, mostly growing up to pines and hickories, and was sold the preceding season for eight dollars and eight cents an acre. One farmer said that it was "good for nothing but to raise cheeping squirrels on." I put no manure whatever on this land, not being the owner, but merely a squatter, and not expecting to cultivate so much again, and I did not quite hoe it all once. I got out several cords of stumps in ploughing, which supplied me with fuel for a long time, and left small circles of virgin mould, easily distinguishable through the summer by the greater luxuriance of the beans there. The dead and for the most part unmerchantable wood behind my house, and the driftwood from the pond, have supplied the remainder of my fuel. I was obliged to hire a team and a man for the ploughing, though I held the plough myself. My farm outgoes for the first season were, for implements, seed, work, etc., $14.72½. The seed corn was given me. This never costs anything to speak of, unless you plant more than enough. I got twelve bushels of beans, and eighteen bushels of potatoes, beside some peas and sweet corn. The yellow corn and turnips were too late to come to anything. My whole income from the farm was

	$23.44
Deducting the outgoes . . .	14.72½
There are left	$8.71½,

beside produce consumed and on hand at the time this estimate was made of the value of $4.50—the amount on hand much more than balancing a little grass which I did not raise. All things considered, that is, considering the importance of a man's soul and of today, notwithstanding the short time occupied by my experiment, nay, partly even because of its transient character, I believe that that was doing better than any farmer in Concord did that year.

The next year I did better still, for I spaded up all the land which I required, about a third of an acre, and I learned from the experience of both years, not being in the least awed by many celebrated works on husbandry, Arthur Young[1] among the rest, that if one would live simply and eat only the crop which he raised, and raise no more than he ate, and not exchange it for an insufficient quantity of more luxurious and expensive things, he would need to cultivate only a few rods[2] of ground, and that it would be cheaper to spade up that than to use oxen to plough it, and to select a fresh spot from time to time than to manure the old, and he could do all his necessary farm work as it were with his left hand at odd hours in the summer; and thus he would not be tied to an ox, or horse, or cow, or pig, as at present. I desire to speak impartially on this point, and as one not interested in the success or failure of the present economical and social arrangements. I was more independent than any farmer in Concord, for I was not anchored to a house or farm, but could follow the bent of my genius, which is a very crooked one, every moment. Beside being better off than they already, if my house had been burned or my crops had failed, I should have been nearly as well off as before.

I am wont to think that men are not so much the keepers of herds as herds are the keepers of men, the former are so much the freer. Men and oxen exchange work; but if we consider necessary work only, the oxen will be seen to have greatly the advantage, their farm is so much the larger. Man does some of his part of the exchange work in his six weeks of haying, and it is no boy's play. Certainly no nation that lived simply in all respects, that is, no nation of philosophers, would commit so great a blunder as to use the labor of animals. True, there never was and is not likely soon to be a nation of philosophers, nor am I certain it is desirable that there should be. However, *I* should never have broken a horse or bull and taken him to board for any work he might do for me, for fear I should become a horse-man or a herds-man merely; and if society seems to be the gainer by so doing, are we certain that what is one man's gain is not another's loss, and that the stable-boy has equal cause with his master to be satisfied? Granted that some public works would not have been constructed without this aid, and let man share the glory of such with the ox and horse; does it follow that he could not have accomplished works yet more worthy of himself in that case? When men begin to do, not merely unnecessary or artistic, but luxurious and idle work, with their assistance, it is inevitable that a few do all the exchange work with the oxen, or, in other words, become the slaves of the strongest. Man thus not only works for the animal within him, but, for a symbol of this, he works for the animal without him. Though we have many substantial houses of brick or stone, the prosperity of the farmer is still measured by the degree to which the barn overshadows the house. This town is said to have the largest houses for oxen, cows, and horses hereabouts, and it is not behindhand in its public buildings; but there are very few halls for free worship or free speech in this county. It should not be by their architecture, but why not even by their power of abstract thought, that nations should seek to commemorate themselves? How much more admirable the Bhagvat-Geeta[3] than all the ruins of the East! Towers and temples are the luxury of princes. A simple and independent mind does not toil at the bidding of any prince. Genius is not a retainer to any emperor, nor is its material silver, or gold, or marble, except to a trifling extent. To what end, pray, is so much stone hammered? In Arcadia,[4] when I was there, I did not see any hammering stone. Nations are possessed with an insane ambition to perpetuate the memory of themselves by the amount of hammered stone they leave. What if equal pains were taken to smooth and polish their manners? One piece of good sense would be more memorable than a monument as high as the moon. I love better to see stones in place. The grandeur of Thebes[5] was a vulgar grandeur. More sensible is a rod of stone wall that bounds an honest man's field than a hundred-gated Thebes that has wandered farther from the true end of life. The religion and civilization which are barbaric and heathenish build splendid temples;

---

[1] *Arthur Young* English writer on agriculture (1741–1820).

[2] *rods* Units of measurement equivalent to about 5.5 yards.

[3] *Bhagvat-Geeta* The *Bhagavad Gita*, important work of Hindu scripture.

[4] *Arcadia* Mythic, pastoral paradise.

[5] *Thebes* Ancient Egyptian capital, known as a place of wealth and architectural grandeur.

but what you might call Christianity does not. Most of the stone a nation hammers goes toward its tomb only. It buries itself alive. As for the Pyramids, there is nothing to wonder at in them so much as the fact that so many men could be found degraded enough to spend their lives constructing a tomb for some ambitious booby, whom it would have been wiser and manlier to have drowned in the Nile, and then given his body to the dogs. I might possibly invent some excuse for them and him, but I have no time for it. As for the religion and love of art of the builders, it is much the same all the world over, whether the building be an Egyptian temple or the United States Bank. It costs more than it comes to. The mainspring is vanity, assisted by the love of garlic and bread and butter. Mr. Balcom, a promising young architect, designs it on the back of his Vitruvius,[1] with hard pencil and ruler, and the job is let out to Dobson & Sons, stonecutters. When the thirty centuries begin to look down on it, mankind begin to look up at it. As for your high towers and monuments, there was a crazy fellow once in this town who undertook to dig through to China, and he got so far that, as he said, he heard the Chinese pots and kettles rattle; but I think that I shall not go out of my way to admire the hole which he made. Many are concerned about the monuments of the West and the East—to know who built them. For my part, I should like to know who in those days did not build them—who were above such trifling. But to proceed with my statistics.

By surveying, carpentry, and day-labor of various other kinds in the village in the meanwhile, for I have as many trades as fingers, I had earned $13.34. The expense of food for eight months, namely, from July 4th to March 1st, the time when these estimates were made, though I lived there more than two years—not counting potatoes, a little green corn, and some peas, which I had raised, nor considering the value of what was on hand at the last date—was

Rice . . . . . $ 1.73 ½
Molasses . . .   1.73   Cheapest form of the
                                     saccharine.
Rye meal . . .   1.04 ¾
Indian meal . . 0.99 ¾} Cheaper than rye.

Pork	0.22	
Flour	0.88	Costs more than Indian meal, both money and trouble.
Sugar	0.80	
Lard	0.65	
Apples	0.25	
Dried apple . .	0.22	
Sweet potatoes .	0.10	
One pumpkin .	0.06	
One watermelon .	0.02	
Salt	0.03	

All experiments which failed.

Yes, I did eat $8.74, all told; but I should not thus unblushingly publish my guilt, if I did not know that most of my readers were equally guilty with myself, and that their deeds would look no better in print. The next year I sometimes caught a mess of fish for my dinner, and once I went so far as to slaughter a woodchuck which ravaged my bean-field—effect his transmigration, as a Tartar would say[2]—and devour him, partly for experiment's sake; but though it afforded me a momentary enjoyment, notwithstanding a musky flavor, I saw that the longest use would not make that a good practice, however it might seem to have your woodchucks ready dressed by the village butcher.

Clothing and some incidental expenses within the same dates, though little can be inferred from this item, amounted to

$8.40 ¾
Oil and some household utensils   2.00

So that all the pecuniary outgoes, excepting for washing and mending,[3] which for the most part were done out of the house, and their bills have not yet been received—and these are all and more than all the ways by which money necessarily goes out in this part of the world—were

---

[1] *Vitruvius* Ancient Roman architect (c. 70 BCE–c. 15 BCE), author of *De architectura*.

[2] *effect … would say* "Transmigration" refers to the transmigration of the soul into a new body after death, a principle important to the belief systems of many cultures; the Tatars are a Turkic ethnic group of eastern Europe and northwestern Asia.

[3] *excepting for washing and mending* These tasks were done by Thoreau's mother and sisters.

House	$28.12½
Farm one year	14.72½
Food eight months . . .	8.74
Clothing, etc., eight months .	8.40¾
Oil, etc., eight months . . .	2.00
In all, ...	$61.99¾

I address myself now to those of my readers who have a living to get. And to meet this I have for farm produce sold

	$23.44
Earned by day-labor . . .	13.34
In all	$36.78,

which subtracted from the sum of the outgoes leaves a balance of $25.21¾ on the one side—this being very nearly the means with which I started, and the measure of expenses to be incurred—and on the other, beside the leisure and independence and health thus secured, a comfortable house for me as long as I choose to occupy it.

These statistics, however accidental and therefore uninstructive they may appear, as they have a certain completeness, have a certain value also. Nothing was given me of which I have not rendered some account. It appears from the above estimate, that my food alone cost me in money about twenty-seven cents a week.[1] It was, for nearly two years after this, rye and Indian meal without yeast, potatoes, rice, a very little salt pork, molasses, and salt, and my drink water. It was fit that I should live on rice, mainly, who loved so well the philosophy of India. To meet the objections of some inveterate cavillers,[2] I may as well state, that if I dined out occasionally, as I always had done, and I trust shall have opportunities to do again, it was frequently to the detriment of my domestic arrangements. But the dining out, being, as I have stated, a constant element, does not in the least affect a comparative statement like this.

I learned from my two years' experience that it would cost incredibly little trouble to obtain one's necessary food, even in this latitude; that a man may use as simple a diet as the animals, and yet retain health and strength. I have made a satisfactory dinner, satisfactory on several accounts, simply off a dish of purslane[3] (*Portulaca oleracea*) which I gathered in my cornfield, boiled and salted. I give the Latin on account of the savoriness of the trivial name. And pray what more can a reasonable man desire, in peaceful times, in ordinary noons, than a sufficient number of ears of green sweet-corn boiled, with the addition of salt? Even the little variety which I used was a yielding to the demands of appetite, and not of health. Yet men have come to such a pass that they frequently starve, not for want of necessaries, but for want of luxuries; and I know a good woman who thinks that her son lost his life because he took to drinking water only.

The reader will perceive that I am treating the subject rather from an economic than a dietetic point of view, and he will not venture to put my abstemiousness to the test unless he has a well-stocked larder.

Bread I at first made of pure Indian meal and salt, genuine hoe-cakes, which I baked before my fire out of doors on a shingle or the end of a stick of timber sawed off in building my house; but it was wont to get[4] smoked and to have a piny flavor. I tried flour also; but have at last found a mixture of rye and Indian meal most convenient and agreeable. In cold weather it was no little amusement to bake several small loaves of this in succession, tending and turning them as carefully as an Egyptian his hatching eggs.[5] They were a real cereal fruit which I ripened, and they had to my senses a fragrance like that of other noble fruits, which I kept in as long as possible by wrapping them in cloths. I made a study of the ancient and indispensable art of bread-making, consulting such authorities as offered, going back to the primitive days and first invention of the unleavened kind, when from the wildness of nuts and meats men first reached the mildness and refinement of this diet, and travelling gradually down in my studies through that accidental souring of the dough

---

[1]   *twenty-seven cents a week*   Though exact comparisons are impossible, the equivalent buying power today would probably require something close to $10.

[2]   *cavillers*   People raising frivolous objections.

[3]   *purslane*   Leafy green vegetable.

[4]   *was wont to get*   Had a tendency to become.

[5]   *an Egyptian his hatching eggs*   Reference to the artificial incubation of eggs said to have been practiced by Ancient Egyptians.

which, it is supposed, taught the leavening process, and through the various fermentations thereafter, till I came to "good, sweet, wholesome bread," the staff of life. Leaven, which some deem the soul of bread, the *spiritus* which fills its cellular tissue, which is religiously preserved like the vestal fire[1]—some precious bottle-full, I suppose, first brought over in the Mayflower, did the business for America, and its influence is still rising, swelling, spreading, in cerealian[2] billows over the land—this seed I regularly and faithfully procured from the village, till at length one morning I forgot the rules, and scalded my yeast; by which accident I discovered that even this was not indispensable—for my discoveries were not by the synthetic but analytic process—and I have gladly omitted it since, though most housewives earnestly assured me that safe and wholesome bread without yeast might not be, and elderly people prophesied a speedy decay of the vital forces. Yet I find it not to be an essential ingredient, and after going without it for a year am still in the land of the living; and I am glad to escape the trivialness of carrying a bottle-full in my pocket, which would sometimes pop and discharge its contents[3] to my discomfiture. It is simpler and more respectable to omit it. Man is an animal who more than any other can adapt himself to all climates and circumstances. Neither did I put any sal-soda, or other acid or alkali,[4] into my bread. It would seem that I made it according to the recipe which Marcus Porcius Cato[5] gave about two centuries before Christ. "*Panem depsticium sic facito. Manus mortariumque bene lavato. Farinam in mortarium indito, aquæ paulatim addito, subigitoque pulchre. Ubi bene subegeris, defingito, coquitoque sub testu.*" Which I take to mean—"Make kneaded bread thus. Wash your hands and trough well. Put the meal into the trough, add water gradually, and knead it thoroughly. When you have kneaded it well, mould it, and bake it under a cover," that is, in a baking-kettle. Not a word about leaven. But I did not always use this staff of life. At one time, owing to the emptiness of my purse, I saw none of it for more than a month.

Every New Englander might easily raise all his own breadstuffs in this land of rye and Indian corn, and not depend on distant and fluctuating markets for them. Yet so far are we from simplicity and independence that, in Concord, fresh and sweet meal is rarely sold in the shops, and hominy and corn in a still coarser form are hardly used by any. For the most part the farmer gives to his cattle and hogs the grain of his own producing, and buys flour, which is at least no more wholesome, at a greater cost, at the store. I saw that I could easily raise my bushel or two of rye and Indian corn, for the former will grow on the poorest land, and the latter does not require the best, and grind them in a hand-mill, and so do without rice and pork; and if I must have some concentrated sweet, I found by experiment that I could make a very good molasses either of pumpkins or beets, and I knew that I needed only to set out a few maples to obtain it more easily still, and while these were growing I could use various substitutes beside those which I have named. "For," as the Forefathers sang,

> we can make liquor to sweeten our lips
> Of pumpkins and parsnips and walnut-tree chips.[6]

Finally, as for salt, that grossest of groceries, to obtain this might be a fit occasion for a visit to the seashore, or, if I did without it altogether, I should probably drink the less water. I do not learn that the Indians ever troubled themselves to go after it.

Thus I could avoid all trade and barter, so far as my food was concerned, and having a shelter already, it would only remain to get clothing and fuel. The pantaloons which I now wear were woven in a farmer's family—thank Heaven there is so much virtue still in man; for I think the fall from the farmer to the operative as great and memorable as that from the man to the farmer—and in a new country, fuel is an encumbrance. As for a habitat, if I were not permitted still to

---

[1] *vestal fire* Fire kept perpetually burning in the Temple of Vesta, goddess of the hearth, in ancient Rome.

[2] *cerealian* Word coined by Thoreau, referencing both cereals (or grains), and the Roman goddess of agriculture.

[3] *bottle-full … its contents* Baker's yeast during this period came in a liquid form, usually obtained from local brewers as a by-product of the beer brewing process.

[4] *sal-soda … alkali* Other chemical leavening agents.

[5] *Marcus Porcius Cato* Also known as Cato the Elder (234 BCE–149 BCE), Roman author of *De Agri Cultura*.

[6] *we can … chips* Lines from a folk song known as the "Forefathers' Song."

squat, I might purchase one acre at the same price for which the land I cultivated was sold—namely, eight dollars and eight cents. But as it was, I considered that I enhanced the value of the land by squatting on it.

There is a certain class of unbelievers who sometimes ask me such questions as, if I think that I can live on vegetable food alone; and to strike at the root of the matter at once—for the root is faith—I am accustomed to answer such, that I can live on board nails. If they cannot understand that, they cannot understand much that I have to say. For my part, I am glad to hear of experiments of this kind being tried; as that a young man tried for a fortnight to live on hard, raw corn on the ear, using his teeth for all mortar. The squirrel tribe tried the same and succeeded. The human race is interested in these experiments, though a few old women who are incapacitated for them, or who own their thirds in mills, may be alarmed.

My furniture—part of which I made myself, and the rest cost me nothing of which I have not rendered an account—consisted of a bed, a table, a desk, three chairs, a looking-glass three inches in diameter, a pair of tongs and andirons, a kettle, a skillet, and a frying-pan, a dipper, a wash-bowl, two knives and forks, three plates, one cup, one spoon, a jug for oil, a jug for molasses, and a japanned[1] lamp. None is so poor that he need sit on a pumpkin. That is shiftlessness. There is a plenty of such chairs as I like best in the village garrets to be had for taking them away. Furniture! Thank God, I can sit and I can stand without the aid of a furniture warehouse. What man but a philosopher would not be ashamed to see his furniture packed in a cart and going up country exposed to the light of heaven and the eyes of men, a beggarly account of empty boxes?[2] That is Spaulding's furniture.[3] I could never tell from inspecting such a load whether it belonged to a so called rich man or a poor one; the owner always seemed poverty-stricken. Indeed, the more you have of such things the poorer you are. Each load looks as if it contained the contents of a dozen shanties; and if one shanty is poor, this is a dozen times as poor. Pray, for what do we *move* ever but to get rid of our furniture, our *exuviæ*;[4] at last to go from this world to another newly furnished, and leave this to be burned? It is the same as if all these traps were buckled to a man's belt, and he could not move over the rough country where our lines are cast without dragging them—dragging his trap. He was a lucky fox that left his tail in the trap.[5] The muskrat will gnaw his third leg off to be free. No wonder man has lost his elasticity. How often he is at a dead set! "Sir, if I may be so bold, what do you mean by a dead set?" If you are a seer, whenever you meet a man you will see all that he owns, ay, and much that he pretends to disown, behind him, even to his kitchen furniture and all the trumpery which he saves and will not burn, and he will appear to be harnessed to it and making what headway he can. I think that the man is at a dead set who has got through a knot hole or gateway where his sledge load of furniture cannot follow him. I cannot but feel compassion when I hear some trig,[6] compact-looking man, seemingly free, all girded and ready, speak of his "furniture," as whether it is insured or not. "But what shall I do with my furniture?" My gay[7] butterfly is entangled in a spider's web then. Even those who seem for a long while not to have any, if you inquire more narrowly you will find have some stored in somebody's barn. I look upon England today as an old gentleman who is travelling with a great deal of baggage, trumpery which has accumulated from long housekeeping, which he has not the courage to burn; great trunk, little trunk, bandbox[8] and bundle. Throw away the first three at least. It would surpass the powers of a well man nowadays to take up his bed and walk, and I should certainly advise a sick one to lay down his bed and run. When I have met an immigrant tottering under a bundle which contained his all—looking like an enormous wen[9] which had grown out of the nape of

---

1 *japanned* Decorated and finished in lacquer (in Japanese style).

2 *beggarly account of empty boxes* See Shakespeare's *Romeo and Juliet* 5.1.48.

3 *Spaulding's furniture* Commercially-fabricated furniture (perhaps referencing Elbridge G. Spaulding, later to be credited with the invention of the greenback. Spaulding's Exchange in Buffalo, founded in 1845, was an emporium housing numerous retail outlets and offering a wide variety of commercial goods for sale).

4 *exuviæ* Latin: castoffs.

5 *He was … the trap* Allusion to one of Aesop's fables, in which a fox escapes a trap by leaving behind his tail.

6 *trig* Secure, steady.

7 *gay* Brightly colored.

8 *bandbox* Small box for storing hats and millinery accessories.

9 *wen* Protuberance.

his neck—I have pitied him, not because that was his all, but because he had all that to carry. If I have got to drag my trap, I will take care that it be a light one and do not nip me in a vital part. But perchance it would be wisest never to put one's paw into it.

I would observe, by the way, that it costs me nothing for curtains, for I have no gazers to shut out but the sun and moon, and I am willing that they should look in. The moon will not sour milk nor taint meat of mine, nor will the sun injure my furniture or fade my carpet, and if he is sometimes too warm a friend, I find it still better economy to retreat behind some curtain which nature has provided, than to add a single item to the details of housekeeping. A lady once offered me a mat, but as I had no room to spare within the house, nor time to spare within or without to shake it, I declined it, preferring to wipe my feet on the sod before my door. It is best to avoid the beginnings of evil.

Not long since I was present at the auction of a deacon's effects, for his life had not been ineffectual:

The evil that men do lives after them.[1]

As usual, a great proportion was trumpery which had begun to accumulate in his father's day. Among the rest was a dried tapeworm. And now, after lying half a century in his garret and other dust holes, these things were not burned; instead of a *bonfire*, or purifying destruction of them, there was an *auction*, or increasing of them. The neighbors eagerly collected to view them, bought them all, and carefully transported them to their garrets and dust holes, to lie there till their estates are settled, when they will start again. When a man dies he kicks the dust.

The customs of some savage nations might, perchance, be profitably imitated by us, for they at least go through the semblance of casting their slough annually; they have the idea of the thing, whether they have the reality or not. Would it not be well if we were to celebrate such a "busk," or "feast of first fruits," as Bartram[2] describes to have been the custom of the Mucclasse Indians? "When a town celebrates the busk," says he, "having previously provided themselves

with new clothes, new pots, pans, and other household utensils and furniture, they collect all their worn out clothes and other despicable things, sweep and cleanse their houses, squares, and the whole town of their filth, which with all the remaining grain and other old provisions they cast together into one common heap, and consume it with fire. After having taken medicine, and fasted for three days, all the fire in the town is extinguished. During this fast they abstain from the gratification of every appetite and passion whatever. A general amnesty is proclaimed; all malefactors may return to their town."

"On the fourth morning, the high priest, by rubbing dry wood together, produces new fire in the public square, from whence every habitation in the town is supplied with the new and pure flame."

They then feast on the new corn and fruits, and dance and sing for three days, "and the four following days they receive visits and rejoice with their friends from neighboring towns who have in like manner purified and prepared themselves."

The Mexicans also practised a similar purification at the end of every fifty-two years, in the belief that it was time for the world to come to an end.

I have scarcely heard of a truer sacrament—that is, as the dictionary defines it, "outward and visible sign of an inward and spiritual grace"—than this, and I have no doubt that they were originally inspired directly from Heaven to do thus, though they have no biblical record of the revelation.

For more than five years I maintained myself thus solely by the labor of my hands, and I found, that by working about six weeks in a year, I could meet all the expenses of living. The whole of my winters, as well as most of my summers, I had free and clear for study. I have thoroughly tried school-keeping, and found that my expenses were in proportion, or rather out of proportion, to my income, for I was obliged to dress and train, not to say think and believe, accordingly, and I lost my time into the bargain. As I did not teach for the good of my fellow-men, but simply for a livelihood, this was a failure. I have tried trade; but I found that it would take ten years to get under way in that, and that then I should probably be on my way to the devil. I was actually afraid that I might by that time be doing

---

[1]   *The evil ... after them*   See Shakespeare's *Julius Caesar* 3.2.84.

[2]   *Bartram*   William Bartram, American botanist and ethnographer, author of *Travels through North and South Carolina* (1791).

what is called a good business. When formerly I was looking about to see what I could do for a living, some sad experience in conforming to the wishes of friends being fresh in my mind to tax my ingenuity, I thought often and seriously of picking huckleberries; that surely I could do, and its small profits might suffice—for my greatest skill has been to want but little—so little capital it required, so little distraction from my wonted moods, I foolishly thought. While my acquaintances went unhesitatingly into trade or the professions, I contemplated this occupation as most like theirs; ranging the hills all summer to pick the berries which came in my way, and thereafter carelessly dispose of them; so, to keep the flocks of Admetus.[1] I also dreamed that I might gather the wild herbs, or carry evergreens to such villagers as loved to be reminded of the woods, even to the city, by hay-cart loads. But I have since learned that trade curses everything it handles; and though you trade in messages from heaven, the whole curse of trade attaches to the business.

As I preferred some things to others, and especially valued my freedom, as I could fare hard and yet succeed well, I did not wish to spend my time in earning rich carpets or other fine furniture, or delicate cookery, or a house in the Grecian or the Gothic style just yet. If there are any to whom it is no interruption to acquire these things, and who know how to use them when acquired, I relinquish to them the pursuit. Some are "industrious," and appear to love labor for its own sake, or perhaps because it keeps them out of worse mischief; to such I have at present nothing to say. Those who would not know what to do with more leisure than they now enjoy, I might advise to work twice as hard as they do—work till they pay for themselves, and get their free papers.[2] For myself I found that the occupation of a day-laborer was the most independent of any, especially as it required only thirty or forty days in a year to support one. The laborer's day ends with the going down of the sun, and he is then free

to devote himself to his chosen pursuit, independent of his labor; but his employer, who speculates[3] from month to month, has no respite from one end of the year to the other.

In short, I am convinced, both by faith and experience, that to maintain one's self on this earth is not a hardship but a pastime, if we will live simply and wisely; as the pursuits of the simpler nations are still the sports of the more artificial. It is not necessary that a man should earn his living by the sweat of his brow, unless he sweats easier than I do.

One young man of my acquaintance, who has inherited some acres, told me that he thought he should live as I did, *if he had the means*. I would not have anyone adopt *my* mode of living on any account; for, beside that before he has fairly learned it I may have found out another for myself, I desire that there may be as many different persons in the world as possible; but I would have each one be very careful to find out and pursue *his own* way, and not his father's or his mother's or his neighbor's instead. The youth may build or plant or sail, only let him not be hindered from doing that which he tells me he would like to do. It is by a mathematical point only that we are wise, as the sailor or the fugitive slave keeps the polestar[4] in his eye; but that is sufficient guidance for all our life. We may not arrive at our port within a calculable period, but we would preserve the true course.

Undoubtedly, in this case, what is true for one is truer still for a thousand, as a large house is not proportionally more expensive than a small one, since one roof may cover, one cellar underlie, and one wall separate several apartments. But for my part, I preferred the solitary dwelling. Moreover, it will commonly be cheaper to build the whole yourself than to convince another of the advantage of the common wall; and when you have done this, the common partition, to be much cheaper, must be a thin one, and that other may prove a bad neighbor, and also not keep his side in repair. The only coöperation which is commonly possible is exceedingly partial and superficial; and what little true coöperation there is, is as if it were not, being a harmony inaudible to men. If a man has faith, he will coöperate with equal faith everywhere; if he has not faith, he will continue

---

[1]   *keep the flocks of Admetus*   King of Pherae in Greek mythology, whose flocks the god Apollo was forced to tend.

[2]   *pay for … free papers*   Reference to a system of indentured servitude, under the terms of which poor immigrants, in order to cover the cost of their voyage to America, were contracted to work without pay for a specified period (usually of at least seven years). The reference may also be to enslaved people who found a way to earn their own money and were thereby able to purchase their own freedom.

[3]   *speculates*   Takes business and investment risks.

[4]   *polestar*   I.e., the North Star.

to live like the rest of the world, whatever company he is joined to. To coöperate, in the highest as well as the lowest sense, means *to get our living together*. I heard it proposed lately that two young men should travel together over the world, the one without money, earning his means as he went, before the mast and behind the plow, the other carrying a bill of exchange in his pocket. It was easy to see that they could not long be companions or coöperate, since one would not *operate* at all. They would part at the first interesting crisis in their adventures. Above all, as I have implied, the man who goes alone can start today; but he who travels with another must wait till that other is ready, and it may be a long time before they get off.

But all this is very selfish, I have heard some of my townsmen say. I confess that I have hitherto indulged very little in philanthropic enterprises. I have made some sacrifices to a sense of duty, and among others have sacrificed this pleasure also. There are those who have used all their arts to persuade me to undertake the support of some poor family in the town; and if I had nothing to do—for the devil finds employment for the idle—I might try my hand at some such pastime as that. However, when I have thought to indulge myself in this respect, and lay their Heaven under an obligation by maintaining certain poor persons in all respects as comfortably as I maintain myself, and have even ventured so far as to make them the offer, they have one and all unhesitatingly preferred to remain poor. While my townsmen and women are devoted in so many ways to the good of their fellows, I trust that one at least may be spared to other and less humane pursuits. You must have a genius for charity as well as for anything else. As for Doing-good, that is one of the professions which are full. Moreover, I have tried it fairly, and, strange as it may seem, am satisfied that it does not agree with my constitution. Probably I should not consciously and deliberately forsake my particular calling to do the good which society demands of me, to save the universe from annihilation; and I believe that a like but infinitely greater steadfastness elsewhere is all that now preserves it. But I would not stand between any man and his genius; and to him who does this work, which I decline, with his whole heart and soul and life, I would say, Persevere, even if the world call it doing evil, as it is most likely they will.

I am far from supposing that my case is a peculiar one; no doubt many of my readers would make a similar defence. At doing something—I will not engage that my neighbors shall pronounce it good—I do not hesitate to say that I should be a capital fellow to hire; but what that is, it is for my employer to find out. What *good* I do, in the common sense of that word, must be aside from my main path, and for the most part wholly unintended. Men say, practically, Begin where you are and such as you are, without aiming mainly to become of more worth, and with kindness aforethought go about doing good. If I were to preach at all in this strain, I should say rather, Set about being good. As if the sun should stop when he had kindled his fires up to the splendor of a moon or a star of the sixth magnitude, and go about like a Robin Goodfellow,[1] peeping in at every cottage window, inspiring lunatics, and tainting meats, and making darkness visible,[2] instead of steadily increasing his genial heat and beneficence till he is of such brightness that no mortal can look him in the face, and then, and in the meanwhile too, going about the world in his own orbit, doing it good, or rather, as a truer philosophy has discovered, the world going about him getting good. When Phaeton,[3] wishing to prove his heavenly birth by his beneficence, had the sun's chariot but one day, and drove out of the beaten track, he burned several blocks of houses in the lower streets of heaven, and scorched the surface of the earth, and dried up every spring, and made the great desert of Sahara, till at length Jupiter[4] hurled him headlong to the earth with a thunderbolt, and the sun, through grief at his death, did not shine for a year.

There is no odor so bad as that which arises from goodness tainted. It is human, it is divine, carrion. If I knew for a certainty that a man was coming to my house with the conscious design of doing me good, I should run for my life, as from that dry and parching

---

1   *Robin Goodfellow*   Sprite who, according to English folk legend, played tricks such as curdling milk.

2   *darkness visible*   See John Milton's *Paradise Lost* 1.62–63: "…yet from those flames / No light, but rather darkness visible."

3   *Phaeton*   In Greek mythology, son of the sun-god Helios, whose chariot pulls the sun across the sky. The story described by Thoreau is prominently featured in Ovid's *Metamorphoses*.

4   *Jupiter*   Latin name for the god known in Greek mythology as Zeus, god of the sky and of thunderstorms.

wind of the African deserts called the simoom, which fills the mouth and nose and ears and eyes with dust till you are suffocated, for fear that I should get some of his good done to me—some of its virus mingled with my blood. No—in this case I would rather suffer evil the natural way. A man is not a good *man* to me because he will feed me if I should be starving, or warm me if I should be freezing, or pull me out of a ditch if I should ever fall into one. I can find you a Newfoundland dog that will do as much. Philanthropy is not love for one's fellow-man in the broadest sense. Howard[1] was no doubt an exceedingly kind and worthy man in his way, and has his reward; but, comparatively speaking, what are a hundred Howards to *us*, if their philanthropy do not help *us* in our best estate, when we are most worthy to be helped? I never heard of a philanthropic meeting in which it was sincerely proposed to do any good to me, or the like of me.

The Jesuits were quite balked by those Indians who, being burned at the stake, suggested new modes of torture to their tormentors. Being superior to physical suffering, it sometimes chanced that they were superior to any consolation which the missionaries could offer; and the law to do as you would be done by fell with less persuasiveness on the ears of those who, for their part, did not care how they were done by, who loved their enemies after a new fashion, and came very near freely forgiving them all they did.

Be sure that you give the poor the aid they most need, though it be your example which leaves them far behind. If you give money, spend yourself with it, and do not merely abandon it to them. We make curious mistakes sometimes. Often the poor man is not so cold and hungry as he is dirty and ragged and gross. It is partly his taste, and not merely his misfortune. If you give him money, he will perhaps buy more rags with it. I was wont to pity the clumsy Irish laborers who cut ice on the pond, in such mean and ragged clothes, while I shivered in my more tidy and somewhat more fashionable garments, till, one bitter cold day, one who had slipped into the water came to my house to warm him, and I saw him strip off three pairs of pants and two pairs of stockings ere he got down to the skin, though they were dirty and ragged enough, it is true,

and that he could afford to refuse the *extra*[2] garments which I offered him, he had so many *intra*[3] ones. This ducking[4] was the very thing he needed. Then I began to pity myself, and I saw that it would be a greater charity to bestow on me a flannel shirt than a whole slop-shop on him. There are a thousand hacking at the branches of evil to one who is striking at the root, and it may be that he who bestows the largest amount of time and money on the needy is doing the most by his mode of life to produce that misery which he strives in vain to relieve. It is the pious slave-breeder devoting the proceeds of every tenth slave to buy a Sunday's liberty for the rest. Some show their kindness to the poor by employing them in their kitchens. Would they not be kinder if they employed themselves there? You boast of spending a tenth part of your income in charity; maybe you should spend the nine tenths so, and done with it. Society recovers only a tenth part of the property then. Is this owing to the generosity of him in whose possession it is found, or to the remissness of the officers of justice?

Philanthropy is almost the only virtue which is sufficiently appreciated by mankind. Nay, it is greatly overrated; and it is our selfishness which overrates it. A robust poor man, one sunny day here in Concord, praised a fellow-townsman to me, because, as he said, he was kind to the poor; meaning himself. The kind uncles and aunts of the race are more esteemed than its true spiritual fathers and mothers. I once heard a reverend lecturer on England, a man of learning and intelligence, after enumerating her scientific, literary, and political worthies, Shakespeare, Bacon, Cromwell, Milton, Newton,[5] and others, speak next of her Christian heroes, whom, as if his profession required it of him, he elevated to a place far above all the rest, as the greatest of the great. They were Penn, Howard, and

---

[1]   *Howard* John Howard, English prison reformer (1726–90).

[2]   *extra* Latin: outer.

[3]   *intra* Latin: inner.

[4]   *ducking* Submersion in water.

[5]   *Bacon* Francis Bacon, English scientist, philosopher, and politician (1561–1626); *Cromwell* Oliver Cromwell, leader of the Parliamentarians during the English Civil War (1642–51) and Lord Protector of the Commonwealth of England from 1653 to 1658; *Milton* John Milton, English poet (1608–74); *Newton* Isaac Newton, English scientist (1642–1727).

Mrs. Fry.[1] Everyone must feel the falsehood and cant of this. The last were not England's best men and women; only, perhaps, her best philanthropists.

I would not subtract anything from the praise that is due to philanthropy, but merely demand justice for all who by their lives and works are a blessing to mankind. I do not value chiefly a man's uprightness and benevolence, which are, as it were, his stem and leaves. Those plants of whose greenness withered we make herb tea for the sick, serve but a humble use, and are most employed by quacks. I want the flower and fruit of a man; that some fragrance be wafted over from him to me, and some ripeness flavor our intercourse. His goodness must not be a partial and transitory act, but a constant superfluity, which costs him nothing and of which he is unconscious. This is a charity that hides a multitude of sins. The philanthropist too often surrounds mankind with the remembrance of his own cast-off griefs as an atmosphere, and calls it sympathy. We should impart our courage, and not our despair, our health and ease, and not our disease, and take care that this does not spread by contagion. From what southern plains comes up the voice of wailing? Under what latitudes reside the heathen to whom we would send light? Who is that intemperate and brutal man whom we would redeem? If anything ail a man, so that he does not perform his functions, if he have a pain in his bowels even—for that is the seat of sympathy—he forthwith sets about reforming—the world. Being a microcosm himself, he discovers—and it is a true discovery, and he is the man to make it—that the world has been eating green apples;[2] to his eyes, in fact, the globe itself is a great green apple, which there is danger awful to think of that the children of men[3] will nibble before it is ripe; and straightway his drastic philanthropy seeks out the Esquimaux and the Patagonian,[4] and embraces the populous Indian and Chinese villages; and thus, by a few years of philanthropic activity, the powers in the meanwhile using him for their own ends, no doubt, he cures himself of his dyspepsia, the globe acquires a faint blush on one or both of its cheeks, as if it were beginning to be ripe, and life loses its crudity and is once more sweet and wholesome to live. I never dreamed of any enormity greater than I have committed. I never knew, and never shall know, a worse man than myself.

I believe that what so saddens the reformer is not his sympathy with his fellows in distress, but, though he be the holiest son of God, is his private ail. Let this be righted, let the spring come to him, the morning rise over his couch, and he will forsake his generous companions without apology. My excuse for not lecturing against the use of tobacco is, that I never chewed it; that is a penalty which reformed tobacco-chewers have to pay; though there are things enough I have chewed, which I could lecture against. If you should ever be betrayed into any of these philanthropies, do not let your left hand know what your right hand does,[5] for it is not worth knowing. Rescue the drowning and tie your shoe-strings. Take your time, and set about some free labor.

Our manners have been corrupted by communication with the saints.[6] Our hymn-books resound with a melodious cursing of God and enduring him forever. One would say that even the prophets and redeemers had rather consoled the fears than confirmed the hopes of man. There is nowhere recorded a simple and irrepressible satisfaction with the gift of life, any memorable praise of God. All health and success does me good, however far off and withdrawn it may appear; all disease and failure helps to make me sad and does me

---

[1] *Penn* William Penn, English-born politician and prominent Quaker who founded the colony of Pennsylvania (1644–1718); *Mrs. Fry* Elizabeth Fry, English Quaker prison reformer and philanthropist (1780–1845).

[2] *eating green apples* Green apples were said to be the cause of a number of illnesses ranging from mild indigestion to cholera, especially in children.

[3] *children of men* Phrase used numerous times in the Old Testament, especially in the Book of Psalms.

[4] *Esquimaux* Arctic peoples, referred to variously today as Eskimo (the term preferred in Alaska) and as Inuit—the term preferred in Canada, where the term "Eskimo" (derived from a French word meaning "one who nets snowshoes") is now widely regarded as offensive; *Patagonian* Indigenous inhabitant of the southern tip of South America.

[5] *left hand … right hand does* See Matthew 6.3–4: "But when thou doest alms, let not thy left hand know what thy right hand doeth: That thine alms may be in secret: and thy Father which seeth in secret himself shall reward thee openly."

[6] *Our manners … the saints* See 1 Corinthians 15.33: "Be not deceived: evil communications corrupt good manners."

evil, however much sympathy it may have with me or I with it. If, then, we would indeed restore mankind by truly Indian, botanic, magnetic,[1] or natural means, let us first be as simple and well as Nature ourselves, dispel the clouds which hang over our own brows, and take up a little life into our pores. Do not stay to be an overseer of the poor, but endeavor to become one of the worthies of the world.

I read in the *Gulistan*, or Flower Garden, of Sheik Sadi of Shiraz,[2] that "They asked a wise man, saying: Of the many celebrated trees which the Most High God has created lofty and umbrageous, they call none *azad*, or free, excepting the cypress, which bears no fruit; what mystery is there in this? He replied: Each has its appropriate produce, and appointed season, during the continuance of which it is fresh and blooming, and during their absence dry and withered; to neither of which states is the cypress exposed, being always flourishing; and of this nature are the *azads*, or religious independents. Fix not thy heart on that which is transitory; for the *Dijlah*, or Tigris, will continue to flow through Bagdad after the race of caliphs is extinct: if thy hand has plenty, be liberal as the date tree; but if it affords nothing to give away, be an *azad*, or free man, like the cypress."

COMPLEMENTAL VERSES[3]

The Pretensions of Poverty

Thou dost presume too much, poor needy wretch,
To claim a station in the firmament[4]
Because thy humble cottage, or thy tub,
Nurses some lazy or pedantic virtue
In the cheap sunshine or by shady springs,
With roots and pot-herbs; where thy right hand,
Tearing those humane passions from the mind,
Upon whose stocks fair blooming virtues flourish,

Degradeth nature, and benumbeth sense,
And, Gorgon-like,[5] turns active men to stone.
We not require the dull society
Of your necessitated temperance,
Or that unnatural stupidity
That knows nor joy nor sorrow; nor your forced
Falsely exalted passive fortitude
Above the active. This low abject brood,
That fix their seats in mediocrity,
Become your servile minds; but we advance
Such virtues only as admit excess,
Brave, bounteous acts, regal magnificence,
All-seeing prudence, magnanimity
That knows no bound, and that heroic virtue
For which antiquity hath left no name,
But patterns only, such as Hercules,
Achilles,[6] Theseus.[7] Back to thy loath'd cell;
And when thou seest the new enlightened sphere,
Study to know but what those worthies were.

T. Carew

Chapter 2
Where I Lived, and What I Lived For

At a certain season of our life we are accustomed to consider every spot as the possible site of a house. I have thus surveyed the country on every side within a dozen miles of where I live. In imagination I have bought all the farms in succession, for all were to be bought, and I knew their price. I walked over each farmer's premises, tasted his wild apples, discoursed on husbandry[8] with him, took his farm at his price, at any price, mortgaging it to him in my mind; even put a higher price on it, took everything but a deed of it—took his word for his deed, for I dearly love to talk—cultivated it, and him too to some extent, I trust, and withdrew when I had enjoyed it long enough, leaving him to carry it on. This experience entitled me to be

---

[1]   *magnetic* I.e., related to animal magnetism, an invisible bodily force believed to exist in the bodies of all living things and to be able to facilitate what was later known as hypnotism.

[2]   *Sheik Sadi of Shiraz* Persian poet (1210–c. 1291), highly admired by many Transcendentalists.

[3]   Poem by English poet Thomas Carew (1595–1640); the title and subtitle are added by Thoreau.

[4]   *firmament* Heavens.

[5]   *Gorgon-like* In Greek mythology, the Gorgons are three sisters with snakes for hair whose appearance turns viewers to stone.

[6]   *Achilles* Mythic hero of the Trojan War and the protagonist of Homer's *Iliad*.

[7]   *Theseus* Mythological founder of Athens who, like Hercules, performed many dangerous labors, including defeating the Minotaur in the Labyrinth.

[8]   *husbandry* Agriculture.

regarded as a sort of real-estate broker by my friends. Wherever I sat, there I might live, and the landscape radiated from me accordingly. What is a house but a *sedes*, a seat? Better if a country seat. I discovered many a site for a house not likely to be soon improved, which some might have thought too far from the village, but to my eyes the village was too far from it. Well, there I might live, I said; and there I did live, for an hour, a summer and a winter life; saw how I could let the years run off, buffet the winter through, and see the spring come in. The future inhabitants of this region, wherever they may place their houses, may be sure that they have been anticipated. An afternoon sufficed to lay out the land into orchard, wood-lot, and pasture, and to decide what fine oaks or pines should be left to stand before the door, and whence each blasted tree could be seen to the best advantage; and then I let it lie, fallow, perchance, for a man is rich in proportion to the number of things which he can afford to let alone.

My imagination carried me so far that I even had the refusal of several farms—the refusal was all I wanted—but I never got my fingers burned by actual possession. The nearest that I came to actual possession was when I bought the Hollowell place, and had begun to sort my seeds, and collected materials with which to make a wheelbarrow to carry it on or off with; but before the owner gave me a deed of it, his wife—every man has such a wife—changed her mind and wished to keep it, and he offered me ten dollars to release him. Now, to speak the truth, I had but ten cents in the world, and it surpassed my arithmetic to tell, if I was that man who had ten cents, or who had a farm, or ten dollars, or all together. However, I let him keep the ten dollars and the farm too, for I had carried it far enough; or rather, to be generous, I sold him the farm for just what I gave for it, and, as he was not a rich man, made him a present of ten dollars, and still had my ten cents, and seeds, and materials for a wheelbarrow left. I found thus that I had been a rich man without any damage to my poverty. But I retained the landscape, and I have since annually carried off what it yielded without a wheelbarrow. With respect to landscapes,

> I am monarch of all I *survey*,
> My right there is none to dispute.[1]

I have frequently seen a poet withdraw, having enjoyed the most valuable part of a farm, while the crusty farmer supposed that he had got a few wild apples only. Why, the owner does not know it for many years when a poet has put his farm in rhyme, the most admirable kind of invisible fence, has fairly impounded it, milked it, skimmed it, and got all the cream, and left the farmer only the skimmed milk.

The real attractions of the Hollowell farm, to me, were: its complete retirement, being about two miles from the village, half a mile from the nearest neighbor, and separated from the highway by a broad field; its bounding on the river, which the owner said protected it by its fogs from frosts in the spring, though that was nothing to me; the gray color and ruinous state of the house and barn, and the dilapidated fences, which put such an interval between me and the last occupant; the hollow and lichen-covered apple trees, gnawed by rabbits, showing what kind of neighbors I should have; but above all, the recollection I had of it from my earliest voyages up the river, when the house was concealed behind a dense grove of red maples, through which I heard the house-dog bark. I was in haste to buy it, before the proprietor finished getting out some rocks, cutting down the hollow apple trees, and grubbing up some young birches which had sprung up in the pasture, or, in short, had made any more of his improvements. To enjoy these advantages I was ready to carry it on; like Atlas,[2] to take the world on my shoulders—I never heard what compensation he received for that—and do all those things which had no other motive or excuse but that I might pay for it and be unmolested in my possession of it; for I knew all the while that it would yield the most abundant crop of the kind I wanted, if I could only afford to let it alone. But it turned out as I have said.

All that I could say, then, with respect to farming on a large scale—I have always cultivated a garden—was,

---

[1]   *I am ... to dispute*   See "Verses Supposed to Be Written by Alexander Selkirk" by William Cowper (1731–1800); Thoreau italicizes "survey" to emphasize his pun on the word.

[2]   *Atlas*   Greek god who was said to hold up the pillars of the universe.

that I had had my seeds ready. Many think that seeds improve with age. I have no doubt that time discriminates between the good and the bad; and when at last I shall plant, I shall be less likely to be disappointed. But I would say to my fellows, once for all, As long as possible live free and uncommitted. It makes but little difference whether you are committed to a farm or the county jail.

Old Cato,[1] whose "De Re Rusticâ" is my "Cultivator,"[2] says—and the only translation I have seen makes sheer nonsense of the passage—"When you think of getting a farm turn it thus in your mind, not to buy greedily; nor spare your pains to look at it, and do not think it enough to go round it once. The oftener you go there the more it will please you, if it is good." I think I shall not buy greedily, but go round and round it as long as I live, and be buried in it first, that it may please me the more at last.

The present was my next experiment of this kind, which I purpose to describe more at length, for convenience putting the experience of two years into one. As I have said, I do not propose to write an ode to dejection, but to brag as lustily as chanticleer[3] in the morning, standing on his roost, if only to wake my neighbors up.

When first I took up my abode in the woods, that is, began to spend my nights as well as days there, which, by accident, was on Independence Day, or the Fourth of July, 1845, my house was not finished for winter, but was merely a defense against the rain, without plastering or chimney, the walls being of rough, weather-stained boards, with wide chinks, which made it cool at night. The upright white hewn studs and freshly planed door and window casings gave it a clean and airy look, especially in the morning, when its timbers were saturated with dew, so that I fancied that by noon some sweet gum would exude from them. To my imagination it retained throughout the day more or less of this auroral[4] character, reminding me of a certain house on a mountain which I had visited a year before. This was an airy and unplastered cabin, fit to entertain a traveling god, and where a goddess might trail her garments. The winds which passed over my dwelling were such as sweep over the ridges of mountains, bearing the broken strains, or celestial parts only, of terrestrial music. The morning wind forever blows, the poem of creation is uninterrupted; but few are the ears that hear it. Olympus[5] is but the outside of the earth everywhere.

The only house I had been the owner of before, if I except a boat, was a tent, which I used occasionally when making excursions in the summer, and this is still rolled up in my garret; but the boat, after passing from hand to hand, has gone down the stream of time. With this more substantial shelter about me, I had made some progress toward settling in the world. This frame, so slightly clad, was a sort of crystallization around me, and reacted on the builder. It was suggestive somewhat as a picture in outlines. I did not need to go outdoors to take the air, for the atmosphere within had lost none of its freshness. It was not so much within doors as behind a door where I sat, even in the rainiest weather. The Harivansa[6] says, "An abode without birds is like a meat without seasoning." Such was not my abode, for I found myself suddenly neighbor to the birds; not by having imprisoned one, but having caged myself near them. I was not only nearer to some of those which commonly frequent the garden and the orchard, but to those wilder and more thrilling songsters of the forest which never, or rarely, serenade a villager—the wood thrush, the veery, the scarlet tanager, the field sparrow, the whip-poor-will, and many others.

I was seated by the shore of a small pond, about a mile and a half south of the village of Concord and somewhat higher than it, in the midst of an extensive wood between that town and Lincoln, and about two miles south of that our only field known to fame, Concord Battle Ground;[7] but I was so low in the woods that the opposite shore, half a mile off, like the rest, covered with wood, was my most distant horizon. For the first

---

[1] *Old Cato* Cato the Elder (234–149 BCE), Roman senator who wrote *De Agricultura* (On Agriculture).

[2] *Cultivator* Monthly journal on farming practices in circulation during the 1800s.

[3] *chanticleer* Literary name for a cockerel; rooster.

[4] *auroral* Dawn-like.

[5] *Olympus* Mount Olympus, home of the gods in Greek mythology.

[6] *Harivansa* Sacred Hindu text.

[7] *Concord Battle Ground* Site of one of the first battles of the American Revolutionary War; it took place on 19 April 1775.

week, whenever I looked out on the pond it impressed me like a tarn[1] high up on the side of a mountain, its bottom far above the surface of other lakes, and, as the sun arose, I saw it throwing off its nightly clothing of mist, and here and there, by degrees, its soft ripples or its smooth reflecting surface was revealed, while the mists, like ghosts, were stealthily withdrawing in every direction into the woods, as at the breaking up of some nocturnal conventicle.[2] The very dew seemed to hang upon the trees later into the day than usual, as on the sides of mountains.

This small lake was of most value as a neighbor in the intervals of a gentle rain-storm in August, when, both air and water being perfectly still, but the sky overcast, mid-afternoon had all the serenity of evening, and the wood thrush sang around, and was heard from shore to shore. A lake like this is never smoother than at such a time; and the clear portion of the air above it being shallow and darkened by clouds, the water, full of light and reflections, becomes a lower heaven itself so much the more important. From a hill-top nearby, where the wood had been recently cut off, there was a pleasing vista southward across the pond, through a wide indentation in the hills which form the shore there, where their opposite sides sloping toward each other suggested a stream flowing out in that direction through a wooded valley, but stream there was none. That way I looked between and over the near green hills to some distant and higher ones in the horizon, tinged with blue. Indeed, by standing on tiptoe I could catch a glimpse of some of the peaks of the still bluer and more distant mountain ranges in the northwest, those true-blue coins from heaven's own mint, and also of some portion of the village. But in other directions, even from this point, I could not see over or beyond the woods which surrounded me. It is well to have some water in your neighborhood, to give buoyancy to and float the earth. One value even of the smallest well is, that when you look into it you see that earth is not continent but insular. This is as important as that it keeps butter cool.[3] When I looked across the pond from this peak toward the Sudbury meadows, which in time of flood I

distinguished elevated perhaps by a mirage in their seething valley, like a coin in a basin, all the earth beyond the pond appeared like a thin crust insulated and floated even by this small sheet of intervening water, and I was reminded that this on which I dwelt was but *dry land*.

Though the view from my door was still more contracted, I did not feel crowded or confined in the least. There was pasture enough for my imagination. The low shrub oak plateau to which the opposite shore arose stretched away toward the prairies of the West and the steppes of Tartary,[4] affording ample room for all the roving families of men. "There are none happy in the world but beings who enjoy freely a vast horizon," said Damodara,[5] when his herds required new and larger pastures.

Both place and time were changed, and I dwelt nearer to those parts of the universe and to those eras in history which had most attracted me. Where I lived was as far off as many a region viewed nightly by astronomers. We are wont to imagine rare and delectable places in some remote and more celestial corner of the system, behind the constellation of Cassiopeia's Chair,[6] far from noise and disturbance. I discovered that my house actually had its site in such a withdrawn, but forever new and unprofaned, part of the universe. If it were worth the while to settle in those parts near to the Pleiades or the Hyades, to Aldebaran or Altair,[7] then I was really there, or at an equal remoteness from the life which I had left behind, dwindled and twinkling with as fine a ray to my nearest neighbor, and to be seen only in moonless nights by him. Such was that part of creation where I had squatted—

There was a shepherd that did live,
And held his thoughts as high
As were the mounts whereon his flocks
Did hourly feed him by.[8]

---

[1] *tarn* Small mountain lake.

[2] *conventicle* Religious gathering.

[3] *keeps butter cool* Referring to the practice of storing butter in wells, prior to the invention of refrigeration.

[4] *steppes of Tartary* Plains of central and northern Asia, including parts of what are now Siberia and Mongolia.

[5] *Damodara* Name for the Hindu god Krishna; Thoreau derives the quotation from a French edition of the *Harivansa*.

[6] *Cassiopeia's Chair* Set of stars in the constellation Cassiopeia, which form the shape of the queen's chair.

[7] *Pleiades ... Altair* Other constellations.

[8] *There was ... him by* Early seventeenth-century verse by an anonymous author, which Thoreau would probably have discovered in Thomas Evans's *Old Ballads* (1810).

What should we think of the shepherd's life if his flocks always wandered to higher pastures than his thoughts?

Every morning was a cheerful invitation to make my life of equal simplicity, and I may say innocence, with Nature herself. I have been as sincere a worshipper of Aurora[1] as the Greeks. I got up early and bathed in the pond; that was a religious exercise, and one of the best things which I did. They say that characters were engraven on the bathing tub of King Tching-thang[2] to this effect: "Renew thyself completely each day; do it again, and again, and forever again." I can understand that. Morning brings back the heroic ages. I was as much affected by the faint hum of a mosquito making its invisible and unimaginable tour through my apartment at earliest dawn, when I was sitting with door and windows open, as I could be by any trumpet that ever sang of fame. It was Homer's[3] requiem; itself an Iliad and Odyssey in the air, singing its own wrath and wanderings. There was something cosmical about it; a standing advertisement, till forbidden, of the everlasting vigor and fertility of the world. The morning, which is the most memorable season of the day, is the awakening hour. Then there is least somnolence in us; and for an hour, at least, some part of us awakes which slumbers all the rest of the day and night. Little is to be expected of that day, if it can be called a day, to which we are not awakened by our Genius, but by the mechanical nudgings of some servitor, are not awakened by our own newly acquired force and aspirations from within, accompanied by the undulations of celestial music, instead of factory bells, and a fragrance filling the air— to a higher life than we fell asleep from; and thus the darkness bear its fruit, and prove itself to be good, no less than the light. That man who does not believe that each day contains an earlier, more sacred, and auroral hour than he has yet profaned, has despaired of life, and is pursuing a descending and darkening way. After a partial cessation of his sensuous life, the soul of man, or its organs rather, are reinvigorated each day, and his Genius tries again what noble life it can make. All memorable events, I should say, transpire in morning time and in a morning atmosphere. The Vedas[4] say, "All intelligences awake with the morning." Poetry and art, and the fairest and most memorable of the actions of men, date from such an hour. All poets and heroes, like Memnon,[5] are the children of Aurora, and emit their music at sunrise. To him whose elastic and vigorous thought keeps pace with the sun, the day is a perpetual morning. It matters not what the clocks say or the attitudes and labors of men. Morning is when I am awake and there is a dawn in me. Moral reform is the effort to throw off sleep. Why is it that men give so poor an account of their day if they have not been slumbering? They are not such poor calculators. If they had not been overcome with drowsiness, they would have performed something. The millions are awake enough for physical labor; but only one in a million is awake enough for effective intellectual exertion, only one in a hundred millions to a poetic or divine life. To be awake is to be alive. I have never yet met a man who was quite awake. How could I have looked him in the face?

We must learn to reawaken and keep ourselves awake, not by mechanical aids, but by an infinite expectation of the dawn, which does not forsake us in our soundest sleep. I know of no more encouraging fact than the unquestionable ability of man to elevate his life by a conscious endeavor. It is something to be able to paint a particular picture, or to carve a statue, and so to make a few objects beautiful; but it is far more glorious to carve and paint the very atmosphere and medium through which we look, which morally we can do. To affect the quality of the day, that is the highest of arts. Every man is tasked to make his life, even in its details, worthy of the contemplation of his most elevated and critical hour. If we refused, or rather used up, such paltry information as we get, the oracles would distinctly inform us how this might be done.

I went to the woods because I wished to live deliberately, to front only the essential facts of life, and see if

---

1   *Aurora* Classical goddess of the dawn.

2   *King Tching-thang* Emperor Tang, founder of the Shang dynasty in China. The quotation that follows is from the Confucian text *The Great Learning*.

3   *Homer* Author of the *Iliad* and *Odyssey*, epic works of Classical Greek poetry.

4   *Vedas* Collection of four texts which comprise some of the most significant scriptures of Hinduism; the actual source of the following quotation is unknown.

5   *Memnon* In Greek mythology, son of Eos (also known as Aurora) and king of the Ethiopians; he was killed by Achilles in the Trojan War.

I could not learn what it had to teach, and not, when I came to die, discover that I had not lived. I did not wish to live what was not life, living is so dear; nor did I wish to practice resignation, unless it was quite necessary. I wanted to live deep and suck out all the marrow of life, to live so sturdily and Spartan-like[1] as to put to rout all that was not life, to cut a broad swath and shave close, to drive life into a corner, and reduce it to its lowest terms, and, if it proved to be mean,[2] why then to get the whole and genuine meanness of it, and publish its meanness to the world; or if it were sublime, to know it by experience, and be able to give a true account of it in my next excursion. For most men, it appears to me, are in a strange uncertainty about it, whether it is of the devil or of God, and have *somewhat hastily* concluded that it is the chief end of man here to "glorify God and enjoy him forever."[3]

Still we live meanly, like ants; though the fable tells us that we were long ago changed into men; like pygmies we fight with cranes;[4] it is error upon error, and clout upon clout, and our best virtue has for its occasion a superfluous and evitable wretchedness. Our life is frittered away by detail. An honest man has hardly need to count more than his ten fingers, or in extreme cases he may add his ten toes, and lump the rest. Simplicity, simplicity, simplicity! I say, let your affairs be as two or three, and not a hundred or a thousand; instead of a million count half a dozen, and keep your accounts on your thumbnail. In the midst of this chopping sea of civilized life, such are the clouds and storms and quicksands and thousand-and-one items to be allowed for, that a man has to live, if he would not founder and go to the bottom and not make his port at all, by dead reckoning, and he must be a great calculator indeed who succeeds. Simplify, simplify. Instead of three meals a day, if it be necessary eat but one; instead of a hundred dishes, five; and reduce other things in proportion. Our life is like a German Confederacy,[5] made up of petty states, with its boundary forever fluctuating, so that even a German cannot tell you how it is bounded at any moment. The nation itself, with all its so-called internal improvements, which, by the way are all external and superficial, is just such an unwieldy and overgrown establishment, cluttered with furniture and tripped up by its own traps, ruined by luxury and heedless expense, by want of calculation and a worthy aim, as the million households in the land; and the only cure for it, as for them, is in a rigid economy, a stern and more than Spartan simplicity of life and elevation of purpose. It lives too fast. Men think that it is essential that the *Nation* have commerce, and export ice, and talk through a telegraph, and ride thirty miles an hour, without a doubt, whether *they* do or not; but whether we should live like baboons or like men, is a little uncertain. If we do not get out sleepers,[6] and forge rails, and devote days and nights to the work, but go to tinkering upon our *lives* to improve *them,* who will build railroads? And if railroads are not built, how shall we get to heaven in season?[7] But if we stay at home and mind our business, who will want railroads? We do not ride on the railroad; it rides upon us. Did you ever think what those sleepers are that underlie the railroad? Each one is a man, an Irishman, or a Yankee man. The rails are laid on them, and they are covered with sand, and the cars run smoothly over them. They are sound sleepers, I assure you. And every few years a new lot is laid down and run over; so that, if some have the pleasure of riding on a rail, others have the misfortune to be ridden upon. And when they run over a man that is walking in his sleep, a supernumerary sleeper in the wrong position, and wake him up, they suddenly stop the cars, and make a hue and cry about it, as if this were an exception. I am glad to know that it takes a gang of men for every five miles to keep the sleepers down and level in their beds as it is, for this is a sign that they may sometime get up again.

---

[1]   *Spartan-like*   Akin to the citizens of the ancient Greek state of Sparta, who were known for their bravery and disciplined simplicity of living.

[2]   *mean*   Base, lowly, undignified.

[3]   *the chief ... him forever*   From the Shorter Catechism in *The New England Primer*. Question: "What is the chief end of man?" Answer: "Man's chief end is to glorify God and enjoy him forever." See also Psalm 86.12: "and I will glorify thy name for evermore."

[4]   *like pygmies ... with cranes*   See Homer's *Iliad*, book 3, in which the warring Trojans are likened to the pygmies, a mythological race of small humans who were said to be at constant war with cranes.

---

[5]   *German Confederacy*   Germany was not unified until 1871; prior to that, it comprised numerous states, which were often at war with one another.

[6]   *sleepers*   Wooden planks upon which train rails are built; also a pun.

[7]   *in season*   In time.

Why should we live with such hurry and waste of life? We are determined to be starved before we are hungry. Men say that a stitch in time saves nine, and so they take a thousand stitches today to save nine tomorrow. As for *work*, we haven't any of any consequence. We have the Saint Vitus' dance,[1] and cannot possibly keep our heads still. If I should only give a few pulls at the parish bell-rope, as for a fire, that is, without setting the bell, there is hardly a man on his farm in the outskirts of Concord, notwithstanding that press of engagements which was his excuse so many times this morning, nor a boy, nor a woman, I might almost say, but would forsake all and follow that sound, not mainly to save property from the flames, but, if we will confess the truth, much more to see it burn, since burn it must, and we, be it known, did not set it on fire—or to see it put out, and have a hand in it, if that is done as handsomely; yes, even if it were the parish church itself. Hardly a man takes a half-hour's nap after dinner, but when he wakes he holds up his head and asks, "What's the news?" as if the rest of mankind had stood his sentinels. Some give directions to be waked every half-hour, doubtless for no other purpose; and then, to pay for it, they tell what they have dreamed. After a night's sleep the news is as indispensable as the breakfast. "Pray tell me anything new that has happened to a man anywhere on this globe,"—and he reads it over his coffee and rolls, that a man has had his eyes gouged out this morning on the Wachito River; never dreaming the while that he lives in the dark unfathomed mammoth cave of this world, and has but the rudiment of an eye himself.

For my part, I could easily do without the post-office. I think that there are very few important communications made through it. To speak critically, I never received more than one or two letters in my life—I wrote this some years ago—that were worth the postage. The penny-post[2] is, commonly, an institution through which you seriously offer a man that penny for his thoughts which is so often safely offered in jest. And I am sure that I never read any memorable news in a newspaper. If we read of one man robbed, or murdered, or killed by accident, or one house burned, or one vessel wrecked, or one steamboat blown up, or one cow run over on the Western Railroad, or one mad dog killed, or one lot of grasshoppers in the winter—we never need read of another. One is enough. If you are acquainted with the principle, what do you care for a myriad instances and applications? To a philosopher all *news*, as it is called, is gossip, and they who edit and read it are old women over their tea. Yet not a few are greedy after this gossip. There was such a rush, as I hear, the other day at one of the offices to learn the foreign news by the last arrival, that several large squares of plate glass belonging to the establishment were broken by the pressure—news which I seriously think a ready wit might write a twelvemonth, or twelve years, beforehand with sufficient accuracy. As for Spain, for instance, if you know how to throw in Don Carlos and the Infanta, and Don Pedro and Seville and Granada,[3] from time to time in the right proportions—they may have changed the names a little since I saw the papers—and serve up a bull-fight when other entertainments fail, it will be true to the letter, and give us as good an idea of the exact state or ruin of things in Spain as the most succinct and lucid reports under this head in the newspapers: and as for England, almost the last significant scrap of news from that quarter was the revolution of 1649;[4] and if you have learned the history of her crops for an average year, you never need attend to that thing again, unless your speculations are of a merely pecuniary character. If one may judge who rarely looks into the newspapers, nothing new does ever happen in foreign parts, a French revolution[5] not excepted.

---

1   *Saint Vitus' dance*   Chorea, a disorder of the nerves causing jerking motions in the face, hands, and feet; named after the patron saint of the disease, Saint Vitus.

2   *penny-post*   Postal service by which letters could be sent for the cost of one penny.

3   *Don Carlos ... and Granada*   Examples of typical figures of Spanish history; Carlos of Spain (1788–1855) was a pretender to the Spanish throne, eventually ousted by the Infante Isabella (1830–1904), the daughter of Carlos's brother and the previous king, Ferdinand VII (1784–1833). "Don Pedro" refers to the Castilian king known as Peter the Cruel (1334–69).

4   *revolution of 1649*   Year in which Charles I of England was executed by the Parliamentarians in the English Civil War, signaling the beginning of the Puritan Commonwealth of England, lasting until 1660.

5   *a French Revolution*   At the time *Walden* was being written, the most recent revolution in France had been that of 1848, which led to the establishment of the Second French Empire under Napoleon III (1808–73).

What news! how much more important to know what that is which was never old! "Kieou-he-yu (great dignitary of the state of Wei) sent a man to Khoung-tseu[1] to know his news. Khoung-tseu caused the messenger to be seated near him, and questioned him in these terms: What is your master doing? The messenger answered with respect: My master desires to diminish the number of his faults, but he cannot come to the end of them. The messenger being gone, the philosopher remarked: What a worthy messenger! What a worthy messenger!" The preacher, instead of vexing the ears of drowsy farmers on their day of rest at the end of the week—for Sunday is the fit conclusion of an ill-spent week, and not the fresh and brave beginning of a new one—with this one other draggle-tail of a sermon, should shout with thundering voice, "Pause! Avast! Why so seeming fast, but deadly slow?"

Shams and delusions are esteemed for soundest truths, while reality is fabulous.[2] If men would steadily observe realities only, and not allow themselves to be deluded, life, to compare it with such things as we know, would be like a fairy tale and the Arabian Nights' Entertainments.[3] If we respected only what is inevitable and has a right to be, music and poetry would resound along the streets. When we are unhurried and wise, we perceive that only great and worthy things have any permanent and absolute existence, that petty fears and petty pleasures are but the shadow of the reality. This is always exhilarating and sublime. By closing the eyes and slumbering, and consenting to be deceived by shows, men establish and confirm their daily life of routine and habit everywhere, which still is built on purely illusory foundations. Children, who play life, discern its true law and relations more clearly than men, who fail to live it worthily, but who think that they are wiser by experience, that is, by failure. I have read in a Hindoo book, that "there was a king's son, who, being expelled in infancy from his native city, was brought up by a forester, and, growing up to maturity in that state, imagined himself to belong to the barbarous race with which he lived. One of his father's ministers having discovered him, revealed to him what he was, and the misconception of his character was removed, and he knew himself to be a prince. So soul," continues the Hindoo philosopher, "from the circumstances in which it is placed, mistakes its own character, until the truth is revealed to it by some holy teacher, and then it knows itself to be *Brahme*."[4] I perceive that we inhabitants of New England live this mean life that we do because our vision does not penetrate the surface of things. We think that that *is* which *appears* to be. If a man should walk through this town and see only the reality, where, think you, would the "Mill-dam"[5] go to? If he should give us an account of the realities he beheld there, we should not recognize the place in his description. Look at a meeting-house, or a court-house, or a jail, or a shop, or a dwelling-house, and say what that thing really is before a true gaze, and they would all go to pieces in your account of them. Men esteem truth remote, in the outskirts of the system, behind the farthest star, before Adam and after the last man. In eternity there is indeed something true and sublime. But all these times and places and occasions are now and here. God himself culminates in the present moment, and will never be more divine in the lapse of all the ages. And we are enabled to apprehend at all what is sublime and noble only by the perpetual instilling and drenching of the reality that surrounds us. The universe constantly and obediently answers to our conceptions; whether we travel fast or slow, the track is laid for us. Let us spend our lives in conceiving then. The poet or the artist never yet had so fair and noble a design but some of his posterity at least could accomplish it.

Let us spend one day as deliberately as Nature, and not be thrown off the track by every nutshell and mosquito's wing that falls on the rails. Let us rise early and fast, or break fast, gently and without perturbation; let company come and let company go, let the bells ring and the children cry, determined to make a day of it. Why should we knock under and go with the stream?

---

[1]   *Khoung-tseu* Antiquated English spelling of the Mandarin name of Confucius; the story is from Book Fourteen of the *Analects*, a collection of sayings traditionally attributed to Confucius.

[2]   *fabulous* Mythical, fictional.

[3]   *Arabian Nights' Entertainments* Also known as *One Thousand and One Nights*, a collection of Arabic, Indian, and Persian folk tales.

[4]   *there was ... be Brahme* Thoreau's source for the story is unclear; *Brahme* likely refers to Brahman, which in Hinduism is the unifying principle that pervades all reality, simultaneously creative and unchanging.

[5]   *Mill-dam* Center in which business was conducted in Concord.

Let us not be upset and overwhelmed in that terrible rapid and whirlpool called a dinner, situated in the meridian shallows. Weather this danger and you are safe, for the rest of the way is downhill. With unrelaxed nerves, with morning vigor, sail by it, looking another way, tied to the mast like Ulysses.[1] If the engine whistles, let it whistle till it is hoarse for its pains. If the bell rings, why should we run? We will consider what kind of music they are like. Let us settle ourselves, and work and wedge our feet downward through the mud and slush of opinion, and prejudice, and tradition, and delusion, and appearance, that alluvion[2] which covers the globe, through Paris and London, through New York and Boston and Concord, through Church and State, through poetry and philosophy and religion, till we come to a hard bottom and rocks in place, which we can call *reality*, and say, This is, and no mistake; and then begin, having a *point d'appui*,[3] below freshet and frost and fire, a place where you might found a wall or a state, or set a lamp-post safely, or perhaps a gauge, not a Nilometer,[4] but a Realometer, that future ages might know how deep a freshet of shams and appearances had gathered from time to time. If you stand right fronting and face to face to a fact, you will see the sun glimmer on both its surfaces, as if it were a scimitar, and feel its sweet edge dividing you through the heart and marrow, and so you will happily conclude your mortal career. Be it life or death, we crave only reality. If we are really dying, let us hear the rattle in our throats and feel cold in the extremities; if we are alive, let us go about our business.

Time is but the stream I go a-fishing in. I drink at it; but while I drink I see the sandy bottom and detect how shallow it is. Its thin current slides away, but eternity remains. I would drink deeper; fish in the sky, whose bottom is pebbly with stars. I cannot count one. I know not the first letter of the alphabet. I have always been regretting that I was not as wise as the day I was born. The intellect is a cleaver; it discerns and rifts its way into the secret of things. I do not wish to be any more busy with my hands than is necessary. My head is hands and feet. I feel all my best faculties concentrated in it. My instinct tells me that my head is an organ for burrowing, as some creatures use their snout and fore paws, and with it I would mine and burrow my way through these hills. I think that the richest vein is somewhere hereabouts; so by the divining-rod and thin rising vapors I judge; and here I will begin to mine.

from CHAPTER 5
SOLITUDE

This is a delicious evening, when the whole body is one sense, and imbibes delight through every pore. I go and come with a strange liberty in Nature, a part of herself. As I walk along the stony shore of the pond in my shirt-sleeves, though it is cool as well as cloudy and windy, and I see nothing special to attract me, all the elements are unusually congenial to me. The bullfrogs trump to usher in the night, and the note of the whip-poor-will is borne on the rippling wind from over the water. Sympathy with the fluttering alder and poplar leaves almost takes away my breath; yet, like the lake, my serenity is rippled but not ruffled. These small waves raised by the evening wind are as remote from storm as the smooth reflecting surface. Though it is now dark, the wind still blows and roars in the wood, the waves still dash, and some creatures lull the rest with their notes. The repose is never complete. The wildest animals do not repose, but seek their prey now; the fox, and skunk, and rabbit, now roam the fields and woods without fear. They are Nature's watchmen—links which connect the days of animated life.

When I return to my house I find that visitors have been there and left their cards, either a bunch of flowers, or a wreath of evergreen, or a name in pencil on a yellow walnut leaf or a chip. They who come rarely to the woods take some little piece of the forest into their hands to play with by the way, which they leave, either intentionally or accidentally. One has peeled a willow wand, woven it into a ring, and dropped it on my table. I could always tell if visitors had called in my absence, either by the bended twigs or grass, or the print of their

---

[1]   *tied to … like Ulysses* In Homer's *Odyssey*, Odysseus (also known by the Roman name Ulysses) ties himself to the mast of his ship so that he can hear the seductive song of the Sirens without succumbing to their call—as they were known in mythology to lead sailors to their deaths.

[2]   *alluvion* Flood.

[3]   *point d'appui* French: point of support.

[4]   *Nilometer* Structure used in ancient Egypt to measure the rising and falling levels of the Nile.

shoes, and generally of what sex or age or quality they were by some slight trace left, as a flower dropped, or a bunch of grass plucked and thrown away, even as far off as the railroad, half a mile distant, or by the lingering odor of a cigar or pipe. Nay, I was frequently notified of the passage of a traveller along the highway sixty rods[1] off by the scent of his pipe.

There is commonly sufficient space about us. Our horizon is never quite at our elbows. The thick wood is not just at our door, nor the pond, but somewhat is always clearing, familiar and worn by us, appropriated and fenced in some way, and reclaimed from Nature. For what reason have I this vast range and circuit, some square miles of unfrequented forest, for my privacy, abandoned to me by men? My nearest neighbor is a mile distant, and no house is visible from any place but the hilltops within half a mile of my own. I have my horizon bounded by woods all to myself; a distant view of the railroad where it touches the pond on the one hand, and of the fence which skirts the woodland road on the other. But for the most part it is as solitary where I live as on the prairies. It is as much Asia or Africa as New England. I have, as it were, my own sun and moon and stars, and a little world all to myself. At night there was never a traveller passed my house, or knocked at my door, more than if I were the first or last man; unless it were in the spring, when at long intervals some came from the village to fish for pouts—they plainly fished much more in the Walden Pond of their own natures, and baited their hooks with darkness—but they soon retreated, usually with light baskets, and left "the world to darkness and to me,"[2] and the black kernel of the night was never profaned by any human neighborhood. I believe that men are generally still a little afraid of the dark, though the witches are all hung, and Christianity and candles have been introduced.

Yet I experienced sometimes that the most sweet and tender, the most innocent and encouraging society may be found in any natural object, even for the poor misanthrope and most melancholy man. There can be no very black melancholy to him who lives in the midst of nature and has his senses still. There was never yet such a storm but it was Aeolian[3] music to a healthy and innocent ear. Nothing can rightly compel a simple and brave man to a vulgar sadness. While I enjoy the friendship of the seasons I trust that nothing can make life a burden to me. The gentle rain which waters my beans and keeps me in the house today is not drear and melancholy, but good for me too. Though it prevents my hoeing them, it is of far more worth than my hoeing. If it should continue so long as to cause the seeds to rot in the ground and destroy the potatoes in the low lands, it would still be good for the grass on the uplands, and, being good for the grass, it would be good for me. Sometimes, when I compare myself with other men, it seems as if I were more favored by the gods than they, beyond any deserts that I am conscious of; as if I had a warrant and surety at their hands which my fellows have not, and were especially guided and guarded. I do not flatter myself, but if it be possible they flatter me. I have never felt lonesome, or in the least oppressed, by a sense of solitude, but once, and that was a few weeks after I came to the woods, when, for an hour, I doubted if the near neighborhood of man was not essential to a serene and healthy life. To be alone was something unpleasant. But I was at the same time conscious of a slight insanity in my mood, and seemed to foresee my recovery. In the midst of a gentle rain while these thoughts prevailed, I was suddenly sensible of such sweet and beneficent society in Nature, in the very pattering of the drops, and in every sound and sight around my house, an infinite and unaccountable friendliness all at once like an atmosphere sustaining me, as made the fancied advantages of human neighborhood insignificant, and I have never thought of them since. Every little pine needle expanded and swelled with sympathy and befriended me. I was so distinctly made aware of the presence of something kindred to me, even in scenes which we are accustomed to call wild and dreary, and also that the nearest of blood to me and humanest was not a person nor a villager, that I thought no place could ever be strange to me again.

---

1   *rods*   Units of measurement, derived from the surveyor's tool; a rod is equivalent to approximately 5.5 yards.

2   *the world … to me*   See Thomas Gray's "Elegy Written in a Country Churchyard" (1751).

3   *Aeolian*   Of Aeolus, the Greek god of the winds; the Aeolian harp, an instrument designed to be "played" by the blowing of the wind, had been popularized during the Romantic era, and was favored by Thoreau.

Mourning untimely consumes the sad;
Few are their days in the land of the living,
Beautiful daughter of Toscar.[1]

Some of my pleasantest hours were during the long rain-storms in the spring or fall, which confined me to the house for the afternoon as well as the forenoon, soothed by their ceaseless roar and pelting, when an early twilight ushered in a long evening in which many thoughts had time to take root and unfold themselves. In those driving northeast rains which tried the village houses so, when the maids stood ready with mop and pail in front entries to keep the deluge out, I sat behind my door in my little house, which was all entry, and thoroughly enjoyed its protection. In one heavy thunder-shower the lightning struck a large pitch pine across the pond, making a very conspicuous and perfectly regular spiral groove from top to bottom, an inch or more deep, and four or five inches wide, as you would groove a walking-stick. I passed it again the other day, and was struck with awe on looking up and beholding that mark, now more distinct than ever, where a terrific and resistless bolt came down out of the harmless sky eight years ago. Men frequently say to me, "I should think you would feel lonesome down there, and want to be nearer to folks, rainy and snowy days and nights especially." I am tempted to reply to such—This whole earth which we inhabit is but a point in space. How far apart, think you, dwell the two most distant inhabitants of yonder star, the breadth of whose disk cannot be appreciated by our instruments? Why should I feel lonely? is not our planet in the Milky Way? This which you put seems to me not to be the most important question. What sort of space is that which separates a man from his fellows and makes him solitary? I have found that no exertion of the legs can bring two minds much nearer to one another. What do we want most to dwell near to? Not to many men surely—the depot, the post-office, the bar-room, the meeting-house, the school-house, the grocery, Beacon Hill,[2] or the Five Points,[3] where men most congregate—but to the perennial source of our life, whence in all our experience we have found that to issue, as the willow stands near the water and sends out its roots in that direction. This will vary with different natures, but this is the place where a wise man will dig his cellar. I one evening overtook one of my townsmen, who has accumulated what is called "a handsome property"—though I never got a *fair* view of it—on the Walden road, driving a pair of cattle to market, who inquired of me how I could bring my mind to give up so many of the comforts of life. I answered that I was very sure I liked it passably well; I was not joking. And so I went home to my bed, and left him to pick his way through the darkness and the mud to Brighton[4]—or Bright-town—which place he would reach some time in the morning.

Any prospect of awakening or coming to life to a dead man makes indifferent all times and places. The place where that may occur is always the same, and indescribably pleasant to all our senses. For the most part we allow only outlying and transient circumstances to make our occasions. They are, in fact, the cause of our distraction. Nearest to all things is that power which fashions their being. *Next* to us the grandest laws are continually being executed. *Next* to us is not the workman whom we have hired, with whom we love so well to talk, but the workman whose work we are.

"How vast and profound is the influence of the subtle powers of Heaven and of Earth!"

"We seek to perceive them, and we do not see them; we seek to hear them, and we do not hear them; identified with the substance of things, they cannot be separated from them."

"They cause that in all the universe men purify and sanctify their hearts, and clothe themselves in their holiday garments to offer sacrifices and oblations to their ancestors. It is an ocean of subtle intelligences. They are everywhere, above us, on our left, on our right; they environ us on all sides."[5]

We are the subjects of an experiment which is not a little interesting to me. Can we not do without the

---

[1] *Mourning ... of Toscar* See the poem "Croma" in *The Genuine Remains of Ossian* (1841) by Patrick MacGregor.

[2] *Beacon Hill* Neighborhood in Boston.

[3] *Five Points* Manhattan district known at the time both for its dense population and for its prevalence of crime.

[4] *Brighton* Town, now part of Boston, known in the nineteenth century for housing farm markets and slaughterhouses.

[5] *How vast ... all sides* Thoreau's translation from Guillaume Pauthier's *Confucius et Mencius*, itself a French translation of the Confucian book *The Doctrine of the Mean*.

society of our gossips a little while under these circumstances—have our own thoughts to cheer us? Confucius says truly, "Virtue does not remain as an abandoned orphan; it must of necessity have neighbors."[1]

With thinking we may be beside ourselves in a sane sense. By a conscious effort of the mind we can stand aloof from actions and their consequences; and all things, good and bad, go by us like a torrent. We are not wholly involved in Nature. I may be either the driftwood in the stream, or Indra[2] in the sky looking down on it. I *may* be affected by a theatrical exhibition; on the other hand, I *may not* be affected by an actual event which appears to concern me much more. I only know myself as a human entity—the scene, so to speak, of thoughts and affections—and am sensible of a certain doubleness by which I can stand as remote from myself as from another. However intense my experience, I am conscious of the presence and criticism of a part of me, which, as it were, is not a part of me, but spectator, sharing no experience, but taking note of it; and that is no more I than it is you. When the play—it may be the tragedy—of life is over, the spectator goes his way. It was a kind of fiction, a work of the imagination only, so far as he was concerned. This doubleness may easily make us poor neighbors and friends sometimes.

I find it wholesome to be alone the greater part of the time. To be in company, even with the best, is soon wearisome and dissipating. I love to be alone. I never found the companion that was so companionable as solitude. We are for the most part more lonely when we go abroad among men than when we stay in our chambers. A man thinking or working is always alone, let him be where he will. Solitude is not measured by the miles of space that intervene between a man and his fellows. The really diligent student in one of the crowded hives of Cambridge College is as solitary as a dervish[3] in the desert. The farmer can work alone in the field or the woods all day, hoeing or chopping, and not feel lonesome, because he is employed; but when he comes home at night he cannot sit down in a room

alone, at the mercy of his thoughts, but must be where he can "see the folks," and recreate, and, as he thinks, remunerate himself for his day's solitude; and hence he wonders how the student can sit alone in the house all night and most of the day without ennui and "the blues"; but he does not realize that the student, though in the house, is still at work in *his* field, and chopping in *his* woods, as the farmer in his, and in turn seeks the same recreation and society that the latter does, though it may be a more condensed form of it.

Society is commonly too cheap. We meet at very short intervals, not having had time to acquire any new value for each other. We meet at meals three times a day, and give each other a new taste of that old musty cheese that we are. We have had to agree on a certain set of rules, called etiquette and politeness, to make this frequent meeting tolerable and that we need not come to open war. We meet at the post-office, and at the sociable, and about the fireside every night; we live thick and are in each other's way, and stumble over one another, and I think that we thus lose some respect for one another. Certainly less frequency would suffice for all important and hearty communications. Consider the girls in a factory—never alone, hardly in their dreams. It would be better if there were but one inhabitant to a square mile, as where I live. The value of a man is not in his skin, that we should touch him.

I have heard of a man lost in the woods and dying of famine and exhaustion at the foot of a tree, whose loneliness was relieved by the grotesque visions with which, owing to bodily weakness, his diseased imagination surrounded him, and which he believed to be real. So also, owing to bodily and mental health and strength, we may be continually cheered by a like but more normal and natural society, and come to know that we are never alone.

I have a great deal of company in my house; especially in the morning, when nobody calls. Let me suggest a few comparisons, that some one may convey an idea of my situation. I am no more lonely than the loon in the pond that laughs so loud, or than Walden Pond itself. What company has that lonely lake, I pray? And yet it has not the blue devils,[4] but the blue angels in it, in the azure tint of its waters. The sun is alone, except in thick weather, when there sometimes appear

---

[1] *Virtue … neighbors* Thoreau's translation of Confucius's *Analects*, again from Pauthier's French translation.

[2] *Indra* Hindu deity associated with the heavens, thunder, and rain.

[3] *dervish* Sufi Muslim ascetic.

[4] *blue devils* Demons that cause melancholy.

to be two, but one is a mock sun.[1] God is alone—but the devil, he is far from being alone; he sees a great deal of company; he is legion. I am no more lonely than a single mullein or dandelion in a pasture, or a bean leaf, or sorrel, or a horse-fly, or a humblebee.[2] I am no more lonely than the Mill Brook, or a weathercock, or the north star, or the south wind, or an April shower, or a January thaw, or the first spider in a new house. …

from CHAPTER 6
VISITORS

I think that I love society as much as most, and am ready enough to fasten myself like a bloodsucker for the time to any full-blooded man that come in my way. I am naturally no hermit, but might possibly sit out the sturdiest frequenter of the bar-room, if my business called me thither.

I had three chairs in my house; one for solitude, two for friendship, three for society. When visitors came in larger and unexpected numbers there was but the third chair for them all, but they generally economized the room by standing up. It is surprising how many great men and women a small house will contain. I have had twenty-five or thirty souls, with their bodies, at once under my roof, and yet we often parted without being aware that we had come very near to one another. Many of our houses, both public and private, with their almost innumerable apartments, their huge halls and their cellars for the storage of wines and other munitions of peace, appear to me extravagantly large for their inhabitants. They are so vast and magnificent that the latter seem to be only vermin which infest them. …

Who should come to my lodge this morning but a true Homeric or Paphlagonian[3] man—he had so suitable and poetic a name[4] that I am sorry I cannot print it here—a Canadian, a woodchopper and postmaker, who can hole fifty posts in a day, who made

his last supper on a woodchuck which his dog caught. He, too, has heard of Homer, and, "if it were not for books," would "not know what to do rainy days," though perhaps he has not read one wholly through for many rainy seasons. Some priest who could pronounce the Greek itself taught him to read his verse in the Testament in his native parish far away; and now I must translate to him, while he holds the book, Achilles' reproof to Patroclus for his sad countenance: "Why are you in tears, Patroclus, like a young girl?"

Or have you alone heard some news from
    Phthia?
They say that Menoetius lives yet, son of Actor,
And Peleus lives, son of Aeacus, among the
    Myrmidons,
Either of whom having died, we should greatly
    grieve.[5]

He says, "That's good." He has a great bundle of white oak bark under his arm for a sick man, gathered this Sunday morning. "I suppose there's no harm in going after such a thing today," says he. To him Homer was a great writer, though what his writing was about he did not know. A more simple and natural man it would be hard to find. Vice and disease, which cast such a sombre moral hue over the world, seemed to have hardly any existence for him. He was about twenty-eight years old, and had left Canada and his father's house a dozen years before to work in the States, and earn money to buy a farm with at last, perhaps in his native country. He was cast in the coarsest mould; a stout but sluggish body, yet gracefully carried, with a thick sunburnt neck, dark bushy hair, and dull sleepy blue eyes, which were occasionally lit up with expression. He wore a flat gray cloth cap, a dingy wool-colored greatcoat, and cowhide boots. He was a great consumer of meat, usually carrying his dinner to his work a couple of miles past my house—for he chopped all summer—in a tin pail; cold meats, often cold woodchucks, and coffee in a stone bottle which dangled by a string from his belt; and sometimes he offered me a drink. He came along early, crossing my bean-field, though without anxiety

---

[1]   *mock sun* Sundog; bright spot appearing next to the sun.

[2]   *humblebee* Bumblebee.

[3]   *Paphlagonian* Of Paphlagonia, an ancient country in present-day Turkey, known for its mountains and forests.

[4]   *so suitable … a name* The man described in these passages is Alek Therien (1812–85), whose surname derived from the French *terrien*, meaning a landowner, or a person of the earth.

[5]   *Or have … grieve* See book 16 of Homer's *Iliad*, translated here by Thoreau himself. Patroclus was the closest friend (and, in some versions of the myths, the lover) of the warrior hero Achilles.

or haste to get to his work, such as Yankees exhibit. He wasn't a-going to hurt himself. He didn't care if he only earned his board. Frequently he would leave his dinner in the bushes, when his dog had caught a woodchuck by the way, and go back a mile and a half to dress it and leave it in the cellar of the house where he boarded, after deliberating first for half an hour whether he could not sink it in the pond safely till nightfall—loving to dwell long upon these themes. He would say, as he went by in the morning, "How thick the pigeons are! If working every day were not my trade, I could get all the meat I should want by hunting—pigeons, woodchucks, rabbits, partridges— by gosh! I could get all I should want for a week in one day." He was a skilful chopper, and indulged in some flourishes and ornaments in his art. He cut his trees level and close to the ground, that the sprouts which came up afterward might be more vigorous and a sled might slide over the stumps; and instead of leaving a whole tree to support his corded wood, he would pare it away to a slender stake or splinter which you could break off with your hand at last.

He interested me because he was so quiet and soli- tary and so happy withal; a well of good humor and contentment which overflowed at his eyes. His mirth was without alloy. Sometimes I saw him at his work in the woods, felling trees, and he would greet me with a laugh of inexpressible satisfaction, and a salutation in Canadian French, though he spoke English as well. When I approached him he would suspend his work, and with half-suppressed mirth lie along the trunk of a pine which he had felled, and, peeling off the inner bark, roll it up into a ball and chew it while he laughed and talked. Such an exuberance of animal spirits had he that he sometimes tumbled down and rolled on the ground with laughter at anything which made him think and tickled him. Looking round upon the trees he would exclaim, "By George! I can enjoy myself well enough here chopping; I want no better sport." Sometimes, when at leisure, he amused himself all day in the woods with a pocket pistol, firing salutes to himself at regular intervals as he walked. In the winter he had a fire by which at noon he warmed his coffee in a kettle; and as he sat on a log to eat his dinner the chickadees would sometimes come round and alight on his arm and peck at the potato in his fingers; and he said that he "liked to have the little *fellers* about him."

In him the animal man chiefly was developed. In physical endurance and contentment he was cousin to the pine and the rock. I asked him once if he was not sometimes tired at night, after working all day; and he answered, with a sincere and serious look, "Gorrappit, I never was tired in my life." But the intellectual and what is called spiritual man in him were slumbering as in an infant. He had been instructed only in that innocent and ineffectual way in which the Catholic priests teach the aborigines, by which the pupil is never educated to the degree of consciousness, but only to the degree of trust and reverence, and a child is not made a man, but kept a child. When Nature made him, she gave him a strong body and contentment for his portion, and propped him on every side with reverence and reliance, that he might live out his three- score years and ten[1] a child. He was so genuine and unsophisticated that no introduction would serve to introduce him, more than if you introduced a wood- chuck to your neighbor. He had got to find him out as you did. He would not play any part. Men paid him wages for work, and so helped to feed and clothe him; but he never exchanged opinions with them. He was so simply and naturally humble—if he can be called humble who never aspires—that humility was no distinct quality in him, nor could he conceive of it. Wiser men were demigods to him. If you told him that such a one was coming, he did as if he thought that anything so grand would expect nothing of himself, but take all the responsibility on itself, and let him be forgotten still. He never heard the sound of praise. He particularly reverenced the writer and the preacher. Their performances were miracles. When I told him that I wrote considerably, he thought for a long time that it was merely the handwriting which I meant, for he could write a remarkably good hand himself. I sometimes found the name of his native parish hand- somely written in the snow by the highway, with the proper French accent, and knew that he had passed. I asked him if he ever wished to write his thoughts. He said that he had read and written letters for those who could not, but he never tried to write thoughts— no, he could not, he could not tell what to put first,

---

[1] *threescore years and ten* I.e., seventy years.

it would kill him, and then there was spelling to be attended to at the same time!

I heard that a distinguished wise man and reformer asked him if he did not want the world to be changed; but he answered with a chuckle of surprise in his Canadian accent, not knowing that the question had ever been entertained before, "No, I like it well enough." It would have suggested many things to a philosopher to have dealings with him. To a stranger he appeared to know nothing of things in general; yet I sometimes saw in him a man whom I had not seen before, and I did not know whether he was as wise as Shakespeare or as simply ignorant as a child, whether to suspect him of a fine poetic consciousness or of stupidity. A townsman told me that when he met him sauntering through the village in his small close-fitting cap, and whistling to himself, he reminded him of a prince in disguise.

His only books were an almanac and an arithmetic, in which last he was considerably expert. The former was a sort of cyclopaedia to him, which he supposed to contain an abstract of human knowledge, as indeed it does to a considerable extent. I loved to sound him on the various reforms of the day, and he never failed to look at them in the most simple and practical light. He had never heard of such things before. Could he do without factories? I asked. He had worn the home-made Vermont gray,[1] he said, and that was good. Could he dispense with tea and coffee? Did this country afford any beverage beside water? He had soaked hemlock leaves[2] in water and drank it, and thought that was better than water in warm weather. When I asked him if he could do without money, he showed the convenience of money in such a way as to suggest and coincide with the most philosophical accounts of the origin of this institution, and the very derivation of the word *pecunia*.[3] If an ox were his property, and he wished to get needles and thread at the store, he thought it would be inconvenient and impossible soon to go on mortgaging some portion of the creature each time to that amount. He could defend many institutions better than any philosopher, because, in describing them as they concerned him, he gave the true reason for their prevalence, and speculation had not suggested to him any other. At another time, hearing Plato's definition of a man—a biped without feathers—and that one exhibited a cock plucked and called it Plato's man,[4] he thought it an important difference that the *knees* bent the wrong way. He would sometimes exclaim, "How I love to talk! By George, I could talk all day!" I asked him once, when I had not seen him for many months, if he had got a new idea this summer. "Good Lord," said he, "a man that has to work as I do, if he does not forget the ideas he has had, he will do well. Maybe the man you hoe with is inclined to race; then, by gorry, your mind must be there; you think of weeds." He would sometimes ask me first on such occasions, if I had made any improvement. One winter day I asked him if he was always satisfied with himself, wishing to suggest a substitute within him for the priest without, and some higher motive for living. "Satisfied!" said he; "some men are satisfied with one thing, and some with another. One man, perhaps, if he has got enough, will be satisfied to sit all day with his back to the fire and his belly to the table, by George!" Yet I never, by any maneuvering, could get him to take the spiritual view of things; the highest that he appeared to conceive of was a simple expediency, such as you might expect an animal to appreciate; and this, practically, is true of most men. If I suggested any improvement in his mode of life, he merely answered, without expressing any regret, that it was too late. Yet he thoroughly believed in honesty and the like virtues.

There was a certain positive originality, however slight, to be detected in him, and I occasionally observed that he was thinking for himself and expressing his own opinion, a phenomenon so rare that I would any day walk ten miles to observe it, and it amounted to the re-origination of many of the institutions of society. Though he hesitated, and perhaps failed to express himself distinctly, he always had a

---

[1]   *Vermont gray*   Rustic, undyed outer garment worn in rural New England; the context here suggests that it was frequently homemade.

[2]   *hemlock leaves*   Presumably meaning the needles of the hemlock spruce (i.e., not the leaves of poison hemlock).

[3]   *derivation ... pecunia*   The Latin word for money is derived from *pecu*, meaning "cattle."

[4]   *Plato's definition ... Plato's man*   In *Politicus*, Plato (c. 428–c. 348 BCE) defines the human being as a "featherless biped." According to legend, the philosopher Diogenes (412–323 BCE) plucked a rooster and presented it before Plato's Academy as "Plato's man"; the Academy then added "with flat nails" to the definition.

presentable thought behind. Yet his thinking was so primitive and immersed in his animal life, that, though more promising than a merely learned man's, it rarely ripened to anything which can be reported. He suggested that there might be men of genius in the lowest grades of life, however permanently humble and illiterate, who take their own view always, or do not pretend to see at all; who are as bottomless even as Walden Pond was thought to be, though they may be dark and muddy. ...

CHAPTER 11
HIGHER LAWS

As I came home through the woods with my string of fish, trailing my pole, it being now quite dark, I caught a glimpse of a woodchuck stealing across my path, and felt a strange thrill of savage delight, and was strongly tempted to seize and devour him raw; not that I was hungry then, except for that wildness which he represented. Once or twice, however, while I lived at the pond, I found myself ranging the woods, like a half-starved hound, with a strange abandonment, seeking some kind of venison which I might devour, and no morsel could have been too savage for me. The wildest scenes had become unaccountably familiar. I found in myself, and still find, an instinct toward a higher, or, as it is named, spiritual life, as do most men, and another toward a primitive rank and savage one, and I reverence them both. I love the wild not less than the good. The wildness and adventure that are in fishing still recommended it to me. I like sometimes to take rank hold on life and spend my day more as the animals do. Perhaps I have owed to this employment and to hunting, when quite young, my closest acquaintance with Nature. They early introduce us to and detain us in scenery with which otherwise, at that age, we should have little acquaintance. Fishermen, hunters, woodchoppers, and others, spending their lives in the fields and woods, in a peculiar sense a part of Nature themselves, are often in a more favorable mood for observing her, in the intervals of their pursuits, than philosophers or poets even, who approach her with expectation. She is not afraid to exhibit herself to them. The traveller on the prairie is naturally a hunter, on the head waters of the Missouri and Columbia a trapper, and at the Falls of St. Mary a fisherman. He who is only a traveller learns things at second-hand and by the halves, and is poor authority. We are most interested when science reports what those men already know practically or instinctively, for that alone is a true *humanity*, or account of human experience.

They mistake who assert that the Yankee has few amusements, because he has not so many public holidays, and men and boys do not play so many games as they do in England, for here the more primitive but solitary amusements of hunting, fishing, and the like have not yet given place to the former. Almost every New England boy among my contemporaries shouldered a fowling-piece between the ages of ten and fourteen; and his hunting and fishing grounds were not limited, like the preserves of an English nobleman, but were more boundless even than those of a savage. No wonder, then, that he did not oftener stay to play on the common. But already a change is taking place, owing, not to an increased humanity, but to an increased scarcity of game, for perhaps the hunter is the greatest friend of the animals hunted, not excepting the Humane Society.

Moreover, when at the pond, I wished sometimes to add fish to my fare for variety. I have actually fished from the same kind of necessity that the first fishers did. Whatever humanity I might conjure up against it was all factitious, and concerned my philosophy more than my feelings. I speak of fishing only now, for I had long felt differently about fowling, and sold my gun before I went to the woods. Not that I am less humane than others, but I did not perceive that my feelings were much affected. I did not pity the fishes nor the worms. This was habit. As for fowling, during the last years that I carried a gun my excuse was that I was studying ornithology, and sought only new or rare birds. But I confess that I am now inclined to think that there is a finer way of studying ornithology than this. It requires so much closer attention to the habits of the birds, that, if for that reason only, I have been willing to omit the gun. Yet notwithstanding the objection on the score of humanity, I am compelled to doubt if equally valuable sports are ever substituted for these; and when some of my friends have asked me anxiously about their boys, whether they should let them hunt, I have answered, yes—remembering that it was one of the best parts of my education—*make them hunters*, though sportsmen only at first, if possible, mighty hunters at last, so that they shall not find game large enough for them in this or any vegetable wilderness—hunters as well as fishers of men.[1] Thus far I am of the opinion of Chaucer's nun, who

> yave not of the text a pulled hen
> That saith that hunters ben not holy men.[2]

There is a period in the history of the individual, as of the race, when the hunters are the "best men," as the Algonquins called them. We cannot but pity the boy who has never fired a gun; he is no more humane, while his education has been sadly neglected. This was my answer with respect to those youths who were bent on this pursuit, trusting that they would soon outgrow it. No humane being, past the thoughtless age of boyhood, will wantonly murder any creature which holds its life by the same tenure that he does. The hare in its extremity cries like a child. I warn you, mothers, that my sympathies do not always make the usual phil-*anthropic*[3] distinctions.

Such is oftenest the young man's introduction to the forest, and the most original part of himself. He goes thither at first as a hunter and fisher, until at last, if he has the seeds of a better life in him, he distinguishes his proper objects, as a poet or naturalist it may be, and leaves the gun and fish-pole behind. The mass of men are still and always young in this respect. In some countries a hunting parson is no uncommon sight. Such a one might make a good shepherd's dog, but is far from being the Good Shepherd. I have been surprised to consider that the only obvious employment, except wood-chopping, ice-cutting, or the like business, which ever to my knowledge detained at Walden Pond for a whole half-day any of my fellow-citizens, whether fathers or children of the town, with

just one exception, was fishing. Commonly they did not think that they were lucky, or well paid for their time, unless they got a long string of fish, though they had the opportunity of seeing the pond all the while. They might go there a thousand times before the sediment of fishing would sink to the bottom and leave their purpose pure; but no doubt such a clarifying process would be going on all the while. The Governor and his Council faintly remember the pond, for they went a-fishing there when they were boys; but now they are too old and dignified to go a-fishing, and so they know it no more forever. Yet even they expect to go to heaven at last. If the legislature regards it, it is chiefly to regulate the number of hooks to be used there; but they know nothing about the hook of hooks with which to angle for the pond itself, impaling the legislature for a bait. Thus, even in civilized communities, the embryo man passes through the hunter stage of development.

I have found repeatedly, of late years, that I cannot fish without falling a little in self-respect. I have tried it again and again. I have skill at it, and, like many of my fellows, a certain instinct for it, which revives from time to time, but always when I have done I feel that it would have been better if I had not fished. I think that I do not mistake. It is a faint intimation, yet so are the first streaks of morning. There is unquestionably this instinct in me which belongs to the lower orders of creation; yet with every year I am less a fisherman, though without more humanity or even wisdom; at present I am no fisherman at all. But I see that if I were to live in a wilderness I should again be tempted to become a fisher and hunter in earnest. Beside, there is something essentially unclean about this diet and all flesh, and I began to see where housework commences, and whence the endeavor, which costs so much, to wear a tidy and respectable appearance each day, to keep the house sweet and free from all ill odors and sights. Having been my own butcher and scullion[4] and cook, as well as the gentleman for whom the dishes were served up, I can speak from an unusually complete experience. The practical objection to animal food in my case was its uncleanness; and besides, when I had caught and cleaned and cooked and eaten my fish, they

---

[1]   *fishers of men*   See Mark 1.17: "And Jesus said unto them, Come ye after me, and I will make you to become fishers of men."

[2]   *yave not … holy men*   Did not give a plucked hen for any text that says hunters are not holy men. See "Prologue" to Geoffrey Chaucer's *The Canterbury Tales*; the lines refer in fact to the monk, not the nun.

[3]   *phil-anthropic*   Thoreau here emphasizes the Greek etymology of the term "philanthropy," from *philos*, "to love," and *anthropos*, "man."

[4]   *scullion*   Low-ranking servant who attends to menial kitchen tasks such as washing the dishes.

seemed not to have fed me essentially. It was insignificant and unnecessary, and cost more than it came to. A little bread or a few potatoes would have done as well, with less trouble and filth. Like many of my contemporaries, I had rarely for many years used animal food, or tea, or coffee, etc.; not so much because of any ill effects which I had traced to them, as because they were not agreeable to my imagination. The repugnance to animal food is not the effect of experience, but is an instinct. It appeared more beautiful to live low and fare hard in many respects; and though I never did so, I went far enough to please my imagination. I believe that every man who has ever been earnest to preserve his higher or poetic faculties in the best condition has been particularly inclined to abstain from animal food, and from much food of any kind. It is a significant fact, stated by entomologists—I find it in Kirby and Spence[1]—that "some insects in their perfect state, though furnished with organs of feeding, make no use of them"; and they lay it down as "a general rule, that almost all insects in this state eat much less than in that of larvae. The voracious caterpillar when transformed into a butterfly, and the gluttonous maggot when become a fly" content themselves with a drop or two of honey or some other sweet liquid. The abdomen under the wings of the butterfly still represents the larva. This is the tidbit which tempts his insectivorous fate. The gross feeder is a man in the larva state; and there are whole nations in that condition, nations without fancy or imagination, whose vast abdomens betray them.

It is hard to provide and cook so simple and clean a diet as will not offend the imagination; but this, I think, is to be fed when we feed the body; they should both sit down at the same table. Yet perhaps this may be done. The fruits eaten temperately need not make us ashamed of our appetites, nor interrupt the worthiest pursuits. But put an extra condiment into your dish, and it will poison you. It is not worth the while to live by rich cookery. Most men would feel shame if caught preparing with their own hands precisely such a dinner, whether of animal or vegetable food, as is every day prepared for them by others. Yet till this is otherwise we are not civilized, and, if gentlemen and ladies, are not true men and women. This certainly suggests

what change is to be made. It may be vain to ask why the imagination will not be reconciled to flesh and fat. I am satisfied that it is not. Is it not a reproach that man is a carnivorous animal? True, he can and does live, in a great measure, by preying on other animals; but this is a miserable way—as anyone who will go to snaring rabbits, or slaughtering lambs, may learn—and he will be regarded as a benefactor of his race who shall teach man to confine himself to a more innocent and wholesome diet. Whatever my own practice may be, I have no doubt that it is a part of the destiny of the human race, in its gradual improvement, to leave off eating animals, as surely as the savage tribes have left off eating each other when they came in contact with the more civilized.

If one listens to the faintest but constant suggestions of his genius, which are certainly true, he sees not to what extremes, or even insanity, it may lead him; and yet that way, as he grows more resolute and faithful, his road lies. The faintest assured objection which one healthy man feels will at length prevail over the arguments and customs of mankind. No man ever followed his genius till it misled him. Though the result were bodily weakness, yet perhaps no one can say that the consequences were to be regretted, for these were a life in conformity to higher principles. If the day and the night are such that you greet them with joy, and life emits a fragrance like flowers and sweet-scented herbs, is more elastic, more starry, more immortal—that is your success. All nature is your congratulation, and you have cause momentarily to bless yourself. The greatest gains and values are farthest from being appreciated. We easily come to doubt if they exist. We soon forget them. They are the highest reality. Perhaps the facts most astounding and most real are never communicated by man to man. The true harvest of my daily life is somewhat as intangible and indescribable as the tints of morning or evening. It is a little star-dust caught, a segment of the rainbow which I have clutched.

Yet, for my part, I was never unusually squeamish; I could sometimes eat a fried rat with a good relish, if it were necessary. I am glad to have drunk water so long, for the same reason that I prefer the natural sky to an opium-eater's heaven. I would fain keep sober always; and there are infinite degrees of drunkenness. I believe that water is the only drink for a wise man;

---

[1]   *Kirby and Spence*   William Kerby and William Spence, authors of *An Introduction to Entomology* (1815).

wine is not so noble a liquor; and think of dashing the hopes of a morning with a cup of warm coffee, or of an evening with a dish of tea! Ah, how low I fall when I am tempted by them! Even music may be intoxicating. Such apparently slight causes destroyed Greece and Rome, and will destroy England and America. Of all ebriosity,[1] who does not prefer to be intoxicated by the air he breathes? I have found it to be the most serious objection to coarse labors long continued, that they compelled me to eat and drink coarsely also. But to tell the truth, I find myself at present somewhat less particular in these respects. I carry less religion to the table, ask no blessing; not because I am wiser than I was, but, I am obliged to confess, because, however much it is to be regretted, with years I have grown more coarse and indifferent. Perhaps these questions are entertained only in youth, as most believe of poetry. My practice is "nowhere," my opinion is here. Nevertheless I am far from regarding myself as one of those privileged ones to whom the Ved[2] refers when it says, that "he who has true faith in the Omnipresent Supreme Being may eat all that exists," that is, is not bound to inquire what is his food, or who prepares it; and even in their case it is to be observed, as a Hindoo commentator has remarked, that the Vedant limits this privilege to "the time of distress."

Who has not sometimes derived an inexpressible satisfaction from his food in which appetite had no share? I have been thrilled to think that I owed a mental perception to the commonly gross sense of taste, that I have been inspired through the palate, that some berries which I had eaten on a hillside had fed my genius. "The soul not being mistress of herself," says Thseng-tseu, "one looks, and one does not see; one listens, and one does not hear; one eats, and one does not know the savor of food."[3] He who distinguishes the true savor of his food can never be a glutton; he who does not cannot be otherwise. A puritan may go to his brown-bread crust with as gross an appetite as ever an alderman

to his turtle.[4] Not that food which entereth into the mouth defileth a man,[5] but the appetite with which it is eaten. It is neither the quality nor the quantity, but the devotion to sensual savors; when that which is eaten is not a viand[6] to sustain our animal, or inspire our spiritual life, but food for the worms that possess us. If the hunter has a taste for mud-turtles, muskrats, and other such savage tidbits, the fine lady indulges a taste for jelly made of a calf's foot, or for sardines from over the sea, and they are even. He goes to the mill-pond, she to her preserve-pot. The wonder is how they, how you and I, can live this slimy, beastly life, eating and drinking.

Our whole life is startlingly moral. There is never an instant's truce between virtue and vice. Goodness is the only investment that never fails. In the music of the harp which trembles round the world it is the insisting on this which thrills us. The harp is the travelling patterer for the Universe's Insurance Company, recommending its laws, and our little goodness is all the assessment that we pay. Though the youth at last grows indifferent, the laws of the universe are not indifferent, but are forever on the side of the most sensitive. Listen to every zephyr[7] for some reproof, for it is surely there, and he is unfortunate who does not hear it. We cannot touch a string or move a stop but the charming moral transfixes us. Many an irksome noise, go a long way off, is heard as music, a proud, sweet satire on the meanness of our lives.

We are conscious of an animal in us, which awakens in proportion as our higher nature slumbers. It is reptile and sensual, and perhaps cannot be wholly expelled; like the worms which, even in life and health, occupy our bodies. Possibly we may withdraw from it, but never change its nature. I fear that it may enjoy a certain health of its own; that we may be well, yet not pure. The other day I picked up the lower jaw of a hog, with white and sound teeth and tusks, which suggested

---

[1] *ebriosity* Habitual drunkenness.

[2] *the Ved* I.e., the Vedas, a large body of Hindu scripture. Thoreau quotes in the following lines from the translations by Rajah Ram Mohan Roy (1772–1833).

[3] *The soul … of food* From Guillaume Pauthier's translation of the Confucian text *The Great Learning*. Zengzi (Tseng-tzu) was an important disciple of Confucius.

[4] *an alderman to his turtle* Turtle soup was considered during this period to be a delicacy; it was commonly served to aldermen and other civic leaders.

[5] *Not that … a man* See Matthew 15.11: "Not that which goeth into the mouth defileth a man; but that which cometh out of the mouth, this defileth a man."

[6] *a viand* Food.

[7] *zephyr* Gentle wind.

that there was an animal health and vigor distinct from the spiritual. This creature succeeded by other means than temperance and purity. "That in which men differ from brute beasts," says Mencius, "is a thing very inconsiderable; the common herd lose it very soon; superior men preserve it carefully."[1] Who knows what sort of life would result if we had attained to purity? If I knew so wise a man as could teach me purity I would go to seek him forthwith. "A command over our passions, and over the external senses of the body, and good acts, are declared by the Ved to be indispensable in the mind's approximation to God." Yet the spirit can for the time pervade and control every member and function of the body, and transmute what in form is the grossest sensuality into purity and devotion. The generative energy, which, when we are loose, dissipates and makes us unclean, when we are continent invigorates and inspires us. Chastity is the flowering of man; and what are called Genius, Heroism, Holiness, and the like, are but various fruits which succeed it. Man flows at once to God when the channel of purity is open. By turns our purity inspires and our impurity casts us down. He is blessed who is assured that the animal is dying out in him day by day, and the divine being established. Perhaps there is none but has cause for shame on account of the inferior and brutish nature to which he is allied. I fear that we are such gods or demigods only as fauns and satyrs,[2] the divine allied to beasts, the creatures of appetite, and that, to some extent, our very life is our disgrace.

How happy's he who hath due place assigned
To his beasts and disafforested his mind!

* * * * * * * * * * * * *

Can use this horse, goat, wolf, and every beast,
And is not ass himself to all the rest!
Else man not only is the herd of swine,
But he's those devils too which did incline
Them to a headlong rage, and made them worse.[3]

---

[1] *That in … it carefully* Thoreau's translation from the French of a passage from Pauthier's *Confucius and Mencius*.

[2] *fauns and satyrs* Roman and Greek names, respectively, for mythological creatures with the torsos of men and the lower bodies of goats.

[3] *How happy's … worse* See "To Sir Edward Herbert at Iulyers" by John Donne (1572–1631); *disafforested* Said of land: changed in legal status from forest to common land.

All sensuality is one, though it takes many forms; all purity is one. It is the same whether a man eat, or drink, or cohabit, or sleep sensually. They are but one appetite, and we only need to see a person do any one of these things to know how great a sensualist he is. The impure can neither stand nor sit with purity. When the reptile is attacked at one mouth of his burrow, he shows himself at another. If you would be chaste, you must be temperate. What is chastity? How shall a man know if he is chaste? He shall not know it. We have heard of this virtue, but we know not what it is. We speak conformably to the rumor which we have heard. From exertion come wisdom and purity; from sloth ignorance and sensuality. In the student sensuality is a sluggish habit of mind. An unclean person is universally a slothful one, one who sits by a stove, whom the sun shines on prostrate, who reposes without being fatigued. If you would avoid uncleanness, and all the sins, work earnestly, though it be at cleaning a stable. Nature is hard to be overcome, but she must be overcome. What avails it that you are Christian, if you are not purer than the heathen, if you deny yourself no more, if you are not more religious? I know of many systems of religion esteemed heathenish whose precepts fill the reader with shame, and provoke him to new endeavors, though it be to the performance of rites merely.

I hesitate to say these things, but it is not because of the subject—I care not how obscene my *words* are—but because I cannot speak of them without betraying my impurity. We discourse freely without shame of one form of sensuality, and are silent about another. We are so degraded that we cannot speak simply of the necessary functions of human nature. In earlier ages, in some countries, every function was reverently spoken of and regulated by law. Nothing was too trivial for the Hindoo lawgiver, however offensive it may be to modern taste. He teaches how to eat, drink, cohabit, void excrement and urine, and the like, elevating what is mean, and does not falsely excuse himself by calling these things trifles.

Every man is the builder of a temple, called his body, to the god he worships, after a style purely his own, nor can he get off by hammering marble instead. We are all sculptors and painters, and our material is our own flesh and blood and bones. Any nobleness begins at once to refine a man's features, any meanness or sensuality to imbrute them.

John Farmer sat at his door one September evening, after a hard day's work, his mind still running on his labor more or less. Having bathed, he sat down to recreate his intellectual man. It was a rather cool evening, and some of his neighbors were apprehending a frost. He had not attended to the train of his thoughts long when he heard someone playing on a flute, and that sound harmonized with his mood. Still he thought of his work; but the burden of his thought was, that though this kept running in his head, and he found himself planning and contriving it against his will, yet it concerned him very little. It was no more than the scurf[1] of his skin, which was constantly shuffled off. But the notes of the flute came home to his ears out of a different sphere from that he worked in, and suggested work for certain faculties which slumbered in him. They gently did away with the street, and the village, and the state in which he lived. A voice said to him—Why do you stay here and live this mean moiling[2] life, when a glorious existence is possible for you? Those same stars twinkle over other fields than these. But how to come out of this condition and actually migrate thither? All that he could think of was to practise some new austerity, to let his mind descend into his body and redeem it, and treat himself with ever increasing respect.

from CHAPTER 12
BRUTE NEIGHBORS

… I was witness to events of a less peaceful character. One day when I went out to my wood-pile, or rather my pile of stumps, I observed two large ants, the one red, the other much larger, nearly half an inch long, and black, fiercely contending with one another. Having once got hold they never let go, but struggled and wrestled and rolled on the chips incessantly. Looking farther, I was surprised to find that the chips were covered with such combatants, that it was not a *duellum*, but a *bellum*,[3] a war between two races of ants, the red always pitted against the black, and frequently two red

ones to one black. The legions of these Myrmidons[4] covered all the hills and vales in my wood-yard, and the ground was already strewn with the dead and dying, both red and black. It was the only battle which I have ever witnessed, the only battlefield I ever trod while the battle was raging; internecine[5] war; the red republicans on the one hand, and the black imperialists on the other. On every side they were engaged in deadly combat, yet without any noise that I could hear, and human soldiers never fought so resolutely. I watched a couple that were fast locked in each other's embraces, in a little sunny valley amid the chips, now at noonday prepared to fight till the sun went down, or life went out. The smaller red champion had fastened himself like a vice to his adversary's front, and through all the tumblings on that field never for an instant ceased to gnaw at one of his feelers near the root, having already caused the other to go by the board; while the stronger black one dashed him from side to side, and, as I saw on looking nearer, had already divested him of several of his members. They fought with more pertinacity than bulldogs. Neither manifested the least disposition to retreat. It was evident that their battle-cry was "Conquer or die." In the meanwhile there came along a single red ant on the hillside of this valley, evidently full of excitement, who either had dispatched his foe, or had not yet taken part in the battle; probably the latter, for he had lost none of his limbs; whose mother had charged him to return with his shield or upon it. Or perchance he was some Achilles, who had nourished his wrath apart, and had now come to avenge or rescue his Patroclus.[6] He saw this unequal combat from afar—for the blacks were nearly twice the size of the red—he drew near with rapid pace till he stood on his guard within half an inch of the combatants; then, watching his opportunity, he sprang upon the black warrior, and commenced his operations near the root of his right foreleg, leaving the foe to select among his own members; and so there were three united for life, as if a new kind of attraction had been invented which

---

[1] *scurf* Outermost layer of skin.

[2] *moiling* Toiling; fatiguing.

[3] *duellum … bellum* Latin for "duel" and "war," respectively.

[4] *Myrmidons* Ancient warriors from Thessaly, who fought in the Trojan War.

[5] *internecine* Devastating.

[6] *some Achilles … Patroclus* In the *Iliad*, the great warrior Achilles resists fighting in the Trojan War until Patroclus has been killed in the fighting.

put all other locks and cements to shame. I should not have wondered by this time to find that they had their respective musical bands stationed on some eminent chip, and playing their national airs the while, to excite the slow and cheer the dying combatants. I was myself excited somewhat even as if they had been men. The more you think of it, the less the difference. And certainly there is not the fight recorded in Concord history, at least, if in the history of America, that will bear a moment's comparison with this, whether for the numbers engaged in it, or for the patriotism and heroism displayed. For numbers and for carnage it was an Austerlitz or Dresden.[1] Concord Fight! Two killed on the patriots' side, and Luther Blanchard[2] wounded! Why here every ant was a Buttrick[3]—"Fire! for God's sake fire!"—and thousands shared the fate of Davis and Hosmer.[4] There was not one hireling there. I have no doubt that it was a principle they fought for, as much as our ancestors, and not to avoid a three-penny tax on their tea; and the results of this battle will be as important and memorable to those whom it concerns as those of the battle of Bunker Hill,[5] at least.

I took up the chip on which the three I have particularly described were struggling, carried it into my house, and placed it under a tumbler on my window-sill, in order to see the issue. Holding a microscope[6] to the first-mentioned red ant, I saw that, though he was assiduously gnawing at the near fore leg of his enemy, having severed his remaining feeler, his own breast was all torn away, exposing what vitals he had there to the jaws of the black warrior, whose breastplate was apparently too thick for him to pierce; and the dark carbuncles of the sufferer's eyes shone with ferocity such as war only could excite. They struggled half

an hour longer under the tumbler, and when I looked again the black soldier had severed the heads of his foes from their bodies, and the still living heads were hanging on either side of him like ghastly trophies at his saddle-bow, still apparently as firmly fastened as ever, and he was endeavoring with feeble struggles, being without feelers and with only the remnant of a leg, and I know not how many other wounds, to divest himself of them; which at length, after half an hour more, he accomplished. I raised the glass, and he went off over the window-sill in that crippled state. Whether he finally survived that combat, and spent the remainder of his days in some Hôtel des Invalides,[7] I do not know; but I thought that his industry would not be worth much thereafter. I never learned which party was victorious, nor the cause of the war; but I felt for the rest of that day as if I had had my feelings excited and harrowed by witnessing the struggle, the ferocity and carnage, of a human battle before my door.

Kirby and Spence tell us that the battles of ants have long been celebrated and the date of them recorded, though they say that Huber[8] is the only modern author who appears to have witnessed them. "Aeneas Sylvius,"[9] say they, "after giving a very circumstantial account of one contested with great obstinacy by a great and small species on the trunk of a pear tree," adds that "'this action was fought in the pontificate of Eugenius the Fourth, in the presence of Nicholas Pistoriensis, an eminent lawyer, who related the whole history of the battle with the greatest fidelity.' A similar engagement between great and small ants is recorded by Olaus Magnus,[10] in which the small ones, being victorious, are said to have buried the bodies of their own soldiers, but left those of their giant enemies a prey to the birds. This event happened previous to the expulsion of the tyrant Christiern the Second[11] from Sweden." The battle which I witnessed took place in

[1] *Austerlitz or Dresden* Sites of significant and devastating battles in the Napoleonic Wars, in 1805 and 1813, respectively.

[2] *Luther Blanchard* Soldier who was reputedly the first person to be wounded at the Battle of Concord on 19 April 1775.

[3] *Buttrick* John Buttrick, leader of the Concord militia during the Battle of Concord; he commanded soldiers to begin shooting after the British Army began their offensive.

[4] *Davis and Hosmer* Isaac Davis and Abner Hosmer, the only American soldiers killed during this battle.

[5] *battle of Bunker Hill* Fought in Charlestown, Massachusetts on 17 June 1775.

[6] *microscope* Probably referring to a magnifying glass.

[7] *Hôtel des Invalides* Allusion to the Parisian veterans' hospital built in the 1670s.

[8] *Huber* Swiss entomologist Pierre Huber (1750–1831).

[9] *Aeneas Sylvius* Latin name of Pope Pius II (1405–64).

[10] *Olaus Magnus* Swedish historian and archbishop of Uppsala (1490–1558).

[11] *Christiern the Second* Tyrant king of Norway, Denmark, and Sweden (1481–1559), who was deposed in a rebellion in 1532.

the Presidency of Polk,[1] five years before the passage of Webster's Fugitive-Slave Bill.[2] ...

CHAPTER 17
SPRING

The opening of large tracts by the ice-cutters[3] commonly causes a pond to break up earlier; for the water, agitated by the wind, even in cold weather, wears away the surrounding ice. But such was not the effect on Walden that year, for she had soon got a thick new garment to take the place of the old. This pond never breaks up so soon as the others in this neighborhood, on account both of its greater depth and its having no stream passing through it to melt or wear away the ice. I never knew it to open in the course of a winter, not excepting that of '52–3, which gave the ponds so severe a trial. It commonly opens about the first of April, a week or ten days later than Flint's Pond and Fair-Haven, beginning to melt on the north side and in the shallower parts where it began to freeze. It indicates better than any water hereabouts the absolute progress of the season, being least affected by transient changes of temperature. A severe cold of a few days' duration in March may very much retard the opening of the former ponds, while the temperature of Walden increases almost uninterruptedly. A thermometer thrust into the middle of Walden on the 6th of March, 1847, stood at 32°, or freezing point; near the shore at 33°; in the middle of Flint's Pond, the same day, at 32½°; at a dozen rods from the shore, in shallow water, under ice a foot thick, at 36°. This difference of three and a half degrees between the temperature of the deep water and the shallow in the latter pond, and the fact that a great proportion of it is comparatively shallow, show why it should break up so much sooner than Walden. The ice in the shallowest part was at this time several inches thinner than in the middle. In midwinter the middle had been the warmest and the ice thinnest there. So,

also, everyone who has waded about the shores of the pond in summer must have perceived how much warmer the water is close to the shore, where only three or four inches deep, than a little distance out, and on the surface where it is deep, than near the bottom. In spring the sun not only exerts an influence through the increased temperature of the air and earth, but its heat passes through ice a foot or more thick, and is reflected from the bottom in shallow water, and so also warms the water and melts the underside of the ice, at the same time that it is melting it more directly above, making it uneven, and causing the air bubbles which it contains to extend themselves upward and downward until it is completely honeycombed, and at last disappears suddenly in a single spring rain. Ice has its grain as well as wood, and when a cake begins to rot or "comb," that is, assume the appearance of honeycomb, whatever may be its position, the air cells are at right angles with what was the water surface. Where there is a rock or a log rising near to the surface the ice over it is much thinner, and is frequently quite dissolved by this reflected heat; and I have been told that in the experiment at Cambridge to freeze water in a shallow wooden pond, though the cold air circulated underneath, and so had access to both sides, the reflection of the sun from the bottom more than counterbalanced this advantage. When a warm rain in the middle of the winter melts off the snow-ice from Walden, and leaves a hard dark or transparent ice on the middle, there will be a strip of rotten though thicker white ice, a rod or more wide, about the shores, created by this reflected heat. Also, as I have said, the bubbles themselves within the ice operate as burning-glasses to melt the ice beneath.

The phenomena of the year take place every day in a pond on a small scale. Every morning, generally speaking, the shallow water is being warmed more rapidly than the deep, though it may not be made so warm after all, and every evening it is being cooled more rapidly until the morning. The day is an epitome of the year. The night is the winter, the morning and evening are the spring and fall, and the noon is the summer. The cracking and booming of the ice indicate a change of temperature. One pleasant morning after a cold night, February 24th, 1850, having gone to Flint's Pond to spend the day, I noticed with surprise,

---

[1]   *Polk*   James K. Polk, President from 1845 to 1849.

[2]   *Webster's Fugitive-Slave Bill*   The 1850 Fugitive Slave Act, widely abhorred by abolitionists for its severe provisions requiring fugitive enslaved people to be returned to slavery, even from "free" states, was supported by Massachusetts senator Daniel Webster.

[3]   *ice-cutters*   Referring to the harvesting of ice from Walden Pond.

that when I struck the ice with the head of my axe, it resounded like a gong for many rods around, or as if I had struck on a tight drum-head. The pond began to boom about an hour after sunrise, when it felt the influence of the sun's rays slanted upon it from over the hills; it stretched itself and yawned like a waking man with a gradually increasing tumult, which was kept up three or four hours. It took a short siesta at noon, and boomed once more toward night, as the sun was withdrawing his influence. In the right stage of the weather a pond fires its evening gun with great regularity. But in the middle of the day, being full of cracks, and the air also being less elastic, it had completely lost its resonance, and probably fishes and muskrats could not then have been stunned by a blow on it. The fishermen say that the "thundering of the pond" scares the fishes and prevents their biting. The pond does not thunder every evening, and I cannot tell surely when to expect its thundering; but though I may perceive no difference in the weather, it does. Who would have suspected so large and cold and thick-skinned a thing to be so sensitive? Yet it has its law to which it thunders obedience when it should as surely as the buds expand in the spring. The earth is all alive and covered with papillae. The largest pond is as sensitive to atmospheric changes as the globule of mercury in its tube.

One attraction in coming to the woods to live was that I should have leisure and opportunity to see the Spring come in. The ice in the pond at length begins to be honeycombed, and I can set my heel in it as I walk. Fogs and rains and warmer suns are gradually melting the snow; the days have grown sensibly longer; and I see how I shall get through the winter without adding to my wood-pile, for large fires are no longer necessary. I am on the alert for the first signs of spring, to hear the chance note of some arriving bird, or the striped squirrel's chirp, for his stores must be now nearly exhausted, or see the woodchuck venture out of his winter quarters. On the 13th of March, after I had heard the bluebird, song sparrow, and red-wing, the ice was still nearly a foot thick. As the weather grew warmer it was not sensibly worn away by the water, nor broken up and floated off as in rivers, but, though it was completely melted for half a rod in width about the shore, the middle was merely honeycombed and

saturated with water, so that you could put your foot through it when six inches thick; but by the next day evening, perhaps, after a warm rain followed by fog, it would have wholly disappeared, all gone off with the fog, spirited away. One year I went across the middle only five days before it disappeared entirely. In 1845 Walden was first completely open on the 1st of April; in '46, the 25th of March; in '47, the 8th of April; in '51, the 28th of March; in '52, the 18th of April; in '53, the 23d of March; in '54, about the 7th of April.

Every incident connected with the breaking up of the rivers and ponds and the settling of the weather is particularly interesting to us who live in a climate of so great extremes. When the warmer days come, they who dwell near the river hear the ice crack at night with a startling whoop as loud as artillery, as if its icy fetters were rent from end to end, and within a few days see it rapidly going out. So the alligator comes out of the mud with quakings of the earth. One old man, who has been a close observer of Nature, and seems as thoroughly wise in regard to all her operations as if she had been put upon the stocks when he was a boy, and he had helped to lay her keel—who has come to his growth, and can hardly acquire more of natural lore if he should live to the age of Methuselah[1]—told me—and I was surprised to hear him express wonder at any of Nature's operations, for I thought that there were no secrets between them—that one spring day he took his gun and boat, and thought that he would have a little sport with the ducks. There was ice still on the meadows, but it was all gone out of the river, and he dropped down without obstruction from Sudbury, where he lived, to Fair-Haven Pond, which he found, unexpectedly, covered for the most part with a firm field of ice. It was a warm day, and he was surprised to see so great a body of ice remaining. Not seeing any ducks, he hid his boat on the north or back side of an island in the pond, and then concealed himself in the bushes on the south side, to await them. The ice was melted for three or four rods from the shore, and there was a smooth and warm sheet of water, with a muddy bottom, such as the ducks love, within, and he thought it likely that some would be along pretty soon. After he had lain still there about an hour he heard a low

---

[1]   *Methuselah*   According to Genesis 5.27, Methuselah lived to be 969 years old.

and seemingly very distant sound, but singularly grand and impressive, unlike anything he had ever ·heard, gradually swelling and increasing as if it would have a universal and memorable ending, a sullen rush and roar, which seemed to him all at once like the sound of a vast body of fowl coming in to settle there, and, seizing his gun, he started up in haste and excited; but he found, to his surprise, that the whole body of the ice had started while he lay there, and drifted in to the shore, and the sound he had heard was made by its edge grating on the shore—at first gently nibbled and crumbled off, but at length heaving up and scattering its wrecks along the island to a considerable height before it came to a standstill.

At length the sun's rays have attained the right angle, and warm winds blow up mist and rain and melt the snowbanks, and the sun dispersing the mist smiles on a checkered landscape of russet and white smoking with incense, through which the traveler picks his way from islet to islet, cheered by the music of a thousand tinkling rills and rivulets whose veins are filled with the blood of winter which they are bearing off.

Few phenomena gave me more delight than to observe the forms which thawing sand and clay assume in flowing down the sides of a deep cut on the railroad through which I passed on my way to the village, a phenomenon not very common on so large a scale, though the number of freshly exposed banks of the right material must have been greatly multiplied since railroads were invented. The material was sand of every degree of fineness and of various rich colors, commonly mixed with a little clay. When the frost comes out in the spring, and even in a thawing day in the winter, the sand begins to flow down the slopes like lava, sometimes bursting out through the snow and overflowing it where no sand was to be seen before. Innumerable little streams overlap and interlace one with another, exhibiting a sort of hybrid product, which obeys half way the law of currents, and half way that of vegetation. As it flows it takes the forms of sappy leaves or vines, making heaps of pulpy sprays a foot or more in depth, and resembling, as you look down on them, the laciniated, lobed, and imbricated thalluses[1] of some lichens; or you are reminded of coral, of leopards' paws

or birds' feet, of brains or lungs or bowels, and excrements of all kinds. It is a truly *grotesque* vegetation, whose forms and color we see imitated in bronze, a sort of architectural foliage more ancient and typical than acanthus, chiccory, ivy, vine, or any vegetable leaves; destined perhaps, under some circumstances, to become a puzzle to future geologists. The whole cut impressed me as if it were a cave with its stalactites laid open to the light. The various shades of the sand are singularly rich and agreeable, embracing the different iron colors, brown, gray, yellowish, and reddish. When the flowing mass reaches the drain at the foot of the bank it spreads out flatter into *strands*, the separate streams losing their semi-cylindrical form and gradually becoming more flat and broad, running together as they are more moist, till they form an almost flat *sand*, still variously and beautifully shaded, but in which you can trace the original forms of vegetation; till at length, in the water itself, they are converted into *banks*, like those formed off the mouths of rivers, and the forms of vegetation are lost in the ripple marks on the bottom.

The whole bank, which is from twenty to forty feet high, is sometimes overlaid with a mass of this kind of foliage, or sandy rupture, for a quarter of a mile on one or both sides, the produce of one spring day. What makes this sand foliage remarkable is its springing into existence thus suddenly. When I see on the one side the inert bank—for the sun acts on one side first—and on the other this luxuriant foliage, the creation of an hour, I am affected as if in a peculiar sense I stood in the laboratory of the Artist who made the world and me—had come to where he was still at work, sporting on this bank, and with excess of energy strewing his fresh designs about. I feel as if I were nearer to the vitals of the globe, for this sandy overflow is something such a foliaceous mass as the vitals of the animal body. You find thus in the very sands an anticipation of the vegetable leaf. No wonder that the earth expresses itself outwardly in leaves, it so labors with the idea inwardly. The atoms have already learned this law, and are pregnant by it. The overhanging leaf sees here its prototype. *Internally*, whether in the globe or animal body, it is a moist thick *lobe*, a word especially applicable to the liver and lungs and the *leaves* of fat ($\lambda\varepsilon\iota\beta\omega$, *labor, lapsus*, to

---

[1] *laciniated* Divided into irregular lobes; *imbricated* Overlapping; *thalluses* Plant structures (such as those of mosses and

lichens) which have no differentiation between leaf and stem and lack true roots.

flow or slip downward, a lapsing; λοβός, *globus*, lobe, globe; also lap, flap, and many other words); *externally* a dry thin *leaf*, even as the *f* and *v* are a pressed and dried *b*. The radicals of *lobe* are *lb*, the soft mass of the *b* (single lobed, or B, double lobed), with the liquid *l* behind it pressing it forward. In globe, *glb*, the guttural *g* adds to the meaning the capacity of the throat. The feathers and wings of birds are still drier and thinner leaves. Thus, also, you pass from the lumpish grub in the earth to the airy and fluttering butterfly. The very globe continually transcends and translates itself, and becomes winged in its orbit. Even ice begins with delicate crystal leaves, as if it had flowed into moulds which the fronds of water plants have impressed on the watery mirror. The whole tree itself is but one leaf, and rivers are still vaster leaves whose pulp is intervening earth, and towns and cities are the ova of insects in their axils.

When the sun withdraws the sand ceases to flow, but in the morning the streams will start once more and branch and branch again into a myriad of others. You here see perchance how blood-vessels are formed. If you look closely you observe that first there pushes forward from the thawing mass a stream of softened sand with a drop-like point, like the ball of the finger, feeling its way slowly and blindly downward, until at last with more heat and moisture, as the sun gets higher, the most fluid portion, in its effort to obey the law to which the most inert also yields, separates from the latter and forms for itself a meandering channel or artery within that, in which is seen a little silvery stream glancing like lightning from one stage of pulpy leaves or branches to another, and ever and anon swallowed up in the sand. It is wonderful how rapidly yet perfectly the sand organizes itself as it flows, using the best material its mass affords to form the sharp edges of its channel. Such are the sources of rivers. In the silicious matter which the water deposits is perhaps the bony system, and in the still finer soil and organic matter the fleshy fiber or cellular tissue. What is man but a mass of thawing clay? The ball of the human finger is but a drop congealed. The fingers and toes flow to their extent from the thawing mass of the body. Who knows what the human body would expand and flow out to under a more genial heaven? Is not the hand a spreading *palm* leaf with its lobes and veins? The ear

may be regarded, fancifully, as a lichen, *umbilicaria*, on the side of the head, with its lobe or drop. The lip—*labium*, from *labor* (?)—laps or lapses from the sides of the cavernous mouth. The nose is a manifest congealed drop or stalactite. The chin is a still larger drop, the confluent dripping of the face. The cheeks are a slide from the brows into the valley of the face, opposed and diffused by the cheek bones. Each rounded lobe of the vegetable leaf, too, is a thick and now loitering drop, larger or smaller; the lobes are the fingers of the leaf; and as many lobes as it has, in so many directions it tends to flow, and more heat or other genial influences would have caused it to flow yet farther.

Thus it seemed that this one hillside illustrated the principle of all the operations of Nature. The Maker of this earth but patented a leaf. What Champollion[1] will decipher this hieroglyphic for us, that we may turn over a new leaf at last? This phenomenon is more exhilarating to me than the luxuriance and fertility of vineyards. True, it is somewhat excrementitious in its character, and there is no end to the heaps of liver, lights,[2] and bowels, as if the globe were turned wrong side outward; but this suggests at least that Nature has some bowels, and there again is mother of humanity. This is the frost coming out of the ground; this is Spring. It precedes the green and flowery spring, as mythology precedes regular poetry. I know of nothing more purgative of winter fumes and indigestions. It convinces me that Earth is still in her swaddling-clothes, and stretches forth baby fingers on every side. Fresh curls spring from the baldest brow. There is nothing inorganic. These foliaceous heaps lie along the bank like the slag[3] of a furnace, showing that Nature is "in full blast" within. The earth is not a mere fragment of dead history, stratum upon stratum like the leaves of a book, to be studied by geologists and antiquaries chiefly, but living poetry like the leaves of a tree, which precede flowers and fruit—not a fossil earth, but a living earth; compared with whose great central life all animal and

---

1   *Champollion* Jean-François Champollion (1790–1832), French scholar responsible for deciphering the hieroglyphics carved onto the Rosetta Stone, thereby providing the means for understanding ancient Egyptian writing.

2   *lights* Lungs.

3   *slag* Refuse created as a by-product during the process of smelting metal.

vegetable life is merely parasitic. Its throes will heave our exuviæ from their graves. You may melt your metals and cast them into the most beautiful molds you can; they will never excite me like the forms which this molten earth flows out into. And not only it, but the institutions upon it are plastic like clay in the hands of the potter.

Ere long, not only on these banks, but on every hill and plain and in every hollow, the frost comes out of the ground like a dormant quadruped from its burrow, and seeks the sea with music, or migrates to other climes in clouds. Thaw with his gentle persuasion is more powerful than Thor[1] with his hammer. The one melts, the other but breaks in pieces.

When the ground was partially bare of snow, and a few warm days had dried its surface somewhat, it was pleasant to compare the first tender signs of the infant year just peeping forth with the stately beauty of the withered vegetation which had withstood the winter— life-everlasting, goldenrods, pinweeds, and graceful wild grasses, more obvious and interesting frequently than in summer even, as if their beauty was not ripe till then; even cotton-grass, cat-tails, mulleins, johnswort, hard-hack, meadow-sweet, and other strong-stemmed plants, those unexhausted granaries which entertain the earliest birds—decent weeds, at least, which widowed Nature wears.[2] I am particularly attracted by the arching and sheaf-like top of the wool-grass; it brings back the summer to our winter memories, and is among the forms which art loves to copy, and which, in the vegetable kingdom, have the same relation to types already in the mind of man that astronomy has. It is an antique style, older than Greek or Egyptian. Many of the phenomena of Winter are suggestive of an inexpressible tenderness and fragile delicacy. We are accustomed to hear this king described as a rude and boisterous tyrant; but with the gentleness of a lover he adorns the tresses of Summer.

At the approach of spring the red squirrels got under my house, two at a time, directly under my feet as I sat reading or writing, and kept up the queerest chuckling and chirruping and vocal pirouetting and gurgling sounds that ever were heard; and when I stamped they only chirruped the louder, as if past all fear and respect in their mad pranks, defying humanity to stop them. No, you don't—chickaree—chickaree. They were wholly deaf to my arguments, or failed to perceive their force, and fell into a strain of invective that was irresistible.

The first sparrow of spring! The year beginning with younger hope than ever! The faint silvery warblings heard over the partially bare and moist fields from the bluebird, the song sparrow, and the red-wing, as if the last flakes of winter tinkled as they fell! What at such a time are histories, chronologies, traditions, and all written revelations? The brooks sing carols and glees to the spring. The marsh hawk, sailing low over the meadow, is already seeking the first slimy life that awakes. The sinking sound of melting snow is heard in all dells, and the ice dissolves apace in the ponds. The grass flames up on the hillsides like a spring fire, "*et primitus oritur herba imbribus primoribus evocata*,"[3] as if the earth sent forth an inward heat to greet the returning sun; not yellow but green is the color of its flame; the symbol of perpetual youth, the grass-blade, like a long green ribbon, streams from the sod into the summer, checked indeed by the frost, but anon pushing on again, lifting its spear of last year's hay with the fresh life below. It grows as steadily as the rill oozes out of the ground. It is almost identical with that, for in the growing days of June, when the rills are dry, the grass-blades are their channels, and from year to year the herds drink at this perennial green stream, and the mower draws from it betimes their winter supply. So our human life but dies down to its root, and still puts forth its green blade to eternity.

Walden is melting apace. There is a canal two rods wide along the northerly and westerly sides, and wider still at the east end. A great field of ice has cracked off from the main body. I hear a song sparrow singing from the bushes on the shore—*olit*, *olit*, *olit*—*chip*, *chip*, *chip*, *che char*—*che wiss*, *wiss*, *wiss*. He too is helping to crack it. How handsome the great sweeping curves in the edge of the ice, answering somewhat to those of the

---

[1]   *Thor*   Norse god of thunder, often depicted with his fearsome hammer, Mjolnir.

[2]   *decent weeds … Nature wears*   Punning on a secondary use of the word "weeds," meaning the clothing worn by a widow.

[3]   *et primitus … primoribus evocata*   From *Rerum Rusticarum* by Marcus Terentius Varro (116–27 BCE), Roman scholar: "and the grass which is called forth by the early rains is just growing."

shore, but more regular! It is unusually hard, owing to the recent severe but transient cold, and all watered or waved like a palace floor. But the wind slides eastward over its opaque surface in vain, till it reaches the living surface beyond. It is glorious to behold this ribbon of water sparkling in the sun, the bare face of the pond full of glee and youth, as if it spoke the joy of the fishes within it, and of the sands on its shore—a silvery sheen as from the scales of a leuciscus,[1] as it were all one active fish. Such is the contrast between winter and spring. Walden was dead and is alive again. But this spring it broke up more steadily, as I have said.

The change from storm and winter to serene and mild weather, from dark and sluggish hours to bright and elastic ones, is a memorable crisis which all things proclaim. It is seemingly instantaneous at last. Suddenly an influx of light filled my house, though the evening was at hand, and the clouds of winter still overhung it, and the eaves were dripping with sleety rain. I looked out the window, and lo! where yesterday was cold gray ice there lay the transparent pond already calm and full of hope as in a summer evening, reflecting a summer evening sky in its bosom, though none was visible overhead, as if it had intelligence with some remote horizon. I heard a robin in the distance, the first I had heard for many a thousand years, methought, whose note I shall not forget for many a thousand more—the same sweet and powerful song as of yore. O the evening robin, at the end of a New England summer day! If I could ever find the twig he sits upon! I mean *he*; I mean *the twig*. This at least is not the *Turdus migratorius*.[2] The pitch pines and shrub oaks about my house, which had so long drooped, suddenly resumed their several characters, looked brighter, greener, and more erect and alive, as if effectually cleansed and restored by the rain. I knew that it would not rain any more. You may tell by looking at any twig of the forest, ay, at your very wood-pile, whether its winter is past or not. As it grew darker, I was startled by the honking of geese flying low over the woods, like weary travelers getting in late from Southern lakes, and indulging at last in unrestrained complaint and mutual consolation. Standing at my door, I could hear the rush of their wings; when, driving toward my house, they suddenly

spied my light, and with hushed clamor wheeled and settled in the pond. So I came in, and shut the door, and passed my first spring night in the woods.

In the morning I watched the geese from the door through the mist, sailing in the middle of the pond, fifty rods off, so large and tumultuous that Walden appeared like an artificial pond for their amusement. But when I stood on the shore they at once rose up with a great flapping of wings at the signal of their commander, and when they had got into rank circled about over my head, twenty-nine of them, and then steered straight to Canada, with a regular *honk* from the leader at intervals, trusting to break their fast in muddier pools. A "plump" of ducks rose at the same time and took the route to the north in the wake of their noisier cousins.

For a week I heard the circling, groping clangor of some solitary goose in the foggy mornings, seeking its companion, and still peopling the woods with the sound of a larger life than they could sustain. In April the pigeons were seen again flying express in small flocks, and in due time I heard the martins twittering over my clearing, though it had not seemed that the township contained so many that it could afford me any, and I fancied that they were peculiarly of the ancient race that dwelt in hollow trees ere white men came. In almost all climes the tortoise and the frog are among the precursors and heralds of this season, and birds fly with song and glancing plumage, and plants spring and bloom, and winds blow, to correct this slight oscillation of the poles and preserve the equilibrium of nature.

As every season seems best to us in its turn, so the coming in of spring is like the creation of Cosmos out of Chaos and the realization of the Golden Age.[3]

Eurus ad Auroram, Nabathaeaque regna recessit,
Persidaque, et radiis juga subdita matutinis.

---

[1] *leuciscus* Genus of freshwater fish.

[2] *Turdus migratorius* The American robin.

[3] *the creation … Golden Age* In Classical mythology, Cosmos, or the universe, was created out of the primordial state of Chaos, ushering in the peaceful and prosperous Golden Age of human history. The myth was recounted by many Classical authors; the quotations here are from the *Metamorphoses*, by the Roman writer Ovid (43 BCE–c. 17 CE), translated by Thoreau. The two quotations are of 1.61–62 and 1.78–81. (Oddly, Thoreau provides the Latin for only the first of these.)

The East-Wind withdrew to Aurora and the
    Nabathæan kingdom,
And the Persian, and the ridges placed under the
    morning rays.

*   *   *   *   *   *   *   *   *   *   *

Man was born. Whether that Artificer of things,
The origin of a better world, made him from the
    divine seed;
Or the earth, being recent and lately sundered from
    the high
Ether, retained some seeds of cognate heaven.

A single gentle rain makes the grass many shades greener. So our prospects brighten on the influx of better thoughts. We should be blessed if we lived in the present always, and took advantage of every accident that befell us, like the grass which confesses the influence of the slightest dew that falls on it; and did not spend our time in atoning for the neglect of past opportunities, which we call doing our duty. We loiter in winter while it is already spring. In a pleasant spring morning all men's sins are forgiven. Such a day is a truce to vice. While such a sun holds out to burn, the vilest sinner may return. Through our own recovered innocence we discern the innocence of our neighbors. You may have known your neighbor yesterday for a thief, a drunkard, or a sensualist, and merely pitied or despised him, and despaired of the world; but the sun shines bright and warm this first spring morning, recreating the world, and you meet him at some serene work, and see how his exhausted and debauched veins expand with still joy and bless the new day, feel the spring influence with the innocence of infancy, and all his faults are forgotten. There is not only an atmosphere of good will about him, but even a savor of holiness groping for expression, blindly and ineffectually perhaps, like a new-born instinct, and for a short hour the south hill-side echoes to no vulgar jest. You see some innocent fair shoots preparing to burst from his gnarled rind and try another year's life, tender and fresh as the youngest plant. Even he has entered into the joy of his Lord. Why the jailer does not leave open his prison doors—why the judge does not dismiss his case—why the preacher does not dismiss his congregation! It is because they do not obey the hint which

God gives them, nor accept the pardon which he freely offers to all.

"A return to goodness produced each day in the tranquil and beneficent breath of the morning, causes that in respect to the love of virtue and the hatred of vice, one approaches a little the primitive nature of man, as the sprouts of the forest which has been felled. In like manner the evil which one does in the interval of a day prevents the germs of virtues which began to spring up again from developing themselves and destroys them.

"After the germs of virtue have thus been prevented many times from developing themselves, then the beneficent breath of evening does not suffice to preserve them. As soon as the breath of evening does not suffice longer to preserve them, then the nature of man does not differ much from that of the brute. Men seeing the nature of this man like that of the brute, think that he has never possessed the innate faculty of reason. Are those the true and natural sentiments of man?"[1]

The Golden Age was first created, which without any
    avenger
Spontaneously without law cherished fidelity and
    rectitude.
Punishment and fear were not; nor were threatening
    words read
On suspended brass; nor did the suppliant crowd fear
The words of their judge; but were safe without an
    avenger.
Not yet the pine felled on its mountains had descended
To the liquid waves that it might see a foreign world,
And mortals knew no shores but their own.

*   *   *   *   *   *   *   *   *   *   *

There was eternal spring, and placid zephyrs with
    warm
Blasts soothed the flowers born without seed.[2]

---

[1] *A return ... of man* Quotation from the *Works* by Chinese philosopher Mencius or Meng-tzu (372–289 BCE).

[2] *The Golden ... without seed* See Ovid's *Metamorphoses* 1.89–96, 1.107–08.

On the 29th of April, as I was fishing from the bank of the river near the Nine-Acre-Corner bridge, standing on the quaking grass and willow roots, where the muskrats lurk, I heard a singular rattling sound, somewhat like that of the sticks which boys play with their fingers, when, looking up, I observed a very slight and graceful hawk, like a nighthawk, alternately soaring like a ripple and tumbling a rod or two over and over, showing the underside of its wings, which gleamed like a satin ribbon in the sun, or like the pearly inside of a shell. This sight reminded me of falconry and what nobleness and poetry are associated with that sport. The Merlin it seemed to me it might be called: but I care not for its name. It was the most ethereal flight I had ever witnessed. It did not simply flutter like a butterfly, nor soar like the larger hawks, but it sported with proud reliance in the fields of air; mounting again and again with its strange chuckle, it repeated its free and beautiful fall, turning over and over like a kite, and then recovering from its lofty tumbling, as if it had never set its foot on *terra firma*.[1] It appeared to have no companion in the universe, sporting there alone, and to need none but the morning and the ether with which it played. It was not lonely, but made all the earth lonely beneath it. Where was the parent which hatched it, its kindred, and its father in the heavens? The tenant of the air, it seemed related to the earth but by an egg hatched sometime in the crevice of a crag; or was its native nest made in the angle of a cloud, woven of the rainbow's trimmings and the sunset sky, and lined with some soft midsummer haze caught up from earth? Its eyrie now some cliffy cloud.

Beside this I got a rare mess of golden and silver and bright cupreous[2] fishes, which looked like a string of jewels. Ah! I have penetrated to those meadows on the morning of many a first spring day, jumping from hummock to hummock, from willow root to willow root, when the wild river valley and the woods were bathed in so pure and bright a light as would have waked the dead, if they had been slumbering in their graves, as some suppose. There needs no stronger proof of immortality. All things must live in such a light. O Death, where was thy sting? O Grave, where was thy victory, then?[3]

Our village life would stagnate if it were not for the unexplored forests and meadows which surround it. We need the tonic of wildness—to wade sometimes in marshes where the bittern and the meadow-hen lurk, and hear the booming of the snipe; to smell the whispering sedge where only some wilder and more solitary fowl builds her nest, and the mink crawls with its belly close to the ground. At the same time that we are earnest to explore and learn all things, we require that all things be mysterious and unexplorable, that land and sea be infinitely wild, unsurveyed and unfathomed by us because unfathomable. We can never have enough of nature. We must be refreshed by the sight of inexhaustible vigor, vast and titanic features, the sea-coast with its wrecks, the wilderness with its living and its decaying trees, the thundercloud, and the rain which lasts three weeks and produces freshets.[4] We need to witness our own limits transgressed, and some life pasturing freely where we never wander. We are cheered when we observe the vulture feeding on the carrion which disgusts and disheartens us, and deriving health and strength from the repast. There was a dead horse in the hollow by the path to my house, which compelled me sometimes to go out of my way, especially in the night when the air was heavy, but the assurance it gave me of the strong appetite and inviolable health of Nature was my compensation for this. I love to see that Nature is so rife with life that myriads can be afforded to be sacrificed and suffered to prey on one another; that tender organizations can be so serenely squashed out of existence like pulp—tadpoles which herons gobble up, and tortoises and toads run over in the road; and that sometimes it has rained flesh and blood! With the liability to accident, we must see how little account is to be made of it. The impression made on a wise man is that of universal innocence. Poison is not poisonous after all, nor are any wounds fatal. Compassion is a very untenable ground. It must be expeditious. Its pleadings will not bear to be stereotyped.

Early in May, the oaks, hickories, maples, and other trees, just putting out amidst the pine woods around

[1] *terra firma* Latin: solid land.

[2] *cupreous* Copper-colored.

[3] *O Death ... victory, then?* See 1 Corinthians 15.55: "O death, where is thy sting? O grave, where is thy victory?"

[4] *freshets* Freshwater streams.

the pond, imparted a brightness like sunshine to the landscape, especially in cloudy days, as if the sun were breaking through mists and shining faintly on the hillsides here and there. On the third or fourth of May I saw a loon in the pond, and during the first week of the month I heard the whippoorwill, the brown-thrasher, the veery, the wood-pewee, the chewink, and other birds. I had heard the wood-thrush long before. The phoebe had already come once more and looked in at my door and window, to see if my house was cavern-like enough for her, sustaining herself on humming wings with clinched talons, as if she held by the air, while she surveyed the premises. The sulphur-like pollen of the pitch-pine soon covered the pond and the stones and rotten wood along the shore, so that you could have collected a barrelful. This is the "sulphur showers" we hear of. Even in Calidas' drama of Sacontala,[1] we read of "rills dyed yellow with the golden dust of the lotus." And so the seasons went rolling on into summer, as one rambles into higher and higher grass.

Thus was my first year's life in the woods completed; and the second year was similar to it. I finally left Walden September 6th, 1847.

CHAPTER 18
CONCLUSION

To the sick the doctors wisely recommend a change of air and scenery. Thank Heaven, here is not all the world. The buck-eye[2] does not grow in New England, and the mockingbird is rarely heard here. The wild goose is more of a cosmopolite[3] than we; he breaks his fast in Canada, takes a luncheon in the Ohio, and plumes himself for the night in a southern bayou. Even the bison, to some extent, keeps pace with the seasons, cropping the pastures of the Colorado only till a greener and sweeter grass awaits him by the Yellowstone. Yet we think that if rail fences are pulled down, and stone walls piled up on our farms, bounds are henceforth set to our lives and our fates decided. If you are chosen town clerk, forsooth, you cannot go to

Tierra del Fuego[4] this summer: but you may go to the land of infernal fire nevertheless. The universe is wider than our views of it.

Yet we should oftener look over the tafferel[5] of our craft, like curious passengers, and not make the voyage like stupid sailors picking oakum.[6] The other side of the globe is but the home of our correspondent. Our voyaging is only great-circle sailing, and the doctors prescribe for diseases of the skin merely. One hastens to southern Africa to chase the giraffe; but surely that is not the game he would be after. How long, pray, would a man hunt giraffes if he could? Snipes and woodcocks also may afford rare sport; but I trust it would be nobler game to shoot one's self.

> Direct your eye right inward, and you'll find
> A thousand regions in your mind
> Yet undiscovered. Travel them, and be
> Expert in home-cosmography.[7]

What does Africa, what does the West stand for? Is not our own interior white on the chart? black though it may prove, like the coast, when discovered. Is it the source of the Nile, or the Niger, or the Mississippi, or a Northwest Passage around this continent, that we would find? Are these the problems which most concern mankind? Is Franklin the only man who is lost, that his wife should be so earnest to find him?[8] Does Mr. Grinnell[9] know where he himself is? Be rather the

---

[1] *Calidas' drama of Sacontala* Referring to a Sanskrit play *Shakuntala* by Kalidasa.

[2] *buck-eye* Chestnut tree.

[3] *cosmopolite* Citizen of the world; person at home in a wide variety of different environments.

[4] *Tierra del Fuego* Archipelago off the southwest coast of South America; Thoreau puns on the Spanish translation of the name, "Land of Fire."

[5] *tafferel* Upper part of a ship's stern.

[6] *picking oakum* Picking apart the ship's ropes in order to use their fibers to make caulking for the ship—painstaking and tedious work often assigned to prisoners, or to sailors when there was nothing better to do.

[7] *Direct your … home-cosmography* From "To My Honoured Friend Sir Ed. P. Knight" by English poet William Habington (1605–54).

[8] *Is Franklin … find him?* Referring to the lost Arctic expedition of English explorer Sir John Franklin (1786–1847); his wife Jane Franklin launched one of many searches to find him and his crewmembers.

[9] *Mr. Grinnell* Henry Grinnell (1799–1874), New York merchant who spent much of his retirement after 1850 participating in efforts to find Franklin's remains.

Mungo Park, the Lewis and Clark and Frobisher,[1] of your own streams and oceans; explore your own higher latitudes, with shiploads of preserved meats to support you, if they be necessary; and pile the empty cans sky-high for a sign. Were preserved meats invented to preserve meat merely? Nay, be a Columbus to whole new continents and worlds within you, opening new channels, not of trade, but of thought. Every man is the lord of a realm beside which the earthly empire of the Czar is but a petty state, a hummock left by the ice. Yet some can be patriotic who have no *self*-respect, and sacrifice the greater to the less. They love the soil which makes their graves, but have no sympathy with the spirit which may still animate their clay.[2] Patriotism is a maggot in their heads. What was the meaning of that South-Sea Exploring Expedition,[3] with all its parade and expense, but an indirect recognition of the fact that there are continents and seas in the moral world to which every man is an isthmus or an inlet, yet unexplored by him, but that it is easier to sail many thousand miles through cold and storm and cannibals, in a government ship, with five hundred men and boys to assist one, than it is to explore the private sea, the Atlantic and Pacific Ocean of one's being alone.

> *Erret, et extremos alter scrutetur Iberos.*
> *Plus habet hic vitae, plus habet ille viae.*[4]

Let them wander and scrutinize the outlandish
   Australians.
I have more of God, they more of the road.

It is not worth the while to go round the world to count the cats in Zanzibar.[5] Yet do this even till you can do better, and you may perhaps find some "Symmes'

Hole"[6] by which to get at the inside at last. England and France, Spain and Portugal, Gold Coast and Slave Coast, all front on this private sea; but no bark[7] from them has ventured out of sight of land, though it is without doubt the direct way to India. If you would learn to speak all tongues and conform to the customs of all nations, if you would travel farther than all travelers, be naturalized in all climes, and cause the Sphinx[8] to dash her head against a stone, even obey the precept of the old philosopher, and Explore thyself.[9] Herein are demanded the eye and the nerve. Only the defeated and deserters go to the wars, cowards that run away and enlist. Start now on that farthest western way, which does not pause at the Mississippi or the Pacific, nor conduct toward a worn-out China or Japan, but leads on direct, a tangent to this sphere, summer and winter, day and night, sun down, moon down, and at last earth down too.

It is said that Mirabeau[10] took to highway robbery "to ascertain what degree of resolution was necessary in order to place one's self in formal opposition to the most sacred laws of society." He declared that "a soldier who fights in the ranks does not require half so much courage as a foot-pad,"—"that honor and religion have never stood in the way of a well-considered and a firm resolve." This was manly, as the world goes; and yet it was idle, if not desperate. A saner man would have found himself often enough "in formal opposition" to what are deemed "the most sacred laws of society," through obedience to yet more sacred laws, and so have tested his resolution without going out of his way. It is not for a man to put himself in such an attitude to society, but to maintain himself in whatever attitude he find himself through obedience to the laws of his

---

[1] *Mungo Park ... and Frobisher* Mungo Park (1771–1806); Meriwether Lewis (1774–1809) and William Clark (1770–1838); and Martin Frobisher (c. 1535–94), all famous explorers.

[2] *clay* I.e., bodies.

[3] *South-Sea Exploring Expedition* Led by Charles Wilkes (1798–1877), American expedition of the Pacific Ocean and Antarctica undertaken from 1838 to 1842.

[4] *Erret, et ... ille viae* From "The Old Man of Verona" by Latin poet Claudian (c. 370–c. 404); the following is Thoreau's rather loose translation of the lines.

[5] *cats in Zanzibar* Allusion to *The Races of Man* (1851) by American anthropologist Charles Pickering; the book describes his travels in Africa, and his study of the domestic cats of Zanzibar.

[6] *Symmes' Hole* Referring to the theory expanded upon by John Symmes (1780–1829), which posits that the Earth is hollow and that its "habitable" interior can be accessed through holes at the North and South Poles.

[7] *bark* Ship.

[8] *Sphinx* In Greek mythology, the winged guardian of Thebes, who killed those who could not answer her riddles; when Oedipus did solve her riddle, she dashed her head against a stone.

[9] *the precept ... Explore thyself* Allusion to the ancient Greek aphorism "know thyself," made famous in particular by its use in works by Plato (c. 427–c. 347 BCE).

[10] *Mirabeau* French Revolutionary leader Honoré Gabriel Riqueti, comte de Mirabeau (1749–91).

being, which will never be one of opposition to a just government, if he should chance to meet with such.

I left the woods for as good a reason as I went there. Perhaps it seemed to me that I had several more lives to live, and could not spare any more time for that one. It is remarkable how easily and insensibly we fall into a particular route, and make a beaten track for ourselves. I had not lived there a week before my feet wore a path from my door to the pond-side; and though it is five or six years since I trod it, it is still quite distinct. It is true, I fear that others may have fallen into it, and so helped to keep it open. The surface of the earth is soft and impressible by the feet of men; and so with the paths which the mind travels. How worn and dusty, then, must be the highways of the world, how deep the ruts of tradition and conformity! I did not wish to take a cabin passage, but rather to go before the mast and on the deck of the world, for there I could best see the moonlight amid the mountains. I do not wish to go below now.

I learned this, at least, by my experiment; that if one advances confidently in the direction of his dreams, and endeavors to live the life which he has imagined, he will meet with a success unexpected in common hours. He will put some things behind, will pass an invisible boundary; new, universal, and more liberal laws will begin to establish themselves around and within him; or the old laws be expanded, and interpreted in his favor in a more liberal sense, and he will live with the license of a higher order of beings. In proportion as he simplifies his life, the laws of the universe will appear less complex, and solitude will not be solitude, nor poverty poverty, nor weakness weakness. If you have built castles in the air, your work need not be lost; that is where they should be. Now put the foundations under them.

It is a ridiculous demand which England and America make, that you shall speak so that they can understand you. Neither men nor toadstools grow so. As if that were important, and there were not enough to understand you without them. As if Nature could support but one order of understandings, could not sustain birds as well as quadrupeds, flying as well as creeping things, and *hush* and *who*, which Bright[1] can understand, were the best English. As if there were safety in stupidity alone. I fear chiefly lest my expression may not be *extra-vagant*[2] enough, may not wander far enough beyond the narrow limits of my daily experience, so as to be adequate to the truth of which I have been convinced. *Extra vagance!* it depends on how you are yarded. The migrating buffalo, which seeks new pastures in another latitude, is not extravagant like the cow which kicks over the pail, leaps the cowyard fence, and runs after her calf, in milking time. I desire to speak somewhere *without* bounds; like a man in a waking moment, to men in their waking moments; for I am convinced that I cannot exaggerate enough even to lay the foundation of a true expression. Who that has heard a strain of music feared then lest he should speak extravagantly anymore forever? In view of the future or possible, we should live quite laxly and undefined in front, our outlines dim and misty on that side; as our shadows reveal an insensible perspiration toward the sun. The volatile truth of our words should continually betray the inadequacy of the residual statement. Their truth is instantly *translated*; its literal monument alone remains. The words which express our faith and piety are not definite; yet they are significant and fragrant like frankincense to superior natures.

Why level downward to our dullest perception always, and praise that as common sense? The commonest sense is the sense of men asleep, which they express by snoring. Sometimes we are inclined to class those who are once-and-a-half-witted with the half-witted, because we appreciate only a third part of their wit. Some would find fault with the morning red, if they ever got up early enough. "They pretend," as I hear, "that the verses of Kabir have four different senses; illusion, spirit, intellect, and the exoteric doctrine of the Vedas";[3] but in this part of the world it is considered a ground for complaint if a man's writings admit of more than one interpretation. While England endeavors to cure the potato-rot,[4] will not any

---

[1]   *Bright*   Common name for an ox.

[2]   *extra-vagant*   Play on the Latin origins of the word: *extra* meaning "outside," *vagant* meaning "to wander."

[3]   *They pretend ... the Vedas* From *Histoire de la literature hindoui et hindoustani* (1839) by French scholar Garcin de Tassy; *Kabir* Indian poet and mystic of the fifteenth century, influenced by both Hinduism and Islam.

[4]   *potato-rot* Potato blight, which affected much of Europe in the 1840s but especially Ireland, then under the rule of England, where it caused a devastating famine; close to one million people are estimated to have died between 1845 and 1848.

endeavor to cure the brain-rot, which prevails so much more widely and fatally?

I do not suppose that I have attained to obscurity, but I should be proud if no more fatal fault were found with my pages on this score than was found with the Walden ice. Southern customers objected to its blue color, which is the evidence of its purity, as if it were muddy, and preferred the Cambridge ice, which is white, but tastes of weeds. The purity men love is like the mists which envelop the earth, and not like the azure ether beyond.

Some are dinning in our ears that we Americans, and moderns generally, are intellectual dwarfs compared with the ancients, or even the Elizabethan men. But what is that to the purpose? A living dog is better than a dead lion.[1] Shall a man go and hang himself because he belongs to the race of pygmies, and not be the biggest pygmy that he can? Let everyone mind his own business, and endeavor to be what he was made.

Why should we be in such desperate haste to succeed and in such desperate enterprises? If a man does not keep pace with his companions, perhaps it is because he hears a different drummer. Let him step to the music which he hears, however measured or far away. It is not important that he should mature as soon as an apple tree or an oak. Shall he turn his spring into summer? If the condition of things which we were made for is not yet, what were any reality which we can substitute? We will not be shipwrecked on a vain reality. Shall we with pains erect a heaven of blue glass over ourselves, though when it is done we shall be sure to gaze still at the true ethereal heaven far above, as if the former were not?

There was an artist in the city of Kouroo[2] who was disposed to strive after perfection. One day it came into his mind to make a staff. Having considered that in an imperfect work time is an ingredient, but into a perfect work time does not enter, he said to himself, It shall be perfect in all respects, though I should do nothing else in my life. He proceeded instantly to the forest for wood, being resolved that it should not be made of unsuitable material; and as he searched for and rejected stick after stick, his friends gradually deserted him, for they grew old in their works and died, but he grew not older by a moment. His singleness of purpose and resolution, and his elevated piety, endowed him, without his knowledge, with perennial youth. As he made no compromise with Time, Time kept out of his way, and only sighed at a distance because he could not overcome him. Before he had found a stock in all respects suitable the city of Kouroo was a hoary ruin, and he sat on one of its mounds to peel the stick. Before he had given it the proper shape the dynasty of the Candahars was at an end, and with the point of the stick he wrote the name of the last of that race in the sand, and then resumed his work. By the time he had smoothed and polished the staff Kalpa was no longer the pole-star; and ere he had put on the ferule and the head adorned with precious stones, Brahma[3] had awoke and slumbered many times. But why do I stay to mention these things? When the finishing stroke was put to his work, it suddenly expanded before the eyes of the astonished artist into the fairest of all the creations of Brahma. He had made a new system in making a staff, a world with full and fair proportions; in which, though the old cities and dynasties had passed away, fairer and more glorious ones had taken their places. And now he saw by the heap of shavings still fresh at his feet, that, for him and his work, the former lapse of time had been an illusion, and that no more time had elapsed than is required for a single scintillation from the brain of Brahma to fall on and inflame the tinder of a mortal brain. The material was pure, and his art was pure; how could the result be other than wonderful?

No face which we can give to a matter will stead us so well at last as the truth. This alone wears well. For the most part, we are not where we are, but in a false position. Through an infinity of our natures, we suppose a case, and put ourselves into it, and hence are in two cases at the same time, and it is doubly difficult to get out. In sane moments we regard only the facts, the case that is. Say what you have to say, not what you ought. Any truth is better than make-believe. Tom Hyde, the tinker, standing on the gallows, was asked if he had anything to say. "Tell the tailors," said he, "to remember to make a knot in their thread before

---

[1] *A living ... dead lion* See Ecclesiastes 9.4.

[2] *There was ... of Kouroo* The source of the following fable is unclear; though influences from Hindu texts are evident, Thoreau likely made up the substance of the tale himself.

---

[3] *Brahma* Hindu creator god.

they take the first stitch." His companion's prayer is forgotten.[1]

However mean your life is, meet it and live it; do not shun it and call it hard names. It is not so bad as you are. It looks poorest when you are richest. The fault-finder will find faults even in paradise. Love your life, poor as it is. You may perhaps have some pleasant, thrilling, glorious hours, even in a poor-house. The setting sun is reflected from the windows of the alms-house as brightly as from the rich man's abode; the snow melts before its door as early in the spring. I do not see but a quiet mind may live as contentedly there, and have as cheering thoughts, as in a palace. The town's poor seem to me often to live the most independent lives of any. Maybe they are simply great enough to receive without misgiving. Most think that they are above being supported by the town; but it oftener happens that they are not above supporting themselves by dishonest means, which should be more disreputable. Cultivate poverty like a garden herb, like sage. Do not trouble yourself much to get new things, whether clothes or friends. Turn the old; return to them. Things do not change; we change. Sell your clothes and keep your thoughts. God will see that you do not want society. If I were confined to a corner of a garret all my days, like a spider, the world would be just as large to me while I had my thoughts about me. The philosopher said: "From an army of three divisions one can take away its general, and put it in disorder; from the man the most abject and vulgar one cannot take away his thought."[2] Do not seek so anxiously to be developed, to subject yourself to many influences to be played on; it is all dissipation. Humility like darkness reveals the heavenly lights. The shadows of poverty and meanness gather around us, "and lo! creation widens to our view."[3] We are often reminded that if there were bestowed on us the wealth of Croesus,[4] our aims must still be the same, and our means essentially the same.

Moreover, if you are restricted in your range by poverty, if you cannot buy books and newspapers, for instance, you are but confined to the most significant and vital experiences; you are compelled to deal with the material which yields the most sugar and the most starch. It is life near the bone where it is sweetest. You are defended from being a trifler. No man loses ever on a lower level by magnanimity on a higher. Superfluous wealth can buy superfluities only. Money is not required to buy one necessary of the soul.

I live in the angle of a leaden wall, into whose composition was poured a little alloy of bell metal. Often, in the repose of my mid-day, there reaches my ears a confused *tintinnabulum* from without. It is the noise of my contemporaries. My neighbors tell me of their adventures with famous gentlemen and ladies, what notabilities they met at the dinner-table; but I am no more interested in such things than in the contents of the Daily Times. The interest and the conversation are about costume and manners chiefly; but a goose is a goose still, dress it as you will. They tell me of California and Texas, of England and the Indies, of the Hon. Mr. —— of Georgia or of Massachusetts, all transient and fleeting phenomena, till I am ready to leap from their courtyard like the Mameluke bey.[5] I delight to come to my bearings—not walk in procession with pomp and parade, in a conspicuous place, but to walk even with the Builder of the universe, if I may—not to live in this restless, nervous, bustling, trivial Nineteenth Century, but stand or sit thoughtfully while it goes by. What are men celebrating? They are all on a committee of arrangements, and hourly expect a speech from somebody. God is only the president of the day, and Webster[6] is his orator. I love to weigh, to settle, to gravitate toward that which most strongly and rightfully attracts me—not hang by the beam of the scale and try to weigh less, not suppose a case, but take the case that is; to travel the only path I can, and that on which no power can resist me. It affords me no

---

1   *Tom Hyde … is forgotten*   Thoreau's source for this story and figure is unclear.

2   *The philosopher … his thought*   From the *Analects* of Confucius 9.26.

3   *and lo! … our view*   Slight misquotation from "Night and Day" or "To Night" by Spanish-born poet and theologian Joseph Blanco White (1775–1841).

4   *Croesus*   Famously affluent king of Lydia (r. c. 585–c. 546 BCE), whose name came to be applied to anyone of great wealth.

5   *Mameluke bey*   Reference to the massacre of the Mamluks, an Egyptian military caste, in 1811; according to legend, all died but for one "bey" or officer, who leapt from the citadel with his horse.

6   *Webster*   Massachusetts senator Daniel Webster (1782–1852), renowned for his oratorical skill and admired by many but often criticized by Thoreau, who disliked Webster for his willingness to compromise with supporters of slavery (notably in the Compromise of 1850).

satisfaction to commence to spring an arch before I have got a solid foundation. Let us not play at kittly-benders.[1] There is a solid bottom everywhere. We read that the traveler asked the boy if the swamp before him had a hard bottom. The boy replied that it had. But presently the traveler's horse sank in up to the girths, and he observed to the boy, "I thought you said that this bog had a hard bottom." "So it has," answered the latter, "but you have not got half way to it yet." So it is with the bogs and quicksands of society; but he is an old boy that knows it. Only what is thought, said, or done at a certain rare coincidence is good. I would not be one of those who will foolishly drive a nail into mere lath and plastering; such a deed would keep me awake nights. Give me a hammer, and let me feel for the furring.[2] Do not depend on the putty. Drive a nail home and clinch it so faithfully that you can wake up in the night and think of your work with satisfaction—a work at which you would not be ashamed to invoke the Muse. So will help you God, and so only. Every nail driven should be as another rivet in the machine of the universe, you carrying on the work.

Rather than love, than money, than fame, give me truth. I sat at a table where were rich food and wine in abundance, and obsequious attendance, but sincerity and truth were not; and I went away hungry from the inhospitable board. The hospitality was as cold as the ices. I thought that there was no need of ice to freeze them. They talked to me of the age of the wine and the fame of the vintage; but I thought of an older, a newer, and purer wine, of a more glorious vintage, which they had not got, and could not buy. The style, the house and grounds and "entertainment" pass for nothing with me. I called on the king, but he made me wait in his hall, and conducted like a man incapacitated for hospitality. There was a man in my neighborhood who lived in a hollow tree. His manners were truly regal. I should have done better had I called on him.

How long shall we sit in our porticoes practicing idle and musty virtues, which any work would make impertinent? As if one were to begin the day with long-suffering, and hire a man to hoe his potatoes; and in the afternoon go forth to practice Christian meekness and charity with goodness aforethought! Consider the China pride[3] and stagnant self-complacency of mankind. This generation inclines a little to congratulate itself on being the last of an illustrious line; and in Boston and London and Paris and Rome, thinking of its long descent, it speaks of its progress in art and science and literature with satisfaction. There are the Records of the Philosophical Societies, and the public Eulogies of *Great Men*! It is the good Adam contemplating his own virtue. "Yes, we have done great deeds, and sung divine songs, which shall never die,"—that is, as long as *we* can remember them. The learned societies and great men of Assyria,[4] where are they? What youthful philosophers and experimentalists we are! There is not one of my readers who has yet lived a whole human life. These may be but the spring months in the life of the race. If we have had the seven-years' itch,[5] we have not seen the seventeen-year locust yet in Concord. We are acquainted with a mere pellicle[6] of the globe on which we live. Most have not delved six feet beneath the surface, nor leaped as many above it. We know not where we are. Beside, we are sound asleep nearly half our time. Yet we esteem ourselves wise, and have an established order on the surface. Truly, we are deep thinkers, we are ambitious spirits! As I stand over the insect crawling amid the pine needles on the forest floor, and endeavoring to conceal itself from my sight, and ask myself why it will cherish those humble thoughts, and hide its head from me who might, perhaps, be its benefactor, and impart to its race some cheering information, I am reminded of the greater Benefactor and Intelligence that stands over me the human insect.

There is an incessant influx of novelty into the world, and yet we tolerate incredible dullness. I need only suggest what kind of sermons are still listened to in the most enlightened countries. There are such words as joy and sorrow, but they are only the burden

---

1   *kittlybenders*   Game of trying to run atop thin ice without breaking through.

2   *furring*   Thin boards nailed to a surface in order to raise it to be lathed.

3   *China pride*   Tensions arose between China and Britain in the 1830s, when the Chinese government refused to relax its longstanding isolationist foreign policy; thereafter, a widespread stereotype of the Chinese as proud and arrogant took root in the West.

4   *Assyria*   Empire of ancient Mesopotamia.

5   *seven-years' itch*   Scabies.

6   *pellicle*   Surface; skin.

of a psalm, sung with a nasal twang, while we believe in the ordinary and mean. We think that we can change our clothes only. It is said that the British Empire is very large and respectable, and that the United States are a first-rate power. We do not believe that a tide rises and falls behind every man which can float the British Empire like a chip, if he should ever harbor it in his mind. Who knows what sort of seventeen-year locust will next come out of the ground? The government of the world I live in was not framed, like that of Britain, in after-dinner conversations over the wine.

The life in us is like the water in the river. It may rise this year higher than man has ever known it, and flood the parched uplands; even this may be the eventful year, which will drown out all our muskrats. It was not always dry land where we dwell. I see far inland the banks which the stream anciently washed, before science began to record its freshets. Everyone has heard the story which has gone the rounds of New England, of a strong and beautiful bug which came out of the dry leaf of an old table of apple-tree wood, which had stood in a farmer's kitchen for sixty years, first in Connecticut, and afterward in Massachusetts, from an egg deposited in the living tree many years earlier still, as appeared by counting the annual layers beyond it; which was heard gnawing out for several weeks, hatched perchance by the heat of an urn. Who does not feel his faith in a resurrection and immortality strengthened by hearing of this? Who knows what beautiful and winged life, whose egg has been buried for ages under many concentric layers of woodenness in the dead dry life of society, deposited at first in the alburnum[1] of the green and living tree, which has been gradually converted into the semblance of its well-seasoned tomb—heard perchance gnawing out now for years by the astonished family of man, as they sat round the festive board—may unexpectedly come forth from amidst society's most trivial and handselled[2] furniture, to enjoy its perfect summer life at last!

I do not say that John or Jonathan[3] will realize all this; but such is the character of that morrow which mere lapse of time can never make to dawn. The light which puts out our eyes is darkness to us. Only that day dawns to which we are awake. There is more day to dawn. The sun is but a morning star.

—1854

In Context

The Photographs of Herbert Wendell Gleason

At the age of 44, Congregationalist minister Herbert Wendell Gleason (1855–1937) gave up his position in order to pursue a new calling—studying, photographing, and writing about the natural world. In subsequent decades he became well known as a photographer as he traveled throughout North America, but he was known above all as a photographer of the New England landscapes that Thoreau had made famous half a century earlier. When Houghton Mifflin reproduced his photographs in their 1906 *Works of Henry David Thoreau*, the publisher described Gleason's contribution in glowing terms:

> Mr. Gleason has made a careful study of all Thoreau's writings … and has explored with equal thoroughness the woods and fields of Concord, visiting the localities mentioned in the Journal and getting photographs, not only of the places themselves, but also of many of the fleeting phenomena of the natural year in the very spots where Thoreau observed them.

In 1917 Gleason published *Through the Year with Thoreau*, in which he included many more of his photographs of Thoreau-related landscapes. A small selection is included here.

---

[1]   *alburnum*   Sapwood.
[2]   *handselled*   Unwanted.
[3]   *John or Jonathan*   John Bull or Brother Jonathan, common personifications of England and America, respectively.

Thoreau's Cove, Walden Pond, 11 June 1901.

Fitchburg Railroad Train with Walden Pond in Winter, 24 March 1920.

Skunk Cabbage, from *Through the Year with Thoreau* (1917).

Eastern Shore, Walden Pond, 6 November 1899.

Ferns in the area Thoreau named Clintonia Swamp, just north of Walden Pond.

Cairn marking the site of Thoreau's cabin at Walden Pond. In 1881, Walt Whitman described this scene in his *Specimen Days*: "On the spot in the woods where Thoreau had his solitary house is now quite a cairn of stones, to mark the place; I too carried one and deposited on the heap." Elsewhere, Whitman declared that Thoreau, who had been a friend of his, "is not easily grasped— is elusive: yet he is one of the native forces—stands for a fact, a movement, an upheaval: Thoreau belongs to America, to the transcendental, to the protestors. … Thoreau was not so precious, tender, a personality as Emerson: but he was a force—he looms up bigger and bigger[.]"

Frederick Douglass

1818 – 1895

Author of the most powerfully written and most widely read slave narrative of the antebellum era, Frederick Douglass became the foremost voice in the abolitionist movement, and, following the Civil War, one of the foremost critics of the horrors of the new "Jim Crow" system of oppression. He spoke up too against the oppression of women and against all forms of prejudice and inequality, and he spoke up consistently in favor of speaking up—in favor of resistance. "Power concedes nothing without a demand," he famously wrote. "It never did and it never will." He occupies a unique place in American literature, American history, and American political thought.

Douglass was born Frederick Augustus Washington Bailey in Talbot County, Maryland. A degree of mystery surrounds the circumstances of Douglass's birth; like many enslaved people, he was denied full knowledge of his parentage or date of birth. He inherited the enslavement of his mother, Harriet Bailey, but his father was almost certainly a white man, quite likely his enslaver, Aaron Anthony (though other possibilities have been suggested). Douglass came to accept a tentative birth year of 1817; however, we now know that he was born in February 1818.

In 1826 Douglass was acquired by the slaveholder Thomas Auld, and was sent to live in Baltimore with Auld's brother and sister-in-law. In 1833 Douglass was removed from his situation in Baltimore and forced to work on Thomas Auld's plantation. Emboldened by his growing consciousness of slavery's injustice, Douglass grew increasingly rebellious, and was sent to work for a man named Edward Covey, locally famous as a so-called slave-breaker. Douglass attempted escape twice. In 1836 he was part of a failed plot organized by several enslaved companions, and was briefly jailed for his participation. Two years later, Douglass's second attempt was successful. Douglass left unexplained in the first and second versions of his autobiography any of the details of this escape, on the grounds—as he explains in Chapter 11—that telling the story would probably cause "difficulties" for those who helped him and "would most undoubtedly induce greater vigilance on the part of slaveholders"; it is only the third and final version—the 1881 *Life and Times of Frederick Douglass*—that includes the story of his escape.

Douglass presents the escape very largely as a solo endeavor; as we now know, he was in fact aided by several people—very much including the free black woman Anna Murray, to whom he had become engaged shortly before the escape. It was largely from Anna that Douglass obtained the funds that enabled him to travel from slavery in Baltimore to freedom in New York on 3 September 1838. Anna made the same trip a week later, and on 15 September the two were married in the home of David Ruggles, a black grocer and printer who led an organization devoted to assisting fugitive slaves. It was Ruggles who suggested that Frederick Bailey change his name—as was often done by those wishing to minimize the chances of being captured and returned to bondage. For a few days Douglass called himself Frederick Johnson, and it was under that name that he and Anna were married.

Ruggles also suggested that the couple move to New Bedford, Massachusetts, a community more friendly than was New York to fugitives who had been enslaved, and one where he felt Douglass would be able to find employment. There the Douglasses stayed initially at the home of an abolitionist named Nathan Johnson—evidently one of many Johnsons in New Bedford. Feeling that another name was necessary to distinguish himself from the other Johnsons, Frederick asked Nathan Johnson to suggest a new name; according to the narrative, it was Johnson who suggested the name under which Douglass would become famous.

In the North Douglass found a land of remarkable prosperity but also of profound contradiction; though an ordinary white laborer might enjoy a more luxurious existence and higher education level than an upper-class southern slaveholder, a free black citizen could expect continual discrimination from employers, church congregations, and other groups. Eventually Douglass—whose religious conversion experiences are given more emphasis in his two later memoirs—found employment as a licensed preacher in the African Methodist Episcopal Zion Church. Douglass also became a regular reader of the *Liberator*, an antislavery newspaper founded by leading white abolitionist William Lloyd Garrison. Douglass began attending antislavery meetings, where he soon began to share his own story and to make a local name for himself. In August 1841 he delivered his first formal speech before an antislavery audience in Nantucket. His moving story and evident oratorical talents caught Garrison's attention; Douglass became a valued contributor to the *Liberator*, and was appointed to a paid position with the Massachusetts Anti-Slavery Society not long thereafter.

Over the following years Douglass traveled widely and delivered speech after speech to audiences throughout the Northern states; he came to occupy a central place in the abolitionist movement. When Emerson was invited to deliver a major speech on slavery in August 1844, for example, Frederick Douglass was among the three others rounding out the program. People everywhere found something extraordinary about him. Nathaniel P. Rogers, editor of the *Herald of Freedom* abolitionist newspaper, described in 1843 the effect of Douglass's words when the speaker was in full flight as "sterner, darker, deeper" than oratory or eloquence. "It was the volcanic outbreak of human nature, long pent up in slavery and at last bursting its imprisonment. It was the storm of insurrection."

Douglass's celebrated status also often made him a target; he endured egg- and brick-throwing and, in Pennsylvania in 1843, a mob attack resulted in a permanent injury to his right hand. Even those who ostensibly supported Douglass's goals were often unable or unwilling to reconcile the distinguished and eloquent speaker they saw with the enslaved life he described, and insisted that his story must have been falsified. (Douglass averred in the second version of his autobiography that "prejudice against color is stronger in the north than [in the] south; it hangs around my neck like a heavy weight.")

Emboldened rather than intimidated by the challenges to his story, Douglass began work on an autobiography in which he would provide factual details to corroborate his claims. Written in the space of just a few months beginning in December 1844, *Narrative of the Life of Frederick Douglass, an American Slave. Written by Himself*, was published in the spring of 1845 by the Anti-Slavery Office in Boston. The book was welcomed with enthusiasm in the abolitionist press; most notably, the *New York Tribune* on 10 June 1845 printed on its front page a long and highly favorable review (written by Margaret Fuller), along with a substantial excerpt from the book. By contrast, the *New York Herald* accorded it only a few words—"a neatly printed volume, which abolitionists may find interesting"—and most mainstream newspapers in northern states ignored it altogether. (In most southern states the dissemination of such works was strictly prohibited; a *Richmond Enquirer* article from April 1849 details a case in which a preacher named Jarvis C. Bacon was prosecuted for having circulated copies of Douglass's *Narrative* and another antislavery publication.)

By the 1840s the "slave narrative" was a well-established literary genre; in America alone at least ten such volumes were published between 1830 and 1845. Douglass's *Narrative* closely follows the conventions of the genre in several respects. The inclusion of a prefatory address by a white activist attesting to the book's authorship; the repeated assertions, near the beginning of the text, of un-hyperbolic truthfulness; the visceral descriptions of whippings, auction blocks, and other gruesome realities of enslaved life—all these are typical of the genre. Yet from the beginning Douglass's work was recognized as extraordinary in the quality of its writing and the depth of feeling it conveys; Fuller was not alone in finding the *Narrative* to be "glowing with … life and fertile in invention," "more simple, true, coherent, and warm with genuine feeling" than any other work of its kind. Writing in the 1860s, black abolitionist William Wells Brown reminisced that "the narrative of [Douglass's] life … gave a new impetus to the black man's literature. All other stories of fugitive slaves faded away before the beautifully written, highly descriptive, and thrilling memoir of Frederick Douglass." Within less than four months the *Narrative* had sold almost 5,000 copies, and by 1850 some 30,000 copies had been printed.

The book's broad readership and Douglass's increasing fame, however, did nothing to alter his legal status. With the threat of discovery and capture by fugitive-slave hunters in mind, Douglass embarked in late 1845 on a lecture tour of Great Britain—a tour that broadened Douglass's readership and led to several European editions of his *Narrative*. While he was abroad a group of English friends purchased his manumission for a sum of £150; Douglass returned to the United States a legally free man in 1847, and moved with his family to Rochester, New York.

That same year Douglass established a new antislavery weekly newspaper, *The North Star* (a collaboration with the free-born black abolitionist Martin Delany). The ideals emblazoned on its masthead—"Right is of no Sex—Truth is of no Color—God is the Father of us all, and we are all Brethren"—may seem unexceptionable today, but in 1847 they were revolutionary on several fronts. Douglass struggled to build a readership (in 1851 he merged *The North Star* with another weekly to form *Frederick Douglass' Paper*, and in 1858 he began to publish monthly rather than weekly), but he managed in one form or another to keep publishing a newspaper until 1863, and each issue is believed to have had several thousand readers.

William Lloyd Garrison did not entirely welcome the competition with his *Liberator*. By 1851, Douglass and Garrison had reached a formal parting of the ways, with issues of principle having come to separate the two. Garrison was an uncompromising believer in "immediatism"—the doctrine that slavery should be abolished immediately rather than gradually—but he remained reluctant to countenance the use of force to overcome the evils of slavery; Douglass, by contrast, was more and more strongly convinced that the use of force in certain circumstances was entirely justified. Douglass's revised and expanded 1855 autobiography, *My Bondage and My Freedom*, puts forward even more powerfully than the *Narrative* the case for forceful resistance to such evils as slavery. (A passage from the 1855 autobiography is provided for comparison in the online component of this anthology.)

Douglass had also begun to feel a desire to distance himself from the sometimes patronizing guidance of white abolitionists such as Garrison; his declared goal in founding *The North Star* had been to provide "a printing-press and paper, permanently established, under the complete control and direction of the immediate victims of slavery and oppression." Increasingly, questions about the appropriate means of resisting oppression became matters not only of the moral imperatives involved, but also matters of character formation; like Emerson, Douglass took the idea of self-reliance very much to heart. As early as 1848, in an essay entitled "What Are the Colored People Doing for Themselves?," Douglass had written against "that lazy, mean, and cowardly spirit that robs us of all self-reliance, and teaches us to depend upon others for the accomplishment of that which we should achieve with our own hands." For Douglass, the principle of self-reliance had a special resonance for African Americans.

In many of Douglass's writings, self-reliance (and self-fashioning) appears to be heavily gendered; "manhood" is given a central place. But Douglass was also involved in the fight for women's rights. In 1848 he spoke at both the Rochester and the Seneca Falls Women's Rights Conventions. One of Douglass's most celebrated speeches, commonly titled "What to the Slave Is the Fourth of July?," was given at an Independence Day event hosted by the Rochester Ladies' Anti-Slavery Society. During this period, then, Douglass saw activism on behalf of African Americans and activism for women's rights as connected causes. "When the true history of the antislavery cause shall be written," he wrote, "woman will occupy a large space in its pages, for the cause of the slave has been peculiarly a woman's cause." In the wake of the Civil War, however, there was for some years a significant rift between Douglass and leading campaigners for women's rights such as Elizabeth Cady Stanton and Susan B. Anthony, as debate intensified over the 1868 Fourteenth Amendment (affirming citizenship for all people born in the United States, regardless of color, but affirming the right to vote only for *male* citizens) and the 1870 Fifteenth Amendment (affirming that the right to vote was not to "be denied ... on account of race"). Anthony and Stanton were among those who opposed the Fifteenth Amendment; they saw no reason why the vote should be granted to black men before it had been granted to white women. Douglass, on the other hand, was outspoken in his belief that the former was a more urgent imperative than the latter. (Throughout the controversy, the voices of black women activists such as Frances Harper and Mary Ann Shadd Cary were too seldom heard.)

In addition to his autobiographical writings, Douglass published hundreds of speeches and essays—and one novella, *The Heroic Slave* (1852). After the war he became a prominent member of the Republican Party (which remained for many decades after Lincoln's death a party sympathetic to and supportive of African Americans). He received several government appointments, including United States Marshall for the District of Columbia and Minister (ambassador) to Haiti. In 1884, two years after Anna Murray-Douglass's death, he married Helen Pitts, a college-educated activist who had been working with Douglass in the office of the Recorder of Deeds. That she was white and he black led to accusations of betrayal and to her estrangement from several members of her family, but the two weathered the storm, and their marriage was a happy one.

Douglass lived for thirty years after the end of the Civil War, received many honors, and continued to speak out powerfully on a wide variety of topics. But in the years following the Compromise of 1887 and the rebirth of legalized oppression in the southern states, the tide was running against Douglass. His eloquence could do little to stop the spread of revisionist versions of the Civil War that downplayed the centrality of slavery to the struggle and framed the Confederacy as a noble "lost cause." As the years went by the genre of 'slave narrative' received less and less attention. Douglass's final great act of self-fashioning—his 1881 *Life and Times of Frederick Douglass*—sold poorly. By 1900 such writing had been nearly forgotten by mainstream white America. That year saw the publication of *A Literary History of America* by Harvard Professor of English Barrett Wendell; Wendell's eighteen-page chapter on the literature of the antislavery movement makes no mention whatsoever of Douglass—or of any other African American author. Douglass remained more consistently renowned among black readers in the late-nineteenth and early-twentieth centuries. He was honored in a long elegy by popular African American poet Paul Laurence Dunbar upon his death in 1895, and in 1899 was the subject of a biography written by black novelist Charles Chesnutt for the popular series Beacon Biographies of Eminent Americans; in 1906 Booker T. Washington wrote, "No negro can read and study the life of Frederick Douglass without deriving from it courage to look up and forward."

Nevertheless, in the first half of the twentieth century Douglass's *Narrative* went out of print. Not until 1960 did Harvard University Press bring out a new edition of the work—and even then with some timidity, the editor suggesting in his introduction that "perhaps Douglass seemed to protest too much in making slavery out as a 'soul-killing' institution." Only in the twenty-first century has Douglass come once again to be acknowledged without apology or equivocation as a uniquely towering presence, of enduring importance to America.

NOTE ON THE TEXTS: The texts of the works presented here are based on their first published editions. Spelling and punctuation have been modernized in accordance with the practices of this anthology.

⌘ ⌘ ⌘

Narrative of the Life of Frederick Douglass, an American Slave. Written by Himself

PREFACE[1]

In the month of August, 1841, I attended an anti-slavery convention in Nantucket, at which it was my happiness to become acquainted with Frederick Douglass, the writer of the following Narrative. He was a stranger to nearly every member of that body; but, having recently made his escape from the southern prison-house of bondage, and feeling his curiosity excited to ascertain the principles and measures of the abolitionists—of whom he had heard a somewhat vague description while he was a slave—he was induced to give his attendance, on the occasion alluded to, though at that time a resident in New Bedford.[2]

Fortunate, most fortunate occurrence!—fortunate for the millions of his manacled brethren, yet panting for deliverance from their awful thraldom!—fortunate for the cause of negro emancipation, and of universal liberty!—fortunate for the land of his birth, which he has already done so much to save and bless!—fortunate for a large circle of friends and acquaintances, whose sympathy and affection he has strongly secured by the many sufferings he has endured, by his virtuous traits of character, by his ever-abiding remembrance of those who are in bonds, as being bound with them!—fortunate for the multitudes, in various parts of our republic, whose minds he has enlightened on the subject of slavery, and who have been melted to tears by his pathos, or roused to virtuous indignation by his stirring eloquence against the enslavers of men!—fortunate for himself, as it at once brought him into the field of public usefulness, "gave the world assurance of a MAN,"[3] quickened the slumbering energies of his soul, and consecrated him to the great work of breaking the rod of the oppressor, and letting the oppressed go free!

I shall never forget his first speech at the convention—the extraordinary emotion it excited in my own mind—the powerful impression it created upon a crowded auditory, completely taken by surprise—the applause which followed from the beginning to the end of his felicitous remarks. I think I never hated slavery so intensely as at that moment; certainly, my perception of the enormous outrage which is inflicted by it, on the godlike nature of its victims, was rendered far more clear than ever. There stood one, in physical proportion and stature commanding and exact—in intellect richly endowed—in natural eloquence a prodigy—in soul manifestly "created but a little lower than the angels"[4]—yet a slave, ay, a fugitive slave—trembling for his safety, hardly daring to believe that on the American soil, a single white person could be found who would befriend him at all hazards, for the love of God and humanity! Capable of high attainments as an intellectual and moral being—needing nothing but a comparatively small amount of cultivation to make him an ornament to society and a blessing to his race—by the law of the land, by the voice of the people, by the terms of the slave code, he was only a piece of property, a beast of burden, a chattel[5] personal, nevertheless!

A beloved friend[6] from New Bedford prevailed on Mr. DOUGLASS to address the convention: He came forward to the platform with a hesitancy and embarrassment, necessarily the attendants of a sensitive mind in such a novel position. After apologizing for his ignorance, and reminding the audience that slavery was a poor school for the human intellect and heart, he proceeded to narrate some of the facts in his own history as a slave, and in the course of his speech gave utterance to many noble thoughts and thrilling reflections. As soon as he had taken his seat, filled with hope and admiration, I rose, and declared that PATRICK HENRY,[7]

---

1 *PREFACE* Written by prominent white abolitionist William Lloyd Garrison (1805–79). It was common practice for the slave narratives of black authors to be prefaced by white authors, whose testimonials were thought to authenticate the text. This practice was not followed with Douglass's two subsequent autobiographies.

2 *New Bedford* Douglass settled in New Bedford, Massachusetts with his wife after his self-emancipation in 1838.

3 *gave the world ... a MAN* See Shakespeare's *Hamlet* 3.4.72.

4 *created but ... the angels* See Psalm 8.5: "For thou hast made him [humankind] a little lower than the angels"; and Hebrews 2.7: "But we see Jesus, who was made a little lower than the angels."

5 *chattel* Property.

6 *A beloved friend* William C. Coffin, prominent white abolitionist in and around New Bedford and a supporter of Douglass.

7 *PATRICK HENRY* American revolutionary orator and Founding Father (1736–99), famous for the speech in which he proclaimed: "Forbid it, Almighty God! I know not what course others may take; but as for me, give me liberty or give me death!"

of revolutionary fame, never made a speech more eloquent in the cause of liberty, than the one we had just listened to from the lips of that hunted fugitive. So I believed at that time—such is my belief now. I reminded the audience of the peril which surrounded this self-emancipated young man at the North—even in Massachusetts, on the soil of the Pilgrim Fathers, among the descendants of revolutionary sires;[1] and I appealed to them, whether they would ever allow him to be carried back into slavery—law or no law, constitution or no constitution. The response was unanimous and in thunder-tones—"NO!" "Will you succor and protect him as a brother-man—a resident of the old Bay State?"[2] "YES!" shouted the whole mass, with an energy so startling, that the ruthless tyrants south of Mason and Dixon's line[3] might almost have heard the mighty burst of feeling, and recognized it as the pledge of an invincible determination, on the part of those who gave it, never to betray him that wanders, but to hide the outcast, and firmly to abide the consequences.

It was at once deeply impressed upon my mind, that, if Mr. DOUGLASS could be persuaded to consecrate his time and talents to the promotion of the anti-slavery enterprise, a powerful impetus would be given to it, and a stunning blow at the same time inflicted on northern prejudice against a colored complexion. I therefore endeavored to instil hope and courage into his mind, in order that he might dare to engage in a vocation so anomalous and responsible for a person in his situation; and I was seconded in this effort by warm-hearted friends, especially by the late General Agent of the Massachusetts Anti-Slavery Society, Mr. JOHN A. COLLINS,[4] whose judgment in this instance entirely coincided with my own. At first, he could give no encouragement; with unfeigned diffidence, he expressed his conviction that he was not adequate to the performance of so great a task; the path marked out was wholly an untrodden one; he was sincerely apprehensive that he should do more harm than good. After much deliberation, however, he consented to make a trial; and ever since that period, he has acted as a lecturing agent, under the auspices either of the American or the Massachusetts Anti-Slavery Society.[5] In labors he has been most abundant; and his success in combating prejudice, in gaining proselytes, in agitating the public mind, has far surpassed the most sanguine expectations that were raised at the commencement of his brilliant career. He has borne himself with gentleness and meekness, yet with true manliness of character. As a public speaker, he excels in pathos, wit, comparison, imitation, strength of reasoning, and fluency of language. There is in him that union of head and heart, which is indispensable to an enlightenment of the heads and a winning of the hearts of others. May his strength continue to be equal to his day! May he continue to "grow in grace, and in the knowledge of God,"[6] that he may be increasingly serviceable in the cause of bleeding humanity, whether at home or abroad!

It is certainly a very remarkable fact, that one of the most efficient advocates of the slave population, now before the public, is a fugitive slave, in the person of FREDERICK DOUGLASS; and that the free colored population of the United States are as ably represented by one of their own number, in the person of CHARLES LENOX REMOND,[7] whose eloquent appeals have extorted the highest applause of multitudes on both sides of the Atlantic. Let the calumniators[8] of the colored race despise themselves for their baseness and illiberality of spirit, and henceforth cease to talk of the natural inferiority of those who require nothing but time and opportunity to attain to the highest point of human excellence.

---

[1] *Pilgrim Fathers ... revolutionary sires* "Pilgrim Fathers" refers to the English colonists who arrived in Plymouth, Massachusetts in 1620; *revolutionary sires* Ancestors who participated in the American Revolution.

[2] *old Bay State* Massachusetts.

[3] *Mason and Dixon's line* Drawn in the 1760s by English surveyors Charles Mason and Jeremiah Dixon, the Mason-Dixon line separated parts of Pennsylvania and Delaware from parts of Maryland and Virginia; it came to signify the border between the American North and South, and thereby the literal and symbolic border between the free states and the slave states.

[4] *JOHN A. COLLINS* White antislavery activist (1810–79).

[5] *American or ... Society* The Massachusetts Anti-Slavery Society was an auxiliary of the American Anti-Slavery Society; both were associated with William Lloyd Garrison.

[6] *grow in grace ... of God* See 2 Peter 3.18: "But grow in grace, and in the knowledge of our Lord and Saviour Jesus Christ."

[7] *CHARLES LENOX REMOND* Free-born African American abolitionist from Salem, Massachusetts (1810–73), a close friend of Douglass after whom Douglass named his youngest son.

[8] *calumniators* Slanderers.

It may, perhaps, be fairly questioned, whether any other portion of the population of the earth could have endured the privations, sufferings and horrors of slavery, without having become more degraded in the scale of humanity than the slaves of African descent. Nothing has been left undone to cripple their intellects, darken their minds, debase their moral nature, obliterate all traces of their relationship to mankind; and yet how wonderfully they have sustained the mighty load of a most frightful bondage, under which they have been groaning for centuries! To illustrate the effect of slavery on the white man—to show that he has no powers of endurance, in such a condition, superior to those of his black brother—DANIEL O'CONNELL,[1] the distinguished advocate of universal emancipation, and the mightiest champion of prostrate but not conquered Ireland, relates the following anecdote in a speech delivered by him in the Conciliation Hall, Dublin, before the Loyal National Repeal Association,[2] March 31, 1845. "No matter," said Mr. O'CONNELL, "under what specious term it may disguise itself, slavery is still hideous. It has a natural, an inevitable tendency to brutalize every noble faculty of man. An American sailor, who was cast away on the shore of Africa, where he was kept in slavery for three years, was, at the expiration of that period, found to be imbruted and stultified—he had lost all reasoning power; and having forgotten his native language, could only utter some savage gibberish between Arabic and English, which nobody could understand, and which even he himself found difficulty in pronouncing. So much for the humanizing influence of THE DOMESTIC INSTITUTION!" Admitting this to have been an extraordinary case of mental deterioration, it proves at least that the white slave can sink as low in the scale of humanity as the black one.

Mr. DOUGLASS has very properly chosen to write his own Narrative, in his own style, and according to the best of his ability, rather than to employ someone else. It is, therefore, entirely his own production; and, considering how long and dark was the career he had

to run as a slave—how few have been his opportunities to improve his mind since he broke his iron fetters—it is, in my judgment, highly creditable to his head and heart. He who can peruse it without a tearful eye, a heaving breast, an afflicted spirit—without being filled with an unutterable abhorrence of slavery and all its abettors, and animated with a determination to seek the immediate overthrow of that execrable system—without trembling for the fate of this country in the hands of a righteous God, who is ever on the side of the oppressed, and whose arm is not shortened that it cannot save—must have a flinty heart, and be qualified to act the part of a trafficker "in slaves and the souls of men."[3] I am confident that it is essentially true in all its statements; that nothing has been set down in malice, nothing exaggerated, nothing drawn from the imagination; that it comes short of the reality, rather than overstates a single fact in regard to SLAVERY AS IT IS.[4] The experience of FREDERICK DOUGLASS, as a slave, was not a peculiar one; his lot was not especially a hard one; his case may be regarded as a very fair specimen of the treatment of slaves in Maryland, in which State it is conceded that they are better fed and less cruelly treated than in Georgia, Alabama, or Louisiana. Many have suffered incomparably more, while very few on the plantations have suffered less, than himself. Yet how deplorable was his situation! what terrible chastisements were inflicted upon his person! what still more shocking outrages were perpetrated upon his mind! with all his noble powers and sublime aspirations, how like a brute was he treated, even by those professing to have the same mind in them that was in Christ Jesus! to what dreadful liabilities was he continually subjected! how destitute of friendly counsel and aid, even in his greatest extremities! how heavy was the midnight of woe which shrouded in blackness the last ray of hope, and filled the future with terror and gloom! what longings after freedom took possession of his breast, and how his misery augmented, in proportion as he grew reflective and intelligent—thus demonstrating that a happy slave is an extinct man! how he thought, reasoned, felt, under the lash of the

---

1   *DANIEL O'CONNELL* Irish politician (1775–1847) who fought to obtain equal rights for Catholics (a goal that was partially achieved with the so-called "Catholic Emancipation" of 1829) and to obtain for Ireland a degree of independence from English rule.

2   *Repeal Association* Founded by O'Connell to call for repeal of the 1800 Acts of Union (which had abolished the Irish Parliament in order to bring Ireland under the direct control of Britain).

3   *in slaves ... souls of men* See Revelation 18.13.

4   *SLAVERY AS IT IS* Allusion to white abolitionist Theodore Dwight Weld's influential 1839 antislavery book *American Slavery as It Is: A Testimony of a Thousand Witnesses.*

driver, with the chains upon his limbs! what perils he encountered in his endeavors to escape from his horrible doom! and how signal have been his deliverance and preservation in the midst of a nation of pitiless enemies!

This Narrative contains many affecting incidents, many passages of great eloquence and power; but I think the most thrilling one of them all is the description Douglass gives of his feelings, as he stood soliloquizing respecting his fate, and the chances of his one day being a freeman, on the banks of the Chesapeake Bay—viewing the receding vessels as they flew with their white wings before the breeze, and apostrophizing[1] them as animated by the living spirit of freedom. Who can read that passage, and be insensible to its pathos and sublimity? Compressed into it is a whole Alexandrian library[2] of thought, feeling, and sentiment—all that can, all that need be urged, in the form of expostulation, entreaty, rebuke, against that crime of crimes—making man the property of his fellowman! O, how accursed is that system, which entombs the godlike mind of man, defaces the divine image, reduces those who by creation were crowned with glory and honor to a level with four-footed beasts, and exalts the dealer in human flesh above all that is called God! Why should its existence be prolonged one hour? Is it not evil, only evil, and that continually? What does its presence imply but the absence of all fear of God, all regard for man, on the part of the people of the United States? Heaven speed its eternal overthrow!

So profoundly ignorant of the nature of slavery are many persons, that they are stubbornly incredulous whenever they read or listen to any recital of the cruelties which are daily inflicted on its victims. They do not deny that the slaves are held as property; but that terrible fact seems to convey to their minds no idea of injustice, exposure to outrage, or savage barbarity. Tell them of cruel scourgings, of mutilations and brandings, of scenes of pollution and blood, of the banishment of all light and knowledge, and they affect to be greatly indignant at such enormous exaggerations, such wholesale misstatements, such abominable libels on the character of the southern planters! As if all these direful outrages were not the natural results of slavery! As if it were less cruel to reduce a human being to the condition of a thing, than to give him a severe flagellation, or to deprive him of necessary food and clothing! As if whips, chains, thumb-screws, paddles, blood-hounds, overseers, drivers, patrols, were not all indispensable to keep the slaves down, and to give protection to their ruthless oppressors! As if, when the marriage institution is abolished, concubinage, adultery, and incest, must not necessarily abound; when all the rights of humanity are annihilated, any barrier remains to protect the victim from the fury of the spoiler; when absolute power is assumed over life and liberty, it will not be wielded with destructive sway! Skeptics of this character abound in society. In some few instances, their incredulity arises from a want of reflection; but, generally, it indicates a hatred of the light, a desire to shield slavery from the assaults of its foes, a contempt of the colored race, whether bond or free. Such will try to discredit the shocking tales of slaveholding cruelty which are recorded in this truthful Narrative; but they will labor in vain. Mr. Douglass has frankly disclosed the place of his birth, the names of those who claimed ownership in his body and soul, and the names also of those who committed the crimes which he has alleged against them. His statements, therefore, may easily be disproved, if they are untrue.

In the course of his Narrative, he relates two instances of murderous cruelty—in one of which a planter deliberately shot a slave belonging to a neighboring plantation, who had unintentionally gotten within his lordly domain in quest of fish; and in the other, an overseer blew out the brains of a slave who had fled to a stream of water to escape a bloody scourging. Mr. Douglass states that in neither of these instances was any thing done by way of legal arrest or judicial investigation. *The Baltimore American*, of March 17, 1845, relates a similar case of atrocity, perpetrated with similar impunity—as follows: "Shooting a slave.—We learn, upon the authority of a letter from Charles County, Maryland, received by a gentleman of this city, that a young man, named Matthews, a nephew of General Matthews, and whose father, it is believed, holds an office at Washington, killed one of the slaves upon his

---

[1]   *apostrophizing* Addressing inanimate objects directly in a poetic fashion.

[2]   *Alexandrian library* Renowned ancient library located in Alexandria, Egypt.

father's farm by shooting him. The letter states that young Matthews had been left in charge of the farm; that he gave an order to the servant, which was disobeyed, when he proceeded to the house, obtained a gun, and, returning, shot the servant. He immediately, the letter continues, fled to his father's residence, where he still remains unmolested." Let it never be forgotten, that no slaveholder or overseer can be convicted of any outrage perpetrated on the person of a slave, however diabolical it may be, on the testimony of colored witnesses, whether bond or free. By the slave code, they are adjudged to be as incompetent to testify against a white man, as though they were indeed a part of the brute creation. Hence, there is no legal protection in fact, whatever there may be in form, for the slave population; and any amount of cruelty may be inflicted on them with impunity. Is it possible for the human mind to conceive of a more horrible state of society?

The effect of a religious profession on the conduct of southern masters is vividly described in the following Narrative, and shown to be anything but salutary. In the nature of the case, it must be in the highest degree pernicious. The testimony of Mr. DOUGLASS, on this point, is sustained by a cloud of witnesses, whose veracity is unimpeachable. "A slaveholder's profession of Christianity is a palpable imposture. He is a felon of the highest grade. He is a man-stealer. It is of no importance what you put in the other scale."

Reader! are you with the man-stealers in sympathy and purpose, or on the side of their down-trodden victims? If with the former, then are you the foe of God and man. If with the latter, what are you prepared to do and dare in their behalf? Be faithful, be vigilant, be untiring in your efforts to break every yoke, and let the oppressed go free. Come what may—cost what it may—inscribe on the banner which you unfurl to the breeze, as your religious and political motto—"NO COMPROMISE WITH SLAVERY! NO UNION WITH SLAVEHOLDERS!"

WM. LLOYD GARRISON.
BOSTON, May 1, 1845.

LETTER FROM WENDELL PHILLIPS,[1] ESQ

BOSTON, April 22, 1845

My Dear Friend

You remember the old fable of "The Man and the Lion,"[2] where the lion complained that he should not be so misrepresented "when the lions wrote history."

I am glad the time has come when the "lions write history." We have been left long enough to gather the character of slavery from the involuntary evidence of the masters. One might, indeed, rest sufficiently satisfied with what, it is evident, must be, in general, the results of such a relation, without seeking farther to find whether they have followed in every instance. Indeed, those who stare at the half-peck of corn a week, and love to count the lashes on the slave's back, are seldom the "stuff" out of which reformers and abolitionists are to be made. I remember that, in 1838, many were waiting for the results of the West India experiment,[3] before they could come into our ranks. Those "results" have come long ago; but, alas! few of that number have come with them, as converts. A man must be disposed to judge of emancipation by other tests than whether it has increased the produce of sugar—and to hate slavery for other reasons than because it starves men and whips women—before he is ready to lay the first stone of his anti-slavery life.

I was glad to learn, in your story, how early the most neglected of God's children waken to a sense of their rights, and of the injustice done them. Experience is a keen teacher; and long before you had mastered your A

---

[1]   WENDELL PHILLIPS   Massachusetts-based abolitionist and social activist (1811–84).

[2]   The Man and the Lion   Allusion to one of Aesop's Fables, in which a man gestures towards a sculpture of a male figure conquering a lion as evidence of human superiority; the lion counters that if lions could sculpt, they would be the ones depicted as victorious. Tradition has long held that the Greek storyteller Aesop was himself enslaved.

[3]   West India experiment   Referring to the British West Indies Emancipation Act that formally abolished slavery in the British West Indies. It was enacted in 1833, and began to take effect a year later, but its provisions were for a phased abolition; until at least 1838 many previously enslaved people were still bound to their former enslavers as apprentices.

B C, or knew where the "white sails" of the Chesapeake were bound, you began, I see, to gauge the wretchedness of the slave, not by his hunger and want, not by his lashes and toil, but by the cruel and blighting death which gathers over his soul.

In connection with this, there is one circumstance which makes your recollections peculiarly valuable, and renders your early insight the more remarkable. You come from that part of the country where we are told slavery appears with its fairest features. Let us hear, then, what it is at its best estate—gaze on its bright side, if it has one; and then imagination may task her powers to add dark lines to the picture, as she travels southward to that (for the colored man) Valley of the Shadow of Death,[1] where the Mississippi sweeps along.

Again, we have known you long, and can put the most entire confidence in your truth, candor, and sincerity. Everyone who has heard you speak has felt, and, I am confident, every one who reads your book will feel, persuaded that you give them a fair specimen of the whole truth. No one-sided portrait—no wholesale complaints—but strict justice done, whenever individual kindliness has neutralized, for a moment, the deadly system with which it was strangely allied. You have been with us, too, some years, and can fairly compare the twilight of rights, which your race enjoy at the North, with that "noon of night" under which they labor south of Mason and Dixon's line. Tell us whether, after all, the half-free colored man of Massachusetts is worse off than the pampered slave of the rice swamps!

In reading your life, no one can say that we have unfairly picked out some rare specimens of cruelty. We know that the bitter drops, which even you have drained from the cup, are no incidental aggravations, no individual ills, but such as must mingle always and necessarily in the lot of every slave. They are the essential ingredients, not the occasional results, of the system.

After all, I shall read your book with trembling for you. Some years ago, when you were beginning to tell me your real name and birthplace, you may remember I stopped you, and preferred to remain ignorant of all. With the exception of a vague description, so I continued, till the other day, when you read me your memoirs. I hardly knew, at the time, whether to thank you or not for the sight of them, when I reflected that it was still dangerous, in Massachusetts, for honest men to tell their names! They say the fathers, in 1776, signed the Declaration of Independence with the halter about their necks. You, too, publish your declaration of freedom with danger compassing you around. In all the broad lands which the Constitution of the United States overshadows, there is no single spot—however narrow or desolate—where a fugitive slave can plant himself and say, "I am safe." The whole armory of Northern Law has no shield for you. I am free to say that, in your place, I should throw the MS.[2] into the fire.

You, perhaps, may tell your story in safety, endeared as you are to so many warm hearts by rare gifts, and a still rarer devotion of them to the service of others. But it will be owing only to your labors, and the fearless efforts of those who, trampling the laws and Constitution of the country under their feet, are determined that they will "hide the outcast,"[3] and that their hearths shall be, spite of the law, an asylum for the oppressed, if, some time or other, the humblest may stand in our streets, and bear witness in safety against the cruelties of which he has been the victim.

Yet it is sad to think, that these very throbbing hearts which welcome your story, and form your best safeguard in telling it, are all beating contrary to the "statute in such case made and provided." Go on, my dear friend, till you, and those who, like you, have been saved, so as by fire, from the dark prison-house, shall stereotype these free, illegal pulses into statutes; and New England, cutting loose from a blood-stained Union, shall glory in being the house of refuge for the oppressed—till we no longer merely "hide the outcast," or make a merit of standing idly by while he is hunted in our midst; but, consecrating anew the soil of the Pilgrims as an asylum for the oppressed, proclaim our welcome to the slave so loudly, that the tones shall reach every hut in the Carolinas, and make the broken-hearted bondman leap up at the thought of old Massachusetts.

God speed the day!

Till then, and ever,
Yours truly,
WENDELL PHILLIPS

---

[1] *Valley of the Shadow of Death* See Psalms 23.4.

[2] *MS* Manuscript.

[3] *hide the outcast* See Isaiah 16.3.

CHAPTER I

I was born in Tuckahoe, near Hillsborough, and about twelve miles from Easton, in Talbot county, Maryland. I have no accurate knowledge of my age, never having seen any authentic record containing it. By far the larger part of the slaves know as little of their ages as horses know of theirs, and it is the wish of most masters within my knowledge to keep their slaves thus ignorant. I do not remember to have ever met a slave who could tell of his birthday. They seldom come nearer to it than planting-time, harvest-time, cherry-time, spring-time, or fall-time. A want of information concerning my own was a source of unhappiness to me even during childhood. The white children could tell their ages. I could not tell why I ought to be deprived of the same privilege. I was not allowed to make any inquiries of my master concerning it. He deemed all such inquiries on the part of a slave improper and impertinent, and evidence of a restless spirit. The nearest estimate I can give makes me now between twenty-seven and twenty-eight years of age. I come to this, from hearing my master say, some time during 1835, I was about seventeen years old.[1]

My mother was named Harriet Bailey. She was the daughter of Isaac and Betsey Bailey, both colored, and quite dark. My mother was of a darker complexion than either my grandmother or grandfather.

My father was a white man. He was admitted to be such by all I ever heard speak of my parentage. The opinion was also whispered that my master was my father; but of the correctness of this opinion, I know nothing; the means of knowing was withheld from me. My mother and I were separated when I was but an infant—before I knew her as my mother. It is a common custom, in the part of Maryland from which I ran away, to part children from their mothers at a very early age. Frequently, before the child has reached its twelfth month, its mother is taken from it, and hired out on some farm a considerable distance off, and the child is placed under the care of an old woman, too old for field labor. For what this separation is done, I do not know, unless it be to hinder the development of the child's affection toward its mother, and to blunt and destroy the natural affection of the mother for the child. This is the inevitable result.

I never saw my mother, to know her as such, more than four or five times in my life; and each of these times was very short in duration, and at night. She was hired by a Mr. Stewart,[2] who lived about twelve miles from my home. She made her journeys to see me in the night, travelling the whole distance on foot, after the performance of her day's work. She was a field hand, and a whipping is the penalty of not being in the field at sunrise, unless a slave has special permission from his or her master to the contrary—a permission which they seldom get, and one that gives to him that gives it the proud name of being a kind master. I do not recollect of ever seeing my mother by the light of day. She was with me in the night. She would lie down with me, and get me to sleep, but long before I waked she was gone. Very little communication ever took place between us. Death soon ended what little we could have while she lived, and with it her hardships and suffering. She died when I was about seven years old, on one of my master's farms, near Lee's Mill. I was not allowed to be present during her illness, at her death, or burial. She was gone long before I knew any thing about it. Never having enjoyed, to any considerable extent, her soothing presence, her tender and watchful care, I received the tidings of her death with much the same emotions I should have probably felt at the death of a stranger.

Called thus suddenly away, she left me without the slightest intimation of who my father was. The whisper that my master was my father, may or may not be true; and, true or false, it is of but little consequence to my purpose whilst the fact remains, in all its glaring odiousness, that slaveholders have ordained, and by law established, that the children of slave women shall in all cases follow the condition of their mothers; and this is done too obviously to administer to their own lusts, and make a gratification of their wicked desires profitable as well as pleasurable; for by this cunning arrangement, the slaveholder, in cases not a few, sustains to his slaves the double relation of master and father.

---

[1] *I have no accurate knowledge … years old* Records made available after Douglass's death reveal that he was born in February 1818 (though the exact date remains unknown).

[2] *hired by a Mr. Stewart* I.e., her owner hired her out to a Mr. Stewart; the transaction would not have involved Douglass's mother being paid.

I know of such cases; and it is worthy of remark that such slaves invariably suffer greater hardships, and have more to contend with, than others. They are, in the first place, a constant offence to their mistress. She is ever disposed to find fault with them; they can seldom do anything to please her; she is never better pleased than when she sees them under the lash, especially when she suspects her husband of showing to his mulatto children favors which he withholds from his black slaves. The master is frequently compelled to sell this class of his slaves, out of deference to the feelings of his white wife; and, cruel as the deed may strike anyone to be, for a man to sell his own children to human flesh-mongers, it is often the dictate of humanity for him to do so; for, unless he does this, he must not only whip them himself, but must stand by and see one white son tie up his brother, of but few shades darker complexion than himself, and ply the gory lash to his naked back; and if he lisp one word of disapproval, it is set down to his parental partiality, and only makes a bad matter worse, both for himself and the slave whom he would protect and defend.

Every year brings with it multitudes of this class of slaves. It was doubtless in consequence of a knowledge of this fact, that one great statesman of the south predicted the downfall of slavery by the inevitable laws of population. Whether this prophecy is ever fulfilled or not, it is nevertheless plain that a very different-looking class of people are springing up at the south, and are now held in slavery, from those originally brought to this country from Africa; and if their increase do no other good, it will do away the force of the argument, that God cursed Ham, and therefore American slavery is right.[1] If the lineal descendants of Ham are alone to be scripturally enslaved, it is certain that slavery at the south must soon become unscriptural; for thousands are ushered into the world, annually, who, like myself, owe their existence to white fathers, and those fathers most frequently their own masters.

I have had two masters. My first master's name was Anthony. I do not remember his first name. He was generally called Captain Anthony—a title which, I presume, he acquired by sailing a craft on the Chesapeake Bay. He was not considered a rich slaveholder. He owned two or three farms, and about thirty slaves. His farms and slaves were under the care of an overseer. The overseer's name was Plummer. Mr. Plummer was a miserable drunkard, a profane swearer, and a savage monster. He always went armed with a cowskin[2] and a heavy cudgel. I have known him to cut and slash the women's heads so horribly, that even master would be enraged at his cruelty, and would threaten to whip him if he did not mind himself. Master, however, was not a humane slaveholder. It required extraordinary barbarity on the part of an overseer to affect him. He was a cruel man, hardened by a long life of slaveholding. He would at times seem to take great pleasure in whipping a slave. I have often been awakened at the dawn of day by the most heart-rending shrieks of an own aunt of mine, whom he used to tie up to a joist, and whip upon her naked back till she was literally covered with blood. No words, no tears, no prayers, from his gory victim, seemed to move his iron heart from its bloody purpose. The louder she screamed, the harder he whipped; and where the blood ran fastest, there he whipped longest. He would whip her to make her scream, and whip her to make her hush; and not until overcome by fatigue, would he cease to swing the blood-clotted cowskin. I remember the first time I ever witnessed this horrible exhibition. I was quite a child, but I well remember it. I never shall forget it whilst I remember anything. It was the first of a long series of such outrages, of which I was doomed to be a witness and a participant. It struck me with awful force. It was the blood-stained gate, the entrance to the hell of slavery, through which I was about to pass. It was a most terrible spectacle. I wish I could commit to paper the feelings with which I beheld it.

This occurrence took place very soon after I went to live with my old master, and under the following circumstances. Aunt Hester went out one night—where or for what I do not know—and happened to be absent when my master desired her presence. He had ordered her not to go out evenings, and warned her that she must never let him catch her in company with a young man, who was paying attention to her, belonging to Colonel Lloyd. The young man's name was Ned

---

[1]   *God cursed Ham ... is right*   Some proslavery apologists claimed that a biblical justification for slavery could be found in Genesis 9.25, in which God curses Canaan, the son of Ham, declaring that "a servant of servants shall he be unto his brethren."

[2]   *cowskin*   Whip made from cowhide.

Roberts, generally called Lloyd's Ned. Why master was so careful of her, may be safely left to conjecture. She was a woman of noble form, and of graceful proportions, having very few equals, and fewer superiors, in personal appearance, among the colored or white women of our neighborhood.

Aunt Hester had not only disobeyed his orders in going out, but had been found in company with Lloyd's Ned; which circumstance, I found, from what he said while whipping her, was the chief offence. Had he been a man of pure morals himself, he might have been thought interested in protecting the innocence of my aunt; but those who knew him will not suspect him of any such virtue. Before he commenced whipping Aunt Hester, he took her into the kitchen, and stripped her from neck to waist, leaving her neck, shoulders, and back, entirely naked. He then told her to cross her hands, calling her at the same time a d——d b——h. After crossing her hands, he tied them with a strong rope, and led her to a stool under a large hook in the joist, put in for the purpose. He made her get upon the stool, and tied her hands to the hook. She now stood fair for his infernal purpose. Her arms were stretched up at their full length, so that she stood upon the ends of her toes. He then said to her, "Now, you d——d b——h, I'll learn[1] you how to disobey my orders!" and after rolling up his sleeves, he commenced to lay on the heavy cowskin, and soon the warm, red blood (amid heart-rending shrieks from her, and horrid oaths from him) came dripping to the floor. I was so terrified and horror-stricken at the sight, that I hid myself in a closet, and dared not venture out till long after the bloody transaction was over. I expected it would be my turn next. It was all new to me. I had never seen anything like it before. I had always lived with my grandmother on the outskirts of the plantation, where she was put to raise the children of the younger women. I had therefore been, until now, out of the way of the bloody scenes that often occurred on the plantation.

CHAPTER 2

My master's family consisted of two sons, Andrew and Richard; one daughter, Lucretia, and her husband, Captain Thomas Auld. They lived in one house, upon the home plantation of Colonel Edward Lloyd. My master was Colonel Lloyd's clerk and superintendent. He was what might be called the overseer of the overseers. I spent two years of childhood on this plantation in my old master's family. It was here that I witnessed the bloody transaction recorded in the first chapter; and as I received my first impressions of slavery on this plantation, I will give some description of it, and of slavery as it there existed. The plantation is about twelve miles north of Easton, in Talbot county, and is situated on the border of Miles River. The principal products raised upon it were tobacco, corn, and wheat. These were raised in great abundance; so that, with the products of this and the other farms belonging to him, he was able to keep in almost constant employment a large sloop,[2] in carrying them to market at Baltimore. This sloop was named Sally Lloyd, in honor of one of the colonel's daughters. My master's son-in-law, Captain Auld, was master of the vessel; she was otherwise manned by the colonel's own slaves. Their names were Peter, Isaac, Rich, and Jake. These were esteemed very highly by the other slaves, and looked upon as the privileged ones of the plantation; for it was no small affair, in the eyes of the slaves, to be allowed to see Baltimore.

Colonel Lloyd kept from three to four hundred slaves on his home plantation, and owned a large number more on the neighboring farms belonging to him. The names of the farms nearest to the home plantation were Wye Town and New Design. "Wye Town" was under the overseership of a man named Noah Willis. New Design was under the overseership of a Mr. Townsend. The overseers of these, and all the rest of the farms, numbering over twenty, received advice and direction from the managers of the home plantation. This was the great business place. It was the seat of government for the whole twenty farms. All disputes among the overseers were settled here. If a slave was convicted of any high misdemeanor, became unmanageable, or evinced a determination to run away, he was brought immediately here, severely whipped, put on board the sloop, carried to Baltimore, and sold to Austin Woolfolk, or some other slave-trader, as a warning to the slaves remaining.

---

[1]   *learn*   Teach.

[2]   *sloop*   Small, single-masted sailing vessel.

Here, too, the slaves of all the other farms received their monthly allowance of food, and their yearly clothing. The men and women slaves received, as their monthly allowance of food, eight pounds of pork, or its equivalent in fish, and one bushel of corn meal. Their yearly clothing consisted of two coarse linen shirts, one pair of linen trousers, like the shirts, one jacket, one pair of trousers for winter, made of coarse negro cloth,[1] one pair of stockings, and one pair of shoes; the whole of which could not have cost more than seven dollars. The allowance of the slave children was given to their mothers, or the old women having the care of them. The children unable to work in the field had neither shoes, stockings, jackets, nor trousers, given to them; their clothing consisted of two coarse linen shirts per year. When these failed them, they went naked until the next allowance-day. Children from seven to ten years old, of both sexes, almost naked, might be seen at all seasons of the year.

There were no beds given the slaves, unless one coarse blanket be considered such, and none but the men and women had these. This, however, is not considered a very great privation. They find less difficulty from the want of beds, than from the want of time to sleep; for when their day's work in the field is done, the most of them having their washing, mending, and cooking to do, and having few or none of the ordinary facilities for doing either of these, very many of their sleeping hours are consumed in preparing for the field the coming day; and when this is done, old and young, male and female, married and single, drop down side by side, on one common bed—the cold, damp floor—each covering himself or herself with their miserable blankets; and here they sleep till they are summoned to the field by the driver's horn. At the sound of this, all must rise, and be off to the field. There must be no halting; everyone must be at his or her post; and woe betides them who hear not this morning summons to the field; for if they are not awakened by the sense of hearing, they are by the sense of feeling: no age nor sex finds any favor. Mr. Severe, the overseer, used to stand by the door of the quarter, armed with a large hickory stick[2] and heavy cowskin, ready to whip anyone who

was so unfortunate as not to hear, or, from any other cause, was prevented from being ready to start for the field at the sound of the horn.

Mr. Severe was rightly named: he was a cruel man. I have seen him whip a woman, causing the blood to run half an hour at the time; and this, too, in the midst of her crying children, pleading for their mother's release. He seemed to take pleasure in manifesting his fiendish barbarity. Added to his cruelty, he was a profane swearer. It was enough to chill the blood and stiffen the hair of an ordinary man to hear him talk. Scarce a sentence escaped him but that was commenced or concluded by some horrid oath. The field was the place to witness his cruelty and profanity. His presence made it both the field of blood and of blasphemy. From the rising till the going down of the sun, he was cursing, raving, cutting, and slashing among the slaves of the field, in the most frightful manner. His career was short. He died very soon after I went to Colonel Lloyd's; and he died as he lived, uttering, with his dying groans, bitter curses and horrid oaths. His death was regarded by the slaves as the result of a merciful providence.

Mr. Severe's place was filled by a Mr. Hopkins. He was a very different man. He was less cruel, less profane, and made less noise, than Mr. Severe. His course was characterized by no extraordinary demonstrations of cruelty. He whipped, but seemed to take no pleasure in it. He was called by the slaves a good overseer.

The home plantation of Colonel Lloyd wore the appearance of a country village. All the mechanical operations for all the farms were performed here. The shoemaking and mending, the blacksmithing, cartwrighting, coopering,[3] weaving, and grain-grinding, were all performed by the slaves on the home plantation. The whole place wore a business-like aspect very unlike the neighboring farms. The number of houses, too, conspired to give it advantage over the neighboring farms. It was called by the slaves the Great House Farm. Few privileges were esteemed higher, by the slaves of the out-farms, than that of being selected to do errands at the Great House Farm. It was associated in their minds with greatness. A representative could not be prouder of his election to a seat in the American Congress, than a slave on one of the out-farms would

---

[1]   *negro cloth*   General term referring to the poor-quality fabric used to make clothing for enslaved people.

[2]   *hickory stick*   Made from the tough wood of the hickory tree.

[3]   *cartwrighting* Carpentry; *coopering* Making of wooden casks, barrels, and other vessels for storing goods.

be of his election to do errands at the Great House Farm. They regarded it as evidence of great confidence reposed in them by their overseers; and it was on this account, as well as a constant desire to be out of the field from under the driver's lash, that they esteemed it a high privilege, one worth careful living for. He was called the smartest and most trusty fellow, who had this honor conferred upon him the most frequently. The competitors for this office sought as diligently to please their overseers, as the office-seekers in the political parties seek to please and deceive the people. The same traits of character might be seen in Colonel Lloyd's slaves, as are seen in the slaves of the political parties.

The slaves selected to go to the Great House Farm, for the monthly allowance for themselves and their fellow-slaves, were peculiarly enthusiastic. While on their way, they would make the dense old woods, for miles around, reverberate with their wild songs, revealing at once the highest joy and the deepest sadness. They would compose and sing as they went along, consulting neither time nor tune. The thought that came up, came out—if not in the word, in the sound; and as frequently in the one as in the other. They would sometimes sing the most pathetic sentiment in the most rapturous tone, and the most rapturous sentiment in the most pathetic tone. Into all of their songs they would manage to weave something of the Great House Farm. Especially would they do this, when leaving home. They would then sing most exultingly the following words:

"I am going away to the Great House Farm!
O, yea! O, yea! O!"

This they would sing, as a chorus, to words which to many would seem unmeaning jargon, but which, nevertheless, were full of meaning to themselves. I have sometimes thought that the mere hearing of those songs would do more to impress some minds with the horrible character of slavery, than the reading of whole volumes of philosophy on the subject could do.

I did not, when a slave, understand the deep meaning of those rude and apparently incoherent songs. I was myself within the circle; so that I neither saw nor heard as those without might see and hear. They told

a tale of woe which was then altogether beyond my feeble comprehension; they were tones loud, long, and deep; they breathed the prayer and complaint of souls boiling over with the bitterest anguish. Every tone was a testimony against slavery, and a prayer to God for deliverance from chains. The hearing of those wild notes always depressed my spirit, and filled me with ineffable sadness. I have frequently found myself in tears while hearing them. The mere recurrence to those songs, even now, afflicts me; and while I am writing these lines, an expression of feeling has already found its way down my cheek. To those songs I trace my first glimmering conception of the dehumanizing character of slavery. I can never get rid of that conception. Those songs still follow me, to deepen my hatred of slavery, and quicken my sympathies for my brethren in bonds. If any one wishes to be impressed with the soul-killing effects of slavery, let him go to Colonel Lloyd's plantation, and, on allowance-day, place himself in the deep pine woods, and there let him, in silence, analyze the sounds that shall pass through the chambers of his soul—and if he is not thus impressed, it will only be because "there is no flesh in his obdurate heart."[1]

I have often been utterly astonished, since I came to the north, to find persons who could speak of the singing, among slaves, as evidence of their contentment and happiness. It is impossible to conceive of a greater mistake. Slaves sing most when they are most unhappy. The songs of the slave represent the sorrows of his heart; and he is relieved by them, only as an aching heart is relieved by its tears. At least, such is my experience. I have often sung to drown my sorrow, but seldom to express my happiness. Crying for joy,

---

[1]   *there is … obdurate heart*   Douglass is quoting from an approximately 50-line passage dealing with slavery (sometimes printed as if it were a separate poem, and given the title "Slavery") that appears in Book 2 of English poet William Cowper's long poem *The Task* (1785). It reads in part as follows:

> My soul is sick, with every day's report
> Of wrong and outrage with which earth is filled·
> There is no flesh in man's obdurate heart…;
> He finds his fellow guilty of a skin
> Not colored like his own[.] …

In America as well as in Britain, editions of Cowper's poetic works remained very widely read well into the second half of the nineteenth century, often outselling poets such as Milton and Wordsworth; it is likely that many of Douglass's readers would have been familiar with this quotation.

and singing for joy, were alike uncommon to me while in the jaws of slavery. The singing of a man cast away upon a desolate island might be as appropriately considered as evidence of contentment and happiness, as the singing of a slave; the songs of the one and of the other are prompted by the same emotion.

CHAPTER 3

Colonel Lloyd kept a large and finely cultivated garden, which afforded almost constant employment for four men, besides the chief gardener, (Mr. M'Durmond). This garden was probably the greatest attraction of the place. During the summer months, people came from far and near—from Baltimore, Easton, and Annapolis—to see it. It abounded in fruits of almost every description, from the hardy apple of the north to the delicate orange of the south. This garden was not the least source of trouble on the plantation. Its excellent fruit was quite a temptation to the hungry swarms of boys, as well as the older slaves, belonging to the colonel, few of whom had the virtue or the vice to resist it. Scarcely a day passed, during the summer, but that some slave had to take the lash for stealing fruit. The colonel had to resort to all kinds of stratagems to keep his slaves out of the garden. The last and most successful one was that of tarring his fence all around; after which, if a slave was caught with any tar upon his person, it was deemed sufficient proof that he had either been into the garden, or had tried to get in. In either case, he was severely whipped by the chief gardener. This plan worked well; the slaves became as fearful of tar as of the lash. They seemed to realize the impossibility of touching tar without being defiled.

The colonel also kept a splendid riding equipage. His stable and carriage-house presented the appearance of some of our large city livery[1] establishments. His horses were of the finest form and noblest blood. His carriage-house contained three splendid coaches, three or four gigs, besides dearborns and barouches[2] of the most fashionable style.

This establishment was under the care of two slaves—old Barney and young Barney—father and son. To attend to this establishment was their sole work. But it was by no means an easy employment; for in nothing was Colonel Lloyd more particular than in the management of his horses. The slightest inattention to these was unpardonable, and was visited upon those, under whose care they were placed, with the severest punishment; no excuse could shield them, if the colonel only suspected any want of attention to his horses—a supposition which he frequently indulged, and one which, of course, made the office of old and young Barney a very trying one. They never knew when they were safe from punishment. They were frequently whipped when least deserving, and escaped whipping when most deserving it. Every thing depended upon the looks of the horses, and the state of Colonel Lloyd's own mind when his horses were brought to him for use. If a horse did not move fast enough, or hold his head high enough, it was owing to some fault of his keepers. It was painful to stand near the stable-door, and hear the various complaints against the keepers when a horse was taken out for use. "This horse has not had proper attention. He has not been sufficiently rubbed and curried, or he has not been properly fed; his food was too wet or too dry; he got it too soon or too late; he was too hot or too cold; he had too much hay, and not enough of grain; or he had too much grain, and not enough of hay; instead of old Barney's attending to the horse, he had very improperly left it to his son." To all these complaints, no matter how unjust, the slave must answer never a word. Colonel Lloyd could not brook any contradiction from a slave. When he spoke, a slave must stand, listen, and tremble; and such was literally the case. I have seen Colonel Lloyd make old Barney, a man between fifty and sixty years of age, uncover his bald head, kneel down upon the cold, damp ground, and receive upon his naked and toil-worn shoulders more than thirty lashes at the time. Colonel Lloyd had three sons—Edward, Murray, and Daniel—and three sons-in-law, Mr. Winder, Mr. Nicholson, and Mr. Lowndes. All of these lived at the Great House Farm, and enjoyed the luxury of whipping the servants when they pleased, from old Barney down to William Wilkes, the coach-driver. I have seen Winder make one of the house-servants stand off from

---

[1] *livery* Stable.

[2] *gigs* Light two-wheeled, one-horse carriages; *dearborns* Light four-wheeled carriages; *barouches* Heavier, four-wheeled carriages, considered quite luxurious.

him a suitable distance to be touched with the end of his whip, and at every stroke raise great ridges upon his back.

To describe the wealth of Colonel Lloyd would be almost equal to describing the riches of Job.[1] He kept from ten to fifteen house-servants. He was said to own a thousand slaves, and I think this estimate quite within the truth. Colonel Lloyd owned so many that he did not know them when he saw them; nor did all the slaves of the out-farms know him. It is reported of him, that, while riding along the road one day, he met a colored man, and addressed him in the usual manner of speaking to colored people on the public highways of the south: "Well, boy, whom do you belong to?" "To Colonel Lloyd," replied the slave. "Well, does the colonel treat you well?" "No, sir," was the ready reply. "What, does he work you too hard?" "Yes, sir." "Well, don't he give you enough to eat?" "Yes, sir, he gives me enough, such as it is."

The colonel, after ascertaining where the slave belonged, rode on; the man also went on about his business, not dreaming that he had been conversing with his master. He thought, said, and heard nothing more of the matter, until two or three weeks afterwards. The poor man was then informed by his overseer that, for having found fault with his master, he was now to be sold to a Georgia trader. He was immediately chained and handcuffed; and thus, without a moment's warning, he was snatched away, and forever sundered, from his family and friends, by a hand more unrelenting than death. This is the penalty of telling the truth, of telling the simple truth, in answer to a series of plain questions.

It is partly in consequence of such facts, that slaves, when inquired of as to their condition and the character of their masters, almost universally say they are contented, and that their masters are kind. The slaveholders have been known to send in spies among their slaves, to ascertain their views and feelings in regard to their condition. The frequency of this has had the effect to establish among the slaves the maxim, that a still tongue makes a wise head. They suppress the truth rather than take the consequences of telling it, and in

so doing prove themselves a part of the human family. If they have anything to say of their masters, it is generally in their masters' favor, especially when speaking to an untried man. I have been frequently asked, when a slave, if I had a kind master, and do not remember ever to have given a negative answer; nor did I, in pursuing this course, consider myself as uttering what was absolutely false; for I always measured the kindness of my master by the standard of kindness set up among slaveholders around us. Moreover, slaves are like other people, and imbibe prejudices quite common to others. They think their own better than that of others. Many, under the influence of this prejudice, think their own masters are better than the masters of other slaves; and this, too, in some cases, when the very reverse is true. Indeed, it is not uncommon for slaves even to fall out and quarrel among themselves about the relative goodness of their masters, each contending for the superior goodness of his own over that of the others. At the very same time, they mutually execrate their masters when viewed separately. It was so on our plantation. When Colonel Lloyd's slaves met the slaves of Jacob Jepson, they seldom parted without a quarrel about their masters; Colonel Lloyd's slaves contending that he was the richest, and Mr. Jepson's slaves that he was the smartest, and most of a man. Colonel Lloyd's slaves would boast his ability to buy and sell Jacob Jepson. Mr. Jepson's slaves would boast his ability to whip Colonel Lloyd. These quarrels would almost always end in a fight between the parties, and those that whipped were supposed to have gained the point at issue. They seemed to think that the greatness of their masters was transferable to themselves. It was considered as being bad enough to be a slave; but to be a poor man's slave was deemed a disgrace indeed!

Chapter 4

Mr. Hopkins remained but a short time in the office of overseer. Why his career was so short, I do not know, but suppose he lacked the necessary severity to suit Colonel Lloyd. Mr. Hopkins was succeeded by Mr. Austin Gore, a man possessing, in an eminent degree, all those traits of character indispensable to what is called a first-rate overseer. Mr. Gore had served Colonel Lloyd, in the capacity of overseer, upon one of

---

[1]　*riches of Job*　The biblical figure Job is best known for the brutal test of faith he is put under by God, but prior to these events he is described as wealthy and prosperous.

the out-farms, and had shown himself worthy of the high station of overseer upon the home or Great House Farm.

Mr. Gore was proud, ambitious, and persevering. He was artful, cruel, and obdurate. He was just the man for such a place, and it was just the place for such a man. It afforded scope for the full exercise of all his powers, and he seemed to be perfectly at home in it. He was one of those who could torture the slightest look, word, or gesture, on the part of the slave, into impudence, and would treat it accordingly. There must be no answering back to him; no explanation was allowed a slave, showing himself to have been wrongfully accused. Mr. Gore acted fully up to the maxim laid down by slaveholders, "It is better that a dozen slaves should suffer under the lash, than that the overseer should be convicted, in the presence of the slaves, of having been at fault." No matter how innocent a slave might be—it availed him nothing, when accused by Mr. Gore of any misdemeanor. To be accused was to be convicted, and to be convicted was to be punished; the one always following the other with immutable certainty. To escape punishment was to escape accusation; and few slaves had the fortune to do either, under the overseership of Mr. Gore. He was just proud enough to demand the most debasing homage of the slave, and quite servile enough to crouch, himself, at the feet of the master. He was ambitious enough to be contented with nothing short of the highest rank of overseers, and persevering enough to reach the height of his ambition. He was cruel enough to inflict the severest punishment, artful enough to descend to the lowest trickery, and obdurate enough to be insensible to the voice of a reproving conscience. He was, of all the overseers, the most dreaded by the slaves. His presence was painful; his eye flashed confusion; and seldom was his sharp, shrill voice heard, without producing horror and trembling in their ranks.

Mr. Gore was a grave man, and, though a young man, he indulged in no jokes, said no funny words, seldom smiled. His words were in perfect keeping with his looks, and his looks were in perfect keeping with his words. Overseers will sometimes indulge in a witty word, even with the slaves; not so with Mr. Gore. He spoke but to command, and commanded but to be obeyed; he dealt sparingly with his words, and bountifully with his whip, never using the former where the latter would answer as well. When he whipped, he seemed to do so from a sense of duty, and feared no consequences. He did nothing reluctantly, no matter how disagreeable; always at his post, never inconsistent. He never promised but to fulfil. He was, in a word, a man of the most inflexible firmness and stone-like coolness.

His savage barbarity was equalled only by the consummate coolness with which he committed the grossest and most savage deeds upon the slaves under his charge. Mr. Gore once undertook to whip one of Colonel Lloyd's slaves, by the name of Demby. He had given Demby but few stripes,[1] when, to get rid of the scourging, he ran and plunged himself into a creek, and stood there at the depth of his shoulders, refusing to come out. Mr. Gore told him that he would give him three calls, and that, if he did not come out at the third call, he would shoot him. The first call was given. Demby made no response, but stood his ground. The second and third calls were given with the same result. Mr. Gore then, without consultation or deliberation with anyone, not even giving Demby an additional call, raised his musket to his face, taking deadly aim at his standing victim, and in an instant poor Demby was no more. His mangled body sank out of sight, and blood and brains marked the water where he had stood.

A thrill of horror flashed through every soul upon the plantation, excepting Mr. Gore. He alone seemed cool and collected. He was asked by Colonel Lloyd and my old master, why he resorted to this extraordinary expedient. His reply was (as well as I can remember) that Demby had become unmanageable. He was setting a dangerous example to the other slaves—one which, if suffered to pass without some such demonstration on his part, would finally lead to the total subversion of all rule and order upon the plantation. He argued that if one slave refused to be corrected, and escaped with his life, the other slaves would soon copy the example; the result of which would be, the freedom of the slaves, and the enslavement of the whites. Mr. Gore's defence was satisfactory. He was continued in his station as overseer upon the home plantation. His fame as an overseer went abroad. His horrid crime was not even submitted to judicial investigation. It was

---

[1] *stripes* I.e., lash-marks.

committed in the presence of slaves, and they of course could neither institute a suit, nor testify against him; and thus the guilty perpetrator of one of the bloodiest and most foul murders goes unwhipped of justice, and uncensured by the community in which he lives. Mr. Gore lived in St. Michael's, Talbot county, Maryland, when I left there; and if he is still alive, he very probably lives there now; and if so, he is now, as he was then, as highly esteemed and as much respected as though his guilty soul had not been stained with his brother's blood.

I speak advisedly when I say this—that killing a slave, or any colored person, in Talbot county, Maryland, is not treated as a crime, either by the courts or the community. Mr. Thomas Lanman, of St. Michael's, killed two slaves, one of whom he killed with a hatchet, by knocking his brains out. He used to boast of the commission of the awful and bloody deed. I have heard him do so laughingly, saying, among other things, that he was the only benefactor of his country in the company, and that when others would do as much as he had done, we should be relieved of "the d——d niggers."

The wife of Mr. Giles Hicks, living but a short distance from where I used to live, murdered my wife's cousin, a young girl between fifteen and sixteen years of age, mangling her person in the most horrible manner, breaking her nose and breastbone with a stick, so that the poor girl expired in a few hours afterward. She was immediately buried, but had not been in her untimely grave but a few hours before she was taken up and examined by the coroner, who decided that she had come to her death by severe beating. The offence for which this girl was thus murdered was this: She had been set that night to mind Mrs. Hicks's baby, and during the night she fell asleep, and the baby cried. She, having lost her rest for several nights previous, did not hear the crying. They were both in the room with Mrs. Hicks. Mrs. Hicks, finding the girl slow to move, jumped from her bed, seized an oak stick of wood by the fireplace, and with it broke the girl's nose and breastbone, and thus ended her life. I will not say that this most horrid murder produced no sensation in the community. It did produce sensation, but not enough to bring the murderess to punishment. There was a warrant issued for her arrest, but it was never served.

Thus she escaped not only punishment, but even the pain of being arraigned before a court for her horrid crime.

Whilst I am detailing bloody deeds which took place during my stay on Colonel Lloyd's plantation, I will briefly narrate another, which occurred about the same time as the murder of Demby by Mr. Gore.

Colonel Lloyd's slaves were in the habit of spending a part of their nights and Sundays in fishing for oysters, and in this way made up the deficiency of their scanty allowance. An old man belonging to Colonel Lloyd, while thus engaged, happened to get beyond the limits of Colonel Lloyd's, and on the premises of Mr. Beal Bondly. At this trespass, Mr. Bondly took offence, and with his musket came down to the shore, and blew its deadly contents into the poor old man.

Mr. Bondly came over to see Colonel Lloyd the next day, whether to pay him for his property, or to justify himself in what he had done, I know not. At any rate, this whole fiendish transaction was soon hushed up. There was very little said about it at all, and nothing done. It was a common saying, even among little white boys, that it was worth a half-cent to kill a "nigger," and a half-cent to bury one.

CHAPTER 5

As to my own treatment while I lived on Colonel Lloyd's plantation, it was very similar to that of the other slave children. I was not old enough to work in the field, and there being little else than field work to do, I had a great deal of leisure time. The most I had to do was to drive up the cows at evening, keep the fowls out of the garden, keep the front yard clean, and run of errands for my old master's daughter, Mrs. Lucretia Auld. The most of my leisure time I spent in helping Master Daniel Lloyd in finding his birds, after he had shot them. My connection with Master Daniel was of some advantage to me. He became quite attached to me, and was a sort of protector of me. He would not allow the older boys to impose upon me, and would divide his cakes with me.

I was seldom whipped by my old master, and suffered little from anything else than hunger and cold. I suffered much from hunger, but much more from cold. In hottest summer and coldest winter, I was kept almost naked—no shoes, no stockings, no jacket, no trousers, nothing on but a coarse tow linen[1] shirt, reaching only to my knees. I had no bed. I must have perished with cold, but that, the coldest nights, I used to steal a bag which was used for carrying corn to the mill. I would crawl into this bag, and there sleep on the cold, damp, clay floor, with my head in and feet out. My feet have been so cracked with the frost, that the pen with which I am writing might be laid in the gashes.

We were not regularly allowanced. Our food was coarse corn meal boiled. This was called mush. It was put into a large wooden tray or trough, and set down upon the ground. The children were then called, like so many pigs, and like so many pigs they would come and devour the mush; some with oyster-shells, others with pieces of shingle, some with naked hands, and none with spoons. He that ate fastest got most; he that was strongest secured the best place; and few left the trough satisfied.

I was probably between seven and eight years old when I left Colonel Lloyd's plantation. I left it with joy. I shall never forget the ecstasy with which I received the intelligence that my old master (Anthony) had determined to let me go to Baltimore, to live with Mr. Hugh Auld, brother to my old master's son-in-law, Captain Thomas Auld. I received this information about three days before my departure. They were three of the happiest days I ever enjoyed. I spent the most part of all these three days in the creek, washing off the plantation scurf, and preparing myself for my departure.

The pride of appearance which this would indicate was not my own. I spent the time in washing, not so much because I wished to, but because Mrs. Lucretia had told me I must get all the dead skin off my feet and knees before I could go to Baltimore; for the people in Baltimore were very cleanly, and would laugh at me if I looked dirty. Besides, she was going to give me a pair of trousers, which I should not put on unless I got all the dirt off me. The thought of owning a pair of trousers was great indeed! It was almost a sufficient motive, not only to make me take off what would be called by pig-drovers the mange, but the skin itself. I went at it in good earnest, working for the first time with the hope of reward.

The ties that ordinarily bind children to their homes were all suspended in my case. I found no severe trial in my departure. My home was charmless; it was not home to me; on parting from it, I could not feel that I was leaving anything which I could have enjoyed by staying. My mother was dead, my grandmother lived far off, so that I seldom saw her. I had two sisters and one brother, that lived in the same house with me; but the early separation of us from our mother had well nigh blotted the fact of our relationship from our memories. I looked for home elsewhere, and was confident of finding none which I should relish less than the one which I was leaving. If, however, I found in my new home hardship, hunger, whipping, and nakedness, I had the consolation that I should not have escaped any one of them by staying. Having already had more than a taste of them in the house of my old master, and having endured them there, I very naturally inferred my ability to endure them elsewhere, and especially at Baltimore; for I had something of the feeling about Baltimore that is expressed in the proverb, that "being hanged in England is preferable to dying a natural death in Ireland." I had the strongest desire to see Baltimore. Cousin Tom, though not fluent in speech, had inspired me with that desire by his eloquent description of the place. I could never point out anything at the Great House, no matter how beautiful or powerful, but that he had seen something at Baltimore far exceeding, both in beauty and strength, the object which I pointed out to him. Even the Great House itself, with all its pictures, was far inferior to many buildings in Baltimore. So strong was my desire, that I thought a gratification of it would fully compensate for whatever loss of comforts I should sustain by the exchange. I left without a regret, and with the highest hopes of future happiness.

We sailed out of Miles River for Baltimore on a Saturday morning. I remember only the day of the week, for at that time I had no knowledge of the days of the month, nor the months of the year. On setting sail, I walked aft, and gave to Colonel Lloyd's plantation what I hoped would be the last look. I then placed myself in the bows of the sloop, and there spent the remainder of the day in looking ahead, interesting myself in what was in the distance rather than in things near by or behind.

---

[1]   *tow linen* Material made from shorter, unworked strands of flax fibers, resulting in a coarser cloth than regular linen.

In the afternoon of that day, we reached Annapolis, the capital of the State. We stopped but a few moments, so that I had no time to go on shore. It was the first large town that I had ever seen, and though it would look small compared with some of our New England factory villages, I thought it a wonderful place for its size—more imposing even than the Great House Farm!

We arrived at Baltimore early on Sunday morning, landing at Smith's Wharf, not far from Bowley's Wharf. We had on board the sloop a large flock of sheep; and after aiding in driving them to the slaughterhouse of Mr. Curtis on Louden Slater's Hill, I was conducted by Rich, one of the hands belonging on board of the sloop, to my new home in Alliciana Street, near Mr. Gardner's shipyard, on Fells Point.

Mr. and Mrs. Auld were both at home, and met me at the door with their little son Thomas, to take care of whom I had been given. And here I saw what I had never seen before; it was a white face beaming with the most kindly emotions; it was the face of my new mistress, Sophia Auld. I wish I could describe the rapture that flashed through my soul as I beheld it. It was a new and strange sight to me, brightening up my pathway with the light of happiness. Little Thomas was told, there was his Freddy—and I was told to take care of little Thomas; and thus I entered upon the duties of my new home with the most cheering prospect ahead.

I look upon my departure from Colonel Lloyd's plantation as one of the most interesting events of my life. It is possible, and even quite probable, that but for the mere circumstance of being removed from that plantation to Baltimore, I should have today, instead of being here seated by my own table, in the enjoyment of freedom and the happiness of home, writing this Narrative, been confined in the galling chains of slavery. Going to live at Baltimore laid the foundation, and opened the gateway, to all my subsequent prosperity. I have ever regarded it as the first plain manifestation of that kind providence which has ever since attended me, and marked my life with so many favors. I regarded the selection of myself as being somewhat remarkable. There were a number of slave children that might have been sent from the plantation to Baltimore. There were those younger, those older, and those of the same age. I was chosen from among them all, and was the first, last, and only choice.

I may be deemed superstitious, and even egotistical, in regarding this event as a special interposition of divine Providence in my favor. But I should be false to the earliest sentiments of my soul, if I suppressed the opinion. I prefer to be true to myself, even at the hazard of incurring the ridicule of others, rather than to be false, and incur my own abhorrence. From my earliest recollection, I date the entertainment of a deep conviction that slavery would not always be able to hold me within its foul embrace; and in the darkest hours of my career in slavery, this living word of faith and spirit of hope departed not from me, but remained like ministering angels to cheer me through the gloom. This good spirit was from God, and to him I offer thanksgiving and praise.

CHAPTER 6

My new mistress proved to be all she appeared when I first met her at the door—a woman of the kindest heart and finest feelings. She had never had a slave under her control previously to myself, and prior to her marriage she had been dependent upon her own industry for a living. She was by trade a weaver; and by constant application to her business, she had been in a good degree preserved from the blighting and dehumanizing effects of slavery. I was utterly astonished at her goodness. I scarcely knew how to behave towards her. She was entirely unlike any other white woman I had ever seen. I could not approach her as I was accustomed to approach other white ladies. My early instruction was all out of place. The crouching servility, usually so acceptable a quality in a slave, did not answer when manifested toward her. Her favor was not gained by it; she seemed to be disturbed by it. She did not deem it impudent or unmannerly for a slave to look her in the face. The meanest slave was put fully at ease in her presence, and none left without feeling better for having seen her. Her face was made of heavenly smiles, and her voice of tranquil music.

But, alas! this kind heart had but a short time to remain such. The fatal poison of irresponsible power was already in her hands, and soon commenced its infernal work. That cheerful eye, under the influence of slavery, soon became red with rage; that voice, made all of sweet accord, changed to one of harsh and horrid discord; and that angelic face gave place to that of a demon.

Very soon after I went to live with Mr. and Mrs. Auld, she very kindly commenced to teach me the A, B, C. After I had learned this, she assisted me in learning to spell words of three or four letters. Just at this point of my progress, Mr. Auld found out what was going on, and at once forbade Mrs. Auld to instruct me further, telling her, among other things, that it was unlawful, as well as unsafe, to teach a slave to read. To use his own words, further, he said, "If you give a nigger an inch, he will take an ell.[1] A nigger should know nothing but to obey his master—to do as he is told to do. Learning would spoil the best nigger in the world. Now," said he, "if you teach that nigger (speaking of myself) how to read, there would be no keeping him. It would forever unfit him to be a slave. He would at once become unmanageable, and of no value to his master. As to himself, it could do him no good, but a great deal of harm. It would make him discontented and unhappy." These words sank deep into my heart, stirred up sentiments within that lay slumbering, and called into existence an entirely new train of thought. It was a new and special revelation, explaining dark and mysterious things, with which my youthful understanding had struggled, but struggled in vain. I now understood what had been to me a most perplexing difficulty—to wit, the white man's power to enslave the black man. It was a grand achievement, and I prized it highly. From that moment, I understood the pathway from slavery to freedom. It was just what I wanted, and I got it at a time when I the least expected it. Whilst I was saddened by the thought of losing the aid of my kind mistress, I was gladdened by the invaluable instruction which, by the merest accident, I had gained from my master. Though conscious of the difficulty of learning without a teacher, I set out with high hope, and a fixed purpose, at whatever cost of trouble, to learn how to read. The very decided manner with which he spoke, and strove to impress his wife with the evil consequences of giving me instruction, served to convince me that he was deeply sensible of the truths he was uttering. It gave me the best assurance that I might rely with the utmost confidence on the results which, he said, would flow from teaching me to read.

What he most dreaded, that I most desired. What he most loved, that I most hated. That which to him was a great evil, to be carefully shunned, was to me a great good, to be diligently sought; and the argument which he so warmly urged, against my learning to read, only served to inspire me with a desire and determination to learn. In learning to read, I owe almost as much to the bitter opposition of my master, as to the kindly aid of my mistress. I acknowledge the benefit of both.

I had resided but a short time in Baltimore before I observed a marked difference, in the treatment of slaves, from that which I had witnessed in the country. A city slave is almost a freeman, compared with a slave on the plantation. He is much better fed and clothed, and enjoys privileges altogether unknown to the slave on the plantation. There is a vestige of decency, a sense of shame, that does much to curb and check those outbreaks of atrocious cruelty so commonly enacted upon the plantation. He is a desperate slaveholder, who will shock the humanity of his non-slaveholding neighbors with the cries of his lacerated slave. Few are willing to incur the odium attaching to the reputation of being a cruel master; and above all things, they would not be known as not giving a slave enough to eat. Every city slaveholder is anxious to have it known of him, that he feeds his slaves well; and it is due to them to say, that most of them do give their slaves enough to eat. There are, however, some painful exceptions to this rule. Directly opposite to us, on Philpot Street, lived Mr. Thomas Hamilton. He owned two slaves. Their names were Henrietta and Mary. Henrietta was about twenty-two years of age, Mary was about fourteen; and of all the mangled and emaciated creatures I ever looked upon, these two were the most so. His heart must be harder than stone, that could look upon these unmoved. The head, neck, and shoulders of Mary were literally cut to pieces. I have frequently felt her head, and found it nearly covered with festering sores, caused by the lash of her cruel mistress. I do not know that her master ever whipped her, but I have been an eye-witness to the cruelty of Mrs. Hamilton. I used to be in Mr. Hamilton's house nearly every day. Mrs. Hamilton used to sit in a large chair in the middle of the room, with a heavy cowskin always by her side, and scarce an hour passed during the day but was marked by the blood of one of these slaves. The girls seldom

---

[1]   *an ell* Approximately 45 inches.

passed her without her saying, "Move faster, you black gip!" at the same time giving them a blow with the cowskin over the head or shoulders, often drawing the blood. She would then say, "Take that, you black gip!" continuing, "If you don't move faster, I'll move you!" Added to the cruel lashings to which these slaves were subjected, they were kept nearly half-starved. They seldom knew what it was to eat a full meal. I have seen Mary contending with the pigs for the offal thrown into the street. So much was Mary kicked and cut to pieces, that she was oftener called "pecked" than by her name.

Chapter 7

I lived in Master Hugh's family about seven years. During this time, I succeeded in learning to read and write. In accomplishing this, I was compelled to resort to various stratagems. I had no regular teacher. My mistress, who had kindly commenced to instruct me, had, in compliance with the advice and direction of her husband, not only ceased to instruct, but had set her face against my being instructed by anyone else. It is due, however, to my mistress to say of her, that she did not adopt this course of treatment immediately. She at first lacked the depravity indispensable to shutting me up in mental darkness. It was at least necessary for her to have some training in the exercise of irresponsible power, to make her equal to the task of treating me as though I were a brute.

My mistress was, as I have said, a kind and tender-hearted woman; and in the simplicity of her soul she commenced, when I first went to live with her, to treat me as she supposed one human being ought to treat another. In entering upon the duties of a slaveholder, she did not seem to perceive that I sustained to her the relation of a mere chattel, and that for her to treat me as a human being was not only wrong, but dangerously so. Slavery proved as injurious to her as it did to me. When I went there, she was a pious, warm, and tender-hearted woman. There was no sorrow or suffering for which she had not a tear. She had bread for the hungry, clothes for the naked, and comfort for every mourner that came within her reach. Slavery soon proved its ability to divest her of these heavenly qualities. Under its influence, the tender heart became stone, and the

lamblike disposition gave way to one of tiger-like fierceness. The first step in her downward course was in her ceasing to instruct me. She now commenced to practise her husband's precepts. She finally became even more violent in her opposition than her husband himself. She was not satisfied with simply doing as well as he had commanded; she seemed anxious to do better. Nothing seemed to make her more angry than to see me with a newspaper. She seemed to think that here lay the danger. I have had her rush at me with a face made all up of fury, and snatch from me a newspaper, in a manner that fully revealed her apprehension. She was an apt woman; and a little experience soon demonstrated, to her satisfaction, that education and slavery were incompatible with each other.

From this time I was most narrowly[1] watched. If I was in a separate room any considerable length of time, I was sure to be suspected of having a book, and was at once called to give an account of myself. All this, however, was too late. The first step had been taken. Mistress, in teaching me the alphabet, had given me the inch, and no precaution could prevent me from taking the ell.

The plan which I adopted, and the one by which I was most successful, was that of making friends of all the little white boys whom I met in the street. As many of these as I could, I converted into teachers. With their kindly aid, obtained at different times and in different places, I finally succeeded in learning to read. When I was sent of errands, I always took my book with me, and by going one part of my errand quickly, I found time to get a lesson before my return. I used also to carry bread with me, enough of which was always in the house, and to which I was always welcome; for I was much better off in this regard than many of the poor white children in our neighborhood. This bread I used to bestow upon the hungry little urchins, who, in return, would give me that more valuable bread of knowledge. I am strongly tempted to give the names of two or three of those little boys, as a testimonial of the gratitude and affection I bear them; but prudence forbids;—not that it would injure me, but it might embarrass them; for it is almost an unpardonable offence to teach slaves to read in this Christian country. It is enough to say of the dear little fellows, that they

---

1   *narrowly* Closely.

lived on Philpot Street, very near Durgin and Bailey's ship-yard. I used to talk this matter of slavery over with them. I would sometimes say to them, I wished I could be as free as they would be when they got to be men. "You will be free as soon as you are twenty-one, but I am a slave for life! Have not I as good a right to be free as you have?" These words used to trouble them; they would express for me the liveliest sympathy, and console me with the hope that something would occur by which I might be free.

I was now about twelve years old, and the thought of being a slave for life began to bear heavily upon my heart. Just about this time, I got hold of a book entitled "The Columbian Orator."[1] Every opportunity I got, I used to read this book. Among much of other interesting matter, I found in it a dialogue between a master and his slave. The slave was represented as having run away from his master three times. The dialogue represented the conversation which took place between them, when the slave was retaken the third time. In this dialogue, the whole argument in behalf of slavery was brought forward by the master, all of which was disposed of by the slave. The slave was made to say some very smart as well as impressive things in reply to his master—things which had the desired though unexpected effect; for the conversation resulted in the voluntary emancipation of the slave on the part of the master.

In the same book, I met with one of Sheridan's[2] mighty speeches on and in behalf of Catholic emancipation. These were choice documents to me. I read them over and over again with unabated interest. They gave tongue to interesting thoughts of my own soul, which had frequently flashed through my mind, and died away for want of utterance. The moral which I

gained from the dialogue was the power of truth over the conscience of even a slaveholder. What I got from Sheridan was a bold denunciation of slavery, and a powerful vindication of human rights. The reading of these documents enabled me to utter my thoughts, and to meet the arguments brought forward to sustain slavery; but while they relieved me of one difficulty, they brought on another even more painful than the one of which I was relieved. The more I read, the more I was led to abhor and detest my enslavers. I could regard them in no other light than a band of successful robbers, who had left their homes, and gone to Africa, and stolen us from our homes, and in a strange land reduced us to slavery. I loathed them as being the meanest as well as the most wicked of men. As I read and contemplated the subject, behold! that very discontentment which Master Hugh had predicted would follow my learning to read had already come, to torment and sting my soul to unutterable anguish. As I writhed under it, I would at times feel that learning to read had been a curse rather than a blessing. It had given me a view of my wretched condition, without the remedy. It opened my eyes to the horrible pit, but to no ladder upon which to get out. In moments of agony, I envied my fellow-slaves for their stupidity. I have often wished myself a beast. I preferred the condition of the meanest reptile to my own. Anything, no matter what, to get rid of thinking! It was this everlasting thinking of my condition that tormented me. There was no getting rid of it. It was pressed upon me by every object within sight or hearing, animate or inanimate. The silver trump of freedom had roused my soul to eternal wakefulness. Freedom now appeared, to disappear no more forever. It was heard in every sound, and seen in every thing. It was ever present to torment me with a sense of my wretched condition. I saw nothing without seeing it, I heard nothing without hearing it, and felt nothing without feeling it. It looked from every star, it smiled in every calm, breathed in every wind, and moved in every storm.

I often found myself regretting my own existence, and wishing myself dead; and but for the hope of being free, I have no doubt but that I should have killed myself, or done something for which I should have been killed. While in this state of mind, I was eager to hear anyone speak of slavery. I was a ready listener.

---

1   *The Columbian Orator*   Anthology of speeches and essays collected by New England educator Caleb Bingham (1757–1817), popular as a schoolbook.

2   *Sheridan*   Douglass is misremembering here. Richard Brinsley Sheridan (1751–1816) was an Irish poet, playwright, and politician; a short Parliamentary speech by Sheridan is included in the contents of the *Orator*, but it bears little resemblance to what Douglass describes here. The text to which he likely meant to refer is the speech for Catholic Emancipation given by United Irishman Arthur O'Connor in 1795, which directly follows the "Dialogue between a Master and Slave." (This speech is often further misidentified as having been given by Daniel O'Connell.)

Every little while, I could hear something about the abolitionists. It was some time before I found what the word meant. It was always used in such connections as to make it an interesting word to me. If a slave ran away and succeeded in getting clear, or if a slave killed his master, set fire to a barn, or did anything very wrong in the mind of a slaveholder, it was spoken of as the fruit of abolition. Hearing the word in this connection very often, I set about learning what it meant. The dictionary afforded me little or no help. I found it was "the act of abolishing"; but then I did not know what was to be abolished. Here I was perplexed. I did not dare to ask anyone about its meaning, for I was satisfied that it was something they wanted me to know very little about. After a patient waiting, I got one of our city papers, containing an account of the number of petitions from the north, praying for the abolition of slavery in the District of Columbia, and of the slave trade between the States. From this time I understood the words abolition and abolitionist, and always drew near when that word was spoken, expecting to hear something of importance to myself and fellow-slaves. The light broke in upon me by degrees. I went one day down on the wharf of Mr. Waters; and seeing two Irishmen unloading a scow of stone, I went, unasked, and helped them. When we had finished, one of them came to me and asked me if I were a slave. I told him I was. He asked, "Are ye a slave for life?" I told him that I was. The good Irishman seemed to be deeply affected by the statement. He said to the other that it was a pity so fine a little fellow as myself should be a slave for life. He said it was a shame to hold me. They both advised me to run away to the north; that I should find friends there, and that I should be free. I pretended not to be interested in what they said, and treated them as if I did not understand them; for I feared they might be treacherous. White men have been known to encourage slaves to escape, and then, to get the reward, catch them and return them to their masters. I was afraid that these seemingly good men might use me so; but I nevertheless remembered their advice, and from that time I resolved to run away. I looked forward to a time at which it would be safe for me to escape. I was too young to think of doing so immediately; besides, I wished to learn how to write, as I might have occasion to write my own pass. I consoled myself with the hope

that I should one day find a good chance. Meanwhile, I would learn to write.

The idea as to how I might learn to write was suggested to me by being in Durgin and Bailey's shipyard, and frequently seeing the ship carpenters, after hewing, and getting a piece of timber ready for use, write on the timber the name of that part of the ship for which it was intended. When a piece of timber was intended for the larboard[1] side, it would be marked thus—"L." When a piece was for the starboard side, it would be marked thus—"S." A piece for the larboard side forward, would be marked thus—"L. F." When a piece was for starboard side forward, it would be marked thus—"S. F." For larboard aft, it would be marked thus—"L. A." For starboard aft, it would be marked thus—"S. A." I soon learned the names of these letters, and for what they were intended when placed upon a piece of timber in the ship-yard. I immediately commenced copying them, and in a short time was able to make the four letters named. After that, when I met with any boy who I knew could write, I would tell him I could write as well as he. The next word would be, "I don't believe you. Let me see you try it." I would then make the letters which I had been so fortunate as to learn, and ask him to beat that. In this way I got a good many lessons in writing, which it is quite possible I should never have gotten in any other way. During this time, my copy-book was the board fence, brick wall, and pavement; my pen and ink was a lump of chalk. With these, I learned mainly how to write. I then commenced and continued copying the italics in Webster's Spelling Book,[2] until I could make them all without looking on the book. By this time, my little Master Thomas had gone to school, and learned how to write, and had written over a number of copy-books. These had been brought home, and shown to some of our near neighbors, and then laid aside. My mistress used to go to class meeting at the Wilk Street meetinghouse every Monday afternoon, and leave me to take care of the house. When left thus, I used to spend the time in writing in the spaces left in Master

---

1   *larboard*   Left (or "port") side of a ship; the right side is referred to as the "starboard."

2   *Webster's Spelling Book*   Refers to *The American Spelling Book* by American educator Noah Webster (1758–1843); first published in 1783, the book was a steady bestseller into the second half of the nineteenth century.

Thomas's copy-book, copying what he had written. I continued to do this until I could write a hand very similar to that of Master Thomas. Thus, after a long, tedious effort for years, I finally succeeded in learning how to write.

CHAPTER 8

In a very short time after I went to live at Baltimore, my old master's youngest son Richard died; and in about three years and six months after his death, my old master, Captain Anthony, died, leaving only his son, Andrew, and daughter, Lucretia, to share his estate. He died while on a visit to see his daughter at Hillsborough. Cut off thus unexpectedly, he left no will as to the disposal of his property. It was therefore necessary to have a valuation of the property, that it might be equally divided between Mrs. Lucretia and Master Andrew. I was immediately sent for, to be valued with the other property. Here again my feelings rose up in detestation of slavery. I had now a new conception of my degraded condition. Prior to this, I had become, if not insensible to my lot, at least partly so. I left Baltimore with a young heart overborne with sadness, and a soul full of apprehension. I took passage with Captain Rowe, in the schooner Wild Cat, and, after a sail of about twenty-four hours, I found myself near the place of my birth. I had now been absent from it almost, if not quite, five years. I, however, remembered the place very well. I was only about five years old when I left it, to go and live with my old master on Colonel Lloyd's plantation; so that I was now between ten and eleven years old.

We were all ranked together at the valuation. Men and women, old and young, married and single, were ranked with horses, sheep, and swine. There were horses and men, cattle and women, pigs and children, all holding the same rank in the scale of being, and were all subjected to the same narrow examination. Silvery-headed age and sprightly youth, maids and matrons, had to undergo the same indelicate inspection. At this moment, I saw more clearly than ever the brutalizing effects of slavery upon both slave and slaveholder.

After the valuation, then came the division. I have no language to express the high excitement and deep anxiety which were felt among us poor slaves during this time. Our fate for life was now to be decided. We had no more voice in that decision than the brutes among whom we were ranked. A single word from the white men was enough—against all our wishes, prayers, and entreaties—to sunder forever the dearest friends, dearest kindred, and strongest ties known to human beings. In addition to the pain of separation, there was the horrid dread of falling into the hands of Master Andrew. He was known to us all as being a most cruel wretch—a common drunkard, who had, by his reckless mismanagement and profligate dissipation, already wasted a large portion of his father's property. We all felt that we might as well be sold at once to the Georgia traders, as to pass into his hands; for we knew that that would be our inevitable condition—a condition held by us all in the utmost horror and dread.

I suffered more anxiety than most of my fellow-slaves. I had known what it was to be kindly treated; they had known nothing of the kind. They had seen little or nothing of the world. They were in very deed men and women of sorrow, and acquainted with grief. Their backs had been made familiar with the bloody lash, so that they had become callous; mine was yet tender; for while at Baltimore I got few whippings, and few slaves could boast of a kinder master and mistress than myself; and the thought of passing out of their hands into those of Master Andrew—a man who, but a few days before, to give me a sample of his bloody disposition, took my little brother by the throat, threw him on the ground, and with the heel of his boot stamped upon his head till the blood gushed from his nose and ears—was well calculated to make me anxious as to my fate. After he had committed this savage outrage upon my brother, he turned to me, and said that was the way he meant to serve me one of these days—meaning, I suppose, when I came into his possession.

Thanks to a kind Providence, I fell to the portion of Mrs. Lucretia, and was sent immediately back to Baltimore, to live again in the family of Master Hugh. Their joy at my return equalled their sorrow at my departure. It was a glad day to me. I had escaped a worse than lion's jaws. I was absent from Baltimore, for the purpose of valuation and division, just about one month, and it seemed to have been six.

Very soon after my return to Baltimore, my mistress, Lucretia, died, leaving her husband and one child,

Amanda; and in a very short time after her death, Master Andrew died. Now all the property of my old master, slaves included, was in the hands of strangers—strangers who had had nothing to do with accumulating it. Not a slave was left free. All remained slaves, from the youngest to the oldest. If any one thing in my experience, more than another, served to deepen my conviction of the infernal character of slavery, and to fill me with unutterable loathing of slaveholders, it was their base ingratitude to my poor old grandmother. She had served my old master faithfully from youth to old age. She had been the source of all his wealth; she had peopled his plantation with slaves; she had become a great grandmother in his service. She had rocked him in infancy, attended him in childhood, served him through life, and at his death wiped from his icy brow the cold death-sweat, and closed his eyes forever. She was nevertheless left a slave—a slave for life—a slave in the hands of strangers; and in their hands she saw her children, her grandchildren, and her great-grandchildren, divided, like so many sheep, without being gratified with the small privilege of a single word, as to their or her own destiny. And, to cap the climax of their base ingratitude and fiendish barbarity, my grandmother, who was now very old, having outlived my old master and all his children, having seen the beginning and end of all of them, and her present owners finding she was of but little value, her frame already racked with the pains of old age, and complete helplessness fast stealing over her once active limbs, they took her to the woods, built her a little hut, put up a little mud-chimney, and then made her welcome to the privilege of supporting herself there in perfect loneliness; thus virtually turning her out to die! If my poor old grandmother now lives, she lives to suffer in utter loneliness; she lives to remember and mourn over the loss of children, the loss of grandchildren, and the loss of great-grandchildren. They are, in the language of the slave's poet, Whittier,[1]

> Gone, gone, sold and gone
> To the rice swamp dank and lone,
> Where the slave-whip ceaseless swings,

> Where the noisome insect stings,
> Where the fever-demon strews
> Poison with the falling dews,
> Where the sickly sunbeams glare
> Through the hot and misty air:—
>   Gone, gone, sold and gone
>   To the rice swamp dank and lone,
>   From Virginia hills and waters—
>   Woe is me, my stolen daughters!

The hearth is desolate. The children, the unconscious children, who once sang and danced in her presence, are gone. She gropes her way, in the darkness of age, for a drink of water. Instead of the voices of her children, she hears by day the moans of the dove, and by night the screams of the hideous owl. All is gloom. The grave is at the door. And now, when weighed down by the pains and aches of old age, when the head inclines to the feet, when the beginning and ending of human existence meet, and helpless infancy and painful old age combine together—at this time, this most needful time, the time for the exercise of that tenderness and affection which children only can exercise towards a declining parent—my poor old grandmother, the devoted mother of twelve children, is left all alone, in yonder little hut, before a few dim embers. She stands—she sits—she staggers—she falls—she groans—she dies—and there are none of her children or grandchildren present, to wipe from her wrinkled brow the cold sweat of death, or to place beneath the sod her fallen remains. Will not a righteous God visit for these things?[2]

In about two years after the death of Mrs. Lucretia, Master Thomas married his second wife. Her name was Rowena Hamilton. She was the eldest daughter of Mr. William Hamilton. Master now lived in St. Michael's. Not long after his marriage, a misunderstanding took place between himself and Master Hugh; and as a means of punishing his brother, he took me from him to live with himself at St. Michael's. Here I underwent another most painful separation. It, however, was not so severe as the one I dreaded at the division of property; for, during this interval, a great change had taken

---

[1] *the slave's poet, Whittier*   John Greenleaf Whittier (1807–92), white Quaker poet and abolitionist who was associated with William Lloyd Garrison. The quotation is from "The Farewell of a Virginia Slave Mother to Her Daughters Sold into Southern Bondage."

[2] *Will not ... these things?*   See Jeremiah 5.29: "Shall I not visit for these things? saith the Lord: shall not my soul be avenged on such a nation as this?"

place in Master Hugh and his once kind and affectionate wife. The influence of brandy upon him, and of slavery upon her, had effected a disastrous change in the characters of both; so that, as far as they were concerned, I thought I had little to lose by the change. But it was not to them that I was attached. It was to those little Baltimore boys that I felt the strongest attachment. I had received many good lessons from them, and was still receiving them, and the thought of leaving them was painful indeed. I was leaving, too, without the hope of ever being allowed to return. Master Thomas had said he would never let me return again. The barrier betwixt himself and brother he considered impassable.

I then had to regret that I did not at least make the attempt to carry out my resolution to run away; for the chances of success are tenfold greater from the city than from the country.

I sailed from Baltimore for St. Michael's in the sloop Amanda, Captain Edward Dodson. On my passage, I paid particular attention to the direction which the steamboats took to go to Philadelphia. I found, instead of going down, on reaching North Point they went up the bay, in a north-easterly direction. I deemed this knowledge of the utmost importance. My determination to run away was again revived. I resolved to wait only so long as the offering of a favorable opportunity. When that came, I was determined to be off.

CHAPTER 9

I have now reached a period of my life when I can give dates. I left Baltimore, and went to live with Master Thomas Auld, at St. Michael's, in March, 1832. It was now more than seven years since I lived with him in the family of my old master, on Colonel Lloyd's plantation. We of course were now almost entire strangers to each other. He was to me a new master, and I to him a new slave. I was ignorant of his temper and disposition; he was equally so of mine. A very short time, however, brought us into full acquaintance with each other. I was made acquainted with his wife not less than with himself. They were well matched, being equally mean¹ and cruel. I was now, for the first time

during a space of more than seven years, made to feel the painful gnawings of hunger—a something which I had not experienced before since I left Colonel Lloyd's plantation. It went hard enough with me then, when I could look back to no period at which I had enjoyed a sufficiency. It was tenfold harder after living in Master Hugh's family, where I had always had enough to eat, and of that which was good. I have said Master Thomas was a mean man. He was so. Not to give a slave enough to eat, is regarded as the most aggravated development of meanness even among slaveholders. The rule is, no matter how coarse the food, only let there be enough of it. This is the theory; and in the part of Maryland from which I came, it is the general practice—though there are many exceptions. Master Thomas gave us enough of neither coarse nor fine food. There were four slaves of us in the kitchen—my sister Eliza, my aunt Priscilla, Henny, and myself; and we were allowed less than a half of a bushel of corn-meal per week, and very little else, either in the shape of meat or vegetables. It was not enough for us to subsist upon. We were therefore reduced to the wretched necessity of living at the expense of our neighbors. This we did by begging and stealing, whichever came handy in the time of need, the one being considered as legitimate as the other. A great many times have we poor creatures been nearly perishing with hunger, when food in abundance lay mouldering in the safe and smoke-house,² and our pious mistress was aware of the fact; and yet that mistress and her husband would kneel every morning, and pray that God would bless them in basket and store!

Bad as all slaveholders are, we seldom meet one destitute of every element of character commanding respect. My master was one of this rare sort. I do not know of one single noble act ever performed by him. The leading trait in his character was meanness; and if there were any other element in his nature, it was made subject to this. He was mean; and, like most other mean men, he lacked the ability to conceal his meanness. Captain Auld was not born a slaveholder. He had been a poor man, master only of a Bay craft. He came into possession of all his slaves by marriage; and of all men, adopted slaveholders are the worst. He was cruel, but cowardly. He commanded without firmness. In the enforcement of his rules, he was at times rigid,

---

¹ *mean* Lowly and undignified; also, miserly.

² *safe and smoke-house* Storage-places for meat.

and at times lax. At times, he spoke to his slaves with the firmness of Napoleon and the fury of a demon; at other times, he might well be mistaken for an inquirer who had lost his way. He did nothing of himself. He might have passed for a lion, but for his ears. In all things noble which he attempted, his own meanness shone most conspicuous. His airs, words, and actions, were the airs, words, and actions of born slaveholders, and, being assumed, were awkward enough. He was not even a good imitator. He possessed all the disposition to deceive, but wanted the power. Having no resources within himself, he was compelled to be the copyist of many, and being such, he was forever the victim of inconsistency; and of consequence he was an object of contempt, and was held as such even by his slaves. The luxury of having slaves of his own to wait upon him was something new and unprepared for. He was a slaveholder without the ability to hold slaves. He found himself incapable of managing his slaves either by force, fear, or fraud. We seldom called him "master"; we generally called him "Captain Auld," and were hardly disposed to title him at all. I doubt not that our conduct had much to do with making him appear awkward, and of consequence fretful. Our want of reverence for him must have perplexed him greatly. He wished to have us call him master, but lacked the firmness necessary to command us to do so. His wife used to insist upon our calling him so, but to no purpose. In August, 1832, my master attended a Methodist camp-meeting[1] held in the Bay-side, Talbot county, and there experienced religion. I indulged a faint hope that his conversion would lead him to emancipate his slaves, and that, if he did not do this, it would, at any rate, make him more kind and humane. I was disappointed in both these respects. It neither made him to be humane to his slaves, nor to emancipate them. If it had any effect on his character, it made him more cruel and hateful in all his ways; for I believe him to have been a much worse man after his conversion than before. Prior to his conversion, he relied upon his own depravity to shield and sustain him in his savage barbarity; but after his conversion, he found religious sanction and support for his slaveholding cruelty. He made the greatest pretensions to piety. His house was the house of prayer. He prayed morning, noon, and night. He

very soon distinguished himself among his brethren, and was soon made a class-leader and exhorter. His activity in revivals was great, and he proved himself an instrument in the hands of the church in converting many souls. His house was the preachers' home. They used to take great pleasure in coming there to put up; for while he starved us, he stuffed them. We have had three or four preachers there at a time. The names of those who used to come most frequently while I lived there, were Mr. Storks, Mr. Ewery, Mr. Humphry, and Mr. Hickey. I have also seen Mr. George Cookman[2] at our house. We slaves loved Mr. Cookman. We believed him to be a good man. We thought him instrumental in getting Mr. Samuel Harrison, a very rich slaveholder, to emancipate his slaves; and by some means got the impression that he was laboring to effect the emancipation of all the slaves. When he was at our house, we were sure to be called in to prayers. When the others were there, we were sometimes called in and sometimes not. Mr. Cookman took more notice of us than either of the other ministers. He could not come among us without betraying his sympathy for us, and, stupid as we were, we had the sagacity to see it.

While I lived with my master in St. Michael's, there was a white young man, a Mr. Wilson, who proposed to keep a Sabbath school for the instruction of such slaves as might be disposed to learn to read the New Testament. We met but three times, when Mr. West and Mr. Fairbanks, both class-leaders, with many others, came upon us with sticks and other missiles, drove us off, and forbade us to meet again. Thus ended our little Sabbath school in the pious town of St. Michael's.

I have said my master found religious sanction for his cruelty. As an example, I will state one of many facts going to prove the charge. I have seen him tie up a lame young woman, and whip her with a heavy cowskin upon her naked shoulders, causing the warm red blood to drip; and, in justification of the bloody deed, he would quote this passage of Scripture—"He that knoweth his master's will, and doeth it not, shall be beaten with many stripes."[3]

---

[1]   *camp-meeting*   Outdoor meeting.

[2]   *Mr. George Cookman*   Methodist minister (1800–41) who served as Chaplain to the Senate and promoted emancipation.

[3]   *He that knoweth … many stripes*   See Luke 12.47.

Master would keep this lacerated young woman tied up in this horrid situation four or five hours at a time. I have known him to tie her up early in the morning, and whip her before breakfast; leave her, go to his store, return at dinner, and whip her again, cutting her in the places already made raw with his cruel lash. The secret of master's cruelty toward "Henny" is found in the fact of her being almost helpless. When quite a child, she fell into the fire, and burned herself horribly. Her hands were so burnt that she never got the use of them. She could do very little but bear heavy burdens. She was to master a bill of expense; and as he was a mean man, she was a constant offence to him. He seemed desirous of getting the poor girl out of existence. He gave her away once to his sister; but, being a poor gift, she was not disposed to keep her. Finally, my benevolent master, to use his own words, "set her adrift to take care of herself." Here was a recently-converted man, holding on upon the mother, and at the same time turning out her helpless child, to starve and die! Master Thomas was one of the many pious slaveholders who hold slaves for the very charitable purpose of taking care of them.

My master and myself had quite a number of differences. He found me unsuitable to his purpose. My city life, he said, had had a very pernicious effect upon me. It had almost ruined me for every good purpose, and fitted me for every thing which was bad. One of my greatest faults was that of letting his horse run away, and go down to his father-in-law's farm, which was about five miles from St. Michael's. I would then have to go after it. My reason for this kind of carelessness, or carefulness, was, that I could always get something to eat when I went there. Master William Hamilton, my master's father-in-law, always gave his slaves enough to eat. I never left there hungry, no matter how great the need of my speedy return. Master Thomas at length said he would stand it no longer. I had lived with him nine months, during which time he had given me a number of severe whippings, all to no good purpose. He resolved to put me out, as he said, to be broken; and, for this purpose, he let me for one year to a man named Edward Covey. Mr. Covey was a poor man, a farm-renter. He rented the place upon which he lived, as also the hands with which he tilled it. Mr. Covey had acquired a very high reputation for breaking young slaves, and this reputation was of immense value

to him. It enabled him to get his farm tilled with much less expense to himself than he could have had it done without such a reputation. Some slaveholders thought it not much loss to allow Mr. Covey to have their slaves one year, for the sake of the training to which they were subjected, without any other compensation. He could hire young help with great ease, in consequence of this reputation. Added to the natural good qualities of Mr. Covey, he was a professor of religion—a pious soul—a member and a class-leader in the Methodist church. All of this added weight to his reputation as a "nigger-breaker." I was aware of all the facts, having been made acquainted with them by a young man who had lived there. I nevertheless made the change gladly; for I was sure of getting enough to eat, which is not the smallest consideration to a hungry man.

CHAPTER 10

I had left Master Thomas's house, and went to live with Mr. Covey, on the 1st of January, 1833. I was now, for the first time in my life, a field hand. In my new employment, I found myself even more awkward than a country boy appeared to be in a large city. I had been at my new home but one week before Mr. Covey gave me a very severe whipping, cutting my back, causing the blood to run, and raising ridges on my flesh as large as my little finger. The details of this affair are as follows: Mr. Covey sent me, very early in the morning of one of our coldest days in the month of January, to the woods, to get a load of wood. He gave me a team of unbroken oxen. He told me which was the in-hand ox, and which the off-hand one.[1] He then tied the end of a large rope around the horns of the in-hand ox, and gave me the other end of it, and told me, if the oxen started to run, that I must hold on upon the rope. I had never driven oxen before, and of course I was very awkward. I, however, succeeded in getting to the edge of the woods with little difficulty; but I had got a very few rods into the woods, when the oxen took fright, and started full tilt, carrying the cart against trees, and over stumps, in the most frightful manner. I expected every moment that my brains would be dashed out against the trees. After running thus for a considerable

---

[1]   *in-hand ox ... off-hand one*   Oxen on the right- and left-hand sides of a pair, respectively.

distance, they finally upset the cart, dashing it with great force against a tree, and threw themselves into a dense thicket. How I escaped death, I do not know. There I was, entirely alone, in a thick wood, in a place new to me. My cart was upset and shattered, my oxen were entangled among the young trees, and there was none to help me. After a long spell of effort, I succeeded in getting my cart righted, my oxen disentangled, and again yoked to the cart. I now proceeded with my team to the place where I had, the day before, been chopping wood, and loaded my cart pretty heavily, thinking in this way to tame my oxen. I then proceeded on my way home. I had now consumed one half of the day. I got out of the woods safely, and now felt out of danger. I stopped my oxen to open the woods gate; and just as I did so, before I could get hold of my ox-rope, the oxen again started, rushed through the gate, catching it between the wheel and the body of the cart, tearing it to pieces, and coming within a few inches of crushing me against the gate-post. Thus twice, in one short day, I escaped death by the merest chance. On my return, I told Mr. Covey what had happened, and how it happened. He ordered me to return to the woods again immediately. I did so, and he followed on after me. Just as I got into the woods, he came up and told me to stop my cart, and that he would teach me how to trifle away my time, and break gates. He then went to a large gum-tree, and with his axe cut three large switches, and, after trimming them up neatly with his pocketknife, he ordered me to take off my clothes. I made him no answer, but stood with my clothes on. He repeated his order. I still made him no answer, nor did I move to strip myself. Upon this he rushed at me with the fierceness of a tiger, tore off my clothes, and lashed me till he had worn out his switches, cutting me so savagely as to leave the marks visible for a long time after. This whipping was the first of a number just like it, and for similar offences.

I lived with Mr. Covey one year. During the first six months, of that year, scarce a week passed without his whipping me. I was seldom free from a sore back. My awkwardness was almost always his excuse for whipping me. We were worked fully up to the point of endurance. Long before day we were up, our horses fed, and by the first approach of day we were off to the field with our hoes and ploughing teams. Mr. Covey gave us enough to eat, but scarce time to eat it. We were often less than five minutes taking our meals. We were often in the field from the first approach of day till its last lingering ray had left us; and at saving-fodder time, midnight often caught us in the field binding blades.[1]

Covey would be out with us. The way he used to stand it, was this. He would spend the most of his afternoons in bed. He would then come out fresh in the evening, ready to urge us on with his words, example, and frequently with the whip. Mr. Covey was one of the few slaveholders who could and did work with his hands. He was a hard-working man. He knew by himself just what a man or a boy could do. There was no deceiving him. His work went on in his absence almost as well as in his presence; and he had the faculty of making us feel that he was ever present with us. This he did by surprising us. He seldom approached the spot where we were at work openly, if he could do it secretly. He always aimed at taking us by surprise. Such was his cunning, that we used to call him, among ourselves, "the snake." When we were at work in the cornfield, he would sometimes crawl on his hands and knees to avoid detection, and all at once he would rise nearly in our midst, and scream out, "Ha, ha! Come, come! Dash on, dash on!" This being his mode of attack, it was never safe to stop a single minute. His comings were like a thief in the night. He appeared to us as being ever at hand. He was under every tree, behind every stump, in every bush, and at every window, on the plantation. He would sometimes mount his horse, as if bound to St. Michael's, a distance of seven miles, and in half an hour afterwards you would see him coiled up in the corner of the wood-fence, watching every motion of the slaves. He would, for this purpose, leave his horse tied up in the woods. Again, he would sometimes walk up to us, and give us orders as though he was upon the point of starting on a long journey, turn his back upon us, and make as though he was going to the house to get ready; and, before he would get half way thither, he would turn short and crawl into a fence-corner, or behind some tree, and there watch us till the going down of the sun.

---

[1] *saving-fodder time* Harvest time; *binding blades* Binding wheat sheaves.

Mr. Covey's *forte*[1] consisted in his power to deceive. His life was devoted to planning and perpetrating the grossest deceptions. Every thing he possessed in the shape of learning or religion, he made conform to his disposition to deceive. He seemed to think himself equal to deceiving the Almighty. He would make a short prayer in the morning, and a long prayer at night; and, strange as it may seem, few men would at times appear more devotional than he. The exercises of his family devotions were always commenced with singing; and, as he was a very poor singer himself, the duty of raising the hymn generally came upon me. He would read his hymn, and nod at me to commence. I would at times do so; at others, I would not. My non-compliance would almost always produce much confusion. To show himself independent of me, he would start and stagger through with his hymn in the most discordant manner. In this state of mind, he prayed with more than ordinary spirit. Poor man! such was his disposition, and success at deceiving, I do verily believe that he sometimes deceived himself into the solemn belief, that he was a sincere worshipper of the most high God; and this, too, at a time when he may be said to have been guilty of compelling his woman slave to commit the sin of adultery. The facts in the case are these: Mr. Covey was a poor man; he was just commencing in life; he was only able to buy one slave; and, shocking as is the fact, he bought her, as he said, for a breeder. This woman was named Caroline. Mr. Covey bought her from Mr. Thomas Lowe, about six miles from St. Michael's. She was a large, able-bodied woman, about twenty years old. She had already given birth to one child, which proved her to be just what he wanted. After buying her, he hired a married man of Mr. Samuel Harrison, to live with him one year; and him he used to fasten up with her every night! The result was, that, at the end of the year, the miserable woman gave birth to twins. At this result Mr. Covey seemed to be highly pleased, both with the man and the wretched woman. Such was his joy, and that of his wife, that nothing they could do for Caroline during her confinement was too good, or too hard, to be done. The children were regarded as being quite an addition to his wealth.

If at any one time of my life more than another, I was made to drink the bitterest dregs of slavery, that time was during the first six months of my stay with Mr. Covey. We were worked in all weathers. It was never too hot or too cold; it could never rain, blow, hail, or snow, too hard for us to work in the field. Work, work, work, was scarcely more the order of the day than of the night. The longest days were too short for him, and the shortest nights too long for him. I was somewhat unmanageable when I first went there, but a few months of this discipline tamed me. Mr. Covey succeeded in breaking me. I was broken in body, soul, and spirit. My natural elasticity was crushed, my intellect languished, the disposition to read departed, the cheerful spark that lingered about my eye died; the dark night of slavery closed in upon me; and behold a man transformed into a brute!

Sunday was my only leisure time. I spent this in a sort of beast-like stupor, between sleep and wake, under some large tree. At times I would rise up, a flash of energetic freedom would dart through my soul, accompanied with a faint beam of hope, that flickered for a moment, and then vanished. I sank down again, mourning over my wretched condition. I was sometimes prompted to take my life, and that of Covey, but was prevented by a combination of hope and fear. My sufferings on this plantation seem now like a dream rather than a stern reality.

Our house stood within a few rods of the Chesapeake Bay, whose broad bosom was ever white with sails from every quarter of the habitable globe. Those beautiful vessels, robed in purest white, so delightful to the eye of freemen, were to me so many shrouded ghosts, to terrify and torment me with thoughts of my wretched condition. I have often, in the deep stillness of a summer's Sabbath, stood all alone upon the lofty banks of that noble bay, and traced, with saddened heart and tearful eye, the countless number of sails moving off to the mighty ocean. The sight of these always affected me powerfully. My thoughts would compel utterance; and there, with no audience but the Almighty, I would pour out my soul's complaint, in my rude way, with an apostrophe[2] to the moving multitude of ships:

---

[1]   *forte*   Italian: strength; particular ability.

[2]   *apostrophe*   Exclamatory speech made either to one or more people who are unable to respond (whether because they are not present or because they are not alive) or to one or more inanimate objects.

"You are loosed from your moorings, and are free; I am fast in my chains, and am a slave! You move merrily before the gentle gale, and I sadly before the bloody whip! You are freedom's swift-winged angels, that fly round the world; I am confined in bands of iron! O that I were free! O, that I were on one of your gallant decks, and under your protecting wing! Alas! betwixt me and you, the turbid waters roll. Go on, go on. O that I could also go! Could I but swim! If I could fly! O, why was I born a man, of whom to make a brute! The glad ship is gone; she hides in the dim distance. I am left in the hottest hell of unending slavery. O God, save me! God, deliver me! Let me be free! Is there any God? Why am I a slave? I will run away. I will not stand it. Get caught, or get clear, I'll try it. I had as well die with ague as the fever.[1] I have only one life to lose. I had as well be killed running as die standing. Only think of it; one hundred miles straight north, and I am free! Try it? Yes! God helping me, I will. It cannot be that I shall live and die a slave. I will take to the water. This very bay shall yet bear me into freedom. The steamboats steered in a north-east course from North Point. I will do the same; and when I get to the head of the bay, I will turn my canoe adrift, and walk straight through Delaware into Pennsylvania. When I get there, I shall not be required to have a pass; I can travel without being disturbed. Let but the first opportunity offer, and, come what will, I am off. Meanwhile, I will try to bear up under the yoke. I am not the only slave in the world. Why should I fret? I can bear as much as any of them. Besides, I am but a boy, and all boys are bound to someone. It may be that my misery in slavery will only increase my happiness when I get free. There is a better day coming."

Thus I used to think, and thus I used to speak to myself; goaded almost to madness at one moment, and at the next reconciling myself to my wretched lot.

I have already intimated that my condition was much worse, during the first six months of my stay at Mr. Covey's, than in the last six. The circumstances leading to the change in Mr. Covey's course toward me form an epoch in my humble history. You have seen how a man was made a slave; you shall see how a slave was made a man. On one of the hottest days of the month of August, 1833, Bill Smith, William Hughes, a slave named Eli, and myself, were engaged in fanning wheat.[2] Hughes was clearing the fanned wheat from before the fan. Eli was turning, Smith was feeding, and I was carrying wheat to the fan. The work was simple, requiring strength rather than intellect; yet, to one entirely unused to such work, it came very hard. About three o'clock of that day, I broke down; my strength failed me; I was seized with a violent aching of the head, attended with extreme dizziness; I trembled in every limb. Finding what was coming, I nerved myself up, feeling it would never do to stop work. I stood as long as I could stagger to the hopper with grain. When I could stand no longer, I fell, and felt as if held down by an immense weight. The fan of course stopped; every one had his own work to do; and no one could do the work of the other, and have his own go on at the same time.

Mr. Covey was at the house, about one hundred yards from the treading-yard where we were fanning. On hearing the fan stop, he left immediately, and came to the spot where we were. He hastily inquired what the matter was. Bill answered that I was sick, and there was no one to bring wheat to the fan. I had by this time crawled away under the side of the post and rail-fence by which the yard was enclosed, hoping to find relief by getting out of the sun. He then asked where I was. He was told by one of the hands. He came to the spot, and, after looking at me awhile, asked me what was the matter. I told him as well as I could, for I scarce had strength to speak. He then gave me a savage kick in the side, and told me to get up. I tried to do so, but fell back in the attempt. He gave me another kick, and again told me to rise. I again tried, and succeeded in gaining my feet; but, stooping to get the tub with which I was feeding the fan, I again staggered and fell. While down in this situation, Mr. Covey took up the hickory slat with which Hughes had been striking off the half-bushel measure, and with it gave me a heavy blow upon the head, making a large wound, and the blood ran freely; and with this again told me to get up. I made no effort to comply, having now made up my mind to let him do his worst. In a short time after

---

[1]   *ague ... fever* The point here is that there is little difference between the two; "ague" was a term given to a range of infectious maladies for which a high fever was a key symptom.

[2]   *fanning wheat* Separating chaff from the wheat by means of a large fanning mill.

receiving this blow, my head grew better. Mr. Covey had now left me to my fate. At this moment I resolved, for the first time, to go to my master, enter a complaint, and ask his protection. In order to [do] this, I must that afternoon walk seven miles; and this, under the circumstances, was truly a severe undertaking. I was exceedingly feeble; made so as much by the kicks and blows which I received, as by the severe fit of sickness to which I had been subjected. I, however, watched my chance, while Covey was looking in an opposite direction, and started for St. Michael's. I succeeded in getting a considerable distance on my way to the woods, when Covey discovered me, and called after me to come back, threatening what he would do if I did not come. I disregarded both his calls and his threats, and made my way to the woods as fast as my feeble state would allow; and thinking I might be overhauled by him if I kept the road, I walked through the woods, keeping far enough from the road to avoid detection, and near enough to prevent losing my way. I had not gone far before my little strength again failed me. I could go no farther. I fell down, and lay for a considerable time. The blood was yet oozing from the wound on my head. For a time I thought I should bleed to death; and think now that I should have done so, but that the blood so matted my hair as to stop the wound. After lying there about three quarters of an hour, I nerved myself up again, and started on my way, through bogs and briers, barefooted and bareheaded, tearing my feet sometimes at nearly every step; and after a journey of about seven miles, occupying some five hours to perform it, I arrived at master's store. I then presented an appearance enough to affect any but a heart of iron. From the crown of my head to my feet, I was covered with blood. My hair was all clotted with dust and blood; my shirt was stiff with blood. I suppose I looked like a man who had escaped a den of wild beasts, and barely escaped them. In this state I appeared before my master, humbly entreating him to interpose his authority for my protection. I told him all the circumstances as well as I could, and it seemed, as I spoke, at times to affect him. He would then walk the floor, and seek to justify Covey by saying he expected I deserved it. He asked me what I wanted. I told him, to let me get a new home; that as sure as I lived with Mr. Covey again, I should live with but to die with him;

that Covey would surely kill me; he was in a fair way for it. Master Thomas ridiculed the idea that there was any danger of Mr. Covey's killing me, and said that he knew Mr. Covey; that he was a good man, and that he could not think of taking me from him; that, should he do so, he would lose the whole year's wages; that I belonged to Mr. Covey for one year, and that I must go back to him, come what might; and that I must not trouble him with any more stories, or that he would himself get hold of me. After threatening me thus, he gave me a very large dose of salts,[1] telling me that I might remain in St. Michael's that night (it being quite late), but that I must be off back to Mr. Covey's early in the morning; and that if I did not, he would get hold of me, which meant that he would whip me. I remained all night, and, according to his orders, I started off to Covey's in the morning (Saturday morning), wearied in body and broken in spirit. I got no supper that night, or breakfast that morning. I reached Covey's about nine o'clock; and just as I was getting over the fence that divided Mrs. Kemp's fields from ours, out ran Covey with his cowskin, to give me another whipping. Before he could reach me, I succeeded in getting to the cornfield; and as the corn was very high, it afforded me the means of hiding. He seemed very angry, and searched for me a long time. My behavior was altogether unaccountable. He finally gave up the chase, thinking, I suppose, that I must come home for something to eat; he would give himself no further trouble in looking for me. I spent that day mostly in the woods, having the alternative before me—to go home and be whipped to death, or stay in the woods and be starved to death. That night, I fell in with Sandy Jenkins, a slave with whom I was somewhat acquainted. Sandy had a free wife[2] who lived about four miles from Mr. Covey's; and it being Saturday, he was on his way to see her. I told him my circumstances, and he very kindly invited me to go home with him. I went home with him, and talked this whole matter over, and got his advice as to what course

---

1   *large dose of salts*   I.e., smelling salts, comprising a mixture of carbonate of ammonia and other scented components, used to restore people from spells of fainting or dizziness.

2   *a free wife*   Because slavery often resulted in spouses being sold to different slaveowners, it sometimes occurred that one would be granted their freedom while the other remained enslaved.

it was best for me to pursue. I found Sandy an old adviser. He told me, with great solemnity, I must go back to Covey; but that before I went, I must go with him into another part of the woods, where there was a certain root, which, if I would take some of it with me, carrying it always on my right side, would render it impossible for Mr. Covey, or any other white man, to whip me. He said he had carried it for years; and since he had done so, he had never received a blow, and never expected to while he carried it. I at first rejected the idea, that the simple carrying of a root in my pocket would have any such effect as he had said, and was not disposed to take it; but Sandy impressed the necessity with much earnestness, telling me it could do no harm, if it did no good. To please him, I at length took the root, and, according to his direction, carried it upon my right side. This was Sunday morning. I immediately started for home; and upon entering the yard gate, out came Mr. Covey on his way to meeting. He spoke to me very kindly, bade me drive the pigs from a lot near by, and passed on towards the church. Now, this singular conduct of Mr. Covey really made me begin to think that there was something in the root which Sandy had given me; and had it been on any other day than Sunday, I could have attributed the conduct to no other cause than the influence of that root; and as it was, I was half inclined to think the root to be something more than I at first had taken it to be. All went well till Monday morning. On this morning, the virtue of the root was fully tested. Long before daylight, I was called to go and rub, curry,[1] and feed, the horses. I obeyed, and was glad to obey. But whilst thus engaged, whilst in the act of throwing down some blades from the loft, Mr. Covey entered the stable with a long rope; and just as I was half out of the loft, he caught hold of my legs, and was about tying me. As soon as I found what he was up to, I gave a sudden spring, and as I did so, he holding to my legs, I was brought sprawling on the stable floor. Mr. Covey seemed now to think he had me, and could do what he pleased; but at this moment—from whence came the spirit I don't know—I resolved to fight; and, suiting my action to the resolution, I seized Covey hard by the throat; and as I did so, I rose. He held on to me, and I to him. My resistance was so entirely unexpected that

Covey seemed taken all aback. He trembled like a leaf. This gave me assurance, and I held him uneasy, causing the blood to run where I touched him with the ends of my fingers. Mr. Covey soon called out to Hughes for help. Hughes came, and, while Covey held me, attempted to tie my right hand. While he was in the act of doing so, I watched my chance, and gave him a heavy kick close under the ribs. This kick fairly sickened Hughes, so that he left me in the hands of Mr. Covey. This kick had the effect of not only weakening Hughes, but Covey also. When he saw Hughes bending over with pain, his courage quailed. He asked me if I meant to persist in my resistance. I told him I did, come what might; that he had used me like a brute for six months, and that I was determined to be used so no longer. With that, he strove to drag me to a stick that was lying just out of the stable door. He meant to knock me down. But just as he was leaning over to get the stick, I seized him with both hands by his collar, and brought him by a sudden snatch to the ground. By this time, Bill came. Covey called upon him for assistance. Bill wanted to know what he could do. Covey said, "Take hold of him, take hold of him!" Bill said his master hired him out to work, and not to help to whip me; so he left Covey and myself to fight our own battle out. We were at it for nearly two hours. Covey at length let me go, puffing and blowing at a great rate, saying that if I had not resisted, he would not have whipped me half so much. The truth was, that he had not whipped me at all. I considered him as getting entirely the worst end of the bargain; for he had drawn no blood from me, but I had from him. The whole six months afterwards, that I spent with Mr. Covey, he never laid the weight of his finger upon me in anger. He would occasionally say, he didn't want to get hold of me again. "No," thought I, "you need not; for you will come off worse than you did before."

This battle with Mr. Covey was the turning-point in my career as a slave. It rekindled the few expiring embers of freedom, and revived within me a sense of my own manhood. It recalled the departed self-confidence, and inspired me again with a determination to be free. The gratification afforded by the triumph was a full compensation for whatever else might follow, even death itself. He only can understand the deep satisfaction which I experienced, who has himself repelled by

---

1   *curry*   Brush.

force the bloody arm of slavery. I felt as I never felt before. It was a glorious resurrection, from the tomb of slavery, to the heaven of freedom. My long-crushed spirit rose, cowardice departed, bold defiance took its place; and I now resolved that, however long I might remain a slave in form, the day had passed forever when I could be a slave in fact. I did not hesitate to let it be known of me, that the white man who expected to succeed in whipping, must also succeed in killing me.

From this time I was never again what might be called fairly whipped, though I remained a slave four years afterwards. I had several fights, but was never whipped.

It was for a long time a matter of surprise to me why Mr. Covey did not immediately have me taken by the constable to the whipping-post, and there regularly whipped for the crime of raising my hand against a white man in defence of myself. And the only explanation I can now think of does not entirely satisfy me; but such as it is, I will give it. Mr. Covey enjoyed the most unbounded reputation for being a first-rate overseer and negro-breaker. It was of considerable importance to him. That reputation was at stake; and had he sent me—a boy about sixteen years old—to the public whipping-post, his reputation would have been lost; so, to save his reputation, he suffered me to go unpunished.

My term of actual service to Mr. Edward Covey ended on Christmas day, 1833. The days between Christmas and New Year's Day are allowed as holidays; and, accordingly, we were not required to perform any labor, more than to feed and take care of the stock. This time we regarded as our own, by the grace of our masters; and we therefore used or abused it nearly as we pleased. Those of us who had families at a distance, were generally allowed to spend the whole six days in their society. This time, however, was spent in various ways. The staid, sober, thinking and industrious ones of our number would employ themselves in making corn-brooms, mats, horse-collars, and baskets; and another class of us would spend the time in hunting opossums, hares, and coons. But by far the larger part engaged in such sports and merriments as playing ball, wrestling, running foot-races, fiddling, dancing, and drinking whisky; and this latter mode of spending the time was by far the most agreeable to the feelings of our masters. A slave who would work during the holidays was considered by our masters as scarcely deserving them. He was regarded as one who rejected the favor of his master. It was deemed a disgrace not to get drunk at Christmas; and he was regarded as lazy indeed, who had not provided himself with the necessary means, during the year, to get whisky enough to last him through Christmas.

From what I know of the effect of these holidays upon the slave, I believe them to be among the most effective means in the hands of the slaveholder in keeping down the spirit of insurrection. Were the slaveholders at once to abandon this practice, I have not the slightest doubt it would lead to an immediate insurrection among the slaves. These holidays serve as conductors, or safety-valves, to carry off the rebellious spirit of enslaved humanity. But for these, the slave would be forced up to the wildest desperation; and woe betide the slaveholder, the day he ventures to remove or hinder the operation of those conductors! I warn him that, in such an event, a spirit will go forth in their midst, more to be dreaded than the most appalling earthquake.

The holidays are part and parcel of the gross fraud, wrong, and inhumanity of slavery. They are professedly a custom established by the benevolence of the slaveholders; but I undertake to say, it is the result of selfishness, and one of the grossest frauds committed upon the down-trodden slave. They do not give the slaves this time because they would not like to have their work during its continuance, but because they know it would be unsafe to deprive them of it. This will be seen by the fact, that the slaveholders like to have their slaves spend those days just in such a manner as to make them as glad of their ending as of their beginning. Their object seems to be, to disgust their slaves with freedom, by plunging them into the lowest depths of dissipation. For instance, the slaveholders not only like to see the slave drink of his own accord, but will adopt various plans to make him drunk. One plan is, to make bets on their slaves, as to who can drink the most whisky without getting drunk; and in this way they succeed in getting whole multitudes to drink to excess. Thus, when the slave asks for virtuous freedom, the cunning slaveholder, knowing his ignorance, cheats him with a dose of vicious dissipation, artfully labelled with the name of liberty. The most of us used to drink it down, and the result was just what might be supposed; many of us were led to think that there was little to choose between liberty and slavery. We felt, and very properly too, that we had almost as well be slaves to man as to rum. So, when the holidays ended, we staggered up from the filth of our wallowing, took a long breath, and marched to the field—feeling, upon the whole, rather glad to go, from what our master had deceived us into a belief was freedom, back to the arms of slavery.

I have said that this mode of treatment is a part of the whole system of fraud and inhumanity of slavery. It is so. The mode here adopted to disgust the slave with freedom, by allowing him to see only the abuse of it, is carried out in other things. For instance, a slave loves molasses; he steals some. His master, in many cases, goes off to town, and buys a large quantity; he returns, takes his whip, and commands the slave to eat the molasses, until the poor fellow is made sick at the very mention of it. The same mode is sometimes adopted to make the slaves refrain from asking for more food than their regular allowance. A slave runs through his allowance, and applies for more. His master is enraged at him; but, not willing to send him off without food, gives him more than is necessary, and compels him to eat it within a given time. Then, if he complains that he cannot eat it, he is said to be satisfied neither full nor fasting, and is whipped for being hard to please! I have an abundance of such illustrations of the same principle, drawn from my own observation, but think the cases I have cited sufficient. The practice is a very common one.

On the first of January, 1834, I left Mr. Covey, and went to live with Mr. William Freeland, who lived about three miles from St. Michael's. I soon found Mr. Freeland a very different man from Mr. Covey. Though not rich, he was what would be called an educated southern gentleman. Mr. Covey, as I have shown, was a well-trained negro-breaker and slave-driver. The former (slaveholder though he was) seemed to possess some regard for honor, some reverence for justice, and some respect for humanity. The latter seemed totally insensible to all such sentiments. Mr. Freeland had many of the faults peculiar to slaveholders, such as being very

passionate and fretful; but I must do him the justice to say, that he was exceedingly free from those degrading vices to which Mr. Covey was constantly addicted. The one was open and frank, and we always knew where to find him. The other was a most artful deceiver, and could be understood only by such as were skilful enough to detect his cunningly-devised frauds. Another advantage I gained in my new master was, he made no pretensions to, or profession of, religion; and this, in my opinion, was truly a great advantage. I assert most unhesitatingly, that the religion of the south is a mere covering for the most horrid crimes—a justifier of the most appalling barbarity—a sanctifier of the most hateful frauds—and a dark shelter under, which the darkest, foulest, grossest, and most infernal deeds of slaveholders find the strongest protection. Were I to be again reduced to the chains of slavery, next to that enslavement, I should regard being the slave of a religious master the greatest calamity that could befall me. For of all slaveholders with whom I have ever met, religious slaveholders are the worst. I have ever found them the meanest and basest, the most cruel and cowardly, of all others. It was my unhappy lot not only to belong to a religious slaveholder, but to live in a community of such religionists. Very near Mr. Freeland lived the Rev. Daniel Weeden, and in the same neighborhood lived the Rev. Rigby Hopkins. These were members and ministers in the Reformed Methodist Church. Mr. Weeden owned, among others, a woman slave, whose name I have forgotten. This woman's back, for weeks, was kept literally raw, made so by the lash of this merciless, religious wretch. He used to hire hands. His maxim was, Behave well or behave ill, it is the duty of a master occasionally to whip a slave, to remind him of his master's authority. Such was his theory, and such his practice.

Mr. Hopkins was even worse than Mr. Weeden. His chief boast was his ability to manage slaves. The peculiar feature of his government was that of whipping slaves in advance of deserving it. He always managed to have one or more of his slaves to whip every Monday morning. He did this to alarm their fears, and strike terror into those who escaped. His plan was to whip for the smallest offences, to prevent the commission of large ones. Mr. Hopkins could always find some excuse for whipping a slave. It would astonish one, unaccustomed to a slaveholding life, to see with what wonderful ease a slaveholder can find things, of which to make occasion to whip a slave. A mere look, word, or motion—a mistake, accident, or want of power—are all matters for which a slave may be whipped at any time. Does a slave look dissatisfied? It is said, he has the devil in him, and it must be whipped out. Does he speak loudly when spoken to by his master? Then he is getting high-minded, and should be taken down a button-hole lower. Does he forget to pull off his hat at the approach of a white person? Then he is wanting in reverence, and should be whipped for it. Does he ever venture to vindicate his conduct, when censured for it? Then he is guilty of impudence—one of the greatest crimes of which a slave can be guilty. Does he ever venture to suggest a different mode of doing things from that pointed out by his master? He is indeed presumptuous, and getting above himself; and nothing less than a flogging will do for him. Does he, while ploughing, break a plough—or, while hoeing, break a hoe? It is owing to his carelessness, and for it a slave must always be whipped. Mr. Hopkins could always find something of this sort to justify the use of the lash, and he seldom failed to embrace such opportunities. There was not a man in the whole county, with whom the slaves who had the getting their own home, would not prefer to live, rather than with this Rev. Mr. Hopkins. And yet there was not a man anywhere round, who made higher professions of religion, or was more active in revivals—more attentive to the class, love-feast, prayer and preaching meetings, or more devotional in his family—that prayed earlier, later, louder, and longer—than this same reverend slave-driver, Rigby Hopkins.

But to return to Mr. Freeland, and to my experience while in his employment. He, like Mr. Covey, gave us enough to eat; but, unlike Mr. Covey, he also gave us sufficient time to take our meals. He worked us hard, but always between sunrise and sunset. He required a good deal of work to be done, but gave us good tools with which to work. His farm was large, but he employed hands enough to work it, and with ease, compared with many of his neighbors. My treatment, while in his employment, was heavenly, compared with what I experienced at the hands of Mr. Edward Covey.

Mr. Freeland was himself the owner of but two slaves. Their names were Henry Harris and John Harris. The rest of his hands he hired. These consisted of myself, Sandy Jenkins,[1] and Handy Caldwell. Henry and John were quite intelligent, and in a very little while after I went there, I succeeded in creating in them a strong desire to learn how to read. This desire soon sprang up in the others also. They very soon mustered up some old spelling-books, and nothing would do but that I must keep a Sabbath school. I agreed to do so, and accordingly devoted my Sundays to teaching these my loved fellow-slaves how to read. Neither of them knew his letters when I went there. Some of the slaves of the neighboring farms found what was going on, and also availed themselves of this little opportunity to learn to read. It was understood, among all who came, that there must be as little display about it as possible. It was necessary to keep our religious masters at St. Michael's unacquainted with the fact, that, instead of spending the Sabbath in wrestling, boxing, and drinking whisky, we were trying to learn how to read the will of God; for they had much rather see us engaged in those degrading sports, than to see us behaving like intellectual, moral, and accountable beings. My blood boils as I think of the bloody manner in which Messrs. Wright Fairbanks and Garrison West, both class-leaders, in connection with many others, rushed in upon us with sticks and stones, and broke up our virtuous little Sabbath school, at St. Michael's—all calling themselves Christians! humble followers of the Lord Jesus Christ! But I am again digressing.

I held my Sabbath school at the house of a free colored man, whose name I deem it imprudent to mention; for should it be known, it might embarrass him greatly, though the crime of holding the school was committed ten years ago. I had at one time over forty scholars, and those of the right sort, ardently desiring to learn. They were of all ages, though mostly men and women. I look back to those Sundays with an amount of pleasure not to be expressed. They were great days to my soul. The work of instructing my dear fellow-slaves was the sweetest engagement with which I was ever blessed. We loved each other, and to leave them at the

---

1   [Douglass's note]   This is the same man who gave me the roots to prevent my being whipped by Mr. Covey. He was "a clever soul." We used frequently to talk about the fight with Covey, and as often as we did so, he would claim my success as the result of the roots which he gave me. This superstition is very common among the more ignorant slaves. A slave seldom dies but that his death is attributed to trickery.

close of the Sabbath was a severe cross indeed. When I think that these precious souls are today shut up in the prison-house of slavery, my feelings overcome me, and I am almost ready to ask, "Does a righteous God govern the universe? and for what does he hold the thunders in his right hand, if not to smite the oppressor, and deliver the spoiled out of the hand of the spoiler?"[1] These dear souls came not to Sabbath school because it was popular to do so, nor did I teach them because it was reputable to be thus engaged. Every moment they spent in that school, they were liable to be taken up, and given thirty-nine lashes. They came because they wished to learn. Their minds had been starved by their cruel masters. They had been shut up in mental darkness. I taught them, because it was the delight of my soul to be doing something that looked like bettering the condition of my race. I kept up my school nearly the whole year I lived with Mr. Freeland; and, beside my Sabbath school, I devoted three evenings in the week, during the winter, to teaching the slaves at home. And I have the happiness to know, that several of those who came to Sabbath school learned how to read; and that one, at least, is now free through my agency.

The year passed off smoothly. It seemed only about half as long as the year which preceded it. I went through it without receiving a single blow. I will give Mr. Freeland the credit of being the best master I ever had, till I became my own master. For the ease with which I passed the year, I was, however, somewhat indebted to the society of my fellow-slaves. They were noble souls; they not only possessed loving hearts, but brave ones. We were linked and interlinked with each other. I loved them with a love stronger than anything I have experienced since. It is sometimes said that we slaves do not love and confide in each other. In answer to this assertion, I can say, I never loved any or confided in any people more than my fellow-slaves, and especially those with whom I lived at Mr. Freeland's. I believe we would have died for each other. We never undertook to do anything, of any importance, without a mutual consultation. We never moved separately. We were one; and as much so by our tempers and

dispositions, as by the mutual hardships to which we were necessarily subjected by our condition as slaves.

At the close of the year 1834, Mr. Freeland again hired me of my master, for the year 1835. But, by this time, I began to want to live upon free land as well as with Freeland; and I was no longer content, therefore, to live with him or any other slaveholder. I began, with the commencement of the year, to prepare myself for a final struggle, which should decide my fate one way or the other. My tendency was upward. I was fast approaching manhood, and year after year had passed, and I was still a slave. These thoughts roused me—I must do something. I therefore resolved that 1835 should not pass without witnessing an attempt, on my part, to secure my liberty. But I was not willing to cherish this determination alone. My fellow-slaves were dear to me. I was anxious to have them participate with me in this, my life-giving determination. I therefore, though with great prudence, commenced early to ascertain their views and feelings in regard to their condition, and to imbue their minds with thoughts of freedom. I bent myself to devising ways and means for our escape, and meanwhile strove, on all fitting occasions, to impress them with the gross fraud and inhumanity of slavery. I went first to Henry, next to John, then to the others. I found, in them all, warm hearts and noble spirits. They were ready to hear, and ready to act when a feasible plan should be proposed. This was what I wanted. I talked to them of our want of manhood, if we submitted to our enslavement without at least one noble effort to be free. We met often, and consulted frequently, and told our hopes and fears, recounted the difficulties, real and imagined, which we should be called on to meet. At times we were almost disposed to give up, and try to content ourselves with our wretched lot; at others, we were firm and unbending in our determination to go. Whenever we suggested any plan, there was shrinking—the odds were fearful. Our path was beset with the greatest obstacles; and if we succeeded in gaining the end of it, our right to be free was yet questionable—we were yet liable to be returned to bondage. We could see no spot, this side of the ocean, where we could be free. We knew nothing about Canada. Our knowledge of the north did not extend farther than New York; and to go there, and be forever harassed with the frightful liability of

---

[1]   *Does a righteous … the spoiler*   These lines contain allusions to several biblical passages, including Exodus 15 and Isaiah 33.1.

being returned to slavery—with the certainty of being treated tenfold worse than before—the thought was truly a horrible one, and one which it was not easy to overcome. The case sometimes stood thus: At every gate through which we were to pass, we saw a watchman—at every ferry a guard—on every bridge a sentinel—and in every wood a patrol. We were hemmed in upon every side. Here were the difficulties, real or imagined—the good to be sought, and the evil to be shunned. On the one hand, there stood slavery, a stern reality, glaring frightfully upon us—its robes already crimsoned with the blood of millions, and even now feasting itself greedily upon our own flesh. On the other hand, away back in the dim distance, under the flickering light of the north star, behind some craggy hill or snow-covered mountain, stood a doubtful freedom—half frozen—beckoning us to come and share its hospitality. This in itself was sometimes enough to stagger us; but when we permitted ourselves to survey the road, we were frequently appalled. Upon either side we saw grim death, assuming the most horrid shapes. Now it was starvation, causing us to eat our own flesh; now we were contending with the waves, and were drowned; now we were overtaken, and torn to pieces by the fangs of the terrible bloodhound. We were stung by scorpions, chased by wild beasts, bitten by snakes, and finally, after having nearly reached the desired spot—after swimming rivers, encountering wild beasts, sleeping in the woods, suffering hunger and nakedness—we were overtaken by our pursuers, and, in our resistance, we were shot dead upon the spot! I say, this picture sometimes appalled us, and made us

> rather bear those ills we had,
> Than fly to others, that we knew not of.[1]

In coming to a fixed determination to run away, we did more than Patrick Henry, when he resolved upon liberty or death. With us it was a doubtful liberty at most, and almost certain death if we failed. For my part, I should prefer death to hopeless bondage. Sandy, one of our number, gave up the notion, but still encouraged us. Our company then consisted of Henry Harris, John Harris, Henry Bailey, Charles

Roberts, and myself. Henry Bailey was my uncle, and belonged to my master. Charles married my aunt: he belonged to my master's father-in-law, Mr. William Hamilton.

The plan we finally concluded upon was, to get a large canoe belonging to Mr. Hamilton, and upon the Saturday night previous to Easter holidays, paddle directly up the Chesapeake Bay. On our arrival at the head of the bay, a distance of seventy or eighty miles from where we lived, it was our purpose to turn our canoe adrift, and follow the guidance of the north star till we got beyond the limits of Maryland. Our reason for taking the water route was, that we were less liable to be suspected as runaways; we hoped to be regarded as fishermen; whereas, if we should take the land route, we should be subjected to interruptions of almost every kind. Anyone having a white face, and being so disposed, could stop us, and subject us to examination.

The week before our intended start, I wrote several protections, one for each of us. As well as I can remember, they were in the following words, to wit:

> This is to certify that I, the undersigned, have given the bearer, my servant, full liberty to go to Baltimore, and spend the Easter holidays. Written with mine own hand, &c., 1835.
> WILLIAM HAMILTON,
>   Near St. Michael's, in Talbot county, Maryland

We were not going to Baltimore; but, in going up the bay, we went toward Baltimore, and these protections were only intended to protect us while on the bay

As the time drew near for our departure, our anxiety became more and more intense. It was truly a matter of life and death with us. The strength of our determination was about to be fully tested. At this time, I was very active in explaining every difficulty, removing every doubt, dispelling every fear, and inspiring all with the firmness indispensable to success in our undertaking; assuring them that half was gained the instant we made the move; we had talked long enough; we were now ready to move; if not now, we never should be; and if we did not intend to move now, we had as well fold our arms, sit down, and acknowledge ourselves fit only to be slaves. This, none of us were

---

[1]   *rather bear ... knew not of*   See Shakespeare's *Hamlet* 3.1.89–90.

prepared to acknowledge. Every man stood firm; and at our last meeting, we pledged ourselves afresh, in the most solemn manner, that, at the time appointed, we would certainly start in pursuit of freedom. This was in the middle of the week, at the end of which we were to be off. We went, as usual, to our several fields of labor, but with bosoms highly agitated with thoughts of our truly hazardous undertaking. We tried to conceal our feelings as much as possible; and I think we succeeded very well.

After a painful waiting, the Saturday morning, whose night was to witness our departure, came. I hailed it with joy, bring what of sadness it might. Friday night was a sleepless one for me. I probably felt more anxious than the rest, because I was, by common consent, at the head of the whole affair. The responsibility of success or failure lay heavily upon me. The glory of the one, and the confusion of the other, were alike mine. The first two hours of that morning were such as I never experienced before, and hope never to again. Early in the morning, we went, as usual, to the field. We were spreading manure; and all at once, while thus engaged, I was overwhelmed with an indescribable feeling, in the fulness of which I turned to Sandy, who was near by, and said, "We are betrayed!" "Well," said he, "that thought has this moment struck me." We said no more. I was never more certain of anything.

The horn was blown as usual, and we went up from the field to the house for breakfast. I went for the form, more than for want of anything to eat that morning. Just as I got to the house, in looking out at the lane gate, I saw four white men, with two colored men. The white men were on horseback, and the colored ones were walking behind, as if tied. I watched them a few moments till they got up to our lane gate. Here they halted, and tied the colored men to the gate-post. I was not yet certain as to what the matter was. In a few moments, in rode Mr. Hamilton, with a speed betokening great excitement. He came to the door, and inquired if Master William was in. He was told he was at the barn. Mr. Hamilton, without dismounting, rode up to the barn with extraordinary speed. In a few moments, he and Mr. Freeland returned to the house. By this time, the three constables rode up, and in great haste dismounted, tied their horses, and met Master William and Mr. Hamilton returning from

the barn; and after talking awhile, they all walked up to the kitchen door. There was no one in the kitchen but myself and John. Henry and Sandy were up at the barn. Mr. Freeland put his head in at the door, and called me by name, saying, there were some gentlemen at the door who wished to see me. I stepped to the door, and inquired what they wanted. They at once seized me, and, without giving me any satisfaction, tied me—lashing my hands closely together. I insisted upon knowing what the matter was. They at length said, that they had learned I had been in a "scrape," and that I was to be examined before my master; and if their information proved false, I should not be hurt.

In a few moments, they succeeded in tying John. They then turned to Henry, who had by this time returned, and commanded him to cross his hands. "I won't!" said Henry, in a firm tone, indicating his readiness to meet the consequences of his refusal. "Won't you?" said Tom Graham, the constable. "No, I won't!" said Henry, in a still stronger tone. With this, two of the constables pulled out their shining pistols, and swore, by their Creator, that they would make him cross his hands or kill him. Each cocked his pistol, and, with fingers on the trigger, walked up to Henry, saying, at the same time, if he did not cross his hands, they would blow his damned heart out. "Shoot me, shoot me!" said Henry; "you can't kill me but once. Shoot, shoot—and be damned! I won't be tied!" This he said in a tone of loud defiance; and at the same time, with a motion as quick as lightning, he with one single stroke dashed the pistols from the hand of each constable. As he did this, all hands fell upon him, and, after beating him some time, they finally overpowered him, and got him tied.

During the scuffle, I managed, I know not how, to get my pass out, and, without being discovered, put it into the fire. We were all now tied; and just as we were to leave for Easton jail, Betsy Freeland, mother of William Freeland, came to the door with her hands full of biscuits, and divided them between Henry and John. She then delivered herself of a speech, to the following effect: addressing herself to me, she said, "You devil! You yellow devil! it was you that put it into the heads of Henry and John to run away. But for you, you long-legged mulatto devil! Henry nor John would never have thought of such a thing." I made no reply, and was immediately hurried off towards St. Michael's. Just a moment previous to the scuffle with Henry, Mr. Hamilton suggested the propriety of making a search for the protections which he had understood Frederick had written for himself and the rest. But, just at the moment he was about carrying his proposal into effect, his aid was needed in helping to tie Henry; and the excitement attending the scuffle caused them either to forget, or to deem it unsafe, under the circumstances, to search. So we were not yet convicted of the intention to run away.

When we got about half way to St. Michael's, while the constables having us in charge were looking ahead, Henry inquired of me what he should do with his pass. I told him to eat it with his biscuit, and own nothing; and we passed the word around, "Own nothing"; and "Own nothing!" said we all. Our confidence in each other was unshaken. We were resolved to succeed or fail together, after the calamity had befallen us as much as before. We were now prepared for anything. We were to be dragged that morning fifteen miles behind horses, and then to be placed in the Easton jail. When we reached St. Michael's, we underwent a sort of examination. We all denied that we ever intended to run away. We did this more to bring out the evidence against us, than from any hope of getting clear of being sold; for, as I have said, we were ready for that. The fact was, we cared but little where we went, so we went together. Our greatest concern was about separation. We dreaded that more than anything this side of death. We found the evidence against us to be the testimony of one person; our master would not tell who it was; but we came to a unanimous decision among ourselves as to who their informant was. We were sent off to the jail at Easton. When we got there, we were delivered up to the sheriff, Mr. Joseph Graham, and by him placed in jail. Henry, John, and myself, were placed in one room together—Charles, and Henry Bailey, in another. Their object in separating us was to hinder concert.

We had been in jail scarcely twenty minutes, when a swarm of slave traders, and agents for slave traders, flocked into jail to look at us, and to ascertain if we were for sale. Such a set of beings I never saw before! I felt myself surrounded by so many fiends from perdition.[1] A band of pirates never looked more like their father, the devil. They laughed and grinned over us, saying, "Ah, my boys! we have got you, haven't we?" And after taunting us in various ways, they one by one went into an examination of us, with intent to ascertain our value. They would impudently ask us if we would not like to have them for our masters. We would make them no answer, and leave them to find out as best they could. Then they would curse and swear at us, telling us that they could take the devil out of us in a very little while, if we were only in their hands.

While in jail, we found ourselves in much more comfortable quarters than we expected when we went there. We did not get much to eat, nor that which was very good; but we had a good clean room, from the windows of which we could see what was going on in the street, which was very much better than though we had been placed in one of the dark, damp cells. Upon the whole, we got along very well, so far as the jail and its keeper were concerned. Immediately after the holidays were over, contrary to all our expectations, Mr. Hamilton and Mr. Freeland came up to Easton, and took Charles, the two Henrys, and John, out of jail, and carried them home, leaving me alone. I regarded this separation as a final one. It caused me more pain than anything else in the whole transaction. I was ready for anything rather than separation. I supposed that they had consulted together, and had decided that, as I was the whole cause of the intention of the others to run away, it was hard to make the innocent suffer with the guilty; and that they had, therefore, concluded to take the others home, and sell me, as a warning to the others that remained. It is due to the noble Henry to say, he seemed almost as reluctant at leaving the prison as at leaving home to come to the prison. But we knew we should, in all probability, be separated, if we were sold; and since he was in their hands, he concluded to go peaceably home.

I was now left to my fate. I was all alone, and within the walls of a stone prison. But a few days before, and I was full of hope. I expected to have been safe in a land of freedom; but now I was covered with gloom, sunk down to the utmost despair. I thought the possibility of freedom was gone. I was kept in this way about one week, at the end of which, Captain Auld, my master, to my surprise and utter astonishment, came up, and took me out, with the intention of sending me, with

---

[1] *perdition* Hell.

a gentleman of his acquaintance, into Alabama. But, from some cause or other, he did not send me to Alabama, but concluded to send me back to Baltimore, to live again with his brother Hugh, and to learn a trade.

Thus, after an absence of three years and one month, I was once more permitted to return to my old home at Baltimore. My master sent me away, because there existed against me a very great prejudice in the community, and he feared I might be killed.

In a few weeks after I went to Baltimore, Master Hugh hired me to Mr. William Gardner, an extensive ship-builder, on Fell's Point. I was put there to learn how to caulk.[1] It, however, proved a very unfavorable place for the accomplishment of this object. Mr. Gardner was engaged that spring in building two large man-of-war brigs, professedly for the Mexican government. The vessels were to be launched in the July of that year, and in failure thereof, Mr. Gardner was to lose a considerable sum; so that when I entered, all was hurry. There was no time to learn anything. Every man had to do that which he knew how to do. In entering the shipyard, my orders from Mr. Gardner were, to do whatever the carpenters commanded me to do. This was placing me at the beck and call of about seventy-five men. I was to regard all these as masters. Their word was to be my law. My situation was a most trying one. At times I needed a dozen pair of hands. I was called a dozen ways in the space of a single minute. Three or four voices would strike my ear at the same moment. It was—"Fred., come help me to cant[2] this timber here."—"Fred., come carry this timber yonder."—"Fred., bring that roller here."—"Fred., go get a fresh can of water."—"Fred., come help saw off the end of this timber."—"Fred., go quick, and get the crowbar."—"Fred., hold on the end of this fall."[3]—"Fred., go to the blacksmith's shop, and get a new punch."—"Hurra, Fred! run and bring me a cold chisel."—"I say, Fred., bear a hand, and get up a fire as quick as lightning under that steam-box."—"Halloo, nigger! come, turn this grindstone."—"Come, come!

move, move! and bowse[4] this timber forward."—"I say, darky, blast your eyes, why don't you heat up some pitch?"—"Halloo! halloo! halloo!" (Three voices at the same time.) "Come here!—Go there!—Hold on where you are! Damn you, if you move, I'll knock your brains out!"

This was my school for eight months; and I might have remained there longer, but for a most horrid fight I had with four of the white apprentices, in which my left eye was nearly knocked out, and I was horribly mangled in other respects. The facts in the case were these: Until a very little while after I went there, white and black ship-carpenters worked side by side, and no one seemed to see any impropriety in it. All hands seemed to be very well satisfied. Many of the black carpenters were freemen. Things seemed to be going on very well. All at once, the white carpenters knocked off, and said they would not work with free colored workmen. Their reason for this, as alleged, was, that if free colored carpenters were encouraged, they would soon take the trade into their own hands, and poor white men would be thrown out of employment. They therefore felt called upon at once to put a stop to it. And, taking advantage of Mr. Gardner's necessities, they broke off, swearing they would work no longer, unless he would discharge his black carpenters. Now, though this did not extend to me in form, it did reach me in fact. My fellow-apprentices very soon began to feel it degrading to them to work with me. They began to put on airs, and talk about the "niggers" taking the country, saying we all ought to be killed; and, being encouraged by the journeymen, they commenced making my condition as hard as they could, by hectoring me around, and sometimes striking me. I, of course, kept the vow I made after the fight with Mr. Covey, and struck back again, regardless of consequences; and while I kept them from combining, I succeeded very well; for I could whip the whole of them, taking them separately. They, however, at length combined, and came upon me, armed with sticks, stones, and heavy handspikes. One came in front with a half brick. There was one at each side of me, and one behind me. While I was attending to those in front, and on either side, the one behind ran up with the handspike, and struck me a heavy blow upon the head. It stunned me. I fell, and

---

[1]   *caulk*   Seal the wooden seams of a boat against leakage with oakum and melted tar.

[2]   *cant*   Smoothen a sharp angle.

[3]   *fall*   Free end of a rope used for hauling.

[4]   *bowse*   Haul.

with this they all ran upon me, and fell to beating me with their fists. I let them lay on for a while, gathering strength. In an instant, I gave a sudden surge, and rose to my hands and knees. Just as I did that, one of their number gave me, with his heavy boot, a powerful kick in the left eye. My eyeball seemed to have burst. When they saw my eye closed, and badly swollen, they left me. With this I seized the handspike, and for a time pursued them. But here the carpenters interfered, and I thought I might as well give it up. It was impossible to stand my hand against so many. All this took place in sight of not less than fifty white ship-carpenters, and not one interposed a friendly word; but some cried, "Kill the damned nigger! Kill him! kill him! He struck a white person." I found my only chance for life was in flight. I succeeded in getting away without an additional blow, and barely so; for to strike a white man is death by Lynch law[1]—and that was the law in Mr. Gardner's shipyard; nor is there much of any other out of Mr. Gardner's shipyard.

I went directly home, and told the story of my wrongs to Master Hugh; and I am happy to say of him, irreligious as he was, his conduct was heavenly, compared with that of his brother Thomas under similar circumstances. He listened attentively to my narration of the circumstances leading to the savage outrage, and gave many proofs of his strong indignation at it. The heart of my once overkind mistress was again melted into pity. My puffed-out eye and blood-covered face moved her to tears. She took a chair by me, washed the blood from my face, and, with a mother's tenderness, bound up my head, covering the wounded eye with a lean piece of fresh beef. It was almost compensation for my suffering to witness, once more, a manifestation of kindness from this, my once affectionate old mistress. Master Hugh was very much enraged. He gave expression to his feelings by pouring out curses upon the heads of those who did the deed. As soon as I got a little the better of my bruises, he took me with him

to Esquire Watson's, on Bond Street, to see what could be done about the matter. Mr. Watson inquired who saw the assault committed. Master Hugh told him it was done in Mr. Gardner's ship-yard at midday, where there were a large company of men at work. "As to that," he said, "the deed was done, and there was no question as to who did it." His answer was, he could do nothing in the case, unless some white man would come forward and testify. He could issue no warrant on my word. If I had been killed in the presence of a thousand colored people, their testimony combined would have been insufficient to have arrested one of the murderers. Master Hugh, for once, was compelled to say this state of things was too bad. Of course, it was impossible to get any white man to volunteer his testimony in my behalf, and against the white young men. Even those who may have sympathized with me were not prepared to do this. It required a degree of courage unknown to them to do so; for just at that time, the slightest manifestation of humanity toward a colored person was denounced as abolitionism, and that name subjected its bearer to frightful liabilities. The watchwords of the bloody-minded in that region, and in those days, were, "Damn the abolitionists!" and "Damn the niggers!" There was nothing done, and probably nothing would have been done if I had been killed. Such was, and such remains, the state of things in the Christian city of Baltimore.

Master Hugh, finding he could get no redress, refused to let me go back again to Mr. Gardner. He kept me himself, and his wife dressed my wound till I was again restored to health. He then took me into the ship-yard of which he was foreman, in the employment of Mr. Walter Price. There I was immediately set to calking, and very soon learned the art of using my mallet and irons. In the course of one year from the time I left Mr. Gardner's, I was able to command the highest wages given to the most experienced caulkers. I was now of some importance to my master. I was bringing him from six to seven dollars per week. I sometimes brought him nine dollars per week: my wages were a dollar and a half a day. After learning how to caulk, I sought my own employment, made my own contracts, and collected the money which I earned. My pathway became much more smooth than before; my condition was now much more comfortable. When I

---

[1]   *is death by Lynch law*   Will lead inevitably to being lynched (i.e., killed by a vigilante mob falsely claiming to be administering justice). Though some lynchings targeted Jews and other minorities, the vast majority were racially motivated murders of black persons by white mobs; the practice became increasingly widespread following the end of Reconstruction in 1877, and remained common throughout the early decades of the twentieth century, during the Jim Crow era of segregation.

could get no calking to do, I did nothing. During these leisure times, those old notions about freedom would steal over me again. When in Mr. Gardner's employment, I was kept in such a perpetual whirl of excitement, I could think of nothing, scarcely, but my life; and in thinking of my life, I almost forgot my liberty. I have observed this in my experience of slavery—that whenever my condition was improved, instead of its increasing my contentment, it only increased my desire to be free, and set me to thinking of plans to gain my freedom. I have found that, to make a contented slave, it is necessary to make a thoughtless one. It is necessary to darken his moral and mental vision, and, as far as possible, to annihilate the power of reason. He must be able to detect no inconsistencies in slavery; he must be made to feel that slavery is right; and he can be brought to that only when he ceases to be a man.

I was now getting, as I have said, one dollar and fifty cents per day. I contracted for it; I earned it; it was paid to me; it was rightfully my own; yet, upon each returning Saturday night, I was compelled to deliver every cent of that money to Master Hugh. And why? Not because he earned it—not because he had any hand in earning it—not because I owed it to him—nor because he possessed the slightest shadow of a right to it; but solely because he had the power to compel me to give it up. The right of the grim-visaged pirate upon the high seas is exactly the same.

CHAPTER 11

I now come to that part of my life during which I planned, and finally succeeded in making, my escape from slavery. But before narrating any of the peculiar circumstances, I deem it proper to make known my intention not to state all the facts connected with the transaction. My reasons for pursuing this course may be understood from the following: First, were I to give a minute statement of all the facts, it is not only possible, but quite probably, that others would thereby be involved in the most embarrassing difficulties. Secondly, such a statement would most undoubtedly induce greater vigilance on the part of slaveholders than has existed heretofore among them; which would, of course, be the means of guarding a door whereby some dear brother bondsman might escape his galling chains. I deeply regret the necessity that impels me to suppress anything of importance connected with my experience in slavery. It would afford me great pleasure indeed, as well as materially add to the interest of my narrative, were I at liberty to gratify a curiosity, which I know exists in the minds of many, by an accurate statement of all the facts pertaining to my most fortunate escape. But I must deprive myself of this pleasure, and the curious of the gratification which such a statement would afford. I would allow myself to suffer under the greatest imputations which evil-minded men might suggest, rather than exculpate myself, and thereby run the hazard of closing the slightest avenue by which a brother slave might clear himself of the chains and fetters of slavery.

I have never approved of the very public manner in which some of our western friends have conducted what they call the underground railroad,[1] but which I think, by their open declarations, has been made most emphatically the upper-ground railroad. I honor those good men and women for their noble daring, and applaud them for willingly subjecting themselves to bloody persecution, by openly avowing their participation in the escape of slaves. I, however, can see very little good resulting from such a course, either to themselves or the slaves escaping; while, upon the other hand, I see and feel assured that those open declarations are a positive evil to the slaves remaining, who are seeking to escape. They do nothing towards enlightening the slave, whilst they do much towards enlightening the master. They stimulate him to greater watchfulness, and enhance his power to capture his slave. We owe something to the slave south of the line as well as to those north of it; and in aiding the latter on their way to freedom, we should be careful to do nothing which would be likely to hinder the former from escaping from slavery. I would keep the merciless slaveholder profoundly ignorant of the means of flight adopted by the slave. I would leave him to imagine himself surrounded by myriads of invisible tormentors, ever ready to snatch from his infernal grasp his trembling prey. Let him be left to feel his way in the dark; let darkness commensurate with his crime hover

---

[1]   *underground railroad*   Secret network of people and safe-houses by means of which many enslaved persons escaped to the North.

over him; and let him feel that at every step he takes, in pursuit of the flying bondman, he is running the frightful risk of having his hot brains dashed out by an invisible agency. Let us render the tyrant no aid; let us not hold the light by which he can trace the footprints of our flying brother. But enough of this. I will now proceed to the statement of those facts, connected with my escape, for which I am alone responsible, and for which no one can be made to suffer but myself.

In the early part of the year 1838, I became quite restless. I could see no reason why I should, at the end of each week, pour the reward of my toil into the purse of my master. When I carried to him my weekly wages, he would, after counting the money, look me in the face with a robber-like fierceness, and ask, "Is this all?" He was satisfied with nothing less than the last cent. He would, however, when I made him six dollars, sometimes give me six cents, to encourage me. It had the opposite effect. I regarded it as a sort of admission of my right to the whole. The fact that he gave me any part of my wages was proof, to my mind, that he believed me entitled to the whole of them. I always felt worse for having received anything; for I feared that the giving me a few cents would ease his conscience, and make him feel himself to be a pretty honorable sort of robber. My discontent grew upon me. I was ever on the look-out for means of escape; and, finding no direct means, I determined to try to hire my time, with a view of getting money with which to make my escape. In the spring of 1838, when Master Thomas came to Baltimore to purchase his spring goods, I got an opportunity, and applied to him to allow me to hire my time. He unhesitatingly refused my request, and told me this was another stratagem by which to escape. He told me I could go nowhere but that he could get me; and that, in the event of my running away, he should spare no pains in his efforts to catch me. He exhorted me to content myself, and be obedient. He told me, if I would be happy, I must lay out no plans for the future. He said, if I behaved myself properly, he would take care of me. Indeed, he advised me to complete thoughtlessness of the future, and taught me to depend solely upon him for happiness. He seemed to see fully the pressing necessity of setting aside my intellectual nature, in order to contentment in slavery. But in spite of him, and even in spite of myself, I continued to think, and to think about the injustice of my enslavement, and the means of escape.

About two months after this, I applied to Master Hugh for the privilege of hiring my time. He was not acquainted with the fact that I had applied to Master Thomas, and had been refused. He too, at first, seemed disposed to refuse; but, after some reflection, he granted me the privilege, and proposed the following terms: I was to be allowed all my time, make all contracts with those for whom I worked, and find my own employment; and, in return for this liberty, I was to pay him three dollars at the end of each week; find myself in calking tools, and in board and clothing. My board was two dollars and a half per week. This, with the wear and tear of clothing and calking tools, made my regular expenses about six dollars per week. This amount I was compelled to make up, or relinquish the privilege of hiring my time. Rain or shine, work or no work, at the end of each week the money must be forthcoming, or I must give up my privilege. This arrangement, it will be perceived, was decidedly in my master's favor. It relieved him of all need of looking after me. His money was sure. He received all the benefits of slaveholding without its evils; while I endured all the evils of a slave, and suffered all the care and anxiety of a freeman. I found it a hard bargain. But, hard as it was, I thought it better than the old mode of getting along. It was a step towards freedom to be allowed to bear the responsibilities of a freeman, and I was determined to hold on upon it. I bent myself to the work of making money. I was ready to work at night as well as day, and by the most untiring perseverance and industry, I made enough to meet my expenses, and lay up a little money every week. I went on thus from May till August. Master Hugh then refused to allow me to hire my time longer. The ground for his refusal was a failure on my part, one Saturday night, to pay him for my week's time. This failure was occasioned by my attending a camp meeting about ten miles from Baltimore. During the week, I had entered into an engagement with a number of young friends to start from Baltimore to the camp ground early Saturday evening; and being detained by my employer, I was unable to get down to Master Hugh's without disappointing the company. I knew that Master Hugh was in no special need of the money that night. I therefore decided to go to camp meeting, and upon my return pay him the three dollars. I stayed at the camp meeting one day longer than I intended when I left. But as soon as I returned, I called upon him to pay him what he considered his due. I found him very angry; he could scarce restrain his wrath. He said he had a great mind to give me a severe whipping. He wished to know how I dared to go out of the city without asking his permission. I told him I hired my time and while I paid him the price which he asked for it, I did not know that I was bound to ask him when and where I should go. This reply troubled him; and, after reflecting a few moments, he turned to me, and said I should hire my time no longer; that the next thing he should know of, I would be running away. Upon the same plea, he told me to bring my tools and clothing home forthwith. I did so; but instead of seeking work, as I had been accustomed to do previously to hiring my time, I spent the whole week without the performance of a single stroke of work. I did this in retaliation. Saturday night, he called upon me as usual for my week's wages. I told him I had no wages; I had done no work that week. Here we were upon the point of coming to blows. He raved, and swore his determination to get hold of me. I did not allow myself a single word; but was resolved, if he laid the weight of his hand upon me, it should be blow for blow. He did not strike me, but told me that he would find me in constant employment in future. I thought the matter over during the next day, Sunday, and finally resolved upon the third day of September, as the day upon which I would make a second attempt to secure my freedom. I now had three weeks during which to prepare for my journey. Early on Monday morning, before Master Hugh had time to make any engagement for me, I went out and got employment of Mr. Butler, at his ship-yard near the drawbridge, upon what is called the City Block, thus making it unnecessary for him to seek employment for me. At the end of the week, I brought him between eight and nine dollars. He seemed very well pleased, and asked why I did not do the same the week before. He little knew what my plans were. My object in working steadily was to remove any suspicion he might entertain of my intent to run away; and in this I succeeded admirably. I suppose he thought I was never better satisfied with

my condition than at the very time during which I was planning my escape. The second week passed, and again I carried him my full wages; and so well pleased was he, that he gave me twenty-five cents (quite a large sum for a slaveholder to give a slave), and bade me to make a good use of it. I told him I would.

Things went on without very smoothly indeed, but within there was trouble.[1] It is impossible for me to describe my feelings as the time of my contemplated start drew near. I had a number of warmhearted friends in Baltimore—friends that I loved almost as I did my life—and the thought of being separated from them forever was painful beyond expression. It is my opinion that thousands would escape from slavery, who now remain, but for the strong cords of affection that bind them to their friends. The thought of leaving my friends was decidedly the most painful thought with which I had to contend. The love of them was my tender point, and shook my decision more than all things else. Besides the pain of separation, the dread and apprehension of a failure exceeded what I had experienced at my first attempt. The appalling defeat I then sustained returned to torment me. I felt assured that, if I failed in this attempt, my case would be a hopeless one—it would seal my fate as a slave forever. I could not hope to get off with anything less than the severest punishment, and being placed beyond the means of escape. It required no very vivid imagination to depict the most frightful scenes through which I should have to pass, in case I failed. The wretchedness of slavery, and the blessedness of freedom, were perpetually before me. It was life and death with me. But I remained firm, and, according to my resolution, on the third day of September, 1838, I left my chains, and succeeded in reaching New York without the slightest interruption of any kind. How I did so—what means I adopted, what direction I travelled, and by what mode of conveyance—I must leave unexplained, for the reasons before mentioned.

I have been frequently asked how I felt when I found myself in a free State. I have never been able to answer the question with any satisfaction to myself. It was a moment of the highest excitement I ever experienced. I suppose I felt as one may imagine the unarmed mariner to feel when he is rescued by a friendly man-of-war[2]

---

1   *within there was trouble*   I felt troubled within myself.

2   *man-of-war*   Large warship.

from the pursuit of a pirate. In writing to a dear friend, immediately after my arrival at New York, I said I felt like one who had escaped a den of hungry lions. This state of mind, however, very soon subsided; and I was again seized with a feeling of great insecurity and loneliness. I was yet liable to be taken back, and subjected to all the tortures of slavery.[1] This in itself was enough to damp the ardor of my enthusiasm. But the loneliness overcame me. There I was in the midst of thousands, and yet a perfect stranger; without home and without friends, in the midst of thousands of my own brethren—children of a common Father, and yet I dared not to unfold to any one of them my sad condition. I was afraid to speak to anyone for fear of speaking to the wrong one, and thereby falling into the hands of money-loving kidnappers, whose business it was to lie in wait for the panting fugitive, as the ferocious beasts of the forest lie in wait for their prey. The motto which I adopted when I started from slavery was this—"Trust no man!" I saw in every white man an enemy, and in almost every colored man cause for distrust. It was a most painful situation; and, to understand it, one must needs experience it, or imagine himself in similar circumstances. Let him be a fugitive slave in a strange land—a land given up to be the hunting-ground for slaveholders—whose inhabitants are legalized kidnappers—where he is every moment subjected to the terrible liability of being seized upon by his fellowmen, as the hideous crocodile seizes upon his prey!—I say, let him place himself in my situation—without home or friends—without money or credit—wanting[2] shelter, and no one to give it—wanting bread, and no money to buy it—and at the same time let him feel that he is pursued by merciless men-hunters, and in total darkness as to what to do, where to go, or where to stay— perfectly helpless both as to the means of defence and means of escape—in the midst of plenty, yet suffering the terrible gnawings of hunger—in the midst of houses, yet having no home—among fellow-men, yet feeling as if in the midst of wild beasts, whose greediness to swallow up the trembling and half-famished fugitive is only equalled by that with which the monsters of the deep swallow up the helpless fish upon which they subsist—I say, let him be placed in this most trying situation—the situation in which I was placed—then, and not till then, will he fully appreciate the hardships of, and know how to sympathize with, the toil-worn and whip-scarred fugitive slave.

Thank Heaven, I remained but a short time in this distressed situation. I was relieved from it by the humane hand of Mr. David Ruggles,[3] whose vigilance, kindness, and perseverance, I shall never forget. I am glad of an opportunity to express, as far as words can, the love and gratitude I bear him. Mr. Ruggles is now afflicted with blindness, and is himself in need of the same kind offices which he was once so forward in the performance of toward others. I had been in New York but a few days, when Mr. Ruggles sought me out, and very kindly took me to his boarding-house at the corner of Church and Lespenard Streets. Mr. Ruggles was then very deeply engaged in the memorable Darg case,[4] as well as attending to a number of other fugitive slaves, devising ways and means for their successful escape; and, though watched and hemmed in on almost every side, he seemed to be more than a match for his enemies.

Very soon after I went to Mr. Ruggles, he wished to know of me where I wanted to go; as he deemed it unsafe for me to remain in New York. I told him I was a caulker, and should like to go where I could get work. I thought of going to Canada; but he decided against it, and in favor of my going to New Bedford, thinking I should be able to get work there at my trade. At this time, Anna,[5] my intended wife, came on; for I wrote to her immediately after my arrival at New York (notwithstanding my homeless, houseless, and helpless condition), informing her of my successful flight, and wishing her to come on forthwith. In a few days after her arrival, Mr. Ruggles called in the Rev. J.W.C.

---

1   *I was yet liable ... tortures of slavery*   When an enslaved person escaped, under the provisions of the Fugitive Slave Act of 1793 a slaveholder was guaranteed the right to seek out, capture, and return that person to enslavement. (Later, the Fugitive Slave Act of 1850 made these provisions even harsher.)

2   *wanting*   Lacking.

3   *Mr. David Ruggles*   Free-born black abolitionist from Connecticut (1810–49), who aided fugitives via the Underground Railroad.

4   *Darg case*   In 1838, Ruggles had been involved in assisting the enslaved man Thomas Hughes in escaping from the enslaver John P. Darg, for which involvement Ruggles was briefly imprisoned.

5   [Douglass's note]   She was free.

Pennington,[1] who, in the presence of Mr. Ruggles, Mrs. Michaels, and two or three others, performed the marriage ceremony, and gave us a certificate, of which the following is an exact copy:

This may certify, that I joined together in holy matrimony Frederick Johnson[2] and Anna Murray, as man and wife, in the presence of Mr. David Ruggles and Mrs. Michaels.
                    JAMES W.C. PENNINGTON
                         New York, Sept. 15, 1838

Upon receiving this certificate, and a five-dollar bill from Mr. Ruggles, I shouldered one part of our baggage, and Anna took up the other, and we set out forthwith to take passage on board of the steamboat John W. Richmond for Newport, on our way to New Bedford. Mr. Ruggles gave me a letter to a Mr. Shaw in Newport, and told me, in case my money did not serve me to New Bedford, to stop in Newport and obtain further assistance; but upon our arrival at Newport, we were so anxious to get to a place of safety, that, notwithstanding we lacked the necessary money to pay our fare, we decided to take seats in the stage,[3] and promise to pay when we got to New Bedford. We were encouraged to do this by two excellent gentlemen, residents of New Bedford, whose names I afterward ascertained to be Joseph Ricketson and William C. Taber. They seemed at once to understand our circumstances, and gave us such assurance of their friendliness as put us fully at ease in their presence. It was good indeed to meet with such friends, at such a time. Upon reaching New Bedford, we were directed to the house of Mr. Nathan Johnson, by whom we were kindly received, and hospitably provided for. Both Mr. and Mrs. Johnson took a deep and lively interest in our welfare. They proved themselves quite worthy of the name of abolitionists. When the stage-driver found us unable to pay our fare, he held on upon our baggage as security for the debt. I had but to mention the fact to Mr. Johnson, and he forthwith advanced the money.

We now began to feel a degree of safety, and to prepare ourselves for the duties and responsibilities of a life of freedom. On the morning after our arrival at New Bedford, while at the breakfast-table, the question arose as to what name I should be called by. The name given me by my mother was, "Frederick Augustus Washington Bailey." I, however, had dispensed with the two middle names long before I left Maryland so that I was generally known by the name of "Frederick Bailey." I started from Baltimore bearing the name of "Stanley." When I got to New York, I again changed my name to "Frederick Johnson," and thought that would be the last change. But when I got to New Bedford, I found it necessary again to change my name. The reason of this necessity was, that there were so many Johnsons in New Bedford, it was already quite difficult to distinguish between them. I gave Mr. Johnson the privilege of choosing me a name, but told him he must not take from me the name of "Frederick." I must hold on to that, to preserve a sense of my identity. Mr. Johnson had just been reading the "Lady of the Lake,"[4] and at once suggested that my name be "Douglass." From that time until now I have been called "Frederick Douglass"; and as I am more widely known by that name than by either of the others, I shall continue to use it as my own.

I was quite disappointed at the general appearance of things in New Bedford. The impression which I had received respecting the character and condition of the people of the north, I found to be singularly erroneous. I had very strangely supposed, while in slavery, that few of the comforts, and scarcely any of the luxuries, of life were enjoyed at the north, compared with what were enjoyed by the slaveholders of the south. I probably came to this conclusion from the fact that northern people owned no slaves. I supposed that they were about upon a level with the non-slaveholding population of the south. I knew they were exceedingly poor, and I had been accustomed to regard their poverty as the necessary consequence of their being non-slaveholders. I had somehow imbibed the opinion that, in the absence of slaves, there could be no wealth, and

---

[1]   *J.W.C. Pennington*   Formerly enslaved abolitionist and minister (1807–70).

[2]   [Douglass's note] I had changed my name from Frederick *Bailey* to that of *Johnson*.

[3]   *stage*   Stagecoach.

[4]   *Lady of the Lake*   Narrative poem by Scottish author Sir Walter Scott (1771–1832). Two of the main characters are James Douglas, an exiled former mentor of King James V of Scotland, and Douglas's daughter Ellen Douglas.

very little refinement. And upon coming to the north, I expected to meet with a rough, hard-handed, and uncultivated population, living in the most Spartan-like[1] simplicity, knowing nothing of the ease, luxury, pomp, and grandeur of southern slaveholders. Such being my conjectures, anyone acquainted with the appearance of New Bedford may very readily infer how palpably I must have seen my mistake.

In the afternoon of the day when I reached New Bedford, I visited the wharves, to take a view of the shipping. Here I found myself surrounded with the strongest proofs of wealth. Lying at the wharves, and riding in the steam, I saw many ships of the finest model, in the best order, and of the largest size. Upon the right and left, I was walled in by granite warehouses of the widest dimensions, stowed to their utmost capacity with the necessaries and comforts of life. Added to this, almost every body seemed to be at work, but noiselessly so, compared with what I had been accustomed to in Baltimore. There were no loud songs heard from those engaged in loading and unloading ships. I heard no deep oaths or horrid curses on the laborer. I saw no whipping of men; but all seemed to go smoothly on. Every man appeared to understand his work, and went at it with a sober, yet cheerful earnestness, which betokened the deep interest which he felt in what he was doing, as well as a sense of his own dignity as a man. To me this looked exceedingly strange. From the wharves I strolled around and over the town, gazing with wonder and admiration at the splendid churches, beautiful dwellings, and finely-cultivated gardens; evincing an amount of wealth, comfort, taste, and refinement, such as I had never seen in any part of slaveholding Maryland.

Every thing looked clean, new, and beautiful. I saw few or no dilapidated houses, with poverty-stricken inmates; no half-naked children and barefooted women, such as I had been accustomed to see in Hillsborough, Easton, St. Michael's, and Baltimore. The people looked more able, stronger, healthier, and happier, than those of Maryland. I was for once made glad by a view of extreme wealth, without being saddened by seeing extreme poverty. But the most astonishing as well as the most interesting thing to me was the condition of the colored people, a great many of whom, like myself, had escaped thither as a refuge from the hunters of men. I found many, who had not been seven years out of their chains, living in finer houses, and evidently enjoying more of the comforts of life, than the average slaveholders in Maryland. I will venture to assert, that my friend Mr. Nathan Johnson (of whom I can say with a grateful heart, "I was hungry, and he gave me meat; I was thirsty, and he gave me drink; I was a stranger, and he took me in"[2]) lived in a neater house; dined at a better table; took, paid for, and read, more newspapers; better understood the moral, religious, and political character of the nation—than nine tenths of the slaveholders in Talbot county, Maryland. Yet Mr. Johnson was a working man. His hands were hardened by toil, and not his alone, but those also of Mrs. Johnson. I found the colored people much more spirited than I had supposed they would be. I found among them a determination to protect each other from the blood-thirsty kidnapper, at all hazards. Soon after my arrival, I was told of a circumstance which illustrated their spirit. A colored man and a fugitive slave were on unfriendly terms. The former was heard to threaten the latter with informing his master of his whereabouts. Straightway a meeting was called among the colored people, under the stereotyped[3] notice, "Business of importance!" The betrayer was invited to attend. The people came at the appointed hour, and organized the meeting by appointing a very religious old gentleman as president, who, I believe, made a prayer, after which he addressed the meeting as follows: "Friends, we have got him here, and I would recommend that you young men just take him outside the door, and kill him!" With this, a number of them bolted at him; but they were intercepted by some more timid than themselves, and the betrayer escaped their vengeance, and has not been seen in New Bedford since. I believe there have been no more such threats, and should there be hereafter, I doubt not that death would be the consequence.

---

[1] *Spartan-like* Resembling the Spartans, who were known for their militaristic self-discipline and material plainness of living.

[2] *I was hungry ... took me in* See Matthew 25.35.

[3] *stereotyped* Printed. (Stereotyping was a then-new method of printing identical copies using metal plates.)

I found employment, the third day after my arrival, in stowing a sloop with a load of oil.[1] It was new, dirty, and hard work for me; but I went at it with a glad heart and a willing hand. I was now my own master. It was a happy moment, the rapture of which can be understood only by those who have been slaves. It was the first work, the reward of which was to be entirely my own. There was no Master Hugh standing ready, the moment I earned the money, to rob me of it. I worked that day with a pleasure I had never before experienced. I was at work for myself and newly-married wife. It was to me the starting-point of a new existence. When I got through with that job, I went in pursuit of a job of calking; but such was the strength of prejudice against color, among the white caulkers, that they refused to work with me, and of course I could get no employment.[2] Finding my trade of no immediate benefit, I threw off my calking habiliments, and prepared myself to do any kind of work I could get to do. Mr. Johnson kindly let me have his wood-horse and saw, and I very soon found myself a plenty of work. There was no work too hard—none too dirty. I was ready to saw wood, shovel coal, carry wood, sweep the chimney, or roll oil casks—all of which I did for nearly three years in New Bedford, before I became known to the anti-slavery world.

In about four months after I went to New Bedford, there came a young man to me, and inquired if I did not wish to take the "Liberator."[3] I told him I did; but, just having made my escape from slavery, I remarked that I was unable to pay for it then. I, however, finally became a subscriber to it. The paper came, and I read it from week to week with such feelings as it would be quite idle for me to attempt to describe. The paper became my meat and my drink. My soul was set all on fire. Its sympathy for my brethren in bonds—its scathing denunciations of slaveholders—its faithful exposures of slavery—and its powerful attacks upon the upholders of the institution—sent a thrill of joy through my soul, such as I had never felt before!

I had not long been a reader of the "Liberator" before I got a pretty correct idea of the principles, measures, and spirit of the anti-slavery reform. I took right hold of the cause. I could do but little; but what I could, I did with a joyful heart, and never felt happier than when in an anti-slavery meeting. I seldom had much to say at the meetings, because what I wanted to say was said so much better by others. But, while attending an anti-slavery convention at Nantucket, on the 11th of August, 1841, I felt strongly moved to speak, and was at the same time much urged to do so by Mr. William C. Coffin, a gentleman who had heard me speak in the colored people's meeting at New Bedford.[4] It was a severe cross, and I took it up reluctantly. The truth was, I felt myself a slave, and the idea of speaking to white people weighed me down. I spoke but a few moments, when I felt a degree of freedom, and said what I desired with considerable ease. From that time until now, I have been engaged in pleading the cause of my brethren—with what success, and with what devotion, I leave those acquainted with my labors to decide.

Appendix

I find, since reading over the foregoing Narrative, that I have, in several instances, spoken in such a tone and manner, respecting religion, as may possibly lead those unacquainted with my religious views to suppose me an opponent of all religion. To remove the liability of such misapprehension, I deem it proper to append the following brief explanation. What I have said respecting and against religion, I mean strictly to apply to the slaveholding religion of this land, and with no possible reference to Christianity proper; for, between the Christianity of this land, and the Christianity of Christ, I recognize the widest possible difference—so wide, that to receive the one as good, pure, and holy, is of necessity to reject the other as bad, corrupt, and wicked. To be the friend of the one, is of necessity to be the enemy of the other. I love the pure, peaceable, and impartial Christianity of Christ: I therefore hate

---

[1] *stowing a sloop with a load of oil* Loading casks of [whale] oil onto a cargo sailing ship.

[2] [Douglass's note] I am told that colored persons can now get employment at caulking in New Bedford—a result of anti-slavery effort.

[3] *take* Subscribe to; *the "Liberator"* Radical abolitionist newspaper established in 1831 and published by William Lloyd Garrison.

[4] *colored people's … New Bedford* I.e., at the meeting of the African Methodist Episcopal Zion Church, where Douglass had begun preaching in 1839.

the corrupt, slaveholding, women-whipping, cradle-plundering, partial and hypocritical Christianity of this land. Indeed, I can see no reason, but the most deceitful one, for calling the religion of this land Christianity. I look upon it as the climax of all misnomers, the boldest of all frauds, and the grossest of all libels. Never was there a clearer case of "stealing the livery of the court of heaven to serve the devil in."[1] I am filled with unutterable loathing when I contemplate the religious pomp and show, together with the horrible inconsistencies, which everywhere surround me. We have men-stealers for ministers, women-whippers for missionaries, and cradle-plunderers for church members. The man who wields the blood-clotted cowskin during the week fills the pulpit on Sunday, and claims to be a minister of the meek and lowly Jesus. The man who robs me of my earnings at the end of each week meets me as a class-leader on Sunday morning, to show me the way of life, and the path of salvation. He who sells my sister, for purposes of prostitution, stands forth as the pious advocate of purity. He who proclaims it a religious duty to read the Bible denies me the right of learning to read the name of the God who made me. He who is the religious advocate of marriage robs whole millions of its sacred influence, and leaves them to the ravages of wholesale pollution. The warm defender of the sacredness of the family relation is the same that scatters whole families—sundering husbands and wives, parents and children, sisters and brothers—leaving the hut vacant, and the hearth desolate. We see the thief preaching against theft, and the adulterer against adultery. We have men sold to build churches, women sold to support the gospel, and babes sold to purchase Bibles for the Poor Heathen! All For The Glory Of God And The Good Of Souls! The slave auctioneer's bell and the church-going bell chime in with each other, and the bitter cries of the heart-broken slave are drowned in the religious shouts of his pious master. Revivals of religion and revivals in the slave-trade go hand in hand together. The slave prison and the church stand near each other. The clanking of fetters and the rattling of chains in the prison, and the pious psalm and solemn prayer in the church, may be heard at the same time. The dealers in the bodies and souls of men erect their stand in the presence of the pulpit, and they mutually help each other. The dealer gives his blood-stained gold to support the pulpit, and the pulpit, in return, covers his infernal business with the garb of Christianity. Here we have religion and robbery the allies of each other—devils dressed in angels' robes, and hell presenting the semblance of paradise.

Just God! and these are they,
    Who minister at thine altar, God of right!
Men who their hands, with prayer and blessing, lay
    On Israel's ark of light.[2]

What! preach, and kidnap men?
    Give thanks, and rob thy own afflicted poor?
Talk of thy glorious liberty, and then
    Bolt hard the captive's door?

What! servants of thy own
    Merciful Son, who came to seek and save
The homeless and the outcast, fettering down
    The tasked and plundered slave!

Pilate and Herod[3] friends!
    Chief priests and rulers, as of old, combine!
Just God and holy! is that church which lends
    Strength to the spoiler thine?[4]

The Christianity of America is a Christianity, of whose votaries it may be as truly said, as it was of the ancient scribes and Pharisees,[5] "They bind heavy burdens, and grievous to be borne, and lay them on men's shoulders, but they themselves will not move them

---

[1] *stealing the livery ... devil in* From Book 8 of Scottish poet Robert Pollok's popular poem *The Course of Time* (1827).

[2] *Israel's ark of light* I.e., the Ark of the Covenant, containing the two stone tablets upon which the Ten Commandments were written, and thus symbolizing religious law as a whole.

[3] *Pilate and Herod* Pontius Pilate, the Roman ruler who approved Jesus' crucifixion; and the Galilean ruler Herod Antipas, who was involved in the executions both of John the Baptist and Jesus.

[4] *Just God ... spoiler thine?* The above comprises the first four stanzas of John Greenleaf Whittier's poem "Clerical Oppressors" (1835).

[5] *ancient scribes and Pharisees* The scribes were professional scholars of religious law, while the Pharisees were a sect whose members insisted on strict adherence to oral and written religious laws; the lines that follow are taken from Matthew 23.4–28, wherein Jesus denounces the scribes and Pharisees for hypocrisy.

with one of their fingers. All their works they do for to be seen of men. They love the uppermost rooms at feasts, and the chief seats in the synagogues, ... and to be called of men, Rabbi, Rabbi. But woe unto you, scribes and Pharisees, hypocrites! for ye shut up the kingdom of heaven against men; for ye neither go in yourselves, neither suffer ye them that are entering to go in. Ye devour widows' houses, and for a pretence make long prayers; therefore ye shall receive the greater damnation. Ye compass sea and land to make one proselyte, and when he is made, ye make him twofold more the child of hell than yourselves. Woe unto you, scribes and Pharisees, hypocrites! for ye pay tithe of mint, and anise, and cumin, and have omitted the weightier matters of the law, judgment, mercy, and faith; these ought ye to have done, and not to leave the other undone. Ye blind guides! which strain at a gnat, and swallow a camel. Woe unto you, scribes and Pharisees, hypocrites! for ye make clean the outside of the cup and of the platter; but within, they are full of extortion and excess. Woe unto you, scribes and Pharisees, hypocrites! for ye are like unto whited sepulchres, which indeed appear beautiful outward, but are within full of dead men's bones, and of all uncleanness. Even so ye also outwardly appear righteous unto men, but within ye are full of hypocrisy and iniquity."

Dark and terrible as is this picture, I hold it to be strictly true of the overwhelming mass of professed Christians in America. They strain at a gnat, and swallow a camel. Could anything be more true of our churches? They would be shocked at the proposition of fellowshipping a sheep-stealer; and at the same time they hug to their communion a man-stealer, and brand me with being an infidel, if I find fault with them for it. They attend with Pharisaical strictness to the outward forms of religion, and at the same time neglect the weightier matters of the law, judgment, mercy, and faith. They are always ready to sacrifice, but seldom to show mercy. They are they who are represented as professing to love God whom they have not seen, whilst they hate their brother whom they have seen. They love the heathen on the other side of the globe. They can pray for him, pay money to have the Bible put into his hand, and missionaries to instruct him; while they despise and totally neglect the heathen at their own doors.

Such is, very briefly, my view of the religion of this land; and to avoid any misunderstanding, growing out of the use of general terms, I mean by the religion of this land, that which is revealed in the words, deeds, and actions, of those bodies, north and south, calling themselves Christian churches, and yet in union with slaveholders. It is against religion, as presented by these bodies, that I have felt it my duty to testify.

I conclude these remarks by copying the following portrait of the religion of the south (which is, by communion and fellowship, the religion of the north), which I soberly affirm is "true to the life," and without caricature or the slightest exaggeration. It is said to have been drawn, several years before the present anti-slavery agitation began, by a northern Methodist preacher, who, while residing at the south, had an opportunity to see slaveholding morals, manners, and piety, with his own eyes. "Shall I not visit for these things? saith the Lord. Shall not my soul be avenged on such a nation as this?"[1]

A PARODY

Come, saints and sinners, hear me tell
How pious priests whip Jack and Nell,
And women buy and children sell,
And preach all sinners down to hell,
    And sing of heavenly union.

They'll bleat and baa, dona like goats,
Gorge down black sheep, and strain at motes,
Array their backs in fine black coats,
Then seize their negroes by their throats,
    And choke, for heavenly union.

They'll church you if you sip a dram,
And damn you if you steal a lamb;
Yet rob old Tony, Doll, and Sam,
Of human rights, and bread and ham;
    Kidnapper's heavenly union.

---

1   *Shall I not ... as this?* See Jeremiah 5.9. The identity of the preacher to whom Douglass refers is unknown; the following poem, which parodies the popular Southern hymn "Heavenly Union," seems to have been written by Douglass himself.

They'll talk loudly of Christ's reward,
And bind his image with a cord,
And scold, and swing the lash abhorred,
And sell their brother in the Lord
   To handcuffed heavenly union.

They'll read and sing a sacred song,
And make a prayer both loud and long,
And teach the right and do the wrong,
Hailing the brother, sister throng,
   With words of heavenly union.

We wonder how such saints can sing,
Or praise the Lord upon the wing,
Who roar, and scold, and whip, and sting,
And to their slaves and mammon cling,
   In guilty conscience union.

They'll raise tobacco, corn, and rye,
And drive, and thieve, and cheat, and lie,
And lay up treasures in the sky,
By making switch and cowskin fly,
   In hope of heavenly union.

They'll crack old Tony on the skull,
And preach and roar like Bashan bull,[1]
Or braying ass, of mischief full,
Then seize old Jacob by the wool,
   And pull for heavenly union.

A roaring, ranting, sleek man-thief,
Who lived on mutton, veal, and beef,
Yet never would afford relief
To needy, sable sons of grief,
   Was big with heavenly union.

"Love not the world," the preacher said,
And winked his eye, and shook his head;
He seized on Tom, and Dick, and Ned,
Cut short their meat, and clothes, and bread,
   Yet still loved heavenly union.

Another preacher whining spoke
Of One whose heart for sinners broke:
He tied old Nanny to an oak,

And drew the blood at every stroke,
   And prayed for heavenly union.

Two others oped their iron jaws,
And waved their children-stealing paws;
There sat the children in gewgaws;[2]
By stinting negroes' backs and maws,
   They kept up heavenly union.

All good from Jack another takes,
And entertains their flirts and rakes[3]
Who dress as sleek as glossy snakes,
And cram their mouths with sweetened cakes;
   And this goes down for union.

Sincerely and earnestly hoping that this little book may do something toward throwing light on the American slave system, and hastening the glad day of deliverance to the millions of my brethren in bonds— faithfully relying upon the power of truth, love, and justice, for my success in my humble efforts—and solemnly pledging my self anew to the sacred cause— I subscribe myself,

      FREDERICK DOUGLASS
      LYNN, Mass., April 28, 1845

—1845

---

[1] *Bashan bull* Strong bull mentioned in Psalm 22.12–13.

[2] *gewgaws* Ornamental or showy clothing.

[3] *rakes* Licentious or immoral men.

IN CONTEXT:

Responses to Frederick Douglass's *Narrative*

Margaret Fuller, Review of *Narrative of the Life of Frederick Douglass, an American Slave*, from *The New York Tribune* (10 June 1845)

Douglass's *Narrative* was welcomed with enthusiasm in the abolitionist press; most notably, the *New York Tribune* on 10 June 1845 printed on its front page a long and highly favorable review written by prominent feminist and Transcendentalist Margaret Fuller. Like many of her contemporaries, Fuller saw parallels between the fight for women's rights and the fight for racial equality, which she saw as linked by a "natural following out of principles." Yet the extent of Fuller's support for abolitionism as a movement has also been the source of substantial disagreement among readers, even among her contemporaries. According to English sociologist Harriet Martineau, Fuller regarded "the anti-slavery subject as simply a low and disagreeable one, which should be left to unrefined persons to manage, while others were occupied with higher things" (*Harriet Martineau's Autobiography*, 1877). Martineau continued: "The difference between us was that while [Fuller] was living and moving in an ideal world ... she looked down upon persons who acted instead of talking finely, and devoted their fortunes, their peace, their repose, and their very lives to the preservation of the principles of the republic." Whether entirely fair or not, the same criticism could have been made of numerous Transcendentalists in the 1830s and 40s, including Emerson and Thoreau—both of whom became ardent abolitionists in the years leading up to the Civil War. Fuller herself died in a shipwreck in 1850, leaving forever unanswered the question of whether or not she would have immersed herself deeper into the antislavery movement later in life.

Frederick Douglass has been for some time a prominent member of the Abolition party. He is said to be an excellent speaker—can speak from a thorough personal experience—and has upon the audience, beside, the influence of a strong character and uncommon talents. In the book before us he has put into the story of his life the thoughts, the feelings and the adventures that have been so affecting through the living voice; nor are they less so from the printed page. He has had the courage to name the persons, times and places, thus exposing himself to obvious danger, and setting the seal on his deep convictions as to the religious need of speaking the whole truth. Considered merely as a narrative, we have never read one more simple, true, coherent, and warm with genuine feeling. It is an excellent piece of writing, and on that score to be prized as a specimen of the powers of the Black Race, which Prejudice persists in disputing. We prize highly all evidence of this kind, and it is becoming more abundant. The Cross of the Legion of Honor has just been conferred in France on Dumas and Soulié,[1] both celebrated in the paths of light literature. Dumas, whose father was a General in the French Army, is a Mulatto; Soulié, a Quadroon.[2] He went from New-Orleans, where, though to the eye a white man, yet, as known to have African blood in his veins, he could never have enjoyed the privileges due to a human being. Leaving the Land of Freedom, he found himself free to develop the powers that God had given.

---

[1]   *Dumas and Soulié*   Alexandre Dumas (1802–70) and Frédéric Soulié (1800–47), widely read French novelists; Dumas's paternal grandmother, Marie-Cessette Dumas, was an enslaved woman of African descent who lived in the French colony of Saint-Domingue (present-day Haiti).

[2]   *Mulatto ... Quadroon*   Terms commonly used in the nineteenth century to classify individuals of mixed racial background; while "mulatto" generally meant a person with one white parent and one parent of African descent, and "quadroon" a person with one grandparent of African descent, the terms were often used rather loosely and might refer more to a person's physical appearance than to his or her actual known ancestry. Persons who were known to have African ancestry or who appeared mixed-race often had more limited social and legal opportunities than those who could "pass" for white.

Two wise and candid thinkers—the Scotchman, Kinment,[1] prematurely lost to this country, of which he was so faithful and generous a student, and the late Dr. Channing[2]—both thought that the African Race had in them a peculiar element, which, if it could be assimilated with those imported among us from Europe, would give to genius a development, and to the energies of character a balance and harmony beyond what has been seen heretofore in the history of the world. Such an element is indicated in their lowest estate by a talent for melody, a ready skill at imitation and adaptation, an almost indestructible elasticity of nature. It is to be remarked in the writings both of Soulié and Dumas, full of faults but glowing with plastic life and fertile in invention. The same torrid energy and saccharine fulness may be felt in the writings of this Douglass, though his life being one of action or resistance, was less favorable to *such* powers than one of a more joyous flow might have been.

The book is prefaced by two communications—one from Garrison, and one from Wendell Phillips[.] That from the former is in his usual over emphatic style. His motives and his course have been noble and generous. We look upon him with high respect, but he has indulged in violent invective and denunciation till he has spoiled the temper of his mind. Like a man who has been in the habit of screaming himself hoarse to make the deaf hear, he can no longer pitch his voice on a key agreeable to common ears. Mr. Phillips's remarks are equally decided, without this exaggeration in the tone. Douglass himself seems very just and temperate[.] We feel that his view, even of those who have injured him most, may be relied upon. He knows how to allow for motives and influences. Upon the subject of Religion, he speaks with great force, and not more than our own sympathies can respond to. The inconsistencies of Slaveholding professors of religion[3] cry to Heaven. We are not disposed to detest, or refuse communion with them. Their blindness is but one form of that prevalent fallacy which substitutes a creed for a faith, a ritual for a life. We have seen too much of this system of atonement not to know that those who adopt it often began with good intentions, and are, at any rate, in their mistakes worthy of the deepest pity. But that is no reason why the truth should not be uttered, trumpet-tongued, about the thing. "Bring no more vain oblations"; sermons must daily be preached anew on that text. Kings, five hundred years ago, built churches with the spoils of war; clergymen today command slaves to obey a Gospel which they will not allow them to read, and call themselves Christians amid the curses of their fellow men. The world ought to get on a little faster than that, if there be really any principle of improvement in it. The Kingdom of Heaven may not at the beginning have dropped seed larger than a mustard-seed, but even from that we had a right to expect a fuller growth than can be believed to exist,[4] when we read such a book as this of Douglass. Unspeakably affecting is the fact that he never saw his mother at all by daylight. ...

Copies of the work may be had of W.H. Graham, Tribune Buildings. Price, 50 cents.

A.C.C. Thompson, "TO THE PUBLIC. FALSEHOOD REFUTED," *The Liberator* (12 December 1845)

It was common practice for antislavery publications to reprint in their pages articles in support of slavery—in order to refute their claims. Thus was this piece, originally from *The Delaware Republican*, reprinted in *The Liberator*, the abolitionist paper run by Douglass's friend and supporter, William Lloyd Garrison.

---

[1] *Kinment* Alexander Kinmont (1799–1838), Scottish philosopher and educator who taught in Cincinnati for several years.

[2] *Dr. Channing* William Ellery Channing (1780–1842), American Unitarian preacher who became an abolitionist late in life (but nevertheless maintained a rather paternalistic form of racism in his writings).

[3] *professors of religion* I.e., those who profess, or pretend, to embrace religious values.

[4] *The Kingdom of Heaven ... to exist* See Matthew 13.31–32: "The kingdom of heaven is like to a grain of mustard seed, which a man took, and sowed in his field: Which indeed is the least of all seeds: but when it is grown, it is the greatest among herbs, and becometh a tree, so that the birds of the air come and lodge in the branches thereof."

It is with considerable regret that I find myself measurably compelled to appear before the public; but my attention has lately been arrested by a pamphlet which has been freely circulated in Wilmington and elsewhere, with the following superscription: *Extract from a Narrative of Frederick Douglass, an American Slave, written by himself.*

And although I am aware that no sensible, unprejudiced person will credit such a ridiculous publication, which bears the glaring impress of falsehood on every page, yet I deem it expedient that I should give the public some information respecting the validity of this narrative, because I was for many years a citizen of the section of country where the scenes of the above mentioned narrative are laid; and am intimately acquainted with most of the gentlemen whose characters are so shamefully traduced; and I am also aware, that the Narrative was not written by the professed author, but from statements of this runaway slave, some evil designed[1] person or persons have composed this catalogue of lies to excite the indignation of the public opinion against the slaveholders of the South; and have even attempted to plunge their venomous fangs in the vitals of the church.

I shall, therefore, briefly notice some of the most glaring falsehoods contained in the aforesaid Narrative, and give a true representation of the character of those gentlemen, who have been censured in such an uncharitable manner, as murderers, hypocrites, and everything else that is vile.

I indulge no animosity against the fabricators and circulators of the Narrative, neither do I know them; but I positively declare the whole to be a bucket of falsehoods, from beginning to end.

1st. The identity of the author. About eight years ago, I knew this recreant[2] slave by the name of Frederick Bailey (instead of Douglass). He then lived with Mr. Edward Covy, and was an unlearned, and rather an ordinary negro, and [I] am confident he was not capable of writing the Narrative alluded to; for none but an educated man, and one who had some knowledge of the rules of grammar, could write so correctly. Although, to make the imposition at all creditable, the composer has labored to write it in as plain a style as possible: consequently, the detection of this first falsehood proves the whole production to be notoriously untrue.

Again. "It is a common custom in the part of Maryland from which I ran away, to separate children from their mothers at a very early age."[3]

This also I know to be false. There is no such custom prevalent in that section of the country; but, on the contrary, the children are raised with their mothers, and generally live with them in the same house, except in some few instances where the mother is hired out as a cook or laborer in some other family.

The gentlemen whose names are so prominently set forth in the said Narrative are Col. Edward Lloyd, Capt. Anthony, Austin Gore, Thomas Lamdin (not Lanman), Giles Hicks, Thomas Auld, and Edward Covy. Most of these persons I am intimately acquainted with and shall give a brief sketch of their characters as follows:

Col. Edward Lloyd was one of the most wealthy and respectable planters in the State of Maryland. He was at one time the Governor of the State, and for several years, a member of the Legislature. He owned several thousand acres of land, and between 4 and 500 slaves. He died before I had much knowledge of him; but I know that he was a kind and charitable man, and in every respect an honorable and worthy citizen.

Most of the same slaves are now owned by his three sons, and they manage their servants in the same manner as did their father; and I know there are no such barbarities committed on their plantations.

Could it be possible that charitable feeling men could murder human beings, with as little remorse of conscience, as the narrative of this infamous libel wishes to make us believe; and that the laws of Maryland, which operate *alike upon black and white*, bond or free, could permit such foul murders to pass unnoticed? No! it is impossible; and every sensible man knows that these false accusations are the ebullition of an unchristian prejudice.

---

1   *evil designed* I.e., with evil intentions.

2   *recreant* Disobedient.

3   *It is … early age* Quotation from Douglass's *Narrative*.

Captain Anthony and Giles Hicks, I know but little of. The accused murderer, Mr. Gore, is a respectable citizen, living near St. Michaels, and I believe a worthy member of the Methodist Episcopal Church; he was formerly an overseer for Col. Lloyd, and at this time, all who know him, think him anything but a murderer.

Thomas Lamdin, who, it is said (in the Narrative), boasted so frequently of his murders, is at this time an honest school teacher in the District where I formerly lived; and all the harm that can be said of him is, that he is too good-natured and harmless to injure any person but himself.

Capt. Thomas Auld, whose hypocritical meanness is so strongly depicted in the aforesaid Narrative, was for many years a respectable merchant in the town of St. Michaels, and an honorable and worthy member of the Methodist E. Church, and only notable for his integrity and irreproachable Christian character. He is now retired from the turmoil of a mercantile life, and engaged in the worthy occupation of tilling the soil, little dreaming of the foul accusations that are circulated against him.

Edward Covy, the renowned "negro breaker," is also a plain, honest farmer, and a tried and faithful member of the Methodist E. Church. Mr. Covy lived for several years on a farm adjoining my father's, at which time this runaway negro lived with him, and I am well aware that no such bloody tragedy as is recorded in that lying Narrative ever occurred on Mr. Covy's farm. All that can be said of Mr. Covy is that he is a good Christian, and a hard working man, and makes every one around him work and treats them well. By his honest industry, he has purchased a fine farm, and is now reaping the reward of his labor.

Such are the characters of the men whom the imposers of this dirty Narrative have so uncharitably traduced, and by blending these false accusations with the Methodist religion of the South, they wish to lacerate her already bleeding wounds.

I was raised among slaves, and have also owned them, and am well aware that the slaves live better and fare better in many respects than the free blacks.

Yet, I am positively opposed to slavery, for I know it is a great evil; but *the evil falls not upon the slave*, but on the owner.

Intrigue and false accusations will never liberate the slave of the South; but, on the contrary, every such attempt will only forge for them new and stronger fetters.

Let the tender-hearted philanthropists of the North speak truth and love towards their southern brethren, and make a liberal application of their gold for the removing the blacks from the country, and their chance of success will be more flattering.

I have given a true representation of the persons connected with the aforesaid Narrative, and I respectfully submit the facts to the judgment of an impartial public.

A.C.C. THOMPSON
No. 101 Market-st. Wilmington, Del.

☞ This attempt to invalidate the Narrative of Frederick Douglass, only confirms its correctness, as Mr. Thompson admits everything but the cruelty described by Douglass—and on that point the latter speaks from experience and knowledge.

Frederick Douglass, "Reply to Mr. A.C.C. Thompson," *The Liberator*
(27 February 1846)

To the Editor of the Liberator

DEAR FRIEND—For the sake of our righteous cause, I was delighted to see, by an extract copied into the *Liberator* of 12th Dec. 1845, from *The Delaware Republican*, that Mr. A.C.C. Thompson, No. 101, Market-street, Wilmington, has undertaken to invalidate my testimony against the slaveholders, whose names I have made prominent in the narrative of my experience while in slavery.

Slaveholders and slave-traders never betray greater indiscretion, than when they venture to defend themselves, or their system of plunder, in any other community than a slaveholding one. Slavery has its own standard of morality, humanity, justice, and Christianity. Tried by that standard, it is a system of the greatest kindness to the slave—sanctioned by the purest morality—in perfect agreement with justice—and, of course, not inconsistent with Christianity. But, tried by any other, it is doomed to condemnation. The naked relation of master and slave is one of those monsters of darkness, to whom the light of truth is death! The wise ones among the slaveholders know this, and they studiously avoid doing anything, which, in their judgment, tends to elicit truth. They seem fully to understand, that their safety is in their silence. They may have learned this wisdom from Junius, who counselled his opponent, Sir William Draper, when defending Lord Granby,[1] never to attract attention to a character, which would only pass without condemnation, when it passed without observation.

I am now almost too far away[2] to answer this attempted refutation by Mr. Thompson. I fear his article will be forgotten, before you get my reply. I, however, think the whole thing worth reviving, as it is seldom we have so good a case for dissection. In any country but the United States, I might hope to get a hearing[3] through the columns of the paper in which I was attacked. But this would be inconsistent with American usage and magnanimity. It would be folly to expect such a hearing. They might possibly advertise me as a runaway slave, and share the reward of my apprehension; but on no other conditions would they allow my reply a place in their columns.

In this, however, I may judge the "Republican" harshly. It may be that, having admitted Mr. Thompson's article, the editor will think it but fair—negro though I am—to allow my reply an insertion.

In replying to Mr. Thompson, I shall proceed as I usually do in preaching the slaveholder's sermon,—dividing the subject under two general heads, as follows:

1st. The statement of Mr. Thompson, in confirmation of the truth of my narrative.

2ndly. His denials of its truthfulness.

Under the first, I beg Mr. Thompson to accept my thanks for his full, free and unsolicited testimony, in regard to my identity. There now need be no doubt on that point, however much there might have been before. Your testimony, Mr. Thompson, has settled the question forever. I give you the fullest credit for the deed, saying nothing of the motive. But for you, sir, the pro-slavery people in the North might have persisted, with some show of reason, in representing me as being an imposter—a free negro who had never been south of Mason & Dixon's line—one whom the abolitionists, acting on the jesuitical principle, that the end justifies the means, had educated and sent forth to attract attention to their faltering cause. I am greatly indebted to you, sir, for silencing those truly prejudicial insinuations. I wish I could make you understand the amount of service you have done me. You have completely tripped up the heels of your pro-slavery friends, and laid them flat at my feet. You have done a piece of anti-slavery work, which no anti-slavery man could do. Our cautious and truth-loving people in New England would never have believed this testimony, in proof of my identity, had it been borne by an abolitionist. Not that they really think an abolitionist capable of bearing false witness intentionally; but such persons are thought fanatical, and to look at everything through a distorted medium. They will believe you—they will believe a slaveholder. They have, somehow or other, imbibed (and, I confess, strangely enough) the idea that persons such as yourself are dispassionate, impartial and disinterested, and therefore capable of giving a fair representation of things connected with slavery. Now, under these circumstances, your testimony is of the utmost importance. It will serve to give effect to my exposures of slavery, both at home and abroad. I hope I shall not administer to your vanity when I tell you that you seem to have been raised up for this purpose! I came to this land with the highest testimonials from some of the most intelligent

---

[1]   *Junius ... Lord Granby*   "Junius" was the pseudonym of a writer of anonymous letters to the London newspaper *Public Advertiser* in 1769–72, which aimed to publicly expose various failures of the British government at that time. In particular, Douglass refers to an instance in which military officer William Draper attempted to defend Member of Parliament John Manners, Lord Granby, from accusations of heavy drinking and unscrupulousness leveled by Junius, only to inadvertently confirm those accusations through his defense.

[2]   *I am ... far away*   Douglass was living in the United Kingdom (which then included both Britain and all of Ireland) at this time, in part to avoid capture by people who hunted fugitives from slavery.

[3]   *get a hearing*   I.e., take Thompson to court for libel.

and distinguished abolitionists in the United States; yet some here have entertained and expressed doubt as to whether I have ever been a slave. You may easily imagine the perplexing and embarrassing nature of my situation, and how anxious I must have been to be relieved from it. You, sir, have relieved me. I now stand before both the American and British public, endorsed by you as being just what I have ever represented myself to be—to wit, an *American slave*.

You say, "I knew this recreant slave by the name of Frederick Bailey (instead of Douglass)." Yes, that was my name; and, leaving out the term recreant, which savors a little of bitterness, your testimony is direct and perfect—just what I have long wanted. But you are not yet satisfied. You seem determined to bear the most ample testimony in my favor. You say you knew me when I lived with Mr. Covey. "And with most of the persons" mentioned in my narrative, "you are intimately acquainted." This is excellent. Then Mr. Edward Covey is not a creature of my imagination, but really did, and may yet exist.

You thus brush away the miserable insinuation of my northern pro-slavery enemies, that I have used fictitious not real names. You say—"Col. Lloyd was a wealthy planter. Mr. Gore was once an overseer for Col. Lloyd, but is now living near St. Michael's, is respected and [you] believe he is a member of the Methodist Episcopal Church. Mr. Thomas Auld is an honorable and worthy member of the Methodist Episcopal Church. Mr. Covey, too, is a member of the Methodist church, and all that can be said of him is, that he is a good Christian," &c. &c. Do allow me, once more, to thank you for this triumphant vindication of the truth of my statements; and to show you how highly I value your testimony, I will inform you that I am now publishing a second edition of my narrative in this country,[1] having already disposed of the first. I will insert your article with my reply as an appendix to the edition now in progress. If you find any fault with my frequent thanks, you may find some excuse for me in the fact, that I have serious fears that you will be but poorly thanked by those whose characters you have felt it your duty to defend. I am almost certain they will regard you as running before you were sent, and as having spoken when you should have been silent. Under these trying circumstances, it is evidently the duty of those interested in your welfare to extend to you such words of consolation as may ease, if not remove, the pain of your sad disappointment! But enough of this.

Now, then, to the second part—or your denials. You are confident I did not write the book; and the reason of your confidence is, that when you knew me, I was an unlearned and rather an ordinary negro. Well, I have to admit I was rather an ordinary negro when you knew me, and I do not claim to be a very extraordinary one now. But you knew me under very unfavorable circumstances. It was when I lived with Mr. Covey, the negro-breaker, *and member of the Methodist Church*. I had just been living with master Thomas Auld, where I had been reduced by hunger. Master Thomas did not allow me enough to eat. Well, when I lived with Mr. Covey, I was driven so hard, and whipped so often, that my soul was crushed and my spirits broken. I was a mere wreck. The degradation to which I was then subjected, as I now look back to it, seems more like a dream than a horrible reality. I can scarcely realize how I ever passed through it, without quite losing all my moral and intellectual energies. I can easily understand that you sincerely doubt if I wrote the narrative; for if any one had told me, seven years ago, I should ever be able to write such an one, I should have doubted as strongly as you now do. You must not judge me now by what I then was—a change of circumstances has made a surprising change in age. Frederick Douglass, the *freeman*, is a very different person from Frederick Bailey,[2] the *slave*. I feel myself almost a new man— freedom has given me new life. I fancy you would scarcely know me. I think I have altered very much in my general appearance, and know I have in my manners. You remember when I used to meet you on the road to St. Michael's, or near Mr. Covey's lane gate, I hardly dared to lift my head, and look up at you. If I should meet you now, amid the free hills of old Scotland, where the ancient "black Douglass"[3] once met his foes, I presume I might summon sufficient fortitude to look you full in the face; and were you to

---

[1]   *this country*   I.e., the United Kingdom.

[2]   [Douglass's note]   My former name.

[3]   *black Douglass*   Douglass's chosen namesake, a character from Walter Scott's loosely historical poem "The Lady of the Lake" (1810). The historical "black Douglas" was James Douglas, Lord of Douglas (c. 1286–1330), an important leader in the fight for Scottish independence.

attempt to make a slave of me, it is possible you might find me almost as disagreeable a subject, as was the Douglass to whom I have just referred. Of one thing, I am certain—you would see *a great change* in me!

I trust I have now explained away your reason for thinking I did not write the narrative in question.

You next deny the existence of such cruelty in Maryland as I reveal in my narrative; and ask, with truly marvellous simplicity, "could it be possible that charitable, feeling men could murder human beings with as little remorse as the narrative of this infamous libeller would make us believe; and that the laws of Maryland, which operate alike upon black and white, bond and free, could permit such four murders to pass unnoticed?" "No," you say, "it is impossible." I am not to determine what charitable, feeling men can do; but, to show what Maryland slaveholders actually do, their charitable feeling is to be determined by their deeds, and not their deeds by their charitable feelings. The cowskin[1] makes as deep a gash in my flesh, when wielded by a professed saint, as it does when wielded by an open sinner. The deadly musket does as fatal execution when its trigger is pulled by Austin Gore, the Christian, as when the same is done by Beal Bondly,[2] the infidel. The best way to ascertain what those charitable, feeling men can do, will be to point you to the laws made by them, and which you say operate alike upon the white and the black, the bond and the free. By consulting the statute laws of Maryland, you will find the following: "Any slave for rambling in the night, or riding horses in the day time without leave, or running away, may be punished by whipping, cropping,[3] branding in the cheek, or otherwise—not rendering him unfit for labor."—p. 337.

Then another: "Any slave convicted of petty treason, murder, or wilful burning of dwelling-houses, may be sentenced to have the right hand cut off, to be hanged in the usual way—his head severed from his body—the body divided into four quarters, and the head and quarters set up in the most public place where such act was committed."—Page 190.

Now, Mr. Thompson, when you consider with what ease a slave may be convicted of any one or all of these crimes, how bloody and atrocious do those laws appear! Yet, sir, they are but the breath of those pious and charitable feeling men, whom you would defend. I am sure I have recorded in my narrative, nothing so revoltingly cruel, murderous, and infernal, as may be found in your own statute book.

You say that the laws of Maryland operate alike upon the white and black, the bond and free. If you mean by this, that the parties named are all equally protected by law, you perpetrate a falsehood as big as that told by President Polk in his inaugural address.[4] It is a notorious fact, even on this side the Atlantic, that a black man cannot testify against a white in any court in Maryland, or any other slave State. If you do not know this, you are more than ordinarily ignorant, and are to be pitied rather than censured. I will not say "that the detection of this falsehood proves all you have said to be false"—for I wish to avail myself of your testimony, in regard to my identity—but I will say, you have made yourself very liable to suspicion.

I will close these remarks by saying, your positive opposition to slavery is fully explained, and will be well understood by anti-slavery men, when you say the evil of the system does not fall upon the slave, but the slaveholder. This is like saying that the evil of being burnt is not felt by the person burnt, but by him who kindles up the fire about him.

FREDERICK DOUGLASS
Perth, (Scotland,) 27th Jan. 1846

---

1   *cowskin*   Whip made of cowhide.

2   *Austin Gore ... Beal Bondly*   Cruel enslavers mentioned in Douglass's *Narrative*.

3   *cropping*   Cutting off one's ears.

4   *President Polk ... inaugural address*   Douglass is likely referring to the following statement made by President James Polk in his inaugural address of March 1845: "All distinctions of birth or rank have been abolished. All citizens, whether native or adopted, are placed upon terms of precise equality. All are entitled to equal rights and equal protection." Polk was a slaveholder throughout most of his adult life.

from *To My Old Master*

Douglass published this as an open letter in the 8 September 1848 issue of the *North Star*; the letter was reprinted in William Lloyd Garrison's abolitionist newspaper *The Liberator* two weeks later, and Douglass also included it, with minor revisions, in the appendices to his second autobiography, *My Bondage and My Freedom* (1855).

THOMAS AULD—SIR:

... I have often thought I should like to explain to you the grounds upon which I have justified myself in running away from you. I am almost ashamed to do so now, for by this time you may have discovered them yourself. I will, however, glance at them. When yet but a child about six years old, I imbibed the determination to run away. The very first mental effort that I now remember on my part, was an attempt to solve the mystery, Why am I a slave? and with this question my youthful mind was troubled for many days, pressing upon me more heavily at times than others. When I saw the slave-driver whip a slave-woman, cut the blood out of her neck, and heard her piteous cries, I went away into the corner of the fence, wept and pondered over this mystery. I had, through some medium, I know not what, got some idea of God, the Creator of all mankind, the black and the white, and that he had made the blacks to serve the whites as slaves. How he could do this and be *good*, I could not tell. I was not satisfied with this theory, which made God responsible for slavery, for it pained me greatly, and I have wept over it long and often. At one time, your first wife, Mrs. Lucretia, heard me singing and saw me shedding tears, and asked of me the matter, but I was afraid to tell her. I was puzzled with this question, till one night, while sitting in the kitchen, I heard some of the old slaves talking of their parents having been stolen from Africa by white men, and were sold here as slaves. The whole mystery was solved at once. Very soon after this, my aunt Jinny and uncle Noah ran away, and the great noise made about it by your father-in-law, made me for the first time acquainted with the fact, that there were free States as well as slave States. From that time, I resolved that I would someday run away. The morality

of the act, I dispose of as follows: I am myself; you are yourself; we are two distinct persons, equal persons. What you are I am. You are a man, so am I. God created both, and made us separate beings. I am not by nature bound to you, or you to me. Nature does not make your existence depend upon me, or mine to depend upon yours. I cannot walk upon your legs, or you upon mine. I cannot breathe for you, or you for me; I must breathe for myself, and you for yourself. We are distinct persons, and are each equally provided with faculties necessary to our individual existence. In leaving you, I took nothing but what belonged to me, and in no way lessened your means of obtaining an *honest* living. Your faculties remained yours, and mine became useful to their rightful owner. I therefore see no wrong in any part of the transaction. It is true, I went off secretly, but that was more your fault than mine. Had I let you into the secret, you would have defeated the enterprise entirely; but for this, I should have been really glad to have made you acquainted with my intention to leave.

You may perhaps want to know how I like my present condition. I am free to say, I greatly prefer it to that which I occupied in Maryland. I am, however, by no means prejudiced against that State as such. Its geography, climate, fertility, and products, are such as to make it a very desirable abode for any man; and but for the existence of slavery there, it is not impossible that I might again take up my abode in that State. It is not that I love Maryland less, but freedom more.[1] You will be surprised to learn that people at the North labor under the strange delusion that if the slaves were emancipated at the South, they would all flock to the North. So far from this being the case, in that event, you would see many old and familiar faces back again at the South. The fact is, there are few here who would not return to the South in the event of emancipation. We want to live in the land of our birth, and to lay our bones by the side of our fathers'; and nothing short of an intense love of personal freedom keeps us from the South. For the sake of this, most of us would live on a crust of bread and a cup of cold water.

---

1   *not that ... freedom more*   See Shakespeare's *Julius Caesar* 3.2.21–24: "If then that friend demand why Brutus rose against Caesar, this is my answer: not that I loved Caesar less, but that I loved Rome more."

Since I left you, I have had a rich experience. I have occupied stations which I never dreamed of when a slave. Three out of the ten years since I left you, I spent as a common laborer on the wharves of New Bedford, Massachusetts. It was there I earned my first free dollar. It was mine. I could spend it as I pleased. I could buy hams or herring with it, without asking any odds of anybody. That was a precious dollar to me. You remember when I used to make seven or eight, and even nine dollars a week in Baltimore, you would take every cent of it from me every Saturday night, saying that I belonged to you, and my earnings also. I never liked this conduct on your part—to say the best, I thought it a little mean.[1] I would not have served you so. But let that pass. I was a little awkward about counting money in New Bedford. I like to have betrayed myself several times. I caught myself saying phip,[2] for four pence; and one time a man actually charged me with being a runaway, whereupon I was silly enough to become one by running away from him, for I was greatly afraid he might adopt measures to get me again into slavery, a condition I then dreaded more than death.

I soon, however, learned to count money as well as to make it, and got on swimmingly. I married soon after leaving you:[3] in fact, I was engaged to be married before I left you; and instead of finding my companion a burden, she was truly a helpmeet. She went to live—at service, and I to work on the wharf, and though we toiled hard the first winter, we never lived more happily. After remaining in New Bedford for three years, I met with Wm. Lloyd Garrison,[4] a person of whom you have *possibly* heard, as he is pretty generally known among slaveholders. He put it into my head that I might make myself serviceable to the cause of the slave by devoting a portion of my time to telling my own sorrows, and those of other slaves which had come under my observation. This was the commencement

of a higher state of existence than any to which I had ever aspired. I was thrown into society the most pure, enlightened and benevolent that the country affords. Among these, I have never forgotten you, but have invariably made you the topic of conversation—thus giving you all the notoriety I could do. I need not tell you that the opinion formed of you in these circles, is far from being favorable. They have little respect for your honesty, and less for your religion.

But I was going on to relate to you something of my interesting experience. I had not long enjoyed the excellent society to which I have referred, before the light of its excellence exerted a beneficial influence on my mind and heart. Much of my early dislike of white persons was removed, and their manners, habits and customs, so entirely unlike what I have been used to in the kitchen-quarters on the plantations of the South, fairly charmed me, and gave me a strong disrelish for the coarse and degrading customs of my former condition. I therefore made an effort so to improve my mind and deportment, as to be somewhat fitted to the station to which I seemed almost Providentially called. The transition from degradation to respectability was indeed great, and to get from one to the other without carrying some marks of one's former condition, is truly a difficult matter. I would not have you think that I am now entirely clear of all plantation peculiarities, but my friends here, while they entertain the strongest dislike to them, regard me with that charity to which my past life somewhat entitles me, so that my condition in this respect is exceedingly pleasant. So far as my domestic affairs are concerned, I can boast of as comfortable a dwelling as your own. I have an industrious and neat companion, and four dear children—the oldest a girl of nine years, and three fine boys, the oldest eight, the next six, and the youngest four years old. The three oldest are now going regularly to school—two can read and write, and the other can spell with tolerable correctness words of two syllables. Dear fellows! they are all in comfortable beds, and are sound asleep, perfectly secure under my own roof. There are no slaveholders here to rend my heart by snatching them from my arms, or blast a proud mother's dearest hopes by tearing them from her bosom. These dear children are ours—not to work up into rice, sugar, and tobacco, but to watch over, regard,

---

[1]   *mean*   Ungenerous; ignoble.

[2]   *phip*   Maryland slang for a four-pence coin.

[3]   *I married ... leaving you*   Douglass's first wife, Anna Murray-Douglass (1813–82) was born free in Maryland, and provided Douglass with crucial aid in his self-emancipation.

[4]   *Wm. Lloyd Garrison*   Among the most prominent white abolitionists of the era, William Lloyd Garrison (1805–79) founded the abolitionist newspaper *The Liberator* as well as the American Anti-Slavery Society.

and protect, and to rear them up in the nurture and admonition of the gospel—to train them up in the paths of wisdom and virtue, and, as far as we can, to make them useful to the world and to themselves. Oh! sir, a slaveholder never appears to me so completely an agent of hell, as when I think of and look upon my dear children. It is then that my feelings rise above my control. I meant to have said more with respect to my own prosperity and happiness, but thoughts and feelings which this recital has quickened, unfits me to proceed further in that direction. The grim horrors of slavery rise in all their ghastly terror before me, the wails of millions pierce my heart, and chill my blood. I remember the chain, the gag, the bloody whip, the deathlike gloom overshadowing the broke spirit of the fettered bondman, the appalling liability of his being torn away from wife and children and sold like a beast in the market. Say not this is a picture of fancy.[1] You well know that I wear stripes[2] on my back inflicted by your direction; and that you, while we were brothers in the same church, caused this right hand, with which I am now penning this letter, to be closely tied to my left, and my person dragged at the pistol's mouth, fifteen miles, from the Bay side to Easton, to be sold like a beast in the market, for the alleged crime of intending to escape from your possession. All this and more you remember, and know to be perfectly true, not only of yourself, but of nearly all of the slaveholders around you.

At this moment, you are probably the guilty holder of at least three of my own dear sisters, and my only brother in bondage. These you regard as your property. They are recorded on your ledger, or perhaps have been sold to human flesh mongers, with a view to filling your own ever-hungry purse. Sir, I desire to know how and where these dear sisters are. Have you sold them? or are they still in your possession? What has become of them? are they living or dead? And my dear old grandmother, whom you turned out like an old horse, to die in the woods—is she still alive? Write and let me know all about them. If my grandmother be still alive, she is of no service to you, for by this time she must be nearly eighty years old—too old to be cared for by one to whom she has ceased to be of service; send her to me at Rochester,[3] or bring her to Philadelphia,[4] and it shall be the crowning happiness of my life to take care of her in her old age. Oh! she was to me a mother, and a father, so far as hard toil for my comfort could make her such. Send me my grandmother! that I may watch over and take care of her in her old age. And my sisters, let me know all about them. I would write to them, and learn all I want to know of them, without disturbing you in any way, but that, through your unrighteous conduct, they have been entirely deprived of the power to read and write. You have kept them in utter ignorance, and have therefore robbed them of the sweet enjoyments of writing or receiving letters from absent friends and relatives. Your wickedness and cruelty committed in this respect on your fellow-creatures, are greater than all the stripes you have laid upon my back, or theirs. It is an outrage upon the soul—a war upon the immortal spirit, and one for which you must give account at the bar of our common Father and Creator.

The responsibility which you have assumed in this regard is truly awful—and how you could stagger under it these many years is marvellous. Your mind must have become darkened, your heart hardened, your conscience seared and petrified, or you would have long since thrown off the accursed load and sought relief at the hands of a sin forgiving God. How, let me ask, would you look upon me, were I some dark night in company with a band of hardened villains, to enter the precincts of your own elegant dwelling and seize the person of your own lovely daughter Amanda, and carry her off from your family, friends, and all the loved ones of her youth—make her my slave—compel her to work, and I take her wages—place her name on my ledger as property—disregard her personal rights—fetter the powers of her immortal soul by denying her the right and privilege of learning to read and write—feed her coarsely—clothe her scantily, and whip her on the naked back occasionally; more and still more horrible, leave her unprotected—a degraded

---

1 *fancy* Imagination; a fiction.

2 *stripes* I.e., scars from having been whipped.

3 *Rochester* The home of Douglass and his family, in New York.

4 *Philadelphia* One of Douglass's first stops on his way to freedom, Philadelphia was largely populated by Quakers, who generally opposed slavery. (Though Pennsylvania was the first state to pass an act abolishing slavery in 1780, its gradual nature meant that there were still people living enslaved in the state well into the early 19th century.)

victim to the brutal lust of fiendish overseers who would pollute, blight, and blast her fair soul—rob her of all dignity—destroy her virtue, and annihilate all in her person the graces that adorn the character of virtuous womanhood? I ask how would you regard me, if such were my conduct? Oh! the vocabulary of the damned would not afford a word sufficiently infernal, to express your idea of my God-provoking wickedness. Yet sir, your treatment of my beloved sisters is in all essential points, precisely like the case I have now supposed. Damning as would be such a deed on my part, it would be no more so than that which you have committed against me and my sisters.

I will now bring this letter to a close; you shall hear from me again unless you let me hear from you. I intend to make use of you as a weapon with which to assail the system of slavery—as a means of concentrating public attention on the system, and deepening the horror of trafficking in the souls and bodies of men. I shall make use of you as a means of exposing the character of the American church and clergy—and as a means of bringing this guilty nation with yourself to repentance. In doing this I entertain no malice towards you personally. There is no roof under which you would be more safe than mine, and there is nothing in my house which you might need for your comfort, which I would not readily grant. Indeed, I should esteem it a privilege, to set you an example as to how mankind ought to treat each other.

I am your fellow man but not your slave,
FREDERICK DOUGLASS

P.S. I send a copy of the paper containing this letter, to save postage.—F.D.

—1848

What to the Slave Is the Fourth of July?

In 1852, Douglass was invited by the Rochester Ladies' Anti-Slavery Society to deliver an oration before the citizenry of Rochester, as part of the local Independence Day celebrations. He did not give the resulting speech a title; it is often referred to as "What to the Slave Is the Fourth of July?" and often, in excerpted form, given the title "The Hypocrisy of American Slavery." The full speech was issued in pamphlet form later in 1852, titled simply "Oration, Delivered in Corinthian Hall, Rochester." In 1855 Douglass published an extract from the speech in the appendices to *My Bondage and My Freedom*. That extract omits some of the speech's more inflammatory passages.

Mr. President, Friends and Fellow Citizens: He who could address this audience without a quailing sensation has stronger nerves than I have. I do not remember ever to have appeared as a speaker before any assembly more shrinkingly, nor with greater distrust of my ability, than I do this day. A feeling has crept over me, quite unfavorable to the exercise of my limited powers of speech. The task before me is one which requires much previous thought and study for its proper performance. I know that apologies of this sort are generally considered flat and unmeaning. I trust, however, that mine will not be so considered. Should I seem at ease, my appearance would much misrepresent me. The little experience I have had in addressing public meetings, in country schoolhouses, avails me nothing on the present occasion.

The papers and placards say that I am to deliver a 4th of July oration. This certainly sounds large and out of the common way for me. It is true that I have often had the privilege to speak in this beautiful Hall, and to address many who now honor me with their presence. But neither their familiar faces, nor the perfect gage I think I have of Corinthian Hall, seems to free me from embarrassment.

The fact is, ladies and gentlemen, the distance between this platform and the slave plantation, from which I escaped, is considerable—and the difficulties to be overcome in getting from the latter to the former, are by no means slight. That I am here today is, to me, a matter of astonishment as well as of gratitude. You will not, therefore, be surprised, if in what I have to say I evince no elaborate preparation, nor grace my speech with any high sounding exordium.[1] With little experience and with less learning, I have been able to throw my thoughts hastily and imperfectly together; and trusting to your patient and generous indulgence, I will proceed to lay them before you.

---

1   *exordium* Introduction.

This, for the purpose of this celebration, is the 4th of July.[1] It is the birthday of your National Independence, and of your political freedom. This, to you, is what the Passover[2] was to the emancipated people of God. It carries your minds back to the day, and to the act of your great deliverance, and to the signs, and to the wonders, associated with that act, and that day. This celebration also marks the beginning of another year of your national life, and reminds you that the Republic of America is now 76 years old. I am glad, fellow-citizens, that your nation is so young. Seventy-six years, though a good old age for a man, is but a mere speck in the life of a nation. Three score years and ten is the allotted time for individual men; but nations number their years by thousands. According to this fact, you are, even now, only in the beginning of your national career, still lingering in the period of childhood. I repeat, I am glad this is so. There is hope in the thought, and hope is much needed, under the dark clouds which lower above the horizon. The eye of the reformer is met with angry flashes, portending disastrous times; but his heart may well beat lighter at the thought that America is young, and that she is still in the impressible stage of her existence. May he not hope that high lessons of wisdom, of justice and of truth, will yet give direction to her destiny? Were the nation older, the patriot's heart might be sadder, and the reformer's brow heavier. Its future might be shrouded in gloom, and the hope of its prophets go out in sorrow. There is consolation in the thought that America is young. Great streams are not easily turned from channels, worn deep in the course of ages. They may sometimes rise in quiet and stately majesty, and inundate the land, refreshing and fertilizing the earth with their mysterious properties. They may also rise in wrath and fury, and bear away, on their angry waves, the accumulated wealth of years of toil and hardship. They, however, gradually flow back to the same old channel, and flow on as serenely as ever. But, while

the river may not be turned aside, it may dry up, and leave nothing behind but the withered branch, and the unsightly rock, to howl in the abyss-sweeping wind, the sad tale of departed glory. As with rivers so with nations.

Fellow citizens, I shall not presume to dwell at length on the associations that cluster about this day. The simple story of it is that, 76 years ago, the people of this country were British subjects. The style and title of your "sovereign people" (in which you now glory) was not then born. You were under the British Crown. Your fathers esteemed the English Government as the home government, and England as the fatherland. This home government, you know, although a considerable distance from your home, did, in the exercise of its parental prerogatives, impose upon its colonial children such restraints, burdens and limitations as, in its mature judgment, it deemed wise, right and proper.

But your fathers, who had not adopted the fashionable idea of this day of the infallibility of government, and the absolute character of its acts, presumed to differ from the home government in respect to the wisdom and the justice of some of those burdens and restraints. They went so far in their excitement as to pronounce the measures of government unjust, unreasonable, and oppressive, and altogether such as ought not to be quietly submitted to. I scarcely need say, fellow citizens, that my opinion of those measures fully accords with that of your fathers. Such a declaration of agreement on my part would not be worth much to anybody. It would, certainly, prove nothing, as to what part I might have taken, had I lived during the great controversy of 1776. To say *now* that America was right, and England wrong, is exceedingly easy. Everybody can say it; the dastard, not less than the noble brave, can flippantly descant on[3] the tyranny of England towards the American Colonies. It is fashionable to do so; but there was a time when to pronounce against England, and in favor of the cause of the colonies, tried men's souls. They who did so were accounted in their day plotters of mischief, agitators and rebels, dangerous men. To side with the right against the wrong, with the weak against the strong, and with the oppressed against the oppressor!

[1] *This ... 4th of July* Though the address was part of the Independence Day festivities, it was delivered on the 5th of July rather than the 4th.

[2] *Passover* Event described in the Book of Exodus in which God frees the Israelites from slavery in Egypt by punishing the Egyptians with ten plagues, the last of which is the death of all the first-born children. God passes over the homes of the Israelites when he brings this final plague.

[3] *descant on* Discuss.

here lies the merit, and the one which, of all others, seems unfashionable in our day. The cause of liberty may be stabbed by the men who glory in the deeds of your fathers. But, to proceed.

Feeling themselves harshly and unjustly treated by the home government, your fathers, like men of honesty, and men of spirit, earnestly sought redress. They petitioned and remonstrated; they did so in a decorous, respectful, and loyal manner. Their conduct was wholly unexceptionable. This, however, did not answer the purpose. They saw themselves treated with sovereign indifference, coldness and scorn. Yet they persevered. They were not the men to look back.

As the sheet anchor takes a firmer hold, when the ship is tossed by the storm, so did the cause of your fathers grow stronger, as it breasted the chilling blasts of kingly displeasure. The greatest and best of British statesmen admitted its justice, and the loftiest eloquence of the British Senate came to its support. But, with that blindness which seems to be the unvarying characteristic of tyrants, since Pharaoh and his hosts were drowned in the Red Sea,[1] the British Government persisted in the exactions complained of.

The madness of this course, we believe, is admitted now, even by England; but we fear the lesson is wholly lost on our present rulers.

Oppression makes a wise man mad. Your fathers were wise men, and if they did not go mad, they became restive under this treatment. They felt themselves the victims of grievous wrongs, wholly incurable in their colonial capacity. With brave men there is always a remedy for oppression. Just here, the idea of a total separation of the colonies from the crown was born! It was a startling idea, much more so, than we, at this distance of time, regard it. The timid and the prudent (as has been intimated) of that day, were, of course, shocked and alarmed by it.

Such people lived then, had lived before, and will, probably, ever have a place on this planet; and their course, in respect to any great change (no matter how great the good to be attained, or the wrong to be redressed by it), may be calculated with as much

precision as can be the course of the stars. They hate all changes, but silver, gold and copper change! Of this sort of change they are always strongly in favor.

These people were called Tories[2] in the days of your fathers; and the appellation probably conveyed the same idea that is meant by a more modern, though a somewhat less euphonious term,[3] which we often find in our papers, applied to some of our old politicians.

Their opposition to the then dangerous thought was earnest and powerful; but, amid all their terror and affrighted vociferations against it, the alarming and revolutionary idea moved on, and the country with it.

On the 2d of July, 1776, the old Continental Congress, to the dismay of the lovers of ease, and the worshipers of property, clothed that dreadful idea with all the authority of national sanction.[4] They did so in the form of a resolution; and as we seldom hit upon resolutions, drawn up in our day, whose transparency is at all equal to this, it may refresh your minds and help my story if I read it.

> Resolved, That these united colonies are, and of right, ought to be free and Independent States; that they are absolved from all allegiance to the British Crown; and that all political connection between them and the State of Great Britain is, and ought to be, dissolved.

Citizens, your fathers made good that resolution. They succeeded; and today you reap the fruits of their success. The freedom gained is yours; and you, therefore, may properly celebrate this anniversary. The 4th of July is the first great fact in your nation's history—the very ringbolt in the chain of your yet undeveloped destiny.

---

[1]   *since Pharaoh ... Red Sea*   Douglass refers to the crossing of the Red Sea in the Book of Exodus, when God parts the sea to allow the Israelites to pass through and then drowns the pursuing Egyptian army.

[2]   *Tories*   Term used in Britain and elsewhere to refer to Conservative politicians and their supporters; it came during the American Revolutionary War to refer to Loyalists to the British cause.

[3]   *somewhat ... term*   Douglass is likely alluding to the term "hunker," which was often applied to conservative politicians in the United States in the mid-nineteenth century; *euphonious*   Pleasant-sounding.

[4]   *On the 2d ... sanction*   The Declaration of Independence was passed by the Second Continental Congress on the 2nd of July, and ratified on the 4th.

Pride and patriotism, not less than gratitude, prompt you to celebrate and to hold it in perpetual remembrance. I have said that the Declaration of Independence is the RINGBOLT to the chain of your nation's destiny; so, indeed, I regard it. The principles contained in that instrument are saving principles. Stand by those principles, be true to them on all occasions, in all places, against all foes, and at whatever cost.

From the round top of your ship of state, dark and threatening clouds may be seen. Heavy billows, like mountains in the distance, disclose to the leeward[1] huge forms of flinty rocks! That *bolt* drawn, that *chain* broken, and all is lost. *Cling to this day—cling to it*, and to its principles, with the grasp of a storm-tossed mariner to a spar[2] at midnight.

The coming into being of a nation, in any circumstances, is an interesting event. But, besides general considerations, there were peculiar circumstances which make the advent of this republic an event of special attractiveness.

The whole scene, as I look back to it, was simple, dignified and sublime.

The population of the country, at the time, stood at the insignificant number of three millions. The country was poor in the munitions of war. The population was weak and scattered, and the country a wilderness unsubdued. There were then no means of concert[3] and combination such as exist now. Neither steam nor lightning[4] had then been reduced to order and discipline. From the Potomac to the Delaware was a journey of many days. Under these, and innumerable other disadvantages, your fathers declared for liberty and independence and triumphed.

Fellow Citizens, I am not wanting[5] in respect for the fathers of this republic. The signers of the Declaration of Independence were brave men. They were great men too—great enough to give fame to a great age. It does not often happen to a nation to raise, at one time, such a number of truly great men. The point from which I am compelled to view them is not, certainly, the most favorable; and yet I cannot contemplate their great deeds with less than admiration. They were statesmen, patriots and heroes, and for the good they did, and the principles they contended for, I will unite with you to honor their memory.

They loved their country better than their own private interests; and, though this is not the highest form of human excellence, all will concede that it is a rare virtue, and that when it is exhibited, it ought to command respect. He who will, intelligently, lay down his life for his country, is a man whom it is not in human nature to despise. Your fathers staked their lives, their fortunes, and their sacred honor, on the cause of their country. In their admiration of liberty, they lost sight of all other interests.

They were peace men; but they preferred revolution to peaceful submission to bondage. They were quiet men; but they did not shrink from agitating against oppression. They showed forbearance; but that they knew its limits. They believed in order; but not in the order of tyranny. With them, nothing was "*settled*" that was not right. With them, justice, liberty and humanity were "*final*"; not slavery and oppression. You may well cherish the memory of such men. They were great in their day and generation. Their solid manhood stands out the more as we contrast it with these degenerate times.

How circumspect, exact and proportionate were all their movements! How unlike the politicians of an hour! Their statesmanship looked beyond the passing moment, and stretched away in strength into the distant future. They seized upon eternal principles, and set a glorious example in their defense. Mark them!

Fully appreciating the hardship to be encountered, firmly believing in the right of their cause, honorably inviting the scrutiny of an onlooking world, reverently appealing to heaven to attest their sincerity, soundly comprehending the solemn responsibility they were about to assume, wisely measuring the terrible odds against them, your fathers, the fathers of this republic, did, most deliberately, under the inspiration of a glorious patriotism, and with a sublime faith in the great principles of justice and freedom, lay deep the cornerstone of the national superstructure, which has risen and still rises in grandeur around you.

---

[1] *leeward* Side facing away from the wind.

[2] *spar* Mast or other pole used to support a ship's sails.

[3] *concert* Coming together.

[4] *steam nor lightning* I.e., neither steam power nor electricity.

[5] *wanting* Lacking.

Of this fundamental work, this day is the anniversary. Our eyes are met with demonstrations of joyous enthusiasm. Banners and pennants[1] wave exultingly on the breeze. The din of business, too, is hushed. Even mammon[2] seems to have quitted his grasp on this day. The ear-piercing fife and the stirring drum unite their accents with the ascending peal of a thousand church bells. Prayers are made, hymns are sung, and sermons are preached in honor of this day; while the quick martial tramp of a great and multitudinous nation, echoed back by all the hills, valleys and mountains of a vast continent, bespeak the occasion one of thrilling and universal interest—a nation's jubilee.

Friends and citizens, I need not enter further into the causes which led to this anniversary. Many of you understand them better than I do. You could instruct me in regard to them. That is a branch of knowledge in which you feel, perhaps, a much deeper interest than your speaker. The causes which led to the separation of the colonies from the British crown have never lacked for a tongue. They have all been taught in your common schools, narrated at your firesides, unfolded from your pulpits, and thundered from your legislative halls, and are as familiar to you as household words. They form the staple of your national poetry and eloquence.

I remember, also, that, as a people, Americans are remarkably familiar with all facts which make in their own favor. This is esteemed by some as a national trait—perhaps a national weakness. It is a fact that whatever makes for the wealth or for the reputation of Americans—and can be had *cheap*!—will be found by Americans. I shall not be charged with slandering Americans, if I say I think the American side of any question may be safely left in American hands.

I leave, therefore, the great deeds of your fathers to other gentlemen whose claim to have been regularly descended will be less likely to be disputed than mine!

THE PRESENT

My business, if I have any here today, is with the present. The accepted time with God and his cause is the ever-living now.

Trust no future, however pleasant,
  Let the dead past bury its dead;
Act, act in the living present,
  Heart within, and God overhead.[3]

We have to do with the past only as we can make it useful to the present and to the future. To all inspiring motives, to noble deeds which can be gained from the past, we are welcome. But now is the time, the important time. Your fathers have lived, died, and have done their work, and have done much of it well. You live and must die, and you must do your work. You have no right to enjoy a child's share in the labor of your fathers, unless your children are to be blessed by your labors. You have no right to wear out and waste the hard-earned fame of your fathers to cover your indolence. Sydney Smith[4] tells us that men seldom eulogize the wisdom and virtues of their fathers, but to excuse some folly or wickedness of their own. This truth is not a doubtful one. There are illustrations of it near and remote, ancient and modern. It was fashionable, hundreds of years ago, for the children of Jacob to boast, we have "Abraham to our father," when they had long lost Abraham's faith and spirit.[5] That people contented themselves under the shadow of Abraham's great name, while they repudiated the deeds which made his name great. Need I remind you that a similar thing is being done all over this country today? Need I tell you that the Jews are not the only people who built the tombs of the prophets, and garnished the sepulchres of the righteous? Washington could not die till he had broken the chains of his slaves. Yet his monument is built up by the price of human blood,[6] and the traders in the bodies

---

1   *pennants*   Narrow, triangular flags.

2   *mammon*   Wealth and profit (regarded as a false god).

---

3   *Trust no … God overhead*   See Henry Wadsworth Longfellow's "A Psalm of Life" (1838).

4   *Sydney Smith*   English humorist and Anglican minister (1771–1845).

5   *children of Jacob … spirit*   See Matthew 3.9; Jacob, a biblical patriarch and grandson of Abraham, appears in the Book of Genesis.

6   *Washington … human blood*   At the time of his death in 1799, George Washington owned 124 enslaved people, all of whom were freed under the terms of his will. The monument to which Douglass refers is the Washington Monument, construction of which had begun in 1848 (though it was not completed until 1884); given that slavery in Washington, D.C. did not end until 1862, it is highly likely that enslaved people played a large role in the early stages of construction.

and souls of men, shout—"We have Washington to '*our father.*'" Alas! that it should be so; yet so it is.

> The evil that men do, lives after them,
> The good is oft' interred with their bones.[1]

Fellow citizens, pardon me, allow me to ask, why am I called upon to speak here today?[2] What have I, or those I represent, to do with your national independence? Are the great principles of political freedom and of natural justice, embodied in that Declaration of Independence, extended to us? and am I, therefore, called upon to bring our humble offering to the national altar, and to confess the benefits and express devout gratitude for the blessings resulting from your independence to us?

Would to God, both for your sakes and ours, that an affirmative answer could be truthfully returned to these questions! Then would my task be light, and my burden easy and delightful. For *who* is there so cold that a nation's sympathy could not warm him? Who so obdurate and dead to the claims of gratitude, that would not thankfully acknowledge such priceless benefits? Who so stolid and selfish, that would not give his voice to swell the hallelujahs of a nation's jubilee, when the chains of servitude had been torn from his limbs? I am not that man. In a case like that, the dumb[3] might eloquently speak, and the "lame man leap as an hart."[4]

But such is not the state of the case. I say it with a sad sense of the disparity between us. I am not included within the pale of this glorious anniversary! Your high independence only reveals the immeasurable distance between us. The blessings in which you, this day, rejoice, are not enjoyed in common. The rich inheritance of justice, liberty, prosperity and independence, bequeathed by your fathers, is shared by you, not by me. The sunlight that brought life and healing to you, has brought stripes[5] and death to me. This Fourth July is *yours*, not *mine. You* may rejoice, *I* must mourn. To

drag a man in fetters into the grand illuminated temple of liberty, and call upon him to join you in joyous anthems, were inhuman mockery and sacrilegious irony. Do you mean, citizens, to mock me, by asking me to speak today? If so, there is a parallel to your conduct.[6] And let me warn you that it is dangerous to copy the example of a nation whose crimes, towering up to heaven, were thrown down by the breath of the Almighty, burying that nation in irrecoverable ruin![7] I can today take up the plaintive lament of a peeled[8] and woe-smitten people!

> By the rivers of Babylon, there we sat down. Yea! we wept when we remembered Zion. We hanged our harps upon the willows in the midst thereof. For there, they that carried us away captive, required of us a song; and they who wasted us required of us mirth, saying, Sing us one of the songs of Zion. How can we sing the Lord's song in a strange land? If I forget thee, O Jerusalem, let my right hand forget her cunning. If I do not remember thee, let my tongue cleave to the roof of my mouth.

Fellow citizens; above your national, tumultuous joy, I hear the mournful wail of millions! whose chains, heavy and grievous yesterday, are today rendered more intolerable by the jubilee shouts that reach them. If I do forget, if I do not faithfully remember those bleeding children of sorrow this day, "may my right hand forget her cunning, and may my tongue cleave to the roof of my mouth"! To forget them, to pass lightly over their wrongs, and to chime in with the popular theme, would be treason most scandalous and shocking, and would make me a reproach before God and the world. My subject, then fellow citizens, is American Slavery. I shall see this day, and its popular characteristics,

---

1   *The evil ... their bones*   See Shakespeare's *Julius Caesar* 3.2.84–85.

2   *Fellow citizens ... today?*   Douglass begins his 1855 "Extract" here.

3   *dumb*   Mute.

4   *lame man ... hart*   See Isaiah 35.6: "Then shall the lame man leap as an hart, and the tongue of the dumb sing: for in the wilderness shall waters break out, and streams in the desert";   *hart*   Stag.

5   *stripes*   I.e., wounds caused by being whipped.

6   *there is ... your conduct*   Douglass alludes to the treatment of the Israelites during their period as captives of the Babylonian King Nebuchadnezzar. Psalm 137 (quoted from below) describes how the Israelites refuse their captor's demand that they "sing the Lord's song in a strange land."

7   *a nation ... irrevocable ruin*   The destruction of the kingdom of Babylon is prophesied in the Old Testament, and described in the Book of Revelations, where the kingdom's sinful history is symbolized by the figure of the "Whore of Babylon."

8   *peeled*   Wretched.

from the slave's point of view. Standing, there, identified with the American bondman, making his wrongs mine, I do not hesitate to declare, with all my soul, that the character and conduct of this nation never looked blacker to me than on this 4th of July! Whether we turn to the declarations of the past, or to the professions of the present, the conduct of the nation seems equally hideous and revolting. America is false to the past, false to the present, and solemnly binds herself to be false to the future. Standing with God and the crushed and bleeding slave on this occasion, I will, in the name of humanity which is outraged, in the name of liberty which is fettered, in the name of the constitution and the Bible, which are disregarded and trampled upon, dare to call in question and to denounce, with all the emphasis I can command, everything that serves to perpetuate slavery—the great sin and shame of America! "I will not equivocate; I will not excuse";[1] I will use the severest language I can command; and yet not one word shall escape me that any man, whose judgment is not blinded by prejudice, or who is not at heart a slaveholder, shall not confess to be right and just.

But I fancy I hear some one of my audience say, it is just in this circumstance that you and your brother abolitionists fail to make a favorable impression on the public mind. Would you argue more, and denounce less,[2] would you persuade more, and rebuke less, your cause would be much more likely to succeed. But, I submit, where all is plain, there is nothing to be argued. What point in the anti-slavery creed would you have me argue? On what branch of the subject do the people of this country need light? Must I undertake to prove that the slave is a man? That point is conceded already. Nobody doubts it. The slaveholders themselves acknowledge it in the enactment of laws for their government. They acknowledge it when they punish disobedience on the part of the slave. There are seventy-two crimes in the State of Virginia, which, if committed by a black man (no matter how ignorant he be), subject him to the punishment of death; while only two of the same crimes will subject a white man to the like punishment. What is this but the acknowledgement that the slave is a moral, intellectual and responsible being? The manhood of the slave is conceded. It is admitted in the fact that Southern statute books are covered with enactments forbidding, under severe fines and penalties, the teaching of the slave to read or to write. When you can point to any such laws, in reference to the beasts of the field, then I may consent to argue the manhood of the slave. When the dogs in your streets, when the fowls of the air, when the cattle on your hills, when the fish of the sea, and the reptiles that crawl, shall be unable to distinguish the slave from a brute, *then* will I argue with you that the slave is a man!

For the present, it is enough to affirm the equal manhood of the negro race. Is it not astonishing that, while we are ploughing, planting and reaping, using all kinds of mechanical tools, erecting houses, constructing bridges, building ships, working in metals of brass, iron, copper, silver and gold; that, while we are reading, writing and cyphering,[3] acting as clerks, merchants and secretaries, having among us lawyers, doctors, ministers, poets, authors, editors, orators and teachers; that, while we are engaged in all manner of enterprises common to other men, digging gold in California, capturing the whale in the Pacific, feeding sheep and cattle on the hill-side, living, moving, acting, thinking, planning, living in families as husbands, wives and children, and, above all, confessing and worshipping the Christian's God, and looking hopefully for life and immortality beyond the grave, we are called upon to prove that we are men!

Would you have me argue that man is entitled to liberty? that he is the rightful owner of his own body? You have already declared it. Must I argue the wrongfulness of slavery? Is that a question for republicans?[4] Is it to be settled by the rules of logic and argumentation, as a matter beset with great difficulty, involving a doubtful application of the principle of justice, hard to be understood? How should I look today, in the presence of Americans, dividing and subdividing a discourse, to show that men have a natural right to freedom? speaking of it relatively, and positively, negatively, and

1   *I will ... not excuse*   Douglass here quotes from William Lloyd Garrison's opening article in the first issue of *The Liberator* (1831), an influential antislavery newspaper.

2   *argue ... less*   I.e., present more arguments in favor of your goals, and make fewer denunciations of the present state.

3   *cyphering*   Doing calculations.

4   *republicans*   I.e., citizens of a republic.

affirmatively? To do so would be to make myself ridiculous, and to offer an insult to your understanding. There is not a man beneath the canopy of heaven, that does not know that slavery is wrong *for him*.

What, am I to argue that it is wrong to make men brutes, to rob them of their liberty, to work them without wages, to keep them ignorant of their relations to their fellow men, to beat them with sticks, to flay their flesh with the lash, to load their limbs with irons, to hunt them with dogs, to sell them at auction, to sunder their families, to knock out their teeth, to burn their flesh, to starve them into obedience and submission to their masters? Must I argue that a system thus marked with blood, and stained with pollution, is *wrong*? No I will not. I have better employment for my time and strength than such arguments would imply.

What, then, remains to be argued? Is it that slavery is not divine; that God did not establish it; that our doctors of divinity are mistaken? There is blasphemy in the thought. That which is inhuman, cannot be divine! *Who* can reason on such a proposition? They that can, may; I cannot. The time for such argument is past.

At a time like this, scorching irony, not convincing argument, is needed. O! had I the ability, and could I reach the nation's ear, I would, today, pour out a fiery stream of biting ridicule, blasting reproach, withering sarcasm, and stern rebuke. For it is not light that is needed, but fire; it is not the gentle shower, but thunder. We need the storm, the whirlwind, and the earthquake. The feeling of the nation must be quickened; the conscience of the nation must be roused; the propriety of the nation must be startled; the hypocrisy of the nation must be exposed; and its crimes against God and man must be proclaimed and denounced.

What, to the American slave, is your 4th of July? I answer: a day that reveals to him, more than all other days in the year, the gross injustice and cruelty to which he is the constant victim. To him, your celebration is a sham; your boasted liberty, an unholy license; your national greatness, swelling vanity; your sounds of rejoicing are empty and heartless; your denunciations of tyrants, brass fronted impudence; your shouts of liberty and equality, hollow mockery; your prayers and hymns, your sermons and thanksgivings, with all your religious parade, and solemnity, are, to him, mere bombast, fraud, deception, impiety, and hypocrisy—a thin veil to cover up crimes which would disgrace a nation of savages. There is not a nation on the earth guilty of practices more shocking and bloody than are the people of these United States, at this very hour.

Go where you may, search where you will, roam through all the monarchies and despotisms of the old world, travel through South America, search out every abuse, and when you have found the last, lay your facts by the side of the everyday practices of this nation, and you will say with me, that, for revolting barbarity and shameless hypocrisy, America reigns without a rival.[1]

The Internal Slave Trade

Take the American slave-trade, which, we are told by the papers, is especially prosperous just now. Ex-Senator Benton[2] tells us that the price of men was never higher than now. He mentions the fact to show that slavery is in no danger. This trade is one of the peculiarities of American institutions. It is carried on in all the large towns and cities in one-half of this confederacy; and millions are pocketed every year by dealers in this horrid traffic. In several states, this trade is a chief source of wealth. It is called (in contradistinction to the foreign slave-trade) *"the internal slave-trade."* It is, probably, called so, too, in order to divert from it the horror with which the foreign slave-trade is contemplated. That trade has long since been denounced by this government, as piracy.[3] It has been denounced with burning words, from the high places of the nation, as an execrable traffic. To arrest it, to put an end to it, this nation keeps a squadron, at immense cost, on the coast of Africa. Everywhere, in this country, it is safe to speak of this foreign slave-trade as a most inhuman traffic, opposed alike to the laws of God and of man. The duty to extirpate and destroy it, is admitted even by our Doctors of Divinity. In order to put an end to it, some of these last have consented that their colored brethren (nominally free)

---

1   *without a rival*   The "Extract" in Douglass's *My Bondage and My Freedom* ends here.

2   *Ex-Senator Benton*   Thomas Hart Benton (1782–1858), Democratic senator who, though he owned enslaved people for much of his life, came to oppose the institution.

3   *That trade … as piracy*   The Atlantic slave trade was abolished by the United States in 1808.

should leave this country, and establish themselves on the western coast of Africa![1] It is, however, a notable fact that, while so much execration is poured out by Americans upon those engaged in the foreign slave-trade, the men engaged in the slave-trade between the states pass without condemnation, and their business is deemed honorable.

Behold the practical operation of this internal slave-trade, the American slave-trade, sustained by American politics and American religion. Here you will see men and women, reared like swine for the market. You know what is a swine-drover? I will show you a man-drover.[2] They inhabit all our Southern States. They perambulate the country, and crowd the highways of the nation, with droves of human stock. You will see one of these human flesh jobbers,[3] armed with pistol, whip and bowie-knife,[4] driving a company of a hundred men, women, and children, from the Potomac to the slave market at New Orleans. These wretched people are to be sold singly, or in lots, to suit purchasers. They are food for the cotton-field, and the deadly sugar-mill. Mark the sad procession, as it moves wearily along, and the inhuman wretch who drives them. Hear his savage yells and his blood-chilling oaths, as he hurries on his affrighted captives! There, see the old man, with locks thinned and gray. Cast one glance, if you please, upon that young mother, whose shoulders are bare to the scorching sun, her briny tears falling on the brow of the babe in her arms. See, too, that girl of thirteen, weeping, *yes*! weeping, as she thinks of the mother from whom she has been torn! The drove moves tardily. Heat and sorrow have nearly consumed their strength; suddenly you hear a quick snap, like the discharge of a rifle; the fetters clank, and the chain rattles simultaneously; your ears are saluted with a scream, that seems to have torn its way to the centre of your soul! The

crack you heard, was the sound of the slave-whip; the scream you heard, was from the woman you saw with the babe. Her speed had faltered under the weight of her child and her chains! that gash on her shoulder tells her to move on. Follow the drove to New Orleans. Attend the auction; see men examined like horses; see the forms of women rudely and brutally exposed to the shocking gaze of American slave-buyers. See this drove sold and separated forever; and never forget the deep, sad sobs that arose from that scattered multitude. Tell me citizens, where, under the sun, you can witness a spectacle more fiendish and shocking. Yet this is but a glance at the American slave-trade, as it exists, at this moment, in the ruling part of the United States.

I was born amid such sights and scenes. To me the American slave-trade is a terrible reality. When a child, my soul was often pierced with a sense of its horrors. I lived on Philpot Street, Fell's Point, Baltimore, and have watched from the wharves, the slave ships in the Basin, anchored from the shore, with their cargoes of human flesh, waiting for favorable winds to waft them down the Chesapeake. There was, at that time, a grand slave mart kept at the head of Pratt Street, by Austin Woldfolk. His agents were sent into every town and county in Maryland, announcing their arrival, through the papers, and on flaming "*hand-bills*," headed cash for negroes. These men were generally well dressed men, and very captivating in their manners. Ever ready to drink, to treat, and to gamble. The fate of many a slave has depended upon the turn of a single card; and many a child has been snatched from the arms of its mother, by bargains arranged in a state of brutal drunkenness.

The flesh-mongers gather up their victims by dozens, and drive them, chained, to the general depot at Baltimore. When a sufficient number have been collected here, a ship is chartered, for the purpose of conveying the forlorn crew to Mobile, or to New Orleans. From the slave prison to the ship, they are usually driven in the darkness of night; for since the antislavery agitation, a certain caution is observed.

In the deep still darkness of midnight, I have been often aroused by the dead heavy footsteps, and the piteous cries of the chained gangs that passed our door. The anguish of my boyish heart was intense; and I was often consoled, when speaking to my mistress in

---

[1] *In order ... of Africa* Douglass alludes to the colonization movement, led chiefly by the American Colonization Society, whose members (many of whom were clergymen, and all of whom were white) advocated for the relocation of free African Americans to the African continent. This movement was widely condemned by many—though not all—abolitionists in the nineteenth century.

[2] *drover* Herder; one who is in charge of moving a herd (or "drove") of animals from place to place.

[3] *jobbers* Dealers.

[4] *bowie-knife* Short fighting-knife often associated with the American South.

the morning, to hear her say that the custom was very wicked; that she hated to hear the rattle of the chains, and the heart-rending cries. I was glad to find one who sympathized with me in my horror.

Fellow citizens, this murderous traffic is, today, in active operation in this boasted republic. In the solitude of my spirit, I see clouds of dust raised on the highways of the South; I see the bleeding footsteps; I hear the doleful wail of fettered humanity, on the way to the slave-markets, where the victims are to be sold like *horses*, *sheep*, and *swine*, knocked off to the highest bidder. There I see the tenderest ties ruthlessly broken, to gratify the lust, caprice and rapacity of the buyers and sellers of men. My soul sickens at the sight.

Is this the land your Fathers loved,
    The freedom which they toiled to win?
Is this the earth whereon they moved?
    Are these the graves they slumber in?[1]

But a still more inhuman, disgraceful, and scandalous state of things remains to be presented.

By an act of the American Congress, not yet two years old, slavery has been nationalized in its most horrible and revolting form. By that act, Mason & Dixon's line has been obliterated; New York has become as Virginia; and the power to hold, hunt, and sell men, women, and children as slaves remains no longer a mere state institution, but is now an institution of the whole United States.[2] The power is co-extensive with the star-spangled banner, and American Christianity. Where these go, may also go the merciless slave-hunter. Where these are, man is not sacred. He is a bird for the

sportsman's gun. By that most foul and fiendish of all human decrees, the liberty and person of every man are put in peril. Your broad republican domain is hunting ground for *men*. *Not* for thieves and robbers, enemies of society, merely, but for men guilty of no crime. Your lawmakers have commanded all good citizens to engage in this hellish sport. Your President, your Secretary of State, your *lords*, *nobles*, and ecclesiastics, enforce, as a duty you owe to your free and glorious country, and to your God, that you do this accursed thing. Not fewer than forty Americans have, within the past two years, been hunted down, and, without a moment's warning, hurried away in chains, and consigned to slavery and excruciating torture. Some of these have had wives and children, dependent on them for bread; but of this, no account was made. The right of the hunter to his prey stands superior to the right of marriage, and to *all* rights in this republic, the rights of God included! For black men there are neither law, justice, humanity, nor religion. The Fugitive Slave *Law* makes mercy to them, a crime; and bribes the judge who tries them. An American Judge gets ten dollars for every victim he consigns to slavery, and five, when he fails to do so. The oath of any two villains is sufficient, under this hell-black enactment, to send the most pious and exemplary black man into the remorseless jaws of slavery! His own testimony is nothing. He can bring no witnesses for himself. The minister of American justice is bound, by the law, to hear but *one* side; and *that* side, is the side of the oppressor. Let this damning fact be perpetually told. Let it be thundered around the world, that, in tyrant-killing, king-hating, people-loving, democratic, Christian America, the seats of justice are filled with judges, who hold their offices under an open and palpable *bribe*, and are bound, in deciding in the case of a man's liberty, *to hear only his accusers*!

In glaring violation of justice, in shameless disregard of the forms of administering law, in cunning arrangement to entrap the defenseless, and in diabolical intent, this Fugitive Slave Law stands alone in the annals of tyrannical legislation. I doubt if there be another nation on the globe, having the brass and the baseness to put such a law on the statute-book. If any man in this assembly thinks differently from me in this matter, and feels able to disprove my statements, I will gladly confront him at any suitable time and place he may select.

---

[1]   *Is this ... slumber in?*   See "Stanzas for the Times" by antislavery poet John Greenleaf Whittier.

[2]   *By an act ... United States*   Douglass refers to the Fugitive Slave Act of 1850 (a part of the Compromise of 1850), under the terms of which it became illegal for anyone, whether in the North or the South, to give aid to people escaping slavery; citizens throughout the country were expected to actively participate in the apprehension and return of such fugitives. Given that the testimony of captured African Americans was not accepted in court, the Act inevitably resulted in the capture and enslavement of many free African Americans, as well as of many who had been previously enslaved; *Mason & Dixon's line*   Line separating parts of Pennsylvania and Delaware from parts of Maryland and Virginia; the phrase was used as shorthand for the boundary between the Northern free states and the Southern slave states.

RELIGIOUS LIBERTY

I take this law to be one of the grossest infringements of Christian Liberty, and, if the churches and ministers of our country were not stupidly blind, or most wickedly indifferent, they, too, would so regard it.

At the very moment that they are thanking God for the enjoyment of civil and religious liberty, and for the right to worship God according to the dictates of their own consciences, they are utterly silent in respect to a law which robs religion of its chief significance, and makes it utterly worthless to a world lying in wickedness. Did this law concern the "*mint, anise and cumin*"[1]—abridge the right to sing psalms, to partake of the sacrament, or to engage in any of the ceremonies of religion, it would be smitten by the thunder of a thousand pulpits. A general shout would go up from the church, demanding *repeal, repeal, instant repeal*! And it would go hard with that politician who presumed to solicit the votes of the people without inscribing this motto on his banner. Further, if this demand were not complied with, another Scotland would be added to the history of religious liberty, and the stern old covenanters[2] would be thrown into the shade. A John Knox would be seen at every church door, and heard from every pulpit, and Fillmore would have no more quarter than was shown by Knox to the beautiful but treacherous queen Mary of Scotland.[3] The fact that the church of our country (with fractional exceptions) does not esteem "the Fugitive Slave Law" as a declaration of war against religious liberty, implies that that church regards religion simply as a form of worship, an empty ceremony, and *not* a vital principle, requiring active benevolence, justice, love and good will towards man. It esteems sacrifice above mercy; psalm-singing above right doing; solemn meetings above practical righteousness. A worship that can be conducted by persons who refuse to give shelter to the houseless, to give bread to the hungry, clothing to the naked, and who enjoin obedience to a law forbidding these acts of mercy, is a curse, not a blessing to mankind. The Bible addresses all such persons as "scribes, pharisees, hypocrites, who pay tithe of *mint, anise*, and *cumin*, and have omitted the weightier matters of the law, judgment, mercy and faith."

THE CHURCH RESPONSIBLE

But the church of this country is not only indifferent to the wrongs of the slave, it actually takes sides with the oppressors. It has made itself the bulwark of American slavery, and the shield of American slavehunters. Many of its most eloquent Divines, who stand as the very lights of the church, have shamelessly given the sanction of religion, and the Bible, to the whole slave system. They have taught that man may, properly, be a slave; that the relation of master and slave is ordained of God; that to send back an escaped bondman to his master is clearly the duty of all the followers of the Lord Jesus Christ; and this horrible blasphemy is palmed off upon the world for Christianity.

For my part, I would say, welcome infidelity! welcome atheism! welcome anything! in preference to the gospel, *as preached by those Divines*! They convert the very name of religion into an engine of tyranny, and barbarous cruelty, and serve to confirm more infidels, in this age, than all the infidel writings of Thomas Paine, Voltaire, and Bolingbroke,[4] put together, have done! These ministers make religion a cold and flinty-hearted thing, having neither principles of right action,

---

[1]   *mint, anise and cumin*   See Matthew 23.23: "Woe unto you, scribes and Pharisees, hypocrites! for ye pay tithe of mint and anise and cumin, and have omitted the weightier matters of the law, judgment, mercy, and faith: these ought ye to have done, and not to leave the other undone."

[2]   *covenanters*   Name given to the Scottish Presbyterians who signed the National Covenant in 1638, seeking to uphold the Presbyterian Church in Scotland in the face of persecution by King Charles I.

[3]   *A John Knox ... Scotland*   John Knox (1514–72), religious dissenter and founder of the Scottish Presbyterian Church, was an ardent opponent of the Catholic Mary Queen of Scots, who was executed for treason in 1587. Millard Fillmore, who was President of the United States at the time of Douglass's speech, was instrumental in the passage of the Fugitive Slave Act.

[4]   *Thomas Paine*   English-born political theorist whose *Common Sense* (1776) was profoundly influential during the time of the American Revolution, and whose *The Age of Reason* (1794–1807) was highly critical of organized religion; *Voltaire* French Enlightenment philosopher (1694–1778) who advocated freedom of speech and the separation of church and state, and was often accused of atheism; *Bolingbroke* Henry St. John, 1st Viscount Bolingbroke (1678–1751), English political philosopher whose antireligious views were influential on Voltaire as well as on numerous key figures of the American Revolution.

nor bowels of compassion. They strip the love of God of its beauty, and leave the throng of religion a huge, horrible, repulsive form. It is a religion for oppressors, tyrants, man-stealers, and *thugs*. It is not that "*pure and undefiled religion*"[1] which is from above, and which is "*first pure, then peaceable, easy to be entreated*, full of mercy and good fruits, *without partiality, and without hypocrisy*." But a religion which favors the rich against the poor; which exalts the proud above the humble; which divides mankind into two classes, tyrants and slaves; which says to the man in chains, *stay there*; and to the oppressor, *oppress on*; it is a religion which may be professed and enjoyed by all the robbers and enslavers of mankind; it makes God a respecter of persons,[2] denies his fatherhood of the race, and tramples in the dust the great truth of the brotherhood of man. All this we affirm to be true of the popular church, and the popular worship of our land and nation—a religion, a church, and a worship which, on the authority of inspired wisdom, we pronounce to be an abomination in the sight of God. In the language of Isaiah, the American church might be well addressed, "Bring no more vain oblations; incense is an abomination unto me: the new moons and Sabbaths, the calling of assemblies, I cannot away with; it is iniquity, even the solemn meeting. Your new moons, and your appointed feasts my soul hateth. They are a trouble to me; I am weary to bear them; and when ye spread forth your hands I will hide mine eyes from you. Yea! when ye make many prayers, I will not hear. YOUR HANDS ARE FULL OF BLOOD; cease to do evil, learn to do well; seek judgment; relieve the oppressed; judge for the fatherless; plead for the widow."[3]

The American church is guilty, when viewed in connection with what it is doing to uphold slavery; but it is superlatively guilty when viewed in connection with its ability to abolish slavery.

The sin of which it is guilty is one of omission as well as of commission. Albert Barnes[4] but uttered what the common sense of every man at all observant of the actual state of the case will receive as truth, when he declared that "There is no power out of the church that could sustain slavery an hour, if it were not sustained in it."

Let the religious press, the pulpit, the Sunday school, the conference meeting, the great ecclesiastical, missionary, Bible and tract associations of the land array their immense powers against slavery, and slave-holding; and the whole system of crime and blood would be scattered to the winds; and that they do not do this involves them in the most awful responsibility of which the mind can conceive.

In prosecuting the anti-slavery enterprise, we have been asked to spare the church, to spare the ministry; but *how*, we ask, could such a thing be done? We are met on the threshold of our efforts for the redemption of the slave, by the church and ministry of the country, in battle arrayed against us; and we are compelled to fight or flee. From *what* quarter, I beg to know, has proceeded a fire so deadly upon our ranks, during the last two years, as from the Northern pulpit? As the champions of oppressors, the chosen men of American theology have appeared—men, honored for their so-called piety, and their real learning. The Lords of Buffalo, the Springs of New York, the Lathrops of Auburn, the Coxes and Spencers of Brooklyn, the Gannets and Sharps of Boston, the Deweys of Washington,[5] and other great religious lights of the land, have, in utter denial of the authority of *Him*, by whom they professed to be called to the ministry, deliberately taught us, against the example of the Hebrews, and against the remonstrance of the Apostles, they teach *that we ought to obey man's law before the law of God.*[6]

My spirit wearies of such blasphemy; and how such men can be supported, as the "standing types and representatives of Jesus Christ," is a mystery which I leave others to penetrate. In speaking of the American church, however, let it be distinctly understood that I mean the *great mass* of the religious organizations of

---

[1]   *pure and undefiled religion*   See James 1.27.

[2]   *respecter of persons*   In Acts 10.34, Peter claims that "God is no respecter of persons"; i.e., that he does not favor people of higher status.

[3]   *In the language ... the widow*   See Isaiah 1.13–17.

[4]   *Albert Barnes*   American antislavery theologian (1798–1870) who wrote numerous books on the subject of slavery and religion.

[5]   *The Lords ... of Washington*   Douglass alludes to a number of religious leaders who were either explicitly proslavery or who were morally opposed to slavery but favored not interfering with the institution.

[6]   *that we ... of God*   See Acts 5.29: "Then Peter and the other apostles answered and said, We ought to obey God rather than men."

our land. There are exceptions, and I thank God that there are. Noble men may be found, scattered all over these Northern States, of whom Henry Ward Beecher of Brooklyn, Samuel J. May[1] of Syracuse, and my esteemed friend[2] on the platform, are shining examples; and let me say further, that, upon these men lies the duty to inspire our ranks with high religious faith and zeal, and to cheer us on in the great mission of the slave's redemption from his chains.

RELIGION IN ENGLAND AND RELIGION IN AMERICA

One is struck with the difference between the attitude of the American church towards the anti-slavery movement, and that occupied by the churches in England towards a similar movement in that country. There, the church, true to its mission of ameliorating, elevating, and improving the condition of mankind, came forward promptly, bound up the wounds of the West Indian slave, and restored him to his liberty. There, the question of emancipation was a high religious question. It was demanded, in the name of humanity, and according to the law of the living God. The Sharps, the Clarksons, the Wilberforces, the Buxtons, and Burchells and the Knibbs,[3] were alike famous for their piety, and for their philanthropy. The anti-slavery movement *there* was not an anti-church movement, for the reason that the church took its full share in prosecuting that movement: and the anti-slavery movement in this country will cease to be an anti-church movement, when the church of this country shall assume a favorable, instead of a hostile position towards that movement.

Americans! your republican politics, not less than your republican religion, are flagrantly inconsistent. You boast of your love of liberty, your superior civilization, and your pure Christianity, while the whole political power of the nation, as embodied in the two great political parties, is solemnly pledged to support and perpetuate the enslavement of three millions of your countrymen. You hurl your anathemas at the crowned headed tyrants of Russia and Austria, and pride yourselves on your Democratic institutions, while you yourselves consent to be the mere *tools* and *bodyguards* of the tyrants of Virginia and Carolina. You invite to your shores fugitives of oppression from abroad, honor them with banquets, greet them with ovations, cheer them, toast them, salute them, protect them, and pour out your money to them like water; but the fugitives from your own land, you advertise, hunt, arrest, shoot and kill. You glory in your refinement, and your universal education; yet you maintain a system as barbarous and dreadful, as ever stained the character of a nation—a system begun in avarice, supported in pride, and perpetuated in cruelty. You shed tears over fallen Hungary,[4] and make the sad story of her wrongs the theme of your poets, statesmen and orators, till your gallant sons are ready to fly to arms to vindicate her cause against her oppressors; but, in regard to the ten thousand wrongs of the American slave, you would enforce the strictest silence, and would hail him as an enemy of the nation who dares to make those wrongs the subject of public discourse! You are all on fire at the mention of liberty for France or for Ireland; but are as cold as an iceberg at the thought of liberty for the enslaved of America. You discourse eloquently on the dignity of labor; yet you sustain a system which, in its very essence, casts a stigma upon labor. You can bare your bosom to the storm of British artillery, to throw off a three-penny tax on tea;[5] and yet wring the last hard-earned farthing from the grasp of the black laborers of your country. You profess to believe "that, of one blood, God made all nations of men to dwell on the face of all the earth,"[6] and hath commanded all men, everywhere to love one another; yet you notoriously hate (and glory in your hatred) all men whose

---

[1]   *Henry Ward Beecher* American Congregationalist minister (1813–87) and antislavery activist; *Samuel J. May* American Unitarian minister (1797–1871) and abolitionist.

[2]   [Douglass's note] Rev. R.R. Raymond. [Baptist minister and abolitionist who contributed to Julia Griffiths's 1853 abolitionist collection *Autographs for Freedom*.]

[3]   *The Sharps ... the Knibbs* Douglass alludes to numerous English abolitionists active in the eighteenth and early nineteenth centuries, among them the influential politician William Wilberforce (1759–1833).

[4]   *fallen Hungary* The Hungarian Revolution, which many Americans supported, took place in 1848; it was violently suppressed by the Austrian Empire.

[5]   *throw off ... on tea* Douglass alludes to the Boston Tea Party of 1773, in which colonists protested the British Tea Act on the grounds that they would not tolerate taxation without representation.

[6]   *that ... the earth* See Acts 17.26.

skins are not colored like your own. You declare, before the world, and are understood by the world to declare, that you "*hold these truths to be self evident, that all men are created equal; and are endowed by their Creator with certain inalienable rights; and that, among these are, life, liberty, and the pursuit of happiness*";[1] and yet, you hold securely, in a bondage which, according to your own Thomas Jefferson, "*is worse than ages of that which your fathers rose in rebellion to oppose*,"[2] a *seventh part* of the inhabitants of your country.

Fellow-citizens! I will not enlarge further on your national inconsistencies. The existence of slavery in this country brands your republicanism as a sham, your humanity as a base pretence, and your Christianity as a lie. It destroys your moral power abroad; it corrupts your politicians at home. It saps the foundation of religion; it makes your name a hissing, and a by word to a mocking earth. It is the antagonistic force in your government, the only thing that seriously disturbs and endangers your *Union*. It fetters your progress; it is the enemy of improvement, the deadly foe of education; it fosters pride; it breeds insolence; it promotes vice; it shelters crime; it is a curse to the earth that supports it; and yet, you cling to it, as if it were the sheet anchor of all your hopes. Oh! be warned! be warned! a horrible reptile is coiled up in your nation's bosom; the venomous creature is nursing at the tender breast of your youthful republic; *for the love of God, tear away*, and fling from you the hideous monster, and *let the weight of twenty millions crush and destroy it forever*!

THE CONSTITUTION

But it is answered in reply to all this, that precisely what I have now denounced is, in fact, guaranteed and sanctioned by the Constitution of the United States; that the right to hold, and to hunt slaves is a part of that Constitution framed by the illustrious Fathers of this Republic.

Then, I dare to affirm, notwithstanding all I have said before, your fathers stooped, basely stooped.

> To palter with us in a double sense:
> And keep the word of promise to the ear,
> But break it to the heart.[3]

And instead of being the honest men I have before declared them to be, they were the veriest imposters that ever practiced on mankind. *This* is the inevitable conclusion, and from it there is no escape; but I differ from those who charge this baseness on the framers of the Constitution of the United States.[4] *It is a slander upon their memory*, at least, so I believe. There is not time now to argue the constitutional question at length; nor have I the ability to discuss it as it ought to be discussed. The subject has been handled with masterly power by Lysander Spooner, Esq., by William Goodell, by Samuel E. Sewall, Esq., and last, though not least, by Gerritt Smith, Esq.[5] These gentlemen have, as I think, fully and clearly vindicated the Constitution from any design to support slavery for an hour.

Fellow citizens! there is no matter in respect to which the people of the North have allowed themselves to be so ruinously imposed upon, as that of the pro-slavery character of the Constitution. In *that* instrument I hold there is neither warrant, license, nor sanction of the hateful thing; but, interpreted as it *ought* to be interpreted, the Constitution is a Glorious Liberty Document. Read its preamble, consider its purposes. Is slavery among them? Is it at the gateway? or is it in the temple? It is neither. While I do not intend to argue this question on the present occasion, let me ask, if it be not somewhat singular that, if the Constitution were intended to be, by its framers and adopters, a slave-holding instrument, why neither *slavery*, *slaveholding*, nor *slave* can anywhere be found in it. What would be thought of an instrument, drawn

---

1 *hold these truths ... of happiness* From the Declaration of Independence.

2 *Thomas Jefferson ... to oppose* Douglass paraphrases text included in a letter sent by Thomas Jefferson to Jean-Nicolas Démeunier in 1786, in which he decried the hypocrisy of American slavery. (Jefferson was himself a slaveholder.)

3 *To palter ... heart* Paraphrase from Shakespeare's *Macbeth* 5.8.24–26.

4 *but I differ ... United States* This disagreement was among the factors that led to Douglass's falling-out with his former colleague William Lloyd Garrison, who strongly believed the Constitution to be an inherently proslavery document.

5 *Lysander ... Esq.* Douglass names several abolitionists who argued that slavery was unconstitutional.

up, *legally* drawn up, for the purpose of entitling the city of Rochester to a track of land, in which no mention of land was made? Now, there are certain rules of interpretation, for the proper understanding of all legal instruments. These rules are well established. They are plain, common-sense rules, such as you and I, and all of us, can understand and apply, without having passed years in the study of law. I scout the idea that the question of the constitutionality, or unconstitutionality of slavery, is not a question for the people. I hold that every American citizen has a right to form an opinion of the constitution, and to propagate that opinion, and to use all honorable means to make his opinion the prevailing one. Without this right, the liberty of an American citizen would be as insecure as that of a Frenchman. Ex-Vice-President Dallas[1] tells us that the constitution is an object to which no American mind can be too attentive, and no American heart too devoted. He further says, the constitution, in its words, is plain and intelligible, and is meant for the home-bred, unsophisticated understandings of our fellow-citizens. Senator Berrien[2] tell us that the Constitution is the fundamental law, that which controls all others. The charter of our liberties, which every citizen has a personal interest in understanding thoroughly. The testimony of Senator Breese, Lewis Cass,[3] and many others that might be named, who are everywhere esteemed as sound lawyers, so regard the constitution. I take it, therefore, that it is not presumption in a private citizen to form an opinion of that instrument.

Now, take the constitution according to its plain reading, and I defy the presentation of a single pro-slavery clause in it. On the other hand it will be found to contain principles and purposes, entirely hostile to the existence of slavery.

I have detained my audience entirely too long already. At some future period I will gladly avail myself of an opportunity to give this subject a full and fair discussion.

Allow me to say, in conclusion, notwithstanding the dark picture I have this day presented of the state of the nation, I do not despair of this country. There are forces in operation, which must inevitably work the downfall of slavery. "*The arm of the Lord is not shortened*,"[4] and the doom of slavery is certain. I, therefore, leave off where I began, with *hope*. While drawing encouragement from the "Declaration of Independence," the great principles it contains, and the genius of American Institutions, my spirit is also cheered by the obvious tendencies of the age. Nations do not now stand in the same relation to each other that they did ages ago. No nation can now shut itself up, from the surrounding world, and trot round in the same old path of its fathers without interference. The time *was* when such could be done. Long established customs of hurtful character could formerly fence themselves in, and do their evil work with social impunity. Knowledge was then confined and enjoyed by the privileged few, and the multitude walked on in mental darkness. But a change has now come over the affairs of mankind. Walled cities and empires have become unfashionable. The arm of commerce has borne away the gates of the strong city. Intelligence is penetrating the darkest corners of the globe. It makes its pathway over and under the sea, as well as on the earth. Wind, steam, and lightning are its chartered agents. Oceans no longer divide, but link nations together. From Boston to London is now a holiday excursion. Space is comparatively annihilated. Thoughts expressed on one side of the Atlantic, are distinctly heard on the other.

The far off and almost fabulous[5] Pacific rolls in grandeur at our feet. The Celestial Empire, the mystery of ages, is being solved. The fiat of the Almighty, "*Let there be Light*,"[6] has not yet spent its force. No abuse, no outrage whether in taste, sport or avarice, can now hide itself from the all-pervading light. The iron shoe, and crippled foot of China must be seen, in contrast

---

[1] *Ex-Vice-President Dallas* George Dallas (1792–1864), Vice President to James K. Polk.

[2] *Senator Berrien* John Berrien (1781–1856), Georgia Senator who argued that slavery was fundamental to the Constitution.

[3] *Senator Breese* Sidney Breese (1800–78), Illinois Senator who favored the rule of popular sovereignty on the question of slavery; *Lewis Cass* Michigan Senator who campaigned for the Presidency in 1848 and was opposed to limiting the spread of slavery.

[4] *The arm ... not shortened* See Isaiah 59.1.

[5] *fabulous* I.e., fabled; of mythological reputation.

[6] *Let there be Light* See Genesis 1.3.

with nature. *Afric must rise and put on her yet unwoven garment. "Ethiopia shall stretch out her hand unto God."*[1] In the fervent aspirations of William Lloyd Garrison, I say, and let every heart join in saying it:

God speed the year of jubilee
    The wide world o'er!
When from their galling chains set free,
Th' oppressed shall vilely bend the knee,
And wear the yoke of tyranny
    Like brutes no more.
That year will come, and freedom's reign,
To man his plundered rights again
    Restore.

God speed the day when human blood
    Shall cease to flow!
In every clime be understood,
The claims of human brotherhood,
And each return for evil, good,
    Not blow for blow;
That day will come all feuds to end,

And change into a faithful friend
    Each foe.

God speed the hour, the glorious hour,
    When none on earth
Shall exercise a lordly power,
Nor in a tyrant's presence cower;
But all to manhood's stature tower,
    By equal birth!
THAT HOUR WILL COME, to each, to all,
And from his prison-house, the thrall
    Go forth.

Until that year, day, hour, arrive,
With head, and heart, and hand I'll strive,
To break the rod, and rend the gyve,[2]
The spoiler of his prey deprive—
    So witness Heaven!
And never from my chosen post,
Whate'er the peril or the cost,
    Be driven.[3]

—1852

---

[1] *Ethiopia ... unto God* See Psalms 68.31; in the nineteenth century, Ethiopia was often thought of as symbolizing all Africa and all people of African descent.

[2] *gyve* Shackle.

[3] *God speed ... Be driven* See William Lloyd Garrison's "The Triumph of Freedom" (1852).

IN CONTEXT

Photographs of Frederick Douglass

Frederick Douglass was a great proponent of the new art of photography. He saw it as a fundamentally democratic medium as well as a crucial tool in the fight to end slavery and racial discrimination. Douglass used photography as a means to assert greater control over his public image as a black man, sitting for at least 160 distinct portraits over the course of his life (as identified by John Stauffer, Zoe Trodd, and Celeste-Marie Bernier in their 2015 *Picturing Frederick Douglass*). By contrast, there are only 126 photographs of Abraham Lincoln known to exist, and only 127 of Walt Whitman.

Daguerreotype taken c. 1841, artist unknown. This is the first known photograph of Douglass.

Daguerreotype taken in July or August 1843, two years before the publication of Douglass's *Narrative*, artist unknown.

Daguerreotype taken in May 1848 by Edward White Gallery.

Daguerreotype taken c. 1853, two years before the publication of Douglass's second autobiography, *My Bondage and My Freedom*. Artist unknown.

Engraving of a photograph taken by John Howe Kent on 3 November 1882, used as the frontispiece to Douglass's revised third autobiography, *The Life and Times of Frederick Douglass* (1893).

Photograph taken on 31 October 1894 by Phineas C. Headley, Jr. and James E. Reed, a few months before Douglass's death. Douglass very rarely smiled in his photographs.

Portrait of Douglass seated with his second wife, Helen Pitts (right). Helen's sister, Eva Pitts, stands in the center. Taken c. 1884, shortly after their marriage, artist unknown.

Engraving used as the frontispiece to the first edition of Douglass's 1845 *Narrative*, artist unknown.

Cover of an 1847 anti-abolitionist pamphlet reprinting one of Douglass's speeches. The pamphlet described Douglass as a "presumptive negro" and as a "runaway slave from Baltimore," despite the fact that he had been manumitted some months before.

THE CIVIL WAR AND ITS LITERATURE

CONTEXTS

By 1861, decades of polarizing debate over the issue of slavery had led many Americans, in both the North and the South, to see the other half of the country as a direct threat to their way of life. Attitudes toward slavery, however, were not as clearly divided along North-South lines as they are often assumed to have been. When the Civil War broke out, a view of slavery as a benign or even positive institution was common not only among slaveholding Southerners but also—despite the strenuous efforts of Northern abolitionists—among a considerable number of white Northerners. A prime example of this romanticized view of Southern slavery, and of the racist representation of African Americans that went hand-in-hand with it, is "I Wish I Was in Dixie's Land," now better-known as "Dixie": a song that is today indelibly associated with the South, due to its adoption by the secessionist states as a quasi-national anthem, but that was actually composed by a Northern musician for an originally Northern audience, with whom it was a hit.

The degree to which slavery was tolerated or even supported by many Northerners made the secession crisis of 1860–61, and the conflict it gave rise to, more complex than just a confrontation between Northern opponents of slavery and Southern defenders of it. As is made clear by documents such as the South Carolina Secession Convention's justification of secession and the infamous "Cornerstone" speech given by Alexander Stephens (the vice-president of the secessionist government), the maintenance of slavery was the central, overriding aim of Southern secessionists. In the North, by contrast, the New York lawyer George Templeton Strong spoke for the majority of his compatriots when, in the February 1861 diary entry included below, he emphatically condemned secession—to the extent of calling for war to suppress it—while also disavowing "abolitionism." Conversely, the diary entries of white Southerner Mary Chesnut record both her strong support for the secessionist cause and her professed dislike for slavery as an institution—albeit also for what she called the "undeveloped savage Africans" whom her society subjugated.

As war commenced, all the parties involved—Southerners, Northern Unionists, Northern abolitionists, and the African Americans at the center of it all—laid claim to the rhetoric of freedom. Adherents of the secessionist cause and the initially distinct Northern causes (Unionism and abolitionism) all proclaimed theirs to be the cause of freedom, and therefore to inherit the mantle of America's Revolutionary origins and to carry the blessing of God. However, the "freedom" invoked in these causes meant importantly different things, as is illustrated by three poems from early in the war included in either the bound book or website components of this section: "The Southern Cross," by the secessionist sympathizer Ellen Key Blunt; "The Nineteenth of April," by the Northerner Lucy Larcom; and "The Battle Hymn of the Republic," by the abolitionist Julia Ward Howe. African Americans, of course, saw the war largely in terms of their own freedom, as the currency during the war of spirituals about escaping slavery such as "Let My People Go" (first recorded in 1861) indicates, but their conception of their spiritual and physical agency in that struggle differed significantly even from that of sympathetic abolitionists such as Howe. This multivalency of "freedom" during the Civil War is exemplified by the career of "The Battle Cry of Freedom," one of the war's foremost anthems, which was crafted to appeal ambiguously to both Unionist and abolitionist camps in the North and was later, with suitable modifications, adopted by the South as well.

Both the North and the South initially expected a quick and easy victory. By 1862, however, the war's initial battles—culminating in the two-day Battle of Shiloh, a bloodbath described in this section's excerpts from the memoirs of the rebel private Sam Watkins and the federal general Ulysses S. Grant—had made it clear to both sides that a long, hard, costly conflict was at hand. This realization spurred changes in thinking regarding what the war was about and what was required to win it, especially in the

North. Abolitionists and black activists argued with increasing urgency and power that the North needed to commit itself openly to the cause of ending slavery—and to include African Americans, the people for whom the stakes in such a struggle were highest, in its war effort. James Madison Bell's poem "What Shall We Do with the Contrabands?" and John Bingham's speech "The New Magna Carta" exemplify such arguments. Opponents of abolition pushed back; Samuel Cox's "Emancipation and Its Results" is one example. In September 1862, President Lincoln ended this debate by issuing his Emancipation Proclamation (though only after another battlefield bloodbath, Antietam, had resulted in a strategic victory that gave him sufficient political cover). It declared most enslaved people in rebel territory free, and it authorized the recruitment of African American troops.

The Emancipation Proclamation revolutionized the nature and meaning of the war for African Americans in particular. The war for the Union was now also a war for their liberation, and African American men were now able to fight that war on their own behalf as soldiers in the U.S. Army (albeit segregated in all-black regiments, commanded by white officers, and paid, at first, considerably less than their white counterparts). Frederick Douglass's "Men of Color, to Arms!" expresses what the legal ability to fight in their own cause meant for black men—in part by situating their participation in the federal war effort in a long tradition of armed African American resistance to slavery—while George Henry Boker's "The Black Regiment" attests to the effect that the heroism of black soldiers had on many white Northerners, a significant number of whom had doubted African Americans' capacity to fight effectively. As "The Song of the First of Arkansas" bears witness, military service also fostered further aspirations among black troops—as well as among some of their white officers—for full racial equality and restitution for slavery's injustices. Meanwhile, as Mattie Jackson and L.S. Thompson's co-authored *The Story of Mattie J. Jackson* illustrates, numerous black women did whatever they could during the war years to free themselves and their families, independent of the federal government or the U.S. Army.

By its very nature as an internal conflict that pitted Americans against each other and in many cases brought combat or destruction to their very doorsteps, the war from its outset had an especially deep and wide-ranging impact on the American population. From the very beginning of the conflict, women sought to aid their sides' cause in every capacity, from the home front through military hospitals to the battle lines themselves; the extracts included in this section from the memoirs of Mary Livermore and Louisa May Alcott capture some of their contributions. Thousands upon thousands of the wounded and maimed were left with enduring physical and psychological impairments, as George Bagby's "The Empty Sleeve" recounts, while innumerable friends and family members of the dead struggled to come to terms with their loved ones' loss—a struggle on display in poems as different as Caroline Ball's "The Jacket of Gray" and Emily Dickinson's "When I was small, a Woman died." These and other works from both sides demonstrate not only how deeply and widely the war affected Americans as it dragged on, but also the diversity of perspectives this wide-ranging involvement gave rise to. Some civilian reflections on the conflict, such as those by Alcott, Ball, Bagby, and Henry Wadsworth Longfellow, are strongly partisan, while other civilians, such as the songwriter Charles C. Sawyer and the poet Ellen Flagg, wrote about the war in an apolitical, sentimental vein that emphasized common humanity and shared suffering.

Also caught up in the war were hundreds of thousands of foreign-born Americans; about a quarter of the white soldiers who fought in the federal army were immigrants. Many held decidedly racist views on slavery and the status of African Americans—views that persisted among federal soldiers even after the Emancipation Proclamation. The song "Pat Murphy of Meagher's Brigade," for example, voices the hostility to both secession and abolition felt by many Irish immigrants, whose resistance to fighting for emancipation contributed to the deadly New York draft riots in 1863. The conscription of mainly immigrant or lower-class men that helped spark the riots is the subject of another Irish immigrant song included in this section, "By the Hush, Me Boys." Other federal soldiers, such as the German-born Jewish officer Marcus Spiegel, changed their opinions about slavery, if often grudgingly, as military service in the South brought them face-to-face with the realities of the institution. President Lincoln himself summed up such changing views about the war and the issues underlying it in his 1864 Sanitary Fair address, which also aptly encapsulates the different ideas held by the contending sides as to the meaning of freedom. Not all Northerners' views changed, though, and many whose thinking did shift in some respects (including Spiegel, who continued to see black people as "naturally lazy and indolent") remained unmoved in others.

The war's conclusion in 1865 settled, or at least appeared to settle, the burning questions—including the relationship between the states and the federal government, and especially the status and future of slavery—that had caused it. At the same time, the end of the war also raised an array of new, similarly urgent and difficult questions. How was the defeated South to be reincorporated into the Union? How was its society to be reorganized in the wake of slavery's collapse? And how would the rest of America's population, North as well as South, respond to the demands of African Americans for full equality in a post-slavery nation? Such questions underlie the poems from the war's ending and aftermath that conclude this section: the anonymous Northern "Voices of the Guns," the black poet Sarah E. Shuften's "Ethiopia's Dead," the white South Carolinian Henry Timrod's "Ode," and the postwar poems of Sarah Piatt. In the years after the war, the different understandings of the war's course, meaning, and outcome on display in these poems would combine, compete, and collide in American politics and culture—as indeed they continue to do into the twenty-first century.

⌘ ⌘ ⌘

Two-panel illustration by the pioneering political cartoonist Thomas Nast, published in the 5 August 1865 issue of *Harper's Weekly*. The illustration questions why former secessionists—such as those depicted in the left-hand panel begging for forgiveness from Columbia, the allegorical personification of the United States—should be able to possess voting and other civil rights in the aftermath of the Civil War when those rights are not available to African Americans—including those, such as the black U.S. Army veteran with an amputated leg depicted in the right-hand panel, who fought for the federal government against the secessionists. The caption of the left-hand panel reads "PARDON. Columbia—'Shall I trust these men'"; the caption of the right-hand panel reads "FRANCHISE. 'And not this man?'"

from South Carolina Secession Convention, "Declaration of the Immediate Causes which Induce and Justify the Secession of South Carolina from the Federal Union" (1860)

In November 1860, Abraham Lincoln, the Republican candidate, won the U.S. presidential election on a platform opposing the expansion of slavery into U.S. territories. Viewing this outcome as a direct threat to the future of slavery as an institution, the state of South Carolina organized a convention to consider whether the state should secede from the Union. On 20 December 1860, the convention adopted an ordinance of secession announcing the dissolution of the union between South Carolina and the rest of the United States. Four days later, this was followed by a statement, the majority of which is given below, explaining the perceived legal grounds for secession.

... [T]he State of South Carolina having resumed her separate and equal place among nations, deems it due to herself, to the remaining United States of America, and to the nations of the world, that she should declare the immediate causes which have led to this act.

In the year 1765, that portion of the British Empire embracing Great Britain, undertook to make laws for the government of that portion composed of the thirteen American Colonies. A struggle for the right of self-government ensued, which resulted, on the 4th July, 1776, in a Declaration, by the Colonies, "that they are, and of right ought to be, FREE AND INDEPENDENT STATES; and that, as free and independent States, they have full power to levy war, conclude peace, contract alliances, establish commerce, and to do all other acts and things which independent States may of right do."

They further solemnly declared that whenever any "form of government becomes destructive of the ends for which it was established, it is the right of the people to alter or abolish it, and to institute a new government." Deeming the Government of Great Britain to have become destructive of these ends, they declared that the Colonies "are absolved from all allegiance to the British Crown, and that all political connection between them and the State of Great Britain is, and ought to be, totally dissolved."

In pursuance of this Declaration of Independence, each of the thirteen States proceeded to exercise its separate sovereignty; adopted for itself a Constitution, and appointed officers for the administration of government in all its departments—Legislative, Executive and Judicial. For purposes of defense, they united their arms and their counsels; and, in 1778, they entered into a League known as the Articles of Confederation, whereby they agreed to entrust the administration of their external relations to a common agent, known as the Congress of the United States, expressly declaring, in the first article, "that each State retains its sovereignty, freedom and independence, and every power, jurisdiction and right which is not, by this Confederation, expressly delegated to the United States in Congress assembled." ...

Thus were established the two great principles asserted by the Colonies, namely: the right of a State to govern itself; and the right of a people to abolish a Government when it becomes destructive of the ends for which it was instituted. ...

In 1787, Deputies were appointed by the States to revise the Articles of Confederation, and on 17th September, 1787, these Deputies recommended for the adoption of the States, the Articles of Union, known as the Constitution of the United States.

The parties to whom this Constitution was submitted, were the several sovereign States; they were to agree or disagree, and when nine of them agreed the compact was to take effect among those concurring; and the General Government, as the common agent, was then to be invested with their authority.

If only nine of the thirteen States had concurred, the other four would have remained as they then were—separate, sovereign States, independent of any of the provisions of the Constitution. In fact, two of the States did not accede to the Constitution until long after it had gone into operation among the other eleven;[1] and during that interval, they each exercised the functions of an independent nation.

---

1   *two ... eleven*   Of the thirteen original states, eleven ratified the Constitution within a year of its completion in September 1787. The remaining two, North Carolina and Rhode Island, did not ratify it until November 1789 and May 1790, respectively.

By this Constitution, certain duties were imposed upon the several States, and the exercise of certain of their powers was restrained, which necessarily implied their continued existence as sovereign States. But, to remove all doubt, an amendment was added, which declared that the powers not delegated to the United States by the Constitution, nor prohibited by it to the States, are reserved to the States, respectively, or to the people.[1] On the 23d May, 1788, South Carolina, by a Convention of her People, passed an Ordinance assenting to this Constitution, and afterwards altered her own Constitution, to conform herself to the obligations she had undertaken.

Thus was established, by compact between the States, a Government, with defined objects and powers, limited to the express words of the grant. This limitation left the whole remaining mass of power subject to the clause reserving it to the States or to the people, and rendered unnecessary any specification of reserved rights.

We hold that the Government thus established is subject to the two great principles asserted in the Declaration of Independence; and we hold further, that the mode of its formation subjects it to a third fundamental principle, namely: the law of compact. We maintain that in every compact between two or more parties, the obligation is mutual; that the failure of one of the contracting parties to perform a material part of the agreement, entirely releases the obligation of the other; and that where no arbiter is provided, each party is remitted to his own judgment to determine the fact of failure, with all its consequences.

In the present case, that fact is established with certainty. We assert that fourteen of the States have deliberately refused, for years past, to fulfill their constitutional obligations, and we refer to their own Statutes for the proof.

The Constitution of the United States, in its 4th Article, provides as follows:

"No person held to service or labor in one State, under the laws thereof, escaping into another, shall, in consequence of any law or regulation therein, be discharged from such service or labor, but shall be delivered up, on claim of the party to whom such service or labor may be due."

This stipulation was so material to the compact, that without it that compact would not have been made. The greater number of the contracting parties held slaves, and they had previously evinced their estimate of the value of such a stipulation by making it a condition in the Ordinance for the government of the territory ceded by Virginia, which now composes the States north of the Ohio River.[2]

The same article of the Constitution stipulates also for rendition by the several States of fugitives from justice from the other States.

The General Government, as the common agent, passed laws to carry into effect these stipulations of the States.[3] For many years these laws were executed. But an increasing hostility on the part of the non-slaveholding States to the institution of slavery, has led to a disregard of their obligations, and the laws of the General Government have ceased to effect the objects of the Constitution. The States of Maine, New Hampshire, Vermont, Massachusetts, Connecticut, Rhode Island, New York, Pennsylvania, Illinois, Indiana, Michigan, Wisconsin and Iowa, have enacted laws which either nullify the Acts of Congress or render useless any attempt to execute them. In many of these States the fugitive is discharged from service or labor claimed, and in none of them has the State Government complied with the stipulation made in the Constitution. The State of New Jersey, at an early day, passed a law in conformity with her constitutional obligation; but the current of anti-slavery feeling has led her more recently to enact laws which render inoperative the remedies provided by her own law and by the laws of Congress. In the State of New York even the right of transit for a

---

[1] *an amendment ... the people* The Tenth Amendment, the final amendment in the Bill of Rights.

[2] *a condition ... Ohio River* Article 6 of the Northwest Ordinance of 1787, which organized the administration of the Northwest Territory (the territory that became the present-day states of Ohio, Indiana, Illinois, Michigan, and Wisconsin, as well as part of Minnesota), prohibited slavery in the region but also specified that "any person escaping into the [territory], from whom labor or service is lawfully claimed in any one of the original States, such fugitive may be lawfully reclaimed and conveyed to the person claiming his or her labor or service as aforesaid."

[3] *The General ... the States* The U.S. Congress passed two fugitive slave laws, in 1793 and 1850; the 1850 law, designed to close loopholes in the 1793 law, was more stringent, and contributed to growing antislavery sentiment in the North over the ensuing decade.

slave[1] has been denied by her tribunals; and the States of Ohio and Iowa have refused to surrender to justice fugitives charged with murder, and with inciting servile insurrection in the State of Virginia. Thus the constituted compact has been deliberately broken and disregarded by the non-slaveholding States, and the consequence follows that South Carolina is released from her obligation.

The ends for which the Constitution was framed are declared by itself to be "to form a more perfect union, establish justice, insure domestic tranquility, provide for the common defence, promote the general welfare, and secure the blessings of liberty to ourselves and our posterity."

These ends it endeavored to accomplish by a Federal Government, in which each State was recognized as an equal, and had separate control over its own institutions. The right of property in slaves was recognized by giving to free persons distinct political rights, by giving them the right to represent, and burdening them with direct taxes for three-fifths of their slaves; by authorizing the importation of slaves for twenty years; and by stipulating for the rendition of fugitives from labor.

We affirm that these ends for which this Government was instituted have been defeated, and the Government itself has been made destructive of them by the action of the non-slaveholding States. Those States have assumed the right of deciding upon the propriety of our domestic institutions; and have denied the rights of property established in fifteen of the States and recognized by the Constitution; they have denounced as sinful the institution of slavery; they have permitted open establishment among them of societies, whose avowed object is to disturb the peace and to eloign[2] the property of the citizens of other States. They have encouraged and assisted thousands of our slaves to leave their homes; and those who remain, have been incited by emissaries, books and pictures to servile insurrection.

For twenty-five years this agitation has been steadily increasing, until it has now secured to its aid the power of the common Government. Observing the *forms* of the Constitution, a sectional party[3] has found within that article establishing the Executive Department, the means of subverting the Constitution itself. A geographical line has been drawn across the Union, and all the States north of that line have united in the election of a man to the high office of President of the United States, whose opinions and purposes are hostile to slavery. He is to be entrusted with the administration of the common Government, because he has declared that that "Government cannot endure permanently half slave, half free," and that the public mind must rest in the belief that Slavery is in the course of ultimate extinction.[4]

This sectional combination for the submersion of the Constitution, has been aided in some of the States by elevating to citizenship, persons who, by the supreme law of the land, are incapable of becoming citizens;[5] and their votes have been used to inaugurate a new policy, hostile to the South, and destructive of its beliefs and safety.

On the 4th day of March next, this party will take possession of the Government. It has announced that the South shall be excluded from the common territory,[6] that the judicial tribunals shall be made sectional, and that a war must be waged against slavery until it shall cease throughout the United States.

---

1   *the right of transit for a slave*   I.e., the right of enslavers to bring enslaved people into a state while in transit to another state. An 1841 New York state law explicitly prohibited enslavers from doing this and mandated the liberation of any enslaved people so brought; the law was upheld by the New York Court of Appeals in March 1860.

2   *eloign*   Carry away.

3   *a sectional party*   I.e., the recently-founded Republican Party, an exclusively Northern party that developed out of opposition to the prospect of slavery being extended to the western territories. In the presidential election of 1860, Lincoln, the Republican candidate, won every free state but not a single slave state.

4   *Government … extinction*   Reference to Lincoln's famous "House Divided" speech, given in 1858, in which he declared "I believe this government cannot endure, permanently half *slave* and half *free*" and spoke of the possibility that "the *opponents* of slavery, will arrest the further spread of it, and place it where the public mind shall rest in the belief that it is in course of ultimate extinction."

5   *persons who … citizens*   I.e., African Americans. The U.S. Supreme Court's 1857 *Dred Scott* ruling had held that black people, whether free or enslaved, were not recognized as citizens under the U.S. Constitution and "had no rights which the white man was bound to respect."

6   *the South … territory*   I.e., that slavery would be excluded from all U.S. territories (areas under federal control that had not yet become states). Opposition to the extension of slavery into the territories was a cornerstone of the Republican Party.

The guaranties of the Constitution will then no longer exist; the equal rights of the States will be lost. The slaveholding States will no longer have the power of self-government, or self-protection, and the Federal Government will have become their enemy.

Sectional interest and animosity will deepen the irritation, and all hope of remedy is rendered vain, by the fact that public opinion at the North has invested a great political error with the sanctions of more erroneous religious belief.

We, therefore, the people of South Carolina, by our delegates, in Convention assembled, appealing to the Supreme Judge of the world for the rectitude of our intentions, have solemnly declared that the Union heretofore existing between this State and the other States of North America, is dissolved, and that the State of South Carolina has resumed her position among the nations of the world, as a separate and independent State; with full power to levy war, conclude peace, contract alliances, establish commerce, and to do all other acts and things which independent States may of right do.

from George Templeton Strong, Diary, 13 February 1861

Born and raised in New York City, George Templeton Strong (1820–75) became a lawyer in his father's law practice (a firm that is now one of the oldest continuously operating law firms in the United States). He began keeping a diary when he was fifteen and wrote in it practically every day for the next forty years. Strong's diary, discovered in the 1930s and published in the 1950s, is today considered a valuable historical source—especially for its detailed account of Strong's life during the Civil War. By no means a committed abolitionist, Strong initially wrestled with his decision to vote for Lincoln in the 1860 presidential election, but the subsequent secession crisis clarified where he stood. He went on to make numerous contributions to the Northern war effort (although he avoided military service himself), including funding a U.S. Army regiment and helping to found the United States Sanitary Commission, which organized care for sick and wounded soldiers.

The text of the entry from Strong's diary presented below is based on the digitized version of the manuscript of the diary available on the website of the New-York Historical Society.

Feb. 13.

Ash-Wednesday. Weather bland enough for April. … After dinner, Ellie read Haydn[1] for me—and Ehninger and George Anthon[2] came in for a few minutes. Jack thinks he and his associates (80 or thereabouts) who have been diligently drilling for six weeks will not be required at Washington on March 4 after all. Probably he's right. Seizing that city by a coup-de-main[3] was certainly on the conspirators' program, but Scott's preparations[4] to receive them and the unexpected attitude assumed by the Border States[5] have brought that project to naught. The electoral votes were counted today, and as I hear no extras in the streets, they were probably counted in due form, and the results announced without disturbance. This was the critical day for the peace of the capital. A foray of Virginia gents with Gov. Wise at their head and Gov. Floyd[6] at their tail could have done infinite mischief

---

[1] *Ellie* Strong's wife, Ellen Ruggles Strong; *Haydn* Franz Joseph Haydn (1732–1809), Austrian composer. Both Strong and his wife were talented amateur musicians.

[2] *Ehninger and George Anthon* Friends of Strong's. John ("Jack") Ehninger (1827–89) was an artist and illustrator of some repute.

[3] *coup-de-main* French: stroke of hand, i.e., a swift, strong attack.

[4] *Scott's preparations* General Winfield Scott (1786–1866), the commander of the U.S. Army in 1861, was a Virginian who remained loyal to the Union while his native state moved toward secession. In response to secessionist threats in February 1861 to raid Washington, D.C. and disrupt the certification of Abraham Lincoln's electoral college victory, Scott stationed troops around the Capitol building and threatened that any intruder would "be lashed to the muzzle of a twelve-pounder [cannon] and fired out the window of the Capitol." These measures were largely successful in preventing the planned assault.

[5] *Border States* I.e., Missouri, Kentucky, Delaware, and Maryland—states in which slavery was legal but that did not join the slave states further south in seceding.

[6] *Gov. Wise … Gov. Floyd* Henry A. Wise (1806–76) and John B. Floyd (1806–63) were both former governors of Virginia; Floyd also served as Secretary of War in the administration of James Buchanan, the U.S. president from 1857 to 1861. Both Wise and Floyd supported secession and went on to become Confederate [continued …]

by destroying the legal evidence of Lincoln's election (after they had killed and beaten General Scott and his Flying Artillery, that is) but preventing Lincoln from taking the oath of office at the usual place and in the usual way on the 4th of March would be so inconsiderable of a result, comparatively, that I do not believe they will try for it. One feature of the conspiracy seems to have been anticipated and suppressed. ...

This revelation of the gallant Floyd's gigantic larcenies[1] must weaken the cause of secession—for many Southerners possess a moral sense and must distrust a leader who steals. Certainly Floyd & Co. have more villainy on smaller provocation than any gang on record. The deluded mobs of Charleston and Savannah[2] have some excuse for their criminal outrages. There is none for the Floyds, Cobbs, Davises,[3] and other false prophets who have deliberately stimulated their ignorance to crime by malicious lies, and who have stuck at nothing from theft to treason and civil war—that they might hold political power a little longer.

These men want hanging—badly.[4] But they will reap deadly fruit yet from *their own* treason. The devil they have raised will turn and rend them unless he be laid at once—and that is beyond the magic of Jeff Davis. The inflammation has run its course. It has produced morbid changes of structure on the Gulf—those unhappy States are sphacelated,[5] gangrenous, dead to the Nation. But the Nation itself has passed its crisis and entered on convalescence. It is sorely shattered, though—convalescence will be slow and precarious. Trifling accident may produce relapse. The peaceable accession of the new Administration, its legal control of the National Government, will be sedative and mollifying. Many Virginian secessionists will be less inclined to rebel when they find that a "Black Republican"[6] regime is not abolitionism after all. But then comes the ugly question of peace or war with the seceded States.

My voice is for war and gunpowder.

> Krieg! Ist das der Name?
> Der Krieg ist schrecklich, wie des Himmels Plagen.
> Doch ist er gut, ist ein Geschick, wie sie.[7]

The youthful life of a great Nation is worth saving, though its only salvation be in such remedies as battle, murder, and sudden death—Minie rifles, Columbiads,[8] devastation and insolvency.

from Alexander Stephens, The "Cornerstone" Speech, 21 March 1861

Alexander H. Stephens (1812–83), a Georgia politician and former congressional representative, was sworn in as vice-president of the Confederate States of America—as the government organized by the secessionist states in rebellion against the U.S. government called itself—on 11 February 1861, although he had

---

generals. At the time of this diary entry, Virginia had not yet seceded; it eventually did so in April 1861, in response to President Lincoln's call for volunteers from all states still in the Union to put down the Southern rebellion.

[1] *gallant ... larcenies*   John B. Floyd was forced to resign as Secretary of War in December 1860 because of a scandal involving the embezzlement of $870,000 in state bonds that had been under his supervision.

[2] *Charleston and Savannah*   Charleston, South Carolina, and Savannah, Georgia, were secessionist hubs.

[3] *Floyds, Cobbs, Davises*   I.e., Southern politicians encouraging and abetting secession. (Howell Cobb, from Georgia, played a major role in the founding of the Confederacy; Jefferson Davis, from Mississippi, was sworn in as Confederate president a few days after the date of this diary entry.)

[4] *want hanging—badly*   I.e., very much deserve to be hanged.

[5] *the Gulf*   I.e., the Gulf of Mexico; *sphacelated* Afflicted by necrosis (tissue death)—i.e., corrupted, decayed.

[6] *Black Republican*   Derogatory term for supporters of the Republican Party that implied that the party—which, in 1861, opposed the extension of slavery into the nation's Western territories but had not yet formally endorsed abolition—was beholden to African Americans.

[7] *Krieg ... sie*   From *Wallenstein's Death* (1799), a play by the German poet and dramatist Friedrich Schiller. The German text can be translated as: "War! Is that the right word? / A war's a dreadful thing, like plagues of Heaven. / And it is good, a godsend, just like plagues."

[8] *Minie rifles*   I.e., rifled muskets—muskets which have been "rifled" by the addition of spiral grooves inside their barrels; rifling imparts spin to the bullet and greatly increases the weapon's range and accuracy. The Minié ball, so-called after its inventor, French military officer Claude-Étienne Minié, was a new type of bullet designed for use in rifled muskets. The higher muzzle velocity and greater range and accuracy of such rifles made them much deadlier than previous infantry weapons; *Columbiads* Very heavy and powerful cannons.

voted against Georgia's secession while a delegate to the state secession convention. On 21 March 1861, Stephens gave a speech explaining the rebel government's new constitution (which had been adopted ten days before) to an enthusiastic overflow crowd in Savannah, Georgia. The speech—which, after the war, Stephens attempted to revise and downplay—became known as the "Cornerstone" speech because of its declaration that slavery and white supremacy together formed the "cornerstone" on which the Confederacy was founded. The text of the speech given here, including the transcriptions of applause, is based on that printed in *Alexander H. Stephens, in Public and Private: With Letters and Speeches, Before, During, and Since the War*, by Henry Cleveland (1866).

... [W]e are passing through one of the greatest revolutions in the annals of the world. Seven States have within the last three months thrown off an old government and formed a new.[1] This revolution has been signally marked, up to this time, by the fact of its having been accomplished without the loss of a single drop of blood. [Applause.]

This new constitution, or form of government, constitutes the subject to which your attention will be partly invited. In reference to it, I make this first general remark: it amply secures all our ancient rights, franchises, and liberties. All the great principles of Magna Charta[2] are retained in it. No citizen is deprived of life, liberty, or property, but by the judgment of his peers under the laws of the land. The great principle of religious liberty, which was the honor and pride of the old constitution, is still maintained and secured. All the essentials of the old constitution, which have endeared it to the hearts of the American people, have been preserved and perpetuated. [Applause.] Some changes

have been made. Of these I shall speak presently. Some of these I should have preferred not to have seen made; but, these, perhaps, meet the cordial approbation of a majority of this audience, if not an overwhelming majority of the people of the Confederacy. Of them, therefore, I will not speak. But other important changes do meet my cordial approbation. They form great improvements upon the old constitution. So, taking the whole new constitution, I have no hesitancy in giving it as my judgment that it is decidedly better than the old. [Applause.] ...

But not to be tedious in enumerating the numerous changes for the better, allow me to allude to one other—though last, not least. The new constitution has put at rest, *forever*, all the agitating questions relating to our peculiar institution—African slavery as it exists amongst us—the proper *status* of the negro in our form of civilization. This was the immediate cause of the late rupture and present revolution. Jefferson in his forecast, had anticipated this, as the "rock upon which the old Union would split."[3] He was right. What was conjecture with him, is now a realized fact. But whether he fully comprehended the great truth upon which that rock *stood* and *stands*, may be doubted. The prevailing ideas entertained by him and most of the leading statesmen at the time of the formation of the old constitution, were that the enslavement of the African was in violation of the laws of nature; that it was wrong in *principle*, socially, morally, and politically. It was an evil they knew not well how to deal with, but the general opinion of the men of that day was that, somehow or other in the order of Providence, the institution would be evanescent and pass away. This idea, though not incorporated in the constitution, was the prevailing idea at that time. The constitution, it is true, secured every essential guarantee to the institution while it should last, and hence no argument can be justly urged against the constitutional guarantees thus secured, because of the common sentiment of the day. Those ideas, however, were fundamentally wrong. They rested upon the assumption of the equality of races. This was an error. It was a sandy foundation,

---

[1]   *Seven states ... new*   Between 20 December 1860 and 1 February 1861, South Carolina, Mississippi, Florida, Alabama, Georgia, Louisiana, and Texas all left the Union; they declared themselves the Confederate States of America on 4 February. Four more states—Virginia, Arkansas, North Carolina, and Tennessee—would join the Confederacy after Stephens's speech.

[2]   *Magna Charta*   Latin: Great Charter; the charter of rights granted to the English nobles by King John in 1215, widely revered in the United States as well as Britain as one of the documents that had provided the basis for individual rights, popular sovereignty, and constitutional government.

[3]   *Jefferson ... split*   Thomas Jefferson seems never to have used the precise words Stephens attributes to him here, but he did voice anxiety, late in his life, as to whether the Union would be able to withstand the divisions slavery was causing.

and the government built upon it fell when the "storm came and the wind blew."[1]

Our new government is founded upon exactly the opposite idea; its foundations are laid, its cornerstone rests, upon the great truth, that the negro is not equal to the white man; that slavery—subordination to the superior race—is his natural and normal condition. [Applause.]

This, our new government, is the first, in the history of the world, based upon this great physical, philosophical, and moral truth. This truth has been slow in the process of its development, like all other truths in the various departments of science. It has been so even amongst us. Many who hear me, perhaps, can recollect well, that this truth was not generally admitted, even within their day. The errors of the past generation still clung to many as late as twenty years ago. Those at the North, who still cling to these errors, with a zeal above knowledge, we justly denominate fanatics. All fanaticism springs from an aberration of the mind—from a defect in reasoning. It is a species of insanity. One of the most striking characteristics of insanity, in many instances, is forming correct conclusions from fancied or erroneous premises; so with the anti-slavery fanatics; their conclusions are right if their premises were. They assume that the negro is equal, and hence conclude that he is entitled to equal privileges and rights with the white man. If their premises were correct, their conclusions would be logical and just—but their premise being wrong, their whole argument fails. I recollect once of having heard a gentleman from one of the northern States, of great power and ability, announce in the House of Representatives, with imposing effect, that we of the South would be compelled, ultimately, to yield upon this subject of slavery, that it was as impossible to war successfully against a principle in politics, as it was in physics or mechanics. That the principle would ultimately prevail. That we, in maintaining slavery as it exists with us, were warring against a principle, a principle founded in nature, the principle of the equality of men. The reply I made to him was, that upon his own grounds, we should, ultimately, succeed, and that he and his associates, in this crusade against our institutions, would ultimately fail. The truth announced, that it was as impossible to war successfully against a principle in politics as it was in physics and mechanics, I admitted; but told him that it was he, and those acting with him, who were warring against a principle. They were attempting to make things equal which the Creator had made unequal.

In the conflict thus far, success has been on our side, complete throughout the length and breadth of the Confederate States. It is upon this, as I have stated, our social fabric is firmly planted; and I cannot permit myself to doubt the ultimate success of a full recognition of this principle throughout the civilized and enlightened world.

As I have stated, the truth of this principle may be slow in development, as all truths are and ever have been, in the various branches of science. It was so with the principles announced by Galileo—it was so with Adam Smith and his principles of political economy. It was so with Harvey, and his theory of the circulation of the blood.[2] It is stated that not a single one of the medical profession, living at the time of the announcement of the truths made by him, admitted them. Now, they are universally acknowledged. May we not, therefore, look with confidence to the ultimate universal acknowledgment of the truths upon which our system rests? It is the first government ever instituted upon the principles in strict conformity to nature, and the ordination of Providence, in furnishing the materials of human society. Many governments have been founded upon the principle of the subordination and serfdom of certain classes of the same race; such were and are in violation of the laws of nature. Our system commits no such violation of nature's laws. With us,

---

[1]   *It was ... blew*   See Matthew 7.24–27, in which Jesus compares those who listen to his teachings and act accordingly to a wise man who builds his house upon a rock, whereas those who listen without acting accordingly are like "a foolish man, which built his house upon the sand: And the rain descended, and the floods came, and the winds blew, and beat upon that house; and it fell: and great was the fall of it."

[2]   *Galileo ... blood*   Italian astronomer Galileo Galilei (1564–1642) was famously prosecuted by the Catholic Church for proposing that the Sun, not the Earth, was the center of the solar system; the British philosopher and economist Adam Smith generated controversy for breaking with the economic orthodoxy of his day in *The Wealth of Nations* (1776), which laid the groundwork for modern free market economic theory; the English physician William Harvey (1578–1657), the first person to fully describe the circulation of blood through the body and the heart's role in it, met with intense resistance from the medical establishment at the time.

all of the white race, however high or low, rich or poor, are equal in the eye of the law. Not so with the negro. Subordination is his place. He, by nature, or by the curse against Canaan,[1] is fitted for that condition which he occupies in our system. The architect, in the construction of buildings, lays the foundation with the proper material—the granite; then comes the brick or the marble. The substratum of our society is made of the material fitted by nature for it, and by experience we know, that it is best, not only for the superior, but for the inferior race, that it should be so. It is, indeed, in conformity with the ordinance of the Creator. It is not for us to inquire into the wisdom of his ordinances, or to question them. For his own purposes, he has made one race to differ from another, as he has made "one star to differ from another star in glory."[2]

The great objects of humanity are best attained when there is conformity to his laws and decrees, in the formation of governments as well as in all things else. Our confederacy is founded upon principles in strict conformity with these laws. This stone which was rejected by the first builders "is become the chief of the corner"[3]—the real "cornerstone"—in our new edifice. [Applause.]

I have been asked, what of the future? It has been apprehended by some that we would have arrayed against us the civilized world. I care not who or how many they may be against us, when we stand upon the eternal principles of truth, *if we are true to ourselves and the principles for which we contend*, we are obliged to, and must triumph. [Immense applause.] …

---

[1] *curse against Canaan* See Genesis 9.20–27, in which Noah's son Ham sees his father lying drunk and naked and alerts his two brothers, who cover their father without looking at him. Upon awakening, Noah curses Canaan, Ham's son, for his father's impropriety: "Cursed be Canaan; a servant of servants shall he be unto his brethren." Because Africa was believed to have been peopled by descendants of Ham, the curse against Canaan was frequently cited in the nineteenth century as one of the supposed biblical justifications for the enslavement of black people.

[2] *one star … glory* See 1 Corinthians 15.41.

[3] *This stone … corner* See Psalm 118.22: "The stone which the builders refused is become the head stone of the corner." On the basis of Jesus' two quotations of it in the New Testament, this passage has frequently been interpreted in the Christian tradition as referring to Jesus himself.

from Mary Chesnut, Diary (1861–65, 1905)

Mary Boykin Miller Chesnut (1823–86) was born into one prominent South Carolina enslaving family and married into another. During the Civil War, her husband, James Chesnut Jr. (1815–85), became a general in the rebel army and served as an aide to Confederate President Jefferson Davis; as a result, the Chesnuts moved in the highest circles of the secessionist South during the war. Mary chronicled her wartime experiences in a diary she kept throughout the war. She heavily revised this diary in the 1880s with the aim of publishing it, but died before she could accomplish this goal. An extensively edited and abridged version of the work appeared in 1905 under the title *A Diary from Dixie*, and the novelist Ben Ames Williams published a longer version, reworked for readability, in 1949. These two publications won Chesnut widespread admiration for the novelistic skill with which she depicted the war's events and personalities, as she perceived them. Not until an authoritative scholarly edition of Chesnut's diary was published in 1981, however, did much of her wartime writing appear in print.

The selections presented below, which give a sample of Chesnut's opinions about slavery and the war from throughout the war's duration, are based the text of the diary's 1905 publication.

Tuesday [12 or 19 March 1861]. … In the hotel parlor[4] we had a scene. Mrs. Scott[5] was describing Lincoln, who is of the cleverest Yankee type. She said: "Awfully ugly, even grotesque in appearance, the kind who are always at the corner stores, sitting on boxes, whittling sticks, and telling stories as funny as they are vulgar." Here I interposed: "But Stephen A.

---

[4] *the hotel parlor* In Montgomery, Alabama, where the Chesnuts were staying while James Chesnut Jr., attended the Provisional Confederate Congress and helped draft the Confederate Constitution.

[5] *Mrs. Scott* Anne (Vivian) Scott, wife of Charles Lewis Scott, a Virginia-born member of congress from California who had left Congress and returned South to side with the Confederacy.

Douglas[1] said one day to Mr. Chesnut, 'Lincoln is the hardest fellow to handle I have ever encountered yet.'" Mr. Scott is from California, and said Lincoln is "an utter American specimen, coarse, rough, and strong; a good-natured, kind creature; as pleasant-tempered as he is clever, and if this country can be joked and laughed out of its rights he is the kind-hearted fellow to do it. Now if there is a war and it pinches the Yankee pocket instead of filling it—"

Here a shrill voice came from the next room (which opened upon the one we were in by folding doors thrown wide open) and said: "Yankees are no more mean and stingy than you are. People at the North are as good as people at the South." The speaker advanced upon us in great wrath.

Mrs. Scott apologized and made some smooth, polite remark, though evidently much embarrassed. But the vinegar face and curly pate refused to receive any concessions, and replied: "That comes with a very bad grace after what you were saying," and she harangued us loudly for several minutes. Someone in the other room giggled outright, but we were quiet as mice. Nobody wanted to hurt her feelings. She was one against so many. If I were at the North, I should expect them to belabor us, and should hold my tongue. We separated North from South because of incompatibility of temper. We are divorced because we hated each other so. If we could only separate, a "*separation à l'agréable*," as the French say it, and not have a horrid fight for divorce.

This poor exile had already been insulted, she said. She was playing "Yankee Doodle" on the piano before breakfast to soothe her wounded spirit, and the Judge[2] came in and calmly requested her to "leave out the Yankee while she played the Doodle." The Yankee end of it did not suit our climate, he said; was totally out of place and had got out of its latitude. …

April 12 [1861]. Anderson will not capitulate.[3] Yesterday's was the merriest, maddest dinner we have had yet. Men were audaciously wise and witty. We had an unspoken foreboding it was to be our last pleasant meeting. … Mrs. Henry King rushed in saying, "The news, I come for the latest news. All of the men of the King family are on the Island,"[4] of which fact she seemed proud.

While she was here our peace negotiator, or envoy, came in—that is, Mr. Chesnut returned.[5] His interview with Colonel Anderson had been deeply interesting, but Mr. Chesnut was not inclined to be communicative. He wanted his dinner. He felt for Anderson and had telegraphed to President Davis[6] for instructions— what answer to give Anderson, etc. He has gone back to Fort Sumter with additional instructions. …

I do not pretend to go to sleep. How can I? If Anderson does not accept terms at four, the orders are, he shall be fired upon. I count four, St. Michael's bells[7] chime out and I begin to hope. At half-past four the heavy booming of a cannon. I sprang out of bed, and on my knees prostrate I prayed as I never prayed before.

There was a sound of stir all over the house, pattering of feet in the corridors. All seemed hurrying one way. I put on my double-gown and a shawl and went, too. It was to the housetop. The shells were bursting. In the dark I heard a man say, "Waste of ammunition." I knew my husband was rowing about in a boat somewhere in that dark bay, and that the shells were roofing it over, bursting toward the fort. If Anderson

---

1   *Stephen A. Douglas*   Democratic politician from Illinois who was Lincoln's political rival: he defeated Lincoln in the 1858 U.S. Senate election in Illinois (known for the Lincoln–Douglas debates) and unsuccessfully contested the 1860 presidential election with Lincoln as one of two Democratic candidates.

2   *the Judge*   Thomas Jefferson Withers (1804–65), a common-law judge, delegate to the South Carolina secession convention, and member of the Provisional Confederate Congress who was Mary Chesnut's uncle and former guardian.

3   *Anderson will not capitulate*   Major Robert Anderson (1805–71) commanded Fort Sumter, a federal military installation in the harbor of Charleston, South Carolina. Confederate authorities considered the fort a threat to their recently-declared independence and demanded its surrender, but were refused.

4   *the island*   Morris Island, an uninhabited island in Charleston harbor, on which one of the Confederate artillery batteries aimed at Fort Sumter was located.

5   *our peace … returned*   James Chesnut Jr. in his capacity as colonel in the South Carolina militia, conveyed the Confederate demands for Fort Sumter's surrender to Major Anderson.

6   *President Davis*   Jefferson Davis (1808–89), Kentucky-born politician who served as President of the Confederate States of America from 18 February 1861.

7   *St. Michael's bells*   I.e., the bells of St. Michael's Episcopal Church in Charleston.

was obstinate, Colonel Chesnut was to order the fort on one side to open fire. Certainly fire had begun. The regular roar of the cannon, there it was. And who could tell what each volley accomplished of death and destruction?

The women were wild there on the housetop. Prayers from the women and imprecations from the men. And then a shell would light up the scene. Tonight they say the forces are to attempt to land. ...

April 15 [1861]. I did not know that one could live such days of excitement. Someone called: "Come out! There is a crowd coming." A mob it was, indeed, but it was headed by Colonels Chesnut and Manning. The crowd was shouting and showing these two as messengers of good news. They were escorted to Beauregard's[1] head-quarters. Fort Sumter had surrendered! Those up on the housetop shouted to us "The fort is on fire." That had been the story once or twice before. ...

RICHMOND, Va., *June 27, 1861*. ... Mr. Lamar,[2] who does not love slavery more than Sumner does, nor than I do, laughs at the compliment New England pays us. We want to separate from them; to be rid of the Yankees forever at any price. And they hate us so, and would clasp us, or grapple us, as Polonius has it, to their bosoms "with hooks of steel."[3] We are an unwilling bride. I think incompatibility of temper began when it was made plain to us that we got all the opprobrium of slavery and they all the money there was in it with their tariff.[4]

Mr. Lamar says, the young men are light-hearted because there is a fight on hand, but those few who look ahead, the clear heads, they see all the risk, the loss of land, limb, and life, home, wife, and children. As in "the brave days of old,"[5] they take it for their country's sake. They are ready and willing, come what may. But not so light-hearted as the *jeunesse dorée*.[6]

September 19 [1861]. A painful piece of news came to us yesterday—our cousin, Mrs. Witherspoon, of Society Hill, was found dead in her bed. She was quite well the night before. Killed, people say, by family sorrows.[7] She was a proud and high-strung woman. Nothing shabby in word, thought, or deed ever came nigh her. She was of a warm and tender heart, too; truth and uprightness itself. Few persons have ever been more loved and looked up to. She was a very handsome old lady, of fine presence, dignified and commanding. ...

The high and disinterested[8] conduct our enemies seem to expect of us is involuntary and unconscious praise. They pay us the compliment to look for from us (and execrate us for the want[9] of it) a degree of virtue they were never able to practise themselves. It is a crowning misdemeanor for us to hold still in slavery those Africans whom they brought here from Africa, or sold to us when they found it did not pay to own them themselves. Gradually, they slid or sold them off down here; or freed them prospectively, giving themselves years in which to get rid of them in a remunerative way. We want to spread them over other lands, too—West and South, or Northwest, where the climate would free them or kill them, or improve them out of the

---

1   *Beauregard* Pierre Gustave Toutant Beauregard (1818–93), Confederate officer who commanded the siege and bombardment of Fort Sumter and later became an important Confederate general.

2   *Mr. Lamar* Lucius Quintus Cincinnatus Lamar (1825–93), politician from Mississippi and Confederate official.

3   *grapple ... steel* In Act 1, Scene 3 of Shakespeare's *Hamlet*, Polonius advises his son Laertes—in the text of the play as typically printed in nineteenth-century editions—to "grapple [his friends] to thy soul with hooks of steel" (1.3.69).

4   *tariff* The tariff, or tax on imports, was a cause of frequent tension between the Northern and Southern states during the early nineteenth century. Northern states tended to support high tariffs on imported manufactures in order to protect and encourage their developing industrial sectors, while Southern states, which generally had little industrial capacity and thus had to import most of their manufactured goods, believed that the tariff imposed an unfair tax burden on them. The dispute led to a major sectional crisis in

1832–33, when South Carolina declared it had the right to "nullify" the tariff, which it held to be unconstitutional, within its borders.

5   *the brave ... old* Reference to "Horatius," one of the *Lays of Ancient Rome* (1842) by the English writer and politician Thomas Babington Macaulay. The ballad describes the Roman hero Horatius's defense of the city against invasion "in the brave days of old."

6   *jeunesse dorée* Fashionable young people (the French phrase literally means "gilded youth").

7   *Killed ... sorrows* In an entry from two days later that was not included in the 1905 publication of her diary, Chesnut describes learning that this cousin "did not die peacefully, as we supposed, in her bed" but was in fact "murdered by her own people. Her negroes."

8   *disinterested* Not motivated by self-interest.

9   *want* Lack.

world, as our friends up North do the Indians. If they had been forced to keep the negroes in New England, I dare say the negroes might have shared the Indians' fate, for they are wise in their generation, these Yankee children of light.[1] Those pernicious Africans! So have just spoken Mr. Chesnut and Uncle John,[2] both *ci-devant*[3] Union men, now utterly for State rights.

July 8 [1862]. … Table-talk today: This war was undertaken by us to shake off the yoke of foreign invaders. So we consider our cause righteous. The Yankees, since the war has begun, have discovered it is to free the slaves they are fighting. So their cause is noble. They also expect to make the war pay. Yankees do not undertake anything that does not pay. They think we belong to them. We have been good milk cows—milked by the tariff, or skimmed. We let them have all of our hard earnings. We bear the ban[4] of slavery; they get the money. Cotton pays everybody who handles it, sells it, manufactures it, but rarely pays the man who grows it. Second hand the Yankees received the wages of slavery. They grew rich. We grew poor. The receiver is as bad as the thief. That applies to us, too, for we received the savages they stole from Africa and brought to us in their slave-ships. As with the Egyptians, so it shall be with us: if they let us go, it must be across a Red Sea—but one made red by blood.[5] …

April 19 [1865]. Just now, when Mr. Clay dashed upstairs, pale as a sheet, saying, "General Lee has capitulated,"[6] I saw it reflected in Mary Darby's face before I heard him speak. She staggered to the table, sat down, and wept aloud. Mr. Clay's eyes were not dry. Quite beside herself Mary shrieked, "Now we belong to negroes and Yankees!" Buck said, "I do not believe it."

How different from ours of them is their estimate of us. How contradictory is their attitude toward us. To keep the despised and iniquitous South within their borders, as part of their country, they are willing to enlist millions of men at home and abroad, and to spend billions, and we know they do not love fighting *per se*, nor spending money. They are perfectly willing to have three killed for our one. We hear they have all grown rich, through "shoddy,"[7] whatever that is. Genuine Yankees can make a fortune trading jack-knives.

"Somehow it is borne in on me that we will have to pay the piper," was remarked today. "No; blood cannot be squeezed from a turnip. You cannot pour anything out of an empty cup. We have no money even for taxes or to be confiscated." …

We are to stay here. Running is useless now; so we mean to bide a Yankee raid, which they say is imminent. Why fly? They are everywhere, these Yankees, like red ants, like the locusts and frogs which were the plagues of Egypt.[8]

The plucky way in which our men keep us is beyond praise. There is no howling, and our poverty is made a matter of laughing. We deride our own penury. Of the country we try not to speak at all.

---

[1] *for they … light*   See Jesus' Parable of the Unjust Steward (Luke 16.1–13), in which Jesus tells a story of a household steward who, knowing he is about to be fired, writes off some of the debts of his employer's debtors to curry favor with them and is then praised by his master for doing so: "And the lord commended the unjust steward, because he had done wisely: for the children of this world are in their generation wiser than the children of light. And I say to you, Make to yourselves friends of the mammon of unrighteousness [i.e., unrighteous wealth]; that, when ye fail, they may receive you into everlasting habitations."

[2] *Uncle John*   John Boykin, the brother of Mary Chesnut's mother.

[3] *ci-devant*   French: from before, i.e., former. (In its original French context, the term was used for members of the French nobility after the French Revolution stripped them of their titles and privileges, and carried a negative connotation.)

[4] *ban*   Curse.

[5] *As with … blood*   Allusion to the biblical story of the Exodus, in which the Israelites escape from slavery in Egypt through the Red Sea, which drowns their Egyptian pursuers. See Exodus 14.

[6] *General Lee has capitulated*   Robert E. Lee, the main Confederate commander, surrendered his army to the Union General Grant at Appomattox, Virginia, on 9 April 1865, effectively bringing the war to an end.

[7] *shoddy*   I.e., inferior or worthless manufactures or supplies sold to the U.S. government by unscrupulous military contractors. The term—which originally referred to a kind of cheap woolen cloth made from rags, supposedly used in army uniforms—first became common in the United States during the Civil War.

[8] *like the locusts … Egypt*   In the Book of Exodus, God inflicts ten plagues on Egypt, including all-encompassing infestations of frogs and locusts, because of the Egyptian Pharaoh's refusal to release the enslaved Israelites. See Exodus 7–12.

from anonymous, "Let My People Go: A Song of the 'Contrabands'" (1861)

This song, the first African American "sorrow song" to appear in print, was recorded by Reverend Lewis Lockwood, a clergyman who heard it being sung by formerly enslaved people at the Union Army base at Fortress Monroe, Virginia, in September 1861. ("Contrabands" was a term for enslaved people who sought refuge with the U.S. Army; because rebel Southerners claimed enslaved people as property, U.S. Army commanders declared that any enslaved people who reached their lines were "contraband of war," i.e., confiscated rebel "property" that they were not obliged to return.)

Lockwood's transcription of the song was published by the *New York Tribune* and then by the *National Anti-Slavery Standard* in December 1861; the text presented below is based on a reprint of the latter. According to the introductory note accompanying the first published versions of the song, it was "said to have been sung for at least fifteen or twenty years in Virginia and Maryland, and perhaps in all the slave States, though stealthily, for fear of the lash." The song has since become one of the most famous African American spirituals.

When Israel was in Egypt's land,[1]
    O let my people go!
Oppressed so hard they could not stand,
    O let my people go!

5 *Chorus:* O go down,[2] Moses,
          Away down to Egypt's land,
          And tell King Pharaoh
          To let my people go!

10 Thus saith the Lord, bold Moses said,
    O let my people go!
If not, I'll smite your first born dead,
    O let my people go!

No more shall they in bondage toil,
    O let my people go!
15 Let them come out with Egypt's spoil,
    O let my people go! …

O 'twas a dark and dismal night,
    O let my people go!
When Moses led the Israelites,
20   O let my people go! …

The Lord told Moses what to do,
    O let my people go!
To lead the children of Israel through,
    O let my people go!

25 O come along, Moses, you won't get lost,
    O let my people go!
Stretch out your rod and come across,
    O let my people go!

As Israel stood by the water side,
30   O let my people go!
At the command of God it did divide,
    O let my people go!

When they had reached the other shore,
    O let my people go!
35 They sang a song of triumph o'er!
    O let my people go!

Pharaoh said he would go across,
    O let my people go!
But Pharaoh and his host were lost,
40   O let my people go! …

O let us all from bondage flee,
    O let my people go!
And let us all in Christ be free,
    O let my people go!

---

[1] *When Israel … land* This song retells the biblical story of the Exodus, the Israelites' escape from slavery in Egypt, as related in the first fourteen chapters of the Book of Exodus.

[2] *go down* The Hebrew Bible (the Old Testament) frequently describes arriving in Egypt as "going down" to it and departing from it as "going up" from it; see, for example, Genesis 42.2 and Exodus 1.10. For enslaved people, "going down" also suggested being "sold down the river" (i.e., the Mississippi) to the Deep South, where enslavement was considered to be particularly brutal.

45 We need not always weep and mourn,
        O let my people go!
    And wear these Slavery chains forlorn,
        O let my people go! …

What a beautiful morning that will be!
50   O let my people go!
    When time breaks up in eternity,
        O let my people go!

African American laborers in Alexandria, Virginia, just across the Potomac River from Washington, D.C. This photograph was taken by Mathew Brady—or more likely by one of his assistants—sometime after U.S. Army troops occupied Alexandria in May 1861.

Julia Ward Howe, "Battle Hymn of the Republic" (1862)

Julia Ward Howe (1819–1910), an abolitionist writer and activist, wrote "The Battle Hymn of the Republic" while visiting Washington, D.C., in November 1861. During an excursion, she joined a group of U.S. Army soldiers in singing the popular marching song "John Brown's Body," whereupon one of her companions suggested that she "write some good words for that stirring tune." (Howe's husband had helped to fund Brown's failed raid on Harpers Ferry, Virginia, in 1859.) By her own account, she wrote her new lyrics for the tune in a burst of midnight inspiration that night. "The Battle Hymn of the Republic" was first published as a poem in the *Atlantic Monthly* in February 1862; the text presented below is based on this first publication. When sung, the chorus consists of "Glory, glory, hallelujah," repeated three times (a carryover from "John Brown's Body"), plus the final line of the preceding stanza. "The Battle Hymn of the Republic" became quickly and enduringly popular—though more among civilians than with the army.

Mine eyes have seen the glory of the coming of the Lord:
He is trampling out the vintage where the grapes of
    wrath are stored;[1]
He hath loosed the fateful lightning of His terrible
    swift sword:
               His truth is marching on.

5 I have seen Him in the watch-fires of a hundred
    circling camps,
They have builded Him an altar in the evening dews
    and damps;
I can read His righteous sentence by the dim and
    flaring lamps:
               His day is marching on.

I have read a fiery Gospel writ in burnished rows of
    steel:
10 "As ye deal with my contemners,[2] so with you my
    grace shall deal;
Let the Hero, born of woman, crush the serpent with
    his heel,[3]
               Since God is marching on."

He has sounded forth the trumpet that shall never call
    retreat;
He is sifting out the hearts of men before His
    judgment-seat:
15 Oh, be swift, my soul, to answer Him! be jubilant,
    my feet!
               Our God is marching on.

In the beauty of the lilies Christ was born across the
    sea,
With a glory in his bosom that transfigures you and
    me:
As he died to make men holy, let us die to make men
    free,
20   While God is marching on.

---

1 *Mine eyes ... stored* See Isaiah 63.1–4: "Who is this that cometh from Edom, with dyed garments from Bozrah? this that is glorious in his apparel, travelling in the greatness of his strength? I that speak in righteousness, mighty to save. Wherefore art thou red in thine apparel, and thy garments like him that treadeth in the winefat? I have trodden the winepress alone; and of the people there was none with me: for I will tread them in mine anger, and trample them in my fury; and their blood shall be sprinkled upon my garments, and I will stain all my raiment. For the day of vengeance is in mine heart, and the year of my redeemed is come." See also Revelation 14.19–20: "And the angel thrust in his sickle into the earth, and gathered the vine of the earth, and cast it into the great winepress of the wrath of God. And the winepress was trodden without the city, and blood came out of the winepress."

2 *contemners* People demonstrating contempt or disobedience.

3 *Let ... heel* See Genesis 3.15, in which God curses the serpent for tempting Adam and Eve into eating the forbidden fruit: "I will put enmity between thee and the woman, and between thy seed and her seed; it shall bruise [also translated "crush"] thy head, and thou shalt bruise his heel." In Christianity, this verse has traditionally been interpreted as the earliest prophecy of Christ's redemption of humanity, in which Christ—born of a virgin and thus the "seed" of Eve, the first woman—defeats sin and death, the products of Satan (crushes the serpent's head) at the cost of his own life, before rising again (his heel being bruised).

Frederick Douglass, "Men of Color, to Arms!" (1863)

Besides declaring the freedom of all enslaved people in areas of the South designated as being in rebellion against the federal government, President Lincoln's Emancipation Proclamation, issued on 1 January 1863, authorized the recruitment of African Americans to the U.S. Army. Foremost among the public figures who promptly began urging blacks to enlist was Frederick Douglass, who had been petitioning the government to allow black enlistment since the start of the war. On 2 March 1863, Douglass issued the following call for recruits for the 54th Massachusetts Infantry Regiment, one of the first units of black troops (commanded by white officers) to be organized in the North in the wake of the Emancipation Proclamation. Two of Douglass's own sons were among the many who responded, and the 54th Massachusetts went on to win a reputation for battlefield heroism that paved the way for further mass African American recruitment.

The text below is based on the published broadside included in the Rare Books and Special Collections Division of the Library of Congress.

When first the rebel cannon shattered the walls of Sumter and drove away its starving garrison,[1] I predicted that the war then and there inaugurated would not be fought out entirely by white men. Every month's experience during these dreary years has confirmed that opinion. A war undertaken and brazenly carried on for the perpetual enslavement of colored men, calls logically and loudly for colored men to help suppress it. Only a moderate share of sagacity was needed to see that the arm of the slave was the best defense against the arm of the slaveholder. Hence with every reverse to the national arms, with every exulting shout of victory raised by the slaveholding rebels, I have implored the imperiled nation to unchain against her foes her powerful black hand. Slowly and reluctantly that appeal is beginning to be heeded. Stop not now to complain that it was not heeded sooner. It may or it may not have been best that it should not. This is not the time to discuss that question. Leave it to the future. When the war is over, the country is saved, peace is established, and the black man's rights are secured, as they will be, history with an impartial hand will dispose of that and sundry other questions. Action! action! not criticism, is the plain duty of this hour. Words are now useful only as they stimulate to blows. The office of speech now is only to point out when, where, and how to strike to the best advantage. There is no time to delay. The tide is at its flood that leads on to fortune. From East to West, from North to South, the sky is written all over with "now or never." Liberty won by white men would lack half its lustre. "Who would be free themselves must strike the blow." "Better even die free, than to live slaves." This is the sentiment of every brave colored man amongst us. There are weak and cowardly men in all nations. We have them among us. They will tell you that this is the "white man's war"; that you will be "no better off after than before the war"; that the getting of you into the army is to "sacrifice you on the first opportunity." Believe them not—cowards themselves, they do not wish to have their cowardice shamed by your brave example. Leave them to their timidity, or to whatever motive may hold them back.

I have not thought lightly of the words I am now addressing to you. The counsel I give comes of close observation of the great struggle now in progress—and of the deep conviction that this is your hour and mine.

In good earnest, then, and after the best deliberation, I, now, for the first time during this war, feel at liberty to call and counsel you to arms. By every consideration which binds you to your enslaved fellow countrymen, and the peace and welfare of your country; by every aspiration which you cherish for the freedom and equality of yourselves and your children; by all the ties of blood and identity which make us one with the brave black men now fighting our battles in Louisiana and in South Carolina,[2] I urge you to fly to

---

[1] *When first ... garrison* Reference to the First Battle of Fort Sumter on 12–13 April 1861, in which Confederate forces in Charleston, South Carolina, bombarded Fort Sumter, a federal military installation in Charleston harbor. Short on men and supplies, the garrison of the fort was forced to surrender. Although neither side suffered any casualties, these were the first shots fired between the South and the North.

[2] *the brave ... South Carolina* Douglass refers to two black Union units which had already been formed in the South, the 1st Louisiana Native Guard and the 1st South Carolina Volunteers, both of which consisted largely or entirely of formerly enslaved people.

arms, and smite with death the power that would bury the government and your liberty in the same hopeless grave. I wish I could tell you that the State of New York calls you to this high honor. For the moment her constituted authorities are silent on the subject. They will speak by and by, and doubtless on the right side; but we are not compelled to wait for her. We can get at the throat of treason and slavery through the State of Massachusetts.

She was first in the War of Independence; first to break the chains of her slaves; first to make the black man equal before the law; first to admit colored children to her common schools, and she was first to answer with her blood the alarm cry of the nation—when its capital was menaced by rebels. You know her patriotic governor, and you know Charles Sumner[1]—I need add no more.

Massachusetts now welcomes you to arms as soldiers. She has but a small colored population from which to recruit. She has full leave of the general government to send one regiment to the war, and she has undertaken to do it. Go quickly and help fill up this first colored regiment from the North. I am authorized to assure you that you will receive the same wages,[2] the same rations, the same equipments, the same protection, the same treatment, and the same bounty[3] secured to the white soldiers. You will be led by able and skillful officers—men who will take special pride in your efficiency

and success. They will be quick to accord to you all the honor you shall merit by your valor—and see that your rights and feelings are respected by other soldiers. I have assured myself on these points—and can speak with authority. More than twenty years of unswerving devotion to our common cause may give me some humble claim to be trusted at this momentous crisis.

I will not argue. To do so implies hesitation and doubt, and you do not hesitate. You do not doubt. The day dawns—the morning star is bright upon the horizon! The iron gate of our prison stands half open. One gallant rush from the North will fling it wide open, while four millions of our brothers and sisters shall march out into liberty! The chance is now given you to end in a day the bondage of centuries, and to rise in one bound from social degradation to the plane of common equality with all other varieties of men. Remember Denmark Vesey of Charleston. Remember Nathaniel Turner of Southampton; remember Shields Green and Copeland, who followed noble John Brown, and fell as glorious martyrs for the cause of the slaves.[4] Remember that in a contest with oppression, the Almighty has no attribute which can take sides with oppressors.[5] The case is before you. This is our golden opportunity—let us accept it—and forever wipe out the dark reproaches unsparingly hurled against us by our enemies. Let us win for ourselves the gratitude of our country—and the best blessings of our posterity through all time. The nucleus of this first regiment is now in camp at Readville, a short distance from Boston. I will undertake to forward to Boston all persons adjudged fit to be mustered into this regiment who shall apply to me at any time within the next two weeks.

[1] *first to break ... the law* In legal cases decided in the years 1781–83, slavery was found to be inconsistent with the 1780 Massachusetts Constitution's declaration that "All men are born free and equal"; *first to admit ... schools* Massachusetts outlawed school assignment by race in 1855; *she was first ... rebels* The 6th Massachusetts Militia Regiment was the first unit of Union volunteers to arrive in Washington, D.C., at the start of the Civil War in April 1861; *her patriotic governor* John A. Andrew, abolitionist Governor of Massachusetts from 1861 to 1866; *Charles Sumner* U.S. senator for Massachusetts noted for his fervent opposition to slavery (1811–74).

[2] *the same wages* In fact, the men of the 54th Massachusetts were paid only $7 a month, whereas white Union soldiers were paid $13 a month. When this was announced, the officers and enlisted men of the regiment chose to serve without pay as a protest. The disparity was remedied over a year later.

[3] *bounty* Volunteers on both sides of the Civil War were frequently offered a monetary payment, or "bounty," as incentive to enlist; in the North, this could amount to up to $300. As with wages, the provision of bounties to African American volunteers was frequently unfair by comparison with those offered to white recruits.

[4] *Denmark Vesey ... slaves* Douglass lists several African American organizers of, or participants in, armed resistance to slavery, all of whom were killed for their actions. Denmark Vesey helped plan an uprising by enslaved people in Charleston, South Carolina, in 1822; the plot was discovered and he was executed before the uprising could begin. Nat Turner, an enslaved man in Southampton County, Virginia, was hanged for leading an antislavery uprising in 1831. Shields Green, a fugitive enslaved man, and John A. Copeland, Jr., a free black man, were both hanged in 1859 for their participation in John Brown's failed raid on Harpers Ferry, Virginia.

[5] *Remember ... oppressors* In *Notes on the State of Virginia* (1781, published 1785), Thomas Jefferson wrote, regarding the possibility of a conflict between enslaved blacks and white enslavers like himself, "The Almighty has no attribute which can take side with us in such a contest."

William Morris Smith, *District of Columbia. Company E, 4th U.S. Colored Infantry, at Fort Lincoln,* date unknown.

George Henry Boker, "The Black Regiment" (1863)

This poem, by the white Philadelphian poet and playwright George Henry Boker (1823–90), describes the widely-publicized attack made by black U.S. troops from Louisiana, many of whom had escaped enslavement, on rebel fortifications at Port Hudson, Louisiana, on 27 May 1863. Though the attack failed, it did much to dispel the prejudice, held by many white Northerners, that black men could not be brave and effective soldiers, and thereby helped facilitate the further mass recruitment of African Americans into the U.S. Army. "The Black Regiment" is one of many poems from this era that drew on "The Charge of the Light Brigade" (1854), a poem by the renowned English poet Alfred, Lord Tennyson describing an incident in the Crimean War; Boker's poem is written in the same distinctive dactylic dimeter that Tennyson employed. The poem was published in 1863 by the Supervisory Committee for Recruiting Colored Regiments and republished in Boker's collection *Poems of the War* in 1864; the text presented here is based on the first published version.

May 27th, 1863

Dark as the clouds of even,°   *evening*
Ranked in the western heaven,
Waiting the breath that lifts
All the dread mass, and drifts
5 Tempest and falling brand°   *lightning*
Over a ruined land—
So still and orderly,
Arm to arm, knee to knee,
Waiting the great event,
10 Stands the black regiment.

Down the long dusky line
Teeth gleam and eyeballs shine;
And the bright bayonet,
Bristling and firmly set,
15 Flashed with a purpose grand,
Long ere the sharp command
Of the fierce rolling drum
Told them their time had come,
Told them what work was sent
20 For the black regiment.

"Now," the flag-sergeant cried,
"Though death and hell betide,°   befall
Let the whole nation see
If we are fit to be
25 Free in this land; or bound
Down, like the whining hound—
Bound with red stripes of pain
In our old chains again!"
Oh, what a shout there went
30 From the black regiment!

"Charge!" Trump and drum awoke,
Onward the bondmen broke;
Bayonet and sabre-stroke
Vainly opposed their rush.
35 Through the wild battle's crush,
With but one thought aflush,
Driving their lords like chaff,
In the guns' mouths they laugh;
Or at the slippery brands°   swords
40 Leaping with open hands,
Down they tear man and horse,
Down in their awful course;
Tramping with bloody heel
Over the crashing steel,
45 All their eyes forward bent,
Rushed the black regiment.

"Freedom!" their battle-cry—
"Freedom! or leave° to die!"   permission
Ah! And they meant the word,
50 Not as with us 'tis heard,
Not a mere party-shout:°   partisan slogan
They gave their spirits out;

Trusted the end to God,
And on the gory sod
55 Rolled in triumphant blood.
    Glad to strike one free blow,
Whether for weal° or woe;   well-being
Glad to breathe one free breath,
Though on the lips of death.
60 Praying—alas! in vain!—
That they might fall again,
So they could once more see
That burst to liberty!
This was what "freedom" lent°   granted
65 To the black regiment.

Hundreds on hundreds fell;
But they are resting well;
Scourges and shackles strong
Never shall do them wrong.
70   Oh, to the living few,
Soldiers, be just and true!
Hail them as comrades tried;
Fight with them side by side;
Never, in field or tent,
75 Scorn the black regiment.

Caroline A. Ball, "The Jacket of Gray" (1863)

Caroline A. Ball (1823–1913) wrote poetry from an early age but never published under her own name until the Civil War. Her collection *The Jacket of Gray and Other Fugitive Poems* was published in Charleston, South Carolina, her birthplace, in 1866. The collection's title poem was immensely popular in the South and was set to music at least twice in the years following the end of the war. The title "The Jacket of Gray" refers to a color widely used during the Civil War for Southern military uniforms.

Fold it up carefully, lay it aside;
Tenderly touch it, look on it with pride;
For dear to our hearts must it be evermore,
The jacket of gray our loved soldier-boy wore.

5 Can we ever forget when he joined the brave band
That rose in defense of our dear Southern land,

And in his bright youth hurried on to the fray,
How proudly he donned it—the jacket of gray?

His fond mother blessed him and looked up above,
10   Commending to heaven the child of her love;
What anguish was hers mortal tongue cannot say,
When he passed from her sight in the jacket of gray.

But her country had called and she would
        not repine,°   complain
Though costly the sacrifice placed on its shrine;
15   Her heart's dearest hopes on its altar she lay,
When she sent out her boy in the jacket of gray.

Months passed, and war's thunders rolled over the land,
Unsheathed was the sword and lighted the brand;°torch
We heard in the distance the sound of the fray,
20   And prayed for our boy in the jacket of gray.

Ah, vain, all in vain, were our prayers and our tears,
The glad shout of victory rang in our ears;
But our treasured one on the red battle-field lay,
While the life-blood oozed out of the jacket of gray.

25   His young comrades found him, and tenderly bore
The cold lifeless form to his home by the shore;
Oh, dark were our hearts on that terrible day,
When we saw our dead boy in the jacket of gray.

Ah, spotted and tattered, and stained now with gore,
30   Was the garment which once he so proudly wore;
We bitterly wept as we took it away,
And replaced with death's white robe the jacket of gray.

We laid him to rest in his cold narrow bed,
And graved° on the marble we placed o'er   engraved
        his head
35   As the proudest tribute our sad hearts could pay—
"He never disgraced it, the jacket of gray."

Then fold it up carefully, lay it aside,
Tenderly touch it, look on it with pride;
For dear must it be to our hearts evermore,
40   The jacket of gray our loved soldier-boy wore!

Charles R. Rees, *Private Edward A. Cary of Company I, 44th Virginia Infantry Regiment, in Uniform and His Sister, Emma J. Garland née Cary,* 1861 or 1862.

Emily Dickinson, "When I was small, a Woman died" (1861–63)

Emily Dickinson wrote voluminously during the Civil War. Much of her poetry can be interpreted as indirectly reflecting the war's violence, suffering, and grief, but little of it refers to the war directly. This poem, written sometime between 1861 and 1863, is one of the apparent exceptions. The text presented here is based on the manuscript of the poem.

When I was small, a Woman died –
    Today – her Only Boy
Went up from the Potomac[1] –
His face all Victory

---

[1] *Potomac* River that forms the border between Virginia, to the south, and Maryland and the District of Columbia, to the north. As such, it was strategically significant during the Civil War; several battles were fought near it, including the Battle of Ball's Bluff, Virginia, in October 1861, at which Dickinson's distant cousin Francis H. Dickinson was killed.

5   To look at her – How slowly
    The Seasons must have turned
    Till Bullets clipt an Angle
    And He passed quickly round –

    If pride shall be in Paradise –
10   Ourself cannot decide –
    Of their imperial conduct –
    No person testified –

    But, proud in Apparition –
    That Woman and her Boy
15   Pass back and forth, before my Brain[1]
    As even in the sky –

    I'm confident, that Bravoes –
    Perpetual break abroad
    For Braveries, remote as this
20   In Yonder Maryland –

Timothy H. O'Sullivan, *A Harvest of Death: Gettysburg, July, 1863*. O'Sullivan's famous photograph of dead soldiers following the Battle of Gettysburg was published in a collection entitled *Photographic Sketch Book of the War* (1866), edited by fellow-photographer Andrew Gardner. See the anthology website for more on this and its companion photograph.

---

1   *Pass … Brain* Compare Dickinson's words in a letter she wrote about the death in battle in March 1862 of Frazer Stearns, a close friend of her brother Austin: "Austin is chilled – by Frazer's murder – he says – his brain keeps saying over 'Frazer is killed' – 'Frazer is killed,' just as Father told it – to Him."

from Louisa May Alcott, *Hospital Sketches* (1863)

Louisa May Alcott worked for six weeks in December 1862 and January 1863 as a volunteer nurse in the Union Hospital in Georgetown, D.C., before falling seriously ill with typhoid. She documented her experiences in four sketches, based on letters to her family, that were serialized in May and June 1863 and then published in book form as *Hospital Sketches* later that year. Chapter 3 of the book, excerpted below, depicts the aftermath of the federal defeat at Fredericksburg, Virginia, in December 1862; the text is based on that of the 1863 book publication.

The sight of several stretchers, each with its legless, armless, or desperately wounded occupant, entering my ward, admonished me that I was there to work, not to wonder or weep; so I corked up my feelings, and returned to the path of duty, which was rather "a hard road to travel"[1] just then. The house had been a hotel before hospitals were needed, and many of the doors still bore their old names; some not so inappropriate as might be imagined, for my ward was in truth a *ball-room,* if gun-shot wounds could christen it.[2] Forty beds were prepared, many already tenanted by tired men who fell down anywhere, and drowsed till the smell of food roused them. Round the great stove was gathered the dreariest group I ever saw— ragged, gaunt and pale, mud to the knees, with bloody bandages untouched since put on days before; many bundled up in blankets, coats being lost or useless; and all wearing that disheartened look which proclaimed defeat, more plainly than any telegram of the Burnside blunder.[3] I pitied them so much, I dared not speak to them, though, remembering all they had been through since the route[4] at Fredericksburg, I yearned to serve the dreariest of them all. Presently, Miss Blank tore me from my refuge behind piles of one-sleeved shirts, odd socks, bandages and lint; put basin, sponge, towels, and a block of brown soap into my hands, with these appalling directions:

"Come, my dear, begin to wash as fast as you can. Tell them to take off socks, coats and shirts, scrub them well, put on clean shirts, and the attendants will finish them off, and lay them in bed."

If she had requested me to shave them all, or dance a hornpipe on the stove funnel, I should have been less staggered; but to scrub some dozen lords of creation at a moment's notice, was really—really——. However, there was no time for nonsense, and, having resolved when I came to do everything I was bid, I drowned my scruples in my wash-bowl, clutched my soap manfully, and, assuming a business-like air, made a dab at the

James Gardner, *Kearney's men wounded at Fredericksburg,* 20 May 1864. The woman seated in the doorway has been identified as volunteer nurse Abby Gibbons, from New York City.

---

1   *a hard road to travel*   Possibly a reference to "Jordan Is a Hard Road to Travel," a popular blackface minstrel song written in 1853 by Dan Emmett (the writer of "Dixie").

2   *a ball-room … christen it*   Alcott here puns on "ball" as a nineteenth-century synonym for "bullet."

3   *the Burnside blunder*   On 13 December 1862, as part of the Battle of Fredericksburg, Union General Ambrose Burnside ordered a series of doomed frontal attacks on entrenched Confederate positions; the attacking Union troops suffered massive casualties.

4   *route*   I.e., rout; resounding defeat.

first dirty specimen I saw, bent on performing my task *vi et armis*[1] if necessary. ...

"I say, Mrs.!" called a voice behind me; and, turning, I saw a rough Michigander, with an arm blown off at the shoulder, and two or three bullets still in him—as he afterwards mentioned, as carelessly as if gentlemen were in the habit of carrying such trifles about with them. I went to him, and, while administering a dose of soap and water, he whispered, irefully:

"That red-headed devil, over yonder, is a reb, damn him! You'll agree to that, I'll bet? He's got shet of a foot, or he'd a cut[2] like the rest of the lot. Don't you wash him, nor feed him, but jest let him holler till he's tired. It's a blasted shame to fetch them fellers in here, along side of us; and so I'll tell the chap that bosses this concern; cuss me if I don't."

I regret to say that I did not deliver a moral sermon upon the duty of forgiving our enemies, and the sin of profanity, then and there; but, being a red-hot Abolitionist, stared fixedly at the tall rebel, who was a copperhead, in every sense of the word,[3] and privately resolved to put soap in his eyes, rub his nose the wrong way, and excoriate his cuticle generally, if I had the washing of him.

My amiable intentions, however, were frustrated; for, when I approached, with as Christian an expression as my principles would allow, and asked the question—"Shall I try to make you more comfortable, sir?" all I got for my pains was a gruff—

"No; I'll do it myself."

"Here's your Southern chivalry, with a witness," thought I, dumping the basin down before him, thereby quenching a strong desire to give him a summary baptism, in return for his ungraciousness; for my angry passions rose, at this rebuff, in a way that would have scandalized good Dr. Watts. He was a disappointment in all respects (the rebel, not the blessed Doctor) for he was neither fiendish, romantic, pathetic, or anything interesting; but a long, fat man, with a head like a burning bush,[4] and a perfectly expressionless face: so I could hate him without the slightest drawback, and ignored his existence from that day forth. One redeeming trait he certainly did possess, as the floor speedily testified; for his ablutions were so vigorously performed, that his bed soon stood like an isolated island, in a sea of soap-suds, and he resembled a dripping merman, suffering from the loss of a fin. If cleanliness is a near neighbor to godliness, then was the big rebel the godliest man in my ward that day.

Having done up our human wash, and laid it out to dry, the second syllable of our version of the word warfare was enacted with much success. Great trays of bread, meat, soup and coffee appeared; and both nurses and attendants turned waiters, serving bountiful rations to all who could eat. I can call my pinafore to testify to my good will in the work, for in ten minutes it was reduced to a perambulating bill of fare, presenting samples of all the refreshments going or gone. It was a lively scene; the long room lined with rows of beds, each filled by an occupant, whom water, shears, and clean raiment, had transformed from a dismal ragamuffin into a recumbent hero, with a cropped head. To and fro rushed matrons, maids, and convalescent "boys," skirmishing with knives and forks; retreating with empty plates; marching and counter-marching, with unvaried success, while the clash of busy spoons made most inspiring music for the charge of our Light Brigade:[5]

Beds to the front of them,
Beds to the right of them,
Beds to the left of them,
    Nobody blundered.
Beamed at by hungry souls,
Screamed at with brimming bowls,
Steamed at by army rolls,
    Buttered and sundered.
With coffee not cannon plied,
Each must be satisfied,

1   *vi et armis* Latin: by force and arms, a term in civil law that derives from "Pro Caecina," a speech by the Roman politician and orator Marcus Tullius Cicero (106–43 BCE).

2   *cut* Run.

3   *a copperhead ... word* "Copperhead," the name for a kind of venomous snake common to the eastern U.S., was a term used by Northern supporters of the war for anti-war Democrats. Alcott is here extending the term, applying it to an actual Confederate.

4   *burning bush* In Chapter 3 of the Book of Exodus, God speaks to Moses out of a burning bush.

5   *the charge of our Light Brigade* "The Charge of the Light Brigade" (1854) is a famous poem by the British poet Alfred, Lord Tennyson that describes a misguided and costly frontal attack by the Light Brigade of British cavalry during the Crimean War (1853–56). Alcott parodies one of the stanzas of the poem.

Whether they lived or died;
    All the men wondered.

Very welcome seemed the generous meal, after a week of suffering, exposure, and short commons;[1] soon the brown faces began to smile, as food, warmth, and rest, did their pleasant work; and the grateful "Thankee's" were followed by more graphic accounts of the battle and retreat, than any paid reporter could have given us. Curious contrasts of the tragic and comic met one everywhere; and some touching as well as ludicrous episodes, might have been recorded that day. A six foot New Hampshire man, with a leg broken and perforated by a piece of shell, so large that, had I not seen the wound, I should have regarded the story as a Munchausenism,[2] beckoned me to come and help him, as he could not sit up, and both his bed and beard were getting plentifully anointed with soup. As I fed my big nestling with corresponding mouthfuls, I asked him how he felt during the battle.

"Well, 'twas my fust, you see, so I aint ashamed to say I was a trifle flustered in the beginnin', there was such an allfired racket; for ef there's anything I do spleen agin,[3] it's noise. But when my mate, Eph Sylvester, caved, with a bullet through his head, I got mad, and pitched in, licketty cut. Our part of the fight didn't last long; so a lot of us larked round Fredericksburg, and give some of them houses a pretty consid'able of a rummage, till we was ordered out of the mess. Some of our fellows cut like time; but I warn't a-goin to run for nobody; and, fust thing I knew, a shell bust, right in front of us, and I keeled over, feelin' as if I was blowed higher'n a kite. I sung out, and the boys come back for me, double quick; but the way they chucked me over them fences was a caution, I tell you. Next day I was most as black as that darkey yonder, lickin' plates on the sly. This is bully coffee, ain't it? Give us another pull at it, and I'll be obleeged to you."

---

[1] *short commons* Short rations; insufficient food.

[2] *Munchausenism* Extravagant tall tale. The term derives from the narrator and protagonist of *Baron Munchausen's Narrative of His Marvellous Travels and Campaigns in Russia* (1785), a book by the German writer Rudolf Erich Raspe. The book's title character, like his real-life inspiration, is a military adventurer who tells wildly exaggerated or outright impossible stories about his supposed experiences.

[3] *do spleen agin* Get angry at.

I did; and, as the last gulp subsided, he said, with a rub of his old handkerchief over eyes as well as mouth: "Look a here; I've got a pair a earbobs and a handkercher pin I'm a goin' to give you, if you'll have them; for you're the very moral o' Lizy Sylvester, poor Eph's wife: that's why I signalled you to come over here. They aint much, I guess, but they'll do to memorize[4] the rebs by."

Burrowing under his pillow, he produced a little bundle of what he called "truck," and gallantly presented me with a pair of earrings, each representing a cluster of corpulent grapes, and the pin a basket of astonishing fruit, the whole large and coppery enough for a small warming-pan. Feeling delicate about depriving him of such valuable relics, I accepted the earrings alone, and was obliged to depart, somewhat abruptly, when my friend stuck the warming-pan in the bosom of his night-gown, viewing it with much complacency, and, perhaps, some tender memory, in that rough heart of his, for the comrade he had lost.

Observing that the man next him had left his meal untouched, I offered the same service I had performed for his neighbor, but he shook his head.

"Thank you, ma'am; I don't think I'll ever eat again, for I'm shot in the stomach. But I'd like a drink of water, if you aint too busy."

I rushed away, but the water-pails were gone to be refilled, and it was some time before they reappeared. I did not forget my patient patient, meanwhile, and, with the first mugful, hurried back to him. He seemed asleep; but something in the tired white face caused me to listen at his lips for a breath. None came. I touched his forehead; it was cold: and then I knew that, while he waited, a better nurse than I had given him a cooler draught, and healed him with a touch. I laid the sheet over the quiet sleeper, whom no noise could now disturb; and, half an hour later, the bed was empty. It seemed a poor requital for all he had sacrificed and suffered—that hospital bed, lonely even in a crowd; for there was no familiar face for him to look his last upon; no friendly voice to say, Good bye; no hand to lead him gently down into the Valley of the Shadow;[5]

---

[4] *memorize* I.e., memorialize, commemorate.

[5] *Valley of the Shadow* See Psalm 23.4: "Yea, though I walk through the valley of the shadow of death, I will fear no evil: for thou [God] art with me."

and he vanished, like a drop in that red sea upon whose shores so many women stand lamenting. For a moment I felt bitterly indignant at this seeming carelessness of the value of life, the sanctity of death; then consoled myself with the thought that, when the great muster roll was called, these nameless men might be promoted above many whose tall monuments record the barren honors they have won.

from Mattie Jackson and L.S. Thompson, *The Story of Mattie J. Jackson* (1866)

Mattie Jane Jackson (1847–1910) was born into slavery in St. Louis, Missouri. Her father escaped via the Underground Railroad when she was a young child; when her mother Ellen attempted to follow him with their children, the family was sold to William Lewis, a "very severe master," in Jackson's words, to whom they were still enslaved when the Civil War began. After the war, Jackson was invited by her mother's second husband (who had also escaped from slavery) to live with him and his new wife, a botanical physician named Lucy Susan Thompson, in Lawrence, Massachusetts, where Jackson—who could read a little but not write—dictated her and her family's story to Thompson, who also arranged for the story's publication. Jackson later returned to St. Louis and married a U.S. Army veteran, William Dyer, with whom she spent the rest of her life.

The Story of Mattie J. Jackson is a rare example of a slave narrative produced through the collaboration of two African American women. It commands interest for its detailed account of an enslaved family struggling to stay together and resist enslavement before and during the Civil War, and for its depiction of the war from the perspective of an enslaved person.

THE SOLDIERS, AND OUR TREATMENT DURING THE WAR

Soon after the war commenced the rebel soldiers encamped near Mr. Lewis' residence, and remained there one week. They were then ordered by General Lyons[1] to surrender, but they refused. There were seven thousand Union and seven hundred rebel soldiers. The Union soldiers surrounded the camp and took them and exhibited them through the city and then confined them in prison.[2] I told my mistress that the Union soldiers were coming to take the camp. She replied that it was false, that it was General Kelly coming to re-enforce Gen. Frost.[3] In a few moments the alarm was heard. I told Mrs. L. the Unionists had fired upon the rebels. She replied it was only the salute of Gen. Kelly. At night her husband came home with the news that Camp Jackson was taken and all the soldiers prisoners. Mrs. Lewis asked how the Union soldiers could take seven hundred men when they only numbered the same. Mr. L. replied they had seven thousand. She was much astonished, and cast her eye around to us for fear we might hear her. Her suspicion was correct; there was not a word passed that escaped our listening ears. My mother and myself could read enough to make out the news in the papers. The Union soldiers took much delight in tossing a paper over the fence to us. It aggravated my mistress very much. My mother used to sit up nights and read to keep posted about the war. In a few days my mistress came down to the kitchen again with another bitter complaint that it was a sad affair that the Unionists had taken their delicate citizens who had enlisted and made prisoners of them—that they were babes. My mother reminded

---

[1]   *General Lyons*   Nathaniel Lyon (1818–61), Union general whose actions early in the Civil War, before his death in battle in August 1861, helped prevent Missouri from joining the Confederacy.

[2]   *Soon after … prison*   In the spring of 1861, General Lyon, the commander of Union troops in Missouri, learned that an ostensibly-neutral unit of Missouri state militia stationed at Camp Jackson, just outside St. Louis, in fact supported the Confederacy and intended to seize the St. Louis Arsenal, a major federal weapons depository. Lyon forced the militia to surrender on 10 May 1861 and then marched his prisoners through St. Louis; a clash ensued between the Union troops and secessionist St. Louis civilians, in which 28 civilians were killed and many more wounded. The "Camp Jackson affair," as it became known, kept Missouri in the Union but deepened the divide between Unionist and secessionist factions in the state.

[3]   *General Kelly … Gen. Frost*   John H. Kelly (1840–64) and Daniel M. Frost (1823–1900) were both Confederate generals; Frost commanded the militia forces that were taken prisoner at Camp Jackson.

her of taking Fort Sumpter and Major Anderson[1] and serving them the same and that turn about was fair play. She then hastened to her room with the speed of a deer, nearly unhinging every door in her flight, replying as she went that the Niggers[2] and Yankees were seeking to take the country. One day, after she had visited the kitchen to superintend some domestic affairs, as she pretended, she became very angry without a word being passed, and said—"I think it has come to a pretty pass, that old Lincoln, with his long legs, an old rail splitter, wishes to put the Niggers on an equality with the whites; that her children should never be on an equal footing with a Nigger. She had rather see them dead." As my mother made no reply to her remarks, she stopped talking, and commenced venting her spite on my companion servant. On one occasion Mr. Lewis searched my mother's room and found a picture of President Lincoln, cut from a newspaper, hanging in her room. He asked her what she was doing with old Lincoln's picture. She replied it was there because she liked it. He then knocked her down three times, and sent her to the trader's yard[3] for a month as punishment. My mistress indulged some hopes till the victory of New Orleans[.][4] …

The days of sadness for mistress were days of joy for us. We shouted and laughed to the top of our voices. My mistress was more enraged than ever—nothing pleased her. One evening, after I had attended to my usual duties, and I supposed all was complete, she, in a terrible rage, declared I should be punished that night. I did not know the cause, neither did she. She went immediately and selected a switch. She placed it in the

Alexandria, Virginia. Slave pen. Exterior view. The date this photograph was taken, and the name of its photographer, are both unknown.

corner of the room to await the return of her husband at night for him to whip me. As I was not pleased with the idea of a whipping I bent the switch in the shape of W, which was the first letter of his name, and after I had attended to the dining room my fellow servant and myself walked away and stopped with an aunt of mine during the night. In the morning we made our way to the Arsenal, but could gain no admission. While we were wandering about seeking protection, the girl's father overtook us and persuaded us to return home. We finally complied. All was quiet. Not a word was spoken respecting our sudden departure. All went on as usual. I permitted to attend to my work without interruption until three weeks after. One morning I entered Mrs. Lewis' room, and she was in a room adjoining, complaining of something I had neglected. Mr. L. then enquired if I had done my work. I told him I had. She then flew into a rage and told him I was saucy, and to strike me, and he immediately gave me a severe blow with a stick of wood, which inflicted a deep wound upon my head. The blood ran over my clothing, which gave me a frightful appearance. Mr. Lewis then ordered me to change my clothing immediately. As I did not obey he became more enraged, and pulled me into another room and threw me on

---

[1]   *Fort Sumpter … Major Anderson*   The Confederate capture of Fort Sumter—a federal military installation in the harbor of Charleston, South Carolina, commanded by Major Robert Anderson (1805–71)—on 13 April 1861 began the Civil War.

[2]   *Niggers*   As the context makes clear, this word had, by the time of the Civil War, achieved its current, emphatically pejorative meaning in white American vernacular.

[3]   *trader's yard*   I.e., the establishment of a slave trader. One especially notorious such "slave pen" in St. Louis was run by the slave trader Bernard M. Lynch from the late 1850s until the Union Army confiscated it in 1861.

[4]   *victory of New Orleans*   The Union capture, in late April 1862, of New Orleans, the Confederacy's largest city and most important port, was a major strategic victory and crucial turning point in the war.

the floor, placed his knee on my stomach, slapped me on the face and beat me with his fist, and would have punished me more had not my mother interfered. He then told her to go away or he would compel her to, but she remained until he left me. I struggled mightily, and stood him a good test for a while, but he was fast conquering me when my mother came. He was aware my mother could usually defend herself against one man, and both of us would overpower him, so after giving his wife strict orders to take me up stairs and keep me there, he took his carriage and drove away. But she forgot it, as usual. She was highly gratified with my appropriate treatment, as she called it, and retired to her room, leaving me to myself. I then went to my mother and told her I was going away. She bid me go, and added "May the Lord help you." I started for the Arsenal again and succeeded in gaining admittance and seeing the Adjutant. He ordered me to go to another tent, where there was a woman in similar circumstances, cooking. When the General found I was there he sent me to the boarding house. I remained there three weeks, and when I went I wore the same stained clothing as when I was so severely punished, which has left a mark on my head which will ever remind me of my treatment while in slavery. Thanks be to God, though tortured by wrong and goaded by oppression, the hearts that would madden with misery have broken the iron yoke. ...

[Jackson's enslaver eventually sells her and several other members of her family to the captain of a Mississippi River steamboat, who in turn sells them separately to new enslavers in Louisville, Kentucky.]

THE FARE AT THEIR NEW HOMES

My mother was sold to Captain Plasio, my sister to Benj. Board, and myself to Capt. Ephraim Frisbee. ... This was in 1863. ... I fared worse than either of the family. I was not allowed enough to eat, exposed to the cold, and not allowed through the cold winter to thoroughly warm myself once a month. The house was very large, and I could gain no access to the fire. I was kept constantly at work of the heaviest kind, compelled to move heavy trunks and boxes, many times to wash till ten and twelve o'clock at night. There were three deaths in the family while I remained there, and the entire burden was put upon me. I often felt to exclaim as the Children of Israel did: "O Lord, my burden is greater than I can bear." I was then seventeen years of age. My health has been impaired from that time to the present. I have a severe pain in my side by the slightest overexertion. In the Winter I suffer intensely with cold, and cannot get warm unless in a room heated to eighty degrees. I am infirm and burdened with the influence of slavery, whose impress will ever remain on my mind and body. For six months I tried to make my escape. I used to rise at four o'clock in the morning to find some one to assist me, and at last I succeeded. I was allowed two hours once in two weeks to go and return three miles. I could contrive no other way than to improve one of those opportunities, in which I was finally successful. I became acquainted with some persons who assisted slaves to escape by the underground railroad. They were colored people. I was to pretend going to church, and the man who was to assist and introduce me to the proper parties was to linger on the street opposite the house, and I was to follow at a short distance. On Sunday evening I begged leave to attend church, which was reluctantly granted if I completed all my work, which was no easy task. It appeared as if my mistress used every possible exertion to delay me from church, and I concluded that her old cloven-footed companion[1] had impressed his intentions on her mind. Finally, when I was ready to start, my mistress took a notion to go out to ride, and desired me to dress her little boy, and then get ready for church. Extensive hoops were then worn, and as I had attached my whole wardrobe under mine by a cord around my waist, it required considerable dexterity and no small amount of maneuvering to hide the fact from my mistress. While attending to the child I had managed to stand in one corner of the room, for fear she might come in contact with me, and thus discover that my hoops were not so elastic as they usually are. I endeavored to conceal my excitement by backing and edging very genteelly out of the door. I had nine pieces of clothing thus concealed on my person, and as the string which fastened them was small it caused me considerable discomfort. To my great satisfaction I at last passed into the street, and my master and mistress

---

[1]   *her old ... companion* I.e., the devil.

drove down the street in great haste and were soon out of sight. I saw my guide patiently awaiting me. I followed him at a distance until we arrived at the church, and there met two young ladies, one of whom handed me a pass and told me to follow them at a square's distance. It was now twilight. There was a company of soldiers about to take passage across the ferry, and I followed. I showed my pass, and proceeded up the stairs on the boat. While thus ascending the stairs, the cord which held my bundle of clothing broke, and my feet became entangled in my wardrobe, but by proceeding, the first step released one foot and the next the other. This was observed only by a few soldiers, who were too deeply engaged in their own affairs to interfere with mine. I seated myself in a remote corner of the boat, and in a few moments I landed on free soil for the first time in my life[.] … I was now under my own control. The cars were waiting in Jefferson City[1] for the passengers for Indianapolis, where we arrived about nine o'clock.

MATTIE IN INDIANAPOLIS—THE GLORY OF FREEDOM—PRESIDENT LINCOLN'S REMAINS EXHIBITED

My first business, after my arrival at Indianapolis, was to find a boarding place in which I at once succeeded, and in a few hours thereafter was at a place of service of my own choice. I had always been under the yoke of oppression, compelled to submit to its laws, and not allowed to advance a rod[2] from the house, or even out of call, without a severe punishment. Now this constant fear and restless yearning was over. It appeared as though I had emerged into a new world, or had never lived in the old one before. The people I lived with were Unionists, and became immediately interested in teaching and encouraging me in my literary advancement and all other important improvements, which precisely met the natural desires for which my soul had ever yearned since my earliest recollection. I could read a little, but was not allowed to learn in slavery. I was obliged to pay twenty-five cents for every letter written for me. I now began to feel that as I was free

I could learn to write, as well as others; consequently Mrs. Harris, the lady with whom I lived, volunteered to assist me. I was soon enabled to write quite a legible hand, which I find a great convenience. I would advise all, young, middle-aged or old, in a free country, to learn to read and write. If this little book should fall into the hands of one deficient of the important knowledge of writing I hope they will remember the old maxim: "Never too old to learn." Manage your own secrets, and divulge them by the silent language of your own pen. Had our blessed President considered it too humiliating to learn in advanced years, our race would yet have remained under the galling yoke of oppression. After I had been with Mrs. Harris seven months, the joyful news came of the surrender of Lee's army and the capture of Richmond.[3] …

On the Saturday after the assassination of the President[4] there was a meeting held on the Common, and a vote taken to have the President's body brought through Indianapolis,[5] for the people to see his dear dead face. The vote was taken by raising the hands, and when the question was put in favor of it a thousand black hands were extended in the air, seemingly higher and more visible than all the rest. Nor were their hands alone raised, for in their deep sorrow and gloom they raised their hearts to God, for well they knew that He, through martyred blood, had made them free. It was some time before the remains reached Indianapolis, as it was near the last of the route. The body was placed in the centre of the hall of the State House, and we marched in by fours, and divided into twos on each side of the casket, and passed directly through the Hall. It was very rainy—nothing but umbrellas were to be seen in any direction. The multitude were passing in and out from eight o'clock in the morning till four o'clock in the afternoon. His body remained until

---

1   *Jefferson City*   Jeffersonville, Indiana, a town directly across the Ohio River from Louisville, Kentucky.

2   *rod*   Unit of measurement equaling about 5.5 yards.

3   *the surrender … Richmond*   The Union capture of Richmond, Virginia, the Confederate capital, on 3 April 1865, followed a few days later by the surrender of the army of General Robert E. Lee, the main Confederate commander, brought the Civil War to an effective end.

4   *the assassination of the President*   President Lincoln was assassinated on 14 April 1865.

5   *to have … Indianapolis*   The funeral train carrying Lincoln's body to Springfield, Illinois, for burial after his assassination stopped at a dozen cities on the way, in each of which the body was put on public display. This took place in Indianapolis on 30 April 1865.

twelve o'clock in the evening, many distinguished persons visiting it, when amid the booming of cannon, it moved on its way to Springfield, its final resting-place. The death of the President was like an electric shock to my soul. I could not feel convinced of his death until I gazed upon his remains, and heard the last roll of the muffled drum and the farewell boom of the cannon. I was then convinced that though we were left to the tender mercies of God, we were without a leader. ...

SISTER LOST—MOTHER'S ESCAPE

In two or three weeks after the body of the President was carried through, my sister made her escape, but by some means we entirely lost trace of her. We heard she was in a free State. In three months my mother also escaped. She rose quite early in the morning, took my little brother, and arrived at my place of service in the afternoon. I was much surprised, and asked my mother how she came there. She could scarcely tell me for weeping, but I soon found out the mystery. After so many long years and so many attempts, for this was her seventh, she at last succeeded, and we were now all free. My mother had been a slave for more than forty-three years, and liberty was very sweet to her. The sound of freedom was music in our ears; the air was pure and fragrant; the genial rays of the glorious sun burst forth with a new lustre upon us, and all creation resounded in responses of praise to the author and creator of him who proclaimed life and freedom to the slave. I was overjoyed with my personal freedom, but the joy at my mother's escape was greater than anything I had ever known. It was a joy that reaches beyond the tide and anchors in the harbor of eternal rest. While in oppression, this eternal life-preserver had continually wafted her toward the land of freedom, which she was confident of gaining, whatever might betide. Our joy that we were permitted to mingle together our earthly bliss in glorious strains of freedom was indescribable. My mother responded with the children of Israel—"The Lord is my strength and my song. The Lord is a man of war, and the Lord is his name."[1] We left Indianapolis the day after my mother arrived, and took the cars at eleven o'clock the following evening for St. Louis, my native State. We

were then free, and instead of being hurried along, bare headed and half naked, through cars and boats, by a brutal master with a bill of sale in his pocket, we were our own, comfortably clothed, and having the true emblems of freedom.

from Mary A. Livermore, *My Story of the War: A Woman's Narrative of Four Years Personal Experience* (1887)

Mary Livermore (1820–1905) was a significant figure in several of the great movements of the nineteenth century. Born and raised in Massachusetts, she spent a formative year in 1839 tutoring the children of a Virginia plantation owner, an experience which made her an active abolitionist. She was also involved in the temperance movement and, later in the century, in the movement for women's rights. During the Civil War she served as an associate member of the U.S. Sanitary Commission; *My Story of the War*, one of several books she wrote, was well reviewed and highly successful. (A much larger set of excerpts from the volume is included in the anthology's website component.)

FROM CHAPTER 2: LOYAL WOMEN OF THE NORTH

... The number of women who actually bore arms and served in the ranks during the war was greater than is supposed. Sometimes they followed the army as nurses, and divided their services between the battlefield and hospital. I remember Annie Etheridge, of Michigan, who was with the Third Michigan in every battle in which it was engaged. When their three years' service was ended, the re-enlisted veterans joined the Fifth Michigan, and Annie went with them. Through the whole four years of the war she was found in the field, often in the thickest of the fight, always inspiring the men to deeds of valor, always respected for her correctness of life. Soldiers and officers vied with one another in their devotion to her.

---

1   *The Lord ... his name*   See Exodus 15.2–3.

Engraving by John J. Cade from a drawing by F.O.C. Daley, *A Woman in Battle—"Michigan Bridget" Carrying the Flag*, 1887.

Bridget Devens,[1] known as "Michigan Bridget," went to the field with the First Michigan Cavalry, in which her husband was a private, and served through the war. Sometimes when a soldier fell she took his place, fighting in his stead with unquailing courage. Sometimes she rallied retreating troops—sometimes she brought off the wounded from the field—always fearless and daring, always doing good service as a soldier. Her love of army life continued after the war ended, and with her husband she joined a regiment of the regular army, stationed on the Plains.

Mrs. Kady Brownell was, like Madame Turchin,[2] born in camp, her father being attached to the British army. She accompanied the Fifth Rhode Island Infantry to the war, of which regiment her husband was a non-commissioned officer. She was the color-bearer of the regiment, and was a skilful sharpshooter

and expert swordsman. She marched with the men, and asked no favors as a woman, but bore the brunt of the battle, on occasion, as fearlessly as her comrades. She was in General Burnside's expedition to Roanoke Island and Newbern, where her husband was severely wounded. When he was pronounced unfit for further service, and discharged, she also sought a discharge, and retired with him to private life and domestic duty.

The Plattville, Wisconsin *Witness*, of March, 1864, records, as if it were nothing unusual, "the return from the army of Miss Georgianna Peterman." Says the local paragrapher,[3] "Miss Peterman has been for two years a drummer in the Seventh Wisconsin. She lives in Ellenboro', Wis., is about twenty years old, wears soldier clothes, and is quiet and reserved." Similar paragraphs appeared occasionally in other Western papers all through the war. These half-soldier heroines generally adopted a semi-military dress, and became expert in the use of the rifle, and skilful shots.

Some one has stated the number of women soldiers known to the service as little less than four hundred. I cannot vouch for the correctness of this estimate, but I am convinced that a larger number of women disguised themselves and enlisted in the service, for

---

[1] *Bridget Devens* There are several, sometimes conflicting accounts of the exploits of Devens, whose name is spelled in several different ways (among them "Diver" and "Divers") in different sources.

[2] *Madame Turchin* Nadine Lvova Turchin (1826–1904), the daughter of a Russian army officer and wife of a Union general (also Russian-born). She traveled with her husband on campaigns and sometimes commanded his troops in his place.

[3] *paragrapher* Journalist.

one cause or other, than was dreamed of. Entrenched in secrecy, and regarded as men, they were sometimes revealed as women, by accident or casualty. Some startling histories of these military women were current in the gossip of army life; and extravagant and unreal as were many of the narrations, one always felt that they had a foundation in fact.

Such service was not the noblest that women rendered the country during its four years' struggle for life, and no one can regret that these soldier women were exceptional and rare. It is better to heal a wound than to make one. And it is to the honor of American women, not that they led hosts to the deadly charge, and battled amid contending armies, but that they confronted the horrid aspects of war with mighty love and earnestness. They kept up their own courage and that of their households. They became ministering angels to their countrymen who perilled health and life for the nation. They sent the love and impulses of home into the extended ranks of the army, through the unceasing correspondence they maintained with "the boys in blue." They planned largely, and toiled untiringly, and with steady persistence to the end, that the horrors of the battlefield might be mitigated, and the hospitals abound in needed comforts. The men at the front were sure of sympathy from the homes, and knew that the women remembered them with sleepless interest. "This put heroic fibre into their souls," said Dr. Bellows,[1] "and restored us our soldiers with their citizen hearts beating normally under their uniforms, as they dropped them off at the last drum-tap." ...

anonymous, "By the Hush, Me Boys"

During the two decades leading up to the Civil War, well over 1.5 million Irish immigrated to the United States, driven mainly by the economic deprivation caused by Britain's ongoing colonial rule over Ireland, and especially by the devastating Great Famine of 1845–49 and its aftermath. Irish immigrants fought on both sides in the Civil War, but because most Irish settled in the North, a much larger number served in the federal forces: close to 200,000 federal soldiers and sailors had been born in Ireland. One perspective on the Irish immigrant experience of fighting in the U.S. Army is provided by the following song (also known as "Paddy's Lamentation"), which is a folk song preserved in Canada. (A different take on Irish American participation in the Civil War, the song "Pat Murphy of Meagher's Brigade," can be found in the website portion of this Contexts section.)

Oh, it's by the hush,[2] me boys, I'm sure that's to hold your noise,
And listen to poor Paddy's narration.
I was by hunger pressed and in poverty distressed,
So I took a thought I'd leave the Irish nation.

5   *Chorus:* Here's to you, boys, do take my advice,
        To Americay I'd have yous not be coming.
        There is nothing here but war where the
            murdering cannons roar,
        And I wish I was at home in dear old Erin.[3]

Then I sold my horse and plough, me little pigs and cow,
10 And me little farm of land and I parted,
And me sweetheart Biddy Magee I'm afeared I'll never see
For I left her that morning brokenhearted.

Then meself and a hundred more to Americay sailed o'er,
Our fortune to be making we were thinking.
15 When we landed in Yankee land, shoved a gun into our hand,
Saying, "Paddy, you must go and fight for Lincoln."

General Mahar[4] to us said, "If you get shot or lose your head,

---

[1]   *Dr. Bellows*   Henry Whitney Bellows (1814–82), Massachusetts clergyman who served as president of the U.S. Sanitary Commission.

[2]   *by the hush*   Anglicization of the Irish *Bí i do thost*, meaning "Be quiet."

[3]   *Erin*   Romantic name for Ireland, based on a version of the Irish word for the country.

[4]   *General Mahar*   Thomas Francis Meagher (1823–67), commander of the Irish Brigade, the most famous Irish American unit in the Union Army. His last name is pronounced "Ma-harr."

Every murdered soul of you will get a pension."
In the war I lost me leg; all I've now is a wooden peg;
20 By me soul it is the truth to you I mention.

Now I think meself in luck to be fed upon Indian
    buck[1]
In old Ireland, the country I delight in,
And with the devil I do say, "Curse Americay,"
For I'm sure I've got enough of their hard fighting.

Lindley Miller and Men of the 1st Arkansas Infantry Regiment (African Descent), "Song of the First of Arkansas" (1864)

The 1st Arkansas Infantry Regiment (African Descent), later redesignated the 46th Regiment, United States Colored Infantry, was a U.S. Army regiment consisting of African Americans from Arkansas. This regimental anthem, more commonly known as "Marching Song of the First Arkansas Regiment," was credited when first published to Captain Lindley Miller (1834–64), one of the regiment's white officers; however, it likely represents a collaboration between Miller and the regiment's black troops. The song reworks Julia Ward Howe's well-known "Battle Hymn of the Republic" (itself a rewriting of the even more popular marching song "John Brown's Body"). It was first published as a lyric sheet by the Supervisory Committee for Recruiting Colored Regiments, on which the version presented here is based. The African American abolitionist and women's rights activist Sojourner Truth subsequently composed a revised and abbreviated version of the song, retitled "The Valiant Soldiers," which she performed to help recruit black troops and later included in postwar editions of her autobiography, *Narrative of Sojourner Truth: A Northern Slave.*

The first publication of this song in 1864 printed it in dialect (as the second and third stanzas are rendered here), but many modern reprintings present it in standard English— arguably, an approach that allows the modern reader an unfiltered experience of its radicalism.

Oh! we're the bully° soldiers of the   *admirable, elite*
    "First of Arkansas."
We are fightin' for the Union, we are fightin' for the
    law;
We can hit a rebel further than a white man ever saw,
        As we go marching on.
5   Glory, glory, hallelujah, etc.

See dar! above de centre, where de flag is wavin'
    bright;
We are goin' out of slavery; we're bound for freedom's
    light;
We mean to show Jeff Davis[2] how the Africans can
    fight,
        As we go marching on.

10 We hab done wid hoein' cotton, we hab done with
    hoein' corn,
We are colored Yankee soldiers now, as sure as you are
    born;
When de massas hear us yellin' dey'll tink it's Gabriel's
    horn,[3]
        As we go marching on.

They will have to pay us wages, the wages of their sin,[4]
15 They will have to bow their foreheads to their colored
    kith and kin,[5]
They will have to give us house-room, or the roof
    shall tumble in,
        As we go marching on.

We heard the proclamation,[6] master hush it as he will;
The bird he sing it to us, hoppin' on the cotton hill,
20 And the possum up the gum tree, he couldn't keep it
    still,
        As he went climbing on.

---

1 *Indian buck* Variety of buckwheat, a grain used to make cakes.

2 *Jeff Davis* Jefferson Davis (1808–89), Confederate president.

3 *Gabriel's horn* In Christian tradition, the second coming of Christ, and the consequent Last Judgment, will be heralded by a trumpet blown by the archangel Gabriel; this motif appears frequently in African American spirituals.

4 *the wages of their sin* According to Romans 6.23, "the wages of sin is death."

5 *kith and kin* Literally, "friends and family," here used as a general phrase meaning "relatives."

6 *proclamation* I.e., the Emancipation Proclamation.

They said, "Now colored brethren, you shall be
   forever free,
From the first of January, eighteen hundred 'n
   sixty-three";
We heard it in the river goin' rushin' to the sea,
25   As it went sounding on.

Father Abraham[1] has spoken, and the message has
   been sent,
The prison doors he opened, and out the pris'ners
   went,

To join the sable[2] army of the "African descent,"
            As we go marching on.

30 Then fall in, colored brethren, you'd better do it soon,
Don't you hear the drum a-beatin' the Yankee
   Doodle[3] tune?
We are with you now this mornin', we'll be far away
   at noon,
            As we go marching on.

David Bustill Bowser, flag of the 22nd Regiment U.S. Colored Troops, an African American U.S. Army unit, 1864. Bowser (1820–1900), a free black Pennsylvanian artist, designed and painted this battle flag (one of several he created during the war), which depicts an African American U.S. soldier bayoneting a rebel officer. The Latin motto at the top, *Sic semper tyrannis*, meaning "Thus always to tyrants," appears on the official seal of the state of Virginia; it was later made famous (in a very different context) when John Wilkes Booth supposedly shouted it after assassinating Abraham Lincoln.

---

1 *Father Abraham* I.e., Abraham Lincoln, here associated with the biblical patriarch Abraham, traditionally considered the progenitor of the Israelites and the spiritual ancestor of all Christians, Jews, and Muslims.

2 *sable* I.e., black.

3 *Yankee Doodle* Famous Revolutionary-era marching song, originally sung by the British to mock colonial American troops and later appropriated by Americans as a patriotic anthem.

Abraham Lincoln, Address at Sanitary Fair, Baltimore, Maryland, 18 April 1864

> Sanitary Fairs were fundraising events on behalf of the United States Sanitary Commission, an organization dedicated to helping sick and wounded U.S. Army soldiers. President Lincoln gave the speech excerpted here at a Sanitary Fair in Baltimore—the biggest city in the border state of Maryland, a slave state that had remained in the Union—on 18 April 1864, seven months before he faced and won re-election.

Ladies and Gentlemen—Calling to mind that we are in Baltimore, we cannot fail to note that the world moves. Looking upon these many people, assembled here, to serve, as they best may, the soldiers of the Union, it occurs at once that three years ago, the same soldiers could not so much as pass through Baltimore.[1] The change from then till now is both great, and gratifying. Blessings on the brave men who have wrought the change, and the fair women who strive to reward them for it.

But Baltimore suggests more than could happen within Baltimore. The change within Baltimore is part only of a far wider change. When the war began, three years ago, neither party, nor any man, expected it would last till now. Each looked for the end, in some way, long ere today. Neither did any anticipate that domestic slavery would be much affected by the war. But here we are; the war has not ended, and slavery has been much affected—how much needs not now to be recounted. So true is it that man proposes, and God disposes.

But we can see the past, though we may not claim to have directed it; and seeing it, in this case, we feel more hopeful and confident for the future.

The world has never had a good definition of the word liberty, and the American people, just now, are much in want of one. We all declare for liberty; but in using the same *word* we do not all mean the same *thing*. With some the word liberty may mean for each man to do as he pleases with himself, and the product of his labor; while with others the same word may mean for some men to do as they please with other men, and the product of other men's labor. Here are two, not only different, but incompatible things, called by the same name—liberty. And it follows that each of the things is, by the respective parties, called by two different and incompatible names—liberty and tyranny.

The shepherd drives the wolf from the sheep's throat, for which the sheep thanks the shepherd as a *liberator*, while the wolf denounces him for the same act as the destroyer of liberty, especially as the sheep was a black one. Plainly the sheep and the wolf are not agreed upon a definition of the word liberty; and precisely the same difference prevails today among us human creatures, even in the North, and all professing to love liberty. Hence we behold the processes by which thousands are daily passing from under the yoke of bondage, hailed by some as the advance of liberty, and bewailed by others as the destruction of all liberty. Recently, as it seems, the people of Maryland have been doing something to define liberty; and thanks to them that, in what they have done, the wolf's dictionary has been repudiated.

It is not very becoming for one in my position to make speeches at great length; but there is another subject upon which I feel that I ought to say a word. A painful rumor, true I fear, has reached us of the massacre, by the rebel forces, at Fort Pillow, in the West end of Tennessee, on the Mississippi River, of some three hundred colored soldiers and white officers, who had just been overpowered by their assailants.[2] There seems to be some anxiety in the public mind whether the government is doing its duty to the colored soldier, and to the service, at this point. At the beginning of the war, and for some time, the use of colored troops

---

[1]   *three years ... Baltimore*   Because Maryland was a slave state, much of its population—especially at the start of the Civil War—sympathized with the Confederacy and opposed military action against it. On 19 April 1861 (almost exactly three years before Lincoln's speech), an anti-war and pro-Confederate mob of Baltimore citizens attacked the 6th Massachusetts Militia, a Union unit on its way to Washington, D.C. in response to Lincoln's initial call for troops to put down the Southern rebellion, as it was passing through the city. In the ensuing violence, four soldiers and twelve Baltimore civilians were killed—the first deaths of the Civil War.

[2]   *the massacre ... assailants*   On 12 April 1864, Confederates under General Nathan Bedford Forrest (later one of the first leaders of the Ku Klux Klan) captured Fort Pillow, a Union fortification garrisoned by both white and black troops. The majority of the fort's garrison surrendered; most of the white Union troops were taken prisoner, most of the black troops (and some of their white officers) massacred.

was not contemplated; and how the change of purpose was wrought, I will not now take time to explain. Upon a clear conviction of duty I resolved to turn that element of strength to account; and I am responsible for it to the American people, to the Christian world, to history, and on my final account to God. Having determined to use the negro as a soldier, there is no way but to give him all the protection given to any other soldier. The difficulty is not in stating the principle, but in practically applying it. It is a mistake to suppose the government is indifferent to this matter, or is not doing the best it can in regard to it. We do not today *know* that a colored soldier, or white officer commanding colored soldiers, has been massacred by the rebels when made a prisoner. We fear it, believe it, I may say, but we do not *know* it. To take the life of one of their prisoners, on the assumption that they murder ours, when it is short of certainty that they do murder ours, might be too serious, too cruel a mistake. We are having the Fort Pillow affair thoroughly investigated; and such investigation will probably show conclusively how the truth is. If, after all that has been said, it shall turn out that there has been no massacre at Fort Pillow, it will be almost safe to say there has been none, and will be none elsewhere. If there has been the massacre of three hundred there, or even the tenth part of three hundred, it will be conclusively proved; and being so proved, the retribution shall as surely come. It will be matter of grave consideration in what exact course to apply the retribution; but in the supposed case, it must come.

anonymous, "The Voices of the Guns" (c. 1865)

This poem's author and date of composition are unknown; however, the reconciliatory sentiments it expresses were common in the work of white Northern writers at the end of the war and in its aftermath. The text given here is based on that printed in *Bugle-Echoes: A Collection of the Poetry of the Civil War, Northern and Southern* (1886).

Within a green and shadowy wood,
  Circled with Spring, alone I stood:
The nook was peaceful, fair, and good.

The wild-plum blossoms lured the bees,
5 The birds sang madly in the trees,
Magnolia scents were on the breeze.

All else was silent; but the ear
Caught sounds of distant bugle clear,
And heard the bullets whistle near—

10 When from the winding river's shore
The Rebel guns began to roar,
And ours to answer, thundering o'er;

And, echoed from the wooded hill,
Repeated and repeated still,
15 Through all my soul they seemed to thrill;

For, as their rattling storm awoke,
And loud and fast the discord broke,
In rude° and trenchant *words* they spoke: *harsh, rough*

"*We hate!*" boomed fiercely o'er the tide;
20 "*We fear not!*" from the other side;
"*We strike!*" the Rebel guns replied.

Quick roared our answer: "We defend!"
"*Our rights!*" the battle-sounds contend;
"The rights of all!" we answer send.

25 "*We conquer!*" rolled across the wave;
"We persevere!" our answer gave;
"*Our chivalry!*" they wildly rave.

"*Ours are the brave!*" "Be ours the free!"
"*Be ours the slave, the masters we!*"
30 "On us their blood no more shall be!"

As when some magic word is spoken
By which a wizard spell is broken,
There was a silence at that token.

The wild birds dared once more to sing,
35 I heard the pine bough's whispering,

And trickling of a silver spring.

Then, crashing forth with smoke and din,
Once more the rattling sounds begin;
Our iron lips roll forth: "We win!"

40 And dull and wavering in the gale
That rushed in gusts across the vale
Came back the faint reply: "*We fail!*"

And then a word, both stern and sad,
From throat of huge Columbiad:[1]
45 "Blind fools and traitors! Ye are mad!"

Again the Rebel answer came,
Muffled and slow, as if in shame:
"*All, all is lost!*" in smoke and flame.

Now bold and strong and stern as Fate
50 The Union guns sound forth: "We wait!"
Faint comes the distant cry: "*Too late!*"

"Return, return!" our cannon said;
And, as the smoke rolled overhead,
"*We dare not!*" was the answer dread.

55 Then came a sound both loud and clear,
A Godlike word of hope and cheer:
"Forgiveness!" echoed far and near;

As when beside some death-bed still
We watch, and wait God's solemn will,
60 A bluebird warbles his soft trill.

I clenched my teeth at that blessed word,
And, angry, muttered, "Not so, Lord!
The only answer is the sword!"

I thought of Shiloh's[2] tainted air,

65 Of Richmond's prisons,[3] foul and bare,
And murdered heroes, young and fair—

Of block[4] and lash and overseer,
And dark, mild faces pale with fear,
Of baying hell-hounds panting near.

70 But then the gentle story told
My childhood in the days of old
Rang out its lessons manifold.

O prodigal and lost! arise,
And read the welcome blessed that lies
75 In a kind Father's patient eyes!

Thy elder brother grudges not
The lost and found should share his lot,
And wrong in concord be forgot.[5]

Thus mused I, as the hours went by,
80 Till the relieving guard drew nigh,
And there was challenge and reply.[6]

And as I hastened back to line,
It seemed an omen half divine
That "Concord" was the countersign.

---

1   *Columbiad* Type of heavy cannon. The name also evokes "Columbia," the female personification of the United States, as well as the title of several epic poems about America written in the late eighteenth or early nineteenth centuries, including Joel Barlow's *The Columbiad* (1807).

2   *Shiloh* Site of a bloody two-day battle in Tennessee in April 1862—the battle that first made clear to both sides how hard and costly the war would be.

3   *Richmond's prisons* Several Confederate prisoner-of-war camps were located in Richmond, Virginia; they gained notoriety in the North for their harsh conditions, which caused the deaths of many of the Union soldiers imprisoned there.

4   *block* I.e., auction block for selling enslaved people.

5   *But then … forgot* Reference to Jesus' famous Parable of the Prodigal Son, which Jesus tells after being criticized for receiving and eating with sinners. The parable concerns the younger son of a wealthy landowner, who squanders his inheritance on dissolute living. He repents and returns home, telling his father "I have sinned against heaven, and in thy sight, and am no more worthy to be called your son" and requesting to be treated like a hired servant, but his father greets him joyfully and arranges a banquet to celebrate his return. This, however, angers the prodigal's older brother, who has been working loyally for their father without reward; in response, the father tells him that it is right for them to celebrate, because "this thy brother … was lost, and is found." See Luke 15.11–32.

6   *challenge and reply* I.e., the speaker was challenged by the relieving guard to prove that he was on the same side and had to respond with the correct password ("the countersign").

Sarah E. Shuften, "Ethiopia's Dead" (1865)

Sarah E. Shuften was the wife of John T. Shuften (born 1840), who in 1865, in his hometown of Augusta, Georgia, founded *The Colored American*—the first African American newspaper published in the state. "Ethiopia's Dead" was printed in *The Colored American* on 30 December 1865.

A tribute to the memory of her sons who have fallen in the great struggle for liberty and independence.

Brave hearts! brave Ethiopia's[1] dead
On hills, in valleys lie,
On every field of strife, made red
   With gory victory.

5 Each valley, where the battle poured
   Its purple swelling tide,
Beheld brave Ethiopia's sword
   With slaughter deeply dyed.

Their bones bleach on the Southern hill,
10   And on the Southern plain,
By brook and river, lake and rill,°   *stream*
   And by the roaring main.°   *ocean*

The land is holy where they fought,
   And holy where they fell;
15 For by their blood, that land was bought,
   That land they loved so well—
Then glory to that valiant band,
   The honored saviors of the land.

Oh! few and weak their numbers were,
20   A handful of brave men,
But up to God they sent their prayer,
   And rushed to battle, then
The God of battle heard their cry,
   And crowned their deeds with victory.

25 From east to west, from hill to vale,
   Then be their names adored—

Europe, with all thy millions, hail!
   The Peace bought by their sword.

Asia, and Africa shall ring
30   From shore to shore, their fame;
And fair Columbia[2] shall sing,
   Their glory, and their name.

Peace, with her olive branch, shall spread
   Her wings, o'er sea and shore,
35 And hearts no more with terror dread
   The battle's clashing roar.

Fair Afric's° *free* and valiant sons,   *Africa's*
   Shall join with Europe's band,[3]
To celebrate in varied tongues,
40   Our *free* and happy land

Till freedom's golden fingers trace,
   A line that knows no end,
And man shall meet in every face,
   A brother and a friend.

Henry Timrod, "Ode Sung on the Occasion of Decorating the Graves of the Confederate Dead, at Magnolia Cemetery, Charleston, S.C." (1866)

Born in Charleston, South Carolina, Henry Timrod (1828–67) published in 1859 a volume of poems that was well-received in both the North and the South. After South Carolina's secession, however, he became one of the primary poetic voices for the secessionist cause. Unable to serve in the military because of poor health, he instead contributed fiery pro-Southern poems that led to him being dubbed the "Poet Laureate of the Confederacy." The secessionist states' defeat, together with the death of his infant son in the fall of 1865, devastated Timrod and contributed to his early death in 1867.

---

1 *Ethiopia* In the mid-nineteenth century, the name "Ethiopia" was used to refer generally to all of Africa, and to all people of African descent.

2 *Columbia* Personification of America.

3 *Europe's band* I.e., the collective body of Americans of European descent.

This poem was first published in the *Charleston Daily Courier* on 18 June 1866; the text given below is based on the revised version of the poem that was printed in the same paper, at Timrod's request, on 23 July.

Sleep sweetly in your humble graves,
  Sleep, martyrs of a fallen cause!—
Though yet no marble column craves
  The pilgrim here to pause.

5 In seeds of laurels[1] in the earth,
  The garlands of your fame are sown;
And, somewhere, waiting for its birth,
  The shaft is in the stone.[2]

Meanwhile, your sisters for the years
10   Which hold in trust your storied° tombs,   *inscribed*
Bring all they now can give you—tears,
  And these memorial blooms.

Small tributes, but your shades will smile
  As proudly on these wreaths today,
15 As when some cannon-moulded[3] pile°   *large edifice*
  Shall overlook this Bay.[4]

Stoop, angels, hither from the skies!
  There is no holier spot of ground,
Than where defeated valor lies
20   By mourning beauty crowned.

---

[1] *laurels* In ancient Greece and Rome, laurel wreaths were given in recognition of high achievement in poetic or athletic competition and in battle.

[2] *The shaft is in the stone* I.e., the shaft of the future memorial column that will be raised for the dead soldiers already exists within the stone out of which it will be carved.

[3] *cannon-moulded* I.e., featuring images of cannon on its mouldings (decorative strips commonly found, in classical architecture, on or just above the columns of a building or monument).

[4] *this Bay* Charleston Harbor, where the Civil War began on 12 April 1861 when Confederate artillery fired on Fort Sumter, a federal military installation in the harbor.

Sarah Piatt, Poems

Although she was largely forgotten for many decades after her death in 1919, Sarah Morgan Bryan Piatt (1836–1919) was, during her lifetime, a prolific and widely read writer; she published eighteen volumes of poetry (two coauthored with her husband), and her work was printed in leading literary magazines on both sides of the Atlantic. Born and raised in Kentucky to a family that owned enslaved people, she married a Northerner, the Ohioan John James Piatt, in the summer of 1861 and settled with him in Washington, D.C., where he worked for the U.S. Treasury Department and where the couple lived for the duration of the Civil War. Piatt's consequent ambivalence and divided loyalties, as a Southern-born writer married to a Northerner and living and working in the federal capital, influenced much of the poetry she wrote about the war and its aftermath, including the examples printed below.

Piatt is increasingly recognized as a major figure in nineteenth-century American poetry, for the complexity and depth of the feelings her poems give voice to as well as for their formal qualities. Her dialogue poems and dramatic monologues have been particularly praised for their subtle yet powerful expressiveness, and her handling of rhythm and rhyme—though often lacking in conventionally "musical" qualities—is extraordinarily assured. In her own time Piatt's sometimes "wayward, abrupt, and enigmatic" way with words made some reviewers uncomfortable—as did the bleak views she often voiced regarding marriage and family, and the overarching pessimism she frequently expressed about life itself. Twenty-first-century readers have been more open to that pessimism, and have embraced the enigmatic quality of much of her poetry; the Piatt poems that make readers uncomfortable today are not her more bleak or enigmatic works, but rather the handful of her poems—"The Old Slave-Music" among them—that give voice to what many feel to be highly inappropriate or misguided feelings of nostalgia regarding the lives of enslaved and formerly enslaved black people.

A much larger selection of Piatt's poems can be found in the website portion of this anthology volume.

Hearing the Battle—July 21, 1861[1] (1864)

One day in the dreamy summer,
   On the Sabbath hills, from afar
We heard the solemn echoes
   Of the first fierce words of war.

5 Ah, tell me, thou veilèd Watcher
   Of the storm and the calm to come,
How long by the sun or shadow
   Till these noises again are dumb.°   *silent*

And soon in a hush and glimmer
10   We thought of the dark, strange fight,
Whose close in a ghastly quiet
   Lay dim in the beautiful night.

Then we talked of coldness and pallor,
   And of things with blinded eyes
15 That stared at the golden stillness
   Of the moon in those lighted skies;

And of souls, at morning wrestling
   In the dust with passion and moan,
So far away at evening
20   In the silence of worlds unknown.

But a delicate wind beside us
   Was rustling the dusky hours,
As it gathered the dewy odors
   Of the snowy jessamine-flowers.

25 And I gave you a spray of the blossoms,
   And said: "I shall never know
How the hearts in the land are breaking,
   My dearest, unless you go."

Army of Occupation (1866)
At Arlington,[2] 1866

The summer blew its little drifts of sound—
   Tangled with wet leaf-shadows and the light
Small breath of scattered morning buds—around
The yellow path through which our footsteps wound.
5   Below, the Capitol rose glittering white.

There stretched a sleeping army. One by one,
   They took their places until thousands met;
No leader's stars flashed on before, and none
Leaned on his sword or staggered with his gun—
10   I wonder if their feet have rested yet!

They saw the dust, they joined the moving mass,
   They answered the fierce music's cry for blood,
Then straggled here and lay down in the grass—
Wear flowers for such, shores whence their feet did
   pass;
15   Sing tenderly; O river's haunted flood!

They had been sick, and worn, and weary, when
   They stopped on this calm hill beneath the trees:
Yet if, in some red-clouded dawn, again
The country should be calling to her men,
20   Shall the reveille[3] not remember these?

Around them underneath the mid-day skies
   The dreadful phantoms of the living walk,
And by low moons and darkness with their cries—
The mothers, sisters, wives with faded eyes,
25   Who call still names amid their broken talk.

And there is one who comes alone and stands
   At his dim fireless hearth—chilled and oppressed

---

[2] *Arlington* Arlington County, Virginia, just across the Potomac River from Washington, D.C., was the location, before the Civil War, of the plantation of Mary Anna Randolph Custis Lee, the daughter of George Washington's adopted son, and her husband Robert E. Lee, who during the Civil War became the secessionist states' main military commander. The U.S. Army occupied the plantation early in the war, and in 1864 it was chosen as the site of a new cemetery for the U.S. Army's war dead—partly so that Lee and his family could never again live there. This cemetery formed the basis for the present-day Arlington National Cemetery.

[3] *reveille* Drum beat or bugle call to awaken troops.

---

[1] *July 21, 1861* Date of the First Battle of Bull Run (called the First Battle of Manassas in the South), the first major military engagement of the Civil War; it ended in a resounding federal defeat.

By Something he had summoned to his lands,
While the weird pallor of its many hands
30   Points to his rusted sword in his own breast!

The Old Slave-Music (1873)

Blow back the breath of the bird,
    Scatter the song through the air,
There was music you never heard,
    And cannot hear anywhere.

5 It was not the sob of the vain
    In the old, old dark so sweet
(I shall never hear it again),
    Nor the coming of fairy feet.

It was music and music alone,
10   Not a sigh from a lover's mouth;
Now it comes in a phantom moan
    From the dead and buried South.

It was savage and fierce and glad,
    It played with the heart at will;

15 Oh, what a wizard° touch it had—   *magic*
    Oh, if I could hear it still!

Were they slaves? They were not then;
    The music had made them free.
They were happy women and men—
20   What more do we care to be?

There is blood and blackness and dust,
    There are terrible things to see,
There are stories of swords that rust,
    Between that music and me.

25 Dark ghosts with your ghostly tunes
    Come back till I laugh through tears;
Dance under the sunken moons,
    Dance over the grassy years!

Hush, hush—I know it, I say;
30   Your armies were bright and brave,
But the music they took away
    Was worth—whatever they gave.

WALT WHITMAN
1819 – 1892

Walt Whitman forged a radical and fundamentally American poetics that would come to inspire generations of writers and social reformers. His work communicates a democratic vision that is at once spiritual, sexual, and political, one that embraces the dignity of the human body and the dignity of working-class labor. His poetic "I" claimed to speak for and to channel the full swath of society—plants and animals as well as all people, including, especially, the marginalized. During Whitman's life, public reception of his work was frequently mixed; while many readers applauded him for his innovative style and bold choice of subject matter, those same innovations of form and theme caused many more conservative readers to take affront, and Whitman frequently faced the threat of obscenity charges throughout his career. Today, he is broadly considered one of the most influential writers in American literary history, as well as one of the most beloved. While readers and critics across the world continue to connect passionately with Whitman's democratic vision and linguistic virtuosity, since the late-twentieth century they have also brought nuanced criticism to bear on his poetry, journalism, and correspondence, particularly on the subjects of race and American expansionism.

Walter Whitman was born into a Long Island family with Quaker ties in May 1819, the second of Walter and Louisa Van Velsor Whitman's eight surviving children. The family moved to Brooklyn in 1823, as Walter Sr., a carpenter and farmer by trade, undertook to engage in the city's booming real estate market. As a young man, Whitman had a somewhat strained relationship with his father, an enthusiastic Democrat and free thinker whom he respected but also found to be stern and occasionally tyrannical. Whitman's relationship to his mother was much warmer; they would remain close well into Whitman's adulthood.

Whitman received only minimal formal schooling in Brooklyn before beginning a series of apprenticeships at the age of eleven, first with a stint as a lawyer's assistant and later as a printer for the Long Island *Patriot*, a Democrat newspaper. His experience at the *Patriot* helped cultivate his commitment to the Northern Democratic Party and to its urban, working-class (and mostly white) constituency. His early newspaper work also trained him in the art of typesetting—which he would later put to use in self-publishing *Leaves of Grass*—and granted him a platform for his first articles and short stories. Whitman developed a strong attachment to the city and remained in Brooklyn even after the rest of his family returned to rural Long Island in 1833. In his free time, he attended the theater and public lectures, visited museums and galleries, and read widely from circulating libraries, developing a taste in particular for popular novelists such as James Fenimore Cooper and the Scottish Sir Walter Scott. Still, it was journalism, which he came to see as the lifeblood of a healthy democracy, that would be the formative influence on his early career.

Strained financial circumstances, stemming in part from the national recession of 1837, induced Whitman to switch careers at the age of seventeen, when he moved back to Long Island to work as a schoolteacher. This initiated a period of profound depression: Whitman didn't enjoy being cut off from the intellectual energy of Brooklyn, and he felt lonely, describing himself to a friend as "forsaken of all God's creation." While teaching, Whitman maintained his connection to the literary world by writing poems and short stories, some of which he published in a variety of periodicals (and some of which he seems to have taught in his classes). Little in this early work indicates the stylistic and thematic innovation that would be a hallmark of his later work; much of it is sentimental, moralistic, and stylistically conventional. His first novel, *Franklin Evans, or the Inebriate*, was published in 1842; a temperance novel, the work was later dismissed by Whitman as having been written during a fit of drunkenness. Whatever its origin, the novel proved quite successful; in fact, it sold more copies than any individual edition of *Leaves of Grass* ever would during Whitman's lifetime.

By 1841, Whitman was able to quit teaching and again leave Long Island, first for New York City and later for his beloved Brooklyn. He attended lectures by the likes of Ralph Waldo Emerson, and it was also during this period that Whitman became enamored of the opera, which he would later describe as a foundational influence on his poetry. Throughout much of the duration of the Mexican–American War (1846–48), Whitman was chief editor of the Brooklyn *Eagle*, a daily aligned with the presiding Democratic Party. In that role, Whitman wrote numerous editorials in support of the controversial conflict, through which the United States aimed to expand its territorial claims into the southwest. Though Whitman shared the fears of many northerners that a U.S. victory in the war would result in the further expansion of slavery into the newly acquired territories, his enthusiasm for western expansion and the ideals of Manifest Destiny dominated; as he put it in an 1846 editorial: "Mexico must be thoroughly chastised!"

By 1848 Whitman had become a supporter of the new Free Soil Party, established by northern Democrats disenchanted with their party's refusal to challenge slavery. Whitman's increasingly vocal condemnations of the institution led the *Eagle* to dismiss him from his editorial role in early 1848. Mere weeks later, a chance encounter with a Louisiana journalist resulted in an offer of work at the *Crescent*, a newly established New Orleans paper. Whitman ventured south in February. Though his time at the *Crescent* ultimately lasted only a few months, the experience was, by all accounts, personally transformative. Basking in the racially, culturally, linguistically, and religiously diverse community of New Orleans, Whitman also witnessed at close range the unforgettable horrors of the domestic slave trade—for which New Orleans functioned as a key port. Many biographers have also speculated that Whitman's New Orleans experience included a passionate love affair with a man, suggested most strongly by the unpublished manuscript version of the poem eventually titled "Once I Pass'd Through a Populous City."

Scholars have long puzzled over the origins of *Leaves of Grass*, for whose stylistic innovations there appears to have been little precedent in Whitman's writing prior to 1855; for some, the New Orleans experience is a plausible answer to part of the mystery. Some scholars have also suggested that the tense social climate growing out of the Compromise of 1850 and the Fugitive Slave Law—widely seen by even proslavery northerners as an unacceptable concession to the southern slave states—led to Whitman's political and creative ideals becoming more radical in the early 1850s; his new poetry would feature a more active imaginative engagement with the theme of racial equality. Later in life Whitman remembered his literary development as follows: "At the age of thirty-one to thirty-three, a desire that had been flitting through my previous life, or hovering on the flanks, mostly indefinite hitherto, had steadily advanced to the front, defined itself, and finally dominated everything else."

The first edition of *Leaves of Grass* was published, at Whitman's expense, in late June 1855. It featured a lengthy prose preface, clearly influenced by Emerson's 1844 essay "The Poet," establishing his cultural project and his conviction that "the United States themselves are essentially the greatest poem." The volume included twelve as-yet untitled poems, whose unrhymed, unmetered, and expansively long lines were unlike almost anything that had been seen in English literature to that date. Whitman's name appeared neither on the book's elegantly leather-bound and embossed cover nor on its title page, but only in the body of the opening poem eventually titled "Song of Myself," in which the speaker declares himself to be "Walt Whitman, an American, one of the roughs, a kosmos."

Reviews were relatively slow to appear—though they were not, as has often been assumed, predominantly negative. The first, by prominent critic Charles A. Dana, was moderately positive. An anonymous reviewer for *Life Illustrated* enthusiastically described *Leaves of Grass* as "like no other book that ever was written," describing its poems as "lines of rhythmical prose, or a series of *utterances* (we know not what else to call them), unconnected, curious, and original." Still, dissatisfied with the book's initial reception,

Whitman soon took matters into his own hands and began submitting anonymous reviews himself: "Not a borrower from other lands, but a prodigal user of his own land is Walt Whitman," declares one he wrote for the *American Phrenological Journal* in October. Another memorably opens, "An American bard at last!" Whitman also sent a copy of the collection to Emerson, who gratified the poet with an enthusiastic and congratulatory letter, calling *Leaves of Grass* "the most extraordinary piece of wit and wisdom that America has yet contributed." The first truly negative review came in November from the notoriously harsh critic Rufus Griswold, who described the book as "a mass of stupid filth," and as the literary culmination of a transcendental philosophy that was "fast rotting the healthy core of all the social virtues." The book's transgressions were thematic at least as much as formal: Whitman's eagerness to express the poetic beauties of the human body, bodily functions, and sex provoked substantial controversy. On this front, the popular journalist and novelist Fanny Fern defended Whitman, declaring that "I extract no poison from these *Leaves*—to me they have brought only healing."

Whitman had begun writing additional material almost as soon as the first edition was released, and a second edition came out in autumn 1856. The new edition dispensed with the preface but added twenty new poems, expanding the previous ninety-five pages to well over three hundred. The poems were now given titles, and the back of the book contained a selection of reviews of the first edition—including Emerson's letter of congratulations (which was reprinted without Emerson's permission). The second edition still sold poorly, and Whitman's financial situation became strained, instigating a temporary return to journalism. During this period he also wrote the pamphlet *The Eighteenth Presidency!*, not published until 1928, which reveals his increasing anger at contemporary politics and at the continuation of slavery, calling on members of the white working class to "abolish slavery, or it will abolish you." He also penned a series of newspaper articles in September 1858 entitled "Manly Health and Training," a health manual and political manifesto arguing for the vitality of the body as the bedrock of a healthy democracy.

A third edition of *Leaves of Grass* appeared in 1860, this time initiated by an offer of publication from Thayer & Eldridge, Boston publishers with close ties to the abolitionist movement. With this edition Whitman aimed more than ever to make the work marketable, arranging his poems into thematic clusters and including several illustrations throughout the volume. The thematic clusters included "Enfans d'Adam" (later renamed "Children of Adam"), a sequence of poems centered on heterosexual love and procreation, which prompted new accusations of obscenity from more conservative readers, who were outraged at this frank discussion of women's desire that was not clearly contained within marriage. The new "Calamus" sequence, meanwhile, was a celebration of what Whitman called "manly love"—of what modern readers usually interpret as a romance. Some biographers have speculated that the "Calamus" poems originated from a love affair Whitman had with a man in the late 1850s, but the sequence provoked less controversy in a society that, while it condemned overt sexuality between men, was nonetheless accustomed to passionate expressions of male friendship. The poems today remain widely cherished for their moving depictions of emotional passion and physical affection between men. For all the controversy it did provoke, the third edition of *Leaves of Grass* was by far Whitman's most successful, selling upwards of four thousand copies.

The onset of the Civil War in 1861 prompted a swift change in the trajectory of Whitman's career and personal life. His first attempt at war poetry was "Beat! Beat! Drums!," a propagandistic piece intended to encourage new recruits to the Union Army; the poem was published in several prominent papers in September 1861. But Whitman's involvement in the war effort became substantially more direct after his brother George was wounded while fighting for the Union in December 1862. Whitman traveled to Virginia to find his brother, later describing his search among the wounded as "the greatest suffering I ever experienced in my life." George's wounds turned out to be minor, but the horror of the hospital environment was transformative for Whitman. He soon moved to Washington, D.C., taking on a part-time job as a clerk in the Union paymaster's office that allowed him to spend the rest of his time volunteering at nearby military hospitals. Whitman offered practical service as a nurse but also endeavored to offer friendship and emotional support to the wounded, reading to them, helping them write letters home, and developing in many cases passionate attachments. His experiences deeply informed a new work of poetry, *Drum-Taps*, first published as an independent volume in 1865 and incorporated into later editions of *Leaves of Grass*. Whitman later published prose accounts of his time in the military hospitals, which he collected under the title *Memoranda During the War* (1875) and later incorporated into the autobiographical *Specimen Days & Collect* (1882), a narrative composed of personal sketches, essays, and notes touching on the poet's life from childhood to the year 1880.

Drum-Taps was already at press when the news broke of Lincoln's assassination in April 1865. Whitman, who had by then developed (if at first grudgingly) a profound admiration for the Republican president, wrote several elegies for him, including "When Lilacs Last in the Dooryard Bloom'd." These were added to *Sequel to Drum-Taps*, published shortly after the first volume. Whitman remained in Washington after the end of the war, where he maintained government employment until the 1870s, while continuing to expand and revise *Leaves of Grass*, which was reissued in further editions in 1867 and 1871.

In 1867 Whitman began composing the essays that would eventually form the pamphlet *Democratic Vistas* (1871). The work expressed his frustration at the inequality and cultural vapidity he saw at the heart of Reconstruction-era America, as well as his enduring hopes that literature would ultimately lift the nation out of moral and political stagnation. On some of the central questions of the Reconstruction, however—namely, African American citizenship and suffrage—Whitman adopted a highly conservative stance, describing universal suffrage as a "danger" and expressing doubts about the ability of African Americans to participate fully in American society; he appears also to have had little to say about the dramatic upsurge of racial violence that began in the late 1860s. While Whitman was a committed abolitionist, and while he embraced and promoted the idea that America should be open to immigrants of all backgrounds, he did express in his journalism and correspondence racist views about African Americans and about America's Indigenous peoples, who he imagined would gradually disappear as their lands were colonized, giving way to a United States shaped by, and belonging to, the white working class. Twenty-first-century scholars working with the critical lenses of race, gender, sexuality, ability, and the environment, have contributed to a reassessment of Whitman that acknowledges his limitations, revealing a poet who broke through many—but not all—of the prejudices of his own time. Before his death Whitman reflected upon, and regretted, some of his earlier views: "After all I may have been tainted a bit, just a little bit," he wrote, with the pernicious racism that suffused his culture, "yet I have been anti-slavery always—was then and am now: and to all and any other slaveries, too, black or white, mental or physical." Whitman suffered a stroke in 1873, prompting him to travel to New Jersey, where many of his family members now resided. Whitman's mother died only days after his arrival, an event that devastated him. Physically weakened, he moved in with his brother George and his wife in a working-class neighborhood in Camden, where he would reside for the following decade.

Personal tragedies notwithstanding, as an artist and public figure Whitman's prospects had by now improved substantially. Over the course of the 1870s and 80s he became a regular correspondent of various intellectuals both at home and abroad, having developed an enthusiastic following in Britain in particular. In the early 1870s his correspondents included English critic John Addington Symonds, an early scholar of homosexuality and one of the first writers to prominently suggest that the "Calamus" poems were expressive of what he termed "Greek love"—a suggestion that Whitman ardently denied. Despite his increased prominence, Whitman was wounded by the omission of his work from a number of prominent literary anthologies around this time, most notably from Emerson's collection *Parnassus* (1874). Such omissions prompted his anonymous submission in 1876 of "Walt Whitman's Actual American Position" to the *West Jersey Press*, which claimed that his work had been systematically vilified and ignored by the American literary establishment.

The poems in the 1881–82 edition of *Leaves of Grass* appeared in their final versions and arrangement. Whitman suffered another stroke in 1888, after which his physical condition deteriorated significantly. In his final year he worked on what is commonly termed the "Deathbed Edition" of *Leaves of Grass* (1891), identical to the 1881 edition but for the inclusion of two more poem clusters, which he termed "annexes," at the end of the volume; he also worked on compiling his *Complete Prose Works*, published in 1892. Whitman died of complications resulting from pneumonia in March 1892, at the age of seventy-two.

During his lifetime and after his death, Whitman became an icon of democratic poetics and politics, the quintessential "outsider," a queer, working-class writer who made his own books and worked on the margins of elite literary culture. In the words of poet June Jordan, he is "the one white father who shares the systematic disadvantages of his heterogenous offspring." He became a central figure in emerging Anglo-American gay culture, with British writers such as Edward Carpenter and John Addington Symonds viewing him as a prophet heralding a new, modern sexuality that would be divested of shame and would include the liberation of homoerotic desire. In the twentieth century he was revered as a radical, inclusive, antiracist poet who celebrated the working class. He had a profound influence, for example, on many Harlem Renaissance, modernist, Beat, and queer writers, such as Langston Hughes, Alain Locke, Jean Toomer, T.S. Eliot, H.D., Wallace Stevens, Hart Crane, Adrienne Rich, and Allen Ginsberg, who wrote that "Whitman's exposure of a new self of man or woman empowered every particular soul who heard his long breathed inspiration." Whitman's influence has also stretched to poets around the world, particularly in Latin and South America and in Europe, including Federico García Lorca and Pablo Neruda. While our understanding of Whitman as a person and writer grows ever more nuanced and complex, his poems continue to act as a catalyst for a new generation of artists, which was just what Whitman himself called for: "I am a man who, sauntering along without fully stopping, turns a casual look upon you and then averts his face, / Leaving it to you to prove and define it, / Expecting the main things from you."

———

NOTE ON THE TEXTS: The texts of the poems presented below are based on the 1881 version of *Leaves of Grass*, with two exceptions: the poem later titled "Song of Myself," which we have included in its untitled 1855 version, and the sequence "Live Oak, with Moss," which was not published in Whitman's lifetime and which is here presented based on the notebook manuscript of 1859. By 1881, "Song of Myself" had undergone numerous revisions, including being divided by Whitman into fifty-two numbered sections; for ease of reference, and to accommodate those readers more familiar with the 1881 text, we include section numbers in the left-hand margins of the 1855 text roughly where they appear in the 1881 version.

Given the evidence of intentional idiosyncrasies of spelling and punctuation on Whitman's part, we have in his case departed from this anthology's conventional practice of modernizing spelling and punctuation. We have departed as well from our usual two-column format for Whitman's poetry; printing Whitman's often very long lines in two-column format would lead to a distracting number of line breaks.

We are deeply indebted to the Whitman Archive (whitmanarchive.org) for making facsimiles of *Leaves of Grass* in the various editions published during Whitman's lifetime freely available online.

⌘ ⌘ ⌘

from *1855 Leaves of Grass* [*Preface*]

America does not repel the past or what it has produced under its forms or amid other politics or the idea of castes[1] or the old religions . . . . accepts the lesson with calmness . . . is not so impatient as has been supposed that the slough[2] still sticks to opinions and manners and literature while the life which served its requirements has passed into the new life of the new forms . . . perceives that the corpse is slowly borne from the eating and sleeping rooms of the house . . . perceives that it waits a little while in the door . . . that it was fittest for its days . . . that its action has descended to the stalwart and wellshaped heir who approaches . . . and that he shall be fittest for his days.

The Americans of all nations at any time upon the earth have probably the fullest poetical nature. The United States themselves are essentially the greatest poem. In the history of the earth hitherto the largest and most stirring appear tame and orderly to their ampler largeness and stir. Here at last is something in the doings of man that corresponds with the broadcast doings of the day and night. Here is not merely a nation but a teeming nation of nations. Here is action untied from strings necessarily blind to particulars and details magnificently moving in vast masses. Here is the hospitality which forever indicates heroes . . . . Here

———

[1] *castes* Hereditary social hierarchies.

[2] *slough* Mud, or the dead tissue that forms over a wound.

are the roughs and beards and space and ruggedness and nonchalance that the soul loves. Here the performance disdaining the trivial unapproached in the tremendous audacity of its crowds and groupings and the push of its perspective spreads with crampless and flowing breadth and showers its prolific and splendid extravagance. One sees it must indeed own the riches of the summer and winter, and need never be bankrupt while corn grows from the ground or the orchards drop apples or the bays contain fish or men beget children upon women.

Other states indicate themselves in their deputies . . . . but the genius of the United States is not best or most in its executives or legislatures, nor in its ambassadors or authors or colleges or churches or parlors, nor even in its newspapers or inventors . . . but always most in the common people. Their manners speech dress friendships—the freshness and candor of their physiognomy[1]—the picturesque looseness of their carriage . . . their deathless attachment to freedom—their aversion to anything indecorous or soft or mean[2]—the practical acknowledgment of the citizens of one state by the citizens of all other states—the fierceness of their roused resentment—their curiosity and welcome of novelty—their self-esteem and wonderful sympathy—their susceptibility to a slight[3]—the air they have of persons who never knew how it felt to stand in the presence of superiors—the fluency of their speech—their delight in music, the sure symptom of manly tenderness and native elegance of soul . . . their good temper and openhandedness—the terrible[4] significance of their elections—the President's taking off his hat to them not they to him—these too are unrhymed poetry. It awaits the gigantic and generous treatment worthy of it.

The largeness of nature or the nation were monstrous without a corresponding largeness and generosity of the spirit of the citizen. Not nature nor swarming states nor streets and steamships nor prosperous business nor farms nor capital nor learning may suffice for the ideal of man . . . nor suffice the poet. No reminiscences may suffice either. A live nation can always cut a deep

mark and can have the best authority the cheapest . . . namely from its own soul. This is the sum of the profitable uses of individuals or states and of present action and grandeur and of the subjects of poets.—As if it were necessary to trot back generation after generation to the eastern records! As if the beauty and sacredness of the demonstrable must fall behind that of the mythical! As if men do not make their mark out of any times! As if the opening of the western continent by discovery and what has transpired since in North and South America were less than the small theatre of the antique or the aimless sleepwalking of the middle ages! The pride of the United States leaves the wealth and finesse of the cities and all returns of commerce and agriculture and all the magnitude of geography or shows of exterior victory to enjoy the breed of full sized men or one full sized man unconquerable and simple.

The American poets are to enclose old and new for America is the race of races. Of them a bard[5] is to be commensurate with a people. To him the other continents arrive as contributions . . . he gives them reception for their sake and his own sake. His spirit responds to his country's spirit . . . . he incarnates its geography and natural life and rivers and lakes. Mississippi with annual freshets[6] and changing chutes, Missouri and Columbia and Ohio and Saint Lawrence with the falls and beautiful masculine Hudson, do not embouchure[7] where they spend themselves more than they embouchure into him. The blue breadth over the inland sea of Virginia and Maryland and the sea off Massachusetts and Maine and over Manhattan bay and over Champlain and Erie and over Ontario and Huron and Michigan and Superior, and over the Texan and Mexican and Floridian and Cuban seas and over the seas off California and Oregon, is not tallied by the blue breadth of the waters below more than the breadth of above and below is tallied by him. When the long Atlantic coast stretches longer and the Pacific coast stretches longer he easily stretches with them

---

[1] *physiognomy* Facial appearance (especially as considered to reveal one's personality).

[2] *mean* Small-minded.

[3] *slight* Insult.

[4] *terrible* I.e., awe-inspiring.

[5] *bard* Wandering poet or minstrel who records the important events of the day in verse.

[6] *freshets* Flooded areas or streams caused by heavy rainfall.

[7] *embouchure* As a noun, "embouchure" can refer to the mouth of a river or to the part of a wind instrument that touches the mouth of the player; Whitman here may be using it as a verb to mean "flow out."

north or south. He spans between them also from east to west and reflects what is between them. On him rise solid growths that offset the growths of pine and cedar and hemlock and liveoak[1] and locust and chestnut and cypress and hickory and limetree and cottonwood and tuliptree and cactus and wildvine and tamarind and persimmon . . . . and tangles as tangled as any canebrake[1] or swamp . . . . and forests coated with transparent ice and icicles hanging from the boughs and crackling in the wind . . . . and sides and peaks of mountains . . . . and pasturage sweet and free as savannah or upland or prairie . . . . with flights and songs and screams that answer those of the wildpigeon and highhold[2] and orchard-oriole and coot and surf-duck and redshouldered-hawk and fish-hawk and white-ibis and indian-hen and cat-owl and water-pheasant and qua-bird and pied-sheldrake[3] and blackbird and mockingbird and buzzard and condor and night-heron and eagle. To him the hereditary countenance descends both mother's and father's. To him enter the essences of the real things and past and present events—of the enormous diversity of temperature and agriculture and mines—the tribes of red aborigines—the weatherbeaten vessels entering new ports or making landings on rocky coasts—the first settlements north or south—the rapid stature and muscle—the haughty defiance of '76,[4] and the war and peace and formation of the constitution . . . . the union always surrounded by blatherers and always calm and impregnable—the perpetual coming of immigrants—the wharf hem'd cities and superior marine—the unsurveyed interior—the loghouses and clearings and wild animals and hunters and trappers . . . . the free commerce—the fisheries and whaling and gold-digging—the endless

gestation of new states—the convening of Congress every December,[5] the members duly coming up from all climates and the uttermost parts . . . . the noble character of the young mechanics and of all free American workmen and workwomen . . . . the general ardor and friendliness and enterprise—the perfect equality of the female with the male . . . . . the large amativeness[6]—the fluid movement of the population—the factories and mercantile life and laborsaving machinery—the Yankee swap[7]—the New-York firemen and the target excursion[8]—the southern plantation life—the character of the northeast and of the northwest and southwest—slavery and the tremulous spreading of hands to protect it, and the stern opposition to it which shall never cease till it ceases or the speaking of tongues and the moving of lips cease. For such the expression of the American poet is to be transcendant and new. It is to be indirect and not direct or descriptive or epic. Its quality goes through these to much more. Let the age and wars of other nations be chanted and their eras and characters be illustrated and that finish the verse. Not so the great psalm of the republic. Here the theme is creative and has vista. Here comes one among the wellbeloved stonecutters and plans with decision and science and sees the solid and beautiful forms of the future where there are now no solid forms.

Of all nations the United States with veins full of poetical stuff most needs poets and will doubtless have the greatest and use them the greatest. Their Presidents shall not be their common referee so much as their poets shall. Of all mankind the great poet is the equable man. Not in him but off from him things are grotesque or eccentric or fail of their sanity. Nothing out of its place is good and nothing in its place is bad. He bestows on every object or quality its fit proportions neither more nor less. He is the arbiter of the diverse

---

[1]   *liveoak* Evergreen oaks, primarily found in the southeastern United States; they often are draped with Spanish moss; *limetree* More commonly known as basswood or linden trees; *wildvine* Species of grapevine, also known as the fox grape; *tamarind* Grown commercially in southern Florida; *persimmon* American persimmon; *canebrake* Thicket of sugarcane.

[2]   *highhold* The northern flicker, a species of woodpecker.

[3]   *surf-duck* Surf scoter; *indian-hen* Pileated woodpecker; *cat-owl* Long-eared owl; *qua-bird* Black-crowned night heron; *pied-sheldrake* Likely a reference to the common shelduck.

[4]   *haughty defiance of '76* I.e., the signing of the Declaration of Independence in 1776.

[5]   *convening … December* Before 1933, Congress would convene on the first Monday in December.

[6]   *amativeness* Love, especially sexual love; the term is derived from the pseudo-science of phrenology, and in that context refers to an individual's alleged propensity for sexual passion.

[7]   *the Yankee swap* Trade of two dissimilar things, typically in which the item given away turns out to be worth considerably less than the one received.

[8]   *target excursion* Day-long excursion by the members of a local militia or gun-club for the purposes of target practice (often also an occasion for general merry-making).

and he is the key. He is the equalizer of his age and land . . . . he supplies what wants supplying and checks what wants checking. If peace is the routine out of him speaks the spirit of peace, large, rich, thrifty, building vast and populous cities, encouraging agriculture and the arts and commerce—lighting the study of man, the soul, immortality—federal, state or municipal government, marriage, health, freetrade, intertravel by land and sea . . . . nothing too close, nothing too far off . . . the stars not too far off. In war he is the most deadly force of the war. Who recruits him recruits horse and foot . . . he fetches parks of artillery[1] the best that engineer ever knew. If the time becomes slothful and heavy he knows how to arouse it . . . he can make every word he speaks draw blood. Whatever stagnates in the flat of custom or obedience or legislation he never stagnates. Obedience does not master him, he masters it. High up out of reach he stands turning a concentrated light . . . he turns the pivot with his finger[2] . . . he baffles the swiftest runners as he stands and easily overtakes and envelops them. The time straying toward infidelity and confections and persiflage[3] he withholds by his steady faith . . . he spreads out his dishes . . . he offers the sweet firmfibred meat that grows men and women. His brain is the ultimate brain. He is no arguer . . . he is judgment. He judges not as the judge judges but as the sun falling around a helpless thing. As he sees the farthest he has the most faith. His thoughts are the hymns of the praise of things. In the talk on the soul and eternity and God off of his equal plane he is silent. He sees eternity less like a play with a prologue and denouement . . . . he sees eternity in men and women . . . he does not see men and women as dreams or dots. Faith is the antiseptic of the soul . . . it pervades the common people and preserves them . . . they never give up believing and expecting and trusting. There is that indescribable freshness and unconsciousness about an illiterate person that humbles and mocks the power of the noblest expressive genius. The poet sees for a certainty how one not a great artist may be just as sacred and perfect as the greatest artist. . . . . . The power to destroy or remould is freely used by him but never the power of attack. What is past is past. If he does not expose superior models and prove himself by every step he takes he is not what is wanted. The presence of the greatest poet conquers . . . not parleying or struggling or any prepared attempts. Now he has passed that way see after him! there is not left any vestige of despair or misanthropy or cunning or exclusiveness or the ignominy of a nativity or color or delusion of hell or the necessity of hell . . . . . and no man thenceforward shall be degraded for ignorance or weakness or sin.

The greatest poet hardly knows pettiness or triviality. If he breathes into any thing that was before thought small it dilates with the grandeur and life of the universe. He is a seer . . . . he is individual . . . he is complete in himself . . . . the others are as good as he, only he sees it and they do not. He is not one of the chorus[4] . . . . he does not stop for any regulation . . . he is the president of regulation. What the eyesight does to the rest he does to the rest. Who knows the curious mystery of the eyesight? The other senses corroborate themselves, but this is removed from any proof but its own and foreruns the identities of the spiritual world. A single glance of it mocks all the investigations of man and all the instruments and books of the earth and all reasoning. What is marvellous? what is unlikely? what is impossible or baseless or vague? after you have once just opened the space of a peachpit and given audience to far and near and to the sunset and had all things enter with electric swiftness softly and duly without confusion or jostling or jam.

The land and sea, the animals fishes and birds, the sky of heaven and the orbs, the forests mountains and rivers, are not small themes . . . but folks expect of the poet to indicate more than the beauty and dignity which always attach to dumb[5] real objects . . . . they expect him to indicate the path between reality and their souls. Men and women perceive the beauty well enough . . probably as well as he. The passionate tenacity of hunters, woodmen, early risers, cultivators of gardens and orchards and fields, the love of healthy women for the manly form, seafaring persons, drivers of horses, the passion for light and the open

---

[1] *parks of artillery*   Artillery units.

[2] *High up . . . his finger* American poets are here likened to lighthouse keepers, who guide beams of light to illumine sections of dark sea and sky.

[3] *persiflage* Banter or light mockery.

[4] *chorus* In classical Greek theater, a group of performers who comment collectively on the action of the play.

[5] *dumb* Incapable of speech; silent.

air, all is an old varied sign of the unfailing perception of beauty and of a residence of the poetic in outdoor people. They can never be assisted by poets to perceive . . . . some may but they never can. The poetic quality is not marshalled in rhyme or uniformity or abstract addresses to things nor in melancholy complaints or good precepts, but is the life of these and much else and is in the soul. The profit of rhyme is that it drops seeds of a sweeter and more luxuriant rhyme, and of uniformity that it conveys itself into its own roots in the ground out of sight. The rhyme and uniformity of perfect poems show the free growth of metrical laws and bud from them as unerringly and loosely as lilacs or roses on a bush, and take shapes as compact as the shapes of chestnuts and oranges and melons and pears, and shed the perfume impalpable to form. The fluency and ornaments of the finest poems or music or orations or recitations are not independent but dependent. All beauty comes from beautiful blood and a beautiful brain. If the greatnesses are in conjunction in a man or woman it is enough . . . . the fact will prevail through the universe . . . . but the gaggery and gilt[1] of a million years will not prevail. Who troubles himself about his ornaments or fluency is lost. This is what you shall do: Love the earth and sun and the animals, despise riches, give alms to every one that asks, stand up for the stupid and crazy, devote your income and labor to others, hate tyrants, argue not concerning God, have patience and indulgence toward the people, take off your hat to nothing known or unknown or to any man or number of men, go freely with powerful uneducated persons and with the young and with the mothers of families, read these leaves in the open air every season of every year of your life, reexamine all you have been told at school or church or in any book, dismiss whatever insults your own soul, and your very flesh shall be a great poem and have the richest fluency not only in its words but in the silent lines of its lips and face and between the lashes of your eyes and in every motion and joint of your body . . . . The poet shall not spend his time in unneeded work. He shall know that the ground is always ready ploughed and manured . . . . others may not know it but he shall. He shall go directly to the creation. His trust shall master the trust of everything he touches . . . . and shall master all attachment.

The known universe has one complete lover and that is the greatest poet. He consumes an eternal passion and is indifferent which chance happens and which possible contingency of fortune or misfortune and persuades daily and hourly his delicious pay. What balks or breaks others is fuel for his burning progress to contact and amorous joy. Other proportions of the reception of pleasure dwindle to nothing to his proportions. All expected from heaven or from the highest he is rapport with in the sight of the daybreak or a scene of the winter woods or the presence of children playing or with his arm round the neck of a man or woman. His love above all love has leisure and expanse . . . . he leaves room ahead of himself. He is no irresolute or suspicious lover . . . he is sure . . . he scorns intervals. His experience and the showers and thrills are not for nothing. Nothing can jar him . . . . suffering and darkness cannot—death and fear cannot. To him complaint and jealousy and envy are corpses buried and rotten in the earth . . . . he saw them buried. The sea is not surer of the shore or the shore of the sea than he is of the fruition of his love and of all perfection and beauty.

The fruition of beauty is no chance of hit or miss . . . it is inevitable as life . . . . it is exact and plumb as gravitation. From the eyesight proceeds another eyesight and from the hearing proceeds another hearing and from the voice proceeds another voice eternally curious of the harmony of things with man. To these respond perfections not only in the committees that were supposed to stand for the rest but in the rest themselves just the same. These understand the law of perfection in masses and floods . . . that its finish is to each for itself and onward from itself . . . that it is profuse and impartial . . . that there is not a minute of the light or dark nor an acre of the earth or sea without it—nor any direction of the sky nor any trade or employment nor any turn of events. This is the reason that about the proper expression of beauty there is precision and balance . . . one part does not need to be thrust above another. The best singer is not the one who has the most lithe and powerful organ[2] . . . the pleasure of

---

[1] *gaggery* Deceit; *gilt* Thin layer of gold.

[2] *organ* I.e., organ of singing; voice.

poems is not in them that take the handsomest measure and similes and sound.

Without effort and without exposing in the least how it is done the greatest poet brings the spirit of any or all events and passions and scenes and persons some more and some less to bear on your individual character as you hear or read. To do this well is to compete with the laws that pursue and follow time. What is the purpose must surely be there and the clue of it must be there . . . . and the faintest indication is the indication of the best and then becomes the clearest indication. Past and present and future are not disjoined but joined. The greatest poet forms the consistence of what is to be from what has been and is. He drags the dead out of their coffins and stands them again on their feet . . . . he says to the past, Rise and walk before me that I may realize you. He learns the lesson . . . . he places himself where the future becomes present. The greatest poet does not only dazzle his rays over character and scenes and passions . . . he finally ascends and finishes all . . . he exhibits the pinnacles that no man can tell what they are for or what is beyond . . . . he glows a moment on the extremest verge. He is most wonderful in his last half-hidden smile or frown . . . by that flash of the moment of parting the one that sees it shall be encouraged or terrified afterward for many years. The greatest poet does not moralize or make applications of morals . . . he knows the soul. The soul has that measureless pride which consists in never acknowledging any lessons but its own. But it has sympathy as measureless as its pride and the one balances the other and neither can stretch too far while it stretches in company with the other. The inmost secrets of art sleep with the twain. The greatest poet has lain close betwixt both and they are vital in his style and thoughts.

The art of art, the glory of expression and the sunshine of the light of letters is simplicity. Nothing is better than simplicity . . . . nothing can make up for excess or for the lack of definiteness. To carry on the heave of impulse and pierce intellectual depths and give all subjects their articulations are powers neither common nor very uncommon. But to speak in literature with the perfect rectitude and insousiance[1] of the movements of animals and the unimpeachableness of the sentiment of trees in the woods and grass by the roadside is the flawless triumph of art. If you have looked on him who has achieved it you have looked on one of the masters of the artists of all nations and times. You shall not contemplate the flight of the graygull over the bay or the mettlesome[2] action of the blood horse or the tall leaning of sunflowers on their stalk or the appearance of the sun journeying through heaven or the appearance of the moon afterward with any more satisfaction than you shall contemplate him. The greatest poet has less a marked style and is more the channel of thoughts and things without increase or diminution, and is the free channel of himself. He swears to his art, I will not be meddlesome, I will not have in my writing any elegance or effect or originality to hang in the way between me and the rest like curtains. I will have nothing hang in the way, not the richest curtains. What I tell I tell for precisely what it is. Let who may exalt or startle or fascinate or sooth I will have purposes as health or heat or snow has and be as regardless of observation. What I experience or portray shall go from my composition without a shred of my composition. You shall stand by my side and look in the mirror with me.

The old red blood and stainless gentility of great poets will be proved by their unconstraint. A heroic person walks at his ease through and out of that custom or precedent or authority that suits him not. Of the traits of the brotherhood of writers savans[3] musicians inventors and artists nothing is finer than silent defiance advancing from new free forms. In the need of poems philosophy politics mechanism science behaviour, the craft of art, an appropriate native grand-opera, shipcraft, or any craft, he is greatest forever and forever who contributes the greatest original practical example. The cleanest expression is that which finds no sphere worthy of itself and makes one.

The messages of great poets to each man and woman are, Come to us on equal terms, Only then can you understand us, We are no better than you, What we enclose you enclose, What we enjoy you may enjoy. Did you suppose there could be only one Supreme? We affirm there can be unnumbered Supremes, and that one does not countervail another any more than one eyesight countervails another . . and that men

---

[1]   *insousiance* Indifference.

[2]   *mettlesome* Spirited or playful.

[3]   *savans* Learned people (savants).

can be good or grand only of the consciousness of their supremacy within them. What do you think is the grandeur of storms and dismemberments and the deadliest battles and wrecks and the wildest fury of the elements and the power of the sea and the motion of nature and of the throes of human desires and dignity and hate and love? It is that something in the soul which says, Rage on, Whirl on, I tread master here and everywhere, Master of the spasms of the sky and of the shatter of the sea, Master of nature and passion and death, And of all terror and all pain.

The American bards shall be marked for generosity and affection and for encouraging competitors . . They shall be kosmos . . without monopoly or secrecy . . glad to pass any thing to any one . . hungry for equals night and day. They shall not be careful of riches and privilege . . . . they shall be riches and privilege . . . . they shall perceive who the most affluent man is. The most affluent man is he that confronts all the shows he sees by equivalents out of the stronger wealth of himself. The American bard shall delineate no class of persons nor one or two out of the strata of interests nor love most nor truth most nor the soul most nor the body most . . . . and not be for the eastern states more than the western or the northern states more than the southern.

Exact science and its practical movements are no checks on the greatest poet but always his encouragement and support. The outset and remembrance are there . . there the arms that lifted him first and brace him best . . . . there he returns after all his goings and comings. The sailor and traveler . . the anatomist chemist astronomer geologist phrenologist[1] spiritualist mathematician historian and lexicographer[2] are not poets, but they are the lawgivers of poets and their construction underlies the structure of every perfect poem. No matter what rises or is uttered they sent the seed of the conception of it . . . of them and by them stand the visible proofs of souls . . . . . always of their fatherstuff must be begotten the sinewy races of bards. If there shall be love and content between the father and the son and if the greatness of the son is the exuding of the greatness of the father there shall be love between the poet and the man of demonstrable science. In the beauty of poems are the tuft and final applause of science.

Great is the faith of the flush of knowledge and of the investigation of the depths of qualities and things. Cleaving and circling here swells the soul of the poet yet it [is] president of itself always. The depths are fathomless and therefore calm. The innocence and nakedness are resumed . . . they are neither modest nor immodest. The whole theory of the special and supernatural and all that was twined with it or educed out of it departs as a dream. What has ever happened . . . . what happens and whatever may or shall happen, the vital laws enclose all . . . . they are sufficient for any case and for all cases . . . none to be hurried or retarded . . . . any miracle of affairs or persons inadmissible in the vast clear scheme where every motion and every spear of grass and the frames and spirits of men and women and all that concerns them are unspeakably perfect miracles all referring to all and each distinct and in its place. It is also not consistent with the reality of the soul to admit that there is anything in the known universe more divine than men and women.

Men and women and the earth and all upon it are simply to be taken as they are, and the investigation of their past and present and future shall be unintermitted and shall be done with perfect candor. Upon this basis philosophy speculates ever looking toward the poet, ever regarding the eternal tendencies of all toward happiness never inconsistent with what is clear to the senses and to the soul. For the eternal tendencies of all toward happiness make the only point of sane philosophy. Whatever comprehends less than that . . . whatever is less than the laws of light and of astronomical motion . . . or less than the laws that follow the thief the liar the glutton and the drunkard through this life and doubtless afterward . . . . . . or less than vast stretches of time or the slow formation of density or the patient upheaving of strata—is of no account. Whatever would put God in a poem or system of philosophy as contending against some being or influence is also of no account. Sanity and ensemble characterise the great master . . . spoilt in one principle all is spoilt. The great master has nothing to do with miracles. He

---

[1] *phrenologist* One who practices the pseudo-science phrenology, according to which the shape of an individual's head is indicative of certain personality traits; phrenology was very influential in the nineteenth century and was a subject of fascination to Whitman.

[2] *lexicographer* Compiler of dictionaries.

sees health for himself in being one of the mass . . . . he sees the hiatus in singular eminence. To the perfect shape comes common ground. To be under the general law is great for that is to correspond with it. The master knows that he is unspeakably great and that all are unspeakably great . . . . that nothing for instance is greater than to conceive children and bring them up well . . . that to be is just as great as to perceive or tell.

In the make of the great masters the idea of political liberty is indispensible. Liberty takes the adherence of heroes wherever men and women exist . . . . but never takes any adherence or welcome from the rest more than from poets. They are the voice and exposition of liberty. They out of ages are worthy the grand idea . . . . to them it is confided and they must sustain it. Nothing has precedence of it and nothing can warp or degrade it. The attitude of great poets is to cheer up slaves and horrify despots. The turn of their necks, the sound of their feet, the motions of their wrists, are full of hazard to the one and hope to the other. Come nigh them awhile and though they neither speak or advise you shall learn the faithful American lesson. Liberty is poorly served by men whose good intent is quelled from one failure or two failures or any number of failures, or from the casual indifference or ingratitude of the people, or from the sharp show of the tushes[1] of power, or the bringing to bear soldiers and cannon or any penal statutes. Liberty relies upon itself, invites no one, promises nothing, sits in calmness and light, is positive and composed, and knows no discouragement. The battle rages with many a loud alarm and frequent advance and retreat . . . . the enemy triumphs . . . . the prison, the handcuffs, the iron necklace and anklet, the scaffold, garrote[2] and leadballs do their work . . . . the cause is asleep . . . . the strong throats are choked with their own blood . . . . the young men drop their eyelashes toward the ground when they pass each other . . . . and is liberty gone out of that place? No never. When liberty goes it is not the first to go nor the second or third to go . . it waits for all the rest to go . . it is the last. . . When the memories of the old martyrs are faded utterly away . . . . when the large names of patriots are laughed at in the public halls from the lips of the orators . . . . when the boys are no more christened after the same but christened after tyrants and traitors instead . . . . when the laws of the free are grudgingly permitted and laws for informers and bloodmoney are sweet to the taste of the people . . . . when I and you walk abroad upon the earth stung with compassion at the sight of numberless brothers answering our equal friendship and calling no man master—and when we are elated with noble joy at the sight of slaves . . . . when the soul retires in the cool communion of the night and surveys its experience and has much extasy over the word and deed that put back a helpless innocent person into the gripe of the gripers or into any cruel inferiority . . . . when those in all parts of these states who could easier realize the true American character but do not yet—when the swarms of cringers, suckers, doughfaces,[3] lice of politics, planners of sly involutions for their own preferment to city offices or state legislatures or the judiciary or congress or the presidency, obtain a response of love and natural deference from the people whether they get the offices or no . . . . when it is better to be a bound booby and rogue in office at a high salary than the poorest free mechanic or farmer with his hat unmoved from his head and firm eyes and a candid and generous heart . . . . and when servility by town or state or the federal government or any oppression on a large scale or small scale can be tried on without its own punishment following duly after in exact proportion against the smallest chance of escape . . . . or rather when all life and all the souls of men and women are discharged from any part of the earth—then only shall the instinct of liberty be discharged from that part of the earth.

As the attributes of the poets of the kosmos concentre[4] in the real body and soul and in the pleasure of things they possess the superiority of genuineness over all fiction and romance. As they emit themselves facts are showered over with light . . . . the daylight is lit with more volatile light . . . . also the deep between the setting and rising sun goes deeper many fold. Each precise object or condition or combination or process

---

[1] *tushes* Dismissive exclamations that express contempt or disapproval.

[2] *garrote* Implement for execution via strangulation.

[3] *doughfaces* Politicians who are overly willing to be led by the ideas or interests of others; at this period, the term often referred in particular to Northerners who were seen as being overly sympathetic with the South in political matters.

[4] *concentre* Concentrate.

exhibits a beauty . . . . the multiplication table its—old age its—the carpenter's trade its—the grand-opera its . . . . the hugehulled cleanshaped New-York clipper at sea under steam or full sail gleams with unmatched beauty . . . . the American circles and large harmonies of government gleam with theirs . . . . and the commonest definite intentions and actions with theirs. The poets of the kosmos advance through all interpositions and coverings and turmoils and stratagems to first principles. They are of use . . . . they dissolve poverty from its need and riches from its conceit. You large proprietor they say shall not realize or perceive more than any one else. The owner of the library is not he who holds a legal title to it having bought and paid for it. Anyone and every one is owner of the library who can read the same through all the varieties of tongues and subjects and styles, and in whom they enter with ease and take residence and force toward paternity and maternity, and make supple and powerful and rich and large. . . . . These American states strong and healthy and accomplished shall receive no pleasure from violations of natural models and must not permit them. In paintings or mouldings or carvings in mineral or wood, or in the illustrations of books or newspapers, or in any comic or tragic prints, or in the patterns of woven stuffs or any thing to beautify rooms or furniture or costumes, or to put upon cornices or monuments or on the prows or sterns of ships, or to put anywhere before the human eye indoors or out, that which distorts honest shapes or which creates unearthly beings or places or contingencies is a nuisance and revolt. Of the human form especially it is so great it must never be made ridiculous. Of ornaments to a work nothing outre[1] can be allowed . . but those ornaments can be allowed that conform to the perfect facts of the open air and that flow out of the nature of the work and come irrepressibly from it and are necessary to the completion of the work. Most works are most beautiful without ornament. . . Exaggerations will be revenged in human physiology. Clean and vigorous children are jetted and conceived only in those communities where the models of natural forms are public every day. . . . . . Great genius and the people of these states must never be demeaned to romances.

As soon as histories are properly told there is no more need of romances.

The great poets are also to be known by the absence in them of tricks and by the justification of perfect personal candor. Then folks echo a new cheap joy and a divine voice leaping from their brains: How beautiful is candor! All faults may be forgiven of him who has perfect candor. Henceforth let no man of us lie, for we have seen that openness wins the inner and outer world and that there is no single exception, and that never since our earth gathered itself in a mass have deceit or subterfuge or prevarication attracted its smallest particle or the faintest tinge of a shade—and that through the enveloping wealth and rank of a state or the whole republic of states a sneak or sly person shall be discovered and despised . . . . and that the soul has never been once fooled and never can be fooled . . . . and thrift without the loving nod of the soul is only a fœtid[2] puff . . . . and there never grew up in any of the continents of the globe nor upon any planet or satellite or star, nor upon the asteroids, nor in any part of ethereal space, nor in the midst of density, nor under the fluid wet of the sea, nor in that condition which precedes the birth of babes, nor at any time during the changes of life, nor in that condition that follows what we term death, nor in any stretch of abeyance or action afterward of vitality, nor in any process of formation or reformation anywhere, a being whose instinct hated the truth.

Extreme caution or prudence, the soundest organic health, large hope and comparison and fondness for women and children, large alimentiveness and destructiveness and causality,[3] with a perfect sense of the oneness of nature and the propriety of the same spirit applied to human affairs . . these are called up of the float[4] of the brain of the world to be parts of the greatest poet from his birth out of his mother's womb and from her birth out of her mother's. Caution seldom goes far enough. It has been thought that the prudent citizen was the citizen who applied himself to solid

---

1 *outre* French: unusual, unorthodox, or extravagant.

2 *fœtid* Rank, stinking.

3 *large alimentiveness … destructiveness … causality* Phrenological terms that suggest pronounced development of certain personality traits: appetite for food, energy and self-preservation, and logical thinking (respectively).

4 *float* For Whitman, the word "float" often suggests the life-giving cosmos before bodies take form and become matter.

gains and did well for himself and his family and completed a lawful life without debt or crime. The greatest poet sees and admits these economies as he sees the economies of food and sleep, but has higher notions of prudence than to think he gives much when he gives a few slight attentions at the latch of the gate. The premises of the prudence of life are not the hospitality of it or the ripeness and harvest of it. Beyond the independence of a little sum laid aside for burial-money, and of a few clapboards around and shingles overhead on a lot of American soil owned, and the easy dollars that supply the year's plain clothing and meals, the melancholy prudence of the abandonment of such a great being as a man is to the toss and pallor of years of moneymaking with all their scorching days and icy nights and all their stifling deceits and underhanded dodgings, or infinitessimals[1] of parlors, or shameless stuffing while others starve . . and all the loss of the bloom and odor of the earth and of the flowers and atmosphere and of the sea and of the true taste of the women and men you pass or have to do with in youth or middle age, and the issuing sickness and desperate revolt at the close of a life without elevation or naivete, and the ghastly chatter of a death without serenity or majesty, is the great fraud upon modern civilization and forethought, blotching the surface and system which civilization undeniably drafts, and moistening with tears the immense features it spreads and spreads with such velocity before the reached kisses of the soul . . . Still the right explanation remains to be made about prudence. The prudence of the mere wealth and respectability of the most esteemed life appears too faint for the eye to observe at all when little and large alike drop quietly aside at the thought of the prudence suitable for immortality. What is wisdom that fills the thinness of a year or seventy or eighty years to wisdom spaced out by ages and coming back at a certain time with strong reinforcements and rich presents and the clear faces of wedding-guests as far as you can look in every direction running gaily toward you? Only the soul is of itself . . . . all else has reference to what ensues. All that a person does or thinks is of consequence. Not a move can a man or woman make that affects him or her in a day or a month or any part of the direct lifetime or the hour of death but the same affects him or her onward afterward through the indirect lifetime. The indirect is always as great and real as the direct. The spirit receives from the body just as much as it gives to the body. Not one name of word or deed . . not of venereal sores[2] or discolorations . . not the privacy of the onanist[3] . . not of the putrid veins of gluttons or rumdrinkers . . . not peculation[4] or cunning or betrayal or murder . . no serpentine poison of those that seduce women . . not the foolish yielding of women . . not prostitution . . not of any depravity of young men . . not of the attainment of gain by discreditable means . . not any nastiness of appetite . . not any harshness of officers to men or judges to prisoners or fathers to sons or sons to fathers or of husbands to wives or bosses to their boys . . not of greedy looks or malignant wishes . . . nor any of the wiles practised by people upon themselves . . . ever is or ever can be stamped on the programme but it is duly realized and returned, and that returned in further performances . . . and they returned again. Nor can the push of charity or personal force ever be any thing else than the profoundest reason, whether it bring arguments to hand or no. No specification is necessary . . to add or subtract or divide is in vain. Little or big, learned or unlearned, white or black, legal or illegal, sick or well, from the first inspiration down the windpipe to the last expiration out of it, all that a male or female does that is vigorous and benevolent and clean is so much sure profit to him or her in the unshakable order of the universe and through the whole scope of it forever. If the savage or felon is wise it is well . . . . if the greatest poet or savan is wise it is simply the same . . if the President or chief justice is wise it is the same . . . if the young mechanic or farmer is wise it is no more or less . . if the prostitute is wise it is no more nor less. The interest will come round . . all will come round. All the best actions of war and peace . . . all help given to relatives and strangers and the poor and old and sorrowful and young children and widows and the sick, and to all shunned persons . . all furtherance of fugitives and of the escape of slaves . . all the self-denial that stood steady and aloof on wrecks and saw others take the seats of the boats . . .

---

1   *infinitessimals* Minutiae, trivialities.

2   *venereal sores* I.e., sores arising from a sexually transmitted infection, here most likely referring to syphilis.

3   *onanist* Masturbator.

4   *peculation* Embezzlement.

all offering of substance or life for the good old cause, or for a friend's sake or opinion's sake . . . all pains of enthusiasts scoffed at by their neighbors . . all the vast sweet love and precious suffering of mothers . . . all honest men baffled in strifes recorded or unrecorded . . . . all the grandeur and good of the few ancient nations whose fragments of annals we inherit . . and all the good of the hundreds of far mightier and more ancient nations unknown to us by name or date or location . . . . all that was ever manfully begun, whether it succeeded or no . . . . all that has at any time been well suggested out of the divine heart of man or by the divinity of his mouth or by the shaping of his great hands . . and all that is well thought or done this day on any part of the surface of the globe . . or on any of the wandering stars[1] or fixed stars by those there as we are here . . or that is henceforth to be well thought or done by you whoever you are, or by any one—these singly and wholly inured at their time and inure now and will inure always to the identities from which they sprung or shall spring . . . Did you guess any of them lived only its moment? The world does not so exist . . no parts palpable or impalpable so exist . . . no result exists now without being from its long antecedent result, and that from its antecedent, and so backward without the farthest mentionable spot coming a bit nearer the beginning than any other spot. . . . . Whatever satisfies the soul is truth. The prudence of the greatest poet answers at last the craving and glut of the soul, is not contemptuous of less ways of prudence if they conform to its ways, puts off nothing, permits no let-up for its own case or any case, has no particular sabbath or judgment-day, divides not the living from the dead or the righteous from the unrighteous, is satisfied with the present, matches every thought or act by its correlative, knows no possible forgiveness or deputed atonement . . knows that the young man who composedly periled his life and lost it has done exceeding well for himself, while the man who has not periled his life and retains it to old age in riches and ease has perhaps achieved noth-ing for himself worth mentioning . . and that only that person has no great prudence to learn who has learnt to prefer real longlived things, and favors body and soul the same, and perceives the indirect assuredly

following the direct, and what evil or good he does leaping onward and waiting to meet him again—and who in his spirit in any emergency whatever neither hurries or avoids death.

The direct trial of him who would be the greatest poet is today. If he does not flood himself with the immedi-ate age as with vast oceanic tides . . . . . and if he does not attract his own land body and soul to himself and hang on its neck with incomparable love and plunge his semitic muscle[2] into its merits and demerits . . . and if he be not himself the age transfigured . . . . and if to him is not opened the eternity which gives similitude to all periods and locations and processes and animate and inanimate forms, and which is the bond of time, and rises up from its inconceivable vagueness and infi-niteness in the swimming shape of today, and is held by the ductile anchors of life, and makes the present spot the passage from what was to what shall be, and commits itself to the representation of this wave of an hour and this one of the sixty beautiful children of the wave—let him merge in the general run and wait his developement . . . . Still the final test of poems or any character or work remains. The prescient poet projects himself centuries ahead and judges performer or performance after the changes of time. Does it live through them? Does it still hold on untired? Will the same style and the direction of genius to similar points be satisfactory now? Has no new discovery in science or arrival at superior planes of thought and judgment and behaviour fixed him or his so that either can be looked down upon? Have the marches of tens and hundreds and thousands of years made willing detours to the right hand and the left hand for his sake? Is he beloved long and long after he is buried? Does the young man think often of him? and the young woman think often of him? and do the middleaged and the old think of him?

A great poem is for ages and ages in common and for all degrees and complexions and all departments and sects and for a woman as much as a man and a man as much as a woman. A great poem is no finish to a man or woman but rather a beginning. Has any one fancied he could sit at last under some due authority and rest

---

[1]   *wandering stars*   I.e., the planets, which, unlike the immobile "fixed stars," change their positions in the night sky.

[2]   *semitic muscle*   I.e., penis; in a later version of "A Woman Waits for Me," which also uses this phrase, Whitman corrects "semitic" to "seminal."

satisfied with explanations and realize and be content and full? To no such terminus does the greatest poet bring . . . he brings neither cessation or sheltered fatness and ease. The touch of him tells in action. Whom he takes he takes with firm sure grasp into live regions previously unattained . . . . thenceforward is no rest . . . . they see the space and ineffable sheen that turn the old spots and lights into dead vacuums. The companion of him beholds the birth and progress of stars and learns one of the meanings. Now there shall be a man cohered out of tumult and chaos . . . . the elder encourages the younger and shows him how . . . they two shall launch off fearlessly together till the new world fits an orbit for itself and looks unabashed on the lesser orbits of the stars and sweeps through the ceaseless rings and shall never be quiet again.

There will soon be no more priests. Their work is done. They may wait awhile . . perhaps a generation or two . . dropping off by degrees. A superior breed shall take their place . . . . the gangs of kosmos and prophets en masse shall take their place. A new order shall arise and they shall be the priests of man, and every man shall be his own priest. The churches built under their umbrage shall be the churches of men and women. Through the divinity of themselves shall the kosmos and the new breed of poets be interpreters of men and women and of all events and things. They shall find their inspiration in real objects today, symptoms of the past and future . . . . They shall not deign to defend immortality or God or the perfection of things or liberty or the exquisite beauty and reality of the soul. They shall arise in America and be responded to from the remainder of the earth.

The English language befriends the grand American expression . . . . it is brawny enough and limber and full enough. On the tough stock of a race who through all change of circumstance was never without the idea of political liberty, which is the animus[1] of all liberty, it has attracted the terms of daintier and gayer and subtler and more elegant tongues. It is the powerful language of resistance . . . it is the dialect of common sense. It is the speech of the proud and melancholy races and of all who aspire. It is the chosen tongue to express growth faith self-esteem freedom justice equality friendliness amplitude prudence decision and courage. It is the medium that shall well nigh express the inexpressible.

No great literature nor any like style of behaviour or oratory or social intercourse or household arrangements or public institutions or the treatment by bosses of employed people, nor executive detail or detail of the army or navy, nor spirit of legislation or courts or police or tuition or architecture or songs or amusements or the costumes of young men, can long elude the jealous and passionate instinct of American standards. Whether or no the sign appears from the mouths of the people, it throbs a live interrogation in every freeman's and freewoman's heart after that which passes by or this built to remain. Is it uniform with my country? Are its disposals without ignominious distinctions? Is it for the evergrowing communes of brothers and lovers, large, well-united, proud beyond the old models, generous beyond all models? Is it something grown fresh out of the fields or drawn from the sea for use to me today here? I know that what answers for me an American must answer for any individual or nation that serves for a part of my materials. Does this answer? or is it without reference to universal needs? or sprung of the needs of the less developed society of special ranks? or old needs of pleasure overlaid by modern science and forms? Does this acknowledge liberty with audible and absolute acknowledgement, and set slavery at nought for life and death? Will it help breed one goodshaped and wellhung man, and a woman to be his perfect and independent mate? Does it improve manners? Is it for the nursing of the young of the republic? Does it solve readily with the sweet milk of the nipples of the breasts of the mother of many children? Has it too the old ever-fresh forbearance and impartiality? Does it look with the same love on the last born and on those hardening toward stature, and on the errant, and on those who disdain all strength of assault outside of their own?

The poems distilled from other poems will probably pass away. The coward will surely pass away. The expectation of the vital and great can only be satisfied by the demeanor of the vital and great. The swarms of the polished deprecating and reflectors and the polite float off and leave no remembrance. America prepares with composure and goodwill for the visitors that have sent

---

[1]   *animus* Motivating impulse.

word. It is not intellect that is to be their warrant[1] and welcome. The talented, the artist, the ingenious, the editor, the statesman, the erudite .. they are not unappreciated .. they fall in their place and do their work. The soul of the nation also does its work. No disguise can pass on it .. no disguise can conceal from it. It rejects none, it permits all. Only toward as good as itself and toward the like of itself will it advance halfway. An individual is as superb as a nation when he has the qualities which make a superb nation. The soul of the largest and wealthiest and proudest nation may well go half-way to meet that of its poets. The signs are effectual. There is no fear of mistake. If the one is true the other is true. The proof of a poet is that his country absorbs him as affectionately as he has absorbed it. —1855

from *1855 Leaves of Grass* [*Song of Myself*]

[1]   I celebrate myself,
      And what I assume you shall assume,
      For every atom belonging to me as good belongs to you.

      I loafe and invite my soul,
5   I lean and loafe at my ease .... observing a spear of summer grass.

[2]   Houses and rooms are full of perfumes .... the shelves are crowded with perfumes,
      I breathe the fragrance myself, and know it and like it,
      The distillation would intoxicate me also, but I shall not let it.

      The atmosphere is not a perfume .... it has no taste of the distillation .... it is odorless,
10   It is for my mouth forever .... I am in love with it,
      I will go to the bank by the wood and become undisguised and naked,
      I am mad for it to be in contact with me.

      The smoke of my own breath,
      Echos, ripples, and buzzed whispers .... loveroot,[2] silkthread, crotch and vine,
15   My respiration and inspiration .... the beating of my heart .... the passing of blood and air
          through my lungs,
      The sniff of green leaves and dry leaves, and of the shore and darkcolored sea-rocks, and of
          hay in the barn,
      The sound of the belched words of my voice .... words loosed to the eddies of the wind,
      A few light kisses .... a few embraces .... a reaching around of arms,
      The play of shine and shade on the trees as the supple boughs wag,
20   The delight alone or in the rush of the streets, or along the fields and hillsides,
      The feeling of health .... the full-noon trill .... the song of me rising from bed and meet-
          ing the sun.

---

[1]   *warrant*   Guarantee.

[2]   *loveroot*   White wildflower of the American Southwest.

Have you reckoned a thousand acres much? Have you reckoned the earth much?
Have you practiced so long to learn to read?
Have you felt so proud to get at the meaning of poems?

25 Stop this day and night with me and you shall possess the origin of all poems,
You shall possess the good of the earth and sun . . . . there are millions of suns left,
You shall no longer take things at second or third hand . . . . nor look through the eyes of the
     dead . . . . nor feed on the spectres in books,
You shall not look through my eyes either, nor take things from me,
You shall listen to all sides and filter them from yourself.

[3] I have heard what the talkers were talking . . . . the talk of the beginning and the end,
But I do not talk of the beginning or the end.

There was never any more inception than there is now,
Nor any more youth or age than there is now;
And will never be any more perfection than there is now,
35 Nor any more heaven or hell than there is now.

Urge and urge and urge,
Always the procreant urge of the world.

Out of the dimness opposite equals advance . . . . Always substance and increase,
Always a knit of identity . . . . always distinction . . . . always a breed of life.

40 To elaborate is no avail . . . . Learned and unlearned feel that it is so.

Sure as the most certain sure . . . . plumb in the uprights, well entretied,[1] braced in the beams,
Stout as a horse, affectionate, haughty, electrical,
I and this mystery here we stand.

Clear and sweet is my soul . . . . and clear and sweet is all that is not my soul.

45 Lack one lacks both . . . . and the unseen is proved by the seen,
Till that becomes unseen and receives proof in its turn.

Showing the best and dividing it from the worst, age vexes age,
Knowing the perfect fitness and equanimity of things, while they discuss I am silent, and go
     bathe and admire myself.

Welcome is every organ and attribute of me, and of any man hearty and clean,
50 Not an inch nor a particle of an inch is vile, and none shall be less familiar than the rest.

I am satisfied . . . . I see, dance, laugh, sing;
As God comes a loving bedfellow and sleeps at my side all night and close on the peep of the
     day,

---

[1] *entretied* Plastered.

And leaves for me baskets covered with white towels bulging the house with their plenty,
Shall I postpone my acceptation and realization and scream at my eyes,
55   That they turn from gazing after and down the road,
And forthwith cipher[1] and show me to a cent,
Exactly the contents of one, and exactly the contents of two, and which is ahead?

[4]   Trippers and askers surround me,
People I meet . . . . . the effect upon me of my early life . . . . of the ward and city I live in . . . .
      of the nation,
60   The latest news . . . . discoveries, inventions, societies . . . . authors old and new,
My dinner, dress, associates, looks, business, compliments, dues,
The real or fancied indifference of some man or woman I love,
The sickness of one of my folks—or of myself . . . . or ill-doing . . . . or loss or lack of money
      . . . . or depressions or exaltations,
They come to me days and nights and go from me again,
65   But they are not the Me myself.

Apart from the pulling and hauling stands what I am,
Stands amused, complacent, compassionating, idle, unitary,
Looks down, is erect, bends an arm on an impalpable certain rest,
Looks with its sidecurved head curious what will come next,
70   Both in and out of the game, and watching and wondering at it.

Backward I see in my own days where I sweated through fog with linguists and contenders,
I have no mockings or arguments . . . . I witness and wait.

[5]   I believe in you my soul . . . . the other I am must not abase itself to you,
And you must not be abased to the other.

75   Loafe with me on the grass . . . . loose the stop from your throat,
Not words, not music or rhyme I want . . . . not custom or lecture, not even the best,
Only the lull I like, the hum of your valved voice.

I mind how we lay in June, such a transparent summer morning;
You settled your head athwart my hips and gently turned over upon me,
80   And parted the shirt from my bosom-bone, and plunged your tongue to my barestript heart,
And reached till you felt my beard, and reached till you held my feet.

Swiftly arose and spread around me the peace and joy and knowledge that pass all the art and
      argument of the earth;[2]
And I know that the hand of God is the elderhand[3] of my own,
And I know that the spirit of God is the eldest brother of my own,

---

1   *cipher* Calculate.

2   *peace … earth* See Philippians 4.7: "And the peace of God, which passeth all understanding, shall keep your hearts and minds through Jesus Christ."

3   *elderhand* Guiding hand, pattern; in card-playing, the "elder hand" is a term used for the first player.

85   And that all the men ever born are also my brothers . . . . and the women my sisters and
        lovers,
      And that a kelson[1] of the creation is love;
      And limitless are leaves stiff or drooping in the fields,
      And brown ants in the little wells beneath them,
      And mossy scabs of the wormfence,[2] and heaped stones, and elder and mullen[3] and pokeweed.

[6]   A child said, What is the grass? fetching it to me with full hands;
      How could I answer the child? . . . . I do not know what it is any more than he.

      I guess it must be the flag of my disposition, out of hopeful green stuff woven.

      Or I guess it is the handkerchief of the Lord,
      A scented gift and remembrancer designedly dropped,
95   Bearing the owner's name someway in the corners,[4] that we may see and remark, and say
        Whose?

      Or I guess the grass is itself a child . . . . the produced babe of the vegetation.

      Or I guess it is a uniform hieroglyphic,
      And it means, Sprouting alike in broad zones and narrow zones,
      Growing among black folks as among white,
100   Kanuck, Tuckahoe, Congressman, Cuff,[5] I give them the same, I receive them the same.

      And now it seems to me the beautiful uncut hair of graves.

      Tenderly will I use you curling grass,
      It may be you transpire from the breasts of young men,
      It may be if I had known them I would have loved them;
105   It may be you are from old people and from women, and from offspring taken soon out of
        their mothers' laps,
      And here you are the mothers' laps.

      This grass is very dark to be from the white heads of old mothers,
      Darker than the colorless beards of old men,
      Dark to come from under the faint red roofs of mouths.

110   O I perceive after all so many uttering tongues!
      And I perceive they do not come from the roofs of mouths for nothing.

_____

1   *kelson* Foundational piece of a ship's structure: the timber that connects the keel and the floor-timbers together.

2   *wormfence* Also known as a "snake-fence," a rough fence made with rails put together in a zigzag pattern.

3   *mullen* I.e., mullein plants, which grow along roadsides and in empty fields (as do elderberries and pokeweed).

4   *designedly ... corners* I.e., a handkerchief dropped on purpose as a gift or love-token, with the owner's initials embroidered on one of the corners.

5   *Kanuck* American slang term for a French Canadian; *Tuckahoe* Person living in Lower Virginia; *Cuff* Slang term, often derogatory, for an African American.

I wish I could translate the hints about the dead young men and women,
And the hints about old men and mothers, and the offspring taken soon out of their laps.

What do you think has become of the young and old men?
115   And what do you think has become of the women and children?

They are alive and well somewhere;
The smallest sprout shows there is really no death,
And if ever there was it led forward life, and does not wait at the end to arrest it,
And ceased the moment life appeared.

120   All goes onward and outward . . . . and nothing collapses,
And to die is different from what any one supposed, and luckier.

[7]   Has any one supposed it lucky to be born?
I hasten to inform him or her it is just as lucky to die, and I know it.

I pass death with the dying, and birth with the new-washed babe . . . . and am not contained
        between my hat and boots,
125   And peruse manifold objects, no two alike, and every one good,
The earth good, and the stars good, and their adjuncts all good.

I am not an earth nor an adjunct of an earth,
I am the mate and companion of people, all just as immortal and fathomless as myself;
They do not know how immortal, but I know.

130   Every kind for itself and its own . . . . for me mine male and female,
For me all that have been boys and that love women,
For me the man that is proud and feels how it stings to be slighted,
For me the sweetheart and the old maid . . . . for me mothers and the mothers of mothers,
For me lips that have smiled, eyes that have shed tears,
135   For me children and the begetters of children.

Who need be afraid of the merge?
Undrape . . . . you are not guilty to me, nor stale nor discarded,
I see through the broadcloth and gingham[1] whether or no,
And am around, tenacious, acquisitive, tireless . . . . and can never be shaken away.

[8]   The little one sleeps in its cradle,
I lift the gauze and look a long time, and silently brush away flies with my hand.

The youngster and the redfaced girl turn aside up the bushy hill,
I peeringly view them from the top.

---

[1]   *broadcloth* Fine wool fabric, often used for men's jackets and trousers; *gingham* Checked cotton fabric, commonly used for dresses, aprons, and shirts.

The suicide sprawls on the bloody floor of the bedroom,
145 It is so . . . . I witnessed the corpse . . . . there the pistol had fallen.

The blab of the pave . . . . the tires of carts and sluff of bootsoles and talk of the promenaders,
The heavy omnibus,[1] the driver with his interrogating thumb, the clank of the shod horses on the granite floor,
The carnival of sleighs, the clinking and shouted jokes and pelts of snowballs;
The hurrahs for popular favorites . . . . the fury of roused mobs,
150 The flap of the curtained litter[2]—the sick man inside, borne to the hospital,
The meeting of enemies, the sudden oath,[3] the blows and fall,
The excited crowd—the policeman with his star quickly working his passage to the centre of the crowd;
The impassive stones that receive and return so many echoes,
The souls moving along . . . . are they invisible while the least atom of the stones is visible?
155 What groans of overfed or half-starved who fall on the flags sunstruck or in fits,
What exclamations of women taken suddenly, who hurry home and give birth to babes,
What living and buried speech is always vibrating here . . . . what howls restrained by decorum,
Arrests of criminals, slights, adulterous offers made, acceptances, rejections with convex lips,
I mind them or the resonance of them . . . . I come again and again.

[9] The big doors of the country-barn stand open and ready,
The dried grass of the harvest-time loads the slow-drawn wagon,
The clear light plays on the brown gray and green intertinged,
The armfuls are packed to the sagging mow:[4]
I am there . . . . I help . . . . I came stretched atop of the load,
165 I felt its soft jolts . . . . one leg reclined on the other,
I jump from the crossbeams, and seize the clover and timothy,[5]
And roll head over heels, and tangle my hair full of wisps.

[10] Alone far in the wilds and mountains I hunt,
Wandering amazed at my own lightness and glee,
170 In the late afternoon choosing a safe spot to pass the night,
Kindling a fire and broiling the freshkilled game,
Soundly falling asleep on the gathered leaves, my dog and gun by my side.

The Yankee clipper is under her three skysails . . . . she cuts the sparkle and scud,[6]
My eyes settle the land . . . . I bend at her prow or shout joyously from the deck.

---

1 *omnibus* Bus.

2 *litter* Frame supporting a couch or bed; used to carry a sick person from one place to another.

3 *oath* Utterance of an expletive; swearing.

4 *mow* Place where hay is stacked in the barn.

5 *timothy* Timothy grass, a popular cultivar for hay.

6 *clipper* Fast sailing ship, with a sharp bow; *skysails* Light sails located above the royal sails; *scud* Ocean spray.

175 The boatmen and clamdiggers arose early and stopped for me,
I tucked my trowser-ends in my boots and went and had a good time,
You should have been with us that day round the chowder-kettle.

I saw the marriage of the trapper in the open air in the far-west . . . . the bride was a red girl,
Her father and his friends sat near by crosslegged and dumbly[1] smoking . . . . they had moccasins to their feet and large thick blankets hanging from their shoulders;
180 On a bank lounged the trapper . . . . he was dressed mostly in skins . . . . his luxuriant beard
and curls protected his neck,
One hand rested on his rifle . . . . the other hand held firmly the wrist of the red girl,
She had long eyelashes . . . . her head was bare . . . . her coarse straight locks descended upon
her voluptuous limbs and reached to her feet.[2]

The runaway slave came to my house and stopped outside,
I heard his motions crackling the twigs of the woodpile,
185 Through the swung half-door of the kitchen I saw him limpsey[3] and weak,
And went where he sat on a log, and led him in and assured him,
And brought water and filled a tub for his sweated body and bruised feet,
And gave him a room that entered from my own, and gave him some coarse clean clothes,
And remember perfectly well his revolving eyes and his awkwardness,
190 And remember putting plasters on the galls[4] of his neck and ankles;
He staid with me a week before he was recuperated and passed north,
I had him sit next me at table . . . . . my firelock[5] leaned in the corner.

[11] Twenty-eight young men bathe by the shore,
Twenty-eight young men, and all so friendly,
195 Twenty-eight years of womanly life, and all so lonesome.

She owns the fine house by the rise of the bank,
She hides handsome and richly drest aft[6] the blinds of the window.

Which of the young men does she like the best?
Ah the homeliest of them is beautiful to her.

200 Where are you off to, lady? for I see you,
You splash in the water there, yet stay stock still in your room.

Dancing and laughing along the beach came the twenty-ninth bather,
The rest did not see her, but she saw them and loved them.

---

1 *dumbly* Silently.

2 *I saw … her feet* This passage describes the scene depicted in *The Trapper's Bride*, a painting by Alfred Jacob Miller
(1810–74).

3 *limpsey* Limp.

4 *plasters* Bandages, dressings; *galls* Wounds caused by chafing.

5 *firelock* Gun.

6 *aft* Behind.

The beards of the young men glistened with wet, it ran from their long hair,
205   Little streams passed all over their bodies.

An unseen hand also passed over their bodies,
It descended tremblingly from their temples and ribs.

The young men float on their backs, their white bellies swell to the sun . . . . they do not ask
    who seizes fast to them,
They do not know who puffs and declines with pendant and bending arch,
210   They do not think whom they souse¹ with spray.

[12]   The butcher-boy puts off his killing-clothes, or sharpens his knife at the stall in the market,
I loiter enjoying his repartee and his shuffle and breakdown.²

Blacksmiths with grimed and hairy chests environ³ the anvil,
Each has his main-sledge⁴ . . . . they are all out . . . . there is a great heat in the fire.

215   From the cinder-strewed threshold I follow their movements,
The lithe sheer of their waists plays even with their massive arms,
Overhand the hammers roll—overhand so slow—overhand so sure,
They do not hasten, each man hits in his place.

[13]   The negro holds firmly the reins of his four horses . . . . the block swags underneath on its
    tied-over chain,
220   The negro that drives the huge dray of the stoneyard . . . . steady and tall he stands poised on
    one leg on the stringpiece,⁵
His blue shirt exposes his ample neck and breast and loosens over his hipband,
His glance is calm and commanding . . . . he tosses the slouch of his hat away from his
    forehead,
The sun falls on his crispy hair and moustache . . . . falls on the black of his polish'd and
    perfect limbs.

I behold the picturesque giant and love him . . . . and I do not stop there,
225   I go with the team also.

---

¹ *souse* Soak.

² *repartee* Clever and witty questions and replies; *shuffle* Slow, sliding dance; *breakdown* Riotous, exuberant dance. Both dances had origins in the folkdance traditions of African Americans, and had been adapted by white performers for use in popular entertainments—including blackface minstrel shows.

³ *environ* Surround.

⁴ *main-sledge* Large hammer used by blacksmiths.

⁵ *dray* Low cart used for carrying or dragging heavy loads; *stoneyard* Place where stone is cut; *stringpiece* Connecting piece of timber used in the framework of the cart.

In me the caresser of life wherever moving . . . . backward as well as forward slueing,[1]
To niches aside and junior bending.

Oxen that rattle the yoke or halt in the shade, what is that you express in your eyes?
It seems to me more than all the print I have read in my life.

230 My tread scares the wood-drake[2] and wood-duck on my distant and daylong ramble,
They rise together, they slowly circle around.
. . . . I believe in those winged purposes,
And acknowledge the red yellow and white playing within me,
And consider the green and violet and the tufted crown[3] intentional;
235 And do not call the tortoise unworthy because she is not something else,
And the mockingbird in the swamp never studied the gamut,[4] yet trills pretty well to me,
And the look of the bay mare shames silliness out of me.

[14] The wild gander leads his flock through the cool night,
Ya-honk! he says, and sounds it down to me like an invitation;
240 The pert[5] may suppose it meaningless, but I listen closer,
I find its purpose and place up there toward the November sky.

The sharphoofed moose of the north, the cat on the housesill, the chickadee, the prairie-dog,
The litter of the grunting sow as they tug at her teats,
The brood of the turkeyhen, and she with her halfspread wings,
245 I see in them and myself the same old law.

The press of my foot to the earth springs a hundred affections,
They scorn the best I can do to relate them.

I am enamoured of growing outdoors,
Of men that live among cattle or taste of the ocean or woods,
250 Of the builders and steerers of ships, of the wielders of axes and mauls,[6] of the drivers of
       horses,
I can eat and sleep with them week in and week out.

What is commonest and cheapest and nearest and easiest is Me,
Me going in for my chances, spending for vast returns,
Adorning myself to bestow myself on the first that will take me,
255 Not asking the sky to come down to my goodwill,
Scattering it freely forever.

---

1 *slueing* Turning or twisting.

2 *wood-drake* Male of the wood duck.

3 *red ... tufted crown* The male wood duck has all these colors in his plumage, and he has tufted white feathers
flaring from his crown down his neck.

4 *gamut* Complete series of notes in a formal musical scale.

5 *pert* Saucy or impertinent person.

6 *mauls* Sledgehammers.

[15] The pure contralto sings in the organloft,
      The carpenter dresses his plank . . . . the tongue of his foreplane[1] whistles its wild ascending lisp,
      The married and unmarried children ride home to their thanksgiving dinner,

260   The pilot seizes the king-pin,[2] he heaves down with a strong arm,
      The mate stands braced in the whaleboat, lance and harpoon are ready,
      The duck-shooter walks by silent and cautious stretches,
      The deacons are ordained with crossed hands at the altar,
      The spinning-girl[3] retreats and advances to the hum of the big wheel,

265   The farmer stops by the bars of a Sunday and looks at the oats and rye,
      The lunatic is carried at last to the asylum a confirmed case,
      He will never sleep any more as he did in the cot in his mother's bedroom;
      The jour printer with gray head and gaunt jaws works at his case,[4]
      He turns his quid of tobacco,[5] his eyes get blurred with the manuscript;

270   The malformed limbs are tied to the anatomist's table,
      What is removed drops horribly in a pail;
      The quadroon[6] girl is sold at the stand . . . . the drunkard nods by the barroom stove,
      The machinist rolls up his sleeves . . . . the policeman travels his beat . . . . the gate-keeper
         marks who pass,
      The young fellow drives the express-wagon . . . . I love him though I do not know him;

275   The half-breed[7] straps on his light boots to compete in the race,
      The western turkey-shooting draws old and young . . . . some lean on their rifles, some sit on
         logs,
      Out from the crowd steps the marksman and takes his position and levels his piece;[8]
      The groups of newly-come immigrants cover the wharf or levee,
      The woollypates[9] hoe in the sugarfield, the overseer views them from his saddle;

280   The bugle calls in the ballroom, the gentlemen run for their partners, the dancers bow to
         each other;
      The youth lies awake in the cedar-roofed garret and harks[10] to the musical rain,
      The Wolverine sets traps on the creek that helps fill the Huron,[11]
      The reformer ascends the platform, he spouts with his mouth and nose,

---

[1] *foreplane*   Carpenter's tool used to smooth the wood after it has been cut.

[2] *pilot*   Person who steers a ship; the navigator;   *king-pin*   Central bolt used to pivot an axle; in this context, the steering wheel of the ship's helm.

[3] *spinning-girl*   I.e., girl at work making yarn or thread on a spinning wheel.

[4] *jour printer*   Journeyman printer, one who has finished an apprenticeship but still works as the employee of someone else;   *case*   Tray divided into sections to hold printing type.

[5] *turns*   Chews;   *quid of tobacco*   Lump of chewing tobacco.

[6] *quadroon*   Term (now considered offensive) for a person who has three white grandparents and one black grandparent.

[7] *half-breed*   Offensive term for a person of mixed ethnic origin (in the U.S., this term was usually applied to a person with one black or white parent and one Indigenous parent).

[8] *piece*   Gun.

[9] *woollypates*   I.e., wooly-haired, offensive term applied to African Americans.

[10] *harks*   Listens.

[11] *Wolverine*   Person from Michigan;   *the Huron*   Any one of three Huron rivers in Michigan or Lake Huron.

The company returns from its excursion, the darkey brings up the rear and bears the well-riddled[1] target,

285 The squaw[2] wrapt in her yellow-hemmed cloth is offering moccasins and beadbags for sale,

The connoisseur peers along the exhibition-gallery with halfshut eyes bent sideways,

The deckhands make fast the steamboat, the plank is thrown for the shoregoing passengers,

The young sister holds out the skein,[3] the elder sister winds it off in a ball and stops now and then for the knots,

The one-year wife is recovering and happy, a week ago she bore her first child,

290 The cleanhaired Yankee girl works with her sewing-machine or in the factory or mill,

The nine months' gone is in the parturition chamber,[4] her faintness and pains are advancing;

The pavingman leans on his twohanded rammer[5]—the reporter's lead[6] flies swiftly over the notebook—the signpainter is lettering with red and gold,

The canal-boy trots on the towpath[7]—the bookkeeper counts at his desk—the shoemaker waxes his thread,

The conductor beats time for the band and all the performers follow him,

295 The child is baptised—the convert is making the first professions,[8]

The regatta is spread on the bay . . . . how the white sails sparkle!

The drover watches his drove,[9] he sings out to them that would stray,

The pedlar sweats with his pack on his back—the purchaser higgles about the odd cent,

The camera and plate are prepared, the lady must sit for her daguerreotype,

300 The bride unrumples her white dress, the minutehand of the clock moves slowly,

The opium eater reclines with rigid head and just-opened lips,

The prostitute draggles her shawl, her bonnet bobs on her tipsy and pimpled neck,

The crowd laugh at her blackguard oaths,[10] the men jeer and wink to each other,

(Miserable! I do not laugh at your oaths nor jeer you,)

305 The President holds a cabinet council, he is surrounded by the great secretaries,

On the piazza walk five friendly matrons with twined arms;

The crew of the fish-smack[11] pack repeated layers of halibut in the hold,

The Missourian crosses the plains toting his wares and his cattle,

The fare-collector goes through the train—he gives notice by the jingling of loose change,

310 The floormen are laying the floor—the tinners are tinning the roof—the masons are calling for mortar,

---

1   *well-riddled*   Shot through (containing many bullet holes).

2   *squaw*   Offensive term for an Indigenous woman; while it carried negative connotations by this point, the term continued to be used frequently by English speakers well into the nineteenth century, even by those who did not intend it derogatorily.

3   *skein*   Large coil of thread or yarn.

4   *parturition chamber*   Birthing room.

5   *rammer*   Instrument used to set paving stones.

6   *lead*   Pencil.

7   *towpath*   Path that runs alongside a canal.

8   *professions*   Statements of faith.

9   *drover*   Cattle dealer; *drove*   Herd of cattle.

10 *blackguard oaths*   Coarse swearing.

11 *fish-smack*   Single-masted sailing ship used for fishing.

In single file each shouldering his hod[1] pass onward the laborers;

Seasons pursuing each other the indescribable crowd is gathered . . . . it is the Fourth of July
. . . . what salutes of cannon and small arms!

Seasons pursuing each other the plougher ploughs and the mower mows and the wintergrain
falls in the ground;

Off on the lakes the pikefisher watches and waits by the hole in the frozen surface,

315   The stumps stand thick round the clearing, the squatter[2] strikes deep with his axe,

The flatboatmen make fast toward dusk near the cottonwood or pekantrees,[3]

The coon-seekers go now through the regions of the Red river, or through those drained by
the Tennessee, or through those of the Arkansas,

The torches shine in the dark that hangs on the Chattahoochee or Altamahaw;[4]

Patriarchs sit at supper with sons and grandsons and great grandsons around them,

320   In walls of abode,[5] in canvass tents, rest hunters and trappers after their day's sport.

The city sleeps and the country sleeps,

The living sleep for their time . . . . the dead sleep for their time,

The old husband sleeps by his wife and the young husband sleeps by his wife;

And these one and all tend inward to me, and I tend outward to them,

325   And such as it is to be of these more or less I am.

[16]   I am of old and young, of the foolish as much as the wise,

Regardless of others, ever regardful of others,

Maternal as well as paternal, a child as well as a man,

Stuffed with the stuff that is coarse, and stuffed with the stuff that is fine,

330   One of the great nation, the nation of many nations—the smallest the same and the largest
the same,

A southerner soon as a northerner, a planter nonchalant and hospitable,

A Yankee bound my own way . . . . ready for trade . . . . my joints the limberest joints on
earth and the sternest joints on earth,

A Kentuckian walking the vale of the Elkhorn in my deerskin leggings,

A boatman over the lakes or bays or along coasts . . . . a Hoosier, a Badger, a Buckeye,[6]

335   A Louisianian or Georgian, a poke-easy[7] from sandhills and pines,

At home on Canadian snowshoes or up in the bush, or with fishermen off Newfoundland,

At home in the fleet of iceboats, sailing with the rest and tacking,

At home on the hills of Vermont or in the woods of Maine or the Texan ranch,

Comrade of Californians . . . . comrade of free northwesterners, loving their big proportions,

340   Comrade of raftsmen and coalmen—comrade of all who shake hands and welcome to drink
and meat;

---

1   *hod*   Open container used to carry mortar or bricks.

2   *squatter*   Settler with no formal title to the land, or a settler on land that the government has not yet surveyed.

3   *pekantrees*   I.e., pecan trees, which grow in the southern United States, particularly near the Mississippi River.

4   *Chattahoochee*   River that stretches from northern Georgia to the Florida panhandle; *Altamahaw*   River that stretches from central to southeastern Georgia.

5   *abode*   Whitman changed this to "adobe" in the 1856 edition of *Leaves of Grass*.

6   *Hoosier ... Badger ... Buckeye*   Residents of Indiana, Wisconsin, and Ohio, respectively.

7   *poke-easy*   Easy-going person that takes it slow (regional term used chiefly in the Southern U.S.).

A learner with the simplest, a teacher of the thoughtfulest,
A novice beginning experient[1] of myriads of seasons,
Of every hue and trade and rank, of every caste and religion,
Not merely of the New World but of Africa Europe or Asia . . . . a wandering savage,
345   A farmer, mechanic, or artist . . . . a gentleman, sailor, lover or quaker,[2]
A prisoner, fancy-man,[3] rowdy, lawyer, physician or priest.

I resist anything better than my own diversity,
And breathe the air and leave plenty after me,
And am not stuck up, and am in my place.

350   The moth and the fisheggs are in their place,
The suns I see and the suns I cannot see are in their place,
The palpable is in its place and the impalpable is in its place.

[17]   These are the thoughts of all men in all ages and lands, they are not original with me,
If they are not yours as much as mine they are nothing or next to nothing,
355   If they do not enclose everything they are next to nothing,
If they are not the riddle and the untying of the riddle they are nothing,
If they are not just as close as they are distant they are nothing.

This is the grass that grows wherever the land is and the water is,
This is the common air that bathes the globe.

[18]   This is the breath of laws and songs and behaviour,
This is the tasteless water of souls . . . . this is the true sustenance,
It is for the illiterate . . . . it is for the judges of the supreme court . . . . it is for the federal
    capitol and the state capitols,
It is for the admirable communes of literary men and composers and singers and lecturers
    and engineers and savans,[4]
It is for the endless races of working people and farmers and seamen.

365   This is the trill of a thousand clear cornets and scream of the octave flute[5] and strike of
    triangles.

I play not a march for victors only . . . . I play great marches for conquered and slain persons.

Have you heard that it was good to gain the day?
I also say it is good to fall . . . . battles are lost in the same spirit in which they are won.

---

1   *experient*   Having knowledge of, experience in.

2   *quaker*   One that trembles from love or from religious zeal; Whitman could also mean a Quaker, a member of the religious sect the Society of Friends.

3   *fancy-man*   A sweetheart; alternatively, a man who lives on the earnings of a prostitute.

4   *savans*   Learned people (savants).

5   *octave flute*   Also known as a piccolo, a small flute that plays an octave higher than the typical flute.

I sound triumphal drums for the dead . . . . I fling through my embouchures[1] the loudest
    and gayest music to them,

370 Vivas[2] to those who have failed, and to those whose war-vessels sank in the sea, and those
    themselves who sank in the sea,
And to all generals that lost engagements, and all overcome heroes, and the numberless
    unknown heroes equal to the greatest heroes known.

[19] This is the meal pleasantly set . . . . this is the meat and drink for natural hunger,
It is for the wicked just the same as the righteous . . . . I make appointments with all,
I will not have a single person slighted or left away,

375 The keptwoman and sponger[3] and thief are hereby invited . . . . the heavy-lipped slave is
    invited . . . . the venerealee[4] is invited,
There shall be no difference between them and the rest.

This is the press of a bashful hand . . . . this is the float and odor of hair,
This is the touch of my lips to yours . . . . this is the murmur of yearning,
This is the far-off depth and height reflecting my own face,

380 This is the thoughtful merge of myself and the outlet again.

Do you guess I have some intricate purpose?
Well I have . . . . for the April rain has, and the mica on the side of a rock has.

Do you take it I would astonish?
Does the daylight astonish? or the early redstart[5] twittering through the woods?

385 Do I astonish more than they?

This hour I tell things in confidence,
I might not tell everybody but I will tell you.

[20] Who goes there! hankering, gross, mystical, nude?
How is it I extract strength from the beef I eat?

390 What is a man anyhow? What am I? and what are you?
All I mark as my own you shall offset it with your own,
Else it were time lost listening to me.

I do not snivel that snivel the world over,
That months are vacuums and the ground but wallow and filth,

395 That life is a suck and a sell, and nothing remains at the end but threadbare crape[6] and tears.

---

[1] *embouchures*   In music, the part of the instrument that touches the mouth of the player.

[2] *Vivas*   Cheers of applause.

[3] *keptwoman*   Woman who is "kept" (i.e., supported financially) in exchange for sexual services; a mistress; *sponger*   Someone living at another person's expense.

[4] *venerealee*   Person who has a venereal disease (sexually transmitted infection).

[5] *redstart*   Migratory eastern North American wood warbler.

[6] *suck*   Deception; *sell*   Hoax, disappointment; *crape*   Thin fabric often dyed black and used for mourning garments.

Whimpering and truckling fold with powders[1] for invalids . . . . conformity goes to the
    fourth-removed,
I cock my hat as I please indoors or out.

Shall I pray? Shall I venerate and be ceremonious?
I have pried through the strata and analyzed to a hair,
400 And counselled with doctors and calculated close and found no sweeter fat than sticks to my
    own bones.

In all people I see myself, none more and not one a barleycorn[2] less,
And the good or bad I say of myself I say of them.

And I know I am solid and sound,
To me the converging objects of the universe perpetually flow,
405 All are written to me, and I must get what the writing means.

And I know I am deathless,
I know this orbit of mine cannot be swept by a carpenter's compass,
I know I shall not pass like a child's carlacue cut with a burnt stick at night.[3]

I know I am august,[4]
410 I do not trouble my spirit to vindicate itself or be understood,
I see that the elementary laws never apologize,
I reckon I behave no prouder than the level I plant my house by after all.

I exist as I am, that is enough,
If no other in the world be aware I sit content,
415 And if each and all be aware I sit content.

One world is aware, and by far the largest to me, and that is myself,
And whether I come to my own today or in ten thousand or ten million years,
I can cheerfully take it now, or with equal cheerfulness I can wait.

My foothold is tenoned and mortised[5] in granite,
420 I laugh at what you call dissolution,
And I know the amplitude of time.

---

[1] *truckling* Servile, submissive behavior; *powders* Medicinal powders. Doses were wrapped in a folded piece of
paper.

[2] *barleycorn* A grain of barley, but also a unit of measurement equivalent to one third of an inch.

[3] *carlacue ... night* Usually spelled "curlicue," which is a curl or twist. In American slang, "to cut a carlicue" was to
pull off a boyish caper or trick—in this case, the child perhaps is writing something with a charred stick, which would
wash away with the first rain.

[4] *august* Respected, eminent, reverenced.

[5] *tenoned and mortised* Securely fixed together. In carpentry, a tenon—a projection at the end of the wooden
piece—is fixed into the mortise—a hole or cavity in another piece of wood. Together they form a strong joint.

[21]   I am the poet of the body,
And I am the poet of the soul.

The pleasures of heaven are with me, and the pains of hell are with me,
425   The first I graft and increase upon myself . . . . the latter I translate into a new tongue.

I am the poet of the woman the same as the man,
And I say it is as great to be a woman as to be a man,
And I say there is nothing greater than the mother of men.

I chant a new chant of dilation[1] or pride,
430   We have had ducking[2] and deprecating about enough,
I show that size is only development.

Have you outstript the rest? Are you the President?
It is a trifle . . . . they will more than arrive there every one, and still pass on.

I am he that walks with the tender and growing night;
435   I call to the earth and sea half-held by the night.

Press close barebosomed night! Press close magnetic nourishing night!
Night of south winds! Night of the large few stars!
Still nodding night! Mad naked summer night!

Smile O voluptuous coolbreathed earth!
440   Earth of the slumbering and liquid trees!
Earth of departed sunset! Earth of the mountains misty-topt!
Earth of the vitreous[3] pour of the full moon just tinged with blue!
Earth of shine and dark mottling the tide of the river!
Earth of the limpid gray of clouds brighter and clearer for my sake!
445   Far-swooping elbowed earth! Rich apple-blossomed earth!
Smile, for your lover comes!

Prodigal![4] you have given me love! . . . . therefore I to you give love!
O unspeakable passionate love!

Thruster holding me tight and that I hold tight!
450   We hurt each other as the bridegroom and the bride hurt each other.

[22]   You sea! I resign myself to you also . . . . I guess what you mean,
I behold from the beach your crooked inviting fingers,

---

1   *dilation*   Expansion.

2   *ducking*   Evading, side-stepping.

3   *vitreous*   Glass-like.

4   *Prodigal*   Christ's Parable of the Prodigal Son is told in Luke 15.11–32. The story focuses on redemption: a wayward son who has wasted his inheritance is welcomed home by his father without reproach.

I believe you refuse to go back without feeling of me;
We must have a turn together . . . . I undress . . . . hurry me out of sight of the land,
455   Cushion me soft . . . . rock me in billowy drowse,
Dash me with amorous wet . . . . I can repay you.

Sea of stretched ground-swells!
Sea breathing broad and convulsive breaths!
Sea of the brine of life! Sea of unshovelled and always-ready graves!
460   Howler and scooper of storms! Capricious and dainty sea!
I am integral with you . . . . I too am of one phase and of all phases.

Partaker of influx and efflux . . . . extoler of hate and conciliation,
Extoler of amies[1] and those that sleep in each others' arms.

I am he attesting sympathy;
465   Shall I make my list of things in the house and skip the house that supports them?

I am the poet of commonsense and of the demonstrable and of immortality;
And am not the poet of goodness only . . . . I do not decline to be the poet of wickedness also.
Washes and razors for foofoos[2] . . . . for me freckles and a bristling beard.

What blurt is it about virtue and about vice?
470   Evil propels me, and reform of evil propels me . . . . I stand indifferent,
My gait is no faultfinder's or rejecter's gait,
I moisten the roots of all that has grown.

Did you fear some scrofula out of the unflagging[3] pregnancy?
Did you guess the celestial laws are yet to be worked over and rectified?

475   I step up to say that what we do is right and what we affirm is right . . . . and some is only
     the ore[4] of right,
Witnesses of us . . . . one side a balance and the antipodal side a balance,
Soft doctrine as steady help as stable doctrine,
Thoughts and deeds of the present our rouse and early start.

This minute that comes to me over the past decillions,
480   There is no better than it and now.

What behaved well in the past or behaves well today is not such a wonder,
The wonder is always and always how there can be a mean man or an infidel.

---

[1]   *amies* Friends, lovers.

[2]   *foofoos* Offensive slang term for men who fussed over their appearance.

[3]   *scrofula* Swelling of the lymph glands: a type of tuberculosis; *unflagging* Untiring, energetic.

[4]   *ore* Material mined from the earth containing valuable metal that has not yet been refined.

[23]   Endless unfolding of words of ages!
        And mine a word of the modern . . . . a word en masse.

485   A word of the faith that never balks,
        One time as good as another time . . . . here or henceforward it is all the same to me.

        A word of reality . . . . materialism first and last imbueing.

        Hurrah for positive science! Long live exact demonstration!
        Fetch stonecrop[1] and mix it with cedar and branches of lilac;
490   This is the lexicographer or chemist . . . . this made a grammar of the old cartouches,[2]
        These mariners put the ship through dangerous unknown seas,
        This is the geologist, and this works with the scalpel, and this is a mathematician.

        Gentlemen I receive you, and attach and clasp hands with you,
        The facts are useful and real . . . . they are not my dwelling . . . . I enter by them to an area of
            the dwelling.

495   I am less the reminder of property or qualities, and more the reminder of life,
        And go on the square[3] for my own sake and for others' sakes,
        And make short account of neuters and geldings,[4] and favor men and women fully equipped,
        And beat the gong of revolt, and stop with fugitives and them that plot and conspire.

[24]   Walt Whitman, an American, one of the roughs, a kosmos,
500   Disorderly fleshy and sensual . . . . eating drinking and breeding,
        No sentimentalist . . . . no stander above men and women or apart from them . . . . no more
            modest than immodest.

        Unscrew the locks from the doors!
        Unscrew the doors themselves from their jambs!

        Whoever degrades another degrades me . . . . and whatever is done or said returns at last to me,
505   And whatever I do or say I also return.

        Through me the afflatus[5] surging and surging . . . . through me the current and index.

        I speak the password primeval . . . . I give the sign of democracy;
        By God! I will accept nothing which all cannot have their counterpart of on the same terms.

---

[1]   *stonecrop*   Sedum plant with small flowers that grows on rocks and old stone walls.

[2]   *cartouches*   Circled areas in Egyptian hieroglyphs containing images that denote a royal name; inscribed tablets
made to look like a scroll of paper are also referred to as cartouches.

[3]   *go on the square*   Act and speak honestly and openly.

[4]   *neuters and geldings*   Castrated or spayed animals; by extension, people perceived to be unsexed or sexually
repressed.

[5]   *afflatus*   Divine inspiration, the passing on of spiritual wisdom.

Through me many long dumb voices,
510 Voices of the interminable generations of slaves,
Voices of prostitutes and of deformed persons,
Voices of the diseased and despairing, and of thieves and dwarfs,
Voices of cycles of preparation and accretion,
And of the threads that connect the stars—and of wombs, and of the fatherstuff,
515 And of the rights of them the others are down upon,
Of the trivial and flat and foolish and despised,
Of fog in the air and beetles rolling balls of dung.

Through me forbidden voices,
Voices of sexes and lusts . . . . voices veiled, and I remove the veil,
520 Voices indecent by me clarified and transfigured.

I do not press my finger across my mouth,
I keep as delicate around the bowels as around the head and heart,
Copulation is no more rank to me than death is.

I believe in the flesh and the appetites,
525 Seeing hearing and feeling are miracles, and each part and tag of me is a miracle.

Divine am I inside and out, and I make holy whatever I touch or am touched from;
The scent of these arm-pits is aroma finer than prayer,
This head is more than churches or bibles or creeds.

If I worship any particular thing it shall be some of the spread of my body;
530 Translucent mould of me it shall be you,
Shaded ledges and rests, firm masculine coulter,[1] it shall be you,
Whatever goes to the tilth[2] of me it shall be you,
You my rich blood, your milky stream pale strippings of my life;
Breast that presses against other breasts it shall be you,
535 My brain it shall be your occult convolutions,
Root of washed sweet-flag, timorous pond-snipe,[3] nest of guarded duplicate eggs, it shall be
     you,
Mixed tussled hay of head and beard and brawn it shall be you,
Trickling sap of maple, fibre of manly wheat, it shall be you;
Sun so generous it shall be you,
540 Vapors lighting and shading my face it shall be you,
You sweaty brooks and dews it shall be you,
Winds whose soft-tickling genitals rub against me it shall be you,

---

1   *coulter*   Blade on a plough that cuts the soil.

2   *tilth*   Cultivation, ploughing.

3   *sweet-flag*   Flowering wetland plant, also called the calamus, which produces a striking, phallic spadix when in flower, and which has long been symbolically associated (in Greek mythology and elsewhere) with love between men;   *pond-snipe*   Shorebird, likely the Wilson's snipe or the common snipe, both of which catch worms and insects along the muddy shores of ponds and in wet fields.

Broad muscular fields, branches of liveoak,[1] loving lounger in my winding paths, it shall be you,
Hands I have taken, face I have kissed, mortal I have ever touched, it shall be you.

545   I dote on myself . . . . there is that lot of me, and all so luscious,
Each moment and whatever happens thrills me with joy.

I cannot tell how my ankles bend . . . . nor whence the cause of my faintest wish,
Nor the cause of the friendship I emit . . . . nor the cause of the friendship I take again.

To walk up my stoop is unaccountable . . . . . I pause to consider if it really be,
550   That I eat and drink is spectacle enough for the great authors and schools,
A morning-glory at my window satisfies me more than the metaphysics of books.

To behold the daybreak!
The little light fades the immense and diaphanous shadows,
The air tastes good to my palate.

555   Hefts of the moving world at innocent gambols, silently rising, freshly exuding,
Scooting obliquely high and low.

Something I cannot see puts upward libidinous prongs,
Seas of bright juice suffuse heaven.

The earth by the sky staid with . . . . the daily close of their junction,
560   The heaved challenge from the east that moment over my head,
The mocking taunt, See then whether you shall be master!

[25]   Dazzling and tremendous how quick the sunrise would kill me,
If I could not now and always send sunrise out of me.

We also ascend dazzling and tremendous as the sun,
565   We found our own my soul in the calm and cool of the daybreak.

My voice goes after what my eyes cannot reach,
With the twirl of my tongue I encompass worlds and volumes of worlds.

Speech is the twin of my vision . . . . it is unequal to measure itself.

It provokes me forever,
570   It says sarcastically, Walt, you understand enough . . . . why don't you let it out then?

Come now I will not be tantalized . . . . you conceive too much of articulation.

Do you not know how the buds beneath are folded?
Waiting in gloom protected by frost,

---

[1]   *liveoak*   Evergreen oaks, primarily found in the southeastern United States.

The dirt receding before my prophetical screams,
575   I underlying causes to balance them at last,
My knowledge my live parts . . . . it keeping tally with the meaning of things,
Happiness . . . . which whoever hears me let him or her set out in search of this day.

My final merit I refuse you . . . . I refuse putting from me the best I am.

Encompass worlds but never try to encompass me,
580   I crowd your noisiest talk by looking toward you.

Writing and talk do not prove me,
I carry the plenum[1] of proof and every thing else in my face,
With the hush of my lips I confound the topmost skeptic.

[26]   I think I will do nothing for a long time but listen,
585   And accrue what I hear into myself . . . . and let sounds contribute toward me.

I hear the bravuras of birds . . . . the bustle of growing wheat . . . . gossip of flames . . . . clack
      of sticks cooking my meals.

I hear the sound of the human voice . . . . a sound I love,
I hear all sounds as they are tuned to their uses . . . . sounds of the city and sounds out of the
      city . . . . sounds of the day and night;
Talkative young ones to those that like them . . . . the recitative[2] of fish-pedlars and fruit-
      pedlars . . . . the loud laugh of workpeople at their meals,
590   The angry base of disjointed friendship . . . . the faint tones of the sick,
The judge with hands tight to the desk, his shaky lips pronouncing a death-sentence,
The heave'e'yo of stevedores[3] unlading ships by the wharves . . . . the refrain of the
      anchor-lifters;
The ring of alarm-bells . . . . the cry of fire . . . . the whirr of swift-streaking engines and hose-
      carts with premonitory tinkles and colored lights,
The steam-whistle . . . . the solid roll of the train of approaching cars;
595   The slow-march played at night at the head of the association,
They go to guard some corpse . . . . the flag-tops are draped with black muslin.

I hear the violincello or man's heart's complaint,
And hear the keyed cornet or else the echo of sunset.

I hear the chorus . . . . it is a grand-opera . . . . this indeed is music!

---

[1]   *plenum*   Entirety of space filled with matter.

[2]   *recitative*   Type of musical utterance that lies between speaking and singing, often used in religious services and
in oratorios and operas.

[3]   *stevedores*   Laborers who load and unload merchant ships.

600　A tenor large and fresh as the creation fills me,
　　　The orbic[1] flex of his mouth is pouring and filling me full.

　　　I hear the trained soprano . . . . she convulses me like the climax of my love-grip;
　　　The orchestra whirls me wider than Uranus flies,
　　　It wrenches unnamable ardors from my breast,
605　It throbs me to gulps of the farthest down horror,
　　　It sails me . . . . I dab with bare feet . . . . they are licked by the indolent waves,
　　　I am exposed . . . . cut by bitter and poisoned hail,
　　　Steeped amid honeyed morphine . . . . my windpipe squeezed in the fakes of death,[2]
　　　Let up again to feel the puzzle of puzzles,
610　And that we call Being.

[27]　To be in any form, what is that?
　　　If nothing lay more developed the quahaug[3] and its callous shell were enough.

　　　Mine is no callous shell,
　　　I have instant conductors all over me whether I pass or stop,
615　They seize every object and lead it harmlessly through me.

　　　I merely stir, press, feel with my fingers, and am happy,
　　　To touch my person to some one else's is about as much as I can stand.

[28]　Is this then a touch? . . . . quivering me to a new identity,
　　　Flames and ether[4] making a rush for my veins,
620　Treacherous tip of me reaching and crowding to help them,
　　　My flesh and blood playing out lightning, to strike what is hardly different from myself,
　　　On all sides prurient provokers stiffening my limbs,
　　　Straining the udder of my heart for its withheld drip,
　　　Behaving licentious toward me, taking no denial,
625　Depriving me of my best as for a purpose,
　　　Unbuttoning my clothes and holding me by the bare waist,
　　　Deluding my confusion with the calm of the sunlight and pasture fields,
　　　Immodestly sliding the fellow-senses away,
　　　They bribed to swap off with touch, and go and graze at the edges of me,
630　No consideration, no regard for my draining strength or my anger,
　　　Fetching the rest of the herd around to enjoy them awhile,
　　　Then all uniting to stand on a headland and worry[5] me.

1　*orbic*　Round, spherical.

2　*fakes of death*　"Fakes" is a nautical term for coils of rope, so this phrase likely suggests the "coils" (or snares) of death.

3　*quahaug*　Narraganset: Atlantic clam.

4　*ether*　Flammable liquid made by combining sulfuric acid and ethanol.

5　*worry*　Take by the throat and injure or kill by biting and shaking (said of dogs or wolves when they catch a sheep). Also used to refer to greedy, excessively fond kisses and hugs and, more generally, to physical harassment and distress.

The sentries desert every other part of me,
They have left me helpless to a red marauder,
635   They all come to the headland to witness and assist against me.

I am given up by traitors;
I talk wildly . . . . I have lost my wits . . . . I and nobody else am the greatest traitor,
I went myself first to the headland . . . . my own hands carried me there.

You villain touch! what are you doing? . . . . my breath is tight in its throat;
640   Unclench your floodgates! you are too much for me.

[29]   Blind loving wrestling touch! Sheathed hooded sharptoothed touch!
Did it make you ache so leaving me?

Parting tracked by arriving . . . . perpetual payment of the perpetual loan,
Rich showering rain, and recompense richer afterward.

645   Sprouts take and accumulate . . . . stand by the curb prolific and vital,
Landscapes projected masculine full-sized and golden.

[30]   All truths wait in all things,
They neither hasten their own delivery nor resist it,
They do not need the obstetric forceps of the surgeon,
650   The insignificant is as big to me as any,
What is less or more than a touch?

Logic and sermons never convince,
The damp of the night drives deeper into my soul.

Only what proves itself to every man and woman is so,
655   Only what nobody denies is so.

A minute and a drop of me settle my brain;
I believe the soggy clods shall become lovers and lamps,
And a compend[1] of compends is the meat of a man or woman,
And a summit and flower there is the feeling they have for each other,
660   And they are to branch boundlessly out of that lesson until it becomes omnific,[2]
And until every one shall delight us, and we them.

[31]   I believe a leaf of grass is no less than the journeywork[3] of the stars,
And the pismire[4] is equally perfect, and a grain of sand, and the egg of the wren,

---

1   *compend*   Compendium, a condensed embodiment.

2   *omnific*   All-making; having the power to create everything.

3   *journeywork*   Work done for pay.

4   *pismire*   Ant.

And the tree-toad is a chef-d'oeuvre[1] for the highest,
665 And the running blackberry would adorn the parlors of heaven,
And the narrowest hinge in my hand puts to scorn all machinery,
And the cow crunching with depressed[2] head surpasses any statue,
And a mouse is miracle enough to stagger sextillions of infidels,
And I could come every afternoon of my life to look at the farmer's girl boiling her iron tea-
    kettle and baking shortcake.

670 I find I incorporate gneiss and coal and long-threaded moss and fruits and grains and escu-
    lent[3] roots,
And am stucco'd with quadrupeds and birds all over,
And have distanced what is behind me for good reasons,
And call any thing close again when I desire it.

In vain the speeding or shyness,
675 In vain the plutonic rocks[4] send their old heat against my approach,
In vain the mastadon[5] retreats beneath its own powdered bones,
In vain objects stand leagues off and assume manifold shapes,
In vain the ocean settling in hollows and the great monsters lying low,
In vain the buzzard houses herself with the sky,
680 In vain the snake slides through the creepers and logs,
In vain the elk takes to the inner passes of the woods,
In vain the razorbilled auk[6] sails far north to Labrador,
I follow quickly . . . . I ascend to the nest in the fissure of the cliff.

[32] I think I could turn and live awhile with the animals . . . . they are so placid and
    self-contained,
685 I stand and look at them sometimes half the day long.

They do not sweat and whine about their condition,
They do not lie awake in the dark and weep for their sins,
They do not make me sick discussing their duty to God,
Not one is dissatisfied . . . . not one is demented with the mania of owning things,
690 Not one kneels to another nor to his kind that lived thousands of years ago,
Not one is respectable or industrious over the whole earth.

So they show their relations to me and I accept them;
They bring me tokens of myself . . . . they evince them plainly in their possession.

---

1 *chef-d'oeuvre* French: masterpiece.

2 *depressed* Lowered.

3 *gneiss* Granite-like rock composed of quartz, feldspar, and mica; *esculent* Edible.

4 *plutonic rocks* Rocks created by heat at great depths in the earth (as opposed to volcanic rocks, which are created at the earth's surface). "Plutonic" can also mean "infernal" or "hellish" (because of the association with the Roman god of the underworld, Pluto).

5 *mastadon* Extinct elephant-like mammal.

6 *razorbilled auk* North Atlantic seabird.

I do not know where they got those tokens,
695 I must have passed that way untold times ago and negligently dropt them,
Myself moving forward then and now and forever,
Gathering and showing more always and with velocity,
Infinite and omnigenous[1] and the like of these among them;
Not too exclusive toward the reachers of my remembrancers,
700 Picking out here one that shall be my amie,
Choosing to go with him on brotherly terms.

A gigantic beauty of a stallion, fresh and responsive to my caresses,
Head high in the forehead and wide between the ears,
Limbs glossy and supple, tail dusting the ground,
705 Eyes well apart and full of sparkling wickedness . . . . ears finely cut and flexibly moving.

His nostrils dilate . . . . my heels embrace him . . . . his well built limbs tremble with pleasure
    . . . . we speed around and return.

I but use you a moment and then I resign you stallion . . . . and do not need your paces, and
    outgallop them,
And myself as I stand or sit pass faster than you.

[33] Swift wind! Space! My Soul! Now I know it is true what I guessed at;
710   What I guessed when I loafed on the grass,
What I guessed while I lay alone in my bed . . . . and again as I walked the beach under the
    paling stars of the morning.

My ties and ballasts[2] leave me . . . . I travel . . . . I sail . . . . my elbows rest in the sea-gaps,
I skirt the sierras . . . . my palms cover continents,
I am afoot with my vision.

715 By the city's quadrangular houses . . . . in log-huts, or camping with lumbermen,
Along the ruts of the turnpike[3] . . . . along the dry gulch and rivulet bed,
Hoeing my onion-patch, and rows of carrots and parsnips . . . . crossing savannas . . . trailing
    in forests,
Prospecting . . . . gold-digging . . . . girdling the trees of a new purchase,
Scorched ankle-deep by the hot sand . . . . hauling my boat down the shallow river;
720 Where the panther walks to and fro on a limb overhead . . . . where the buck turns furiously
    at the hunter,
Where the rattlesnake suns his flabby length on a rock . . . . where the otter is feeding on fish,
Where the alligator in his tough pimples sleeps by the bayou,
Where the black bear is searching for roots or honey . . . . where the beaver pats the mud
    with his paddle-tail;
Over the growing sugar . . . . over the cottonplant . . . . over the rice in its low moist field;

---

1   *omnigenous* Infinitely diverse.
2   *ballasts* Weights placed in the holds of a ship to keep it steadier on the sea.
3   *turnpike* Toll road, usually a main road or highway.

725 Over the sharp-peaked farmhouse with its scalloped scum[1] and slender shoots from the
      gutters;
Over the western persimmon[2] . . . . over the longleaved corn and the delicate blue-flowered
      flax;
Over the white and brown buckwheat, a hummer and a buzzer there with the rest,
Over the dusky green of the rye as it ripples and shades in the breeze;
Scaling mountains . . . . pulling myself cautiously up . . . . holding on by low scragged[3] limbs,
730 Walking the path worn in the grass and beat through the leaves of the brush;
Where the quail is whistling betwixt the woods and the wheatlot,
Where the bat flies in the July eve . . . . where the great goldbug[4] drops through the dark;
Where the flails[5] keep time on the barn floor,
Where the brook puts out of the roots of the old tree and flows to the meadow,
735 Where cattle stand and shake away flies with the tremulous shuddering of their hides,
Where the cheese-cloth hangs in the kitchen, and andirons[6] straddle the hearth-slab, and
      cobwebs fall in festoons from the rafters;
Where triphammers[7] crash . . . . where the press is whirling its cylinders;
Wherever the human heart beats with terrible throes out of its ribs;
Where the pear-shaped balloon is floating aloft . . . . floating in it myself and looking com-
      posedly down;
740 Where the life-car is drawn on the slipnoose[8] . . . . where the heat hatches pale-green eggs in
      the dented sand,
Where the she-whale swims with her calves and never forsakes them,
Where the steamship trails hindways its long pennant of smoke,
Where the ground-shark's[9] fin cuts like a black chip out of the water,
Where the half-burned brig[10] is riding on unknown currents,
745 Where shells grow to her slimy deck, and the dead are corrupting below;
Where the striped and starred flag is borne at the head of the regiments;
Approaching Manhattan, up by the long-stretching island,
Under Niagara, the cataract falling like a veil over my countenance;
Upon a door-step . . . . upon the horse-block[11] of hard wood outside,
750 Upon the race-course, or enjoying pic-nics or jigs or a good game of base-ball,

---

1   *scum*   Froth or sediment on the rainwater that has gathered in the house's gutters.

2   *persimmon*   American persimmon, a tree that grows as far west as Texas and Oklahoma.

3   *scragged*   Thin, rough, scraggly.

4   *great goldbug*   Unclear, but likely the golden tortoise beetle.

5   *flails*   Instruments used to thresh grain.

6   *andirons*   Pair of iron bars used to support wood in a fireplace.

7   *triphammers*   Huge hammers that work by triggering a tripping device, usually a wheel that raises the hammer
and then allows it to fall.

8   *life-car*   Type of watertight life-boat attached to a rope and used to pull people through heavy seas to safety;
slipnoose   Noose that tightens and loosens with a slip-knot.

9   *ground-shark*   Also known as the Greenland shark.

10   *brig*   Ship with two square-rigged masts.

11   *horse-block*   Cement or wooden structure with steps, used to help climb up onto a horse.

At he-festivals with blackguard jibes and ironical license and bull-dances[1] and drinking and laughter,

At the cider-mill, tasting the sweet of the brown sqush[2] . . . . sucking the juice through a straw,

At apple-pealings,[3] wanting kisses for all the red fruit I find,

At musters and beach-parties and friendly bees and huskings and house-raisings;[4]

755 Where the mockingbird sounds his delicious gurgles, and cackles and screams and weeps,

Where the hay-rick stands in the barnyard, and the dry-stalks are scattered, and the brood cow[5] waits in the hovel,

Where the bull advances to do his masculine work, and the stud to the mare, and the cock is treading the hen,

Where the heifers browse, and the geese nip their food with short jerks;

Where the sundown shadows lengthen over the limitless and lonesome prairie,

760 Where the herds of buffalo make a crawling spread of the square miles far and near;

Where the hummingbird shimmers . . . . where the neck of the longlived swan is curving and winding;

Where the laughing-gull scoots by the slappy shore and laughs her near-human laugh;

Where beehives range on a gray bench in the garden half-hid by the high weeds;

Where the band-necked partridges roost in a ring on the ground with their heads out;

765 Where burial coaches enter the arched gates of a cemetery;

Where winter wolves bark amid wastes of snow and icicled trees;

Where the yellow-crowned heron comes to the edge of the marsh at night and feeds upon small crabs;

Where the splash of swimmers and divers cools the warm noon;

Where the katydid works her chromatic reed[6] on the walnut-tree over the well;

770 Through patches of citrons[7] and cucumbers with silver-wired leaves,

Through the salt-lick[8] or orange glade . . . . or under conical furs;

Through the gymnasium . . . . through the curtained saloon . . . . through the office or public hall;

Pleased with the native and pleased with the foreign . . . . pleased with the new and old,

Pleased with women, the homely as well as the handsome,

---

1   *he-festivals* A coinage of Whitman's; *jibes* Taunts, jeers; *bull-dances* Dances with only men present (typically these were dances held by sailors aboard ship). Also called stag-dances.

2   *sqush* Colloquial term for a pulpy, squeezed-out mush.

3   *apple-pealings* Social gatherings at apple-harvest time to bring in the apples and prepare them for cider-making and other uses. Also called an apple-bee.

4   *musters* Social gatherings of firefighters in which skill competitions were held; *bees* Neighborhood gatherings that bring people together to complete labor-heavy tasks, such as gathering in harvests or building houses and barns. There was often a festival atmosphere to lighten the work; *huskings* Gatherings held to husk the corn harvest; *house-raisings* Gatherings held to build homes.

5   *brood cow* Cow ready to conceive calves.

6   *katydid works her chromatic reed* Reference to the sound of the katydid, or bush cricket, a type of grasshopper common to the central and eastern parts of the U.S.

7   *citrons* Lemons.

8   *salt-lick* Place where animals come to lick salt (either a place built by humans for this purpose or a place with naturally-occurring salt).

775   Pleased with the quakeress as she puts off her bonnet and talks melodiously,[1]
     Pleased with the primitive tunes of the choir of the whitewashed church,
     Pleased with the earnest words of the sweating Methodist preacher, or any preacher . . . .
          looking seriously at the camp-meeting;[2]
     Looking in at the shop-windows in Broadway the whole forenoon . . . . pressing the flesh of
          my nose to the thick plate-glass,[3]
     Wandering the same afternoon with my face turned up to the clouds;
780   My right and left arms round the sides of two friends and I in the middle;
     Coming home with the bearded and dark-cheeked bush-boy . . . . riding behind him at the
          drape[4] of the day;
     Far from the settlements studying the print of animals' feet, or the moccasin print;
     By the cot in the hospital reaching lemonade to a feverish patient,
     By the coffined corpse when all is still, examining with a candle;
785   Voyaging to every port to dicker[5] and adventure;
     Hurrying with the modern crowd, as eager and fickle as any,
     Hot toward one I hate, ready in my madness to knife him;
     Solitary at midnight in my back yard, my thoughts gone from me a long while,
     Walking the old hills of Judea[6] with the beautiful gentle god by my side;
790   Speeding through space . . . . speeding through heaven and the stars,
     Speeding amid the seven satellites and the broad ring and the diameter of eighty thousand miles,[7]
     Speeding with tailed meteors . . . . throwing fire-balls like the rest,
     Carrying the crescent child that carries its own full mother in its belly;
     Storming enjoying planning loving cautioning,
795   Backing and filling, appearing and disappearing,
     I tread day and night such roads.

     I visit the orchards of God and look at the spheric product,
     And look at quintillions ripened, and look at quintillions green.

     I fly the flight of the fluid and swallowing soul,
800   My course runs below the soundings of plummets.

     I help myself to material and immaterial,
     No guard can shut me off, no law can prevent me.

---

[1] *the quakeress ... talks melodiously* The Quakers, or Society of Friends, were known for the gender equality of their religious services and for encouraging women to speak in church and become ministers. Quakers also employed an old-fashioned, and many would say musical and charming, style of speech.

[2] *camp-meeting* Religious meeting that takes place outside, usually over the course of several days. Attendees would set up camp at the location for the duration of the meeting.

[3] *plate-glass* High-quality glass used in shop windows to allow passers-by a clear view.

[4] *bush-boy* Usually a term that was applied to an Indigenous boy from Australia or South Africa who lives in the wilderness (here transferred to the American scene); *drape* I.e., close.

[5] *dicker* Bargain, set up deals.

[6] *Judea* Biblical location of Bethlehem, the birthplace of Jesus Christ.

[7] *seven ... miles* I.e., the planet Saturn, of whose numerous moons seven were known by the mid-1800s, and which has a diameter of 72,367 miles.

I anchor my ship for a little while only,
My messengers continually cruise away or bring their returns to me.

805   I go hunting polar furs and the seal . . . . leaping chasms with a pike-pointed staff . . . . cling-
     ing to topples[1] of brittle and blue.

I ascend to the foretruck . . . . I take my place late at night in the crow's nest[2] . . . . we sail
     through the arctic sea . . . . it is plenty light enough,
Through the clear atmosphere I stretch around on the wonderful beauty,
The enormous masses of ice pass me and I pass them . . . . the scenery is plain in all
     directions,
The white-topped mountains point up in the distance . . . . I fling out my fancies toward
     them;
810   We are about approaching some great battlefield in which we are soon to be engaged,
We pass the colossal outposts of the encampments . . . . we pass with still feet and caution;
Or we are entering by the suburbs some vast and ruined city . . . . the blocks and fallen
     architecture more than all the living cities of the globe.

I am a free companion . . . . I bivouac[3] by invading watchfires.

I turn the bridegroom out of bed and stay with the bride myself,
815   And tighten her all night to my thighs and lips.

My voice is the wife's voice, the screech by the rail of the stairs,
They fetch my man's body up dripping and drowned.

I understand the large hearts of heroes,
The courage of present times and all times;
820   How the skipper[4] saw the crowded and rudderless wreck of the steamship, and death chasing
     it up and down the storm,
How he knuckled tight and gave not back one inch, and was faithful of days and faithful of
     nights,
And chalked in large letters on a board, Be of good cheer, We will not desert you;
How he saved the drifting company at last,
How the lank loose-gowned women looked when boated from the side of their prepared
     graves,
825   How the silent old-faced infants, and the lifted sick, and the sharp-lipped unshaved men;
All this I swallow and it tastes good . . . . I like it well, and it becomes mine,
I am the man . . . . I suffered . . . . I was there.[5]

---

1   *topples*   High crests or ledges (here presumably referring to ice formations).

2   *foretruck*   The top of the foremast (in the front of the vessel);   *crow's nest*   Sheltered lookout at the top of a ship's masthead.

3   *bivouac*   Sleep in the open air.

4   *skipper*   Captain of a small ship.

5   *I understand ... was there*   This stanza describes a naval disaster that took place in late December 1853; the steamship *San Francisco* departed New York for San Francisco on 22 December 1853 and was devastated by a storm [continued …]

The disdain and calmness of martyrs,
The mother condemned for a witch and burnt with dry wood, and her children gazing on;
830   The hounded slave that flags[1] in the race and leans by the fence, blowing and covered with
        sweat,
The twinges that sting like needles his legs and neck,
The murderous buckshot and the bullets,
All these I feel or am.

I am the hounded slave . . . . I wince at the bite of the dogs,
835   Hell and despair are upon me . . . . crack and again crack the marksmen,
I clutch the rails of the fence . . . . my gore dribs thinned with the ooze[2] of my skin,
I fall on the weeds and stones,
The riders spur their unwilling horses and haul close,
They taunt my dizzy ears . . . . they beat me violently over the head with their whip-stocks.[3]

840   Agonies are one of my changes of garments;
I do not ask the wounded person how he feels . . . . I myself become the wounded person,
My hurt turns livid upon me as I lean on a cane and observe.

I am the mashed fireman with breastbone broken . . . . tumbling walls buried me in their
        debris,
Heat and smoke I inspired . . . . I heard the yelling shouts of my comrades,
845   I heard the distant click of their picks and shovels;
They have cleared the beams away . . . . they tenderly lift me forth.

I lie in the night air in my red shirt . . . . the pervading hush is for my sake,
Painless after all I lie, exhausted but not so unhappy,
White and beautiful are the faces around me . . . . the heads are bared of their fire-caps,
850   The kneeling crowd fades with the light of the torches.

Distant and dead resuscitate,
They show as the dial or move as the hands of me . . . . and I am the clock myself.

I am an old artillerist, and tell of some fort's bombardment . . . . and am there again.

Again the reveille of drummers . . . . again the attacking cannon and mortars and howitzers,[4]
855   Again the attacked send their cannon responsive.

---

that began on the night of the 24th. Approximately two hundred passengers were swept overboard in the initial storm; others died by suicide or from disease in the following days as they awaited rescue. The survivors were rescued by the *Kilby* on the 28th, though, due to the violent weather, they were not able to disembark in New York until mid-January.

[1]   *flags*   Loses speed.

[2]   *gore*   Blood;   *ooze*   Sweat.

[3]   *whip-stocks*   Handles of whips, or the sticks to which whips are attached.

[4]   *reveille*   Music played to wake people up in the morning;   *mortars*   Artillery guns that fire missiles at high angles;   *howitzers*   Light-weight artillery guns.

I take part . . . . I see and hear the whole,
The cries and curses and roar . . . . the plaudits for well aimed shots,
The ambulanza[1] slowly passing and trailing its red drip,
Workmen searching after damages and to make indispensible repairs,
860 The fall of grenades through the rent[2] roof . . . . the fan-shaped explosion,
The whizz of limbs heads stone wood and iron high in the air.

Again gurgles the mouth of my dying general . . . . he furiously waves with his hand,
He gasps through the clot . . . . Mind not me . . . . mind . . . . the entrenchments.

[34] I tell not the fall of Alamo[3] . . . . not one escaped to tell the fall of Alamo,
865 The hundred and fifty are dumb yet at Alamo.

Hear now the tale of a jetblack sunrise,
Hear of the murder in cold blood of four hundred and twelve young men.[4]

Retreating they had formed in a hollow square with their baggage for breastworks,[5]
Nine hundred lives out of the surrounding enemy's nine times their number was the price
    they took in advance,
870 Their colonel was wounded and their ammunition gone,
They treated[6] for an honorable capitulation, received writing and seal, gave up their arms,
    and marched back prisoners of war.

They were the glory of the race of rangers,[7]
Matchless with a horse, a rifle, a song, a supper or a courtship,
Large, turbulent, brave, handsome, generous, proud and affectionate,
875 Bearded, sunburnt, dressed in the free costume of hunters,
Not a single one over thirty years of age.

The second Sunday morning they were brought out in squads and massacred . . . . it was
    beautiful early summer,
The work commenced about five o'clock and was over by eight.

None obeyed the command to kneel,
880 Some made a mad and helpless rush . . . . some stood stark and straight,

1   *ambulanza*   Italian: ambulance.

2   *rent*   Torn.

3   *Alamo*   The Battle of the Alamo (1836) took place in San Antonio, Texas, during the Texas Revolution. Close to two hundred Texans were killed by the Mexican Army.

4   *murder ... young men*   From here to line 889, Whitman is describing the events of the Goliad Massacre, which took place during the Texas Revolution on 27 March 1836. Between 423 and 445 Texian prisoners were killed by the Mexican Army in the town of Goliad. The prisoners were killed by firing squad and by being beaten and stabbed to death.

5   *breastworks*   Temporary chest-high military barriers.

6   *treated*   Negotiated.

7   *rangers*   Organized group of armed individuals dedicated to protecting a certain area of land.

A few fell at once, shot in the temple or heart . . . . the living and dead lay together,
The maimed and mangled dug in the dirt . . . . the new-comers saw them there;
Some half-killed attempted to crawl away,
These were dispatched[1] with bayonets or battered with the blunts of muskets;

885 A youth not seventeen years old seized his assassin till two more came to release him,
The three were all torn, and covered with the boy's blood.

At eleven o'clock began the burning of the bodies;
And that is the tale of the murder of the four hundred and twelve young men,
And that was a jetblack sunrise.

[35] Did you read in the seabooks of the oldfashioned frigate-fight?[2]
Did you learn who won by the light of the moon and stars?

Our foe was no skulk in his ship, I tell you,
His was the English pluck, and there is no tougher or truer, and never was, and never will be;
Along the lowered eve he came, horribly raking[3] us.

895 We closed with him . . . . the yards[4] entangled . . . . the cannon touched,
My captain[5] lashed fast with his own hands.

We had received some eighteen-pound shots under the water,
On our lower-gun-deck two large pieces had burst at the first fire, killing all around and
    blowing up overhead.

Ten o'clock at night, and the full moon shining and the leaks on the gain, and five feet of
    water reported,
900 The master-at-arms[6] loosing the prisoners confined in the after-hold to give them a chance
    for themselves.

The transit to and from the magazine[7] was now stopped by the sentinels,
They saw so many strange faces they did not know whom to trust.

---

1 *dispatched* Killed.

2 *oldfashioned frigate-fight* The naval war scene that follows describes the events of the Battle of Flamborough Head, which took place on 23 September 1779 during the American Revolutionary War. The battle occurred in the North Sea, between the Franco-American alliance and the British navy, which was protecting a convoy of merchant ships. The battle ended in a victory for the Franco-American side, though the merchant convoy escaped without harm.

3 *raking* Sweeping the ship from bow to stern with gunfire.

4 *yards* Wooden supports for sails on the masts.

5 *captain* Reference to Navy captain John Paul Jones (1747–92), who is often referred to as the "father of the American Navy." His bravery and persistence in the Battle of Flamborough Head became legendary.

6 *master-at-arms* Officer in charge of discipline aboard ship.

7 *magazine* Area of a warship where ammunition, arms, and explosives were kept.

Our frigate was afire . . . . the other asked if we demanded quarters? if our colors were struck[1]
    and the fighting done?

I laughed content when I heard the voice of my little captain,
905 We have not struck, he composedly cried, We have just begun our part of the fighting.

Only three guns were in use,
One was directed by the captain himself against the enemy's mainmast,
Two well-served with grape and canister[2] silenced his musketry and cleared his decks.

The tops alone seconded the fire of this little battery, especially the maintop,[3]
910 They all held out bravely during the whole of the action.

Not a moment's cease,
The leaks gained fast on the pumps . . . . the fire eat toward the powder-magazine,[4]
One of the pumps was shot away . . . . it was generally thought we were sinking.

Serene stood the little captain,
915 He was not hurried . . . . his voice was neither high nor low,
His eyes gave more light to us than our battle-lanterns.

Toward twelve at night, there in the beams of the moon they surrendered to us.

[36] Stretched and still lay the midnight,
Two great hulls motionless on the breast of the darkness,
920 Our vessel riddled and slowly sinking . . . . preparations to pass to the one we had conquered,
The captain on the quarter deck coldly giving his orders through a countenance white as a
    sheet,
Near by the corpse of the child that served in the cabin,
The dead face of an old salt with long white hair and carefully curled whiskers,
The flames spite of all that could be done flickering aloft and below,
925 The husky voices of the two or three officers yet fit for duty,
Formless stacks of bodies and bodies by themselves . . . . dabs of flesh upon the masts and
    spars,
The cut of cordage and dangle of rigging . . . . the slight shock of the soothe of waves,
Black and impassive guns, and litter of powder-parcels, and the strong scent,
Delicate sniffs of the seabreeze . . . . smells of sedgy grass and fields by the shore . . . death-
    messages given in charge to survivors,
930 The hiss of the surgeon's knife and the gnawing teeth of his saw,
The wheeze, the cluck, the swash of falling blood . . . . the short wild scream, the long dull
    tapering groan,
These so . . . . these irretrievable.

---

1 *colors were struck*   To lower the ship's flag—a symbol of surrender.

2 *grape and canister*   I.e., grapeshot and canister-shot, two types of iron balls that were shot from cannons.

3 *tops ... maintop*   Sailors stationed at the tops of the masts.

4 *eat*   Ate;   *powder-magazine*   Place where the gunpowder was stored.

[37]   O Christ! My fit is mastering me!
        What the rebel said gaily adjusting his throat to the rope-noose,
935   What the savage at the stump, his eye-sockets empty, his mouth spirting whoops and
            defiance,
        What stills the traveler come to the vault at Mount Vernon,[1]
        What sobers the Brooklyn boy as he looks down the shores of the Wallabout and remembers
            the prison ships,[2]
        What burnt the gums of the redcoat at Saratoga when he surrendered his brigades,[3]
        These become mine and me every one, and they are but little,
940   I become as much more as I like.

        I become any presence or truth of humanity here,
        And see myself in prison shaped like another man,
        And feel the dull unintermitted pain.

        For me the keepers of convicts shoulder their carbines[4] and keep watch,
945   It is I let out in the morning and barred at night.

        Not a mutineer walks handcuffed to the jail, but I am handcuffed to him and walk by his
            side,
        I am less the jolly one there, and more the silent one with sweat on my twitching lips.

        Not a youngster is taken for larceny, but I go up too and am tried and sentenced.

        Not a cholera patient lies at the last gasp, but I also lie at the last gasp,
950   My face is ash-colored, my sinews gnarl . . . . away from me people retreat.

        Askers embody themselves in me, and I am embodied in them,
        I project my hat and sit shamefaced and beg.

[38]   I rise extatic through all, and sweep with the true gravitation,
        The whirling and whirling is elemental within me.

955   Somehow I have been stunned. Stand back!
        Give me a little time beyond my cuffed head and slumbers and dreams and gaping,
        I discover myself on a verge of the usual mistake.

----

1   *vault at Mount Vernon*   Where George Washington (1732–99) is buried.

2   *Brooklyn boy … prison ships*   Whitman himself grew up near Wallabout Bay and the Brooklyn Naval Yard. During
the Revolutionary War British prison ships were moored at Wallabout, where the terrible conditions resulted in over
10,000 American prisoner-of-war deaths.

3   *redcoat at Saratoga*   British General John Burgoyne led the British army during the Battles of Saratoga (19
September and 7 October 1777);   *surrendered his brigades*   The British surrendered to the Americans on 17 October
1777.

4   *carbines*   Medium-sized firearms.

That I could forget the mockers and insults!
That I could forget the trickling tears and the blows of the bludgeons and hammers!
960   That I could look with a separate look on my own crucifixion and bloody crowning![1]

I remember . . . . I resume the overstaid fraction,
The grave of rock multiplies what has been confided to it . . . . or to any graves,
The corpses rise . . . . the gashes heal . . . . the fastenings roll away.[2]

I troop forth replenished with supreme power, one of an average unending procession,
965   We walk the roads of Ohio and Massachusetts and Virginia and Wisconsin and New
          York and New Orleans and Texas and Montreal and San Francisco and Charleston and
          Savannah and Mexico,
Inland and by the seacoast and boundary lines . . . . and we pass the boundary lines.

Our swift ordinances[3] are on their way over the whole earth,
The blossoms we wear in our hats are the growth of two thousand years.

Eleves[4] I salute you,
970   I see the approach of your numberless gangs . . . . I see you understand yourselves and me,
And know that they who have eyes are divine, and the blind and lame are equally divine,
And that my steps drag behind yours yet go before them,
And are aware how I am with you no more than I am with everybody.

[39]   The friendly and flowing savage . . . . Who is he?
975   Is he waiting for civilization or past it and mastering it?

Is he some southwesterner raised outdoors? Is he Canadian?
Is he from the Mississippi country? or from Iowa, Oregon or California? or from the moun-
          tains? or prairie life or bush-life? or from the sea?

Wherever he goes men and women accept and desire him,
They desire he should like them and touch them and speak to them and stay with them.

980   Behaviour lawless as snow-flakes . . . . words simple as grass . . . . uncombed head and laugh-
          ter and naivete;
Slowstepping feet and the common features, and the common modes and emanations,
They descend in new forms from the tips of his fingers,
They are wafted with the odor of his body or breath . . . . they fly out of the glance of his
          eyes.

---

[1]   *bloody crowning*   Christ was given a crown of thorns to wear during his crucifixion.

[2]   *fastenings roll away*   See Luke 24.1–12, which describes the resurrection of Christ, particularly the moment when the body of Christ is discovered to be missing from the grave: "And they found the stone rolled away from the sepulchre" (24.2).

[3]   *ordinances*   Decrees, commands.

[4]   *Eleves*   French: Students.

[40]   Flaunt of the sunshine I need not your bask . . . . lie over,[1]
985   You light surfaces only . . . . I force the surfaces and the depths also.

Earth! you seem to look for something at my hands,
Say old topknot![2] what do you want?

Man or woman! I might tell how I like you, but cannot,
And might tell what it is in me and what it is in you, but cannot,
990   And might tell the pinings I have . . . . the pulse of my nights and days.

Behold I do not give lectures or a little charity,
What I give I give out of myself.

You there, impotent, loose in the knees, open your scarfed chops[3] till I blow grit within you,
Spread your palms and lift the flaps of your pockets,
995   I am not to be denied . . . . I compel . . . . I have stores plenty and to spare,
And any thing I have I bestow.

I do not ask who you are . . . . that is not important to me,
You can do nothing and be nothing but what I will infold you.

To a drudge of the cottonfields or emptier of privies I lean . . . . on his right cheek I put the
        family kiss,
1000   And in my soul I swear I never will deny him.

On women fit for conception I start bigger and nimbler babes,
This day I am jetting the stuff of far more arrogant republics.

To any one dying . . . . thither I speed and twist the knob of the door,
Turn the bedclothes toward the foot of the bed,
1005   Let the physician and the priest go home.

I seize the descending man . . . . I raise him with resistless will.

O despairer, here is my neck,
By God! you shall not go down! Hang your whole weight upon me.

I dilate you with tremendous breath . . . . I buoy you up;
1010   Every room of the house do I fill with am armed[4] force . . . . lovers of me, bafflers of graves:
Sleep! I and they keep guard all night;
Not doubt, not decease shall dare to lay finger upon you,

---

1   *lie over*   Wait, defer until later.

2   *topknot*   Slang term to refer to an Indigenous person—or, simply, to mean "head."

3   *scarfed chops*   Jaws and mouth wrapped in a scarf.

4   *am armed*   Whitman changed this in the 1856 edition to "an armed."

I have embraced you, and henceforth possess you to myself,
And when you rise in the morning you will find what I tell you is so.

[41] I am he bringing help for the sick as they pant on their backs,
And for strong upright men I bring yet more needed help.

I heard what was said of the universe,
Heard it and heard of several thousand years;
It is middling well as far as it goes . . . . but is that all?

1020 Magnifying and applying come I,
Outbidding at the start the old cautious hucksters,[1]
The most they offer for mankind and eternity less than a spirt of my own seminalwet,
Taking myself the exact dimensions of Jehovah[2] and laying them away,
Lithographing Kronos and Zeus his son, and Hercules[3] his grandson,
1025 Buying drafts of Osiris and Isis and Belus and Brahma and Adonai,[4]
In my portfolio placing Manito[5] loose, and Allah on a leaf, and the crucifix engraved,
With Odin, and the hideous-faced Mexitli,[6] and all idols and images,
Honestly taking them all for what they are worth, and not a cent more,
Admitting they were alive and did the work of their day,
1030 Admitting they bore mites as for unfledged birds who have now to rise and fly and sing for
        themselves,
Accepting the rough deific sketches to fill out better in myself . . . . bestowing them freely on
        each man and woman I see,
Discovering as much or more in a framer framing a house,
Putting higher claims for him there with his rolled-up sleeves, driving the mallet and chisel;
Not objecting to special revelations . . . . considering a curl of smoke or a hair on the back of
        my hand as curious as any revelation;
1035 Those ahold of fire-engines and hook-and-ladder ropes more to me than the gods of the
        antique wars,
Minding their voices peal through the crash of destruction,
Their brawny limbs passing safe over charred laths[7] . . . . their white foreheads whole and
        unhurt out of the flames;

---

1 *hucksters* Pedlars, people selling goods at stalls or booths.

2 *Jehovah* Latinized Hebrew word for God.

3 *Kronos* In Greek mythology, the ruler of the Titans and father of Zeus; *Zeus* Greek god of the sky and thunderbolt who rules the gods as king; *Hercules* Greek hero and son of Zeus.

4 *drafts* Plans, sketches; *Osiris* Egyptian fertility god of the dead and the underworld; *Isis* Egyptian goddess of the sky and natural world, sister and wife of Osiris; *Belus* Babylonian god of war; *Brahma* Hindu god of creation; *Adonai* Another Hebrew name for god.

5 *Manito* Algonquian name for the lifeforce—the great spirit—that infuses all things.

6 *Odin* In Norse mythology, the supreme god, associated with wisdom, death, poetry, war, and healing; *Mexitli* Legendary Aztec leader and priest.

7 *laths* Strips of wood that hold up the plaster on walls and ceilings.

By the mechanic's wife with her babe at her nipple interceding for every person born;[1]

Three scythes at harvest whizzing in a row from three lusty angels with shirts bagged out at
    their waists;

1040 The snag-toothed hostler[2] with red hair redeeming sins past and to come,

Selling all he possesses and traveling on foot to fee[3] lawyers for his brother and sit by him
    while he is tried for forgery:

What was strewn in the amplest strewing the square rod[4] about me, and not filling the
    square rod then;

The bull and the bug never worshipped half enough,

Dung and dirt more admirable than was dreamed,

1045 The supernatural of no account . . . . myself waiting my time to be one of the supremes,

The day getting ready for me when I shall do as much good as the best, and be as prodigious,

Guessing when I am it will not tickle me much to receive puffs[5] out of pulpit or print;

By my life-lumps![6] becoming already a creator!

Putting myself here and now to the ambushed womb of the shadows!

[42]   . . . . A call in the midst of the crowd,

My own voice, orotund[7] sweeping and final.

Come my children,

Come my boys and girls, and my women and household and intimates,

Now the performer launches his nerve . . . . he has passed his prelude on the reeds within.

1055 Easily written loose fingered chords! I feel the thrum[8] of their climax and close.

My head evolves on my neck,

Music rolls, but not from the organ . . . . folks are around me, but they are no household of
    mine.

Ever the hard and unsunk ground,

Ever the eaters and drinkers . . . . ever the upward and downward sun . . . . ever the air and
    the ceaseless tides,

1060 Ever myself and my neighbors, refreshing and wicked and real,

Ever the old inexplicable query . . . . ever that thorned thumb—that breath of itches and
    thirsts,

Ever the vexer's hoot! hoot! till we find where the sly one hides and bring him forth;

---

1   *interceding . . . born*   In Catholic tradition the Virgin Mary acts as an intercessor—one that mediates between God
and humankind to answer the prayers of the faithful.

2   *hostler*   Person who stables horses at an inn.

3   *fee*   Pay.

4   *square rod*   Unit of land measuring 30¼ square yards.

5   *puffs*   Extravagant words of praise in reviews or comments.

6   *life-lumps*   Perhaps a reference to the pseudo-science phrenology, which seeks to trace a person's character and fate
by interpreting the shapes of various parts of the head.

7   *orotund*   Resonant, powerful.

8   *thrum*   Tones made by thrumming—playing—a stringed instrument.

Ever love . . . . ever the sobbing liquid of life,
Ever the bandage under the chin . . . . ever the tressels[1] of death.

1065 Here and there with dimes on the eyes walking,[2]
To feed the greed of the belly the brains liberally spooning,
Tickets buying or taking or selling, but in to the feast never once going;
Many sweating and ploughing and thrashing, and then the chaff[3] for payment receiving,
A few idly owning, and they the wheat continually claiming.

1070 This is the city . . . . and I am one of the citizens;
Whatever interests the rest interests me . . . . politics, churches, newspapers, schools,
Benevolent societies, improvements, banks, tariffs, steamships, factories, markets,
Stocks and stores and real estate and personal estate.

They who piddle[4] and patter here in collars and tailed coats . . . . I am aware who they are . . . .
     and that they are not worms or fleas,
1075 I acknowledge the duplicates of myself under all the scrape-lipped and pipe-legged[5]
     concealments.

The weakest and shallowest is deathless with me,
What I do and say the same waits for them,
Every thought that flounders in me the same flounders in them.

I know perfectly well my own egotism,
1080 And know my omniverous words, and cannot say any less,
And would fetch you whoever you are flush with myself.

My words are words of a questioning, and to indicate reality;
This printed and bound book . . . . but the printer and the printing-office boy?
The marriage estate and settlement . . . . but the body and mind of the bridegroom? also
     those of the bride?
1085 The panorama of the sea . . . . but the sea itself?

The well-taken photographs . . . . but your wife or friend close and solid in your arms?
The fleet of ships of the line[6] and all the modern improvements . . . . but the craft and pluck
     of the admiral?
The dishes and fare and furniture . . . . but the host and hostess, and the look out of their
     eyes?
The sky up there . . . . yet here or next door or across the way?

---

1 *tressels* Trestles—wooden supports—were used to hold up coffins during funerals and wakes.

2 *dimes … walking* Reference to ancient burial practices, particularly in Greece and Rome, in which coins are placed on the eyes or mouths of the dead so they can pay for their passage to the underworld.

3 *thrashing* Process of separating grains from the husks and straw; *chaff* Husks.

4 *piddle* Waste time.

5 *scrape-lipped* Shaved; *pipe-legged* Likely a reference to those who wear suit pants.

6 *ships of the line* Steam and wind-powered naval warships designed to hold a line in battle.

1090   The saints and sages in history . . . . but you yourself?
        Sermons and creeds and theology . . . . but the human brain, and what is called reason, and
            what is called love, and what is called life?

[43]   I do not despise you priests;
        My faith is the greatest of faiths and the least of faiths,
        Enclosing all worship ancient and modern, and all between ancient and modern,
1095   Believing I shall come again upon the earth after five thousand years,
        Waiting responses from oracles . . . . honoring the gods . . . . saluting the sun,
        Making a fetish of the first rock or stump . . . . powowing with sticks in the circle of obis,[1]
        Helping the lama or brahmin[2] as he trims the lamps of the idols,
        Dancing yet through the streets in a phallic procession . . . . rapt and austere in the woods, a
            gymnosophist,[3]
1100   Drinking mead from the skull-cup . . . . to shasta and vedas admirant[4] . . . . minding the
            koran,
        Walking the teokallis, spotted with gore from the stone and knife—beating the serpent-skin
            drum;[5]
        Accepting the gospels, accepting him that was crucified, knowing assuredly that he is divine,
        To the mass kneeling—to the puritan's prayer rising—sitting patiently in a pew,
        Ranting and frothing in my insane crisis—waiting dead-like till my spirit arouses me;
1105   Looking forth on pavement and land, and outside of pavement and land,
        Belonging to the winders of the circuit of circuits.[6]

        One of that centripetal and centrifugal gang,
        I turn and talk like a man leaving charges before a journey.

        Down-hearted doubters, dull and excluded,
1110   Frivolous sullen moping angry affected disheartened atheistical,
        I know every one of you, and know the unspoken interrogatories,
        By experience I know them.

---

1   *powowing* Participating in a powwow, a ceremony held in many Indigenous communities that involves feasting,
dancing, and music; *obis* Igbo word that can mean both "house" and "chief."

2   *lama* In Tibetan Buddhism, the title of a teacher; *brahmin* Hindu priest and teacher.

3   *gymnosophist* Hindu mystic who is dedicated to prayer and lives ascetically.

4   *skull-cup* Vessel made out of a skull (used perhaps by religious devotees as a "momento mori," a reminder of
death); *shasta* Usually spelled "shastra," a name for any of the Hindu sacred texts; *vedas* The four sacred texts
of the Hindus; *admirant* Admiring.

5   *teokallis* A teocalli is a four-sided pyramid built for religious purposes by ancient Mexicans and Central
Americans, including the Aztecs; *spotted with gore* Likely a reference to the practice of human sacrifice, which
would occur on top of the teocalli; *serpent-skin drum* Aztec drums, called "huehuetls," were covered with a skin
and would be played by priests during religious rituals. Snakes were sacred to the Aztecs, as they were associated
symbolically with their god Quetzalcoatl, so a drum made from snake-skin would be appropriate for ceremonies.

6   *winders ... circuits* Preachers in the nineteenth century would follow a travel circuit so they could speak at
churches or outdoors at predetermined locations in a wide area; such preachers were known as "circuit winders."

How the flukes[1] splash!
How they contort rapid as lightning, with spasms and spouts of blood!

1115 Be at peace bloody flukes of doubters and sullen mopers,
I take my place among you as much as among any;
The past is the push of you and me and all precisely the same,
And the day and night are for you and me and all,
And what is yet untried and afterward is for you and me and all.

1120 I do not know what is untried and afterward,
But I know it is sure and alive and sufficient.

Each who passes is considered, and each who stops is considered, and not a single one can it
    fail.

It cannot fail the young man who died and was buried,
Nor the young woman who died and was put by his side,
1125 Nor the little child that peeped in at the door and then drew back and was never seen again,
Nor the old man who has lived without purpose, and feels it with bitterness worse than gall,
Nor him in the poorhouse tubercled by rum and the bad disorder,[2]
Nor the numberless slaughtered and wrecked . . . . nor the brutish koboo,[3] called the ordure
    of humanity,
Nor the sacs merely floating with open mouths for food to slip in,
1130 Nor any thing in the earth, or down in the oldest graves of the earth,
Nor any thing in the myriads of spheres, nor one of the myriads of myriads that inhabit them,
Nor the present, nor the least wisp that is known.

[44] It is time to explain myself . . . . let us stand up.

What is known I strip away . . . . I launch all men and women forward with me into the
    unknown.

1135 The clock indicates the moment . . . . but what does eternity indicate?

Eternity lies in bottomless reservoirs . . . . its buckets are rising forever and ever,
They pour and they pour and they exhale away.

We have thus far exhausted trillions of winters and summers;
There are trillions ahead, and trillions ahead of them.

1140 Births have brought us richness and variety,
And other births will bring us richness and variety.

---

[1]   *flukes* Whale's tail (which extends horizontally on both sides).

[2]   *tubercled* I.e., afflicted with tuberculosis; *bad disorder* Slang or euphemism for a venereal disease (sexually
transmitted infection).

[3]   *koboo* Offensive Malay name for the Orang Batin Sembilan or Anak Dalam people of southeast Sumatra.

I do not call one greater and one smaller,
That which fills its period and place is equal to any.

Were mankind murderous or jealous upon you my brother or my sister?
1145   I am sorry for you . . . . they are not murderous or jealous upon me;
All has been gentle with me . . . . . . I keep no account with lamentation;
What have I to do with lamentation?

I am an acme of things accomplished, and I an encloser of things to be.

My feet strike an apex of the apices[1] of the stairs,
1150   On every step bunches of ages, and larger bunches between the steps,
All below duly traveled—and still I mount and mount.

Rise after rise bow the phantoms behind me,
Afar down I see the huge first Nothing, the vapor from the nostrils of death,
I know I was even there . . . . I waited unseen and always,
1155   And slept while God carried me through the lethargic mist,
And took my time . . . . and took no hurt from the fœtid[2] carbon.

Long I was hugged close . . . . long and long.

Immense have been the preparations for me,
Faithful and friendly the arms that have helped me.

1160   Cycles ferried my cradle, rowing and rowing like cheerful boatmen;
For room to me stars kept aside in their own rings,
They sent influences to look after what was to hold me.

Before I was born out of my mother generations guided me,
My embryo has never been torpid . . . . nothing could overlay it;
1165   For it the nebula cohered to an orb . . . . the long slow strata piled to rest it on . . . . vast
      vegetables gave it sustenance,
Monstrous sauroids[3] transported it in their mouths and deposited it with care.

All forces have been steadily employed to complete and delight me,
Now I stand on this spot with my soul.

[45]   Span of youth! Ever-pushed elasticity! Manhood balanced and florid and full!

1170   My lovers suffocate me!
Crowding my lips, and thick in the pores of my skin,

---

1   *apices*   Plural for "apex."
2   *fœtid*   Rank, stinking.
3   *sauroids*   Lizard-like creatures.

Jostling me through streets and public halls . . . . coming naked to me at night,
Crying by day Ahoy from the rocks of the river . . . . swinging and chirping over my head,
Calling my name from flowerbeds or vines or tangled underbrush,
1175   Or while I swim in the bath . . . . or drink from the pump at the corner . . . . or the curtain is
        down at the opera . . . . or I glimpse at a woman's face in the railroad car;
Lighting on every moment of my life,
Bussing my body with soft and balsamic[1] busses,
Noiselessly passing handfuls out of their hearts and giving them to be mine.

Old age superbly rising! Ineffable grace of dying days!

1180   Every condition promulges not only itself . . . . it promulges what grows after and out of
        itself,
And the dark hush promulges as much as any.

I open my scuttle[2] at night and see the far-sprinkled systems,
And all I see, multiplied as high as I can cipher, edge but the rim of the farther systems.

Wider and wider they spread, expanding and always expanding,
1185   Outward and outward and forever outward.

My sun has his sun, and round him obediently wheels,
He joins with his partners a group of superior circuit,
And greater sets follow, making specks of the greatest inside them.

There is no stoppage, and never can be stoppage;
1190   If I and you and the worlds and all beneath or upon their surfaces, and all the palpable life,
        were this moment reduced back to a pallid float,[3] it would not avail in the long run,
We should surely bring up again where we now stand,
And as surely go as much farther, and then farther and farther.

A few quadrillions of eras, a few octillions of cubic leagues, do not hazard the span, or make
    it impatient,
They are but parts . . . . any thing is but a part.

1195   See ever so far . . . . there is limitless space outside of that,
Count ever so much . . . . there is limitless time around that.

Our rendezvous is fitly appointed . . . . God will be there and wait till we come.

---

1   *Bussing* Kissing; *balsamic* Fragrant, delicious, healing, restorative.

2   *scuttle* Opening in a ship's side or deck with a moveable lid.

3   *float* For Whitman, the word "float" often suggests the life-giving cosmos before bodies take form and become
matter.

[46]   I know I have the best of time and space—and that I was never measured, and never will be
        measured.

1200   I tramp a perpetual journey,
My signs are a rain-proof coat and good shoes and a staff cut from the woods;
No friend of mine takes his ease in my chair,
I have no chair, nor church nor philosophy;
I lead no man to a dinner-table or library or exchange,
1205   But each man and each woman of you I lead upon a knoll,
My left hand hooks you round the waist,
My right hand points to landscapes of continents, and a plain public road.

Not I, not any one else can travel that road for you,
You must travel it for yourself.

1210   It is not far . . . . it is within reach,
Perhaps you have been on it since you were born, and did not know,
Perhaps it is every where on water and on land.

Shoulder your duds,[1] and I will mine, and let us hasten forth;
Wonderful cities and free nations we shall fetch as we go.

1215   If you tire, give me both burdens, and rest the chuff[2] of your hand on my hip,
And in due time you shall repay the same service to me;
For after we start we never lie by again.

This day before dawn I ascended a hill and looked at the crowded heaven,
And I said to my spirit, When we become the enfolders of those orbs and the pleasure and
        knowledge of every thing in them, shall we be filled and satisfied then?
1220   And my spirit said No, we level that lift to pass and continue beyond.

You are also asking me questions, and I hear you;
I answer that I cannot answer . . . . you must find out for yourself.

Sit awhile wayfarer,
Here are biscuits to eat and here is milk to drink,
1225   But as soon as you sleep and renew yourself in sweet clothes I will certainly kiss you with my
        goodbye kiss and open the gate for your egress hence.

Long enough have you dreamed contemptible dreams,
Now I wash the gum from your eyes,
You must habit[3] yourself to the dazzle of the light and of every moment of your life

---

1   *duds*   Clothes; here the word implies clothes and personal things packed in a bag or satchel.
2   *chuff*   This term usually means a swollen cheek; here it seems to refer to the raised curve of the palm below the
thumb.
3   *habit*   Habituate, accustom.

Long have you timidly waded, holding a plank by the shore,
1130   Now I will you to be a bold swimmer,
To jump off in the midst of the sea, and rise again and nod to me and shout, and laughingly
     dash with your hair.

[47]   I am the teacher of athletes,
He that by me spreads a wider breast than my own proves the width of my own,
He most honors my style who learns under it to destroy the teacher.

1135   The boy I love, the same becomes a man not through derived power but in his own right,
Wicked, rather than virtuous out of conformity or fear,
Fond of his sweetheart, relishing well his steak,
Unrequited love or a slight cutting him worse than a wound cuts,
First rate to ride, to fight, to hit the bull's eye, to sail a skiff, to sing a song or play on the
     banjo,
1140   Preferring scars and faces pitted with smallpox over all latherers and those that keep out of
     the sun.

I teach straying from me, yet who can stray from me?
I follow you whoever you are from the present hour;
My words itch at your ears till you understand them.

I do not say these things for a dollar, or to fill up the time while I wait for a boat;
1145   It is you talking just as much as myself . . . . I act as the tongue of you,
It was tied in your mouth . . . . . in mine it begins to be loosened.

I swear I will never mention love or death inside a house,
And I swear I never will translate myself at all, only to him or her who privately stays with
     me in the open air.

If you would understand me go to the heights or water-shore,
1150   The nearest gnat is an explanation and a drop or the motion of waves a key,
The maul the oar and the handsaw second my words.

No shuttered room or school can commune with me,
But roughs and little children better than they.

The young mechanic is closest to me . . . . he knows me pretty well,
1155   The woodman that takes his axe and jug with him shall take me with him all day,
The farmboy ploughing in the field feels good at the sound of my voice,
In vessels that sail my words must sail . . . . I go with fishermen and seamen, and love them,
My face rubs to the hunter's face when he lies down alone in his blanket,
The driver thinking of me does not mind the jolt of his wagon,
1160   The young mother and old mother shall comprehend me,
The girl and the wife rest the needle a moment and forget where they are,
They and all would resume what I have told them.

[48]   I have said that the soul is not more than the body,
        And I have said that the body is not more than the soul,
1165   And nothing, not God, is greater to one than one's-self is,
        And whoever walks a furlong[1] without sympathy walks to his own funeral, dressed in his
            shroud,
        And I or you pocketless of a dime may purchase the pick of the earth,
        And to glance with an eye or show a bean in its pod confounds the learning of all times,
        And there is no trade or employment but the young man following it may become a hero,
1170   And there is no object so soft but it makes a hub for the wheeled universe,
        And any man or woman shall stand cool and supercilious before a million universes.

        And I call to mankind, Be not curious about God,
        For I who am curious about each am not curious about God,
        No array of terms can say how much I am at peace about God and about death.

1175   I hear and behold God in every object, yet I understand God not in the least,
        Nor do I understand who there can be more wonderful than myself.

        Why should I wish to see God better than this day?
        I see something of God each hour of the twenty-four, and each moment then,
        In the faces of men and women I see God, and in my own face in the glass;
1180   I find letters from God dropped in the street, and every one is signed by God's name,
        And I leave them where they are, for I know that others will punctually come forever and ever.

[49]   And as to you death, and you bitter hug of mortality . . . . it is idle to try to alarm me.

        To his work without flinching the accoucheur[2] comes,
        I see the elderhand pressing receiving supporting,
1185   I recline by the sills of the exquisite flexible doors . . . . and mark the outlet, and mark the
            relief and escape.

        And as to you corpse I think you are good manure, but that does not offend me,
        I smell the white roses sweetscented and growing,
        I reach to the leafy lips . . . . I reach to the polished breasts of melons.

        And as to you life, I reckon you are the leavings of many deaths,
1190   No doubt I have died myself ten thousand times before.

        I hear you whispering there O stars of heaven,
        O suns . . . . O grass of graves . . . . O perpetual transfers and promotions . . . . if you do not
            say anything how can I say anything?

---

1   *furlong*   Unit of measurement that varies historically but is now stated to be 220 yards.
2   *accoucheur*   Midwife.

Of the turbid pool that lies in the autumn forest,
Of the moon that descends the steeps of the soughing[1] twilight,
1195   Toss, sparkles of day and dusk . . . . toss on the black stems that decay in the muck,
Toss to the moaning gibberish of the dry limbs.

I ascend from the moon . . . . I ascend from the night,
And perceive of the ghastly glitter the sunbeams reflected,
And debouch[2] to the steady and central from the offspring great or small.

[50]   There is that in me . . . . I do not know what it is . . . . but I know it is in me.

Wrenched and sweaty . . . . calm and cool then my body becomes;
I sleep . . . . I sleep long.

I do not know it . . . . it is without name . . . . it is a word unsaid,
It is not in any dictionary or utterance or symbol.

1205   Something it swings on more than the earth I swing on,
To it the creation is the friend whose embracing awakes me.

Perhaps I might tell more . . . . Outlines! I plead for my brothers and sisters.

Do you see O my brothers and sisters?
It is not chaos or death . . . . it is form and union and plan . . . . it is eternal life . . . . it is
    happiness.

[51]   The past and present wilt . . . . I have filled them and emptied them,
And proceed to fill my next fold of the future.

Listener up there! Here you . . . . what have you to confide to me?
Look in my face while I snuff the sidle[3] of evening,
Talk honestly, for no one else hears you, and I stay only a minute longer.

1215   Do I contradict myself?
Very well then . . . . I contradict myself;
I am large . . . . I contain multitudes.

I concentrate toward them that are nigh . . . . I wait on the door-slab.

Who has done his day's work and will soonest be through with his supper?
1220   Who wishes to walk with me?

Will you speak before I am gone? Will you prove already too late?

---

1   *soughing* Rustling, sighing.

2   *debouch* Emerge from a narrow to a wider space.

3   *sidle* Shy approach.

[52]   The spotted hawk swoops by and accuses me . . . . he complains of my gab and my loitering.

I too am not a bit tamed . . . . I too am untranslatable,
I sound my barbaric yawp over the roofs of the world.

1225   The last scud[1] of day holds back for me,
It flings my likeness after the rest and true as any on the shadowed wilds,
It coaxes me to the vapor and the dusk.

I depart as air . . . . I shake my white locks at the runaway sun,
I effuse my flesh in eddies and drift it in lacy jags.[2]

1230   I bequeath myself to the dirt to grow from the grass I love,
If you want me again look for me under your bootsoles.

You will hardly know who I am or what I mean,
But I shall be good health to you nevertheless,
And filter and fibre your blood.

1235   Failing to fetch me at first keep encouraged,
Missing me one place search another,
I stop some where waiting for you.[3]
        —1855

---

1   *scud*   Hurry; quick movement of light clouds before the wind.

2   *jags*   Fragments, shreds.

3   The 1855 ["Song of Myself"] has generally been printed without a period at the end, as the period is missing in some extant copies of the 1855 *Leaves of Grass*. However, Ed Folsom's "Census of the 1855 *Leaves of Grass*" (2006) shows that many other copies *did* in fact include a period, proving that the missing punctuation in other copies was a simple printing error, and that in all likelihood Whitman intended to have a period close the poem.

IN CONTEXT

1855 *Leaves of Grass* [*Song of Myself*]¹

Alfred Jacob Miller, *The Trapper's Bride*, 1845. Whitman describes a striking scene in lines 178–82 of the 1855 *Leaves of Grass* [*Song of Myself*] that closely resembles the details of this painting by Baltimore artist Alfred Jacob Miller. Miller had taken an expedition in 1837 into what is now western Wyoming, where he recorded his observations of the culture surrounding the Western fur trade. In 1856 he made notes for a sketch of the scene that is depicted in this earlier painting: "The scene represents a trapper taking a wife, or purchasing one. The prices varying in accordance with circumstance. He (the trapper) is seated with his friend, to the left of the sketch, his hand extended to his promised wife, supported by her father and accompanied by a chief, who holds the calumet, an article indispensable in all grand ceremonies. ... A free trapper (white or half-breed), being ton² or upper circle, is a most desirable match, but it is conceded that he is a ruined man after such an investment, the lady running into unheard of extravagancies. She wants a dress, horse, gorgeous saddle, trappings, and the deuce³ knows what besides. For this the poor devil trapper sells himself, body and soul, to the Fur Company for a number of years. He traps beaver, hunts the buffalo and bear, elk and etc. The fur and robes of which the company credit to his account."

Common-law marriages between Indigenous women and trappers were not unusual in the seventeenth to early-nineteenth centuries—they were known as marriage "à la façon du pays" ("in the style of the country")—and they forged important trade and diplomatic alliances. Indigenous women helped the American and European fur traders survive and acted as intermediaries between the fur companies and the Indigenous populations; the Métis people are considered the descendants of these inter-cultural alliances.

---

¹ Materials relating to the battle of the Alamo and the Goliad Massacre—both of which Whitman describes in the 1855 *Leaves of Grass*—can be found in this anthology's "Expansion, Native American Expulsion, and 'Manifest Destiny'" contexts section.

² *ton* High society.

³ *deuce* Devil.

THE WRECK OF THE STEAM SHIP "SAN FRANCISCO"

The Wreck of the Steam Ship "San Francisco," c. 1854. The caption reads: "The ships ANTARCTIC of New York, Captain Stouffer, and THREE BELLS of Glasgow, Captain Creighton, rescuing the passengers and crew from the wreck of the steamship SAN FRANCISCO, disabled and sinking on her voyage from New York to San Francisco, 24 December 1853. The bark KILBY of Bunten, Captain Low, had previously fallen in with the wreck and taken off some passengers but, during a gale in the night, was separated from SAN FRANCISCO and could not find her again." The storm that disabled the *San Francisco* made the rescue extraordinarily risky, but of the 800 passengers (most of whom were U.S. Army members and their families) around 500 were saved. Whitman describes in lines 818–27 the moment when Captain Creighton arrived to save the passengers from the *San Francisco* and told them "Be of good cheer, We will not desert you." The dramatic rescue—and the heroism of the captains who participated in it—was the compelling subject of countless newspaper articles; personal accounts by survivors of the incident were also widely published. The captains Stouffer, Creighton, and Low were given Congressional Life Saving Medals in 1866.

John Paul Jones During the Battle, from James C. Bradford's *The Reincarnation of John Paul Jones: The Navy Discovers Its Professional Roots* (c. 1896). On 23 September 1779, Commodore John Paul Jones led the Continental Navy (American and French forces) into battle against the British at Flamborough Head, off the coast of northeastern England. During the battle, and after his ship had been severely damaged, Jones was asked if he was ready to strike the colors (i.e., surrender, by lowering the new American flag). Jones famously replied that "I have not yet begun to fight." In the end, the Continental Navy prevailed in the battle.

In the nineteenth century, Jones was remembered as a dashing, fearless American naval hero, and he was frequently portrayed as such in works of fiction—among them James Fenimore Cooper's *The Pilot* (1824) and Herman Melville's *Israel Potter* (1854–55). Whitman describes scenes from the Battle of Flamborough Head in lines 890–917 of the 1855 *Leaves of Grass* [*Song of Myself*].

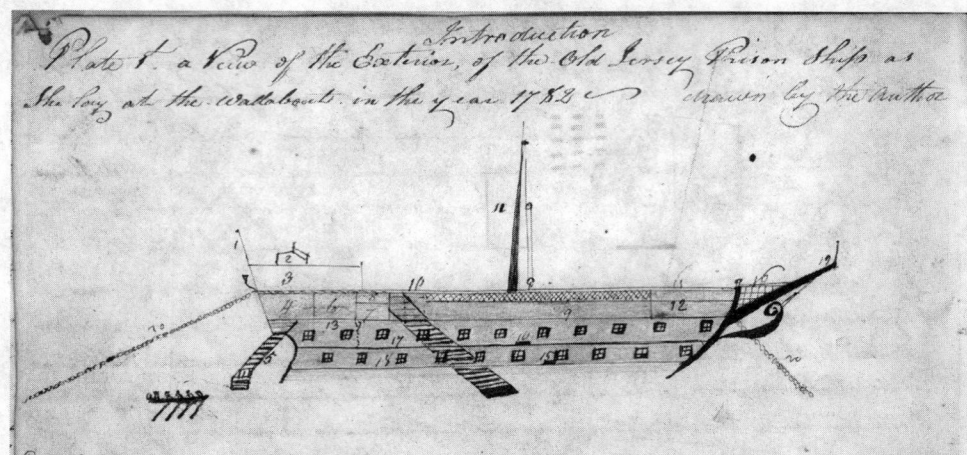

Thomas Dring, *The Jersey Prison Ship as Moored at the Wallabout Near Long Island, in the Year 1782* from *Recollections of Life on the Prison Ship* Jersey, 1829. During the Revolutionary War, British ships anchored in Wallabout Bay, Brooklyn, served as prisons for American prisoners of war. The conditions onboard these ships were unspeakably awful, and it is estimated that between 8,000 and 11,000 American prisoners died while confined, mainly of disease and starvation—more casualties than were incurred on land during the war. Bodies of the dead were either thrown overboard or buried in shallow graves along the sandy shore; human bones were found in the bay for many decades afterwards. Most notorious of all the ships was the HMS *Jersey*, nicknamed "The Hell Afloat," pictured above. Whitman grew up near Wallabout Bay and describes, in line 937 of [*Song of Myself*], what it felt like to live in proximity to such a gruesome history: "What sobers the Brooklyn boy as he looks down the shores of the Wallabout and remembers the prison ships."

The following account of imprisonment aboard the *Jersey* in the autumn of 1780 is by Captain Silas Talbot, as recorded in Danske Dandridge's book *American Prisoners of the Revolution* (1910): "All her port holes were closed. … There were about 1,100 prisoners on board. There were no berths or seats, to lie down on, not a bench to sit on. Many were almost without clothes. The dysentery, fever, phrenzy and despair prevailed among them, and filled the place with filth, disgust and horror. The scantiness of the allowance, the bad quality of the provisions, the brutality of the guards, and the sick, pining for comforts they could not obtain, altogether furnished continually one of the greatest scenes of human distress and misery ever beheld. It was now the middle of October, the weather was cool and clear, with frosty nights, so that the number of deaths per day was reduced to an average of ten, and this number was considered by the survivors a small one, when compared with the terrible mortality that had prevailed for three months before. The human bones and skulls, yet bleaching on the shore of Long Island, and daily exposed, by the falling down of the high bank on which the prisoners were buried, is a shocking sight, and manifestly demonstrates that the *Jersey* prison ship had been as destructive as a field of battle."

from *1881 Leaves of Grass*

from INSCRIPTIONS

One's Self I Sing

One's self I sing, a simple separate person,
  Yet utter the word Democratic, the word En-Masse.

Of physiology from top to toe I sing,
Not physiognomy[1] alone nor brain alone is worthy for the Muse, I say the Form complete is
  worthier far,
5 The Female equally with the Male I sing.

Of Life immense in passion, pulse, and power,
Cheerful, for freest action form'd under the laws divine,
The Modern Man I sing.
—1867, 1881

from CHILDREN OF ADAM

I Sing the Body Electric

1

I sing the body electric,
  The armies of those I love engirth[2] me and I engirth them,
They will not let me off till I go with them, respond to them,
And discorrupt them, and charge them full with the charge of the soul.

5 Was it doubted that those who corrupt their own bodies conceal themselves?
And if those who defile the living are as bad as they who defile the dead?
And if the body does not do fully as much as the soul?
And if the body were not the soul, what is the soul?

2

The love of the body of man or woman balks account,[3] the body itself balks account,
10 That of the male is perfect, and that of the female is perfect.

The expression of the face balks account,
But the expression of a well-made man appears not only in his face,

---

1 *physiognomy*   Facial appearance (especially as considered to reveal one's personality).
2 *engirth*   Surround.
3 *balks account*   Resists description; cannot be explained.

It is in his limbs and joints also, it is curiously in the joints of his hips and wrists,
It is in his walk, the carriage of his neck, the flex of his waist and knees, dress does not hide him,
15   The strong sweet quality he has strikes through the cotton and broadcloth,[1]
To see him pass conveys as much as the best poem, perhaps more,
You linger to see his back, and the back of his neck and shoulder-side.

The sprawl and fulness of babes, the bosoms and heads of women, the folds of their dress, their style as we pass in the street, the contour of their shape downwards,
The swimmer naked in the swimming-bath, seen as he swims through the transparent green-shine, or lies with his face up and rolls silently to and fro in the heave of the water,
20   The bending forward and backward of rowers in row-boats, the horseman in his saddle,
Girls, mothers, house-keepers, in all their performances,
The group of laborers seated at noon-time with their open dinner-kettles, and their wives waiting,
The female soothing a child, the farmer's daughter in the garden or cow-yard,
The young fellow hoeing corn, the sleigh-driver driving his six horses through the crowd,
25   The wrestle of wrestlers, two apprentice-boys, quite grown, lusty, good-natured, native-born, out on the vacant lot at sun-down after work,
The coats and caps thrown down, the embrace of love and resistance,
The upper-hold and under-hold, the hair rumpled over and blinding the eyes;
The march of firemen in their own costumes, the play of masculine muscle through clean-setting trowsers and waist-straps,
The slow return from the fire, the pause when the bell strikes suddenly again, and the listening on the alert,
30   The natural, perfect, varied attitudes, the bent head, the curv'd neck and the counting;
Such-like I love—I loosen myself, pass freely, am at the mother's breast with the little child,
Swim with the swimmers, wrestle with wrestlers, march in line with the firemen, and pause, listen, count.

3

I knew a man, a common farmer, the father of five sons,
And in them the fathers of sons, and in them the fathers of sons.
35   This man was of wonderful vigor, calmness, beauty of person,
The shape of his head, the pale yellow and white of his hair and beard, the immeasurable meaning of his black eyes, the richness and breadth of his manners,
These I used to go and visit him to see, he was wise also,
He was six feet tall, he was over eighty years old, his sons were massive, clean, bearded, tan-faced, handsome,
They and his daughters loved him, all who saw him loved him,
40   They did not love him by allowance, they loved him with personal love,
He drank water only, the blood show'd like scarlet through the clear-brown skin of his face,

---

[1]   *broadcloth* Fine wool fabric, often used to make men's pants and jackets.

He was a frequent gunner and fisher, he sail'd his boat himself, he had a fine one presented to
    him by a ship-joiner, he had fowling-pieces[1] presented to him by men that loved him,
When he went with his five sons and many grand-sons to hunt or fish, you would pick him
    out as the most beautiful and vigorous of the gang,
You would wish long and long to be with him, you would wish to sit by him in the boat that
    you and he might touch each other.

4

45   I have perceiv'd that to be with those I like is enough,
To stop in company with the rest at evening is enough,
To be surrounded by beautiful, curious, breathing, laughing flesh is enough,
To pass among them or touch any one, or rest my arm ever so lightly round his or her neck
    for a moment, what is this then?
I do not ask any more delight, I swim in it as in a sea.

50   There is something in staying close to men and women and looking on them, and in the
    contact and odor of them, that pleases the soul well,
All things please the soul, but these please the soul well.

5

This is the female form,
A divine nimbus[2] exhales from it from head to foot,
It attracts with fierce undeniable attraction,
55   I am drawn by its breath as if I were no more than a helpless vapor, all falls aside but myself
    and it,
Books, art, religion, time, the visible and solid earth, and what was expected of heaven or
    fear'd of hell, are now consumed,
Mad filaments, ungovernable shoots play out of it, the response likewise ungovernable,
Hair, bosom, hips, bend of legs, negligent falling hands all diffused, mine too diffused,
Ebb stung by the flow and flow stung by the ebb, love-flesh swelling and deliciously aching,
60   Limitless limpid jets of love hot and enormous, quivering jelly of love, white-blow and deliri-
    ous juice,
Bridegroom night of love working surely and softly into the prostrate dawn,
Undulating into the willing and yielding day,
Lost in the cleave of the clasping and sweet-flesh'd day.

This the nucleus—after the child is born of woman, man is born of woman,
65   This the bath of birth, this the merge of small and large, and the outlet again.

Be not ashamed women, your privilege encloses the rest, and is the exit of the rest,
You are the gates of the body, and you are the gates of the soul.

---

1   *fowling-pieces* Shotguns for hunting fowl.
2   *nimbus* Halo.

The female contains all qualities and tempers them,
She is in her place and moves with perfect balance,
70   She is all things duly veil'd, she is both passive and active,
She is to conceive daughters as well as sons, and sons as well as daughters.

As I see my soul reflected in Nature,
As I see through a mist, One with inexpressible completeness, sanity, beauty,
See the bent head and arms folded over the breast, the Female I see.

6

75   The male is not less the soul nor more, he too is in his place,
He too is all qualities, he is action and power,
The flush of the known universe is in him,
Scorn becomes him well, and appetite and defiance become him well,
The wildest largest passions, bliss that is utmost, sorrow that is utmost become him well,
    pride is for him,
80   The full-spread pride of man is calming and excellent to the soul,
Knowledge becomes him, he likes it always, he brings every thing to the test of himself,
Whatever the survey, whatever the sea and the sail he strikes soundings at last only here,
(Where else does he strike soundings except here?)

The man's body is sacred and the woman's body is sacred,
85   No matter who it is, it is sacred—is it the meanest[1] one in the laborers' gang?
Is it one of the dull-faced immigrants just landed on the wharf?
Each belongs here or anywhere just as much as the well-off, just as much as you,
Each has his or her place in the procession.

(All is a procession,
90   The universe is a procession with measured and perfect motion.)

Do you know so much yourself that you call the meanest ignorant?
Do you suppose you have a right to a good sight, and he or she has no right to a sight?
Do you think matter has cohered together from its diffuse float,[2] and the soil is on the
    surface, and water runs and vegetation sprouts,
For you only, and not for him and her?

7

95   A man's body at auction,
(For before the war I often go to the slave-mart and watch the sale,)
I help the auctioneer, the sloven[3] does not half know his business.

_____

1   *meanest*   Lowliest (especially in terms of social or financial status).

2   *float*   For Whitman, the word "float" often suggests the life-giving cosmos before bodies take form and become
matter.

3   *sloven*   Untidy person.

Gentlemen look on this wonder,
Whatever the bids of the bidders they cannot be high enough for it,
100 For it the globe lay preparing quintillions of years without one animal or plant,
For it the revolving cycles truly and steadily roll'd.

In this head the all-baffling brain,
In it and below it the makings of heroes.

Examine these limbs, red, black, or white, they are cunning in tendon and nerve,
105 They shall be stript that you may see them.

Exquisite senses, life-lit eyes, pluck,[1] volition,
Flakes of breast-muscle, pliant backbone and neck, flesh not flabby, good-sized arms and legs,
And wonders within there yet.

Within there runs blood,
110 The same old blood! the same red-running blood!
There swells and jets a heart, there all passions, desires, reachings, aspirations,
(Do you think they are not there because they are not express'd in parlors and lecture-rooms?)

This is not only one man, this the father of those who shall be fathers in their turns,
In him the start of populous states and rich republics,
115 Of him countless immortal lives with countless embodiments and enjoyments.

How do you know who shall come from the offspring of his offspring through the centuries?
(Who might you find you have come from yourself, if you could trace back through the
    centuries?)

8

A woman's body at auction,
She too is not only herself, she is the teeming mother of mothers,
120 She is the bearer of them that shall grow and be mates to the mothers.

Have you ever loved the body of a woman?
Have you ever loved the body of a man?
Do you not see that these are exactly the same to all in all nations and times all over the
    earth?

If any thing is sacred the human body is sacred,
125 And the glory and sweet of a man is the token of manhood untainted,
And in man or woman a clean, strong, firm-fibred body, is more beautiful than the most
    beautiful face.

---

1   *pluck* In the sense of courage or spiritedness.

Have you seen the fool that corrupted his own live body? or the fool that corrupted her own live body?

For they do not conceal themselves, and cannot conceal themselves.

9

O my body! I dare not desert the likes of you in other men and women, nor the likes of the parts of you,

130 I believe the likes of you are to stand or fall with the likes of the soul, (and that they are the soul,)

I believe the likes of you shall stand or fall with my poems, and that they are my poems,

Man's, woman's, child's, youth's, wife's, husband's, mother's, father's, young man's, young woman's poems,

Head, neck, hair, ears, drop and tympan of the ears,[1]

Eyes, eye-fringes, iris of the eye, eyebrows, and the waking or sleeping of the lids,

135 Mouth, tongue, lips, teeth, roof of the mouth, jaws, and the jaw-hinges,

Nose, nostrils of the nose, and the partition,

Cheeks, temples, forehead, chin, throat, back of the neck, neck-slue,[2]

Strong shoulders, manly beard, scapula, hind-shoulders, and the ample side-round of the chest,

Upper-arm, armpit, elbow-socket, lower-arm, arm-sinews, arm-bones,

140 Wrist and wrist-joints, hand, palm, knuckles, thumb, forefinger, finger-joints, finger-nails,

Broad breast-front, curling hair of the breast, breast-bone, breast-side,

Ribs, belly, backbone, joints of the backbone,

Hips, hip-sockets, hip-strength, inward and outward round, man-balls, man-root,

Strong set of thighs, well carrying the trunk above,

145 Leg-fibres, knee, knee-pan, upper-leg, under-leg,

Ankles, instep, foot-ball, toes, toe-joints, the heel;

All attitudes, all the shapeliness, all the belongings of my or your body or of any one's body, male or female,

The lung-sponges, the stomach-sac, the bowels sweet and clean,

The brain in its folds inside the skull-frame,

150 Sympathies, heart-valves, palate-valves, sexuality, maternity,

Womanhood, and all that is a woman, and the man that comes from woman,

The womb, the teats, nipples, breast-milk, tears, laughter, weeping, love-looks, love-perturbations and risings,

The voice, articulation, language, whispering, shouting aloud,

Food, drink, pulse, digestion, sweat, sleep, walking, swimming,

155 Poise on the hips, leaping, reclining, embracing, arm-curving and tightening,

The continual changes of the flex of the mouth, and around the eyes,

The skin, the sunburnt shade, freckles, hair,

The curious sympathy one feels when feeling with the hand the naked meat of the body,

The circling rivers the breath, and breathing it in and out,

160 The beauty of the waist, and thence of the hips, and thence downward toward the knees,

---

[1] *tympan of the ears* Eardrum.

[2] *neck-slue* I.e., the turn of the neck.

The thin red jellies within you or within me, the bones and the marrow in the bones,
The exquisite realization of health;
O I say these are not the parts and poems of the body only, but of the soul,
O I say now these are the soul!
—1855, 1881

A Woman Waits for Me

A woman waits for me, she contains all, nothing is lacking,
Yet all were lacking if sex were lacking, or if the moisture of the right man were lacking.

Sex contains all, bodies, souls,
Meanings, proofs, purities, delicacies, results, promulgations,
5 Songs, commands, health, pride, the maternal mystery, the seminal milk,
All hopes, benefactions, bestowals, all the passions, loves, beauties, delights of the earth,
All the governments, judges, gods, follow'd persons of the earth,
These are contain'd in sex as parts of itself and justifications of itself.

Without shame the man I like knows and avows the deliciousness of his sex,
10 Without shame the woman I like knows and avows hers.

Now I will dismiss myself from impassive women,
I will go stay with her who waits for me, and with those women that are warm-blooded and
    sufficient for me,
I see that they understand me and do not deny me,
I see that they are worthy of me, I will be the robust husband of those women.

15 They are not one jot less than I am,
They are tann'd in the face by shining suns and blowing winds,
Their flesh has the old divine suppleness and strength,
They know how to swim, row, ride, wrestle, shoot, run, strike, retreat, advance, resist, defend
    themselves,
They are ultimate in their own right—they are calm, clear, well-possess'd of themselves.

20 I draw you close to me, you women,
I cannot let you go, I would do you good,
I am for you, and you are for me, not only for our own sake, but for others' sakes,
Envelop'd in you sleep greater heroes and bards,
They refuse to awake at the touch of any man but me.

25 It is I, you women, I make my way,
I am stern, acrid, large, undissuadable, but I love you,
I do not hurt you any more than is necessary for you,
I pour the stuff to start sons and daughters fit for these States, I press with slow rude muscle,

I brace myself effectually, I listen to no entreaties,
30 I dare not withdraw till I deposit what has so long accumulated within me.

Through you I drain the pent-up rivers of myself,
In you I wrap a thousand onward years,
On you I graft the grafts of the best-beloved of me and America,
The drops I distil upon you shall grow fierce and athletic girls, new artists, musicians, and
      singers,
35 The babes I beget upon you are to beget babes in their turn,
I shall demand perfect men and women out of my love-spendings,
I shall expect them to interpenetrate with others, as I and you interpenetrate now,
I shall count on the fruits of the gushing showers of them, as I count on the fruits of the
      gushing showers I give now,
I shall look for loving crops from the birth, life, death, immortality, I plant so lovingly now.
—1867, 1881

Once I Pass'd Through a Populous City[1]

Once I pass'd through a populous city imprinting my brain for future use with its shows,
      architecture, customs, traditions,
Yet now of all that city I remember only a woman I casually met there who detain'd me for
      love of me,
Day by day and night by night we were together—all else has long been forgotten by me,
I remember I say only that woman who passionately clung to me,
5   Again we wander, we love, we separate again,
Again she holds me by the hand, I must not go,
I see her close beside me with silent lips sad and tremulous.
—1860, 1881

Crossing Brooklyn Ferry[2]

1

Flood-tide[3] below me! I see you face to face!
Clouds of the west—sun there half an hour high—I see you also face to face.

----

[1]   This poem was first published in the 1860–61 edition of *Leaves of Grass*, where it appeared untitled as the ninth poem in the "Enfans d'Adam" section. The undated manuscript version of the poem reveals that it was originally addressed to a man rather than a woman.

[2]   This poem was added to *Leaves of Grass* in the second edition (1856), where it was entitled "Sun-Down Poem." It was renamed "Crossing Brooklyn Ferry" in 1860. In the 1881 edition of *Leaves of Grass*, the poem appears independently rather than within a cluster of other poems.

[3]   *Flood-tide*   Incoming tide.

Crowds of men and women attired in the usual costumes, how curious you are to me!
On the ferry-boats the hundreds and hundreds that cross, returning home, are more curious
    to me than you suppose,
And you that shall cross from shore to shore years hence are more to me, and more in my
    meditations, than you might suppose.

2

The impalpable sustenance of me from all things at all hours of the day,
The simple, compact, well-join'd scheme, myself disintegrated, every one disintegrated yet
    part of the scheme,
The similitudes of the past and those of the future,
The glories strung like beads on my smallest sights and hearings, on the walk in the street and
    the passage over the river,
The current rushing so swiftly and swimming with me far away,
The others that are to follow me, the ties between me and them,
The certainty of others, the life, love, sight, hearing of others.

Others will enter the gates of the ferry and cross from shore to shore,
Others will watch the run of the flood-tide,
Others will see the shipping of Manhattan north and west, and the heights of Brooklyn to
    the south and east,
Others will see the islands large and small;
Fifty years hence, others will see them as they cross, the sun half an hour high,
A hundred years hence, or ever so many hundred years hence, others will see them,
Will enjoy the sunset, the pouring-in of the flood-tide, the falling-back to the sea of the
    ebb-tide.

3

It avails not, time nor place—distance avails not,
I am with you, you men and women of a generation, or ever so many generations hence,
Just as you feel when you look on the river and sky, so I felt,
Just as any of you is one of a living crowd, I was one of a crowd,
Just as you are refresh'd by the gladness of the river and the bright flow, I was refresh'd,
Just as you stand and lean on the rail, yet hurry with the swift current, I stood yet was
    hurried,
Just as you look on the numberless masts of ships and the thick-stemm'd pipes of steamboats,
    I look'd.

I too many and many a time cross'd the river of old,
Watched the Twelfth-month[1] sea-gulls, saw them high in the air floating with motionless
    wings, oscillating their bodies,
Saw how the glistening yellow lit up parts of their bodies and left the rest in strong shadow,
Saw the slow-wheeling circles and the gradual edging toward the south,

---

1   *Twelfth-month* I.e., December (Quakers followed what they call the "plain calendar," naming the months of the year in this numerical manner).

Saw the reflection of the summer sky in the water,
Had my eyes dazzled by the shimmering track of beams,
Look'd at the fine centrifugal spokes of light round the shape of my head in the sunlit water,
Look'd on the haze on the hills southward and south-westward,
35   Look'd on the vapor as it flew in fleeces tinged with violet,
Look'd toward the lower bay to notice the vessels arriving,
Saw their approach, saw aboard those that were near me,
Saw the white sails of schooners and sloops, saw the ships at anchor,
The sailors at work in the rigging or out astride the spars,[1]
40   The round masts, the swinging motion of the hulls, the slender serpentine pennants,[2]
The large and small steamers in motion, the pilots in their pilot-houses,[3]
The white wake left by the passage, the quick tremulous whirl of the wheels,
The flags of all nations, the falling of them at sunset,
The scallop-edged waves in the twilight, the ladled cups, the frolicsome crests and glistening,
45   The stretch afar growing dimmer and dimmer, the gray walls of the granite storehouses by
        the docks,
On the river the shadowy group, the big steam-tug closely flank'd on each side by the barges,
        the hay-boat, the belated lighter,[4]
On the neighboring shore the fires from the foundry[5] chimneys burning high and glaringly
        into the night,
Casting their flicker of black contrasted with wild red and yellow light over the tops of
        houses, and down into the clefts of streets.

4

These and all else were to me the same as they are to you,
50   I loved well those cities, loved well the stately and rapid river,
The men and women I saw were all near to me,
Others the same—others who look back on me because I look'd forward to them,
(The time will come, though I stop here to-day and to-night.)

5

What is it then between us?
55   What is the count of the scores or hundreds of years between us?

Whatever it is, it avails not—distance avails not, and place avails not,
I too lived, Brooklyn of ample hills was mine,
I too walk'd the streets of Manhattan island, and bathed in the waters around it,
I too felt the curious abrupt questionings stir within me,
60   In the day among crowds of people sometimes they came upon me,

---

[1]   *spars*   Yards, booms, and gaffs—wooden beams—supporting the sails of a ship.

[2]   *pennants*   Flags.

[3]   *pilots*   Those who steer the ship, navigators;   *pilot-house*   Place where the ship's steering-wheel is located.

[4]   *lighter*   Flat-bottomed barge used to load and unload larger ships at harbor.

[5]   *foundry*   Factory where metal and glass are melted and cast into molds.

In my walks home late at night or as I lay in my bed they came upon me,
I too had been struck from the float[1] forever held in solution,
I too had receiv'd identity by my body,
That I was I knew was of my body, and what I should be I knew I should be of my body.

6

65 It is not upon you alone the dark patches fall,
The dark threw its patches down upon me also,
The best I had done seem'd to me blank and suspicious,
My great thoughts as I supposed them, were they not in reality meagre?
Nor is it you alone who know what it is to be evil,
70 I am he who knew what it was to be evil,
I too knitted the old knot of contrariety,
Blabb'd, blush'd, resented, lied, stole, grudg'd,
Had guile, anger, lust, hot wishes I dared not speak,
Was wayward, vain, greedy, shallow, sly, cowardly, malignant,
75 The wolf, the snake, the hog, not wanting in me,
The cheating look, the frivolous word, the adulterous wish, not wanting,
Refusals, hates, postponements, meanness, laziness, none of these wanting,
Was one with the rest, the days and haps[2] of the rest,
Was call'd by my nighest[3] name by clear loud voices of young men as they saw me approaching or passing,
80 Felt their arms on my neck as I stood, or the negligent leaning of their flesh against me as I sat,
Saw many I loved in the street or ferry-boat or public assembly, yet never told them a word,
Lived the same life with the rest, the same old laughing, gnawing, sleeping,
Play'd the part that still looks back on the actor or actress,
The same old role, the role that is what we make it, as great as we like,
85 Or as small as we like, or both great and small.

7

Closer yet I approach you,
What thought you have of me now, I had as much of you—I laid in my stores in advance,
I consider'd long and seriously of you before you were born.

Who was to know what should come home to me?
90 Who knows but I am enjoying this?
Who knows, for all the distance, but I am as good as looking at you now, for all you cannot see me?

---

[1] *float* For Whitman, the word "float" often suggests the life-giving cosmos before bodies take form and become matter. The word can also suggest a boat, a wave, or a crowd of people (among other things).

[2] *haps* Chances, luck.

[3] *nighest* Closest, most intimate.

8

Ah, what can ever be more stately and admirable to me than mast-hemm'd Manhattan?
River and sunset and scallop-edg'd waves of flood-tide?
The sea-gulls oscillating their bodies, the hay-boat in the twilight, and the belated lighter?

95   What gods can exceed these that clasp me by the hand, and with voices I love call me
        promptly and loudly by my nighest name as I approach?
What is more subtle than this which ties me to the woman or man that looks in my face?
Which fuses me into you now, and pours my meaning into you?

We understand then do we not?
What I promis'd without mentioning it, have you not accepted?
100   What the study could not teach—what the preaching could not accomplish is accomplish'd,
        is it not?

9

Flow on, river! flow with the flood-tide, and ebb with the ebb-tide!
Frolic on, crested and scallop-edg'd waves!
Gorgeous clouds of the sunset! drench with your splendor me, or the men and women
        generations after me!
Cross from shore to shore, countless crowds of passengers!
105   Stand up, tall masts of Mannahatta![1] stand up, beautiful hills of Brooklyn!
Throb, baffled and curious brain! throw out questions and answers!
Suspend here and everywhere, eternal float of solution!
Gaze, loving and thirsting eyes, in the house or street or public assembly!
Sound out, voices of young men! loudly and musically call me by my nighest name!
110   Live, old life! play the part that looks back on the actor or actress!
Play the old role, the role that is great or small according as one makes it!
Consider, you who peruse me, whether I may not in unknown ways be looking upon you;
Be firm, rail over the river, to support those who lean idly, yet haste with the hasting current;
Fly on, sea-birds! fly sideways, or wheel in large circles high in the air;
115   Receive the summer sky, you water, and faithfully hold it till all downcast eyes have time to
        take it from you!
Diverge, fine spokes of light, from the shape of my head, or any one's head, in the sunlit
        water!
Come on, ships from the lower bay! pass up or down, white-sail'd schooners, sloops, lighters!
Flaunt away, flags of all nations! be duly lower'd at sunset!
Burn high your fires, foundry chimneys! cast black shadows at nightfall! cast red and yellow
        light over the tops of the houses!

120   Appearances, now or henceforth, indicate what you are,
You necessary film,[2] continue to envelop the soul,
About my body for me, and your body for you, be hung our divinest aromas,

---

1   *Mannahatta*   Leni Lenape name for Manhattan, which means "land of many hills."

2   *film*   Thin membrane, covering.

Thrive, cities—bring your freight, bring your shows, ample and sufficient rivers,
Expand, being than which none else is perhaps more spiritual,
125 Keep your places, objects than which none else is more lasting.

You have waited, you always wait, you dumb,[1] beautiful ministers,
We receive you with free sense at last, and are insatiate henceforward,
Not you any more shall be able to foil us, or withhold yourselves from us,
We use you, and do not cast you aside—we plant you permanently within us,
130 We fathom you not—we love you—there is perfection in you also,
You furnish your parts toward eternity,
Great or small, you furnish your parts toward the soul.
—1856, 1881

Song of the Redwood-Tree[2]

I

ACalifornia song,
A prophecy and indirection, a thought impalpable to breathe as air,
A chorus of dryads, fading, departing, or hamadryads[3] departing,
A murmuring, fateful, giant voice, out of the earth and sky,
5 Voice of a mighty dying tree in the redwood forest dense.

Farewell my brethren,
Farewell O earth and sky, farewell ye neighboring waters,
My time has ended, my term has come.

Along the northern coast,
10 Just back from the rock-bound shore and the caves,
In the saline air from the sea in the Mendocino country,[4]
With the surge for base and accompaniment low and hoarse,
With crackling blows of axes sounding musically driven by strong arms,
Riven deep by the sharp tongues of the axes, there in the redwood forest dense,
15 I heard the mighty tree its death-chant chanting.

The choppers heard not, the camp shanties echoed not,
The quick-ear'd teamsters and chain and jack-screw[5] men heard not,

---

[1] *dumb* Silent.

[2] This poem was first published in *Harper's Magazine* in 1874; it was then included in the 1876 *Two Rivulets*, and was later incorporated into the 1881 edition of *Leaves of Grass*, where it appears independently rather than within a cluster of other poems.

[3] *dryads … hamadryads* Dryads are a class of tree-nymphs in Greek mythology; a hamadryad is intimately connected with the tree it inhabits, dying if the tree is cut down.

[4] *Mendocino country* County in northwestern California, known for its scenic coastlines and redwood forests.

[5] *jack-screw* Tool used for lifting that consists of a large threaded screw-column, which is turned by a handle at the base.

As the wood-spirits came from their haunts of a thousand years to join the refrain,
But in my soul I plainly heard.

20   Murmuring out of its myriad leaves,
Down from its lofty top rising two hundred feet high,
Out of its stalwart trunk and limbs, out of its foot-thick bark,
That chant of the seasons and time, chant not of the past only but the future.

You untold life of me,
25   *And all you venerable and innocent joys,*
Perennial hardy life of me with joys 'mid rain and many a summer sun,
And the white snows and night and the wild winds;
O the great patient rugged joys, my soul's strong joys unreck'd[1] by man,
(For know I bear the soul befitting me, I too have consciousness, identity,
30   *And all the rocks and mountains have, and all the earth,)*
Joys of the life befitting me and brothers mine,
Our time, our term has come.

Nor yield we mournfully majestic brothers,
We who have grandly fill'd our time;
35   *With Nature's calm content, with tacit huge delight,*
We welcome what we wrought for through the past,
And leave the field for them.

For them predicted long,
For a superber race, they too to grandly fill their time,
40   *For them we abdicate, in them ourselves ye forest kings!*
In them these skies and airs, these mountain peaks, Shasta, Nevadas,[2]
These huge precipitous cliffs, this amplitude, these valleys, far Yosemite,
To be in them absorb'd, assimilated.

Then to a loftier strain,
45   *Still prouder, more ecstatic rose the chant,*
As if the heirs, the deities of the West,
Joining with master-tongue bore part.

Not wan from Asia's fetiches,[3]
Nor red from Europe's old dynastic slaughter-house,
50   *(Area of murder-plots of thrones, with scent left yet of wars and scaffolds everywhere,)*
But come from Nature's long and harmless throes, peacefully builded thence,

---

[1]   *unreck'd* Unreckoned; not noticed or understood.

[2]   *Shasta* Volcanic mountain in northern California, at the southern tip of the Cascade range; *Nevadas* I.e., the Sierra Nevada mountain range, located primarily in California (though the Carson Range extends into western Nevada).

[3]   *wan* Pale, sickly; *fetiches* Fetishes; inanimate objects seen as reverential or possessed of magical properties; the term was often used by Europeans to denote spiritual beliefs seen as irrational, barbaric, or otherwise "exotic."

These virgin lands, lands of the Western shore,
To the new culminating man, to you, the empire new,
You promis'd long, we pledge, we dedicate.

55   *You occult deep volitions,*
You average spiritual manhood, purpose of all, pois'd on yourself, giving not taking law,
You womanhood divine, mistress and source of all, whence life and love and aught that comes
*   from life and love,*
You unseen moral essence of all the vast materials of America, (age upon age working in death the
*   same as life,)*
You that, sometimes known, oftener unknown, really shape and mould the New World, adjusting
*   it to Time and Space,*
60   *You hidden national will lying in your abysms, conceal'd but ever alert,*
You past and present purposes tenaciously pursued, may-be unconscious of yourselves,
Unswerv'd by all the passing errors, perturbations of the surface;
You vital, universal, deathless germs,[1] *beneath all creeds, arts, statutes, literatures,*
Here build your homes for good, establish here, these areas entire, lands of the Western shore,
65   *We pledge, we dedicate to you.*

For man of you, your characteristic race,
Here may he hardy, sweet, gigantic grow, here tower proportionate to Nature,
Here climb the vast pure spaces unconfined, uncheck'd by wall or roof,
Here laugh with storm or sun, here joy, here patiently inure,
70   *Here heed himself, unfold himself (not others' formulas heed,) here fill his time,*
To duly fall, to aid, unreck'd at last,
To disappear, to serve.

Thus on the northern coast,
In the echo of teamsters' calls and the clinking chains, and the music of choppers' axes,
75   The falling trunk and limbs, the crash, the muffled shriek, the groan,
Such words combined from the redwood-tree, as of voices ecstatic, ancient and rustling,
The century-lasting, unseen dryads, singing, withdrawing,
All their recesses of forests and mountains leaving,
From the Cascade range to the Wahsatch,[2] or Idaho far, or Utah,
80   To the deities of the modern henceforth yielding,
The chorus and indications, the vistas of coming humanity, the settlements, features all,
In the Mendocino woods I caught.

2

The flashing and golden pageant of California,
The sudden and gorgeous drama, the sunny and ample lands,
85   The long and varied stretch from Puget sound[3] to Colorado south,

---

1   *germs*   Seeds ready for germination; beginnings.

2   *Wahsatch*   Mountain range extending southwards from the Idaho-Utah border.

3   *Puget sound*   Inlet in the pacific northwest, on the coast of which Seattle is located.

Lands bathed in sweeter, rarer, healthier air, valleys and mountain cliffs,
The fields of Nature long prepared and fallow,[1] the silent, cyclic chemistry,
The slow and steady ages plodding, the unoccupied surface ripening, the rich ores forming
   beneath;
At last the New arriving, assuming, taking possession,
100   A swarming and busy race settling and organizing everywhere,
Ships coming in from the whole round world, and going out to the whole world,
To India and China and Australia and the thousand island paradises of the Pacific,
Populous cities, the latest inventions, the steamers on the rivers, the railroads, with many a
   thrifty farm, with machinery,
And wool and wheat and the grape, and diggings of yellow gold.

3

105   But more in you than these, lands of the Western shore,
(These but the means, the implements, the standing-ground),
I see in you, certain to come, the promise of thousands of years, till now deferr'd,
Promis'd to be fulfill'd, our common kind, the race.

The new society at last, proportionate to Nature,
110   In man of you, more than your mountain peaks or stalwart trees imperial,
In woman more, far more, than all your gold or vines, or even vital air.

Fresh come, to a new world indeed, yet long prepared,
I see the genius of the modern, child of the real and ideal,
Clearing the ground for broad humanity, the true America, heir of the past so grand,
115   To build a grander future.
   —1874, 1881

from SEA-DRIFT

Out of the Cradle Endlessly Rocking

Out of the cradle endlessly rocking,
   Out of the mocking-bird's throat, the musical shuttle,[2]
Out of the Ninth-month[3] midnight,
Over the sterile sands[4] and the fields beyond, where the child leaving his bed wander'd alone,
   bareheaded, barefoot,
5   Down from the shower'd halo,
Up from the mystic play of shadows twining and twisting as if they were alive,

---

[1] *fallow* Uncultivated.

[2] *shuttle* Tool used in weaving that moves the thread across the cloth and interweaves it, from one edge to the other. The sound of a shuttle moving across the loom is rhythmic, as well as ascending and descending.

[3] *Ninth-month* I.e., September (Quakers followed what they call the "plain calendar," naming the months of the year in this numerical manner).

[4] *sterile sands* Beach with no vegetation.

Out from the patches of briers and blackberries,
From the memories of the bird that chanted to me,
From your memories sad brother, from the fitful risings and fallings I heard,
10   From under that yellow half-moon late-risen and swollen as if with tears,
From those beginning notes of yearning and love there in the mist,
From the thousand responses of my heart never to cease,
From the myriad thence-arous'd words,
From the word stronger and more delicious than any,
15   From such as now they start the scene revisiting,
As a flock, twittering, rising, or overhead passing,
Borne hither, ere all eludes me, hurriedly,
A man, yet by these tears a little boy again,
Throwing myself on the sand, confronting the waves,
20   I, chanter of pains and joys, uniter of here and hereafter,
Taking all hints to use them, but swiftly leaping beyond them,
A reminiscence sing.

Once Paumanok,[1]
When the lilac-scent was in the air and Fifth-month grass was growing,
25   Up this seashore in some briers,
Two feather'd guests from Alabama, two together,
And their nest, and four light-green eggs spotted with brown,
And every day the he-bird to and fro near at hand,
And every day the she-bird crouch'd on her nest, silent, with bright eyes,
30   And every day I, a curious boy, never too close, never disturbing them,
Cautiously peering, absorbing, translating.

Shine! shine! shine!
Pour down your warmth, great sun!
While we bask, we two together.

35   *Two together!*
Winds blow south, or winds blow north,
Day come white, or night come black,
Home, or rivers and mountains from home,
Singing all time, minding no time,
40   *While we two keep together.*

Till of a sudden,
May-be kill'd, unknown to her mate,
One forenoon the she-bird crouch'd not on the nest,
Nor return'd that afternoon, nor the next,
45   Nor ever appear'd again.

And thenceforward all summer in the sound of the sea,

---

1   *Paumanok*   Indigenous name for Long Island.

And at night under the full of the moon in calmer weather,
Over the hoarse surging of the sea,
Or flitting from brier to brier by day,
50   I saw, I heard at intervals the remaining one, the he-bird,
The solitary guest from Alabama.

Blow! blow! blow!
Blow up sea-winds along Paumanok's shore;
I wait and I wait till you blow my mate to me.

55   Yes, when the stars glisten'd,
All night long on the prong of a moss-scallop'd stake,
Down almost amid the slapping waves,
Sat the lone singer wonderful causing tears.

He call'd on his mate,
60   He pour'd forth the meanings which I of all men know.

Yes my brother I know,
The rest might not, but I have treasur'd every note,
For more than once dimly down to the beach gliding,
Silent, avoiding the moonbeams, blending myself with the shadows,
65   Recalling now the obscure shapes, the echoes, the sounds and sights after their sorts,
The white arms out in the breakers tirelessly tossing,
I, with bare feet, a child, the wind wafting my hair,
Listen'd long and long.

Listen'd to keep, to sing, now translating the notes,
70   Following you my brother.

Soothe! soothe! soothe!
Close on its wave soothes the wave behind,
And again another behind embracing and lapping, every one close,
But my love soothes not me, not me.

75   *Low hangs the moon, it rose late,*
It is lagging—O I think it is heavy with love, with love.

O madly the sea pushes upon the land,
With love, with love.

O night! do I not see my love fluttering out among the breakers?
80   *What is that little black thing I see there in the white?*

Loud! loud! loud!
Loud I call to you, my love!

High and clear I shoot my voice over the waves,
Surely you must know who is here, is here,
85   You must know who I am, my love.

Low-hanging moon!
What is that dusky spot in your brown yellow?
O it is the shape, the shape of my mate!
O moon do not keep her from me any longer.

90   Land! land! O land!
Whichever way I turn, O I think you could give me my mate back again if you only would,
For I am almost sure I see her dimly whichever way I look.
O rising stars!
Perhaps the one I want so much will rise, will rise with some of you.

95   O throat! O trembling throat!
Sound clearer through the atmosphere!
Pierce the woods, the earth,
Somewhere listening to catch you must be the one I want.

Shake out carols!
100   Solitary here, the night's carols!
Carols of lonesome love! Death's carols!
Carols under that lagging, yellow, waning moon!
O under that moon where she droops almost down into the sea!
O reckless despairing carols.

105   But soft! sink low!
Soft! let me just murmur,
And do you wait a moment you husky-nois'd sea,
For somewhere I believe I heard my mate responding to me,
So faint, I must be still, be still to listen,
110   But not altogether still, for then she might not come immediately to me.

Hither my love!
Here I am! here!
With this just-sustain'd note I announce myself to you,
This gentle call is for you my love, for you.

115   Do not be decoy'd elsewhere,
That is the whistle of the wind, it is not my voice,
That is the fluttering, the fluttering of the spray,
Those are the shadows of leaves.
O darkness! O in vain!
120   O I am very sick and sorrowful.

O brown halo in the sky near the moon, drooping upon the sea!
O troubled reflection in the sea!
O throat! O throbbing heart!
And I singing uselessly, uselessly all the night.

125 *O past! O happy life! O songs of joy!*
In the air, in the woods, over fields,
Loved! loved! loved! loved! loved!
But my mate no more, no more with me!
We two together no more.

130 The aria sinking,
All else continuing, the stars shining,
The winds blowing, the notes of the bird continuous echoing,
With angry moans the fierce old mother incessantly moaning,
On the sands of Paumanok's shore gray and rustling,
135 The yellow half-moon enlarged, sagging down, drooping, the face of the sea almost touching,
The boy ecstatic, with his bare feet the waves, with his hair the atmosphere dallying,
The love in the heart long pent, now loose, now at last tumultuously bursting,
The aria's meaning, the ears, the soul, swiftly depositing,
The strange tears down the cheeks coursing,
140 The colloquy there, the trio, each uttering,
The undertone, the savage old mother incessantly crying,
To the boy's soul's questions sullenly timing, some drown'd secret hissing,
To the outsetting bard.

Demon or bird! (said the boy's soul,)
145 Is it indeed toward your mate you sing? or is it really to me?
For I, that was a child, my tongue's use sleeping, now I have heard you,
Now in a moment I know what I am for, I awake,
And already a thousand singers, a thousand songs, clearer, louder and more sorrowful than
     yours,
A thousand warbling echoes have started to life within me, never to die.

150 O you singer solitary, singing by yourself, projecting me,
O solitary me listening, never more shall I cease perpetuating you,
Never more shall I escape, never more the reverberations,
Never more the cries of unsatisfied love be absent from me,
Never again leave me to be the peaceful child I was before what there in the night,
155 By the sea under the yellow and sagging moon,
The messenger there arous'd, the fire, the sweet hell within,
The unknown want, the destiny of me.

O give me the clew![1] (it lurks in the night here somewhere,)
O if I am to have so much, let me have more!

---

[1]   *clew* Clue.

160 A word then, (for I will conquer it,)
  The word final, superior to all,
  Subtle, sent up—what is it?—I listen;
  Are you whispering it, and have been all the time, you sea-waves?
  Is that it from your liquid rims and wet sands?

165 Whereto answering, the sea,
  Delaying not, hurrying not,
  Whisper'd me through the night, and very plainly before daybreak,
  Lisp'd to me the low and delicious word death,
  And again death, death, death, death,
170 Hissing melodious, neither like the bird nor like my arous'd child's heart,
  But edging near as privately for me rustling at my feet,
  Creeping thence steadily up to my ears and laving[1] me softly all over,
  Death, death, death, death, death.

  Which I do not forget,
175 But fuse the song of my dusky demon and brother,
  That he sang to me in the moonlight on Paumanok's gray beach,
  With the thousand responsive songs at random,
  My own songs awaked from that hour,
  And with them the key, the word up from the waves,
180 The word of the sweetest song and all songs,
  That strong and delicious word which, creeping to my feet,
  (Or like some old crone rocking the cradle, swathed in sweet garments, bending aside,)
  The sea whisper'd me.
  —1859, 1881

from BY THE ROADSIDE

When I Heard the Learn'd Astronomer

When I heard the learn'd astronomer,
 When the proofs, the figures, were ranged in columns before me,
When I was shown the charts and diagrams, to add, divide, and measure them,
When I sitting heard the astronomer where he lectured with much applause in the
  lecture-room,
5 How soon unaccountable I became tired and sick,
Till rising and gliding out I wander'd off by myself,
In the mystical moist night-air, and from time to time,
Look'd up in perfect silence at the stars.
  —1865, 1881

---

[1] *laving* Washing, bathing.

from DRUM-TAPS[1]

The Wound-Dresser[2]

1

An old man bending I come among new faces,
    Years looking backward resuming in answer to children,
Come tell us old man, as from young men and maidens that love me,
(Arous'd and angry, I'd thought to beat the alarum, and urge relentless war,
5 But soon my fingers fail'd me, my face droop'd and I resign'd myself,
To sit by the wounded and soothe them, or silently watch the dead);
Years hence of these scenes, of these furious passions, these chances,
Of unsurpass'd heroes (was one side so brave? the other was equally brave);
Now be witness again, paint the mightiest armies of earth,
10 Of those armies so rapid so wondrous what saw you to tell us?
What stays with you latest and deepest? of curious panics,
Of hard-fought engagements or sieges tremendous what deepest remains?

2

O maidens and young men I love and that love me,
What you ask of my days those the strangest and sudden your talking recalls,
15 Soldier alert I arrive after a long march cover'd with sweat and dust,
In the nick of time I come, plunge in the fight, loudly shout in the rush of successful charge,
Enter the captur'd works[3]—yet lo, like a swift-running river they fade,
Pass and are gone they fade—I dwell not on soldiers' perils or soldiers' joys,
(Both I remember well—many the hardships, few the joys, yet I was content).

20 But in silence, in dreams' projections,
While the world of gain and appearance and mirth goes on,
So soon what is over forgotten, and waves wash the imprints off the sand,
With hinged knees returning I enter the doors (while for you up there,
Whoever you are, follow without noise and be of strong heart).

25 Bearing the bandages, water and sponge,
Straight and swift to my wounded I go,
Where they lie on the ground after the battle brought in,
Where their priceless blood reddens the grass the ground,
Or to the rows of the hospital tent, or under the roof'd hospital,
30 To the long rows of cots up and down each side I return,

---

[1]   Inspired by Whitman's experience as a volunteer nurse during the Civil War, *Drum-Taps* was first published as
an independent volume in October 1865. Already at press at the time of Lincoln's assassination, it was followed later
that same month by *Sequel to Drum-Taps*, which included several elegies for the late President. The poems from both
volumes were incorporated into subsequent editions of *Leaves of Grass*.

[2]   In the 1865, 1867, and 1871 editions, this poem was entitled "The Dresser."

[3]   *works* Fortifications.

To each and all one after another I draw near, not one do I miss,
An attendant follows holding a tray, he carries a refuse pail,
Soon to be fill'd with clotted rags and blood, emptied, and fill'd again.

I onward go, I stop,
35 With hinged knees and steady hand to dress wounds,
I am firm with each, the pangs are sharp yet unavoidable,
One turns to me his appealing eyes—poor boy! I never knew you,
Yet I think I could not refuse this moment to die for you, if that would save you.

3

On, on I go (open doors of time! open hospital doors!),
40 The crush'd head I dress (poor crazed hand tear not the bandage away),
The neck of the cavalry-man with the bullet through and through I examine,
Hard the breathing rattles, quite glazed already the eye, yet life struggles hard
(Come sweet death! be persuaded O beautiful death!
In mercy come quickly).

45 From the stump of the arm, the amputated hand,
I undo the clotted lint, remove the slough,[1] wash off the matter and blood,
Back on his pillow the soldier bends with curv'd neck and side-falling head,
His eyes are closed, his face is pale, he dares not look on the bloody stump,
And has not yet look'd on it.

50 I dress a wound in the side, deep, deep,
But a day or two more, for see the frame all wasted and sinking,
And the yellow-blue countenance see.

I dress the perforated shoulder, the foot with the bullet-wound,
Cleanse the one with a gnawing and putrid gangrene, so sickening, so offensive,
55 While the attendant stands behind aside me holding the tray and pail.

I am faithful, I do not give out,
The fractur'd thigh, the knee, the wound in the abdomen,
These and more I dress with impassive hand (yet deep in my breast a fire, a burning flame).

4

Thus in silence in dreams' projections,
60 Returning, resuming, I thread my way through the hospitals,
The hurt and wounded I pacify with soothing hand,
I sit by the restless all the dark night, some are so young,
Some suffer so much, I recall the experience sweet and sad,
(Many a soldier's loving arms about this neck have cross'd and rested,
65 Many a soldier's kiss dwells on these bearded lips.)
        —1865, 1881

---

1   *slough* Layer of dead tissue forming over a wound.

from MEMORIES OF PRESIDENT LINCOLN[1]

When Lilacs Last in the Dooryard Bloom'd

1

When lilacs last in the dooryard bloom'd,
　　And the great star[2] early droop'd in the western sky in the night,
I mourn'd, and yet shall mourn with ever-returning spring.

Ever-returning spring, trinity sure to me you bring,
5　Lilac blooming perennial and drooping star in the west,
And thought of him I love.

2

O powerful western fallen star!
O shades of night—O moody, tearful night!
O great star disappear'd—O the black murk that hides the star!
10　O cruel hands that hold me powerless—O helpless soul of me!
O harsh surrounding cloud that will not free my soul.

3

In the dooryard fronting an old farm-house near the white-wash'd palings,
Stands the lilac-bush tall-growing with heart-shaped leaves of rich green,
With many a pointed blossom rising delicate, with the perfume strong I love,
15　With every leaf a miracle—and from this bush in the dooryard,
With delicate-color'd blossoms and heart-shaped leaves of rich green,
A sprig with its flower I break.

4

In the swamp in secluded recesses,
A shy and hidden bird is warbling a song.

20　Solitary the thrush,
The hermit[3] withdrawn to himself, avoiding the settlements,
Sings by himself a song.

---

[1]　This title was first applied to a group of four poems in the 1881 edition of *Leaves of Grass*; the poems had appeared in the 1871 *Passage to India* under the title *President Lincoln's Burial Hymn*. "When Lilacs Last in the Dooryard Bloom'd" and "O Captain! My Captain!" had first been published in *Sequel to Drum-Taps* in October 1865.

　　President Lincoln died on 15 April 1865 after being shot by Confederate loyalist and spy, John Wilkes Booth; after lying in state in Washington until 21 April, Lincoln's body was brought on a tour aboard the *Lincoln Special*, a funeral train, stopping in major cities along the way, before being buried in Springfield, Illinois. Mourners gathered along the tracks and at the official stops; the shock and sorrow following Lincoln's death were profound.

[2]　*great star*　I.e., Venus, which at certain times of the year can be seen low in the sky just after sunset.

[3]　*hermit*　The hermit thrush, a reclusive bird with a beautiful, melancholy song, heard only in the early morning or late evening during the spring and early summer.

Song of the bleeding throat,
Death's outlet song of life, (for well dear brother I know,
25 If thou wast not granted to sing thou would'st surely die.)

5

Over the breast of the spring, the land, amid cities,
Amid lanes and through old woods, where lately the violets peep'd from the ground, spotting
    the gray debris,
Amid the grass in the fields each side of the lanes, passing the endless grass,
Passing the yellow-spear'd wheat, every grain from its shroud in the dark-brown fields
    uprisen,
30 Passing the apple-tree blows[1] of white and pink in the orchards,
Carrying a corpse to where it shall rest in the grave,
Night and day journeys a coffin.

6

Coffin that passes through lanes and streets,
Through day and night with the great cloud darkening the land,
35 With the pomp of the inloop'd flags with the cities draped in black,
With the show of the States themselves as of crape-veil'd[2] women standing,
With processions long and winding and the flambeaus[3] of the night,
With the countless torches lit, with the silent sea of faces and the unbared heads,
With the waiting depot, the arriving coffin, and the sombre faces,
40 With dirges through the night, with the thousand voices rising strong and solemn,
With all the mournful voices of the dirges pour'd around the coffin,
The dim-lit churches and the shuddering organs—where amid these you journey,
With the tolling tolling bells' perpetual clang,
Here, coffin that slowly passes,
45 I give you my sprig of lilac.

7

(Nor for you, for one alone,
Blossoms and branches green to coffins all I bring,
For fresh as the morning, thus would I chant a song for you O sane and sacred death.

All over bouquets of roses,
50 O death, I cover you over with roses and early lilies,
But mostly and now the lilac that blooms the first,
Copious I break, I break the sprigs from the bushes,
With loaded arms I come, pouring for you,
For you and the coffins all of you O death.)

---

1   *blows* Blossomings.

2   *crape-veil'd* I.e., wearing veils of crape, a fabric traditionally used for mourning garments.

3   *flambeaus* Torches, but also referring here to the bonfires that the mourners lit as they waited for the funeral train
to come.

8

55   O western orb sailing the heaven,
Now I know what you must have meant as a month since I walk'd,
As I walk'd in silence the transparent shadowy night,
As I saw you had something to tell as you bent to me night after night,
As you droop'd from the sky low down as if to my side, (while the other stars all look'd on,)
60   As we wander'd together the solemn night, (for something I know not what kept me from sleep,)
As the night advanced, and I saw on the rim of the west how full you were of woe,
As I stood on the rising ground in the breeze in the cool transparent night,
As I watch'd where you pass'd and was lost in the netherward black of the night,
As my soul in its trouble dissatisfied sank, as where you sad orb,
65   Concluded, dropt in the night, and was gone.

9

Sing on there in the swamp,
O singer bashful and tender, I hear your notes, I hear your call,
I hear, I come presently, I understand you,
But a moment I linger, for the lustrous star has detain'd me,
70   The star my departing comrade holds and detains me.

10

O how shall I warble myself for the dead one there I loved?
And how shall I deck my song for the large sweet soul that has gone?
And what shall my perfume be for the grave of him I love?

Sea-winds blown from east and west,
75   Blown from the Eastern sea and blown from the Western sea, till there on the prairies meeting,
These and with these and the breath of my chant,
I'll perfume the grave of him I love.

11

O what shall I hang on the chamber walls?
And what shall the pictures be that I hang on the walls,
80   To adorn the burial-house of him I love?

Pictures of growing spring and farms and homes,
With the Fourth-month[1] eve at sundown, and the gray smoke lucid and bright,
With floods of the yellow gold of the gorgeous, indolent, sinking sun, burning, expanding the air,
With the fresh sweet herbage under foot, and the pale green leaves of the trees prolific,
85   In the distance the flowing glaze, the breast of the river, with a wind-dapple here and there,

---

1   *Fourth-month*   I.e., April (Quakers followed what they call the "plain calendar," naming the months of the year in this numerical manner).

With ranging hills on the banks, with many a line against the sky, and shadows,
And the city at hand with dwellings so dense, and stacks of chimneys,
And all the scenes of life and the workshops, and the workmen homeward returning.

12

Lo, body and soul—this land,
90 My own Manhattan with spires, and the sparkling and hurrying tides, and the ships,
The varied and ample land, the South and the North in the light, Ohio's shores and flashing
    Missouri,
And ever the far-spreading prairies cover'd with grass and corn.

Lo, the most excellent sun so calm and haughty,
The violet and purple morn with just-felt breezes,
95 The gentle soft-born measureless light,
The miracle spreading bathing all, the fulfill'd noon,
The coming eve delicious, the welcome night and the stars,
Over my cities shining all, enveloping man and land.

13

Sing on, sing on you gray-brown bird,
100 Sing from the swamps, the recesses, pour your chant from the bushes,
Limitless out of the dusk, out of the cedars and pines.

Sing on dearest brother, warble your reedy song,
Loud human song, with voice of uttermost woe.

O liquid and free and tender!
105 O wild and loose to my soul—O wondrous singer!
You only I hear—yet the star holds me, (but will soon depart,)
Yet the lilac with mastering odor holds me.

14

Now while I sat in the day and look'd forth,
In the close of the day with its light and the fields of spring, and the farmers preparing their
    crops,
110 In the large unconscious scenery of my land with its lakes and forests,
In the heavenly aerial beauty, (after the perturb'd winds and the storms,)
Under the arching heavens of the afternoon swift passing, and the voices of children and
    women,
The many-moving sea-tides, and I saw the ships how they sail'd,
And the summer approaching with richness, and the fields all busy with labor,
115 And the infinite separate houses, how they all went on, each with its meals and minutia of
    daily usages,
And the streets how their throbbings throbb'd, and the cities pent—lo, then and there,
Falling upon them all and among them all, enveloping me with the rest,

Appear'd the cloud, appear'd the long black trail,
And I knew death, its thought, and the sacred knowledge of death.

120   Then with the knowledge of death as walking one side of me,
And the thought of death close-walking the other side of me,
And I in the middle as with companions, and as holding the hands of companions,
I fled forth to the hiding receiving night that talks not,
Down to the shores of the water, the path by the swamp in the dimness,
125   To the solemn shadowy cedars and ghostly pines so still.

And the singer so shy to the rest receiv'd me,
The gray-brown bird I know receiv'd us comrades three,
And he sang the carol of death, and a verse for him I love.

From deep secluded recesses,
130   From the fragrant cedars and the ghostly pines so still,
Came the carol of the bird.

And the charm of the carol rapt me,
As I held as if by their hands my comrades in the night,
And the voice of my spirit tallied the song of the bird.

135   *Come lovely and soothing death,*
Undulate round the world, serenely arriving, arriving,
In the day, in the night, to all, to each,
Sooner or later delicate death.

Prais'd be the fathomless universe,
140   *For life and joy, and for objects and knowledge curious,*
And for love, sweet love—but praise! praise! praise!
For the sure-enwinding arms of cool-enfolding death.

Dark mother always gliding near with soft feet,
Have none chanted for thee a chant of fullest welcome?
145   *Then I chant it for thee, I glorify thee above all,*
I bring thee a song that when thou must indeed come, come unfalteringly.

Approach strong deliveress,
When it is so, when thou hast taken them I joyously sing the dead,
Lost in the loving floating ocean of thee,
150   *Laved[1] in the flood of thy bliss O death.*
From me to thee glad serenades,
Dances for thee I propose saluting thee, adornments and feastings for thee,
And the sights of the open landscape and the high-spread sky are fitting,
And life and the fields, and the huge and thoughtful night.

---

[1]   *Laved* Bathed, washed.

155   *The night in silence under many a star,*
     The ocean shore and the husky whispering wave whose voice I know,
     And the soul turning to thee O vast and well-veil'd death,
     And the body gratefully nestling close to thee.

     Over the tree-tops I float thee a song,
160   *Over the rising and sinking waves, over the myriad fields and the prairies wide,*
     Over the dense-pack'd cities all and the teeming wharves and ways,
     I float this carol with joy, with joy to thee O death.

15

     To the tally of my soul,
     Loud and strong kept up the gray-brown bird,
165   With pure deliberate notes spreading filling the night.

     Loud in the pines and cedars dim,
     Clear in the freshness moist and the swamp-perfume,
     And I with my comrades there in the night.

     While my sight that was bound in my eyes unclosed,
170   As to long panoramas of visions.

     And I saw askant the armies,
     I saw as in noiseless dreams hundreds of battle-flags,
     Borne through the smoke of the battles and pierc'd with missiles I saw them,
     And carried hither and yon through the smoke, and torn and bloody,
175   And at last but a few shreds left on the staffs, (and all in silence,)
     And the staffs all splinter'd and broken.

     I saw battle-corpses, myriads of them,
     And the white skeletons of young men, I saw them,
     I saw the debris and debris of all the slain soldiers of the war,
180   But I saw they were not as was thought,
     They themselves were fully at rest, they suffer'd not,
     The living remain'd and suffer'd, the mother suffer'd,
     And the wife and the child and the musing comrade suffer'd,
     And the armies that remain'd suffer'd.

16

185   Passing the visions, passing the night,
     Passing, unloosing the hold of my comrades' hands,
     Passing the song of the hermit bird and the tallying song of my soul,
     Victorious song, death's outlet song, yet varying ever-altering song,
     As low and wailing, yet clear the notes, rising and falling, flooding the night,
190   Sadly sinking and fainting, as warning and warning, and yet again bursting with joy,

Covering the earth and filling the spread of the heaven,
As that powerful psalm in the night I heard from recesses,
Passing, I leave thee lilac with heart-shaped leaves,
I leave thee there in the door-yard, blooming, returning with spring.

195   I cease from my song for thee,
From my gaze on thee in the west, fronting the west, communing with thee,
O comrade lustrous with silver face in the night.

Yet each to keep and all, retrievements out of the night,
The song, the wondrous chant of the gray-brown bird,
200   And the tallying chant, the echo arous'd in my soul,
With the lustrous and drooping star with the countenance full of woe,
With the holders holding my hand nearing the call of the bird,
Comrades mine and I in the midst, and their memory ever to keep, for the dead I loved so well,
For the sweetest, wisest soul of all my days and lands—and this for his dear sake,
205   Lilac and star and bird twined with the chant of my soul,
There in the fragrant pines and the cedars dusk and dim.
      —1865, 1881

O Captain! My Captain!

O Captain! my Captain! our fearful trip is done,
    The ship has weather'd every rack,[1] the prize we sought is won,
The port is near, the bells I hear, the people all exulting,
While follow eyes the steady keel, the vessel grim and daring;
5   But O heart! heart! heart!
            O the bleeding drops of red,
                Where on the deck my Captain lies,
                    Fallen cold and dead.

O Captain! my Captain! rise up and hear the bells;
10   Rise up—for you the flag is flung—for you the bugle trills,
For you bouquets and ribbon'd wreaths—for you the shores a-crowding,
For you they call, the swaying mass, their eager faces turning;
        Here Captain! dear father!
            This arm beneath your head!
15   It is some dream that on the deck,
                You've fallen cold and dead.

My Captain does not answer, his lips are pale and still,
My father does not feel my arm, he has no pulse nor will,
The ship is anchor'd safe and sound, its voyage closed and done,

---

1   *rack* Storm.

20   From fearful trip the victor ship comes in with object won;
              Exult O shores, and ring O bells!
                    But I with mournful tread,
                          Walk the deck my Captain lies,
                                Fallen cold and dead.
          —1865, 1881

This Dust Was Once the Man

This dust was once the man,
   Gentle, plain, just and resolute, under whose cautious hand,
Against the foulest crime in history known in any land or age,
We saved the Union of these States.
—1865, 1881

In Context

Nineteenth-Century Reviews of *Leaves of Grass*[1]

from Charles Eliot Norton, *Putnam's Monthly* (September 1855)

From the 1860s through to the early twentieth century, Charles Eliot Norton (1827–1908) was among the most well-respected public intellectuals in America; he was highly regarded as a translator, travel writer, cultural commentator, and art historian. Norton was still in his twenties when he reviewed *Leaves of Grass* for *Putnam's Monthly Magazine*, a literary and cultural publication founded two years earlier by book publisher George Palmer Putnam (1814–72).

Our account of the last month's literature would be incomplete without some notice of a curious and lawless collection of poems, called *Leaves of Grass*, and issued in a thin quarto[2] without the name of publisher or author. The poems, twelve in number, are neither in rhyme nor blank verse, but in a sort of excited prose broken into lines without any attempt at measure or regularity, and, as many readers will perhaps think, without any idea of sense or reason. The writer's scorn for the wonted[3] usages of good writing, extends to the vocabulary he adopts; words usually banished from polite society are here employed without reserve and with perfect indifference to their effect on the reader's mind; and not only is the book one not to be read aloud to a mixed[4] audience, but the introduction of terms, never before heard or seen, and of slang expressions, often renders an otherwise striking passage altogether laughable. …

---

[1]   A more extensive selection of reviews is available in the website component of this anthology.

[2]   *quarto*   Book composed of quarto pages, which are created when a printer folds a large sheet of paper twice to make four leaves.

[3]   *wonted*   Usual.

[4]   *mixed*   Including both men and women.

[Whitman's poems] may briefly be described as a compound of the New England transcendentalist[1] and New York rowdy. A fireman or omnibus driver, who had intelligence enough to absorb the speculations of that school of thought which culminated at Boston some fifteen or eighteen years ago, and resources of expression to put them forth again in a form of his own, with sufficient self-conceit and contempt for public taste to affront all usual propriety of diction, might have written this gross yet elevated, this superficial yet profound, this preposterous yet somehow fascinating book. As we say, it is a mixture of Yankee transcendentalism and New York rowdyism, and, what must be surprising to both these elements, they here seem to fuse and combine with the most perfect harmony. The vast and vague conceptions of the one, lose nothing of their quality in passing through the coarse and odd intellectual medium of the other; while there is an original perception of nature, a manly brawn, and an epic directness in our new poet, which belong to no other adept of the transcendental school. ...

As seems very proper in a book of transcendental poetry, the author withholds his name from the title page, and presents his portrait, neatly engraved on steel, instead. This, no doubt, is upon the principle that the name is merely accidental; while the portrait affords an idea of the essential being from whom these utterances proceed. We must add, however, that this significant reticence does not prevail throughout the volume, for we learn on p. 29, that our poet is "Walt Whitman, an American, one of the roughs, a kosmos." That he was an American, we knew before, for, aside from America, there is no quarter of the universe where such a production could have had a genesis. That he was one of the roughs was also tolerably plain; but that he was a kosmos, is a piece of news we were hardly prepared for. Precisely what a kosmos is, we trust Mr. Whitman will take an early occasion to inform the impatient public.

anonymous, "A Strange Blade," *Punch Magazine* (26 April 1856)

The London weekly magazine *Punch* rose to popularity in the 1840s and 1850s, developing a reputation for its satirical cartoons and commentary on current affairs, generally known for their conservative bent.

An American Rough, whose name is WALT WHITMAN, and who calls himself a "Kosmos," has been publishing a mad book under the title of *Leaves of Grass*. We can only say that these *Leaves of Grass* are fully worthy to be put on a level with that heap of rubbish called *Fern Leaves*,[2] by FANNY FERN, and similarly "green stuff." The fields of American literature want weeding dreadfully.

from Fanny Fern, "Leaves of Grass," *The New York Ledger* (10 May 1856)

The New York Ledger's columnist Fanny Fern (1811–72) had risen to celebrity and renown in the early 1850s with her honest and witty journalism and short fiction, as well as with her 1854 rags-to-riches novel *Ruth Hall*. Many of her early newspaper pieces were published in the 1853 collection *Fern Leaves from Fanny's Portfolio*—whose title and frontispiece design many scholars have acknowledged as a clear influence on the design of the first edition of *Leaves of Grass*. Fern's public support of Whitman's poetry instigated a brief period of friendship between the two writers; the relationship apparently ended when Whitman failed to repay a debt to Fern's

---

[1]   *New England transcendentalist*   Transcendentalism was an influential but often controversial literary, philosophical, and social movement originating in New England in the 1830s with the work of writers such as Ralph Waldo Emerson and Margaret Fuller. Its adherents emphasised values such as spiritual self-reliance, often rejecting traditional conceptions of God while emphasizing the innate divinity of the human individual.

[2]   *Fern Leaves*   1853 collection of prose stories and sketches by the highly popular American writer Fanny Fern; a short excerpt from Fern's own review of *Leaves of Grass* appears below.

husband, editor James Parton. Further excerpts from Fern's review are included in the website component of this anthology.

Fresh "Leaves of Grass!" not submitted by the self-reliant author to the fingering of any publisher's critic,[1] to be arranged, re-arranged and disarranged to his circumscribed liking, till they hung limp, tame, spiritless, and scentless. No. It were a spectacle worth seeing, this glorious Native American, who, when the daily labor of chisel and plane was over, himself, with toil-hardened fingers, handled the types to print the pages which wise and good men have since delighted to endorse and to honor. Small critics, whose contracted vision could see no beauty, strength, or grace, in these "Leaves," have long ago repented that they so hastily wrote themselves down shallow by such a premature confession. Where an Emerson, and a Howitt[2] have commended, my woman's voice of praise may not avail; but happiness was born a twin, and so I would fain share with others the unmingled delight which these "Leaves" have given me.

I say unmingled; I am not unaware that the charge of coarseness and sensuality has been affixed to them. My moral constitution may be hopelessly tainted or—too sound to be tainted, as the critic wills, but I confess that I extract no poison from these "Leaves"—to me they have brought only healing. Let him who can do so, shroud the eyes of the nursing babe lest it should see its mother's breast. Let him look carefully between the gilded covers of books, backed by high-sounding names, and endorsed by parson and priest, lying unrebuked upon his own family table; where the asp[3] of sensuality lies coiled amid rhetorical flowers. Let him examine well the paper dropped weekly at his door, in which virtue and religion are rendered disgusting, save when they walk in satin slippers, or, clothed in purple and fine linen, kneel on a damask "*prie-dieu*."[4]

---

[1]   *not submitted ... publisher's critic*   Whitman self-published the first edition of *Leaves of Grass*, and was also responsible for much of its typesetting.

[2]   *Emerson*   Transcendental philosopher, lecturer, and poet Ralph Waldo Emerson (1803–82), one of the most prominent public intellectuals in nineteenth-century America, whose private commendations of *Leaves of Grass* became widely known throughout the literary community; see "In Context: Whitman's Correspondence with Emerson" in the website component of this anthology;   *Howitt*   English writer William Howitt (1792–1879); his positive review of *Leaves of Grass* was published in *The London Weekly Dispatch* on 9 March 1856.

[3]   *asp*   Poisonous snake.

[4]   *clothed in purple*   Reference to the historical association of purple fabrics with royalty;   *prie-dieu*   Table for prayer, often highly ornamental.

In Context

The Design of *Leaves of Grass*, 1855–60[1]

Cover of the 1855 edition; Whitman designed the binding and pages himself. Its 795 copies were printed and released in batches between June 1855 and January 1856, with each batch receiving a different binding. Only a fraction of them received the expensive treatment pictured above, with green, embossed leather, gilding on the paper's edges, and gilded text on both the front and back cover—a design bearing a distinct resemblance to that of *Fern Leaves*, the extremely popular prose collection published by Fanny Fern in 1853. Some copies were bound in the same leather but had gilding only on the front cover; others received only a cheap paper wrapping. The costs of these editions ranged widely, from fifty-eight cents to around two dollars. Recent scholarship has uncovered numerous minute differences—small changes of wording, printer's errors corrected and missed—within the texts of these different editions as well, which further attest to Whitman's direct and immediate involvement in the process of printing the work.

---

[1]   The editors are indebted for the information provided in this section to the wealth of scholarship freely available on the Whitman Archive, and especially to Ed Folsom's excellent article "Whitman Making Books/Books Making Whitman: A Catalog and Commentary" (2005).

The portrait of Whitman that appeared opposite the frontispiece of the 1855 edition. The original daguerreotype, likely taken by Gabriel Harrison around July 1854, has now been lost; this engraving was made either by Samuel Hollyer or John C. McRae, in collaboration with Whitman. In the early 2000s, Ted Genoways discovered that the variations between copies of the 1855 edition included two distinct versions of this engraving: in later printings, the engraving had been altered so as to increase the bulging at Whitman's crotch.

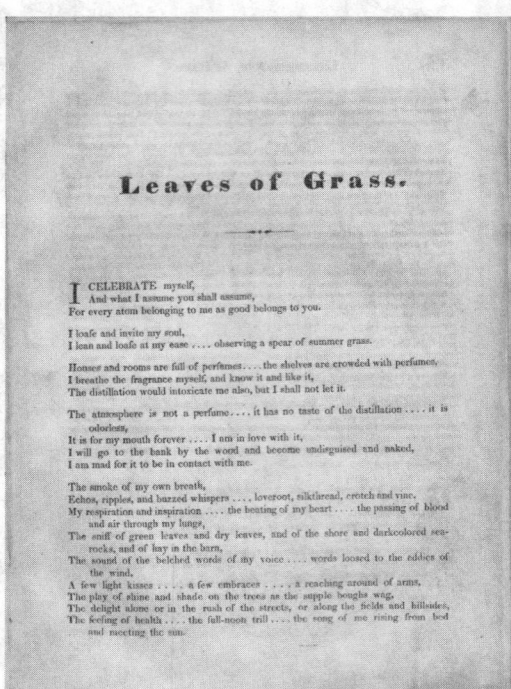

First page of the poem eventually titled "Song of Myself," in the 1855 edition. The typesetting and printing of the text was a collaboration between Whitman and a Brooklyn printer friend, Andrew Rome, whose small firm worked primarily with legal documents and pamphlets. Whitman chose the typeface and helped set some of the type for the edition. The unusually large (approximately eleven inches by eight inches) format of the first edition—which was remarked upon by many of its initial reviewers—may not have been an intentional choice of Whitman's, but rather a consequence of the legal-sized paper Andrew Rome then had available.

First page of "Poem of Walt Whitman, an American" (later titled "Song of Myself") in the 1856 edition. This edition was printed as a "pocket size" book that would be easy to carry around and that caused the long lines of verse to overflow more often (sometimes over several lines); Whitman wrote that "to put a book in your pocket and off to the seashore or the forest—that is an ideal pleasure." The spine of the 1856 edition features an extract from Ralph Waldo Emerson's congratulatory letter: "I greet you at the beginning of a great career."

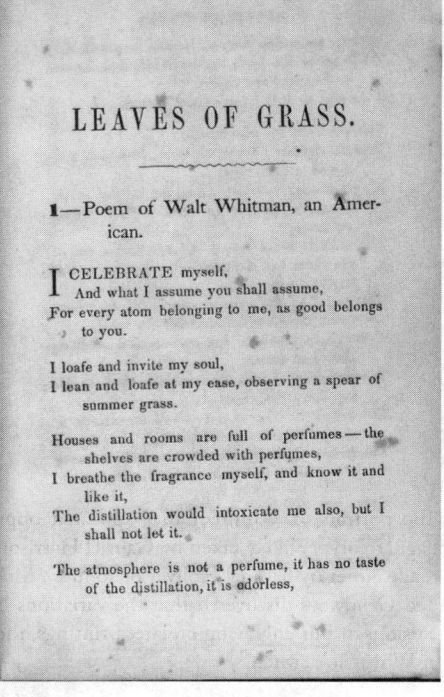

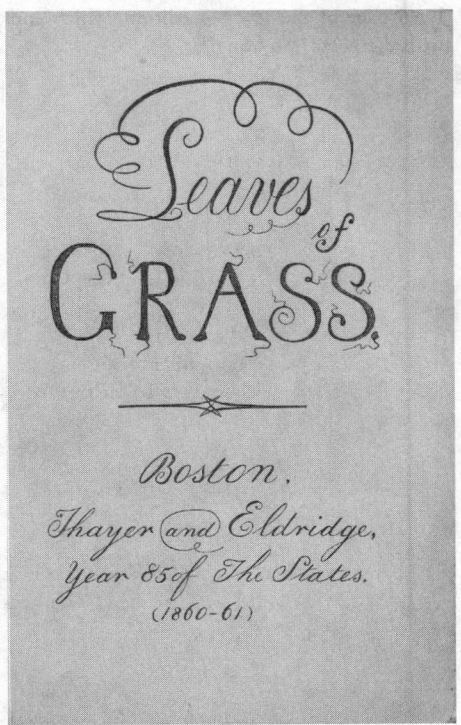

Frontispiece of the 1860–61 edition, which features stylized illustrations of spermatozoa surrounding the word "Grass." In an 1858 essay published in *The Atlantic Monthly*, Ralph Waldo Emerson had claimed, "I find certain books vital and spermatic, not leaving the reader what he was: he shuts the book a richer man." This edition was bound in a red-brown leather rather than the green of the previous two editions. Note also that Whitman begins with this edition to date his books using the "American calendar," for which year one is 1776, the date of the Declaration of Independence.

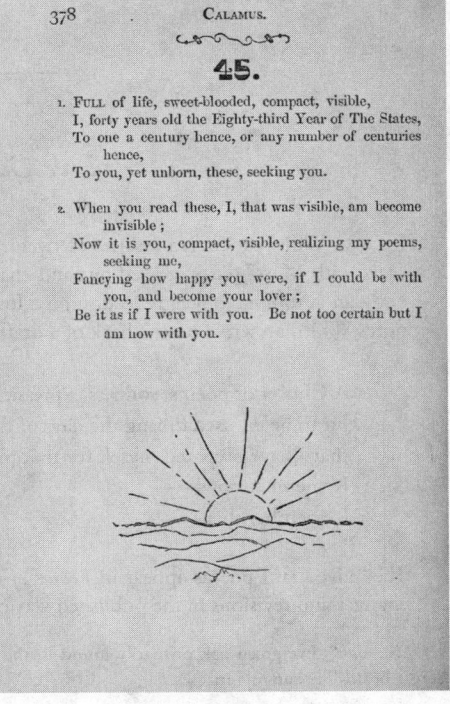

Final page of the *Calamus* cluster in the 1860–61 edition. This illustration of the rising (or setting) sun appears several times throughout the edition, as do illustrations of a perched butterfly (see the following page) and a globe featuring the Western hemisphere. These pages show the design work and variety of typefaces that Whitman chose for this edition, a process he later described in a letter to his brother: "The printers and foremen thought I was crazy, and there were all sorts of supercilious squints (about the typography I ordered, I mean)—but since it has run through the press, they have simmered down. Yesterday the foreman of the press-room . . . pronounced it, in plain terms, the freshest and handsomest piece of typography that had ever passed through his mill—I like it, I think, first rate—though I think I could improve much upon it now. It is quite 'odd,' of course."

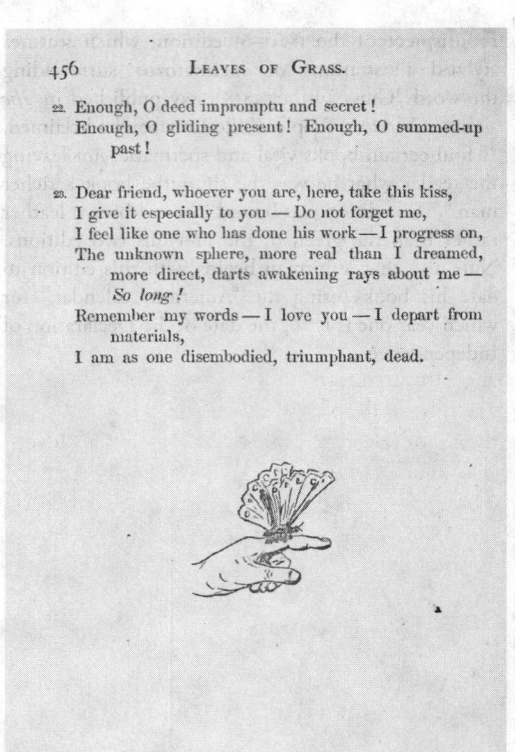

Final page of the 1860–61 edition, which ends with the poem "So Long!"

Live Oak,[1] with Moss

In 1859, Whitman copied a series of twelve poems into a small notebook under the title "Live Oak, with Moss" (later crossed out and changed to "Calamus-Leaves"). The sequence is apparently an autobiographical reflection on a love affair with a man—a possibility supported by the notes Whitman wrote on the back of a draft of the title poem:

> A Cluster of poems, sonnets expressing the thoughts, pictures, aspirations &c.
> Fit to be perused during the days of the approach of Death.
> that I have prepared myself for that purpose—
> Remember now——
> Remember then——

The "Live Oak" poems appear in *Leaves of Grass* as part of the *Calamus* cluster; there are some changes and revisions in the published versions, but by far the most significant change is that the

---

[1] *Live Oak* Evergreen oak primarily found in the southeastern United States. The tree is often overgrown with dense, beard-like hanging mosses.

poems are split up and reordered to an extent that obscures the narrative implied in the original sequence. It is unclear whether Whitman's motivations were purely artistic, or whether, as many critics speculate, he felt the need to partially censor such an explicit portrayal of same-sex love. The poems were not reprinted in their "Live Oak" order until 1953, and were not commonly available in that form until the late twentieth century. The text provided below is based on the notebook manuscript; versions that appeared in *Leaves of Grass* in the *Calamus* cluster are included in the anthology's website component.

1

Not the heat flames up and consumes,
Not the sea-waves hurry in and out,
Not the air, delicious and dry, the air of the ripe summer, bears lightly along white down-
balls of myriads of seeds, wafted, sailing gracefully, to drop where they may,
Not these—O none of these, more than the flames of me, consuming, burning for his love
whom I love—O none, more than I, hurrying in and out;
5   Does the tide hurry, seeking something, and never give up?—O I, the same, to seek my life-
long lover;
O nor down-balls, nor perfumes, nor the high rain-emitting clouds, are borne through the
open air, more than my copious soul is borne through the open air, wafted in all directions,
for friendship, for love.—

2

I saw in Louisiana a live-oak growing,
All alone stood it, and the moss hung down from the branches,
Without any companion it grew there, glistening out with joyous leaves of dark green,
10   And its look, rude,[1] unbending, lusty, made me think of myself;
But I wondered how it could utter joyous leaves, standing alone there without its friend, its
lover—For I knew I could not;
And I plucked a twig with a certain number of leaves upon it, and twined around it a little
moss, and brought it away—And I have placed it in sight in my room,
It is not needed to remind me as of my friends, (for I believe lately I think of little else than
of them,)
Yet it remains to me a curious token—it makes me think of manly love,
15   For all that, and though the live oak glistens there in Louisiana, solitary in a wide flat space,
uttering joyous leaves all its life, without a friend, a lover, near—I know very well I could
not.

3

When I heard at the close of the day how I had been praised in the Capitol, still it was not a
happy night for me that followed;
Nor when I caroused—Nor when my favorite plans were accomplished—was I really happy;
But that day I rose at dawn from the bed of perfect health, electric, inhaling sweet breath,
When I saw the full moon in the west grow pale and disappear in the morning light,

---

[1]   *rude*   Rough or uncultivated.

When I heard at the close of
the Day how I had been
praised in the Capitol, still
it was not a happy night
for me that followed;
And else, when I caroused—Or
when my plans were accom-
plished—it was well enough—
Still I was not happy;
But that Day when I rose
at dawn from the bed of
perfect health, electric, inhaling sweet breath,
When I saw the full moon
in the west grow pale and
disappear in the morning light,
When I wandered alone over the
beach, and undressing, bathed,
laughing with the waters, and
saw the sun rise,

20   When I wandered alone over the beach, and undressing, bathed, laughing with the waters,
       and saw the sun rise,
     And when I thought how my friend, my lover, was coming, then O I was happy;
     Each breath tasted sweeter—and all that day my food nourished me more—And the beauti-
       ful day passed well,
     And the next came with equal joy—And with the next, at evening, came my friend,
     And that night, while all was still, I heard the waters roll slowly continually up the shores

25 I heard the hissing rustle of the liquid and sands, as directed to me, whispering, to congratu-
    late me,—For the friend I love lay sleeping by my side,
    In the stillness his face was inclined towards me, while the moon's clear beams shone, And his
    arm lay lightly over my breast—And that night I was happy.

4

This moment as I sit alone, yearning and pensive, it seems to me there are other men, in
    other lands, yearning and pensive.
It seems to me I can look over and behold them, in Germany, France, Spain—Or far away in
    China, India, or Russia—talking other dialects,
And it seems to me if I could know those men I should love them as I love men in my own
    lands;
30 It seems to me they are as wise, beautiful, benevolent, as any in my own lands;
    O I think we should be brethren—I think I should be happy with them.

5

Long I thought that knowledge alone would suffice me—O if I could but obtain knowledge!
Then the Land of the Prairies engrossed me—the south savannas engrossed me—For them I
    would live—I would be their orator;
Then I met the examples of old and new heroes—I heard of warriors, sailors, and all daunt-
    less persons—And it seemed to me I too had it in me to be as dauntless as any, and would
    be so;
35 And then to finish all, it came to me to strike up the songs of the New World—And then I
    believed my life must be spent in singing;
But now take notice, Land of the prairies, Land of the south savannas, Ohio's land,
Take notice, you Kanuck[1] woods—and you, Lake Huron—and all that with you roll toward
    Niagara—and you Niagara also,
And you, Californian mountains—that you all find some one else that he be your singer of
    songs,
For I can be your singer of songs no longer—I have ceased to enjoy them.
40 I have found him who loves me, as I him in perfect love,
    With the rest I dispense—I sever from all that I thought would suffice me, for it does not—it
    is now empty and tasteless to me,
I heed knowledge, and the grandeur of The States, and the examples of heroes, no more,
I am indifferent to my own songs—I am to go with him I love, and he is to go with me,
It is to be enough for each of us that we are together—We never separate again.—

6

45 What think you I have taken my pen to record?
    Not the battle-ship, perfect-model'd, majestic, that I saw to day arrive in the offing,[2] under
    full sail,

---

1   *Kanuck* American slang meaning "French Canadian."

2   *offing* Area of the sea that is some distance from the shoreline but can be seen from land.

Nor the splendors of the past day—nor the splendors of the night that envelopes me—Nor
   the glory and growth of the great city spread around me,
But the two men I saw to-day on the pier, parting the parting of dear friends.
The one to remain hung on the other's neck and passionately kissed him—while the one to
   depart tightly prest the one to remain in his arms.

7

50   You bards of ages hence! when you refer to me, mind not so much my poems,
Nor speak to me that I prophesied of The States and led them the way of their glories,
But come, I will inform you who I was underneath that impassive exterior—I will tell you
   what to say of me,
Publish my name and hang up my picture as that of the tenderest lover,
The friend, the lover's portrait, of whom his friend, his lover was fondest,
55   Who was not proud of his songs, but of the measureless ocean of love within him—and
   freely poured it forth,
Who often walked lonesome walks thinking of his dearest friends, his lovers,
Who pensive, away from one he loved, often lay sleepless and dissatisfied at night,
Who, dreading lest the one he loved might after all be indifferent to him, felt the sick
   feeling—O sick! sick!
Whose happiest days were those, far away through fields, in woods, on hills, he and another,
   wandering hand in hand, they twain,[1] apart from other men.
60   Who ever, as he sauntered the streets, curved with his arm the manly shoulder of his friend—
   while the curving arm of his friend rested upon him also.

8

Hours continuing long, sore and heavy-hearted,
Hours of the dusk, when I withdraw to a lonesome and unfrequented spot, seating myself,
   leaning my face in my hands,
Hours sleepless, deep in the night, when I go forth, speeding swiftly the country roads, or
   through the city streets, or pacing miles and miles, stifling plaintive cries,
Hours discouraged, distracted—For he, the one I cannot content myself without—soon I
   saw him content himself without me,
65   Hours when I am forgotten—(O weeks and months are passing, but I believe I am never to
   forget!)
Sullen and suffering hours—(I am ashamed—but it is useless—I am what I am;)
Hours of my torment—I wonder if other men ever have the like out of the like feelings?
Is there even one other like me—distracted—his friend, his lover, lost to him?
Is he too as I am now? Does he still rise in the morning, dejected, thinking who is lost to
   him? And at night, awaking, think who is lost?
70   Does he too harbor his friendship silent and endless? Harbor his anguish and passion?
Does some stray reminder, or the casual mention of a name, bring the fit back upon him,
   taciturn and deprest?
Does he see himself reflected in me? In these hours does he see the face of his hours reflected?

---

[1]   *twain*   Two; paired.

9

I dreamed in a dream of a city where all the men were like brothers,
75 O I saw them tenderly love each other—I often saw them, in numbers, walking hand in
     hand;
    I dreamed that was the city of robust friends—Nothing was greater there than manly love—
     it led the rest,
    It was seen every hour in the actions of the men of that city, and in all their looks and
     words.—

10

O you whom I often and silently come where you are, that I may be with you,
As I walk by your side, or sit near, or remain in the same room with you,
80 Little you know the subtle electric fire that for your sake is playing within me.—

11

Earth! Though you look so impassive, ample and spheric there—I now suspect that is not all,
I now suspect there is something terrible in you, ready to break forth,
For an athlete loves me, and I him—But toward him there is something fierce and terrible in
 me,
I dare not tell it in words—not even in these songs.

12

85 To the young man, many things to absorb, to engraft, to develop, I teach, that he be my
     eleve,[1]
    But if through him speed not the blood of friendship, hot and red—If he be not silently
     selected by lovers, and do not silently select lovers—of what use were it for him to seek to
     become eleve of mine?
    —WRITTEN 1858–59 (PUBLISHED 1953)

---

[1] *eleve* Student.

HERMAN MELVILLE

1819 – 1891

Herman Melville is widely acknowledged to be one of America's most significant literary figures, a formidable writer of the sea, and a strong voice for the quintessentially American ideals of democracy, freedom, and equality; he was also fierce in condemning the forces that impeded the fulfillment of those ideals. Though Melville died in relative obscurity, his novels and short fiction have become enduringly popular and highly acclaimed for their narrative power, philosophical depth, thematic richness, and stylistic innovation. One biographer wrote of *Moby-Dick* (1851) that it is "the most daring and prolonged aesthetic adventure that had ever been conducted in the hemisphere in the English language." A persistent and eloquent defender of those who suffer within hierarchical, patriarchal, and racist power structures, Melville wrote about the lives of sailors, enslaved people, office clerks, and factory workers, defying dominant ideologies of masculinity, capitalism, "whiteness," and colonialism.

Herman Melvill was born in 1819 to Allan Melvill and Maria Gansevoort Melvill (the "e" was added later). He was descended on both sides from prominent families: his paternal grandfather played a part in the Boston Tea Party, and his maternal grandfather, General Peter Gansevoort, was a Revolutionary War hero. The Melvill children were raised in Maria's Dutch Reformed Calvinist faith, with its emphasis on original sin, damnation, and predestination; while Melville came to reject this interpretation of Christianity, it had a profound effect on his imagination. Melville began his education in New York City, but when Allan Melvill's importing business failed, the family moved to Albany, where Herman was enrolled at Albany Academy. He was educated there only for a year, before he was withdrawn for financial reasons. When Herman was twelve, his father died after descending into madness, leaving the family in debt, and in 1832 the twelve-year-old Herman began work as a clerk in the New York State Bank. It was at this time that Maria added the "e" to the family name, perhaps in an effort to distance themselves from Allan Melvill's bankruptcy.

Over the next five years, Melville worked at his brother Gansevoort's fur store and attended the Albany Academy again. In 1837, he took up a teaching post near Pittsfield, and in 1838 enrolled at the Lansingburgh Academy to study engineering, but in the following year he changed course dramatically by signing up as a cabin boy on the merchant ship *St. Lawrence*, which sailed from New York to Liverpool and back. On his return, Melville took up teaching, first in Greenbush and then in Brunswick, New York. In 1840 he decided to go to sea again, this time aboard a whaling ship, the *Acushnet*, which sailed from New Bedford to the South Seas on 3 January 1841. After sailing for over a year, Melville jumped ship on 9 July 1842 with his friend Richard Tobias Greene at the Marquesas Islands, where he lived with the islanders of the Taipi Valley for four weeks before joining an Australian whaling crew aboard the *Lucy Ann*. He shortly afterwards went to shore in Tahiti, where he was imprisoned as a mutineer; after escaping in October 1842, he signed on with a Nantucket whaling ship, the *Charles and Henry*. Upon completing the cruise in 1843, Melville spent time in the Hawaiian Islands, where he worked various jobs, including as a pin setter in a bowling alley. Later that year, Melville enlisted in the United States Navy and sailed on a frigate, the *United States*, until 1844, when he landed in Boston and was discharged.

In 1846, Melville published *Typee,* an account of his time among the Marquesas islanders; the book was first printed in London and then in New York. This travel narrative, and its sequel, *Omoo*, which recounts Melville's adventures in Tahiti, were very popular in America and Britain, establishing the young Melville as a literary celebrity known for sultry, action-packed adventure stories. While successes,

Typee and *Omoo* were also controversial: in both books, Melville attacked the Christian missionaries who sought to "civilize" the Indigenous peoples of the islands. While Melville's depiction of the islanders partook of the racial stereotypes of his day, he asserted very clearly that the barbarism of white people far exceeded any that could be found among the islanders: "the fiend-like skill we display in the invention of all manner of death-dealing engines, the vindictiveness with which we carry on our wars, and the misery and desolation that follow in their train, are enough of themselves to distinguish the white civilized man as the most ferocious animal on the face of the earth." Such statements proved provocative enough that the publishers of *Typee* chose to soften the book's comments on missionaries in the second printing.

    Typee was dedicated to Lemuel Shaw, Chief Justice of the Massachusetts Supreme Court and father of Elizabeth Shaw, whom Melville married in 1847; the couple would in time have four children. Melville and Elizabeth settled first in New York City, and most of Melville's family moved in with them: his mother Maria, his four sisters, and his brother and sister-in-law. Melville's early fame brought him into the literary circle of the Duyckinck brothers in New York, from whose libraries Melville borrowed many books. He entered on a course of intense reading, which in turn exerted a profound influence over his future writing; in addition to the Old Testament prophets, he read Shakespeare with increasing wonderment, as well as Defoe, Milton, Rabelais, Swift, Mary Shelley, Byron, Montaigne, and Sir Thomas Browne.

    In 1849, Melville turned from writing semi-autobiographical travel narratives to more inventive forms of fiction, as he felt an "invincible distaste" for facts and "a longing to plume my pinions for flight." Looking to engage a more sophisticated audience in addition to the "superficial skimmer of pages" whom he believed had enjoyed his earlier works, Melville's first fully fictional novel, *Mardi* (1849), shifted away from the realist mode to engage in a philosophical allegory that emphasizes the supreme importance of freedom and equality. The book sold poorly and was rejected by critics, and Melville responded by writing two more books in quick succession: *Redburn* in 1849 and *White-Jacket* in 1850. In a letter to his father-in-law, Melville wrote of these books that "they are two jobs, which I have done for money—being forced to it, as other men are to sawing wood." These two novels, which were in many ways a return to his earlier style, found a wide readership. After members of Congress read Melville's scathing denunciation of flogging in *White-Jacket*, as well as his depiction of the authoritarian, unequal conditions of naval life, they banned flogging on all American ships. *Redburn*, which delves into themes of sexuality, nationalism, and the place of refugees in antebellum society, has been receiving increased critical attention, with one scholar deeming it "one of the great nineteenth-century works about race and emigration."

    In September 1850, Melville and his growing family moved out of New York City to Arrowhead, a farm in Pittsville, Massachusetts, which Melville bought with money borrowed from his father-in-law. While in the area earlier in the summer, Melville had met Nathaniel Hawthorne, and the two quickly became friends. In late August 1850, Melville published "Hawthorne and His Mosses" in the *Literary World* magazine, in which he praises Hawthorne's genius, as well as his originality, darkness, and Americanness: "the smell of your beeches and hemlocks is upon him; your own prairies are in his soul … you will hear the far roar of his Niagara." Viewed as an early expression of the Young America movement, the essay argues for the excellence and potential of American writers, with Hawthorne as an exemplary figure "who breathe[s] that unshackled, democratic spirit of Christianity in all things."

    Melville's friendship with Hawthorne, and Hawthorne's literary influence on Melville, came at a time of great creativity—he was in the process of writing *Moby-Dick*. His passionate letters to Hawthorne, as well as the frequent expression of homoerotic desire in his work, have led many to suppose the friendship between the two writers was a romantic one. If so, evidence for it is one-sided: while Melville was clearly passionately attached to Hawthorne, and while Hawthorne very much admired Melville and his work, only one letter from Hawthorne to Melville exists, and it is a request for Melville to pick up some mail. Though there is no clear biographical proof that Melville had sexual relationships with men, his work certainly celebrates homoerotic desire, linking it with, among other things, creativity and resistance to conventional power structures based on heterosexual norms. For this reason, Melville is frequently hailed as a trailblazer, one of the most significant early writers in the queer American literary tradition.

At Arrowhead during the winter of 1850–51, Melville worked on *Moby-Dick* from early in the morning through to the afternoon. His sister Augusta would every day copy out the work from the day before, and she wrote in a letter that she found the book "very fine." After finishing the manuscript, Melville wrote to Hawthorne that "I have written a wicked book, and feel spotless as a lamb." Unfortunately, though British reviews contained favorable impressions of the novel, American critics at the time were unappreciative and overwhelmed, complaining that the book was too long, too mystical, and overwrought. A reviewer for *The New York Evangelist* wrote in 1851 that "oddity is the governing character [of *Moby-Dick*]" and that Melville "has reached the very limbo of eccentricity." In the wake of the public dismissal of both *Mardi* and *Moby-Dick*, Melville grew increasingly embittered with his readers and reviewers, but continued writing fiction, publishing the novel *Pierre; or, the Ambiguities* in 1852. Critics were even more bewildered by this novel, calling it "morbid and unhealthy…[like] a horrid fit of the night-mare." *Pierre* did not increase Melville's income or reputation, and neither did his final novel, *The Confidence-Man* (1857). Now considered a masterly, metafictional tour-de-force, *The Confidence-Man* confused Melville's contemporary readership, confirming critics in their opinion that Melville had not developed his potential. He himself knew he had; in a letter to Hawthorne he wrote: "Though I wrote the Gospels in this century, I should die in the gutter."

Between 1853 and 1855, Melville turned to a form of fiction that was, at that time, often more lucrative than novels by contributing short stories to *Putnam's Monthly*. Melville was a keen reader of periodicals, and he created works for *Putnam's* that reflected the influence of contemporary writers of short fiction, including Hawthorne, Edgar Allan Poe, and Charles Dickens. Melville continued, in these stories, to explore themes from his novels—the dehumanizing effects of capitalist, patriarchal social structures, the inhumanity of white supremacist attitudes, the mystery of the sea, and the draw of travel. He collected six of his stories and published them as *The Piazza Tales* (1856), including the now well-known tales *Benito Cereno*, "Bartleby, the Scrivener," and "The Encantadas." Reviews for the volume were quite positive, but sales were not, and this disappointment, when paired with the discouraging reception of *Mardi*, *Moby-Dick*, and *Pierre*, contributed to Melville's decision to stop writing fiction for the foreseeable future.

The ensuing decade in Melville's life was a dark one, and one that coincided with the national crisis of the Civil War. In 1856–57, he took a trip to Europe and the Middle East in an attempt to regain his spirits, but things did not improve, and he struggled to support his family on his return. In 1866 he took a job at the New York Custom House, a position he worked for nineteen years, earning four dollars a day. Melville's mental state deteriorated to a point where his wife Elizabeth nearly left him in 1867; that same year Melville's eldest son, Malcolm, died by suicide at the age of eighteen.

Melville did not stop writing, however; instead of fiction, he turned to poetry. *Battle-Pieces*, a collection of poems reflecting on the Civil War, was published in 1866; in an appendix, Melville urged the North to treat the South with mercy. His next work, *Clarel* (1876), was a seven-thousand-line poem inspired by his spiritual crisis and by his trip to the Middle East. *Clarel* was Melville's last publication during his lifetime. Two more books of poetry, *John Marr and Other Sailors* (1888) and *Timoleon* (1891), were printed in runs of twenty-five copies each and circulated privately. Melville's poetry has, until recently, been largely absent from accounts of American literary history, which long held Walt Whitman and Emily Dickinson to be the only great post-bellum nineteenth-century poets. The formal innovations of Melville's poems are being increasingly recognized, including their shift away from Romantic subjectivity, and scholars are integrating Melville's three decades of poetic output into a more nuanced history of nineteenth-century American poetry. In addition to another book of poems, *Weeds and Wildings Chiefly*, an unfinished novella, *Billy Budd*, was found in manuscript after Melville's death in 1891; it was not published until 1924. At once hailed as a masterpiece by Thomas Mann, among others, the story of the execution of the beautiful young sailor has taken its place alongside *Moby-Dick* as one of Melville's most critically acclaimed and often adapted works.

When Melville died, the *North American Review* printed a notice, which said that he "wrote out of his heart … [but] his books are now but little read. When he died the other day … men who could give you the names of fifty living poets and perhaps a hundred living American novelists owned that they had never heard of Herman Melville." The *New York Times* encapsulated Melville's obscurity when it printed a brief article in honor of his life entitled "The Late Hiram Melville." It was not until the height of the Modernist movement in the 1920s that the so-called "Melville Revival" brought Melville's work, particularly *Moby-Dick*, into prominence. Raymond Weaver's *Herman Melville: Mariner and Mystic* (1921) launched the revival, and writers such as Virginia Woolf, D.H. Lawrence, and Lewis Mumford wrote essays highlighting Melville's formal and linguistic innovations. His influence on these writers, and on many writers that followed in the twentieth and twenty-first centuries, has been profound; poets such as W.H. Auden and Hart Crane have commemorated Melville in verse, and Ralph Ellison's groundbreaking novel *Invisible Man* (1952) creatively interprets aspects of *The Confidence-Man* and bears an epigraph drawn from *Benito Cereno*. Melville's reputation among readers and critics has only increased in the century that followed the Revival, but for a long time his fame was based almost solely on *Moby-Dick*, and to a lesser extent *Billy Budd*; it was not until the 1960s that critics and readers began engaging with the short fiction, and not until even more recently that his poetry has found an appreciative audience.

Twenty-first-century scholars have continued to explore the aesthetic, generic, and formal dimensions of Melville's work, and his fiction and poetry are essential to discourses in American literary studies on sexuality, transatlanticism, ecocriticism, and race, as well as to conversations around settler colonialism, imperialism, and the excesses of capitalism—his story "Bartleby, the Scrivener," for example, was an inspirational text for the Occupy Wall Street movement. As American literary studies move away from a nationalist approach and towards a more hemispheric one, Melville has taken on a more global identity—one anticipated, in the 1950s, by the Trinidadian anticolonial activist C.L.R. James's enthusiastic admiration for him. Melville's "ruthless democracy," as he himself called it, made him a voice for the displaced and oppressed; his unwavering commitment to depict the "meanest mariners, and renegades, and castaways" and "weave around them tragic graces" continues to forge connections with new generations of readers, who come to his allusive, complex texts again and again for their sheer linguistic power, but also for their unique ability to bring the reader to the outer edges of perception, where change becomes possible.

NOTE ON THE TEXTS: The texts of Melville's works presented here are based on their earliest printings. The text of *Moby-Dick* has been prepared while consulting the first American edition of *Moby-Dick*, the first British edition (*The Whale*), and the authoritative Northwestern-Newberry edition (1998). This anthology's usual practices of modernization have not been followed in the case of *Moby-Dick*; spelling and punctuation from the original printings have been retained. The shorter stories "Bartleby, the Scrivener" and *Benito Cereno* are based on Brian Yothers's Broadview edition of *The Piazza Tales*, which is in turn based on the 1856 first edition of *The Piazza Tales* published by Dix & Edwards. Where the first edition and the initial magazine publication of the stories in *Putnam's Monthly* are in substantial conflict, Yothers followed the versions in *The Piazza Tales* (1856). The texts from *Battle-Pieces* are based on the first edition printed in New York by Harper & Brothers in 1866.

⌘⌘⌘

from *Moby-Dick, or The Whale*

CHAPTER 42. THE WHITENESS OF THE WHALE.

What the white whale was to Ahab,[1] has been hinted; what, at times, he was to me, as yet remains unsaid.

Aside from those more obvious considerations touching Moby Dick, which could not but occasionally awaken in any man's soul some alarm, there was another thought, or rather vague, nameless horror concerning him, which at times by its intensity completely overpowered all the rest; and yet so mystical and well nigh ineffable was it, that I almost despair of putting it in a comprehensible form. It was the whiteness of the whale that above all things appalled me. But how can I hope to explain myself here; and yet, in some dim, random way, explain myself I must, else all these chapters might be naught.

Though in many natural objects, whiteness refiningly enhances beauty, as if imparting some special virtue of its own, as in marbles, japonicas,[2] and pearls; and though various nations have in some way recognised a certain royal preeminence in this hue; even the barbaric, grand old kings of Pegu[3] placing the title "Lord of the White Elephants" above all their other magniloquent ascriptions of dominion; and the modern kings of Siam[4] unfurling the same snow-white quadruped in the royal standard; and the Hanoverian flag[5] bearing the one figure of a snow-white charger; and the great Austrian Empire, Cæsarian heir to overlording Rome,[6] having for the imperial colour the same impe-rial hue; and though this pre-eminence in it applies to the human race itself, giving the white man ideal mastership over every dusky tribe; and though, besides all this, whiteness has been even made significant of gladness, for among the Romans a white stone marked a joyful day; and though in other mortal sympathies and symbolizings, this same hue is made the emblem of many touching, noble things—the innocence of brides, the benignity of age; though among the Red Men of America the giving of the white belt of wampum[7] was the deepest pledge of honor; though in many climes, whiteness typifies the majesty of Justice in the ermine of the Judge, and contributes to the daily state of kings and queens drawn by milk-white steeds; though even in the higher mysteries of the most august religions it has been made the symbol of the divine spotlessness and power; by the Persian fire worshippers,[8] the white forked flame being held the holiest on the altar; and in the Greek mythologies, Great Jove himself being made incarnate in a snow-white bull; and though to the noble Iroquois, the midwinter sacrifice of the sacred White Dog was by far the holiest festival of their theology, that spotless, faithful creature being held the purest envoy they could send to the Great Spirit with the annual tidings of their own fidelity; and though directly from the Latin word for white, all Christian priests derive the name of one part of their sacred vesture, the alb or tunic, worn beneath the cassock; and though among the holy pomps of the Romish faith, white is specially employed in the celebration of the Passion of our Lord; though in the Vision of St. John, white robes are given to the redeemed, and the four-and-twenty elders stand clothed in white before the great white throne, and the Holy One that sitteth there white like wool;[9] yet for all these accumulated asso-

---

[1] *Ahab*   Captain of the *Pequod*, the whaling ship on which the speaker, Ishmael, is embarked as a member of the crew. A grim mystery surrounds Captain Ahab, who lost his leg to a legendary white sperm whale known as Moby Dick and is now obsessed with hunting down and killing the whale. Ahab is described in the Bible as a wicked king who did "evil in the sight of the Lord above all that were before him" (1 Kings 16.30).

[2] *japonicas*   Flowering camellia plants from Japan.

[3] *Pegu*   Region that is located in what is now south-central Myanmar.

[4] *Siam*   Thailand.

[5] *Hanoverian flag*   Flag of the Electorate (later Kingdom) of Hanover, a German state from 1692–1807 and again from 1814–37.

[6] *Austrian Empire … overlording Rome*   The Austrian Empire (1804–1918) evolved from the Holy Roman Empire, the emperor of which claimed his legitimacy from the ancient Roman emperors or "Caesars."

[7] *wampum*   Shell beads used by various Indigenous peoples for purposes including gifts, record-keeping, and trade.

[8] *Persian fire worshippers*   Zoroastrians. Members of this faith pray in the presence of fire due to its association with wisdom and spiritual insight. A "fire worshipper" named Fedallah plays a significant role in *Moby-Dick* as Ahab's sinister "shadow" and voice of the fate that supposedly awaits him.

[9] *Vision of St. John … wool*   See the Book of Revelation (traditionally believed to have been written by St. John), especially 7.9–14, 4.4, and 1.14.

ciations, with whatever is sweet, and honorable, and sublime, there yet lurks an elusive something in the innermost idea of this hue, which strikes more of panic to the soul than that redness which affrights in blood.

This elusive quality it is, which causes the thought of whiteness, when divorced from more kindly associations, and coupled with any object terrible in itself, to heighten that terror to the furthest bounds. Witness the white bear of the poles, and the white shark of the tropics; what but their smooth, flaky whiteness makes them the transcendent horrors they are? That ghastly whiteness it is which imparts such an abhorrent mildness, even more loathsome than terrific, to the dumb gloating of their aspect. So that not the fierce-fanged tiger in his heraldic coat can so stagger courage as the white-shrouded bear or shark.[1]

Bethink thee of the albatross, whence come those clouds of spiritual wonderment and pale dread, in which that white phantom sails in all imaginations? Not Coleridge first threw that spell;[2] but God's great, unflattering laureate, Nature.[3]

Most famous in our Western annals and Indian traditions is that of the White Steed of the Prairies; a magnificent milk-white charger, large-eyed, small-headed, bluff-chested, and with the dignity of a thousand monarchs in his lofty, overscorning carriage. He was the elected Xerxes[4] of vast herds of wild horses, whose pastures in those days were only fenced by the Rocky Mountains and the Alleghanies. At their flaming head he westward trooped it like that chosen star which every evening leads on the hosts of light. The flashing cascade of his mane, the curving comet of his tail, invested him with housings[5] more resplendent than gold and silver-beaters could have furnished him. A most imperial and archangelical apparition of that

embrace some holy ark. Wondrous flutterings and throbbings shook it. Though bodily unharmed, it uttered cries, as some king's ghost in supernatural distress. Through its inexpressible, strange eyes, methought I peeped to secrets which took hold of God. As Abraham before the angels, I bowed myself [see Genesis 18.2]; the white thing was so white, its wings so wide, and in those for ever exiled waters, I had lost the miserable warping memories of traditions and of towns. Long I gazed at that prodigy of plumage. I cannot tell, can only hint, the things that darted through me then. But at last I awoke; and turning, asked a sailor what bird was this. A goney, he replied. Goney! I never had heard that name before; is it conceivable that this glorious thing is utterly unknown to men ashore! never! But some time after, I learned that goney was some seaman's name for albatross. So that by no possibility could Coleridge's wild Rhyme have had aught to do with those mystical impressions which were mine, when I saw that bird upon our deck. For neither had I then read the Rhyme, nor knew the bird to be an albatross. Yet, in saying this, I do but indirectly burnish a little brighter the noble merit of the poem and the poet.

I assert, then, that in the wondrous bodily whiteness of the bird chiefly lurks the secret of the spell; a truth the more evinced in this, that by a solecism of terms there are birds called grey albatrosses; and these I have frequently seen, but never with such emotions as when I beheld the Antarctic fowl.

But how had the mystic thing been caught? Whisper it not, and I will tell; with a treacherous hook and line, as the fowl floated on the sea. At last the Captain made a postman of it; tying a lettered, leathern tally [stick with carved messages] round its neck, with the ship's time and place; and then letting it escape. But I doubt not, that leathern tally, meant for man, was taken off in Heaven, when the white fowl flew to join the wing-folding, the invoking, and adoring cherubim!

---

[1] [Melville's note] With reference to the Polar bear, it may possibly be urged by him who would fain go still deeper into this matter, that it is not the whiteness, separately regarded, which heightens the intolerable hideousness of that brute; for, analysed, that heightened hideousness, it might be said, only rises from the circumstance, that the irresponsible ferociousness of the creature stands invested in the fleece of celestial innocence and love; and hence, by bringing together two such opposite emotions in our minds, the Polar bear frightens us with so unnatural a contrast. But even assuming all this to be true; yet, were it not for the whiteness, you would not have that intensified terror.

As for the white shark, the white gliding ghostliness of repose in that creature, when beheld in his ordinary moods, strangely tallies with the same quality in the Polar quadruped. This peculiarity is most vividly hit by the French in the name they bestow upon that fish. The Romish mass for the dead begins with "Requiem eternam" (eternal rest), whence Requiem denominating the mass itself, and any other funeral music. Now, in allusion to the white, silent stillness of death in this shark, and the mild deadliness of his habits, the French call him *Requin*.

[2] *Coleridge ... spell* Melville is referring to Samuel Taylor Coleridge's famous poem featuring an albatross, *The Rime of the Ancient Mariner* (1798).

[3] [Melville's note] I remember the first albatross I ever saw. It was during a prolonged gale, in waters hard upon the Antarctic seas. From my forenoon watch below, I ascended to the overclouded deck; and there, dashed upon the main hatches, I saw a regal, feathery thing of unspotted whiteness, and with a hooked, Roman bill sublime. At intervals, it arched forth its vast archangel wings, as if to

[4] *Xerxes* King of Persia (c. 518–465 BCE) who gained inherited, not elected, power.

[5] *housings* Trappings or ornaments that extend from the horse's saddle over its back and sides.

unfallen, western world,[1] which to the eyes of the old trappers and hunters revived the glories of those primeval times when Adam walked majestic as a god, bluff-browed and fearless as this mighty steed. Whether marching amid his aides and marshals in the van[2] of countless cohorts that endlessly streamed it over the plains, like an Ohio; or whether with his circumambient subjects browsing all around at the horizon, the White Steed gallopingly reviewed them with warm nostrils reddening through his cool milkiness; in whatever aspect he presented himself, always to the bravest Indians he was the object of trembling reverence and awe. Nor can it be questioned from what stands on legendary record of this noble horse, that it was his spiritual whiteness chiefly, which so clothed him with divineness; and that this divineness had that in it which, though commanding worship, at the same time enforced a certain nameless terror.

But there are other instances where this whiteness loses all that accessory and strange glory which invests it in the White Steed and Albatross.

What is it that in the Albino man so peculiarly repels and often shocks the eye, as that sometimes he is loathed by his own kith[3] and kin! It is that whiteness which invests him, a thing expressed by the name he bears.[4] The Albino is as well made as other men—has no substantive deformity—and yet this mere aspect of all-pervading whiteness makes him more strangely hideous than the ugliest abortion.[5] Why should this be so?

Nor, in quite other aspects, does Nature in her least palpable but not the less malicious agencies, fail to enlist among her forces this crowning attribute of the terrible. From its snowy aspect, the gauntleted ghost of the Southern Seas has been denominated the White Squall. Nor, in some historic instances, has the art of human malice omitted so potent an auxiliary. How wildly it heightens the effect of that passage in Froissart, when, masked in the snowy symbol of their faction, the desperate White Hoods of Ghent murder their bailiff in the market-place![6]

Nor, in some things, does the common, hereditary experience of all mankind fail to bear witness to the supernaturalism of this hue. It cannot well be doubted, that the one visible quality in the aspect of the dead which most appals the gazer, is the marble pallor lingering there; as if indeed that pallor were as much like the badge of consternation in the other world, as of mortal trepidation here. And from that pallor of the dead, we borrow the expressive hue of the shroud in which we wrap them. Nor even in our superstitions do we fail to throw the same snowy mantle round our phantoms; all ghosts rising in a milk-white fog—Yea, while these terrors seize us, let us add, that even the king of terrors, when personified by the evangelist, rides on his pallid horse.[7]

Therefore, in his other moods, symbolize whatever grand or gracious thing he will by whiteness, no man can deny that in its profoundest idealized significance it calls up a peculiar apparition to the soul.

But though without dissent this point be fixed, how is mortal man to account for it? To analyse it, would seem impossible. Can we, then, by the citation of some of those instances wherein this thing of whiteness—though for the time either wholly or in great part stripped of all direct associations calculated to impart to it aught fearful, but nevertheless, is found to exert over us the same sorcery, however modified;—can we thus hope to light upon some chance clue to conduct us to the hidden cause we seek?

Let us try. But in a matter like this, subtlety appeals to subtlety, and without imagination no man can follow another into these halls. And though, doubtless, some at least of the imaginative impressions about to be presented may have been shared by most men,

---

1   *unfallen, western world*   North America before European colonial encroachment.

2   *van*   Forefront.

3   *kith*   Friends and acquaintances.

4   *Albino ... name he bears*   "Albino" is a borrowing from Portuguese, referring to a person lacking the pigment melanin; the term is based on the Latin "albus," meaning "white."

5   *abortion*   In this context, a person imperfectly made, a monstrosity.

6   *Froissart ... market-place*   This description is from the *Chronicles* (written c. 1379–c. 1405) of the medieval French historian Jean Froissart. The White Hoods were a militia in medieval Ghent and Bruges; in the incident referred to here, a city bailiff was sent to arrest the leaders of the White Hoods, but the White Hoods kill the bailiff before he can do so.

7   *king of terrors ... pallid horse*   See Revelation 6.8, attributed to St. John the Evangelist: "And I looked, and behold a pale horse: and his name that sat on him was Death, and Hell followed with him."

yet few perhaps were entirely conscious of them at the time, and therefore may not be able to recall them now.

Why to the man of untutored ideality,[1] who happens to be but loosely acquainted with the peculiar character of the day, does the bare mention of Whitsuntide[2] marshal in the fancy such long, dreary, speechless processions of slow-pacing pilgrims, down-cast and hooded with new-fallen snow? Or, to the unread, unsophisticated Protestant of the Middle American States, why does the passing mention of a White Friar or a White Nun,[3] evoke such an eyeless statue in the soul?

Or what is there apart from the traditions of dungeoned warriors and kings (which will not wholly account for it) that makes the White Tower of London tell so much more strongly on the imagination of an untravelled American, than those other storied structures, its neighbors—the Byward Tower, or even the Bloody?[4] And those sublimer towers, the White Mountains of New Hampshire, whence, in peculiar moods, comes that gigantic ghostliness over the soul at the bare mention of that name, while the thought of Virginia's Blue Ridge is full of a soft, dewy, distant dreaminess? Or why, irrespective of all latitudes and longitudes, does the name of the White Sea exert such a spectralness over the fancy, while that of the Yellow Sea[5] lulls us with mortal thoughts of long lacquered mild afternoons on the waves, followed by the gaudiest and yet sleepiest of sunsets? Or, to choose a wholly unsubstantial instance, purely addressed to the fancy, why, in reading the old fairy tales of Central Europe, does "the tall pale man" of the Hartz forests, whose changeless pallor unrustlingly glides through the green of the groves—why is this phantom more terrible than all the whooping imps of the Blocksburg?[6]

Nor is it, altogether, the remembrance of her cathedral-toppling earthquakes; nor the stampedoes of her frantic seas; nor the tearlessness of arid skies that never rain;[7] nor the sight of her wide field of leaning spires, wrenched cope-stones, and crosses all adroop (like canted yards[8] of anchored fleets); and her suburban avenues of house-walls lying over upon each other, as a tossed pack of cards;[9]—it is not these things alone which make tearless Lima, the strangest, saddest city thou can'st see. For Lima has taken the white veil;[10] and there is a higher horror in this whiteness of her woe. Old as Pizarro,[11] this whiteness keeps her ruins for ever new; admits not the cheerful greenness of complete decay; spreads over her broken ramparts the rigid pallor of an apoplexy[12] that fixes its own distortions.

I know that, to the common apprehension, this phenomenon of whiteness is not confessed to be the prime agent in exaggerating the terror of objects otherwise terrible; nor to the unimaginative mind is there aught of terror in those appearances whose awfulness to another mind almost solely consists in this one phenomenon, especially when exhibited under any form at all approaching to muteness or universality. What I

---

[1]   *ideality*   Imaginativeness.

[2]   *Whitsuntide*   Church season of Pentecost, beginning on Whitsunday (a contraction of "White Sunday"), that celebrated the descent of the Holy Spirit upon the Apostles. Confirmation and baptismal ceremonies are frequently held on Pentecost, for which white robes are traditionally worn.

[3]   *White Friar … White Nun*   Ghostly nuns and friars are common motifs in Gothic fiction.

[4]   *White Tower … Byward Tower … Bloody*   Individual towers in the fortress known as the Tower of London. The White Tower, built between 1078 and 1097, is the keep of the castle and housed soldiers and acted as a prison. It was whitewashed inside and out in 1240 on the orders of Henry III. The Bloody Tower was built between 1238 and 1272 and was thought to be the site of the murder of the two "Princes in the Tower"—Edward V and his brother the Duke of York—as well as the site of the death of Henry VI. Byward Tower, also built between 1238 and 1272, was the gatehouse to the Outer Ward of the fortress.

[5]   *White Sea*   Inlet of the Barents Sea off the northwest Russian coast; *Yellow Sea*   Inlet off the Pacific Ocean between China and the Korean peninsula.

[6]   *tall pale man … Hartz forests*   Der Grossman, or the "Tall Man" or "Slenderman" is a medieval folktale figure who lives in the Black Forest, luring children to the woods; *imps of the Blocksburg*   Blocksberg is the highest mountain in the Harz range in Germany; the mountain has long been thought to be peopled with devils and witches.

[7]   *never rain*   Lima, Peru, receives less than two inches of rain per year.

[8]   *canted yards*   Supports for the sails that are tilted while a vessel is at anchor.

[9]   *wrenched … cards*   An earthquake in 1746 caused extensive damage to Lima, which was still evident when Melville visited in 1844.

[10]   *Lima … white veil*   Some of the most prominent architecture in Lima at this time was made with white stone (the Presidential Palace, the Cathedral of Lima, the Archbishop's Palace, and Aliaga House, for example). When initiates become nuns, they "take the white veil" as a symbolic representation of their marriage with Christ.

[11]   *Pizarro*   Francisco Pizarro (c. 1470–1541) founded Lima in 1535.

[12]   *apoplexy*   Sudden loss of consciousness, a stroke.

mean by these two statements may perhaps be respectively elucidated by the following examples.

First: The mariner, when drawing nigh the coasts of foreign lands, if by night he hear the roar of breakers, starts to vigilance, and feels just enough of trepidation to sharpen all his faculties; but under precisely similar circumstances, let him be called from his hammock to view his ship sailing through a midnight sea of milky whiteness—as if from encircling headlands shoals of combed white bears were swimming round him, then he feels a silent, superstitious dread; the shrouded phantom of the whitened waters is horrible to him as a real ghost; in vain the lead assures him he is still off soundings;[1] heart and helm they both go down; he never rests till blue water is under him again. Yet where is the mariner who will tell thee, "Sir, it was not so much the fear of striking hidden rocks, as the fear of that hideous whiteness that so stirred me"?

Second: To the native Indian of Peru, the continual sight of the snow-howdahed[2] Andes conveys naught of dread, except, perhaps, in the mere fancying of the eternal frosted desolateness reigning at such vast altitudes, and the natural conceit of what a fearfulness it would be to lose oneself in such inhuman solitudes. Much the same is it with the backwoodsman of the West, who with comparative indifference views an unbounded prairie sheeted with driven snow, no shadow of tree or twig to break the fixed trance of whiteness. Not so the sailor, beholding the scenery of the Antarctic seas; where at times, by some infernal trick of legerdemain[3] in the powers of frost and air, he, shivering and half shipwrecked, instead of rainbows speaking hope and solace to his misery, views what seems a boundless church-yard grinning upon him with its lean ice monuments and splintered crosses.

But thou sayest, methinks that white-lead[4] chapter about whiteness is but a white flag hung out from a craven soul; thou surrenderest to a hypo,[5] Ishmael.

Tell me, why this strong young colt, foaled in some peaceful valley of Vermont, far removed from all beasts of prey—why is it that upon the sunniest day, if you but shake a fresh buffalo robe behind him, so that he cannot even see it, but only smells its wild animal muskiness—why will he start, snort, and with bursting eyes paw the ground in phrensies[6] of affright? There is no remembrance in him of any gorings of wild creatures in his green northern home, so that the strange muskiness he smells cannot recall to him anything associated with the experience of former perils; for what knows he, this New England colt, of the black bisons of distant Oregon?

No: but here thou beholdest even in a dumb brute, the instinct of the knowledge of the demonism in the world. Though thousands of miles from Oregon, still when he smells that savage musk, the rending, goring bison herds are as present as to the deserted wild foal of the prairies, which this instant they may be trampling into dust.

Thus, then, the muffled rollings of a milky sea; the bleak rustlings of the festooned frosts of mountains; the desolate shiftings of the windrowed[7] snows of prairies; all these, to Ishmael, are as the shaking of that buffalo robe to the frightened colt!

Though neither knows where lie the nameless things of which the mystic sign gives forth such hints; yet with me, as with the colt, somewhere those things must exist. Though in many of its aspects this visible world seems formed in love, the invisible spheres were formed in fright.

But not yet have we solved the incantation of this whiteness, and learned why it appeals with such power to the soul; and more strange and far more portentous—why, as we have seen, it is at once the most meaning symbol of spiritual things, nay, the very veil of the Christian's Deity; and yet should be as it is, the intensifying agent in things the most appalling to mankind.

Is it that by its indefiniteness it shadows forth the heartless voids and immensities of the universe, and thus stabs us from behind with the thought of annihilation, when beholding the white depths of the milky way? Or is it, that as in essence whiteness is not so much

---

[1]   *off soundings*   In water deep enough that the soundings—the lines and weights used to test the depth of surrounding water—do not hit bottom.

[2]   *snow-howdahed*   Snow-topped (a howdah is the structure placed on top of an elephant's back to seat riders).

[3]   *legerdemain*   Sleight of hand.

[4]   *white-lead*   Carbonate of lead used to make white pigments.

[5]   *hypo*   Episode of anxiety or hypochondria.

[6]   *phrensies*   I.e., frenzies.

[7]   *windrowed*   Blown into rows by the wind.

a color as the visible absence of color; and at the same time the concrete of all colors; is it for these reasons that there is such a dumb blankness, full of meaning, in a wide landscape of snows—a colorless, all-color of atheism from which we shrink? And when we consider that other theory of the natural philosophers,[1] that all other earthly hues—every stately or lovely emblazoning—the sweet tinges of sunset skies and woods; yea, and the gilded velvets of butterflies, and the butterfly cheeks of young girls; all these are but subtile deceits, not actually inherent in substances, but only laid on from without; so that all deified Nature absolutely paints like the harlot, whose allurements cover nothing but the charnel-house within;[2] and when we proceed further, and consider that the mystical cosmetic which produces every one of her hues, the great principle of light, for ever remains white or colorless in itself, and if operating without medium upon matter, would touch all objects, even tulips and roses, with its own blank tinge—pondering all this, the palsied universe lies before us a leper; and like wilful travellers in Lapland, who refuse to wear colored and coloring glasses[3] upon their eyes, so the wretched infidel gazes himself blind at the monumental white shroud that wraps all the prospect around him. And of all these things the Albino whale was the symbol. Wonder ye then at the fiery hunt?

—1851

---

[1] *natural philosophers* Those studying the physical and natural world, precursors to today's scientists. Some, such as John Locke (1628–1704), believed that "secondary" qualities in physical objects (like color) are painted on by the mind and are not inherent in the object itself.

[2] *allurements ... within* See Matthew 23.27: "Woe unto you, scribes and Pharisees, hypocrites! for ye are like unto whited sepulchres, which indeed appear beautiful outward, but are within full of dead men's bones, and of all uncleanness."

[3] *colored and coloring glasses* I.e., sunglasses.

IN CONTEXT

Nineteenth-Century Images of Whales and Whaling

The Essex Struck by a Whale, from *The Mariner's Chronicle*, 1834. New Bedford Whaling Museum. This is one of the earliest images depicting the *Essex* disaster to be printed in the United States.

William James Linton, *Boats Attacking Whales*, 1830–39. Alexander Turnbull Library, Wellington, New Zealand.

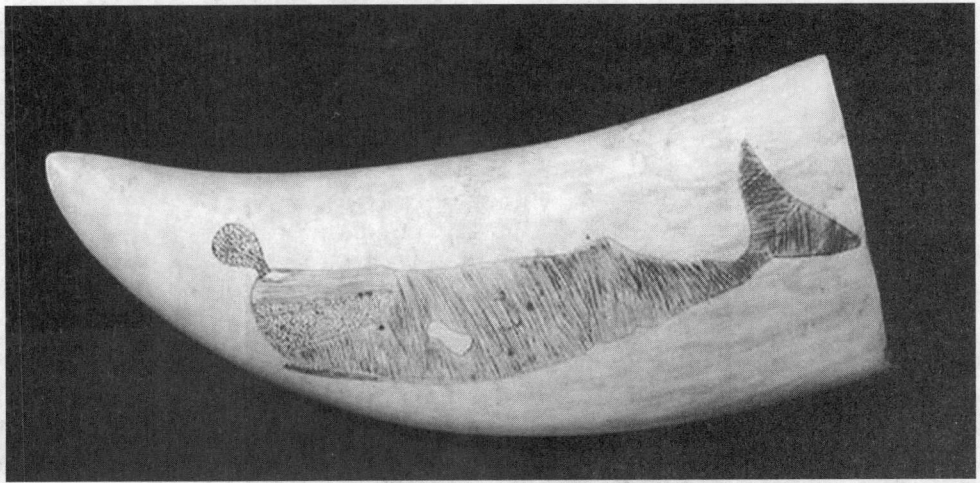

Unknown artist, engraved sperm whale tooth (skrimshander), depicting large sperm whale spouting blood, c. mid-nineteenth century. Nantucket Historical Association.

In the Whale's Jaw, frontispiece from William S. Davis, *Nimrod of the Sea: or, The American Whaleman*, 1874.

There She Blows, illustration from William S. Davis, *Nimrod of the Sea: or, The American Whaleman*, 1874.

Cutting In, illustration from William S. Davis, *Nimrod of the Sea: or, The American Whaleman*, 1874.

Bartleby, the Scrivener

I am a rather elderly man. The nature of my avocations, for the last thirty years, has brought me into more than ordinary contact with what would seem an interesting and somewhat singular set of men, of whom, as yet, nothing, that I know of, has ever been written—I mean, the law-copyists, or scriveners.[1] I have known very many of them, professionally and privately, and, if I pleased, could relate diverse histories, at which good-natured gentlemen might smile, and sentimental souls might weep. But I waive the biographies of all other scriveners, for a few passages in the life of Bartleby, who was a scrivener, the strangest I ever saw, or heard of. While, of other law-copyists, I might write the complete life, of Bartleby nothing of that sort can be done. I believe that no materials exist, for a full and satisfactory biography of this man. It is an irreparable loss to literature. Bartleby was one of those beings of whom nothing is ascertainable, except from the original sources, and, in his case, those are very small. What my own astonished eyes saw of Bartleby, *that* is all I know of him, except, indeed, one vague report, which will appear in the sequel.[2]

Ere introducing the scrivener, as he first appeared to me, it is fit I make some mention of myself, my *employés*,[3] my business, my chambers, and general surroundings; because some such description is indispensable to an adequate understanding of the chief character about to be presented. Imprimis:[4] I am a man who, from his youth upwards, has been filled with a profound conviction that the easiest way of life is the best. Hence, though I belong to a profession proverbially energetic and nervous, even to turbulence, at times, yet nothing of that sort have I ever suffered to invade my peace. I am one of those unambitious lawyers who never addresses a jury, or in any way draws down public applause; but, in the cool tranquility of a snug retreat, do a snug business among rich men's bonds, and mortgages, and title-deeds. All who know me, consider me an eminently *safe* man. The late John Jacob Astor,[5] a personage little given to poetic enthusiasm, had no hesitation in pronouncing my first grand point to be prudence; my next, method. I do not speak it in vanity, but simply record the fact, that I was not unemployed in my profession by the late John Jacob Astor; a name which, I admit, I love to repeat; for it hath a rounded and orbicular sound to it, and rings like unto bullion.[6] I will freely add, that I was not insensible to the late John Jacob Astor's good opinion.

Some time prior to the period at which this little history begins, my avocations had been largely increased. The good old office, now extinct in the State of New York, of a Master in Chancery,[7] had been conferred upon me. It was not a very arduous office, but very pleasantly remunerative. I seldom lose my temper; much more seldom indulge in dangerous indignation at wrongs and outrages; but, I must be permitted to be rash here, and declare, that I consider the sudden and violent abrogation of the office of Master in Chancery, by the new Constitution, as a ——[8] premature act; inasmuch as I had counted upon a life-lease of the profits, whereas I only received those of a few short years. But this is by the way.

My chambers were up stairs, at No. —— Wall street. At one end, they looked upon the white wall of the interior of a spacious skylight shaft, penetrating the building from top to bottom.

This view might have been considered rather tame than otherwise, deficient in what landscape painters call "life." But, if so, the view from the other end of my chambers offered, at least, a contrast, if nothing more. In that direction, my windows commanded an

---

[1] *avocations* Employments, vocations; *scriveners* People employed to copy or write documents.

[2] *sequel* Refers not to a follow-up story, but to the "vague report" that is relayed to the reader at the end of this story.

[3] *employés* French: employees.

[4] *Imprimis* Latin: In the first place; often used by lawyers to introduce the first in a list of items (in a will, for instance).

[5] *John Jacob Astor* Wealthy American businessperson (1763–1848) who made his fortune in the fur trade.

[6] *orbicular* Spherical; *bullion* Raw gold or silver.

[7] *Master in Chancery* Senior supervisory role at the Court of Chancery. The New York Chancery Court, which existed from 1701 to 1847, dealt with equity matters and functioned as a court of appeals for the state Supreme Court.

[8] *abrogation ... new Constitution* The Court of Chancery was abolished in 1847 when the New York state judicial system was overhauled in accordance with the State Constitutional Convention of 1846; —— The dashes are marking an expletive.

unobstructed view of a lofty brick wall, black by age and everlasting shade; which wall required no spy-glass[1] to bring out its lurking beauties, but, for the benefit of all near-sighted spectators, was pushed up to within ten feet of my window panes. Owing to the great height of the surrounding buildings, and my chambers being on the second floor, the interval between this wall and mine not a little resembled a huge square cistern.[2]

At the period just preceding the advent of Bartleby, I had two persons as copyists in my employment, and a promising lad as an office-boy. First, Turkey; second, Nippers; third, Ginger Nut. These may seem names, the like of which are not usually found in the Directory. In truth, they were nicknames, mutually conferred upon each other by my three clerks, and were deemed expressive of their respective persons or characters. Turkey was a short, pursy[3] Englishman, of about my own age—that is, somewhere not far from sixty. In the morning, one might say, his face was of a fine florid hue, but after twelve o'clock, meridian[4]—his dinner hour—it blazed like a grate full of Christmas coals; and continued blazing—but, as it were, with a gradual wane—till six o'clock, P.M., or thereabouts; after which, I saw no more of the proprietor of the face, which, gaining its meridian with the sun, seemed to set with it, to rise, culminate, and decline the following day, with the like regularity and undiminished glory. There are many singular coincidences I have known in the course of my life, not the least among which was the fact, that, exactly when Turkey displayed his fullest beams from his red and radiant countenance, just then, too, at that critical moment, began the daily period when I considered his business capacities as seriously disturbed for the remainder of the twenty-four hours. Not that he was absolutely idle, or averse to business, then; far from it. The difficulty was, he was apt to be altogether too energetic. There was a strange, inflamed, flurried, flighty recklessness of activity about him. He would be incautious in dipping his pen into his ink-stand. All his blots upon my documents were dropped there after twelve o'clock, meridian. Indeed, not only

would he be reckless, and sadly given to making blots in the afternoon, but, some days, he went further, and was rather noisy. At such times, too, his face flamed with augmented blazonry, as if cannel coal had been heaped on anthracite.[5] He made an unpleasant racket with his chair; spilled his sand-box;[6] in mending his pens, impatiently split them all to pieces, and threw them on the floor in a sudden passion; stood up, and leaned over his table, boxing his papers about in a most indecorous manner, very sad to behold in an elderly man like him. Nevertheless, as he was in many ways a most valuable person to me, and all the time before twelve o'clock, meridian, was the quickest, steadiest creature, too, accomplishing a great deal of work in a style not easily to be matched—for these reasons, I was willing to overlook his eccentricities, though, indeed, occasionally, I remonstrated with him. I did this very gently, however, because, though the civilest, nay, the blandest and most reverential of men in the morning, yet, in the afternoon, he was disposed, upon provocation, to be slightly rash with his tongue—in fact, insolent. Now, valuing his morning services as I did, and resolved not to lose them—yet, at the same time, made uncomfortable by his inflamed ways after twelve o'clock—and being a man of peace, unwilling by my admonitions to call forth unseemly retorts from him, I took upon me, one Saturday noon (he was always worse on Saturdays)[7] to hint to him, very kindly, that, perhaps, now that he was growing old, it might be well to abridge his labors; in short, he need not come to my chambers after twelve o'clock, but, dinner over, had best go home to his lodgings, and rest himself till tea-time.[8] But no; he insisted upon his afternoon devotions. His countenance became intolerably fervid, as he oratorically assured me—gesticulating with a long ruler at the other end of the room—that if his services

---

[1]   *spy-glass*   Telescope.

[2]   *cistern*   Water tank (often these were set high up on a building to supply it with water).

[3]   *pursy*   Fat.

[4]   *meridian*   Noon.

[5]   *blazonry*   The art of depicting armorial symbols, but in this case used figuratively to mean "coloring";   *cannel coal*   Hard coal with a bright flame;   *anthracite*   Hard, high-quality coal that burns with little flame or smoke.

[6]   *sand-box*   Box filled with sand used to blot ink.

[7]   *on Saturdays*   It was customary to work a six-day work week in the nineteenth century (the five-day work week was only instituted in the U.S. in the mid-twentieth century).

[8]   *tea-time*   Four or five o'clock in the afternoon.

in the morning were useful, how indispensable, then, in the afternoon?

"With submission, sir," said Turkey, on this occasion, "I consider myself your right-hand man. In the morning I but marshal and deploy my columns; but in the afternoon I put myself at their head, and gallantly charge the foe, thus"—and he made a violent thrust with the ruler.

"But the blots, Turkey," intimated I.

"True; but, with submission, sir, behold these hairs! I am getting old. Surely, sir, a blot or two of a warm afternoon is not to be severely urged against gray hairs. Old age—even if it blot the page—is honorable. With submission, sir, we *both* are getting old."

This appeal to my fellow-feeling was hardly to be resisted. At all events, I saw that go he would not. So, I made up my mind to let him stay, resolving, nevertheless, to see to it that, during the afternoon, he had to do with my less important papers.

Nippers, the second on my list, was a whiskered, sallow, and, upon the whole, rather piratical-looking young man, of about five and twenty. I always deemed him the victim of two evil powers—ambition and indigestion. The ambition was evinced by a certain impatience of the duties of a mere copyist, an unwarrantable usurpation of strictly professional affairs, such as the original drawing up of legal documents. The indigestion seemed betokened in an occasional nervous testiness and grinning irritability, causing the teeth to audibly grind together over mistakes committed in copying; unnecessary maledictions, hissed, rather than spoken, in the heat of business; and especially by a continual discontent with the height of the table where he worked. Though of a very ingenious mechanical turn, Nippers could never get this table to suit him. He put chips under it, blocks of various sorts, bits of pasteboard, and at last went so far as to attempt an exquisite adjustment, by final pieces of folded blotting-paper. But no invention would answer.[1] If, for the sake of easing his back, he brought the table lid at a sharp angle well up towards his chin, and wrote there like a man using the steep roof of a Dutch house for his desk, then he declared that it stopped the circulation in his arms. If now he lowered the table to his waistbands, and stooped over it in writing, then there was

a sore aching in his back. In short, the truth of the matter was, Nippers knew not what he wanted. Or, if he wanted anything, it was to be rid of a scrivener's table altogether. Among the manifestations of his diseased ambition was a fondness he had for receiving visits from certain ambiguous-looking fellows in seedy coats, whom he called his clients. Indeed, I was aware that not only was he, at times, considerable of a ward-politician, but he occasionally did a little business at the Justices' courts, and was not unknown on the steps of the Tombs.[2] I have good reason to believe, however, that one individual who called upon him at my chambers, and who, with a grand air, he insisted was his client, was no other than a dun,[3] and the alleged title-deed, a bill. But, with all his failings, and the annoyances he caused me, Nippers, like his compatriot Turkey, was a very useful man to me; wrote a neat, swift hand; and, when he chose, was not deficient in a gentlemanly sort of deportment. Added to this, he always dressed in a gentlemanly sort of way; and so, incidentally, reflected credit upon my chambers. Whereas, with respect to Turkey, I had much ado to keep him from being a reproach to me. His clothes were apt to look oily, and smell of eating-houses. He wore his pantaloons very loose and baggy in summer. His coats were execrable; his hat not to be handled. But while the hat was a thing of indifference to me, inasmuch as his natural civility and deference, as a dependent[4] Englishman, always led him to doff it the moment he entered the room, yet his coat was another matter. Concerning his coats, I reasoned with him; but with no effect. The truth was, I suppose, that a man with so small an income could not afford to sport such

---

[1]   *answer* Suffice.

[2]   *considerable of a ward-politician* Of importance to a local politician; this phrase can also be interpreted to mean that Nippers has ambitions of becoming a local politician; *Justices' courts* I.e., the courts of the State judges;   *the Tombs* Informal name for the city prison, known formally as the New York City Halls of Justice and House of Detention. Built in the Egyptian Revival style, the prison was situated on what had been the Collect Pond. The area had been drained and filled in, but not very successfully, and soon after the Tombs was built it began to sink into the ground, creating damp and unhealthy conditions for the inmates. After visiting the prison in 1842, Charles Dickens wrote that "such indecent and disgusting dungeons as these cells, would bring disgrace upon the most despotic empire in the world."

[3]   *dun* Debt collector.

[4]   *dependent* Subordinate.

a lustrous face and a lustrous coat at one and the same time. As Nippers once observed, Turkey's money went chiefly for red ink.[1] One winter day, I presented Turkey with a highly respectable-looking coat of my own—a padded gray coat, of a most comfortable warmth, and which buttoned straight up from the knee to the neck. I thought Turkey would appreciate the favor, and abate his rashness and obstreperousness of afternoons. But no; I verily believe that buttoning himself up in so downy and blanket-like a coat had a pernicious effect upon him—upon the same principle that too much oats are bad for horses. In fact, precisely as a rash, restive horse is said to feel his oats, so Turkey felt his coat. It made him insolent. He was a man whom prosperity harmed.

Though, concerning the self-indulgent habits of Turkey, I had my own private surmises, yet, touching Nippers, I was well persuaded that, whatever might be his faults in other respects, he was, at least, a temperate[2] young man. But, indeed, nature herself seemed to have been his vintner, and, at his birth, charged him so thoroughly with an irritable, brandy-like disposition, that all subsequent potations[3] were needless. When I consider how, amid the stillness of my chambers, Nippers would sometimes impatiently rise from his seat, and stooping over his table, spread his arms wide apart, seize the whole desk, and move it, and jerk it, with a grim, grinding motion on the floor, as if the table were a perverse voluntary agent, intent on thwarting and vexing him, I plainly perceive that, for Nippers, brandy-and-water were altogether superfluous.

It was fortunate for me that, owing to its peculiar cause—indigestion—the irritability and consequent nervousness of Nippers were mainly observable in the morning, while in the afternoon he was comparatively mild. So that, Turkey's paroxysms only coming on about twelve o'clock, I never had to do with their eccentricities at one time. Their fits relieved each other, like guards. When Nippers's was on, Turkey's was off; and *vice versa*. This was a good natural arrangement, under the circumstances.

Ginger Nut, the third on my list, was a lad, some twelve years old. His father was a car-man,[4] ambitious of seeing his son on the bench instead of a cart, before he died. So he sent him to my office, as student at law, errand-boy, cleaner and sweeper, at the rate of one dollar a week. He had a little desk to himself, but he did not use it much. Upon inspection, the drawer exhibited a great array of the shells of various sorts of nuts. Indeed, to this quick-witted youth, the whole noble science of the law was contained in a nut-shell. Not the least among the employments of Ginger Nut, as well as one which he discharged with the most alacrity, was his duty as cake and apple purveyor for Turkey and Nippers. Copying law-papers being proverbially a dry, husky[5] sort of business, my two scriveners were fain to moisten their mouths very often with Spitzenbergs,[6] to be had at the numerous stalls nigh the Custom House and Post Office. Also, they sent Ginger Nut very frequently for that peculiar cake—small, flat, round, and very spicy—after which he had been named by them. Of a cold morning, when business was but dull, Turkey would gobble up scores of these cakes, as if they were mere wafers—indeed, they sell them at the rate of six or eight for a penny—the scrape of his pen blending with the crunching of the crisp particles in his mouth. Of all the fiery afternoon blunders and flurried rashnesses of Turkey, was his once moistening a ginger-cake between his lips, and clapping it on to a mortgage, for a seal. I came within an ace[7] of dismissing him then. But he mollified me by making an oriental bow, and saying—

"With submission, sir, it was generous of me to find you in stationery on my own account."

Now my original business—that of a conveyancer and title hunter,[8] and drawer-up of recondite documents of all sorts—was considerably increased by receiving the master's office. There was now great work for scriveners. Not only must I push the clerks already with me, but I must have additional help.

---

[1]   *red ink*   Wine.

[2]   *temperate*   Moderate, avoiding alcohol.

[3]   *vintner*   Seller of wine;   *potations*   Alcoholic drinks.

[4]   *car-man*   A person who drives a cart.

[5]   *husky*   Tough and dry like husks.

[6]   *Spitzenbergs*   Variety of apple.

[7]   *came within an ace*   Was on the point of.

[8]   *conveyancer*   Lawyer who prepares documents for the exchange of property;   *title hunter*   Lawyer who investigates the legal ownership of land and property.

In answer to my advertisement, a motionless young man one morning stood upon my office threshold, the door being open, for it was summer. I can see that figure now—pallidly neat, pitiably respectable, incurably forlorn! It was Bartleby.

After a few words touching his qualifications, I engaged him, glad to have among my corps of copyists a man of so singularly sedate an aspect, which I thought might operate beneficially upon the flighty temper of Turkey, and the fiery one of Nippers.

I should have stated before that ground glass folding-doors divided my premises into two parts, one of which was occupied by my scriveners, the other by myself. According to my humor, I threw open these doors, or closed them. I resolved to assign Bartleby a corner by the folding-doors, but on my side of them, so as to have this quiet man within easy call, in case any trifling thing was to be done. I placed his desk close up to a small side-window in that part of the room, a window which originally had afforded a lateral view of certain grimy backyards and bricks, but which, owing to subsequent erections, commanded at present no view at all, though it gave some light. Within three feet of the panes was a wall, and the light came down from far above, between two lofty buildings, as from a very small opening in a dome. Still further to a satisfactory arrangement, I procured a high green folding screen, which might entirely isolate Bartleby from my sight, though not remove him from my voice. And thus, in a manner, privacy and society were conjoined.

At first, Bartleby did an extraordinary quantity of writing. As if long famishing for something to copy, he seemed to gorge himself on my documents. There was no pause for digestion. He ran a day and night line,[1] copying by sun-light and by candle-light. I should have been quite delighted with his application, had he been cheerfully industrious. But he wrote on silently, palely, mechanically.

It is, of course, an indispensable part of a scrivener's business to verify the accuracy of his copy, word by word. Where there are two or more scriveners in an office, they assist each other in this examination, one reading from the copy, the other holding the original. It is a very dull, wearisome, and lethargic affair. I can readily imagine that, to some sanguine[2] temperaments, it would be altogether intolerable. For example, I cannot credit that the mettlesome poet, Byron,[3] would have contentedly sat down with Bartleby to examine a law document of, say five hundred pages, closely written in a crimpy[4] hand.

Now and then, in the haste of business, it had been my habit to assist in comparing some brief document myself, calling Turkey or Nippers for this purpose. One object I had, in placing Bartleby so handy to me behind the screen, was, to avail myself of his services on such trivial occasions. It was on the third day, I think, of his being with me, and before any necessity had arisen for having his own writing examined, that, being much hurried to complete a small affair I had in hand, I abruptly called to Bartleby. In my haste and natural expectancy of instant compliance, I sat with my head bent over the original on my desk, and my right hand sideways, and somewhat nervously extended with the copy, so that, immediately upon emerging from his retreat, Bartleby might snatch it and proceed to business without the least delay.

In this very attitude did I sit when I called to him, rapidly stating what it was I wanted him to do—namely, to examine a small paper with me. Imagine my surprise, nay, my consternation, when, without moving from his privacy, Bartleby, in a singularly mild, firm voice, replied, "I would prefer not to."

I sat awhile in perfect silence, rallying my stunned faculties. Immediately it occurred to me that my ears had deceived me, or Bartleby had entirely misunderstood my meaning. I repeated my request in the clearest tone I could assume; but in quite as clear a one came the previous reply, "I would prefer not to."

"Prefer not to," echoed I, rising in high excitement, and crossing the room with a stride. "What do you mean? Are you moon-struck?[5] I want you to help me compare this sheet here—take it," and I thrust it towards him.

---

1 *ran ... line* I.e., he copied both day and night.

2 *sanguine* Brave and amorous.

3 *Byron* George Gordon, Lord Byron (1788–1824), a Romantic poet famous for his passionate and energetic personality as well as for his verse.

4 *crimpy* Wobbly.

5 *moon-struck* Insane (the moon was long thought to unsettle the mental faculties).

"I would prefer not to," said he.

I looked at him steadfastly. His face was leanly composed; his gray eye dimly calm. Not a wrinkle of agitation rippled him. Had there been the least uneasiness, anger, impatience or impertinence in his manner; in other words, had there been anything ordinarily human about him, doubtless I should have violently dismissed him from the premises. But as it was, I should have as soon thought of turning my pale plaster-of-paris bust of Cicero[1] out of doors. I stood gazing at him awhile, as he went on with his own writing, and then reseated myself at my desk. This is very strange, thought I. What had one best do? But my business hurried me. I concluded to forget the matter for the present, reserving it for my future leisure. So calling Nippers from the other room, the paper was speedily examined.

A few days after this, Bartleby concluded four lengthy documents, being quadruplicates of a week's testimony taken before me in my High Court of Chancery. It became necessary to examine them. It was an important suit, and great accuracy was imperative. Having all things arranged, I called Turkey, Nippers and Ginger Nut, from the next room, meaning to place the four copies in the hands of my four clerks, while I should read from the original. Accordingly, Turkey, Nippers, and Ginger Nut had taken their seats in a row, each with his document in his hand, when I called to Bartleby to join this interesting group.

"Bartleby! quick, I am waiting."

I heard a slow scrape of his chair legs on the uncarpeted floor, and soon he appeared standing at the entrance of his hermitage.

"What is wanted?" said he, mildly.

"The copies, the copies," said I, hurriedly. "We are going to examine them. There"—and I held towards him the fourth quadruplicate.

"I would prefer not to," he said, and gently disappeared behind the screen.

For a few moments I was turned into a pillar of salt,[2] standing at the head of my seated column of clerks.

Recovering myself, I advanced towards the screen, and demanded the reason for such extraordinary conduct.

"*Why* do you refuse?"

"I would prefer not to."

With any other man I should have flown outright into a dreadful passion, scorned all further words, and thrust him ignominiously from my presence. But there was something about Bartleby that not only strangely disarmed me, but, in a wonderful[3] manner, touched and disconcerted me. I began to reason with him.

"These are your own copies we are about to examine. It is labor saving to you, because one examination will answer for your four papers. It is common usage. Every copyist is bound to help examine his copy. Is it not so? Will you not speak? Answer!"

"I prefer not to," he replied in a flutelike tone. It seemed to me that, while I had been addressing him, he carefully revolved every statement that I made; fully comprehended the meaning; could not gainsay the irresistible conclusion; but, at the same time, some paramount consideration prevailed with him to reply as he did.

"You are decided, then, not to comply with my request—a request made according to common usage and common sense?"

He briefly gave me to understand, that on that point my judgment was sound. Yes: his decision was irreversible.

It is not seldom the case that, when a man is browbeaten in some unprecedented and violently unreasonable way, he begins to stagger in his own plainest faith. He begins, as it were, vaguely to surmise that, wonderful as it may be, all the justice and all the reason is on the other side. Accordingly, if any disinterested persons are present, he turns to them for some reinforcement for his own faltering mind.

"Turkey," said I, "what do you think of this? Am I not right?"

"With submission, sir," said Turkey, in his blandest tone, "I think that you are."

"Nippers," said I, "what do *you* think of it?"

"I think I should kick him out of the office."

---

1   *Cicero* Marcus Tullius Cicero (106–43 BCE) was a Roman lawyer and consul admired for his intellect, oratorical skills, and integrity.

2   *pillar of salt* In chapter 15 of the book of Genesis, God rains fire and brimstone on Sodom and Gomorrah, but angels warn Lot and

his wife and daughters to flee to the mountains without looking back before the destruction comes. Lot's wife does look back and is turned into a pillar of salt.

3   *wonderful* Astonishing, unusual.

(The reader, of nice[1] perceptions, will here perceive that, it being morning, Turkey's answer is couched in polite and tranquil terms, but Nippers replies in ill-tempered ones. Or, to repeat a previous sentence, Nippers's ugly mood was on duty, and Turkey's off.)

"Ginger Nut," said I, willing to enlist the smallest suffrage in my behalf, "what do *you* think of it?"

"I think, sir, he's a little *luny*,"[2] replied Ginger Nut, with a grin.

"You hear what they say," said I, turning towards the screen, "come forth and do your duty."

But he vouchsafed no reply. I pondered a moment in sore perplexity. But once more business hurried me. I determined again to postpone the consideration of this dilemma to my future leisure. With a little trouble we made out to examine the papers without Bartleby, though at every page or two Turkey deferentially dropped his opinion, that this proceeding was quite out of the common; while Nippers, twitching in his chair with a dyspeptic[3] nervousness, ground out, between his set teeth, occasional hissing maledictions against the stubborn oaf behind the screen. And for his (Nippers's) part, this was the first and the last time he would do another man's business without pay.

Meanwhile Bartleby sat in his hermitage, oblivious to everything but his own peculiar business there.

Some days passed, the scrivener being employed upon another lengthy work. His late remarkable conduct led me to regard his ways narrowly. I observed that he never went to dinner; indeed, that he never went anywhere. As yet I had never, of my personal knowledge, known him to be outside of my office. He was a perpetual sentry in the corner. At about eleven o'clock though, in the morning, I noticed that Ginger Nut would advance toward the opening in Bartleby's screen, as if silently beckoned thither by a gesture invisible to me where I sat. The boy would then leave the office, jingling a few pence, and reappear with a handful of ginger-nuts, which he delivered in the hermitage, receiving two of the cakes for his trouble.

He lives, then, on ginger-nuts, thought I; never eats a dinner, properly speaking; he must be a vegetarian, then; but no; he never eats even vegetables, he eats nothing but ginger-nuts. My mind then ran on in reveries concerning the probable effects upon the human constitution of living entirely on ginger-nuts. Ginger-nuts are so called, because they contain ginger as one of their peculiar constituents, and the final flavoring one. Now, what was ginger? A hot, spicy thing. Was Bartleby hot and spicy? Not at all. Ginger, then, had no effect upon Bartleby. Probably, he preferred it should have none.

Nothing so aggravates an earnest person as a passive resistance. If the individual so resisted be of a not inhumane temper, and the resisting one perfectly harmless in his passivity, then, in the better moods of the former, he will endeavor charitably to construe to his imagination what proves impossible to be solved by his judgment. Even so, for the most part, I regarded Bartleby and his ways. Poor fellow! thought I, he means no mischief; it is plain he intends no insolence; his aspect sufficiently evinces that his eccentricities are involuntary. He is useful to me. I can get along with him. If I turn him away, the chances are he will fall in with some less-indulgent employer, and then he will be rudely treated, and perhaps driven forth miserably to starve. Yes. Here I can cheaply purchase a delicious self-approval. To befriend Bartleby; to humor him in his strange willfulness, will cost me little or nothing, while I lay up in my soul what will eventually prove a sweet morsel for my conscience. But this mood was not invariable, with me. The passiveness of Bartleby sometimes irritated me. I felt strangely goaded on to encounter him in new opposition—to elicit some angry spark from him answerable to my own. But, indeed, I might as well have essayed to strike fire with my knuckles against a bit of Windsor soap.[4] But one afternoon the evil impulse in me mastered me, and the following little scene ensued:

"Bartleby," said I, "when those papers are all copied, I will compare them with you."

"I would prefer not to."

"How? Surely you do not mean to persist in that mulish vagary?"

No answer.

I threw open the folding-doors near by, and, turning upon Turkey and Nippers, exclaimed:

---

[1]   *nice* Accurate, discerning, discriminating.

[2]   *luny* I.e., loony, the shortened form of lunatic, which is another way of saying "moon-struck" ("luna" means "moon" in Latin).

[3]   *dyspeptic* Uneasy, uncomfortable (resulting from indigestion).

[4]   *Windsor soap* Brown, scented soap.

"Bartleby a second time says, he won't examine his papers. What do you think of it, Turkey?"

It was afternoon, be it remembered. Turkey sat glowing like a brass boiler; his bald head steaming; his hands reeling among his blotted papers.

"Think of it?" roared Turkey; "I think I'll just step behind his screen, and black his eyes for him!"

So saying, Turkey rose to his feet and threw his arms into a pugilistic[1] position. He was hurrying away to make good his promise, when I detained him, alarmed at the effect of incautiously rousing Turkey's combativeness after dinner.

"Sit down, Turkey," said I, "and hear what Nippers has to say. What do you think of it, Nippers? Would I not be justified in immediately dismissing Bartleby?"

"Excuse me, that is for you to decide, sir. I think his conduct quite unusual, and, indeed, unjust, as regards Turkey and myself. But it may only be a passing whim."

"Ah," exclaimed I, "you have strangely changed your mind, then—you speak very gently of him now."

"All beer," cried Turkey; "gentleness is effects of beer—Nippers and I dined together to-day. You see how gentle *I* am, sir. Shall I go and black his eyes?"

"You refer to Bartleby, I suppose. No, not to-day, Turkey," I replied; "pray, put up[2] your fists."

I closed the doors, and again advanced towards Bartleby. I felt additional incentives tempting me to my fate. I burned to be rebelled against again. I remembered that Bartleby never left the office.

"Bartleby," said I, "Ginger Nut is away; just step around to the Post Office, won't you? (it was but a three minutes' walk), and see if there is anything for me."

"I would prefer not to."

"You *will* not?"

"I *prefer* not."

I staggered to my desk, and sat there in a deep study. My blind inveteracy[3] returned. Was there any other thing in which I could procure myself to be ignominiously repulsed by this lean, penniless wight?[4]—my hired clerk? What added thing is there, perfectly reasonable, that he will be sure to refuse to do?

"Bartleby!"

No answer.

"Bartleby," in a louder tone.

No answer.

"Bartleby," I roared.

Like a very ghost, agreeably to the laws of magical invocation, at the third summons, he appeared at the entrance of his hermitage.

"Go to the next room, and tell Nippers to come to me."

"I prefer not to," he respectfully and slowly said, and mildly disappeared.

"Very good, Bartleby," said I, in a quiet sort of serenely-severe self-possessed tone, intimating the unalterable purpose of some terrible retribution very close at hand. At the moment I half intended something of the kind. But upon the whole, as it was drawing towards my dinner-hour, I thought it best to put on my hat and walk home for the day, suffering much from perplexity and distress of mind.

Shall I acknowledge it? The conclusion of this whole business was, that it soon became a fixed fact of my chambers, that a pale young scrivener, by the name of Bartleby, had a desk there; that he copied for me at the usual rate of four cents a folio (one hundred words); but he was permanently exempt from examining the work done by him, that duty being transferred to Turkey and Nippers, out of compliment, doubtless, to their superior acuteness; moreover, said Bartleby was never, on any account, to be dispatched on the most trivial errand of any sort; and that even if entreated to take upon him such a matter, it was generally understood that he would "prefer not to"—in other words, that he would refuse point-blank.

As days passed on, I became considerably reconciled to Bartleby. His steadiness, his freedom from all dissipation, his incessant industry (except when he chose to throw himself into a standing revery behind his screen), his great stillness, his unalterableness of demeanor under all circumstances, made him a valuable acquisition. One prime thing was this—*he was always there*—first in the morning, continually through the day, and the last at night. I had a singular confidence in his honesty. I felt my most precious papers perfectly safe in his hands. Sometimes, to be sure, I could not, for the very soul of me, avoid falling

---

[1] *pugilistic* Ready-to-fight.

[2] *put up* Put away.

[3] *inveteracy* Hostility.

[4] *wight* Person, but can also be used to refer to a ghost.

into sudden spasmodic passions with him. For it was exceeding difficult to bear in mind all the time those strange peculiarities, privileges, and unheard of exemptions, forming the tacit stipulations on Bartleby's part under which he remained in my office. Now and then, in the eagerness of dispatching pressing business, I would inadvertently summon Bartleby, in a short, rapid tone, to put his finger, say, on the incipient tie of a bit of red tape[1] with which I was about compressing some papers. Of course, from behind the screen the usual answer, "I prefer not to," was sure to come; and then, how could a human creature, with the common infirmities of our nature, refrain from bitterly exclaiming upon such perverseness—such unreasonableness. However, every added repulse of this sort which I received only tended to lessen the probability of my repeating the inadvertence.

Here it must be said, that according to the custom of most legal gentlemen occupying chambers in densely-populated law buildings, there were several keys to my door. One was kept by a woman residing in the attic, which person weekly scrubbed and daily swept and dusted my apartments. Another was kept by Turkey for convenience sake. The third I sometimes carried in my own pocket. The fourth I knew not who had.

Now, one Sunday morning I happened to go to Trinity Church,[2] to hear a celebrated preacher, and finding myself rather early on the ground I thought I would walk round to my chambers for a while. Luckily I had my key with me; but upon applying it to the lock, I found it resisted by something inserted from the inside. Quite surprised, I called out; when to my consternation a key was turned from within; and thrusting his lean visage at me, and holding the door ajar, the apparition of Bartleby appeared, in his shirt sleeves, and otherwise in a strangely tattered dishabille,[3] saying quietly that he was sorry, but he was deeply engaged just then, and—preferred not admitting me at present. In a brief word or two, he moreover added, that perhaps I had better walk round the block two or three times, and by that time he would probably have concluded his affairs.

Now, the utterly unsurmised[4] appearance of Bartleby, tenanting my law-chambers of a Sunday morning, with his cadaverously gentlemanly *nonchalance*, yet withal firm and self-possessed, had such a strange effect upon me, that incontinently[5] I slunk away from my own door, and did as desired. But not without sundry twinges of impotent rebellion against the mild effrontery of this unaccountable scrivener. Indeed, it was his wonderful mildness chiefly, which not only disarmed me, but unmanned me as it were. For I consider that one, for the time, is a sort of unmanned when he tranquilly permits his hired clerk to dictate to him, and order him away from his own premises. Furthermore, I was full of uneasiness as to what Bartleby could possibly be doing in my office in his shirt sleeves, and in an otherwise dismantled condition of a Sunday morning. Was anything amiss going on? Nay, that was out of the question. It was not to be thought of for a moment that Bartleby was an immoral person. But what could he be doing there?—copying? Nay again, whatever might be his eccentricities, Bartleby was an eminently decorous person. He would be the last man to sit down to his desk in any state approaching to nudity. Besides, it was Sunday; and there was something about Bartleby that forbade the supposition that he would by any secular occupation violate the proprieties of the day.[6]

Nevertheless, my mind was not pacified; and full of a restless curiosity, at last I returned to the door. Without hindrance I inserted my key, opened it, and entered. Bartleby was not to be seen. I looked round anxiously, peeped behind his screen; but it was very plain that he was gone. Upon more closely examining the place, I surmised that for an indefinite period Bartleby must have ate, dressed, and slept in my office, and that, too without plate, mirror, or bed. The cushioned seat of a ricketty old sofa in one corner bore the faint impress of a lean, reclining form. Rolled away under his desk, I found a blanket; under the empty grate, a blacking

---

[1] *put his finger ... red tape* The speaker is tying up legal documents in the typical red or pink tape that was customarily used for such purposes.

[2] *Trinity Church* Episcopal church near Wall Street that catered to wealthy and money-minded New Yorkers.

[3] *dishabille* Disheveled style of dress.

[4] *unsurmised* Unimagined, unexpected.

[5] *incontinently* Lacking in resolution.

[6] *proprieties of the day* Nineteenth-century American Protestants, following the Puritan tradition, treated Sunday (the Sabbath) as a day of rest, when no secular work could take place.

box[1] and brush; on a chair, a tin basin, with soap and a ragged towel; in a newspaper a few crumbs of ginger-nuts and a morsel of cheese. Yes, thought I, it is evident enough that Bartleby has been making his home here, keeping bachelor's hall all by himself. Immediately then the thought came sweeping across me, what miserable friendlessness and loneliness are here revealed! His poverty is great; but his solitude, how horrible! Think of it. Of a Sunday, Wall-street is deserted as Petra;[2] and every night of every day it is an emptiness. This building, too, which of week-days hums with industry and life, at nightfall echoes with sheer vacancy, and all through Sunday is forlorn. And here Bartleby makes his home; sole spectator, of a solitude which he has seen all populous—a sort of innocent and transformed Marius brooding among the ruins of Carthage![3]

For the first time in my life a feeling of overpowering stinging melancholy seized me. Before, I had never experienced aught but a not unpleasing sadness. The bond of a common humanity now drew me irresistibly to gloom. A fraternal melancholy! For both I and Bartleby were sons of Adam.[4] I remembered the bright silks and sparkling faces I had seen that day, in gala trim, swan-like sailing down the Mississippi of Broadway; and I contrasted them with the pallid copy-ist, and thought to myself, Ah, happiness courts the light, so we deem the world is gay; but misery hides aloof, so we deem that misery there is none. These sad fancyings—chimeras, doubtless, of a sick and silly brain—led on to other and more special thoughts, con-cerning the eccentricities of Bartleby. Presentiments of strange discoveries hovered round me. The scrivener's pale form appeared to me laid out, among uncaring strangers, in its shivering winding sheet.[5]

Suddenly I was attracted by Bartleby's closed desk, the key in open sight left in the lock.

I mean no mischief, seek the gratification of no heart-less curiosity, thought I; besides, the desk is mine, and its contents, too, so I will make bold to look within. Everything was methodically arranged, the papers smoothly placed. The pigeon holes were deep, and removing the files of documents, I groped into their recesses. Presently I felt something there, and dragged it out. It was an old bandanna handkerchief, heavy and knotted. I opened it, and saw it was a savings' bank.

I now recalled all the quiet mysteries which I had noted in the man. I remembered that he never spoke but to answer; that, though at intervals he had consid-erable time to himself, yet I had never seen him read-ing—no, not even a newspaper; that for long periods he would stand looking out, at his pale window behind the screen, upon the dead brick wall; I was quite sure he never visited any refectory[6] or eating house; while his pale face clearly indicated that he never drank beer like Turkey, or tea and coffee even, like other men; that he never went anywhere in particular that I could learn; never went out for a walk, unless, indeed, that was the case at present; that he had declined telling who he was, or whence he came, or whether he had any relatives in the world; that though so thin and pale, he never complained of ill health. And more than all, I remembered a certain unconscious air of pallid—how shall I call it?—of pallid haughtiness, say, or rather an austere reserve about him, which had positively awed me into my tame compliance with his eccentricities, when I had feared to ask him to do the slightest inci-dental thing for me, even though I might know, from his long-continued motionlessness, that behind his screen he must be standing in one of those dead-wall reveries of his.

Revolving all these things, and coupling them with the recently discovered fact, that he made my office his constant abiding place and home, and not forget-ful of his morbid moodiness; revolving all these things, a prudential feeling began to steal over me. My first emotions had been those of pure melancholy and sin-cerest pity; but just in proportion as the forlornness of Bartleby grew and grew to my imagination, did that same melancholy merge into fear, that pity into

---

[1]   *blacking box*   Box containing shoe polish.

[2]   *Petra*   Deserted city in what is now Jordan.

[3]   *Marius ... Carthage*   When Roman general Gaius Marius was exiled in 88 CE, he went to Carthage (which had been destroyed by Rome in the Punic Wars, between 264–146 BCE). There is a well-known Neoclassical painting of Marius "brooding" in Carthage by Dutch-American painter John Vanderlyn, entitled "Marius Amid the Ruins of Carthage" (1808).

[4]   *sons of Adam*   I.e., human beings, sharing the fate of Adam, who, in the book of Genesis, eats from the tree of knowledge and is punished with loss of paradise, a life of toil, and mortality.

[5]   *winding sheet*   Burial shroud.

[6]   *refectory*   Communal dining hall.

repulsion. So true it is, and so terrible, too, that up to a certain point the thought or sight of misery enlists our best affections; but, in certain special cases, beyond that point it does not. They err who would assert that invariably this is owing to the inherent selfishness of the human heart. It rather proceeds from a certain hopelessness of remedying excessive and organic ill. To a sensitive being, pity is not seldom pain. And when at last it is perceived that such pity cannot lead to effectual succor, common sense bids the soul be rid of it. What I saw that morning persuaded me that the scrivener was the victim of innate and incurable disorder. I might give alms[1] to his body; but his body did not pain him; it was his soul that suffered, and his soul I could not reach.

I did not accomplish the purpose of going to Trinity Church that morning. Somehow, the things I had seen disqualified me for the time from church-going. I walked homeward, thinking what I would do with Bartleby. Finally, I resolved upon this—I would put certain calm questions to him the next morning, touching his history, etc., and if he declined to answer them openly and unreservedly (and I supposed he would prefer not), then to give him a twenty dollar bill over and above whatever I might owe him, and tell him his services were no longer required; but that if in any other way I could assist him, I would be happy to do so, especially if he desired to return to his native place, wherever that might be, I would willingly help to defray the expenses. Moreover, if, after reaching home, he found himself at any time in want of aid, a letter from him would be sure of a reply.

The next morning came.

"Bartleby," said I, gently calling to him behind his screen.

No reply.

"Bartleby," said I, in a still gentler tone, "come here; I am not going to ask you to do anything you would prefer not to do—I simply wish to speak to you."

Upon this he noiselessly slid into view.

"Will you tell me, Bartleby, where you were born?"

"I would prefer not to."

"Will you tell me *anything* about yourself?"

"I would prefer not to."

"But what reasonable objection can you have to speak to me? I feel friendly towards you."

He did not look at me while I spoke, but kept his glance fixed upon my bust of Cicero, which, as I then sat, was directly behind me, some six inches above my head.

"What is your answer, Bartleby," said I, after waiting a considerable time for a reply, during which his countenance remained immovable, only there was the faintest conceivable tremor of the white attenuated mouth.

"At present I prefer to give no answer," he said, and retired into his hermitage.

It was rather weak in me I confess, but his manner, on this occasion, nettled me. Not only did there seem to lurk in it a certain calm disdain, but his perverseness seemed ungrateful, considering the undeniable good usage and indulgence he had received from me.

Again I sat ruminating what I should do. Mortified as I was at his behavior, and resolved as I had been to dismiss him when I entered my office, nevertheless I strangely felt something superstitious knocking at my heart, and forbidding me to carry out my purpose, and denouncing me for a villain if I dared to breathe one bitter word against this forlornest of mankind. At last, familiarly drawing my chair behind his screen, I sat down and said: "Bartleby, never mind, then, about revealing your history; but let me entreat you, as a friend, to comply as far as may be with the usages of this office. Say now, you will help to examine papers to-morrow or next day: in short, say now, that in a day or two you will begin to be a little reasonable:—say so, Bartleby."

"At present I would prefer not to be a little reasonable," was his mildly cadaverous reply.

Just then the folding-doors opened, and Nippers approached. He seemed suffering from an unusually bad night's rest, induced by severer indigestion than common. He overheard those final words of Bartleby.

"*Prefer not*, eh?" gritted Nippers—"I'd *prefer* him, if I were you, sir," addressing me—"I'd *prefer* him; I'd give him preferences, the stubborn mule! What is it, sir, pray, that he *prefers* not to do now?"

Bartleby moved not a limb.

"Mr. Nippers," said I, "I'd prefer that you would withdraw for the present."

---

[1]   *give alms* Offer charity.

Somehow, of late, I had got into the way of involuntarily using this word "prefer" upon all sorts of not exactly suitable occasions. And I trembled to think that my contact with the scrivener had already and seriously affected me in a mental way. And what further and deeper aberration might it not yet produce? This apprehension had not been without efficacy in determining me to summary[1] measures.

As Nippers, looking very sour and sulky, was departing, Turkey blandly and deferentially approached.

"With submission, sir," said he, "yesterday I was thinking about Bartleby here, and I think that if he would but prefer to take a quart of good ale every day, it would do much towards mending him, and enabling him to assist in examining his papers."

"So you have got the word, too," said I, slightly excited.

"With submission, what word, sir," asked Turkey, respectfully crowding himself into the contracted space behind the screen, and by so doing, making me jostle the scrivener. "What word, sir?"

"I would prefer to be left alone here," said Bartleby, as if offended at being mobbed in his privacy.

"*That's* the word, Turkey," said I—"*that's* it."

"Oh, *prefer*? oh yes—queer word. I never use it myself. But, sir, as I was saying, if he would but prefer—"

"Turkey," interrupted I, "you will please withdraw."

"Oh certainly, sir, if you prefer that I should."

As he opened the folding-door to retire, Nippers at his desk caught a glimpse of me, and asked whether I would prefer to have a certain paper copied on blue paper or white. He did not in the least roguishly accent the word prefer. It was plain that it involuntarily rolled from his tongue. I thought to myself, surely I must get rid of a demented man, who already has in some degree turned the tongues, if not the heads of myself and clerks. But I thought it prudent not to break the dismission[2] at once.

The next day I noticed that Bartleby did nothing but stand at his window in his dead-wall revery. Upon asking him why he did not write, he said that he had decided upon doing no more writing.

"Why, how now? what next?" exclaimed I, "do no more writing?"

"No more."

"And what is the reason?"

"Do you not see the reason for yourself," he indifferently replied.

I looked steadfastly at him, and perceived that his eyes looked dull and glazed. Instantly it occurred to me, that his unexampled diligence in copying by his dim window for the first few weeks of his stay with me might have temporarily impaired his vision.

I was touched. I said something in condolence with him. I hinted that of course he did wisely in abstaining from writing for a while; and urged him to embrace that opportunity of taking wholesome exercise in the open air. This, however, he did not do. A few days after this, my other clerks being absent, and being in a great hurry to dispatch certain letters by the mail, I thought that, having nothing else earthly to do, Bartleby would surely be less inflexible than usual, and carry these letters to the post-office. But he blankly declined. So, much to my inconvenience, I went myself.

Still added days went by. Whether Bartleby's eyes improved or not, I could not say. To all appearance, I thought they did. But when I asked him if they did, he vouchsafed no answer. At all events, he would do no copying. At last, in reply to my urgings, he informed me that he had permanently given up copying.

"What!" exclaimed I; "suppose your eyes should get entirely well—better than ever before—would you not copy then?"

"I have given up copying," he answered, and slid aside.

He remained as ever, a fixture in my chamber. Nay—if that were possible—he became still more of a fixture than before. What was to be done? He would do nothing in the office; why should he stay there? In plain fact, he had now become a millstone[3] to me, not only useless as a necklace, but afflictive to bear. Yet I was sorry for him. I speak less than truth when I say that, on his own account, he occasioned me uneasiness. If he would but have named a single relative or friend, I would instantly have written, and urged

---

1   *summary*   Quick and determined.

2   *dismission*   Dismissal.

3   *millstone*   Heavy stone used to grind corn; a "millstone around one's neck" is a common saying, meaning that one is burdened by a heavy problem.

their taking the poor fellow away to some convenient retreat. But he seemed alone, absolutely alone in the universe. A bit of wreck in the mid Atlantic. At length, necessities connected with my business tyrannized over all other considerations. Decently as I could, I told Bartleby that in six days time he must unconditionally leave the office. I warned him to take measures, in the interval, for procuring some other abode. I offered to assist him in this endeavor, if he himself would but take the first step towards a removal. "And when you finally quit me, Bartleby," added I, "I shall see that you go not away entirely unprovided. Six days from this hour, remember."

At the expiration of that period, I peeped behind the screen, and lo! Bartleby was there.

I buttoned up my coat, balanced myself; advanced slowly towards him, touched his shoulder, and said, "The time has come; you must quit this place; I am sorry for you; here is money; but you must go."

"I would prefer not," he replied, with his back still towards me.

"You *must*."

He remained silent.

Now I had an unbounded confidence in this man's common honesty. He had frequently restored to me sixpences and shillings carelessly dropped upon the floor, for I am apt to be very reckless in such shirt-button affairs.[1] The proceeding, then, which followed will not be deemed extraordinary.

"Bartleby," said I, "I owe you twelve dollars on account; here are thirty-two; the odd twenty are yours—Will you take it?" and I handed the bills towards him.

But he made no motion.

"I will leave them here, then," putting them under a weight on the table. Then taking my hat and cane and going to the door, I tranquilly turned and added— "After you have removed your things from these offices, Bartleby, you will of course lock the door—since everyone is now gone for the day but you—and if you please, slip your key underneath the mat, so that I may have it in the morning. I shall not see you again; so good-by to you. If, hereafter, in your new place of abode, I can be of any service to you, do not fail to advise me by letter. Good-by, Bartleby, and fare you well."

But he answered not a word; like the last column of some ruined temple, he remained standing mute and solitary in the middle of the otherwise deserted room.

As I walked home in a pensive mood, my vanity got the better of my pity. I could not but highly plume[2] myself on my masterly management in getting rid of Bartleby. Masterly I call it, and such it must appear to any dispassionate thinker. The beauty of my procedure seemed to consist in its perfect quietness. There was no vulgar bullying, no bravado of any sort, no choleric[3] hectoring, and striding to and fro across the apartment, jerking out vehement commands for Bartleby to bundle himself off with his beggarly traps.[4] Nothing of the kind. Without loudly bidding Bartleby depart—as an inferior genius might have done—I *assumed* the ground that depart he must; and upon that assumption built all I had to say. The more I thought over my procedure, the more I was charmed with it. Nevertheless, next morning, upon awakening, I had my doubts— I had somehow slept off the fumes of vanity. One of the coolest and wisest hours a man has, is just after he awakes in the morning. My procedure seemed as sagacious as ever—but only in theory. How it would prove in practice—there was the rub.[5] It was truly a beautiful thought to have assumed Bartleby's departure; but, after all, that assumption was simply my own, and none of Bartleby's. The great point was, not whether I had assumed that he would quit me, but whether he would prefer so to do. He was more a man of preferences than assumptions.

After breakfast, I walked down town, arguing the probabilities *pro* and *con*. One moment I thought it would prove a miserable failure, and Bartleby would be found all alive at my office as usual; the next moment it seemed certain that I should find his chair empty. And so I kept veering about. At the corner of Broadway and Canal street, I saw quite an excited group of people standing in earnest conversation.

---

1   *reckless ... affairs*   I.e., careless about such small things.

2   *plume*   Congratulate.

3   *choleric*   Angry.

4   *traps*   Belongings.

5   *there was the rub*   See Shakespeare's *Hamlet* (1609) Act 3, Scene 1, where Hamlet considers what might follow after death: "To die, To sleep; / To sleep, perchance to dream—ay, there's the rub, / For in that sleep of death what dreams may come / When we have shuffled off this mortal coil, / Must give us pause" (65–69).

"I'll take odds he doesn't," said a voice as I passed.

"Doesn't go?—done!" said I, "put up your money."

I was instinctively putting my hand in my pocket to produce my own, when I remembered that this was an election day. The words I had overheard bore no reference to Bartleby, but to the success or non-success of some candidate for the mayoralty. In my intent frame of mind, I had, as it were, imagined that all Broadway shared in my excitement, and were debating the same question with me. I passed on, very thankful that the uproar of the street screened my momentary absent-mindedness.

As I had intended, I was earlier than usual at my office door. I stood listening for a moment. All was still. He must be gone. I tried the knob. The door was locked. Yes, my procedure had worked to a charm; he indeed must be vanished. Yet a certain melancholy mixed with this: I was almost sorry for my brilliant success. I was fumbling under the door mat for the key, which Bartleby was to have left there for me, when accidentally my knee knocked against a panel, producing a summoning sound, and in response a voice came to me from within—"Not yet; I am occupied."

It was Bartleby.

I was thunderstruck. For an instant I stood like the man who, pipe in mouth, was killed one cloudless afternoon long ago in Virginia, by summer lightning; at his own warm open window he was killed, and remained leaning out there upon the dreamy afternoon till someone touched him, when he fell.

"Not gone!" I murmured at last. But again obeying that wondrous ascendancy which the inscrutable scrivener had over me, and from which ascendancy, for all my chafing, I could not completely escape, I slowly went down stairs and out into the street, and while walking round the block, considered what I should next do in this unheard-of perplexity. Turn the man out by an actual thrusting I could not; to drive him away by calling him hard names would not do; calling in the police was an unpleasant idea; and yet, permit him to enjoy his cadaverous triumph over me—this, too, I could not think of. What was to be done? or, if nothing could be done, was there anything further that I could *assume* in the matter? Yes, as before I had prospectively assumed that Bartleby would depart, so now I might retrospectively assume that departed he

was. In the legitimate carrying out of this assumption, I might enter my office in a great hurry, and pretending not to see Bartleby at all, walk straight against him as if he were air. Such a proceeding would in a singular degree have the appearance of a home-thrust.[1] It was hardly possible that Bartleby could withstand such an application of the doctrine of assumptions. But upon second thoughts the success of the plan seemed rather dubious. I resolved to argue the matter over with him again.

"Bartleby," said I, entering the office, with a quietly severe expression, "I am seriously displeased. I am pained, Bartleby. I had thought better of you. I had imagined you of such a gentlemanly organization, that in any delicate dilemma a slight hint would suffice—in short, an assumption. But it appears I am deceived. Why," I added, unaffectedly starting, "you have not even touched that money yet," pointing to it, just where I had left it the evening previous.

He answered nothing.

"Will you, or will you not, quit me?" I now demanded in a sudden passion, advancing close to him.

"I would prefer *not* to quit you," he replied gently emphasizing the *not*.

"What earthly right have you to stay here? Do you pay any rent? Do you pay my taxes? Or is this property yours?"

He answered nothing.

"Are you ready to go on and write now? Are your eyes recovered? Could you copy a small paper for me this morning? or help examine a few lines? or step round to the post-office? In a word, will you do anything at all, to give a coloring to your refusal to depart the premises?"

He silently retired into his hermitage.

I was now in such a state of nervous resentment that I thought it but prudent to check myself at present from further demonstrations. Bartleby and I were alone. I remembered the tragedy of the unfortunate Adams and the still more unfortunate Colt in the solitary office of the latter; and how poor Colt, being dreadfully incensed by Adams, and imprudently permitting himself to get wildly excited, was at unawares hurried into his fatal act—an act which certainly no

---

1   *home-thrust* I.e., move that strikes home (hits its target).

man could possibly deplore more than the actor him-self.[1] Often it had occurred to me in my ponderings upon the subject, that had that altercation taken place in the public street, or at a private residence, it would not have terminated as it did. It was the circumstance of being alone in a solitary office, upstairs, of a build-ing entirely unhallowed by humanizing domestic asso-ciations—an uncarpeted office, doubtless, of a dusty, haggard sort of appearance—this it must have been, which greatly helped to enhance the irritable despera-tion of the hapless Colt.

But when this old Adam[2] of resentment rose in me and tempted me concerning Bartleby, I grappled him and threw him. How? Why, simply by recalling the divine injunction: "A new commandment give I unto you, that ye love one another."[3] Yes, this it was that saved me. Aside from higher considerations, charity often operates as a vastly wise and prudent principle—a great safeguard to its possessor. Men have commit-ted murder for jealousy's sake, and anger's sake, and hatred's sake, and selfishness' sake, and spiritual pride's sake; but no man, that ever I heard of, ever commit-ted a diabolical murder for sweet charity's sake. Mere self-interest, then, if no better motive can be enlisted, should, especially with high-tempered men, prompt all beings to charity and philanthropy. At any rate, upon the occasion in question, I strove to drown my exas-perated feelings towards the scrivener by benevolently construing his conduct.—Poor fellow, poor fellow! thought I, he don't mean anything; and besides, he has seen hard times, and ought to be indulged.

I endeavored, also, immediately to occupy myself, and at the same time to comfort my despondency. I tried to fancy, that in the course of the morning, at such time as might prove agreeable to him, Bartleby, of his own free accord, would emerge from his her-mitage and take up some decided line of march in the

direction of the door. But no. Half-past twelve o'clock came; Turkey began to glow in the face, overturn his inkstand, and become generally obstreperous; Nippers abated down into quietude and courtesy; Ginger Nut munched his noon apple; and Bartleby remained stand-ing at his window in one of his profoundest dead-wall reveries. Will it be credited? Ought I to acknowledge it? That afternoon I left the office without saying one further word to him.

Some days now passed, during which, at leisure intervals I looked a little into "Edwards on the Will," and "Priestley on Necessity."[4] Under the circumstances, those books induced a salutary feeling. Gradually I slid into the persuasion that these troubles of mine, touch-ing the scrivener, had been all predestinated[5] from eternity, and Bartleby was billeted[6] upon me for some mysterious purpose of an allwise Providence, which it was not for a mere mortal like me to fathom. Yes, Bartleby, stay there behind your screen, thought I; I shall persecute you no more; you are harmless and noiseless as any of these old chairs; in short, I never feel so private as when I know you are here. At last I see it, I feel it; I penetrate to the predestinated purpose of my life. I am content. Others may have loftier parts to enact; but my mission in this world, Bartleby, is to furnish you with office-room for such period as you may see fit to remain.

I believe that this wise and blessed frame of mind would have continued with me, had it not been for the unsolicited and uncharitable remarks obtruded upon me by my professional friends who visited the rooms. But thus it often is, that the constant friction of illiberal minds wears out at last the best resolves of the more generous. Though to be sure, when I reflected upon it, it was not strange that people entering my office should be struck by the peculiar aspect of the unaccountable Bartleby, and so be tempted to throw out some sinister

---

[1]   *tragedy ... himself* The story that the lawyer alludes to here is one of the more infamous murder cases in New York City. John Caldwell Colt (1810–42), brother of the firearms inventor Samuel Colt (1814–62), murdered a printer named Samuel Adams with a hatchet, covered up the crime, and died by suicide on the day he was scheduled to be executed.

[2]   *Adam* I.e., sin, human weakness. Adam, as the original sinner, stands here for the sinful tendencies of all humanity.

[3]   *A new ... another* See John 13.34; these words are spoken by Christ to his disciples after the Last Supper.

[4]   *Edwards on the Will* Calvinist theologian Jonathan Edwards's *Freedom of the Will* (1754) argues that human will is depraved, and that humanity is consequently reliant on God's grace for sal-vation; *Priestley on Necessity* Joseph Priestley was an eminent English materialist philosopher. In his *Doctrine of Philosophical Necessity* (1777) he denies the reality of both the soul and free will.

[5]   *predestinated* Edwards was a vigorous proponent of the doc-trine of predestination: that God predestined people to salvation or damnation without reference to their own works.

[6]   *billeted* Lodged.

observations concerning him. Sometimes an attorney, having business with me, and calling at my office, and finding no one but the scrivener there, would undertake to obtain some sort of precise information from him touching my whereabouts; but without heeding his idle talk, Bartleby would remain standing immovable in the middle of the room. So after contemplating him in that position for a time, the attorney would depart, no wiser than he came.

Also, when a reference[1] was going on, and the room full of lawyers and witnesses, and business driving fast, some deeply-occupied legal gentleman present, seeing Bartleby wholly unemployed, would request him to run round to his (the legal gentleman's) office and fetch some papers for him. Thereupon, Bartleby would tranquilly decline, and yet remain idle as before. Then the lawyer would give a great stare, and turn to me. And what could I say? At last I was made aware that all through the circle of my professional acquaintance, a whisper of wonder was running round, having reference to the strange creature I kept at my office. This worried me very much. And as the idea came upon me of his possibly turning out a long-lived man, and keep occupying my chambers, and denying my authority; and perplexing my visitors; and scandalizing my professional reputation; and casting a general gloom over the premises; keeping soul and body together to the last upon his savings (for doubtless he spent but half a dime a day), and in the end perhaps outlive me, and claim possession of my office by right of his perpetual occupancy: as all these dark anticipations crowded upon me more and more, and my friends continually intruded their relentless remarks upon the apparition in my room; a great change was wrought in me. I resolved to gather all my faculties together, and forever rid me of this intolerable incubus.[2]

Ere revolving any complicated project, however, adapted to this end, I first simply suggested to Bartleby the propriety of his permanent departure. In a calm and serious tone, I commanded the idea to his careful and mature consideration. But, having taken three days to meditate upon it, he apprised me, that his original determination remained the same; in short, that he still preferred to abide with me.

What shall I do? I now said to myself, buttoning up my coat to the last button. What shall I do? what ought I to do? what does conscience say I *should* do with this man, or, rather, ghost. Rid myself of him, I must; go, he shall. But how? You will not thrust him, the poor, pale, passive mortal—you will not thrust such a helpless creature out of your door? you will not dishonor yourself by such cruelty? No, I will not, I cannot do that. Rather would I let him live and die here, and then mason up his remains in the wall.[3] What, then, will you do? For all your coaxing, he will not budge. Bribes he leaves under your own paper-weight on your table; in short, it is quite plain that he prefers to cling to you.

Then something severe, something unusual must be done. What! surely you will not have him collared by a constable, and commit his innocent pallor to the common jail? And upon what ground could you procure such a thing to be done?—a vagrant, is he? What! he a vagrant, a wanderer, who refuses to budge? It is because he will *not* be a vagrant, then, that you seek to count him *as* a vagrant. That is too absurd. No visible means of support: there I have him. Wrong again: for indubitably he *does* support himself, and that is the only unanswerable proof that any man can show of his possessing the means so to do. No more, then. Since he will not quit me, I must quit him. I will change my offices; I will move elsewhere, and give him fair notice, that if I find him on my new premises I will then proceed against him as a common trespasser.

Acting accordingly, next day I thus addressed him: "I find these chambers too far from the City Hall; the air is unwholesome. In a word, I propose to remove my offices next week, and shall no longer require your services. I tell you this now, in order that you may seek another place."

He made no reply, and nothing more was said.

On the appointed day I engaged carts and men, proceeded to my chambers, and, having but little furniture, everything was removed in a few hours. Throughout, the scrivener remained standing behind the screen, which I directed to be removed the last thing. It was

---

[1]   *reference*   Meeting to resolve a legal matter or dispute.

[2]   *incubus*   Demon who has sexual intercourse with sleeping victims, usually women; it can also mean "nightmare," and is often used to describe an oppressive or parasitic person.

---

[3]   *mason up ... wall*   In Edgar Allan Poe's story "The Cask of Amontillado" (1846), the murderer buries his victim alive by immurement (bricking him up behind a wall).

withdrawn; and, being folded up like a huge folio, left him the motionless occupant of a naked room. I stood in the entry watching him a moment, while something from within me upbraided me.

I re-entered, with my hand in my pocket—and—and my heart in my mouth.

"Good-by, Bartleby; I am going—good-by, and God some way bless you; and take that," slipping something in his hand. But it dropped upon the floor, and then—strange to say—I tore myself from him whom I had so longed to be rid of.

Established in my new quarters, for a day or two I kept the door locked, and started at every footfall in the passages. When I returned to my rooms, after any little absence, I would pause at the threshold for an instant, and attentively listen, ere applying my key. But these fears were needless. Bartleby never came nigh me.

I thought all was going well, when a perturbed-looking stranger visited me, inquiring whether I was the person who had recently occupied rooms at No. —— Wall street.

Full of forebodings, I replied that I was.

"Then, sir," said the stranger, who proved a lawyer, "you are responsible for the man you left there. He refuses to do any copying; he refuses to do anything; he says he prefers not to; and he refuses to quit the premises."

"I am very sorry, sir," said I, with assumed tranquility, but an inward tremor, "but, really, the man you allude to is nothing to me—he is no relation or apprentice of mine, that you should hold me responsible for him."

"In mercy's name, who is he?"

"I certainly cannot inform you. I know nothing about him. Formerly I employed him as a copyist; but he has done nothing for me now for some time past."

"I shall settle him, then—good morning, sir."

Several days passed, and I heard nothing more; and, though I often felt a charitable prompting to call at the place and see poor Bartleby, yet a certain squeamishness, of I know not what, withheld me.

All is over with him, by this time, thought I, at last, when, through another week, no further intelligence reached me. But, coming to my room the day after, I found several persons waiting at my door in a high state of nervous excitement.

"That's the man—here he comes," cried the foremost one, whom I recognized as the lawyer who had previously called upon me alone.

"You must take him away, sir, at once," cried a portly person among them, advancing upon me, and whom I knew to be the landlord of No. —— Wall street. "These gentlemen, my tenants, cannot stand it any longer; Mr. B——," pointing to the lawyer, "has turned him out of his room, and he now persists in haunting the building generally, sitting upon the banisters of the stairs by day, and sleeping in the entry by night. Everybody is concerned; clients are leaving the offices; some fears are entertained of a mob; something you must do, and that without delay."

Aghast at this torrent, I fell back before it, and would fain have locked myself in my new quarters. In vain I persisted that Bartleby was nothing to me—no more than to anyone else. In vain—I was the last person known to have anything to do with him, and they held me to the terrible account. Fearful, then, of being exposed in the papers (as one person present obscurely threatened), I considered the matter, and, at length, said, that if the lawyer would give me a confidential interview with the scrivener, in his (the lawyer's) own room, I would, that afternoon, strive my best to rid them of the nuisance they complained of.

Going up stairs to my old haunt, there was Bartleby silently sitting upon the banister at the landing.

"What are you doing here, Bartleby?" said I.

"Sitting upon the banister," he mildly replied.

I motioned him into the lawyer's room, who then left us.

"Bartleby" said I, "are you aware that you are the cause of great tribulation to me, by persisting in occupying the entry after being dismissed from the office?"

No answer.

"Now one of two things must take place. Either you must do something, or something must be done to you. Now what sort of business would you like to engage in? Would you like to re-engage in copying for some one?"

"No; I would prefer not to make any change."

"Would you like a clerkship in a dry-goods store?"

"There is too much confinement about that. No, I would not like a clerkship; but I am not particular."

"Too much confinement," I cried, "why you keep yourself confined all the time!"

"I would prefer not to take a clerkship," he rejoined, as if to settle that little item at once.

"How would a bar-tender's business suit you? There is no trying of the eye-sight in that."

"I would not like it at all; though, as I said before, I am not particular."

His unwonted wordiness inspirited me. I returned to the charge.

"Well, then, would you like to travel through the country collecting bills for the merchants? That would improve your health."

"No, I would prefer to be doing something else."

"How, then, would going as a companion to Europe, to entertain some young gentleman with your conversation—how would that suit you?"

"Not at all. It does not strike me that there is anything definite about that. I like to be stationary. But I am not particular."

"Stationary you shall be, then," I cried, now losing all patience, and, for the first time in all my exasperating connection with him, fairly flying into a passion. "If you do not go away from these premises before night, I shall feel bound—indeed, I *am* bound—to—to—to quit the premises myself!" I rather absurdly concluded, knowing not with what possible threat to try to frighten his immobility into compliance. Despairing of all further efforts, I was precipitately leaving him, when a final thought occurred to me—one which had not been wholly unindulged before.

"Bartleby," said I, in the kindest tone I could assume under such exciting circumstances, "will you go home with me now—not to my office, but my dwelling—and remain there till we can conclude upon some convenient arrangement for you at our leisure? Come, let us start now, right away."

"No: at present I would prefer not to make any change at all."

I answered nothing; but, effectually dodging every one by the suddenness and rapidity of my flight, rushed from the building, ran up Wall street towards Broadway, and, jumping into the first omnibus, was soon removed from pursuit. As soon as tranquility returned, I distinctly perceived that I had now done all that I possibly could, both in respect to the demands of the landlord and his tenants, and with regard to my own desire and sense of duty, to benefit Bartleby, and shield him from rude persecution, I now strove to be entirely care-free and quiescent; and my conscience justified me in the attempt; though, indeed, it was not so successful as I could have wished. So fearful was I of being again hunted out by the incensed landlord and his exasperated tenants, that, surrendering my business to Nippers, for a few days, I drove about the upper part of the town and through the suburbs, in my rockaway;[1] crossed over to Jersey City and Hoboken, and paid fugitive visits to Manhattanville and Astoria.[2] In fact, I almost lived in my rockaway for the time.

When again I entered my office, lo, a note from the landlord lay upon the desk. I opened it with trembling hands. It informed me that the writer had sent to the police, and had Bartleby removed to the Tombs as a vagrant. Moreover, since I knew more about him than anyone else, he wished me to appear at that place, and make a suitable statement of the facts. These tidings had a conflicting effect upon me. At first I was indignant; but, at last, almost approved. The landlord's energetic, summary disposition, had led him to adopt a procedure which I do not think I would have decided upon myself; and yet, as a last resort, under such peculiar circumstances, it seemed the only plan.

As I afterwards learned, the poor scrivener, when told that he must be conducted to the Tombs, offered not the slightest obstacle, but, in his pale, unmoving way, silently acquiesced.

Some of the compassionate and curious bystanders joined the party; and headed by one of the constables arm in arm with Bartleby, the silent procession filed its way through all the noise, and heat, and joy of the roaring thoroughfares at noon.

The same day I received the note, I went to the Tombs, or, to speak more properly, the Halls of Justice. Seeking the right officer, I stated the purpose of my call, and was informed that the individual I described was, indeed, within. I then assured the functionary that Bartleby was a perfectly honest man, and greatly

---

1   *rockaway* Carriage.

2   *Jersey City … Hoboken* Cities in New Jersey, both located on the Hudson River; *Manhattanville* Neighborhood in Manhattan, also called West Harlem; *Astoria* Neighborhood in the borough of Queens, New York.

to be compassionated, however unaccountably eccentric. I narrated all I knew and closed by suggesting the idea of letting him remain in as indulgent confinement as possible, till something less harsh might be done—though, indeed, I hardly knew what. At all events, if nothing else could be decided upon, the alms-house[1] must receive him. I then begged to have an interview.

Being under no disgraceful charge, and quite serene and harmless in all his ways, they had permitted him freely to wander about the prison, and, especially, in the inclosed grass-platted yards thereof. And so I found him there, standing all alone in the quietest of the yards, his face towards a high wall, while all around, from the narrow slits of the jail windows, I thought I saw peering out upon him the eyes of murderers and thieves.

"Bartleby!"

"I know you," he said, without looking round—"and I want nothing to say to you."

"It was not I that brought you here, Bartleby," said I, keenly pained at his implied suspicion. "And to you, this should not be so vile a place. Nothing reproachful attaches to you by being here. And see, it is not so sad a place as one might think. Look, there is the sky, and here is the grass."

"I know where I am," he replied, but would say nothing more, and so I left him.

As I entered the corridor again, a broad meat-like man, in an apron, accosted me, and, jerking his thumb over his shoulder, said—"Is that your friend?"

"Yes."

"Does he want to starve? If he does, let him live on the prison fare, that's all."

"Who are you?" asked I, not knowing what to make of such an unofficially speaking person in such a place.

"I am the grub-man. Such gentlemen as have friends here, hire me to provide them with something good to eat."

"Is this so?" said I, turning to the turnkey.

He said it was.

"Well, then," said I, slipping some silver into the grub-man's hands (for so they called him), "I want you to give particular attention to my friend there; let him have the best dinner you can get. And you must be as polite to him as possible."

"Introduce me, will you?" said the grub-man, looking at me with an expression which seem to say he was all impatience for an opportunity to give a specimen of his breeding.

Thinking it would prove of benefit to the scrivener, I acquiesced; and, asking the grub-man his name, went up with him to Bartleby.

"Bartleby, this is a friend; you will find him very useful to you."

"Your sarvant, sir, your sarvant," said the grub-man, making a low salutation behind his apron. "Hope you find it pleasant here, sir; nice grounds—cool apartments—hope you'll stay with us some time—try to make it agreeable. What will you have for dinner to-day?"

"I prefer not to dine to-day," said Bartleby, turning away. "It would disagree with me; I am unused to dinners." So saying, he slowly moved to the other side of the inclosure, and took up a position fronting the dead-wall.

"How's this?" said the grub-man, addressing me with a stare of astonishment. "He's odd, ain't he?"

"I think he is a little deranged," said I, sadly.

"Deranged? deranged is it? Well, now, upon my word, I thought that friend of yourn was a gentleman forger; they are always pale, and genteel-like, them forgers. I can't help pity 'em—can't help it, sir. Did you know Monroe Edwards?[2] he added, touchingly, and paused. Then, laying his hand piteously on my shoulder, sighed, "he died of consumption at Sing-Sing.[3] So you weren't acquainted with Monroe?"

"No, I was never socially acquainted with any forgers. But I cannot stop longer. Look to my friend yonder. You will not lose by it. I will see you again."

Some few days after this, I again obtained admission to the Tombs, and went through the corridors in quest of Bartleby; but without finding him.

"I saw him coming from his cell not long ago," said a turnkey, "may be he's gone to loiter in the yards."

So I went in that direction.

---

[1]   *alms-house*   Charitable house or building that offered shelter to the poor.

[2]   *Monroe Edwards*   Infamous slave trader and forger (1808–47) whose trial gained considerable prominence in the years preceding Melville's writing of "Bartleby."

[3]   *Sing-Sing*   Prison in New York state.

"Are you looking for the silent man?" said another turnkey, passing me. "Yonder he lies—sleeping in the yard there. 'Tis not twenty minutes since I saw him lie down."

The yard was entirely quiet. It was not accessible to the common prisoners. The surrounding walls, of amazing thickness, kept off all sounds behind them. The Egyptian character of the masonry weighed upon me with its gloom. But a soft imprisoned turf grew under foot. The heart of the eternal pyramids, it seemed, wherein, by some strange magic, through the clefts, grass-seed, dropped by birds, had sprung.

Strangely huddled at the base of the wall, his knees drawn up, and lying on his side, his head touching the cold stones, I saw the wasted Bartleby. But nothing stirred. I paused; then went close up to him; stooped over, and saw that his dim eyes were open; otherwise he seemed profoundly sleeping. Something prompted me to touch him. I felt his hand, when a tingling shiver ran up my arm and down my spine to my feet.

The round face of the grub-man peered upon me now. "His dinner is ready. Won't he dine to-day, either? Or does he live without dining?"

"Lives without dining," said I, and closed the eyes.

"Eh!—He's asleep, ain't he?"

"With kings and counselors,"[1] murmured I.

* * * * * *

There would seem little need for proceeding further in this history. Imagination will readily supply the meagre recital of poor Bartleby's interment. But, ere parting with the reader, let me say, that if this little narrative has sufficiently interested him, to awaken curiosity as to who Bartleby was, and what manner of life he led prior to the present narrator's making his acquaintance, I can only reply, that in such curiosity I fully share, but am wholly unable to gratify it. Yet here I hardly know whether I should divulge one little item of rumor, which came to my ear a few months after the scrivener's decease. Upon what basis it rested, I could never ascertain; and hence, how true it is I cannot now tell. But, inasmuch as this vague report has not been without a certain suggestive interest to me, however sad, it may prove the same with some others; and so I will briefly mention it. The report was this: that Bartleby had been a subordinate clerk in the Dead Letter Office[2] at Washington, from which he had been suddenly removed by a change in the administration. When I think over this rumor, hardly can I express the emotions which seize me. Dead letters! does it not sound like dead men? Conceive a man by nature and misfortune prone to a pallid hopelessness, can any business seem more fitted to heighten it than that of continually handling these dead letters, and assorting them for the flames? For by the cart-load they are annually burned. Sometimes from out the folded paper the pale clerk takes a ring—the finger it was meant for, perhaps, moulders in the grave; a banknote sent in swiftest charity—he whom it would relieve, nor eats nor hungers anymore; pardon for those who died despairing; hope for those who died unhoping; good tidings for those who died stifled by unrelieved calamities. On errands of life, these letters speed to death.

Ah, Bartleby! Ah, humanity!

—1853

---

[1]   *With kings and counselors*   See the book of Job, Chapter 3, where Job curses the day he was born: "'Why died I not from the womb? ... For now should I have lain still and been quiet ... / With kings and counsellors of the earth, who built desolate places for themselves'" (3.11–14). The full chapter appears as an In Context section below.

---

[2]   *Dead Letter Office*   Place where undeliverable mail is stored and eventually destroyed.

In Context

The Book of Job

Melville alludes to the Bible frequently in his work, most often to the books of the Old Testament. The Job story, which grapples with the problem of evil in a complex, ambiguous way, had a powerful influence on Melville's imagination and on "Bartleby the Scrivener" in particular. After Bartleby dies in the Tombs, the narrator directly references the Book of Job, Chapter 3, which is reproduced below from the King James Version of the Bible.

Job 3

3 After this opened Job his mouth, and cursed his day.

2 And Job spake, and said,

3 Let the day perish wherein I was born, and the night in which it was said, There is a man child conceived.

4 Let that day be darkness; let not God regard it from above, neither let the light shine upon it.

5 Let darkness and the shadow of death stain it; let a cloud dwell upon it; let the blackness of the day terrify it.

6 As for that night, let darkness seize upon it; let it not be joined unto the days of the year, let it not come into the number of the months.

7 Lo, let that night be solitary, let no joyful voice come therein.

8 Let them curse it that curse the day, who are ready to raise up their mourning.

9 Let the stars of the twilight thereof be dark; let it look for light, but have none; neither let it see the dawning of the day:

10 Because it shut not up the doors of my mother's womb, nor hid sorrow from mine eyes.

11 Why died I not from the womb? why did I not give up the ghost when I came out of the belly?

12 Why did the knees prevent me? or why the breasts that I should suck?

13 For now should I have lain still and been quiet, I should have slept: then had I been at rest,

14 With kings and counsellors of the earth, which build desolate places for themselves;

15 Or with princes that had gold, who filled their houses with silver:

16 Or as an hidden untimely birth I had not been; as infants which never saw light.

17 There the wicked cease from troubling; and there the weary be at rest.

18 There the prisoners rest together; they hear not the voice of the oppressor.

19 The small and great are there; and the servant is free from his master.

20 Wherefore is light given to him that is in misery, and life unto the bitter in soul;

21 Which long for death, but it cometh not; and dig for it more than for hid treasures;

22 Which rejoice exceedingly, and are glad, when they can find the grave?

23 Why is light given to a man whose way is hid, and whom God hath hedged in?

24 For my sighing cometh before I eat, and my roarings are poured out like the waters.

25 For the thing which I greatly feared is come upon me, and that which I was afraid of is come unto me.

26 I was not in safety, neither had I rest, neither was I quiet; yet trouble came.

Benito Cereno

An important context for *Benito Cereno* is the history of the Haitian Revolution, which was underway in 1799, the year the story is set. Beginning in 1791 and ending in 1804, the Haitian Revolution led to the foundation of a black state free from slavery.

In August 1791, the enslaved people of what was then the French colony of St. Domingue rose in revolt against their white enslavers—whom they outnumbered by at least a ten to one ratio—killing the whites and burning their plantations. In the following years the rebel army defeated not only French forces, but also those sent by Britain to seize control of the lucrative colony. By 1801, the formerly enslaved population controlled the entire island (Saint Domingue as well as the neighboring Spanish colony of Santo Domingo), and Toussaint Louverture, the commander of the rebel army, created a new constitution that abolished slavery across the territory. In 1802, French forces renewed efforts to retake the colony and reinstitute slavery. Toussaint was captured and imprisoned in France, but the fighting continued, with the French perpetrating mass executions of captured soldiers. Toussaint died in prison in 1803; in November of that year, the rebel army, now under the leadership of Jean-Jacques Dessalines, drove the French off the island. Dessalines declared independence for Haiti on 1 January 1804. He then ordered the massacre of the remaining white population.

In America, news of the Haitian Revolution elicited mixed responses. Many abolitionists were supportive and saw the conflict as further proof that societies built on slavery were inherently unstable, whereas Southern enslavers and their supporters reacted in terror that similar events would occur on their plantations. Haiti became a source of hope to enslaved people across the world, and to black resistance in America particularly. As Frederick Douglass said in 1893, "Until [Haiti] spoke no Christian nation had abolished Negro slavery. Until she spoke no Christian nation had given to the world an organized effort to abolish slavery. Until she spoke the slave ship, followed by hungry sharks, greedy to devour the dead and dying slaves flung overboard to feed them, ploughed in peace the South Atlantic, painting the sea with the Negro's blood." Melville sets his story mid-way through the Haitian Revolution, before Louverture created a constitution but after the enslaved population had taken the upper hand in the conflict.

In the year 1799, Captain Amasa Delano,[1] of Duxbury, in Massachusetts, commanding a large sealer[2] and general trader, lay at anchor with a valuable cargo, in the harbor of St. Maria—a small, desert, uninhabited island toward the southern extremity of the long coast of Chili.[3] There he had touched[4] for water.

On the second day, not long after dawn, while lying in his berth, his mate came below, informing him that a strange sail was coming into the bay. Ships were then not so plenty in those waters as now. He rose, dressed, and went on deck.

The morning was one peculiar to that coast. Everything was mute and calm; everything gray. The sea, though undulated into long roods[5] of swells, seemed fixed, and was sleeked at the surface like waved lead that has cooled and set in the smelter's mould. The sky seemed a gray surtout.[6] Flights of troubled gray fowl, kith and kin[7] with flights of troubled gray vapors among which they were mixed, skimmed low and fitfully over the waters, as swallows over meadows before storms.

Shadows present, foreshadowing deeper shadows to come.

To Captain Delano's surprise, the stranger, viewed through the glass, showed no colors; though to do so upon entering a haven, however uninhabited in its shores, where but a single other ship might be lying, was the custom among peaceful seamen of all nations. Considering the lawlessness and loneliness of the spot, and the sort of stories, at that day, associated with those seas, Captain Delano's surprise might have deepened into some uneasiness had he not been a person of a singularly undistrustful good-nature, not liable, except on extraordinary and repeated incentives, and hardly then, to indulge in personal alarms, any way involving

---

1   *Amasa Delano*   This character is based on a real American sea captain, best known for his book *Narrative of Voyages and Travels in the Northern and Southern Hemispheres, Comprising Three Voyages Round the World* (1817).

2   *sealer*   Seal-hunting vessel.

3   *Chili*   Modern-day Chile.

4   *touched*   Landed.

5   *roods*   Units of land measurement, each equivalent to a quarter of an acre. A rood can also be a Christian cross.

6   *surtout*   Overcoat.

7   *kith and kin*   Friends and family.

the imputation of malign evil in man. Whether, in view of what humanity is capable, such a trait implies, along with a benevolent heart, more than ordinary quickness and accuracy of intellectual perception, may be left to the wise to determine.

But whatever misgivings might have obtruded on first seeing the stranger, would almost, in any seaman's mind, have been dissipated by observing that, the ship, in navigating into the harbor, was drawing too near the land; a sunken reef making out off her bow. This seemed to prove her a stranger, indeed, not only to the sealer, but the island; consequently, she could be no wonted freebooter[1] on that ocean. With no small interest, Captain Delano continued to watch her—a proceeding not much facilitated by the vapors partly mantling[2] the hull, through which the far matin light[3] from her cabin streamed equivocally enough; much like the sun—by this time hemisphered on the rim of the horizon, and, apparently, in company with the strange ship entering the harbor—which, wimpled by the same low, creeping clouds, showed not unlike a Lima intriguante's one sinister eye peering across the Plaza from the Indian loop-hole of her dusk *saya-y-manta*.[4]

It might have been but a deception of the vapors, but, the longer the stranger was watched the more singular appeared her manoeuvres. Ere long it seemed hard to decide whether she meant to come in or no— what she wanted, or what she was about. The wind, which had breezed up a little during the night, was now extremely light and baffling,[5] which the more increased the apparent uncertainty of her movements. Surmising, at last, that it might be a ship in distress, Captain Delano ordered his whale-boat to be dropped, and, much to the wary opposition of his mate, prepared to board her, and, at the least, pilot[6] her in. On

the night previous, a fishing-party of the seamen had gone a long distance to some detached rocks out of sight from the sealer, and, an hour or two before daybreak, had returned, having met with no small success. Presuming that the stranger might have been long off soundings,[7] the good captain put several baskets of the fish, for presents, into his boat, and so pulled away. From her continuing too near the sunken reef, deeming her in danger, calling to his men, he made all haste to apprise those on board of their situation. But, some time ere the boat came up, the wind, light though it was, having shifted, had headed the vessel off, as well as partly broken the vapors from about her.

Upon gaining a less remote view, the ship, when made signally visible on the verge of the leaden-hued swells, with the shreds of fog here and there raggedly furring her, appeared like a white-washed monastery after a thunder-storm, seen perched upon some dun cliff among the Pyrenees. But it was no purely fanciful resemblance which now, for a moment, almost led Captain Delano to think that nothing less than a ship-load of monks was before him. Peering over the bulwarks were what really seemed, in the hazy distance, throngs of dark cowls; while, fitfully revealed through the open port-holes, other dark moving figures were dimly descried, as of Black Friars[8] pacing the cloisters.

Upon a still nigher approach, this appearance was modified, and the true character of the vessel was plain—a Spanish merchantman of the first class, carrying negro slaves, amongst other valuable freight, from one colonial port to another. A very large, and, in its time, a very fine vessel, such as in those days were at intervals encountered along that main;[9] sometimes superseded Acapulco treasure-ships,[10] or retired frigates of the Spanish king's navy, which, like

---

1 *wonted freebooter* Practiced pirate.

2 *mantling* Cloaking; covering.

3 *matin light* Morning light, but with the suggestion of morning prayer-time (matins).

4 *wimpled* Veiled; *Lima* Capital of Peru; *intriguante* Woman who engages in an intrigue—here, perhaps, an extramarital affair; *saya-y-manta* Dress with a hood that partially covers the face, which women wore in colonial Peru and could conceal their identities.

5 *baffling* Variable, shifting.

6 *pilot* Steer, guide.

7 *off soundings* In waters so deep that the soundings—the line and lead used by a ship to ascertain water depth—could not reach the bottom. When in water so deep there are few fish to be caught; shallower seas contain more sea life.

8 *Black Friars* Members of the Order of Preachers, or Dominicans, who wear black cloaks.

9 *main* Sea.

10 *Acapulco treasure-ships* Also known as Manila Galleons, ships that for over two centuries (1565–1815) moved between Acapulco and the Philippines (both were part of what was known as New Spain). This trade route brought the treasures of the Far East to the Americas.

superannuated Italian palaces, still, under a decline of masters, preserved signs of former state.

As the whale-boat drew more and more nigh, the cause of the peculiar pipe-clayed aspect[1] of the stranger was seen in the slovenly neglect pervading her. The spars,[2] ropes, and great part of the bulwarks,[3] looked woolly, from long unacquaintance with the scraper, tar, and the brush. Her keel[4] seemed laid, her ribs put together, and she launched, from Ezekiel's Valley of Dry Bones.[5]

In the present business in which she was engaged, the ship's general model and rig appeared to have undergone no material change from their original warlike and Froissart pattern.[6] However, no guns were seen.

The tops[7] were large, and were railed about with what had once been octagonal net-work, all now in sad disrepair. These tops hung overhead like three ruinous aviaries, in one of which was seen, perched, on a ratlin, a white noddy,[8] a strange fowl, so called from its lethargic, somnambulistic character, being frequently caught by hand at sea. Battered and mouldy, the castellated forecastle[9] seemed some ancient turret, long ago taken by assault, and then left to decay. Toward the stern, two high-raised quarter galleries—the balustrades here and there covered with dry, tindery sea-moss—opening out from the unoccupied state-cabin, whose dead-lights,[10] for all the mild weather, were hermetically closed and calked—these tenantless balconies hung over the sea as if it were the grand Venetian canal. But the principal relic of faded grandeur was the ample oval of the shield-like stern-piece,[11] intricately carved with the arms of Castile and Leon,[12] medallioned about by groups of mythological or symbolical devices; uppermost and central of which was a dark satyr[13] in a mask, holding his foot on the prostrate neck of a writhing figure, likewise masked.

Whether the ship had a figure-head, or only a plain beak,[14] was not quite certain, owing to canvas wrapped about that part, either to protect it while undergoing a re-furbishing, or else decently to hide its decay. Rudely painted or chalked, as in a sailor freak,[15] along the forward side of a sort of pedestal below the canvas, was the sentence, "*Seguid vuestro jefe*" (follow your leader); while upon the tarnished headboards,[16] near by, appeared, in stately capitals, once gilt, the ship's name, "SAN DOMINICK,"[17] each letter streakingly corroded with tricklings of copper-spike rust; while, like mourning weeds, dark festoons of sea-grass slimily swept to and fro over the name, with every hearse-like roll of the hull.

---

[1]   *pipe-clayed aspect*   Look of having been whitened (pipes were made of white clay).

[2]   *spars*   Wooden masts, and the wooden parts of sails (booms and yards).

[3]   *bulwarks*   Sides of the ship above the level of the deck.

[4]   *keel*   Bottom centerline structure of a ship; the rest of the hull is built around the keel.

[5]   *Ezekiel's ... Bones*   Ezekiel 37.1–14 recounts the prophet's vision of a valley of dry human bones, which God tells Ezekiel are the exiled bones of the people of Israel, waiting to be resurrected in their homeland.

[6]   *Froissart pattern*   Jean Froissart (1337–1405) was a French historian of the Hundred Years' War (1337–1453) who celebrated chivalry and the feudal aristocracy. Illustrated editions of Froissart's *Chronicles* (c. 1391)—one of which was published in New York in 1854, shortly before the publication of *Benito Cereno*—contain stylized illustrations of medieval warships, which typically contain one mast and sail and a high turreted forecastle and after castle. By the time Melville's story takes place, this style of shipbuilding had been obsolete for a century and a half.

[7]   *tops*   Topsails.

[8]   *ratlin*   Small rope used in forming a ship's ladder; *white noddy*   Small seabird, also known as a tern.

[9]   *castellated forecastle*   Forecastle (the raised deck at the front of a ship) that is built like a castle wall for defensive purposes (the ships in the Froissart illustrations have this appearance).

[10]   *dead-lights*   Shutters placed over port-holes and cabin-windows to keep water out in a storm.

[11]   *stern-piece*   Flat piece of wood at the stern, to which the side planks are attached.

[12]   *arms of Castile and Leon*   The symbols (arms) of the Spanish region of Castile and León are two lions and two castles.

[13]   *satyr*   Woodland deity; often represented as part human, part animal, and in a state of sexual arousal.

[14]   *figure-head*   Ornamental sculpture, usually a woman's figure, that is placed at the head of a ship;   *plain beak*   Undecorated projection at the head of the ship (beak-shaped).

[15]   *freak*   Eccentric behavior.

[16]   *headboards*   Planking between the headrails—the timbers that extend on each side from the head of the ship.

[17]   *SAN DOMINICK*   Name suggestive of the Roman Catholic Order of Preachers, or Dominicans, who took their name from St. Dominic, and also of the Haitian Revolution: "Saint-Domingue" is the name of the French colony in which the revolution took place. Melville invented this name for the ship.

As, at last, the boat was hooked from the bow along toward the gangway[1] amidship, its keel, while yet some inches separated from the hull, harshly grated as on a sunken coral reef. It proved a huge bunch of conglobated[2] barnacles adhering below the water to the side like a wen[3]—a token of baffling airs and long calms passed somewhere in those seas.

Climbing the side, the visitor was at once surrounded by a clamorous throng of whites and blacks, but the latter outnumbering the former more than could have been expected, negro transportation-ship as the stranger in port was. But, in one language, and as with one voice, all poured out a common tale of suffering; in which the negresses, of whom there were not a few, exceeded the others in their dolorous vehemence. The scurvy,[4] together with the fever, had swept off a great part of their number, more especially the Spaniards. Off Cape Horn they had narrowly escaped shipwreck;[5] then, for days together, they had lain tranced[6] without wind; their provisions were low; their water next to none; their lips that moment were baked.

While Captain Delano was thus made the mark[7] of all eager tongues, his one eager glance took in all faces, with every other object about him. Always upon first boarding a large and populous ship at sea, especially a foreign one, with a nondescript crew such as Lascars or Manilla men,[8] the impression varies in a peculiar way from that produced by first entering a strange house with strange inmates in a strange land. Both house and ship—the one by its walls and blinds, the other by its high bulwarks like ramparts—hoard from view their interiors till the last moment: but in the case of the ship there is this addition; that the living spectacle it contains, upon its sudden and complete disclosure, has, in contrast with the blank ocean which zones it, something of the effect of enchantment. The ship seems unreal; these strange costumes, gestures, and faces, but a shadowy tableau just emerged from the deep, which directly must receive back what it gave.

Perhaps it was some such influence, as above is attempted to be described, which, in Captain Delano's mind, heightened whatever, upon a staid scrutiny, might have seemed unusual; especially the conspicuous figures of four elderly grizzled negroes, their heads like black, doddered[9] willow tops, who, in venerable contrast to the tumult below them, were couched, sphynx-like, one on the starboard cat-head, another on the larboard, and the remaining pair face to face on the opposite bulwarks above the main-chains.[10] They each had bits of unstranded old junk in their hands, and, with a sort of stoical self-content, were picking the junk into oakum,[11] a small heap of which lay by their sides. They accompanied the task with a continuous, low, monotonous, chant; droning and drilling away like so many gray-headed bag-pipers playing a funeral march.

The quarter-deck rose into an ample elevated poop,[12] upon the forward verge of which, lifted, like the oakum-pickers, some eight feet above the general throng, sat along in a row, separated by regular spaces, the cross-legged figures of six other blacks; each with a rusty hatchet in his hand, which, with a bit of brick and a rag, he was engaged like a scullion in scouring;[13] while between each two was a small stack of hatchets, their rusted edges turned forward awaiting a like operation. Though occasionally the four oakum-pickers would briefly address some person or persons in the crowd

---

[1] *gangway*   Passage between stowed cargo in the hold.

[2] *conglobated*   Gathered together in a round mass.

[3] *wen*   Tumor.

[4] *scurvy*   A disease caused by vitamin C deficiency, once common among sailors.

[5] *Off Cape … shipwreck*   Rounding Cape Horn (the southern-most tip of South America) was one of the more dangerous tasks that mariners could confront, as the seas are particularly rough, and storms are common.

[6] *tranced*   I.e., entranced, becalmed.

[7] *mark*   Target.

[8] *Lascars*   Sailors from Asia, especially the Indian subcontinent; *Manilla men*   Filipinos.

[9] *doddered*   Made unsteady, trembling.

[10] *cat-head*   Beam that sticks out from the ship's bows and is used to raise and lower the anchor without hitting the bows; *main-chains*   Tackle that is either near or attached to the mainmast.

[11] *junk*   Old ropes; *oakum*   Fibers from hemp ropes that have been unwound and separated, often used as a caulking material on ships. Picking ropes to make oakum was a painful job.

[12] *quarter-deck*   Upper deck behind the mainmast; *poop*   Stern of the ship.

[13] *bit of brick … scouring*   These men were using bricks of pumice stone to polish (scour) the rust from the hatchets. A "scullion" was the lowest rank of servant, who was given the worst jobs in the household.

below, yet the six hatchet-polishers neither spoke to others, nor breathed a whisper among themselves, but sat intent upon their task, except at intervals, when, with the peculiar love in negroes of uniting industry with pastime, two and two they sideways clashed their hatchets together, like cymbals, with a barbarous din. All six, unlike the generality, had the raw aspect of unsophisticated Africans.

But that first comprehensive glance which took in those ten figures, with scores less conspicuous, rested but an instant upon them, as, impatient of the hubbub of voices, the visitor turned in quest of whomsoever it might be that commanded the ship.

But as if not unwilling to let nature make known her own case among his suffering charge, or else in despair of restraining it for the time, the Spanish captain, a gentlemanly, reserved-looking, and rather young man to a stranger's eye, dressed with singular richness, but bearing plain traces of recent sleepless cares and disquietudes, stood passively by, leaning against the mainmast, at one moment casting a dreary, spiritless look upon his excited people, at the next an unhappy glance toward his visitor. By his side stood a black of small stature, in whose rude face, as occasionally, like a shepherd's dog, he mutely turned it up into the Spaniard's, sorrow and affection were equally blended.

Struggling through the throng, the American advanced to the Spaniard, assuring him of his sympathies, and offering to render whatever assistance might be in his power. To which the Spaniard returned for the present but grave and ceremonious acknowledgments, his national formality dusked by the saturnine[1] mood of ill-health.

But losing no time in mere compliments, Captain Delano, returning to the gangway, had his basket of fish brought up; and as the wind still continued light, so that some hours at least must elapse ere the ship could be brought to the anchorage, he bade his men return to the sealer, and fetch back as much water as the whale-boat could carry, with whatever soft bread the steward might have, all the remaining pumpkins on board, with a box of sugar, and a dozen of his private bottles of cider.

Not many minutes after the boat's pushing off, to the vexation of all, the wind entirely died away, and the tide turning, began drifting back the ship helplessly seaward. But trusting this would not long last, Captain Delano sought, with good hopes, to cheer up the strangers, feeling no small satisfaction that, with persons in their condition, he could—thanks to his frequent voyages along the Spanish main—converse with some freedom in their native tongue.

While left alone with them, he was not long in observing some things tending to heighten his first impressions; but surprise was lost in pity, both for the Spaniards and blacks, alike evidently reduced from scarcity of water and provisions; while long-continued suffering seemed to have brought out the less good-natured qualities of the negroes, besides, at the same time, impairing the Spaniard's authority over them. But, under the circumstances, precisely this condition of things was to have been anticipated. In armies, navies, cities, or families, in nature herself, nothing more relaxes good order than misery. Still, Captain Delano was not without the idea, that had Benito Cereno been a man of greater energy, misrule would hardly have come to the present pass. But the debility,[2] constitutional or induced by hardships, bodily and mental, of the Spanish captain, was too obvious to be overlooked. A prey to settled dejection, as if long mocked with hope he would not now indulge it, even when it had ceased to be a mock, the prospect of that day, or evening at furthest, lying at anchor, with plenty of water for his people, and a brother captain to counsel and befriend, seemed in no perceptible degree to encourage him. His mind appeared unstrung, if not still more seriously affected. Shut up in these oaken walls, chained to one dull round of command, whose unconditionality cloyed him, like some hypochondriac abbot he moved slowly about, at times suddenly pausing, starting, or staring, biting his lip, biting his fingernail, flushing, paling, twitching his beard, with other symptoms of an absent or moody mind. This distempered spirit was lodged, as before hinted, in as distempered a frame. He was rather tall, but seemed never to have been robust, and now with nervous suffering was almost worn to a skeleton. A tendency to some pulmonary complaint appeared to have been lately confirmed. His voice was like that of one with lungs half gone—hoarsely suppressed, a husky whisper. No

---

1 *saturnine* Gloomy.

2 *debility* Weakness.

wonder that, as in this state he tottered about, his private servant apprehensively followed him. Sometimes the negro gave his master his arm, or took his handkerchief out of his pocket for him; performing these and similar offices with that affectionate zeal which transmutes into something filial or fraternal acts in themselves but menial; and which has gained for the negro the repute of making the most pleasing body-servant in the world; one, too, whom a master need be on no stiffly superior terms with, but may treat with familiar trust; less a servant than a devoted companion.

Marking the noisy indocility[1] of the blacks in general, as well as what seemed the sullen inefficiency of the whites it was not without humane satisfaction that Captain Delano witnessed the steady good conduct of Babo.

But the good conduct of Babo, hardly more than the ill-behavior of others, seemed to withdraw the half-lunatic Don Benito from his cloudy languor. Not that such precisely was the impression made by the Spaniard on the mind of his visitor. The Spaniard's individual unrest was, for the present, but noted as a conspicuous feature in the ship's general affliction. Still, Captain Delano was not a little concerned at what he could not help taking for the time to be Don Benito's unfriendly indifference towards himself. The Spaniard's manner, too, conveyed a sort of sour and gloomy disdain, which he seemed at no pains to disguise. But this the American in charity ascribed to the harassing effects of sickness, since, in former instances, he had noted that there are peculiar natures on whom prolonged physical suffering seems to cancel every social instinct of kindness; as if, forced to black bread themselves, they deemed it but equity that each person coming nigh them should, indirectly, by some slight or affront, be made to partake of their fare.

But ere long Captain Delano bethought him that, indulgent as he was at the first, in judging the Spaniard, he might not, after all, have exercised charity enough. At bottom it was Don Benito's reserve which displeased him; but the same reserve was shown towards all but his faithful personal attendant. Even the formal reports which, according to sea-usage, were, at stated times, made to him by some petty underling, either a white, mulatto or black, he hardly had patience

enough to listen to, without betraying contemptuous aversion. His manner upon such occasions was, in its degree, not unlike that which might be supposed to have been his imperial countryman's, Charles V., just previous to the anchoritish retirement[2] of that monarch from the throne. This splenetic[3] disrelish of his place was evinced in almost every function pertaining to it. Proud as he was moody, he condescended to no personal mandate. Whatever special orders were necessary, their delivery was delegated to his body-servant, who in turn transferred them to their ultimate destination, through runners, alert Spanish boys or slave boys, like pages or pilot-fish[4] within easy call continually hovering round Don Benito. So that to have beheld this undemonstrative invalid gliding about, apathetic and mute, no landsman could have dreamed that in him was lodged a dictatorship beyond which, while at sea, there was no earthly appeal.

Thus, the Spaniard, regarded in his reserve, seemed the involuntary victim of mental disorder. But, in fact, his reserve might, in some degree, have proceeded from design. If so, then here was evinced the unhealthy climax of that icy though conscientious policy, more or less adopted by all commanders of large ships, which, except in signal emergencies, obliterates alike the manifestation of sway with every trace of sociality; transforming the man into a block, or rather into a loaded cannon, which, until there is call for thunder, has nothing to say.

Viewing him in this light, it seemed but a natural token of the perverse habit induced by a long course of such hard self-restraint, that, notwithstanding the present condition of his ship, the Spaniard should still persist in a demeanor, which, however harmless, or, it may be, appropriate, in a well-appointed vessel, such as the San Dominick might have been at the outset of the voyage, was anything but judicious now. But the Spaniard, perhaps, thought that it was with captains as with gods: reserve, under all events, must still be

---

[1]   *indocility*   Unruliness, lack of submissiveness.

[2]   *anchoritish retirement*   In 1556, Charles V (1500–58) abdicated his throne as Holy Roman Emperor and joined a monastery. An anchorite is a person who withdraws from society to lead a life of religious seclusion.

[3]   *splenetic*   Melancholic, grumpy.

[4]   *pages*   Attendants on a person of high-rank;   *pilot-fish*   Fish that swim alongside, and eat parasites from, sharks. They also eat leftover bits from a shark's kill.

their cue. But probably this appearance of slumbering dominion might have been but an attempted disguise to conscious imbecility—not deep policy, but shallow device. But be all this as it might, whether Don Benito's manner was designed or not, the more Captain Delano noted its pervading reserve, the less he felt uneasiness at any particular manifestation of that reserve towards himself.

Neither were his thoughts taken up by the captain alone. Wonted to the quiet orderliness of the sealer's comfortable family of a crew, the noisy confusion of the San Dominick's suffering host repeatedly challenged his eye. Some prominent breaches, not only of discipline but of decency, were observed. These Captain Delano could not but ascribe, in the main, to the absence of those subordinate deck-officers to whom, along with higher duties, is intrusted what may be styled the police department of a populous ship. True, the old oakum-pickers appeared at times to act the part of monitorial constables to their countrymen, the blacks; but though occasionally succeeding in allaying trifling outbreaks now and then between man and man, they could do little or nothing toward establishing general quiet. The San Dominick was in the condition of a transatlantic emigrant ship, among whose multitude of living freight are some individuals, doubtless, as little troublesome as crates and bales; but the friendly remonstrances of such with their ruder companions are of not so much avail as the unfriendly arm of the mate. What the San Dominick wanted was, what the emigrant ship has, stern superior officers. But on these decks not so much as a fourth-mate was to be seen.

The visitor's curiosity was roused to learn the particulars of those mishaps which had brought about such absenteeism, with its consequences; because, though deriving some inkling of the voyage from the wails which at the first moment had greeted him, yet of the details no clear understanding had been had. The best account would, doubtless, be given by the captain. Yet at first the visitor was loth to ask it, unwilling to provoke some distant rebuff. But plucking up courage, he at last accosted Don Benito, renewing the expression of his benevolent interest, adding, that did he (Captain Delano) but know the particulars of the ship's misfortunes, he would, perhaps, be better able in the end to relieve them. Would Don Benito favor him with the whole story.

Don Benito faltered; then, like some somnambulist suddenly interfered with, vacantly stared at his visitor, and ended by looking down on the deck. He maintained this posture so long, that Captain Delano, almost equally disconcerted, and involuntarily almost as rude, turned suddenly from him, walking forward to accost one of the Spanish seamen for the desired information. But he had hardly gone five paces, when, with a sort of eagerness, Don Benito invited him back, regretting his momentary absence of mind, and professing readiness to gratify him.

While most part of the story was being given, the two captains stood on the after part of the main-deck, a privileged spot, no one being near but the servant.

"It is now a hundred and ninety days," began the Spaniard, in his husky whisper, "that this ship, well officered and well manned, with several cabin passengers—some fifty Spaniards in all—sailed from Buenos Ayres bound to Lima, with a general cargo, hardware, Paraguay tea[1] and the like—and," pointing forward, "that parcel of negroes, now not more than a hundred and fifty, as you see, but then numbering over three hundred souls. Off Cape Horn we had heavy gales. In one moment, by night, three of my best officers, with fifteen sailors, were lost, with the main-yard; the spar snapping under them in the slings, as they sought, with heavers,[2] to beat down the icy sail. To lighten the hull, the heavier sacks of mata were thrown into the sea, with most of the water-pipes[3] lashed on deck at the time. And this last necessity it was, combined with the prolonged detentions[4] afterwards experienced, which eventually brought about our chief causes of suffering. When—"

Here there was a sudden fainting attack of his cough, brought on, no doubt, by his mental distress. His servant sustained him, and drawing a cordial from his pocket placed it to his lips. He a little revived. But

---

[1] *Paraguay tea* I.e., yerba mate, a major export from Paraguay in the nineteenth century.

[2] *slings* Middle part of a yard; *heavers* Wooden bars used to tighten ropes.

[3] *mata* I.e., the yerba mate; *water-pipes* Barrels of drinking water.

[4] *detentions* Periods of being delayed (in this case, becalmed).

unwilling to leave him unsupported while yet imperfectly restored, the black with one arm still encircled his master, at the same time keeping his eye fixed on his face, as if to watch for the first sign of complete restoration, or relapse, as the event might prove.

The Spaniard proceeded, but brokenly and obscurely, as one in a dream.

—"Oh, my God! rather than pass through what I have, with joy I would have hailed the most terrible gales; but—"

His cough returned and with increased violence; this subsiding; with reddened lips and closed eyes he fell heavily against his supporter.

"His mind wanders. He was thinking of the plague that followed the gales," plaintively sighed the servant; "my poor, poor master!" wringing one hand, and with the other wiping the mouth. "But be patient, Señor," again turning to Captain Delano, "these fits do not last long; master will soon be himself."

Don Benito reviving, went on; but as this portion of the story was very brokenly delivered, the substance only will here be set down.

It appeared that after the ship had been many days tossed in storms off the Cape, the scurvy broke out, carrying off numbers of the whites and blacks. When at last they had worked round into the Pacific, their spars and sails were so damaged, and so inadequately handled by the surviving mariners, most of whom were become invalids, that, unable to lay her northerly course by the wind, which was powerful, the unmanageable ship, for successive days and nights, was blown northwestward, where the breeze suddenly deserted her, in unknown waters, to sultry calms. The absence of the water-pipes now proved as fatal to life as before their presence had menaced it. Induced, or at least aggravated, by the more than scanty allowance of water, a malignant fever followed the scurvy; with the excessive heat of the lengthened calm, making such short work of it as to sweep away, as by billows, whole families of the Africans, and a yet larger number, proportionably, of the Spaniards, including, by a luckless fatality, every remaining officer on board. Consequently, in the smart west winds eventually following the calm, the already rent sails, having to be simply dropped, not furled, at need, had been gradually reduced to the beggars' rags they were now. To procure substitutes for

his lost sailors, as well as supplies of water and sails, the captain, at the earliest opportunity, had made for Baldivia, the southernmost civilized port of Chili and South America; but upon nearing the coast the thick weather had prevented him from so much as sighting that harbor. Since which period, almost without a crew, and almost without canvas and almost without water, and, at intervals giving its added dead to the sea, the San Dominick had been battle-dored[1] about by contrary winds, inveigled by currents, or grown weedy in calms. Like a man lost in woods, more than once she had doubled upon her own track.

"But throughout these calamities," huskily continued Don Benito, painfully turning in the half embrace of his servant, "I have to thank those negroes you see, who, though to your inexperienced eyes appearing unruly, have, indeed, conducted themselves with less of restlessness than even their owner could have thought possible under such circumstances."

Here he again fell faintly back. Again his mind wandered; but he rallied, and less obscurely proceeded.

"Yes, their owner was quite right in assuring me that no fetters[2] would be needed with his blacks; so that while, as is wont in this transportation, those negroes have always remained upon deck—not thrust below, as in the Guinea-men[3]—they have, also, from the beginning, been freely permitted to range within given bounds at their pleasure."

Once more the faintness returned—his mind roved—but, recovering, he resumed:

"But it is Babo here to whom, under God, I owe not only my own preservation, but likewise to him, chiefly, the merit is due, of pacifying his more ignorant brethren, when at intervals tempted to murmurings."

"Ah, master," sighed the black, bowing his face, "don't speak of me; Babo is nothing; what Babo has done was but duty."

"Faithful fellow!" cried Captain Delano. "Don Benito, I envy you such a friend; slave I cannot call him."

As master and man stood before him, the black upholding the white, Captain Delano could not but

---

[1]   *battle-dored*   Shunted back and forth like a shuttlecock between battledores (the rackets used in badminton).

[2]   *fetters*   Shackles, restraints.

[3]   *Guinea-men*   Slave ships used in the transatlantic slave trade.

bethink him of the beauty of that relationship which could present such a spectacle of fidelity on the one hand and confidence on the other. The scene was heightened by the contrast in dress, denoting their relative positions. The Spaniard wore a loose Chili jacket of dark velvet; white small-clothes[1] and stockings, with silver buckles at the knee and instep; a high-crowned sombrero, of fine grass; a slender sword, silver mounted, hung from a knot in his sash—the last being an almost invariable adjunct, more for utility than ornament, of a South American gentleman's dress to this hour. Excepting when his occasional nervous contortions brought about disarray, there was a certain precision in his attire curiously at variance with the unsightly disorder around; especially in the belittered Ghetto,[2] forward of the main-mast, wholly occupied by the blacks.

The servant wore nothing but wide trowsers, apparently, from their coarseness and patches, made out of some old topsail; they were clean, and confined at the waist by a bit of unstranded rope, which, with his composed, deprecatory air at times, made him look something like a begging friar of St. Francis.[3]

However unsuitable for the time and place, at least in the blunt-thinking American's eyes, and however strangely surviving in the midst of all his afflictions, the toilette[4] of Don Benito might not, in fashion at least, have gone beyond the style of the day among South Americans of his class. Though on the present voyage sailing from Buenos Ayres, he had avowed himself a native and resident of Chili, whose inhabitants had not so generally adopted the plain coat and once plebeian pantaloons; but, with a becoming modification, adhered to their provincial costume, picturesque as any in the world. Still, relatively to the pale history of the voyage, and his own pale face, there seemed something so incongruous in the Spaniard's apparel, as almost to suggest the image of an invalid courtier tottering about London streets in the time of the plague.

The portion of the narrative which, perhaps, most excited interest, as well as some surprise, considering the latitudes in question, was the long calms spoken of, and more particularly the ship's so long drifting about. Without communicating the opinion, of course, the American could not but impute at least part of the detentions both to clumsy seamanship and faulty navigation. Eying Don Benito's small, yellow hands, he easily inferred that the young captain had not got into command at the hawse-hole, but the cabin-window;[5] and if so, why wonder at incompetence, in youth, sickness, and gentility united?

But drowning criticism in compassion, after a fresh repetition of his sympathies, Captain Delano, having heard out his story, not only engaged, as in the first place, to see Don Benito and his people supplied in their immediate bodily needs, but, also, now farther promised to assist him in procuring a large permanent supply of water, as well as some sails and rigging; and, though it would involve no small embarrassment to himself, yet he would spare three of his best seamen for temporary deck officers; so that without delay the ship might proceed to Conception,[6] there fully to refit for Lima, her destined port.

Such generosity was not without its effect, even upon the invalid. His face lighted up; eager and hectic, he met the honest glance of his visitor. With gratitude he seemed overcome.

"This excitement is bad for master," whispered the servant, taking his arm, and with soothing words gently drawing him aside.

When Don Benito returned, the American was pained to observe that his hopefulness, like the sudden kindling in his cheek, was but febrile[7] and transient.

---

1   *small-clothes*   Knee-breeches.

2   *Ghetto*   Area of the ship likened to a segregated ghetto in a city (in the nineteenth century a "ghetto" referred most often to the Jewish quarter of a European city).

3   *unstranded* Unbroken; *friar of St. Francis* Franciscans are mendicant friars; their iconic habit is a brown woolen robe belted with a white rope, which is knotted three times to remind the wearer of the three central vows of Franciscan life: poverty, chastity, and obedience. The Franciscans and Dominicans were frequent rivals during the Middle Ages.

4   *toilette*   Style of dress.

5   *got into … cabin-window*   I.e., he is a landsman who gained his captaincy through connections rather than through experience at sea. When one "climbs through the hawse-hole" one rises through the ranks from the bottom up (the hawse-hole is one of two small holes that the ship's cable runs through); climbing through the "cabin window," on the other hand, means gaining command of a ship by jumping straight into the captain's cabin (by virtue of one's wealth and connections).

6   *Conception*   Port in south-central Chile.

7   *febrile*   Feverish.

Ere long, with a joyless mien, looking up towards the poop, the host invited his guest to accompany him there, for the benefit of what little breath of wind might be stirring.

As during the telling of the story, Captain Delano had once or twice started at the occasional cymballing of the hatchet-polishers, wondering why such an interruption should be allowed, especially in that part of the ship, and in the ears of an invalid; and moreover, as the hatchets had anything but an attractive look, and the handlers of them still less so, it was, therefore, to tell the truth, not without some lurking reluctance, or even shrinking, it may be, that Captain Delano, with apparent complaisance, acquiesced in his host's invitation. The more so, since, with an untimely caprice of punctilio,[1] rendered distressing by his cadaverous aspect, Don Benito, with Castilian bows, solemnly insisted upon his guest's preceding him up the ladder leading to the elevation; where, one on each side of the last step, sat for armorial supporters and sentries two of the ominous file.[2] Gingerly enough stepped good Captain Delano between them, and in the instant of leaving them behind, like one running the gauntlet, he felt an apprehensive twitch in the calves of his legs.

But when, facing about, he saw the whole file, like so many organ-grinders, still stupidly intent on their work, unmindful of everything beside, he could not but smile at his late fidgety panic.

Presently, while standing with his host, looking forward upon the decks below, he was struck by one of those instances of insubordination previously alluded to. Three black boys, with two Spanish boys, were sitting together on the hatches, scraping a rude wooden platter, in which some scanty mess had recently been cooked. Suddenly, one of the black boys, enraged at a word dropped by one of his white companions, seized a knife, and, though called to forbear by one of the oakum-pickers, struck the lad over the head, inflicting a gash from which blood flowed.

In amazement, Captain Delano inquired what this meant. To which the pale Don Benito dully muttered, that it was merely the sport of the lad.

"Pretty serious sport, truly," rejoined Captain Delano. "Had such a thing happened on board the Bachelor's Delight, instant punishment would have followed."

At these words the Spaniard turned upon the American one of his sudden, staring, half-lunatic looks; then, relapsing into his torpor, answered, "Doubtless, doubtless, Señor."

Is it, thought Captain Delano, that this hapless man is one of those paper captains I've known, who by policy wink at what by power they cannot put down? I know no sadder sight than a commander who has little of command but the name.

"I should think, Don Benito," he now said, glancing towards the oakum-picker who had sought to interfere with the boys, "that you would find it advantageous to keep all your blacks employed, especially the younger ones, no matter at what useless task, and no matter what happens to the ship. Why, even with my little band, I find such a course indispensable. I once kept a crew on my quarter-deck thrumming mats[3] for my cabin, when, for three days, I had given up my ship— mats, men, and all—for a speedy loss, owing to the violence of a gale, in which we could do nothing but helplessly drive before it."

"Doubtless, doubtless," muttered Don Benito.

"But," continued Captain Delano, again glancing upon the oakum-pickers and then at the hatchet-polishers, near by, "I see you keep some, at least, of your host employed."

"Yes," was again the vacant response.

"Those old men there, shaking their pows[4] from their pulpits," continued Captain Delano, pointing to the oakum-pickers, "seem to act the part of old dominies[5] to the rest, little heeded as their admonitions are at times. Is this voluntary on their part, Don Benito, or have you appointed them shepherds to your flock of black sheep?"

"What posts they fill, I appointed them," rejoined the Spaniard, in an acrid tone, as if resenting some supposed satiric reflection.

---

[1] *punctilio* Politeness, adherence to formal etiquette.

[2] *file* Line of workers polishing the hatchets.

[3] *thrumming mats* Sewing rope over mats or sails to create a rough thick surface that could be used to stop leaks.

[4] *pows* Scottish word meaning "heads."

[5] *dominies* Preachers within the Dutch Reformed Church, in which denomination Melville was brought up; alternatively, schoolmasters.

"And these others, these Ashantee[1] conjurors here," continued Captain Delano, rather uneasily eying the brandished steel of the hatchet-polishers, where, in spots, it had been brought to a shine, "this seems a curious business they are at, Don Benito?"

"In the gales we met," answered the Spaniard, "what of our general cargo was not thrown overboard was much damaged by the brine. Since coming into calm weather, I have had several cases of knives and hatchets daily brought up for overhauling and cleaning."

"A prudent idea, Don Benito. You are part owner of ship and cargo, I presume; but none of the slaves, perhaps?"

"I am owner of all you see," impatiently returned Don Benito, "except the main company of blacks, who belonged to my late friend, Alexandro Aranda."

As he mentioned this name, his air was heart-broken; his knees shook; his servant supported him.

Thinking he divined the cause of such unusual emotion, to confirm his surmise, Captain Delano, after a pause, said: "And may I ask, Don Benito, whether—since awhile ago you spoke of some cabin passengers—the friend, whose loss so afflicts you, at the outset of the voyage accompanied his blacks?"

"Yes."

"But died of the fever?"

"Died of the fever. Oh, could I but—"

Again quivering, the Spaniard paused.

"Pardon me," said Captain Delano, lowly, "but I think that, by a sympathetic experience, I conjecture, Don Benito, what it is that gives the keener edge to your grief. It was once my hard fortune to lose, at sea, a dear friend, my own brother, then supercargo.[2] Assured of the welfare of his spirit, its departure I could have borne like a man; but that honest eye, that honest hand—both of which had so often met mine—and that warm heart; all, all—like scraps to the dogs—to throw all to the sharks! It was then I vowed never to have for fellow-voyager a man I loved, unless, unbeknown to him, I had provided every requisite, in case of a fatality, for embalming his mortal part for interment on shore.

Were your friend's remains now on board this ship, Don Benito, not thus strangely would the mention of his name affect you."

"On board this ship?" echoed the Spaniard. Then, with horrified gestures, as directed against some spectre, he unconsciously fell into the ready arms of his attendant, who, with a silent appeal toward Captain Delano, seemed beseeching him not again to broach a theme so unspeakably distressing to his master.

This poor fellow now, thought the pained American, is the victim of that sad superstition which associates goblins with the deserted body of man, as ghosts with an abandoned house. How unlike are we made! What to me, in like case, would have been a solemn satisfaction, the bare suggestion, even, terrifies the Spaniard into this trance. Poor Alexandro Aranda! what would you say could you here see your friend—who, on former voyages, when you, for months, were left behind, has, I dare say, often longed, and longed, for one peep at you—now transported with terror at the least thought of having you anyway nigh him.

At this moment, with a dreary grave-yard toll, betokening a flaw, the ship's forecastle bell, smote by one of the grizzled oakum-pickers, proclaimed ten o'clock, through the leaden calm; when Captain Delano's attention was caught by the moving figure of a gigantic black, emerging from the general crowd below, and slowly advancing towards the elevated poop. An iron collar was about his neck, from which depended a chain, thrice wound round his body; the terminating links padlocked together at a broad band of iron, his girdle.

"How like a mute Atufal moves," murmured the servant.

The black mounted the steps of the poop, and, like a brave prisoner, brought up to receive sentence, stood in unquailing muteness before Don Benito, now recovered from his attack.

At the first glimpse of his approach, Don Benito had started, a resentful shadow swept over his face; and, as with the sudden memory of bootless[3] rage, his white lips glued together.

This is some mulish mutineer, thought Captain Delano, surveying, not without a mixture of admiration, the colossal form of the negro.

---

[1]   *Ashantee*   The Ashanti or Asante people are among the Akan peoples of West Africa. They resisted British colonization and had a reputation for martial prowess in the nineteenth century.

[2]   *supercargo*   A representative of the ship's owner who sails aboard the ship to guard the cargo.

[3]   *bootless*   Unavailing.

"See, he waits your question, master," said the servant.

Thus reminded, Don Benito, nervously averting his glance, as if shunning, by anticipation, some rebellious response, in a disconcerted voice, thus spoke:—

"Atufal, will you ask my pardon, now?"

The black was silent.

"Again, master," murmured the servant, with bitter upbraiding eying his countryman, "Again, master; he will bend to master yet."

"Answer," said Don Benito, still averting his glance, "say but the one word, *pardon*, and your chains shall be off."

Upon this, the black, slowly raising both arms, let them lifelessly fall, his links clanking, his head bowed; as much as to say, "no, I am content."

"Go," said Don Benito, with inkept[1] and unknown emotion.

Deliberately as he had come, the black obeyed.

"Excuse me, Don Benito," said Captain Delano, "but this scene surprises me; what means it, pray?"

"It means that that negro alone, of all the band, has given me peculiar cause of offense. I have put him in chains; I—"

Here he paused; his hand to his head, as if there were a swimming there, or a sudden bewilderment of memory had come over him; but meeting his servant's kindly glance seemed reassured, and proceeded:—

"I could not scourge[2] such a form. But I told him he must ask my pardon. As yet he has not. At my command, every two hours he stands before me."

"And how long has this been?"

"Some sixty days."

"And obedient in all else? And respectful?"

"Yes."

"Upon my conscience, then," exclaimed Captain Delano, impulsively, "he has a royal spirit in him, this fellow."

"He may have some right to it," bitterly returned Don Benito, "he says he was king in his own land."

"Yes," said the servant, entering a word, "those slits in Atufal's ears once held wedges of gold; but poor Babo here, in his own land, was only a poor slave; a black man's slave was Babo, who now is the white's."

Somewhat annoyed by these conversational familiarities, Captain Delano turned curiously upon the attendant, then glanced inquiringly at his master; but, as if long wonted to these little informalities, neither master nor man seemed to understand him.

"What, pray, was Atufal's offense, Don Benito?" asked Captain Delano; "if it was not something very serious, take a fool's advice, and, in view of his general docility, as well as in some natural respect for his spirit, remit him his penalty."

"No, no, master never will do that," here murmured the servant to himself, "proud Atufal must first ask master's pardon. The slave there carries the padlock, but master here carries the key."

His attention thus directed, Captain Delano now noticed for the first,[3] that, suspended by a slender silken cord, from Don Benito's neck, hung a key. At once, from the servant's muttered syllables, divining the key's purpose, he smiled, and said:—"So, Don Benito—padlock and key—significant symbols, truly."

Biting his lip, Don Benito faltered.

Though the remark of Captain Delano, a man of such native simplicity as to be incapable of satire or irony, had been dropped in playful allusion to the Spaniard's singularly evidenced lordship over the black; yet the hypochondriac seemed some way to have taken it as a malicious reflection upon his confessed inability thus far to break down, at least, on a verbal summons, the entrenched will of the slave. Deploring this supposed misconception, yet despairing of correcting it, Captain Delano shifted the subject; but finding his companion more than ever withdrawn, as if still sourly digesting the lees[4] of the presumed affront above-mentioned, by-and-by Captain Delano likewise became less talkative, oppressed, against his own will, by what seemed the secret vindictiveness of the morbidly sensitive Spaniard. But the good sailor, himself of a quite contrary disposition, refrained, on his part, alike from the appearance as from the feeling of resentment, and if silent, was only so from contagion.

---

[1]   *inkept*   Suppressed.

[2]   *scourge*   Whip, torture.

[3]   *the first*   The *Putnam's* edition of "Benito Cereno" reads "for the first time," but the later *Piazza Tales* edition omits the word "time."

[4]   *lees*   Dregs.

Presently the Spaniard, assisted by his servant somewhat discourteously crossed over[1] from his guest; a procedure which, sensibly enough, might have been allowed to pass for idle caprice of ill-humor, had not master and man, lingering round the corner of the elevated skylight, began whispering together in low voices. This was unpleasing. And more; the moody air of the Spaniard, which at times had not been without a sort of valetudinarian[2] stateliness, now seemed anything but dignified; while the menial familiarity of the servant lost its original charm of simple-hearted attachment.

In his embarrassment, the visitor turned his face to the other side of the ship. By so doing, his glance accidentally fell on a young Spanish sailor, a coil of rope in his hand, just stepped from the deck to the first round of the mizzen-rigging.[3] Perhaps the man would not have been particularly noticed, were it not that, during his ascent to one of the yards, he, with a sort of covert intentness, kept his eye fixed on Captain Delano, from whom, presently, it passed, as if by a natural sequence, to the two whisperers.

His own attention thus redirected to that quarter, Captain Delano gave a slight start. From something in Don Benito's manner just then, it seemed as if the visitor had, at least partly, been the subject of the withdrawn consultation going on—a conjecture as little agreeable to the guest as it was little flattering to the host.

The singular alternations of courtesy and ill-breeding in the Spanish captain were unaccountable, except on one of two suppositions—innocent lunacy, or wicked imposture.

But the first idea, though it might naturally have occurred to an indifferent observer, and, in some respect, had not hitherto been wholly a stranger to Captain Delano's mind, yet, now that, in an incipient way, he began to regard the stranger's conduct something in the light of an intentional affront, of course the idea of lunacy was virtually vacated.

But if not a lunatic, what then? Under the circumstances, would a gentleman, nay, any honest boor, act the part now acted by his host? The man was an impostor. Some low-born adventurer, masquerading as an oceanic grandee; yet so ignorant of the first requisites of mere gentlemanhood as to be betrayed into the present remarkable indecorum.

That strange ceremoniousness, too, at other times evinced, seemed not uncharacteristic of one playing a part above his real level. Benito Cereno—Don Benito Cereno—a sounding name. One, too, at that period, not unknown, in the surname, to super-cargoes and sea captains trading along the Spanish Main, as belonging to one of the most enterprising and extensive mercantile families in all those provinces; several members of it having titles; a sort of Castilian Rothschild,[4] with a noble brother, or cousin, in every great trading town of South America. The alleged Don Benito was in early manhood, about twenty-nine or thirty. To assume a sort of roving cadetship in the maritime affairs of such a house, what more likely scheme for a young knave of talent and spirit? But the Spaniard was a pale invalid. Never mind. For even to the degree of simulating mortal disease, the craft of some tricksters had been known to attain. To think that, under the aspect of infantile weakness, the most savage energies might be couched—those velvets of the Spaniard but the silky paw to his fangs.

From no train of thought did these fancies come; not from within, but from without; suddenly, too, and in one throng, like hoar frost; yet as soon to vanish as the mild sun of Captain Delano's good-nature regained its meridian.

Glancing over once more towards his host—whose side-face, revealed above the skylight, was now turned towards him—he was struck by the profile, whose clearness of cut was refined by the thinness, incident to ill-health, as well as ennobled about the chin by the beard. Away with suspicion. He was a true off-shoot of a true hidalgo[5] Cereno.

Relieved by these and other better thoughts, the visitor, lightly humming a tune, now began indifferently pacing the poop, so as not to betray to Don Benito that

---

[1] *discourteously crossed over* Rudely walked away across the poop deck without excusing themselves from the conversation.

[2] *valetudinarian* Invalid.

[3] *mizzen-rigging* Rigging on the smaller mast in the aft (rear) portion of the ship.

[4] *Rothschild* Major European banking family in the nineteenth century.

[5] *hidalgo* Member of the Spanish nobility.

he had at all mistrusted incivility, much less duplicity; for such mistrust would yet be proved illusory, and by the event; though, for the present, the circumstance which had provoked that distrust remained unexplained. But when that little mystery should have been cleared up, Captain Delano thought he might extremely regret it, did he allow Don Benito to become aware that he had indulged in ungenerous surmises. In short, to the Spaniard's black-letter text, it was best, for awhile, to leave open margin.[1]

Presently, his pale face twitching and overcast, the Spaniard, still supported by his attendant, moved over towards his guest, when, with even more than his usual embarrassment, and a strange sort of intriguing intonation in his husky whisper, the following conversation began:—

"Señor, may I ask how long you have lain at this isle?"

"Oh, but a day or two, Don Benito."

"And from what port are you last?"

"Canton."

"And there, Señor, you exchanged your sealskins for teas and silks, I think you said?"

"Yes. Silks, mostly."

"And the balance you took in specie,[2] perhaps?"

Captain Delano, fidgeting a little, answered—

"Yes; some silver; not a very great deal, though."

"Ah—well. May I ask how many men have you, Señor?"

Captain Delano slightly started, but answered—

"About five-and-twenty, all told."

"And at present, Señor, all on board, I suppose?"

"All on board, Don Benito," replied the Captain, now with satisfaction.

"And will be to-night, Señor?"

At this last question, following so many pertinacious[3] ones, for the soul of him Captain Delano could not but look very earnestly at the questioner, who, instead of meeting the glance, with every token of craven discomposure dropped his eyes to the deck; presenting

an unworthy contrast to his servant, who, just then, was kneeling at his feet, adjusting a loose shoe-buckle; his disengaged face meantime, with humble curiosity, turned openly up into his master's downcast one.

The Spaniard, still with a guilty shuffle, repeated his question:

"And—and will be to-night, Señor?"

"Yes, for aught I know," returned Captain Delano— "but nay," rallying himself into fearless truth, "some of them talked of going off on another fishing party about midnight."

"Your ships generally go—go more or less armed, I believe, Señor?"

"Oh, a six-pounder[4] or two, in case of emergency," was the intrepidly indifferent reply, "with a small stock of muskets, sealing-spears, and cutlasses, you know."

As he thus responded, Captain Delano again glanced at Don Benito, but the latter's eyes were averted; while abruptly and awkwardly shifting the subject, he made some peevish allusion to the calm, and then, without apology, once more, with his attendant, withdrew to the opposite bulwarks, where the whispering was resumed.

At this moment, and ere Captain Delano could cast a cool thought upon what had just passed, the young Spanish sailor, before mentioned, was seen descending from the rigging. In act of stooping over to spring inboard to the deck, his voluminous, unconfined frock, or shirt, of coarse woolen, much spotted with tar, opened out far down the chest, revealing a soiled under garment of what seemed the finest linen, edged, about the neck, with a narrow blue ribbon, sadly faded and worn. At this moment the young sailor's eye was again fixed on the whisperers, and Captain Delano thought he observed a lurking significance in it, as if silent signs, of some Freemason sort, had that instant been interchanged.

This once more impelled his own glance in the direction of Don Benito, and, as before, he could not but infer that himself formed the subject of the conference. He paused. The sound of the hatchet-polishing fell on his ears. He cast another swift side-look at the two. They had the air of conspirators. In connection with the late questionings, and the incident of the young sailor, these things now begat such return of

---

1   *black-letter text … open margin* A black-letter text is a heavy Gothic typeface. To leave open margin is to leave space for more text to be added to a page—i.e., Captain Delano is leaving space for Cereno to redeem his rude behavior.

2   *specie* Coins (currency).

3   *pertinacious* Annoyingly persistent.

4   *six-pounder* Cannon that shoots balls weighing six pounds.

involuntary suspicion, that the singular guilelessness of the American could not endure it. Plucking up a gay and humorous expression, he crossed over to the two rapidly, saying:—"Ha, Don Benito, your black here seems high in your trust; a sort of privy-counselor, in fact."

Upon this, the servant looked up with a good-natured grin, but the master started as from a venomous bite. It was a moment or two before the Spaniard sufficiently recovered himself to reply; which he did, at last, with cold constraint:—"Yes, Señor, I have trust in Babo."

Here Babo, changing his previous grin of mere animal humor into an intelligent smile, not ungratefully eyed his master.

Finding that the Spaniard now stood silent and reserved, as if involuntarily, or purposely giving hint that his guest's proximity was inconvenient just then, Captain Delano, unwilling to appear uncivil even to incivility itself, made some trivial remark and moved off; again and again turning over in his mind the mysterious demeanor of Don Benito Cereno.

He had descended from the poop, and, wrapped in thought, was passing near a dark hatchway, leading down into the steerage, when, perceiving motion there, he looked to see what moved. The same instant there was a sparkle in the shadowy hatchway, and he saw one of the Spanish sailors, prowling there hurriedly placing his hand in the bosom of his frock, as if hiding something. Before the man could have been certain who it was that was passing, he slunk below out of sight. But enough was seen of him to make it sure that he was the same young sailor before noticed in the rigging.

What was that which so sparkled? thought Captain Delano. It was no lamp—no match—no live coal. Could it have been a jewel? But how come sailors with jewels?—or with silk-trimmed under-shirts either? Has he been robbing the trunks of the dead cabin-passengers? But if so, he would hardly wear one of the stolen articles on board ship here. Ah, ah—if, now, that was, indeed, a secret sign I saw passing between this suspicious fellow and his captain awhile since; if I could only be certain that, in my uneasiness, my senses did not deceive me, then—

Here, passing from one suspicious thing to another, his mind revolved the strange questions put to him concerning his ship.

By a curious coincidence, as each point was recalled, the black wizards of Ashantee would strike up with their hatchets, as in ominous comment on the white stranger's thoughts. Pressed by such enigmas and portents, it would have been almost against nature, had not, even into the least distrustful heart, some ugly misgivings obtruded.

Observing the ship, now helplessly fallen into a current, with enchanted sails, drifting with increased rapidity seaward; and noting that, from a lately intercepted projection of the land, the sealer was hidden, the stout mariner began to quake at thoughts which he barely durst confess to himself. Above all, he began to feel a ghostly dread of Don Benito. And yet, when he roused himself, dilated his chest, felt himself strong on his legs, and coolly considered it—what did all these phantoms amount to?

Had the Spaniard any sinister scheme, it must have reference not so much to him (Captain Delano) as to his ship (the Bachelor's Delight). Hence the present drifting away of the one ship from the other, instead of favoring any such possible scheme, was, for the time, at least, opposed to it. Clearly any suspicion, combining such contradictions, must need be delusive. Beside, was it not absurd to think of a vessel in distress—a vessel by sickness almost dismanned of her crew—a vessel whose inmates were parched for water—was it not a thousand times absurd that such a craft should, at present, be of a piratical character; or her commander, either for himself or those under him, cherish any desire but for speedy relief and refreshment? But then, might not general distress, and thirst in particular, be affected? And might not that same undiminished Spanish crew, alleged to have perished off to a remnant, be at that very moment lurking in the hold? On heart-broken pretense of entreating a cup of cold water, fiends in human form had got into lonely dwellings, nor retired until a dark deed had been done. And among the Malay pirates,[1] it was no unusual thing to lure ships after them into their treacherous harbors, or

---

[1] *Malay pirates* Piracy in the Straight of Malacca (between the Malay Peninsula and the island of Sumatra) was particularly prevalent in the eighteenth and nineteenth centuries.

entice boarders from a declared enemy at sea, by the spectacle of thinly manned or vacant decks, beneath which prowled a hundred spears with yellow arms ready to upthrust them through the mats. Not that Captain Delano had entirely credited such things. He had heard of them—and now, as stories, they recurred. The present destination of the ship was the anchorage. There she would be near his own vessel. Upon gaining that vicinity, might not the San Dominick, like a slumbering volcano, suddenly let loose energies now hid?

He recalled the Spaniard's manner while telling his story. There was a gloomy hesitancy and subterfuge about it. It was just the manner of one making up his tale for evil purposes, as he goes. But if that story was not true, what was the truth? That the ship had unlawfully come into the Spaniard's possession? But in many of its details, especially in reference to the more calamitous parts, such as the fatalities among the seamen, the consequent prolonged beating about, the past sufferings from obstinate calms, and still continued suffering from thirst; in all these points, as well as others, Don Benito's story had corroborated not only the wailing ejaculations of the indiscriminate multitude, white and black, but likewise—what seemed impossible to be counterfeit—by the very expression and play of every human feature, which Captain Delano saw. If Don Benito's story was, throughout, an invention, then every soul on board, down to the youngest negress, was his carefully drilled recruit in the plot: an incredible inference. And yet, if there was ground for mistrusting his veracity, that inference was a legitimate one.

But those questions of the Spaniard. There, indeed, one might pause. Did they not seem put with much the same object with which the burglar or assassin, by day-time, reconnoitres the walls of a house? But, with ill purposes, to solicit such information openly of the chief person endangered, and so, in effect, setting him on his guard; how unlikely a procedure was that? Absurd, then, to suppose that those questions had been prompted by evil designs. Thus, the same conduct, which, in this instance, had raised the alarm, served to dispel it. In short, scarce any suspicion or uneasiness, however apparently reasonable at the time, which was not now, with equal apparent reason, dismissed.

At last he began to laugh at his former forebodings; and laugh at the strange ship for, in its aspect, someway siding with them, as it were; and laugh, too, at the odd-looking blacks, particularly those old scissors-grinders, the Ashantees; and those bed-ridden old knitting women, the oakum-pickers; and almost at the dark Spaniard himself, the central hobgoblin of all.

For the rest, whatever in a serious way seemed enigmatical, was now good-naturedly explained away by the thought that, for the most part, the poor invalid scarcely knew what he was about; either sulking in black vapors, or putting idle questions without sense or object. Evidently for the present, the man was not fit to be intrusted with the ship. On some benevolent plea withdrawing the command from him, Captain Delano would yet have to send her to Conception, in charge of his second mate, a worthy person and good navigator—a plan not more convenient for the San Dominick than for Don Benito; for, relieved from all anxiety, keeping wholly to his cabin, the sick man, under the good nursing of his servant, would, probably, by the end of the passage, be in a measure restored to health, and with that he should also be restored to authority.

Such were the American's thoughts. They were tranquilizing. There was a difference between the idea of Don Benito's darkly pre-ordaining Captain Delano's fate, and Captain Delano's lightly arranging Don Benito's. Nevertheless, it was not without something of relief that the good seaman presently perceived his whale-boat in the distance. Its absence had been prolonged by unexpected detention at the sealer's side, as well as its returning trip lengthened by the continual recession of the goal.

The advancing speck was observed by the blacks. Their shouts attracted the attention of Don Benito, who, with a return of courtesy, approaching Captain Delano, expressed satisfaction at the coming of some supplies, slight and temporary as they must necessarily prove.

Captain Delano responded; but while doing so, his attention was drawn to something passing on the deck below: among the crowd climbing the landward bulwarks, anxiously watching the coming boat, two blacks, to all appearances accidentally incommoded by one of the sailors, violently pushed him aside, which the sailor someway resenting, they dashed him to the deck, despite the earnest cries of the oakum-pickers.

"Don Benito," said Captain Delano quickly, "do you see what is going on there? Look!"

But, seized by his cough, the Spaniard staggered, with both hands to his face, on the point of falling. Captain Delano would have supported him, but the servant was more alert, who, with one hand sustaining his master, with the other applied the cordial. Don Benito restored, the black withdrew his support, slipping aside a little, but dutifully remaining within call of a whisper. Such discretion was here evinced as quite wiped away, in the visitor's eyes, any blemish of impropriety which might have attached to the attendant, from the indecorous conferences before mentioned; showing, too, that if the servant were to blame, it might be more the master's fault than his own, since, when left to himself, he could conduct thus well.

His glance called away from the spectacle of disorder to the more pleasing one before him, Captain Delano could not avoid again congratulating his host upon possessing such a servant, who, though perhaps a little too forward now and then, must upon the whole be invaluable to one in the invalid's situation.

"Tell me, Don Benito," he added, with a smile— "I should like to have your man here, myself—what will you take for him? Would fifty doubloons be any object?"

"Master wouldn't part with Babo for a thousand doubloons," murmured the black, overhearing the offer, and taking it in earnest, and, with the strange vanity of a faithful slave, appreciated by his master, scorning to hear so paltry a valuation put upon him by a stranger. But Don Benito, apparently hardly yet completely restored, and again interrupted by his cough, made but some broken reply.

Soon his physical distress became so great, affecting his mind, too, apparently, that, as if to screen the sad spectacle, the servant gently conducted his master below.

Left to himself, the American, to while away the time till his boat should arrive, would have pleasantly accosted some one of the few Spanish seamen he saw; but recalling something that Don Benito had said touching their ill conduct, he refrained; as a shipmaster indisposed to countenance cowardice or unfaithfulness in seamen.

While, with these thoughts, standing with eye directed forward towards that handful of sailors, suddenly he thought that one or two of them returned the glance and with a sort of meaning. He rubbed his eyes, and looked again; but again seemed to see the same thing. Under a new form, but more obscure than any previous one, the old suspicions recurred, but, in the absence of Don Benito, with less of panic than before. Despite the bad account given of the sailors, Captain Delano resolved forthwith to accost one of them. Descending the poop, he made his way through the blacks, his movement drawing a queer cry from the oakum-pickers, prompted by whom, the negroes, twitching each other aside, divided before him; but, as if curious to see what was the object of this deliberate visit to their Ghetto, closing in behind, in tolerable order, followed the white stranger up. His progress thus proclaimed as by mounted kings-at-arms, and escorted as by a Caffre[1] guard of honor, Captain Delano, assuming a good-humored, off-handed air, continued to advance; now and then saying a blithe word to the negroes, and his eye curiously surveying the white faces, here and there sparsely mixed in with the blacks, like stray white pawns venturously involved in the ranks of the chess-men opposed.

While thinking which of them to select for his purpose, he chanced to observe a sailor seated on the deck engaged in tarring the strap of a large block, a circle of blacks squatted round him inquisitively eying the process.

The mean employment of the man was in contrast with something superior in his figure. His hand, black with continually thrusting it into the tar-pot held for him by a negro, seemed not naturally allied to his face, a face which would have been a very fine one but for its haggardness. Whether this haggardness had aught to do with criminality, could not be determined; since, as intense heat and cold, though unlike, produce like sensations, so innocence and guilt, when, through casual association with mental pain, stamping any visible impress, use one seal—a hacked one.

---

1   *Caffre*   Variant on caffer or kaffir, a racial slur usually applied to a black person from southern Africa. Since the mid-twentieth century, this term has been considered highly offensive (and in South Africa its use is legally actionable).

Not again that this reflection occurred to Captain Delano at the time, charitable man as he was. Rather another idea. Because observing so singular a haggardness combined with a dark eye, averted as in trouble and shame, and then again recalling Don Benito's confessed ill opinion of his crew, insensibly he was operated upon by certain general notions which, while disconnecting pain and abashment from virtue, invariably link them with vice.

If, indeed, there be any wickedness on board this ship, thought Captain Delano, be sure that man there has fouled his hand in it, even as now he fouls it in the pitch. I don't like to accost him. I will speak to this other, this old Jack here on the windlass.[1]

He advanced to an old Barcelona tar,[2] in ragged red breeches and dirty night-cap, cheeks trenched and bronzed, whiskers dense as thorn hedges. Seated between two sleepy-looking Africans, this mariner, like his younger shipmate, was employed upon some rigging—splicing a cable—the sleepy-looking blacks performing the inferior function of holding the outer parts of the ropes for him.

Upon Captain Delano's approach, the man at once hung his head below its previous level; the one necessary for business. It appeared as if he desired to be thought absorbed, with more than common fidelity, in his task. Being addressed, he glanced up, but with what seemed a furtive, diffident air, which sat strangely enough on his weather-beaten visage, much as if a grizzly bear, instead of growling and biting, should simper and cast sheep's eyes. He was asked several questions concerning the voyage—questions purposely referring to several particulars in Don Benito's narrative, not previously corroborated by those impulsive cries greeting the visitor on first coming on board. The questions were briefly answered, confirming all that remained to be confirmed of the story. The negroes about the windlass joined in with the old sailor; but, as they became talkative, he by degrees became mute, and at length quite glum, seemed morosely unwilling to answer more questions, and yet, all the while, this ursine[3] air was somehow mixed with his sheepish one.

Despairing of getting into unembarrassed talk with such a centaur,[4] Captain Delano, after glancing round for a more promising countenance, but seeing none, spoke pleasantly to the blacks to make way for him; and so, amid various grins and grimaces, returned to the poop, feeling a little strange at first, he could hardly tell why, but upon the whole with regained confidence in Benito Cereno.

How plainly, thought he, did that old whiskerando yonder betray a consciousness of ill desert.[5] No doubt, when he saw me coming, he dreaded lest I, apprised by his Captain of the crew's general misbehavior, came with sharp words for him, and so down with his head. And yet—and yet, now that I think of it, that very old fellow, if I err not, was one of those who seemed so earnestly eying me here awhile since. Ah, these currents spin one's head round almost as much as they do the ship. Ha, there now's a pleasant sort of sunny sight; quite sociable, too.

His attention had been drawn to a slumbering negress, partly disclosed through the lacework of some rigging, lying, with youthful limbs carelessly disposed, under the lee of the bulwarks, like a doe in the shade of a woodland rock. Sprawling at her lapped breasts, was her wide-awake fawn, stark naked, its black little body half lifted from the deck, crosswise with its dam's; its hands, like two paws, clambering upon her; its mouth and nose ineffectually rooting to get at the mark; and meantime giving a vexatious half-grunt, blending with the composed snore of the negress.

The uncommon vigor of the child at length roused the mother. She started up, at a distance facing Captain Delano. But as if not at all concerned at the attitude in which she had been caught, delightedly she caught the child up, with maternal transports, covering it with kisses.

There's naked nature, now; pure tenderness and love, thought Captain Delano, well pleased.

This incident prompted him to remark the other negresses more particularly than before. He was gratified with their manners: like most uncivilized women, they seemed at once tender of heart and tough of constitution; equally ready to die for their infants or fight

---

1   *windlass* An instrument—a roller on supports—used on a ship to wind rope or chain (for example to haul an anchor up and down).

2   *tar* Sailor.

3   *ursine* Bear-like.

4   *centaur* Hybrid creature; in Greek mythology, centaurs were half-human, half-horse.

5   *desert* Merit.

for them. Unsophisticated as leopardesses; loving as doves. Ah! thought Captain Delano, these, perhaps, are some of the very women whom Ledyard[1] saw in Africa, and gave such a noble account of.

These natural sights somehow insensibly deepened his confidence and ease. At last he looked to see how his boat was getting on; but it was still pretty remote. He turned to see if Don Benito had returned; but he had not.

To change the scene, as well as to please himself with a leisurely observation of the coming boat, stepping over into the mizzen-chains,[2] he clambered his way into the starboard quarter-gallery—one of those abandoned Venetian-looking water-balconies[3] previously mentioned—retreats cut off from the deck. As his foot pressed the half-damp, half-dry sea-mosses matting the place, and a chance phantom cats-paw[4]—an islet of breeze, unheralded, unfollowed—as this ghostly cats-paw came fanning his cheek; as his glance fell upon the row of small, round dead-lights—all closed like coppered eyes of the coffined—and the state-cabin door, once connecting with the gallery, even as the dead-lights had once looked out upon it, but now calked fast like a sarcophagus[5] lid; and to a purple-black tarred-over, panel, threshold, and post; and he bethought him of the time, when that state-cabin and this state-balcony had heard the voices of the Spanish king's officers, and the forms of the Lima viceroy's daughters had perhaps leaned where he stood—as these and other images flitted through his mind, as the cats-paw through the calm, gradually he felt rising a dreamy inquietude, like that of one who alone on the prairie feels unrest from the repose of the noon.

He leaned against the carved balustrade, again looking off toward his boat; but found his eye falling upon the ribbon grass, trailing along the ship's water-line, straight as a border of green box;[6] and parterres of seaweed, broad ovals and crescents, floating nigh and far, with what seemed long formal alleys between, crossing the terraces of swells, and sweeping round as if leading to the grottoes below. And overhanging all was the balustrade by his arm, which, partly stained with pitch and partly embossed with moss, seemed the charred ruin of some summer-house in a grand garden long running to waste.

Trying to break one charm, he was but becharmed anew. Though upon the wide sea, he seemed in some far inland country; prisoner in some deserted château, left to stare at empty grounds, and peer out at vague roads, where never wagon or wayfarer passed.

But these enchantments were a little disenchanted as his eye fell on the corroded main-chains. Of an ancient style, massy and rusty in link, shackle and bolt, they seemed even more fit for the ship's present business than the one for which she had been built.

Presently he thought something moved nigh the chains. He rubbed his eyes, and looked hard. Groves of rigging were about the chains; and there, peering from behind a great stay, like an Indian from behind a hemlock, a Spanish sailor, a marlingspike[7] in his hand, was seen, who made what seemed an imperfect gesture towards the balcony, but immediately as if alarmed by some advancing step along the deck within, vanished into the recesses of the hempen forest, like a poacher.

What meant this? Something the man had sought to communicate, unbeknown to any one, even to his captain. Did the secret involve aught unfavorable to his captain? Were those previous misgivings of Captain Delano's about to be verified? Or, in his haunted mood at the moment, had some random, unintentional motion of the man, while busy with the stay, as if repairing it, been mistaken for a significant beckoning?

Not unbewildered, again he gazed off for his boat. But it was temporarily hidden by a rocky spur of the isle. As with some eagerness he bent forward, watching for the first shooting view of its beak, the balustrade gave way before him like charcoal. Had he not clutched an outreaching rope he would have fallen into the sea.

---

[1] *Ledyard* American explorer John Ledyard (1751–89). In the *Putnam*'s publication of *Benito Cereno*, Melville mentions the Scottish explorer Mungo Park (1771–1806) here instead, who led more extensive explorations into West Africa.

[2] *mizzen-chains* Set of chains used to work the mizzen-sail (attached to the mizzen-mast, which is located to the rear of the main mast).

[3] *water-balconies* Balconies in Venice overlook canals, as these do the sea. Balconies in Venice were also often used as settings in popular nineteenth-century Gothic tales.

[4] *cats-paw* Wind that slightly and momentarily ruffles the sea.

[5] *sarcophagus* Ancient stone coffin.

[6] *box* I.e., box-hedges.

[7] *marlingspike* Tool used in when splicing rope (to separate the strands).

The crash, though feeble, and the fall, though hollow, of the rotten fragments, must have been overheard. He glanced up. With sober curiosity peering down upon him was one of the old oakum-pickers, slipped from his perch to an outside boom; while below the old negro, and, invisible to him, reconnoitering from a port-hole like a fox from the mouth of its den, crouched the Spanish sailor again. From something suddenly suggested by the man's air, the mad idea now darted into Captain Delano's mind, that Don Benito's plea of indisposition, in withdrawing below, was but a pretense: that he was engaged there maturing his plot, of which the sailor, by some means gaining an inkling, had a mind to warn the stranger against; incited, it may be, by gratitude for a kind word on first boarding the ship. Was it from foreseeing some possible interference like this, that Don Benito had, beforehand, given such a bad character of his sailors, while praising the negroes; though, indeed, the former seemed as docile as the latter the contrary? The whites, too, by nature, were the shrewder race. A man with some evil design, would he not be likely to speak well of that stupidity which was blind to his depravity, and malign that intelligence from which it might not be hidden? Not unlikely, perhaps. But if the whites had dark secrets concerning Don Benito, could then Don Benito be any way in complicity with the blacks? But they were too stupid. Besides, who ever heard of a white so far a renegade as to apostatize from his very species almost, by leaguing in against it with negroes? These difficulties recalled former ones. Lost in their mazes, Captain Delano, who had now regained the deck, was uneasily advancing along it, when he observed a new face; an aged sailor seated cross-legged near the main hatchway. His skin was shrunk up with wrinkles like a pelican's empty pouch; his hair frosted; his countenance grave and composed. His hands were full of ropes, which he was working into a large knot. Some blacks were about him obligingly dipping the strands for him, here and there, as the exigencies of the operation demanded.

Captain Delano crossed over to him, and stood in silence surveying the knot; his mind, by a not uncongenial transition, passing from its own entanglements to those of the hemp. For intricacy, such a knot he had never seen in an American ship, nor indeed any other. The old man looked like an Egyptian priest, making Gordian knots for the temple of Ammon.[1] The knot seemed a combination of double-bowline-knot, treble-crown-knot, back-handed-well-knot, knot-in-and-out-knot, and jamming-knot.

At last, puzzled to comprehend the meaning of such a knot, Captain Delano addressed the knotter:—

"What are you knotting there, my man?"

"The knot," was the brief reply, without looking up.

"So it seems; but what is it for?"

"For some one else to undo," muttered back the old man, plying his fingers harder than ever, the knot being now nearly completed.

While Captain Delano stood watching him, suddenly the old man threw the knot towards him, saying in broken English—the first heard in the ship—something to this effect: "Undo it, cut it, quick." It was said lowly, but with such condensation of rapidity, that the long, slow words in Spanish, which had preceded and followed, almost operated as covers to the brief English between.

For a moment, knot in hand, and knot in head, Captain Delano stood mute; while, without further heeding him, the old man was now intent upon other ropes. Presently there was a slight stir behind Captain Delano. Turning, he saw the chained negro, Atufal, standing quietly there. The next moment the old sailor rose, muttering, and, followed by his subordinate negroes, removed to the forward part of the ship, where in the crowd he disappeared.

An elderly negro, in a clout[2] like an infant's, and with a pepper and salt head, and a kind of attorney air, now approached Captain Delano. In tolerable Spanish, and with a good-natured, knowing wink, he informed him that the old knotter was simple-witted, but harmless; often playing his odd tricks. The negro concluded by begging the knot, for of course the stranger would not care to be troubled with it. Unconsciously, it was handed to him. With a sort of congé,[3] the negro received it, and, turning his back, ferreted into it like a detective custom-house officer after smuggled laces. Soon, with some African word, equivalent to pshaw, he tossed the knot overboard.

---

[1]   *Gordian knots*   Knots too complex to be untangled, but they can be cut;   *Ammon*   Amun-Ra, chief Egyptian deity.

[2]   *clout*   Scrap of clothing.

[3]   *congé*   Ceremonious departure.

All this is very queer now, thought Captain Delano, with a qualmish sort of emotion; but, as one feeling incipient sea-sickness, he strove, by ignoring the symptoms, to get rid of the malady. Once more he looked off for his boat. To his delight, it was now again in view, leaving the rocky spur astern.

The sensation here experienced, after at first relieving his uneasiness, with unforeseen efficacy soon began to remove it. The less distant sight of that well-known boat—showing it, not as before, half blended with the haze, but with outline defined, so that its individuality, like a man's, was manifest; that boat, Rover by name, which, though now in strange seas, had often pressed the beach of Captain Delano's home, and, brought to its threshold for repairs, had familiarly lain there, as a Newfoundland dog; the sight of that household boat evoked a thousand trustful associations, which, contrasted with previous suspicions, filled him not only with lightsome confidence, but somehow with half humorous self-reproaches at his former lack of it.

"What, I, Amasa Delano—Jack of the Beach, as they called me when a lad—I, Amasa; the same that, duck-satchel in hand, used to paddle along the water-side to the school-house made from the old hulk[1]—I, little Jack of the Beach, that used to go berrying with cousin Nat and the rest; I to be murdered here at the ends of the earth, on board a haunted pirate-ship by a horrible Spaniard? Too nonsensical to think of! Who would murder Amasa Delano? His conscience is clean. There is some one above. Fie, fie, Jack of the Beach! you are a child indeed; a child of the second childhood, old boy; you are beginning to dote and drule,[2] I'm afraid."

Light of heart and foot, he stepped aft, and there was met by Don Benito's servant, who, with a pleasing expression, responsive to his own present feelings, informed him that his master had recovered from the effects of his coughing fit, and had just ordered him to go present his compliments to his good guest, Don Amasa, and say that he (Don Benito) would soon have the happiness to rejoin him.

There now, do you mark that? again thought Captain Delano, walking the poop. What a donkey I was. This kind gentleman who here sends me his kind compliments, he, but ten minutes ago, dark-lantern in hand, was dodging round some old grind-stone in the hold, sharpening a hatchet for me, I thought. Well, well; these long calms have a morbid effect on the mind, I've often heard, though I never believed it before. Ha! Glancing towards the boat; there's Rover; good dog; a white bone in her mouth. A pretty big bone though, seems to me.—What? Yes, she has fallen afoul of the bubbling tide-rip there. It sets her the other way, too, for the time. Patience.

It was now about noon, though, from the grayness of everything, it seemed to be getting towards dusk.

The calm was confirmed. In the far distance, away from the influence of land, the leaden ocean seemed laid out and leaded up, its course finished, soul gone, defunct. But the current from landward, where the ship was, increased; silently sweeping her further and further towards the tranced waters beyond.

Still, from his knowledge of those latitudes, cherishing hopes of a breeze, and a fair and fresh one, at any moment, Captain Delano, despite present prospects, buoyantly counted upon bringing the San Dominick safely to anchor ere night. The distance swept over was nothing; since, with a good wind, ten minutes' sailing would retrace more than sixty minutes, drifting. Meantime, one moment turning to mark "Rover" fighting the tide-rip, and the next to see Don Benito approaching, he continued walking the poop.

Gradually he felt a vexation arising from the delay of his boat; this soon merged into uneasiness; and at last—his eye falling continually, as from a stage-box into the pit, upon the strange crowd before and below him, and, by-and-by, recognizing there the face—now composed to indifference—of the Spanish sailor who had seemed to beckon from the main-chains—something of his old trepidations returned.

Ah, thought he—gravely enough—this is like the ague:[3] because it went off, it follows not that it won't come back.

Though ashamed of the relapse, he could not altogether subdue it; and so, exerting his good-nature to the utmost, insensibly he came to a compromise.

---

1 *duck-satchel* Bag made of linen canvas ("duck canvas"), a thick, heavy cotton. Sailors often had a bag made of this material to move personal items from ship to shore; *hulk* Dismantled ship that is still afloat but put to other uses (in this case as a school-house).

2 *drule* I.e., drool.

3 *ague* Fever.

Yes, this is a strange craft; a strange history, too, and strange folks on board. But—nothing more.

By way of keeping his mind out of mischief till the boat should arrive, he tried to occupy it with turning over and over, in a purely speculative sort of way, some lesser peculiarities of the captain and crew. Among others, four curious points recurred:

First, the affair of the Spanish lad assailed with a knife by the slave boy; an act winked at by Don Benito. Second, the tyranny in Don Benito's treatment of Atufal, the black; as if a child should lead a bull of the Nile[1] by the ring in his nose. Third, the trampling of the sailor by the two negroes; a piece of insolence passed over without so much as a reprimand. Fourth, the cringing submission to their master, of all the ship's underlings, mostly blacks; as if by the least inadvertence they feared to draw down his despotic displeasure.

Coupling these points, they seemed somewhat contradictory. But what then, thought Captain Delano, glancing towards his now nearing boat—what then? Why, Don Benito is a very capricious commander. But he is not the first of the sort I have seen; though it's true he rather exceeds any other. But as a nation—continued he in his reveries—these Spaniards are all an odd set; the very word Spaniard has a curious, conspirator, Guy-Fawkish[2] twang to it. And yet, I dare say, Spaniards in the main are as good folks as any in Duxbury, Massachusetts. Ah good! At last "Rover" has come.

As, with its welcome freight, the boat touched the side, the oakum-pickers, with venerable gestures, sought to restrain the blacks, who, at the sight of three gurried[3] water-casks in its bottom, and a pile of wilted pumpkins in its bow, hung over the bulwarks in disorderly raptures.

Don Benito, with his servant, now appeared; his coming, perhaps, hastened by hearing the noise. Of him Captain Delano sought permission to serve out the water, so that all might share alike, and none injure themselves by unfair excess. But sensible, and, on Don Benito's account, kind as this offer was, it was received with what seemed impatience; as if aware that he lacked energy as a commander, Don Benito, with the true jealousy of weakness, resented as an affront any interference. So, at least, Captain Delano inferred.

In another moment the casks were being hoisted in, when some of the eager negroes accidentally jostled Captain Delano, where he stood by the gangway; so that, unmindful of Don Benito, yielding to the impulse of the moment, with good-natured authority he bade the blacks stand back; to enforce his words making use of a half-mirthful, half-menacing gesture. Instantly the blacks paused, just where they were, each negro and negress suspended in his or her posture, exactly as the word had found them—for a few seconds continuing so—while, as between the responsive posts of a telegraph, an unknown syllable ran from man to man among the perched oakum-pickers. While the visitor's attention was fixed by this scene, suddenly the hatchet-polishers half rose, and a rapid cry came from Don Benito.

Thinking that at the signal of the Spaniard he was about to be massacred, Captain Delano would have sprung for his boat, but paused, as the oakum-pickers, dropping down into the crowd with earnest exclamations, forced every white and every negro back, at the same moment, with gestures friendly and familiar, almost jocose, bidding him, in substance, not be a fool. Simultaneously the hatchet-polishers resumed their seats, quietly as so many tailors, and at once, as if nothing had happened, the work of hoisting in the casks was resumed, whites and blacks singing at the tackle.

Captain Delano glanced towards Don Benito. As he saw his meagre form in the act of recovering itself from reclining in the servant's arms, into which the agitated invalid had fallen, he could not but marvel at the panic by which himself had been surprised, on the darting supposition that such a commander, who, upon a legitimate occasion, so trivial, too, as it now appeared, could lose all self-command, was, with energetic iniquity, going to bring about his murder.

The casks being on deck, Captain Delano was handed a number of jars and cups by one of the steward's aids, who, in the name of his captain, entreated

---

[1] *bull of the Nile* In Ancient Egypt, sacred bulls were worshipped as manifestations of the god Apis.

[2] *Guy-Fawkish* Guy Fawkes (1570–1606) was a leader of the Gunpowder Plot of 1605, which aimed to blow up Parliament and restore Catholicism in England. Fawkes also fought in the Spanish army during the Eighty Years' War against the Protestant Dutch.

[3] *gurried* Slimed with fish waste.

him to do as he had proposed—dole out the water. He complied, with republican impartiality as to this republican element, which always seeks one level, serving the oldest white no better than the youngest black; excepting, indeed, poor Don Benito, whose condition, if not rank, demanded an extra allowance. To him, in the first place, Captain Delano presented a fair pitcher of the fluid; but, thirsting as he was for it, the Spaniard quaffed not a drop until after several grave bows and salutes. A reciprocation of courtesies which the sight-loving Africans hailed with clapping of hands.

Two of the less wilted pumpkins being reserved for the cabin table, the residue were minced up on the spot for the general regalement. But the soft bread, sugar, and bottled cider, Captain Delano would have given the whites alone, and in chief Don Benito; but the latter objected; which disinterestedness not a little pleased the American; and so mouthfuls all around were given alike to whites and blacks; excepting one bottle of cider, which Babo insisted upon setting aside for his master.

Here it may be observed that as, on the first visit of the boat, the American had not permitted his men to board the ship, neither did he now; being unwilling to add to the confusion of the decks.

Not uninfluenced by the peculiar good-humor at present prevailing, and for the time oblivious of any but benevolent thoughts, Captain Delano, who, from recent indications, counted upon a breeze within an hour or two at furthest, dispatched the boat back to the sealer, with orders for all the hands that could be spared immediately to set about rafting casks to the watering-place and filling them. Likewise he bade word be carried to his chief officer, that if, against present expectation, the ship was not brought to anchor by sunset, he need be under no concern; for as there was to be a full moon that night, he (Captain Delano) would remain on board ready to play the pilot, come the wind soon or late.

As the two Captains stood together, observing the departing boat—the servant, as it happened, having just spied a spot on his master's velvet sleeve, and silently engaged rubbing it out—the American expressed his regrets that the San Dominick had no boats; none, at least, but the unseaworthy old hulk of the long-boat, which, warped as a camel's skeleton in the desert, and almost as bleached, lay pot-wise inverted amidships, one side a little tipped, furnishing a subterraneous sort of den for family groups of the blacks, mostly women and small children; who, squatting on old mats below, or perched above in the dark dome, on the elevated seats, were descried, some distance within, like a social circle of bats, sheltering in some friendly cave; at intervals, ebon[1] flights of naked boys and girls, three or four years old, darting in and out of the den's mouth.

"Had you three or four boats now, Don Benito," said Captain Delano, "I think that, by tugging at the oars, your negroes here might help along matters some. Did you sail from port without boats, Don Benito?"

"They were stove in the gales, Señor."

"That was bad. Many men, too, you lost then. Boats and men. Those must have been hard gales, Don Benito."

"Past all speech," cringed the Spaniard.

"Tell me, Don Benito," continued his companion with increased interest, "tell me, were these gales immediately off the pitch of Cape Horn?"

"Cape Horn?—who spoke of Cape Horn?"

"Yourself did, when giving me an account of your voyage," answered Captain Delano, with almost equal astonishment at this eating of his own words, even as he ever seemed eating his own heart, on the part of the Spaniard. "You yourself, Don Benito, spoke of Cape Horn," he emphatically repeated.

The Spaniard turned, in a sort of stooping posture, pausing an instant, as one about to make a plunging exchange of elements, as from air to water.

At this moment a messenger-boy, a white, hurried by, in the regular performance of his function carrying the last expired half hour forward to the forecastle, from the cabin time-piece, to have it struck at the ship's large bell.

"Master," said the servant, discontinuing his work on the coat sleeve, and addressing the rapt Spaniard with a sort of timid apprehensiveness, as one charged with a duty, the discharge of which, it was foreseen, would prove irksome to the very person who had imposed it, and for whose benefit it was intended, "master told me never mind where he was, or how engaged, always to remind him to a minute, when shaving-time comes.

---

[1]   *ebon*   Black (like ebony).

Miguel has gone to strike the half-hour afternoon. It is *now*, master. Will master go into the cuddy?"[1]

"Ah—yes," answered the Spaniard, starting, as from dreams into realities; then turning upon Captain Delano, he said that ere long he would resume the conversation.

"Then if master means to talk more to Don Amasa," said the servant, "why not let Don Amasa sit by master in the cuddy, and master can talk, and Don Amasa can listen, while Babo here lathers and strops."[2]

"Yes," said Captain Delano, not unpleased with this sociable plan, "yes, Don Benito, unless you had rather not, I will go with you."

"Be it so, Señor."

As the three passed aft, the American could not but think it another strange instance of his host's capriciousness, this being shaved with such uncommon punctuality in the middle of the day. But he deemed it more than likely that the servant's anxious fidelity had something to do with the matter; inasmuch as the timely interruption served to rally his master from the mood which had evidently been coming upon him.

The place called the cuddy was a light deck-cabin formed by the poop, a sort of attic to the large cabin below. Part of it had formerly been the quarters of the officers; but since their death all the partitioning had been thrown down, and the whole interior converted into one spacious and airy marine hall; for absence of fine furniture and picturesque disarray of odd appurtenances, somewhat answering to the wide, cluttered hall of some eccentric bachelor-squire in the country, who hangs his shooting-jacket and tobacco-pouch on deer antlers, and keeps his fishing-rod, tongs, and walking-stick in the same corner.

The similitude was heightened, if not originally suggested, by glimpses of the surrounding sea; since, in one aspect, the country and the ocean seem cousins-german.[3]

The floor of the cuddy was matted. Overhead, four or five old muskets were stuck into horizontal holes along the beams. On one side was a claw-footed old table lashed to the deck; a thumbed missal[4] on it, and over it a small, meagre crucifix attached to the bulkhead. Under the table lay a dented cutlass or two, with a hacked harpoon, among some melancholy old rigging, like a heap of poor friars' girdles.[5] There were also two long, sharp-ribbed settees of Malacca cane,[6] black with age, and uncomfortable to look at as inquisitors' racks, with a large, misshapen arm-chair, which, furnished with a rude barber's crotch[7] at the back, working with a screw, seemed some grotesque engine of torment. A flag locker was in one corner, open, exposing various colored bunting,[8] some rolled up, others half unrolled, still others tumbled. Opposite was a cumbrous washstand, of black mahogany, all of one block, with a pedestal, like a font, and over it a railed shelf, containing combs, brushes, and other implements of the toilet.[9] A torn hammock of stained grass swung near; the sheets tossed, and the pillow wrinkled up like a brow, as if who ever slept here slept but illy, with alternate visitations of sad thoughts and bad dreams.

The further extremity of the cuddy, overhanging the ship's stern, was pierced with three openings, windows or port-holes, according as men or cannon might peer, socially or unsocially, out of them. At present neither men nor cannon were seen, though huge ring-bolts and other rusty iron fixtures of the wood-work hinted of twenty-four-pounders.[10]

Glancing towards the hammock as he entered, Captain Delano said, "You sleep here, Don Benito?"

"Yes, Señor, since we got into mild weather."

"This seems a sort of dormitory, sitting-room, sail-loft, chapel, armory, and private closet all together, Don Benito," added Captain Delano, looking round.

---

1   *cuddy* Cabin near the stern, often used to serve the officers' meals. It can also refer to the captain's cabin.

2   *strops* Sharpens the razor for shaving.

3   *cousins-german* First cousins.

4   *missal* Catholic book of devotional prayers, often richly decorated.

5   *girdles* Belts. Franciscan mendicant friars tied their habits with rope.

6   *settees of Malacca cane* Sofas made with interwoven pieces of Malacca cane, a type of rattan palm from Sumatra.

7   *barber's crotch* Forked peg on which the barber could hang implements.

8   *flag locker* Locker on a ship used for storing various flags; *bunting* Flags.

9   *toilet* Process of grooming and dressing.

10   *twenty-four-pounders* I.e., cannons that fire twenty-four-pound balls of shot.

"Yes, Señor; events have not been favorable to much order in my arrangements."

Here the servant, napkin on arm, made a motion as if waiting his master's good pleasure. Don Benito signified his readiness, when, seating him in the Malacca arm-chair, and for the guest's convenience drawing opposite one of the settees, the servant commenced operations by throwing back his master's collar and loosening his cravat.

There is something in the negro which, in a peculiar way, fits him for avocations about one's person. Most negroes are natural valets and hair-dressers; taking to the comb and brush congenially as to the castinets,[1] and flourishing them apparently with almost equal satisfaction. There is, too, a smooth tact about them in this employment, with a marvelous, noiseless, gliding briskness, not ungraceful in its way, singularly pleasing to behold, and still more so to be the manipulated subject of. And above all is the great gift of good-humor. Not the mere grin or laugh is here meant. Those were unsuitable. But a certain easy cheerfulness, harmonious in every glance and gesture; as though God had set the whole negro to some pleasant tune.

When to this is added the docility arising from the unaspiring contentment of a limited mind and that susceptibility of blind attachment sometimes inhering in indisputable inferiors, one readily perceives why those hypochondriacs, Johnson and Byron[2]—it may be, something like the hypochondriac Benito Cereno—took to their hearts, almost to the exclusion of the entire white race, their serving men, the negroes, Barber and Fletcher.[3] But if there be that in the negro which exempts him from the inflicted sourness of the morbid or cynical mind, how, in his most prepossessing aspects, must he appear to a benevolent one? When at ease with respect to exterior things, Captain Delano's nature was not only benign, but familiarly and humorously so. At home, he had often taken rare satisfaction in sitting in his door, watching some free man of color at his work or play. If on a voyage he chanced to have a black sailor, invariably he was on chatty and half-gamesome terms with him. In fact, like most men of a good, blithe heart, Captain Delano took to negroes, not philanthropically, but genially, just as other men to Newfoundland dogs.

Hitherto, the circumstances in which he found the San Dominick had repressed the tendency. But in the cuddy, relieved from his former uneasiness, and, for various reasons, more sociably inclined than at any previous period of the day, and seeing the colored servant, napkin on arm, so debonair about his master, in a business so familiar as that of shaving, too, all his old weakness for negroes returned.

Among other things, he was amused with an odd instance of the African love of bright colors and fine shows, in the black's informally taking from the flag-locker a great piece of bunting of all hues, and lavishly tucking it under his master's chin for an apron.

The mode of shaving among the Spaniards is a little different from what it is with other nations. They have a basin, specifically called a barber's basin, which on one side is scooped out, so as accurately to receive the chin, against which it is closely held in lathering; which is done, not with a brush, but with soap dipped in the water of the basin and rubbed on the face.

In the present instance salt-water was used for lack of better; and the parts lathered were only the upper lip, and low down under the throat, all the rest being cultivated beard.

The preliminaries being somewhat novel to Captain Delano, he sat curiously eying them, so that no conversation took place, nor, for the present, did Don Benito appear disposed to renew any.

Setting down his basin, the negro searched among the razors, as for the sharpest, and having found it, gave it an additional edge by expertly strapping[4] it on the firm, smooth, oily skin of his open palm; he then made a gesture as if to begin, but midway stood suspended for an instant, one hand elevating the razor, the other professionally dabbling among the bubbling

---

1   *castinets*   Pair of instruments made of concave shells that are attached to the thumbs and hit by the middle fingers to produce a rattling sound; they are traditionally used in Spanish dances.

2   *Johnson*   Samuel Johnson (1709–84), British intellectual of the eighteenth century; *Byron*   George Gordon, Lord Byron (1788–1824), Romantic poet.

3   *Barber*   Jamaican-born Francis Barber (c. 1742/43–1801) was Samuel Johnson's servant and literary assistant for over 30 years; *Fletcher*   William Fletcher (c. 1775–1839) was Byron's valet for nearly two decades; contrary to what Melville suggests here, he was a white Englishman.

4   *strapping*   I.e., "stropping," sharpening a razor on a piece of leather (in this case on Babo's hand).

suds on the Spaniard's lank neck. Not unaffected by the close sight of the gleaming steel, Don Benito nervously shuddered; his usual ghastliness[1] was heightened by the lather, which lather, again, was intensified in its hue by the contrasting sootiness of the negro's body. Altogether the scene was somewhat peculiar, at least to Captain Delano, nor, as he saw the two thus postured, could he resist the vagary, that in the black he saw a headsman,[2] and in the white a man at the block. But this was one of those antic conceits,[3] appearing and vanishing in a breath, from which, perhaps, the best regulated mind is not always free.

Meantime the agitation of the Spaniard had a little loosened the bunting from around him, so that one broad fold swept curtain-like over the chair-arm to the floor, revealing, amid a profusion of armorial bars and ground-colors—black, blue, and yellow—a closed castle in a blood red field diagonal with a lion rampant in a white.[4]

"The castle and the lion," exclaimed Captain Delano—"why, Don Benito, this is the flag of Spain you use here. It's well it's only I, and not the King, that sees this," he added, with a smile, "but"—turning towards the black—"it's all one, I suppose, so the colors be gay"; which playful remark did not fail somewhat to tickle the negro.

"Now, master," he said, readjusting the flag, and pressing the head gently further back into the crotch of the chair; "now, master," and the steel glanced nigh the throat.

Again Don Benito faintly shuddered.

"You must not shake so, master. See, Don Amasa, master always shakes when I shave him. And yet master knows I never yet have drawn blood, though it's true, if master will shake so, I may some of these times. Now master," he continued. "And now, Don Amasa, please go on with your talk about the gale, and all that; master can hear, and, between times, master can answer."

"Ah yes, these gales," said Captain Delano; "but the more I think of your voyage, Don Benito, the more I wonder, not at the gales, terrible as they must have been, but at the disastrous interval following them. For here, by your account, have you been these two months and more getting from Cape Horn to St. Maria, a distance which I myself, with a good wind, have sailed in a few days. True, you had calms, and long ones, but to be becalmed for two months, that is, at least, unusual. Why, Don Benito, had almost any other gentleman told me such a story, I should have been half disposed to a little incredulity."

Here an involuntary expression came over the Spaniard, similar to that just before on the deck, and whether it was the start he gave, or a sudden gawky roll of the hull in the calm, or a momentary unsteadiness of the servant's hand, however it was, just then the razor drew blood, spots of which stained the creamy lather under the throat: immediately the black barber drew back his steel, and, remaining in his professional attitude, back to Captain Delano, and face to Don Benito, held up the trickling razor, saying, with a sort of half humorous sorrow, "See, master—you shook so—here's Babo's first blood."

No sword drawn before James the First of England,[5] no assassination in that timid King's presence, could have produced a more terrified aspect than was now presented by Don Benito.

Poor fellow, thought Captain Delano, so nervous he can't even bear the sight of barber's blood; and this unstrung, sick man, is it credible that I should have imagined he meant to spill all my blood, who can't endure the sight of one little drop of his own? Surely, Amasa Delano, you have been beside yourself this day. Tell it not when you get home, sappy Amasa. Well, well, he looks like a murderer, doesn't he? More like as if himself were to be done for. Well, well, this day's experience shall be a good lesson.

Meantime, while these things were running through the honest seaman's mind, the servant had taken the napkin from his arm, and to Don Benito had

---

[1] *ghastliness* Paleness.

[2] *vagary* Momentary play of the imagination; *headsman* Executioner (one that kills by beheading).

[3] *conceits* Imaginings, fancies.

[4] *armorial bars* In heraldry, lines drawn horizontally across a shield (or in this case flag); *ground-colors* Background colors; *closed castle … white* Describes the heraldic symbols on the flag of Castile and León.

[5] *James the First of England* James I of England (r. 1603–25) was also James VI of Scotland (r. 1567–1625). Known for his vivid belief in the supernatural, he survived several conspiracies and assassination attempts, including Guy Fawkes's Gunpowder Plot (see note above).

said—"But answer Don Amasa, please, master, while I wipe this ugly stuff off the razor, and strop it again."

As he said the words, his face was turned half round, so as to be alike visible to the Spaniard and the American, and seemed, by its expression, to hint, that he was desirous, by getting his master to go on with the conversation, considerably to withdraw his attention from the recent annoying accident. As if glad to snatch the offered relief, Don Benito resumed, rehearsing to Captain Delano, that not only were the calms of unusual duration, but the ship had fallen in with obstinate currents; and other things he added, some of which were but repetitions of former statements, to explain how it came to pass that the passage from Cape Horn to St. Maria had been so exceedingly long; now and then, mingling with his words, incidental praises, less qualified than before, to the blacks, for their general good conduct. These particulars were not given consecutively, the servant, at convenient times, using his razor, and so, between the intervals of shaving, the story and panegyric went on with more than usual huskiness.

To Captain Delano's imagination, now again not wholly at rest, there was something so hollow in the Spaniard's manner, with apparently some reciprocal hollowness in the servant's dusky comment of silence, that the idea flashed across him, that possibly master and man, for some unknown purpose, were acting out, both in word and deed, nay, to the very tremor of Don Benito's limbs, some juggling[1] play before him. Neither did the suspicion of collusion lack apparent support, from the fact of those whispered conferences before mentioned. But then, what could be the object of enacting this play of the barber before him? At last, regarding the notion as a whimsy, insensibly suggested, perhaps, by the theatrical aspect of Don Benito in his harlequin ensign,[2] Captain Delano speedily banished it.

The shaving over, the servant bestirred himself with a small bottle of scented waters, pouring a few drops on the head, and then diligently rubbing; the vehemence of the exercise causing the muscles of his face to twitch rather strangely.

His next operation was with comb, scissors, and brush; going round and round, smoothing a curl here, clipping an unruly whisker-hair there, giving a graceful sweep to the temple-lock, with other impromptu touches evincing the hand of a master; while, like any resigned gentleman in barber's hands, Don Benito bore all, much less uneasily, at least than he had done the razoring; indeed, he sat so pale and rigid now, that the negro seemed a Nubian[3] sculptor finishing off a white statue-head.

All being over at last, the standard[4] of Spain removed, tumbled up, and tossed back into the flag-locker, the negro's warm breath blowing away any stray hair, which might have lodged down his master's neck; collar and cravat readjusted; a speck of lint whisked off the velvet lapel; all this being done; backing off a little space, and pausing with an expression of subdued self-complacency, the servant for a moment surveyed his master, as, in toilet at least, the creature of his own tasteful hands.

Captain Delano playfully complimented him upon his achievement; at the same time congratulating Don Benito.

But neither sweet waters, nor shampooing, nor fidelity, nor sociality, delighted the Spaniard. Seeing him relapsing into forbidding gloom, and still remaining seated, Captain Delano, thinking that his presence was undesired just then, withdrew, on pretense of seeing whether, as he had prophesied, any signs of a breeze were visible.

Walking forward to the main-mast, he stood awhile thinking over the scene, and not without some undefined misgivings, when he heard a noise near the cuddy, and turning, saw the negro, his hand to his cheek. Advancing, Captain Delano perceived that the cheek was bleeding. He was about to ask the cause, when the negro's wailing soliloquy enlightened him.

"Ah, when will master get better from his sickness; only the sour heart that sour sickness breeds made him serve Babo so; cutting Babo with the razor, because, only by accident, Babo had given master one little scratch; and for the first time in so many a day, too. Ah, ah, ah," holding his hand to his face.

---

[1]   *juggling* Deceptive.

[2]   *harlequin ensign* Multicolored costume (like the fabric worn by clowns) covered in heraldic symbols (i.e., the flag).

[3]   *Nubian* Person from Nubia, a region in north-east Africa along the Nile river.

[4]   *standard* Flag.

Is it possible, thought Captain Delano; was it to wreak in private his Spanish spite against this poor friend of his, that Don Benito, by his sullen manner, impelled me to withdraw? Ah this slavery breeds ugly passions in man.—Poor fellow!

He was about to speak in sympathy to the negro, but with a timid reluctance he now re-entered the cuddy.

Presently master and man came forth; Don Benito leaning on his servant as if nothing had happened.

But a sort of love-quarrel, after all, thought Captain Delano.

He accosted Don Benito, and they slowly walked together. They had gone but a few paces, when the steward—a tall, rajah-looking mulatto, orientally set off with a pagoda turban formed by three or four Madras handkerchiefs wound about his head, tier on tier—approaching with a salaam,[1] announced lunch in the cabin.

On their way thither, the two captains were preceded by the mulatto, who, turning round as he advanced, with continual smiles and bows, ushered them on, a display of elegance which quite completed the insignificance of the small bare-headed Babo, who, as if not unconscious of inferiority, eyed askance the graceful steward. But in part, Captain Delano imputed his jealous watchfulness to that peculiar feeling which the full-blooded African entertains for the adulterated one. As for the steward, his manner, if not bespeaking much dignity of self-respect, yet evidenced his extreme desire to please; which is doubly meritorious, as at once Christian and Chesterfieldian.[2]

Captain Delano observed with interest that while the complexion of the mulatto was hybrid, his physiognomy was European—classically so.

"Don Benito," whispered he, "I am glad to see this usher-of-the-golden-rod[3] of yours; the sight refutes an ugly remark once made to me by a Barbadoes planter;[4] that when a mulatto has a regular European face, look out for him; he is a devil. But see, your steward here has features more regular than King George's of England; and yet there he nods, and bows, and smiles; a king, indeed—the king of kind hearts and polite fellows. What a pleasant voice he has, too?"

"He has, Señor."

"But tell me, has he not, so far as you have known him, always proved a good, worthy fellow?" said Captain Delano, pausing, while with a final genuflexion[5] the steward disappeared into the cabin; "come, for the reason just mentioned, I am curious to know."

"Francesco is a good man," a sort of sluggishly responded Don Benito, like a phlegmatic[6] appreciator, who would neither find fault nor flatter.

"Ah, I thought so. For it were strange, indeed, and not very creditable to us white-skins, if a little of our blood mixed with the African's, should, far from improving the latter's quality, have the sad effect of pouring vitriolic acid[7] into black broth; improving the hue, perhaps, but not the wholesomeness."

"Doubtless, doubtless, Señor, but"—glancing at Babo—"not to speak of negroes, your planter's remark I have heard applied to the Spanish and Indian inter-mixtures in our provinces. But I know nothing about the matter," he listlessly added.

And here they entered the cabin.

The lunch was a frugal one. Some of Captain Delano's fresh fish and pumpkins, biscuit and salt beef,

---

1   *rajah-looking* Resembling Indian nobility; *mulatto* One of the terms commonly used in the nineteenth century to classify individuals of mixed racial background; "mulatto" generally meant a person with one white parent and one parent of African descent; *pagoda* Temple; *Madras handkerchiefs* Traditional, colorful head-wraps made of madras (Indian) cotton; *salaam* Bow.

2   *Chesterfieldian* Allusion to Philip Stanhope, Earl of Chesterfield (1694–1773), whose posthumously published *Letters to His Son* (1774) contained extensive advice for gentlemen on topics including what he called "the art of pleasing" as well as ways to seduce women. Chesterfield emphasized the idea that gentlemen often need to make moral compromises in order to thrive in society.

3   *usher-of-the-golden-rod* The Usher of the Black Rod keeps order in the House of Lords in the U.K. Parliament; other ushers (stewards) have different colored rods associated with their duties, though there is no usher of the golden rod. Francesco's light pigmentation causes Delano to use "golden" rather than "black" to describe him.

4   *Barbadoes planter* I.e., plantation owner and enslaver on the island of Barbados, a British colony in the Caribbean. By the time *Benito Cereno* was published, slavery on Barbados (and throughout the British Empire) had been abolished, but it was still legal at the time the story takes place.

5   *genuflexion* Bow.

6   *phlegmatic* Inexpressive, indifferent.

7   *vitriolic acid* I.e., sulphuric acid (to call a person "vitriolic" suggests rebelliousness and ill-temper).

the reserved bottle of cider, and the San Dominick's last bottle of Canary.[1]

As they entered, Francesco, with two or three colored aids, was hovering over the table giving the last adjustments. Upon perceiving their master they withdrew, Francesco making a smiling congé, and the Spaniard, without condescending to notice it, fastidiously remarking to his companion that he relished not superfluous attendance.

Without companions, host and guest sat down, like a childless married couple, at opposite ends of the table, Don Benito waving Captain Delano to his place, and, weak as he was, insisting upon that gentleman being seated before himself.

The negro placed a rug under Don Benito's feet, and a cushion behind his back, and then stood behind, not his master's chair, but Captain Delano's. At first, this a little surprised the latter. But it was soon evident that, in taking his position, the black was still true to his master; since by facing him he could the more readily anticipate his slightest want.

"This is an uncommonly intelligent fellow of yours, Don Benito," whispered Captain Delano across the table.

"You say true, Señor."

During the repast, the guest again reverted to parts of Don Benito's story, begging further particulars here and there. He inquired how it was that the scurvy and fever should have committed such wholesale havoc upon the whites, while destroying less than half of the blacks. As if this question reproduced the whole scene of plague before the Spaniard's eyes, miserably reminding him of his solitude in a cabin where before he had had so many friends and officers round him, his hand shook, his face became hueless, broken words escaped; but directly the sane memory of the past seemed replaced by insane terrors of the present. With starting eyes he stared before him at vacancy. For nothing was to be seen but the hand of his servant pushing the Canary over towards him. At length a few sips served partially to restore him. He made random reference to the different constitution of races, enabling one to offer more resistance to certain maladies than another. The thought was new to his companion.

Presently Captain Delano, intending to say something to his host concerning the pecuniary part of the business he had undertaken for him, especially—since he was strictly accountable to his owners—with reference to the new suit of sails, and other things of that sort; and naturally preferring to conduct such affairs in private, was desirous that the servant should withdraw; imagining that Don Benito for a few minutes could dispense with his attendance. He, however, waited awhile; thinking that, as the conversation proceeded, Don Benito, without being prompted, would perceive the propriety of the step.

But it was otherwise. At last catching his host's eye, Captain Delano, with a slight backward gesture of his thumb, whispered, "Don Benito, pardon me, but there is an interference with the full expression of what I have to say to you."

Upon this the Spaniard changed countenance; which was imputed to his resenting the hint, as in some way a reflection upon his servant. After a moment's pause, he assured his guest that the black's remaining with them could be of no disservice; because since losing his officers he had made Babo (whose original office, it now appeared, had been captain of the slaves) not only his constant attendant and companion, but in all things his confidant.

After this, nothing more could be said; though, indeed, Captain Delano could hardly avoid some little tinge of irritation upon being left ungratified in so inconsiderable a wish, by one, too, for whom he intended such solid services. But it is only his querulousness, thought he; and so filling his glass he proceeded to business.

The price of the sails and other matters was fixed upon. But while this was being done, the American observed that, though his original offer of assistance had been hailed with hectic animation, yet now when it was reduced to a business transaction, indifference and apathy were betrayed. Don Benito, in fact, appeared to submit to hearing the details more out of regard to common propriety, than from any impression that weighty benefit to himself and his voyage was involved.

Soon, his manner became still more reserved. The effort was vain to seek to draw him into social talk. Gnawed by his splenetic mood, he sat twitching his

---

[1] *Canary* White wine from the Canary Islands.

beard, while to little purpose the hand of his servant, mute as that on the wall, slowly pushed over the Canary.

Lunch being over, they sat down on the cushioned transom;[1] the servant placing a pillow behind his master. The long continuance of the calm had now affected the atmosphere. Don Benito sighed heavily, as if for breath.

"Why not adjourn to the cuddy," said Captain Delano; "there is more air there." But the host sat silent and motionless.

Meantime his servant knelt before him, with a large fan of feathers. And Francesco coming in on tiptoes, handed the negro a little cup of aromatic waters, with which at intervals he chafed his master's brow; smoothing the hair along the temples as a nurse does a child's. He spoke no word. He only rested his eye on his master's, as if, amid all Don Benito's distress, a little to refresh his spirit by the silent sight of fidelity.

Presently the ship's bell sounded two o'clock; and through the cabin windows a slight rippling of the sea was discerned; and from the desired direction.

"There," exclaimed Captain Delano, "I told you so, Don Benito, look!"

He had risen to his feet, speaking in a very animated tone, with a view the more to rouse his companion. But though the crimson curtain of the stern-window near him that moment fluttered against his pale cheek, Don Benito seemed to have even less welcome for the breeze than the calm.

Poor fellow, thought Captain Delano, bitter experience has taught him that one ripple does not make a wind, any more than one swallow a summer.[2] But he is mistaken for once. I will get his ship in for him, and prove it.

Briefly alluding to his weak condition, he urged his host to remain quietly where he was, since he (Captain Delano) would with pleasure take upon himself the responsibility of making the best use of the wind.

Upon gaining the deck, Captain Delano started at the unexpected figure of Atufal, monumentally fixed at the threshold, like one of those sculptured porters of black marble guarding the porches of Egyptian tombs.

But this time the start was, perhaps, purely physical. Atufal's presence, singularly attesting docility even in sullenness, was contrasted with that of the hatchet-polishers, who in patience evinced their industry; while both spectacles showed, that lax as Don Benito's general authority might be, still, whenever he chose to exert it, no man so savage or colossal but must, more or less, bow.

Snatching a trumpet which hung from the bulwarks, with a free step Captain Delano advanced to the forward edge of the poop, issuing his orders in his best Spanish. The few sailors and many negroes, all equally pleased, obediently set about heading the ship towards the harbor.

While giving some directions about setting a lower stu'n'-sail,[3] suddenly Captain Delano heard a voice faithfully repeating his orders. Turning, he saw Babo, now for the time acting, under the pilot, his original part of captain of the slaves. This assistance proved valuable. Tattered sails and warped yards were soon brought into some trim. And no brace or halyard was pulled but to the blithe songs of the inspirited negroes.

Good fellows, thought Captain Delano, a little training would make fine sailors of them. Why see, the very women pull and sing too. These must be some of those Ashantee negresses that make such capital soldiers, I've heard. But who's at the helm. I must have a good hand there.

He went to see.

The San Dominick steered with a cumbrous tiller, with large horizontal pullies attached. At each pully-end stood a subordinate black, and between them, at the tiller-head, the responsible post, a Spanish seaman, whose countenance evinced his due share in the general hopefulness and confidence at the coming of the breeze.

He proved the same man who had behaved with so shame-faced an air on the windlass.

"Ah,—it is you, my man," exclaimed Captain Delano—"well, no more sheep's-eyes now;—look straight forward and keep the ship so. Good hand, I trust? And want to get into the harbor, don't you?"

---

[1]   *transom*   Seat built into the side of a ship's cabin.

[2]   *one swallow a summer*   From the proverb "One swallow does not a summer make"—i.e., the arrival of one migrating swallow does not mean summer has arrived.

[3]   *stu'n'-sail*   An additional sail set to increase the ship's speed.

The man assented with an inward chuckle, grasping the tiller-head firmly. Upon this, unperceived by the American, the two blacks eyed the sailor intently.

Finding all right at the helm, the pilot went forward to the forecastle, to see how matters stood there.

The ship now had way[1] enough to breast the current. With the approach of evening, the breeze would be sure to freshen.[2]

Having done all that was needed for the present, Captain Delano, giving his last orders to the sailors, turned aft to report affairs to Don Benito in the cabin; perhaps additionally incited to rejoin him by the hope of snatching a moment's private chat while the servant was engaged upon deck.

From opposite sides, there were, beneath the poop, two approaches to the cabin; one further forward than the other, and consequently communicating with a longer passage. Marking the servant still above, Captain Delano, taking the nighest entrance—the one last named, and at whose porch Atufal still stood—hurried on his way, till, arrived at the cabin threshold, he paused an instant, a little to recover from his eagerness. Then, with the words of his intended business upon his lips, he entered. As he advanced toward the seated Spaniard, he heard another footstep, keeping time with his. From the opposite door, a salver[3] in hand, the servant was likewise advancing.

"Confound the faithful fellow," thought Captain Delano; "what a vexatious coincidence."

Possibly, the vexation might have been something different, were it not for the brisk confidence inspired by the breeze. But even as it was, he felt a slight twinge, from a sudden indefinite association in his mind of Babo with Atufal.

"Don Benito," said he, "I give you joy; the breeze will hold, and will increase. By the way, your tall man and time-piece, Atufal, stands without.[4] By your order, of course?"

Don Benito recoiled, as if at some bland satirical touch,[5] delivered with such adroit garnish of apparent good breeding as to present no handle for retort.

He is like one flayed alive, thought Captain Delano; where may one touch him without causing a shrink?

The servant moved before his master, adjusting a cushion; recalled to civility, the Spaniard stiffly replied: "you are right. The slave appears where you saw him, according to my command; which is, that if at the given hour I am below, he must take his stand and abide my coming."

"Ah now, pardon me, but that is treating the poor fellow like an ex-king indeed. Ah, Don Benito," smiling, "for all the license you permit in some things, I fear lest, at bottom, you are a bitter hard master."

Again Don Benito shrank; and this time, as the good sailor thought, from a genuine twinge of his conscience.

Again conversation became constrained. In vain Captain Delano called attention to the now perceptible motion of the keel gently cleaving the sea; with lack-lustre eye, Don Benito returned words few and reserved.

By-and-by, the wind having steadily risen, and still blowing right into the harbor bore the San Dominick swiftly on. Sounding a point of land, the sealer at distance came into open view.

Meantime Captain Delano had again repaired to the deck, remaining there some time. Having at last altered the ship's course, so as to give the reef a wide berth, he returned for a few moments below.

I will cheer up my poor friend, this time, thought he.

"Better and better, Don Benito," he cried as he blithely re-entered: "there will soon be an end to your cares, at least for awhile. For when, after a long, sad voyage, you know, the anchor drops into the haven, all its vast weight seems lifted from the captain's heart. We are getting on famously, Don Benito. My ship is in sight. Look through this side-light here; there she is; all a-taunt-o![6] The Bachelor's Delight, my good friend. Ah, how this wind braces one up. Come, you must take a cup of coffee with me this evening. My old

---

[1] *way* Momentum.

[2] *freshen* Strengthen.

[3] *salver* Tray.

[4] *without* Outside.

---

[5] *touch* Rebuke.

[6] *a-taunt-o* With all sails rigged.

steward will give you as fine a cup as ever any sultan tasted. What say you, Don Benito, will you?"

At first, the Spaniard glanced feverishly up, casting a longing look towards the sealer, while with mute concern his servant gazed into his face. Suddenly the old ague of coldness returned, and dropping back to his cushions he was silent.

"You do not answer. Come, all day you have been my host; would you have hospitality all on one side?"

"I cannot go," was the response.

"What? it will not fatigue you. The ships will lie together as near as they can, without swinging foul. It will be little more than stepping from deck to deck; which is but as from room to room. Come, come, you must not refuse me."

"I cannot go," decisively and repulsively repeated Don Benito.

Renouncing all but the last appearance of courtesy, with a sort of cadaverous sullenness, and biting his thin nails to the quick, he glanced, almost glared, at his guest, as if impatient that a stranger's presence should interfere with the full indulgence of his morbid hour. Meantime the sound of the parted waters came more and more gurglingly and merrily in at the windows; as reproaching him for his dark spleen; as telling him that, sulk as he might, and go mad with it, nature cared not a jot; since, whose fault was it, pray?

But the foul mood was now at its depth, as the fair wind at its height.

There was something in the man so far beyond any mere unsociality or sourness previously evinced, that even the forbearing good-nature of his guest could no longer endure it. Wholly at a loss to account for such demeanor, and deeming sickness with eccentricity, however extreme, no adequate excuse, well satisfied, too, that nothing in his own conduct could justify it, Captain Delano's pride began to be roused. Himself became reserved. But all seemed one to the Spaniard. Quitting him, therefore, Captain Delano once more went to the deck.

The ship was now within less than two miles of the sealer. The whale-boat was seen darting over the interval.

To be brief, the two vessels, thanks to the pilot's skill, ere long neighborly style lay anchored together.

Before returning to his own vessel, Captain Delano had intended communicating to Don Benito the smaller details of the proposed services to be rendered. But, as it was, unwilling anew to subject himself to rebuffs, he resolved, now that he had seen the San Dominick safely moored, immediately to quit her, without further allusion to hospitality or business. Indefinitely postponing his ulterior plans, he would regulate his future actions according to future circumstances. His boat was ready to receive him; but his host still tarried below. Well, thought Captain Delano, if he has little breeding, the more need to show mine. He descended to the cabin to bid a ceremonious, and, it may be, tacitly rebukeful adieu. But to his great satisfaction, Don Benito, as if he began to feel the weight of that treatment with which his slighted guest had, not indecorously, retaliated upon him, now supported by his servant, rose to his feet, and grasping Captain Delano's hand, stood tremulous; too much agitated to speak. But the good augury hence drawn was suddenly dashed, by his resuming all his previous reserve, with augmented gloom, as, with half-averted eyes, he silently reseated himself on his cushions. With a corresponding return of his own chilled feelings, Captain Delano bowed and withdrew.

He was hardly midway in the narrow corridor, dim as a tunnel, leading from the cabin to the stairs, when a sound, as of the tolling for execution in some jail-yard, fell on his ears. It was the echo of the ship's flawed bell, striking the hour, drearily reverberated in this subterranean vault. Instantly, by a fatality not to be withstood, his mind, responsive to the portent, swarmed with superstitious suspicions. He paused. In images far swifter than these sentences, the minutest details of all his former distrusts swept through him.

Hitherto, credulous good-nature had been too ready to furnish excuses for reasonable fears. Why was the Spaniard, so superfluously punctilious at times, now heedless of common propriety in not accompanying to the side his departing guest? Did indisposition forbid? Indisposition had not forbidden more irksome exertion that day. His last equivocal demeanor recurred. He had risen to his feet, grasped his guest's hand, motioned toward his hat; then, in an instant, all was eclipsed in sinister muteness and gloom. Did this imply one brief, repentant relenting at the final moment, from some iniquitous plot, followed by remorseless return to it? His last glance seemed to express a calamitous, yet acquiescent farewell to Captain Delano forever. Why decline the invitation to visit the sealer that evening? Or was the Spaniard less hardened than the Jew, who refrained not from supping at the board of him whom the same night he meant to betray?[1] What imported all those day-long enigmas and contradictions, except they were intended to mystify, preliminary to some stealthy blow? Atufal, the pretended rebel, but punctual shadow, that moment lurked by the threshold without. He seemed a sentry, and more. Who, by his own confession, had stationed him there? Was the negro now lying in wait?

The Spaniard behind—his creature before: to rush from darkness to light was the involuntary choice.

The next moment, with clenched jaw and hand, he passed Atufal, and stood unharmed in the light. As he saw his trim ship lying peacefully at anchor, and almost within ordinary call; as he saw his household boat, with familiar faces in it, patiently rising and falling, on the short waves by the San Dominick's side; and then, glancing about the decks where he stood, saw the oakum-pickers still gravely plying their fingers; and heard the low, buzzing whistle and industrious hum of the hatchet-polishers, still bestirring themselves over their endless occupation; and more than all, as he saw the benign aspect of nature, taking her innocent repose in the evening; the screened sun in the quiet camp of the west shining out like the mild light from Abraham's tent;[2] as charmed eye and ear took in all these, with the chained figure of the black, clenched jaw and hand relaxed. Once again he smiled at the phantoms which had mocked him, and felt something like a tinge of remorse, that, by harboring them even for a moment, he should, by implication, have betrayed an atheist doubt of the ever-watchful Providence above.

There was a few minutes' delay, while, in obedience to his orders, the boat was being hooked along to the gangway. During this interval, a sort of saddened satisfaction stole over Captain Delano, at thinking of the kindly offices he had that day discharged for a stranger. Ah, thought he, after good actions one's conscience is never ungrateful, however much so the benefited party may be.

Presently, his foot, in the first act of descent into the boat, pressed the first round of the side-ladder, his face presented inward upon the deck. In the same moment, he heard his name courteously sounded; and, to his pleased surprise, saw Don Benito advancing—an unwonted energy in his air, as if, at the last moment, intent upon making amends for his recent discourtesy. With instinctive good feeling, Captain Delano, withdrawing his foot, turned and reciprocally advanced. As he did so, the Spaniard's nervous eagerness increased, but his vital energy failed; so that, the better to support him, the servant, placing his master's hand on his naked shoulder, and gently holding it there, formed himself into a sort of crutch.

When the two captains met, the Spaniard again fervently took the hand of the American, at the same time casting an earnest glance into his eyes, but, as before, too much overcome to speak.

I have done him wrong, self-reproachfully thought Captain Delano; his apparent coldness has deceived me: in no instance has he meant to offend.

Meantime, as if fearful that the continuance of the scene might too much unstring his master, the servant seemed anxious to terminate it. And so, still presenting himself as a crutch, and walking between the two captains, he advanced with them towards the gangway; while still, as if full of kindly contrition, Don Benito would not let go the hand of Captain Delano, but retained it in his, across the black's body.

Soon they were standing by the side, looking over into the boat, whose crew turned up their curious eyes. Waiting a moment for the Spaniard to relinquish his hold, the now embarrassed Captain Delano lifted his foot, to overstep the threshold of the open gangway; but still Don Benito would not let go his hand. And yet, with an agitated tone, he said, "I can go no further; here I must bid you adieu. Adieu, my dear, dear Don Amasa. Go—go!" suddenly tearing his hand loose, "go, and God guard you better than me, my best friend."

Not unaffected, Captain Delano would now have lingered; but catching the meekly admonitory eye of

---

[1]   *Jew ... betray*   See John 13.2, where Judas Iscariot, after sharing the Last Supper with Jesus, betrays him. While Jesus and all his disciples were Jews, Judas' Jewishness is often emphasized in anti-Semitic rhetoric.

[2]   *mild light ... Abraham's tent*   In Genesis 18, God visits Abraham and Sarah in their tent on the plains of Mamre and tells Sarah she will bear a child in her old age.

the servant, with a hasty farewell he descended into his boat, followed by the continual adieus of Don Benito, standing rooted in the gangway.

Seating himself in the stern, Captain Delano, making a last salute, ordered the boat shoved off. The crew had their oars on end. The bowsmen pushed the boat a sufficient distance for the oars to be lengthwise dropped. The instant that was done, Don Benito sprang over the bulwarks, falling at the feet of Captain Delano; at the same time calling towards his ship, but in tones so frenzied, that none in the boat could understand him. But, as if not equally obtuse, three sailors, from three different and distant parts of the ship, splashed into the sea, swimming after their captain, as if intent upon his rescue.

The dismayed officer of the boat eagerly asked what this meant. To which, Captain Delano, turning a disdainful smile upon the unaccountable Spaniard, answered that, for his part, he neither knew nor cared; but it seemed as if Don Benito had taken it into his head to produce the impression among his people that the boat wanted to kidnap him. "Or else—give way for your lives," he wildly added, starting at a clattering hubbub in the ship, above which rang the tocsin[1] of the hatchet-polishers; and seizing Don Benito by the throat he added, "this plotting pirate means murder!" Here, in apparent verification of the words, the servant, a dagger in his hand, was seen on the rail overhead, poised, in the act of leaping, as if with desperate fidelity to befriend his master to the last; while, seemingly to aid the black, the three white sailors were trying to clamber into the hampered bow. Meantime, the whole host of negroes, as if inflamed at the sight of their jeopardized captain, impended in one sooty avalanche over the bulwarks.

All this, with what preceded, and what followed, occurred with such involutions of rapidity, that past, present, and future seemed one.

Seeing the negro coming, Captain Delano had flung the Spaniard aside, almost in the very act of clutching him, and, by the unconscious recoil, shifting his place, with arms thrown up, so promptly grappled the servant in his descent, that with dagger presented at Captain Delano's heart, the black seemed of purpose to have leaped there as to his mark. But the weapon was wrenched away, and the assailant dashed down into

the bottom of the boat, which now, with disentangled oars, began to speed through the sea.

At this juncture, the left hand of Captain Delano, on one side, again clutched the half-reclined Don Benito, heedless that he was in a speechless faint, while his right foot, on the other side, ground the prostrate negro; and his right arm pressed for added speed on the after oar, his eye bent forward, encouraging his men to their utmost.

But here, the officer of the boat, who had at last succeeded in beating off the towing sailors, and was now, with face turned aft, assisting the bowsman at his oar, suddenly called to Captain Delano, to see what the black was about; while a Portuguese oarsman shouted to him to give heed to what the Spaniard was saying.

Glancing down at his feet, Captain Delano saw the freed hand of the servant aiming with a second dagger—a small one, before concealed in his wool—with this he was snakishly writhing up from the boat's bottom, at the heart of his master, his countenance lividly vindictive, expressing the centred purpose of his soul; while the Spaniard, half-choked, was vainly shrinking away, with husky words, incoherent to all but the Portuguese.

That moment, across the long-benighted mind of Captain Delano, a flash of revelation swept, illuminating, in unanticipated clearness, his host's whole mysterious demeanor, with every enigmatic event of the day, as well as the entire past voyage of the San Dominick. He smote Babo's hand down, but his own heart smote him harder. With infinite pity he withdrew his hold from Don Benito. Not Captain Delano, but Don Benito, the black, in leaping into the boat, had intended to stab.

Both the black's hands were held, as, glancing up towards the San Dominick, Captain Delano, now with scales dropped from his eyes, saw the negroes, not in misrule, not in tumult, not as if frantically concerned for Don Benito, but with mask torn away, flourishing hatchets and knives, in ferocious piratical revolt. Like delirious black dervishes, the six Ashantees danced on the poop. Prevented by their foes from springing into the water, the Spanish boys were hurrying up to the topmost spars, while such of the few Spanish sailors, not already in the sea, less alert, were descried, helplessly mixed in, on deck, with the blacks.

---

[1] *tocsin* Signal, alarm.

Meantime Captain Delano hailed his own vessel, ordering the ports up, and the guns run out. But by this time the cable of the San Dominick had been cut; and the fag-end,[1] in lashing out, whipped away the canvas shroud about the beak, suddenly revealing, as the bleached hull swung round towards the open ocean, death for the figure-head, in a human skeleton; chalky comment on the chalked words below, "*Follow your leader.*"

At the sight, Don Benito, covering his face, wailed out: "'Tis he, Aranda! my murdered, unburied friend!"

Upon reaching the sealer, calling for ropes, Captain Delano bound the negro, who made no resistance, and had him hoisted to the deck. He would then have assisted the now almost helpless Don Benito up the side; but Don Benito, wan as he was, refused to move, or be moved, until the negro should have been first put below out of view. When, presently assured that it was done, he no more shrank from the ascent.

The boat was immediately dispatched back to pick up the three swimming sailors. Meantime, the guns were in readiness, though, owing to the San Dominick having glided somewhat astern of the sealer, only the aftermost one could be brought to bear. With this, they fired six times; thinking to cripple the fugitive ship by bringing down her spars. But only a few inconsiderable ropes were shot away. Soon the ship was beyond the gun's range, steering broad out of the bay; the blacks thickly clustering round the bowsprit, one moment with taunting cries towards the whites, the next with upthrown gestures hailing the now dusky moors of ocean—cawing crows escaped from the hand of the fowler.[2]

The first impulse was to slip the cables and give chase. But, upon second thoughts, to pursue with whale-boat and yawl[3] seemed more promising.

Upon inquiring of Don Benito what firearms they had on board the San Dominick, Captain Delano was answered that they had none that could be used; because, in the earlier stages of the mutiny, a cabin-passenger, since dead, had secretly put out of order the locks of what few muskets there were. But with all his remaining strength, Don Benito entreated the American not to give chase, either with ship or boat; for the negroes had already proved themselves such desperadoes, that, in case of a present assault, nothing but a total massacre of the whites could be looked for. But, regarding this warning as coming from one whose spirit had been crushed by misery the American did not give up his design.

The boats were got ready and armed. Captain Delano ordered his men into them. He was going himself when Don Benito grasped his arm.

"What! have you saved my life, Señor, and are you now going to throw away your own?"

The officers also, for reasons connected with their interests and those of the voyage, and a duty owing to the owners, strongly objected against their commander's going. Weighing their remonstrances a moment, Captain Delano felt bound to remain; appointing his chief mate—an athletic and resolute man, who had been a privateer's-man[4]—to head the party. The more to encourage the sailors, they were told, that the Spanish captain considered his ship good as lost; that she and her cargo, including some gold and silver, were worth more than a thousand doubloons. Take her, and no small part should be theirs. The sailors replied with a shout.

The fugitives had now almost gained an offing.[5] It was nearly night; but the moon was rising. After hard, prolonged pulling, the boats came up on the ship's quarters, at a suitable distance laying upon their oars to discharge their muskets. Having no bullets to return, the negroes sent their yells. But, upon the second volley, Indian-like, they hurtled their hatchets. One took off a sailor's fingers. Another struck the whale-boat's bow, cutting off the rope there, and remaining stuck in the gunwale like a woodman's axe. Snatching it, quivering from its lodgment, the mate hurled it back. The returned gauntlet now stuck in the ship's broken quarter-gallery, and so remained.

The negroes giving too hot a reception, the whites kept a more respectful distance. Hovering now just out of reach of the hurtling hatchets, they, with a view to

---

[1]   *fag-end*   End of a loose rope.

[2]   *fowler*   Bird-catcher.

[3]   *yawl*   Small ship's boat with four to six oars.

[4]   *privateer's-man*   Person who worked on a privateer, a ship privately owned but commissioned by a government to capture enemy merchant ships. Sailors on privateers were thus familiar with armed conflict on the sea.

[5]   *offing*   Safe distance.

the close encounter which must soon come, sought to decoy the blacks into entirely disarming themselves of their most murderous weapons in a hand-to-hand fight, by foolishly flinging them, as missiles, short of the mark, into the sea. But, ere long, perceiving the stratagem, the negroes desisted, though not before many of them had to replace their lost hatchets with handspikes; an exchange which, as counted upon, proved, in the end, favorable to the assailants.

Meantime, with a strong wind, the ship still clove the water; the boats alternately falling behind, and pulling up, to discharge fresh volleys.

The fire was mostly directed towards the stern, since there, chiefly, the negroes, at present, were clustering. But to kill or maim the negroes was not the object. To take them, with the ship, was the object. To do it, the ship must be boarded; which could not be done by boats while she was sailing so fast.

A thought now struck the mate. Observing the Spanish boys still aloft, high as they could get, he called to them to descend to the yards, and cut adrift the sails. It was done. About this time, owing to causes hereafter to be shown, two Spaniards, in the dress of sailors, and conspicuously showing themselves, were killed; not by volleys, but by deliberate marksman's shots; while, as it afterwards appeared, by one of the general discharges, Atufal, the black, and the Spaniard at the helm likewise were killed. What now, with the loss of the sails, and loss of leaders, the ship became unmanageable to the negroes.

With creaking masts, she came heavily round to the wind; the prow slowly swinging into view of the boats, its skeleton gleaming in the horizontal moonlight, and casting a gigantic ribbed shadow upon the water. One extended arm of the ghost seemed beckoning the whites to avenge it.

"Follow your leader!" cried the mate; and, one on each bow, the boats boarded. Sealing-spears and cutlasses crossed hatchets and hand-spikes. Huddled upon the long-boat amidships, the negresses raised a wailing chant, whose chorus was the clash of the steel.

For a time, the attack wavered; the negroes wedging themselves to beat it back; the half-repelled sailors, as yet unable to gain a footing, fighting as troopers in the saddle, one leg sideways flung over the bulwarks, and one without, plying their cutlasses like carters' whips.

But in vain. They were almost overborne, when, rallying themselves into a squad as one man, with a huzza, they sprang inboard, where, entangled, they involuntarily separated again. For a few breaths' space, there was a vague, muffled, inner sound, as of submerged sword-fish rushing hither and thither through shoals of black-fish. Soon, in a reunited band, and joined by the Spanish seamen, the whites came to the surface, irresistibly driving the negroes toward the stern. But a barricade of casks and sacks, from side to side, had been thrown up by the main-mast. Here the negroes faced about, and though scorning peace or truce, yet fain would have had respite. But, without pause, overleaping the barrier, the unflagging sailors again closed. Exhausted, the blacks now fought in despair. Their red tongues lolled, wolf-like, from their black mouths. But the pale sailors' teeth were set; not a word was spoken; and, in five minutes more, the ship was won.

Nearly a score of the negroes were killed. Exclusive of those by the balls,[1] many were mangled; their wounds—mostly inflicted by the long-edged sealing-spears, resembling those shaven ones of the English at Preston Pans,[2] made by the poled scythes of the Highlanders. On the other side, none were killed, though several were wounded; some severely, including the mate. The surviving negroes were temporarily secured, and the ship, towed back into the harbor at midnight, once more lay anchored.

Omitting the incidents and arrangements ensuing, suffice it that, after two days spent in refitting, the ships sailed in company for Conception, in Chili, and thence for Lima, in Peru; where, before the vice-regal courts, the whole affair, from the beginning, underwent investigation.

Though, midway on the passage, the ill-fated Spaniard, relaxed from constraint, showed some signs of regaining health with free-will; yet, agreeably to his own foreboding, shortly before arriving at Lima, he relapsed, finally becoming so reduced as to be carried ashore in arms. Hearing of his story and plight, one of the many religious institutions of the City of Kings opened an hospitable refuge to him, where both

---

[1] *balls* Bullets.

[2] *Preston Pans* Rebel victory in the Jacobite rising of 1745, when Catholic Scottish Highlanders loyal to the Stuart dynasty attempted—and ultimately failed—to restore Charles Stuart to the throne of Great Britain.

physician and priest were his nurses, and a member of the order volunteered to be his one special guardian and consoler, by night and by day.

The following extracts, translated from one of the official Spanish documents, will, it is hoped, shed light on the preceding narrative, as well as, in the first place, reveal the true port of departure and true history of the San Dominick's voyage, down to the time of her touching at the island of St. Maria.

But, ere the extracts come, it may be well to preface them with a remark.

The document selected, from among many others, for partial translation, contains the deposition of Benito Cereno; the first taken in the case. Some disclosures therein were, at the time, held dubious for both learned and natural reasons. The tribunal inclined to the opinion that the deponent, not undisturbed in his mind by recent events, raved of some things which could never have happened. But subsequent depositions of the surviving sailors, bearing out the revelations of their captain in several of the strangest particulars, gave credence to the rest. So that the tribunal, in its final decision, rested its capital sentences upon statements which, had they lacked confirmation, it would have deemed it but duty to reject.

————————

I, DON JOSE DE ABOS AND PADILLA, His Majesty's Notary for the Royal Revenue, and Register of this Province, and Notary Public of the Holy Crusade of this Bishopric, etc.

Do certify and declare, as much as is requisite in law, that, in the criminal cause commenced the twenty-fourth of the month of September, in the year seventeen hundred and ninety-nine, against the negroes of the ship San Dominick, the following declaration before me was made:

Declaration of the first witness, DON BENITO CERENO.

The same day, and month, and year, His Honor, Doctor Juan Martinez de Rozas, Councilor of the Royal Audience of this Kingdom, and learned in the law of this Intendency,[1] ordered the captain of the ship San Dominick, Don Benito Cereno, to appear; which

he did, in his litter, attended by the monk Infelez; of whom he received the oath, which he took by God, our Lord, and a sign of the Cross; under which he promised to tell the truth of whatever he should know and should be asked;—and being interrogated agreeably to the tenor of the act commencing the process, he said, that on the twentieth of May last, he set sail with his ship from the port of Valparaiso, bound to that of Callao;[2] loaded with the produce of the country beside thirty cases of hardware and one hundred and sixty blacks, of both sexes, mostly belonging to Don Alexandro Aranda, gentleman, of the city of Mendoza;[3] that the crew of the ship consisted of thirty-six men, beside the persons who went as passengers; that the negroes were in part as follows:

[*Here, in the original, follows a list of some fifty names, descriptions, and ages, compiled from certain recovered documents of Aranda's, and also from recollections of the deponent, from which portions only are extracted.*]

—One, from about eighteen to nineteen years, named José, and this was the man that waited upon his master, Don Alexandro, and who speaks well the Spanish, having served him four or five years; * * * a mulatto, named Francesco, the cabin steward, of a good person and voice, having sung in the Valparaiso churches, native of the province of Buenos Ayres, aged about thirty-five years. * * * A smart negro, named Dago, who had been for many years a grave-digger among the Spaniards, aged forty-six years. * * * Four old negroes, born in Africa, from sixty to seventy, but sound, calkers[4] by trade, whose names are as follows:— the first was named Muri, and he was killed (as was also his son named Diamelo); the second, Nacta; the third, Yola, likewise killed; the fourth, Ghofan; and six full-grown negroes, aged from thirty to forty-five, all raw,[5] and born among the Ashantees—Matiluqui, Yan, Lecbe, Mapenda, Yambaio, Akim; four of whom were killed; * * * a powerful negro named Atufal, who being

————————

[1]   *Intendency*   Administration (those in charge of the province).

[2]   *Valparaiso*   Port in Chile;   *Callao*   Port in Peru.

[3]   *Mendoza*   City in Argentina.

[4]   *calkers*   Caulkers—those who waterproof the seams of ships by stuffing them with oakum (shredded hemp) and sealing them with pitch.

[5]   *raw*   I.e., from Africa.

supposed to have been a chief in Africa, his owner set great store by him. * * * And a small negro of Senegal, but some years among the Spaniards, aged about thirty, which negro's name was Babo; * * * that he does not remember the names of the others, but that still expecting the residue of Don Alexandro's papers will be found, will then take due account of them all, and remit to the court; * * * and thirty-nine women and children of all ages.

[*The catalogue over, the deposition goes on.*]

* * * That all the negroes slept upon deck, as is customary in this navigation, and none wore fetters, because the owner, his friend Aranda, told him that they were all tractable; * * * that on the seventh day after leaving port, at three o'clock in the morning, all the Spaniards being asleep except the two officers on the watch, who were the boatswain, Juan Robles, and the carpenter, Juan Bautista Gayete, and the helmsman and his boy, the negroes revolted suddenly, wounded dangerously the boatswain and the carpenter, and successively killed eighteen men of those who were sleeping upon deck, some with hand-spikes and hatchets, and others by throwing them alive overboard, after tying them; that of the Spaniards upon deck, they left about seven, as he thinks, alive and tied, to manoeuvre the ship, and three or four more, who hid themselves, remained also alive. Although in the act of revolt the negroes made themselves masters of the hatchway, six or seven wounded went through it to the cockpit, without any hindrance on their part; that during the act of revolt, the mate and another person, whose name he does not recollect, attempted to come up through the hatchway, but being quickly wounded, were obliged to return to the cabin; that the deponent resolved at break of day to come up the companion-way, where the negro Babo was, being the ringleader, and Atufal, who assisted him, and having spoken to them, exhorted them to cease committing such atrocities, asking them, at the same time, what they wanted and intended to do, offering, himself, to obey their commands; that notwithstanding this, they threw, in his presence, three men, alive and tied, overboard; that they told the deponent to come up, and that they would not kill him; which having done, the negro

Babo asked him whether there were in those seas any negro countries where they might be carried, and he answered them, No; that the negro Babo afterwards told him to carry them to Senegal, or to the neighboring islands of St. Nicholas;[1] and he answered, that this was impossible, on account of the great distance, the necessity involved of rounding Cape Horn, the bad condition of the vessel, the want of provisions, sails, and water; but that the negro Babo replied to him he must carry them in any way; that they would do and conform themselves to everything the deponent should require as to eating and drinking; that after a long conference, being absolutely compelled to please them, for they threatened to kill all the whites if they were not, at all events, carried to Senegal, he told them that what was most wanting for the voyage was water; that they would go near the coast to take it, and thence they would proceed on their course; that the negro Babo agreed to it; and the deponent steered towards the intermediate ports, hoping to meet some Spanish, or foreign vessel that would save them; that within ten or eleven days they saw the land, and continued their course by it in the vicinity of Nasca;[2] that the deponent observed that the negroes were now restless and mutinous, because he did not effect the taking in of water, the negro Babo having required, with threats, that it should be done, without fail, the following day; he told him he saw plainly that the coast was steep, and the rivers designated in the maps were not to be found, with other reasons suitable to the circumstances; that the best way would be to go to the island of Santa Maria, where they might water easily, it being a solitary island, as the foreigners did; that the deponent did not go to Pisco,[3] that was near, nor make any other port of the coast, because the negro Babo had intimated to him several times, that he would kill all the whites the

---

[1] *islands of St. Nicholas* Probably the Cabo Verde (Cape Verde) Islands, an archipelago located approximately 400 miles off the coast of Senegal in West Africa, one of which is named São Nicolau (St. Nicholas). The town of Tarrafal on São Nicolau was an anchorage for whaling ships in the nineteenth century, which may be the basis for Melville's familiarity with it. Senegal and the Cabo Verde Islands were both major sites of embarkation in the transatlantic slave trade; the Cabo Verde Islands also served as a penal colony for their Portuguese colonizers and were the site of several anticolonial revolts.

[2] *Nasca* Province in southern Peru.

[3] *Pisco* Port city in southern Peru.

very moment he should perceive any city, town, or settlement of any kind on the shores to which they should be carried: that having determined to go to the island of Santa Maria, as the deponent had planned, for the purpose of trying whether, on the passage or near the island itself, they could find any vessel that should favor them, or whether he could escape from it in a boat to the neighboring coast of Arruco,[1] to adopt the necessary means he immediately changed his course, steering for the island; that the negroes Babo and Atufal held daily conferences, in which they discussed what was necessary for their design of returning to Senegal, whether they were to kill all the Spaniards, and particularly the deponent; that eight days after parting from the coast of Nasca, the deponent being on the watch a little after day-break, and soon after the negroes had their meeting, the negro Babo came to the place where the deponent was, and told him that he had determined to kill his master, Don Alexandro Aranda, both because he and his companions could not otherwise be sure of their liberty, and that to keep the seamen in subjection, he wanted to prepare a warning of what road they should be made to take did they or any of them oppose him; and that, by means of the death of Don Alexandro, that warning would best be given; but, that what this last meant, the deponent did not at the time comprehend, nor could not, further than that the death of Don Alexandro was intended; and moreover the negro Babo proposed to the deponent to call the mate Raneds, who was sleeping in the cabin, before the thing was done, for fear, as the deponent understood it, that the mate, who was a good navigator, should be killed with Don Alexandro and the rest; that the deponent, who was the friend, from youth, of Don Alexandro, prayed and conjured, but all was useless; for the negro Babo answered him that the thing could not be prevented, and that all the Spaniards risked their death if they should attempt to frustrate his will in this matter, or any other; that, in this conflict, the deponent called the mate, Raneds, who was forced to go apart, and immediately the negro Babo commanded the Ashantee Martinqui and the Ashantee Lecbe to go and commit the murder; that those two went down with hatchets to the berth of Don Alexandro; that, yet half alive and mangled, they dragged him on deck; that they were going to throw him overboard in that state, but the negro Babo stopped them, bidding the murder be completed on the deck before him, which was done, when, by his orders, the body was carried below, forward; that nothing more was seen of it by the deponent for three days; * * * that Don Alonzo Sidonia, an old man, long resident at Valparaiso, and lately appointed to a civil office in Peru, whither he had taken passage, was at the time sleeping in the berth opposite Don Alexandro's; that awakening at his cries, surprised by them, and at the sight of the negroes with their bloody hatchets in their hands, he threw himself into the sea through a window which was near him, and was drowned, without it being in the power of the deponent to assist or take him up; * * * that a short time after killing Aranda, they brought upon deck his german-cousin, of middle-age, Don Francisco Masa, of Mendoza, and the young Don Joaquin, Marques de Aramboalaza, then lately from Spain, with his Spanish servant Ponce, and the three young clerks of Aranda, José Mozairi, Lorenzo Bargas, and Hermenegildo Gandix, all of Cadiz; that Don Joaquin and Hermenegildo Gandix, the negro Babo, for purposes hereafter to appear, preserved alive; but Don Francisco Masa, José Mozairi, and Lorenzo Bargas, with Ponce the servant, beside the boatswain, Juan Robles, the boatswain's mates, Manuel Viscaya and Roderigo Hurta, and four of the sailors, the negro Babo ordered to be thrown alive into the sea, although they made no resistance, nor begged for anything else but mercy; that the boatswain, Juan Robles, who knew how to swim, kept the longest above water, making acts of contrition, and, in the last words he uttered, charged this deponent to cause mass to be said for his soul to our Lady of Succor:[2] * * * that, during the three days which followed, the deponent, uncertain what fate had befallen the remains of Don Alexandro, frequently asked the negro Babo where they were, and, if still on board, whether they were to be preserved for interment ashore, entreating him so to order it; that the negro Babo answered nothing till the fourth day, when at sunrise, the deponent coming on deck, the negro Babo showed him a skeleton, which had been substituted for the ship's proper figure-head—the

---

1   *Arruco*   I.e., Araucanía, a region in Chile.

2   *our Lady of Succor*   An epithet of the Virgin Mary.

image of Christopher Colon,[1] the discoverer of the New World; that the negro Babo asked him whose skeleton that was, and whether, from its whiteness, he should not think it a white's; that, upon discovering his face, the negro Babo, coming close, said words to this effect: "Keep faith with the blacks from here to Senegal, or you shall in spirit, as now in body, follow your leader," pointing to the prow; * * * that the same morning the negro Babo took by succession each Spaniard forward, and asked him whose skeleton that was, and whether, from its whiteness, he should not think it a white's; that each Spaniard covered his face; that then to each the negro Babo repeated the words in the first place said to the deponent; * * * that they (the Spaniards), being then assembled aft, the negro Babo harangued them, saying that he had now done all; that the deponent (as navigator for the negroes) might pursue his course, warning him and all of them that they should, soul and body, go the way of Don Alexandro, if he saw them (the Spaniards) speak, or plot anything against them (the negroes)—a threat which was repeated every day; that, before the events last mentioned, they had tied the cook to throw him overboard, for it is not known what thing they heard him speak, but finally the negro Babo spared his life, at the request of the deponent; that a few days after, the deponent, endeavoring not to omit any means to preserve the lives of the remaining whites, spoke to the negroes peace and tranquillity, and agreed to draw up a paper, signed by the deponent and the sailors who could write, as also by the negro Babo, for himself and all the blacks, in which the deponent obliged himself to carry them to Senegal, and they not to kill any more, and he formally to make over to them the ship, with the cargo, with which they were for that time satisfied and quieted. * * But the next day, the more surely to guard against the sailors' escape, the negro Babo commanded all the boats to be destroyed but the long-boat, which was unseaworthy, and another, a cutter[2] in good condition, which knowing it would yet be wanted for towing the water casks, he had it lowered down into the hold.

* * * * * *

[*Various particulars of the prolonged and perplexed navigation ensuing here follow, with incidents of a calamitous calm, from which portion one passage is extracted, to wit:*]

—That on the fifth day of the calm, all on board suffering much from the heat, and want of water, and five having died in fits, and mad, the negroes became irritable, and for a chance gesture, which they deemed suspicious—though it was harmless—made by the mate, Raneds, to the deponent in the act of handing a quadrant,[3] they killed him; but that for this they afterwards were sorry, the mate being the only remaining navigator on board, except the deponent.

* * * * * *

—That omitting other events, which daily happened, and which can only serve uselessly to recall past misfortunes and conflicts, after seventy-three days' navigation, reckoned from the time they sailed from Nasca, during which they navigated under a scanty allowance of water, and were afflicted with the calms before mentioned, they at last arrived at the island of Santa Maria, on the seventeenth of the month of August, at about six o'clock in the afternoon, at which hour they cast anchor very near the American ship, Bachelor's Delight, which lay in the same bay, commanded by the generous Captain Amasa Delano; but at six o'clock in the morning, they had already descried the port, and the negroes became uneasy, as soon as at distance they saw the ship, not having expected to see one there; that the negro Babo pacified them, assuring them that no fear need be had; that straightway he ordered the figure on the bow to be covered with canvas, as for repairs, and had the decks a little set in order; that for a time the negro Babo and the negro Atufal conferred; that the negro Atufal was for sailing away, but the negro Babo would not, and, by himself, cast about what to do; that at last he came to the deponent, proposing to him to say and do all that the deponent declares to have said and done to the American captain; * * * * * * * * that the negro Babo warned him that if

---

[1] *Christopher Colon* Christopher Columbus.

[2] *cutter* Boat kept on a warship and typically used for carrying stores and passengers from ship to shore.

[3] *quadrant* Instrument for making measurements of angles up to 90 degrees; used for navigation.

he varied in the least, or uttered any word, or gave any look that should give the least intimation of the past events or present state, he would instantly kill him, with all his companions, showing a dagger, which he carried hid, saying something which, as he understood it, meant that that dagger would be alert as his eye; that the negro Babo then announced the plan to all his companions, which pleased them; that he then, the better to disguise the truth, devised many expedients, in some of them uniting deceit and defense; that of this sort was the device of the six Ashantees before named, who were his bravoes; that them he stationed on the break of the poop, as if to clean certain hatchets (in cases, which were part of the cargo), but in reality to use them, and distribute them at need, and at a given word he told them; that, among other devices, was the device of presenting Atufal, his right hand man, as chained, though in a moment the chains could be dropped; that in every particular he informed the deponent what part he was expected to enact in every device, and what story he was to tell on every occasion, always threatening him with instant death if he varied in the least: that, conscious that many of the negroes would be turbulent, the negro Babo appointed the four aged negroes, who were calkers, to keep what domestic order they could on the decks; that again and again he harangued the Spaniards and his companions, informing them of his intent, and of his devices, and of the invented story that this deponent was to tell; charging them lest any of them varied from that story; that these arrangements were made and matured during the interval of two or three hours, between their first sighting the ship and the arrival on board of Captain Amasa Delano; that this happened about half-past seven o'clock in the morning, Captain Amasa Delano coming in his boat, and all gladly receiving him; that the deponent, as well as he could force himself, acting then the part of principal owner, and a free captain of the ship, told Captain Amasa Delano, when called upon, that he came from Buenos Ayres, bound to Lima, with three hundred negroes; that off Cape Horn, and in a subsequent fever, many negroes had died; that also, by similar casualties, all the sea officers and the greatest part of the crew had died.

*   *   *   *   *   *

[*And so the deposition goes on, circumstantially recounting the fictitious story dictated to the deponent by Babo, and through the deponent imposed upon Captain Delano; and also recounting the friendly offers of Captain Delano, with other things, but all of which is here omitted. After the fictitious story, etc. the deposition proceeds:*]

*   *   *   *   *   *

—that the generous Captain Amasa Delano remained on board all the day, till he left the ship anchored at six o'clock in the evening, deponent speaking to him always of his pretended misfortunes, under the fore-mentioned principles, without having had it in his power to tell a single word, or give him the least hint, that he might know the truth and state of things; because the negro Babo, performing the office of an officious servant with all the appearance of submission of the humble slave, did not leave the deponent one moment; that this was in order to observe the deponent's actions and words, for the negro Babo understands well the Spanish; and besides, there were thereabout some others who were constantly on the watch, and likewise understood the Spanish; * * * that upon one occasion, while deponent was standing on the deck conversing with Amasa Delano, by a secret sign the negro Babo drew him (the deponent) aside, the act appearing as if originating with the deponent; that then, he being drawn aside, the negro Babo proposed to him to gain from Amasa Delano full particulars about his ship, and crew, and arms; that the deponent asked "For what?" that the negro Babo answered he might conceive; that, grieved at the prospect of what might overtake the generous Captain Amasa Delano, the deponent at first refused to ask the desired questions, and used every argument to induce the negro Babo to give up this new design; that the negro Babo showed the point of his dagger; that, after the information had been obtained the negro Babo again drew him aside, telling him that that very night he (the deponent) would be captain of two ships, instead of one, for that, great part of the American's ship's crew being to be absent fishing, the six Ashantees, without any one else, would easily take it; that at this time he said other things to the same purpose; that no entreaties availed; that, before Amasa Delano's coming on board, no hint had been given touching the capture of the American ship: that to prevent this project the deponent was powerless; * * *—that in some things his memory is confused, he cannot distinctly recall every event; * * * —that as soon as they had cast anchor at six of the clock in the evening, as has before been stated, the American Captain took leave, to return to his vessel; that upon a sudden impulse, which the deponent believes to have come from God and his angels, he, after the farewell had been said, followed the generous Captain Amasa Delano as far as the gunwale, where he stayed, under pretense of taking leave, until Amasa Delano should have been seated in his boat; that on shoving off, the deponent sprang from the gunwale into the boat, and fell into it, he knows not how, God guarding him; that—

* * * * * *

[*Here, in the original, follows the account of what further happened at the escape, and how the San Dominick was retaken, and of the passage to the coast; including in the recital many expressions of "eternal gratitude" to the "generous Captain Amasa Delano." The deposition then proceeds with recapitulatory remarks, and a partial renumeration of the negroes, making record of their individual part in the past events, with a view to furnishing, according to command of the court, the data whereon to found the criminal sentences to be pronounced. From this portion is the following;*]

—That he believes that all the negroes, though not in the first place knowing to the design of revolt, when it was accomplished, approved it. * * * That the negro, José, eighteen years old, and in the personal service of Don Alexandro, was the one who communicated the information to the negro Babo, about the state of things in the cabin, before the revolt; that this is known, because, in the preceding midnight, he used to come from his berth, which was under his master's, in the cabin, to the deck where the ringleader and his associates were, and had secret conversations with the negro Babo, in which he was several times seen by the mate; that, one night, the mate drove him away twice; * * that this same negro José was the one who, without being commanded to do so by the negro Babo, as Lecbe and Martinqui were, stabbed his master, Don Alexandro, after he had been dragged half-lifeless to

the deck; * * that the mulatto steward, Francesco, was of the first band of revolters, that he was, in all things, the creature and tool of the negro Babo; that, to make his court, he, just before a repast in the cabin, proposed, to the negro Babo, poisoning a dish for the generous Captain Amasa Delano; this is known and believed, because the negroes have said it; but that the negro Babo, having another design, forbade Francesco; * * that the Ashantee Lecbe was one of the worst of them; for that, on the day the ship was retaken, he assisted in the defense of her, with a hatchet in each hand, with one of which he wounded, in the breast, the chief mate of Amasa Delano, in the first act of boarding; this all knew; that, in sight of the deponent, Lecbe struck, with a hatchet, Don Francisco Masa, when, by the negro Babo's orders, he was carrying him to throw him overboard, alive, beside participating in the murder, before mentioned, of Don Alexandro Aranda, and others of the cabin-passengers; that, owing to the fury with which the Ashantees fought in the engagement with the boats, but this Lecbe and Yan survived; that Yan was bad as Lecbe; that Yan was the man who, by Babo's command, willingly prepared the skeleton of Don Alexandro, in a way the negroes afterwards told the deponent, but which he, so long as reason is left him, can never divulge; that Yan and Lecbe were the two who, in a calm by night, riveted the skeleton to the bow; this also the negroes told him; that the negro Babo was he who traced the inscription below it; that the negro Babo was the plotter from first to last; he ordered every murder, and was the helm and keel of the revolt; that Atufal was his lieutenant in all; but Atufal, with his own hand, committed no murder; nor did the negro Babo; * * that Atufal was shot, being killed in the fight with the boats, ere boarding; * * that the negresses, of age, were knowing to the revolt, and testified themselves satisfied at the death of their master, Don Alexandro; that, had the negroes not restrained them, they would have tortured to death, instead of simply killing, the Spaniards slain by command of the negro Babo; that the negresses used their utmost influence to have the deponent made away with; that, in the various acts of murder, they sang songs and danced—not gaily, but solemnly; and before the engagement with the boats, as well as during the action, they sang melancholy songs to the negroes, and that this melancholy tone was more inflaming than a different one would have been, and was so intended; that all this is believed, because the negroes have said it.—that of the thirty-six men of the crew, exclusive of the passengers (all of whom are now dead), which the deponent had knowledge of, six only remained alive, with four cabin-boys and ship-boys, not included with the crew; * *—that the negroes broke an arm of one of the cabin-boys and gave him strokes with hatchets.

[*Then follow various random disclosures referring to various periods of time. The following are extracted;*]

—That during the presence of Captain Amasa Delano on board, some attempts were made by the sailors, and one by Hermenegildo Gandix, to convey hints to him of the true state of affairs; but that these attempts were ineffectual, owing to fear of incurring death, and, furthermore, owing to the devices which offered contradictions to the true state of affairs, as well as owing to the generosity and piety of Amasa Delano incapable of sounding such wickedness; * * * that Luys Galgo, a sailor about sixty years of age, and formerly of the king's navy, was one of those who sought to convey tokens to Captain Amasa Delano; but his intent, though undiscovered, being suspected, he was, on a pretense, made to retire out of sight, and at last into the hold, and there was made away with. This the negroes have since said; * * * that one of the ship-boys feeling, from Captain Amasa Delano's presence, some hopes of release, and not having enough prudence, dropped some chance-word respecting his expectations, which being overheard and understood by a slave-boy with whom he was eating at the time, the latter struck him on the head with a knife, inflicting a bad wound, but of which the boy is now healing; that likewise, not long before the ship was brought to anchor, one of the seamen, steering at the time, endangered himself by letting the blacks remark some expression in his countenance, arising from a cause similar to the above; but this sailor, by his heedful after conduct, escaped; * * * that these statements are made to show the court that from the beginning to the end of the revolt, it was impossible for the deponent and his men to act otherwise than they did; * * *—that the third clerk, Hermenegildo Gandix, who before had been forced to live among the seamen, wearing a seaman's habit, and in all respects appearing to be one for the time; he, Gandix, was killed by a musket ball fired through mistake from the boats before boarding; having in his fright run up the mizzen-rigging, calling to the boats—"don't board," lest upon their boarding the negroes should kill him; that this inducing the Americans to believe he some way favored the cause of the negroes, they fired two balls at him, so that he fell wounded from the rigging, and was drowned in the sea; * * *—that the young Don Joaquin, Marques de Aramboalaza, like Hermenegildo Gandix, the third clerk, was degraded to the office and appearance of a common seaman; that upon one occasion when Don Joaquin shrank, the negro Babo commanded the Ashantee Lecbe to take tar and heat it, and pour it upon Don Joaquin's hands; * * *—that Don Joaquin was killed owing to another mistake of the Americans, but one impossible to be avoided, as upon the approach of the boats, Don Joaquin, with a hatchet tied edge out and upright to his hand, was made by the negroes to appear on the bulwarks; whereupon, seen with arms in his hands and in a questionable attitude, he was shot for a renegade seaman; * * *—that on the person of Don Joaquin was found secreted a jewel, which, by papers that were discovered, proved to have been meant for the shrine of our Lady of Mercy in Lima; a votive offering, beforehand prepared and guarded, to attest his gratitude, when he should have landed in Peru, his last destination, for the safe conclusion of his entire voyage from Spain; * * *—that the jewel, with the other effects of the late Don Joaquin, is in the custody of the brethren of the Hospital de Sacerdotes,[1] awaiting the disposition of the honorable court; * * *—that, owing to the condition of the deponent, as well as the haste in which the boats departed for the attack, the Americans were not forewarned that there were, among the apparent crew, a passenger and one of the clerks disguised by the negro Babo; * * *—that, beside the negroes killed in the action, some were killed after the capture and re-anchoring at night, when shackled to the ring-bolts on deck; that these deaths were committed by the sailors, ere they could be prevented. That so soon as informed of it, Captain Amasa Delano used all his

---

[1]   *Hospital de Sacerdotes*   A place where priests would take care of the sick or needy ("sacerdotes" means "priests" in Spanish).

authority, and, in particular with his own hand, struck down Martinez Gola, who, having found a razor in the pocket of an old jacket of his, which one of the shackled negroes had on, was aiming it at the negro's throat; that the noble Captain Amasa Delano also wrenched from the hand of Bartholomew Barlo a dagger, secreted at the time of the massacre of the whites, with which he was in the act of stabbing a shackled negro, who, the same day, with another negro, had thrown him down and jumped upon him; * * *—that, for all the events, befalling through so long a time, during which the ship was in the hands of the negro Babo, he cannot here give account; but that, what he has said is the most substantial of what occurs to him at present, and is the truth under the oath which he has taken; which declaration he affirmed and ratified, after hearing it read to him.

He said that he is twenty-nine years of age, and broken in body and mind; that when finally dismissed by the court, he shall not return home to Chili, but betake himself to the monastery on Mount Agonia without; and signed with his honor, and crossed himself, and, for the time, departed as he came, in his litter, with the monk Infelez, to the Hospital de Sacerdotes.

BENITO CERENO.

DOCTOR ROZAS.

If the Deposition have served as the key to fit into the lock of the complications which precede it, then, as a vault whose door has been flung back, the San Dominick's hull lies open to-day.

Hitherto the nature of this narrative, besides rendering the intricacies in the beginning unavoidable, has more or less required that many things, instead of being set down in the order of occurrence, should be retrospectively, or irregularly given; this last is the case with the following passages, which will conclude the account:

During the long, mild voyage to Lima, there was, as before hinted, a period during which the sufferer a little recovered his health, or, at least in some degree, his tranquillity. Ere the decided relapse which came, the two captains had many cordial conversations—their fraternal unreserve in singular contrast with former withdrawments.

Again and again it was repeated, how hard it had been to enact the part forced on the Spaniard by Babo.

"Ah, my dear friend," Don Benito once said, "at those very times when you thought me so morose and ungrateful, nay, when, as you now admit, you half thought me plotting your murder, at those very times my heart was frozen; I could not look at you, thinking of what, both on board this ship and your own, hung, from other hands, over my kind benefactor. And as God lives, Don Amasa, I know not whether desire for my own safety alone could have nerved me to that leap into your boat, had it not been for the thought that, did you, unenlightened, return to your ship, you, my best friend, with all who might be with you, stolen upon, that night, in your hammocks, would never in this world have wakened again. Do but think how you walked this deck, how you sat in this cabin, every inch of ground mined into honey-combs under you. Had I dropped the least hint, made the least advance towards an understanding between us, death, explosive death—yours as mine—would have ended the scene."

"True, true," cried Captain Delano, starting, "you have saved my life, Don Benito, more than I yours; saved it, too, against my knowledge and will."

"Nay, my friend," rejoined the Spaniard, courteous even to the point of religion, "God charmed your life, but you saved mine. To think of some things you did—those smilings and chattings, rash pointings and gesturings. For less than these, they slew my mate, Raneds; but you had the Prince of Heaven's safe-conduct through all ambuscades."[1]

"Yes, all is owing to Providence, I know: but the temper of my mind that morning was more than commonly pleasant, while the sight of so much suffering, more apparent than real, added to my good-nature, compassion, and charity, happily interweaving the three. Had it been otherwise, doubtless, as you hint, some of my interferences might have ended unhappily enough. Besides, those feelings I spoke of enabled me to get the better of momentary distrust, at times when acuteness might have cost me my life, without saving another's. Only at the end did my suspicions get the better of me, and you know how wide of the mark they then proved."

---

[1]   *ambuscades* Ambushes.

"Wide, indeed," said Don Benito, sadly; "you were with me all day; stood with me, sat with me, talked with me, looked at me, ate with me, drank with me; and yet, your last act was to clutch for a monster, not only an innocent man, but the most pitiable of all men. To such degree may malign machinations and deceptions impose. So far may even the best man err, in judging the conduct of one with the recesses of whose condition he is not acquainted. But you were forced to it; and you were in time undeceived. Would that, in both respects, it was so ever, and with all men."

"You generalize, Don Benito; and mournfully enough. But the past is passed; why moralize upon it? Forget it. See, yon bright sun has forgotten it all, and the blue sea, and the blue sky; these have turned over new leaves."

"Because they have no memory," he dejectedly replied; "because they are not human."

"But these mild trades[1] that now fan your cheek, do they not come with a human-like healing to you? Warm friends, steadfast friends are the trades."

"With their steadfastness they but waft me to my tomb, Señor," was the foreboding response.

"You are saved," cried Captain Delano, more and more astonished and pained; "you are saved: what has cast such a shadow upon you?"

"The negro."

There was silence, while the moody man sat, slowly and unconsciously gathering his mantle about him, as if it were a pall.[2]

There was no more conversation that day.

But if the Spaniard's melancholy sometimes ended in muteness upon topics like the above, there were others upon which he never spoke at all; on which, indeed, all his old reserves were piled. Pass over the worst, and, only to elucidate let an item or two of these be cited. The dress, so precise and costly, worn by him on the day whose events have been narrated, had not willingly been put on. And that silver-mounted sword, apparent symbol of despotic command, was not, indeed, a sword, but the ghost of one. The scabbard, artificially stiffened, was empty.

As for the black—whose brain, not body, had schemed and led the revolt, with the plot—his slight frame, inadequate to that which it held, had at once yielded to the superior muscular strength of his captor, in the boat. Seeing all was over, he uttered no sound, and could not be forced to. His aspect seemed to say, since I cannot do deeds, I will not speak words. Put in irons in the hold, with the rest, he was carried to Lima. During the passage, Don Benito did not visit him. Nor then, nor at any time after, would he look at him. Before the tribunal he refused. When pressed by the judges he fainted. On the testimony of the sailors alone rested the legal identity of Babo.

Some months after, dragged to the gibbet[3] at the tail of a mule, the black met his voiceless end. The body was burned to ashes; but for many days, the head, that hive of subtlety, fixed on a pole in the Plaza, met, unabashed, the gaze of the whites; and across the Plaza looked towards St. Bartholomew's church, in whose vaults slept then, as now, the recovered bones of Aranda: and across the Rimac bridge looked towards the monastery, on Mount Agonia without; where, three months after being dismissed by the court, Benito Cereno, borne on the bier, did, indeed, follow his leader.

—1856

---

[1]   *trades*   Trade winds.

[2]   *pall*   A cloth spread over a coffin, or a shroud over a dead body.

[3]   *gibbet*   Gallows; place of execution.

from *Battle-Pieces and Aspects of the War*[1]

THE PORTENT
(1859)

Hanging from the beam,
  Slowly swaying (such the law),
Gaunt the shadow on your green,
  Shenandoah!²
5 The cut is on the crown
    (Lo, John Brown),³
And the stabs shall heal no more.

Hidden in the cap
  Is the anguish none can draw;
10 So your future veils its face,

---

1   Melville added the following dedication: "The Battle-Pieces in this volume are dedicated to the memory of the three hundred thousand who in the war for the maintenance of the union fell devotedly under the flag of their fathers." An authorial note also follows the title page:

With few exceptions, the Pieces in this volume originated in an impulse imparted by the fall of Richmond [Sunday April 2, 1865; Richmond, Virginia, was the Confederate capital]. They were composed without reference to collective arrangement, but, being brought together in review, naturally fall into the order assumed.

The events and incidents of the conflict—making up a whole, in varied amplitude, corresponding with the geographical area covered by the war—from these but a few themes have been taken, such as for any cause chanced to imprint themselves upon the mind.

The aspects which the strife as a memory assumes are as manifold as are the moods of involuntary meditation—moods variable, and at times widely at variance. Yielding instinctively, one after another, to feelings not inspired from any one source exclusively, and unmindful, without purposing to be, of consistency, I seem, in most of these verses, to have but placed a harp in a window [an "aeolian" harp, that sounds out music passively when wind blows across it], and noted the contrasted airs which wayward winds have played upon the strings.

2   *Shenandoah* River that runs through Virginia and joins the Potomac at Harpers Ferry.

3   *John Brown* Abolitionist who initiated a planned campaign against slavery in the Southern states by raiding the U.S. arsenal at Harpers Ferry in Virginia (now West Virginia) on 16–18 October 1859. Brown was tried and hanged for treason on 2 December 1859; his last words were written down on a scrap of paper: "I John Brown am now quite certain that the crimes of this guilty land will never be purged away; but with Blood. I had as I now think vainly flattered myself that without very much bloodshed; it might be done." The raid on Harpers Ferry is widely seen by historians as a prelude to the Civil War that erupted in 1861.

Shenandoah!
But the streaming beard is shown
(Weird° John Brown),   *uncanny, fateful*
The meteor⁴ of the war.
—1866

Misgivings
(1860)

When ocean-clouds over inland hills
  Sweep storming in late autumn brown,
And horror the sodden valley fills,
  And the spire falls crashing in the town,
5 I muse upon my country's ills—
  The tempest bursting from the waste of Time
On the world's fairest hope linked with man's foulest
  crime.

Nature's dark side is heeded now—
  (Ah! optimist-cheer disheartened flown)—
10 A child may read the moody brow
    Of yon black mountain lone.
With shouts the torrents down the gorges go,
  And storms are formed behind the storm we feel:
The hemlock shakes in the rafter, the oak in the driv-
  ing keel.
—1866

*The March into Virginia, Ending in the First Manassas*⁵
(JULY, 1861)

Did all the lets° and bars appear   *obstructions*
  To every just or larger end,

---

4   *meteor* Meteors and other atmospheric phenomena were often interpreted as presaging conflict and death; see also Henry David Thoreau's essay "The Last Days of John Brown" (1860): "John Brown's career for the last six weeks of his life was meteor-like, flashing through the darkness in which we live."

5   *First Manassas* First major battle of the Civil War, fought on 21 July 1861 (also called the First Battle of Bull Run). The battle was a Confederate victory, with the Union army suffering close to 3,000 casualties. The Union army, on its march to battle, was accompanied by civilian supporters who, assuming an easy victory, cheerfully came to watch, even bringing picnics with them.

Whence should come the trust and cheer?
　　Youth must its ignorant impulse lend—
5　Age finds place in the rear.
　　　All wars are boyish, and are fought by boys,
　The champions and enthusiasts of the state:
　　　Turbid ardors and vain joys
　　　　Not barrenly abate—
10　　　Stimulants to the power mature,
　　　　Preparatives of fate.

　Who here forecasteth the event?
　What heart but spurns at precedent
　And warnings of the wise,
15　Contemned foreclosures of surprise?
　The banners play, the bugles call,
　The air is blue and prodigal.°　　　　　　　*reckless, lavish*
　　　No berrying party, pleasure-wooed,
　No picnic party in the May,
20　Ever went less loth than they
　　　Into that leafy neighborhood.
　In Bacchic[1] glee they file toward Fate,
　Moloch's uninitiate;[2]
　Expectancy, and glad surmise
25　Of battle's unknown mysteries.
　All they feel is this: 'tis glory,
　A rapture sharp, though transitory,
　Yet lasting in belaureled story.
　So they gayly go to fight,
30　Chatting left and laughing right.

　But some who this blithe mood present,
　　　As on in lightsome files they fare,
　Shall die experienced ere three days are spent—
　　　Perish, enlightened by the vollied glare;[3]
35　Or shame survive, and, like to adamant,[4]
　　　The throe° of Second Manassas,[5] share.　　　*agony*
　　—1866

---

[1]　*Bacchic*　Wild, unrestrained.

[2]　*Moloch*　Ancient Canaanite god to whom children were sacrificed; *uninitiate*　I.e., one who has yet to be initiated.

[3]　*vollied glare*　I.e., the glare caused by the exchange of fire in battle.

[4]　*adamant*　Very hard and impenetrable rock.

[5]　*Second Manassas*　Also known as the Second Battle of Bull Run, fought on 29–30 August, 1862; it was a Confederate victory, with 14,000 Union soldiers wounded and killed.

Dupont's Round Fight[6]
(November, 1861)

In time and measure perfect moves
　All Art whose aim is sure;
Evolving rhyme and stars divine
　Have rules, and they endure.

5　Nor less the Fleet that warred for Right,
　　And, warring so, prevailed,
In geometric beauty curved,
　　And in an orbit sailed.

The rebel at Port Royal felt
10　　The Unity overawe,
And ruled the spell. A type° was here,　　　*symbol, ideal*
　　And victory of Law.
—1866

A Utilitarian View of the Monitor's Fight[7]

Plain be the phrase, yet apt the verse,
　More ponderous than nimble;
For since grimed War here laid aside
His Orient pomp,[8] 'twould ill befit
5　　　Overmuch to ply
　　　The rhyme's barbaric cymbal.

---

[6]　*Dupont's Round Fight*　In 1861, Samuel Francis Du Pont, Rear Admiral in the U.S. Navy, was put in charge of the South Atlantic Blockading Squadron, a large fleet of ships charged with the mission of blocking trade between the Confederacy and Europe. Du Pont's ships attacked Port Royal harbor in South Carolina on 7 November 1861; the harbor was guarded by two Confederate forts, and Du Pont directed his ships to circle round and round the harbor, firing on both forts along the way, until they both capitulated. The victory at Port Royal secured the blockade of Confederate waters on the southeast coast.

[7]　*Utilitarian*　Materialistic, practical; *Monitor's Fight*　Battle of Hampton Roads, a naval battle fought on 8–9 March 1862 where the Elizabeth, Nansemond, and James Rivers meet before flowing out into Chesapeake Bay in Virginia. The battle was the first in which armored, steam-powered warships fought each other (the *USS Monitor* vs. the *CSS Virginia*); neither ship was able to defeat the other, and the battle ended indecisively. The battle had a significant impact on navies around the world, triggering an arms race in which every navy sought to develop ironclad warships.

[8]　*Orient pomp*　Luxurious and splendid show.

Hail to victory without the gaud°   *showiness*
    Of glory; zeal that needs no fans
Of banners; plain mechanic power
10 Plied cogently in War now placed—
    Where War belongs—
    Among the trades and artisans.

Yet this was battle, and intense—
    Beyond the strife of fleets heroic;
15 Deadlier, closer, calm 'mid storm;
No passion; all went on by crank,
    Pivot, and screw,
    And calculations of caloric.°   *heat*

Needless to dwell; the story's known.
20   The ringing of those plates on plates
Still ringeth round the world—
The clangor of the blacksmiths' fray.
    The anvil-din
    Resounds this message from the Fates:

25 War yet shall be, and to the end;
    But war-paint shows the streaks of weather;
War yet shall be, but warriors
Are now but operatives; War's made
    Less grand than Peace,
30   And a singe runs through lace and feather.
    —1866

Shiloh[1]
A Requiem
(APRIL, 1862)

Skimming lightly, wheeling still,
    The swallows fly low
Over the field in clouded days,
    The forest-field of Shiloh—
5 Over the field where April rain

---

[1] *Shiloh* The Battle of Shiloh was fought on 6–7 April 1862 in southwestern Tennessee. This battle resulted in the highest casualties of the Civil War up to that time, including the death of General Albert Sidney Johnston, the commander of the Confederate western armies; while the Union army won the battle, it also lost the most soldiers.

Solaced the parched ones stretched in pain
Through the pause of night
That followed the Sunday fight
    Around the church of Shiloh—
10 The church so lone, the log-built one,
That echoed to many a parting groan
    And natural prayer
    Of dying foemen mingled there—
Foemen at morn, but friends at eve—
15   Fame or country least their care:
(What like a bullet can undeceive!)
    But now they lie low,
While over them the swallows skim,
    And all is hushed at Shiloh.
—1866

Malvern Hill[2]
(JULY, 1862)

Ye elms that wave on Malvern Hill
    In prime of morn and May,
Recall ye how McClellan's men
    Here stood at bay?
5 While deep within yon forest dim
    Our rigid comrades lay—
Some with the cartridge in their mouth,
Others with fixed arms lifted South—
    Invoking so
10 The cypress glades? Ah wilds of woe!

The spires of Richmond, late beheld
    Through rifts in musket-haze,
Were closed from view in clouds of dust
    On leaf-walled ways,
15 Where streamed our wagons in caravan;
    And the Seven Nights and Days
Of march and fast, retreat and fight,

---

[2] *Malvern Hill* The Battle of Malvern Hill was fought on 1 July 1862 and was the last of the so-called Seven Days Battles, in which Confederate general Robert E. Lee pushed back Union forces under George B. McClellan that had been threatening Richmond, Virginia. The Union army won the battle of Malvern Hill, but its drive for Richmond had been halted. Casualties in the battle were heavy, particularly on the Confederate side, which lost close to 6,000 soldiers in one day.

Pinched our grimed faces to ghastly plight—
    Does the elm wood
20 Recall the haggard beards of blood?

The battle-smoked flag, with stars eclipsed,
    We followed (it never fell!)—
In silence husbanded our strength—
    Received their yell;[1]
25 Till on this slope we patient turned
    With cannon ordered well;
Reverse we proved was not defeat;
But ah, the sod what thousands meet!—
    Does Malvern Wood
30 Bethink itself, and muse and brood?

    We elms of Malvern Hill
      Remember every thing;
    But sap the twig will fill:
    Wag the world how it will,[2]
35   *Leaves must be green in Spring.*
    —1866

The House-top
A Night Piece
(JULY, 1863)

No sleep. The sultriness pervades the air
And binds the brain—a dense oppression, such
As tawny tigers feel in matted shades,
Vexing their blood and making apt for ravage.
5 Beneath the stars the roofy desert spreads
Vacant as Libya.[3] All is hushed near by.
Yet fitfully from far breaks a mixed surf
Of muffled sound, the Atheist roar of riot.[4]

Yonder, where parching Sirius[5] set in drought,
10 Balefully glares red Arson—there—and there.
The Town is taken by its rats—ship-rats
And rats of the wharves.[6] All civil charms
And priestly spells which late held hearts in awe—
Fear-bound, subjected to a better sway
15 Than sway of self; these like a dream dissolve,
And man rebounds whole aeons back in nature.
Hail to the low dull rumble, dull and dead,
And ponderous drag that shakes the wall.
Wise Draco[7] comes, deep in the midnight roll
20 Of black artillery; he comes, though late;
In code corroborating Calvin's creed[8]
And cynic tyrannies of honest kings;
He comes, nor parlies; and the Town redeemed,
Gives thanks devout; nor, being thankful, heeds
25 The grimy slur on the Republic's faith implied,
Which holds that Man is naturally good,
And—more—is Nature's Roman, never to be scourged.[9]
—1866

---

[1] *their yell* I.e., the "rebel yell," the noise made by Confederate soldiers when they charged into battle.

[2] *Wag … will* Proverbial phrase suggesting that world events will happen when and as they happen (and are of little concern to the speaker).

[3] *Vacant as Libya* Reference is to the northeastern part of the Sahara desert, which is in Libya.

[4] *roar of riot* Between 13 and 16 July, 1863, rioting erupted in Manhattan over the Union army draft. What started as a white working-class uprising to protest being drafted turned into a race riot: buildings were destroyed—the homes of abolitionists and black

people were particularly targeted—and eleven black people were lynched by white rioters. By 16 July there were thousands of Federal and State militia troops in the city to restore order, and the draft was postponed, which helped calm the violence. This riot is widely considered one of the most damaging incidents of civil unrest in American history. Many black families left Manhattan after the riot, moving instead to Brooklyn and New Jersey.

[5] *parching Sirius* The period of time when the bright star Sirius rises over the horizon line in summer is traditionally known as the "dog days" of summer—the hottest days, when drought, heat, and storms are common.

[6] *rats of the wharves* During the riot, violence was particularly fierce at the midtown docks, where white workers attacked black coworkers, as well as businesses that catered to black customers.

[7] *Draco* Ancient Greek legislator (fl. 7th century BCE) who replaced an oral judicial system based on blood feud with a strict written system of laws characterized by harsh punishments. It is also a constellation in the northern sky.

[8] *Calvin's creed* Calvinists believe that each person is born in a state of sinfulness and must rely entirely on God's grace for salvation.

[9] *Nature's Roman … scourged* I.e., in a republic, where individuals have what are considered natural and inalienable rights, there should not be punishment before a trial. See Acts 22.25: "As they bound him [the Apostle Paul] with thongs, Paul said unto the centurion that stood by, Is it lawful for you to scourge a man that is a Roman, and uncondemned?"

The Apparition
(A Retrospect)

Convulsions came; and, where the field
　Long slept in pastoral green,
A goblin-mountain was upheaved[1]
(Sure the scared sense was all deceived),
5　　Marl-glen and slag-ravine.[2]

The unreserve of Ill was there,
　The clinkers[3] in her last retreat;
But, ere the eye could take it in,
Or mind could comprehension win,
10　　It sunk!—and at our feet.

So, then, Solidity's a crust—
　The core of fire below;
All may go well for many a year,
But who can think without a fear
15　　Of horrors that happen so?
—1866

America

1.

Where the wings of a sunny Dome expand
　I saw a Banner in gladsome air—
Starry, like Berenice's Hair[4]—
Afloat in broadened bravery there;
5　With undulating long-drawn flow,
As rolled Brazilian billows go
Voluminously o'er the Line.°　　*equator*
The Land reposed in peace below;
　The children in their glee
10　Were folded to the exulting heart
　　Of young Maternity.

2.

Later, and it streamed in fight
　When tempest mingled with the fray,
And over the spear-point of the shaft
15　　I saw the ambiguous lightning play.
Valor with Valor strove, and died:
Fierce was Despair, and cruel was Pride;
And the lorn Mother speechless stood,
Pale at the fury of her brood.

3.

20　Yet later, and the silk did wind
　Her fair cold form;
Little availed the shining shroud,[5]
　Though ruddy in hue, to cheer or warm.
A watcher looked upon her low, and said—
25　She sleeps, but sleeps, she is not dead.
　　But in that sleep contortion showed
The terror of the vision there—
　A silent vision unavowed,
Revealing earth's foundation bare,
30　　And Gorgon[6] in her hidden place.
It was a thing of fear to see

1　*Convulsions ... upheaved*　Reference to an episode known as the Battle of the Crater, which took place on 30 July 1864, during the Siege of Petersburg (1864–65). The Union army had dug a tunnel underneath the Confederate line and filled it with explosives, with the intention of blowing a hole in the line to break the siege. The resulting explosion immediately killed several hundred Confederate soldiers and created a huge crater, which then became a battlefield—Union soldiers entered the crater and were then shot at by rallied Confederate troops. Approximate casualties for that day were 3,798 Union and 1,500 Confederate; Ulysses S. Grant called it "the saddest affair I have witnessed in the war."

2　*Marl-glen*　A rocky valley; marl is a sedimentary rock made of clay and limestone. In his epic *Paradise Lost* (1667), John Milton describes the ground of hell as "burning Marle" (1.296); *slag-ravine*　A ravine composed of the lumpy, rocky waste that results from refining metal.

3　*clinkers*　Masses of solidified volcanic lava.

4　*Berenice's Hair*　Constellation seen from the northern hemisphere; Queen Berenice II of Egypt (267/66–221 BCE) cut her hair as an offering for her husband's safe return, but the hair was stolen and placed up in the sky.

5　*shroud*　Cloth used to cover a dead body.

6　*Gorgon*　In Greek mythology, a creature with snakes for hair and a face that, when looked upon, turns its victims to stone.

So foul a dream upon so fair a face,
And the dreamer lying in that starry shroud.

4.

But from the trance she sudden broke—
35   The trance, or death into promoted life;
At her feet a shivered° yoke,   shattered
And in her aspect turned to heaven
        No trace of passion or of strife—
A clear calm look. It spake of pain,
40 But such as purifies from stain—

Sharp pangs that never come again—
        And triumph repressed by knowledge
            meet,°   appropriate
Power delicate,[1] and hope grown wise,
        And youth matured for age's seat—
45 Law on her brow and empire in her eyes.
        So she, with graver air and lifted flag;
While the shadow, chased by light,
Fled along the far-drawn height,
        And left her on the crag.
—1866

---

[1] *delicate* "Dedicate" in the first edition, but many subsequent
editors have interpreted this as a typo.

POPULAR LITERATURE AND PRINT CULTURE

This section adopts a broad definition of "popular," including not only works that manifestly reached a vast audience (songs such as Payne's "Home, Sweet Home"; plays such as *Fashion, or Life in New York*; novels such as *The Quaker City* and *Ragged Dick*; and magazine articles such as those in *Godey's Lady's Book*) but also works (such as "Theresa, A Haytien Tale," the poems and stories included in the *Lowell Offering*, and Wilhelm Weitling's "Der Kleine Kommunist") that *aimed* in one way or another at a broad audience, even if they may not have achieved a vast readership. We are mindful too of the etymology of popular ("belonging to the people") and for that reason we place some emphasis on works written by members of the working classes and/or in the interests of the working classes—"the common folk."

The vast growth of popular literature and of print culture during the 1820–Reconstruction period was driven by several engines. The country's population increased from just under 10 million in 1820 to almost 50 million in the late 1870s. Elementary schools proliferated, and by 1870 the overall illiteracy rate, as measured by formal schooling, had fallen to 20 per cent (a percentage that masks extraordinary levels of inequality—the illiteracy rate for white Americans was under 12 per cent while almost 80 per cent of black Americans were unable to read or write). The introduction of the "penny press" in 1833 (whereby newspapers began to be priced at one cent apiece, compared to the previous norm of six cents) brought about a dramatic change. Technological developments continued throughout the period to create greater efficiencies in the printing of books, magazines, and newspapers (all of which became far less expensive over the period). At the same time, changes in transportation and postal service revolutionized distribution systems.

If there were powerful forces driving the growth of popular literature and print culture, there were also powerful forces holding back growth. While the number of elementary schools grew exponentially, growth at the more advanced levels was much slower. Secondary schools were rare (and almost always fee-based rather than free), and, while the number of colleges and universities did grow substantially, by 1860 there were still only 241 degree-granting institutions[1]—almost all of them offering an education only to white males of substantial means. (Not surprisingly, the growth in readership for dime novels far outstripped the growth in the market for more highbrow publications.) The barriers to education for women and—even more so—for Indigenous people, black Americans, and other racialized groups continued to be all but insurmountable even after the Civil War. Under slavery Southern blacks were typically forbidden to learn how to write; during Reconstruction some schools did open to black students, but they were few in number and typically poorly funded.

Though it is the practice of this anthology to include special sections focused on popular literature and print culture, readers should be aware that there are works throughout the anthology that were extremely popular in their own era. The fiction of Sedgwick, Cooper, Child, Stowe, Alcott, Southworth, and Ridge; the nonfiction of Emerson, Fern, and Douglass; the poems of Sigourney, Bryant, Longfellow, and Whittier—all these (and more) found a very wide nineteenth-century readership. Particular attention should be drawn to the section "African American Oral Literature." And we should note, too, that many other culturally distinct communities produced forms of popular expression—shared oral, performance, and material cultures, for example—that lie beyond the reach of this volume.

⌘ ⌘ ⌘

---

[1]   By comparison, there are today well over 5,000 such institutions.

John Howard Payne, "Home, Sweet Home!"

"Home, Sweet Home!" may well have been the most popular song in nineteenth-century America. The song originated as part of an opera first performed on 8 May 1823 at the Covent Garden Opera house in London: *Clari, or The Maid of Milan*. The song's music was by the British composer Henry R. Bishop, its lyrics by the American poet and actor John Howard Payne (1791–1852). By the early 1830s (as the excerpt below from "Evening Music at Sea" attests) the song had become extremely well known, and its popularity only increased as the century wore on. Various versions added stanzas, and in some others alterations were made (such as the substitution of "I" for "we" in the first line).

'Mid pleasures and palaces though we may roam,
Be it ever so humble, there's no place like home!
A charm from the skies seems to hallow us there
Which, seek through the world, is ne'er met with elsewhere.

5   Home! Home, sweet, sweet home!
There's no place like home!
There's no place like home!

An exile from home splendour dazzles in vain!
Oh! give me my lowly thatched cottage again!
10 The birds singing gently that came at my call
Give me them with the peace of mind dearer than all.

Home! Home, sweet, sweet home!
There's no place like home!
There's no place like home!
            —1823

In Context

The Reception of "Home, Sweet Home!"

from anonymous ("A Quondam Sailor"), "Evening Music at Sea" (1833)

This piece describing the effect of "Home, Sweet Home!" on a group of sailors was first published in *The Western Monthly Magazine and Literary Journal* and widely reprinted, including in the 23 May issue of the *Lancaster Examiner* (Lancaster, Pennsylvania), the 10 July issue of the *Knoxville Republican* (Knoxville, Tennessee), and the August 1833 issue of *The Military and Naval Magazine of the United States*.

One of the delicious afternoons of February, peculiar to the West Indies, as the sun was declining below the western horizon, the beautiful *Hornet* lay in a calm near the island of Cuba. ... At this hour a few of the officers assembled on the forecastle to contemplate the scene; and, recalling the joys of other days, to hold that converse which, in a small degree, alleviates the privations of a seaman's life. ...

Then it was the remembrance of the past crowded up like odors from a bed of flowers, lulling the feelings to that delicious calmness which pleasant memories always inspire. ... The father dwelt in tenderness on his distant family; the brother recalled the unbidden assiduities of a sister's love; and the son, as he leaned against the mast, his features set in the sedateness of sober reflection, felt his heart softened by the recollection of a mother's care. But few remarks were made. All felt that the stillness which reigned above, beneath, and around, should not be disturbed. Each one had retired to the recesses of his own heart—a sanctuary too sacred to be violated.

Such was the state of feeling when a clear, melodious voice slowly poured forth the first line of that exquisite song "Home, Sweet home!" As the words "Mid pleasures and palaces" swelled upon the air, a single exclamation of pleasure escaped the hearers, and then they again relapsed into silence. We had often heard the song, but never had it come so thrillingly as then. Had it been sung by even an ordinary performer, its effect would have been great, but breathed as it was, with a fervor and feeling I have never known excelled, in a voice full, manly, and touching, it could but produce a powerful impression. ... The man whose locks were whitened, equally with the boy whose features were unmarked by the furrows of time and care, seemed to drink in the beautiful words as a healing draught.

Winslow Homer, *Home, Sweet Home!*, 1863. This painting (which now hangs in the National Gallery of Art in Washington, D.C.) did much to establish Winslow Homer's reputation when it was first exhibited in 1863. It depicts two infantrymen in the Union army listening to their regimental band play the famous song. The previous year General Nelson A. Miles had described how the playing of this song affected both Union and Confederate forces:

> Late in the afternoon our bands were accustomed to play the most spirited martial and national airs,[1] as "Columbia," "America," "E. Pluribus Unum," "The Star-spangled Banner," etc., to be answered along the Confederate lines by bands playing, with equal enthusiasm, "The Bonny Blue Flag," "Southern Rights," and "Dixie." These demonstrations frequently aroused the hostile sentiments of the two armies, yet the animosity disappeared when at the close some band would strike up that melody which comes nearest the hearts of all true men, "Home, Sweet Home," and every band within hearing would join in that sacred anthem with unbroken accord and enthusiasm.

By the time the war ended, however, the song was no longer played in such contexts; as John Funchion notes, "it became banned on the front lines because Union and Confederate doctors feared it would afflict soldiers with potentially deadly nostalgia."

---

[1] *airs* Songs.

anonymous ("Yankee"), "A Song Written for the Fourth of July 1828, Addressed to the Working Classes"

Though the formation of American labor unions (or "trade societies," as they were often called) first occurred at the end of the eighteenth century, the labor movement suffered a series of setbacks in the second decade of the nineteenth century as several strikes failed and various court decisions went against labor. Following the depression of 1819–22, however, labor began again to flex its organizational muscles in New Orleans, New York, Philadelphia, and other centers. An 1827 "stand-out" (as strikes were then called) by carpenters in Philadelphia called for a reduction of the workday from sixteen to ten hours—and an influential pamphlet published in April 1827 in Philadelphia called for workingmen to school themselves in political economy so as to be better able to argue their case and exert real power politically. In his "Address to the Members of Trade Societies," William Heighton (1800–73) called for the formation of a workingmen's library and a workingmen's press in every community. By the end of the year the various Philadelphia labor groups had formed the Mechanics' Union of Trade Associations. The Mechanics' Library Company had also been formed, and had began publishing the *Mechanics' Free Press*, a pioneering labor newspaper that became widely circulated. The poem reprinted here was first published in the 5 July 1828 issue of the *Mechanics' Free Press*.

When Freedom waved her signal high,
O'er this fav'rite chosen land—
"To arms! to arms!" was heard the cry
Throughout the faithful fearless band.

5   With patriotic fire they burned,
And 'roused to flame by freedom's breath,
They on their country's tyrants turned,
Resolved on "Liberty or Death."[1]

Each heart was joined to aid the cause
10   Of liberty and sacred right;
To give Columbia[2] equal laws,
No longer yield to foreign might.

The God of justice viewed the strife,
And lent a force of freemen's blows;
15   While they, despising slavish life,
Rushed fearless on their vet'ran foes.

They fought, they conquered, and then gained
Sweet liberty and high renown;
And shall their sons e'en now be chained,
20   And tremble at th' oppressor's frown!

Awake! ye humble men who toil,
Remember what our sires have done;
Remember this is freedom's soil—
Our fathers have the blessing won.

25   Shall we then bow to haughty pride,
Built on the labour of our hands!
Or shall we for ourselves provide,
And proudly spurn unjust demands!

The bright example of our sires,
30   Is still before our mental eyes;
Then may we feel those sacred fires,
Which bid them on their tyrants rise.

Freedom is ours—and shall we yield
To haughty speculator's claims!
35   Dare we not enter freedom's field?
Shall we still wear these humbling chains?

Come, let us rise in wisdom's might,
And firm united in the cause,
We'll boldly claim our sacred right,
40   Nor longer stand in doubtful pause.
—1828

---

[1]   *Liberty or Death*   The sentence "Give me liberty, or give me death!" was spoken during a speech delivered at the Second Virginia Convention on 23 March 1775, most often attributed to the revolutionary Patrick Henry.

[2]   *Columbia*   I.e., America.

anonymous, "The Mill Has Shut Down"

The severe economic downturn known as the "Panic of 1837" left vast numbers of working people unemployed or partially employed, and many who kept their jobs were forced to work for much lower wages than they had earned just a few years earlier. Many trade societies and a number of labor newspapers folded. The song reproduced below was published by St. Clair Smith in Philadelphia as an undated broadside.

"The mill has shut down! Good God, shut down!"
  Like the cry of flood or fire the cry
Runs swifter than lightning through the town.
"The mill has shut down! Good God, shut down!"
5 Men wring their hands and look at the sky;
Women fall fainting; like dead they lie.
At the very best they earned but bread,
With the mill shut down they'd better be dead.

Last year with patience a lessened wage
10 They helplessly took—better than none;
More children worked, at tender age—
Even their mite° helped the lessened   *small contribution*
    wage.
The babies were left at their home alone.
'Twas enough to break a heart of stone
15 To see how these people worked for bread!
With the mill shut down they'd better be dead!

"The mill has shut down! Good God, shut down!"
It has run at loss this many a day.
Far worse than flood or fire in the town
20 Will be famine, now the mill has shut down.
But to shut mills down is the only way,
When they run at a loss, the mill owners say.
God help the hands to whom it meant bread!
With the mill shut down they'd better be dead!
—?1830s–1850s

Factory Girls, the Lowell Mills, and the *Lowell Offering*

As discussed in the overview introduction to the 1820–Reconstruction period, one of the first templates for factory employment in the United States was the system developed by Francis Cabot Lowell, which was innovative in terms both of technology and of labor. The system increased efficiency by combining within each textile factory the operations of spinning and weaving. It took a different approach where the workforce was concerned as well; under the Lowell system, young women on family farms were encouraged to take up paid employment in the city. Factories that made use of this scheme—initially, the Boston Manufacturing Company factory in Waltham, Massachusetts, that opened in 1814, and, famously, the various textile mills in Lowell, Massachusetts, that opened soon afterwards—initially promised their employees relatively good wages, clean and comfortable housing (the vast majority of female employees lived communally in on-site boarding houses), and a companionable environment in which the "mill girls" were given broader educational and cultural opportunities than would normally have been available to them.

By February of 1834, however, conditions at several of the Lowell mills were so poor and wages so low that the factory girls staged a "turn-out" (i.e., went on strike) after their pay had been reduced by 15 per cent They issued a statement proclaiming "Union Is Power," and some 1,200 joined the strike, but it was soon broken—as was a similar effort in 1836. The song "The Lowell Factory Girl" likely dates from this period. Numerous versions of this song exist with slight variants, published as broadsides between the 1830s and the 1850s; several bear the title "A Factory Girl" and make no reference to any particular location, while one published in Lewiston, Maine, is entitled "The Factory Girl's Come-All-Ye."

Conditions in the Lowell mills appeared to have improved somewhat in the 1840s. That the mills attracted a great many educated and intelligent workers was a point driven home by the writers of the *Lowell Offering*, a periodical launched in October 1840 and published through to 1845 that consisted entirely of pieces written by factory "operatives." The editing of the magazine was largely the work of Harriet Farley, a clergyman's daughter who had briefly been a teacher before, in 1837, becoming a mill worker. (If "A Factory Girl" is to be believed, the wages of mill workers—low though they were—were "greater than those of many domestics, seamstresses, and schoolteachers.")

Farley's publication was criticized for the degree to which it emphasized the positive when describing the lives of the factory workers; the "In Context" materials that follow the *Lowell Offering* selections may help to balance the picture.

anonymous, "The Lowell Factory Girl"

When I set out for Lowell,
 Some factory for to find,
I left my native country,
And all my friends behind.

 [Refrain]
5 Then I sing hit-re-i-re-a-re-o
 Then I sing hit-re-i-re-a-re-o

But now I am in Lowell,
And summoned by the bell,[1]
I think less of the factory
10 Than of my native dell.°   *valley*

The factory bell begins to ring,
And we must all obey,
And to our old employment go,
Or else be turned away.

15 Come all ye weary factory girls,
I'll have you understand,
I'm going to leave the factory
And return to my native land.

No more I'll put my bonnet on
20 And hasten to the mill,
While all the girls are working hard,
Here I'll be lying still.

No more I'll lay my bobbins up,
No more I'll take them down;
25 No more I'll clean my dirty work,
For I'm going out of town.

No more I'll take my piece of soap,
No more I'll go to wash,
No more my overseer shall say,
30 "Your frames are stopped to doff."[2]

Come all you little doffers
That work in the spinning room;
Go wash your face and comb your hair,
Prepare to leave the room.

35 No more I'll oil my picker rods,
No more I'll brush my loom,
No more I'll scour my dirty floor
All in the weaving room.

No more I'll draw these threads
40 All through the harness eye;
No more I'll say to my overseer,
Oh! dear me, I shall die.

No more I'll get my overseer
To come and fix my loom,
45 No more I'll say to my overseer,
Can't I stay out 'till noon?

Then since they've cut my wages down,
To nine shillings[3] per week,

---

1 *the bell* Tolled to call workers to their stations; in some New England factories, the bell was rung for a total of ten minutes, after which the factory doors were shut and any workers who were late would have to pay a fee to enter.

2 *Your frames are stopped to doff* I.e., the machine has paused operations in order for the doffers to "doff," or remove, bobbins full of spun fibers and replace them with empty ones.

3 *nine shillings* The American banking system remained in disarray through the 1830s and 1840s, and the coins most commonly in circulation were in many areas denominations of Spanish dollars that had circulated in that country's colonies. To add to the confusion, these coins were given different names and exchanged at different values in the different states. In Massachusetts a "shilling" was

If I cannot better wages make,
50 Some other place I'll seek.

No more he'll find me reading,
No more he'll see me sew,
No more he'll come to me and say,
"Such works I can't allow."

55 I do not like my overseer,
I do not mean to stay,
I mean to hire a depot-boy[1]
To carry me away.

The dress-room[2] girls, they needn't think
60 Because they higher go,
That they are better than the girls
That work in the rooms below.

The overseers they need not think,
Because they higher stand,
65 That they are better than the girls
That work at their command.

'Tis wonder how the men
Can such machinery make,
A thousand wheels together roll
70 Without the least mistake.

Now soon you'll see me married
To a handsome little man,
'Tis then I'll say to you factory girls,
Come and see me when you can.
—c. 1830s

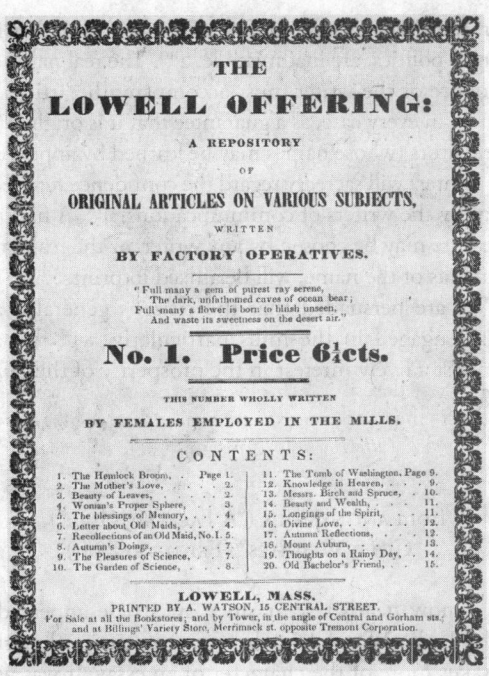

Title page from the first issue of the *Lowell Offering*, October 1840.

from the *Lowell Offering*

from "EDITORIAL CORNER" (OCTOBER 1840)

The *Lowell Offering* is strictly what it purports to be, a "repository of original articles on various subjects, written by factory operatives." The objects of its publication are, to encourage the cultivation of talent; to preserve such articles as are deemed most worthy of preservation; and to correct an erroneous idea which generally prevails in relation to the intelligence of persons employed in the mills. This number is wholly the offering of females.

The editors solicit communications from operatives of both sexes for the second number of the *Offering*, to be published in the early part of December.[3] 1st.

---

the equivalent of 16.67 cents. Nine shillings per week was thus the equivalent of $1.50 per week.

1 *hire a depot-boy*   This idiomatic reference is not entirely clear. Perhaps "hire a boy from the railroad depot" [to take her to the station].

2 *dress-room*   Part of the factory where the yarn is "dressed," or cleaned and prepared for weaving. Conditions in the dress room were generally better, and the wages for dress-room workers were higher.

3 *The editors solicit … December*   The 25 December 1840 issue, however, carried this notice: "We have concluded, for the present, to publish none other than articles written by females, and we hope the several male friends who have furnished us communications will not attribute this conclusion to any unworthy influence."

Communications of a sectarian character, in either religion or politics, are inadmissible. 2nd. The real name and residence of the writer must accompany the article furnished, in every case, as a guarantee that it is original. 3rd. The editors (whose names may be learned by applying to the printer) will sacredly regard the confidence reposed in them by the writers of communications. 4th. A fictitious signature may be chosen by any writer, or the real name, or initials of the name, will be affixed in print. …

We are persuaded that the citizens generally, and those engaged in the mills particularly, will feel and manifest a lively interest in the prosperity of the *Lowell Offering*. …

—1840

from ANONYMOUS ("A FACTORY GIRL"), "GOLD WATCHES" (FEBRUARY 1841)

It is now nearly a year since an article appeared in the Ladies' Book,[1] in the form of a tale, though it partakes more of the character of an essay. It was written by Mrs. Hale and exhibits her usual judgement and talent. Her object evidently was, to correct the many erroneous impressions which exist in society, with regard to the folly of extravagance in dress, and all outward show. I was much pleased with all of it, with the exception of a single sentence. Speaking of the impossibility of considering dress a mark of distinction, she observed (addressing herself, I presume, to the *ladies* of New England), "How stands the difference now? Many of the factory girls wear gold watches, and an imitation, at least, of all the ornaments which grace the daughters of our most opulent citizens."

O, the times! O, the manners! Alas! how very sadly the world has changed! The time was when the *lady* could be distinguished from the *no-lady* by her dress, as far as the eye could reach; but now, you might stand in the same room, and, judging by their outward appearance, you could not tell "which was which." Even gold watches are now no *sure* indication—for they have been worn by the lowest, even by "many of the factory girls." No *lady* need carry one now, for any other than

the simple purpose of easily ascertaining the time of day, or night, if she so please!

But seriously: why is the idea so prevalent that dress appears more objectionable in the factory girl than in any other female? Extravagance should be objected to in anyone; but the exercise of taste in dress, should not be denied to *them*, more than to other young females.

A gentleman may receive a thousand dollars per annum, and have half a dozen daughters, who all think they should dress in a style superior to that of the factory girl, who receives one or two hundred dollars per year. And when they find this impossible, they say, "O dear! How the factory girls do rig up! We cannot get anything but they will imitate us." What a dreadful evil! But it is a part of my belief that out of evil good may eventually come; and if the impossibility of making dress a mark of distinction, induces the conviction that *ladies* must attain some higher distinctive trait, this deplorable evil must result in a great benefit.

Those who do not labor for their living, have more time for the improvement of their minds, for the cultivation of conversational powers, and graceful manners; but if, with these advantages, they still need richer dress to distinguish them from *us*, the fault must be their own, and they should at least learn to honor merit, and acknowledge talent wherever they see it.

I pity the girl who cannot take pleasure in wearing the new and beautiful bonnet which her father has presented her, because, forsooth, she sees that some factory girl has, with her hard-won earnings, procured one just like it. I said I pitied the girl; but I fear there is too much of contempt and indignation in the feeling which swells my heart, to render it worthy of the gentle name of pity. Yet such things are said by Lowell girls, whose fathers are as dependent on the factories as any female operatives in the city, and who, if deprived of them, would perhaps be obliged to labor themselves.

And now I will address myself to my sister operatives in the Lowell factories. Good advice should be taken, from whatever quarter it may come, whether from friend or foe; and part of the advice which Mrs. Hale has given to the readers of the Ladies' Book, may be of advantage to us. Is there not among us, as a class, too much of this striving for distinction in dress? Is it not the only aim and object of too many of us, to wear something a little better than others can obtain? Do

---

[1]   *the Ladies' Book* I.e., *Godey's Lady's Book*, a popular magazine printed in Philadelphia and edited during most of its years of circulation (1830–78) by Sarah Josepha Hale.

we not sometimes see the girl who has half a dozen silk gowns, toss her head, as if she felt herself six times better than her neighbor who has none? Oh, how they will sometimes walk, "mincing as they go,"[1] as if the ground was hardly good enough for them. And many of them can put on an air of haughty contempt, which would do honor (or disgrace) to the proudest lady in the court of Victoria. And all this, because their Florence bonnet is finer, and their shawl much more costly, than is usually worn! I have often been reminded of the words of the Scottish bard—

> O wad some power the giftie gie us,
> To see oursels as ithers see us,—
> It wad frae mony a blunder free us,
>   An' foolish notion;
> Sic airs in dress an' gait was lea'e us,
>   An' e'en devotion.[2]

I have often thought that *we* should have more common sense about such things, than those who have been brought up in higher circles. We cannot expect all girls to overcome educational prejudice. The mind which can do that is of a higher order than is common. But we have not this to do. We see things more as they really are, and not through the false medium which misleads the aristocracy. Oh, how foolish is the feeling which prompts some among us to neglect or ridicule the poorly clad girl, who has just come from her country home, to seek among strangers a toilsome subsistence! Too often the first things she learns are, that she must assume an air of self-confidence or impudence, and buy fine clothes as fast as she can earn them; or she must hang her head with a feeling of inferiority, and submit to the insolence of the vain and worthless. I do not say that this is often the case, but *too often*—for it is sometimes so—and even once is too often.

We all have many opportunities for the exercise of the kindly affections, and more than most females. We should look upon one another something as a band of orphans should do. We are fatherless and motherless: we are alone and surrounded by temptation. Let us caution each other; let us watch over and endeavor to improve each other; and both at our boarding-houses and in the Mill, let us strive to promote each other's comfort and happiness. Above all, let us endeavor to improve ourselves by making good use of the many advantages we here possess. I say, let us at least strive to do this; and if we succeed, it will finally be acknowledged that Factory Girls shine forth in ornaments far more valuable than *Gold Watches*.

—1841

ANONYMOUS ("A.M.S.") "HOME" (FEBRUARY 1845)

I dream of home, and much rejoice,
For then I hear my father's voice,
    Ascend again in prayer;
I see again my mother's face,
Return each sister's kind embrace,   [5]
    And meet a brother there.

And then I wake alone, alone,
And hear no kind familiar tone,
    Nor form of kindred see;
They vanish all with that sweet dream,   [10]
For hills and vales now lie between
    My distant home and me.

And Autumn winds shall cease to wail
Among the groves of that fair vale
    Where rolls the Chicopee;[3]   [15]
And Winter stern, all pale and cold,
About the earth his robe shall fold,
    Ere I my home shall see.

But when shall come the vernal queen,
With floral crown and mantle green,   [20]
    To bid rude Winter flee,
Then all my weary exile o'er,
I'll seek with joy my home, where roar
    The falls of Chicopee.

—1845

---

[1]   *mincing as they go*   See Isaiah 3.16: "The daughters of Zion are haughty, and walk with stretched forth necks and wanton eyes, walking and mincing as they go, and making a tinkling with their feet"; *mincing*   Walking with affected daintiness.

[2]   *O wad ... e'en devotion*   See Robert Burns's "To a Louse, On Seeing One on a Lady's Bonnet at Church" (1786).

[3]   *Chicopee*   River in central Massachusetts, near Springfield; the large Chicopee Falls Dam, referenced in the final line of the poem, was constructed in the 1820s.

IN CONTEXT

Factory Girls

from anonymous ("Pi"), "Testimony of Females to the Evils of the Factory System" (1844)

The following questions were proposed to women of probity, by a friend of the factory girls: Miss W., a worthy woman, who has labored in the factory seventeen years, and acquired property, was asked, does the mill disqualify a woman for housework? "Why, la!" said she, "I know nothing about housework—I cannot even attend to the sick." She then described a visit to her sister's, at whose house she attempted to make a shortcake, and met with an entire failure, plastering the cookstove hearth all over.

Miss M., a female of several years' experience in factory life, was asked how the labor of the mill affected her? Oh, says she, when I come to eat I have to hurry so much that it hurts me. At night, instead of going to meeting,[1] when I have sat down in my chair, I feel as if I cannot rise again. And I cannot rest until time to go to work in the morning, for fear of being too late. I frequently rise hours before the time, *to listen for the bell*.

Miss B. is an experienced weaver. Not far from twenty years she has worked in factories. She too is a pious woman. She was asked, what do you think of the factory? "Oh," said she, with an emphasis that made me feel, "it gets worse and worse. The language used by most of the overseers is exceedingly profane—it makes one tremble. If we be too late, they will say, d—n you, if you do not come sooner, you shall not work here. We are worried all the time—we live all the time in fear of their abuse."

Miss S. is a fine girl. Her family is wealthy, and she has no need to work in the factory. However, she is fond of dress and pocket money, and for half the year, she toils in the mill. Well, Miss, I said, are you abused in the mill? "O yes," said she, "very much." How do you like it? "I bear it as well as I can." But why do you not as girls rise up against such abuse? She replied, "I know we ought to do, but there is no union among us. If we were to turn out against these evils, a part would soon go in and begin work again." Can you, I asked, give us any instance of the way in which they treat you for being too late? "Why," said she, "today I was a little too late at dinner, and the overseer asked me what I had to dinner, to which I replied herring. Well, says he, tell your folks to pick all the bones out, for you cannot be allowed to come behind the time."

Miss A. has spent many years in factories. She was asked if the factory life tends to make women negligent in domestic duties? The question awaked in her all the feelings of a woman, but after a moment's consideration, she replied, "How can it be otherwise, seeing that we have not time do anything otherwise than *hurriedly*."

A mother whose children are employed in the factory was asked if she knew whether factory life had any tendency to unfit females for domestic life. "Yes," she says, "there are many of them know nothing about it. Next door to us, a fine-looking woman, who dresses well, did not know, when she was put to it, how to wash her handkerchief."

---

[1]   *meeting*   I.e., an evening church service.

These are a few facts instituted as introductory to others which we hope the factory help will furnish themselves, in their language and with their own feelings. The community has no idea of the brutal and profane treatment which girls have to take from their overseers. The cruel usage which many worthy women have locked up in their own bosoms, would make our ears tingle, and our blood both chill and boil. These acts of cruelty, profanity, and oppression, we hope to publish in the reports of the committees of the several State Legislatures. God speed the cause of humanity.

Sarah Mapps Douglass, "The Stranger in America"

The teacher, writer, and abolitionist Sarah Mapps Douglass (1806–82) belonged to a prominent black family in Philadelphia and became an important figure in the city's African American literary and cultural scene. In the course of a career as an educator that spanned more than four decades, she first ran her own school for African American girls and then, after this school merged with Philadelphia's Institute for Colored Youth (which continues today as Cheyney University, the oldest historically black higher education institution in the U.S.), led the Institute's primary department. Douglass also helped found the Philadelphia Female Anti-Slavery Society (1833), an interracial abolitionist organization, and the Female Literary Association (1831), a reading and writing group for black Philadelphian women. Douglass's role in this latter group helped inspire her own writing, which she published in abolitionist and African American newspapers under a variety of pseudonyms. The poem by Douglass presented below was printed in 1836, under the name "Ella," in the *National Enquirer*, a Philadelphia newspaper founded by the Quaker abolitionist Benjamin Lundy and sponsored by the Pennsylvania Anti-Slavery Society.

"They tie our feet, and seal our mouths, and then exclaim,
'See how superior we are to these people!'" – J. Forten, Jr.[1]

---

[1]   *They tie … J. Forten, Jr.*   From *An Address Delivered Before the Ladies' Anti-Slavery Society of Philadelphia*, an 1836 speech by James Forten Jr., an orator and writer who belonged to one of the leading free black families in Philadelphia.

I come from a far country, where I dwelt
With friends and kindred in a quiet vale.
Of distant scenes we knew not; and I now
Find some *most* strange—incomprehensible.
5   I hear the Negro spoken of, as one
Who wears the form of man, but who has not
His intellectual powers. Can this be so?
    "*It is*! 'Tis true he wears the form of man,
Else could he not perform the labor done
10   *Here* by the grov'ling whites. He was so formed,
To execute the tasks allotted him.
The work your horses and your oxen do,
Is done by him; but walking upright, he
Can other tasks perform."
                                        And is that all;
15   Has he not intellect—a mind—a heart?
    "*He has no intellect*! Phrenologists[2]
Will tell you that his skull is not like ours:
He is a link between us and the brutes,
Found more than half way down."[3]

---

[2]   *Phrenologists*   Practitioners of phrenology, a pseudo-science, very popular and influential during the nineteenth century, that held that a person's character was shaped by several "organs" found in the brain. Phrenologists claimed to be able to measure the degree of development of these "organs," based on observations of the shape of the head, and draw conclusions therefrom about the individual's personality and capacities. Phrenology was frequently invoked to justify belief in the inherent superiority of some people over others, often reinforcing racist beliefs, among other forms of prejudice.

[3]   *He is … down*   Ideas regarding how human beings were related to supposedly "lower" forms of animal life were already widespread in the early and mid-nineteenth century, even before Charles Darwin gave evolutionary thinking a firm scientific basis in his *Origin of Species* (1859). Early nineteenth-century proponents of these ideas also frequently used them—as Douglass's imaginary interlocutor does in this poem, and as "scientific" racists would continue to do after Darwin—to justify sorting and hierarchizing various human races in terms of their supposed position on this evolutionary scale.

'Tis very strange!
No intellect—no mind—and has he not
A *soul* to save, or lose?
                              "Young stranger, come,
Such enquiries may not be answered *here*,
Where gloomy superstition[1] reigns.
Come with me to the *South*, where freedom dwells,
25   There shall you see the truth of all I've told."
Oh! can it be, that I have lived till now,
Nor known of such misery and crime—
Such stain upon a world I deemed so fair?
The Negro—why his limbs are manacled!
30   He can but use them as a tyrant wills;
And on his mind, his senses, and his soul,
Are fetters heavier still. Proud Southron,[2] yes!
He *has* a soul; but he will not be judged,
Surely unerring justice will not judge
35   *His* soul as thine—*he* knows not what he does;
The voice of conscience silenced by the lash,
Will not the crimes that he may perpetrate,
Be charged to *thy* account?
—1836

anonymous, "Know Ye Not That Ye Are Men?"

In 1840 just 11 per cent of the American population lived in urban areas; the remaining 89 per cent lived on farms or in small rural communities. (Even in 1880 only 28 per cent were city dwellers.) Not surprisingly, a good deal of space in many newspapers and magazines was devoted to items concerning farm life—poems and stories as well as information about crops, agricultural innovations, agricultural society meetings, and so on. As with other newspaper and magazine content, pieces were often reprinted in many different publications, with various attributions. The poem below appeared in the 15 June 1844 issue of the *Poughkeepsie Journal* under the heading "The Poet" (a regular feature in that newspaper at the time), with the credit line "from the *Boston Post*"; the same poem appeared, among other places, in the December 1844 issue of the *New York Farmer and Mechanic*, with the credit line "from the *Barre Gazette*."

Know ye not that ye are men,
    Ye laboring throngs of earth?
Must ye be told and told again
    That Truth and Toil are worth?

5   Why do you look upon the ground,
        No fire within the eye,
When noble born are all around,
        And Wealth and Rank go by?

For have ye not a heart within,
10   And sense and soul as they?
And more—have ye not toiled to win
        The bread ye eat today?

Do ye despise your sunburnt hands—
        So hard and brown with toil,
15   That have made fair the forest lands,
        And turned the forest soil?

What! Do you fear the haughty gaze
        Of men in rich array?
'Tis said, Pride hath not many days,
20   And Riches fly away.

Up, heart and hand, and persevere,
        And overcome the scorn—
The haughty hate and heartless sneer
        Of this world's gentle-born!

25   Fear not—shrink not—to you is given
        The guardianship of earth;
And on the record-book of heaven
        Is writ your honest worth!

---

[1]   *gloomy superstition* I.e., restrictive or depressing religious beliefs, such as the ideas of salvation and damnation that the speaker has just been expressing. Douglass's imagined interlocutor is here voicing a common Southern criticism of the North as a region in thrall to supposedly judgmental or puritanical forms of Christianity, such as those represented, in the seventeenth and eighteenth centuries, by the actual Puritans of New England.

[2]   *Southron* Originally a Scottish term for an English person, this synonym for "Southerner" took hold in American literary writing, beginning in the 1820s, due to the influence of Sir Walter Scott, in whose popular historical novels about Scottish life the term appears frequently.

Honor yourselves! Be honest, true,
30   And willing, firm, and strong;
Do well whate'er your hands may do,
      Though praise may linger long!

A high and holy work is yours,
      And yours should be a fame
35 That lives for ages and endures
      Beyond the hero's name!

Go, with your hands upon the plough,
      And the plough beneath the sod;
Pity the heart that scorns, and bow
40   To nothing but your God!
—?1844

from Anna Cora Mowatt, *Fashion: Or Life in New York*

When Anna Cora Mowatt (1819–70) discovered in 1841 that her husband was ruined financially, she began to give public readings of poems and dramatic excerpts, and tried her hand at writing of all sorts—magazine articles, advice books, and novels as well as plays. Her first play for the professional stage, *Fashion*, opened at New York's Park Theatre on 26 March 1845. It enjoyed a successful run there, and—as the preface to the London edition of the play published in 1850 put it—"was afterwards received with the same indulgence in all the principal cities of the United States." (See "In Context" below for excerpts of a review of the play's opening night.)

Anna Cora Mowatt, c. 1850.

At the comic center of *Fashion* is Mrs. Tiffany, a former milliner who has married a New York merchant and fancies herself to have become a member of fashionable society; her hapless attempts to adopt "sophisticated" foreign phrases and manners are the source of continual amusement. The play also features a good deal of what at the time was considered comic byplay involving the Tiffanys' black servant, Zeke—most of which reads today as substantially tainted by racism.

Mrs. Tiffany would like her daughter Seraphina to marry the man who purports to be Count Jolimaitre. Mr. Tiffany's Confidential Clerk, however (Snobson, by name), has discovered that Tiffany has been engaging in forgery and other unscrupulous business practices, and Snobson is blackmailing him—asking not only for continual increases in salary but also for the hand of Seraphina in marriage. A good deal of the unfolding story revolves around the ball that Mrs. Tiffany is intent on hosting for the "Count" (despite her husband's objections that they can't afford the expense); the commentary of the young poet T. Tennyson Twinkle is also a source of comedy. In the end it is the straightforward Yankee farmer Adam Trueman who sorts matters out between Mr. Tiffany and Snobson, reveals the true identity of the supposed Count, and promises to assist the Tiffanys financially—provided that they sell the fashionable house they cannot afford; that Tiffany "let moderation" be his counselor, and ... "let *honesty* be [his] confidential clerk"; and that he "bundle [his] wife and daughter off to the country," where they can "learn economy, true independence, and home virtues, instead of foreign follies."

from ACT 1, SCENE 1

(*A splendid drawing room in the house of Mrs. Tiffany. Open folding door, discovering a conservatory. On either side glass windows down to the ground. Doors on right and left. Mirror, couches, ottomans, a table with albums, etc., beside it an armchair. Millinette dusting furniture, etc., Zeke in a dashing livery,*[1] *scarlet coat, etc.*)

... MRS. TIFFANY. This mode of receiving visitors only upon one specified day of the week is a most convenient custom! It saves the trouble of keeping the house continually in order and of being always dressed. I flatter myself that *I*
5 was the first to introduce it amongst the New York

---
1 *livery* Servants' uniform.

ee-light. You are quite sure that it is strictly a Parisian mode, Millinette?

MILLINETTE.   Oh, *oui,* Madame; entirely *mode de Paris.*

MRS. TIFFANY.   This girl is worth her weight in gold (*aside*). Millinette, how do you say *armchair* in French?

MILLINETTE.   *Fauteuil,* Madame.

MRS. TIFFANY.   *Fo-tool!* That has a foreign—an out-of-the-wayish sound that is perfectly charming—and so genteel! There is something about our American words decidedly vulgar. *Fowtool!* how refined. *Fowtool! Armchair!* what a difference!

MILLINETTE.   Madame have one charmante pronunciation. *Fow-tool!* (*mimicking aside*) Charmante, Madame!

MRS. TIFFANY.   Do, you think so, Millinette? Well, I believe I have. But a woman of refinement and of fashion can always accommodate herself to everything foreign! And a week's study of that invaluable work—*French without a Master*—has made me quite at home in the court language of Europe! But where is the new valet? I'm rather sorry that he is black, but to obtain a white American for a domestic is almost impossible; and they call this a free country! What did you say was the name of this new servant, Millinette?

MILLINETTE.   He do say his name is Monsieur Zeke.

MRS. TIFFANY.   Ezekiel, I suppose. Zeke! Dear me, such a vulgar name will compromise the dignity of the whole family. Can you not suggest something more aristocratic, Millinette? Something *French!*

MILLINETTE.   Oh, *oui,* Madame; *Adolph* is one very fine name.

MRS. TIFFANY.   A-dolph! Charming! Ring the bell, Millinette! (*Millinette rings the bell.*) I will change his name immediately, besides giving him a few directions.

(*Enter Zeke.*)

(*Mrs. Tiffany addresses him with great dignity.*)

Your name, I hear, is *Ezekiel.* I consider it too plebeian an appellation to be uttered in my presence. In future you are called A-dolph. Don't reply—never interrupt me when I am speaking. A-dolph, as my

guests arrive, I desire that you will inquire the name of every person, and then announce it in a loud, clear tone. *That* is the fashion in Paris.

(*Millinette retires up the stage.*)

ZEKE.   Consider de office discharged, Missus. (*speaking very loudly*)

MRS. TIFFANY.   Silence! Your business is to obey and not to talk.

ZEKE.   I'm dumb,[1] Missus!

MRS. TIFFANY.   (*pointing up stage*) A-dolph, place that *fow-tool* behind me.

ZEKE.   (*looking about him*)   I hab'nt got dat far in de dictionary yet. No matter, a genus gets his learning by nature.   (*takes up the table and places it behind Mrs. Tiffany, then expresses in dumb show great satisfaction. Mrs. Tiffany, as she goes to sit, discovers the mistake.*)

MRS. TIFFANY.   You dolt! Where have you lived not to know that *fow-tool* is the French for *armchair?* What ignorance! Leave the room this instant.

(*Mrs. Tiffany draws forward an armchair and sits. Millinette comes forward, suppressing her merriment at Zeke's mistake and removes the table.*)

ZEKE.   Dem's de defects ob not having a libery[2] education.   (*Exit.*)

(*Prudence peeps in.*)

PRUDENCE.   I wonder if any of the fine folks have come yet. Not a soul—I knew they hadn't. There's Betsy all alone (*walks in*). Sister Betsy!

MRS. TIFFANY.   Prudence! how many times have I desired you to call me *Elizabeth? Betsy* is the height of vulgarity.

PRUDENCE.   Oh! I forgot. Dear me, how spruce we do look here, to be sure—everything in first rate style now, Betsy.

(*Mrs. T. looks at her angrily.*)

---

1   *dumb* Silent (a pun may have been intended; the use of *dumb* to mean *foolish* or *stupid* was by the 1840s becoming more common).

2   *libery* Liberal.

Elizabeth I mean. Who would have thought, when you and I were sitting behind that little mahogany-colored counter, in Canal Street, making up flashy hats and caps—

80   MRS. TIFFANY.   Prudence, what *do* you mean? Millinette, leave the room.

MILLINETTE.   Oui, Madame.

(*Millinette pretends to arrange the books upon a side table, but lingers to listen.*)

PRUDENCE.   But I always predicted it—I always told you so, Betsy—I always said you were destined to
85   rise above your station!

MRS. TIFFANY.   Prudence! Prudence! have I not told you that—

PRUDENCE.   No, Betsy, it was *I* that told *you*, when we used to buy our silks and ribbons of Mr. Antony
90   Tiffany—"*talking Tony*," you know we used to call him—and when you always put on the finest bonnet

in our shop to go to his—and when you stayed so long smiling and chattering with him, I always told you that *something* would grow out of it—and didn't
95   it?

MRS. TIFFANY.   Millinette, send Seraphina here instantly. Leave the room.

MILLINETTE.   Oui, Madame. So dis Americaine ladi of fashion vas one *milliner*? Oh, vat a fine country
100   for *les merchandes des modes*! I shall send for all my relation by de next packet![1] (*aside*)

(*Exit Millinette.*)

MRS. TIFFANY.   Prudence! never let me hear you mention this subject again. Forget what we *have* been, it is enough to remember that we *are* of the
105   *upper ten thousand*![2]

—1845

[Additional excerpts from *Fashion* are included in the website component of this anthology.]

---

1   *packet*   Ship that transports mail.

2   *upper ten thousand*   In a widely noticed 1844 newspaper piece, New York writer Nathaniel Parker Willis had declared that "at present there is no distinction between the upper ten thousand of the city. ... There are five or ten thousand men who dress as well as the millionaire's son; five or ten thousand ladies for whom milliners and mantua-makers do their best. ... New York is ... the largest republic of "first quality" people that the world ever saw." The phrase "upper ten thousand" (sometimes shortened to "upper ten") continued to be used for many decades.

IN CONTEXT

The Success of *Fashion*

from "The New Comedy at the Park Theatre," *New York Herald* (27 March 1845)

The much-talked of new comedy, "Fashion," by Mrs. Mowatt, was produced at the Park last night. It was one of the best houses we have ever seen; boxes, pit, and galleries were crowded. All the literati of the city were there, with a tolerable sprinkling of the *elite*, and the greatest curiosity and excitement appeared to prevail throughout the house relative to the probable success or failure of the first attempt to exhibit on the American stage a picture of American society and manners. …

[The play] was received last night with the greatest favor, and was announced for repetition this evening amid loud applause. It has been put upon the stage in a really superb manner, and the various characters were sustained in a manner highly creditable. Thus far it may be said that *Fashion* has been quite successful, but whether it will have a long or a short run is yet to be seen. We have no doubt, however, that, if possible, the Park will be still more crowded tonight than it was last night; and, from the peculiar character of the comedy, we expect some very singular developments amongst the playgoing people of the city.

---

from George Lippard, *The Quaker City; or The Monks of Monk-Hall: A Romance of Philadelphia Life, Mystery, and Crime*

George Lippard (1822–54) was among the most popular American writers of the first half of the nineteenth century. In the course of his ten-year career he wrote well over twenty novels, most notable among them *The Quaker City*, which, some claim, was the best-selling American novel before *Uncle Tom's Cabin* (1852). A lurid account of crime and debauchery in Philadelphia, the novel was inspired by the sensational trial of Singleton Mercer for the murder of a man Mercer claimed had violently raped his sister. *The Quaker City* is often considered the first American incarnation of the "city-mystery" genre, a genre developed in Europe whose novels purport to reveal the worlds of crime and moral debauchery that underlie the respectable exteriors of well-known cities. Like many authors of city mysteries, Lippard had both a commercial and social agenda, simultaneously exploiting the popular taste for sensation and appealing to the sense of moral indignation that—it was claimed—readers would feel at the actions depicted. The novel enjoyed extraordinary popularity throughout this period; as an 1876 edition summarized it, "no American novel has ever commanded so widespread an interest as this work. … On one hand, it has been denounced as a work of the most immoral and incendiary character; on the other, it has been elaborately praised as a painfully vivid picture of Life in the Great City." The novel's title is an ironic and pointed reference to the historical reputation of Quaker-founded Philadelphia as a bastion of American morality and fellow-feeling. (Like many of the progressive social reformers of his day, Lippard, though not a Quaker, had a deep admiration for Quaker spirituality and morality.)

THE ORIGIN AND OBJECT OF THIS BOOK

One winter night I was called to the bedside of a dying friend. I found him sitting up in his death-couch, pale and trembling yet unawed by the gathering shadows of the tomb. His white hairs fell over his clammy brow, his dark grey eye glared with the unnatural light, which heralds the approach of death. Old K—— had been a singular man. He had been a profound lawyer, without fame or judgeship. In quiet he pursued his dreamy way, deriving sufficient from his profession to support him in decency and honor. In a city where no man has a friend that has not money to back him, the good lawyer had been my friend. He was one of those old-fashioned lawyers who delight to bury themselves among their books, who love the law for its theory, and not for its trick and craft and despicable chicanery. Old K—— had been my friend, and now I sat by his bedside in his last hour.

"Death is coming," he said with a calm smile, "but I dread him not. My accounts with God are settled; my face is clammy with the death-sweat, but I have no fear. When I am gone, you will find in yonder desk a large packet inscribed with your name. This packet contains the records of my experience as a private councillor and a lawyer for the last thirty years. You are young and friendless, but you have a pen, which will prove your best friend. I bequeath these papers to you; they may be made serviceable to yourself and to the world—"

In a faint voice, I asked the good old lawyer, concerning the nature of these records.

"They contain a full and terrible development of the Secret Life of Philadelphia. In that packet you will find records of crimes that never came to trial, murders that have never been divulged; there you will discover the results of secret examinations, held by official personages, in relation to atrocities almost too horrible for belief—"

"Then," said I, "Philadelphia is not so pure as it looks!"

"Alas, alas, that I should have to say it," said the old man with an expression of deep sorrow, "but whenever I behold its regular streets and formal look, I think of The White Sepulchre,[1] without all purity, within, all rottenness and dead men's bones. Have you courage to write a book from those papers?"

"Courage?"

"Aye, courage, for the day has come, when a man dare not speak a plain truth, without all the pitiful things of this world rising up against him, with adder's tongues and treacherous hands. Write a book, with all your heart bent on some good object, and for every word you write, you will find a low-bred calumniator,[2] eager to befoul you with his slanders. Have you courage to write a book from the materials, which I leave you, which shall be devoted to these objects: To defend the sanctity of female honor; to show how miserable and corrupt is that Pseudo-Christianity which tramples on every principle ever preached or practiced by the Saviour Jesus; to lay bare vice in high places, and strip gilded crimes of their tinsel. Have you courage for this?"

I could only take the old man's hand within my own, and murmur faintly, "I'll try!"

"Have you courage to lift the cover from the White Sepulchre, and, while the world is crying honor to its outward purity, to show the festering corruption that rankles in its depths? Then those records are yours!"

I sat beside the deathbed of the old man all night long. His last hours were passed in calm converse, full of hope and trust in God. Near the break of day, he died. God bless him! He was my friend, when I had nothing but an orphan's gratitude, to tender in return for his friendship. He was a lawyer, and *honest*; a Christian and yet no bigot; a philosopher and yet no sceptic.

After his funeral, I received the packet of papers, inscribed with my name, and endorsed, REVELATIONS OF THE SECRET LIFE OF PHILADELPHIA, *being the records of thirty years practice as a councillor, by * * * K——.*

The present book is founded upon those portions of the Revelations, more intimately connected with the present day.

With the same sincerity with which I have written this Book of the Quaker City, I now give it to my countrymen, as an illustration of the life, mystery and crime of Philadelphia.

It was commenced on the 5th of September 1844, and published in ten numbers, with a success almost without parallel in the annals of our literature. Since its first publication, near 40,000 numbers of the book have been sold. Whether this success is owing to the merits of the work, or the malignant persecution of a few paltry enemies, I leave the reader to determine.

I now present the work to the public in complete form, after nine editions in numbers have met with a

---

1 *The White Sepulchre* See Matthew 23.27: "Woe unto you, scribes and Pharisees, hypocrites! for ye are like unto whited sepulchres, which indeed appear beautiful outward, but are within full of dead men's bones, and of all uncleanness."

2 *calumniator* Slanderer.

rapid sale.[1] And as a matter of some small chronological interest, I must here make the record, that—

On the night, November eleventh, 1844, a play taken from this book was withdrawn by the managers of the Chestnut Street Theatre, because the same mob who with characteristic cowardice threatened to murder the author, declared their intention to destroy or burn the building in case the piece was played.[2] The mayor, finding the arm of the civil power too weak to

protect the theatre, in a city where churches had been laid in ashes by a mob,[3] preferred the more convenient method of requesting the non-performance of the play, *because a riot was threatened.*

—1845

[Excerpts from Chapters 13 and 14 are included in the website component of this anthology.]

F.O.C. Darley, *The Quaker City* title page, 1876.

---

[1] *I now present ... rapid sale* The novel was first published as a series of nine forty-eight-page installments, similar to pamphlets.

[2] *On the night ... played* Lippard himself adapted *The Quaker City* for the stage while the novel was still being published serially. The rioters he describes here were hired by Singleton Mercer, whose trial inspired Lippard's story; Mercer was almost arrested, but, fearing violence, the mayor of Philadelphia called for the production to be canceled instead.

---

[3] *in a city where ... mob* The St. Augustine Catholic Church was burned down on 8 May 1844 during one of a series of anti-Catholic riots led by members of Philadelphia's Protestant community.

anonymous, Davy Crockett Tales

In 1835, a year before Davy Crockett's death during the Texas Revolution, a Nashville company called Snag and Sawyer published *Davy Crockett's Almanac*, a short book that combined astronomical information (times of sunrise and sunset, dates of full and new moons, etc.) with essays regarding wildlife, and stories about Crockett and other figures. The *Almanac* became a regular annual publication, at first through Snag and Sawyer and then in the 1840s through the publishing firm of Turner and Fisher, with offices in Philadelphia and New York and nationwide distribution. The early editions may have exaggerated the facts to some extent in their telling of tales about Crockett, but they remained largely factual—as they did in their essays on such topics as "Methods of Catching Wild Horses on the Prairies of Texas." Under the Turner and Fisher imprint, however, the tall tales became more and more detached from reality, with Crockett portrayed in light-hearted fashion as an almost mythical figure— the nineteenth-century equivalent of a Marvel superhero in the twenty-first century. The tall tales featuring Crockett include "Crockett's Wonderful Escape Up Niagara Falls" (1844), "Crockett among the Cannibals" (1854), and "Crockett and the (Black) Emperor of Haiti" (1856). Later issues also include tall tales featuring other heroic figures—Kit Carson notable among them.

The tales reproduced on the following pages are from *Crockett's Almanac, 1846: Scenes in River Life, Feats on the Lakes, Manners in the Backwoods, Adventures in Texas, Etc. Etc.*

Crockett himself seems to have been a figure very different from that portrayed in many of the tall tales. Though renowned for his exploits as a "frontiersman," he also made a strong impression as a politician, serving in the U.S. House of Representatives from 1827 to 1831 and again from 1833 to 1835. Something of his character comes through in the report published in the 28 June 1830 issue of the Raleigh, North Carolina *Raleigh Register*, describing Crockett delivering a speech against Andrew Jackson's Indian Removal Act of 1830.

There have been so many queer stories told of this gentleman, and so many quaint sayings attributed to him, that most persons … have taken up the idea that he is one of those rough bears. … Whoever reads these remarks will be soon convinced that he possesses qualities both of the head and heart which would do credit to any man, whatever may be the want of polish in his manners, or the homeliness of his language.

The speech itself is a powerful indictment of the provisions of an act designed to ensure that "the Indians were to have no privileges allowed them while the white men were to have all—now, if this was not oppression with a vengeance, he did not know what was."

For more on the Texas Revolution and the attack on the Alamo, in which Crockett likely died, see the "Contexts: Expansion, Native American Expulsion, and 'Manifest Destiny'" section elsewhere in this volume.

Chester Harding, *David Crockett*, 1834 (detail).

"I LEAVE THIS RULÆ FOR OTHERS, WHEN I'M DEAD,
BE ALWAYS SURE YOU'RE RIGHT, THEN GO-AHEAD."

CROCKETT'S
18 | ALMANAC. | 46

Scenes in River Life, Feats on the Lakes, Manners in the Back
Woods, Adventures in Texas, &c. &c.

Crockett's wonderful escape up the Niagara Falls, on his Pet Alligator.

PUBLISHED BY TURNER & FISHER:
No. 15 NORTH SIXTH STREET, PHILADELPHIA;
AND 74 CHATHAM STREET, NEW YORK.

Toy Books, Song Books, Almanacs, Colored Prints, Juvenile Works, Valentines, &c.

Cover, *Crockett's 1846 Almanac.*

CROCKETT DRINKING UP THE GULF
BETWEEN THE UNITED STATES AND TEXAS.

You see, I told you in my last year's speech, that I go in for Texas and Annexation, clar up to the very gravel stone, in spite o' all the Mixy Mexican Spanish brown an red niggars; an the Malgamation party in Uncle Sam's lands, who go in for Annexation with the blackies. I've heard all the four mile speeches, an ten mile petitions on the subject, an' I have come to the clar conclusion that the only thing that raley prevents the annexation, is the leetle deep bellied pond called a Gulf between Uncle Sam an Texas; it stands like the Gulf between the rich man and Lazarus in the big book. It struck me like a thunderbolt, that if we war only to take that are deep Alligator water out o' the way, it would put an end to all no-go-ciation legislation, an all that sort o' national nonsense, for then little Texas an the States would annex themselves jist us nat'ral as two pumpkin vines, or as a gal o' seventeen annexes herself to a walken sprout o' lightnin, without the advice an consent o' the old folks. So in order to remove this one little liquid obstacle out o' the way o' sich a great national wedding, I've jist straddled across the neck o' this pond, an like Captain Colossus straddlen the Roads, an commence drinkin it up instanter. You see, when I open my flesh tunnel, it must come like a walken water spout, swaller arter swaller, till the bottom walks up as bair as a pumpkin, an then, if any human critter, Yankee, Texian or Mexican, dare's to oppose instanter annexation, saw me up if I don't swallow them too, an' arter that I'll jist mount my alligator, travel into the middle o' Mexico, lick all the tarnal Royalists out o' thar tarnal mustaches, strip Santa Anna of his powership, show him all naked in his villany, an' wooden-legged ambition; teach the natives, red niggers, creoles, and the true bred Yankee Independence an Republicanism; an, then run for President myself, an if a better man beat me, why it will be all the better for human natur, an' I'll jist treat him to as much hog snappen jelly and whiskey as he can eat for a bull term, and hold myself ready to lick all traitors an dishonest politicians into true Republican decency, an if the critturs can't get along arter that, why I'll drink every spoonful of water between her an the United States, and annex her myself, in spite o' old Spain, an all the monkies called monarchs in creation.

In addition to "Crockett Drinking Up the Gulf" and "Crockett Catching a Mexican Tigress" (see facing page), the 1846 issue of the *Almanac* included a variety of other tall tales featuring Davy Crockett, among them "Crockett Riding His Pet Bear Up a Tree," "Crockett Dancing Fire out of a Rock, and Burning the Indians," "Crockett and Ben Hardin Skating a Party of Indians into an Air Hole" and "Crockett Splitting the Great Mississippi Snag Alligator."

CROCKETT CATCHING A MEXICAN TIGRESS.

While I was in Texas, I met my old friend General Jimmy Raymond, the wild beast collector for all creation; he wanted about fifty men to go into Mexico, to catch an all tearin she tiger, an her young cubs for his great Zoological Institute. Well, soon as he spoke o' fifty men, I broke out instinctively into a horse laugh fit that lasted nearly an hour, It fairly shook the clothes off my back. "Fifty men," says I? "Yes," says he "Why," says I, "fist you foller me, to the haunt of the critter, you want, an if I don't kidnap the hull tiger family, then call me a sucken fawn." "Agreed," says he, an off we started; we soon got near the tarnal night swamp spot; I walked into it about a hundred yards, feelin my way, till I saw a couple o' small lights which turned out to be a he tiger's eyes keepin watch for his wife an family; he was just springin at me when I caught hold of the two paws of the critter, twisted 'em, an tied 'em around his neck so tarnal tight, that he died an choked instanter. I then walked up to the nest, grabbed Mrs. Tiger by the throat, pared off her nails, an held her till I choked half of her temper out, put her four young ones in my great skin cap, an marched out to the General, draggen their mommy arter me by the throat as docile as a kitten.

anonymous, *Crockett Catching a Mexican Tigress*, 1846.

Phoebe Cary, "Homes for All"

Phoebe Cary (1824–71) and her sister Alice Cary (1820–71) were both respected poets in mid-nineteenth-century America. Born into an Ohio farming family, Phoebe was the sixth of nine children. Largely self-educated, she began to publish poetry in the early 1840s, a few years after her sister had done the same. The reputation of the pair was established when they were included in an 1849 anthology, *The Female Poets of America*, and with the proceeds from the volume they published the following year, *The Poems of Alice and Phoebe Cary*, they were able to relocate to New York City, where Alice became a regular contributor to the *New York Ledger* and president of the New York Women's Club. Both sisters were devoted to the abolitionist cause. Phoebe later worked for the *Revolution*, a suffrage newspaper edited by Susan B. Anthony. In *The Female Poets of America*, editor Rufus Griswold described Phoebe as a poet who "refers more than Alice to the common experience, and has perhaps a deeper sympathy with … those movements of the day which look for a nearer approach to equality, in culture, fortune, and social relations."

Columbia,[1] fairest nation of the world,
  Sitting in queenly beauty in the west,
With all thy banners round about thee furled,
  Nursing the cherub Peace upon thy breast;
5 Never did daughter of a kingly line
Look on a lovelier heritage than thine!

Thou hast deep forests stretching far away,
  The giant growth of the long centuries,
From whose dim shadows to the light of day
10   Come forth the mighty rivers toward the seas,
To walk like happy lovers, hand in hand,
Down through the green vales of our pleasant land.

Thou hast broad prairies, where the lovely flowers
  Blossom and perish with the changing year;
15 Where harvests wave not through the summer hours,
  Nor with the autumn ripen in the ear;
And beautiful lakes that toss their milky spray
Where the strong ship hath never cleaved its way.

And yet with all thy broad and fertile land,
20   Where hands sow not, nor gather in the grain,
Thy children come and round about thee stand,
  Asking the blessing of a home in vain—
Still lingering, but with feet that long to press
Through the green windings of the wilderness.

25 In populous cities do men live and die,
  That never breathe the pure and liberal[2] air;
Down where the damp and desolate rice-swamps lie,
  Wearying the ear of Heaven with constant prayer,
Are souls that never yet have learned to raise
30 Under God's equal sky the psalm of praise.

Turn not, Columbia! from their pleading eyes;
  Give to thy sons that ask of thee a home;
So shall they gather round thee, not with sighs,
  But as young children to their mother come;
35 And brightly to the centuries shall go down
The glory that thou wearest like a crown.
—1850

Wilhelm Weitling, undated photograph.

---

1   *Columbia*   Common personification of America.

2   *liberal*   Ample, open, generously distributed.

Wilhelm Weitling, "Der Kleine Kommunist" ("The Little Communist")[1]

Of the many Germans who immigrated to the United States during this period, the "48ers"—those who had left Germany following the attempted revolution of 1848—were particularly active in political and cultural circles. Prominent among them was Wilhelm Weitling (1808–71), a leading socialist theorist and activist who had until 1846 been a close colleague of Karl Marx. Weitling embarked on various cooperative workers' projects in America, and in 1850 founded *Die Republik der Arbeiter* (*The Republic of Workers*), a German-language socialist newspaper. The paper enjoyed some success initially (its circulation was close to 5,000 by the end of 1850), but was unable to sustain that readership; it folded in 1855.

The poem below was published anonymously in the 1 January 1853 issue of *Die Republik der Arbeiter*. (William Frederick Kamman identifies Weitling as the author in his *Socialism in German American Literature*.)

Ich bin ein kleiner Kommunist
Und brauche niemals mehr
Als mir zum Leben nötig ist,
Das andre geb' ich her.

5 Ich bin ein kleiner Kommunist
Der seine Brüder liebt
Und alles, was sein eigen ist,
A'uch gerne Anderen gibt.

Ich bin ein kleiner Kommunist
10 Und frage nicht nach Geld,
Da unser Meister Jesus Christ
Davon ja auch nichts halt.

Ich bin ein kleiner Kommunist,
Ich bin's mit Lieb und Treu.
15 Und trete einst als treuer Christ
Dem Arbeitsbunde bei.
—1853

I am a little communist[2]—what for?
I need what I need to live
And no more, nothing more;
All else to others I give.

5 A little communist I am—for who?
For the brothers I love,
And for others; to all of you
I'll give all that I have.

A little communist I am—for us;
10 Let's not care about money,
Any more than did Christ Jesus—
He who never wanted any.

I am a little Communist—for good:
Love and faith for me,
15 And as a true Christ-follower should,
With the workers' association I'll be.
—TRANSLATION 2022

---

[1] Translated for this anthology by Don LePan and Maureen Okun; translation copyright © Broadview Press 2022.

[2] *communist* The word "communist" dates from the early 1840s. German philosophers Karl Marx and Friedrich Engels published the original German edition of their *Communist Manifesto* in 1848 in London; the first English translation was published in 1850.

from *Godey's Lady's Book* (October 1857)

Godey's Lady's Book (1830–78) was among the most popular magazines in America during the period in which it was published. Its innovative format included all manner of material that was considered likely to be of interest to its largely female readership: hand-tinted fashion plates, sewing and knitting patterns, poetry, sheet music, art engravings, short fiction, and nonfiction articles. (It stayed deliberately far from politics or other controversial subjects; the decision to try to avoid controversy was likely a factor in the magazine's gradual demise during and after the Civil War.) Among white, middle-class women, the magazine was one of the most influential arbiters of popular taste at mid-century.

Many of the era's most influential poets and short story writers (including Nathaniel Hawthorne and Edgar Allan Poe) published work in *Godey's*, as did many lesser-known writers. For this anthology we have included a sampling of the pieces that appeared in a single issue—that of October 1857.

For most of its existence, the magazine was edited by Sarah Josepha Hale, one of the first female magazine editors in America; excerpts from her editorial column for this issue are included below.

Virginia De Forrest, "The Sisters"

My heroine lived in a pretty village in Massachusetts. You could come from the city, within a mile of it, with a locomotive and train of cars; but, after you left the panting monster to carry his burden further on, you could turn from the track up a shaded path, and be in the country. It was a pretty house, small, but large enough for the wants of the occupants. It stood back from the road, with the trees planted so thickly in front of it that, but for the neat fence and little gate, you would never have dreamed of looking for a house in among the foliage; but there it was, a white cottage, covered with creeping plants, roses, honeysuckles, eglantine, and jasmine; and there, in the little porch, is the large chair for an hour's rest, under the vines, after the day's labor is over. When my story commences, there were six inmates of the pretty cottage: Mr. Grant, a tall, stately old gentleman, with white hair, and many, many wrinkles, but erect and unbent, even by the weight of the seventy years that had passed over him. There was his wife, Mary Grant, much younger than her husband, but, at thirty-six, pale, feeble, and moving with a languid step, looking actually older than her stately lord. Next came the two children, Meta, the eldest, just completing her fifteenth year, and Lily, a tiny baby, only a few weeks old. Earnest Lovel, a guest of Mr. Grant's, and his ward, was the son of an old friend, the heir of an immense fortune, and attending an academy about a mile from the cottage, previous to entering college. These, with one servant, Martha, were the family at this pleasant home.

Mrs. Grant was so much of an invalid that the entire charge of the baby fell upon Meta. Under her mother's directions, she tended and cared for the child, until Mary Grant herself scarcely loved her babe more tenderly than Meta. Lily was only two years old when Mrs. Grant laid down the weary burden of her earthly life, to enter into life eternal; and Lily became indeed Meta's charge. Faithfully and tenderly the loving elder sister supplied a mother's place to the bereaved little one. Lily became the sunshine of the cottage. Her pale, waxen complexion, golden hair, and large, expressive blue eyes, with her fragile figure, made her name singularly appropriate. If Mr. Grant, shut up in his study, refused all comfort, denied admittance to the weeping Meta, and closed the door against Earnest, one accent of Lily's sweet, silvery voice, calling "Papa," was sure to open the door, and bring the heart-broken old man to his darling. Was Meta's heart heavy, brooding over her loss, Lily could cheer her, and, by her winning ways, bring a smile to her lips. Did Earnest pore too long over his books, Lily's invitation for a walk brought him into the garden; and, with Meta and Lily, many a pleasant hour was passed among the flowers and trees.

After his wife's death, a great change passed over Mr. Grant. The tall, erect figure, which had stood against the storms of seventy winters, was bowed by the weight of this great sorrow; the dark, piercing eye was dimmed; and old age came rapidly. Meta, the loving daughter, watched her father with love, and strove, by every means in her power, to supply her mother's place in the household. Poor Meta! It was no easy task that lay before her. Lily, though lovely and patient, was a delicate child, requiring constant care. The little house must be kept in the beautiful order her mother had delighted in; and, when weary with care, the poor child had no gentle bosom to rest upon, no loving voice to cheer, comfort, and direct her, as her dear mother's had been wont to do.

Earnest watched Meta with a brother's anxiety, and loved to chat with and comfort her. Many a pleasant hour they passed together, talking of Mrs. Grant, to whom Earnest had been as a son, contriving plans for drawing Mr. Grant from the contemplation of his sorrow, and discussing Lily's education. There was no talk of love, no protestations; but Earnest vowed in his heart to win Meta for his wife; and Meta felt sorrowful and heavy whenever the thought of Earnest's departure for college occurred to her.

A year passed away, and Meta was packing Earnest's trunk for a long voyage. He had determined to finish his education at a German college, and was to start the next morning. She lingered over her task, the last she could do for him for many weary months; and the scalding tears fell more than once upon the nicely folded clothes she was packing. A strong arm was passed around her waist; her head was drawn down upon Earnest's breast; and then he spoke to her.

"Meta, you are weeping for me. I must speak again. One little week ago, you told me you could not marry me until Lily was old enough to take your place and be a companion to your father. How can I wait so long, Meta? Say you will be mine in three years when I come home."

"Oh, I cannot promise, Earnest! My poor father would be so lonely, and he positively refuses to leave the cottage and live with us. He is old, feeble, and sorrowful. Surely, my first duty is to him. You will find others more lovable than Meta. It would be better to go unfettered by any engagement, and forget me."

"You would not have me do so. You are pale and trembling now at the idea of being forgotten. No! no! you will not promise; but I shall not forget. Darling, I shall never forget you—never love another."

After Earnest left, Mr. Grant seemed to fail even more rapidly. He missed the recreation of assisting the young man in his studies. He missed his cheerful voice and delicate attentions, for Earnest had ever been

a tender and respectful ward; and Meta was occupied with Lily and house cares, and unable, much as she desired it, fully to supply Earnest's place. Lily seemed to grow more frail as she grew older; and her golden head often rested on Meta's breast, while the elder sister sang to her, when a more robust child would have been playing.

Oh, the agony it was to the affectionate Meta to see her father fail before her eyes! Six weeks after Earnest left them, he was unable to leave his chair; and, in four months more, they laid him in the graveyard beside his wife.

After her father's death, Lily seemed to cling more and more to Meta. Excepting the servant, they were alone in the cottage. The small income they had always found sufficient for their simple wants ceased at their father's death, and poverty was added to Meta's cares. The neighbors were very friendly; and she was able to keep the cottage, and clothe herself and Lily by the liberal prices paid for her exquisite embroidery. The rich people of the village petted[1] the pretty child; and Meta was filled with gratitude for many kinds of attentions to her frail little sister, such as a long ride in the open country, which would bring the roses to the pale cheeks, and make the blue eyes dance with delight.

Another year passed away. Earnest's letters were Meta's greatest comfort. He promised to return faithfully at the end of the three years, and, calling Meta his dear wife, bade her be ready to receive her lord and master. He would be Lily's brother; and, after all her troubles, bright days were surely in store for her. But Meta's troubles were not yet over. The landlord of the little cottage, a hard man, had been offered a higher rent for it, and gave her warning that, unless she could bring the rent up to the sum he was offered, she must leave her home. She could not. It had taken all her time and constant labor to pay the present rent, and support herself and her sister; and, with a bursting heart, Meta prepared to leave the place where her parents died, and herself and sister been born. It is a bitter parting to leave a house so dear by association as this one was to the orphan girl, and she felt the keenest anguish at the prospect. Her friends advised her to leave the village and go to the city, where her embroidery would command high prices; and her mother's

---

[1]   *petted* I.e., showed attention and affection toward.

aunt wrote to her, offering her a home. So the furniture was sold, everything, even her father's chair and the low couch upon which her mother had breathed her last sigh; and, with the money thus raised, Meta went to her aunt's. She wrote to Earnest, telling him of her removal; but the letter never reached him, for, on that very day, he too removed, and left Germany to make the tour of Europe. He wrote to tell her of this change of plan; and the letter lay in the little village post office until the post-master, finding the person to whom it was directed had left the place, sent it to Washington to the Dead-Letter Office. So, in addition to her other sorrows, Earnest's letters failed her.

Little Lily pined in her city home, pined for the green fields and bright flowers, and for her accustomed walks and rides. Daily her step grew more languid, and she asked often to be cradled in Meta's arms and hear the sweet songs she loved so well. "Meta," she would say— "I love you, Meta. Sing to me, sister."

"Aunt Mary," said Meta, one day, when her aunt came in, and found Lily asleep on her bosom, "I want to see a doctor about Lily. She is not well; she was never strong, and now she seems wasting away. Her weight is scarcely more than half of what it was, and see how pale she looks. I cannot lose her, aunt. All the rest have gone; but I feel certain God will spare me Lily."

The doctor came. To Meta, he advised country air for the child. To her aunt, he said only one word— "Consumption!" One of Meta's kind friends, near her old home, cordially invited her to pass the summer with her; and she accepted the invitation.

Lily did not profit, as Meta had expected, by change of air. I must pass over the last scenes of the little one's life, and Meta's terrible grief and despair, as she let this last treasure go from her. A long, severe illness followed the loss of her sister; and Meta seemed about to follow her loved ones to heaven. But youth and a good constitution triumphed over sorrow and sickness. Again she was able to move about; but the weight of trouble pressed heavily, and she murmured. One evening, she went to visit the little grave beside her parents. Her heart was sore, and she was filled with bitter repinings. Bowing her head upon her knees, she wept uncontrollably. A low voice seemed sighing in her ears, "Sister"; and, looking up, Lily appeared to be hovering above her, pointing upwards, no longer thin and pale, but

radiant and lovely. "Sister, mourn not; look up; God is good, and tries us but to guide us aright. Those whom the Lord loveth, he chasteneth."[1]

Meta sat gazing upwards, until the lovely vision vanished, and the shades of evening fell around her. Was it a dream? If so, it was a comforting one, for her heart was filled with a new peace, as she retraced her steps to the farmhouse. "God is good. Those whom he loveth, he chasteneth." The words seemed still ringing in her ears, and she eagerly hailed the comforters.

A light was burning in the parlor; and, dreading to see strangers, she hastened to her own room. The window was open; and she heard, from the room below: "I must try to find her. It is very late, and I have waited very patiently."

The blood rushed to Meta's cheeks; and, with a quick step, she sprang downstairs and entered the parlor. She found what she sought.

"Earnest!"

"Meta!"

Now, reader, you and I will not intrude, just now; but I will tell you what happened later.

A week ago, we drove by the little cottage, and accepted the invitation to stop and rest. Earnest and Meta consider themselves an old married couple, for it is now six years since they were wedded in the little village church. They are rich, but prefer passing their summers in the dear little cottage to building a finer residence. There were two children playing on the porch, Mary and Lily, the latter having her aunt's golden curls and blue eyes, but as healthy and beautiful a child of two years as one would desire to see. And, after all her trials, Meta is happy.

—1857

---

1   *Those whom ... he chasteneth*   This sentiment appears several times throughout the Old and New Testaments, including in the Book of Job, which tells of the suffering of a righteous man: "Behold, happy is the man whom God correcteth: therefore despise not thou the chastening of the Almighty" (Job 5.17).

ENIGMAS[1]

15

Nature, though cattle have me not, provides
I shall belong to man and beast besides;
Giving me also to dear woman too,
As the offending have had cause to rue—
5 And not a learned board or company
Exists without—while some are made for me.

Strange, too, though liked, I'm very often cut
And knocked upon the head, and sometimes put
Far within prison walls—and over-driven
10 Like weary beasts—and sometimes, too, am bitten
By the unthinking and unfeeling one,
Who, if blood flows not, heeds not what is done.

16

'Tis found that everywhere I am
Characteristic of both beasts and man;
15 Of the former, perhaps, the patient cat
Who lies in ambush for a thieving rat—

And of the latter a coast-guardsman, who
Is ever on a telescopic view,
Serve to depict me—for the poor old men
20 Who once were me, will ne'er exist again.

I am besides a substance, as they know
Who only deem me useful when I go—
And if I change not, but remain the same,
Find me of no more value than a name.

18

25 Horses, men, and boys have me,
I'm used to take in custody—
And girls who haven't much to do
Make me—and bore themselves and you—
Deeming that I'm most admired
30 When their patience most I've tried.
—1857

---

[1] ENIGMAS Riddles; the answers were provided in the following month's issue. (For this anthology we have provided them in the anthology's website component.)

SELECTED FASHION ILLUSTRATIONS

The illustrations in *Godey's Lady's Book and Magazine* were typically interspersed through the second half of each issue. In the October 1857 issue they included designs for embroidery and for needlework, an illustration and description of a "bead candlestick ornament," and an illustration of "crochet boots for an infant," as well as three large illustrations of women's fashions, two of which are included here.

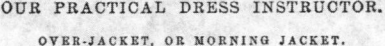

OUR PRACTICAL DRESS INSTRUCTOR.
OVER-JACKET, OR MORNING JACKET.

For outdoor wear, this jacket should be made of a light gray or lavender cloth, bound with silk braid of the same color. The girdle should be of rich silk to correspond. Every scallop is ornamented with a flat silk button. It will be found a particularly comfortable shape for a morning wrapper, in muslin or cambric.

THE ANDALUSIAN.

[From the establishment of G. Brodie, 51 Canal Street, New York.   Drawn by L. T. Voigt, from actual articles of costume.]

This is drawn from a magnificent velvet garment. It would require us to be professional dressmakers to explain the peculiarity of its construction, as its *cut* is, in several important respects, quite different from that employed in fitting basques,[1] the seams being novel and ingenious, and calculated to occasion great fulness in the drapery of the skirt. Indeed, to make ourselves understood, we would be compelled to have diagrams prepared of the pattern. This and similar styles will be much in fashion. There is a peculiar piquancy in their graceful and bewitching contour, which must render them immensely popular. The ornament consists of a rich lace *berth,* and a passementerie,[2] composed of drop buttons, falling from a rich braid.
—1857

---

[1] *basques* Fitted jackets, often designed to flare out dramatically over the skirts.

[2] *passementerie* Elaborate decorative trimming involving braids, tassels, beads, etc.

from SARAH HALE, "EDITOR'S TABLE"

The art of amusing children in a manner that shall be beneficial to health, manners, and morals, is a desideratum yet to be discovered. Little children are always active. It is a necessity of their nature. This perpetual unrest, of which their attendants so often complain, is the instinct that God, for wise purposes, has implanted in the young of all animals. That lambs skip and bound; kittens and puppies seem wild with the joy of life; and little children naturally run, leap, dance and shout in the exuberance of that capacity for happiness, which the young human heart feels as instinctively as the flower-buds open to the sun.

To repress this natural joyousness, not to direct and train it for good, seems to be the object of most parents. So the merry little children are often sent to the hot schoolroom, there confined in the close, impure atmosphere, and subjected to a routine of instruction which they are utterly unable to comprehend. But then they are kept quiet until this painful lesson is impressed, that to be active is to be very naughty; and then, if they are not troublesome, their indolence passes for goodness.

We are certainly of opinion that education, or instruction, rather, should commence early. The child should, from the first, be trained rightly. In proportion to his faculties, the boy (or girl) should begin that lesson of mental discipline and industry which is rarely acquired thoroughly, if not undertaken in the pliancy of early childhood.

What we wish is that, after the severe studies of A B C (severe to a child) have been duly attended to, and the character invigorated by a half-hour of the self-control required in "keeping still," some suitable direction should be provided for the playful activity and genial affections of the little folks that are to become, in a very few years, young men and women. Besides the usual plays and games that children invent for themselves, or find on record, handed down from the memories of the past, and which boys enjoy most in the open air, there should be indoor amusements also. We do not mean to exclude little girls from the outdoor plays. Children of both sexes should be kept, while exercising in the daytime, as much as possible in the free, pure air of heaven, and in sight of the cheerful face of nature. But, in the long winter evenings, and on festive occasions, there should be means of amusement provided for children and youth at home, where their parents and elders can witness and moderate the mirth, if too wild, and enjoy the happiness of promoting this innocent recreation. …

THANKSGIVING DAY[1]—We hope the Governors will unite on November 26th, the last Thursday in the month. Then the war of politics will be over for the year; and all elections, State and National, will be closed, the harvests of the country gathered in, the preparations for winter made; and the crowning glory of all the blessings God has, during the year, bestowed on our great nation, would be the union of all our States and Territories in a *day* of National Thanksgiving. The peoples of the Old World would thus be taught that freedom from man's tyranny brings us nearer to God—that, while rejecting earthly lords, we willingly acknowledge our dependence on the Lord of heaven and earth. The celebration of the Fourth of July has marked effect on our national character. The American citizen dwelling in foreign countries feels the influence of observing that day. It gives him an increase of honor among the millions who are pining in vain for such high privileges as his national birthright bestows; and he is proud of the title, "American citizen."

The Day of Thanksgiving would, if observed nationally, soon be celebrated in every part of the world where an American family was settled. If the *last Thursday in November* could be established as the Day, and known to be the time in each year when, from Maine to New Mexico, and from Plymouth Rock to the Pacific sands, the great American people united in this festival of gladness and gratitude, the whole world might be moved to join in the rejoicing, and bless God for his goodness to the children of men.

Last year, nearly all the States and Territories united on that day. This year, we trust, there will be no blank

in the number, nor a seat left vacant at the Table of the Nation.
—1857

---

anonymous, "The Beautiful Snow"

This poem was published in numerous American newspapers from 1859 through to the early 1910s, attributed to a variety of different authors—or, in many cases, to no author at all. An 1873 issue of *The Irish Nationalist* attributed the work to Annie Keely, an Irish-born emigrant to the United States, while an article in the 1 January 1911 *Los Angeles Times* suggests that, while its authorship is uncertain, its most likely author was James W. Watson. The same 1911 article states that "some years ago the London *Spectator*, a most worthy and very high authority, printed ['The Beautiful Snow'] and pronounced it the finest poem ever written in America." The 1882 textbook *Common School Elocutionary Selections* provides the following summary before its text of the poem:

> A beautiful legend connected with this poem gives it historic interest. It is related that during a visit to Cincinnati of the late Thomas Buchanan Read, author of many heroic poems, a woman was found dead in the streets, having perished in the night from cold and neglect. Upon a crumpled piece of paper, found in her bosom, was the manuscript of "Beautiful Snow." Supposing her to be the author of these most exquisite lines, prophetic of her fate, Mr. Read had the body decently prepared at his own expense, and followed it, the soul mourner, to the grave.

Regardless of its true authorship, the piece is a remarkable example of the "fallen woman" poem, an exceptionally popular genre in the late nineteenth century; the vast majority of such poems were authored by men. The present text is taken from the February 1859 *Knickerbocker*, where the poem is printed without attribution.

---

[1]   THANKSGIVING DAY At the time that this article was written, Thanksgiving was not an official federal holiday, though thanksgiving days were sometimes declared by the government. Hale began campaigning in the late 1840s for the adoption of Thanksgiving as a federal holiday; the holiday was officially adopted in 1863 following a declaration by Abraham Lincoln. For more on the evolution of Thanksgiving, see the "Civilizations in Contact" section of Volume A of this anthology.

Oh! the snow, the beautiful snow,
Filling the sky and the earth below;
Over the house-tops, over the street,
Over the heads of the people you meet,
5   Dancing,
                        Flirting,
                              Skimming along,
Beautiful snow! it can do nothing wrong,
Flying to kiss a fair lady's cheek;
10   Clinging to lips in a frolicksome freak,
Beautiful snow from the heavens above,
Pure as an angel, and fickle as love!

Oh! the snow, the beautiful snow!
How the flakes gather and laugh as they go!
15   Whirling about in its maddening fun,
It plays in its glee with everyone,
                   Chasing,
                        Laughing,
                              Hurrying by,
20   It lights up the face, and it sparkles the eye;
And even the dogs, with a bark and a bound,
Snap at the crystals that eddy around;
The town is alive, and its heart in a glow,
To welcome the coming of beautiful snow.

25   How wild the crowd goes swaying along,
Hailing each other with humor and song!
How the gay sledges, like meteors flash by,
Bright for a moment, then lost to the eye;
                   Ringing,
30   Swinging,
                              Dashing they go
Over the crust of the beautiful snow:
Snow so pure when it falls from the sky,
To be trampled in mud by the crowd rushing by:
35   To be trampled and tracked by the thousands of feet
Till it blends with the filth in the horrible street.

Once I was pure as the snow—but I fell:
Fell, like the snow-flakes, from Heaven—to hell:
Fell, to be trampled as filth of the street:
40   Fell, to be scoffed, to be spit on and beat,
                   Pleading,
                        Cursing,
                              Dreading to die,

Selling my soul to whoever would buy,
45   Dealing in shame for a morsel of bread,
Hating the living and fearing the dead.
Merciful GOD! have I fallen so low?
And yet I was once like this beautiful snow.

Once I was fair as the beautiful snow,
50   With an eye like its crystals, a heart like its glow:
Once I was loved for my innocent grace—
Flattered and sought for the charm of my face.
                   Father,
                        Mother,
55   Sister, all,
GOD, and myself I have lost by my fall.
The veriest wretch that goes shivering by
Will take a wide sweep, lest I wander too nigh:
For of all that is on or about me, I know
60   There is nothing that's pure but the beautiful snow.

How strange it should be that this beautiful snow
Should fall on a sinner with nowhere to go!
How strange it would be, when the night comes again,
If the snow and the ice struck my desperate brain!
65   *Fainting,*
                     Freezing,
                           Dying alone!
Too wicked for prayer, too weak for my moan
To be heard in the crash of the crazy town,
70   *Gone mad in their joy at the snow's coming down;*
To lie and to die in my terrible woe,
With a bed and a shroud of the beautiful snow!
—1859

from William J. Wilson, Speech Delivered at Newark, New Jersey, 1 August 1859

William J. Wilson was an abolitionist and black rights activist, who published frequently (often under the pen name "Ethiop") in the various African American-run newspapers of the mid-nineteenth century. The following speech was delivered on "August First Day" in 1859. August First Day, marking the anniversary of the dates on which the Slavery Abolition Act in Britain and its colonies had gone into effect—1 August 1834 and 1 August 1838 (see the In Context material below)—was widely celebrated by both blacks and abolitionist whites in mid-century America. Speeches continued to be made and celebrations held on this date for some decades even after slavery was abolished in the United States. As the twenty-fifth anniversary, August First Day in 1859 was of particular significance. Wilson's speech was published on 20 August 1859 in *The Weekly Anglo-African*.

An excerpt from Wilson's well-known *Afric-American Picture Gallery* is included in the website component of this anthology.

Ladies and Gentlemen: ... [A] few days ago, our ears were greeted with the roar of cannon, and our eyes beheld the vast heavens red with the light of patriotic fires, and the hills and vales were vocal with the voice of the orator. And why these demonstrations of patriotism? The answer comes to us from the same warm gush of feeling that everywhere pervaded that day: "It is the return of the day on which our national independence had its birth." Just eighty-three years had rolled away since that event. Just twenty-five years this day, 800,000 bondmen[1] lifted up their hands to the God of Heaven, and exclaimed, "We are free!" If, as American citizens, we found cause of rejoicing because of emancipation from oppressive laws, shall we not as such find far greater because of the restoration to freedom of 800,000 fellow-beings, our brethren—not restored to freedom merely, but to citizenship, to manhood? If the disenthralment from a foreign power was so great an achievement, and is hailed with so much joy, is not the unloosening of thousands of hard-pressed bondmen an achievement still greater? And can it ever be forgotten by us? I trust not.

A dark cloud once hung over those beautiful islands of the sea. No single ray of light penetrated the gloom. Go back with me to the time before even a Wilberforce or a Clarkson[2] appeared, when the dusky inhabitants of these West India Islands might be seen with uplifted

hands—shackled though they were—pleading for deliverance. ...

... The British West Indies are this day free, and are not only free, but prosperous and happy. I am aware that slave-holders and their abettors, the servile press, and paid menials, have endeavored to distort this truth so as to show an adverse condition of these islands since emancipation, for these reasons: If slaves could be emancipated in the British West Indies without the shedding of blood, and support themselves thereafter without dependence upon some other than their own arm, and the islands were still profitable in a commercial sense, why, then, the whole argument, or rather the whole tirade as to either the propriety, necessity, or rightfulness of slavery, must fall to the pit of oblivion. If the emancipated could sustain these positions, then the patriarchal institution of the *South* must be shorn of its entire support. The first howl set up by these infamous dogs, long before the Act of Emancipation passed, was that blood would be shed. The bill passed, the day for emancipation arrived, and in spite of their fears, and tremblings, and howlings, no *butcherings* occurred, no blood flowed down the hillside and through the ravines of those beautiful islands. All was peace and ecstasies of joy. Then came the old and flimsy resort, that negroes could not, and these would not (unaided), take care of themselves. But the emancipated obtained, by purchase or otherwise, lands, and commenced labor for themselves—for their own wives and little ones. Homes were formed, wants supplied, and comforts produced. The plantation and the master began to sink into neglect. The once haughty, insolent, indolent master became reduced to his proper level, while the once trembling slave, by his own efforts, raises himself to the dignity of a man—an humble man, if you will, yet a MAN.

... [T]he charge that because less is exported from these islands than previous to emancipation, they are less prosperous, is as weak as it is infamous.[3] By every rule or test of political economy, they are in a far more prosperous condition now than formerly. Such are the facts, and I challenge any man of respectable information to successfully contradict them. ...

---

[1] *800,000 bondmen* The enslaved population of the British colonies in 1833 totaled approximately 800,000.

[2] *a Wilberforce or a Clarkson* Reference to the prominent English politicians William Wilberforce (1759–1833) and Thomas Clarkson (1760–1846), leaders of the movement to abolish slavery in the British Empire.

---

[3] *infamous* Harmful; wicked.

… A beautiful incident connected with the Danish West India emancipation, of recent date (1848),[1] illustrative of this truth, may not be out of place to briefly relate here. In the island of St. Croix, under the guidance of one of God's noblemen, one Moses Bourd, the germ of liberty was nurtured in all its purity and simple grandeur. This wonderful man, like Moses in the history of the past, seems to have been raised up in the Providence of God for the express medium through which deliverance was to come to this people. He digested well his plans, arranged them, and then went from estate to estate, laying down, among the oppressed, regulations and rules for their guidance, enforcing commands, giving council and encouragement. Under his skillful hand the trembling slave was taught to know himself, and each rose from his posture as a slave and stood erect, and, in the strength of their united manhood, demanded their liberty. Their shackles they had thrown aside, and arming themselves as best they could, they repaired to the town where the authorities were. These fled. These stalwart men, with liberty in their breasts and determination in their faces, marched forth. A lady stepped out upon the balcony, and begged and besought that there should be no violence—no slaughter. Now mark the grand but simple reply of these men: "*Madam, we want to hurt no one; we want and will have liberty!*" The noble and sublime response rang throughout the lines of this bronzed army back even to the estates. The *authorities* heard and granted the demand, and *St. Croix was free.*

I cannot conclude these remarks without expressing my confidence that, under the guidance of judicious but able and fearless leaders, the time is coming—yea, nigh at hand—when all our brethren held in the unlawful bonds of our country shall also be able to exclaim, "*We want and will have liberty!*" and by a judicious and energetic use of our time, talents, and opportunities, shall be able with our own unaided but strong arms to obtain it.

… Wield rightly and well what strength you have, and each successive stride towards the goal of our ambition will, by its own action, give new and increased accessions of strength, till, on and on, we at length reach the high object of our pursuit. Up, up, then, fellow-citizens, and be doing! Linger not nor tarry. Let us leave nothing to be done by others that should be done by ourselves. …

—1859

In Context

The First of August

from anonymous ("E.Q."), "The First of August," *The Liberator* (1843)

The editorial excerpted here appeared in the 21 July 1843 issue of *The Liberator*; at the time, August First was starting to be more and more widely celebrated as the anniversary of emancipation in British colonies.

The editorial identifies 1 August 1838 as the date being celebrated, whereas 1 August 1834 is very often identified as the relevant date (including by Wilson in the piece above). In fact, both dates are significant. The Slavery Abolition Act of 1833 came into effect 1 August 1834, but it did not immediately free all those who had been enslaved; the status of enslaved people older than six years of age was altered to "apprentice," and they were forced to work without pay for their former slaveholders for a further four years, as

---

[1]   *the Danish … (1848)*   The Danish government had originally proposed a plan of gradual abolition for the Danish West Indies, to begin in 1847, but widespread protests by the enslaved in the colonies forced the government to declare the immediate emancipation of all enslaved people in 1848.

compensation to the former slaveholders. There was good reason, then, to celebrate the anniversary of both 1 August 1838 and 1 August 1834.

[N.B. James M. Whitfield's 1849 poem "Stanzas for the First of August" appears under Whitfield's author entry elsewhere in this anthology.]

The fifth anniversary of a past event in the world's history—the deliverance of the West India slave—is at hand. It is fitting that it should be welcomed and celebrated with hearts full of grateful remembrances and glad anticipations. ...

The "iron tongue of Time" that proclaimed at midnight, from the cathedral towers of the Antilles, that slavery was no more within their borders, at the same time sounded the death knell of slavery throughout the world. ... Every year that has since rolled by free from the bloodshed and violence has been an angel messenger of good tidings of great joy to those pining in bondage, and to those who feel as if bound with them in their chains. ... De Tocqueville[1] has well remarked that slavery is one of those institutions which may exist for a thousand years if no one questions its rightful existence, but cannot endure long after the question has once been asked. ... Revolutions never go backwards—and of all the revolutions that the world has ever seen, the one that is now in progress for the overthrow of the most gross and hateful form of human oppression is the most certain of a prosperous issue[2]—though it may be after much toil and tribulation. ...

Under whatever aspect we may regard the West India Emancipation, it is an event that deserves our hearty joy and glad commemoration. Whether we look on it merely as the deliverance of eight hundred thousand of our fellow men from the woes of slavery, or whether we view it as only one of the earlier victories of the revolutionary struggle in which we are engaged, auspicious of still higher and more glorious successes yet in store for the champions of freedom, it well deserves to be freshly remembered and joyfully commemorated. It is not often that the American abolitionists have an occasion for a general thanksgiving. ... While awaiting, and doing what we can to hasten this happy event, it is right—it is wise—to refresh ourselves once in a year by assembling ourselves and holding a glad Jubilee in memory of the sublime doings of the First of August, 1838. From such a joyful communing one with another we shall derive fresh strength and new encouragement for the prosecution of our long, but never tedious, conflict with our own slavery. ...

It is well done, therefore, on the part of the abolitionists in various parts of the country, the setting apart this day for celebrations of a festival character. It becomes us to rejoice with those that do rejoice, as well as to weep with those that do weep. ... The novelty of the measure, and the mode of celebration—the attractions of the blue sky, the overarching groves, "God's first temples," the processions, the addresses in the open air, may attract many who have held themselves aloof from the vulgar[3] anti-slavery lecture. ... If arrangements have not yet been made by the abolitionists in any town for the due celebration of this illustrious day, let no time be lost in making them. Let the friends in every town decide whether they will have a Pic Nic[4] of their own, or whether they will join with those in some other place who have a celebration[.] ... Let the country be alive on the first of August with parties flocking together to spend a long and happy day in innocent festivity, and a joyful interchange of congratulations and of hopes. The abolitionists of Boston intend celebrating the day by a Pic Nic at Dedham, with the friends in that and the neighboring towns. There is to be a large gathering of the abolitionists of Middlesex at Lowell. Another meeting will be held at Weymouth. Others will, no doubt, be arranged in due time. There is yet time for arrangements to be made everywhere—let them not be neglected. ...

---

[1] *De Tocqueville* French sociologist Alexis de Tocqueville, whose study of American politics and society, *Democracy in America*, was published in two parts in 1835 and 1840.

[2] *issue* Result.

[3] *vulgar* Common; ordinary.

[4] *Pic Nic* When first imported into English, this term was used to refer to a large social gathering (not necessarily out of doors) to which the guests would all bring food; by the mid-nineteenth century the meaning was shifting, such that an outdoors gathering was usually implied.

William Dean Howells, "The Poet's Friends"

Howells (1837–1920) is best known for his late-nineteenth-century fiction in the realist mode—and, as a literary critic, for his advocacy of realism. He was active on many literary fronts for over fifty years; as a twenty-three-year-old he wrote Abraham Lincoln's campaign biography and published poems such as that below in the February 1860 issue of *The Atlantic Monthly* (a magazine he edited from 1871 to 1881). Little is

known of "Mrs. Frances Sophia Stoughton Pratt," whose poem responding to Howells' presumption of stupidity among cows was published in the July 1860 issue.

The robin sings in the elm;
        The cattle stand beneath,
Sedate and grave, with great brown eyes
        And fragrant meadow-breath.
5   They listen to the flattered bird,
        The wise-looking, stupid things!
And they never understand a word
        Of all the robin sings.
    —1860

Frances Sophia Stoughton Pratt, "The 'Cattle' to the 'Poet'"

How do *you* know what the cow may know,
        As under the tasselled bough she lies,
When earth is a-beat with the life below,
When the orient mornings redden and glow,
5   When the silent butterflies come and go—
        The dreamy cow with the Juno eyes?

How do *you* know that she may not know
        That the meadow all over is lettered, "Love,"
Or hear the mystic syllable low
10 In the grasses' growth and the waters' flow?
How do *you* know that she may not know
        What the robin sings on the twig above?
    —1860

Covers of Ann S. Stephens's *Malaeska: The Indian Wife of the White Hunter* (1860), the first in Beadle's series of dime novels; and of Edward S. Ellis, *Seth Jones; or, The Captives of the Frontier* (1860). Stephens's novel had been serialized over twenty years earlier (in the *Ladies' Companion*); reissued in this new format, it now became a great success in book form—and inexpensive novels printed on cheap paper became a staple of popular American literature. (By comparison, a one-volume novel printed and bound conventionally was typically priced in 1860 at 75 cents or more.)

Whereas *Malaeska* is focused on the experience of an Indigenous woman, Ellis's *Seth Jones* (published later in the same year by Beadle's) is a male-focused tale of a white hunter saving white captives from Mohawk warriors. The editor at Beadle's, Orville J. Victor, termed it "the perfect Dime Novel"; it was marketed to achieve even greater popularity than *Malaeska*, and stories of male heroism soon came to dominate the genre.

[The first chapter of *Malaeska* and the first chapter of *Seth Jones* are both included in the website component of this anthology.]

anonymous, "Right Names"

Like many other newspapers in mid nineteenth-century America, the New Orleans *Daily Picayune* had a custom of printing a poem in a conspicuous location in many of its issues. The poem below appeared at the top of the center column of the newspaper's second page.

Of old a "spade" was called a "spade"[1]
　　By simples[2] and by sages
A "workman" did his honest "work,"
　　And "servants" earned their "wages."
5　A "man" was title of respect,
　　Whenever virtue named it;
There was but one of higher worth,
　　And lovely "woman" claimed it;
But now we masquerade with words,
10　　The truth a great offence is,
And desecrate our English tongue
　　By pride and false pretenses.

We shame the language of our sires—
　　We talk so mild and meekly;
15　We've "operatives" for working-men
　　And draw our "salaries" weekly.
Our "lady" takes the place of "wife"—
　　That word so true and hearty;
And every "man's" a "gentleman,"
20　　Unless we call him "party."
The "shopman" hates the name of shop,
　　And, by perversion later,
The man who digs a railway trench
　　Is called a "navigator."

25　O give us back our honest speech!
　　It had a soul of beauty;

And let us do our daily "work,"
　　And think it pleasant duty;
Let's earn our "wages" as of yore—
30　　The work can never harm us;
Let's love our "sweethearts" and our "wives,"
　　And own° that women charm us.　　　　*admit*
So shall our actions, like our words,
　　Be void of affectation,
35　And "spade" be "spade" and "man" be "man,"
　　Throughout the entire nation.
　　　—1855, 1863

anonymous ("A Mechanic's[3] Wife"), "Capital and Labor"

This poem seems to have been first printed in Bridgeport, Connecticut in the 11 October 1866 issue of the *Coach Makers' International Journal*. Among the publications in which it was subsequently reprinted were the December 1866 issue of the *Molders' International Journal* and the 12 June 1867 issue of the Greensboro, Alabama newspaper, the *Alabama Beacon*.

"The autumn winds blow shrill and cold,
　　Bleak winter soon will come;
Heaven help the poor—protect the old—
　　And give us all a home."
5　Thus often does the rich man pray,
　　With solemn tone and word;
But, oh! how seldom does he say,
　　"I'll be thy agent, Lord.

"The needy that around me live
10　　Shall have my daily care,
And from thy treasure lent, I'll give
　　To all who need a share,
And as this wealth is fast increased,
　　By laboring, needy men,
15　I will not grudgingly withhold
　　The profits due to them."

1　*a "spade" was called a "spade"*　The phrase "to call a spade a spade" (meaning to call a thing by its plain name, not by some ornamental or euphemistic name—such as "digging implement," for example) has a long history in several languages; its first known use in written English dates from 1542. The use of the word "spade" as a derogatory term for a black person took root in the 1920s; the fact that the latter usage is now rightly considered to be offensive and unacceptable has inevitably complicated use of the phrase "call a spade a spade."

2　*simples*　In the nineteenth century, a term commonly used to denote people of limited intelligence.

3　*Mechanic*　During this period the term had a broader meaning than it does today, often referring to any skilled manual laborer.

But, no! he has no goods to waste;
    He has no time to spare;
So offering them to Heaven for help,
20   His conscience eased, he leaves them there
And turns his thoughts to earth again,
    His factory or his farm,
And studies how to increase his wealth
    By the laborer's sinewy arm.

25 And how to get from labor most,
    And in return give least,
He cares not if his workmen starve,
    If he can only feast.
And so he'll make their wages less,
30   Grind down with iron heel,
Until in poverty's distress
    E'en manhood scarce they feel.
Men with God's impress in their soul,
    His likeness in their brow,
35 Obeying Heaven's command to toil,
    Must slaves before him bow.

Arouse ye laborers! Take a new
    And nobler view of life;
Cast off these base, degrading chains,
40   Be manly in the strife;

Unite with brotherly accord,
    In love, sincere and true,
Ah, standing firm, demand the rights
    So long and justly due.

45 What are those rights? For every hour
    Of toil, sufficient pay
To make your home less comfortless,
    And keep grim Want° away;   *poverty*
To lighten the too heavy load
50   We weary wives now bear;
To feed and clothe your little ones,
    And have some time to spare,
Neglected minds to cultivate,
    To study and reflect,
55 And fit yourselves for usefulness,
    Where duty may direct.

But struggle not for this alone—
    For Principle contend;
Make Labor honored and revered,
60   Be this your aim and end,
And raise the humblest laborers,
    At least to stand beside
The men who live from off their toil,
    In indolence and pride.
—1866

Eastman Johnson, *Whittier's Barefooted Boy*, 1868. Eastman Johnson was among the most well-known American painters of his generation, respected both for his scenes of rural life and for his portraits of prominent Americans. The poem that inspired this painting—"The Barefoot Boy," by John Greenleaf Whittier—is included in the website component of this anthology.

from Horatio Alger, *Ragged Dick; or, Street Life in New York with the Boot Blacks*

The writing career of Horatio Alger Jr. (1832–99) began with an 1855 collection of sentimental tales and poems entitled *Bertha's Christmas Vision*. Over the next decade Alger tried his hand at several other sorts of fiction; his short sensation novel *The Mad Heiress* was serialized in 1860, and his first novel for young people, *Frank's Campaign* (on the ways in which boys could be of service "in assisting to put down the Rebellion") appeared in 1864. But it was *Ragged Dick* (serialized in the magazine *Student and Schoolmate* in 1867, and published in book form the following year) that made his reputation. The novel tells the tale of an enterprising young man who, through hard work, pluck, and a bit of good luck, makes good in the world of work while also resisting attempts to swindle him, and resisting as well the temptations of vice. A conduct book for young males as well as a page-turning story of success, *Ragged Dick* became the template for dozens of subsequent Alger novels—and for an entire sub-genre of fiction.

While Alger's juvenile novels enjoyed substantial success during his lifetime (he estimated not long before he died that his approximately one hundred books for juvenile readers had sold approximately 800,000 copies), they became even more successful after his death—so much so that by 1910 they were estimated to be selling more than a million copies each year. It was at that point that the phrase "a Horatio Alger story" became a widely used shorthand for a certain sort of life story—that of any American white male who had risen virtuously from poverty and hardship to respectability and success. (A common misperception was and is that Alger's heroes usually become rich as well as respectable; in fact, Horatio Alger stories often end as *Ragged Dick* does, with the hero attaining a middle-class job—in Dick's case, as an accountant—rather than achieving great wealth.)

Included here is the preface to the novel; the first chapter of *Ragged Dick* is included in the anthology's online component.

PREFACE

"Ragged Dick" was contributed as a serial story to the pages of the *Schoolmate*, a well-known juvenile magazine, during the year 1867. While in course of publication, it was received with so many evidences of favor that it has been rewritten and considerably enlarged, and is now presented to the public as the first volume of a series intended to illustrate the life and experiences of the friendless and vagrant children who are now numbered by thousands in New York and other cities.

Several characters in the story are sketched from life. The necessary information has been gathered mainly from personal observation and conversations with the boys themselves. The author is indebted also to the excellent Superintendent of the Newsboys' Lodging House, in Fulton Street, for some facts of which he has been able to make use. Some anachronisms may be noted. Wherever they occur, they have been admitted, as aiding in the development of the story, and will probably be considered as of little importance in an unpretending[1] volume, which does not aspire to strict historical accuracy.

The author hopes that, while the volumes in this series may prove interesting stories, they may also have the effect of enlisting the sympathies of his readers in behalf of the unfortunate children whose life is described, and of leading them to co-operate with the praiseworthy efforts now making by the Children's Aid Society and other organizations to ameliorate their condition.

New York, April, 1868

—1868

---

[1]   *unpretending*   Humble; also, lacking pretense (i.e., in this case, of historical accuracy).

Following the novel's initial success, the A.K. Loring book publishing company made *Ragged Dick* the first volume in the "Ragged Dick Series," using the above illustration in each. The four boys pictured include two boot-blacks (center and bottom right), a luggage boy (left), and a newspaper hawker (upper right). The "Ragged Dick Series" was followed by several other series of novels, including the "Luck and Pluck Series" (1871–75) and the "Ways to Success Series" (1887–90).

HARRIET WILSON

1825 – 1900

For well over a century after its 1859 publication, *Our Nig*, Harriet Wilson's first and only book, languished in obscurity, and its author received no recognition for it. Wilson and her work only reentered literary history when the book was republished and its writer's identity confirmed in the 1980s. The profound consequences of this rediscovery for American literature were aptly described by the novelist Alice Walker: "I sat up most of the night reading and pondering the enormous significance of Harriet Wilson's *Our Nig*. It is as if we'd just discovered Phillis Wheatley—or Langston Hughes." Today, Wilson is widely credited with having written the first novel by an African American woman to be published in North America. Yet the importance of *Our Nig*—or to give it its full title, *Our Nig; or, Sketches from the Life of a Free Black, in a Two-Story White House, North. Showing that Slavery's Shadows Fall Even There*—goes beyond its status as a "first" anything. Wilson's portrayal of a black girl's abusive servitude in a white New England home vividly captures the entanglement of race, gender, and class relations in mid-nineteenth-century America and challenges deep-seated assumptions, both in its own time and today, about what parts of the country were and were not implicated in the racism and slavery that underpinned the country as a whole.

Since *Our Nig*'s rediscovery, a series of scholars have unearthed detailed information about Harriet Wilson, recovering her life as an entrepreneur and religious speaker as well as an author. Still, much of what is known about her early life depends on *Our Nig* itself, which is heavily autobiographical. Wilson was born in Milford, New Hampshire, in 1825. Like Frado, her fictionalized surrogate in *Our Nig*, she was the daughter of a white woman, Margaret Smith, and a black man, Joshua Green; after her father's death, her mother abandoned her at about age six with a local white family, with whom she lived as an indentured servant for over a decade. Scholars have plausibly identified this family as the Haywards, a Milford clan with connections to a nationally-popular musical troupe at the time, the Hutchinson Family Singers. The fact that the Hutchinsons, and possibly also their relatives the Haywards, held abolitionist views lends extra force to *Our Nig*'s condemnations of the hypocritical racism of many "professed abolitionists."

After the end of her indenture, Wilson—who at the time went by the surname Adams—worked as a domestic servant, seamstress, and hatmaker while also furthering her own education, despite frequent ill health due to years of mistreatment. As *Our Nig* puts it of Frado, she learned "the value of useful books," because of which she "felt herself capable of elevation." She married in 1851 and gave birth to her son George the following year; however, her husband, Thomas Wilson—who, she writes, posed as a fugitive from slavery—left the family soon afterwards to look for work, never to return. In order to support herself and her son, Wilson started selling her own hair care products door to door. This enterprise soon flourished into a business that spread throughout the Northeast; bottles of Wilson's merchandise with her name embossed on them still exist. She also wrote *Our Nig*, which she composed, according to the book's preface, to "aid in maintaining myself and child." The book was published in 1859—either at Wilson's own expense or via a subsidy—by George Rand, a Boston printer with ties to the city's abolitionist community; it appeared anonymously, but Wilson is known to be its author because she had previously registered the copyright for it in her own name.

One of the foremost questions that confronts *Our Nig*'s readers is the question of how to categorize it. The book's autobiographical basis, amply documented by present-day scholarship, is also something the book calls attention to directly: its early chapter titles refer to its protagonist in the first person, and one of the "testimonials" included at the end of the book (likely written by Wilson herself) explicitly calls it an "autobiography." Yet the book also fictionalizes many names and numerous other details, and some of its key sequences, such as its opening scenes depicting how Frado's parents came to be married, are beyond the scope of Wilson's historical knowledge. Accordingly, scholars have debated whether *Our Nig* is best seen as an originator of the African American novel or as an innovation within an already extant tradition of African American life writing, exemplified by the slave narrative. Others have contended that the book's complex position in between fiction and autobiography demands reassessment of the usefulness of these conventional generic categories, or at least modern understandings of them, for describing and interpreting nineteenth-century literature.

Our Nig has also been read in terms of, or shown to engage with, an array of other, more specific genres, including the slave narrative, the conversion narrative, domestic fiction, and sentimental fiction. However, in the same way that the book complicates straightforward categorization as novel or autobiography, it also confounds or subverts these other genres: it lacks the slave narrative's focus on formal enslavement, the conversion narrative's unambiguous embrace of religion, domestic fiction's exaltation of the home, and sentimental fiction's clear-cut resolution. *Our Nig* is subversive in other ways, too. By making its protagonist's primary abuser a white woman, it subverts its readers' expectations about white femininity, and by focusing on the racist subordination and violence faced by a nominally "free" black person in New England, it refutes the way in which that region, by the mid-nineteenth century, had come to mythologize itself as both uniformly free of connection with slavery and uniformly white. Instead, *Our Nig* emphasizes African Americans' persistent, deep-rooted presence in New England, as well as what the book's subtitle calls slavery's enduring "shadows" in the region—New England's own history of slavery, its ongoing ties to the institution, and the racism that slavery fostered and was fostered by.

Our Nig's scathing depiction of Northern racism, including the racism of many Northern abolitionists, likely explains why the book met with a cold reception from New England's literary and cultural establishment. No contemporary reviews of the book have ever been found; it seems to have passed completely without notice. The book's evident failure with abolitionists—black as well as white—may also be due to a perception that it would harm the abolitionist movement by lending credence to proslavery arguments: for example, the argument that conditions for free blacks in the North were no better, and frequently worse, than those of enslaved people in the South. (Indeed, on the few occasions when *Our Nig* was noticed at all by literary scholars before the 1980s, it was sometimes misread as a work of proslavery propaganda.) In lieu of any endorsement by the New England literary scene, Wilson apparently marketed the book herself during her commercial travels: most of the extant first editions of *Our Nig* have been traced back to the same areas that Wilson visited to sell her hair products. A disproportionate number of copies seem to have ended up in the hands of young readers, likely because the book is both about a child and was written to support a child, and many of these readers seem to have valued it: some went on to give the book as a gift to siblings or other acquaintances, and one owner wrote "a good book" twice in his copy of it.

Tragically, the publication of this book meant to help support Wilson's son was followed, a few months later, by his death. The loss of her child may have prompted Wilson's turn, in the second half of her life, to a new career: that of spiritualist medium. Instead of being defeated by her early years in bondage and her son's death, Wilson moved to Boston in the 1860s, remarried in 1870, and soon became well-known in the city's Spiritualist circles. She eventually gained enough of a reputation to be referred to as "Dr. Hattie Wilson" (though also, more condescendingly, as "the colored medium"), traveling as far as Chicago to give lectures, frequently while "entranced," that were abundantly documented in Spiritualist periodicals such as the *Banner of Light* and *Spiritual Scientist*. Wilson also gave talks on issues of labor reform, especially child labor, and on children's education. She remained deeply involved in the Boston Spiritualist community until her death in 1900.

Our Nig was not completely forgotten from 1859 to the 1980s, but the rare scholarly mentions of it during this period misunderstood and mischaracterized it in a way that was possibly even worse than outright neglect. One 1954 study, for example, misidentified Wilson as a white Southern woman who wrote to defend slavery and even mistitled her book, possibly on purpose, as *Our Meg*. The scholarly verification of Wilson's identity in 1982, and *Our Nig*'s republication in 1983, were thus not just a rediscovery but a reclamation. Scholars have since filled in some of the gaps of Wilson's life and energetically explored and debated her work. This ongoing scholarly discussion has fed into broader efforts to preserve and promote

Wilson's legacy. The Harriet Wilson Project, founded in 2003, sponsors discussions about Wilson, facilitates artistic and dramatic depictions of her work, and advocates the teaching of *Our Nig*. Under the project's auspices, a sculpture of Wilson by the artist Fern Cunningham was unveiled in Milford in 2006.

NOTE ON THE TEXT: The excerpts from *Our Nig* presented here are based on the 1859 first edition, the only edition of the book published during the nineteenth century. Spelling and punctuation have been modernized according to the practices of this anthology.

⌘ ⌘ ⌘

from *Our Nig;*[1] *or, Sketches from the Life of a Free Black, in a Two-Story White House, North*

PREFACE

In offering to the public the following pages, the writer confesses her inability to minister to the refined and cultivated, the pleasure supplied by abler pens. It is not for such these crude narrations appear. Deserted by kindred, disabled by failing health, I am forced to some experiment which shall aid me in maintaining myself and child without extinguishing this feeble life. I would not from these motives even palliate[2] slavery at the South, by disclosures of its appurtenances[3] North. My mistress was wholly imbued with *southern* principles. I do not pretend to divulge every transaction in my own life, which the unprejudiced would declare unfavorable in comparison with treatment of legal bondmen;[4] I have purposely omitted what would most provoke shame in our good anti-slavery friends at home.

My humble position and frank confession of errors will, I hope, shield me from severe criticism. Indeed, defects are so apparent it requires no skilful hand to expose them.

I sincerely appeal to my colored brethren universally for patronage, hoping they will not condemn this attempt of their sister to be erudite, but rally around me a faithful band of supporters and defenders.

H.E.W.

CHAPTER 1. MAG SMITH, MY MOTHER.

Oh, Grief beyond all other griefs, when fate
First leaves the young heart lone and desolate
In the wide world, without that only tie
For which it loved to live or feared to die;
Lorn° as the hung-up lute, that ne'er   *forlorn*
    hath spoken
Since the sad day its master-chord was broken!
                                          Moore.[5]

Lonely Mag Smith! See her as she walks with downcast eyes and heavy heart. It was not always thus. She *had* a loving, trusting heart. Early deprived of parental guardianship, far removed from relatives, she was left to guide her tiny boat over life's surges alone and inexperienced. As she merged into womanhood, unprotected, uncherished, uncared for, there fell on her ear the music of love, awakening an intensity of emotion long dormant. It whispered of an elevation before unaspired to; of ease and plenty her simple heart had never dreamed of as hers. She knew the voice of her charmer, so ravishing, sounded far above her. It seemed like an angel's, alluring her upward and onward. She thought she could ascend to him and become an

---

1   *Nig*   Abbreviated but equally pejorative form of the "n-word," which, by the mid-nineteenth century, had achieved its current, emphatically derogatory meaning in white American vernacular.

2   *palliate*   Minimize or excuse.

3   *appurtenances*   Appendages, adjuncts.

4   *legal bondmen*   I.e., formally enslaved people.

5   *Oh, Grief ... Moore*   From *Lalla Rookh* (1817), a popular Orientalist romance by the Irish poet Thomas Moore, consisting of four narrative poems linked by a prose frame narrative.

equal. She surrendered to him a priceless gem, which he proudly garnered as a trophy, with those of other victims, and left her to her fate. The world seemed full of hateful deceivers and crushing arrogance. Conscious that the great bond of union to her former companions was severed, that the disdain of others would be insupportable, she determined to leave the few friends she possessed, and seek an asylum among strangers. Her offspring came unwelcomed, and before its nativity numbered weeks, it passed from earth, ascending to a purer and better life.

"God be thanked," ejaculated[1] Mag, as she saw its breathing cease; "no one can taunt *her* with my ruin."

Blessed release! may we all respond. How many pure, innocent children not only inherit a wicked heart of their own, claiming life-long scrutiny and restraint, but are heirs also of parental disgrace and calumny,[2] from which only long years of patient endurance in paths of rectitude can disencumber them.

Mag's new home was soon contaminated by the publicity of her fall; she had a feeling of degradation oppressing her; but she resolved to be circumspect, and try to regain in a measure what she had lost. Then some foul tongue would jest of her shame, and averted looks and cold greetings disheartened her. She saw she could not bury in forgetfulness her misdeed, so she resolved to leave her home and seek another in the place she at first fled from.

Alas, how fearful are we to be first in extending a helping hand to those who stagger in the mires of infamy; to speak the first words of hope and warning to those emerging into the sunlight of morality! Who can tell what numbers, advancing just far enough to hear a cold welcome and join in the reserved converse[3] of professed reformers, disappointed, disheartened, have chosen to dwell in unclean places, rather than encounter these "holier-than-thou" of the great brotherhood of man!

Such was Mag's experience; and disdaining to ask favor or friendship from a sneering world, she resolved to shut herself up in a hovel she had often passed in better days, and which she knew to be untenanted. She vowed to ask no favors of familiar faces; to die

neglected and forgotten before she would be dependent on any. Removed from the village, she was seldom seen except as upon your introduction, gentle reader, with downcast visage, returning her work to her employer, and thus providing herself with the means of subsistence. In two years many hands craved the same avocation; foreigners who cheapened toil and clamored for a livelihood, competed with her, and she could not thus sustain herself. She was now above no drudgery. Occasionally old acquaintances called to be favored with help of some kind, which she was glad to bestow for the sake of the money it would bring her; but the association with them was such a painful reminder of bygones, she returned to her hut morose and revengeful, refusing all offers of a better home than she possessed. Thus she lived for years, hugging her wrongs, but making no effort to escape. She had never known plenty, scarcely competency; but the present was beyond comparison with those innocent years when the coronet[4] of virtue was hers.

Every year her melancholy increased, her means diminished. At last no one seemed to notice her, save a kind-hearted African, who often called to inquire after her health and to see if she needed any fuel, he having the responsibility of furnishing that article, and she in return mending or making garments.

"How much you earn dis week, Mag?" asked he one Saturday evening.

"Little enough, Jim. Two or three days without any dinner. I washed for the Reeds, and did a small job for Mrs. Bellmont; that's all. I shall starve soon, unless I can get more to do. Folks seem as afraid to come here as if they expected to get some awful disease. I don't believe there is a person in the world but would be glad to have me dead and out of the way."

"No, no, Mag! don't talk so. You shan't starve so long as I have barrels to hoop.[5] Peter Greene boards me cheap. I'll help you, if nobody else will."

A tear stood in Mag's faded eye. "I'm glad," she said, with a softer tone than before, "if there is *one* who isn't glad to see me suffer. I b'lieve all Singleton wants to see me punished, and feel as if they could tell when

---

[1]   *ejaculated*   Uttered suddenly and with emotion.

[2]   *calumny*   Slander.

[3]   *reserved converse*   Chilly, distant conversation.

[4]   *coronet*   Small crown.

[5]   *barrels to hoop*   To "hoop" a barrel is to fasten a metal hoop around the individual wooden staves comprising it in order to bind them together.

I've been punished long enough. It's a long day ahead they'll set it, I reckon."

After the usual supply of fuel was prepared, Jim returned home. Full of pity for Mag, he set about devising measures for her relief. "By golly!" said he to himself one day—for he had become so absorbed in Mag's interest that he had fallen into a habit of musing aloud—"By golly! I wish she'd *marry* me."

"Who?" shouted Pete Greene, suddenly starting from an unobserved corner of the rude shop.

"Where you come from, you sly nigger!"[1] exclaimed Jim.

"Come, tell me, who is't?" said Pete; "Mag Smith, you want to marry?"

"Git out, Pete! and when you come in dis shop again, let a nigger know it. Don't steal in like a thief."

Pity and love know little severance. One attends the other. Jim acknowledged the presence of the former, and his efforts in Mag's behalf told also of a finer principle.

This sudden expedient which he had unintentionally disclosed, roused his thinking and inventive powers to study upon the best method of introducing the subject to Mag.

He belted his barrels,[2] with many a scheme revolving in his mind, none of which quite satisfied him, or seemed, on the whole, expedient. He thought of the pleasing contrast between her fair face and his own dark skin; the smooth, straight hair, which he had once, in expression of pity, kindly stroked on her now wrinkled but once fair brow. There was a tempest gathering in his heart, and at last, to ease his pent-up passion, he exclaimed aloud, "By golly!" Recollecting his former exposure, he glanced around to see if Pete was in hearing again. Satisfied on this point, he continued: "She'd be as much of a prize to me as she'd fall short of coming up to the mark with white folks. I don't care for past things. I've done things 'fore now I's 'shamed of. She's good enough for me, any how."

One more glance about the premises to be sure Pete was away.

The next Saturday night brought Jim to the hovel again. The cold was fast coming to tarry[3] its apportioned time. Mag was nearly despairing of meeting its rigor.

"How's the wood, Mag?" asked Jim.

"All gone; and no more to cut, any how," was the reply.

"Too bad!" Jim said. His truthful reply would have been, I'm glad.

"Anything to eat in the house?" continued he.

"No," replied Mag.

"Too bad!" again, orally, with the same *inward* gratulation[4] as before.

"Well, Mag," said Jim, after a short pause, "you's down low enough. I don't see but I've got to take care of ye. 'Sposin' we marry!"

Mag raised her eyes, full of amazement, and uttered a sonorous "What?"

Jim felt abashed for a moment. He knew well what were her objections.

"You's had trial of white folks, any how. They run off and left ye, and now none of 'em come near ye to see if you's dead or alive. I's black outside, I know, but I's got a white heart inside. Which you rather have, a black heart in a white skin, or a white heart in a black one?"

"Oh, dear!" sighed Mag; "Nobody on earth cares for *me*—"

"I do," interrupted Jim.

"I can do but two things," said she, "beg my living, or get it from you."

"Take me, Mag. I can give you a better home than this, and not let you suffer so."

He prevailed; they married. You can philosophize, gentle reader, upon the impropriety of such unions, and preach dozens of sermons on the evils of amalgamation.[5] Want is a more powerful philosopher and preacher. Poor Mag. She has sundered another bond which held her to her fellows. She has descended another step down the ladder of infamy. …

---

1 *nigger* By the mid-nineteenth century, as noted above, this word, when used by white people of black people, had acquired the extremely derogatory connotations it carries today, but it had also become a term used by African Americans for and among themselves in a neutral or positive way, as Jim's use of it here and in his following statement demonstrates.

2 *belted his barrels* I.e., fastened hoops around the wooden staves comprising them.

3 *tarry* Reside.

4 *gratulation* Rejoicing.

5 *amalgamation* I.e., the mingling of races—what, a few years after *Our Nig* was published, would be pejoratively termed "miscegenation."

[A few years after Jim's marriage to Mag, he dies of tuberculosis, leaving her with two children. Mag subsequently cohabits with Jim's business partner Seth Shipley; facing penury and hunger and unable to support both children, they resolve to give away Mag's daughter Frado. Mag leaves Frado with the Bellmonts, a well-to-do local white family whose mother Mag considers "a right she-devil," on the pretence that she will return for her at the end of the day; however, Frado never sees her again.]

CHAPTER 3. A NEW HOME FOR ME.

Oh! did we but know of the shadows so nigh,
    The world would indeed be a prison of gloom;
All light would be quenched in youth's eloquent eye,
    And the prayer-lisping[1] infant would ask for the
    tomb.

For if Hope be a star that may lead us astray,
    And "deceiveth the heart," as the aged ones preach;
Yet 'twas Mercy that gave it, to beacon our way,
    Though its halo illumes° where it   illuminates
    never can reach.

Eliza Cook.[2]

As the day closed and Mag did not appear, surmises were expressed by the family that she never intended to return. Mr. Bellmont was a kind, humane man, who would not grudge hospitality to the poorest wanderer, nor fail to sympathize with any sufferer, however humble. The child's desertion by her mother appealed to his sympathy, and he felt inclined to succor her. To do this in opposition to Mrs. Bellmont's wishes, would be like encountering a whirlwind charged with fire, daggers and spikes. She was not as susceptible of fine emotions as her spouse. Mag's opinion of her was not without foundation. She was self-willed, haughty, undisciplined, arbitrary and severe. In common parlance, she was a *scold*, a thorough one. Mr. B. remained silent during the consultation which follows, engaged

in by mother, Mary and John, or Jack, as he was familiarly called.

"Send her to the County House,"[3] said Mary, in reply to the query what should be done with her, in a tone which indicated self-importance in the speaker. She was indeed the idol of her mother, and more nearly resembled her in disposition and manners than the others.

Jane, an invalid daughter, the eldest of those at home, was reclining on a sofa apparently uninterested.

"Keep her," said Jack. "She's real handsome and bright, and not very black, either."

"Yes," rejoined Mary; "that's just like you, Jack. She'll be of no use at all these three years, right under foot all the time."

"Poh! Miss Mary; if she should stay, it wouldn't be two days before you would be telling the girls about *our* nig, *our* nig!" retorted Jack.

"I don't want a nigger 'round *me*, do you, mother?" asked Mary.

"I don't mind the nigger in the child. I should like a dozen better than one," replied her mother. "If I could make her do my work in a few years, I would keep her. I have so much trouble with girls I hire, I am almost persuaded if I have one to train up in my way from a child, I shall be able to keep them awhile. I am tired of changing every few months."

"Where could she sleep?" asked Mary. "I don't want her near me."

"In the L chamber," answered the mother.

"How'll she get there?" asked Jack. "She'll be afraid to go through that dark passage, and she can't climb the ladder safely."

"She'll have to go there; it's good enough for a nigger," was the reply.

Jack was sent on horseback to ascertain if Mag was at her home. He returned with the testimony of Pete Greene that they were fairly departed, and that the child was intentionally thrust upon their family.

The imposition was not at all relished by Mrs. B., or the pert, haughty Mary, who had just glided into her teens.

"Show the child to bed, Jack," said his mother. "You seem most pleased with the little nigger, so you may introduce her to her room."

---

1   *prayer-lisping*   Uttering prayers in a childlike, imperfect way.

2   *Oh! did we ... Eliza Cook*   From "The Future," by Eliza Cook (1818–89), a popular English poet and journalist known for her political advocacy on behalf of women and the working class.

3   *County House*   Local poorhouse.

He went to the kitchen, and, taking Frado gently by the hand, told her he would put her in bed now; perhaps her mother would come the next night after her.

It was not yet quite dark, so they ascended the stairs without any light, passing through nicely furnished rooms, which were a source of great amazement to the child. He opened the door which connected with her room by a dark, unfinished passageway. "Don't bump your head," said Jack, and stepped before to open the door leading into her apartment—an unfinished chamber over the kitchen, the roof slanting nearly to the floor, so that the bed could stand only in the middle of the room. A small half window furnished light and air. Jack returned to the sitting room with the remark that the child would soon outgrow those quarters.

"When she *does*, she'll outgrow the house," remarked the mother.

"What can she do to help you?" asked Mary. "She came just in the right time, didn't she? Just the very day after Bridget left," continued she.

"I'll see what she can do in the morning," was the answer.

While this conversation was passing below, Frado lay, revolving in her little mind whether she would remain or not until her mother's return. She was of wilful, determined nature, a stranger to fear, and would not hesitate to wander away should she decide to. She remembered the conversation of her mother with Seth, the words "given away" which she heard used in reference to herself; and though she did not know their full import, she thought she should, by remaining, be in some relation to white people she was never favored with before. So she resolved to tarry,[1] with the hope that mother would come and get her some time. The hot sun had penetrated her room, and it was long before a cooling breeze reduced the temperature so that she could sleep.

Frado was called early in the morning by her new mistress. Her first work was to feed the hens. She was shown how it was *always* to be done, and in no other way; any departure from this rule to be punished by a whipping. She was then accompanied by Jack to drive the cows to pasture, so she might learn the way. Upon her return she was allowed to eat her breakfast, consisting of a bowl of skimmed milk, with brown bread crusts, which she was told to eat, standing, by the kitchen table, and must not be over ten minutes about it. Meanwhile the family were taking their morning meal in the dining-room. This over, she was placed on a cricket[2] to wash the common dishes; she was to be in waiting always to bring wood and chips,[3] to run hither and thither from room to room.

A large amount of dish-washing for small hands followed dinner. Then the same after tea and going after the cows finished her first day's work. It was a new discipline to the child. She found some attractions about the place, and she retired to rest at night more willing to remain. The same routine followed day after day, with slight variation; adding a little more work, and spicing the toil with "words that burn," and frequent blows on her head. These were great annoyances to Frado, and had she known where her mother was, she would have gone at once to her. She was often greatly wearied, and silently wept over her sad fate. At first she wept aloud, which Mrs. Bellmont noticed by applying a rawhide,[4] always at hand in the kitchen. It was a symptom of discontent and complaining which must be "nipped in the bud," she said.

Thus passed a year. No intelligence of Mag. It was now certain Frado was to become a permanent member of the family. Her labors were multiplied; she was quite indispensable, although but seven years old. She had never learned to read, never heard of a school until her residence in the family.

Mrs. Bellmont was in doubt about the utility of attempting to educate people of color, who were incapable of elevation. This subject occasioned a lengthy discussion in the family. Mr. Bellmont, Jane and Jack arguing for Frado's education; Mary and her mother objecting. At last Mr. Bellmont declared decisively that she *should* go to school. He was a man who seldom decided controversies at home. The word once spoken admitted of no appeal; so, notwithstanding Mary's objection that she would have to attend the same school she did, the word became law.

It was to be a new scene to Frado, and Jack had many queries and conjectures to answer. He was himself too far advanced to attend the summer school, which

---

1 *tarry* Linger.

2 *cricket* Footstool.

3 *wood and chips* For the fire.

4 *rawhide* Whip made of untreated cattle hide.

Frado regretted, having had too many opportunities of witnessing Miss Mary's temper to feel safe in her company alone.

The opening day of school came. Frado sauntered on far in the rear of Mary, who was ashamed to be seen "walking with a nigger." As soon as she appeared, with scanty clothing and bared feet, the children assembled, noisily published[1] her approach: "See that nigger," shouted one. "Look! look!" cried another. "I won't play with her," said one little girl. "Nor I neither," replied another.

Mary evidently relished these sharp attacks, and saw a fair prospect of lowering Nig where, according to her views, she belonged. Poor Frado, chagrined and grieved, felt that her anticipations of pleasure at such a place were far from being realized. She was just deciding to return home, and never come there again, when the teacher appeared, and observing the downcast looks of the child, took her by the hand, and led her into the school-room. All followed, and, after the bustle of securing seats was over, Miss Marsh inquired if the children knew "any cause for the sorrow of that little girl?" pointing to Frado. It was soon all told. She then reminded them of their duties to the poor and friendless; their cowardice in attacking a young innocent child; referred them to one who looks not on outward appearances, but on the heart.[2] "She looks like a good girl; I think *I* shall love her, so lay aside all prejudice, and vie with each other in showing kindness and goodwill to one who seems different from you," were the closing remarks of the kind lady. Those kind words! The most agreeable sound which ever meets the ear of sorrowing, grieving childhood.

Example rendered her words efficacious. Day by day there was a manifest change of deportment towards "Nig." Her speeches often drew merriment from the children; no one could do more to enliven their favorite pastimes than Frado. Mary could not endure to see her thus noticed, yet knew not how to prevent it. She could not influence her schoolmates as she wished. She had not gained their affections by winning ways and yielding points of controversy. On the contrary, she was self-willed, domineering; every day reported "mad" by some of her companions. She availed herself of the only alternative, abuse and taunts, as they returned from school. This was not satisfactory; she wanted to use physical force "to subdue her," to "keep her down."

There was, on their way home, a field intersected by a stream over which a single plank was placed for a crossing. It occurred to Mary that it would be a punishment to Nig to compel her to cross over; so she dragged her to the edge, and told her authoritatively to go over. Nig hesitated, resisted. Mary placed herself behind the child, and, in the struggle to force her over, lost her footing and plunged into the stream. Some of the larger scholars being in sight, ran, and thus prevented Mary from drowning and Frado from falling. Nig scampered home fast as possible, and Mary went to the nearest house, dripping, to procure a change of garments. She came loitering home, half crying, exclaiming, "Nig pushed me into the stream!" She then related the particulars. Nig was called from the kitchen. Mary stood with anger flashing in her eyes. Mr. Bellmont sat quietly reading his paper. He had witnessed too many of Miss Mary's outbreaks to be startled. Mrs. Bellmont interrogated Nig.

"I didn't do it! I didn't do it!" answered Nig, passionately, and then related the occurrence truthfully.

The discrepancy greatly enraged Mrs. Bellmont. With loud accusations and angry gestures she approached the child. Turning to her husband, she asked,

"Will you sit still, there, and hear that black nigger call Mary a liar?"

"How do we know but she has told the truth? I shall not punish her," he replied, and left the house, as he usually did when a tempest threatened to envelop him. No sooner was he out of sight than Mrs. B. and Mary commenced beating her inhumanly; then propping her mouth open with a piece of wood, shut her up in a dark room, without any supper. For employment, while the tempest raged within, Mr. Bellmont went for the cows, a task belonging to Frado, and thus unintentionally prolonged her pain. At dark Jack came in, and seeing Mary, accosted her with, "So you thought you'd vent your spite on Nig, did you? Why can't you let her alone? It was good enough for you to get a ducking,[3] only you did not stay in half long enough."

---

[1]   *published*   Announced, reported.

[2]   *one who … heart*   See 1 Samuel 16.7: "the Lord seeth not as man seeth; for man looketh on the outward appearance, but the Lord looketh on the heart."

[3]   *ducking*   I.e., dunking.

"Stop!" said his mother. "You shall never talk so before me. You would have that little nigger trample on Mary, would you? She came home with a lie; it made Mary's story false."

"What was Mary's story?" asked Jack.

It was related.

"Now," said Jack, sallying into a chair, "the school-children happened to see it all, and they tell the same story Nig does. Which is most likely to be true, what a dozen agree they saw, or the contrary?"

"It is very strange you will believe what others say against your sister," retorted his mother, with flashing eye. "I think it is time your father subdued you."

"Father is a sensible man," argued Jack. "He would not wrong a dog. Where *is* Frado?" he continued.

"Mother gave her a good whipping and shut her up," replied Mary.

Just then Mr. Bellmont entered, and asked if Frado was "shut up yet."

The knowledge of her innocence, the perfidy of his sister, worked fearfully on Jack. He bounded from his chair, searched every room till he found the child; her mouth wedged apart, her face swollen, and full of pain.

How Jack pitied her! He relieved her jaws, brought her some supper, took her to her room, comforted her as well as he knew how, sat by her till she fell asleep, and then left for the sitting room. As he passed his mother, he remarked, "If that was the way Frado was to be treated, he hoped she would never wake again!" He then imparted her situation to his father, who seemed untouched, till a glance at Jack exposed a tearful eye. Jack went early to her next morning. She awoke sad, but refreshed. After breakfast Jack took her with him to the field, and kept her through the day. But it could not be so generally. She must return to school, to her household duties. He resolved to do what he could to protect her from Mary and his mother. He bought her a dog, which became a great favorite with both. The invalid, Jane, would gladly befriend her; but she had not the strength to brave the iron will of her mother. Kind words and affectionate glances were the only expressions of sympathy she could safely indulge in. The men employed on the farm were always glad to hear her prattle;[1] she was a great favorite with them. Mrs. Bellmont allowed them the privilege of talking with her in the kitchen. She did not fear but she should have ample opportunity of subduing her when they were away. Three months of schooling, summer and winter, she enjoyed for three years. Her winter over-dress was a cast-off overcoat, once worn by Jack, and a sun-bonnet. It was a source of great merriment to the scholars, but Nig's retorts were so mirthful, and their satisfaction so evident in attributing the selection to "Old Granny Bellmont," that it was not painful to Nig or pleasurable to Mary. Her jollity was not to be quenched by whipping or scolding. In Mrs. Bellmont's presence she was under restraint; but in the kitchen, and among her schoolmates, the pent up fires burst forth. She was ever at some sly prank when unseen by her teacher, in school hours; not unfrequently some outburst of merriment, of which she was the original, was charged upon some innocent mate, and punishment inflicted which she merited. They enjoyed her antics so fully that any of them would suffer wrongfully to keep open the avenues of mirth. She would venture far beyond propriety, thus shielded and countenanced.

The teacher's desk was supplied with drawers, in which were stored his books and other *et ceteras*[2] of the profession. The children observed Nig very busy there one morning before school, as they flitted in occasionally from their play outside. The master came; called the children to order; opened a drawer to take the book the occasion required; when out poured a volume of smoke. "Fire! fire!" screamed he, at the top of his voice. By this time he had become sufficiently acquainted with the peculiar odor, to know he was imposed upon. The scholars shouted with laughter to see the terror of the dupe, who, feeling abashed at the needless fright, made no very strict investigation, and Nig once more escaped punishment. She had provided herself with cigars, and puffing, puffing away at the crack of the drawer, had filled it with smoke, and then closed it tightly to deceive the teacher, and amuse the scholars. The interim of terms was filled up with a variety of duties new and peculiar. At home, no matter how powerful the heat when sent to rake hay or guard the grazing herd, she was never permitted to shield her skin from the sun. She was not many shades darker than Mary now; what a calamity it would be ever to hear the contrast spoken of. Mrs. Bellmont was determined the

---

[1] *prattle* Chatter, banter.

[2] *et ceteras* Additional things.

sun should have full power to darken the shade which nature had first bestowed upon her as best befitting. ...

[When Frado reaches the age of nine, Mrs. Bellmont stops her schooling. During the following years, Frado is befriended by Mr. Bellmont's unmarried sister, Abby, and James Bellmont, a grown son of the family who has returned home to attempt to recover from illness.]

CHAPTER 7. SPIRITUAL CONDITION OF NIG.

What are our joys but dreams? and what our hopes
But goodly shadows in the summer cloud?
                                        H.K.W.[1]

James did not improve as was hoped. Month after month passed away, and brought no prospect of returning health. He could not walk far from the house for want of strength; but he loved to sit with Aunt Abby in her quiet room, talking of unseen glories, and heart-experiences, while planning for the spiritual benefit of those around them. In these confidential interviews, Frado was never omitted. They would discuss the prevalent opinion of the public, that people of color are really inferior; incapable of cultivation and refinement. They would glance at the qualities of Nig, which promised so much if rightly directed. "I wish you would take her, James, when you are well, home with *you*," said Aunt Abby, in one of these seasons.

"Just what I am longing to do, Aunt Abby. Susan[2] is just of my mind, and we intend to take her; I have been wishing to do so for years."

"She seems much affected by what she hears at the evening meetings, and asks me many questions on serious things; seems to love to read the Bible; I feel hopes of her."

"I hope she *is* thoughtful; no one has a kinder heart, one capable of loving more devotedly. But to think how prejudiced the world is towards her people; that she must be reared in such ignorance as to drown all the finer feelings. When I think of what she might

be, of what she will be, I feel like grasping time till opinions change, and thousands like her rise into a noble freedom. I have seen Frado's grief, because she is black, amount to agony. It makes me sick to recall these scenes. Mother pretends to think she don't know enough to sorrow for anything; but if she could see her as I have, when she supposed herself entirely alone, except her little dog Fido, lamenting her loneliness and complexion, I think, if she is not past feeling, she would retract. In the summer I was walking near the barn, and as I stood I heard sobs. 'Oh! oh!' I heard, 'why was I made? why can't I die? Oh, what have I to live for? No one cares for me only to get my work. And I feel sick; who cares for that? Work as long as I can stand, and then fall down and lay there till I can get up. No mother, father, brother or sister to care for me, and then it is, You lazy nigger, lazy nigger—all because I am black! Oh, if I could die!'

"I stepped into the barn, where I could see her. She was crouched down by the hay with her faithful friend Fido, and as she ceased speaking, buried her face in her hands, and cried bitterly; then, patting Fido, she kissed him, saying, 'You love me, Fido, don't you? but we must go work in the field.' She started on her mission; I called her to me, and told her she need not go, the hay was doing well.

"She has such confidence in me that she will do just as I tell her; so we found a seat under a shady tree, and there I took the opportunity to combat the notions she seemed to entertain respecting the loneliness of her condition and want of sympathizing friends. I assured her that mother's views were by no means general; that in our part of the country there were thousands upon thousands who favored the elevation of her race, disapproving of oppression in all its forms; that she was not unpitied, friendless, and utterly despised; that she might hope for better things in the future. Having spoken these words of comfort, I rose with the resolution that if I recovered my health I would take her home with me, whether mother was willing or not."

"I don't know what your mother would do without her; still, I wish she was away."

Susan now came for her long absent husband, and they returned home to their room.

The month of November was one of great anxiety on James's account. He was rapidly wasting away.

---

[1]   *What are ... H.K.W.* From "On Time," by the English poet Henry Kirke White (1785–1806).

[2]   *Susan*   James's wife.

A celebrated physician was called, and performed a surgical operation, as a last means. Should this fail, there was no hope. Of course he was confined wholly to his room, mostly to his bed. With all his bodily suffering, all his anxiety for his family, whom he might not live to protect, he did not forget Frado. He shielded her from many beatings, and every day imparted religious instructions. No one, but his wife, could move[1] him so easily as Frado; so that in addition to her daily toil she was often deprived of her rest at night.

Yet she insisted on being called; she wished to show her love for one who had been such a friend to her. Her anxiety and grief increased as the probabilities of his recovery became doubtful.

Mrs. Bellmont found her weeping on his account, shut her up, and whipped her with the raw-hide, adding an injunction never to be seen snivelling again because she had a little work to do. She was very careful never to shed tears on his account, in her presence, afterwards. ...

[As James's health continues to decline, Frado starts attending church with Aunt Abby.]

from CHAPTER 8. VISITOR AND DEPARTURE.

... Frado, under the instructions of Aunt Abby and the minister, became a believer in a future existence—one of happiness or misery. Her doubt was, *is* there a heaven for the black? She knew there was one for James, and Aunt Abby, and all good white people; but was there any for blacks? She had listened attentively to all the minister said, and all Aunt Abby had told her; but then it was all for white people.

As James approached that blessed world, she felt a strong desire to follow, and be with one who was such a dear, kind friend to her.

While she was exercised with these desires and aspirations, she attended an evening meeting with Aunt Abby, and the good man urged all, young or old, to accept the offers of mercy, to receive a compassionate Jesus as their Saviour. "Come to Christ," he urged, "all, young or old, white or black, bond or free, come all to Christ for pardon; repent, believe."

This was the message she longed to hear; it seemed to be spoken for her. But he had told them to repent; "what was that?" she asked. She knew she was unfit for any heaven, made for whites or blacks. She would gladly repent, or do anything which would admit her to share the abode of James.

Her anxiety increased; her countenance bore marks of solicitude[2] unseen before; and though she said nothing of her inward contest, they all observed a change.

James and Aunt Abby hoped it was the springing of good seed sown by the Spirit of God. Her tearful attention at the last meeting encouraged his aunt to hope that her mind was awakened, her conscience aroused. Aunt Abby noticed that she was particularly engaged in reading the Bible; and this strengthened her conviction that a heavenly Messenger was striving with her. The neighbors dropped in to inquire after the sick, and also if Frado was "*serious?*" They noticed she seemed very thoughtful and tearful at the meetings. Mrs. Reed was very inquisitive; but Mrs. Bellmont saw no appearance of change for the better. She did not feel responsible for her spiritual culture,[3] and hardly believed she had a soul.

Nig was in truth suffering much; her feelings were very intense on any subject, when once aroused. She read her Bible carefully, and as often as an opportunity presented, which was when entirely secluded in her own apartment, or by Aunt Abby's side, who kindly directed her to Christ, and instructed her in the way of salvation.

Mrs. Bellmont found her one day quietly reading her Bible. Amazed and half crediting the reports of officious neighbors, she felt it was time to interfere. Here she was, reading and shedding tears over the Bible. She ordered her to put up the book, and go to work, and not be snivelling about the house, or stop to read again.

But there was one little spot seldom penetrated by her mistress' watchful eye: this was her room, uninviting and comfortless; but to herself a safe retreat. Here she would listen to the pleadings of a Saviour, and try to penetrate the veil of doubt and sin which clouded her soul, and long to cast off the fetters of sin, and rise to the communion of saints.

Mrs. Bellmont, as we before said, did not trouble herself about the future destiny of her servant. If she

---

1   *move*   Influence or persuade.

2   *solicitude*   Disquiet, concern.

3   *culture*   Cultivation, development.

did what she desired for *her* benefit, it was all the responsibility she acknowledged. But she seemed to have great aversion to the notice Nig would attract should she become pious. How could she meet this case? She resolved to make her complaint to John.[1] Strange, when she was always foiled in this direction, she should resort to him. It was time something was done; she had begun to read the Bible openly.

The night of this discovery, as they were retiring, Mrs. Bellmont introduced the conversation, by saying:

"I want your attention to what I am going to say. I have let Nig go out to evening meetings a few times, and, if you will believe it, I found her reading the Bible today, just as though she expected to turn pious nigger, and preach to white folks. So now you see what good comes of sending her to school. If she should get converted she would have to go to meeting: at least, as long as James lives. I wish he had not such queer notions about her. It seems to trouble him to know he must die and leave her. He says if he should get well he would take her home with him, or educate her here. Oh, how awful! What can the child mean? So careful, too, of her! He says we shall ruin her health making her work so hard, and sleep in such a place. O, John! do you think he is in his right mind?"

"Yes, yes; she is slender."

"Yes, *yes!*" she repeated sarcastically, "you know these niggers are just like black snakes; you *can't* kill them. If she wasn't tough she would have been killed long ago. There was never one of my girls could do half the work."

"Did they ever try?" interposed her husband. "I think she can do more than all of them together."

"What a man!" said she, peevishly. "But I want to know what is going to be done with her about getting pious?"

"Let her do just as she has a mind to. If it is a comfort to her, let her enjoy the privilege of being good. I see no objection."

"I should think *you* were crazy, sure. Don't you know that every night she will want to go toting off to meeting? and Sundays, too? and you know we have a great deal of company Sundays, and she can't be spared."

"I thought you Christians held to going to church," remarked Mr. B.

"Yes, but who ever thought of having a nigger go, except to drive others there? Why, according to you and James, we should very soon have her in the parlor, as smart as our own girls. It's of no use talking to you or James. If you should go on as you would like it would not be six months before she would be leaving me; and that won't do. Just think how much profit she was to us last summer. We had no work hired out; she did the work of two girls—"

"And got the whippings for two with it!" remarked Mr. Bellmont.

"I'll beat the money out of her, if I can't get her worth any other way," retorted Mrs. B. sharply. While this scene was passing, Frado was trying to utter the prayer of the publican, "God be merciful to me a sinner."[2] …

[In Chapter 9, James dies and the far-flung Bellmont family assembles to mourn him.]

CHAPTER 10. PERPLEXITIES—ANOTHER DEATH.

'Neath the billows of the ocean,
Hidden treasures wait the hand,
That again to light shall raise them
With the diver's magic wand.

G.W. Cook.[3]

The family, gathered by James's decease, returned to their homes. Susan and Charles[4] returned to Baltimore. Letters were received from the absent, expressing their sympathy and grief. The father bowed like a "bruised reed,"[5] under the loss of his beloved son. He felt

---

1   *John*   I.e., her husband.

2   *the prayer … sinner*   In Luke 18, Jesus tells a parable of a Pharisee and a tax collector—or, in the language of the King James Bible, a "publican"—who both go to the temple to pray. While the Pharisee, in his prayer, thanks God that he is not like the publican, "the publican, standing afar off, would not lift up so much as his eyes unto heaven, but smote upon his breast, saying, God be merciful to me a sinner" (Luke 18.13). Jesus concludes that the publican rather than the Pharisee "went down to his house justified," because "every one that exalteth himself shall be abased; and he that humbleth himself shall be exalted."

3   *'Neath … Cook*   The source of this quotation has not been identified.

4   *Charles*   James's son.

5   *bruised reed*   See Matthew 12.20, which quotes a prophecy from the Book of Isaiah concerning the Messiah: "A bruised reed shall he

desirous to die the death of the righteous; also, conscious that he was unprepared, he resolved to start on the narrow way, and some time solicit entrance through the gate which leads to the celestial city.[1] He acknowledged his too ready acquiescence with Mrs. B., in permitting Frado to be deprived of her only religious privileges for weeks together. He accordingly asked his sister to take her to meeting once more, which she was ready at once to do.

The first opportunity they once more attended meeting together. The minister conversed faithfully with every person present. He was surprised to find the little colored girl so solicitous, and kindly directed her to the flowing fountain where she might wash and be clean.[2] He inquired of the origin of her anxiety, of her progress up to this time, and endeavored to make Christ, instead of James, the attraction of Heaven. He invited her to come to his house, to speak freely her mind to him, to pray much, to read her Bible often.

The neighbors, who were at meeting—among them Mrs. Reed—discussed the opinions Mrs. Bellmont would express on the subject. Mrs. Reed called[3] and informed Mrs. B. that her colored girl "related her experience the other night at the meeting."

"What experience?" asked she, quickly, as if she expected to hear the number of times she had whipped Frado, and the number of lashes set forth in plain Arabic numbers.

"Why, you know she is serious, don't you? She told the minister about it."

Mrs. B. made no reply, but changed the subject adroitly. Next morning she told Frado she "should not go out of the house for one while, except on errands; and if she did not stop trying to be religious, she would whip her to death."

Frado pondered; her mistress was a professor[4] of religion; was *she* going to heaven? then she did not wish to go. If she should be near James, even, she could not be happy with those fiery eyes watching her ascending path. She resolved to give over all thought of the future world, and strove daily to put her anxiety far from her.

Mr. Bellmont found himself unable to do what James or Jack could accomplish for her. He talked with her seriously, told her he had seen her many times punished undeservedly; he did not wish to have her saucy or disrespectful, but when she was *sure* she did not deserve a whipping, to avoid it if she could. "You are looking sick," he added, "you cannot endure beating as you once could."

It was not long before an opportunity offered of profiting by his advice. She was sent for wood, and not returning as soon as Mrs. B. calculated, she followed her, and, snatching from the pile a stick, raised it over her.

"Stop!" shouted Frado, "strike me, and I'll never work a mite more for you"; and throwing down what she had gathered, stood like one who feels the stirring of free and independent thoughts.

By this unexpected demonstration, her mistress, in amazement, dropped her weapon, desisting from her purpose of chastisement. Frado walked towards the house, her mistress following with the wood she herself was sent after. She did not know, before, that she had a power to ward off assaults. Her triumph in seeing her enter the door with *her* burden, repaid her for much of her former suffering.

It was characteristic of Mrs. B. never to rise in her majesty, unless she was sure she should be victorious.

This affair never met with an "after clap," like many others.

Thus passed a year. The usual amount of scolding, but fewer whippings. Mrs. B. longed once more for Mary's return,[5] who had been absent over a year; and she wrote imperatively for her to come quickly to her. A letter came in reply, announcing that she would comply as soon as she was sufficiently recovered from an illness which detained her.

---

not break, and smoking flax shall he not quench, till he send forth judgment unto victory."

[1] *he resolved … city* Reference to *The Pilgrim's Progress* (1678), an allegorical narrative by the English writer and preacher John Bunyan that was widely and enduringly popular in both Britain and America. The narrative concerns the difficult journey undertaken by a character called "Christian" on the "straight and narrow way" that leads to the "Celestial City" (i.e., Heaven). Bunyan and Wilson both also echo Matthew 7.14: "Because strait is the gate, and narrow is the way, which leadeth unto life, and few there be that find it."

[2] *the flowing … clean* I.e., Christ.

[3] *called* I.e., visited.

---

[4] *professor* Believer, adherent.

[5] *Mary's return* Mary had earlier moved away to live with another Bellmont son, Lewis.

No serious apprehensions were cherished by either parent, who constantly looked for notice of her arrival, by mail. Another letter brought tidings that Mary was seriously ill; her mother's presence was solicited.

She started without delay. Before she reached her destination, a letter came to the parents announcing her death.

No sooner was the astounding news received, than Frado rushed into Aunt Abby's, exclaiming:

"She's dead, Aunt Abby!"

"Who?" she asked, terrified by the unprefaced announcement.

"Mary; they've just had a letter."

As Mrs. B. was away, the brother and sister could freely sympathize, and she sought him in this fresh sorrow, to communicate such solace as she could, and to learn particulars of Mary's untimely death, and assist him in his journey thither.

It seemed a thanksgiving to Frado. Every hour or two she would pop into Aunt Abby's room with some strange query:

"She got into the *river* again, Aunt Abby, didn't she; the Jordan[1] is a big one to tumble into, anyhow. S'posen she goes to hell, she'll be as black as I am. Wouldn't mistress be mad to see her a nigger!" and others of a similar stamp, not at all acceptable to the pious, sympathetic dame; but she could not evade them.

The family returned from their sorrowful journey, leaving the dead behind. Nig looked for a change in her tyrant; what could subdue her, if the loss of her idol could not?

Never was Mrs. B. known to shed tears so profusely, as when she reiterated to one and another the sad particulars of her darling's sickness and death. There was, indeed, a season of quiet grief; it was the lull of the fiery elements. A few weeks revived the former tempests, and so at variance did they seem with chastisement sanctified, that Frado felt them to be unbearable. She determined to flee. But where? Who would take

her? Mrs. B. had always represented her[2] ugly. Perhaps every one thought her so. Then no one would take her. She was black, no one would love her. She might have to return, and then she would be more in her mistress's power than ever.

She remembered her victory at the wood-pile. She decided to remain to do as well as she could; to assert her rights when they were trampled on; to return once more to her meeting in the evening, which had been prohibited. She had learned how to conquer; she would not abuse the power while Mr. Bellmont was at home.

But had she not better run away? Where? She had never been from the place far enough to decide what course to take. She resolved to speak to Aunt Abby. *She* mapped the dangers of her course, her liability[3] to fail in finding so good friends as John and herself. Frado's mind was busy for days and nights. She contemplated administering poison to her mistress, to rid herself and the house of so detestable a plague.

But she was restrained by an overruling Providence; and finally decided to stay contentedly through her period of service,[4] which would expire when she was eighteen years of age.

In a few months Jane returned home with her family,[5] to relieve her parents, upon whom years and affliction had left the marks of age. The years intervening since she had left her home, had, in some degree, softened the opposition to her unsanctioned marriage with George. The more Mrs. B. had about her, the more energetic seemed her directing capabilities, and her fault-finding propensities. Her own, she had full power over; and Jane after vain endeavors, became disgusted, weary, and perplexed, and decided that, though her mother might suffer, she could not endure her home. They followed Jack to the West.[6] Thus vanished all hopes of sympathy or relief from this source to Frado. There seemed no one capable of enduring

---

[1] *Jordan*   The Jordan River, which today forms the boundary between Israel and the West Bank on one side and the nation of Jordan on the other, possesses a great deal of symbolic significance in the Jewish and Christian traditions. Because in the Bible the Israelites entered the Promised Land by crossing the Jordan, the river was frequently used to symbolize the transition from this world to the next.

[2] *represented her*   Characterized her as.

[3] *liability*   Likelihood.

[4] *period of service*   I.e., as an indentured servant—Frado's legal status with the Bellmonts.

[5] *Jane … family*   In Chapter 5, Jane Bellmont defies her mother by rejecting a wealthy suitor and marrying a poorer but kinder man instead, with whom she moves away.

[6] *They followed … West*   Jack Bellmont has earlier gone West to seek his fortune.

the oppressions of the house but her. She turned to the darkness of the future with the determination previously formed, to remain until she should be eighteen. Jane begged her to follow her so soon as she should be released; but so wearied out was she by her mistress, she felt disposed to flee from any and every one having her similitude of name or feature.

[Frado fulfills her intention to remain with the Bellmonts until the end of her term as an indentured servant and then leaves. She fends for herself for a number of years until her health breaks down, partially due to her years of mistreatment, whereupon she returns to the Bellmont home. Abby cares for her there. Frado subsequently works as a domestic for a time and then supports herself by sewing and bonnet making; she suffers from chronic ill-health but is aided by the charity of friends whose esteem she has won.]

CHAPTER 12. THE WINDING UP OF THE MATTER.

Nothing new under the sun.

Solomon.[1]

A few years ago, within the compass of my narrative, there appeared often in some of our New England villages, professed fugitives from slavery, who recounted their personal experience in homely phrase, and awakened the indignation of non-slaveholders against brother Pro.[2] Such a one appeared in the new home of Frado; and as people of color were rare there, was it strange she should attract her dark brother; that he should inquire her out; succeed in seeing her; feel a strange sensation in his heart towards her; that he should toy with her shining curls, feel proud to provoke her to smile and expose the ivory concealed by thin, ruby lips; that her sparkling eyes should fascinate; that he should propose; that they should marry? A short acquaintance was indeed an objection, but she

saw him often, and thought she knew him. He never spoke of his enslavement to her when alone, but she felt that, like her own oppression, it was painful to disturb oftener than was needful.

He was a fine, straight negro, whose back showed no marks of the lash, erect as if it never crouched beneath a burden. There was a silent sympathy which Frado felt attracted her, and she opened her heart to the presence of love—that arbitrary and inexorable tyrant.

She removed to Singleton, her former residence, and there was married. Here were Frado's first feelings of trust and repose on human arm. She realized, for the first time, the relief of looking to another for comfortable support. Occasionally he would leave her to "lecture."

Those tours were prolonged often to weeks. Of course he had little spare money. Frado was again feeling her self-dependence, and was at last compelled to resort alone to that. Samuel was kind to her when at home, but made no provision for his absence, which was at last unprecedented.

He left her to her fate—embarked at sea, with the disclosure that he had never seen the South, and that his illiterate harangues[3] were humbugs for hungry abolitionists. Once more alone! Yet not alone. A still newer companionship would soon force itself upon her. No one wanted her with such prospects. Herself was burden enough; who would have an additional one?

The horrors of her condition nearly prostrated her, and she was again thrown upon the public for sustenance. Then followed the birth of her child. The long absent Samuel unexpectedly returned, and rescued her from charity. Recovering from her expected illness, she once more commenced toil for herself and child, in a room obtained of a poor woman, but with better fortune. One so well known would not be wholly neglected. Kind friends watched her when Samuel was from home, prevented her from suffering, and when the cold weather pinched the warmly clad, a kind friend took them in, and thus preserved them. At last Samuel's business became very engrossing, and after long desertion, news reached his family that he had become a victim of yellow fever, in New Orleans.

So much toil as was necessary to sustain Frado, was more than she could endure. As soon as her babe

---

[1] *Nothing ... Solomon* See Ecclesiastes 1.9: "The thing that hath been, it is that which shall be; and that which is done is that which shall be done: and there is no new thing under the sun." The Book of Ecclesiastes was traditionally believed to have been written by the Israelite King Solomon, famous in the Bible for his wisdom.

[2] *Pro* I.e., proslavery.

[3] *harangues* I.e., his lectures.

could be nourished without his mother, she left him in charge of a Mrs. Capon, and procured an agency,[1] hoping to recruit[2] her health, and gain an easier livelihood for herself and child. This afforded her better maintenance than she had yet found. She passed into the various towns of the State she lived in, then into Massachusetts. Strange were some of her adventures. Watched by kidnappers,[3] maltreated by professed abolitionists, who didn't want slaves at the South, nor niggers in their own houses, North. Faugh! to lodge one; to eat with one; to admit one through the front door; to sit next one; awful!

Traps slyly laid by the vicious to ensnare her, she resolutely avoided. In one of her tours, Providence favored her with a friend who, pitying her cheerless lot, kindly provided her with a valuable recipe, from which she might herself manufacture a useful article for her maintenance. This proved a more agreeable, and an easier way of sustenance.

And thus, to the present time, may you see her busily employed in preparing her merchandise; then sallying forth to encounter many frowns, but some kind friends and purchasers. Nothing turns her from her steadfast purpose of elevating herself. Reposing on God, she has thus far journeyed securely. Still an invalid, she asks your sympathy, gentle reader. Refuse not, because some part of her history is unknown, save by the Omniscient God. Enough has been unrolled to demand your sympathy and aid.

Do you ask the destiny of those connected with her *early* history? A few years only have elapsed since Mr. and Mrs. B. passed into another world. As age increased, Mrs. B. became more irritable, so that no one, even her own children, could remain with her; and she was accompanied by her husband to the home of Lewis, where, after an agony in death unspeakable, she passed away. Only a few months since, Aunt Abby entered heaven. Jack and his wife rest in heaven, disturbed by no intruders; and Susan and her child are yet with the living. Jane has silver locks in place of auburn tresses, but she has the early love of Henry[4] still, and has never regretted her exchange of lovers. Frado has passed from their memories, as Joseph from the butler's,[5] but she will never cease to track them till beyond mortal vision.

—1859

---

1   *procured an agency*   Obtained a job as traveling agent (representative) of a business.

2   *recruit*   Recuperate.

3   *kidnappers*   Under the provisions of the Fugitive Slave Act of 1850, adopted as part of a compromise to appease the Southern slave states, law enforcement officials in the North were required to arrest black people suspected or accused of having escaped slavery. Because those accused of being fugitives had no legal recourse, the law also enabled the kidnapping and enslavement of free Northern blacks.

4   *Henry*   An apparent textual discrepancy: Henry Reed is the name of the alternative suitor Jane rejects in Chapter 5, whereas the man she marries is George Means.

5   *as Joseph … butler's*   In Chapter 40 of the Book of Genesis, Joseph, an Israelite sold into slavery in Egypt and imprisoned there, interprets a dream of the Egyptian Pharaoh's chief butler, who has also been imprisoned after falling into disfavor. On the basis of the butler's dream, Joseph predicts that the butler will soon be restored to his position and requests that the butler remember him afterwards; however, after the butler is restored, he "did not … remember Joseph, but forgat him" (Genesis 40.23).

Frances Ellen Watkins Harper

1825 – 1911

One of the most important and most popular African American poets and novelists of the nineteenth century, Frances Ellen Watkins Harper was also among the century's most influential political activists; both through her writing and through her activism she was deeply involved in the antebellum and the post–Civil War struggles for black rights and for women's rights. As a speaker, Harper identified the interconnectedness of the injustices of nineteenth-century American society, declaring: "We are all bound up together in one great bundle of humanity, and society cannot trample on the weakest and feeblest of its members without receiving the curse in its own soul. … Society cannot afford to neglect the enlightenment of any class of its members."

Harper was born Frances Ellen Watkins to free parents in Baltimore, Maryland, then a slaveholding state. Her parents both died when she was about three years old, leaving her to be raised by an uncle, the abolitionist educator, minister, and doctor William Watkins. Harper received a remarkably thorough education at the institution run by her uncle, the William Watkins Academy for Negro Youth, where she studied until the age of thirteen. She subsequently found employment as a seamstress and domestic servant in the home of a wealthy family, where she was encouraged to read from their extensive book collection in her spare time, and, as the years went on, to write her own poetry. By the age of about twenty Harper had written enough poems to fill a volume; *Forest Leaves* was published in the mid-to-late 1840s. (For many years this volume was deemed lost, but in May 2013 one extant, undated copy was discovered in the library of the Maryland Historical Society.) Many of the poems in this early collection would later be reworked and republished in periodicals and in Harper's later collections.

Harper left Maryland in 1850, shortly after the passage of the Fugitive Slave Act. Her first stop was Ohio, where she taught sewing at the Columbus Union Seminary; she then moved to Pennsylvania, where she continued to work as a teacher but also became more engaged in the antislavery movement (and, more broadly, in the struggle against racial prejudice). Following the passage of a law in Maryland in 1853 forbidding free African Americans from re-entering the state—making her effectively an exile—Harper decided to abandon her teaching post and become fully involved in the abolitionist cause. She began a lifelong friendship with William Still (later a renowned historian of the Underground Railroad) and was invited to live with him and his wife, where she continued to write poetry to support herself, submitting pieces to abolitionist newspapers such as *The Liberator* and *Frederick Douglass' Paper*. In 1854, Harper traveled to Massachusetts and delivered her first antislavery speech in New Bedford; she then traveled to Maine, where she found employment as an official paid lecturer for the Maine Anti-Slavery Society.

That same year, Harper released the collection *Poems on Miscellaneous Subjects*. The 48-page pamphlet was immensely successful; it was sold at Harper's lectures and went through about twenty editions over the next twenty years, selling 10,000 individual copies by 1857. The collection touched on themes such as Christian faith, alcoholism, and poverty as well as on slavery, and concluded with a number of short essays; in the final piece, "The Colored People in America," Harper comments on the oppression experienced by both free and enslaved African Americans across the country.

Harper ardently supported the abolitionist raid led by John Brown in 1859; she sent letters of support to his imprisoned followers, and sent her poem "Bury Me in a Free Land" (earlier published in the *Anti-Slavery Bugle*) to a man awaiting execution for his participation in the raid. That year Harper also published the story "The Two Offers" in the *Anglo-American Magazine*. Touching on themes such as class, marriage, and domestic abuse, the story featured a protagonist who, much like Harper, was unmarried and was trying to make a living as a writer. Harper herself did marry Fenton Harper, a widower, shortly after the story's publication, temporarily slowing the pace of her public antislavery career to adapt to her new role as a homemaker and as stepmother to his three children. The Harpers had one child together, Mary, before Fenton died in 1864. He left behind significant debts, and (although Frances had herself purchased the farm on which they'd lived) all her property as well as his was seized by authorities to pay off these debts. She was left almost destitute—a demeaning experience that helped to fuel Harper's passion for the cause of women's rights. "They left me one thing—and that was a looking glass!" she memorably proclaimed in a ground-breaking speech delivered in New York at the Eleventh National Women's Rights Convention in 1866 that has come to be known by the title "We Are All Bound Up Together." Though the speech was well received at the convention, it received little or no mention in nineteenth-century accounts of the suffrage movement; not until the twenty-first century has its importance as a statement of principles now associated with the concept of intersectionality become fully acknowledged.

During the early years of Reconstruction Harper traveled extensively in the South, where she lectured and helped establish educational institutions for freed men and women. She became highly renowned for her lectures, which were often very long and delivered extemporaneously, and in which she commented frequently on her hopes for the future of African Americans: "If we have had no past, it is well for us to look hopefully to the future—for the shadows bear the promise of a brighter coming day." In 1869 she returned to Pennsylvania—where she would live with her daughter Mary for the rest of her life—and began work on a new poetry collection, *Sketches of Southern Life* (1872). The collection included a cycle of poems featuring the character Aunt Chloe, a formerly enslaved woman whose reminiscences of slavery and of Reconstruction in the South presented a challenge to stereotypical literary portrayals of enslaved people, and would influence poetic portrayals of slavery and of African American vernacular speech for decades to come.

Between 1869 and 1882 Harper published three novels in serial form—*Minnie's Sacrifice* (1869), *Sowing and Reaping* (1876–77), and *Trial and Triumph* (1888–89)—while continuing to fight to better the lives of African Americans and of women. Harper's work was affected by the schism that occurred in the women's movement in the years leading up to the Fifteenth Amendment. Many white feminists, including Stanton and Anthony, decried the decision implicit in the Fifteenth Amendment to put the interests of African Americans—and of African American men in particular—ahead of those of women; their rhetoric in many cases became increasingly shaded with racism. For her own part, Harper supported the Fifteenth Amendment, predicting that black women would not receive justice under the law as women until they began to receive justice under the law as black.

Harper's fourth and final work of fiction, *Iola Leroy; or, Shadows Uplifted* (1892), explored themes such as mixed-race identity, racial "passing," and the sexual violence experienced by enslaved women. For many years *Iola Leroy* was thought to have been the first full-length novel published by a black woman in the United States. (*Our Nig*, which had been published anonymously in 1859 and long assumed to have been written by a white author, is now recognized as having been written by black author Harriet Wilson; Harper's first three novels, meanwhile, had escaped the attention of scholars until their rediscovery by literary historian Frances Smith Foster in the mid-1990s.) *Iola Leroy* received largely favorable reviews; it was praised not least of all for pleading "the cause of a race whose needs were never more pressing … and whose destiny is now more closely interwoven with those of the nation than ever." Its significance, however, was downplayed in the twentieth century by various male African American authorities and white women scholars. Like her other work, it has received renewed attention in the twenty-first century.

Harper remained politically engaged until her death in 1911. Her reputation suffered considerably for many decades following her death. The sentimentalism of much of her poetry had fallen out of fashion, as had poetry that dealt explicitly with social, political, and moral concerns. The general neglect of black authors and activists by white scholars played a part as well; it is perhaps telling that in the multi-volume *History of Woman Suffrage* (1881–1922), authored in part by Stanton and Anthony, Harper is not mentioned once.

———————————

NOTE ON THE TEXTS: Most of the texts included here are the versions that first appeared in collected editions of Harper's poetry. To that generalization there is a notable exception; the text of "Bury Me in a Free Land" is taken from the 20 November 1858 issue of *The Anti-Slavery Bugle*. The text of "The Colored People in America," which was likely first delivered as a speech in the early 1850s, is taken from its appearance near the end of *Poems on Miscellaneous Subjects*, while the text of "We Are All Bound Up Together" is taken from the transcription included in *Proceedings of the Eleventh Woman's Rights Convention, May 1866*. The text of "The Triumph of Freedom—A Dream" is taken from the 1860 volume of *The Anglo-African Magazine*, and the selection from Harper's *Fancy Sketches* column is taken from its appearance in the 15 January 1874 issue of the *Christian Recorder*. The text of the letter titled "Breathing the Air of Freedom" is taken from *Poems on Miscellaneous Subjects*; the text of Harper's letter to John Brown is taken from its appearance in James Redpath's volume *Echoes of Harper's Ferry* (1860); and the text of Harper's 1871 letter to William Still is taken from its appearance in Still's *The Underground Rail Road* (1872). Spelling and punctuation have been modernized in accordance with the practices of this anthology.

⌘ ⌘ ⌘

The Slave Mother

Heard you that shriek? It rose
    So wildly on the air,
It seemed as if a burdened heart
    Was breaking in despair.

5 Saw you those hands so sadly clasped—
    The bowed and feeble head—
The shuddering of that fragile form—
    That look of grief and dread?

Saw you the sad, imploring eye?
10   Its every glance was pain,
As if a storm of agony
    Were sweeping through the brain.

She is a mother pale with fear,
    Her boy clings to her side,
15 And in her kirtle° vainly tries   *dress*
    His trembling form to hide.

He is not hers, although she bore
    For him a mother's pains;
He is not hers, although her blood
20   Is coursing through his veins!

He is not hers, for cruel hands
    May rudely tear apart
The only wreath of household love
    That binds her breaking heart.

25 His love has been a joyous light
    That o'er her pathway smiled,
A fountain gushing ever new,
    Amid life's desert wild.

His lightest word has been a tone
30   Of music round her heart,
Their lives a streamlet blent in° one—   *blended into*
    Oh, Father! must they part?

They tear him from her circling arms,
    Her last and fond embrace:
35 Oh! never more may her sad eyes
    Gaze on his mournful face.

No marvel, then, these bitter shrieks
    Disturb the listening air;
She is a mother, and her heart
40   Is breaking in despair.
    —1854

Bible Defense of Slavery

Take sackcloth[1] of the darkest dye,
    And shroud the pulpits round!
Servants of him that cannot lie,
     Sit mourning on the ground.

5   Let holy horror blanch each cheek,
     Pale every brow with fears;
And rocks and stones, if ye could speak,
     Ye well might melt to tears!

Let sorrow breathe in every tone,
10   In every strain ye raise;
Insult not God's majestic throne
     With th' mockery of praise.

A "reverend" man, whose light should be
     The guide of age and youth,
15   Brings to the shrine of Slavery
     The sacrifice of truth!

For the direst wrong by man imposed,
     Since Sodom's[2] fearful cry,
The word of life has been unclosed,
20   To give your God the lie.

Oh! when ye pray for heathen lands,
     And plead for their dark shores,
Remember Slavery's cruel hands
     Make heathens at your doors!
      —1854

Eliza Harris[3]

Like a fawn from the arrow, startled and wild,
A woman swept by us, bearing a child;
In her eye was the night of a settled despair,
And her brow was o'ershaded with anguish and care.

5   She was nearing the river—in reaching the brink,
She heeded no danger, she paused not to think;
For she is a mother—her child is a slave—
And she'll give him his freedom, or find him a grave!

It was a vision to haunt us, that innocent face—
10   So pale in its aspect, so fair in its grace;
As the tramp of the horse and the bay of the hound,
With the fetters that gall,° were   *chafe*
     trailing the ground!

She was nerved by despair, and strengthened by woe,
As she leaped o'er the chasms that yawned from below;
15   Death howled in the tempest, and raved in the blast,
But she heard not the sound till the danger was past.

Oh! how shall I speak of my proud country's shame?
Of the stains on her glory, how give them their name?
How say that her banner in mockery waves—
20   Her "star spangled banner"—o'er millions of slaves?

How say that the lawless may torture and chase
A woman whose crime is the hue of her face?
How the depths of the forest may echo around
With the shrieks of despair, and the bay of the hound?

25   With her step on the ice, and her arm on her child,
The danger was fearful, the pathway was wild;
But, aided by Heaven, she gained a free shore,
Where the friends of humanity opened their door.

So fragile and lovely, so fearfully pale,
30   Like a lily that bends to the breath of the gale,

---

1   *sackcloth*   Coarse fabric traditionally used for mourning or penitential garments.

2   *Sodom*   City destroyed by God in the Book of Genesis as punishment for the sinfulness of its inhabitants.

---

3   The poem takes inspiration from the character of the same name in Harriet Beecher Stowe's 1852 *Uncle Tom's Cabin*; Eliza Harris, a young enslaved woman, decides to flee her enslavers when she finds out they intend on selling her young son Harry. Stowe's version of events is in turn said to have been inspired by that of a real woman who had escaped slavery.

Save the heave of her breast, and the sway of her hair,
You'd have thought her a statue of fear and despair.

In agony close to her bosom she pressed
The life of her heart, the child of her breast—
35 Oh! love from its tenderness gathering might,
Had strengthened her soul for the dangers of flight.

But she's free! yes, free from the land where the slave
From the hand of oppression must rest in the grave;
Where bondage and torture, where scourges and chains
40 Have placed on our banner indelible stains.

The bloodhounds have missed the scent of her way;
The hunter is rifled and foiled of his prey;
Fierce jargon and cursing, with clanking of chains,
Make sounds of strange discord on Liberty's plains.

45 With the rapture of love and fulness of bliss,
She placed on his brow a mother's fond kiss:
Oh! poverty, danger and death she can brave,
For the child of her love is no longer a slave!
—1854

Ethiopia[1]

Yes! Ethiopia yet shall stretch
    Her bleeding hands abroad;
Her cry of agony shall reach
    The burning throne of God.[2]

5 The tyrant's yoke from off her neck,
    His fetters from her soul,
The mighty hand of God shall break,
    And spurn the base control.

Redeemed from dust and freed from chains,
10   Her sons shall lift their eyes;
From cloud-capped hills and verdant plains
    Shall shouts of triumph rise.

Upon her dark, despairing brow,
    Shall play a smile of peace;
15 For God shall bend unto her woe,
    And bid her sorrows cease.

'Neath sheltering vines and stately palms
    Shall laughing children play,
And aged sires with joyous psalms
20   Shall gladden every day.

Secure by night, and blessed by day,
    Shall pass her happy hours;
Nor human tigers hunt for prey
    Within her peaceful bowers.

25 Then, Ethiopia! stretch, oh! stretch
    Thy bleeding hands abroad;
Thy cry of agony shall reach
    And find redress from God.
—1854

The Drunkard's Child

He stood beside his dying child,
    With a dim and bloodshot eye;
They'd won him from the haunts of vice
    To see his first-born die.
5 He came with a slow and staggering tread,
    A vague, unmeaning stare,
And, reeling, clasped the clammy hand,
    So deathly pale and fair.

In a dark and gloomy chamber,
10   Life ebbing fast away,
On a coarse and wretched pallet,
    The dying sufferer lay:
A smile of recognition
    Lit up the glazing eye;
15 "I'm very glad," it seemed to say,
    "You've come to see me die."

---

[1] The present text is the version that appeared in Harper's 1854 collection, *Poems on Miscellaneous Subjects*; a slightly different version had appeared in Harper's earlier collection, *Forest Leaves*. Throughout much of European history, the term "Ethiopia" often functioned as a metonym for the African continent or to represent people of African descent.

[2] *Ethiopia … of God* See Psalm 68.31: "Ethiopia shall soon stretch out her hands unto God."

That smile reached to his callous heart,
    Its sealèd fountains stirred;
He tried to speak, but on his lips
20   Faltered and died each word.
And burning tears like rain
    Poured down his bloated face,
Where guilt, remorse and shame
    Had scathed, and left their trace.

25 "My father!" said the dying child,
    (His voice was faint and low,)
"Oh! clasp me closely to your heart,
    And kiss me ere I go.
Bright angels beckon me away,
30   To the holy city fair—
Oh! tell me, father, ere I go,
    Say, will you meet me there?"

He clasped him to his throbbing heart,
    "I will! I will!" he said;
35 His pleading ceased—the father held
    His first-born and his dead!
The marble brow, with golden curls,
    Lay lifeless on his breast;
Like sunbeams on the distant clouds
40   Which line the gorgeous west.
    —1854

The Revel

"*He knoweth not that the dead are there.*"[1]

In yonder halls reclining
    Are forms surpassing fair,[2]
And brilliant lights are shining,
    But, oh! the dead are there!

5 There's music, song and dance,
    There's banishment of care,
And mirth in every glance,
    But, oh! the dead are there!

The wine cup's sparkling glow
10   Blends with the viands° rare,   foods
There's a revelry and show,
    But still, the dead are there!

'Neath that flow of song and mirth
    Runs the current of despair,
15 But the simple sons of earth
    Know not the dead are there!

They'll shudder start and tremble,
    They'll weep in wild despair
When the solemn truth breaks on them,
20   That the dead, the dead are there!
    —1854

Advice to the Girls

Nay, do not blush! I only heard
    You had a mind to marry;
I thought I'd speak a friendly word,
    So just one moment tarry.

5 Wed not a man whose merit lies
    In things of outward show,
In raven hair or flashing eyes,
    That please your fancy so.

But marry one who's good and kind,
10   And free from all pretence;
Who, if without a gifted mind,
    At least has common sense.
    —1854

---

[1] *He knoweth ... are there* See Proverbs 9.13–18: "A foolish woman is clamorous: she is simple, and knoweth nothing. For she sitteth at the door of her house, on a seat in the high places of the city, To call passengers who go right on their ways: Whoso is simple, let him turn in hither: and as for him that wanteth understanding, she saith to him, Stolen waters are sweet, and bread eaten in secret is pleasant. But he knoweth not that the dead are there; and that her guests are in the depths of hell."

[2] *surpassing fair* Exceedingly beautiful.

A Mother's Heroism

When the noble mother of Lovejoy heard of her son's
death, she said, "It is well! I had rather he should die
so than desert his principles."[1]

The murmurs of a distant strife
    Fell on a mother's ear;
Her son had yielded up his life,
    Mid scenes of wrath and fear.

5 They told her how he'd spent his breath
    In pleading for the dumb,°   *mute*
And how the glorious martyr wreath
    Her child had nobly won.

They told her of his courage high,
10   Mid brutal force and might;
How he had nerved himself to die
    In battling for the right.

It seemed as if a fearful storm
    Swept wildly round her soul;
15 A moment, and her fragile form
    Bent 'neath its fierce control.

From lip and brow the color fled—
    But light flashed to her eye:
"'Tis well! 'tis well!" the mother said,
20   "That thus my child should die.

"'Tis well that, to his latest breath,
    He plead for liberty;
Truth nerved him for the hour of death,
    And taught him how to die.

25 "It taught him how to cast aside
    Earth's honors and renown;
To trample on her fame and pride,
    And win a martyr's crown."
    —1854

---

1 *When the noble … principles* The reference is to the case of
abolitionist newspaper editor Elijah Parish Lovejoy, whose murder
by a proslavery mob in 1837 sent shockwaves throughout the United
States and spurred many abolitionists to further commit to the
cause; his mother was Elizabeth Pattee Lovejoy.

The Fugitive's Wife

It was my sad and weary lot
    To toil in slavery;
But one thing cheered my lowly cot—
    My husband was with me.

5 One evening, as our children played
    Around our cabin door,
I noticed on his brow a shade
    I'd never seen before;

And in his eyes a gloomy night
10   Of anguish and despair—
I gazed upon their troubled light,
    To read the meaning there.

He strained me to his heaving heart—
    My own beat wild with fear;
15 I knew not, but I sadly felt
    There must be evil near.

He vainly strove to cast aside
    The tears that fell like rain:
Too frail, indeed, is manly pride,
20   To strive with grief and pain.

Again he clasped me to his breast,
    And said that we must part:
I tried to speak—but, oh! it seemed
    An arrow reached my heart.

25 "Bear not," I cried, "unto your grave,
    The yoke you've borne from birth;
No longer live a helpless slave,
    The meanest[2] thing on earth!"
—1854

Bury Me in a Free Land

You may make my grave wherever you will,
    In a lowly vale or a lofty hill;
You may make it among earth's humblest graves,
    But not in a land where men are slaves.

---

2 *meanest* Lowliest.

5 I could not sleep if around my grave
        I heard the steps of a trembling slave;
His shadow above my silent tomb
        Would make it a place of fearful gloom.

I could not rest if I heard the tread
10   Of a coffle-gang to the shambles¹ led,
And the mother's shriek of wild despair
        Rise like a curse on the trembling air.

I could not rest if I heard the lash
        Drinking her blood at each fearful gash,
15 And I saw her babes torn from her breast
        Like trembling doves from their parent nest.

I'd shudder and start, if I heard the bay
        Of the bloodhounds seizing their human prey;
If I heard the captive plead in vain
20   As they tightened afresh his galling chain.

If I saw young girls, from their mothers' arms
        Bartered and sold for their youthful charms
My eye would flash with a mournful flame,
        My death-paled cheek grow red with shame.

25 I would sleep, dear friends, where bloated might
        Can rob no man of his dearest right;
My rest shall be calm in any grave.
        Where none calls his brother a slave.

I ask no monument proud and high
30   To arrest the gaze of passers by;
All that my spirit yearning craves,
        Is—bury me not in the land of slaves.²
        —1858

---

¹ *coffle-gang* Group of people, especially enslaved people or prisoners, chained together; *shambles* Literally, a slaughterhouse, but
in this instance symbolizing a place of violence or suffering, likely a
slave-market.

² *I ask … of slaves* The words of this final stanza are reproduced
as an epitaph on Harper's gravestone.

*Vashti*³

She leaned her head upon her hand
    And heard the king's decree—
"My lords are feasting in my halls,
        Bid Vashti come to me.

5 "I've shown the treasures of my house,
        My costly jewels rare,
But with the glory of her eyes
        No rubies can compare.

"Adorned and crowned I'd have her come,
10   With all her queenly grace,
And, 'mid my lords and mighty men,
        Unveil her lovely face.

"Each gem that sparkles in my crown,
        Or glitters on my throne,
15 Grows poor and pale when she appears,
        My beautiful, my own!"

All waiting stood the chamberlains
        To hear the Queen's reply,
They saw her cheek grow deathly pale,
20   But light flashed to her eye:

"Go, tell the King," she proudly said,
        "That I am Persia's Queen,
And by his crowds of merry men
        I never will be seen.

25 "I'll take their crown from off my head
        And tread it 'neath my feet
Before their rude and careless gaze
        My shrinking eyes shall meet.

"A queen unveiled before the crowd!
30   Upon each lip my name!
Why, Persia's women all would blush
        And weep for Vashti's shame!

"Go back!" she cried, and waived her hand,
        And grief was in her eye:

---

³ *Vashti* Persian queen whose story is recounted in the Book of
Esther.

35   "Go, tell the King," she sadly said,
      "That I would rather die."

They brought her message to the King,
    Dark flashed his angry eye;
'Twas as the lightning ere the storm
40   Hath swept in fury by.

Then bitterly outspoke the King,
    Through purple lips of wrath—
"What shall be done to her who dares
    To cross your monarch's path?"

45 Then spake his wily counsellors—
    "O King of this fair land!
From distant Ind to Ethiop,[1]
    All bow to thy command.

"But if, before thy servants' eyes,
50   This thing they plainly see,
That Vashti doth not heed thy will
    Nor yield herself to thee,

"The women, restive 'neath our rule,
    Would learn to scorn our name,
55 And from her deed to us would come
    Reproach and burning shame.

"Then, gracious King, sign with thy hand
    This stern but just decree
That Vashti lay aside her crown,
60   Thy Queen no more to be."

She heard again the King's command,
    And left her high estate,
Strong in her earnest womanhood,
    She calmly met her fate,

65 And left the palace of the King,
    Proud of her spotless name—
A woman who could bend to grief,
    But would not bow to shame.
    —1871

---

1 *Ind* Term used in the nineteenth century to denote India, or for the East generally; *Ethiop* Term widely used in the nineteenth century to denote the African continent.

Learning to Read[2]

Very soon the Yankee teachers
    Came down and set up school;
But, oh! how the Rebs[3] did hate it—
    It was agin' their rule.

5 Our masters always tried to hide
    Book learning from our eyes;
Knowledge didn't agree with slavery—
    'Twould make us all too wise.

But some of us would try to steal
10   A little from the book,
And put the words together,
    And learn by hook or crook.

I remember Uncle Caldwell,
    Who took pot-liquor fat[4]
15 And greased the pages of his book,
    And hid it in his hat.

And had his master ever seen
    The leaves upon his head,
He'd have thought them greasy papers,
20   But nothing to be read.

And there was Mr. Turner's Ben,
    Who heard the children spell,
And picked the words right up by heart,
    And learned to read 'em well.

25 Well, the Northern folks kept sending
    The Yankee teachers down;
And they stood right up and helped us,
    Though Rebs did sneer and frown.

---

2 *Learning to Read* This is the fourth of six poems in the "Aunt Chloe" cycle in *Sketches of Southern Life*, narrated from the perspective of a formerly enslaved woman on a plantation in the post-Civil War South; the full "Aunt Chloe" poem cycle is included in the website component of this anthology.

3 *Rebs* Rebels; i.e., Confederates; supporters of the rebellion against the Union.

4 *pot-liquor fat* Grease skimmed from cooking broth.

And, I longed to read my Bible,
30   For precious words it said;
But when I begun to learn it,
        Folks just shook their heads,

And said there is no use trying,
        Oh! Chloe, you're too late;
35 But as I was rising sixty,
        I had no time to wait.

So I got a pair of glasses,
        And straight to work I went,
And never stopped till I could read
40   The hymns and Testament.

Then I got a little cabin
        A place to call my own—
And I felt as independent
        As the queen upon her throne.
                                        —1872

In Context

Learning to Read and Write before Emancipation

from Elijah P. Marrs, *Life and History of the Rev. Elijah P. Marrs, First Pastor of Beargrass Baptist Church, and Author* (1885)

> Elijah P. Marrs (1840–1910) was born into slavery in Kentucky, and served in the Union Army during the final months of the Civil War. Following the war he worked as a Baptist minister and a teacher, and also organized and led various groups for the defense of African Americans against the Ku Klux Klan.

Very early in life I took up the idea that I wanted to learn to read and write. I was convinced that there would be something for me to do in the future that I could not accomplish by remaining in ignorance. I had heard so much about freedom, and of the colored people running off and going to Canada, that my mind was busy with this subject even in my young days. I sought the aid of the white boys, who did all they could in teaching me. They did not know that it was dangerous for a slave to read and write. I availed myself of every opportunity, daily I carried my book in my pocket, and every chance that offered would be learning my A, B, C's. Soon I learned to read. After this the white people would send me daily to the post office, at Simpsonville, K[entuck]y, a distance of two miles, when I would read the address of the letters; I also would read the newspapers the best I could. There was an old colored man on the place by the name of Ham Graves, who opened a night school, beginning at 10 o'clock at night. I attended his school one year and learned how to write my name and read writing. On every gatepost around the stable, as on the plow handles, you could see where I had been trying to write. Of course, I did not know the danger of it, and that fools' names, like fools' faces, are always seen in public places.

from Susie King Taylor, *Reminiscences of My Life in Camp with the 33d United States Colored Troops, late 1st S.C. Volunteers* (1902)

> Susie King Taylor (1848–1912) worked as a nurse, laundress, and teacher for the black freedmen of the 1st South Carolina Volunteers (which was later renamed the 33rd United States Colored Infantry Regiment). She continued to work as an educator after the end of the Civil War, dividing most of the rest of her life between Boston, where she found employment, and the South, where much of her family remained.

from CHAPTER 2
MY CHILDHOOD

I was born under the slave law in Georgia, in 1848, and was brought up by my grandmother in Savannah. There were three of us with her, my younger sister and brother. My brother and I being the two eldest, we were sent to a friend of my grandmother, Mrs. Woodhouse, a widow, to learn to read and write. She was a free woman and lived on Bay Lane, between Habersham and Price streets, about half a mile from my house. We went every day about nine o'clock, with our books wrapped in paper to prevent the police or white persons from seeing them. We went in, one at a time, through the gate, into the yard to the L kitchen, which was the schoolroom. She had twenty-five or thirty children whom she taught, assisted by her daughter, Mary Jane. The neighbors would see us going in sometimes, but they supposed we were there learning trades, as it was the custom to give children a trade of some kind. After school we left the same way we entered, one by one, when we would go to a square, about a block from the school, and wait for each other. We would gather laurel leaves and pop them on our hands, on our way home. I remained at her school for two years or more, when I was sent to a Mrs. Mary Beasley, where I continued until May 1860, when she told my grandmother she had taught me all she knew, and grandmother had better get someone else who could teach me more, so I stopped my studies for a while.

I had a white playmate about this time, named Katie O'Connor, who lived on the next corner of the street from my house, and who attended a convent. One day she told me, if I would promise not to tell her father, she would give me some lessons. On my promise not to do so, and getting her mother's consent, she gave me lessons about four months, every evening. At the end of this time she was put into the convent permanently, and I have never seen her since.

A month after this, James Blouis, our landlord's son, was attending the High School, and was very fond of grandmother, so she asked him to give me a few lessons, which he did until the middle of 1861, when the Savannah Volunteer Guards, to which he and his brother belonged, were ordered to the front under General Barton. In the first battle of Manassas,[1] his brother Eugene was killed, and James deserted over to the Union side, and at the close of the war went to Washington, D.C., where he has since resided.

The Rallying Cry

O children of the tropics,
    Amid our pain and wrong,
Have you no other mission
    Than music, dance and song?

5 While through the weary ages
    Our dripping tears still fall;
Is this a time to dally
    With pleasure's silken thrall?°   *enslavement*

Go muffle all your viols,[2]
10   As heroes learn to stand

With faith in God's great justice;
    Nerve every heart and hand.

Dream not of ease nor pleasure,
    Nor honor, wealth nor fame,
15 Till from the dust you've lifted
    Our long-dishonored name.

And crown that name with glory
    By deeds of holy worth;
To shine in light emblazoned
20   The noblest name on earth.

Engrave upon your banners,
    In words of golden light;

---

[1] *first battle of Manassas* First major battle of the Civil War, fought on 21 July 1861.
[2] *viols* The viol, a now-archaic stringed instrument (larger than today's viola, but smaller than a cello), was often played to accompany dances.

That mercy, truth and justice
    Are more than godless might.

25 Count life a dismal failure
    Unblessing and unblessed,
That seeks in ceaseless ease
    For pleasure or for rest.

With courage, strength and valor
30   Your lives and actions brace;
Shrink not from pain and hardship
    And dangers bravely face.

Above earth's pain and sorrow
    Christ's dying face I see
35 I hear the cry of anguish
    Why'st Thou forsaken me?[1]

The pallor of that anguish
    Reveals the only light
To flood with joy and gladness
40   Earth's sorrow, pain and night.

Arrayed in Christly armor,
    'Gainst error, crime and sin;
The victory can't be doubtful
    For God is sure to win.
    —1891

A Double Standard

Do you blame me that I loved him?
    If when standing all alone
I cried for bread a careless world
    Pressed to my lips a stone.

5 Do you blame me that I loved him,
    That my heart beat glad and free,
When he told me in the sweetest tones
    He loved but only me?

Can you blame me that I did not see
10   Beneath his burning kiss
The serpent's wiles, nor even hear
    The deadly adder hiss?

Can you blame me that my heart grew cold
    That the tempted, tempter turned;
15 When he was feted° and caressed   *celebrated*
    And I was coldly spurned?

Would you blame him, when you draw from me
    Your dainty robes aside,
If he with gilded baits should claim
20   Your fairest as his bride?

Would you blame the world if it should press
    On him a civic crown;
And see me struggling in the depth
    Then harshly press me down?

25 Crime has no sex and yet today
    I wear the brand of shame;
Whilst he amid the gay and proud
    Still bears an honored name.

Can you blame me if I've learned to think
    Your hate of vice a sham,
30 When you so coldly crushed me down
    And then excused the man?

Would you blame me if tomorrow
    The coroner should say,
35 A wretched girl, outcast, forlorn,
    Has thrown her life away?

Yes, blame me for my downward course,
    But oh! remember well,
Within your homes you press the hand
40   That led me down to hell.

I'm glad God's ways are not our ways,
    He does not see as man;
Within His love I know there's room
    For those whom others ban.

---

[1] *Why'st Thou forsaken me?* Question addressed to God by Jesus when he was dying on the cross, as related in Matthew 27.46 and Mark 15.34.

45 I think before His great white throne,
        His throne of spotless light,
That whited sepulchers[1] shall wear
        The hue of endless night.

That I who fell, and he who sinned,
50   Shall reap as we have sown;
That each the burden of his loss
        Must bear and bear alone.

No golden weights can turn the scale
        Of justice in His sight;
55 And what is wrong in woman's life
        In man's cannot be right.
—1894

The Colored People in America

Having been placed by a dominant race in circumstances over which we have had no control, we have been the butt of ridicule and the mark of oppression. Identified with a people over whom weary ages of degradation have passed, whatever concerns them, as a race, concerns me. I have noticed among our people a disposition to censure and upbraid each other, a disposition which has its foundation rather, perhaps, in a want[2] of common sympathy and consideration, than mutual hatred, or other unholy passions. Born to an inheritance of misery, nurtured in degradation, and cradled in oppression, with the scorn of the white man upon their souls, his fetters upon their limbs, his scores upon their flesh, what can be expected from their offspring, but a mournful reaction of that accursed system which spreads its baneful influence over body and soul; which dwarfs the intellect, stunts its development, debases the spirit, and degrades the soul? Place any nation in the same condition which has been our hapless[3] lot, fetter their limbs and degrade their souls, debase their sons and corrupt their daughters, and when the restless yearnings for liberty shall burn through heart and brain—when, tortured by wrong

and goaded by oppression, the hearts that would madden with misery, or break in despair, resolve to break their thrall, and escape from bondage, then let the bay of the bloodhound and the scent of the human tiger be upon their track—let them feel that, from the ceaseless murmur of the Atlantic to the sullen roar of the Pacific, from the thunders of the rainbow-crowned Niagara to the swollen waters of the Mexican gulf, they have no shelter for their bleeding feet, or resting-place for their defenceless heads; let them, when nominally[4] free, feel that they have only exchanged the iron yoke of oppression for the galling fetters of a vitiated[5] public opinion; let prejudice assign them the lowest places and the humblest positions, and make them "hewers of wood and drawers of water";[6] let their income be so small that they must from necessity bequeath to their children an inheritance of poverty and a limited education—and tell me, revealer of our race! censurer of our people! if there is a nation in whose veins runs the purest Caucasian blood, upon whom the same causes would not produce the same effects; whose social condition, intellectual and moral character, would present a more favorable aspect than ours? But there is hope; yes, blessed be God! for our downtrodden and despised race. Public and private schools accommodate our children; and in my own southern home, I see women, whose lot is unremitted labor, saving a pittance from their scanty wages to defray the expense of learning to read. We have papers edited by colored editors, which we may consider it an honor to possess, and a credit to sustain. We have a church that is extending itself from east to west, from north to south, through poverty and reproach, persecution and pain. We have our faults, our want of union and concentration of purpose; but are they are not extenuating circumstances around our darkest faults—palliating excuses for our most egregious errors? and shall we not hope, that the mental and moral aspect which we present is but the first step of a mighty advancement, the faintest coruscations[7] of

---

1 *whited sepulchers* Tombs that have been bleached white.

2 *want* Lack.

3 *hapless* Unfortunate.

4 *nominally* In name; legally.

5 *vitiated* False or corrupt.

6 *hewers of ... water* Biblical phrase used to refer to menial labor; see Joshua 9.21–23, in which the Israelites conquer the Gibeonites and sentence them to become "hewers of wood and drawers of water."

7 *coruscations* Flashes of light.

the day that will dawn with unclouded splendor upon our downtrodden and benighted race, and that ere long we may present to the admiring gaze of those who wish us well, a people to whom knowledge has given power, and righteousness exaltation?

—1857

We Are All Bound Up Together

I feel I am something of a novice upon this platform.[1] Born of a race whose inheritance has been outrage and wrong, most of my life had been spent in battling against those wrongs. But I did not feel as keenly as others, that I had these rights, in common with other women, which are now demanded. About two years ago, I stood within the shadows of my home. A great sorrow had fallen upon my life. My husband had died suddenly, leaving me a widow, with four children, one my own, and the others stepchildren. I tried to keep my children together. But my husband died in debt; and before he had been in his grave three months, the administrator had swept the very milk crocks and wash tubs from my hands. I was a farmer's wife and made butter for the Columbus market; but what could I do, when they had swept all away? They left me one thing—and that was a looking-glass! Had I died instead of my husband, how different would have been the result! By this time he would have had another wife, it is likely; and no administrator would have gone into his house, broken up his home, and sold his bed, and taken away his means of support.

I took my children in my arms, and went out to seek my living. While I was gone, a neighbor to whom I had once lent five dollars, went before a magistrate and swore that he believed I was a non-resident, and laid an attachment on my very bed. And I went back to Ohio with my orphan children in my arms, without a single feather bed in this wide world, that was not in the custody of the law. I say, then, that justice is not fulfilled so long as woman is unequal before the law.

We are all bound up together in one great bundle of humanity, and society cannot trample on the weakest and feeblest of its members without receiving the curse in its own soul. You tried that in the case of the negro. You pressed him down for two centuries; and in so doing you crippled the moral strength and paralyzed the spiritual energies of the white men of the country. When the hands of the black were fettered, white men were deprived of the liberty of speech and the freedom of the press. Society cannot afford to neglect the enlightenment of any class of its members. At the South, the legislation of the country was in behalf of the rich slaveholders, while the poor white man was neglected. What is the consequence today? From that very class of neglected poor white men comes the man who stands today with his hand upon the helm of the nation.[2] He fails to catch the watchword of the hour, and throws himself, the incarnation of meanness,[3] across the pathway of the nation. My objection to Andrew Johnson is not that he has been a poor white man; my objection is that he keeps "poor whits"[4] all the way through. (Applause.) That is the trouble with him.

This grand and glorious revolution which has commenced, will fail to reach its climax of success until throughout the length and breadth of the American Republic the nation shall be so color-blind as to know no man by the color of his skin or the curl of his hair. It will then have no privileged class, trampling upon and outraging the unprivileged classes, but will be then one great privileged nation, whose privilege will be to produce the loftiest manhood and womanhood that humanity can attain.

I do not believe that giving the woman the ballot is immediately going to cure all the ills of life. I do not believe that white women are dew-drops just exhaled from the skies. I think that like men they may be divided into three classes, the good, the bad, and the

---

[1] *this platform* I.e., the cause of women's rights; Harper had dedicated most of her activism prior to this point to the causes of abolition and anti-racism.

[2] *From that very ... the nation* Harper refers to Andrew Johnson (1808–75), who had been vice president at the time of Lincoln's assassination in 1865 and thereafter assumed the Presidency. Johnson had been born into poverty in North Carolina, and had received no formal education. As President, Johnson was notoriously resistant to improving the civil and legal conditions of African Americans in the aftermath of the Civil War (for instance, he refused to interfere with the "Black Codes" passed by various state legislatures, which restricted black freedom to such an extent that they effectively re-established slavery).

[3] *meanness* Inferiority of character; stinginess.

[4] *keeps "poor whits"* Has unvaryingly displayed a lack of intelligence.

indifferent. The good would vote according to their convictions and principles; the bad, as dictated by prejudice or malice; and the indifferent will vote on the strongest side of the question, with the winning party.

You white women speak here of rights. I speak of wrongs. I, as a colored woman, have had in this country an education which has made me feel as if I were in the situation of Ishmael,[1] my hand against every man, and every man's hand against me. Let me go tomorrow morning and take my seat in one of your street cars—I do not know that they will do it in New York, but they will in Philadelphia—and the conductor will put up his hand and stop the car rather than let me ride.

A Lady—They will not do that here.

Mrs. Harper—They do in Philadelphia. Going from Washington to Baltimore this Spring, they put me in the smoking car. (Loud Voices—"Shame.") Aye, in the capital of the nation, where the black man consecrated himself to the nation's defence, faithful when the white man was faithless, they put me in the smoking car! They did it once; but the next time they tried it, they failed; for I would not go in. I felt the fight in me; but I don't want to have to fight all the time. Today I am puzzled where to make my home. I would like to make it in Philadelphia, near my own friends and relations. But if I want to ride in the streets of Philadelphia, they send me to ride on the platform with the driver. (Cries of "Shame.") Have women nothing to do with this? Not long since, a colored woman took her seat in an Eleventh Street car in Philadelphia, and the conductor stopped the car, and told the rest of the passengers to get out, and left the car with her in it alone, when they took it back to the station. One day I took my seat in a car, and the conductor came to me and told me to take another seat. I just screamed "murder." The man said if I was black I ought to behave myself. I knew that if he was white he was not behaving himself. Are there not wrongs to be righted?

In advocating the cause of the colored man, since the Dred Scott decision,[2] I have sometimes said I thought the nation had touched bottom. But let me tell you there is a depth of infamy lower than that. It is when the nation, standing upon the threshold of a great peril, reached out its hands to a feebler race, and asked that race to help it, and when the peril was over, said, You are good enough for soldiers, but not good enough for citizens.[3] When Judge Taney[4] said that the men of my race had no rights which the white man was bound to respect, he had not seen the bones of the black man bleaching outside of Richmond. He had not seen the thinned ranks and the thickened graves of the Louisiana Second, a regiment which went into battle nine hundred strong, and came out with three hundred. He had not stood at Olustee and seen defeat and disaster crushing down the pride of our banner, until words was brought to Col. Hallowell, "The day is lost; go in and save it"; and black men stood in the gap, beat back the enemy, and saved your army.[5] (Applause.)

We have a woman in our country who has received the name of "Moses," not by lying about it, but by acting it out (applause)—a woman who has gone down into the Egypt of slavery and brought out hundreds of our people into liberty.[6] The last time I saw that

---

[1] *Ishmael* In the Book of Genesis, Ishmael is the son of Abraham by his wife's handmaid, Hagar. Abraham's wife, Sarai, casts out the expectant Hagar, who wanders the parched desert until God says to her, "Behold, thou art with child and shalt bear a son, and shalt call his name Ishmael; because the Lord hath heard thy affliction. And he will be a wild man; his hand will be against every man, and every man's hand against him" (Genesis 16.11–12).

[2] *Dred Scott decision* 1857 Supreme Court decision in which it was determined that persons of African descent, whether free or enslaved, could not be considered American citizens, and thereby had no legal standing in court. The decision came after the formerly enslaved Dred Scott attempted to secure the court's further confirmation of his freedom so that the children of his deceased former owner could not claim inherited ownership of Scott's daughters.

[3] *It is when … for citizens* Harper alludes to the participation of black soldiers in the Union Army during the Civil War, and especially following the Emancipation Proclamation (1863), which called for newly emancipated black men to join the Army.

[4] *Judge Taney* Author of the majority decision in the Dred Scott case.

[5] *Olustee … saved your army* Though the 1864 Battle of Olustee in Florida resulted in a Confederate victory, regiments comprised of African American soldiers, including the famous 54th Massachusetts Infantry, performed feats of bravery that prevented the total destruction of Union forces. The 54th Massachusetts was at the time under the command of Colonel Edward Needles Hallowell (1836–71).

[6] *We have … into liberty* Harper refers to Harriet Tubman, who escaped slavery in 1849 and subsequently became a dedicated Underground Railroad agent, helping to free hundreds of people; she also worked as a spy for the Union Army during the Civil War. Tubman was affectionately called "Moses" by her [continued...]

woman, her hands were swollen. That woman who had led one of Montgomery's most successful expeditions,[1] who was brave enough and secretive enough to act as a scout for the American army, had her hands all swollen from a conflict with a brutal conductor, who undertook to eject her from her place. That woman, whose courage and bravery won a recognition from our army and from every black man in the land, is excluded from every thoroughfare of travel. Talk of giving women the ballot-box? Go on. It is a normal school,[2] and the white women of this country need it. While there exists this brutal element in society which tramples upon the feeble and treads down the weak, I tell you that if there is any class of people who need to be lifted out of their airy nothings and selfishness, it is the white women of America. (Applause.)
—1866

The Triumph of Freedom—A Dream

It was a beautiful day in spring. The green sward[3] stretched beneath my feet like a velvet carpet, fair flowers sprung up in my path, and peaceful streams swept laughingly by to gain their ocean home. Above me the heavens were eloquent with the praise of God, around me the earth was poetic with His ideas. It was one of those days when Nature, in the excess of her happiness, leans on the bosom of the balmy sunshine, listening to the gentle voices of the wooing winds. I had fallen into a state of dreamy, delicious languor, when I was roused to sudden consciousness by a startling shriek. I looked up, and, bending over me, I saw a spirit gazing upon me with a look of unmistakable sadness. "Come with me?" said she, laying her hand upon me and drawing me along with an irresistible impulse.

Silently I followed, awed by her strange manner. "I wish," said she, after a few moments silence, "to show you the goddess of this place." Surely, thought I, that must be a welcome sight, for the loveliness of the place suggested to my mind a presiding genius of glorious beauty. "It is now her hour of worship, and I want to show you some of her rites and ceremonies, and also the priests of her shrine." Just then we came in sight of the goddess. She was seated on a glittering throne, all sparkling with precious gems and rubies; and, indeed, so bright was her throne, it threw a dazzling radiance over her sallow countenance. She wore a robe of flowing white, but it was not pure white, and I noticed that upon its hem and amid its seams and folds were great spots of blood. It was the hour of worship, and her priests were standing by, with their sacred books in their hands; it was one of their rites to search them for texts and passages to spread over the stains on her garment. When this was done, they bowed down their heads and worshipped, saying: "Thou art the handmaid of Christianity; thy mission is heaven-appointed and divine." And all the people said "Amen." But during this worship I saw a young man arise, his face pale with emotion and horror, and he said, "It is false." That one word, so sublime in its brevity, sent a thrill of indignant fear through the hearts of the crowd. It lashed them into a tumultuous fury. Some of them dashed madly after the intruder, and hissed in his ears, "Fanatic, madman, traitor, and infidel." But the efforts they made to silence him only gained him a better hearing. They forced him into prison, but they had no chains strong enough to bind his freeborn spirit. A number of adherents gathered around the young man, and asked to know his meaning. "Come with me," said he, "and I will show you," and while they still chanted the praises of the goddess, he drew them to the spot, where they might view the base and inside of the throne, and the foundation of her altar. I looked (for I had joined them, led on by my guide), and I saw a number of little hearts all filed together and quivering. "What," said I, "are these?" My guide answered, "They are the hearts of a hundred thousand newborn babes." I turned deathly sick, a fearful faintness swept over me, and I was about to fall, but she caught me in her arms, and said, "Look here," and beneath the throne were piles of hearts laid layer upon layer. I noticed that

supporters, referring to the story in the Book of Exodus in which Moses leads the Israelites out of Egyptian slavery.

[1] *one of … successful expeditions* In 1863 Tubman, alongside Colonel James Montgomery, helped lead the Combahee Ferry raid, which resulted in the emancipation of over 700 people.

[2] *normal school* Institution for training schoolteachers. The implication is that suffrage for white women will only further empower them in what is already a socially accepted role, that of teachers and moral guides.

[3] *sward* Surface of the earth; grass.

they seemed rocking to and fro, as if smitten with a great agony. "What are these?" said I, gazing horror-stricken upon them. "They are the hearts of desolate slave mothers, robbed of their little ones." I looked a little higher, and saw a row of poor, bruised and seared hearts. "What are these?" "These are the hearts out of which the manhood has been crushed; and these," said she, pointing to another pile of young, fresh hearts, from which the blood was constantly streaming, "are the hearts of young girls, sold from the warm clasp of their mothers' arms to the brutal clutches of a libertine or a profligate[1]—from the temples of Christ to the altars of shame. And these," said she, looking sadly at a row of withered hearts, from which the blood still dropped, "are the hearts in which the manhood has never been developed." I turned away, heart-sickened, the blood almost freezing in my veins, and I saw the young man standing on an eminence, pointing to the throne and altar, his lips trembling with the burden of a heaven-sent message. He reminded me of the ancient seers, robed in the robes of prophecy, pronouncing the judgments of God against the oppressors of olden times. Some listened earnestly, and were roused by his words to deeds of noble daring. Others, within whose shrunken veins all noble blood was pale and thin, mocked him and breathed out their hatred against him; they set a price upon his head and tracked his steps with bitter malice, but he had awakened the spirit of Agitation, that would not slumber at their bidding.

The blood-stained goddess felt it shaking her throne, its earnest eye searching into the very depths of her guilty soul, and she said to her worshippers: "Hide me beneath your constitutions and laws—shield me beneath your parchments and opinions." And it was done; but the restless eye of Agitation pierced through all of them, as through the most transparent glass. "Hide me," she cried to the priests, "beneath the shadow of your pulpits; throw around me the robes of your religion; spread over me your altar clothes, and dye my lips with sacramental blood." And yet, into the recesses of her guilty soul came the eye of this Agitation, and she trembled before its searching glance.

Then I saw an aged man standing before her altars; his gray hair floated in the air, a solemn radiance lit up his eye, and a lofty purpose sat enthroned upon his brow. He fixed his eye upon the goddess, and she cowered beneath his unfaltering gaze. He laid his aged hands upon her blood-cemented throne, and it shook and trembled to its base; her cheeks blanched with dread, her hands fell nerveless by her side. It seemed to me as if his fiery gaze would have almost annihilated her; but just then I saw, bristling with bayonets, a blood-stained ruffian, named the General Government, and he caught the hands of the aged man and fettered them, and he was then led to prison. I know not whether the angels of the living God walked to and fro in his prison—that, amid the silent watches of the night, he heard the rustling of their garments—I only know that the old man was a host within himself. The goddess gathered courage when she knew that she could rely on the arm of her ruffian accomplice; the old man offered her freedom, but she answered him with a scaffold—the gallows bent beneath his aged form. Her minions drained the blood from his veins, and they thought they had conquered him, but it was a delusion. From the prison came forth a cry of victory; from the gallows a shout of triumph over that power whose ethics are robbery of the weak and oppression of the feeble; the trophies of whose chivalry are a plundered cradle and a scourged and bleeding woman. I saw the green sward stained with his blood, but every drop of it was like the terrible teeth sown by Cadmus;[2] they woke up armed men to smite the terror-stricken power that had invaded his life. It seemed as if his blood had been instilled into the veins of freemen and given them fresh vigor to battle against the hoary forms of gigantic Error and colossal Theory, who stood as sentinels around the throne of the goddess. His blood was a new baptism of Liberty. I noticed that they fought against her till she tottered and fell, amid the shouts of men who had burst their chains, and the rejoicings of women newly freed, and Freedom, like a glorified angel, smiled over the glorious jubilee and stood triumphant on the very spot where the terrible goddess had reigned for centuries. I saw Truth and Justice crown her radiant brow, from joyful lips floated anthems of praise and songs of deliverance—just such songs as one might expect to

---

[1]   *libertine or a profligate*   Sexually licentious man.

[2]   *the terrible ... by Cadmus*   In Greek mythology, Cadmus founds the city of Thebes with the help of five men born from the teeth of a dragon Cadmus had defeated, which he had strewn over the ground like seeds.

hear if a thousand rainbows would melt into speech, or the music of the spheres would translate itself into words. Peace, like light dew, descended where Slavery had spread ruin and desolation, and the guilty goddess, cowering beneath the clear, open gaze of Freedom, and ashamed of the meanness and guilt, skulked from the habitations of men, and ceased to curse the land with her presence; but the first stepping-stones of Freedom to power, were the lifeless bodies of the old man and his brave companions.

—1860

from *Fancy*[1] *Sketches*

"Why Aunty, what makes you look so serious this morning? You look as sober as if some dear old widower had made you an offer to take care of him and his six motherless children. Let me inquire in poetic parlance—'Why that shadow on thy brow?'"

"I am a little puzzled, Jenny, to know how to answer a letter from a dear young friend of mine. She is a girl who has surmounted difficulties, and borne quite an amount of privation in obtaining an education, but owing to the bill which has lately passed in her state[2] she has lost her school."

"What does she say and what does she intend doing?"

"She writes to me saying, 'My dear friend, the tidal wave of progress has reached us here and I feel that the ground has suddenly slidden from under my feet. The authorities have closed my school, and like Othello "my occupation is gone."[3] Some of my friends say, "Go South," but I am the mainstay of my widowed mother, and so necessary am I to her comfort that I cannot think of leaving her. The wide field of domestic duty is before me, but perhaps you will call it false pride, but I do not feel that I have either inclination or aptitude for that mode of life; and to learn any trade or business now would consume months which I feel I cannot well afford to give. Now what am I to do?' This is the question, Jenny; which has been ringing in my mind all this morning. What am I to do?"

"Well, Aunty, while I cannot help rejoicing at the passage of this bill, I cannot fail to sympathise with those young girls who have fitted themselves for the position of teachers and who feel as she does that the ground is about to slip from under their feet. Aunty, I do wish we women could vote. It seems to me that the men who vote find that vote increased advantage, and I do wish that at the late National civil rights meeting,[4] some women had been sent as delegates."

"What for? to have kept better order?"

"No, but to have given them an opportunity to present unto that convention some views of vital importune to the future of our woman."

"Would you have opposed the civil rights, on the plea that mixed schools would close up a number of avenues against many of our girls?"

"No Aunty, I would not have done that, for I look upon such measures as mixing the children as one of those reformatory or revolutionary schemes, which, while it causes present pain eventuates in permanent good."

---

1   *Fancy* Fanciful; fictional. *Fancy Sketches* was the title of a series of short stories published by Harper in the *Christian Recorder* throughout the 1870s. (The series was sometimes titled *Fancy Etchings*.)

2   *the bill … her state* It is not clear exactly what bill is being referred to here. Before the Civil War it had been illegal in most Southern states to teach black people how to read or write. Reconstruction brought change; states allowed schools for black people to operate and in some cases funded their operation (though typically at much lower levels than schools for whites). The Freedman's Bureau set up more than a thousand schools, and close to 100,000 students enrolled in them. But financial support from the Freedman's Bureau for setting up and maintaining schools ended in the early 1870s. A few states continued to require support for black education; Maryland, for example, passed a law in 1872 requiring that a public school for African Americans be set up in every district. But in most Southern states the tide was running in the other direction. In the early 1870s, states such as Kentucky (1873), Tennessee (1873), and West Virginia (1872) passed laws making it illegal for blacks and whites to be educated together, and in some cases making it more difficult to operate separate schools for black students (Kentucky, for example, mandated that no "colored school" could operate within one mile of a school for whites). It is likely

legislation of that sort that would have resulted in the closure of the school referred to here.

3   *my occupation is gone* Paraphrase spoken by the eponymous Moorish protagonist of Shakespeare's *Othello* when he begins (mistakenly) to suspect his wife's fidelity, 3.3.409.

4   *late National civil rights meeting* The National Civil Rights Convention, held in Washington in December 1873; *late* Recent.

"I think, Jenny, that just such a closing up of the gates should make us more earnest to open up avenues in other directions."

"Aunty, I was just thinking (though the thought may seem Utopian) that it would be an excellent plan if some of our colored men who possessed money could only unite upon some plan by which we could build up some thriving industries of our own. Suppose we had a large number of persons personally interested in building up a cotton factory, could not this thing be effected among us by the power of combination? We can combine together for pleasure, could we not do the same for business?"

"We could, Jenny, provided we had firm faith in each other's honesty, and ability to carry on business."

"Well, Aunty I am not surprised if colored men are a little slow to combine in civil associations. That men who acquire slowly and painfully will be somewhat timid in risking what it has cost them so much to attain is quite natural. I don't know what can be done for our young women, but I do wish some of the most thoughtful men and women of our race would take into consideration some plan for opening the fields of occupation for us. If white women feel that they are limited by their sex, how must it be with us who have the shadows of the past still projected into our lives? What they call limitation would be to us broad liberty. The most that I dread is that some of our girls will be discouraged, and missing the stimulus of hope will not struggle as earnestly as they might to get a thorough education."

"I hope that instead of abating heart and hope, that they will strive to reach the highest point of efficiency as teachers; believing as Daniel Webster[1] once said, 'There is always room in the upper story.'"

"And though prejudice has not died out of the American mind, and you cannot legislate hatred and contempt out of people's hearts, you may so change the condition of things, as to create a new class of associations; and as patience, industry and skill can change the 'Mulberry leaf into satin'[2] so united, earnest and

faithful endeavor may yet change the world's dread into admiring recognition."

"I think Aunty that after the civil rights bill is passed that the cap sheaf will have been placed on the temple of our liberties, and that the most important thing then for us to consider, is not simply what this party will do for us, or the other one against us; but what are we going to do as for ourselves, to diversify our industry, build up our character, better our condition, and intensify our spiritual life. Congress may make its statute books black with laws for our defence, but all the help that comes from without is not like the help that comes from within and this is the force we must generate if we take our place fairly and squarely alongside the other branches of the human race in this Western Hemisphere."
—1874

Letters

Niagara Falls
September 12, 1856

My Dear Friend,

I have just returned from Canada today. I gave one lecture at Toronto, which was well attended. Well, I have gazed for the first time upon Free Land! And would you believe it, tears sprang to my eyes, and I wept. Oh! it was a glorious sight to gaze for the first time on a land where a poor slave, flying from our glorious land of liberty (!), would in a moment find his fetters broken, his shackles loosed, and whatever he was in the land of Washington, beneath the shadow

---

[1] *Daniel Webster* American lawyer and politician (1782–1852); the quotation (sometimes given as "There's always room at the top") has often been attributed to Webster, though its source is unclear.

[2] *industry ... into satin* Common proverb, possibly derived by Harper from a similar line in Ralph Waldo Emerson's famous oration

"The American Scholar" (1837); silkworms are known to prefer feeding off of mulberry leaves.

[3] This letter is reproduced in William Still's history *The Underground Rail Road* (1872), in which it is given the present title.

of Bunker Hill Monument,[1] or even Plymouth Rock,[2] *here* he becomes "a man and a brother."[3]

I had gazed on Harper's Ferry, or rather the Rock at the Ferry,[4] towering up in simple grandeur with the gentle Potomac gliding peacefully by its feet, and felt that that was God's masonry; and my soul had expanded in gazing on its sublimity. I had seen the Ocean, singing its wild chorus of sounding waves, and ecstasy had thrilled upon the living chords of my heart. I have since then seen the rainbow-crowned Niagara, girdled with grandeur, and robed with glory, chanting the choral hymn of Omnipotence, but none of the sights have melted me as the first sight of Free Land.

Towering mountains, lifting their hoary summits to catch the first faint flush of day when the sunbeams kiss the shadows from morning's drowsy face, may expand and exalt your soul. The first view of the ocean may fill you with strange ecstasy and delight. Niagara, the great, the glorious Niagara, may hush your spirit with its ceaseless thunder; it may charm you with its robe of crested spray and rainbow crown; but the land of Freedom has a lesson of deeper significance than foaming waves or towering mountains.

It carries the heart back to that heroic struggle for emancipation, in Great Britain, in which the great heart of the people throbbed for liberty, and the mighty pulse of the nation beat for freedom till nearly 800,000 men, women and children arose redeemed from bondage and freed from chains.[5]

LETTER TO JOHN BROWN[6]

Kendallville, Indiana
[25 November 1859]

Dear Friend,

Although the hands of Slavery throw a barrier between you and me, and it may not be my privilege to see you in your prison-house, Virginia has no bolts or bars through which I dread to send you my sympathy. In the name of the young girl sold from the warm clasp of a mother's arms to the clutches of a libertine[7] or a profligate—in the name of the slave mother, her heart rocked to and fro by the agony of her mournful separations—I thank you, that you have been brave enough to reach out your hands to the crushed and blighted of my race. You have rocked the bloody Bastille;[8] and I hope that from your sad fate great good may arise to the cause of freedom. Already from your prison has come a shout of triumph against the giant sin of our country. The hemlock is distilled with victory when it is pressed to the lips of Socrates.[9] The Cross becomes a glorious ensign when Calvary's page-browed sufferer yields up his life upon it.[10] And, if Universal Freedom is ever to be the dominant power of the land, your bodies may be only her first stepping stones to dominion. I would prefer to see Slavery go down peaceably by men breaking off their sins by righteousness and their iniquities by showing justice and mercy to the poor; but we cannot tell what the

---

[1] *Bunker Hill Monument*   Site of the Battle of Bunker Hill (1775) in Massachusetts, a significant event of the Revolutionary War.

[2] *Plymouth Rock*   On the coast of Massachusetts, purported site of the disembarking of the Pilgrims from the *Mayflower* in 1620.

[3] *a man and a brother*   Allusion to the slogan of many abolitionists, "Am I Not a Man and a Brother?," popularized in particular by its use on a medallion designed by English potter and abolitionist Josiah Wedgwood in 1787.

[4] *the Rock at the Ferry*   Jefferson Rock, a rock formation located in the town of Harpers Ferry (then in Virginia, now in West Virginia).

[5] *that heroic struggle ... chains*   Harper alludes to the Slavery Abolition Act of 1833, which abolished slavery throughout most of the British Empire.

[6] *JOHN BROWN*   In October 1859, white abolitionist John Brown led a raid on the town of Harpers Ferry, as part of his endeavor to begin a slave revolution. The raid was quashed within two days by a company of U.S. Marines, and Brown was tried for treason and sentenced to death, as were several of his accomplices. Brown's actions were extremely controversial at the time; while pacifist abolitionists condemned his actions, many others saw him as a hero and martyr.

[7] *libertine*   Morally—especially sexually—licentious man.

[8] *rocked the bloody Bastille*   Allusion to a key moment at the onset of the French Revolution: the storming of the Bastille, an important political prison in Paris, by civil insurgents in July 1789.

[9] *The hemlock ... of Socrates*   Reference to the execution of the philosopher Socrates by the administration of poison hemlock in 399 BCE.

[10] *The Cross ... upon it*   Reference to the execution of Jesus upon the Cross at the site known as Calvary.

future may bring forth. God writes national judgments upon national sins; and what may be slumbering in the storehouse of divine justice we do not know. We may earnestly hope that your fate will not be a vain lesson, that it will intensify our hatred of Slavery and love of freedom, and that your martyr grave will be a sacred altar upon which men will record their vows of undying hatred to that system which tramples on man and bids defiance to God. I have written to your dear wife, and sent her a few dollars, and I pledge myself to you that I will continue to assist her. May the ever-blessed God shield you and your fellow-prisoners in the darkest hour. Send my sympathy to your fellow-prisoners; tell them to be of good courage; to seek a refuge in the Eternal God, and lean upon His everlasting arms for a sure support. If any of them, like you, have a wife or children that I can help, let them send me word.

LETTER TO WILLIAM STILL[1]

Mobile
July 5, 1871

My Dear Friend,

It is said that truth is stranger than fiction; and if ten years since[2] someone had entered my humble log house and seen me kneading bread and making butter, and said that in less than ten years you will be in the lecture field, you will be a welcome guest under the roof of the President of the Confederacy, though not by special invitation from him,[3] that you will see his brother's former slave a man of business and influence, that hundreds of colored men will congregate on the old baronial possessions, that a school will spring up there like a well in the desert dust, that this former slave will be a magistrate upon that plantation, that labor will be organized upon a new basis, and that

under the sole auspices and moulding hands of this man and his sons will be developed a business whose transactions will be numbered in hundreds of thousands of dollars, would you not have smiled incredulously? And I have lived to see the day when the plantation has passed into new hands, and these hands once wore the fetters of slavery. Mr. Montgomery, the present proprietor by contract of between five and six thousand acres of land, has one of the most interesting families that I have ever seen in the South. They are building up a future which if exceptional now I hope will become more general hereafter. Every hand of his family is adding its quota to the success of this experiment of a colored man both trading and farming on an extensive scale. Last year his wife took on her hands about 130 acres of land, and with her force she raised about 107 bales of cotton. She has a number of orphan children employed, and not only does she supervise their labor, but she works herself. One daughter, an intelligent young lady, is postmistress and I believe assistant bookkeeper. One son attends to the planting interest, and another daughter attends to one of the stores. The business of this firm of Montgomery & Sons has amounted, I understand, to between three and four hundred thousand dollars in a year. I stayed on the place several days and was hospitably entertained and kindly treated. When I come, if nothing prevents, I will tell you more about them. Now for the next strange truth. Enclosed I send you a notice from one of the leading and representative papers of rebeldom. The editor has been, or is considered, one of the representative men of the South. I have given a lecture since this notice, which brought out some of the most noted rebels, among whom was Admiral Semmes.[4] In my speech I referred to the Alabama sweeping away our commerce, and his son sat near him and seemed to receive it with much good humor. I don't know what the papers will say today; perhaps they will think that I dwelt upon the past too much. Oh, if you had seen the rebs[5] I had out last night, perhaps you would have felt a little nervous for me. However, I lived through it, and gave them more gospel truth than perhaps some of them have heard for some time.

---

[1] WILLIAM STILL African American abolitionist and historian. Still included this letter in his historical work *The Underground Rail Road* (1872).

[2] *since* Ago.

[3] *you will be … from him* Harper means that she is legally welcome in the states of the former Confederacy, regardless of the opinions of Confederate leaders such as the Confederacy's former president, Jefferson Davis.

[4] *Admiral Semmes* Confederate officer Raphael Semmes (1809–77).

[5] *rebs* Rebels; i.e., supporters of the Confederacy.

John Rollin Ridge / Yellow Bird

1827 – 1867

Among the most widely read Native American writers of the mid-nineteenth century, John Rollin Ridge—who usually published as Yellow Bird—played a key role in the development of Californian literature and the literature of the "West." His only novel, *The Life and Adventures of Joaquín Murieta, The Celebrated California Bandit* (1854), adapted the formulae of the era's popular dime novels to the rapidly changing social landscape of Gold Rush-era California, developing the genre sometimes referred to today as "borderland literature"; it is generally considered the first published novel by an Indigenous author. Ridge was also an accomplished poet and a prolific journalist.

John Rollin Ridge, or Chees-quat-a-law-ny (Yellow Bird), was born in 1827 into a prominent Cherokee family, the son of John Ridge and Sarah Bird Northrup Ridge, a white woman. Both his father and his grandfather, Major Ridge, were powerful members of the Cherokee National Council. Over the preceding decades, the Cherokee Nation had adopted Anglo-American agricultural practices, social and political structures, and forms of religious worship, with Major Ridge having been, among others, at the forefront of this cultural transition. Rollin Ridge's early childhood was spent on his family's sizeable plantation in New Echota, Georgia, then the capital of the Cherokee Nation. The family plantation held a number of enslaved people; Ridge would be a determined anti-abolitionist throughout his adulthood.

In the mid-1830s, Ridge's family was at the center of a heated dispute within the Nation about how best to respond to the increasing numbers of white settlers encroaching upon Cherokee territory. Many Cherokee were subjected to property theft and physical violence from these settlers, and the federal government, particularly following passage of the Indian Removal Act of 1830, pressured the Cherokee to relocate to the area west of the Mississippi that had been designated as "Indian Territory." Initially, most Cherokee were vehemently opposed to removal; the Ridges, however, came to view removal as inevitable, and began to speak out in its favor. In 1835, several members of the Ridge family and their supporters signed the Treaty of New Echota, a controversial document ceding much of the Cherokee's land to the federal government. The Ridges subsequently moved to Honey Creek, in the northwest corner of the Cherokee Nation (now the southwestern point of Missouri). Anti-Removal Cherokee, including Principal Chief John Ross, argued that the Ridges did not have the authority to enter into agreements with the U.S. and declared the treaty invalid, but the federal government enforced the expulsion of all remaining Cherokee to Indian Territory in the summer of 1838. A key episode in the series of forced removals now known as the Trail of Tears, this expulsion led to thousands of deaths.

The resultant enmity between the "Treaty Party" and the "Ross Party" culminated in 1839 with the assassination of several members of the Treaty Party, including Major Ridge and John Ridge. Rollin Ridge, who witnessed his father's death, was traumatized by the assassination and would later describe it as "a scene of agony the sight of which might make one regret that the human race had ever been created." Fearing for the safety of her remaining family, Sarah fled with her children to Fayetteville, Arkansas.

In his mid-teens Ridge was sent to school in Massachusetts, though he remained only briefly before returning to Fayetteville, where he then studied the law. In 1847, Ridge married Elizabeth Wilson, a white woman he had met during his time in New England, and they had their first and only child, Alice Bird, the following year. Around this time, Ridge began publishing poetry in local newspapers. In 1849, Ridge was involved in a fight likely related to the Ross-Ridge conflict, killing a man named David Kell. Forced into exile again, Ridge fled with his wife and daughter to Springfield, Missouri.

Gold had been discovered at Sutter's Mill, California in January 1848, and by 1849 the California Gold Rush was well underway. Ridge joined the westward migration of "forty-niners" in early 1850, accompanied by his brother Aeneas and an enslaved man, Wacooli, and temporarily leaving Elizabeth and Alice in Arkansas with his mother. In California—which had become part of the U.S. following the end of the Mexican–American War in 1848—Ridge found a land fraught with racial tensions, as white American fortune seekers sought to stake their claims over the territory at the expense of Indigenous Californians, Mexicans, and the thousands of international immigrants who had begun to arrive. Ridge's own experience appears to have been relatively untainted by the racism and nativism of the forty-niners, but he nevertheless found little success in the search for gold; instead, he soon took to journalism, writing for and editing a variety of California periodicals.

Much of Ridge's journalism expressed his rage at the violence perpetrated by white settlers against Indigenous Californians, including groups such as the Maidu, Miwok, Monache, Pomo, and Northern Paiute (all of whom were indiscriminately referred to with the pejorative "Diggers" by most English speakers, Ridge included). Such violence was often explicitly condoned by the state; California's first governor, Peter Burnett, called for the "extermination" of Indigenous Californians, and offered financial rewards for the murder of Indigenous men and the capture and enslavement of Indigenous women and children. Ridge acted as an advocate on behalf of these groups, but he also regularly suggested assimilation to Eurocentric culture or removal to Indian reservations as the solution to colonial violence.

By 1854, Ridge had conceived an ambition to "contribute [his] mite to those materials out of which the early history of California shall one day be composed." That year saw the publication of his first and only novel, *The Life and Adventures of Joaquín Murieta, The Celebrated California Bandit*, widely believed to be the first novel published in California. The work tells of the eponymous Murieta, an initially kind-hearted Mexican who turns to violence and banditry after a series of abuses at the hands of white Americans (including the rape of his lover and the murder of his brother). Inspired by widespread accounts of Mexican banditry throughout the mining regions of California—including accounts of several prominent bandits named "Joaquín"—the novel was taken by many readers to be at least partly nonfictional. It now seems clear, however, that the work is more heavily informed by the conventions of contemporary popular fiction and dime novels than it is by any knowledge on the part of Ridge of actual bandits. *The Life and Adventures* proved extremely popular throughout both North America and Europe; widespread piracy, however, together with financial difficulties on the part of the book's publishers, resulted in Ridge receiving next to no remuneration for his work.

In the late 1850s, Ridge was rejoined by his wife and daughter, with whom he eventually settled in Grass Valley. During this period Ridge became increasingly well-respected as a poet, and was invited to compose and recite poems on various public occasions. By 1864, his work was of sufficient renown that the *Daily Alta California* dubbed him "*the* poet of California." Throughout the Civil War, Ridge remained outspoken as a journalist, and became affiliated with the "Copperheads," a faction of Union Democrats who sought a quick resolution to the war and the continuation of slavery in the states of the Confederacy. At the end of the conflict, he was chosen to lead the Southern Cherokee delegation in treaty negotiations in Washington; Ridge hoped to have the Cherokee Nation granted statehood, but this did not come to pass.

Ridge died in 1867; his wife oversaw the publication of a volume of his *Poems* the following year. The edition did not sell well, and within a few years Ridge's work as a poet had been largely forgotten by the American public. For many decades Ridge attracted little attention from critics, either—though in a 1932 study published in the *Southwest Review* Angie Debo concluded that "nearly all of Ridge's poetry shows that his teachers had done their full duty in 'civilizing' him," but that he had perhaps learned their lessons too well. In Debo's view, Ridge "failed to realize in his poems his ambitious plans for presenting to the world the case of the oppressed Indian tribes, and became instead tritely conventional in the white man's manner."

Academic critics such as Debo ignored Ridge's prose fiction entirely, but the character of Joaquín Murieta continued to live on in the public imagination, reinvented and reinterpreted by countless novelists, historians, playwrights, and eventually even filmmakers in the late nineteenth and early twentieth centuries; the novel's 1955 editor credited Ridge with "creat[ing] California's most enduring myth." And in recent decades Ridge has attracted considerable attention from academics as well; the race-related complexities in much of Ridge's work—including his simultaneous advocacy for the better treatment of Indigenous peoples and his promotion of assimilation, slavery, and the ideals of American expansionism—continue to fascinate and trouble scholars today.

NOTE ON THE TEXT: The text of Ridge's *The Life and Adventures of Joaquín Murieta, The Celebrated California Bandit*, is based on that first published in 1854. Spelling and punctuation have been modernized in accordance with the practices of this anthology.

⌘ ⌘ ⌘

from *The Life and Adventures of Joaquín Murieta*

In the early 1850s, California newspapers were replete with sensational reports of Mexican bandits terrorizing white and Chinese miners around California's gold country. By 1853, most of these incidents were alleged to be linked to a group known as the "Five Joaquíns": Joaquín Ocomorenia, Joaquín Valenzuela, Joaquín Botellier, Joaquín Carillo, and Joaquín Murrieta (the typical Spanish spelling of the name). That year, Mexican–American War veteran and bounty hunter Harry Love (1810–68) was appointed leader of the California Rangers and tasked with hunting down the suspected bandits. On 25 July, after several months of unsuccessful searching, the rangers encountered a band of horse thieves and initiated a fight that led to the deaths of several men, including two they identified as Murrieta and his associate Three-Fingered Jack. The head of the former and the hand of the latter were each cut off and preserved in a jar of alcohol, and exhibited around the state by Love. Though the truth of Love's claims about the men's identities was almost immediately questioned by journalists, he and his rangers were nevertheless awarded six thousand dollars for the feat.

Ridge's novel, published the following year, takes inspiration from these sensational events. The novel was taken by many contemporaries to be a truthful history of Murrieta's life, and continued to be taken as such by historians later in the century, adding further layers to the mystery surrounding these legendary figures of early California.

I sit down to write somewhat concerning the life and character of *Joaquín Murieta*, a man as remarkable in the annals of crime as any of the renowned robbers of the Old or New World who have preceded him; and I do this, not for the purpose of ministering to any depraved taste for the dark and horrible in human action, but rather to contribute my mite[1] to those materials out of which the early history of California shall one day be composed. The character of this truly wonderful[2] man was nothing more than a natural production of the social and moral condition of the country in which he lived, acting upon certain peculiar circumstances favorable to such a result, and, consequently, his individual history is a part of the most valuable history of the State.

There were two Joaquíns, bearing the various surnames of Murieta, O'Comorenia, Valenzuela, Botellier, and Carillo—so that it was supposed there were no less than five sanguinary devils ranging the country at one and the same time. It is now fully ascertained that there were only two, whose proper names were Joaquín Murieta and Joaquín Valenzuela, the latter being nothing more than a distinguished subordinate to the first, who is the Rinaldo Rinaldini[3] of California.

Joaquín Murieta was a Mexican, born in the province of Sonora of respectable parents and educated

---

1   *mite* Small donation.

2   *wonderful* Extraordinary; to be wondered at (with no suggestion of a positive connotation).

3   *Rinaldo Rinaldini* Character created by German novelist Christian August Vulpius for his successful 1797 dime novel *Rinaldo Rinaldini, the Robber Captain*. The novel is set in the Kingdom of Naples and was likely based loosely on the lives of various historical Italian brigands.

in the schools of Mexico. While growing up, he was remarkable for a very mild and peaceable disposition, and gave no sign of that indomitable and daring spirit which afterwards characterized him. Those who knew him in his schoolboy days speak affectionately of his generous and noble nature at that period of his life and can scarcely credit the fact that the renowned and bloody bandit of California was one and the same being. At an early age of his manhood—indeed, while he was yet scarcely more than a boy—he became tired of the uncertain state of affairs in his own country, the usurpations and revolutions which were of such common occurrence, and resolved to try his fortunes among the American people, of whom he had formed the most favorable opinion from an acquaintance with the few whom he had met in his own native land. The war with Mexico had been fought, and California belonged to the United States.[1] Disgusted with the conduct of his degenerate countrymen and fired with enthusiastic admiration of the American character, the youthful Joaquín left his home with a buoyant heart and full of the exhilarating spirit of adventure. The first that we hear of him in the Golden State is that, in the spring of 1850, he is engaged in the honest occupation of a miner in the Stanislaus placers,[2] then reckoned among the richest portions of the mines. He was then eighteen years of age, a little over the medium height, slenderly but gracefully built, and active as a young tiger. His complexion was neither very dark or very light, but clear and brilliant, and his countenance is pronounced to have been, at that time, exceedingly handsome and attractive. His large black eyes, kindling with the enthusiasm of his earnest nature, his firm and well-formed mouth, his well-shaped head from which the long, glossy, black hair hung down over his shoulders, his silvery voice full of generous utterance, and

the frank and cordial bearing which distinguished him made him beloved by all with whom he came in contact. He had the confidence and respect of the whole community around him, and was fast amassing a fortune from his rich mining claim. He had built him a comfortable mining residence in which he had domiciled his heart's treasure—a beautiful Sonorian girl, who had followed the young adventurer in all his wanderings with that devotedness of passion which belongs to the dark-eyed damsels of Mexico. It was at this moment of peace and felicity that a blight came over the young man's prospects. The country was then full of lawless and desperate men, who bore the name of Americans but failed to support the honor and dignity of that title. A feeling was prevalent among this class of contempt for any and all Mexicans, whom they looked upon as no better than conquered subjects of the United States, having no rights which could stand before a haughtier and superior race. They made no exceptions. If the proud blood of the Castilians[3] mounted to the cheek of a partial descendant of the Mexiques, showing that he had inherited the old chivalrous spirit of his Spanish ancestry, they looked upon it as a saucy presumption in one so inferior to them. The prejudice of color, the antipathy of races, which are always stronger and bitterer with the ignorant and unlettered, they could not overcome, or if they could, would not, because it afforded them a convenient excuse for their unmanly cruelty and oppression. A band of these lawless men, having the brute power to do as they pleased, visited Joaquín's house and peremptorily bade him leave his claim, as they would allow no Mexicans to work in that region. Upon his remonstrating against such outrageous conduct, they struck him violently over the face, and, being physically superior, compelled him to swallow his wrath. Not content with this, they tied him hand and foot and ravished[4] his mistress before his eyes. They left him, but the soul of the young man was from that moment darkened. It was the first injury he had ever received at the hands of the Americans, whom he had always hitherto respected, and it wrung him to the soul as a deeper and deadlier wrong from that very circumstance. He departed with his weeping and almost heart-broken

---

1 *The war ... United States* The Mexican–American War (1846–48) ended with the Treaty of Guadalupe Hidalgo, which granted territorial ownership to the U.S. of California and much of what is now Arizona, New Mexico, Nevada, Utah, and Colorado. Mexicans who chose to continue living in the relevant territory were to be granted full American citizenship, though many were nevertheless antagonized by white American settlers, especially following the beginning of the gold rush and California's admission to the Union in 1850.

2 *Stanislaus* River in central California, important site of gold panning during the Gold Rush; *placers* Sand or soil deposits containing gold.

3 *Castilians* I.e., the Spanish.

4 *ravished* Raped.

mistress for a more northern portion of the mines; and the next we hear of him, he is cultivating a little farm on the banks of a beautiful stream that watered a fertile valley, far out in the seclusion of the mountains. Here he might hope for peace—here he might forget the past, and again be happy. But his dream was not destined to last. A company of unprincipled Americans—shame that there should be such bearing the name!—saw his retreat, coveted his little home surrounded by its fertile tract of land, and drove him from it, with no other excuse than that he was "an infernal Mexican intruder!" Joaquín's blood boiled in his veins, but his spirit was still unbroken, nor had the iron so far entered his soul as to sear up the innate sensitiveness to honor and right which reigned in his bosom. Twice broken up in his honest pursuit of fortune, he resolved still to labor on with unflinching brow and with that true *moral* bravery, which throws its redeeming light forward upon his subsequently dark and criminal career. How deep must have been the anguish of that young heart and how strongly rooted the native honesty of his soul, none can know or imagine but they who have been tried in a like manner. He bundled up his little movable property, still accompanied by his faithful bosom-friend, and again started forth to strike once more, like a brave and honest man, for fortune and for happiness. He arrived at "Murphy's Diggings" in Calaveras County, in the month of April, and went again to mining, but, meeting with nothing like his former success, he soon abandoned that business and devoted his time to dealing "monte," a game which is common in Mexico, and has been almost universally adopted by gamblers in California. It is considered by the Mexican in no manner a disreputable employment, and many well-raised young men from the Atlantic States have resorted to it as a profession in this land of luck and chances. It was then in much better odor[1] than it is now, although it is at present a game which may be played on very fair and honest principles; provided, anything can be strictly honest or fair which allows the taking of money without a valuable consideration. It was therefore looked upon as no departure from rectitude on the part of Joaquín, when he commenced the business of dealing "monte." Having a very pleasing exterior and being, despite of all his sorrows,

very gay and lively in disposition, he attracted many persons to his table, and won their money with such skill and grace, or lost his own with such perfect good humor that he was considered by all the very beau ideal[2] of a gambler and the prince of clever fellows. His sky seemed clear and his prospects bright, but Fate was weaving her mysterious web around him, and fitting him to be by the force of circumstances what nature never intended to make him.

He had gone a short distance from Murphy's Diggings to see a half-brother, who had been located in that vicinity for several months, and returned to Murphy's upon a horse which his brother had lent him. The animal proved to have been stolen, and being recognized by a number of individuals in town, an excitement was raised on the subject. Joaquín suddenly found himself surrounded by a furious mob and charged with the crime of theft. He told them how it happened that he was riding the horse and in what manner his half-brother had come in possession of it. They listened to no explanation, but bound him to a tree, and publicly disgraced him with the lash. They then proceeded to the house of his half-brother and hung him without judge or jury. It was then that the character of Joaquín changed, suddenly and irrevocably. Wanton cruelty and the tyranny of prejudice had reached their climax. His soul swelled beyond its former boundaries, and the barriers of honor, rocked into atoms by the strong passion which shook his heart like an earthquake, crumbled around him. Then it was that he declared to a friend that he would live henceforth for revenge and that his path should be marked with blood. Fearfully did he keep his promise, as the following pages will show.

It was not long after this unfortunate affair that an American was found dead in the vicinity of Murphy's Diggings, having been cut to pieces with a knife. Though horribly mangled, he was recognized as one of the mob engaged in whipping Joaquín. A doctor, passing in the neighborhood of this murder, was met, shortly afterward, by two men on horseback, who fired their revolvers at him, but, owing to his speed on foot, and the unevenness of the ground, he succeeded in escaping with no further injury than having a bullet shot through his hat within an inch of the top of his

---

1   *odor* Favor.

2   *beau ideal* French: perfect model.

head! A panic spread among the rash individuals who had composed that mob, and they were afraid to stir out on their ordinary business. Whenever any one of them strayed out of sight of his camp or ventured to travel on the highway, he was shot down suddenly and mysteriously. Report after report came into the villages that Americans had been found dead on the highways, having been either shot or stabbed, and it was invariably discovered, for many weeks, that the murdered men belonged to the mob who publicly whipped Joaquín. It was fearful and it was strange to see how swiftly and mysteriously those men disappeared. "Murieta's revenge was very nearly complete," said an eyewitness of these events, in reply to an inquiry which I addressed him. "I am inclined to think he *wiped out* the most of those prominently engaged in whipping him."

Thus far, who can blame him? But the iron had entered too deeply in his soul for him to stop here. He had contracted a hatred to the whole American race, and was determined to shed their blood, whenever and wherever an opportunity occurred. It was no time now for him to retrace his steps. He had committed deeds which made him amenable to the law, and his only safety lay in a persistence in the unlawful course which he had begun. It was necessary that he should have horses and that he should have money. These he could not obtain except by robbery and murder, and thus he became an outlaw and a bandit on the verge of his nineteenth year.

The year 1850 rolled away, marked with the eventful history of this young man's wrongs and trials, his bitter revenge on those who had perpetrated the crowning act of his deep injury and disgrace; and, as it closed, it shut him away forever from his peace of mind and purity of heart. He walked forth into the future a dark, determined criminal, and his proud nobility of soul existed only in memory.

It became generally known in 1851 that an organized banditti was ranging the country; but it was not yet ascertained who was the leader. Travelers, laden with the produce of the mines, were met upon the roads by well-dressed men who politely invited them to "stand and deliver"; persons riding alone in the many wild and lonesome regions, which form a large portion of this country, were skillfully noosed with the lasso (which the Mexicans throw with great accuracy, being able thus to capture wild cattle, elk, and sometimes even grizzly bears, upon the plains), dragged from their saddles, and murdered in the adjacent thickets. Horses of the finest mettle[1] were stolen from the ranches, and, being tracked up, were found in the possession of a determined band of men, ready to retain them at all hazards and fully able to stand their ground. The scenes of murder and robbery shifted with the rapidity of lightning. At one time, the northern countries would be suffering slaughters and depredations, at another the southern, and, before one would have imagined it possible, the east and the west, and every point of the compass would be in trouble. There had never been before this, either in '49 or '50,[2] any such as an organized banditti, and it had been a matter of surprise to every one, since the country was so well adapted to a business of this kind—the houses scattered at such distances along the roads, the plains so level and open in which to ride with speed, and the mountains so rugged with their ten thousand fastnesses[3] in which to hide. Grass was abundant in the far-off valleys which lay hidden in the rocky gorges; cool, delicious streams made music at the feet of the towering peaks, or came leaping down in gladness from their sides; game abounded on every hand, and nine unclouded months of the year made a climate so salubrious that nothing could be sweeter than a day's rest under the tall pines or a night's repose under the open canopy of Heaven. Joaquín knew his advantages. His superior intelligence and education gave him the respect of his comrades, and, appealing to the prejudice against the "Yankees," which the disastrous results of the Mexican war had not tended to lessen in their minds, he soon assembled around him a powerful band of his countrymen, who daily increased, as he ran his career of almost magical success. Among the number was Manuel Garcia, more frequently known as "Three-Fingered Jack," from the fact of his having had one of his fingers shot off in a skirmish with an American party during the Mexican war. He was a man of unflinching bravery, but cruel and sanguinary. His form was large and

1   *mettle* Disposition.

2   *either in '49 or '50* Years during which the California Gold Rush was at its height.

3   *fastnesses* Fortresses.

rugged and his countenance so fierce that few liked to look upon it. He was different from his more youthful leader, in possessing nothing of his generous, frank, and cordial disposition, and in being utterly destitute of one merciful trait of humanity. His delight was in murder for its own diabolical sake, and he gloated over the agonies of his unoffending victims. He would sacrifice policy, the safety and interests of the band for the mere gratification of this murderous propensity, and it required all Joaquín's firmness and determination to hold him in check. The history of this monster was well known before he joined Joaquín. He was known to be the same man who, in 1846, surrounded with his party two Americans, young men by the name of Cowie and Fowler, as they were traveling on the road between Sonoma and Bodega, stripped them entirely naked, and, binding them each to a tree, slowly tortured them to death. He began by throwing knives at their bodies, as if he were practicing at a target; he then cut out their tongues, punched out their eyes with his knife, gashed their bodies in numerous places, and, finally, flaying them alive, left them to die. A thousand cruelties like these had he been guilty of, and, long before Joaquín knew him, he was a hardened, experienced, and detestable monster. When it was necessary for the young chief to commit some peculiarly horrible and cold-blooded murder, some deed of hellish ghastliness at which his soul revolted, he deputed this man to do it. And well was it executed, with certainty and to the letter.

Another member of this band was Reyes Feliz, a youth of sixteen years of age, who had read the wild romantic lives of the chivalrous robbers of Spain and Mexico until his enthusiastic spirit had become imbued with the same sentiments which actuated them, and he could conceive of nothing grander than to throw himself back upon the strictly natural rights of man and hurl defiance at society and its law. He also was a Sonorian, and the beautiful mistress of Joaquín was his sister. He was a devoted follower of his chief; like him, brave, impulsive, and generous.

A third member was Claudio, a man about thirty-five years of age, of lean but vigorous constitution, a dark complexion, and possessing a somewhat savage but lively and expressive countenance. He was indisputably brave, but exceedingly cautious and cunning, springing upon his prey at an unexpected moment and executing his purposes with the greatest possible secrecy as well as precision. He was a deep calculator, a wily schemer, and could wear the appearance of an honest man with the same grace and ease that he would show in throwing around his commanding figure the magnificent cloak in which he prided. In disposition, he was revengeful, tenacious in his memory of a wrong, sly and secret in his windings as a serpent, and, with less nobility than the rattlesnake, he gave no warning before he struck. Yet, as I have said before, he was brave when occasion called it forth, and, although ever ready to take an advantage, he never flinched in the presence of danger. This extreme caution, united with a strong will and the courage to do, made him an exceedingly formidable man.

A fourth member was Joaquín Valenzuela, who has been frequently confounded with Joaquín Murieta, from the fact that the latter threw upon him much responsibility in the government of the band and entrusted him with important expeditions, requiring in their execution a great amount of skill and experience. Valenzuela was a much older man than his leader and had acted for many years in Mexico as a bandit under the famous guerilla chief, Padre Jurata.[1]

Another distinguished member was Pedro Gonzalez, less brave than many others, but a skillful spy and expert horse-thief, and as such, an invaluable adjunct to a company of mounted men, who required a continual supply of fresh horses as well as a thorough knowledge of the state of affairs around them.

There were many others belonging to this organization whom it is not necessary to describe. It is sufficient to say that they composed as formidable a force of outlaws as ever gladdened the eye of an acknowledged leader. Their number, at this early period, is not accurately known, but a fair estimate would not place it at a lower figure than fifty, with the advantage of a continual and steady increase.

Such was the unsettled condition of things, so distant and isolated were the different mining regions, so lonely and uninhabited the sections through which the

---

1 *Padre Jurata* Allusion to the Spanish priest Celedonio Dómeco de Jarauta (1814–48), who emigrated to Mexico during the Mexican–American War and became a guerilla leader; he was captured and executed by Mexican troops following his refusal to acknowledge the Treaty of Guadalupe Hidalgo.

roads and trails were cut, and so numerous the friends and acquaintances of the bandits themselves that these lawless men carried on their operations with almost absolute impunity. It was a rule with them to injure no man who ever extended them a favor, and, whilst they plundered every one else and spread devastation in every other quarter, they invariably left those ranches and houses unharmed whose owners and inmates had afforded them shelter or assistance. Many persons, who were otherwise honestly inclined, bought the safety of their lives and property by remaining scrupulously silent in regard to Joaquín and neutral in every attempt to do him an injury. Further than this, there were many large rancheros who were secretly connected with the banditti, and stood ready to harbor them in times of danger and to furnish them with the best animals that fed on their extensive pastures. The names of several of these wealthy and highly respectable individuals are well known, and will transpire in the course of this history.

At the head of this most powerful combination of men, Joaquín ravaged the State in various quarters during the year 1851, without at that time being generally known as the leader; his subordinates, Claudio, Valenzuela, and Pedro Gonzalez being alternately mistaken for the actual chief. Except to few persons, even his name was unknown, and many were personally acquainted with him and frequently saw him in the different towns and villages, without having the remotest idea that he stood connected with the bloody events which were then filling the country with terror and dismay. He resided for weeks at a time in different localities, ostensibly engaged in gambling, or employed as a vaquero,[1] a packer, or in some other apparently honest avocation, spending much of his time in the society of that sweetest of all companions, the woman that he loved.

While living in a secluded part of the town of San José, sometime in the summer of '51, he one night became violently engaged in a row at a fandango,[2] was arrested for a breach of the peace, brought up before a magistrate, and fined twelve dollars. He was in the charge of Mr. Clark, the deputy sheriff of Santa Clara County, who had made himself particularly obnoxious to the banditti by his rigorous scrutiny into their conduct and his determined attempts to arrest some of this number. Joaquín had the complete advantage of him, inasmuch as the deputy was totally ignorant of the true character of the man with whom he had to deal. With the utmost frankness in his manner, Joaquín requested him to walk down to his residence in the skirts of the town, and he would pay him the money. They proceeded together, engaged in a pleasant conversation, until they reached the edge of a thicket when the young bandit suddenly drew a knife and informed Clark that he had brought him there to kill him, at the same instant stabbing him to the heart before he could draw his revolver. Though many persons knew the author of this most cool and bloody deed by sight, yet it was a long time before it was ascertained that the escaped murderer was no less a personage than the leader of the daring cut-throats who were then infesting the country.

In the fall of the same year, Joaquín moved up in the more northern part of the State and settled himself down with his mistress at the Sonorian Camp, a cluster of tents and cloth houses situated about three miles from the city of Marysville, in Yuba County. It was not long before the entire country rung with the accounts of frequent, startling, and diabolical murders. *The Marysville Herald* of November 13, 1851, speaking of the horrible state of affairs, has the following remarkable paragraph:

"Seven men have been murdered within three or four days in a region of country not more than twelve miles in extent."

Shortly after the murders thus mentioned, two men who were traveling on the road that leads up Feather River, near to the Honcut Creek, which puts into that stream, discovered just ahead of them four Mexicans, one of whom was dragging at his saddlebow by a lariat[3] an American whom they had just lassoed around the neck. The two travelers did not think it prudent to interfere, and so hurried on to a place of safety, and reported what they had seen. Legal search being made upon this information, six other men were found murdered near the same place, bearing upon their throats the fatal mark of the lariat.

---

[1]   *vaquero*   Cattle driver.

[2]   *fandango*   Spanish form of couples' dance; by extension, a gathering at which the fandango or other related dances are performed.

[3]   *lariat*   Rope used to form a lasso.

Close upon these outrages, reports came that several inividuals had been killed and robbed at Bidwel's Bar,[1] some ten or fifteen miles up the river. Consternation spread like fire—fear thrilled through the hearts of hundreds, and all dreaded to travel the public roads.

Suspicion was directed to the Sonorian Camp, it being occupied exclusively by Mexicans, many of whom had no ostensible employment, and yet rode fine horses and spent money freely. This suspicion was confirmed by a partial confession obtained from a Mexican thief who had fallen into the hands of the "Vigilance Committee" of Marysville and had been run up with a rope several times to the limb of a tree, by order of that formidable body. The sheriff of Yuba county, R. B. Buchanan, went out on a moonlight night with his *posse* (which, to say the truth, consisted of one man only, widely and familiarly known as Ike Bowen) to examine the premise and to arrest three suspicious characters, who were known to be lurking in that neighborhood. While getting through the bars of a fence, they were attacked from behind by three Mexicans who had been hid, and the sheriff was severely wounded with a pistol-ball, which struck him near the spine, and passing through his body, came out in the front near the navel. The Mexicans escaped, and Buchanan was finally taken back to Marysville, where he lay a long time in a very dangerous situation but eventually recovered—much to the gratification of the community, who admired the devotion and courage with which he had well-nigh sacrificed his life in the discharge of his duties. He, in common with everyone else, was, for a long time afterward, in ignorance that he had received his wound in a personal encounter with the redoubtable Joaquín himself.

The bandits did not remain long in the vicinity of Marysville after this occurrence but rode off into the coast range of mountains to the west of Mount Shasta, a conspicuous landmark in the northern portion of the State, which rears its white shaft at all seasons of the year high about every other peak, and serves at a distance of two hundred miles to direct the course of the mountain-traveler, being to him as the polar star to the mariner. Gazing at it from the Sacramento Valley at a distance of one hundred and fifty miles, it rises in its garments of snow like some mighty archangel, filling the heaven with his solemn presence.

MOUNT SHASTA, SEEN FROM A DISTANCE[2]

Behold the dread Mount Shasta, where it stands,
Imperial midst the lesser height, and like
Some mighty, unimpassioned mind, companionless
And cold. The storms of Heaven may beat in wrath
Against it, but it stands in unpolluted
Grandeur still; and from the rolling mists up-heaves
Its tower of pride e'en purer than before.
Each wintry shower, and white-winged tempest leave
Their frozen tributes on its brow, and it
Doth make of them an everlasting crown.
Thus doth it day by day, and age by age,
Defy each stroke of time—still rising higher
Into Heaven!

Aspiring to the eagle's cloudless height,
No human foot hath stained its snowy side,
Nor human breath has dimmed the icy mirror
Which it holds unto the moon, and stars, and sov'reign
Sun. We may not grow familiar with the secret
Of its hoary top, whereon the Genius
Of that mountain builds his glorious throne!
Far-lifted in the boundless blue, he doth
Encircle, with his gaze supreme, the broad
Dominions of the West, that lie beneath
His feet, in pictures of sublime repose
No artist ever drew. He sees the tall,
Gigantic hills arise in silentness
And peace, and in the long review of distance
Range themselves in order grand. He sees the sunlight
Play upon the golden streams that through the valleys
Glide. He hears the music of the great and solemn
Sea, and over-looks the huge old western wall,
To view the birth-place of undying Melody!

Itself, all light, save when some loftiest cloud
Doth for a while embrace its cold forbidding

---

[1]   *Bidwel's Bar* Butte county gold mining camp.

[2]   Ridge composed this poem in 1852, some time before he started work on the novel. It was later published in a number of California newspapers, and was included as the opening poem in Ridge's posthumous collection *Poems* (1868).

Form—that monarch-mountain casts its mighty
Shadows down upon the crownless peaks below,
That, like inferior minds to some great
Spirit, stand in strong contrasted littleness!
All through the long and summery months of our
Most tranquil year, it points its icy shaft
On high, to catch the dazzling beams that fall
In showers of splendor round that crystal cone,
And roll, in floods of far magnificence,
Away from that lone vast Reflector in
The dome of Heaven.

*   Still watchful of the fertile*
Vale, and undulating plains below, the grass
Grows greener in its shade, and sweeter bloom
The flowers. Strong Purifier! From its snowy
Side the breezes cool are wafted to "the peaceful
Homes of men," who shelter at its feet, and love
To gaze upon its honored form; aye, standing
There, the guarantee of health and happiness!
Well might it win communities so blest
To loftier feelings, and to nobler thoughts—
The great material symbol of eternal
Things! And well, I ween, in after years, how,
In the middle of his furrowed track, the plowman,
In some sultry hour, will pause, and, wiping
From his brow the dusty sweat, with reverence
Gaze upon that hoary peak. The herdsman
Oft will rein his charger[1] in the plain, and drink
Into his inmost soul the calm sublimity;
And little children, playing on the green, shall
Cease their sport, and, turning to that mountain
Old, shall, of their mother ask, "Who made it?"
And she shall answer, "God!"
And well this Golden State shall thrive, if, like
Its own Mount Shasta, sovereign law shall lift
Itself in purer atmosphere—so high
That human feeling, human passion, at its base
Shall lie subdued; e'en pity's tears shall on
Its summit freeze; to warn it, e'en the sunlight
Of deep sympathy shall fail—
Its pure administration shall be like
The snow, immaculate upon that mountain's brow!

In the rugged fastness of the wild range lying to the west of this huge mount, a range inhabited only by human savages and savage beasts, did the outlaws hide themselves for several long months, descending into the valleys at intervals with no further purpose than to steal horses, of which they seemed determined to keep a good supply. They induced the Indians to aid them in this *laudable* purpose, and so efficiently did these simple people render their assistance that the rancheros of that region loaded the very air with their curses of the "naked devils," who tormented them to such an intolerable degree! On one occasion, during these depredations upon locomotive property, an exasperated party of Americans, who had been on [the] track of their stolen animals, came up with the Indian thieves and managed to hem them between a perpendicular wall of bluffs and a deep river, so that there was no escape for them but to swim the stream, which swept by in a mad and foaming torrent. They fired upon the Indians, who leaped into the water, many of them dyeing it with their blood, and a few successfully swimming across. In the midst of the firing, a tall Mexican, mounted upon a fine horse, dashed down the banks, firing his revolver as he went, and plunged into the stream. His horse struck boldly with him for the opposite shore, and he gained the middle of the current in a distance of a hundred yards from his pursuers, before any effectual shot at him was made. He was about to escape, and nothing would now avail but a dead aim and a steady nerve. The best marksman in the crowd, a lank Missourian, dismounted from his horse, drew his rifle to his shoulder while the other looked anxiously on, and taking a long "bead,"[2] fired. The Mexican leaned forward a moment, and the next instant floated from the saddle and sunk, while his fine charger breasted the waves and ascended the bank with a snorting nostril and dripping mane. No one was willing to risk the dangerous passage even to possess so noble an animal, and they returned with their recovered property to their homes. This tall Mexican was, without doubt, a member of Joaquín's band, who had led the Indians in that very unsuccessful thieving expedition.

In that desolate region, through which, at long intervals, only a few straggling miners passed on their lonesome prospecting tours, human skeletons were

---

[1] *charger* Horse.

[2] *bead* Aiming device of a gun.

found bleaching in the sun, some leaving no trace of the manner in which they perished, while others plainly showed by the perforated skull that the leaden ball had suddenly and secretly done its work. The ignorant Indians suffered for many a deed which had been perpetrated by civilized hands. It will be recollected by many persons who resided at Yreka and on Scott's River in the fall and winter of 1851 how many "prospecters" were lost in the mountains and never again heard from; how many were found dead, supposed to have been killed by the Indians, and yet bearing upon their bodies the marks of knives and bullets quite as frequently as arrows.

As soon as the spring opened in 1852, Joaquín and his party descended from the mountains, and, by forced marches in the night, drove some two or three hundred horses which they had collected at their winter rendezvous down through the southern portion of the state into the province of Sonora. Returning in a few weeks, they took up their headquarters at Arroyo Cantooya,[1] a fine tract of rich pasturage, containing seven or eight thousand acres, beautifully watered, and fenced in by a circular wall of mountains through which an entrance was afforded by a narrow gate or pass, at which a very formidable force could be stayed in their progress by a small body of men. This rich and fertile basin lies halfway between the Tejon and the Pacheco Pass, to the east of the Coast Range and to the west of the great Tulare Lake, thoroughly embosomed in its rugged boundaries and the more valuable as a retreat that it was distant at least one hundred and fifty miles from any human habitation. From the surrounding eminences, an approaching enemy could be seen for a long way off. This region was, in one respect in particular, adapted to the purpose for which it was chosen, and that is, it abounded in game of every kind: elk, antelope, deer, grizzly bears, quails, grouse, and every species of smaller animals most desirable for food. Here Joaquín selected a clump of evergreen oaks for his residence, and many a pleasant day found him and his still blooming companion roofed by the rich foliage of the trees and reclining upon a more luxurious carpet than ever blossomed, with its imitative flowers, beneath the satin-slippered feet of the fairest daughters of San Francisco. The brow of his sweet and faithful friend would sometimes grow sad as she recurred to the happy and peaceful lives which they had once lived, but with a woman's true nature, she loved him in spite of all his crimes, and her soul was again lighted up as she gazed into those dark and glorious eyes which had never quailed before mortal man, and lost their fierceness only when they looked on her. Besides, in her tender heart she made for him many allowances; she saw many strong palliations of his conduct in the treatment which he had received—she knew the secret history of his soul, his sufferings, and his struggles with an evil fate, and the long agony which rent up by the roots the original honesty of his high-born nature. More than this, he had told her that he would soon finish his dangerous career, when, having completed his revenge, and, having accumulated an equivalent for the fortune of which he had been robbed by the Americans, he would retire into a peaceful portion of the State of Sonora, build him a pleasant home, and live alone for love and her. She believed him, for he spoke truly of his intentions, and—wonder not, ye denizens of cities!—she was happy even in the wilderness. It matter not how the world regarded him; to her he was all that is noble, generous, and beautiful.

After spending a few weeks at the rendezvous, Joaquín divided his party, then consisting of about seventy men, into different bands headed by Claudio, Three-Fingered Jack, and Valenzuela, and dispatched them to various quarters with orders to devote themselves chiefly to stealing horses and mules, as he had a purpose to effect which required at least fifteen hundred or two thousand animals. He himself started on a separate course, accompanied by Reyes Feliz, Pedro Gonzales, and Juan. Three females, who were dressed in male attire and well armed, were also in company; that is to say Joaquín's mistress, and the wives of Reyes Feliz and Pedro Gonzalez. All the party were well mounted, and rode, no one knew whither, except Joaquín himself. Arriving at Mokelumne Hill[2] in Calaveras County, they took up quarters with some of their Mexican acquaintances in that place, and, passing through the streets, or visiting the saloons, were looked

---

[1]   *Arroyo Cantooya* Today known as Cantua Creek; an *arroyo* is a creek or gulch that is normally dry but that occasionally fills during flash floods.

[2]   *Mokelumne Hill* Approximately fifty miles southeast of Sacramento.

upon as nothing more than peaceful Mexicans, residing in the town. This was in the month of April. While here, the women appeared in their proper attire, and were admired for their exceedingly modest and quiet deportment. The men issued forth at night upon no praiseworthy missions, and, mounted upon their magnificent chargers, scoured an extent of many miles ere they returned stealthily back to their hiding place and the arms of their languishing loves. Joaquín bore the appearance and character of an elegant and successful gambler, being amply provided with means from his night excursions.

In the meantime his men were, in different directions, prosecuting with ardor the business upon which they had been sent, and there was a universal cry throughout the lower country that horse-thieves were very nearly impoverishing the ranchos. Joaquín gathered a pretty good knowledge of what his followers were about from the newspapers, which made a very free use of his own name in the accounts of these transactions and handled his character in no measured terms. In the various outbreaks in which he had been personally engaged, he had worn different disguises, and was actually disguised the most when he showed his real features. No man who had met him on the highway would be apt to recognize him in the cities. He frequently stood very unconcernedly in a crowd and listened to long and earnest conversations in relation to himself, and laughed in his sleeve at the many conjectures which were made as to his whereabouts and intentions.

After remaining as long as he desired at Mokelumne Hill, about the first of May he prepared to take his departure, which he resolved to do at the hour of midnight. His horses were saddled, the women dressed in their male clothes, and everything ready, when Joaquín sauntered out into the streets, according to his custom, and visited the various drinking and gambling saloons, with which every California town and village abound. While sitting·at a monte table, at which he carelessly put down a dollar or two to while away the time, his attention was suddenly arrested by the distinct pronunciation of his name just opposite to where he sat. Looking up, he observed three or four Americans engaged in loud and earnest conversation in relation to his identical self, in which one of them, a tall fellow

armed with a revolver, remarked that he "would just like once in his life to come across Joaquín and that he would kill him as quick as he would a snake." The daring bandit, upon hearing this speech, jumped on the monte table in view of the whole house, and, drawing his six-shooter, shouted out, "I am Joaquín! if there is any shooting to do, I am in." So sudden and startling was this movement that everyone quailed before him, and, in the midst of the consternation and confusion which reigned, he gathered his cloak about him and walked out unharmed. After his bold avowal of himself, it was necessary for him to make his stay quite short in that vicinity. Mounting his horse, therefore, with expedition,[1] he dashed off with his party at his heels, sending back a whoop of defiance which rung out thrillingly upon the night air. The extreme chagrin of the citizens can be imagined when they found, for the first time, that they had unwittingly tolerated in their very midst the man whom, above all others, they would have wished to get hold of.

Returning to his rendezvous at Arroyo Cantoova, he found that his marauding bands had collected some two or three hundred heads of horses and were patiently waiting his further orders. He detached a portion of them to take the animals into Sonora for safe keeping and made remittances of money at the same time to a secret partner of his in that State.

Towards the last of May, becoming again restless and tired of an inactive life, he started forth upon the highroads, attended as before, when on his visit to Mokelumne Hill, simply by Reyes Feliz, Pedro Gonzalez, Juan, and the three bright-eyed girls, who, mounted on very elegant chargers, appeared as charming a trio of handsome cavaliers as ever delighted the visions of romantic damsels. Meeting with no one for a week or two but impoverished Frenchmen and dilapidated Germans in search of "diggings,"[2] and having sent very nearly all his money to Sonora, Joaquín's purse was getting pretty low, and he resolved to attack the first man or men he might meet, who appeared to be supplied. He was at this time on the road to San Luis Gonzagos, to which place a young American, named Allen Ruddle, was at the same time driving a wagon, loaded with groceries. Overtaking this young man on

---

1   *expedition*   Great speed.

2   *diggings*   Promising sites at which to dig in search of gold.

an open plain, Joaquín, leaving his party behind, rode up to him where he sat on one of his wheel-horses, and, politely bidding him "good morning," requested to him the loan of what small change he might have about him, remarking at the same moment:

"It is true, I am a robber, but, as sure as I live, I merely wish to *borrow* this money, and I will as certainly pay it back to you as my name is Joaquín. It is not often that I am without funds, but such is my situation at present."

Ruddle, without replying, made a sudden motion to draw his pistol, upon which Joaquín exclaimed:

"Come, don't be foolish—I have no wish to kill you, and let us have no fight."

Ruddle made another effort to get his pistol, which, from excitement, or perhaps from its hanging in the holster, he could not instantly draw, when the bandit, with a muttered oath, slashed him across the neck with his bowie-knife[1] and dashed him from the saddle. Searching his pockets, he found about three hundred dollars. His party coming up, he rode on, leaving the murdered man where he lay and his wagon and team standing by the road. Joaquín's conscience smote him for this deed, and he regretted the necessity of killing so honest and hardworking a man as Ruddle seemed to be.

It happened that just at this period Capt. Harry Love, whose own history is one of equal romance with that of Joaquín but marked only with events which redound[2] to his honor, was at the head of a small party gotten up on his own responsibility in search of this outrageous bandit. Love had served as an express rider in the Mexican war and had borne dispatches from one military post to another over the most dangerous tracts of Mexico. He had traveled alone for hundreds of miles over mountains and deserts, beset with no less danger than the dreaded "guerillas" who hung upon the skirts of the American army, laid-in-wait at mountain-passes and watering-places, and made it their business to murder every unfortunate straggler that fell into their hands. Riding fleet horses and expert in the use of the lasso, it required a well-mounted horseman to escape them on the open plains, and many a hard race with them has the Captain had to save his neck and the

valuable papers in his charge. He had been, moreover, from his early youth, a hardy pioneer, experienced in all the dangers and hardships of a border-life. Having these antecedents in his favor and possessing the utmost coolness in the presence of danger, he was a man well-fitted to contend with a person like Joaquín, than whom the lightning was not quicker and surer in the execution of a deadly errand. Love was on the direct trail of Joaquín when Ruddle was murdered. With the utmost speed consistent with the caution necessary to a surprise of the bandit, he pursued him by his murders and robberies, which left a bloody trail behind him to the rancho of San Luis Gonzagos, which is now well known to have been a place which regularly harbored the banditti. Arriving at that place at night, he ascertained by certain spies whom he had employed that the party of whom he was in search were staying in a canvas-house on the edge of the rancho.

Proceeding cautiously to this house with his men, the Captain had just reached the door when the alarm was given by a woman in a neighboring tent, and, in an instant, Joaquín, Gonzalez, Reyes Feliz, and Juan had cut their way through the back part and escaped into the darkness. Upon entering, no one was to be seen but the women, three of whom, then dressed in their proper garments, were the bandits' mistresses, of which fact, however, Love was ignorant. Leaving the women to shift for themselves, the fugitives went to their horses, which were hitched in an adjacent thicket, mounted them, and rode directly over to Oris Timbers, a distance of eight miles, where they immediately stole twenty head of horses and drove them off into the neighboring mountains. They remained concealed all the next day but at night came back (a movement wholly unanticipated by Love) to the cloth-house where they had left their women, who quickly doffed[3] their female attire and rode off with their companions into the hills from which they had just come. Driving the stolen horses before them, the party started in high glee across the Tulare Plains for Los Angeles. Love followed them no further, having business which recalled him. The owner of Oris Timbers Rancho, however, attended by a few Americans, fell upon their trail, indicated by the Captain, and pursued them without

---

1   *bowie-knife*   Short-handled fighting knife.

2   *redound*   Add, contribute.

3   *doffed*   Removed.

much difficulty into the country of the Tejon Indians.[1] Not coming up with them, and perhaps not very anxious to do so, the owner of the horses proceeded with his attendants to the seat of government of the Tejon Nation in order to see the old Chief, Sapatarra, and, if possible, to make an arrangement with him by which to recover his property. They soon reached the capital, which consisted of twenty or thirty very picturesque-looking bark huts scattered along the side of a hill, in front of the largest of which they found old Sapatarra, seated upon his haunches in all the grandeur of "naked majesty," enjoying a very luxurious repast[2] of roasted acorns and dried angle-worms. His swarthy subjects were scattered in various directions around him, engaged for the most part in the very arduous task of doing nothing. The little smoky-looking children were sporting, like a black species of water-fowl, in the creek which ran a short distance below, while the women were pounding with stone pestles in stone mortars, industriously preparing their acorn bread. The delicacies of the chief's table were soon spread before his guests, which, though tempting, they respectfully declined and entered immediately upon their business. Sapatarra was informed that a party of Mexican horse-thieves had sought shelter in his boundaries; that they were only a few in number, and that they had in their possession twenty splendid horses, one-half of which should belong to the chief if he recovered the whole number. This arrangement was speedily effected, and the high contracting parties separated with great satisfaction and mutual assurances of their distinguished regard.

Sapatarra held a council of state, which resulted in sending spies over his dominions to discover traces of the marauding band. Information was returned in a day or two that seven Mexicanos, superbly dressed, and covered with splendid jewelry, and having a large number of fine horses, were camped on a little stream about fifteen miles from the capital. The cupidity[3] of the old chief and his right-hand men was raised to the

highest pitch, and they resolved to manage the matter in hand with great skill and caution; which last, by the way, is a quality that particularly distinguished the California Indians, amounting to so extreme a degree that it might safely be called cowardice. Joaquín and party, having ascertained that they were no longer pursued by the Oris Timbers Ranchero, and feeling perfectly secure amongst so harmless a people as the Tejons, disencumbered themselves of their weapons and resolved to spend a few days in careless repose and genuine rural enjoyment. Juan was, one evening, lying in the grass, watching the horses as they fed around him, while Gonzalez, Feliz, and Murieta were each of them separately seated under a live-oak tree, enjoying a private *tête-à-tête*[4] with their beloved and loving partners. The evening shades were softly stealing around them, and all nature seemed to lull their unquiet spirits to security and repose. Just at this moment, a few dark figures might have been seen, but, unfortunately, were not, creeping cat-like in the direction of the unsuspecting Juan and the equally unconscious Murieta, Gonzalez, and the rest. It was well managed. By a sudden and concerted movement, the whole party were seized, overpowered, and securely bound before they were aware of what was going on. The Indians were in ecstasies at this almost unhoped-for success, for, had the least resistance been made, a single pistol cocked, or a knife drawn, they would have left the ground on the wings of the wind—so largely developed is the bump of caution on the head[5] of a California Indian! But cunning is equally developed, and serves their purposes quite as well sometimes as downright courage. As soon as this feat was accomplished, the woods became alive with forms, faces, and voices. A triumphal march was made with the captives to the capital. They were stripped entirely naked, and their rich clothing covered the weather-beaten backs and scaly legs of the Tejons; but great was the astonishment of the natives when they discovered the sex of

---

1 *Tejon Indians* An error: the land in question is in fact that of the Miwok, whom Ridge refers to as the Tejon throughout the novel. "Tejon" is a colonial name for the Kitanemuk, some of whose members are today part of the federally recognized Tejon Tribe.

2 *repast* Meal.

3 *cupidity* Greed.

4 *tête-à-tête* French: literally, "head to head"; private conversation between two people.

5 *largely developed ... the head* Reference to the pseudo-science of phrenology, according to which a person's personality and abilities are indicated by the relative size and shapes of certain bumps or "organs" on the head. The pseudo-science was often used to justify a variety of racist stereotypes, as certain races were thought to share certain phrenological features.

three youthful cavaliers, who were kindly permitted, in pity for their modesty, to wear some of the old cast-off shirts that lay around in the dirt. The women were robbed of their jewelry to the amount of three thousand dollars and the men of seven thousand dollars in gold dust, besides their riding animals and the stolen horses. They were left also without a solitary weapon. Never were men so completely humiliated. The poor, miserable, cowardly Tejons had achieved a greater triumph over them than all the Americans put together! Joaquín looked grim for a while, but finally bust out into a loud laugh at his ridiculous position, and ever afterwards endured his captivity with a quiet smile. The most potent, grave, and reverend Señor Sapatarra immediately dispatched one-half of the stolen horses to the Oris Timbers, while he retained the other according to agreement. He kept his prisoners of war in custody for a week or two, debating in his mind whether to make targets of them for his young men to practice archery upon, or to hang, burn, or drown them. He finally sent word to "The Great Capitan," the county judge of Los Angeles, that he had a party of Mexicans in custody and wanted his advice on what to do with them. The judge, supposing that the capture was the result of a little feud between some "greasers"[1] and the Tejons, advised him to release them. Accordingly, one fine morning, the prisoners, under the supervision of Sapatarra surrounded by his guard, who were armed with the revolvers and knives which they had taken from the bandits, were led forth from the village with such solemnity that they imagined they were going to no other than a place of execution. Arrived at a group of live-oaks, they were stripped entirely naked and bound each to a tree. Sapatarra made a long speech upon the merits of the important transaction which was about to occur, enlarging upon the enormity of the crime which had been committed (although it looked very much like self-condemnation in him to denounce stealing), and went off into extreme glorification over the magnanimity which would allow such great rascals to escape with their lives. He then gave orders to have them whipped. Seven large, stout fellows stepped out with a bunch of willow rods, each to his place, and gave the unfortunate party a very decent and thorough flogging. Sapatarra then declared the ends of justice satisfied and dismissed the prisoners from custody.

Poor fellows! They went forth into the wilderness as naked as on the day that they were born and stricken with a blanker poverty than the veriest beggar upon the streets of London, or New York, or any other proud city that raises its audacious head above its sea of crime and wretchedness into the pure light of Heaven. The biters were bit. The robbers were robbed, and loud and deep were the curses which Feliz, Juan, and Gonzalez pronounced upon Sapatarra and the whole Tejon Nation; but Joaquín rubbed his smarting back and laughed prodigiously—declaring upon his honor as a man that not a hair of old Sapatarra's head should be harmed. That night they slept without a stitch of covering; but, fortunately, it was near summer, and the air possessed a merely pleasant coolness. The next day, in passing through an *arroyo*, Reyes Feliz, who was behind, was attacked by a grizzly bear, and, utterly defenceless, was horribly mangled. He begged his companions to leave him, as he must certainly die, and they could do him no good. After removing him to a shady place among some rocks and near to a stream of water, they left him to die—all but his sorrowing mistress, who resolved to remain with him whatever might befall. They turned to look as they departed, and the last they saw was the faithful girl with her lover's head upon her lap, pouring her tears upon him like a healing balm from her heart. Give me not a sneer, thou rigid righteous! for the love of woman is beautiful at all times, whether she smiles under gilded canopies in her satin garments or weeps over a world-hated criminal alone and naked in a desert. ...

On the following morning, Joaquín collected his bands around him, numbering, from a late accession of new "fighting members" as he called them, one hundred men, and explained to them fully his views and purposes.

"I am at the head of an organization," said he, "of two thousand men whose ramifications[2] are in Sonora, Lower California, and in this state.[3] I have money in abundance deposited in a safe place. I intend to arm and equip fifteen hundred or two thousand men and

---

[1]   *greasers*   Derogatory term for Mexicans. The term was widely used by Anglo-Americans in California during this period.

[2]   *ramifications*   Divisions or branches.

[3]   *Lower California*   I.e., Baja California, a state of Mexico;   *this state*   I.e., California (originally known as Upper California).

make a clean sweep of the southern countries. I intend to kill the Americans by 'wholesale,' burn their ranchos, and run off their property at one single swoop so rapidly that they will not have time to collect an opposing force before I will have finished the work and found safety in the mountains of Sonora. When I do this, I shall wind up my career. My brothers, we will then be revenged for our wrongs, and some little, too, for the wrongs of our poor, bleeding country. We will divide our substance and spend the rest of our days in peace. I am now preparing for this grand climax, and this is the reason, Valenzuela, that I have kept you so busy collecting horses."

The banditti shouted in loud applause of their gallant leader. Their eyes kindled with enthusiasm at the magnificent prospect which he presented to them, and they could scarcely contain themselves in view of the astounding revelations which he had made. They had entertained no adequate idea of the splendid genius which belonged to their chief, although they had loved and admired him throughout his dangerous career. They were fired with new energy, and more than ever willing and anxious to obey him at all hazards and under the most disadvantageous circumstances.

On this same day he dispatched a remittance of $50,000 to his secret partner in Sonora under a strong force commanded by Valenzuela and directed Three-Fingered Jack, with fifty men, to drive off to the same state a thousand head of the horses which had been collected. Joaquín was accordingly left at the rendezvous with twenty-five men, who had nothing to do but kill game, and attend to their horses, and clean their arms. The wife of Gonzalez was there, who had consoled her widowhood by accepting a huge fellow as her husband, by the name of Guerra, who looked like a grizzly bear more than a human being. He was not so kind to her as Gonzalez had been, and, one night while he was asleep, she was about to cut his throat when Joaquín, who was lying in the same tent, fiercely told her to behave herself and assured her with an emphasis that he would hold her responsible if Guerra was ever found dead about camp. She threw her knife spitefully towards Joaquín and laid down again by her adorable spouse, who snored in blissful ignorance of his wife's affectionate purpose.

Lounging in his tent one misty day—for the rainy season had set in—Joaquín was aroused from the luxurious lap of his mistress by one of his sentinels, who galloped up and informed him that he had just discovered a fresh trail through the grass, about a mile and a half below on the Cantoova Creek, and, from appearances, he should judge there were eight or ten men. It was important to keep a sharp lookout and to allow no Americans to leave that valley with the knowledge that it was occupied by any body of men whatever, as such a circumstance would materially interfere with the gigantic plans projected. Accordingly, it was not long before Joaquín was mounted upon one of his swiftest horses and accompanied by fifteen picked men. They proceeded to the trail indicated by the sentinel and rode rapidly for two hours, which brought them in sight of ten Americans, who halted in curious surprise and waited for them to come up.

"Who are you?" said Joaquín, "and what is your business in these parts?"

They replied that they were hunters in search of bears and deer.

"We are hunters, also," rejoined the bandit, "and are camped just across the plain here. Come over with us, and let us have a chat. Besides, we have some first-rate liquor at our camp."

Suspecting nothing wrong, the hunters accompanied them, and, having dismounted at the tents and turned out their horses to graze, found themselves suddenly in a very doubtful position. They were surrounded by a company more than double their own who made demonstrations not at all grateful to their sight,[1] and in a few moments, they realized the bitter fact that they were driven to the extremity of a hopeless struggle for their lives. They remonstrated with Joaquín against so shameless an act as the cold-blooded murder of men who had never injured him.

"You have found me here," he replied, "and I have no guarantee that you will not betray me. If I do not tell you who I am, you will think it no harm to say that you have seen a man of my description; and, if I do tell you, then you will be certain to mention it at the first opportunity."

At this moment a young man, originally from the wilds of Arkansas, not more than eighteen years of age, advanced in front of his trembling comrades and,

---

[1] *not at all … their sight* I.e., that they were not grateful to see.

standing face to face with the robber-chief, addressed him in a firm voice to the following effect:

"I suspect strongly who you are, sir. I am satisfied that you are Joaquín Murieta. I am also satisfied that you are a brave man, who would not unnecessarily commit murder. You would not wish to take our lives, unless your own safety demanded it. I do not blame you, following the business you do, for desiring to put an effectual seal of silence on our tongues. But listen to me just a moment. You see that I am no coward. I do not look at you with the aspect of a man who would tell a falsehood to save his life. I promise you faithfully for myself, and in behalf of my companions, that if you spare our lives, which are completely in your power, not a word shall be breathed of your whereabouts. I will myself kill the first man who says a word in regard to it. Under different circumstances, I should take a different course, but *now,* I am conscious that to spare our lives will be an act of magnanimity on your part, and I stake my honor, not as an American citizen, but as a man, who is simply bound by justice to himself, under circumstances in which no other consideration can prevail, that you shall not be betrayed. If you say you will spare us, we thank you. If you say no, we can only fight until we die, and you must lose some of your lives in the conflict."

Joaquín drew his hand across his brow, and looked thoughtful and undecided. A beautiful female approached him from the tent near by and touched him on the shoulder.

"Spare them, Joaquín," she tremulously whispered, and, looking at him with pleading eyes, retired softly to her seat again.

Raising his fine head with a lofty look, he bent his large clear eyes upon the young American, as if he would read him like an outspread page. He answered his glance with a look so royally sincere that Joaquín exclaimed with sudden energy:

"I will spare you. Your countrymen have injured me, they have made me what I am, but I scorn to take the advantage of so brave a man. I will risk a look and a voice like yours, if it should lead to perdition. Saddle their horses for them," he said to his followers, "and let them depart in peace."

The party were very soon mounted again, and, showering blessings on Joaquín, who had become suddenly transformed into an angel in their estimation, they took their leave. I have never learned that the young man, or any of his party, broke their singular compact, and, indeed, it seems to me that it would have been very questionable morality in them to have done so, for certainly, however much they owed to society, it would have been a suicidal act to refuse to enter into such an agreement, and, as nothing but a firm conviction that they intended to keep their word could have induced Joaquín to run so great a risk, they were bound to preserve their faith inviolate. If they had a right to purchase their lives at the price of silence, they had an equal right, and not only that, but were morally bound, to stand up to their bargain. It would be well if men were never forced into such a position, but society has no right, after it has happened, to wring from them a secret which belongs to *them* and not to the world. In such matters God is the only judge.

The month of December was drawing to a close, and the busy brain of the accomplished chief had mapped out the full plan of his operations for the new year just at hand. It was the year which would close his short and tragical career with a crowning glory—a deed of daring and of power which would redeem with its refulgent light the darkness of his previous history and show him to aftertimes, not as a mere outlaw, committing petty depredations and robberies, but as a *hero* who has revenged his country's wrongs and washed out her disgrace in the blood of her enemies.

It was time for Three-Fingered Jack and Valenzuela to return from Sonora, and Joaquín waited patiently for their arrival in order to replenish his purse largely during the first months of the new year so that he might execute his magnificent purpose without embarrassment or obstruction. In a few days, Garcia and Valenzuela returned, accompanied by an old guerrilla comrade of the latter, named Luis Vulvia. The two had lost five men from their bands, killed in several skirmishes on their way back, with the citizens of Los Angeles County. Further than this, they had received no injury, and were in fine health and spirits, although their horses were somewhat jaded. Each leader handed to Joaquín a well-filled purse of gold coin. Having rested two days, the major portion of the banditti mounted fresh horses and, leaving the remainder, numbering twenty-five men, at the rendezvous under the command of Guerra, with whom they also left the females, not thinking it prudent, in view of the bloody scenes which would be enacted, to take them along, they set out for Calaveras County.

They had not been gone more than three days before a quarrel arose between Guerra and his affectionate wife, which ended in his giving her a wholesale thrashing. She submitted to the infliction with great apparent humility, but the next morning at breakfast time when Guerra was called and did not come, several of his companions went into his tent to arouse him and found him stone-dead. There was no sign of violence on his body, and it remained a complete mystery how he died. He had been a hard drinker, and, finally, his death was attributed to an over-indulgence the night before. But the fact of the case was, that unconscious sleeper had received at midnight just one drop of hot lead into his ear, tipped from a ladle by a small and skillful hand. Byron has said in one of his misanthropic verses:

> Woman's tears, produced at will,
> Deceive in life, unman in death.[1]

and the truth of this bitter asseveration was partially illustrated when the inconsolable widow wept so long and well over the husband whom she, like a second, nay, the thousandth jezebel,[2] had made a corpse. It is barely possible, however, that her tears were those of remorse. She accepted for her third husband a young fellow in the band at the rendezvous named Isidora Conejo, who loved her much more tenderly than did the brutal Guerra, whom she so skillfully put out of the way. This young man was a few years her junior, but she looked as youthful as himself. Twice widowed, her sorrows had not dimmed the lustre of her eyes, or taken the gloss from her rich dark hair, or the rose from her cheeks. Her step was as buoyant as ever, the play of her limbs as graceful, the heave of her impulsive bosom as entrancing, and her voice full of music as if she had never lost Gonzalez or murdered Guerra. There are some women who seem never to grow old. As each successive spring renews the plumage of the birds, so with them the passing year adds fresh beauty to their forms, and decay long lingers ere he has the heart to touch their transcendent loveliness with his cold and withering fingers. The fascinating Margarita was one of these.

Joaquín with his party, fully bent on the most extensive mischief, entered Calaveras County about the middle of December. This country was then, as it is now, one of the richest in the state of California. Its mountains were veined with gold—the beds of its clear and far-rushing streams concealed the yellow grains in abundance—and the large quartz-leads, like the golden tree of the Hesperides,[3] spread their fruitful branches abroad through the hills. Its fertile valleys bloomed with voluptuous flowers over which you might walk as on a carpet woven of rainbows—or waved with the green and mellow harvests, whose ready music charmed the ear. The busy wheels of the sawmills with their glittering teeth rived[4] the mighty pines, which stood like green and spiral towers, one above another, from base to summit of the majestic peaks. Long tunnels, dimly lighted with swinging lamps or flickering candles, searched far into the bowels of the earth for her hidden secrets. Those which were abandoned served as dens for the cougar and wolf, or, more frequently, the dens of thieves.

Over this attractive field for his enterprizes, Joaquín scattered his party in different directions. He entrusted Reis with the command of twenty men, Luis Vulvia with that of twenty-five, retaining about fifteen for his own use, among whom was the terrible Three-Fingered Jack and the no less valuable Valenzuela, and employed the remainder as spies and bearers of news from one point of action to another. Reis went up to the headwaters of the Stanislaus River between whose forks the rich valleys, covered with horses, afforded a fine theater for his operations. On all the mountain-fed branches and springs of these forks, the picks and shovels of a thousand miners were busy, and the industrious Chinese had pitched their little cloth villages in a hundred spots, and each day hurried to and fro like innumerable ants, picking up the small but precious grains.

---

[1] *Woman's tears ... in death* See English poet Lord Byron's "Euthanasia" (1811).

[2] *jezebel* Immoral woman, especially one considered to be seductive or sexually promiscuous; the name is derived from that of the biblical queen who promoted the worship of Baal.

[3] *golden tree of the Hesperides* In Greek mythology, a group of nymphs called the Hesperides guard a tree of golden apples.

[4] *rived* Tore apart.

Luis Vulvia—as daring a man as Claudio and as cunning—proceeded to the headwaters of the Mokelumne River; and detached portions of these two bands, at intervals, ranged the intermediate space. Joaquín himself had no particular sphere but chose his ground according to circumstances. Keeping Three-Fingered Jack with him most of the time, he yet, once in a while, gave him the charge of a small party with liberty to do as he pleased—a favor which the bloody monster made good use of; so much so that scarcely a man whom he ever met, rich or poor, escaped with his life. The horse which this hideous fellow rode might have rivaled *Bucephalus*[1] in breadth of chest, high spirit, and strength of limb, united with swiftness. No one but a powerful man could have rode him; the Three-Fingered Jack, with a fine Mexican saddle (the best saddles in the world) fastened securely with a broad girth made of horse hair as strong as a band of iron, and curbing him with a huge Spanish bit—with which he might have rent[2] his jaw—managed the royal animal with ease. To see this man, with his large and rugged frame in which the strength of a dozen common men slumbered—his face and forehead scarred with bullets and grooved with the wrinkles of grim thoughts, and his intensely lighted eyes glaring maliciously, like caverned demons, under his shaggy brows—to see such a man mounted upon a raven-black horse whose nostrils drew the air like a gust of wind into his broad chest, whose wrathful hoof pawed the ground as if the spirit of his rider inspired him, and whose wild orbs rolled from side to side in untameable fire—would aptly remind one of old Satan himself, mounted upon a hell-born beast, after he had been "let loose for a thousand years."[3]

Among the many thrilling instances of the daring and recklessness of spirit which belonged to Joaquín, there is one which I do not feel at liberty to omit—especially as it comes naturally and properly in this connection. Shortly after he parted from Reis and Luis Vulvia, he went up into the extreme north of the country.

There, at the head of a branch of the South Fork of the Mokelumne River, in a wild and desolate region near the boundary line of Calaveras and El Dorado Counties, were located a company of miners, consisting of twenty-five men. They were at a long distance from any neighbors, having gone there well-armed on a prospecting tour which resulted in their finding diggings so rich that they were persuaded to put their tents and remain. One morning while they were eating their breakfast on a flat rock—a natural table which stood in front of their tents—armed as usual with their revolvers, a young fellow with very dark hair and eyes rode up and saluted them. He spoke very good English and they could scarcely make out whether he was a Mexican or an American. They requested him to get down and eat with them, but he politely declined. He sat with one leg crossed over his horse's neck very much at his ease, conversing very freely on various subjects, until Jim Boyce, one of the partners who had been to the spring after water, appeared in sight. At the first glance on him, the young horseman flung his reclining leg back over the saddle and spurred his horse. Boyce roared out:

"Boys, that fellow is *Joaquín*; d—n it, shoot him!" At the same instant, he himself fired without effect.

Joaquín dashed down to the creek below with headlong speed and crossed with the intention, no doubt, to escape over the hills which ran parallel with the stream, but his way was blocked up by perpendicular rocks, and his only practicable path was a narrow digger-trail which led along the side of a huge mountain, directly over a ledge of rocks a hundred yards in length, which hung beetling[4] over the rushing stream beneath in a direct line with the hill upon which the miners had pitched their tents, and not more than forty yards distant. It was a fearful gauntlet for any man to run. Not only was there danger of falling a hundred feet from the rocks, but he must run in a parallel line with his enemies, and in pistol-range, for a hundred yards. In fair view of him stood the whole company with their revolvers drawn. He dashed along that fearful trail as if he had been mounted upon a spirit-steed, shouting as he passed:

"I am Joaquín! kill me if you can!"

---

[1]   *Bucephalus*   Horse of Macedonian conqueror Alexander the Great.

[2]   *rent*   Torn.

[3]   *Satan himself ... thousand years*   Slight misremembering of Revelation 20.6–7: "they shall be priests of God and of Christ, and shall reign with him a thousand years. And when the thousand years are expired, Satan shall be loosed out of his prison."

---

[4]   *beetling*   Hanging precariously.

Shot after shot came clanging around his head, and bullet after bullet flattened on the wall of slate at his right. In the midst of the first firing, his hat was knocked from his head, and left his long black hair streaming behind him. He had no time to use his own pistol, but, knowing that his only chance lay in the swiftness of his sure-footed animal, he drew his keenly polished bowie-knife in proud defiance of the danger and waved it in scorn as he rode on. It was perfectly sublime to see such a super-human daring and recklessness. At each report,[1] which came fast and thick, he kissed the flashing blade and waved it at his foes. He passed the ordeal, as awful and harrowing to a man's nerves as can be conceived, untouched by a ball and otherwise unharmed. In a few moments, a loud whoop rang out in the woods a quarter of a mile distant, and the bold rider was safe!

—1854

In Context

Sensational News of Joaquín Murieta!

Rumors and unsubstantiated reports concerning Joaquín Murieta and his associates were fodder for sensational news stories in all parts of America; the excerpt below from a long round-up piece on California news that appeared in a Virginia newspaper is a good example. The report in *The San Joaquín Republican* employs similarly sensationalistic language—but without the italics.

from *The San Joaquín Republican* (29 January 1853)

It is well known that during the winter months a band of Mexican marauders have infested Calaveras county, and weekly we receive the details of dreadful murders and outrages committed in the lonely gulches and solitary outposts of that region. The farmers lost their cattle and horses, the trader's tent was pillaged, and the life of every traveler was insecure. ... The band is led by a robber, named Joaquín, a very desperate man, who was concerned in the murder of four Americans, sometime ago, at Turnerville.

from "California News," *The Richmond Dispatch* (29 September 1853)

A young man named Mark T. Howe, a native of Maine, was murdered near Angel's camp recently. It was supposed that Joaquin's band were the perpetrators.

A California paper has the following, relative to the alleged capture of Joaquin:

The citizens of Los Angeles have a curious story that the capture and decapitation of Joaquín Murieta did not take place on the *person of the bandit!* It is stated that the portion of Joaquín's gang alleged to have been surprised and routed was none other than a party of native Californians and Sonorians who had gone to the Tulare valley for the express and avowed purpose of "running mustangs." Three of the party, our correspondent states, "have returned to Los Angeles and report that they were attacked by a party of Americans, and that the balance of their party, four in number, had been killed, and that Joaquín Valenzuela, one of the party, *was killed and his head cut off by one of his captors!*" This is a very singular statement and will bear looking into.

---

[1]   *report*   Sound of gunfire.

Artist's depiction of "Joaquin, the Mountain Robber," first published in the Sacramento *Union Steamer Edition* for 22 April 1853, and subsequently used in later versions of Ridge's novel.

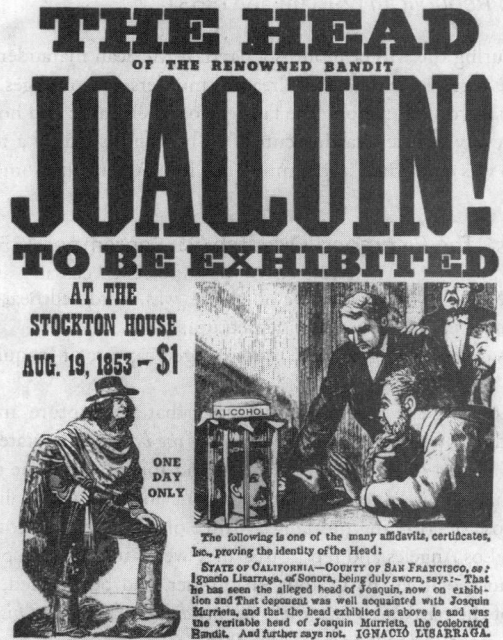

Advertisement for the exhibition of the alleged head of Joaquín Murieta in Stockton, California, including a short testimonial to the head's authenticity from a person claiming to have known Murieta, and an illustration of the bandit that was subsequently used in pirated versions of Ridge's novel.

GENDER AND SEXUALITY
CONTEXTS

In early to mid-nineteenth-century America, anyone who did not fully adhere to gender and sexual norms faced social, economic, and sometimes legal consequences, though the extent of these consequences generally depended on who and where one was. Yet there were many people who could not or would not live according to the prescribed norms, and whose very existence challenged the dominant ideologies of gender—such as, for example, the middle- and upper-class notion of "separate spheres," whereby men were expected to find fulfillment in public spaces and women exclusively in the home. Enslaved people, working-class people, and men seeking their fortunes on ships or in Gold Rush camps were among those for whom the separate spheres ideology was, to varying degrees, difficult or impossible to enact. People who formed their most important relationships with those of the same sex—or whose understanding of their own gender did not match that imposed by their community—also struggled to find space to live their lives within the social expectations of the period. And some women resisted oppressive gender norms by instigating a national debate about women's rights: about whether equality between the sexes was naturally ordained, whether the presence of women in the public sphere was socially permissible, what forms the implementation of gender equality would take, and what impact these changes might have on domestic life and on American society as a whole.

The proliferation of conduct manuals and marriage advice published in the 1820s and 30s testifies to the conscious effort that went into ensuring that people were well instructed in what were considered their essential virtues and duties in life. Generally speaking, advice for married women centered on their roles as family caregivers and household managers, while the (less ubiquitous but still common) advice for married men centered on their duty to provide for and rule their families. Works such as T.S. Arthur's *The Young Wife's Book* (1836) highlight the imbalance in marriage relations, explaining that while "matrimonial duties are reciprocal … [t]hose of a wife are the most strongly enforced, for to hers are added by Divine command, that of obedience also." Advice manuals such as Matthew Hale Smith's *Counsels Addressed to Young Ladies and Young Men* (1846) focus on unmarried as well as married life—and much of the advice to young unmarried women centers on their need to protect their sexual purity. Hale's seemingly melodramatic assertion that young women "are always in peril" reflects the profound anxiety that existed in the nineteenth century around the specter of the "fallen woman," whose sexual transgression—a relationship out of wedlock, an adulterous affair, or an act of prostitution—caused her to be cast out of her family and society.

The ideal of the sexually pure, domestically dutiful wife was interpreted in myriad ways by the individuals whose lives it dominated during the early to mid-nineteenth century. Some of the most successful women writers of the period argued that the right to engage in intellectual and literary pursuits was not incompatible with what they nevertheless accepted (at least in their published writings) as the highest duties for women: marriage and caring for the family. Literary celebrities such as the poet Lydia Sigourney and the novelist Lydia Maria Child did not find that their gender disqualified them from tremendous popularity. Sigourney, whose writings in many ways embodied the ideals of white middle-class femininity, nevertheless faced severe disapproval from her husband, whose condemnatory letter asking her to become "less of a poet" and more of a wife is excerpted below. Women published their writing in large numbers and in all genres during the nineteenth century, but critics and readers tended to associate them with particular subjects and genres—especially sentimental novels and poetry. One anonymous contributor to *The New York Observer* lamented in 1857 that "the country has been flooded with novels mostly written by women" and encouraged women writers to

Go out washing, take in sewing, attend to the children, nurse the sick, do anything honest and useful, but do stop writing wishy-washy, namby-pamby, milk-and-water, sentimental love stories.

Such views were not universal but were certainly commonplace; Nathaniel Hawthorne has in recent decades become notorious for his 1855 complaints about the "damned mob of scribbling women." (He did entertain exceptions such as Fanny Fern, who he said in the same letter "writes as if the Devil was in her; and that is the only condition under which a woman ever writes anything worth reading.")

The more radical ideas that had been heralded by feminist writings of the eighteenth century were taken up again in the 1830s, which saw the growth of women's rights activism as a movement. Influenced especially by writers of the 1790s, such as Olympe de Gouges and Mary Wollstonecraft, women's rights activists often invoked the language of revolution, often gesturing to the hypocrisy with which the ideals of the American Revolution had been implemented in a way that left out women. Maria W. Chapman's poem "The Times that Try Men's Souls" (1837) invokes Thomas Paine's *The American Crisis* (1776–83), while the "Declaration of Sentiments" presented at the 1848 Seneca Falls Convention on women's rights is a pointed revision of the Declaration of Independence. Criticism of women's rights activists often took the form of satirical cartoons, which expressed derision for the movement by depicting women wearing men's clothing, or engaging in masculine activities—smoking pipes, reading newspapers, discussing politics in the street, and leaving their husbands at home with the children. Such cartoons were designed to humiliate their targets—and, viewed in retrospect, point to the profound fear felt by many in America that reform was a threat to the categories by which social life was understood.

In its early days, the women's rights movement was closely tied to the abolitionist movement. Many women abolitionists were drawn to fight for women's rights because of the heavily gendered criticism they received in response to their antislavery activism—criticism that sometimes came from within the abolitionist movement itself. Some black women, such as the "Mrs. Sanford" whose speech at the 1848 Colored National Convention is included below, argued persuasively for the right to be heard in the highly male-dominated circles of the black rights movement. Others, such as Sojourner Truth and Frances Ellen Watkins Harper (whose works are included elsewhere in this anthology), found renown through navigating both movements. Lucretia Mott (whose 1849 *Discourse on Women* is excerpted below) and Angelina and Sarah Moore Grimké (whose antislavery public speaking tour was a target of heavily gendered criticism) were among those white women who sought actively to synthesize their women's rights activism with their antislavery activism. Yet many others—especially later in the century as the debate over suffrage equality was increasingly present in mainstream discourse—came to prioritize the fight for *white* women's rights over that for black rights. Much as the ideals of the American Revolution had left women and African Americans behind, the women's suffrage movement often left behind African American women.

As the women's rights movement gained momentum, the norms surrounding masculinity, too, were changing in the decades leading up to the Civil War. Most white Americans had long believed that men should, as the marriage advice manuals suggested, provide for and hold authority over their families. Also prevalent during the century was the popular ideal of the independent, high-achieving "Self-Made Man"—encapsulated by Frederick Douglass in his speech "Self-Made Men," below. Both of these ideals sat uneasily with the changing realities of labor for middle-class men in American cities, as men became less likely to run their own businesses and more likely to work for wages. Anxieties around this change found a focal point in the figure of the "counter jumper" or shop clerk, who was satirized as effeminate and vain with an aura of sexual immorality. For enslaved men, the ideals of self-actualization through work and of providing for and ruling one's family were both almost entirely unachievable, and some abolitionists described slavery as an attack on masculinity. As the formerly enslaved abolitionist Lewis Clarke famously and emphatically phrased it, "A SLAVE CAN'T BE A MAN!"

Portrayals of black masculinity—and especially of the masculinity of enslaved men—were replete with dehumanizing and often contradictory stereotypes. Proslavery writings tended to depict black men as childlike and adoringly obedient to the enslavers they depended on for guidance or, less often, as brutish and prone to animalistic violence. Abolitionist writings by white authors tended to draw on the same set of tropes, attempting to invoke the pity of white readers by portraying enslaved men as dependents in need of aid—or, occasionally, attempting to inspire fear of the violent retribution enslavers might face if they persisted in their ways. Within this climate of expectations, black men writing slave narratives and other antislavery works faced a daunting rhetorical task as they attempted to present their full humanity without alienating white readers.

As some people struggled to embody the gender roles idealized in the period, others fought to break free of them. Selections included below testify to the existence of women who wore men's clothes, men who wore women's clothes, and people who had to conceal their biological sex in order to pass as women or men in their daily lives. In encountering this material, it can often be difficult to tell whether a given individual's gender expression should be interpreted as a way of pushing back against restrictive gender roles, as a means of opening up different opportunities for work, or as an expression of gender identity.

Fiction and news articles of the nineteenth century reflect a particular fascination with the figure of the cross-dressing woman—especially women who clearly identified as women but adopted masculine attire to perform heroic acts in war, to pursue lost lovers, or for other adventurous purposes. But apart from this media phenomenon, women who adopted masculine garments or behaved in what were considered masculine ways were largely condemned by American society; this contempt is clearly illustrated by the public response to the "Bloomer" costume worn by some female reformers for a brief period in the 1850s (see the general introduction to this volume). And while stories of cross-dressing men were far less common, men who dressed or behaved in traditionally feminine ways were often, too, the subjects of mockery and derision. In the second half of the nineteenth century, many cities passed laws that explicitly or effectively criminalized anyone appearing in public wearing clothes "not belonging to his or her sex."

But there were also spaces within American culture where a perhaps surprising degree of gender fluidity was welcome. In the overwhelmingly male-dominated communities of the mid-century California Gold Rush settlements, for example, some men attended dances wearing handkerchiefs or other markers to identify themselves as "women" for the purpose of partnered dancing, while women apparently cross-dressed to pursue their fortunes so frequently that the author of one "help wanted" ad felt the need to specify that "no young women in disguise need apply." And many Indigenous communities across America continued, as they had before contact, to include more than two gender roles in their cultural practices—though in most cases these roles were increasingly threatened by colonization as white American governments and religious institutions imposed their gender ideology on Indigenous communities.

While terms such as "lesbian" existed by the nineteenth century, and underground communities of men who loved other men existed in some cities, the concepts of "heterosexuality" and "homosexuality" as descriptors of innate identity did not develop until the last decades of the century. The landscape of same-sex desire and connection was thus shaped less by identity categories than by social rules regarding what practices were accepted and prohibited. Chief among the accepted practices was that of romantic friendship, which was condoned both between men and between women, and could be practiced with passionate intensity—albeit within prescribed limits. Eliza Farrar, author of the advice manual *The Lady's Friend* (1837), defines the boundaries of propriety for young women engaged in such friendships:

> there is a custom among young ladies of holding each other's hands, and fondling them before company, which had much better be dispensed with. All kissing and caressing of your female friends should be kept for your hours of privacy, and never be indulged in before gentlemen.

Both women and men were expected to marry and to let such friendships take a subordinate place to their opposite-sex marriages, and for the most part same-sex relationships were permitted only to the extent that they were understood to be at least plausibly platonic. But this expansive view of friendship provided effective cover for some same-sex couples to pursue physically as well as emotionally intimate relationships while raising minimal suspicion; it can also, in some cases, make it difficult to determine from surviving writings whether or not individuals involved in a given passionate connection perceived it as a sexual one at all. This ideology of friendship also created space for the mainstream acceptance of works that would come to be considered watershed moments in the development of queer American literature—works such as Bayard Taylor's *Joseph and His Friend* (1870), a novel about two men in love, or Walt Whitman's meditations on "manly love" in his *Calamus* sequence.

Generally speaking, the consequences for those caught engaging in same-sex sexuality differed dramatically depending on one's circumstances. For women, there could be significant economic and social consequences, but the practice was not illegal—in part because many in the nineteenth century posited that women experienced less sexual desire than men and that sexuality between women was an impossibility. For men, penetrative sex was criminalized by laws against sodomy, a term that grouped together a number of sex acts considered "unnatural," including anal sex and bestiality. The application of such laws varied widely. In the all-male environment of the U.S. Navy, for example, same-sex sexuality was very common and generally not punished; on Southern plantations, where enslaved people were often forced to live in a gender-segregated environment, the sentence for enslaved men convicted of sodomy could be execution. Overall, criminal punishments for sodomy became less draconian and less frequent in the decades leading up to the Civil War—at least for people who were not enslaved—with a number of states reducing the sentence from capital punishment to imprisonment. Legal and social persecution of men engaging in same-sex sexuality would, however, escalate after Reconstruction.

⌘ ⌘ ⌘

Women in the Public Sphere

from Charles Sigourney, letter to Lydia Sigourney, October 1827

Lydia Huntley was already a published author by the time she married entrepreneur Charles Sigourney in 1819; initially, he encouraged her writing in a limited way, but as her fame increased so did his disapproval. When she published her collection *Poems* (1827) without his knowledge or consent, Charles was furious and wrote the following letter. Sigourney tried and failed to convince Charles to agree to a formal separation, and in the end agreed to his demands that she slow down her literary activity and focus on performing the duties of a wife. Many of her subsequent published works center on themes of feminine virtue and women's domestic roles.

My beloved wife,

I come to you in the spirit of deep self-abasement. I come to you in the spirit of kindness, and conjugal affection. I come to you, my wife, in the spirit of prayer; for on my knees have I implored, and repeatedly, the direction and blessing of the Almighty on the application I am about to make to you. ...

The first years of our marriage, may it *yet* be blessed, you may remember that, in addition to the sentiments of love, and esteem I entertained for you, I took a pride in admiring the talents with which your mind was adorned, and the efforts, then only occasional, of your poetical imagination. You may remember too, not only my admiration of the powers of your mind, but the satisfaction, and patience, with which I cooperated with you in preparing your "Traits," and your "Sketch,"[1] and the pleasure, with which, in the former work, I anticipated, what did not follow, an honourable, and successful sale. This, my wife, pardon me if I say it, was the more meritorious, as, in both cases, I surrendered my own opinions, as regarded the *publication* of the works, to your wishes. Nevertheless, our minds, to a certain degree, to the period of the publication of the

"Traits," were one; and I endeavoured, by every means in my power, not merely to uphold your character, but to extend your reputation. To this time, however, you restrained, within the limits of what I deemed propriety, your desire of public attention. But when, afterwards, I began to perceive your great susceptibility of[2] praise, and, as I thought, your passion for literary distinction increasing, I perceived also that it led you occasionally, without any motive I agree beyond self-gratification for the moment, and thinking no evil, into conduct I could not reconcile with my ideas of the delicate propriety which should ever mark the female character—that, at first it occupied, as appeared to me, too large a share of your thoughts—then excluded other duties, and feelings, as of inferior importance—and, finally, like avarice, growing by what it fed on, usurped, and engrossed *your whole mind. Then* it was that I, by degrees, drew back and feeling, as well as perceiving, the injurious operation of this passion on the feminine part of your character, on your conjugal affections, and domestic habits, I gradually abstained from administering fuel to a fire I believed would consume your happiness; and finally did, indirectly, what I could to check its progress, and thereby prevent the growth of habits which, however they might augment your individual reputation and interest, I was convinced would not contribute to *domestic* quiet.

These, then, being my opinions on this subject generally, in your own case, my dear wife, what is it I think I have to regret, and complain of? ... It is, that the ambition for literary distinction seems now to be occupying nearly all your thoughts, and threatens to destroy your conjugal character—that the apparently unconquerable passion of displaying yourself is the secret principle which of late influences your conduct, and may be traced in very much which you do—that it begets a lust of praise which, like the appetite of the cormorant, is not to be satisfied—that it leads you to prefer the flatteries of the parasites who hang upon you, to the good opinion, and plain but steady esteem of your husband—that it leads you to despise, as you have repeatedly avowed, the conversation and society of your own sex, and will lead you, probably, for the next step (if not already the case) to despise that of your husband—and, on the other hand, that it leads

---

[1]   *your "Traits," and your "Sketch"*   Lydia Sigourney's *Traits of the Aborigines of North America* (1822) and *A Sketch of Connecticut Forty Years Since* (1824).

[2]   *susceptibility of*   Weakness for.

you to prefer, and, in defiance of that modesty, and reserve, which should ever be the ornament of your sex, to court, to make advances to, to solicit the notice, and correspondence, or in another word the praise of, literary men, whose civilities, and flatteries (to a lady especially) may most surely be obtained by the bribe of flattery to begin with. …

I have thought, my dear wife, if you could hear it without pain, and without taking offence, it might be the part[1] of a friend to inform you the public are already taking the liberty to pass those criticisms on your character, which your placing yourself on the conspicuous point of observation you have chosen has in fact *invited them to do*. I have heard, within a year past, and without either soliciting, or going out of my way for them, of remarks made concerning you, by respected persons, but some of whose names I do not know although represented as friends of us both, which, perhaps, it were proper should be repeated to you. A lady and gentleman, visiting us, some years since, "saw enough to satisfy them all was not right," in reference to the appearance of the children: A lady declining to visit you alleged as a reason, "you were always in the clouds"; another thought you had "been very much injured by flattery"; a gentleman, making some comments on the publication of your book, and circumstances connected with it, observed "he shall not like it, if you were his wife"; another expressed the opinion I had "run a great risk in marrying a woman so wise in her own conceit as to think she could never do wrong"; while another uttered the exclamation "the Lord deliver me from marrying a Poetess." …

I do object that you sink the *woman*, and the *wife*, in the *writer*; that you appear to be more anxious, and better pleased to be known for talents as an author, than for virtues as a wife and a mother; that those who will flatter the first have more influence with you, and seem to occupy higher ground in your regard, than your husband. …

… Is it, I say, to be wondered at if, by degrees, my own mind became weaned from its first inclination to indulge and aid you in your peculiar pursuits, which occupying so undue a proportion of your thoughts, I began to consider as the bar to my domestic comfort and happiness, and poetry itself as my enemy? and to

say to myself were you *less of a poet*, how much *more valuable* would you be *as a wife*?

… There may be a spiritual seduction, as well as a corporeal one—a seduction of the mind and affections, as well as of the person. And the public may be the seducer, as well as an individual. Who wants, or would value, a wife, who is to be the public property of the whole community? She who *wishes to belong* to the *public* never should consent to be the private possession of any individual man. She, who is infatuated with the ambition of literary eminence, and to whose happiness popular applause becomes in consequence indispensable, bows down to the God of her idolatry elevated in her own breast, and can neither "love, honour, or obey" a common mortal. It is a most dangerous situation for a married woman, where she yields but her person, and the exterior concessions of married life, to her husband, and goes elsewhere to seek her *chief* pleasures and gratifications, from the society and flatteries of others, and from sources foreign to the domestic fireside. It requires not the spirit of prophecy to foresee the result of such a course. The small remains of affection will soon be weaned from *him* from whom you seek not your happiness. Indifference will succeed. Distaste and dislike ensues—then aversion—domestic discord—hatred——!——!——

Turn then, my dear wife, ere it be too late, and escape from the gulf which is threatening to draw you into its vortex. Return to the affections of your husband, and he will receive you, will cherish, and "comfort, honour, and keep you, forsaking all others"—for none other does he love, as he loves you. …

your husband, who ever loves you,

C. Sigourney.

from Pastoral Letter of the General Association of Congregational Ministers of Massachusetts, July 1837

The following pastoral letter, written by a body of Massachusetts Congregational ministers, was an implicit condemnation of an important speaking tour the Southern antislavery activists Angelina and Sarah Moore Grimké undertook in New England in 1837. The letter condemns any form of antislavery activism that, they

---

1   *part* Role or duty.

argue, undermines "deference to the pastoral office," but it especially castigates women who engage in public speaking. The letter created a stir and was part of an outpouring of antifeminist criticism that prompted the Grimkés to take up as an additional cause women's right to participate in the public sphere. The pastoral letter was reprinted in abolitionist papers along with defenses of the Grimkés; the text below is based on that appearing in *The Liberator* in August 1837.

We invite your attention to the dangers which at present seem to threaten the female character with widespread and permanent injury.

The appropriate duties and influence of woman are clearly stated in the New Testament. Those duties and that influence are unobtrusive and private, but the source of mighty power. When the mild, dependent, softening influence of woman upon the sternness of man's opinions is fully exercised, society feels the effects of it in a thousand forms. The power of woman is in her dependence, flowing from the consciousness of that weakness which God has given her for her protection, and which keeps her in those departments of life that form the character of individuals and of the nation. There are social influences which females use in promoting piety and the great objects of Christian benevolence which we cannot too highly commend. We appreciate the unostentatious prayers and efforts of woman in advancing the cause of religion at home and abroad: in Sabbath-schools; in leading religious inquirers to the pastors for instruction; and in all such associated effort as becomes the modesty of her sex; and earnestly hope that she may abound more and more in these labors of piety and love.

But when she assumes the place and tone of man as a public reformer, our care and protection of her seem unnecessary; we put ourselves in self-defence against her; she yields the power which God has given her for protection, and her character becomes unnatural. If the vine, whose strength and beauty is to lean upon the trellis-work and half conceal its clusters, thinks to assume the independence and the over-shadowing nature of the elm, it will not only cease to bear fruit, but fall in shame and dishonor into the dust. We cannot, therefore, but regret the mistaken conduct of those who encourage females

to bear an obtrusive and ostentatious part in measures of reform, and countenance any of that sex who so far forget themselves as to itinerate[1] in the character of public lecturers and teachers. We especially deplore the intimate acquaintance and promiscuous[2] conversation of females with regard to things "which ought not to be named";[3] by which that modesty and delicacy which is the charm of domestic life, and which constitutes the true influence of woman in society, is consumed, and the way opened, as we apprehend, for degeneracy and ruin. We say these things, not to discourage proper influences against sin, but to secure such reformation as we believe is Scriptural, and will be permanent.

Maria W. Chapman, "The Times That Try Men's Souls"[4] (1839)

Maria Weston Chapman (1806–85) was a prominent abolitionist, and one who was vocal in the controversial fight for women to be included in the antislavery movement. She wrote the following poem in response to the 1837 open letter by the Congregational Ministers of Massachusetts excerpted above. Chapman's poem was later read aloud at the monumental 1848 Seneca Falls women's rights convention.

LANGUAGE OF THE REVOLUTION

Confusion has seized us, and all things go wrong—
The women have leaped from "their spheres";[5]

---

1   *itinerate* Travel.

2   *promiscuous* Undiscriminating; disorderly; mixed.

3   *which ought ... named* See Ephesians 5.3: "But fornication and all uncleanness or covetousness, let it not even be named among you, as is fitting for saints."

4   The poem's title alludes to the first line of Thomas Paine's *The American Crisis* (1776–83), a pamphlet series published in support of the American Revolution.

5   *The women ... "their spheres"* Reference to the earth-centered model of the solar system, according to which the stars are fixed in place on a "celestial sphere" that encircles the earth. Planets and other celestial bodies that move relative to one another in the sky were sometimes referred to as unfixed or wandering stars. See also Shakespeare's *Hamlet* 1.5.22: "Make thy two eyes, like stars, start from their spheres."

And, instead of *fixed* stars, shoot as comets along,
   And, are setting the world by the ears!
5 In courses erratic, they're wheeling through space,
In brainless confusion and meaningless chase.

In vain do our knowing ones try to compute
   Their return to the orbit *designed*;°   *intended*
They're glanced at a moment, then, onward they
   shoot,
10 And are "neither to hold nor to bind";[1]
So freely they move in their chosen ellipse,[2]
The "lords of creation"[3] do fear an eclipse.

They've taken a notion to *speak for themselves*,
   And are wielding the tongue and the pen;
15 They've mounted the rostrum, (the termagant elves!)[4]
   And, (oh horrid!) are talking *to men!*
With faces unblanched in our presence they come,
To harangue us, they say, in behalf of the dumb.[5]

They insist on their *right* to petition and pray;—
20   That St. Paul, in Corinthians, has given them rules
For appearing in public;[6] despite what those say
   Whom we've trained to instruct them in orthodox
      schools.
But vain *such* instructions, if *women* may scan
And quote texts of scripture to favor their plan.

25 Our grandmothers' learning consisted, of yore,
   In spreading their generous boards;°   *tables*

In twisting the distaff,[7] or mopping the floor,
   And *obeying the will of their lords.*
Now, *misses* may reason, and think, and debate,
30 Till unquestioned submission is quite out of date.

Our clergy have preached on the sin and the shame
   Of woman when out of "her sphere,"
And labored *divinely* to ruin her fame,
   And shorten this horrid career.
35 But for spiritual guidance no longer they look
To Folsom, or Winslow, or learned Parson Cooke.[8]

Our *wise* men have tried to exorcise, in vain—
   The turbulent spirit's abroad;
As well might we deal with the fetterless main[9]
40   Or conquer ethereal essence with sword.
Like the devils of Milton,[10] they rise from each blow,
With spirit unbroken insulting the foe.

Our patriot fathers, of eloquent fame,
   Waged war against tangible forms;
45 Ay, *their* foes were men—and if ours were the same,
   We might speedily quiet their storms.
But, ah! their descendants enjoy not such bliss—
The assumptions[11] of Britain were nothing to this.

Could *we* but array all our force in the *field*,
50   We'd teach these usurpers of power
That their bodily safety demands they should yield,
   And in presence of manhood should cower.
But, alas! for our tethered and impotent state—
Chained by notions of knighthood—we can but
   debate.

---

1   *neither ... to bind*   Proverbial: ungovernable.

2   *ellipse*   I.e., oval-shaped orbit.

3   *lords of creation*   Phrase used sarcastically to refer to men, derived from a comment in Samuel Richardson's novel *Clarissa* (1748).

4   *termagant elves*   Overbearing, malicious creatures.

5   *dumb*   Mute; unable to speak.

6   [Chapman's note]   But every woman that prayeth or prophesieth with her head uncovered, dishonoreth her head: for that is even all one as if she were shaven. 1 Corinthians 11.5. [The First Epistle to the Corinthians (traditionally attributed to Paul the Apostle) has several passages dictating how women should comport themselves in public and in the church. The instruction quoted above from 1 Corinthians 11.5 may appear to contradict that given in 1 Corinthians 14.34, which asserts that women should "keep silence in the churches: for it is not permitted unto them to speak."]

7   *distaff*   Tool used for spinning wool or other fibers into thread.

8   *Folsom ... Cooke*   A.A. Folsom, Hubbard Winslow, and Parsons Cooke were among a number of church officials whose sermons opposing women's public speaking were excerpted in the 1837 *Annual Report of the Boston Female Anti-Slavery Society.*

9   *fetterless main*   Unchained ocean.

10   *Milton*   English poet John Milton, best known for his 1667 biblical epic *Paradise Lost*, which tells of the war waged by Satan and his fellow fallen angels against God in heaven.

11   *assumptions*   Unwarranted claims of power.

55 Oh! shade° of the prophet Mahomet, arise![1]   *ghost*
     Place woman again in "her sphere";
And teach that her soul was not born for the skies,
     But to flutter a brief moment here.
The doctrine of Jesus, as preached up by Paul,[2]
60 If embraced in its spirit, will ruin us all.
                                   LORDS OF CREATION

from *Report of the Proceedings of the Colored National Convention Held at Cleveland, Ohio, on Wednesday, September 6, 1848* (1848)

The degree to which the fight for African American rights would include fighting for the rights of African American women was a matter of occasional dispute among black leaders. At the 1848 Colored National Convention all delegates were male, but at least one woman was allowed to speak—Rebecca Sanford, a white Quaker.

... [T]he Rules were suspended[3] to hear remarks from a lady who wished to say something on the subject of the Rights of Woman. The President[4] then introduced to the audience Mrs. Sanford, who made some eloquent remarks, of which the following is a specimen:

> From the birth-day of Eve, the then prototype of woman's destiny, to the flash of the star of Bethlehem,[5] she had been the slave of power and passion. If raised by courage and ambition to the proud trial of heroism, she was still the marred model of her first innocence; if thrown by beauty into the ordeal of temptation, man lost his own dignity in contemning her intellectual weight, and refusing the right to exercise her moral powers; if led by inclination to the penitential life of a recluse, the celestial effulgence of a virtuous innocence was lost, and she only lived out woman's degradation!

> But the day of her regeneration dawned. The Son of God had chosen a mother from among the daughters of Eve! A Saviour, who could have come into this a God-man, ready to act, to suffer, and be·crucified, came in the helplessness of infancy, for woman to cherish and direct. Her *exaltation was consummated!* * * * * *

> True, we ask for the Elective Franchise:[6] for right of property in the marriage covenant, whether earned or bequeathed. True, we pray to co-operate in making the laws we obey; but it is not to domineer, to dictate or assume. We ask it, for it is a right granted by a higher disposer of human events than man. We pray for it now, for there are duties around us, and we weep at our inability.

> And to the delegates, officers, people and spirit of this Convention, I would say, God speed you in your efforts for elevation and freedom; stop not; shrink not; look not back till you have justly secured an *unqualified citizenship of the United States, and those inalienable rights granted you by an impartial Creator.*

Convention passed a vote of thanks to Mrs. Sanford, and also requested a synopsis of her, from which the above are extracts.

A vote of thanks was here passed to John M. Sterling, Esq., of Cleveland, for the presentation of a bundle of books entitled "Slavery as it is."[7]

---

[1] *Oh! shade ... arise* Reference to the false belief, commonly held by Christian Americans in the nineteenth century, that Islam is inherently more sexist than Christianity.

[2] [Chapman's note] There is neither Jew nor Greek, there is neither bond nor free, there is neither male nor female: for ye are all one in Christ Jesus. Galatians 3.28.

[3] *Rules were suspended* I.e., the usual rules governing participation in the convention were momentarily set aside.

[4] *The President* Frederick Douglass.

[5] *the flash ... of Bethlehem* I.e., the birth of Christ.

[6] *Elective Franchise* Right to vote.

[7] *Slavery as it is* Monumental antislavery work *American Slavery as It Is* published in 1839 and written by Theodore Dwight Weld, Angelina Grimké Weld, and Sarah Moore Grimké, which includes hundreds of testimonials to the cruelties of slavery taken from contemporary newspapers and other sources.

Discussion was resumed on the indefinite postponement of the Resolution as to Woman's Right.[1] Objection was made to the resolution, and in favor of its postponement, by Messrs. Langston and Day, on the ground that we had passed one similar, making all colored persons present, delegates to this Convention, and they considered *women persons*.

Frederick Douglass[2] moved to amend the 33d Resolution, by saying that the word *persons* used in the resolution designating delegates, be understood to include *woman*. On the call for the previous question, the Resolution was not indefinitely postponed. Mr. Douglass' amendment was seconded and carried, with three cheers for woman's rights.

from the abstract of Richard Henry Dana Sr., *Woman*, 4 December 1849[3]

Writer, critic, and orator Richard Henry Dana Sr. delivered a series of popular lectures on Shakespeare in a number of American cities; he included in the series a lecture on women in which he articulates a view of gender roles that was commonplace in the mid-nineteenth century. When he delivered this lecture in Philadelphia in 1849, antislavery and women's rights orator Lucretia Mott was in the audience and responded to Dana's claims with a rebuttal lecture of her own, delivered the following week; that lecture, titled *Discourse on Women*, is excerpted below.

The full text of Dana's lecture was not published; the excerpts below are from a newspaper summary of his speech.

Mr. Dana announced, as the subject of his third lecture, woman—the characteristics of the sex, and the essential difference between the nature of man and woman. These differences he considered as grounded in nature, not arbitrary nor the result of accident. ...

The distinctions of sex designate certain indestructible relations, such as that of father, mother etc. These imply an order of beings pre-ordained to such relations, possessing mental as well as physical differences. ... Each sex is peculiar,[4] and has its limited attributes. Woman has hers, and whenever ambition leads her to attempt to act the man, she, so far, ceases to be a woman. ...

Much scorn has been expressed at the doctrine of man's supremacy. No true woman, however, will refuse to acknowledge it. There is a sense of reverence in all of us. It is called into action by beauty, by the innocent face of a child. It makes the strong man gentle before a child, and yielding as a woman in the presence of woman. It gives to woman the power of man in the presence of man. That woman is wanting[5] in something essential who has not this feeling of reverence.

If there is lack of it towards man, there is danger that it may be feeble towards God. Many women have married, but none have loved, without this reverence. ...

... If woman leave the fireside, and turn political reformers, what a fearful state we should be in! Man would be branded[6] by her at the ballot-box—outtalked by her in the marketplace. Such a change would be monstrous. Love would become brutalized—woman would become gross[7] as man; and there would be no longer man and woman, but a new race of moral and mental hybrids. ...

Let woman seek and do that for which she is physically and spiritually pre-configured. To the general rule of man's supremacy there are exceptions. Genius is one, but it is independent, and only makes the individual in whom it resides its organ. Woman need not be lost sight of; but many seek notoriety, and, if they can write a love-tale, or pen half-a-dozen stanzas, are pleased to become the gaudy centre of the public gaze. There is too great a propensity among them to make duties

---

1   [Editor's note]   33rd Resolution: Whereas, we fully believe in the equality of the sexes, therefore, Resolved, That we hereby invite females hereafter to take part in our deliberations.

2   *Frederick Douglass* Influential abolitionist orator and writer, who had fled slavery in 1838.

3   The abstract excerpted here first appeared in the *Evening Bulletin* in December 1849; the present text is based upon that reprinted in Francis Brewster's book *The Philosophy of Human Nature* (1851).

4   *peculiar* Distinct (i.e., from the other sex).

5   *wanting* Lacking.

6   *branded* Disgraced.

7   *gross* Vulgar; unrefined.

abroad,[1] and the womanly attributes are sacrificed to this desire for notoriety. A refined man then feels that something of beauty has gone forth from her. Woman should only cultivate whatever is distinctly womanly. When she begins to talk of rights, she becomes, not manly, but *man-ish*. She seeks notoriety; man seeks fame. …

The true woman is a beautiful being. I pray she may not turn iconoclast, and break the image of man's lower worship. Let her be content to be the softener of the manlier soul, and not come with us into the strife of the world. Let her not come into the glare of the sun; but when the sun goes down, let her appear to grow brighter, like the stars, as the sun recedes. Let her not strive to be the sun, but rather the gentle moon, with face veiled at first, but growing brighter. We watch for her coming, and still call her the new moon.

from Lucretia Mott, *Discourse on Women*, 17 December 1849

Prominent Quaker activist Lucretia Mott was renowned for her oratorical skill, which she employed in favor of a number of causes including abolition and women's rights. Her speech excerpted here, *Discourse on Women*, was framed as a rebuttal to a lecture on women's roles (excerpted above) that had been delivered by popular critic Richard Henry Dana Sr. earlier in the month. Mott's rebuttal lecture was so successful that it was published in pamphlet form the following year.

… Why should not woman seek to be a reformer? If she is to shrink from being such an iconoclast as shall "break the image of man's lower worship," as so long held up to view; if she is to fear to exercise her reason, and her noblest powers, lest she should be thought to "attempt to act the man," and not "acknowledge his supremacy"; if she is to be satisfied with the narrow sphere assigned her by man, nor aspire to a higher, lest she should transcend the bounds of female delicacy; truly it is a mournful prospect for woman. We would admit all the difference that our great and beneficent Creator has made in the relation of man and woman, nor would we seek to disturb this relation; but we deny that the present position of woman is her true sphere of usefulness: nor will she attain to this sphere until the disabilities and disadvantages, religious, civil, and social, which impede her progress, are removed out of her way. These restrictions have enervated her mind and paralysed her powers. … As it is desirable that man should act a manly and generous part, not "mannish," so let woman be urged to exercise a dignified and womanly bearing, not womanish. Let her cultivate all the graces and proper accomplishments of her sex, but let not these degenerate into a kind of effeminacy in which she is satisfied to be the mere plaything or toy of society, content with her outward adornings, and with the tone of flattery and fulsome adulation too often addressed to her. True, nature has made a difference in her configuration, her physical strength, her voice—and we ask no change, we are satisfied with nature. But how has neglect and mismanagement increased this difference! It is our duty to develop these natural powers, by suitable exercise, so that they may be strengthened "by reason of use." In the ruder[2] state of society, woman is made to bear heavy burdens, while her "lord and master" walks idly by her side. In the civilization to which we have attained, if cultivated and refined woman would bring all her powers into use, she might engage in pursuits which she now shrinks from as beneath her proper vocation. The energies of men need not then be wholly devoted to the counting house and common business of life, in order that women in fashionable society may be supported in their daily promenades and nightly visits to the theatre and ball room. …

The question is often asked, "What does woman want, more than she enjoys? What is she seeking to obtain? Of what rights is she deprived? What privileges are withheld from her?" I answer, she asks nothing as favor, but as right; she wants to be acknowledged a moral, responsible being. She is seeking not to be governed by laws in the making of which she has no voice. She is deprived of almost every right in civil society, and is a cypher[3] in the nation, except in the right of presenting a petition. In religious society

---

1   *make duties abroad*   Engage in activities outside the home.

2   *ruder*   Less refined; uncivilized.

3   *cypher*   Zero; useless or nonexistent thing.

her disabilities, as already pointed out, have greatly retarded her progress. Her exclusion from the pulpit or ministry—her duties marked out for her by her equal brother man, subject to creeds, rules, and disciplines made for her by him—this is unworthy her true dignity. In marriage, there is assumed superiority, on the part of the husband, and admitted inferiority, with a promise of obedience, on the part of the wife. This subject calls loudly for examination, in order that the wrong may be redressed. Customs suited to darker ages in Eastern countries are not binding upon enlightened society. The solemn covenant of marriage may be entered into without these lordly assumptions, and humiliating concessions and promises. …

It is with reluctance that I make the demand for the political rights of woman, because this claim is so distasteful to the age. Woman shrinks, in the present state of society, from taking any interest in politics. …

Walker, of Cincinnati, in his *Introduction to American Law*,[1] says:

> With regard to political rights, females form a positive exception to the general doctrine of equality. They have no part or lot in the formation or administration of government. They cannot vote or hold office. We require them to contribute their share in the way of taxes, to the support of government, but allow them no voice in its direction. We hold them amenable to the laws when made, but allow them no share in making them. This language, applied to males, would be the exact definition of political slavery; applied to females, custom does not teach us so to regard it.

Woman, however, is beginning so to regard it. …

… [T]he demand for a more extended education will not cease until girls and boys have equal instruction in all the departments of useful knowledge. We have as yet no high school for girls in this state. …

Women's property has been taxed, equally with that of men's, to sustain colleges endowed by the states; but they have not been permitted to enter those high seminaries of learning. Within a few years, however, some colleges have been instituted, where young women are admitted, nearly upon equal terms with young men; and numbers are availing themselves of their long denied rights. This is among the signs of the times, indicative of an advance for women. The book of knowledge is not opened to her in vain. Already is she aiming to occupy important posts of honor and profit in our country. We have three female editors in our state—some in other states of the Union. Numbers are entering the medical profession—one received a diploma last year;[2] others are preparing for a like result.

Let woman then go on—not asking as favor, but claiming as right, the removal of all the hindrances to her elevation in the scale of being—let her receive encouragement for the proper cultivation of all her powers, so that she may enter profitably into the active business of life; employing her own hands, in ministering to her necessities, strengthening her physical being by proper exercise, and observance of the laws of health. Let her not be ambitious to display a fair hand, and to promenade the fashionable streets of our city, but rather, coveting earnestly the best gifts, let her strive to occupy such walks in society, as will befit her true dignity in all the relations of life. …

"Woman's Emancipation" and "Fashions for August," *Harper's New Monthly Magazine* (August 1851)

The influential *Harper's New Monthly Magazine* was founded in June 1850, and for the first few years of its existence much of its content was reprinted from British periodicals. The following cartoon and accompanying article first appeared in *Punch*, a popular London satirical publication with a generally conservative bent. In this satire of the women's rights movement, the women are depicted wearing exaggerated versions of the "Bloomer" costume, a short-skirt-and-pants combination worn by a small number of reformers for a brief period in the early 1850s.

---

[1]   *Introduction to American Law*   1837 law textbook by Timothy Walker.

[2]   *one received … last year*   In 1849, Elizabeth Blackwell became the first woman to receive a medical degree in the United States, having attended Geneva Medical College.

WOMAN'S EMANCIPATION.
(BEING A LETTER ADDRESSED TO MR. PUNCH, WITH A DRAWING, BY A STRONG-MINDED AMERICAN WOMAN.)

IT is quite easy to realize the considerable difficulty that the natives of this old country are like to have in estimating the rapid progress of ideas on all subjects among us, the Anglo-Saxons of the Western World. Mind travels with us on a rail-car, or a high-pressure river-boat. The snags and sawyers of prejudice, which render so dangerous the navigation of Time's almighty river, whose water-power has toppled over these giant-growths of the world, without being able to detach them from the congenial mud from which they draw their nutriment, are dashed aside or run down in the headlong career of the United States mind.

We laugh to scorn the dangers of popular effervescence. Our almighty-browed and cavernous-eyed statesmen sit, heroically, on the safety-valve, and the mighty ark of our vast Empire of the West moves on at a pressure on the square inch which would rend into shivers the rotten boiler-plates of your outworn states of the Old World.

To use a phrase which the refined manners of our ladies have banished from the drawing-room, and the saloon of the boarding-house, we go ahead. And our progress is the progress of all—not of high and low, for we have abolished the odious distinction—but of man, woman, and child, each in his or her several sphere.

Our babies are preternaturally sharp, and highly independent from the cradle. The high-souled American boy will not submit to be whipped at school. That punishment is confined to the lower animals.

But it is among our sex—among women (for I am a woman, and my name is THEODOSIA EUDOXIA BANG, of Boston, U.S., Principal of the Homeopathic and Collegiate Thomsonian Institute for developing the female mind in that intellectual city) that the stranger may realize, in the most convincing manner, the progressional influences of the democratic institutions it is our privilege to live under.

An American female—for I do not like the term Lady, which suggests the outworn distinctions of feudalism—can travel alone from one end of the States to the other; from the majestic waters of Niagara to the mystic banks of the Yellowstone, or the rolling prairies of Texas. The American female delivers lectures, edits newspapers, and similar organs of opinion, which exert so mighty a leverage on the national mind of our great people, is privileged to become a martyr to her principles, and to utter her soul from the platform, by the side of the gifted POE or the immortal PEABODY. All this in these old countries is the peculiar privilege of man, as opposed to woman. The female is consigned to the slavish duties of the house. In America the degrading cares of the household are comparatively unknown to our sex. The American wife resides in a boarding-house, and, consigning the petty cares of daily life to the helps of the establishment, enjoys leisure for higher pursuits, and can follow her vast aspirations upward, or in any other direction.

We are emancipating ourselves, among other badges of the slavery of feudalism, from the inconvenient dress of the European female. With man's functions, we have asserted our right to his garb, and especially to that part of it which invests the lower extremities. With this great symbol, we have adopted others—the hat, the cigar, the paletot or round jacket. And it is generally calculated that the dress of the Emancipated American female is quite pretty—as becoming in all points as it is manly and independent. I inclose a drawing made by my gifted fellow-citizen, INCREASEN TARBOX, of Boston, U.S., for the Free Woman's Banner, a periodical under my conduct, aided by several gifted women of acknowledged progressive opinions.

I appeal to my sisters of the Old World, with confidence, for their sympathy and their countenance in the struggle in which we are engaged, and which will soon be found among them also. For I feel that I have a mission across the broad Atlantic, and the steamers are now running at reduced fares. I hope to rear the standard of Female Emancipation on the roof of the Crystal Palace, in London Hyde Park. (Empty wit may sneer at its form, which is bifurcate. And why not? MOHAMMED warred under the Petticoat of his wife KADIGA. The American female Emancipist marches on her holy war under the distinguishing garment of her husband. In the compartment devoted to the United States in your Exposition, my sisters of the old country may see this banner by the side of a uniform of female freedom—such as my drawing represents—the garb of martyrdom for a month; the trappings of triumph for all ages of the future!

THEODOSIA E. BANG, M.A.,
M.C.P., Φ.Δ.K., K.L.M., &c., &c. (of Boston, U.S.)

Marriage and Domestic Life

from T.S. Arthur, *The Young Wife's Book; A Manual of Moral, Religious and Domestic Duties* (1836)

A prolific and popular author primarily of moralistic fiction, T.S. Arthur was best-known for his influential temperance novel *Ten Nights in a Bar-Room and What I Saw There* (1854). His first book, *The Young Wife's Book*, is an advice manual offering the sort of conventional wisdom that was typical of such guides in the mid-nineteenth century. It was sufficiently successful that Arthur followed it with a sequel, *The Young Husband's Book* (1836).

from THE DUTIES OF A WIFE

... What is in that solemn moment pledged to the object who receives at the altar a woman's plighted faith? Do you not promise to obey, to serve, love, and honour him? To comfort him in sickness and in health, and to forsake all others for him alone?

After a vow thus made, the duties of a wife, like her affections, must be unalienable. No longer seeking individual enjoyment, her pleasures must spring from participation, and her happiness be the reflected bliss arising from sharing the peace of another. Her cares also, reposing in another bosom, are divested of half their thorns, and her comforts, springing from the same cause, are multiplied in enjoyment, and sweet in remembrance.

The matrimonial duties are reciprocal—they consist in mutual forbearance and mutual offices of love and kindness. Those of a wife are the most strongly enforced, for to hers are added by Divine command, that of obedience also. *Obedience!* start not at the word which generally sounds so harsh to a female ear, but rather ask yourself if it be difficult to pay it to the commands of affection, to the wishes of tenderness, to the looks of love? May no other obedience be ever exacted from you; but remember that the matrimonial path is not, any more than another, strewn with thornless roses; and if fate should decree that some of them are to be pointed at our bosom, recollect also that religion, fortitude, and patience will blunt their edge, although they may not be able to heal entirely the wounds inflicted by them. ...

from Matthew Hale Smith, *Counsels Addressed to Young Ladies and Young Men* (1846)

The book excerpted below is based on a lecture given by prominent Unitarian minister and author Matthew Hale Smith in April 1846, and in its full form includes advice for young unmarried women, young unmarried men, "young married persons," and young parents. Such lectures were widely popular during the mid-nineteenth century; the published *Counsels* opens with a testimonial from former president John Quincy Adams, who believed that its content would be "eminently useful in promoting the cause of religion and good morals."

MOMENTOUS CONSIDERATIONS

You are always in peril. Attending dangers, which never leave you a moment, demand of you great watchfulness and prudence. You possess not that variety of occupation which is allowed to young men. You cannot, like them, change your place often, or your calling. Temptations from which they are exempt, meet you on every side. The result of imprudence, or folly, or indiscretion, can be repaired much more easily in them than in you. The principle is unnatural and wrong, yet it is nevertheless true, that the world is more ready to forgive and forget the wrong doings of a young man than of a young woman. They will sooner restore a young man, who has erred from the path of right, than overlook or extenuate the fault of a young woman. One false step blasts her forever. With scorn her name is mentioned. Coldly is she passed by former associates and intimate friends. Circles that once she adorned are barred forever against her. Upon her vows of reformation and sighs of penitence, little reliance is placed. Yet into those very circles from which she is forever to be an outcast, a young man, stained with sin and familiar with those steps that take hold on hell, will be admitted in favor, and welcomed with smiles.

A young man may lose his good name in one country, and then fly to another. In that distant land, no reports of his deeds may be heard. In exile he may wear off the stain thrown upon his character; he may traverse continents; oceans may roll between him and his conduct. By great diligence and circumspection, by years of undeviating propriety and great moral honesty, he can regain public confidence. The past will be forgiven, and all against him will be blotted from memory. High honor will reward his virtuous exertions, and a warm welcome await his return to a moral and religious life.

One Misstep. It is not thus with a young woman. Her deeds of wrong are not forgotten. The stains upon her character and reputation cannot be removed. As in a rock, with the pen of a diamond, are they written. No distant time will obliterate, no abject penitence will atone. For female degradation no redeeming power on earth can be found. No fount below can, by its flow, wipe out the spot. When she falls, she falls to rise no more. No change of place—no distant future—no holy life can efface the remembrance of her deeds, or bring her back to stations of respect. The reproach of friends must she bear, and bear it while life endures. The jeers of the world—the stings of an accusing conscience—all must be met day by day. Her refuge is in the grave—which is but the avenue to the Judgment and the retributions of the Eternal World. …

from COUNSELS TO A YOUNG HUSBAND

RESPECT THE RIGHTS OF YOUR WIFE

A wife has rights and feelings. She yielded neither in marriage. The wife is the crown of her husband; and her position and her honor must, in a great measure, decide his own. Few families are prosperous in which a wife is either a slave or a cipher.[1] …

MAKE A SUITABLE PROVISION FOR YOUR HOUSEHOLD

"If any man provide not for his own, even for those of his own house, he has denied the faith, and is worse than an infidel"[2]—so important is this duty in the sight of God. A married man no longer lives to himself. His time, his talents, his best energies, belong to his wife and family. Custom makes the wife dependent; and no mark of detestation should be deeper or more broad than that placed upon the man who is unmindful of the wants of his family. A woman must toil hard to secure the necessaries of life when the support of the family falls upon her. For the same work, she receives a compensation much below that allotted to a man. …

from COUNSELS TO A YOUNG WIFE

BE OBEDIENT

So God expressly commands. To love, cherish, and obey, was your bridal vow, voluntarily imposed upon yourself. This law does not resolve you into a slave, or your husband into a despot. Your relation has mutual rights, as well as mutual duties. But "the head of the woman is the man":[3] he must control and direct. In the kind of business he pursues, in the place in which he will pursue that business, it becomes the wife to submit at once and cheerfully. No doubt, this often involves great sacrifice on your part: but to leave father and mother, is a part of the marriage contract; and, if oceans roar between you and those you love, you must obey, if duty calls. In the style of living, and in the expenditures incident to your home, his will, and not your simple taste or wish, must prevail. A prompt and ready acquiescence in the desires and all the reasonable and right wishes of your husband, is for your peace as well as your duty. …

---

1   *cipher* Zero; nothing.

2   *If any man … infidel* 1 Timothy 5.8.

3   *the head … the man* See 1 Corinthians 11.3: "But I would have you know, that the head of every man is Christ; and the head of the woman is the man; and the head of Christ is God."

Armand Lanusse, "Epigram" (1845)

Armand Lanusse (1810–68) was one of seventeen contributors to *Les Cenelles*, an 1845 volume generally considered the first anthology of poetry written by African Americans. Catholic, French-speaking residents of New Orleans, the authors were "free people of color," a designation that generally applied to people of mixed racial background who occupied an uncertain social position between white and enslaved black society. Many of the poems in *Les Cenelles* express anxiety about the extralegal practice of *placage*, by which free mixed-race women entered into informal, marriage-like relationships with wealthy white men. The following poem is a 1949 translation from the French by American poet Langston Hughes.

"Do you not wish to renounce the Devil?"
   Asked a good priest of a woman of evil
Who had so many sins that every year
They cost her endless remorse and fear.
5 "I wish to renounce him forever," she said,
"But that I may lose every urge to be bad,
Before pure grace takes me in hand,
Shouldn't I show my daughter how to get a man?"

from Catharine Beecher, *A Treatise on Domestic Economy, for the Use of Young Ladies at Home and at School* (1841, 1856)

Catharine Beecher (1800–78) was a leading figure in the reform of women's education that took place in the early nineteenth century. The Hartford Female Seminary she founded in 1823 was one of many similar institutions that offered students a novel blend of academic, moral, domestic, and physical education. While the existence of such institutions allowed a small number of middle-class girls a much greater degree of education than they would have been able to attain in the previous century, these schools also tended to emphasize the goal of training students to become proper mothers and homemakers, rendering intellectual pursuits subservient to the ideals of domestic

femininity. In her *Treatise on Domestic Economy*, Beecher provides a practical guide on household management, elaborating in its preface on her theory of women's education—especially domestic education—as essential to the collective happiness of the home.

from PREFACE TO THE THIRD EDITION

The author of this work was led to attempt it by discovering, in her extensive travels, the deplorable sufferings of multitudes of young wives and mothers, from the combined influence of *poor health, poor domestics, and a defective domestic education*. The number of young women whose health is crushed, ere the first few years of married life are past, would seem incredible to one who has not investigated this subject, and it would be vain to attempt to depict the sorrow, discouragement, and distress experienced in most families where the wife and mother is a perpetual invalid.

The writer became early convinced that this evil results mainly from the fact that young girls, especially in the more wealthy classes, *are not trained for their profession*. In early life, they go through a course of school training which results in great debility of constitution, while, at the same time, their physical and domestic education is almost wholly neglected. Thus they enter on their most arduous and sacred duties so inexperienced and uninformed, and with so little muscular and nervous strength, that probably there is not *one chance in ten* that young women of the present day will pass through the first years of married life without such prostration of health and spirits as makes life a burden to themselves, and, it is to be feared, such as seriously interrupts the confidence and happiness of married life.

The measure which, more than any other, would tend to remedy this evil, would be to place *domestic economy* on an equality with the other sciences in female schools. This should be done because it *can* be properly and systematically taught (not *practically*, but as a *science*), as much so as *political economy* or *moral* science, or any other branch of study; because it embraces knowledge, which will be needed by young women at all times and in all places; because this science can never be *properly* taught until it is made a branch of *study*; and because this method will secure a dignity and importance in the estimation of young girls, which can never be accorded while they perceive their teachers and parents practically attaching more value to every other department of science than this. When young ladies are taught the construction of their own bodies, and all the causes in domestic life which tend to weaken the constitution; when they are taught rightly to appreciate and learn the most convenient and economical modes of performing all family duties, and of employing time and money; and when they perceive the true estimate accorded to these things by teachers and friends, the grand cause of this evil will be removed. Women will be trained to secure, as of first importance, a strong and healthy constitution, and all those rules of thrift and economy that will make domestic duty easy and pleasant.

Gender Crossing

anonymous, "The Man Who Thought Himself a Woman," *The Knickerbocker* (December 1857)

> While fictional accounts of cross-dressing and gender passing in which characters pass as men were common in the nineteenth century, similar accounts in which characters cross-dress or pass as women are far less so. The following short story appeared anonymously in *The Knickerbocker*, a literary periodical that frequently published the work of such prominent authors as Washington Irving, Henry Wadsworth Longfellow, and Lydia Maria Child.

Japhet Colbones was a very odd individual. All his ancestors were odd individuals, as far back as they can be remembered. His great-grandfather, at the age of seventy-one, built a hut in a patch of thick woods, leaving a handsome and comfortable home, a wife, children, and grand-children, to live alone by himself. He even forbade the visits of his family, though a favorite daughter ventured sometimes to present herself on the forbidden premises, till one day he brought out his gun and threatened to shoot her if she came again. At long intervals he would return to his old home, but he required to be received in all respects as a stranger. Dire was his wrath if anyone called him "father"; and the little tow-headed[1] urchins on the premises were taught, with their catechism, not to notice the old man whenever they should see him, nor, on peril of their lives, to call him by the endearing cognomen of grand-daddy.

Nobody could account for this freak[2] taken in his old age. His forest residence was uncouth, irregular—lighted by an unsheltered opening, filled with logs and coarse contrivances for furniture. There, in his rude[3] fire-place, he cooked the game that he killed with his own hands. Whenever he was out of necessary food he supplied himself from his well-filled larder at home, the servants or the daughters knowing what provision he wanted by the particular basket or utensil he carried.

It was useless for the old wife, poor thing! to follow him mutely, the longing in her heart to comfort and to live with him, plainly written on her face. He deigned to take no notice of her whatever, except to frown if he met her eye; and thus he lived till he died.

The son, grandfather to Japhet, was not a whit behind his father in his oddities. He caused a coat to be made wherein were introduced seven different colors, and would not kill or allow to be killed on his premises anything that had life. Consequently his family were Grahamites[4] against their will. Cats and dogs swarmed in all directions, and it took nearly everything that was raised to keep his constantly-multiplying herds. None who lived in Rattle-Snake Village can have forgotten the extraordinary sensation caused by his death, nor with what gusto scores of useless animals were sacrificed to the manes[5] of the departed oddity.

Number three, father of Japhet, was in his way an original and an eccentric. His tastes travelled bookward. Not an auction took place in the neighboring city that he did not attend, and purchase every leather-covered and worm-eaten volume that could be found,

---

[1] *tow-headed* Having light-colored and messy hair.

[2] *freak* Whim.

[3] *rude* Crude.

[4] *Grahamites* Reference to the "Graham diet," developed in the early nineteenth century by the minister and social reformer Sylvester Graham (1794–1851), which advocated the consumption of only plain, vegetable-based foods, such as the crackers that have since come to be known as graham crackers.

[5] *manes* Spirit, especially of an ancestor.

oftentimes paying the most ridiculous prices, extorted by those who took advantage of his weakness. He is living now, a pale, loose-jointed man, a little weak in the knees, with an abundant shock of iron-gray locks; large, flatulent-looking[1] blue-white eyes, a prominent nose, and a peaked chin. In his house books abounded. Not a closet, chest, trunk, drawer, or shelf but was filled with flapping leaves. The children kicked and tore them about the premises, for the old man seemed to set no store by them after he had made them his own by way of purchase. All the sentimental maids and youths came to Squire Colbones for mental aliment, and I am not sure that the collection was the choicest in the world. Many of them were never returned; and as Mrs. Colbones said, when the Squire grumbled, she was sure it was a mercy, for they eat, and drank, and slept on books now; and if they were all returned they'd have to build additions every year for the sake of getting a room to themselves.

All the male members of the Colbones family were, as it is generally expressed, "lacking somewhere." The women were generally good, harmless creatures, with few idiosyncrasies, and feeble mental constitutions, willing to put up with the queer freaks of the masculines, and always ready with a defence or an excuse when they were particularly disagreeable. They did hope, however, the four maiden aunts belonging to the last generation but one, that Japhet, the most promising scion of the family and the only son of his father (seven daughters preceding him), would be free from all singularities, queerities, quips, quirks, and oddities; and while they watched him with fearful misgivings, they yet said to themselves and to each other: "He looks so different from the Colbones, and so much like the Rashers (his mother's side), that I guess there won't be any streaks in him." Japhet was rather a fine-looking boy. The only draw-back to his good appearance was a head of somewhat unwieldy size, and whitish blue eyes, exactly like his father's. With books, of course, he was on intimate terms, they having been his playthings from his earliest years—indeed, he was seldom seen without them. Manfully he mastered his "abs" and "ebs,"[2] and hurried forward to the first class in the primary school. So rapid was his progress, that everybody marvelled, and an itinerant phrenologist[3] examined his cranium for nothing, because, he said: "One did not often meet with such splendid development of brain." Forthwith he declared that Japhet must go to college; that he shouldn't wonder if the boy was a marvel; yes, indeed, he fully expected to ask him for an office when he should advance to the dignity of being President of the United States. The elder Colbones was in raptures, and almost went to the city heels over head in his anxiety to buy more books, that the sciences and ologies might be crammed into that capacious brain. Only one person professed to have no faith in the predictions of the man with the skulls, old goody[4] Granger—the matron of the poor-house.

"La!" she would say, putting her thumbs on her hips, "do you s'pose a Colbones'll ever come to anything? Talk about his brain; anybody might see it was rickety. Take my word for 't, he'll be as much of a fool as the rest on 'em."

Suddenly, when he was fourteen, Master Japhet refused to go to school any longer. His mother coaxed him, his father beat him, but all to no purpose. He had learning enough, he said; he meant to go to farming, or anything else he liked. He had his way; left the red schoolhouse; made up faces at the teacher when he asked him why; bought himself yarn and knitting-needles, and pestered his mother till she taught him how to knit. From knitting he went to embroidery, and during the long winter evenings made fancy seats for chairs, table-covers, and everything else he could think of, saying that he was preparing himself for future housekeeping. His family grew accustomed to his odd ways, and his sisters happy that instead of teasing them as other brothers did their sisters, he sat down with them like a real good boy, and when they were in a quandary, helped them out. Japhet was something of a genius, in his way, in devising patterns and drawing them; and he often made a sixpence in this manner. As he grew older he became more and more fond of his needle and of indoor employment. The moment his labor was over

---

1   *flatulent-looking*   I.e., puffy.

2   *"abs" and "ebs"*   Reference to a form of pronunciation exercise found in spelling books of the period.

3   *phrenologist*   Practitioner of the pseudo-science of phrenology, which proposed that one's intellectual and psychological qualities could be ascertained based on the shape of one's head.

4   *goody*   Old-fashioned term of address for a respectable older woman.

in the field, he would hie to his own little room, and there, cutting out articles to please his fancy, stitch away at them with all the ardor of a young mother shaping a dress for her first-born. Singular as it may seem, he was not ashamed to have his handiwork shown at the county fair, with his name attached, and contemplated a handsome quilt, which he had contributed, with as much satisfaction as a first-rate machinist gazes at his complicated cogs and wheels, shafts and pulleys.

Everybody laughed at Japhet, though they said it was to be expected, coming from so odd a family. The girls made all manner of sport of him, especially Nanny Halliday and Nelly Gray, two young ladies who were quite near neighbors of the odd family, and to whom Japhet distributed his smiles and nodded his capacious head.

"Don't you say another word to me about Japhet Colbones," cried Nanny, in great wrath, to someone who quizzed her. "Good laws! ketch me to have a woman for a husband when there are plenty of men about."

"But jest see what a grand farm you'd get, Nanny," pursued her tormentor; "and if ever you got tired cutting out, makin' and mendin', why, you could jest hand the needle-book over to your husband, and he'd do it tidy as a mitten."

"Oh! do hush," cried Nanny with spirit, her red cheeks growing redder; "I wouldn't have Japhet Colbones if there wasn't another fellow in the world."

Just then Tiddy Grant came into the little cottage. Tiddy was twenty-four, lean, poor, and worked very hard. Her face had a sort of sharp prettiness that sometimes falls to the lot of thin people. She had been washing, and came to rest herself in talking with her neighbors.

"Poh!" she exclaimed, overhearing the last remark, "you're a great fool then, if he's asked you, I'm sure. Catch me to refuse a young man that's got nothing suspicious about him but a few little oddities. I'm sure Japhet's a very good farmer, and a very good-looking man too; and as for his sewing propensities, I know some men that had better be using needle and thread than be lounging in bar-rooms and making their wives miserable."

Little she thought that Japhet, now a young man of nineteen, was hidden in the next room, and that he

had indulged in another odd freak in prevailing upon an old friend to propose for him in this novel manner.

"Bless us, Japhet!" exclaimed his sisters as he came down the next morning in his newest suit of blue, with bright buttons, "an't you going to work?"

"I'm going to get married," said Japhet shortly.

Such a look of consternation! The girls caught their breath and stared at him stupidly.

"For pity's sake, who to?" queried the oldest.

"Tiddy Grant," he responded, pulling up his dicky[1] before the little glass.

"Oh! g-r-a-c-i-o-u-s!" cried his eldest sister again. "Why she's an old maid."

"So are you!" responded the young man quietly.

"Well, if I am, I arn't going to get married to a little boy," retorted his sister sharply.

"Nor an't she," replied Japhet, giving a final look at the glass.

"I don't believe it; it's only one of his odd freaks," said another sister, watching him as he went down the road.

"It'll be just like him exactly, to bring that mean, poor-spirited thing here this very day," exclaimed another; "and we can't have a wedding, or company, or anything."

"Like's not he'll find her at the wash-tub, and marry her in a check apron," said the younger sister, who had never liked Tiddy, because she was poor and mean[2] in her appearance.

Off posted[3] Japhet to the little brown cottage where lived Tiddy Grant. At a long table her mother and herself were ironing, for they took in washing for their living. Both paused when they saw the young man; and Tiddy, bethinking herself of yesterday's speech, blushed till she looked almost handsome.

"It's a nice day!" said Japhet.

"Very," echoed mother and daughter.

"A fine day to be married in," suggested the young man.

Tiddy looked up in astonishment and then looked down in confusion.

---

[1]   *dicky*   Stiff, false shirt front that was worn as part of male formal attire.

[2]   *mean*   Lowly or unpleasant.

[3]   *posted*   Hurried.

"If you'll have me Tiddy, say 'Yes,' and put your bonnet on; we'll go right to the minister's."

The poor girl was confounded; she never had received an offer before in her life. So she stood awkwardly, catching by the table; then in her consternation, took hold of a hot iron, cried, "Oh!" and sank upon a seat paralyzed.

"I an't got much time," said Japhet very coolly, rising; "and I'm determined to be married today or never. If you'll have me, here I am; but you must make haste or we shan't be home in time for dinner."

"Law, Tiddy, are you dumb?"[1] exclaimed old Mrs. Grant in an agony of fear that her daughter would lose the chance; "do say 'Yes!' and done with it."

"Yes, and done with it," murmured Tiddy faintly.

"Well, now don't lose any time; I've got some hoeing to do to that patch of corn at the left of the house. I'll wait till you put on your bonnet and shawl."

Tiddy walked in a dream to the door to go upstairs. Then turning irresolutely, she said, timidly: "What will your sisters think?"

"Law! Tiddy, do hurry!" cried old Mrs. Grant, while Japhet said quite coolly: "I never ask them what they think, or anybody else."

Another moment of indecision, and Tiddy was arraying herself in her best gown—a shilling print[2]—trembling, half-laughing, half-crying. It was so strange! so odd! but then everybody knew Japhet came of an odd family.

Japhet got home with his wife just as his father drove up with a new cart-load of books. Sisters and mother looked daggers at the double infliction. Old Mr. Colbones glanced suspiciously at Tiddy Grant, now Tiddy Colbones.

"Now you can all have your look, and say your say," exclaimed Japhet; "Tiddy is my wife. I've jest been and married her, and brought her home to dinner; I hope it's most ready."

The elder Colbones spoke not a word, but sending for someone to unload his books, he went complacently into the house. Poor Mrs. Colbones, on the contrary, fretted and fumed. "What did Japhet want to be such a confounded fool for? Wasn't the house

already full from cellar floor to clapboard with trash? and now he must go to bringing more."

Tiddy had not been in her new home a week before the sisters of the new bridegroom held a consultation, with the doors shut.

"I'm sure no such thing ever happened before," whispered the eldest, "and I'm almost confident that hussy has taken it."

"And don't you think," said Sarah, the next eldest, "two pair of my very finest stockings are gone."

"And my nicest, newest flannel petticoat," chimed in another. "And my blue and green striped calico!"

"Did mother tell you she missed two of her best caps?"

"No! the laws, you don't say so!"

"Yes, and like's not the hussy has carried them to the old woman's, at home," chimed in another.

"Well, I declare! to think that our Japhet should go and marry a thief!"

All this while, poor Tiddy was scrubbing away downstairs (for work was her life), helping her new mother-in-law. She had really found in Japhet a tolerable companion and a very industrious husband. She had not yet become sufficiently accustomed to her sisters to like their ways; she even felt nervous and uncomfortable in their presence. How would her indignation have been roused could she have known that they suspected her of stealing! She noticed their growing coldness, their avoidance of her, and spoke to her husband about it. His only reply was: "I'm going to build a house; wait awhile."

With his father's aid, Japhet set himself to work in earnest, and near the close of the harvest he had ready a pretty little cottage, with a garden spot attached, and a fine orchard in the rear. The land was his father's gift; the house he built with his own money, and furnished it neatly. By this time Tiddy was looked upon with less suspicion by the members of the odd family. They had searched her drawers in her absence, and found means to inspect even the old widow's wardrobe. Finding none of the missing clothes, they contented themselves with calling it a mystery, or supposing that in their absence some strolling thief had robbed them. As the family was over large, Tiddy suggested to her husband, that two of his sisters should come and stay with them, adding that "she might be glad of their services before a great while."

---

[1]   *dumb*   Mute; unable to speak.

[2]   *shilling print*   Inexpensive printed fabric.

"Do just as you please," was his reply.

So Drusy, the eldest, and Fanny, the next in age, were invited to become inmates of the new house. The girls very willingly accepted the offer, as their father was disclosing some new freak of eccentricity every day. He had recently had every door taken from its hinges, and the house was uncomfortably cold, until he had a mind to put them on again.

Some years had passed, and Tiddy had often congratulated herself on her good fortune. She was the mother of two handsome little girls, who were the delight of their parents; and Japhet, though very odd and singular, had developed no very unusual trait of character. Drusy and Fanny, still unmarried, lived with them yet.

One pleasant morning Drusy came down stairs in no very amiable mood.

"I can't find my best black silk!" she cried in consternation; "the one I earned myself. I've looked for it high and low. And my nice tucked[1] skirt is gone, too; and Fanny's pink pelerine[2] and best bonnet. What shall we do? I'm sure they were all in my drawers yesterday!"

Tiddy was astonished as well as they. She left her work, and commenced searching. In every nook and corner of the house they hunted, turned chests wrong side out, emptied drawers, stripped closets, but nothing could they find of the missing articles. There was no other recourse for Drusy, the poor thing, but to cry; and at it she went, bemoaning her ill-fortune in the most extravagant manner.

It certainly was very mysterious. None but the usual inmates had been in the house. Tiddy searched her own part of the premises as faithfully as every other. But what would she want of the dress or the vandyke?[3] She could get such things whenever she wished; and Drusy did not even suspect her this time: but how had it happened? By witchcraft? The Colbones were very superstitious, and they shuddered to go to bed after this strange mishap. Drusy declared that she heard footsteps every night; and waking up her sister the night after the accident, both lay listening and trembling, for there certainly was a sound as of someone moving around the house.

"As sure as you live, Fanny, the house is haunted," whispered Drusy.

"For pity's sake, don't!" cried Fanny, pulling the bed-quilt over her head.

"I've heard that sometimes them that's gone get a spite against you, and torment you almost to—"

"Drusy! hold your tongue! I wish you hadn't waked me up," chattered Fanny under the bed-clothes.

"I was only wondering," persisted Drusy, who had a love for the horrible, "if old Grandpa Colbones—"

"I'll scream murder if you don't keep still!" cried Fanny, now trembling so that the bed shook.

"Well, anyhow, there's a noise downstairs. There, don't you hear it? Like somebody marching."

Poor Fanny was striving to be oblivious to everything, but it would not do; she was thoroughly frightened.

"O Drusy!" she moaned, "if there should be robbers! Japhet has got money in the house; and they might come in and murder us in our beds. O Drusy! did you lock the door?"

Yes: Drusy never went to bed without locking doors and windows, and shaking every dress and stocking out, to be sure there was nobody inside. She would have gone to her brother's room, but that it was across the entry, and she was a coward. Beside, she was sure she had heard the same sounds before, and they were yet unharmed.

Fanny declared the next day that she would go back to her father's house, for she was scared almost out of her seven senses. Tiddy was astonished. Tiddy had heard nothing; but then, she added, with a laugh, a whole regiment of soldiers might come in the house, and she never should know it, she was so sound a sleeper.

It was very strange, she said, an hour after, she could not find her best shawl, high nor low; and two very fine night-dresses were gone. She had been hunting for them quietly, though she very well knew where she had left them. She had but one place for them. Wasn't it strange?

Drusy wondered, Fanny wondered; but Japhet said not a word, and soon went out as usual.

"How dreadfully stupid Japhet looks of mornings!" said Drusy, who began to question and to be suspicious of everybody.

"He's such a hard sleeper!" responded Tiddy; "why, I can hardly get him awake by breakfast-time! I have to pound him and pull him and turn him!"

"He used to be up earlier," said Drusy thoughtfully.

In the course of the day a neighbor came in and brought her knitting-work.

"Has Japhet taken to peddling?" she asked with a little laugh. "Taken to peddling!" echoed Tiddy and both the sisters: "what can you mean?"

"Why, he goes through the village every day with a great tin box," replied the woman; "and actually as many as a dozen people have asked me if he has gone to peddling."

"I'm sure I don't know what you mean!" said Tiddy; "I didn't know he carried any box of the kind."

"Very strange!" said Drusy and Fanny; but they determined to "wait for the wagon." When they heard it coming they hurried to a chamber at the back of the house, overlooking the barn. Sure enough, there was Japhet, just lifting from his wagon with no little difficulty a great tin box such as peddlers carry. The sisters looked at each other: what did it mean?

"Between you and me," whispered Drusy, "I shouldn't wonder if he grew strange as he grew older; you know they say all the others did: but what can he have in that box?"

"I'm sure I can't think," replied Fanny; "and do look: if he arnt locking up the carriage-house! Laws, Drusy! I thought of going in and trying to find out what it can be."

"So did I," responded Drusy; "but it's no use now. He's got some odd idea in his head, and I suppose he'll keep it there."

Tiddy Colbones manifested no little astonishment when Drusy and Fanny told her what they had seen, and what they had heard; and for the moment seemed a little uneasy.

"Perhaps it's empty, and he's only taken the notion to carry the box with him because it looks sort of business-like," she suggested.

"I'm sure it isn't empty!" exclaimed Drusy, "for he lifted it as if it was a heft. Dear me! what can it be?"

"Did you bring anything from town, Japhet?" asked Tiddy that evening at supper.

He looked up as if astonished at the question.

"To be sure I did: I brought myself," he answered.

"Oh!" and his wife made no other reply; only Drusy and Fanny exchanged glances with her.

That night, by previous arrangement, Drusy and Fanny were to occupy the chamber adjoining Tiddy's sleeping-room. A small window or movable frame opened from one chamber to the other, and under that Tiddy had affixed a string in such a way that a slight pull upon it would awaken her, if her slumber were ever so deep. For a long while the redoubtable spinster kept awake, her fears excited at the slightest sound; but finally drowsiness overcame her, and her eyes obstinately refused to keep open.

For some hours she slept heavily; but at the accustomed time awoke, as had become a usual habit with her.

There were the sounds again; the going down-stairs, lifting the latch, the fumbling and stepping about. Drusy pulled the string. In a few moments Tiddy's night-capped head appeared at the door.

"It is Japhet, as I suspected," she said, whispering. "He's not in my room. Come; we won't light a lamp, but go softly down-stairs. You foolish thing, to tremble so! it's only one of his freaks, and harmless, I suppose, at that. Come; are you ready?"

Drusy delayed as long as she could, fidgeting about the shawl she had prepared beforehand, and shivering, she said, at the cold; then, taking care to keep behind Tiddy, crept downstairs.

There seemed to be an illumination. The hall was quite light. Tiddy stood on the stair, and reached over to the glass top of the door. For a moment she stood gazing; then, sinking back, she began laughing immoderately to herself; her queer contortions, as she beckoned Drusy to look, and the efforts she made to keep from betraying herself, making her, in her night-cap and uncouth attire, appear quite ridiculous.

Drusy stood on tip-toe, taking in the whole scene and its ludicrousness at a glance. Japhet was standing before the looking-glass, his box open beside him. He was arrayed in woman's clothes almost from head to foot, and was just then pulling and straightening out the ruffles on a cap which Drusy recognized as the one her mother had lost some years before. The gown, with its bright blue and white pattern, was familiar to her; and now he was throwing over the pelerine that they had missed so lately. Everything he had on seemed to have undergone a change—to have been widened, enlarged, and otherwise altered. After he had sufficiently admired himself, he spread out his gown, took his handkerchief in his hand, and began to walk back and forth with as much of the air and gait of a woman as he could assume. Then he would take out his knitting, smile amicably, sit down with finikin niceness,[1] and knit, holding his head affectedly now this way, now that, with many an accomplished smirk.

Poor Drusy did not feel like laughing, for she saw now where her nice black silk had gone, and sundry other of her valuables, and she began forming a plan in her mind how she should avail herself of them, when Japhet arose, and appeared to be coming toward the door, whereupon the two women fled upstairs.

The next night, and the next, they watched, and saw the same scene acted over with but few variations. Sometimes the beautiful black silk, altered and disfigured; sometimes other missing dresses were donned; and the imaginary woman kept on knitting, smirking, and smiling, till the two hours he had allotted himself were over.

Many were the plans the three women formed to get possession of the box, but they could seem to make none of them available;[2] and they dared not hint to Japhet what they knew.

One beautiful bright day in August, when the rich harvests, rudely wrested from the bosom of nature, covered the land, and the heavens smiled in a blue and quiet serenity, Japhet lingered about the house till the breakfast-dishes were placed away, and the usual domestic work was begun. All at once the man of few words spoke:

"Tiddy! take the children, and go and spend the day at father's."

"Oh! I can't, Japhet; there's the churning, and little bits of things to do that I have let go till now. But I'll get them all through, and go tomorrow, Japhet."

"Drusy and Fanny," said the oddity, looking about, "dress the children, and go with Tiddy to spend the day at father's."

Nothing more was to be said. Tiddy had never dreamed of having a way of her own; so she smothered down her disappointment, and prepared for the visit. They all set off very soon, Japhet standing at the door as they went, saying, that if he didn't call for them before dark they needn't come home that night.

"If you don't come for me by five," spoke up Tiddy with more self-will than she had ever dared before, "I shall come home."

He jerked his head in his odd way, and off they went.

The day passed, pleasantly. The old man and his old wife were social in their queerness; for association with her husband for over forty years had made Mrs. Colbones almost as strange as he. But toward five Tiddy began to grow uneasy.

"I feel worried and unhappy," she said to Drusy; "I wish Japhet would come."

"Why should you feel worried?" asked Drusy, her own face somewhat clouded.

"I don't know," was the reply; "but just as I got up from the dinner-table, something seemed to choke me: did you see me catch hold of my throat? and I have had a peculiar feeling ever since."

"And just then I grew dizzy, too," said Drusy; "I didn't like to tell you, but I've felt queer ever since."

"How foolish we are," said Tiddy, trying to laugh; "there's the cart now: and there's—oh! no, it isn't; it's a neighbor. Let us get the children and ourselves ready; for if he isn't here by five, I shall certainly go home."

They all sat waiting till after the clock struck five. Then they started, Tiddy saying, in a faint sort of way, that they should probably meet Japhet on the road, and they might as well be occupied with something: it was only half a mile.

Quite silent, listening to the pretty prattle of the little girls, they arrived at the house. It was shut up, and looked strangely lonesome. They rapped at the door. No answer. Pretty soon the girl they had left at home came flying over from a neighbor's.

"Mr. Colbones told me I might go for the day, after you were gone," she said, laughing. Apparently she had been enjoying herself very much.

"But the work?" said Tiddy reproachfully.

"I know: but he wouldn't let me stay. When I told him what you expected, he just took me by the arm and put me out."

"Where in the world is he?" cried Tiddy, now alarmed, shaking the door.

---

[1] *finikin niceness* Dainty neatness.

[2] *available* I.e., effective.

"I'm sure I don't know," replied the girl; "gone off somewhere, I suppose. I'll get in the cellar-way, and let you in." And so she did.

Once in the house, Tiddy felt oppressed with a strange awe. She went into the parlor, and started back with a scream. All the chairs in the house had been brought in and ranged in double rows around the room, as if for a funeral, while the large hall-table was set in the centre, spread with a white cloth, and occupied only by the great Bible and hymn-book.

"What does this mean?" asked Tiddy, sinking down, her strength entirely gone. The children laughed with glee, and began to play meeting.

"It's surely a sign!" cried Drusy, her cheeks whitening, while Fanny shivered as with an ague.[1]

"Where *is* that man? oh! dear! where *can* he be?" cried Tiddy, in great distress. "Drusy! you go hunt. Mary! (to the girl) go round to all the neighbors." Then, proceeding to the foot of the stairs, she shouted his name; but there was no answer.

"I don't know why, but I dread to go upstairs," said Tiddy falteringly. "Look; he has shut up every blind."

"There's no use in feeling so; we might as well go up," said Drusy, summoning a show of courage. "I don't believe he's in the house, nor haven't from the first. That fixing in the parlor, and shutting up the blinds, was just one of his freaks. I knew he would grow odder as he grew older; all the Colbones do. Come; we might as well have it over with." So saying, she resolutely mounted into the chamber.

Everything there was in scrupulous order; though the rooms, upon such an unexpected summons, had been left somewhat untidy. He was in none of the sleeping-apartments, and Tiddy breathed more freely. Drusy now boldly opened the door leading to the great garret. The red rays of the fast-setting sun streamed down the narrow stairs. She went up slowly, one at a time, and when well at the top, gave one sweeping glance about. Then, in a loud voice she cried: "Here he is, Tiddy: the wicked fellow! trying to scare us all out of our senses. O Japhet!"

By this time Tiddy had flown up with Fanny, and now approached the figure that sat in the shadow. Bonnet, cap, pelerine, gloves, black-silk gown, a bag in its hand, fantastic bows pinned all over it: it was a most fearfully grotesque object. Tiddy, calling him by name, went nearer and nearer, and still nearer; then, with a shriek: "O Drusy!" she cried, "he's stone dead!" and fell down fainting.

It was quite true. This was the oddest freak yet, of the odd man. He had managed to hang himself in a sitting posture, and his face was calm and placid. In the bag in his hand was a paper on which were written the words:

I think I am a woman. I have been seven years making me a perfect suit of garments appropriate for my sex. As I have passed so long, falsely, for a man, I am ashamed to show myself in my true colors; therefore, I hang myself. The property all to go to the woman I have called my wife. It is now twelve o'clock. I have prepared everything for the funeral, and desire that I may be laid out in the clothes I have on.

JAPHET COLBONES.

Poor Tiddy was almost distracted.[2] In spite of his strange ways, she had loved her husband deeply, and the manner of his death made the bereavement much more dreadful. Crowds came flocking to see the strange sight; and the wonder grew when it was seen that he had taken the greatest pains to leave out not the smallest minutia of a woman's wearing-apparel.

And thus, according to the term of his singular request, he was placed in his coffin in Drusy's black silk; the only difference in the terms being that the bonnet and shawl were taken off, and the gold rings and jewelry with which he had adorned his neck and fingers.

"There's the last of the Colbones, likely," whispered one neighbor to another. "The women will die old maids, and Tiddy's two children are girls: an't it lucky?"

Tiddy was left with a handsome property; but she could no longer bear to live in the house where he had died. So she bought a little cottage for herself and her mother, and very kindly took Drusy and Fanny to live with her.

Old Mr. Colbones still mourns that he has no sons to leave his books to; and it is whispered that if he should die before his wife, there will probably be a great bonfire somewhere in the vicinity.

---

[1]   *ague* Fever.

[2]   *distracted* Insane.

The Man-Monster, 1836. Working under the name Mary Jones and using a prosthetic vagina to disguise their biology, an African American prostitute in New York City made headlines in 1836 when they were arrested for stealing their clients' wallets. They appeared in court in women's attire. "I am a man," they stated when questioned, and when asked why they dressed in women's clothes, gave the following account:

> I have been in the practice of waiting upon girls of ill fame … and they induced me to dress in women's clothes, saying I looked so much better in them, and I have always attended parties among the people of my own color dressed in this way—and in New Orleans I always dressed in this way.

The accused was sentenced to five years' imprisonment for grand larceny. Cross-dressing was not yet illegal in New York, but they were mocked viciously during the court proceedings and in the press; the lithograph reproduced here was printed the week after the sensational trial.

from J.D. Borthwick, *Three Years in California* (1857)

In some respects, the overwhelmingly male-dominated mining communities of the California Gold Rush (1848–55) provided an unusually permissive space for the crossing of gender boundaries. The following account of a ball for men is drawn from the Scottish miner John David Borthwick's travel memoir *Three Years in California*.

In the evening, a ball took place at the hotel … I was staying at where, though none of the fair sex were present, dancing was kept up with great spirit for several hours. For music the company were indebted to two amateurs, one of whom played the fiddle and the other the flute. It is customary in the mines for the fiddler to take the responsibility of keeping the dancers all right. He goes through the dance orally, and at the proper intervals his voice is heard above the music and the conversation, shouting loudly his directions to the dancers, "Lady's chain," "Set to your partner," with other dancing-school words of command; and after all the legitimate figures of the dance had been performed, out of consideration for the thirsty appetites of the dancers, and for the good of the house, he always announced, in a louder voice than usual, the supplementary finale of "Promenade to the bar, and treat your partners." This injunction, as may be supposed, was most rigorously obeyed, and the "ladies," after their fatigues, tossed off their cocktails and lighted their pipes just as in more polished circles they eat ice-creams and sip lemonade.

It was a strange sight to see a party of long-bearded men, in heavy boots and flannel shirts, going through all the steps and figures of the dance with so much spirit, and often with a great deal of grace, hearty enjoyment depicted on their dried-up sunburned faces, and revolvers and bowie-knives glancing in their belts; while a crowd of the same rough-looking customers stood around, cheering them on to greater efforts, and occasionally dancing a step or two quietly on their own account. Dancing parties such as these were very common, especially in small camps where there was no such general resort as the gambling-saloons of the larger towns. Wherever a fiddler could be found to play, a dance was got up. Waltzes and polkas were not so much in fashion as the "Lancers"[1] which appeared to be very generally known, and, besides, gave plenty of exercise to the light fantastic toes of the dancers; for here men danced, as they did everything else, with all their might; and to go through the "Lancers" in such company was a very severe gymnastic exercise. The absence of ladies was a difficulty which was very easily overcome by a simple arrangement whereby it was understood that every gentleman who had a patch on a certain part of his inexpressibles[2] should be considered a lady for the time being. These patches were rather fashionable, and were usually large squares of canvas, showing brightly on a dark ground, so that the "ladies" of the party were as conspicuous as if they had been surrounded by the usual quantity of white muslin. …

Images: Charlotte Cushman

Advertisement for Cushman's "farewell" performance as Hamlet in Washington, D.C., before her departure for Rome in 1861. (Cushman would in fact return to Washington in 1863, performing in the role of Lady Macbeth before President Abraham Lincoln, who praised the performance highly.) Cushman was one of dozens of women actors who played Hamlet in the nineteenth century.

---

1   *Lancers* Type of square dance.

2   *inexpressibles* Trousers.

Charlotte Cushman (1816–76) made her acting debut in 1835 in the role of Lady Macbeth, and thereafter established a career as one of the most celebrated tragic actors in antebellum America. Her deep contralto voice (she had initially trained to become an opera singer), supposedly masculine facial features, and powerful stage presence were considered to lend themselves particularly well to masculine roles, and she was celebrated for the unique erotic intensity of her portrayal of Romeo as well as her mastery of the famously difficult role of Hamlet—both characters that some critics felt were better portrayed by women because of the figures' supposedly feminine qualities. Cushman never married and had numerous romantic attachments with women, including at least two long-term relationships: first with the English writer and translator Matilda Hays, who was her romantic partner for ten years, and subsequently with American sculptor Emma Stebbins, with whom Cushman lived from 1857 until her death in 1876.

Cushman and her sister, actor Susan Webb Cushman, in the respective roles of Romeo and Juliet, 1846. The success of this London performance established Cushman as an international celebrity, and Cushman reprised the role several times in her career—sometimes with a real-life romantic interest playing opposite her as Juliet.

Cushman (sitting, left) and her partner Matilda Hays (right), c. 1855. English poet Elizabeth Barrett Browning referred to the women's relationship as a "female marriage." The marriage ended in 1857.

from Loreta Velázquez, *The Woman in Battle: A Narrative of the Exploits, Adventures, and Travels of Madame Loreta Janeta Velázquez, Otherwise Known as Lieutenant Harry T. Buford, Confederate States Army* (1876)

Loreta Janeta Velázquez's (1842–1923) expansive memoir *The Woman in Battle* tells the extraordinary tale of her year spent fighting and spying for the Confederate Army. Born in Cuba to well-off parents, at the age of fourteen Velázquez eloped to the United States with a Texan named William, whose itinerant life as a soldier would bring her closer to the traditionally masculine world of battles and heroics that she had dreamt of since childhood. According to her memoir, at the outbreak of the Civil War in April 1861, she quickly entered the Confederate Army—initially without William's knowledge—as Harry T. Buford. For about a year, she participated under this name in several battles, worked as a Confederate spy, and mingled in Southern society—frequently engaging in flirtations and affairs with young women along the way. She doffed her disguise intermittently, allowing her to remarry following William's early death in battle. Velázquez's adventures ended in the spring of 1862, after an injury she sustained in the Battle of Shiloh led to the discovery of her sex—though she apparently continued to work as a Confederate spy, presenting as a woman, for some time thereafter.

Velázquez published her memoir in 1876, intending its sales to support herself and her young child following the death of her third husband. Yet her account immediately roused suspicion from various quarters, with Confederate general Jubal Early being among the most prominent figures to declare *The Woman in Battle* an outright fabrication. Modern historians continue to be divided on the question—though for most, the question of whether or not Velázquez's narrative is factually true remains of less interest than its vibrant exploration of gender performance and sexual non-normativity in mid-nineteenth-century Southern society.

from CHAPTER 5
from AN ARKANSAS BELLE

The idea of having a mild little flirtation with this fair flower of the Arkansas forest rather grew upon me as I noticed the impression I was making upon her susceptible imagination. I had some curiosity to know how love-making[1] went from the masculine standpoint, and thought that the present would be a good opportunity to gain some valuable experience in that line; for it occurred to me that if I was to figure successfully in the rôle of a dashing young Confederate officer, it would be necessary for me to learn how to make myself immensely agreeable to the ladies. I knew how to make myself agreeable to the men, or thought I did, and I could, if I chose, be agreeable to women in a feminine sort of fashion; but I had never studied the masculine carriage towards my sex critically, with a view of imitating it, and it was important, therefore, that I should begin at once to do so, in order that when compelled to associate with women, as I assuredly would be to a greater or less extent, I might not belie my outward appearances by my conduct. I flatter myself that during the time I passed for a man I was tolerably successful with the women; and I had not a few curious and most amusing adventures, which gave me an insight into some of the peculiarities of feminine human nature which had not impressed themselves on my mind before, perhaps because I was a woman.

My flirtation with Miss Sadie Giles was not a very savage one, and I hope that it did not inflict more damage on her heart than it did on mine. It was immensely amusing to me while it lasted, and I presume, if not exactly amusing, it might at least be deemed entertaining to her. At any rate, I succeeded not only in having a little sly fun at her expense, but I picked up an idea or two that I subsequently found useful.

Noticing that Miss Sadie was developing a marked partiality for me, but was much too bashful to give me any encouragement, except some shy glances out of the corners of her eyes, I commenced to ogle her and, whenever I had an opportunity, to pay her

---

1   *love-making* Flirtation, not necessarily with a sexual connotation.

some delicate attentions, for the purpose of making her think I was just a bit fascinated with her. It soon became very evident that the heart which beat under that yellow calico dress was in a great state of excitement, and Miss Sadie, while not encouraging me by any direct advances, made it very plainly understood that my little attentions were appreciated. …

Supper was now announced, and we all sat down to a tolerably plentiful repast, the principal features of which were bacon, cabbage, and fried chickens—the latter having been prepared in my honor. Miss Sadie managed to place herself by my side, by a dexterous little manoeuvre, which escaped the attention of the family, but which I understood perfectly. I, for my part, strove to play the gallant by helping her bountifully to the bacon, cabbage, and chicken, and by endeavoring

MADAM VELASQUEZ IN FEMALE ATTIRE.

These two portraits of Velázquez/Buford were included in the original edition of *The Woman in Battle*.

to induce her to join in the conversation. She undoubtedly appreciated my attentions at their full value, but was not sufficiently self-possessed to do much talking; indeed, during the supper I could scarcely get anything out of her except a timid yes or no. …

from MY MUSTACHE IN DANGER

Before the supper was over I had a terrible fright, and for a few moments fancied that I was on the brink of a discovery that would upset all my plans, and nip my enterprise in the bud. While drinking a glass of buttermilk, which I greatly enjoyed, for it was the best thing on the table, and was most refreshing, my mustache got full of the fluid, and when I attempted to wipe this ornament, which my Memphis friend had so carefully glued upon my upper lip, and which added so much to the manliness of my countenance, I fancied that it was loose and was about to fall off. Here was a terrible situation, and I cannot undertake to describe what I felt. To say that I was frightened, scarcely gives an idea of the cold chills that ran down my back. The ridicule of my entertainers, and especially of Miss Sadie, was the least thing that I feared, and I would rather brave any number of perils at the cannon's mouth than to repeat the emotions of that dreadful moment. Such a situation as this is ludicrous enough, but it was not a bit funny for me at that time; and I was on pins and needles until I could get away, and take means to secure the mustache firmly on again. I managed, however, to keep a straight countenance,[1] and to join in the conversation with a tolerable degree of equanimity, keeping my hand up to my mouth all the time though, and doing my best to hold the mustache on. My fright, after all, was causeless, for on examination I found that the hair was too firmly glued to my lip to be easily removed; indeed, I subsequently discovered that it was practically impossible to move it without the aid of alcohol. …

A PRETTY WIDOW

During the brief time I had been in Pensacola I had formed the acquaintance of a number of officers who were going to the front, and, as they intended to leave

---

[1]   *countenance* Expression.

for Richmond shortly, I concluded that it would be better to go in their company, especially as several of them were first-rate fellows, and one or two particular friends of my late husband. I also became acquainted with a good many ladies, one of whom, a dashing young widow, paid my masculine charms the compliment of falling desperately in love with them. This lady did not require any encouragement from me; but finding that, while polite to her, I was rather shy and reserved, and apparently insensible to her attractions, she made a dead set at me, and took pains to let me know, in terms that could not be misunderstood, the sentiments she felt for me.

I was really in no mood for nonsense of this kind, and, to tell the truth, I was not particularly pleased with the decidedly unfeminine advances that were made towards me. The necessity of playing the character I had assumed, however, in a successful manner, pressed upon me, and I felt that diversion of some kind was requisite to divert my mind from the sad and gloomy thoughts caused by my bereavement. I accordingly determined to meet my fair one half way, and paid her numerous attentions, such as taking her to the theatre, and to drive upon the beach. I, however, resolutely refused to accept any of the numerous very broad hints she threw out, to the effect that a little more love-making would be more than agreeable, at which she seemed considerably surprised. Finding, at length, that I either could not or would not understand what she was driving at, she bluntly reproached me for not being more tender in my demonstrations towards her. I put on the innocent air of a green schoolboy, perfectly nonplussed with the advances of a pretty woman, and assured her that I had never courted a lady in my life, and really did not know how to begin. The eagerness with which the widow undertook to instruct me was decidedly comical, and I learned more about some of the fine points of feminine human nature from her in a week, than I had picked up for myself in twenty years. The courting was pretty much all on her side, and I really had not imagined before that it was possible for a lady to take such an important matter so entirely out of the gentleman's hands. For the fun of the thing I pretended to soften to her, and by the time I was ready to start for Virginia, we were the best possible friends; and although I was careful to make no

definite promises, the widow parted from me with the understanding that when the war was over we were to be something more than friends to each other. If I were a man, it would be absurd for me to tell all this, but being a woman, this and other of my love adventures have a comical interest for me, as I doubt not they will have for the reader. If they do not show some of the members of my own sex in the best possible light, it is their fault and not mine.

"Thirty Years in Disguise," *The New York Times* (9 January 1880)

> The following obituary for the celebrated stage-coach driver Charley Parkhurst first appeared in the *San Francisco Call* before its reprinting in *The New York Times*.

A NOTED OLD CALIFORNIAN STAGE-DRIVER DISCOVERED AFTER DEATH TO BE A WOMAN.
CORRESPONDENCE OF THE SAN FRANCISCO CALL.

Watsonville, Cal., Dec. 31. There is hardly a city or town or hamlet of the Pacific coast that includes among its citizens a few of the gold-hunters of the early days where at least one person cannot be found who will remember Charley Parkhurst. For in the early days the gold-hunters were, by rapidly-succeeding gold discoveries, drawn back to San Francisco as a head-quarters, and again distributed from it to the most recently found diggings and in those same early days Charley Parkhurst was a stage-driver on the more important routes leading out from the city. He was in his day one of the most dexterous and celebrated of the famous California drivers, ranking with Foss, Hank Monk, and George Gordon,[1] and it was an honor to be striven for to occupy the spare end of the driver's seat when the fearless Charley Parkhurst held the reins of a four or six in hand. California coaching had, and has even yet, one exciting adjunct that was wanting[2] in all preceding coaching. It was when the organized bands of highwaymen waylaid the coaches, leaped to

---

[1] *Foss ... George Gordon* Famous stagecoach drivers of the nineteenth-century West.

[2] *wanting* Lacking.

the leaders' heads, and, over leveled shot-guns, issued the grim command made so often that it has crystallized into the felonious formula of "Throw down the box." Drivers of a phlegmatic[1] temperament become accustomed to these interruptions, expertly reckon up the killing capacity of the gun-barrels leveled at them, accept the inevitable, throw down the treasure-box to get his coach and passengers clear. But he did it, even under the "drop" of the robbers' fire-arms, with all ill-grace, and he defiantly told the highwaymen that he would "break even with them." He was as good as his word, for, being subsequently stopped on a return trip from Mariposa to Stockton, he watched his opportunity, and, contemporaneously, turned his wild mustangs and his wicked revolver loose, and brought everything through safe. That his shooting was to the mark was subsequently ascertained by the confession of "Sugarfoot," a notorious highwayman, who, mortally wounded, found his way to a miner's cabin in the hills, and *in articulo mortis*[2] told how he had been shot by Charley Parkhurst, the famous driver, in a desperate attempt, with others, to stop his stage.

Charley Parkhurst also afterward drove on the great stage route from Oakland to San José, and later, and for a long time, he was "the boss of the road" between San Juan and Santa Cruz, when San Francisco was reached by way of San Juan. But Parkhurst was of both an energetic and a thrifty nature, and when rapid improvements in the means of locomotion relegated coaches further out toward the frontiers, and made the driving of them less profitable, it was not sufficient for him that he was acknowledged as one of the three or four crack whips of the coast. He resolutely abandoned driving and went to farming. For 15 years he prosecuted this calling, varying it in the winter times by working in the woods, where he was known as one of the most skillful and powerful of choppers and lumbermen, and where his services were eagerly sought for, and always commanded the highest wages. Although, in his stage-coaching days, he was a hale fellow well met[3] with the migratory miners, and during the succeeding years of his life as farmer and lumberman he was social and generous with his fellows, he was never intemperate,

immoral, or reckless, and the sure result was that his years of labor had been rewarded with a competency[4] of several thousands of dollars. For several years past he had been so severely afflicted with rheumatism as not only to be unable to do physical labor, but the malady had even resulted in partial shriveling and distortion of some of his limbs. He was also attacked by a cancer on his tongue. As the combined diseases became more aggressive, the genial Charley Parkhurst became, not morose, but less and less communicative, till of late he has conversed with no one except on the ordinary topics of the day.

Last Sunday, in a little cabin on the Moss Ranch, about six miles from Watsonville, Charley Parkhurst, the famous coachman, the fearless fighter, the industrious farmer, and expert woodman, died of the cancer on his tongue. He knew that death was approaching, but he did not relax the reticence of his later years other than to express a few wishes as to certain things to be done at his death. Then, when the hands of the kind friends who had ministered to his dying wants came to lay out the dead body of the adventurous Argonaut,[5] a discovery was made that was literally astounding. Charley Parkhurst was a woman. The discoveries of the successful concealment for protracted periods of the female sex under the disguise of the masculine are not infrequent, but the case of Charley Parkhurst may fairly claim to rank as by all odds the most astonishing of all of them. That a young woman should assume man's attire and, friendless and alone, defy the dangers of the voyage of 1849, to the then almost mythical California—dangers over which hardy pioneers still grow boastful—has in it sufficient of the wonderful.[6] That she should achieve distinction in an occupation above all professions calling for the best physical qualities of nerve, courage, coolness, and endurance, and that she should add to them the almost romantic personal bravery that enables one to fight one's way through the ambush of an enemy, seems almost fabulous,[7] and that

---

1   *phlegmatic* Calm.

2   *in articulo mortis* Latin: at the moment of death.

3   *met* Matched.

4   *competency* Amount of wealth sufficient to provide for oneself.

5   *Argonaut* In Greek mythology, the Argonauts are a group of heroic men who embark on a journey to find the Golden Fleece; the term was often applied to participants in the California Gold Rush (1848–55).

6   *wonderful* I.e., inspiring wonder.

7   *fabulous* Mythical, fictional.

for 30 years she should be in constant and intimate association with men and women, and that her true sex should never have been even suspected, and that she should finally go knowingly down to her death, without disclosing by word or deed who she was, or why she had assumed man's dress and responsibilities, are things that a reader might be justified in doubting, if the proof of their exact truth was not so abundant and conclusive. On the great register of Santa Cruz County for the year 1867 appears this entry: "Parkhurst, Charles Durkee, 55, New-Hampshire, farmer, Soquel," where he then lived. It is said by several who knew her intimately, that she came from Providence, R.I.

Images: Two-Spirit People

In the nineteenth century, many Indigenous societies incorporated third and sometimes fourth gender roles, offering space for people who occupied the middle of a gender spectrum or who suited a social role not usually assigned to their biological sex. In Zuni communities, for example, Lhamana performed both men's and women's roles, while in Ojibwe communities ikwekaazo were seen as male-bodied people occupying women's roles and ininiikaazo were seen as female-bodied people in men's roles. Each culture that incorporated these genders did so in its own way, but often third and fourth genders were respected and associated with spiritual power. Adoption of these gender roles did not necessarily suggest any particular sexual orientation, but was a reflection of the personal qualities and vocation of the individuals who embodied them. In the twenty-first century, the wide variety of Indigenous third and fourth gender roles are sometimes grouped under the umbrella term "two-spirit," a term coined by Indigenous activists in 1990 to replace the earlier "berdache," which is today generally considered offensive; some Indigenous people consider themselves two-spirit, while others prefer to use only the designations specific to their nation.

The photograph below depicts an individual known as Old Doctor, a member of the Tolowa people of what is now northwestern California. Their clothing includes garments worn by both men and women among the Tolowa and other nearby peoples, and indicates that Old Doctor was a shaman. Census records suggest that they lived in the village of Cushion Creek in a large household including their wife, son, and sister.

Two-spirit individuals were often viewed with suspicion or even disgust by white observers. The white painter George Catlin, who traveled widely throughout the West and became famous for his portraits of Native Americans, observed in an 1841 account that rituals centered on "berdaches" among the Sac and Meskwaki (Fox) peoples were among "the most unaccountable and disgusting that [he had] ever met in the Indian country." His 1830 painting, *Dance to the Berdache*, depicts one such ceremony. In Catlin's *Letters and Notes on the Manners, Customs, and Condition of the North American Indians* (1841), a sketch of the painting is accompanied by a wish that such practices "might be extinguished before [they] be more fully recorded." Indeed, colonizing officials in the nineteenth century made a concerted effort to impose Western gender ideology on Indigenous people, and, in many communities, Indigenous gender practices were nearly or entirely stamped out; scholars and knowledge-keepers continue to work to recover and rebuild these practices.

Photograph of Old Doctor, c. 1871, photographer unknown.

George Catlin, *Dance to the Berdache*, 1830.

Masculinity, Race, and Class

from Joseph Holt Ingraham, *Lafitte: The Pirate of the Gulf* (1836)

Born in Maine, Joseph Holt Ingraham spent most of his life in Mississippi, where he wrote more than seventy novels. One of the first was *Lafitte: The Pirate of the Gulf*, in which the character of Cudjoe offers a typical example of the way black men were often characterized in proslavery fiction of the 1830s. At the end of the novel, Cudjoe murders several people.

from BOOK 3
from CHAPTER I

... Cudjoe ... was a young slave about four feet high, with a glossy black skin, ivory white teeth, two of which, flanking his capacious jaws, projected outwards, with the dignity of the embryo tusks of a young elephant. His lips were of ample dimensions, and of the brightest vermillion, the lower one hanging down, and resting familiarly upon his short, retreating chin. His nose, which surmounted, or rather stood in the rear of these formidable appendages to his mouth, was of vast dimensions, terminating in a magnificent expansion of the nostril, and threatening to encroach upon the province of his ears, which hung down in enormous lapels, as if welcoming the expected proximity.

His eyes were small, restless, and almost deficient in that generous display of white, characteristic of his race. One of these organs he kept at all times hermetically sealed, while the other enjoyed that obliquity of vision which rendered it difficult for the beholder to decide certainly as to the particular point their owner was directing his visual orb.

His neck, short, thick, and bull-like, was set into broad shoulders, from which depended long arms hanging by his side like those of the ourang-outang and terminating in short stunted fingers, of which useful ornaments two and a half were wanting.[1] His feet were broad and flat, of equal longitude either way from the base of his short legs, which were placed

exactly in their centre; so that he seemed to enjoy the enviable facility of progressing in opposite directions without the trouble of turning his body.

His forehead, lined with innumerable fine wrinkles, was very high and round, down to the centre of which the reddish wool curled barrenly to a point, displaying a physiognomical[2] feature, which was the mere mockery of that intellect it indicated. His voice—or rather his voices, for nature, charitably making up his deficiencies, had bestowed two upon him—in ordinary conversation was sharp and wiry, and pitched upon a shrill, discordant key; but when he sung, as he often did, the soft airs[3] of his tribe for the amusement of his master, the melody of a siren[4] seemed floating around the enraptured listener.

His natural disposition was gentle and affectionate; but when roused to revenge, he was more terrible than the uncaged hyena. Gratitude to his master, who captured him from a slaver, and subsequently saved him from an imminent and revolting death, had bound him to him with a faithfulness and attachment nothing could diminish, and death only terminate; while the shrewdness, activity and animal courage of the young and deformed African, rendered him a useful and necessary appendage to the person[5] of his master. ...

from Harriet Beecher Stowe, *Dred: A Tale of the Great Dismal Swamp* (1856)

Harriet Beecher Stowe (1811–96) is by far best known for her sentimental antislavery novel *Uncle Tom's Cabin* (1852), but she revisited the subject four years later with the less successful *Dred*, a more radical take on antislavery. The novel's title character, introduced in the passage below, was clearly inspired by black slave revolt leaders such as Nat Turner and Denmark Vesey. Both *Dred* and *Uncle Tom's Cabin*, though they

---

1   *wanting* Lacking.

2   *physiognomical* The term "physiognomy" here refers to one's facial appearance, especially when considered as indicating one's inner character.

3   *airs* Songs.

4   *siren* In Greek mythology, female monsters who lured sailors to their deaths with their beautiful singing.

5   *person* Body.

advocate passionately for black rights, also reveal Stowe's deep-set racial prejudices.

... He was a tall black man, of magnificent stature and proportions. His skin was intensely black, and polished like marble. A loose shirt of red flannel, which opened very wide at the breast, gave a display of a neck and chest of herculean strength. The sleeves of the shirt, rolled up nearly to the shoulders, showed the muscles of a gladiator. The head, which rose with an imperial air from the broad shoulders, was large and massive, and developed with equal force both in the reflective and perceptive department.[1] The perceptive organs jutted like dark ridges over the eyes, while that part of the head which phrenologists attribute to the moral and intellectual sentiments, rose like an ample dome above them. The large eyes had that peculiar and solemn effect of unfathomable blackness and darkness which is often a striking characteristic of the African eye. But there burned in them, like tongues of flame in a black pool of naphtha,[2] a subtle and restless fire, that betokened habitual excitement to the verge of insanity. If any organs were predominant in the head, they were those of ideality, wonder, veneration, and firmness; and the whole combination was such as might have formed one of the wild old warrior prophets of the heroic ages. He wore a fantastic sort of turban, apparently of an old scarlet shawl, which added to the outlandish effect of his appearance. His nether garments, of coarse negro-cloth,[3] were girded round the waist by a strip of scarlet flannel, in which was thrust a bowie-knife and hatchet. Over one shoulder he carried a rifle, and a shot-pouch was suspended to his belt. A rude[4] game-bag hung upon his arm. ...

from Austin Steward, *Twenty-Two Years a Slave, and Forty Years a Freeman* (1857)

Author, activist, and entrepreneur Austin Steward's memoir *Twenty-Two Years a Slave, and Forty Years a Freeman* (1857) details his experiences of enslavement in Virginia and New York and his efforts, after his escape, to establish a free colony in Canada. The following brief passage discusses the experience of married enslaved men forced to witness the punishment of their wives.

from CHAPTER 1
SLAVE LIFE ON THE PLANTATION

... The slave husband must submit without a murmur, to see the fore of his cherished, but wretched wife, not only exposed to the rude gaze of a beastly tyrant, but he must unresistingly see the heavy cowhide descend upon her shrinking flesh, and her manacled limbs writhe in inexpressible torture, while her piteous cries for help ring through his ears unanswered. The wild throbbing of his heart must be suppressed, and his righteous indignation find no voice, in the presence of the human monster who holds dominion over him. ...

---

[1] *developed ... perceptive department* Stowe's description in this passage alludes to the popular pseudo-science of phrenology, which posited that one could determine a person's inner character through the shape of their head, with the size of certain bumps or "organs" indicating certain mental capacities.

[2] *naphtha* Petroleum.

[3] *negro-cloth* Generic term for the poor-quality fabric often used for the garments of enslaved people.

[4] *rude* Crude or simple.

from Frederick Douglass, *Self-Made Men* (1859, 1895)

The following lecture was first given by the prominent formerly enslaved abolitionist Frederick Douglass in 1859; he repeated it many more times over the course of his career.

... I am here to speak to you of a peculiar type of manhood under the title of *Self-Made Men*. ...

On the first point I may say that, by the term "self-made men," I mean especially what, to the popular mind, the term itself imports. Self-made men are the men who, under peculiar difficulties and without the ordinary helps of favoring circumstances, have attained knowledge, usefulness, power and position and have learned from themselves the best uses to which life can be put in this world, and in the exercises of these uses to build up worthy character. They are the men who owe little or nothing to birth, relationship, friendly surroundings; to wealth inherited or to early approved means of education; who are what they are, without the aid of any favoring conditions by which other men usually rise in the world and achieve great results. In fact they are the men who are not brought up but who are obliged to come up, not only without the voluntary assistance or friendly co-operation of society, but often in open and derisive defiance of all the efforts of society and the tendency of circumstances to repress, retard and keep them down. They are the men who, in a world of schools, academies, colleges

Am I Not a Man and a Brother?, broadside illustration, 1837. Originally developed in the 1780s as the seal of the Society for the Abolition of Slavery in England, this image became an icon of the antislavery movements on both sides of the Atlantic. The version reproduced here is from an 1837 broadside of abolitionist John Greenleaf Whittier's poem "Our Countrymen in Chains."

John Quincy Adams Ward, *The Freedman*, 1863. John Quincy Adams Ward is best known for his monumental statues of figures such as George Washington, but this piece is a smaller sculpture about a foot and a half high. Ward, a white abolitionist, created this work to mark the Emancipation Proclamation (1863). A *New York Times* critic described it as follows:

> It is the full-length figure of a Negro, modelled from select specimens of the race, and shows that the African shares with the European the exalted proportions of the human figure.

and other institutions of learning, are often compelled by unfriendly circumstances to acquire their education elsewhere and, amidst unfavorable conditions, to hew out for themselves a way to success, and thus to become the architects of their own good fortunes. They are, in a peculiar sense, indebted to themselves for themselves. If they have travelled far, they have made the road on which they have travelled. If they have ascended high, they have built their own ladder. From the depths of poverty such as these have often come. From the heartless pavements of large and crowded cities; barefooted, homeless, and friendless, they have come. From hunger, rags and destitution, they have come; motherless and fatherless, they have come, and may come. Flung overboard in the midnight storm on the broad and tempest-tossed ocean of life; left without ropes, planks, oars or life-preservers, they have bravely buffeted the frowning billows and have risen in safety and life where others, supplied with the best appliances for safety and success, have fainted, despaired and gone down forever.

Such men as these, whether found in one position or another, whether in the college or in the factory; whether professors or plowmen; whether Caucasian or Indian; whether Anglo-Saxon or Anglo-African, are self-made men and are entitled to a certain measure of respect for their success and for proving to the world the grandest possibilities of human nature, of whatever variety of race or color.

Though a man of this class need not claim to be a hero or to be worshiped as such, there is genuine heroism in his struggle and something of sublimity and glory in his triumph. Every instance of such success is an example and a help to humanity. It, better than any mere assertion, gives us assurance of the latent powers and resources of simple and unaided manhood. …

From these remarks it will be evident that, allowing only ordinary ability and opportunity, we may explain success mainly by one word and that word is WORK! WORK!! WORK!!! WORK!!!! Not transient and fitful effort, but patient, enduring, honest, unremitting and indefatigable work into which the whole heart is put, and which, in both temporal and spiritual affairs, is the true miracle worker. Everyone may avail himself of this marvelous power, if he will. There is no royal road to perfection. Certainly no one must wait for some kind

of friend to put a springing board under his feet, upon which he may easily bound from the first round of their ladder onward and upward to its highest round. If he waits for this, he may wait long, and perhaps forever. He who does not think himself worth saving from poverty and ignorance by his own efforts, will hardly be thought worth the efforts of anybody else.

The lesson taught at this point by human experience is simply this, that the man who will get up will be helped up; and the man who will not get up will be allowed to stay down. This rule may appear somewhat harsh, but in its general application and operation it is wise, just and beneficent. I know of no other rule which can be substituted for it without bringing social chaos. Personal independence is a virtue and it is the soul out of which comes the sturdiest manhood. But there can be no independence without a large share of self-dependence, and this virtue cannot be bestowed. It must be developed from within.

I have been asked "How will this theory affect the negro?" and "What shall be done in his case?" My general answer is "Give the negro fair play and let him alone. If he lives, well. If he dies, equally well. If he cannot stand up, let him fall down." …

I meant all that I said and a good deal more than some understand by fair play. It is not fair play to start the negro out in life, from nothing and with nothing, while others start with the advantage of a thousand years behind them. He should be measured, not by the heights others have obtained, but from the depths from which he has come. For any adjustment of the scale of comparison, fair play demands that to the barbarism from which the negro started shall be added two hundred years heavy with human bondage. Should the American people put a school house in every valley of the South and a church on every hillside and supply the one with teachers and the other with preachers, for a hundred years to come, they would not then have given fair play to the negro. …

The Counter-Jumper

In the mid-nineteenth century, the urban stereotype of the effeminate "counter-jumper"— a man, typically white, who worked as a shopkeeper's assistant—was a frequent object of derision and of anxiety surrounding men's roles in the changing urban economy. The examples below of this short-lived but significant genre of satire are drawn from the New York satirical weekly *Vanity Fair* (published from 1859 to 1863), which included the stereotype with particular frequency in its articles and caricatures. The first piece is a description of the counter-jumper written in the style of a naturalist describing a new species; the second is a parody of the Walt Whitman poem eventually titled "Song of Myself" (first published in 1855, and included in the Whitman author section in this anthology). Today acknowledged by virtually all literary scholars as an important queer writer, Whitman frequently celebrated masculinity and affection between men in his poetry—though the degree to which the homoeroticism of his verse was acknowledged as such by readers in the 1850s and 60s is unclear. The fact that Whitman had friendly connections both with *Vanity Fair* and with this poem's probable author, Fitz-James O'Brien, makes his relationship to the following piece all the more intriguing.

from anonymous, "Natural History. The Counter-Jumper," *Vanity Fair* (February 1860)

Genus *Homo*: Species, *Counter-jumperii*.

This truly singular and beautiful animal exists throughout the civilized world, but is only found in perfection in large cities. ... It is generally about the size of the human species, and bears a resemblance to man, as well as to the ape tribe, with which it is often classified, I think erroneously. So far as my studies go, I consider the COUNTER-JUMPER no more an ape than a man; but belonging to a distinct tribe, somewhere between the two.

In external appearance, this is one of the prettiest subjects of the Animal Kingdom. Its hair, which grows luxuriantly upon the head and face, is long, glossy, often curled gracefully, and of different colors in different individuals. Its eyes are rather small, but have a beautiful languishing expression. Its skin is exceedingly white, soft, and fine in texture, particularly upon its paws, or hands, of which it takes the most scrupulous

care, as it also does of its hair and teeth. Indeed, its principal characteristic is an excessive neatness and love of personal adornment—a trait which places it considerably above the ape.

A great peculiarity with the Counter-jumper, and one which would be almost impossible to believe, were it not firmly established as a fact, is its total want[1] of sex. It is neither male nor female, though its manners are more feminine than masculine, for which reason, probably, it is a much greater favorite with the ladies than with us. [Can the learned Professor intend a bit of sly sarcasm, here? Eds. Vanity Fair.] Another curious peculiarity of this animal is, that it is endowed with neither heart nor brain, those organs having, apparently, no function to perform in its economy. ...

anonymous [probably Fitz-James O'Brien], "Counter-Jumps," *Vanity Fair* (March 1860)

A POEMETTINA.—AFTER WALT WHITMAN.

Am the Counter-jumper, weak and effeminate.
   I love to loaf and lie about dry-goods.[2]
I loaf and invite the Buyer.
I am the essence of retail. The sum and result of small
   profits and quick returns.
5 The Picayune[3] is part of me, and so is the half cent,
   and the mill[4] only arithmetically appreciable.
The shining, cheap-woven sarsnet[5] is of me, and I am
   of it.
And the white bobinet,[6]
And the moire[7] antique, thickly webbed and strown
   with impossible flowers,
And the warm winter gloves lined with fur,
10 And the delicate summer gloves of silk threads,

---

1   *want*   Lack.

2   *dry-goods*   Textile and other clothing-related merchandise.

3   *Picayune*   Coin of small value, originally currency in Spanish Louisiana.

4   *mill*   One-tenth of a cent.

5   *sarsnet*   Type of silk fabric.

6   *bobinet*   Fine, lacy cotton fabric with an open weave.

7   *moire*   Silk woven to produce a wavy, fluid effect.

And the intermediate ones built of the hide of the
   Swedish rat,
All these things are of me, and many more also,
For I am the shop, and the counter, and the till,
But particularly the last.
15 And I explore and rummage the till, and am at home
   in it.
And I am the shelves on which lie the damaged
   goods;
The damaged goods themselves I am,

And I ask what's the damage?
I am the crate, and the hamper, and the yard-wand,
   and the box of silks fresh from France,
20 And when I came into the world I paid duty,
And I never did my duty,
And never intend to do it,
For I am the creature of weak depravities;
I am the Counter-jumper;
25 I sound my feeble yelp over the woofs[1] of the World.

"Dry Good Clerk," mid-nineteenth century. In the mid-nineteenth century, comic valentines were as popular as earnest ones; here, the subject of mockery is a shop clerk who is short on "tin" (money).

Cover page for the sheet music to "The Gay Young Clerk in the Dry Goods Store" (1868). The song describes a "handsome man" who is "proud and poor," satirically presenting him as ripe for marriage. In the mid-nineteenth century, "gay" carried a range of meanings, including "carefree," "well-dressed," and "sexually immoral."

_____

1   *woofs* Fabrics (with reference to the intersecting "woof" and "warp" threads that make up a woven fabric).

Same-Sex Friendship, Sex, and Love

From 1807 until 1851, Charity Bryant and Sylvia Drake lived together in the rural village of Weybridge, Vermont, as a married couple. Their relationship appears to have turned very few heads in their community, among whom it was generally accepted that Bryant was the "husband"—officially considered the head of her household on tax and census documents—and Drake her "wife" and "help-meet." The couple ran a successful tailoring business out of their Weybridge home, which Bryant left to Drake upon her death; when Drake died in 1868, she was buried next to Bryant, under a headstone engraved with both of their names. The silhouette portrait reproduced here, framed by locks of the women's hair, was likely produced some time in the 1810s, in the early years of their marriage.

from Philip Van Buskirk, Diary (1852–1903)

The son of a prominent Maryland politician, Philip Van Buskirk (1834–1903) entered the Marine Corps in 1845 after the death of his father and his family's subsequent financial crisis. His career included many years with the Marines as well as periods spent traveling independently around the United States, working as a farmer, and fighting in the Confederate Army. From the age of seventeen until his death, Van Buskirk kept a detailed diary in which he reflected on his own experiences, his reading, and the social practices he observed among the people he worked with, most of whom were of a much less affluent background. Perhaps most remarkably, the diaries provide a frank and vivid picture of the sexual lives of Van Buskirk and his fellow marines, as the excerpts below reveal.

[19 October 1853]

James Keenan, or "Jimmy," has been an object of interest to me from the first time of my seeing him. He joined us from the Mississippi, and had not passed a night in his new home before Coleman tried every art to engage him in mutual self-pollution[1] (or not self-pollution, but paederasty,[2] or, as it is learned in the technical language of iniquity, "the act of going 'chaw for chaw'"), but Coleman did not succeed. And several men likewise failed who tried to draw him into their practice of pollution. Berry the Captain of

---

[1]   *self-pollution* Masturbation.

[2]   *paederasty* Usually, this term refers to sexual intercourse between an older man and a boy, particularly as it was practiced in ancient Greece, but for Van Buskirk (as he explains in the diary entry below) it refers to "the practice of sodomy between two males where the hand of each is used to pollute the other."

the Afterguard, who has argus eyes,[1] and from whom very little of our practical iniquity can be concealed, who emphatically, "knows all the moves, and besides that, the movers," told me of Keenan, in answer to my enquiry, "He is one of the right sort—one of your sort—he won't do anything of that kind; O! By Hokee, he has been tried." In the night watches of our passage from Loo Choo[2] here I have availed myself of opportunity to ascertain the leading points of his history, and to investigate the condition of his mind and morals. Accomplishing this by the instrumentality of private and free conversation. I had long ago caused him to have respect for me and confidence in the friendliness of my feelings towards him. I had slept under the same coats with him and forbore (I doubt not to his surprise) taking any criminal liberties with his person. After strict enquiry and a laborious examination of evidence, I can say of Keenan what cannot be said of any other boy in the ship, that he is not addicted to the practice of paederasty. But I have one sentence to write unfavorably to the brave little fellow, and that I regret to do, but I must, and it shall be in his own words: "Buskirk, I don't deny but that I have done it [committed paederasty]; I won't deny it; I got entrapped into it once; I will never do it again though!" And these last words were spoken with earnestness. I venture to say, or rather to repeat and endorse the common saying, "That no boy can ever remain a year on board of an American man-of-war without being led or forced to commit this crime" (which by the way is not regarded as a crime in a man-of-war). I cheerfully accept Keenan on the list of those who have my friendly esteem.

PAEDERASTY—SODOMY. To prevent confusion of meaning which might in future ensue upon a wrong use of the terms paederasty and sodomy in these Notes, I will now as clearly as possible define the meaning I have thought belonging to them. I first met with "paederasty" in Gibbon's *Rome* where the crime is charged upon the Bishops of Rhodes and Diospolis.[3] I understand the word to mean the practice of sodomy between two males where the hand of each is used to pollute the other, or where one performs with the hand this horrid office for another. On board of ships, paederasty (called "shaking") is not looked upon as a form of sodomy, but considered innocent and undeserving of reproach. I extend the signification of sodomy to embrace every horrid unnatural use of the organs of generation: and as such, embracing paederasty, where one must act for another, onanism,[4] where one acts for himself, and lastly the laying down of a male to act as a woman to another male, which form alone sailors call "sodomy."

[12 May 1855]

… All the kindness that I have shown to Bones has been wasted; I have failed signally in attempting to attach himself to my person, or detach him from any of the vices, as drinking brandy, chewing tobacco, smoking, associating (or rather fraternizing) with noted sodomites, and lying. After it became known that Jack gave McDonald a yanckum, I cautioned Evans to not be seen in his company, but instead of showing a natural abhorrence of the crime by shunning the criminal, he rather courted his society; and by the brotherly intimacy that now subsists between the two, I should judge that no repugnance to, or abhorrence of, sodomy exists on either side. Bones may go! He has deliberately rejected my friendship and sided against me with those who would effect his ruin. I begin to feel that he carries a treacherous and foul heart under a fair and pleasant exterior. I have once loved him—I once smiled upon—I kissed his cheek with the fervor of affection—; I can never hate him—never frown upon him—and palsied[5] may that hand of mine be that should smite him, treacherous, and vile as he is; but he may go, nor look to me hereafter for kindness or countenance. By an effort I have erased his image from my heart. When

---

[1] *who has argus eyes* I.e., who sees everything; the phrase originates with the Greek mythological figure Argus, who was said to have a hundred eyes.

[2] *Loo Choo* Antiquated English name for the Ryukyu Islands, an archipelago that stretches between Japan and Taiwan.

[3] *Gibbon's Rome … Diospolis* In *The History of the Decline and Fall of the Roman Empire* (1776–89), Edward Gibbon describes the brutal punishment of two sixth-century bishops, Isaiah of Rhodes and Alexander of Diospolis, for the crime of what Gibbon terms "paederasty" or "unmanly lust."

[4] *onanism* Masturbation.

[5] *palsied* Paralyzed.

affliction comes upon him, he may look to Charley, to the Pirate, and to Jack for sympathy and help. Go! I have said it. It is the decree of my heart; a bitter tear has sealed it. Go!

Bayard Taylor, "To a Persian Boy, in the Bazaar at Smyrna"[1] (1855)

> Bayard Taylor (1825–78) was widely known during the mid-nineteenth century as a poet and translator. His travels took him throughout Europe as well as to northern Africa and central and east Asia, journeys that inspired both prose and poetry, often reflecting the nineteenth-century Euro-American fascination with the "Orient." Though Taylor was married, many of his works explore the idea of love between men. Taylor's 1870 novel *Joseph and His Friend* is today often cited as a landmark in the history of gay American literature for its forthright, passionate depiction of a romantic connection between two men. (Excerpts from that novel are included in the website component of this anthology.)

The gorgeous blossoms of that magic tree
    Beneath whose shade I sat a thousand nights,
Breathed from their opening petals all delights
Embalmed in spice of Orient Poesy,
When first, young Persian, I beheld thine eyes,
5   And felt the wonder of the beauty grow
Within my brain, as some fair planet's glow
Deepens, and fills the summer evening skies.
From under thy dark lashes shone on me
The rich, voluptuous soul of Eastern land,
10   Impassioned, tender, calm, serenely sad—
Such as immortal Hafiz felt when he
Sang by the fountain-streams of Rocnabad,
Or in the bowers of blissful Samarcand.[2]

---

[1]   *Smyrna* Ancient Greek port city on the west coast of what is now Turkey.

[2]   *Hafiz ... Samarcand* Reference to the poem "Shirazi Turk" by the fourteenth-century Persian poet Hafez, in which the speaker expresses his love for a Turkish youth, invoking the beautiful stream of Roknabad in the Persian city of Shiraz and the wealth of the Persian city of Samarkand. The gender of the youth is not made

from Rev. William Alger, "The Literature of Friendship" (1856)

> Boston-based Unitarian minister and author, William Alger wrote widely on the subjects of theology, comparative religion, and Eastern literature, and his lectures around New England were widely attended by intellectual figures of the day. This essay lamenting the relative absence of intimate friendships among men in nineteenth-century America was first published in the well-known literary journal *The North America Review*; he returned to the subject of friendship in his 1868 study *The Friendships of Women*.

... The instances in which friendship between men rises to the height of a controlling passion seem to be few, as we look around us. There have been times when such an experience was both more frequent and more prominent than now. There are still lands where it is far more common than with us. The prosaic sternness and literalness, the unsentimental spirit and frigid manners, of the Puritan type of character, are still influential in New England. We are an undemonstrative people. The understanding is exhibited, the heart concealed. Brazen sense lords it over modest sentiment. Iron-handed morality thrusts the graces aside. The glowing coals on the hearth stone of the breast are hidden under the ashes of a chill and formal exterior. Business and gossip are garrulous; friendship and poetry are silent. The endearing phrases, the meeting and parting kiss, the close embrace, the numerous spontaneous signs and endearments of manly affection, so natural and copious with the Italians, Germans, French, Persians, Arabs, Hindoos, are not cherished, are scarcely tolerated, here. ...

A reflective observer is astonished, when he thinks of the incomparable preciousness of friendship, to see how generally its culture is neglected. It is here as elsewhere; the real ends of the spirit, the true aims of life, are left to chance and to incidental side-play, while mere secular affairs—the routine of traffic,[3] toil,

---

explicit in the original Persian text of the poem; many translators have interpreted the youth as being male.

[3]   *traffic* I.e., trade.

and fashion—exhaust the serious labors and hours of men. Why, it seems to be asked, should we search for a friend, and earnestly strive to secure his heart? The lodestone attracts its related atoms amidst the jostle of matter. Yes, but man is not a lodestone. He has free will and contingent duties. He can seek or avoid, neglect or foster, many relations with persons. And friendship, above all things, thrives on smiling attentions, and in slight and carelessness perishes. It is a visitor which, though it may look in at the door of common courtesy, will not stay except where it is treated as a royal guest. Men struggle with frenzied energy and unflagging perseverance for money, position, reputation, power. Why should they not study, with as much greater painstaking as the prize is more valuable and essential, to found and nurture consummate friendships with the worthiest persons? One may become a millionaire, move in the selectest society, hold exalted office, and yet be none the better, none the wiser, none the happier; but when he finds a true friend, then, in this life-stadium, his chariot rounds the goal of success, and he snatches the surmounting wreath. Let us not, then, live friendless in the world, but give the laws of attraction free scope, and cordially embrace our fellows. ...

What fond and generous friendships are often bred among youthful companions in the bright epoch of school-day life! Then the innocence, gayety, and hope of unsophisticated hearts create sky and land anew, and robe the scene in their own soft hues. No cynic frost has fallen on our disinterested sympathies. The world has not laid its icy hand on our throbbing pulses. Our faith in each other, in whatever is lovely, virtuous, heroic, knows no limits. Then how frequent it is for attachments to grow up, at whose stainless sincerity and tender romance we smile in after years, when, alas! in too many cases, time has hardly brought enough to compensate for what it has taken away! Together we wander through the fields as through enchanted grounds. We dream dreams resplendent with the triumphs we fondly vow and think to win. In the artlessness of that pure time our secret souls are transparent, and in the unflawed clearness of our communion we look through each other. Our joys, our griefs, our whole hearts, are united in a free friendship whose strength and closeness foretell a sweeter and nobler life than the fairest passages of history have as yet realized. These

halcyon[1] unions rarely survive a full entrance upon the common pursuits of life. But they are prophetic. And when the cares of the world, the deceitfulness of riches, and many sins, come upon us and alienate us, still their glorious oracles are never all forgotten. They haunt us like voices from fairy land. And oft the cliffs and shores of memory reverberate the plaintive echoes of our love, calling after many a beautiful Hylas[2] vanished from beside the fountain of youth. How often the remembrances of the friends and the friendships of other days come back from the bygone times when we knew them, and fill our hearts as with the wild, sad melodies of an Aeolian harp![3] Who, as he reviews the hallowed hours that went so swiftly in the morning of life, and recalls the dear, familiar faces laid so early in the dust of the grave, would be ashamed to shed a tear to their mingled memory? ...

Friendship inspires those who are possessed by it. It is a perpetual fire, kindling brave thoughts and noble deeds. To deepen his friend's regard for him, a man strives to heighten his merits and multiply his achievements. Love adorns itself, that it may win its meed.[4] One desires to appear beautiful, heroic, wise, divine, to his friend. Together we can do what we should never have dared, and endure what would have crushed us, alone. ...

from Anna Cora Mowatt, "Woman-Friendship," *Women of the South Distinguished in Literature* (1861)

Best-known as the author of the hit play *Fashion* (1845), Anna Cora Mowatt was a novelist, essayist, and actor as well as a playwright. Her essay excerpted below was included in the anthology *Women of the South Distinguished in Literature*, edited by Julia Deane Freeman; it later appeared

---

1   *halcyon*   Peaceful; carefree.

2   *Hylas*   In Greek mythology, the dear companion of the hero Heracles. Heracles is distraught when Hylas disappears with a group of beautiful female nymphs; some myths suggest he went willingly, while others claim he was kidnapped and that the nymphs stifled his screams for Heracles.

3   *Aeolian harp*   Stringed instrument designed to make music when touched by a breeze.

4   *meed*   Reward.

in Mowatt's own collection *The Clergyman's Wife, and Other Sketches* (1867). (Excerpts from *Fashion* are included elsewhere in this anthology in the omnibus section "Popular Literature and Print Culture.")

All the world gives ready credence to the possibility of friendship between man and man—some people are even inclined to believe that the immutable attachment of Orestes and Pylades, of Aeneas and Achates,[1] may be repeated among men in these inconstant modern times; but the devotion of woman to one of her own sex, the sincerity with which she clasps the hand or presses the lip of woman, the genuineness of her self-sacrifices daily made for a beloved sister, are subjects of a vast amount of skepticism. Philosophic writers, poets, wits, have openly declared their disbelief in the existence of the strange phenomena of woman-friendships. Even Dinah Mulock,[2] who has written so many lines of woman which bear the impress of truth and wisdom—who has solved so many of the enigmas inseparable from woman's nature—gravely shakes her head when she touches upon "female friendships," and calls up such a doubting host of "ifs" and "buts" to usher in the possibility of perfect love between women, that we inevitably draw the inference that she sides with the unbelievers. …

… [N]ot only have we perfect faith in the possibility of a thoroughly unselfish, all-absorbing attachment between two women, but we entertain the belief that there are certain female minds so constituted that a tender friendship with one of the same sex is positively *indispensable to happiness*. Such natures experience an irresistible impulse to confide in one who, enlightened by her own yearnings and failings, can understand feminine wants and frailties—who can look upon feminine insufficiencies, not from a strong, manly, but a weak, womanly point of view.

A woman may be the most irreproachable of wives to the best of husbands, and yet feel a void in her affections, a chamber in her large heart unfilled—a something needful lacking, if there be no Celia[3] into whose ear she can pour the history of her joys and sorrows—to whom she can turn for advice, and lenient judgment, and comprehending sympathy.

There are trivial domestic difficulties, petty annoyances, perplexing positions with which no woman of tact will trouble and bewilder her husband by relating to him. If he is a man of decided intellect, he will not attach any importance to these small crosses, will not even understand these minor miseries, and the wife is thrown back upon her own resources, vexed and disheartened by her failing attempt to enlist his aid or sympathy. If he is a man of limited mental powers, he will be more annoyed than she, and will only increase her vexations without disentangling a single thread of the fine web of dilemmas into which she is snared. But to a sympathetic female companion, a woman may enter into all the details of these insignificant trials, and, clasping a friend's hand, she may search for and discover the clue that can guide her out of her domestic labyrinth.

The higher love—the love for man—neither absorbs nor forbids the lower, the friendship for woman. They are distinct, emotional capacities which may be coexistent in one heart. They are evidences of rich, spiritual organization. If they dwell together in pristine purity, one affection strengthens rather than weakens the other.

Who can deny that two women, through a mysterious affinity, may become, and recognize each other as, sisters in heart? Who can doubt that there is a bond of sisterhood between their spirits, as real and as strong as the tie of blood between sisters? And if this be true, must not that internal kinship outlive even the dissevering stroke of death, and proclaim them *true sisters* in the great hereafter? But in this lower sphere, what name can we give to their attachment but that of "woman-friendship"?

---

[1] *Orestes and Pylades … Aeneas and Achates* Examples of intimate friendships between men in classical mythology; the friendship between Orestes and Pylades in particular is often discussed as being potentially homoerotic in nature, though, as with many similar friendships in ancient myth, interpretations have varied greatly throughout history.

[2] *Dinah Mulock* English novelist Dinah Maria Mulock Craik, whose comments on the differences between male and female friendship in *A Woman's Thoughts about Women* (1858) are included in the online portion of this Contexts section.

[3] *Celia* Possible reference to the character of this name in Shakespeare's *As You Like It*, who is a cousin and beloved friend of the play's heroine Rosalind.

Addie Brown, letter to Rebecca Primus, 20 August 1859

The correspondence between Addie Brown and Rebecca Primus reveals much about the lives of free African American women in the mid-nineteenth century. The daughter of a relatively well-off grocer and seamstress, Primus was born in 1836 in Hartford, Connecticut; following the Civil War, she traveled to the South to establish schools for black children. Brown was born in Philadelphia in 1841 and received no formal education. She entered the Primus household as a domestic servant sometime in the 1850s. The two women clearly became deeply attached, and their written correspondence began in 1859, after Brown left to work in another household. Primus's letters to Brown do not appear to have survived, but Brown's letters to Primus reveal a passionately loving relationship. In presenting the following excerpt, the editors have foregone this anthology's usual practice of modernizing spelling and punctuation.

Waterbury Aug. 30 1859

My ever Dear Friend
I no doubt you will be surprise to received a letter so soon I think it will be received with just as much pleasure this week as you will nexe my <u>Dearest Dearest Rebecca</u> my heart it allmost broke I don't know that I ever spent such hours as I have my loving friend it goes harder with me now then it ever did I am more acquainted with you is seem to me this very moments if I only had the wings of a <u>dove</u> I would not remain long in Waterbury although we cant allway be together O it tis hard

O Dear I am so lonesome I barelly know how to contain myself if I was only near you and having of those <u>sweet</u> kisses. Man appoint and God disappoints.[1] There is not much news here worthy to attention there is going to be a picnic tomorry the Childrens temperance Jubilee. The hand of hope will be celebrated to it will be a grand affair. Mr. Pete Sinclair the well known apostle of temperance will address the Gathering I supose it tis quit gay in Hartford [...]

O my <u>Dear</u> Friend how I did miss you last night I did not have any one to hug me and to kiss. Rebecca dont you think I am very foolish I dont want anyone to kiss me now I turn Mr Games away this morning no <u>kisses</u> is like yours [...]

You are the first Girl that I ever <u>love</u> so it you are the <u>last</u> one Dear Rebecca do not say anything against me <u>loving</u> you so for I mean just what I say O Rebecca it seem I can see you now casting those loving eyes at me if you was a man what would things come to they would after come to something very quick what do you think the matter dont laugh at me [...] I must say I dont know that I every injoyed myself any better than I did when I was at your parents house. I was treated so rich by all the Family I hope I may have the extreme pleasure returning the same pleasure to you all each will remember the visit as for your self Dear H[enrietta] there is no one like her if you was to travel all over united states
[...] Affectionate Friend Addie
PS give my love to all the Family and kiss also to your Mo. Addie
please write to soon

---

[1] *Man appoint and God disappoints* Proverbial expression.

EMILY DICKINSON

1830 – 1886

Emily Dickinson wrote in a letter to a friend that "Biography first convinces us of the fleeing of the Biographied—." And indeed, as several generations of critics and biographers have approached this enigmatic poet's work and life, the poet herself remains elusive, though legends about her abound. Widely considered one of America's greatest writers, Dickinson has attracted a dedicated and passionate readership, as well as worldwide critical acclaim. Working entirely in compact poetic forms, she left us close to 1,800 poems, among which are some of the most incisive and psychologically powerful lyrics in English on the subjects of death, love, nature, and religion.

Emily Elizabeth Dickinson was born in Amherst, in the Connecticut Valley of Massachusetts, on 10 December 1830, and for most of her life she continued to live with her family in an Amherst mansion called the Homestead. She was the second of three children to Edward and Emily Norcross Dickinson. Edward Dickinson was a locally prominent lawyer and politician, who entered the United States House of Representatives in 1853. He was also a pious man who regularly read to his children from the Bible; Dickinson later said of him that "his heart was pure and terrible, and I think no other like it exists." Dickinson's mother, Emily Norcross Dickinson, came from a family that valued education for women, and she herself studied the sciences intently while at school. She suffered ill health throughout her life, and seems to have been emotionally distant; Dickinson said to Thomas Wentworth Higginson in 1870 that she "never had a mother. I suppose a mother is one to whom you hurry when you are troubled."

In 1840, Dickinson and her sister Lavinia were both enrolled at Amherst Academy, a converted boys' school with progressive educational ideals; here they studied subjects such as botany, chemistry, languages, and art, and attended lectures by visiting academics. By all accounts Dickinson was an engaged scholar, respected for her sense of humor and the strength of her intellect; she was also passionate about music and enjoyed dancing. In 1847, she began her secondary education at Mount Holyoke Female Seminary, where there was more emphasis on religious faith. Dickinson, who had not been baptized and who even at a young age maintained her distance from the established Puritanism of her community, publicly upheld her nonconformity. A fellow student, Clara Turner, remembered a day when the director of the school "asked all those who wanted to be Christians to rise." Dickinson remained in her seat and said to Clara: "They thought it queer I didn't rise—I thought a lie would be queerer." For reasons that remain somewhat unclear but that likely had to do with ill health, Dickinson left Mount Holyoke after a year, returning home in 1848.

In her time at school, Dickinson had developed several significant and intense friendships with both men and women. While at Amherst Academy, she became close to Leonard Humphrey, the principal of the school, who nurtured her love of reading. He was the first of a series of older male friends that Dickinson would refer to variously as "Tutor" or "Preceptor." The second was an attorney, Benjamin Franklin Newton, who worked with her father, and who introduced her to the works of William Wordsworth, Henry Wadsworth Longfellow, Ralph Waldo Emerson, and Lydia Maria Child. In the late 1840s, Dickinson met Susan Gilbert (later Susan Gilbert Dickinson), who was to become a life-long friend and eventually sister-in-law; the two formed a close bond and carried on a passionate correspondence; their letters have been interpreted by some later scholars as evidence of a romantic relationship. Dickinson wrote at least ninety-four poems to Susan, who—intelligent, sensitive, and open-minded—became very dear to the poet.

Dickinson's early life was also repeatedly marked by tragic loss. Her cousin and friend, Sophia Holland, died of typhus fever in 1844, and Dickinson's grief and ensuing depression were so deep that she was sent to Boston to recover. In May 1848, another friend, Jacob Holt, died, and two years later, Leonard Humphrey died of a brain aneurysm at the age of twenty-five. Three years later, Benjamin Newton died of tuberculosis when he was thirty-two. These were deep emotional blows to Dickinson, whose sensibility was marked by this series of young deaths; her poetry returns again and again to the themes of death, loss, and separation: "Parting is all we know of heaven / And all we need of hell."

When Dickinson returned home from school, she felt acutely the contrast between the relative freedom of school life and the constrictions of a home life in which a young woman was expected to devote her time to domestic duties. As she wrote to her friend Abiah Root in 1850, "God keep me from what they call households." Dickinson nonetheless took on many of these duties—and continued to do so throughout her life. She was a dedicated and gifted gardener; she baked the family desserts and bread; and she took care of her often-ailing mother. Dickinson also took steps, however, to secure some hours to herself, and she began in 1849 to write poetry. She refused to accept many of the social demands typically placed on the women of a prominent family like hers, withdrawing from the custom of "visiting" and receiving visitors; she saw only her family and closest friends.

Her need to preserve freedom may also have had a good deal to do with her decision not to marry. She wrote to Susan in 1852 about the merits of a single life: "How dull our lives must seem to the bride, and the plighted maiden, whose days are fed with gold, and who gathers pearls every evening; but to the *wife*, Susie, sometimes the *wife forgotten*, our lives perhaps seem dearer than all others in the world." Dickinson's choice to remain single did not mean that she lived without passionate attachments, however. She had intense relationships with both men and women throughout her life, mainly carried on through written correspondence (with the Reverend Charles Wadsworth, Benjamin Newton, and Susan Dickinson, among others). It is not clear to what degree these relationships were sexual, but it is abundantly clear that they could be passionate—and that, as the poet Adrienne Rich put it, Dickinson "was attracted by and interested in" men and women "whose minds had something to offer her."

In 1850 the Great Revival swept through Amherst, and Dickinson's father, sister, and many of her friends joined the local Congregationalist Church and declared themselves "for Christ." Dickinson did not join the church, as she had trouble accepting some of the tenets of the Congregationalist faith—particularly those surrounding predestination and hell. As she began to write more and more poetry, Dickinson often voiced religious concerns, but her spirituality was individual; she refused to adhere to a prescribed form of Christianity. In a letter to Jane Humphrey in 1850, she wrote: "Christ is calling everyone here, all my companions have answered … and I am standing alone in rebellion, and growing very careless. … I can't tell you *what* they have found, but *they* think it is something precious. I wonder if it *is*?"

At the Homestead, Dickinson continued to read widely in British and American literature, particularly the novelists and poets of her own century. She was also fond of the early modern poets—especially of William Shakespeare, of whose works she wrote to a friend, "Why is any other book needed?" Dickinson's own verse carries echoes of all these sources—as well as of the King James Bible, to whose rhetorical structures and poetic language she had been thoroughly introduced as a child.

However much she drew on literary traditions, Dickinson's own use of language, and the poetic forms she shaped, are unique. Most of her poetry is loosely organized according to stanzaic and metrical forms commonly used in Christian hymns—forms with relatively short rhymed lines, typically grouped in four-line stanzas. But Dickinson experiments with and transforms these traditional structures, using enjambment, imperfect and suspended rhymes, iconoclastic punctuation, and unusual word order to disrupt expectations and present compressed thoughts and feelings in extraordinarily suggestive ways.

Over the course of the 1850s the group of friends with whom Dickinson corresponded grew into something of a literary network. During her lifetime this was the primary audience for her poems, a quarter of which she sent to her friends in letters—letters which often also included reflections in prose that could be almost as cryptically expressive and fascinating as the poems themselves. "A letter," she wrote, "always feels to me like immortality because it is the mind alone without corporeal friend."

In the 1850s, Dickinson began to write to several correspondents from the literary world; these included two editors of the abolitionist newspaper *Springfield Republican*, Samuel Bowles and Josiah Holland. Bowles published seven of her lyrics in his paper, smoothing out a good deal of what he saw as Dickinson's idiosyncratic punctuation, rhymes, line breaks, and rhythms—a practice her other early editors also followed. Dickinson does not appear to have made any attempt to prevent such publication, and there is evidence in her letters with Susan that the two young women were looking forward to seeing "Safe in Their Alabaster Chambers" in print. In other letters and poems, however, such as "A Narrow fellow in the Grass" (1863) and "Publication – is the Auction" (1865), the speaker expresses highly ambivalent views toward the ideas of publicity and fame.

Dickinson's most prolific period of writing began in the late 1850s and continued to the mid-1860s, by which time she had written over a thousand poems. In 1858, she began making fair copies, organizing the poems into groups later called "fascicles," which she sewed together by hand. In the spring of 1862, Dickinson read an article in *The Atlantic Monthly* by the literary critic Thomas Wentworth Higginson. Wanting an educated opinion on her work, she sent him four poems, asking if her poetry "breathed." This letter prompted the beginning of a correspondence with Higginson that would last until Dickinson's death. Though he offered her some criticism and some poetic advice, Higginson greatly admired the poetry and was sensitive to the power of her personality; he became a great support to her (she later told him that he had saved her life by responding to her query). Though she wrote to him in the language of a student to her teacher, she maintained a confident independence about her work; rarely if ever did she take his advice. For his part, Higginson may have suggested regularizing a good deal of her grammar and punctuation, but he described her poetry as "woven out of the heart's own atoms," and later acknowledged that "when a thought takes one's breath away, a lesson in grammar seems an impertinence."

In the early 1860s, Dickinson's reclusiveness increased, as did her creativity and poetic output. Her poems became even more experimental and dynamic, and she began increasingly to add variants to her manuscripts—alternative word choices that she wrote down in footnotes or in marginalia, allowing for at times radically different readings to coexist within a given poem. Scholars have noted that her most productive period coincided with the Civil War. She wrote in a letter that "Sorrow seems more general than it did, and not the estate of a few persons, since the war began; and if the anguish of others helped one with one's own, now would be many medicines. ..."

The loss of Dickinson's father in 1874 caused prolonged grief, as her letters attest. "I dream about father every night," she wrote, "always a different dream, and forget what I am doing daytimes, wondering where he is. Without any body, I keep thinking. What kind can that be?" Her mother had a stroke the following year and broke her hip, and Dickinson became the primary caregiver until her mother's death in 1882. After a period of increasing ill health, Dickinson herself died on 15 May 1886, of kidney disease; she was buried beside her parents in Amherst.

The story of how the bulk of Dickinson's poems first saw publication after her death is complicated by a family disagreement. It began with the arrival in Amherst of David Todd, an astronomy professor, and his talented wife, Mabel Loomis Todd, in 1881. Dickinson's brother Austin and his wife, Susan Dickinson, both befriended Mabel. Dickinson also took an interest in her, albeit from afar: she would listen to Mabel sing and speak to her through a door, but the two never met. (Mabel, however, took a deep interest in Dickinson, and felt assured of her poetic genius.) The web of friendship frayed, however, when Austin and Mabel fell in love; the two began an affair that lasted for the remainder of Austin's life. After Dickinson's death, her sister Lavinia found a large cache of poems in Emily's chest of drawers; Lavinia eventually gave these to Mabel Todd to prepare for publication. Susan Dickinson, meanwhile, had a separate collection of poems and letters that Emily had given her over the course of their lifetime of friendship. The ensuing feud between Susan and Mabel over Dickinson's legacy continued down through their daughters' generation.

Mabel Todd, together with Higginson, edited the first two editions of Dickinson's verse, *Poems* (1890) and *Poems* (1891); these editions did not include any of the material from Susan Dickinson's collection. Todd and Higginson added titles to the poems, grouped them thematically—Dickinson did not title or number her work—and standardized much of her grammar and punctuation, with the intent of making the poetry more accessible. Their interventions received considerable censure in the late twentieth and early twenty-first centuries; the uncomplicated view that Helen McNeil expressed in the introduction to her 1986 edition—that Dickinson's "works were mangled by editors"—was widely shared. More recent scholarship has been less censorious and more alive to historical context—alive both to the extent that Dickinson's approach to poetry was ahead of her time, and to the sort of reception that her work would likely have received in the late nineteenth century had it been published with her manuscript capitalization, punctuation, and grammar intact. Even in Todd and Higginson's "cleaned up" versions, Dickinson's style met with a hostile reception from not a few critics; the reviewer for the popular *Scribner's Monthly*, for example, complained of her "neglect of form" and her "perverseness and eccentricity," while the famous British critic Andrew Lang was more caustic, writing in the *Daily News* that Dickinson "reminds us of no sane nor educated writer." Other critics were far more positive, however. The reviewer for the *New York Commercial Advertiser* termed Dickinson "the poet in quintessence," and in *Harper's*, William Dean Howells (perhaps the leading American arbiter of literary taste during the period) praised her "short, quick impulses of intense feeling or poignant thought," and concluded that her "strange poetry" constituted "a distinctive addition to the literature of the world." The poems were popular with the public as well—particularly among female readers; eleven editions were issued by the end of 1892.

After Susan Dickinson's death, her daughter, Martha Dickinson Bianchi, decided to publish the Dickinson poems and letters that had been in her mother's possession, under the title *The Single Hound* (1914). This volume sparked another surge of interest in Dickinson's poetry, one that launched her as a proto-modernist. In a review of *The Single Hound*, Harriet Monroe called Dickinson "an unconscious and uncatalogued Imagiste." This marked a moment in the history of Dickinson criticism when scholars began situating the poet within larger intellectual contexts—in relation not only to New England Transcendentalism and Puritanism, but also to international movements such as Imagism, the early-twentieth-century literary movement that valued concision, clarity, and formal experimentation. Modernist critics also placed Dickinson within the tradition of seventeenth-century Metaphysical poets such as Henry Vaughan and John Donne. By the early 1920s, Dickinson was firmly established as a significant American poet. In Conrad Aiken's introduction to *Selected Poems of Emily Dickinson* (1924), he describes her poetry as "perhaps the finest, by a woman, in the English language." Interestingly, however, Dickinson remained marginalized in many conventional narratives of the development of American literature; neither the 1924 *Short History of American Literature* nor the 1925 *Literary History of America* include any mention of her at all.

In 1955, the scholar Thomas H. Johnson collected all the Dickinson poems and letters that were, at that time, known to exist; his edition presented the poems for the first time in an approximation of their original state, and in an attempt at chronological order. Johnson's edition sparked renewed interest in her poetry—and that interest has never let up in the intervening decades. Scholars in the 1960s focused largely on thematic and linguistic concerns, those in the 1970s largely on feminist and psychoanalytic readings. Scholars continued as well to research her life and build her biography, as well as to consider her within wider nineteenth-century contexts. In 1998 came another major editorial achievement, Ralph Franklin's edition of the poems, which offered a more reliable order and chronology than had that of Johnson (Franklin was able to trace, from watermarks and pinholes, the original order of poems in Dickinson's fascicles). In 2013, the online open-access Emily Dickinson Archive was launched, allowing all interested readers and scholars to engage with images of the manuscripts. And in 2016, Cristanne Miller published a ground-breaking new edition, *Emily Dickinson's Poems: As She Preserved Them*, presenting all the poems in Dickinson's canon as they were copied down—those that were sewn into her forty fascicles, and those that she had kept in draft form.

In the twenty-first century, critical approaches to Dickinson have emphasized the materiality of her manuscripts and probed into the history of her various editors, with a focus on gender politics. Critics have also been considering Dickinson's poetry from the perspectives of ecocriticism, animal studies, queer theory, disability studies, race studies, and digital humanities. Dickinson's influence on American and world literatures has been profound. Readers, poets, and critics alike return to Dickinson for her ability to push the boundaries of language and poetic form, and for her articulation of a vision of human experience that is unique in its suggestive power, its compressed emotion, and its ability to prompt questions. As Dickinson biographer Richard B. Sewall has put it, "We still are not quite sure of her. We ask and ask."

NOTE ON THE TEXTS: As do the editors of almost all anthologies, we make an exception in the case of Emily Dickinson to several of our usual practices. It is by this time a commonplace to acknowledge that Dickinson's style is so idiosyncratic as to make it entirely appropriate to suspend an anthology's conventions regarding modernizing or regularizing punctuation, and capitalization—as we have done in these pages. We have also suspended the anthology's conventions regarding the dating of works; our normal practice is to foreground the date of first publication of each work; in Dickinson's case it is for obvious reasons the date of composition that appears after each poem.

The texts printed in these pages are based on the handwritten manuscripts themselves, in the facsimile form in which the Emily Dickinson Archive, in cooperation with the Houghton Library at Harvard University (and other institutions holding the manuscripts), now makes the vast majority of Dickinson's manuscript versions available to the general public. (Like all editors—and all readers of Dickinson—we are greatly in their debt for the opportunity to experience her manuscripts directly.)

In preparing the texts of the poems included in this anthology we have also consulted the three major editions that are based directly on the manuscripts: Thomas H. Johnson's *The Complete Poems of Emily Dickinson* (1955); R.W. Franklin's *The Poems of Emily Dickinson* (1998); and Cristanne Miller's *Emily Dickinson's Poems: As She Preserved Them* (2016). In many cases where the transcriptions of these editors differ from one another, we provide information in the notes as to those differences, often indicating our reasoning in siding with one editor over another or—in a very few cases—in offering a reading different from those of any of the three.

We also in these pages provide examples of the manuscripts themselves in facsimile form. As those examples show very clearly, *any* transcription of Dickinson's poems into a printed form entails judgment calls as to what constitutes a dash and what a period; as to whether or not a letter is capitalized; as to where line breaks occur, and so on. Following Johnson, Franklin, and Miller, we standardize all marks perceived to be dashes (Johnson standardizes using an em dash; we, like Franklin and Miller, employ a spaced en dash). But as all editors acknowledge—and as anyone reading the manuscripts for themselves can plainly see—those marks in a substantial number of poems[1] vary very widely indeed. Some are high in the line, some in the middle, some well below the line; some are very long and emphatically rendered, others are so short as to make it difficult to be sure if they are intended as dashes or as periods. A great many marks—especially at the ends of lines—have a downwards left to right slant to them, and are distinctly below the line. Miller conjectures that, "like many of her contemporaries, [Dickinson] probably quite often wrote elongated periods—in a kind of rolling stop. She may also have written commas both high within her row of script and slanting right rather than left." Miller nevertheless decides not to "thoroughly revise earlier interpretations of these marks." Such decisions are entirely defensible; they have the merit of simplicity, and do not risk confusing readers who have, over the decades since the publication of Johnson's edition, become familiar with the convention of representing a wide variety of Dickinson's marks in the same way. (For that very reason we have maintained the "one-size dash" convention in the transcriptions found in these pages.) But such decisions implicitly concede that print transcriptions of Dickinson's handwritten manuscripts inevitably entail a good deal of interpretation. The reality is that it is simply not known, for example, whether Dickinson intended a mark that resembles a right-slanting comma to be read as some form of dash, as a comma, or as a mark with some other, special meaning. In recognition of these realities, we have also, in the case of a small number of the poems presented in these pages, presented alternative transcriptions alongside the conventional ones. (As part of the anthology's website component we present several more such alternative transcriptions.)

In the case of several poems, we have also provided examples of early editing practice; this anthology's two-column format allows us conveniently to place different versions side by side, providing a convenient portfolio for the purposes of comparison.

In these pages we order the poems chronologically, taking the lead of Johnson and Franklin (and drawing as well on the scholarship of Miller). As one other part of the website component of this anthology, however, we present one complete fascicle—Fascicle 13—for the benefit of those who wish to study a group of Dickinson's poems "as she preserved them," to use Miller's phrase. Miller's edition has many merits, not the least of which is the degree to which it encourages scholars, students, and readers generally, to think of Dickinson afresh; we hope that the various ways in which Dickinson is presented in these pages will, in much more modest fashion, serve a similar end.

⌘ ⌘ ⌘

---

[1]   Much as the transcription issues are of considerable interest and real significance, it is important too to make clear that they are not ubiquitous. A poem such as "These are the days when Birds come back" is in this respect not typical. Indeed, a great many of Dickinson's poems present few transcription issues, or none at all; all editors are in agreement as to what is capitalized, what is a dash and what is a comma, etc.

[*It's all I have to bring today –*][1]

It's all I have to bring today –
This, and my heart beside –
This, and my heart, and all the fields –
And all the meadows wide –
5 Be sure you count – sh'd I forget
Some one the sum could tell[2] –
This, and my heart, and all the Bees
Which in the Clover dwell.
—1858

[*I never lost as much but twice –*][3]

I never lost as much but[4] twice –
And that was in the sod.
Twice have I stood a beggar
Before the door of God!

5 Angels – twice descending
Reimbursed my store –
Burglar! Banker – Father!
I am poor once more!
—1858

[*I robbed the woods –*][5]

I robbed the Woods –
The trusting Woods –
The unsuspecting Trees
Brought out their
5 Burs[6] and mosses
My fantasy to please.
I scanned their trinkets curious –
I grasped – I bore away –
What will the solemn Hemlock[7] –
10 What will the Oak tree say?
—1859

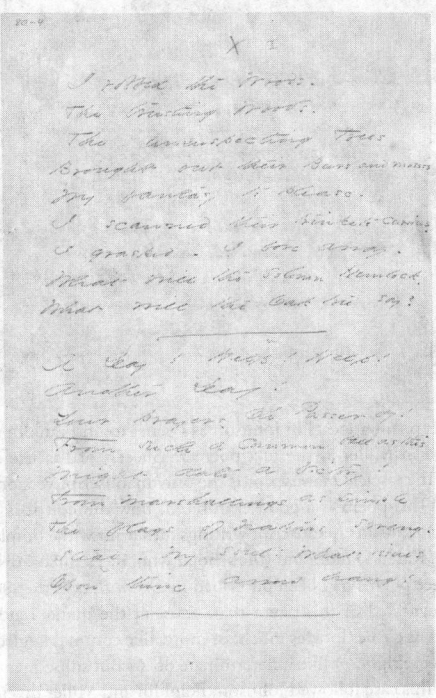

1 This poem appears in Johnson as Poem 26; in Franklin as Poem 17; and in Miller as the second poem in Sheet 3 of Fascicle 1, page 38. The present text is in complete accord with the transcriptions of Franklin and Miller; the marks after "fields" and after "count," however, could plausibly be transcribed as right-slanting commas.

2 *the sum could tell*   I.e., it would be reflected in the total number.

3 This poem appears in Johnson as Poem 49; in Franklin as Poem 39; and in Miller as the second poem in Sheet 3 of Fascicle 3, page 57. There are no transcription issues.

It is worth noting that Sheets 3 and 4 of this fascicle are made up of poems composed in 1858, whereas the fascicle's first two sheets are made up of poems dating from 1859.

4 *but*   Except.

5 This poem appears in Johnson as Poem 41; in Franklin as Poem 57; and in Miller as the fourth poem in Sheet 3 of Fascicle 2, page 47. The present text is in agreement with Johnson in reading the mark at the end of the sixth line as a period, but in agreement with Franklin and Miller in reading the mark at the end of line 2 as a dash. The marks at the ends of lines 7, 8, and 9 could all plausibly be transcribed as right-slanting commas. A facsimile of the manuscript appears above.

6 *Burs*   Acorns from the bur oak tree.

7 *Hemlock*   The reference is to the North American hemlock pine, not to the poisonous plant of the same name.

[*These are the days when Birds come back*]¹

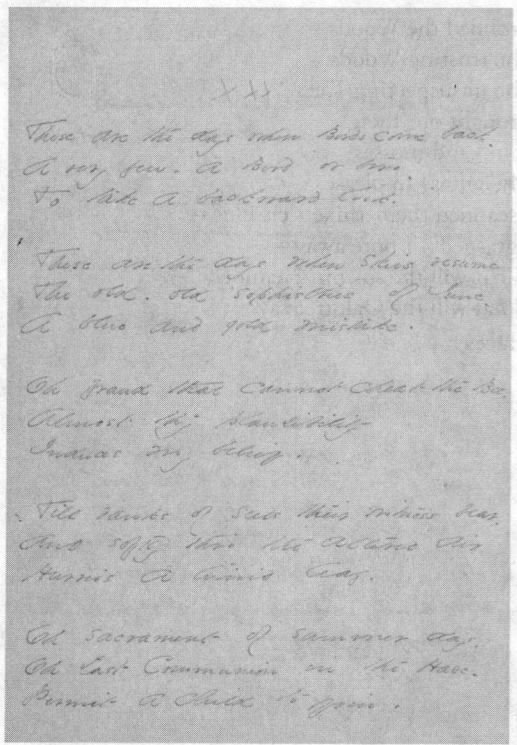

[*These are the days when Birds come back*]

These are the days when Birds come back
A very few – a Bird or two
To take a backward look.

These are the days when skies resume
5   The old . old sophistries² of June
A blue and gold mistake.

Oh fraud that cannot cheat the Bee.
Almost thy plausibility
Induces my belief,

10   Till ranks of seeds their witness bear –
And softly thro' the altered air
Hurries a timid leaf.

Oh sacrament of summer days,
Oh Last Communion³ in the Haze
15   Permit a child to join,

Thy sacred emblems to partake
Thy consecrated bread to take
And thine immortal wine!
—1859

1   This poem appears in Johnson as Poem 130; in Franklin as Poem 122; and in Miller as the first poem in Sheet 3 of Fascicle 6, pages 81–82. The fascicle manuscript is the only manuscript version extant.

   This poem is a good example of how difficult it is to transcribe Dickinson's manuscript writings into print with complete confidence. Karen Dandurand (the scholar who, in the 1980s, discovered that three poems had been published in *Drum Beat* in the 1860s) has fairly suggested of this poem that "most of the marks rendered by Johnson as dashes look as much, or more, like commas angled downward to the right, or like indeterminate dots." But subsequent editors have in this case followed Johnson; Franklin and Miller diverge from Johnson only in how they reproduce the mark at the end of one line ("Permit a child to join"), which Johnson prints as a period, Franklin prints as a dash, and Miller prints as a comma.

   A facsimile of the first page of the 1859 manuscript version appears to the left. In the next column we offer a transcription that endeavors to present the marks more-or-less as they appear in the manuscript. In the third column a conventional transcription is provided, with the right-slanting marks interpreted as dashes. The fourth column prints the text as it was published (from a now-lost manuscript) in *Drum Beat*, 11 March 1864.

   A version of the poem was included in Todd and Higginson's *Poems* (1890) under the title "Indian Summer."

2   *sophistries*   Deceptive reasonings.

3   *Last Communion*   Christian sacrament administered to the dying; the recipient eats bread and drinks wine in remembrance of Christ's sacrifice. The ritual is thought to bind the departing soul with Christ and thus with the promise of eternal life.

[*These are the days when Birds come back –*]

These are the days when Birds come back –
A very few – a Bird or two –
To take a backward look.

These are the days when skies resume
5 The old – old sophistries of June –
A blue and gold mistake.

Oh fraud that cannot cheat the Bee,
Almost thy plausibility
Induces my belief,

10 Till ranks of seeds their witness bear –
And softly thro' the altered air
Hurries a timid leaf.

Oh sacrament of summer days,
Oh Last Communion in the Haze –
15 Permit a child to join –

Thy sacred emblems to partake –
Thy consecrated bread to take
And thine immortal wine!
—1859

[*October*]

These are the days when birds come back,
A very few, a bird or two,
To take a backward look.

These are the days when skies resume
5 The old, old sophistries of June,—
A blue and gold mistake.

Oh, fraud that cannot cheat the bee!
Almost thy plausibility
Induces my belief,

10 Till ranks of seeds their witness bear,
And softly, through the altered air,
Hurries a timid leaf.

Oh, sacrament of summer days,
Oh last communion in the haze,
15 Permit a child to join!

Thy sacred emblems to partake,
Thy consecrated bread to take,
And thine immortal wine!
—1864

[*Success is counted sweetest*][1]

Success is counted sweetest
By those who ne'er succeed.
To comprehend a nectar
Requires sorest need.

5   Not one of all the purple Host
Who took the Flag[2] today
Can tell the definition
So clear of Victory

As he defeated – dying –
10 On whose forbidden ear
The distant strains of triumph
Burst agonized and clear!
—1859

SUCCESS.

SUCCESS is counted sweetest
   By those who ne'er succeed.
To comprehend a Nectar
Requires the sorest need.
Not one of all the Purple Host
Who took the flag to-day,
Can tell the definition,
So plain, of Victory,
As he defeated, dying,
On whose forbidden ear
The distant strains of triumph
Break, agonizing clear.

---

[1] This poem appears in Johnson as Poem 67; in Franklin as Poem 112; and in Miller as the third poem in Sheet 1 of Fascicle 5, page 69. The present transcription is in complete agreement with those of all three of these editors. The fascicle version probably dates from the summer of 1859; variant manuscript versions (in which the poem is not divided into stanzas) were sent to Susan Dickinson in 1859 and to Thomas Wentworth Higginson in July of 1862. The poem was first published in the *Brooklyn Daily Union*, 27 April 1862; that version (the source of which is presumed to have been a now-lost manuscript copy) was reprinted in 1878 in the anthology *A Masque of Poets*. Higginson and Todd made slight revisions for *Poems* (1890); this is the poem that opens that volume.

[2] *took the Flag* Won the battle.

[*Safe in their Alabaster Chambers –*][1]

Safe in their Alabaster[2] Chambers –
Untouched by Morning
And untouched by Noon –
Sleep the meek members of the Resurrection[3] –
5 Rafter of satin,
And Roof of stone.

Light laughs the breeze
In her Castle above them –
Babbles the Bee in a stolid Ear,
10 Pipe the Sweet Birds in ignorant cadence –
Ah, what sagacity perished here!
　　—1859 VERSION

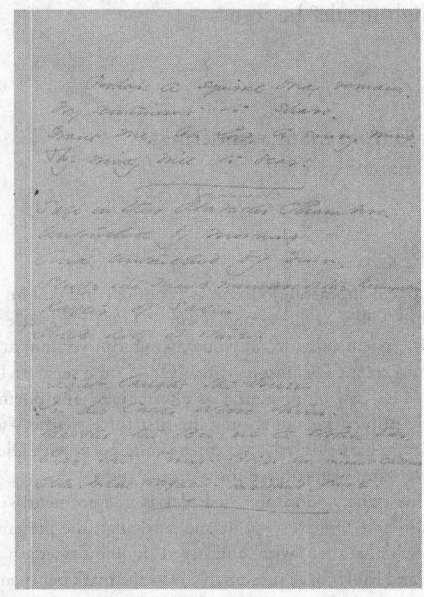

ORIGINAL POETRY.
The Sleeping.

Safe in their alabaster chambers,
Untouched by morning,
  And untouched by noon,
Sleep the meek members of the Resurrection,
  Rafter of satin, and roof of stone.

Light laughs the breeze
In her castle above them,
  Babbles the bee in a stolid ear,
Pipe the sweet birds in ignorant cadences:
  Ah! what sagacity perished here!
Pelham Hill, June, 1861.

[*Safe in their Alabaster Chambers,*][4]

Safe in their Alabaster Chambers,
Untouched by Morning –
And untouched by Noon –
Lie the meek members of the Resurrection –
5 Rafter of Satin and Roof of Stone –

Grand go the Years – in the Crescent – above them –
Worlds scoop their Arcs –
And Firmaments – row –
Diadems – drop – and Doges[5] – surrender –
10 Soundless as dots – on a Disc of snow –
　　—1861 VERSION

---

[1] This poem appears in Johnson as Poem 216; in Franklin as Poem 124; and in Miller as the third poem in Sheet 3 of Fascicle 6, page 83 [the 1859 version] and also as the third poem in Sheet 4 of Fascicle 10, page 122 [the 1861 version]. The present transcription is in agreement with those of Franklin and Miller—though it is worth noting that the marks at the ends of lines 1, 3, and 4 may plausibly be read as right-slanting commas rather than dashes.
　　A variant of this 1859 version was published (with the title "The Sleeping") in the *Springfield Daily Republican*, 1 March 1862.

[2] *Alabaster* Smooth, translucent white stone, frequently used for carving and statuary.

[3] *members of the Resurrection* I.e., the dead; those awaiting Judgment Day and the resurrection of the body.

[4] This 1861 version of the poem appears in Johnson as a variant of Poem 216; in Franklin as a variant of Poem 124; and in Miller as the third poem in Sheet 4 of Fascicle 10, page 122. The present transcription of the 1861 fascicle manuscript is in agreement with those of Franklin and Miller, except in two particulars: with Franklin, we read "Chambers" in line 1 as upper case; and, with Miller, we read "Noon" in line 3 as upper case. (Both can plausibly be read either way.)
　　An additional 1861 trial version of the second stanza is available under the heading *Dickinson's Personal Correspondence*, page 11, in the online component of this anthology.

[5] *Doges* Magistrates holding high civil office in the Venetian Republic from the seventh to the eighteenth centuries; the republic of Genoa also had a similar office.

[*Besides the Autumn poets sing*][1]

Besides[2] the Autumn poets sing
A few prosaic days
A little this side of the snow
And that side of the Haze.

5 A few incisive mornings –
A few Ascetic[3] eves –
Gone – Mr Bryant's "Golden Rod" –
And Mr Thomson's "sheaves."[4]

Still, is the bustle in the Brook –
10 Sealed are the spicy valves[5] –
Mesmeric fingers softly touch
The eyes of many Elves –

Perhaps a squirrel may remain –
My sentiments to share –
15 Grant me, Oh Lord, a sunny mind –
Thy windy will to bear!
—1859

[*All overgrown by cunning moss,*][6]

All overgrown by cunning[7] moss,
All interspersed with – weed,
The little cage of "Currer Bell"
In quiet "Haworth"[8] laid.

5 This Bird — observing others
When frosts too sharp became
Retire to other latitudes –
Quietly did the same –

But differed in returning –
10 Since Yorkshire hills are green –
Yet not in all the nests I meet –
Can Nightingale[9] be seen –

Or –

Gathered from many wanderings –
15 Gethsemane[10] can tell

---

[1] This poem appears in Johnson as Poem 131; in Franklin as Poem 123; and in Miller as the second poem in Sheet 3 of Fascicle 6, page 82. The present transcription has been made according to conventional principles and, except for reading the mark after "Haze" as a period, is in accord with those of Johnson, Franklin, and Miller (all of whom print the poem with a dash after "Gone" in line 7, and with dashes at the ends of lines 5, 6, 7, 9, 10, 13, 14, and 15). These marks could all plausibly be read differently, however—the mark after "Gone" as a period; and the other marks as right-slanting commas. An alternative transcription appears in the website component of this anthology.

    The poem appears in Todd and Higginson's *Poems* (1891) as Poem 49; they assign to it the title "November."

[2] *Besides* In addition to, beyond.

[3] *Ascetic* Austere, self-denying; Christian Ascetics withdrew from society and practiced abstinence and fasting, adhering to rigorous schedules of work and prayer.

[4] *Mr Bryant's "Golden Rod"* See "The Death of the Flowers," line 15, by American poet William Cullen Bryant (1794–1878); *Mr Thomson's "sheaves"* See "Autumn," a section of the longer work *The Seasons*, by Scottish poet James Thomson (1700–48), lines 168 and 180.

[5] *spicy valves* I.e., flowers or seed pods that open or split like valves or doors; may refer more specifically to the "valves" of the flower's nectaries (which release scent as well as nectar).

[6] This poem appears in Johnson as Poem 148; in Franklin as Poem 146; and in Miller as the second poem in Sheet 1, Fascicle 7, pages 86–87. The poem exists in only one manuscript version; at the end of the third stanza Dickinson writes "Or –" on a separate line, and then provides two more stanzas as alternatives. The poem is thus frequently printed including only the first three stanzas—although some editions have printed it as a three-stanza poem with Dickinson's alternative stanzas substituted for stanzas 2 and 3.

    The transcription provided here is in agreement with those of Franklin and Miller except in one particular; the present editors read the mark between "with" and "weed" in line 2 as a dash, whereas Franklin and Miller have presumably read the mark between the two words as the cross from the "t" in "with." Dickinson certainly often places the crosses for her "t"s well beyond where the letter itself appears, but rarely so far forward as here—and rarely so low.

[7] *cunning* Skillful and crafty, as well as quaint, attractive.

[8] *Currer Bell* Pseudonym of English novelist and poet Charlotte Brontë (1816–55); *Haworth* Name of the parsonage where the Brontë family lived in Yorkshire, England (the graveyard attached to the church was directly adjacent to the parsonage house).

[9] *Nightingale* Migratory thrush whose beautiful, haunting song and habit of night-time singing have led to a symbolic association with poets and singers.

[10] *Gethsemane* Garden in Jerusalem where Christ prayed and endured agony of mind before his arrest and crucifixion.

Thro' what transporting anguish
She reached the Asphodel![1]

Soft fall the sounds of Eden
Upon her puzzled ear –
20 Oh what an afternoon for Heaven,
When "Bronte" entered there!
—1860

[*I'm "wife" – I've finished that –*][2]

I'm "wife" – I've finished that –
That other state –
I'm Czar[3] – I'm "Woman" now –
It's safer so –

5 How odd the Girl's life looks
Behind this soft Eclipse –
I think that Earth feels so
To folks in Heaven – now –

This being comfort – then
10 That other kind – was pain –
But why compare?
I'm "Wife"! Stop there!
—1861

[*Title divine – is mine!*][4]

Title divine – is mine!
The Wife – without the Sign!
Acute Degree – conferred on me –
Empress of Calvary![5]
5 Royal – all but the Crown!
Betrothed – without the swoon
God sends us Women –
When you – hold – Garnet to Garnet –
Gold – to Gold –
10 Born – Bridalled[6] – Shrouded –
In a Day –
Tri Victory
"My Husband" – women say –
Stroking the Melody –
15 Is this – the way?
—c. 1861

---

[1] *Asphodel* In Greek mythology, this white flower covers the Elysian Fields, where heroes and virtuous souls rested after death.

[2] This poem appears in Johnson as Poem 199; in Franklin as Poem 225; and in Miller as the fourth poem in Sheet 6, Fascicle 9, pages 112–13. There are few transcription issues—though the "dash" following "kind" in line 10 arguably might be better represented by a dot than a line of any length.

Todd and Higginson included the poem under the title "Apocalypse" in their edition of *Poems* (1890); aside from differences in punctuation, the version there includes two word changes in the second stanza; "feels" to "seems" and "folks" to "those."

[3] *Czar* Title of the emperor of Russia.

---

[4] This poem appears in Johnson as Poem 1072; in Franklin as Poem 194; and in Miller under "Poems Not Retained" on page 701. The poem exists in two manuscript versions (one to Samuel Bowles, the other to Susan Dickinson), both sent by Dickinson as letters, and both including this message following the poem itself: "Here's what I had to 'tell you' –you will tell no other: – Honor – is its own pawn." (Dickinson uses the "Honor is its own pawn" appeal in her 16 April 1862 letter to Thomas Wentworth Higginson.)

One line appears only in the version sent to Susan Dickinson; the Bowles version does not include the line "Tri Victory." In the Bowles version (but not in the Susan Dickinson) the word "this" in the final line is underlined. The present transcription is from the Susan Dickinson letter; Miller transcribes from the Bowles letter, while both Johnson (in *Final Harvest*) and Franklin (in *The Poems of Emily Dickinson: Reading Edition*) offer a composite version, including the "Tri Victory" line from the Susan Dickinson version and the underlining of "this" from the Bowles version.

An alternative transcription (in which this mark ˏ is used for "dashes" that have the form of right-slanting commas) appears in the website component of this anthology.

[5] *Calvary* Place where Christ was crucified.

[6] *Bridalled* I.e., married (with a pun on "bridled").

[*Faith is a fine invention*][1]

Faith is a fine invention
For Gentlemen who *see*.
But *Microscopes* are prudent
In an Emergency!
—1861

[*"Faith" is a fine invention*]

"Faith" is a fine invention
For Gentlemen who <u>see</u>!
But Microscopes are prudent
In an Emergency!
—1861

[*Some keep the Sabbath going to Church —*][2]

Some keep the Sabbath going to Church –
I keep it, staying at Home –
With a Bobolink[3] for a Chorister –
And an Orchard, for a Dome –

5　Some keep the Sabbath in Surplice[4] –
I just wear my Wings –
And instead of tolling the Bell, for Church,
Our little Sexton[5] – sings.

God preaches, a noted Clergyman –
10　And the sermon is never long,
So instead of getting to Heaven, at last –
I'm going, all along.
—1861

---

[1]　The earliest extant version of this poem is that which appears in a letter to Samuel Bowles (dating probably from late 1860 or early 1861):

> Dear Mr Bowles
> Thank you.
>> "Faith" is a fine invention
>> When Gentlemen can see –
>> But Microscopes are prudent
>> In an Emergency.
> You spoke of the "East." I have thought about it this winter.
> Don't you think you and I should be shrewder, to take the <u>Mountain Road</u>?
>> That <u>Bareheaded life</u> – under the grass – worries one like a wasp.
> The Rose is for Mary.
>> Emily.

Dickinson included a revised version of the poem in Fascicle 10 (printed first above), and included a slightly different version in Fascicle 12 the next year (also printed above). The standard editions take different approaches to the poem: Johnson prints a transcription of the 1860 Bowles letter version as Poem 185; Franklin prints a transcription of the Fascicle 12 version as Poem 202; and Miller prints both fascicle versions (Fascicle 10, Sheet 1, page 119; Fascicle 12, Sheet 1, page 137), while noting in a footnote the existence of the Bowles letter version. Miller reads the punctuation at the end of the second line of the Fascicle 10 version as a dash; in other respects the present transcriptions are in accord with hers.

[2]　This poem appears in Johnson as Poem 324; in Franklin as Poem 236; and in Miller as the final poem of Fascicle 9, Sheet 7, page 115. In their one-volume editions, both Johnson and Franklin print the version that Dickinson sent to Thomas Wentworth Higginson in July of 1861; that version is also used as the base text here. Miller prints the fascicle version (believed to date from the spring of 1861).

The poem was published (from a now-lost manuscript copy) in *Round Table*, 12 March 1864, under the title "My Sabbath," and was published by Todd and Higginson in *Poems* (1890) under the title "A Service of Song." As was standard practice when Dickinson's poems were published in her lifetime, capitalization, and punctuation were regularized; this resulted in the removal of most of the dashes—but also in the addition of one dash (both the *Round Table* version and the *Poems* [1890] version add a comma after "preaches" in line 9).

An alternative transcription (in which this mark ˌ is used for marks that have the form of right-slanting commas) appears in the website component of this anthology; the "dashes" at the ends of lines 2, 3, and 6 take this form, and the mark after "Heaven" is represented as a dot in the middle of the line rather than a comma, or, as it is sometimes transcribed, a dash.

[3]　*Bobolink*　North American songbird with a cheerful, tinkling song; its black and white plumage gives the bird a clerical look.

[4]　*Surplice*　Type of vestment worn by ministers, choristers, and other church officials.

[5]　*Sexton*　Caretaker of a church who traditionally rang the church bells.

[*The Lamp burns sure – within –*][1]

The Lamp burns sure – within –
Tho' Serfs[2] – supply the Oil –
It matters not the busy Wick –
At her phosphoric[3] toil!

5 The Slave – forgets – to fill –
The Lamp – burns golden – on –
Unconscious that the oil is out –
As that the Slave – is gone.
—1861

[*I came to buy a smile – today –*][4]

I came to buy a smile – today –
But just a single smile –
The smallest one upon your cheek
Will suit me just as well –
5 The one that no one else would miss
It shone so very small –
I'm pleading at the counter – sir –
Could you afford to sell?

I've Diamonds – on my fingers –
10 You know what Diamonds are!
I've Rubies – like the Evening Blood –
And Topaz – like the star!
'Twould be a bargain for a Jew![5]
Say – may I have it – Sir?
—1861

---

[1] This poem appears in Johnson as Poem 233; in Franklin as Poem 247; and in Miller as the fourth poem in Sheet 1 of Fascicle 10, page 117. The present text is in complete accord with the transcriptions of Johnson, Franklin, and Miller; the mark at the end of line 3, however, could plausibly be transcribed as a right-slanting comma.

[2] *Serf* Person in servitude; slave.

[3] *phosphoric* Phosphorescent, glowing in the dark.

[4] This poem appears in Johnson as Poem 223; in Franklin as Poem 258; and in Miller as the only poem in Sheet 2 of Fascicle 11, page 127. The present text is in agreement with Franklin and Miller regarding the punctuation of the poem, and with Miller in emending "opon" to "upon" in line 3.

[5] *'Twould ... Jew* I.e., you would get a good deal (Dickinson is referring to the racist stereotype that Jewish people get the better of others in financial dealings).

[*I'm Nobody! Who are you?*][6]

I'm Nobody! Who are you?
Are you – Nobody – too?
Then there's a pair of us!
Don't tell! they'd banish us – you know!

5 How dreary – to be – Somebody!
How public – like a Frog –
To tell your name – the livelong June –
To an admiring Bog!
—1861

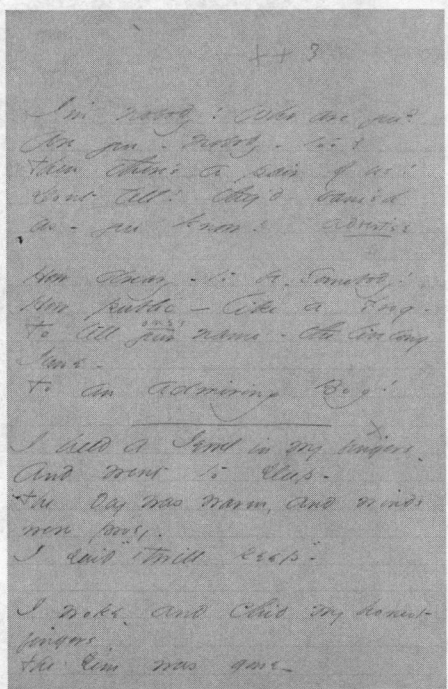

---

[6] This poem appears in Johnson as Poem 288; in Franklin as Poem 260; and in Miller as part of Fascicle 11, Sheet 4, page 128. The poem was printed by Todd and Higginson in *Poems* (1891), with "Don't tell" printed at the end of the third line rather than the beginning of the fourth. There is only one manuscript version extant; transcriptions of the fourth line vary. The present editors follow Johnson in emending "Dont" to "Don't," while printing "they'd" in lower case; Franklin transcribes the line as-is ("Dont … they'd"), while Miller emends "Dont" to "Don't" and capitalizes "They'd."

Dickinson provides two variant word choices in the manuscript: "advertise" for "banish" in line 4, and "one's" for "your" in line 7.

A facsimile of the manuscript appears above.

X 2

Wild nights - Wild nights!
Were I with thee
Wild nights - should be
Our luxury!

Futile - the winds -
To a Heart in port -
Done with the Compass -
Done with the Chart -!

Rowing in Eden -
Ah - the Sea!
Might I but moor -
Tonight -
In thee!

[*Wild nights – Wild nights!*][1]

Wild nights – Wild nights!
Were I with thee
Wild nights should[2] be
Our luxury!

5   Futile – the winds –
To a Heart in port –
Done with the Compass –
Done with the Chart!

Rowing in Eden –
10 Ah – the Sea!
Might I but moor – tonight –
In thee!
—1861

[*Wild nights – Wild nights!*]

Wild nights – Wild nights!
Were I with thee
Wild nights should be
Our luxury!

5   Futile – the winds –
To a Heart in port –
Done with the Compass –
Done with the Chart!

Rowing in Eden –
10 Ah! the Sea!
Might I but moor –
Tonight –
In thee!
—1861

---

[1] This poem appears in Johnson as Poem 249; in Franklin as Poem 269; and in Miller as part of Fascicle 11, Sheet 8, page 133. Here we present first a facsimile of the only manuscript version (see the facing page). Next is a conventional transcription of the poem, according to the principles followed by both Franklin and Miller—with the mark after "Ah" interpreted as a dash, and with "tonight" interpreted as the final word of the eleventh line, written in lower case. The next column presents an alternative transcription, with the mark after "Ah" interpreted as an exclamation mark missing its dot, and "Tonight" read as a capitalized word, forming a line on its own. Given that Dickinson capitalized with great frequency, and that she did not generally indent so as to make it clear if a word at the beginning of a line was intended to be carried over from the previous line or to begin a new line, other readings seem possible as well. Johnson reads the mark after "Ah" as a comma and capitalizes "Tonight," while keeping it as part of the eleventh line.

   Todd and Higginson include the poem in their edition of *Poems*, second series (1891), with "To-night" capitalized and printed at the beginning of the twelfth line rather than at the end of the eleventh; their version is reproduced here on the following page.

[2] *should* Would.

[*Wild nights – Wild nights!*]

Wild nights! Wild nights!
Were I with thee,
Wild nights should be
Our luxury!

5   Futile the winds
To a heart in port,
Done with the compass,
Done with the chart.

Rowing in Eden!
10 Ah! the sea!
Might I but moor
To-night in thee!
—1891

[*Over the fence –*][1]

Over the fence –
Strawberries – grow –
Over the fence –
I could climb – if I tried, I know –
5   Berries are nice!

But – if I stained my Apron –
God would certainly scold!
Oh, dear, – I guess if He were a Boy –
He'd – climb – if He could!
—1861

---

1   This poem appears in Johnson as Poem 251; in Franklin as Poem 271; and in Miller as the last poem of Fascicle 11, page 134. The present transcription is in agreement with those of all three; it is worth noting, however, that the marks on either side of "dear" could plausibly be read as single quotation marks rather than commas—and that the following mark could easily be read as a comma rather than a dash.

[*I taste a liquor never brewed –*][1]

I taste a liquor never brewed –
From tankards scooped in Pearl –
Not all the Frankfort Berries[2]
Yield such an alcohol!

5 Inebriate of air – am I –
And Debauchee of Dew –
Reeling, thro' endless summer days,
From inns of molten Blue –

When "Landlords" turn the drunken Bee
10 Out of the foxglove's door –
When Butterflies – renounce their "drams"[3] –
I shall but drink the more!

Till Seraphs[4] swing their snowy Hats –
And Saints – to windows run –
15 To see the little Tippler
From Manzanilla[5] come!
—1861

The May-Wine.

I taste a liquor never brewed,
  From tankards scooped in pearl;
Not Frankfort berries yield the sense
  Such a delirious whirl.

Inebriate of air am I,
  And debauchee of dew;—
Reeling through endless summer days,
  From inns of molten blue.

When landlords turn the drunken bee
  Out of the Fox-glove's door,
When butterflies renounce their drams,
  I shall but drink the more;

Till seraphs swing their snowy hats,
  And saints to windows run,
To see the little tippler
  Come staggering toward the sun.

---

[1] This poem appears in Johnson as Poem 214; in Franklin as Poem 207; and in Miller as the first poem in Sheet 1 of Fascicle 12, page 135 [the 1859 version] and also as the third poem in Sheet 4 of Fascicle 10, pages 122–23 [the 1861 version]. The fascicle manuscripts are the only manuscript versions extant. Dickinson provides two variant readings: "Vats upon the Rhine" for "Frankfort Berries" and "Leaning against the – Sun –" as an alternative last line (Franklin adopts the variant last line in his *Poems of Emily Dickinson*). The present transcription is in agreement with those of Franklin and Miller, except in one particular; we read the small mark at the end of line 7 (which resembles a right-slanting comma) as a comma rather than a dash.

    A variant of this poem (from a now-lost manuscript copy, with a different last line) was published in the *Springfield Daily Republican*, 4 May 1861, under the title "The May-Wine."

[2] *Frankfort Berries* Grapes grown in Germany's Rhine Valley.

[3] *drams* Small cups of liquor or wine.

[4] *Seraphs* Angels.

[5] *Tippler* Habitual drinker, but not a full-fledged alcoholic; *Manzanilla* Spanish sherry.

[*There's a certain Slant of light,*][1]

There's a certain Slant of light,
Winter Afternoons –
That oppresses, like the Heft
Of Cathedral Tunes –

5 Heavenly Hurt, it gives us –
We can find no scar,
But internal difference –
Where the Meanings, are –

None may teach it – Any –
10 'Tis the Seal Despair –
An imperial affliction
Sent us of the Air –

When it comes, the Landscape listens –
Shadows – hold their breath –
15 When it goes, 'tis like the Distance
On the look of Death –
—1862

---

[1] This poem appears in Johnson as Poem 258; in Franklin as Poem 320; and in Miller as the fourth poem in Sheet 3, Fascicle 13, page 153. A facsimile of the only manuscript version extant appears to the left. Above is a conventional transcription of the poem following the principles established by Johnson, Franklin, and Miller; both Franklin and Miller read the poem as having thirteen dashes. (Johnson reads the mark after "difference" as a comma; in other respects his transcription is identical to those of Franklin and Miller.) The left column on the following page offers an alternative transcription, with this mark , used to designate punctuation that takes a form resembling a right-slanting comma.

Todd and Higginson edited the poem for their edition of *Poems* (1890), with "weight" replacing "heft" in line 3, and with only one dash; that version is reproduced on the following page in the right column.

[*There's a certain Slant of light,*]

There's a certain Slant of light,
Winter Afternoons ˎ
That oppresses, like the Heft
Of Cathedral Tunes –

5 Heavenly Hurt, it gives us –
We can find no scar,
But internal difference ˎ
Where the Meanings, are –

None may teach it ˎ Any –
10 'Tis the Seal Despair –
An imperial affliction
Sent us of the Air –

When it comes, the Landscape listens ˎ
Shadows – hold their breath –
15 When it goes, 'tis like the Distance
On the look of Death –
—1862

[*There's a certain Slant of light,*]

There's a certain slant of light,
On winter afternoons,
That oppresses, like the weight
Of cathedral tunes.

5 Heavenly hurt it gives us;
We can find no scar,
But internal difference
Where the meanings are.

None may teach it anything,
10 'Tis the seal, despair, –
An imperial affliction
Sent us of the air.

When it comes, the landscape listens,
Shadows hold their breath;
15 When it goes, 't is like the distance
On the look of death.
—1890

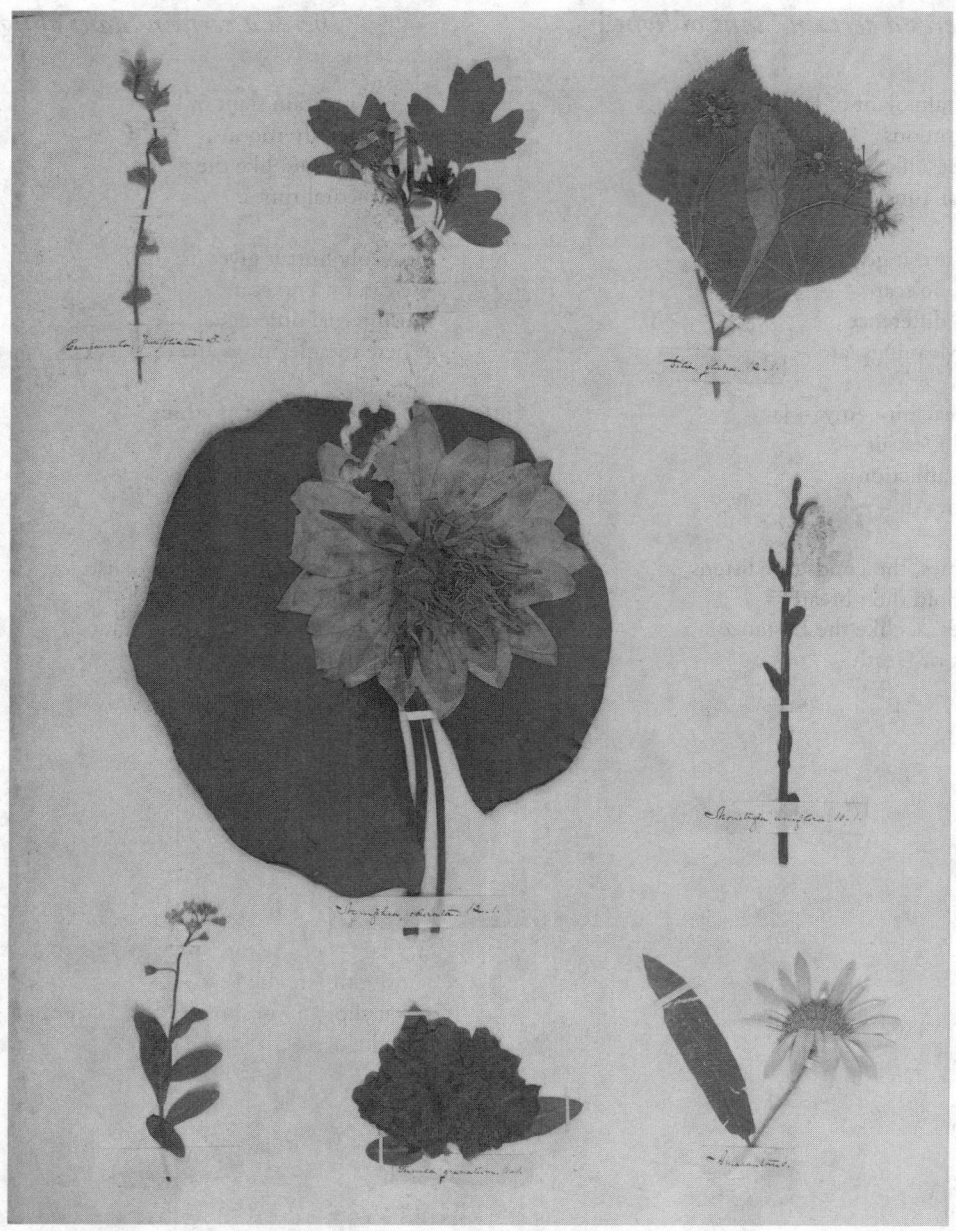

Emily Dickinson, *Herbarium*, c. 1839–46, Seq. 35. Between the ages of about nine and sixteen, Dickinson created a book of pressed flower specimens labeled with their Latin names. Among the plants included on this page is a flower that came to hold significance for Dickinson, the *Monotropa uniflora* (center right), commonly known as the Indian pipe (a name no longer in use), the ghost plant, and the ghost pipe. When Mabel Loomis Todd sent her a drawing of the ghost plant in 1882, Dickinson wrote a letter back, saying: "That without suspecting it you should send me the preferred flower of life, seems almost supernatural, and the sweet glee that I felt at meeting it, I could confide to none" (L769). The ghost plant also features in the 1879 poem "'Tis whiter than an Indian Pipe—". For an additional page from Dickinson's herbarium, see this volume's color insert.

[*"Hope" is the thing with feathers –*][1]

"Hope" is the thing with feathers –
That perches in the soul –
And sings the tune without the words –
And never stops – at all –

5   And sweetest – in the Gale – is heard –
And sore must be the storm –
That could abash the little Bird
That kept so many warm –

I've heard it in the chilliest land
10   And on the strangest Sea –
Yet, never, in Extremity,
It asked a crumb – of Me.
—1862

[*Your Riches – taught me – Poverty.*][2]

Your Riches – taught me – Poverty.
Myself – a Millionaire
In little Wealths, as Girls could boast
Till broad as Buenos Ayre[3] –

5   You drifted your Dominions –
A Different Peru –
And I esteemed All Poverty
For Life's Estate with you –

Of Mines, I little know – myself –
10   But just the names, of Gems –
The Colors of the Commonest –
And scarce of Diadems –

So much, that did I meet the Queen –
Her Glory I should know –
15   But this, must be a different Wealth –
To miss it – beggars so –

I'm sure 'tis India – all Day –
To those who look on You –
Without a stint – without a blame,
20   Might I – but be the Jew[4] –

I'm sure it is Golconda[5] –
Beyond my power to deem –
To have a smile for Mine – each Day,
How better, than a Gem!

25   At least, it solaces to know
That there exists – a Gold –
Altho' I prove it, just in time
It's distance – to behold –

It's far – far Treasure to surmise –
30   And estimate the Pearl –
That slipped my simple[6] fingers through –
While just a Girl at school.
—1862

1   This poem appears in Johnson as Poem 254; in Franklin as Poem 314; and in Miller within Fascicle 13, Sheet 2, page 150. All three of those editors punctuate the poem identically, as have the editors of this anthology—which is an entirely defensible reading, though alternative readings are certainly possible in lines 6, 11, and 12, and perhaps line 4 as well.

2   This poem appears in Johnson as Poem 299; in Franklin as Poem 418; and in Miller as the first poem in Sheet 5 of Fascicle 14, pages 165–66. The present text is in agreement with Johnson, Franklin, and Miller regarding the punctuation of the fascicle manuscript of the poem, and with Franklin and Miller in transcribing the "m" in "mine" in line 23 and the "S" in "school" in the poem's final line as lower case rather than capital letters. The marks at the ends of lines 4, 18, 21, and 22 could plausibly be read as right-slanting commas.

This poem was originally sent as a letter to Dickinson's sister-in-law and dear friend, Susan Gilbert Dickinson. "Dear Sue" was inscribed above the poem, and following it was a simple note: "Dear Sue – You see I remember. Emily." Dickinson also copied the poem into Fascicle 14 and sent a copy to Thomas Wentworth Higginson.

3   *Buenos Ayre* Buenos Aires, here representing the wealth of South America, whose mines of gems and silver had been much

discussed in American periodicals during this period; the other place names of this poem, "Peru" and "India," share this association with riches and splendor and were considered sources of exotic luxuries.

4   *Jew* Stereotypes in Dickinson's day often depicted Jewish people as merchants of precious gems.

5   *Golconda* Region in India known for its diamond mines.

6   *simple* Innocent, foolish.

[*I found the words to every thought*][1]

I found the words to every thought
I ever had – but One –
And that – defies me –
As a Hand did try to chalk[2] the Sun

5 To Races – nurtured in the Dark –
How would your own – begin?
Can Blaze be shown in Cochineal[3] –
Or Noon – in Mazarin?[4]
—1862

[*I like a look of Agony,*][5]

I like a look of Agony,
Because I know it's true –
Men do not sham Convulsion,
Nor simulate, a Throe –

5 The eyes glaze once – and that is Death –
Impossible to feign
The Beads upon the Forehead
By homely Anguish strung.
—1862

[*I felt a Funeral, in my Brain,*][6]

I felt a Funeral, in my Brain,
And Mourners to and fro
Kept treading – treading – till it seemed
That Sense[7] was breaking through –

5 And when they all were seated,
A Service, like a Drum –
Kept beating – beating – till I thought
My Mind was going numb –

And then I heard them lift a Box
10 And creak across my Soul
With those same Boots of Lead, again,
Then Space – began to toll,

As all the Heavens were a Bell,
And Being, but an Ear,
15 And I, and Silence, some strange Race
Wrecked, solitary, here –

And then a Plank in Reason, broke,
And I dropped down, and down –
And hit a World, at every plunge,
20 And Finished knowing – then –
—1862

---

1 This poem appears in Johnson as Poem 581; in Franklin as Poem 436; and in Miller as the last poem in Sheet 5 of Fascicle 15, page 175. Dickinson provides two variant word choices in the fascicle manuscript: "phrase" for "words" in line 1; and "done" for "shown" in line 7.

2 *chalk* Sketch, but also "make pale" or whiten.

3 *Cochineal* Lustrous scarlet color, made from a dye composed of the desiccated bodies of an insect, the *coccus cacti*, commonly found in Mexico.

4 *Mazarin* Deep shade of blue.

5 This poem appears in Johnson as Poem 339; in Franklin as Poem 241; and in Miller as the second poem in Sheet 2 of Fascicle 16, page 179. All three transcribe the poem in the same way—as is done here.

---

6 This poem appears in Johnson as Poem 280; in Franklin as Poem 340; and in Miller as the third poem in Sheet 2 of Fascicle 16, page 179. The present transcription of the fascicle manuscript is in complete agreement with those of Johnson, Franklin, and Miller. There are few transcription issues with the punctuation of the poem; the mark at the end of line 6 could plausibly be read as a right-slanting comma, and the mark at the end of line 8 as a period. Dickinson provides two variant word choices in the manuscript: "Crash" for "plunge" in line 19, and "Got through" for "Finished" in line 20. The poem was first published by Todd and Higginson in *Poems: Third Series* (1896), with the final stanza omitted and numerous smaller changes.

7 *Sense* Meaning, but also sensory perception, consciousness.

[*It was not Death, for I stood up,*][1]

It was not Death, for I stood up,
And all the Dead, lie down –
It was not Night, for all the Bells
Put Out their Tongues, for Noon.

5 It was not Frost, for on my Flesh
I felt Siroccos[2] – crawl –
Nor Fire – for just my Marble feet
Could keep a Chancel,[3] cool –

And yet, it tasted, like them all,
10 The Figures I have seen
Set orderly, for Burial,
Reminded me, of mine –

As if my life were shaven,
And fitted to a frame,
15 And could not breathe without a key,
And 'twas like Midnight, some –

When everything that ticked – has stopped –
And Space stares, all around,
Or Grisly frosts – first Autumn morns,
20 Repeal the Beating Ground –

But, most, like Chaos – Stopless – cool –
Without a Chance, or Spar[4] –
Or even a Report of Land –
To justify – Despair.
    —1862

[*A Bird came down the Walk –*][5]

A Bird came down the Walk –
He did not know I saw.
He bit an Angleworm[6] in halves
And ate the fellow, raw,

5 And then he drank a Dew
From a convenient Grass –
And then hopped sidewise to the Wall
To let a Beetle pass –

He glanced with rapid eyes
10 That hurried all around –
They looked like frightened Beads, I thought –
He stirred his Velvet Head

Like one in danger, Cautious,
I offered him a Crumb
15 And he unrolled his feathers
And rowed him softer home –

Than Oars divide the Ocean,
Too silver[7] for a seam –
Or Butterflies, off Banks of Noon
20 Leap, plashless as they swim.
    —1862

---

[1] This poem appears in Johnson as Poem 510; in Franklin as Poem 355; and in Miller as the first poem in Sheet 4 of Fascicle 17, pages 187–88. There is only one manuscript version extant; two alternative readings are written in the margins: "Knees" for "Flesh" in line 5, and "two" for "my" in line 7. Other than in line 18, the transcription here is in accord with the three standard editions. Miller and Johnson both transcribe the punctuation in line 18 as two dashes, while Franklin reads the line as having a dash at the end and no punctuation after "stares." In the manuscript the marks that appear after "stares" and after "around" are similar—both shaped like right-slanting commas.

[2] *Siroccos* Hot, dry winds from North Africa that sweep across the Mediterranean to Southern Europe.

[3] *Chancel* Section of a church where the services are performed.

[4] *Spar* Piece of timber, often used for supportive wooden structures on a ship, such as masts, booms, or gaffs.

[5] This poem appears in Johnson as Poem 328; in Franklin as Poem 359; and in Miller as the third and last poem in Sheet 5 of Fascicle 17, pages 189–90. There are two manuscript versions extant, both evidently from 1862; the punctuation of the two differs in several respects, beginning with the comma that appears after "Bird" in the first line of the version that both Franklin and Miller take as their primary copy text. The present text is (like that in Johnson's edition) transcribed from the variant manuscript; the transcriptions are identical except for the punctuation at the end of the second line, which Johnson reads as a dash. It is one of several points of uncertainty; several of the other dashes could well be read as right-slanting commas.

Another now-lost manuscript version was sent to Higginson, who printed the full poem in his October 1891 *Atlantic Monthly* article on Dickinson (see the website component of this anthology); Todd and Dickinson edited the poem for *Poems* (1890), giving it the title "In the Garden."

[6] *Angleworm* Earthworm (like those used by "anglers," or fishers).

[7] *silver* Glistening and in motion, like quicksilver (mercury), as well as silver in color. Dickinson describes the ocean in similar terms elsewhere, for example as an "everywhere of silver."

[*I know that He exists.*][1]

I know that He exists.
Somewhere – in Silence –
He has hid his rare life
From our gross eyes.

5 'Tis an instant's play.
'Tis a fond Ambush –
Just to make Bliss
Earn her own surprise!

But – should the play
10 Prove piercing earnest –
Should the glee – glaze –
In Death's – stiff – stare –

Would not the fun
Look too expensive!
15 Would not the jest –
Have crawled too far!
—1862

[*After great pain, a formal feeling comes –*][2]

After great pain, a formal feeling comes –
The Nerves sit ceremonious, like Tombs –
The stiff Heart questions 'was it He, that bore,'
And 'Yesterday, or Centuries before'?

5 The Feet, mechanical, go round –
A Wooden way
Of Ground, or Air, or Ought –
Regardless grown,
A Quartz contentment, like a stone –

10 This is the Hour of Lead –
Remembered, if outlived,
As Freezing persons, recollect the Snow –
First – Chill – then Stupor – then the letting go –
—1862

[*This World is not conclusion.*][3]

This World is not conclusion.
A Species[4] stands beyond –
Invisible, as Music –
But positive, as Sound –
5 It beckons, and it baffles –
Philosophy, don't know –
And through a Riddle, at the last –
Sagacity, must go –
To guess it, puzzles scholars –
10 To gain it, Men have borne
Contempt of Generations
And Crucifixion, shown –
Faith slips – and laughs, and rallies –
Blushes, if any see –
15 Plucks at a twig of Evidence –
And asks a Vane,[5] the way –

---

1 This poem appears in Johnson as Poem 338; in Franklin as Poem 365; and in Miller as the first poem in Sheet 2 of Fascicle 18, pages 193–94. There is one manuscript version extant, with little disagreement over the transcription. The present text agrees with Johnson in transcribing the mark at the end of line 5 as a period; both Franklin and Miller transcribe it as a dash.

2 This poem appears in Johnson as Poem 341; in Franklin as Poem 372; and in Miller as the third poem in Sheet 4 of Fascicle 18, page 198. The manuscript transcriptions by Franklin and Miller diverge in several respects from that by Johnson—most notably in that Johnson does not transcribe the quotation marks, and ignores the manuscript marks regarding the ordering of the lines in the second stanza. The present text agrees with those of Franklin and of Miller in every particular; it may be worth noting, however, that the mark at the end of line 7 could perhaps more plausibly be read as a right-slanting comma than as a dash, and that the mark after "First" in the last line appears to be a dot rather than a dash.

3 This poem appears in Johnson as Poem 501; in Franklin as Poem 373; and in Miller as the fourth poem in Sheet 4 of Fascicle 18, pages 198–99. There are several alternatives indicated in the manuscript: "sequel" for "Species" in line 2; "prove" for "guess" in line 9; "Sure" for "Strong" in line 18; and "Mouse" for "Tooth" in line 19. The transcriptions by Johnson, Franklin, and Miller are in agreement except in one particular; Franklin does not emend "dont" to "don't" in line 6. The present text agrees with those of Franklin and of Miller; it is worth noting, however, that several of the marks at the ends of lines could plausibly be read as right-slanting commas, and at least two others as periods.

4 *Species* Metaphysical ideal or vision.

5 *Vane* Weather-vane.

Much Gesture, from the Pulpit –
Strong Hallelujahs roll –
Narcotics cannot still the – Tooth
20   That nibbles at the soul –
—1862

[*I like to see it lap the Miles* –][1]

I like to see it lap the Miles –
And lick the Valleys up –
And stop to feed itself at Tanks[2] –
And then – prodigious step

5   Around a Pile of Mountains –
And supercilious peer
In Shanties – by the sides of Roads –
And then a Quarry pare

To fit its sides
10   And crawl between
Complaining all the while
In horrid – hooting stanza –
Then chase itself down Hill –

And neigh like Boanerges[3] –
15   Then – prompter than a Star
Stop – docile and omnipotent
At its own stable door –
—1862

[*The Soul selects her own Society* –][4]

The Soul selects her own Society –
Then – shuts the Door –
To her divine Majority –
Present no more –

5   Unmoved – she notes the Chariots – pausing –
At her low Gate –
Unmoved – an Emperor be kneeling
Upon her Mat

I've known her – from an ample nation –
10   Choose One –
Then – close the Valves of her attention –
Like Stone –
—1862

[*One need not be a Chamber – to be Haunted* –][5]

One need not be a Chamber – to be Haunted –
One need not be a House –

---

[1]   This poem appears in Johnson as Poem 585; in Franklin as Poem 383; and in Miller as the second poem in Sheet 2 of Fascicle 19, page 204. Franklin leaves "it's" uncorrected both in line 9 and in line 17; Dickinson provides several alternative readings in the fascicle manuscript: "hear it" for "see it" in line 1; "Ribs" for "sides" in line 9; "then" for "And" in line 14; and "punctual" for "prompter" in line 15. Todd and Higginson edited the poem for *Poems* (1890), giving it the title "The Railway Train."

[2]   *Tanks* Water stations (also called "water stops") for steam engines, where they could replenish their supply of water.

[3]   *Boanerges* Loud, denunciatory preacher.

[4]   This poem appears in Johnson as Poem 303; in Franklin as Poem 409; and in Miller as the last poem in Sheet 4 of Fascicle 20, page 218. The present transcription of the fascicle manuscript is in complete agreement with those of the three standard editions; it is worth noting, however, that several of the marks at the ends of lines (notably, at the ends of lines 1, 3, 5, and 11) could plausibly be read as a right-slanting commas—as could the marks after "Chariots" in line 5 and "her" in line 9. Todd and Higginson include the poem under the title "Exclusion" in *Poems* (1890); they adopt the variant word choices Dickinson provides for lines 3 and 4: "On" for "To" in line 3, and "Obtrude" for "Present" in line 4. Dickinson also provides manuscript variant readings for line 8 ("On her Rush mat") and line 11 ("lids" for "Valves").

[5]   This poem appears in Johnson as Poem 670; in Franklin as Poem 407; and in Miller as the first poem in Sheet 4 of Fascicle 20, page 217. The present editors follow Johnson and Franklin in transcribing from the 1864 variant that Dickinson sent to Susan Dickinson; it differs in several small particulars from the 1862 fascicle text, and in one large one: the fascicle text ends with "More near" rather than "Or More." The fascicle manuscript also includes numerous variants. Like Johnson (but unlike Franklin), we emend "it's" to "its" in line 7. Todd and Higginson include the poem in *Poems* (1891) under the title "Ghosts," evidently using the fascicle manuscript as their base text, but adopting Dickinson's variant word choice for line 8 ("Whiter" for "cooler").

The Brain has Corridors – surpassing
Material Place –

5 Far safer, of a Midnight Meeting
External Ghost
Than its interior Confronting –
That Cooler Host.

Far safer, through an Abbey gallop,[1]
10 The Stones a'chase –
Than Unarmed, one's a'self encounter –
In lonesome Place –

Ourself behind ourself, concealed –
Should startle most –
15 Assassin hid in our Apartment
Be Horror's least.

The Body – borrows a Revolver –
He bolts the Door –
O'erlooking a superior spectre –
20 Or More –
    —1862, 1864

[*They shut me up in Prose* –][2]

They shut me up in Prose –
As when a little Girl
They put me in the Closet –
Because they liked me "still" –

5 Still! Could themself have peeped –
And seen my Brain – go round –

They might as wise have lodged a Bird
For Treason – in the Pound –

Himself[3] has but to will
10 And easy as a Star
Look down upon Captivity –
And laugh – No more have I –
    —1862

[*This was a Poet* –][4]

This was a Poet –
It is That
Distills amazing sense
From ordinary Meanings –
5 And Attar[5] so immense

From the familiar species
That perished by the Door –
We wonder it was not Ourselves
Arrested[6] it – before –

10 Of Pictures, the Discloser –
The Poet – it is He –
Entitles Us – by Contrast –
To ceaseless Poverty –

Of Portion – so unconscious –
15 The Robbing – could not harm –
Himself – to Him – a Fortune –
Exterior – to Time –
    —1862

---

1 *through an Abbey gallop* Abbeys—usually haunted—are common settings in Gothic literature.

2 This poem appears in Johnson as Poem 613; in Franklin as Poem 445; and in Miller as the last poem in Sheet 2 of Fascicle 21, page 223. The present transcription of the fascicle manuscript is in complete agreement with those of Johnson and Miller; Franklin prints "opon" (for "upon") in line 11, rather than silently correcting, as is done by other editors. It is worth noting that several of the marks at the ends of lines (notably, at the ends of lines 1, 3, 5, 6, and 11) could plausibly be read as right-slanting commas. The manuscript provides a variant of line 11: "Abolish his Captivity" for "Look down upon Captivity."

3 *Himself* I.e., the bird.

4 This poem appears in Johnson as Poem 448; in Franklin as Poem 446; and in Miller as the first poem in Sheet 3 of Fascicle 21, page 224. The present transcription of the fascicle manuscript is in complete agreement with those of Franklin and Miller; Johnson reads what appear in the manuscript to be the poem's first two lines as one, thus regularizing the poem into stanzas of four lines each. It is worth noting that several of the marks at the ends of lines (notably, at the ends of lines 1, 4, 10, and 12) could plausibly be read as right-slanting commas.

5 *Attar* Essential oil made from roses.

6 *Arrested* Caught, laid hold of.

[*I died for Beauty – but was scarce*][1]

I died for Beauty – but was scarce
Adjusted in the Tomb
When One who died for Truth, was lain
In an adjoining Room

5 He questioned softly "Why I failed"?
"For Beauty", I replied –
"And I – for Truth – Themself are One –
We Brethren, are", He said –

And so, as Kinsmen, met a Night –
10 We talked between the Rooms –
Until the Moss had reached our lips –
And covered up – our names –
—1862

[*The Malay – took the Pearl –*][2]

The Malay[3] – took the Pearl –
Not – I – the Earl –
I – feared the Sea – too much
Unsanctified – to touch –

5 Praying that I might be
Worthy – the Destiny –
The Swarthy fellow swam –
And bore my Jewel – Home –

Home to the Hut! What lot
10 Had I – the Jewel – got –
Borne on a Dusky Breast –
I had not deemed a Vest
Of Amber – fit –

The Negro[4] never knew
15 I – wooed it – too –
To gain, or be undone –
Alike to Him – One –
—1862

---

[1] This poem appears in Johnson as Poem 449; in Franklin as Poem 448; and in Miller as the third poem in Sheet 3 of Fascicle 21, page 225. The present transcription of the fascicle manuscript is in complete agreement with that of Johnson, who emends "bretheren" to "brethren." (Franklin and Miller print the word with the additional "e.") The word was spelled (and presumably pronounced) with three syllables in late medieval times ("bretheryn"), though by Shakespeare's time it had become standardized as a two-syllable word. It is certainly possible that Dickinson intended the archaic spelling and pronunciation, but it seems at least as likely that this was an inadvertent misspelling; Dickinson was, as Miller says, "an erratic speller." It is also worth noting that, with the two-syllable "brethren," the line scans as iambic trimeter—as do the last lines of the other two stanzas.

There are few transcription issues with the punctuation of the poem, though the marks at the ends of lines 10 and 11 could plausibly be read as right-slanting commas.

---

[2] This poem appears in Johnson as Poem 452; in Franklin as Poem 451; and in Miller as the third poem in Sheet 4 of Fascicle 21, page 226. The present text is in agreement with Johnson, Franklin, and Miller regarding the punctuation of the poem—though the mark at the end of line 7 could plausibly be read as a right-slanting comma.

[3] *Malay* Person from the Malay Peninsula. Prior to the industrialization of the pearl industry, many pearls were harvested by divers in Southeast Asia.

[4] *Negro* In the nineteenth century, this term could be used to refer to any person perceived as having dark skin.

[*Our journey had advanced –*][1]

Our journey had advanced –
Our feet were almost come
To that odd Fork in Being's Road –
Eternity – by Term

5   Our pace took sudden awe –
Our feet – reluctant – led –
Before – were Cities – but Between –
The Forest of the Dead –

Retreat – was Out of Hope –
10   Behind – a Sealed Route –
Eternity's White Flag – Before –
And God – at every Gate –
    —1862

[*Because I could not stop for Death –*][2]

Because I could not stop for Death –
He kindly stopped for me –
The Carriage held but just Ourselves –
And Immortality.

5   We slowly drove – He knew no haste
And I had put away
My labor and my leisure too,
For His Civility –

We passed the School, where Children strove[3]
10   At Recess – in the Ring –
We passed the Fields of Gazing Grain –
We passed the Setting Sun –

Or rather – He passed Us –
The Dews drew quivering and Chill –
15   For only Gossamer,[4] my Gown –
My Tippet – only Tulle[5] –

We paused before a House that seemed
A Swelling of the Ground –
The Roof was scarcely visible –
20   The Cornice[6] – in the Ground –

Since then – 'tis Centuries – and yet
Feels shorter than the Day
I first surmised the Horses' Heads
Were toward Eternity –
    —1862

---

[1]   This poem appears in Johnson as Poem 615; in Franklin as Poem 453; and in Miller as the first poem in Sheet 5 of Fascicle 21, page 227. The present text is in full accord with the transcriptions of Johnson, Franklin, and Miller—though it may be noted that the mark at the end of line 7 could plausibly be read as a right-slanting comma. The poem was first published by Todd and Higginson in *Poems* (1891), under the title "The Journey."

[2]   This poem appears in Johnson as Poem 712; in Franklin as Poem 479; and in Miller as the opening poem in Fascicle 23, Sheet 1, page 239. The fascicle version (reproduced on the following pages) is the only manuscript version extant. The transcriptions in the Johnson, Franklin, and Miller editions are in complete accord, interpreting the marks at the ends of lines 3, 12, 13, and 24 as dashes, and the mark after "Centuries" in line 21 as a dash as well; the transcription here takes the same approach. In the "Alternative Readings" section that appears as part of the website component of this anthology we present an alternative transcription, in which the same marks are read as reverse or right-slanting commas (ˎ).

    The Todd and Higginson edition of *Poems* (1890) includes a version of this poem, under the title "The Chariot," in which there are several substantive changes—including the omission of the fourth stanza.

---

[3]   *strove*   Fought or quarreled.

[4]   *Gossamer*   Extremely fine material.

[5]   *Tippet*   Small shawl or capelet;   *Tulle*   Fine, netted fabric.

[6]   *Cornice*   Decorative molding that runs along the base of a building's roof.

31

2

Because I could not
stop for Death —
He kindly stopped for me —
The Carriage held but our-
self — Ourselves —
And Immortality.

We slowly drove — He
knew no haste
And I had put away
My labor and my leisure
too,
For His Civility —

We passed the School,
where Children strove
At Recess — in the Ring —
We passed the Fields
of Gazing Grain —
We passed the Setting Sun —

Or rather - He passed
Us -
The Dews drew quivering
and Chill -
For Only Gossamer, My
Gown -
My Tippet - only Tulle -

We paused before a
House that seemed
A Swelling of the Ground -
The Roof was scarcely
visible -
The Cornice - in the Ground -

Since then - 'tis Centuries -
and yet
Feels shorter than the Day
I first surmised the
Horses Heads
Were toward Eternity -

[*I dwell in Possibility –*][1]

I dwell in Possibility –
A fairer House than Prose –
More numerous of Windows –
Superior – for Doors –

5   Of Chambers as the Cedars –
Impregnable of Eye –
And for an Everlasting Roof
The Gambrels[2] of the Sky –

Of Visitors – the fairest –
10 For Occupation – This –
The spreading wide my narrow Hands
To gather Paradise –
—1862

[*He fumbles at your Soul*][3]

He fumbles at your Soul
As Players at the Keys[4]
Before they drop full Music on –
He stuns you by degrees –
5   Prepares your brittle nature
For the ethereal Blow
By fainter Hammers – further heard –
Then nearer – Then so slow
Your Breath has time to straighten –
10 Your Brain – to bubble Cool –
Deals – One – imperial – Thunderbolt –
That scalps your naked Soul –

When Winds take Forests in their Paws –
The Universe – is still –
—1862

[*It feels a shame to be Alive –*][5]

It feels a shame to be Alive –
When Men so brave – are dead –
One envies the Distinguished Dust –
Permitted – such a Head –

---

1   This poem appears in Johnson as Poem 657; in Franklin as Poem 466; and in Miller as the first poem in Sheet 4 of Fascicle 22, page 233. The present transcription of the fascicle manuscript is in complete agreement with those of all three of these editors—all of whom silently emend "visiters" in line 9. There are few transcription issues with the punctuation of the poem, though the mark at the end of line 5 could plausibly be read as a right-slanting comma. Dickinson provides one alternative reading in the manuscript—"Gables" for "Gambrels" in line 8.

2   *Gambrels*   Roofs with two slopes on each side. (This variety of roof was common in the northeastern states.)

3   This poem appears in Johnson as Poem 315; in Franklin as Poem 477; and in Miller as the third poem in Sheet 6 of Fascicle 22, pages 237–38. Miller transcribes from the fascicle manuscript, in which "substance" appears instead of "nature" in line 5; "chance" instead of "time" in line 9; "peels" instead of "scalps" in line 12; and "Firmaments – are" instead of "Universe – is" in line 14. The variant readings are included in the fascicle manuscript, and were adopted in the manuscript version sent to Susan Dickinson (also believed to date from late 1862), which is the basis for the present text. The first 12 lines in the fascicle version are organized into three four-line stanzas. Franklin's Poem 477 adopts all the variant readings of the Susan Dickinson version, but adopts the stanza structure of the fascicle version. Both Franklin and Miller retain the misspelling of "ethereal" as "etherial," which appears in both versions. There are few transcription issues with the punctuation of this poem.

4   *Keys*   I.e., piano keys.

5   This poem appears in Johnson as Poem 444; in Franklin as Poem 524; and in Miller as the second poem in Sheet 6 of Fascicle 24, pages 257–58. The present text is in agreement with the transcriptions of both Franklin and Miller. It is perhaps worth noting that nineteenth-century reading habits in a poetic context such as line 15 of this poem would almost certainly have taken "dissolved" as having three syllables (dis-sol-ved).

5 The Stone – that tells defending Whom
   This Spartan put away[1]
   What little of Him we – possessed
   In Pawn for Liberty

   The price is great – Sublimely paid –
10 Do we deserve – a Thing –
   That lives – like Dollars – must be piled
   Before we may obtain?

   Are we that wait – sufficient worth –
   That such Enormous Pearl
15 As life – dissolved be[2] – for Us –
   In Battle's – horrid Bowl?

   It may be – a Renown to live –
   I think the Men who die –
   Those unsustained – Saviors –
20 Present Divinity –
   —1863

[*This is my letter to the World*][3]

   This is my letter to the World
   That never wrote to Me –
   The simple News that Nature told –
   With tender Majesty

5 Her Message is committed
   To Hands I cannot see –
   For love of Her – Sweet – countrymen –
   Judge tenderly – of Me
   —1863

[*I'm sorry for the Dead – Today –*][4]

   I'm sorry for the Dead – Today –
   It's such congenial times
   Old Neighbors have at fences –
   It's time o' year for Hay.

5 And Broad – Sunburned Acquaintance
   Discourse between the Toil –
   And laugh, a homely species
   That makes the Fences smile –

   It seems so straight to lie away
10 From all the noise of Fields –
   The Busy Carts – the fragrant Cocks[5] –
   The Mower's Metre[6] – Steals

   A Trouble lest they're homesick –
   Those Farmers – and their Wives –
15 Set separate from the Farming –
   And all the Neighbor's lives –

   A Wonder if the Sepulchre
   Don't feel a lonesome way –
   When Men – and Boys – and Carts – and June,
20 Go down the Fields to "Hay" –
   —1863

---

1   *The Stone ... put away* Allusion to the famous epitaph at the site of the Battle of Thermopylae (480 BCE), where all 300 of the Spartan soldiers who were sent to defend Greece against the Persian army died; one translation of the epitaph reads, "Go tell the Spartans, thou who passest by, / That here, obedient to their laws, we lie."

2   *Enormous Pearl ... dissolved be* Reference to the commonly held belief that pearls dissolve in strongly acidic solutions. See also Matthew 13.45–46: "Again, the kingdom of heaven is like unto a merchant man, seeking goodly pearls: Who, when he had found one pearl of great price, went and sold all that he had, and bought it."

3   This poem appears in Johnson as Poem 441; in Franklin as Poem 519; and in Miller as the second poem in Sheet 4 of Fascicle 24, page 254. The present transcription of the fascicle manuscript is in complete agreement with those of all three of these editors. There are few transcription issues with the punctuation of the poem, though the marks at the ends of lines 2 and 6 could plausibly be read as periods rather than dashes.

4   This poem appears in Johnson as Poem 529; in Franklin as Poem 582; and in Miller as the first poem in Sheet 5 of Fascicle 25, page 266. Franklin leaves "Dont" uncorrected in line 18, whereas Miller emends to "Don't"; in other respects the present text is in agreement with the transcriptions of both Franklin and Miller. It is worth noting, however, that many of the dashes in the last two stanzas of the poem could plausibly be read as right-slanting commas.

5   *Cocks* I.e., haycocks, or piles of hay.

6   *The Mower's Metre* I.e., the rhythm of the scythe.

[*I heard a Fly buzz – when I died –*][1]

I heard a Fly buzz – when I died –
The Stillness in the Room
Was like the Stillness in the Air –
Between the Heaves of Storm –

5   The Eyes around – had wrung them dry –
And Breaths were gathering firm
For that last Onset – when the King
Be witnessed – in the Room –

I willed my Keepsakes – Signed away
10 What portion of me be
Assignable – and then it was
There interposed a Fly –

With Blue – uncertain stumbling Buzz –
Between the light – and me –
15 And then the Windows failed – and then
I could not see to see –
    —1863

[*The Brain – is wider than the Sky –*][2]

The Brain – is wider than the Sky –
For – put them side by side –
The one the other will contain
With ease – and You – beside –

5   The Brain is deeper than the sea –
For – hold them – Blue to Blue –
The one the other will absorb –
As Sponges – Buckets – do –

The Brain is just the weight of God –
10 For – Heft them – Pound for Pound –
And they will differ – if they do –
As Syllable from Sound –
    —1863

[*There's been a Death, in the Opposite House,*][3]

There's been a Death, in the Opposite House,
As lately as Today –
I know it, by the numb look
Such Houses have – alway[4] –

5   The Neighbors rustle in and Out –
The Doctor – drives away –
A Window opens like a Pod –
Abrupt – mechanically –

Somebody flings a Mattress Out –
10 The Children hurry by –
They wonder if it died – on that –
I used to – when a Boy

The Minister – goes stiffly in –
As if the House were His –
15 And He owned all the Mourners – now –
And little Boys – besides –

---

1   This poem appears in Johnson as Poem 465; in Franklin as Poem 591; and in Miller as the third poem in Sheet 1 of Fascicle 26, page 270. The present transcription of the fascicle manuscript is in complete agreement with those of Franklin and Miller. There are few transcription issues with the punctuation of the poem, though the marks at the ends of lines 3 and 12 could plausibly be read as right-slanting commas. The second dash in line 13—if dash it is—takes the form of an underline mark beneath the "s" of "stumbling"; Johnson does not read there as being any punctuation mark here.

2   This poem appears in Johnson as Poem 632; in Franklin as Poem 598; and in Miller as the third poem in Sheet 3 of Fascicle 26, page 273. The present transcription of the fascicle manuscript is in complete agreement with those of Johnson, Franklin, and Miller. There are few transcription issues with the punctuation of the poem; the mark at the end of line 11 could plausibly be read as a right-slanting comma, and the mark at the end of line 12 as a period. Dickinson provides one variant word choice in the manuscript: "include" for "contain" in line 3.

3   This poem appears in Johnson as Poem 389; in Franklin as Poem 547; and in Miller as the first poem in Sheet 1 of Fascicle 27, page 279. The present transcription of the fascicle manuscript is in complete agreement with those of Johnson, Franklin, and Miller, except in one particular; Franklin spells "mattrass" just as the word appears in Dickinson's manuscript, whereas other editors correct the spelling error. There are few transcription issues with the punctuation of the poem; the marks at the end of lines 11, 20, and 23 could plausibly be read as right-slanting commas, as could the mark after "Milliner" in line 17. Dickinson does not provide any variant words in the manuscript.

4   *alway* Always.

And then the Milliner[1] – and the Man
Of the Appalling Trade[2] –
To take the measure of the House –
20 There'll be that Dark Parade –

Of Tassels – and of Coaches – soon –
It's easy as a Sign –
The Intuition of the News –
In just a Country Town –
        —1863

[I measure every Grief I meet][3]

I measure every Grief I meet
With narrow, probing, Eyes –
I wonder if It weighs like Mine –
Or has an Easier size.

5 I wonder if They bore it long –
Or did it just begin –
I could not tell the Date of Mine –
It feels so old a pain –

I wonder if it hurts to live –
10 And if They have to try –
And whether – could They choose between –
It would not be – to die –

I note that Some – gone patient long –
At length, renew their smile –

15 An imitation of a Light
That has so little Oil[4] –

I wonder if when Years have piled –
Some Thousands – on the Harm –
That hurt them early – such a lapse
20 Could give them any Balm[5] –

Or would they go on aching still
Through Centuries of Nerve –
Enlightened to a larger Pain –
In Contrast with the Love –

25 The Grieved – are many – I am told –
There is the various Cause –
Death – is but one – and comes but once –
And only nails the eyes –

There's Grief of Want – and Grief of Cold –
30 A sort they call "Despair" –
There's Banishment from native Eyes –
In sight of Native Air –

And though I may not guess the kind –
Correctly – yet to me
35 A piercing Comfort it affords
In passing Calvary[6] –

To note the fashions – of the Cross –
And how they're mostly worn –
Still fascinated to presume
40 That Some – are like My Own –
        —1863

---

[1] *Milliner* Maker of hats and other clothing accessories (in this context, to measure for mourning garments).

[2] *the Man … Appalling Trade* I.e., the undertaker.

[3] This poem appears in Johnson as Poem 561; in Franklin as Poem 550; and in Miller as the first poem in Sheet 2 of Fascicle 27, pages 280–81. There are few transcription issues with the punctuation of the poem, though there are several with its capitalization. Franklin reads "eyes" in line 2, while both Franklin and Miller read "my own" in the poem's final line; in all those cases the present reading agrees with that of Johnson. Johnson, however, includes a dash between "my" and "own" in the final line, a point at which no punctuation is apparent in the manuscript. Dickinson provides one variant phrase: "With analytic eyes" in line 2.

---

[4] *so little Oil* Reference to an oil lamp in which the fuel is running low.

[5] *Balm* Soothing ointment.

[6] *Calvary* Site where Jesus was crucified.

[*Much Madness is divinest Sense —*][1]

Much Madness is divinest Sense —
To a discerning Eye —
Much Sense — the starkest Madness —
'Tis the Majority
5   In this, as all, prevail —
Assent — and you are sane —
Demur — you're straightway dangerous —
And handled with a Chain —
—1863

[*I started Early – Took my Dog –*][2]

I started Early – Took my Dog –
And visited the Sea –
The Mermaids in the Basement
Came out to look at me –

5   And Frigates – in the Upper Floor
Extended Hempen[3] Hands –
Presuming Me to be a Mouse –
Aground – upon the Sands –

But no Man moved Me – till the Tide
10 Went past my simple Shoe –

And past my Apron – and my Belt
And past my Boddice – too –

And made as He would eat me up –
As wholly as a Dew
15 Upon a Dandelion's Sleeve –
And then – I started – too –

And He – He followed – close behind –
I felt His Silver Heel
Upon my Ankle – Then my Shoes
20 Would overflow with Pearl –

Until We met the Solid Town –
No One He seemed to know –
And bowing – with a Mighty look –
At me – The Sea withdrew –
—1863

[*That I did always love*][4]

That I did always love
I bring thee Proof
That till I loved
I never lived – Enough –

5   That I shall love alway[5] –
I argue thee
That love is life –
And life hath Immortality –

This – dost thou doubt – Sweet –
10 Then have I
Nothing to show
But Calvary[6]
—1863

---

1   This poem appears in Johnson as Poem 435; in Franklin as Poem 620; and in Miller as the fourth poem in Sheet 3 of Fascicle 29, page 304. Johnson and Franklin read "All" rather than "all" in line 5; a comparison of Dickinson's rendering in line 6 of a capital "A" followed by lower case letters (in "Assent") lends support to Miller's reading of the "a" in "all" as lower case.

2   This poem appears in Johnson as Poem 520; in Franklin as Poem 656; and in Miller as the first poem in Sheet 2 of Fascicle 30, pages 311–12. The present text follows Johnson in emending all three of the obvious misspellings in the manuscript: "opon" in line 8, and again in line 19; and "Ancle" in line 19. Franklin leaves all three uncorrected, while Miller emends "opon" but not "Ancle." The present text is in agreement with Johnson, Franklin, and Miller regarding the punctuation of the poem. The mark in the middle of line 11 could plausibly be read as a right-slanting comma, and the mark at the end of line 4 could plausibly be read as a period.

3   *Hempen*   Hemp fiber was and is commonly used to make ropes; in the nineteenth century it was also (somewhat less commonly) used to make ships' sails.

4   This poem appears in Johnson as Poem 549; in Franklin as Poem 652; and in Miller as the last poem in Sheet 6 of Fascicle 31, page 329. The present text is in complete agreement with the transcriptions of Johnson, Franklin, and Miller. Dickinson provides three variant phrases in the fascicle manuscript: "did not live" for "never lived" in line 4; "offer" for "argue" in line 6; and "be" for "is" in line 7.

5   *alway*   Always.

6   *Calvary*   Site of Jesus' crucifixion.

[*What Soft – Cherubic Creatures –*][1]

What Soft – Cherubic Creatures –
These Gentlewomen are –
One would as soon assault a Plush –
Or violate a Star –

5   Such Dimity[2] Convictions –
A Horror so refined
Of freckled Human Nature –
Of Deity – Ashamed –

It's such a common – Glory –
10 A Fisherman's – Degree –
Redemption – Brittle Lady –
Be so – ashamed of Thee.
—1863

[*My Life had stood – a Loaded Gun –*][3]

My Life had stood – a Loaded Gun –
In Corners – till a Day
The Owner passed – identified –
And carried Me away –

5   And now We roam in Sovreign Woods –
And now We hunt the Doe –
And every time I speak for Him –
The Mountains straight reply –

And do I smile, such cordial light
10 Upon the Valley glow –
It is as a Vesuvian[4] face
Had let its pleasure through –

And when at Night – Our good Day done –
I guard My Master's Head –
15 'Tis better than the Eider-Duck's[5]
Deep Pillow – to have shared –

To foe of His – I'm deadly foe –
None stir the second time –
On whom I lay a Yellow Eye –
20 Or an emphatic Thumb –

Though I than He – may longer live
He longer must – than I –
For I have but the power to kill,
Without – the power to die –
—1863

---

1   This poem appears in Johnson as Poem 401; in Franklin as Poem 675; and in Miller as the third poem in Sheet 1 of "Unbound Sheets," page 418. Johnson and Miller read "Ashamed" as lower case both in line 8 and in line 12; Franklin reads the word as capitalized in line 8 but lowercase in line 12. Johnson, Franklin, and Miller all read a dash rather than a period at the end of the poem.

2   *Dimity* Lightweight cotton.

3   This poem appears in Johnson as Poem 754; in Franklin as Poem 764; and in Miller as the first poem in Sheet 4 of Fascicle 34, pages 354–55. The present transcription of the fascicle manuscript is with two exceptions in agreement with those of Johnson, Franklin, and Miller: Franklin spells "it's" in line 12 just as the word appears in Dickinson's manuscript, whereas other editors correct the error; Franklin and Miller both omit the mark that appears between "Eider" and "Duck" in line 15, whereas (like Johnson) the present editors transcribe it as a hyphen. There are a few other possible transcription issues with the punctuation of the poem; the marks at the end of lines 14 and 19 could plausibly be read as right-slanting commas, while the mark at the end of line 22 could very plausibly be read as a period. Dickinson provides four alternative readings in the manuscript: "the" for "in" in line 5; "Low" for "Deep" in line 16; "harm" for "stir" in line 18; and "art" for "power" in line 23.

4   *Vesuvian* The southern Italian volcano Mount Vesuvius erupted in 79 CE, killing well over one thousand people, primarily in the city of Pompeii.

5   *Eider-Duck* Genus of sea ducks, whose feathers are commonly used to stuff quilts and pillows.

["Nature" is what We see –][1]

"Nature" is what We see –
The Hill – the Afternoon –
Squirrel – Eclipse – the Bumble bee –
Nay – Nature is Heaven –

5   Nature is what We hear –
The Bobolink[2] – the Sea –
Thunder – the Cricket –
Nay – Nature is Harmony –

"Nature" is what We know –
10 Yet have no art to say –
So impotent Our Wisdom is
To Her Sincerity –
—1863

[I could bring You Jewels – had I a mind to –][3]

I could bring You Jewels – had I a mind to –
But You have enough – of those –
I could bring You Odors from St Domingo[4] –

Colors – from Vera Cruz[5] –

5   Berries[6] of the Bahamas – have I –
But this little Blaze
Flickering to itself – in the Meadow –
Suits Me – more than those –

Never a Fellow matched this Topaz –
10 And his Emerald Swing –
Dower[7] itself – for Bobadilo[8] –
Better – Could I bring?
—1863

[Publication – is the Auction][9]

Publication – is the Auction
Of the Mind of Man –
Poverty – be justifying
For so foul a thing

5   Possibly – but We – would rather
From Our Garret go
White – Unto the White Creator –
Than invest – Our Snow –

Thought belong to Him who gave it –
10 Then – to Him Who bear
It's Corporeal illustration – Sell
The Royal Air –

---

1   This poem appears in Johnson as Poem 668; in Franklin as Poem 721; and in Miller as the third poem in Sheet 2 of Fascicle 35, page 361. Johnson transcribes from a variant that Dickinson sent to Susan Dickinson; it differs in several small particulars and two large ones: the poem is not divided into stanzas, and "Simplicity" is substituted for "Sincerity" in the final line. The present text follows Franklin and Miller in transcribing from the fascicle manuscript version, and is in agreement with their readings.

2   *Bobolink*   Species of blackbird native to the Americas.

3   This poem appears in Johnson as Poem 697; in Franklin as Poem 726; and in Miller as the second poem in Sheet 4 of Fascicle 35, page 364. The present text is in complete accord with the transcriptions of Franklin and Miller; it may be worth noting, however, that the mark at the end of line 5 could plausibly be read as a period.

4   *Odors*   I.e., fragrant ointments or perfumes; *St Domingo*   While "Santo Domingo" is the name of the capital city of the Dominican Republic, it is more likely that Dickinson means to refer to the newly independent Haiti, which had been known as Saint Domingue under the French colonial regime. The Haitian Revolution of the late-eighteenth century had been led by a coalition of free and enslaved black Haitians, resulting in the abolition of slavery and the expulsion of most white colonials from the country. To many white Americans in the nineteenth century, "Domingo" remained shorthand both for Haiti itself and for the violence of revolution (though the success of the Haitian Revolution also remained an inspiration to many black abolitionists).

5   *Colors*   I.e., pigments or dyes;   *Vera Cruz*   State in Mexico, located on the coast of the Gulf of Mexico.

6   *Berries*   Here likely referring to melons, which botanically speaking are a type of berry.

7   *Dower*   Dowry; money brought by a bride into her marriage.

8   *Bobadilo*   Francisco de Bobadilla, Spanish-born governor of the colony of Saint Domingue (1499–1502).

9   This poem appears in Johnson as Poem 709; in Franklin as Poem 788; and in Miller as the second poem in Sheet 5 of Fascicle 37, pages 386–87. The present text is in complete accord with the transcriptions of Johnson, Franklin, and Miller; it may be noted, however, that the mark at the end of line 7 could plausibly be read as a right-slanting comma.

In the Parcel – Be the Merchant
Of the Heavenly Grace –
15   But reduce no Human Spirit
To Disgrace of Price –
         —1863

[*Truth – is as old as God –*][1]

Truth – is as old as God –
His Twin identity
And will endure as long as He
A Co-Eternity –

5   And perish on the Day
Himself is borne away
From Mansion of the Universe
A lifeless Deity.
         —1864, 1865

[*I never saw a Moor –*][2]

I never saw a Moor –
I never saw the Sea –
Yet know I how the Heather looks
And what a Billow[3] be.

5   I never spoke with God
Nor visited in Heaven –
Yet certain am I of the spot
As if the Checks[4] were given –
         —1864

[*Color – Caste – Denomination –*][5]

Color – Caste – Denomination –
These – are Time's Affair –
Death's diviner Classifying
Does not know they are –

5   As in sleep – All Hue forgotten –
Tenets – put behind –
Death's large – Democratic fingers
Rub away the Brand.[6]

If Circassian[7] – He is careless –
10   If He put away
Chrysalis of Blonde – or Umber –
Equal Butterfly –

They emerge from His Obscuring –
What Death – knows so well –
15   Our minuter intuitions –
Deem unplausible
         —1864

---

[1]   This poem appears in Johnson as Poem 836; in Franklin as Poem 795; and in Miller under "Unbound Sheets," page 447. The version here is that which Dickinson retained, and is believed to date from 1865; the transcription here is entirely in accord with those of Johnson, Franklin, and Miller. Dickinson sent a variant to Josiah Holland in 1864; the latter is more heavily punctuated, with a dash (or, arguably, a right-slanting comma) after "identity," a comma after "perish," and dashes after "He" and "Universe."

[2]   This poem appears in Johnson as Poem 1052; in Franklin as Poem 800; and in Miller under "Loose Poems," page 532. The present text is in agreement with the transcriptions of Johnson, Franklin, and Miller.

[3]   *Billow*   Wave.

[4]   *Checks*   Train tickets.

[5]   This poem appears in Johnson as Poem 970; in Franklin as Poem 836; and in Miller as the first poem in Sheet 6 of Fascicle 40, page 412. The present text is in agreement with the transcriptions of Johnson, Franklin, and Miller except in one particular; we read the mark at the end of line 8 as a period rather than a dash. (It may also be worth noting that the mark at the end of the first line could plausibly be read as a right-slanting comma.) Dickinson provides one variant word choice in the manuscript: "incredible" for "unplausible" in the final line.

[6]   *Brand*   Physical identifying mark, possibly with reference to a brand burned into the skin of an enslaved person.

[7]   *Circassian*   Of Circassia, a region in the North Caucasus in what is now southwestern Russia.

[*She rose to His Requirement – dropt*][1]

She rose to His Requirement – dropt
The Playthings of Her Life
To take the honorable Work
Of Woman, and of Wife –

5 If ought[2] She missed in Her new Day,
Of Amplitude, or Awe –
Or first Prospective – Or the Gold
In using, wear away,

It lay unmentioned – as the Sea
10 Develope Pearl, and Weed,
But Only to Himself – be known
The Fathoms they abide –
    —1864

[*The Poets light but Lamps –*][3]

The Poets light but Lamps –
Themselves – go out –
The Wicks they stimulate
If vital Light

5 Inhere as do the Suns –
Each Age a Lens
Disseminating their
Circumference –
    —1865

[*A Man may make a Remark –*][4]

A Man may make a Remark –
In itself – a quiet thing
That may furnish the Fuse unto a Spark
In dormant nature – lain –

5 Let us divide – with skill –
Let us discourse – with care –
Powder exists in Charcoal –
Before it exists in Fire.
    —1865

[*Banish Air from Air –*][5]

Banish Air from Air –
Divide Light if you dare –
They'll meet
While Cubes in a Drop
5 Or Pellets of Shape
Fit.
Films[6] cannot annul
Odors return whole
Force Flame
10 And with a Blonde push
Over your impotence
Flits Steam.
    —1865

---

1   This poem appears in Johnson as Poem 732; in Franklin as Poem 857; and in Miller as part of Fascicle 38, Sheet 4, pages 393–94. The present transcription of the manuscript is in agreement with those of Franklin and Miller—though it may be noted that the marks at the end of line 6 and after "unmentioned" in line 9 could plausibly be read as right-slanting commas.

    The poem was published under the title "The Wife" in Todd and Higginson's *Poems* (1890); in that version "Develops" is substituted for "Develope" in line 10 and "is" for "be" in line 11.

2   *ought*   Aught.

3   This poem appears in Johnson as Poem 883; in Franklin as Poem 930; and in Miller under "Unbound Sheets," as the first poem on Sheet 15, page 436. The present transcription of the manuscript is in agreement with those of Franklin and Miller; Johnson reads the mark at the end of line 3 as a dash, but it seems more plausible to read it as the crossing of the final "t" in "stimulate."

4   This poem appears in Johnson as Poem 952; in Franklin as Poem 913; and in Miller under "Unbound Sheets," page 430. Except in taking the small mark at the end of the final line to be a period (as does Johnson) rather than a dash, the present text is in agreement with the transcriptions of Franklin and Miller. Dickinson provides alternative readings in every line except the fourth.

5   This poem appears in Johnson as Poem 854; in Franklin as Poem 963; and in Miller under "Unbound Sheets," pages 446–47. Editors differ over the transcription of the mark after "Fit"; Franklin and Miller transcribe it as a dash rather than a period.

6   *Films*   In the sense of thin coverings.

[*As imperceptibly as Grief*][1]

As imperceptibly as Grief
The Summer lapsed away –
Too imperceptible at last
To feel like Perfidy[2] –

5   A Quietness distilled –
As Twilight long begun –
Or Nature – spending with Herself
Sequestered Afternoon –

Sobriety inhered
10 Though gaudy influence
The Maple lent unto the Road
And graphic Consequence

Invested sombre place –
As suddenly be worn
15 By sober Individual
A Homogeneous Gown –

Departed was the Bird –
And scarcely had the Hill
A flower to help His straightened face
20 In stress of Burial –

The Winds came closer up –
The Cricket spoke so clear
Presumption was – His Ancestors
Inherited the Floor –

25 The Dusk drew earlier in –
The Morning foreign shone –
The courteous – but harrowing Grace
Of Guest who would be gone –

And thus, without a Wing
30 Or Service of a Keel –
Our Summer made Her light Escape
Unto the Beautiful –
—c. 1865

[*The Heart has narrow Banks*][3]

The Heart has narrow Banks
It measures like the Sea
In mighty – unremitting Bass
And Blue monotony

5 Till Hurricane bisect
And as itself discerns
Its insufficient Area
The Heart convulsive learns

That Calm is but a Wall
10 Of Unattempted Gauze
An instant's Push demolishes
A Questioning – dissolves.
—c. 1865

---

1 This poem appears in Johnson as Poem 1540; in Franklin as Poem 935; and in Miller as the first poem in Sheet 16 of "Unbound Sheets," page 437. A variant version includes only the first eight and the final eight lines, without any stanza breaks. The present text is in agreement with the transcriptions of Franklin and Miller—though it may be noted that the marks following "distilled" in line 5, "begun" in line 6, "courteous" in line 27, and "Keel" in line 30 could all plausibly be read as forward-slanting commas. Dickinson provides one alternative in the manuscript—"into" for "Unto" in the final line.

2 *Perfidy* Treachery.

---

3 This poem appears in Johnson as Poem 928; in Franklin as Poem 960; and in Miller as the second poem of Sheet 21 in "Unbound Sheets," page 445. The present text, like those of Miller and Johnson, emends "It's" to "Its" in line 7. We agree with both Miller and Franklin in reading "monotony" in line 4 as lower case and "Unattempted" in line 10 as upper case (whereas Johnson reads the words as "Monotony" and "unattempted"). Dickinson provides one variant word choice in the manuscript—"paces" for "measures" in line 2.

[*Could I but ride indefinite*][1]

Could I but ride indefinite
As doth the Meadow Bee
And visit only where I liked
And no one visit me

5 And flirt all Day with Buttercups
And marry whom I may
And dwell a little everywhere
Or better, run away

With no Police to follow
10 Or chase Him if He do
Till He should jump Peninsulas
To get away from me –

I said "But just to be a Bee"
Upon a Raft of Air
15 And row in Nowhere all Day long
And anchor "off the Bar"

What Liberty! So Captives deem
Who tight in Dungeons are.
—c. 1865

Detail (buttercup) from Dickinson's *Herbarium*, Seq. 26.
Facsimile pages from the *Herbarium* are reproduced above
and in this volume's color insert.

---

1 This poem appears in Johnson as Poem 661; in Franklin as Poem
1056; and in Miller as the first poem in Sheet 43 under "Unbound
Sheets," page 474. The present text is in agreement with the transcriptions of Franklin and Miller except in one particular; like Miller,
we emend "Opon" to "Upon" in line 14.

[*As the Starved Maelstrom laps the Navies*][2]

As the Starved Maelstrom[3] laps the Navies
As the Vulture teazed
Forces the Broods[4] in lonely Valleys
As the Tiger eased

5 By but a Crumb of Blood, fasts Scarlet
Till he meet a Man
Dainty adorned with Veins and Tissues
And partakes – his Tongue

Cooled by the Morsel for a moment
10 Grows a fiercer thing
Till he esteem his Dates and Cocoa
A Nutrition mean

I, of a finer Famine
Deem my Supper dry
15 For but a Berry of Domingo[5]
And a Torrid[6] Eye.
—1865

---

2 This poem appears in Johnson as Poem 872; in Franklin as
Poem 1064; and in Miller as the second poem in Sheet 45, under
"Unbound Sheets," page 477. The present text is in agreement with
the transcriptions of Johnson, Franklin, and Miller except in two
particulars; we side with Franklin and Miller in retaining Dickinson's
archaic variant spelling of "teazed," and with Johnson in reading the
mark at the end of the poem as a period rather than a dash (though
either reading is certainly defensible).

3 *Maelstrom* Whirlpool.

4 *Forces* I.e., overpowers; *Broods* Young birds.

5 *Berry* In this context, a melon; *Domingo* Possibly a reference to Saint Domingo, the capital city of the Dominican Republic,
but more likely to Saint Domingue, the colonial name of Haiti
prior to the 1791 Haitian Revolution, which had been led by free
and enslaved black Haitians. Throughout the nineteenth century,
"Domingo" remained common shorthand (especially to white
Americans) both for Haiti itself and for the violence of revolution.

6 *Torrid* Hot; also possibly a reference to the torrid zone, another
name for the Tropics.

[*A narrow Fellow in the Grass*]

This poem was first published on 14 February 1866, in the *Springfield Republican*, a newspaper edited by Dickinson's friend Samuel Bowles. Dickinson did not submit the poem for publication, however; it has been plausibly conjectured that Susan Dickinson passed along to Bowles a now-lost manuscript copy which Dickinson had given her. A facsimile of the 1865 manuscript page appears on the facing page, followed by a transcription. Next appears the 1866 published version, and finally a transcription of the 1872 manuscript version.

This is the only known instance in which Dickinson complained of any of the specifics relating to the publication of one of her poems; in a 17 March 1866 letter to Higginson she commented as follows on the publication of the poem in the *Springfield Republican* (it is presumed that she enclosed a clipping of the newspaper's printed version with her letter):

Lest you meet my Snake and suppose I deceive it was robbed of me—defeated too of the third line by the punctuation. The third and fourth were one—I had told you I did not print—I feared you might think me ostensible.[1] If I still entreat you to teach me, are you much displeased?

As is often the case with Dickinson's letters, it is difficult to be entirely clear of her meaning here. She does not want Higginson to think that she has deceived him—presumably in her protestations that she has not sought to have her work printed; she assures him that this poem was stolen from her. She asserts too that her intentions were "defeated" by the punctuation of the third line in the newspaper version, which retains the dash in the middle of the line but adds a question mark at the end of the line—whereas in the 1865 manuscript Dickinson has no punctuation. (Interestingly, Dickinson herself includes a question mark in her 1872 manuscript version—but in the middle of the line, not at its end.) On that point her complaint seems clear—but what does she mean by "The third and fourth were one"? Could she mean that the third and fourth [lines of the poem] were [intended to be set out as] one [line]? That would mean a line like this—

You may have met Him – did you not His notice sudden is –

which seems highly implausible. The alternative is that she means that the third and fourth [lines of the poem] were [wrongly made into] one [by the newspaper editors], when Dickinson herself had intended them to be separate lines—in other words, that Dickinson had intended the first stanza to have five lines. That appears to be how she writes the stanza in the 1872 version she sent to Susan Dickinson, in which she capitalizes the first letter of Did. With Dickinson it is frequently difficult to be sure of her intentions regarding line breaks, given that she so often capitalized words in the middle of lines, but in the 1872 version it seems clear that there would have been ample room on the page for Dickinson to write the word "Did," after "him?" if she had intended "You may have met him? Did you not" to form just one line. But here again, it is impossible to be entirely sure of Dickinson's intentions.

---

[1]   *ostensible*   Seeking visibility; ostentatious.

88-13

A narrow fellow in
the Grass
Occasionally rides -
You may have met Him -
Did you not -
His notice sudden is -

The Grass divides as
with a Comb.
A spotted shaft is
seen.
And then it closes
at your feet.
And opens further On -

He likes a Boggy
Acre
A Floor too Cool
for Corn
Yet when a Boy, and
Barefoot.

[*A narrow Fellow in the Grass*][1]

A narrow Fellow in the Grass
Occasionally rides –
You may have met Him – did you not
His notice sudden is –

5   The Grass divides as with a Comb –
A spotted shaft is seen –
And then it closes at your feet
And opens further on –

He likes a Boggy Acre
10 A Floor too cool for Corn
Yet when a Boy, and Barefoot –
I more than once at Noon

Have passed, I thought, a Whip lash
Unbraiding in the Sun
15 When stooping to secure it
It wrinkled, and was gone –

Several of Nature's People
I know, and they know me –
I feel for them a transport[2]
20 Of cordiality –

But never met this Fellow
Attended, or alone
Without a tighter breathing
And Zero at the Bone –
—1865

THE SNAKE.

A narrow fellow in the grass
Occasionally rides;
You may have met him—did you not?
His notice instant is,
The grass divides as with a comb,
A spotted shaft is seen,
And then it closes at your feet,
And opens further on.

He likes a boggy acre,
A floor too cool for corn,
Yet when a boy and barefoot,
I more than once at noon
Have passed, I thought, a whip-lash,
Unbraiding in the sun,
When stooping to secure it,
It wrinkled and was gone.

Several of nature's people
I know, and they know me;
I feel for them a transport
Of cordiality.
Yet never met this fellow,
Attended or alone,
Without a tighter breathing,
And zero at the bone.

---

[1] This poem appears in Johnson as Poem 986; in Franklin as Poem 1096; and in Miller as part of Unbound Sheet 54, pages 489–90. There are two manuscript versions extant; the first dates from 1865, while the second is included in an 1872 letter to Susan Dickinson. Johnson and Miller transcribe from the 1865 version; the two differ only slightly (the first two lines of the third stanza are punctuated differently, with Miller reading a dash at the end of the first line and Johnson reading a dash at the end of the second line). The image in the righthand column shows the version printed under the title "The Snake" in the *Springfield Daily Republican* on 14 February 1866.

[2] *transport* Rush of emotion.

[*A narrow Fellow in the Grass*]

A narrow Fellow in the Grass
Occasionally rides –
You may have met him?
Did you not
5 His notice instant is –

The Grass divides as with a Comb –
A spotted Shaft is seen,
And then it closes at your Feet
And opens further on –

10 He likes a Boggy Acre –
A Floor too cool for Corn –
But when a Boy and Barefoot
I more than once at Noon

Have passed I thought a Whip Lash
15 Unbraiding in the Sun
When stooping to secure it
It wrinkled
And was gone –

Several of Nature's People
20 I know and they know me
I feel for them a transport
Of Cordiality

But never met this Fellow
Attended or alone
25 Without a tighter Breathing
And Zero at the Bone.
—1872

[*The Bustle in a House*][1]

The Bustle in a House
The Morning after Death
Is solemnest of industries
Enacted upon Earth –

5 The Sweeping up the Heart
And putting Love away
We shall not want to use again
Until Eternity –
—1865

[*A Spider sewed at Night*][2]

A Spider sewed at Night
Without a Light
Upon an Arc of White –

If Ruff it was of Dame
5 Or Shroud of Gnome
Himself himself inform –

Of Immortality
His strategy
Was physiognomy[3] –
—1868

---

[1] This poem appears in Johnson as Poem 1078; in Franklin as Poem 1108; and in Miller as the third poem in Sheet 57, under "Unbound Sheets," page 494. The present text is in agreement with the transcriptions of Johnson, Franklin, and Miller except in one particular; we side with Franklin and Miller in reading the mark at the end of the poem as a dash rather than (as Johnson reads it) a period.

[2] This poem appears in Johnson as Poem 1138; in Franklin as Poem 1163; and in Miller under "Poems Not Retained," pages 705–06. The present text is in agreement with the transcriptions of Franklin and Miller except in one particular; like Miller, we emend "Opon" to "Upon" in line 3. The dashes in the manuscript sent to Susan Dickinson very much resemble commas.

[3] *physiognomy* Study of a person's facial features to determine his or her character.

The manuscript of "Tell all the Truth but tell it slant" (Amherst College, Amherst - Amherst Manuscript # 372 - Tell all the truth but tell it slant - asc:12240 - p. 1). Dickinson's handwriting varied considerably both from one manuscript to another and over time.

[*Tell all the Truth but tell it slant –*][1]

Tell all the Truth but tell it slant –
Success in Circuit lies
Too bright for our infirm Delight
The Truth's superb surprise
5 As Lightning to the Children eased
With explanation kind
The Truth must dazzle gradually
Or every man be blind –
—1872

[*To pile like Thunder to its close*][2]

To pile like Thunder to its close
Then crumble grand away
While Everything created hid
This – would be Poetry –

5 Or Love – the two coeval[3] come –
We both and neither prove –
Experience either and consume –
For None see God and live –
—c. 1875

[*Apparently with no surprise*][4]

Apparently with no surprise
To any happy Flower
The Frost beheads it at its play –
In accidental power –
5 The blonde Assassin passes on –
The Sun proceeds unmoved
To measure off another Day
For an Approving God –
—c. 1884

[*A Word made Flesh is seldom*][5]

A Word made Flesh[6] is seldom
And tremblingly partook
Nor then perhaps reported
But have I not mistook
5 Each one of us has tasted
With ecstasies of stealth
The very food debated
To our specific strength –

A Word that breathes distinctly
10 Has not the power to die
Cohesive as the Spirit
It may expire if He –

---

1   This poem appears in Johnson as Poem 1129; in Franklin as Poem 1263; and in Miller under "Loose Poems," pages 563–64. The present transcription of the manuscript is in complete agreement with those of Johnson, Franklin, and Miller. Dickinson provides two variant word choices in the manuscript: "bold" for "bright" in line 3, and "moderately" for "gradually" in line 7.

2   This poem appears in Johnson as Poem 1247; in Franklin as Poem 1353; and in Miller under "Poems Not Retained," page 713. The present text is in agreement with the transcriptions of Franklin and Miller except in one particular; like Miller, we emend "it's" to "its" in line 1.

3   *coeval* Of contemporaneous duration or existence.

4   This poem appears in Johnson as Poem 1624; in Franklin as Poem 1668; and in Miller under "Loose Poems," page 654. The present text is in agreement with the transcriptions of Johnson, Franklin, and Miller except in two particulars; like Johnson and Miller, we emend "it's" to "its" in line 3, and like Franklin and Miller we read the mark at the end of the poem as a dash rather than a period. Todd and Higginson edited the poem for *Poems* (1890), giving it the title "Death and Life."

5   This poem appears in Johnson as Poem 1651; in Franklin as Poem 1715; and in Miller under "Poems Transcribed by Others," page 671. No Dickinson manuscript appears to have survived, and the date of composition is not known; a transcription by Susan Dickinson has survived, and the poem appears in *Poems: Third Series* (1896). Johnson reads the manuscript as having three stanzas rather than two (with a stanza break after "He –").

6   *A Word made Flesh* See John 1.1–14: "In the beginning was the Word, and the Word was with God, and the Word was God. ... And the Word was made flesh, and dwelt among us (and we beheld his glory, the glory as of the only begotten of the Father), full of grace and truth."

"Made Flesh and dwelt among us"
Could condescension be
15 Like this consent of Language
This loved Philology

—DATE OF COMPOSITION UNKNOWN (FIRST PUBLISHED
1896)

[*My life closed twice before its close;*][1]

My life closed twice before its close;
It yet remains to see
If Immortality unveil
A third event to me,

5 So huge, so hopeless to conceive
As these that twice befell.
Parting is all we know of heaven,
And all we need of hell.

—DATE OF COMPOSITION UNKNOWN (FIRST PUBLISHED
1896)

[*To make a prairie it takes a clover and one bee,*][2]

To make a prairie it takes a clover and one bee,
One clover, and a bee,
And revery.
The revery alone will do,
5 If bees are few.

—DATE OF COMPOSITION UNKNOWN (FIRST PUBLISHED
1896)

---

[1]   This poem appears in Johnson as Poem 1732; in Franklin as Poem 1773; and in Miller under "Poems Transcribed by Others," page 686. No Dickinson manuscript appears to have survived; a transcription by Mabel Todd has survived, and the poem appears in *Poems: Third Series* (1896). Franklin retains the spelling "it's" in line 1.

[2]   This poem appears in Johnson as Poem 1755; in Franklin as Poem 1779; and in Miller under "Poems Transcribed by Others," page 688. No Dickinson manuscript appears to have survived; a transcription by Mabel Todd has survived, and the poem appears in *Poems: Third Series* (1896).

Rebecca Harding Davis

1831 – 1910

Rebecca Harding Davis became an overnight literary celebrity with the publication of her first major short story, "Life in the Iron-Mills." Immediately hailed as a work of outstanding strength and insight, the story has since been identified as an early and important contribution to literary realism, a movement that would not properly take hold in American fiction until two decades later, with the works of writers such as Mark Twain. Davis herself continued to develop her brand of realism over a long, prolific, and popularly successful career in which she strove, as she wrote, "to dig into this commonplace, this vulgar American life, and see what is in it." In addition to these realist works of pathos and social observation, she worked in a remarkable range of genres both highbrow and lowbrow, including serialized gothic and mystery fiction, children's stories, memoir, and essays. Raised in what is now West Virginia with ties to the South and to the North, Davis considered herself a "Westerner" and took an iconoclastic approach to the political issues of her day; her stance on matters from marriage to the Civil War did not align fully with either Southern or Northern intellectual traditions.

Born in Washington, Pennsylvania, in 1831, Rebecca Blaine Harding was the eldest of five children born to Rachel Leet Wilson and English-born Richard W. Harding. Washington was her mother's hometown, but the family's permanent residence at the time was in Alabama, after which they settled in 1836 in Wheeling, Virginia. The family was comfortably middle class; Richard, a great reader, stocked an ample library with British classics, which comprised Harding's first exposure to literature. She read widely, enjoying novels by the likes of Maria Edgeworth, John Bunyan, and Sir Walter Scott. Despite her father's bias against American literature, however, Harding was deeply influenced by the short fiction of American author Nathaniel Hawthorne, whom she credited with inspiring her initial interest in fiction that centered on "commonplace folk and things."

The Harding children all received an extensive home education, provided by their mother and various tutors; in 1844, Harding returned to her mother's hometown to attend the Washington Female Seminary, a prestigious girls' educational institution whose curriculum blended conventionally "feminine" topics such as music and drawing with the study of literature, philosophy, theology, mathematics, and various sciences. Students were exposed to lectures by prominent literary figures, and Washington society provided opportunities for Harding to attend abolitionist lectures by activists such as Horace Greeley and Francis LeMoyne.

Harding graduated from the seminary as valedictorian in 1848; despite this academic achievement, as a woman her prospects were limited. For the next fourteen years she lived at her family home, where, despite the extensive household duties expected of her, she began to build a writing career. Over the course of those years she published numerous—mostly anonymous—reviews, essays, stories, and poems in the local *Wheeling Intelligencer*, of which she also served as editor for a brief period in 1859. Her breakthrough came in the winter of 1861, when she had a story accepted by the *Atlantic Monthly*, a periodical which had been founded only a few years previously but had already become one of the most eminent literary publications in the country. Harding was paid fifty dollars for "Life in the Iron-Mills," which was printed anonymously in the April volume of the magazine that year (the same month in which the Civil War broke out). Written following a series of highly publicized workers' strikes across the country, the story is socially provocative: the protagonist is an industrial laborer who, despite his innate artistic abilities, lacks the means of escaping the hardships and injustice of the nineteenth-century class system.

"Life in the Iron-Mills" was an immediate success, its grim realism a distinguishing feature amidst the sentimental and romantic fiction that dominated the American literary scene.

Davis soon visited Boston and Concord, where she met Hawthorne and Ralph Waldo Emerson, and where she formed a long-lived friendship with Louisa May Alcott. Davis found, however, that her objections to Transcendentalism and to New England elitism were reaffirmed by her experience in Massachusetts. She would later write of "Emerson, Hawthorne, and the other members of the 'Atlantic' coterie" that "while they thought they were guiding the real world, they stood quite outside of it, and never would see it as it was."

Among the many letters of admiration Davis received for her first story was one from a man named L. Clarke Davis, a lawyer and newspaper editor from Philadelphia. The two met in Wheeling in 1862, and they became engaged that summer, marrying the following year and moving to Philadelphia, where their home would become a meeting place for local intellectuals. In 1864 Davis gave birth to the first of their three children, Richard Harding Davis.

Davis's writing provided the family's main income, and she continued to publish prolifically throughout the next decades. But although the realism of Davis's writing was largely well-received, she nevertheless faced a degree of editorial censorship when editors or publishers considered her sobering tone and political subject matter to be too much for readers' tastes. This pattern began with her second submission to the *Atlantic*: editor James T. Fields initially rejected the piece, a long story titled "The Deaf and the Dumb." His recommendations—which Davis followed—included changing the title and inserting a happier ending; the story was then serialized as "A Story of To-day" in 1862 (and later published as a single novel, *Margaret Howth*).

While she continued to publish with the *Atlantic* and to accept Fields's interventions in her work, Davis also began a long-term relationship with *Peterson's Magazine*, an inexpensive publication intended for middle-class women readers. It was far less prestigious than the *Atlantic*, but *Peterson's* paid significantly better and offered one of the largest audiences of any periodical of the era. Over the following decades, she would publish fourteen serialized novels and more than eighty short stories in the magazine, many of them works drawing on the gothic, mystery, and other popular genres.

Davis's work consistently tackled difficult social and political questions: "The Wife's Story" (1864), for instance, is an impassioned account of the anguish experienced by a new wife torn between domestic responsibilities and a desire to pursue an artistic career; and *Waiting for the Verdict* (1868), Davis's most ambitious novel, addresses the question of persisting systemic racism in postwar America. (Race was a topic of vital importance to Davis, though her fiction often presented a mixed bag of socially progressive ideals and pervasive racial stereotyping.) The same questions of class, race, and gender that inform her fiction also emerged repeatedly throughout her distinguished career as an editorial correspondent, during which she also reported on topics such as prostitution and asylum reform. For many years her primary journalistic relationship was with the *New York Tribune*, until she resigned from the paper when it tried to suppress her essay series criticizing some of its advertisers; later she wrote most frequently for the *New York Independent*, in addition to contributing to other publications such as Harriet Beecher Stowe's periodical *Hearth and Home*. Davis became at least as celebrated for her journalism as for her stories and novels; all in all, it is estimated that she published more than five hundred pieces of fiction and nonfiction.

At the age of seventy-three, Davis completed the memoir *Bits of Gossip* (1904), whose self-effacing title belies the greater ambition expressed in its opening line: "It has always seemed to me that each human being, before going out into the silence, should leave behind him, not the story of his own life, but of the time in which he lived." Davis died six years later. She was largely forgotten in the years following her death, perhaps in part overshadowed by the success of her son Richard, who had become a literary celebrity in his own right. In the early 1970s, however, a volume of Davis's stories was discovered in a junk shop by the feminist writer and activist Tillie Olsen, who was immediately taken by the power of "Life in the Iron-Mills." The story was re-published in 1972 by the Feminist Press, as the first of their series of rediscovered classics by women authors. Since then, the story has been considered a staple of the American literary canon, though many scholars of the late twentieth century felt that the quality of the rest of her work had been compromised by editorial intervention and a desire to appeal to a broad audience. Some twenty-first-century critics argue, however, that the quality of her oeuvre has been significantly underestimated, citing its political complexity, its deft deployment of genre conventions, and its pioneering achievement in American realism. As one critic wrote in 1868, "[t]he festering spots of society, from which so many writers shrink, she probes with the unerring blade."

NOTE ON THE TEXT: Except where otherwise noted, the text presented below is based on that printed in the *Atlantic Monthly* in 1861, with references to both the original manuscript version and the version later included in *Atlantic Tales* (1865) where relevant. Spelling and punctuation have been modernized in accordance with the practices of this anthology.

⌘ ⌘ ⌘

Life in the Iron-Mills

"Is this the end?
O Life, as futile, then, as frail!
What hope of answer or redress?"[1]

A cloudy day: do you know what that is in a town[2] of iron-works? The sky sank down before dawn, muddy, flat, immovable. The air is thick, clammy with the breath of crowded human beings. It stifles me. I open the window, and, looking out, can scarcely see through the rain the grocer's shop opposite, where a crowd of drunken Irishmen are puffing Lynchburg[3] tobacco in their pipes. I can detect the scent through all the foul smells ranging loose in the air.

The idiosyncrasy of this town is smoke. It rolls sullenly in slow folds from the great chimneys of the iron-foundries, and settles down in black, slimy pools on the muddy streets. Smoke on the wharves, smoke on the dingy boats, on the yellow river—clinging in a coating of greasy soot to the house-front, the two faded poplars, the faces of the passers-by. The long train of mules, dragging masses of pig-iron[4] through

the narrow street, have a foul vapor hanging to their reeking sides. Here, inside, is a little broken figure of an angel pointing upward from the mantel-shelf; but even its wings are covered with smoke, clotted and black. Smoke everywhere! A dirty canary chirps desolately in a cage beside me. Its dream of green fields and sunshine is a very old dream—almost worn out, I think.

From the back-window I can see a narrow brick-yard sloping down to the river-side, strewed with rain-butts[5] and tubs. The river, dull and tawny-colored, (*la belle rivière!*[6]) drags itself sluggishly along, tired of the heavy weight of boats and coal-barges. What wonder? When I was a child, I used to fancy a look of weary, dumb[7] appeal upon the face of the negro-like river slavishly bearing its burden day after day. Something of the same idle notion comes to me today, when from the street-window I look on the slow stream of human life creeping past, night and morning, to the great mills. Masses of men, with dull, besotted[8] faces bent to the ground, sharpened here and there by pain or cunning; skin and muscle and flesh begrimed with smoke and ashes; stooping all night over boiling cauldrons of metal, laired by day in dens of drunkenness and infamy; breathing from infancy to death an air saturated with fog and grease and soot, vileness for soul and body. What do you make of a case like that,

---

[1] *Is this ... or redress?* Lines adapted from Alfred, Lord Tennyson's *In Memoriam A.H.H.* (1850).

[2] *town* Though the town is never named in the text, it appears to be Davis's hometown of Wheeling, Virginia (now West Virginia).

[3] *drunken Irishmen* Nineteenth-century discourse was rife with negative stereotypes of the Irish, including an association between Irish people and drunkenness; *Lynchburg* Virginian city known for the production of inferior-quality dark-leaf tobacco.

[4] *pig-iron* Small blocks of crude iron.

[5] *rain-butts* Vessels designed to catch rainwater for various uses.

[6] *la belle rivière* French: the beautiful river, a name used by French explorers to refer to the Ohio River, which runs through Wheeling.

[7] *dumb* Silent.

[8] *besotted* Dull, stupefied.

amateur psychologist? You call it an altogether serious thing to be alive: to these men it is a drunken jest, a joke—horrible to angels perhaps, to them commonplace enough. My fancy about the river was an idle one: it is no type of such a life. What if it be stagnant and slimy here? It knows that beyond there waits for it odorous[1] sunlight—quaint old gardens, dusky with soft, green foliage of apple-trees, and flushing crimson with roses—air, and fields, and mountains. The future of the Welsh puddler[2] passing just now is not so pleasant. To be stowed away, after his grimy work is done, in a hole in the muddy graveyard, and after that—*not* air, nor green fields, nor curious roses.

Can you see how foggy the day is? As I stand here, idly tapping the window-pane, and looking out through the rain at the dirty back-yard and the coal-boats below, fragments of an old story float up before me—a story of this old house into which I happened to come today. You may think it a tiresome story enough, as foggy as the day, sharpened by no sudden flashes of pain or pleasure. I know: only the outline of a dull life, that long since, with thousands of dull lives like its own, was vainly lived and lost: thousands of them—massed, vile, slimy lives, like those of the torpid lizards in yonder stagnant water-butt. Lost? There is a curious point for you to settle, my friend, who study psychology in a lazy, *dilettante* way. Stop a moment. I am going to be honest. This is what I want you to do. I want you to hide your disgust, take no heed to your clean clothes, and come right down with me—here, into the thickest of the fog and mud and foul effluvia. I want you to hear this story. There is a secret down here, in this nightmare fog, that has lain dumb for centuries: I want to make it a real thing to you. You, Egoist, or Pantheist, or Arminian,[3] busy in making straight paths for your feet on the hills, do not see it clearly—this terrible question which men here have gone mad and died trying to answer. I dare

not put this secret into words. I told you it was dumb. These men, going by with drunken faces and brains full of unawakened power, do not ask it of Society or of God. Their lives ask it; their deaths ask it. There is no reply. I will tell you plainly that I have a great hope; and I bring it to you to be tested. It is this: that this terrible dumb question is its own reply; that it is not the sentence of death we think it, but, from the very extremity of its darkness, the most solemn prophecy which the world has known of the Hope to come. I dare make my meaning no clearer, but will only tell my story. It will, perhaps, seem to you as foul and dark as this thick vapor about us, and as pregnant with death; but if your eyes are free as mine are to look deeper, no perfume-tinted dawn will be so fair with promise of the day that shall surely come.

My story is very simple—only what I remember of the life of one of these men—a furnace-tender in one of Kirby & John's rolling-mills—Hugh Wolfe. You know the mills? They took the great order for Lower Virginia railroads there last winter; run usually with about a thousand men. I cannot tell why I choose the half-forgotten story of this Wolfe more than that of myriads of these furnace-hands. Perhaps because there is a secret underlying sympathy between that story and this day with its impure fog and thwarted sunshine—or perhaps simply for the reason that this house is the one where the Wolfes lived. There were the father and son—both hands,[4] as I said, in one of Kirby & John's mills for making railroad-iron—and Deborah, their cousin, a picker[5] in some of the cotton-mills. The house was rented then to half a dozen families. The Wolfes had two of the cellar-rooms. The old man, like many of the puddlers and feeders[6] of the mills, was Welsh—had spent half of his life in the Cornish tin-mines. You may pick the Welsh emigrants, Cornish miners, out of the throng passing the windows, any day. They are a trifle more filthy; their muscles are not so brawny; they stoop more. When they are drunk, they neither yell, nor shout, nor stagger, but skulk along like beaten hounds. A pure, unmixed blood,

---

[1] *odorous* Fragrant; sweet-smelling.

[2] *puddler* Worker who converts pig iron into steel or wrought iron by means of a labor-intensive process of melting and stirring.

[3] *Egoist* One who believes the pursuit of self-interest will lead to universal improvement; *Pantheist* One who believes that God is inherently present in all nature; *Arminian* Follower of the religious doctrines of Jacobus Arminius (1560–1607), which oppose the doctrines of Calvinism and assert that salvation can be attained through the performance of good works.

[4] *hands* I.e., workers.

[5] *picker* Worker who operated the machine, also called a picker, that separated cotton fibers in preparation for spinning.

[6] *feeders* Workers who feed molten metal into the iron-casting form.

I fancy: shows itself in the slight angular bodies and sharply-cut facial lines. It is nearly thirty years since the Wolfes lived here. Their lives were like those of their class: incessant labor, sleeping in kennel-like rooms, eating rank pork and molasses, drinking—God and the distillers only know what; with an occasional night in jail, to atone for some drunken excess. Is that all of their lives?—of the portion given to them and these their duplicates swarming the streets today?—nothing beneath?—all? So many a political reformer will tell you—and many a private reformer, too, who has gone among them with a heart tender with Christ's charity, and come out outraged, hardened.

One rainy night, about eleven o'clock, a crowd of half-clothed women stopped outside of the cellar-door. They were going home from the cotton-mill.

"Good-night, Deb," said one, a mulatto,[1] steadying herself against the gas-post. She needed the post to steady her. So did more than one of them.

"Dah's a ball to Miss Potts' tonight. Ye'd best come."

"Inteet, Deb, if hur'll[2] come, hur'll hef fun," said a shrill Welsh voice in the crowd.

Two or three dirty hands were thrust out to catch the gown of the woman, who was groping for the latch of the door.

"No."

"No? Where's Kit Small then?"

"Begorra![3] on the spools.[4] Alleys behint,[5] though we helped her, we dud. An wid ye! Let Deb alone! It's ondacent[6] frettin' a quite body. Be the powers, an' we'll have a night of it! there'll be lashin's o' drink—the Vargent[7] be blessed and praised for 't!"

They went on, the mulatto inclining for a moment to show fight, and drag the woman Wolfe off with them; but, being pacified, she staggered away.

Deborah groped her way into the cellar, and, after considerable stumbling, kindled a match, and lighted a tallow dip,[8] that sent a yellow glimmer over the room. It was low, damp—the earthen floor covered with a green, slimy moss—a fetid air smothering the breath. Old Wolfe lay asleep on a heap of straw, wrapped in a torn horse-blanket. He was a pale, meek little man, with a white face and red rabbit-eyes. The woman Deborah was like him; only her face was even more ghastly, her lips bluer, her eyes more watery. She wore a faded cotton gown and a slouching bonnet. When she walked, one could see that she was deformed, almost a hunchback. She trod softly, so as not to waken him, and went through into the room beyond. There she found by the half-extinguished fire an iron saucepan filled with cold boiled potatoes, which she put upon a broken chair with a pint-cup of ale. Placing the old candlestick beside this dainty repast, she untied her bonnet, which hung limp and wet over her face, and prepared to eat her supper. It was the first food that had touched her lips since morning. There was enough of it, however: there is not always. She was hungry—one could see that easily enough—and not drunk, as most of her companions would have been found at this hour. She did not drink, this woman—her face told that, too—nothing stronger than ale. Perhaps the weak, flaccid wretch had some stimulant in her pale life to keep her up—some love or hope, it might be, or urgent need. When that stimulant was gone, she would take to whiskey. Man cannot live by work alone. While she was skinning the potatoes, and munching them, a noise behind her made her stop.

"Janey!" she called, lifting the candle and peering into the darkness. "Janey, are you there?"

A heap of ragged coats was heaved up, and the face of a young girl emerged, staring sleepily at the woman.

"Deborah," she said, at last, "I'm here the night."

"Yes, child. Hur's welcome," she said, quietly eating on.

The girl's face was haggard and sickly; her eyes were heavy with sleep and hunger: real Milesian[9] eyes they were, dark, delicate blue, glooming out from black shadows with a pitiful fright.

"I was alone," she said, timidly.

"Where's the father?" asked Deborah, holding out a potato, which the girl greedily seized.

---

1 **mulatto** Antiquated term for a person of mixed race.

2 **hur'll** Throughout the story, "hur" is frequently used as a dialectical pronoun meaning him, her, she, he, or you.

3 **Begorra** Irish-English expression meaning "by God."

4 **spools** In a cotton mill, spindles on which cotton is stretched, spun, and wound.

5 **Alleys behint** Always behind.

6 **ondacent** Indecent.

7 **Vargent** Virgin; i.e., the Virgin Mary.

8 **tallow dip** Cheap candle.

9 **Milesian** Irish.

"He's beyant[1]—wid Haley—in the stone house." (Did you ever hear the word *jail* from an Irish mouth?) "I came here. Hugh told me never to stay me-lone."

"Hugh?"

"Yes."

A vexed frown crossed her face. The girl saw it, and added quickly—

"I have not seen Hugh the day, Deb. The old man says his watch[2] lasts till the mornin'."

The woman sprang up, and hastily began to arrange some bread and flitch[3] in a tin pail, and to pour her own measure of ale into a bottle. Tying on her bonnet, she blew out the candle.

"Lay ye down, Janey dear," she said, gently, covering her with the old rags. "Hur can eat the potatoes, if hur's hungry."

"Where are ye goin', Deb? The rain's sharp."

"To the mill, with Hugh's supper."

"Let him bide till th' morn. Sit ye down."

"No, no," sharply pushing her off. "The boy'll starve."

She hurried from the cellar, while the child wearily coiled herself up for sleep. The rain was falling heavily, as the woman, pail in hand, emerged from the mouth of the alley, and turned down the narrow street, that stretched out, long and black, miles before her. Here and there a flicker of gas lighted an uncertain space of muddy footwalk and gutter; the long rows of houses, except an occasional lager-bier shop, were closed; now and then she met a band of mill hands skulking to or from their work.

Not many even of the inhabitants of a manufacturing town know the vast machinery of system by which the bodies of workmen are governed, that goes on unceasingly from year to year. The hands of each mill are divided into watches that relieve each other as regularly as the sentinels of an army. By night and day the work goes on, the unsleeping engines groan and shriek, the fiery pools of metal boil and surge. Only for a day in the week, in half-courtesy to public censure, the fires are partially veiled; but as soon as the clock strikes midnight, the great furnaces break forth with renewed fury, the clamor begins with fresh, breathless vigor, the engines sob and shriek like "gods in pain."

As Deborah hurried down through the heavy rain, the noise of these thousand engines sounded through the sleep and shadow of the city like far-off thunder. The mill to which she was going lay on the river, a mile below the city-limits. It was far, and she was weak, aching from standing twelve hours at the spools. Yet it was her almost nightly walk to take this man his supper, though at every square she sat down to rest, and she knew she should receive small word of thanks.

Perhaps, if she possessed an artist's eye, the picturesque oddity of the scene might have made her step stagger less, and the path seem shorter; but to her the mills were only "summat deilish[4] to look at by night."

The road leading to the mills had been quarried from the solid rock, which rose abrupt and bare on one side of the cinder-covered road, while the river, sluggish and black, crept past on the other. The mills for rolling iron are simply immense tent-like roofs, covering acres of ground, open on every side. Beneath these roofs Deborah looked in on a city of fires, that burned hot and fiercely in the night. Fire in every horrible form: pits of flame waving in the wind; liquid metal-flames writhing in tortuous streams through the sand; wide cauldrons filled with boiling fire, over which bent ghastly wretches stirring the strange brewing; and through all, crowds of half-clad men, looking like revengeful ghosts in the red light, hurried, throwing masses of glittering fire. It was like a street in Hell. Even Deborah muttered, as she crept through, "'T looks like t' Devil's place!" It did—in more ways than one.

She found the man she was looking for, at last, heaping coal on a furnace. He had not time to eat his supper; so she went behind the furnace, and waited. Only a few men were with him, and they noticed her only by a "Hyur comes t' hunchback, Wolfe."

Deborah was stupid with sleep; her back pained her sharply; and her teeth chattered with cold, with the rain that soaked her clothes and dripped from her at every step. She stood, however, patiently holding the pail, and waiting.

"Hout, woman! ye look like a drowned cat. Come near to the fire," said one of the men, approaching to scrape away the ashes.

She shook her head. Wolfe had forgotten her. He turned, hearing the man, and came closer.

---

[1]   *beyant* Beyond.

[2]   *watch* Shift.

[3]   *flitch* Bacon.

[4]   *deilish* Devilish.

"I did no' think; gi' me my supper, woman."

She watched him eat with a painful eagerness. With a woman's quick instinct, she saw that he was not hungry—was eating to please her. Her pale, watery eyes began to gather a strange light.

"Is't good, Hugh? T' ale was a bit sour, I feared."

"No, good enough." He hesitated a moment. "Ye're tired, poor lass! Bide here till I go. Lay down there on that heap of ash, and go to sleep."

He threw her an old coat for a pillow, and turned to his work. The heap was the refuse of the burnt iron, and was not a hard bed; the half-smothered warmth, too, penetrated her limbs, dulling their pain and cold shiver.

Miserable enough she looked, lying there on the ashes like a limp, dirty rag—yet not an unfitting figure to crown the scene of hopeless discomfort and veiled crime: more fitting, if one looked deeper into the heart of things—at her thwarted woman's form, her colorless life, her waking stupor that smothered pain and hunger— even more fit to be a type[1] of her class. Deeper yet if one could look, was there nothing worth reading in this wet, faded thing, half-covered with ashes? no story of a soul filled with groping passionate love, heroic unselfishness, fierce jealousy? of years of weary trying to please the one human being whom she loved, to gain one look of real heart-kindness from him? If anything like this were hidden beneath the pale, bleared eyes, and dull, washed-out-looking face, no one had ever taken the trouble to read its faint signs: not the half-clothed furnace-tender, Wolfe, certainly. Yet he was kind to her: it was his nature to be kind, even to the very rats that swarmed in the cellar: kind to her in just the same way. She knew that. And it might be that very knowledge had given to her face its apathy and vacancy more than her low, torpid life. One sees that dead, vacant look steal sometimes over the rarest, finest of women's faces—in the very midst, it may be, of their warmest summer's day; and then one can guess at the secret of intolerable solitude that lies hid beneath the delicate laces and brilliant smile. There was no warmth, no brilliancy, no summer for this woman; so the stupor and vacancy had time to gnaw into her face perpetually. She was young, too, though no one guessed it; so the gnawing was the fiercer.

She lay quiet in the dark corner, listening, through the monotonous din and uncertain glare of the works, to the dull plash of the rain in the far distance—shrinking back whenever the man Wolfe happened to look towards her. She knew, in spite of all his kindness, that there was that in her face and form which made him loathe the sight of her. She felt by instinct, although she could not comprehend it, the finer nature of the man, which made him among his fellow-workmen something unique, set apart. She knew, that, down under all the vileness and coarseness of his life, there was a groping passion for whatever was beautiful and pure—that his soul sickened with disgust at her deformity, even when his words were kindest. Through this dull consciousness, which never left her, came, like a sting, the recollection of the dark blue eyes and lithe figure of the little Irish girl she had left in the cellar. The recollection struck through even her stupid intellect with a vivid glow of beauty and of grace. Little Janey, timid, helpless, clinging to Hugh as her only friend: that was the sharp thought, the bitter thought, that drove into the glazed eyes a fierce light of pain. You laugh at it? Are pain and jealousy less savage realities down here in this place I am taking you to than in your own house or your own heart—your heart, which they clutch at sometimes? The note is the same, I fancy, be the octave high or low.

If you could go into this mill where Deborah lay, and drag out from the hearts of these men the terrible tragedy of their lives, taking it as a symptom of the disease of their class, no ghost Horror would terrify you more. A reality of soul-starvation, of living death, that meets you every day under the besotted faces on the street—I can paint nothing of this, only give you the outside outlines of a night, a crisis in the life of one man: whatever muddy depth of soul-history lies beneath you can read according to the eyes God has given you.

Wolfe, while Deborah watched him as a spaniel its master, bent over the furnace with his iron pole, unconscious of her scrutiny, only stopping to receive orders. Physically, Nature had promised the man but little. He had already lost the strength and instinct vigor of a man, his muscles were thin, his nerves weak, his face (a meek, woman's face) haggard, yellow with consumption.[2] In the mill he was known as one of the girl-men: "Molly Wolfe"

---

[1] *type* Symbol; representative model.

[2] *consumption* Extreme wasting of the body, typically due to tuberculosis. In reality, it is unlikely a person of Wolfe's physical weakness would have been capable of performing the demanding work of puddling.

was his *sobriquet*.[1] He was never seen in the cockpit, did not own a terrier,[2] drank but seldom; when he did, desperately. He fought sometimes, but was always thrashed, pommeled to a jelly. The man was game enough, when his blood was up: but he was no favorite in the mill; he had the taint of school-learning on him—not to a dangerous extent, only a quarter or so in the free-school in fact, but enough to ruin him as a good hand in a fight.

For other reasons, too, he was not popular. Not one of themselves, they felt that, though outwardly as filthy and ash-covered; silent, with foreign thoughts and longings breaking out through his quietness in innumerable curious ways: this one, for instance. In the neighboring furnace-buildings lay great heaps of the refuse from the ore after the pig-metal is run. *Korl* we call it here: a light, porous substance, of a delicate, waxen, flesh-colored tinge. Out of the blocks of this korl, Wolfe, in his off hours from the furnace, had a habit of chipping and moulding figures—hideous, fantastic enough, but sometimes strangely beautiful: even the mill-men saw that, while they jeered at him. It was a curious fancy in the man, almost a passion. The few hours for rest he spent hewing and hacking with his blunt knife, never speaking, until his watch came again—working at one figure for months, and, when it was finished, breaking it to pieces perhaps, in a fit of disappointment. A morbid, gloomy man, untaught, unled, left to feed his soul in grossness and crime, and hard, grinding labor.

I want you to come down and look at this Wolfe, standing there among the lowest of his kind, and see him just as he is, that you may judge him justly when you hear the story of this night. I want you to look back, as he does every day, at his birth in vice, his starved infancy; to remember the heavy years he has groped through as boy and man—the slow, heavy years of constant, hot work. So long ago he began, that he thinks sometimes he has worked there for ages. There is no hope that it will ever end. Think that God put into this man's soul a fierce thirst for beauty—to know it, to create it; to *be*—something, he knows not what—other than he is. There are moments when a

passing cloud, the sun glinting on the purple thistles, a kindly smile, a child's face, will rouse him to a passion of pain—when his nature starts up with a mad cry of rage against God, man, whoever it is that has forced this vile, slimy life upon him. With all this groping, this mad desire, a great blind intellect stumbling through wrong, a loving poet's heart, the man was by habit only a coarse, vulgar laborer, familiar with sights and words you would blush to name. Be just: when I tell you about this night, see him as he is. Be just—not like man's law, which seizes on one isolated fact, but like God's judging angel, whose clear, sad eye saw all the countless cankering days of this man's life, all the countless nights, when, sick with starving, his soul fainted in him, before it judged him for this night, the saddest of all.

I called this night the crisis of his life. If it was, it stole on him unawares. These great turning-days of life cast no shadow before, slip by unconsciously. Only a trifle, a little turn of the rudder, and the ship goes to heaven or hell.

Wolfe, while Deborah watched him, dug into the furnace of melting iron with his pole, dully thinking only how many rails the lump would yield. It was late—nearly Sunday morning; another hour, and the heavy work would be done—only the furnaces to replenish and cover for the next day. The workmen were growing more noisy, shouting, as they had to do, to be heard over the deep clamor of the mills. Suddenly they grew less boisterous—at the far end, entirely silent. Something unusual had happened. After a moment, the silence came nearer; the men stopped their jeers and drunken choruses. Deborah, stupidly lifting up her head, saw the cause of the quiet. A group of five or six men were slowly approaching, stopping to examine each furnace as they came. Visitors often came to see the mills after night: except by growing less noisy, the men took no notice of them. The furnace where Wolfe worked was near the bounds of the works; they halted there hot and tired: a walk over one of these great foundries is no trifling task. The woman, drawing out of sight, turned over to sleep. Wolfe, seeing them stop, suddenly roused from his indifferent stupor, and watched them keenly. He knew some of them: the overseer, Clarke; a son of Kirby, one of the mill-owners; and a Doctor May, one of the town-physicians. The other two were strangers.

---

[1]   *sobriquet* Nickname.

[2]   *cockpit* Arena in which roosters are made to fight one another to the death, for entertainment; *terrier* Some terrier breeds were commonly kept for the purpose of dogfighting.

Wolfe came closer. He seized eagerly every chance that brought him into contact with this mysterious class that shone down on him perpetually with the glamour of another order of being. What made the difference between them? That was the mystery of his life. He had a vague notion that perhaps tonight he could find it out. One of the strangers sat down on a pile of bricks, and beckoned young Kirby to his side.

"This *is* hot, with a vengeance. A match, please?"—lighting his cigar. "But the walk is worth the trouble. If it were not that you must have heard it so often, Kirby, I would tell you that your works look like Dante's Inferno."[1]

Kirby laughed.

"Yes. Yonder is Farinata[2] himself in the burning tomb,"—pointing to some figure in the shimmering shadows.

"Judging from some of the faces of your men," said the other, "they bid fair to try the reality of Dante's vision, some day."

Young Kirby looked curiously around, as if seeing the faces of his hands[3] for the first time.

"They're bad enough, that's true. A desperate set, I fancy. Eh, Clarke?"

The overseer did not hear him. He was talking of net profits just then—giving, in fact, a schedule of the annual business of the firm to a sharp peering little Yankee, who jotted down notes on a paper laid on the crown of his hat: a reporter for one of the city-papers, getting up a series of reviews of the leading manufactories. The other gentlemen had accompanied them merely for amusement. They were silent until the notes were finished, drying their feet at the furnaces, and sheltering their faces from the intolerable heat. At last the overseer concluded with—

"I believe that is a pretty fair estimate, Captain."

"Here, some of your men!" said Kirby, "bring up those boards. We may as well sit down, gentlemen, until the rain is over. It cannot last much longer at this rate."

"Pig-metal,"—mumbled the reporter, "um!—coal facilities—um!—hands employed, twelve hundred—bitumen—um!—all right, I believe, Mr. Clarke; sinking-fund[4]—what did you say was your sinking-fund?"

"Twelve hundred hands?" said the stranger, the young man who had first spoken. "Do you control their votes, Kirby?"

"Control? No." The young man smiled complacently. "But my father brought seven hundred votes to the polls for his candidate last November. No force-work, you understand—only a speech or two, a hint to form themselves into a society, and a bit of red and blue bunting to make them a flag. The Invincible Roughs—I believe that is their name. I forget the motto: 'Our country's hope,' I think."

There was a laugh. The young man talking to Kirby sat with an amused light in his cool gray eye, surveying critically the half-clothed figures of the puddlers, and the slow swing of their brawny muscles. He was a stranger in the city, spending a couple of months in the borders of a Slave State,[5] to study the institutions of the South—a brother-in-law of Kirby's—Mitchell. He was an amateur gymnast, hence his anatomical eye; a patron, in a *blasé* way, of the prize-ring; a man who sucked the essence out of a science or philosophy in an indifferent, gentlemanly way; who took Kant, Novalis, Humboldt,[6] for what they were worth in his own scales; accepting all, despising nothing, in heaven, earth, or hell, but one-idead men; with a temper yielding and brilliant as summer water, until his Self was touched, when it was ice, though brilliant still. Such men are not rare in the States.

As he knocked the ashes from his cigar, Wolfe caught with a quick pleasure the contour of the white hand, the blood-glow of a red ring he wore. His voice, too, and that of Kirby's, touched him like music—low, even, with chording cadences. About this man Mitchell hung the impalpable atmosphere belonging

---

[1] *Dante's Inferno* Hell, as described by the Italian poet Dante Alighieri (1265–1321) in *Inferno*, the first part of his epic three-part poem *The Divine Comedy*.

[2] *Farinata* Farinata degli Uberti, an aristocrat who in the *Inferno* is described as one among many heretics whose eternal torment is to be entombed in sepulchres surrounded by fire (see Cantos 9–10).

[3] *hands* I.e., workers.

[4] *sinking-fund* Money set aside for the purpose of paying down the principle of a company debt.

[5] *borders of a Slave State* The story was written prior to the establishment of West Virginia as a free state separate from the slave state of Virginia.

[6] *Kant* Immanuel Kant (1724–1804), German philosopher; *Novalis* Pen name of German poet and mystic philosopher Friedrich von Hardenberg (1772–1801); *Humboldt* German explorer and naturalist Alexander von Humboldt (1769–1859).

to the thorough-bred gentleman. Wolfe, scraping away the ashes beside him, was conscious of it, did obeisance to it with his artist sense, unconscious that he did so.

The rain did not cease. Clarke and the reporter left the mills; the others, comfortably seated near the furnace, lingered, smoking and talking in a desultory way. Greek would not have been more unintelligible to the furnace-tenders, whose presence they soon forgot entirely. Kirby drew out a newspaper from his pocket and read aloud some article, which they discussed eagerly. At every sentence, Wolfe listened more and more like a dumb, hopeless animal, with a duller, more stolid look creeping over his face, glancing now and then at Mitchell, marking acutely every smallest sign of refinement, then back to himself, seeing as in a mirror his filthy body, his more stained soul.

Never! He had no words for such a thought, but he knew now, in all the sharpness of the bitter certainty, that between them there was a great gulf never to be passed.[1] Never!

The bell of the mills rang for midnight. Sunday morning had dawned. Whatever hidden message lay in the tolling bells floated past these men unknown. Yet it was there. Veiled in the solemn music ushering the risen Savior was a key-note to solve the darkest secrets of a world gone wrong—even this social riddle which the brain of the grimy puddler grappled with madly tonight.

The men began to withdraw the metal from the cauldrons. The mills were deserted on Sundays, except by the hands who fed the fires, and those who had no lodgings and slept usually on the ash-heaps. The three strangers sat still during the next hour, watching the men cover the furnaces, laughing now and then at some jest of Kirby's.

"Do you know," said Mitchell, "I like this view of the works better than when the glare was fiercest? These heavy shadows and the amphitheatre of smothered fires are ghostly, unreal. One could fancy these red smouldering lights to be the half-shut eyes of wild beasts, and the spectral figures their victims in the den."

Kirby laughed. "You are fanciful. Come, let us get out of the den. The spectral figures, as you call them, are a little too real for me to fancy a close proximity in the darkness—unarmed, too."

The others rose, buttoning their overcoats, and lighting cigars.

"Raining, still," said Doctor May, "and hard. Where did we leave the coach, Mitchell?"

"At the other side of the works. Kirby, what's that?"

Mitchell started back, half-frightened, as, suddenly turning a corner, the white figure of a woman faced him in the darkness—a woman, white, of giant proportions, crouching on the ground, her arms flung out in some wild gesture of warning.

"Stop! Make that fire burn there!" cried Kirby, stopping short.

The flame burst out, flashing the gaunt figure into bold relief.

Mitchell drew a long breath.

"I thought it was alive," he said, going up curiously. The others followed.

"Not marble, eh?" asked Kirby, touching it.

One of the lower overseers stopped.

"Korl, Sir."

"Who did it?"

"Can't say. Some of[2] the hands; chipped it out in off-hours."

"Chipped to some purpose, I should say. What a flesh-tint the stuff has! Do you see, Mitchell?"

"I see."

He had stepped aside where the light fell boldest on the figure, looking at it in silence. There was not one line of beauty or grace in it: a nude woman's form, muscular, grown coarse with labor, the powerful limbs instinct[3] with some one poignant longing. One idea: there it was in the tense, rigid muscles, the clutching hands, the wild, eager face, like that of a starving wolf's. Kirby and Doctor May walked around it, critical, curious. Mitchell stood aloof, silent. The figure touched him strangely.

"Not badly done," said Doctor May. "Where did the fellow learn that sweep of the muscles in the arm and

---

[1]   *a great gulf ... be passed*   See Luke 16.25–26, where Abraham addresses a rich man who suffers in hell while Lazarus, who was a beggar in life, resides in heaven with Abraham: "Son, remember that thou in thy lifetime receivedst thy good things, and likewise Lazarus evil things: but now he is comforted, and thou art tormented. And beside all this, between us and you there is a great gulf fixed: so that they which would pass from hence to you cannot; neither can they pass to us, that would come from thence."

[2]   *Some of*   I.e., one of.

[3]   *instinct*   Charged, animated.

hand? Look at them! They are groping—do you see? clutching: the peculiar action of a man dying of thirst."

"They have ample facilities for studying anatomy," sneered Kirby, glancing at the half-naked figures.

"Look," continued the Doctor, "at this bony wrist, and the strained sinews of the instep! A working-woman—the very type of her class."

"God forbid!" muttered Mitchell.

"Why?" demanded May. "What does the fellow intend by the figure? I cannot catch the meaning."

"Ask him," said the other, dryly.

"There he stands," pointing to Wolfe, who stood with a group of men, leaning on his ash-rake.

The Doctor beckoned him with the affable smile which kind-hearted men put on, when talking to these people.

"Mr. Mitchell has picked you out as the man who did this—I'm sure I don't know why. But what did you mean by it?"

"She be hungry."

Wolfe's eyes answered Mitchell, not the Doctor.

"Oh-h! But what a mistake you have made, my fine fellow! You have given no sign of starvation to the body. It is strong—terribly strong. It has the mad, half-despairing gesture of drowning."

Wolfe stammered, glanced appealingly at Mitchell, who saw the soul of the thing, he knew. But the cool, probing eyes were turned on himself now—mocking, cruel, relentless.

"Not hungry for meat," the furnace-tender said at last.

"What then? Whiskey?" jeered Kirby, with a coarse laugh.

Wolfe was silent a moment, thinking.

"I dunno," he said, with a bewildered look. "It mebbe.[1] Summat to make her live, I think—like you. Whiskey ull do it, in a way."

The young man laughed again. Mitchell flashed a look of disgust somewhere—not at Wolfe.

"May," he broke out impatiently, "are you blind? Look at that woman's face! It asks questions of God, and says, 'I have a right to know.' Good God, how hungry it is!"

They looked a moment; then May turned to the mill-owner:

"Have you many such hands as this? What are you going to do with them? Keep them at puddling iron?"

Kirby shrugged his shoulders. Mitchell's look had irritated him.

"Ce n'est pas mon affaire.[2] I have no fancy for nursing infant geniuses. I suppose there are some stray gleams of mind and soul among these wretches. The Lord will take care of his own; or else they can work out their own salvation.[3] I have heard you call our American system a ladder which any man can scale. Do you doubt it? Or perhaps you want to banish all social ladders, and put us all on a flat table-land—eh, May?"

The Doctor looked vexed, puzzled. Some terrible problem lay hid in this woman's face, and troubled these men. Kirby waited for an answer, and, receiving none, went on, warming with his subject.

"I tell you, there's something wrong that no talk of 'Liberté' or 'Egalité'[4] will do away. If I had the making of men, these men who do the lowest part of the world's work should be machines—nothing more—hands. It would be kindness. God help them! What are taste, reason, to creatures who must live such lives as that?" He pointed to Deborah, sleeping on the ash-heap. "So many nerves to sting them to pain. What if God had put your brain, with all its agony of touch, into your fingers, and bid you work and strike with that?"

"You think you could govern the world better?" laughed the Doctor.

"I do not think at all."

"That is true philosophy. Drift with the stream, because you cannot dive deep enough to find bottom, eh?"

"Exactly," rejoined Kirby. "I do not think. I wash my hands of all social problems—slavery, caste, white or black. My duty to my operatives has a narrow limit— the pay-hour on Saturday night. Outside of that, if they cut korl, or cut each other's throats (the more popular amusement of the two), I am not responsible."

The Doctor sighed—a good honest sigh, from the depths of his stomach.

---

[1] *mebbe* May be.

[2] *Ce n'est ... mon affaire* French: This is none of my business.

[3] *work out their own salvation* See Philippians 2.12, where Paul urges the people of Philippi to "not as in my presence only, but now much more in my absence, work out your own salvation with fear and trembling."

[4] *'Liberté' or 'Egalité'* Allusion to the national motto of France, originating in the French Revolution: "Liberty, Equality, Fraternity."

"God help us! Who is responsible?"

"Not I, I tell you," said Kirby, testily. "What has the man who pays them money to do with their souls' concerns, more than the grocer or butcher who takes it?"

"And yet," said Mitchell's cynical voice, "look at her! How hungry she is!"

Kirby tapped his boot with his cane. No one spoke. Only the dumb face of the rough image looking into their faces with the awful question, "What shall we do to be saved?" Only Wolfe's face, with its heavy weight of brain, its weak, uncertain mouth, its desperate eyes, out of which looked the soul of his class—only Wolfe's face turned towards Kirby's. Mitchell laughed—a cool, musical laugh.

"Money has spoken!" he said, seating himself lightly on a stone with the air of an amused spectator at a play. "Are you answered?"—turning to Wolfe his clear, magnetic face.

Bright and deep and cold as Arctic air, the soul of the man lay tranquil beneath. He looked at the furnace-tender as he had looked at a rare mosaic in the morning; only the man was the more amusing study of the two.

"Are you answered? Why, May, look at him! *De profundis clamavi.*[1] Or, to quote in English, 'Hungry and thirsty, his soul faints in him.'[2] And so Money sends back its answer into the depths through you, Kirby! Very clear the answer, too! I think I remember reading the same words somewhere: washing your hands in Eau de Cologne, and saying, 'I am innocent of the blood of this man.[3] See ye to it!'"

Kirby flushed angrily.

"You quote Scripture freely."

"Do I not quote correctly? I think I remember another line, which may amend my meaning: 'Inasmuch as ye did it unto one of the least of these, ye did it unto me.'[4]

Deist?[5] Bless you, man, I was raised on the milk of the Word. Now, Doctor, the pocket of the world having uttered its voice, what has the heart to say? You are a philanthropist, in a small way—*n'est ce pas*?[6] Here, boy, this gentleman can show you how to cut korl better—or your destiny. Go on, May!"

"I think a mocking devil possesses you tonight," rejoined the Doctor, seriously.

He went to Wolfe and put his hand kindly on his arm. Something of a vague idea possessed the Doctor's brain that much good was to be done here by a friendly word or two: a latent genius to be warmed into life by a waited-for sunbeam. Here it was: he had brought it. So he went on complacently:

"Do you know, boy, you have it in you to be a great sculptor, a great man?—do you understand?" (talking down to the capacity of his hearer: it is a way people have with children, and men like Wolfe), "to live a better, stronger life than I, or Mr. Kirby here? A man may make himself anything he chooses. God has given you stronger powers than many men—me, for instance."

May stopped, heated, glowing with his own magnanimity. And it was magnanimous. The puddler had drunk in every word, looking through the Doctor's flurry, and generous heat, and self-approval, into his will, with those slow, absorbing eyes of his.

"Make yourself what you will. It is your right."

"I know," quietly. "Will you help me?"

Mitchell laughed again. The Doctor turned now, in a passion—

"You know, Mitchell, I have not the means. You know, if I had, it is in my heart to take this boy and educate him for—"

"The glory of God, and the glory of John May."

May did not speak for a moment; then, controlled, he said,

"Why should one be raised, when myriads are left? I have not the money, boy," to Wolfe, shortly.

"Money?" He said it over slowly, as one repeats the guessed answer to a riddle, doubtfully. "That is it? Money?"

---

[1]   *De profundis clamavi*   First words of the Latin version of Psalm 130; in English, the Psalm begins, "Out of the depths have I cried unto thee, O Lord."

[2]   *Hungry and ... in him*   See Psalm 107.5.

[3]   *I am innocent ... this man*   See Matthew 27.24, where Pontius Pilate, the Roman governor who has consented to the crucifixion of Jesus, washes his hands before the mob and refuses to take personal responsibility for Jesus' death.

[4]   *Inasmuch as ... unto me*   See Matthew 25.40, where Jesus thanks the blessed for assisting him when he was in poverty and need, explaining that "Inasmuch as ye have done it unto one of the least of these my brethren, ye have done it unto me."

[5]   *Deist*   One who believes in a God who was the first cause and creator of the universe, but who has had little or no influence on the world and its inhabitants since. Deism became prominent in the United States in the eighteenth century, especially among scientists, philosophers, and those who were skeptical of organized religion.

[6]   *n'est ce pas*   French: isn't that so.

"Yes, money, that is it," said Mitchell, rising, and drawing his furred coat about him. "You've found the cure for all the world's diseases. Come, May, find your good-humor, and come home. This damp wind chills my very bones. Come and preach your Saint-Simonian[1] doctrines tomorrow to Kirby's hands. Let them have a clear idea of the rights of the soul, and I'll venture next week they'll strike for higher wages. That will be the end of it."

"Will you send the coach-driver to this side of the mills?" asked Kirby, turning to Wolfe.

He spoke kindly: it was his habit to do so. Deborah, seeing the puddler go, crept after him. The three men waited outside. Doctor May walked up and down, chafed. Suddenly he stopped.

"Go back, Mitchell! You say the pocket and the heart of the world speak without meaning to these people. What has its head to say? Taste, culture, refinement? Go!"

Mitchell was leaning against a brick wall. He turned his head indolently, and looked into the mills. There hung about the place a thick, unclean odor. The slightest motion of his hand marked that he perceived it, and his insufferable disgust. That was all. May said nothing, only quickened his angry tramp.

"Besides," added Mitchell, giving a corollary to his answer, "it would be of no use. I am not one of them."

"You do not mean"—said May, facing him.

"Yes, I mean just that. Reform is born of need, not pity. No vital movement of the people's has worked down, for good or evil; fermented, instead, carried up the heaving, cloggy mass. Think back through history, and you will know it. What will this lowest deep—thieves, Magdalens,[2] negroes—do with the light filtered through ponderous Church creeds, Baconian theories,

Goethe schemes?[3] Some day, out of their bitter need will be thrown up their own light-bringer—their Jean Paul, their Cromwell,[4] their Messiah."

"Bah!" was the Doctor's inward criticism. However, in practice, he adopted the theory; for, when, night and morning, afterwards, he prayed that power might be given these degraded souls to rise, he glowed at heart, recognizing an accomplished duty.

Wolfe and the woman had stood in the shadow of the works as the coach drove off. The Doctor had held out his hand in a frank, generous way, telling him to "take care of himself, and to remember it was his right to rise." Mitchell had simply touched his hat, as to an equal, with a quiet look of thorough recognition. Kirby had thrown Deborah some money, which she found, and clutched eagerly enough. They were gone now, all of them. The man sat down on the cinder-road, looking up into the murky sky.

"'T be late, Hugh. Wunnot hur come?"

He shook his head doggedly, and the woman crouched out of his sight against the wall. Do you remember rare moments when a sudden light flashed over yourself, your world, God? when you stood on a mountain-peak, seeing your life as it might have been, as it is? one quick instant, when custom lost its force and everyday usage? when your friend, wife, brother, stood in a new light? your soul was bared, and the grave—a foretaste of the nakedness of the Judgment-Day? So it came before him, his life, that night. The slow tides of pain he had borne gathered themselves up and surged against his soul. His squalid daily life, the brutal coarseness eating into his brain, as the ashes into his skin: before, these things had been a dull aching

---

[1] *Saint-Simonian* Saint-Simonism was a Christian proto-socialist movement in France based on the doctrines of the philosopher Henri, comte de Saint-Simon (1760–1825). Saint-Simon argued that the application of reason and scientific industry in conjunction with social cooperation could bring an end to poverty, war, and other excesses of capitalism; he also advocated a reformation of Christianity that would be centered on brotherly love.

[2] *Magdalens* Prostitutes or former prostitutes (the term references Mary Magdalene, a follower of Jesus in the New Testament, apocryphally considered by some Christians to have been a repentant prostitute).

---

[3] *Baconian theories* Sir Francis Bacon (1561–1624) was an English philosopher, jurist, and powerful political figure best known for his contributions to the development of the scientific method; *Goethe schemes* Johann Wolfgang von Goethe (1749–1832) was a German poet and philosopher who exerted a great influence on Romanticism.

[4] *Jean Paul* Influential German novelist (1763–1825) associated with the Romantic movement; *Cromwell* Oliver Cromwell (1599–1658), English Puritan who was a leader in the uprising that overthrew King Charles I; he eventually established himself as Lord Protector of the nation, ruling for five years. He is a controversial figure, considered a violent dictator by some and a revolutionary hero by others.

into his consciousness; tonight, they were reality. He gripped the filthy red shirt that clung, stiff with soot, about him, and tore it savagely from his arm. The flesh beneath was muddy with grease and ashes—and the heart beneath that! And the soul? God knows.

Then flashed before his vivid poetic sense the man who had left him—the pure face, the delicate, sinewy limbs, in harmony with all he knew of beauty or truth. In his cloudy fancy he had pictured a Something like this. He had found it in this Mitchell, even when he idly scoffed at his pain: a Man all-knowing, all-seeing, crowned by Nature, reigning—the keen glance of his eye falling like a sceptre on other men. And yet his instinct taught him that he too—He! He looked at himself with sudden loathing, sick, wrung his hands with a cry, and then was silent. With all the phantoms of his heated, ignorant fancy, Wolfe had not been vague in his ambitions. They were practical, slowly built up before him out of his knowledge of what he could do. Through years he had day by day made this hope a real thing to himself—a clear, projected figure of himself, as he might become.

Able to speak, to know what was best, to raise these men and women working at his side up with him: sometimes he forgot this defined hope in the frantic anguish to escape—only to escape—out of the wet, the pain, the ashes, somewhere, anywhere—only for one moment of free air on a hill-side, to lie down and let his sick soul throb itself out in the sunshine. But tonight he panted for life. The savage strength of his nature was roused; his cry was fierce to God for justice.

"Look at me!" he said to Deborah, with a low, bitter laugh, striking his puny chest savagely. "What am I worth, Deb? Is it my fault that I am no better? My fault? My fault?"

He stopped, stung with a sudden remorse, seeing her hunchback shape writhing with sobs. For Deborah was crying thankless tears, according to the fashion of women.

"God forgi' me, woman! Things go harder wi' you nor me. It's a worse share."

He got up and helped her to rise; and they went doggedly down the muddy street, side by side.

"It's all wrong," he muttered, slowly—"all wrong! I dunnot understan'. But it'll end some day."

"Come home, Hugh!" she said, coaxingly; for he had stopped, looking around bewildered.

"Home—and back to the mill!" He went on saying this over to himself, as if he would mutter down every pain in this dull despair.

She followed him through the fog, her blue lips chattering with cold. They reached the cellar at last. Old Wolfe had been drinking since she went out, and had crept nearer the door. The girl Janey slept heavily in the corner. He went up to her, touching softly the worn white arm with his fingers. Some bitterer thought stung him, as he stood there. He wiped the drops from his forehead, and went into the room beyond, livid, trembling. A hope, trifling, perhaps, but very dear, had died just then out of the poor puddler's life, as he looked at the sleeping, innocent girl—some plan for the future, in which she had borne a part. He gave it up that moment, then and forever. Only a trifle, perhaps, to us: his face grew a shade paler—that was all. But, somehow, the man's soul, as God and the angels looked down on it, never was the same afterwards.

Deborah followed him into the inner room. She carried a candle, which she placed on the floor, closing the door after her. She had seen the look on his face, as he turned away: her own grew deadly. Yet, as she came up to him, her eyes glowed. He was seated on an old chest, quiet, holding his face in his hands.

"Hugh!" she said, softly.

He did not speak.

"Hugh, did hur hear what the man said—him with the clear voice? Did hur hear? Money, money—that it wud do all?"

He pushed her away—gently, but he was worn out; her rasping tone fretted him.

"Hugh!"

The candle flared a pale yellow light over the cobwebbed brick walls, and the woman standing there. He looked at her. She was young, in deadly earnest; her faded eyes, and wet, ragged figure caught from their frantic eagerness a power akin to beauty.

"Hugh, it is true! Money ull do it! Oh, Hugh, boy, listen till me! He said it true! It is money!"

"I know. Go back! I do not want you here."

"Hugh, it is t'last time. I'll never worrit[1] hur again."

---

[1]   *worrit* Worry; bother.

There were tears in her voice now, but she choked them back.

"Hear till me only tonight! If one of t' witch people wud come, them we heard of t' home, and gif hur all hur wants, what then? Say, Hugh!"

"What do you mean?"

"I mean money."

Her whisper shrilled through his brain.

"If one of t' witch dwarfs wud come from t' lane moors tonight, and gif hur money, to go out—*out*, I say—out, lad, where t' sun shines, and t' heath grows, and t' ladies walk in silken gownds, and God stays all t' time—where t' man lives that talked to us tonight—Hugh knows—Hugh could walk there like a king!"

He thought the woman mad, tried to check her, but she went on, fierce in her eager haste.

"If *I* were t' witch dwarf, if I had t' money, wud hur thank me? Wud hur take me out o' this place wid hur and Janey? I wud not come into the gran' house hur wud build, to vex hur wid t' hunch—only at night, when t' shadows were dark, stand far off to see hur."

Mad? Yes! Are many of us mad in this way?

"Poor Deb! poor Deb!" he said, soothingly.

"It is here," she said, suddenly jerking into his hand a small roll. "I took it! I did it! Me, me! not hur! I shall be hanged, I shall be burnt in hell, if anybody knows I took it! Out of his pocket, as he leaned against t' bricks. Hur knows?"

She thrust it into his hand, and then, her errand done, began to gather chips together to make a fire, choking down hysteric sobs.

"Has it come to this?"

That was all he said. The Welsh Wolfe blood was honest. The roll was a small green pocket-book containing one or two gold pieces, and a check for an incredible amount, as it seemed to the poor puddler. He laid it down, hiding his face again in his hands.

"Hugh, don't be angry wud me! It's only poor Deb—hur knows?"

He took the long skinny fingers kindly in his.

"Angry? God help me, no! Let me sleep. I am tired."

He threw himself heavily down on the wooden bench, stunned with pain and weariness. She brought some old rags to cover him.

It was late on Sunday evening before he awoke. I tell God's truth, when I say he had then no thought of keeping this money. Deborah had hid it in his pocket. He found it there. She watched him eagerly, as he took it out.

"I must gif it to him," he said, reading her face.

"Hur knows," she said with a bitter sigh of disappointment. "But it is hur right to keep it."

His right! The word struck him. Doctor May had used the same. He washed himself, and went out to find this man Mitchell. His right! Why did this chance word cling to him so obstinately? Do you hear the fierce devils whisper in his ear, as he went slowly down the darkening street?

The evening came on, slow and calm. He seated himself at the end of an alley leading into one of the larger streets. His brain was clear tonight, keen, intent, mastering. It would not start back, cowardly, from any hellish temptation, but meet it face to face. Therefore the great temptation of his life came to him veiled by no sophistry,[1] but bold, defiant, owning its own vile name, trusting to one bold blow for victory.

He did not deceive himself. Theft! That was it. At first the word sickened him; then he grappled with it. Sitting there on a broken cart-wheel, the fading day, the noisy groups, the church-bells' tolling passed before him like a panorama,[2] while the sharp struggle went on within. This money! He took it out, and looked at it. If he gave it back, what then? He was going to be cool about it.

People going by to church saw only a sickly mill-boy watching them quietly at the alley's mouth. They did not know that he was mad, or they would not have gone by so quietly: mad with hunger; stretching out his hands to the world, that had given so much to them, for leave to live the life God meant him to live. His soul within him was smothering to death; he wanted so much, thought so much, and *knew*—nothing. There was nothing of which he was certain, except the mill and things there. Of God and heaven he had heard so little, that they were to him what fairy-land is to a child: something real, but not here; very far off. His brain, greedy, dwarfed, full of thwarted energy and

---

1 *sophistry* Clever but fallacious reasoning.

2 *panorama* Long painting broken up into contiguous scenes, which would be unrolled or otherwise unveiled before audiences, sometimes with musical accompaniment; panoramas were popular entertainments during the nineteenth century.

unused powers, questioned these men and women going by, coldly, bitterly, that night. Was it not his right to live as they—a pure life, a good, true-hearted life, full of beauty and kind words? He only wanted to know how to use the strength within him. His heart warmed, as he thought of it. He suffered himself to think of it longer. If he took the money?

Then he saw himself as he might be, strong, helpful, kindly. The night crept on, as this one image slowly evolved itself from the crowd of other thoughts and stood triumphant. He looked at it. As he might be! What wonder, if it blinded him to delirium—the madness that underlies all revolution, all progress, and all fall?

You laugh at the shallow temptation? You see the error underlying its argument so clearly—that to him a true life was one of full development rather than self-restraint? that he was deaf to the higher tone in a cry of voluntary suffering for truth's sake than in the fullest flow of spontaneous harmony? I do not plead his cause. I only want to show you the mote in my brother's eye: then you can see clearly to take it out.[1]

The money—there it lay on his knee, a little blotted slip of paper, nothing in itself; used to raise him out of the pit; something straight from God's hand. A thief! Well, what was it to be a thief? He met the question at last, face to face, wiping the clammy drops of sweat from his forehead. God made this money—the fresh air, too—for his children's use. He never made the difference between poor and rich. The Something who looked down on him that moment through the cool gray sky had a kindly face, he knew—loved his children alike. Oh, he knew that!

There were times when the soft floods of color in the crimson and purple flames, or the clear depth of amber in the water below the bridge, had somehow given him a glimpse of another world than this—of an infinite depth of beauty and of quiet somewhere—somewhere—a depth of quiet and rest and love. Looking up now, it became strangely real. The sun had sunk quite below the hills, but his last rays struck upward, touching the zenith. The fog had risen, and the town and river were steeped in its thick, gray damp;

but overhead, the sun-touched smoke-clouds opened like a cleft ocean—shifting, rolling seas of crimson mist, waves of billowy silver veined with blood-scarlet, inner depths unfathomable of glancing light. Wolfe's artist-eye grew drunk with color. The gates of that other world! Fading, flashing before him now! What, in that world of Beauty, Content, and Right, were the petty laws, the mine and thine, of mill-owners and mill-hands?

A consciousness of power stirred within him. He stood up. A man, he thought, stretching out his hands—free to work, to live, to love! Free! His right! He folded the scrap of paper in his hand. As his nervous fingers took it in, limp and blotted, so his soul took in the mean temptation, lapped it in fancied rights, in dreams of improved existences, drifting and endless as the cloud-seas of color. Clutching it, as if the tightness of his hold would strengthen his sense of possession, he went aimlessly down the street. It was his watch at the mill. He need not go, need never go again, thank God!—shaking off the thought with unspeakable loathing.

Shall I go over the history of the hours of that night? how the man wandered from one to another of his old haunts, with a half-consciousness of bidding them farewell—lanes and alleys and backyards where the mill-hands lodged—noting, with a new eagerness, the filth and drunkenness, the pig-pens, the ash-heaps covered with potato-skins, the bloated, pimpled women at the doors—with a new disgust, a new sense of sudden triumph, and, under all, a new, vague dread, unknown before, smothered down, kept under, but still there? It left him but once during the night, when, for the second time in his life, he entered a church. It was a sombre Gothic pile, where the stained light lost itself in far-retreating arches; built to meet the requirements and sympathies of a far other class than Wolfe's. Yet it touched, moved him uncontrollably. The distances, the shadows, the still, marble figures, the mass of silent kneeling worshippers, the mysterious music, thrilled, lifted his soul with a wonderful pain. Wolfe forgot himself, forgot the new life he was going to live, the mean terror gnawing underneath. The voice of the speaker strengthened the charm; it was clear, feeling full, strong. An old man, who had lived much, suffered much; whose brain was keenly alive, dominant; whose

---

1   *the mote ... take it out*   See Matthew 7.3–5: "And why beholdest thou the mote that is in thy brother's eye, but considerest not the beam [i.e., of timber] that is in thine own eye? ... Thou hypocrite, first cast out the beam out of thine own eye; and then shalt thou see clearly to cast out the mote out of thy brother's eye."

heart was summer-warm with charity. He taught it tonight. He held up Humanity in its grand total; showed the great world-cancer to his people. Who could show it better? He was a Christian reformer; he had studied the age thoroughly; his outlook at man had been free, world-wide, over all time. His faith stood sublime upon the Rock of Ages;[1] his fiery zeal guided vast schemes by which the gospel was to be preached to all nations. How did he preach it tonight? In burning, light-laden words he painted the incarnate Life, Love, the universal Man: words that became reality in the lives of these people, that lived again in beautiful words and actions, trifling, but heroic. Sin, as he defined it, was a real foe to them; their trials, temptations, were his. His words passed far over the furnace-tender's grasp, toned to suit another class of culture; they sounded in his ears a very pleasant song in an unknown tongue. He meant to cure this world-cancer with a steady eye that had never glared with hunger, and a hand that neither poverty nor strychnine-whiskey[2] had taught to shake. In this morbid, distorted heart of the Welsh puddler he had failed.

Years ago,[3] a mechanic[4] tried reform in the alleys of a city as swarming and vile as this mill town, who did

---

1 *Rock of Ages* Common metaphor for Christ.

2 *strychnine-whiskey* Slang term for cheap whiskey, to which poisons such as strychnine were sometimes added to allow producers to dilute the alcohol but achieve similar intoxicating effects.

3 *Years ago* The following paragraph was censored from the original 1861 publication of the story; a revised form of it was restored when the text was reprinted in the 1865 anthology *Atlantic Tales*. Janice Milner Lasseter has persuasively argued that the manuscript version of the paragraph better reflects Davis's artistic vision; that version is reproduced above. In 1865, the paragraph was revised as follows:

> Eighteen centuries ago, the Master of this man tried reform in the streets of a city as crowded and vile as this, and did not fail. His disciple, showing Him to-night to cultured hearers, showing the clearness of the God-power acting through Him, shrank back from one coarse fact; that in birth and habit the man Christ was thrown up from the lowest of the people: his flesh, their flesh; their blood, his blood; tempted like them, to brutalize day by day; to lie, to steal: the actual slime and want of their hourly life, and the wine-press he trod alone.
>
> Yet, is there no meaning in this perpetually covered truth? If the son of the carpenter had stood in the church that night, as he stood with the fishermen and harlots by the sea of Galilee, before His Father and their Father, despised and rejected of men, without a place to lay His head, wounded for their iniquities, bruised for their transgressions, would not that hungry

not fail. Could Wolfe have seen him as He was, that night, what then? A social Pariah, a man of the lowest caste, thrown up from among them, dying with their pain, starving with their hunger, tempted as they are to drink, to steal, to curse God and die. Theirs by blood, by birth. The son, they said, of Joseph the carpenter, his mother and sisters there among them. Terribly alone, one who loved and was not loved, and suffered from that pain; who dared to be pure and honest in that devil's den; who dared to die for us though he was a physical coward and feared death. If He had stood in the church that night, would not the wretch in the torn shirt there in the pew have "known the man"?[5] His brother first. And then, unveiled his God.

Wolfe rose at last, and turned from the church down the street. He looked up; the night had come on foggy, damp; the golden mists had vanished, and the sky lay dull and ash-colored. He wandered again aimlessly down the street, idly wondering what had become of the cloud-sea of crimson and scarlet. The trial-day of this man's life was over, and he had lost the victory. What followed was mere drifting circumstance—a quicker walking over the path—that was all. Do you want to hear the end of it? You wish me to make a tragic story out of it? Why, in the police-reports of the morning paper you can find a dozen such tragedies: hints of shipwrecks unlike any that ever befell on the high seas; hints that here a power was lost to heaven— that there a soul went down where no tide can ebb or flow. Commonplace enough the hints are—jocose sometimes, done up in rhyme.

Doctor May, a month after the night I have told you of, was reading to his wife at breakfast from this fourth column of the morning-paper: an unusual thing, these police-reports not being, in general, choice reading for ladies; but it was only one item he read.

"Oh, my dear! You remember that man I told you of, that we saw at Kirby's mill?—that was arrested for robbing Mitchell? Here he is; just listen: 'Circuit Court. Judge Day. Hugh Wolfe, operative in Kirby &

> mill-boy at least, in the back seat, have "known the man"? That Jesus did not stand there.

4 *mechanic* Tradesperson; manual worker. Jesus is often described as a carpenter (also the trade of his mother's husband, Joseph).

5 *known the man* See Matthew 26.72, where Peter denies that he was Jesus' disciple, saying "I do not know the man."

John's Loudon Mills. Charge, grand larceny. Sentence, nineteen years hard labor in penitentiary.' Scoundrel! Serves him right! After all our kindness that night! Picking Mitchell's pocket at the very time!"

His wife said something about the ingratitude of that kind of people, and then they began to talk of something else.

Nineteen years! How easy that was to read! What a simple word for Judge Day to utter! Nineteen years! Half a lifetime!

Hugh Wolfe sat on the window-ledge of his cell, looking out. His ankles were ironed. Not usual in such cases; but he had made two desperate efforts to escape. "Well," as Haley, the jailer, said, "small blame to him! Nineteen years' imprisonment was not a pleasant thing to look forward to." Haley was very good-natured about it, though Wolfe had fought him savagely.

"When he was first caught," the jailer said afterwards, in telling the story, "before the trial, the fellow was cut down at once—laid there on that pallet like a dead man, with his hands over his eyes. Never saw a man so cut down in my life. Time of the trial, too, came the queerest dodge[1] of any customer I ever had. Would choose no lawyer. Judge gave him one, of course. Gibson it was. He tried to prove the fellow crazy; but it wouldn't go. Thing was plain as daylight: money found on him. 'Twas a hard sentence, all the law allows; but it was for 'xample's sake. These millhands are gettin' onbearable. When the sentence was read, he just looked up, and said the money was his by rights, and that all the world had gone wrong. That night, after the trial, a gentleman came to see him here, name of Mitchell—him as he stole from. Talked to him for an hour. Thought he came for curiosity, like. After he was gone, thought Wolfe was remarkable quiet, and went into his cell. Found him very low; bed all bloody. Doctor said he had been bleeding at the lungs. He was as weak as a cat; yet, if ye'll b'lieve me, he tried to get a-past me and get out. I just carried him like a baby, and threw him on the pallet. Three days after, he tried it again: that time reached the wall. Lord help you! he fought like a tiger—giv' some terrible blow. Fightin' for life, you see; for he can't live long, shut up in the stone crib down yonder. Got a death-cough now. 'T took two of us to bring him down that day; so I just

put the irons on his feet. There he sits, in there. Goin' tomorrow, with a batch more of 'em. That woman, hunchback, tried with him—you remember?—she's only got three years. 'Complice. But *she's* a woman, you know. He's been quiet ever since I put on irons: giv' up, I suppose. Looks white, sick-lookin'. It acts different on 'em, bein' sentenced. Most of 'em gets reckless, devilish-like. Some prays awful, and sings them vile songs of the mills, all in a breath. That woman, now, she's desper't'. Been beggin' to see Hugh, as she calls him, for three days. I'm a-goin' to let her in. She don't go with him. Here she is in this next cell. I'm a-goin' now to let her in."

He let her in. Wolfe did not see her. She crept into a corner of the cell, and stood watching him. He was scratching the iron bars of the window with a piece of tin which he had picked up, with an idle, uncertain, vacant stare, just as a child or idiot would do.

"Tryin' to get out, old boy?" laughed Haley. "Them irons will need a crowbar beside your tin, before you can open 'em."

Wolfe laughed, too, in a senseless way.

"I think I'll get out," he said.

"I believe his brain's touched," said Haley, when he came out.

The puddler scraped away with the tin for half an hour. Still Deborah did not speak. At last she ventured nearer, and touched his arm.

"Blood?" she said, looking at some spots on his coat with a shudder.

He looked up at her. "Why, Deb!" he said, smiling—such a bright, boyish smile, that it went to poor Deborah's heart directly, and she sobbed and cried out loud.

"Oh, Hugh, lad! Hugh! dunnot look at me, when it wur my fault! To think I brought hur to it! And I loved hur so! Oh, lad, I dud!"

The confession, even in this wretch, came with the woman's blush through the sharp cry.

He did not seem to hear her, scraping away diligently at the bars with the bit of tin.

Was he going mad? She peered closely into his face. Something she saw there made her draw suddenly back, something which Haley had not seen, that lay beneath the pinched, vacant look it had caught since the trial, or the curious gray shadow that rested on it. That gray

---

[1]   *dodge*   Scheme; trick.

shadow—yes, she knew what that meant. She had often seen it creeping over women's faces for months, who died at last of slow hunger or consumption. That meant death, distant, lingering: but this——Whatever it was the woman saw, or thought she saw, used as she was to crime and misery, seemed to make her sick with a new horror. Forgetting her fear of him, she caught his shoulders, and looked keenly, steadily, into his eyes.

"Hugh!" she cried, in a desperate whisper, "oh, boy, not that! for God's sake, not *that*!"

The vacant laugh went off his face, and he answered her in a muttered word or two that drove her away. Yet the words were kindly enough. Sitting there on his pallet, she cried silently a hopeless sort of tears, but did not speak again. The man looked up furtively at her now and then. Whatever his own trouble was, her distress vexed him with a momentary sting.

It was market-day. The narrow window of the jail looked down directly on the carts and wagons drawn up in a long line, where they had unloaded. He could see, too, and hear distinctly the clink of money as it changed hands, the busy crowd of whites and blacks shoving, pushing one another, and the chaffering[1] and swearing at the stalls. Somehow, the sound, more than anything else had done, wakened him up—made the whole real to him. He was done with the world and the business of it. He let the tin fall, and looked out, pressing his face close to the rusty bars. How they crowded and pushed! And he—he should never walk that pavement again! There came Neff Sanders, one of the feeders at the mill, with a basket on his arm. Sure enough, Neff was married the other week. He whistled, hoping he would look up; but he did not. He wondered if Neff remembered he was there—if any of the boys thought of him up there, and thought that he never was to go down that old cinder-road again. Never again! He had not quite understood it before; but now he did. Not for days or years, but never!—that was it.

How clear the light fell on that stall in front of the market! and how like a picture it was, the dark-green heaps of corn, and the crimson beets, and golden melons! There was another with game: how the light flickered on that pheasant's breast, with the purplish blood dripping over the brown feathers! He could see the red shining of the drops, it was so near. In one minute he could be down there. It was just a step. So easy, as it seemed, so natural to go! Yet it could never be—not in all the thousands of years to come—that he should put his foot on that street again! He thought of himself with a sorrowful pity, as of some one else. There was a dog down in the market, walking after his master with such a stately, grave look!—only a dog, yet he could go backwards and forwards just as he pleased: he had good luck! Why, the very vilest cur, yelping there in the gutter, had not lived his life, had been free to act out whatever thought God had put into his brain; while he—No, he would not think of that! He tried to put the thought away, and to listen to a dispute between a countryman and a woman about some meat; but it would come back. He, what had he done to bear this?

Then came the sudden picture of what might have been, and now. He knew what it was to be in the penitentiary, how it went with men there. He knew how in these long years he should slowly die, but not until soul and body had become corrupt and rotten—how, when he came out, if he lived to come, even the lowest of the mill-hands would jeer him—how his hands would be weak, and his brain senseless and stupid. He believed he was almost that now. He put his hand to his head, with a puzzled, weary look. It ached, his head, with thinking. He tried to quiet himself. It was only right, perhaps; he had done wrong. But was there right or wrong for such as he? What was right? And who had ever taught him? He thrust the whole matter away. A dark, cold quiet crept through his brain. It was all wrong; but let it be! It was nothing to him more than the others. Let it be!

The door grated, as Haley opened it.

"Come, my woman! Must lock up for t' night. Come, stir yerself!"

She went up and took Hugh's hand.

"Good-night, Deb," he said, carelessly.

She had not hoped he would say more; but the tired pain on her mouth just then was bitterer than death. She took his passive hand and kissed it.

"Hur'll never see Deb again!" she ventured, her lips growing colder and more bloodless.

What did she say that for? Did he not know it? Yet he would not be impatient with poor old Deb. She had trouble of her own, as well as he.

---

[1] *chaffering* Bartering, haggling.

"No, never again," he said, trying to be cheerful.

She stood just a moment, looking at him. Do you laugh at her, standing there, with her hunchback, her rags, her bleared, withered face, and the great despised love tugging at her heart?

"Come, you!" called Haley, impatiently.

She did not move.

"Hugh!" she whispered.

It was to be her last word. What was it?

"Hugh, boy, not THAT!"

He did not answer. She wrung her hands, trying to be silent, looking in his face in an agony of entreaty. He smiled again, kindly.

"It is best, Deb. I cannot bear to be hurted any more."

"Hur knows," she said, humbly.

"Tell my father good-bye; and—and kiss little Janey."

She nodded, saying nothing, looked in his face again, and went out of the door. As she went, she staggered.

"Drinkin' today?" broke out Haley, pushing her before him. "Where the Devil did you get it? Here, in with ye!" and he shoved her into her cell, next to Wolfe's, and shut the door.

Along the wall of her cell there was a crack low down by the floor, through which she could see the light from Wolfe's. She had discovered it days before. She hurried in now, and, kneeling down by it, listened, hoping to hear some sound. Nothing but the rasping of the tin on the bars. He was at his old amusement again. Something in the noise jarred on her ear, for she shivered as she heard it. Hugh rasped away at the bars. A dull old bit of tin, not fit to cut korl with.

He looked out of the window again. People were leaving the market now. A tall mulatto girl, following her mistress, her basket on her head, crossed the street just below, and looked up. She was laughing; but, when she caught sight of the haggard face peering out through the bars, suddenly grew grave, and hurried by. A free, firm step, a clear-cut olive face, with a scarlet turban tied on one side, dark, shining eyes, and on the head the basket poised, filled with fruit and flowers, under which the scarlet turban and bright eyes looked out half-shadowed. The picture caught his eye. It was good to see a face like that. He would try tomorrow, and cut one like it. *Tomorrow*! He threw down the tin,

trembling, and covered his face with his hands. When he looked up again, the daylight was gone.

Deborah, crouching nearby on the other side of the wall, heard no noise. He sat on the side of the low pallet, thinking. Whatever was the mystery which the woman had seen on his face, it came out now slowly, in the dark there, and became fixed—a something never seen on his face before. The evening was darkening fast. The market had been over for an hour; the rumbling of the carts over the pavement grew more infrequent: he listened to each, as it passed, because he thought it was to be for the last time. For the same reason, it was, I suppose, that he strained his eyes to catch a glimpse of each passer-by, wondering who they were, what kind of homes they were going to, if they had children—listening eagerly to every chance word in the street, as if—(God be merciful to the man! what strange fancy was this?)—as if he never should hear human voices again.

It was quite dark at last. The street was a lonely one. The last passenger, he thought, was gone. No—there was a quick step: Joe Hill, lighting the lamps. Joe was a good old chap; never passed a fellow without some joke or other. He remembered once seeing the place where he lived with his wife. "Granny Hill" the boys called her. Bedridden she was; but so kind as Joe was to her! kept the room so clean!—and the old woman, when he was there, was laughing at "some of t' lad's foolishness." The step was far down the street; but he could see him place the ladder, run up, and light the gas. A longing seized him to be spoken to once more.

"Joe!" he called, out of the grating. "Good-bye, Joe!"

The old man stopped a moment, listening uncertainly; then hurried on. The prisoner thrust his hand out of the window, and called again, louder; but Joe was too far down the street. It was a little thing; but it hurt him, this disappointment.

"Good-bye, Joe!" he called, sorrowfully enough.

"Be quiet!" said one of the jailers, passing the door, striking on it with his club.

Oh, that was the last, was it?

There was an inexpressible bitterness on his face, as he lay down on the bed, taking the bit of tin, which he had rasped to a tolerable degree of sharpness, in his hand—to play with, it may be. He bared his arms, looking intently at their corded veins and sinews. Deborah, listening in the next cell, heard a slight clicking sound, often repeated. She shut her lips tightly, that she might not scream; the cold drops of sweat broke over her, in her dumb agony.

"Hur knows best," she muttered at last, fiercely clutching the boards where she lay.

If she could have seen Wolfe, there was nothing about him to frighten her. He lay quite still, his arms outstretched, looking at the pearly stream of moonlight coming into the window. I think in that one hour that came then he lived back over all the years that had gone before. I think that all the low, vile life, all his wrongs, all his starved hopes, came then, and stung him with a farewell poison that made him sick unto death. He made neither moan nor cry, only turned his worn face now and then to the pure light, that seemed so far off, as one that said, "How long, O Lord? how long?"

The hour was over at last. The moon, passing over her nightly path, slowly came nearer, and threw the light across his bed on his feet. He watched it steadily, as it crept up, inch by inch, slowly. It seemed to him to carry with it a great silence. He had been so hot and tired there always in the mills! The years had been so fierce and cruel! There was coming now quiet and coolness and sleep. His tense limbs relaxed, and settled in a calm languor. The blood ran fainter and slow from his heart. He did not think now with a savage anger of what might be and was not; he was conscious only of deep stillness creeping over him. At first he saw a sea of faces: the mill-men—women he had known, drunken and bloated—Janeys timid and pitiful—poor old Debs: then they floated together like a mist, and faded away, leaving only the clear, pearly moonlight.

Whether, as the pure light crept up the stretched-out figure, it brought with it calm and peace, who shall say? His dumb soul was alone with God in judgment. A Voice may have spoken for it from far-off Calvary, "Father, forgive them, for they know not what they do!"[1] Who dare say? Fainter and fainter the heart rose and fell, slower and slower the moon floated from behind a cloud, until, when at last its full tide of white splendor swept over the cell, it seemed to wrap and fold into a deeper stillness the dead figure that never should move again. Silence deeper than the Night!

Nothing that moved, save the black, nauseous stream of blood dripping slowly from the pallet to the floor!

There was outcry and crowd enough in the cell the next day. The coroner and his jury, the local editors, Kirby himself; and boys with their hands thrust knowingly into their pockets and heads on one side, jammed into the corners. Coming and going all day. Only one woman. She came late, and outstayed them all. A Quaker,[2] or Friend, as they call themselves. I think this woman was known by that name in heaven. A homely body, coarsely dressed in gray and white. Deborah (for Haley had let her in) took notice of her. She watched them all—sitting on the end of the pallet, holding his head in her arms—with the ferocity of a watch-dog, if any of them touched the body. There was no meekness, no sorrow, in her face; the stuff out of which murderers are made, instead. All the time Haley and the woman were laying straight the limbs and cleaning the cell, Deborah sat still, keenly watching the Quaker's face. Of all the crowd there that day, this woman alone had not spoken to her—only once or twice had put some cordial to her lips. After they all were gone, the woman, in the same still, gentle way, brought a vase of wood-leaves and berries, and placed it by the pallet, then opened the narrow window. The fresh air blew in, and swept the woody fragrance over the dead face. Deborah looked up with a quick wonder.

"Did hur know my boy wud like it? Did hur know Hugh?"

"I know Hugh now."

The white fingers passed in a slow, pitiful way over the dead, worn face. There was a heavy shadow in the quiet eyes.

"Did hur know where they'll bury Hugh?" said Deborah in a shrill tone, catching her arm.

This had been the question hanging on her lips all day.

"In t' town-yard? Under t' mud and ash? T' lad'll smother, woman! He war born on t' lane[3] moor, where

---

[1] *Calvary* Site of Jesus' crucifixion; *Father, forgive … they do* Jesus' words at the crucifixion, referring to his persecutors; see Luke 23.34.

[2] *Quaker* Member of the Religious Society of Friends, a Christian movement that has historically been associated with philanthropy and the pursuit of social justice causes such as abolitionism and prison reform. Quakers were also historically known for wearing simple, modest clothing, and for their use of what had originally been considered "plain speech," retaining the usage of words such as "thee" and "thou" after they had come to be considered antiquated.

[3] *lane* Lone; lonely.

t' air is frick[1] and strong. Take hur out, for God's sake, take hur out where t' air blows!"

The Quaker hesitated, but only for a moment. She put her strong arm around Deborah and led her to the window.

"Thee sees the hills, friend, over the river? Thee sees how the light lies warm there, and the winds of God blow all the day? I live there, where the blue smoke is, by the trees. Look at me." She turned Deborah's face to her own, clear and earnest. "Thee will believe me? I will take Hugh and bury him there tomorrow."

Deborah did not doubt her. As the evening wore on, she leaned against the iron bars, looking at the hills that rose far off through the thick sodden clouds, like a bright, unattainable calm. As she looked, a shadow of their solemn repose fell on her face: its fierce discontent faded into a pitiful, humble quiet. Slow, solemn tears gathered in her eyes: the poor weak eyes turned so hopelessly to the place where Hugh was to rest, the grave heights looking higher and brighter and more solemn than ever before. The Quaker watched her keenly. She came to her at last, and touched her arm.

"When thee comes back," she said, in a low, sorrowful tone, like one who speaks from a strong heart deeply moved with remorse or pity, "thee shall begin thy life again—there on the hills. I came too late; but not for thee—by God's help, it may be."

Not too late. Three years after, the Quaker began her work. I end my story here. At evening-time it was light. There is no need to tire you with the long years of sunshine, and fresh air, and slow, patient Christ-love, needed to make healthy and hopeful this impure body and soul. There is a homely pine house, on one of these hills, whose windows overlook broad, wooded slopes and clover-crimsoned meadows—niched into the very place where the light is warmest, the air freest. It is the Friends' meeting-house.[2] Once a week they sit there, in their grave, earnest way, waiting for the Spirit of Love to speak, opening their simple hearts to receive His words. There is a woman, old, deformed, who takes a humble place among them: waiting like them: in

her gray dress, her worn face, pure and meek, turned now and then to the sky. A woman much loved by these silent, restful people; more silent than they, more humble, more loving. Waiting: with her eyes turned to hills higher and purer than these on which she lives—dim and far off now, but to be reached some day. There may be in her heart some latent hope to meet there the love denied her here—that she shall find him whom she lost, and that then she will not be all-unworthy. Who blames her? Something is lost in the passage of every soul from one eternity to the other—something pure and beautiful, which might have been and was not: a hope, a talent, a love, over which the soul mourns, like Esau deprived of his birthright.[3] What blame to the meek Quaker, if she took her lost hope to make the hills of heaven more fair?

Nothing remains to tell that the poor Welsh puddler once lived, but this figure of the mill-woman cut in korl. I have it here in a corner of my library. I keep it hid behind a curtain—it is such a rough, ungainly thing. Yet there are about it touches, grand sweeps of outline, that show a master's hand. Sometimes—tonight, for instance, the curtain is accidentally drawn back, and I see a bare arm stretched out imploringly in the darkness, and an eager, wolfish face watching mine: a wan, woeful face, through which the spirit of the dead korl-cutter looks out, with its thwarted life, its mighty hunger, its unfinished work. Its pale, vague lips seem to tremble with a terrible question. "Is this the End?" they say, "nothing beyond? no more?" Why, you tell me you have seen that look in the eyes of dumb brutes[4]—horses dying under the lash. I know.

The deep of the night is passing while I write. The gas-light wakens from the shadows here and there the objects which lie scattered through the room: only faintly, though; for they belong to the open sunlight. As I glance at them, they each recall some task or pleasure of the coming day. A half-moulded child's head; Aphrodite;[5] a bough of forest-leaves; music; work; homely fragments, in which lie the secrets of all eternal truth and beauty. Prophetic all! Only this dumb,

---

1   *frick* Fresh.

2   *Friends' meeting-house* Instead of holding conventional church services, some Quakers practice a form of unprogrammed worship in which they gather in meeting places and remain in contemplative silence, speaking to the group if compelled by divine inspiration.

3   *like Esau … his birthright* See Genesis 25.33–34, where the starving Esau, a firstborn son, sells his inheritance to his younger brother Jacob in exchange for a bowl of food.

4   *dumb brutes* Speechless animals.

5   *Aphrodite* Greek goddess of love.

woeful face seems to belong to and end with the night. I turn to look at it. Has the power of its desperate need commanded the darkness away? While the room is yet steeped in heavy shadow, a cool, gray light suddenly touches its head like a blessing hand, and its groping arm points through the broken cloud to the far East, where, in the flickering, nebulous crimson, God has set the promise of the Dawn.

—1861

This 1870s photo of the First Point Bridge gives some sense of the degree to which smoke from the mills affected air quality in Pittsburgh, a city approximately eighty miles up the Ohio River from Wheeling, Virginia (where Davis's story is likely set) and likewise known in the mid-nineteenth century for its booming iron industry. (See the website component of this anthology for more material on the mills of Pittsburgh in the nineteenth century.)

LOUISA MAY ALCOTT

1832 – 1888

The author of one of the most perennially popular children's novels of all time, Louisa May Alcott worked in an extraordinarily diverse number of genres (though she famously dismissed her juvenile writing as "moral pap for the young"). Throughout her career, Alcott's literary output included sentimental romances, amusing sketches, and sensational thrillers, much of it peopled by unconventional female characters and distinguished by astute, regionally tinted, and often humorous observations on human behavior. It was one book in particular, however, that brought Alcott fortune and renown—the gentle but subtly subversive coming-of-age story *Little Women* (1868–69). Hailed by many reviewers at the time as a sign of changing tides in the realm of literature for young people, *Little Women* has remained, in every generation since, Alcott's most widely read and most celebrated work.

Louisa was born in 1832 to Abigail and Amos Bronson Alcott. Alcott's was an unusual childhood: her father a prominent Transcendentalist philosopher and teacher, she and her sisters grew up in a family that counted some of the most well-known New England figures of the age among their friends and acquaintances, including Nathaniel Hawthorne, Margaret Fuller, Elizabeth Peabody, Ralph Waldo Emerson, and Henry David Thoreau. Alcott's boisterous and "boyish" personality likely found a better home among this extraordinary group than it would have in more conventional New England society, but she nevertheless often struggled against the behavioral standards of her loving but perfectionist father. In 1843, Bronson's impractical idealism culminated in the establishment of Fruitlands, a self-sufficient farming community founded in collaboration with two English philosophers even more eccentric than himself and governed by the philosophical principles of Transcendentalism. Fruitlands suffered from mismanagement and community conflicts from the beginning; after an unsuccessful first harvest the project was declared a failure, and the Alcotts returned to Concord, where they boarded with acquaintances. Thirty years later, Alcott would pen the semi-fictional story "Transcendental Wild Oats" (1873), a lively and satirical account of the Fruitlands scheme.

Following the Fruitlands disaster the Alcotts lived in transient poverty for years, with Abigail Alcott becoming the primary wage earner as a social worker. As an adolescent, Louisa also worked to support the family; her employments ranged from sewing and teaching to washing laundry and working as a domestic servant. In her spare time, Alcott also wrote extensively. Alcott's publishing ambitions were probably inspired at least as much by financial need as by literary aspirations. Her first success came at the age of twenty, when the story "The Rival Painters" (1852) was published in a local paper. This was followed by *Flower Fables* (1854), a volume of fairy stories Alcott had written as a teenager for Emerson's daughter Ellen. *Flower Fables* was a modest success; critical reviews, though few, were positive, and the book's printing of sixteen hundred sold well (though Alcott herself earned relatively little for her contribution, thanks to poorly established copyright practices). In 1860 Alcott had a story published in the prestigious journal *The Atlantic Monthly*; over the next year-and-a-half she worked on two novels, *Moods* (published 1865) and *Work* (published 1873), the latter inspired by her own varied work experiences.

In 1862 Alcott traveled to D.C. to contribute to the war effort as a nurse, having previously lamented in her journals that she could not, as a woman, contribute to the fighting. Her nursing career would prove brief—within a matter of weeks in the unsanitary conditions of the Union Hotel Hospital (which Alcott nicknamed "Hurly-burly House") she had contracted a serious bout of typhoid fever; although she recovered, the mercury-laden medicine with which she had been treated left her weakened for life. Alcott's hospital experience was not wholly unproductive, however: in 1863 her Civil War story "The Brothers" (later republished as "My Contraband") was published in *The Atlantic*, and the following year would see the publication of her first longer work to earn serious attention, *Hospital Sketches* (1863), a barely fictionalized version of her own hospital journals.

Following her return to Massachusetts, Alcott published several more stories about the Civil War, and also began publishing thrillers, some under the pseudonym A.M. Barnard. These pieces took up subjects such as unhappy marriages, violence, drug addiction, and the supernatural, and often featured female protagonists who in various ways challenged the era's accepted gender roles. Alcott's influences for these stories ranged from the English Gothic tradition (she deeply admired Charlotte Brontë), to American writers such as Washington Irving and Nathaniel Hawthorne, to the popular fiction proliferated by the cheap tabloid periodicals in which many of her own stories were published.

In 1867, Alcott was approached by the publishing house Roberts Brothers to write something of a very different sort: a "girls' book." Alcott was not initially enthusiastic at this prospect; "Never liked girls," she wrote in her journal, "or knew many, except my sisters." But her mother and sisters encouraged her in the venture, and—acknowledging that "lively, simple books are very much needed for girls, and perhaps I can supply the need"—Alcott soon set herself to the task. The first part of what became *Little Women* was published in late 1868. The novel's central character, the tomboyish and literary Josephine "Jo" March, was a close likeness of a younger Louisa May Alcott, and indeed the novel as a whole was heavily autobiographical (although Bronson was all but erased from the family portrait). "Not a bit sensational," Alcott reflected of her creation, "but simple and true, for we really lived most of it; and if it succeeds that will be the reason of it."

To say the novel did succeed would be an understatement. *Little Women* sold remarkably well, and reviews were almost unanimously positive (excepting some of the most conservatively Christian perspectives, and those which disapproved of the characters' "slangy" dialogue); many critics reflected that not only was *Little Women* a very wholesome and moral novel, but that it was also interesting, genuinely entertaining, and refreshingly realistic in its execution. "Verily there is a new era in this country in the literature for children," a writer for *Putnam's Magazine* declared in December 1868, while a critic for *The Galaxy* remarked that "Good books for children are so rare that we welcome one which is so marked an exception to the general rule as Louisa M. Alcott's 'Little Women.'"

Readers clamored for a second part to the novel—with a particular interest in finding out how the March sisters would marry. Alcott somewhat reluctantly obliged, although she defied expectations by marrying Jo off not to her charming girlhood companion, but to an older German philosophy professor. (Alcott herself remained unmarried all her life; of her sister Anna's marriage in 1860, she famously wrote: "Very sweet and pretty, but I'd rather be a free spinster and paddle my own canoe.") The sequel was published in January 1869; today the two volumes are usually published in North America as a single novel. Both parts of *Little Women* were soon bestsellers in England—where the sequel was retitled *Good Wives*—as well, and were translated into many languages. Within this short period Alcott had become a household name, and nearly a millionaire by modern standards; she was well able to support her family financially.

The story of the March sisters eventually spawned two more sequels—*Little Men* (1871) and *Jo's Boys* (1886)—and Alcott published numerous volumes of stories under the title *Aunt Jo's Scrap-Bag* (1872–82). Alcott's renown as an author led numerous groups and institutions to invite her to do public readings or to lecture on various topics, and she steadily became more and more involved in the women's rights movement, becoming the first woman in Concord to register to vote (following an 1879 reform in Massachusetts election laws that allowed women to vote in certain local elections—notably, for school committee members).

By the late 1880s Alcott had published nearly 300 written works, including over ten novels. By 1886 her chronic health problems had resurfaced dangerously, and in 1888 she died of a stroke, mere days after the death of her father. Her writings continued to be popular in the decades following her death; an 1893 poll in the periodical *The Critic* counted *Little Women* twentieth in a list of "Best American Books," one space below Benjamin Franklin's *Autobiography* (it was one of only four books by women to make it onto that list). Never out of print, *Little Women* remains one of the most widely read English-language novels of all time, and continues to inspire readers and provoke conversation among those interested in children's literature, women's history, and middle-class life in nineteenth-century New England.

NOTE ON THE TEXTS: The text of "My Contraband" (first published as "The Brothers") presented below is based on that included in Alcott's 1869 collection *Hospital Sketches and Camp and Fireside Stories*. The text of "Transcendental Wild Oats" is based on that included in Clara Endicott Sears' 1915 compilation *Bronson Alcott's Fruitlands, with Transcendental Wild Oats*. Spelling and punctuation have been modernized in accordance with the practices of this anthology.

⌘ ⌘ ⌘

My Contraband[1]

Doctor Franck came in as I sat sewing up the rents[2] in an old shirt, that Tom might go tidily to his grave. New shirts were needed for the living, and there was not wife or mother to "dress him handsome when he went to meet the Lord," as one woman said, describing the fine funeral she had pinched herself[3] to give her son.

"Miss Dane, I'm in a quandary," began the Doctor, with that expression of countenance which says as plainly as words, "I want to ask a favor, but I wish you'd save me the trouble."

"Can I help you out of it?"

"Faith! I don't like to propose it, but you certainly can, if you please."

"Then give it a name, I beg."

"You see a Reb[4] has just been brought in crazy with typhoid; a bad case every way; a drunken, rascally little captain somebody took the trouble to capture, but whom nobody wants to take the trouble to cure. The wards are full, the ladies worked to death, and willing to be for our own boys, but rather slow to risk their lives for a Reb. Now, you've had the fever,[5] you like queer patients, your mate will see to your ward for a while, and I will find you a good attendant. The fellow won't last long, I fancy; but he can't die without some sort of care, you know. I've put him in the fourth story of the west wing, away from the rest. It is airy, quiet, and comfortable there. I'm on that ward, and will do my best for you in every way. Now, then, will you go?"

"Of course I will, out of perversity,[6] if not common charity; for some of these people think that because I'm an abolitionist I am also a heathen, and I should rather like to show them that, though I cannot quite love my enemies, I am willing to take care of them."

"Very good; I thought you'd go; and speaking of abolition reminds me that you can have a contraband for servant, if you like. It is that fine mulatto[7] fellow who was found burying his rebel master after the fight, and, being badly cut over the head, our boys brought him along. Will you have him?"

---

[1] This story was first published as "The Brothers" in the November 1863 edition of *The Atlantic*. That title had been chosen by *Atlantic* editor James T. Fields, apparently without input from Alcott; in 1869 the story was republished in *Hospital Sketches and Camp and Fireside Stories* under Alcott's preferred title, "My Contraband"; *Contraband* Fugitive from slavery—especially, in the Civil War context, a fugitive taken in by the Union Army.

[2] *rents* Rips.

[3] *pinched herself* I.e., made penny-pinching efforts; saved money.

[4] *Reb* Rebel; member of the Confederate Army.

[5] *had the fever* I.e., the narrator had survived the typhoid fever in the past, meaning she had developed an immunity.

[6] *perversity* Contrariness.

[7] *mulatto* Term for a person with one white and one black parent; or, more loosely, a person with the appearance of being mixed-race. (The designation is today considered offensive.)

"By all means—for I'll stand to my guns on that point, as on the other; these black boys are far more faithful and handy than some of the white scamps given me to serve, instead of being served by. But is this man well enough?"

"Yes, for that sort of work, and I think you'll like him. He must have been a handsome fellow before he got his face slashed; not much darker than myself; his master's son, I dare say, and the white blood makes him rather high and haughty about some things. He was in a bad way when he came in, but vowed he'd die in the street rather than turn in with the black fellows below; so I put him up in the west wing, to be out of the way, and he's seen to the captain all the morning. When can you go up?"

"As soon as Tom is laid out, Skinner moved, Haywood washed, Marble dressed, Charley rubbed, Downs taken up, Upham laid down, and the whole forty fed."

We both laughed, though the Doctor was on his way to the dead-house and I held a shroud on my lap. But in a hospital one learns that cheerfulness is one's salvation; for, in an atmosphere of suffering and death, heaviness of heart would soon paralyze usefulness of hand, if the blessed gift of smiles had been denied us.

In an hour I took possession of my new charge, finding a dissipated-looking boy of nineteen or twenty raving in the solitary little room, with no one near him but the contraband in the room adjoining. Feeling decidedly more interest in the black man than in the white, yet remembering the Doctor's hint of his being "high and haughty," I glanced furtively at him as I scattered chloride of lime[1] about the room to purify the air, and settled matters to suit myself. I had seen many contrabands, but never one so attractive as this. All colored men are called "boys," even if their heads are white; this boy was five-and-twenty at least, strong-limbed and manly, and had the look of one who never had been cowed by abuse or worn with oppressive labor. He sat on his bed doing nothing; no book, no pipe, no pen or paper anywhere appeared, yet anything less indolent or listless than his attitude and expression I never saw. Erect he sat, with a hand on either knee, and eyes fixed on the bare wall opposite, so rapt in some absorbing

thought as to be unconscious of my presence, though the door stood wide open and my movements were by no means noiseless. His face was half averted, but I instantly approved the Doctor's taste, for the profile which I saw possessed all the attributes of comeliness belonging to his mixed race. He was more quadroon[2] than mulatto, with Saxon[3] features, Spanish complexion darkened by exposure, color in lips and cheek, waving hair, and an eye full of the passionate melancholy which in such men always seems to utter a mute protest against the broken law that doomed them at their birth. What could he be thinking of? The sick boy cursed and raved, I rustled to and fro, steps passed the door, bells rang, and the steady rumble of army-wagons came up from the street, still he never stirred. I had seen colored people in what they call "the black sulks," when, for days, they neither smiled nor spoke, and scarcely ate. But this was something more than that, for the man was not dully brooding over some small grievance; he seemed to see an all-absorbing fact or fancy recorded on the wall, which was a blank to me. I wondered if it were some deep wrong or sorrow, kept alive by memory and impotent regret; if he mourned for the dead master to whom he had been faithful to the end; or if the liberty now his were robbed of half its sweetness by the knowledge that someone near and dear to him still languished in the hell from which he had escaped. My heart warmed to him at that idea; I wanted to know and comfort him; and, following the impulse of the moment, I went in and touched him on the shoulder.

In an instant the man vanished and the slave appeared. Freedom was too new a boon to have wrought its blessed changes yet; and as he started up, with his hand at his temple, and an obsequious "Yes, Missis," any romance that had gathered round him fled away, leaving the saddest of all sad facts in living guise before me. Not only did the manhood seem to die out of him, but the comeliness that first attracted me; for, as he turned, I saw the ghastly wound that had laid open cheek and forehead. Being partly healed, it was no longer bandaged, but held together with strips of that transparent plaster

---

[1] *chloride of lime*   Calcium hypochlorite, a white powder used as a disinfectant.

[2] *quadroon*   Term for a person with one grandparent of African ancestry. (Like "mulatto," the term is today considered outdated and offensive.)

[3] *Saxon*   I.e., English (or, more broadly, white).

which I never see without a shiver, and swift recollections of the scenes with which it is associated in my mind. Part of his black hair had been shorn away, and one eye was nearly closed; pain so distorted, and the cruel sabre-cut so marred that portion of his face, that, when I saw it, I felt as if a fine medal had been suddenly reversed, showing me a far more striking type of human suffering and wrong than Michelangelo's bronze prisoner.[1] By one of those inexplicable processes that often teach us how little we understand ourselves, my purpose was suddenly changed; and, though I went in to offer comfort as a friend, I merely gave an order as a mistress.

"Will you open these windows? This man needs more air."

He obeyed at once, and, as he slowly urged up the unruly sash, the handsome profile was again turned toward me, and again I was possessed by my first impression so strongly that I involuntarily said,

"Thank you."

Perhaps it was fancy, but I thought that in the look of mingled surprise and something like reproach which he gave me, there was also a trace of grateful pleasure. But he said, in that tone of spiritless humility these poor souls learn so soon,

"I isn't a white man, Missis, I'se a contraband."

"Yes, I know it; but a contraband is a free man, and I heartily congratulate you."

He liked that; his face shone, he squared his shoulders, lifted his head, and looked me full in the eye with a brisk—

"Thank ye, Missis; anything more to do fer yer?"

"Doctor Franck thought you would help me with this man, as there are many patients and few nurses or attendants. Have you had the fever?"

"No, Missis."

"They should have thought of that when they put him here; wounds and fevers should not be together. I'll try to get you moved."

He laughed a sudden laugh: if he had been a white man, I should have called it scornful; as he was a few shades darker than myself, I suppose it must be considered an insolent, or at least an unmannerly one.

"It don't matter, Missis. I'd rather be up here with the fever than down with those niggers; and there isn't no other place fer me."

Poor fellow! that was true. No ward in all the hospital would take him in to lie side by side with the most miserable white wreck there. Like the bat in Aesop's fable,[2] he belonged to neither race; and the pride of one and the helplessness of the other, kept him hovering alone in the twilight a great sin has brought to overshadow the whole land.

"You shall stay, then; for I would far rather have you than my lazy Jack. But are you well and strong enough?"

"I guess I'll do, Missis."

He spoke with a passive sort of acquiescence—as if it did not much matter if he were not able, and no one would particularly rejoice if he were.

"Yes, I think you will. By what name shall I call you?"

"Bob, Missis."

Every woman has her pet whim; one of mine was to teach the men self-respect by treating them respectfully. Tom, Dick and Harry would pass, when lads rejoiced in those familiar abbreviations; but to address men often old enough to be my father in that style did not suit my old-fashioned ideas of propriety. This "Bob" would never do; I should have found it as easy to call the chaplain "Gus" as my tragical-looking contraband by a title so strongly associated with the tail of a kite.[3]

"What is your other name?" I asked. "I like to call my attendants by their last names rather than by their first."

"I'se got no other, Missis; we have our master's names, or do without. Mine's dead, and I won't have anything of his 'bout me."

---

1   *Michelangelo's bronze prisoner* The reference may be to a series of four unfinished sculptures (in stone rather than bronze) by Florentine Renaissance artist Michelangelo (1475–1564), known as the "Prisoners" or "Slaves," depicting four suffering male figures who appear to be trapped in the stone from which they are carved. Michelangelo is today known to have occasionally worked in bronze, though only two of his bronzes have survived, both of which were only attributed to him in 2018.

2   *the bat in Aesop's fable* Aesop's fable of "The Bat, The Birds, and The Beasts" tells of a war that arose between the birds and the beasts. The bat refused to join either side, declaring himself to be neither bird nor beast; in turn, when the war was over, neither side would accept his friendship.

3   *the tail of a kite* The weights or ribbons at the end of a kite's tail are sometimes referred to as the "bob."

"Well, I'll call you Robert, then, and you may fill this pitcher for me, if you will be so kind."

He went; but, through all the tame obedience years of servitude had taught him, I could see that the proud spirit his father gave him was not yet subdued, for the look and gesture with which he repudiated his master's name were a more effective declaration of independence than any Fourth-of-July orator[1] could have prepared.

We spent a curious week together. Robert seldom left his room, except upon my errands; and I was a prisoner all day, often all night, by the bedside of the rebel. The fever burned itself rapidly away, for there seemed little vitality to feed it in the feeble frame of this old young man, whose life had been none of the most righteous, judging from the revelations made by his unconscious lips; since more than once Robert authoritatively silenced him, when my gentler hushings were of no avail, and blasphemous wanderings or ribald camp-songs made my cheeks burn and Robert's face assume an aspect of disgust. The captain was a gentleman in the world's eye, but the contraband was the gentleman in mine; I was a fanatic, and that accounts for such depravity of taste, I hope. I never asked Robert of himself, feeling that somewhere there was a spot still too sore to bear the lightest touch; but, from his language, manner, and intelligence, I inferred that his color had procured for him the few advantages within the reach of a quick-witted, kindly-treated slave. Silent, grave, and thoughtful, but most serviceable, was my contraband; glad of the books I brought him, faithful in the performance of the duties I assigned to him, grateful for the friendliness I could not but feel and show toward him. Often I longed to ask what purpose was so visibly altering his aspect with such daily deepening gloom. But I never dared, and no one else had either time or desire to pry into the past of this specimen of one branch of the chivalrous "F.F.V.s."[2]

---

1   *Fourth-of-July orator*   Reference to the popular Independence Day tradition of public oratory. It is possible that Alcott was aware of the influential Fourth of July oration delivered in 1852 by the renowned abolitionist Frederick Douglass, who had escaped slavery in 1838. That oration—included in this anthology under its popular title "What to the Slave Is the Fourth of July?"—addressed the hypocrisy of celebrating Independence Day in a slaveholding nation.

2   *F.F.Vs*   First Families of Virginia; colloquial term for Virginia's wealthy, plantation-owning families.

On the seventh night, Dr. Franck suggested that it would be well for someone, besides the general watchman of the ward, to be with the captain, as it might be his last. Although the greater part of the two preceding nights had been spent there, of course I offered to remain—for there is a strange fascination in these scenes, which renders one careless of fatigue and unconscious of fear until the crisis is past.

"Give him water as long as he can drink, and if he drops into a natural sleep, it may save him. I'll look in at midnight, when some change will probably take place. Nothing but sleep or a miracle will keep him now. Goodnight."

Away went the Doctor; and, devouring a whole mouthful of gapes, I lowered the lamp, wet the captain's head, and sat down on a hard stool to begin my watch. The captain lay with his hot, haggard face turned toward me, filling the air with his poisonous breath, and feebly muttering, with lips and tongue so parched that the sanest speech would have been difficult to understand. Robert was stretched on his bed in the inner room, the door of which stood ajar, that a fresh draught from his open window might carry the fever-fumes away through mine. I could just see a long, dark figure, with the lighter outline of a face, and, having little else to do just then, I fell to thinking of this curious contraband, who evidently prized his freedom highly, yet seemed in no haste to enjoy it. Doctor Franck had offered to send him on to safer quarters, but he had said, "No, thank yer, sir, not yet," and then had gone away to fall into one of those black moods of his, which began to disturb me, because I had no power to lighten them. As I sat listening to the clocks from the steeples all about us, I amused myself with planning Robert's future, as I often did my own, and had dealt out to him a generous hand of trumps wherewith to play this game of life which hitherto had gone so cruelly against him, when a harsh choked voice called—

"Lucy!"

It was the captain, and some new terror seemed to have gifted him with momentary strength.

"Yes, here's Lucy," I answered, hoping that by the following fancy I might quiet him—for his face was damp with the clammy moisture, and his frame shaken with the nervous tremor that so often precedes death.

His dull eye fixed upon me, dilating with a bewildered look of incredulity and wrath, till he broke out fiercely—

"That's a lie! She's dead—and so's Bob, damn him!"

Finding speech a failure, I began to sing the quiet tune that had often soothed delirium like this; but hardly had the line—

See gentle patience smile on pain,[1]

passed my lips, when he clutched me by the wrist, whispering like one in mortal fear—

"Hush! She used to sing that way to Bob, but she never would to me. I swore I'd whip the Devil out of her, and I did; but you know before she cut her throat she said she'd haunt me, and there she is!"

He pointed behind me with an aspect of such pale dismay, that I involuntarily glanced over my shoulder and started as if I had seen a veritable ghost; for, peering from the gloom of that inner room, I saw a shadowy face, with dark hair all about it, and a glimpse of scarlet at the throat. An instant showed me that it was only Robert leaning from his bed's foot, wrapped in a gray army-blanket, with his red shirt just visible above it, and his long hair disordered by sleep. But what a strange expression was on his face! The unmarred side was toward me, fixed and motionless as when I first observed it—less absorbed now, but more intent. His eye glittered, his lips were apart like one who listened with every sense, and his whole aspect reminded me of a hound to which some wind had brought the scent of unsuspected prey.

"Do you know him, Robert? Does he mean you?"

"Laws, no, Missis; they all own half-a-dozen Bobs: but hearin' my name woke me; that's all."

He spoke quite naturally, and lay down again, while I returned to my charge, thinking that this paroxysm was probably his last. But by another hour I perceived a hopeful change; for the tremor had subsided, the cold dew was gone, his breathing was more regular, and Sleep, the healer, had descended to save or take him gently away. Doctor Franck looked in at midnight, bade me keep all cool and quiet, and not fail to administer a certain draught as soon as the captain woke. Very much relieved, I laid my head on my arms,

uncomfortably folded on the little table, and fancied I was about to perform one of the feats which practice renders possible, "sleeping with one eye open," as we say: a half-and-half doze, for all senses sleep but that of hearing; the faintest murmur, sigh, or motion will break it, and give one back one's wits much brightened by the brief permission to "stand at ease." On this night, the experiment was a failure, for previous vigils, confinement, and much care had rendered naps a dangerous indulgence. Having roused half-a-dozen times in an hour to find all quiet, I dropped my heavy head on my arms, and, drowsily resolving to look up again in fifteen minutes, fell fast asleep.

The striking of a deep-voiced clock awoke me with a start. "That is one," thought I; but, to my dismay, two more strokes followed, and in remorseful haste I sprang up to see what harm my long oblivion had done. A strong hand put me back into my seat, and held me there. It was Robert. The instant my eye met his, my heart began to beat, and all along my nerves tingled that electric flash which foretells a danger that we cannot see. He was very pale, his mouth grim, and both eyes full of sombre fire; for even the wounded one was open now, all the more sinister for the deep scar above and below. But his touch was steady, his voice quiet, as he said,

"Sit still, Missis; I won't hurt yer, nor scare yer, ef I can help it, but yer waked too soon."

"Let me go, Robert—the captain is stirring—I must give him something."

"No, Missis, yer can't stir an inch. Look here!"

Holding me with one hand, with the other he took up the glass in which I had left the draught, and showed me it was empty.

"Has he taken it?" I asked, more and more bewildered.

"I flung it out o'winder, Missis; he'll have to do without."

"But why, Robert? Why did you do it?"

"'Kase I hate him!"

Impossible to doubt the truth of that; his whole face showed it, as he spoke through his set teeth, and launched a fiery glance at the unconscious captain. I could only hold my breath and stare blankly at him, wondering what mad act was coming next. I suppose I shook and turned white, as women have a foolish habit

---

[1]   *See gentle … on pain*   Line of a Christian hymn.

of doing when sudden danger daunts them; for Robert released my arm, sat down upon the bedside just in front of me, and said, with the ominous quietude that made me cold to see and hear,

"Don't yer be frightened, Missis; don't try to run away, fer the door's locked and the key in my pocket; don't yer cry out, fer yer'd have to scream a long while, with my hand on yer mouth, 'efore yer was heard. Be still, an' I'll tell yer what I'm gwine to do."

"Lord help us! He has taken the fever in some sudden, violent way, and is out of his head. I must humor him till someone comes"; in pursuance of which swift determination, I tried to say, quite composedly,

"I will be still and hear you; but open the window. Why did you shut it?"

"I'm sorry I can't do it, Missis; but yer'd jump out, or call, if I did, an' I'm not ready yet. I shut it to make yer sleep, an' heat would do it quicker'n anything else I could do."

The captain moved, and feebly muttered "Water!" Instinctively I rose to give it to him, but the heavy hand came down upon my shoulder, and in the same decided tone Robert said—

"The water went with the physic;[1] let him call."

"Do let me go to him! He'll die without care!"

"I mean he shall; don't yer meddle, if yer please, Missis."

In spite of his quiet tone and respectful manner, I saw murder in his eyes, and turned faint with fear; yet the fear excited me, and, hardly knowing what I did, I seized the hands that had seized me, crying,

"No, no; you shall not kill him! It is base to hurt a helpless man. Why do you hate him? He is not your master?"

"He's my brother."

I felt that answer from head to foot, and seemed to fathom what was coming, with a prescience vague, but unmistakable. One appeal was left to me, and I made it.

"Robert, tell me what it means? Do not commit a crime and make me accessory to it. There is a better way of righting wrong than by violence—let me help you find it."

My voice trembled as I spoke, and I heard the frightened flutter of my heart; so did he, and if any little act

of mine had ever won affection or respect from him, the memory of it served me then. He looked down, and seemed to put some question to himself; whatever it was, the answer was in my favor, for when his eyes rose again, they were gloomy, but not desperate.

"I *will* tell yer, Missis; but mind, this makes no difference; the boy is mine. I'll give the Lord a chance to take him fust: if He don't, I shall."

"Oh, no! Remember, he is your brother."

An unwise speech; I felt it as it passed my lips, for a black frown gathered on Robert's face, and his strong hands closed with an ugly sort of grip. But he did not touch the poor soul gasping there behind him, and seemed content to let the slow suffocation of that stifling room end his frail life.

"I'm not like to forget dat, Missis, when I've been thinkin' of it all this week. I knew him when they fetched him in, an' would 'a' done it long 'fore this, but I wanted to ask where Lucy was; he knows—he told tonight—an' now he's done for."

"Who is Lucy?" I asked hurriedly, intent on keeping his mind busy with any thought but murder.

With one of the swift transitions of a mixed temperament like this, at my question Robert's deep eyes filled, the clenched hands were spread before his face, and all I heard were the broken words—

"My wife—he took her—"

In that instant every thought of fear was swallowed up in burning indignation for the wrong, and a perfect passion of pity for the desperate man so tempted to avenge an injury for which there seemed no redress but this. He was no longer slave or contraband, no drop of black blood marred him in my sight, but an infinite compassion yearned to save, to help, to comfort him. Words seemed so powerless I offered none, only put my hand on his poor head, wounded, homeless, bowed down with grief for which I had no cure, and softly smoothed the long, neglected hair, pitifully wondering the while where was the wife who must have loved this tender-hearted man so well.

The captain moaned again, and faintly whispered, "Air!" but I never stirred. God forgive me! Just then I hated him as only a woman thinking of a sister woman's wrong could hate. Robert looked up; his eyes were dry again, his mouth grim. I saw that, said, "Tell me

---

[1]   *physic* Medicine.

more," and he did; for sympathy is a gift the poorest may give, the proudest stoop to receive.

"Yer see, Missis, his father—I might say ours, ef I warn't ashamed of both of 'em—his father died two years ago, an' left us all to Marster Ned—that's him here, eighteen then. He always hated me, I looked so like old Marster: he don't—only the light skin an' hair. Old Marster was kind to all of us, me 'specially, an' bought Lucy off the next plantation down there in South Car'lina, when he found I liked her. I married her, all I could; it warn't much, but we was true to one another till Marster Ned come home a year after an' made hell fer both of us. He sent my old mother to be used up in his rice-swamp in Georgy; he found me with my pretty Lucy, an' though young Miss cried, an' I prayed to him on my knees, an' Lucy run away, he wouldn't have no mercy; he brought her back, an'—took her."

"Oh, what did you do?" I cried, hot with helpless pain and passion.

How the man's outraged heart sent the blood flaming up into his face and deepened the tones of his impetuous voice, as he stretched his arm across the bed, saying, with a terribly expressive gesture,

"I half murdered him, an' tonight I'll finish."

"Yes, yes—but go on now; what came next?"

He gave me a look that showed no white man could have felt a deeper degradation in remembering and confessing these last acts of brotherly oppression.

"They whipped me till I couldn't stand, an' then they sold me further South. Yer thought I was a white man once—look here!"

With a sudden wrench he tore the shirt from neck to waist, and on his strong, brown shoulders showed me furrows deeply ploughed, wounds which, though healed, were ghastlier to me than any in that house. I could not speak to him, and, with the pathetic dignity a great grief lends the humblest sufferer, he ended his brief tragedy by simply saying,

"That's all, Missis. I'se never seen her since, an' now I never shall in this world—maybe not in t'other."

"But, Robert, why think her dead? The captain was wandering when he said those sad things; perhaps he will retract them when he is sane. Don't despair; don't give up yet."

"No, Missis, I'spect he's right; she was too proud to bear that long. It's like her to kill herself. I told her to, if there was no other way; an' she always minded me, Lucy did. My poor girl! Oh, it warn't right! No, by God, it warn't!"

As the memory of this bitter wrong, this double bereavement, burned in his sore heart, the devil that lurks in every strong man's blood leaped up; he put his hand upon his brother's throat, and, watching the white face before him, muttered low between his teeth,

"I'm lettin' him go too easy; there's no pain in this; we a'n't even yet. I wish he knew me. Marster Ned! it's Bob; where's Lucy?"

From the captain's lips there came a long faint sigh, and nothing but a flutter of the eyelids showed that he still lived. A strange stillness filled the room as the elder brother held the younger's life suspended in his hand, while wavering between a dim hope and a deadly hate. In the whirl of thoughts that went on in my brain, only one was clear enough to act upon. I must prevent murder, if I could—but how? What could I do up there alone, locked in with a dying man and a lunatic? for any mind yielded utterly to any unrighteous impulse is mad while the impulse rules it. Strength I had not, nor much courage, neither time nor wit for stratagem, and chance only could bring me help before it was too late. But one weapon I possessed—a tongue—often a woman's best defence; and sympathy, stronger than fear, gave me power to use it. What I said Heaven only knows, but surely Heaven helped me; words burned on my lips, tears streamed from my eyes, and some good angel prompted me to use the one name that had power to arrest my hearer's hand and touch his heart. For at that moment I heartily believed that Lucy lived, and this earnest faith roused in him a like belief.

He listened with the lowering look of one in whom brute instinct was sovereign for the time—a look that makes the noblest countenance base. He was but a man—a poor, untaught, outcast, outraged man. Life had few joys for him; the world offered him no honors, no success, no home, no love. What future would this crime mar? and why should he deny himself that sweet, yet bitter morsel called revenge? How many white men, with all New England's freedom, culture, Christianity, would not have felt as he felt then? Should I have reproached him for a human anguish, a human longing for redress, all now left him from the ruin of his few poor hopes? Who had taught him that self-control, self-sacrifice, are attributes that make men masters of the earth, and lift them nearer heaven? Should I have urged the beauty of forgiveness, the duty of devout submission? He had no religion, for he was no saintly "Uncle Tom,"[1] and Slavery's black shadow seemed to darken all the world to him, and shut out God. Should I have warned him of penalties, of judgments, and the potency of law? What did he know of justice, or the mercy that should temper that stern virtue, when every law, human and divine, had been broken on his hearthstone? Should I have tried to touch him by appeals to filial duty, to brotherly love? How had his appeals been answered? What memories had father and brother stored up in his heart to plead for either now? No—all these influences, these associations, would have proved worse than useless, had I been calm enough to try them. I was not; but instinct, subtler than reason, showed me the one safe clue by which to lead this troubled soul from the labyrinth in which it groped and nearly fell. When I paused, breathless, Robert turned to me, asking, as if human assurances could strengthen his faith in Divine Omnipotence—

"Do you believe, if I let Marster Ned live, the Lord will give me back my Lucy?"

"As surely as there is a Lord, you will find her here or in the beautiful hereafter, where there is no black or white, no master and no slave."

He took his hand from his brother's throat, lifted his eyes from my face to the wintry sky beyond, as if searching for that blessed country, happier even than the happy North. Alas, it was the darkest hour before the dawn! there was no star above, no light below but the pale glimmer of the lamp that showed the brother who had made him desolate. Like a blind man who believes there is a sun, yet cannot see it, he shook his head, let his arms drop nervelessly upon his knees, and sat there dumbly asking that question which many a soul whose faith is firmer fixed than his had asked in hours less dark than this—"Where is God?" I saw the tide had turned, and strenuously tried to keep this

rudderless life-boat from slipping back into the whirlpool wherein it had been so nearly lost.

"I have listened to you, Robert; now hear me, and heed what I say, because my heart is full of pity for you, full of hope for your future, and a desire to help you now. I want you to go away from here, from the temptation of this place, and the sad thoughts that haunt it. You have conquered yourself once, and I honor you for it, because, the harder the battle, the more glorious the victory; but it is safer to put a greater distance between you and this man. I will write you letters, give you money, and send you to good old Massachusetts to begin your new life a freeman—yes, and a happy man; for when the captain is himself again, I will learn where Lucy is, and move heaven and earth to find and give her back to you. Will you do this, Robert?"

Slowly, very slowly, the answer came; for the purpose of a week, perhaps a year, was hard to relinquish in an hour.

"Yes, Missis, I will."

"Good! Now you are the man I thought you, and I'll work for you with all my heart. You need sleep, my poor fellow; go, and try to forget. The captain is still alive, and as yet you are spared that sin. No, don't look there; I'll care for him. Come, Robert, for Lucy's sake."

Thank Heaven for the immortality of love! for when all other means of salvation failed, a spark of this vital fire softened the man's iron will, until a woman's hand could bend it. He let me take from him the key, let me draw him gently away, and lead him to the solitude which now was the most healing balm I could bestow. Once in his little room, he fell down on his bed and lay there, as if spent with the sharpest conflict of his life. I slipped the bolt across his door, and unlocked my own, flung up the window, steadied myself with a breath of air, then rushed to Doctor Franck. He came; and till dawn we worked together, saving one brother's life, and taking earnest thought how best to secure the other's liberty. When the sun came up as blithely as if it shone only upon happy homes, the Doctor went to Robert. For an hour I heard the murmur of their voices; once I caught the sound of heavy sobs, and for a time reverent hush, as if in the silence that good man were ministering to soul as well as body. When he departed, he took Robert with him, pausing to tell

---

[1]   *saintly "Uncle Tom"*   Enslaved title character of white author Harriet Beecher Stowe's abolitionist novel *Uncle Tom's Cabin* (1852), depicted as pious, kind hearted, and long suffering. (Excerpts from that novel are included elsewhere in this anthology.)

me he should get him off as soon as possible, but not before we met again.

Nothing more was seen of them all day; another surgeon came to see the captain, and another attendant came to fill the empty place. I tried to rest, but could not, with the thought of poor Lucy tugging at my heart, and was soon back at my post again, anxiously hoping that my contraband had not been too hastily spirited away. Just as night fell there came a tap, and, opening, I saw Robert literally "clothed, and in his right mind."[1] The Doctor had replaced the ragged suit with tidy garments, and no trace of that tempestuous night remained but deeper lines upon the forehead, and the docile look of a repentant child. He did not cross the threshold, did not offer me his hand—only took off his cap, saying, with a traitorous falter in his voice—

"God bless yer, Missis! I'm gwine."[2]

I put out both my hands, and held his fast.

"Goodbye, Robert! Keep up good heart, and when I come home to Massachusetts, we'll meet in a happier place than this. Are you quite ready, quite comfortable for your journey?"

"Yes, Missis, yes; the Doctor's fixed everything; I'se gwine with a friend of his; my papers are all right, an' I'm as happy as I can be till I find"—

He stopped there; then went on, with a glance into the room—

"I'm glad I didn't do it, an' I thank yer, Missis, fer hinderin' me—thank yer hearty; but I'm afraid I hate him jest the same."

Of course he did; and so did I; for these faulty hearts of ours cannot turn perfect in a night, but need frost and fire, wind and rain, to ripen and make them ready for the great harvest-home. Wishing to divert his mind, I put my poor mite[3] into his hand, and, remembering the magic of a certain little book, I gave him mine, on whose dark cover whitely shone the Virgin Mother and the Child, the grand history of whose life the book contained. The money went into Robert's pocket with

a grateful murmur, the book into his bosom, with a long look and a tremulous—

"I never saw *my* baby, Missis."

I broke down then; and though my eyes were too dim to see, I felt the touch of lips upon my hands, heard the sound of departing feet, and knew my contraband was gone.

When one feels an intense dislike, the less one says about the subject of it the better; therefore I shall merely record that the captain lived; in time was exchanged; and that, whoever the other party was, I am convinced the Government got the best of the bargain. But long before this occurred, I had fulfilled my promise to Robert; for as soon as my patient recovered strength of memory enough to make his answer trustworthy, I asked, without any circumlocution,

"Captain Fairfax, where is Lucy?"

And too feeble to be angry, surprised, or insincere, he straightway answered,

"Dead, Miss Dane."

"And she killed herself when you sold Bob?"

"How the devil did you know that?" he muttered, with an expression half-remorseful, half-amazed; but I was satisfied, and said no more.

Of course this went to Robert, waiting far away there in a lonely home—waiting, working, hoping for his Lucy. It almost broke my heart to do it; but delay was weak, deceit was wicked; so I sent the heavy tidings, and very soon the answer came—only three lines; but I felt that the sustaining power of the man's life was gone.

"I tort I'd never see her anymore; I'm glad to know she's out of trouble. I thank yer, Missis; an' if they let us, I'll fight fer yer till I'm killed, which I hope will be 'fore long."

Six months later he had his wish, and kept his word. Everyone knows the story of the attack on Fort Wagner;[4] but we should not tire yet of recalling how our Fifty-Fourth, spent with three sleepless nights, a day's fast, and a march under the July sun, stormed the fort as night fell, facing death in many shapes, following their brave leaders through a fiery rain of shot

---

[1]   *clothed ... right mind*   See Luke 8.35: "Then they went out to see what was done; and came to Jesus, and found the man, out of whom the devils were departed, sitting at the feet of Jesus, clothed, and in his right mind: and they were afraid."

[2]   *gwine*   Going.

[3]   *mite*   Small donation of money.

[4]   *attack on Fort Wagner*   Attack on the Confederate fortress at Fort Wagner, led by the Union Army's 54th Massachusetts Regiment—an entirely African American regiment—on 18 July 1863; the ensuing battle resulted in a sweeping Confederate victory with hundreds of Union casualties.

and shell, fighting valiantly for "God and Governor Andrew,"[1]—how the regiment that went into action seven hundred strong, came out having had nearly half its number captured, killed, or wounded, leaving their young commander[2] to be buried, like a chief of earlier times, with his body-guard around him, faithful to the death. Surely, the insult turns to honor, and the wide grave needs no monument but the heroism that consecrates it in our sight; surely, the hearts that held him nearest, see through their tears a noble victory in the seeming sad defeat; and surely, God's benediction was bestowed, when this loyal soul answered, as Death called the roll, "Lord, here am I, with the brothers Thou has given me!"

The future must show how well that fight was fought; for though Fort Wagner once defied us, public prejudice is down; and through the cannon-smoke of that black night, the manhood of the colored race shines before many eyes that would not see, rings in many ears that would not hear, wins many hearts that would not hitherto believe.

When the news came that we were needed, there was none so glad as I to leave teaching contrabands, the new work I had taken up, and go to nurse "our boys," as my dusky[3] flock so proudly called the wounded of the Fifty-Fourth. Feeling more satisfaction, as I assumed my big apron and turned up my cuffs, than if dressing for the President's levee,[4] I fell to work in Hospital No. 10 at Beaufort. The scene was most familiar, and yet strange; for only dark faces looked up at me from the pallets so thickly laid along the floor, and I missed the sharp accent of my Yankee boys in the slower, softer voices calling cheerily to one another, or answering my questions with a stout, "We'll never give it up, Missis, till the last Reb's dead," or, "If our people's free, we can afford to die."

Passing from bed to bed, intent on making one pair of hands do the work of three, at least, I gradually washed, fed, and bandaged my way down the long line of sable[5] heroes, and coming to the very last, found that he was my contraband. So old, so worn, so deathly weak and wan, I never should have known him but for the deep scar on his cheek. That side lay uppermost, and caught my eye at once; but even then I doubted, such an awful change had come upon him, when, turning to the ticket just above his head, I saw the name, "Robert Dane." That both assured and touched me, for, remembering that he had no name, I knew that he had taken mine. I longed for him to speak to me, to tell how he had fared since I lost sight of him, and let me perform some little service for him in return for many he had done for me; but he seemed asleep; and as I stood reliving that strange night again, a bright lad, who lay next him softly waving an old fan across both beds, looked up and said,

"I guess you know him, Missis?"

"You are right. Do you?"

"As much as any one was able to, Missis."

"Why do you say 'was,' as if the man were dead and gone?"

"I s'pose because I know he'll have to go. He's got a bad jab in the breast, an' is bleedin' inside, the Doctor says. He don't suffer any, only gets weaker 'n' weaker every minute. I've been fannin' him this long while, an' he's talked a little; but he don't know me now, so he's most gone, I guess."

There was so much sorrow and affection in the boy's face, that I remembered something, and asked, with redoubled interest,

"Are you the one that brought him off? I was told about a boy who nearly lost his life in saving that of his mate."

I dare say the young fellow blushed, as any modest lad might have done; I could not see it, but I heard the chuckle of satisfaction that escaped him, as he glanced from his shattered arm and bandaged side to the pale figure opposite.

"Lord, Missis, that's nothin'; we boys always stan' by one another, an' I warn't goin' to leave him to be tormented any more by them cussed Rebs. He's been a slave once, though he don't look half so much like it as me, an' I was born in Boston."

---

1   *Governor Andrew*   Reference to John Albion Andrew (1818–67), Governor of Massachusetts, who helped to organize the formation of the 54th Massachusetts Infantry Regiment.

2   *their young commander*   Robert Gould Shaw (1837–63), white commander of the 54th Massachusetts Regiment, who was killed during the Battle of Fort Wagner.

3   *dusky*   I.e., dark-skinned.

4   *levee*   Formal reception ceremony.

5   *sable*   Dark-skinned.

He did not; for the speaker was as black as the ace of spades—being a sturdy specimen, the knave[1] of clubs would perhaps be a fitter representative—but the dark freeman looked at the white slave with the pitiful, yet puzzled expression I have so often seen on the faces of our wisest men, when this tangled question of Slavery presented itself, asking to be cut or patiently undone.

"Tell me what you know of this man; for, even if he were awake, he is too weak to talk."

"I never saw him till I joined the regiment, an' no one 'peared to have got much out of him. He was a shut-up sort of feller, an' didn't seem to care for anything but gettin' at the Rebs. Some say he was the fust man of us that enlisted; I know he fretted till we were off, an' when we pitched into old Wagner, he fought like the devil."

"Were you with him when he was wounded? How was it?"

"Yes, Missis. There was somethin' queer about it; for he 'peared to know the chap that killed him, an' the chap knew him. I don't dare to ask, but I rather guess one owned the other some time; for, when they clinched, the chap sung out, 'Bob!' an' Dane, 'Marster Ned!'—then they went at it."

I sat down suddenly, for the old anger and compassion struggled in my heart, and I both longed and feared to hear what was to follow.

"You see, when the Colonel—Lord keep an' send him back to us!—it a'n't certain yet, you know, Missis, though it's two days ago we lost him—well, when the Colonel shouted, 'Rush on, boys, rush on!' Dane tore away as if he was goin' to take the fort alone; I was next him, an' kept close as we went through the ditch an' up the wall. Hi! warn't that a rusher!" and the boy flung up his well arm with a whoop, as if the mere memory of that stirring moment came over him in a gust of irrepressible excitement.

"Were you afraid?" I said, asking the question women often put, and receiving the answer they seldom fail to get.

"No, Missis!"—emphasis on the "Missis"—"I never thought of anything but the damn' Rebs, that scalp, slash, an' cut our ears off, when they git us. I was bound to let daylight into one of 'em at least, an' I did. Hope he liked it!"

"It is evident that you did. Now go on about Robert, for I should be at work."

"He was one of the fust up; I was just behind, an' though the whole thing happened in a minute, I remember how it was, for all I was yellin' an' knockin' round like mad. Just where we were, some sort of an officer was wavin' his sword an' cheerin' on his men; Dane saw him by a big flash that come by; he flung away his gun, give a leap, an' went at that feller as if he was Jeff, Beauregard, an' Lee,[2] all in one. I scrabbled after as quick as I could, but was only up in time to see him git the sword straight through him an' drop into the ditch. You needn't ask what I did next, Missis, for I don't quite know myself; all I'm clear about is that I managed somehow to pitch that Reb into the fort as dead as Moses, git hold of Dane, an' bring him off. Poor old feller! We said we went in to live or die; he said he went in to die, an' he's done it."

I had been intently watching the excited speaker; but as he regretfully added those last words I turned again, and Robert's eyes met mine—those melancholy eyes, so full of an intelligence that proved he had heard, remembered, and reflected with that preternatural power which often outlives all other faculties. He knew me, yet gave no greeting; was glad to see a woman's face, yet had no smile wherewith to welcome it; felt that he was dying, yet uttered no farewell. He was too far across the river to return or linger now; departing thought, strength, breath, were spent in one grateful look, one murmur of submission to the last pang he could ever feel. His lips moved, and, bending to them, a whisper chilled my cheek, as it shaped the broken words,

"I'd 'a' done it—but it's better so—I'm satisfied."

Ah! well he might be—for, as he turned his face from the shadow of the life that was, the sunshine of the life to be touched it with a beautiful content, and in the drawing of a breath my contraband found wife and home, eternal liberty and God.

—1869

---

[1] *knave* Jack.

[2] *Jeff, Beauregard, an' Lee* Reference to Jefferson Davis (1808–89), President of the Confederate States; P.G.T. Beauregard (1818–93), Confederate general; and Robert E. Lee (1807–70), Commander of the Confederate Army.

Transcendental Wild Oats

In 1843, Louisa May Alcott's father, Amos Bronson Alcott, brought his wife and four young children to a run-down farm newly christened "Fruitlands," and, along with English philosophers Charles Lane and Henry Wright, embarked upon a project to found a self-sufficient Transcendentalist farming community. The men advocated strict vegetarianism (what would today be called veganism), avoidance of cotton or other products reliant on enslaved labor, the rejection of money, and aimed to live a spiritual life in which they would work hard—but only when the spirit called. Perhaps unsurprisingly, much of the actual work fell to the community's women and children. If Louisa Alcott's childhood journals, which she began to keep while living at Fruitlands, are to be believed, she indeed enjoyed her time at the community, as it afforded her ample time to run freely about the surrounding countryside. But thirty years after the failure of the short-lived project—which left her father in a profound depression for months—Alcott returned to Fruitlands with a matured eye, and the result was published as "Transcendental Wild Oats" in *The Independent* in 1873.

In the edition of the story included in the volume *Bronson Alcott's Fruitlands* (1915), the following cast of characters was included before the text of the story:

TIMON LION . . . . *Charles Lane.*
HIS SON . . . . *William Lane.*
ABEL LAMB . . . . *A. Bronson Alcott.*
SISTER HOPE . . . . *Mrs. Alcott.*
HER DAUGHTERS . . . . . . *The Alcott girls.*
JOHN PEASE . . . . *Samuel Bower.*
FOREST ABSALOM . . . . . . *Abram Everett.*
MOSES WHITE . . . . *Joseph Palmer.*
JANE GAGE . . . . *Anna Page.*

A CHAPTER FROM AN UNWRITTEN ROMANCE

On the first day of June, 184–, a large wagon, drawn by a small horse and containing a motley[1] load, went lumbering over certain New England hills, with the pleasing accompaniments of wind, rain, and hail.

A serene man with a serene child upon his knee was driving, or rather being driven, for the small horse had it all his own way. A brown boy with a William Penn style of countenance sat beside him, firmly embracing a bust of Socrates.[2] Behind them was an energetic-looking woman, with a benevolent brow, satirical mouth, and eyes brimful of hope and courage. A baby reposed upon her lap, a mirror leaned against her knee, and a basket of provisions danced about at her feet, as she struggled with a large, unruly umbrella. Two blue-eyed little girls, with hands full of childish treasures, sat under one old shawl, chatting happily together.

In front of this lively party stalked a tall, sharp-featured man, in a long blue cloak; and a fourth small girl trudged along beside him and through the mud as if she rather enjoyed it.

The wind whistled over the bleak hills; the rain fell in a despondent drizzle, and twilight began to fall. But the calm man gazed as tranquilly into the fog as if he beheld a radiant bow of promise spanning the gray sky. The cheery woman tried to cover every one but herself with the big umbrella. The brown boy pillowed his head on the bald pate[3] of Socrates and slumbered peacefully. The little girls sang lullabies to their dolls in soft, maternal murmurs. The sharp-nosed pedestrian marched steadily on, with the blue cloak streaming out behind him like a banner; and the lively infant splashed through the puddles with a duck-like satisfaction pleasant to behold.

Thus these modern pilgrims journeyed hopefully out of the old world, to found a new one in the wilderness.

The editors of *The Transcendental Tripod*[4] had received from Messrs. Lion & Lamb (two of the aforesaid pilgrims) a communication from which the following statement is an extract:

"We have made arrangements with the proprietor of an estate of about a hundred acres which liberates this

---

[1] *motley* Varied and incongruous.

[2] *William Penn style* Penn (1644–1718) was a Quaker colonist and founder of Pennsylvania; Penn had a reputation for having been optimistic, kind hearted, and benevolent, and that is generally reflected in eighteenth- and nineteenth-century portraits (no verified image of Penn from his lifetime is known to have survived); *Socrates* Greek philosopher of the fifth century BCE.

[3] *pate* Scalp.

[4] *The Transcendental Tripod* Reference to *The Dial*, a literary and philosophical journal edited by members of the Transcendentalist movement between 1840 and 1844.

tract from human ownership. Here we shall prosecute our effort to initiate a Family in harmony with the primitive instincts of man.

"Ordinary secular farming is not our object. Fruit, grain, pulse, herbs, flax, and other vegetable products, receiving assiduous attention, will afford ample manual occupation, and chaste supplies for the bodily needs. It is intended to adorn the pastures with orchards, and to supersede the labor of cattle by the spade and the pruning-knife.

"Consecrated to human freedom, the land awaits the sober culture of devoted men. Beginning with small pecuniary means, this enterprise must be rooted in a reliance on the succors of an ever-bounteous Providence, whose vital affinities being secured by this union with uncorrupted field and unworldly persons, the cares and injuries of a life of gain are avoided.

"The inner nature of each member of the Family is at no time neglected. Our plan contemplates all such disciplines, cultures, and habits as evidently conduce to the purifying of the inmates.

"Pledged to the spirit alone, the founders anticipate no hasty or numerous addition to their numbers. The kingdom of peace is entered only through the gates of self-denial; and felicity is the test and the reward of loyalty to the unswerving law of Love."

This prospective Eden at present consisted of an old red farm-house, a dilapidated barn, many acres of meadow-land, and a grove. Ten ancient apple-trees were all the "chaste supply" which the place offered as yet; but, in the firm belief that plenteous orchards were soon to be evoked from their inner consciousness, these sanguine founders had christened their domain Fruitlands.

Here Timon Lion intended to found a colony of Latter Day Saints, who, under his patriarchal sway, should regenerate the world and glorify his name forever. Here Abel Lamb, with the devoutest faith in the high ideal which was to him a living truth, desired to plant a Paradise, where Beauty, Virtue, Justice, and Love might live happily together, without the possibility of a serpent entering in.[1] And here his wife, unconverted but faithful to the end, hoped, after many

wanderings over the face of the earth, to find rest for herself and a home for her children.

"There is our new abode," announced the enthusiast, smiling with a satisfaction quite undamped by the drops dripping from his hat-brim, as they turned at length into a cart-path that wound along a steep hillside into a barren-looking valley.

"A little difficult of access," observed his practical wife, as she endeavored to keep her various household gods from going overboard with every lurch of the laden ark.

"Like all good things. But those who earnestly desire and patiently seek will soon find us," placidly responded the philosopher from the mud, through which he was now endeavoring to pilot the much-enduring horse.

"Truth lies at the bottom of a well,[2] Sister Hope," said Brother Timon, pausing to detach his small comrade from a gate, whereon she was perched for a clearer gaze into futurity.

"That's the reason we so seldom get at it, I suppose," replied Mrs. Hope, making a vain clutch at the mirror, which a sudden jolt sent flying out of her hands.

"We want no false reflections here," said Timon, with a grim smile, as he crunched the fragments under foot in his onward march.

Sister Hope held her peace, and looked wistfully through the mist at her promised home. The old red house with a hospitable glimmer at its windows cheered her eyes; and, considering the weather, was a fitter refuge than the sylvan bowers[3] some of the more ardent souls might have preferred.

The new-comers were welcomed by one of the elect precious—a regenerate farmer, whose ides of reform consisted chiefly in wearing white cotton raiment and shoes of untanned leather.[4] This costume, with a snowy beard, gave him a venerable, and at the same time a somewhat bridal appearance.

---

1   *serpent entering in*   Alluding to the serpent who enters the Garden of Eden in the Book of Genesis and leads to Adam and Eve's downfall.

2   *Truth lies … a well*   Proverb attributed to Greek philosopher Democritus (c. 460–c. 370 BCE).

3   *sylvan bowers*   Woodland dwellings; i.e., unsheltered forest.

4   *a regenerate … untanned leather*   This is Joseph Palmer (1791–1873), the only member of the Fruitlands community who had significant farming experience. Palmer had become infamous in Concord for wearing a full beard, which was then unfashionable to the point of being socially unacceptable; *untanned leather*   Leather that has not been treated in the standard way; untanned leather is less durable and paler in color.

The goods and chattels[1] of the Society not having arrived, the weary family reposed before the fire on blocks of wood, while Brother Moses White regaled them with roasted potatoes, brown bread and water, in two plates, a tin pan, and one mug; his table service[2] being limited. But, having cast the forms and vanities of a depraved world behind them, the elders welcomed hardship with the enthusiasm of new pioneers, and the children heartily enjoyed this foretaste of what they believed was to be a sort of perpetual picnic.

During the progress of this frugal meal, two more brothers appeared. One a dark, melancholy man, clad in homespun, whose peculiar mission was to turn his name hind part before and use as few words as possible.[3] The other was a bland, bearded Englishman, who expected to be saved by eating uncooked food and going without clothes.[4] He had not yet adopted the primitive costume, however; but contented himself with meditatively chewing dry beans out of a basket.

"Every meal should be a sacrament, and the vessels used should be beautiful and symbolical," observed Brother Lamb, mildly, righting the tin pan slipping about on his knees. "I priced a silver service when in town, but it was too costly; so I got some graceful cups and vases of Britannia ware."[5]

"Hardest things in the world to keep bright. Will whiting[6] be allowed in the community?" inquired Sister Hope, with a housewife's interest in labor-saving institutions.

"Such trivial questions will be discussed at a more fitting time," answered Brother Timon, sharply, as he burnt his fingers with a very hot potato. "Neither

sugar, molasses,[7] milk, butter, cheese, nor flesh are to be used among us, for nothing is to be admitted which has caused wrong or death to man or beast."

"Our garments are to be linen till we learn to raise our own cotton[8] or some substitute for woollen fabrics," added Brother Abel, blissfully basking in an imaginary future as warm and brilliant as the generous fire before him.

"Haou abaout shoes?" asked Brother Moses, surveying his own with interest.

"We must yield that point till we can manufacture an innocent substitute for leather. Bark, wood, or some durable fabric will be invented in time. Meanwhile, those who desire to carry out our idea to the fullest extent can go barefooted," said Lion, who liked extreme measures.

"I never will, nor let my girls," murmured rebellious Sister Hope, under her breath.

"Haou do you cattle'ate to treat the ten-acre lot? Ef things ain't 'tended to right smart, we shan't hev no crops," observed the practical patriarch in cotton.

"We shall spade it," replied Abel, in such perfect good faith that Moses said no more, though he indulged in a shake of the head as he glanced at hands that had held nothing heavier than a pen for years. He was a paternal old soul and regarded the younger men as promising boys on a new sort of lark.[9]

"What shall we do for lamps, if we cannot use any animal substance? I do hope light of some sort is to be thrown upon the enterprise," said Mrs. Lamb, with anxiety, for in those days kerosene and camphene were not, and gas unknown in the wilderness.

"We shall go without till we have discovered some vegetable oil or wax to serve us," replied Brother Timon, in a decided tone, which caused Sister Hope to resolve that her private lamp should be always trimmed,[10] if not burning.

"Each member is to perform the work for which experience, strength, and taste best fit him," continued Dictator Lion. "Thus drudgery and disorder will be

---

[1] *chattels*   Property.

[2] *table service*   Dishes, utensils, and other dining implements.

[3] *One a dark … as possible*   This is Abraham Everett, who was also known as Abraham Woods and also had a tendency to call himself "Woods Abraham"; he had spent a period in a mental institution before coming to Fruitlands; *homespun*   Clothing made from yarn or thread spun at home.

[4] *The other … without clothes*   Samuel Bower.

[5] *Britannia ware*   Metal alloy produced in England, known for its lustrous surface (resembling silver but less expensive to produce).

[6] *whiting*   Powdered white chalk, used for polishing surfaces such as metal.

[7] *sugar, molasses*   Sugar production was heavily reliant on the labor of enslaved workers on Southern plantations.

[8] *cotton*   Also heavily reliant on enslaved plantation laborers for its production.

[9] *lark*   Adventure or frolic.

[10] *trimmed*   Well-maintained and prepared for use.

avoided and harmony prevail. We shall rise at dawn, begin the day by bathing, followed by music, and then a chaste repast of fruit and bread. Each one finds congenial occupation till the meridian meal; when some deep-searching conversation gives rest to the body and development to the mind. Healthful labor again engages us till the last meal, when we assemble in social communion, prolonged till sunset, when we retire to sweet repose, ready for the next day's activity."

"What part of the work do you incline to yourself?" asked Sister Hope, with a humorous glimmer in her keen eyes.

"I shall wait till it is made clear to me. Being in preference to doing is the great aim, and this comes to us rather by a resigned willingness than a wilful activity, which is a check to all divine growth," responded Brother Timon.

"I thought so." And Mrs. Lamb sighed audibly, for during the year he had spent in her family Brother Timon had so faithfully carried out his idea of "being, not doing," that she had found his "divine growth" both an expensive and unsatisfactory process.

Here her husband struck into the conversation, his face shining with the light and joy of the splendid dreams and high ideals hovering before him.

"In these steps of reform, we do not rely so much on scientific reasoning or physiological skill as on the spirit's dictates. The greater part of man's duty consists in leaving alone much that he now does. Shall I stimulate with tea, coffee, or wine? No. Shall I consume flesh? Not if I value health. Shall I subjugate cattle? Shall I claim property in any created thing? Shall I trade? Shall I adopt a form of religion? Shall I interest myself in politics? To how many of these questions—could we ask them deeply enough and could they be heard as having relation to our eternal welfare—would the response be 'Abstain'?"

A mild snore seemed to echo the last word of Abel's rhapsody, for Brother Moses had succumbed to mundane slumber and sat nodding like a massive ghost. Forest Absalom, the silent man, and John Pease, the English member, now departed to the barn; and Mrs. Lamb led her flock to a temporary fold, leaving the founders of the "Consociate Family" to build castles in the air till the fire went out and the symposium ended in smoke.

The furniture arrived next day, and was soon bestowed; for the principal property of the community consisted in books. To this rare library was devoted the best room in the house, and the few busts and pictures that still survived many flittings were added to beautify the sanctuary, for here the family was to meet for amusement, instruction, and worship.

Any housewife can imagine the emotions of Sister Hope, when she took possession of a large, dilapidated kitchen, containing an old stove and the peculiar stores out of which food was to be evolved for her little family of eleven. Cakes of maple sugar, dried peas and beans, barley and hominy, meal of all sorts, potatoes, and dried fruit. No milk, butter, cheese, tea, or meat appeared. Even salt was considered a useless luxury and spice entirely forbidden by these lovers of Spartan simplicity. A ten years' experience of vegetarian vagaries had been good training for this new freak, and her sense of the ludicrous supported her through many trying scenes.

Unleavened bread, porridge, and water for breakfast; bread, vegetables, and water for dinner; bread, fruit, and water for supper was the bill of fare ordained by the elders. No teapot profaned that sacred stove, no gory steak cried aloud for vengeance from her chaste gridiron; and only a brave woman's taste, time, and temper were sacrificed on that domestic altar.

The vexed question of light was settled by buying a quantity of bayberry wax for candles; and, on discovering that no one knew how to make them, pine knots[1] were introduced, to be used when absolutely necessary. Being summer, the evenings were not long, and the weary fraternity found it no great hardship to retire with the birds. The inner light was sufficient for most of them. But Mrs. Lamb rebelled. Evening was the only time she had to herself, and while the tired feet rested the skilful hands mended torn frocks and little stockings, or anxious heart forgot its burden in a book.

So "mother's lamp" burned steadily, while the philosophers built a new heaven and earth by moonlight; and through all the metaphysical mists and philanthropic pyrotechnics of that period Sister Hope played her own little game of "throwing light," and none but the moths were the worse for it.

---

[1] *pine knots* Knots from pitch-pine trees, burned to provide light.

Such farming probably was never seen before since Adam delved.[1] The band of brothers began by spading garden and field; but a few days of it lessened their ardor amazingly. Blistered hands and aching backs suggested the expediency of permitting the use of cattle till the workers were better fitted for noble toil by a summer of the new life.

Brother Moses brought a yoke of oxen from his farm—at least, the philosophers thought so till it was discovered that one of the animals was a cow; and Moses confessed that he "must be let down easy, for he couldn't live on garden sarse[2] entirely."

Great was Dictator Lion's indignation at this lapse from virtue. But time pressed, the work must be done; so the meek cow was permitted to wear the yoke and the recreant brother continued to enjoy forbidden draughts in the barn, which dark proceeding caused the children to regard him as one set apart for destruction.

The sowing was equally peculiar, for, owing to some mistake, the three brethren, who devoted themselves to this graceful task, found when about half through the job that each had been sowing a different sort of grain in the same field; a mistake which caused so much perplexity, as it could not be remedied; but, after a long consultation and a good deal of laughter, it was decided to say nothing and see what would come of it.

The garden was planted with a generous supply of useful roots and herbs; but, as manure was not allowed to profane the virgin soil, few of these vegetable treasures ever came up. Purslane[3] reigned supreme, and the disappointed planters ate it philosophically, deciding that Nature knew what was best for them, and would generously supply their needs, if they could only learn to digest her "sallets" and wild roots.

The orchard was laid out, a little grafting done, new trees and vines set, regardless of the unfit season and entire ignorance of the husbandmen, who honestly believed that in the autumn they would reap a bounteous harvest.

Slowly things got into order, and rapidly rumors of the new experiment went abroad, causing many strange spirits to flock thither, for in those days communities were the fashion and transcendentalism raged wildly. Some came to look on and laugh, some to be supported in poetic idleness, a few to believe sincerely and work heartily. Each member was allowed to mount his favorite hobby[4] and ride it to his heart's content. Very queer were some of the riders, and very rampant some of the hobbies.

One youth, believing that language was of little consequence if the spirit was only right, startled new-comers by blandly greeting them with "Good-morning, damn you," and other remarks of an equally mixed order. A second irrepressible being held that all the emotions of the soul should be freely expressed, and illustrated his theory by antics that would have sent him to a lunatic asylum, if, as an unregenerate wag said, he had not already been in one. When his spirit soared, he climbed trees and shouted; when doubt assailed him, he lay upon the floor and groaned lamentably. At joyful periods, he raced, leaped, and sang; when sad, he wept aloud; and when a great thought burst upon him in the watches of the night, he crowed like a jocund cockerel, to the great delight of the children and the great annoyance of the elders. One musical brother fiddled whenever so moved, sang sentimentally to the four little girls, and put a music-box on the wall when he hoed corn.

Brother Pease ground away at his uncooked food, or browsed over the farm on sorrel, mint, green fruit, and new vegetables. Occasionally he took his walks abroad, airily attired in an unbleached cotton *poncho*, which was the nearest approach to the primeval costume he was allowed to indulge in. At midsummer he retired to the wilderness, to try his plan where the woodchucks were without prejudices and huckleberry-bushes were hospitably full. A sunstroke unfortunately spoilt his plan, and he returned to semi-civilization a sadder and wiser man.

Forest Absalom preserved his Pythagorean silence,[5] cultivated his fine dark locks, and worked like a beaver, setting an excellent example of brotherly love, justice, and fidelity by his upright life. He it was who helped

---

1   *since Adam delved*   Since the age of Adam and Eve; *delved* Dug; i.e., tilled the soil.

2   *garden sarse*   Fruits and vegetables.

3   *Purslane*   Sour-tasting, low-growing edible succulent.

4   *mount his favorite hobby*   Speak on topics of special interest to him.

5   *Pythagorean silence*   The disciples of the Greek philosopher and mathematician Pythagoras (c. fifth century BCE) took a vow of silence.

overworked Sister Hope with her heavy washes, kneaded the endless succession of batches of bread, watched over the children, and did the many tasks left undone by the brethren, who were so busy discussing and defining great duties that they forgot to perform the small ones.

Moses White placidly plodded about, "chorin' raound," as he called it, looking like an old-time patriarch, with his silver hair and flowing beard, and saving the community from many a mishap by his thrift and Yankee shrewdness.

Brother Lion domineered over the whole concern; for, having put the most money into the speculation, he was resolved to make it pay—as if anything founded on an ideal basis could be expected to do so by any but enthusiasts.

Abel Lamb simply revelled in the Newness, firmly believing that his dream was to be beautifully realized and in time not only little Fruitlands, but the whole earth, be turned into a Happy Valley. He worked with every muscle of his body, for *he* was in deadly earnest. He taught with his whole head and heart; planned and sacrificed, preached and prophesied, with a soul full of the purest aspirations, most unselfish purposes, and desires for a life devoted to God and man, too high and tender to bear the rough usage of this world.

It was a little remarkable that only one woman ever joined this community. Mrs. Lamb merely followed wheresoever her husband led, "as ballast for his balloon," as she said, in her bright way.

Miss Jane Gage was a stout lady of mature years, sentimental, amiable, and lazy. She wrote verses copiously, and had vague yearnings and graspings after the unknown, which led her to believe herself fitted for a higher sphere than any she had yet adorned.

Having been a teacher, she was set to instructing the children in the common branches. Each adult member took a turn at the infants; and, as each taught in his own way, the result was a chronic state of chaos in the minds of these much-afflicted innocents.

Sleep, food, and poetic musings were the desires of dear Jane's life, and she shirked all duties as clogs upon her spirit's wings. Any thought of lending a hand with the domestic drudgery never occurred to her; and when to the question, "Are there any beasts of burden on the place?" Mrs. Lamb answered, with a face that

told its own tale, "Only one woman!" the buxom Jane took no shame to herself, but laughed at the joke, and let the stout-hearted sister tug on alone.

Unfortunately, the poor lady hankered after the flesh-pots,[1] and endeavored to stay herself with private sips of milk, crackers, and cheese, and on one dire occasion she partook of fish at a neighbor's table.

One of the children reported this sad lapse from virtue, and poor Jane was publicly reprimanded by Timon.

"I only took a little bit of the tail," sobbed the penitent poetess.

"Yes, but the whole fish had to be tortured and slain that you might tempt your carnal appetite with that one taste of the tail. Know ye not, consumers of flesh meat, that ye are nourishing the wolf and tiger in your bosoms?"

At this awful question and the peal of laughter which arose from some of the younger brethren, tickled by the ludicrous contrast between the stout sinner, the stern judge, and the naughty satisfaction of the young detective, poor Jane fled from the room to pack her trunk and return to a world where fishes' tails were not forbidden fruit.

Transcendental wild oats were sown broadcast that year, and the fame thereof has not yet ceased in the land; for, futile as this crop seemed to outsiders, it bore an invisible harvest, worth much to those who planted in earnest. As none of the members of this particular community have ever recounted their experiences before, a few of them may not be amiss, since the interest in these attempts has never died out and Fruitlands was the most ideal of all these castles in Spain.

A new dress was invented, since cotton, silk, and wool were forbidden as the product of slave-labor, worm-slaughter, and sheep-robbery. Tunics and trousers of brown linen were the only wear. The women's skirts were longer, and their straw hat-brims wider than the men's, and this was the only difference. Some persecution lent a charm to the costume, and the

---

1   *flesh-pots* Pots for the cooking of meat, used figuratively to refer to luxuries and indulgent bodily pleasures; see Exodus 16.3: "And the children of Israel said unto them, Would to God we had died by the hand of the Lord in the land of Egypt, when we sat by the flesh pots, and when we did eat bread to the full; for ye have brought us forth into this wilderness, to kill this whole assembly with hunger."

long-haired, linen-clad reformers quite enjoyed the mild martyrdom they endured when they left home.

Money was abjured, as the root of all evil. The produce of the land was to supply most of their wants, or be exchanged for the few things they could not grow. This idea had its inconveniences; but self-denial was the fashion, and it was surprising how many things one can do without. When they desired to travel, they walked, if possible, begged the loan of a vehicle, or boldly entered car or coach, and, stating their principles to the officials, took the consequences. Usually their dress, their earnest frankness, and gentle resolution won them a passage; but now and then they met with hard usage, and had the satisfaction of suffering for their principles.

On one of these penniless pilgrimages they took passage on a boat, and, when fare was demanded, artlessly offered to talk, instead of pay. As the boat was well under way and they actually had not a cent, there was no help for it. So Brothers Lion and Lamb held forth to the assembled passengers in their most eloquent style. There must have been something effective in this conversation, for the listeners were moved to take up a contribution for these inspired lunatics, who preached peace on earth and good-will to man so earnestly, with empty pockets. A goodly sum was collected; but when the captain presented it the reformers proved that they were consistent even in their madness, for not a penny would they accept, saying, with a look at the group about them, whose indifference or contempt had changed to interest and respect, "You see how well we get on without money"; and so went serenely on their way, with their linen blouses flapping airily in the cold October wind.

They preached vegetarianism everywhere and resisted all temptations of the flesh, contentedly eating apples and bread at well-spread tables, and much afflicting hospitable hostesses by denouncing their food and taking away their appetites, discussing the "horrors of shambles,"[1] the "incorporation[2] of the brute in man," and "on elegant abstinence the sign of a pure soul." But, when the perplexed or offended ladies asked what they should eat, they got in reply a bill of fare consisting of "bowls of sunrise for breakfast," "solar seeds of the sphere," "dishes from Plutarch's[3] chaste table," and other viands[4] equally hard to find in any modern market.

Reform conventions of all sorts were haunted by these brethren, who said many wise things and did many foolish ones. Unfortunately, these wanderings interfered with their harvest at home; but the rule was to do what the spirit moved, so they left their crops to Providence and went a-reaping in wider and, let us hope, more fruitful fields than their own.

Luckily, the earthly providence who watched over Abel Lamb was at hand to glean the scanty crop yielded by the "uncorrupted land," which, "consecrated to human freedom," had received "the sober culture of devout men."

About the time the grain was ready to house, some call of the Oversoul[5] wafted all the men away. An easterly storm was coming up and the yellow stacks were sure to be ruined. Then Sister Hope gathered her forces. Three little girls, one boy (Timon's son), and herself, harnessed to clothes-baskets and Russia-linen sheets, were the only teams she could command; but with these poor appliances the indomitable woman got in the grain and saved food for her young, with the instinct and energy of a mother-bird with a brood of hungry nestlings to feed.

This attempt at regeneration had its tragic as well as comic side, though the world only saw the former.

With the first frosts, the butterflies, who had sunned themselves in the new light through the summer, took flight, leaving the few bees to see what honey they had stored for winter use. Precious little appeared beyond the satisfaction of a few months of holy living.

At first it seemed as if a chance to try holy dying also was to be offered them. Timon, much disgusted with the failure of the scheme, decided to retire to the

---

[1]   *shambles* Slaughterhouses.

[2]   *incorporation* I.e., absorbing into the body.

[3]   *Plutarch* Greek biographer and essayist (c. 45–125 CE). Some less well-known elements of his thought include his support of Pythagorean vegetarianism and his argument that some non-human animals can be considered rational beings.

[4]   *viands* Foods.

[5]   *Oversoul* Term first used by Transcendentalist leader Ralph Waldo Emerson in an essay of the same name (1841), the Oversoul or Over-soul refers to a supreme or underlying spirit that pervades all reality, transcending and unifying human individuality.

Shakers,[1] who seemed to be the only successful community going.

"What is to become of us?" asked Mrs. Hope, for Abel was heart-broken at the bursting of his lovely bubble.

"You can stay here, if you like, till a tenant is found. No more wood must be cut, however, and no more corn ground. All I have must be sold to pay the debts of the concern, as the responsibility rests with me," was the cheering reply.

"Who is to pay us for what we have lost? I gave all I had—furniture, time, strength, six months of my children's lives—and all are wasted. Abel gave himself body and soul, and is almost wrecked by hard work and disappointment. Are we to have no return for this, but leave to starve and freeze in an old house, with winter at hand, no money, and hardly a friend left; for this wild scheme has alienated nearly all we had. You talk much about justice. Let us have a little, since there is nothing else left."

But the woman's appeal met with no reply but the old one: "It was an experiment. We all risked something, and must bear our losses as we can."

With this cold comfort, Timon departed with his son, and was absorbed into the Shaker brotherhood, where he soon found the order of things was reversed, and it was all work and no play.

Then the tragedy began for the forsaken little family. Desolation and despair fell upon Abel. As his wife said, his new beliefs had alienated many friends. Some thought him mad, some unprincipled. Even the most kindly thought him a visionary, whom it was useless to help till he took more practical views of life. All stood aloof, saying: "Let him work out his own ideas, and see what they are worth."

He had tried, but it was a failure. The world was not ready for Utopia yet, and those who attempted to found it only got laughed at for their pains. In other days, men could sell all and give to the poor, lead lives devoted to holiness and high thought, and, after the persecution was over, find themselves honored as saints or martyrs. But in modern times these things are out of fashion. To live for one's principles, at all costs, is a dangerous speculation; and the failure of an ideal, no matter how humane and noble, is harder for the world to forgive and forget than bank robbery or the grand swindles of corrupt politicians.

Deep waters now for Abel, and for a time there seemed no passage through. Strength and spirits were exhausted by hard work and too much thought. Courage failed when, looking about for help, he saw no sympathizing face, no hand outstretched to help him, no voice to say cheerily,

"We all make mistakes, and it takes many experiences to shape a life. Try again, and let us help you."

Every door was closed, every eye averted, every heart cold, and no way open whereby he might earn bread for his children. His principles would not permit him to do many things that others did; and in the few fields where conscience would allow him to work, who would employ a man who had flown in the face of society, as he had done?

Then this dreamer, whose dream was the life of his life, resolved to carry out his idea to the bitter end. There seemed no place for him here—no work, no friend. To go begging conditions was as ignoble as to go begging money. Better perish of want than sell one's soul for the sustenance of his body. Silently he lay down upon his bed, turned his face to the wall, and waited with pathetic patience for death to cut the knot which he could not untie. Days and nights went by, and neither food nor water passed his lips. Soul and body were dumbly struggling together, and no word of complaint betrayed what either suffered.

His wife, when tears and prayers were unavailing, sat down to wait the end with a mysterious awe and submission; for in this entire resignation of all things there was an eloquent significance to her who knew him as no other human being did.

"Leave all to God," was his belief; and in this crisis the loving soul clung to this faith, sure that the Allwise Father would not desert this child who tried to live so near to Him. Gathering her children about her, she waited the issue of the tragedy that was being enacted

---

[1] *Shakers* Members of a millenarian Christian sect (more properly called the United Society of Believers in Christ's Second Appearing) that emerged in eighteenth-century England and had its peak in the mid-nineteenth century; the colloquial name stems from their dancing and eccentric behavior during worship services. Among the Shakers' doctrines were a belief in complete celibacy and in a certain degree of gender equality. A community of Shakers had been established in the same township as Fruitlands.

in that solitary room, while the first snow fell outside, untrodden by the footprints of a single friend.

But the strong angels who sustain and teach perplexed and troubled souls came and went, leaving no trace without, but working miracles within. For, when all other sentiments had faded into dimness, all other hopes died utterly; when the bitterness of death was nearly over, when body was past any pang of hunger or thirst, and soul stood ready to depart, the love that outlives all else refused to die. Head had bowed to defeat, hand had grown weary with too heavy tasks, but heart could not grow cold to those who lived in its tender depths, even when death touched it.

"My faithful wife, my little girls—they have not forsaken me, they are mine by ties that none can break. What right have I to leave them alone? What right to escape from the burden and the sorrow I have helped to bring? This duty remains to me, and I must do it manfully. For their sakes, the world will forgive me in time; for their sakes, God will sustain me now."

Too feeble to rise, Abel groped for the food that always lay within his reach, and in the darkness and solitude of that memorable night ate and drank what was to him the bread and wine of a new communion, a new dedication of heart and life to the duties that were left him when the dreams fled.

In the early dawn, when that sad wife crept fearfully to see what change had come to the patient face on the pillow, she found it smiling at her, saw a wasted hand outstretched to her, and heard a feeble voice cry bravely, "Hope!"

What passed in that little room is not to be recorded except in the hearts of those who suffered and endured much for love's sake. Enough for us to know that soon the wan shadow of a man came forth, leaning on the arm that never failed him, to be welcomed and cherished by the children, who never forgot the experiences of that time.

"Hope" was the watchword now; and, while the last logs blazed on the hearth, the last bread and apples covered the table, the new commander, with recovered courage, said to her husband—

"Leave all to God—and me. He has done his part; now I will do mine."

"But we have no money, dear."

"Yes, we have. I sold all we could spare, and have enough to take us away from this snowbank."

"Where can we go?"

"I have engaged four rooms at our good neighbor, Lovejoy's. There we can live cheaply till spring. Then for new plans and a home of our own, please God."

"But, Hope, your little store won't last long, and we have no friends."

"I can sew and you can chop wood. Lovejoy offers you the same pay as he gives his other men; my old friend, Mrs. Truman, will send me all the work I want; and my blessed brother stands by us to the end. Cheer up, dear heart, for while there is work and love in the world we shall not suffer."

"And while I have my good angel Hope, I shall not despair, even if I wait another thirty years before I step beyond the circle of the sacred little world in which I still have a place to fill."

So one bleak December day, with their few possessions piled on a ox-sled, the rosy children perched atop, and the parents trudging arm in arm behind, the exiles left their Eden and faced the world again.

"Ah, me! my happy dream. How much I leave behind that never can be mine again," said Abel, looking back at the lost Paradise, lying white and chill in its shroud of snow.

"Yes, dear; but how much we bring away," answered brave-hearted Hope, glancing from husband to children.

"Poor Fruitlands! The name was as great a failure as the rest!" continued Abel, with a sigh, as a frostbitten apple fell from a leafless bough at his feet.

But the sigh changed to a smile as his wife added, in a half-tender, half-satirical tone—

"Don't you think Apple Slump[1] would be a better name for it, dear?"

—1873

---

1   *Apple Slump*   This was the name Alcott herself gave Orchard House, the home in which her family eventually settled after the Fruitlands disaster. In addition to its ordinary meaning, a "slump" or more specifically an "apple slump" is a traditional New England dessert of which Alcott was particularly fond.

Glossary of Terms

Abolitionism: a social and political movement in the pre-Civil War era that sought to bring an end to the institution of slavery.

Accent: the natural emphasis (or stress) that speakers place on a syllable.

Accentual-Syllabic Verse: the most common metrical system in traditional English verse, in which a line is measured by the number of syllables and by the pattern of accented (stressed) and unaccented (unstressed) syllables.

Allegory: a narrative with both a literal meaning and secondary, often symbolic meaning or meanings, in which nearly every element, including such things as setting, characters, objects, and plot lines, may contribute to that symbolic meaning. See, for example, Nathaniel Hawthorne's "Young Goodman Brown."

Alliteration: the grouping of words with the same initial consonant (e.g., Longfellow's "In the world's broad field of battle / In the bivouac of Life"). The repetition of sound acts as a connector and adds auditory (and sometimes also thematic) emphasis.

Allusion: a reference, often indirect or unidentified, to a person, thing, or event. A reference in one literary work to another literary work, whether to its content or its form, also constitutes an allusion.

Almanac: an annual publication compiling information on many subjects, such as weather predictions for the year, cures for ailments, lists of roads, lists of government officials, poetry, and essays on current topics of interest.

Ambiguity: an "opening" of language created by the writer to allow for multiple meanings or differing interpretations. In literature, ambiguity may be deliberately employed by the writer to enrich meaning; this differs from any unintentional, unwanted ambiguity in non-literary prose.

Analogy: a broad term that refers to our processes of noting similarities among things or events. Specific forms of analogy in poetry include *simile* and *metaphor* (see below).

Antebellum: before, or existing before, a war; in American usage, particularly the period before American Civil War. See also *postbellum*.

Antinomian Controversy / Free Grace Controversy: a conflict that took place from 1636 to 1638 involving religious and political leaders in the Massachusetts Bay Colony. The dispute originated with a difference in interpretation of the relationship between "works" (an individual's good acts) and "grace" (bestowed by God) as markers of spiritual salvation. Puritans generally agreed that salvation came through God's grace alone—people could not bring about their own salvation through good works—but most thought that a person who had been saved would necessarily think and act in accordance with the rules set out in the Bible. Proponents of "free grace" (called *antinomians* by their opponents) took the more extreme position that individuals who had been saved would simply know it, and that one's actions should not be treated as evidence of salvation—including one's adherence to civil or biblical law. Political and religious leaders responded to this challenge to their authority by banishing some of the movement's leaders—including, most famously, Anne Hutchinson—from the colony.

Aphorism: a pithy observation or saying that contains a general truth. For example: "Three may keep a secret, if two of them are dead" (Benjamin Franklin).

Apostrophe: a figure of speech (a trope; see *figures of speech* below) in which a writer directly addresses an object—or a dead or absent person—as if the imagined audience were actually listening. For example, James Monroe Whitfield's "America, it is to thee / Thou boasted land of liberty, / It is to thee I raise my song."

Archetype: in literature and mythology, a recurring idea, symbol, motif, character, or place. To some scholars and psychologists, an archetype represents universal human thought-patterns or experiences.

Arminianism: the theological doctrine that grew in opposition to the idea of predestination in Calvinism, holding instead that salvation was available to those who had faith in God and practiced good works; the movement influenced Methodism and, later, Unitarianism.

Autobiography: an account of a person's life, or portions of it, as written by that person and presumed to be factual.

Ballad: a folk song, or a poem originally recited to an audience, which tells a dramatic story based on legend or history. See, for example, Longfellow's "Paul Revere's Ride."

Ballad Stanza: a quatrain with alternating four-stress and three-stress lines, rhyming abcb. A variant is "common measure," in which the alternating lines are strictly iambic, and rhyme abab. Emily Dickinson used the technique to great effect; see, for example, "There is no Frigate like a Book."

Baptist: a member of a Protestant denomination that tends to adhere to Calvinist doctrine and advocates baptism for adult believers only—by total immersion, and after a confession of faith—in contrast to the practice of infant baptism among other denominations. See *Calvinism, Separatists.*

Bathos: an anticlimactic effect brought about by a writer's descent from an elevated subject or tone to the ordinary or trivial.

Bildungsroman: from the German words *Bildung* (education) and *Roman* (novel), a narrative (often a novel) of personal development as a young or innocent person grows through a series of social, sexual, and political experiences, among others.

Blank Verse: unrhymed lines written in iambic pentameter. See George Moses Horton's "Division of an Estate."

Bombast: inappropriately inflated or grandiose language.

Broadside: individual sheet of paper printed on only one side. Broadsides of a variety of different sorts (e.g., ballads, political tracts, short satires) were sold on the streets; they were also used to distribute information or as advertisements.

Brownists: a group of Separatists from the Church of England who adhered to the principles of church government espoused by Robert Browne (1550–1633), the founder of Congregationalism. See *Congregationalism.*

Burlesque: satire of a particularly exaggerated sort, particularly that which mocks its subject by emphasizing its vulgar or ridiculous aspects.

Calvinism: a branch of Protestantism based on the teachings of John Calvin (1509–64), stressing the absolute power of God and humanity's total depravity; central to Calvinist doctrine is the idea that human beings are innately and irreversibly sinful, and that only those who are predestined at birth to be saved—the elect—will be granted salvation. Many of the Separatists and Puritans who first settled in America followed Calvinist doctrine. See also *Protestantism.*

Canon: in literature, those works that are commonly accepted as possessing authority or importance. In practice, "canonical" texts or authors are those that are discussed most frequently by scholars and taught most frequently in university courses.

Canto: a sub-section of a long (usually epic) poem. See Melville's *Clarel* and Ezra Pound's *The Cantos.*

Captivity Narrative: a genre of literature that relates the experiences of a person who has been kidnapped; in American literature, the "Indian captivity narrative" was especially popular from the seventeenth through the nineteenth centuries. Conventions of this genre include a focus on the perspective of white captives, usually women; an emphasis on the subject's piety during the captivity; a tendency toward dehumanizing representations of Indigenous people; and detailed but prejudiced descriptions of Indigenous ways of life. *A Narrative of the Captivity and Restoration of Mrs. Mary Rowlandson* (1682) serves as an excellent example.

Catharsis: the arousal through the performance of a dramatic tragedy of "emotions of pity and fear" to a point where "purgation" or "purification" occurs and the feelings are released or transformed. The concept was developed by Aristotle in his *Poetics* from an ancient Greek medical concept, and adapted by him into an aesthetic principle.

Chiasmus: a figure of speech (a scheme) that reverses word order in successive parallel clauses; if the word order is A-B-C in the first clause, it becomes C-B-A in the second. See, for example, Frederick Douglass's phrase: "You have seen how a man was made a slave; you shall see how a slave was made a man."

Church of England/Anglican Church: Christian church established in the 1530s when the English King Henry VIII broke from the Roman Catholic Church and papal authority. In the sixteenth and seventeenth centuries, there was substantial conflict over whether or not the Anglican Church was sufficiently Protestant in its ideology and aesthetics; Puritans, Separatists, and related groups argued that the Church retained too much of what they saw as Catholic corruption. Some of the reforms advocated by the Puritans were taken up by the Anglican Church, but different factions within the Church continue to express a wide range of opinions on rituals and organization, from elaborate ceremony and a strict hierarchy to relatively informal religious services and more egalitarian governance. After the American Revolution, Anglican churches in America separated from the Church of England and, eventually, formed the Episcopal Church.

Civil Disobedience: title commonly applied to an 1849 essay by Henry David Thoreau ("Resistance to Civil Government"); more generally, a political view that recommends passive resistance to authority whenever laws or social obligations contradict individual beliefs.

Classical: originating in or relating to ancient Greek or Roman culture. As commonly conceived, classical implies a strong sense of formal order. The term neoclassical is often used with reference to literature (particularly of the eighteenth century) that was strongly influenced by ancient Greek and Roman models.

Closet Drama: a play (typically in verse) written for private performance. The term came into use in the first half of the nineteenth century.

Colonialism/Colonization: the system or policy by which a nation acquires control of another nation or nations by means of settlement, economic exploitation, and the subjugation of the region's original inhabitants. The term "colonization" may also refer to the idea, popular among white Americans in the early and mid-nineteenth century, of transporting freed enslaved people to Africa.

Colony: a settled area that is connected with a parent, often distant, country; the community of people in that area, and their descendants.

Color Line: a reference to the division between blacks and whites after the abolition of slavery, so named after an 1881 article by Frederick Douglass.

Colored Narrative: alternative term for *free indirect discourse.*

Comedy: as a literary term, used originally to denote that class of ancient Greek drama in which the action ends happily. More broadly the term has been used to describe a wide variety of literary forms of a more or less light-hearted or humorous character.

Conceit: an unusually elaborate metaphor or simile that presents a striking parallel between two apparently dissimilar things (see, for example, Edward Taylor's poem "Huswifery," in which God is cast as a cloth-maker and the speaker His spinning wheel). Ingenious or fanciful images and comparisons were especially popular with the metaphysical poets of seventeenth-century England, giving rise to the term "metaphysical conceit."

Confederacy: a group of people or nations joined together in political or social union for a particular purpose or mutual support; as, for example, the Iroquois Confederacy. The term is also used to denote the Confederate States of America, the self-proclaimed national government formed by the southern states that supported slavery and seceded from the United States.

Congregationalism: a Protestant religious movement in the Calvinist tradition in which each congregation runs its own affairs, independently from others. See also *Protestantism, Calvinism.*

Connotation: the implied, often unspoken meaning(s) of a given word, as distinct from its denotation, or literal meaning. Connotations may have highly emotional undertones and are usually culturally specific.

Contact: a reference to the physical and cultural meeting between European explorers and Indigenous peoples of North America, the repercussions of which included extensive loss of land and epidemic disease and death for the Indigenous population.

Convention: aesthetic approach, technique, or practice accepted as characteristic and appropriate for a particular form. It is a convention of certain sorts of plays, for example, that the characters speak in blank verse, of other sorts of plays that characters speak in rhymed couplets, and of still other sorts of dramatic performances that characters frequently break into song to express their feelings.

Coverture: a common-law doctrine stipulating that a married woman had no legal identity separate from that of her husband, and so was "covered" or controlled by him in the eyes of the law, with no property or economic rights of her own.

Creation Story: a story that narrates the origins of the world and its first inhabitants; creation stories may present a culture's fundamental worldview, including its moral and spiritual values; some may also chronicle significant geographical or historical events. The telling of creation stories is an act of great importance in many Indigenous cultures.

Creole: originally, a person of European descent who was born in the West Indies or Latin America; also, an enslaved person of African descent born in the colonies. These diverse groups of people settled in a variety of regions and established distinct social and political identities, and the term today can be defined variously; in Louisiana, the term refers to people who are descended from (mainly French) colonial settlers of the Louisiana region before the Louisiana Purchase in 1803. "Creole" may also refer to the hybrid language that develops as a result of the mixing of two or more such groups who speak a different parent language.

Declaration of Independence: the pronouncement adopted on 4 July 1776 that sets out to explain why the Thirteen Colonies felt it necessary to leave the British Empire and declare themselves independent states.

Deism: a school of religious and philosophical thought that grew to prominence during the Enlightenment, proposing that God exists only as the creator of the universe, and has had little or no influence on the world since creation; more generally, deists deny the literal truth of the Bible and other teachings of formal religion.

Democratic Party: a political party established in 1828; led by Andrew Jackson, the party supported a somewhat limited federal government, states' rights, and the removal of the central banking system. See also *Democratic-Republican Party*, *Whig Party*.

Democratic-Republican Party: one of the first two political parties of the United States; established in 1792 and led by Thomas Jefferson and James Madison, the party advocated a limited, decentralized federal government, agrarian and anti-aristocratic policies, and stronger ties to France in foreign affairs. Originally known as just the Republican Party, or the Jeffersonian Republicans, the party embraced the "Democratic-Republican Party" label in 1798, a name that had been intended by Federalist opponents to link them to the radicalism of the French Revolution. The party grew enormously during and after Jefferson's presidency—so much so that in 1824 it ran four candidates for the presidency; however, political division ensued, and the party eventually split in two, giving rise over the next decade to the Democratic Party and the Whig Party.

Denotation: See *connotation* above.

Dialogue: words spoken by characters to one another. (When a character is addressing themselves or the audience directly, the words spoken are referred to as a *monologue*.)

Diaspora: a group of people with a similar heritage or homeland who disperse across the globe to different locations, especially involuntarily; or, the dispersion itself.

Diction: word choice; the diction of a literary work (or of a literary character), whether colloquial, conversational, formal, or of some other type, contributes significantly to the tone of the text as well as to characterization.

Didacticism: aesthetic approach emphasizing moral instruction. See, for example, Harriet Beecher Stowe's novel, *Uncle Tom's Cabin*, or Frances Harper's temperance poems.

Disenfranchisement: the state of being deprived of civil privileges, especially the right to vote.

Doppelgänger: a look-alike (from the German *doppel-* double + *-gänger* walker); in folklore and literature, often an apparition of a living person, the sight of which spells doom or bad luck.

Dramatic Irony: This form of irony occurs when the audience's reception of a speech by a character on the stage is affected by the possession by the audience of information not available to the character.

Dred Scott v. Sandford: an 1857 Supreme Court decision in which the Court held that people of African descent were not United States citizens and so were not entitled to the rights and privileges laid out in the U.S. Constitution. The decision also held that the Missouri Compromise was unconstitutional, nullifying Congress's power to prevent the spread of slavery into new states. The decision came after the formerly enslaved Dred Scott attempted to secure the court's further confirmation of his freedom so that the children of his deceased former enslaver could not claim inherited ownership of Scott's daughters.

Elegy: a poem or other similar form of expression which formally mourns the death of a particular person (e.g., Whitman's "When Lilacs Last in the Dooryard Bloom'd") or in which the poet or speaker meditates on other serious subjects (e.g., Chief Seattle's 1854 speech concerning Indigenous worldviews and the environment).

Ellipsis: the omission of a word or words necessary for the complete grammatical construction of a sentence, but not necessary for our understanding of the sentence.

End-Stopped: a line of poetry is said to be end-stopped when the end of the line coincides with a natural pause in the syntax, such as the conclusion of a sentence; an end-stopped line is usually but not always marked by punctuation. For example, the first two lines of Longfellow's "The Arrow and the Song": "I shot an arrow into the air, / It fell to earth, I knew not where." Compare *enjambement*.

Enjambement: the "running-on" of the sense from one line of poetry to the next, with no pause created by punctuation or syntax. Longfellow's poem "The Arrow and the Song" provides an example, which follows on the heels of an end-stopped line: "For, so swiftly it flew, the sight / Could not follow it in its flight." Compare *end-stopped*.

Enlightenment: an intellectual movement of the seventeenth and eighteenth centuries broadly characterized by radically new scientific, political, and philosophical ideas that ushered in a wholesale reappraisal of society. Also referred to as the "Age of Reason," the period placed great stock in empirical observation and in the belief that human rationality, rather than faith and religious doctrine, would improve society. Enlightenment thinkers frequently called for the reform of existing political, religious, and social institutions, extending to—in the case of more radical figures—the separation of church and state, constitutional government, freedom of expression, and other kindred individual liberties. Enlightenment ideals directly inspired the American and other national revolutions.

Epic: a lengthy narrative poem, often divided into sections, that generally celebrates heroic deeds or events, and the style of which tends to be lofty and grand. Examples include Anne Bradstreet's *The Four Monarchies* and Michael Wigglesworth's *The Day of Doom*.

Epigraph: a quotation placed at the beginning of a discourse to indicate or foreshadow the theme.

Epiphany: a moment at which matters of significance are suddenly illuminated for a literary character (or for the reader), typically triggered by something small and seemingly of little import.

Episodic Plot: plot comprising a variety of episodes that are only loosely connected by threads of story material (as opposed to plots that present one or more continually unfolding narratives where successive episodes build one on another).

Eulogy: text expressing praise, especially for a distinguished person recently deceased. While not necessarily typical of the form, William Apess's *Eulogy on King Philip* provides an example.

Euphemism: mode of expression through which aspects of reality considered to be vulgar, crudely physical, or unpleasant are referred to indirectly rather than named explicitly. A variety of euphemisms exist for the processes of urination and defecation; *passed away* is often used as a euphemism for *died*.

Exposition: the setting out of material in an ordered form, either in speech or in writing. In a play those parts of the action that do not occur on stage but are rather recounted by the characters are frequently described as being presented in exposition. Similarly, when the background narrative is filled in near the beginning of a novel, such material is often described as having been presented in exposition.

Federalist Party: one of the first two political parties of the United States; led by Alexander Hamilton, George Washington, and John Adams, and favored by conservatives and business owners, the party dominated the national government from 1791 to 1801. Federalists advocated a strong centralized federal government, a national bank, and stronger ties to Britain in foreign affairs. The party faded after 1801 and dissolved soon thereafter. See also *Democratic-Republican Party*.

Fifteenth Amendment: an 1870 amendment to the U.S. Constitution guaranteeing that the right to vote could not be denied to anyone based on "race, color, or previous condition of servitude." Even after the amendment passed, threats, violence, and poll taxes continued to prevent some populations from voting in many places, and women were excluded from the amendment.

Figures of Speech: deliberate, highly concentrated uses of language intended to achieve particular purposes or effects on an audience. There are two kinds of figures: schemes and tropes. Schemes involve changes in word-sound and word-order, such as *alliteration* and *chiasmus*. Tropes play on our understandings of words to extend, alter, or transform meaning, as in *metaphor* and *personification*.

Fireside Poets: a group of nineteenth-century American poets who became widely popular especially in the latter half of the century, including Henry Wadsworth Longfellow, John Greenleaf Whittier, James Russell Lowell, William Cullen Bryant, and Oliver Wendell Holmes Sr. Their fame stemmed from their tendency to write in conventional meter on domestic themes and familiar moral and political issues.

First Great Awakening: the period of increased religious fervor that swept through the American colonies beginning in the 1730s. Having originated in Europe, the movement was introduced to New England through the preaching of figures like George Whitefield and Jonathan Edwards; it influenced many denominations, and led to, among other things, the emergence of evangelical Christianity. Proponents reinvigorated concepts of Calvinism as a reaction against the confidence placed in science and reason during the Age of Enlightenment and as an antidote to the prevailing materialism in the colonies. See also *Second Great Awakening*.

First-Person Narrative: narrative recounted using *I* and *me*. See also *narrative perspective*.

Folklore: the traditions and cultural artifacts shared by a given group of people; these include such things as tales and proverbs, handmade items and building styles, rituals and celebratory practices, and so on.

Folktale: a story that is passed down through generations orally and that, while often featuring fictional elements or characters, can communicate key aspects of a culture's knowledge, history, or beliefs; a genre of folklore.

Foot: a unit of a line of verse which contains a particular combination of stressed and unstressed syllables. Dividing a line into metrical feet (*iambs*, *trochees*, etc.), then counting the number of feet per line, is part of *scansion*. See also *meter*.

Founders/Founding Fathers: the leading figures in the founding of the United States who worked to unite the Thirteen Colonies, draft the Declaration of Independence and Constitution, lead the war for independence in various capacities, and build the ideological and functional framework of the country's democratic government.

Fourteenth Amendment: an 1868 amendment to the U.S. Constitution that granted citizenship to formerly enslaved people and guaranteed them "equal protection of the laws," thereby nullifying the Supreme Court's 1857 *Dred Scott* decision that had prevented people of African descent from becoming citizens. The amendment also gave the federal government authority to punish states for restricting citizens' right to vote; introduced hurdles that made it difficult for former Confederate leaders to hold office; invalidated federal and state debts owed to the now defunct Confederate states; and prohibited compensation to be paid to former enslavers.

Free Indirect Discourse: in prose fiction, third-person narration in which a seemingly objective and omniscient narrative voice assumes the point of view of one or more characters, and in which the thoughts and expressions are not typically set apart with indicators such as "he said" or "she thought"; the term may also be applied to situations in which it may not be entirely clear if the thoughts expressed emanate from the character, the narrator, or some combination of the two. When we hear through the third-person narrative voice of Melville's *Benito Cereno*, for example, the unsettling description of enslaved black sailors, we are likely to take it as being the view of the character Captain Delano. The narrator ascribes to the sailors the traits of "docility," "good-humour," and "cheerfulness"—"as though God had set the whole negro to some pleasant tune"—but it is difficult to imagine that the extreme incongruity between their enslavement and the narrator's description of their disposition is an objective statement of perceived truth on the part of the novel's third-person narrative voice.

Free Verse: poetry that does not follow any regular meter, line length, or rhyming scheme. In many respects, though, free verse follows the complex natural "rules" and rhythmic patterns (or cadences) of speech. Walt Whitman's long poetic lines provide a fine example.

Frontier: an extreme limit of settled land; as a concept in American history and culture, the frontier was an imagined border in the west beyond which lay wilderness. To many colonists, the idea of the frontier represented the opportunity for leading a new and better life; however, this idea frequently distorted the reality of the conditions in the frontier territory and either minimized or dismissed outright the Indigenous people who already inhabited it.

Fugitive Slave Acts: two federal laws, enacted in 1793 and 1850, that provided for the capture and return of escapees from slavery and imposed penalties on anyone who harbored or helped them; both acts were meant to quell the unrest emerging in southern states as a result of increasing antislavery sentiment in the north.

Genre: a particular literary form. The concept of genre may be used with different levels of generality. At the most general, poetry, drama, and prose fiction are distinguished as separate genres. At a lower level of generality various subgenres are frequently distinguished, such as (within drama) comedy and tragedy, or, at a still lower level of generality, minstrelsy, puppetry, burlesque, and so on.

Gilded Age: a period between the end of the Civil War and the start of the twentieth century in which tremendous industrial and technological growth led to extreme economic disparity between wealthy industrialists and financiers, on one hand, and the working class and immigrants, on the other; the term was coined by Mark Twain in reference to the façade of respectability that masked the era's greed and corruption.

Gold Coast: a region in West Africa named by imperial nations after its chief export, gold; modern-day Ghana. It was one of many coastal regions from Senegambia (modern-day Senegal) to Angola that were exploited during the era of the transatlantic slave trade.

Goodman/Goodwife: polite terms of address used in colonial America, generally in reference to those of lower or middling social status—laborers or farmers (and their wives)—as opposed to merchants and others of the wealthier classes.

Gospel: historically, the first four books of the New Testament, which narrate the life and relate the teachings of Jesus Christ, or the biblical message of Christ in general; also, a genre of music in which songs echo and elevate Christian worship, often featuring evangelical lyrics. See also *spiritual*.

Gothic: in literature, a term used to describe work with a sinister or grotesque tone that seeks to evoke a sense of terror on the part of the reader or audience. The term was used originally to describe styles prevalent in architecture and the visual arts in late Medieval Europe; Gothic literature originated in eighteenth-century England as a distinct genre in which works often featured medieval settings or themes, supernatural elements, and fantastic, macabre plots. Examples in American literature include much of Edgar

Allan Poe's work, Charles Brockden Brown's *Edgar Huntly*, and "The Legend of Sleepy Hollow" by Washington Irving.

Gullah/Geechee: a distinct group of African Americans who live in parts of Georgia, North Carolina, South Carolina, and Florida; the culture developed as various ethnic groups of enslaved people from Africa were forced to work on large and relatively isolated plantations in the region; also, the creole language that they speak.

Haitian Revolution: a large-scale revolution in Haiti that began in 1791 and was led by black and mixed-race Haitians, many of whom were enslaved; it ultimately resulted in the expulsion of French colonial forces and the establishment of Haiti as an independent nation in 1804. The revolution's success, along with Haiti's proximity to the fledgling United States, had a profound impact on American racial, social, and political history.

Homestead Act: a law enacted by Congress during the Civil War in 1862 that granted public lands to any private citizen or citizens-to-be who had not taken up arms against the Federal government; the law dealt a severe blow to Indigenous peoples.

Hoodoo: a set of spiritual practices and folk magic based in part on traditions and beliefs of enslaved Africans, including African spiritualism and Christianity. Hoodoo practice is also known as conjure or rootwork. See also *Obeah, Voodoo*.

Hudson River School: a group of New York-based landscape artists in the nineteenth century who were influenced by the ideas of Romanticism.

Humors: The four humors were believed until the sixteenth and seventeenth centuries to be elements in the makeup of all humans; a person's temperament was thought to be determined by the way in which the humors were combined. When the *choleric* humor was dominant, the person would tend toward anger; when the *sanguine* humor was dominant, toward pleasant affability; when the *phlegmatic* humor was dominant, toward a cool and calm attitude and/or a lack of feeling or enthusiasm; and when the *melancholic* humor was dominant, toward withdrawal and melancholy.

Hymn: a song whose theme is usually religious, in praise of divinity. Literary hymns may praise more secular subjects. African American spirituals provide abundant examples; see, for instance, "Swing Low, Sweet Chariot."

Hyperbole: a *figure of speech* (a trope) that deliberately exaggerates or inflates meaning to achieve particular effects, such as the theatrical tale of Pocahontas by John Smith, who describes her as laying her own head upon his to prevent him

from being clubbed to death (see Smith's *General History of Virginia*), or, to more humorous effect, when Joel Chandler Harris's Uncle Remus describes sleep as an old man "ridin' on my eyeleds."

Iamb: the most common metrical foot in English verse, containing one unstressed syllable followed by a stressed syllable (e.g., between, achieve).

Idyll: traditionally, a short pastoral poem that idealizes country life, conveying impressions of innocence and happiness. See, for example, Longfellow's "The Village Blacksmith."

Image: the recreation in words of objects perceived by the senses, sometimes thought of as "pictures," although other senses besides sight are involved. Besides this literal application, the term also refers more generally to the descriptive effects of figurative language, especially in *metaphor* and *simile*.

Incantation: a chant or recitation of words that are believed to have magical power. A poem can achieve an "incantatory" effect through a compelling rhyme scheme and other repetitive patterns. For example, see Edgar Allan Poe's "The Raven."

Indentured Servant/Apprentice: a person who was bound to work without pay for a fixed period of time; indentures were usually at least somewhat voluntary, but the contracts were often liable to be sold to different employers with little to no consultation with the servant or apprentice in question.

Indian Expulsion: the forced removal of Indigenous people from their homes to facilitate settlement by predominantly white settlers, codified in the 1830 Indian Removal Act; also called Indian Removal.

Indian Territory: areas in modern-day Oklahoma, Missouri, and Kansas designated by the Federal government for Indigenous nations who had been forcibly removed from their homes; the territory shifted continuously throughout the eighteenth and nineteenth centuries, decreasing over time.

Indigenous people: the inhabitants of a region who are the descendants of the people who lived there prior to another ethnic group settling or colonizing that region.

Individualism: an ideology that emphasizes self-reliance, independence, and the value of one's own instincts and intelligence, especially with respect to aesthetic, social, or ethical judgments; in religion, an ideology that affirms the individual as the sole source of an authentic relationship with God, and the sole arbiter of one's social and intellectual responsibilities.

Irony: a subtle form of humor in which a statement is understood to convey a quite different (and often entirely opposite) meaning. A writer achieves this by carefully making sure that the statement occurs in a context which undermines or twists the statement's "literal" meaning. *Hyperbole* and *litotes* are often used for ironic effect. *Sarcasm* is a particularly strong or crude form of irony (usually spoken), in which the meaning is conveyed largely by the tone of voice adopted; something said sarcastically is meant clearly to imply its opposite.

See, for example, Washington Irving's *History of New York*, in which the narrator employs irony to relate one of the more disastrous effects that European colonization had on Indigenous people:

> ... no sooner did the benevolent inhabitants of Europe behold their sad condition than they immediately went to work to ameliorate and improve it. They ... made known to them a thousand remedies, by which the most inveterate diseases are alleviated and healed, and that they might comprehend the benefits and enjoy the comforts of these medicines, they previously introduced among them the diseases, which they were calculated to cure. By these and a variety of other methods was the condition of these poor savages, wonderfully improved. ...

Künstlerroman: from the German for *Künstler* (artist) and *Roman* (novel), a narrative (often in novel form) about the personal and aesthetic growth of an artist, as he or she apprentices in an art form (music, literature, painting, or sculpture). See, for example, Louisa May Alcott's *Little Women*.

Jacksonian Democracy: a nineteenth-century political movement associated with the presidency of Andrew Jackson; the movement saw expanded suffrage (for white men), a hands-off approach to the economy, and aggressive expansionism. While the movement had an egalitarian drive, many changes came at the expense of black and Indigenous people.

Jeffersonian Democracy: a late eighteenth-century and early nineteenth-century political movement named after Thomas Jefferson whose advocates staunchly supported the common people and ideas of republicanism, the tenets of which underpinned the values of the Democratic-Republican Party. See also *Democratic-Republican Party*, *Republicanism*.

Jeremiad: a literary work, often a sermon or speech, that expresses mourning, sorrow, or moral and spiritual disapproval; the form laments or decries perceived social or moral evils and prophesies doom unless the supposedly more wholesome spirit of an earlier time can be reawakened.

Jesuit: a member of the Society of Jesus, an order of the Roman Catholic Church; founded in the mid-sixteenth century during the rise of Protestantism, the order professed total obedience to the pope and sought to advance the Catholic faith, often by education or missionary activity.

Jim Crow: comic character commonly depicted by blackface performers in minstrel shows in the mid-nineteenth century; due to the popularity of such shows, "Jim Crow" was often used as a racist epithet for African Americans, and in the late nineteenth century the term came to refer to the legal and social systems that enforced racial segregation in southern states.

Know-Nothing Movement: an anti-immigrant and anti-Catholic movement that formed in the mid-nineteenth century in opposition to widespread German and Irish immigration.

Ku Klux Klan: a white supremacist group that emerged in the South in the wake of the Civil War and whose early members used organized violence, terror, and murder as a way to intimidate and abuse formerly enslaved people; the initial Klan's activities declined by the early 1880s, but there have been various resurgences throughout the twentieth and twenty-first centuries.

Ledger Art/Ledger Drawing: narrative drawings developed by the Indigenous nations of the Great Plains as a means of historical representation; made with pencil, ink, crayon, and/or watercolor, and drawn on the pages of old ledgers (i.e., account books) that had earlier been used by white settlers. The practice flourished from the 1860s to the 1920s, continuing a long history of recording oral histories pictorially.

Litotes: a *figure of speech* (a trope) in which a writer deliberately uses understatement to paradoxically highlight significance, or, conversely, to convey an ironic attitude; this is often accomplished by affirming something through the negation of the opposite thing. For example, when the narrator of Melville's "Bartleby, the Scrivener" states that he was "not unemployed" by John Jacob Astor and "not insensible" to Astor's good opinion, the oddly constructed understatements cause the reader to pause, even stumble, and to call the narrator's reliability or purpose into question.

Local Color: a style of writing from the latter half of the nineteenth century that captures the character of a specific locale and the people who live there; practitioners sought to reproduce regional dialects and to give color to distinctive features of landscape, custom, and folklore. See also *Regionalism*.

Loyalist: a colonist who remained loyal to Britain in the American War of Independence. See also *Tory*.

Lyric: a poem, usually short, expressing an individual speaker's feelings or private thoughts. Originally a song performed with accompaniment on a lyre, the lyric poem is often noted for musicality of rhyme and rhythm. The lyric genre includes a variety of forms, including the *sonnet*, the *elegy*, the *ode*, and the *hymn*.

Manifest Destiny: a term, originating in the 1840s, used to communicate the belief that the United States was destined to expand westward across the North American continent; the doctrine of expansionism was couched in the terms of moral duty and God-given destiny, and its implementation had dire consequences for Indigenous and Hispanic people.

Mason-Dixon Line: Eighteenth-century survey line separating Pennsylvania and Delaware from Maryland and Virginia. In the *antebellum* United States, it and the Ohio River formed much of the dividing line between free and slave states and hence between North and South.

Mass: within Christianity, a church service that includes the sacrament of the Eucharist (Holy Communion), in which bread and wine are consumed; these are believed by those of many Christian denominations, especially Roman Catholics, to have been transubstantiated into the body and blood of Christ. Protestants do not generally use the term "Mass" and are more likely to believe that the bread and wine merely symbolize the body and blood.

Mayflower Compact: a document signed in 1620 aboard the *Mayflower* before it landed at Plymouth that committed the settlers to majority-rule government.

Melodrama: originally a term used to describe nineteenth-century plays featuring sensational story lines and a crude separation of characters into moral categories, with the pure and virtuous pitted against evil villains. Early melodramas employed background music throughout the action of the play as a means of heightening the emotional response of the audience. By extension, certain sorts of prose fictions or poems are often described as having melodramatic elements.

Mesoamerica: cultural region of Mexico and most of Central America where the Maya, Aztec, and other Indigenous peoples flourished before the Spanish Conquest. While the peoples of the region shared some cultural traits, geographical and linguistic differences were many.

Mestizo: a term used in Spanish America for a person of mixed Indigenous and European ancestry; from the Spanish word, meaning "mixed."

Metaphor: a *figure of speech* (in this case, a trope) in which a comparison is made or identity is asserted between two unrelated things or actions without the use of "like" or "as." The primary subject is known as the *tenor*; to illuminate its nature, the writer links it to wholly different images, ideas, or actions referred to as the *vehicle*. Unlike a *simile*, which is a direct comparison of two things, a metaphor "fuses" the separate qualities of two things, creating a new idea. For example, Dickinson's "'Hope' is the thing with feathers" is a metaphorical statement. The tenor, or primary subject, is "hope"; the vehicle of the metaphor is the image of an initially unnamed "thing with feathers," a bird. The line fuses the idea of hope with the qualities of a delicate bird perched in the soul and forever singing.

Meter: the pattern of stresses, syllables, and pauses that constitutes the regular rhythm of a line of verse. The meter of a poem is determined by identifying the stressed and unstressed syllables in a line of verse, and grouping them into recurring units known as feet. See also *accent*, *accentual-syllabic verse*, *foot*, and *scansion*.

Methodist: a member of a Protestant denomination formed in the eighteenth century as part of the religious movement led by John and Charles Wesley. Originally a sect within the Church of England, Methodism entailed enthusiastic evangelism, a strong emphasis on free will, and a strict, methodical regimen of Christian worship and living.

Metonymy: a *figure of speech* (a trope), meaning "change of name," in which a writer refers to an object or idea by substituting the name of another object or idea closely associated with it: for example, the substitution of "crown" for monarchy, "the press" for journalism, or "the pen" for writing. *Synecdoche* (see below) is a kind of metonymy.

Middle Passage: in the slave trade, the transatlantic journey from the coasts of Africa to the Americas and the West Indies; for the enslaved people in the slave ships, the one- to two-month voyage was horrific, brutal, and often deadly.

Minstrel Show/Minstrelsy: a form of Vaudeville theater popularized in the mid-nineteenth century that featured entertainers performing in blackface.

Miscegenation: the mixing of different racial or ethnic groups, or sexual relationships or reproduction between individuals of those groups, especially between white and non-white people; the term was coined in 1863.

Missouri Compromise: a deal made by Congress in 1820 to resolve the political imbalance that would have resulted if Missouri was admitted as a slave state; Maine was admitted as a free state, and slavery was prohibited thereafter anywhere north of Missouri's southern border.

Monologue: words spoken by a character to him or herself or to an audience directly.

Mood: This can describe the writer's attitude, implied or expressed, toward the subject (see *tone* below); or it may refer to the atmosphere that a writer creates in a passage of description or narration.

Mormonism: the teachings and doctrines of the Latter-Day Saint movement; started by Joseph Smith in the 1820s, Mormon theology embraces as sacred scripture both the Bible and the Book of Mormon, the latter of which Smith claimed to have translated from an ancient record shown to him by an angel.

Motif: an idea, image, action, or plot element that recurs throughout a literary work, creating new levels of meaning and strengthening structural coherence. The term is taken from music, where it describes recurring melodies or themes. See also *theme*.

Mulatto: term for a person with one white and one black parent; more loosely, a person with the appearance of being mixed-race. The designation is today considered offensive.

Myth: a traditional story that provides an explanation for a society or culture's early history or spiritual beliefs, or features of the natural world, usually involving a supernatural element of some kind.

Narrative Perspective: in fiction, the point of view from which the story is narrated. A first-person narrative is recounted using *I* and *me*, whereas a third-person narrative is recounted using *he*, *she*, *they*, and so on. When a narrative is written in the third person and the narrative voice evidently "knows" all that is being done and thought, the story is typically described as being recounted by an "omniscient narrator."

Neoclassical: adapted from or substantially influenced by the cultures of ancient Greece and Rome. The term *neoclassical* is often used to describe the ideals of eighteenth-century writers, thinkers, and artists who looked to ancient Greek and Roman civilization for models.

Non-Alphabetic Literature: a transmission or recording of knowledge, or a literary expression, that is inscribed without employing an alphabet; Indigenous literacies of this sort include objects such as baskets, wampum, pottery, tattoos, textiles, pictographs, and rock art.

Nonconformist: general term used to describe one who does not subscribe to the Church of England.

Obeah: a practice of spiritual healing and witchcraft, or folk medicine, originating among enslaved West Africans and developed in the Caribbean; the practice is more individual than it is collective. See also *Hoodoo*, *Voodoo*.

Ode: in English poetry, a long lyric poem of some gravity that is typically elevated in tone and complex in structure. Originally a classical poetic form, the ode was used by the Greeks and Romans to convey serious themes; later imitations of the form stemmed from the examples set by the Greek poet Pindar and the Roman poet Horace.

Onomatopoeia: a *figure of speech* (a scheme) in which a word "imitates" a sound, or in which the sound of a word seems to reflect its meaning.

Oral Literature: a form of literature communicated by spoken word and passed down from generation to generation; often taking the form of stories, oral literature may serve as a repository of history, mythology, spiritual belief, etc.

Oratory: the formal art of public speaking, especially with eloquence and with an eye toward persuasion.

Over-Soul: all-encompassing spiritual "unity" that animates the universe and resides in each human soul, and through which all of humanity is connected. The term was coined in 1841 by Ralph Waldo Emerson, but the concept is also a central principle in a number of Eastern religions.

Oxymoron: a *figure of speech* (a trope) in which two words whose meanings seem contradictory are placed together: for example, Fitzgerald's description in *The Great Gatsby* of Wolfsheim eating with "ferocious delicacy."

Parliament: in Britain, the combined legislative body, comprising both the House of Commons (the "lower house," made up of elected officials) and the House of Lords (the "upper house," comprised of members of the aristocracy). Unlike the American system, the British parliamentary system does not separate the executive and legislative functions of government.

Parody: a close, usually mocking imitation of a particular literary work, or of the well-known style of a particular author, in order to expose or magnify weaknesses. Parody is a form of satire—that is, humor that may ridicule and scorn its object. The poem "Counter-Jumps" parodies Whitman's sprawling "Song of Myself":   "I am the shop, and the counter, and the till, / But particularly the last. / And I explore and rummage the till, and am at home in it."

Pastiche: a discourse which borrows or imitates other writers' characters, forms, style, or ideas. Unlike a parody, a pastiche is usually intended as a compliment to the original writer.

Pastoral: in general, pertaining to country life; in prose, drama, and poetry, a stylized type of writing that idealizes the lives and innocence of country people, particularly shepherds and shepherdesses. See *idyll*.

Pathetic Fallacy: a form of personification in which inanimate objects are given human emotions: for example, rain clouds "weeping." The word "fallacy" in this connection is intended to suggest the distortion of reality or the false emotion that may result from an exaggerated use of personification.

Pathos: the emotional quality of a discourse; or the ability of a discourse to appeal to our emotions. It is usually applied to the mood conveyed by images of pain, suffering, or loss that arouse feelings of pity or sorrow in the reader.

Persona: the assumed identity or "speaking voice" that a writer projects in a discourse. The term "persona" literally means "mask." Even when a writer speaks in the first person, we should be aware that the attitudes or opinions we hear may not necessarily be those of the writer in real life. Much of Herman Melville's shorter fiction and essays, especially "Bartleby, the Scrivener" and *Benito Cereno*, makes extensive use of personas.

Personification: a *figure of speech* (a trope) in which a writer refers to inanimate objects, ideas, or animals as if they were human, or creates a human figure to represent an abstract entity such as Philosophy or Peace. For example, see Allen Ginsberg's "America": "America, when will you be angelic? / When will you take off your clothes?"

Picaresque: a genre of fiction that deals with the adventures of an unscrupulous but charismatic individual.

Pilgrims: Puritans who broke with the Church of England and settled the Plymouth Colony in 1620; their break from the church led to them being labeled Separatists. See also *Separatists*.

Pioneer: a person who is (or is deemed to be) among the first to explore or settle a new or unknown region or territory; the term is often used without considering prior Indigenous habitation.

Plantation: a large-scale agricultural enterprise that produces cash crops; in the American south, plantations varied greatly in size, but all relied on the forced labor of enslaved people. The term was also used in the seventeenth and eighteenth centuries to refer to the American colonies themselves.

Plot: the organization of story materials within a literary work. The order in which story material is presented (especially causes and consequences); the inclusion of elements that allow or encourage the reader or audience to form expectations as to what is likely to happen; the decision to present some story material through exposition rather than in more extended form as part of the main action of the narrative—all these are matters of plotting.

Postbellum: after, or existing after, a war; in American usage, especially the American Civil War. See also *antebellum*.

Predestination: the Calvinist belief that God has predetermined who is saved and who is damned. The belief thereby advances a doctrine of grace (rather than a doctrine of works): the actions, or works, of a person while alive have no influence on their fate. Rather, their salvation comes as a predetermined gift from God. See also *Calvinism*.

Presbyterian: term applied to a group of Protestants who advocated replacing the traditional hierarchy of the church (in which bishops and archbishops governed lower-level members of the clergy) with a system in which all presbyters, or ministers, would be equal; the Presbyterians were strongly influenced by Calvinism.

Prosody: the study and analysis of meter, rhythm, rhyme, stanzaic pattern, and other devices of versification.

Protagonist: the central character in a literary work.

Protestant Reformation/Reformation: a religious movement of the sixteenth century that set out to reform the Roman Catholic Church, and which resulted in the establishment of various Protestant churches throughout Europe and Britain and, eventually, its colonies; the movement effected a profound religious, political, intellectual, and cultural upheaval. See also *Protestantism*.

Protestantism: a branch of Christianity that formed as a result of the Protestant Reformation in the early sixteenth century. Protestant denominations reject the authority of the pope and of the Catholic Church, and they tend to place a greater emphasis than the Catholic Church on the Bible as the primary or sole source of religious doctrine.

Pun: a play on words, in which a word with two or more distinct meanings, or two words with similar sounds, may create humorous ambiguities.

Puritan: term applied to sixteenth- and seventeenth-century Protestants who felt that the Anglican Church was too similar to the Catholic Church and required further reform. Puritans played a leading role in the settlement of many New England colonies, including the Massachusetts Bay Colony in 1630. See also *Separatists*.

Quakerism/Religious Society of Friends: a Protestant sect committed to pacifism and the spiritual equality of all worshippers, and whose members stressed a direct relationship with God through Jesus Christ; many Quakers were also abolitionists and advocates of various social reforms.

Radical Republican: a mid-nineteenth century group within the Republican Party that, prior to the Civil War, was vehemently opposed to slavery and any form of compromise with the south; the group later advocated equal civil and political rights for former enslaved people during Reconstruction. See also *Republican Party*.

Realism: a literary movement that gained in prominence with the rise of social reform movements of the late nineteenth century. Proponents rejected the grandeur, sentimentalism, and idealism of Romanticism in favor of logic, fact, and objectivity; works feature a candid and detailed treatment of ordinary people living everyday lives. Rebecca Harding Davis's "Life in the Iron-Mills" (1861) provides a prime early example.

Reconstruction: the period from 1865 to 1877 during which the states that had seceded from the United States during the Civil War were readmitted to the federal system of government and reorganized; also, the process by which this reorganization was effected. The reorganization of the former secessionist states prominently featured efforts to secure the rights and promote the welfare of formerly enslaved people, including the ratification of the Fourteenth and Fifteenth Amendments. These efforts, however, were largely negated by the violent reimposition of white supremacy throughout the South and by the federal government's abandonment of Reconstruction in 1877.

Regionalism: a category of literature that emerged after the Civil War and that centers on the distinctiveness of regional, or local, culture and geography, rather than on broader national themes and issues. Bret Harte's coverage of the California Gold Rush in "The Luck of Roaring Camp" (1868) is an example. See also *local color*.

Renaissance, American: a term coined by literary critic F.O. Matthiessen to refer to the period in American literature between 1830 and 1865 during which, in Matthiessen's opinion, five main writers—Ralph Waldo Emerson, Nathaniel Hawthorne, Herman Melville, Henry David Thoreau, and Walt Whitman—helped to forge a literary style that was unique to the national spirit of the United States. Subsequent critics have taken Matthiessen to task for his exclusion of women and of African American and Indigenous writers, and have much broadened the list of those responsible for defining a national literature of the period. Some have also questioned whether such a uniform literature even exists. See also *Transcendentalism*, *Romanticism*.

Republican Party: a political party established in 1854 by a group of Whigs, Democrats, and other politicians who left their respective parties to form a party opposed to slavery's expansion. The Republicans nominated Abraham Lincoln as their presidential candidate in 1860; after the Civil War, the party sought for a time to protect and promote the rights of newly emancipated African Americans during Reconstruction, but the party gradually became more oriented toward economic and industrial growth. Not to be confused with the earlier political party of the same name that formed in opposition to the Federalist Party in the early 1790s. See also *Democratic-Republican Party*.

Republicanism: a political philosophy of the eighteenth century that rejected aristocracies and monarchies, and instead stressed liberty, the virtue of common citizens, and the uninfringeable rights of individuals. See also *Jeffersonian democracy*.

Reservation: an area of land set aside for a special purpose; in the context of America's Indigenous peoples, reservations were created by treaty, legislation, or executive order, and very often involved the forcible removal of Indigenous populations from their homelands.

Rhetoric: in classical Greece and Rome, the art of persuasion and public speaking. From the Middle Ages onwards, the study of rhetoric gave greater attention to style, particularly figures of speech. Today in poetics, the term rhetoric may encompass not only figures of speech, but also the persuasive effects of forms, sounds, and word choices.

Rhyme: the repetition of identical or similar sounds, usually in pairs and generally at the ends of metrical lines.

> **End-Rhyme:**   a rhyming word or syllable at the end of a line.
>
> **Eye-Rhyme:**   rhyming that pairs words whose spellings are alike but whose pronunciations are different: for example, move/love.
>
> **Feminine Rhyme:**   a two-syllable (also known as "double") rhyme. The first syllable is stressed and the second unstressed: for example, hasty/tasty. See also *triple rhyme*.

Interlocking Rhyme: the repetition of rhymes from one stanza to the next, creating links that add to the poem's continuity and coherence.

Internal Rhyme: the placement of rhyming words within lines so that at least two words in a line rhyme with each other.

Masculine Rhyme: a correspondence of sound between the final stressed syllables at the end of two or more lines, as in grieve/leave, arr-ive/sur-vive.

Slant Rhyme: an imperfect or partial rhyme (also known as "near" or "half" rhyme) in which the final consonants of stressed syllables match but the vowel sounds do not. E.g., spoiled/spilled, taint/stint.

Triple Rhyme: a three-syllable rhyme in which the first syllable of each rhyme-word is stressed and the other two unstressed (e.g., greenery/scenery).

True Rhyme: a rhyme in which everything but the initial consonant matches perfectly in sound and spelling.

Rhythm: in speech, the arrangement of stressed and unstressed syllables creates units of sound. In song or verse, these units usually form a regular rhythmic pattern, a kind of beat, described in prosody as *meter*.

Romanticism: a major social and cultural movement that originated in Europe as a reaction against the rationalism of the Enlightenment and that shaped much of Western artistic thought in the late eighteenth and nineteenth centuries; the movement emphasized the essential roles played by subjectivity and emotion in knowing and experiencing the world. Romantic works in literature tend to elevate the individual, to disparage the conventional, and to stress the value of contact with the natural world. Examples include William Cullen Bryant's poem "Thanatopsis" (1817). See also *Transcendentalism*.

Sarcasm: See *irony*.

Satire: literary work designed to make fun of or seriously criticize its subject. According to many literary theories of the Renaissance and neoclassical periods, the ridicule through satire of a certain sort of behavior may function for the reader or audience as a corrective of such behavior.

Scansion: the formal analysis of patterns of rhythm and rhyme in poetry. Each line of verse will have a certain number of fairly regular "beats" consisting of alternating stressed and unstressed syllables. To "scan" a poem is to count the beats in each line, to mark stressed and unstressed syllables and

indicate their combination into "feet," to note pauses, and to identify rhyme schemes with letters of the alphabet.

Scheme: See *figures of speech*.

Secession: the action of withdrawing from membership of a political state, religious organization, or other similar alliance; in the United States, the insurrectionist withdrawal of eleven Southern states from the federal government that brought about the Civil War.

Second Great Awakening: a widespread Protestant religious revival during the early nineteenth century; the heart of the new evangelical movement stressed God's benevolence and humans' ability to endeavor to save themselves (where earlier Calvinist tradition emphasized the deep depravity of humanity, the inability to alter our fate, and salvation through God). See *Great Awakening*.

Sermon: a discourse based upon scripture for the purpose of giving religious instruction or encouragement.

Seneca Falls Convention: 1848 New York convention often viewed as having launched the women's suffrage movement in America.

Separatists: a Protestant group in the Calvinist tradition whose members believed that the Church of England was too corrupt to be reformed and that it was necessary to separate from it; the Pilgrims aboard the *Mayflower* were Separatists. See also *Calvinism*, *Pilgrims*.

Simile: a *figure of speech* (a trope) which makes an explicit comparison between a particular object and another object or idea that is similar in some (often unexpected) way. A simile always uses "like" or "as" to signal the connection. Compare with *metaphor*.

Slave Narrative: an autobiographical account of the experiences of an enslaved person; numerous slave narratives were published in the United States from the late-eighteenth to the mid-nineteenth century, and they contributed greatly to the rise of the abolitionist movement and the spread of opposition to slavery.

Sonnet: a highly structured lyric poem, which normally has fourteen lines of iambic pentameter. See the glossary of poetic terms in this anthology's online component.

Sons of Liberty: a loosely connected group of underground, grassroots organizations in Colonial America that formed in response to the Stamp Act with the goal of undermining British rule through acts of radical civil disobedience.

Spiritual: a genre of religious song that grew out of the collective experience of enslaved people and was adopted by black Christians of the southern United States especially; blending African, American, and African American musical elements, spirituals often express ideals of hope, justice, and salvation in the face of the oppressive experience of enslavement. See also *gospel*, *work song*.

Spiritualism: a nineteenth-century religious movement, especially popular among the upper and middle classes, whose adherents believed it was possible for the living to communicate with the spirits of the dead. It was closely linked to widely discussed scientific and pseudoscientific ideas.

Stanza: any lines of verse that are grouped together in a poem and separated from other similarly structured groups by a space.

Stress: See *accent*.

Sublime: a concept of the qualities of grandeur, power, and awe that may be inherent in or produced by undomesticated nature or great art. The sublime is generally thought of as higher and loftier than something that is merely beautiful; the concept plays a central role in many Romantic works.

Subplot: a line of story that is subordinate to the main storyline of a narrative. (Note that properly speaking a subplot is a category of story material, not of plot.)

Subtext: implied or suggested meaning of a passage of text, or of an entire work.

Suffrage: the right to vote.

Sun Dance: a large annual ceremony practiced primarily by Plains Indigenous cultures to honor the earth and sun, prove bravery, and pray for prowess in, for example, hunting or fighting; over several days, individuals endure exhaustion and self-torture as a path to spiritual renewal and enhanced prestige, or to establish stronger personal or tribal relationships.

Syllable: vocal sound or group of sounds forming a unit of speech; a syllable may be formed with a single effort of articulation. Some syllables consist of a single phoneme (e.g., the word *I*, or the first syllable in the word *u-ni-ty*) but others may be made up of several phonemes (as with one-syllable words such as *lengths*, *splurged*, and *through*). By contrast, the much shorter words *ago*, *any*, and *open* each have two syllables.

Symbol: a word, image, or idea that represents something more, or other, than for what it at first appears to stand. Like metaphor, the symbol extends meaning; but while the components of a metaphor are bound in a specific relationship, a

symbol may have a range of connotations. For example, the image of a rose may call forth associations of love, passion, transience, fragility, youth, and beauty, among others. Often, such meaning is implied rather than explicitly stated; indeed, much of the power of symbolic language lies in the reader's ability to make meaningful sense of it.

Synecdoche: a kind of *metonymy* in which a writer substitutes the name of a part of something to signify the whole: for example, "sail" for ship or "hand" for a member of the ship's crew.

Tall Tale: a form of folktale in which unbelievably exaggerated details are related as though they are historically factual. Tall tales may describe one's own supposed adventures or the adventures of a larger-than-life folk hero; examples of the latter include narratives about figures such as Davy Crockett and Johnny Appleseed, as well as African American oral stories such as "Big Sixteen."

Theme: the governing idea of a discourse, conveyed through the development of the subject, and through the recurrence of certain words, sounds, or metrical patterns. See also *motif*.

Third-Person Narrative: See *narrative perspective*.

Thirteenth Amendment: an 1865 amendment to the U.S. Constitution that abolished slavery throughout the nation; it was the first of three Reconstruction amendments following the Civil War that attempted to secure equal status and rights for African Americans.

Three-Fifths Clause: a provision in the U.S. Constitution that allowed for three-fifths of the enslaved population to be counted when determining each state's representation in the House of Representatives, thereby bolstering southern states' political power.

Tone: the writer's attitude toward a given subject or audience, as expressed through an authorial persona or "voice." Tone can be projected through particular choices of wording, imagery, figures of speech, and rhythmic devices. Compare *mood*.

Tory: a person who supported the British Crown; more generally, a political conservative who supports traditional political and social institutions. See also *Loyalist*.

Tragedy: in the traditional definition originating in discussions of ancient Greek drama, a serious narrative recounting the downfall of the protagonist. More loosely, the term has been applied to a wide variety of literary forms in which the tone is predominantly a dark one and the narrative does not end happily.

Trail of Tears: the expression used generally to invoke the suffering that Indigenous nations experienced when forcibly removed from their ancestral lands and driven, despite the threats of disease, exposure, starvation, and death, to "Indian Territory" west of the Mississippi; more specifically, the route traversed by the Cherokee nation during its expulsion in 1838 and 1839. See also *Indian Expulsion*, *Indian Territory*.

Transcendentalism: a philosophical and literary movement, centered mainly in New England, that flourished in the 1830s and 1840s; linked with the Romantic movement, its adherents held to a mystical, idealistic belief in the unity of all creation and the innate goodness of nature and of people, as well as a trust in one's own insight and intellect as a pathway to the deepest truths. Its members included Margaret Fuller, Ralph Waldo Emerson, and Henry David Thoreau. See also *Romanticism*.

Trickster: a figure in the mythology or oral literature of many cultures, including Indigenous peoples and African Americans, that turns its intelligence toward playing tricks or breaking rules and challenging conventions; in different cultures the figure takes different forms—often an animal such as Coyote or Raven (in various Indigenous cultures) or Brer Rabbit (in African American folklore).

Trope: any figure of speech that plays on our understandings of words to extend, alter, or transform "literal" meaning. Common tropes include *metaphor*, *simile*, *personification*, *hyperbole*, *metonymy*, *oxymoron*, *synecdoche*, and *irony*. See also *figures of speech*.

Uncle Sam: a personification of the United States and its people, typically represented as a white man with a severe gaze, white hair and chin whiskers, dressed in red, white, and blue; a symbol of American patriotism.

Uncle Tom: the enslaved title character of Harriet Beecher Stowe's 1852 novel; theatrical adaptations of the novel frequently transformed Uncle Tom into a subservient apologist for slavery, and the term "Uncle Tom" subsequently became a derogatory epithet for someone who accepts or willingly participates in their own subordination.

Underground Railroad: the secret network of support and safehouses by means of which many enslaved people escaped to the North, to Canada, or (in some cases) to Mexico.

Union: the United States; specifically, the group of northern states that were opposed to slavery and that remained loyal to the Federal government during the Civil War.

Unitarianism: a Christian movement beginning in the late eighteenth century that emphasized free will and universal salvation: the idea that all human beings can and will be saved, regardless of whether or not they belong to or accept the beliefs of a particular church. The movement was particularly influential upon Transcendentalists in the early nineteenth century (though it was also criticized by several of them, including by Emerson, himself a former Unitarian minister).

Verse: a general term for works of poetry, usually referring to poems that incorporate some kind of metrical structure. The term may also describe a line of poetry, though more frequently it is applied to a stanza.

Visual Literature: a form of literature in which images make up the primary means of communication, for example, sign language, rock art, winter counts, ledger art, etc.

Voodoo, or Vodou: a religion developed in the sixteenth century in Hispaniola (now Haiti) by enslaved Africans that blends elements from African religions with aspects of Roman Catholicism. See also *Hoodoo*, *Obeah*.

Wampum: beads made from shells, often threaded together in strings or belts, used by Indigenous peoples for ornamental, ceremonial, and record-keeping purposes.

Whig: during the American Revolution, a supporter of American independence; more generally, a supporter of the British or American Whig Party or its principles.

Whig Party: a political party that emerged in 1834 in opposition to the political platform of Andrew Jackson and his strong executive power; the party splintered in the 1850s over the issue of slavery, the northern faction joining with antislavery Democrats to form the Republican Party. See also *Democratic Party*, *Democratic-Republican Party*.

Winter Count: a pictographic record or calendar that records the major events in the history of an Indigenous community, especially Indigenous nations of the Plains.

Work Song: a song sung by physical laborers, especially enslaved people, as they worked, and usually linked rhythmically to the work being done. See also *spiritual*.

Yankee: a New Englander or, more generally, a person from a Northern state; outside of the United States, the term is often used to refer to any American.

Zeugma: a *figure of speech* (trope) in which one word links or "yokes" two others in the same sentence, often to comic or ironic effect. For example, a verb may govern two objects, as when Twain describes the fight between Tom Sawyer and the "new boy": "They ... covered themselves with dust and glory."

MAPS

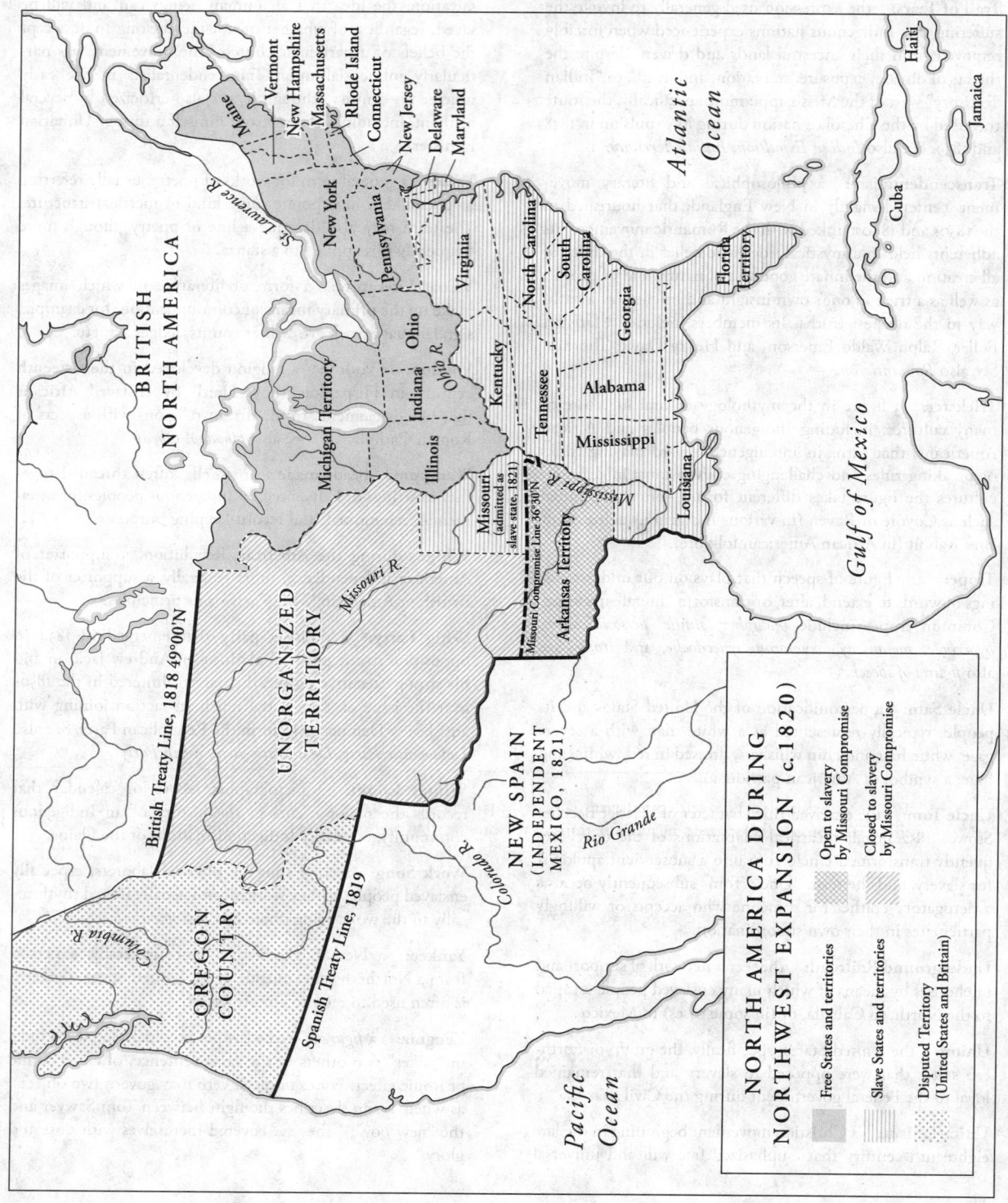

NORTH AMERICA DURING NORTHWEST EXPANSION (c. 1820)

Free States and territories

Slave States and territories

Disputed Territory (United States and Britain)

Open to slavery by Missouri Compromise

Closed to slavery by Missouri Compromise

BRITISH NORTH AMERICA

Atlantic Ocean

Gulf of Mexico

Pacific Ocean

OREGON COUNTRY

UNORGANIZED TERRITORY

NEW SPAIN (INDEPENDENT MEXICO, 1821)

British Treaty Line, 1818 49°00'N

Spanish Treaty Line, 1819

Columbia R.

Colorado R.

Rio Grande

Missouri R.

Mississippi R.

St. Lawrence R.

Ohio R.

Maine

Vermont

New Hampshire

Massachusetts

Rhode Island

Connecticut

New York

New Jersey

Pennsylvania

Delaware

Maryland

Ohio

Virginia

North Carolina

South Carolina

Georgia

Florida Territory

Michigan Territory

Indiana

Illinois

Kentucky

Tennessee

Alabama

Mississippi

Louisiana

Missouri (admitted as slave state, 1821)

Arkansas Territory

Missouri Compromise Line 36°30'N

Cuba

Haiti

Jamaica

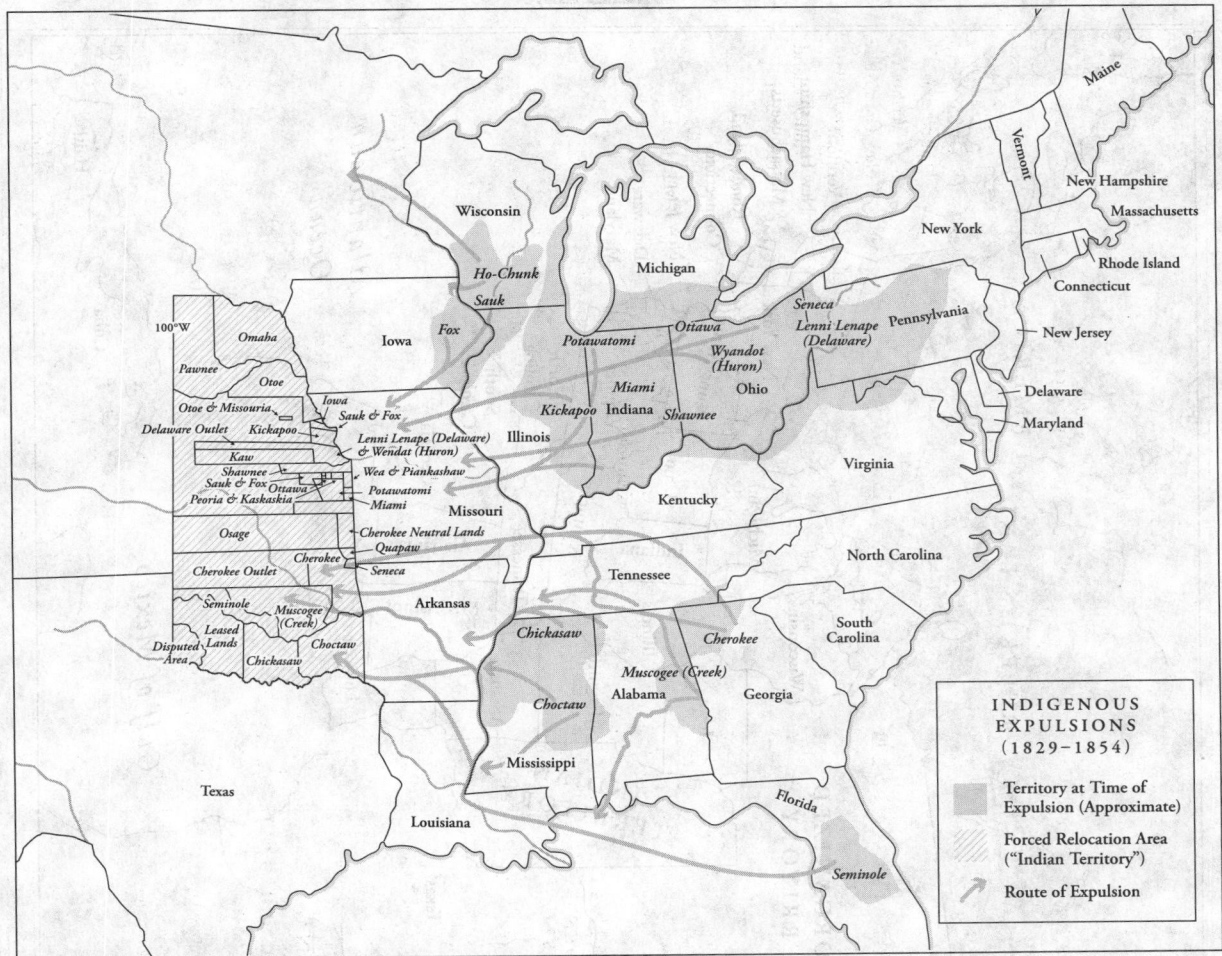

The push westward by U.S. settlers led eventually to the passage in 1830 of the Indian Removal Act, which effectively forced all eastern Indigenous nations to relocate in what was designated as "Indian Territory" west of the Mississippi River. The boundaries of the federally designated territory (and the individual reservations within it) were not static. The territory expanded at first as more and more Indigenous nations were expelled from their homelands; but settler colonization continued, legitimized by government legislation, and the Indian Territory diminished through the remainder of the nineteenth century. It ceased to exist as a legal entity in 1907, when Oklahoma became a state.

In the interest of legibility, the routes of expulsion shown on the map are simplified and mostly uniform. However, this was not usually the case; there were diversions to city centers or forts; not all members of Indigenous nations followed the same route; expulsions happened at different times across decades (including dates before and after those represented here); and some routes were complicated by returns.

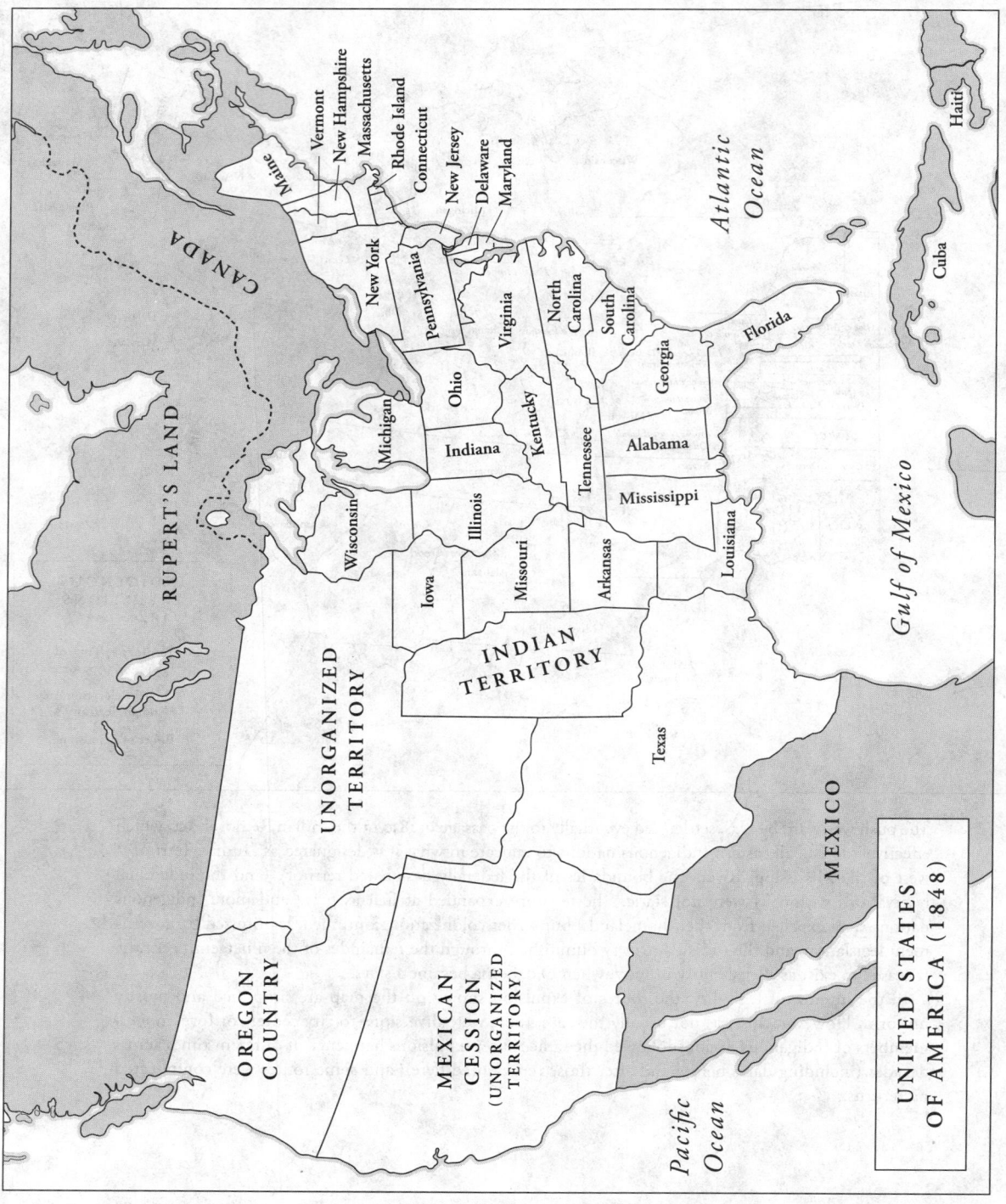

CANADA

RUPERT'S LAND

Maine

Vermont
New Hampshire
Massachusetts
Rhode Island
Connecticut
New Jersey
Delaware
Maryland

New York

Pennsylvania

Virginia

North Carolina

South Carolina

Georgia

Florida

Atlantic Ocean

Haiti

Cuba

Gulf of Mexico

Michigan

Ohio

Indiana

Kentucky

Tennessee

Alabama

Mississippi

Louisiana

Wisconsin

Illinois

Missouri

Arkansas

Iowa

UNORGANIZED TERRITORY

INDIAN TERRITORY

Texas

OREGON COUNTRY

MEXICAN CESSION
(UNORGANIZED TERRITORY)

MEXICO

Pacific Ocean

UNITED STATES
OF AMERICA (1848)

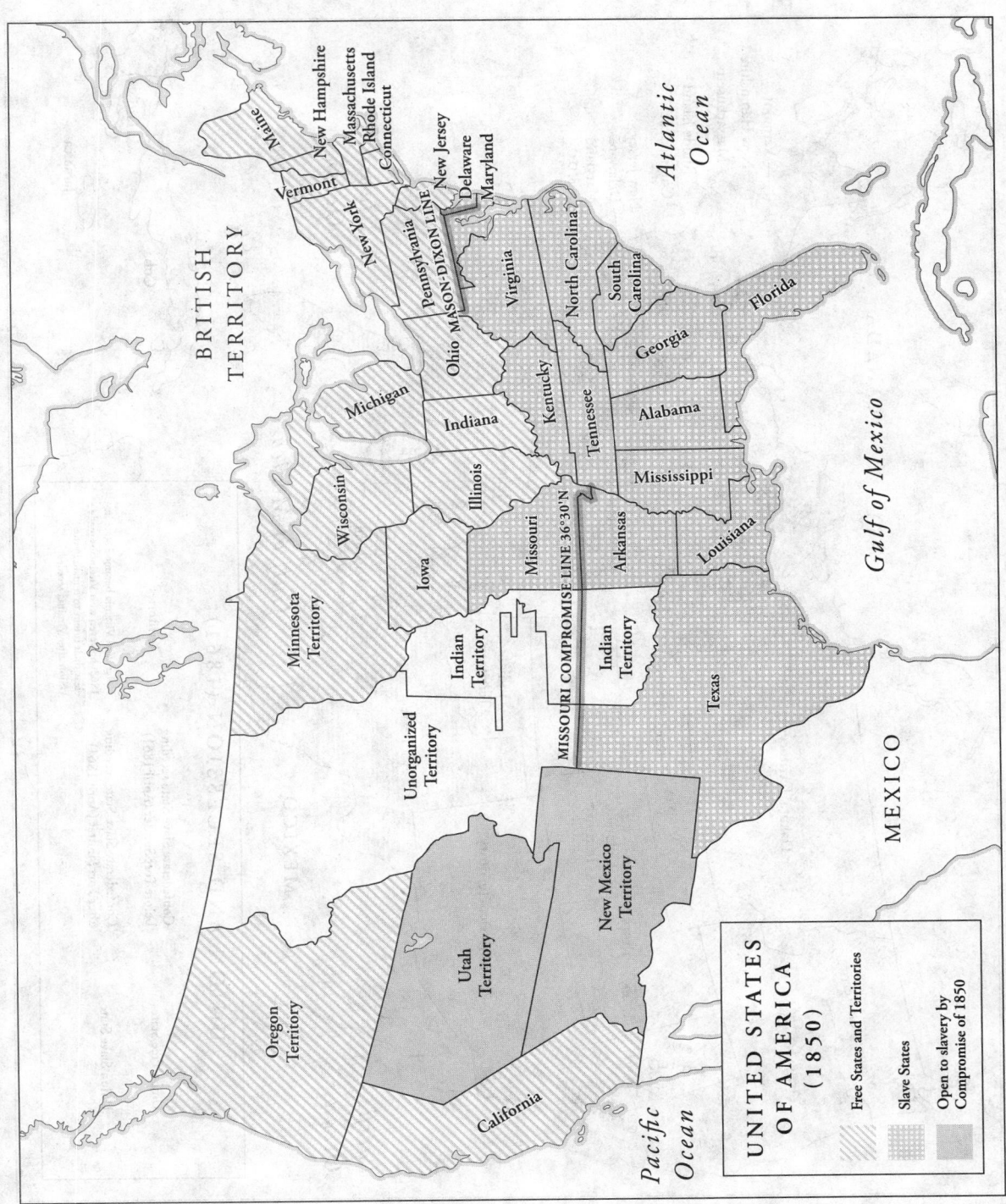

BRITISH TERRITORY

Maine

New Hampshire
Massachusetts
Rhode Island
Connecticut

Vermont

New York

New Jersey
Delaware
Maryland

Pennsylvania

MASON-DIXON LINE

Ohio

Virginia

North Carolina

South Carolina

Georgia

Florida

Atlantic Ocean

Michigan

Indiana

Kentucky

Tennessee

Alabama

Mississippi

Gulf of Mexico

Wisconsin

Illinois

Missouri

Arkansas

Louisiana

Iowa

Minnesota Territory

Indian Territory

MISSOURI COMPROMISE LINE 36°30'N

Indian Territory

Texas

Unorganized Territory

New Mexico Territory

MEXICO

Utah Territory

Oregon Territory

California

Pacific Ocean

UNITED STATES
OF AMERICA
(1850)

Free States and Territories

Slave States

Open to slavery by
Compromise of 1850

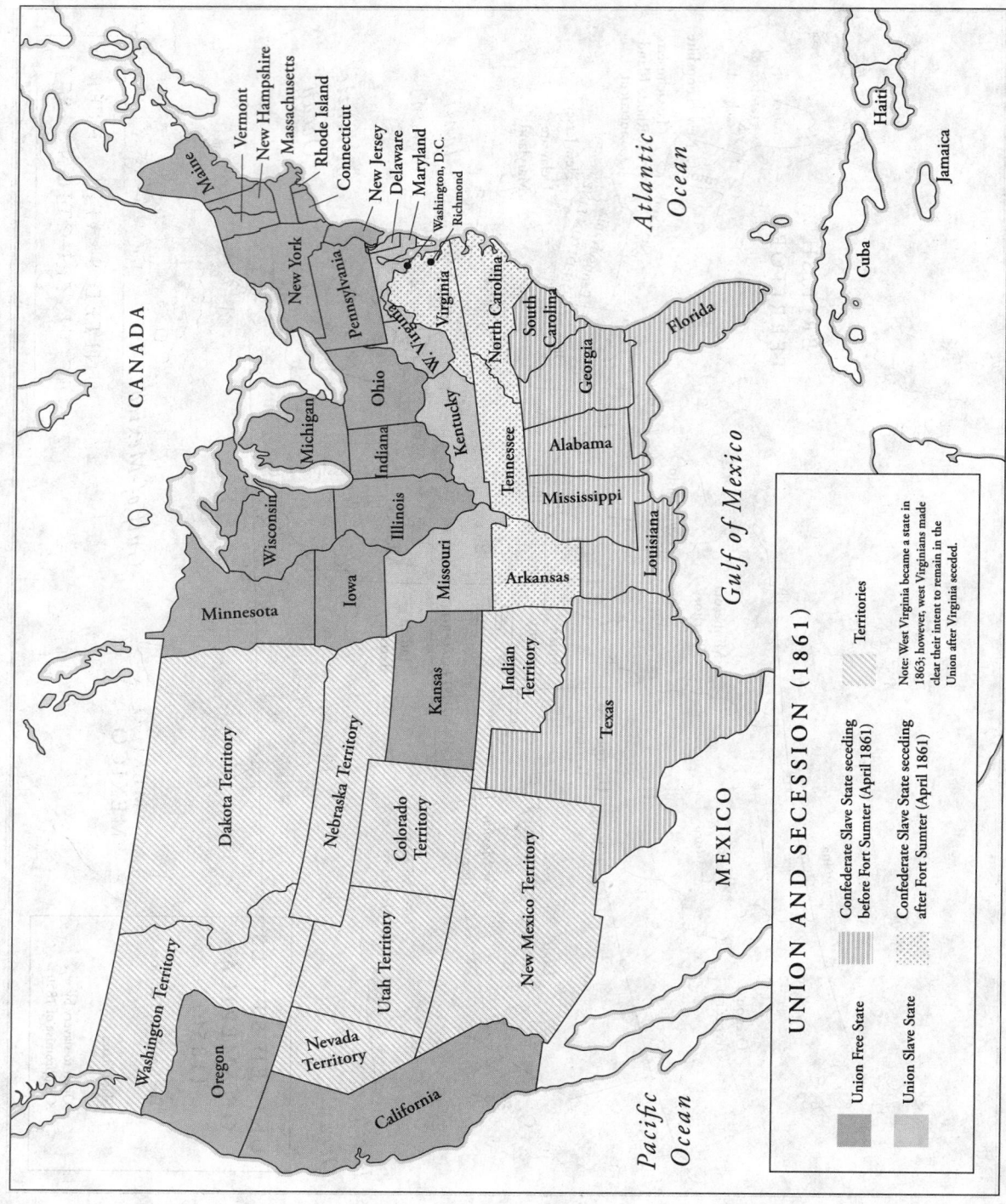

UNION AND SECESSION (1861)

Union Free State

Union Slave State

Confederate Slave State seceding before Fort Sumter (April 1861)

Confederate Slave State seceding after Fort Sumter (April 1861)

Territories

Note: West Virginia became a state in 1863; however, west Virginians made clear their intent to remain in the Union after Virginia seceded.

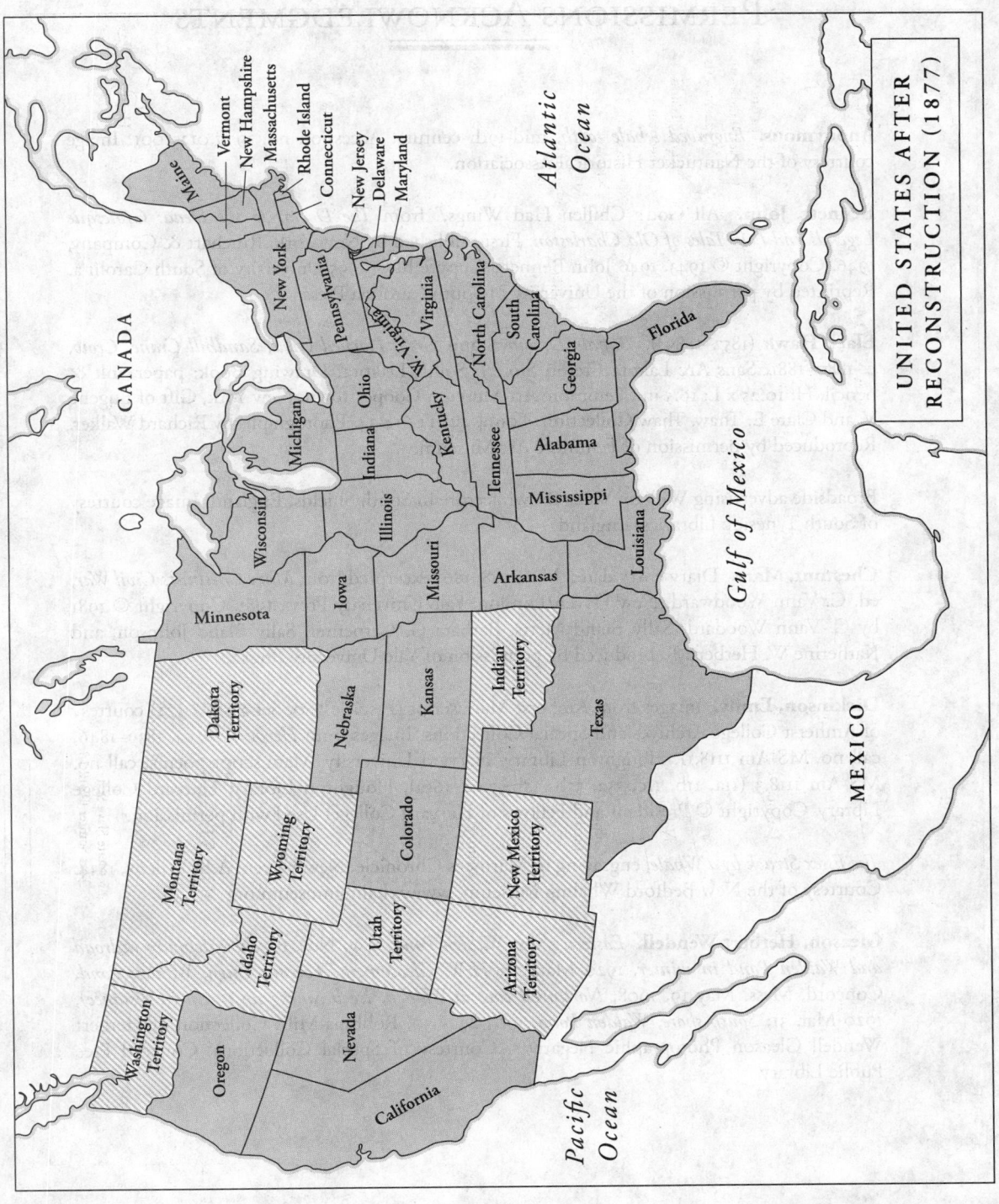

UNITED STATES AFTER RECONSTRUCTION (1877)

CANADA

Maine
Vermont
New Hampshire
Massachusetts
Rhode Island
Connecticut
New York
New Jersey
Delaware
Maryland
Pennsylvania
Virginia
W. Virginia
North Carolina
South Carolina
Georgia
Florida
Michigan
Ohio
Kentucky
Tennessee
Alabama
Indiana
Illinois
Mississippi
Wisconsin
Missouri
Arkansas
Louisiana
Iowa
Minnesota

Dakota
Territory
Nebraska
Kansas
Indian
Territory
Texas

Montana
Territory
Wyoming
Territory
Colorado
New Mexico
Territory

Idaho
Territory
Utah
Territory
Arizona
Territory

Washington
Territory
Oregon
Nevada
California

MEXICO

Atlantic
Ocean

Gulf of Mexico

Pacific
Ocean

Permissions Acknowledgments

Anonymous. *Engraved whale tooth*, mid-19th century. Accession no. 1977.0127.001. Image courtesy of the Nantucket Historical Association.

Bennett, John. "All God's Chillen Had Wings," from *The Doctor to the Dead: Grotesque Legends and Folk Tales of Old Charleston*. First published by New York: Rinehart & Company, 1946. Copyright © 1943, 1946 John Bennett. Copyright © 1995 University of South Carolina. Reprinted by permission of the University of South Carolina Press.

Black Hawk (1852–1889?). *Buffalo Dreamers* and *Great Horned Owls, Sandhill Crane, Crow*, c. 1880–1881, Sans Arc Lakota (Teton Sioux), South Dakota, Drawing Book: paper, ink & pencil, H: 10.25 x L: 16.5 in., Fenimore Art Museum Cooperstown, New York, Gift of Eugene V. and Clare E. Thaw. Thaw Collection. T0614-44, T0614-34. Photographs by Richard Walker. Reproduced by permission of Fenimore Art Museum.

Broadside advertising William Wells Brown lecture in South Shields, England. Image courtesy of South Tyneside Libraries, England.

Chestnut, Mary. Diary entry dated March 18, 1861 excerpted from *Mary Chestnut's Civil War*, ed. C. Vann Woodward. New Haven/London: Yale University Press, 1981. Copyright © 1981 by C. Vann Woodard, Sally Bland Metts, Barbara G. Carpenter, Sally Bland Johnson, and Katherine W. Herbert. Reproduced by permission of Yale University Press.

Dickinson, Emily. Images from Amherst Manuscript (Fascicle #80, Set # 88, # 372) courtesy of Amherst College Archives and Special Collections. Images from *Herbarium*, ca. 1839–1846, call no. MS Am 1118.11, Houghton Library, Harvard University. Manuscript poems, call no. MS Am 1118.3 (11a, 11b, 11c, 35a, 35b, 38b, 74d, 165a), Houghton Library, Harvard College Library. Copyright © President and Fellows of Harvard College. Used with permission.

The Essex Struck by a Whale, engraving in Mariner's Chronicle, New Haven: A.B. Wilcox, 1834. Courtesy of the New Bedford Whaling Museum. www.whalingmuseum.org

Gleason, Herbert Wendell. *Eastern shore, Walden Pond*, 1899 Nov. 6; *The Fitchburg railroad and Walden Pond in winter*, 1920 Mar. 24; *H.W. Gleason at Thoreau's cairn, Walden Pond*, Concord, Mass. May 19, 1908; *Northwest cove of Walden, ice breaking up (train in distance)*, 1920 Mar. 31; *South shore, Walden Pond*, 1903 May 30. Robbins-Mills Collection of Herbert Wendell Gleason Photographic Negatives. Courtesy of Special Collections, Concord Free Public Library.

Color Insert

Index of Authors and Titles

From the Publisher

A name never says it all, but the word "Broadview" expresses a good deal of the philosophy behind our company. We are open to a broad range of academic approaches and political viewpoints. We pay attention to the broad impact book publishing and book printing has in the wider world; for some years now we have used 100% recycled paper for most titles. Our publishing program is internationally oriented and broad-ranging. Our individual titles often appeal to a broad readership too; many are of interest as much to general readers as to academics and students.

Founded in 1985, Broadview remains a fully independent company owned by its shareholders—not an imprint or subsidiary of a larger multinational.

To order our books or obtain up-to-date information, please visit broadviewpress.com.

broadview press

www.broadviewpress.com